ORCHESTRAL MUSIC IN PRINT

1994 SUPPLEMENT

Edited by

Margaret K. Farish

Music-In-Print Series, Vol. 5t

MUSICDATA, INC.
Philadelphia, 1994

The Music-In-Print Series to date:

Vols. 1a,b. Sacred Choral Music In Print, Second Edition (1985)

Vol 1c. Sacred Choral Music In Print, Second Edition: Arranger Index (1987)

Vol. 1s. Sacred Choral Music In Print: 1988 Supplement

Vol. 1t. Sacred Choral Music In Print: 1992 Supplement

Vol. 1x. Sacred Choral Music In Print: Master Index 1992

Vols. 2a,b. Secular Choral Music In Print, Second Edition (1987)

Vol. 2c. Secular Choral Music In Print, Second Edition: Arranger Index (1987)

Vol. 2s. Secular Choral Music In Print: 1991 Supplement

Vol. 2t. Secular Choral Music In Print: 1993 Supplement

Vol. 2x. Secular Choral Music In Print: Master Index 1993

Vol. 3. Organ Music In Print, Second Edition (1984)

Vol. 3s. Organ Music In Print, 1990 Supplement

Vol. 4. Classical Vocal Music In Print (1976) (out of print)

Vol. 4s. Classical Vocal Music In Print: 1985 Supplement

Vol. 5. Orchestral Music In Print (1979)

Vol. 5s. Orchestral Music In Print: 1983 Supplement

Vol. 5t. Orchestral Music In Print: 1994 Supplement

Vol. 6. String Music In Print, Second Edition (1973) (out of print)

Vol. 6s. String Music In Print: 1984 Supplement

Vol. 7. Classical Guitar Music In Print (1989)

Vol. XC. Music-In-Print Master Composer Index 1988

Vol. XT. Music-In-Print Master Title Index 1988

Music-In-Print Series: ISSN 0146-7883

Printed by Port City Press, Baltimore, Maryland

Musicdata, Inc.
P.O. Box 48010
Philadelphia, Pennsylvania 19144-8010

Library of Congress Cataloging-in-Publication Data

Farish, Margaret K.
    Orchestral music in print. 1994 supplement/edited by Margaret
K. Farish.
        p.   cm. -- (Music-in-print series, ISSN 0146-7883 ; vol. 5t)
    ISBN 0-88478-033-3
    1. Orchestral music--Bibliography.   I. Title. II. Series.
ML128.O5F33   1994
016.7842'0263--dc20   94-16889
                                                                          CIP
                                                                          MN

Contents

Preface

This volume is the second supplement to *Orchestral Music in Print*, published in 1979. It contains listings obtained since the first supplement of 1983. The publisher is, of course, the only dependable source of information on music currently in print. The entries in this supplement were compiled from catalogs and lists sent by publishers in this country and abroad. As in *Orchestral Music in Print*, all works for eleven or more players are included, with the exception of those scored solely for wind instruments. Music for solo instruments or voices with orchestra is listed, but not works for chorus and orchestra. For information on these publications, see *Choral Music in Print*.

In *Orchestral Music in Print* a main entry appears under the name of the composer and includes, whenever possible, the instrumentation and duration. If the work is available from more than one publisher, all editions are listed under one uniform title. This system has been followed in this volume. However, since it is a supplement, instrumentation and duration are not shown for new editions of works listed in the base volume.

Although most publishers send excellent catalogs, some do not provide all of the information needed for a complete entry. Often the missing elements can be added by the editor, if the composer and the title can be identified. Unfortunately, this is not always possible. Without the full name and dates it is difficult to know which member of a musical family is the composer and, even more frequently, which work is offered. For example, if "Concerto in D" by a prolific 18th century composer is listed by half a dozen publishers, it is impossible to tell whether six different concertos or six editions of one concerto are available. In these circumstances, each is listed separately with a Musicdata Identification Number (MIN) for the benefit of the computer which is programmed to treat all works with identical titles as multiple editions. A similar system is used for common titles, such as "Minuet". The repetition of identical titles indicates lack of information. The works may be the same; only an examination of the scores will provide proof.

The works of each composer are listed alphabetically by title. Because the computer-based system does not permit changes in this order, entries for collections will not always precede those for individual works, as they do in most music library files. Symphonies will come before Symphony, but Suites will follow Suite. For most titles of this nature, the English form of the plural has been used but there are, inevitably, a few exceptions. The most important of these is Concerto. The Italian plural has been adopted in this case to accomodate the unalterable *Concerti Grossi*.

Once again, it is a pleasure to thank Northwestern University and the staff of the Music Library for invaluable assistance, and to acknowledge my debt to all who participated in the preparation of this volume: Mark Daugherty, Susan H. Simon, Noah Simon, Kathe Jacoby, Joseph Pluciennik and Mark Resnick.

In addition, Musicdata would like to express its appreciation to Irving Herman of Cedar Falls, Iowa, who supplied the idea that made possible the reprinting of *Orchestral Music in Print* in February, 1991, thereby paving the way for the current supplement.

Evanston, Illinois
February 1994

Margaret K. Farish

Guide to Use

THE MUSIC-IN-PRINT SERIES

The Music-In-Print series is an ongoing effort to locate and catalog all music in print throughout the world. The intention is to cover all areas of music as rapidly as resources permit, as well as to provide a mechanism for keeping the information up to date.

Since 1973, Musicdata, Inc. has solicited catalogs and listings from music publishers throughout the world. Using the information supplied by co-operating publishers, the series lists specific editions which are available from a publisher either for sale or on a rental basis in appropriate categories. The volumes in the series are basically organized by the primary performing force, instrument or instrumental family, such as Sacred Choral Music, Organ Music or String Music.

It is often difficult to define the boundaries between the various broad areas of music covered by the volumes in the series. The definition of sacred and secular choral music varies from publisher to publisher; some major choral works are no longer listed in Orchestral Music, reflecting changing editorial practice; some solo vocal music is in Orchestral Music; etc. The user is advised to consult the preface to individual volumes for greater definition of scope. Use of more than one volume may well be necessary to locate an edition or all editions of a work.

Editorial policy is to include as much information as the publisher supplies, within the limits of practicality. An important goal of the series is to try to bring together different editions of a composition under a single title.

VOLUME FORMAT

The volumes of the Music-In-Print series have two basic formats: unified or structured. Reference to the editor's preface and the table of contents will assist in determining how a given volume is organized.

The unified volumes (e.g., Organ Music, Orchestral Music) are arranged in a single alphabetical interfiling of composers' names, titles of works and cross references. The title under a composer's name serves as the focus for major information on each composition. In the absence of a composer, the title in the main alphabet becomes the focal point for this information.

The structured volumes (e.g., String Music) are arranged by an imposed framework: instrumentation, time period, type of work or other categorization. Within each section, entries are alphabetized by composer name or, in the absence of a composer, by title. Entries will be repeated in all appropriate sections. A structured volume also contains a Composer/Title Index and, in some cases, other specialized indexes. The Composer/Title Index is a single alphabetical list of composers' names, composition titles and cross references, with a reference to the section(s) of the volume in which complete edition information will be found. The running heads on each page of the catalog enable the user to quickly find the proper section.

ENTRY TYPES

Two basic types of entries appear in the Music-In-Print series: normal and collection. A normal entry describes a single piece of music. A collection consists of any two or more associated pieces.

NORMAL ENTRY CONTENT

In order to bring together all different editions of a composition under a uniform and/or structured title, many musical form titles are translated into English (so, Konzert becomes Concerto, Fantaisie becomes Fantasy, etc.).

For each title there are two types of information: a) generic information about the composition and b) specific information pertaining to the editions which are in print. Included in the generic information category are the uniform title of the composition, a structured title for the work (e.g., Concerto No. 2 In D Minor; Cantata No. 140), a thematic catalog number or opus and number designation, the larger source from which the work was taken, and remarks.

Following the generic information about the piece is the information about the individual editions. This information includes the arranger, the published title of the edition if different from the uniform title, the language of the text (for vocal works), instrumentation required for performance, the duration of the work in minutes (') and seconds ("), a difficulty rating assigned to the edition by the publisher or editor, the format of the publication, publisher, publisher's number, and price or rental information concerning the edition.

Following is an example of a typical entry under a composer:

MOZART, WOLFGANG AMADEUS (1756-1791)
   Nozze Di Figaro, Le: Overture
     [4']
      2.2.2.2. 2.2.0.0. timp,strings
    sc,parts RICORDI-IT rental   (M1)
    "Marriage of Figaro, The: Overture"
     sc,parts BREITKOPF-W f.s.   (M2)

In this entry under the composer, Wolfgang Amadeus Mozart, the title of an excerpt, "Overture", follows the original title of the complete work, "Nozze Di Figaro, Le". It is scored for 2 flutes, 2 oboes, 2 clarinets, 2 bassoons, 2 horns, 2 trumpets, timpani and strings. Duration is approximately 4 minutes. The code RICORDI-IT indicates the publisher of the first listed edition; score and parts are offered by this publisher on rental. The sequence number (M1) marks the end of the information on this edition. The English title "Marriage Of Figaro, The: Overture" is given for the next edition which is published by BREITKOPF-W; score and parts for this edition are for sale.

The full names and addresses of all publishers or U.S. agents are given in the publisher list which follows the list of editions at the end of the book.

Following is an example of an entry with a structured title:

MOZART, WOLFGANG AMADEUS (1756-1791)
   Symphony No. 25, [excerpt]
    (Gordon, Philip) 2.1.2.1.al-
      sax. ten-sax. 2.2.1.1.timp,perc,
      strings [3'] (Menuetto, [arr.])
    PRESSER sets $7.50, and up, sc
    $1.50   (M3)

Here a structured title "Symphony No. 25," requires a different form of listing. The excerpt, "Menuetto", has been arranged by Philip Gordon for 2 flutes, oboe, 2 clarinets, bassoon, alto saxophone, tenor saxophone, 2 horns, 2 trumpets, trombone, tuba, timpani, percussion and strings. Du-

ration is three minutes. The publisher, PRESSER, offers sets of parts priced at $7.50 and up. A separate score is available for $1.50.

INSTRUMENTATION

Instrumentation is given in the customary order. When a work is scored for full orchestra, the number of wind players required is indicated by two groups of numbers—four for woodwinds (flute, oboe, clarinet, bassoon) and four for brass (horn, trumpet, trombone, tuba). Other instruments are listed by name, or abbreviated name. A number placed before a named instrument indicates the number of players. A slash is used for alternate instrumentation.

The common auxiliary wind instruments are not mentioned by most publishers. For example, 2.2.3.3. for woodwinds indicates the work is scored for two flutes, but it *may* include a piccolo part which can be played by one of the flutists. Similarly, it is possible that parts for English horn, bass clarinet and contrabassoon are provided but no additional players will be required. If the publisher does specify the auxiliary instruments required, this information is given either in parentheses (the number of players is not affected) or after a plus sign (an additional player is needed).

Example:

   2(pic).2+opt ob.3(opt bass-clar).2+contrabsn.
   4.2.3.0+opt tuba.timp,2-3perc,harp,cel/pno,
   strings

This example is scored for 2 flutes and piccolo (played by one of the flutists), 2 oboes plus an optional third oboe, 3 clarinets (one may play the optional bass clarinet part), 2 bassoons plus contrabassoon (additional player required), 4 horns, 2 trumpets, 3 trombones, optional tuba, timpani, percussion (2 or 3 players), harp, celeste or piano, and strings.

The term "orch" may be substituted for a detailed listing if the publisher has not provided the instrumentation for orchestral works.

Solo instrumental parts are listed following the complete orchestration of a work.

Choral parts are given as a list of voices (e.g., SATB, TTBB, etc.). The term "cor" (and similar terms) may be substituted when the publisher has not listed the specific voices.

Solo vocal parts are given as a list of voices followed by the term "solo" or "soli." The term "solo voice(s)" is used when the publisher does not specify the voice(s). (No attempt has been made to give equivalents for scale ranges listed by publishers.)

REMARKS

The remarks are a series of codes or abbreviations giving information on the seasonal or other usage of the piece, the type of music, and the national origin and century for folk or anonymous pieces. (These codes also make it possible to retrieve, from the data base developed for the Music-In-Print series, specialized listings of music for particular seasons, types, etc.) Following this Guide to Use will be found a complete List of Abbreviations.

PRICES

Only U.S. dollar prices are given, and we can give no assurance of their accuracy. They are best used for making rough comparisons. The publishers should be consulted directly for current prices.

SEQUENCE NUMBERS

An alphanumeric number, appearing on the right margin, has been assigned to each edition represented in this catalog. These are for the purpose of easing identification and location of specific entries.

COLLECTION ENTRY CONTENT

An attempt has been made to provide the user with access to pieces contained within collections, while still keeping the work within reasonable bounds of time and space. Accordingly, the following practices have been adopted:

If the members of a collection are published separately, they are listed individually, regardless of the number of pieces involved. If the collection is only published as a whole, the members are listed only if they do not exceed six in number. For larger collections, a code is given indicating the number of pieces and whether or not the contents are listed in the publisher's catalog. For example,

CC18L indicates a collection of 18 pieces which are *listed* in the publisher's catalog

CC101U indicates a collection of 101 pieces which are *unlisted* in the publisher's catalog

CCU indicates a collection of an unknown number of pieces

Whenever the members are listed, they are also cross-referenced to the collection. For example, consider the following entry:

FIVE VOLUNTARIES, [ARR.]
  (Davies, Peter Maxwell) 3.3.2.1, 3.3.0.0.
    timp,perc,strings,cont sc,parts
    SCHOTT 10994 f.s.
    contains: Attaignant, Pierre,
      Magnificat; Clarke, Jeremiah,
      King William's March; Clarke,
      Jeremiah, Serenade; Couperin,
      Louis, Sarabande; Croft, William,
      March Tune   (F1)

Published by Schott, edition number 10994, this collection edited by Peter Maxwell Davies contains five members, which are not published separately. Under each of the members there is a cross reference saying 'see FIVE VOLUNTARIES, [ARR.]'.

Collection entries also contain many of the elements of information found in normal entries. For example, the entry shown above contains arranger, instrumentation, format of publication, publisher and publisher number.

Collections of several pieces published as a whole, but having no overall title, create another problem. In this case the complete publication information is given under the composer or title of the first piece listed, together with the comment 'contains also,' followed by titles of the other collection members.

CROSS REFERENCES

In order to provide the user with as many points of access as possible, the Music-In-Print series has been heavily cross referenced. In the unified volumes, the cross references are interfiled with the composers' names and the titles. In the structured volumes, cross references only appear in the Composer/Title Index.

Works may be located by title, with or without knowing the name of the composer. Using the first example by Mozart above, this composition may be located under either its Italian or English title in the main alphabet, as well as under the composer.

To make this possible the following cross references would exist in the main alphabet:

    NOZZE DI FIGARO, LE: OVERTURE
      see Mozart, Wolfgang Amadeus

and

    MARRIAGE OF FIGARO, THE: OVERTURE see
      Mozart, Wolfgang Amadeus, Nozze Di
      Figaro, Le: Overture

and in addition, the following cross reference would be found under the composer's name:

    Marriage of Figaro, The: Overture
      *see Nozze Di Figaro, Le: Overture

Cross references are employed also to assist in the search for works frequently identified by popular names or subtitles, such as the "Surprise" Symphony of Haydn and the "Jupiter" Symphony of Mozart.

Numerous cross references have been made from unused and variant forms of composer names to assist the user in finding the form of name chosen for the series.

COLLECTION CROSS REFERENCES

Whenever the members of a collection are listed, they are cross referenced to the collection. In unified volumes, these are interfiled with composers' names and titles. In structured volumes, these cross references only occur in the Composer/Title Index.

Using the above example, FIVE VOLUNTARIES, [ARR.], there is a cross reference under each of the composers saying 'see FIVE VOLUNTARIES, [Arr.]'. (If a collection member lacks a composer, the cross reference will occur at the title.)

When collections are also published separately, the cross references in both directions read 'see also'. If the members are only published separately (i.e., the collection were not published as a whole) then the cross reference under the collection would read 'see' and under the members, 'see from'. Thus, 'see' and 'see also' direct the user to information concerning publication, while 'see from' provides access to the collection of which a given publication is a part.

With untitled collections, which are listed under the first composer and/or title, the cross reference 'see' under each of the other collection members directs the user to the full entry under the first member, at which point complete edition information will be found.

COMPOSER/TITLE INDEX

The Composer/Title Index is a single alphabetical listing of composer names, composition titles and cross references. This index is used to identify the location of a specific entry in a structured volume.

The actual reference is usually under the composer name, and only under a title when a work is not attributable to a person. The reference is to the chapter and/or section of the volume which contains the entry for the music sought.

For example, in String Music, IV.1 refers the user to Chapter IV, Section 1: String Quartets. Similarly, VIII refers to Chapter VIII: Music for Eight Instruments. Reference to the table of contents and the head of each page of the volume will assist the user in finding the appropriate section containing the information sought.

ARRANGER INDEX

The Arranger Index lists in alphabetical order all arrangers and editors cited in a specific volume. The arranger's or editor's name is listed in all capital letters. In the case of multiple arrangers, the arranger names appear together, separated by semi-colons. The listing under each arranger name gives the composer and title of each arranged (edited) work, in alphabetical order. If a work has no composer, it is listed by title. In the case of uniform and translated titles, the uniform titles are the ones appearing in the index.

This arrangement allows the user to look up any desired arranger or editor and then scan for the composers and titles of desired works. Once the composer and title have been determined, the work may then be looked up in the catalog itself to obtain complete bibliographic and ordering information.

MASTER INDEX

The Music-In-Print Master Index provides a single place to look in order to locate any composer or title listed in the Music-In-Print series. The Master Index eliminates all problems of knowing whether a specific piece of music is listed in a base volume, supplementary volumes, or not at all.

The Master Composer Index lists all composers found within the Music-In-Print series. Under each composer's name is a complete alphabetical listing of the titles of works by that composer to be found in the series. Next to each title is a number or series of numbers referring the user to the volume or volumes containing the specific piece. A key explaining these numbers and the volumes to which they correspond is to be found on the reverse side of the title page. Once the user has located the correct volume, it is easy to find the specific piece in the volume's alphabetical sequence. In the case of structured volumes, reference should be made to the Composer/Title Index in each volume.

The Master Title Index lists in a single alphabetical listing all titles of works within the Music-In-Print series. Each title is followed by a reference number or series of numbers, directing the user to the volume or volumes containing the specific title as explained above.

Additionally, as more supplementary volumes are added to the Music-In-Print series, certain volumes may update the Master Index in a specific area from time to time, through the publication of a specialized Master Index. In this way, the user can easily locate a piece of music within the volumes dealing with a specific area.

List of Abbreviations

The following is a general list of abbreviations developed for the Music-In-Print series. Therefore, all of the abbreviations do not necessarily occur in the present volume. Also, it should be noted that terms spelled out in full in the catalog, e.g. woodwinds, tuba, Easter, Passover, folk, Swiss, do not appear in this list.

A	alto
acap	a cappella
accomp	accompaniment
acord	accordion
Adv	Advent
Afr	African
Agnus	Agnus Dei
al-clar	alto clarinet
al-fl	alto flute
al-sax	alto saxophone
Allelu	Alleluia
AmInd	American Indian
ampl	amplified
Anh.	Anhang (supplement)
anti	antiphonal
app	appendix, appendices
arr.	arranged
Asc	Ascension
ASD	All Saints' Day
aud	audience
Austral	Australian
B	bass
Bald	Baldwin organ
Bar	baritone
bar horn	baritone horn
bar-sax	baritone saxophone
bass-clar	bass clarinet
bass-fl	bass flute
bass-sax	bass saxophone
bass-trom	bass trombone
bass-trp	bass trumpet
bds	boards
Belg	Belgian
Benton	thematic catalog of the works of Ignace Pleyel by Rita Benton
Bibl	Biblical
bk	book
Boh	Bohemian
boy cor	boys' chorus
Braz	Brazilian
Bryan	thematic catalog of the symphonies of Johann Wanhal by Paul Bryan
bsn	bassoon
BVM	Blessed Virgin Mary
BWV	Bach-Werke-Verzeichnis; thematic catalog of the works of J.S. Bach by Wolfgang Schmieder
BuxWV	Buxtehude-Werke-Verzeichnis; thematic catalog of the works of Dietrich Buxtehude by G. Kärstadt (Wiesbaden, 1974)

C&W	Country & Western
C.Landon	numbering of the keyboard sonatas of Joseph Haydn by Christa Landon
camb	cambiata
Can	Canadian
cant	cantata
Carib	Caribbean
CC	collection
CCU	collection, unlisted
CCUL	collection, partially listed
cel	celesta
Cen Am	Central American
cent	century
cf.	compare
Chin	Chinese
chord	chord organ
Circum	Circumcision
clar	clarinet
cloth	clothbound
cmplt ed	complete edition
Cnfrm	Confirmation
Commun	Communion
cong	congregation
Conn	Conn organ
cont	continuo
contrabsn	contrabassoon
copy	ed produced to order by a copy process
cor	chorus
cor pts	choral parts
cor-resp	choral response
Corpus	Corpus Christi
cradle	cradle song
cym	cymbals
D.	thematic catalog of the works of Franz Schubert by Otto Erich Deutsch
Dan	Danish
db	double bass
db-tuba	double-bass tuba
dbl cor	double chorus
Ded	Dedication
degr.	degree, 1-9 (difficulty), assigned by editor
desc	descant
diag	diagram(s)
diff	difficult

Dounias	thematic catalog of the violin concertos of Giuseppe Tartini by Minous Dounias
Doxol	Doxology
ea.	each
ECY	End of Church Year
ed	edition
educ	educational material
elec	electric
Ember	Ember Days
Eng	English
enl	enlarged
Epiph	Epiphany
eq voices	equal voices
Eur	European
evang	evangelistic
Eve	Evening
F.	thematic catalog of the instrumental works of Antonio Vivaldi by Antonio Fanna
f(f)	following
f.s.	for sale
fac ed	facsimile edition
facsim	facsimile(s)
Fest	festivals
film	music from film score
Finn	Finnish
fl	flute
Fr	French
Gd.Fri.	Good Friday
Ge.	thematic catalog of the works of Luigi Boccherini by Yves Gerard
Gen	general
Ger	German
Giegling	thematic catalog of the works of Giuseppe Torelli by Franz Giegling
girl cor	girls' chorus
glock	glockenspiel
gr. I-V	grades I-V, assigned by publisher
Greg	Gregorian chant
gtr	guitar
Gulbransen	Gulbransen organ

Hamm — Hammond organ
Harv — Harvest
Heb — Hebrew
Helm — thematic catalog of the works of C.P.E. Bach by Eugene Helm
Hill — thematic catalog of the works of F.L. Gassmann by George Hill
Hob. — thematic catalog of the works of Joseph Haydn by Anthony van Hoboken
Holywk — Holy Week
horn — French horn
hpsd — harpsichord
Hung — Hungarian
HWC — Healey Willan Catalogue

ill — illustrated, illustrations
Ind — Indian
inst — instruments
intro — introduction
ipa — instrumental parts available
ipr — instrumental parts for rent
Ir — Irish
Isr — Israeli
It — Italian

J-C — thematic catalog of the works of G.B. Sammartini by Newell Jenkins and Bathia Churgin
Jap — Japanese
Jew — Jewish
jr cor — junior chorus
Jubil — Jubilate Deo

K. — thematic catalog of the works of W.A. Mozart by Ludwig, Ritter von Köchel; thematic catalog of the works of J.J. Fux by the same author
Kaul — thematic catalog of the instrumental works of F.A. Rosetti by Oskar Kaul
kbd — keyboard
Kirkpatrick — thematic catalog of the sonatas of Domenico Scarlatti by Ralph Kirkpatrick
Kor — Korean
Krebs — thematic catalog of the works of Karl Ditters von Dittersdorf by Karl Krebs

L — listed
Landon — numbering of the keyboard trios of Joseph Haydn by H.C.R. Landon
Lat — Latin
liturg — liturgical
Longo — thematic catalog of the sonatas of Domenico Scarlatti by Alessandro Longo
Lowery — Lowery organ

Magnif — Magnificat
maj — major
man — manualiter; on the manuals alone
mand — mandolin
manuscript — manuscript (handwritten)
med — medium
mel — melody
men cor — mens' chorus
Mex — Mexican
Mez — mezzo-soprano
MIN — Musicdata Identification Number
min — minor
min sc — miniature score
mix cor — mixed chorus
Morav — Moravian
Morn — Morning
mot — motet

Neth — Netherlands
NJ — Name of Jesus
No. — number
Nor Am — North American
Norw — Norwegian
Nos. — numbers
Nunc — Nunc Dimittis

ob — oboe
oct — octavo
offer — offertory
Op. — Opus
Op. Posth. — Opus Posthumous
opt — optional, ad lib
ora — oratorio
orch — orchestra
org — organ
org man — organ, manuals only
orig — original

P., P.S. — thematic catalogs of the orchestral works of Antonio Vivaldi by Marc Pincherle
p(p) — page(s)
Palm — Palm Sunday
pap — paperbound

Paymer — thematic catalog of the works of G.B. Pergolesi by Marvin Paymer
pce, pcs — piece, pieces
Pent — Pentecost
perc — percussion
perf mat — performance material
perf sc — performance score
Perger — thematic catalog of the instrumental works of Michael Haydn by Lothar Perger
pic — piccolo
pic-trp — piccolo trumpet
pipe — pipe organ
pno — piano
pno-cond sc — piano-conducting score
pno red — piano reduction
Pol — Polish
Polynes — Polynesian
pop — popular
Port — Portuguese
pos — position
PreClass — Pre-Classical
pref — preface
Proces — processional
Psntd — Passiontide
pt, pts — part, parts

quar — quartet
quin — quintet
Quinqua — Quinquagesima

rec — recorder
Reces — recessional
Refm — Reformation
rent — for rent
repr — reprint
Req — Requiem
rev — revised, revision
Royal — royal occasion
Rum — Rumanian
Russ — Russian
RV — Ryom-Verzeichnis; thematic catalog of the works of Antonio Vivaldi by Peter Ryom

S — soprano
s.p. — separately published
Sab — Sabbath
sac — sacred
sax — saxophone
sc — score
Scot — Scottish
sec — secular

Septua	Septuagesima
Sexa	Sexagesima
show	music from musical show score
So Am	South American
sop-clar	soprano clarinet
sop-sax	soprano saxophone
Span	Spanish
speak cor	speaking chorus
spir	spiritual
sr cor	senior chorus
study sc	study score
suppl	supplement
Swed	Swedish
SWV	Schütz-Werke-Verzeichnis; thematic catalog of the works of Heinrich Schütz by W. Bittinger (Kassel, 1960)
T	tenor
tamb	tambourine
temp blks	temple blocks
ten-sax	tenor saxophone
Thanks	Thanksgiving
Thomas	Thomas organ
TI	Tárrega Index; thematic catalog of the Preludes, Studies, and Exercises of Francisco Tárrega by Mijndert Jape
timp	timpani
transl	translation
treb	treble
Trin	Trinity

trom	trombone
trp	trumpet
TV	music from television score
TWV	Telemann-Werke-Verzeichnis; thematic catalog of the works of G.P. Telemann by Mencke and Ruhncke
U	unlisted
UL	partially listed
unis	unison
US	United States
vcl	violoncello
vibra	vibraphone
vla	viola
vln	violin
voc pt	vocal part
voc sc	vocal score
VOCG	Robert de Visée, Oeuvres Completes pour Guitare edited by Robert Strizich
vol(s)	volume(s)
Whitsun	Whitsuntide
WO	without opus number; used in thematic catalog of the works of Muzio Clementi by Alan Tyson

Wolf	thematic catalog of the symphonies of Johann Stamitz by Eugene Wolf
wom cor	womens' chorus
WoO.	work without opus number; used in thematic catalogs of the works of Beethoven by Kinsky and Halm and of the works of J.N. Hummel by Dieter Zimmerscheid
Wq.	thematic catalog of the works of C.P.E. Bach by Alfred Wotquenne
Wurlitzer	Wurlitzer organ
WV	Wagenseil-Verzeichnis; thematic catalog of the works of G.C. Wagenseil by Helga Scholz-Michelitsch
Xmas	Christmas
xylo	xylophone
Z.	thematic catalog of the works of Henry Purcell by Franklin Zimmerman

ORCHESTRAL MUSIC

A

A BERENICE; SOL NASCENTE, FOR SOLO
VOICE AND ORCHESTRA see Mozart,
Wolfgang Amadeus

A CARLO SCARPA ARCHITETTO, AI SUOI
INFINITI POSSIBILI see Nono, Luigi

A DAY - THE DAYS see Sandström, Sven-
David

A. DE MAHLER, FOR SOLO VOICES AND
ORCHESTRA see Koering, Rene

A FOR ORKESTER see Berge, Sigurd

A GIACOMO LEOPARDI, FOR SOLO VOICE AND
ORCHESTRA see Mascagni, Pietro

A LA BUSCA DEL MAS ALLA see Rodrigo,
Joaquín

A LA FENETRE RECELANT see Garuti, Mario

À LA MÉMOIRE DE BÉLA BARTÓK see Arma,
Paul (Pál) (Imre Weisshaus)

A L'ALLEMANDE see Lagana, Ruggero

A L'ILE DE GOREE, FOR HARPSICHORD AND
INSTRUMENTAL ENSEMBLE see Xenakis,
Yannis (Iannis)

A MON FILS, FOR SOLO VOICE AND
ORCHESTRA see Vellones, Pierre

A-PIC, FOR BASSOON AND INSTRUMENTAL
ENSEMBLE see Devillers, Jean
Baptiste

A QUESTO SENO DEH VIENI, FOR SOLO VOICE
AND ORCHESTRA see Mozart, Wolfgang
Amadeus

A SA RODBLOND, FOR SOLO VOICE AND
ORCHESTRA see Groven, Eivind

A SPASSO CON LA FIGLIA DEL TAMBURO
MAGGIORE, FOR SOLO VOICE AND
ORCHESTRA [ARR.] see Offenbach,
Jacques

A UNE DAME CREOLE, FOR SOLO VOICE AND
ORCHESTRA see Aliprandi, Paul

A UNE OMBRE see Tisne, Antoine

AAMULAULU, FOR SOLO VOICE AND STRING
ORCHESTRA [ARR.] see Kuula, Toivo

ABACO, EVARISTO FELICE DALL'
(1675-1742)
Concerto, Op. 2, No. 4, in A minor
(Bonelli) KALMUS A7346 sc $8.00,
set $7.50, pts $1.50, ea.   (A1)

ABBADO, MARCELLO (1926-   )
Concerto for Piano, Violin, Viola,
Violoncello and Orchestra
2.2.2.2. 2.2.2.0. timp,3perc,
strings,pno solo,vln solo,vla
solo,vcl solo
RICORDI-IT 132132 perf mat rent
(A2)
Fasce Sonore, For 2 Pianos And
Chamber Orchestra [8'10"]
1.1.1.1. 1.1.0.0. perc,12vln,
6vla,3vcl,3db,2pno soli
RICORDI-IT 132313 perf mat rent
(A3)

ABBOTT, ALAIN (1938-   )
Folie Et Mort D'ophelie, For Solo
Voices And Orchestra [23']
2.2.2.2. 2.2.2.0. timp,perc,harp,
strings,SBar soli
BILLAUDOT perf mat rent   (A4)

Music for Accordion and String
Orchestra [19']
string orch,acord solo
BILLAUDOT perf mat rent   (A5)

ABBRUCHE see Ruzicka, Peter

ABDELAZAR: SUITE, [ARR.] see Purcell,
Henry

ABDELAZER: INCIDENTAL MUSIC see
Purcell, Henry

ABDELAZER: SPIELMUSIK see Purcell,
Henry

ABE, KOMEI (1911-   )
Piccola Sinfonia [20']
string orch
JAPAN 8503   (A6)

ABEILLE, L', FOR VIOLONCELLO AND STRING
ORCHESTRA [ARR.] see Schubert,
Franz

ABEL, CARL FRIEDRICH (1723-1787)
Six Selected Symphonies
(Helm, Sanford) sc A-R ED
ISBN 0-89579-094-7 f.s.
contains: Symphony, Op. 1, No. 4,
in E flat; Symphony, Op. 4, No.
2, in B flat; Symphony, Op. 7,
No. 1, in G; Symphony, Op. 10,
No. 1, in E; Symphony, Op. 14,
No. 2, in E flat; Symphony, Op.
17, No. 1, in E flat   (A7)

Symphonies, Six *CC12U
(Zimmerman; Warbutron; Maunder) sc
GARLAND ISBN 0-8240-3825-8 $90.00
"The Symphony" Vol. E-II: also
contains Six Symphonic Works by
Johann Christian Bach   (A8)

Symphony, Op. 1, No. 4, in E flat
see Six Selected Symphonies

Symphony, Op. 1, No. 6, in G
(Hockner) KALMUS A5881 sc $6.00,
set $12.00, perf mat rent   (A9)

Symphony, Op. 4, No. 2, in B flat
see Six Selected Symphonies

Symphony, Op. 5, No. 1, in F
(Hockner) KALMUS A5575 sc $6.00,
set $12.00, pts $1.00, ea.   (A10)

Symphony, Op. 7, No. 1, in G
see Six Selected Symphonies

Symphony, Op. 7, No. 6, in E flat
BREITKOPF-W perf mat rent   (A11)

Symphony, Op. 10, No. 1, in E
see Six Selected Symphonies

Symphony, Op. 14, No. 2, in E flat
see Six Selected Symphonies

Symphony, Op. 17, No. 1, in E flat
see Six Selected Symphonies

ABENCERAGES, LES: OVERTURE see
Cherubini, Luigi

ABENDEMPFINDUNG, FOR SOLO VOICE AND
ORCHESTRA, [ARR.] see Mozart,
Wolfgang Amadeus

ABENDSTERN see Strauss, Josef

ABENTEUER DES BRAVEN SOLDATEN SCHWEJK,
DIE, FOR NARRATOR AND ORCHESTRA see
Zytovich, Vladimir

ABFUHR see Campana, Jose Luis

ABGEWANDT see Rihm, Wolfgang

ABKEHR see Rihm, Wolfgang

ABLEBLOMST, FOR SOLO VOICE AND
ORCHESTRA, [ARR.] see Nielsen, Carl

ABLOSUNG IM SOMMER see Mahler, Gustav

ABONNENTEN WALZER see Strauss, Eduard

ABRAHAMSEN, HANS (1952-   )
Lied In Fall, For Violoncello And
Orchestra [10']
0+alto fl(pic).1(English
horn).1. 1.1.1.0. perc,pno,
2vln,vla,vcl,db,vcl solo
HANSEN-DEN perf mat rent   (A12)

Marchenbilder [14']
1(pic).1.1(clar in E flat).1.
1.1.1.0. perc,pno,string quar,
db
HANSEN-DEN perf mat rent   (A13)

Nacht Und Trompeten [10']
2(alto fl).2(English horn).2.2.
2.3.0.0. 2perc,pno,strings
HANSEN-DEN perf mat rent   (A14)

Stratifications [8']
2(pic).2.2.1. 2.2.1.0. timp,
2perc,pno,strings
sc HANSEN-DEN f.s., perf mat rent
(A15)
Symphony in C [10']
3(pic).3.3.3. 4.3.3.1. 3perc,pno,
strings
HANSEN-DEN perf mat rent   (A16)

Symphony No. 1 [10']
2(pic).2.2.2. 4.2.3.0. timp,
3perc,strings
HANSEN-DEN perf mat rent   (A17)

ABRIL, A. GARCÍA
see GARCIA-ABRIL, ANTON

ABSCHIED see Trojahn, Manfred

ABSENCE DE DULCINEE, L', FOR SOLO
VOICES AND ORCHESTRA see Rodrigo,
Joaquín

ABSIL, JEAN (1893-1974)
Fantaisie Caprice, For Alto Saxophone
And String Orchestra *Op.152
string orch,alto sax solo
LEMOINE perf mat rent   (A18)

Petite Suite *Op.20
1.1.1.1. 2.0.0.0. timp,strings
ESCHIG perf mat rent   (A19)

Rhapsody for Horn and Orchestra, Op.
120 [7']
1.1.2.1. 2.1.1.0. timp,perc,harp,
strings,horn solo
LEMOINE perf mat rent   (A20)

ABSTR'ACTE see Couroupos, Georges

ABU HASSAN: OVERTURE see Weber, Carl
Maria von

ABYSS, FOR SOLO VOICE, BASS FLUTE AND
INSTRUMENTAL ENSEMBLE see Donatoni,
Franco

ABYSSAL, FOR 2 GUITARS AND INSTRUMENTAL
ENSEMBLE see Ibarrondo, Felix

ACADEMIC OVERTURE see Suben, Joel Eric

ACANTE ET CEPHISE: SUITE see Rameau,
Jean-Philippe

ACCANTO, FOR CLARINET AND ORCHESTRA see
Lachenmann, Helmut Friedrich

ACCART-BECKER, EVELYNE (1921-   )
Concert Pour Cuivres Et Cordes [15']
2horn,2trp,2trom,strings
BILLAUDOT perf mat rent   (A21)

ACH HERR, LASS DEINE LIEBEN ENGELEIN,
FOR SOLO VOICE AND STRING ORCHESTRA
see Tunder, Franz

ACH, TRAURIGER MOND, FOR PERCUSSION AND
STRING ORCHESTRA see Brandmüller,
Theo

ACH UM DEINE FEUCHTEN SCHWINGEN see
Schubert, Franz (Peter), Suleika
II, For Solo Voice And
Orchestra[arr.]

ACHILLE A SYROS: AIR D'ULYSSE, FOR SOLO
VOICE AND ORCHESTRA see Jommelli,
Niccolo, Achille In Sciro: Aria
d'Ulisse, For Solo Voice And
Orchestra

ACHILLE A SYROS: DUO ACHILLE ET ULYSSE,
FOR SOLO VOICES AND ORCHESTRA see
Jommelli, Niccolo, Achille In
Sciro: Duo Achille E Ulisse, For
Solo Voices And Orchestra

ACHILLE A SYROS: RECIT ET AIR
D'ACHILLE, FOR SOLO VOICE AND
ORCHESTRA see Jommelli, Niccolo,
Achille In Sciro: Recitativo E Aria
d'Achille, For Solo Voice And
Orchestra

ACHILLE IN SCIRO: ARIA D'ULISSE, FOR
SOLO VOICE AND ORCHESTRA see
Jommelli, Niccolo

ACHILLE IN SCIRO: DUO ACHILLE E ULISSE,
FOR SOLO VOICES AND ORCHESTRA see
Jommelli, Niccolo

ACHILLE IN SCIRO: OVERTURE see
Jommelli, Niccolo

ACHILLE IN SCIRO: RECITATIVO E ARIA
D'ACHILLE, FOR SOLO VOICE AND
ORCHESTRA see Jommelli, Niccolo

ACHT GEDICHTE VON HERMANN HESSE, FOR
SOLO VOICE AND ORCHESTRA see
Raphael, Günther

ACHT KORTE KARAKTERSCHETSEN see Osieck,
Hans

ACHT LIEDER AUS DEM "REISEBUCH", FOR
SOLO VOICE AND ORCHESTRA see
Krenek, Ernst

ACHT VARIATIONEN UND CODA UBER "O DU
LIEBER AUGUSTIN" see Hummel, Johann
Nepomuk

ACINTYAS see Sandström, Jan

ACIS AND GALATEA: AS WHEN THE DOVE, FOR
  SOLO VOICE AND ORCHESTRA see
  Handel, George Frideric

ACIS AND GALATEA: I RAGE, I MELT, I
  BURN; O RUDDIER THAN THE CHERRY,
  FOR SOLO VOICE AND ORCHESTRA see
  Handel, George Frideric

ACIS AND GALATEA: 'TIS DONE; HEART,
  THE SEAT OF SOFT DELIGHT, FOR SOLO
  VOICE AND ORCHESTRA see Handel,
  George Frideric

ACIS UND GALATEA: O SCHMACH, O WUT; O
  ROSIG WIE DIE PFIRSCHE, FOR SOLO
  VOICE AND ORCHESTRA see Handel,
  George Frideric, Acis And Galatea:
  I Rage, I Melt, I Burn; O Ruddier
  Than The Cherry, For Solo Voice And
  Orchestra

ACIS UND GALATEA: SO SEI'S; HERZ, DER
  LIEBE SÜSSER BORN, FOR SOLO VOICE
  AND ORCHESTRA see Handel, George
  Frideric, Acis And Galatea: 'Tis
  Done; Heart, The Seat Of Soft
  Delight, For Solo Voice And
  Orchestra

ACIS UND GALATEA: SO WIE DIE TAUBE,
  FOR SOLO VOICE AND ORCHESTRA see
  Handel, George Frideric, Acis And
  Galatea: As When The Dove, For Solo
  Voice And Orchestra

ACKER, DIETER (1940-   )
  Concerto for Bassoon and Orchestra
    [25']
    2(pic).1+English horn.2(bass
      clar).0. 3.2.1.0. 2perc,harp,
      pno,strings,bsn solo
    study sc BOTE f.s., perf mat rent
                                  (A22)
  Concerto for Violin and Orchestra,
    No. 1
    study sc BREITKOPF-W PB 5103 f.s.
                                  (A23)
ACQUAINTED WITH NIGHT, FOR SOLO VOICE
  AND ORCHESTRA see Burgon, Geoffrey

ACROPOLIS see Charpentier, Jacques

ACROSS THE WIDE MISSOURI see Amram,
  David Werner

ACTIONEN WALZER see Strauss, Josef

ACTIONS SIMULTANEES see Prin, Yves

ACTUS see Guerrero, Francisco

ACUARELAS VALENCIANAS see Chavarri,
  Eduardo López

AD ASTRA see Hauksson, Thorsteinn

AD MARGINEM see Holliger, Heinz

ADAGIO AND FUGE IN C MINOR, K.546 see
  Mozart, Wolfgang Amadeus

ADAGIO AND RONDO, FOR HORN AND
  ORCHESTRA see Holloway, Robin

ADAGIO CANTABILE see Ferrero, Lorenzo

ADAGIO CON VARIAZIONI see Ágústsson,
  Herbert Hriberschek

ADAGIO ET ALLEGRO DE "FAUBLAS" see
  Cimarosa, Domenico

ADAGIO ET ALLEGRO MOLTO, FOR HORN,
  TROMBONE AND ORCHESTRA see Haydn,
  [Johann] Michael

ADAGIO LAMENTOSO, FOR FLUTE, CLARINET
  AND ORCHESTRA see Ajdic, Alojz

ADAGIO NACH KELTISCHEN MELODIEN, FOR
  VIOLONCELLO AND ORCHESTRA see
  Bruch, Max

ADAGIO ON CELTIC MELODIES, FOR
  VIOLONCELLO AND ORCHESTRA see
  Bruch, Max, Adagio Nach Keltischen
  Melodien, For Violoncello And
  Orchestra

ADAM, ADOLPHE-CHARLES (1803-1856)
  Ah! Vous Dirai-Je, Maman, For Solo
    Voice And Orchestra
    1.2.2.2. 2.0.0.0. strings,S solo
    "Bravour-Variationen. "Ach, Mama,
    Ich Sag Es Dir", For Solo Voice
    And Orchestra" BREITKOPF-L perf
    mat rent   (A24)

  Bravour-Variationen. "Ach, Mama, Ich
    Sag Es Dir", For Solo Voice And
    Orchestra
    see Ah! Vous Dirai-Je, Maman, For
    Solo Voice And Orchestra

ADAM, ADOLPHE-CHARLES (cont'd.)

  Postillon De Longjumeau, Le: Mes Amis
    Écoutez l'Histoire, For Solo
    Voice And Orchestra
    2.2.2.2. 4.2.3.0. perc,strings,T
      solo
    BREITKOPF-L perf mat rent   (A25)

ADAM, CLAUS (1917-1983)
  Concerto Variations '76 [20']
    3.1+English horn.3.2. 2.2.2.1.
      timp,2perc,pno,strings
    MARGUN BP 1060 perf mat rent (A26)

ADAM IN BALLINGSCHAP, FOR NARRATOR AND
  ORCHESTRA see Roos, Robert de

ADAMS, JOHN (1947-   )
  Chairman Dances, The [12']
    2(pic).2.2(bass clar).2. 4.2.2.1.
      timp,3perc,pno,harp,strings
    sc AMP 50480014 $30.00, perf mat
    rent   (A27)

  Common Tones In Simple Time [19']
    3(pic).2.3(clar in A).2. 2.2.0.0.
      2perc,2pno,strings
    sc AMP f.s., perf mat rent   (A28)

  Eros Piano, For Piano And Orchestra
    [14']
    2(pic).2.2(bass clar).2. 2.0.0.0.
      perc,opt synthesizer,strings
    HENDON perf mat rent   (A29)

  Fearful Symmetries [27']
    2(pic).2(English horn).2+bass
      clar.1.4sax. 2.3.3.0. timp,
      synthesizer,pno,strings
    HENDON perf mat rent   (A30)

  Harmonielehre [40']
    4(pic).3(English horn).4(bass
      clar).3+contrabsn. 4.4.3.2.
      timp,4perc,2harp,pno,cel,
      strings
    sc AMP f.s., perf mat rent   (A31)

  Shaker Loops [28']
    string orch
    sc AMP 50488934 $30.00, perf mat
    rent   (A32)

  Short Ride In A Fast Machine [4']
    2+pic.2+English horn.4.3+
      contrabsn. 4.4.3.1. 3perc,
      strings,opt synthesizer
    HENDON   (A33)

  Tromba Lontana [4']
    2+pic.2.2.0. 4.2.0.0. 3perc,
      strings
    HENDON   (A34)

  Wound-Dresser, The, For Solo Voice
    And Orchestra [19']
    2(pic).2.1+bass clar.2. 2.1.0.0.
      timp,synthesizer,strings,Bar
      solo
    HENDON perf mat rent   (A35)

ADAMS, LESLIE (1932-   )
  Blake: Prelude [6']
    2+pic.2.2.2. 4.2.3.1. timp,perc,
      harp,strings
    AM.COMP.AL. perf mat rent   (A36)

  Concerto for Piano and Orchestra
    [24']
    2.2+English horn.1.2. 4.2.3.1.
      timp,perc,cel,strings,pno solo
    AM.COMP.AL.   (A37)

  Ode To Life [12']
    2.2.2.2. 4.3.3.1. timp,perc,cel,
      strings
    sc AM.COMP.AL. $56.85, perf mat
    rent   (A38)

  Symphony No. 1
    2+pic.2+English horn.2+bass
      clar.2. 4.3.3.1. timp,perc,
      harp,cel,strings
    sc AM.COMP.AL. f.s.   (A39)

ADASKIN, MURRAY (1906-   )
  Divertimento No. 6 for Percussion and
    Orchestra
    2.2.2.2. 2.2.1.1. strings,perc
      solo
    CAN.MUS.CENT. MI 1340 A221D   (A40)

  T'filat Shalom, For Violin And
    Orchestra [7']
    2ob,2trp,strings,vln solo
    CAN.MUS.CENT. MI 1311 A221T   (A41)

ADDIO, L' see Ullman, Bo

ADDISON, JOHN MERVYN (1920-   )
  Concertante For Oboe, Clarinet, Horn
    And Orchestra
    2.0.0.2. 2.2.3.0. timp,perc,
      strings,ob solo,clar solo,horn
      solo

ADDISON, JOHN MERVYN (cont'd.)

    OXFORD perf mat rent   (A42)

ADDRESS FOR ORCHESTRA see Walker,
  George Theophilus

ADDRESS: PASSACAGLIA see Walker, George
  Theophilus

ADELAIDE: SINFONIA see Porpora, Nicola
  Antonio

ADEPTEN WALZER, DIE see Strauss,
  Johann, [Sr.]

ADESTE FIDELIS [ARR.]
  (Scott, Earl) 2fl,clar,strings
    [1'30"] KALMUS A4585 set $3.00, pts
    $6.00, $.75, ea.   (A43)

ADHESIONS see Silverman, Faye-Ellen

ADJUSTABLE WRENCH see Torke, Michael

ADLER, JAMES R. (1950-   )
  Suite Moderne [10'30"]
    string orch
    BELWIN perf mat rent   (A44)

ADLER, RICHARD (1921-   )
  Damn Yankees: A Little Brains, A
    Little Talent, For Solo Voice And
    Orchestra
    0.0.4+bass clar.0. 0.3.3.0. perc,
      strings,S solo
    FRANK perf mat rent   (A45)

  Damn Yankees: A Man Doesn't Know, For
    Solo Voice And Orchestra
    0.1(English horn).3+bass clar.0.
      0.3.1.0. perc,gtr,strings,male
      solo
    FRANK perf mat rent   (A46)

  Damn Yankees: Overture
    1+pic.0.3.0.2alto sax.2tenor
      sax.baritone sax. 1.3.3.0.
      perc,gtr,strings
    FRANK perf mat rent   (A47)

  Pajama Game: A New Town Is A Blue
    Town, For Solo Voice And
    Orchestra
    0+opt fl.0+English horn.3+bass
      clar.0. 0.3.3.0. timp,perc,gtr,
      strings,male solo
    FRANK perf mat rent   (A48)

  Pajama Game: Entr'acte
    2alto sax,2tenor sax,baritone
      sax,3trp,3trom,timp,perc,gtr,
      strings
    FRANK perf mat rent   (A49)

  Pajama Game: Hernando's Hideaway, For
    Solo Voice And Orchestra
    1(pic).0.2+bass clar.1.tenor sax.
      0.3.3.0. timp,perc,gtr,strings,
      female solo
    FRANK perf mat rent   (A50)

  Pajama Game: Hey There, For Solo
    Voice And Orchestra
    1.0.3+bass clar.0. 0.3.3.0. timp,
      perc,gtr,strings,male solo
    FRANK perf mat rent   (A51)

  Pajama Game: Overture
    alto sax/clar,alto sax,2tenor
      sax/2clar,baritone sax,3trp,
      3trom,timp,perc,gtr,strings
    FRANK perf mat rent   (A52)

  Pajama Game: Small Town, For Solo
    Voices And Orchestra
    2.0.3+bass clar.1. 0.3.3.0. perc,
      gtr,strings,female solo&male
      solo
    FRANK perf mat rent   (A53)

  Pajama Game: There Once Was A Man,
    For Solo Voices And Orchestra
    4clar,bass clar,3trp,3trom,perc,
      gtr,strings,female solo&male
      solo
    FRANK perf mat rent   (A54)

ADLER, SAMUEL HANS (1928-   )
  Concertino No. 2 [8']
    string orch
    set LUDWIG CSO-13 $30.00   (A55)

  Concerto for Flute and Orchestra
    SOUTHERN rent   (A56)

  Concerto for Piano and Orchestra
    [22']
    2+pic.2.2.2. 4.3.3.1. timp,3perc,
      strings,pno solo
    SCHIRM.G perf mat rent   (A57)

  Four Early American Tunes
    SCHIRM.G f.s.   (A58)

ADLER, SAMUEL HANS (cont'd.)

In Just Spring [8']
PRESSER perf mat rent   (A59)

Joi, Amor & Cortezia [17']
2(pic).2(English horn).2.2.
2.0.0.0. 2perc,strings
SCHIRM.G perf mat rent   (A60)

Symphony No. 5 for Solo Voice and
Orchestra [22']
2+pic.2+English horn.2+bass
clar.2+contrabsn. 4.3.3.1.
timp,3perc,pno,strings,Mez solo
(We are the echoes) sc BOOSEY
$25.00, perf mat rent   (A61)

Symphony No. 6
PRESSER perf mat rent   (A62)

ADOLESCENT, THE see Hively, Wells

ADOLPHE, BRUCE (1955-   )
Dream Of My Parents Dancing, A [12']
1.1.1.1. 2.1.0.0. pno,strings
sc AM.COMP.AL. $19.10   (A63)

Night Journey [15']
2.2.2.0. 4.2.2.0. perc,harp,
strings
sc AM.COMP.AL. $46.90, perf mat
rent   (A64)

ADOLPHUS, MILTON (1913-   )
Cape Cod Suite *Op.200 [16']
2.2.2.2. 4.2.2.0. timp,strings
sc AM.COMP.AL. $16.20   (A65)

Suite No. 2, Op. 62 [20']
2.2.3.2. 4.4.4.0. timp,strings
AM.COMP.AL. perf mat rent   (A66)

ADOMIAN, LAN (1905-1979)
Balada De Terezin, La, For Flute And
Chamber Orchestra [9']
timp,2perc,strings,fl solo
SCHIRM.G perf mat rent   (A67)

Canto [9']
string orch
SCHIRM.G perf mat rent   (A68)

Cinque Canciones D'Espagne
2.2.2.2. 2.2.2.0. timp,strings
SCHIRM.G perf mat rent   (A69)

Clavurenito, For Piano And Orchestra
[15']
2.2.2.2. 2.4.2.1. perc,strings,
pno solo
SCHIRM.G perf mat rent   (A70)

Interplay I [12']
4.4.4.4. 4.4.4.1. timp,perc,pno&
cel,elec gtr,strings
SCHIRM.G perf mat rent   (A71)

Interplay II [16']
4.4.4.4. 4.4.4.1. timp,perc,pno&
cel,elec gtr,strings
SCHIRM.G perf mat rent   (A72)

Israel [18']
2.2.2.2. 2.3.3.0. timp,perc,
strings
SCHIRM.G perf mat rent   (A73)

Lincoln's Gettysburg Address, For
Solo Voice And Orchestra [18']
2(pic).2(English horn).2.2.
2.3.3.0. timp,perc,strings,Bar
solo
SCHIRM.G perf mat rent   (A74)

Little Serenade [7']
1(pic).1.1.1. 1.1.0.0. strings
SCHIRM.G perf mat rent   (A75)

Matin Des Magiciens, Le [17']
2(pic)+alto fl.3+English horn.3+
bass clar.3+contrabsn. 4.4.4.1.
timp,3-4perc,2pno,strings
SCHIRM.G perf mat rent   (A76)

Notturno Patetico [15']
3(pic).3(English horn).2+bass
clar.2. 4.3.3.0. timp,perc,pno,
strings
SCHIRM.G perf mat rent   (A77)

Pantomime [6']
2(pic).2(English horn).2.2.
2.2.2.0. timp,perc,pno,strings
SCHIRM.G perf mat rent   (A78)

Para Ninos [7']
1.1.1.1. 2.1.1.0. perc,cel,
strings
SCHIRM.G perf mat rent   (A79)

Symphony No. 1 [23']
2(pic).2(English horn).2(clar in
A).2. 2.2.2.0. timp,perc,
strings
(Sinfonia Lirica) SCHIRM.G perf mat

ADOMIAN, LAN (cont'd.)

rent   (A80)

Symphony No. 2 [19']
4.4.4.4. 4.4.4.1. timp,2perc,pno,
strings
(Espanola) SCHIRM.G perf mat rent
(A81)

Symphony No. 3 [23']
2+pic.2+English horn.2+bass
clar.2+contrabsn. 4.3.3.1.
timp,2perc,pno,strings
SCHIRM.G perf mat rent   (A82)

Symphony No. 4 [16']
3.3.3.2. 2.2.2.0. timp,2perc,pno,
strings
(Une Petite Musique Pour Sachenk)
SCHIRM.G perf mat rent   (A83)

Symphony No. 5 [23']
3.3.3.3. 4.4.4.1. timp,perc,
strings
(Version II) SCHIRM.G perf mat rent
(A84)

Symphony No. 6 [22']
3.3.3.3. 4.3.3.1. timp,2perc,
strings
(La Cadeau De La Vie) SCHIRM.G perf
mat rent   (A85)

Symphony No. 7 [13']
3(pic).3(English horn).2+bass
clar.2+contrabsn. 4.4.4.1.
timp,perc,pno,strings
SCHIRM.G perf mat rent   (A86)

Symphony No. 8 [19']
3.3.3.3. 4.3.3.1. timp,2perc,pno,
strings
SCHIRM.G perf mat rent   (A87)

Tamayana [19']
4.4.4.4. 4.3.3.1. timp,3perc,pno,
cel,strings
SCHIRM.G perf mat rent   (A88)

Tempo Di Marcia, Version I [6']
3.3.3.2. 4.3.3.1. timp,perc,
strings
SCHIRM.G perf mat rent   (A89)

Tempo Di Marcia, Version II [8']
3.3.3.2. 4.3.3.1. timp,perc,
strings
SCHIRM.G perf mat rent   (A90)

Una Vida [7']
clar,bsn,horn,strings
SCHIRM.G perf mat rent   (A91)

ADRIAN
Soledades [12']
1.1.1.1. 1.0.0.0. timp,perc,pno,
strings,vln/vla/vcl solo
SCHIRM.G perf mat rent   (A92)

ADRIANA LECOUVREUR: ECCO IL MONOLOGO,
FOR SOLO VOICE AND ORCHESTRA see
Ciléa, Francesco

ADRIANA LECOUVREUR: GIUSTO CIELO, FOR
SOLO VOICE AND ORCHESTRA see Ciléa,
Francesco

ADRIANA LECOUVREUR: IO SONO L'UMILE
ANCELLA, FOR SOLO VOICE AND
ORCHESTRA see Ciléa, Francesco

ADRIANA LECOUVREUR: MA, DUNQUE, E VERO?
FOR SOLO VOICES AND ORCHESTRA see
Ciléa, Francesco

ADRIANA LECOUVREUR: MAURIZIO! SIGNORE!
FOR SOLO VOICES AND ORCHESTRA see
Ciléa, Francesco

ADRIANA LECOUVREUR: NON
RISPONDE...APRITE, FOR SOLO VOICES
AND ORCHESTRA see Ciléa, Francesco

ADRIANA LECOUVREUR: OGNI ECO; O
VAGABONDA, FOR SOLO VOICE AND
ORCHESTRA see Ciléa, Francesco

ADRIANA LECOUVREUR: POVERI FIORI, FOR
SOLO VOICE AND ORCHESTRA see Ciléa,
Francesco

ADRIANO IN SIRIA: SINFONIA see
Pergolesi, Giovanni Battista

ADRIENNE LECOUVREUR see Schierbeck,
Poul

ADVENTURA see Read, Thomas Lawrence

ADVENTURE ON EARTH [ARR.] see Williams,
John T.

ADVENTURES OF IAN THE OBOE, THE, FOR
OBOE AND CHAMBER ORCHESTRA see
Raum, Elizabeth

ADVENTURES OF ROBIN HOOD: SYMPHONIC
SUITE see Korngold, Erich Wolfgang

ADVERTISEMENTS, FOR SOLO VOICE AND
ORCHESTRA [ARR.] see Mossolov,
Alexander

AEON see Pernaiachi, Gianfranco

AERE DET EVIGE FOR SOLO SOLOAAR I
LEVET, FOR VOICE AND ORCHESTRA see
Eggen, Arne

AFFIRMATION see Rovics, Howard

AFORISMI II see Pernaiachi, Gianfranco

AFORISMI IN MODO FRIGIO see Grisoni,
Renato

AFRICA see Still, William Grant

AFRICAN ODE see Forsyth, Malcolm

AFRIKANERIN QUADRILLE, DIE see Strauss,
Johann, [Jr.]

AFRO-CONCERTO, FOR PERCUSSION AND
ORCHESTRA see Ishii, Maki

AFTENVINDEN see Strom, Alf Gotlin

AFTER-INTERMISSION OVERTURE, AN see
Hoag, Charles K.

AFTER LONG SILENCE, FOR SOLO VOICE,
OBOE AND STRING ORCHESTRA see
Rorem, Ned

AFTER SPRING RAIN see Swafford, Jan

AFTERIMAGES see Consoli, Marc-Antonio

AFTERLIGHT see Peaslee, Richard

AFTERTHOUGHTS see Samama, Leo

AFTERTHOUGHTS, FOR DOUBLE BASS AND
ORCHESTRA see Brown, Ray

AFTERWARDS EVERYTHING IS TOO LATE, FOR
SOLO VOICE AND ORCHESTRA see Kvam,
Oddvar S., Att Doda Ett Barn, For
Solo Voice And Orchestra

AGAFONNIKOV, VLADISLAV (1936-   )
Concerto for Piano and Orchestra
[20']
2.2.2.0. 4.3.3.0. timp,perc,
strings, flexaton, pno solo
VAAP perf mat rent   (A93)

AGAINST ODDS see Samama, Leo

AGAINST THAT TIME, FOR SOLO VOICE AND
ORCHESTRA see DeFotis, William

AGAM see Samuel, Gerhard

AGITATO, FOR PIANO AND ORCHESTRA see
Sandström, Sven-David

AGNUS DEI, FOR SOLO VOICE AND ORCHESTRA
see Bizet, Georges

AGOPOV, VLADIMIR (1953-   )
Concerto for Violoncello and
Orchestra [24']
3.3.3.3. 4.3.3.1. 3perc,harp,pno,
strings,vcl solo
sc SUOMEN f.s.   (A94)

AGRELL, JOHAN JOACHIM (1701-1765)
Symphonies, Five
(Sheerin; Bebbington; Davis; Hill)
("The Symphony" Vol. C-I) sc
GARLAND ISBN 0-8240-3833-9 $90.00
contains also: Graun, Johann
Gottlieb, Symphonic Works, Three;
Graun, Carl Heinrich, Overtures,
Two; Lang, Johann Georg,
Symphonies,Three   (A95)

AGUILA, MIGUEL DEL
Hexen, For Bassoon And String
Orchestra [12']
string orch,bsn solo
"Witches, For Bassoon And String
Orchestra" PEER perf mat rent
(A96)

Toccata [6']
2(pic).2.2.2. 2.1.1.1. perc,pno,
strings
PEER perf mat rent   (A97)

Witches, For Bassoon And String
Orchestra
see Hexen, For Bassoon And String
Orchestra

ÁGÚSTSSON, HERBERT HRIBERSCHEK
(1926-   )
Adagio Con Variazioni *Op.21
[15'35"]
1.1.1.1. 1.0.0.0. cel,strings
ICELAND 009-023   (A98)

ÁGÚSTSSON, HERBERT HRIBERSCHEK
(cont'd.)

Andante for Horn and String Orchestra
[5']
string orch,horn solo
ICELAND 009-017   (A99)

Concerto for Horn and Orchestra
[13'45"]
ICELAND 009-002   (A100)

Refuge, For Solo Voice And Orchestra
[18'25"]
3.3.3.3. 4.3.3.1. timp,2perc,
strings,S solo
ICELAND 009-001   (A101)

Rondo for Horn and String Orchestra
[8'50"]
string orch,horn solo
ICELAND 009-018   (A102)

Structure II, For Violin And
Orchestra [18']
2.2.2.2. 2.2.3.1. timp,perc,
strings,vln solo
ICELAND 009-022   (A103)

Three Spiritual Songs, For Solo Voice
And Orchestra [9'30"]
2.2.2.2. 4.2.2.0. timp,perc,
strings,solo voice
ICELAND 009-004   (A104)

Two Images
3.2.2.2.sax. 4.4.4.1. timp,5perc,
pno,strings
ICELAND 009-026   (A105)

Variations for Orchestra [10'25"]
3.3.2.2. 4.3.3.1. timp,perc,pno,
strings
ICELAND 009-003   (A106)

AH! CRUDEL, NEL PIANTO MIO, FOR SOLO
VOICE AND ORCHESTRA see Handel,
George Frideric

AH LO PREVIDI, FOR SOLO VOICE AND
ORCHESTRA see Mozart, Wolfgang
Amadeus

AH! PERFIDO, FOR SOLO VOICE AND
ORCHESTRA, OP. 65 see Beethoven,
Ludwig van

AH SE IN CIEL, BENIGNE STELLE, FOR SOLO
VOICE AND ORCHESTRA see Mozart,
Wolfgang Amadeus

AH! VOUS DIRAI-JE, MAMAN, FOR SOLO
VOICE AND ORCHESTRA see Adam,
Adolphe-Charles

AHLIN, SVEN (1951-)
Al Fresco, For Piano And Orchestra
*Op.6 [20']
3.2.3.2. 4.2.2.0. timp,perc,harp,
strings,pno solo
STIM perf mat rent   (A107)

AHNUNG, FOR VIOLIN AND ORCHESTRA see
Lampersberg, Gerhard

AHNUNG DES ENDES see Meijering, Chiel

AHO, KALEVI (1949-)
Concerto for Violoncello and
Orchestra [30']
2.2.3.2.alto sax.
2.2.1.1.baritone horn. timp,
perc,harp,acord,mand,org/cel,
strings,vcl solo
sc SUOMEN f.s.   (A108)

AHVENAINEN, VEIKKO (1929-)
Concert Walz [arr.]
(Katajev, Igor) 3.2.2.2. 4.2.2.1.
timp,perc,harp/pno,strings
[8'30"] FAZER perf mat rent
        (A109)

Finnish Dance No. 1 [4']
2.1.2.1. 2.2.2.1. timp,perc,
strings
FAZER perf mat rent   (A110)

Kallavesi [14']
2.2.2.2. 4.2.3.1. timp,perc,
strings
FAZER perf mat rent   (A111)

Nocturne [7'30"]
2.1.1.1. 4.2.0.0. timp,perc,harp,
pno,strings
FAZER perf mat rent   (A112)

AIDA: MARCIA see Verdi, Giuseppe

AÏDA: SINFONIA 1872 see Verdi, Giuseppe

AIDA: TRIUMPHAL MARCH see Verdi,
Giuseppe, Aida: Marcia

AIGA see Lunde, Ivar

AIN MI see Mitrea-Celarianu, Mihai

AIOLOS see Holm, Mogens Winkel

AION, FOR TIMPANI, PERCUSSION AND
ORCHESTRA see Scelsi, Giacinto

AIR DE BALLET see Herbert, Victor

AIR-METAL see Lalonde, Alain

AIR MIT SPHINXES see Huber, Nicolaus A.

AIR MUSIC see Rorem, Ned

AIRE CLARO, L' see Hultqvist, Anders

AIS, FOR SOLO VOICE AND ORCHESTRA see
Xenakis, Yannis (Iannis)

AISHIHIK, FOR PIANO AND ORCHESTRA see
Ware, Peter

AITKEN, HUGH (1924-)
Concerto for Violin and Orchestra
[21']
PRESSER perf mat rent   (A113)

AIUTO see Monnet, Marc

AJDIC, ALOJZ (1939-)
Adagio Lamentoso, For Flute, Clarinet
And Orchestra [10']
3(pic).2.2(bass clar).2. 4.2.3.0.
timp,perc,strings,fl solo,clar
solo
DRUSTVO DSS 1062 perf mat rent
        (A114)

Fantasy [14']
2(pic).2(English horn).2(soprano
clar in E flat,bass clar).2.
4.2.3.1. timp,perc,harp,strings
DRUSTVO DSS 1060 perf mat rent
        (A115)

Vision Of Colours
see Vizija Barv

Vizija Barv [9']
2(pic).2(English horn).2(soprano
clar in E flat,bass
clar).2(contrabsn).4sax.
4.2.3.1. timp,perc,vibra,xylo,
cel,pno,6vcl,4db
"Vision Of Colours" DRUSTVO
DSS 1061 perf mat rent   (A116)

AKA AKA TO I, II, III, FOR SOLO VOICE
AND INSTRUMENTAL ENSEMBLE see
Sciarrino, Salvatore

AKADEMISCHE-BURGER WALZER see Strauss,
Eduard

AKADEMISCHE FESTOUVERTURE see Brahms,
Johannes

AKASHA, SKY see Buhr, Glenn

AKHMATOVA: REQUIEM, FOR SOLO VOICES AND
ORCHESTRA see Tavener, John

AKHNATON: DANCE see Glass, Philip

AKROASIS FOR SOLO VOICES AND ORCHESTRA
see Fritsch, Johannes Georg

AKROSTICHON see Schultheiss, Ulrich

AKUTAGAWA, YASUSHI (1925-1988)
Concerto Ostinato, For Violoncello
And Orchestra [17']
2.2.2.2. 2.2.2.1. timp,perc,harp,
hpsd,strings,vcl solo
ZEN-ON perf mat rent   (A117)

Prima Sinfonia [28']
3(pic).3(English horn).3(bass
clar).3(contrabsn). 6.3.3.1.
timp,perc,harp,strings
ZEN-ON perf mat rent   (A118)

Sounds, For Organ And Orchestra [16']
4(pic).3(English horn).3(bass
clar).3(contrabsn). 6.3.3.1.
timp,perc,harp,pno,strings,org
solo
JAPAN 8701   (A119)
ZEN-ON perf mat rent   (A120)

Trinita Sinfonica [25']
2.2.2.2. 4.2.2.0. timp,perc,pno,
strings
ZEN-ON perf mat rent   (A121)

AL COMPONER, FOR VIOLA, VIOLONCELLO,
DOUBLE BASS AND ORCHESTRA see
Hidalgo, Manuel

AL DESIO, DI CHI T'ADORA, FOR SOLO
VOICE AND ORCHESTRA see Mozart,
Wolfgang Amadeus

AL FRESCO, FOR PIANO AND ORCHESTRA see
Ahlin, Sven

ALABASTER see Matsushita, Isao

ALADDIN see Hornemann, Christian Emil

ALADDIN: SEVEN PIECES see Nielsen, Carl

ALANDIA, EDGAR (1950-)
Pampa, For Clarinet And Orchestra
[13']
2.2.0.2. 4.2.1.0. timp,perc,
vibra,strings,clar solo
RICORDI-IT 132934 perf mat rent
        (A122)

Sajsayhuaman [15']
3.0.2.0. 3.2.1.0. perc,pno,
strings
RICORDI-IT 133634 perf mat rent
        (A123)

ALAP see Sackman, Nicholas

ALAX see Xenakis, Yannis (Iannis)

ALBA see Leeuw, Ton de

ALBA, FOR SOLO VOICE AND CHAMBER
ORCHESTRA see Osborne, Nigel

ALBADA, INTERLUDI I DANSA see Gerhard,
Roberto

ALBAM, MANNY (1922-)
Concerto For Jazz Alto And Orchestra
[18'50"]
3.2.3.2.alto sax. 4.4.4.1. timp,
perc,kbd,harp,elec bass,
strings,alto sax solo
NEWAM 19003 perf mat rent   (A124)

ALBÉNIZ, ISAAC (1860-1909)
Arbol Azpian
3(pic).2.2.2. 4.2.3.0. timp,perc,
strings
UNION ESP. perf mat rent   (A125)

Asturias, For Guitar, Harp And String
Orchestra [arr.]
(Behrend, Siegfried) string orch,
gtr solo,harp solo/pno solo [4']
SIKORSKI perf mat rent   (A126)

Automne, L'
1+pic.2.2.2. 4.2.3.1. timp,perc,
strings
UNION ESP. perf mat rent   (A127)

Concerto for Piano and Orchestra, Op.
78, [arr.]
(Trayter) 2.2.2.2. 2.2.3.0. timp,
strings,pno solo [26'] (Concierto
Fantastico) min sc UNION ESP.
f.s., perf mat rent   (A128)

Piezas Caracteristicas
2+pic.2.2.2. 4.2.3.0. timp,harp,
strings
UNION ESP. perf mat rent   (A129)

Rapsodia Espanola, For Piano And
Orchestra [arr]
(Enesco, Georges) 3.3.2.2. 4.2.3.1.
timp,perc,harp,strings,pno solo
[15'] SALABERT perf mat rent
        (A130)

Seguidillas (from Cantos De Espana)
1.1.2.1. 2.2.2.0. harp,strings
UNION ESP. perf mat rent   (A131)

Suite Espanola [arr.]
(Fruehbeck De Burgos) 3(pic,alto
fl).2+English horn.2+bass clar.2+
contrabsn. 4.3.3.1. timp,4perc,
harp,cel,strings [42'] UNION ESP.
perf mat rent   (A132)

Variaciones [arr.]
(Halffter, Christobal) 3+pic.2+
English horn.2.2. 4.2.3.1. timp,
perc,strings (Ballet After
"Rapsodia Espanola") UNION ESP.
perf mat rent   (A133)

ALBERO DEI VIVI, L' see Renosto, Paolo

ALBERT, STEPHEN JOEL (1941-)
Anthem And Processionals [16']
3(pic).2+English horn.3(bass
clar).2(contrabsn). 4.3.3.1.
timp,2perc,harp,pno,strings
SCHIRM.G perf mat rent   (A134)

Concerto for Violoncello and
Orchestra [20']
2.2.2.2. 2.2.0.0. perc,harp,pno,
strings,vcl solo
SCHIRM.G perf mat rent   (A135)

Distant Hills Coming Nigh, For Solo
Voices And Instrumental Ensemble
[31']
1.1.1.1. 1.0.0.0. pno,2vln,vla,
vcl,db,ST soli
SCHIRM.G perf mat rent   (A136)

ALBERT, STEPHEN JOEL (cont'd.)

Flower Of The Mountain, For Solo
    Voice And Orchestra [16']
    2.2.2.2. 2.2.0.0. perc,harp,pno,
    strings,S solo
    study sc SCHIRM.G 50488736 f.s.,
    perf mat rent   (A137)

In Concordiam, For Violin And
    Orchestra [18']
    2(pic,alto fl).2(English
    horn).2(bass
    clar).2(contrabsn). 2.2.0.0.
    timp,3perc,strings,vln solo
    SCHIRM.G perf mat rent   (A138)

Into Eclipse, For Solo Voice And
    Orchestra [30']
    2.2.2.2(contrabsn). 4.2.3.1.
    perc,harp,pno&cel,strings,T
    solo, alternate wind scoring:
    1(pic) 01(clref)0 1100
    SCHIRM.G perf mat rent   (A139)

Rivering Waters (from Riverrun) [18']
    3(pic,alto fl).2+English
    horn.2(clar in E flat)+bass
    clar.1+contrabsn.alto sax.
    4.3.3.1. timp,perc,2harp,pno,
    strings
    SCHIRM.G perf mat rent   (A140)

Riverrun [33']
    3(pic,alto fl).2+English
    horn.2(clar in E flat)+bass
    clar.1+contrabsn.alto sax.
    4.3.3.1. timp,perc,vibra,2harp,
    pno,strings
    study sc SCHIRM.G 50480096 $40.00,
    perf mat rent   (A141)

Sun's Heat, For Solo Voice And
    Instrumental Ensemble (from
    Distant Hills Coming Nigh) [15']
    1.1.1.1. 1.0.0.0. pno,2vln,vla,
    vcl,db,T solo
    SCHIRM.G perf mat rent   (A142)

Treestone, For Solo Voices And
    Chamber Orchestra [45']
    1.0.1.0. 1.1.0.0. perc,harp,pno,
    string quin,ST soli
    SCHIRM.G perf mat rent   (A143)

ALBERTSEN, PER HJORT (1919-   )
Capriccio Giovanile *Op.57 [7']
    3.3.3.3. 4.3.3.1. timp,perc,harp,
    strings
    NORGE   (A144)

Concertino for Flute and Orchestra,
    Op. 7 [12']
    0.1.1.1. 2.0.0.0. strings,fl solo
    NORGE   (A145)

Concerto for Piano and Orchestra, Op.
    33
    2.2.2.2. 2.3.2.0. timp,perc,
    strings,pno solo
    NORGE   (A146)

Concerto Piccolo For Violin And
    Amateur String Orchestra
    see Concerto Piccolo For Violin Og
    Amator-Strykeorkester

Concerto Piccolo For Violin Og
    Amator-Strykeorkester *Op.23
    [9']
    string orch,vln solo
    "Concerto Piccolo For Violin And
    Amateur String Orchestra" NORGE
                                     (A147)

Liten Suite For Strykeorkester
    *Op.14 [10']
    string orch
    "Small Suite For String Orchestra"
    NORGE   (A148)

Notturno E Danza *Op.22 [9']
    2.2.2.2. 2.2.2.1. timp,perc,
    strings
    NORGE   (A149)

Presentasjon Ouverture *Op.20 [10']
    2.2.2.2. 3.3.3.1. timp,perc,
    strings
    NORGE   (A150)

Small Suite For String Orchestra
    see Liten Suite For Strykeorkester

Symfonisk Forspill *Op.10 [7']
    2.1.2.2. 3.3.2.0. timp,strings
    "Symphonic Prelude" NORGE (A151)

Symphonic Prelude
    see Symfonisk Forspill

Tordenskioldiana *Op.39 [12']
    2.2.2.2. 3.3.3.0. perc,harp,
    strings
    NORGE   (A152)

ALBERTSEN, PER HJORT (cont'd.)

Two Orchestral Pieces *Op.35
    2.1.2.2. 2.2.2.0. timp,perc,harp,
    strings
    NORGE   (A153)

ALBICASTRO, HENRICUS (? -ca. 1738)
Concerto, Op. 7, No. 6, in F
    (Zulauf) KALMUS A7069 sc $8.00, set
    $10.00, pts $2.00, ea.   (A154)

Concerto, Op. 7, No. 7, in B minor
    (Zulauf) KALMUS A7070 sc $5.00,
    $10.00, pts $2.00, ea.   (A155)

ALBIN, ROGER (1920-   )
Chantefables, For Solo Voice And
    Orchestra [10'18"]
    1(pic).1(English horn).1+bass
    clar.1+contrabsn. 1.1.1.0.
    timp,perc,pno,cel,harp,strings,
    S solo
    RIDEAU perf mat rent   (A156)

Tre Pezzi Pazzi, For Solo Voice And
    Orchestra [23'25"]
    2+pic.2+bass clar.2+contrabsn.
    3.2.2.1. 4perc,strings,A solo
    RIDEAU perf mat rent   (A157)

ALBINONI, TOMASO (1671-1750)
Concerto in B flat, MIN 170, [arr.]
    (Thilde, J.) string orch,trp solo
    [9'35"] sc BILLAUDOT f.s., perf
    mat rent   (A158)

Concerto in D minor, MIN 172, [arr.]
    (Thilde, J.) string orch,trp solo
    [12'20"] BILLAUDOT perf mat rent
                                     (A159)
Concerto, Op. 5, No. 7, in D minor
    (Bonelli) KALMUS A7345 sc $7.00,
    set $9.00, pts $1.50, ea.   (A160)

Concerto, Op. 7, No. 6, in D
    (Kolneder, W.) KUNZEL GM 344 sc
    $12.00, pts $3.00, ea.   (A161)

Concerto, Op. 7, No. 8, in D
    string orch,cont,2ob soli
    (Kolneder, W.) KUNZEL GM 346 sc
    $12.00, pts $3.00, ea.   (A162)

Concerto, Op. 7, No. 9, in F
    (Kolneder, W.) KUNZEL GM 347 sc
    $12.00, pts $3.00, ea.   (A163)

Concerto, Op. 7, No. 11, in C
    string orch,cont,2ob soli
    (Kolneder, W.) KUNZEL GM 349 sc
    $12.00, pts $3.00, ea.   (A164)

Concerto, Op. 7, No. 12, in C
    (Kolneder, W.) KUNZEL GM 350 sc
    $12.00, pts $3.00, ea.   (A165)

Concerto, Op. 9, No. 2, in D minor,
    [arr.]
    (Thilde, J.) string orch,trp solo
    [6'40"] sc BILLAUDOT f.s., perf
    mat rent   (A166)

Sinfonia, Op. 2, No. 1
    string orch,cont
    (Kolneder, W.) KUNZEL GM 305 sc
    $12.00, pts $3.00, ea.   (A167)

Sinfonia, Op. 2, No. 2
    string orch,cont
    (Kolneder, W.) KUNZEL GM 306 sc
    $12.00, pts $3.00, ea.   (A168)

Sinfonia, Op. 2, No. 3
    string orch,cont
    (Kolneder, W.) KUNZEL GM 307 sc
    $12.00, pts $3.00, ea.   (A169)

ALBION POLKA see Strauss, Johann, [Jr.]

ALBJERG, H.C.
Divertimento
    string orch [7'] HANSEN-DEN perf
    mat rent   (A170)

ALBRECHTSBERGER, JOHANN GEORG
    (1736-1809)
Concerto for Horn and String
    Orchestra
    (Leloir, E.) string orch,horn solo
    [15'] sc BILLAUDOT f.s., perf mat
    rent   (A171)

ALBRIGHT, WILLIAM H. (1944-   )
Bacchanal, For Organ And Orchestra
    [15']
    3.3.3(opt contrabass clar).3.
    4.4.3.1. timp,3perc,harp,cel,
    strings,org solo
    PETERS P66918 perf mat rent (A172)

ALBUM DE LOS DUENDECITOS, EL see
    Grantham, Donald

ALBUM DE MADAME BOVARY see Milhaud,
    Darius

ALBUM D'ENFANTS [ARR.] see Telemann,
    Georg Philipp

ALBUM FOR THE YOUNG [ARR.] see
    Telemann, Georg Philipp, Album
    D'enfants [arr.]

ALBUM SUITE FOR MATHILDE WESENDONK
    [ARR.] see Wagner, Richard

ALBUMBLATT see Sigurbjörnsson, Thorkell

ALBUMBLATT, EIN, FOR VIOLIN AND
    ORCHESTRA [ARR.] see Wagner,
    Richard

ALCANDRO, LO CONFESSO, FOR SOLO VOICE
    AND ORCHESTRA see Mozart, Wolfgang
    Amadeus

ALCANDRO, LO CONFESSO (I), FOR SOLO
    VOICE AND ORCHESTRA see Mozart,
    Wolfgang Amadeus

ALCANDRO, LO CONFESSO (II), FOR SOLO
    VOICE AND ORCHESTRA see Mozart,
    Wolfgang Amadeus

ALCAPHANTE POUR FLUTES, FOR FLUTE AND
    ORCHESTRA see Tisne, Antoine

ALCAZAR, MIGUEL (1942-   )
Hommage A Webern
    1.1.1.1. 1.1.1.1. cel,strings
    LIGA   (A173)

ALCESTE: DIE IHR IM HADES HERRSCHT, FOR
    SOLO VOICE AND ORCHESTRA see Gluck,
    Christoph Willibald, Ritter von,
    Alceste: Divinites Du Styx, For
    Solo Voice And Orchestra

ALCESTE: DIVINITES DU STYX, FOR SOLO
    VOICE AND ORCHESTRA see Gluck,
    Christoph Willibald, Ritter von

ALCESTE: OÙ SUIS-JE? NON, CE N'EST
    POINT UN SACRIFICE, FOR SOLO VOICE
    AND ORCHESTRA see Gluck, Christoph
    Willibald, Ritter von

ALCESTE: WO BIN ICH? NEIN, NICHT EIN
    OPFER WERD ICH'S NENNEN, FOR SOLO
    VOICE AND ORCHESTRA see Gluck,
    Christoph Willibald, Ritter von,
    Alceste: Où Suis-Je? Non, Ce N'est
    Point Un Sacrifice, For Solo Voice
    And Orchestra

ALCOCK, JOHN
Concerti Grossi, Six *see THREE
    CENTURIES OF MUSIC IN SCORE, VOL.
    3: CONCERTO II, ENGLAND

ALCYONE, FOR SOLO VOICES AND ORCHESTRA
    see Ravel, Maurice

ALDATZA, FOR SOLO VOICE AND CHAMBER
    ORCHESTRA see Larrauri, Anton

ALDATZA, FOR SOLO VOICE AND ORCHESTRA
    see Larrauri, Anton

ALEF. HOMMAGE À SCHÖNBERG see Jeney,
    Zoltan

ALEGRIAS, FOR PIANO AND CHAMBER
    ORCHESTRA see Hidalgo, Manuel

ALEKO: SUITE see Rachmaninoff, Sergey
    Vassilievich

ALEPH, FOR SOLO VOICES AND ORCHESTRA
    see Manoury, Philippe

ALEPH. SINFONIA SACRA see Werner, Jean-
    Jacques

ALESSANDRO, RAFAELE D' (1911-1959)
Concerto for Bassoon and String
    Orchestra, Op. 75
    string orch,bsn solo
    (Meylan) sc AMADEUS BP 386 f.s.,
    perf mat rent   (A174)

ALEXANDER BALU: HORCH, ER SCHLÄGT DAS
    GOLDNE SPIEL, FOR SOLO VOICE AND
    ORCHESTRA see Handel, George
    Frideric, Alexander Balus: Hark! He
    Strikes The Golden Lyre, For Solo
    Voice And Orchestra

ALEXANDER BALUS: HARK! HE STRIKES THE
    GOLDEN LYRE, FOR SOLO VOICE AND
    ORCHESTRA see Handel, George
    Frideric

ALEXANDER IN INDIA, FOR SOLO VOICE AND
    ORCHESTRA see Kozeluch, Johann
    Anton (Jan Evangelista)

ALEXANDRIAN SEQUENCE, THE see Hamilton, Iain

ALEXANDRINE POLKA see Strauss, Johann, [Jr.]

ALFVÉN, HUGO (1872-1960)
Symphony No. 2, Op. 11, in D [55']
3(pic).2+English horn.2+bass
clar.2+contrabsn. 4.2.3.1.
timp,perc,strings
HANSEN-DEN perf mat rent   (A175)

Tva Folkmelodier [4']
string orch
GEHRMANS sc 6017P f.s., pts 6017S
f.s.   (A176)

ALIA see Guarnieri, Adriano

ALICE NEL PAESE DELLE MERAVIGLIE:
WONDERLAND VARIATIONS see Testoni,
Giampaolo

ALICE SYMPHONY, AN, FOR SOLO VOICE AND
ORCHESTRA see Del Tredici, David

ALIPRANDI, PAUL (1925-   )
A Une Dame Creole, For Solo Voice And
Orchestra [2']
2.1.2.1. 2.2.2.1. perc,harp,pno,
strings,S solo
BILLAUDOT perf mat rent   (A177)

Ouverture Pour Un Drame Lyrique [10']
3.3.3.3. 4.3.3.1. timp,perc,harp,
cel,strings
BILLAUDOT perf mat rent   (A178)

Prelude Pour Rebecca [5']
2.1.2.2. 2.0.0.0. perc,strings
BILLAUDOT perf mat rent   (A179)

Reversibilite, For Solo Voice And
Orchestra
2.1.2.1. 2.2.2.0. perc,harp,
strings,S solo
[4'40"] BILLAUDOT perf mat rent
(A180)

ALIRULI-ALIZADE, AKSHIN (1937-   )
Symphony No. 4 for Solo Voice and
String Orchestra [23']
string orch,T solo
VAAP perf mat rent   (A181)

ALIS, ROMAN (1931-   )
Impresion, For Solo Voice And Chamber
Orchestra
1+pic.1.1.1. 0.0.0.0. perc,pno,
strings,S solo
ALPUERTO   (A182)

Invocacion, For Solo Voice And
Orchestra
ALPUERTO   (A183)

Musica Para Un Festival En Sevilla
*Op.60 [12'50"]
2.2.2.2. 4.2.3.1. timp,perc,xylo,
strings
ALPUERTO   (A184)

Reverberaciones *Op.85 [12'15"]
2+2pic.3.3+2bass clar.3+
contrabsn. 6.4.3.1. timp,perc,
pno,cel,2harp,strings
ALPUERTO   (A185)

ALIX, RENÉ (1907-1966)
Prelude, Barcarolle, Valse A La
Maniere De Chopin [7']
pno,strings
BILLAUDOT perf mat rent   (A186)

ALKAN, CHARLES-HENRI VALENTIN
(1813-1888)
Concerto Da Camera, For Piano And
String Orchestra, No. 2
string orch,pno solo
BILLAUDOT perf mat rent   (A187)

Festin d'Esope, Le [arr]
(Starr, Mark) 2+pic.2.2+bass
clar.2+contrabsn. 4.3.3.1. perc,
harp,pno&cel,strings [10']
FISCHER,C perf mat rent   (A188)

Ouverture De Concert [arr.]
(Starr, Mark) 2+pic.2.2.2+
contrabsn. 4.3.3.1. timp,perc,
strings [18'] FISCHER,C perf mat
rent   (A189)

Symphony, Op. 39, [arr.]
(Starr, Mark) 3(pic).2.2.3+
contrabsn. 4.3.3.1. timp,perc,
harp,strings [30'] FISCHER,C perf
mat rent   (A190)
(Stover, Franklin) COMPOSER'S GR
(A191)

ALKEMA, HENK (1944-   )
Sinfonia [15']
2.1.1.1. 1.1.1.0. perc,harp,
strings
DONEMUS perf mat rent   (A192)

ALL IN THE GOLDEN AFTERNOON, FOR SOLO
VOICE AND ORCHESTRA see Del
Tredici, David

ALL MY INSTINCTS see Gupta, Rolf

ALL PRAISE TO MUSIC see Nelson, Ronald
J. (Ron)

ALLA MARCIA see Blacher, Boris see
Gropp, Johann-Maria

ALLANBROOK, DOUGLAS PHILLIPS
(1921-   )
Serenade [30']
3(pic).2+English horn.2+bass
clar.2. 2.1.0.0. timp,pno,
strings
BOOSEY perf mat rent   (A193)

Symphony No. 5 [20']
2+pic.2.2.2. 0.0.0.0. timp,perc,
strings,brass quin soli
BOOSEY perf mat rent   (A194)

ALLE MEINE ENTCHEN, FOR SOLO VOICE AND
STRING ORCHESTRA see Volkmann,
Joachim

ALLEGORIA DELLA NOTTE, FOR VIOLIN AND
ORCHESTRA see Sciarrino, Salvatore

ALLEGORIES D'EXIL I: EXERGUE, FOR
VIOLONCELLO AND INSTRUMENTAL
ENSEMBLE see Lenot, Jacques

ALLEGORIES D'EXIL IV: DOLCEZZE IGNOTE
ALL'ESTASI see Lenot, Jacques

ALLEGORIES D'EXIL X: EPILOGUE see
Lenot, Jacques

ALLEGRETTO, FOR BASSOON AND ORCHESTRA
see Szalowski, Antoni

ALLEGRETTO GIOCOSO see Hesselberg,
Eyvind

ALLEGRETTO PASTORALE, FOR OBOE AND
STRING ORCHESTRA see Arnita,
Salvador

ALLEGRO ALLA TALA, FOR VIOLONCELLO AND
ORCHESTRA see Okamoto, Masami

ALLEGRO APPASSIONATO, FOR PIANO AND
ORCHESTRA see Saint-Saëns, Camille

ALLEGRO ENERGICO [ARR.] see Grieg,
Edvard Hagerup

ALLEGRO FESTIVO E SOLENNE NORVEGESE see
Andersen, Karl August

ALLEGRO MODERATO see Bridge, Frank

ALLEMAN see Ketting, Otto

ALLEMANDA 1 ET 2 [ARR.] see Dumont,
Henri

ALLEN'S LANDING see Tull, Fisher Aubrey

ALLES REDET JETZT UND SINGET, FOR SOLO
VOICES AND ORCHESTRA see Telemann,
Georg Philipp

ALLIK, KRISTI (1952-   )
Three Textures, For Violoncello And
String Orchestra
string orch,vcl solo
CAN.MUS.CENT. MI 1613 A436TH (A195)

ALLMACHT, DIE, "GROSS IST JEHOVA", FOR
SOLO VOICE AND ORCHESTRA, [ARR.]
see Schubert, Franz (Peter)

ALLOEIDEA see Rouse, Christopher

ALLTAGLICHE, DAS, FOR SOLO VOICES AND
ORCHESTRA see Bredemeyer, Reiner

ALMA GRANDE E NOBIL CORE, FOR SOLO
VOICE AND ORCHESTRA see Mozart,
Wolfgang Amadeus

ALMACKS QUADRILLE see Strauss, Johann,
[Sr.]

ALMILA, ATSO (1953-   )
Concerto for Tuba and String
Orchestra [16']
string orch,tuba solo
sc SUOMEN f.s.   (A196)

Concerto for Violin and Orchestra
[24']
2.2.2.2. 4.2.2.0. perc,strings,
vln solo
sc SUOMEN f.s.   (A197)

Symphony for Brass Quintet and
Orchestra [25']
2(pic).2(English horn).2(bass
clar.)2(contrabsn). 4.0.0.0.
2perc,strings,brass quin soli

ALMILA, ATSO (cont'd.)

sc SUOMEN f.s.   (A198)

ALMZAUBER IDYLLE, FOR TRUMPET AND
ORCHESTRA see Tanterl, H.

ALNADOS DE ESPANA, LOS see Still,
William Grant

ALNAES, EYVIND (1872-1932)
Februarmorgen Ved Golfen, For Solo
Voice And Orchestra *Op.28,No.3
[4']
4horn,harp,strings,Mez solo
"February Morning At The Gulf, For
Solo Voice And Orchestra" HANSEN-
DEN perf mat rent   (A199)

February Morning At The Gulf, For
Solo Voice And Orchestra
see Februarmorgen Ved Golfen, For
Solo Voice And Orchestra

Three Songs, For Solo Voice And
Orchestra, Op. 17 [12']
2.2.2.2. 4.2.3.1. timp,harp,
strings,Mez/Bar solo
HANSEN-DEN perf mat rent   (A200)

Three Songs, For Solo Voice And
Orchestra, Op. 26, No. 2, Op. 30,
No. 2, Op.31, No. 3 [10']
2.2.2.2. 4.0.0.0. timp,harp,
strings,Mez/Bar solo
HANSEN-DEN perf mat rent   (A201)

ALO-AHE see Danczak, Jul

ALONGSIDE see Finnissy, Michael

ALONSO, MIGUEL (1925-   )
Nube-Musica, For Solo Voice And
Chamber Orchestra [11'5"]
2bsn,2horn,perc,pno,strings,S
solo
sc ALPUERTO f.s.   (A202)

ALPENLANDISCHE SUITE see Grabner,
Hermann

ALPENSINFONIE, EINE [ARR.] see Strauss,
Richard

ALPHA CENTAURE see Durville, Philippe

ALPHA ES ET O see Werner, Jean-Jacques

ALPHORN CONCERTO "IN THE CELTIC MANNER"
see Schwertsik, Kurt

ALSO NORWAY see Hyla, Leon (Lee)

ALT VANDRER MAANEN, FOR SOLO VOICE AND
ORCHESTRA see Sjögren, (Johan
Gustaf) Emil

ALTAR, FOR SOLO VOICE AND STRING
ORCHESTRA see Jensen, Ludwig Irgens

ALTBERLINER LUSTPIEL OUVERTURE see
Bruchmann, Klaus Peter

ALTDEUTSCHE SUITE see Höffner, Paul
Marx

ALTDORFER-PASSION, FOR SOLO VOICES AND
INSTRUMENTAL ENSEMBLE see
Kropfreiter, Augustinus Franz

ALTE NIEDERDEUTSCHE VOLKSTANZE see
Niemann, Walter

ALTERED STATES BALLET see Corigliano,
John

ALTERNANZE see Bettinelli, Bruno

ALTERNATING NOTES FOR ORCHESTRA see
Persen, John, Dreieitoner For
Orkester

ALTISSIMO see Einaudi, Ludovico

ALTO-SEPTUOR see Masson, Gerard

ALTO TAMBOUR, FOR 2 VIOLAS AND STRING
ORCHESTRA see Masson, Gerard

ALUCINACION see Ibarrondo, Felix

ALVORADA see Hartke, Stephen Paul

ALVORADA NA FLORESTA TROPICAL see
Villa-Lobos, Heitor

ALYSSA, FOR SOLO VOICES AND ORCHESTRA
see Ravel, Maurice

ÅM, MAGNAR (1952-   )
And Let The Boat Slip Quietly Out,
For Solo Voice And Orchestra
[9'30"]
4.2.4.4. 4.2.3.1. timp,2perc,pno,
synthesizer,strings,solo voice
(winds may be reduced to 3.1.2.2.

ÅM, MAGNAR (cont'd.)

4.2.3.0.) NORGE   (A203)

If We Lift As One [7'5"]
  4.3.4.4. 4.3.3.1. timp,2perc,pno,
  strings
NORGE   (A204)

Min Klode Mi Sjel (Symphony) [27']
  2.2.2.3. 3.2.2.0. timp,perc,harp,
  strings,S solo
NORGE   (A205)

Studie Over Ein Salmetone Fra Luster
  [9']
  string orch
  "Study On A Norwegian Hymn" NORSK
                                   (A206)
Study On A Norwegian Hymn
  see Studie Over Ein Salmetone Fra
  Luster

Symphony
  see Min Klode Mi Sjel

Tvers Gjennom Alt Dette [20'30"]
  2.2.2.3. 2.3.2.0. timp,perc,harp,
  pno&harmonium,strings
NORGE   (A207)

AMADIGI: PENA TIRANNA, FOR SOLO VOICE
  AND ORCHESTRA see Handel, George
  Frideric

AMADIGI: QUALEN OHNE ENDE, FOR SOLO
  VOICE AND ORCHESTRA see Handel,
  George Frideric, Amadigi: Pena
  Tiranna, For Solo Voice And
  Orchestra

AMAZON II see Tower, Joan

AMAZONEN QUADRILLE see Strauss, Josef

AMBER WAVES, FOR BRASS QUARTET AND
  ORCHESTRA see Peck, Russell James

AMBROSI, ALEARCO (1931-)
  Divertimento Su Temi Del XVI Secolo,
  For Orchestra [11']
  2.2.1.1. 2.2.2.0. timp,perc,xylo,
  cel,harp,strings
SONZOGNO perf mat rent   (A208)

Divertimento Su Temi Del XVI Secolo,
  For String Orchestra [11']
  string orch
SONZOGNO perf mat rent   (A209)

AMBROSIUS, HERMANN (1897- ?)
  Eleusisches Fest, Ein *Op.8 [15']
  2.2.2.2. 2.2.0.0. timp,perc,harp,
  strings
KAHNT perf mat rent   (A210)

AMBUSH ON ALL SIDES, FOR PIPA AND
  ORCHESTRA see Mut, Man-Chung

AMDAHL, MAGNE (1943-)
  Concerto for Piano and Orchestra, No.
  1 [19']
  3.2.4.3.sax. 4.3.3.1. timp,3perc,
  elec gtr,strings,pno solo
NORGE   (A211)

Sailing
  see Seiling

Seiling [4']
  2.2.2.2. 3.3.3.0. timp,perc,pno/
  acord,strings
  "Sailing" NORGE   (A212)

AMEN II see Sjöberg, Johan Magnus

AMENDMENT I, FOR ORCHESTRA AND TAPE see
  Brandon, Seymour (Sy)

AMERICA: A VISION [ARR.] see Bean,
  Mabel

AMERICA(N) (DAY)DREAMS, FOR SOLO VOICE
  AND ORCHESTRA see Kernis, Aaron Jay

AMERICAN ACCENTS see Stock, David
  Frederick

AMERICAN CARNIVAL OVERTURE see Kraft,
  William

AMERICAN CONCERTO, FOR VIOLIN AND
  ORCHESTRA [ARR.] see Gusikoff,
  Michel

AMERICAN DANCE NO. 1, NO. 2 AND NO. 3
  see Goeb, Roger

AMERICAN DANCE NO. 4 see Goeb, Roger

AMERICAN DANCE NO. 5 see Goeb, Roger

AMERICAN DANCE SUITE see Amram, David
  Werner

AMERICAN FOLK SONG SUITE see Biggs,
  John

AMERICAN HYMN see Schuman, William
  Howard

AMERICAN INVENTION see Martland, Steve

AMERICAN ODE, AN see Kountz, G.

AMERICAN OVERTURE see Knight, Eric see
  Murray, Lyn

AMERICAN OVERTURE, AN see Britten,
  [Sir] Benjamin

AMERICAN RHAPSODY see Delius, Frederick

AMERICAN SCENE, THE see Still, William
  Grant

AMERICAN SERENADE see Dorati, Antal

AMERICAN SYMPHONY NO. 5 see Kaufman,
  Fredrick

AMERICANA see Kolar, Victor

AMERIKA: ORCHESTRA SUITE see Kohs,
  Ellis Bonoff

AMERIKANERIN, DIE, FOR SOLO VOICE AND
  STRING ORCHESTRA see Bach, Johann
  Christoph Friedrich

AMERS see Arcuri, Serge

AMES, WILLIAM T. (1901-)
  Concerto for Clarinet and Chamber
  Orchestra [25']
  1.1.1.1. 1.1.1.0. timp,strings,
  clar solo
sc AM.COMP.AL. $30.10   (A213)

Excursion II [12']
  2.2.2.2. 2.2.0.0. timp,strings
sc AM.COMP.AL. $9.60   (A214)

Morning [20']
  2.2.2.2. 4.2.2.0. timp,perc,
  strings
sc AM.COMP.AL. $15.30   (A215)

Nocturne And Scherzo For 2 Pianos And
  String Orchestra [5']
  string orch without db,2pno soli
AM.COMP.AL. sc $9.15, pts $6.90,
  perf mat rent   (A216)

Prelude [2']
  string orch
sc AM.COMP.AL. $3.85   (A217)

Symphony No. 1 [20']
  2.2.2.2. 2.2.2.1. perc,strings
sc AM.COMP.AL. $40.40   (A218)

AMICO FRITZ, L': DUET AND SUZEL'S
  LAMENT "NON MI RESTA CHE IL PIANTO
  ED IL DOLORE", FOR SOLO VOICES AND
  ORCHESTRA see Mascagni, Pietro

AMICO FRITZ, L': ED ANCHE BEPPE AMO; O
  AMORE, FOR SOLO VOICE AND ORCHESTRA
  see Mascagni, Pietro

AMICO FRITZ, L': IL PADRONE FRA POCO
  SARA DESTO, FOR SOLO VOICES AND
  ORCHESTRA see Mascagni, Pietro

AMICO FRITZ, L': LACERI MISERI, FOR
  SOLO VOICE AND ORCHESTRA see
  Mascagni, Pietro

AMICO FRITZ, L': O PALLIDA CHE UN
  GIORNO MI GUARDASTI, FOR SOLO VOICE
  AND ORCHESTRA see Mascagni, Pietro

AMICO FRITZ, L': PER VOI, FOR SOLO
  VOICE AND ORCHESTRA see Mascagni,
  Pietro

AMICO FRITZ, L': SON POCHI FIORI, FOR
  SOLO VOICE AND ORCHESTRA see
  Mascagni, Pietro

AMID NATURE see Dvořák, Antonín

AMISTAD see Roosevelt, [Joseph] Willard

AMON, JOHANN ANDREAS (1763-1825)
  Concerto For Viola And Orchestra, Op.
  10, In G *see THREE CENTURIES OF
  MUSIC IN SCORE, VOL. 5: CONCERTO
  IV, CLASSICAL STRINGS AND WINDS

AMOR BRUJO, EL, FIRST VERSION see
  Falla, Manuel de

AMOR ET LABOR see Søderlind, Ragnar

AMORE MEDICO, L': OVERTURE see Wolf-
  Ferrari, Ermanno

AMOUR DES TROIS ORANGES, L': SUITE see
  Prokofiev, Serge, Love Of Three
  Oranges: Suite

AMPHITRYON 4: MINIATURE OVERTURE see
  Blumenfeld, Harold

AMPHITRYON: SUITE, [ARR.] see Purcell,
  Henry

AMRAM, DAVID WERNER (1930-)
  Across The Wide Missouri [10']
  2.2(English horn).2.2. 4.2.3.1.
  timp,2-3perc,harp,strings
PETERS P67011 $17.50, perf mat rent
                                   (A219)

American Dance Suite [20']
  2.2.2.2. 2.2.1.1. perc,strings
sc PETERS P67151 $30.00, perf mat
  rent   (A220)

Aya Zehn, For Oboe Or Trumpet And
  Orchestra [5']
  2.2.2.2. 4.2.2.2. 3perc,strings,
  ob/trp solo
PETERS P67073 perf mat rent   (A221)

Fox Hunt, The [2']
  2.2.2.2. 4.2.3.1. perc,strings
PETERS P67037 perf mat rent   (A222)

Honor Song, For Violoncello And
  Orchestra [25']
  2(pic).2(English horn).2(bass
  clar).2. 2.2.2.0. 4perc,
  strings,vcl solo
PETERS P66955 perf mat rent   (A223)

Travels, For Trumpet And Orchestra
  [15']
  2(pic).2(English horn).2.2.
  4.2.2.0. timp,3perc,strings,trp
  solo
PETERS P67063 perf mat rent   (A224)

AMUSEMENT PARK SUITE see Horwood,
  Michael

AMUSEMENT PATHETIQUE, FOR VIOLIN AND
  ORCHESTRA see Donizetti, Gaetano

AMY, GILBERT (1936-)
  Refrains
  4.3.3.3. 4.3.3.1. timp,3perc,
  marimba,harp,elec gtr,cel,pno,
  strings
sc UNIVER. UE 15753 f.s., perf mat
  rent   (A225)

Shin'anim Sha'ananim, For Solo Voice,
  Violoncello And Instrumental
  Ensemble [15']
  3.0.3.0. 0.1.0.0. 2perc,harp,cel,
  pno,4vcl,2db,vcl solo,Mez solo
sc UNIVER. UE17106 $25.00, perf mat
  rent   (A226)

Variation Ajoutee, La [17']
  2pic,English horn,2basset horn,
  bsn,2perc,pno,harp,vln,vla,vcl,
  db,electronic tape
AMPHION perf mat rent   (A227)

AN DER MOLDAU POLKA see Strauss,
  Johann, [Jr.]

AN DER WOLGA POLKA see Strauss, Johann,
  [Jr.]

AN DIE HOFFNUNG, SOLO VOICE AND
  ORCHESTRA, [ARR.] see Beethoven,
  Ludwig van

AN DIE MUSIK, FOR SOLO VOICE AND
  CHAMBER GROUP see Birtwistle,
  Harrison

AN DIE MUSIK, FOR SOLO VOICE AND
  ORCHESTRA, [ARR.] see Schubert,
  Franz (Peter)

AN EINE AOLSHARFE, FOR GUITAR AND
  INSTRUMENTAL ENSEMBLE see Henze,
  Hans Werner

AN MAGRIT see Jordan, Sverre

AN MEINE SEELE, FOR SOLO VOICE AND
  ORCHESTRA see Ebel, Arnold

ANA ET L'ALBATROS: INTERLUDE see
  Bondon, Jacques

ANABASIS see Roosendael, Jan Rokus van

ANACREON: OVERTURE see Cherubini, Luigi

ANACRUSI see Tykesson, Nils

ANAGAMIN see Scelsi, Giacinto

ANAHATA see Levinson, Gerald

ANAHIT, FOR VIOLIN AND INSTRUMENTAL
  ENSEMBLE see Scelsi, Giacinto

ANAKREONS GRAB, FOR SOLO VOICE AND
   ORCHESTRA see Wolf, Hugo

ANALOGIE see DuBois, Pierre-Max

ANAMORPHOSE see Eder, Helmut

ANAMORPHOSE, FOR PIANO AND CHAMBER
   ORCHESTRA see Tanaka, Karen

ANANDA, JOY, FOR SOLO VOICE AND
   INSTRUMENTAL ENSEMBLE see Buhr,
   Glenn

ANANKE see Bergman, Erik

ANAO see Houdy, Pierick

ANAPHORES, FOR PIANO AND ORCHESTRA see
   Zinsstag, Gérard

ANBRUCH DES TAGES, DER see Su, Cong

ANCELIN, PIERRE (1934-   )
   Capriccio for String Orchestra [20']
      string orch
      sc BILLAUDOT $50.75, perf mat rent
                        (A228)

   Concerto for Flute and Orchestra
     [18']
      perc,pno,strings,fl solo
      BILLAUDOT perf mat rent   (A229)

   Hommage A Ghirlandaio, For
     Violoncello And Orchestra
     CHOUDENS perf mat rent   (A230)

   Ouverture Pour Les Achariens [6']
      2.2.2.2. 2.2.2.1. timp,perc,cel,
       strings
      BILLAUDOT perf mat rent   (A231)

   Silene, For Bassoon And Instrumental
     Ensemble [14']
      1.1.1.0. 0.0.0.0. pno,cel,string
       quin,bsn solo
      BILLAUDOT perf mat rent   (A232)

   Sinfonietta for String Orchestra
     [15']
      string orch
      BILLAUDOT perf mat rent   (A233)

ANCIENT DANCES see Asgeirsson, Jon

ANCIENT GREEK MELODIES see Harris,
   Matthew

ANCIENT MUSIC, FOR PIANO AND CHAMBER
   ORCHESTRA see Grahn, Ulf

AND ALL THE FLAVOURS AROUND see
   Sandström, Sven-David

AND IN THESE TIMES: SEASON'S GREETINGS
   see Ward-Steinman, David

AND LET THE BOAT SLIP QUIETLY OUT, FOR
   SOLO VOICE AND ORCHESTRA see Åm,
   Magnar

AND MARSYAS, FOR SOLO VOICE AND
   INSTRUMENTAL ENSEMBLE see Samuel,
   Gerhard

AND STILL..., FOR HORN AND ORCHESTRA
   see Cowles, Darleen

AND THE GREAT DAY THAT DAWNS see
   Raminsh, Imant

AND THEN WE SAW A SEA LION, FOR MARIMBA
   AND ORCHESTRA see Yavelow,
   Christopher Johnson

ANDANDO NEL SOLE CHE ABBAGLIA see
   Cappelli, Gilberto

ANDANTE CANTABILE ET RONDO, FOR TRUMPET
   AND STRING ORCHESTRA [ARR.] see
   Mozart, Wolfgang Amadeus

ANDANTE CON MOTO see Hjellemo, Ole

ANDANTE E PRESTO IN D [ARR.] see
   Tartini, Giuseppe

ANDANTE FESTIVO see Sibelius, Jean

ANDANTE FUNEBRE see Olsen, Sparre

ANDANTE SOSTENUTO see Pennisi,
   Francesco

ANDANTE, VARIATIONEN UND BOLERO, FOR
   FLUTE AND ORCHESTRA see
   Lindpainter, Peter Joseph

ANDANTINO see Bizet, Georges see
   Hoemsnes, Bjørn Korsan

ANDANTINO FOR OBOE AND STRING ORCHESTRA
   see Dittersdorf, Karl Ditters von

ANDERS, CHRISTIAN (1944-   )
   Malibu-Sinfonie [25']
      2.0.2.0. 3.4.3.0. timp,perc,harp,
       pno,elec gtr,strings,opt wom
       cor
      SIKORSKI perf mat rent   (A234)

ANDERSEN, KARL AUGUST (1903-1970)
   Allegro Festivo E Solenne Norvegese
     [11']
      3.3.3.2. 4.3.3.1. timp,perc,
       strings
      NORGE   (A235)

   Humoreske [8']
      1.0.1.0. 1.1.1.0. pno,harmonium,
       strings
      NORGE   (A236)

   Pilemonsteret: Suite [40']
      2.2.2.2. 2.2.2.0. perc,strings
      NORGE   (A237)

   Suite [30']
      1.1.1.1. 2.2.1.1. timp,perc,
       strings
      NORGE   (A238)

   Symphony for Chamber Orchestra [28']
      1.1.1.1. 1.1.1.1. strings
      NORGE   (A239)

   To Norske Danser [7']
      1.0.1.0. 1.1.1.0. pno,harmonium,
       strings
      "Two Norwegian Dances" NORGE (A240)

   Two Norwegian Dances
     see To Norske Danser

ANDERSEN-WINGAR, ALFRED (1869-1952)
   Suite No. 2 [14']
      2.2.2.2. 4.2.3.1. timp,perc,harp,
       strings
      NORGE   (A241)

ANDERSON, BETH
   Revel [8']
      1.1.1.1. 2.2.1.1. perc,harp,
       strings
      sc AM.COMP.AL. $27.15, perf mat
       rent   (A242)

   Revelation [12']
      1.2.1.2. 2.1.0.0. timp,perc,pno,
       strings
      sc AM.COMP.AL. $25.90   (A243)

ANDERSON, JEAN (1939-   )
   Theme and Variations [5']
      2.2.2.2. 2.2.1.0. timp,perc,
       strings
      CAN.MUS.CENT. MI 1200 A547T (A244)

ANDERSON, LEROY (1908-1975)
   Classical Jukebox [2'30"]
      2+pic.2+English horn.2+bass
       clar.2+contrabsn. 4.3.3.1.
       timp,perc,harp,opt pno,strings
      WOODBURY perf mat rent   (A245)

   Concerto for Piano and Orchestra in C
     [16']
      2+pic.2.2.2. 4.3.3.1. perc,
       strings,pno solo
      (available from Theodore Presser
       Co.) WOODBURY perf mat rent
                        (A246)

ANDERSON, RUTH (1928-   )
   Fugue [7']
      string orch
      sc AM.COMP.AL. $4.60, perf mat rent
                        (A247)

   Two Movements [6']
      string orch
      sc AM.COMP.AL. $9.15, perf mat rent
                        (A248)

   Two Pieces [10']
      string orch
      sc AM.COMP.AL. $9.95, perf mat rent
                        (A249)

ANDERSON, THOMAS JEFFERSON (1928-   )
   Horizons '76, For Solo Voice And
     Orchestra [50']
      3.3.3.3.sax. 4.3.3.1. timp,harp,
       pno&cel,strings,S solo
      sc AM.COMP.AL. $55.05, perf mat
       rent   (A250)

   In Memoriam Malcolm X, For Solo Voice
     And Orchestra [10']
      2+pic.2.2.2.alto sax. 4.3.3.1.
       perc,pno,strings,med solo
      sc AM.COMP.AL. $16.90, perf mat
       rent   (A251)

ANDERSSON, GERT OVE
   Conflicts
     see Konflikter

   Impression, For Violin And Orchestra
     [4'10"]
      2.0.2(bass clar).0. 3.3.0.0.
       harp,cel,strings,vln solo
      BUSCH HBM 016 perf mat rent (A252)

ANDERSSON, GERT OVE (cont'd.)

   Konflikter [11'55"]
      2(alto fl).2(English horn).2(bass
       clar).2. 4.3.3.0. timp,perc,
       harp,cel,strings
      "Conflicts" BUSCH HBM 014 perf mat
       rent   (A253)

   Zick-Zack [3'5"]
      2.2.2.2. 3.3.3.0. timp,perc,harp,
       gtr,pno,strings
      "Zig-Zag" BUSCH perf mat rent
                        (A254)

   Zig-Zag
     see Zick-Zack

ANDERSSON, MAGNUS F. (1953-   )
   Vasca Da Bagno [13']
      3.3.3.3. 4.3.3.1. timp,3perc,
       harp,pno,strings
      STIM   (A255)

ANDREAS WOLFIUS: MONOLOG DES WOLFIUS,
   FOR SOLO VOICE AND ORCHESTRA see
   Walter, Fried

ANDREASIAN, OVSEP (1933-   )
   Concertino for Clarinet and Orchestra
     [14']
      1.1.1.0. 1.1.1.0. timp,perc,harp,
       strings,clar solo
      BELAIEFF   (A256)

   Symphony No. 1 [17']
      2.2.2.2. 4.2.3.1. timp,perc,harp,
       strings
      BELAIEFF   (A257)

   Symphony No. 2 [20']
      1.1.1.1. 2.1.1.0. timp,perc,
       strings,MezT soli,mix cor
      BELAIEFF   (A258)

ANDRESEN, ERIK (1941-   )
   Dialogue
      alto sax,gtr,db,drums,strings
      NORGE   (A259)

ANDRIESSEN, HENDRIK (1892-1981)
   Ballade Van Den Merel, For Narrator
     And Orchestra
      1.2.1.1. 0.0.0.0. 16vln,4vla,4vcl,
       2db,narrator [8'] sc DONEMUS f.s.
                        (A260)

ANDRIESSEN, JURRIAAN (1925-   )
   Hommage A Milhaud [8']
      1.1.1.alto sax. 1.1.1.0. vln,
       vla,vcl
      sc,pts DONEMUS f.s.   (A261)

   Monomania E Policromia [7']
      1.1.1.1. 2.1.1.0. harp,pno,
       strings
      DONEMUS perf mat rent   (A262)

   Time Suspended [35']
      3.3.3.3. 4.3.3.1. 4-5perc,harp,
       pno,strings
      DONEMUS perf mat rent   (A263)

ANDRIESSEN, LOUIS (1939-   )
   Snelheid, De [18']
      3.0.0.0.2alto sax.2soprano sax.
       4.4.4.2. 3-6perc,2pno,bass gtr,
       Hamm,strings, 2elec harp
      "Velocity" DONEMUS   (A264)

   Velocity
     see Snelheid, De

ANDROMAQUE: OVERTURE see Saint-Saëns,
   Camille

ANDROMEDE ET PERSEE, FOR SOLO VOICE AND
   STRING ORCHESTRA see Mouret, Jean
   Joseph

ANFOSSI, PASQUALE (1727-1797)
   Concerto for Violoncello and
     Orchestra
      2horn,strings without vla,cont,
       vcl solo
      sc,pts KUNZEL 10228 f.s. (A265)

   Sinfonie, Two
     see Martini, [Padre] Giovanni
     Battista, Sinfonie, Four

   Sinfonie, Two *see Martini, [Padre]
     Giovanni Battista, Sinfonie, Four

ANGELFIRE see Lieuwen, Peter

ANGELICUM see Fongaard, Bjørn

ANGELUS see Fujita, Masanori

ANGERER, PAUL (1927-   )
   Concerto for Viola and Orchestra
     [18']
      mand,hpsd,harp,perc,strings
       without vla,vla solo
      (1975 version) DOBLINGER perf mat
       rent   (A266)

ANGERER, PAUL (cont'd.)

"Ire In Orbem" [17']
string orch
study sc DOBLINGER STP 516 f.s.,
perf mat rent (A267)

Luctus Et Gaudium, For Trombone And
String Orchestra [11']
string orch,trom solo
DOBLINGER perf mat rent (A268)

Musica Conquisita Pro Fidicina Et
Cordarum Sonus, For Harp And
String Orchestra [14']
string orch,harp solo
DOBLINGER perf mat rent (A269)

Musica Exanimata, For Violoncello And
Chamber Orchestra
1.1.1.1. 1.1.1.0. strings,vcl
solo
[10'] DOBLINGER perf mat rent
(A270)

"Quicquam", For Double Bass And
Strings [18']
strings,db solo
DOBLINGER perf mat rent (A271)

ANGOT QUADRILLE see Strauss, Eduard

ANGULO, MANUEL (1930-   )
Cuatro Movimentos Para Orquesta [18']
2+pic.2+English horn.2+bass
clar.2+contrabsn. 4.3.3.1.
8perc,cel,harp,strings
ALPUERTO (A272)

ANHALT, ISTVÁN (1919-   )
Foci
sc BERANDOL BER 1430 $20.00 (A273)

Simulacrum [24']
2(alto fl).2.2(clar in E flat).2.
2+opt 2horn.2+opt trp.0+opt
2trom.0. perc,opt 1-2kbd,opt
harp,strings
CAN.MUS.CENT. MI 1100 A596SI (A274)

Sonance-Resonance: Welche Tone?
3(pic).3(English horn).3(bass
clar,clar in E
flat).3(contrabsn). 4.3.3.1.
baritone horn,timp,4perc,kbd,
strings
CAN.MUS.CENT. MI 1100 A596SO (A275)

Sparkskraps
2.2.2.2. 2.2.2.1. 2perc,pno&elec
org&cel,harp,strings
CAN.MUS.CENT. MI 1100 A596SP (A276)

ANIMA, FOR VIOLA AND ORCHESTRA see
Connolly, Justin [Riveagh]

ANIMA DEL FILOSOFO OSSIA ORFEO ET
EURIDICE, L': OVERTURE see Haydn,
[Franz] Joseph

ANIMA LATIMA see Brouwer, Leo

ANIMAUX MODELES, LES: SUITE see
Poulenc, Francis

ANNA see Guy, Barry

ANNA BOLENA: AH! PAREA CHE PER INCANTO,
FOR SOLO VOICE AND ORCHESTRA see
Donizetti, Gaetano

ANNA BOLENA: AL DOLCE GUIDAMI CASTEL
NATIO, FOR SOLO VOICE AND ORCHESTRA
see Donizetti, Gaetano

ANNA BOLENA: COME INNOCENTE GIOVANE,
FOR SOLO VOICE AND ORCHESTRA see
Donizetti, Gaetano

ANNA BOLENA: DA QUEL DI CHE LEI
PERDUTA, FOR SOLO VOICE AND
ORCHESTRA see Donizetti, Gaetano

ANNA BOLENA: DEH! NON VOLER
COSTRINGERE, FOR SOLO VOICE AND
ORCHESTRA see Donizetti, Gaetano

ANNA BOLENA: FAMA! SI L'AVRETE, FOR
SOLO VOICES AND ORCHESTRA see
Donizetti, Gaetano

ANNA BOLENA: PER QUESTA FIAMMA
INDOMITA, FOR SOLO VOICE AND
ORCHESTRA see Donizetti, Gaetano

ANNA BOLENA: S'EI T'ABBOREE, IO T' AMO
ANCORA, FOR SOLO VOICES AND
ORCHESTRA see Donizetti, Gaetano

ANNA BOLENA: SUL SUO CAPO AGGRAVI UN
DIO, FOR SOLO VOICES AND ORCHESTRA
see Donizetti, Gaetano

ANNA BOLENA: VIVI TU, TE NE SCONGIURO,
FOR SOLO VOICE AND ORCHESTRA see
Donizetti, Gaetano

ANNA KARENINA: ROMANTIC MUSIC FOR
ORCHESTRA see Shchedrin, Rodion

ANNA LA BONNE, FOR SOLO VOICE AND
ORCHESTRA see Israel-Meyer, Pierre

ANNAHERUNG UND STILLE, FOR PIANO AND
STRINGS see Ruzicka, Peter

ANNE OF THE INDES OVERTURE see Waxman,
Franz

ANNEES DE PELERINAGE: SPOSALIZIO, IL
PENSEROSO [ARR.] see Liszt, Franz

ANNINA, FOR SOLO VOICE AND ORCHESTRA
[ARR.] see Merikanto, Oskar

ANNIVERSARIES see Bennett, Richard
Rodney

ANNONCIER POLKA see Keler-Bela
(Adalbert Paul von Keler)

ANOTHER SYMPHONY see Tomasson, Jonas

ANSINK, CAROLINE (1959-   )
Concerto for Violin and Orchestra
[18']
3.2.2.3.alto sax.tenor sax.
3.0.3.0. 3perc,harp,pno,
strings,vln solo
DONEMUS perf mat rent (A277)

Night And Day [30']
1.1.1.1. 1.1.1.0. perc,harp,
strings
sc DONEMUS f.s., perf mat rent
(A278)

ANTCHAR, FOR SOLO VOICE AND ORCHESTRA
see Rimsky-Korsakov, Nikolai

ANTE MI see Fernandez Alvez, Gabriel

ANTECEDENTS OF THE SYMPHONY *CC25L
(Green, Douglass M.; Lazarevich,
Gordana) sc GARLAND
ISBN 0-8240-3828-2 $90.00 "The
Symphony" Vol. A-I (A279)

ANTHEIL, GEORGE (1900-1959)
Jazz Symphony, A, 1925 Version [12']
2ob,2alto sax,soprano sax&tenor
sax,3trp,3trom,tuba,perc,
2banjo,2pno,strings,pno solo
WEINTRB perf mat rent (A280)

Jazz Symphony, A, 1955 Version [8']
1.0.3.0. 0.3.3.0. perc,pno,
strings
WEINTRB perf mat rent (A281)

McKonkey's Ferry [8']
3+pic.2+English horn.2+bass
clar.2+contrabsn. 4.3.3.1.
timp,perc,harp,strings
WEINTRB perf mat rent (A282)

Over The Plains [8']
2+pic.2+bass clar.2. 4.3.3.1.
timp,perc,harp,strings
WEINTRB perf mat rent (A283)

Serenade for Strings [12']
string orch
WEINTRB perf mat rent (A284)

Symphony No. 6 [20']
2+pic.2+English horn.2+bass
clar.2+contrabsn. 4.3.3.1.
perc,pno,strings
WEINTRB perf mat rent (A285)

ANTHEM AND PROCESSIONALS see Albert,
Stephen Joel

ANTICHAOS see Lipovsek, Marijan

ANTIFONIA PASCUAL A LA VIRGEN, FOR SOLO
VOICES AND ORCHESTRA see Halffter,
Cristobal

ANTIGONE see Brandmüller, Theo see
Hvoslef, Ketil

ANTIKHTHON see Xenakis, Yannis (Iannis)

ANTILL, JOHN HENRY (1904-   )
Five Australian Lyrics, For Solo
Voice And Orchestra [13']
harp,strings,med solo
BOOSEY perf mat rent (A286)

ANTILLAS see Ortiz, William

ANTINOMIE see Hetu, Jacques

ANTIPHONAE NO. 1 see Csemiczky, M.

ANTIPHONE, FOR SOLO VOICE AND ORCHESTRA
see Killmayer, Wilhelm

ANTIPHONIE, FOR ORGAN AND ORCHESTRA see
Kelemen, Milko

ANTIPHYSIS, FOR FLUTE AND ORCHESTRA see
Dufourt, Hugues

ANTITHESES see Constantinides, Dinos
Demetrios

ANTONIANA see Turok, Paul Harris

ANTONINI, ALFREDO (1901-1983)
My Little Mule
SHAWNEE perf mat rent (A287)

Why Reach For The Moon
SHAWNEE perf mat rent (A288)

World's Fair March, The [3'30"]
2.2.2.2. 4.3.3.0. timp,perc,harp,
gtr,strings
BOURNE perf mat rent (A289)

ANTONIOU, THEODORE (1935-   )
Cheironomiës
"Gesten" variable instrumentation
study sc BÄREN. BA 6127 $12.75,
perf mat rent (A290)

Double Concerto For Percussion And
Orchestra [16']
1(pic).1.1+bass clar.1. 2.2.1.1.
harp,pno,strings,2perc soli
BÄREN. BA 6747 perf mat rent (A291)

Epilog Nach Homers Odyssee, For Solo
Voices And Orchestra [10']
0.1.0.0. 1.0.0.0. 1-3perc,gtr,
pno,strings,Mez&speaking voice
study sc BÄREN. BA 4379 $12.75,
perf mat rent (A292)

Fluxus 1 [16']
4(pic,alto fl).2+English horn.2+
bass clar.2+contrabsn. 6.4.4.1.
4perc,harp,pno&Hamm&cel,strings
BÄREN. BA 6735 perf mat rent (A293)

Fluxus 2, For Piano And Chamber
Orchestra [18']
1(alto fl).1(English horn).1(bass
clar).1. 1.1.1.0. perc,strings,
pno solo
BÄREN. BA 6739 perf mat rent (A294)

GBYSO Music, the [16']
3.3.3.3. 4.3.3.1. 4perc,harp,pno,
strings
GUNMAR MP1075 perf mat rent (A295)

Gesten
see Cheironomiës

Klagelied, The Memory Of Igor
Stravinsky
see Threnos

Klima Tis Apussias, For Solo Voice
And Chamber Orchestra [10']
1.1.1.1. 0.0.0.0. perc,pno,
strings,med solo
"Sense Of Absence, For Solo Voice
And Chamber Orchestra" [Greek/
Eng] study sc BÄREN. BA 6048
f.s., perf mat rent (A296)

Paean [8']
4.4.4.4. 6.4.3.1. timp,4perc,
harp,pno,strings
GUNMAR MP1067 perf mat rent (A297)

Sense Of Absence, For Solo Voice And
Chamber Orchestra
see Klima Tis Apussias, For Solo
Voice And Chamber Orchestra

Skolion [15']
3.3.3.3. 4.3.3.1. 3perc,harp,pno,
strings
GUNMAR MP1079 perf mat rent (A298)

Threnos [12'30"]
2.1.2.2. 2.2.3.1. perc,pno,db
"Klagelied, The Memory Of Igor
Stravinsky" BÄREN. BA 6287 perf
mat rent (A299)

ANTWORT OHNE FRAGE see Gubaidulina,
Sofia

ANUTA: SUITE see Gavrilin, Valery

ANYTHING GOES see Porter, Cole

ANYWAY... see Hellermann, William

APERGHIS, GEORGES (1945-   )
Ascoltare Stanca [10']
fl&pic,2ob,2horn,pno&hpsd,6vln,
2vla,2vcl,db
SALABERT perf mat rent (A300)

B.W.V., For Solo Voices And
Instrumental Ensemble [17']
2rec,2clar,2bass clar,4trom,pno,
hpsd,org,vla,vcl,4db,
SMezTBarBar&countertenor
study sc SALABERT f.s., perf mat
rent (A301)

APERGHIS, GEORGES (cont'd.)

Contrepoint [10']
　　trom,perc,pno,strings
　　BILLAUDOT perf mat rent　　(A302)

Parentheses [15']
　　2.0.2.1. 1.1.1.0. 3perc,harp,pno,
　　vln,vla,vcl,db
　　SALABERT perf mat rent　　(A303)

Variations Pour Quatorze Instruments
　　[12']
　　1.1.1.1. 1.0.0.0. perc,gtr,harp,
　　pno,2vln,vla,vcl,db
　　SALABERT perf mat rent　　(A304)

Walls Have Ears, The
　　see Wande Haben Ohren, Die

Wande Haben Ohren, Die [17']
　　3(pic).3.3.3. 4.3.3.1. 2perc,
　　strings
　　"Walls Have Ears, The" SALABERT
　　perf mat rent　　(A305)

APEX II see Zbar, Michel

APHORISMS see Lombardo, Robert M.

APHRODITE see Chadwick, George
Whitefield

API, LE, FOR OBOE AND STRING ORCHESTRA
[ARR.] see Pasculli, Antonio

APOKALYPTISCHES FRAGMENT, EIN, FOR SOLO
VOICE, PIANO AND ORCHESTRA
ORCHESTRA see Reimann, Aribert

APOLLO & HYACINTH see Samuel, Gerhard

APOLLO UND DAPHNE: DIE FREIHEIT GAB ICH
DIR WIEDER, FOR SOLO VOICES AND
ORCHESTRA see Handel, George
Frideric

APONTE-LEDEE, RAFAEL (1938-　　)
Impulsos
　　3(pic).3.3.3. 4.2.3.1. perc,
　　strings
　　PEER perf mat rent　　(A306)

APPALACHIAN FOLK TALE, AN, FOR NARRATOR
AND ORCHESTRA see Whear, Paul
William

APPARITIONS see Sitsky, Larry

APPEL DE LA MONTAGNE, L' see Honegger,
Arthur

APPLE BLOSSOM, FOR SOLO VOICE AND
ORCHESTRA, [ARR.] see Nielsen,
Carl, Ableblomst, For Solo Voice
And Orchestra, [arr.]

APPLEBAUM, ALLYSON BROWN (1955-　　)
Symphony In Two Movements [25']
　　3(pic).3(English horn).3(bass
　　clar).3(contrabsn). 4.3.3.1.
　　timp,2perc,pno&cel,harp,strings
　　NORRUTH perf mat rent　　(A307)

APPLEBAUM, EDWARD (1937-　　)
Night Waltz, For Guitar And Orchestra
　　[14']
　　2(pic).2(English horn).2(bass
　　clar).2(contrabsn). 4.2.2.1.
　　3perc,pno&cel,strings,gtr solo
　　NORRUTH perf mat rent　　(A308)

Princess In The Garden, The [6']
　　string orch
　　NORRUTH perf mat rent　　(A309)

Waltz In Two, For Narrator And
　　Orchestra [12']
　　2(pic).2.2(clar in E flat,bass
　　clar).2. 4.2.2.1. timp,2perc,
　　harp,strings,narrator
　　NORRUTH perf mat rent　　(A310)

APPLEBAUM, STANLEY (1922-　　)
Concert Aria, For Violoncello And
　　Orchestra [12']
　　2(pic).1.2(clar in E flat,bass
　　clar).1.soprano sax(alto sax,
　　baritone sax). 2.2.1.0. perc,
　　harp,8vln,3vla,3vcl,db,vcl solo
　　NORRUTH perf mat rent　　(A311)

Concerto for Piano and Orchestra
　　[19']
　　3(pic).3(English horn).2+bass
　　clar.3(contrabsn). 4.3.3.1.
　　timp,perc,harp,strings,pno solo
　　(Dreams and Voyage) NORRUTH perf
　　mat rent　　(A312)

Lost Hour, The: Theme
　　SHAWNEE perf mat rent　　(A313)

Symphony No. 2 [15']
　　3(pic,alto fl,bass fl).3(English
　　horn).3(soprano clar in E flat,

APPLEBAUM, STANLEY (cont'd.)

　　bass clar).3(contrabsn).
　　4.4.4.1. perc,harp,pno&cel,
　　strings
　　NORRUTH perf mat rent　　(A314)

APPRENTI SORCIER, L' see Dukas, Paul

APPROACHES TO DUN AENGUS, FOR
VIOLONCELLO AND ORCHESTRA see
Brettingham Smith, Jolyon

APRESLUDE see Vogt, Hans

APRIL I CHOOSE see Bangert, Emil, Jeg
Vaelger Mig April

AQUARELLE see Denisov, Edison
Vasilievich

AQUARELLE [ARR.] see Cleve, Cissi

AQUARELLES [ARR.] see Gade, Niels
Wilhelm

AQUARIA see Mobberley, James

AQUATHEME see Malec, Ivo

ARABESCO see Kielland, Olav

ARABESK see Arnestad, Finn

ARABESKE see Heimerl, Chr.

ARABESQUE see Kroll, William

ARABESQUE, FOR PIANO AND CHAMBER GROUP
see Krauze, Zygmunt

ARABESQUE, FOR SAXOPHONE AND CHAMBER
ORCHESTRA see Smith, Leland C.

ARABESQUE NO. 1 IN E [ARR.] see
Debussy, Claude

ARABESQUE NO. 2 IN G [ARR.] see
Debussy, Claude

ARAMBARRI, JESÚS (1902-1960)
Cuatro Impromtus
　　0+pic.2.2.2. 2.2.0.0. timp,perc,
　　harp,strings
　　UNION ESP. perf mat rent　　(A315)

Fantasia Espanola
　　0+pic.2+English horn.2(bass
　　clar).2(contrabsn). 4.3.3.1.
　　timp,perc,harp,pno,strings
　　UNION ESP. perf mat rent　　(A316)

Gabon Zar Sorignak [10']
　　2.1.2.1. 2.2.0.0. timp,perc,harp,
　　strings
　　UNION ESP. perf mat rent　　(A317)

In Memoriam [10']
　　3+pic.2.3(bass clar).2. 4.2.3.1.
　　timp,perc,harp,strings
　　UNION ESP. perf mat rent　　(A318)

Minueto Y Rondo
　　string orch
　　UNION ESP. perf mat rent　　(A319)

Ofrenda A Falla, For English Horn And
　　String Orchestra
　　string orch,English horn solo
　　UNION ESP. perf mat rent　　(A320)

ARAPOV, BORIS (1905-　　)
Choreographic Poem
　　sc MEZ KNIGA f.s.　　(A321)

Concerto for Violin, Piano,
　　Percussion and Chamber Orchestra
　　[28']
　　1.2.2.1. 1.1.1.0. perc,strings,
　　vln solo,pno solo
　　SIKORSKI perf mat rent　　(A322)
　　VAAP perf mat rent　　(A323)

ARBOL AZPIAN see Albéniz, Isaac

ARBOR COSMICA see Panufnik, Andrzej

ARBOS see Pärt, Arvo

ARBRE DES SONGES, L', FOR VIOLIN AND
ORCHESTRA see Dutilleux, Henri

ARC, PART I, FOR PIANO AND ORCHESTRA
see Takemitsu, Toru

ARC, PART II, FOR PIANO AND ORCHESTRA
see Takemitsu, Toru

ARC FOR STRINGS see Takemitsu, Toru

ARCADE II, FOR VIOLA AND INSTRUMENTAL
ENSEMBLE see Levinas, Michael

ARCADE III: LE CHOEUR DES ARCHES see
Levinas, Michael

ARCADES see Stroe, Aurel

ARCH, L', FOR SOLO VOICE AND CHAMBER
ORCHESTRA see Tabachnik, Michel

ARCHAEOPTERYX see Riisager, Knudage

ARCHAIC RITUAL see Still, William Grant

ARCHE, FOR VIOLA AND CHAMBER ORCHESTRA
see Shatin, Judith

ARCHE NOAH, FOR NARRATOR AND ORCHESTRA
see Weiner, Stanley

ARCHER, VIOLET (1913-　　)
Concertino for Clarinet and Orchestra
　　sc BERANDOL BER 1790 $10.00　　(A324)

Concerto for Piano and Orchestra, No.
　　1
　　sc BERANDOL BER 1784 $20.00　　(A325)

Concerto for Violin and Orchestra
　　sc BERANDOL BER 1794 $20.00　　(A326)

Divertimento for Piano and String
　　Orchestra [15']
　　string orch,pno solo
　　CAN.MUS.CENT. MI 1361 A672D　　(A327)

Evocations, For 2 Pianos And
　　Orchestra
　　2.2.2.2. 4.2.3.1. timp,3perc,
　　strings,2pno soli
　　CAN.MUS.CENT. MI 1461 A672EV　　(A328)

Fantasia Concertante
　　sc BERANDOL BER 1792 $8.00　　(A329)

Fantasy On A Ground
　　sc BERANDOL BER 1789 $8.00　　(A330)

Improvisation On A Name
　　1.0.2.2. 2.0.0.0. strings
　　CAN.MUS.CENT. MI 1200 A672IM　　(A331)

Poem
　　sc BERANDOL BER 1793 $8.00　　(A332)

ARCHES DE LUMIERE see Tisne, Antoine

ARCHETYPON see Kelemen, Milko

ARCHIBALD DOUGLAS, FOR SOLO VOICE AND
ORCHESTRA see Loewe, Carl Gottfried

ARCHIBALD DOUGLAS [ARR.] see Loewe,
Carl Gottfried

ARCHIPELAGO see Reynolds, Roger

ARCHIPELAGO ISLE, FOR SOLO VOICE AND
ORCHESTRA see Haquinius, Algot

ARCHITEKTUR DER EBENE see Emmerik, Ivo
Van

ARCHITESTO, L', FOR SOLO VOICE AND
ORCHESTRA see Pasquotti, Corrado

ARCHITETTURA PER MUSICA see Beyer,
Frank Michael

ARCO-22 see Malec, Ivo

ARCURI, SERGE (1954-　　)
Amers [5']
　　2.2.2.2. 2.2.2.0. 2perc,strings
　　CAN.MUS.CENT. MI 1100 A 675AM
　　　　　　　　　　　　(A333)

ARCUS see Pade, Steen

ARDEN COURT [ARR.] see Boyce, William

ARENDS, H. (1855-1924)
Salammbo: Suite
　　3.3.2.3. 3.4.3.1. timp,perc,harp,
　　strings
　　VAAP perf mat rent　　(A334)

ARENSKY, ANTON STEPANOVICH (1861-1906)
Concerto for Violin and Orchestra in
　　A minor
　　KALMUS A5832 sc $25.00, set $35.00,
　　perf mat rent　　(A335)

Egyptian Nights: Suite
　　sc MEZ KNIGA f.s.　　(A336)

ARES UND APHRODITE see Fritsch,
Johannes Georg

ARGENTO, DOMINICK (1927-　　)
Bravo Mozart! [30']
　　2(pic).1.2(bass clar).0. 1.2.2.0.
　　perc,cel,pno,strings
　　min sc BOOSEY 940 $21.00, perf mat
　　rent　　(A337)

Capriccio for Clarinet and Orchestra
　　see Rossini In Paris, For Clarinet
　　And Orchestra

ARGENTO, DOMINICK (cont'd.)

Casa Guidi, For Solo Voice And
Orchestra [20']
3+pic+alto fl.2+English horn.2+
bass clar.2. 4.3.3.1. perc,
harp,pno,strings,Mez solo
BOOSEY perf mat rent   (A338)

Fire Variations [22']
3(pic).2+English horn.3(bass
clar).3. 4.3.3.1. timp,2perc,
harp,pno,cel,strings
min sc BOOSEY $17.50, perf mat rent
(A339)

Rossini In Paris, For Clarinet And
Orchestra (Capriccio for Clarinet
and Orchestra) [20']
2+pic.2+English horn.2+bass
clar.2+contrabsn. 4.3.3.1.
timp,3perc,harp,strings,clar
solo
BOOSEY perf mat rent   (A340)

Tombeau d'Edgar Poe, Le [16']
2+pic.2+English horn.2+bass
clar.2+contrabsn. 4.3.3.1.
timp,3perc,harp,strings, offstage soprano and tenor
BOOSEY perf mat rent   (A341)

ARI-TA-ARI see Larrauri, Anton

ARIA AND TOCCATA, FOR PIANO AND
ORCHESTRA see Hartig, Heinz
Friedrich

ARIA BRAVURA, FOR SOLO INSTRUMENT AND
ORCHESTRA see Ford, Ronald

ARIA DI CERERE, FOR SOLO VOICE AND
ORCHESTRA see Bellini, Vincenzo

ARIA DI FARNASPE, FOR SOLO VOICE AND
STRING ORCHESTRA see Pergolesi,
Giovanni Battista

ARIA DI SAMMETE "SE D'AMOR SE DI
CONTENTO", FOR SOLO VOICE AND
STRING ORCHESTRA see Traetta,
Tommaso (Michele Francesco Saverio)

ARIA HEBRAIQUE see Stein, Leon

ARIA SCHIAVONA see Veracini, Francesco
Maria

ARIADNA ON NAXOS, FOR SOLO VOICES AND
ORCHESTRA see Benda, Georg Anton
(Jiří Antonín)

ARIADNE, FOR SOLO VOICE AND ORCHESTRA
see Maconchy, Elizabeth

ARIANE ET BACCHUS: SUITE see Marais,
Marin

ARIANE ET BARBE-BLEUE: INTRODUCTION,
ACT III see Dukas, Paul

ARIANNA A NAXOS, FOR SOLO VOICE AND
ORCHESTRA see Haydn, [Franz] Joseph

ARIANNA A NAXOS, FOR SOLO VOICE AND
ORCHESTRA, [ARR.] see Haydn,
[Franz] Joseph

ARIAS, EMMANUEL (1935-   )
Sonoralia, Opus 2
string orch,pno
LIGA   (A342)

Sonoralia, Opus 3
string orch
LIGA   (A343)

ARIBLA see Vea, Ketil

ARIE, FOR SOLO VOICE AND ORCHESTRA see
Donatoni, Franco

ARIE DISSOLUTE, FOR VIOLA AND
INSTRUMENTAL ENSEMBLE see Hübler,
Klaus-K.

ARIEL see D'amico, Matteo see Gerhard,
Roberto see Legg, James

ARIELS GESANG AUS SHAKESPEARES "STURM"
see Braunfels, Walter

ARIETTA see Dello Joio, Norman

ARIETTEN, FOR PIANO AND ORCHESTRA see
Einem, Gottfried von

ARIODANTE: BRAMO HAVER MILLE VITE, FOR
SOLO VOICES AND ORCHESTRA see
Handel, George Frideric

ARIOSO see Ferrero, Lorenzo

ARIOSO [ARR.] see Bach, Johann
Sebastian

ARIOSO E FURIOSO see Koch, Erland von

ARIOSO E TOCCATA II, FOR PIANO AND
ORCHESTRA see Glaser, Werner Wolf

ARIOSO MOBILE, FOR FLUTE AND ORCHESTRA
see Pennisi, Francesco

ARKANSAS TRAVELER see Guion, David
Wendall Fentress

ARKHANGELSKY, G.
D'Après Ecrits Sur Toiles [15']
2(pic,alto fl).2(English
horn).2.2. 2.0.0.0. 12vln,4vla,
4vcl,2db
AMPHION perf mat rent   (A344)

ARKIHUOLESI HEITA, FOR SOLO VOICE AND
ORCHESTRA [ARR.] see Madetoja,
Leevi

ARLEN, HAROLD (1905-   )
Blues In The Night [3'10"]
WARNER perf mat rent   (A345)

ARLEQUIN see Lalo, Edouard see Stirn,
D.

ARLESIENNE, L': SUITE [ARR.] see Bizet,
Georges

ARMA, PAUL (PÁL) (IMRE WEISSHAUS)
(1904-1987)
À La Mémoire De Béla Bartók
perc,strings sc EMB 12154 f.s.
(A346)

Cinq Resonances [15']
2.2.2.2. 2.2.2.0. timp,2perc,
strings
BILLAUDOT perf mat rent   (A347)

Onze Convergences
string orch sc EMB 12153 f.s.
(A348)

Polydiaphonie [26']
3.2.3.3. 4.2.3.1. timp,3perc,
xylo,cel,pno,strings
BILLAUDOT perf mat rent   (A349)

Variations for String Orchestra
[8'30"]
string orch
BILLAUDOT perf mat rent   (A350)

ARMEN BALL POLKA see Strauss, Johann,
[Jr.]

ARMENIAN RHAPSODY see Ippolitov-Ivanov,
Mikhail Mikhailovich

ARMESTIC CHIMES see Lund, Signe

ARMIDA ABBANDONATA, FOR SOLO VOICE AND
STRING ORCHESTRA see Handel, George
Frideric

ARMIDA: OVERTURE see Cherubini, Luigi
see Dvorák, Antonín

ARMIDE: ACH SOLL DIES FREIE HERZ, FOR
SOLO VOICE AND ORCHESTRA see Gluck,
Christoph Willibald, Ritter von

ARMIDE ET RENAUD: THREE INSTRUMENTAL
PIECES see Lully, Jean-Baptiste
(Lulli)

ARMIES OF THE NIGHT, THE see Milburn,
Ellsworth

ARMONIA see Keulen, Geert van

ARMSTRONG, JOHN
Circle's End, For Guitar And
Orchestra [10']
1.1.1.1. 1.0.0.0. strings,gtr
solo
CAN.MUS.CENT. MI 1315 A736C   (A351)

Three Pieces For Guitar And String
Orchestra [10']
string orch,gtr solo
CAN.MUS.CENT. MI 1615 A736T   (A352)

ARNE, THOMAS AUGUSTINE (1710-1778)
Artaxerxes: Overture [arr.]
(Warrack, Guy) 0.2.0.2. 0.0.0.0.
strings [7'] BOOSEY perf mat rent
(A353)

Concerto for Keyboard Instrument and
Orchestra, No. 1, in C [14']
2ob,strings,kbd solo,opt 2horn,
opt 2trp, opt timp
(Langley, Robin) sc OXFORD 32.175
$25.00, perf mat rent   (A354)

Concerto for Keyboard Instrument and
Orchestra, No. 2, in G [10']
2ob,strings,kbd solo
(Langley, Robin) sc OXFORD 32.176
$25.00, perf mat rent   (A355)

Concerto for Keyboard Instrument and
Orchestra, No. 3, in A [18']
2ob,strings,kbd solo

ARNE, THOMAS AUGUSTINE (cont'd.)

(Langley, Robin) sc OXFORD 32.177
$25.00, perf mat rent   (A356)

Concerto for Keyboard Instrument and
Orchestra, No. 4, in B flat [12']
2ob,strings,kbd solo
(Langley, Robin) sc OXFORD 32.178
$25.00, perf mat rent   (A357)

Concerto for Keyboard Instrument and
Orchestra, No. 5, in G minor
[12']
2ob,strings,kbd solo
(Langley, Robin) sc OXFORD 32.179
$18.00, perf mat rent   (A358)

Concerto for Keyboard Instrument and
Orchestra, No. 6, in B flat [12']
2ob,strings,kbd solo
(Langley, Robin) sc OXFORD 32.180
$19.95, perf mat rent   (A359)

Overture in B flat, MIN 1, [arr.]
(Herbage, Julian) 2ob,bsn,strings
[6'] BOOSEY perf mat rent   (A360)

Rule, Britannia
0.2.0.1. 0.2.0.0. timp,cont,
strings
OXFORD perf mat rent   (A361)

Rule, Britannia [arr]
(Sargent, M.) 3.3.3.3. 4.4.3.1.
timp,perc,strings [3'] OXFORD
perf mat rent   (A362)

Suite Of Dances [arr.]
(Collins, Anthony) 1.1.1.1.
1.0.0.0. strings [16'] FOX,S perf
mat rent   (A363)

ARNESTAD, FINN (1916-   )
Arabesk [10']
3.2.3.3. 4.2.2.1. timp,perc,harp,
strings
NORGE   (A364)

Blacksmith And The Baker, The, For
Solo Voice And Chamber Orchestra
see Smeden Og Bageren, For Solo
Voice And Chamber Orchestra

Cavatina Cambiata [8']
2.2.2.2. 3.2.2.1. perc,strings
NORGE   (A365)

Concerto for Piano and Orchestra
[15']
2.1.2.1. 3.1.0.0. timp,strings,
pno solo
NORGE   (A366)

Concerto for Violin and Orchestra
[27']
2.0.2.2. 2.2.0.0. timp,strings,
vln solo
NORGE   (A367)

Constellation [7']
2.2.2.2. 4.2.2.0. timp,perc,harp,
strings
NORGE   (A368)

Conversation, For Piano And Orchestra
[4']
2.2.2.2. 2.2.0.0. timp,perc,
strings,pno solo
NORGE   (A369)

Inri [26']
3.2.3.3. 4.3.3.1. timp,perc,harp,
strings
NORGE   (A370)

Meditation [5']
1.2.2.2. 4.2.2.0. timp,perc,harp,
strings
NORGE   (A371)

Mouvement Concertant, For Double Bass
And Orchestra [6']
1.1.1.1. 2.1.2.0. timp,strings,db
solo
NORGE   (A372)

Overture [5']
2.2.3.2. 4.3.2.1. timp,perc,
strings
NORGE   (A373)

Smeden Og Bageren, For Solo Voice And
Chamber Orchestra [35']
fl,ob,hpsd,strings,Bar solo
"Blacksmith And The Baker, The, For
Solo Voice And Chamber Orchestra"
NORGE   (A374)

Suite I Gamle Danserytmer [20']
fl,ob,hpsd,strings
"Suite In Old Dance Rhythms" NORGE
(A375)

Suite In Old Dance Rhythms
see Suite I Gamle Danserytmer

ARNESTAD, FINN (cont'd.)

Toccata [6']
  2.2.2.2. 3.2.3.0. timp,strings
  NORGE   (A376)

ARNIC, BLAZ (1901-1970)
Concerto for Orchestra [14']
  fl,harp,cel,strings
  DRUSTVO DSS 982 perf mat rent
                  (A377)

ARNITA, SALVADOR (1915-   )
Allegretto Pastorale, For Oboe And
  String Orchestra [3'30"]
  string orch,ob solo
  sc BILLAUDOT f.s., perf mat rent
                  (A378)

ARNOLD, MALCOLM (1921-   )
Commonwealth Christmas Overture
  *Op.64 [15']
  3.2.2.2. 4.3.3.1. timp,4perc,cel,
    harp,strings
  LENGNICK perf mat rent   (A379)

Concerto for Clarinet and Orchestra,
  No. 2, Op. 115
  2.2.2.0. 2.0.0.0. timp,perc,
    strings,clar solo
  sc FABER 023-00150 $17.50 (A380)

Concerto for Horn and Orchestra, No.
  1, Op. 11 [22']
  3.2.2.2. 0.0.0.0. timp,strings,
    horn solo
  LENGNICK perf mat rent   (A381)

Concerto for Piano 4-Hands and String
  Orchestra, Op. 32 [22']
  string orch,pno 4-hands soli
  LENGNICK perf mat rent   (A382)

Concerto for 2 Pianos and Orchestra,
  Op. 104 [13']
  3.2.2.2. 4.3.3.1. timp,2perc,
    harp,strings,2pno soli
  (reduced scoring: 2222 2211, timp,
    perc, str) sc FABER f.s., perf
    mat rent   (A383)

Concerto for Trumpet and Orchestra,
  Op. 125
  study sc FABER 023-00186 $15.50
                  (A384)
  sc FABER F0658 $15.50   (A385)

Divertimento No. 2, Op. 24 [9']
  PATERSON perf mat rent   (A386)

Four Irish Dances *Op.126 [11']
  3.2.2.2. 4.3.3.1. timp,2perc,
    harp,strings
  sc FABER $16.00, perf mat rent
                  (A387)

Hobsons Choice
  PATERSON perf mat rent   (A388)

Larch Trees *Op.3
  2.2.2.2. 4.0.0.0. strings
  sc FABER F0864 $6.95, perf mat rent
                  (A389)

Philharmonic Concerto *Op.120 [13']
  2+pic.2+English horn.2+
    contrabsn. 4.3.3.1. timp,3perc,
    harp,strings
  sc FABER F0827 f.s., perf mat rent
                  (A390)

Serenade for Guitar and String
  Orchestra, Op. 50 [6']
  string orch,gtr solo
  PATERSON perf mat rent   (A391)

Sinfonietta No. 2, Op. 65
  study sc PATERSON 60302 f.s. (A392)

Sinfonietta No. 3, Op. 81 [15']
  PATERSON perf mat rent   (A393)

Solitaire: Saraband And Polka [4']
  PATERSON perf mat rent   (A394)

Sound Barrier, The *Op.38 [7']
  PATERSON perf mat rent   (A395)

Sweeney Todd: Suite (from Op. 68a)
  [12']
  2.1.2.1. 2.2.2.0. timp,perc,harp,
    pno&cel,strings
  sc FABER f.s., perf mat rent (A396)

Symphonic Study, "Machines" *Op.30
  sc FABER 023-00150 $17.50 (A397)

Symphony No. 5
  study sc PATERSON 60405 f.s. (A398)

Symphony, No. 7, Op. 113 [33']
  2+pic.2.2.2+contrabsn. 4.3.3.1.
    timp,2perc,harp,strings
  FABER perf mat rent   (A399)

Symphony No. 8, Op. 121
  sc FABER F0638 $36.00   (A400)

Variations, Op. 122 [13']
  2.2.2.2. 2.2.0.0. timp,strings
  FABER perf mat rent   (A401)

AROLDO: AH DA ME FUGGI, INVOLATI, FOR
  SOLO VOICES AND ORCHESTRA see
  Verdi, Giuseppe

AROLDO: AH! DAGLI SCANNI ETEREI, FOR
  SOLO VOICE AND ORCHESTRA see Verdi,
  Giuseppe

AROLDO: DITE CHE IL FALLO A TERGERE,
  FOR SOLO VOICES AND ORCHESTRA see
  Verdi, Giuseppe

AROLDO: ERA VERO?...AH NO... E
  IMPOSSIBLE, FOR SOLO VOICES AND
  ORCHESTRA see Verdi, Giuseppe

AROLDO: MINA, PENSAI CHE UN ANGELO, FOR
  SOLO VOICE AND ORCHESTRA see Verdi,
  Giuseppe

AROLDO: OPPOSTO E IL CALLE, CHE IN
  AVVENIRE, FOR SOLO VOICES AND
  ORCHESTRA see Verdi, Giuseppe

AROLDO: SALVAMI TU, GRAN DIO, FOR SOLO
  VOICE AND ORCHESTRA see Verdi,
  Giuseppe

AROLDO: SOTTO IL SOL DI SIRIA ARDENTE,
  FOR SOLO VOICE AND ORCHESTRA see
  Verdi, Giuseppe

AROUND THE BLUES see Hodeir, Andre

AROURA see Xenakis, Yannis (Iannis)

ARPEGGIONE-SONATE, FOR VIOLONCELLO AND
  ORCHESTRA [ARR.] see Schubert,
  Franz (Peter)

ARPEGGIONE-SONATE, FOR VIOLONCELLO AND
  STRING ORCHESTRA, [ARR.] see
  Schubert, Franz (Peter)

ARRACHART, J.M.
Emkahesa
  CHOUDENS perf mat rent   (A402)

ARRAY see Crosse, Gordon

ARRIAGA, JUAN CRISÓSTOMO (1806-1826)
Pastorale [5']
  2+pic.2.2.2. 4.2.3.1. timp,perc,
    strings
  KALMUS A5876 sc $5.00, set $20.00,
    perf mat rent   (A403)

ARRIEU, CLAUDE (1903-   )
Mois De Mai, Le, For Solo Voice And
  Orchestra (from Chansons Du
  Folklore De France) [2'50"]
  2fl,bsn,strings,solo voice
  BILLAUDOT perf mat rent   (A404)

Trois Jolis Tambours, For Solo Voice
  And Orchestra (from Chansons Du
  Folklore De France) [3']
  fl,ob,clar,perc,strings,solo
    voice
  BILLAUDOT perf mat rent   (A405)

ARRIGO, GIROLAMO (1930-   )
Nel Fuggir Del Tempo, For Solo Voices
  And Orchestra [28']
  3.2.3.2. 4.2.3.1. timp,2perc,org,
    harp,strings,TBarB soli
  sc RICORDI-IT 132383 f.s., perf mat
    rent   (A406)

Solarium [37']
  5.3.4.3. 6.4.4.2. timp,3perc,
    2harp,cel,elec org,strings
  RICORDI-IT 132869 perf mat rent
                  (A407)

ARRIGONI, CARLO (1697-1744)
Concerto for Mandolin and String
  Orchestra in C
  (Gladd) string orch without vla,
    hpsd,mand solo sc,pts PLUCKED STR
    PSE 023 $10.00   (A408)

ARRIVAL OF THE QUEEN OF SHEBA see
  Handel, George Frideric, Solomon:
  Entrance Of The Queen Of Sheba

ARRIVO DELL' UNICORNO, L', FOR HARP AND
  INSTRUMENTAL ENSEMBLE see Pennisi,
  Francesco

ARROWS OF SAINT SEBASTIAN, THE see
  Fowler, Jennifer

ARSENEAULT, RAYNALD (1945-   )
Prelude A L'infini [7']
  3(alto fl).3(Heckelphone).3.3.
    4.4.3.1. 2perc,strings
  CAN.MUS.CENT. MI 1100 A781PR (A409)

Symphony [10']
  4.4.4.4. 8.6.4.2. timp,6perc,pno
    4-hands,org,2harp,strings
  CAN.MUS.CENT. MI 1100 A781SY (A410)

ARSTIDSSTYCKEN, FOR SOLO VOICE AND
  STRING ORCHESTRA see Hedwall,
  Lennart

ARTAXERXES: OVERTURE [ARR.] see Arne,
  Thomas Augustine

ARTEAGA, ANGEL (1928-   )
Cueva De Nerja, La [14']
  2+pic.2+English horn.2+bass
    clar.2+contrabsn. 4.4.3.1.
    3perc,pno,2harp,strings
  ALPUERTO   (A411)

Eloges, For Solo Voice And Orchestra
  [12']
  3.2.2+bass clar.2+contrabsn.
    2.2.3.1. timp,perc,harp,cel,
    strings,T solo
  ALPUERTO   (A412)

Improvisacion Y Canon [10']
  string orch
  ALPUERTO   (A413)

Musica De Don Quijote [22']
  2rec,fl,2ob,bsn,2trp,timp,perc,
    cel,harp,strings, cromorno
    bajo, 2 viellas
  ALPUERTO   (A414)

Musica Para Un Festival [12']
  2fl,clar,2horn,strings
  ALPUERTO   (A415)

Sinfonietta
  2fl,2clar,horn,strings
  ALPUERTO   (A416)

Toccata for Orchestra [8']
  4.2.2+bass clar.2+contrabsn.
    4.4.3.1. strings
  ALPUERTO   (A417)

ARTEMISIA: OVERTURE see Cimarosa,
  Domenico

ARTICULATIONS see Wilson, Richard
  (Edward)

ARTIST'S LIFE see Strauss, Johann,
  [Jr.], Kunstlerleben Walzer

ARTYOMOV, VYACHESLAV (1940-   )
Concerto for Violin and Orchestra
  [15']
  3.3.3.3. 4.3.3.1. 5perc,harp,cel,
    pno,strings,vln solo
  SIKORSKI perf mat rent   (A418)

Elegiac Symphony [40']
  6perc,strings,2vln soli
  "Elegiensinfonie" SIKORSKI perf mat
    rent   (A419)

Elegiac Symphony: Elegy III [18']
  6perc,9vln,vln solo
  SIKORSKI perf mat rent   (A420)
  VAAP perf mat rent   (A421)

Elegiensinfonie
  see Elegiac Symphony

Girlande Von Rezitationen [12'-25']
  1.1.1.1.sax. 0.0.0.0. perc,harp,
    hpsd,pno,9vln,3vla,2vcl,db
  SIKORSKI perf mat rent   (A422)

Tempo Constante [15']
  fl,ob,perc,hpsd,strings
  SIKORSKI perf mat rent   (A423)
  VAAP perf mat rent   (A424)

Way To Olympus, The [20']
  4.3.4.3.2sax. 4.4.3.1. 7perc,
    2harp,org,strings
  VAAP perf mat rent   (A425)
  "Weg Zum Olymp, Der" SIKORSKI perf
    mat rent   (A426)

Weg Zum Olymp, Der
  see Way To Olympus, The

ARUTIUNIAN, ALEXANDER (1920-   )
Concerto for Flute and Orchestra
  [12']
  harp,bells,strings,fl solo
  VAAP perf mat rent   (A427)

Concerto for Oboe and Orchestra [14']
  2.0.2.2. 3.0.0.0. timp,perc,
    strings,ob solo
  SIKORSKI perf mat rent   (A428)
  VAAP perf mat rent   (A429)

Concerto for Oboe and String
  Orchestra
  string orch,ob solo
  VAAP perf mat rent   (A430)

Poem for Violoncello and Orchestra
  [19']
  3.2.3.2. 4.4.3.1. timp,harp,
    strings,vcl solo
  SIKORSKI perf mat rent   (A431)

Sinfonietta for String Orchestra
  [17']
  string orch
  SIKORSKI perf mat rent   (A432)

ARUTIUNIAN, ALEXANDER (cont'd.)

Theme and Variations for Trumpet and
Orchestra
3.3.3.2. 4.2.3.1. timp,xylo,harp,
strings,trp solo
SIKORSKI perf mat rent   (A433)
VAAP perf mat rent   (A434)

AS IMPERCEPTIBLY AS GRIEF, FOR
PERCUSSION AND ORCHESTRA see
Samuel, Gerhard

AS LONG AS IT ISN'T LOVE, FOR SOLO
VOICE AND ORCHESTRA see Babbitt,
Milton Byron

AS MANY AS see Thommessen, Olav Anton,
Flest

AS THE BEAST DIES, FOR SOLO VOICE AND
CHAMBER ORCHESTRA see
Sigurbjornsson, Hrodmar Ingi

AS YOU LIKE IT, FOR SOLO VOICE AND
ORCHESTRA [ARR.] see Walton, [Sir]
William (Turner)

ASAFIEV, BORIS (1884-1949)
Concerto for Guitar and Chamber
Orchestra [25']
clar,timp,strings,gtr solo
SIKORSKI perf mat rent   (A435)

Fairy's Gift, The. Tyrolienne No. 5
1.2.2.2. 4.0.0.0. perc,harp,
strings
VAAP perf mat rent   (A436)

Symphony No. 1 in C [34']
3.3.3.2. 4.3.3.1. timp,perc,harp,
strings
VAAP perf mat rent   (A437)

ASCHERMITTWOCH, FOR SOLO VOICE AND
CHAMBER ORCHESTRA see Gonzalez
Acilu, Agustin

ASCOLTARE STANCA see Aperghis, Georges

ASGEIRSSON, JON (1928-   )
Ancient Dances
2.2.2.2. 4.2.3.1. perc,strings
ICELAND 010-004   (A438)

Ballet Suite: Blind Man's Buff
2.2.2.2. 4.3.2.1. timp,perc,harp,
strings
ICELAND 010-024   (A439)

Concerto for Violoncello and
Orchestra
2.2.3.2. 4.2.0.0. timp,strings,
vcl solo
ICELAND 010-028   (A440)

Icelandic Folk Songs, For Solo Voice
And Orchestra
1.1.1.1. 1.2.1.0. perc,strings,
solo voice
ICELAND 010-009   (A441)

Poem Of Seven Strings, A [10'30"]
string orch
ICELAND 010-008   (A442)

Rhapsody [5'40"]
2.2.2.2. 4.3.3.1. timp,2perc,
strings
ICELAND 010-002   (A443)

ASH see Torke, Michael

ASH WEDNESDAY, FOR SOLO VOICE AND
STRING ORCHESTRA see Orrego-Salas,
Juan A.

ASHEIM, NILS HENRIK (1960-   )
Mirror
3.3.3.3. 4.3.3.2. euphonium,perc,
harp,pno,org,synthesizer,
strings
NORGE   (A444)

Opening [6']
3.3.3.3. 4.4.3.1. timp,perc,harp,
strings
NORGE   (A445)

ASHKENAZY, BENJAMIN (1940-   )
Concerto for Trombone and Orchestra
[20']
3.3.4.3. 4.3.3.1. timp,3perc,
2harp,pno,strings,trom solo
sc,solo pt DONEMUS f.s., perf mat
rent   (A446)

Concerto for Vibraphone, Marimba and
Chamber Orchestra [17']
1.1.1.1.alto sax. 1.1.1.1. perc,
pno,acord,strings,vibra solo,
marimba solo
DONEMUS perf mat rent   (A447)

ASHKENAZY, BENJAMIN (cont'd.)

Izkor, For English Horn, Piano And
Orchestra [27']
2.2.2.2. 2.1.1.0. perc,marimba&
xylo,vibra,pno,cel,strings,
English horn solo,pno solo
DONEMUS perf mat rent   (A448)

ASIOLI, BONIFAZIO (1769-1832)
Sinfonia A Grand' Orchestra
(Gallarani, Massimo) (Monumenta,
Serie I, Vol. VII) MONTEVERDI
f.s.   (A449)

ASKESIS see Castaldo, Joseph F.

ASPIRATIONES PRINCIPIS, FOR SOLO VOICES
AND ORCHESTRA see Farkas, Ferenc

ASPLMAYR, FRANZ (1728-1786)
Symphonies, Three
(Monk; Kimball; Agee; Zakin; Eisen)
("The Symphony" Vol. B-VII) sc
GARLAND ISBN 0-8240-3854-1 $90.00
contains also: Hofmann, Leopold,
Symphonies, Four; Pichl, Wenzel
(Vaclav), Symphonies, Three;
Mozart, Leopold, Symphonies,
Three   (A450)

ASSAI see Dusapin, Pascal

ASSONANZEN see Bialas, Günter

ASTERION, FOR PIANO AND ORCHESTRA see
Kobayashi, Akira

ASTRUP SUITE see Tveitt, Geirr

ASTURIAS, FOR GUITAR, HARP AND STRING
ORCHESTRA [ARR.] see Albéniz, Isaac

ASTURIAS, RODRIGO (1942-   )
Banquete De Las Nubes, El, For Solo
Voice And Orchestra [40']
APNM   (A451)

Concerto for Violoncello and
Orchestra
[30'] sc APNM $40.00, perf mat rent
(A452)

Jardin De Los Senderos Que Se
Bifurcan, El, For Piano And
Orchestra [28']
sc APNM $50.00, perf mat rent
(A453)

Livre Pour Orchestra [108']
5.5.5.5. 8.5.3.2. 3perc,2harp,
pno,strings
APNM   (A454)

ASTUZIE FEMMINILI, LE: OVERTURE see
Cimarosa, Domenico

ASYMPTOPIA I see Hunt, Michael

ASYMPTOPIA II see Hunt, Michael

AT FIRST LIGHT see Benjamin, George

AT RIVERS, ON MOUNTAINS AND IN VALLEYS
see Sköld, Sven, Vid Alvom, Pa Berg
Och I Dalom

AT THE BIER OF A YOUNG ARTIST see
Nielsen, Carl

AT THE CIRCUS see Khachaturian, Karen

AT THE TOMB see Rimsky-Korsakov,
Nikolai

AT THE TOMB OF CHARLES IVES see
Harrison, Lou

AT THE WELL see Hageman, Richard

AT THE WHITE EDGE OF PHRYGIA see
Montague, Stephen

ATA see Xenakis, Yannis (Iannis)

ATALANTA: OVERTURE see Handel, George
Frideric

ATAYOSKEWIN see Forsyth, Malcolm

ATE see Toovey, Andrew

ATHABASCAN DANCES see Foley, Daniel

ATHALIA: KRIEGSMARSCH DER PRIESTER see
Mendelssohn-Bartholdy, Felix

ATHANEAL THE TRUMPETER, FOR TRUMPET AND
ORCHESTRA see Waxman, Franz

ATHANOR see Druckman, Jacob Raphael

ATHENA see Calmel, Roger

ATLAS see Cowie, Edward

ATMOSPHERE, FOR OBOE AND INSTRUMENTAL
ENSEMBLE see Barraine, Elsa

ATT DODA ETT BARN, FOR SOLO VOICE AND
ORCHESTRA see Kvam, Oddvar S.

ATTAQUE DU MOULIN, L': SUITE see
Bruneau, Alfred

ATTERBERG, KURT (1887-1974)
Rhapsody for Piano and Orchestra, Op.
1 [11']
2.2.2.2. 4.2.3.1. timp,perc,
strings,pno solo
STIM   (A455)

ATTILA: OH! NEL FUGGENTE NUVOLO, FOR
SOLO VOICE AND ORCHESTRA see Verdi,
Giuseppe

ATTRAVERSO I CANCELLI see Sciarrino,
Salvatore

ATYS: OVERTURE see Piccinni, Niccolo

AU BORD D'ABIMES see Ibarrondo, Felix

AU BOUT DU CHAGRIN UNE FENETRE OUVERTE,
FOR TRUMPET AND ORCHESTRA see
Landowski, Marcel

AU LIEU DES FLEURS see Minard, Robin

AU PAYS DU TENDRE see Vellones, Pierre

AU SOUFFLE D'UNE VOIX, FOR SOLO VOICES
AND ORCHESTRA see Prin, Yves

AU TOMBEAU DU MARTYR JUIF INCONNU, FOR
HARP AND STRING ORCHESTRA see
Williamson, Malcolm

AU VILLAGE see Mouquet, Jules

AUBADE see Tanaka, Karen

AUBAIN, JEAN (1928-   )
Concerto for Clarinet and Orchestra
[19']
2.2.2.2. 2.2.0.0. timp,perc,
strings,clar solo
BILLAUDOT perf mat rent   (A456)

AUBE DES BLEUETS see Mantero, Ajmone

AUBER, DANIEL-FRANÇOIS-ESPRIT
(1782-1871)
Concerto For Violin And Orchestra In
D *see THREE CENTURIES OF MUSIC
IN SCORE, VOL. 6: CONCERTO V,
LATE CLASSICAL STRINGS AND WINDS

Grand Pas Classique [arr.]
(Stirn, D.) 2.2.2.2. 4.2.3.1. timp,
perc,harp,strings [12'] BOIS perf
mat rent   (A457)

Rendezvous, Les [arr.]
(Lambert, Constant) 2.2.2.2.
4.2.3.1. timp,perc,strings [24']
BOOSEY perf mat rent   (A458)

Rondo for Violoncello and Orchestra
[7']
1.2.2.2. 2.1.3.0. strings,vcl
solo
(Jaffe, Ramon) SIKORSKI perf mat
rent   (A459)

AUBERT, JACQUES (1689-1753)
Concerto, Op. 17, No. 1, in D. [arr.]
(Blanchard, R.) string orch,cont
[10'] sc BILLAUDOT f.s., perf mat
rent   (A460)

Concerto, Op. 17, No. 2, in G, [arr.]
(Blanchard, R.) string orch,cont
[10'] sc BILLAUDOT f.s., perf mat
rent   (A461)

Concerto, Op. 17, No. 3, in A, [arr.]
(Blanchard, R.) string orch,cont
[10'] sc BILLAUDOT f.s., perf mat
rent   (A462)

Concerto, Op. 17, No. 4, in E minor,
[arr.]
(Blanchard, R.) string orch,cont
[10'] sc BILLAUDOT f.s., perf mat
rent   (A463)

Concerto, Op. 17, No. 5, in F, [arr.]
(Blanchard, R.) string orch,cont
[10'] sc BILLAUDOT f.s., perf mat
rent   (A464)

Concerto, Op. 17, No. 6, in G minor,
[arr.]
(Blanchard, R.) string orch,cont
[10'] sc BILLAUDOT f.s., perf mat
rent   (A465)

Concerto, Op. 26, No. 1, in E, [arr.]
(Blanchard, R.) string orch,cont
[10'] sc BILLAUDOT f.s., perf mat
rent   (A466)

AUBERT, JACQUES (cont'd.)

Concerto, Op. 26, No. 2, in F, [arr.]
(Blanchard, R.) string orch,cont
[10'] sc BILLAUDOT f.s., perf mat
rent   (A467)

Concerto, Op. 26, No. 3, in D, [arr.]
(Blanchard, R.) string orch,cont
[10'] sc BILLAUDOT f.s., perf mat
rent   (A468)

Concerto, Op. 26, No. 4, in E minor,
[arr.]
(Blanchard, R.) string orch,cont
[10'] sc BILLAUDOT f.s., perf mat
rent   (A469)

Symphony No. 5, [arr.]
(Boulay, L.) string orch [10']
BILLAUDOT perf mat rent   (A470)

AUBES INCENDIEES, FOR SPEAKER AND
INSTRUMENTAL ENSEMBLE see Decoust,
Michel

AUBIN, FRANCINE (1938-   )
Concerto for Organ and Orchestra
[15'30"]
3.3.3.3. 4.3.3.1. timp,perc,harp,
strings,org solo
BILLAUDOT perf mat rent   (A471)

Concerto Pour Ariane, For Double Bass
And Orchestra [15']
3.2.3.2. 3.3.3.0. timp,2perc,
harp,strings,db solo
BILLAUDOT perf mat rent   (A472)

Fantasy for Clarinet and Orchestra
[15']
2.1.0.1. 1.1.0.0. timp,2perc,
strings,clar solo
BILLAUDOT perf mat rent   (A473)

AUBIN, TONY (1907-1981)
Chant D'amour, Chant De Mort De
Troilus, For Solo Voice And
Orchestra [14'30"]
3.3.3.2. 4.2.3.1. timp,perc,cel,
harp,strings,T solo
BILLAUDOT perf mat rent   (A474)

AUDIANE, FOR SOLO VOICE AND ORCHESTRA
see Hoemsnes, Bjørn Korsan

AUDRAN, EDMOND (1840-1901)
Mascotte, La: Ballet Music [12']
CHOUDENS perf mat rent   (A475)

Miss Helyett: Valse Celebre
CHOUDENS perf mat rent   (A476)

AUDUBON, NO. 1: APPLE WALTZES see
Gould, Morton

AUDUBON, NO. 2: BIRD MOVEMENTS see
Gould, Morton

AUDUBON, NO. 3: CHORALES AND RAGS see
Gould, Morton

AUDUBON, NO. 4: CONCERTO GROSSO see
Gould, Morton

AUDUBON, NO. 5: FIRE MUSIC see Gould,
Morton

AUDUBON, NO. 6: INDIAN ATTACK see
Gould, Morton

AUDUBON, NO. 7: NIGHT MUSIC see Gould,
Morton

AUDUBON, NO. 8: SCHERZO see Gould,
Morton

AUDUBON, NO. 9: SERENADE see Gould,
Morton

AUDUBON, NO. 10: TRIBAL DANCE see
Gould, Morton

AUF DER GALERIE see Febel, Reinhard

AUF EIN ALTES BILD "IN GRUNER
LANDSCHAFT", FOR SOLO VOICE AND
ORCHESTRA see Wolf, Hugo

AUF FERIENREISEN see Strauss, Josef

AUF MEINES KINDES TOD "VON FERN DIE
UHREN SCHLAGEN", FOR SOLO VOICE AND
ORCHESTRA see Schoeck, Othmar

AUF- UND ABLEHNUNG see Krenek, Ernst

AUF ZUM TANZE see Strauss, Johann,
[Jr.]

AUFBRUCH see Glanert, Detlev

AUFERSTEHUNG UND HIMMELFAHRT JESU: IHR
TORE EROFFNET EUCH, FOR SOLO VOICE
AND ORCHESTRA see Bach, Carl
Philipp Emanuel

AUFFORDERUNG ZUM TANZ [ARR.] see Weber,
Carl Maria von

AUFZEICHNUNG: DAMMERUNG UND UMRISS see
Rihm, Wolfgang

AUGENSPRACHE see Strauss, Eduard

AUGURI see Stranz, Ulrich

AUGUST, FOR SOLO VOICE AND ORCHESTRA
see Hovland, Egil

AUGUSTE IAM COELESTIUM, D.488 see
Schubert, Franz (Peter)

AULA-LIEDER WALZER see Strauss, Eduard

AULODIE MIORITICA, FOR DOUBLE BASS AND
ORCHESTRA see Dumitrescu, Iancu

AURA see Shatin, Judith see Verbey,
Theo

AUREOLE see Druckman, Jacob Raphael

AURIC, GEORGES (1899-1983)
Fontaine De Jouvence, La [7']
1.1.1.1. 0.1.0.0. perc,pno/cel,
2vln,2vla,2vcl,db
ESCHIG perf mat rent   (A477)

Overture [7']
3.3.3.3. 4.3.3.1. timp,perc,
2harp,cel,strings
SIKORSKI perf mat rent   (A478)

AURIOL, HUBERT (1913-1980)
Phrenologie [15']
1.1.2.1. 0.0.0.0. timp,perc,
strings
BILLAUDOT perf mat rent   (A479)

AURORA see Cerchio, Bruno see Nilsson,
Anders see Powers, Anthony see
Wigglesworth, Frank

AURORA-GIOVE see Willi, Herbert

AURORA IV, FOR PIANO AND ORCHESTRA see
Fujita, Masanori

AURORAS see Erickson, Robert

AUS DEM MORGENLANDE see Heuberger,
Richard

AUS DEM RECHTSLEBEN WALZER see Strauss,
Eduard

AUS DEM TAGEBUCH DES ALTEN see Baur,
Jürg

AUS DEN BERGEN WALZER see Strauss,
Johann, [Jr.]

AUS DER FERNE see Strauss, Josef

AUS DER STUDIENZEIT WALZER see Strauss,
Eduard

AUS DER TIEFE RUFE ICH, HERR, ZU DIR,
FOR SOLO VOICE AND STRING ORCHESTRA
see Stölzel, Gottfried Heinrich

AUS JIDDISCHER VOLKSPOESIE, FOR SOLO
VOICES AND ORCHESTRA see
Shostakovich, Dmitri, From Jewish
Folk Poetry, For Solo Voices And
Orchestra

AUS LIEB' ZU IHR POLKA see Strauss,
Eduard

AUSKLANG, FOR PIANO AND ORCHESTRA see
Lachenmann, Helmut Friedrich

AUSSER RAND UND BAND POLKA see Strauss,
Eduard

AUSSTRAHLUNG, FOR SOLO VOICE AND
ORCHESTRA see Maderna, Bruno

AUSSTRAHLUNGEN W.A. MOZART'SCHER THEMEN
see Wimberger, Gerhard

AUSTIN, JOHN
Prelude, Fugue And Chorale [14']
2.3.3.3. 2.2.3.1. strings
sc AM.COMP.AL. $18.30   (A480)

Triple Play [7']
2.2.2.2. 2.2.2.0. timp,strings
sc AM.COMP.AL. $12.10   (A481)

AUSTIN, LARRY (1930-   )
Canadian Coastlines, For Solo Voice
And Chamber Orchestra [11']
fl,rec,bsn,trom,marimba,gtr,hpsd,
harp,vln,vla,vcl,db,electronic
tape,med solo
sc AM.COMP.AL. $18.80, perf mat
rent   (A482)

AUSTIN, LARRY (cont'd.)

Improvisations For Orchestra And Jazz
Soloists [15']
2(alto fl,pic).2.2(clar in E
flat,bass clar).2. 4.3.3.1.
timp,4perc,pno&cel,strings,trp
solo,alto sax solo,clar solo,
tenor sax solo,bass sax solo
sc,pts MJQ rent   (A483)

Sinfonia Concertante [17']
1.1.1.1. 1.1.0.0. timp,harp,pno,
strings,electronic tape
(Mozartean Episode, A) sc
AM.COMP.AL. $62.40, perf mat rent   (A484)

AUSTRALIS, FOR FLUTE AND STRING
ORCHESTRA see Horban, Walter

AUTODAFE, FOR PIANO AND INSTRUMENTAL
ENSEMBLE see Marco, Tomas

AUTOGRAPH WALTZES see Strauss, Johann,
[Jr.]

AUTOMNE, FOR CLARINET AND ORCHESTRA see
Francois, Renaud

AUTOMNE, L' see Albéniz, Isaac see
Koechlin, Charles

AUTORITRATTO NELLA NOTTE see Sciarrino,
Salvatore

AUTUMN, FOR BIWA, SHAKUHACHI, AND
ORCHESTRA see Takemitsu, Toru

AUTUMN, FOR SOLO VOICE AND STRING
ORCHESTRA see Eggen, Arne, Host,
For Solo Voice And String Orchestra

AUTUMN, FOR SOLO VOICE AND ORCHESTRA
see Lutoslawski, Witold, Jesien,
For Solo Voice And Orchestra

AUTUMN LYRICS, FOR SOLO VOICE AND
ORCHESTRA see Lilja, Bernhard

AUTUMN MUSIC see Huba, Volodymyr

AUTUMN NOCTURNE see Prokofiev, Serge,
Autumnal Sketch

AUTUMN PLAY see Thorarinsson, Leifur

AUTUMN SONG, THE, FOR SOLO VOICE AND
ORCHESTRA see Groven, Eivind,
Hostsangen, For Solo Voice And
Orchestra

AUTUMN SONG [ARR.] see Tchaikovsky,
Piotr Ilyich

AUTUMN SYMPHONY see Coulthard, Jean

AUTUMN THOUGHTS see Du, Ming-Xin

AUTUMNAL SKETCH see Prokofiev, Serge

AUTUNNO, L' see Trojahn, Manfred

AUX ETOILES see Duparc, Henri

AUX MENDIANTS DU CIEL, FOR SOLO VOICE
AND ORCHESTRA see Landowski, Marcel

AUX RIVES ULTERIEURES, FOR VIOLIN AND
INSTRUMENTAL ENSEMBLE see Lenot,
Jacques

AV "TUE BENTSONS VISER", FOR SOLO VOICE
AND ORCHESTRA see Jordan, Sverre

AVANTI see Kucera, Václav

AVE MARIA see Ekimovsky, Viktor

AVE MARIA, FOR VIOLONCELLO AND
ORCHESTRA see Bruch, Max

AVEN, L', FOR FLUTE AND ORCHESTRA see
Dusapin, Pascal

AVENTURE DE LA GUIMARD, UNE: DANSES
ANCIENNES see Messager, Andre

AVENTURES DE MERCURE [ARR.] see Satie,
Erik

AVERITT, WILLIAM EARL (1948-   )
Gentle, Into That Night [12']
2+pic.2.2+bass clar.2. 4.3.3.1.
timp,2perc,harp,strings
MMB perf mat rent   (A485)

AVISON, CHARLES (1709-1770)
Concerto in G minor
(Milner) string orch,cont OXFORD
perf mat rent   (A486)

AVONDZANG, FOR SOLO VOICE AND ORCHESTRA
see Diepenbrock, Alphons

AXIS see Yavelow, Christopher Johnson

AXMAN, EMIL (1887-1949)
  Concerto for Violoncello and
    Orchestra
    3.2.2.2. 4.2.1.0. timp,perc,harp,
      cel,strings,vcl solo
    SUPRAPHON   (A487)

AYA ZEHN, FOR OBOE OR TRUMPET AND
  ORCHESTRA see Amram, David Werner

AZIONI MUSICALI see Badings, Henk

AZZURRI ABISSI, FOR CLARINET AND
  ORCHESTRA see Gentilucci, Armando

B

B FOR ORKESTER see Berge, Sigurd

B.W.V., FOR SOLO VOICES AND
  INSTRUMENTAL ENSEMBLE see Aperghis,
  Georges

BA ME VIETNAM, FOR DOUBLE BASS AND
  INSTRUMENTAL ENSEMBLE see Dao,
  Nguyen Thien

BAAL-GESANGE, FOR SOLO VOICE AND
  ORCHESTRA see Cerha, Friedrich

BABBITT, MILTON BYRON (1916-   )
  As Long As It Isn't Love, For Solo
    Voice And Orchestra (from Three
    Theatrical Songs)
    2(pic).1.2.1. 2.1.1.1. perc,pno&
      cel,strings,solo voice
    (Schuller, Gunther) PETERS P66842
      $7.75 contains also: Now You See
      It, For Solo Voice And Orchestra
                                       (B1)
  Concerto for Piano and Orchestra
    [20']
    2(pic).2(English horn).3(clar in
      E flat,bass clar).2(contrabsn).
      3.2.3.1. perc,harp,strings,pno
      solo
    PETERS P67087 perf mat rent   (B2)

  Now You See It, For Solo Voice And
    Orchestra
    see As Long As It Isn't Love, For
    Solo Voice And Orchestra

  Transfigured Notes [19']
    string orch
    PETERS P67194 perf mat rent   (B3)

BABCOCK, DAVID (1956-   )
  Symphony No. 2 [15']
    2+pic.2(English horn).2(bass
      clar).2(contrabsn). 4.3.3.1.
      perc,harp,strings
    DOBLINGER perf mat rent   (B4)

BABEL see Manneke, Daan

BABES IN TOYLAND: MARCH OF THE TOYS,
  [ARR.] see Herbert, Victor

BABY SERENADE see Korngold, Erich
  Wolfgang

BACA LOCATION NO. 1 see Ware, Peter

BACCHANAL, FOR ORGAN AND ORCHESTRA see
  Albright, William H.

BACCHANALES ROMAINES see Bozza, Eugène

BACH, CARL PHILIPP EMANUEL (1714-1788)
  Auferstehung Und Himmelfahrt Jesu:
    Ihr Tore Eröffnet Euch, For Solo
    Voice And Orchestra
    0.2.0.0. 2.2.0.0. strings,B solo
    sc,pts BREITKOPF-L rent   (B5)

  Concerto for Flute and Orchestra in D
    minor, MIN 146
    string orch,fl solo
    KUNZEL 10163 sc $14.00, pts $3.00,
      ea.   (B6)

  Concerto for Harpsichord and
    Orchestra in D, Wq. 27
    (Kulukundis, Elias N.) (Collegium
      Musicum Series of Yale
      University) sc A-R ED
    ISBN 0-89579-024-6 $19.95   (B7)

  Concerto for Harpsichord and String
    Orchestra in A minor, Wq. 26
    [25']
    string orch,hpsd solo
    KAHNT perf mat rent   (B8)

  Concerto for Harpsichord and String
    Orchestra in F, Wq. 33
    (Oberdorffer) KALMUS A7329 sc
      $20.00, set $12.50, pts $2.50,
      ea.   (B9)

  Concerto for Harpsichord and String
    Orchestra in G minor, Wq. 6
    (Oberdorffer) KALMUS A7328 sc
      $20.00, set $12.50, pts $2.50,
      ea.   (B10)

  Concerto for Harpsichord, Piano and
    Orchestra in E flat, Wq. 47
    2.0.0.0. 2.0.0.0. strings,hpsd
      solo,pno solo
    (Jacobi) KALMUS A6995 sc $20.00,
      set $18.00, pts $2.00, ea., perf
      mat rent   (B11)

BACH, CARL PHILIPP EMANUEL (cont'd.)

  Concerto for Oboe and String
    Orchestra, Wq. 164
    KUNZEL 10164 sc $20.00, pts $3.00,
      ea.   (B12)

  Concerto for Oboe and String
    Orchestra, Wq. 165
    KUNZEL 10177 sc $18.00, pts $3.00,
      ea.   (B13)

  Concerto for Violoncello and String
    Orchestra in B flat, Wq. 171
    (Schulz) KALMUS A5564 sc $12.00,
      set $12.00, pts $2.00, ea.   (B14)

  Keyboard Concertos, Nos 38, 39
    (Kulukundis, Elias; Wiley, Paul)
      (C.P.E. Bach Edition, Ser. II,
      Vol. 15) sc OXFORD f.s.   (B15)

  Klopstocks Morgengesang Am
    Schöpfungsfeste "Noch Kommt Sie
    Nicht, Die Sonne", For Solo
    Voices And Orchestra
    2fl,ob,strings,hpsd,SS soli
    BREITKOPF-L perf mat rent   (B16)

  Magnificat: Fecit Potentiam, For Solo
    Voice And Orchestra
    3trp,timp,strings,B solo
    BREITKOPF-L perf mat rent   (B17)

  Symphony, Wq. 182, No. 2, in B flat
    (Schmid) KALMUS A5588 sc $7.00, set
      $5.00, pts $1.00, ea.   (B18)

  Symphony, Wq. 182, No. 5, in B minor
    (Scmid) KALMUS A7400 sc $10.00, set
      $7.50, pts $1.50, ea.   (B19)

  Symphony, Wq. 183, No. 1, in D [14']
    2.2.0.1+opt bsn. 2.0+opt
      2trp.0.0. opt timp,strings
    BREITKOPF-W perf mat rent   (B20)

  Symphony, Wq. 183, No. 2, in E flat
    KALMUS A5742 sc $12.00, set $20.00,
      perf mat rent   (B21)

BACH, JAN MORRIS (1937-   )
  Gala Fanfare
    sc HIGHGATE 7.0284 $9.50   (B22)

  Happy Prince, The, For Narrator And
    Chamber Orchestra
    sc HIGHGATE $17.50   (B23)

BACH, JOHANN BERNHARD (1676-1749)
  Overture, No. 1, in G minor
    string orch,cont
    (Bergmann) CARUS 40.527   (B24)

  Overture, No. 2, in G
    string orch,cont
    (Bergmann) CARUS 40.528   (B25)

  Overture, No. 3, in E minor
    string orch,cont
    (Bergmann) CARUS 40.529   (B26)

  Overture, No. 4, in D
    string orch,cont
    (Bergmann) CARUS 40.530   (B27)

BACH, JOHANN CHRISTIAN (1735-1782)
  Clemenza Di Scipione, La: Overture
    SONZOGNO perf mat rent   (B28)

  Collected Works, Vol. 26: Symphonies
    I *CCU
    sc GARLAND ISBN 0-8240-6075-X
      $82.00   (B29)

  Collected Works, Vol. 27: Symphonies
    II *CCU
    sc GARLAND ISBN 0-8240-6076-8
      $92.00   (B30)

  Collected Works, Vol. 28: Symphonies
    III *CCU
    sc GARLAND ISBN 0-8240-6077-6
      $110.00   (B31)

  Collected Works, Vol. 29: Symphonies
    IV *CCU
    sc GARLAND ISBN 0-8240-6078-4 f.s.
                                   (B32)
  Collected Works, Vol. 30: Symphonies
    Concertantes I *CCU
    sc GARLAND ISBN 0-8240-6079-2
      $100.00   (B33)

  Collected Works, Vol. 31: Symphonies
    Concertantes II *CCU
    sc GARLAND ISBN 0-8240-6080-6
      $102.00   (B34)

  Collected Works, Vol. 32: Keyboard
    Concertos I *CCU
    sc GARLAND ISBN 0-8240-6081-4
      $82.00   (B35)

BACH, JOHANN CHRISTIAN (cont'd.)

Collected Works, Vol. 33: Keyboard
    Concertos II *CCU
    sc GARLAND ISBN 0-8240-6082-2
    $62.00   (B36)

Collected Works, Vol. 34: Keyboard
    Concertos III *CCU
    sc GARLAND ISBN 0-8240-6083-0
    $77.00   (B37)

Collected Works, Vol. 35: Keyboard
    Concertos IV *CCU
    sc GARLAND ISBN 0-8240-6084-9
    $85.00   (B38)

Collected Works, Vol. 36: Other Solo
    Concertos *CC5U
    sc GARLAND ISBN 0-8240-6085-7
    $77.00 contains 5 solo concertos
    for woodwind instruments   (B39)

Concerto for Harpsichord and
    Orchestra in E flat, MIN 147
    2horn,strings,hpsd solo
    sc KUNZEL 10147 $16.00, ipa   (B40)

Concerto for Harpsichord and
    Orchestra, Op. 13, No. 2, in D
    (Landshoff) KALMUS A7382 sc $10.00,
    set $20.00, pts $2.00, ea., perf
    mat rent   (B41)

Concerto for Harpsichord and
    Orchestra, Op. 13, No. 4, in B
    flat
    KALMUS A7383 sc $12.00, set $15.00,
    pts $2.00, ea.   (B42)

Concerto for Harpsichord and String
    Orchestra in E flat
    (Praetorius) KALMUS A5585 sc
    $12.00, set $5.00, pts $1.00, ea.
                                   (B43)

Concerto for Harpsichord and String
    Orchestra in F minor, MIN 45
    (Martini, E.) KALMUS A4142 sc
    $12.00, set $10.00   (B44)

Concerto for Harpsichord and String
    Orchestra, Op. 7, No. 5, in E
    flat
    (Dobereiner) KALMUS A7381 sc
    $12.00, set $6.00, pts $1.50, ea.
                                   (B45)

Meiner Allerliebsten Schönen, For
    Solo Voice And Orchestra
    see Zwei Weltliche Arien, For Solo
    Voice And Orchestra

Sinfonia Concertante in A
    (Einstein) KALMUS A5586 sc $12.00,
    set $22.00, pts $2.00, ea. (B46)

Sinfonia in E flat, MIN 167
    (McAlister) 2ob,2horn,cont,
    strings [13'] (periodical
    overture no. 44) KALMUS A5637 sc
    $12.00, set $20.00, perf mat rent
                                   (B47)

Sinfonia, Op. 9, No. 2, in E flat
    (Stein) KALMUS A5898 sc $10.00, set
    $18.00, perf mat rent   (B48)

Sinfonia, Op. 9, No. 3, in B flat
    sc,pts BREITKOPF-W PB-OB 5059 f.s.
                                   (B49)

Sinfonia, Op. 18, No. 1, in E flat
    SONZOGNO perf mat rent   (B50)
    (Landshof) KALMUS A5566 sc $10.00,
    set $30.00, pts $2.00, ea.   (B51)
    (Stein) KALMUS A7149 sc $12.00, set
    $30.00, pts $3.00, ea.   (B52)

Sinfonia, Op. 18, No. 2, in B flat
    (Landshof) KALMUS A5567 sc $10.00,
    set $15.00, pts $1.00, ea. (B53)

Sinfonia, Op. 18, No. 3, in D
    (Stein) KALMUS A5568 sc $10.00, set
    $30.00, pts $2.00, ea.   (B54)

Sinfonia, Op. 18, No. 4, in D
    (Einstein) KALMUS A5569 sc $12.00,
    set $25.00, pts $2.00, ea. (B55)

Wenn Nach Der Stürme Toben, For Solo
    Voice And Orchestra
    see Zwei Weltliche Arien, For Solo
    Voice And Orchestra

Zwei Weltliche Arien, For Solo Voice
    And Orchestra
    (Walter) 2fl/ob,strings,hpsd,T solo
    BREITKOPF-L perf mat rent
    contains: Meiner Allerliebsten
    Schönen, For Solo Voice And
    Orchestra; Wenn Nach Der Stürme
    Toben, For Solo Voice And
    Orchestra   (B56)

BACH, JOHANN CHRISTOPH (1642-1703)
    Lamento "Ach, Dass Ich Wassers Gnug
    Hätte", For Solo Voice And
    Orchestra
    (Schneider) BREITKOPF-L perf mat
    rent   (B57)

Wie Bist Du Denn, O Gott, In Zorn
    Entbrannt, For Solo Voice And
    Orchestra
    ob,strings,hpsd,B solo
    BREITKOPF-L perf mat rent   (B58)

BACH, JOHANN CHRISTOPH FRIEDRICH
    (1732-1795)
    Amerikanerin, Die, For Solo Voice And
    String Orchestra [9']
    string orch,hpsd,B/T solo
    BREITKOPF-L perf mat rent   (B59)
    (Walter, G.) BREITKOPF-W perf mat
    rent   (B60)

Four Early Sinfonias
    (Nolte, Ewald V.) sc A-R ED
    ISBN 0-89579-170-6 $27.95
    contains: Sinfonia in B flat;
    Sinfonia in D minor; Sinfonia
    in E; Sinfonia in F   (B61)

Four Late Sinfonias *CC4U
    (Nolte, Ewald V.) sc A-R ED $27.95,
    perf mat rent   (B62)

Sinfonia in B flat
    see Four Early Sinfonias

Sinfonia in D minor
    see Four Early Sinfonias

Sinfonia in E
    see Four Early Sinfonias

Sinfonia in F
    see Four Early Sinfonias

Sinfonia No. 20 in B flat
    1.0.2.1. 2.0.0.0. strings
    sc,pts HANSSLER f.s.   (B63)

BACH, JOHANN LUDWIG (1677-1741)
    Suite in G
    opt 2ob,strings,cont
    (Hofmann, K.) HANSSLER 30.051 f.s.
                                   (B64)

BACH, JOHANN SEBASTIAN (1685-1750)
    Arioso [arr.]
    (Balazs, Frederic) 2.3.3.2.
    4.3.3.1. timp,harp,strings [6']
    AM.COMP.AL. perf mat rent   (B65)

Bach Suite, A [arr.] (from Piano
    Suites)
    (Williams) 1.1.1.1. 0.1.0.0. timp,
    strings [23'] KALMUS A7372 sc
    $15.00, set $25.00, pts $2.50,
    ea., perf mat rent   (B66)

Bach Works For Strings
    see Werke Fur Streicher Und Basso
    Continuo

Brandenburg Concerti Nos.1-3, BWV
    1046-1048
    min sc KALMUS K00741 $5.25   (B67)

Brandenburg Concerti Nos. 1-6, BWV
    1046-1051
    (Soldan; Landshoff) sc,cloth PETERS
    577 f.s.   (B68)

Brandenburg Concerti Nos. 4-6, BWV
    1049-1051
    min sc KALMUS K00742 $5.25   (B69)

Brandenburg Concerti Nos. 1-6, BWV
    1046-1051
    (Mariassy) study sc EMB 40089 f.s.
                                   (B70)

Brandenburg Concerto No. 1 In F, BWV
    1046
    (Máriássy) sc EMB 8103 f.s.   (B71)

Brandenburg Concerto No. 2 in F, BWV
    1047
    MMB perf mat rent   (B72)
    (Máriássy) sc EMB 8104 f.s.   (B73)

Brandenburg Concerto No. 3 In G, BWV
    1048
    (Máriássy) sc EMB 8481 f.s.   (B74)

Brandenburg Concerto No. 4 In G, BWV
    1049
    (Máriássy) sc EMB 8482 f.s.   (B75)

Brandenburg Concerto No. 5 In D, BWV
    1050
    (Máriássy) sc EMB 8835 f.s.   (B76)

Brandenburg Concerto No. 6 In B Flat,
    BWV 1051
    (Máriássy) sc EMB 8836 f.s.   (B77)

Cantata No. 35: Geist Und Seele Wird
    Virwirret, For Solo Voice And
    Orchestra

BACH, JOHANN SEBASTIAN (cont'd.)

    BREITKOPF-L perf mat rent   (B78)

Cantata No. 49: Ich Geh' Und Suche
    Mit Verlangen, For Solo Voices
    And Orchestra
    sc,pts BREITKOPF-L EB 7049 KIA rent
                                   (B79)
Cantata No. 49: Ich Geh' Und Suche
    Mit Verlangen, For Solo Voices
    And Orchestra
    KALMUS A4498 sc $12.00, set $14.00,
    pts $2.00, ea.   (B80)

Cantata No. 51: Jauchzet Gott In
    Allen Landen, For Solo Voice And
    Orchestra
    sc,pts BREITKOPF-L EB 7051 KIA rent
                                   (B81)

Cantata No. 53: Schlage Doch
    Gewunschte Stunde, For Solo Voice
    And Orchestra
    [Ger/Eng] (attributed to Bach;
    actually composed by Georg
    Melchior Hoffmann) min sc PHILH
    PH. 102 $3.00   (B82)

Cantata No. 54: Widerstehe Doch Der
    Sünde, For Solo Voice And
    Orchestra
    sc,pts BREITKOPF-L EB 7054 KIA rent
                                   (B83)

Cantata No. 58: Ach Gott, Wie Manches
    Herzeleid, For Solo Voices And
    Orchestra
    sc,pts BREITKOPF-L EB 7058 KIA rent
                                   (B84)

Cantata No. 82: Ich Habe Genug, For
    Solo Voice And Orchestra
    BREITKOPF-L pts EB 7082 KIA f.s.,
    sc rent   (B85)

Cantata No. 152: Tritt Auf Die
    Glaubensbahn, For Solo Voices And
    Orchestra
    sc BREITKOPF-L EB 7152 KIA f.s.,
    perf mat rent   (B86)

Cantata No. 170: Vergnügte Ruh,
    Beliebte Seelenlust, For Solo
    Voice And Orchestra
    sc,pts BREITKOPF-L EB 7170 KIA rent
                                   (B87)

Cantata No. 199: Mein Herze Schwimmt
    Im Blut: For Solo Voice And
    Orchestra
    sc,pts BREITKOPF-L EB 7199 KIA rent
                                   (B88)

Cantata No. 202: Weichet Nur,
    Betrübte Schatten, For Solo Voice
    And Orchestra
    sc BREITKOPF-L EB 7202 KIA f.s.,
    perf mat rent   (B89)

Cantata No. 204: Ich Bin In Mir
    Vergnügt, For Solo Voice And
    Orchestra
    sc,pts BREITKOPF-L EB 7204 KIA rent
                                   (B90)

Cantata No. 209: Non Sa Che Sia
    Dolore, For Solo Voice And
    Orchestra
    sc BREITKOPF-L EB 7209 KIA f.s.,
    perf mat rent   (B91)

Cantata No. 210: O Holder Tag,
    Erwünschte Zeit, For Solo Voice
    And Orchestra
    sc,pts BREITKOPF-L EB 7210 KIA rent
                                   (B92)

Cantata No. 211: Schweigt Stille,
    Plaudert Nicht, For Solo Voices
    And Orchestra
    [Ger/Eng] min sc PHILH PH. 103
    $3.00   (B93)
    BREITKOPF-L sc EB 7211 KIA f.s.,
    pts EB 7211 KIA f.s.   (B94)

Choral Preludes, Two [arr.]
    see Choralvorspiele, Zwei [arr.]

Choral Variation
    see Wachet Auf, Ruft Uns Die Stimme
    [arr.]

Choralvorspiele, Zwei [arr.]
    (Gui) "Choral Preludes, Two [arr.]"
    (contains: In Dir Ist Freude
    [arr.] and O Mensch, Bewein Dein
    Sunde Gross [arr.]) KALMUS A4280
    sc $5.00, set $20.00, perf mat
    rent   (B95)

Concerti For Harpsichord, 16 *CC16U
    min sc LEA LPS0069 $4.00   (B96)

Concerti For Solo Keyboard And
    Orchestra, Seven *CC7U
    sc DOVER 249298 $8.95 reprint of
    Bach Gesellschaft edition   (B97)

Concerto for 2 Harpsichords and
    String Orchestra, No. 1, in C,
    BWV 1060
    (Reger) BREITKOPF-L perf mat rent

BACH, JOHANN SEBASTIAN (cont'd.)

(B98)

Concerto for 2 Harpsichords and
String Orchestra, No. 2, in C,
BWV 1061
(Reger) BREITKOPF-L perf mat rent
(B99)

Concerto for Oboe and String
Orchestra, BWV 1059a
*reconstruction
(Mehl, Arnold) string orch,cont,ob
solo sc KUNZEL 10209 $20.00, perf
mat rent (B100)

Concerto for Oboe and String
Orchestra in C, [arr.] (from
Concerto For Harpsichord And
String Orchestra, BWV 1055)
(Hausler) string orch,cont,ob solo
[14'] sc,pts SIKORSKI 1035 f.s.
(B101)

Concerto for Oboe d'Amore and String
Orchestra in D, BWV 1053
*reconstruction
(Mehl, Arnold) string orch,cont,ob
d'amore solo sc KUNZEL 10208
$20.00, perf mat rent (B102)

Concerto for String Orchestra, No. 2,
in E, BWV 1042
see Concerto for Violin and String
Orchestra, No. 1, in A minor, BWV
1041

Concerto for Violin and Orchestra in
F, [arr.] (from Brandenburg
Concerto No. 2)
(Mottl) 3.3.2.2. 2.2.0.0. strings,
vln solo [15'] KALMUS A6772 sc
$20.00, set $20.00, pts $1.25,
ea., perf mat rent (B103)

Concerto for Violin and String
Orchestra, No. 1, in A minor, BWV
1041
min sc KALMUS K00908 $5.25 contains
also: Concerto for String
Orchestra, No. 2, in E, BWV 1042;
Concerto Movement For Violin,
Orchestra In D; Concerto for 2
Violins and String Orchestra in D
minor, BWV 1043 (B104)
(Killan, Dietrich) study sc BAREN.
$7.50 contains also: Concerto for
Violin and String Orchestra, No.
2, in E, BWV 1042 (B105)

Concerto for Violin and String
Orchestra, No. 2, in E, BWV 1042
see Concerto for Violin and String
Orchestra, No. 1, in A minor, BWV
1041

Concerto for 2 Violins and String
Orchestra in D minor, BWV 1043
BAREN. sc,pts BA 5188 f.s., min sc
TP 284 f.s. (B106)
see Concerto for Violin and String
Orchestra, No. 1, in A minor, BWV
1041

Concerto for 2 Violins and String
Orchestra in D minor, BWV 1043,
[arr.]
(Zinn, William) string orch
EXCELSIOR sc 494-01304 $7.50, pts
494-01305-01309 $2.50, ea. (B107)

Concerto Movement For Violin,
Orchestra In D
see Concerto for Violin and String
Orchestra, No. 1, in A minor, BWV
1041

Concerto No. 1 in G for Violoncello
and String Orchestra, [arr.]
string orch,hpsd,vcl solo [7'20"]
INTERNAT. perf mat rent (B108)

Fantasia And Fugue [arr.]
(Zinn, William) string orch
EXCELSIOR sc 494-01316 $7.00, pts
494-01317-01321 $2.50, ea. (B109)

Fantasia And Fugue In G Minor [arr.]
(Goedicke, Alexander) 3.3.3.3.
4.3.3.1. timp,perc,strings [11']
VAAP perf mat rent (B110)

Fantasia And Fugue No. 6 [arr.]
(Villa-Lobos, Heitor) 3.3.3.3.
4.2.3.1. timp,strings AMP perf
mat rent (B111)

Fantasia In G [arr.]
(Volkel, George) string orch VAAP
perf mat rent (B112)

Feste Burg Ist Unser Gott, Ein'
[arr.]
(Damrosch, Walter) "Mighty Fortress
Is Our God, A [arr.]" 2+
pic.2.2. 4.3.3.1. timp,chimes,
strings [5'] WARNER perf mat rent
(B113)

BACH, JOHANN SEBASTIAN (cont'd.)

Fugue, BWV 857, [arr.]
(Dimitrakopoulos, Apostolo) [4']
STIM (B114)

Fugue in G minor, BWV 542, [arr.]
string orch
(Sanford, Ruth) (The "Great")
WARNER perf mat rent (B115)

Fugue in G minor, BWV 578, [arr.]
[3'14"]
(Damrosch, Walter) 2.2+English
horn.2+bass clar.2. 4.2.3.1.
timp,triangle,strings [3'] WARNER
perf mat rent (B116)
(Demerest, Clifford) (The "Lesser")
WARNER perf mat rent (B117)

Funf Geistliche Lieder, For Solo
Voice And Orchestra [arr.]
(Schnebel, Dieter) 2.2.2.2.
2.2.2.1. harp,strings,solo voice
SCHOTTS perf mat rent
contains: Ich Liebe Jesum In Der
Not; Ich Steh An Deiner Krippen
Hier; Komm Susser Tod; Kommt
Wieder Aus Der Finstren Gruft;
O Du Liebe Meiner Liebe (B118)

Gavotte En Rondeau [arr.] (from
Partita, Bwv 1006)
(Reuter) 2.1.0.1. 2.2.1.0. pno,
strings [4'] KALMUS A5684 sc
$5.00, set $15.00 (B119)

Ich Liebe Jesum In Der Not
see Funf Geistliche Lieder, For
Solo Voice And Orchestra [arr.]

Ich Steh An Deiner Krippen Hier
see Funf Geistliche Lieder, For
Solo Voice And Orchestra [arr.]

In Dir Ist Freude, [arr.]
(Medek, Tilo) 0.1.3.1. 3.3.2.1.
timp,perc,vla,vcl [13'] HANSEN-
GER perf mat rent (B120)
*see Bach, Johann Sebastian,
Choralvorspiele, Zwei

Komm Susser Tod
see Funf Geistliche Lieder, For
Solo Voice And Orchestra [arr.]

Kommt Wieder Aus Der Finstren Gruft
see Funf Geistliche Lieder, For
Solo Voice And Orchestra [arr.]

Kunst Der Fuge, Die [arr]
(Stiedry, Fritz) 3.3(ob d'amore,
English horn).2.3(contrabsn).
2.2.1.0. 2pno,strings [70'] BOTE
perf mat rent (B121)

Menuet From A Serenata [arr.]
see Menuette Aus Einer Serenata
[arr.]

Menuette Aus Einer Serenata [arr.]
"Menuet From A Serenata [arr.]"
2fl,strings [4'] KALMUS A7454 sc
$7.00, set $10.00, pts $1.50, ea.
(B122)

Mighty Fortress Is Our God, A [arr.]
see Feste Burg Ist Unser Gott, Ein'
[arr.]

Musical Offering [arr.]
see Musikalisches Opfer [arr.]

Musikalisches Opfer [arr.] *BWV 1079
(Adomian, Lan) "Musical Offering
[arr.]" 3.3.3.3. 4.3.3.1. strings
[50'] SCHIRM.G perf mat rent
(B123)
(David, J.N.) 1.1+ob da caccia.0.1.
0.0.0.0. hpsd,strings BREITKOPF-W
perf mat rent (B124)

Musikalisches Opfer: Ricercare A 3
Und 8 Kanons [arr]
(Beyer, Frank Michael) 1.2(English
horn).2(bass clar).1. 1.1.1.0.
harp,strings [21'] BOTE perf mat
rent (B125)

O Du Liebe Meiner Liebe
see Funf Geistliche Lieder, For
Solo Voice And Orchestra [arr.]

O Mensch, Bewein Dein Sunde Gross
[arr.] *see Bach, Johann
Sebastian, Choralvorspiele, Zwei

O Mensch, Bewein Sein Sunde Gross
[arr.]
(Reger) KALMUS A4282 sc $3.00, set
$3.75 (B126)

Overtures, Four
see Suites Nos. 1-4, BWV 1066-1069

BACH, JOHANN SEBASTIAN (cont'd.)

Passion Chorale, The [arr.]
(Besly, Maurice) string orch [5']
BOOSEY perf mat rent (B127)

Prelude and Fugue in C minor, [arr.]
(Villa-Lobos, Heitor) 3.2.2.3.
4.1.2.1. timp,harp,strings [5']
ESCHIG perf mat rent (B128)

Prelude and Fugue in D minor, [arr.]
(Villa-Lobos, Heitor) string orch
[5'] ESCHIG perf mat rent (B129)

Prelude in C minor, [arr.]
(Goldberg, Norman) 2.2.2+bass
clar.2. 4.3.3.1. timp,strings
[7'] MMB perf mat rent (B130)

Schafe Konnen Sicher Weiden [arr.]
(from Cantata No.208)
(Wittaker) "Sheep May Safely Graze
[arr.]" string orch,opt 2fl,opt
pno [7'] OXFORD 77.020 sc $6.00,
pts $1.50, ea. (B131)

Sheep May Safely Graze [arr.]
see Schafe Konnen Sicher Weiden
[arr.]

Sinfonias, Three (from Cantatas Nos.
196, 61, 209)
(Hoffmann) fl,strings [11'] KALMUS
A7447 sc $10.00, set $9.00, pts
$1.50, ea. (B132)

Sinfonien Und Ritornell (from
Kantaten 4, 68, 76, 150, 196)
string orch sc,pts PELIKAN PE 851
f.s. (B133)

Sonata in E minor, BWV 1023, [arr.]
(Respighi) KALMUS A4283 sc $7.00,
set $10.00 (B134)

Suite, [arr.] (from Bwv 1067 And Bwv
1068)
(Mahler) 1.2.0.0. 0.3.0.0. timp,
pno,org,strings [8'] KALMUS A6065
sc $15.00, set $35.00, perf mat
rent (B135)

Suite in G, MIN 373, [arr.] (from
French Suite, Bwv 816)
(Goossens, E.) KALMUS A5008 sc
$12.00, set $35.00, perf mat rent
(B136)

Suite in G minor, MIN 162, [arr.]
(from English Suite No.3)
(Raff, Erdmansdorfer) 2.2.2.2.
2.2.0.0. timp,strings [25']
KALMUS A5891 sc $15.00, set
$30.00, perf mat rent (B137)
(Raff, Joachim) 2.2.2.2. 2.2.0.0.
timp,strings RIES perf mat rent
(B138)

Suite No. 1 in C, BWV 1066
(Gruss, Hans) BAREN. sc,pts BA 5157
f.s., min sc TP 192 f.s. (B139)
(Gruss, Hans) DEUTSCHER sc 1726
f.s., pts 2726 f.s. (B140)

Suite No. 2 in B minor, BWV 1067
(Gruss, Hans) BAREN. sc,pts BA 5158
f.s., min sc TP 193 f.s. (B141)
(Gruss, Hans) DEUTSCHER sc 1727
f.s., pts 2727 f.s. (B142)
(Mariassy) study sc EMB 40079 f.s.
(B143)

Suite No. 3 in D, BWV 1068
(Gruss, Hans) sc,pts BAREN. BA 5159
f.s. (B144)
(Gruss, Hans) DEUTSCHER sc 1728
f.s., pts 2728 f.s. (B145)
(Newstone, Harry) min sc EULENBURG
EU00818 $3.75 (B146)

Suite No. 4 in D, BWV 1069
(Gruss, Hans) BAREN. sc,pts BA 5160
f.s., min sc TP 195 f.s. (B147)
(Gruss, Hans) sc DEUTSCHER 1729
f.s. (B148)

Suites Nos. 1-4, BWV 1066-1069
"Overtures, Four" min sc KALMUS
K00779 $5.25 (B149)

Toccata And Fugue, [arr.]
(Villa-Lobos, Heitor) 3.2.2.3.
4.2.2.1. timp,strings [5'] ESCHIG
perf mat rent (B150)

Wachet Auf, Ruft Uns Die Stimme
[arr.] (from Cantata No. 140)
(Bantock, G.) "Choral Variation"
KALMUS A2624 sc $3.00, set $10.00
(B151)

Werke Fur Streicher Und Basso
Continuo
(Hoffmann) "Bach Works For Strings"
KALMUS 7110 sc $10.00, set
$10.00, pts $2.00, ea. (B152)

"BACH, P.D.Q." (PETER SCHICKELE)
see also SCHICKELE, PETER

　Breakfast Antiphonies [22']
　　(restricted for Peter Schickele's
　　personal appearances) PRESSER
　　perf mat rent　　　　　　　　　(B153)

　Gross Concerto No. 2
　　(restricted for Peter Schickele's
　　personal appearances) PRESSER
　　perf mat rent　　　　　　　　　(B154)

　Preachers Of Crimetheus [14']
　　(restricted for Peter Schickele's
　　personal appearances) PRESSER
　　perf mat rent　　　　　　　　　(B155)

　Royal Firewater Musick [17']
　　2.1.0.0. 2.0.0.0. perc,strings,
　　　bottles
　　PRESSER perf mat rent　　　　　(B156)

　1712 Overture [10']
　　(restricted for Peter Schickele's
　　personal appearances) PRESSER
　　perf mat rent　　　　　　　　　(B157)

　Should, S. 365, A Chorale Prelude For
　　The New Year [2']
　　2trp,timp,strings
　　PRESSER perf mat rent　　　　　(B158)

BACH, WILHELM FRIEDEMANN (1710-1784)
　Concerto for Harpsichord and String
　　Orchestra in E minor
　　(Upmeyer) KALMUS A5618 sc $15.00,
　　set $10.00, pts $2.00, ea. (B159)

　Sinfonia On The Birthday Of Frederick
　　The Great [11']
　　2fl,strings
　　(Prieger) KALMUS A5587 sc $5.00,
　　set $7.00, pts $1.00, ea. (B160)

BACH, WILHELM FRIEDRICH ERNST
　(1759-1845)
　Concerto For 2 Harpsichords And
　　String Orchestra In E Flat *see
　　THREE CENTURIES OF MUSIC IN
　　SCORE, VOL. 4: CONCERTO III,
　　KEYBOARD

　Concerto For Harpsichord And String
　　Orchestra In G Minor *see THREE
　　CENTURIES OF MUSIC IN SCORE, VOL.
　　4: CONCERTO III, KEYBOARD

BACH PORTRAIT, FOR NARRATOR AND
　ORCHESTRA see Schickele, Peter

BACH SUITE, A [ARR.] see Bach, Johann
　Sebastian

BACH WORKS FOR STRINGS see Bach, Johann
　Sebastian, Werke Fur Streicher Und
　Basso Continuo

BACHBURG CONCERTO NO. 2, FOR ALTO
　SAXOPHONE, PIANO AND ORCHESTRA see
　Brandon, Seymour (Sy)

BACHBURG CONCERTO NO. 3, FOR 2 OBOES,
　BASSOON, AND STRING ORCHESTRA see
　Brandon, Seymour (Sy)

BACHFLUSSIGKEIT see Rosse, Francois

BACIO DI MANO, UN, FOR SOLO VOICE AND
　ORCHESTRA see Mozart, Wolfgang
　Amadeus

BÄCK, SVEN-ERIK (1919-　　)
　Ciclos, For Piano And Orchestra [15']
　　perc,timp,strings,pno solo
　　NORDISKA perf mat rent　　　　(B161)

　Concerto for Violin and Orchestra,
　　No. 2, Op. 136 [30']
　　2+pic.2+English horn.2+bass
　　　clar.2+contrabsn. 4.3.3.1.
　　　timp,perc,harp,strings,vln solo
　　HANSEN-DEN perf mat rent　　　(B162)

　Ekvator
　　3.3.3.3. 4.3.3.1. alto sax,timp,
　　　3perc,harp,pno&cel,strings,
　　　electronic tape
　　STIM　　　　　　　　　　　　　(B163)

　Four Motets For Orchestra [21']
　　2.2.2.2. 4.2.2.0. timp,perc,harp,
　　　strings
　　NORDISKA perf mat rent　　　　(B164)

　Four Motets For Strings [16']
　　string orch
　　NORDISKA perf mat rent　　　　(B165)

　Ikaros [12']
　　timp,perc,pno,cel,strings
　　NORDISKA perf mat rent　　　　(B166)

　String Symphony [26']
　　string orch
　　NORDISKA perf mat rent　　　　(B167)

BÄCK, SVEN-ERIK (cont'd.)

　Sumerkei [15']
　　string orch NORDISKA perf mat rent
　　　　　　　　　　　　　　　　　(B168)

　Three Dialogue Motets, For
　　Violoncello And String Orchestra
　　[25']
　　string orch,vcl solo
　　NORDISKA perf mat rent　　　　(B169)

BACK TO BASS-ICS see Stock, David
　Frederick

BACKER-LUNDE, JOHAN (1874-1958)
　Prelude And Rondo [5']
　　3(pic).2.2.2. 4.3.2.1. timp,perc,
　　　harp,cel,strings
　　NORSK perf mat rent　　　　　　(B170)

BACKOFEN, JOHANN GEORG HEINRICH
　(1768-1830)
　Sinfonia Concertante for 2 Clarinets
　　and Orchestra, Op. 10
　　MUS. RARA perf mat rent　　　　(B171)

BADEN, CONRAD (1908-1989)
　By The Vala Lake, For Solo Voice And
　　Orchestra
　　see Pa Valasjoen, For Solo Voice
　　And Chamber Orchestra

　Concertino for Clarinet and String
　　Orchestra, Op. 37 [12']
　　string orch,clar solo
　　NORGE　　　　　　　　　　　　　(B172)

　Concerto for Bassoon and String
　　Orchestra, Op. 126 [23']
　　string orch,bsn solo
　　NORGE　　　　　　　　　　　　　(B173)

　Concerto for Orchestra [13']
　　2.2.2.3. 4.3.3.1. timp,perc,harp,
　　　strings
　　NORGE　　　　　　　　　　　　　(B174)

　Concerto for Piano and Orchestra, Op.
　　118 [21']
　　2.2.2.2. 4.2.3.1. timp,strings,
　　　pno solo
　　NORGE　　　　　　　　　　　　　(B175)

　Concerto for Viola and Orchestra, Op.
　　99 [23']
　　2.2.2.2. 4.2.0.0. timp,perc,cel,
　　　strings,vla solo
　　NORGE　　　　　　　　　　　　　(B176)

　Concerto for Violoncello and
　　Orchestra, Op. 142
　　2.2.2.2. 4.2.3.1. timp,strings,
　　　vcl solo
　　NORGE　　　　　　　　　　　　　(B177)

　Divertimento, Op. 30 [15']
　　2.2.2.2. 4.3.3.0. timp,strings
　　NORGE　　　　　　　　　　　　　(B178)

　Eventyr Suite *Op.49 [14']
　　3.2.2.3. 4.3.3.1. timp,perc,harp,
　　　pno,strings
　　"Fairy Tale Suite" NORGE　　　(B179)

　Fairy Tale Suite
　　see Eventyr Suite

　Fantasia Breve *Op.65 [10']
　　3.2.2.3. 4.3.3.1. timp,perc,harp,
　　　cel,strings
　　NORGE　　　　　　　　　　　　　(B180)

　Intrada Sinfonica *Op.78 [10']
　　2.2.2.2. 4.3.3.1. timp,perc,harp,
　　　cel,strings
　　NORGE　　　　　　　　　　　　　(B181)

　Overtura Gioia *Op.32 [6']
　　2.2.2.2. 4.2.3.1. timp,perc,
　　　strings
　　NORGE　　　　　　　　　　　　　(B182)

　Pa Valasjoen, For Solo Voice And
　　Chamber Orchestra *Op.14,No.1
　　[2']
　　1.1.1.0. 2.0.0.0. strings,S solo
　　"By The Vala Lake, For Solo Voice
　　And Orchestra" NORGE　　　　　(B183)

　Pastorale [6']
　　1.1.1.1. 2.0.0.0. harp,strings
　　NORGE　　　　　　　　　　　　　(B184)

　Pastorale Og Fuge *Op.46 [12']
　　1.1.1.1. 2.0.0.0. strings
　　NORGE　　　　　　　　　　　　　(B185)

　Rondo [5']
　　1.1.2.1. 2.0.0.0. harp,strings
　　NORGE　　　　　　　　　　　　　(B186)

　Symphony No. 1, Op. 34 [25']
　　2.2.2.2. 4.3.3.1. timp,perc,
　　　strings
　　NORGE　　　　　　　　　　　　　(B187)

BADEN, CONRAD (cont'd.)

　Symphony No. 2, Op. 42 [27']
　　2.2.2.2. 4.3.3.1. timp,perc,
　　　strings
　　NORGE　　　　　　　　　　　　　(B188)

　Symphony No. 3, Op. 48 [13']
　　2.2.2.2. 4.3.4.0. timp,perc,
　　　strings
　　(Sinfonia Piccola) NORGE　　　(B189)

　Symphony No. 4, Op. 85 [14']
　　2.2.2.2. 4.3.3.1. harp,cel,
　　　strings
　　NORGE　　　　　　　　　　　　　(B190)

　Symphony No. 5, Op. 109 [12']
　　2.2.2.2. 4.3.3.0. perc,harp,cel,
　　　strings
　　(Sinfonia Voluntatis) NORGE　(B191)

　Symphony No. 6, Op. 124 [20']
　　2.2.2.2. 4.3.3.1. timp,perc,harp,
　　　cel,strings
　　(Sinfonia Espressiva) NORGE　(B192)

　Variations, Op. 60 [10']
　　3.2.2.2. 4.3.2.1. timp,perc,harp,
　　　cel,strings
　　NORGE　　　　　　　　　　　　　(B193)

BADINAGE see Damase, Jean-Michel

BADINGS, HENK (1907-1987)
　Azioni Musicali [23']
　　2.2.2.2. 2.0.0.0. vcl,db
　　DONEMUS perf mat rent　　　　　(B194)

　Concerto for Orchestra [21']
　　3.3.4.3.alto sax. 4.3.3.1. timp,
　　　perc,harp,strings
　　sc DONEMUS f.s., perf mat rent
　　　　　　　　　　　　　　　　　(B195)

　Concerto for 4 Saxophones and
　　Orchestra [20']
　　3.2.3.2. 4.3.3.1. timp,4perc,
　　　strings,4sax soli
　　DONEMUS perf mat rent　　　　　(B196)

　Coninckskinderen [9']
　　2.2.2.2. 4.3.3.0. timp,2perc,
　　　harp,strings
　　sc DONEMUS f.s., perf mat rent
　　　　　　　　　　　　　　　　　(B197)

　Elfes, Les, For Narrator And
　　Orchestra [8']
　　3.2.2.2. 3.3.3.0. timp,perc,harp,
　　　cel,strings,narrator sc DONEMUS
　　　f.s.　　　　　　　　　　　　(B198)

　Serenade for Strings [12']
　　string orch without db
　　DONEMUS perf mat rent　　　　　(B199)

　Westenwind, De, For Narrator And
　　Orchestra [9']
　　2.2.2.1. 4.2.2.1. timp,perc,harp,
　　　pno,cel,15vln,5vla,4vcl,3db,
　　　narrator sc DONEMUS f.s.　　(B200)

BADLANDS see McBeth, William Francis

BAERMANN, HEINRICH JOSEPH
　see BARMANN, HEINRICH JOSEPH

BAGATELLEN see Spannheimer, Franz
　Erasmus

BAGATELLES see Kogoj, Marij, Bagatelle

BAGATELLES, 5, [ARR] see Dvorák,
　Antonin

BAGGIANI, GUIDO (1932-　　)
　Double [14']
　　2.2+English horn.2+bass clar.2.
　　　2.0.0.0. 2db
　　SALABERT perf mat rent　　　　(B201)

　Memoria [12']
　　1(pic).1.1+clar in E flat.1.
　　　1.1.2.0+db tuba. marimba,pno,
　　　3vln,vla,vcl,db,electronic
　　　equipment
　　SALABERT perf mat rent　　　　(B202)

BAHK, JUNSANG (1938-　　)
　Parinama [30']
　　3.3.3.2.alto sax. 3.3.2.1. timp,
　　　4perc,strings
　　PETERS　　　　　　　　　　　　(B203)

BAILE see Chavez, Carlos

BAILLY, JEAN GUY (1925-　　)
　Tombeau De Rainer Maria Rilke, Le,
　　For Solo Voice And Orchestra
　　[19']
　　1.1.1.1. 2.2.2.0. 2perc,harp,pno,
　　　strings,S solo
　　BILLAUDOT perf mat rent　　　　(B204)

BAINBRIDGE, SIMON
  Concertante In Moto Perpetuo
    fl,ob,clar,horn,pno,strings
    sc UNITED MUS $16.25   (B205)

  Fantasy
    UNITED MUS   (B206)

BAIRD, TADEUSZ (1928-1981)
  Colas Breugnon, For Flute And String
    Orchestra [15']
    string orch,fl solo
    HANSEN-GER perf mat rent   (B207)

  Quartet for Strings, [arr.]
    string orch [18'] HANSEN-GER perf
    mat rent   (B208)

BAJAJA THE PRINCE see Sommer, Vladimír

BAJURA, KEITH V.A.
  Forest Songs
    PHOEBUS PA 9 sc $6.95, set $29.95,
    pts $2.95, ea.   (B209)

  Mount Olympus
    PHOEBUS PA 8 sc $10.95, set $49.95,
    pts $3.95, ea.   (B210)

  Sabbat De Sorciere, Le
    PHOEBUS PA 4 sc $6.95, set $29.95,
    pts $2.95, ea.   (B211)

  Tempest, The
    PHOEBUS PA 7 sc $7.95, set $39.95,
    pts $3.95, ea.   (B212)

BAKER, DAVID N. (1931-   )
  Concerto For 2 Pianos, Jazz Band,
    Strings And Percussion [23']
    5sax,5trp,3trom,bass trom,tuba,
    pno,drums,db,5perc,strings,2pno
    soli
    NORRUTH perf mat rent   (B213)

  Concerto For Cello And Jazz Band
    [26']
    5sax,5trp,3trom,bass trom,tuba,
    pno,drums,db,vcl solo
    NORRUTH perf mat rent   (B214)

  Concerto For Trumpet, String
    Orchestra And Jazz Band [21']
    5sax,5trp,3trom,bass trom,tuba,
    pno,drums,db,strings,trp solo
    NORRUTH perf mat rent   (B215)

  Concerto For Violin And Jazz Band
    [22']
    5sax,5trp,3trom,bass trom,tuba,
    pno,drums,db,vln solo
    NORRUTH perf mat rent   (B216)

  Concerto for Violoncello and Chamber
    Orchestra [15']
    1.1.1.1. 2.0.0.0. timp,perc,
    strings without vcl,vcl solo
    AMP perf mat rent   (B217)

  Cycles Of Life, For Solo Voice, Horn
    And String Orchestra [20']
    string orch,horn solo,T solo
    NORRUTH perf mat rent   (B218)

  Homage: Bartok, Bird, Duke [16']
    1.1.1.1. 0.2.1.1. 2perc,2harp,
    strings
    NORRUTH perf mat rent   (B219)

  Kosbro [13']
    3.3.3.3. 4.3.3.1. timp,perc,xylo,
    pno,strings
    AMP perf mat rent   (B220)

BAKER, MICHAEL CONWAY (1941-   )
  Capriccio, Op. 78
    2.1.2.2. 4.2.3.1. timp,perc,pno/
    synthesizer,harp,strings,inst
    solo
    (solo instrument may be fl, ob,
    clar, sax, horn, vln, vcl, bsn,
    or pno) CAN.MUS.CENT.
    MI 1321 B168CA   (B221)

  Chanson Joyeuse *Op.78
    3.2.2(clar in E flat).2. 4.2.3.1.
    timp,perc,pno,harp,strings
    CAN.MUS.CENT. MI 1100 B168CH (B222)

  Étude for Piano and String Orchestra
    string orch,pno solo
    CAN.MUS.CENT. MI 1661 B168ET (B223)

  Fanfare To Expo 86
    3.3.3.3. 4.4.3.1. timp,perc,
    strings
    CAN.MUS.CENT. MI 1100 B168F (B224)

  Four Songs For Ann, For Solo Voice
    And Orchestra
    pno,harp,strings,solo voice,opt
    fl,opt bsn,opt clar,opt brass
    CAN.MUS.CENT. MV 1300 B168F (B225)

BAKER, MICHAEL CONWAY (cont'd.)

  Pacific Suite *Op.85 [8']
    2(S rec).1.1.2. 4.2.3.1. timp,
    perc,harp,pno&synthesizer,
    strings
    CAN.MUS.CENT. MI 1100 B168PA (B226)

  Planet For The Taking [7']
    1.1.1.1. 4.2.2.0. timp,perc,
    synthesizer,strings
    CAN.MUS.CENT. MI 1200 B158PL (B227)

  Reflections On A Lost Dream, For
    Violin And String Orchestra
    *Op.84
    string orch,vln solo
    CAN.MUS.CENT. MI 1611 B168RE (B228)

  Sinfonia for Strings
    string orch
    CAN.MUS.CENT. MI 1500 B168S (B229)

  Technophrenia *Op.88 [8']
    3(pic).2.2.2. 4.3.3.1. timp,perc,
    pno&synthesizer,strings
    CAN.MUS.CENT. MI 1100 B168TE (B230)

  Through The Lions' Gate *Op.83 [15']
    2(pic).2.2.2. 4.2.3.1. timp,perc,
    pno&cel,harp,strings
    CAN.MUS.CENT. MI 1100 B168TH (B231)

  Vocalise, For Solo Voice And Chamber
    Orchestra
    clar,pno,harp,strings,low solo
    CAN.MUS.CENT. MV 1300 B168V (B232)

  Washington Square: Suite [16']
    2(pic).2.2.2. 4.2.3.1. perc,cel,
    pno,harp,strings
    CAN.MUS.CENT. MI 1100 B168WAS
                                  (B233)

BAKKE, RUTH (1947-   )
  Chromocumuli [14']
    3.3.4.3.alto sax. 4.3.3.1. timp,
    perc,strings
    NORGE   (B234)

BAKSA, ROBERT FRANK (1938-   )
  Meditation
    SHAWNEE perf mat rent   (B235)

BAL CHAMPETRE QUADRILLE see Strauss,
Johann, [Jr.]

BAL MIRO, LE: SUITE NO. 1 see Bussotti,
Sylvano

BALADA, LEONARDO (1933-   )
  Concerto for Violin and Orchestra
    [20']
    2(pic).2.2(bass clar).2. 2.2.1+
    bass trom.0. timp,perc,strings,
    vln solo
    study sc SCHIRM.G f.s., perf mat
    rent   (B236)

  Persistencias, For Guitar And
    Orchestra [22']
    2(pic).2.2.2. 2.2.2+bass trom.0.
    perc,pno,strings,gtr solo
    SCHIRM.G perf mat rent   (B237)

  Quasi Un Pasadoble [13']
    2+pic.2+opt English horn.2+opt
    bass clar.2+contrabsn. 4+opt
    horn.3+opt trp.2+bass trom.1.
    3perc,harp,pno&cel,strings
    SCHIRM.G perf mat rent   (B238)

  Sardana [15']
    2+pic.2+English horn.2(clar in E
    flat)+bass clar.2. 4.3.3.1.
    4perc,harp,pno,cel,strings
    SCHIRM.G perf mat rent   (B239)

  Three Anecdotes, For Percussion And
    Chamber Orchestra [8']
    1(pic).1.1(bass clar).1. 1.1.0.0.
    strings,perc solo
    sc SCHIRM.G 006-48518 $16.00, perf
    mat rent   (B240)

BALADA DE TEREZIN, LA, FOR FLUTE AND
CHAMBER ORCHESTRA see Adomian, Lan

BALADE see Srebotnjak, Alojz F.

BALAKAUSKAS, OSVALDAS (1937-   )
  Opera Strumentale [40']
    3.3.3.3. 4.3.3.1. timp,perc,harp,
    cel,pno,strings
    SIKORSKI perf mat rent   (B241)

BALAKIREV, MILY ALEXEYEVICH (1837-1910)
  Concerto for Piano and Orchestra in E
    flat
    KALMUS A6113 sc $50.00, set $75.00,
    perf mat rent   (B242)

  Islamey [arr.]
    (Casella) 3+pic.2+English horn.2+
    clar in E flat.3+contrabsn.
    4.3.3.1. timp,perc,2harp,strings
    [12'] KALMUS A6075 sc $25.00, set

BALAKIREV, MILY ALEXEYEVICH (cont'd.)

    $60.00, perf mat rent   (B243)

  Symphony No. 1 in C
    min sc KALMUS K01504 $14.25   (B244)

  Symphony No. 2 in D minor
    min sc KALMUS K01505 $14.25   (B245)

  Tamara
    min sc EULENBURG EU00598 $12.50
                                  (B246)

BALANCHIVADZE, ANDREI (1906-   )
  Concerto for Piano and Orchestra, No.
    4 [32']
    3.3.3.3. 4.3.3.1. timp,perc,
    strings,pno solo
    SIKORSKI perf mat rent   (B247)
    VAAP perf mat rent   (B248)

  Concerto for Piano and String
    Orchestra, No. 3 [11']
    string orch,pno solo
    SIKORSKI perf mat rent   (B249)

  Symphony No. 4 [28']
    3.3.3.3. 4.4.3.1. timp,perc,harp,
    pno,strings,electronic tape,cor
    VAAP perf mat rent   (B250)

BALASSA, SÁNDOR (1935-   )
  Calls And Cries *Op.33
    sc EMB 10248 f.s.   (B251)

  Cantata Y, For Solo Voice And
    Orchestra *Op.21
    [Hung/Eng] orch,S solo sc EMB 10204
    f.s.   (B252)

  Chant Of Glarus *Op.29
    sc EMB 10226 f.s.   (B253)

  Day-Dreamer's Diary, A *Op.35
    3(pic,alto fl).2(English horn).2+
    bass clar.2. 2.2.0.0. cel,harp,
    strings
    sc EMB 10268 f.s., perf mat rent
                                  (B254)

  Island Of Everlasting Youth, The
    *Op.32
    sc EMB 10237 f.s.   (B255)

  Three Fantasies *Op.36
    sc EMB 13050 f.s., perf mat rent
                                  (B256)

  Tresses, For Solo Voice And Chamber
    Orchestra *Op.2
    [Hung/Eng] orch,S solo sc EMB 8908
    f.s.   (B257)

BALAZS, FREDERIC (1920-   )
  Sonnets After E.B. Browning, For Solo
    Voice And Orchestra [25']
    1.1.1.1. 0.0.0.0. harp,strings,
    high solo
    sc AM.COMP.AL. $15.30   (B258)

BALDISSERA, LIVID (1947-   )
  Generative Cells [20']
    2fl,2ob,strings
    RICORDI-IT 133112 perf mat rent
                                  (B259)

BALES, GERALD (1919-   )
  Rhapsody for Organ and Orchestra
    CAN.MUS.CENT. MI 1364 B184RH (B260)

BALES, RICHARD HORNER (1915-   )
  Elegy For A Master [8']
    string orch
    PEER perf mat rent   (B261)

BALL, MICHAEL (1946-   )
  Resurrection Symphonies *Op.18
    NOVELLO perf mat rent   (B262)

BALL GESCHICHTEN WALZER see Strauss,
Johann, [Jr.]

BALL PROMESSEN WALZER see Strauss,
Eduard

BALL SUITE see Lachner, Franz

BALLABILI see Dello Joio, Norman

BALLAD ABOUT THE MOTHERLAND, FOR SOLO
VOICE AND ORCHESTRA see
Khachaturian, Aram Ilyich

BALLAD ABOUT TOSCANA, THE, FOR SOLO
VOICE AND ORCHESTRA see Groven,
Eivind, Balladen Om Toscanaland,
For Solo Voice And Orchestra

BALLAD FOR A SUMMER'S DAY see Woodard,
James

BALLAD OF READING GAOL, THE, FOR SOLO
VOICE AND CHAMBER ORCHESTRA see
Nielson, Lewis

BALLAD OF THE BLACK SORROW, FOR SOLO
VOICES AND CHAMBER ORCHESTRA see
Holt, Simon

BALLADE AND ALLEGRO, FOR 2 VIOLINS AND
STRING ORCHESTRA see Weiner,
Stanley

BALLADE CONCERTANTE, FOR PIANO AND
ORCHESTRA see Delannoy, Marcel

BALLADE DE BALLET see Templeton, Alec

BALLADE VAN DEN BOER, FOR NARRATOR AND
ORCHESTRA see Mengelberg, Kurt
Rudolf

BALLADE VAN DEN MEREL, FOR NARRATOR AND
ORCHESTRA see Andriessen, Hendrik

BALLADEN OM TOSCANALAND, FOR SOLO VOICE
AND ORCHESTRA see Groven, Eivind

BALLADS see Srebotnjak, Alojz F.,
Balade

BALLARD, LOUIS WAYNE (1931-   )
Scenes From Indian Life [4'45"]
2.2.2.2. 4.2.2.0. timp,perc,
strings
BOURNE perf mat rent   (B263)

Why The Duck Has A Short Tail, For
Narrator And Orchestra [15']
2.2.2.2. 4.3.3.1. timp,perc,harp,
pno,strings,narrator
BOURNE perf mat rent   (B264)

BALLCHRONIK WALZER see Strauss, Eduard

BALLET see Taub, Bruce J.H.

BALLET DES MUSES [ARR.] see Lully,
Jean-Baptiste (Lulli)

BALLET EGYPTIEN: SUITES NOS. 1 AND 2
see Luigini, Alexandre

BALLET SUITE see Leopold, Bohuslav

BALLET SUITE: BLIND MAN'S BUFF see
Asgeirsson, Jon

BALLET SUITE NO.1 see Shostakovich,
Dmitri

BALLET SUITE NO. 2 see Shostakovich,
Dmitri

BALLET SUITE NO. 3 see Shostakovich,
Dmitri

BALLET SUITE NO. 4 see Shostakovich,
Dmitri

BALLETSUITE see Hemel, Oscar van

BALLETTI À 6 see Biber, Heinrich Ignaz
Franz von

BALLETTI IN C see Poglietti, Alessandro

BALLETTO, FOR ORCHESTRA see Ferrero,
Lorenzo

BALLI see Rota, Nino

BALLIANA, FRANCO (1954-   )
Dove La Luce [10']
1.1.1.1. 1.0.1.0. perc,pno,2vln,
vla,vcl,db
SONZOGNO perf mat rent   (B265)

BALLOU, ESTHER WILLIAMSON (1915-1973)
Early American Portrait, For Solo
Voice And Orchestra [20']
2.1.1.1. 2.1.1.0. perc,harp,
strings,S solo
sc AM.COMP.AL. $26.00, perf mat
rent   (B266)

BALLOU, PHILIP
Music Box [12']
fl,English horn,clar,bsn,horn,
trom,perc,2vln,vla,vcl,db
sc APNM $7.75, perf mat rent (B267)

BALLSIRENEN see Lehar, Franz

BALLSTRAUSSCHEN POLKA see Strauss,
Johann, [Jr.]

BALMER, LUC (1898-   )
Concertino for Piano and Orchestra
[19']
0.2(English horn).1.1. 2.0.0.0.
strings,pno solo
HUG GH 11268 perf mat rent   (B268)

BALTIN, ALEXANDER (1931-   )
Concerto for Harpsichord and
Orchestra in F minor
1.1.2.1. 2.2.0.0. timp,perc,harp,
strings,hpsd solo
VAAP perf mat rent   (B269)

Concerto for Solo Voice and Orchestra
[10']
3.2.3.2. 4.2.1.0. timp,perc,
strings,Mez solo

BALTIN, ALEXANDER (cont'd.)

SIKORSKI perf mat rent   (B270)

Concerto for Violin and Orchestra
[15']
3.2.3.2. 4.2.3.0. timp,perc,harp,
strings,vln solo
SIKORSKI perf mat rent   (B271)

Concerto for Violoncello and
Orchestra [17']
3.2.3.2. 4.2.0.1. timp,2perc,
harp,cel,strings,vcl solo
SIKORSKI perf mat rent   (B272)

BAMBINO PERDUTO, IL see Gorli, Sandro

BAMBOULA BEACH see Wuorinen, Charles

BAMBOULA SQUARED see Wuorinen, Charles

BAMERT, MATTHIAS (1942-   )
Circus Parade, For Narrator And
Orchestra [12']
2.2.2.2. 4.2.2.0. perc,harp,pno,
strings,narrator sc EUR.AM.MUS.
01436 $30.00, perf mat rent
(B273)

BANCHETTO MUSICALE: SUITE NO. 7 see
Schein, Johann Hermann

BANCHETTO MUSICALE: SUITE NO. 8 see
Schein, Johann Hermann

BANCHETTO MUSICALE: SUITE NO. 14 see
Schein, Johann Hermann

BANCQUART, ALAIN (1934-   )
Fragments d'Apocalypse, For Solo
Voices And Orchestra (Symphony
No. 3) [40']
4.4.4.0. 4.4.4.0. 6perc,elec gtr,
strings,TBB soli
RICORDI-FR perf mat rent   (B274)

Magique- Circonstancielle, For Solo
Voices And Orchestra
3.3.5.3. 5.5.3.1. 2perc,pno,
2harp,strings,2 narrators&Mez
solo
BILLAUDOT perf mat rent   (B275)

Symphony No. 3
see Fragments d'Apocalypse, For
Solo Voices And Orchestra

BANDITEN GALOPP POLKA see Strauss,
Johann, [Jr.]

BANFIELD, RAFFAELLO DE (1922-   )
Liebes Lied, For Solo Voice And
Orchestra
2.2.2.2. 2.2.0.0. timp,perc,harp,
strings,S solo
SALABERT perf mat rent   (B276)

Serale, For Solo Voice And Orchestra
2.1.2.2. 2.0.2.1. perc,harp,org,
strings,S solo
SALABERT perf mat rent   (B277)

Sturm, Der, For Solo Voice And
Orchestra
2(pic).2(English horn).2.2.
4.3.3.1. timp,3perc,harp,
strings,S solo
SALABERT perf mat rent   (B278)

Tod Der Geliebten, Der, For Solo
Voice And Orchestra [8']
2(pic).2.2.2. 2.2.0.0. cym,harp,
strings,S solo
SALABERT perf mat rent   (B279)

BANGERT, EMIL
April I Choose
see Jeg Vaelger Mig April

Jeg Vaelger Mig April
"April I Choose" sc,pts SAMFUNDET
f.s.   (B280)

BANK, JACQUES (1943-   )
Thomas, For Tape And 19 Instruments
[10']
2.1.1.1.4sax. 0.2.1.0. 2perc,elec
org,pno,4db,electronic tape
sc DONEMUS f.s., perf mat rent
(B281)

BANKS, DON (1923-   )
Trilogy [26']
2(pic,alto fl).2(English
horn).2(bass
clar).2(contrabsn). 4.2.3.0.
harp,pno&cel,timp,perc,strings
sc CHESTER CH 55380 f.s.   (B282)
CHESTER JWC578 perf mat rent (B283)

BANQUETE DE LAS NUBES, EL, FOR SOLO
VOICE AND ORCHESTRA see Asturias,
Rodrigo

BANTOCK, [SIR] GRANVILLE (1868-1946)
Old English Suite
KALMUS A6114 sc $20.00, set $30.00,
perf mat rent   (B284)

Pierrot Of The Minute, The
KALMUS A5901 sc $20.00, set $65.00,
perf mat rent   (B285)

BARAB, SEYMOUR (1921-   )
Concerto Grosso [20']
string orch
SCHIRM.G perf mat rent   (B286)

G.A.G.E., For Narrator And Orchestra
[20']
2.2.2.2. 2.2.2.0. timp,2perc,
harp,pno,strings,narrator
voc sc SCHIRM.G f.s., perf mat rent
(B287)

BARATI, GEORGE (1913-   )
Branches Of Time, For 2 Pianos And
Orchestra [22']
2.2.2.2. 2.2.2.0. timp,perc,
strings,2pno soli
AM.COMP.AL. sc $19.85, pts $13.80,
perf mat rent   (B288)

Concerto for Guitar and Chamber
Orchestra [20']
1.0.1.0. 1.0.0.0. timp,perc,
strings,gtr solo
AM.COMP.AL. sc $38.15, pts $4.60,
perf mat rent   (B289)

Concerto for Violin and Orchestra
2.2.2.2. 4.2.3.0. timp,perc,xylo,
harp,strings,vln solo
sc AM.COMP.AL. $76.80, perf mat
rent   (B290)

Confluence [12']
3.3.3.3. 4.3.3.1. timp,perc,harp,
pno,cel,strings
sc AM.COMP.AL. $15.25, perf mat
rent   (B291)

Fragment From "Cities Of The
Interior", For Solo Voice And
Orchestra [7']
1.1.1.1. 1.1.1.0. perc,strings,S
solo
sc AM.COMP.AL. $6.15, perf mat rent
(B292)

Noelani's Aria, For Solo Voice And
Orchestra [4']
2.2.2.2. 0.0.0.0. timp,harp,
strings,A solo
sc AM.COMP.AL. $4.60   (B293)

BARBARA ALLEN *see TWO SONGS WITHOUT
WORDS [arr.]

BARBAUD, PIERRE (1911-   )
Cogitationes Symbolicae [10']
string orch
BILLAUDOT perf mat rent   (B294)

French Gagaku [13']
30strings
BILLAUDOT perf mat rent   (B295)

BARBE-BLEUE: OVERTURE [ARR.] see
Offenbach, Jacques

BARBER, SAMUEL (1910-1981)
Canzonetta, For Oboe And String
Orchestra [arr.]
(Turner, Charles) string orch,ob
solo [8'] SCHIRM.G perf mat rent
(B296)

Essay No. 3 *Op.47 [14']
2+pic.2+English horn.2+bass
clar.1. 4.3.3.1+euphonium.
timp,2harp,pno,strings
SCHIRM.G perf mat rent   (B297)

Medea *Op.23 [20']
2.2.2.2. 2+opt 2horn.2.2.1. timp,
perc,harp,pno,strings
SCHIRM.G perf mat rent   (B298)

Vanessa: Anatol's Aria, For Solo
Voice And Orchestra
2+pic.2+English horn.2+bass
clar.2. 4.3.3.0. timp,perc,
harp,strings,solo voice
SCHIRM.G perf mat rent   (B299)

Vanessa: Do Not Utter A Word, For
Solo Voice And Orchestra
2+pic.2+English horn.2.2.
4.3.3.1. timp,perc,harp,
strings,solo voice
SCHIRM.G perf mat rent   (B300)

Vanessa: Must Winter Come So Soon,
For Solo Voice And Orchestra
3(pic).2+English horn.2+bass
clar.2. 4.3.3.1. timp,perc,
harp,strings,solo voice
SCHIRM.G perf mat rent   (B301)

BARBERINE, FOR SOLO VOICE AND
ORCHESTRA, [ARR.] see Lekeu,
Guillaume

BARBIER VON BAGDAD, DER: OVERTURE see Cornelius, Peter

BARBIER VON SEVILLA, DER: DIE VERLEUMDUNG, FOR SOLO VOICE AND ORCHESTRA see Rossini, Gioacchino, Barbiere Di Siviglia, Il: La Calunnia, For Solo Voice And Orchestra

BARBIER VON SEVILLA, DER: FRAG ICH MEIN BEKLOMMEN HERZ, FOR SOLO VOICE AND ORCHESTRA see Rossini, Gioacchino, Barbiere Di Siviglia, Il: Una Voce Poco Fa, For Solo Voice And Orchestra

BARBIER VON SEVILLA, DER: GLÜCK UND HULD, MEIN HERR, ZUM GRUSSE, FOR SOLO VOICES AND ORCHESTRA see Rossini, Gioacchino

BARBIER VON SEVILLA, DER: ICH BIN DAS FAKTOTUM, FOR SOLO VOICE AND ORCHESTRA see Rossini, Gioacchino, Barbiere Di Siviglia, Il: Largo Al Factotum, For Solo Voice And Orchestra

BARBIERE DI SIVIGLIA, IL: AH ROSINA! VOI LINDORO? FOR SOLO VOICES AND ORCHESTRA see Paisiello, Giovanni

BARBIERE DI SIVIGLIA, IL: DIAMO ALLO NOIA IL BANDO, FOR SOLO VOICES AND ORCHESTRA see Paisiello, Giovanni

BARBIERE DI SIVIGLIA, IL: GIA RIEDE PRIMAVERA, FOR SOLO VOICE AND ORCHESTRA see Paisiello, Giovanni

BARBIERE DI SIVIGLIA, IL: GIUSTO CIEL, CHE CONOSCETE, FOR SOLO VOICE AND ORCHESTRA see Paisiello, Giovanni

BARBIERE DI SIVIGLIA, IL: LA CALUNNIA, MIO SIGNOR, FOR SOLO VOICE AND ORCHESTRA see Paisiello, Giovanni

BARBIERE DI SIVIGLIA, IL: LA CALUNNIA, FOR SOLO VOICE AND ORCHESTRA see Rossini, Gioacchino

BARBIERE DI SIVIGLIA, IL: LARGO AL FACTOTUM, FOR SOLO VOICE AND ORCHESTRA see Rossini, Gioacchino

BARBIERE DI SIVIGLIA, IL: LODE AL CIEL, FOR SOLO VOICES AND ORCHESTRA see Paisiello, Giovanni

BARBIERE DI SIVIGLIA, IL: MA DOV' ERI TU, STORDITO, FOR SOLO VOICES AND ORCHESTRA see Paisiello, Giovanni

BARBIERE DI SIVIGLIA, IL: NON DUBITAR, O FIGARO, FOR SOLO VOICES AND ORCHESTRA see Paisiello, Giovanni

BARBIERE DI SIVIGLIA, IL: OH CHE UMORE, FOR SOLO VOICES AND ORCHESTRA see Paisiello, Giovanni

BARBIERE DI SIVIGLIA, IL: OVERTURE see Rossini, Gioacchino

BARBIERE DI SIVIGLIA, IL: SAPER BRAMATE, FOR SOLO VOICE AND ORCHESTRA see Paisiello, Giovanni

BARBIERE DI SIVIGLIA, IL: SCORSI GIA MOLTI PAESI, FOR SOLO VOICE AND ORCHESTRA see Paisiello, Giovanni

BARBIERE DI SIVIGLIA, IL: UNA VOCE POCO FA, FOR SOLO VOICE AND ORCHESTRA see Rossini, Gioacchino

BARBIERE DI SIVIGLIA, IL: VERAMENTE HA TORTO, E VERO, FOR SOLO VOICE AND ORCHESTRA see Paisiello, Giovanni

BARBIERE DI SIVIGLIA, IL: VUOI TU, ROSINA, FOR SOLO VOICE AND ORCHESTRA see Paisiello, Giovanni

BARBOTEAU, G.
Limites, For Horn And Orchestra [17']
CHOUDENS perf mat rent (B302)

BARCE, RAMÓN (1928-)
Concierto De Lizara No. 1, For Oboe, Trumpet, Percussion, And String Orchestra [13']
string orch,ob solo,trp solo,perc solo
ALPUERTO (B303)

Concierto De Lizara No. 4 [13']
3.0+English horn.1+bass clar.0. 1.1.0.1. perc,harp,strings
sc ALPUERTO f.s. (B304)

BARCHET, SIEGFRIED (1918-1982)
Symphony in C
string orch
HÄNSSLER (B305)

BARDWELL
Concerto for Mandolin and Orchestra
2ob,2bsn,2horn,strings,mand solo
sc PLUCKED STR PSSE 2022 $40.00, perf mat rent (B306)

BARENHAUTER, DIE: OVERTURE see Wagner, Siegfried

BARKAUSKAS, VYTAUTAS (1931-)
Concerto for Viola and Chamber Orchestra [20']
hpsd/pno,strings,vla solo
SIKORSKI perf mat rent (B307)
VAAP perf mat rent (B308)

Symphony No. 2 [24']
3.3.3.3. 4.3.3.1. 4perc,harp,cel, pno,strings
SIKORSKI perf mat rent (B309)
VAAP perf mat rent (B310)

Toccamento [18']
11vln,4vla,3vcl,db,pno solo
SIKORSKI perf mat rent (B311)

BARKIN, ELAINE R. (1932-)
Plus Ca Change [12']
perc,strings
AM.COMP.AL. sc $18.30, pts $38.00, perf mat rent (B312)

BARLOW, FRED (1881-1951)
Saisons, Les (Sinfonietta)
timp,strings
ESCHIG perf mat rent (B313)

Sinfonietta
see Saisons, Les

BARLOW, KLARENS (1945-)
Im Januar Am Nil [17']
2soprano sax,perc,pno,4vln,2vcl, db
sc FEEDBACK FB 8407 f.s. (B314)

BÄRMANN, HEINRICH JOSEPH (1784-1847)
Concerto for Clarinet and Orchestra, Op. 23
(Strebel, Harald) opt 2horn, strings,clar solo SCHOTTS sc CON 205 $20.00, set CON 205-50 $65.00 (B315)

BARNES, MILTON (1931-)
Channuka Suite No. 1, For Chamber Orchestra [9']
1.1.0.0. 1.0.0.0. strings
CAN.MUS.CENT. MI 1200 B261C (B316)

Concerto for 2 Guitars and String Orchestra [23']
string orch,2gtr soli
CAN.MUS.CENT. MI 1715 B261DO (B317)

Fanfare Populaire, For 3 Trumpets And Orchestra [3']
3.2.2.2. 4.3.3.1. timp,4perc,opt org,strings,3trp soli
CAN.MUS.CENT. MI 1436 B261F (B318)

Follies Overture [4']
2.2.2.2. 4.2.3.1. timp,3perc, strings
CAN.MUS.CENT. MI 1100 B261F (B319)

Legends [17']
3.3.2.2. 4.3.3.1. timp,3perc, harp,strings
CAN.MUS.CENT. MI 1100 B261L (B320)

Papageno Variations, For Doublebass And String Orchestra [10']
string orch,db solo
CAN.MUS.CENT. MI 1614 B261PA (B321)

BARONE, MICHAEL (1936-)
Theme and Variations [25'40"]
1+alto fl+pic.1+English horn.2+ bass clar+contrabass clar.1+ contrabsn. 4.4.4.1. timp,perc, 2pno,strings, Fender-Rhodes
NEWAM 19004 perf mat rent (B322)

BARONE AVARO, IL: PRELUDIO see Napoli, Jacopo

BAROQUE CONCERTO FOR TROMBONE AND STRING ORCHESTRA see Hidas, Frigyes

BARQUE SUR L'OCEAN, UNE [ARR.] see Ravel, Maurice

BARRAINE, ELSA (1910-)
Atmosphere, For Oboe And Instrumental Ensemble [15']
2perc,4vln,2vla,2vcl,ob solo
sc BILLAUDOT f.s., perf mat rent (B323)

BARRAUD, HENRY (1900-)
Fantasy for Piano and Orchestra [22']
2.2.2.2. 2.2.2.0. timp,perc,harp, strings,pno solo
BOOSEY perf mat rent (B324)

Lavinia: Overture [5']
1(pic).1(English horn).1.1. 1.1.1.0. timp,perc,harp,pno, cel,strings
BOOSEY perf mat rent (B325)

Ouverture Pour Un Opera Interdit [9'50"]
CHOUDENS perf mat rent (B326)

Saison En Enfer, Une [23']
2+pic.2+English horn.2+bass clar.2+contrabsn. 4.3.3.1. timp,perc,harp,cel,pno,strings
BOOSEY perf mat rent (B327)

Variations A Treize [12']
1.0.1(bass clar).1. 1.1.1.0. 2perc,harp,cel,pno,vln,vcl
BOOSEY perf mat rent (B328)

BARREAU, GISELE (1948-)
Piano-Piano [17']
2(pic).0+English horn.2.0+ contrabsn. 1.1.1.0. 3perc,2pno, 2vln,vla,vcl,db
SALABERT perf mat rent (B329)

BARRY, GERALD (1952-)
Cheveaux-De-Frise
2.2.2.2. 4.3.3.1. glock,pno, strings
sc OXFORD $49.95 (B330)

Children Aged 10-17 [7']
2.2.2.2. 0.2.0.0. perc,2harp, strings
OXFORD perf mat rent (B331)

Diner
2.2.2.2. 4.2.3.1. perc,pno, strings
sc OXFORD $23.95 (B332)

Of Queens' Gardens [10']
1.1.1.1. 1.1.1.0. perc,pno, strings
OXFORD perf mat rent (B333)

BARTA, JOSEF (ca. 1746-1787)
Symphonies, Two
see Laube, Antonin, Symphony

BARTERED BRIDE, THE: DEAREST SON, FOR SOLO VOICE AND ORCHESTRA see Smetana, Bedrich

BARTERED BRIDE, THE: GLADLY WILL I BE BELIEVING, FOR SOLO VOICE AND ORCHESTRA see Smetana, Bedrich

BARTERED BRIDE, THE: HA, THAT HIT LIKE A LIGHTNING BLAST, FOR SOLO VOICES AND ORCHESTRA see Smetana, Bedrich

BARTERED BRIDE, THE: HE WOULD HAVE COME HERE, FOR SOLO VOICES AND ORCHESTRA see Smetana, Bedrich

BARTERED BRIDE, THE: HERE SHE COMES WITHOUT SUSPICION, FOR SOLO VOICES AND ORCHESTRA see Smetana, Bedrich

BARTERED BRIDE, THE: HE'S BLESSED, SO BLESSED WHO LOVES AND CAN BELIEVE, FOR SOLO VOICES AND ORCHESTRA see Smetana, Bedrich

BARTERED BRIDE, THE: I KNOW A GIRL SO SWEET AND DEAR, FOR SOLO VOICES AND ORCHESTRA see Smetana, Bedrich

BARTERED BRIDE, THE: IT IS SUCCEEDING, FOR SOLO VOICE AND ORCHESTRA see Smetana, Bedrich

BARTERED BRIDE, THE: JUST ONE WORD WILL BE ENOUGH, FOR SOLO VOICES AND ORCHESTRA see Smetana, Bedrich

BARTERED BRIDE, THE: MY DEAREST LOVE, I BEG YOU PLEASE, FOR SOLO VOICES AND ORCHESTRA see Smetana, Bedrich

BARTERED BRIDE, THE: OH, I FEEL SO QUEASY, FOR SOLO VOICE AND ORCHESTRA see Smetana, Bedrich

BARTERED BRIDE, THE: OVERTURE see Smetana, Bedrich

BARTERED BRIDE, THE: SO NOW ALL IS DECIDED, FOR SOLO VOICES AND ORCHESTRA see Smetana, Bedrich

BARTERED BRIDE, THE: THE WORLD IS DEAD AND BLACKER THAN NIGHT, FOR SOLO VOICE AND ORCHESTRA see Smetana, Bedrich

BARTERED BRIDE, THE: THERE'S NO NEED TO
    WORRY, FOR SOLO VOICES AND
    ORCHESTRA see Smetana, Bedrich

BARTERED BRIDE, THE: WITH MY MOTHER
    HOPE WAS ENDED, FOR SOLO VOICES AND
    ORCHESTRA see Smetana, Bedrich

BARTHOLOMÉE, PIERRE (1937-   )
    Fancy As A Ground [20']
        0.1.1.1. 1.1.1.0. 2perc,harp,cel,
        2vln,2vla,vcl,db
    sc UNIVER. UE17485 f.s., perf mat
        rent   (B334)

    Politophonie [12']
        4.4.4.4. 4.4.3.1. timp,2perc,
        strings
    SALABERT perf mat rent   (B335)

BARTLES, ALFRED H. (1930-   )
    Music For Symphony Orchestra And Jazz
        Ensemble *Op.4 [21']
        3.3.3.3. 4.3.2.1. 2perc,harp,
        strings,2alto sax soli,tenor sax
        solo,bass sax solo,4trp soli,
        3trom soli,bass trom solo,pno
        solo,db solo,drums solo sc,pts
    MJQ rent   (B336)

BARTÓK, BÉLA (1881-1945)
    Four Orchestral Pieces *Op.12
    min sc BOOSEY 1112 $22.50   (B337)

    Rhapsody for Piano and Orchestra, Op.
        1
    KALMUS A5589 sc $25.00, set $50.00,
        perf mat rent   (B338)

    Rumanian Dance
        (Dille) EMB f.s. sc 5033, study sc
        40032   (B339)

    Scherzo for Piano and Orchestra
        (Dille) min sc EMB 3556 f.s. (B340)

    Suite, No. 1, Op. 3
    min sc KALMUS K01465 $14.25   (B341)

BARTOS, A.
    Strahlende Sterne, For Solo Voice And
        Orchestra
    KRENN   (B342)

    Verliebte Serenade, For Solo Voice
        And Orchestra
    KRENN   (B343)

BARTOŠ, JAN ZDENEK (1908-1981)
    Concerto Da Camera, For Viola And
        String Orchestra [16']
        string orch,vla solo
    BÄREN. BA 6616   (B344)

BARUFFE CHIOZZOTTE, LE: OVERTURE see
    Sinigaglia, Leone

BAS RELIEFS ASSYRIENS see Martelli,
    Henri

BASHMAKOV, LEONID (1927-   )
    Concerto for Violin and Orchestra,
        No. 2 [18']
        1.1.2.2. 2.2.3.0. timp,4perc,
        harp,pno,strings,vln solo
    sc SUOMEN f.s.   (B345)

BASOCHE, LA: PASSEPIED see Messager,
    Andre

BASSE DANSE see McCabe, John

BASSETT, LESLIE (1923-   )
    Concerto Lirico, For Trombone And
        Orchestra [15']
        3.2.3.2. 4.2.3.1. 4perc,harp,pno&
        cel,trom solo
    PETERS P66980 perf mat rent   (B346)

    From A Source Evolving [13']
        3.3.3.3. 4.3.3.1. 4perc,harp,pno,
        strings
    PETERS P67118 perf mat rent   (B347)

BASTA! TI CREDO! see Reicha, Anton

BASTA, VINCESTI, FOR SOLO VOICE AND
    ORCHESTRA see Mozart, Wolfgang
    Amadeus

BASTET see Berkeley, Michael

BASUN, FOR SOLO VOICE AND ORCHESTRA see
    Tveitt, Geirr

BATA see Leon, Tania Justina

BATASHOV, KONSTANTIN
    Concerto for Violin and Orchestra
        [13'15"] min sc MUZYKA f.s. (B348)

BATNUN, FOR DOUBLE BASS AND CHAMBER
    ORCHESTRA see Olivero, Betty

BATTAGLIA DI LEGNANO, LA: AH! D'UN
    CONSORTE, O PERFIDI, FOR SOLO
    VOICES AND ORCHESTRA see Verdi,
    Giuseppe

BATTAGLIA DI LEGNANO, LA: AH!
    M'ABBRACCIA...D' ESULTANZA, FOR
    SOLO VOICE AND ORCHESTRA see Verdi,
    Giuseppe

BATTAGLIA DI LEGNANO, LA: BEN VI SCORGO
    NEL SEMBIANTE, FOR SOLO VOICES AND
    ORCHESTRA see Verdi, Giuseppe

BATTAGLIA DI LEGNANO, LA: DIGLI CH' E
    SANGUE ITALICO, FOR SOLO VOICES AND
    ORCHESTRA see Verdi, Giuseppe

BATTAGLIA DI LEGNANO, LA: LA PIA
    MATERNA MANO, FOR SOLO VOICE AND
    ORCHESTRA see Verdi, Giuseppe

BATTAGLIA DI LEGNANO, LA: QUANTE VOLTE
    COME IN DONO, FOR SOLO VOICE AND
    ORCHESTRA see Verdi, Giuseppe

BATTAGLIA DI LEGNANO, LA: SE AL NUOVO
    DI PUGNANDO, FOR SOLO VOICE AND
    ORCHESTRA see Verdi, Giuseppe

BATTISTELLI, GIORGIO
    Racconto Di Monsieur B., Il [7'30"]
        2.2.2.2. 4.4.3.0. 3perc,strings
    RICORDI-IT 134326 perf mat rent
                                    (B349)

BATTLE OF STALINGRAD, THE see
    Khachaturian, Aram Ilyich

BATTLE OF THE HUNS see Liszt, Franz,
    Hunnenschlacht

BATTLESHIP POTEMKIN, THE: SUITE see
    Tchaikovsky, Alexander

BATTLESTAR GALACTICA: SUITE see
    Phillips, Stu

BATUQUE see Fernandez, Oscar Lorenzo

BAUDRIER, YVES (1906-1989)
    Raz De Sein [8']
        3.3.3.2. 4.3.3.1. timp,perc,harp,
        strings
    ESCHIG perf mat rent   (B350)

BAUER, JERZY (1936-   )
    Czerwone I Czarne, For Piano And
        Orchestra [6'30"]
        3.0.3.0. 4.3.3.0. perc,strings,
        pno solo
    "Red And Black, For Piano And
        Orchestra" sc POLSKIE f.s. (B351)

    Red And Black, For Piano And
        Orchestra
    see Czerwone I Czarne, For Piano
        And Orchestra

BAUER, MARION EUGENIE (1887-1955)
    Concerto for Piano and Orchestra
        2.2.2.2. 4.2.2.0. timp,perc,
        strings,pno solo
    SCHIRM.G perf mat rent   (B352)

BAUER, ROSS
    Neon [9']
        3.3.3.3. 4.3.3.1. 3perc,harp,pno&
        cel,strings
    sc AM.COMP.AL. $54.65, perf mat
        rent   (B353)

    Sospenso [9']
        string orch
    sc AM.COMP.AL. $24.85, perf mat
        rent   (B354)

BAUERN POLKA see Strauss, Johann, [Jr.]

BAUERSACHS, FRED M. (1930-   )
    Capriccio, Op. 50
    BOHM perf mat rent   (B355)

BAULD, ALISON (1944-   )
    One Pearl, For Solo Voice And
        Orchestra [16']
        1.0.0.0. 0.0.0.0. strings,S solo
    NOVELLO perf mat rent   (B356)

BAUM-FELS-EISWASSER- UND FISCHSTUCKE,
    FOR PIANO AND ORCHESTRA see Gasser,
    Ulrich

BAUMGARTNER, JEAN-PAUL (1932-   )
    Chemin De La Croix, Le, For Solo
        Voices And Orchestra [22']
    CHOUDENS perf mat rent   (B357)

    Concerto for Orchestra, No. 1 [25']
    CHOUDENS perf mat rent   (B358)

    Polyphonie 4 [10']
    CHOUDENS perf mat rent   (B359)

    Suite Symphonique No. 1 [35']
    CHOUDENS perf mat rent   (B360)

BAUMGARTNER, JEAN-PAUL (cont'd.)

    Symphonie Concertante for Viola and
        Orchestra [23']
    CHOUDENS perf mat rent   (B361)

BAUR, JÜRG (1918-   )
    Aus Dem Tagebuch Des Alten (Symphony
        No. 2) [22']
        2+pic.2+English horn.2+bass
        clar.2+contrabsn. 4.3.3.1.
        timp,3-4perc,harp,strings
    BREITKOPF-W perf mat rent   (B362)

    Fresken
        string orch
    BREITKOPF-W perf mat rent   (B363)

    Konzertante Fantasie, For Organ And
        String Orchestra
        string orch,org solo
    BREITKOPF-W perf mat rent   (B364)

    Sinfonie Einer Stadt [25']
        2+pic.2+English horn.2+bass
        clar.2+contrabsn. 4.3.3.1.
        timp,perc,harp,strings
    study sc BREITKOPF-W f.s., perf mat
        rent   (B365)

    Sinfonische Metamorphosen Uber
        Gesualdo
    study sc BREITKOPF-W PB 5105 f.s.
                                    (B366)

    Symphony No. 2
    see Aus Dem Tagebuch Des Alten

BAYAYA, FOR SOLO VOICE AND ORCHESTRA
    see Trojan, Václav

BAYLE, FRANCOIS (1932-   )
    Opera-Bus, Chapitre I: Prologue [5']
        1.1.1.0. 1.1.1.0. 6perc,pno,harp,
        strings,electronic tape
    BILLAUDOT perf mat rent   (B367)

    Pluriel [8']
        2.1.1.1. 2.1.1.0. 2perc,harp,
        strings,electronic tape
    BILLAUDOT perf mat rent   (B368)

BAZAR see Dandelot, Georges

BAZELON, IRWIN ALLEN (1922-   )
    Fusions
        2.2.2.1. 1.2.1.0. perc,pno,vla,db
    sc NOVELLO $54.50   (B369)

    Junctures For Orchestra [17']
        3.2.4.3. 4.3.3.1. timp,4perc,pno,
        strings,S solo
    NOVELLO perf mat rent   (B370)

    Phenomena, For Solo Voice And Chamber
        Orchestra [15']
        1(pic).1.3(bass
        clar).1(contrabsn). 1.1.1.0.
        2perc,pno,strings,S solo
    NOVELLO perf mat rent   (B371)

    Sinfonia Concertante [20']
        3.2.4.2. 4.3.3.1. timp,4perc,
        prepared pno,strings,clar solo,
        trp solo,marimba solo
    NOVELLO perf mat rent   (B372)

    Spirits Of The Night [18']
        3.3.4.3. 4.3.3.1. timp,4perc,pno,
        strings
    NOVELLO perf mat rent   (B373)

BAZIN, FRANÇOIS-EMANUEL-JOSEPH
    (1816-1878)
    Maitre Pathelin: Je Pense A Vous, For
        Solo Voice And Orchestra
    LEMOINE perf mat rent   (B374)

    Voyage En Chine: Overture
        1.1.1.1. 4.1.3.0. timp,perc,harp,
        strings
    LEMOINE perf mat rent   (B375)

BÁZLIK, MIROSLAV (1931-   )
    Concert Music
    see Koncertna Hudba

    Koncertna Hudba
    "Concert Music" SLOV.HUD.FOND
                                    (B376)

BE NOT AFEARD, FOR SOLO VOICES AND
    ORCHESTRA see Nordheim, Arne

BEALE, JAMES (1924-   )
    Music for Solo Voice and Orchestra,
        Op. 34 [15']
        2.2+English horn.2+bass clar.2.
        2.3.3.1. perc,cel,strings,S
        solo
    sc AM.COMP.AL. $13.80, perf mat
        rent   (B377)

    Suite, Op. 42 [20']
        string orch
    sc AM.COMP.AL. $12.10   (B378)

BEAN, MABEL
America: A Vision [arr.]
(Still, William Grant) 3.2+English
horn.3.2. 4.3.3.0. timp,drums,
harp,pno,strings sc STILL $7.90
(B379)

BEARDS OF A FATHER see Lieberman, Glenn

BEATRICE ET BENEDICT: OVERTURE see
Berlioz, Hector (Louis)

BEAU BRUMMEL: MINUET see Elgar, [Sir]
Edward (William)

BEAU IDEAL MARCH, THE see Sousa, John
Philip

BEAU MONDE QUADRILLE, LE see Strauss,
Johann, [Jr.]

BEAUBOURG MUSIQUE see Haubenstock-
Ramati, Roman

BECERRA SCHMIDT, GUSTAVO (1925-)
Concerto for 2 Guitars and Orchestra
[20']
2.2.0.2. 0.2.0.0. perc,strings,
2gtr soli
PEER MUSIK perf mat rent (B380)

Concerto for Percussion and Orchestra
[20']
3.3.3.3. 3.4.3.3.1. harp,strings,
perc solo
PEER MUSIK perf mat rent (B381)

BECHERT, ERNST (1958-)
Concerto for Violoncello and
Orchestra [15']
2.1.2.1. 2.2.1.1. 2perc,hpsd,
8vln,4vla,3db,vcl solo
SIKORSKI perf mat rent (B382)

BECK, CONRAD (1901-1989)
Nachklange [16']
2.2.2.2. 4.2.0.0. timp,perc,
strings
SCHOTTS perf mat rent (B383)

BECK, FRANZ (1731-1809)
Sinfonia, Op. 3, No. 5, in D minor
(Landon, H.C.R.) KALMUS A7282 sc
$20.00, set $12.00, pts $2.50,
ea. (B384)

BECK, JOHN NESS (1930-1987)
Variants On An Irish Hymn Tune
(Tatgenhorst) BECKEN set $20.00, sc
$2.00, pts $1.00, ea. (B385)

BECKER, FRANK (1944-)
Messenger RNA [8']
6vln,3vla,2vcl,db
SALABERT perf mat rent (B386)

Philiapaideia [16']
3(pic).3.3(bass clar).3. 4.3.3.0.
timp,4perc,pno,strings
SALABERT perf mat rent (B387)

BECKER, GÜNTHER (1924-)
Un Poco Giocoso, For Tuba And Chamber
Orchestra [20']
1(pic).1.1.1. 1.1.1.0. perc,harp,
pno,vln,vla,vcl,db,tuba solo
BREITKOPF-W perf mat rent (B388)

BECKER, JOHN JOSEPH (1886-1961)
Concerto In One Movement, For Violin
And Orchestra [30']
2.2.2.3. 4.2.3.1. timp,perc,
strings,vln solo
PETERS P66438 perf mat rent (B389)

Rain Down Death [30']
1.1.1.1. 1.1.0.0. timp,perc,pno,
strings
sc AM.COMP.AL. $21.35, perf mat
rent (B390)

Satiro, For Piano And Orchestra [15']
2.2.2.2. 4.2.2.1. perc,strings,
pno solo
sc AM.COMP.AL. $21.35 (B391)

Symphony No. 5 [15']
1.1.0.0. 2.2.0.0. strings
AM.COMP.AL. perf mat rent (B392)

When The Willow Nods (from Stagework
No. 5b) [20']
1.1.1.1. 1.1.0.0. timp,perc,pno,
strings
PETERS P66439 perf mat rent (B393)

BECKMESSER VARIATIONEN ÜBER THEMEN AUS
RICHARD WAGNERS "MEISTERSINGER VON
NURNBERG" see Korn, Peter Jona

BECKWITH, JOHN (1927-)
Flower Variations And Wheels
sc BERANDOL BER 1785 $20.00 (B394)

BECOMING PERFECTLY ONE see Stearns,
Peter Pindar

BEDFORD, DAVID (1937-)
Prelude For A Maritime Nation [6'30"]
3(pic).3.3.3. 4.4.3.1. timp,
3perc,org,strings
UNIVER. perf mat rent (B395)

Symphony For 12 Musicians [8']
1.2.1.1. 1.0.0.0. perc,2vln,vla,
vcl,db
UNIVER. perf mat rent (B396)

Symphony No. 1
3.3.3.3. 4.3.3.1. timp,perc,
strings
sc UNIVER. UE 17933 f.s. (B397)

Transfiguration, The [12']
2.2.0.0. 0.0.0.0. 3perc,pno,8vln,
2vla,2vcl,db
UNIVER. perf mat rent (B398)

Valley-Sleeper, The Children, The
Snakes And The Giant, The [18']
2(pic).2.2.2. 2.2.0.0. perc,
strings
sc UNIVER. UE 17663 $19.50, perf
mat rent (B399)

BEDMAR, LUIS (1931-)
Concerto for 2 Horns and Orchestra
ALPUERTO (B400)

BEECROFT, NORMA (1934-)
Jeu De Bach, For Oboe, Trumpet And
String Orchestra [10']
string orch,electronic tape,ob
solo,piccolo trp solo
CAN.MUS.CENT. MI 9343 B414J (B401)

BEERMAN, BURTON (1943-)
Moments 1977 [21']
2.2.2.2. 2.2.2.0. perc,strings
sc AM.COMP.AL. $19.10 (B402)

Night Dances, For Clarinet, Dancer
And Orchestra [21']
2(pic).2.2.2. 2.1.1.0. perc,
strings,clar solo
sc AM.COMP.AL. $16.10, perf mat
rent (B403)

BEETHOVEN, LUDWIG VAN (1770-1827)
Ah! Perfido, For Solo Voice And
Orchestra, Op. 65
SONZOGNO perf mat rent (B404)
BREITKOPF-L perf mat rent (B405)

An Die Hoffnung, Solo Voice And
Orchestra, [arr.]
(Mottl) BREITKOPF-L perf mat rent
(B406)

Concerti for Piano and Orchestra,
Nos. 1-3
(Beethoven Werke, Series III,
Vol.2) HENLE pap 4081 $124.25,
cloth 4082 $132.50 (B407)

Concerti for Piano and Orchestra,
Nos. 1-5
min sc KALMUS K00302 $20.00 (B408)
(reprint of Breitkopf and Hartel
edition) sc DOVER 245632 $12.95
(B409)
Concerto for Piano and Orchestra in D
(Hess) 1.2.0.2. 2.2.0.0. timp,
strings,pno solo [12'] KALMUS
A6793 sc $10.00, set $15.00, pts
$1.00, ea., perf mat rent (B410)

Concerto for Piano and Orchestra in E
flat, WoO. 4
(Hess) KALMUS A6245 sc $35.00, set
$18.00, pts $2.00, ea., perf mat
rent (B411)

Concerto for Piano and Orchestra, No.
1, Op. 15, in C
(Kuthen, Hans-Werner) sc BÄREN.
$8.10 (B412)

Concerto for Piano and Orchestra, No.
2, Op. 19, in B flat
(Kuthen, Hans-Werner) sc BÄREN.
$6.30 (B413)

Concerto for Piano and Orchestra, No.
3, Op. 37, in C minor
(Kuthen, Hans-Werner) sc BÄREN.
$6.90 (B414)

Concerto for Violin and Orchestra,
Op. 61, in D
sc MUZYKA f.s. (B415)
(Darvas) study sc EMB 40060 f.s.
(B416)
(Kojima, Shin Augustinus) sc BÄREN.
$6.00 (B417)
(Sommer, J.; Schneiderhan, W.) sc
HENLE 325 $27.50 (B418)
*see GREAT ROMANTIC VIOLIN
CONCERTOS

Concerto for Violin, Violoncello,
Piano and Orchestra, Op. 56, in C
(van der Linde, Bernard) sc BÄREN.
$10.50 (B419)

BEETHOVEN, LUDWIG VAN (cont'd.)

Contretanze, Zwolf, WOo.14
SONZOGNO perf mat rent (B420)

Coriolan Overture *Op.62
HENLE sc HN 40440 f.s., pts
HN 40442-40447 f.s. (B421)
see Overtures, Four
see Overtures, Six
see Overtures, Vol. 2

Deutsche Tänze, Zwölf, WoO. 8
(Kovács) sc EMB 6540 f.s. (B422)

Ecossaises [arr.]
(Cruft, Adrian) 2.2.2.2. 2.0.0.0.
timp,strings [3'30"] sc JOAD
f.s., perf mat rent (B423)

Egmont *Op.84
min sc KALMUS K01002 $5.25 (B424)
sc PETERS 2006 $19.50 (B425)

Egmont: Overture
SONZOGNO perf mat rent (B426)
see Overtures, Four
see Overtures, Six
see Overtures, Vol. 2

Es War Einmal Ein Konig, For Solo
Voice And Orchestra [arr.]
*Op.75,No.3
(Shostakovich, D.) "Flohlied Aus
Goethes "Faust", For Solo Voice
And Orchestra [arr.]" 3.2.2.2.
2.0.0.0. strings,B solo [3']
SIKORSKI perf mat rent (B427)
(Stravinsky, Igor) "Mephistopheles'
Song Of The Flea, For Solo Voice
And Orchestra [arr.]" KALMUS
A6952 sc $8.00, set $12.00, pts
$1.00, ea. (B428)

Fidelio: Abscheulicher, Wo Eilst Du
Hin, For Solo Voice And Orchestra
BREITKOPF-L perf mat rent (B429)

Fidelio: Gott, Welch' Dunkel Hier,
For Solo Voice And Orchestra
2.2.2.2. 4.0.0.0. timp,strings,T
solo
BREITKOPF-L perf mat rent (B430)

Fidelio: Gott, Welch' Dunkel Hier,
For Solo Voice And Orchestra,
First Version
2.2.2.3. 4.0.2.0. timp,strings,T
solo
BREITKOPF-L perf mat rent (B431)

Fidelio: Hat Man Nicht Auch Gold
Beineben, For Solo Voice And
Orchestra
BREITKOPF-L perf mat rent (B432)

Fidelio: Jetzt Schatzchen, Jetzt Sind
Wir Allein, For Solo Voices And
Orchestra
1.2.2.2. 2.0.0.0. strings,ST soli
KALMUS A6202 sc $5.00, set $12.00,
pts $1.00, ea. (B433)
BREITKOPF-L perf mat rent (B434)

Fidelio: Mir Ist So Wunderbar, For
Solo Voices And Orchestra [5']
2.0.2.2. 2.0.0.0. strings,SSTB
soli
BREITKOPF-W perf mat rent (B435)
BREITKOPF-L perf mat rent (B436)

Fidelio: O, War Ich Schon Mit Dir
Vereint, For Solo Voice And
Orchestra [5']
1.2.2.2. 2.0.0.0. strings,S solo
BREITKOPF-W perf mat rent (B437)
BREITKOPF-L perf mat rent (B438)

Fidelio: Overture
SONZOGNO perf mat rent (B439)
see Overtures, Six
see Overtures, Vol. 2

Flohlied Aus Goethes "Faust", For
Solo Voice And Orchestra [arr.]
see Es War Einmal Ein Konig, For
Solo Voice And Orchestra [arr.]

Geschopfe Des Prometheus, Die *Op.43
[48']
2.2.2.2. 2.2.0.0. timp,harp,
strings
KALMUS A1267 sc $40.00, set
$100.00, pts $6.00, ea., perf mat
rent (B440)

Geschopfe Des Prometheus, Die:
Overture
see Overtures, Four
see Overtures, Vol. 2

Grosse Fuge [arr.]
(Weingartner, F.) string orch [17']
KALMUS A1008 sc $7.00, set
$12.00, pts $2.50, ea. (B441)

BEETHOVEN, LUDWIG VAN (cont'd.)

Konig Stephan Overture
  see Overtures, Four

Kontretänze, Zwölf, WoO. 14
  (Mezö) sc EMB 6541 f.s.   (B442)

Leonore Overture No. 1
  see Overtures, Six
  see Overtures, Vol. 1

Leonore Overture No.2 *Op.72
  sc,pts BREITKOPF-W PB-OB 5142 f.s.
                                 (B443)
  see Overtures, Six
  see Overtures, Vol. 1

Leonore Overture No. 3
  see Overtures, Four
  see Overtures, Six
  see Overtures, Vol. 1

Menuette, Zwolf, WoO. 12
  (Hess) "Twelve Minuets" KALMUS
  A6418 sc $12.00, set $28.00, pts
  $2.00, ea., perf mat rent (B444)

Mephistopheles' Song Of The Flea, For
  Solo Voice And Orchestra [arr.]
  see Es War Einmal Ein Konig, For
  Solo Voice And Orchestra [arr.]

Mit Mädeln Sich Vertragen, For Solo
  Voice And Orchestra
  see Zwei Arien, For Solo Voice And
  Orchestra

Namensfeier Overture *Op.115
  HENLE sc HN 40450 f.s., pts
  HN 40452-40457 f.s.   (B445)
  see Overtures, Four

No, Non Turbati!, For Solo Voice And
  String Orchestra
  string orch/string quar,S solo
  KALMUS A6635 sc $5.00, set $5.00,
  pts $1.00, ea.   (B446)
  sc,pts MCGIN-MARX $12.00   (B447)

O Welch Ein Leben, For Solo Voice And
  Orchestra
  see Zwei Arien Zu Ignaz Umlaufs
  Singspiel "Die Schöne Schusterin"

Overtures, Four
  min sc KALMUS K00441 $8.75
    contains: Coriolan Overture;
    Egmont: Overture; Geschopfe Des
    Prometheus, Die: Overture;
    Leonore Overture No. 3   (B448)

Overtures, Four
  min sc KALMUS K00028 $5.50
    contains: Konig Stephan Overture;
    Namensfeier Overture; Ruinen
    Von Athen Overture; Weihe Des
    Hauses, Die   (B449)

Overtures, Six
  sc DOVER 247899 $9.95 reprint of
    Breitkopf and Hartel edition
    contains: Coriolan Overture;
    Egmont: Overture; Fidelio:
    Overture; Leonore Overture No.
    1; Leonore Overture No. 2;
    Leonore Overture No. 3   (B450)

Overtures, Vol. 1
  sc PETERS 1021A f.s.
    contains: Leonore Overture No. 1;
    Leonore Overture No. 2; Leonore
    Overture No. 3   (B451)

Overtures, Vol. 2
  sc PETERS 1021B f.s.
    contains: Coriolan Overture;
    Egmont: Overture; Fidelio:
    Overture; Geschöpfe Des
    Prometheus, Die: Overture
                               (B452)
Prelude and Fugue in F
  (Hess) string orch [5'] KALMUS
  A6976 sc $5.00, set $6.00, pts
  $1.25, ea.   (B453)

Primo Amore Piacer Del Ciel, For Solo
  Voice And Orchestra
  1.2.0.2. 2.0.0.0. strings,S solo
  BREITKOPF-L perf mat rent   (B454)

Prüfung Des Küssens, For Solo Voice
  And Orchestra
  see Zwei Arien, For Solo Voice And
  Orchestra

Romance for Violin and Orchestra, No.
  1, Op. 40, in G
  sc BÄREN. $4.20 contains also:
  Romance for Violin and Orchestra,
  No. 2, Op. 50, in F   (B455)
  BROUDE BR. sc $5.00, set $12.50,
  pts $1.00, ea.   (B456)
  HENLE sc HN 41050 f.s., pts
  HN 41052-41057 f.s. contains
  also: Romance for Violin and

BEETHOVEN, LUDWIG VAN (cont'd.)

  Orchestra, No. 2, Op. 50, in F
                               (B457)
  (Orban) study sc EMB 40111 f.s.
  contains also: Romance for Violin
  and Orchestra, No. 2, Op. 50, in
  F   (B458)

Romance for Violin and Orchestra, No.
  2, Op. 50, in F
  BROUDE BR. sc $7.50, set $17.50,
  pts $1.50, ea.   (B459)
  see Romance for Violin and
  Orchestra, No. 1, Op. 40, in G

Ruinen Von Athen Overture
  see Overtures, Four

Soll Ein Schuh Nicht Drücken, For
  Solo Voice And Orchestra
  see Zwei Arien Zu Ignaz Umlaufs
  Singspiel "Die Schöne Schusterin"

Sonata, Op. 106, in B flat, [arr.]
  (Weingartner, F.) 2+pic.2.2.3.
  4.2.3.0. timp,strings [49']
  BREITKOPF-W perf mat rent (B460)

Symphonies Nos. 1-4
  min sc KALMUS K00309 $14.25 (B461)
Symphonies Nos. 1-9, Vols. 1 And 2
  (Markevitch) sc PETERS 9610 f.s.
                               (B462)
Symphonies Nos.5-7
  min sc KALMUS K00310 $14.25 (B463)
Symphonies, Nos.6-8
  (Beethoven Werke, Series I, Vol.3)
  HENLE pap 4021 f.s., cloth 4022
  f.s.   (B464)
Symphonies Nos.8-9
  min sc KALMUS K00311 $14.25 (B465)
Symphony No. 1, Op. 21, in C
  (Darvas) study sc EMB 40003 f.s.
                               (B466)
  (Hauschild) sc PETERS 9601 f.s.
                               (B467)
Symphony No. 2, Op. 36, in D
  SONZOGNO perf mat rent   (B468)
  (Darvas) study sc EMB 40004 f.s.
                               (B469)
Symphony No. 3, Op. 55, in E flat
  (Darvas) study sc EMB 40005 f.s.
                               (B470)
Symphony No. 4, Op. 60, in B flat
  (Darvas) study sc EMB 40011 f.s.
                               (B471)
Symphony No. 5, Op. 67, in C minor
  sc MUZYKA f.s.   (B472)
  (Darvas) study sc EMB 40019 f.s.
                               (B473)
Symphony No. 6, Op. 68, in F
  (Darvas) study sc EMB 40020 f.s.
                               (B474)
  (Hauschild, Peter) sc PETERS P9606
  f.s.   (B475)
Symphony No. 7, [arr.]
  (Wellmann, O.) strings,harmonium,
  pno [37'] KALMUS A4169 set
  $26.00, pts $3.50, ea., perf mat
  rent   (B476)
Symphony No. 7, Op. 92, in A
  (Darvas) study sc EMB 40022 f.s.
                               (B477)
Symphony No. 8, Op. 93, in F
  (Darvas) study sc EMB 40023 f.s.
                               (B478)
Symphony No. 9, Op. 125, in D minor
  (Darvas) study sc EMB 40036 f.s.
                               (B479)
Tremate, Empi, Tremate, For Solo
  Voices And Orchestra, Op. 116
  BREITKOPF-L perf mat rent   (B480)
Turkish March [arr.]
  (Denisov, Edison) VAAP perf mat
  rent   (B481)
Twelve Minuets
  see Menuette, Zwolf, WoO. 12

Two Arias, For Solo Voice And
  Orchestra
  see Zwei Arien, For Solo Voice And
  Orchestra

Vestas Feuer: Scene, For Solo Voices
  And Orchestra
  (Hess) KALMUS A6632 sc $10.00, set
  $15.00, pts $1.00, ea.   (B482)

Vestas Feuer: Scene, For Solo Voices
  And Orchestra [arr.]
  (Westermann, Clayton) 2.2.2.2.
  2.0.0.0. strings,STTBar soli
  [20'] voc sc SCHIRM.G f.s., perf
  mat rent   (B483)

BEETHOVEN, LUDWIG VAN (cont'd.)

  Wachtelschlag, Der, "Horch Wie
  Schallts Dorten", For Solo Voice
  And Orchestra, [arr.]
  2.2.2.2. 2.2.0.0. timp,strings
  (Mottl) sc,pts BREITKOPF-L rent
                               (B484)
  Weihe Des Hauses, Die
  see Overtures, Four

Wellingtons Sieg *Op.91
  "Wellington's Victory or The Battle
  Of Vittoria" min sc EULENBURG
  EU01367 f.s.   (B485)

Wellington's Victory or The Battle Of
  Vittoria
  see Wellingtons Sieg

Zwei Arien, For Solo Voice And
  Orchestra
  1.2.0.0. 2.0.0.0. strings,B solo
  BREITKOPF-L perf mat rent
    contains: Mit Mädeln Sich
    Vertragen, For Solo Voice And
    Orchestra; Prüfung Des Küssens,
    For Solo Voice And Orchestra
                               (B486)
Zwei Arien, For Solo Voice And
  Orchestra
  "Two Arias, For Solo Voice And
  Orchestra" KALMUS A3391 sc $6.00,
  set $9.00, pts $1.00, ea.   (B487)

Zwei Arien Zu Ignaz Umlaufs Singspiel
  "Die Schöne Schusterin"
  BREITKOPF-L perf mat rent
    contains: O Welch Ein Leben, For
    Solo Voice And Orchestra
    (1.2.0.2. 2.0.0.0. strings,T
    solo); Soll Ein Schuh Nicht
    Drücken, For Solo Voice And
    Orchestra (1.2.0.2. 2.0.0.0.
    strings,S solo)   (B488)

BEFORE ALLINE see Miller, Michael R.

BEGGAR'S CONCERTO, THE, FOR CLARINET
  AND STRING ORCHESTRA see
  Tischhauser, Franz

BEGINNINGS see Liptak, David

BEHOLD, I BRING YOU GLAD TIDINGS: TWO
  PIECES see Purcell, Henry

BEHOLD THAT STAR, FOR SOLO VOICE AND
  ORCHESTRA [ARR.]
  (Burleigh, Harry T.) 2.1.2.1.
  2.2.1.0. timp,harp,strings,low solo
  COLOMBO perf mat rent   (B489)

BEHREND, SIEGFRIED (1933-1990)
  Spanische Impressionen, For Guitar
  And Orchestra, [arr.] [6']
  2.1.2.0. 2.4.4.0. timp,perc,
  castanets,elec bass,strings,gtr
  solo
  (Schmitz-Steinberg, Chr.) ZIMMER.
                               (B490)
  Spanisches Konzert, For Guitar And
  Orchestra
  1(pic).1+English horn.2.2.
  4.4.4.0. triangle,tamb,bongos,
  perc,strings,gtr solo
  ZIMMER.   (B491)

  Stierkampfmusik, For Guitar And
  Orchestra, [arr.] [2'45"]
  1+pic.1.2.1. 2.4.4.0. timp,perc,
  castanets,elec bass,strings,gtr
  solo
  (Schmitz-Steinberg, Chr.) ZIMMER.
                               (B492)
BEI UNS Z'HAUS see Strauss, Johann,
  [Jr.]

BEKKU, SADAO (1922-)
  Concerto for Piano and Orchestra
  [32']
  2(pic).2.2.2. 4.2.3.0. timp,harp,
  strings,pno solo
  sc ZEN-ON 899210 f.s., perf mat
  rent   (B493)

BELAUBRE, LOUIS-NOËL (1932-)
  Concerto for 2 Pianos and Orchestra
  [25']
  2.2.2.2. 2.2.2.0. timp,strings,
  2pno soli
  BILLAUDOT perf mat rent   (B494)

BELKIN, ALAN (1951-)
  Symphony No. 2 [10']
  3(pic).3.3(bass
  clar).3(contrabsn). 4.3.3.1.
  timp,3perc,harp,cel,strings
  CAN.MUS.CENT. MI 1100 B432SY (B495)

BELL, ALLAN (1953-)
  Concerto for Percussion and Orchestra
  [16']
  2.2.2.2. 4.2.1.0. harp,strings,
  perc solo
  CAN.MUS.CENT. MI 1340 B433CO (B496)

BELL, ELIZABETH (1928-)
Concerto for Orchestra [10']
2.2.2.2. 4.2.3.1. perc,strings
sc AM.COMP.AL. $52.95, perf mat
rent (B497)

Rituals For Orchestra [10']
3.3.3.3. 4.3.3.1. timp,4perc,
strings
sc AM.COMP.AL. $52.05, perf mat
rent (B498)

Symphony No. 1 [20']
3.3.3.3. 4.3.3.1. 3perc,strings
sc AM.COMP.AL. $139.95, perf mat
rent (B499)

BELL, LARRY
Continuum For Orchestra [8']
1(pic).1+English horn.2.1+
contrabsn. 1.2.1.1. perc,harp,
pno,strings
sc AM.COMP.AL. $18.60, perf mat
rent (B500)

BELLA, JÁN LEVOSLAV (1843-1936)
Serenade in E flat
string orch
SLOV.HUD.FOND (B501)

BELLA FIAME DEL MIO CORE, FOR SOLO
VOICE AND ORCHESTRA [ARR.] see
Suppe, Franz von

BELLA MIA FIAMMA, FOR SOLO VOICE AND
ORCHESTRA see Mozart, Wolfgang
Amadeus

BELLE AU BOIS DORMANT, LA: PAS DE DEUX
see Tchaikovsky, Piotr Ilyich,
Sleeping Beauty, The: Pas De Deux

BELLE AU BOIS DORMANT, LA: PAS DE DEUX,
ACT III [ARR.] see Tchaikovsky,
Piotr Ilyich, Sleeping Beauty, The:
Pas De Deux, Act III [arr.]

BELLE AU BOIS DORMANT, LA: PAS DE DEUX,
"L'OISEAU BLEU" [ARR.] see
Tchaikovsky, Piotr Ilyich, Sleeping
Beauty, The: Pas De Deux,
"Bluebird" [arr.]

BELLE EXCENTRIQUE, LA see Satie, Erik

BELLE MUSIQUE NO. 3, LA see
Rabinowitch, Alexandre

BELLE OF CHICAGO MARCH, THE see Sousa,
John Philip

BELLE PIERRETTE, LA see Foulds, John
Herbert

BELLINI, VINCENZO (1801-1835)
Aria Di Cerere, For Solo Voice And
Orchestra [6']
2fl,2clar,2horn,strings,S solo
sc BSE 11 f.s., perf mat rent
(B502)

Capuleti Ed I Montecchi, I: E Serbato
A Questo Acciaro, For Solo Voice
And Orchestra
KALMUS A4667 sc $12.00, set $30.00,
pts $2.00, ea., perf mat rent
(B503)

Capuleti Ed I Montecchi, I: Morte Io
Non Temo, For Solo Voice And
Orchestra
KALMUS A4673 sc $12.00, set $30.00,
pts $2.00, ea., perf mat rent
(B504)

Capuleti Ed I Montecchi, I: Oh Quante
Volte, Oh Quante, For Solo Voice
And Orchestra
KALMUS A4669 sc $5.00, set $20.00,
pts $1.00, ea., perf mat rent
(B505)

Capuleti Ed I Montecchi, I: Se Romeo
T' Uccise Un Figlio, For Solo
Voice And Orchestra
KALMUS A4668 sc $15.00, set $30.00,
pts $2.00, ea., perf mat rent
(B506)

Capuleti Ed I Montecchi, I: Si,
Fuggire: A Noi Non Resta, For
Solo Voices And Orchestra
KALMUS A4670 sc $20.00, set $50.00,
pts $2.50, ea., perf mat rent
(B507)

Capuleti Ed I Montecchi, I: Stolto!
Ad Un Sol Mio Grido, For Solo
Voices And Orchestra
KALMUS A4674 sc $21.00, set $45.00,
pts $3.00, ea., perf mat rent
(B508)

E Nello Stringerti A Questo Core, For
Solo Voice And Orchestra [6']
2.2.2.2. 2.0.0.0. strings,S solo
sc BSE 3 f.s., perf mat rent (B509)

Gratias Agimus, For Solo Voice And
Orchestra [5']
2fl,2clar,2horn,strings,S solo
sc BSE 9 f.s., perf mat rent (B510)

BELLINI, VINCENZO (cont'd.)
Pirata, Il: Cedo Al Destin Orrible,
For Solo Voices And Orchestra
KALMUS A4690 sc $12.00, set $20.00,
pts $1.00, ea., perf mat rent
(B511)

Pirata, Il: Col Sorriso D'innocenza,
For Solo Voice And Orchestra
KALMUS A4693 sc $18.00, set $30.00,
pts $2.00, ea., perf mat rent
(B512)

Pirata, Il: Lo Sognai Ferito,
Esangue, For Solo Voice And
Orchestra
KALMUS A4680 sc $12.00, set $32.00,
pts $2.00, ea., perf mat rent
(B513)

Pirata, Il: Nel Furor Della Tempeste,
For Solo Voice And Orchestra
KALMUS A4679 sc $12.00, set $30.00,
pts $2.00, ea., perf mat rent
(B514)

Pirata, Il: Si, Vincemmo, E Il Pregio
Io Sento, For Solo Voice And
Orchestra
KALMUS A4684 sc $9.00, set $22.00,
pts $1.00, ea., perf mat rent
(B515)

Pirata, Il: Tu M' Apristi In Cor
Ferita, For Solo Voices And
Orchestra
KALMUS A4689 sc $18.00, set $30.00,
pts $2.00, ea., perf mat rent
(B516)

Pirata, Il: Tu Sciagurato! Ah! Fuggi,
For Solo Voices And Orchestra
KALMUS A4682 sc $18.00, set $30.00,
pts $2.00, ea., perf mat rent
(B517)

Pirata, Il: Tu Vedrai La Sventurata,
For Solo Voice And Orchestra
KALMUS A4692 sc $12.00, set $30.00,
pts $2.00, ea., perf mat rent
(B518)

Puritani, I: Ah, Per Sempre Io Ti
Perdei, For Solo Voice And
Orchestra
KALMUS A4696 sc $9.00, set $30.00,
pts $2.00, ea., perf mat rent
(B519)

Puritani, I: Cinta Di Fiori, For Solo
Voice And Orchestra
KALMUS A4703 sc $7.00, set $12.00,
pts $1.00, ea., perf mat rent
(B520)

Puritani, I: Il Rival Salvar Tu Dei,
For Solo Voices And Orchestra
KALMUS A4704 sc $12.00, set $27.00,
pts $2.00, ea., perf mat rent
(B521)

Puritani, I: Nel Mirati Un Solo
Istante, For Solo Voices And
Orchestra
KALMUS A4707 sc $8.00, set $30.00,
pts $2.00, ea., perf mat rent
(B522)

Puritani, I: Sai Com'arde In Petto
Mio, For Solo Voices And
Orchestra
KALMUS A4697 sc $18.00, set $30.00,
pts $2.50, ea., perf mat rent
(B523)

Quando Incise Su Quel Marmo, For Solo
Voice And Orchestra [7']
2.2.2.2. 2.0.0.0. strings,S solo
sc BSE 7 f.s., perf mat rent (B524)

Si Per Te, Gran Nume Eterno, For Solo
Voice And Orchestra [6']
2fl,2clar,2horn,strings,S solo
sc BSE 1 f.s., perf mat rent (B525)

Sinfonia Breve In D
(Di Stefano) KALMUS A7336 sc $7.00,
set $13.00, pts $1.50, ea. (B526)

Sonnambula, La: Ah! Non Credea
Mirati, For Solo Voice And
Orchestra
KALMUS A4734 sc $12.00, set $30.00,
pts $1.50, ea., perf mat rent
(B527)

Sonnambula, La: Son Geloso Del
Zeffiro Errante, For Solo Voices
And Orchestra
KALMUS A4728 sc $6.00, set $30.00,
pts $2.00, ea., perf mat rent
(B528)

Sonnambula, La: Tutto E Sciolto, For
Solo Voice And Orchestra
KALMUS A4731 sc $12.00, set $30.00,
pts $1.50, ea., perf mat rent
(B529)

Straniera, La: Ah! Se Non M' Ami Piu,
For Solo Voice And Orchestra
KALMUS A4718 sc $12.00, set $30.00,
pts $2.00, ea., perf mat rent
(B530)

Straniera, La: Io La Vidi, For Solo
Voices And Orchestra
KALMUS A4710 sc $15.00, set $30.00,
pts $2.00, ea., perf mat rent
(B531)

BELLINI, VINCENZO (cont'd.)
Straniera, La: Serba, Serba I Tuoi
Segreti, For Solo Voices And
Orchestra
KALMUS A4712 sc $14.00, set $30.00,
pts $2.00, ea., perf mat rent
(B532)

Straniera, La: Si Li Sciogliete, O
Giudici, For Solo Voice And
Orchestra
KALMUS A4716 sc $12.00, set $30.00,
pts $2.00, ea., perf mat rent
(B533)

Straniera, La: Si! Sulla Salma Del
Fratello, For Solo Voices And
Orchestra
KALMUS A4717 sc $12.00, set $30.00,
pts $2.00, ea., perf mat rent
(B534)

Straniera, La: Sventurato Il Cor Che
Fida, For Solo Voice And
Orchestra
KALMUS A4711 sc $4.00, set $20.00,
pts $1.00, ea., perf mat rent
(B535)

Symphony in E flat [10']
2.2.2.0. 2.2.2.0. strings
sc BSE 13 f.s., perf mat rent
(B536)

Tecum Principium, For Solo Voice And
Orchestra [5']
2.2.2.2. 2.0.0.0. strings,S solo
sc BSE 5 f.s., perf mat rent (B537)

BELLISARIO, ANGELO (1932-)
Overture Su Tema Di I. Pizzetti
*Op.52 [10']
3.3.3.2. 4.3.3.1. timp,perc,harp,
strings
sc SONZOGNO f.s., perf mat rent
(B538)

Zagare, Le [9']
2.2.2.2. 2.2.0.0. timp,perc,harp,
strings
SONZOGNO perf mat rent (B539)

BELLMAN-SOIREE see Nilo, Calle

BELLS, THE see Milhaud, Darius

BELLS RINGING see Shchedrin, Rodion,
Concerto for Orchestra, No. 2

BELSHAZZAR'S FEAST: SUITE see Sibelius,
Jean

BEMBE see García-Caturla, Alejandro

BEN HUR: SUITE see Rozsa, Miklos

BENCHARONG see Boyd, Anne

BENDA, FRANZ (FRANTIŠEK) (1709-1786)
Concerti For Flute And String
Orchestra
sc SUPRAPHON MAB 80 f.s.
contains: Concerto for Flute and
String Orchestra, No. 1, in G;
Concerto for Flute and String
Orchestra, No. 2, in E minor;
Concerto for Flute and String
Orchestra, No. 3, in A (B540)

Concerto for Flute and String
Orchestra, No. 1, in G
see Concerti For Flute And String
Orchestra

Concerto for Flute and String
Orchestra, No. 2, in E minor
see Concerti For Flute And String
Orchestra

Concerto for Flute and String
Orchestra, No. 3, in A
see Concerti For Flute And String
Orchestra

Sinfonia in C, MIN 30 [7']
string orch
KALMUS A1094 sc $4.50, set $6.25,
pts $1.25, ea. (B541)

Sinfonia in D, MIN 31 [7']
fl,2horn,hpsd,strings
SUPRAPHON (B542)

Sinfonia No. 1 in G [8']
string orch
SUPRAPHON (B543)

Sinfonia No. 2 in G [8']
string orch
SUPRAPHON (B544)

Sinfonia No. 4 in B flat [10']
string orch
SUPRAPHON (B545)

Sinfonia No. 12 in A [9']
string orch
SUPRAPHON (B546)

BENDA, GEORG ANTON (JIŘÍ ANTONÍN)
(1722-1795)
Aria for Solo Voice and String
Orchestra [4']
string orch,solo voice
SUPRAPHON   (B547)

Ariadna On Naxos, For Solo Voices And
Orchestra [35']
2.2.0.2. 2.4.0.0. timp,hpsd,
strings,3 speaking voices
SUPRAPHON   (B548)

Benda's Complaint, For Solo Voice And
Chamber Orchestra [11']
2fl,hpsd,strings,S solo
SUPRAPHON   (B549)

Concerti For Harpsichord And String
Orchestra, Two
sc SUPRAPHON MAB 77 f.s.
contains: Concerto for
Harpsichord and String
Orchestra, No. 1, in F;
Concerto for Harpsichord and
String Orchestra, No. 2, in G
(B550)

Concerto for Harpsichord and String
Orchestra in G [18']
(Bethan) string orch,hpsd solo
KALMUS A7298 sc $20.00, set
$12.50, pts $2.50, ea.   (B551)

Concerto for Harpsichord and String
Orchestra, No. 1, in F
see Concerti For Harpsichord And
String Orchestra, Two

Concerto for Harpsichord and String
Orchestra, No. 2, in G
see Concerti For Harpsichord And
String Orchestra, Two

BENDA, KARL HERMANN HEINRICH
(1748-1836)
Sinfonia in D
2ob,2horn,strings
sc,pts MOSELER M 40.145 f.s. (B552)

BENDA'S COMPLAINT, FOR SOLO VOICE AND
CHAMBER ORCHESTRA see Benda, Georg
Anton (Jiří Antonín)

BENDIK OG AROLILJA see Hurum, Alf

BENDL, KAREL (1838-1897)
Yugoslav Rhapsody *Op.60
4.2.2.2. 4.2.3.1. timp,perc,harp,
strings
SIMROCK perf mat rent   (B553)

BENEDICT, [SIR] JULIUS (1804-1885)
Capinera, La, For Solo Voice And
Orchestra [arr.]
1.1.2.1.alto sax.tenor sax.
2.2.1.0. timp,strings,solo
voice
(Clark, Tom) "Wren, The, For Solo
Voice And Orchestra, [arr.]"
SCHIRM.G perf mat rent   (B554)

Wren, The, For Solo Voice And
Orchestra, [arr.]
see Capinera, La, For Solo Voice
And Orchestra [arr.]

BENES, JURAJ (1940-   )
Hudba Pre J.S.
"Music For J.S." SLOV.HUD.FOND
(B555)

Music For J.S.
see Hudba Pre J.S.

BENGUEREL, XAVIER (1931-   )
Concerto for Percussion and Orchestra
[22']
2.2.2.2. 2.2.2.0. pno,strings,
perc solo
ZIMMER.   (B556)

Concerto for Violoncello and
Orchestra [23']
3.3.3.3. 4.3.3.1. pno,perc,vcl
solo
HANSEN-GER perf mat rent   (B557)

Fotomontage *Op.27 [10']
2+pic.0.2+clar in E flat.2.
3.2.3.1. 2perc,strings
HANSEN-GER perf mat rent   (B558)

Raises Hispanicas [23']
2+pic.2+English horn.2+bass
clar.2+contrabsn. 4.3.3.1.
perc,pno,strings
HANSEN-GER perf mat rent   (B559)

BENI MORA see Holst, Gustav

BENJAMIN, ARTHUR (1893-1960)
Jamaican Rumba
see Two Jamaican Pieces

Jamaican Song
see Two Jamaican Pieces

BENJAMIN, ARTHUR (cont'd.)

Two Jamaican Pieces
1.1.2.1.opt alto sax. 2.1.0.0. opt
timp,perc,pno,strings BOOSEY perf
mat rent
contains: Jamaican Rumba;
Jamaican Song   (B560)

BENJAMIN, GEORGE
At First Light [20']
1(pic,alto fl).1.1(bass
clar).1(contrabsn). 1.1.1.0.
perc,pno&cel,2vln,vla,vcl,db
sc FABER F0718 f.s., perf mat rent
(B561)

Fanfare For Aquarius [40']
1(pic).1.1.1. 1.1.1.0. perc,harp,
pno,vln,vla,vcl,db
FABER perf mat rent   (B562)

Mind Of Winter, A, For Solo Voice And
Orchestra [9']
2.1+English horn.2.2. 2.2.0.0.
perc,strings,S solo
sc FABER F0654 $34.00, perf mat
rent   (B563)

Ringed By The Flat Horizon [18']
3.3.3.3. 4.3.3.1. 5perc,cel,harp,
pno,strings
sc FABER F0625 $32.00, perf mat
rent   (B564)

BENKER, HEINZ (1921-   )
Mobile Concertante
SCHOTTS sc CON 181 $31.00, set
CON 181-50 $68.00   (B565)

BENNETT, FRANK
Carnival Scenes [15']
2+pic.2.2.2. 4.3.3.1. timp,2perc,
strings
AMP perf mat rent   (B566)

BENNETT, RICHARD RODNEY (1936-   )
Anniversaries [17']
3.3.3.3. 4.3.3.1. timp,perc,pno,
harp,strings
study sc NOVELLO $21.50, perf mat
rent   (B567)

Concerto for Guitar and Chamber
Orchestra
1(pic).1(English horn).0+bass
clar.0. 1.1.0.0. 2perc,cel,vln,
vla,vcl,gtr solo
min sc UNIVER. 15406 $14.50, perf
mat rent   (B568)

Love Spells, For Solo Voice And
Orchestra (from Spells) [14']
2(pic).2(English horn).2(bass
clar).2(contrabsn). 4.3.3.1.
timp,3perc,pno&cel,harp,
strings,S solo
NOVELLO perf mat rent   (B569)

Music for Strings [13']
string orch
NOVELLO perf mat rent   (B570)

Reflections On A Theme Of William
Walton
11strings soli
NOVELLO perf mat rent   (B571)

Sonnet Sequence, For Solo Voice And
String Orchestra [13']
string orch,T solo
NOVELLO perf mat rent   (B572)

Sonnets To Orpheus, For Violoncello
And Orchestra [33']
2(pic).2(English horn).2(bass
clar).2(contrabsn). 2.2.2.1.
timp,3perc,pno&cel,2harp,
strings,vcl solo
study sc NOVELLO 2971-90 $38.25,
perf mat rent   (B573)

BENNETT, ROBERT RUSSELL (1894-1981)
Four Freedoms Symphony, The [18'30"]
2.2(English horn).3(bass clar).2.
4.3.3.1. timp,3perc,strings
ROBBINS perf mat rent   (B574)

BENNETT, [SIR] WILLIAM STERNDALE
(1816-1875)
Concerto for Piano and Orchestra, No.
4, Op. 19
KISTNER perf mat rent   (B575)

BENOLIEL, BERNARD (1943-   )
Black Tower, The, For Solo Voice And
Orchestra [11']
1.0+English horn.0+bass clar.1.
1.2.1.0. strings,S solo
HANSEN-GER perf mat rent   (B576)

Symphony [26']
4(pic).2+3English horn.2+2bass
clar.3+contrabsn. 4+4Wagner
tuba.3+bass trp.4.1. timp,perc,
strings
HANSEN-GER perf mat rent   (B577)

BENTZON, JØRGEN (1897-1951)
Fotomontage *Op.27 [10']
2(pic).0.2+clar in E flat.2.
3.2.3.1. 2perc,strings
HANSEN-DEN perf mat rent   (B578)

Introduction, Variations And Rondo,
For Alto Saxophone And String
Orchestra [10']
string orch,alto sax solo
HANSEN-DEN perf mat rent   (B579)

Sinfonia Buffa *Op.37 [5']
trp,pno,perc,strings
HANSEN-DEN perf mat rent   (B580)

Symphonic Trio
study sc SAMFUNDET f.s.   (B581)

Symphony No. 1, Op. 37 [34']
2.2.2.2. 4.2.3.1. timp,perc,
strings
HANSEN-DEN perf mat rent   (B582)

Variations, Op. 28 [10']
1(pic).1.2.1. 2.1.1.0. timp,perc,
strings
HANSEN-DEN perf mat rent   (B583)

BENTZON, NIELS VIGGO (1919-   )
Capriccio for Tuba and Orchestra, Op.
396 [7']
trp,pno,perc,strings,tuba solo
HANSEN-DEN perf mat rent   (B584)

Climatic Changes, For Saxophone,
Piano And Orchestra *Op.474
[20']
1.1.1.1. 1.1.1.1. perc,string
quar,baritone sax solo,pno solo
HANSEN-DEN perf mat rent   (B585)

Concerto for Clarinet and Orchestra,
Op. 375 [15']
2.2.2+bass clar.2+contrabsn.
4.3.3.1. timp,perc,harp,
strings,clar solo
HANSEN-DEN perf mat rent   (B586)

Concerto for Flute and Orchestra, No.
2, Op. 388 [15']
0.1+English horn.1+bass clar.1.
2.1.1.1. timp,4perc,harp,
strings,fl solo
HANSEN-DEN perf mat rent   (B587)

Concerto for Flute and String
Orchestra, Op. 386 [12']
string orch,fl solo
HANSEN-DEN perf mat rent   (B588)

Concerto for Horn and Orchestra [15']
2(pic).2+English horn.2+bass
clar.2+contrabsn. 4.3.3.1.
timp,perc,strings,horn solo
HANSEN-DEN perf mat rent   (B589)

Concerto for Piano and Orchestra, No.
8 [18']
2+pic.2+English horn.2+bass
clar.2+contrabsn. 4.3.3.1.
timp,3perc,strings,pno solo
HANSEN-DEN perf mat rent   (B590)

Concerto for 2 Pianos and Orchestra,
Op. 482
2+pic.2+English horn.2+bass
clar.2+contrabsn. 4.3.3.1.
timp,5perc,harp,cel,strings,
2pno soli
HANSEN-DEN perf mat rent   (B591)

Concerto for Strings, Op. 488 [12']
string orch
HANSEN-DEN perf mat rent   (B592)

Concerto for Tuba and Orchestra, Op.
373 [20']
2+pic.2+English horn.2+bass
clar.2+contrabsn. 4.3.3.1.
timp,perc,strings,tuba solo
HANSEN-DEN perf mat rent   (B593)

Concerto for Viola and Orchestra, Op.
303 [30']
2.2.2.2. 4.3.3.1. timp,harp,perc,
strings,vla solo
HANSEN-DEN perf mat rent   (B594)

Concerto for Violin and Orchestra,
No. 4, Op. 374
1+2pic.2+English horn.2+bass
clar.2+contrabsn. 4.3.3.1.
timp,3perc,harp,strings,vln
solo
HANSEN-DEN perf mat rent   (B595)

Concerto for Violoncello and
Orchestra, No. 3, Op. 444 [26']
2+pic.2+English horn.2+bass
clar.2+contrabsn. 4.3.3.1.
timp,3perc,strings,vcl solo
HANSEN-DEN perf mat rent   (B596)

BENTZON, NIELS VIGGO (cont'd.)

Concerto for Violoncello and
Orchestra, Op. 311 [23']
2(pic).2.2.2. 2.2.0.0. timp,perc,
strings,vcl solo
HANSEN-DEN perf mat rent   (B597)

Epitaph *Op.272 [8']
3(pic).2+English horn.2+bass
clar.2+contrabsn. 4.3.3.1.
timp,perc,harp,strings
HANSEN-DEN perf mat rent   (B598)

Feature On René Descartes *Op.357
[27']
3+pic.3+English horn.3+bass
clar.3+contrabsn. 6.4.4.1.
2timp,perc,cel,harp,pno,strings
HANSEN-DEN perf mat rent   (B599)

Leipziger Tag, For Piano And String
Orchestra *Op.383 [15']
string orch,pno solo
HANSEN-DEN perf mat rent   (B600)

Sinfonia Concertante for Wind Quintet
and Orchestra, Op. 390 [20']
0.0+English horn.0+bass clar.0+
contrabsn. 0.1.1.1. timp,5perc,
strings,wind quin soli HANSEN-DEN
perf mat rent   (B601)

Sinfonia, Op. 402 [25']
2.2.2.2. 2.2.1.0. timp,strings
HANSEN-DEN perf mat rent   (B602)

Symphonic Fantasy, For Two Pianos And
Orchestra *Op.119
2+pic.2+English horn.2+bass
clar.2. 4.3.3.1. timp,3perc,
strings,2pno soli
HANSEN-DEN perf mat rent   (B603)

Symphony No. 15, Op. 432
3(pic).2+English horn.2+bass
clar.2+contrabsn. 4.3.3.1.
timp,3perc,harp,cel,strings
(Marrakesh) HANSEN-DEN perf mat
rent   (B604)

Symphony No. 16, Op. 509 [22']
2+pic.2+English horn.2+bass
clar.2+contrabsn. 4.3.3.1.
timp,4perc,cel,harp,strings
HANSEN-DEN perf mat rent   (B605)

Symphony No. 17, Op. 522 [33']
3.2+English horn.2+bass clar.2+
contrabsn. 4.3.3.1. 5perc,cel,
harp,strings
HANSEN-DEN perf mat rent   (B606)

Symphony No. 18, Op. 523 [27']
3.2+English horn.2+bass clar.2+
contrabsn. 4.3.3.1. timp,3perc,
cel,harp,strings
HANSEN-DEN perf mat rent   (B607)

Symphony No. 19, Op. 524 [30']
3.2+English horn.2+bass clar.2+
contrabsn. 4.3.3.1. 3perc,harp,
cel,strings
HANSEN-DEN perf mat rent   (B608)

Variazioni Senza Tema, For Piano And
Orchestra *Op.438 [14']
2.2.2.2. 4.2.3.0. timp,perc,
strings,pno solo
HANSEN-DEN perf mat rent   (B609)

BENVENUTO CELLINI: OVERTURE see
Berlioz, Hector (Louis)

BENVENUTO CELLINI: SEUL POUR LUTTER,
FOR SOLO VOICE AND ORCHESTRA see
Berlioz, Hector (Louis)

BERBIGUIER, BENOIT-TRANQUILLE
(1782-1838)
Concerto for Flute and Orchestra, No.
7, in E flat [24']
0.2.1.1. 2.0.0.0. strings,fl solo
BREITKOPF-W perf mat rent   (B610)

BERCEUSE, LA see Strauss, Johann, [Jr.]

BERCEUSE D'AMERIQUE see Brucken-Fock,
Gerard H.G. von

BERCEUSE DU PAYSAN, FOR SOLO VOICE AND
ORCHESTRA [ARR] see Mussorgsky,
Modest Petrovich

BERCEUSE ELEGIAQUE see Busoni,
Ferruccio Benvenuto

BERCEUSE ELEGIAQUE [ARR.] see Busoni,
Ferruccio Benvenuto

BEREAU, J.S.
Triptyque, For Bassoon And Orchestra
[20']
CHOUDENS perf mat rent   (B611)

BERENHOLTZ, JIM
March To Battle, For Solo Voice And
Orchestra [5']
2.3.3.3. 3.3.3.1. perc,strings,
synthesizer,S solo
sc AM.COMP.AL. $8.45   (B612)

BERENICE CHE FAI, FOR SOLO VOICE AND
ORCHESTRA see Haydn, [Franz] Joseph

BEREZOWSKY, NICOLAI T. (1900-1953)
Fantasy for 2 Pianos and Orchestra,
Op. 9
2(pic).2.2.2. 4.2.3.1. timp,perc,
strings,2pno soli
AMP perf mat rent   (B613)

BERG, ALBAN (1885-1935)
Kammerkonzert, For Piano, Violin And
Winds
pic,fl,ob,English horn,clar in E
flat,clar in A,bass clar,bsn,
contrabsn,2horn,trp,trom,pno
solo,vln solo
min sc PHILH PH. 423 $18.00   (B614)
sc UNIVER. 8393 $130.00   (B615)

BERG, CHRISTOPHER (1949-   )
Not Waving But Drowning, For Solo
Voice And Orchestra [20']
1(pic).1.1.1. 1.1.1.0. timp,perc,
harp,pno/cel,strings,med solo
PEER perf mat rent   (B616)

BERG, NATANAËL (1879-1957)
Concerto for Piano and Orchestra
[28']
3.3.3.3. 4.2.3.0. timp,strings,
pno solo
STIM   (B617)

BERG, OLAV (1949-   )
Concerto for Clarinet and Orchestra
[17']
2.2.2.2. 4.2.3.0. timp,2perc,
harp,strings,clar solo
NORGE   (B618)

Epilog [12'30"]
3.3.3.3. 4.3.3.1. timp,perc,harp,
pno,strings
NORGE   (B619)

Etyde
2.2.2.2. 4.3.3.1. timp,perc,
strings
NORGE   (B620)

Kveita, For Narrator And Chamber
Orchestra [30']
1.1.1.1. 1.0.0.0. pno,strings,
narrator
NORGE   (B621)

Mot En Fanfare [5']
3.2.2.2. 4.3.3.1. timp,perc,
strings
NORGE   (B622)

Pezzo Per Orchestra [9']
2.2.2.2. 2.0.0.0. strings
NORGE   (B623)

Poseidon [12']
3(pic).3(English horn).3(bass
clar).3(contrabsn). 4.3.3.1.
timp,perc,harp,strings
NORSK   (B624)

BERGAMO, PETAR (1930-   )
Musica Concertante
3.3.3.3. 4.3.3.1. timp,perc,harp,
cel,pno,strings
sc UNIVER. $83.00   (B625)
min sc UNIVER. PH00499 $23.00
                                   (B626)

BERGE, HÅKON (1954-   )
Landscape; Open; Quiet
see Landskap; Apent; Stille

Landskap; Apent; Stille [7']
3.2.2.2. 4.3.3.1. timp,perc,
strings
"Landscape; Open; Quiet" NORGE   (B627)

Signal For Chamber Orchestra And
Magnetic Tape [11']
1.1.1.1. 1.1.1.0. 2perc,2pno,
strings,Mez solo,electronic
tape
NORGE   (B628)

BERGE, SIGURD (1929-   )
A For Orkester [11']
3.3.3.3. 4.3.3.1. timp,perc,
strings
NORGE   (B629)

B For Orkester [6']
3.3.3.3. 4.3.3.0. timp,perc,
strings
NORGE   (B630)

Between Mirrors, For Violin And
String Orchestra
see Mellom Speil, For Violin And

BERGE, SIGURD (cont'd.)

String Orchestra

Mellom Speil, For Violin And String
Orchestra [14']
string orch,vln solo
"Between Mirrors, For Violin And
String Orchestra" NORGE   (B631)

Music for Orchestra [15']
3.3.3.3. 4.3.3.0. perc,strings
NORGE   (B632)

Pezzo Orchestrale [11']
3.2.2.2. 4.3.3.1. timp,perc,
strings
NORGE   (B633)

Raga, For Oboe And Orchestra [18']
2.2.2.2. 4.3.3.0. timp,perc,
strings,ob solo
NORGE   (B634)

Sinus [9']
timp,perc,strings
NORGE   (B635)

Ta Den Springar [1']
2.2.2.2. 2.2.2.0. perc,pno,acord,
strings
NORGE   (B636)

Tamburo Piccolo [5']
timp,perc,strings
NORGE   (B637)

BERGEN, DE see Mengelberg, Karel

BERGER, ARTHUR VICTOR (1912-   )
Prelude, Aria And Waltz [9']
string orch
sc PETERS P66953 f.s., perf mat
rent   (B638)

BERGER, JEAN (1909-   )
Sinfonietta
string orch
SCHIRM.G sc 50348000 $6.00, set
50347990 $18.00   (B639)

Three Dances For Strings
string orch
set SCHIRM.G 50347850 $16.00   (B640)

BERGH, SVERRE (1915-1980)
Bjonnes'n: Norsk Dans No. 1 [3']
2.1.1.2. 1.2.2.0. perc,strings
NORGE   (B641)

Concertino for Clarinet and String
Orchestra
string orch,clar solo
sc LYCHE 863 f.s.   (B642)

Eva Before The Fall Of Man
see Eva For Syndefallet

Eva For Syndefallet
1.1.2.1. 2.1.1.0. timp,perc,
acord,strings
"Eva Before The Fall Of Man" NORGE
                                   (B643)

Intrata [7']
1.1.2.1.2sax. 0.2.2.0. perc,pno,
strings
NORGE   (B644)

BERGLIOT, FOR NARRATOR AND ORCHESTRA
see Grieg, Edvard Hagerup

BERGMAN, ERIK (1911-   )
Ananke
NOVELLO perf mat rent   (B645)

Colori Ed Improvisazioni *Op.72
[19'30"]
3.3.3.3. 4.4.3.1. timp,4perc,
harp,cel,strings
sc FAZER f.s., perf mat rent   (B646)

Concerto for Violin and Orchestra,
Op. 99
2.2.2.2. 4.3.3.0. perc,harp,
strings,vln solo
sc NOVELLO $52.50   (B647)

Dualis, For Violoncello And Orchestra
*Op.86
NOVELLO perf mat rent   (B648)

BERGMANNEN, FOR SOLO VOICE AND
ORCHESTRA see Johnsen, Hallvard

BERICHT VOM MENSCHEN see Pirckmayer,
Georg

BERIO, LUCIANO (1925-   )
Calmo, For Solo Voice And Chamber
Orchestra [20']
0+pic+alto fl.0.2+clar in E flat+
bass clar.1.alto sax. 1.1.1.0.
perc,harp,3vla,3vcl,2db,Mez
solo
UNIVER. perf mat rent   (B649)

BERIO, LUCIANO (cont'd.)

Concerto for Piano and Orchestra, No.
2 [25']
3+pic.2+English horn.4+bass
clar.2+contrabsn.alto sax.tenor
sax. 3.4.3.1. cel,elec org,
3vla,3vcl,3db,pno solo
(Echoing curves, for piano and two
instrumental groups) UNIVER. perf
mat rent   (B650)

Continuo [20']
4.2+English horn.3+bass clar.2+
contrabsn.alto sax.tenor sax.
6.4.4.2. vibra,marimba,2harp,
cel,pno,elec org,strings
UNIVER. perf mat rent   (B651)

Corale (from Sequenza VIII) [15']
2horn,12vln,4vla,4vcl,3db,vln
solo
sc UNIVER. 17545 $22.00   (B652)

Encore Per Orchestra
4.3.4.3.2sax. 3.3.3.1. timp,perc,
harp,cel,pno,strings
sc UNIVER. $24.00   (B653)

Entrata [3']
4.2+English horn.4.3. 3.3.3.1.
3perc,harp,pno,strings
sc UNIVER. 17256 f.s.   (B654)

Fanfara [2']
2+2pic.2+English horn.2+bass
clar.2+contrabsn. 4.4.3.1.
timp,2perc,cel,strings without
vln
UNIVER. perf mat rent   (B655)

Festum [2']
2+2pic.2+English horn.2+bass
clar.2+contrabsn. 6.5.3.1.
timp,perc,elec org,strings
UNIVER. perf mat rent   (B656)

Formazioni [20']
4(pic).2+English horn.2+bass
clar.2+contrabsn.alto sax.tenor
sax. 6.4.4.2. timp,2harp,cel&
elec org,strings
UNIVER. perf mat rent   (B657)

Requies [13']
1+pic.1+English horn.1+clar in E
flat+bass clar.2. 2.2.1.0.
marimba,harp,cel,strings
sc UNIVER. UE19149 f.s., perf mat
rent   (B658)

Voci, For Viola And Two Instrumental
Groups [30']
3.2.4.2. 2.2.2.1. 3perc,cel&elec
org,strings,vla solo
sc UNIVER. UE18201 f.s., perf mat
rent   (B659)

BERKELEY, [SIR] LENNOX (1903-1989)
Concerto for Piano and String
Orchestra [23']
string orch,pno solo
CHESTER perf mat rent   (B660)

Concerto for Violoncello and
Orchestra [20']
2.2.2.2. 4.2.3.1. timp,perc,
strings,vcl solo
CHESTER perf mat rent   (B661)

Divertimento, Op. 18, in B flat [19']
2.2.2.2. 2.2.1.0. timp,strings
KALMUS A7475 sc $35.00, set $60.00,
pts $3.50, ea., perf mat rent
                                      (B662)

Elegy [3']
string orch CHESTER JWC511 perf mat
rent   (B663)

Overture For Light Orchestra [7']
2.2.2.2. 4.2.3.0. timp,perc,harp,
strings
CHESTER perf mat rent   (B664)

Palm Court Music [8']
2(pic).2.2.2. 4.2.3.1. timp,perc,
harp,strings
CHESTER perf mat rent   (B665)

Serenade [14']
string orch
KALMUS A7042 sc $10.00, set $17.50,
pts $3.50, ea.   (B666)

Suite for Orchestra
2+pic.2+English horn.2+bass
clar.2+contrabsn. 4.3.3.1.
timp,perc,harp,strings
CHESTER perf mat rent   (B667)

Symphony No. 4 [30']
2+pic.2+English horn.2+bass
clar.2+contrabsn. 4.3.3.1.
harp,timp,perc,strings
CHESTER JWC513 perf mat rent (B668)

BERKELEY, MICHAEL
Bastet
2(pic).2(English horn).2(bass
clar).2(contrabsn). 4.2.3.1.
timp,perc,harp,strings
[35'] OXFORD perf mat rent   (B669)

Chamber Symphony [20']
1.1.1.0. 1.0.0.0. pno,strings
OXFORD perf mat rent   (B670)

Concerto for Horn and String
Orchestra [20']
string orch,horn solo
OXFORD perf mat rent   (B671)

Concerto for Organ and Orchestra
2.2.2.0. 4.3.2.1. timp,perc,
strings,org solo
sc OXFORD $49.95, perf mat rent
                                      (B672)

Concerto for Violoncello and
Orchestra [12']
2.2.0.2. 2.0.0.0. strings,vcl
solo
OXFORD perf mat rent   (B673)

Coronach [6']
string orch
OXFORD perf mat rent   (B674)

Daybreak And A Candle End [7']
2.2.2.2. 4.2.3.0. timp,perc,harp,
strings
OXFORD perf mat rent   (B675)

Fanfare And British National Anthem
[5']
2.2.2.2. 4.3.3.1. timp,3perc,
harp,opt org,strings
OXFORD perf mat rent   (B676)

For Mrs. Tomoyasu, For Solo Voice And
Orchestra [6']
1(pic).2(English horn).0.2.
2.0.0.0. strings,S solo
OXFORD perf mat rent   (B677)

Gregorian Variations
3.3.3.3.alto sax. 4.3.3.1. timp,
perc,harp,pno&cel,strings
sc OXFORD $32.00, perf mat rent
                                      (B678)

Romance Of The Rose, The
1(pic).1.1.1. 1.0.0.0. strings,
woodblock [13'] OXFORD sc
362046-4 $9.95, set 362047-2
$35.00   (B679)

Songs Of Awakening Love, For Solo
Voice And Orchestra [26']
1.2.0.2. 2.0.0.0. strings,S solo
OXFORD perf mat rent   (B680)

Vision Of Piers The Ploughman [12']
2horn,perc,pno,strings
OXFORD perf mat rent   (B681)

BERLINER MOMENTE see Boudreau, Walter

BERLINSKY, SERGEI (1946-   )
Concerto-Symphony For Violin And
Orchestra [34']
3.2.4.3. 4.3.3.1. timp,perc,harp,
cel,pno,strings, flexaton, vln
solo
VAAP perf mat rent   (B682)

BERLIOZ, HECTOR (LOUIS) (1803-1869)
Beatrice Et Benedict: Overture
2(pic).2.2.2. 4.3.3.0. timp,perc,
gtr,2harp,strings
(Macdonald, Hugh) BÄREN. BA 5443
                                      (B683)
see Overtures, Five

Benvenuto Cellini: Overture [10']
2(pic).2.2(bass clar).4. 4.4.3.1.
timp,perc,strings
CHOUDENS perf mat rent   (B684)

Benvenuto Cellini: Seul Pour Lutter,
For Solo Voice And Orchestra
KALMUS A4228 sc $5.00, set $22.00,
pts $1.00, ea., perf mat rent
                                      (B685)

Captive, La, For Solo Voice And
Orchestra *Op.12 [8']
2.2.2.2. 2.0.0.0. timp,perc,
strings,A/Mez solo
"Gefangene, Die, For Solo Voice And
Orchestra" BREITKOPF-W perf mat
rent   (B686)

Carnaval Romain, Le *Op.9
SONZOGNO perf mat rent   (B687)

Collected Works. Malherbe Edition,
Leipzig, 1900-1907
(microfiche reprint) UNIV.MUS.ED.
$185.00   (B688)

Corsaire, Le
see Overtures, Five

BERLIOZ, HECTOR (LOUIS) (cont'd.)

Damnation De Faust, La: Marche
Hongroise, Ballet Des Sylphes,
Menuet Des Follets
"Damnation Of Faust: Hungarian
March, Dance Of The Sylphs, Dance
Of The Sprites" min sc KALMUS
K00175 $4.00   (B689)

Damnation De Faust, La:
Mephistopheles' Song, For Solo
Voice And Orchestra
KALMUS A3423 sc $4.00, set $8.00,
pts $1.00, ea.   (B690)

Damnation Of Faust: Hungarian March,
Dance Of The Sylphs, Dance Of The
Sprites
see Damnation De Faust, La: Marche
Hongroise, Ballet Des Sylphes,
Menuet Des Follets

Death Of Ophelia, For Solo Voice And
Orchestra[arr.]
see Mort D'ophelie, La, For Solo
Voice And Orchestra [arr.]

Enfance Du Christ, L': Prelude, Part
II, "La Fuite En Egypte"
"Flight Into Egypt" SCHIRM.G perf
mat rent   (B691)

Femerichter, Die: Overture
see Francs-Juges, Les: Overture

Flight Into Egypt
see Enfance Du Christ, L': Prelude,
Part II, "La Fuite En Egypte"

Francs-Juges, Les: Overture [12']
2(pic).2.2.2+contrabsn. 4.2+
cornet.3.2. timp,perc,strings
"Femerichter, Die: Overture"
BREITKOPF-W perf mat rent   (B692)
see Overtures, Five

Gefangene, Die, For Solo Voice And
Orchestra
see Captive, La, For Solo Voice And
Orchestra

Harold En Italie
see Symphonie Fantastique

Herminie, For Solo Voice And
Orchestra
2.2.2.2. 4.2.0.0. timp,perc,
strings,solo voice
KALMUS A2762 sc $18.00, set $30.00,
pts $3.50, ea., perf mat rent
                                      (B693)
min sc KALMUS K00511 $4.75   (B694)

Jeune Patre Breton, Le, For Solo
Voice And Orchestra *Op.13,No.4
"Young Breton Shepherd, The, For
Solo Voice And Orchestra"
1.2.2.1. 2.0.0.0. string orch
without db,Mez/T solo KALMUS
A2763 sc $4.00, set $10.00, pts
$1.00, ea.   (B695)

King Lear Overture
see Overtures, Five

Mort De Cleopatre, La, For Solo Voice
And Orchestra
min sc KALMUS K00512 $8.75   (B696)

Mort D'ophelie, La, For Solo Voice
And Orchestra [arr.]
(Malcolm) "Death Of Ophelia, For
Solo Voice And Orchestra[arr.]"
2.0(English horn).2.0. 3.0.0.0.
strings,S solo [7'30"] KALMUS
A7075 pno-cond sc $5.00, set
$15.00, pts $1.50, ea., perf mat
rent   (B697)

Nuits D'ete, Les, For Solo Voice And
Orchestra *Op.7
min sc KALMUS K01230 $5.50   (B698)
SONZOGNO perf mat rent   (B699)

Nuits D'ete, Les: L'ile Inconnue, For
Solo Voice And Orchestra [arr]
(Constant, Marius) 1.1.1.1.
1.1.1.0. timp,gtr,cel,2pno,2vln,
vla,vcl,db,S/T solo SALABERT perf
mat rent   (B700)

Nuits D'ete, Les: Sur Les Lagunes,
For Solo Voice And Orchestra
[arr]
(Koering, Rene) 1.1.1.1. 1.1.1.0.
timp,gtr,cel,2pno,2vln,vla,vcl,
db,S/T solo SALABERT perf mat
rent   (B701)

Nuits D'ete, Les: Villanelle, For
Solo Voice And Orchestra [arr]
(Levinas, Michael) 1.1.1.1.
1.1.1.0. timp,gtr,cel,2pno,2vln,
vla,db,S/T solo SALABERT perf mat
rent   (B702)

BERLIOZ, HECTOR (LOUIS) (cont'd.)

Overtures, Five
min sc KALMUS K00090 $11.50
contains: Beatrice Et Benedict:
Overture; Corsaire, Le; Francs-
Juges, Les: Overture; King Lear
Overture; Waverly Overture
(B703)

Romeo Et Juliette: Grande Fête Chez
Capulet
"Romeo Und Julia: Grosses Fest Bei
Capulet" sc BREITKOPF-L PB 1747
f.s. (B704)

Romeo Et Juliette: La Reine Mab,
Scherzo
"Romeo Und Julia: Königin Mab" sc
BREITKOPF-L PB 1646 f.s. (B705)

Romeo Et Juliette: Scene d'Amour
"Romeo Und Julia: Liebesszene" sc
BREITKOPF-L PB 1670 f.s. (B706)

Romeo Und Julia: Grosses Fest Bei
Capulet
see Romeo Et Juliette: Grande Fête
Chez Capulet

Romeo Und Julia: Königin Mab
see Romeo Et Juliette: La Reine
Mab, Scherzo

Romeo Und Julia: Liebesszene
see Romeo Et Juliette: Scene
d'Amour

Serenade, Hymn And Toccata [arr.]
(Matthews, Colin) 1.1.1.1. 1.1.0.0.
strings [10'] FABER perf mat rent
(B707)

Symphonie Fantastique *Op.14
sc DOVER 246574 $11.95 contains
also: Harold En Italie (B708)
SONZOGNO perf mat rent (B709)

Trojans, The: Hail, All Hail To The
Queen
3.2.2.2. 4.2.3.1(ophicleide).
2cornet,perc,strings OXFORD perf
mat rent (B710)

Troyens, Les: Chasse Et Orage [10']
2+pic.2.2.4. 4.2+2cornet.3.1.
timp,perc,strings,opt cor
(Macdonald, Hugh) BÄREN. BA 5783
(B711)

Waverly Overture
see Overtures, Five

Young Breton Shepherd, The, For Solo
Voice And Orchestra
see Jeune Patre Breton, Le, For
Solo Voice And Orchestra

Zaide, For Solo Voice And Orchestra
*Op.19,No.1
1.2.2.2. 4.0.0.0. perc,strings,S
solo
KALMUS A2574 sc $7.00, set $15.00,
pts $1.25, ea., perf mat rent
(B712)

BERNAOLA, CARMELO (1929-   )
Impulsos [18']
ALPUERTO (B713)

Juegos
1.1.1.1. 0.2.2.0. perc,pno,
strings
ALPUERTO (B714)

Mixturas [9']
1.1.1.1. 2.1.0.0. timp,strings
ALPUERTO (B715)

Relatividades [18'20"]
2(pic).1.1+bass clar.1. 1.2.1.0.
xylo,vibra,harp,pno,strings
ALPUERTO (B716)

Symphony in C [19']
3.2.3.3. 6.3.3.0. perc,pno,cel,
harp,strings
ALPUERTO (B717)

BERNARD, FILIP (1896-1984)
Bilecanka [13']
3(pic).2.(English horn).2(bass
clar).2(contrabsn). 4.3.3.1.
timp,perc,harp,strings
DRUSTVO DSS 603 perf mat rent
(B718)

BERNARD, ROBERT (1900-1971)
Concert Aile Dans Les Jardins
Nocturnes [14']
2harp,pno,strings
BILLAUDOT perf mat rent (B719)

Danse Devant L'arche, La [22']
4.3.3.3.alto sax.tenor sax.
4.4.3.1. timp,3perc,2harp,pno,
strings
BILLAUDOT perf mat rent (B720)

BERNERS, LORD (GERALD TYRWHITT)
(1883-1950)
Fantasie Espagnole
KALMUS A5690 sc $20.00, set $50.00,
perf mat rent (B721)

For A Statesman (from Three Little
Funeral Marches) [3']
1(pic).1.2.1. 2.2.1.0. timp,perc,
strings
CHESTER JWC567 perf mat rent (B722)

Nickleby, Nicholas: Suite [arr]
(Irving, Ernest) 2(pic).2.2+bass
clar.2. 4.2.3.1. timp,perc,harp,
strings [11'] CHESTER perf mat
rent (B723)

Three Orchestral Pieces
KALMUS A5689 sc $15.00, set $50.00,
perf mat rent (B724)

Triumph Of Neptune, The: Suite [25']
3(pic).2+English horn.2+bass
clar.2+contrabsn. 4.3.3.1.
harp,pno,cel,timp,perc,strings
CHESTER JWC55A perf mat rent (B725)

Triumph Of Neptune, The: Suite,
[arr.]
(Douglas) 2(pic).1+English horn.2+
bass clar.2. 4.3.3.1. harp,pno&
cel,timp,perc,strings [19']
CHESTER JWC60 perf mat rent
(B726)

BERNSTEIN, DAVID (1942-   )
Variations On A Symphonic Landscape
[10']
3(pic).3.3.2+contrabsn. 4.3.3.1.
timp,perc,harp,cel,pno,strings
SCHIRM.G perf mat rent (B727)

BERNSTEIN, LEONARD (1918-1990)
Divertimento [15']
2+pic.2+English horn.2+clar in E
flat+bass clar.2+contrabsn.
4.3.3.1. timp,5perc,harp,pno,
strings
min sc BOOSEY $15.00, perf mat rent
(B728)

Halil, For Flute And Orchestra [16']
harp,perc,timp,strings,fl solo
min sc BOOSEY 972 $14.00, perf mat
rent (B729)

Mass: Three Meditations, For
Violoncello And Orchestra [19']
perc,org,pno,harp,strings,vcl
solo
sc BOOSEY $18.00, perf mat rent
(B730)

Mass: Two Meditations [7']
perc,org,pno,harp,strings
BOOSEY perf mat rent (B731)

Musical Toast, A [2']
2+pic.2+English horn.2+clar in E
flat(bass clar).2+contrabsn.
4.3.3.1. timp,5perc,harp,pno,
opt org,opt elec gtr,strings
min sc BOOSEY 976 $10.25, perf mat
rent (B732)

Take Care Of This House, For Solo
Voice And Orchestra [4']
1.1.2+bass clar.1. 2.2.2.1.
2perc,harp,gtr,pno,strings,solo
voice
BOOSEY perf mat rent (B733)

West Side Story: A Boy Like That, For
Solo Voices And Orchestra
1.0.1+bass clar.1. 2.3.2.0. perc,
gtr,pno,strings,SA soli
SCHIRM.G perf mat rent (B734)

West Side Story: Balcony Scene
"Tonight", For Solo Voices And
Orchestra
1.1.2+bass clar.1. 2.3.2.0. perc,
pno,cel,strings,ST soli
SCHIRM.G perf mat rent (B735)

West Side Story: Ballet Sequence
1+pic.1+English horn.1(clar in E
flat)+bass clar.1. 2.3.2.0.
perc,pno,cel,strings
SCHIRM.G perf mat rent (B736)

West Side Story: Dance Sequence
1+pic.1.1(clar in E flat)+bass
clar.1.4sax. 2.3.2.0. perc,gtr,
pno,strings
SCHIRM.G perf mat rent (B737)

West Side Story: Finale, For Solo
Voices And Orchestra
2.0.2.1. 2.3.2.0. perc,gtr,
strings,ST soli
SCHIRM.G perf mat rent (B738)

West Side Story: I Feel Pretty, For
Solo Voice And Orchestra
1.0.1.1. 2.3.2.0. perc,pno,
strings,S solo
SCHIRM.G perf mat rent (B739)

BERNSTEIN, LEONARD (cont'd.)

West Side Story: Maria, For Solo
Voice And Orchestra
1.1.2.1. 2.3.2.0. perc,gtr,pno,
strings,T solo
SCHIRM.G perf mat rent (B740)

West Side Story: One Hand, One Heart,
For Solo Voices And Orchestra
1.1.2+bass clar.1. 2.3.2.0. perc,
cel,pno,strings,ST soli
SCHIRM.G perf mat rent (B741)

West Side Story: Overture
1+pic.0.2+bass clar.1. 2.3.2.0.
perc,gtr,pno,strings
SCHIRM.G perf mat rent (B742)

West Side Story: Prologue
1+pic.0.1(clar in E flat)+bass
clar.1.4sax. 2.3.2.0. perc,gtr,
pno,strings
SCHIRM.G perf mat rent (B743)

West Side Story: Something's Coming,
For Solo Voice And Orchestra
3.0.3+bass clar.1. 2.3.3.0. perc,
gtr,pno,strings,T solo
SCHIRM.G perf mat rent (B744)

West Side Story: Somewhere, For Solo
Voices And Orchestra
1.1.1+bass clar.1. 2.3.2.0. perc,
pno,gtr,strings,ST soli
SCHIRM.G perf mat rent (B745)

BERTOMEU, AGUSTIN (1929-   )
Concierto Galante [13'15"]
1+alto fl.1+English horn.1+bass
clar.1. 0.0.0.0. perc,hpsd,
strings
ALPUERTO (B746)

BERTONI, FERDINANDO (GIUSEPPE)
(1725-1813)
Sinfonia in C, MIN 73
(Bonelli) KALMUS A7388 sc $8.00,
set $13.50, pts $1.50, ea. (B747)

BERTOTTO, DANIELE (1947-   )
Regions Inconnues, Les [10']
3.0.3.2. 4.2.2.1. timp,strings
SONZOGNO perf mat rent (B748)

BERTRAND DE BORN: SUITE see Casadesus,
Francis

BERWALD, FRANZ (ADOLF) (1796-1868)
Concerto for Piano and Orchestra in D
[20']
1.0.2.2. 2.1.0.0. timp,strings,
pno solo
sc,solo pt BÄREN. BA 4906 f.s.,
perf mat rent (B749)

Concerto for Violin and Orchestra,
Op. 2, in C sharp minor
KALMUS A6116 sc $25.00, set $45.00,
perf mat rent (B750)

Sinfonie Capricieuse (Symphony No. 4)
min sc KALMUS K01516 $11.50 (B751)

Sinfonie Naive (Symphony in E flat)
sc BÄREN. BA 4904 f.s., perf mat
rent (B752)

Sinfonie Sérieuse [29']
2.2.2.2. 4.2.3.0. timp,strings
(Hedwall, Lennart) (G min) sc
BÄREN. BA 4901 f.s., perf mat
rent (B753)

Sinfonie Singuliere (Symphony No. 5
in C)
min sc KALMUS K01521 $8.75 (B754)
MMB perf mat rent (B755)

Symphony in E flat
see Sinfonie Naive

Symphony No. 4
see Sinfonie Capricieuse

Symphony No. 5 in C
see Sinfonie Singuliere

BESCH, OTTO (1885-1966)
Divertimento [12']
2(pic).1.2.2. 2.2.0.0. timp,
strings
BOTE perf mat rent (B756)

BESCHWINGTES VORSPIEL see Schlemm,
Gustav Adolf

BESOZZI
Concerto for Bassoon and Orchestra in
B flat
WORLDWIDE perf mat rent (B757)

BESSERE ZEITEN WALZER see Strauss,
Eduard

BEST OF THE BIG BANDS, THE
  (Sultanof, Jeff) 3(pic).2+English
  horn.2+bass clar.2.alto sax.tenor
  sax.baritone sax. 4.4.4.1. timp,
  perc,pno&cel,harp,gtr,strings [8']
  WARNER perf mat rent   (B758)

BESTIAIRE, LE, FOR SOLO VOICE AND
  ORCHESTRA see Durey, Louis

BETLEHEM, FOR SOLO VOICE AND STRING
  ORCHESTRA see Parviainen, Jarmo

BETTINELLI, BRUNO (1913-   )
  Alternanze [22']
    4.3.3.3. 4.3.3.1. timp,3perc,
    harp,pno,strings
    RICORDI-IT 133700 perf mat rent
                                    (B759)
  Cantata No. 2 for Solo Voice and
    Orchestra
    see In Nativitate Domini, For Solo
    Voice And Orchestra

  Concerto for Violin and Orchestra
    [25']
    2.2.2.2. 2.2.1.0. timp,perc,
    strings,vln solo
    RICORDI-IT 133517 perf mat rent
                                    (B760)
  Contrasti [20']
    4.3.3.3. 4.3.3.1. timp,3perc,
    harp,pno,strings
    RICORDI-IT 132969 perf mat rent
                                    (B761)
  In Nativitate Domini, For Solo Voice
    And Orchestra (Cantata No. 2 for
    Solo Voice and Orchestra) [12']
    2.2.2.2. 2.1.0.0. timp,perc,
    strings,S solo
    RICORDI-IT 133396 perf mat rent
                                    (B762)
  Omaggio A Stravinsky [14']
    1.1.1.1. 1.0.0.0. strings
    RICORDI-IT 133876 perf mat rent
                                    (B763)
  Quadruplum [15']
    2.2.2.2. 2.2.1.0. timp,3perc,pno,
    strings
    sc RICORDI-IT 133208 f.s., perf mat
    rent   (B764)

  Sinfonia No. 7 [20']
    2.2.2.2. 2.2.0.0. timp,perc,
    strings
    sc RICORDI-IT 132708 f.s., perf mat
    rent   (B765)

  Strutture [12']
    2.2.2.2. 2.2.0.0. timp,perc,
    strings
    RICORDI-IT 133972 f.s., perf mat
    rent   (B766)

BETTY, FOR TROMBONE AND ORCHESTRA see
  Rose, David

BETTY'S POLKA see Smetana, Bedrich

BETWEEN MIRRORS, FOR VIOLIN AND STRING
  ORCHESTRA see Berge, Sigurd, Mellom
  Speil, For Violin And String
  Orchestra

BEURDEN, BERNARD VAN (1933-   )
  Concertino for 4 Saxophones and
    Orchestra [15']
    perc,pno,harp,strings,4sax soli
    DONEMUS perf mat rent   (B767)

  Divertimento Ostinato [24']
    1.1.1.0.alto sax. 0.1.1.0. 4perc,
    harp,vln,vla,vcl
    sc DONEMUS f.s., perf mat rent
                                    (B768)
  Konsertante Muziek II, For Violin,
    Viola And Winds [16']
    winds,vln solo,vla solo
    DONEMUS perf mat rent   (B769)

BEURRIERES DE PARIS, LES see Duchemin,
  Lucien

BEYER, FRANK MICHAEL (1928-   )
  Architettura Per Musica [15']
    1.1.1.1. 1.1.0.0. string quin
    BOTE perf mat rent   (B770)

  Deutsche Tanze, For Violoncello,
    Doublebass And Orchestra [12']
    1(pic).2.1.2. 1.1.0.0. strings,
    vcl solo,db solo
    BOTE perf mat rent   (B771)

  Geburt Des Tanzes (from Orphische
    Scene) [30']
    4(pic,bass fl).3(English
    horn).3(clar in E flat,bass
    clar).3(contrabsn). 4.3.3.1.
    timp,2perc,harp,pno,strings
    BOTE perf mat rent   (B772)

  Griechenland
    string orch sc BOTE f.s.   (B773)

BEYER, FRANK MICHAEL (cont'd.)
  Mysteriensonate [18']
    3(pic,alto fl).3(English
    horn).3(bass
    clar).3(contrabsn). 4.3.3.0.
    timp,perc,harp,pno,strings,vla
    solo
    BOTE perf mat rent   (B774)

  Notre-Dame Musik [16']
    3(pic).3(English horn).2+bass
    clar.3. 4.3.3.1. timp,perc,
    harp,strings
    BOTE perf mat rent   (B775)

  Streicherfantasien Zu Einem Motiv Von
    J.S. Bach
    string orch sc BOTE f.s.   (B776)

BEYOND MCBEAN, FOR VIOLIN AND CHAMBER
  ORCHESTRA see Samuel, Gerhard

BEYOND NEON; POSTCOMMERCIAL SOUND
  SCULPTURES FOR HORN AND ORCHESTRA
  see Thommessen, Olav Anton

BEYOND THE REALM OF BIRD, FOR SOLO
  VOICE AND ORCHESTRA see Lerdahl,
  Fred

BEYOND WINTERLOCK see Fox, Frederick
  Alfred (Fred)

BEZANSON, PHILIP (1916-1975)
  Songs Of Innocence, For Solo Voice
    And Orchestra [15']
    1.1.1.1. 2.0.0.0. strings,high
    solo
    sc AM.COMP.AL. $26.00   (B777)

BHAJAN, FOR VIOLONCELLO AND STRING
  ORCHESTRA see Grant, Stewart

BHAKTI see Harvey, Jonathan

BIALAS, GÜNTER (1907-   )
  Assonanzen [10']
    12vcl BÄREN. BA 6746   (B778)

  Kammerkonzert, For Harpsichord Or
    Piano And String Orchestra [18']
    7vln,3vla,2vcl,db,hpsd/pno solo
    BÄREN. BA 6085   (B779)

  Lamento Di Orlando, For Solo Voice
    And Orchestra [28']
    3+pic.2.2(bass clar).2+contrabsn.
    4.3.4.1. timp,3perc,harp,
    harmonium&elec org,pno,strings,
    Bar solo,opt cor
    BÄREN. BA 7136   (B780)

  Landler-Fantasie [15']
    2+pic.2.2+contrabsn. 4.3.3.1.
    timp,3perc,harp,strings
    study sc BÄREN. BA 7316 f.s.   (B781)

  Marsch-Fantasie [18']
    2+pic.2.2+contrabsn. 4.4.4.2.
    timp,4perc,pno,strings
    study sc BÄREN. BA 7304 f.s.   (B782)

  Waldmusik [17']
    2+pic.2.2.2(contrabsn). 4.3.3.1.
    timp,2perc,harp,strings
    study sc BÄREN. BA 6729 f.s. (B783)

BIANCHERA, SILVIA
  Varianti, For Bassoon And Strings
    11strings,bsn solo
    sc CURCI 10297 perf mat rent (B784)

BIANCHI, GIOVANNI
  Concerti Grossi, Op. 2, Six *see
    THREE CENTURIES OF MUSIC IN
    SCORE, VOL. 2: CONCERTO I, ITALY

BIBALO, ANTONIO (1922-   )
  Pour "Marguerite Infante" [10']
    1.1.1.1. 0.0.0.0. cel,harp,
    strings
    HANSEN-DEN perf mat rent   (B785)

  Symphony No. 2 [44']
    2(pic).2(English horn).2(bass
    clar).2(contrabsn). 4.3.3.0.
    timp,2perc,harp,strings
    HANSEN-DEN perf mat rent   (B786)

BIBER, HEINRICH IGNAZ FRANZ VON
  (1644-1704)
  Balletti À 6
    2trp,hpsd,strings
    MUS. RARA 1711B $13.75   (B787)

  Sonata À 6 In B Flat
    trp,kbd,strings
    MUS. RARA 2075 $8.75   (B788)

BIBIK, VALENTIN (1940-   )
  Concerto for Flute and Chamber
    Orchestra, No. 2
    VAAP perf mat rent   (B789)

BIBIK, VALENTIN (cont'd.)
  Concerto for Violin and Chamber
    Orchestra
    VAAP perf mat rent   (B790)

  Seven Miniatures [18']
    string orch
    VAAP perf mat rent   (B791)

  Symphony No. 4
    fl,horn,3perc,harp,2pno,org,8vln,
    4vla,3vcl,db
    VAAP perf mat rent   (B792)

  Symphony No. 7
    VAAP perf mat rent   (B793)

  Triptych, For Viola And Chamber
    Orchestra
    VAAP perf mat rent   (B794)

BIBLICAL SONGS, FOR SOLO VOICE AND
  ORCHESTRA see Dvořák, Antonín

BICENTENNIAL FANFARE see Piston, Walter

BICHES, LES: SUITE see Poulenc, Francis

BIEBL, FRANZ (1906-   )
  Concertino for Flute and String
    Orchestra [14']
    string orch,pno,fl solo
    ORLANDO perf mat rent   (B795)

BIENE, DIE, FOR VIOLONCELLO AND STRING
  ORCHESTRA [ARR.] see Schubert,
  Franz, Abeille, L', For Violoncello
  And String Orchestra [arr.]

BIENVENU, LILY (1920-   )
  Mere, For Solo Voices And Orchestra
    [19'30"]
    1.1.0.1. 1.0.0.0. perc,cel,harp,
    strings,SBar soli
    BILLAUDOT perf mat rent   (B796)

BIG BANG AND BEYOND, THE see Mackey,
  Steven

BIG CITY BALLADS, FOR 3 SAXOPHONES AND
  ORCHESTRA see McLean, Edwin

BIG CITY BLUES see Gould, Morton

BIG MARBLE see Henneman, Ig

BIG NIGHT, THE see Schelle, Michael

BIG SUR see Simons, Netty

BIG VARIATIONS see McLean, Edwin

BIGGS, JOHN (1932-   )
  American Folk Song Suite [15']
    2.2.2.2. 4.3.3.1. timp,3perc,
    harp,strings,opt men cor
    CONSORT PR 308 perf mat rent (B797)

  Concerto for Oboe and String
    Orchestra [18']
    string orch,ob solo
    CONSORT PR 300 perf mat rent (B798)

  Concerto for Orchestra [20']
    2.2.2.2. 4.3.3.1. timp,3perc,
    harp,strings
    CONSORT PR 311 perf mat rent (B799)

  Concerto for Violin and Orchestra
    [26']
    2.2.2.2. 2.2.0.0. timp,strings,
    vln solo
    CONSORT PR 310 perf mat rent (B800)

  Little Suite, For 2 Violins And
    Chamber Orchestra [17']
    2.2.2.2. 2.2.0.0. timp,strings,
    2vln soli
    CONSORT PR 306 perf mat rent (B801)

  Passacaglia [9'30"]
    2.2.2.2. 4.2.2.1. timp,2perc,
    strings
    CONSORT PR 303 perf mat rent (B802)

  Songs Of Laughter, Love And Tears,
    For Solo Voice And String
    Orchestra [20']
    string orch,T solo
    CONSORT PR CP 309 perf mat rent
                                    (B803)
  Symphony No. 1 [26']
    2.2.2.2. 4.2.2.1. timp,2perc,
    harp,strings
    CONSORT PR 302 perf mat rent (B804)

  Triple Concerto, For Trumpet, Horn,
    Trombone And String Orchestra
    [18']
    string orch,trp solo,horn solo,
    trom solo
    CONSORT PR 301 perf mat rent (B805)

BIGGS, JOHN (cont'd.)

Variations On A Theme Of
Shostakovich, For Piano And
Orchestra [21']
2.2.2.2. 4.2.2.1. timp,3perc,
harp,strings
CONSORT PR 307 perf mat rent   (B806)

BIHOR DANCES see Silvestri, Constantin

BIJOUX POLKA see Strauss, Johann, [Jr.]

BILDER AUS OSTEN [ARR.] see Schumann,
Robert (Alexander)

BILDER DER JAHRESZEIT, FOR SOLO VOICE
AND STRING ORCHESTRA see Füssl,
Karl-Heinz

BILDER EINER AUSSTELLUNG [ARR.] see
Mussorgsky, Modest Petrovich,
Pictures At An Exhibition [arr.]

BILDNISSE I see Kirchner, Volker David

BILDNISSE II see Kirchner, Volker David

BILECANKA see Bernard, Filip

BILLY AND THE CARNIVAL, FOR NARRATOR
AND ORCHESTRA see Dorff, Daniel Jay

BILLY ASCENDS, FOR SOLO VOICE AND
ORCHESTRA see Evett, Robert

BILUCAGLIA, CLAUDIO (1946-   )
Solitudine Del Giorno Martedi [10']
2.2.2.2. 2.2.0.0. timp,perc,
strings
RICORDI-IT 132104 perf mat rent
(B807)

BING, BANG, BONG see Gillis, Don E.

BIONI, ANTONIO (1698- ?)
Issipile: So Che Riduce A Piangere,
For Solo Voice And Orchestra [7']
2ob,bsn,hpsd,strings,T solo
SUPRAPHON   (B808)

BIRD FLEW HIGH, A, FOR SOLO VOICE AND
STRING ORCHESTRA see Brimberg, Jack

BIRD OF YEARNING see Richter, Marga

BIRD SERMON OF ST. FRANCIS OF ASSISI
[ARR.] see Liszt, Franz, St.
Francois D'assise: La Predication
Aux Oiseaux [arr.]

BIRDS OF SORROW see Chihara, Paul Seiko

BIRGINGU see Tveitt, Geirr

BIRGISSON, SNORRI SIGFUS (1954-   )
Hymn
string orch
ICELAND 040-014   (B809)

Songs And Places [9'30"]
2.2.3.2. 4.2.2.1. perc,pno,
strings
ICELAND 040-007   (B810)

BIRNSTEIN, RENATE M. (1946-   )
Scatola [10']
2.1.3.2. 2.1.1.0. strings
SIKORSKI perf mat rent   (B811)

BIRTHDAY BOUQUET, A see Druckman, Jacob
Raphael

BIRTHDAY CHORDS see Ekizian, Michelle

BIRTHDAY MUSIC FOR RRB see Saxton,
Robert

BIRTHDAY SURPRISE see Dickinson, Peter

BIRTHDAY WAVES see Tanenbaum, Elias

BIRTWISTLE, HARRISON (1934-   )
An Die Musik, For Solo Voice And
Chamber Group [5']
1(pic).1.1.1. 0.0.0.0. tamb,
vibra,2vln,vla,vcl,db,S solo
UNIVER. perf mat rent   (B812)

Earth Dances [38']
3.3.3.3. 4.2.4.2. 5perc,harp,pno,
strings
UNIVER. perf mat rent   (B813)

Imaginary Landscape, An
0.0.0.0. 4.4.3.1. 4perc,8db
min sc UNIVER. 15476 $22.00 (B814)

Machaut A Ma Maniere [10']
2.2.2.2. 4.2.3.1. 2perc,strings
sc UNIVER. UE19152 $45.00, perf mat
rent   (B815)

Secret Theatre [28'45"]
1.1.1.1. 1.1.1.0. perc,pno,string
quin
UNIVER. perf mat rent   (B816)

BIRTWISTLE, HARRISON (cont'd.)

Still Movement [14']
8vln,2vla,2vcl,db
UNIVER. perf mat rent   (B817)

Words Overheard, For Solo Voice And
Chamber Orchestra [8']
fl,ob,bsn,strings,S solo
sc UNIVER. UE17982 f.s., perf mat
rent   (B818)

BISCHOF, RAINER (1947-   )
Come Uno Sviluppo...Stracci *Op.25
[10']
0+alto fl.0+English horn.1.1.
1.1.1.0+tenor tuba. timp,cel,
strings
DOBLINGER perf mat rent   (B819)

Concerto for Flute and Orchestra, Op.
11, No. 1 [17']
string orch,fl solo
study sc DOBLINGER STP 508 f.s.,
perf mat rent   (B820)

Concerto for Organ and Orchestra, Op.
19 [20']
2.2+English horn.2.2. 2.2.2.0+
tenor tuba. timp,perc,cel,
strings,org solo
DOBLINGER perf mat rent   (B821)

Concerto for Violin, Violoncello and
Orchestra, Op. 13 [20']
2(alto fl).2(English
horn).2(contrabsn). 2.2.2.0.
timp,perc,cel,strings,vln solo,
vcl solo
DOBLINGER perf mat rent   (B822)

Deduktionen *Op.7 [13']
string orch
study sc DOBLINGER STP 503 f.s.
(B823)

Largo Desolato *Op.20 [4']
string orch
study sc DOBLINGER STP 611 f.s.,
perf mat rent   (B824)

Orchesterstucke *Op.10 [11']
2+alto fl.2+English horn.2+bass
clar.2+contrabsn. 4.4.4.0.
timp,perc,strings
DOBLINGER perf mat rent   (B825)

BISHOP THOMAS' SONG OF FREEDOM, FOR
SOLO VOICE AND ORCHESTRA see
Nordqvist, Gustaf see Rangström,
Ture

BIST DU! MILD WIE EIN LUFTHAUCH, FOR
SOLO VOICE AND ORCHESTRA [ARR.] see
Liszt, Franz

BITSCH, MARCEL (1921-   )
Suite Symphonique [14']
2.2.2.2. 2.2.2.0. timp,2perc,
harp,strings
BILLAUDOT perf mat rent   (B826)

Trois Images [6'30"]
3.1.0.0.2alto sax.2tenor
sax.baritone sax. 0.4.4.1.
timp,2perc,harp,pno,9vcl,db
BILLAUDOT perf mat rent   (B827)

BITTE SCHÖN POLKA see Strauss, Johann,
[Jr.]

BIZET, GEORGES (1838-1875)
Agnus Dei, For Solo Voice And
Orchestra [8']
0.0.2.2.sax. 2.0.0.0. harp,
strings,solo voice
SONZOGNO perf mat rent   (B828)

Andantino *Op.22
string orch
sc,pts WOLLENWEBER WW 904 f.s.
(B829)

Arlesienne, L': Suite [arr.]
(Zani, G.) 2.1.1.2.sax. 2.0.0.0.
timp,pno,7vln,vla,5vcl,2db [20']
SONZOGNO perf mat rent   (B830)

Carmen: Prelude
CHOUDENS perf mat rent   (B831)

Fantaisie Brillante On Themes From
"Carmen", For Flute And Orchestra
[arr.]
(Borne, Francois; Galway, James)
2.2.2.2. 2.2.3.0. timp,2perc,
harp,strings,fl solo [11']
SCHIRM.G perf mat rent   (B832)

Ivan IV: Prelude [4']
CHOUDENS perf mat rent   (B833)

Jolie Fille De Perth, La: Scenes
Bohemiennes [12'20"]
2(pic).2(English horn).2.2.
4.2.3.0. timp,perc,harp,strings
CHOUDENS perf mat rent   (B834)

BIZET, GEORGES (cont'd.)

Marche Funebre [10']
CHOUDENS perf mat rent   (B835)

Symphony No. 1 in C
min sc KALMUS K00397 $8.75 (B836)

Variations Chromatiques [arr.]
(Weingartner) min sc KALMUS K01468
$6.00   (B837)

BJELIK, MARTIN (1940-   )
Mobile [14'30"]
2.2.2.2. 4.2.3.0. timp,strings
DOBLINGER perf mat rent   (B838)

Nachtstuck [12']
2.2.2.2. 4.2.3.0. timp,strings
DOBLINGER perf mat rent   (B839)

Relief [12']
2.2.2.2. 4.2.3.0. timp,strings
DOBLINGER perf mat rent   (B840)

BJELINSKI, BRUNO (1909-   )
Musica Tonalis
ob,bsn,strings
sc UNIVER. 15751 $23.50   (B841)

Pinocchio: Suite No. 1 [15']
2.2.2.2. 2.2.0.0. timp,2perc,pno,
strings
sc BREITKOPF-W f.s., perf mat rent
(B842)

Pinocchio: Suite No. 2 [15']
2.2.2.2. 2.2.0.0. timp,2perc,pno,
strings
sc BREITKOPF-W f.s., perf mat rent
(B843)

BJONNES'N: NORSK DANS NO. 1 see Bergh,
Sverre

BJÖRKANDER, NILS (1893-1972)
Cavatina, For Violin And Orchestra
[5']
2fl,2clar,strings,vln solo
NORDISKA perf mat rent   (B844)

Intermezzo And Gavotte Caprice [5']
string orch
NORDISKA perf mat rent   (B845)

BJÖRKLUND, NILS
Romance [5']
2.2.2.2. 2.2.1.0. timp,strings
NORDISKA perf mat rent   (B846)

BJÖRKLUND, STAFFAN (1944-   )
Mountaineerings [19']
2.2.2.3. 4.2.2.0. timp,perc,harp,
elec pno,strings
STIM   (B847)

Music For Psychopaths [12']
2.2.3.3. 4.4.3.2. timp,perc,harp,
pno,Hamm,strings
STIM   (B848)

BJORKLUND, TERJE (1945-   )
Contrasts For Symphony Orchestra And
Jazz Group
see Kontraster For Symfoniorkester
Og Jazzgruppe

Kontraster For Symfoniorkester Og
Jazzgruppe
2.1.2.1. 2.2.3.0. timp,perc,
strings, jazz group: 2 tenor
sax, gtr, pno, electric pno,
double bass, perc
"Contrasts For Symphony Orchestra
And Jazz Group" NORGE   (B849)

Morene
2.1.2.2. 2.2.3.0. perc,harp,
strings
NORGE   (B850)

Sarek, For Violin And String
Orchestra [10']
string orch,vln solo
NORGE   (B851)

BJÖRNSSON, ARNI (1905-   )
Festive March
1+pic.1.2.1. 2.2.1.0. timp,
strings
ICELAND 001-021A   (B852)

In The Mountains *Op.5
2.2.2.2.alto sax.tenor sax.
2.2.3.1. timp,perc,strings
ICELAND 001-011   (B853)

Little Suite *Op.12
string orch
ICELAND 001-010   (B854)

Overture, New Year's Eve
2+pic.2.2.2. 3.2.3.1. timp,perc,
strings
ICELAND 001-017   (B855)

BJÖRNSSON, ARNI (cont'd.)

Two Romances For Violin And Orchestra [arr.] *Op.6,Op.14 (Sveinsson, Atli Heimir) 3.3.3.3. 4.3.3.0. timp,perc,harp,strings, vln solo ICELAND 001-009B (B856)

Variations On A Rhyme Song *Op.7 2.2.2.1. 2.2.1.0. timp,perc, strings ICELAND 001-012 (B857)

BLA FOLKET, DET see Rypdal, Terje

BLACHER, BORIS (1903-1975)
Alla Marcia [3'] 2.2.2.2. 4.3.3.1. timp,perc, strings BOTE perf mat rent (B858)

Dance Suite No. 2 (from Dance Scenes) [13'] 2(pic).2.2.2. 2.2.2.0. timp,perc, strings (Drew) BOOSEY perf mat rent (B859)

Prelude Und Konzertarie, For Solo Voice And Orchestra [15'] 2.1.2.1. 2.1.1.0. perc,harp, strings,Mez solo BOTE perf mat rent (B860)

Preussisches Marchen: Concordia Walzer [arr] (Richter, Caspar) 2+pic.2.2.2. 4.3.3.1. timp,harp,strings [3'30"] BOTE perf mat rent (B861)

BLACK, CHARLES
Teserac [21'50"] 3(pic).2+English horn.3+bass clar.2.soprano sax.alto sax.tenor sax.baritone sax. 4.4(flügelhorn).4.1. perc,gtr, kbd,harp,strings NEWAM 19005 perf mat rent (B862)

BLACK & WHITE see Torke, Michael

BLACK BOTTOM see Still, William Grant

BLACK, BROWN & BEIGE [ARR.] see Ellington, Edward Kennedy (Duke)

BLACK LIGHT see Toovey, Andrew

BLACK MAN DANCES, THE see Still, William Grant

BLACK PENTECOST, FOR SOLO VOICES AND ORCHESTRA see Davies, Peter Maxwell

BLACK PIERROT, A see Still, William Grant

BLACK TOWER, THE, FOR SOLO VOICE AND ORCHESTRA see Benoliel, Bernard

BLACKBERRY VINES AND WINTER FRUIT see Richter, Marga

BLACKFORD, RICHARD
Music For Carlow [6'] string orch study sc OXFORD 19 362062 6 f.s., perf mat rent (B863)

BLACKSMITH AND THE BAKER, THE, FOR SOLO VOICE AND CHAMBER ORCHESTRA see Arnestad, Finn, Smeden Og Bageren, For Solo Voice And Chamber Orchestra

BLACKWOOD, EASLEY RUTLAND (1933-)
Symphony No. 4 [33'] 4+pic.4(ob d'amore)+English horn.3+clar in E flat.4+ contrabsn. 8.5+bass trp.3+bass trom.2. timp,perc,strings SCHIRM.G perf mat rent (B864)

BLAKE, DAVID (1936-)
Bones Of Chuang Tzu, The, For Solo Voice And Orchestra [17'] 1(pic).1.2.1. 1.0.0.0. harp,pno, cel,perc,strings,Bar solo NOVELLO perf mat rent (B865)

From The Mattress Grave, For Solo Voice And Orchestra [29'] 1(pic).1.2(bass clar).1. 1.0.0.0. strings,high solo NOVELLO perf mat rent (B866)

In Praise Of Krishna, For Solo Voice And Orchestra [24'] 1.0.2.0. 1.0.0.0. harp,strings,S solo NOVELLO perf mat rent (B867)

Nine Poems Of Heine, For Solo Voice And Orchestra [24'] 1(pic).1.2(bass clar).1. 1.0.0.0. strings,high solo NOVELLO perf mat rent (B868)

BLAKE, DAVID (cont'd.)

Sonata Alla Marcia [12'] 0.2.0.0. 2.0.0.0. strings sc NOVELLO $11.00, perf mat rent (B869)

Toussaint: Song Of The Common Wind, For Solo Voice And Orchestra [10'] 3(pic).2(English horn).3(bass clar).0. 1.0.0.0. 2perc,cel, pno,harp,strings,Mez solo NOVELLO perf mat rent (B870)

Toussaint: Suite, For Solo Voices And Orchestra [36'] 3(pic).3(English horn).3(bass clar).3(contrabsn). 4.4.3.1. timp,4perc,pno&cel,harp, strings,MezBar soli NOVELLO perf mat rent (B871)

BLAKE, HOWARD (1938-)
Concert Dances, For Piano And Orchestra [15'] 2.1.2.1. 2.1.1.0. 2perc,harp, strings,pno solo FABER perf mat rent (B872)

Concerto for Clarinet and Orchestra [23'] 1.2.0.2. 2.0.0.0. strings,clar solo FABER perf mat rent (B873)

Divertimento for Violoncello and Orchestra [22'] 2.2.2.2. 2.2.2.0. timp,perc, strings,vcl solo FABER perf mat rent (B874)

Heartbeat [20'] tenor sax,perc,strings FABER perf mat rent (B875)

Snowman, The, For Solo Voices And Orchestra [26'] 2.1.2.1. 2.1.0.0. timp,perc,pno, opt cel,harp,strings,narrator& boy solo sc FABER 023-00355 $45.00, perf mat rent (B876)

Toccata [22'] 3.2.2.3. 4.3.3.1. 4perc,org,harp, cel,strings FABER perf mat rent (B877)

Up And Down Man, The [12'] 2.1.2.1. 2.1.1.0. 2perc,pno&cel, harp,strings FABER perf mat rent (B878)

BLAKE: PRELUDE see Adams, Leslie

BLANK, ALLAN (1925-)
Concertino for Bassoon and String Orchestra [15'] string orch,bsn solo sc AM.COMP.AL. $18.85, perf mat rent (B879)

Concertino for String Orchestra [10'] string orch sc AM.COMP.AL. $18.85, perf mat rent (B880)

Overture For A Happy Occasion [5'] 3.2.3.2. 4.3.4.1. timp,4perc,pno& cel,strings sc AM.COMP.AL. $47.05, perf mat rent (B881)

Six Significant Landscapes, For Solo Voice And Chamber Orchestra [15'] 1.1.2.1. 1.1.1.0. perc,harp,mand, vln,vla,vcl,db,S solo sc AM.COMP.AL. $28.90, perf mat rent (B882)

BLANK, WILLIAM (1957-)
Omaggi *Op.7 3.3.3.3. 4.3.3.1. timp,3perc,cel, 2harp,pno,strings [20'] study sc GUILYS f.s., perf mat rent (B883)

BLANQUER, AMANDO (1935-)
Concerto for Bassoon and String Orchestra [17'] string orch,bsn solo BILLAUDOT perf mat rent (B884)

Concerto for Horn and Orchestra [12'] 2.2.2.2. 0.0.0.0. timp,strings, horn solo BILLAUDOT perf mat rent (B885)

Concierto De Camera [16'] 1(pic,alto fl).1(English horn).1(bass clar).1. 1.0.0.0. perc,glock,xylo,marimba,6vln, 2vla,2vcl,db sc ALPUERTO f.s. (B886)

BLANQUER, AMANDO (cont'd.)

Oda A Manuel De Falla, For Harpsichord And Orchestra [11'] 2perc,strings,hpsd/pno solo sc REAL RM-16-1003 f.s., perf mat rent (B887)

BLAUBART QUADRILLE see Strauss, Josef

BLAUSTEIN, SUSAN
Canzo, For Solo Voice And Orchestra [11'] 1.1.1.1. 1.1.1.0. 2perc,pno,2vln, vla,vcl,db,S solo sc APNM $10.00, perf mat rent (B888)

Concerto for Violoncello and Chamber Orchestra [26'] 2.2.2.2. 1.1.1.0. 2perc,harp,pno, 2vln,vla,2vcl,db,vcl solo sc APNM $24.00, perf mat rent (B889)

Song Of Songs, For Solo Voices And Orchestra [23'] 2.2.2.1. 1.1.1.0. 2perc,harp,pno, strings,MezT soli sc APNM $21.00, perf mat rent (B890)

BLEAK HOUSE SUITE see Burgon, Geoffrey

BLEND see Nowak, Alison

BLENDINGER, HERBERT (1936-)
Concerto for Piano and Orchestra, Op. 42 [20'] 2(pic).2.2.2. 2.2.2.1. timp,perc, strings,pno solo DOBLINGER perf mat rent (B891)

Divertimento Concertante *Op.41 [23'] string orch ORLANDO perf mat rent (B892)

Praludium Und Meditation, For Violoncello And Orchestra [15'] perc,strings,vcl solo ORLANDO perf mat rent (B893)

BLESSURE-SOLEIL I, FOR CLARINET AND ORCHESTRA see Dao, Nguyen Thien

BLESSURE-SOLEIL II see Dao, Nguyen Thien

BLEU DU CIEL, LE see Sato, Kimi

BLEU LOIN see Masson, Gerard

BLEUSE, MARC (1937-)
Concerto for Violin and String Orchestra [18'] string orch,vln solo BILLAUDOT perf mat rent (B894)

Concerto for Violoncello and Orchestra [23'] 2.2.2.2. 4.2.1.1. timp,perc, strings,vcl solo BILLAUDOT perf mat rent (B895)

Koimeterion (Hommage A André Jolivet) [9'] 6vln,2vla,2vcl,db BILLAUDOT perf mat rent (B896)

BLEYLE, KARL (1880-1969)
Flagellantenzug *Op.9 KISTNER perf mat rent (B897)

Gnomentanz *Op.16 KISTNER (B898)

Symphony, Op. 6, in F KISTNER perf mat rent (B899)

BLICK see Rihm, Wolfgang

BLIR VACKERT DAR DU GAR, DET, FOR SOLO VOICE AND ORCHESTRA see Jonsson, Josef [Petrus]

BLISS, [SIR] ARTHUR (DRUMMOND) (1891-1975)
Lady Of Shalott, The [17'] 2(pic).2(English horn).2.2. 4.3.3.1. timp,2perc,harp, strings NOVELLO perf mat rent (B900)

March Of Homage [4'] 2(pic).2.2.2. 4.2.3.1. 4perc, timp,strings NOVELLO perf mat rent (B901)

Melee Fantasque [12'] 3.3.3.3. 4.3.3.1. timp,perc,harp, strings CURWEN perf mat rent (B902)

Rout For Solo Voice And Orchestra [7'] 2.1.2.2. 4.2.0.0. timp,perc,harp, strings,S solo sc CURWEN f.s., perf mat rent

BLISS, [SIR] ARTHUR (DRUMMOND)
(cont'd.)

Things To Come: Music, [arr.] [22']   (B903)
(Palmer) 3(pic).3(English
horn).3(bass clar).3. 4.4.4.1.
timp,4perc,pno,2harp,org,strings
NOVELLO perf mat rent   (B904)

Two Studies [12']
2(pic).2(English horn).3(bass
clar).3(contrabsn). 4.2.3.1.
perc,timp,harp,cel,strings
NOVELLO perf mat rent   (B905)

BLISWORTH TUNNEL BLUES, FOR SOLO VOICE
AND CHAMBER ORCHESTRA see
Nicholson, George

BLOCH, ERNEST (1880-1959)
Concerto Grosso No. 1
BROUDE BR. sc $15.00, set $38.50
                                                             (B906)

Deux Psaumes, For Solo Voice And
Orchestra
study sc SCHIRM.G $30.00   (B907)

Four Episodes [14']
1.1.1.1. 1.1.0.0. perc,pno,
strings
BROUDE BR. perf mat rent   (B908)

Helvetia, The Land Of Mountains And
Its People [23']
4.3+English horn.3+bass clar.3+
contrabsn. 6.4.3.1. timp,perc,
cel,2harp,strings,opt cor
BROUDE BR. perf mat rent   (B909)

Symphony in C sharp minor
KALMUS A5584 sc $75.00, perf mat
rent, set $200.00, pts $8.00, ea.
                                                             (B910)

BLOCH, WALDEMAR (1906-1984)
Concerto for 2 Trumpets and Orchestra
[20']
2.0.2.2. 2.0.0.0. timp,perc,
strings,2trp soli
DOBLINGER perf mat rent   (B911)

BLOCK see Godøy, Rolf Inge, Blokk

BLOCK, HANS VOLKER (1940-1979)
Concerto for Piano and Orchestra
[25']
2+pic.2+English horn.3.2.
4.3.2.1. timp,perc,strings,pno
solo
DOBLINGER perf mat rent   (B912)

Euphonie, For String Quintet And
String Orchestra [15']
string orch,2vln,vla,vcl,db soli
DOBLINGER perf mat rent   (B913)

Moments Musicaux [15']
3(pic).2+English horn.3(clar in E
flat,clar in A).2+contrabsn.
4.3.2.1. timp,perc,pno,harp,
strings
DOBLINGER perf mat rent   (B914)

BLOCS EN VRAC DE BRIC ET DE BROC see
Singier, Jean Marc

BLOKK see Godøy, Rolf Inge

BLOMBERG, ERIK (1922-   )
Symphony No. 6 [26']
2.2.2.2. 2.2.2.1. timp,perc,
strings
STIM   (B915)

BLOOD WEDDING see Surinach, Carlos,
Bodas De Sangre

BLUE GAL see Carpenter, John Alden

BLUE NOCTURNE see Oganesian, Edgar

BLUE SCARECROW, THE [ARR.] see Ludwig,
Norbert

BLUE TOWERS see Fine, Irving

BLUE YONDER see Hopkins, John

BLUEBEARD: OVERTURE [ARR.] see
Offenbach, Jacques, Barbe-Bleue:
Overture [arr.]

BLUES, THE see Still, William Grant

BLUES IN THE NIGHT see Arlen, Harold

BLUETTE POLKA see Strauss, Johann,
[Jr.]

BLUM, ROBERT (1900-   )
Musik Uber Drei Altdeutsche
Volkslieder [20']
string orch,2vln soli,vcl solo
HUG GH 11110 perf mat rent   (B916)

BLUMENFELD, HAROLD (1923-   )
Amphitryon 4: Miniature Overture [4']
2(pic).1.2.1. 2.0.0.0. timp,
2perc,harp,cel,strings
MCA perf mat rent   (B917)

Miniature Overture [5']
2(pic).1.2.1(contrabsn). 3.2.2.0.
timp,3perc,cel,harp,strings
MMB perf mat rent   (B918)

Scenes From Rimbaud [19']
3(pic,alto fl).2+English
horn.3(clar in E flat,bass
clar).2+contrabsn. 4.3.3.1.
timp,4perc,pno,cel,harp,strings
MMB perf mat rent   (B919)

Starfires, For Solo Voices And
Orchestra [20']
3horn,trp,trom,tuba,timp,3perc,
cel,6vla,6vcl,4db,MezT soli
MMB perf mat rent   (B920)

Voix Reconnue, La, For Solo Voices
And Orchestra [21']
1.1.1.1. 1.0.0.0. 2perc,cel,2vla,
2vcl,db,TS soli
MMB perf mat rent   (B921)

BLUMENFEST POLKA see Strauss, Johann,
[Jr.]

BO, SONIA (1960-   )
Da Una Lettura Di Husserl [11']
2.2.2.2. 2.2.0.0. 2perc,cel,harp,
pno,strings
RICORDI-IT 134081 perf mat rent
                                                             (B922)

BOCCACCIO: MENUETT UND TARANTELLA
[ARR.] see Suppe, Franz von

BOCCACCIO QUADRILLE see Strauss, Eduard

BOCCHERINI, LUIGI (1743-1805)
Concerto for Flute and String
Orchestra, Op. 27, in D, Ge. 489
(Redel, K.) (incorrectly attributed
to Boccherini) LEUCKART   (B923)

Concerto for Violoncello and
Orchestra in C, Ge. 473 [20']
2ob,2horn,strings,vcl solo
BSE 122 perf mat rent   (B924)

Concerto for Violoncello and
Orchestra in C, Ge. 477 [20']
2horn,strings,vcl solo
sc BSE 21 f.s., perf mat rent
                                                             (B925)

Concerto For Violoncello And
Orchestra In D *see THREE
CENTURIES OF MUSIC IN SCORE, VOL.
5: CONCERTO IV, CLASSICAL STRINGS
AND WINDS

Concerto for Violoncello and
Orchestra in D, Ge. 476 [20']
2ob,2horn,strings,vcl solo
BSE 121 perf mat rent   (B926)

Concerto for Violoncello and
Orchestra in D, Ge. 479 [20']
string orch,vcl solo
BSE 133 perf mat rent   (B927)

Concerto for Violoncello and
Orchestra in D, Ge. 483 [20']
2ob,2horn,strings,vcl solo
BSE 151 perf mat rent   (B928)
(Pais, Aldo) ZANIBON sc 6020 rent,
pts 6021 rent   (B929)

Concerto for Violoncello and
Orchestra in D, MIN 131
(Respighi) sc RICORDI-IT 133110
$14.75   (B930)

Concerto for Violoncello and
Orchestra in E flat, Ge. 474
[20']
2ob,2horn,strings,vcl solo
BSE 140 perf mat rent   (B931)

Concerto for Violoncello and String
Orchestra in G, Ge. 480 [20']
string orch,vcl solo
BSE 134 perf mat rent   (B932)

Concerto for Violoncello and String
Orchestra, No. 2, in B flat,
[arr.]
(Aslamasjan, S.) string orch,vcl
solo [18'] SIKORSKI perf mat rent   (B933)

Concerto in D minor for 2 Flutes and
Orchestra, [arr.]
(Jenkins, N.) 2ob,2horn,strings,2fl
soli SCHIRM.G perf mat rent
                                                             (B934)

Gioco Di Minuetti Ballabili, Un [25']
2ob,2bsn,2horn,strings
sc BSE 14 f.s., perf mat rent
                                                             (B935)

BOCCHERINI, LUIGI (cont'd.)

Sinfonia, Ge. 493, Op. 21, No. 1, in
B flat
sc BSE 15 f.s., perf mat rent
                                                             (B936)
(Hockner) KALMUS A6410 sc $12.00,
set $9.00, pts $1.00, ea.   (B937)

Sinfonia, Ge. 494, Op. 21, No. 2, in
E flat
sc BSE 16 f.s., perf mat rent
                                                             (B938)

Sinfonia, Ge. 495, Op. 21, No. 3, in
C
sc BSE 17 f.s., perf mat rent
                                                             (B939)

Sinfonia, Ge. 496, Op. 21, No. 4, in
D
sc BSE 18 f.s., perf mat rent
                                                             (B940)

Sinfonia, Ge. 497, Op. 21, No. 5, in
B flat
sc BSE 19 f.s., perf mat rent
                                                             (B941)

Sinfonia, Ge. 498, Op. 21, No. 6, in
A
sc BSE 20 f.s., perf mat rent
                                                             (B942)

Sinfonia, Ge. 506, Op. 12, No. 4, in
D minor
BSE 83 perf mat rent   (B943)

Sinfonia, Ge. 510, Op. 35, No. 2, in
E flat
sc BSE 97 f.s., perf mat rent
                                                             (B944)

Sinfonia, Ge. 511, Op. 35, No. 3, in
A
(This edition listed as op. 1, no.
3) KALMUS A7385 sc $8.00, set
$25.00, pts $2.50, ea., perf mat
rent   (B945)

Sinfonia, Ge. 514, Op. 35, No. 6, in
B flat
(Bonelli) KALMUS A7335 sc $7.00,
set $15.00, pts $1.50, ea., perf
mat rent   (B946)

Sinfonia, Ge. 515, Op. 37, No. 1, in
C
BSE 104 perf mat rent   (B947)

Sinfonia, Ge. 519, Op. 41, in C
minor, [arr.] [10']
1.1.0.1. 1.0.0.0. strings without
db
(Haas) NOVELLO perf mat rent   (B948)

Sinfonia, Ge. 522, Op. 45, in D minor
BSE 105 perf mat rent   (B949)

Sinfonie, Six
see Martini, [Padre] Giovanni
Battista, Sinfonie, Four

Sinfonie, Six *see Martini, [Padre]
Giovanni Battista, Sinfonie, Four

BOCHSA, ROBERT-NICOLAS-CHARLES
(1789-1856)
Concerto for Harp and Orchestra, No.
1, Op. 15, in D minor
1.2.2.2. 2.0.0.0. strings,harp
solo
COSTALL C.3452 perf mat rent   (B950)

Heritier De Paimpol, L'
2(pic).2.2.2. 2.0.0.0. strings
COSTALL perf mat rent   (B951)

BODAS DE SANGRE see Surinach, Carlos

BODENSOHN, ERNST FRIEDRICH WILHELM
Concerto for Alto Flute and String
Orchestra in G
string orch,alto fl solo
sc,pts BODENS E 56 f.s.   (B952)

Fantasie Uber Barockthemen Von J.
Baston, For Soprano Recorder And
Chamber Orchestra
hpsd,strings,S rec solo
sc,pts BODENS E 83 f.s.   (B953)

BODY, JACK
Little Elegies [13']
3.3.3.3. 4.3.3.1. 4perc,cel,pno,
harp,strings
sc WAI-TE-ATA f.s.   (B954)

Poems Of Solitary Delights, For
Narrator And Orchestra [11']
1.1.1.1. 2.1.1.0. 3perc,pno/hpsd,
harp,strings without db,
narrator
sc WAI-TE-ATA f.s.   (B955)

"...BODY AND SHADOW..." see Rands,
Bernard

BOEHMER, KONRAD (1941-   )
  Concert-Ouverture Dr. Faustus [7']
    4.4.5.3. 4.4.4.2. timp,3-4perc,
    2harp,gtr,elec org,pno,strings
  sc DONEMUS f.s., perf mat rent
                                    (B956)
  Lied Aus Der Ferne, For Solo Voice
    And Orchestra
    2.2.4.2. 4.2.0.1. timp,perc,pno,
    elec gtr,strings,S solo
  TONOS perf mat rent   (B957)

BOER, ED DE (1957-   )
  Eris *Op.10 [10']
    2.2.2.2. 2.0.0.0. vcl,db
  sc DONEMUS f.s., perf mat rent
                                    (B958)
  Foxtrot (On A Dutch Folksong) *Op.7,
    No.1 [1'45"]
    1.1.2.1. 1.0.3.0. perc,strings,
    opt pno
  sc DONEMUS f.s., perf mat rent   (B959)

BOESMANS, PHILIPPE (1936-   )
  Concerto for Violin and Orchestra
  JOBERT   (B960)

  Conversions
    4.2.3+bass clar.2. 4.4.3.1.
    3perc,vibra,marimba,harp,pno,
    strings
  JOBERT   (B961)

BOGILJA see Ekström, Lars

BOGUSLAWSKI, EDWARD (1940-   )
  Pro Varsovia [17']
    4.4.3.3. 6.4.3.0. perc,harp,pno,
    strings
  POLSKIE   (B962)

BOHÁC, JOSEF (1929-   )
  Suita Drammatica [14']
    timp,strings
  SUPRAPHON   (B963)

BOHDANOWICZ, BAZYLI (1754-1819)
  Symphony in D
    2ob,2horn,strings
    (Swierczek) POLSKIE   (B964)

BOHEMIAN-DANISH FOLK SONG see Nielsen,
  Carl

BOHEMIAN SONGS AND DANCES, NO. 1 see
  Weinberger, Jaromir

BOHEMIAN SONGS AND DANCES, NO. 2 see
  Weinberger, Jaromir

BOHEMIAN SONGS AND DANCES, NO. 3 see
  Weinberger, Jaromir

BOHEMIAN SONGS AND DANCES, NO. 4 see
  Weinberger, Jaromir

BOHEMIAN SONGS AND DANCES, NO. 5 see
  Weinberger, Jaromir

BOHEMIAN SONGS AND DANCES, NO. 6 see
  Weinberger, Jaromir

BOHME, OSKAR
  Concerto for Trumpet and Orchestra in
    E minor
    2.2.2.2. 4.2.2.1. timp,strings,
    trp solo
  UNICORN 3.9999.7 perf mat rent
                                    (B965)
BOHMLER, CRAIG (1956-   )
  Celebre, For Flute And Chamber
    Orchestra [17']
    1(pic).1(English horn).1.1.
    2.1.1.1. timp,perc,harp,
    strings,fl solo
  NORRUTH perf mat rent   (B966)

BOHREN, GEIR (1951-   )
  Ice Palace, The: Suite [arr.]
    (composed with Aserud, Bent)
    [15']
    (Soderlind, Ragnar) 3.3.3.3.
    4.3.3.1. timp,perc,2harp,strings
  NORGE   (B967)

BOIS, ROB DU (1934-   )
  Luna, For Alto Flute And Orchestra
    [9']
    2.1.3.1. 1.1.1.1. perc,harp,
    strings,alto fl solo
  DONEMUS perf mat rent   (B968)

BOISMORTIER, JOSEPH BODIN DE
    (1689-1755)
  Concerto, Op. 21, No. 4, in B minor,
    [arr.]
    (Ruf, Hugo) string orch,cont,fl
    solo/vln solo/2fl soli/fl solo/ob
    solo sc,pts BÄREN. HM 253 f.s.
                                    (B969)
  Sonata, Op. 34, No. 2
    string orch
    (Petit, J.L.) [7'] BILLAUDOT
    576-00030 sc $3.25, pts $20.00
                                    (B970)

BOITE DE NUIT see Tomasi, Henri

BOITO, ARRIGO (1842-1918)
  Mefistofele: Ave, Signor, For Solo
    Voice And Orchestra
    KALMUS A4736 sc $7.00, set $20.00,
    pts $1.00, ea., perf mat rent
                                    (B971)
  Mefistofele: Dai Campi, Dai Prati,
    For Solo Voice And Orchestra
    KALMUS A4741 sc $4.00, set $12.00,
    pts $.75, ea., perf mat rent
                                    (B972)
  Mefistofele: Epilogue- The Death Of
    Faust, For Solo Voice And
    Orchestra
    KALMUS A4749 sc $12.00, set $25.00,
    pts $1.50, ea., perf mat rent
                                    (B973)
  Mefistofele: La Luna Immobile, For
    Solo Voices And Orchestra
    KALMUS A4748 sc $5.00, set $15.00,
    pts $.75, ea., perf mat rent
                                    (B974)
  Mefistofele: Lontano, Lontano, For
    Solo Voices And Orchestra
    KALMUS A4746 sc $6.00, set $20.00,
    pts $1.00, ea., perf mat rent
                                    (B975)
  Mefistofele: Son Lo Spirito, For Solo
    Voice And Orchestra
    KALMUS A4742 sc $7.00, set $18.00,
    pts $1.00, ea., perf mat rent
                                    (B976)
  Mefistofele: Spunta L'aurora Pallida,
    For Solo Voice And Orchestra
    KALMUS A4747 sc $4.00, set $15.00,
    pts $.75, ea.   (B977)
  Mefistofele: Strano Figlio Del Caos,
    For Solo Voices And Orchestra
    KALMUS A4743 sc $7.00, set $22.00,
    pts $1.00, ea., perf mat rent
                                    (B978)
  Mefistofele: Su Cammina, Cammina, For
    Solo Voices And Orchestra
    KALMUS A4745 sc $6.00, set $18.00,
    pts $1.00, ea., perf mat rent
                                    (B979)

BOIVEN, PHILIPPE (1954-   )
  Concerto for Viola and Chamber
    Orchestra [15']
    1+pic.1+English horn.1+clar in E
    flat.2. 2.0.0.0. strings,vla
    solo
  SALABERT perf mat rent   (B980)

BOLCOM, WILLIAM ELDEN (1938-   )
  Ragomania [10']
    3(pic).3(English horn).3(bass
    clar).3(contrabsn). 4.3.3.1.
    timp,3perc,pno,opt harp,strings
  MARKS perf mat rent   (B981)

  Symphony for Chamber Orchestra [35']
    1(pic,alto fl).2(English
    horn).1(clar in E flat,bass
    clar).2. 2.0.0.0. pno&cel,
    strings
  MARKS perf mat rent   (B982)

BOLDEMANN, LACI (1921-1969)
  Concerto for Piano and Orchestra, Op.
    13 [21']
    2.2.2.2. 4.3.3.1. timp,strings,
    pno solo
  STIM   (B983)

  Four Epitaphs, For Solo Voice And
    String Orchestra *Op.10 [16']
    string orch,Mez solo
    sc GEHRMANS 6656P f.s., perf mat
    rent   (B984)

BOLERO see Cremer, Curt see Ravel,
  Maurice

BOLERO, FOR GUITAR AND ORCHESTRA see
  Geese, Heinz

BOLLELATEN see Söderlundh, Lille Bror

BOLT, THE: SUITE see Shostakovich,
  Dmitri

BOLZONI, GIOVANNI (1841-1919)
  Corno Inopportuno, Un, For Horn And
    String Orchestra [5'30"]
    string orch,horn solo
    KALMUS A5580 sc $6.00, set $6.00
                                    (B985)
  Serenata Romantica No. 2 (from Al
    Castello Medioevale)
    KALMUS A5755 sc $5.00, set $5.00
                                    (B986)

BOMBI BITT see Nilsson, Bo

BON, ANDRE (1946-   )
  D'un Chant Perdu, For Solo Voice And
    Chamber Orchestra [15']
    4(pic).0+English horn+ob
    d'amore.4(bass clar).2+
    contrabsn.alto sax.tenor sax.
    4.4.3.1. 3perc,harp,pno,string
    quin,S solo
  AMPHION perf mat rent   (B987)

BON, ANDRE (cont'd.)

  Emergence [13']
    3.0.3.0.sax. 0.2.1.0. perc,pno,
    strings
  AMPHION perf mat rent   (B988)
  Ode II [15']
    2.2.0.1. 2.0.0.0. timp,strings
  AMPHION perf mat rent   (B989)
  Ricercare [16']
    fl,English horn,2clar,alto sax,
    horn,trp,tuba,perc,harp,pno,
    strings
  sc JOBERT 576-00421S $36.00   (B990)

BON, MAARTEN (1933-   )
  Boreal IV [6']
    3.3.3.3. 4.3.0.1. 2harp,strings
  sc DONEMUS f.s., perf mat rent
                                    (B991)
  Display V [16']
    12vcl
  DONEMUS perf mat rent   (B992)
  Thalia [7']
    3.3.3.3. 4.3.3.1. strings
  sc DONEMUS f.s., perf mat rent
                                    (B993)

BON, WILLEM FREDERIK (1940-1983)
  Symphony for Strings [20']
    string orch
  sc DONEMUS f.s., perf mat rent
                                    (B994)

BONAMPAK: SUITE see Sandi, Luis

BOND, VICTORIA (1945-   )
  Frog Prince, The, For Narrator And
    Orchestra [24']
    2(pic).2.2(bass clar).2. 4.3.3.1.
    timp,3perc,strings,narrator
  SCHIRM.G perf mat rent   (B995)

BONDON, JACQUES (1927-   )
  Ana Et L'Albatros: Interlude [8']
    3.2.2.2. 4.2.2.1. strings
  ESCHIG perf mat rent   (B996)

  Chant Et Danse, For Trombone And
    Orchestra [7']
    1.1.1.1. 1.1.1.0. perc,strings,
    trom solo
  ESCHIG perf mat rent   (B997)

  Concerto Con Fuoco, For Guitar And
    String Orchestra
    string orch,gtr solo
  study sc ESCHIG $8.95, perf mat
    rent   (B998)

  Concerto Pour Un Ballet, For Flute
    And Orchestra [23']
    2.2.2.2. 4.2.2.0. perc,strings,fl
    solo
  ESCHIG perf mat rent   (B999)

  Concerto Solaire For Brass Ensemble
    And Orchestra [23']
    4.4.4.4. 4.2.2.1. timp,4perc,
    strings, soli: 2 horn, 2trp, 2
    trom, tuba
  sc ESCHIG f.s., perf mat rent
                                   (B1000)

  Ivanhoe [20']
    2.2.2.2. 2.2.2.0. timp,perc,harp,
    strings
  ESCHIG perf mat rent   (B1001)

  Lumieres Et Formes Animees, For
    Orchestra
    3.3.3.3. 4.3.3.1. 3perc,strings
    [20'] ESCHIG perf mat rent
                                   (B1002)
  Lumieres Et Formes Animees, For
    String Orchestra [20']
    string orch
  sc ESCHIG f.s., perf mat rent
                                   (B1003)
  Monts De L'Etoile, Les, For Solo
    Voice And Orchestra [23']
    2.2.2.2. 2.2.2.0. 2perc,strings,S
    solo
  ESCHIG perf mat rent   (B1004)

  Suite Pour Les Dixiemes Jeux [30']
    4.4.4.4. 6.4.3.2. timp,6perc,cel,
    Ondes Martenot,strings
  ESCHIG perf mat rent   (B1005)

  Symphonie Latine [18']
    2.2.2.2. 2.2.1.0. timp,perc,
    strings
  ESCHIG perf mat rent   (B1006)

  Trois Images Concertantes, For
    Bassoon And Orchestra [18']
    2.2.2.2. 2.2.2.0. perc,strings,
    bsn solo
  ESCHIG perf mat rent   (B1007)

BONDT, CORNELIS DE (1953-   )
  Gebroken Oor, Het [20']
    1.1.2.1. 1.0.0.0. 2pno,2vln,vla,
    vcl,db
  DONEMUS perf mat rent   (B1008)

BONES OF CHUANG TZU, THE, FOR SOLO
VOICE AND ORCHESTRA see Blake,
David

BONIFACIO, MAURO (1957-   )
Musica Da Concerto, For Harpsichord
And Chamber Orchestra [16']
1.1.2.2. 2.2.0.0. timp,strings,
hpsd solo
SONZOGNO perf mat rent   (B1009)

Undici Tracce [7']
1.1.1.1. 1.0.0.0. harp,2vln,vla,
vcl,db
SONZOGNO perf mat rent   (B1010)

BONN, FOR SOLO VOICE AND STRING
ORCHESTRA see Gulbranson, Eilif

BONNEAU, PAUL (1918-   )
Deux Caprices En Forme De Valse, For
Alto Saxophone And String
Orchestra
string orch,harp,alto sax solo
LEDUC AL 27671-27672 perf mat rent
(B1011)

BONNET, ANTOINE (1958-   )
D'une Source Oubliee [15']
2(pic,alto fl).0.2(clar in E
flat,clar in A,bass clar).0.
1.0.1.0. 2perc,pno,vln,vla,
3vcl,db
SALABERT perf mat rent   (B1012)

BONPORTI, FRANCESCO ANTONIO (1672-1748)
Concerto, Op. 11, No. 6, in F [10']
string orch,cont,vln solo
(Barblan) KALMUS A7405 sc $12.00,
set $17.50, pts $2.50, perf mat
rent   (B1013)

BONS, JOËL (1952-   )
Bref [9']
1.1.3.1. 1.1.1.0. 2perc,vibra,
harp,pno,2vln,vla,vcl,db
sc DONEMUS f.s., perf mat rent
(B1014)

BONSEL, ADRIAAN (1918-   )
Suite For Bamboo Flute Ensemble And
String Orchestra [14']
string orch, bamboo flute
ensemble or recorder ensemble
sc DONEMUS f.s., perf mat rent
(B1015)

BOOG see Heppener, Robert

BOOGAARD, BERNARD VAN DEN (1952-   )
Neutron Sonata [12']
3.3.3.3. 4.3.3.1. 2perc,harp,
strings
sc DONEMUS f.s., perf mat rent
(B1016)
Prisma, For Piano And Orchestra [23']
0.2.0.0. 2.0.0.0. strings,pno
solo
sc DONEMUS f.s., perf mat rent
(B1017)
Symfonie Der Duinen [17']
3.3.3.3. 4.3.3.1. 3perc,1-2harp,
strings
"Symphony Of Dunes" sc DONEMUS
f.s., perf mat rent   (B1018)

Symphony Of Dunes
see Symfonie Der Duinen

BOOGIE IN BRASS see Gillis, Don E.

BOOMERANG, FOR OBOE AND CHAMBER
ORCHESTRA see Nordheim, Arne

BOONE, CHARLES N. (1939-   )
Chinese Texts, For Solo Voice And
Orchestra [15']
2.2.2.2. 3.2.2.1. 3perc,pno,
strings,S solo
sc SALABERT f.s., perf mat rent
(B1019)
Edge Of The Land, The [12']
2(pic).2.2.2. 4.2.2.1. 2perc,pno,
harp,Hamm,strings
SALABERT perf mat rent   (B1020)

Fields-Singing, For Solo Voice And
Instrumental Ensemble [15']
2.1.0.0. 0.1.2.0. 2perc,pno,2vln,
vla,2vcl,db,S solo
SALABERT perf mat rent   (B1021)

First Landscape [15']
4.4(English horn).4(bass
clar).4(contrabsn). 4.4.3.0.
perc,pno,10vla,10vcl,9db
SALABERT perf mat rent   (B1022)

Second Landscape [14']
1.1.1.1(contrabsn). 0.2.0.0.
2perc,pno,strings
sc SALABERT f.s., perf mat rent
(B1023)
String Piece [12']
7vln,2vla,2vcl,db
sc SALABERT f.s., perf mat rent
(B1024)

BOONE, CHARLES N. (cont'd.)

Trace, For Flute And Instrumental
Ensemble [12']
ob,clar,trp,perc,elec org,pno,
vln,vla,vcl,db,fl solo
SALABERT perf mat rent   (B1025)

BOOREN, JO VAN DEN (1935-   )
Passage *Op.66 [11']
2.2.2.2. 4.2.3.1. timp,strings
sc DONEMUS f.s., perf mat rent
(B1026)
Passion De Jeanne d'Arc, La *Op.53
[80']
2.2.2.2. 2.2.2.1. perc,harp,opt
org,strings
DONEMUS perf mat rent   (B1027)

Souvenir De Budapest *Op.57 [5']
string orch
DONEMUS perf mat rent   (B1028)

Symphony No. 2 [17']
3.3.3.3. 4.3.3.1. timp,2perc,
harp,strings
sc DONEMUS f.s., perf mat rent
(B1029)
Symphony No. 3, Op. 66 [11']
2.2.2.2. 4.2.3.1. timp,strings
(Short Symphony) sc DONEMUS f.s.,
perf mat rent   (B1030)

BORDER FORT see Kristoffersen,
Fridthjof, Grensefestning

BOREAL IV see Bon, Maarten

BORGSTRÖM, HJALMAR (1864-1925)
Thought, The
3(pic).2.2.2. 4.2.3.1. timp,perc,
strings
NORSK perf mat rent   (B1031)

BORIS GODUNOV: DEATH OF BORIS, FOR SOLO
VOICE AND ORCHESTRA see Mussorgsky,
Modest Petrovich

BORIS GODUNOV: DIE HÖCHSTE MACHT IST
MEIN, FOR SOLO VOICE AND ORCHESTRA
see Mussorgsky, Modest Petrovich,
Boris Godunov: Monologue Of Boris,
For Solo Voice And Orchestra

BORIS GODUNOV: GESTATTET IHR, DEM
ENSCHEINBAREN KNECHTE GOTTES, FOR
SOLO VOICES AND ORCHESTRA see
Mussorgsky, Modest Petrovich, Boris
Godunov: May A Humble Slave Of God,
For Solo Voices And Orchestra

BORIS GODUNOV: HÖRT, WAS EINST IN DER
STADT KASAN GESCHEHEN, FOR SOLO
VOICE AND ORCHESTRA see Mussorgsky,
Modest Petrovich, Boris Godunov:
Varlaam's Song, For Solo Voice And
Orchestra

BORIS GODUNOV: LEB WOHL, MEIN SOHN, FOR
SOLO VOICE AND ORCHESTRA see
Mussorgsky, Modest Petrovich, Boris
Godunov: Death Of Boris, For Solo
Voice And Orchestra

BORIS GODUNOV: MAY A HUMBLE SLAVE OF
GOD, FOR SOLO VOICES AND ORCHESTRA
see Mussorgsky, Modest Petrovich

BORIS GODUNOV: MONOLOGUE OF BORIS, FOR
SOLO VOICE AND ORCHESTRA see
Mussorgsky, Modest Petrovich

BORIS GODUNOV: VARLAAM'S SONG, FOR SOLO
VOICE AND ORCHESTRA see Mussorgsky,
Modest Petrovich

BORISHANSKY, ELLIOT (1930-   )
In Commemoration [3']
string orch
sc AM.COMP.AL. $3.85   (B1032)

BORKOVEC, PAVEL (1894-1972)
Pied Piper, The [29']
3.2.3.2. 4.2.3.1. timp,perc,xylo,
mand,pno,strings,opt T solo
SUPRAPHON   (B1033)

BORLENGHI, ENZO (1908-   )
Due Impressioni
string orch
sc BONGIOVANI EB 2623 f.s., perf
mat rent   (B1034)

BORN see Nordentoft, Anders

BORNE, FRANCOIS (1840-1920)
Fantaisie Brillante Sur Carmen, For
Flute And Orchestra [12']
2.2.2.2. 4.0.0.0. timp,perc,harp,
strings,fl solo
(Guiot, R.) BILLAUDOT perf mat rent
(B1035)

BORODIN, ALEXANDER PORFIRIEVICH
(1833-1887)
Mer, La, For Solo Voice And Orchestra
[4']
2.2.2.2. 4.2.3.1. timp,strings,
solo voice
(Rimsky-Korsakov) KALMUS A5620 sc
$15.00, set $24.00, pts $1.00,
ea.   (B1036)

Mlada: Finale
(Rimsky-Korsakov) KALMUS A5808 sc
$15.00, set $22.00, perf mat rent
(B1037)
Polovetzian Dances, [arr.] *see
TWELVE POP HITS FROM THE
CLASSICS, VOL. 2

Prince Igor: March
KALMUS A5712 sc $10.00, set $25.00,
perf mat rent   (B1038)

Prince Igor: Polovtsian Dances
sc MEZ KNIGA f.s.   (B1039)

Princesse Endormie, La, For Solo
Voice And Orchestra [arr.]
see Sleeping Princess, For Solo
Voice And Orchestra [arr.]

Quartet No. 2, [arr.] *see TWELVE
POP HITS FROM THE CLASSICS, VOL.
1

Scherzo for Orchestra [6']
0+pic.2.2.2. 4.2.3.0. timp,
strings
BREITKOPF-W perf mat rent   (B1040)

Schlafende Prinzessin, Die, For Solo
Voice And Orchestra[arr.]
see Sleeping Princess, For Solo
Voice And Orchestra [arr.]

Sinfonia for Strings, [arr.] (from
Quartet No. 2)
(Drew, Lucas) string orch [28']
KALMUS A5973 sc $25.00, set
$25.00, perf mat rent   (B1041)

Sleeping Princess, For Solo Voice And
Orchestra [arr.]
(Rimsky-Korsakov) "Princesse
Endormie, La, For Solo Voice And
Orchestra [arr.]" 2.2.2.2.
2.2.1.0. timp,strings,solo voice
KALMUS A4572 sc $5.00, set
$11.00, pts $.75, ea., perf mat
rent   (B1042)
(Rimsky-Korsakov, Nikolai)
"Schlafende Prinzessin, Die, For
Solo Voice And Orchestra[arr.]"
2.2.2.2. 2.2.1.0. timp,strings,
Mez/Bar solo [3'] PETERS (B1043)

BOROFF, EDITH
Concerto for Marimba and Orchestra
[12']
2.2.2.2. 2.2.0.0. perc,strings,
marimba solo
sc AM.COMP.AL. $56.35, perf mat
rent   (B1044)

BOROGYIN, A.P.
see BORODIN, ALEXANDER PORFIREVICH

BØRRESEN, HAKON (1876-1954)
Mod Doden
"Towards Death" sc,pts SAMFUNDET
f.s.   (B1045)

Nordiske Folketoner
sc,pts SAMFUNDET f.s.   (B1046)

Normannerne
"Normans, The" sc,pts SAMFUNDET
f.s.   (B1047)

Normans, The
see Normannerne

Olympisk Hymne
sc,pts SAMFUNDET f.s.   (B1048)

Symphony No. 3
sc SAMFUNDET f.s., perf mat rent
(B1049)
Towards Death
see Mod Doden

BORSARI, AMEDEE (1905-   )
Concerto for Alto Saxophone and
String Orchestra [18'20"]
string orch,alto sax solo
BILLAUDOT perf mat rent   (B1050)

BORSTLAP, JOHN (1950-   )
Concerto for Violin and Orchestra
[20']
2.3.2.3. 3.2.2.0. timp,pno,
strings,vln solo
sc DONEMUS f.s., perf mat rent
(B1051)
Sinfonia [20']
2.3.3.3. 2.0.0.0. strings
sc DONEMUS f.s., perf mat rent

BORSTLAP, JOHN (cont'd.)

(B1052)
Trois Préludes [10']
3.3.3.2. 4.3.3.0. timp,perc,harp,
strings
sc DONEMUS f.s., perf mat rent
(B1053)

BORTBUREN see Jonsson, Reine

BORTE, FOR SOLO VOICE AND ORCHESTRA
[ARR.] see Grieg, Edvard Hagerup

BORTKIEWICZ, SERGEI EDUARDOVICH
(1877-1952)
Concerto for Piano and Orchestra, Op.
16
sc KISTNER f.s.   (B1054)

Othello *Op.19
KISTNER perf mat rent   (B1055)

Russische Tanze *Op.18
KISTNER perf mat rent   (B1056)

BORTNIANSKY, DIMITRI STEPANOVICH
(1751-1825)
Sinfonia Concertante for Piano, Harp
and String Orchestra [22']
string orch,pno solo,harp solo
BELAIEFF   (B1057)

Vespergesang [arr.]
(Riege, E.) 1.1.2.1. 4.2.3.1. timp,
perc,strings [4'] SIKORSKI perf
mat rent   (B1058)

BÖRTZ, DANIEL (1943-)
Concerto for Oboe and Orchestra [17']
2.2.2.2. 2.2.2.1. timp,4perc,
strings,ob solo
sc GEHRMANS 6425P f.s., perf mat
rent   (B1059)

Concerto for Piano and Orchestra
[18']
1.1.1.1. 2.2.2.0. 2perc,strings,
pno solo
sc GEHRMANS 6128P f.s., perf mat
rent   (B1060)

Concerto for Violin and Orchestra
[20']
2.2.2.2. 2.2.1.0. 2perc,strings,
vln solo
sc GEHRMANS 6319P f.s., perf mat
rent   (B1061)

Concerto for Violin, Bassoon and
Chamber Orchestra [20']
2.0.2.0. 2.2.0.0. timp,perc,
strings,vln solo,bsn solo
sc GEHRMANS 6096P f.s., perf mat
rent   (B1062)

Concerto for Violoncello and String
Orchestra [19']
string orch,vcl solo
sc GEHRMANS 6123P f.s., perf mat
rent   (B1063)

Follow-The-Leader Into My Song [11']
1.1.0.0. 1.0.0.0. strings
sc GEHRMANS 6203P f.s., perf mat
rent   (B1064)

Fyra Bagateller For Strakar [11']
string orch
GEHRMANS f.s. sc 6422P, pts 6422S
(B1065)

In Memoria DI... [11']
2.2.2.2. 2.2.1.0. timp,2perc,
harp,pno,strings
sc GEHRMANS 6002P f.s., perf mat
rent   (B1066)

Night Clouds [10']
string orch
sc GEHRMANS 5912P f.s., perf mat
rent   (B1067)

Parodos [12']
4.4.4.4. 4.4.4.1. timp,3perc,
strings
sc GEHRMANS 6589P f.s., perf mat
rent   (B1068)

Sinfonia No. 4 [24']
4.4.4.4. 6.4.4.1. timp,6perc,
harp,pno,strings
sc GEHRMANS 6041P f.s., perf mat
rent   (B1069)

Sinfonia No. 5 [24']
4.4.4.4. 6.4.4.1. timp,6perc,
harp,pno,strings
sc GEHRMANS 6113P f.s., perf mat
rent   (B1070)

Sinfonia No. 6 [30']
4.4.4.4. 6.4.4.1. timp,2perc,
harp,strings,S solo
sc GEHRMANS 6168P f.s., perf mat
rent   (B1071)

BÖRTZ, DANIEL (cont'd.)

Sinfonia No. 7 [27']
4.4.4.4. 4.4.4.1. timp,4perc,pno,
strings
sc GEHRMANS 6440P f.s., perf mat
rent   (B1072)

Sinfonia No. 8 [33']
3.3.3.3. 4.3.3.1. timp,3perc,
strings,MezBar soli
sc GEHRMANS 6655P f.s., perf mat
rent   (B1073)

Summer Elegi, For Flute And String
Orchestra [15']
string orch,fl solo
sc GEHRMANS 6188P f.s., perf mat
rent   (B1074)

BORUP-JORGENSEN, AXEL (1924-)
Marin *Op.60 [22']
3.3.3.3. 4.3.3.1. timp,perc,pno,
strings
sc SAMFUNDET 313 f.s., perf mat
rent   (B1075)

Nordic Summer Pastoral
see Nordisk Sommerpastorale

Nordisk Sommerpastorale
"Nordic Summer Pastoral" sc,pts
SAMFUNDET f.s.   (B1076)

BOSE, HANS JÜRGEN (1923-)
Funf Gesange, For Solo Voice And
Instrumental Ensemble [22']
1.1.1(bass clar).1. 1.0.0.0.
2vln,vla,vcl,db,Bar solo
SCHOTTS perf mat rent   (B1077)

Idyllen [17']
3.3.3.3. 4.3.3.1. timp,perc,harp,
cel&pno,strings
sc ARS VIVA AV 122 $44.00   (B1078)

Labyrinth I [30']
4(pic).4.4(bass
clar).4(contrabsn). 6.4.4.1.
timp,3perc,2harp,elec org&pno,
strings
SCHOTTS perf mat rent   (B1079)

"...other echoes inhabit the garden",
for oboe and orchestra [23']
3(pic).2(ob d'amore,English
horn).3(clar in A,bass clar,
basset
horn).2(contrabsn).soprano sax.
2.2.2.1. timp,3perc,2harp,
strings,ob solo
SCHOTTS perf mat rent   (B1080)

Prozess [12']
1(pic,alto fl).1(English
horn).2.0+contrabsn. 1.1.1.0.
timp,perc,pno,2vln,vla,vcl,db
SCHOTTS perf mat rent   (B1081)

Symbolum, For Organ And Orchestra
[18']
4(pic).4(English horn).4(clar in
E flat,bass clar).4(contrabsn).
6.4(trp in D).4.1. timp,perc,
2harp,elec org,strings,org solo
SCHOTTS perf mat rent   (B1082)

BOSMANS, HENRIËTTE (1895-1952)
Doodenmarsch, For Narrator And
Orchestra [5']
2.2.2.2. 3.3.0.0. perc,strings,
narrator
sc DONEMUS f.s., perf mat rent
(B1083)

BOSQUE HA ECHADO A ANDAR, EL see
Farinas Cantero, Carlos

BOSWELL, ROBERT
My Love's An Arbutus [5']
pno,strings
NOVELLO perf mat rent   (B1084)

BOTANY BAY: SUITE see Waxman, Franz

BOTSCHAFT, DIE see Vasks, Peteris

BOTTARI, G.
Troica *Op.57
1.1.2.1. 2.2.1.0. timp,strings
ZIMMER.   (B1085)

BÖTTCHER, EBERHARD (1934-)
Concerto for Horn and String
Orchestra [18']
string orch,horn solo
RIES   (B1086)

Concerto Ripieno [12']
string orch
NORGE   (B1087)

BOTTENBERG, WOLFGANG (1930-)
Concertino for Saxophone and String
Orchestra [15']
string orch,tenor sax solo
CAN.MUS.CENT. MI 1625 B751CO

BOTTENBERG, WOLFGANG (cont'd.)

(B1088)

BOTTESINI, GIOVANNI (1821-1889)
Concerto for Double Bass and
Orchestra, No. 2, in B minor,
[arr.]
string orch,db solo INTERNAT. perf
mat rent   (B1089)

Concerto for Double Bass and String
Orchestra, No. 2, in A minor
string orch,db solo
YORKE 8.0072 perf mat rent   (B1090)

Elegia And Tarantella, For Double
Bass And Orchestra
2+pic.0.2.2. 4.0.4.0. timp,
strings,db solo
YORKE 8.0060 perf mat rent   (B1091)

Passione Amorose, For 2 Double Basses
And Orchestra [13']
1.2.0.2. 2.0.0.0. strings,2db/db&
vln soli
(Malaric, Rudolf) DOBLINGER perf
mat rent   (B1092)

Tarantelle for Double Bass and String
Orchestra in A minor [5'30"]
(Girard, Andre) string orch,db solo
BILLAUDOT perf mat rent   (B1093)

BOTTJE, WILL GAY (1925-)
Chamber Concerto, For Oboe, Bassoon
And Chamber Orchestra [16']
2.0.2.0. 2.1.1.0. perc,strings,ob
solo,bsn solo
sc AM.COMP.AL. $19.15, perf mat
rent   (B1094)

Commentaries, For Guitar And Chamber
Orchestra [17']
1.1.1+bass clar.1. 1.1.0.0. perc,
strings,gtr solo
sc AM.COMP.AL. $27.50   (B1095)

Concerto for 2 Flutes and Orchestra
[19']
2.1.1.1. 2.1.1.0. harp,strings,
2fl soli
sc AM.COMP.AL. $73.45   (B1096)

Concerto for Tuba and Orchestra [16']
3.2.3.2. 4.3.3.0. timp,perc,
strings,tuba solo
AM.COMP.AL. sc $24.45, pts $3.85
(B1097)

Concerto for Violin, Oboe and Chamber
Orchestra [19']
2.2.0.2. 0.1.1.0. perc,harp,
strings,vln solo,ob solo
sc AM.COMP.AL. $44.75, perf mat
rent   (B1098)

Mutations [16']
2.1.2.1. 2.1.1.0. perc,strings
sc AM.COMP.AL. $22.90   (B1099)

Sounds From The West Shore [16']
3(pic).2.2.2. 4.2.2.1. timp,perc,
strings
sc AM.COMP.AL. $31.10, perf mat
rent   (B1100)

BOUCHARA, FOR SOLO VOICE AND
INSTRUMENTAL ENSEMBLE see Vivier,
Claude

BOUCOURECHLIEV, ANDRÉ (1925-)
Chevelure De Berenice [20']
1.1.1.1. 1.1.1.0. perc,7vln,2vla,
2vcl,db
SALABERT perf mat rent   (B1101)

Concerto for Piano and Orchestra
[21']
2(pic).0.2.2. 2.2.1.0. 2perc,
strings,pno solo
sc SALABERT f.s., perf mat rent
(B1102)

Lit De Neige, For Solo Voice And
Instrumental Ensemble [20']
2.1.2.1. 1.1.1.0. 3perc,harp,pno&
cel,2vln,vla,vcl,db,S solo
SALABERT perf mat rent   (B1103)

Miroir, Le, For Solo Voice And
Orchestra [20']
2.2.2.2. 2.2.2.0. 3perc,harp,pno&
cel,strings,Mez solo
SALABERT perf mat rent   (B1104)

BOUDREAU, WALTER (1947-)
Berliner Momente
2(pic).2(English horn).2(bass
clar).2(contrabsn). 4.2.3.1.
timp,2perc,strings
CAN.MUS.CENT. MI 1100 B756BE
(B1105)

BOUFFONNE, LA see Telemann, Georg
Philipp

BOULEZ, PIERRE (1925-   )
Derive 2 [12']
English horn,clar,bsn,horn,vibra,
marimba,harp,pno,vln,vla,vcl
UNIVER. perf mat rent   (B1106)

Notations I-IV
4.4.5.4. 6.4.4.1. timp,perc,
3harp,cel,strings
sc UNIVER. $67.50   (B1107)

Repons [43']
2.2.3.2. 2.2.2.1. 2pno,harp,
vibra,glock,cimbalom,3vln,2vla,
2vcl,db,electronic equipment
sc UNIVER. UE17487 f.s., perf mat
rent   (B1108)

BOULIANE, DENYS (1955-   )
Cactus Rieur Et La Demoiselle Qui
Souffrait D'une Soif Insatiable,
Le [20']
3.3.3.3. 4.3.3.1. timp,3perc,
harp,pno&cel,strings
CAN.MUS.CENT. MI 1100 B763CA
(B1109)

BOULOGNE, JOSEPH (CHEVALIER DE ST.-
GEORGES)
see SAINT-GEORGES, JOSEPH BOULOGNE DE

BOUR-DRONES see Lanza, Alcides E.

BOURGEOIS, DEREK (1941-   )
Romance for Double Bass and Chamber
Orchestra, Op. 64 [11']
2(pic).0.0.0. 2.0.0.0. strings,db
solo
YORKE 8.0071 $7.50, perf mat rent
(B1110)

BOURREE FANTASQUE see Chabrier,
[Alexis-] Emmanuel

BOURREES BOURBONNAISES see Ropartz,
Joseph Guy (Marie)

BOUSCH, FRANÇOIS (1946-   )
Spirales Insolites [15']
2(pic).0.1+contrabass clar.0.
1.0.0.0. perc,harp,2vln,vla,
vcl,db,synthesizer
SALABERT perf mat rent   (B1111)

BOUTON D'OR: SUITE see Pierne, Gabriel

BOUTRY, ROGER (1932-   )
Fantasy for Trombone and Orchestra
[16']
1.1.2.2. 2.2.0.0. timp,harp,
strings,trom solo
BILLAUDOT perf mat rent   (B1112)

BOWDEN, ROBERT
Fiddler's Medley
SHAWNEE perf mat rent   (B1113)

BOY AND THE DOLPHIN, THE see Oliver,
Stephen

BOY AND THE GLASS VIOLIN, THE see
Hauksson, Thorsteinn

BOYCE, WILLIAM (1711-1779)
Arden Court [arr.]
(Lambert) opt 2fl,opt 2ob,2trp,
timp,strings OXFORD perf mat rent
(B1114)
Overture In D, To "The Cambridge Ode"
[arr.]
(Lambert) string orch OXFORD perf
mat rent   (B1115)
Overture No. 1 in D
(McAllster) KALMUS A5602 sc $7.00,
set $11.00, pts $1.25, ea.
(B1116)
Overture No. 2 in G
(McAllster) KALMUS A5603 sc $7.00,
perf mat rent, set $15.00, pts
$1.25, ea.   (B1117)
Overture No. 3 in B flat
(McAllster) KALMUS A5604 sc $5.00,
set $10.00, pts $1.25, ea.
(B1118)
Overture No. 5 in F
(McAllster) KALMUS A5645 sc $7.00,
set $10.00, pts $1.25, ea.
(B1119)
Overture No. 7 in G
(McAllster) KALMUS A5647 sc $7.00,
set $10.00, pts $1.25, ea.
(B1120)
Overture, Ode For His Majesty's
Birthday, 1772 [7']
2ob,bsn,2horn,strings,cont
STAINER HL273 perf mat rent (B1121)
Overture, Ode For The New Year, 1770
[9']
2ob,bsn,strings,cont
STAINER HL267 perf mat rent (B1122)
Overtures
(Finzi, Gerald) sc STAINER MB13
f.s.   (B1123)

BOYCE, WILLIAM (cont'd.)
Sonata in A minor, [arr.]
see Sonatas, Two

Sonata in F, [arr.]
see Sonatas, Two

Sonatas, Two
(Brown) strings,pno KALMUS A5648 sc
$7.00, set $15.00, pts $2.00, ea.
contains: Sonata in A minor,
[arr.]; Sonata in F, [arr.]
(B1124)
Suite in A, MIN 122
strings,pno
(Adlington) KALMUS A3411 sc $3.00,
set $8.00, pts $1.00, ea. (B1125)

BOYD, ANNE
Bencharong [15']
7vln,2vla,2vcl,db
FABER perf mat rent   (B1126)

Summer Nights, For Solo Voice And
Orchestra [15']
4perc,harp,strings, Alto
orCountertenor Solo
FABER perf mat rent   (B1127)

BOYFRIEND, THE: CONCERT SUITE see
Davies, Peter Maxwell

BOYFRIENDS-GIRLFRIENDS see Quelle,
Ernst August

BOYKAN, MARTIN (1931-   )
Concerto For 13 Players [25']
1(pic).0.1+bass clar.1. 1.1.1.0.
harp,pno,vln,vla,vcl,db
sc APNM $39.75, perf mat rent
(B1128)

BOYLE, RORY (1951-   )
Moel Bryn Divisions [10']
string orch
CHESTER perf mat rent   (B1129)

Night Pictures [12']
1(pic,alto fl).1.1.1. 1.0.0.0.
perc,pno,string quar,db
CHESTER perf mat rent   (B1130)

Winter Music
2(pic).2.2.2. 4.3.3.1. perc,pno,
strings
CHESTER perf mat rent   (B1131)

BOY'S DANCE FROM "MISS SALLY'S PARTY"
see Still, William Grant

BOZAY, ATTILA (1939-   )
Variations for Orchestra
sc EMB 8611 f.s., perf mat rent
(B1132)

BOZIC, DARIJAN (1933-   )
Humoreska, For Horn And String
Orchestra [6']
string orch,horn solo
DRUSTVO DSS 949 perf mat rent
(B1133)

Koncertantna Glasba [7']
2(pic).2.3.1(contrabsn).alto sax.
5.3.3.1. timp,perc,pno,strings
"Music Concertant" DRUSTVO DSS 1084
perf mat rent   (B1134)

Music Concertant
see Koncertantna Glasba

BOZZA, EUGÈNE (1905-   )
Bacchanales Romaines [30']
3.3.3.3. 4.3.3.1. timp,perc,
2harp,pno,strings
study sc ESCHIG f.s., perf mat rent
(B1135)
Prelude Et Invention [15']
1.1.1.1.soprano sax. 1.1.1.0.
timp,perc,cel,pno,strings
study sc ESCHIG f.s., perf mat rent
(B1136)
Symphonie Da Camera [20']
1.1.1.1. 1.0.0.0. perc,harp,pno,
strings
ESCHIG perf mat rent   (B1137)

BRADE, WILLIAM (ca. 1560-1630)
Newe Auserlesene Liebliche Branden
KALMUS A6474 sc $5.00, set $5.00,
pts $1.00, ea.   (B1138)

BRADY, TIMOTHY (1956-   )
Concerto for Piano and Chamber
Orchestra
1.0.1.1. 0.0.0.0. 2perc,strings,
pno solo
CAN.MUS.CENT. MI 1319 B812CH
(B1139)

BRAEIN, EDVARD FLIFLET (1924-1976)
Einsleg, For Solo Voice And String
Orchestra [2']
string orch,solo voice
sc MUSIKK f.s., perf mat rent
(B1140)
Morgon, For Solo Voice And Orchestra
*Op.3,No.3 [3']
2.1.2.1. 2.2.2.0. timp,harp,

BRAEIN, EDVARD FLIFLET (cont'd.)
strings,solo voice
"Morning, For Solo Voice And
Orchestra" NORGE   (B1141)

Morning, For Solo Voice And Orchestra
see Morgon, For Solo Voice And
Orchestra

Symfonisk Forspill *Op.11 [12']
2.2.2.2. 4.3.3.0. timp,perc,
strings
"Symphonic Prelude" NORGE   (B1142)

Symphonic Prelude
see Symfonisk Forspill

Symphony No. 1, Op. 4 [32']
2.2.2.2. 4.2.3.0. timp,perc,
strings
NORGE   (B1143)

Symphony No. 3, Op. 16 [18']
2.2.2.2. 4.2.3.0. timp,perc,
strings
sc MUSIKK f.s., perf mat rent
(B1144)

BRAENDING see Norgaard, Per

BRAGA, ANTONIO (1929-   )
Concerto Gitano, For Violoncello And
Orchestra [28']
CHOUDENS perf mat rent   (B1145)

BRAHMS, JOHANNES (1833-1897)
Akademische Festouverture
see Three Orchestral Works

Complete Concerti
(Mandyczewski, E.) "Sämtliche
Konzerte" study sc BREITKOPF-W
5711114 f.s.   (B1146)

Concerto for Piano and Orchestra, No.
1, Op. 15, in D minor
(Gerdes) (includes variants of
piano solo part) sc PETERS P9825
f.s.   (B1147)

Concerto for Piano and Orchestra, No.
2, Op. 83, in B flat
study sc BREITKOPF-L PB 3695 f.s.
(B1148)
(Darvas) study sc EMB 40083 f.s.
(B1149)
Concerto for Violin and Orchestra,
Op. 77, in D
(Darvas) study sc EMB 40073 f.s.
(B1150)
Concerto for Violin, Violoncello and
Orchestra, Op. 102, in A minor
sc MEZ KNIGA f.s.   (B1151)

Concerto for Violoncello and
Orchestra in E minor, [arr.]
(Mannino, Franco) 2.2.2.1. 0.2.0.0.
timp,perc,strings,vcl solo [30']
sc BSE 1210 f.s., perf mat rent
(B1152)
Feldeinsamkeit, For Solo Voice And
Orchestra [arr.] *Op.86,No.2
(Reger) "Lonely Field, The, For
Solo Voice And Orchestra [arr.]"
2.1.2.1. 2.0.0.0. timp,strings,
high solo [4'] SIMROCK perf mat
rent   (B1153)

Hungarian Dance No. 4 [arr.]
see Ungarischer Tanz No. 4 [arr.]

Hungarian Dance No. 8 [arr.]
see Ungarischer Tanz No. 8 [arr.]

Hungarian Dance No. 9 [arr.]
see Ungarischer Tanz No. 9 [arr.]

Hungarian Dances Nos. 1 And 3 [arr.]
see Ungarische Tanze Nos. 1 And 3
[arr.]

Intermezzo, Op. 116, No. 4, [arr.]
(Klengel, P.) KALMUS A5756 sc
$2.00, set $10.00   (B1154)

Intermezzo, Op. 117, No. 1, [arr.]
(Klengel, P.) KALMUS A5872 sc
$3.00, set $9.00   (B1155)

Lonely Field, The, For Solo Voice And
Orchestra [arr.]
see Feldeinsamkeit, For Solo Voice
And Orchestra [arr.]

Quartet, Op. 60, in C minor, [arr.]
(King, John) 2.2.2.2. 4.2.3.0.
timp,strings [15'] sc AM.COMP.AL.
$22.85   (B1156)

Sämtliche Konzerte
see Complete Concerti

Samtliche Symphonien
see Symphonies, Nos. 1-4

BRAHMS, JOHANNES (cont'd.)

Serenade, Op. 11, in D
min sc KALMUS K0021 $7.00 contains
also: Serenade, Op. 16, in A
(B1157)

Serenade, Op. 16, in A
see Serenade, Op. 11, in D

Sonata for Clarinet and Orchestra,
Op. 120, No. 1, [arr.]
(Berio, Luciano) 2.2.2.2+contrabsn.
3.3.1.0. strings,clar/vla solo
[25'] sc UNIVER. UE18868 $95.00,
perf mat rent
(B1158)

Suite From Waltzes, Op. 39 [arr.]
(Nightingale) 2.2.2.2. 4.2.3.0.
timp,strings [10'] KALMUS A6735
sc $12.00, set $35.00, pts $2.00,
ea., perf mat rent
(B1159)

Symphonies Nos. 1-2
min sc KALMUS K00425 $8.75 (B1160)

Symphonies, Nos. 1-4
(Mandyczewski, E.) "Samtliche
Symphonien" study sc BREITKOPF-W
5711088 f.s.
(B1161)

Symphonies Nos. 3-4
min sc KALMUS K00426 $8.75 (B1162)

Symphony No. 1, Op. 68, in C minor
(reproduction of pierpont morgan
library manuscript) sc DOVER
24976X $9.95
(B1163)

Symphony No. 2, Op. 73, in D
study sc EMB 40044 f.s.
(B1164)

Symphony No. 3, [arr.] *see TWELVE
POP HITS FROM THE CLASSICS, VOL.
1

Three Orchestral Works
sc DOVER 24637X $7.50 reprint of
Breitkopf and Hartel edition
contains: Akademische
Festouverture; Tragische
Ouverture; Variationen Uber Ein
Thema Von Joseph Haydn (B1165)

Tragische Ouverture
see Three Orchestral Works

Ungarische Tanze Nos. 1 And 3 [arr.]
(Riesenfeld) "Hungarian Dances Nos.
1 And 3 [arr.]" 1+pic.1.2.2. 4.1+
cornet.2+bass trom.0. timp,perc,
strings SCHIRM.G perf mat rent
(B1166)

Ungarische Tanze Nos.8 And 9 [arr.]
(Gal, H.) 2.2.2.2. 2.2.0.0. timp,
perc,strings [5'] SIMROCK perf
mat rent
(B1167)

Ungarischer Tanz No. 4 [arr.]
(Juon) "Hungarian Dance No. 4
[arr.]" 2.2.2.2. 4.2.3.0. timp,
harp,strings [5'] KALMUS 6631 sc
$8.00, set $16.00, pts $.75, ea.
(B1168)

Ungarischer Tanz No. 8 [arr.]
(Dennison) "Hungarian Dance No. 8
[arr.]" 2+pic.2.2.2. 4.2.3.1.
timp,perc,strings [2'30"] KALMUS
A4593 sc $10.00, set $40.00, perf
mat rent
(B1169)

Ungarischer Tanz No. 9 [arr.]
(Dennison) "Hungarian Dance No. 9
[arr.]" 2+pic.2+English horn.2+
bass clar.2+contrabsn. 4.3.3.1.
timp,perc,strings [2'] KALMUS
A3614 sc $5.00, set $25.00, perf
mat rent
(B1170)

Variationen Über Ein Thema Von Joseph
Haydn *Op.56a
"Variations On A Theme Of Haydn"
study sc EMB 40046 f.s. (B1171)
see Three Orchestral Works

Variations On A Theme Of Haydn
see Variationen Über Ein Thema Von
Joseph Haydn

Vier Ernste Gesänge, For Solo Voice
And Orchestra, [arr.] *Op.121
(Raphael) 2.2.2.2. 2.2.3.0. timp,
strings,B solo BREITKOPF-L perf
mat rent
(B1172)

Vier Ernste Gesange [arr.] *Op.121
(Hofmann, Wolfgang) 2horn,harp,
strings [16'] PETERS (B1173)

We Strolled, For Solo Voice And
Orchestra [arr.]
see Wir Wandelten, For Solo Voice
And Orchestra [arr.]

Wir Wandelten, For Solo Voice And
Orchestra [arr.] *Op.96,No.2
1.1.2.1. 2.0.0.0. timp,strings,

BRAHMS, JOHANNES (cont'd.)

high solo
(Reger) "We Strolled, For Solo
Voice And Orchestra [arr.]" [4']
SIMROCK perf mat rent (B1174)

Zigeunerlieder [arr.] *Op.103
(Hofmann, Wolfgang) string orch
[16'] PETERS (B1175)
(Molin, Franz) 2.2.2.2. 2.2.0.0.
timp,perc,strings [16'] PETERS
(B1176)

BRAIDING GAME see Palsson, Pall P.

BRANCHES OF TIME, FOR 2 PIANOS AND
ORCHESTRA see Barati, George

BRANDENBURG CONCERTI NOS.1-3, BWV 1046-
1048 see Bach, Johann Sebastian

BRANDENBURG CONCERTI NOS. 1-6, BWV
1046-1051 see Bach, Johann
Sebastian

BRANDENBURG CONCERTI NOS. 4-6, BWV
1049-1051 see Bach, Johann
Sebastian

BRANDENBURG CONCERTI NOS. 1-6, BWV
1046-1051 see Bach, Johann
Sebastian

BRANDENBURG CONCERTO NO. 1 IN F, BWV
1046 see Bach, Johann Sebastian

BRANDENBURG CONCERTO NO. 2 IN F, BWV
1047 see Bach, Johann Sebastian

BRANDENBURG CONCERTO NO. 3 IN G, BWV
1048 see Bach, Johann Sebastian

BRANDENBURG CONCERTO NO. 4 IN G, BWV
1049 see Bach, Johann Sebastian

BRANDENBURG CONCERTO NO. 5 IN D, BWV
1050 see Bach, Johann Sebastian

BRANDENBURG CONCERTO NO. 6 IN B FLAT,
BWV 1051 see Bach, Johann Sebastian

BRANDENBURG GATE, REVISITED, FOR HORN
AND STRING ORCHESTRA see Brubeck,
David (Dave) Warren

BRANDENBURGISCHES KONZERT see
Ekimovsky, Viktor

BRANDMÜLLER, THEO (1948-)
Ach, Trauriger Mond, For Percussion
And String Orchestra [14']
string orch,perc solo
BOTE perf mat rent (B1177)

Antigone [18']
3(pic).2+English horn.2+bass
clar.2(contrabsn). 4.3.3.1.
timp,2perc,harp,pno,strings
BREITKOPF-W perf mat rent (B1178)

Cis-Cantus III [15']
2(pic).2(English horn).2+bass
clar.2(contrabsn). 4.3.3.0.
timp,2perc,hpsd/cel,strings
BREITKOPF-W perf mat rent (B1179)

Concerto for Organ and Orchestra
[17']
3trp,2perc,strings,org solo
BOTE perf mat rent (B1180)

Dramma Per Musica [11'30"]
2+pic.2(English horn).2+bass
clar.2+contrabsn. 4.3.3.1.
timp,2perc,harp,pno&cel,strings
BOTE perf mat rent (B1181)

Fred Astaire Music [11']
string orch
sc BREITKOPF-W f.s., perf mat rent
(B1182)

Si J'etais Domenico, For Harpsichord
And String Orchestra [25']
string orch,hpsd solo
sc BREITKOPF-W f.s., perf mat rent
(B1183)

U(h)r-Tone [14']
2(2pic).2(English
horn).2.2(contrabsn). 4.2.3.0.
2perc,strings,vln solo
BREITKOPF-W perf mat rent (B1184)

Venezianische Schatten [8']
1(pic).0+English
horn.1.1(contrabsn). 2.1.0.0.
2perc,strings
BOTE perf mat rent (B1185)

Zeit-Enden [18']
2+pic.2+bass clar.2. 4.3.3.1.
harp,elec org,strings
BOTE perf mat rent (B1186)

BRANDON, SEYMOUR (SY) (1945-)
Amendment I, For Orchestra And Tape
CO OP perf mat rent (B1187)

Bachburg Concerto No. 2, For Alto
Saxophone, Piano And Orchestra
CO OP perf mat rent (B1188)

Bachburg Concerto No. 3, For 2 Oboes,
Bassoon, And String Orchestra
string orch,2ob soli,bsn solo
CO OP perf mat rent (B1189)

Ricercare
1.1.2.0. 1.1.1.0. 2perc,2vln,vla,
vcl
CO OP $20.00 (B1190)

Symphonic Movements
CO OP perf mat rent (B1191)

BRANDSTRÖM, CHRISTER (1951-)
Sinfonia Umana, For Violoncello And
Orchestra
4.2.3.3. 4.2.3.1. timp,4perc,
harp,strings,vcl solo
STIM (B1192)

BRANZOVSKY, VACLAV (1790-1840)
Merry Poverty: Fucik, For Solo Voice
And Orchestra [5']
2ob,2horn,strings,T solo
SUPRAPHON (B1193)

BRASS, NIKOLAUS (1949-)
Landschaft Der Vergangenheit [25']
4.4.4.4. 4.4.4.1. 3perc,harp,
2pno,strings
RICORDI-GER SY 3033 perf mat rent
(B1194)

BRAUNFELS, WALTER (1882-1954)
Ariels Gesang Aus Shakespeares
"Sturm" *Op.18
KALMUS A7272 sc $7.00, set $25.00,
pts $1.50, ea., perf mat rent
(B1195)

BRAUT VON MESSINA, DIE, OP. 100:
OVERTURE see Schumann, Robert
(Alexander)

BRAUTSCHAU POLKA see Strauss, Johann,
[Jr.]

BRAVNICAR, MATIJA (1897-1977)
King Matthias
see Kralj Matjaz

Kralj Matjaz [8']
2(pic).2(English horn).2.2.
4.2.3.1. timp,perc,strings
"King Matthias" DRUSTVO DSS 931
perf mat rent (B1196)

BRAVO MOZART! see Argento, Dominick

BRAVOUR-VARIATIONEN. "ACH, MAMA, ICH
SAG ES DIR", FOR SOLO VOICE AND
ORCHESTRA see Adam, Adolphe-
Charles, Ah! Vous Dirai-Je, Maman,
For Solo Voice And Orchestra

BREAKFAST ANTIPHONIES see "Bach,
P.D.Q." (Peter Schickele)

BREDEMEYER, REINER (1929-)
Alltagliche, Das, For Solo Voices And
Orchestra [20']
3.2+English horn.2+bass clar.3.
3.2.1.1. timp,harp,pno,strings,
ST soli
PETERS (B1197)

Pointing
11vln,4vla,2vcl,db
sc PETERS $17.00 (B1198)

Schlagstuck 3 Für Schlagzeuge Und
Orchester
2.2.2.1. 1.1.1.1. perc,pno,
strings
sc PETERS $9.00 (B1199)

BREEROO see Dijk, Jan van

BREF see Bons, Joël

BREGENT, MICHEL (1948-)
Swiateo, For Solo Voices And
Orchestra [17']
2.2.2.2. 2.2.0.0. 2perc,cel,
strings,SMezB soli
CAN.MUS.CENT. MV 3400 B833SW
(B1200)

Trad-Sens Concertio, For Piano And
Orchestra [30']
3(pic).3(English horn).3(bass
clar,clar in E
flat).3(contrabsn). 4.2.3.1.
3perc,harp,strings,pno solo
CAN.MUS.CENT. MI 1361 B833TR
(B1201)

BREHM, ALVIN (1925-)
Concerto for Tuba and Orchestra [22']
2.2.2(bass clar). 4.3.3.0.
timp,perc,pno&cel,harp,strings,
tuba solo

BREHM, ALVIN (cont'd.)

SCHIRM.G perf mat rent   (B1202)

BREIMO, BJØRN (1958-   )
Agnus Dei
1.1.1.1. 1.1.1.0. timp,perc,harp,
strings
NORGE   (B1203)

Fantasia Concertante, For Oboe,
Violin, Violoncello, Piano And
String Orchestra [17']
string orch,ob solo,vln solo,vcl
solo,pno solo
NORGE   (B1204)

Fantasia Sinfonica [15']
3.2.2.2. 4.2.3.0. timp,perc,harp,
strings
NORGE   (B1205)

Largo Nostalgico [6']
string orch
NORGE   (B1206)

Quasi Passacaglia [12']
string orch
NORGE   (B1207)

Sinfonia
3.3.3.3. 4.3.3.1. timp,3perc,cel,
harp,strings
NORGE   (B1208)

BREMER STADTMUSIKANTEN, DIE, FOR
NARRATOR AND ORCHESTRA see Soring,
Wolfgang

BRENET, THERESE (1935-   )
Chant Des Mondes, Le, For Solo Voice,
Piano And Orchestra [35']
CHOUDENS perf mat rent   (B1209)

Fragor: For 2 Pianos And Orchestra
[25'15"]
2+pic.2+English horn.2+bass
clar.2+contrabsn. 4.3.3.1.
timp,3perc,strings,2pno soli
RIDEAU perf mat rent   (B1210)

Hapax [16']
CHOUDENS perf mat rent   (B1211)

Hommes Sur La Terre, Les, For Solo
Voices And Orchestra [15'25"]
2.2.2.2. 2.2.2.0. timp,3perc,
harp,cel,strings,TB soli
BILLAUDOT perf mat rent   (B1212)

Pour Un Poeme Inconnu, For Piano And
Orchestra [18']
Ondes Martenot,strings,pno solo
RIDEAU perf mat rent   (B1213)

Rois Mages, Les, For Solo Voices And
Orchestra [15'15"]
2.2.3.2. 2.2.2.1. timp,2perc,cel,
strings,BarB soli
BILLAUDOT perf mat rent   (B1214)

Siderales [9'30"]
CHOUDENS perf mat rent   (B1215)

Vibrations, For Harpe Celtique And
String Orchestra
CHOUDENS perf mat rent   (B1216)

Visions Prophetiques De Cassandre,
Les, For Solo Voices And
Orchestra [15']
2.2.3.2. 2.2.2.0. timp,2perc,
harp,strings,SB soli
BILLAUDOT perf mat rent   (B1217)

BRENNEND, FOR SOLO VOICE AND ORCHESTRA
see Pröve, Bernfried

BRENNENDE LIEBE see Strauss, Josef

BRESGEN, CESAR (1913-1988)
Capriccio for Flute and String
Orchestra [16']
string orch,fl solo
DOBLINGER perf mat rent   (B1218)

Concert Spirituel [22'30"]
2(pic).2(English horn).2(bass
clar).2. 2.2.2.0. timp,perc,
harp,strings
DOBLINGER perf mat rent   (B1219)

Concerto for Clarinet and Orchestra
2(pic).2.0.2. 2.2.2.0. timp,perc,
harp,strings,clar solo
DOBLINGER perf mat rent   (B1220)

Magnalia Dei, For Speaking Voice And
Orchestra [23']
3(pic).2.3(bass
clar).3(contrabsn). 4.2.3.0.
timp,perc,harp,strings,speaking
voice
DOBLINGER perf mat rent   (B1221)

BRESGEN, CESAR (cont'd.)

Tres Retratos [9']
2(pic).2.2.2. 2.2.2.0. strings
study sc DOBLINGER STP 413 f.s.,
perf mat rent   (B1222)

BRETTINGHAM SMITH, JOLYON (1949-   )
Approaches To Dun Aengus, For
Violoncello And Orchestra *Op.37
[13']
3(pic).2+English horn.2+bass
clar.2+contrabsn. 4.3.3.0.
timp,2perc,pno,strings,vcl solo
sc BOTE f.s., perf mat rent (B1223)

BRÉVAL, JEAN BAPTISTE (1756-1825)
Symphonie Concertante in F
0.0.1.1. 1.0.0.0. strings
(Brook, Barry) FRANK perf mat rent
(B1224)

BREVIK, TOR (1932-   )
Andante Cantabile for Violin and
String Orchestra [7']
string orch,vln solo
NORGE   (B1225)

Canto Elegiaco [7']
2.2.2.2. 4.3.3.1. timp,strings
NORGE   (B1226)

Chaconne [8']
2.2.2.2. 4.2.3.1. timp,strings
NORGE   (B1227)

Concertino for Clarinet and String
Orchestra [15']
string orch,clar solo
NORGE   (B1228)

Concertino for Strings [8']
string orch
NORGE   (B1229)

Concerto for Viola and Orchestra
[27']
2.2.2.2. 2.2.0.0. strings,vla
solo
NORGE   (B1230)

Intrada [8']
2.2.3.2. 4.2.3.1. timp,perc,
strings
NORGE   (B1231)

Overture [6']
2.2.2.2. 4.2.3.0. timp,strings
NORGE   (B1232)

Romance for Violin and Orchestra [9']
2.2.2.2. 2.2.0.0. timp,strings,
vln solo
NORGE   (B1233)

Senja Suite
2horn,perc,strings
NORGE   (B1234)

Serenade for String Orchestra [15']
string orch
NORGE   (B1235)

Sinfonietta [21']
2.2.2.2. 3.2.3.1. timp,perc,
strings
NORGE   (B1236)

BRICCIALDI, GIULIO (1818-1881)
Carnival Of Venice, For Flute And
Orchestra, [arr.] [7']
(Galway) 3.2.2.2. 2.2.2.1. timp,
perc,harp,strings,fl solo NOVELLO
perf mat rent   (B1237)

BRIDE OF FRANKENSTEIN, THE: DANCE
MACABRE see Waxman, Franz

BRIDE OF FRANKENSTEIN, THE: SUITE see
Waxman, Franz

BRIDESHEAD VARIATIONS see Burgon,
Geoffrey

BRIDGE, FRANK (1879-1941)
Allegro Moderato [12']
string orch
FABER perf mat rent   (B1238)

Christmas Dance, A [4']
string orch
STAINER HL34 perf mat rent (B1239)

Dance Poem [15']
3.3.3.3. 4.4.3.1. timp,perc,harp,
strings
FABER perf mat rent   (B1240)

Dance Rhapsody [18']
3.2.2.2. 4.2.3.1. timp,perc,cel,
harp,strings
FABER perf mat rent   (B1241)

Day After Day, For Solo Voice And
Orchestra
see Two Songs, For Solo Voice And
Orchestra

BRIDGE, FRANK (cont'd.)

Lament [6']
string orch
KALMUS A4281 sc $3.00, set $5.00
(B1242)
CURWEN perf mat rent   (B1243)

Norse Legend [5']
1.1.2.1. 2.2.1.0. timp,perc,harp,
strings
BOOSEY perf mat rent   (B1244)

Rosemary [arr.]
string orch [2'] BOOSEY perf mat
rent   (B1245)

Scherzetto, For Violoncello And
Orchestra [arr.]
(Cornford, Robert) 1.1.1.1.
2.0.0.0. strings,vcl solo [3']
FABER perf mat rent   (B1246)

Speak To Me, My Love, For Solo Voice
And Orchestra
see Two Songs, For Solo Voice And
Orchestra

Suite for String Orchestra
string orch
sc FABER C90700 f.s.   (B1247)
CURWEN $20.00   (B1248)

Suite for Violoncello and Orchestra,
[arr.]
(Cornford, Robert) 2.2.2.2.
2.0.0.0. harp,strings,vcl solo
[12'] FABER perf mat rent (B1249)

Two Entr'actes: Rosemary; Canzonetta
[7']
1.1.2.1. 2.2.1.0. timp,harp,
strings
BOOSEY perf mat rent   (B1250)

Two Intermezzi (from Threads) [10']
1.1.2.1. 2.2.1.0. timp,perc,
strings
BOOSEY perf mat rent   (B1251)

Two Songs, For Solo Voice And
Orchestra
2.2.2.2. 2.0.0.0. harp,strings,Mez
solo STAINER HL39 perf mat rent
contains: Day After Day, For Solo
Voice And Orchestra; Speak To
Me, My Love, For Solo Voice And
Orchestra   (B1252)

BRIEF, EIN, FOR SOLO VOICE AND
ORCHESTRA see Kagel, Mauricio

BRIEF, TODD
Cantares, For Voice And Orchestra
4.4.5.4. 4.3.4.1. perc,2harp,cel,
pno,strings,S solo [16'] UNIVER.
perf mat rent   (B1253)

BRIEF ELEGY, FOR OBOE AND STRING
ORCHESTRA see Kay, Ulysses Simpson

BRIEFE see Zechlin, Ruth

BRIGG FAIR see Delius, Frederick

BRIGHT BLUE MUSIC see Torke, Michael

BRILLON DE JOUY, ANNE LOUISE
D'HARDANCOURT (1744-1824)
Saratoga Victory March
(Nightingale) 2.2.2.2. 2.3.0.0.
timp,perc,strings [3'] KALMUS
A7222 sc $8.00, set $15.00, pts
$1.00, ea.   (B1254)

BRIMBERG, JACK
Bird Flew High, A, For Solo Voice And
String Orchestra [8']
string orch,pno,med solo
sc AM.COMP.AL. $6.15   (B1255)

BRINGS, ALLEN STEPHEN (1934-   )
Scherzi Musicali [8']
2(pic).2.2.2. 4.2.3.1. timp,
2perc,strings
MIRA sc $25.00, study sc $10.00,
perf mat rent   (B1256)

BRIOSCHI, ANTONIO (fl. 1725-1750)
Symphonies, Three
(Churgin; Russell; Frolich;
Johnson; Moore) ("The Symphony"
Vol. A-III) sc GARLAND
ISBN 0-8240-3858-4 $90.00
contains also: Chelleri,
Fortunato, Symphony; Sacchini,
Antonio (Maria Gasparo
Gioacchino), Symphonies, Two;
Pugnani, Gaetano, Sinfonie, Six
(B1257)

BRITTEN, [SIR] BENJAMIN (1913-1976)
American Overture, An [10']
3(pic).3.3(bass clar).3. 4.3.3.1.
timp,2perc,1-2harp,opt pno&opt
cel,strings
sc FABER F0807 f.s., perf mat rent

BRITTEN, [SIR] BENJAMIN (cont'd.)
                                        (B1258)
    Death In Venice [arr.]
        (Bedford, S.) 2.2.2.2. 2.2.2.1.
        timp,4perc,harp,pno,strings [26']
        sc FABER f.s., perf mat rent
                                        (B1259)
    Men Of Goodwill [8']
        3.2.2.2. 4.2.3.1. timp,2perc,
        harp,strings
        sc FABER F0620 $16.50, perf mat
        rent   (B1260)
    Occasional Overture
        3.3.3.3. 4.3.3.1. timp,3perc,cel,
        harp,strings
        sc FABER F0713 $25.50, perf mat
        rent   (B1261)
    Paul Bunyan: Overture [7']
        2(pic).1.2+bass clar.1. 2.2.2.1.
        timp,2-3perc,harp/pno,strings
        (Matthews, Colin) sc FABER F0571
        $17.25, perf mat rent   (B1262)
    Quatre Chansons Françaises, For Solo
        Voice And Orchestra [15']
        2.1.3.2. 4.0.0.0. perc,harp,pno,
        strings,S solo
        sc FABER F0674 f.s., perf mat rent
                                        (B1263)
    Young Apollo, For Piano, String
        Quartet And String Orchestra
        *Op.16
        string orch,pno solo,string quar
        soli
        sc FABER F0646 $34.00   (B1264)

BRIVIO, GIUSEPPE FERDINANDO (1700- ?)
    Demofonte: Finale, Act III [2']
        2ob,2horn,hpsd,strings
        SUPRAPHON   (B1265)

BRIXHAM OVERTURE see Tate, Brian

BRIXI, FRANZ XAVER (1732-1771)
    Concerti For Organ And Orchestra, Two
        sc SUPRAPHON MAB 75 f.s.
        contains: Concerto No. 1 for
        Organ and Orchestra in D;
        Concerto No. 2 for Organ and
        Orchestra in G   (B1266)
    Concerto No. 1 for Organ and
        Orchestra in D
        see Concerti For Organ And
        Orchestra, Two
    Concerto No. 2 for Organ and
        Orchestra in G
        see Concerti For Organ And
        Orchestra, Two

BROADBENT, ALAN (1947-   )
    Conversation Piece [15'10"]
        3+pic.2+English horn.3+bass
        clar.3+contrabsn.soprano
        sax.alto sax.tenor sax.baritone
        sax. 4.4.4.1. timp,perc,gtr,
        cel,pno,strings
        NEWAM 19007 perf mat rent   (B1267)
    Suite For Orchestra: Songs Of Home
        [21'29"]
        2+pic.2+English horn.3+bass
        clar.2+contrabsn.alto sax. 4.4+
        flügelhorn.4.1. perc,harp,2pno&
        cel, fender-rhodes, strings
        NEWAM 19006 perf mat rent   (B1268)

BROCKLESS, BRIAN (1926-   )
    English Elegy, An [7']
        string orch
        NOVELLO perf mat rent   (B1269)

BRODSGAARD, ANDERS
    Variations for Orchestra [15']
        3.3.4.3. 4.3.3.1. perc,cel,pno,
        harp,strings
        SAMFUNDET perf mat rent   (B1270)

BROEGE, TIMOTHY (1947-   )
    Sinfonia No. 11
        1.2.1.2. 2.1.0.0. perc,pno,
        strings
        BOURNE perf mat rent   (B1271)

BROKIGA BLAD see Sörenson, Torsten
    Napoleon

BRONS, CAREL (1931-1983)
    Springtime Music [22']
        1(pic).1(English horn).1(bass
        clar).0. 0.0.0.0. perc,pno&cel,
        2vln,vla,vcl,db
        DONEMUS perf mat rent   (B1272)
    Symphonic Fantasy, For Organ And
        Orchestra [13']
        3.3.2.2. 3.3.3.1. timp,4perc,
        strings,org solo
        sc DONEMUS f.s., perf mat rent
                                        (B1273)

BRONSART, MAX VON
    Concerto for Piano and Orchestra, Op.
        10
        KISTNER perf mat rent   (B1274)

BROOK GREEN SUITE see Holst, Gustav

BROOKS, RICHARD JAMES (1942-   )
    Chorale Variations, For 2 Horns And
        String Orchestra [15']
        string orch,string quin soli,
        2horn soli
        AM.COMP.AL. sc $7.70, pts $6.55
                                        (B1275)
    Seascape [7']
        3.3.4.3. 4.3.3.1. timp,3perc,
        strings
        (Overture From Moby Dick) sc
        AM.COMP.AL. $36.00   (B1276)
    Symphony In One Movement [20']
        3.2.2.2. 4.3.3.1. perc,strings
        sc AM.COMP.AL. $22.60   (B1277)

BROPHY, GERARD (1953-   )
    Orfeo [13']
        8vln,2vla,2vcl,db
        RICORDI-IT 134156 perf mat rent
                                        (B1278)

BROSCHI, RICCARDO (ca. 1698-1756)
    Merope: Ballet Music [2']
        0.2.0.2. 2.2.0.0. hpsd,strings
        SUPRAPHON   (B1279)

BROTT, ALEXANDER (1915-   )
    Emperor's New Clothes, The, For
        Narrator And Orchestra [19']
        1.1.1.1. 2.1.1.0. timp,perc,
        strings,narrator
        CAN.MUS.CENT. MV 1400 B874E (B1280)
    Invocation And Dance, For Violin And
        Orchestra [11']
        2.2.2.2. 2.2.2.0. timp,perc,harp,
        strings,vln solo
        CAN.MUS.CENT. MI 1311 B874I (B1281)
    Oracle
        3.2.2.2. 4.3.3.1. timp,perc,pno,
        strings
        CAN.MUS.CENT. MI 1100 B874OR
                                        (B1282)
    Symphony
        3.2.3.3. 4.3.3.1. timp,3perc,
        strings
        CAN.MUS.CENT. MI 1100 B874S (B1283)

BROUWER, LEO (1939-   )
    Anima Latima
        4.3.3.3. 6.3.3.0. 3perc,harp,
        strings
        TONOS perf mat rent   (B1284)
    Concerto for Guitar and Orchestra,
        No. 1 [26']
        1.1.1.1. 1.1.0.0. timp,perc,
        strings,gtr solo
        ESCHIG perf mat rent   (B1285)
    Concerto for Guitar and Orchestra,
        No. 3 [25']
        timp,perc,strings,gtr solo
        study sc ESCHIG f.s., perf mat rent
                                        (B1286)
    Retrats Catalans, For Guitar And
        Orchestra [18']
        2fl,timp,perc,pno,strings,gtr
        solo
        sc ESCHIG f.s., perf mat rent
                                        (B1287)
    Tres Danzas Concertantes, For Guitar
        And String Orchestra
        string orch,gtr solo
        sc ESCHIG $19.95, perf mat rent
                                        (B1288)

BROWN, CHRISTOPHER (ROLAND) (1943-   )
    Concerto for Organ and Orchestra, Op.
        49 [15']
        2ob,2horn,timp,strings,org solo
        CHESTER JWC555 perf mat rent
                                        (B1289)
    Festival Variations [8']
        string orch
        CHESTER perf mat rent   (B1290)
    Into The Sun [16']
        string orch
        CHESTER perf mat rent   (B1291)
    Soliloquy, For Solo Voice And
        Orchestra [30']
        2(pic).1+English horn(ob
        d'amore).1+bass clar.2.
        2.2.2.0. harp,pno&cel,timp,
        perc,strings,A/Bar/countertenor
        CHESTER JWC 460 perf mat rent
                                        (B1292)
    Triptych [34']
        3(pic).2+English horn.3(clar in E
        flat,bass clar).2+contrabsn.
        4.3.3.1. harp,pno&cel,timp,
        6perc,strings,opt org
        CHESTER JWC526 perf mat rent
                                        (B1293)

BROWN, JONATHAN BRUCE (1952-   )
    Lyric Variations, For Tuba And String
        Orchestra
        string orch,tuba solo
        SEESAW   (B1294)

BROWN, RAY
    Afterthoughts, For Double Bass And
        Orchestra [13'45"]
        3(pic)+3alto fl.2.2+2bass
        clar.2(contrabsn). 4.4.4.1.
        timp,perc,pno,elec pno,2gtr,
        harp,strings,db solo
        NEWAM 19008 perf mat rent   (B1295)

BROWN, RAYNER (1912-   )
    Concerto for Clarinet and Orchestra
        BROWN,R   (B1296)
    Concerto for Organ and String
        Orchestra, No. 1
        BROWN,R   (B1297)
    Concerto for Organ and String
        Orchestra, No. 2
        BROWN,R   (B1298)
    Concerto for Organ and String
        Orchestra, No. 3
        BROWN,R   (B1299)
    Concerto for Organ and String
        Orchestra, No. 5
        BROWN,R   (B1300)
    Concerto for Organ and String
        Orchestra, No. 7
        BROWN,R   (B1301)
    Concerto for Violin, Harp and
        Orchestra
        BROWN,R   (B1302)
    Symphony No. 1
        BROWN,R   (B1303)
    Symphony No. 2
        BROWN,R   (B1304)
    Symphony No. 3
        BROWN,R   (B1305)
    Symphony No. 6
        BROWN,R   (B1306)
    Variations Of A Hymn
        BROWN,R   (B1307)

BROWNE, PHILIP (1933-   )
    Concerto for Strings
        string orch
        sc EUR.AM.MUS. 01275FS f.s., perf
        mat rent   (B1308)

BROZAK, DANIEL (1947-   )
    Mobiel
        variable instrumentation sc DONEMUS
        f.s.   (B1309)

BRUBECK, DAVID (DAVE) WARREN
    (1920-   )
    Brandenburg Gate, Revisited, For Horn
        And String Orchestra
        string orch,horn solo
        SHAWNEE perf mat rent   (B1310)
    Light In The Wilderness, The:
        Excerpts
        SHAWNEE perf mat rent   (B1311)
    Out Of The Way Of The People (from
        The Gates Of Justice)
        SHAWNEE perf mat rent   (B1312)

BRUCH, MAX (1838-1920)
    Adagio Nach Keltischen Melodien, For
        Violoncello And Orchestra *Op.56
        "Adagio On Celtic Melodies, For
        Violoncello And Orchestra" KALMUS
        A6106 sc $10.00, set $15.00, perf
        mat rent   (B1313)
    Adagio On Celtic Melodies, For
        Violoncello And Orchestra
        see Adagio Nach Keltischen
        Melodien, For Violoncello And
        Orchestra
    Ave Maria, For Violoncello And
        Orchestra (Konzertstück for
        Violoncello and Orchestra, Op.
        61) [8']
        2.2.2.2. 4.2.3.0. timp,strings,
        vcl solo
        SIMROCK perf mat rent   (B1314)
    Canzonetta [5'] Op. Posth.
        2.2.2.2. 4.2.0.0. timp,perc,harp,
        strings
        SIMROCK perf mat rent   (B1315)
    Concerto for Clarinet, Viola and
        Orchestra, Op. 88 [17']
        2.3.2.2. 4.2.0.0. timp,strings,
        clar/vln solo,vla solo
        SIMROCK perf mat rent   (B1316)

BRUCH, MAX (cont'd.)

Concerto for 2 Pianos and Orchestra,
Op. 88a [22']
2.3.2.2. 4.2.3.0. timp,strings,
2pno soli
SIMROCK perf mat rent   (B1317)

Konzertstück for Violin and
Orchestra, Op. 84
KALMUS A6074 sc $25.00, set $40.00,
perf mat rent   (B1318)

Konzertstück for Violoncello and
Orchestra, Op. 61
see Ave Maria, For Violoncello And
Orchestra

Loreley, Die: Einleitung
sc KISTNER f.s.   (B1319)

Serenade Nach Schwedischen
Volksliedern [17']
string orch
SIMROCK perf mat rent   (B1320)

Symphony, Op. 28, in E flat
sc KISTNER f.s., perf mat rent
        (B1321)

BRUCHMANN, KLAUS PETER (1932-   )
Altberliner Lustspiel Ouverture [5']
2.2.2.2. 4.3.4.1. timp,perc,
strings
ORLANDO perf mat rent   (B1322)

BRUCHSTUCK "DIE VORZEICHEN" see Rihm,
Wolfgang

BRUCHSTUCKE see Holliger, Heinz

BRUCKE, DIE, FOR SOLO VOICES AND
ORCHESTRA see Schweinitz, Wolfgang
von

BRUCKEN-FOCK, GERARD H.G. VON
(1859-1935)
Berceuse D'amerique
sc BROEKMANS 199 f.s., perf mat
rent   (B1323)

Suite Bretonne
sc BROEKMANS 216 f.s., perf mat
rent   (B1324)

BRUCKNER, ANTON (1824-1896)
Four Small Orchestral Pieces
see Vier Orchesterstücke

Quintet in F,Third Movement, [arr.]
string orch [6'] KALMUS A1015 set
$5.00, pts $10.00, ea.   (B1325)

Quintet in F, [excerpt]
(Almeida) string orch (Adagio,
arr.) sc BOIS f.s., perf mat rent
        (B1326)
Symphony, No. 1, in C minor
min sc KALMUS K01396 $8.75   (B1327)

Symphony, No. 2, in C minor
min sc KALMUS K01397 $7.00   (B1328)

Symphony No. 4 in E flat
min sc KALMUS K00093 $14.25
contains also: Symphony No. 7 in
E   (B1329)

Symphony, No. 5, in B flat
min sc KALMUS K01467 $14.25   (B1330)
sc KUNZEL 10463 $23.00   (B1331)

Symphony, No. 6, in A
min sc KALMUS K01399 $7.00   (B1332)

Symphony, No. 7, in E
(Haas) KALMUS A7168 sc $50.00, set
$120.00, pts $6.00, ea., perf mat
rent   (B1333)
see Symphony No. 4 in E flat

Vier Orchesterstücke [13']
2.2.2.2. 2.2.3.0. timp,strings
(Orel, Alfred) MUSIKWISS. AOE 10033
        (B1334)
(Schoenzeler) "Four Small
Orchestral Pieces" sc KUNZEL
10068 $11.00, ipr   (B1335)

BRUCKNER ESSAY see Redel, Martin
Christoph

BRUDEMARSJ see Madsen, Trygve

BRUDER STUDIO POLKA see Strauss, Eduard

BRUN, FRITZ (1878-1959)
Symphony No. 2 in B flat [45']
3.2.2.3. 4.2.3.1. timp,strings
HUG GH 7320A   (B1336)

Symphony No. 3 in D minor [59']
2.2.2.3. 4.2.0.0. timp,strings
HUG GH 5975 perf mat rent   (B1337)

BRUN, FRITZ (cont'd.)
Symphony No. 4 in E [45']
2.2.2.3. 4.2.0.0. timp,strings
HUG GH 6933 perf mat rent   (B1338)

BRUNEAU, ALFRED (1857-1934)
Attaque Du Moulin, L': Suite [20'30"]
2(pic).2.2.2. 4.2.3.1. timp,perc,
harp,strings
CHOUDENS perf mat rent   (B1339)

BRUNNER, ADOLF (1901-   )
Concerto for Orchestra [25']
3.3.4.3. 4.3.3.1. timp,2perc,
strings
BÄREN. BA 6083   (B1340)

Konzertante Musik [22']
1(pic).1.1+bass clar.1+
contrabsn.alto sax. 1.2.2.1.
timp,2perc,strings,vla solo
BÄREN. BA 6084   (B1341)

BRUNS, VICTOR (1904-   )
Concerto for Clarinet and Orchestra,
Op. 76
1.1.1.1. 2.0.0.0. timp,perc,
strings,clar solo
BREITKOPF-L perf mat rent   (B1342)

Concerto for Double Bass and String
Orchestra, Op. 73
string orch,db solo
BREITKOPF-L perf mat rent   (B1343)

Concerto for English Horn and
Orchestra, Op. 61
1.1.1.1. 2.0.0.0. perc,strings,
English horn solo
(edition for english horn and
piano- no. eb 7529) BREITKOPF-L
perf mat rent   (B1344)

Concerto for Flute, English Horn and
Orchestra, Op. 74
perc,strings,fl solo,English horn
solo
BREITKOPF-L perf mat rent   (B1345)

Concerto for Horn and Orchestra, Op.
63 [20']
1.1.2.1. 0.0.0.0. timp,perc,
strings,horn solo
BREITKOPF-L perf mat rent   (B1346)

Concerto for Oboe, Bassoon and String
Orchestra, Op. 66
string orch,ob solo,bsn solo
BREITKOPF-L perf mat rent   (B1347)

Concerto for Viola and Orchestra, Op.
69
1.1.1.1. 2.0.0.0. timp,perc,
strings,vla solo
BREITKOPF-L perf mat rent   (B1348)

Concerto for Violin and Orchestra,
Op. 53
1.1.1.1. 2.0.0.0. perc,strings,
vln solo
BREITKOPF-L perf mat rent   (B1349)

Kammersinfonie
string orch
BREITKOPF-L perf mat rent   (B1350)

Minna Von Barnhelm: Overture
2.1.2.2. 2.2.0.0. perc,cel,
strings
BREITKOPF-L perf mat rent   (B1351)

Symphony No. 3, Op. 37 [28']
3.2.2.2. 4.3.3.1. timp,perc,
strings
BREITKOPF-L perf mat rent   (B1352)

Symphony No. 5, Op. 64
3.2.2.2. 4.3.3.1. perc,strings
BREITKOPF-L perf mat rent   (B1353)

Symphony No. 6, Op. 67 [25']
3.2.2.2. 4.3.0.0. timp,perc,
strings
BREITKOPF-L perf mat rent   (B1354)

BRUSTAD, BJARNE (1895-1978)
Berceuse for Solo Voice and Orchestra
[4']
fl,2sax,2horn,harp,strings,S solo
NORGE   (B1355)

Concertino for Viola and Chamber
Orchestra [18']
0.2.0.2. 1.1.0.0. hpsd/pno,
strings,vla solo
NORGE   (B1356)

Concerto Grosso [15']
2.1.2.1. 2.2.3.0. strings
NORGE   (B1357)

Fra Barnets Verden [10']
1.1.2.1. 2.1.1.0. timp,perc,pno,
strings
NORGE   (B1358)

BRUSTAD, BJARNE (cont'd.)
Ouverture Festivo [12']
3.2.2.2. 4.3.3.1. timp,perc,harp,
cel,strings
NORGE   (B1359)

Rhapsody for Violin and Orchestra
[18']
2.2.2.2. 4.2.3.1. timp,perc,harp,
pno,strings,vln solo
NORGE   (B1360)

Suite No. 2 [19']
2.2.2.2. 4.3.3.1. timp,perc,harp,
cel,strings
NORGE   (B1361)

Symphony No. 1 [30']
2.2.2.2. 4.3.3.0. timp,perc,harp,
cel,strings,15 solo voices
NORGE   (B1362)

Symphony No. 3 [27']
2.2.2.2. 4.3.3.0. timp,perc,pno,
cel,strings
NORGE   (B1363)

Symphony No. 5 [17']
2.2.2.2. 4.3.3.0. timp,perc,harp,
pno,strings
NORGE   (B1364)

Symphony No. 6 [18']
2.2.2.2. 4.2.3.0. timp,harp,cel,
pno,strings
NORGE   (B1365)

BRUSTAD, KARSTEN (1959-   )
Kekosmesthai [18']
2.2.1.1. 0.0.0.0. perc,pno,
strings
NORGE   (B1366)

Three Pieces For String Orchestra
[16']
string orch
NORGE   (B1367)

BRUUKS see Janssen, Guus

BRUYERES [ARR] see Debussy, Claude

BRUYNÈL, TON (1934-   )
Phases [13']
2.3.3.2. 4.3.3.1. timp,perc,pno,
xylo,strings,electronic tape
sc DONEMUS f.s., perf mat rent
        (B1368)

BRUZDOWICZ, JOANNA (1943-   )
Concerto for Piano and Orchestra
CHOUDENS perf mat rent   (B1369)

Eclairs [8']
CHOUDENS perf mat rent   (B1370)

BRYLLAUP I SKOGEN see Groven, Eivind

BÜCHTGER, FRITZ (1903-1978)
Music, Op. 9
KISTNER   (B1371)

BUCK, OLE (1945-   )
Granulations [17']
3.3.3.3. 3.3.3.0. perc,pno,
strings
HANSEN-DEN perf mat rent   (B1372)

Pastorals [12']
2.2.2.1. 2.2.0.0. perc,strings
HANSEN-DEN perf mat rent   (B1373)

BUCKLEY, JOHN (1951-   )
Concerto for Chamber Orchestra [23']
1.2.0.2. 2.0.0.0. strings
sc UNIV.CR P01717 f.s.   (B1374)

BUCKLIGE PFERDCHEN, DAS: SUITE NO. 2
see Shchedrin, Rodion, Little
Humpback Horse, The: Suite No. 2

BUCOLICA see Legido, Jesus

BUCOLICS see Pitfield, Thomas Baron see
Schober, Brian

BUCZYNSKI, PAWEL
Fallende Blatter
string orch
TONOS perf mat rent   (B1375)
"Music Of Falling Leaves" (co-
edition with Tonos) POLSKIE
        (B1376)

Litania
3.3.3.3. 4.3.3.1. 3perc,strings
TONOS perf mat rent   (B1377)

Music Of Falling Leaves
see Fallende Blatter

BUCZYNSKI, WALTER (1933-   )
Lyric III, For Violoncello And
Orchestra [18']
2.2.2.2. 2.2.0.0. timp,perc,
strings,vcl solo
CAN.MUS.CENT. MI 1313 B926L3

BUCZYNSKI, WALTER (cont'd.)

                       (B1378)
  Lyric V, For Oboe And String
    Orchestra [20']
    string orch,ob solo
    CAN.MUS.CENT. MI 1622 B926L5
                     (B1379)
  Symphony No. 1 [27']
    3.3.3.3. 4.3.3.1. timp,perc,pno,
    harp,strings
    CAN.MUS.CENT. MI 1100 B926SY1
                     (B1380)

BUFFALO CITY GUARD PARADE MARCH see
Johnson, Francis

BUFFERS-VISA, FOR SOLO VOICE AND
ORCHESTRA [ARR.] see Storbekken,
Egil

BUGAKU see Mayuzumi, Toshiro

BUHR, GLENN
  Akasha, Sky [4']
    2(pic).2.0.0. 2.1.1.0. perc,
    strings
    CAN.MUS.CENT. MI 1100 B931AK
                     (B1381)
  Ananda, Joy, For Solo Voice And
    Instrumental Ensemble [10']
    fl,clar,horn,trom,perc,strings,
    solo voice
    CAN.MUS.CENT. MV 1300 B931AN
                     (B1382)
  Ecstasy [10']
    2.2.2(clar in E flat).2. 4.2.3.1.
    timp,2perc,pno&cel,harp,strings
    CAN.MUS.CENT. MI 1100 B831EC
                     (B1383)
  Jyotir, Brilliance [6']
    1(pic).1.1.1. 2.1.1.0. perc,pno,
    strings
    CAN.MUS.CENT. MI 1200 B931JY
                     (B1384)
  Lure Of The Fallen Seraphim [30']
    3.3.4(bass clar,clar in E
    flat).3. 4.3.3.1. timp,3perc,
    pno&cel,harp,strings,opt
    narrator
    CAN.MUS.CENT. MI 1100 B931LU
                     (B1385)

BUILDING BLOCKS see Ford, Ronald

BUISSON ARDENT, LE see Koechlin,
Charles

BUJARSKI, ZBIGNIEW (1933-   )
  Concerto for Strings
    string orch
    POLSKIE   (B1386)

  Concerto for Violin and String
    Orchestra [18']
    string orch,vln solo
    sc POLSKIE f.s.   (B1387)

  Musica Domestica [12']
    string orch
    POLSKIE   (B1388)

  Similis Greco I [17']
    4.2.3.2. 3.4.2.1. harp,pno,
    strings
    sc POLSKIE f.s.   (B1389)

BUKKERITTET, FOR SOLO VOICES AND
ORCHESTRA see Fladmoe, Arvid

BUKOLLA, FOR CLARINET AND ORCHESTRA see
Sigurbjörnsson, Thorkell

BULL, EDVARD HAGERUP (1922-   )
  Chant d'Hommage A Jean Rivier [8'28"]
    2.2.2.2. 2.2.1.0. timp,perc,harp,
    pno,strings
    BILLAUDOT perf mat rent   (B1390)

  Concerto for Saxophone and Orchestra,
    Op. 52a [17']
    2.2.2.2. 2.2.0.0. timp,perc,harp,
    pno,strings,alto sax solo
    NORGE   (B1391)

  Dialogue, For Violin And Chamber
    Orchestra *Op.18b [18']
    pno,strings,vln solo
    NORGE   (B1392)

  Escapades [10'30"]
    3.3.2.2. 4.2.3.1. timp,perc,harp,
    cel,strings
    sc BILLAUDOT f.s., perf mat rent
                     (B1393)
  Guirlandes, For Solo Voice And String
    Orchestra *Op.5 [6']
    string orch,S solo
    NORGE   (B1394)

  Movimenti *Op.56b
    2.2.2.2. 2.2.2.0. timp,perc,harp,
    pno,strings
    NORGE   (B1395)

  Postlude: Pour L'Epilogue D'Une Monde
    *Op.58b
    2.2.2.2. 2.2.2.1. 2perc,harp,

BULL, EDVARD HAGERUP (cont'd.)

    strings
    NORGE   (B1396)

  Serenade, Op. 8 [14']
    3.2.2.2. 4.2.3.1. timp,perc,harp,
    pno,strings
    NORGE   (B1397)

  Sinfonia Humana *Op.37 [23']
    3.2.2.2. 4.2.3.1. timp,perc,harp,
    pno,cel,strings
    NORGE   (B1398)

  Symphony No. 2, Op. 21 [25']
    3.3.3.3. 4.2.3.1. timp,perc,harp,
    pno,cel,strings
    NORGE   (B1399)

  Symphony No. 3, Op. 30 [22']
    2.2.2.2. 4.2.3.1. timp,perc,harp,
    pno,cel,strings
    (Sinfonia espressiva) NORGE (B1400)

  Trois Morceaux Rapsodiques *Op.7
    [10']
    3.2.2.2. 4.2.3.1. timp,perc,harp,
    cel,pno,strings
    NORGE   (B1401)

BULL MAN, THE see Sigurbjörnsson,
Thorkell

BULL TRANSCENDED, THE see Hartke,
Stephen Paul

BULLER, JOHN (1929-   )
  Procenca, For Solo Voice, Guitar, And
    Orchestra [40']
    3.2+English horn.3.2+contrabsn.
    4.3.4.0. 4perc,harp,strings,gtr
    solo,Mez solo
    sc OXFORD 63.079 $45.00, perf mat
    rent   (B1402)

  Theatre Of Memory, The [40']
    4.3+English horn.3+contrabass
    clar.3+contrabsn. 8.4.4.0.
    6perc,cel,harp,strings
    sc OXFORD 77.037 $65.00, perf mat
    rent   (B1403)

  Towards Aquarius
    1.1.1.1. 2.1.2.0. perc,strings,
    electronic tape
    OXFORD perf mat rent   (B1404)

BUMBERBOOM see Hodkinson, Sydney P.

BUNGE, SAS (1924-1980)
  Overture To William Shakespeare's
    Twelth Night, An [15']
    3.2.2.2. 4.2.3.1. timp,2-3perc,
    harp,strings
    sc DONEMUS f.s., perf mat rent
                     (B1405)
  Symfonie In E Kleine Terts [22']
    2.2.2.2. 4.2.3.1. timp,strings
    sc DONEMUS f.s., perf mat rent
                     (B1406)
  Variaties Over Een Frans Volkslied
    2.2.2.2. 2.2.1.0. timp,2perc,
    strings
    sc DONEMUS f.s., perf mat rent
                     (B1407)
BURCHFIELD GALLERY see Gould, Morton

BUREN, JOHN VAN (1952-   )
  Divertimento [9']
    2.2.2.2. 4.3.3.0. strings
    PEER MUSIK perf mat rent   (B1408)

BURG-SERENADE see Koetsier, Jan

BURGAN, PATRICK (1960-   )
  Vagues [18']
    3.3.3.3. 4.3.3.1. timp,2perc,pno&
    cel,harp,strings
    BILLAUDOT perf mat rent   (B1409)

BURGERS, SIMON (1958-   )
  Synthese [11']
    3.3.4.3.3alto sax. 4.3.3.2. timp,
    3perc,2harp,pno,strings
    sc DONEMUS f.s., perf mat rent
                     (B1410)
BURGERSINN WALZER see Strauss, Johann,
[Jr.]

BURGERWEISEN WALZER see Strauss,
Johann, [Jr.]

BURGMÜLLER, NORBERT (1810-1836)
  Overture, Op. 5
    KISTNER perf mat rent   (B1411)

  Symphony No. 1, Op. 2, in C minor
    KISTNER perf mat rent   (B1412)

  Symphony No. 2, Op. 11, in D
    KISTNER perf mat rent   (B1413)

BURGON, GEOFFREY (1941-   )
  Acquainted With Night, For Solo Voice
    And Orchestra [15']
    timp,harp,strings,B solo
    CHESTER perf mat rent   (B1414)

  Bleak House Suite [15']
    1(pic).0.1(bass clar).1.
    1.1(cornet).0.0. harp,strings
    CHESTER perf mat rent   (B1415)

  Brideshead Variations [18']
    1(pic).1(English horn).0.1.
    1.1.0.0. harp,strings
    CHESTER perf mat rent   (B1416)

  Canciones Del Alma, For Solo Voices
    And Strings
    sc CHESTER CH 55569 perf mat rent
                     (B1417)
  Golden Fish, The [18']
    2.2.2.2. 4.2.3.0. timp,strings
    CHESTER perf mat rent   (B1418)

  May Day Prelude [5']
    1.1.1.0. 1.1.1.0. perc,string
    quin
    CHESTER perf mat rent   (B1419)

  Nunc Dimittis for Solo Voice and
    Orchestra [3']
    trp,strings,S/T solo
    CHESTER JWC 576 perf mat rent
                     (B1420)
  Title Divine, For Solo Voice And
    Orchestra
    2(pic).2+English horn.3(bass
    clar).2+contrabsn. 4.3.3.1.
    timp,2perc,harp,pno&cel,
    strings,S solo
    CHESTER perf mat rent   (B1421)

  Trial Of Prometheus, The [25']
    2+pic.2+English horn.2(clar in E
    flat)+bass clar.2+contrabsn.
    4.3.3.1. timp,3perc,harp,pno,
    strings
    CHESTER perf mat rent   (B1422)

  World Again, The, For Solo Voice And
    Orchestra [23']
    3(pic).3(English horn).3(bass
    clar).3(contrabsn). 4.3.3.1.
    timp,perc,harp,strings,S solo
    CHESTER perf mat rent   (B1423)

BURIAN, EMIL FRANTIŠEK (1904-1959)
  May [50']
    1.1.2.1. 1.1.1.0. timp,perc,cel,
    harp,strings,narrator
    SUPRAPHON   (B1424)

BURLAS, LADISLAV (1927-   )
  Symphony No. 2
    SLOV.HUD.FOND   (B1425)

BURLESK see Sköld, Sven see Söderman,
[Johan] August

BURLESQUE, FOR FLUTE, BASSOON AND
ORCHESTRA see Kosma, Joseph

BURLESQUE, FOR VIOLIN AND ORCHESTRA see
Vacek, Miloš

BURLESQUE OVERTURE see Tarp, Svend Erik

BURN see Norgaard, Per

BURRITT, LLOYD (1940-   )
  Reflection, For Solo Voice And
    Orchestra
    1.1.1.1. 2.1.1.0. perc,pno,
    strings,Mez solo
    CAN.MUS.CENT. MV 1400 B971RE
                     (B1426)
  Symphony [7']
    2.2.2.2. 4.2.3.0. timp,strings
    CAN.MUS.CENT. MI 1100 B971SY
                     (B1427)
  Three Autumn Songs, For Solo Voice
    And Orchestra [8']
    1.1.1.1. 1.0.0.0. perc,pno,
    strings,Mez solo
    CAN.MUS.CENT. MV 1300 B971TH
                     (B1428)
BURSCHENWANDERUNG POLKA see Strauss,
Johann, [Jr.]

BURT, FRANCIS (1926-   )
  Morgana [15']
    1.1.1.1. 1.1.1.0. strings
    UNIVER. perf mat rent   (B1429)

BUS, JAN (1961-   )
  Praefixum [7']
    3.3.3.3. 4.3.3.1. timp,4perc,pno,
    strings
    sc DONEMUS f.s., perf mat rent
                     (B1430)
BUSCH, RICHARD (1947-   )
  In Dulci Jubilo [12']
    1.2.1.2. 2.1.0.0. timp,perc,pno,
    12vln,4vla,4vcl,2db
    MARGUN BP 1049 perf mat rent
                     (B1431)

BUSCH-ORPHAL, ULRICH (1955-   )
Concerto for Violoncello and
Orchestra [18']
2.2.2.2. 4.2.3.1. 3perc,strings,
vcl solo
SIKORSKI perf mat rent   (B1432)

Gegen Den Strom [11']
4.3.3.2. 4.2.3.1. 5perc,harp,
strings
SIKORSKI perf mat rent   (B1433)

Quellen I [5']
4.3.3.3. 4.2.3.1. perc,pno,
strings
(winds may be reduced to .2222
4231. 2.2.2.2. 4.2.3.1.) SIKORSKI
perf mat rent   (B1434)

Quellen II [4']
3.3.3.3. 4.2.3.1. perc,pno,
strings
(winds may be reduced to 2.2.2.2.
4.2.3.1.) SIKORSKI perf mat rent
(B1435)

Quellen III [11']
4.3.3.3. 4.2.3.1. perc,pno,
strings
SIKORSKI perf mat rent   (B1436)

BUSH, ALAN [DUDLEY] (1900-   )
For A Festal Occasion [6']
2.2.2.2. 4.2.3.0. timp,perc,org,
strings
NOVELLO perf mat rent   (B1437)

BUSH, GEOFFREY (1920-   )
Finale For A Concert [5']
2(pic).1.2.1. 2.2.1.0. 2perc,
strings
NOVELLO perf mat rent   (B1438)

Three Little Pieces For Strings [10']
string orch
NOVELLO perf mat rent   (B1439)

BUSONI, FERRUCCIO BENVENUTO (1866-1924)
Berceuse Elegiaque
KALMUS A6186 sc $8.00, set $20.00,
perf mat rent   (B1440)

Berceuse Elegiaque [arr.]
(Adams, John) 2.1.1+bass clar.2.
2.0.0.0. timp,harp,cel&pno,
strings [8'] HENDON perf mat rent
(B1441)

Concerto for Piano and String
Orchestra in D minor
(Sitsky, Larry) string orch,pno
solo BREITKOPF-W sc PB 5160 f.s.,
pts OB 5160 f.s.   (B1442)

Lustspiel-Overture *Op.38
KALMUS A6389 sc $20.00, set $40.00,
pts $2.00, ea., perf mat rent
(B1443)

Nocturne Symphonique *Op.43
KALMUS A3957 sc $10.00, set $25.00,
pts $1.25, ea., perf mat rent
(B1444)

Turandot: Suite
KALMUS A7188 sc $50.00, set $80.00,
pts $3.00, ea., perf mat rent
(B1445)

Turandot: Verzweiflung Und Ergebung
pts BREITKOPF-L OB 2187 f.s.
(B1446)

BUSSER, HENRI-PAUL (1872-1973)
Carosse Du St. Sacrement, Le: Prelude
[2'15"]
CHOUDENS perf mat rent   (B1447)

BUSSOTTI, SYLVANO (1931-   )
Bal Miro, Le: Suite No. 1
4.2.4.3. 4.3.3.1. 5perc,cel,harp,
pno,strings
RICORDI-IT 134204 perf mat rent
(B1448)

Catalogo E Questo No. 1, Il [33'43"]
3.3.3.3. 4.3.2.1. timp,3perc,cel,
harp,pno,strings
(Opus Cygne) sc RICORDI-IT 132971
f.s., perf mat rent   (B1449)

Catalogo E Questo No. 2, Il
3.3.3.3. 4.3.2.1. timp,3perc,
strings
(Raragramma) sc RICORDI-IT 133507
f.s., perf mat rent   (B1450)

Catalogo E Questo No. 2, Il:
Pomeriggio Musicale
2.2.2.2. 2.2.0.0. timp,bass drum,
strings
RICORDI-IT 133301 perf mat rent
(B1451)

Catalogo E Questo No. 3, Il
3.3.3.3. 4.3.2.1. 5perc,cel,pno,
harp,strings
RICORDI-IT 133852 perf mat rent
(B1452)

Catalogo E Questo No. 3, Il:
Intermezzo, For Viola And
Orchestra
3.3.3.3. 4.3.2.1. 5perc,cel,pno,
harp,strings,vla solo

BUSSOTTI, SYLVANO (cont'd.)

RICORDI-IT 133855 perf mat rent
(B1453)

Catalogo E Questo No. 3, Il: La
Fiorentinata [20']
3.3.3.3. 4.3.2.1. 5perc,cel,harp,
strings
RICORDI-IT 133761 perf mat rent
(B1454)

Catalogo E Questo No. 3, Il: Timpani
3.2.3.2. 4.3.2.0. timp,4perc,
harp,cel,strings
RICORDI-IT 134100 perf mat rent
(B1455)

Catalogo E Questo No. 4, Il: H-III
[20']
4.3.3.3.sax. 4.3.2.1. 5perc,cel,
harp,pno,strings
RICORDI-IT 134336 perf mat rent
(B1456)

Dai, Dimmi, Su! [20']
1(pic).1.1.1. 1.0.0.0. timp,perc,
pno 4-hands,cel,vln,vcl
sc RICORDI-IT 132845 f.s., perf mat
rent   (B1457)

Lorenzaccio: Aria Di Mara, For Solo
Voice And Orchestra
clar,horn,3trp,3perc,2gtr,pno,
harmonium,cel,vln,vcl,db,S solo
(Taverna, G.) RICORDI-IT 132077
perf mat rent   (B1458)

Lorenzaccio Symphony I, For Solo
Voice And Orchestra [20']
3.3.4.3. 4.2.3.1. timp,2perc,
vibra,xylo,pno,2gtr,2harp,cel,
harmonium,strings,S solo
RICORDI-IT 132219 perf mat rent
(B1459)

Lorenzaccio Symphony II [20']
5.3.4.3.sax. 4.4.3.1. timp,2perc,
vibra,xylo,pno,2gtr,2harp,cel,
glock,harmonium,strings
RICORDI-IT 132533 perf mat rent
(B1460)

Passion Selon Sade, La: Solo
2(pic).1+ob_d'amore.2(clar in E
flat).2. 2.0.0.0. perc,pno,cel,
harp,vcl
(Gorli, S.) RICORDI-IT 132760 perf
mat rent   (B1461)

Poesia Di De Pisis, For Solo Voice
And Instrumental Ensemble [5']
1.1.3.1. 1.1.0.0. cel,harp,pno,
vln,vla,vcl,db,S solo
RICORDI-IT 132389 perf mat rent
(B1462)

Rosso [6']
3.3.3.3. 4.3.2.1. 5perc,cel,harp,
strings
sc RICORDI-IT 133663 f.s., perf mat
rent   (B1463)

"...BUT THIS IS A LANDSCAPE, MONSIEUR
DALI!" see Merilainen, Usko

BUTLER, MARTIN (1960-   )
Cavalcade
3.3.3.3. 4.3.3.1. perc,strings
sc OXFORD f.s.   (B1464)

Concertino for Chamber Orchestra
[14']
1.1.1.1. 1.1.1.0. perc,pno&cel,
strings
sc OXFORD $27.50, perf mat rent
(B1465)

Fixed Doubles
3.3.3.3. 4.3.3.1. timp,3perc,pno&
cel,strings
OXFORD perf mat rent   (B1466)

Flights Of Col, The
3.3.3.3. 4.3.3.3.1. timp,perc,harp,
pno,strings
sc OXFORD $35.00, perf mat rent
(B1467)

BUTTERCUP, FOR SOLO VOICE AND ORCHESTRA
see Tveitt, Geirr, Smorblomster,
For Solo Voice And Orchestra

BUTTERFLIES see Jacobsen, Julius,
Papillons

BUTTERFLY LOVERS, THE, FOR PIANO AND
ORCHESTRA see Chen, Gang

BUTTERFLY LOVERS, THE, FOR VIOLIN AND
ORCHESTRA see Chen, Gang

BUTTERWORTH, ARTHUR (1923-   )
Concertante *Op.27 [17']
0.2.0.0. 2.0.0.0. strings
NOVELLO perf mat rent   (B1468)

Symphony No. 2 [26']
2(pic)+pic.2+English horn.2+bass
clar.2+contrabsn. 4.3.3.1.
timp,perc,strings
CHESTER JWC-A perf mat rent (B1469)

BUTTERWORTH, GEORGE SAINTON KAYE
(1885-1916)
Shropshire Lad, A [11']
2.2+English horn.2+bass clar.2.
4.2.3.1. timp,harp,strings
min sc EULENBURG UE01382 $5.00
(B1470)
KALMUS A7189 sc $15.00, set $25.00,
pts $1.00, ea., perf mat rent
(B1471)

BUTTING, MAX (1888-1976)
Triptychon
sc PETERS 4658 f.s.   (B1472)

BUTZKO, YURI (1938-   )
Feierlicher Lobgesang [23']
string orch
SIKORSKI perf mat rent   (B1473)

Sinfonie In Vier Fragmenten [31']
3.3.4.3. 6.3.3.1. timp,perc,harp,
pno,strings
SIKORSKI perf mat rent   (B1474)

Sonata-Ricercar, For Violin And
Chamber Orchestra [35']
timp,perc,harp,pno,strings,vln
solo
VAAP perf mat rent   (B1475)

Sonata-Ricercar, For Violoncello And
Chamber Orchestra [24']
timp,5perc,bells,harp,pno,
strings,vcl solo
SIKORSKI perf mat rent   (B1476)

BUXTEHUDE, DIETRICH (ca. 1637-1707)
Canzonetta [arr.]
see Three Pieces

Sonata da Chiesa in C
(Woldike) string orch,cont sc,pts
HANSEN-GER f.s.   (B1477)

Three Pieces
(Margola) string orch KALMUS A7334
sc $5.00, set $7.50, pts $1.50,
ea.
contains: Canzonetta [arr.];
Vater Unser Im Himmelreich,
Chorale [arr.]; Von Gott Will
Ich Nicht Lassen, Chorale
[arr.]   (B1478)

Vater Unser Im Himmelreich, Chorale
[arr.]
see Three Pieces

Von Gott Will Ich Nicht Lassen,
Chorale [arr.]
see Three Pieces

BY THE LAGOON see Reed, Alfred

BY THE SEA, FOR SOLO VOICE AND
ORCHESTRA see Jordan, Sverre, Ved
Havet, For Solo Voice And Orchestra

BY THE TARN see Goossens, [Sir] Eugene

BY THE VALA LAKE, FOR SOLO VOICE AND
ORCHESTRA see Baden, Conrad, Pa
Valasjoen, For Solo Voice And
Chamber Orchestra

BYRD, WILLIAM (1543-1623)
Carman's Whistle, The [arr.]
(Bantock) string orch KALMUS A5870
sc $3.00, set $5.00   (B1479)

Fantasy From Psalms, Songs And
Sonnets Of 1611
string orch [3'] KALMUS A5710 sc
$5.00, set $6.00   (B1480)

Fantasy No. 2
(Fellowes) string orch [3'] KALMUS
A5709 sc $5.00, set $6.00 (B1481)

John Come Kisse Me Now [arr.]
(Jackson) string orch [5'] KALMUS
A7379 sc $5.00, set $7.50, pts
$1.50, ea.   (B1482)

Prelude And Fantasy [arr.]
(Fellowes; McAlister) string orch
[6'] KALMUS A6383 sc $5.00, set
$7.00, pts $1.50, ea., perf mat
rent   (B1483)

C

CABANILLES, JUAN BAUTISTA JOSÉ
(1644-1712)
Tres Piezas [arr.]
(Moreno Gans, Jose) 2.2.0.2.
2.0.0.0. strings [20'] UNION ESP.
perf mat rent   (C1)

CABLE, HOWARD
Quintemento [12']
2.2.2.2. 4.3.3.1. timp,2perc,
harp,strings,gtr solo,string
quar soli
CAN.MUS.CENT. MI 1450 C115QU (C2)

CACAVAS, JOHN (1930-)
Crimson Slipper [4']
2.2.4.2. 4.3.3.0. perc,strings
BOURNE perf mat rent   (C3)

CACCIA see Holten, Bo see Lauermann,
Herbert

CACIOPPO, CURT
Largo [8']
timp,pno,strings
sc APNM $5.75, perf mat rent   (C4)

To A Child Dancing In The Wind, For
Solo Voice And Orchestra [20']
sc APNM $20.00, perf mat rent (C5)

CACTUS RIEUR ET LA DEMOISELLE QUI
SOUFFRAIT D'UNE SOIF INSATIABLE, LE
see Bouliane, Denys

CADENCE MUSIC see McGuire, John

CADENCIAS see Fernandez Alvez, Gabriel

CADENCIAS, FOR VIOLIN AND ORCHESTRA see
Garcia-Abríl, Antón

CADENZA AND DANCE, FOR VIOLIN AND
ORCHESTRA see Sigurbjörnsson,
Thorkell

CADIZ see Gerhard, Roberto

CAEN WOOD see Josephs, Wilfred

CAFE RIO see Gould, Morton

CAFE WALTZES see Waxman, Franz

CAGE, JOHN (1912-1992)
Dance For Four Orchestras
3.3.3.3. 4.3.3.1. timp,3perc,
harp,pno,16vln,6vla,5vcl,3db
PETERS 66911 perf mat rent   (C6)

Etcetera, For 2-4 Orchestras [30']
PETERS P67119 perf mat rent (C7)

Hymnkus, For Solo Voice And Orchestra
alto fl,clar,bsn,alto sax,tenor
sax,trom,2perc,acord,2pno,vln,
vcl,solo voice
PETERS P67158 perf mat rent (C8)

CAGLIOSTRO: OVERTURE see Reicha, Anton

CAGLIOSTRO QUADRILLE see Strauss,
Johann, [Jr.]

CAHUZAC, LOUIS (1880-1960)
Cantilene, For Clarinet And Orchestra
[4'45"]
1.1.0.1. 1.0.0.0. strings,clar
solo
BILLAUDOT perf mat rent   (C9)

Fantaisie Variee Sur Un Vieil Air
Champetre, For Clarinet And
Orchestra [7'20"]
2.2.0.2. 2.2.3.0. timp,strings,
clar solo
BILLAUDOT perf mat rent   (C10)

Pastorale Cevenole, For Clarinet And
String Orchestra [5'30"]
string orch,clar solo
BILLAUDOT perf mat rent   (C11)

CAJKOVSKIJ, PETR ILJIC
see TCHAIKOVSKY, PIOTR ILYICH

CALDARA, ANTONIO (1670-1736)
Verita Nell'ingnanno, La: Nicomedes'
Aria, For Solo Voice And
Orchestra [4']
0.2.0.1. 0.0.0.0. hpsd,strings,T
solo
SUPRAPHON   (C12)

CALIFORNIA MYSTERY PARK: OVERTURE see
Kievman, Carson

CALISTO see Fongaard, Bjørn

CALLAWAY, ANN (1949-)
Concerto for Bass Clarinet and
Chamber Orchestra [16']
1.1.2.1. 2.1.1.0. 2perc,cel,
strings,bass clar solo
AM.COMP.AL. perf mat rent   (C13)

CALLES Y SUENOS see Raxach, Enrique

CALLING ALL TOURISTS see Lunden-Welden,
Gunnar

CALLIRHOE SUITE see Chaminade, Cécile

CALLS AND CRIES see Balassa, Sándor

CALMEL, ROGER (1921-)
Athena [8'50"]
CHOUDENS perf mat rent   (C14)

Concerto Breve, For Violoncello And
Orchestra [17']
CHOUDENS perf mat rent   (C15)

Concerto Mediterraneen, For Trumpet
And Orchestra [15']
perc,strings,trp solo
BILLAUDOT perf mat rent   (C16)

CALMO, FOR SOLO VOICE AND CHAMBER
ORCHESTRA see Berio, Luciano

CALTABIANO, RONALD (1959-)
Medea, For Solo Voice And Orchestra
[18']
1(pic).1.1+bass clar.1. 1.1.0.0.
vln,vla,vcl,db,S solo
AMP perf mat rent   (C17)

Poplars [15']
MERION perf mat rent   (C18)

CALYPSO SOUVENIR see Gould, Morton

CAMARA DE LOBOS see Gjerstrom, Bjorn G.

CAMARGO GUARNIERI
see GUARNIERI, CAMARGO MOZART

CAMBIALE DI MATRIMONIO, LA: ANCH' IO
SON GIOVANE, FOR SOLO VOICE AND
ORCHESTRA see Rossini, Gioacchino

CAMBIALE DI MATRIMONIO, LA: CHI MAI
TROVA IL DRITTO, IL FONDO, FOR SOLO
VOICE AND ORCHESTRA see Rossini,
Gioacchino

CAMBIALE DI MATRIMONIO, LA: DAREI PER
SI BEL FONDO, FOR SOLO VOICES AND
ORCHESTRA see Rossini, Gioacchino

CAMBIALE DI MATRIMONIO, LA: DITE,
PRESTO, DOVE STA, FOR SOLO VOICES
AND ORCHESTRA see Rossini,
Gioacchino

CAMBIALE DI MATRIMONIO, LA: GRAZIE...
GRAZIE, FOR SOLO VOICE AND
ORCHESTRA see Rossini, Gioacchino

CAMBIALE DI MATRIMONIO, LA: NON C'E IL
VECCHIO SUSSURRONE, FOR SOLO VOICES
AND ORCHESTRA see Rossini,
Gioacchino

CAMBIALE DI MATRIMONIO, LA: PORTERO
COSI IL CAPPELLO, FOR SOLO VOICES
AND ORCHESTRA see Rossini,
Gioacchino

CAMBIALE DI MATRIMONIO, LA: QUAL IRA,
OH CIEL, V'ACCENDE, FOR SOLO VOICES
AND ORCHESTRA see Rossini,
Gioacchino

CAMBIALE DI MATRIMONIO, LA: QUELL'
AMABILE VISINO, FOR SOLO VOICES AND
ORCHESTRA see Rossini, Gioacchino

CAMBIALE DI MATRIMONIO, LA: TORNAMI A
DIR CHE M' AMI, FOR SOLO VOICES AND
ORCHESTRA see Rossini, Gioacchino

CAMBIALE DI MATRIMONIO, LA: VORREI
SPIEGARVI IL GIUBILO, FOR SOLO
VOICE AND ORCHESTRA see Rossini,
Gioacchino

CAMBINI, GIOVANNI GIUSEPPE (1746-1825)
Symphonie Concertante No. 4 In D
*see THREE CENTURIES OF MUSIC IN
SCORE, VOL. 6: CONCERTO V, LATE
CLASSICAL STRINGS AND WINDS

CAMBODIAN SUITE see Norodom Sihanouk

CAMELIEN POLKA see Strauss, Johann,
[Jr.]

CAMERLOHER, JOSEPH (1710-1743)
Symphonies, Three
see Graupner, Christoph,
Symphonies, Four

CAMERLOHER, PLACIDUS VON (1718-1782)
Drei Freisinger Sinfonien *CC3U
(Hoffmann) KALMUS A7094 sc $10.00,
set $15.00, pts $3.00, ea. (C19)

CAMILLERI, CHARLES (1931-)
Concerto for Organ and Orchestra
[23']
perc,strings,org solo
ROBERTON 95411   (C20)

CAMPAGNOLI, BARTOLOMMEO (1751-1827)
Symphonie Concertante
see Vogler, [Abbe] Georg Joseph,
Symphony

CAMPANA, JOSE LUIS (1949-)
Abfuhr [18']
1.1.1.1. 1.1.1.1. pno,cel/
synthesizer,2vln,vla,vcl,db
sc BILLAUDOT f.s., perf mat rent
                 (C21)

Circoli Viziosi [17'30"]
1.1.1.1. 1.1.1.0. perc,2vln,vla,
vcl,db
BILLAUDOT perf mat rent   (C22)

Splitting [18']
3(pic,alto fl).3(English
horn).3(bass
clar).3(contrabsn). 4.3.3.1.
2perc,harp,pno,cel,strings
LEMOINE perf mat rent   (C23)

Trieb 1 [10']
3.3.3.3. 4.3.3.1. timp,4perc,
harp,pno,cel,strings
BILLAUDOT perf mat rent   (C24)

Trieb 2, For 4 Percussion And
Orchestra
3.3.3.3. 4.3.3.1. cel,harp,pno,
strings,4perc soli
[13'50"] BILLAUDOT perf mat rent
                 (C25)

CAMPANAE PRAGENSES see Kapr, Jan

CAMPANE DI RAVELLO see Corigliano, John

CAMPANELLO, IL: BELLA COSA, AMICI CARI,
FOR SOLO VOICE AND ORCHESTRA see
Donizetti, Gaetano

CAMPANELLO, IL: DA ME LUNGI ANCOR
VIVENDO, FOR SOLO VOICES AND
ORCHESTRA see Donizetti, Gaetano

CAMPANELLO, IL: HO UNA BELLA, UN'
INFIDELE, FOR SOLO VOICES AND
ORCHESTRA see Donizetti, Gaetano

CAMPANELLO, IL: MESCI, MESCI E SPERDA
IL VENTO, FOR SOLO VOICE AND
ORCHESTRA see Donizetti, Gaetano

CAMPANELLO, IL: MIO SIGNORE VENERATO,
FOR SOLO VOICES AND ORCHESTRA see
Donizetti, Gaetano

CAMPANELLO, IL: NON FUGGIR; T' ARRESTA,
INGRATA, FOR SOLO VOICES AND
ORCHESTRA see Donizetti, Gaetano

CAMPBELL-TIPTON, LOUIS (1877-1921)
Spirit Flower, A, For Solo Voice And
Orchestra
1.1.1.1. 1.1.1.0. timp,strings,
solo voice
SCHIRM.G perf mat rent   (C26)

CAMPO DEI FIORI, IL, FOR TRUMPET AND
ORCHESTRA see Kennan, Kent Wheeler

CAMPO TRAVIESA see Patterson, Michael

CAMPRA, ANDRÉ (1660-1744)
Carnaval De Venise, Le: Suite No. 1
[arr.]
(Blanchard, R.) 2rec,2ob,2bsn,perc,
strings BILLAUDOT perf mat rent
                 (C27)
Carnaval De Venise, Le: Suite No. 2
[arr.]
(Blanchard, R.) 2rec,2ob,2bsn,perc,
strings BILLAUDOT perf mat rent
                 (C28)
Carnaval De Venise, Le: Suite No. 3
[arr.]
(Blanchard, R.) 2rec,2ob,2bsn,2trp,
perc,hpsd,strings BILLAUDOT perf
mat rent   (C29)

Florete Prata, For Solo Voice And
Orchestra
2fl,strings,cont,countertenor
COSTALL C.3407 perf mat rent (C30)

Laudate Dominum, For Solo Voice And
String Orchestra
(Durand, H.A.) string orch,cont,B
solo [11'] COSTALL C.3406 perf

CAMPRA, ANDRÉ (cont'd.)

mat rent (C31)

Noces De Venus, Les: Suite [arr.]
(Vaubourgoin, M.) 2rec,2ob,2bsn,
horn,trp,timp,strings BILLAUDOT
perf mat rent (C32)

O Jesu Amantissime, For Solo Voices
And Orchestra
(Durand, H.A.) 2fl,strings,cont,TB
soli [17'] COSTALL C.3405 perf
mat rent (C33)

CANADIAN COASTLINES, FOR SOLO VOICE AND
CHAMBER ORCHESTRA see Austin, Larry

CANADIAN DANCES: SET 1 see Crawley,
Clifford

CANADIAN TRIBUTE see Knight, Eric

CANADIANA, FOR PIANO AND ORCHESTRA see
Goldberg, Theo

CANAT, ANNE EDITH
Livre D'heures, For Solo Voices And
Orchestra [23']
1.1.1.0. 0.1.0.0. harp,org,perc,
vln,vla,vcl,SATB soli
study sc JOBERT $21.75, perf mat
rent (C34)

CANCION DESESPERADA, FOR SOLO VOICES
AND CHAMBER ORCHESTRA see Otero,
Francisco

CANCION ULTIMA, FOR SOLO VOICE AND
ORCHESTRA see Leyendecker, Ulrich

CANCIONERO DE PEDRELL, FOR SOLO VOICE
AND INSTRUMENTAL ENSEMBLE see
Gerhard, Roberto

CANCIONES DEL ALMA, FOR SOLO VOICES AND
STRINGS see Burgon, Geoffrey

CANCIONES TORERAS, FOR SOLO VOICE AND
ORCHESTRA see Gerhard, Roberto

CANCOES TIPICAS BRASILEIRAS, FOR SOLO
VOICE AND ORCHESTRA see Villa-
Lobos, Heitor

CANCONETA, FOR VIOLIN AND STRING
ORCHESTRA see Rodrigo, Joaquín

CANDIDE: SUITE FOR HARPSICHORD AND
ORCHESTRA see Constant, Marius

CANDLELIGHT, FOR PIANO AND ORCHESTRA
see Silverman, Faye-Ellen

CANIDE-IOUNE-SABATH, FOR SOLO VOICE AND
ORCHESTRA see Villa-Lobos, Heitor

CANONIC OVERTURE: ARMS RACING see
Matthews, Colin

CANSLER, LARRY
Mojave, For Narrator And Orchestra
[17']
2.2.3.2. 4.4.4.1. timp,perc,harp,
pno,strings,narrator
NEWAM 19009 perf mat rent (C35)

CANTABILE see Chailley, Jacques see
Vasks, Peteris

CANTABILE EXPRESSIVO, FOR VIOLONCELLO
AND ORCHESTRA see Maingueneau,
Louis

CANTARES, FOR VOICE AND ORCHESTRA see
Brief, Todd

CANTATA DE NAVIDAD, FOR SOLO VOICE AND
ORCHESTRA see Orrego-Salas, Juan A.

CANTATA, "E QUANDO SARA MAI CHE ALLE
MIE PENE", FOR SOLO VOICE AND
STRING ORCHESTRA [ARR.] see
Jommelli, Niccolo

CANTATA, "GIA LA NOTTE SI AVVICINA",
FOR SOLO VOICE AND STRING
ORCHESTRA, [ARR.] see Jommelli,
Niccolo

CANTATA NO. 35: GEIST UND SEELE WIRD
VIRWIRRET, FOR SOLO VOICE AND
ORCHESTRA see Bach, Johann
Sebastian

CANTATA NO. 49: ICH GEH' UND SUCHE MIT
VERLANGEN, FOR SOLO VOICES AND
ORCHESTRA see Bach, Johann
Sebastian

CANTATA NO. 49: ICH GEH' UND SUCHE MIT
VERLANGEN, FOR SOLO VOICES AND
ORCHESTRA see Bach, Johann
Sebastian

CANTATA NO. 51: JAUCHZET GOTT IN ALLEN
LANDEN, FOR SOLO VOICE AND
ORCHESTRA see Bach, Johann
Sebastian

CANTATA NO. 53: SCHLAGE DOCH GEWUNSCHTE
STUNDE, FOR SOLO VOICE AND
ORCHESTRA see Bach, Johann
Sebastian

CANTATA NO. 54: WIDERSTEHE DOCH DER
SÜNDE, FOR SOLO VOICE AND ORCHESTRA
see Bach, Johann Sebastian

CANTATA NO. 58: ACH GOTT, WIE MANCHES
HERZELEID, FOR SOLO VOICES AND
ORCHESTRA see Bach, Johann
Sebastian

CANTATA NO. 82: ICH HABE GENUG, FOR
SOLO VOICE AND ORCHESTRA see Bach,
Johann Sebastian

CANTATA NO. 152: TRITT AUF DIE
GLAUBENSBAHN, FOR SOLO VOICES AND
ORCHESTRA see Bach, Johann
Sebastian

CANTATA NO. 170: VERGNÜGTE RUH,
BELIEBTE SEELENLUST, FOR SOLO VOICE
AND ORCHESTRA see Bach, Johann
Sebastian

CANTATA NO. 199: MEIN HERZE SCHWIMMT IM
BLUT: FOR SOLO VOICE AND ORCHESTRA
see Bach, Johann Sebastian

CANTATA NO. 202: WEICHET NUR, BETRÜBTE
SCHATTEN, FOR SOLO VOICE AND
ORCHESTRA see Bach, Johann
Sebastian

CANTATA NO. 204: ICH BIN IN MIR
VERGNUGT, FOR SOLO VOICE AND
ORCHESTRA see Bach, Johann
Sebastian

CANTATA NO. 209: NON SA CHE SIA DOLORE,
FOR SOLO VOICE AND ORCHESTRA see
Bach, Johann Sebastian

CANTATA NO. 210: O HOLDER TAG,
ERWÜNSCHTE ZEIT, FOR SOLO VOICE AND
ORCHESTRA see Bach, Johann
Sebastian

CANTATA NO. 211: SCHWEIGT STILLE,
PLAUDERT NICHT, FOR SOLO VOICES AND
ORCHESTRA see Bach, Johann
Sebastian

CANTATA Y, FOR SOLO VOICE AND ORCHESTRA
see Balassa, Sándor

CANTATE CANTICA SOCII see Sonninen,
Ahti

CANTATE POUR CORDES see Prevost, Andre

CAN'TCHA LINE 'EM see Still, William
Grant

CANTELOUBE DE MALARET, MARIE-JOSEPH
(1879-1957)
Chants D'Auvergne, For Solo Voice And
Orchestra, Vol. 1
(contains: Series 1 and 2) sc
HEUGEL HE 33662 f.s. (C36)

Chants D'Auvergne, For Solo Voice And
Orchestra, Vol. 2
(contains: Series 3 and 4) sc
HEUGEL HE 33663 f.s. (C37)

Chants D'Auvergne, For Solo Voice And
Orchestra, Vol. 3
(contains: Series 5) sc HEUGEL
HE 33664 f.s. (C38)

CANTERBURY PILGRIMS, THE: SUITE [ARR.]
see Dyson, George

CANTERVILLE GHOST, THE: SCENES see
Knaifel, Alexander

CANTERVILLE GHOST, THE: SCENES, FOR
SOLO VOICES AND CHAMBER ORCHESTRA
see Knaifel, Alexander

CANTI COMMENTATI see Ullman, Bo

CANTI D'AMORE, FOR SOLO VOICE AND
ORCHESTRA see Hazon, Roberto

CANTI DEL SOLE, FOR SOLO VOICE AND
ORCHESTRA see Rands, Bernard

CANTI DI EURIDICI see Schuback, Peter

CANTI DI MAIAKOVSKI, FOR SOLO VOICES
AND INSTRUMENTAL ENSEMBLE see
Gentilucci, Armando

CANTI E CAPRICCI, FOR VIOLONCELLO AND
ORCH see Kruyf, Ton de

CANTI LUNATICI, FOR SOLO VOICE AND
ORCHESTRA see Rands, Bernard

CANTI SACRI, FOR SOLO VOICE AND
ORCHESTRA see Hazon, Roberto

CANTI SPIRITUALI DI RAGAZZI D'OGGI, FOR
SOLO VOICE AND ORCHESTRA see Hazon,
Roberto

CANTICLE, FOR PERCUSSION AND CHAMBER
ORCHESTRA see Wienhorst, Richard

CANTICLE OF THE EVENING BELLS, FOR
FLUTE AND ORCHESTRA see Schwantner,
Joseph

CANTICLE OF THE SUN, FOR SOLO VOICE AND
INSTRUMENTAL ENSEMBLE see Harris,
Roy Ellsworth

CANTICO DEI CANTICI see Pedini, Carlo

CANTILENA E MARCIA POPULAIRE NO. 1 see
Koch, Erland von

CANTILENAS AND INTERLUDES see Rajna,
Thomas

CANTILENE, FOR CLARINET AND ORCHESTRA
see Cahuzac, Louis

CANTILENE, FOR VIOLIN AND ORCHESTRA see
Simonis, Jean-Marie

CANTIQUE see Lloyd, Jonathan see
Massenet, Jules

CANTIQUE D'AMOUR see Markevitch, Igor

CANTIQUE DES CANTIQUES, LE, FOR SOLO
VOICE AND ORCHESTRA see Chatman,
Stephen, Song Of Solomon, The, For
Solo Voice And Orchestra

CANTIUNCULAE AMORIS, FOR SOLO VOICE AND
STRING ORCHESTRA see Füssl, Karl-
Heinz

CANTO see Adomian, Lan

CANTO CONTINUO [ARR.] see Keizer, Henk

CANTO D'ANTUNNO see Szöllösy, Andras

CANTO DELLE BALENE see Skouen, Synne

CANTO DI SPETTRO, FOR VIOLONCELLO AND
ORCHESTRA see Schuback, Peter

CANTO D'OMAGGIO see Jensen, Ludwig
Irgens

CANTO ELEGIACO see Brevik, Tor

CANTO I see Stroe, Aurel

CANTO II see Stroe, Aurel

CANTO LIRICO, FOR TRUMPET AND ORCHESTRA
see Zaninelli, Luigi

CANTO NOTTURNO, FOR SOLO VOICE AND
CHAMBER ENSEMBLE see Gentilucci,
Armando

CANTON, EDOUARDO (1934-)
D'un Bout A L'autre [8']
1.1.2.0. 2.2.1.0. 3perc,harp,
strings,electronic tape
BILLAUDOT perf mat rent (C39)

Opera-Bus, Chapitres II, III, VI
1.0.1.1. 1.1.1.0. 3perc,harp,pno,
strings,electronic tape,solo
voice
BILLAUDOT perf mat rent (C40)

CANTOS, FOR SAXOPHONE AND ORCHESTRA see
Niculescu, Stefan

CANTUS IN MEMORY OF BENJAMIN BRITTEN
see Pärt, Arvo

CANYON, THE see Glass, Philip

CANZO, FOR SOLO VOICE AND ORCHESTRA see
Blaustein, Susan

CANZONA A 12 see Cavalli, (Pietro)
Francesco

CANZONA, [ARR.] see Gabrieli, Giovanni

CANZONA CONCERTANTE NO. 1, OP. 57, FOR
ENGLISH HORN AND ORCHESTRA see
Turok, Paul Harris

CANZONA CONCERTANTE NO. 2, OP. 63, FOR
TROMBONE AND ORCHESTRA see Turok,
Paul Harris

CANZONA CONCERTANTE NO. 3, OP. 64 see
Turok, Paul Harris

CANZONA DI BAROCCO see Czyz, Henryk

CANZONA FOR DOUBLE STRING ORCHESTRA see
  Gabrieli, Giovanni, Canzona Per
  Doppia Orchestra D'archi

CANZONA, OP. 119C see Lerstad, Terje B.

CANZONA PER DOPPIA ORCHESTRA D'ARCHI
  see Gabrieli, Giovanni

CANZONA SONATA, FOR VIOLA AND STRING
  ORCHESTRA see Kenins, Talivaldis

CANZONE NO. 26 see Schein, Johann
  Hermann

CANZONE PER SONAR see Marez Oyens, Tera
  de

CANZONE QUARTI TONI [ARR.] see
  Gabrieli, Giovanni

CANZONETTA see Bruch, Max see Sibelius,
  Jean

CANZONETTA, FOR OBOE AND STRING
  ORCHESTRA see Kochan, Ernst

CANZONETTA, FOR OBOE AND STRING
  ORCHESTRA [ARR.] see Barber, Samuel

CANZONETTA, FOR VIOLIN AND ORCHESTRA
  see Sköld, Sven

CANZONETTA [ARR.] see Buxtehude,
  Dietrich

CANZONI FOR PRISONERS see Schafer, R.
  Murray

CAPDENAT, PHILIPPE (1934-   )
  Croce È Delizia, For Solo Voice And
    Instrumental Ensemble [20']
    fl,pic,clar,bass clar,trom,
    2marimba,prepared pno,strings,S
    solo
    AMPHION perf mat rent   (C41)

  Palindrome En Chaconne II [15']
    3.3.3.3. 4.3.3.1. timp,2perc,
    strings
    AMPHION perf mat rent   (C42)

CAPDEVIELLE, PIERRE (1906-1969)
  Deux Apologues D'Oscar Wilde, For
    Solo Voices And Orchestra [21']
    3.3.3.2. 4.3.3.1. timp,4perc,cel,
    2harp,pno,strings,MezT soli
    BILLAUDOT perf mat rent   (C43)

CAPE COD SUITE see Adolphus, Milton

CAPINERA, LA, FOR SOLO VOICE AND
  ORCHESTRA [ARR.] see Benedict,
  [Sir] Julius

CAPPELLI, GILBERTO (1952-   )
  Andando Nel Sole Che Abbaglia [15']
    2.2.2.2. 2.2.0.0. timp,strings,
    vln solo,vla solo
    RICORDI-IT 133310 perf mat rent
                                   (C44)

CAPRICCI DEL DOLORE, I see Ullman, Bo

CAPRICCI E CADENZE, FOR HARPSICHORD AND
  ORCHESTRA see Pennisi, Francesco

CAPRICCIO AND FIVE COMMENTS see Ogdon,
  Wilbur L.

CAPRICCIO BRILLANT, FOR PIANO AND
  ORCHESTRA see Mendelssohn-
  Bartholdy, Felix

CAPRICCIO BRILLANT, FOR PIANO AND
  ORCHESTRA see Mendelssohn-
  Bartholdy, Felix

CAPRICCIO CONCERTANTE see Susskind,
  Walter

CAPRICCIO ESPAGNOL see Rimsky-Korsakov,
  Nikolai

CAPRICCIO FOR PIANO AND ORCHESTRA (1929
  VERSION) see Stravinsky, Igor

CAPRICCIO GIOVANILE see Albertsen, Per
  Hjort

CAPRICCIO ITALIEN see Tchaikovsky,
  Piotr Ilyich

CAPRICCIO PIAN' E FORTE see Ruders,
  Poul

CAPRICCIO STRAVAGANTE see Farina, Carlo

CAPRICCIO VIENNESE, FOR VIOLIN AND
  ORCHESTRA see Stuppner, Hubert

CAPRICE, FOR PIANO AND CHAMBER
  ORCHESTRA see Sigurbjörnsson,
  Thorkell

CAPRICE NO. 13, FOR VIOLIN AND
  ORCHESTRA [ARR.] see Paganini,
  Niccolo

CAPRICE NO. 20, FOR VIOLIN AND
  ORCHESTRA [ARR.] see Paganini,
  Niccolo

CAPRICE NO. 24, FOR VIOLIN AND
  ORCHESTRA [ARR.] see Paganini,
  Niccolo

CAPRICE NORVEGIEN, NR. 1, 2 OG 3 see
  Kristoffersen, Fridthjof

CAPRICE VIENNOIS, FOR VIOLIN AND
  ORCHESTRA [ARR.] see Kreisler,
  Fritz

CAPRICES, FIVE, FOR VIOLIN AND STRING
  ORCHESTRA [ARR.] see Paganini,
  Niccolo

CAPRICES ON THE NAME SCHOENBERG, FOR
  PIANO AND ORCHESTRA see Lee, Noel

CAPRICHO INTERIORANO see Cordero, Roque

CAPRICORN CONCERTO, FOR FLUTE AND
  CHAMBER ORCHESTRA see Kocsar,
  Miklos

CAPTAINS COURAGEOUS: SUITE see Waxman,
  Franz

CAPTIVE, LA, FOR SOLO VOICE AND
  ORCHESTRA see Berlioz, Hector
  (Louis)

CAPTIVE, THE, FOR SOLO VOICE AND
  CHAMBER ORCHESTRA see Edwards,
  George

CAPUA, RINALDO DI
  see RINALDO DI CAPUA

CAPULETI ED I MONTECCHI, I: E SERBATO A
  QUESTO ACCIARO, FOR SOLO VOICE AND
  ORCHESTRA see Bellini, Vincenzo

CAPULETI ED I MONTECCHI, I: MORTE IO
  NON TEMO, FOR SOLO VOICE AND
  ORCHESTRA see Bellini, Vincenzo

CAPULETI ED I MONTECCHI, I: OH QUANTE
  VOLTE, OH QUANTE, FOR SOLO VOICE
  AND ORCHESTRA see Bellini, Vincenzo

CAPULETI ED I MONTECCHI, I: SE ROMEO T'
  UCCISE UN FIGLIO, FOR SOLO VOICE
  AND ORCHESTRA see Bellini, Vincenzo

CAPULETI ED I MONTECCHI, I: SI,
  FUGGIRE: A NOI NON RESTA, FOR SOLO
  VOICES AND ORCHESTRA see Bellini,
  Vincenzo

CAPULETI ED I MONTECCHI, I: STOLTO! AD
  UN SOL MIO GRIDO, FOR SOLO VOICES
  AND ORCHESTRA see Bellini, Vincenzo

CARA, SE LE MIE PENE, FOR SOLO VOICE
  AND ORCHESTRA see Mozart, Wolfgang
  Amadeus

CARACTERES see Tisne, Antoine

CARAVANES see Tomasi, Henri

CARCERI D'INVENZIONE I see Ferneyhough,
  Brian

CARDI, MAURO
  Melos, For Solo Voice And Orchestra
    [11']
    3.2.2.2. 4.2.0.0. 2perc,harp,cel,
    strings,S solo
    RICORDI-IT 133593 perf mat rent
                                   (C45)

CARILLONS see Durey, Louis

CARISSIMA see Elgar, [Sir] Edward
  (William)

CARL, ROBERT
  Distant Shore, The [9']
    2.1.1.1. 1.1.1.0. perc,harp,
    strings
    sc AM.COMP.AL. $14.50, perf mat
    rent   (C46)

  Distant Shore II, The, For Solo Voice
    And Chamber Orchestra [12']
    pic,fl,horn,trp,perc,4vln,2vla,
    2vcl,db,S solo
    AM.COMP.AL. sc $10.65, pts $7.60
                                   (C47)

  Images Of Birth [16']
    2.2.2.2. 4.3.3.0. perc,harp,pno&
    cel,strings
    sc AM.COMP.AL. $38.50, perf mat
    rent   (C48)

CARL SANDBURG SUITE see Wilder, Alec

CARLES, MARC (1933-   )
  Images Romanes [19']
    2perc,cel,strings,fl solo,ob
    solo,vcl solo,hpsd solo
    BILLAUDOT perf mat rent   (C49)

CARLSEN, PHILIP
  Fair Seed-Time, For Solo Voice And
    Orchestra [10']
    2.2.2.2. 2.1.1.0. perc,pno,
    strings,T solo
    sc AM.COMP.AL. $31.40   (C50)

  Palette [8']
    1.1.1.1. 1.1.1.0. perc,harp,pno,
    strings
    sc AM.COMP.AL. $16.50   (C51)

CARLSSON, BENGT (1890-1953)
  Suite, Op. 13 [12']
    string orch
    FAZER perf mat rent   (C52)

CARLSTEDT, JAN (1926-   )
  Intrada *Op.43
    2.2.2.2. 2.2.2.0. timp,perc,
    strings
    STIM perf mat rent   (C53)

  Metamorphosi Per Archi *Op.42 [15']
    string orch
    STIM   (C54)

CARLUCCIO, FRANCESCO (1953-   )
  Overture [12']
    3.3.4.3. 4.3.3.0. timp,bass drum,
    harp,strings
    RICORDI-IT 133228 perf mat rent
                                   (C55)

CARMAN'S WHISTLE, THE [ARR.] see Byrd,
  William

CARMEN CRIATURALIS, FOR HORN AND
  INSTRUMENTAL ENSEMBLE see Terzian,
  Alicia

CARMEN FANTASY, A, FOR TRUMPET AND
  ORCHESTRA see Proto, Frank

CARMEN FANTASY, FOR FLUTE AND ORCHESTRA
  see Wilson, Ransom

CARMEN: PRELUDE see Bizet, Georges

CARNAVAL [ARR.] see Schumann, Robert
  (Alexander)

CARNAVAL DE VENISE, LE: SUITE NO. 1
  [ARR.] see Campra, André

CARNAVAL DE VENISE, LE: SUITE NO. 2
  [ARR.] see Campra, André

CARNAVAL DE VENISE, LE: SUITE NO. 3
  [ARR.] see Campra, André

CARNAVAL DES ANIMAUX, LE see Saint-
  Saëns, Camille

CARNAVAL ROMAIN, LE see Berlioz, Hector
  (Louis)

CARNET DE CROQUIS [ARR.] see Satie,
  Erik

CARNEVAL IN ROM: BALLETTMUSIK see
  Strauss, Johann, [Jr.]

CARNEVAL-SPEKTAKEL QUADRILLE see
  Strauss, Johann, [Jr.]

CARNEVALS-BOTSCHAFTER WALZER see
  Strauss, Johann, [Jr.]

CARNIVAL HUMORESQUE see Weiner, Leo,
  Fasching

CARNIVAL IN PARIS see Svendsen, Johan
  (Severin), Karneval I Paris

CARNIVAL OF THE ANIMALS see Saint-
  Saëns, Camille, Carnaval Des
  Animaux, Le

CARNIVAL OF VENICE, FOR FLUTE AND
  ORCHESTRA, [ARR.] see Briccialdi,
  Giulio

CARNIVAL OF WALES see Mathias, William

CARNIVAL OVERTURE see Dvorák, Antonín

CARNIVAL SCENES see Bennett, Frank

CAROLINA SEASONS see Valenti, Michael

CAROSSE DU ST. SACREMENT, LE: PRELUDE
  see Busser, Henri-Paul

CAROUSEL SUITE, FOR NARRATOR AND
  CHAMBER GROUP see Russo, William
  Joseph

CARPENTER, JOHN ALDEN (1876-1951)
Blue Gal
2.2.2.2. 2.2.2.0. perc,pno,
strings
SCHIRM.G perf mat rent   (C56)

Concerto for Violin and Orchestra
2(pic).2(English horn).2.2.
4.3.3.1. timp,perc,harp,cel,
pno,strings,vln solo
SCHIRM.G perf mat rent   (C57)

Home Road, The, For Solo Voice And
Orchestra [arr.]
(De Lamarter, Eric) 2.2.2.2.
4.2.3.1. timp,harp,strings,solo
voice SCHIRM.G perf mat rent
(C58)

Little Indian; Little Dancer
(Strasser) 1.1.2.1.2sax. 2.2.1.0.
timp,perc,strings [3'] KALMUS
A5745 pno-cond sc $2.00, set
$25.00, perf mat rent   (C59)

Serenade
2.2.2.2. 2.0.0.0. perc,harp,pno,
strings
SCHIRM.G perf mat rent   (C60)

Water Colors, For Solo Voice And
Orchestra [10']
2(pic).1.1(bass clar).1. 2.2.0.0.
perc,pno&cel,strings,solo voice
SCHIRM.G perf mat rent   (C61)

CARR, BENJAMIN (1768-1831)
Federal Overture [arr.]
(Franceschini, Romulus)
2(pic).2.2.2. 2.2.2.0. timp,perc,
strings [8'] KALMUS A3988 sc
$27.00, set $40.00, perf mat rent
(C62)

CARR, EDWIN
Symphony No. 1 [18']
3.3.3.3. 4.3.3.1. timp,perc,harp,
pno,strings
sc WAI-TE-ATA f.s.   (C63)

CARRAUD, GASTON (1869-1920)
Nuits, Les [47']
3.3.3.4. 4.4.3.1. perc,cel,2harp,
strings
ESCHIG perf mat rent   (C64)

CARRES MAGIQUES see Philippot, Michel
Paul

CARRIKER, ROB (1954-   )
Mattapan Rag [arr.]
(Schuller, Gunther) 1.1.1.1.
1.1.1.1. perc,banjo,pno,2vln,vla,
vcl,db [4'] MARGUN MP1047 sc
$8.00, set $30.00, pts $22.00
(C65)

CARSON, PHILIPPE
Collages [6']
2.1.1.2. 2.1.2.0. 2perc,harp,
strings,electronic tape
BILLAUDOT perf mat rent   (C66)

CARTASTRACCIA, FOR SAXOPHONE AND
ORCHESTRA see Kinkelder, Dolf de

CARTER, ELLIOTT COOK, JR. (1908-   )
Celebration Of Some 100 X 150 Notes,
A [3']
2+pic.2+English horn.2+bass
clar.2+contrabsn. 4.3.3.1.
timp,perc,pno/cel,strings
HENDON perf mat rent   (C67)

Concerto for Oboe and Orchestra [20']
1(alto fl,pic).0.1(bass clar).0.
1.0.1.0. perc,strings,ob solo,
concertino group: 4vla, perc
HENDON perf mat rent   (C68)

In Sleep, In Thunder, For Solo Voice
And Instrumental Ensemble
1(pic,alto fl).1(English
horn).1(bass clar).1. 1.1.1.0.
perc,pno,2vln,vla,vcl,db,T solo
min sc HENDON 979 $32.00, perf mat
rent   (C69)

Penthode [18']
1(pic,alto fl).1(English
horn).1(clar in E flat)+bass
clar(contrabass clar).1.
1.2.1.1. 3perc,harp,pno,2vln,
vla,vcl,db
HENDON perf mat rent   (C70)

Remembrance [5']
2+pic.2+English horn.2+bass
clar.2+contrabsn. 4.3.3.1.
timp,perc,pno/cel,strings
HENDON perf mat rent   (C71)

Syringa, For Solo Voices And
Instrumental Ensemble
alto fl,English horn,clar&bass
clar,bass trom,perc,pno,gtr,
string quar,MezB soli
sc AMP $60.00   (C72)

CARULLI, FERDINANDO (1770-1841)
Petite Concerto, For Guitar And
Orchestra *Op.140
2ob,2horn,strings,gtr solo
(Riehle) SCHOTTS sc CON 204 $25.00,
set CON 204-50 $48.00   (C73)

CASA GUIDI, FOR SOLO VOICE AND
ORCHESTRA see Argento, Dominick

CASABLANCA: SUITE see Steiner,
Max(imillian Raoul Walter)

CASADESUS, FRANCIS (1870-1954)
Bertrand De Born: Suite
CHOUDENS perf mat rent   (C74)

CASADESUS, ROBERT MARCEL (1899-1972)
Capriccio, Op. 49 for Piano and
String Orchestra [17']
string orch,pno solo
SCHIRM.G perf mat rent   (C75)

CASANOVA see Sylviano, R.

CASANOVA, ANDRÉ (1919-   )
Cinq Melodies, For Solo Voice And
Chamber Orchestra [9']
1.1.1.1. 0.1.1.0. perc,harp,4vla,
4vcl,2db,T solo
BILLAUDOT perf mat rent   (C76)

Prelude for String Orchestra [8']
string orch
min sc BILLAUDOT f.s., perf mat
rent   (C77)

Serenade for Flute and Instrumental
Ensemble [18'30"]
0.0.1.1. 0.1.1.0. xylo,harp,
string quar,fl solo,
clavitimbre
min sc BILLAUDOT f.s., perf mat
rent   (C78)

Strophes [10'30"]
2.2.2.2. 2.1.1.0. timp,xylo,
strings
min sc BILLAUDOT f.s., perf mat
rent   (C79)

CASCANDO, FOR SOLO VOICE, VIOLIN, AND
STRING ORCHESTRA see Lutyens,
Elisabeth

CASE JANICE, THE, FOR SOLO VOICE AND
ORCHESTRA see Germeten, Gunnar,
Tilfellet Janice, For Solo Voice
And Orchestra

CASELLA, ALFREDO (1883-1947)
Italia *Op.11
KALMUS A 6455 sc $25.00, set
$75.00, pts $3.00, ea., perf mat
rent   (C80)

Pupazzetti
KALMUS A3956 sc $20.00, set $40.00,
perf mat rent   (C81)

Suite A Jean Hure *Op.13
KALMUS A6089 sc $35.00, set $80.00,
perf mat rent   (C82)

CASKEN, JOHN (1949-   )
Erin, For Doublebass And Orchestra
[13']
2ob,2horn,strings,db solo
SCHOTT perf mat rent   (C83)

Masque
study sc SCHOTT ED 12156 $39.00,
perf mat rent   (C84)

Orion Over Farne [20']
3(pic).3.3(bass clar).3. 0.0.0.0.
timp,3perc,pno,cel,strings
study sc SCHOTT ED 12335 $50.00,
perf mat rent   (C85)

Vaganza [18']
1(pic,alto fl).1(English
horn).1(clar in E flat,bass
clar).1(contrabsn).soprano sax.
1.1.1.0. perc,harp,org,2vln,
vla,vcl,db
study sc SCHOTT ED 12326 f.s., perf
mat rent   (C86)

CASSANDRE see Leclerc, Sophie

CASSATION NO. 3 IN B-LYDISCH see
Wolter, Detlef

CASSATIONS NOS. 1-2, K. 63, K. 99 see
Mozart, Wolfgang Amadeus

CASSE-NOISETTE: GRAND PAS DE DEUX
[ARR.] see Tchaikovsky, Piotr
Ilyich, Nutcracker: Grand Pas De
Deux [arr.]

CASSE-NOISETTE: PAS DE DEUX see
Tchaikovsky, Piotr Ilyich,
Nutcracker: Pas De Deux

CASSIOPEIA, FOR PERCUSSION AND
ORCHESTRA see Takemitsu, Toru

CASSUTO, ALVARO (1938-   )
In Memoriam: Pedro De Freitas Branco
[12']
4.3.4.2+contrabsn. 6.4.3.1. timp,
perc,strings
SCHIRM.G perf mat rent   (C87)

CASTAGNOLI, GIULIO (1958-   )
Klang [8']
13strings
SONZOGNO perf mat rent   (C88)

CASTALDI, PAOLO (1930-   )
Clap, For Clarinet And Orchestra
1.2.2.2.sax. 2.1.1.0. timp,perc,
harp,strings,clar solo
RICORDI-IT 133452 perf mat rent
(C89)

CASTALDO, JOSEPH F. (1927-   )
Askesis
1.1.1.0. 1.1.1.0. perc,pno,
strings
(all players double on percussion
instruments) PEER perf mat rent
(C90)

Concerto for Violoncello and
Orchestra [23']
2+pic.2.2.2. 2.2.2.0. perc,harp,
strings,vcl solo
KALMUS A7296 sc $40.00, set
$100.00, pts $3.50, ea., perf mat
rent   (C91)
SCHIRM.G perf mat rent   (C92)

Elegy for Solo Voice and Orchestra
[17']
1.1.1.1. 1.1.0.0. perc,harp,pno,
strings,S solo
KALMUS A7295 sc $35.00, set $45.00,
pts $3.50, ea., perf mat rent
(C93)

Eye Of God, The [25']
3.2.3(clar in E flat).3. 4.3.3.1.
4perc,pno,cel,2harp,strings
SCHIRM.G perf mat rent   (C94)

CASTEL DEL MONTE, FOR HORN AND
ORCHESTRA see Rota, Nino

CASTEREDE, JACQUES (1926-   )
Concerto for Piano and Orchestra, No.
2 [24']
2+pic.2(English horn).2.2.
3.3.3.1. timp,4perc,strings,pno
solo
RIDEAU perf mat rent   (C95)

Concerto for Piano and String
Orchestra [23']
string orch,pno solo
SALABERT perf mat rent   (C96)

Figures, For Harpsichord, Violin,
Viola, Violoncello, And Chamber
Orchestra [14'15"]
2.1.2.1. 2.1.1.0. perc,harp,
strings,hpsd solo,vln solo,vla
solo,vcl solo
BILLAUDOT perf mat rent   (C97)

Images Pour Un Jour D'ete, For 2
Pianos And Orchestra [16']
2(pic).2(English horn).2.2.
2.2.2.0. timp,perc,strings,2pno
soli
RIDEAU perf mat rent   (C98)

Rhapsodie Pour Un Jour De Fete, For
Guitar And Orchestra [16']
3.2.2.2. 4.3.3.0. 3perc,strings,
gtr solo
BILLAUDOT perf mat rent   (C99)

CASTIGLIONI, NICCOLÒ (1932-   )
Cavatina, For Piccolo And Orchestra
[10']
1.2.2.0. 0.1.0.0. perc,cel,hpsd,
pno,harp,16vln,pic solo
RICORDI-IT 133333 perf mat rent
(C100)

Comme Io Passo L'estate
(Testoni, G.) 2.2.2.2. 2.2.1.0.
perc,harp,cel,strings [9']
RICORDI-IT 133654 perf mat rent
(C101)

Concerto for 3 Pianos and Orchestra
[15']
5.4.4.0. 3.3.3.0. timp,perc,hpsd,
cel,strings,3pno soli
RICORDI-IT 133681 perf mat rent
(C102)

Couplets, For Harpsichord And
Orchestra [11']
4.2.3.2. 2.3.1.0. timp,perc,harp,
pno,cel,strings,hpsd solo
RICORDI-IT 132921 perf mat rent
(C103)

Dickinson Lieder, For Solo Voice And
Orchestra [10']
2(pic).2.2(clar in E flat).1.
1.2.0.0. perc,pno,harp,cel,
strings,S solo
RICORDI-IT 132674 perf mat rent

CASTIGLIONI, NICCOLÒ (cont'd.)
(C104)
Figure, For Solo Voice And Orchestra
[25']
3.3.3.3. 3.3.3.0. timp,perc,harp,
cel,pno,strings,S solo
RICORDI-IT 133607 perf mat rent
(C105)
Fiori Di Ghiaccio, For Piano And
Orchestra [12']
3.2.2.0. 2.2.0.0. perc,harp,hpsd,
cel,16vln,pno solo
RICORDI-IT 133535 perf mat rent
(C106)
Geistliches Lied, For Solo Voice And
Orchestra [5']
2.2.2.2. 2.2.0.0. timp,perc,
strings,S solo
RICORDI-IT 133547 perf mat rent
(C107)
Moreaux Lyriques, For Oboe And
Orchestra [19']
2.1.2.2. 2.2.1.0. 3perc,harp,pno,
hpsd,cel,strings,ob solo
RICORDI-IT 133515 perf mat rent
(C108)
Petite Suite (from Oberon And The
Lords' Masque) [11']
2.3.2.2. 2.3.3.0. timp,perc,harp,
pno,cel,hpsd,strings
RICORDI-IT 133316 perf mat rent
(C109)
Quodlibet [11'30"]
2.2.2.0. 1.1.0.0. perc,cel,harp,
4vln,3vla,2vcl,db
sc RICORDI-IT 132559 f.s., perf mat
rent
(C110)
Sinfonia Con Giardino [7'30"]
2.2.2.1. 2.2.1.0. perc,harp,hpsd,
cel,pno,strings
sc RICORDI-IT 132828 f.s., perf mat
rent
(C111)
Sinfonietta for Solo Voice and
Orchestra [7']
2.2.2.2. 2.2.1.0. timp,perc,harp,
pno,cel,strings,S solo
RICORDI-IT 133062 perf mat rent
(C112)
Small Is Beautiful [12']
3.3.3.3. 3.3.1.0. timp,perc,harp,
pno,cel,hpsd,strings
RICORDI-IT 133702 perf mat rent
(C113)
Zweihundertfunfzig Jahre [10']
2.2.2.2. 2.2.1.0. timp,perc,harp,
pno,cel,hpsd,strings
RICORDI-IT 133297 perf mat rent
(C114)

CASTILLA see Sanjuan, Pedro

CASTLE HOUSE RAG [ARR.] see Europe,
James Reese

CASTLE WALK, THE [ARR.] see Europe,
James Reese

CASTOR ET POLLUX: SUITE see Rameau,
Jean-Philippe

CATALANI, ALFREDO (1854-1893)
Contemplazione [12']
2.2.2.2. 4.2.3.1. timp,strings
sc BSE 1225 f.s., perf mat rent
(C115)
Loreley: Danza Delle Ondine
set KALMUS A5757 $18.00, perf mat
rent
(C116)
Scherzo [8']
2.2.2.2. 4.2.3.1. timp,strings
sc BSE 1224 f.s., perf mat rent
(C117)
Sinfonia in F [20']
2+pic.2.2.2. 2.2.3.1. timp,
strings
sc BSE 115 f.s., perf mat rent
(C118)
Wally, La: Ebben? Ne Andro Lontana,
For Solo Voice And Orchestra
KALMUS A4751 sc $5.00, set $15.00,
pts $1.00, ea., perf mat rent
(C119)
Wally, La: M' Hai Salvato, For Solo
Voice And Orchestra
KALMUS A4753 sc $6.00, set $25.00,
pts $1.00, ea., perf mat rent
(C120)
Wally, La: Ne Mai Dunque Avro Pace,
For Solo Voice And Orchestra
KALMUS A 4752 sc $3.00, set $25.00,
pts $1.00, ea., perf mat rent
(C121)
Wally, La: T' Amo Ben Io, For Solo
Voice And Orchestra
KALMUS A4750 sc $5.00, set $20.00,
pts $1.00, ea., perf mat rent
(C122)

CATALOGO E QUESTO NO. 1, IL see
Bussotti, Sylvano

CATALOGO E QUESTO NO. 2, IL see
Bussotti, Sylvano

CATALOGO E QUESTO NO. 2, IL: POMERIGGIO
MUSICALE see Bussotti, Sylvano

CATALOGO E QUESTO NO. 3, IL see
Bussotti, Sylvano

CATALOGO E QUESTO NO. 3, IL:
INTERMEZZO, FOR VIOLA AND ORCHESTRA
see Bussotti, Sylvano

CATALOGO E QUESTO NO. 3, IL: LA
FIORENTINATA see Bussotti, Sylvano

CATALOGO E QUESTO NO. 3, IL: TIMPANI
see Bussotti, Sylvano

CATALOGO E QUESTO NO. 4, IL: H-III see
Bussotti, Sylvano

CATALOGUE OF INCIDENTS FROM ROMEO AND
JULIET see Frankel, Benjamin

CATENA see Karlins, M. William

CATENA III, FOR HORN AND ORCHESTRA see
Karlins, M. William

CATURLA, ALEJANDRO GARCIA
see GARCIA-CATURLA, ALEJANDRO

CAUCASIAN SKETCHES, SERIES II see
Ippolitov-Ivanov, Mikhail
Mikhailovich

CAVALCADE see Butler, Martin see
Muczynski, Robert Stanley

CAVALIERS ANDALOUS see Vellones, Pierre

CAVALLI, (PIETRO) FRANCESCO (1602-1676)
Canzona A 12
(Leppard, Raymond) 2cornetto,4trom,
strings,cont [5'] FABER perf mat
rent
(C123)

CAVATINA see Halffter, Ernesto

CAVATINA, FOR PICCOLO AND ORCHESTRA see
Castiglioni, Niccolò

CAVATINA, FOR VIOLIN AND ORCHESTRA see
Björkander, Nils

CAVATINA CAMBIATA see Arnestad, Finn

CAVATINE, FOR HORN AND ORCHESTRA see
Dubois, Theodore

CAVILLO ET CARILLON see Fürst, Paul
Walter

CAZDEN, NORMAN (1914-1980)
Lonely Ones, The *Op.44 [9']
1(pic).1.1.1. 1.1.1.0. perc,
strings
MCA perf mat rent
(C124)

Symphony, Op. 49 [30']
3.3.3.3. 4.3.3.1. timp,pno,
strings
MCA perf mat rent
(C125)

Woodland Valley Sketches *Op.73
[10']
3.1.3.1.opt A rec. 2.1.1.0.
triangle,strings
MCA perf mat rent
(C126)

CE QU'ON ENTEND SUR LA MONTAGNE see
Liszt, Franz

CECCONI, MONIC (1936-   )
Hommage A... [19']
ob,clar,bsn,sax,3vln,2vla,2vcl,db
BILLAUDOT perf mat rent
(C127)

Muse Qui Est La Grace, La, For Solo
Voices And Orchestra [15']
2.2.3.2. 2.2.2.1. timp,2perc,cel,
harp,strings,SBar soli
BILLAUDOT perf mat rent
(C128)

CEDRE ET LE PALMIER, LE see Kabalevsky,
Dmitri Borisovich

CELEBIDACHIANA see Garcia-Abríl, Antón

CELEBRATION see Chase, Bruce see
Daniels, Melvin L. see Ussachevsky,
Vladimir see Zwilich, Ellen Taaffe

CELEBRATION AT VANDERBURGH see Ott,
David

CELEBRATION OF MAY-DAY see Hoffding,
Finn

CELEBRATION OF SOME 100 X 150 NOTES, A
see Carter, Elliott Cook, Jr.

CELEBRATION OVERTURE see Kulesha, Gary

CELEBRATION OVERTURE, VERSION FOR LARGE
ORCHESTRA see Kulesha, Gary

CELEBRATION SEQUENT I see Stalvey,
Dorrance

CELEBRATION STRUT see Gould, Morton

CELEBRATIONS see Ferritto, John E.

CELEBRATIONS - REFLECTIONS see
Schwartz, Elliott Schelling

CELEBRE, FOR FLUTE AND CHAMBER
ORCHESTRA see Bohmler, Craig

CELESTIAL BIRD, THE, FOR PIANO AND
STRING ORCHESTRA see Karkoff,
Ingvar, Himmelska Fageln, Den, For
Piano And String Orchestra

CELESTIAL MECHANICS see Hillborg,
Anders

CELTIC SET see Cowell, Henry Dixon

CELUI QUI EST COURONNE, FOR SOLO VOICE
AND INSTRUMENTAL ENSEMBLE see
Lenot, Jacques

CENERENTOLA, LA: OVERTURE see Rossini,
Gioacchino

CENG-MEN see Oberson, René

CENT TROIS REGARDS DANS L'EAU, FOR
VIOLIN AND INSTRUMENTAL ENSEMBLE
see Constant, Marius

CENT TROIS REGARDS DANS L'EAU, FOR
VIOLIN AND ORCHESTRA see Constant,
Marius

CENTENARY FIREDANCES see Downes, Andrew

CENTENNIAL WALTZ see Strauss, Johann,
[Jr.]

CENTO see Johnson, A. Paul

CERCHIO, BRUNO (1954-   )
Aurora (from Missa Aurea) [20']
3.3.4.3. 4.3.3.1. timp,perc,
2harp,cel,strings
RICORDI-IT 134067 perf mat rent
(C129)
Larmes Des Rochers, Les
2perc,pno,hpsd,harp,10strings
CURCI perf mat rent
(C130)

CERCHIO E GLI INGANNI, IL see Vacchi,
Fabio

CERCLE DU VENT, LE see Reverdy, Michele

CEREMONIAL 1 see Rands, Bernard

CEREMONIAL 2 see Rands, Bernard

CEREMONIAL NOCTURNE see Zbar, Michel

CEREMONIES see Wallace, William

CERHA, FRIEDRICH (1926-   )
Baal-Gesange, For Solo Voice And
Orchestra [55']
2(pic).3+English horn).3.2+
contrabsn.2sax.
4.3(flügelhorn).4.1. timp,
4perc,harp,gtr,acord,elec org,
strings,Bar solo
sc UNIVER. UE18311 $119.00. perf
mat rent
(C131)
Concerto for Flute, Bassoon and
Orchestra [25']
2.2.2.2. 4.2.3.1. timp,4perc,
strings,fl solo,bsn solo
sc UNIVER. UE17795 f.s., perf mat
rent
(C132)
Concerto for String Orchestra [10']
string orch
study sc DOBLINGER STP 557 f.s.,
perf mat rent
(C133)
Keintate I, For Solo Voice And
Instrumental Ensemble [60']
2clar,2horn,perc,acord,2vln,vla,
vcl,db,med solo
UNIVER. perf mat rent
(C134)
Keintate II, For Solo Voice And
Instrumental Ensemble [25']
2clar,2horn,perc,acord,2vln,vla,
vcl,db,med solo
UNIVER. perf mat rent
(C135)
Monumentum Für Karl Pranti [22']
3(pic).3+English horn.2+bass
clar.2+contrabsn.sax. 5.3.4.0.
timp,2perc,org,strings
UNIVER. perf mat rent
(C136)
Nachtgesang, For Solo Voice And
Orchestra [15']
2(pic,alto fl).1+English horn.1+
bass clar.2(contrabsn).sax.
2.2.2.0. 4-5perc,harp,gtr,

CERHA, FRIEDRICH (cont'd.)

    acord,strings,T solo
    UNIVER. perf mat rent   (C137)

    Requiem Für Rikke, For Solo Voice And
      Orchestra [11']
      2(alto fl).2+English horn.2+bass
      clar.2+contrabsn.soprano sax.
      4.3.3.0. baritone horn,perc,
      strings,T solo
    UNIVER. perf mat rent   (C138)

    Triptychon [11']
      1.1.1.0. 1.0.0.0. strings
      study sc DOBLINGER STP 558 f.s.,
      perf mat rent   (C139)

C'ETAIT UN BAISER, FOR SOLO VOICE AND
    ORCHESTRA see Tomasi, Henri

CETRA, LA, OP. 9, VOL. 1 see Vivaldi,
    Antonio

CETRA, LA, OP. 9, VOL. 2 see Vivaldi,
    Antonio

CHABRIER, [ALEXIS-] EMMANUEL
    (1841-1894)
    Bourree Fantasque
      ENOCH perf mat rent   (C140)

    Cortege Burlesque
      2.2.2.2. 4.2.3.1. timp,perc,
      strings
      (Lacome, P.) BILLAUDOT perf mat
      rent   (C141)

    Elegy, [arr.]
      (Francaix, Jean) 1.1.1.1. 1.0.0.0.
      strings [4'] ESCHIG perf mat rent
              (C142)

    Espana [7']
      2+pic.2.2.4. 4.2+2cornet.3.1.
      timp,perc,2harp,strings
      ENOCH perf mat rent   (C143)

    Gwendoline: Overture [6']
      2+pic.1+English horn.2+bass
      clar.2. 4.2+2cornet.3.1. timp,
      perc,2harp,strings
      ENOCH perf mat rent   (C144)

    Gwendoline: Prelude, Act II [6']
      2+pic.1+English horn.1+bass
      clar.2. 4.2.3.1. timp,2harp,
      strings
      ENOCH perf mat rent   (C145)

    Habanera [3']
      2.1.2.1. 2.2+2cornet.0.0. timp,
      triangle,strings
      ENOCH perf mat rent   (C146)

    Joyeuse Marche [4']
      2+pic.2.2.4. 4.2+2cornet.3.1.
      timp,perc,2harp,strings
      ENOCH perf mat rent   (C147)

    Larghetto, For Horn And Orchestra
      2.2.2.2. 2.0.0.0. harp,timp,
      strings,horn solo
      KALMUS A6750 sc $8.00, set $15.00,
      pts $1.00, ea.   (C148)
      [10'] sc BILLAUDOT $30.00, perf mat
      rent   (C149)

    Menuet Pompeux [arr.]
      (Ravel, Maurice) 2(pic).2.2.2.
      4.2.3.1. timp,perc,harp,strings
      [6'] ENOCH perf mat rent   (C150)

    Prelude Pastoral [5']
      2.2.2.2. 2.2.3.0. timp,harp,
      strings
      BILLAUDOT perf mat rent   (C151)

    Roi Malgre Lui, Le: Danse Slave [5']
      1+pic.2.2.2. 2.0+2cornet.3.0.
      timp,perc,strings
      ENOCH perf mat rent   (C152)

    Roi Malgre Lui, Le: Fete Polonaise
      [8']
      1+pic.2.2.2. 2.0+2cornet.3.0.
      timp,perc,strings
      ENOCH perf mat rent   (C153)

    Suite Pastorale [19']
      2(pic).1.2.2. 2.0+2cornet.3.0.
      timp,perc,harp,strings
      ENOCH perf mat rent   (C154)

    Trois Valses Romantiques [15']
      2+pic.2+English horn.2+bass
      clar.4. 4.3.3.3. timp,perc,
      2harp,strings
      ENOCH perf mat rent   (C155)

CHACCONE ON "IAM DULCIS AMICA" see
    Harvey, Jonathan

CHACONNE AND FUGUE ON A NORWEGIAN FOLK
    TUNE see Kjellsby, Erling, Chaconne
    Og Fuga Over Et Norsk Folketonetema

CHACONNE OG FUGA OVER ET NORSK
    FOLKETONETEMA see Kjellsby, Erling

CHACONNE: PASSION OF THE HEART see
    Thorne, Nicholas C.K.

CHADWICK, GEORGE WHITEFIELD (1854-1931)
    Aphrodite [20']
      3.2+English horn.2+bass clar.2+
      contrabsn. 4.4.3.1. timp,perc,
      cel,harp,strings
      KALMUS A6966 sc $40.00, set $75.00,
      pts $3.00, ea., perf mat rent
              (C156)
    Suite Symphonique In E Flat [30']
      2+pic.2.2.2. 4.3.3.1. timp,perc,
      harp,strings
      KALMUS A6086 sc $50.00, set
      $100.00, perf mat rent   (C157)

    Symphonic Sketches
      min sc KALMUS K01526 $14.25 (C158)

CHAGAGORTIAN, EDUARD (1930-1983)
    Concerto for Clarinet and Orchestra
      [14']
      3.0.4.2. 4.2.1.0. timp,perc,pno,
      strings,clar solo
      SIKORSKI perf mat rent   (C159)
      VAAP perf mat rent   (C160)

CHAGALL WINDOWS, THE see McCabe, John

CHAIKIN, NIKOLAI (1915-   )
    Concerto for Accordion and Orchestra
      in B flat [25']
      2.2.2.2. 4.2.1.0. timp,perc,harp/
      pno,strings,acord solo
      SIKORSKI perf mat rent   (C161)

    Concerto For Bayan And Orchestra
      2.2.2.2. 4.2.1.0. timp,perc,harp/
      pno,strings,bayan solo
      VAAP perf mat rent   (C162)

CHAIKOVSKII, PETR IL'ICH
    see TCHAIKOVSKY, PIOTR ILYICH

CHAILLEY, JACQUES (1910-   )
    Cantabile [8']
      string orch
      BILLAUDOT perf mat rent   (C163)

    Symphony in G minor [25']
      3.3.4.4.alto sax.soprano sax.
      4.3.3.1. timp,3perc,2harp,cel,
      strings
      BILLAUDOT perf mat rent   (C164)

CHAILLY, LUCIANO (1920-   )
    ES-Kammerkonzert
      fl,clar,bass clar,perc,strings
      BSE BSM 14 perf mat rent (C165)

    ES-Konzert
      2+pic.2+English horn.2+clar in E
      flat+bass clar.2+contrabsn.
      4.3.3.1. timp,perc,org,Ondes
      Martenot,pno,harp,strings
      BSE BSM 4 perf mat rent   (C166)

    Newton-Variazioni, For Chamber
      Orchestra [23']
      2(pic).2.2.2. 2.2.2.0. timp,perc,
      harp,strings
      RICORDI-IT 132976 perf mat rent
              (C167)
    Newton-Variazioni, For Instrumental
      Ensemble [23']
      1(pic).1.1(clar in E flat,bass
      clar).1. 1.1.1.0. perc,pno&
      glock&xylo&cel,2vln,vla,vcl,db
      RICORDI-IT 132978 perf mat rent
              (C168)

CHAIN 1 see Lutoslawski, Witold

CHAIN 2, FOR VIOLIN AND ORCHESTRA see
    Lutoslawski, Witold

CHAIN 3 see Lutoslawski, Witold

CHAIRMAN DANCES, THE see Adams, John

CHAKA, FOR SOLO VOICE AND ORCHESTRA see
    Holzer, Gerhard

CHALAIEV, SHIRVANI (1936-   )
    Und Die Welt War Dazwischen..., For
      Solo Voice And Orchestra [18']
      1.1.1.3. bells,drums,
      vibra,cel,pno,strings,A solo
      SIKORSKI perf mat rent   (C169)

CHALLENGE, THE see Fry, Gary D.

CHAMBER CANTATA NO. 1, FOR SOLO VOICE
    AND CHAMBER ORCHESTRA see Kiva,
    Oleh

CHAMBER CANTATA NO. 2, FOR SOLO VOICE
    AND CHAMBER ORCHESTRA see
    Zahortsev, Volodomyr

CHAMBER CANTATA NO. 2, FOR SOLO VOICE
    AND ORCHESTRA see Kiva, Oleh

CHAMBER CANTATA NO. 3, FOR SOLO VOICE
    AND CHAMBER ORCHESTRA see Kiva,
    Oleh

CHAMBER CANTATA NO. 4, FOR SOLO VOICES
    AND CHAMBER ORCHESTRA see Kiva,
    Oleh

CHAMBER CONCERTO see Clement, Sheree
    see Emborg, Jens Laurson see
    Hagerty, Mark see Powers, Anthony

CHAMBER CONCERTO, FOR OBOE, BASSOON AND
    CHAMBER ORCHESTRA see Bottje, Will
    Gay

CHAMBER CONCERTO FOR CLARINET AND
    ELEVEN PLAYERS see Frank, Andrew

CHAMBER CONCERTO FOR 11 INSTRUMENTS see
    Milhaud, Darius

CHAMBER CONCERTO IN THE SHAPE OF A
    SUMMER, FOR FLUTE AND CHAMBER
    ORCHESTRA see Samuel, Gerhard

CHAMBER CONCERTO NO. 1 see Zahortsev,
    Volodomyr

CHAMBER CONCERTO NO.1, FOR DOUBLE BASS
    AND CHAMBER ORCHESTRA see Schwartz,
    Elliott Schelling

CHAMBER CONCERTO NO. 1, FOR FLUTE AND
    STRING ORCHESTRA see Firsova, Elena

CHAMBER CONCERTO NO. 2 see Maegaard,
    Jan

CHAMBER CONCERTO NO. 2, FOR VIOLONCELLO
    AND ORCHESTRA see Firsova, Elena

CHAMBER CONCERTO NO. 3 see Zahortsev,
    Volodomyr

CHAMBER CONCERTO NO.3, FOR PIANO AND
    CHAMBER ORCHESTRA see Schwartz,
    Elliott Schelling

CHAMBER CONCERTO NO. 3, FOR PIANO AND
    ORCHESTRA see Firsova, Elena

CHAMBER CONCERTO NO. 4, FOR SAXOPHONE
    AND INSTRUMENTAL ENSEMBLE see
    Schwartz, Elliott Schelling

CHAMBER FANTASY see Goodman, David

CHAMBER MUSIC see Durko, Zsolt see
    Firsova, Elena

CHAMBER MUSIC, FOR INSTRUMENTAL
    ENSEMBLE see Golob, Jani, Komorna
    Glasba, For Instrumental Ensemble

CHAMBER MUSIC, FOR ORCHESTRA see Golob,
    Jani, Komorna Glasba, For Orchestra

CHAMBER MUSIC, FOR SOLO VOICE AND
    CHAMBER ORCHESTRA see Dorati, Antal

CHAMBER MUSIC 1 see Sallinen, Aulis

CHAMBER MUSIC 2 see Sallinen, Aulis

CHAMBER MUSIC 3, FOR VIOLONCELLO AND
    STRING ORCHESTRA see Sallinen,
    Aulis

CHAMBER MUSIC FOR ORCHESTRA see Parris,
    Robert

CHAMBER MUSIC NO. 2, FOR SOLO VOICE AND
    INSTRUMENTAL ENSEMBLE see Rosenman,
    Leonard

CHAMBER PIECE NO.1 see Wolpe, Stefan

CHAMBER PIECE NO. 2 see Wolpe, Stefan

CHAMBER SYMPHONY see Berkeley, Michael
    see Denisov, Edison Vasilievich see
    Ge, Gan-Ru see Hoffman, Joel see
    Koykkar, Joseph see Lazarof, Henri
    see Lee, Eugene see Milner, Anthony
    see Schuller, Gunther see Spinner,
    Leopold see Tchaikovsky, Boris see
    Zur, Menachem

CHAMBER SYMPHONY FOR OBOE, VIOLA AND
    ORCHESTRA see Holmboe, Vagn

CHAMBER SYMPHONY IN B FLAT see Wolf-
    Ferrari, Ermanno

CHAMBER SYMPHONY NO. 1 see Holmboe,
    Vagn see Luedeke, Raymond see
    Stankovich, Evgeny

CHAMBER SYMPHONY NO. 1, OP. 9 see
    Schoenberg, Arnold

CHAMBER SYMPHONY NO. 2 see Stankovich,
    Evgeny

CHAMBER SYMPHONY NO. 3 see Erkanian, Edvand see Stankovich, Evgeny

CHAMBER SYMPHONY, OP. 110A [ARR.] see Shostakovich, Dmitri

CHAMBER SYMPHONY, OP. 118A [ARR.] see Shostakovich, Dmitri

CHAMBER VARIATIONS see Ekimovsky, Viktor

CHAMINADE, CÉCILE (1857-1944)
Callirhoe Suite *Op.37
2+pic.2.2.4. 4.4.3.1. timp,perc,
harp,strings [14'30"] KALMUS
A5823 sc $35.00, set $80.00, perf
mat rent (C170)

Concert Pieces, For Piano And
Orchestra, Op. 40
2+pic.2+English horn.2.2. 4.2+
2cornet.3.1. timp,perc,strings,
pno solo
ENOCH perf mat rent (C171)

Concertino for Flute and Orchestra,
Op. 107 [7']
1.2.2.2. 4.0.3.1. timp,harp,
strings,fl solo
ENOCH perf mat rent (C172)

CHAMPAGNE, CLAUDE (1891-1965)
Paysanna
sc BERANDOL BER 1807 $9.00 (C173)

CHAMPAGNE PARTY [ARR.] see Strauss,
Johann, [Jr.]

CHAN, KA NIN (1949-)
Land Beautiful, The [15']
string orch
CAN.MUS.CENT. MI 1500 C454LA (C174)

Tai Chi
1.1.0.0. 1.0.0.0. 2perc,harp,pno,
vln,vla,vcl,db
CAN.MUS.CENT. MI 9357 C454T (C175)

CHANCE, NANCY LAIRD (1931-)
Elegy [9']
string orch
MMB perf mat rent (C176)

Liturgy [18']
2.2+English horn.2+bass clar.2+
contrabsn. 4.3+trp in C.2.1.
4perc,cel,harp,strings
SCHIRM.G perf mat rent (C177)

Odysseus, For Solo Voice And
Orchestra [32']
PRESSER perf mat rent (C178)

CHANDOSCHKIN, IWAN
see KHANDOSHKIN, IVAN

CHANG, LAO
White-Haired Girl, The: Suite *see
Chu, Wei

CHANGE see Sønstevold, Gunnar,
Forvandling

CHANGING LANDSCAPE, THE see Gotskosik,
Oleg

CHANNUKA SUITE NO. 1, FOR CHAMBER
ORCHESTRA see Barnes, Milton

CHANSON DE MARIN, FOR SOLO VOICE AND
ORCHESTRA see Tomasi, Henri

CHANSON DE MATIN see Elgar, [Sir]
Edward (William)

CHANSON DE MEPHISTOPHELES, FOR SOLO
VOICE AND ORCHESTRA [ARR.] see
Mussorgsky, Modest Petrovich

CHANSON DE MEPHISTOPHELES DANS LE CAVE
D'AUERBACH, FOR SOLO VOICE AND
ORCHESTRA [ARR.] see Mussorgsky,
Modest Petrovich

CHANSON DE NUIT see Elgar, [Sir] Edward
(William)

CHANSON JOYEUSE see Baker, Michael
Conway

CHANSON LOUIS XIII AND PAVANE, FOR
VIOLIN AND ORCHESTRA [ARR.] see
Kreisler, Fritz

CHANSONNETTES QUADRILLE see Strauss,
Johann, [Jr.]

CHANSONNIER see Retzel, Frank

CHANSONS DE JADIS: SIX SONGS OF
LONELINESS, FOR SOLO VOICE AND
ORCHESTRA see Hodkinson, Sydney P.

CHANSONS VILLAGEOISES, FOR SOLO VOICE
AND ORCHESTRA see Poulenc, Francis

CHANT D'ALOUETTE [ARR.] see
Tchaikovsky, Piotr Ilyich

CHANT D'AMOUR, CHANT DE MORT DE
TROILUS, FOR SOLO VOICE AND
ORCHESTRA see Aubin, Tony

CHANT DE LA FEE DES ILES, FOR SOLO
VOICE AND ORCHESTRA see Tomasi,
Henri

CHANT DE LA "VESLEMØY", FOR VIOLIN AND
STRING ORCHESTRA see Halvorsen,
Johan

CHANT DE SOLITUDE, FOR SOLO VOICES AND
ORCHESTRA see Landowski, Marcel

CHANT DES MONDES, LE, FOR SOLO VOICE,
PIANO AND ORCHESTRA see Brenet,
Therese

CHANT D'HOMMAGE A JEAN RIVIER see Bull,
Edvard Hagerup

CHANT DU DESTIN, LE see Glazunov,
Alexander Konstantinovich

CHANT ELEGIAQUE, FOR CELLO AND
ORCHESTRA see Schmitt, Florent

CHANT ET DANSE, FOR TROMBONE AND
ORCHESTRA see Bondon, Jacques

CHANT OF GLARUS see Balassa, Sándor

CHANT POUR UNE AUTRE GALAXIE see Tisne,
Antoine

CHANT SANS PAROLES [ARR.] see
Tchaikovsky, Piotr Ilyich

CHANTEFABLES, FOR SOLO VOICE AND
ORCHESTRA see Albin, Roger

CHANTERELLE see Felderhof, Jan

CHANTEYS see Perera, Ronald Christopher

CHANTS D'AUTOMNE, FOR SOLO VOICE AND
CHAMBER ORCHESTRA see Denhoff,
Michael

CHANTS D'AUVERGNE, FOR SOLO VOICE AND
ORCHESTRA, VOL. 1 see Canteloube de
Malaret, Marie-Joseph

CHANTS D'AUVERGNE, FOR SOLO VOICE AND
ORCHESTRA, VOL. 2 see Canteloube de
Malaret, Marie-Joseph

CHANTS D'AUVERGNE, FOR SOLO VOICE AND
ORCHESTRA, VOL. 3 see Canteloube de
Malaret, Marie-Joseph

CHANTS DE TSE YEH, FOR SOLO VOICE AND
INSTRUMENTAL ENSEMBLE see Denis,
Didier

CHANTS FAEZ, LES, FOR PIANO AND CHAMBER
ORCHESTRA see Pesson, Gerard

CHANTS LAOTIENS, FOR SOLO VOICE AND
ORCHESTRA see Tomasi, Henri

CHANTS NOIRS see Trojahn, Manfred

CHAPPELL, HERBERT
Paddington Bear's First Concert, For
Narrator And Orchestra [28']
2(pic).2(English horn).2.2.alto
sax. 2.2.0.0. 2perc,harp,
strings,narrator
CHESTER perf mat rent (C179)

CHAPPLE, BRIAN (1945-)
Concerto for Piano and Orchestra
[34']
3(pic).3(English horn).3(clar in
E flat,bass clar).2+contrabsn.
4.3.3.1. timp,perc,strings,pno
solo
CHESTER JWC532 perf mat rent (C180)

Delphine [12']
2(pic).2.2(bass clar).2. 4.2.3.0.
timp,2perc,strings
CHESTER perf mat rent (C181)

Little Symphony [12']
1(pic).2(English horn).0.2.
2.0.0.0. strings
CHESTER perf mat rent (C182)

Venus Flytrap [20']
1(pic).1.1(clar in E flat).1.
1.1.1.0. pno,string quar,db
CHESTER JWC556 perf mat rent (C183)

CHARADES see Feron, Alain

CHARBONNIER, JANINE (1926-)
Generateur 1 Et 2 [8'30"]
1.0.2.0. 1.1.1.0. 2perc,pno,vln,
db
BILLAUDOT perf mat rent (C184)

CHARIOTS see Kay, Ulysses Simpson

CHARIOTS OF FIRE: SUITE, [ARR.] see
Vangelis

CHARIVARI see Gruber, Heinz Karl

CHARIVARI QUADRILLE see Strauss,
Johann, [Sr.]

CHARLES, ERNEST (1895-)
Clouds, For Solo Voice And Orchestra
[arr.]
(Clark, Tom) 1.1.2.1.3sax. 2.2.1.0.
timp,strings,solo voice SCHIRM.G
perf mat rent (C185)

Let My Song Fill Your Heart, For Solo
Voice And Orchestra
2.1.2.1. 2.3.2.0. timp,perc,harp,
strings,solo voice SCHIRM.G perf
mat rent (C186)

Sweet Song Of Long Ago, For Solo
Voice And Orchestra [arr.]
(Clark, Tom) 1.1.2.1.3sax. 2.2.1.0.
timp,glock&vibra,strings,solo
voice SCHIRM.G perf mat rent
(C187)

CHARLES, JON
Snapshots [5']
2+pic.2.3.2. 4.4.4.1. perc,pno,
harp,gtr,elec bass,strings
NEWAM 19010 perf mat rent (C188)

CHARLIE RUTLAGE [ARR.] see Ives,
Charles

CHARM BRACELET, THE see Waxman, Franz

CHARPENTIER, GUSTAVE (1860-1956)
Impressions De Voyage: Munich [40']
3.3.6.5.4sax. 6.4.4.1. 2bugle,
2baritone horn,db tuba,timp,
perc,2harp,gtr,strings
ESCHIG perf mat rent (C189)

CHARPENTIER, JACQUES (1933-)
Acropolis (Symphony No. 7)
LEDUC perf mat rent (C190)

Manque De Chance, For Solo Voice And
Orchestra
LEDUC perf mat rent (C191)

Symphony No. 7
see Acropolis

Vitrail Pour Un Temps De Guerre
LEDUC perf mat rent (C192)

CHARPENTIER, MARC-ANTOINE
(ca. 1634-1704)
Prelude Du Te Deum
(Jetvic, I.) 2trp,strings [2']
BILLAUDOT perf mat rent (C193)

Tenebrae Factae Sunt, For Solo Voice
And String Orchestra
(Lambert, G.) string orch,B solo
COSTALL C.3604 f.s. (C194)

CHARPENTIER, RAYMOND (1880-1960)
Suite Francaise [18']
3.2.2.2. 2.2.2.1. timp,3perc,cel,
harp,strings
BILLAUDOT perf mat rent (C195)

CHARTERHOUSE SUITE, THE, [ARR.] see
Vaughan Williams, Ralph

CHASE, BRUCE
Celebration [6']
3(pic).2.2.2. 4.3.3.1. timp,
3perc,cel&pno,strings
MARKS perf mat rent (C196)

CHASSE, LA, FOR VIOLIN AND ORCHESTRA
[ARR.] see Kreisler, Fritz

CHATMAN, STEPHEN (1950-)
Cantique Des Cantiques, Le, For Solo
Voice And Orchestra
see Song Of Solomon, The, For Solo
Voice And Orchestra

Crimson Dream [14']
3.3.3.3. 4.3.3.1. timp,3perc,
harp,strings
CAN.MUS.CENT. MI 1100 C494CR (C197)

Mirage [10']
2.2.2.2. 4.2.3.1. timp,perc,
strings
CAN.MUS.CENT. MI 1100 C494MI (C198)

Song Of Solomon, The, For Solo Voice
And Orchestra [10']
2.2.2.2. 3.2.0.0. 2perc,pno,harp,
strings,high solo/med solo

CHATMAN, STEPHEN (cont'd.)

"Cantique Des Cantiques, Le, For
Solo Voice And Orchestra"
CAN.MUS.CENT. MV 1400 C494S
(C199)

Variations On A Canadian Folk Song,
For 2 Pianos And Orchestra [10']
2.2.2.2. 2.2.0.0. timp,strings,
2pno soli
CAN.MUS.CENT. MI 1461 C494VA (C200)

CHATSCHATURJAN, ARAM
see KHACHATURIAN, ARAM

CHATTERBOX POLKA see Strauss, Josef,
Plappermoulchen Polka

CHAVARRI, EDUARDO LÓPEZ (1871-1970)
Acuarelas Valencianas [15']
string orch
KALMUS A7401 sc $8.00, set $17.50,
pts $3.50, ea., perf mat rent
(C201)

Valencianas [20']
3(pic).2.2+bass clar.2. 4.2.3.1.
timp,perc,2harp,strings
UNION ESP. perf mat rent (C202)

CHAVEZ, CARLOS (1899-1978)
Baile [4']
3.3.2.4. 4.2.3.1. timp,3perc,pno,
strings
CARLAN perf mat rent (C203)

Concerto for Trombone and Orchestra
[18']
2+pic.2+English horn.2+bass
clar.2+contrabsn. 4.3.3.1.
timp,perc,strings,trom solo
SCHIRM.G perf mat rent (C204)

Cuatro Nocturnos, For Solo Voices And
Orchestra [15']
3.3.3.3. 4.3.3.1. timp,3perc,
harp,pno,strings,SA soli
"Four Nocturnes, For Solo Voices
And Orchestra" CARLAN perf mat
rent (C205)

Elatio [14']
3.3.3.3. 4.3.3.1. timp,3perc,
2harp,pno,strings
study sc CARLAN f.s., perf mat rent
(C206)

Four Nocturnes, For Solo Voices And
Orchestra
see Cuatro Nocturnos, For Solo
Voices And Orchestra

Himno Nacional Mexicano [2']
4.3.4.3. 6.3.3.1. timp,6perc,
harp,cel,strings
CARLAN perf mat rent (C207)

Sonante For String Orchestra [10']
string orch
CARLAN perf mat rent (C208)

Symphony [30']
2.2.2.3. 4.3.3.1. timp,strings
CARLAN perf mat rent (C209)

Toccata [8']
3.3.4.3. 4.3.3.1. timp,3perc,
2harp,strings
CARLAN perf mat rent (C210)

CHAYNES, CHARLES (1925-)
Visions Concertantes, For Guitar And
Strings [20']
7vln,2vla,2vcl,db,gtr solo
RIDEAU perf mat rent (C211)

CHE COSA E QUESTA AMORE, FOR SOLO VOICE
AND ORCHESTRA see Kvandal, Johan

CHE SAI GUARDIANO DELLE NOTTE, FOR
CLARINET AND ORCHESTRA see
Sciarrino, Salvatore

CHEERS! A CELEBRATION MARCH see Gould,
Morton

CHEIRONOMIËS see Antoniou, Theodore

CHELLERI, FORTUNATO (ca. 1690-1757)
Symphony
see Brioschi, Antonio, Symphonies,
Three

CHEMIN DE LA CROIX, LE, FOR SOLO VOICES
AND ORCHESTRA see Baumgartner,
Jean-Paul

CHEMIN-PETIT, HANS (1902-1981)
Concerto Symphonico [12']
2(pic).2+English horn.2+bass
clar.2+contrabsn. 4.2.3.0.
timp,2perc,strings
BOTE perf mat rent (C212)

CHEMINS DE LA NUIT, LES, FOR
VIOLONCELLO AND ORCHESTRA see
Francois, Renaud

CHEN, GANG
Butterfly Lovers, The, For Piano And
Orchestra
3.2.2.2. 4.2.3.1. timp,perc,harp,
strings,pno solo
HONG KONG perf mat rent (C213)

Butterfly Lovers, The, For Violin And
Orchestra (composed with He, Zhan
Hao) [28']
2.2.2.2. 4.2.3.0. timp,perc,harp,
pno,strings,vln solo
HONG KONG perf mat rent (C214)

Fantasy On A Sinkiang Folk Song, For
Violin And Orchestra [arr.]
(Manabu Kawai) 2.2.2.2. 4.2.0.0.
timp,perc,harp,strings,vln solo
[9'] HONG KONG perf mat rent
(C215)

CHEN, PEI-XUN
Yellow Crane House, The [15']
3.2+English horn.3.3. 4.3.3.1.
timp,perc,xylo,vibra,harp,cel,
strings
HONG KONG perf mat rent (C216)

CHEN, QIGANG (1951-)
Lumieres De Guang-Ling [15']
2.1.1.1. 0.0.0.0. 2perc,pno,harp,
3vln,vla,vcl,db
BILLAUDOT perf mat rent (C217)

Poeme Lyrique, For Solo Voice And
Instrumental Ensemble [15']
1.1.1.0. 1.0.0.0. perc,harp,2vln,
vla,vcl,db,solo voice
BILLAUDOT perf mat rent (C218)

CHEN, YI
Duo Ye [7']
1.1.1+clar in E flat.1. 1.0.0.0.
perc,strings
HONG KONG perf mat rent (C219)

Yian Shi, For Viola And Orchestra
[14']
3.2.2.2. 4.3.3.0. timp,perc,
strings,vla solo
HONG KONG perf mat rent (C220)

CHENOO WHO STAYED TO DINNER, THE, FOR
NARRATOR AND ORCHESTRA see
Schickele, Peter

CHENOWETH, GERALD
Cracks-Reforms-Bursts [10']
2.2.2.2. 4.3.3.1. 3perc,strings
sc AM.COMP.AL. $43.65, perf mat
rent (C221)

CHENOWETH, WILBUR (1899-)
Vocalise, For Solo Voice And
Orchestra
2.2.2.2. 1.0.0.0. harp,strings,
solo voice
SCHIRM.G perf mat rent (C222)

CHERNEY, BRIAN (1942-)
Illuminations [19']
string orch
CAN.MUS.CENT. MI 1500 C521IL (C223)

CHERUBINI, LUIGI (1760-1842)
Abencerages, Les: Overture
see Overtures, Four

Anacreon: Overture
see Overtures, Four

Armida: Overture [12']
2.2.2.2. 2.2.0.0. timp,strings
sc BSE 92 f.s., perf mat rent
(C224)

Concerto for Horn and String
Orchestra
(Leloir, E.) string orch,horn solo
[12'] sc BILLAUDOT f.s., perf mat
rent (C225)

Crescendo, Le: Overture [16']
2.2.2.2. 4.2.1.0. strings
sc BSE 1233 f.s., perf mat rent
(C226)

Deux Journees, Les: Overture
see Overtures, Four

Epicure: Overture [10']
2.2.2.2. 2.2.1.0. timp,strings
sc BSE 109 f.s., perf mat rent
(C227)

Marche Funebre [10']
0.2.2.2+contrabsn. 2.2.3.0. timp,
perc,strings
min sc BSE 1111 f.s., perf mat rent
(C228)

Marches Pour La Pompe Funebre De
General Hoche [10']
2.2.2.2. 2.2.3.0. timp,perc,
strings
sc BSE 112 f.s., perf mat rent
(C229)

Medee: Overture
see Overtures, Four

CHERUBINI, LUIGI (cont'd.)

Overtures, Four
min sc KALMUS K00044 $7.00
contains: Abencerages, Les:
Overture; Anacreon: Overture;
Deux Journees, Les: Overture;
Medee: Overture (C230)

Prisonniere, La: Overture [10']
1.2.2.2. 2.2.1.0. strings
BSE 82 perf mat rent (C231)
(Beaudoin) KALMUS A7162 sc $25.00,
set $25.00, pts $1.50, ea., perf
mat rent (C232)

Symphony in D [30']
1.2.2.2. 2.2.0.0. timp,strings
sc BSE 85 f.s., perf mat rent
(C233)
(Winter) KALMUS A5577 sc $25.00,
perf mat rent, set $50.00, pts
$3.00, ea. (C234)

CHERVINSKY, NIKOLAI (1925-)
Hamlet: Suite [37']
3.3.4.3. 4.3.3.1. timp,perc,harp,
pno,org,strings
SIKORSKI perf mat rent (C235)

CHETRO KETL see Neikrug, Marc E.

CHEVALIER DE SAINT-GEORGES
see SAINT-GEORGES, JOSEPH BOULOGNE DE

CHEVEAUX-DE-FRISE see Barry, Gerald

CHEVELURE DE BERENICE see
Boucourechliev, André

CHI DELL'ALTRUI SI VESTE: OVERTURE see
Cimarosa, Domenico

CHI SÀ, CHI SÀ, QUAL SIA, FOR SOLO
VOICE AND ORCHESTRA see Mozart,
Wolfgang Amadeus

CHI VIVE AMANTE, FOR SOLO VOICE AND
ORCHESTRA see Haydn, [Franz] Joseph

CHIARORE DELL'UTOPIA, IL, FOR SOLO
VOICE AND ORCHESTRA see Gentilucci,
Armando

CHIAROSCURO see Milburn, Ellsworth see
Sharman, Rodney

CHIFFRE III see Rihm, Wolfgang

CHIFFRE V see Rihm, Wolfgang

CHIFFRE VII see Rihm, Wolfgang

CHIFFRE-ZYKLUS see Rihm, Wolfgang

CHIHARA, PAUL SEIKO (1938-)
Birds Of Sorrow (Symphony No. 2)
[18']
3(pic).2(English
horn).2.2(contrabsn). 4.4.3.1.
timp,3perc,harp,cel,strings
PETERS 66909 perf mat rent (C236)

Concerto for Guitar and Orchestra
[16']
1.1.0.1. 0.1.0.0. strings,gtr
solo
SCHIRM.G perf mat rent (C237)

Concerto for String Quartet and
Orchestra
4horn,2trp,3trom,timp,perc,
harmonica,string quar soli
SCHIRM.G perf mat rent (C238)

Symphony No. 2
see Birds Of Sorrow

Tempest, The: Suite [50']
2(pic).2.2.2(contrabsn). 4.2.3.1.
timp,3perc,harp,pno/cel,
strings,electronic tape
PETERS P66826A perf mat rent (C239)

CHIITI, GIAN PAOLO (1940-)
Per Orchestra [14']
2.2.2.2. 2.2.0.0. timp,pno,
strings
MMB perf mat rent (C240)

Rencontres, For Flute And Strings
[12']
6vln,2vla,2vcl,db,fl solo
MMB perf mat rent (C241)

Ricercare [17']
1.2.0.1. 2.0.0.0. strings
MMB perf mat rent (C242)

CHILD, PETER B. (1953-)
Clare Cycle, For Solo Voice And
Orchestra [18']
fl&alto fl,ob,clar&bass clar,
perc,pno,2vln,vla,vcl,db,S solo
sc APNM $23.75, perf mat rent
(C243)

CHROMOSPHERE, FOR PERCUSSION AND
   ORCHESTRA see Fukushi, Norio

CHRONICA see Goldschmidt, Berthold

CHRONICA: SUITE see Goldschmidt,
   Berthold

CHRONIK EINES SOMMERTAGES, FOR CLARINET
   AND STRING ORCHESTRA see Prado,
   José-Antonio (Almeida)

CHRONOS see Gudmundsen-Holmgreen, Pelle

CHRUDIMSKA OVERTURE see Skroup,
   František

CHU, WEI
   Harvest Scenes [27']
      3.2.2.2. 4.3.3.1. timp,perc,harp,
         strings
      HONG KONG perf mat rent   (C274)

   Hero's Monument [18']
      3.2+English horn.2.2. 4.3.3.1.
         timp,perc,strings
      HONG KONG perf mat rent   (C275)

   Red Lady, The (composed with Wang,
      Jiu-Fang) [13']
      2.2.2.2. 4.3.3.1. timp,perc,harp,
         strings, bamboo flute
      HONG KONG perf mat rent   (C276)

   White-Haired Girl, The: Suite
      (composed with Chang, Lao; Huan,
      Chin; Ma, Ko) [22']
      3.2.2.2. 4.3.3.1. timp,perc,harp,
         strings, bamboo flute
      HONG KONG perf mat rent   (C277)

CHUECA, FEDERICO (1846-1908)
   Golondrinas, Las [arr.] (composed
      with Valverde, Joaquín)
      (Lotter) "Swallows, The [arr.]" 1+
         pic.2.2.2. 4.2.3.0. perc,strings
         [3'] pno-cond sc,set KALMUS A6154
         $12.00   (C278)

   Swallows, The [arr.]
      see Golondrinas, Las [arr.]

CHUKRUM see Scelsi, Giacinto

CIACCONA see Jommelli, Niccolo

CIACCONA, FOR VIOLIN AND STRING
   ORCHESTRA [ARR.] see Vitali,
   Tommaso Antonio

CIACCONNA, FOR VIOLIN AND ORCHESTRA,
   [ARR.] see Vitali, Tommaso Antonio

CIACONNA SINFONICA see Goldschmidt,
   Berthold

CIAIKOVSKI, PIETRO
   see TCHAIKOVSKY, PIOTR ILYICH

CICLOS, FOR PIANO AND ORCHESTRA see
   Bäck, Sven-Erik

CID, LE: OVERTURE see Massenet, Jules

CIFRA, LA: OVERTURE see Salieri,
   Antonio

CIGALE, LA: SUITE see Massenet, Jules

CIGLIC, ZVONIMIR (1921-   )
   Triptih, For Solo Voice And Orchestra
      [15']
      1(pic).1(English horn).2(bass
         clar).1. 1.1.1.1. timp,perc,
         strings,male solo
      DRUSTVO DSS 1078 perf mat rent
                                     (C279)
CILÉA, FRANCESCO (1866-1950)
   Adriana Lecouvreur: Ecco Il Monologo,
      For Solo Voice And Orchestra
      KALMUS A4756 sc $6.00, set $22.00,
         pts $1.00, ea., perf mat rent
                                     (C280)
   Adriana Lecouvreur: Giusto Cielo, For
      Solo Voice And Orchestra
      KALMUS A4762 sc $3.00, set $22.00,
         pts $1.00, ea., perf mat rent
                                     (C281)
   Adriana Lecouvreur: Io Sono L'umile
      Ancella, For Solo Voice And
      Orchestra
      KALMUS A4754 sc $4.00, set $18.00,
         pts $1.00, ea.   (C282)
   Adriana Lecouvreur: Ma, Dunque, E
      Vero? For Solo Voices And
      Orchestra
      KALMUS A4759 sc $4.00, set $15.00,
         pts $.75, ea., perf mat rent
                                     (C283)
   Adriana Lecouvreur: Maurizio!
      Signore! For Solo Voices And
      Orchestra
      KALMUS A4764 sc $6.00, set $22.00,
         pts $1.00, ea., perf mat rent
                                     (C284)

CILÉA, FRANCESCO (cont'd.)
   Adriana Lecouvreur: Non
      Risponde...Aprite, For Solo
      Voices And Orchestra
      KALMUS A4760 sc $7.00, set $25.00,
         pts $2.00, ea., perf mat rent
                                     (C285)
   Adriana Lecouvreur: Ogni Eco; O
      Vagabonda, For Solo Voice And
      Orchestra
      KALMUS A4757 sc $6.00, set $22.00,
         pts $1.00, ea., perf mat rent
                                     (C286)
   Adriana Lecouvreur: Poveri Fiori, For
      Solo Voice And Orchestra
      KALMUS A4763 sc $3.00, set $9.00,
         pts $.75, ea.   (C287)

CILENSEK, JOHANN (1913-   )
   Konzertstück for Horn and Orchestra
      2.2.3.2. 3.3.0.0. timp,perc,harp,
         strings,horn solo
      sc,pt PETERS $50.00   (C288)

CIMAROSA, DOMENICO (1749-1801)
   Adagio Et Allegro De "Faublas"
      2.2.2.2. 2.2.0.0. timp,strings
      BOIS perf mat rent   (C289)

   Artemisia: Overture
      (Toni, A.) KALMUS A7034 sc $8.00,
         set $15.00, pts $1.00, ea. (C290)

   Astuzie Femminili, Le: Overture
      (Toni, A.) "Feminine Wiles:
         Overture" KALMUS A7033 sc $6.00,
         set $12.00, pts $1.00, ea. (C291)

   Chi Dell'Altrui Si Veste: Overture
      [6']
      0.2.0.1. 2.0.0.0. strings
      (Blanchard, R.) BOIS perf mat rent
                                     (C292)
   Concerto for Clarinet and String
      Orchestra in C minor
      (Thilde, J.) string orch,clar solo
         [8'50"] BILLAUDOT perf mat rent
                                     (C293)
   Concerto for 2 Flutes and Orchestra
      in G, MIN 129
      (Wollheim) DOBLINGER sc $40.75, set
         $35.00, pts $6.00, ea.   (C294)

   Feminine Wiles: Overture
      see Astuzie Femminili, Le: Overture

   Frustrated Plans: Overture
      see Trame Deluse, Le: Overture

   Giannina E Bernardone: Overture
      (Toni, A.) KALMUS A7032 sc $10.00,
         set $10.00, pts $1.25, ea. (C295)

   Giorno Felice, Il: Overture
      (Toni, A.) "Happy Day, The:
         Overture" KALMUS A7031 sc $6.00,
         set $12.00, pts $1.00, ea. (C296)

   Happy Day, The: Overture
      see Giorno Felice, Il: Overture

   Mariage Secret: Air De Geronimo, For
      Solo Voice And Orchestra
      see Matrimonio Segreto, Il: Aria Di
         Geronimo, For Solo Voice And
         Orchestra

   Mariage Secret: Overture
      see Matrimonio Segreto, Il:
         Overture

   Marriage By Trickery: Overture
      see Matrimonio Per Raggiro, Il:
         Overture

   Matrimonio Per Raggiro, Il: Overture
      (Toni, A.) "Marriage By Trickery:
         Overture" KALMUS A7029 sc $10.00,
         set $12.00, pts $1.25, ea. (C297)

   Matrimonio Segreto, Il: Aria Di
      Geronimo, For Solo Voice And
      Orchestra [8']
      0.2.0.2. 2.0.0.0. strings,B solo
      "Mariage Secret: Air De Geronimo,
         For Solo Voice And Orchestra"
      BOIS perf mat rent   (C298)
   Matrimonio Segreto, Il: Brillar Mi
      Sento Il Core, For Solo Voice And
      Orchestra
      KALMUS A4772 sc $6.00, set $11.00,
         pts $1.00, ea., perf mat rent
                                     (C299)
   Matrimonio Segreto, Il: Cara Non
      Dubitar, For Solo Voice And
      Orchestra
      KALMUS A4765 sc $6.00, set $18.00,
         pts $2.00, ea., perf mat rent
                                     (C300)
   Matrimonio Segreto, Il: Cosa Farete?,
      For Solo Voices And Orchestra
      KALMUS A4779 sc $7.00, set $7.00,
         pts $.75, ea.   (C301)

CIMAROSA, DOMENICO (cont'd.)
   Matrimonio Segreto, Il: E Vero Che In
      Casa, For Solo Voice And
      Orchestra
      KALMUS 4769 sc $7.00, set $13.00,
         pts $1.00, ea., perf mat rent
                                     (C302)
   Matrimonio Segreto, Il: Il Parlar Di
      Carolina, For Solo Voices And
      Orchestra
      KALMUS 4782 sc $6.00, set $11.00,
         pts $1.00, ea., perf mat rent
                                     (C303)
   Matrimonio Segreto, Il: Io Ti Lascio,
      Perche Uniti, For Solo Voices And
      Orchestra
      KALMUS A4766 sc $6.00, set $11.00,
         pts $1.00, ea., perf mat rent
                                     (C304)
   Matrimonio Segreto, Il: Le Faccio Un
      Inchino, For Solo Voices And
      Orchestra
      KALMUS A 4768 sc $7.00, set $12.00,
         pts $1.00, ea., perf mat rent
                                     (C305)
   Matrimonio Segreto, Il: Overture
      (Clemandh, J.) "Mariage Secret:
         Overture" BILLAUDOT perf mat rent
                                     (C306)
   Matrimonio Segreto, Il: Perdonate
      Signor Mio, For Solo Voice And
      Orchestra
      KALMUS A4774 sc $9.00, set $11.00,
         pts $1.00, ea., perf mat rent
                                     (C307)
   Matrimonio Segreto, Il: Pria Che
      Spunti In Ciel L'aurora, For Solo
      Voice And Orchestra
      KALMUS A4777 sc $9.00, set $13.00,
         pts $1.00, ea., perf mat rent
                                     (C308)
   Matrimonio Segreto, Il: Se Fiato In
      Corpo Avete, For Solo Voice And
      Orchestra
      KALMUS 4775 sc $12.00, set $15.00,
         pts $1.25, ea., perf mat rent
                                     (C309)
   Matrimonio Segreto, Il: Se Non
      Vendicata, For Solo Voice And
      Orchestra
      KALMUS A4781 sc $6.00, set $11.00,
         pts $1.00, ea., perf mat rent
                                     (C310)
   Matrimonio Segreto, Il: Sento In
      Petto Un Freddo Gelo, For Solo
      Voices And Orchestra
      KALMUS 4771 sc $10.00, set $13.00,
         pts $1.00, ea., perf mat rent
                                     (C311)
   Matrimonio Segreto, Il: Sento Ohime!
      Che Mi Vien Male, For Solo Voices
      And Orchestra
      KALMUS 4776 sc $9.00, set $11.00,
         pts $1.00, ea., perf mat rent
                                     (C312)
   Matrimonio Segreto, Il: Senza Tante
      Cerimonie, For Solo Voice And
      Orchestra
      KALMUS A4770 sc $6.00, set $7.00,
         pts $.75, ea.   (C313)
   Matrimonio Segreto, Il: Signor, Deh!
      Concedete, For Solo Voices And
      Orchestra
      KALMUS A4773 sc $9.00, set $11.00,
         pts $1.00, ea., perf mat rent
                                     (C314)
   Matrimonio Segreto, Il: Son Lunatico,
      Bilioso, For Solo Voice And
      Orchestra
      KALMUS A4778 sc $9.00, set $15.00,
         pts $2.00, ea., perf mat rent
                                     (C315)
   Matrimonio Segreto, Il: Udite Tutti,
      Udite, For Solo Voice And
      Orchestra
      KALMUS A4767 sc $9.00, set $15.00,
         pts $2.00, ea., perf mat rent
                                     (C316)
   Traci Amanti, I: Overture
      (Napolitano) KALMUS A7384 sc $7.00,
         set $16.50, pts $1.50, ea. (C317)

   Traci Amanti, I: Overture [arr.]
      (Maione) 0.2.0.2. 2.0.0.0. strings
         [5'50"] sc CURCI 10117 f.s., perf
         mat rent   (C318)

   Trame Deluse, Le: Overture
      (Toni, A.) "Frustrated Plans:
         Overture" KALMUS A7030 sc $8.00,
         set $10.00, pts $1.00, ea. (C319)

CIMAROSIANA, LA see Malipiero, Gian
   Francesco

CINDERELLA: SUITE NO. 2 see Prokofiev,
   Serge

CINQ EPIGRAPHES see Trojahn, Manfred

CINQ FOIS JE T'AIME, FOR SOLO VOICES
   AND ORCHESTRA see Denis, Didier

CINQ MELODIES, FOR SOLO VOICE AND
CHAMBER ORCHESTRA see Casanova,
André

CINQ PIECES, FOR VIOLONCELLO AND STRING
ORCHESTRA see Francaix, Jean

CINQ POEMES, FOR SOLO VOICE AND
ORCHESTRA see Vellones, Pierre

CINQ POEMES DE RENE CHAR, FOR SOLO
VOICE AND ORCHESTRA see Kaipainen,
Jouni

CINQ RESONANCES see Arma, Paul (Pál)
(Imre Weisshaus)

CINQ RONDEAUX DE CHARLES D'ORLEANS, FOR
SOLO VOICE AND INSTRUMENTAL
ENSEMBLE see Devries, Ivan

CINQUANTA VARIAZIONE PICCOLE see
Saeverud, Harald

CINQUE CANCIONES D'ESPAGNE see Adomian,
Lan

CINQUE MOVIMENTI, FOR CLARINET AND
ORCHESTRA see Kocsar, Miklos

CINQUE ROMANZE, FOR VIOLA AND ORCHESTRA
see Mannino, Franco

CIO CHE DICONO I FIORI, FOR SOLO VOICES
AND ORCHESTRA see Rossellini, Renzo

CIRCADIAN RHYTHMS see Josephs, Wilfred

CIRCE, LA: LAVATEVI PRESTO, FOR SOLO
VOICES AND ORCHESTRA see Haydn,
[Franz] Joseph

CIRCLE OF THE MOON, A, FOR OBOE AND
ORCHESTRA see Sermila, Jarmo

CIRCLE'S END, FOR GUITAR AND ORCHESTRA
see Armstrong, John

CIRCLES OF LIGHT see Saxton, Robert

CIRCOLI VIZIOSI see Campana, Jose Luis

CIRCULATING SCENERY, FOR VIOLIN AND
ORCHESTRA see Ichiyanagi, Toshi

CIRCUS, THE see Ranki, György

CIRCUS PARADE, FOR NARRATOR AND
ORCHESTRA see Bamert, Matthias

CIRCUS PICTURES: SMALL SUITE see Hall,
Pauline, Cirkusbilleder: Liten
Suite

CIRIBIRIBIN, FOR SOLO VOICE AND
ORCHESTRA see Pestalozza, A.

CIRKUS see Nordentoft, Anders

CIRKUSBILLEDER: LITEN SUITE see Hall,
Pauline

CIRY, MICHEL (1919-   )
Meditation Symphonique No. 3 [15']
3.3.3.3. 4.4.3.1. timp,3perc,pno,
harp,strings
BILLAUDOT perf mat rent   (C320)

CIS-CANTUS III see Brandmüller, Theo

CITE NOUVELLE, LA see Koechlin, Charles

CITIZEN KANE OVERTURE see Herrmann,
Bernard

CITY MUSIC: SONG AND DANCE see
Stallcop, Glenn

CIURLIONIS, MIKOLAJUS (1875-1911)
Im Wald
see In The Forest

In The Forest [20']
3.3.3.3. 4.2.3.1. harp,strings
VAAP perf mat rent   (C321)
"Im Wald" SIKORSKI perf mat rent
(C322)
Meer, Das, For Organ And Orchestra
see Sea, The, For Organ And
Orchestra

Sea, The, For Organ And Orchestra
[30']
3.3.3.3. 6.4.3.1. timp,perc,harp,
strings,org solo
VAAP perf mat rent   (C323)
"Meer, Das, For Organ And
Orchestra" SIKORSKI perf mat rent
(C324)

CIVIL WARS, THE: COLOGNE see Glass,
Philip

CLAFLIN, [ALAN] AVERY (1898-1979)
Pop Concert Concerto, For Piano And
Orchestra [17']
3.3.2.2. 4.3.3.1. timp,perc,harp,
strings,pno solo
sc AM.COMP.AL. $35.50, perf mat
rent   (C325)

CLAIR DE LUNE, FOR PIANO AND ORCHESTRA
see Sciarrino, Salvatore

CLAIR-OBSCUR, FOR CONTRABASSOON,
DOUBLEBASS AND ORCHESTRA see
Papineau-Couture, Jean

CLAIRIERES DANS LE CIEL, FOR SOLO VOICE
AND ORCHESTRA see Tomasi, Henri

CLAIRS-OBSCURS see Devillers, Jean
Baptiste

CLAP, FOR CLARINET AND ORCHESTRA see
Castaldi, Paolo

CLARAE STELLAE, SCINTILLATE, FOR SOLO
VOICE AND STRING ORCHESTRA see
Vivaldi, Antonio

CLARE CYCLE, FOR SOLO VOICE AND
ORCHESTRA see Child, Peter B.

CLARICE CARA MIA SPOSA, FOR SOLO VOICE
AND ORCHESTRA see Mozart, Wolfgang
Amadeus

CLARINET CLARINA, THE, FOR SOLO VOICE,
CLARINET AND ORCHESTRA see Kvam,
Oddvar S., Klarinetten Klarina, For
Solo Voice, Clarinet And Orchestra

CLARISSA SYMPHONY, FOR SOLO VOICES AND
ORCHESTRA see Holloway, Robin

CLARKE, F.R.C. (1931-   )
Triptych [14']
2.2.2.2. 4.2.3.1. timp,perc,
strings
CAN.MUS.CENT. MI 1100 C597TR (C326)

CLARKE, JEREMIAH (ca. 1673-1707)
Trumpet Tune [arr.]
(Dearnley, C.; Willcocks, D.)
3.3.3.3. 4.3.3.1. timp,perc,org,
strings [5'] OXFORD perf mat rent
(C327)

CLARO-OSCURO, FOR SOLO VOICES AND
CHAMBER ORCHESTRA see Seco De Arpe,
Manuel

CLASSIC FILM THEMES see Waxman, Franz

CLASSIC LOVE THEMES see Waxman, Franz

CLASSICAL CONCERTO, FOR PIANO AND
ORCHESTRA see Rojko, Uroš, Klasicni
Koncert, For Piano And Orchestra

CLASSICAL JUKEBOX see Anderson, Leroy

CLASSICAL ROMANCE see Peck, Russell
James

CLASSICAL SYMPHONY see Lovec, Vladimir,
Klasicna Simfonija

CLASSICAL VARIATIONS ON COLONIAL THEMES
see Gould, Morton

CLAVIER CONCERTOS, TWO see Nichelmann,
Christoph

CLAVURENITO, FOR PIANO AND ORCHESTRA
see Adomian, Lan

CLEA see Taira, Yoshihisa

CLEMENS NON PAPA
see CLEMENS, JACOBUS

CLEMENT, JACOBUS
see CLEMENS, JACOBUS

CLEMENT, SHEREE (1955-   )
Chamber Concerto [15']
pic,fl,clar,bass clar,horn,trp,
trom,tuba,2perc,pno,2vln,vla,
vcl,db
MARGUN BP 1050 perf mat rent (C328)

CLEMENTI, MUZIO (1752-1832)
Symphony
see Crotch, William, Symphony

CLEMENZA DI SCIPIONE, LA: OVERTURE see
Bach, Johann Christian

CLEMENZA DI TITO, LA: ALLEGRO MA NON
TROPPO FROM ACT III see Hasse,
Johann Adolph

CLEMENZA DI TITO, LA: DEH, PER QUESTO
ISTANTE SOLO, FOR SOLO VOICE AND
ORCHESTRA see Mozart, Wolfgang
Amadeus

CLEMENZA DI TITO, LA: ECCO IL PUNTO;
NON PIU DI FIORI, FOR SOLO VOICE
AND ORCHESTRA see Mozart, Wolfgang
Amadeus

CLEMENZA DI TITO, LA: OVERTURE see
Mozart, Wolfgang Amadeus

CLEMENZA DI TITO, LA: PARTO, MA TU BEN
MIO, FOR SOLO VOICE AND ORCHESTRA
see Mozart, Wolfgang Amadeus

CLEMENZA DI TITO, LA: TARDI SAVOEDE
D'UN TRADIMENTO, FOR SOLO VOICE AND
ORCHESTRA see Hasse, Johann Adolph

CLEOPATRA, FOR SOLO VOICE AND ORCHESTRA
see Hamilton, Iain

CLÉRAMBAULT, LOUIS-NICOLAS (1676-1749)
Leandre Et Hero, For Solo Voice And
Instrumental Ensemble
(Geoffroy-Dechaume, A.) 2fl,hpsd,
strings,S solo [17'20"] BILLAUDOT
perf mat rent   (C329)

CLEVE, CISSI (1911-   )
Aquarelle [arr.]
(Soderlind, Ragnar) 2.2.2.2.
4.2.3.0. strings NORGE   (C330)

Dream, The
see Drommen

Drommen
"Dream, The" MUSIKK perf mat rent
(C331)
Kjertegn [arr.]
(Sonderlind, Ragnar) "Love Sign
[arr.]" 2.2.2.2. 4.0.0.0. harp,
strings NORGE   (C332)

Legende [arr.]
(Soderlind, Ragnar) ob,harp,strings
NORGE   (C333)

Love Sign [arr.]
see Kjertegn [arr.]

Manesolv [arr.]
(Soderlind, Ragnar) "Moon Silver
[arr.]" 2.2.2.2. 4.0.0.0. timp,
perc,harp,cel,strings NORGE
(C334)
Moon Silver [arr.]
see Manesolv [arr.]

Nocturne
MUSIKK perf mat rent   (C335)

Nocturne, [arr.]
(Soderlind, Ragnar) harp,strings,ob
solo NORGE   (C336)

Solglott [arr.]
(Soderlind, Ragnar) 2.2.2.2.
4.2.3.1. timp,perc,harp,strings
NORGE   (C337)

Soljevalsen
MUSIKK perf mat rent   (C338)

Soljevalsen [arr.]
(Danielsen, Ragnar) 2.2.2.2.
0.0.0.0. cel,strings NORGE (C339)

Soloppgang [arr.]
(Soderlind, Ragnar) "Sun Rise
[arr.]" 2.2.2.2. 4.2.3.1. timp,
perc,harp,strings [14'] NORGE
(C340)
Spring Yearning [arr.]
see Varlengsel [arr.]

Sun Rise [arr.]
see Soloppgang [arr.]

Theme and Variations, [arr.]
(Bergh, Sverre) 1.1.2.1. 0.0.0.0.
strings NORGE   (C341)

Valse Lyrique
pts MUSIKK f.s.   (C342)

Varlengsel [arr.]
(Soderlind, Ragnar) "Spring
Yearning [arr.]" 2.2.2.2.
4.2.3.0. timp,perc,strings NORGE
(C343)

CLEVE, HALFDAN (1879-1951)
Concerto for Piano and String
Orchestra, No. 3, Op. 9, in E
flat [22']
string orch,pno solo
BREITKOPF-W perf mat rent   (C344)

CLIMATIC CHANGES, FOR SAXOPHONE, PIANO
AND ORCHESTRA see Bentzon, Niels
Viggo

CLIMATS see Rivier, Jean

CLINE, THORNTON
Onemo [7']
2.2.2.2. 2.2.2.0. perc,strings
PEER perf mat rent (C345)

CLOCHE FELEE, LA see Levinas, Michael

CLOCHES, LES see Milhaud, Darius,
Bells, The

CLOCKWORKS see Luedeke, Raymond

CLODAGH, FOR SOLO VOICE AND ORCHESTRA
see Franco, Johan

CLOUD OF UNKNOWING, THE, FOR SOLO VOICE
AND CHAMBER ORCHESTRA see Primosch,
James

CLOUDS, FOR SOLO VOICE AND ORCHESTRA
[ARR.] see Charles, Ernest

CLOUDS AND ECLIPSES see Watkins,
Michael Blake

COAKLEY, DONALD
Serial Set In Four [6']
string orch
KERBY DC 3 (C346)

COALESCENCE, FOR CLARINET AND ORCHESTRA
see Tessier, Roger

COATES, ERIC (1886-1957)
Miniature Suite [13']
2+pic.2.2.2. 2.0.0.0. timp,perc,
strings
KALMUS A6098 sc $20.00, set $30.00,
perf mat rent (C347)

COFFEE HOUSE, THE: OVERTURE see
Schultz, Svend S.

COGITATIONES SYMBOLICAE see Barbaud,
Pierre

COHEN, EDWARD (1940-)
Stone And Earth, For Solo Voice And
String Orchestra [8']
string orch,Mez solo
sc APNM $6.50, perf mat rent (C348)

COHEN, JEROME D. (1936-)
Invincible Bunbury, The [5']
2+pic.2.2.2. 4.3.3.1. timp,4perc,
glock,strings
OXFORD perf mat rent (C349)

COIGNET, ANTOINE (1914-)
Trio Concertante, For Violin, Viola,
Violoncello And String Orchestra
[9']
string orch,vln solo,vla solo,vcl
solo
LYNWD sc $6.00, pts $9.00 (C350)

COINVOLGIMENTO, FOR 2 VIOLINS, VIOLA
AND INSTRUMENTAL ENSEMBLE see
Gentilucci, Armando

COJO ENAMORADO, EL see Halffter,
Ernesto

COLAÇO OSORIO-SWAAB, REINE (1889-1971)
Genezing Van Den Blinde, For Narrator
And Orchestra [15']
3.2.3.2. 2.2.2.0. timp,perc,harp,
cel,strings,narrator (1950
version) sc DONEMUS f.s., perf
mat rent (C351)
2.2.2.1. 1.0.0.0. timp,perc,cel,
strings,narrator (1954 version)
sc DONEMUS f.s., perf mat rent
(C352)

COLAS BREUGNON, FOR FLUTE AND STRING
ORCHESTRA see Baird, Tadeusz

COLD WHEN THE DRUM SOUNDS FOR DAWN see
Samuel, Gerhard

COLDING-JORGENSEN, HENRIK (1944-)
Victoria Gennem Skoven, For Solo
Voice And Orchestra [14']
2.2.2.1. 1.2.1.0. timp,strings,A
solo
"Victoria Through The Forest, For
Solo Voice And Orchestra" sc
SAMFUNDET 309 f.s., perf mat rent
(C353)
Victoria Through The Forest, For Solo
Voice And Orchestra
see Victoria Gennem Skoven, For
Solo Voice And Orchestra

COLERIDGE-TAYLOR, SAMUEL (1875-1912)
Novelette, Op. 52, No. 1, In A
[2'30"]
string orch,tamb,triangle
KALMUS A7258 sc $5.00, set $7.00,
pts $1.25, ea. (C354)

Novelette, Op. 52, No. 2, In C [3']
string orch,tamb,triangle
KALMUS A7259 sc $5.00, set $7.00,
pts $1.25, ea. (C355)

COLERIDGE-TAYLOR, SAMUEL (cont'd.)

Novelette, Op 52, No.3, In A Minor
[3'30"]
string orch,tamb,triangle
KALMUS A7260 sc $5.00, set $7.00,
pts $1.25, ea. (C356)

Novelette, Op 52, No. 4, In D [3']
string orch,tamb,triangle
KALMUS A7261 sc $5.00, set $7.00,
pts $1.25, ea. (C357)

Rhapsodic Dance No. 1: The Bamboula
KALMUS A6072 sc $15.00, set $40.00,
pts $2.00, ea., perf mat rent
(C358)

COLES, GRAHAM (1948-)
Variations On A Mozart Rondo *Op.26
[22']
string orch
CAN.MUS.CENT. MI 1500 C693VA (C359)

COLGRASS, MICHAEL (CHARLES) (1932-)
Chaconne for Viola and Orchestra
[30']
3.2.3.1. 4.3.3.1. timp,4perc,cel&
pno,harp,strings,vla solo
CAN.MUS.CENT. MI 1312 C695C (C360)

Concertmasters, For 3 Violins And
Orchestra [22']
2.2.2.2. 4.3.3.1. perc,2harp,
hpsd&cel,strings,3vln soli
FISCHER,C perf mat rent (C361)

Delta, For Violin, Clarinet,
Percussion And Orchestra [18']
2.2.2.2. 2.2.0.0. strings,vln
solo,clar solo,perc solo
FISCHER,C perf mat rent (C362)

Demon, For Piano And Orchestra [7']
2.0.3.1. 4.3.3.1. timp,perc,
strings,electronic equipment,
amplified pno solo
FISCHER,C perf mat rent (C363)

Divertimento [8']
perc,strings
FISCHER,C perf mat rent (C364)

Letter From Mozart [16']
2.2.2.2. 2.2.2.1. perc,harp,pno&
cel,strings
sc FISCHER,C $25.00, perf mat rent
(C365)
Memento, For 2 Pianos And Orchestra
[17']
3.1.3.3. 4.3.3.0. perc,harp,cel,
strings,2pno soli
FISCHER,C perf mat rent (C366)

Rhapsodic Fantasy, For Percussion And
Orchestra [8']
2(pic,alto fl).1.1.1. 1.1.1.0.
timp,3perc,harp,cel,strings,
perc solo: 15 chromatic roto-
toms
study sc MCA f.s., perf mat rent
(C367)
COLIN ET CHLOE see Denisov, Edison
Vasilievich

COLLAGE see Helmus, Menno

COLLAGE ON B-A-C-H see Pärt, Arvo

COLLAGES see Carson, Philippe

COLLAN, KARL (1828-1871)
Sylvian Joululaulu, For Solo Voice
And Orchestra [arr.]
(Kuusisto, I.) 2fl,strings,solo
voice [4'] FAZER perf mat rent
(C368)
COLLANA see LeFanu, Nicola

COLLECTED FACSIMILE EDITION, VOL. 2:
WORKS FOR SMALL ORCHESTRA see
Holst, Gustav

COLLECTED WORKS. LEIPZIG, 1884-1936 see
Grétry, André Ernest Modeste

COLLECTED WORKS. MALHERBE EDITION,
LEIPZIG, 1900-1907 see Berlioz,
Hector (Louis)

COLLECTED WORKS. PARIS, 1895-1913 see
Rameau, Jean-Philippe

COLLECTED WORKS, VOL. 26: SYMPHONIES I
see Bach, Johann Christian

COLLECTED WORKS, VOL. 27: SYMPHONIES II
see Bach, Johann Christian

COLLECTED WORKS, VOL. 28: SYMPHONIES
III see Bach, Johann Christian

COLLECTED WORKS, VOL. 29: SYMPHONIES IV
see Bach, Johann Christian

COLLECTED WORKS, VOL. 30: SYMPHONIES
CONCERTANTES I see Bach, Johann
Christian

COLLECTED WORKS, VOL. 31: SYMPHONIES
CONCERTANTES II see Bach, Johann
Christian

COLLECTED WORKS, VOL. 32: KEYBOARD
CONCERTOS I see Bach, Johann
Christian

COLLECTED WORKS, VOL. 33: KEYBOARD
CONCERTOS II see Bach, Johann
Christian

COLLECTED WORKS, VOL. 34: KEYBOARD
CONCERTOS III see Bach, Johann
Christian

COLLECTED WORKS, VOL. 35: KEYBOARD
CONCERTOS IV see Bach, Johann
Christian

COLLECTED WORKS, VOL. 36: OTHER SOLO
CONCERTOS see Bach, Johann
Christian

COLLET, HENRI (1885-1951)
Concerto Flammenco No. 2, For Violin
And Orchestra
2+pic.2.0+2clar in A.2. 4.2.3.1.
timp,perc,harp,strings,vln solo
SALABERT perf mat rent (C369)

COLLISIONS see Kucharzyk, Henry

COLLOCATIONS see Nystedt, Knut

COLLOÏDES, FOR FLUTE AND INSTRUMENTAL
ENSEMBLE see Durko, Zsolt

COLOMBE, LA: ENTR'ACTE see Gounod,
Charles François

COLOMBIER, MICHEL
Nightbird, For Saxophone And
Orchestra
see Oiseau De Nuit, For Saxophone
And Orchestra

Oiseau De Nuit, For Saxophone And
Orchestra [20']
3(pic).2(English horn).3(bass
clar).2(contrabsn).
4.4(flügelhorn).3+bass trom.1.
timp,perc,harp,2pno,strings,
gtr, fender-rhodes, sax solo
"Nightbird, For Saxophone And
Orchestra" NEWAM 19011 perf mat
rent (C370)

COLOMBINE POLKA see Strauss, Eduard

COLONIAL SONG see Grainger, Percy
Aldridge

COLONIAL SONGS see Grainger, Percy
Aldridge

COLONNE INFINIE see Olah, Tiberiu

COLONNEN WALZER see Strauss, Johann,
[Jr.]

COLORI ED IMPROVISAZIONI see Bergman,
Erik

COLOURS, FOR HARMONICA AND STRING
ORCHESTRA see Kvam, Oddvar S.

COLUMBIA FALLS see LeFanu, Nicola

COLUMBINE, FOR FLUTE AND STRING
ORCHESTRA see Sigurbjörnsson,
Thorkell

COMBATTIMENTO DI CECCO E LA SUA
COMPAGNIA, IL, FOR VIOLONCELLO AND
STRING ORCHESTRA see Willi, Herbert

COME BACK, LITTLE SHEBA see Waxman,
Franz

COME OCEAN WINDS, COME see Søderlind,
Ragnar, Kom Havsvindar, Kom

COME UNO SVILUPPO...STRACCI see
Bischof, Rainer

COMEDIANS, THE see Kabalevsky, Dmitri
Borisovich

COMES AUTUMN TIME see Sowerby, Leo

COMME IO PASSO L'ESTATE see
Castiglioni, Niccolò

COMMEDIA SENZA PAROLE see Csemiczky, M.

COMMEMORATION AND CELEBRATION OVERTURE
see Ott, David

COMMENCEMENT SUITE: PROCESSIONAL, FOR
STRING ORCHESTRA see Taylor,
Clifford Oliver

COMMENTARIES, FOR GUITAR AND CHAMBER ORCHESTRA see Bottje, Will Gay

COMMON TONES IN SIMPLE TIME see Adams, John

COMMONWEALTH CHRISTMAS OVERTURE see Arnold, Malcolm

COMMOTION see Sigurbjörnsson, Thorkell

COMPLEANNO, IL, FOR ORCHESTRA AND TWO SEXTETS see Hvoslef, Ketil

COMPLETE CONCERTI see Brahms, Johannes

COMPLETE WORKS, CHRYSANDER EDITION, 1858-1894, 1902 see Handel, George Frideric

COMPLETE WORKS. LEIPZIG, 1878-1880, 1902 see Chopin, Frédéric

COMPLEX SIMPLE, FOR 2 ONDES MARTINOT AND INSTRUMENTAL ENSEMBLE see Tamba, Akira

COMPOSE-COMPOSITE see Ferrari, Luc

COMPOSITION FOR ORCHESTRA see Winham, Godfrey

COMPOSITION IN F SHARP see Ogura, Roh

COMPOSITION IV see Philippot, Michel Paul

COMPOSIZIONI PER ORCHESTRA I see Vejvanovsky, Pavel Josef

COMPOSIZIONI PER ORCHESTRA II see Vejvanovsky, Pavel Josef

COMPOSIZIONI PER ORCHESTRA III see Vejvanovsky, Pavel Josef

COMPOSTELLE I see Tremblay, Gilles

COMPRESENZE see Rihm, Wolfgang

COMTE ORY, LE: A LA FAVEUR DE CETTE NUIT OBSCURE, FOR SOLO VOICES AND ORCHESTRA see Rossini, Gioacchino

COMTE ORY, LE: AH QUEL RESPECT, MADAME, FOR SOLO VOICES AND ORCHESTRA see Rossini, Gioacchino

COMTE ORY, LE: UNE DAME DE HAUT PARAGE, FOR SOLO VOICES AND ORCHESTRA see Rossini, Gioacchino

CON CORDES see Hunt, Michael

CON ESPRESSIONE see Leyendecker, Ulrich

CON FUOCO see Nordentoft, Anders

CON OSSEQUIO, CON RISPETTO, FOR SOLO VOICE AND ORCHESTRA see Mozart, Wolfgang Amadeus

CONCENTUS see Godfrey, Daniel

CONCENTUS AD LIBITUM, FOR JAZZ QUINTET AND ORCHESTRA see Hurum, Helge

CONCEPT, THREE see Tautenhahn, Gunther

CONCERT, FOR VIOLIN AND ORCHESTRA see Siohan, Robert

CONCERT, FOR VIOLIN, DOUBLE BASS AND STRING ORCHESTRA see Lancen, Serge

CONCERT AILE DANS LES JARDINS NOCTURNES see Bernard, Robert

CONCERT ARIA, FOR SOLO VOICE AND ORCHESTRA see Winslow, Walter

CONCERT ARIA, FOR VIOLONCELLO AND ORCHESTRA see Applebaum, Stanley

CONCERT CANTATA, FOR SOLO VOICES AND ORCHESTRA see Hafsteinsson, Gudmundur

CONCERT CHAMPÊTRE, FOR VIOLIN AND ORCHESTRA see Lucas, Leighton

CONCERT DANCES, FOR PIANO AND ORCHESTRA see Blake, Howard

CONCERT DES ELEMENTS, LE see DuBois, Pierre-Max

CONCERT EN 3 PARTIES, FOR TRUMPET AND ORCHESTRA see Lantier, Pierre

CONCERT EN TROIS PARTIES see Guezec, Jean-Pierre

CONCERT ETUDE, FOR TRUMPET AND ORCHESTRA see Goedicke, Alexander

CONCERT ETUDE FOR TRUMPET AND STRINGS see Goedicke, Alexander

CONCERT FLAMAND see Jaubert, Maurice

CONCERT FOR CHAMBER ORCHESTRA see Damase, Jean-Michel

CONCERT IN G DANS LE GOUT THEATRAL [ARR] see Couperin, François (le Grand)

CONCERT IN QUARTO, FOR VIOLIN AND STRING ORCHESTRA see Merlet, Michel

CONCERT MUSIC see Bázlik, Miroslav, Koncertna Hudba see Greenburg, Laura

CONCERT NO. 6 [ARR.] see Rameau, Jean-Philippe

CONCERT-OUVERTURE DR. FAUSTUS see Boehmer, Konrad

CONCERT OVERTURE see Hovland, Egil see Lybbert, Donald see Su, Cong

CONCERT OVERTURE - AUSTRALIA see Willcocks, Jonathan

CONCERT PIECES, FOR PIANO AND ORCHESTRA, OP. 40 see Chaminade, Cécile

CONCERT POUR CUIVRES ET CORDES see Accart-Becker, Evelyne

CONCERT POUR UNE BALLERINE, FOR ALTO SAXOPHONE AND CHAMBER ORCHESTRA see Moeschinger, Albert

CONCERT RHAPSODY, FOR PIANO AND ORCHESTRA see Khachaturian, Aram Ilyich

CONCERT SPIRITUEL see Bresgen, Cesar

CONCERT SUITE see Telemann, Georg Philipp

CONCERT WALZ [ARR.] see Ahvenainen, Veikko

CONCERT WORKS, FOR SYMPHONY ORCHESTRA see Mirzoyev, M.

CONCERTANT CHRISTMAS MUSIC *CCU string orch,ob solo,2vln soli,vcl solo KALMUS A6357 sc $10.00, set $15.00, pts $2.00, ea. contains works by Handel, Corelli, Manfredini, and Schiassi   (C371)

CONCERTANT II, FOR BASSOON AND STRING ORCHESTRA see Goeb, Roger

CONCERTANT NO. 1 see Goeb, Roger

CONCERTANT NO. 4, FOR CLARINET AND CHAMBER ORCHESTRA see Goeb, Roger

CONCERTANT-TANZERISCHE MUSIK IN D-MIXOLYDISCH see Wolter, Detlef

CONCERTANTE see Butterworth, Arthur

CONCERTANTE, FOR FLUTE, OBOE AND ORCHESTRA IN F see Moscheles, Ignaz

CONCERTANTE, FOR FLUTE, VIOLIN, AND ORCHESTRA see Reicha, Anton

CONCERTANTE, FOR VIOLIN, STRINGS AND PERCUSSION see Somers, Harry Stewart

CONCERTANTE DANCES see Kelly, Bryan

CONCERTANTE FOR ENGLISH HORN, CLARINET AND ORCHESTRA see Fiala, J.

CONCERTANTE FOR OBOE, CLARINET, HORN AND ORCHESTRA see Addison, John Mervyn

CONCERTANTE FOR 16 STRINGS AND 2 FRENCH HORNS see Lazarof, Henri

CONCERTANTE FOR VIOLIN, VIOLONCELLO AND ORCHESTRA, WOO. 11 see Spohr, Ludwig (Louis)

CONCERTANTE IN MOTO PERPETUO see Bainbridge, Simon

CONCERTANTE LIRICO see Frankel, Benjamin

CONCERTANTE PASTORALE see Rawsthorne, Alan

CONCERTI, FIVE see Vivaldi, Antonio

CONCERTI A DUE CORI, THREE see Handel, George Frideric

CONCERTI FOR FLUTE AND STRING ORCHESTRA see Benda, Franz (František)

CONCERTI FOR FLUTE, FOR OBOE AND FOR BASSOON see Mozart, Wolfgang Amadeus

CONCERTI FOR HARPSICHORD, 16 see Bach, Johann Sebastian

CONCERTI FOR HARPSICHORD AND STRING ORCHESTRA, TWO see Benda, Georg Anton (Jiří Antonín)

CONCERTI FOR OBOE AND ORCHESTRA, FOUR see Handel, George Frideric

CONCERTI FOR ONE WIND INSTRUMENT AND ORCHESTRA see Haydn, [Franz] Joseph

CONCERTI FOR ORGAN AND ORCHESTRA, TWO see Brixi, Franz Xaver

CONCERTI FOR SOLO KEYBOARD AND ORCHESTRA, SEVEN see Bach, Johann Sebastian

CONCERTI FOR WIND INSTRUMENTS see Mozart, Wolfgang Amadeus

CONCERTI GROSSI, FIVE see Handel, George Frideric

CONCERTI, OP. 2, NOS. 1-6 see Stanley, John

CONCERTI, OP. 10, NOS. 1-6 see Stanley, John

CONCERTI, TWELVE, [ARR.] see Marcello, Benedetto

CONCERTINO CARINTICO see Einem, Gottfried von

CONCERTINO CLASSICO, FOR 2 TRUMPETS AND ORCHESTRA see Horovitz, Joseph

CONCERTINO FOR CIMBALOM AND ORCHESTRA see Ranki, György

CONCERTINO FOR JAZZ QUARTET AND ORCHESTRA see Schuller, Gunther

CONCERTINO FOR JAZZ QUARTET AND STRINGS see Prohaska, Miljenko

CONCERTINO GIOCOSO, FOR HARP AND ORCHESTRA see Evensen, Bernt Kasberg

CONCERTINO GRAZIOSO, FOR RECORDER AND STRING ORCHESTRA see Erdmann, Dietrich

CONCERTINO IN MEMORIAM Z.H., FOR HORN AND CHAMBER ORCHESTRA see Kocsar, Miklos

CONCERTINO SERENO, FOR VIOLIN, DOUBLE BASS AND ORCHESTRA see Krol, Bernhard

CONCERTMASTERS, FOR 3 VIOLINS AND ORCHESTRA see Colgrass, Michael (Charles)

CONCERTO, FOR OBOE AND STRING ORCHESTRA [ARR.] see Sammartini, Giovanni Battista

CONCERTO A.B., FOR CHAMBER ORCHESTRA see Eder, Helmut

CONCERTO A.B., FOR ORCHESTRA see Eder, Helmut

CONCERTO A BECCO, FOR RECORDER AND CHAMBER ORCHESTRA see Ramovs, Primoz

CONCERTO A DODICI ("VIAGGI") see Wimberger, Gerhard

CONCERTO A DUE CORI IN B FLAT, HWV 332 see Handel, George Frideric, Concerto Grosso No. 27 in B flat

CONCERTO A DUE CORI IN F, HWV 333 see Handel, George Frideric, Concerto Grosso No. 28 in F

CONCERTO A DUE CORI IN F, HWV 334 see Handel, George Frideric, Concerto Grosso No. 29 in F

CONCERTO AUSTRAL, FOR OBOE AND ORCHESTRA see Marco, Tomas

CONCERTO AVVENTUROSO see Motte, Diether de la

CONCERTO BAROCCO, FOR HORN AND ORCHESTRA see Krol, Bernhard

CONCERTO BREVE, FOR VIOLONCELLO AND ORCHESTRA see Calmel, Roger

CONCERTO BUFFO see Slonimsky, Sergey

CONCERTO CAPRICCIOSO, FOR 2 FLUTES AND ORCHESTRA see Stadlmair, Hans

CONCERTO CLASSICO see Sary, Laszlo

CONCERTO CON FUOCO, FOR GUITAR AND STRING ORCHESTRA see Bondon, Jacques

CONCERTO CONCERTANTE see Thorne, Francis Burritt

CONCERTO CRIOLLO, FOR PIANO AND ORCHESTRA see Leon, Tania Justina

CONCERTO DA CAMERA see Crosse, Gordon see Israel-Meyer, Pierre see Soproni, Jozsef

CONCERTO DA CAMERA, FOR FLUTE AND STRING ORCHESTRA see Tamba, Akira

CONCERTO DA CAMERA, FOR HARP, VIOLONCELLO AND STRING ORCHESTRA see Meyer, Krzysztof

CONCERTO DA CAMERA, FOR PIANO AND STRING ORCHESTRA, NO. 2 see Alkan, Charles-Henri Valentin

CONCERTO DA CAMERA, FOR VIOLA AND STRING ORCHESTRA see Bartoš, Jan Zdenek

CONCERTO DA CAMERA, FOR VIOLONCELLO AND ORCHESTRA see Hess, Ernst

CONCERTO DE LOURMARIN, FOR ORGAN AND STRING ORCHESTRA see Guinot, Georges Leonce

CONCERTO DE NUREMBERG, FOR ALTO SAXOPHONE AND STRINGS see Hasquenoph, Pierre

CONCERTO DI ARIELE, FOR OBOE AND ORCHESTRA see Hazon, Roberto

CONCERTO DUO FOR TROMBONE, GUITAR AND ORCHESTRA see Holman, Bill

CONCERTO ESTIVO see Rapf, Kurt

CONCERTO EVOCATIVO, FOR GUITAR AND ORCHESTRA see Cordero, Ernesto

CONCERTO FESTIVA, FOR BRASS QUINTET AND ORCHESTRA see Schuller, Gunther

CONCERTO FESTIVO see Panufnik, Andrzej

CONCERTO (FIERCE AND COMING FROM FAR AWAY) see Fulkerson, James

CONCERTO FLAMMENCO NO. 2, FOR VIOLIN AND ORCHESTRA see Collet, Henri

CONCERTO FOR 2 PIANOS, JAZZ BAND, STRINGS AND PERCUSSION see Baker, David N.

CONCERTO FOR 3 GUITARS, SOLO INSTRUMENTS AND ORCHESTRA see Slonimsky, Sergey

CONCERTO FOR 13 PLAYERS see Boykan, Martin

CONCERTO FOR BANDONEON AND ORCHESTRA see Piazzolla, Astor

CONCERTO FOR BARREL ORGAN AND ORCHESTRA see Constant, Marius

CONCERTO FOR BAYAN AND ORCHESTRA see Chaikin, Nikolai

CONCERTO FOR BRASS AND ORCHESTRA see Erb, Donald

CONCERTO FOR CELLO AND JAZZ BAND see Baker, David N.

CONCERTO FOR DOUBLE BRASS CHOIR AND ORCHESTRA see Harbison, John

CONCERTO FOR EUPHONIUM AND ORCHESTRA, OP. 55 see Madsen, Trygve

CONCERTO FOR FLUTE, NARRATOR AND CHAMBER ORCHESTRA see Vea, Ketil

CONCERTO FOR 4 SOLO INSTRUMENTS AND ORCHESTRA see Eshpai, Andrey Y.

CONCERTO FOR FOUR GROUPS OF INSTRUMENTS see Lieberson, Peter

CONCERTO FOR JAZZ ALTO AND ORCHESTRA see Albam, Manny

CONCERTO FOR JAZZ CLARINET AND STRING ORCHESTRA see Schneider, Gary M.

CONCERTO FOR JAZZ SOLOIST AND ORCHESTRA (VARIANTS) see Smith, William Overton

CONCERTO FOR JAZZ TRIO AND ORCHESTRA see Tillis, Frederick C.

CONCERTO FOR KEYBOARDS AND ORCHESTRA see Erb, Donald

CONCERTO FOR ORCHESTRA, CHAMBER ORCHESTRA VERSION see Laderman, Ezra

CONCERTO FOR PIANO THREE HANDS see Schuller, Gunther

CONCERTO FOR PIANO WITH SELECTED ORCHESTRA see Harrison, Lou

CONCERTO FOR SYMPHONY ORCHESTRA AND JAZZ BAND see Gubaidulina, Sofia

CONCERTO FOR TRUMPET, STRING ORCHESTRA AND JAZZ BAND see Baker, David N.

CONCERTO FOR VIOLIN AND JAZZ BAND see Baker, David N.

CONCERTO FOR VIOLIN AND ORCHESTRA IN G MINOR, MIN 132
(Rostal) GERIG BG 1168 perf mat rent (C372)

CONCERTO FOR VIOLIN AND ORCHESTRA, OP. 62 see Spohr, Ludwig (Louis)

CONCERTO FOR VIOLIN AND ORCHESTRA, OP. 79 see Spohr, Ludwig (Louis)

CONCERTO FOR WINDS AND STRINGS see Lessard, John Ayres

CONCERTO FOR WINDS AND STRINGS, VERSION 2 see Lessard, John Ayres

CONCERTO GIOCONDO E SEVERO see Holmboe, Vagn

CONCERTO GIOCOSO, FOR PIANO AND ORCHESTRA see Maurice, Paule see Pütz, Eduard

CONCERTO GITANO, FOR VIOLONCELLO AND ORCHESTRA see Braga, Antonio

CONCERTO GRASSO see Pütz, Eduard

CONCERTO "GROOVY", FOR SWING BAND AND ORCHESTRA see Hallberg, Bengt

CONCERTO GROSSO FOR SYMPHONY ORCHESTRA AND JAZZ ENSEMBLE see Eiger, Walter

CONCERTO GROSSO IN C (ALEXANDER'S FEAST) see Handel, George Frideric

CONCERTO IN MEMORIAM JÓZSEF ATTILA see Szervanszky, Endre

CONCERTO IN ONE MOVEMENT, FOR VIOLIN AND ORCHESTRA see Becker, John Joseph

CONCERTO IN TWO UNINTERRUPTED SPEEDS, FOR PIANO AND ORCHESTRA see Perry, Julia

CONCERTO ITINERANT, FOR SOLO VOICE, FLUTE, VIOLIN, AND INSTRUMENTAL ENSEMBLE see Volkonsky, Andrei

CONCERTO L'ENVOI, FOR FLUTE AND STRING ORCHESTRA see Dao, Nguyen Thien

CONCERTO LIRICO see Koch, Erland von

CONCERTO LIRICO, FOR HARP AND STRING ORCHESTRA see Nordal, Jon

CONCERTO LIRICO, FOR TROMBONE AND ORCHESTRA see Bassett, Leslie

CONCERTO LIRICO NO. 5, FOR GUITAR AND CHAMBER ORCHESTRA see Franco, Johan

CONCERTO LYRIQUE, FOR CLARINET AND STRING ORCHESTRA see Gotkovsky, Ida

CONCERTO LYRIQUE, FOR STRING QUARTET AND ORCHESTRA see Martinon, Jean

CONCERTO MEDITERRANEEN, FOR TRUMPET AND ORCHESTRA see Calmel, Roger

CONCERTO MINIATURE, FOR FLUTE AND ORCHESTRA see Grimm, Carl Hugo

CONCERTO MOOGO see Kingsley, Gershon Gary

CONCERTO MOVEMENT FOR VIOLIN, ORCHESTRA IN D see Bach, Johann Sebastian

CONCERTO ON SILESIAN TUNES, FOR VIOLA AND CHAMBER ORCHESTRA see Lewin, Frank

CONCERTO OSTINATO, FOR VIOLONCELLO AND ORCHESTRA see Akutagawa, Yasushi

CONCERTO PASTORALE, FOR HORN AND ORCHESTRA see Rollin, Robert Leon

CONCERTO PATHETIQUE, FOR PIANO AND ORCHESTRA see Liszt, Franz

CONCERTO PATHETIQUE, FOR PIANO AND ORCHESTRA IN E MINOR [ARR] see Liszt, Franz

CONCERTO PER CONTRABBASSO LADRO E ORCHESTRA see Negri, Gino

CONCERTO PER MSTISLAV ROSTROPOVIC, FOR VIOLONCELLO AND ORCHESTRA see Mortari, Virgilio

CONCERTO PER OBOE E ORCHESTRA, SU TEMI DELL'OPERA "I VESPRI SICILIANI" DI G. VERDI [ARR.] see Pasculli, Antonio

CONCERTO PER OBOE E ORCHESTRA, SU TEMI DELL'OPERA "LA FAVORITA" DI G. DONIZETTI [ARR.] see Pasculli, Antonio

CONCERTO PICCOLO see Holm, Mogens Winkel

CONCERTO PICCOLO FOR VIOLIN AND AMATEUR STRING ORCHESTRA see Albertsen, Per Hjort, Concerto Piccolo For Violin Og Amator-Strykeorkester

CONCERTO PICCOLO FOR VIOLIN OG AMATOR-STRYKEORKESTER see Albertsen, Per Hjort

CONCERTO POLONOIS see Telemann, Georg Philipp

CONCERTO POUR 15 INSTRUMENTS SOLISTES, TIMBALES ET CORDES see Francaix, Jean

CONCERTO POUR ALTO ET-OU VIOLON see Philippot, Michel Paul

CONCERTO POUR ARIANE, FOR DOUBLE BASS AND ORCHESTRA see Aubin, Francine

CONCERTO POUR UN BALLET, FOR FLUTE AND ORCHESTRA see Bondon, Jacques

CONCERTO POUR VOIX ELEVEE see Tailleferre, Germaine

CONCERTO QUATERNIO see Schuller, Gunther

CONCERTO RAPSODIE, FOR PIANO AND ORCHESTRA see Lancen, Serge

CONCERTO-RHAPSODY, FOR VIOLIN AND ORCHESTRA see Khachaturian, Aram Ilyich

CONCERTO RIPIENO see Böttcher, Eberhard

CONCERTO ROMANTICO, FOR HARP AND ORCHESTRA see Polgar, Tibor

CONCERTO SACRO, FOR VIOLA AND ORCHESTRA see Klein, Lothar

CONCERTO SOLAIRE FOR BRASS ENSEMBLE AND ORCHESTRA see Bondon, Jacques

CONCERTO SPIRITUOSO NO.4, FOR SOLO VOICE, STRING QUARTET AND ORCHESTRA see Nelhybel, Vaclav

CONCERTO SYMPHONICO see Chemin-Petit, Hans

CONCERTO-SYMPHONY FOR VIOLIN AND ORCHESTRA see Berlinsky, Sergei

CONCERTO TRITTICO see Tomasson, Jonas

CONCERTO 25, FOR GUITAR AND CHAMBER ORCHESTRA see Meranger, Paul

CONCERTO VARIATIONS see Wallace, William

CONCERTO VARIATIONS '76 see Adam, Claus

CONCERTONE FOR FLUTE, TWO CLARINETS, HORN AND ORCHESTRA IN F see Mercadante, G. Saverio

CONCERTONE FOR TWO FLUTES, TWO CLARINETS, HORN AND ORCHESTRA IN F see Mercadante, G. Saverio

CONCERTPIECE, FOR VIOLONCELLO AND
    CHAMBER ORCHESTRA see Van de Vate,
    Nancy Hayes

CONCIERTO AGUEDIANO, FOR GUITAR AND
    ORCHESTRA see Garcia-Abríl, Antón

CONCIERTO BREVE, FOR PIANO AND
    ORCHESTRA see Montsalvatge, Xavier

CONCIERTO COMO UN DIVERTIMENTO, FOR
    VIOLONCELLO AND ORCHESTRA see
    Rodrigo, Joaquín

CONCIERTO DE ARANJUEZ, FOR GUITAR AND
    ORCHESTRA see Rodrigo, Joaquín

CONCIERTO DE ARANJUEZ, FOR HARP AND
    ORCHESTRA see Rodrigo, Joaquín

CONCIERTO DE CAMARA see Orrego-Salas,
    Juan A.

CONCIERTO DE CAMERA see Blanquer,
    Amando

CONCIERTO DE LIZARA NO. 1, FOR OBOE,
    TRUMPET, PERCUSSION, AND STRING
    ORCHESTRA see Barce, Ramón

CONCIERTO DE LIZARA NO. 4 see Barce,
    Ramón

CONCIERTO DE SAMBA, FOR 3 GUITARS AND
    ORCHESTRA see Wüsthoff, Klaus

CONCIERTO DEL ALBAYZIN, FOR HARPSICHORD
    AND ORCHESTRA see Montsalvatge,
    Xavier

CONCIERTO DEL ALMA, FOR VIOLIN AND
    STRING ORCHESTRA see Marco, Tomas

CONCIERTO GALANTE see Bertomeu, Agustin

CONCIERTO HEROICO, FOR PIANO AND
    ORCHESTRA see Rodrigo, Joaquín

CONCIERTO MADRIGAL, FOR 2 GUITARS AND
    ORCHESTRA see Rodrigo, Joaquín

CONCIERTO MUDEJAR, FOR GUITAR AND
    STRING ORCHESTRA see Garcia-Abríl,
    Antón

CONCIERTO PARA UNA FIESTA, FOR GUITAR
    AND ORCHESTRA see Rodrigo, Joaquín

CONCORD see Gudmundsen-Holmgreen, Pelle

CONCORDANZA see Gubaidulina, Sofia

CONCORDIA TANZE see Strauss, Johann,
    [Sr.]

CONCURRENZEN WALZER see Strauss,
    Johann, [Jr.]

CONDUCT (SECOND VERSION) see Trojahn,
    Manfred

CONFESSION: SUITE see Denisov, Edison
    Vasilievich

CONFESSIONS see Korndorf, Nicolai

CONFETTI see Kaper, Bronislaw

CONFIDENCES D'UN JOUEUR DE CLARINETTE,
    LES: GRANDE VALSE DU BAL A LA FETE
    D'ECKERSWIR, FOR CLARINET AND
    ORCHESTRA see Koechlin, Charles

CONFIDENCES D'UN JOUEUR DE CLARINETTE,
    LES: NOCTURNE, FOR VIOLA AND
    ORCHESTRA see Koechlin, Charles

CONFLICTS see Andersson, Gert Ove,
    Konflikter

CONFLUENCE see Barati, George

CONFRONTATIONS see Jørgensen, Erik,
    Konfrontationer

CONFRONTI, FOR HORN AND ORCHESTRA see
    Laman, Wim

CONGRUENCES, FOR FLUTE, OBOE AND
    INSTRUMENTAL ENSEMBLE see Jarrell,
    Michael

CONINCKSKINDEREN see Badings, Henk

CONNOLLY, JUSTIN [RIVEAGH] (1933-   )
    Anima, For Viola And Orchestra [25']
        3.3(English horn).3.3(contrabsn).
        3.2.2.1. 3perc,harp,pno,
        strings,vla solo
    NOVELLO perf mat rent   (C373)

    Diaphony, For Organ And Orchestra
        *Op.31 [20']
        3.3(English horn).3.3(contrabsn).
        4.4.4.1. timp,3perc,pno,
        strings,org solo

CONNOLLY, JUSTIN [RIVEAGH] (cont'd.)

    NOVELLO perf mat rent   (C374)

CONQUEROR, THE: ROMANCE AND TWO DANCES
    see German, [Sir] Edward (Edward
    German Jones)

CONSEQUENZEN WALZER see Strauss, Eduard

CONSERVATI FEDELE, FOR SOLO VOICE AND
    ORCHESTRA see Mozart, Wolfgang
    Amadeus

CONSOLATION see Leifs, Jon

CONSOLATION [ARR] see Schoeck, Othmar

CONSOLAZIONE CONCERTO, FOR ENGLISH HORN
    AND STRING ORCHESTRA see Krol,
    Bernhard

CONSOLI, MARC-ANTONIO (1941-   )
    Afterimages [22']
        3.3.3.3. 4.3.3.1. timp,3perc,
        harp,strings
    MARGUN BP 1051 perf mat rent (C375)

    Naked Masks [20']
        2.2.2.2. 4.2.2.1. timp,perc,pno,
        harp,strings
    sc AM.COMP.AL. perf mat rent (C376)

CONSORT FOR STRINGS see Pleskow, Raoul

CONSORT MUSIC 4 see Rechberger, Herman

CONSORT MUSIC 5 see Rechberger, Herman

CONSORTIEN WALZER see Strauss, Josef

CONSTANT, FRANZ (1910-   )
    Fantasy for Alto Saxophone and
        Orchestra, Op. 41 [12']
        2.2.2.2. 2.2.2.0. timp,perc,
        strings,alto sax solo
    BILLAUDOT perf mat rent   (C377)

CONSTANT, MARIUS (1925-   )
    Candide: Suite For Harpsichord And
        Orchestra [20']
        3.3.4.3. 4.3.3.1. timp,4perc,
        harp,strings,hpsd solo
    SALABERT perf mat rent   (C378)

    Cent Trois Regards Dans L'eau, For
        Violin And Instrumental Ensemble
        [35']
        1.0.1+bass clar.0. 1.0.0.0. perc,
        harp,pno,2vln,vla,vcl,db,vln
        solo
    SALABERT perf mat rent   (C379)

    Cent Trois Regards Dans L'eau, For
        Violin And Orchestra [35']
        3.3.3.3. 4.2.3.1. timp,3perc,
        harp,strings,vln solo
    SALABERT perf mat rent   (C380)

    Concerto For Barrel Organ And
        Orchestra [16']
        2(pic).2.2.2. 2.2.0.0. timp,perc,
        strings, barrel organ solo
    SALABERT perf mat rent   (C381)

    Faciebat Anno, For 24 Violins And
        Orchestra
        3.3.4.3. 4.3.3.1. timp,3perc,
        2harp,24vln,6vla,6vcl,5db
    [14'] SALABERT perf mat rent (C382)

    Perpetuo [6']
        3.3(English horn).2+clar in E
        flat+bass clar.3(contrabsn).
        4.3.3.1. timp,3perc,harp,
        strings
    SALABERT EAS18399P perf mat rent
                                    (C383)
    Piano Personnage, For Piano And
        Instrumental Ensemble [20']
        1.1.1+bass clar+contrabass
        clar.0. 1.1.1.0. 2perc,gtr,elec
        org,cel,vla,vcl,db,pno solo
    sc SALABERT f.s., perf mat rent
                                    (C384)
    Strings For Guitar And Strings [12']
        7vln,2vla,2vcl,db,elec gtr solo
    sc SALABERT f.s., perf mat rent
                                    (C385)
    Strings For Harpsichord And Strings
        [12']
        7vln,2vla,2vcl,db,hpsd solo
    SALABERT perf mat rent   (C386)

    Texas Twilight [2']
        4trp,strings
    SALABERT perf mat rent   (C387)

CONSTANTI see Grabovsky, Leonid

CONSTANTINIDES, DINOS DEMETRIOS
    (1929-   )
    Antitheses
        2fl,ob,3trom,2perc,pno,strings
    SEESAW   (C388)

CONSTANTINIDES, DINOS DEMETRIOS
    (cont'd.)

    Four Songs, For Solo Voice And
        Orchestra
        3.2.3.2. 4.3.3.1. timp,2perc,
        strings
    sc SEESAW $22.00   (C389)

    Kaleidoscope, For Solo Voice And
        Orchestra
        2.1.2.1. 1.1.1.0. perc,harp,pno,
        strings,solo voice
    sc SEESAW $33.00   (C390)

CONSTELLATION see Arnestad, Finn

CONTAGION, LA, FOR SOLO VOICE AND
    ORCHESTRA see Semenoff, Ivan

CONTE FANTASMAGORIQUE see Ford,
    Clifford

CONTE FEERIQUE see Rimsky-Korsakov,
    Nikolai

CONTEMPLATION UPON FLOWERS, A, FOR SOLO
    VOICE AND ORCHESTRA see Hoddinott,
    Alun

CONTEMPLATIONS, FOR SOLO VOICE AND
    CHAMBER ORCHESTRA see Searle,
    Humphrey

CONTEMPLAZIONE see Catalani, Alfredo

CONTERSO see Franzen, Olov

CONTEXTURES II: THE FINAL BEAST, FOR
    SOLO VOICES AND CHAMBER ORCHESTRA
    see Kraft, William

CONTINGENCIAS see Larrauri, Anton

CONTINUO see Berio, Luciano

CONTINUUM FOR ORCHESTRA see Bell, Larry

CONTRA ESTO Y AQUELLO see Garcia Roman,
    Jose

CONTRABANDISTA, EL see Espla, Oscar

CONTRAFACTUM, FOR VIOLONCELLO AND
    ORCHESTRA see Rasmussen, Karl Aage

CONTRAPUNCTI, FOR STRING QUARTET AND
    STRING ORCHESTRA see Payne, Anthony

CONTRARY MOTION see Verbey, Theo,
    Tegenbeweging

CONTRASTI see Bettinelli, Bruno

CONTRASTS see Elgar, [Sir] Edward
    (William) see Morgan, David

CONTRASTS, FOR ENGLISH HORN AND STRING
    ORCHESTRA see Hansen, Theodore Carl

CONTRASTS FOR SYMPHONY ORCHESTRA AND
    JAZZ GROUP see Bjorklund, Terje,
    Kontraster For Symfoniorkester Og
    Jazzgruppe

CONTRASTS: THE WEB AND THE WIND see
    Freedman, Harry

CONTREDANSE see Salieri, Antonio

CONTREES D'UN REVE see Giraud, Suzanne

CONTREPOINT see Aperghis, Georges

CONTRETANZE, ZWOLF, WOO.14 see
    Beethoven, Ludwig van

CONTROVERSEN WALZER see Strauss,
    Johann, [Jr.]

CONUNDRUM see Rieti, Vittorio

CONVERGENCE OF THE TWAIN, THE see
    Nicholson, George

CONVERGENCES see Ratiu, Horia

CONVERSARI PER ORCHESTRA see Di Lotti,
    Silvana

CONVERSATION, FOR PIANO AND ORCHESTRA
    see Arnestad, Finn

CONVERSATION PIECE see Broadbent, Alan

CONVERSE, FREDERICK SHEPHERD
    (1871-1940)
    Mystic Trumpeter, The *Op.18 [12']
        2+pic.2+English horn.2+bass
        clar.2+contrabsn. 4.3.3.1.
        timp,perc,harp,strings
    KALMUS A5686 sc $30.00, set $75.00,
        perf mat rent   (C391)
    SCHIRM.G perf mat rent   (C392)

CONVERSIONS see Boesmans, Philippe

CONVERSIONS, FOR HARP AND STRING
ORCHESTRA see Jarrell, Michael

CONYNGHAM, BARRY (1944-)
Concerto for Double Bass and
Orchestra [18']
2.2.2.2. 2.2.2.0. perc,pno,
strings,db solo
(Shadows of Noh) UNIVER. perf mat
rent (C393)

Concerto for Orchestra [28']
3(pic,alto fl).3(English
horn).3(bass
clar).3(contrabsn). 4.3.3.1.
timp,2perc,harp,pno,strings
(Horizons) UNIVER. perf mat rent
(C394)

Concerto for Violin, Piano and
Orchestra [32']
3(pic,alto fl).3(English
horn).3(bass clar,contrabass
clar).3(contrabsn). 4.3.3.1.
timp,3perc,harp,cel,strings,vln
solo,pno solo
(Southern Cross) UNIVER. perf mat
rent (C395)

Concerto for Violoncello and String
Orchestra [25']
8vln,2vla,vcl,db,vcl solo
sc UNIVER. UE29264 $35.00, perf mat
rent (C396)

Dwellings [25']
1(alto fl).1.1(bass clar).0.
1.1.0.0. perc,harp,pno,gtr,vln,
vla,vcl,db
UNIVER. perf mat rent (C397)

Mirages
2.2.3.2. 4.2.3.1. perc,harp,pno,
strings
study sc UNIVER. 29223 $15.00, perf
mat rent (C398)

Monuments, For Piano And Orchestra
[20']
3(pic,alto fl).3(English horn).2+
bass clar.2+contrabsn. 4.3.3.1.
timp,2perc,harp,cel,strings,
pno/synthesizer solo
UNIVER. perf mat rent (C399)

Recurrences [12']
3.3.2.4. 4.3.3.1. timp,2perc,
harp,org,cel,pno 4-hands,elec
pno,strings
UNIVER. perf mat rent (C400)

Vast I "The Sea" [27']
2.2.2.2. 4.2.3.0. timp,2perc,
harp,pno&cel&synthesizer,
strings
UNIVER. perf mat rent (C401)

Vast II "The Coast" [18']
2.2.2.2. 4.2.3.0. timp,2perc,
harp,pno&cel&synthesizer,
strings
UNIVER. perf mat rent (C402)

Vast III "The Centre" [28']
2.2.2.2. 4.2.3.0. timp,2perc,
harp,pno&cel&synthesizer,
strings,vln solo,vla solo,vcl
solo,db solo
UNIVER. perf mat rent (C403)

Vast IV "The Cities" [23']
2.2.2.2. 4.2.3.0. timp,2perc,
harp,pno&cel&synthesizer,
strings
UNIVER. perf mat rent (C404)

COOKE, ARNOLD (1906-)
Concerto for Clarinet and Orchestra,
No. 2
WORLDWIDE perf mat rent (C405)

Concerto for Violoncello and
Orchestra [25']
2(pic).2.2.2. 4.3.3.1. timp,
3perc,pno,strings,vcl solo
NOVELLO perf mat rent (C406)

Symphony No. 1 [34']
2.2.2.2. 4.3.3.1. timp,strings
NOVELLO perf mat rent (C407)

COOLIDGE, PEGGY STUART (1913-1981)
Evening In New Orleans, An: Suite
[17']
2+pic.1+English horn.2+bass
clar.1+contrabsn.sax. 4.2.2.0.
timp,perc,pno,vibra,harp,
strings
PEER perf mat rent (C408)

New England Autumn [12']
2(pic).2(English horn).2(bass
clar).2. 4.2.2.1.0. timp,perc,
harp,strings
PEER perf mat rent (C409)

COOLIDGE, PEGGY STUART (cont'd.)
Pioneer Dances For Chamber Orchestra
[11'30"]
1.1.2.1. 1.2.1.0. timp,perc,
strings
PEER perf mat rent (C410)

Pioneer Dances For String Orchestra
[11'30"]
string orch
PEER perf mat rent (C411)

Spirituals In Sunshine And Shadow
[13']
2+pic.2.2.2. 4.3.3.1. timp,perc,
harp,strings
PEER perf mat rent (C412)

Voice, The [14']
2+pic.2.2+bass clar.2. 4.3.3.1.
timp,perc,harp,strings
PEER perf mat rent (C413)

COOLS, EUGÈNE (1877-1936)
Mort De Chenier, La [16']
2.3.2.2. 4.2.3.0. perc,harp,
strings
ESCHIG perf mat rent (C414)

Musique Pour Hamlet [35']
3.3.3.3. 4.3.3.0. perc,strings
ESCHIG perf mat rent (C415)

Ouverture Symphonique [7']
3.3.2.2. 4.2.2.1. perc,strings
ESCHIG perf mat rent (C416)

Prelude Pour La Mort De Tintagiles
*Op.92 [40']
0.2.2.2. 4.3.3.0. perc,harp,
strings
ESCHIG perf mat rent (C417)

Symphony, Op. 59, in C minor [40']
3.3.3.3. 4.3.3.0. perc,harp,
strings
ESCHIG perf mat rent (C418)

COOMBES, DOUGLAS
Ting Tang The Elephant, For Narrator
And Orchestra
2(pic).2(English horn).3+bass
clar.2+contrabsn. 4.3.3.1.
timp,3perc,harp,strings,
narrator
LINDSAY (C419)

Ting Tang The Elephant, For Narrator
And Chamber Orchestra
2(pic).1.2.1. 2.2.1.1. timp,
2perc,harp,strings,narrator
LINDSAY (C420)

Treasure Trail, The For Narrator And
Orchestra
1(pic).1.1.1. 2.1.1.1. timp,
2perc,strings,narrator
LINDSAY (C421)

COOPER, PAUL (1926-)
Concerto for Flute and Orchestra
[17']
0.1(English horn).1(bass
clar).1(contrabsn). 1.1.1.0.
timp,perc,pno&cel,strings,fl
solo
HANSEN-NY perf mat rent (C422)

Concerto for Organ and Orchestra
[18']
2.2.2.2. 2.2.2.0. timp,perc,cel,
strings,org solo
HANSEN-NY perf mat rent (C423)

Concerto for Violin and Orchestra,
No. 2 [27']
2.2+English horn.2.2. 2.2.0.0.
perc,harp,strings,vln solo
HANSEN-NY perf mat rent (C424)

Concerto for Violin, Viola and
Orchestra [19']
2.2.2.2. 2.2.0.0. 2perc,harp,cel,
strings,vln solo,vla solo
HANSEN-NY perf mat rent (C425)

Concerto for Violoncello and
Orchestra [21']
2+alto fl.2+English horn.2+bass
clar.2. 4.2.3.1. timp,perc,
2harp,cel,pno,strings,vcl solo
HANSEN-NY perf mat rent (C426)

Coram Morte, For Solo Voice And
Chamber Orchestra [21']
1(alto fl).1(English horn).1(bass
clar).0. 0.0.0.0. 2perc,pno&
cel,2vln,vla,vcl,db,
synthesizer,Mez solo
HANSEN-NY perf mat rent (C427)

Descants, For Viola And Orchestra
[14']
1.1.1.1. 1.1.1.0. pno&cel,timp,
perc,strings,vla solo

COOPER, PAUL (cont'd.)
CHESTER JWC547 perf mat rent (C428)

Duo Concertante, For Violin, Viola
And Orchestra
2.2.2.2. 2.2.0.0. timp,2perc,
harp,cel,strings,vln solo,vla
solo
HANSEN-NY perf mat rent (C429)

Homage [5']
3.2+English horn.2+bass clar.2.
4.3.3.1. harp,cel&pno,timp,
perc,strings
CHESTER JWC481 perf mat rent (C430)

Love Songs And Dances
1(pic,alto fl).1(English
horn).1(bass clar).1. 1.1.1.0.
perc,harp,7vln,2vla,2vcl,db
HANSEN-NY perf mat rent (C431)

Shenandoah, A [8']
2.2+English horn.2+bass clar.2.
4.2.3.1. timp,3perc,harp,pno&
cel,strings,fl solo,trp solo,
vla solo
HANSEN-NY perf mat rent (C432)

Symphony In Two Movements [18']
2+pic.2+English horn.2+bass
clar.2+contrabsn. 4.4.3.1.
3perc,harp,strings
HANSEN-NY perf mat rent (C433)

Symphony No. 6 [26']
2+alto fl.2+English horn.2+bass
clar.2+contrabsn. 4.4.3.1.
2perc,harp,cel,pno,strings
HANSEN-NY perf mat rent (C434)

Variants For Orchestra [15']
2.2.2+bass clar.2. 4.3.3.1. timp,
3perc,pno&cel,strings
HANSEN-NY perf mat rent (C435)

COORDENADAS INFORMALES see Santiago,
Rodrigo de

COPLAND, AARON (1900-1990)
Eight Poems Of Emily Dickinson, For
Solo Voice And Chamber Orchestra
[20']
1.1.1.1. 1.1.1.1. harp,strings,
med solo
min sc BOOSEY 934 $22.75, perf mat
rent (C436)

Proclamation [arr.]
(Ramey, Philip) 3(pic).2.2.2.
4.3.3.1. timp,perc,pno,strings
[2'] BOOSEY perf mat rent (C437)

Three Latin American Sketches [10']
1.1.1.1. 0.1.0.0. perc,2pno,
strings
min sc BOOSEY 814 $7.00, perf mat
rent (C438)

COPPER, FOR BRASS QUINTET AND ORCHESTRA
see Torke, Michael

COPPOLA, PIERO (1888-1971)
Deux Danses Symphoniques
study sc LEDUC 597-00158 $3.50
(C439)

Poem for Piano and Orchestra [30']
2.3.2.3. 4.3.3.1. perc,cel,
strings,pno solo
study sc ESCHIG f.s., perf mat rent
(C440)

Scherzo Fantasque [6']
3.2.2.2. 4.2.3.1. perc,harp,
strings
study sc ESCHIG f.s., perf mat rent
(C441)

COPPOOLSE, DAVID (1960-)
Storia Della Mille E Una Notte, Una
[16']
2.2.2.2. 2.2.2.0. timp,vibra,
harp,pno,strings
DONEMUS perf mat rent (C442)

COPTIC LIGHT see Feldman, Morton

CORAL, GIAMPAOLO (1944-)
Suite for Orchestra [16']
2.2.2.2. 4.3.3.1. timp,3perc,pno,
harp,strings
SONZOGNO perf mat rent (C443)

Tout A Coup Et Comme Par Jeu, For
Flute And Orchestra [15']
3.3.3.3. 4.3.3.1. timp,perc,cel,
pno,harp,strings,fl solo
SONZOGNO perf mat rent (C444)

CORALE see Berio, Luciano

CORALE, INTERLUDIO E ARIA see Knapik,
Eugeniusz

CORAM MORTE, FOR SOLO VOICE AND CHAMBER
ORCHESTRA see Cooper, Paul

CORDERO, ERNESTO (1946-   )
    Concerto Evocativo, For Guitar And
        Orchestra [18']
        1.1.2.1. 2.1.0.0. timp,strings,
            gtr solo
        ESCHIG perf mat rent   (C445)

CORDERO, ROQUE (1917-   )
    Capricho Interiorano [5']
        3.2.3.2. 3.2.3.0. timp,perc,
            strings
        PEER perf mat rent   (C446)

    Momentum Jubilo
        0.0.0.0. 3.3.3.1. timp,perc,
            strings
        (in auditorium: 5 trp, 3 horn,
            chimes) PEER perf mat rent (C447)

    Symphony No. 4 [35']
        2+pic.2+English horn.2+bass
            clar.2. 4.3.3.1. timp,perc,
            strings
        PEER perf mat rent   (C448)

CORELLI, ARCANGELO (1653-1713)
    Christmas Concerto *see Concerto
        Grosso, Op. 6, No. 8, in G Minor

    Concerti Grossi, Op. 6, Nos. 1-6
        min sc KALMUS K01242 $7.00   (C449)

    Concerto Grosso, Op. 6, No. 3, in C
        minor
        (Schering) string orch,kbd,2vln
            soli,vla solo [14'] KAHNT KT 8121
            f.s.   (C450)

    Concerto Grosso, Op. 6, No. 8, in G
        minor
        string orch,cont,2A rec soli
            (version of 1725) sc,pts AMADEUS
            BP 703 f.s.   (C451)
        (Schering) string orch,kbd,2vln
            soli,vcl solo KAHNT KT 6819 f.s.
                                      (C452)
    Sonata da Chiesa, Op. 3, No. 12, in
        A, [arr.]
        (Bruni) string orch [8'] KALMUS
            A7333 sc $7.00, set $7.00, pts
            $1.50, ea.   (C453)

CORIGLIANO, JOHN (1938-   )
    Altered States Ballet [25']
        3(pic).3(English horn).2(bass
            clar).3(contrabsn). 4.3.3.1.
            timp,3perc,harp,pno,strings
        SCHIRM.G perf mat rent   (C454)

    Aria for Oboe and String Orchestra
        (from Concerto For Oboe And
        Orchestra) [6']
        string orch,ob solo
        SCHIRM.G perf mat rent   (C455)

    Campane Di Ravello [3']
        3+pic.3+English horn.3+bass
            clar.3+contrabsn. 4.4.3.1.
            timp,pno,5perc,harp,pno,strings
        SCHIRM.G perf mat rent   (C456)

    Concerto for Clarinet and Orchestra
        study sc SCHIRM.G $42.50, perf mat
        rent   (C457)

    Concerto for Oboe and Orchestra [26']
        3.1.2.2. 2.1.1.0. timp,perc,harp,
            pno&cel,strings,ob solo
        SCHIRM.G perf mat rent   (C458)

    Creations, For Narrator And Chamber
        Orchestra [24']
        1+pic.1+English horn.1+bass
            clar.1. 2.1.1.0. timp,perc,pno,
            harp,strings,narrator
        SCHIRM.G perf mat rent   (C459)

    Fantasia On An Ostinato [14']
        3(pic).3.3.3(contrabsn). 4.4.3.1.
            timp,4perc,harp,pno,strings
        study sc SCHIRM.G 50541080 $18.95,
        perf mat rent   (C460)

    Overture To The Imaginary Invalid
        (from Gazebo Dances) [4']
        2(pic).2.2.2. 4.3.3.1. timp,
            3perc,pno,strings
        SCHIRM.G perf mat rent   (C461)

    Pied Piper Fantasy, For Flute And
        Orchestra [35']
        2(pic).3.3.3(contrabsn). 4.3.3.1.
            timp,5-6perc,harp,pno,cel,
            strings,fl solo, children's
            group: flute, drums
        SCHIRM.G perf mat rent   (C462)

    Promenade Overture [8']
        2+pic.2.2.2+opt contrabsn.
            4.4.3.1. timp,4perc,harp,
            strings
        sc SCHIRM.G 50480020 $15.00, perf
        mat rent   (C463)

CORIGLIANO, JOHN (cont'd.)

    Ritual Dance (from Altered States)
        [3']
        3(pic).3.3(clar in E flat,bass
            clar).3(contrabsn). 4.3.3.1.
            timp,perc,harp,strings
        SCHIRM.G perf mat rent   (C464)

    Soliloquy, For Clarinet And Orchestra
        (from Concerto For Clarinet And
        Orchestra) [9']
        2+pic.2(English horn).0+bass
            clar.2+contrabsn. 1.2.3.1.
            harp,pno,strings,clar solo
        SCHIRM.G perf mat rent   (C465)

    Summer Fanfare [9']
        2+pic.3.3.3. 4+opt 2horn.3+opt
            trp in D.3.3. timp,4perc,pno,
            harp,strings
        SCHIRM.G perf mat rent   (C466)

    Symphony No. 1 [35']
        4(pic).3(English horn).3(clar in
            E flat)+bass clar.3+contrabsn.
            6.5.4.2. timp,5perc,harp,pno,
            4mand,strings
        SCHIRM.G perf mat rent   (C467)

    Three Hallucinations [12']
        2+pic.3.3.3. 4.3.3.1. timp,6perc,
            harp,2pno,org,strings
        study sc SCHIRM.G 50507750 $30.00,
        perf mat rent   (C468)

    Tournaments [12']
        2+pic.2+English horn.2+bass
            clar.2+contrabsn. 4.3.3.1.
            timp,3perc,harp,pno,strings
        SCHIRM.G perf mat rent   (C469)

    Williamsburg Sampler, A [11']
        2.1.0.1. 0.0.0.0. hpsd/harp,
            strings
        SCHIRM.G perf mat rent   (C470)

CORIOLAN OVERTURE see Beethoven, Ludwig
    van

CORNELIUS, PETER (1824-1874)
    Barbier Von Bagdad, Der: Overture
        KALMUS A5132 sc $20.00, set $22.00,
        perf mat rent   (C471)

    Musical Works. Leipzig, 1905-1906
        (microfiche reprint) UNIV.MUS.ED.
        $75.00   (C472)

CORNELIUS MARCH see Mendelssohn-
    Bartholdy, Felix

CORNILIOS, NICOS (1954-   )
    Peupliers [8']
        7vln,2vla,2vcl,db
        SALABERT perf mat rent   (C473)

CORNO INOPPORTUNO, UN, FOR HORN AND
    STRING ORCHESTRA see Bolzoni,
    Giovanni

CORONA see Takemitsu, Toru

CORONA, LA, FOR SOLO VOICES AND CHAMBER
    ORCHESTRA see Rice, Thomas N.

CORONACH see Berkeley, Michael see
    Losh, Werner J.

CORONATION MARCH see Elgar, [Sir]
    Edward (William) see German, [Sir]
    Edward (Edward German Jones) see
    Svendsen, Johan (Severin),
    Kroningsmarsj

CORPO IN LUCE, FOR PIANO AND ORCHESTRA
    see Jansson, Johannes

CORPS DE LOUANGE, UN see Leroux,
    Philippe

CORPUS CUM FIGURIS see Ruders, Poul

CORREGGIA, ENRICO (1933-   )
    Duna [11']
        bass fl,gtr,pno,4vln,2vla,2vcl,db
        SALABERT perf mat rent   (C474)

    Gial'eolia Di Notte [9']
        1.1.1.1. 1.1.1.0. 2perc,pno,2vln,
            vla,vcl,db
        SALABERT perf mat rent   (C475)

CORREGIDOR, DER: VORSPIEL see Wolf,
    Hugo

CORREGIDOR: OVERTURE see Wolf, Hugo,
    Corregidor, Der: Vorspiel

CORREGIDOR Y LA MOLINERA, EL: CONCERT
    SUITE see Falla, Manuel de

CORREGIO see Hartmann, Johan Peder
    Emilius

CORRETTE, MICHEL (1709-1795)
    Concerto for Harpsichord and String
        Orchestra, Op. 26, No. 1 [13'10"]
        string orch,hpsd/org solo
        (Petit, J.L.) sc,pts BILLAUDOT f.s.
                                      (C476)
    Concerto for Trumpet and String
        Orchestra in G
        (Thilde, J.) string orch,trp solo
        [7'] BILLAUDOT perf mat rent
                                      (C477)

CORRIDA, LA see Ferraro, Ralph

CORRO INFRANGIBLE, EL see Reverdy,
    Michele

CORSAIRE, LE see Berlioz, Hector
    (Louis)

CORTEGE BURLESQUE see Chabrier,
    [Alexis-] Emmanuel

CORY, ELEANOR (1943-   )
    Tapestry [15']
        3.2.3.3. 4.3.3.1. perc,strings
        sc AM.COMP.AL. $35.50   (C478)

COSATSCHOQUE, LE see Dargomyzhsky,
    Alexander Sergeyevich, Kasachok

COSI DUNQUE TRADISCI, FOR SOLO VOICE
    AND ORCHESTRA see Mozart, Wolfgang
    Amadeus

COSI FAN TUTTE: AH GUARDA, SORELLA, FOR
    SOLO VOICES AND ORCHESTRA see
    Mozart, Wolfgang Amadeus

COSI FAN TUTTE: DER ODEM DER LIEBE, FOR
    SOLO VOICE AND ORCHESTRA see
    Mozart, Wolfgang Amadeus, Cosi Fan
    Tutte: Un' Aura Amorosa, For Solo
    Voice And Orchestra

COSI FAN TUTTE: DONNE MIE, LA FATE A
    TANTI, FOR SOLO VOICE AND ORCHESTRA
    see Mozart, Wolfgang Amadeus

COSI FAN TUTTE: E AMORE UN LADRONCELLO,
    FOR SOLO VOICE AND ORCHESTRA see
    Mozart, Wolfgang Amadeus

COSI FAN TUTTE: EIN LOSER DIEB IST
    AMOR, FOR SOLO VOICE AND ORCHESTRA
    see Mozart, Wolfgang Amadeus, Cosi
    Fan Tutte: E Amore Un Ladroncello,
    For Solo Voice And Orchestra

COSI FAN TUTTE: MÄDCHEN, SO TREIBT
    IHR'S MIT ALLEN, FOR SOLO VOICE AND
    ORCHESTRA see Mozart, Wolfgang
    Amadeus, Cosi Fan Tutte: Donne Mie,
    La Fate A Tanti, For Solo Voice And
    Orchestra

COSI FAN TUTTE: SCHON EIN MÄDCHEN VON
    FÜNFZEHN JAHREN, FOR SOLO VOICE AND
    ORCHESTRA see Mozart, Wolfgang
    Amadeus, Cosi Fan Tutte: Una Donna
    A Quindici Anni, For Solo Voice And
    Orchestra

COSI FAN TUTTE: UN' AURA AMOROSA, FOR
    SOLO VOICE AND ORCHESTRA see
    Mozart, Wolfgang Amadeus

COSI FAN TUTTE: UNA DONNA A QUINDICI
    ANNI, FOR SOLO VOICE AND ORCHESTRA
    see Mozart, Wolfgang Amadeus

COSMA, EDGAR (1919-   )
    Concerto for Trumpet and Orchestra
        [12'40"]
        1.1.1.1. 2.0.0.0. 2perc,harp,
            strings,trp solo
        BILLAUDOT perf mat rent   (C479)

    Invocation, For Alto Saxophone And
        Orchestra [4']
        2.2.2.2. 3.3.3.0. timp,perc,cel,
            pno,harp,strings,alto sax solo
        BILLAUDOT perf mat rent   (C480)

COSMIC CYCLE see Rudhyar, Dane (Daniel
    Chennevière)

COSMOGONIE see Jolivet, Andre

COSMOGONIES see Tisne, Antoine

COSMOPHONIE see Prevost, Andre

COTILLON POLKA see Strauss, Johann,
    [Jr.]

COULEURS DU TEMPS, VERSION NO. 1 see
    Miereanu, Costin

COULEURS PRINTANIÈRES see Klein,
    Immanuel

COULTHARD, JEAN (1908-   )
    Autumn Symphony [23']
        string orch
        CAN.MUS.CENT. MI 1500 C855AU (C481)

COULTHARD, JEAN (cont'd.)

Meditation And Three Dances, For
Viola And String Orchestra
string orch,vla solo
CAN.MUS.CENT. MI 1612 C855ME (C482)

COUNT UGOLINO, FOR SOLO VOICE AND
CHAMBER ORCHESTRA see Willingham,
Lawrence

COUNTERPOINTS, FOR PIANO AND CHAMBER
ORCHESTRA see Doppmann, William

COUNTRY GARDENS see Grainger, Percy
Aldridge

COUNTRY NIGHT see Reed, Alfred

COUP DE COUPERIN see Hermans, Nico

COUPERIN, FRANÇOIS (LE GRAND)
(1668-1733)
Allemande, [arr.]
(Hoeree, A.) opt fl,opt ob,opt bsn,
strings [7'] BILLAUDOT perf mat
rent (C483)

Concert In G Dans Le Gout Theatral
[arr]
(Oubradous) 2.2.0.1. 0.1.0.0. timp,
strings [16'] KALMUS A 7302 sc
$20.00, set $30.00, pts $2.50,
ea., perf mat rent (C484)

Folies Francaises, Les [arr.]
(McAlister) 2(pic).2(English
horn).2.2. 2.1.0.0. timp,strings
[9'30"] KALMUS A6066 sc $20.00,
set $20.00, perf mat rent (C485)

Paix Du Parnasse, La [arr.]
(Boulay, L.) hpsd,strings [8'25"]
sc BILLAUDOT f.s., perf mat rent
(C486)

Visionnaire, La [arr.]
(Petit, J.L.) string orch [7'45"]
sc,pts BILLAUDOT f.s. (C487)

COUPERIN, LOUIS (ca. 1626-1661)
Sarabande And Chaconne [arr.]
(Cruft, Adrian) string orch [4'30"]
sc JOAD f.s., perf mat rent
(C488)

COUPLET FOR A DESERT SUMMER see
Stallcop, Glenn

COUPLETS, FOR HARPSICHORD AND ORCHESTRA
see Castiglioni, Niccolò

COUROUPOS, GEORGES (1942-)
Abstr'acte *Op.21 [10'15"]
1.1.1.1. 1.1.1.1. tam-tam,org,
vln,vla,vcl
RIDEAU perf mat rent (C489)

COURSE OF NATURE see Hunfeld, Xander

COURSING see Knussen, Oliver

COURTYARD MUSIC see Drew, James M.

COUTURE, GUILLAUME
Reverie [6'25"]
2.2.2.2. 3.0.0.0. timp,harp,
strings
sc,pts CAN.MUS.HER. f.s. (C490)

COVENTRY see Tausky, Vilem

COWBOY'S MEDITATION, FOR SOLO VOICE AND
ORCHESTRA see Guion, David Wendall
Fentress

COWBOY'S OVERTURE, THE see Williams,
John T.

COWELL, HENRY DIXON (1897-1965)
Celtic Set [14']
2.2.2.2. 2.2.1.1. timp,perc,
strings
AMP perf mat rent (C491)

Flirtatious Jig, For Violin And
String Orchestra [2']
string orch,vln solo
sc AMP 50488516 $25.00, perf mat
rent (C492)

Four Irish Tales, For Piano And
Orchestra [13']
2+pic.3.3.3. 4.3.3.1. timp,perc,
strings,pno solo
AMP perf mat rent (C493)

Movement, For String Orchestra
string orch
AMP perf mat rent (C494)

Rhythmicana
1+pic.1.1.1. 4.3.3.1. strings,
rhythmicon
AMP perf mat rent (C495)

COWIE, EDWARD (1943-)
Atlas [35']
3(pic,alto fl).2+English
horn.2(clar in E flat)+bass
clar.2+contrabsn.alto sax.
4.3(flügelhorn,trp in D).3.1.
timp,3perc,harp,pno&hpsd&cel,
strings
SCHOTT perf mat rent (C496)

Endymion Nocturnes, For Solo Voice
And Orchestra [23']
horn,strings,T solo
CHESTER perf mat rent (C497)

Leviathan [26']
4(pic,alto fl).4(English
horn).4(bass
clar).4(contrabsn). 6.4.4.2.
2harp,6perc,strings
CHESTER JWC390 perf mat rent (C498)

Moon, Sea And Stars, The: Nocturnes,
For Solo Voice And Chamber
Orchestra [18']
horn,perc,4vln,2vla,2vcl,2db,T
solo
CHESTER JWC 348 perf mat rent
(C499)

Roof Of Heaven, The, For Solo Voice
And Orchestra [15']
0.2(English horn).0.0. 2.0.0.0.
strings,T solo
SCHOTT perf mat rent (C500)

COWLES, DARLEEN
And Still..., For Horn And Orchestra
[22']
2(pic).2.2.2. 2.2.2(bass trom).0.
perc,strings,horn solo
sc AM.COMP.AL. $28.20 (C501)

COX, HARRY (1923-)
Sinfonietta [15']
1.1.1.1. 1.0.0.0. strings
BILLAUDOT perf mat rent (C502)

CRACKS-REFORMS-BURSTS see Chenoweth,
Gerald

CRADLE SONG [ARR.] see Skinner, J.
Scott

CRAWFORD, PAUL (1947-)
Selkirk Music
2.1.1.0. 0.1.0.0. strings
CAN.MUS.CENT. MI 1200 C899SE (C503)

CRAWLEY, CLIFFORD
Canadian Dances: Set 1 [16']
2.2.2.2. 4.2.3.1. timp,3perc,
harp/pno,strings
CAN.MUS.CENT. MI 1100 C911CA (C504)

Concertino for Piano and Orchestra,
No. 2
2.2.2.2. 4.2.3.1. timp,2perc,
strings,pno solo
CAN.MUS.CENT. MI 1361 C911C2 (C505)

Gemini Dances, For 2 Violins And
Orchestra
2(pic).2(English horn).2.2.
4.2.3.1. timp,2perc,harp,2vln
soli
CAN.MUS.CENT. MI 1411 C911GE (C506)

Group Of Seven, A [15']
string orch,opt kbd
CAN.MUS.CENT. MI 1500 C911GR (C507)

Sinfonietta
2.2.2.2. 2.2.0.0. timp,perc,strings
CAN.MUS.CENT. MI 1200 C911SI
(C508)

Threnody
3.2.2.2. 4.2.3.1. timp,2perc,
strings
CAN.MUS.CENT. MI 1100 C911T (C509)

CREATION, THE, FOR NARRATOR AND
ORCHESTRA see Engel, [A.] Lehmann

CREATIONS, FOR NARRATOR AND CHAMBER
ORCHESTRA see Corigliano, John

CREMER, CURT (1926-)
Bolero [12']
3.3.3.3.alto sax. 4.4.3.1. timp,
perc,harp,elec org,strings
sc SIKORSKI f.s., perf mat rent
(C510)

CRENEAUX see Fontyn, Jacqueline

CREPUSCULE see Massenet, Jules

CRESCENDO, LE: OVERTURE see Cherubini,
Luigi

CRESCENT MOON see Ye, Xiao-Gang, Xin
Yue

CRESSWELL, LYELL
Salm [14']
3.3.3.3. 4.3.3.1. timp,3perc,
harp,strings
sc WAI-TE-ATA f.s. (C511)

CRESTON, PAUL (1906-1985)
Kangaroo Kaper
SHAWNEE perf mat rent (C512)

Sadhana, For Violoncello And
Orchestra *Op.117 [20']
2.2.2.2. 2.2.2.0. timp,perc,harp,
strings,vcl solo
study sc SCHIRM.G 50339920 $24.00,
perf mat rent (C513)

Symphony No. 6, Op. 118 [25']
2.2.2.2. 2.2.2.0. perc,org,
strings
sc SCHIRM.G 006-48523 $25.00 (C514)

CRICKET ON THE HEARTH, THE: PRELUDE,
ACT III see Goldmark, Karl,
Heimchen Am Herd, Das: Prelude, Act
III

CRIES see Holm, Mogens Winkel

CRIMSON DREAM see Chatman, Stephen

CRIMSON SLIPPER see Cacavas, John

CRIN BLANC: SUITE see Le Roux, Maurice

CRIPTOGRAFIA, FOR VIOLA, AND ORCHESTRA
see Gentile, Ada

CRISPINO QUADRILLE see Strauss, Josef

CRISTOFORO COLUMBO see Ortolani, Riz

CROCE E DELIZIA, FOR SOLO VOICE AND
INSTRUMENTAL ENSEMBLE see Capdenat,
Philippe

CROCKETT, DONALD (1951-)
Lyrikos, For Solo Voice And Orchestra
[21']
2(alto fl).2.2(bass clar).2.
2.2.1.0. 2harp,strings,T solo
PEER perf mat rent (C515)

Melting Voice, The [4']
1.1.1.1. 2.1.1.0. 2perc,pno,harp,
3vln,vla,vcl,db
NORRUTH perf mat rent (C516)

Melting Voices
3.3.3.3. 4.3.3.1. harp,pno&cel,
strings
NORRUTH 4.0100.7 perf mat rent
(C517)

Still Life With Bell [15']
1(pic).0+English horn.1(bass
clar).1. 1.1.1.0. perc,pno,
2vln,vla,vcl,db
NORRUTH perf mat rent (C518)

Sun And Moon Dance And Blow Trumpets,
The [4']
3.3.3(clar in E flat,clar in
A).3. 4.3.3.1. 2perc,pno,harp,
strings
NORRUTH perf mat rent (C519)

Tenth Muse, The, For Solo Voice And
Orchestra [30']
2(pic,alto fl).1+English
horn.2(bass clar).2. 2.2.1.0.
timp,perc,strings,S solo
NORRUTH perf mat rent (C520)

CROISADE DES ENFANTS, LA: PRELUDE, PART
II see Pierne, Gabriel

CROSSE, GORDON (1937-)
Array [30']
trp,strings
OXFORD perf mat rent (C521)

Concerto Da Camera (Concerto for
Violin and Orchestra, No. 1, Op.
6) [19']
1.1(English horn).2(bass clar).1.
2.2.1.0. timp,2perc,strings,vln
solo
sc OXFORD 3634526 f.s., perf mat
rent (C522)

Concerto for Violin and Orchestra,
No. 1, Op. 6
see Concerto Da Camera

Elegy And Scherzo Alla Marcia (from
String Quartet, Op. 47) [10']
string orch
OXFORD perf mat rent (C523)

Symphony No. 2 [24']
3.3.3.3. 4.3.3.1. timp,4perc,
harp,cel,strings
OXFORD perf mat rent (C524)

CROSSE, GORDON (cont'd.)

Thel, For Flute And Orchestra [14']
2horn,strings,fl solo
OXFORD perf mat rent   (C525)

Water Music [11']
rec,strings
OXFORD perf mat rent   (C526)

Wildboy [27']
2.2.2.2. 4.2.3.0. 2-3perc,harp,
hpsd/pno/gtr,strings
OXFORD perf mat rent   (C527)

Young Apollo, The
2.2.4.2. 4.3.3.0. timp,perc,harp/
cel,strings,pno solo
[30'] OXFORD perf mat rent   (C528)

CROSSFIRE see Wuorinen, Charles

CROSSING see Einaudi, Ludovico

CROSSINGS see Linkola, Jukka

CROSSWAYS see Prodromides, Jean

CROTCH, WILLIAM (1775-1847)
Symphony
(Temperly; Greenbaum; Hill) ("The
Symphony" Vol. E-IV-V) sc GARLAND
ISBN 0-8240-3825-5 $90.00
contains also: Clementi, Muzio,
Symphony   (C529)

CROWN OF INDIA SUITE see Elgar, [Sir]
Edward (William)

CROWN OF INDIA SUITE: MARCH OF THE
MOGUL EMPERORS see Elgar, [Sir]
Edward (William)

CRUCIFIXUS see Turina De Santos, Jose
Luis

CRUCIFIXUS, FOR SOLO VOICE AND
ORCHESTRA see Smith, Larry Alan

CRUFT, ADRIAN (1921-1987)
Concertino for Clarinet and String
Orchestra, Op. 21 [12']
string orch,clar solo
sc JOAD f.s., perf mat rent (C530)

Diversion "If All The World Were
Paper" [2']
string orch
sc JOAD f.s., perf mat rent (C531)

Impromptu for Clarinet and String
Orchestra, Op. 22a [2'30"]
string orch,clar/vla solo
sc JOAD f.s., perf mat rent (C532)

Meditation On The Passion Chorale
*Op.72a [3'30"]
string orch, string trio soli
sc JOAD f.s., perf mat rent (C533)

Oxford Suite *Op.36 [10']
2.1.2.1. 2.2.1.0. timp,perc,
strings
sc JOAD f.s., perf mat rent (C534)

Prospero's Island *Op.39 [11']
3.3.3.3. 4.3.3.1. timp,2perc,pno,
cel,harp,strings
sc JOAD f.s., perf mat rent (C535)

Scherzetto, For Violin And String
Orchestra *Op.4 [2'30"]
strings,harp/pno,vln/harmonica
solo
sc JOAD f.s., perf mat rent (C536)

Tamburlaine *Op.38 [10']
2.2.2.2. 4.2.0.0. timp,perc,
strings
sc JOAD f.s., perf mat rent (C537)

CRUMB, GEORGE (1929-   )
Haunted Landscape, A [18']
3.3.3.3. 4.3.3.1. timp,4perc,
2harp,pno,strings
sc PETERS P67003 f.s., perf mat
rent   (C538)

CRUSADER MARCH, THE see Sousa, John
Philip

CRUSELL, BERNHARD HENRIK (1775-1838)
Concertino for Bassoon and Orchestra
in B flat
MUS. RARA perf mat rent   (C539)

Concerto for Clarinet and Orchestra,
Op. 11, in B flat
(Bieger) sc KUNZEL 10226 f.s., perf
mat rent   (C540)

Introduktion Und Variationen Uber Ein
Schwedisches Lied *Op.12 [9']
1.2.0.2. 2.2.0.0. timp,strings,
clar solo
(Michaels) SIKORSKI perf mat rent

CRUSELL, BERNHARD HENRIK (cont'd.)
(C541)

CRUX FIDELIS, FOR SOLO VOICE AND
ORCHESTRA see Stout, Alan

CRUZ DE CASTRO, CARLOS (1941-   )
Proceso [20']
20vln,8vla,8vcl,6db
ALPUERTO   (C542)

Proyeccion De La Verical [13']
1+pic+alto fl.2+English horn.1+
clar in E flat+bass
clar.2.soprano sax.tenor sax.
6.3.3.1. perc,pno,2harp,strings
ALPUERTO   (C543)

CRYSTALS, FOR ALTO FLUTE AND ORCHESTRA
see Rypdal, Terje, Krystaller, For
Alto Flute And Orchestra

CSARDAS MACABRE [ARR.] see Liszt, Franz

CSEMICZKY, M.
Antiphonae No. 1
string orch
sc EMB 12862 f.s., perf mat rent
(C544)

Commedia Senza Parole
sc EMB 13246 f.s., perf mat rent
(C545)

Pas A Pas
sc EMB 12813 f.s., perf mat rent
(C546)

Sinfonietta
sc EMB 13086 f.s., perf mat rent
(C547)

CSV: KONKURRANSEMUSIKK see Persen, John

CTION see Stuhec, Igor

CUATRE CANCONS EN LENGUA CATALANA, FOR
SOLO VOICE AND ORCHESTRA see
Rodrigo, Joaquín

CUATRO IMPROMTUS see Arambarri, Jesús

CUATRO MOVIMENTOS PARA ORQUESTA see
Angulo, Manuel

CUATRO NOCTURNOS, FOR SOLO VOICES AND
ORCHESTRA see Chavez, Carlos

CUEVA DE NERJA, LA see Arteaga, Angel

CUI, CÉSAR ANTONOVICH (1835-1918)
Deux Morceaux, For Cello And
Orchestra *Op.36
"Two Pieces For Cello And
Orchestra" KALMUS A7462 sc
$20.00, set $20.00, pts $1.50,
ea., perf mat rent   (C548)

Fils Du Mandarin: Overture
KALMUS A5809 sc $15.00, set $22.00,
perf mat rent   (C549)

Scherzo No. 2, Op. 2, in G minor
2(pic).2.2.2. 4.2.3.1. timp,strings
[7'30"] KALMUS A5813 sc $10.00,
set $20.00, perf mat rent   (C550)

Scherzo, Op. 82, No. 2, in F
3.1.1.1. 4.0.2.1. timp,perc,harp,
strings
VAAP perf mat rent   (C551)

Tarantelle, Op. 12
3(pic).2.2.2. 4.2.3.1. timp,perc,
harp,strings [6'] KALMUS A5815 sc
$15.00, set $25.00, perf mat rent
(C552)
SONZOGNO perf mat rent   (C553)

Two Pieces For Cello And Orchestra
see Deux Morceaux, For Cello And
Orchestra

CUIVRES CELESTES see Miereanu, Costin

CUIVRES DO-RE see Miereanu, Costin

CULMINATIONS see Sandström, Sven-David

CUMNOCK ORCADIAN, THE see Macmillan,
James

CUNIOT, LAURENT (1957-   )
Lice Des Nuits, La [20']
4(pic,alto fl).4(English
horn).4(bass
clar).4(contrabsn). 4.4.3.1.
timp,2perc,strings,2synthesizer
SALABERT perf mat rent   (C554)

CUNNINGHAM, MICHAEL GERALD (1937-   )
Islands
3.3.3.2. 4.3.3.1. timp,perc,harp,
strings
sc SEESAW $16.00   (C555)

Trans Actions
2.2.2.2. 4.2.2.1. cel,harp,
strings
sc SEESAW $24.00, perf mat rent

CUNNINGHAM, MICHAEL GERALD (cont'd.)
(C556)

CURTIS, ERNESTO DE
Torna A Sorrento, For Solo Voice And
Orchestra
KALMUS A6205 sc $4.00, set $9.00,
pts $.75, ea.   (C557)

CURTIS-SMITH, CURTIS O.B. (1941-   )
Great American Symphony [22']
3.3.4.3.sax. 4.4.2.1. timp,perc,
banjo,pno,strings
PIEDMONT perf mat rent   (C558)

CUSATELLI, ALESSANDRO (1956-   )
Elegia D'estate [6']
string orch
SONZOGNO perf mat rent   (C559)

Sei Preludi [19']
3.3.3.2. 3.2.0.0. timp,perc,cel,
harp,strings
SONZOGNO perf mat rent   (C560)

CYCLES OF LIFE, FOR SOLO VOICE, HORN
AND STRING ORCHESTRA see Baker,
David N.

CYCLOIDEN WALZER see Strauss, Johann,
[Jr.]

CYGNE, LE see Ysaye, Eugene

CYGNOLOGY, FOR SOLO VOICE AND ORCHESTRA
see Tanenbaum, Elias

CYRANO DE BERGERAC see Wagenaar, Johan

CYTHEREN QUADRILLE see Strauss, Johann,
[Jr.]

CZECH SUITE see Dvorák, Antonín, Suite,
Op. 39

CZERWONE I CZARNE, FOR PIANO AND
ORCHESTRA see Bauer, Jerzy

CZYZ, HENRYK (1923-   )
Canzona Di Barocco [7']
string orch
sc POLSKIE f.s.   (C561)

D

DA! see Knaifel, Alexander

DA A DA DA see Sciarrino, Salvatore

DA LACHEN JA DIE HUHNER, FOR SOLO VOICE AND ORCHESTRA see Maasz, Gerhard

DA UNA LETTURA DI HUSSERL see Bo, Sonia

DAGEN VAKNAR see Kielland, Olav

DAGENS NYHETER, FOR SOLO VOICE AND CHAMBER ORCHESTRA see Kvam, Oddvar S.

DAI, DIMMI, SU! see Bussotti, Sylvano

DAISSI: SUITE see Paliashvili, Sachari

DAKIN, CHARLES
    Eypa
        2clar,2tenor sax,2trp,2trom,4vla,
            4vcl,2db
        sc,pts DORN $40.00   (D1)

    Suite Concertante, For Saxophone And
        String Orchestra
        string orch,baritone sax solo
        sc,pts DORN $85.00   (D2)

DAL FILO DI ARIANNA, FOR PIANO AND INSTRUMENTAL ENSEMBLE see D'amico, Matteo

DAL FONDO DI UNO SPECCHIO see Gentilucci, Armando

DALASVIT see Söderlundh, Lille Bror

DALBY, MARTIN (1942-   )
    Concerto for Viola and Orchestra
        [17']
        3(pic).1(English horn).3(bass
            clar).1(contrabsn). 3.1.2.2.
            harp,2perc,strings
        NOVELLO perf mat rent   (D3)

    Ruisenor, El [10']
        3.3.3.3. 4.3.3.1. timp,3perc,
            harp,strings
        NOVELLO perf mat rent   (D4)

DALE, BENJAMIN JAMES (1885-1943)
    Flowing Tide, The [28']
        3(pic).2+English horn.3(clar in E
            flat)+bass clar.2+contrabsn.
            4.3.3.1. timp,3perc,2harp,cel,
            strings
        BOOSEY perf mat rent   (D5)

D'ALESSANDRO, RAFAELE
    see ALESSANDRO, RAFAELE D'

DALL'ABACO, EVARISTO FELICE
    see ABACO, EVARISTO FELICE DALL'

DALLINGER, FRIDOLIN (1933-   )
    Lamento [12']
        2.2.2.2. 3.3.3.1. timp,perc,cel,
            strings
        DOBLINGER perf mat rent   (D6)

    Sieben Todsunden, Die [25']
        2(pic).2.2.2.sax. 2.2.3.0. timp,
            perc,acord,cel,pno,strings
        DOBLINGER perf mat rent   (D7)

    Symphonischer Marsch [5']
        2+pic.2+English horn.2+clar in E
            flat.2+contrabsn. 4.3.3.1.
            timp,perc,strings
        DOBLINGER perf mat rent   (D8)

    Symphony No. 1 [35']
        2+pic.2+English horn.2+clar in E
            flat+bass clar.2+contrabsn.
            4.3.3.1. timp,perc,harp,strings
        DOBLINGER perf mat rent   (D9)

    Symphony No. 2 [29']
        2+pic.2+English horn.2+bass
            clar.2+contrabsn. 4.3.3.1.
            timp,perc,strings
        DOBLINGER perf mat rent   (D10)

DAM, HERMAN VAN
    Three Nocturnal Pieces [20']
        3.3.3.2. 4.3.3.1. harp,pno,
            strings
        sc DONEMUS f.s., perf mat rent
                                            (D11)

DAMASE, JEAN-MICHEL (1928-   )
    Badinage [8']
        2.1.2.1. 1.1.0.0. timp,perc,harp,
            strings
        LEMOINE perf mat rent   (D12)

DAMASE, JEAN-MICHEL (cont'd.)
    Concert For Chamber Orchestra [24']
        1.1.1.1. 1.1.1.0. perc,hpsd/harp,
            strings
        LEMOINE perf mat rent   (D13)

    Concertino for Harp and String
        Orchestra [13']
        string orch,harp solo
        LEMOINE perf mat rent   (D14)

    Concertino for Piano and String
        Orchestra [15']
        string orch,pno solo
        BILLAUDOT perf mat rent   (D15)

    Concerto for Double Bass and
        Orchestra [22']
        1.1.1.1. 1.1.1.0. timp,perc,harp,
            strings,db solo
        BILLAUDOT perf mat rent   (D16)

    Danses Du Tresor D'Orphee [8']
        0.1(English horn).1.1. 2.1.0.0.
            timp,perc,2harp,cel,strings
        LEMOINE perf mat rent   (D17)

    Enseigne De Gersaint [8']
        2.2.2.2. 2.2.1.0. timp,perc,harp,
            strings
        LEMOINE perf mat rent   (D18)

    Meandres, For Oboe And String
        Orchestra [11']
        string orch,ob solo
        LEMOINE perf mat rent   (D19)

    Rhapsody for Horn and Orchestra
        2.2.2.2. 0.2.2.0. timp,perc,harp,
            cel,strings,horn solo
        LEMOINE perf mat rent   (D20)

    Rhapsody for Oboe and String
        Orchestra [7']
        string orch,ob solo
        LEMOINE perf mat rent   (D21)

    Silk Rhapsody [20']
        2.2.2.2. 2.2.2.0. 2perc,2harp,
            2cel,strings
        LEMOINE perf mat rent   (D22)

    Suite Concertante, For Oboe And
        Chamber Orchestra [13']
        fl,horn,harp,strings,ob solo
        LEMOINE perf mat rent   (D23)

    Trois Interludes [8']
        1(pic).1.2.1. 2.1.1.0. timp,perc,
            harp,strings
        LEMOINE perf mat rent   (D24)

    Variations Monegasques [13']
        1.1.1.1. 1.1.1.1. timp,perc,harp,
            pno,cel,strings
        LEMOINE perf mat rent   (D25)

    Variations On A Theme Of Gilbert
        Becaud [22']
        2(pic).2.2.2. 4.3.3.1. timp,perc,
            harp,pno,cel,strings
        RIDEAU perf mat rent   (D26)

DAME KOBOLD: OVERTURE see Raff, Joseph Joachim see Reinecke, Carl

DAME KOBOLD: WALZER see Weingartner, (Paul) Felix von

DAMEN SOUVENIR POLKA see Strauss, Johann, [Sr.]

D'AMICO, MATTEO (1955-   )
    Ariel [13'35"]
        3.2.2.2. 2.2.1.0. timp,perc,
            strings
        RICORDI-IT 133813 perf mat rent
                                            (D27)
    Dal Filo Di Arianna, For Piano And
        Instrumental Ensemble [10']
        1.1.1.1. 1.0.0.0. perc,2vln,vla,
            vcl,db,pno solo
        RICORDI-IT 134321 perf mat rent
                                            (D28)
    Jeux Des Masques, For Solo Voice,
        Harpsichord And Orchestra [20']
        3.3.3.3. 4.3.3.1. timp,2perc,
            harp,pno,strings,S solo,hpsd
            solo
        RICORDI-IT 134206 perf mat rent
                                            (D29)

DAMMERUNG see Rihm, Wolfgang

DAMN YANKEES: A LITTLE BRAINS, A LITTLE TALENT, FOR SOLO VOICE AND ORCHESTRA see Adler, Richard

DAMN YANKEES: A MAN DOESN'T KNOW, FOR SOLO VOICE AND ORCHESTRA see Adler, Richard

DAMN YANKEES: OVERTURE see Adler, Richard

DAMNATION DE FAUST, LA: MARCHE HONGROISE, BALLET DES SYLPHES, MENUET DES FOLLETS see Berlioz, Hector (Louis)

DAMNATION DE FAUST, LA: MEPHISTOPHELES' SONG, FOR SOLO VOICE AND ORCHESTRA see Berlioz, Hector (Louis)

DAMNATION OF FAUST: HUNGARIAN MARCH, DANCE OF THE SYLPHS, DANCE OF THE SPRITES see Berlioz, Hector (Louis), Damnation De Faust, La: Marche Hongroise, Ballet Des Sylphes, Menuet Des Follets

DANAE see Soler, Josep

DANAIDES, LES: OVERTURE see Salieri, Antonio

DANA'S PIECE see Kunz, Alfred

DANCA DOS MOSQUITOS see Villa-Lobos, Heitor

DANCA FRENETICA see Villa-Lobos, Heitor

DANCE see Harris, Roy Ellsworth

DANCE BEFORE THE HUT FROM "SAHDJI" see Still, William Grant

DANCE FOR FOUR ORCHESTRAS see Cage, John

DANCE FROM KLOCKRIKEMUSIKEN see Söderlundh, Lille Bror

DANCE GALLERY: SOFT SHOE GAVOTTE see Gould, Morton

DANCE INTERLUDE see MacBride, David Huston

DANCE INTERMEZZO see Sibelius, Jean

DANCE MACABRE see Waxman, Franz

DANCE MACABRE, FOR PIANO AND ORCHESTRA see Liszt, Franz

DANCE NO. 1 see Telfer, Nancy

DANCE NO. 1, FOR VIOLIN AND ORCHESTRA see Koch, Erland von

DANCE NO. 2 see Telfer, Nancy

DANCE NO. 3, FOR VIOLIN AND ORCHESTRA see Koch, Erland von

DANCE NO. 4 see Koch, Erland von

DANCE NO. 5 see Koch, Erland von

DANCE OF THE MARIONETTES see Vinter, Gilbert

DANCE OF THE RAT see Polovinkin, Leonid

DANCE OF THE YAO PEOPLE see Yuen, Mao

DANCE OVERTURE see McKay, Neil

DANCE POEM see Bridge, Frank

DANCE RHAPSODY see Bridge, Frank

DANCE RHAPSODY NO. 2 see Delius, Frederick

DANCE SUITE see Rakov, Nikolai see Svoboda, Tomas see Vinci, Albert see Wallace, William

DANCE SUITE [ARR.] see Tchaikovsky, Piotr Ilyich

DANCE SUITE NO. 2 see Blacher, Boris

DANCE THROUGH THE LAND OF SHADOWS, THE see Germeten, Gunnar

DANCERIES see Fontyn, Jacqueline

DANCES FOR ORCHESTRA see Locklair, Dan Steven

DANCES FROM ARIMINTHA see Starer, Robert

DANCES IN OLD STYLE see Vacek, Miloš

DANCES OF BRITTANY see Pruden, Larry

DANCING IN THE DARK, [ARR.] see Schwartz, Arthur

DANCZAK, JUL (1919-   )
    Alo-Ahe [5']
        2.2.2.1. 2.2.2.0. perc,strings
        SIKORSKI perf mat rent   (D30)

DANCZAK, JUL (cont'd.)

Shanty Potpourri [10']
2.1.2.1. 2.2.2.0. perc,strings
SIKORSKI perf mat rent (D31)

DANDELOT, GEORGES (1895-1975)
Bazar [13']
2.2.2.2. 3.3.2.0. 2perc,cel,harp,
pno,strings
BILLAUDOT perf mat rent (D32)

Concerto for Piano and Orchestra
[22']
3.3.3.3. 4.4.3.1. perc,strings,
pno solo
ESCHIG perf mat rent (D33)

Danses [13'50"]
2.2.2.2. 2.2.1.0. 2perc,strings
BILLAUDOT perf mat rent (D34)

Pieta D'avignon, La [7']
2.2.2.2. 3.3.2.0. timp,2perc,cel,
harp,strings
BILLAUDOT perf mat rent (D35)

Six Chansons De Bilitis, For Solo
Voice And Orchestra [17']
3.2.2.0. 2.0.0.0. triangle,cel,
harp,strings,solo voice
ESCHIG perf mat rent (D36)

Symphony for String Orchestra
string orch
ESCHIG perf mat rent (D37)

DANIELPOUR, RICHARD (1956-)
Concerto for Piano and Orchestra
[27']
2.3.3.3. 4.3.3.1. timp,perc,
strings,pno solo
sc PETERS P66941 f.s., perf mat
rent (D38)

Concerto for Piano and Orchestra, No.
2 [24']
2(pic).2(English horn).2(bass
clar).2. 2.2.2.0. timp,3perc,
harp,strings,pno solo
(Metamorphosis) AMP perf mat rent
(D39)

Elegy for Piano and Orchestra [17']
2.2.3.2. 2.2.2.0. timp,3perc,
harp,strings,pno solo
AMP perf mat rent (D40)

First Light [13']
2.1+English horn.2.2. 2.2.2.0.
timp,3perc,harp,pno,strings
(for chamber version, winds may be
reduced to 1.1.1.1. 2.1.1.0.) AMP
(D41)

Symphony No. 1 [30']
3.3.3.3. 4.3.3.1. timp,2perc,
harp,pno,strings
(Dona Nobis Pacem) PETERS P67201
perf mat rent (D42)

Symphony No. 2 [36']
2.2(English horn).2+bass clar.2.
4.3.3.1. timp,2perc,harp,pno,
strings,ST soli
(visions) AMP (D43)

DANIELS, MELVIN L. (1931-)
Celebration
3(pic).2(English horn).3.2.
4.3.3.1. timp,perc,harp,strings
[10'] (gr. V) SOUTHERN A-30 sc
$7.50, set $55.00, pts $2.50, ea.
(D44)

DANIELSSON, HARRY (1905-)
Leggenda [6']
2.2.2.2. 0.0.0.0. strings
STIM perf mat rent (D45)

Melodi, For Solo Voice And Orchestra
[arr.]
(Kjellberg, Olle) STIM (D46)

Pilen; Skrivet Pa Vandring En Tidig
Vardag, For Solo Voice And
Orchestra
2.2.2.2. 2.2.0.0. strings,solo
voice
STIM perf mat rent (D47)

Ungdom
string orch,opt solo voice
STIM perf mat rent (D48)

DANNA
Concerto for Synthesizer and
Orchestra
HARRIS HI-4 f.s. (D49)

DANNING, CHR.
Dreams
see Dromme

Dromme
"Dreams" sc,pts SAMFUNDET f.s.
(D50)

DANS LE DEUIL DES VAGUES II see Masson,
Gerard

DANS LE TUMULTE DES FLOTS II, FOR
VIOLIN AND INSTRUMENTAL ENSEMBLE
see Lenot, Jacques

DANS L'UNIVERS, L'AMOUR see Lalonde,
Alain

DANSE see Rihm, Wolfgang

DANSE ADAGIO ET FUGATO see Martelli,
Henri

DANSE [ARR.] see Debussy, Claude

DANSE BASQUE, LA see Leopold, Bohuslav

DANSE DE L'AMAZONE see Liadov, Anatol
Konstantinovich

DANSE DEVANT L'ARCHE, LA see Bernard,
Robert

DANSE INCANTATOIRE see Jolivet, Andre

DANSE INDIENNE see Vellones, Pierre

DANSE LENTE see Durufle, Maurice

DANSE POUR ORCHESTRE see El-Khoury,
Bechara

DANSE RITUELLE see Sanjuan, Pedro

DANSE SACREE ET DANSE PROFANE, FOR
HARP, SORCH see Debussy, Claude

DANSE: SUITE NO. 1 see Lumbye, Hans
Christian

DANSE TRIOMPHALE see Hogenhaven, Knud

DANSES see Dandelot, Georges

DANSES DE LA MORT see Hovland, Egil

DANSES DE REVE see Tomasi, Henri

DANSES DU TRESOR D'ORPHEE see Damase,
Jean-Michel

DANSES POPULAIRES FRANCAISES see
Tiersot, (Jean Baptiste Elisee)
Julien

DANSEUSES DE DEGAS, FOR HARP AND STRING
ORCHESTRA see Tomasi, Henri

DANZA see Miller, Franz R.

DANZA, LA see Mercadante, G. Saverio

DANZA, LA, FOR SOLO VOICE AND ORCHESTRA
[ARR.] see Rossini, Gioacchino

DANZA A SOLATIO see Eder, Helmut

DANZA BARBARA see Garlick, Antony

DANZA VIVA see Turok, Paul Harris

DANZA Y TRONIO see Garcia-Abríl, Antón

DANZE PIEMONTESI, NO. 1 see Sinigaglia,
Leone

DANZE PIEMONTESI, NO. 2 see Sinigaglia,
Leone

DANZI, FRANZ (1763-1826)
Concertino for Clarinet, Bassoon and
Orchestra
1.2.0.0. 0.0.0.0. strings,clar
solo,bsn solo
sc KUNZEL 10201 $17.00, ipa (D51)

Concerto for Bassoon and Orchestra in
C, MIN 126
2ob,2horn,strings,bsn solo
(Veit, J.) sc,pts LEUCKART AM 50A
f.s. (D52)

Concerto for Horn and Orchestra in E
flat, MIN 631 [13'55"]
2fl,2horn,strings,horn solo
INTERNAT. perf mat rent (D53)

Phantasie Uber "La Ci Darem La Mano"
Aus Don Giovanni Von W. A.
Mozart, For Clarinet And
Orchestra
(Zorzor, Stefan) fl,2ob,opt 2bsn,
opt 2horn,strings,clar solo
[9'30"] ORLANDO perf mat rent
(D54)

Sinfonia Concertante for Flute,
Clarinet and Orchestra, Op. 41,
in B flat
sc,pts KUNZEL 10175 f.s. (D55)
MUS. RARA 2076 perf mat rent (D56)

Symphonic Works, Three
see Vogler, [Abbe] Georg Joseph,
Symphony

DAO, NGUYEN THIEN
Ba Me Vietnam, For Double Bass And
Instrumental Ensemble [25']
pic,contrabass clar,2trom,elec
org,3perc,7vln,3vcl,2db,db solo
SALABERT perf mat rent (D57)

Blessure-Soleil I, For Clarinet And
Orchestra [25']
2.2.0.0. 2.0.0.0. 2perc,strings,
clar solo
SALABERT perf mat rent (D58)

Blessure-Soleil II [17']
2.2.0.1. 1.0.0.0. perc,7vln,2vla,
2vcl,db
SALABERT perf mat rent (D59)

Concerto for Piano and Orchestra
[20']
3.2+English horn.2+bass clar.2+
contrabsn. 4.3.3.1(db tuba).
3perc,strings,pno solo
SALABERT perf mat rent (D60)

Concerto for 6 Strings and Orchestra
[21']
3.2.3(bass clar).3(contrabsn).
3.2.2.1. 3perc,cel,strings,
6strings soli
SALABERT perf mat rent (D61)

Concerto for Violin and Orchestra
[20']
2.2.2+bass clar.2+contrabsn.
4.2.2.1(db tuba). 3perc,cel,
strings,vln solo
(Thien Thai) SALABERT perf mat rent
(D62)

Concerto L'envoi, For Flute And
String Orchestra [12']
string orch,fl solo
SALABERT perf mat rent (D63)

Hoang Hon, For Solo Voice And
Orchestra [15']
2.2.2.1. 2.1.1.0.+db tuba. 2perc,
harp,strings,S solo
SALABERT perf mat rent (D64)

Koskom [30']
2pic,alto fl,bass fl,ob,2clar in
A,bass clar,contrabass clar,
contrabsn,2trp,2trom,3perc,cel,
strings
SALABERT perf mat rent (D65)

Mai-Sau, For Violin And Strings [42']
12strings,vln solo
SALABERT perf mat rent (D66)

Mau Va Hoa [30']
6(alto fl,bass fl).4.6(bass clar,
contrabass clar).4. 6.4.4.3.
5perc,strings
SALABERT perf mat rent (D67)

Symphonie Pour Pouvoir, For Solo
Voice And Orchestra [24']
3(pic,alto fl).3(English
horn).3(bass
clar).3(contrabsn). 4.2.2.0+db
tuba. 3perc,cel,strings,S solo
SALABERT perf mat rent (D68)

Ten Do Gu, For Percussion And
Orchestra [22']
1+alto fl.2.1+bass clar.0+
contrabsn. 2.2.1.0+db tuba.
strings,perc solo
sc SALABERT f.s., perf mat rent
(D69)

Than Mong, For Violoncello And
Orchestra [30']
3(pic).2.2+bass clar.2+contrabsn.
3.3.2.1. 3perc,harp,strings,vcl
solo
SALABERT perf mat rent (D70)

DAPHNIS ET CHLOE see Ravel, Maurice

DAPHNIS ET CHLOE: SUITE NO. 1 see
Ravel, Maurice

DAPPLED THINGS see Primosch, James

D'APRÉS ECRITS SUR TOILES see
Arkhangelsky, G.

DAR DEN STORA TIGERN LJUGER see
Jonsson, Reine

DARASSE, XAVIER (1934-1992)
Instants Eclates [15']
3.2+English horn.2+bass clar.2+
contrabsn. 4.3.2.1. 4perc,
2harp,strings
SALABERT perf mat rent (D71)

Instants Passes [15']
4(pic).4(English horn).4(bass
clar).4(contrabsn). 6.3.3.1.
timp,4perc,2harp,strings
SALABERT perf mat rent (D72)

DARBY AND JOAN, FOR VIOLIN, VIOLONCELLO
    AND STRING ORCHESTRA see Foulds,
    John Herbert

DARDANUS: SUITE [ARR.] see Rameau,
    Jean-Philippe

DARGOMYZHSKY, ALEXANDER SERGEYEVICH
    (1813-1869)
    Baba Yaga *see RUSSIAN SYMPHONIC
        MUSIC, VOL. 3

    Chukhon Fantasy *see RUSSIAN
        SYMPHONIC MUSIC, VOL. 3

    Cosatschoque, Le
        see Kasachok

    Kasachok
        "Cosatschoque, Le" KALMUS A5811 sc
        $15.00, set $35.00, perf mat rent
                                            (D73)
    Ukrainian Cossack Dance *see RUSSIAN
        SYMPHONIC MUSIC, VOL. 3

DARK NEBULAE see Van de Vate, Nancy
    Hayes

DARKNESS TO DAY, FOR CLARINET AND
    STRING ORCHESTRA see Powers,
    Anthony

DATURA FASTUOSA see Guerrero, Francisco

DAUGHERTY, MICHAEL (1954-   )
    Firecracker, For Oboe And Chamber
        Orchestra [15']
        1(pic).0.1+bass clar.1. 0.0.2.0.
        4vln,2vla,2vcl,db,synthesizer,
        ob solo
        PEER perf mat rent   (D74)

    Mxyzptlk, For 2 Flutes And Chamber
        Orchestra [7']
        0.2.2.2. 2.1.1.0. 1-2perc,
        strings,synthesizer,2fl soli
        PEER perf mat rent   (D75)

    Oh Lois! [5']
        2.2.2.2. 4.3.3.0. timp,2perc,
        synthesizer/kbd,strings
        PEER perf mat rent   (D76)

    Strut [6']
        string orch
        PEER perf mat rent   (D77)

DAUTREMER, MARCEL (1906-   )
    Concerto for Saxophone and String
        Orchestra [16']
        string orch,sax solo
        LEMOINE perf mat rent   (D78)

    Sinfonietta for String Orchestra
        [11']
        string orch
        LEMOINE perf mat rent   (D79)

DAVID, FERDINAND (1810-1873)
    Concertino for Trombone and
        Orchestra, Op. 4
        KALMUS A4274 sc $25.00, set $20.00,
        perf mat rent   (D80)

DAVID, FOR SOLO VOICE AND ORCHESTRA see
    Thorkelsdottir, Mist

DÁVID, GYULA (1913-   )
    Concerto Grosso for Viola and String
        Orchestra
        string orch,vla solo
        sc EMB 13484 f.s., perf mat rent
                                            (D81)
    Overture
        sc EMB 10257 f.s., perf mat rent
                                            (D82)
DAVID, JOHANN NEPOMUK (1895-1977)
    Concerto for Violin and Orchestra,
        No. 3, Op. 56
        study sc BREITKOPF-W PB 5073 f.s.
                                            (D83)
DAVID, THOMAS CHRISTIAN (1925-   )
    Concerto for Double Bass and String
        Orchestra [18']
        string orch,db solo
        DOBLINGER perf mat rent   (D84)

    Concerto for Flute and Orchestra
        [20']
        0.2.0.2. 2.0.0.0. strings,fl solo
        DOBLINGER perf mat rent   (D85)

    Concerto for Violin and Orchestra,
        No. 2 [30']
        2(pic).2.2+contrabsn. 4.2.3.0.
        timp,harp,strings,vln solo
        DOBLINGER perf mat rent   (D86)

    Concerto for Violin, Clarinet, Piano
        and Orchestra [20']
        2.2.0.2. 2.0.0.0. strings,vln
        solo,clar solo,pno solo
        DOBLINGER perf mat rent   (D87)

DAVID, THOMAS CHRISTIAN (cont'd.)
    Concerto for 3 Violins and String
        Orchestra [25']
        string orch,3vln soli
        DOBLINGER perf mat rent   (D88)

    Concerto for Violoncello and
        Orchestra [20']
        2+pic.2.2.2+contrabsn. 4.2.3.0.
        timp,perc,strings,vcl solo
        DOBLINGER perf mat rent   (D89)

    Festlicher Prolog [10']
        2(pic).2.2+bass clar.2+contrabsn.
        4.3.3.1. timp,perc,strings
        DOBLINGER perf mat rent   (D90)

DAVIDOV, CARL (1838-1889)
    Concerto for Violoncello and
        Orchestra, No. 1, Op. 5
        KISTNER perf mat rent   (D91)

DAVIDOVSKY, MARIO (1934-   )
    Divertimento for Violoncello and
        Orchestra [17']
        2(pic,alto fl).2(English
        horn).2(bass
        clar).2(contrabsn). 4.2.2.1.
        2perc,pno,strings,vcl solo
        PETERS P67049 perf mat rent   (D92)

    Pennplay [12']
        2(pic,alto fl).0.2(clar in E
        flat,bass clar).0. 1.1.1.1.
        2perc,pno,vln,vla,vcl,db
        PETERS $21.35, perf mat rent   (D93)

    Scenes From Shir Ha-Shirim, For Solo
        Voices And Chamber Orchestra
        [30']
        1(pic,alto fl).1(ob
        d'amore).1(bass clar).0.
        0.0.0.0. perc,pno,vln,vla,vcl,
        db,STTB soli
        sc PETERS P67007 $40.00, perf mat
        rent   (D94)

DAVIDS VISION see Sheriff, Noam

DAVIES, PETER MAXWELL (1934-   )
    Black Pentecost, For Solo Voices And
        Orchestra [41']
        2+alto fl.2+English horn.2+bass
        clar.2+contrabsn. 4.3.2.0.
        5perc,timp,cel,strings,MezBar
        soli
        sc CHESTER JWC 579 $65.25, perf mat
        rent   (D95)

    Boyfriend, The: Concert Suite [25']
        1.0.2.0.soprano sax(alto
        sax).alto sax(tenor sax).tenor
        sax. 0.2.1.0. perc,pno 4-hands&
        cel,banjo,harp,strings,
        ukelele&mando
        CHESTER perf mat rent   (D96)

    Concerto for Trumpet and Orchestra
        [22']
        2+alto fl.2+English horn.2+bass
        clar.2+contrabsn. 4.3.3.1.
        timp,4perc,strings,trp solo
        BOOSEY perf mat rent   (D97)

    Concerto for Violin and Orchestra
        [30']
        2.2.2.2. 2.2.0.0. timp,strings,
        vln solo
        CHESTER perf mat rent   (D98)

    Devils, The: Suite, For Solo Voice
        And Orchestra [20']
        1(pic,alto fl).0.1(bass clar).0.
        0.1.1.0. Hamm&prepared pno&cel,
        3perc,vcl,db,S solo, vln&vla&
        regal, untuned zither
        CHESTER JWC 581 perf mat rent (D99)

    Into The Labyrinth, For Solo Voice
        And Orchestra [31']
        2.2.2.2. 2.2.0.0. strings,T solo
        CHESTER perf mat rent   (D100)

    Jimmack The Postie [9']
        2(pic,alto fl).2.2(bass clar).2.
        2.2.2.0. timp,strings
        CHESTER CH723 perf mat rent   (D101)

    Orkney Wedding With Sunrise, An [11']
        2.2.2(bass clar).2. 4.2.2.1.
        timp,perc,strings, highland
        bagpipe
        BOOSEY perf mat rent   (D102)

    Salome: Dances [54']
        2(pic,alto fl).2.2.2(bass
        clar).2(contrabsn). 4.2.2.0.
        timp,5perc,harp,cel,strings
        BOOSEY perf mat rent   (D103)

    Sinfonietta Accademica [26']
        2.2.2.2. 2.2.0.0. strings
        CHESTER CH667 perf mat rent   (D104)

DAVIES, PETER MAXWELL (cont'd.)
    Stone Litany: "Runes From A House Of
        The Dead", For Solo Voice And
        Orchestra
        min sc BOOSEY 1110 $13.00   (D105)

    Strathclyde Concerto No. 1, For Oboe
        And Orchestra [28']
        2(pic).0.2(bass clar).0. 2.0.0.0.
        timp,strings,ob solo
        BOOSEY perf mat rent   (D106)

    Strathclyde Concerto No.2, For
        Violoncello And Orchestra [30']
        2(pic).2.1(bass clar).2. 2.2.0.0.
        timp,strings,vcl solo
        CHESTER perf mat rent   (D107)

    Symphonie Concertante [30']
        1.1.1.1. 1.0.0.0. timp,strings
        CHESTER perf mat rent   (D108)

    Symphony No. 2
        3.2.3.3. 4.3.2.0. timp,perc,harp,
        strings
        sc BOOSEY $40.00   (D109)

    Symphony No. 3 [50']
        3(pic,alto fl).2+English horn.2+
        bass clar.2+contrabsn. 4.3.3.1.
        timp,strings
        min sc BOOSEY $61.00, perf mat rent
                                            (D110)
    Symphony No. 4
        BOOSEY perf mat rent   (D111)

    Worldes Blis [37']
        2+pic.2.2+bass clar.2+contrabsn.
        4.3.3.1. timp,5perc,2harp,org,
        strings
        sc BOOSEY $71.00, perf mat rent
                                            (D112)
DAVIES, VICTOR (1939-   )
    Good Times
        1.1.1.1. 2.2.1.1. strings
        (may be performed by strings alone)
        CAN.MUS.CENT. MI 1200 D257G
                                            (D113)
DAVIS, ANTHONY
    Malcolm's Prison Aria, For Solo Voice
        And Orchestra [8']
        2(pic).1.2.1+contrabsn.2sax.
        2.1.2.0. timp,3perc,pno,
        strings,Bar solo
        SCHIRM.G perf mat rent   (D114)

    Maps, For Violin And Orchestra [25']
        timp,perc,harp,strings,vln solo
        SCHIRM.G perf mat rent   (D115)

    Notes From The Underground [9']
        2(pic).2.2.2. 2.2.2.1. perc,
        strings
        SCHIRM.G perf mat rent   (D116)

    Still Waters [17']
        2.1.1.1. 2.0.1.0. timp,3-4perc,
        harp,pno,strings
        SCHIRM.G perf mat rent   (D117)

    Wayang V, For Piano And Orchestra
        [25']
        2(pic).1.2(bass clar).1. 2.1.2.0.
        timp,3perc,strings,pno solo
        SCHIRM.G perf mat rent   (D118)

DAVIS, CURTIS W.
    Four Sonnets, For Solo Voice And
        Orchestra [15']
        2.2.2.2. 4.3.3.1. timp,perc,harp,
        strings,S solo
        NORRUTH perf mat rent   (D119)

DAVISON, PETER (1948-   )
    Eagle Springs, For Keyboard And
        Orchestra [15']
        3+pic.2.2.2. 3.3.3.1. timp,perc,
        gtr,strings,kbd solo
        (the soloist performs on piano,
        celeste and synthesizer) NEWAM
        19012 perf mat rent   (D120)

DAWES, CHARLES G.
    Dawes' Melody Played Around The World
        [6'30"]
        (Wilson, Don) WARNER perf mat rent
                                            (D121)
DAWES' MELODY PLAYED AROUND THE WORLD
    see Dawes, Charles G.

DAWN AT THE SEA, FOR SOLO VOICE AND
    ORCHESTRA see Wohlfart, Karl

DAWN IN A TROPICAL FOREST see Villa-
    Lobos, Heitor, Alvorada Na Floresta
    Tropical

DAY AFTER DAY, FOR SOLO VOICE AND
    ORCHESTRA see Bridge, Frank

DAY-DREAMER'S DIARY, A see Balassa,
    Sándor

DAYBREAK AND A CANDLE END see Berkeley, Michael

DAYDREAMS IN NUMBERS see Hallgrimsson, Haflidi

DE BANFIELD, RAFFAELLO
  see BANFIELD, RAFFAELLO DE

DE CURTIS, ERNESTO
  see CURTIS, ERNESTO DE

DE GLORY ROAD [ARR.] see Wolfe, Jacques

DE GRANDIS, RENATO (1927-   )
  Due Preludi Sinfonici
    2.2.2.2. 4.2.1.0. timp,perc,harp,
    cel,strings
    TONOS   (D122)

DE LA GRAVITATION SUSPENDUE DES
  MEMOIRES see Decoust, Michel

DE LA TERRE A LA VIE, FOR CLARINET AND
  STRINGS see Finzi, Graciane

DE LAMARTER, ERIC (1880-1953)
  Huckleberry Finn Overture [2']
    WARNER perf mat rent   (D123)

DE LAUD'S BAPTIZIN' [ARR.] see Guion,
  David Wendall Fentress

DE PABLO, LUIS
  see PABLO, LUIS DE

DE PROFUNDIS see Larrauri, Anton

DE PROFUNDIS, FOR SOLO VOICE AND
  ORCHESTRA see Gaathaug, Morten see
  Lerstad, Terje B.

DE SABATA, VICTOR (1892-1967)
  Mille E Una Notte [27']
    3.3.3.3. 4.3.3.1. timp,perc,org,
    2pno,2harp,strings
    RICORDI-IT 122074 perf mat rent
                                       (D124)

DE SEVERAC, DEODAT
  see SEVERAC, DEODAT DE

DE TERRE ET DE CIEL see Murail, Tristan

DE VOS MALAN, JACQUES
  Footprints Of The Birds
    3.3.3.3. 4.3.3.1. timp,cel,
    strings
    sc SEESAW $16.00, perf mat rent
                                       (D125)
  Music For Chuang Tzu
    3.3.3.3. 4.2.3.1. perc,strings
    SEESAW perf mat rent   (D126)

  Piano And Orchestra
    3.3.3.3. 4.2.3.1. perc,harp,
    strings,pno solo
    SEESAW perf mat rent   (D127)

  Yin Fire
    2.1.2.2. 2.2.1.1. perc,harp,pno,
    strings
    sc SEESAW $14.00, perf mat rent
                                       (D128)

DEAI see Schuller, Gunther

DEÁK, CSABA (1932-   )
  Vivax [20']
    2.2.2.2. 2.2.2.1. timp,perc,
    strings
    sc GEHRMANS 6280P f.s., perf mat
    rent   (D129)

DEATH IN VENICE [ARR.] see Britten,
  [Sir] Benjamin

DEATH OF OPHELIA, FOR SOLO VOICE AND
  ORCHESTRA[ARR.] see Berlioz, Hector
  (Louis), Mort D'ophelie, La, For
  Solo Voice And Orchestra [arr.]

DEATH VALLEY SUITE [ARR.] see Grofe,
  Ferde (Ferdinand Rudolph von)

D'EAU ET DE PIERRE see Grisey, Gerard

DEBARADEURS QUADRILLE see Strauss,
  Josef

DEBIE, RICK (1955-   )
  Preludium Festivum *Op.17 [6']
    2.2.2.2. 2.2.0.0. timp,2perc,
    strings
    sc DONEMUS f.s., perf mat rent
                                       (D130)

DEBUSSY, CLAUDE (1862-1918)
  Arabesque No. 1 In E [arr.]
    (Mouton) 1.1.2.1. 2.0.0.0. strings
    [4'30"] set KALMUS A4149 $12.00
                                       (D131)
  Arabesque No. 2 In G [arr.]
    (Mouton) 1.1.2.1. 2.0.0.0. perc,
    strings [4'] set KALMUS A4150
    $12.00   (D132)

DEBUSSY, CLAUDE (cont'd.)
  Bruyeres [arr] (from Preludes, Book
    II)
    (Mouton) 1.1.2.1. 2.0.0.0. strings,
    vln solo [4'] set KALMUS A2163
    $10.00, and up   (D133)
  Children's Corner [arr.]
    (Caplet) 2(pic).2.2.2. 4.2.0.0.
    perc,harp,strings [15'] KALMUS
    A6135 sc $30.00, set $40.00, perf
    mat rent   (D134)
  Clair De Lune, [arr.] *see TWELVE
    POP HITS FROM THE CLASSICS, VOL.
    2
  Danse [arr.]
    (Mouton) 1.1.2.1. 2.2.1.0. timp,
    cym,strings [5'30"] KALMUS A5733
    pno-cond sc $5.00, set $30.00,
    perf mat rent   (D135)
  Danse Sacree Et Danse Profane, For
    Harp, Sorch
    (Kluvetasch) PETERS sc P9154 f.s.,
    study sc P9154A f.s.   (D136)
  Douze Préludes, Vol. 1, [arr.]
    (Henkemans, Hans) 3.3.2.3. 4.3.3.1.
    timp,perc,cel,2harp,strings [35']
    WEINBERGER   (D137)
  Fantasy for Piano and Orchestra
    (Pommer, M.) PETERS sc P9352 f.s.,
    study sc P9352A f.s.   (D138)
  Fille Aux Cheveux De Lin, La [arr]
    (from Preludes)
    (Mouton) string orch [3'] KALMUS
    A7263 pno-cond sc $2.00, set
    $17.00, and up   (D139)
  Images
    (Pommer, M.) PETERS sc P9155 f.s.,
    study sc P9155A f.s.   (D140)
  Images, No. 1: Gigues
    KALMUS A6747 sc $15.00, set $60.00,
    pts $2.00, ea., perf mat rent
                                       (D141)
  Images, No. 2: Iberia
    KALMUS A5895 sc $40.00, set
    $110.00, min sc KALMUS K09942 $11.50 (D143)
    min sc KALMUS K09942 $11.50   (D143)
  Images, No. 3: Rondes De Printemps
    KALMUS A5984 sc $25.00, set $80.00,
    perf mat rent   (D144)
  Jeux
    (Nieweg) KALMUS A7239 sc $50.00,
    set $175.00, pts $9.00, ea., perf
    mat rent   (D145)
    (Pommer, M.) PETERS sc P9152 f.s.,
    study sc P9152A f.s.   (D146)
  Marche Ecossaise [arr.]
    (Mouton) 2.1.2.2. 2.2.2.0. timp,
    perc,strings [6'30"] KALMUS A5735
    pno-cond sc $5.00, set $18.00,
    perf mat rent   (D147)
  Marche Ecossaise Sur Un Theme
    Populaire
    2+pic.2+English horn.2.2. 4.2.3.0.
    perc,harp,strings [6'30"] KALMUS
    A5562 sc $15.00, set $30.00, perf
    mat rent   (D148)
  Martyre De Saint Sebastian, Le: Suite
    KALMUS A6452 set $25.00, pts
    $80.00, $3.00, ea., perf mat rent
                                       (D149)
  Mer, La
    study sc EMB 40038 f.s.   (D150)
    see Three Orchestral Works
  Nocturnes
    study sc EMB 40045 f.s.   (D151)
    (Rozhdestvensky, G.) sc MUZYKA f.s.
                                       (D152)
    see Three Orchestral Works
  Petite Suite [arr.]
    min sc KALMUS K01525 $8.75   (D153)
  Plus Que Lent, La [arr.]
    fl,clar,pno,cimbalom,strings
    [4'30"] KALMUS A6442 sc $5.00,
    set $9.00, pts $1.00, ea.   (D154)
  Prélude À l'Après-Midi d'Un Faune
    (Darvas) study sc EMB 40015 f.s.
                                       (D155)
    (Reinisch, Frank) 2.2+English
    horn.2.2. 4.0.0.0. perc,2harp,
    strings [10'] BREITKOPF-W sc
    PB 5169 f.s., pts OB 5169 f.s.
                                       (D156)
    see Three Orchestral Works
  Prelude A L'apres-Midi d'un Faune
    [arr.]
    (Walter, D.) 1.1.1.1. 1.0.0.0.

DEBUSSY, CLAUDE (cont'd.)
    harp,strings [10'] BILLAUDOT perf
    mat rent   (D157)
  Printemps
    sc KUNZEL 10066 $15.00   (D158)
    (Jancsovics) study sc EMB 40001
    f.s.   (D159)
  Reverie [arr.]
    (Mouton) 1.1.2.1. 1.0.0.0. strings
    [4'] KALMUS A5734 pno-cond sc
    $2.00, set $10.00   (D160)
    *see TWELVE POP HITS FROM THE
    CLASSICS, VOL. 2
  Rhapsody, No. 1 for Clarinet and
    Orchestra
    KALMUS A6165 sc $20.00, set $45.00,
    perf mat rent   (D161)
    (Zimmermann) sc PETERS P9353 f.s.
                                       (D162)
  Three Orchestral Works
    sc DOVER 244415 $9.95
    contains: Mer, La; Nocturnes;
    Prelude A L'apres-Midi D'un
    Faune   (D163)
  Triomphe De Bacchus
    KALMUS A5744 sc $10.00, set $25.00,
    perf mat rent   (D164)
  Trois Ballades De Francois Villon,
    For Solo Voice And Orchestra
    KALMUS A6312 sc $15.00, set $20.00,
    perf mat rent   (D165)

DECLAMATORIUM "DE DRUKKUNST", FOR
  NARRATOR AND ORCHESTRA see Paap,
  Wouter

DECORATION DAY see Ives, Charles

DECOUST, MICHEL (1936-   )
  Aubes Incendiees, For Speaker And
    Instrumental Ensemble [20']
    1(pic).0+English horn.1.0+
    contrabsn. 1.0.2.0. perc,pno,
    vln,vla,vcl,db,speaking voice
    SALABERT perf mat rent   (D166)
  De La Gravitation Suspendue Des
    Memoires [25']
    4(pic).4.4.4(contrabsn). 4.4.3.1.
    timp,3perc,strings
    SALABERT perf mat rent   (D167)
  Hommage A Maurice Ravel [6']
    3(pic).2+English horn.3.3.
    4.3.3.1. timp,perc,strings
    SALABERT perf mat rent   (D168)
  Inference [13']
    3.3.3.3. 4.4.3.1. timp,3perc,
    2harp/2pno,strings
    BILLAUDOT perf mat rent   (D169)
  Je, Qui, D'autre, For Solo Voices And
    Orchestra [45']
    1.1(English horn).1.0. 2.0.0+bass
    trom.0. 2perc,harp,vln,vla,
    2vcl,db,STB soli
    SALABERT perf mat rent   (D170)
  Lierre [13']
    string orch
    SALABERT perf mat rent   (D171)
  Polymorphie [20']
    5(pic,alto fl).4(English
    horn).5(clar in E flat,bass
    clar).4(contrabsn). 5.5(piccolo
    trp,bass trp).0.1. 2harp,
    strings
    SALABERT perf mat rent   (D172)
  Sonnet [17']
    1(pic).0+English horn.1.0+
    contrabsn. 1.0.1.0. perc,pno,
    vln,vla,vcl,db
    SALABERT perf mat rent   (D173)
  Synopsis [8']
    2(pic).2(English horn).2.2.2alto
    sax. 2.2.2.0. timp,perc,strings
    SALABERT perf mat rent   (D174)

DECSENYI, JANOS (1927-   )
  Concerto for Violoncello and
    Orchestra
    sc EMB 13292 f.s., perf mat rent
                                       (D175)
  Epitaph From Aquincum, For Solo Voice
    And Orchestra
    elec org,strings,S solo sc EMB
    10245 f.s.   (D176)

DEDALO see Larrauri, Anton

DEDALO II see Turchi, Guido

DEDICA, FOR FLUTE, SOLO VOICE AND
  ORCHESTRA see Manzoni, Giacomo

DEDICATION see Nordal, Jon

DEDICATION TO COURAGE, FOR SOLO VOICE
AND ORCHESTRA see Uspensky,
Vladislav

DEDUKTIONEN see Bischof, Rainer

DEEP see Lorentzen, Bent

DEFAYE, JEAN MICHEL (1932-)
Concerto for Trombone and Orchestra
LEDUC perf mat rent (D177)

DEFILE see Loucheur, Raymond

DEFOTIS, WILLIAM
Against That Time, For Solo Voice And
Orchestra [20']
2(pic).1+English horn.3(bass
clar).3(contrabsn). 4.3.3.1.
perc,harp,cel,strings,S/Mez
solo
sc AM.COMP.AL. $31.40, perf mat
rent (D178)

DEGEN, JOHANNES (1910-)
Var En Gang, Det *Op.66
ob,clar,bsn,strings
STIM (D179)

DEI GAMLE FJELL see Vea, Ketil

DEIDAMIA: ES BIRGT DIE NACHTIGALL, FOR
SOLO VOICE AND STRING ORCHESTRA see
Handel, George Frideric, Deidamia:
Nasconde l'Usignol' In Altri Rami
Il Nido, For Solo Voice And String
Orchestra

DEIDAMIA: NASCONDE L'USIGNOL' IN ALTRI
RAMI IL NIDO, FOR SOLO VOICE AND
STRING ORCHESTRA see Handel, George
Frideric

DEIDRE OVERTURE (AN IRISH LEGEND) see
Whitney, Maurice Cary

DÉJÀ VU, FOR OBOE D'AMORE AND CHAMBER
ORCHESTRA see Stranz, Ulrich

DEL TREDICI, DAVID (1937-)
Alice Symphony, An, For Solo Voice
And Orchestra
sc BOOSEY FSB-495 $35.00 (D180)

All In The Golden Afternoon, For Solo
Voice And Orchestra (from Child
Alice) [35']
3(pic).3(English horn).3(clar in
E flat)+bass clar.3(contrabsn).
4.4.3.1. timp,5perc,2harp,cel,
strings,S solo
BOOSEY perf mat rent (D181)

Final Alice, For Solo Voice And
Orchestra
sc BOOSEY FSB-450 $75.00 (D182)

Haddock's Eyes, For Solo Voice And
Instrumental Ensemble [20']
fl&pic,clar,horn,trp,pno,2vln,
vla,vcl,db,S solo
BOOSEY perf mat rent (D183)

Happy Voices (from Child Alice) [21']
3(pic).3(English horn).2+clar in
E flat+bass clar.3(contrabsn).
4.4.3.1. timp,5perc,2harp,cel,
strings
BOOSEY perf mat rent (D184)

In Memory Of A Summer Day, For Solo
Voice And Orchestra (from Child
Alice) [63']
3(pic).3(English horn).3(clar in
E flat+bass clar.3(contrabsn).
4.4.3.1. 5perc,2harp,cel,
strings,S solo
sc BOOSEY $75.00, perf mat rent
(D185)
March To Tonality [22']
4(pic).3(English horn).2+clar in
E flat+bass clar.3(contrabsn).
4.4.3.1. timp,4perc,strings
BOOSEY perf mat rent (D186)

Night Conjure-Verse, For Solo Voices
And Instrumental Ensemble [18']
1+pic.1.1+bass clar.1. 1.0.0.0.
2vln,vla,vcl,S&countertenor/
SMez soli
min sc BOOSEY $25.00, perf mat rent
(D187)
Quaint Events, For Solo Voice And
Orchestra (from Child Alice)
[25']
3(pic).3(English horn).2+clar in
E flat+bass clar.3(contrabsn).
4.4.3.1. timp,5perc,2harp,cel,
strings,S solo
BOOSEY perf mat rent (D188)

DELAGE, MAURICE (1879-1961)
Four Hindu Poems, For Solo Voice And
Orchestra
see Quatre Poemes Hindous, For Solo
Voice And Orchestra

Mort D'un Samourai, La [7']
2.2.2.2. 2.2.0.0. perc,harp,pno,
strings
ESCHIG perf mat rent (D189)

Quatre Poemes Hindous, For Solo Voice
And Orchestra [6']
2.2.2.0. 0.0.0.0. harp,string
quar,high solo
"Four Hindu Poems, For Solo Voice
And Orchestra" KALMUS A7248 sc
$20.00, set $15.00, pts $1.50,
ea. (D190)

DELALANDE, MICHEL-RICHARD (1657-1726)
Symphonie Des Soupers Du Roi [11']
2.2.0.2. 0.2.0.0. hpsd,strings
BILLAUDOT perf mat rent (D191)

DELANNOY, MARCEL (1898-1962)
Ballade Concertante, For Piano And
Orchestra *Op.59 [13']
1.1.1.1.sax. 0.1.2.0. timp,perc,
cel,vln,db,pno solo
ESCHIG perf mat rent (D192)

Ballade, Op. 39 [13']
2.2.3.2. 4.3.3.0. 3perc,harp,
strings
ESCHIG perf mat rent (D193)

Serenade Concertante, For Violin And
Orchestra [20']
2.2.2.2. 2.2.1.0. timp,perc,harp,
strings,vln solo
ESCHIG perf mat rent (D194)

DELAS, JOSE LUIS DE (1928-)
Paroles Et L'air, Les [22']
2+pic+alto fl.2+English horn.2+
bass clar.2. 4.3.2.2.0. 2perc,
harp,cel,strings
BREITKOPF-W perf mat rent (D195)

DELERUE, GEORGES (1925-)
Concerto for Trombone and String
Orchestra
string orch,trom solo
sc BILLAUDOT f.s., perf mat rent
(D196)
Panique [6'30"]
2.2.2.2. 4.3.3.1. timp,2perc,
harp,pno,strings
BILLAUDOT perf mat rent (D197)

Prelude Et Danse, For Oboe And String
Orchestra [6'45"]
string orch,ob solo
sc BILLAUDOT f.s., perf mat rent
(D198)

DELFT, MARC VAN (1958-)
Capriccio, Op. 11 [12']
3.0.2.0.alto sax. 2.0.2.0. perc,
pno,2vln,vla,vcl,db
DONEMUS perf mat rent (D199)

Orkestsuite De 7 Planeten *Op.6
[24'-31']
3.3.3.3. 4.3.3.1. 5perc,pno&cel,
2harp,strings
DONEMUS perf mat rent (D200)

Orkestvariaties, Chaconne En Fantasie
*Op.18 [17']
3.2.2.2. 4.3.3.1. timp,2-7perc,
opt harp,pno&cel,strings
sc DONEMUS f.s., perf mat rent
(D201)
Symphonisch Gedicht, For Solo Voice
And Orchestra *Op.9 [25']
3.3.3.3. 4.3.3.1. perc,harp,pno&
cel,strings,speaking voice
DONEMUS perf mat rent (D202)

Vier Temperamenten, De *Op.5 [10']
3.3.3.3. 4.3.3.1. timp,5perc,
2harp,cel,strings
DONEMUS perf mat rent (D203)

DELICIOUS SUITE, [ARR.] see Gershwin,
George

DELIUS, FREDERICK (1862-1934)
American Rhapsody [12']
2+pic.2.2.3. 4.2+2cornet.3.1.
timp,perc,2harp,strings
BOOSEY perf mat rent (D204)

Brigg Fair
min sc BOOSEY 981 $10.00 (D205)
KALMUS A4140 sc $20.00, set $60.00,
perf mat rent (D206)

Concerto for Piano and Orchestra
KALMUS A5800 sc $25.00, set $25.00,
perf mat rent (D207)

Concerto for Violin and Orchestra
see Concerto for Violin,
Violoncello and Orchestra

DELIUS, FREDERICK (cont'd.)
Concerto for Violin, Violoncello and
Orchestra
(Beecham, Thomas) sc STAINER B648
f.s. contains also: Concerto for
Violin and Orchestra (D208)

Dance Rhapsody No. 2
see North Country Sketches

Eventyr
see North Country Sketches

Fantastic Dance [4']
2(pic).2+English horn.2.2.
4.2.3.1. timp,perc,2harp,
strings
BOOSEY perf mat rent (D209)

Folkeraadet [20']
2.2.2.2. 4.2.3.1. timp,perc,
strings
BOOSEY perf mat rent (D210)

Hassan: Serenade, For Violoncello And
Orchestra [arr.]
(Fenby, Eric) 2.1+English horn.1+
bass clar.1. 2.0.0.0. harp,
strings,vcl solo [3'] BOOSEY perf
mat rent (D211)

In A Summer Garden
KALMUS A6408 sc $15.00, set $30.00,
pts $1.00, ea., perf mat rent
(D212)
Koanga: Closing Scene, For Solo
Voices And Orchestra [arr.]
(Beecham, Thomas) 3(pic).2+English
horn.2+bass clar.3+contrabsn.
4.2.3.1. timp,2harp,strings,
SSSSSS soli BOOSEY perf mat rent
(D213)
Koanga: Intermezzo [arr.]
(Robinson, Stanford) 3.2+English
horn.2+bass clar.3. 4.2.3.1.
timp,perc,harp,strings [12']
BOOSEY perf mat rent (D214)

Legende, For Violin And Orchestra
[8']
2.2.2.2. 4.0.0.0. timp,harp,
strings,vln solo
BOOSEY perf mat rent (D215)

Life's Dance
KALMUS A7187 sc $25.00, set $75.00,
pts $2.50, ea., perf mat rent
(D216)
(Fenby, Eric) sc STAINER B676 f.s.
(D217)

North Country Sketches
(Beecham, Thomas) sc STAINER B661
f.s. contains also: Dance
Rhapsody No. 2; Eventyr (D218)

On Hearing The First Cuckoo In Spring
see Three Pieces For Small
Orchestra
see Two Pieces For Small Orchestra

Paa Vidderne, For Narrator And
Orchestra [40']
2+pic.2+English horn.2.2.
4.2.3.1. timp,perc,strings,
narrator
BOOSEY perf mat rent (D219)

Paa Vidderne, For Orchestra [15']
2+pic.2.2+bass clar.2. 4.2+
2cornet.3.1. timp,perc,harp,
strings
BOOSEY perf mat rent (D220)

Paris
KALMUS A5900 sc $25.00, set $65.00,
perf mat rent (D221)

Petite Suite For Orchestra [13']
2.2.2.2. 2.1.0.0. timp,strings
BOOSEY perf mat rent (D222)

Sakuntala, For Solo Voice And
Orchestra
3.2+English horn.2+bass clar.2.
4.0.0.0. timp,2harp,strings,T
solo
BOOSEY perf mat rent (D223)

Sonata for String Orchestra [20']
string orch
STAINER HL75 perf mat rent (D224)

Song Before Sunrise, A
see Three Pieces For Small
Orchestra

Songs With Orchestra, Part I, For
Solo Voice And Orchestra
(Beecham, Thomas) sc STAINER B658
f.s. (D225)

Spring Morning [6']
3.2.2.2. 4.2.3.1. timp,strings
BOOSEY perf mat rent (D226)

DELIUS, FREDERICK (cont'd.)

Suite for Violin and Orchestra [20']
3.2.2.2. 4.2.3.1. timp,strings,
vln solo
BOOSEY perf mat rent   (D227)

Summer Night On The River
see Three Pieces For Small
Orchestra
see Two Pieces For Small Orchestra

Summer Nights, For Solo Voice And
Orchestra
see Three Songs, For Solo Voice And
Orchestra

Three Pieces For Small Orchestra
(Beecham, Thomas) sc STAINER B677
f.s.
contains: On Hearing The First
Cuckoo In Spring; Song Before
Sunrise, A; Summer Night On The
River   (D228)

Three Songs, For Solo Voice And
Orchestra
STAINER HL79 perf mat rent
contains: Summer Nights, For Solo
Voice And Orchestra; Through
Long, Long, Years, For Solo
Voice And Orchestra; Wine
Roses, For Solo Voice And
Orchestra   (D229)

Through Long, Long, Years, For Solo
Voice And Orchestra
see Three Songs, For Solo Voice And
Orchestra

Two Pieces For Small Orchestra
KALMUS A7247 sc $6.00, set $15.00,
pts $1.25, ea.
contains: On Hearing The First
Cuckoo In Spring; Summer Night
On The River   (D230)

Village Romeo And Juliet, A: Waltz
[arr.]
(Douglas, Keith) 2(pic).2(English
horn).2. 4.2.3.0. timp,1-2perc,
opt harp/pno,strings [8'] BOOSEY
perf mat rent   (D231)

Wine Roses, For Solo Voice And
Orchestra
see Three Songs, For Solo Voice And
Orchestra

DELLO JOIO, JUSTIN (1954-   )
Musica Humana [20']
3+pic.3+English horn.3+bass
clar.3+contrabsn. 6.8.3.1.
perc,harp,cel,pno,strings
AMP perf mat rent   (D232)

DELLO JOIO, NORMAN (1913-   )
Arietta
string orch MARKS 00006124 $15.00
(D233)

Ballabili [23']
2+pic.2+English horn.2+bass
clar.2. 4.3.3.1. timp,2perc,
harp,strings
AMP perf mat rent   (D234)

Easthampton Sketches
string orch
set AMP 068-35704 $26.00   (D235)

Lyric Dances [11']
fl,ob,clar,horn,trp,strings
AMP perf mat rent   (D236)

Songs Of Remembrance, For Solo Voice
And Orchestra [20']
2+pic.2+English horn.2+bass
clar.2+contrabsn. 4.3.3.1.
timp,perc,harp,strings,Bar solo
AMP perf mat rent   (D237)

Southern Echoes [16']
2.2+English horn.2+bass clar.0.
4.3.3.1. 2perc,strings
AMP perf mat rent   (D238)

Variants On A Bach Chorale
2+pic.2+English horn.2+bass
clar.2. 4.3.3.1. timp,perc,
strings
AMP perf mat rent   (D239)

DELNOOZ, HENRI (1942-   )
Symphony For 21 Players [16']
2.2.2.2.alto sax. 2.2.1.0. perc,
pno,2vln,vla,vcl,db
DONEMUS perf mat rent   (D240)

DELPHINE see Chapple, Brian

DELPHINE "ACH, WAS SOLL ICH BEGINNEN",
FOR SOLO VOICE AND ORCHESTRA,
[ARR.] see Schubert, Franz (Peter)

DELTA, FOR VIOLIN, CLARINET, PERCUSSION
AND ORCHESTRA see Colgrass, Michael
(Charles)

DELTAS see Miroglio, Francis

DEM UNENDLICHEN, FOR SOLO VOICE AND
ORCHESTRA, [ARR.] see Schubert,
Franz (Peter)

DEMAREST, CLIFFORD (1874-1946)
Rhapsody for Piano and Orchestra
1.1.2.1. 2.3.1.0. timp,strings,
pno solo
SCHIRM.G perf mat rent   (D241)

DEMBSKI, STEPHEN (1949-   )
Refraction-Retracja [5']
1.1.1.1. 1.2.1.1. perc,strings
sc AM.COMP.AL. f.s.   (D242)

Spectra [15']
1.1.1.1. 1.1.0.0. perc,strings
sc AM.COMP.AL. $20.25   (D243)

DEMERSSEMAN, JULE AUGUSTE (1833-1866)
Solo for Flute and Orchestra, No. 6,
Op. Posth. [15'30]
1.1.2.2. 2.2.3.0. timp,strings,fl
solo
BILLAUDOT perf mat rent   (D244)

DEMETRIUS AND THE GLADIATORS: SUITE see
Waxman, Franz

DEMI FORTUNE POLKA see Strauss, Johann,
[Jr.]

DEMILLAC
Concerto for Flute and Orchestra
LEDUC perf mat rent   (D245)

DEMOFONTE: FINALE, ACT III see Brivio,
Giuseppe Ferdinando

DEMOLIRER POLKA see Strauss, Johann,
[Jr.]

DEMON, FOR PIANO AND ORCHESTRA see
Colgrass, Michael (Charles)

"...DEN IMPULS ZUM WEITERSPRECHEN ERST
EMPFINGE", FOR VIOLA AND ORCHESTRA
see Ruzicka, Peter

DEN SOM BYGGER PA STEIN see Haugland,
Glenn Erik

DENHOFF, MICHAEL (1955-   )
Chants d'Automne, For Solo Voice And
Chamber Orchestra [25']
2(pic,alto fl).1+English
horn.2(bass clar).1(contrabsn).
2.0.0.0. perc,harp,2vln,vla,
vcl,db,Bar solo
BREITKOPF-W   (D246)

Desastres De La Guerra [17']
3(pic).2+English horn.2(bass
clar).2(contrabsn). 3.3.3.1.
timp,2perc,2harp,strings
BREITKOPF-W   (D247)

Einsamkeit; In Memoriam W. Buchebner
[12']
1(pic).1.1.1. 1.1.1.0. tam-tam,
harp,strings
BREITKOPF-W   (D248)

Melancolia [21']
1+alto fl.1+English horn.1+bass
clar.0+contrabsn. 0.0.0.0.
perc,harp,pno,4vla,4vcl,2db
BREITKOPF-W   (D249)

Mutazioni [10']
2(pic).2.2.2. 2.2.0.0. 2perc,pno,
strings
BREITKOPF-W   (D250)

DENIS, DIDIER (1947-   )
Chants De Tse Yeh, For Solo Voice And
Instrumental Ensemble [10']
fl,ob d'amore,horn,trp,2perc,gtr,
mand,harp,cel,pno,vln,vcl,
speaking voice
RIDEAU perf mat rent   (D251)

Cinq Fois Je T'aime, For Solo Voices
And Orchestra [12']
3(pic).2+English horn.2+bass
clar.2+contrabsn. 4.3.3.1.
5perc,harp,cel,strings,
narrator&coloratura sop
RIDEAU perf mat rent   (D252)

DENISOV, EDISON VASILIEVICH (1929-   )
Aquarelle [9']
14vln,4vla,4vcl,2db
SIKORSKI perf mat rent   (D253)
VAAP perf mat rent   (D254)

Chamber Symphony
clar,bsn,pno,strings
[16'] VAAP perf mat rent   (D255)

DENISOV, EDISON VASILIEVICH (cont'd.)

Children's Suite [7']
2.1.2.2. 2.1.0.0. timp,perc,cel,
pno,strings
VAAP perf mat rent   (D256)
"Kindersuite" SIKORSKI perf mat
rent   (D257)

Colin Et Chloe [36']
3.3.3.3.alto sax.tenor sax.
3.3.3.1. perc,cel,elec gtr,bass
gtr,harp,pno,strings
VAAP perf mat rent   (D258)

Concerto for Bassoon, Violoncello and
Orchestra [30']
1.1.1.0. 2.1.1.0. perc,strings,
bsn solo,vcl solo
RICORDI-IT 133698 perf mat rent
(D259)
SIKORSKI perf mat rent   (D260)
VAAP perf mat rent   (D261)

Concerto for Clarinet and Orchestra
[25']
4.4.4.0. 6.4.3.0. 3perc,harp,cel,
strings,clar solo
SIKORSKI perf mat rent   (D262)

Concerto for Flute, Oboe and
Orchestra [24']
3.0+English horn.3.1. 4.3.3.0.
6perc,harp,cel,strings,fl solo,
ob solo
UNIVER. perf mat rent   (D263)
VAAP perf mat rent   (D264)

Concerto for Oboe and Orchestra [20']
3.0.3+bass clar.3. 3.3.3.0. timp,
perc,harp,cel,strings,ob solo
SIKORSKI perf mat rent   (D265)
VAAP perf mat rent   (D266)

Concerto for Viola and Orchestra
[40']
2.1.3.2. 0.3.3.0. timp,perc,harp,
cel,strings,vla solo
SIKORSKI perf mat rent   (D267)

Concerto for 2 Violas, Harpsichord
and String Orchestra
string orch,2vla soli,hpsd solo
SIKORSKI perf mat rent   (D268)
VAAP perf mat rent   (D269)

Concerto for Violin and Orchestra
[22']
3.2.3.1. 4.3.0.0. perc,cel,harp,
strings,vln solo
VAAP perf mat rent   (D270)

Confession: Suite [35']
2.2.3.2. 4.3.3.0. timp,perc,harp,
cel,pno,strings
VAAP perf mat rent   (D271)

Epitaph [6']
1.1.1.1. 1.1.1.0. perc,pno,vln,
vla,vcl,db
RICORDI-IT 133638 perf mat rent
(D272)
VAAP perf mat rent   (D273)

Glocken Im Nebel [16']
4.1.4.0. 6.4.4.0. perc,harp,cel,
strings
SIKORSKI perf mat rent   (D274)

Hommage A Pierre
2fl,2clar,horn,vibra,harp,pno,
vln,vla,vcl
sc,pts LEDUC AL 27238 f.s.   (D275)

Kindersuite
see Children's Suite

Little Suite [8']
2.1.2.2.sax. 2.1.0.0. timp,perc,
harp,pno,strings
VAAP perf mat rent   (D276)

Ton Image Charmante, For Solo Voice
And Orchestra [19']
2.2.2.2. 3.0.3.0. cel,harp,
strings,solo voice
VAAP perf mat rent   (D277)

Variations On A Theme Of Haydn "Tod
Ist Ein Langer Schlaf", For
Violoncello And Orchestra [12']
2ob,2horn,bells,strings,vcl solo
study sc SIKORSKI f.s., perf mat
rent   (D278)
sc VAAP f.s., perf mat rent   (D279)

DENK ICH AN HAYDN see Winbeck, Heinz

DENNISON, PAUL S. (1954-   )
Concertino for Violin and String
Orchestra [12']
string orch,vln solo
KALMUS A4137 sc $12.00, set $12.00
(D280)

DENNISON, SAM (1926-   )
Adagio for Horn and Chamber Orchestra
[6']
2.2.2.2. 0.0.0.0. timp,strings,
horn solo
KALMUS A5670 sc $5.00, set $17.00,
pts $1.25, ea.   (D281)

Kaleidoscope [3'30"]
2.2+English horn.2+bass clar.2.
4.3.3.1. timp,perc,strings
KALMUS A5175 sc $15.00, set $30.00,
perf mat rent   (D282)

DENVER, JOHN
see DEUTSCHENDORF, HENRY JOHN

DEPLORATION see Joubert, John

DEPRAZ, RAYMOND (1915-   )
Poursuivant, Le, For Solo Voice And
Instrumental Ensemble [15']
1.0.1.1. 1.1.1.0. timp,cel,vln,
vla,db, countertenor solo
BILLAUDOT perf mat rent   (D283)

"...DER DIE GESANGE ZERSCHLUG", FOR
SOLO VOICE AND CHAMBER ORCHESTRA
see Ruzicka, Peter

DER SYNGER INGEN FUGLE, FOR SOLO VOICE
AND ORCHESTRA see Jordan, Sverre

DERIVE 2 see Boulez, Pierre

DERIVE DES CONTINENTS, LA, FOR VIOLA
AND STRING ORCHESTRA see Murail,
Tristan

DERIVES see Grisey, Gerard

DERNIER SOMMEIL DE LA VIERGE, LE, FOR
CELLO AND STRING ORCHESTRA see
Massenet, Jules

DERVAUX, PIERRE JEAN EMILE (1917-   )
Symphony for Strings [20']
string orch
sc BILLAUDOT f.s., perf mat rent
(D284)

DES FÄHRMANNS BRÄUTE, FOR SOLO VOICE
AND ORCHESTRA see Sibelius, Jean,
Koskenlaskian Morsiamet, For Solo
Voice And Orchestra

DES FREUNDES UMNACHTUNG see Incardona,
Federico

DES ILES, FOR SOLO VOICE AND ORCHESTRA
see Tveitt, Geirr

DES KNABEN WUNDERHORN: LIED DES
VERFOLGTEN IM TURM, FOR SOLO VOICE
AND ORCHESTRA see Mahler, Gustav

DES KNABEN WUNDERHORN: LIEDER, VOL. I
see Mahler, Gustav

DES KNABEN WUNDERHORN: LIEDER, VOL. II
see Mahler, Gustav

DES KNABEN WUNDERHORN: LOB DES HOHEN
VERSTANDES, FOR SOLO VOICE AND
ORCHESTRA see Mahler, Gustav

DES KNABEN WUNDERHORN: RHEINLEGENDCHEN,
FOR SOLO VOICE AND ORCHESTRA see
Mahler, Gustav

DES KNABEN WUNDERHORN: TROST IM
UNGLUCK, FOR SOLO VOICE AND
ORCHESTRA see Mahler, Gustav

DES KNABEN WUNDERHORN: TWO SONGS, FOR
SOLO VOICE AND ORCHESTRA see
Mahler, Gustav

DES KNABEN WUNDERHORN: VERLORNE MUH',
FOR SOLO VOICE AND ORCHESTRA see
Mahler, Gustav

DES KNABEN WUNDERHORN: WER HAT DIES
LIEDLEIN ERDACHT? FOR SOLO VOICE
AND ORCHESTRA see Mahler, Gustav

DESASTRES DE LA GUERRA see Denhoff,
Michael

DESCANTS, FOR VIOLA AND ORCHESTRA see
Cooper, Paul

DESCOBRIMENTO DO BRASIL: SUITE NO. 1
see Villa-Lobos, Heitor

DESCOBRIMENTO DO BRASIL: SUITE NO. 2
see Villa-Lobos, Heitor

DESCOBRIMENTO DO BRASIL: SUITE NO. 3
see Villa-Lobos, Heitor

DESENCLOS, ALFRED (1912-1971)
Vitrail [11']
2.2.2.2. 4.0.0.0. 2perc,harp,
strings
BILLAUDOT perf mat rent   (D285)

DESERT SONG, THE, FOR SOLO VOICE AND
ORCHESTRA, [ARR.] see Romberg,
Sigmund

DESERT SONG, THE: ONE ALONE, FOR SOLO
VOICE AND ORCHESTRA, [ARR.] see
Romberg, Sigmund

DESERT SONG, THE: SELECTIONS, [ARR.]
see Romberg, Sigmund

DESERTS see Varese, Edgard

DESILETS, RICHARD (1957-   )
Metamorphose Du Cri [16']
6trp,perc,3vln,2vla,2vcl,db
CAN.MUS.CENT. MI 1200 D475ME (D286)

Oui
CAN.MUS.CENT. MI 1100 D4570U (D287)

DESINTEGRACION MORFOLOGICA DE LA
CHACONA DE J.S. BACH see
Montsalvatge, Xavier

DESINTEGRATIONS see Murail, Tristan

DESOLATE CITY, THE, FOR SOLO VOICE AND
ORCHESTRA see Porter, Quincy

DESPORTES, YVONNE (1907-   )
Hommage A Maurice Emmanuel [33'30"]
2.2.2.2.opt alto sax. 2.2.2.0.
timp,perc,harp,strings
BILLAUDOT perf mat rent   (D288)

DESSAU, PAUL (1894-1979)
Symphonische Adaptationen Des
Quintetts, Kv 614 Von Mozart
[30']
3.2.3.2. 4.2.1.0. timp,perc,
strings
PETERS sc P9061 f.s., study sc
P9061A f.s.   (D289)

DESTAN CONCERTO see Nurymov, Chary

DESTINATION TOKYO see Waxman, Franz

DESTINI see Lewis, Robert Hall

DET ER GANSKE VIST see Hoffding, Finn

DET GULNAR LAUVET, FOR SOLO VOICE AND
STRING ORCHESTRA see Eggen, Arne

DETAILS see Hodeir, Andre

DETTO II, FOR VIOLONCELLO AND
INSTRUMENTAL ENSEMBLE see
Gubaidulina, Sofia

DEUTERONOMIUM, FOR SOLO VOICES AND
INSTRUMENTAL ENSEMBLE see Rebel,
Meeuwis

DEUTLICH LIEGT VOR MIR see Rimsky-
Korsakov, Nikolai, Tsar's Bride,
The: Aria Of Martha, For Solo Voice
And Orchestra

DEUTSCHE GRUSSE WALZER see Strauss,
Josef

DEUTSCHE HERZEN WALZER see Strauss,
Eduard

DEUTSCHE RHAPSODIE, FOR VIOLIN AND
ORCHESTRA see Koch, Friedrich E.

DEUTSCHE TANZE, FOR VIOLONCELLO,
DOUBLEBASS AND ORCHESTRA see Beyer,
Frank Michael

DEUTSCHE TÄNZE, SECHS [ARR.] see Haydn,
[Franz] Joseph

DEUTSCHE TÄNZE, ZWÖLF, WOO. 8 see
Beethoven, Ludwig van

DEUTSCHMEISTER JUBILÄUMS MARSCH see
Strauss, Johann, [Jr.]

DEUX APOLOGUES D'OSCAR WILDE, FOR SOLO
VOICES AND ORCHESTRA see
Capdevielle, Pierre

DEUX AUBADES see Lalo, Edouard

DEUX CAPRICES, FOR FLUTE AND ORCHESTRA
see Ponse, Luctor

DEUX CAPRICES EN FORME DE VALSE, FOR
ALTO SAXOPHONE AND STRING ORCHESTRA
see Bonneau, Paul

DEUX DANSES SYMPHONIQUES see Coppola,
Piero

DEUX ESSAIS SYMPHONIQUES see Thierac,
Jacques

DEUX ETUDES, OP. 43 see Goehr,
Alexander

DEUX IMAGES DE LA BIBLE see Tansman,
Alexandre

DEUX JOURNEES, LES: OVERTURE see
Cherubini, Luigi

DEUX LIEDER, FOR PIANO AND ORCHESTRA
see Koering, Rene

DEUX MELODIES DE PAUL FORT, FOR SOLO
VOICE AND ORCHESTRA see Tomasi,
Henri

DEUX MORCEAUX, FOR CELLO AND ORCHESTRA
see Cui, César Antonovich

DEUX PIGEONS, LES: SUITE see Messager,
Andre

DEUX POEMES SYMPHONIQUES see Koechlin,
Charles

DEUX PRELUDES see Jacob, [Dom] Clement

DEUX PSAUMES, FOR SOLO VOICE AND
ORCHESTRA see Bloch, Ernest

DEUX SKETCHES MONTMARTROIS [ARR.] see
Satie, Erik

DEUXIEME POEME LYRIQUE SUR LE LIVRE DE
JOB, FOR SOLO VOICE AND ORCHESTRA
see Rabaud, Henri

DEVEVEY, PIERRE (1919-   )
Fantasy for Piano and Orchestra
[4'30"]
2.1.2.1. 2.3.2.0. timp,perc,harp,
strings,pno solo
BILLAUDOT perf mat rent   (D290)

DEVIATIES see Janssen, Guus

DEVIENNE, FRANÇOIS (1759-1803)
Concerto for Flute and Orchestra, No.
1, in D [19'40"]
2ob,2horn,strings,fl solo
(Paubon, P.) BILLAUDOT perf mat
rent   (D291)

Concerto for Flute and Orchestra, No.
8, in G [17'40"]
2ob,2horn,strings,fl solo
(Paubon, P.) BILLAUDOT perf mat
rent   (D292)

Concerto for Flute and Orchestra, No.
10, in D [18'20"]
2ob,2horn,strings,fl solo
(Paubon, P.) BILLAUDOT perf mat
rent   (D293)

Concerto for Flute and Orchestra, Op.
Posth., in D [18']
2ob,bsn,2horn,strings,fl solo
(Paubon, P.) BILLAUDOT perf mat
rent   (D294)

Symphonie Concertante for Oboe,
Bassoon and Orchestra, No. 2, in
C
(Máriássy) sc EMB 7187 f.s. (D295)

DEVIL AND DANIEL WEBSTER, THE: SUITE
see Herrmann, Bernard

DEVILLERS, JEAN BAPTISTE (1953-   )
A-Pic, For Bassoon And Instrumental
Ensemble [14']
2(pic,alto fl).2(English
horn).1(bass clar).0. 2.0.0.0.
perc,7vln,2vla,2vcl,db,bsn solo
SALABERT perf mat rent   (D296)

Clairs-Obscurs [18']
1(pic,alto fl).1(English
horn).1(clar in E flat,bass
clar).1(contrabsn). 1.1.2.0.
4perc,harp,pno,2vln,vla,vcl,db
SALABERT perf mat rent   (D297)

Primavera, For Violin And Orchestra
[17']
1.1+English horn.2.2. 2.0.0.0.
perc,hpsd,9vln,3vla,2vcl,db,vln
solo
SALABERT perf mat rent   (D298)

DEVILS, THE: SUITE, FOR SOLO VOICE AND
ORCHESTRA see Davies, Peter Maxwell

DEVIL'S ROUND, THE see Loeffler,
Charles Martin, Villanelle Du
Diable

DEVIL'S TRILL, THE, [ARR.] see Tartini,
Giuseppe, Sonata, "Il Trillo Del
Diavolo" For Violin And Orchestra,
[arr.]

DEVRIES, IVAN (1909-   )
Cinq Rondeaux De Charles d'Orleans,
For Solo Voice And Instrumental
Ensemble [11']
fl,ob,English horn,trp,2harp,
3vla,2vcl,db,solo voice

DEVRIES, IVAN (cont'd.)

    BILLAUDOT perf mat rent   (D299)

DEWANGER, ANTON
  Epilogue Joyeux *Op.71 [8']
    3.3.3.3. 3.3.2.1. timp,perc,
     strings
    BILLAUDOT perf mat rent   (D300)

  Mephisto *Op.60 [17']
    3.3.3.3. 3.3.2.1. timp,perc,
     strings
    BILLAUDOT perf mat rent   (D301)

  Serenade, Op. 63 [25']
    2.1.1.1. 0.0.0.0. strings
    BILLAUDOT perf mat rent   (D302)

  Symphonie Dramatique *Op.68 [65']
    3.3.3.3.2soprano sax.2alto
     sax.2tenor sax.baritone
     sax.2bass sax. 6.9.6.2. timp,
     perc,strings
    BILLAUDOT perf mat rent   (D303)

DHYAN 1 see Sohal, Naresh

DI BALLO: OVERTURE see Sullivan, [Sir]
  Arthur Seymour

DI BARI, MARCO (1958-   )
  Dove Piu Dolce Suono Migra [8']
    2.2.2.2. 2.2.0.0. timp,perc,
     strings
    RICORDI-IT 133878 perf mat rent
                        (D304)
  Eternally Present [10'30"]
    4.3.2.2. 4.0.0.0. timp,perc,cel,
     pno,strings
    RICORDI-IT 133940 perf mat rent
                        (D305)
DI DOMENICA, ROBERT (1927-   )
  Concerto for Piano and Orchestra, No.
    2 [30']
    2(pic).2.2.2. 2.2.3.1. timp,perc,
     harp,cel,strings,pno solo
    MARGUN MP2084 perf mat rent   (D306)

  Concerto for Violin and Chamber
    Orchestra [18']
    1.1.1.1. 1.0.0.0. 2vln,vla,vcl,
     db,vln solo
    sc,pts MJQ rent   (D307)

  Dream Journeys [10']
    3.3.3.3. 4.3.3.1. timp,3perc,
     2harp,pno,strings
    MARGUN BP 2063 perf mat rent (D308)

  Variations And Soliloquies [24']
    3.3.3.3. 4.3.3.1. timp,3perc,
     2harp,strings
    MARGUN MP2083 perf mat rent (D309)

  Variations On A Theme By Gunther
    Schuller, For Tuba And Chamber
    Orchestra [12']
    fl,clar,bass clar,harp,3vln,3vcl,
     2db,tuba solo
    MARGUN BP 2064 perf mat rent (D310)

DI LOTTI, SILVANA (1942-   )
  Conversari Per Orchestra [10']
    3.2.3.2. 2.2.1.0. timp,perc,
     strings
    SONZOGNO perf mat rent   (D311)

  In Nomine Domini [14']
    3.2.3.2. 4.2.2.1. timp,perc,harp,
     strings
    sc SONZOGNO f.s., perf mat rent
                        (D312)
  Serenade [8']
    2.0.1.0. 1.1.1.0. perc,pno,
     strings
    sc SONZOGNO f.s., perf mat rent
                        (D313)
DI RETRO AL SOL see Fanticini, Fabrizio

...DI SUSSULTI E DI TREMORI, FOR PIANO
  AND ORCHESTRA see Guarnieri,
  Adriano

DIA SUCCARI (1938-   )
  Fugue No. 1 for Strings [7'50"]
    string orch
    BILLAUDOT perf mat rent   (D314)

  Fugue No. 2 for Strings [5']
    string orch
    BILLAUDOT perf mat rent   (D315)

DIABOLIN POLKA see Strauss, Johann,
  [Jr.]

DIAFORA see Holmboe, Vagn

DIAGONAL see Fenelon, Philippe

DIALOG AV MARIONETTER, FOR SOLO VOICES
  AND STRING ORCHESTRA see Hallnäs,
  Eyvind

DIALOG MIT HAYDN see Zender, Hans

DIALOGE, FOR 2 PIANOS AND ORCHESTRA see
  Zimmermann, Bernd Alois

DIALOGOS, FOR PIANO AND ORCHESTRA see
  Larrauri, Anton

DIALOGUE see Andresen, Erik

DIALOGUE FOR VIOLIN AND CHAMBER
  ORCHESTRA see Bull, Edvard Hagerup

DIALOGUE FOR PIANO AND ORCHESTRA see
  Hameenniemi, Eero

DIALOGUE FOR SYNCLAVIER AND ORCHESTRA
  see Proto, Frank

DIALOGUE POUR TRIO BASSO ET ORCHESTRE
  see Mather, Bruce

DIALOGUES see Rudhyar, Dane (Daniel
  Chennevière)

DIALOGUES, FOR VIOLIN, VIOLONCELLO AND
  ORCHESTRA see Ward, Robert Eugene

DIALOGUES FOR JAZZ QUINTET AND
  ORCHESTRA see Schifrin, Lalo
  (Boris)

DIALOGUES OF THE MIND AND HEART, FOR
  JAZZ TRIO AND ORCHESTRA see
  Kellaway, Roger

DIALOGUS, FOR VIOLONCELLO AND ORCHESTRA
  see Walker, George Theophilus

DIAMANTS IMAGINAIRES see Hurel,
  Philippe

DIANA'S FAREWELL see Sary, Laszlo

DIAPHANEIS see Lenot, Jacques

DIAPHONY see Sigurbjörnsson, Thorkell

DIAPHONY, FOR ORGAN AND ORCHESTRA see
  Connolly, Justin [Riveagh]

DIARIO '83 see Donatoni, Franco

DIBAK, IGOR (1947-   )
  Concerto for Violoncello and
    Orchestra
    SLOV.HUD.FOND   (D316)

DICKERSON, ROGER DONALD (1934-   )
  New Orleans Concerto, For Piano And
    Orchestra
    3(pic).3(English horn).3(bass
     clar).2. 4.3.3.1. timp,perc,
     strings, s voice, pno solo
    PEER perf mat rent   (D317)

DICKINSON, PETER (1934-   )
  Birthday Surprise [2']
    3(pic).3.3.3. 4.3.3.1. 2perc,
     strings
    NOVELLO perf mat rent   (D318)

  Concerto for Piano and Orchestra
    3.3.3.3. 4.3.3.1. perc,cel,2harp,
     strings,pno solo
    sc NOVELLO $41.75, perf mat rent
                        (D319)
  Concerto for Strings, Percussion and
    Organ [15']
    perc,elec org,strings
    NOVELLO perf mat rent   (D320)

  Monologue For Strings [9']
    string orch
    NOVELLO perf mat rent   (D321)

DICKINSON LIEDER, FOR SOLO VOICE AND
  ORCHESTRA see Castiglioni, Niccolò

DIDO AND AENEAS: SUITE, [ARR.] see
  Purcell, Henry

DIDON: OVERTURE see Piccinni, Niccolo

DIDONE ABBANDONATA see Vinci, Leonardo

DIE IHR DES UNERMESSLICHEN WELTALLS
  SCHÖPFER, FOR SOLO VOICE AND
  ORCHESTRA, [ARR.] see Mozart,
  Wolfgang Amadeus

DIEMER, EMMA LOU (1927-   )
  Concerto for Flute and Orchestra
    SOUTHERN rent   (D322)

  Concerto for Harpsichord and Chamber
    Orchestra
    2.2.3.2. 4.1.1.0. perc,strings,
     hpsd solo
    sc SEESAW $44.00, perf mat rent
                        (D323)
  Serenade for String Orchestra
    string orch
    sc SEESAW $40.00, perf mat rent
                        (D324)

DIEMER, EMMA LOU (cont'd.)

  Suite for Orchestra
    2.2.2.2. 4.2.3.1. timp,perc,pno,
     harp,strings
    SEESAW   (D325)

  Symphony No. 2
    3.3.3.3. 4.3.3.1. timp,perc,pno,
     harp,cel,strings
    SEESAW   (D326)

DIEPENBROCK, ALPHONS (1862-1921)
  Avondzang, For Solo Voice And
    Orchestra [4']
    2.2.3.2. 4.0.0.0. strings,T solo sc
    DONEMUS f.s., perf mat rent
                        (D327)
DIETTER, CHRISTIAN LUDWIG (1757-1822)
  Concerto for 2 Bassoons and Orchestra
    2ob,strings,2bsn soli
    (Angermuller, Rudolph) DOBLINGER
    DM 890 sc $23.20, set $23.20 (D328)

DIFERENCIAS, FOR VIOLONCELLO AND
  ORCHESTRA see Sarmientos, Jorge

DIFERENCIAS PARA ORQUESTA see Halffter,
  Rodolfo

DIFFRACTIONS see Keay, Nigel

DIJK, DE, FOR NARRATOR AND ORCHESTRA
  see Lier, Bertus van

DIJK, JAN VAN (1918-   )
  Breeroo *Op.705 [12']
    3.2.2.1.alto sax. 1.1.0.0. timp,
     perc,opt pno,strings
    DONEMUS perf mat rent   (D329)

  Concert Piece for Piano and Orchestra
    [8']
    2.2.3.2. 3.2.3.0. timp,perc,
     strings,pno solo
    sc,solo pt DONEMUS f.s., perf mat
     rent   (D330)

  Sinfonia No. 7, Op. 770a [14']
    2.2.2.2. 2.3.2.0. timp,2-3perc,
     strings
    (Coutances) sc DONEMUS f.s., perf
     mat rent   (D331)

DILLON, JAMES (1950-   )
  Überschreiten
    1(pic,alto fl).1.2(bass
     clar).1(contrabsn). 1.1.1.1.
     perc,pno/Hamm,2vln,vla,vcl,db
    sc PETERS P7348 $60.00, perf mat
     rent   (D332)

DILLON, SHAUN
  Suite Of Airs And Graces
    string orch
    STAINER HI70 f.s.   (D333)

DILUVIO UNIVERSALE, IL: OVERTURE see
  Donizetti, Gaetano

DIMANCHE BASQUE, UN see Laparra, Raoul

DIMITRAKOPOULOS, APOSTOLO (1955-   )
  Divertimento for Strings [9']
    string orch
    STIM   (D334)

  Speculum Amoris [20']
    3.3.3.3. 4.4.2.2. timp,3perc,pno,
     cel,strings
    STIM   (D335)

DIMITRIEV, GEORGI
  Concerto for Violin and Orchestra
    [26']
    3.2.3.2.2sax. 4.3.3.0. timp,
     3perc,strings,vln solo
    PETERS   (D336)

  Sybille, For Flute And Orchestra
    [21']
    2ob,2horn,timp,perc,hpsd,cel,pno,
     strings,fl solo
    PETERS   (D337)

DIMLER, ANTON (1753-1819)
  Concerto for Clarinet and Orchestra
    in B flat
    (Balassa, Fodor) EMB f.s. sc 6123,
     pts 6124   (D338)

DIMMALIMM see Halldorsson, Skuli

D'INDY, VINCENT
  see INDY, VINCENT D'

DINER see Barry, Gerald

DING see Moser, Roland Olivier

DING, SHAN-DE
  Long March Symphony [67']
    3.2+English horn.3.3. 4.4.3.1.
     timp,perc,harp,pno,strings
    HONG KONG perf mat rent   (D339)

DING, SHAN-DE (cont'd.)

New China Suite [12']
3.2.2.2. 4.2.3.0. timp,perc,xylo,
harp,cel,strings
HONG KONG perf mat rent   (D340)

Overture, Op. 20 [7']
3.3.3.3. 4.3.3.1. timp,perc,xylo,
harp,strings
HONG KONG perf mat rent   (D341)

Sinkiang Dance No. 2, For Orchestra
[6']
3.2+English horn.2.2. 4.3.3.1.
timp,perc,harp,cel,strings
HONG KONG perf mat rent   (D342)

DINORAH QUADRILLE see Strauss, Johann,
[Jr.]

DION see Goodman, David

DION, DENIS (1957-   )
Concerto for Orchestra [12']
2(pic).2(English horn).2.2.
2.2.0.0. perc,strings
CAN.MUS.CENT. MI 1100 D592KO (D343)

Veuillez Agreger Les Sentiments Mes
Plus Distincts, For Harpsichord
And String Orchestra [12']
string orch,hpsd solo
CAN.MUS.CENT. MI 1662 D592VE (D344)

DIONISI, RENATO (1910-   )
Music for Timpani and Chamber
Orchestra
2(pic).2.2.2. 2.2.0.0. timp,perc,
strings
CARISCH   (D345)

DIONYSIA see Trythall, Gilbert

DIOTIMA see Harbison, John

DIPTYCH see Tansman, Alexandre

DIRECTORATE MARCH, THE see Sousa, John
Philip

DIRGE see Howe, Mary

DIRGE BY BACH, A see Yuasa, Joji

DISCANTUS see Vries, Klaas de

DISCOURSE see Downey, John Wilham

DISPA, ROBERT (1929-   )
Concerto for String Orchestra [14']
string orch
DONEMUS perf mat rent   (D346)

DISPLAY V see Bon, Maarten

DISPUTATIONEN WALZER see Strauss, Josef

DISSEMBLER, THE, FOR SOLO VOICE AND
CHAMBER ORCHESTRA see Krenek, Ernst

DISTANT HILLS COMING NIGH, FOR SOLO
VOICES AND INSTRUMENTAL ENSEMBLE
see Albert, Stephen Joel

DISTANT RUNES AND INCANTATIONS, FOR
PIANO AND ORCHESTRA see Schwantner,
Joseph

DISTANT SHORE, THE see Carl, Robert

DISTANT SHORE II, THE, FOR SOLO VOICE
AND CHAMBER ORCHESTRA see Carl,
Robert

DISTINGUISH, FOR VIOLIN AND ORCHESTRA
see Ye, Xiao-Gang

DISTLER, HUGO (1908-1942)
Concerto for Harpsichord and String
Orchestra, Op. 14
KALMUS A6992 sc $35.00, set $30.00,
pts $6.00, ea., perf mat rent
(D347)
Lied Am Herde, For Solo Voice And
Orchestra *Op.21,No.1
KALMUS A7076 sc $15.00, set $15.00,
pts $1.50, ea., perf mat rent
(D348)

DITE ALMENO, FOR SOLO VOICES AND
ORCHESTRA see Mozart, Wolfgang
Amadeus

DITHYRAMBE see Strauss, Josef

DITTERSDORF, KARL DITTERS VON
(1739-1799)
Andantino For Oboe And String
Orchestra
(Kovács) string orch,ob/fl solo sc
EMB 8502 f.s.   (D349)

Concerto for Double Bass and
Orchestra, No. 1, in D
2fl,2ob,2horn,strings,db solo
YORKE 8.0059 perf mat rent   (D350)

DITTERSDORF, KARL DITTERS VON (cont'd.)

Concerto for Double Bass and
Orchestra, No. 2, in D
2ob,2horn,strings,db solo
YORKE 8.0059 perf mat rent   (D351)

Concerto for Flute and String
Orchestra in E minor
(Sonntag) string orch,fl solo [13']
KALMUS A7407 sc $15.00, set
$15.00, pts $2.50, ea.   (D352)

Concerto for Violin and String
Orchestra in G, MIN 5
(Mlynarczyk; Lurman) KALMUS A5611
sc $12.00, set $10.00, pts $2.00,
ea.   (D353)

Sinfonia Concertante for Viola,
Double Bass and Orchestra
INTERNAT. perf mat rent   (D354)
(Altmann) KALMUS A6117 sc $8.00,
set $11.00   (D355)

Sinfonia in C, Krebs 73, [arr.]
(Liebeskind) 1.2.0.2. 2.2.0.0.
timp,strings [17'] ("The Four
Ages Of Man") KALMUS A5722 sc
$15.00, set $30.00, perf mat rent
(D356)
Sinfonia in D, MIN 117
(Murányi) sc EMB 8921 f.s.   (D357)

Sinfonia in G, Krebs 75, [arr.]
(Liebeskind) 2ob,2horn,strings
[14'] ("The Transformation Of
Actaeon") KALMUS A5723 sc $10.00,
set $18.00, perf mat rent   (D358)

Sinfonietta, MIN 118
(Laki) sc EMB 12131 f.s.   (D359)

Symphonies, Six
(Badura-Skoda, Eva; Rudolf, Kenneth
E.) ("The Symphony" Vol. B-I) sc
GARLAND ISBN 0-8240-3859-2 $90.00
contains also: Monn, Georg
Matthias, Symphonies, Five; Mann,
Johann Christoph, Symphony (D360)

DITTO see Strouse, Charles Louis

DIVERSION "IF ALL THE WORLD WERE PAPER"
see Cruft, Adrian

DIVERSIONS see Fine, Irving

DIVERTIMENTI, SIX see Mozart, Wolfgang
Amadeus

DIVERTIMENTI, TEN see Mozart, Wolfgang
Amadeus

DIVERTIMENTO CONCERTANTE see
Blendinger, Herbert

DIVERTIMENTO CONCERTANTE, FOR 2 PIANOS
AND ORCHESTRA, OP. 10 see Evensen,
Bernt Kasberg

DIVERTIMENTO OSTINATO see Beurden,
Bernard van

DIVERTIMENTO - SERENADE NO. 4 see
Martinu, Bohuslav (Jan)

DIVERTIMENTO SU TEMI DEL XVI SECOLO,
FOR ORCHESTRA see Ambrosi, Alearco

DIVERTIMENTO SU TEMI DEL XVI SECOLO,
FOR STRING ORCHESTRA see Ambrosi,
Alearco

DIVERTISSEMENT SUR DES CHANSONS RUSSES
see Rabaud, Henri

DIVERTISSEMENTS see Schober, Brian

DIX, ROBERT (1917-   )
Concertino for Chamber Orchestra [9']
1.1.1.1. 2.1.1.0. pno,strings
DRK 122 sc $15.00, study sc $5.00
(D361)
Concertino for Viola and String
Orchestra [13']
string orch,vla solo
DRK 121 sc $12.00, study sc $4.00
(D362)
Symphony No. 1 [22']
3.3.3.2. 4.3.3.1. timp,3perc,
strings
DRK 113 sc $35.00, study sc $7.00
(D363)
Three Movements For Orchestra [15']
3.3.3.2. 4.3.3.1. timp,2perc,
strings
DRK 109 sc $24.00, study sc $5.00
(D364)
Three Movements For Orchestra-II
[19']
3.3.3.2. 4.2.3.1. timp,3perc,
strings
DRK 123 sc $35.00, study sc $7.00
(D365)

DIX COMMANDEMENTS, LES see Tansman,
Alexandre

DJINNS, FOR SOLO VOICE AND ORCHESTRA
see Vierne, Louis

DJINNS, LES, FOR PIANO AND ORCHESTRA
see Franck, Cesar

DMITRIYEV, GEORGI (1942-   )
Symphony No. 2 [35']
3.3.3.3. 6.3.3.1. timp,6perc,
2harp,cel,strings
SIKORSKI perf mat rent   (D366)

DO IT IVO, FOR TROMBONE AND ORCHESTRA
see Ekström, Lars

DOBROWOLSKI, ANDRZEJ (1921-1990)
Passacaglia [12']
2.2.2.2. 4.3.3.1. strings
POLSKIE   (D367)

DOCE MOVILES PARA CONJUNTO DE CAMERA
see Nova, Jacqueline

DOCTEUR FABRICIUS, LE see Koechlin,
Charles

DOCTRINEN WALZER see Strauss, Eduard

DODECACELLI see Ott, David

DODGSON, STEPHEN (1924-   )
Russian Pieces, Set 1 [8']
2.2.2.0. 2.1.0.0. strings
NOVELLO perf mat rent   (D368)

Russian Pieces, Set 2 [7']
2.2.2.0. 2.1.0.0. strings
NOVELLO perf mat rent   (D369)

DOENDE FJARILEN, DEN, FOR ENGLISH HORN,
SAXOPHONE AND ORCHESTRA see
Wittenberg, Alexander

DOERNBERG, MARTIN (1920-   )
Adagio for String Orchestra [13']
string orch
KAHNT KT 9187 f.s.   (D370)

DÖHL, FRIEDHELM (1936-   )
Passion [20']
2(2pic).1.2.2(contrabsn).
2.3.2.0. perc,strings
study sc BREITKOPF-W PB 5153 f.s.
perf mat rent   (D371)

Tombeau
4.4.4.4. 4.4.4.1. perc,harp,pno,
strings
sc MOECK $31.00   (D372)

DOHNÁNYI, ERNST VON (1877-1960)
Concerto for Violin and Orchestra,
Op. 27
KALMUS A5656 sc $35.00, set $45.00,
perf mat rent   (D373)

Konzertstück for Violoncello and
Orchestra, Op. 12, in D
KALMUS A5802 sc $20.00, set $30.00,
perf mat rent   (D374)

Schleier Der Pierrette, Der, Op. 18:
Hochzeitswalzer
"Veil Of Pierrette, The, Op. 18:
Wedding March" KALMUS A6079 sc
$10.00, set $20.00, perf mat rent
(D375)
Schleier Der Pierrette, Der, Op. 18:
Lustiger Trauermarsch
"Veil Of Pierrette, The, Op. 18:
Jolly Funeral March" KALMUS A6078
sc $3.00, set $13.00   (D376)
Schleier Der Pierrette, Der, Op. 18:
Menuett
"Veil Of Pierrette, The, Op. 18:
Menuett" KALMUS A6080 sc $3.00,
set $10.00   (D377)
Schleier Der Pierrette, Der, Op. 18:
Pierrettens Wahnsinnstanz
"Veil Of Pierrette, The, Op. 18:
Pierrette's Dance Of Madness"
KALMUS A6081 sc $10.00, set
$25.00, perf mat rent   (D378)
Schleier Der Pierrette, Der, Op. 18:
Pierrots Liebesklage
"Veil Of Pierrette, The, Op. 18:
Pierrot's Complaint Of Love"
KALMUS A6076 sc $4.00, set $12.00
(D379)
Schleier Der Pierrette, Der, Op. 18:
Walzer-Reigen
"Veil Of Pierrette, The, Op. 18:
Waltz" KALMUS A6077 sc $3.00, set
$10.00   (D380)

Serenade, Op. 10, [arr.]
(Drew, Lucas) string orch [18']
KALMUS A4145 sc $20.00, set
$20.00, perf mat rent   (D381)

DOHNÁNYI, ERNST VON (cont'd.)

Suite, Op. 19
KALMUS A6090 sc $50.00, set
$100.00, perf mat rent   (D382)

Symphony, Op. 9, in D minor
KALMUS A4345 sc $60.00, set
$110.00, perf mat rent   (D383)

Veil Of Pierrette, The, Op. 18: Jolly
Funeral March
see Schleier Der Pierrette, Der,
Op. 18: Lustiger Trauermarsch

Veil Of Pierrette, The, Op. 18:
Menuett
see Schleier Der Pierrette, Der,
Op. 18: Menuett

Veil Of Pierrette, The, Op. 18:
Pierrette's Dance Of Madness
see Schleier Der Pierrette, Der,
Op. 18: Pierrettens Wahnsinnstanz

Veil Of Pierrette, The, Op. 18:
Pierrot's Complaint Of Love
see Schleier Der Pierrette, Der,
Op. 18: Pierrots Liebesklage

Veil Of Pierrette, The, Op. 18: Waltz
see Schleier Der Pierrette, Der,
Op. 18: Walzer-Reigen

Veil Of Pierrette, The, Op. 18:
Wedding March
see Schleier Der Pierrette, Der,
Op. 18: Hochzeitswalzer

DOLATSHAHI, DARIUSH
From Behind The Glass [12']
pno,strings
sc APNM $11.50, perf mat rent
    (D384)

May 1973 [5']
string orch
sc APNM $7.25, perf mat rent (D385)

Mirages [14']
1.1.1.1. 2.2.2.1. 2perc,strings,
electronic tape
sc APNM $23.50, perf mat rent
    (D386)

Prelude And Rondo [10']
string orch
sc APNM $10.00, perf mat rent
    (D387)

DOLIN, SAMUEL (1917-)
Concerto for Accordion and Orchestra
[21']
1.1.1.1. 2.1.1.0. opt perc,
strings,acord solo
CAN.MUS.CENT. MI 1366 D664CO (D388)

Concerto for Oboe, Violoncello and
Orchestra
2(pic).2.2.2. 4.2.2.0. timp,perc,
strings,ob solo,vcl solo
CAN.MUS.CENT. MI 1450 D 664CO
    (D389)

DOLLARHIDE, THEODORE (1948-)
Fantasy Of Ivory Thoughts And Shallow
Whispers, A [10']
2.2.2.2. 2.0.0.1. strings
sc AM.COMP.AL. $7.70   (D390)

Movements [15']
3.2.3.2. 4.3.3.1. perc,pno,
strings
AM.COMP.AL. perf mat rent   (D391)

Other Dreams, Other Dreamers [10']
3(pic,alto fl).2+English
horn.3(bass clar).3. 4.3.3.1.
4perc,pno,cel,2harp,strings
NORRUTH perf mat rent   (D392)

Pluriels [9']
4(pic).3(English
horn).4.3(contrabsn). 6.4.4.2.
perc,pno,2harp,strings
sc NORRUTH perf mat rent   (D393)

DOLORES see Tomasi, Henri

DOLOROUS SYMPHONY see Karkoff, Maurice

DOM SEBASTIEN: INTRODUCTION, ACT I see
Donizetti, Gaetano

DOMAZLICKY, FRANTISEK (1913-)
Concerto for Horn and Orchestra [17']
2.2.2.2. 0.0.0.0. timp,strings,
horn solo
SUPRAPHON   (D394)

DOMINELLO, LARRY
Tear, The, For Saxophone And
Orchestra [15'45"]
3+pic+alto fl.2+English
horn.3.2. 4.4.4.1. perc,gtr,
elec gtr,elec bass,harp,pno,
strings,tenor sax solo
"Traene, Die, For Saxophone And
Orchestra" NEWAM 19013 perf mat
rent   (D395)

DOMINELLO, LARRY (cont'd.)

Traene, Die, For Saxophone And
Orchestra
see Tear, The, For Saxophone And
Orchestra

DOMINIQUE, CARL-AXEL (1939-)
Global Suite
wind quin,strings
STIM   (D396)

**DON CARLOS: A MEZZA NOTTE, AI GIARDIN
DELLA REGINA, FOR SOLO VOICES AND
ORCHESTRA** see Verdi, Giuseppe

**DON CARLOS: GIUSTIZIA, GIUSTIZIA, SIRE!
FOR SOLO VOICES AND ORCHESTRA** see
Verdi, Giuseppe

**DON CARLOS: IL GRAND' INQUISITOR! FOR
SOLO VOICES AND ORCHESTRA** see
Verdi, Giuseppe

**DON CARLOS: IO VENGO A DOMANDAR GRAZIA
ALLA MIA REGINA, FOR SOLO VOICES
AND ORCHESTRA** see Verdi, Giuseppe

**DON CARLOS: LA REGINA! UNA CANZONE QUI
LIETA, FOR SOLO VOICES AND
ORCHESTRA** see Verdi, Giuseppe

**DON CARLOS: NON PIANGER, MIA COMPAGNA,
FOR SOLO VOICE AND ORCHESTRA** see
Verdi, Giuseppe

**DON CARLOS: O MIO RODRIGO, FOR SOLO
VOICES AND ORCHESTRA** see Verdi,
Giuseppe

**DON CARLOS: PRESSO ALL MIA PERSONA, FOR
SOLO VOICES AND ORCHESTRA** see
Verdi, Giuseppe

**DON CARLOS: TU CHE LE VANITA, FOR SOLO
VOICE AND ORCHESTRA** see Verdi,
Giuseppe

**DON CARLOS: UN DETTO, UN SOL, FOR SOLO
VOICES AND ORCHESTRA** see Verdi,
Giuseppe

DON-ELEGIE [ARR.] see Levitin, Yuri

**DON GIOVANNI: AUF DENN ZUM FESTE, FOR
SOLO VOICE AND ORCHESTRA** see
Mozart, Wolfgang Amadeus, Don
Giovanni: Finch' Han Dal Vino, For
Solo Voice And Orchestra

**DON GIOVANNI: AUF ZU DEM FESTE, FOR
SOLO VOICE AND ORCHESTRA** see
Mozart, Wolfgang Amadeus, Don
Giovanni: Finch' Han Dal Vino, For
Solo Voice And Orchestra

**DON GIOVANNI: BATTI, BATTI, O BEL
MASETTO, FOR SOLO VOICE AND
ORCHESTRA** see Mozart, Wolfgang
Amadeus

**DON GIOVANNI: DALLA SUA PACE, FOR SOLO
VOICE AND ORCHESTRA** see Mozart,
Wolfgang Amadeus

**DON GIOVANNI: DEH VIENI ALLA FINESTRA,
FOR SOLO VOICE AND ORCHESTRA** see
Mozart, Wolfgang Amadeus

**DON GIOVANNI: DON OTTAVIO, ENTSETZLICH;
DU KENNST NUN DEN FREVIER, FOR SOLO
VOICE AND ORCHESTRA** see Mozart,
Wolfgang Amadeus, Don Giovanni: Don
Ottavio, Son Morta; Or Sai Chi
L'onore, For Solo Voice And
Orchestra

**DON GIOVANNI: DON OTTAVIO, SON MORTA;
OR SAI CHI L'ONORE, FOR SOLO VOICE
AND ORCHESTRA** see Mozart, Wolfgang
Amadeus

**DON GIOVANNI: FEINSLIEBCHEN, KOMM ANS
FENSTER, FOR SOLO VOICE AND
ORCHESTRA** see Mozart, Wolfgang
Amadeus, Don Giovanni: Deh Vieni
Alla Finestra, For Solo Voice And
Orchestra

**DON GIOVANNI: FINCH' HAN DAL VINO, FOR
SOLO VOICE AND ORCHESTRA** see
Mozart, Wolfgang Amadeus

**DON GIOVANNI: IN QUALI ECCESSI; MI
TRADI QUELL'ALMA INGRATA, FOR SOLO
VOICE AND ORCHESTRA** see Mozart,
Wolfgang Amadeus

**DON GIOVANNI: IN WELCHE FREVEL; MICH
VERRIET DER UNDANKBARE, FOR SOLO
VOICE AND ORCHESTRA** see Mozart,
Wolfgang Amadeus, Don Giovanni: In
Quali Eccessi; Mi Tradi Quell'alma
Ingrata, For Solo Voice And
Orchestra

**DON GIOVANNI: LA CI DAREM LA MANO, FOR
SOLO VOICES AND ORCHESTRA** see
Mozart, Wolfgang Amadeus

**DON GIOVANNI: MADAMINA! IL CATALOGO,
FOR SOLO VOICE AND ORCHESTRA** see
Mozart, Wolfgang Amadeus

**DON GIOVANNI: NUR IHREM FRIEDEN, FOR
SOLO VOICE AND ORCHESTRA** see
Mozart, Wolfgang Amadeus, Don
Giovanni: Dalla Sua Pace, For Solo
Voice And Orchestra

DON GIOVANNI: OVERTURE see Mozart,
Wolfgang Amadeus

**DON GIOVANNI: REICH MIR DIE HAND, MEIN
LEBEN, FOR SOLO VOICES AND
ORCHESTRA** see Mozart, Wolfgang
Amadeus, Don Giovanni: La Ci Darem
La Mano, For Solo Voices And
Orchestra

**DON GIOVANNI: SCHMÄLE, TOBE, LIEBER
JUNGE, FOR SOLO VOICE AND ORCHESTRA**
see Mozart, Wolfgang Amadeus, Don
Giovanni: Batti, Batti, O Bel
Masetto, For Solo Voice And
Orchestra

**DON GIOVANNI: SCHÖNE DONNA! DIESES
KLEINE REGISTER, FOR SOLO VOICE AND
ORCHESTRA** see Mozart, Wolfgang
Amadeus, Don Giovanni: Madamina! Il
Catalogo, For Solo Voice And
Orchestra

**DON GIOVANNI: VEDRAI CARINO, FOR SOLO
VOICE AND ORCHESTRA** see Mozart,
Wolfgang Amadeus

**DON GIOVANNI: WENN DU FEIN FROMM BIST,
FOR SOLO VOICE AND ORCHESTRA** see
Mozart, Wolfgang Amadeus, Don
Giovanni: Vedrai Carino, For Solo
Voice And Orchestra

DON JUAN: BALLET MUSIC, [ARR.] see
Gluck, Christoph Willibald, Ritter
von

**DON PASQUALE, E RIMASTO LA IMPIETRATO,
FOR SOLO VOICES AND ORCHESTRA** see
Donizetti, Gaetano

**DON PASQUALE: PRENDER MOGLIE, FOR SOLO
VOICES AND ORCHESTRA** see Donizetti,
Gaetano

DON PERLIMPLIN: PROLOGUE see Rieti,
Vittorio

DON QUIXOTE see Gerhard, Roberto see
Karayev, Kara see Rubinstein, Anton

**DON QUIXOTE AND THE SHEEP, FOR SOLO
VOICES AND ORCHESTRA** see Lessard,
John Ayres

DON QUIXOTE: DANCES see Gerhard,
Roberto

DON QUIXOTE: PAS DE DEUX [ARR.] see
Minkus, Léon (Fyodorovich) [Alois;
Louis]

DON QUIXOTE: SYMPHONIC SUITE see
Gerhard, Roberto

DONATONI, FRANCO (1927-)
Abyss, For Solo Voice, Bass Flute And
Instrumental Ensemble [18']
English horn,bass clar,contrabsn,
horn,trom,perc,pno,vla,vcl,db,
female solo,bass fl solo
RICORDI-IT 133642 perf mat rent
    (D397)

Arie, For Solo Voice And Orchestra
[23']
4.4.4.4. 5.3.2.1. 3perc,glock,
cel,vibra,pno,2harp,strings,
solo voice
sc RICORDI-IT 132822 f.s., perf mat
rent   (D398)

Diario '83 [18']
4.0.4.0. 4.4.4.1. 2perc,strings
RICORDI-IT 133704 perf mat rent
    (D399)

Eco [10']
2fl,2ob,2horn,6vln,2vla,2vcl
RICORDI-IT 134127 perf mat rent
    (D400)

Ruisseau Sur l'Escalier, Le, For
Violoncello And Instrumental
Ensemble [13']
4.0.4.1. 0.0.0.1. 2perc,
xylorimba,vibra,pno&cel,3vln,
db,vcl solo
sc RICORDI-IT 031-35861 $20.75,
perf mat rent   (D401)

Sinfonia, Op. 63 [4']
clar,bass clar,2horn,strings
(Anton Webern) sc RICORDI-IT 133565

DONATONI, FRANCO (cont'd.)

    f.s., perf mat rent   (D402)

Tema [15']
  1.1.1.1. 2.0.0.0. 3vln,2vla,vcl
  RICORDI-IT 133236 perf mat rent
    (D403)

DONDEYNE, DESIRE (1921-)
Suite, Tableaux, For Wind Quintet And
  String Orchestra [22']
  string orch,fl solo,ob solo,clar
    solo,bsn solo,horn solo,
    alternate scoring: sop-sax
    solo, 2 al-sax soli, ten-sax
    solo, bar-sax solo
  BILLAUDOT perf mat rent   (D404)

DONIZETTI, GAETANO (1797-1848)
Amusement Pathetique, For Violin And
  Orchestra (from Anna Bolena)
  [12']
  2+pic.2.2.2. 4.2.3.1. timp,perc,
    strings,vln solo
  sc BSE 138 f.s., perf mat rent
    (D405)
Anna Bolena: Ah! Parea Che Per
  Incanto, For Solo Voice And
  Orchestra
  KALMUS A4791 sc $9.00, set $20.00,
    pts $1.00, ea., perf mat rent
    (D406)
Anna Bolena: Al Dolce Guidami Castel
  Natio, For Solo Voice And
  Orchestra
  KALMUS A4800 sc $18.00, set $40.00,
    pts $2.00, ea., perf mat rent
    (D407)
Anna Bolena: Come Innocente Giovane,
  For Solo Voice And Orchestra
  KALMUS A4787 sc $9.00, set $25.00,
    pts $2.00, ea., perf mat rent
    (D408)
Anna Bolena: Da Quel Di Che Lei
  Perduta, For Solo Voice And
  Orchestra
  KALMUS A4789 sc $15.00, set $30.00,
    pts $2.00, ea., perf mat rent
    (D409)
Anna Bolena: Deh! Non Voler
  Costringere, For Solo Voice And
  Orchestra
  KALMUS A4786 sc $5.00, set $19.00,
    pts $1.00, ea., perf mat rent
    (D410)
Anna Bolena: Fama! Si L'avrete, For
  Solo Voices And Orchestra
  KALMUS A4788 sc $20.00, set $35.00,
    pts $2.50, ea., perf mat rent
    (D411)
Anna Bolena: Per Questa Fiamma
  Indomita, For Solo Voice And
  Orchestra
  KALMUS A4797 sc $15.00, set $30.00,
    pts $2.00, ea., perf mat rent
    (D412)
Anna Bolena: S'ei T'abboree, Io T'
  Amo Ancora, For Solo Voices And
  Orchestra
  KALMUS A4792 sc $30.00, set $35.00,
    pts $2.50, ea., perf mat rent
    (D413)
Anna Bolena: Sul Suo Capo Aggravi Un
  Dio, For Solo Voices And
  Orchestra
  KALMUS A4795 sc $15.00, set $30.00,
    pts $2.00, ea., perf mat rent
    (D414)
Anna Bolena: Vivi Tu, Te Ne
  Scongiuro, For Solo Voice And
  Orchestra
  KALMUS A4798 sc $10.00, set $30.00,
    pts $2.00, ea., perf mat rent
    (D415)
Campanello, Il: Bella Cosa, Amici
  Cari, For Solo Voice And
  Orchestra
  KALMUS A4821 sc $10.00, set $20.00,
    pts $1.00, ea., perf mat rent
    (D416)
Campanello, Il: Da Me Lungi Ancor
  Vivendo, For Solo Voices And
  Orchestra
  KALMUS A4827 sc $10.00, set $12.00,
    pts $.75, ea., perf mat rent
    (D417)
Campanello, Il: Ho Una Bella, Un'
  Infidele, For Solo Voices And
  Orchestra
  KALMUS A4825 sc $20.00, set $20.00,
    pts $1.00, ea., perf mat rent
    (D418)
Campanello, Il: Mesci, Mesci E Sperda
  Il Vento, For Solo Voice And
  Orchestra
  KALMUS A4824 sc $9.00, set $15.00,
    pts $.75, ea., perf mat rent
    (D419)
Campanello, Il: Mio Signore Venerato,
  For Solo Voices And Orchestra
  KALMUS A4826 sc $12.00, set $20.00,
    pts $1.00, ea., perf mat rent
    (D420)
Campanello, Il: Non Fuggir, T'
  Arresta, Ingrata, For Solo Voices
  And Orchestra

DONIZETTI, GAETANO (cont'd.)

  KALMUS A4823 sc $15.00, set $35.00,
    pts $2.00, ea., perf mat rent
    (D421)
Concertino for Chamber Orchestra,
  [arr.]
  (Westermann, Clayton) 2fl,2horn,
    strings [10'] SCHIRM.G perf mat
    rent   (D422)
Concerto for Horn and String
  Orchestra in F
  (Leloir, E.) string orch,horn solo
    [9'30"] sc BILLAUDOT f.s., perf
    mat rent   (D423)
Diluvio Universale, Il: Overture
  (Gilardoni, D.) 3.2.2.2. 4.2.3.0.
    timp,perc,strings [9'] SONZOGNO
    perf mat rent   (D424)
Dom Sebastien: Introduction, Act I
  [3']
  2.2.2.2. 4.4.3.1. timp,perc,
    strings
  KALMUS A5889 sc $4.00, set $15.00,
    perf mat rent   (D425)
Don Pasquale, E Rimasto La
  Impietrato, For Solo Voices And
  Orchestra
  KALMUS A 3462 sc $4.00, set $10.00,
    pts $.75, ea.   (D426)
Don Pasquale: Prender Moglie, For
  Solo Voices And Orchestra
  KALMUS A3459 sc $12.00, set $28.00,
    pts $2.00, ea., perf mat rent
    (D427)
Favorita, La: A Tanto Amor, For Solo
  Voices And Orchestra
  KALMUS A4813 sc $9.00, set $25.00,
    pts $1.00, ea., perf mat rent
    (D428)
Favorita, La: Ah! Mio Bene, Un Dio T'
  Invia, For Solo Voices And
  Orchestra
  KALMUS A4807 sc $15.00, set $30.00,
    pts $2.00, ea., perf mat rent
    (D429)
Favorita, La: Ah! Paventa Il Furor,
  For Solo Voices And Orchestra
  KALMUS A4812 sc $25.00, set $35.00,
    pts $2.00, ea., perf mat rent
    (D430)
Favorita, La: Ballet Music [12']
  2+pic.2.2.2. 4.2.3.1. timp,perc,
    strings
  KALMUS A4811 sc $45.00, set $70.00,
    perf mat rent   (D431)
Favorita, La: E Fia Vero, For Solo
  Voices And Orchestra
  KALMUS A 4804 sc $9.00, set $15.00,
    pts $.75, ea., perf mat rent
    (D432)
Favorita, La: Pietoso Al Par Del
  Nume, For Solo Voices And
  Orchestra
  KALMUS A4819 sc $20.00, set $35.00,
    pts $2.00, ea., perf mat rent
    (D433)
Favorita, La: Quando Le Soglie
  Paterne, For Solo Voices And
  Orchestra
  KALMUS A4810 sc $6.00, set $15.00,
    pts $.75, ea., perf mat rent
    (D434)
Favorita, La: Si, Che Un Tuo Solo
  Accento, For Solo Voices And
  Orchestra
  KALMUS A4808 sc $7.00, set $15.00,
    pts $.75, ea., perf mat rent
    (D435)
Favorita, La: Una Vergine, Un Angel
  Di Dio, For Solo Voice And
  Orchestra
  KALMUS A 4803 sc $3.00, set $15.00,
    pts $.75, ea.   (D436)
Favorita, La: Vien Leonora, A Piedi
  Tuoi, For Solo Voice And
  Orchestra
  KALMUS A4809 sc $12.00, set $25.00,
    pts $1.00, ea., perf mat rent
    (D437)
Gianni Di Parigi: Overture [10']
  2.2.2.2. 2.2.3.0. timp,strings
  BSE 107 perf mat rent   (D438)
Libera Me, For Solo Voice And
  Orchestra
  sc KUNZEL 10150 $12.00, perf mat
    rent   (D439)
Linda Chamounix: Al Ben Destin Che
  Attendevi, For Solo Voices And
  Orchestra
  KALMUS A 4835 sc $8.00, set $15.00,
    pts $.75, ea., perf mat rent
    (D440)
Linda Di Chamounix: Ah!
  Dimmi...Dimmi, Io T' Amo, For
  Solo Voices And Orchestra
  KALMUS A4838 sc $12.00, set $18.00,

DONIZETTI, GAETANO (cont'd.)

  pts $1.00, ea., perf mat rent
    (D441)
Linda Di Chamounix: Buona Gente, For
  Solo Voice And Orchestra
  KALMUS A4830 sc $20.00, set $30.00,
    pts $2.00, ea., perf mat rent
    (D442)
Linda Di Chamounix: Cari Luoghi Ov'
  Io Passai, For Solo Voice And
  Orchestra
  KALMUS A 4831 sc $5.00, set $20.00,
    pts $1.00, ea., perf mat rent
    (D443)
Linda Di Chamounix: Ciel, Che Dite?
  Linda E Morta, For Solo Voices
  And Orchestra
  KALMUS A 4841 sc $12.00, set
    $18.00, pts $1.00, ea., perf mat
    rent   (D444)
Linda Di Chamounix: Da Quel Di Che T'
  Incontrai, For Solo Voices And
  Orchestra
  KALMUS A4832 sc $15.00, set $20.00,
    pts $1.00, ea., perf mat rent
    (D445)
Linda Di Chamounix: Di Tue Pene
  Sparve Il Sogno, For Solo Voices
  And Orchestra
  KALMUS A4845 sc $8.00, set $15.00,
    pts $.75, ea., perf mat rent
    (D446)
Linda Di Chamounix: E La Voce Che
  Primiera, For Solo Voice And
  Orchestra
  KALMUS A4843 sc $15.00, set $30.00,
    pts $2.00, ea., perf mat rent
    (D447)
Linda Di Chamounix: Ella E Un Giglio
  Di Puro Candore, For Solo Voice
  And Orchestra
  KALMUS A4842 sc $15.00, set $25.00,
    pts $1.00, ea., perf mat rent
    (D448)
Linda Di Chamounix: Io Vi Dico Che
  Partiate, For Solo Voices And
  Orchestra
  KALMUS A4836 sc $18.00, set $25.00,
    pts $2.00, ea., perf mat rent
    (D449)
Linda Di Chamounix: Overture
  BSE 26 perf mat rent   (D450)
Linda Di Chamounix: Quella Pieta Si
  Provvida, For Solo Voices And
  Orchestra
  KALMUS A4833 sc $15.00, set $23.00,
    pts $1.00, ea., perf mat rent
    (D451)
Linda Di Chamounix: Se Tanto In Ira
  Agli Uomini, For Solo Voice And
  Orchestra
  KALMUS A4837 sc $5.00, set $15.00,
    pts $.75, ea., perf mat rent
    (D452)
Maria Di Rohan: Overture [10']
  2+pic.2.2.2. 2.2.3.1. timp,perc,
    strings
  sc BSE 24 f.s., perf mat rent
    (D453)
Marino Faliero: Overture [10']
  2+pic.2.2.2. 4.2.3.1. timp,perc,
    strings
  sc BSE 25 f.s., perf mat rent
    (D454)
Martyrs, Les: Overture
  BSE 27 perf mat rent   (D455)
Ne Procias Me, For Solo Voice, Horn
  And Orchestra
  sc KUNZEL 10152 $12.00, perf mat
    rent   (D456)
Otto Mesi In Due Ore: Overture [10']
  2+pic.2.2.2. 2.2.3.1. timp,perc,
    strings
  BSE 108 perf mat rent   (D457)
Preludio Funebre [12']
  2+pic.2.2.2. 4.0.3.0. timp,
    strings
  sc BSE 126 perf mat rent   (D458)
Sinfonia *see Martini, [Padre]
  Giovanni Battista, Sinfonie, Four
  see Martini, [Padre] Giovanni
  Battista, Sinfonie, Four
Sinfonia Sopra I Migliori Motivi Di
  Bellini [12']
  2.2.2.2. 4.2.3.0. timp,perc,
    strings
  BSE 40 perf mat rent   (D459)
Tibi Soli Peccari, For Solo Voice,
  Basset Horn And String Orchestra
  basset horn,strings,S solo
  sc KUNZEL 10153 $12.00, perf mat
    rent   (D460)

DONNE, DONNE, CHI VI CREDE see Reicha,
Anton

DONORA, LUIGI (1935-   )
Et Verbum Caro Factum Est [13']
2.2.2.2. 2.2.2.0. timp,strings
SONZOGNO perf mat rent   (D461)

DONOVAN, RICHARD [FRANK] (1891-1970)
Ricercare for Oboe and String
Orchestra [6']
string orch,ob solo
BOOSEY perf mat rent   (D462)

DONUM SACRUM BRANCUSI, FOR SOLO VOICE
AND ORCHESTRA see Miereanu, Costin

DOODENMARSCH, FOR NARRATOR AND
ORCHESTRA see Bosmans, Henriëtte

DOOLITTLE, QUENTIN (1925-   )
Vivaldiana
3.2.2.2. 4.3.3.1. timp,2perc,
harp,strings
(Il Combattimento Dell' Invenzione
E Tonalita) CAN.MUS.CENT.
MI 1100 D691V   (D463)

DOPPEL KONZERT, FOR SAXOPHONE,
PERCUSSION AND CHAMBER ORCHESTRA
see Miereanu, Costin

DOPPELBAUER, JOSEF FRIEDRICH
(1918-1989)
Symphony No. 1 in G [30']
2(pic).2.2.2. 4.2.2.1. timp,
strings
DOBLINGER perf mat rent   (D464)

DOPPLER, FRANZ (1821-1883)
Concerto for 2 Flutes and Orchestra
[20']
2.2.2.2. 4.2.3.0. timp,harp,
strings,2fl soli
(Adorjan, A.) sc BILLAUDOT f.s.,
perf mat rent   (D465)

Fantaisie Pastorale Hongroise, For
Flute And Orchestra, [Arr.]
*Op.26 [10']
(Galway) "Hungarian Fantasy, For
Flute And Orchestra, [arr.]"
1.1.1.1. 2.1.1.0. timp,strings,fl
solo NOVELLO perf mat rent   (D466)
(Klautzsch) 1.1.2.1. 2.2.3.1. timp,
strings,fl solo [12'] KALMUS
A6234 pno-cond sc $5.00, set
$20.00   (D467)

Fantaisie Sur Des Motifs Hongrois,
For 2 Flutes And Orchestra [arr.]
*Op.35 (composed with Doppler,
Karl)
(Adorjan, A.) 1.2.2.2. 4.2.3.0.
timp,perc,strings,2fl soli [10']
sc BILLAUDOT f.s., perf mat rent   (D468)

Hungarian Fantasy, For Flute And
Orchestra, [arr.]
see Fantaisie Pastorale Hongroise,
For Flute And Orchestra, [Arr.]

DOPPMANN, WILLIAM (1933-   )
Counterpoints, For Piano And Chamber
Orchestra [17']
2perc,strings,pno solo
sc GUNMAR MP2090 $40.00, perf mat
rent   (D469)

DORATI, ANTAL (1906-1988)
American Serenade [15']
string orch
BOOSEY perf mat rent   (D470)

Chamber Music, For Solo Voice And
Chamber Orchestra [25']
1.2.1.2. 2.0.0.0. pno,9vln,3vla,
3vcl,db,S solo
CHESTER JWC 553 perf mat rent   (D471)

Concerto for Violoncello and
Orchestra [25']
3(pic).2.2.2(contrabsn). 4.2.3.0.
timp,perc,harp,strings,vcl solo
BOOSEY perf mat rent   (D472)

Divertimento for Oboe and Orchestra
[25']
3(pic).0.3(bass clar).0. 0.3.0.0.
timp,perc,harp,cel,strings,ob
solo
BOOSEY perf mat rent   (D473)

Querela Pacis [28']
4(pic,alto fl).3+English
horn.4(clar in E flat,bass
clar).3(contrabsn). 4.3.3.1.
timp,5perc,harp,pno,strings
BOOSEY perf mat rent   (D474)

Stimmen, Die, For Solo Voice And
Orchestra [40']
2(pic).2.2+bass clar.2+contrabsn.
4.2.3.1. timp,perc,harp,cel,
pno,strings,B solo
"Voices, The, For Solo Voice And
Orchestra" BOOSEY perf mat rent   (D475)

DORATI, ANTAL (cont'd.)

Voices, The, For Solo Voice And
Orchestra
see Stimmen, Die, For Solo Voice
And Orchestra

DORFF, DANIEL JAY (1956-   )
Billy And The Carnival, For Narrator
And Orchestra [12']
PRESSER perf mat rent   (D476)

Lamentations [5']
string orch
PRESSER perf mat rent   (D477)

Rock Rhapsody [10']
4(pic).4(English horn).4(bass
clar).4. 4.3.3.1. perc,harp,
pno,strings
PRESSER perf mat rent   (D478)

DORIAN GRAY: SUITE see Fürst, Paul
Walter

DORISCHE MUSIK see Edler, Robert

DORISCHES STUCK, FOR VIOLONCELLO AND
STRING ORCHESTRA see Müller-Zürich,
Paul

DORMOLEN, JAN WILLEM VAN (1956-   )
Fields And Roads
see Velden En Wegen

Velden En Wegen
8.2.2.0.4sax. 6.6.0.1. 2perc,elec
gtr,2harp,acord,pno,strings
"Fields And Roads" DONEMUS perf mat
rent   (D479)

DORNROSCHEN, FOR SOLO VOICES AND
CHAMBER GROUP see Lampersberg,
Gerhard

DOROTHY AND CARMINE, FOR FLUTE AND
STRING ORCHESTRA see Serebrier,
Jose

DORTMUNDER VARIATIONEN see Halffter,
Cristobal

DORUMSGAARD, ARNE (1921-   )
Four Songs, For Solo Voice And
Orchestra, Op. 17
2.2.2.2. 4.2.3.0. perc,harp,
strings,solo voice NORGE f.s.
contains: Gom Mig, Gom Mig;
Jorden Ar Manniskans Hem; Var
Inte Radd For Morkret; Var
Stilla Hjarta   (D480)

Gom Mig, Gom Mig
see Four Songs, For Solo Voice And
Orchestra, Op. 17

Jorden Ar Manniskans Hem
see Four Songs, For Solo Voice And
Orchestra, Op. 17

Var Inte Radd For Morkret
see Four Songs, For Solo Voice And
Orchestra, Op. 17

Var Stilla Hjarta
see Four Songs, For Solo Voice And
Orchestra, Op. 17

DOS AMBIENTES SONOROS see Halffter,
Rodolfo

DOS BERCEUSES see Rodrigo, Joaquín

DOS DANZAS ESPANOLAS see Rodrigo,
Joaquín

DOS MOVIMENTOS, FOR TIMPANI AND STRING
ORCHESTRA see Halffter, Cristobal

DOS SOLILOQUIOS PARA ORQUESTA see Homs,
Joaquín

DOUBLE see Baggiani, Guido

DOUBLE CONCERTO FOR PERCUSSION AND
ORCHESTRA see Antoniou, Theodore

DOUBLE CONCERTO FOR TWO SOLO
INSTRUMENTS AND ORCHESTRA see
Manduell, John

DOUBLE CONCERTO, OP. 49 see Holst,
Gustav

DOUBLE DEALER, THE see Purcell, Henry

DOUBLE ENTENDRE see Parmentier, F.
Gordon

DOUBLE PLAY, FOR VIOLIN, PIANO AND
CHAMBER ORCHESTRA see Kraft,
William

DOUBLES see Hoddinott, Alun

DOURY, PIERRE
Concerto for 3 Violoncelli and
Orchestra
CHOUDENS perf mat rent   (D481)

DOUW, ANDRE (1951-   )
Downtown, For Violin And Orchestra
[20']
3.3.3.2. 4.2.2.1. 3perc,strings,
vln solo
DONEMUS perf mat rent   (D482)

Symfonie - Het Leger [35']
0.0.0.0. 4.4.2.1. perc,strings
DONEMUS perf mat rent   (D483)

DOUZE EMOTIONS SONORES see Marischal,
Louis

DOUZE PRÉLUDES, VOL. 1, [ARR.] see
Debussy, Claude

DOVE LA LUCE see Balliana, Franco

DOVE PIU DOLCE SUONO MIGRA see Di Bari,
Marco

DOWN AMPNEY, "COME DOWN, O LOVE DIVINE"
[ARR.] see Vaughan Williams, Ralph

DOWN EAST see Schultheiss, Ulrich

DOWNES, ANDREW (1950-   )
Centenary Firedances *Op.43 [20']
LYNWD sc $20.90, pts $55.00 (D484)

Five Movements, For Piano And String
Orchestra *Op.10 [20']
string orch,pno solo
LYNWD sc $20.80, pts $52.00 (D485)

In The Cotswolds *Op.36 [6']
4.3.3.3. 4.3.3.0. 4perc,strings
LYNWD sc $5.40, pts $23.40 (D486)

Overture For St. Cere *Op.8 [12']
2.2.2.2. 3.3.0.0. timp,strings
LYNWD sc $13.40, pts $30.00 (D487)

Symphony No. 1, Op. 27 [35']
0.0.0.0. 4.8.3.1. perc,org,
strings
LYNWD sc $28.00, pts $172.00 (D488)

Symphony No. 2, Op. 30 [20']
2.2.2.0. 2.2.0.0. timp,strings
LYNWD sc $17.80, pts $34.40 (D489)

Symphony No. 3, Op. 45 [30']
3.2.3.2+contrabsn. 4.3.0.1. perc,
strings
LYNWD sc $28.00, pts $200.00 (D490)

Toccata, Op. 26 [4']
2ob,2horn,strings
LYNWD sc $5.80, pts $9.40 (D491)

DOWNEY, JOHN WILHAM (1927-   )
Discourse [18']
ob,hpsd,strings
PRESSER perf mat rent   (D492)

DOWNSTREAM see Hopkins, John

DOWNTOWN, FOR VIOLIN AND ORCHESTRA see
Douw, Andre

DRAESEKE, FELIX (1835-1913)
Concerto for Piano and Orchestra, Op.
36, in E flat
KISTNER perf mat rent   (D493)

Penthesilea *Op.50
KISTNER   (D494)

Serenade, Op. 49
KISTNER perf mat rent   (D495)

Symphonia Tragica *Op.40
KISTNER perf mat rent   (D496)

Symphony No. 1, Op. 12, in G [35']
2.2.2.2. 4.3.0.0. timp,strings
KAHNT perf mat rent   (D497)

Symphony No. 2, Op. 25
KISTNER   (D498)

DRAGNING, FOR CLARINET AND STRING
ORCHESTRA see Sivertsen, Kenneth

DRAGONETTI, DOMENICO (1763-1846)
Concerto for Double Bass and
Orchestra, No. 1, in A [18']
2ob,2horn,timp,strings,db solo
(Malaric, Rudolf) DOBLINGER perf
mat rent   (D499)

Concerto for Double Bass and
Orchestra, No. 3, in A, [arr.]
(Sechter, Simon; Malaric, Rudolf)
2ob,2horn,strings,db solo [15']
DOBLINGER perf mat rent   (D500)

DRAGOSTINOV, STEFAN
    Polytempi No. 4, For Piano And
        Orchestra [20'20"]
        2.2.2.2. 2.2.1.1. timp,perc,cel,
        harp,strings,pno solo
        RICORDI-IT 133224 perf mat rent
                                      (D501)

DRALA see Lieberson, Peter

DRAMAPHONIA, FOR PIANO AND ORCHESTRA
    see Ruders, Poul

DRAMATIC OVERTURE see Dvorák, Antonín,
    Tragic Overture see Goedicke,
    Alexander

DRAMATIC PICTURE see Slimácek, Jan

DRAMATIC SONG see Slonimsky, Sergey

DRAMATISCHES LIED see Slonimsky,
    Sergey, Dramatic Song

DRAMMA PER MUSICA see Brandmüller, Theo

DRAMMATICO, FOR VIOLONCELLO AND
    ORCHESTRA see Kelemen, Milko

DRAZGOSE see Gobec, Radovan

DREAM, THE see Cleve, Cissi, Drommen

DREAM ABOUT "THE HOUSE", A, FOR HARP
    AND STRING ORCHESTRA see
    Thorarinsson, Leifur

DREAM ABOUT THE PAST see Martinu,
    Bohuslav (Jan), Sen O Minulosti

DREAM JOURNEYS see Di Domenica, Robert

DREAM OF MY PARENTS DANCING, A see
    Adolphe, Bruce

DREAM OF THE INFINITE ROOMS, THE, FOR
    VIOLONCELLO AND ORCHESTRA see
    Reynolds, Roger

DREAM OF THE MORNING SKY, FOR SOLO
    VOICE AND ORCHESTRA see Kernis,
    Aaron Jay

DREAM OVERTURE see Schwartz, Elliott
    Schelling

DREAM RAINBOW DREAM THUNDER see
    Schafer, R. Murray

DREAM SEQUENCES see Hellan, Arne

DREAM-WINDOW see Takemitsu, Toru

DREAM WORLD, FOR SOLO VOICE AND
    ORCHESTRA [ARR] see Wolf, Daniel

DREAMBOAT, FOR VIOLIN AND CHAMBER
    ORCHESTRA see Sveinsson, Atli
    Heimir

DREAMPLAY, FOR SOLO VOICE AND ORCHESTRA
    see Höller, York, Traumspiel, For
    Solo Voice And Orchestra

DREAMS see Danning, Chr., Dromme see
    Kulesha, Gary see Prokofiev, Serge,
    Reves see Watkins, Michael Blake

DREAMS, VERSION FOR SMALL ORCHESTRA see
    Kulesha, Gary

DREAMTIME see Erb, Donald see
    Takemitsu, Toru

DREAMWALTZES see Stucky, Steven Edward

DREI FESTLICHE MARSCHE see Gluck,
    Christoph Willibald, Ritter von

DREI FINNISCHE SUITEN see Erdlen,
    Hermann

DREI FREISINGER SINFONIEN see
    Camerloher, Placidus von

DREI GESÄNGE, FOR SOLO VOICE AND
    ORCHESTRA see Trexler, Georg

DREI GESÄNGE DAVIDS, FOR VIOLIN AND
    STRING ORCHESTRA see Sturzenegger,
    Richard

DREI GREICHISCHE TANZE see Müller, Karl
    Franz

DREI HYMNEN AN DIE NACHT, FOR SOLO
    VOICE AND ORCHESTRA see Hausegger,
    Siegmund von

DREI KLEINE STUCKE FUR ORCHESTER see
    Huber, Klaus

DREI KONZERTARIEN, FOR SOLO VOICE AND
    ORCHESTRA see Khachaturian, Aram
    Ilyich, Three Concert Arias, For
    Solo Voice And Orchestra

DREI LIEDER NACH GEDICHTEN VON EDGAR
    ALLAN POE, FOR SOLO VOICE AND
    ORCHESTRA see Reimann, Aribert

DREI MANNHEIMER SINFONIEN see Stamitz,
    Johann Wenzel Anton

DREI MINIATUREN see Schedl, Gerhard

DREI PINTOS, DIE: ENTR'ACTE see Weber,
    Carl Maria von

DREI ROMANZEN NACH GEDICHTEN VON A.
    PUSCHKIN, FOR SOLO VOICE AND
    CHAMBER ORCHESTRA see Shostakovich,
    Dmitri, Three Songs On Poems Of
    Pushkin, For Solo Voice And Chamber
    Orchestra

DREI SATZE FUR STREICHORCHESTER see
    Fheodoroff, Nikolaus

DREI SINFONIEN see Richter, Franz Xaver

DREI STUDIEN FOR 12 VIOLONCELLOS see
    Leitermeyer, Fritz

DREI STUDIEN, FOR ORCHESTRA see
    Leitermeyer, Fritz

DREI SZENEN see Nilsson, Bo

DREI VOLKSTANZE see Höffner, Paul Marx

DREI WALZER see Rihm, Wolfgang

DREI ZIGEUNER, DIE, FOR SOLO VOICE AND
    ORCHESTRA see Liszt, Franz

DREI ZIGEUNER, DIE, "DREI ZIGEUNER FAND
    ICH EINMAL", FOR SOLO VOICE AND
    ORCHESTRA see Schoeck, Othmar

DREIETONER FOR ORKESTER see Persen,
    John

DREIKLANGSKONZERT, FOR VIOLIN,
    VIOLONCELLO AND CHAMBER ORCHESTRA
    see Pärt, Arvo

DREW, JAMES M. (1929-   )
    Courtyard Music [15']
        PRESSER perf mat rent   (D502)

DRIE TANZSKIZZEN, FOR PIANO AND
    ORCHESTRA see Gilse, Jan van

DRIFTWOOD TO THE FLOW see Muldowney,
    Dominic

DRIGO, RICCARDO (1846-1930)
    Millions d'Arlequin, Les: Berceuse
        [3'15"]
        (Walter, Fried) ZIMMER.   (D503)

    Millions d'Arlequin, Les: Die Gute
        Fee
        (Walter, Fried) ZIMMER.   (D504)

    Millions d'Arlequin, Les: Dramatische
        Szene
        (Walter, Fried) ZIMMER.   (D505)

    Millions d'Arlequin, Les: Fliegentanz
        [2'25"]
        (Walter, Fried) ZIMMER.   (D506)

    Millions d'Arlequin, Les: Galopp
        [3'40"]
        (Marszalek, Franz) ZIMMER. (D507)

    Millions d'Arlequin, Les: Harlekin
        Und Die Lerchen [3'40"]
        (Walter, Fried) ZIMMER.   (D508)

    Millions d'Arlequin, Les:
        Lerchenballett [5'40"]
        (Walter, Fried) ZIMMER.   (D509)

    Millions d'Arlequin, Les:
        Maskengesellschaft [2'25"]
        (Walter, Fried) ZIMMER.   (D510)

    Millions d'Arlequin, Les: Pierrot Und
        Pierrette [2'25"]
        (Walter, Fried) ZIMMER.   (D511)

    Millions d'Arlequin, Les: Pizzicato
        [2'40"]
        (Marszalek, Franz) ZIMMER. (D512)

    Millions d'Arlequin, Les: Polonaise
        [3'30"]
        (Marszalek, Franz) ZIMMER. (D513)

    Millions d'Arlequin, Les: Serenade
        [3']
        (Marszalek, Franz) ZIMMER. (D514)

    Millions d'Arlequin, Les: Tanz Der
        Freunde [1'35"]
        (Walter, Fried) ZIMMER.   (D515)

    Millions d'Arlequin, Les: Unterredung
        [3'45"]
        (Walter, Fried) ZIMMER.   (D516)

DRIGO, RICCARDO (cont'd.)

    Millions d'Arlequin, Les: Valse Des
        Alouettes [3']
        (Marszalek, Franz) ZIMMER. (D517)

    Millions d'Arlequin, Les: Vorspiel
        [1'50"]
        (Walter, Fried) ZIMMER.   (D518)

    Reveil De Flore, Le: Apparition
        d'Aurore, Scène Et Valse
        2.2.2.2. 1.2.3.0. timp,vibra,
        harp,strings
        (Walter, Fried) ZIMMER.   (D519)

    Reveil De Flore, Le: Galopp
        1(pic).2.2.2. 4.2.3.0. timp,cym,
        triangle,strings
        (Walter, Fried) ZIMMER.   (D520)

    Reveil De Flore, Le: Marche
        Bacchanale
        1.1.1.1. 4.2.3.0. timp,xylo,
        triangle,cym,harp,strings
        (Walter, Fried) ZIMMER.   (D521)

    Reveil De Flore, Le: Nocturne
        2.2.2.2. 4.2.3.0. timp,harp,
        strings
        (Walter, Fried) ZIMMER.   (D522)

    Reveil De Flore, Le: Scène et Pas
        d'Ensemble
        2.2.2.2. 4.0.0.0. harp,strings,
        vcl solo
        (Walter, Fried) ZIMMER.   (D523)

    Reveil De Flore, Le: Variation De
        Flore
        1.1.2.2. 4.0.0.0. strings
        (Walter, Fried) ZIMMER.   (D524)

DRITTE ABGESANGSSZENE, FOR SOLO VOICE
    AND ORCHESTRA see Rihm, Wolfgang

DROMME see Danning, Chr.

DROMMEN see Cleve, Cissi

DROSTE-HÜLSHOFF, MAXIMILIAN F. VON
    (1764-1840)
    Concerto for 3 Flutes and Orchestra
        [17']
        0.2.0.2. 2.2.0.0. timp,strings,
        3fl soli
        (Adorjan, A.) sc BILLAUDOT f.s.,
        perf mat rent   (D525)

DROTTNINGHOLMSMUSIKEN [ARR.] see Roman,
    Johan Helmich

DROTTNINGHOLMSMUSIKEN: SUITE NO.
    1[ARR.] see Roman, Johan Helmich

DROTTNINGHOLMSMUSIKEN: SUITE NO. 2
    [ARR.] see Roman, Johan Helmich

DROTTNINGHOLMSMUSIKEN: SUITE NO. 3
    [ARR.] see Roman, Johan Helmich

DROTTNINGHOLMSMUSIKEN: SUITES NOS. 1,
    2, 3 [ARR.] see Roman, Johan
    Helmich

DRUCKMAN, JACOB RAPHAEL (1928-   )
    Athanor [23']
        2+alto fl.2+English horn.2+bass
        clar.2. 4.3.3.1. timp,3perc,
        harp,pno,strings,synthesizer
        BOOSEY perf mat rent   (D526)

    Aureole [12']
        2+alto fl.2+English horn.2+bass
        clar.2. 4.3.3.1. timp,3perc,
        harp,pno,strings
        min sc BOOSEY $17.50, perf mat rent
                                      (D527)

    Birthday Bouquet, A [1']
        3(pic).2+English horn.2.2.
        4.3.3.0. timp,3perc,harp,pno,
        strings
        BOOSEY perf mat rent   (D528)

    Prism [22']
        3(pic,alto fl).2+English horn.2+
        bass clar.2. 4.3.3.1. timp,
        3perc,harp,pno,strings,
        electric hpsd
        sc BOOSEY $60.00, perf mat rent
                                      (D529)

DRUSHETZKY, GEORG (1745-1819)
    Concerto for Oboe and Orchestra
        2fl,2horn,strings,ob solo
        sc KUNZEL 10160 $12.00, ipa (D530)

    Symphonies, Two
        see Ivancic, Amandus, Symphonies,
        Two

DRYAD, THE see Sibelius, Jean

DRYADEN, FOR SOLO VOICE AND ORCHESTRA
    see Nordqvist, Gustaf

DU, MING-XIN
  Autumn Thoughts [6']
    3.2+English horn.2.2. 4.3.3.1.
    timp,perc,harp,cel,strings
    HONG KONG perf mat rent   (D531)

  Concerto for Violin and Orchestra
    [26']
    3.2+English horn.2.2. 4.3.3.0.
    timp,perc,harp,cel,strings,vln
    solo
    HONG KONG perf mat rent   (D532)

  Goddess Of River Luo, The [17']
    3.2+English horn.2.2. 4.3.3.1.
    timp,perc,cel,strings
    HONG KONG perf mat rent   (D533)

  Landscape Of Northern Shensi, For
    Harmonica And Orchestra [15']
    3.2.2.2. 4.3.3.0. timp,perc,harp,
    strings,harmonica solo
    HONG KONG perf mat rent   (D534)

  Mermaid Suite (composed with Wu, Ju
    Jiang) [35']
    3.2+English horn.2.2. 4.3.3.1.
    timp,perc,harp,strings
    HONG KONG perf mat rent   (D535)

  Mermaid Suite: Coral Dance [arr.]
    (composed with Wu, Ju Jiang)
    (Manabu Kawai) 2.2.2.2. 2.0.0.0.
    strings [2'] HONG KONG perf mat
    rent   (D536)

  Mermaid Suite: Dance Of Ginseng
    [arr.] (composed with Wu, Ju
    Jiang)
    (Manabu Kawai) 3.2.3.2. 4.3.0.0.
    timp,strings [3'] HONG KONG perf
    mat rent   (D537)

  Mermaid Suite: Dance Of The Seaweed
    [arr.] (composed with Wu, Ju
    Jiang)
    (Manabu Kawai) 3.2.3.2. 4.3.0.0.
    cym,strings [5'] HONG KONG perf
    mat rent   (D538)

  Mermaid Suite: Dance Of Twenty-Four
    Mermaids [arr.] (composed with
    Wu, Ju Jiang)
    (Manabu Kawai) 3.1+English
    horn.3.2. 4.3.3.1. timp,perc,
    strings [8'] HONG KONG perf mat
    rent   (D539)

  Mermaid Suite: Mass Dance At The
    Wedding [arr.] (composed with Wu,
    Ju Jiang)
    (Manabu Kawai) 3.2.3.2. 4.3.3.1.
    timp,perc,strings [2'] HONG KONG
    perf mat rent   (D540)

  Mermaid Suite: Straw Hats Flower
    Dance [arr.] (composed with Wu,
    Ju Jiang)
    (Manabu Kawai) 3.2.3.2. 4.3.0.0.
    perc,strings [3'] HONG KONG perf
    mat rent   (D541)

  Sinkiang Dance No. 1, For Violin And
    Orchestra [6']
    2.2.2.2. 4.3.3.1. timp,perc,harp,
    strings,vln solo
    HONG KONG perf mat rent   (D542)

  Sinkiang Dance No. 2, For Violin And
    Orchestra [4']
    2.2.2.2. 4.3.3.1. timp,perc,
    strings,vln solo
    HONG KONG perf mat rent   (D543)

  Sinkiang Dance No. 3, For Violin And
    Orchestra [5']
    3.2.2.2. 4.3.3.1. timp,perc,harp,
    strings,vln solo
    HONG KONG perf mat rent   (D544)

  Sinkiang Dance No. 4, For Violin And
    Orchestra [4']
    3.2.2.2. 4.3.3.1. timp,perc,
    strings,vln solo
    HONG KONG perf mat rent   (D545)

  Sinkiang Dance No. 5, For Violin And
    Orchestra [5']
    3.2.2.2. 4.0.0.0. perc,harp,
    strings,vln solo
    HONG KONG perf mat rent   (D546)

  Sinkiang Dance No. 6, For Violin And
    Orchestra [4']
    3.2.2.2. 4.3.3.1. perc,strings,
    vln solo
    HONG KONG perf mat rent   (D547)

  Sinkiang Dance No. 7, For Violin And
    Orchestra [4']
    3.2.2.2. 4.3.3.1. timp,perc,harp,
    strings,vln solo
    HONG KONG perf mat rent   (D548)

DU, MING-XIN (cont'd.)

  Sinkiang Dance No. 8, For Violin And
    Orchestra [5']
    3.2.2.2. 4.3.3.1. timp,perc,harp,
    strings,vln solo
    HONG KONG perf mat rent   (D549)

  Sinkiang Dance No. 9, For Violin And
    Orchestra [6']
    2.0.2.0. 3.0.0.0. perc,harp,cel,
    strings,vln solo
    HONG KONG perf mat rent   (D550)

  Sinkiang Dance No. 10, For Violin And
    Orchestra [4']
    3.2.2.2. 4.3.3.1. timp,perc,
    strings,vln solo
    HONG KONG perf mat rent   (D551)

  Southern Sea, The [17']
    3.2+English horn.3.3. 4.3.3.1.
    timp,perc,strings
    HONG KONG perf mat rent   (D552)

  Youth Symphony [21']
    3.2+English horn.2.2. 4.3.3.1.
    timp,perc,harp,cel,strings
    HONG KONG perf mat rent   (D553)

  Youth Waltz [4']
    2.2.2.2. 4.3.3.1. timp,perc,cel,
    strings
    HONG KONG perf mat rent   (D554)

DU BIST DIE RUH, FOR SOLO VOICE AND
  ORCHESTRA, [ARR.] see Schubert,
  Franz (Peter)

DU BLANC LE JOUR SON ESPACE, FOR SOLO
  VOICE AND INSTRUMENTAL ENSEMBLE see
  Fenelon, Philippe

DU BOIS, ROB
  see BOIS, ROB DU

DU CLAIR AU SOMBRE, FOR SOLO VOICE AND
  CHAMBER ORCHESTRA see Nigg, Serge

DU CRISTAL see Saariaho, Kaija

DU SOLEIL ET DE LA LUNE, FOR SOLO
  VOICES AND INSTRUMENTAL ENSEMBLE
  see Monnet, Marc

DUALIS, FOR VIOLONCELLO AND ORCHESTRA
  see Bergman, Erik

DUALISMEN see Müllich, Hermann

DUBEDOUT, BERTRAND (1958-   )
  Maestrazgo [14']
    ob,clar,bass clar,trp,trom,perc,
    2harp,vla,vcl,db
    BILLAUDOT perf mat rent   (D555)

DUBOIS, PIERRE-MAX (1930-   )
  Analogie [13'30"]
    2.1.1.1. 2.1.1.1. timp,perc,
    strings
    BILLAUDOT perf mat rent   (D556)

  Concert Des Elements, Le [26']
    2.2.2.2. 3.3.3.1. timp,perc,cel,
    harp,pno,strings
    ESCHIG perf mat rent   (D557)

  Concerto for Accordion and String
    Orchestra, No. 1 [18'30"]
    string orch,acord solo
    BILLAUDOT perf mat rent   (D558)

  Concerto for Violin and String
    Orchestra, No. 2 [20']
    string orch,vln solo
    ESCHIG perf mat rent   (D559)

  En Taille Douce [28']
    2.2.2.2. 3.2.2.0. timp,2perc,
    harp,strings
    BILLAUDOT perf mat rent   (D560)

  Fantasy For Saxhorn And Orchestra
    [9']
    CHOUDENS perf mat rent   (D561)

  Hommage A Rabelais [7']
    ob,horn,strings
    RIDEAU perf mat rent   (D562)

  Instantanes 1 Et 2, For Clarinet And
    String Orchestra [9']
    string orch,clar solo
    BILLAUDOT perf mat rent   (D563)

  Moments Musicaux, For Alto Saxophone
    And String Orchestra [17']
    string orch,alto sax solo
    BILLAUDOT perf mat rent   (D564)

  Queue Leu Leu [20']
    2.1.2.1. 2.1.1.0. timp,perc,pno,
    strings
    BILLAUDOT perf mat rent   (D565)

DUBOIS, PIERRE-MAX (cont'd.)

  Serieux s'Abstenir [11']
    2.1.2.1.alto sax. 1.1.1.1. timp,
    perc,gtr,pno,acord,strings
    BILLAUDOT perf mat rent   (D566)

  Simard Suite, For Vibraphone, Marimba
    And Orchestra [21'30"]
    2(pic).2.2.2. 2.2.2.0. timp,pno,
    strings,vibra solo,marimba solo
    BILLAUDOT perf mat rent   (D567)

  Six Preludes En Forme De Suite, For
    Violin And Chamber Orchestra
    [15'40"]
    fl,clar,bsn,strings,vln solo
    RIDEAU perf mat rent   (D568)

  Suite Concertante, For Woodwind
    Quintet, Percussion And Orchestra
    [18']
    1.1.1.1. 1.1.1.0. perc,pno,
    strings
    BILLAUDOT perf mat rent   (D569)

  Symphonie Serenade [17']
    string orch
    ESCHIG perf mat rent   (D570)

  Trois Serenades [10']
    0.1.1.1.alto sax. 0.0.0.0. perc,
    vibra,cel,strings
    BILLAUDOT perf mat rent   (D571)

  Visions Liturgiques [22']
    2.2.2.2. 2.2.1.1. timp,2perc,cel,
    pno,strings
    BILLAUDOT perf mat rent   (D572)

DUBOIS, THEODORE (1837-1924)
  Cavatine, For Horn And Orchestra [5']
    1.1.1.1. 0.0.0.0. strings,horn
    solo
    KALMUS A6068 sc $5.00, set $7.00
                                     (D573)

  Fantasy for Harp and Orchestra
    KALMUS A5696 sc $25.00, set $50.00,
    perf mat rent   (D574)

DUBROVAY, LASZLO (1943-   )
  Concerto for Flute and String
    Orchestra
    string orch,fl solo
    sc EMB 12514 f.s., perf mat rent
                                     (D575)

  Concerto for Strings
    11strings sc EMB 10252 f.s. (D576)

  Concerto for Trumpet and Strings
    15strings,trp solo
    sc EMB 13203 f.s., perf mat rent
                                     (D577)

DUCHEMIN, LUCIEN (1909-   )
  Beurrieres De Paris, Les [11'25"]
    harp,pno,strings
    BILLAUDOT perf mat rent   (D578)

DUCLOS, PIERRE (1929-1974)
  Serenade for Strings [17']
    string orch
    BILLAUDOT perf mat rent   (D579)

  Symphonie Pour Les Temps Nouveaux
    [40']
    2.2.2.2. 2.2.2.0. timp,3perc,
    harp,cel,pno,strings
    BILLAUDOT perf mat rent   (D580)

DUCOL, BRUNO (1949-   )
  Metalayi 2
    LEDUC AL 27085-27086 perf mat rent
                                     (D581)

  Metalayi No. 3, For Piano And
    Orchestra *Op.19 [23']
    2(pic,alto fl).2(English
    horn).2(clar in E flat,bass
    clar).2(contrabsn). 2.0.2(bass
    trom).0. timp,2perc,pno&cel,
    elec gtr,strings,pno solo
    SALABERT perf mat rent   (D582)

  Passages *Op.17 [12']
    2.2.2.1. 1.0+cornet.1.0+db tuba.
    2perc,cel,elec gtr,strings
    SALABERT perf mat rent   (D583)

DUE CANZONI NATALIZIE ETNEE see
  Pennisi, Francesco

DUE IMPRESSIONI see Borlenghi, Enzo

DUE INTERMEZZI, FOR ORCHESTRA see
  Tansman, Alexandre

DUE PEZZI: TOCCATA ED ADAGIO DOLOROSO
  see Eklund, Hans

DUE PRELUDI SINFONICI see De Grandis,
  Renato

DUE SONETTI, FOR SOLO VOICE AND STRING
  ORCHESTRA see Wanek, Friedrich K.

DUE SORGENTI, LE see Gorli, Sandro

DUE STUDI see Ziino, Ottavio

DUEL see Xenakis, Yannis (Iannis)

DUEL, FOR SOLO VOICE AND ORCHESTRA see Miyoshi, Akira

DUERMETE, NINO, FOR SOLO VOICES AND ORCHESTRA see Rodrigo, Joaquín

DUESSELDORF CONCERTO see Richter, Marga

DUETTO CONCERTANTE, FOR OBOE, VIOLONCELLO AND STRING ORCHESTRA see Yun, Isang

DUETTO (MUSIQUE DE SCENE) see Scarlatti, Alessandro

DUFOURT, HUGUES (1943-   )
Antiphysis, For Flute And Orchestra
JOBERT   (D584)

Heure Des Traces, L' [17']
2.2.3.1. 1.1.1.0. 3perc,2vln,
2vla,vcl,db
SALABERT perf mat rent   (D585)

Mura Della Citta Di Dite [14']
1(alto fl).1(English horn).1+bass
clar.0. 1.1.1.0. 2perc,harp,
cel,elec org,strings
sc JOBERT 576-00126 $18.75, perf
mat rent   (D586)

DUHAMEL
Tombeau De Philippe d'Orleans, Le
sc BOIS f.s.   (D587)

DUKAS, PAUL (1865-1935)
Apprenti Sorcier, L'
sc PETERS 10514 f.s.   (D588)

Ariane Et Barbe-Bleue: Introduction,
Act III [8']
3.2+English horn.2+bass clar.3.
4.3.3.1. timp,perc,2harp,
strings
KALMUS A6438 sc $5.00, set $25.00,
pts $1.00, ea., perf mat rent
(D589)

Peri, La
KALMUS A6428 sc $45.00, set $90.00,
pts $5.00, ea., perf mat rent
(D590)

Polyeucte
KALMUS A6126 sc $20.00, set $45.00,
perf mat rent   (D591)

Symphony in C
min sc KALMUS K01469 $8.50   (D592)

Villanelle, For Horn And Orchestra
[arr.]
(Henkemans, Hans) 3.3.3.3. 4.3.3.1.
timp,perc,2harp,strings,horn solo
[6'] DONEMUS perf mat rent (D593)
(Miller) 2(pic).2.2.2. 2.2.0.0.
timp,perc,strings,horn solo [6']
KALMUS A7255 sc $10.00, set
$30.00, pts $1.50, ea., perf mat
rent   (D594)

DUKE, VERNON
see DUKELSKY, VLADIMIR

DUKELSKY, VLADIMIR ("VERNON DUKE")
(1903-1969)
Symphony No. 1 [18']
2+pic.2+English horn.2+bass
clar.2+contrabsn. 4.4.3.1.
timp,perc,pno,strings
BOOSEY perf mat rent   (D595)

Symphony No. 2 [17']
3+pic.3+English horn.3+bass
clar.2+contrabsn. 4.3.3.1.
timp,pno,strings
BOOSEY perf mat rent   (D596)

DUKURRAHSCH MONGKHOHR see Heyn, Volker

DUMITRESCU, IANCU (1944-   )
Aulodie Mioritica, For Double Bass
And Orchestra [17']
2.2.2.2. 2.2.2.1. 2perc,4vln,
2vla,2vcl,2db,synthesizer,db
solo
SALABERT perf mat rent   (D597)

DUMKA [ARR.] see Rubinstein, Anton

DUMONT, HENRI (1610-1684)
Allemanda 1 Et 2 [arr.]
(Sanvoisin, M.) hpsd/org,strings
[8'] BILLAUDOT perf mat rent
(D598)
Pavana [arr.]
(Sanvoisin, M.) strings without vla
[4'] BILLAUDOT perf mat rent
(D599)
Symphonia 1 Et 2 [arr.]
(Sanvoisin, M.) hpsd/org,strings
[8'] BILLAUDOT perf mat rent

DUMONT, HENRI (cont'd.)
(D600)

D'UN BOUT A L'AUTRE see Canton,
Edouardo

D'UN CHANT PERDU, FOR SOLO VOICE AND
CHAMBER ORCHESTRA see Bon, Andre

D'UN COEUR QUI T'AIME, FOR SOLO VOICES
AND ORCHESTRA see Gounod, Charles
François

D'UN OPERA DE POUPEE EN SEPT MUSIQUES
see Jolas, Betsy

DUNA see Correggia, Enrico

DUNAYEVSZKY, ISAAK O. (1900-1955)
Snowflakes [arr.]
(Shirley, Charles) 2.2.2.2.
2.2.2.1. timp,perc,harp,pno,
strings VAAP perf mat rent (D601)

D'UNE SOURCE OUBLIEE see Bonnet,
Antoine

DUO CONCERTANTE, FOR FLUTE, HARP AND
ORCHESTRA see Ramovs, Primoz

DUO CONCERTANTE, FOR VIOLIN, VIOLA AND
ORCHESTRA see Cooper, Paul

DUO CONCERTANTE, FOR VIOLONCELLO,
BASSOON AND ORCHESTRA, NO.2 see
Koetsier, Jan

DUO YE see Chen, Yi

DUPARC, HENRI (1848-1933)
Aux Étoiles
KALMUS A6100 sc $8.00, set $11.00
(D602)
Lenore
KALMUS A5759 sc $20.00, set $45.00,
perf mat rent   (D603)

DUPLICATES, FOR 2 PIANOS AND ORCHESTRA
see Powell, Mel

DUPUY, EDOUARD (1770-1822)
Ungdom Og Galskab
"Youth And Folly" sc,pts SAMFUNDET
f.s.   (D604)

Youth And Folly
see Ungdom Og Galskab

DURAND, PIERRE
Passacaglia for Piano and Orchestra
[10']
2.2.2.2. 2.2.2.1. timp,perc,harp,
cel,strings,pno solo
BILLAUDOT perf mat rent   (D605)

DURANTE, FRANCESCO (1684-1755)
Concerto in B flat [10']
string orch
BSE 128 perf mat rent   (D606)

Trois Litanies, For Solo Voices And
String Orchestra [7']
string orch,cont,T&countertenor
(Blanchard, R.) BOIS perf mat rent
(D607)
DUREY, LOUIS (1888-1979)
Bestiaire, Le, For Solo Voice And
Orchestra
2.1.1.1. 1.0.0.0. pno&cel,
strings,med solo
CHESTER JWC 554 perf mat rent
(D608)
Carillons *Op.7,No.1 [4']
3.3.3.3. 4.3.3.1. timp,perc,cel,
2harp,strings
ESCHIG perf mat rent   (D609)

Neige *Op.7,No.2 [5']
4.3.4.3. 4.3.3.1. timp,perc,cel,
2harp,strings
ESCHIG perf mat rent   (D610)

DURIEUX, FREDERIC (1959-   )
Exil II, For Solo Voices And
Instrumental Ensemble [21']
1(alto fl).1(English horn).1.0.
1.1.0.0. 3perc,harp,pno,vln,
vla,vcl,A&coloratura sop
SALABERT perf mat rent   (D611)

Macie [20']
2(pic)+alto fl.2+English
horn.2(clar in A)+bass
clar.3(contrabsn). 4.3.3.1.
6perc,2harp,pno,cel,strings
SALABERT perf mat rent   (D612)

Parcours Pluriel [13']
1.0+English horn.1.0. 0.1.1.0.
vibra,marimba,harp,pno,2vln,
2vla,2vcl,2synthesizer
SALABERT perf mat rent   (D613)

Seuil Deploye [22']
2(alto fl).0.2(bass clar).0.
1.1.1.0. harp,pno,synthesizer,

DURIEUX, FREDERIC (cont'd.)
strings
LEMOINE perf mat rent   (D614)

DURKO, ZSOLT (1934-   )
Chamber Music
2pno,strings
sc EMB 7273 f.s.   (D615)

Colloïdes, For Flute And Instrumental
Ensemble
sc EMB 10084 f.s.   (D616)

Concerto for Piano and Orchestra
sc EMB 10250 f.s.   (D617)

Iconography No. 2, For Horn And
Chamber Orchestra
sc EMB 10132 f.s.   (D618)

Impromptus In F, For Flute And
Orchestra [15']
0.1.1.0. 1.0.0.0. perc,pno&org,
string quar,db,fl solo
CHESTER perf mat rent   (D619)

Ornamenti No. 2 [14']
3(pic).3(English horn).3(bass
clar).3. 3.3.3.1. timp,4perc,
harp,pno&cel,strings
CHESTER perf mat rent   (D620)

Ornamenti No. 1
sc EMB 13282 f.s., perf mat rent
(D621)
Quattro Dialoghi, For Two Percussion
Soloists And Orchestra
sc EMB 10235 f.s.   (D622)

Refrains, For Violin And Orchestra
sc EMB 10241 f.s.   (D623)

Rhapsody
(second version) sc EMB 10238 f.s.
(D624)
DURUFLE, MAURICE (1902-1986)
Danse Lente
see Trois Danses

Divertissement
see Trois Danses

Tambourin
see Trois Danses

Trois Danses
study sc DURAND $20.25
contains: Danse Lente;
Divertissement; Tambourin
(D625)

DURVILLE, PHILIPPE (1957-   )
Alpha Centaure [27']
2.2.2.2. 3.2.2.1. perc,harp,pno,
elec org,strings
BILLAUDOT perf mat rent   (D626)

Espace Du Dedans, L' [10']
2.1.2.1. 1.2.1.0. 2perc,pno,harp,
4vln,2vla,2vcl,db
BILLAUDOT perf mat rent   (D627)

DUSAPIN, PASCAL (1955-   )
Assai [15']
2+pic.3.3.3. 3.2.2.1. timp,
strings
SALABERT perf mat rent   (D628)

Aven, L', For Flute And Orchestra
[9']
2+pic.2+English horn.2+bass
clar.2+contrabsn. 3.3.2.2.
2timp,strings,fl solo
sc SALABERT f.s., perf mat rent
(D629)
Haro [38']
3.2.2.2. 2.2.2.0. timp,perc,
strings
SALABERT perf mat rent   (D630)

Hop [11']
1.1.1+bass clar.1. 2.1.0.0. vln,
vla,vcl,db
SALABERT perf mat rent   (D631)

Riviere, La [11']
2+pic.2+English horn.2+clar in E
flat+bass clar.2+contrabsn.sax.
6.4.3+bass trom.0. strings
SALABERT perf mat rent   (D632)

Tre Scalini [17']
2+2pic.3+English horn.3+clar in E
flat+bass clar.3+contrabsn.
5.4.3+bass trom.0. strings
SALABERT perf mat rent   (D633)

DUSK: A SETTING FOR ORCHESTRA see
Waxman, Franz

DUSSEK, JOHANN LADISLAUS (1760-1812)
Symphonie Concertante
see Gyrowetz, Adalbert (Jirovec),
Symphonies, Four

DUTILLEUX, HENRI (1916-   )
Arbre Des Songes, L', For Violin And
  Orchestra [25']
  3.3(ob d'amore).4.3. 3.3.3.1.
  timp,5perc,harp,cimbalom,pno&
  cel,strings,vln solo
  study sc SCHOTTS ED 627 f.s., perf
  mat rent   (D634)

Six Heures A Perdre
  2.1.2+bass clar.2.alto sax.
  4.3.3.1. timp,perc,harp,pno&
  cel,Ondes Martenot,strings
  SALABERT perf mat rent   (D635)

DUVERNOY, FREDERIC NICOLAS (1765-1838)
Concerto for Horn and Orchestra, No.
  7 [15']
  2.2.0.2. 2.0.0.0. strings,horn
  solo
  (Leloir, E.) sc BILLAUDOT f.s.,
  perf mat rent   (D636)

DUYN, WILLEM (1922-   )
Variations [20']
  2.2.2.2. 3.3.3.1. strings
  sc DONEMUS f.s., perf mat rent
                                (D637)

DVE FANFARY see Novák, Milan

DVE VDOVY: BALLET MUSIC see Smetana,
  Bedrich, Two Widows, The: Ballet
  Music

DVORÁK, ANTONÍN (1841-1904)
Amid Nature *Op.91
  (Sourek) "In Nature's Realm" KALMUS
  A7180 sc $35.00, set $70.00, pts
  $3.00, ea., perf mat rent (D638)

Armida: Overture [6']
  3.3.3.3. 4.4.3.1. timp,perc,harp,
  strings
  SUPRAPHON   (D639)

Bagatelles, 5, [arr] *Op.47
  (Russell Davies, D.) 1.2(English
  horn).1(bass clar).2. 2.0.0.0.
  strings [20'] BREITKOPF-W perf
  mat rent   (D640)

Biblical Songs, For Solo Voice And
  Orchestra *Op.99
  KALMUS A7481 sc $50.00, set $45.00,
  pts $3.00, ea., perf mat rent (D641)

Carnival Overture *Op.92
  (Sourek) KALMUS A7181 sc $30.00,
  set $50.00, pts $2.00, ea., perf
  mat rent   (D642)

Concerto for Piano and Orchestra, Op.
  33, in G minor
  (Sourek) (contains original and
  Kurz versions) KALMUS A7179 sc
  $80.00, set $40.00, pts $3.00,
  ea., perf mat rent   (D643)

Concerto for Violin and Orchestra,
  Op. 53, in A minor
  (Sourek) KALMUS A7172 sc $50.00,
  set $50.00, pts $3.00, perf
  mat rent   (D644)

Concerto for Violoncello and
  Orchestra in A
  (Burghauser, Jarmil) 2.2.2.2.
  2.2.0.0. timp,strings,vcl solo
  [32'] sc SUPRAPHON f.s.   (D645)

Concerto for Violoncello and
  Orchestra, Op. 104, in B minor
  min sc EULENBURG EU00785 $8.00
                                (D646)
  (Pommer) PETERS pts 9584 $55.00,
  study sc 9584A $10.00   (D647)
  (Sourek) KALMUS A7132 sc $50.00,
  set $75.00, pts $3.00, perf
  mat rent   (D648)
  *see GREAT ROMANTIC CELLO
  CONCERTOS

Czech Suite
  see Suite, Op. 39

Dramatic Overture
  see Tragic Overture

Evening Songs, For Solo Voice And
  Orchestra *Op.3
  2.3.2.2. 2.0.0.0. strings,Bar
  solo
  SUPRAPHON   (D649)

From The Bohemian Forest: In The
  Spinning Room [arr.] *Op.68,No.1
  "In Den Spinnstuben [arr.]"
  2(pic).2.2.2. 4.2.3.0. timp,perc,
  harp,strings [4'] KALMUS A6101 sc
  $15.00, set $20.00, perf mat rent
                                (D650)

Gipsy Songs, For Solo Voice And
  Orchestra, [arr.]
  (Cumming, Richard) 2.2+English
  horn.2+bass clar.2+contrabsn.
  4.2.2.1. timp,perc,harp,strings,

DVORÁK, ANTONÍN (cont'd.)

solo voice [15'] BOOSEY perf mat
  rent   (D651)

Golden Spinning Wheel, The *Op.109
  KALMUS A7198 sc $40.00, set $70.00,
  pts $3.00, perf mat rent   (D652)

Hero's Song *Op.111
  KALMUS A7483 sc $50.00, set
  $100.00, pts $5.00, ea., perf mat
  rent   (D653)

Humoresque, For Violin And Orchestra,
  [arr.] [4'40']
  (Waxman, Franz) FIDELIO perf mat
  rent   (D654)

Husitska. Overture *Op.67
  KALMUS A7200 sc $40.00, set $75.00,
  pts $3.00, ea., perf mat rent (D655)

In Den Spinnstuben [arr.]
  see From The Bohemian Forest: In
  The Spinning Room [arr.]

In Nature's Realm
  see Amid Nature

Mazurka for Violin and Orchestra, Op.
  49
  KALMUS A5890 sc $8.00, set $12.00
                                (D656)

Midday Witch *Op.108
  "Noon Witch, The" KALMUS A7199 sc
  $20.00, set $45.00, pts $2.00,
  ea., perf mat rent   (D657)

Noon Witch, The
  see Midday Witch

Othello Overture *Op.93
  min sc KALMUS K01470 $4.00   (D658)
  (Sourek) KALMUS A7182 sc $25.00,
  set $45.00, pts $2.00, ea., perf
  mat rent   (D659)

Peasant A Rogue, The: Overture
  see Roguish Peasant, The: Overture

Polonaise for Violoncello and
  Orchestra in A, Op. Posth. [9']
  1.2.2.2. 1.0.0.0. timp,strings,
  vcl solo
  (Klug) SIMROCK perf mat rent (D660)

Rhapsody in A minor
  KALMUS A6451 sc $30.00, set $40.00,
  pts $2.00, ea., perf mat rent (D661)

Roguish Peasant, The: Overture
  *Op.37
  "Peasant A Rogue, The: Overture"
  KALMUS A5597 sc $25.00, perf mat
  rent, set $22.00, pts $1.00, ea.
                                (D662)

Scherzo Capriccioso *Op.66
  (Sourek) KALMUS A6961 sc $30.00,
  set $50.00, pts $2.00, ea., perf
  mat rent   (D663)

Serenade, Op. 22, in E
  min sc KALMUS K00247 $6.00   (D664)
  SONZOGNO perf mat rent   (D665)
  (Sourek) KALMUS A7176 sc $30.00,
  set $20.00, pts $4.00, perf
  mat rent   (D666)

Serenade, Op. 44, in D minor
  (Sourek) KALMUS A6778 sc $25.00,
  set $22.00, pts $2.00, ea., perf
  mat rent   (D667)

Slavonic Dances, Op. 46
  sc DOVER 253945 $9.95   (D668)

Slavonic Dances, Op. 46, Book I, Nos.
  1-4
  min sc KALMUS K01471 $8.75   (D669)
  (Sourek) KALMUS A6963 sc $50.00,
  set $40.00, pts $2.00, perf
  mat rent   (D670)

Slavonic Dances, Op. 46, Book II,
  Nos. 5-8
  min sc KALMUS K01472 $8.75   (D671)
  (Sourek) KALMUS A6964 sc $50.00,
  set $40.00, pts $2.00, ea., perf
  mat rent   (D672)

Slavonic Dances, Op. 72, Book I, Nos.
  9-12
  (listed in this edition as Op.72,
  Nos. 1-4) min sc KALMUS K01473
  $8.75   (D673)
  (Sourek) KALMUS A7177 sc $40.00,
  set $40.00, pts $2.00, ea., perf
  mat rent   (D674)

Slavonic Dances, Op. 72, Book II,
  Nos. 13-16
  (listed in this edition as Op.72,
  Nos. 5-8) min sc KALMUS K01474
  $8.75   (D675)
  (Sourek) KALMUS A7178 sc $40.00,

DVORÁK, ANTONÍN (cont'd.)

set $60.00, pts $3.00, ea., perf
  mat rent   (D676)

Slavonic Rhapsody, Op. 45, No. 1, In
  D
  KALMUS A7202 sc $30.00, set $40.00,
  pts $2.00, ea., perf mat rent
                                (D677)

Slavonic Rhapsody, Op. 45, No. 2, In
  G Minor
  KALMUS A7203 sc $30.00, set $60.00,
  pts $3.00, ea., perf mat rent
                                (D678)

Slavonic Rhapsody, Op. 45, No. 3, In
  A Flat
  KALMUS A7204 sc $25.00, set $40.00,
  pts $2.00, ea., perf mat rent
                                (D679)

Suite, Op. 39
  (Sourek) "Czech Suite" KALMUS A6962
  sc $25.00, set $45.00, pts $3.00,
  ea., perf mat rent   (D680)

Suite, Op. 98b, in A
  KALMUS A6162 sc $20.00, set $50.00,
  perf mat rent   (D681)
  (Sourek) KALMUS A7175 sc $25.00,
  set $70.00, pts $3.00, ea., perf
  mat rent   (D682)

Symphonic Variations *Op.78
  min sc KALMUS K01412 $11.50   (D683)
  (Sourek) KALMUS A7171 sc $40.00,
  set $80.00, pts $4.00, ea., perf
  mat rent   (D684)

Symphony, Op. 4, in B flat
  (Sourek) KALMUS A7174 sc $100.00,
  set $175.00, pts $9.00, ea., perf
  mat rent   (D685)

Symphony, Op. 10, in E flat
  KALMUS A6304 sc $60.00, set
  $120.00, perf mat rent   (D686)

Symphony, Op. 13, in D minor
  KALMUS A6456 sc $60.00, set $90.00,
  pts $5.00, ea., perf mat rent (D687)

Symphony, Op. 60, in D
  (Bartos; Sourek) KALMUS A6757 sc
  $60.00, set $90.00, pts $6.00,
  ea., perf mat rent   (D688)

Symphony, Op. 70, in D minor
  (Sourek) KALMUS A6774 sc $75.00,
  set $80.00, pts $5.00, ea., perf
  mat rent   (D689)

Symphony, Op. 76, in F
  (Bartos) KALMUS A7482 sc $80.00,
  set $125.00, pts $6.50, ea., perf
  mat rent   (D690)

Symphony, Op. 88, in G
  (reprint of Simrock edition) sc
  DOVER 24749X $10.95 contains
  also: Symphony, Op. 95, in E
  minor   (D691)
  SIMROCK perf mat rent   (D692)
  (Sourek) KALMUS A7183 sc $50.00,
  set $100.00, pts $5.00, ea., perf
  mat rent   (D693)

Symphony, Op. 95, in E minor
  BREITKOPF-W sc PB 5198 f.s., pts
  OB 5198 f.s.   (D694)
  study sc EMB 40080 f.s.   (D695)
  (Doge, Klaus) min sc EULENBURG
  EU00433 $11.75   (D696)
  (Sourek) KALMUS A7064 sc $75.00,
  set $80.00, pts $4.00, ea., perf
  mat rent   (D697)
  see Symphony, Op. 88, in G

Tragic Overture
  "Dramatic Overture" KALMUS A7186 sc
  $25.00, set $50.00, pts $2.00,
  ea., perf mat rent   (D698)
  "Dramatic Overture" SUPRAPHON
                                (D699)

Two Waltzes, Op. 54
  string orch [7'] KALMUS A6133 sc
  $3.00, set $5.00, pts $1.25, ea.,
  perf mat rent   (D700)

Water Goblin, The
  see Watersprite

Watersprite *Op.107
  min sc KALMUS K01401 $5.50   (D701)
  "Water Goblin, The" KALMUS A7201 sc
  $35.00, set $75.00, pts $3.00,
  ea., perf mat rent   (D702)

Wild Dove , The
  see Wood Dove

Wood Dove *Op.110
  "Wild Dove , The" KALMUS A7197 sc
  $30.00, set $50.00, pts $2.00,
  ea., perf mat rent   (D703)

DWELLINGS see Conyngham, Barry

DYCHKO, LIUDMYLA (1939-   )
  Spring Songs
    see Vesnyanky

  Vesnyanky [10']
    3.3.3.2. 4.3.3.1. perc,cel,harp,
      strings
    "Spring Songs" VAAP perf mat rent
                                    (D704)

DYDO, J. STEPHEN (1948-   )
  Capriccio for Piano and Orchestra
    [25']
    2.2.3.2. 4.3.2.1. perc,strings,
      pno solo
    sc AM.COMP.AL. $38.15   (D705)

  Concerto for Violin and Orchestra
    [18']
    2.2.2.2. 2.2.2.1. strings,vln
      solo
    AM.COMP.AL. sc $32.50, pts $3.85
                                    (D706)

DYENS, ROLAND (1955-   )
  Concerto for Guitar and String
    Orchestra
    string orch,gtr solo
    LEMOINE perf mat rent   (D707)

DYING BUTTERFLY, THE, FOR ENGLISH HORN,
  SAXOPHONE AND ORCHESTRA see
  Wittenberg, Alexander, Doende
  Fjarilen, Den, For English Horn,
  Saxophone And Orchestra

DYING TREE, THE, FOR SOLO VOICE AND
  ORCHESTRA see Rangström, Ture

DYNAMICS see Hodkinson, Sydney P.

DYSON, GEORGE (1883-1964)
  Canterbury Pilgrims, The: Suite
    [arr.]
    (Palmer, Christopher) timp,harp,
      org,strings OXFORD perf mat rent
                                    (D708)

DYVEKE SANGE, FOR SOLO VOICE AND
  ORCHESTRA see Nielsen, Svend

E

E, KE JIAN
  Hung Hu, For Violin And Orchestra
    [15']
    3.2.2.2. 4.2.2.0. timp,perc,harp,
      strings,vln solo
    HONG KONG perf mat rent   (E1)

E NELLO STRINGERTI A QUESTO CORE, FOR
  SOLO VOICE AND ORCHESTRA see
  Bellini, Vincenzo

EAGLE SPRINGS, FOR KEYBOARD AND
  ORCHESTRA see Davison, Peter

EAR PIECE FOR ORCHESTRA see Persen,
  John, Øreverk For Orkester

EARLY AMERICAN PORTRAIT, FOR SOLO VOICE
  AND ORCHESTRA see Ballou, Esther
  Williamson

EARLY EVENING see Proto, Frank

EARTH, FOR SOLO VOICE AND ORCHESTRA see
  Strand, Ragnvald, Jord, For Solo
  Voice And Orchestra

EARTH CRY see Sculthorpe, Peter
  [Joshua]

EARTH DANCES see Birtwistle, Harrison

EARTH'S SKETCHES, FOR SOLO VOICE,
  VIOLIN AND STRINGS see Stroman,
  Scott

EASTER ORISONS see Harvey, Jonathan

EASTER TRIPTYCHON, FOR VIOLONCELLO AND
  CHAMBER ORCHESTRA see Mouravieff,
  Leon, Oster-Triptychon, For
  Violoncello And Chamber Orchestra

EASTHAMPTON SKETCHES see Dello Joio,
  Norman

EASTMAN OVERTURE see Walker, George
  Theophilus

EASTWOOD, THOMAS (1922-   )
  Hymn To Pan [9']
    3.3.3.3. 4.2.3.1. timp,2perc,cel,
      strings
    FABER perf mat rent   (E2)

  Ronde Des Saisons, For Solo Voice And
    String Orchestra [18']
    string orch,T solo
    FABER perf mat rent   (E3)

EASY SUITE see Ernst Ludwig, Landgraf
  von Hessen

EATING LIVING MONKEYS see Lang, David

EATON, JOHN C. (1935-   )
  Overture
    SHAWNEE perf mat rent   (E4)

  Remembering Rome [23']
    string orch
    AMP perf mat rent   (E5)

  Songs Of Despair, For Solo Voice And
    Chamber Orchestra [21']
    1(pic).1(English horn).1(bass
      clar).1. 1.1.1.1. 2perc,pno,
      harp,strings,Mez solo
    AMP perf mat rent   (E6)

  Symphony No. 2 [25']
    3.3.3+contrabass clar.3+
      contrabsn. 4.4.3.1. timp,perc,
      2pno,strings, musical saw
    AMP perf mat rent   (E7)

EAU ET LE FEU, L' see Pichaureau,
  Claude

EBEL, ARNOLD (1883-1963)
  An Meine Seele, For Solo Voice And
    Orchestra
    KISTNER perf mat rent   (E8)

EBEN, PETR (1929-   )
  Concerto for Organ and Orchestra, No.
    2
    UNITED MUS   (E9)

  Night Hours, For Woodwind Quintet And
    Orchestra
    study sc PANTON 2142 f.s.   (E10)

EBENHÖH, HORST (1930-   )
  Concerto for Violin, Viola and
    Orchestra, Op. 52
    2.2.2.2+contrabsn. 3.3.3.0. perc,
      harp,strings,vln solo,vla solo
    DOBLINGER perf mat rent   (E11)

EBENHÖH, HORST (cont'd.)
  Concerto, Op. 54 [20']
    trom,perc,strings
    DOBLINGER perf mat rent   (E12)

  Festmusik *Op.45,No.2 [9']
    2+pic.2.2+bass clar.2+contrabsn.
      3.3.3.1. timp,perc,strings
    DOBLINGER perf mat rent   (E13)

  Kolloquium, For Trombone, Percussion
    And Orchestra *Op.42,No.2 [14']
    2.2.2.2. 2.2.1.0. strings,trom
      solo,perc solo
    DOBLINGER perf mat rent   (E14)

  Symphony, Op. 34 [25']
    2+pic.2.2.2+contrabsn. 3.3.3.0.
      timp,perc,strings
    study sc DOBLINGER STP 643 f.s.,
      perf mat rent   (E15)

EBERHARD, DENNIS (1943-   )
  Ephrata, For Four Percussion Soli And
    Orchestra [13']
    3.3.3(clar in E flat).3. 4.3.3.1.
      harp,pno&cel,strings,4perc soli
    MARGUN BP 2062 perf mat rent (E16)

EBERL, ANTON (FRANZ JOSEF) (1765-1807)
  Symphony
    see Witt, Friedrich, Symphony

EBERWEIN, CARL (1786-1868)
  Sinfonia Concertante for Wind Quintet
    and Orchestra, Op. 67
    0.0.2.0. 2.2.0.0. timp,strings,
      wind quin soli
    BREITKOPF-L perf mat rent   (E17)

EBON CHRONICLE see Still, William Grant

ECCE ANCELLA DOMINI see Marie, Jean
  Étienne

ECCE OPUS see Guerrero, Francisco

ECCO! see Smith, William Overton

ECHANGE, FOR CLARINET AND INSTRUMENTAL
  ENSEMBLE see Xenakis, Yannis
  (Iannis)

ECHANGES see Richard, Andre

ÉCHARPPE D'IRIS, L' see Gaudibert, Eric

ECHOES OF OSSIAN OVERTURE see Gade,
  Niels Wilhelm, Nachklange Von
  Ossian: Overture

ECHO'S see Franssens, Joep

ECKERBERG, SIXTEN (1909-   )
  Epilog [18']
    3.2.2.2. 4.4.4.2. 2perc,harp,
      strings
    STIM   (E18)

ECKERT, MICHAEL
  Sea Changes, For Solo Voice And
    Chamber Orchestra [15']
    2fl,2clar,horn,trp,perc,harp,pno&
      cel,vln,vla,vcl,Mez solo
    AM.COMP.AL. sc $23.00, pts $53.60
                                 (E19)

ECKHARDT-GRAMATTE, SOPHIE CARMEN
  (1902-1974)
  Ile, L' [7']
    3.3.3.3. 4.3.3.1. timp,perc,cel,
      2harp,strings
    CAN.MUS.CENT. MI 1100 E19IL (E20)

  Konzertstück for Violin and Orchestra
    2.2.2.2. 2.1.0.0. timp,cel,
      strings,vln solo
    CAN.MUS.CENT. MI 1311 E19CO (E21)

ECLAIRS see Bruzdowicz, Joanna

ECLAT APPROCHANT, L' see Thommessen,
  Olav Anton

ECLIPSES see Fenelon, Philippe

ECLISSE A FLERI, FOR 2 FLUTES AND
  ORCHESTRA see Pennisi, Francesco

ECLISSI see Vianello, Riccardo

ECO see Donatoni, Franco

ECOGRAMAS see Fernandez Alvez, Gabriel

ECOS I see Maiguashca, Mesias

ECOS II see Maiguashca, Mesias

ECOSSAISES [ARR.] see Beethoven, Ludwig
  van

ECRAN see Vieru, Anatol

ECSTASY see Buhr, Glenn see Søderlind, Ragnar

ECSTATIC ORANGE see Torke, Michael

EDEN...JEDEN, FOR SOLO VOICES AND INSTRUMENTAL ENSEMBLE see Zinsstag, Gérard

EDER, HELMUT (1916-   )
  Anamorphose [30']
    1(pic).1.1.1. 1.1.1.0. perc,pno& hpsd,strings
    DOBLINGER perf mat rent   (E22)

  Concert Piece, Op. 83 [7'30"]
    string orch
    study sc DOBLINGER STP 604 f.s., perf mat rent   (E23)

  Concertino, Op. 81 for Orchestra [14']
    2(pic).2.2.2. 2.2.0.0. timp,perc, strings
    study sc DOBLINGER STP 600 f.s., perf mat rent   (E24)

  Concerto A.B., For Chamber Orchestra *Op.78,No.1 [15']
    2ob.2bsn,2horn,strings
    DOBLINGER perf mat rent   (E25)

  Concerto A.B., For Orchestra *Op.78, No.2
    2(pic).2.2(bass clar).2. 2.2.2.0. timp,perc,strings
    DOBLINGER perf mat rent   (E26)

  Concerto for Flute and Orchestra, Op. 82 [20']
    0+pic.2.3.2. 3.2.2.1. timp,perc, strings,fl solo
    study sc DOBLINGER STP 615 f.s., perf mat rent   (E27)

  Concerto for Violin and Orchestra, No. 1, Op. 32 [17']
    1(pic).1.1.1. 1.0.0.0. strings, vln solo
    study sc DOBLINGER STP 619 f.s., perf mat rent   (E28)

  Concerto for Violin and Orchestra, No. 3, Op. 75 [21']
    3.2.2+bass clar.2. 3.2.2.0. timp, perc,strings,vln solo
    DOBLINGER perf mat rent   (E29)

  Danza A Solatio *Op.36 [9']
    2+pic.2.2+bass clar.2. 4.2+opt trp.3.1. perc,pno,strings
    DOBLINGER perf mat rent   (E30)

  Divertimento for Solo Voice and Orchestra, Op. 64 [18']
    4(pic).3(English horn).4(bass clar).4. 6.4.3.1. timp,2perc, cel,harp,strings,coloratura sop
    study sc DOBLINGER STP 388 f.s., perf mat rent   (E31)

  Eine Rose Uberwaltigt Alles, Die, For Solo Voice And Orchestra *Op.88, No.2 [16']
    2(pic).1.2.1. 1.2.0.0. timp,perc, pno,cel,strings,high solo
    DOBLINGER perf mat rent   (E32)

  Notturni, Op.79, No.3 [13']
    fl,ob,strings
    DOBLINGER perf mat rent   (E33)

  Orgel-Sinfonie (Symphony No. 5, Op. 72) [15']
    3(pic,alto fl).2(English horn).3(bass clar).2(contrabsn). 5.2.2.1. timp,perc,cel,pno,org,strings
    study sc DOBLINGER STP 510 f.s., perf mat rent   (E34)

  Pezzo Sereno *Op.27 [5']
    2(pic).0.1.2.alto sax. 4.2.2.1. perc,pno,strings
    DOBLINGER perf mat rent   (E35)

  Prelude And Chorale On "Nun Komm Der Heiden Heiland" *Op.63,No.2
    string orch,ob solo
    DOBLINGER sc $13.50, set $10.50   (E36)

  Schwanengesang, For Violoncello And Chamber Orchestra *Op.90 [10']
    clar,2horn,strings,vcl solo
    study sc DOBLINGER STP 630 f.s., perf mat rent   (E37)

  Symphony No. 2, Op. 24 [32']
    2(pic).2.2.2(contrabsn).alto sax. 3.2.2.1. timp,perc,pno,strings
    DOBLINGER perf mat rent   (E38)

  Symphony No. 5, Op. 72
    see Orgel-Sinfonie

EDER, HELMUT (cont'd.)
  Tanzreihen *Op.22 [20']
    2+pic.2.2.2. 4.3.3.1. timp,perc, pno,strings
    DOBLINGER perf mat rent   (E39)

  Variationen Uber Das Alte Adventlied "O Heiland, Reiss Die Himmel Auf" *Op.63,No.3 [7']
    fl,ob,strings
    sc,pts DOBLINGER 74 208 f.s.   (E40)

EDER DE LASTRA, ERICH (1933-   )
  Concerto for Clarinet and Orchestra [13']
    1+pic.0.1+bass clar.0+contrabsn. 4.2.1.1. timp,perc,harp, strings,clar solo
    DOBLINGER perf mat rent   (E41)

  Serenade [7'30"]
    string orch
    DOBLINGER perf mat rent   (E42)

  Stringendo [13']
    string orch
    DOBLINGER perf mat rent   (E43)

  Symphony No. 1 [35']
    2(pic).2.2.2. 4.3.2.1. timp,perc, strings
    DOBLINGER perf mat rent   (E44)

EDGAR: PRELUDIO see Puccini, Giacomo

EDGE OF THE LAND, THE see Boone, Charles N.

EDGE OF THE OLDE ONE, THE, FOR ENGLISH HORN AND ORCHESTRA see Hodkinson, Sydney P.

EDIFICE IN MEMORIAM see Newell, Robert M.

EDLER, ROBERT (1912-   )
  Dorische Musik
    string orch
    TONOS   (E45)

EDLUND, LARS (1922-   )
  Tracce [22']
    1.1.1.1. 0.0.0.0. timp,perc,harp, strings
    NORDISKA perf mat rent   (E46)

EDUARDO E CRISTINA: OVERTURE see Rossini, Gioacchino

EDWARDS, CLARA (1887-1974)
  Fisher's Widow, The [arr.]
    (Clark, Tom) 1.1.2.1. 2.2.1.0. timp,strings SCHIRM.G perf mat rent   (E47)

EDWARDS, GEORGE (1943-   )
  Captive, The, For Solo Voice And Chamber Orchestra [13']
    fl,ob,clar,bass clar,vibra,hpsd, 2vln,2vla,vcl,db,S solo
    sc AM.COMP.AL. $38.30, perf mat rent   (E48)

  Heraclitean Fire, For String Quartet And String Orchestra [7']
    string orch,string quar soli
    sc AM.COMP.AL. $36.95, perf mat rent   (E49)

  Moneta's Mourn [17']
    2.2.3.2. 4.2.3.0. timp,perc,harp, strings
    sc AM.COMP.AL. $44.65, perf mat rent   (E50)

EDWARDS, ROSS (1943-   )
  Concerto for Piano and Orchestra [20']
    3.3.3.2. 4.3.3.1. 2perc,strings, pno solo
    UNIVER. perf mat rent   (E51)

  Maninyas, For Violin And Orchestra [25']
    3.3.3.3. 4.4.3.1. 2perc,harp,pno, strings,vln solo
    UNIVER. perf mat rent   (E52)

  Mountain Village
    sc FABER F0641 f.s.   (E53)

  Mountain Village In A Clearing Mist [12']
    2.2.2.2. 2.2.3.1. 3perc,harp,pno, strings
    sc UNIVER. UE29307 $20.00, perf mat rent   (E54)

  Yarrageh, For Percussion And Orchestra [15']
    0.0.0.0. 2.2.3.0. pno&cel, strings,perc solo
    UNIVER. perf mat rent   (E55)

EEZY COMMA see Heyn, Volker

EFEBO CON RADIO, FOR SOLO VOICE AND ORCHESTRA see Sciarrino, Salvatore

EFFINGER, CECIL STANLEY (1914-1990)
  Capriccio, Op. 91 [14']
    3(pic).2+English horn.2+bass clar.2+contrabsn. 4.3.3.1. timp,3perc,harp,cel,strings
    SCHIRM.G perf mat rent   (E56)

EFISAES, FOR PIANO AND STRINGS see Hameenniemi, Eero

EFTERSOMMER, FOR SOLO VOICE AND ORCHESTRA see Jordan, Sverre

EG HEV FUNNE MIN FLOYSNE LOKKAR ATT I MITT SVARMERUS, FOR SOLO VOICE AND ORCHESTRA see Søderlind, Ragnar

EGDON HEATH see Holst, Gustav

EGGE, KLAUS (1906-1979)
  Concerto for Piano and Orchestra, No. 1, Op. 9 [25']
    2.1.2.2. 2.1.1.0. timp,harp, strings,pno solo
    NORGE   (E57)

  Fjell-Norig, For Solo Voice And Orchestra *Op.15 [9']
    2.2.2.2. 2.2.0.0. timp,perc, strings,S solo
    "Mountainous Norway, For Solo Voice And Orchestra" NORGE   (E58)

  Mountainous Norway, For Solo Voice And Orchestra
    see Fjell-Norig, For Solo Voice And Orchestra

EGGEN, ARNE (1881-1955)
  Aere Det Evige For Solo Soloaar I Levet, For Voice And Orchestra [3']
    2.1.2.2. 3.2.3.0. timp,strings, solo voice
    "Eternal Spring, For Solo Voice And Orchestra" NORGE   (E59)

  Autumn, For Solo Voice And String Orchestra
    see Host, For Solo Voice And String Orchestra

  Chaconne in G minor [17']
    2.2.2.2. 4.2.3.1. timp,perc, strings
    NORGE   (E60)

  Det Gulnar Lauvet, For Solo Voice And String Orchestra [3']
    string orch,solo voice
    "Yellow Leaves, For Solo Voice And String Orchestra" NORGE   (E61)

  Eternal Spring, For Solo Voice And Orchestra
    see Aere Det Evige For Solo Soloaar I Levet, For Voice And Orchestra

  Hald Ut, Hjarte, For Solo Voices And Orchestra [6']
    2.1.2.2. 3.1.2.0. timp,harp, strings,solo voice
    "My Weary Heart, For Solo Voice And Orchestra" NORGE   (E62)

  Ho Mor Faer Lofotfolket Sitt Heim, For Solo Voice And String Orchestra [3']
    string orch,solo voice
    "Return Of The Lofoten People, The, For Solo Voice And String Orchestra" NORGE   (E63)

  Host, For Solo Voice And String Orchestra [1']
    string orch,solo voice
    "Autumn, For Solo Voice And String Orchestra" NORGE   (E64)

  Ikke Enhver Som Siger Til Mig, For Solo Voice And Orchestra (Psalm for Solo Voice and Orchestra) [3']
    2.2.2.2. 4.3.4.0. timp,strings, solo voice
    NORGE   (E65)

  King Olav: Day Is Brightening, For Solo Voice And Orchestra
    see Kong Olav: Dag Er Pa Himlen Komin, For Solo Voice And Orchestra

  Kong Olav: Dag Er Pa Himlen Komin, For Solo Voice And Orchestra
    2.2.2.2. 4.3.4.0. timp,perc,harp, strings,solo voice
    "King Olav: Day Is Brightening, For Solo Voice And Orchestra" NORGE   (E66)

EGGEN, ARNE (cont'd.)

Liti Kjersti: Little Bird, A, For
Solo Voice And Orchestra
see Liti Kjersti: Og Det Var Litin
Smafugl, For Solo Voice And
Orchestra

Liti Kjersti: Og Det Var Litin
Smafugl, For Solo Voice And
Orchestra [3']
2ob,harp,strings,solo voice
"Liti Kjersti: Little Bird, A, For
Solo Voice And Orchestra" NORGE
(E67)

Liti Kjersti Suite [16']
2.2.2.2. 4.2.3.1. timp,perc,
strings
NORGE   (E68)

Liti Kjersti Suite: Symfonisk
Mellomspill
2.2.2.2. 4.2.3.0. timp,perc,
strings
"Liti Kjersti Suite: Symphonic
Intermezzo" NORGE   (E69)

Liti Kjersti Suite: Symphonic
Intermezzo
see Liti Kjersti Suite: Symfonisk
Mellomspill

My Weary Heart, For Solo Voice And
Orchestra
see Hald Ut, Hjarte, For Solo
Voices And Orchestra

No Sprette Lauvet, For Solo Voice And
Orchestra [3']
2.2.2.2. 4.2.3.1. timp,harp,
strings,T solo
"Spring Tide, For Solo Voice And
Orchestra" NORGE   (E70)

Olav Liljekrans: Fragment From Act
III [20']
2.2.2.2. 4.2.3.1. timp,perc,harp,
strings
NORGE   (E71)

Olav Liljekrans: Min Moders Arvesolv,
For Solo Voice And Orchestra [2']
2.2.2.2. 4.2.3.1. timp,harp,
strings,S solo
"Olav Liljekrans: My Mother's
Silver, For Solo Voice And
Orchestra" NORGE   (E72)

Olav Liljekrans: My Mother's Silver,
For Solo Voice And Orchestra
see Olav Liljekrans: Min Moders
Arvesolv, For Solo Voice And
Orchestra

Olav Liljekrans: Olavs Fortelling,
For Solo Voice And Orchestra
2.2.2.2. 4.2.1.0. cel,harp,
strings,T solo
"Olav Liljekrans: Olav's Story, For
Solo Voice And Orchestra" NORGE
(E73)

Olav Liljekrans: Olavs Monolog Og
Arie, For Solo Voice And
Orchestra [5']
2.2.2.2. 4.2.3.1. timp,perc,harp,
strings,T solo
"Olav Liljekrans: Olav's Monologue
And Aria, For Solo Voice And
Orchestra" NORGE   (E74)

Olav Liljekrans: Olav's Monologue And
Aria, For Solo Voice And
Orchestra
see Olav Liljekrans: Olavs Monolog
Og Arie, For Solo Voice And
Orchestra

Olav Liljekrans: Olav's Story, For
Solo Voice And Orchestra
see Olav Liljekrans: Olavs
Fortelling, For Solo Voice And
Orchestra

Out, Out, That Is Norsemen's
Yearning, For Solo Voice And
Orchestra
see Ut, Ja Ut, Det Var Nordmanns
Traa, For Solo Voice And
Orchestra

Psalm for Solo Voice and Orchestra
see Ikke Enhver Som Siger Til Mig,
For Solo Voice And Orchestra

Return Of The Lofoten People, The,
For Solo Voice And String
Orchestra
see Ho Mor Faer Lofotfolket Sitt
Heim, For Solo Voice And String
Orchestra

Sleep Little Child Jesus, For Solo
Voice And Orchestra
see Sov Barn Jesus Lille, For Solo
Voice And Orchestra

EGGEN, ARNE (cont'd.)

Snjo, For Solo Voice And String
Orchestra [3']
string orch,solo voice
"Snow, For Solo Voice And String
Orchestra" NORGE   (E75)

Snow, For Solo Voice And String
Orchestra
see Snjo, For Solo Voice And String
Orchestra

Solfager, For Solo Voice And
Orchestra [3']
2.1.2.2. 2.0.0.0. timp,harp,
strings,solo voice
"Sunfair, For Solo Voice And
Orchestra" NORGE   (E76)

Sov Barn Jesus Lille, For Solo Voice
And Orchestra [4']
2clar,2bsn,strings,solo voice
"Sleep Little Child Jesus, For Solo
Voice And Orchestra" NORGE   (E77)

Sparrow, The, For Solo Voice And
Orchestra
see Sporven, For Solo Voice And
Orchestra

Sporven, For Solo Voice And Orchestra
[3']
2fl,2clar,perc,strings,solo voice
"Sparrow, The, For Solo Voice And
Orchestra" NORGE   (E78)

Spring Tide, For Solo Voice And
Orchestra
see No Sprette Lauvet, For Solo
Voice And Orchestra

Sunfair, For Solo Voice And Orchestra
see Solfager, For Solo Voice And
Orchestra

Til En Gammel Kirke, For Solo Voice
And Orchestra [3']
clar,strings,solo voice
"To An Old Church, For Solo Voice
And Orchestra" NORGE   (E79)

To An Old Church, For Solo Voice And
Orchestra
see Til En Gammel Kirke, For Solo
Voice And Orchestra

Ut, Ja Ut, Det Var Nordmanns Traa,
For Solo Voice And Orchestra [3']
0.0.2.1. 2.0.0.0. timp,strings,
solo voice
"Out, Out, That Is Norsemen's
Yearning, For Solo Voice And
Orchestra" NORGE   (E80)

Yellow Leaves, For Solo Voice And
String Orchestra
see Det Gulnar Lauvet, For Solo
Voice And String Orchestra

EGGEN, ERIK (1887-1957)
Norwegian Rhapsody
2.2.2.2. 2.2.2.0. timp,perc,
strings
NORGE   (E81)

EGK, WERNER (1901-1983)
Joan Von Zarissa: Suite, For Solo
Voices And Orchestra [30']
3(pic).3(English horn).3(bass
clar).3(contrabsn). 4.3.3.1.
timp,perc,cel,harp,opt org,
strings,2 solo voices,
backstage: 8trp, bells
SCHOTTS perf mat rent   (E82)

Kleine Symphonie [25']
2.3.2.3. 2.2.1.0. timp,perc,pno,
strings
SCHOTTS perf mat rent   (E83)

Music for Strings [12']
string orch
SCHOTTS perf mat rent   (E84)

Nachtanz [4']
2(pic).3.3.3. 4.3.3.0. timp,perc,
harp,strings
SCHOTTS perf mat rent   (E85)

Overture
sc SCHOTTS 71 A6982 $27.00, perf
mat rent   (E86)

EGLOGA see Lang, Istvan see Vantus,
Istvan

EGMONT see Beethoven, Ludwig van

EGMONT: OVERTURE see Beethoven, Ludwig
van

EGYEDÜL AZ ERDÖBEN, FOR SOLO VOICE AND
CHAMBER ORCHESTRA see Petrovics,
Emil

EGYPTIAN NIGHTS: SUITE see Arensky,
Anton Stepanovich

EHEPAAR, DAS, FOR SOLO VOICES AND
INSTRUMENTAL ENSEMBLE see
Lauermann, Herbert

EHRET DIE FRAUEN WALZER see Strauss,
Eduard

EICHHORN
Variations for Orchestra
sc PETERS 9228 $33.00   (E87)

EICHNER, ERNST (1740-1777)
Symphony *see Richter, Franz Xaver,
Symphonies, Five
see Richter, Franz Xaver,
Symphonies, Five

EIDESES II see Lanza, Alcides E.

EIGER, WALTER
Concerto Grosso For Symphony
Orchestra And Jazz Ensemble [28']
2.2.2.2. 4.2.1.1. timp,perc,
strings, Jazz Ensemble: 2 alto
sax, 2 tenor sax, baritone sax,
4 trp, 4 trom, db, perc, opt
gtr
BOURNE perf mat rent   (E88)

EIGHT BAREFOOT SONGS, FOR SOLO VOICE
AND ORCHESTRA see Pettersson, Allan

EIGHT BRITISH AND AMERICAN FOLK SONGS
see Shostakovich, Dmitri

"8 - 80" see Rojko, Uroš

EIGHT LINES see Reich, Steve

EIGHT MOVEMENTS FOR ORCHESTRA see
Thorne, Nicholas C.K.

EIGHT POEMS OF EMILY DICKINSON, FOR
SOLO VOICE AND CHAMBER ORCHESTRA
see Copland, Aaron

EIGHT VARIATIONS AND CODA ON "O DU
LIEBER AUGUSTIN" see Hummel, Johann
Nepomuk, Acht Variationen Und Coda
Uber "O Du Lieber Augustin"

EIN HERZ EIN SINN see Strauss, Johann,
[Jr.]

EINAUDI, LUDOVICO (1955-   )
Altissimo [10']
1.1.1.1. 1.1.1.0. 2perc,pno,elec
org,harp,strings
(version for 17 performers is also
available) RICORDI-IT 133848 perf
mat rent   (E89)

Crossing [7']
fl,ob,bass clar,bsn,2perc,pno,
2vln,vla,vcl,db
RICORDI-IT 134069 perf mat rent
(E90)

Movimento [9']
2.2.2.2. 3.4.2.0. marimba,vibra,
2pno,strings
RICORDI-IT 134280 perf mat rent
(E91)

Per Vie D'acqua [6']
3.3.3.3. 2.2.2.1. 2perc,harp,
strings
RICORDI-IT 133292 perf mat rent
(E92)

Rondo for Solo Voice and Chamber
Orchestra [13']
3.2.3.2. 2.2.2.0. 3perc,harp,
strings,Mez solo
RICORDI-IT 133488 perf mat rent
(E93)

EINE ROSE UBERWALTIGT ALLES, DIE, FOR
SOLO VOICE AND ORCHESTRA see Eder,
Helmut

EINEM, GOTTFRIED VON (1918-   )
Arietten, For Piano And Orchestra
*Op.50 [20']
2.2.2.2. 2.2.1.0. timp,strings,
pno solo
BOOSEY perf mat rent   (E94)

Concertino Carintico *Op.86 [13']
7vln,2vla,2vcl,db
BOTE perf mat rent   (E95)

Concerto for Organ and Orchestra, Op.
62 [30']
3trom,timp,4perc,strings,org solo
sc UNIVER. UE 17572 f.s., perf mat
rent   (E96)

Munich Symphony *Op.70 [22']
2(pic).2.2.2. 2.2.2.0. timp,perc,
strings
sc BOOSEY f.s., perf mat rent (E97)

Prince Chocolat *Op.66
1.1.1.1. 1.1.0.0. timp,perc,
strings,opt speaking voice
sc UNIVER. $30.00   (E98)

EINEM, GOTTFRIED VON (cont'd.)

Rosa Mystica, For Solo Voice And
Orchestra *Op.40 [18']
2+pic.2.2.2. 2.2.1.0. timp,
strings,med solo
BOOSEY perf mat rent (E99)

Symphony No. 4, Op. 80 [35']
2.2.2.2. 2.2.2.1. timp,perc,harp,
strings
study sc UNIVER. UE19303 $30.00,
perf mat rent (E100)

EINFELD(T), DIETER (1935-)
Concerto for Percussion and Orchestra
3.2.2.2. 4.2.3.1. strings,perc
solo
PEER MUSIK perf mat rent (E101)

Imaginationen II, For Alto Saxophone
And Orchestra [18']
2.2.2.2. 4.2.3.1. timp,perc,
strings,alto sax solo
PEER MUSIK perf mat rent (E102)

Sechs Bilder Fur Orchester
2(pic).2.2.2. 2.2.2.0. timp,perc,
strings
"Six Portraits For Orchestra" PEER
MUSIK perf mat rent (E103)

Sinfonia Brevis [20']
2+pic.2.2+English horn.2+bass
clar.2+contrabsn. 4.2.3.1.
timp,perc,harp,strings
PEER MUSIK perf mat rent (E104)

Six Portraits For Orchestra
see Sechs Bilder Fur Orchester

EINLEITUNG UND THEMA MIT VARIATIONEN,
FOR VIOLIN AND STRING ORCHESTRA see
Paganini, Niccolo

EINSAM MANN, FOR SOLO VOICE AND
ORCHESTRA see Kjellsby, Erling

EINSAMKEIT; IN MEMORIAM W. BUCHEBNER
see Denhoff, Michael

EINSLEG, FOR SOLO VOICE AND STRING
ORCHESTRA see Braein, Edvard
Fliflet

EIRIKSDOTTIR, KAROLINA (1951-)
Five Pieces For Chamber Orchestra
1.1.1.1. 1.0.0.0. strings
ICELAND 037-011 (E105)

Notes [9'40"]
3.3.3.3. 4.3.3.1. timp,3perc,
harp,strings
ICELAND 037-003 (E106)

Sinfonietta [14']
2.2.2.2. 4.3.3.1. perc,harp,
strings
ICELAND 037- 016 (E107)

Sonans [15']
2.2.2.2. 4.3.3.0. timp,2perc,
harp,strings
ICELAND 037-008 (E108)

EIS THANATON, FOR SOLO VOICES AND
ORCHESTRA see Tavener, John

EISENMANN, WILL (1906-)
Stadt, Die
string orch
sc UNIVER. 14410 $17.00 (E109)

EISLER, HANNS (1898-1962)
Es Lächelt Der See, For Solo Voices
And Orchestra (from Bühnenmusik
Zu Schillers "Wilhelm Tell")
2.2.2.2. 4.3.3.1. timp,perc,
strings,MezTBar soli
BREITKOPF-L perf mat rent (E110)

Jetzt Hast Du Die Macht, Prolet, For
Solo Voice And Strings
2clar,2bsn,2horn,trp,timp,perc,
strings,speaking voice
BREITKOPF-L perf mat rent (E111)

Mitte Des Jahrhunderts: Präludium,
For Solo Voice And Orchestra
3.2.3.2. 4.0.0.0. perc,strings,S
solo
BREITKOPF-L perf mat rent (E112)

Regimenter Gehn, For Solo Voice And
Orchestra
2.2.2.2. 4.2.0.0. timp,perc,pno,
strings,Bar solo
BREITKOPF-L perf mat rent (E113)

Schweyk Im Zeiten Weltkrieg: In Den
Höheren Regionen No. 1, For Solo
Voices And Strings
8vcl,8db,timp,BarB soli
BREITKOPF-L perf mat rent (E114)

EISLER, HANNS (cont'd.)

Schweyk Im Zeiten Weltkrieg: In Den
Höheren Regionen No. 2, For Solo
Voices And Strings
8vcl,8db,timp,BarBar soli
BREITKOPF-L perf mat rent (E115)

Schweyk Im Zeiten Weltkrieg: In Den
Höheren Regionen No. 3, For Solo
Voices And Strings
8vcl,8db,timp,TBar soli
BREITKOPF-L perf mat rent (E116)

EISMA, WILL (1929-)
Passo Del Diavolo [10']
2.2.2.2. 2.2.1.0. timp,3perc,cel,
harp,strings
sc DONEMUS f.s., perf mat rent
(E117)

Pentathlon, For 5 Violas And
Orchestra [11']
1.2.2.1. 2.1.1.0. marimba,harp,
3vln,3vcl,2db,5vla soli
sc DONEMUS f.s., perf mat rent
(E118)

Silver Plated Bronze, For Doublebass
And Orchestra [15'30"]
1.1.2.1. 1.0.0.0. harp,strings,db
solo
DONEMUS perf mat rent (E119)

EJERCICIO POETICO see Escribano, Maria

EKAYA see Turnage, Mark-Anthony

EKIMOVSKY, VIKTOR (1947-)
Ave Maria [5']
48vln
SIKORSKI perf mat rent (E120)

Brandenburgisches Konzert [12']
hpsd,3vln,3vla,vcl,db,fl solo,ob
solo,vln solo
SIKORSKI perf mat rent (E121)

Chamber Variations [8']
1.1.1.0. 1.1.1.0. timp,perc,harp,
vln,vla,vcl,db
VAAP perf mat rent (E122)
"Kammervariationen" SIKORSKI perf
mat rent (E123)

Kammervariationen
see Chamber Variations

Lyrische Abweichungen, For 10
Violoncelli And Orchestra [18']
2.2.2.2. 4.2.2.0. timp,perc,harp,
strings,10vcl soli
SIKORSKI perf mat rent (E124)

Sublimationen [10']
3.3.3.3. 4.3.3.1. 3perc,strings
SIKORSKI perf mat rent (E125)

EKIZIAN, MICHELLE (1956-)
Birthday Chords [1']
2.2.2.2. 4.2.3.1. perc,strings
AM.COMP.AL. perf mat rent (E126)

Exiled Heart, The [16']
2+pic.2+English horn.2+bass
clar.2+contrabsn. 4.2.2+bass
trom.0. timp,3perc,strings
SCHIRM.G perf mat rent (E127)

EKKEHARD see Schreker, Franz

EKLUND, HANS (1927-)
Concerto Grosso for String Quartet
and String Orchestra
string orch,string quar soli
sc GEHRMANS 6683P f.s., perf mat
rent (E128)

Divertimento for Orchestra [16']
2.2.2.2. 2.2.1.0. timp,strings
STIM (E129)

Due Pezzi: Toccata Ed Adagio Doloroso
3.2.2.2. 4.2.3.1. timp,2perc,pno,
strings
STIM (E130)

Estate, L' [11']
string orch
sc GEHRMANS 6615P f.s., perf mat
rent (E131)

Fantasia Breve
2.2.2.2. 2.2.4.1. timp,2perc,
strings
STIM (E132)

Introduzzione E Allegro, For
Harpsichord And String Orchestra
[10']
string orch,hpsd solo
STIM (E133)

Kammerkonsert, For Violin And String
Orchestra [12']
string orch,vln solo
sc GEHRMANS 5947P f.s., perf mat
rent (E134)

EKLUND, HANS (cont'd.)

Lamento [6']
2fl,2clar,strings
sc GEHRMANS 6001P f.s., perf mat
rent (E135)

Musica Da Camera No.4, For Piano And
Orchestra [14']
1.1.1.1. 2.1.0.0. timp,perc,
strings,pno solo
STIM (E136)

Musica Da Camera No. 6, For Oboe And
Orchestra [15']
timp,perc,xylo,strings,ob solo
sc BUSCH HBM 033 f.s., perf mat
rent (E137)

Symphony No. 6 [25']
2.2.2.2. 4.2.3.1. timp,3perc,
strings
(Sinfonia senza speranza) sc
GEHRMANS 6522P f.s., perf mat
rent (E138)

Symphony No. 8 [23']
3.2.2.2. 4.3.3.1. timp,3perc,
strings
(Sinfonia grave) sc GEHRMANS 6535P
f.s., perf mat rent (E139)

EKSOTISK SUITE see Hurum, Alf

EKSTRÖM, LARS (1956-)
Bogilja
string orch
STIM (E140)

Concerto for Flute and Orchestra
1.1.2.1. 0.0.0.0. timp,3perc,
strings,fl solo
STIM (E141)

Do It Ivo, For Trombone And Orchestra
[20']
2.2.3.2. 3.2.2.1. timp,3perc,
strings,trom solo
STIM (E142)

FluxAska [20']
fl,clar,bass clar,2perc,pno,
strings
STIM (E143)

Jarnnatten [12']
1.2.1.2. 1.2.2.0. perc,pno,
strings
STIM (E144)

Pravda Love [25']
string orch,drums
STIM (E145)

EKVATOR see Bäck, Sven-Erik

EL CID: SUITE see Rozsa, Miklos

EL-DABH, HALIM (1921-)
Ramesses The Great (Symphony No. 9)
[20']
4.3.4.3. 4.4.3.1. 4perc,2harp,
strings
PETERS P67178 perf mat rent (E146)

Symphony No. 9
see Ramesses The Great

EL-KHOURY, BECHARA (1957-)
Concerto for Piano and Orchestra, Op.
36 [25']
3.3.3.3. 4.4.3.1. timp,perc,
strings,pno solo
ESCHIG perf mat rent (E147)

Danse Pour Orchestre *Op.9 [3']
3.2.2.2. 4.4.3.1. timp,perc,
strings
ESCHIG perf mat rent (E148)

Meditation Poetique, For Violin And
Orchestra *Op.41 [8']
2.2.3.2. 3.3.3.0. timp,harp,
strings,vln solo
ESCHIG perf mat rent (E149)

Ouverture Fantaisie *Op.42 [6']
3.3.3.3. 4.4.3.1. timp,perc,harp,
strings
ESCHIG perf mat rent (E150)

Poeme Symphonique No. 3 *Op.34 [17']
3.3.3.3. 4.4.3.1. timp,perc,harp,
strings
ESCHIG perf mat rent (E151)

Requiem, Op. 18 for Orchestra
3.3.3.3. 4.4.3.1. timp,harp,
strings
[20'] ESCHIG perf mat rent (E152)

Symphony, Op. 37 [30']
3.3.3.3. 4.4.3.1. timp,perc,harp,
strings
ESCHIG perf mat rent (E153)

EL Y ELLOS, FOR VIOLIN AND ORCHESTRA
see Enriquez, Manuel

ELATIO see Chavez, Carlos

ELEGIA AND TARANTELLA, FOR DOUBLE BASS
AND ORCHESTRA see Bottesini,
Giovanni

ELEGIA D'ESTATE see Cusatelli,
Alessandro

ELEGIA IN MEMORIAM CARLOS CHAVEZ see
Halffter, Rodolfo

ELEGIAC MUSIC IN MEMORIAM IGOR
STRAVINSKY see Falik, Yuri

ELEGIAC ODE see Stanford, Charles
Villiers

ELEGIAC SUITE, FOR SOLO VOICE AND
STRING ORCHESTRA see Stout, Alan

ELEGIAC SYMPHONY see Artyomov,
Vyacheslav see Harrison, Lou

ELEGIAC SYMPHONY: ELEGY III see
Artyomov, Vyacheslav

ELEGIAC VARIATIONS, FOR VIOLONCELLO AND
ORCHESTRA see Fisher, Alfred

ELEGIE IN MEMORY OF DARIUS MILHAUD see
Tansman, Alexandre

ELEGIE VOOR BIEKE see Eyken, Ernest Van
Der

ELEGIENSINFONIE see Artyomov,
Vyacheslav, Elegiac Symphony

ELEGIES, FOR HARP AND STRING ORCHESTRA
see MacBride, David Huston

ELEGISCHE MUSIK ZUM GEDENKEN AN I.
STRAVINSKY see Falik, Yuri, Elegiac
Music In Memoriam Igor Stravinsky

ELEGY AND SCHERZO ALLA MARCIA see
Crosse, Gordon

ELEGY FOR A MASTER see Bales, Richard
Horner

ELEGY FOR A PRINCE, FOR SOLO VOICE AND
ORCHESTRA see Mathias, William

ELEGY FOR ASTRONAUTS see Ward-Steinman,
David

ELEGY FOR THE LONESOME ONES, FOR
CLARINET AND STRING ORCHESTRA see
Luening, Otto

ELEGY FOR VILHO LAMPI see Nordgren,
Pehr Henrik

ELEGY IN HONOUR OF IVAN SAMARIN see
Tchaikovsky, Piotr Ilyich

ELEGY "IN MEMORIAM WILLIAM MORRIS" see
Holst, Gustav

ELEGY ON THE DEATH AND BURIAL OF COCK
ROBIN, FOR SOLO VOICE AND STRINGS
see Steptoe, Roger

ELEGY, TRANSFORMATION, JUBILATION see
Somers, Harry Stewart

ELEPHANT IN THE DARK see Evangelista,
Jose

ELEUSISCHES FEST, EIN see Ambrosius,
Hermann

ELEVEN MEDITATIONS ON SETTLEMENT see
Tomasson, Jonas

ELEVEN PORTRAITS FOR ORCHESTRA see
Thomson, Virgil Garnett

ELEVEN SONGS "SHROPSHIRE", FOR SOLO
VOICE AND ORCHESTRA see Leichtling,
Alan

ELFEN POLKA see Strauss, Josef

ELFENTANZ see Lehar, Franz

ELFES, LES, FOR NARRATOR AND ORCHESTRA
see Badings, Henk

ELGAR, [SIR] EDWARD (WILLIAM)
(1857-1934)
Beau Brummel: Minuet [4']
2.2.2.2. 2.2.3.0. timp,perc,
strings
NOVELLO perf mat rent   (E154)

Carissima [5']
2.2.2.2. 2.2.3.0. harp,perc,
strings
NOVELLO perf mat rent   (E155)

ELGAR, [SIR] EDWARD (WILLIAM) (cont'd.)

Chanson De Matin
KALMUS A5594 sc $5.00, set $9.00,
pts $.75, ea.   (E156)

Chanson De Nuit
KALMUS A5582 sc $5.00, set $8.00,
pts $.75, ea.   (E157)

Concerto for Violin and Orchestra,
Op. 61
KALMUS A5893 sc $35.00, set $90.00,
perf mat rent   (E158)
min sc KALMUS K01529 $8.75   (E159)

Contrasts *Op.10,No.3
KALMUS A4341 sc $10.00, set $22.00,
perf mat rent
see Three Pieces, Op. 10   (E160)

Coronation March *Op.65
KALMUS A6454 sc $12.00, set $50.00,
pts $2.00, ea., perf mat rent
                             (E161)

Crown Of India Suite
KALMUS A6347 sc $20.00, set $50.00,
pts $2.00, ea., perf mat rent
                             (E162)

Crown Of India Suite: March Of The
Mogul Emperors [5']
2+pic.2.2+bass clar.2+contrabsn.
4.3.3.1. timp,perc,strings
KALMUS A6348 sc $8.00, set $30.00,
pts $1.25, ea., perf mat rent
                             (E163)

Empire March, The [5']
2+pic.2+English horn.2+bass
clar.2+contrabsn. 4.2.3.1.
timp,perc,harp,org,strings
BOOSEY perf mat rent   (E164)

Enigma Variations *Op.36
min sc EULENBURG EU00884 $7.00
                             (E165)

Falstaff *Op.68
KALMUS A6748 sc $50.00, set
$100.00, pts $4.00, ea., perf mat
rent   (E166)

Falstaff: Two Interludes
KALMUS A7240 set $10.00, pts
$20.00, $1.25, ea., perf mat rent
                             (E167)

Froissart Overture
KALMUS A5743 sc $25.00, set $40.00,
perf mat rent   (E168)

Gavotte
(Schmid) 2(pic).2.2.2. 4.2.3.0.
timp,perc,opt harp,strings [5']
KALMUS A4129 sc $5.00, set
$20.00, perf mat rent   (E169)

In The South *Op.50
KALMUS A5596 sc $35.00, perf mat
rent, set $80.00, pts $3.00, ea.
                             (E170)

Introduction And Allegro For String
Quartet And String Orchestra
*Op.47
string orch
min sc EULENBURG $5.95   (E171)
min sc KALMUS K00532 $4.25   (E172)

May Song
KALMUS A5626 sc $5.00, perf mat
rent, set $15.00, pts $1.00, ea.
                             (E173)

Mazurka
see Three Pieces, Op. 10

Minuet, Op. 21
KALMUS A4063 sc $5.00, set $12.00
                             (E174)

Pomp And Circumstance March No. 3 In
C Minor
KALMUS A5636 sc $12.00, perf mat
rent, set $30.00, pts $1.25, ea.
                             (E175)

Pomp And Circumstance March No. 4 In
G
KALMUS A5636 sc $10.00, perf mat
rent, set $25.00, pts $1.00, ea.
                             (E176)

Romance for Bassoon and Orchestra,
Op. 62
KALMUS A6346 sc $6.00, set $20.00,
pts $1.25, ea., perf mat rent
                             (E177)

Rosemary - That's For Remembrance
[3']
2.2.2.2. 2.2.2.0. perc,harp,
strings
NOVELLO perf mat rent   (E178)

Salut D'Amour [arr.] *Op.12
(Fraser, Donald) string orch
FENTONE   (E179)

Sea Pictures, For Solo Voice And
Orchestra
KALMUS A5724 sc $16.00, set $35.00,
pts $2.00, ea., perf mat rent
                             (E180)

ELGAR, [SIR] EDWARD (WILLIAM) (cont'd.)

Serenade Lyrique [2'30"]
2.2.2.2. 2.0.0.0. timp,harp,
strings
KALMUS A5595 sc $8.00, perf mat
rent, set $17.00, pts $1.00, ea.
                             (E181)

Serenade Mauresque
see Three Pieces, Op. 10

Serenade, Op. 20, in E minor
min sc KALMUS K01403 $4.00   (E182)
FENTONE   (E183)

Sospiri *Op.70
KALMUS A7243 sc $5.00, set $7.00,
pts $1.00, ea.   (E184)

Spanish Lady Suite, [arr.] [16']
string orch
(Young, Percy) NOVELLO perf mat
rent   (E185)

Starlight Express, The: Incidental
Music [80']
2(pic).2.2.2. 2.2.2.0. 3perc,
harp,org,strings,SBar soli,
barrel org
NOVELLO perf mat rent   (E186)

Symphony No. 1, Op. 55, in A flat
3.3.3.3. 4.3.3.1. timp,perc,
2harp,strings
sc EULENBURG $20.00   (E187)
KALMUS A5042 sc $60.00, set
$150.00, perf mat rent   (E188)

Symphony No. 2, Op. 63
KALMUS A6120 sc $75.00, set
$175.00, perf mat rent   (E189)

Symphony No. 2, Op. 63, in E flat
3.3.4.3. 4.3.3.1. timp,perc,
2harp,strings
sc EULENBURG $20.00   (E190)
(includes facsimiles of composer's
sketches) sc NOVELLO 2941-90
$132.50   (E191)

Three Bavarian Dances *Op.27
KALMUS A5613 sc $30.00, perf mat
rent, set $50.00, pts $2.00, ea.
                             (E192)

Three Pieces, Op. 10
2(pic).2.2.2. 4.2.3.1. timp,2perc,
strings NOVELLO perf mat rent
contains: Contrasts; Mazurka;
Serenade Mauresque   (E193)

Three Pieces, Op. 10: Mazurka [5']
2(pic).2.2.2. 4.2.3.1. timp,perc,
strings
KALMUS A5583 sc $10.00, perf mat
rent, set $22.00, pts $1.00, ea.
                             (E194)
NOVELLO perf mat rent   (E195)

Three Songs, For Solo Voice And
Orchestra [7']
2.2.2.2. 2.0.3.0. harp,timp,
strings,A solo
NOVELLO perf mat rent   (E196)

Torch, The, For Solo Voice And
Orchestra *Op.60,No.1 [3']
3(pic).2.2.3(contrabsn). 4.3.3.1.
harp,timp,strings,low solo
NOVELLO perf mat rent   (E197)

Voix Dans Le Desert, Une, For Solo
Voice And Orchestra
2.2.2.2. 4.2.3.0. perc,strings,
Mez solo
NOVELLO perf mat rent   (E198)

Wand Of Youth Suite No. 1 *Op.1a
KALMUS A5644 sc $30.00, perf mat
rent, set $50.00, pts $2.00, ea.
                             (E199)

Wand Of Youth Suite No. 2 *Op.1b
KALMUS A5654 sc $35.00, perf mat
rent, set $70.00, pts $3.00, ea.
                             (E200)

ELIAS, BRIAN (1948-   )
Eylah, L' [22']
3.2+English horn.2+bass clar.2+
contrabsn. 4.3.3.1. timp,perc,
2harp,strings
CHESTER perf mat rent   (E201)

Five Songs To Poems By Irina
Ratushinkskaya, For Solo Voice
And Orchestra [28']
4(pic,alto fl).2+English
horn.2(clar in E flat)+bass
clar.2+contrabsn.
4.3(flügelhorn).2+bass trom.1.
timp,5perc,2harp,cel,strings,S
solo
CHESTER perf mat rent   (E202)

Somnia, For Solo Voice And Orchestra
[25']
2(pic).2.1+bass clar.2. 2.2.2.0.
timp,3perc,harp,pno&cel,

ELIAS, BRIAN (cont'd.)

strings,T solo
sc CHESTER f.s., perf mat rent
(E203)

ELIAS: HORE ISRAEL, FOR SOLO VOICE AND
ORCHESTRA see Mendelssohn-
Bartholdy, Felix

ELIASSON, ANDERS (1947-   )
Fantasy for Orchestra
2.2.2.2. 3.2.2.1. timp,perc,pno,
strings
STIM   (E204)

Ostacoli [14']
string orch
STIM   (E205)

Symphony No. 1 [30']
3.3.3.3. 4.3.3.1. timp,4perc,cel,
strings
STIM   (E206)

ELIJAH'S VIOLIN see Saxton, Robert

ELISEN POLKA see Strauss, Johann, [Jr.]

ELKA see Sommerfeldt, Öistein

ELLINGTON, EDWARD KENNEDY (DUKE)
(1899-1974)
Black, Brown & Beige [arr.]
(Ellington, Mercer; Whaley, Thomas)
3(pic).2+English horn.2+bass
clar.3(contrabsn).alto sax.opt
baritone sax. 4.3.3.1. timp,
2perc,harp,strings [38'] SCHIRM.G
perf mat rent   (E207)

Grand Slam Jam, For Piano, Clarinet,
Trumpet And Orchestra [8']
2.2(English horn).2(bass
clar).2.2alto sax.2tenor
sax.opt baritone sax. 4.4.3.1.
timp,2perc,harp,strings,pno
solo,clar solo,trp solo
SCHIRM.G perf mat rent   (E208)

Harlem [18']
2(pic).2.2(bass clar).2.2alto
sax.2tenor sax.opt baritone
sax. 4.3.3.1. timp,2perc,harp,
strings
SCHIRM.G perf mat rent   (E209)

New World A' Comin', For Piano And
Orchestra [arr.]
(Peress, Maurice) 2(pic).2.2+bass
clar.2. 4.4.3.1. timp,perc,harp,
strings,pno solo, opt dance band
[10'] SCHIRM.G perf mat rent
(E210)

Night Creature [17']
2.2.2(bass clar).2.2alto
sax.2tenor sax.opt baritone
sax. 4.4.3.1. timp,2perc,harp,
strings
SCHIRM.G perf mat rent   (E211)

Three Black Kings [15']
2+pic.2+English horn.2+bass
clar.2+contrabsn. 4.4.4.1.
timp,perc,pno,gtr,harp,strings
SCHIRM.G perf mat rent   (E212)

Three Black Kings, Concerto Grosso
Version [arr.]
(Henderson, Luther) 2+pic.2+English
horn.2+bass clar.3(contrabsn).
4.4.3+bass trom.1. timp,perc,pno,
harp,strings, jazz band: 5 reeds,
trap set, jazz bass SCHIRM.G perf
mat rent   (E213)
(Peress, Maurice) 3(pic).2+English
horn.2+bass clar.2(contrabsn).
4.4.3.1. timp,perc,harp,pno,
strings, E Flat Or B Flat Or C,
Solo Instrument [16'] SCHIRM.G
perf mat rent   (E214)

ELLIOTT, JACK
Great Galloping Gottschalk, For Piano
And Orchestra [27'30"]
3(alto fl,pic).2(English
horn).2(clar in E flat)+bass
clar.2. 4.3.3.1. timp,perc,
harp,strings,pno solo
NEWAM 19014 perf mat rent   (E215)

ELLIPSE EN CONCERT, FOR FLUTE AND
INSTRUMENTAL ENSEMBLE see Ferrero,
Lorenzo

ELLIPSIS see Liptak, David

ELLIS, DAVID GRAHAM
Images From A Twisted Dream
UNITED MUS   (E216)

ELM IS SCATTERING, THE, FOR OBOE AND
ORCHESTRA see White, David Ashley

ELMSLY, JOHN
Neither From Nor Towards [8']
string orch
sc WAI-TE-ATA f.s.   (E217)

ELOGES, FOR SOLO VOICE AND ORCHESTRA
see Arteaga, Angel

ELOGIO DE LA SOMBRA see Pernaiachi,
Gianfranco

ELOS, E. GIUSEPPE (1956-   )
Petit Air, For Solo Voice And
Orchestra [9']
3.3.2.2. 4.2.1.0. 3perc,cel,harp,
strings,med solo
SONZOGNO perf mat rent   (E218)

ELOY, JEAN-CLAUDE (1938-   )
Fluctuante-Immuable
4.4.4.4. 4.4.4.4. 2perc,vibra,
marimba,pno,cel,org,2harp,
strings
AMPHION perf mat rent   (E219)

ELWELL, HERBERT (1898-1974)
Pastorale for Solo Voice and
Orchestra
ACCURA perf mat rent   (E220)

EMBORG, JENS LAURSON (1876-1957)
Chamber Concerto
sc,pts SAMFUNDET f.s.   (E221)

Concerto for Organ and Orchestra
sc,pts SAMFUNDET f.s.   (E222)

Concerto for Strings and Piano
sc,pts SAMFUNDET f.s.   (E223)

Concerto Grosso, Op. 51
string orch,ob solo,vln solo,vcl
solo
KISTNER perf mat rent   (E224)

Fire Nordiske Danse
"Four Nordic Dances" sc SAMFUNDET
f.s.   (E225)

Four Nordic Dances
see Fire Nordiske Danse

Tolv Masker, De
"Twelve Masks, The" sc,pts
SAMFUNDET f.s.   (E226)

Twelve Masks, The
see Tolv Masker, De

EMBRACEABLE YOU, [ARR.] see Gershwin,
George

EMERALD REFLECTIONS see Hunt, Michael

EMERGENCE see Bon, Andre

EMERSON, KEITH
Concerto for Piano and Orchestra, No.
1 [18']
3.2.2.3. 4.3.3.1. timp,2perc,
strings,pno solo
PRESSER perf mat rent   (E227)

EMILSSON, ANDERS (1963-   )
Romance for Violin and String
Orchestra [10']
string orch,vln solo
sc GEHRMANS 6274P f.s., perf mat
rent   (E228)

EMIRA: SINFONIA see Leo, Leonardo
(Ortensio Salvatore de)

EMKAHESA see Arrachart, J.M.

EMMANUEL, MAURICE (1862-1938)
Salamine: Overture [5'30"]
CHOUDENS perf mat rent   (E229)

Symphony No. 2 in A [19']
3(pic).3(English horn).3(bass
clar).4(contrabsn). 4.0.3.1.
timp,perc,2harp,strings
(Symphonie Bretonne) LEMOINE perf
mat rent   (E230)

EMMER, HUIB (1951-   )
Reel World, The, For Oboe And
Orchestra [14']
1.0.2.0. 1.2.2.0. perc,pno,Hamm,
strings,ob solo
DONEMUS perf mat rent   (E231)

EMMERIK, IVO VAN (1961-   )
Architektur Der Ebene [7']
3.3.3.3. 2.2.3.1. 2perc,2pno,
strings
sc DONEMUS f.s., perf mat rent
(E232)

EMOTIONEN, FOR VIOLA, DOUBLE BASS AND
STRING ORCHESTRA see Fürst, Paul
Walter

EMPEROR AND GALILEAN see Saeverud,
Harald

EMPEROR AND THE NIGHTINGALE, THE see
Speight, John A.

EMPEROR OF PORTUGALLIA, THE see
Söderlundh, Lille Bror, Kejsarn Av
Portugallien

EMPEROR'S NEW CLOTHES, THE, FOR
NARRATOR AND ORCHESTRA see Brott,
Alexander

EMPFINDSAMES KONZERT, EIN, FOR DOUBLE
BASS AND ORCHESTRA see Schwertsik,
Kurt

EMPIRE MARCH, THE see Elgar, [Sir]
Edward (William)

EMPIRE STRIKES BACK, THE: SYMPHONIC
SUITE see Williams, John T.

EMPIRICAL RAG see Fennelly, Brian

EMPREINTES see Xenakis, Yannis (Iannis)

EN ATTENDANT see Mori, Kurodo

EN ETSI VALTAA LOISTOA, FOR SOLO VOICE
AND STRING ORCHESTRA [ARR.] see
Sibelius, Jean

EN GUISE DE FETE, FOR SOLO VOICE AND
CHAMBER ORCHESTRA see Evangelista,
Jose

EN MER, LA NUIT, VERSION A see
Koechlin, Charles

EN MER, LA NUIT, VERSION B see
Koechlin, Charles

EN MINIATUR POLKA see Strauss, Eduard

EN PASSANT FOR VIOLIN AND ORCHESTRA see
Miyoshi, Akira

EN SOI LOINTAIN see Miyoshi, Akira

EN TAILLE DOUCE see DuBois, Pierre-Max

ENCHANTED FOREST, THE see Gavrilin,
Valery

ENCHANTED LOOM, THE see Kolb, Barbara

ENCHANTED MIDNIGHT, THE see Weber, Ben
Brian

ENCLAVES, FOR VIOLONCELLO AND ORCHESTRA
see Lenot, Jacques

ENCORE CONCERTO, THE see Gillis, Don E.

ENCORE (ON A THEME OF SCOTT JOPLIN) see
Josephs, Wilfred

ENCORE PER ORCHESTRA see Berio, Luciano

ENCOUNTER, FOR PIANO AND ORCHESTRA see
Rudhyar, Dane (Daniel Chennevière)

ENCOUNTERS I-IX see Turner, Robert
[Comrie]

ENDECHA PARA UNA ENCORDADURA see Otero,
Francisco

ENDLER, JOHANN SAMUEL (1694-1762)
Ouverture In D
see Suite in D

Suite in D
"Ouverture In D" ob,3trp,timp,
strings,cont,vln solo sc KUNZEL
10200 f.s., perf mat rent (E233)

Symphonies, Three
see Graupner, Christoph,
Symphonies, Four

ENDO, MASAO (1947-   )
Zephyr With Outstretched Wings, For
Violin And Orchestra [18']
JAPAN 8601   (E234)

ENDYMION NOCTURNES, FOR SOLO VOICE AND
ORCHESTRA see Cowie, Edward

ENESCO, GEORGES (ENESCU) (1881-1955)
Intermezzo, Op. 12, in D
string orch
SALABERT perf mat rent   (E235)

Konzertstück for Viola and Orchestra
[7']
2.2+English horn.2.2. 3.2.2.1.
timp,perc,harp,strings,vla solo
ENOCH perf mat rent   (E236)

Poeme Roumain *Op.1 [26']
3.2+English horn.2.2. 4.2+
2cornet.3.1. timp,perc,2harp,
strings
ENOCH perf mat rent   (E237)

ENESCO, GEORGES (ENESCU) (cont'd.)

Rumanian Rhapsody No. 1 In A [11']
3.2+English horn.2.2. 4.2+
2cornet.3.1. timp,perc,2harp,
strings
ENOCH perf mat rent   (E238)

Rumanian Rhapsody No. 2 In D [7']
3.2+English horn.2.2. 4.2.3.0.
timp,perc,2harp,strings
ENOCH perf mat rent   (E239)

Suite No. 1, Op. 9 [22']
2+pic.2(English horn).2.2.
4.2.3.0. perc,harp,strings
ENOCH perf mat rent   (E240)
KALMUS A5761 sc $40.00, set $90.00,
perf mat rent   (E241)

Symphonie Concertante for Violoncello
and Orchestra, Op. 8 [18']
2.2(English horn).2.2. 4.2.3.0.
timp,strings,vcl solo
ENOCH perf mat rent   (E242)
KALMUS A5862 sc $35.00, set $60.00,
perf mat rent   (E243)

Symphony, Op. 13, in E flat
ENOCH perf mat rent   (E244)
KALMUS A5762 sc $60.00, set
$190.00, perf mat rent   (E245)

ENFANCE DU CHRIST, L': PRELUDE, PART
II, "LA FUITE EN EGYPTE" see
Berlioz, Hector (Louis)

ENFANCES DE LA FONTAINE, FOR SOLO VOICE
AND ORCHESTRA see Tomasi, Henri

ENFANT APPELLE, UN, FOR SOLO VOICE,
VIOLONCELLO AND ORCHESTRA see
Landowski, Marcel

ENFANT ROI, L', FOR SOLO VOICE AND
ORCHESTRA see Gagnon, Alain

ENFANT, SI J'ETAIS ROI, FOR SOLO VOICE
AND ORCHESTRA [ARR.] see Liszt,
Franz

ENGEL, FOR SOLO VOICES AND INSTRUMENTAL
ENSEMBLE see Rihm, Wolfgang

ENGEL, JAN
Symphonies, Vol. 2
(Muchenberg) 0.2.0.1. 2.0.0.0.
strings POLSKIE f.s.
contains: Symphony in B flat;
Symphony in D minor; Symphony
in F   (E246)

Symphony in B flat
see Symphonies, Vol. 2

Symphony in D minor
see Symphonies, Vol. 2

Symphony in F
see Symphonies, Vol. 2

ENGEL, [A.] LEHMANN (1910-1982)
Creation, The, For Narrator And
Orchestra [30']
3.3.3.3. 4.3.3.1. timp,perc,harp,
pno&cel,strings,narrator
sc AMP f.s., perf mat rent   (E247)

ENGEL, PAUL (1949-)
Concerto for Violoncello and
Orchestra [24']
2(pic).1.1.2(contrabsn). 2.1.1.0.
harp,perc,strings,vcl solo
DOBLINGER perf mat rent   (E248)

Kammersinfonie
3(alto fl,pic).2+2English
horn.2.3(contrabsn). 4.2.2.1.
timp,perc,harp,pno&cel&
harmonium,strings
(Ein Sommerspiel) BÄREN. BA 7180
(E249)

Passage, Le [23']
3(pic).3(English horn).3(bass
clar).3(contrabsn). 4.3.3.1.
timp,perc,harp,cel,strings
DOBLINGER perf mat rent   (E250)

Symphony No. 2 for Solo Voice and
Orchestra [65']
3(pic,alto fl).3(English
horn).3(bass clar,clar in E
flat).3(contrabsn).
4.3.3.1.2baritone horn. timp,
perc,harp,pno,cel&harmonium&
org,hpsd,strings,Bar solo
DOBLINGER perf mat rent   (E251)

Symphony No. 3 [50']
4(pic,alto fl).3(English
horn).4(clar in E flat,bass
clar)+contrabass
clar.3(contrabsn). 4+baritone
horn.3.3.1. timp,perc,2harp,
pno,cel,strings,Bar solo,cor
DOBLINGER perf mat rent   (E252)

ENGEL, PAUL (cont'd.)

Widerhall [25']
4(pic,alto fl).3(English horn).3+
clar in E flat+bass
clar.3(contrabsn). 6.4.3.1.
timp,perc,harp,pno,cel,
harmonium&org,strings
DOBLINGER perf mat rent   (E253)

ENGELMANN, HANS ULRICH (1921-)
Sinfonia Da Camera, Op.46 [14']
1.1.1.1. 1.0.0.0. pno,strings
without db
BREITKOPF-W perf mat rent   (E254)

ENGEN, FOR KOTO AND ORCHESTRA see
Ichiyanagi, Toshi

ENGER, ELLING (1905-1979)
Festival Ouverture
see Festspel

Festspel *Op.18 [7']
3.2.2.2. 4.3.3.1. timp,perc,
strings
"Festival Ouverture" NORGE   (E255)

ENGFUHRUNG see Holliger, Heinz

ENGLAND'S CAROL see Lewis, John Aaron

ENGLISH ELEGY, AN see Brockless, Brian

ENGLISH OPERA, AN: OVERTURE see Haydn,
[Franz] Joseph

ENGLISH SUITE, AN see Parry, [Sir]
Charles Hubert Hastings

ENGLISH VIRGINALISTS
(Margola) string orch KALMUS A7320 sc
$7.00, set $7.00, pts $1.50, ea.
contains: Bull, John, Duchesse Of
Brunswick, The; Byrd, William,
Earle Of Oxford's March, The;
Farnaby, Giles, Put Up Thy
Dagger, Jenny; Philips, Peter,
Galiarda   (E256)

ENGLUND, EINAR (1916-)
Concerto for Flute and Orchestra
[22']
3.2.2.2. 4.3.3.0. timp,4perc,
harp,cel&hpsd,strings,fl solo
sc SUOMEN f.s.   (E257)

Symphony No. 4 [23']
2perc,strings
sc FAZER f.s., perf mat rent (E258)

Symphony No. 6
sc FAZER f.s.   (E259)

ENGRAVINGS IN SOUND see Frost, Robert
S.

ENGSTROM, TORBJORN (1963-)
Concertino for Vibraphone, Marimba
and Orchestra
2.2.2.2. 4.2.3.1. timp,strings,
vibra solo,marimba solo
STIM   (E260)

Riverrun [10']
2.2.2.2. 2.2.2.0. timp,strings
STIM   (E261)

ENIGMA VARIATIONS see Elgar, [Sir]
Edward (William)

ENIWETOCK see Travlos, Michael

ENKELIEN JOULULAULU, FOR SOLO VOICE AND
ORCHESTRA [ARR.] see Madetoja,
Leevi

ENLACEMENTS INFINIS, FOR SOLO VOICE AND
INSTRUMENTAL ENSEMBLE see Miereanu,
Costin

ENNEADES, FOR BASSOON AND ORCHESTRA see
Roizenblat, A.

ENRIQUEZ, MANUEL (1926-)
El Y Ellos, For Violin And Orchestra
1.0.1.1. 1.1.1.0. perc,strings,
vln solo
"He And They, For Violin And
Orchestra" MEXICANAS perf mat
rent   (E262)

He And They, For Violin And Orchestra
see El Y Ellos, For Violin And
Orchestra

Raices
2+pic.2+English horn.2+bass
clar.1+contrabsn. 4.4.3.1.
4perc,strings
TONOS   (E263)

ENSEIGNE DE GERSAINT see Damase, Jean-
Michel

ENSEMBLE FOR STRINGS see Otte, Hans

ENSEMBLE-KONZERT see Goldmann,
Friedrich

ENTELECHIAE see Helmschrott, Robert M.

ENTELECHIE II, FOR SOLO VOICE AND
INSTRUMENTAL ENSEMBLE see Schat,
Peter

ENTERTAINER, THE [ARR.] see Joplin,
Scott

ENTFÜHRUNG AUS DEM SERAIL, DIE: DURCH
ZÄRTLICHKEIT, FOR SOLO VOICE AND
ORCHESTRA see Mozart, Wolfgang
Amadeus

ENTFUHRUNG AUS DEM SERAIL, DIE: FRISCH
ZUM KAMPFE! FRISCH ZUM STREITE!,
FOR SOLO VOICE AND ORCHESTRA see
Mozart, Wolfgang Amadeus

ENTFUHRUNG AUS DEM SERAIL, DIE: HA! WIE
WILL ICH TRIUMPHIEREN, FOR SOLO
VOICE AND ORCHESTRA see Mozart,
Wolfgang Amadeus

ENTFUHRUNG AUS DEM SERAIL, DIE: ICH
BAUE GANZ AUF DEINE STARKE, FOR
SOLO VOICE AND ORCHESTRA see
Mozart, Wolfgang Amadeus

ENTFÜHRUNG AUS DEM SERAIL, DIE: MARTERN
ALLER ARTEN, FOR SOLO VOICE AND
ORCHESTRA see Mozart, Wolfgang
Amadeus

ENTFUHRUNG AUS DEM SERAIL, DIE:
OVERTURE see Mozart, Wolfgang
Amadeus

ENTFUHRUNG AUS DEM SERAIL, DIE: WELCHE
WONNE, WELCHE LUST, FOR SOLO VOICE
AND ORCHESTRA see Mozart, Wolfgang
Amadeus

ENTFUHRUNG AUS DEM SERAIL, DIE: WENN
DER FREUDE TRANEN FLIESSEN, FOR
SOLO VOICE AND ORCHESTRA see
Mozart, Wolfgang Amadeus

ENTGEGEN see Nordentoft, Anders

ENTRANCE OF LES PORTEUSES see Still,
William Grant

ENTRATA see Berio, Luciano

ENTUZIAZMI GAMA see Stuhec, Igor

ENTWEDER ODER POLKA see Strauss,
Johann, [Jr.]

ENVOI, FOR PIANO AND INSTRUMENTAL
ENSEMBLE see Tremblay, Gilles

EOLIDES, LES see Franck, Cesar

EOS, FOR DOUBLE BASS AND ORCHESTRA see
Guy, Barry

EÖTVÖS, PÊTER (1944-)
Chinese Opera [35']
2.2.3.2. 2.2.2.1. 3perc,harp,
2vln,2vla,2vcl,db,synthesizer
SALABERT perf mat rent   (E264)

Pierre-Idyll [10']
alto fl,ob d'amore,English horn,
2clar,bass clar,2bsn,2horn,
2perc,pno,2vln,vla,vcl,db
SALABERT perf mat rent   (E265)

EPH-PHATHA see Finnissy, Michael

EPHEMERON see Perlongo, Daniel James

EPHRATA, FOR FOUR PERCUSSION SOLI AND
ORCHESTRA see Eberhard, Dennis

EPICURE: OVERTURE see Cherubini, Luigi

EPICYCLE, FOR VIOLONCELLO, AND
INSTRUMENTAL ENSEMBLE see Xenakis,
Yannis (Iannis)

EPIGRAM see Lillebjerka, Sigmund

EPIGRAMME see Walter, Fried

EPILOG see Berg, Olav see Eckerberg,
Sixten

EPILOG NACH HOMERS ODYSSEE, FOR SOLO
VOICES AND ORCHESTRA see Antoniou,
Theodore

EPILOGUE see Grisey, Gerard see
Wallace, William

EPILOGUE JOYEUX see Dewanger, Anton

EPIONEN TANZE see Strauss, Johann,
[Sr.]

EPIPHYT, FOR FLUTE AND CHAMBER
ORCHESTRA see Hübler, Klaus-K.

EPISODES see Lukaszewski, Wojciech see
Michans, Carlos

EPISODES CONCERTANTES see Srebotnjak,
Alojz F., Koncertantne Epizode

EPISODI see Theorin, Hakan

EPISODI, FOR OBOE AND STRING ORCHESTRA
see Kocsar, Miklos

EPITAFFIO AGITATO see Ullman, Bo

EPITAFFIO IN MEMORIAM SZABÓ FERENC see
Sarai, Tibor

EPITAFION see Nordal, Jon

EPITAPH see Bentzon, Niels Viggo see
Denisov, Edison Vasilievich see
Holmboe, Vagn see Pitfield, Thomas
Baron

EPITAPH FROM AQUINCUM, FOR SOLO VOICE
AND ORCHESTRA see Decsenyi, Janos

EPITAPH FÜR HINGERICHTETE see Schollum,
Robert

EPITAPHE POUR ENESCO see Taranu, Cornel

EPITAPHIUM see Pleskow, Raoul

EPITAPHIUM: STEFAN WOLPE IN MEMORIAM
see Pleskow, Raoul

EPYLLION, FOR VIOLONCELLO AND STRINGS
see Maconchy, Elizabeth

ERA LA NOTTE, FOR SOLO VOICE,
HARPSICHORD AND ORCHESTRA see
Pennisi, Francesco

ERB, DONALD (1927-   )
Concerto For Brass And Orchestra
3.3.3.3. 3.4.3.1. timp,3perc,
harp,kbd,strings
study sc MERION $38.50, perf mat
rent   (E266)

Concerto for Clarinet and Orchestra
[15']
2(pic).2.3.2(contrabsn). 2.2.2.0.
timp,2perc,kbd,harp,strings,
clar solo
MERION perf mat rent   (E267)

Concerto for Contrabassoon and
Orchestra [13']
3.2.3.2. 4.3.3.1. timp,5perc,
harp,pno,cel,org,strings,
contrabsn solo
MERION perf mat rent   (E268)

Concerto for Flute and Orchestra
MERION perf mat rent   (E269)

Concerto For Keyboards And Orchestra
[20']
3.2.3.3. 4.3.3.1. timp,perc,
kbds, harp, strings
MERION perf mat rent   (E270)

Concerto for Orchestra [20']
3.3.3.3. 4.3.3.1. timp,3perc,
harp, kbds, strings
MERION perf mat rent   (E271)

Dreamtime [12']
3.2.3.3. 4.3.3.1. timp,3perc,
harp, kbds, strings
MERION perf mat rent   (E272)

Honor, Honor, For Solo Voice And
String Orchestra [5']
string orch,solo voice
MERION perf mat rent   (E273)

Prismatic Variations [16']
3.3.3.3. 4.3.3.1. timp,3perc,
kbds, harp, strings
MERION perf mat rent   (E274)

ERBSE, HEIMO (1924-   )
Sieben Skizzen In Form Einer Alten
Suite, For Violoncello And
Chamber Orchestra *Op.34a
perc,harp,cel,pno,strings,vcl
solo
[20'] (Alternate scoring: piano,
strings, cello solo) DOBLINGER
perf mat rent   (E275)

ERDLEN, HERMANN (1893-1972)
Drei Finnische Suiten
KISTNER perf mat rent   (E276)

ERDMANN, DIETRICH (1917-   )
Concertino for Violin and Orchestra
[18']
1.1.1.1. 1.0.0.0. perc,strings,
vln solo
BREITKOPF-W perf mat rent   (E277)

Concertino for Violoncello and
Chamber Orchestra [23']
1.1.1.1. 1.0.0.0. perc,vln,vla,
vcl,db,vcl solo
BREITKOPF-W perf mat rent   (E278)

Concertino Grazioso, For Recorder And
String Orchestra [13']
string orch,rec solo
BREITKOPF-W perf mat rent   (E279)

Konzertstück for Alto Saxophone and
Orchestra [6']
BREITKOPF-W perf mat rent   (E280)

Serenita Notturna
string orch
BREITKOPF-W perf mat rent   (E281)

ERGO INTEREST; QUAERE SUPERNA, FOR SOLO
VOICE AND ORCHESTRA see Mozart,
Wolfgang Amadeus

ERHARD, KARL (1928-   )
Invention
BOHM perf mat rent   (E282)

ERICKSON, FRANK WILLIAM (1923-   )
Irish Folk Song Suite [8'30"]
1.1.2.0.alto sax.tenor sax.
1.3.3.1. timp,perc,pno,strings
BOURNE perf mat rent   (E283)

ERICKSON, ROBERT (1917-   )
Auroras
SEESAW   (E284)

Rainbow Rising
SEESAW   (E285)

ERICSSON, HANS-OLA (1958-   )
Musik För En Sjuk Varld
1.1.1.1. 1.0.0.0. pno,strings,vla
solo
STIM   (E286)

ERIDANOS see Xenakis, Yannis (Iannis)

ERIKHTHON, FOR PIANO AND ORCHESTRA see
Xenakis, Yannis (Iannis)

ERIKSON, AKE (1937-   )
Fanfar Till Uppsala Stads 700-
Arsjubileum
STIM   (E287)

ERIN, FOR DOUBLEBASS AND ORCHESTRA see
Casken, John

ERINDRINGER, FOR SOLO VOICE ABD STRING
ORCHESTRA see Lunde, Ivar

ERINNERUNG see Mahler, Gustav

ERINNERUNG AN COVENT GARDEN WALZER see
Strauss, Johann, [Jr.]

ERIS see Boer, Ed de

ERKANIAN, EDVAND (1951-   )
Chamber Symphony No. 3 [12']
1.1.1.1. 2.0.0.0. perc,hpsd,pno,
14strings
SIKORSKI perf mat rent   (E288)
VAAP perf mat rent   (E289)

Orest: Suite [25']
3.3.4.3. 4.3.3.1. timp,perc,harp,
strings
SIKORSKI perf mat rent   (E290)

Symphony No. 1 [18']
4.3.4.3. 4.4.3.1. timp,perc,harp,
pno,strings
SIKORSKI perf mat rent   (E291)

ERKEL, FRANZ (FERENC) (1810-1893)
Hungarian National Anthem
sc,pts EMB 6475 f.s.   (E292)

ERMIONE: OVERTURE see Rossini,
Gioacchino

ERNANI: COME RUGIADA AL CESPITE, FOR
SOLO VOICE AND ORCHESTRA see Verdi,
Giuseppe

ERNANI: ESCI...A TE, FOR SOLO VOICES
AND ORCHESTRA see Verdi, Giuseppe

ERNANI: LO VEDREMO, VEGLIO AUDACE, FOR
SOLO VOICE AND ORCHESTRA see Verdi,
Giuseppe

ERNANI: OH DE' VERD' ANNI MIEI, FOR
SOLO VOICE AND ORCHESTRA see Verdi,
Giuseppe

ERNANI: ORO, QUANT ORO, FOR SOLO VOICES
AND ORCHESTRA see Verdi, Giuseppe

ERNANI: QUI MI TRASSE AMOR POSSENTE,
FOR SOLO VOICES AND ORCHESTRA see
Verdi, Giuseppe

ERNANI: SOLINGO, ERRANTE, MISERO, FOR
SOLO VOICES AND ORCHESTRA see
Verdi, Giuseppe

ERNESTINE: DUO, FOR SOLO VOICES AND
ORCHESTRA see Saint-Georges, Joseph
Boulogne de

ERNST LUDWIG, LANDGRAF VON HESSEN
(1667-1739)
Easy Suite
strings,hpsd [8'] KALMUS A7097 sc
$8.00, set $10.00, pts $2.00, ea.
(E293)

ERNST UND HUMOR WALZER see Strauss,
Josef

ERÖD, IVAN (1936-   )
Konzertante Fantasie, For Viola And
String Orchestra [11']
string orch,vla solo
DOBLINGER perf mat rent   (E294)

Krokodilslieder, For Solo Voice And
Chamber Orchestra [14']
1.1.1.1. 1.1.0.0. perc,pno,
strings,Bar solo
DOBLINGER perf mat rent   (E295)

Rejouissance *Op.48 [7']
2(pic).2.2+clar in E flat.2+
contrabsn. 4.4.3.1. timp,perc,
strings
DOBLINGER perf mat rent   (E296)

Schwarzerde, For Solo Voice And
Orchestra *Op.49 [20']
2(pic)+alto fl.2+English horn.2+
bass clar.2+contrabsn. 4.3.3.1.
timp,perc,harp,strings,Bar solo
study sc DOBLINGER STP 603 f.s.,
perf mat rent   (E297)

Sinfonietta, Op. 51 [15']
3(pic,alto fl).2+English
horn.3(clar in E flat)+bass
clar.2+contrabsn. 4.3.3.1.
timp,perc,harp,strings
(Minnesota Sinfonietta) study sc
DOBLINGER STP 620 f.s., perf mat
rent   (E298)

Soirees Imaginaires [20']
2(pic).2(English horn).2+bass
clar.2. 4.3.3.1. timp,perc,
harp,strings
DOBLINGER perf mat rent   (E299)

Studien [10']
string orch
DOBLINGER perf mat rent   (E300)

Symphonische Szene *Op.46 [13']
2+pic.2+English horn.2+bass
clar.2+contrabsn. 4.3.3.1.
timp,perc,harp,cel,pno,strings
(Hommage A Franz Liszt) study sc
DOBLINGER STP 635 f.s., perf mat
rent   (E301)

Vox Lucis, For Solo Voice, Oboe And
Orchestra *Op.56 [30']
2(pic)+alto fl.0.2+bass clar.2.
2.0.0.1. timp,perc,cel,harp,
strings,Bar solo,ob solo
DOBLINGER perf mat rent   (E302)

EROISMO RIDICOLO, L': OVERTURE see
Spontini, Gaspare

EROS, FOR SOLO VOICE AND ORCHESTRA see
Vierne, Louis

EROS, FOR SOLO VOICES AND ORCHESTRA see
Finke, Fidelio Friedrich (Fritz)

EROS PIANO, FOR PIANO AND ORCHESTRA see
Adams, John

ERSTE ABGESANGSSZENE see Rihm, Wolfgang

ERSTEN CUREN WALZER, DIE see Strauss,
Johann, [Jr.]

ERSTEN UND DIE LETZTEN, DIE see
Strauss, Josef

ERSTER DOPPELGESANG, FOR VIOLA,
VIOLONCELLO AND ORCHESTRA see Rihm,
Wolfgang

ERUPTION AT HEIMAEY see Halldorsson,
Skuli

ERUPTIONS see Kalbfleisch, Rodger

ERYNNIES, LES see Massenet, Jules

ES-KAMMERKONZERT see Chailly, Luciano

ES-KONZERT see Chailly, Luciano

ES LÄCHELT DER SEE, FOR SOLO VOICES AND
ORCHESTRA see Eisler, Hanns

ES LIEGT EIN SCHLOSS IN OSTERREICH, FOR
CLARINET AND CHAMBER ORCHESTRA see
Kubizek, Augustin

ES MUSS EIN WUNDERBARES SEIN, FOR SOLO
VOICE AND ORCHESTRA [ARR.] see
Liszt, Franz

ES WAR EIN KONIG IN THULE, FOR SOLO
VOICE AND ORCHESTRA see Liszt,
Franz

ES WAR EINMAL EIN KONIG, FOR SOLO VOICE
AND ORCHESTRA [ARR.] see Beethoven,
Ludwig van

ESCAPADES see Bull, Edvard Hagerup

ESCAPE see Rossem, Andries van

ESCENAS CAMPESTRAS, FOR SOLO VOICES AND
ORCHESTRA see Gottschalk, Louis
Moreau

ESCENAS DE CORTES Y PASTORES see
Orrego-Salas, Juan A.

ESCENIA Y DANZA CHARRA see Gombau,
Gerardo

ESCHER, RUDOLF GEORGE (1912-1980)
Concerto for String Orchestra, Op. 14
[14']
timp,strings
DONEMUS perf mat rent   (E303)

  Passacaglia [13']
  4.4.4.4.2sax. 4.5.3.1. timp,
  4perc,2harp,cel,org,strings
  DONEMUS perf mat rent   (E304)

  Summer Rites At Noon, For 2
  Orchestras [arr.]
  (Vlijmen, Jan Van) 3.4.5.5.2sax.
  4.5.5.5. 12perc,3pno,2harp,
  strings [22'] sc DONEMUS f.s.,
  perf mat rent   (E305)

ESCORIAL see Marco, Tomas

ESCRIBANO, MARIA (1954-   )
Ejercicio Poetico
1+pic.1.1.1. 1.1.1.1. perc,harp,
vla,vcl,pno
ALPUERTO   (E306)

ESCUDERO, FRANCISCO (1913-   )
Concerto for Violoncello and
Orchestra
2+pic.1.2+bass clar.1. 2.1.1.0.
timp,2perc,harp,cel,strings,vcl
solo
ALPUERTO   (E307)

  Sinfonia Sacra
  ob,English horn,bsn,strings
  ALPUERTO   (E308)

ESHPAI, ANDREY Y. (1925-   )
Concerto For 4 Solo Instruments And
Orchestra [14']
3.2.3.3. 4.3.3.1. timp,perc,harp,
strings,trp solo,pno solo,vibra
solo,db solo
SIKORSKI perf mat rent   (E309)
VAAP perf mat rent   (E310)

  Concerto for Oboe and Orchestra [24']
  4(pic).2.2.2. 4.3.3.1. timp,perc,
  harp,hpsd,pno,strings,ob solo
  VAAP perf mat rent   (E311)

  Concerto for Piano and Orchestra, No.
  1 [21']
  3.3.3.2. 4.3.3.1. timp,perc,harp,
  cel,strings,pno solo
  SIKORSKI perf mat rent   (E312)
  SIKORSKI perf mat rent   (E313)

  Concerto for Piano and Orchestra, No.
  2 [18']
  2+pic+alto fl.2+English horn.2.2+
  contrabsn. 4.3.3.1. timp,perc,
  harp,strings,pno solo
  VAAP perf mat rent   (E314)

  Concerto for Piano and Orchestra, Op.
  4 [28']
  timp,perc,org,strings,pno solo
  VAAP perf mat rent   (E315)

  Concerto for Saxophone and Orchestra
  [25']
  2+pic.2.2+bass clar.2. 4.3.3.1.
  timp,2perc,harp,gtr,strings,sax
  solo
  sc UNIVER. UE18692 f.s., perf mat
  rent   (E316)

ESHPAI, ANDREY Y. (cont'd.)
  Concerto for Viola and Orchestra
  [26']
  sc MUZÝKA f.s.   (E317)

  Concerto for Violin and Orchestra,
  No. 1 [26']
  3(pic).2+English horn.2(clar in
  A).2. 4.3.3.1. timp,perc,harp,
  strings,vln solo
  VAAP perf mat rent   (E318)

  Concerto for Violin and Orchestra,
  No. 2 [26']
  3.2.2.2. 4.3.3.1. timp,perc,harp,
  cel,strings,vln solo
  SIKORSKI perf mat rent   (E319)

  Concerto Grosso
  3.2.3.3. 4.3.3.1. timp,perc,harp,
  pno,strings
  VAAP perf mat rent   (E320)

  Festival Overture For Big Band And
  String Orchestra [6']
  2alto sax,2tenor sax,baritone
  sax,4trp,4trom,perc,pno,gtr,
  strings
  SIKORSKI perf mat rent   (E321)

  Hungarian Tunes, For Violin And
  Orchestra [14']
  3(pic).2+English horn.2.2.
  4.3.3.1. timp,perc,harp,cel,
  pno,strings,vln solo
  VAAP perf mat rent   (E322)

  Songs Of The People Of Marree In
  Mountains And Meads, The [15']
  fl,horn,timp,harp,cel,strings
  VAAP perf mat rent   (E323)

  Symphony No. 1 [18']
  3(pic).3(English horn).3(bass
  clar).3(contrabsn). 4.3.3.1.
  timp,perc,harp,cel,strings
  VAAP perf mat rent   (E324)

  Symphony No. 2 [27']
  3.3.3.3. 4.4.3.1. timp,perc,
  2harp,pno,strings
  VAAP perf mat rent   (E325)

  Symphony No. 3 [22']
  3.2.2.2+contrabsn. 4.3.3.1. timp,
  perc,harp,cel,pno,strings
  VAAP perf mat rent   (E326)

  Symphony No. 4 [37']
  3.2.2.3. 4.3.3.1. timp,perc,cel,
  hpsd,pno,2harp,strings, jazz
  band: 6 sax, 4 trp, 4 trom,
  perc, 2 elec gtr
  SIKORSKI perf mat rent   (E327)
  VAAP perf mat rent   (E328)

  Symphony No. 5 [30']
  3+pic.2.2+bass clar.2+contrabsn.
  4.4.4.1. timp,perc,harp,cel,
  pno,strings
  VAAP perf mat rent   (E329)

ESPACE AU-DELA DU DERNIER see Miereanu,
Costin

ESPACE DU DEDANS, L' see Durville,
Philippe

ESPACE II see Miereanu, Costin

ESPANA see Chabrier, [Alexis-] Emmanuel

ESPANA, FOR VIOLONCELLO AND ORCHESTRA
see Klein, Lothar

ESPANA WALTZ see Waldteufel, Emile

ESPANSIONI see Kelterborn, Rudolf

ESPERANZA FOR SINFONIETTA see
Marcussen, Kjell

ESPLA, OSCAR (1886-1976)
Contrabandista, El [30']
3.3.2.2. 2.2.0.0. timp,perc,
castanets,harp,pno,strings
ESCHIG perf mat rent   (E330)

  Llama Del Amor Viva [20']
  2+pic.2(English horn).2.2.
  4.2.3.0. timp,perc,harp,pno,
  strings
  UNION ESP. perf mat rent   (E331)

  Noche Buena Del Diablo [40']
  3.3.3.3. 4.3.3.1. timp,perc,cel,
  2harp,strings
  ESCHIG perf mat rent   (E332)

  Pirata Cautivo, El
  2+pic.2+English horn.2+bass
  clar.2+contrabsn. 4.2.3.0.
  timp,perc,harp,strings
  UNION ESP. perf mat rent   (E333)

ESPRIT see Tatgenhorst, John

ESQUISSE A LA MEMOIR DE MAURICE RAVEL
see Philippot, Michel Paul

ESQUISSE I see Osborne, Nigel

ESQUISSE II see Osborne, Nigel

ESSAIMS-CRIBLES, FOR BASS CLARINET AND
INSTRUMENTAL ENSEMBLE see Jarrell,
Michael

ESSAY see Goeb, Roger

ESSAY FOR CLARINET AND ORCHESTRA see
Forbes, Sebastian

ESSAY FOR ORCHESTRA see Walker, Gwyneth

ESSAY NO. 3 see Barber, Samuel

ESSENCE AND DISTRACTIONS see Libbey,
Dee

ESSL, KARL HEINZ (1960-   )
O Tiempo Tus Piramides [20']
1(pic).1.1(clar in E flat,bass
clar).1. 1.1.1.0. 2perc,6vln,
3vla,2vcl,db
UNIVER. perf mat rent   (E334)

ESTAMPES JAPONAISES, FOR SOLO VOICE AND
INSTRUMENTAL ENSEMBLE see Mefano,
Paul

ESTAMPIE see Rodriguez, Robert Xavier

ESTANCIAS, FOR SOLO VOICE AND CHAMBER
ORCHESTRA see Fernandez Alvez,
Gabriel

ESTATE, L' see Eklund, Hans

ESTEVEZ, ANTONIO (1916-   )
Concerto for Orchestra [18']
2+pic.2.2+bass clar.2. 4.2.3.1.
timp,perc,pno,strings
sc ESCHIG f.s., perf mat rent
                                  (E335)

ESTEVEZ, FRANCISCO
Loa, For Doublebass And String
Orchestra [15']
string orch,db solo
sc ALPUERTO f.s.   (E336)

ESTHER: TURN NOT, O QUEEN, THY FACE
AWAY, FOR SOLO VOICE AND ORCHESTRA
see Handel, George Frideric

ESTONIAN FOLK DANCES see Tubin, Eduard

ESTRELLITA [ARR.] see Ponce, Manuel
Maria

ESTRO MELODICO, L' see Lajovic,
Aleksander

ET VERBUM CARO FACTUM EST see Donora,
Luigi

ETALAGE see Watkins, Michael Blake

ETAT D'HORIZON 3 see Lemeland, Aubert

ETCETERA, FOR 2-4 ORCHESTRAS see Cage,
John

ETENDRE see Rands, Bernard

ETERNAL CALM, FOR SOLO VOICE AND
CHAMBER ORCHESTRA see Smirnov,
Dmitri

ETERNAL LIGHT, THE, FOR SOLO VOICE AND
ORCHESTRA see Thorne, Francis
Burritt, Luce Eterna, La, For Solo
Voice And Orchestra

ETERNAL SPRING, FOR SOLO VOICE AND
ORCHESTRA see Eggen, Arne, Aere Det
Evige For Solo Soloaar I Levet, For
Voice And Orchestra

ETERNALLY PRESENT see Di Bari, Marco

ETERNITE, FOR SOLO VOICE AND ORCHESTRA
see Gougeon, Denis

ETERNITY'S SUNRISE see Neikrug, Marc E.

ETINCELLE DU SILEX, L' see Succari, Dia

ETLER, ALVIN [DERALD] (1913-1973)
Gehenna
2.1.2.1. 2.1.1.0. perc,pno,
strings
AMP perf mat rent   (E337)

ETRUSCAN CONCERTO, FOR PIANO AND
ORCHESTRA see Glanville-Hicks,
Peggy

ETTI, KARL (1912-   )
　Mozart Variationen, For Trumpet And
　　Orchestra [10']
　　　0.2.2.2. 0.0.0.0. strings,trp
　　　solo
　　DOBLINGER perf mat rent   (E338)

　Tuba Mirum. Mozart Paraphrase, For
　　Trombone And Orchestra [8']
　　　2clar,2bsn,strings,trom solo
　　DOBLINGER perf mat rent   (E339)

　Variationen Und Fuge Uber Ein Menuett
　　Von Paderewski [12']
　　　2(pic).2.2.2. 2.2.0.0. timp,perc,
　　　strings
　　BOTE perf mat rent   (E340)

　Variationen Und Fuge Uber Ein Thema
　　Von Joseph Haydn [11']
　　　1.2.2.2. 2.0.0.0. strings
　　DOBLINGER perf mat rent   (E341)

ETUDE I D'APRES GOYA see Tisne, Antoine

ETUDE SYMPHONIC see Nelhybel, Vaclav

ETUDES ANTIQUES, OP. 46, NO. 1: LES
　TEMPLES see Koechlin, Charles

ETUDES ANTIQUES, OP. 46, NO. 2: LE SOIR
　AU BORD DU LAC see Koechlin,
　Charles

ETUDES ANTIQUES, OP. 46, NO. 3: CORTEGE
　D'AMPHITRITE see Koechlin, Charles

ETUDES ANTIQUES, OP. 46, NO. 4:
　EPITAPHE D'UNE JEUNE FEMME see
　Koechlin, Charles

ETUDES ANTIQUES, OP. 46, NO. 5: LA JOIE
　PAIENNE see Koechlin, Charles

ETUDES [ARR.] see Chopin, Frédéric

ETUDES DE FLUX see Reibel, Guy

ETUDES FOR ORCHESTRA, NO. 1: ON THE
　BEACH see Nash, Peter Paul

ETUDES FOR ORCHESTRA, NO. 2: THE EMPTY
　BEACH see Nash, Peter Paul

ETUDES FOR ORCHESTRA, NO. 3: PARTING
　see Nash, Peter Paul

ETUDES FOR STRINGS see Suslin, Viktor

ETWAS WEITER see Lefebvre, Claude

ETYDE see Berg, Olav

EU TE AMO, FOR SOLO VOICE AND ORCHESTRA
　see Villa-Lobos, Heitor

EUGENE ONEGIN: ARIA OF LENSKI, FOR SOLO
　VOICE AND ORCHESTRA see
　Tchaikovsky, Piotr Ilyich

EUGENE ONEGIN: ARIA OF PRINCE GREMIN,
　FOR SOLO VOICE AND ORCHESTRA see
　Tchaikovsky, Piotr Ilyich

EUGENE ONEGIN: TRIQUET'S SONG, FOR SOLO
　VOICE AND ORCHESTRA see
　Tchaikovsky, Piotr Ilyich

EUGENIE GRANDET see Jurovsky, Vladimir

EUPHONIE, FOR STRING QUINTET AND STRING
　ORCHESTRA see Block, Hans Volker

EURIDICE, FOR FLUTE AND ORCHESTRA see
　Sigurbjörnsson, Thorkell

EUROPE, JAMES REESE (1881-1919)
　Castle House Rag [arr.]
　　(Schuller, Gunther) fl,clar,trp,
　　trom,tuba,drums,gtr,pno,2vln,vla,
　　vcl,db [4'] MARGUN MP2052 perf
　　mat rent   (E342)

　Castle Walk, The [arr.]
　　(Schuller, Gunther) fl,clar,trp,
　　trom,tuba,drums,gtr,pno,2vln,vla,
　　vcl,db [4'] MARGUN MP2053 perf
　　mat rent   (E343)

EUROPHONY see Patterson, Paul

EURYANTHE: GLOCKLEIN IM TALE, FOR SOLO
　VOICE AND ORCHESTRA see Weber, Carl
　Maria von

EVA BEFORE THE FALL OF MAN see Bergh,
　Sverre, Eva For Syndefallet

EVA FOR SYNDEFALLET see Bergh, Sverre

EVANGELISTA, JOSE (1943-   )
　Elephant In The Dark [12']
　　2.2.2.2. 2.0.2.0. vibra,pno,
　　strings
　　CAN.MUS.CENT. MI 1100 E92EL   (E344)

EVANGELISTA, JOSE (cont'd.)
　En Guise De Fete, For Solo Voice And
　　Chamber Orchestra [18']
　　　perc,vibra,harp,pno,4vln,2vla,
　　　2vcl,db,S solo
　　sc ALPUERTO f.s.   (E345)

　Miroir Fugace
　　14strings
　　ALPUERTO   (E346)

　Motionless Move [13']
　　1.1.1.0. 0.0.0.0. 2perc,harp,elec
　　gtr,2pno,2vln,vla,vcl,
　　synthesizer
　　SALABERT perf mat rent   (E347)

　Piano Concertant, For Piano And
　　Orchestra
　　　2.2.2.2. 2.2.0.0. vibra,strings,
　　　pno solo
　　CAN.MUS.CENT. MI 1361 E92PI   (E348)

EVE DREAMS IN PARADISE, FOR SOLO VOICE
　AND ORCHESTRA see Goehr, Alexander

EVE OF ST. JOHN KUPALO, THE see
　Grabovsky, Leonid

EVENING IN NEW ORLEANS, AN: SUITE see
　Coolidge, Peggy Stuart

EVENING SONGS, FOR SOLO VOICE AND
　ORCHESTRA see Dvořák, Antonín

EVENING WITH FRANK LOESSER, AN, PART I
　[ARR.] see Loesser, Frank

EVENING WITH FRANK LOESSER, AN, PART II
　[ARR.] see Loesser, Frank

EVENSEN, BERNT KASBERG (1944-   )
　Concertino Giocoso, For Harp And
　　Orchestra *Op.12 [19']
　　　2.2.2.2. 4.2.3.1. timp,perc,
　　　strings,harp solo
　　NORGE   (E349)

　Divertimento Concertante, For 2
　　Pianos And Orchestra, Op. 10
　　[20']
　　　2.2.2.2. 2.2.2.0. timp,perc,
　　　strings,2pno soli
　　NORGE   (E350)

　Musik Für Johanna *Op.32b [11']
　　string orch
　　NORGE   (E351)

　Notturno for Violin and Orchestra
　　　2.2.2.2. 4.2.3.1. strings,vln
　　　solo
　　NORGE   (E352)

　Und Es Bleibt Uns Unser Zweifel [20']
　　3.3.3.3. 4.3.3.1. harp,strings
　　NORGE   (E353)

EVENTYR see Delius, Frederick

EVENTYR, ET see Oulie, Einar

EVENTYR SUITE see Baden, Conrad

EVENTYRLAND see Hurum, Alf

EVERLASTING LONGINGS see Radulescu,
　Horatio

EVERYTHING RETURNS, FOR SOLO VOICE AND
　ORCHESTRA see Lloyd, Jonathan

EVETT, ROBERT (1922-1975)
　Billy Ascends, For Solo Voice And
　　Orchestra (Symphony No. 2 for
　　Solo Voice and Orchestra) [14']
　　　2.3.3.3. 4.3.3.1. timp,perc,cel,
　　　strings,Bar solo
　　sc AM.COMP.AL. $26.75, perf mat
　　rent   (E354)

　Symphony No. 2 for Solo Voice and
　　Orchestra
　　see Billy Ascends, For Solo Voice
　　And Orchestra

EVOCACION GOYESCA see Gil Serrano, Jose
　M.

EVOCARE see Hartmann, Per Johannes

EVOCATION see Lewin, Frank

EVOCATIONS, FOR 2 PIANOS AND ORCHESTRA
　see Archer, Violet

EVOCATIONS, OP. 15: LA VILLA ROSE see
　Roussel, Albert (Charles Paul)

EVOCATIONS, OP. 15: LES DIEUX DANS
　L'OMBRE DES CAVERNES see Roussel,
　Albert (Charles Paul)

EVOE, FOR HARPSICHORD, FLUTE,
　VIOLONCELLO AND STRING ORCHESTRA
　see Orlinski, Heinz Bernhard

EVOLUTION see Hoffding, Finn see Raum,
　Elizabeth

EVVIVA see Halier, Ronald

EWAZEN, ERIC (1954-   )
　Little Red Schoolhouse
　　3.3.3.2. 4.2.2.1. timp,perc,harp,
　　pno,strings
　　SEESAW perf mat rent   (E355)

EWIGE ZUFLUCHT, FOR SOLO VOICE AND
　CHAMBER ORCHESTRA see Smirnov,
　Dmitri, Eternal Calm, For Solo
　Voice And Chamber Orchestra

EX LIBRIS see Svoboda, Tomas

EXCERPTS see Guarnieri, Adriano

EXCURSION II see Ames, William T.

EXEUNT see Foss, Lukas

EXIL II, FOR SOLO VOICES AND
　INSTRUMENTAL ENSEMBLE see Durieux,
　Frederic

EXILED HEART, THE see Ekizian, Michelle

EXIT see Kruse, Bjørn Howard

EXOTIC BOUQUET, FOR SOLO VOICE AND
　ORCHESTRA see Fernström, John

EXOTIC SUITE see Hurum, Alf, Eksotisk
　Suite

EXOTICA see Legido, Jesus

EXPLORATION, FOR VIOLA AND ORCHESTRA
　see Sveinsson, Atli Heimir

EXPULSIE: PARTS III-IV see Verbey, Theo

EXSULTATE see Nystedt, Knut

EXSULTATE, JUBILATE, FOR SOLO VOICE AND
　ORCHESTRA see Mozart, Wolfgang
　Amadeus

EXTASE PERDU, L', OP. 148 see Lerstad,
　Terje B.

EXTRAVAGANTEN WALZER, DIE see Strauss,
　Johann, [Jr.]

EXULTATE JUBILATE: ALLELUJA, FOR SOLO
　VOICE AND ORCHESTRA [ARR.] see
　Mozart, Wolfgang Amadeus

EYBLER, JOSEPH (1765-1846)
　Symphony
　　see Hoffmeister, Franz Anton,
　　Symphonies, Two

　Symphony in C
　　2ob,bsn,2horn,2trp,strings
　　(Morgan; Paeuler) sc KUNZEL 10126
　　$24.00, perf mat rent   (E356)

　Twelve Minuets
　　see Zwölf Menuette

　Zwölf Menuette
　　"Twelve Minuets" sc KUNZEL 10111
　　$18.00, perf mat rent   (E357)

EYE IN THE PYRAMID, THE see Pierson,
　Tom

EYE OF GOD, THE see Castaldo, Joseph F.

EYES OF THE FOREST, THE see Solås,
　Eyvind, Skogens Oyne

EYKEN, ERNEST VAN DER
　Elegie Voor Bieke [11']
　　string orch
　　sc CBDM f.s.   (E358)

EYLAH, L' see Elias, Brian

EYPA see Dakin, Charles

EZIO: FOLLE È COLUI; NASCE AL BOSCO,
　FOR SOLO VOICE AND ORCHESTRA see
　Handel, George Frideric

F

F MELODIES see Maiguashca, Mesias

FABLES FROM THE DARK WOOD see Siegmeister, Elie

FABRICE-MARSCH see Kretschmer, Edmund

FACCHINETTI, GIANCARLO (1936-   )
Concerto for Orchestra [9']
2.2.2.2. 2.2.0.0. perc,strings
SONZOGNO perf mat rent   (F1)

Notturno for Flute and Orchestra [9']
2.2.2.2. 2.2.0.0. timp,perc,
strings,fl solo
SONZOGNO perf mat rent   (F2)

FACETTEN, FOR SOLO VOICE AND ORCHESTRA see Roosendael, Jan Rokus van

FACIEBAT ANNO, FOR 24 VIOLINS AND ORCHESTRA see Constant, Marius

FACKLOR I STORMEN, FOR SOLO VOICE AND ORCHESTRA see Nordqvist, Gustaf

FAHRES, MICHAEL (1951-   )
Sonnenstruktur [12']
4.4.6.0. 3.3.4.1. 6perc,pno,
strings
sc DONEMUS f.s., perf mat rent (F3)

FAIR AT SOROTCHINSK, THE *see also Jahrmarkt Von Sorotschinzi, Der

FAIR AT SOROTCHINSK, THE: GOPAK [ARR] see Mussorgsky, Modest Petrovich

FAIR SEED-TIME, FOR SOLO VOICE AND ORCHESTRA see Carlsen, Philip

FAIREST LORD JESUS
(Kirkland, Camp) 1.1.0.1. 1.3.3.1.
baritone horn,perc,org,pno,strings
sc,pts BROADMAN 4573-48 $25.00 (F4)

FAIRIES, THE: OVERTURE see Smith, John Christopher

FAIRY QUEEN, THE: TWO SUITES see Purcell, Henry

FAIRY TALE, A see Oulie, Einar, Eventyr, Et

FAIRY TALE SUITE see Baden, Conrad, Eventyr Suite

FAIRYLAND see Hurum, Alf, Eventyrland

FAIRY'S GIFT, THE. TYROLIENNE NO. 5 see Asafiev, Boris

FALB, REMIGIUS
Pastorella Sinfonia, Op. 2, No. 5, In C
org,strings
KUNZEL 10075 sc $15.00, pts $3.00,
ea., kbd pt $8.00   (F5)

FALDAFEYKIR see Groven, Eivind

FALIK, YURI (1936-   )
Concertino for Oboe and Chamber Orchestra [10']
1.0.2.1. 2.1.1.0. tamb,2vln,2vla,
2vcl,db,ob solo
SIKORSKI perf mat rent   (F6)

Concerto for Orchestra, No. 2 see Symphonic Etudes

Concerto for Violin and Orchestra [23']
3.3.3.3. 4.2.2.1. timp,2perc,
harp,cel,10vcl,8db,vln solo
SIKORSKI perf mat rent   (F7)
VAAP perf mat rent   (F8)

Elegiac Music In Memoriam Igor Stravinsky [10']
4trom,8vln,4vla,3vcl,db
"Elegische Musik Zum Gedenken An I.
Stravinsky" SIKORSKI perf mat
rent   (F9)

Elegische Musik Zum Gedenken An I. Stravinsky
see Elegiac Music In Memoriam Igor Stravinsky

Sinfonietta for String Orchestra [15']
string orch
VAAP perf mat rent   (F10)

Symphonic Etudes (Concerto for Orchestra, No. 2) [21']
4.3.4.3. 4.4.4.0. 4perc,harp,pno,

FALIK, YURI (cont'd.)
strings
SIKORSKI perf mat rent   (F11)

Symphony for String Orchestra and Percussion [20']
timp,perc,glock,vibra,xylo,pno,
strings
SIKORSKI perf mat rent   (F12)

Till Eulenspiegel [20']
3.3.2.2. 4.3.3.1. timp,perc,harp,
pno,org,strings
SIKORSKI perf mat rent   (F13)
VAAP perf mat rent   (F14)

FALLA, MANUEL DE (1876-1946)
Amor Brujo, El, First Version
1(pic).1.0.0. 1.0+cornet.0.0.
pno,strings
CHESTER perf mat rent   (F15)

Corregidor Y La Molinera, El: Concert Suite [16']
1(pic).1.1.1. 1.1.0.0. pno,
strings
CHESTER perf mat rent   (F16)

Fuego Fatuo [41']
2.1(English horn).2.2. 2.2.2.0.
timp,perc,harp,strings
CHESTER perf mat rent   (F17)

Noches En Los Jardines De Espana, For Piano And Chamber Orchestra [25']
2.2.2.2. 2.2.0.0. timp,perc,harp,
cel,strings
"Nuits Dans Les Jardins D'Espagne,
For Piano And Chamber Orchestra"
ESCHIG perf mat rent   (F18)

Nuits Dans Les Jardins D'Espagne, For Piano And Chamber Orchestra
see Noches En Los Jardines De Espana, For Piano And Chamber Orchestra

Vida Breve, La: Interlude And Spanish Dance [arr.]
(De Klug, Heinrich) 12vcl [4']
ESCHIG perf mat rent   (F19)

FALLENDE BLATTER see Buczynski, Pawel

FALSTAFF see Elgar, [Sir] Edward (William)

FALSTAFF, OSSIA LE TRE BURLE: OVERTURE see Salieri, Antonio

FALSTAFF: TWO INTERLUDES see Elgar, [Sir] Edward (William)

FAMILLE DE CHARLES IV, LA see Hoérée, Arthur

FANARAPSODI see Kristoffersen, Fridthjof

FANCY AS A GROUND see Bartholomée, Pierre

FANDANCE see Sharman, Rodney

FANDANGO SOBRE UN TEMA DE BOCCHERINI see Garcia-Abríl, Antón

FANDANGO SOPRA UN BASSO DEL PADRE SOLER see Henze, Hans Werner

FANELLI, ERNEST (1860-1917)
Tableaux Symphoniques
4.3.3.4. 4.3.3.4. timp,perc,
2harp,strings
ESCHIG perf mat rent   (F20)

FANFAR TILL UPPSALA STADS 700-ARSJUBILEUM see Erikson, Ake

FANFARA see Berio, Luciano

FANFARE see Foss, Lukas see Holmboe, Vagn see Jarvlepp, Jan see Kropatschek, H. see Luedeke, Raymond

FANFARE AND BRITISH NATIONAL ANTHEM see Berkeley, Michael

FANFARE AND PROCESSION see Hewitt-Jones, Tony

FANFARE FOR A FESTIVE OCCASION see Proto, Frank

FANFARE FOR AMERICAN WAR HEROES see Still, William Grant

FANFARE FOR AQUARIUS see Benjamin, George

FANFARE FOR LARGE ORCHESTRA see Orrego-Salas, Juan A.

FANFARE FOR ORCHESTRA AND ANTIPHONAL BRASS see Tull, Fisher Aubrey

FANFARE FOR THE HOUSTON SYMPHONY see Wuorinen, Charles

FANFARE, FUGUE AND FAST FOUR, FOR 3 TRUMPETS AND ORCHESTRA see Thorne, Francis Burritt

FANFARE POPULAIRE, FOR 3 TRUMPETS AND ORCHESTRA see Barnes, Milton

FANFARE (SALUTE TO BASIE) see Lewis, John Aaron

FANFARE TO EXPO 86 see Baker, Michael Conway

FANFARES AND ARABESQUES see Mostad, Jon

FANFARES AND WHISPERS, FOR TRUMPET AND STRING ORCHESTRA see Leef, Yinam

FANFARRIA PARA LA ALEGRIA POR LA PAZ see Montsalvatge, Xavier

FANFERLIESCHEN SCHONEFUSSCHEN: VERWANDLUNGSMUSIK see Schwertsik, Kurt

FANNI HAGYOMÁNYAI, FOR SOLO VOICE AND CHAMBER ORCHESTRA see Petrovics, Emil

FANTAISIE BRILLANTE ON THEMES FROM "CARMEN", FOR FLUTE AND ORCHESTRA [ARR.] see Bizet, Georges

FANTAISIE BRILLANTE SUR CARMEN, FOR FLUTE AND ORCHESTRA see Borne, Francois

FANTAISIE CAPRICE, FOR ALTO SAXOPHONE AND STRING ORCHESTRA see Absil, Jean

FANTAISIE CREOLE, FOR PIANO AND ORCHESTRA see Lancen, Serge

FANTAISIE DE CONCERT, FOR VIOLIN AND ORCHESTRA see Rimsky-Korsakov, Nikolai

FANTAISIE PASTORALE HONGROISE, FOR FLUTE AND ORCHESTRA, [ARR.] see Doppler, Franz

FANTAISIE RHYTHMIQUE see Poot, Marcel

FANTAISIE SUR DES MOTIFS HONGROIS, FOR 2 FLUTES AND ORCHESTRA [ARR.] see Doppler, Franz

FANTAISIE SUR UN THEME MALGACHE, FOR PIANO AND ORCHESTRA see Martelli, Henri

FANTAISIE VARIEE SUR UN VIEIL AIR CHAMPETRE, FOR CLARINET AND ORCHESTRA see Cahuzac, Louis

FANTASEA see Thorkelsdottir, Mist

FANTASIA AND FUGUE [ARR.] see Bach, Johann Sebastian

FANTASIA AND FUGUE IN G MINOR [ARR.] see Bach, Johann Sebastian

FANTASIA AND FUGUE NO. 6 [ARR.] see Bach, Johann Sebastian

FANTASIA BOREALIS see Søderlind, Ragnar

FANTASIA BREVE see Baden, Conrad see Eklund, Hans

FANTASIA CONCERTANTE see Archer, Violet

FANTASIA CONCERTANTE, FOR OBOE, VIOLIN, VIOLONCELLO, PIANO AND STRING ORCHESTRA see Breimo, Bjørn

FANTASIA CONCERTANTE, FOR ORCHESTRA OF VIOLONCELLOS see Villa-Lobos, Heitor

FANTASIA CONCERTANTE ON A THEME OF CORELLI see Tippett, [Sir] Michael

FANTASIA ESPANOLA see Arambarri, Jesús

FANTASIA FOR STRING ORCHESTRA see Mennin, Peter (Mennini)

FANTASIA HABANERA see Tsontakis, George

FANTASIA IN G [ARR.] see Bach, Johann Sebastian

FANTASIA IV, FOR VIOLIN, PIANO, AND ORCHESTRA see Harper, Edward James

FANTASIA MELODICA, FOR GUITAR AND
  STRING ORCHESTRA see Koch, Erland
  von

FANTASIA ON AN OSTINATO see Corigliano,
  John

FANTASIA ON SUSSEX FOLKSONGS, FOR CELLO
  AND ORCHESTRA see Vaughan Williams,
  Ralph

FANTASIA SINFONICA see Breimo, Bjørn

FANTASIA SINFONICA, SUL CORALE
  "LIEBSTER JESU WIR SIND HIER" DI
  J.S. BACH see Lorenzini, Danilo

FANTASIA SLAVA, FOR PIANO AND ORCHESTRA
  see Respighi, Ottorino

FANTASIA SU UN SOGGETTO CAVATO see
  Suben, Joel Eric

FANTASIA ÜBER EINEN KLANG VON G.F.
  HANDEL, FÜR VIOLONCELLI-GRUPPE UND
  STREICHER see Halffter, Cristobal

FANTASIA V see Harper, Edward James

FANTASIAS see Tircuit, Heuwell (Andrew)

FANTASIE ESPAGNOLE see Berners, Lord
  (Gerald Tyrwhitt)

FANTASIE, K.608, [ARR.] see Mozart,
  Wolfgang Amadeus

FANTASIE UBER BAROCKTHEMEN VON J.
  BASTON, FOR SOPRANO RECORDER AND
  CHAMBER ORCHESTRA see Bodensohn,
  Ernst Friedrich Wilhelm

FANTASIE ÜBER NEURE DEUTSCHE LIEDER see
  Strauss, Eduard

FANTASIE UBER UNGARISCHE VOLKSMELODIEN,
  FOR PIANO AND ORCHESTRA see Liszt,
  Franz

FANTASIES EN FORMA DE CONCERT, FOR
  FLUTE AND ORCHESTRA see Valls
  Gorina

FANTASIES FOR STRINGS see Murto, Matti

FANTASIES IN LINE AND COLOR see
  Siegmeister, Elie

FANTASTIC DANCE see Delius, Frederick

FANTASY see Goeb, Roger

FANTASY AND FUGUE, FOR WOODWIND QUINTET
  AND STRING ORCHESTRA see Rice,
  Thomas N.

FANTASY FOR SAXHORN AND ORCHESTRA see
  DuBois, Pierre-Max

FANTASY FROM PSALMS, SONGS AND SONNETS
  OF 1611 see Byrd, William

FANTASY OF IVORY THOUGHTS AND SHALLOW
  WHISPERS, A see Dollarhide,
  Theodore

FANTASY ON A GROUND see Archer, Violet

FANTASY ON A SINKIANG FOLK SONG, FOR
  VIOLIN AND ORCHESTRA [ARR.] see
  Chen, Gang

FANTASY ON "CARMEN" BY BIZET, FOR
  VIOLIN AND ORCHESTRA see Hubay,
  Jenő see Sarasate, Pablo de

FANTASY ON RUSSIAN THEMES, FOR VIOLIN
  AND ORCHESTRA see Rimsky-Korsakov,
  Nikolai, Fantaisie De Concert, For
  Violin And Orchestra

FANTASY ON SERBIAN THEMES see Rimsky-
  Korsakov, Nikolai

FANTASY PIECE FOR SAXOPHONE AND STRING
  ORCHESTRA see Swanson, Howard

FANTASY PIECE V see Leichtling, Alan

FANTASY VARIATIONS see Fennelly, Brian
  see Kay, Ulysses Simpson

FANTICINI, FABRIZIO (1955-   )
  Di Retro Al Sol [9']
    3.2.3.2. 4.2.2.1. timp,3perc,cel,
    harp,strings
    RICORDI-IT 134194 perf mat rent
                                        (F21)

FANTOME DE L'OPERA, LE: SUITE see
  Landowski, Marcel

FAR CALLS, COMING, FAR, FOR VIOLIN AND
  ORCHESTRA see Takemitsu, Toru

FAR, HVOR FLYVER SVANERNE HEN?, FOR
  SOLO VOICE AND ORCHESTRA see
  Madetoja, Leevi

FARBENSPIEL see Schuller, Gunther

FAREWELL see Suslin, Viktor see Vajda,
  J.

FARINA, CARLO (ca. 1600-ca. 1640)
  Capriccio Stravagante
    string orch
    KUNZEL GM 933 sc,pts $25.00, pts
    $3.50, ea.   (F22)

  Pavana E Gagliarda [arr.]
    (Bonelli) string orch [8'] set
    KALMUS A7332 $17.00, and up (F23)

FARINAS CANTERO, CARLOS (1934-   )
  Bosque Ha Echado A Andar, El
    4.4.4.4. 6.4.4.1. strings
    TONOS perf mat rent   (F24)

FARKAS, FERENC (1905-   )
  Aspirationes Principis, For Solo
    Voices And Orchestra
    orch,TBar soli sc EMB 10217 f.s.
                                        (F25)
  Concertino for Oboe and Orchestra
    sc EMB 12643 f.s., perf mat rent
                                        (F26)
  Concertino for Trumpet and String
    Orchestra
    string orch,trp solo
    sc EMB 13012 f.s., perf mat rent
                                        (F27)
  Marionette's Dance Suite
    sc EMB 889 f.s.   (F28)
    min sc EMB 3193 f.s.   (F29)

  Musica Giocosa
    string orch
    sc EMB 12896 f.s., perf mat rent
                                        (F30)
  Philharmonic Overture
    sc EMB 10230 f.s.   (F31)

FARNABY, GILES (ca. 1560-1640)
  Suite Of Seven Pieces [arr.]
    (Bantock) string orch,pno [7'30"]
    KALMUS A6103 sc $8.00, set $5.00
                                        (F32)

FARNACE: AL VEZZEGGIAR D'UN VOLTO, FOR
  SOLO VOICE AND STRING ORCHESTRA see
  Vivaldi, Antonio

FARNACE: COMBATTONO QUEST'ALMA, FOR
  SOLO VOICE AND ORCHESTRA see
  Vivaldi, Antonio

FARNACE: DA QUEL FERRO CHE HA SVENATO,
  FOR SOLO VOICE AND STRING ORCHESTRA
  see Vivaldi, Antonio

FARNACE: FORSE, O CARO, IN QUESTI
  ACCENTI, FOR SOLO VOICE AND
  ORCHESTRA see Vivaldi, Antonio

FARNACE: GELIDO IN OGNI VENA, FOR SOLO
  VOICE AND ORCHESTRA see Vivaldi,
  Antonio

FARNACE: LASCIA DI SOSPIRAR, FOR SOLO
  VOICE AND STRING ORCHESTRA see
  Vivaldi, Antonio

FARNACE: NELL'INTIMO DEL PETTO, FOR
  SOLO VOICE AND ORCHESTRA see
  Vivaldi, Antonio

FARNACE: RICORDATI CHE SEI, FOR SOLO
  VOICE AND STRING ORCHESTRA see
  Vivaldi, Antonio

FARNACE: ROMA INVITTA, MA CLEMENTE, FOR
  SOLO VOICE AND STRING ORCHESTRA see
  Vivaldi, Antonio

FARNACE: SINFONIA see Vivaldi, Antonio

FARNACE: SORGE L'IRATO NEMBO, FOR SOLO
  VOICES AND ORCHESTRA see Vivaldi,
  Antonio

FARNE see LeFanu, Nicola

FARQUHAR, DAVID (1928-   )
  Ring Round The Moon
    sc WAI-TE-ATA f.s.   (F33)

  Symphony No. 1 [23']
    3.2.3.2. 4.3.3.1. timp,perc,harp,
    strings
    sc WAI-TE-ATA f.s.   (F34)

FASCE SONORE, FOR 2 PIANOS AND CHAMBER
  ORCHESTRA see Abbado, Marcello

FASCH, JOHANN FRIEDRICH (1688-1758)
  Concerto in C, MIN 174
    MUS. RARA perf mat rent   (F35)

  Concerto in D minor [13']
    strings,hpsd,lute solo
    SUPRAPHON   (F36)

FASCH, JOHANN FRIEDRICH (cont'd.)

  Concerto in F, MIN 173
    (Thilde, J.) string orch,2trp soli
    BILLAUDOT perf mat rent   (F37)

  Symphony in A [15']
    string orch,cont
    (Hoffmann) KALMUS A7449 sc $8.00,
    set $12.50, pts $2.50, ea.   (F38)

  Symphony in G [12']
    string orch,cont
    (Hoffmann) KALMUS A7448 sc $7.00,
    set $12.50, pts $2.50, ea.   (F39)

FASCHING see Weiner, Leo

FASER see Hedstrom, Åse

FASETTER AV EN FIGUR see Godøy, Rolf
  Inge

FASHION SHOW see Reed, Alfred

FAST BREAK see Stock, David Frederick

FASTES DE L'IMAGINAIRE see Nigg, Serge

FASTES DE L'IMAGINAIRE, LES see
  Nielsen, Svend

FASTNACHTSTRAUM, FOR SAXOPHONE AND
  ORCHESTRA see Kubinsky, R.

FATA MORGANA see Strauss, Johann, [Jr.]

FATE NOSTALGIA see Nordgren, Pehr
  Henrik

FATINITZA: MARZIALE [ARR.] see Suppe,
  Franz von

FATINITZA QUADRILLE see Strauss, Eduard

FATUM see Tchaikovsky, Piotr Ilyich

FAUNE ET LA BERGERE, LE, FOR SOLO VOICE
  AND ORCHESTRA see Stravinsky, Igor

FAURE, GABRIEL-URBAIN (1845-1924)
  Ballade for Piano and Orchestra, Op.
    19
    min sc EULENBURG EU01384 $7.50
                                        (F40)
    (Lacoste) sc PETERS P9568 f.s.
                                        (F41)
  Berceuse, Op. 16, [arr.]
    (Talmi) clar,strings,fl solo [4']
    KALMUS A6972 sc $5.00, set $8.00,
    pts $1.25, ea.   (F42)

  Concerto for Violin and Orchestra in
    D minor [14']
    2.2.2.2. 4.2.3.0. timp,strings,
    vln solo
    (Spada, Pietro) sc BSE f.s., perf
    mat rent   (F43)

  Fantasy for Flute and Orchestra,
    [arr.] [6']
    (Galway) 0.1.2.1. 1.0.0.0. harp,
    strings,fl solo NOVELLO perf mat
    rent   (F44)
    (Talmi) 0.1.1.1. 0.0.0.0. strings,
    fl solo [5'] KALMUS A6969 sc
    $10.00, set $10.00, pts $1.25,
    ea.   (F45)

  Morceau De Concours, For Flute And
    String Orchestra
    (Talmi) string orch,fl solo [3']
    KALMUS A6971 sc $3.00, set $5.00,
    pts $1.00, ea.   (F46)

  Pavane, Op. 50 [7']
    2.2.2.2. 2.0.0.0. strings,opt cor
    BROUDE BR. sc $7.50, set $25.00,
    pts $1.75, ea.   (F47)

  Penelope
    KALMUS A6752 sc $7.00, set $20.00,
    pts $1.00.. perf mat rent   (F48)

  Shylock: Incidental Music, For Solo
    Voice And Orchestra *Op.57
    [21'30"]
    2.2.2.2. 4.2.0.0. timp,perc,
    2harp,strings,T solo
    KALMUS A5572 sc $30.00, set $60.00,
    pts $3.00, ea.   (F49)

  Sicilienne [arr.] *Op.78
    (Talmi) clar,harp,strings,fl solo
    [3'] KALMUS A6970 sc $5.00, set
    $8.00, pts $1.00, ea.   (F50)

  Symphony in F [12']
    2.2.2.2. 4.0.0.0. strings
    sc BSE 78 f.s., perf mat rent (F51)

FAUST: BALLET MUSIC see Gounod, Charles
  François

FAUST FOR FUN see Stirn, D.

FAUST: INTRODUCTION see Gounod, Charles François

FAUST: OVERTURE see Spohr, Ludwig (Louis) see Wagner, Richard

FAUST-SZENEN: OVERTURE see Schumann, Robert (Alexander)

FAVORITA, LA: A TANTO AMOR, FOR SOLO VOICES AND ORCHESTRA see Donizetti, Gaetano

FAVORITA, LA: AH! MIO BENE, UN DIO T' INVIA, FOR SOLO VOICES AND ORCHESTRA see Donizetti, Gaetano

FAVORITA, LA: AH! PAVENTA IL FUROR, FOR SOLO VOICES AND ORCHESTRA see Donizetti, Gaetano

FAVORITA, LA: BALLET MUSIC see Donizetti, Gaetano

FAVORITA, LA: E FIA VERO, FOR SOLO VOICES AND ORCHESTRA see Donizetti, Gaetano

FAVORITA, LA: PIETOSO AL PAR DEL NUME, FOR SOLO VOICES AND ORCHESTRA see Donizetti, Gaetano

FAVORITA, LA: QUANDO LE SOGLIE PATERNE, FOR SOLO VOICES AND ORCHESTRA see Donizetti, Gaetano

FAVORITA, LA: SI, CHE UN TUO SOLO ACCENTO, FOR SOLO VOICE AND ORCHESTRA see Donizetti, Gaetano

FAVORITA, LA: UNA VERGINE, UN ANGEL DI DIO, FOR SOLO VOICE AND ORCHESTRA see Donizetti, Gaetano

FAVORITA, LA: VIEN LEONORA, A PIEDI TUOI, FOR SOLO VOICE AND ORCHESTRA see Donizetti, Gaetano

FEARFUL SYMMETRIES see Adams, John

FEATURE ON RENÉ DESCARTES see Bentzon, Niels Viggo

FEBEL, REINHARD (1952-   )
Auf Der Galerie [16']
  3vln,3vla,3vcl,2db
  RICORDI-GER SY 2465 perf mat rent
                                        (F52)
Concerto for Percussion and Orchestra [37']
  3.3.3.3. 3.3.3.1. timp,pno&cel, strings,perc solo
  sc RICORDI-GER f.s., perf mat rent
                                        (F53)
Symphony [30']
  3.3.3.3. 3.3.3.1. timp,3perc, harp,pno,strings
  sc RICORDI-GER SY 3019 f.s., perf mat rent
                                        (F54)
Unendliche, Das, For Solo Voices And Orchestra [18']
  3.3.3.3. 3.3.3.1. perc,pno, strings,MezBar soli
  sc RICORDI-GER SY 2437 f.s., perf mat rent
                                        (F55)
Variations for Orchestra [16']
  3(pic).2+English horn.2(bass clar).2+contrabsn. 3.3.3.1. timp,2perc,harp,pno,strings
  sc RICORDI-GER SY 2349 f.s., perf mat rent
                                        (F56)

FEBERDIGTE, FOR SOLO VOICE AND ORCHESTRA see Jordan, Sverre

FEBRUARMORGEN VED GOLFEN, FOR SOLO VOICE AND ORCHESTRA see Alnaes, Eyvind

FEBRUARY MORNING AT THE GULF, FOR SOLO VOICE AND ORCHESTRA see Alnaes, Eyvind, Februarmorgen Ved Golfen, For Solo Voice And Orchestra

FEDERAL OVERTURE [ARR.] see Carr, Benjamin

FEDORA: AMOR TI VIETA, FOR SOLO VOICE AND ORCHESTRA see Giordano, Umberto

FEEMARCHEN WALZER see Strauss, Johann, [Jr.]

FEEN, DIE: OVERTURE see Wagner, Richard

FEEST see Torrenga, Benno

FEIERLICHER EINZUG see Strauss, Richard

FEIERLICHER LOBGESANG see Butzko, Yuri

FEIGIN, LEONID (1923-   )
Concertino for 2 Violins and String Orchestra, Op. 15 [21']
  string orch,2vln soli
  SIKORSKI perf mat rent
                                        (F57)

FELD, JINDRICH (1925-   )
Concerto for Accordion and Orchestra [17']
  1(pic).2.2.2. 2.0.2.0. timp,perc, strings,acord solo
  SCHIRM.G perf mat rent
                                        (F58)
Concerto for Saxophone and Orchestra [24']
  2trp,2trom,perc,xylo,vibra, strings,sax solo
  MMB perf mat rent
                                        (F59)
Concerto for Trombone and Orchestra [16']
  2.2.2.2. 2.2.0.0. timp,4perc, strings,trom solo
  SUPRAPHON
                                        (F60)

FELDEINSAMKEIT, FOR SOLO VOICE AND ORCHESTRA [ARR.] see Brahms, Johannes

FELDERHOF, JAN (1907-   )
Chanterelle [10']
  2.2.2.2. 2.2.2.0. timp,2perc, harp,strings
  DONEMUS perf mat rent
                                        (F61)
Suite Nostalgique [12']
  2.2.2.2. 2.2.2.1. timp,perc, strings
  sc DONEMUS f.s., perf mat rent
                                        (F62)

FELDMAN, MORTON (1926-1987)
Coptic Light [20']
  2.2.2.2. 2.2.2.1. timp,vibra, 2harp,2pno,strings
  sc UNIVER. UE18435 f.s., perf mat rent
                                        (F63)
For Samuel Beckett [60']
  2.2.2.2. 2.2.2.1. vibra,harp,pno, string quin
  UNIVER. perf mat rent
                                        (F64)
Oboe And Orchestra
  4.4.4.4. 3.3.3.1. perc,harp,pno/ cel,strings,ob solo
  sc UNIVER. $25.00
                                        (F65)
Turfan Fragments, The [17']
  2.2.2.2. 2.2.2.0. 6vla,4vcl,4db
  sc UNIVER. UE16495 $49.00, perf mat rent
                                        (F66)
Violin And Orchestra [60']
  3+pic.3+English horn.3+bass clar.3+contrabsn. 3.3.3+bass trom.1. 4perc,2harp,2pno, strings,vln solo
  UNIVER. perf mat rent
                                        (F67)

FELTON, WILLIAM (1715-1769)
Concerto No. 4 for Organ and Orchestra
  2ob,strings,org solo
  HARMONIA 2935 f.s.
                                        (F68)

FELURE see Frenette, Claude

FEMDELT FORM III see Weis, Flemming

FEMERICHTER, DIE: OVERTURE see Berlioz, Hector (Louis), Francs-Juges, Les: Overture

FEMININE WILES: OVERTURE see Cimarosa, Domenico, Astuzie Femminili, Le: Overture

FEMME SANS PASSE, LA see Landowski, Marcel

FEMUND [ARR.] see Storbekken, Egil

FENELON, PHILIPPE (1952-   )
Diagonal [15']
  pic,ob,clar,bass clar,bsn,horn, trp,trom,bass trom,pno&cel&org, harp,vln,vla,vcl
  AMPHION perf mat rent
                                        (F69)
Du Blanc Le Jour Son Espace, For Solo Voice And Instrumental Ensemble [19']
  1+pic+alto fl.1+English horn.1+ bass clar.0. 1.1.1.1. pno,cel, org,2vln,vla,vcl,Bar solo
  AMPHION perf mat rent
                                        (F70)
Eclipses [26']
  4(pic).2(English horn).4(bass clar).3. 4.2.2.1. 3perc,cel, strings
  AMPHION perf mat rent
                                        (F71)

FENNELLY, BRIAN (1937-   )
Concerto for Alto Saxophone and String Orchestra [22']
  string orch,alto sax solo
  sc AM.COMP.AL. $13.80, perf mat rent
                                        (F72)
Empirical Rag [5']
  2.2.2.2. 2.2.2.1. perc,strings
  AM.COMP.AL. perf mat rent   (F73)
Fantasy Variations [22']
  3.3.3.3. 4.3.3.1. 3perc,harp, strings
  sc AM.COMP.AL. $97.20, perf mat rent
                                        (F74)
In Wildness Is The Preservation Of The World [16']
  2.2.2.2. 4.3.3.1. perc,harp, strings
  sc AM.COMP.AL. $39.75, perf mat rent
                                        (F75)
Scintilla Prisca, For Violoncello And Orchestra [14']
  2.2.2.2. 2.0.0.0. perc,harp, strings,vcl solo
  sc AM.COMP.AL. $12.25, perf mat rent
                                        (F76)
Thoreau Fantasy No. 2 [20']
  2(pic).2.2(bass clar).2. 4.3.3.1. timp,perc,pno,strings
  sc AM.COMP.AL. $60.05, perf mat rent
                                        (F77)
Tropes And Echoes, For Clarinet And Chamber Orchestra [15']
  1.1.0+bass clar.1. 1.1.1.0. perc, pno,strings,clar solo
  sc AM.COMP.AL. $16.75   (F78)

FERDAMANN see Kielland, Olav

FERDINAND QUADRILLE see Strauss, Johann, [Sr.]

FERENCZY, OTO (1921-   )
Intrada
  SLOV.HUD.FOND   (F79)

FERNANDEZ, OSCAR LORENZO (1897-1948)
Batuque
  3.3.3.3. 4.3.3.1. timp,perc, strings
  min sc PEER MUSIK 60095-856 $5.00, perf mat rent
                                        (F80)

FERNANDEZ ALVEZ, GABRIEL (1943-   )
Ante Mi [10']
  6vln,3vla,2vcl,2db
  ALPUERTO   (F81)
Cadencias [17']
  1.1.1.1. 1.1.1.0. 2perc,harp,cel, pno,strings
  sc ALPUERTO f.s.   (F82)
Concerto for Violin, Viola, Violoncello, Piano and Orchestra [15']
  perc,strings,vln solo,vla solo, vcl solo,pno solo
  ALPUERTO   (F83)
Ecogramas
  1.1.1.1. 1.0.0.0. perc,pno, strings
  ALPUERTO   (F84)
Estancias, For Solo Voice And Chamber Orchestra [12']
  1.1.1.0. 1.1.1.0. perc,pno, strings,solo voice
  ALPUERTO   (F85)
Penalara
  ob,clar,bsn,2perc,hpsd,org,6vln, 3vla,2vcl,db
  sc ALPUERTO f.s.   (F86)
Symphony [14']
  2.2.2.2. 4.2.3.0. 3perc,harp, strings
  ALPUERTO   (F87)
Symphony No. 2 [11']
  2÷pic.3.3+bass clar.3+contrabsn. 4.3.3.1. 4perc,pno,2harp, strings
  ALPUERTO   (F88)
Tridimensional
  1+pic.1.1.1+contrabsn. 1.1.1.0. perc,strings
  ALPUERTO   (F89)

FERNE KLANG, DER see Holliger, Heinz

FERNEYHOUGH, BRIAN (1943-   )
Carceri D'invenzione I [12']
  1(pic).1(English horn).2(clar in E flat,bass clar).1(contrabsn). 1.1.2.1. perc,pno,strings
  sc PETERS P7291 f.s., perf mat rent

FERNEYHOUGH, BRIAN (cont'd.)

                             (F90)
   Firecycle Beta [23']
     2timp,6perc,2harp,2pno,cimbalom,
     elec org,hpsd,cel,gtr,28vln,
     12vla,12vcl,8db
     sc RICORDI-IT 132492 f.s., perf mat
     rent   (F91)

FERNSTRÖM, JOHN (1897-1961)
   Exotic Bouquet, For Solo Voice And
     Orchestra [10']
     2.1.2.2. 2.2.2.0. perc,strings,
     med solo
     NORDISKA perf mat rent   (F92)

FERON, ALAIN (1954-   )
   Charades [18']
     1.1.1.1. 0.0.0.0. 4perc,2vln,vla,
     vcl
     SALABERT perf mat rent   (F93)

FERRARI, GIORGIO (1925-   )
   Lumina [15']
     3.3.4.2. 4.3.3.1. timp,perc,
     strings
     SONZOGNO perf mat rent   (F94)

   Musica Francescana, For Solo Voice
     And Orchestra [12']
     3.2.2.2. 4.2.2.0. timp,strings,S
     solo
     SONZOGNO perf mat rent   (F95)

   Nora, For 2 Violins And String
     Orchestra [18']
     string orch,2vln soli
     SONZOGNO perf mat rent   (F96)

   Parabole, For Flute, Violoncello,
     Piano And String Orchestra [18']
     string orch,fl solo,vcl solo,pno
     solo
     SONZOGNO perf mat rent   (F97)

FERRARI, LUC (1929-   )
   Compose-Composite [8'24"]
     2.1.2.1. 2.2.1.0. 2perc,harp,
     strings,electronic tape
     BILLAUDOT perf mat rent   (F98)

   Opera-Bus, Chapitre V: La Musique A
     L'envers [10']
     BILLAUDOT perf mat rent   (F99)

FERRARO, RALPH
   Corrida, La [5']
     3(pic).2.3.2. 4.4.4.1. timp,perc,
     pno,harp,gtr,strings
     NEWAM 19015 perf mat rent (F100)

FERRERO, LORENZO (1951-   )
   Adagio Cantabile [12']
     fl,ob,clar,bsn,horn,perc,pno,
     2vln,vla,vcl,db
     RICORDI-IT 132612 perf mat rent
                      (F101)

   Arioso [24']
     3.3.3.3.sax. 4.2.3.1. 4perc,
     strings
     RICORDI-IT 133271 perf mat rent
                      (F102)

   Balletto, For Orchestra [20']
     3.3.4.3.alto sax. 4.3.3.1. timp,
     2perc,harp,pno&cel,strings
     RICORDI-IT 133141 perf mat rent
                      (F103)

   Ellipse En Concert, For Flute And
     Instrumental Ensemble [10']
     fl,ob,clar,bass clar,contrabsn/
     bsn,marimba,cel,harp,2vln,vcl,
     db,fl solo
     RICORDI-IT 133467 perf mat rent
                      (F104)

   Mare Nostro: Intermezzo Notturno [4']
     1.1.1.1. 2.1.0.0. strings,vln
     solo
     RICORDI-IT 134297 perf mat rent
                      (F105)

   Marilyn Suite, For Solo Voices And
     Orchestra [30']
     2.2.3.2.sax. 2.3.2.1. 3perc,pno&
     cel&elec org,harp,strings,ST
     soli
     RICORDI-IT 133122 perf mat rent
                      (F106)

   Movimento [14']
     2.2.2.2. 2.2.0.0. timp,perc,
     12vln,3vla,3vcl,2db
     RICORDI-IT 133213 perf mat rent
                      (F107)

   My Blues [6']
     string orch
     RICORDI-IT 133435 perf mat rent
                      (F108)

   My Rock [10']
     2.2.2.2. 2.2.0.0. perc,strings
     RICORDI-IT 134102 perf mat rent
                      (F109)

   Ombres [15']
     2.1+English horn.1+clar in E
     flat+bass
     clar.2(contrabsn).sax. 1.1.1.0.
     2perc,strings, vocoder
     RICORDI-IT 133598 perf mat rent

FERRERO, LORENZO (cont'd.)

                           (F110)
   Symphony No. 1 [18']
     3.3.3.3. 4.3.3.0. 4perc,2elec
     gtr,elec pno,strings
     (Dance Music) RICORDI-IT 133739
     perf mat rent   (F111)

   Thema 44 (Ad Honorem J. Haydn)
     [11'10"]
     2.2.3.2. 2.2.0.0. 2perc,harp,pno,
     cel,strings
     RICORDI-IT 133372 perf mat rent
                      (F112)

FERRITTO, JOHN E. (1937-   )
   Celebrations *Op.19 [9']
     2+pic.2.2.2. 4.3.3.1. timp,perc,
     harp,strings
     sc AM.COMP.AL. $22.15, perf mat
     rent   (F113)

   Concerto for Violoncello and
     Orchestra, Op. 17 [23']
     3.2.2.2. 4.3.3.1. timp,perc,
     strings,vcl solo
     AM.COMP.AL. sc $50.25, pts $4.10,
     perf mat rent   (F114)

   Sogni, For Solo Voice And Orchestra
     *Op.21
     sc AM.COMP.AL. $26.75   (F115)

   Variations, Op. 16 [13']
     4.3.2.3. 4.3.3.1. timp,perc,harp,
     strings
     sc AM.COMP.AL. $32.50   (F116)

FERRO CANTO see Heyn, Volker

FERVAAL: PRELUDE, ACT I see Indy,
   Vincent d'

FERVAAL: PRELUDE, ACT III see Indy,
   Vincent d'

FEST-MUSIK see Schierbeck, Poul

FEST-OUVERTURE see Koppel, Herman David
   see Nystedt, Knut see Sønstevold,
   Maj

FEST-OUVERTURE, OP. 123 see Schumann,
   Robert (Alexander)

FEST OVERTURE see Nicolai, Otto see
   Reinecke, Carl

FEST QUADRILLE see Strauss, Johann,
   [Sr.]

FESTAL MARCH see Jacob, Gordon

FESTE BURG IST UNSER GOTT, EIN' [ARR.]
   see Bach, Johann Sebastian

FESTFORSPILL see Jordan, Sverre

FESTIN DE L'ARAIGNEE, LE see Roussel,
   Albert (Charles Paul)

FESTIN D'ESOPE, LE [ARR] see Alkan,
   Charles-Henri Valentin

FESTINA LENTE see Pärt, Arvo

FESTING, MICHAEL CHRISTIAN
   (ca. 1680-1752)
   Concerti, Eight *see THREE CENTURIES
     OF MUSIC IN SCORE, VOL. 3:
     CONCERTO II, ENGLAND

FESTIVAL see Ovchinnikov, Viacheslav

FESTIVAL OUVERTURE see Enger, Elling,
   Festspel see Madsen, Trygve

FESTIVAL OVERTURE see Hovland, Egil,
   Festouverture see Isolfsson, Pall
   see Jordan, Sverre, Festforspill
   see Nystedt, Knut, Fest-Ouverture
   see Sønstevold, Maj, Fest-Ouverture
   see Sze, Man-Tsuen

FESTIVAL OVERTURE FOR BIG BAND AND
   STRING ORCHESTRA see Eshpai, Andrey
   Y.

FESTIVAL QUADRILLE see Strauss, Johann,
   [Jr.]

FESTIVAL VARIATIONS see Brown,
   Christopher (Roland)

FESTIVE MARCH see Björnsson, Arni

FESTIVE OVERTURE see Leighton, Kenneth
   see Stein, Leon

FESTIVE PROLOGUE see Vacek, Miloš

FESTKLANGE see Liszt, Franz

FESTLICHER PROLOG see David, Thomas
   Christian

FESTLICHES PRAELUDIUM see Strauss,
   Richard

FESTMUSIK see Ebenhöh, Horst

FESTOUVERTURE see Hovland, Egil

FESTSPEL see Enger, Elling

FESTTAG IN KARTLI see Taktakishvili,
   Otar

FESTUM see Berio, Luciano

FETE A THELEME see Poot, Marcel

FETE DES FLEURS A GENZANO, LA [ARR.]
   see Helsted

FETE GALANTE see Schierbeck, Poul

FETE GALANTE ET PASTORALE see Krauze,
   Zygmunt

FETE SACREE, LA, FOR PICCOLO, 3 FLUTES
   AND STRING ORCHESTRA see Gougeon,
   Denis

FETE SLAVE, UNE see Glazunov, Alexander
   Konstantinovich

FÊTES DU TÊT, FOR PIANO AND ORCHESTRA
   see Nguyen Van Ty, L.

FETLER, PAUL (1920-   )
   Concerto for Violin and Orchestra
     [24']
     1(pic).2.0.2. 2.0.0.0. timp,
     2perc,cel,strings,vln solo
     SCHIRM.G perf mat rent   (F117)

   Three Poems By Walt Whitman, For
     Narrator And Orchestra [18']
     3(pic).2+English horn.2+bass
     clar.2+contrabsn. 4.3.3.1.
     timp,4perc,cel&pno,strings,
     narrator
     SCHIRM.G perf mat rent   (F118)

FETRAS, OSCAR
   Melodies
     (Schlenkermann) 2.1.2.2. 4.3.3.0.
     perc,harp,strings [8'] BENJ perf
     mat rent   (F119)

FEUERSNOT: LOVE SCENE see Strauss,
   Richard, Feuersnot, Op. 50:
   Liebesszene

FEUERSNOT, OP. 50: LIEBESSZENE see
   Strauss, Richard

FEUERWERKSMUSIK see Handel, George
   Frideric, Royal Fireworks Music

FEUILLETON WALZER see Strauss, Johann,
   [Jr.]

FEUX FOLLETS [ARR.] see Liszt, Franz

FEVER POEMS, FOR SOLO VOICE AND
   ORCHESTRA see Jordan, Sverre,
   Feberdigte, For Solo Voice And
   Orchestra

FEW AUTUMN LEAVES, A see Palsson, Pall
   P.

FHEODOROFF, NIKOLAUS (1931-   )
   Drei Satze Fur Streichorchester [8']
     string orch
     sc,pts DOBLINGER 74 107 f.s. (F120)

FIALA, J.
   Concertante For English Horn,
     Clarinet And Orchestra
     MUS. RARA 2048 perf mat rent (F121)

FICHER, JACOBO (1896-   )
   Suite for Chamber Orchestra
     1.1.1.1. 2.1.0.0. timp,strings
     PEER perf mat rent   (F122)

FIDDLER'S CHILD see Janácek, Leoš

FIDDLER'S JOURNEY TO HIS LAST RESTING
   PLACE, THE see Jonsson, Josef
   [Petrus]

FIDDLER'S MEDLEY see Bowden, Robert

FIDELE BURSCHE WALZER see Strauss,
   Eduard

FIDELIO: ABSCHEULICHER, WO EILST DU
   HIN, FOR SOLO VOICE AND ORCHESTRA
   see Beethoven, Ludwig van

FIDELIO: GOTT, WELCH' DUNKEL HIER, FOR
   SOLO VOICE AND ORCHESTRA see
   Beethoven, Ludwig van

FIDELIO: GOTT, WELCH' DUNKEL HIER, FOR
   SOLO VOICE AND ORCHESTRA, FIRST
   VERSION see Beethoven, Ludwig van

FIDELIO: HAT MAN NICHT AUCH GOLD
BEINEBEN, FOR SOLO VOICE AND
ORCHESTRA see Beethoven, Ludwig van

FIDELIO: JETZT SCHATZCHEN, JETZT SIND
WIR ALLEIN, FOR SOLO VOICES AND
ORCHESTRA see Beethoven, Ludwig van

FIDELIO: MIR IST SO WUNDERBAR, FOR SOLO
VOICES AND ORCHESTRA see Beethoven,
Ludwig van

FIDELIO: O, WAR ICH SCHON MIT DIR
VEREINT, FOR SOLO VOICE AND
ORCHESTRA see Beethoven, Ludwig van

FIDELIO: OVERTURE see Beethoven, Ludwig
van

FIELD, JOHN (1782-1837)
Concerti for Piano and Orchestra,
Nos. 1-3
(Merrick, Frank) sc STAINER MB17
f.s.   (F123)

FIELDS AND ROADS see Dormolen, Jan
Willem van, Velden En Wegen

FIELDS OF WONDER, FOR SOLO VOICE AND
STRING ORCHESTRA see Owens, Robert

FIELDS-SINGING, FOR SOLO VOICE AND
INSTRUMENTAL ENSEMBLE see Boone,
Charles N.

FIELITZ, ALEXANDER VON (1860-1930)
Vier Stimmungsbilder *Op.37 [8']
2+pic.2+English horn.2.2.
4.2.3.0. timp,harp,strings
BREITKOPF-W perf mat rent (F124)

FIERA DI VENEZIA, LA: SINFONIA see
Salieri, Antonio

FIGARO POLKA see Strauss, Johann, [Jr.]

FIGLIA DI LORIO, LA: SUITE, FOR SOLO
VOICE AND ORCHESTRA see Hazon,
Roberto

FIGURE, FOR SOLO VOICE AND ORCHESTRA
see Castiglioni, Niccolò

FIGURES, FOR HARPSICHORD, VIOLIN,
VIOLA, VIOLONCELLO, AND CHAMBER
ORCHESTRA see Casterede, Jacques

FILIAE MAESTAE JERUSALEM, FOR SOLO
VOICE AND STRING ORCHESTRA see
Vivaldi, Antonio

FILIGRANFALTER, FOR SOLO VOICE AND
STRINGS see Fritsch, Johannes Georg

FILLE AUX CHEVEUX DE LIN, LA [ARR] see
Debussy, Claude

FILLE QUI CHANTE, LA, FOR SOLO VOICE
AND ORCHESTRA see Philippe, Pierre

FILLING STATION: SUITE see Thomson,
Virgil Garnett

FILLMORE, HENRY (1881-1956)
His Excellency March [3']
1.1.2.1. 2.2.1.0. drums,strings
set KALMUS A4146 $12.00   (F125)

FILMBALL (WALZER) see Kindermann, Ernst

FILS, [JOHANN] ANTON (1733-1760)
Sinfonia in C, MIN 128 [10']
string orch
(Townsend) sc PETERS P6977 f.s.,
perf mat rent   (F126)

Symphonies, Two
see Holzbauer, Ignaz Jakob,
Symphonic Works, Three

FILS DU MANDARIN: OVERTURE see Cui,
César Antonovich

FILTZ, ANTON (ANTONÍN)
see FILS, [JOHANN] ANTON

FIN AL PUNTO see Killmayer, Wilhelm

FINAL ALICE, FOR SOLO VOICE AND
ORCHESTRA see Del Tredici, David

FINALE see Ramovs, Primoz

FINALE FOR A CONCERT see Bush, Geoffrey

FINALMUSIK IN G. K. 63 see Mozart,
Wolfgang Amadeus

FINCH, RONALD (1922-   )
Romance for Viola and String
Orchestra
string orch,vla solo
[10'] CHESTER JWC122 perf mat rent
(F127)

FINE, IRVING (1914-1962)
Blue Towers
3.2.2.2.opt 2alto sax.opt tenor
sax.opt baritone sax. 4.3.3.1.
timp,perc,cel/pno,strings
sc SCHIRM.G $20.00, perf mat rent
(F128)

Diversions
2.3.2.2.opt 2alto sax.opt tenor
sax.opt baritone sax. 4.3.3.1.
timp,perc,cel/pno,strings
sc SCHIRM.G $20.00, perf mat rent
(F129)

Notturno
harp,strings
sc SCHIRM.G $12.00, perf mat rent
(F130)

Partita for Orchestra, [arr.]
(Spiegelman, Joel) 2+pic.2.2.2.
4.3.3.1. timp,2perc,strings
SCHIRM.G perf mat rent   (F131)

Symphony
3.3.3.3. 4.3.3.1. timp,perc,harp,
pno/cel,strings
sc SCHIRM.G $35.00, perf mat rent
(F132)

FINIS CORONAT OPUS, FOR PIANO AND
ORCHESTRA see Miereanu, Costin

FINKE, FIDELIO FRIEDRICH (FRITZ)
(1891-1968)
Eros, For Solo Voices And Orchestra
3.3.3.3. 4.3.3.0. timp,perc,harp,
strings,ST soli
BREITKOPF-L perf mat rent (F133)

Schein Und Sein, For Solo Voice And
Orchestra
3.3.3.3. 4.2.2.1. timp,perc,cel,
harp,strings,A/Bar solo
(edition for voice and piano- no.
EB 5860) sc,pts BREITKOPF-L perf
mat rent   (F134)

Suite No. 6
BREITKOPF-L perf mat rent (F135)

FINKO, DAVID (1936-   )
Moses, For Piano And Orchestra [19']
PRESSER perf mat rent   (F136)

FINNEY, ROSS LEE (1906-   )
Variations On A Memory [6'30"]
2.0.2.0.tenor sax. 2.1.1.0. perc,
strings
PETERS P66659 perf mat rent (F137)

FINNISCHE POLKA see Mohr, Gerhard

FINNISH DANCE NO. 1 see Ahvenainen,
Veikko

FINNISH FOLK TUNES see Pahlman, Emil

FINNISH MYTH, A see Rautavaara,
Einojuhani

FINNISSY, MICHAEL (1946-   )
Alongside
1.1.1.1. 1.1.1.0. perc,pno,2vln,
vla,vcl,db
sc UNIVER. 50 16349 $43.00, perf
mat rent   (F138)

Eph-Phatha [13']
2.1.1.1. 1.1.1.0. perc,harp,
strings
study sc OXFORD f.s., perf mat rent
(F139)

Jeanne D'Arc, For Solo Voices And
Chamber Group [20']
1.1.1.0. 1.1.1.0. 3perc,harp,
string quin,ST soli
UNIVER. perf mat rent   (F140)

Offshore [11']
3.3.3.3. 4.3.3.1. 3perc,2harp,
hpsd,pno,strings
UNIVER. perf mat rent   (F141)

Red Earth
3.3.3.0. 3.3.0.0. timp,4perc,
2harp,strings, 2 didjeridus
sc OXFORD $49.95   (F142)

Sea And Sky [24']
4.3.4.3. 4.4.4.1. timp,4perc,
2harp,2cel,strings
UNIVER. perf mat rent   (F143)

FINTA GIARDINIERA, LA: OVERTURE see
Mozart, Wolfgang Amadeus

FINTA SEMPLICE, LA: ELLA VUOLE ED IO
TORREI, FOR SOLO VOICE AND STRING
ORCHESTRA see Mozart, Wolfgang
Amadeus

FINTA SEMPLICE, LA: OVERTURE see
Mozart, Wolfgang Amadeus

FINTA SEMPLICE, LA: SONO IN AMORE, FOR
SOLO VOICE AND ORCHESTRA see
Mozart, Wolfgang Amadeus

FINZI, GERALD (1901-1956)
Introit, For Violin And Orchestra
*Op.6 [8']
1.1+English horn.2.1. 2.0.0.0.
strings,vln solo
BOOSEY perf mat rent   (F144)

Prelude, Op. 25 [4']
string orch
BOOSEY perf mat rent   (F145)

Severn Rhapsody, A *Op.3 [6']
1.1(English horn).1(bass clar).0.
1.0.0.0. strings
BOOSEY perf mat rent   (F146)
KALMUS A6127 sc $5.00, set $9.00
(F147)

Two Milton Sonnets, For Solo Voice
And Orchestra *Op.12 [8']
2.1+English horn.2.2. 2.0.0.0.
strings,T/S solo
BOOSEY perf mat rent   (F148)

FINZI, GRACIANE (1945-   )
De La Terre A La Vie, For Clarinet
And Strings [15']
12strings,clar solo
BILLAUDOT perf mat rent   (F149)

FIOCCO, JOSEPH-HECTOR (1703-1741)
Laudate Pueri, For Solo Voice And
Orchestra [15']
2ob,bsn,org,strings,S solo
COSTALL C.3474 perf mat rent (F150)

FIORI DI GHIACCIO, FOR PIANO AND
ORCHESTRA see Castiglioni, Niccolò

FIORILLO, FEDERIGO (1755-1823)
Concerto for Violin and Orchestra,
No. 1, in F
(Mezo) sc EMB 7235 f.s., perf mat
rent   (F151)

FIRAT, ERTUGRUL
Vision Of Days Past
vla,clar,trp,pno,strings
sc SEESAW $41.00, perf mat rent
(F152)

FIRE AND EARTH AND WATER AND AIR see
Roussakis, Nicolas

FIRE AND ICE SUITE see Kraft, William

FIRE FROM WITHIN, THE see Ware, Peter

FIRE GAMMELTESTAMENTLIGE SANGE, FOR
SOLO VOICE AND ORCHESTRA see
Koppel, Herman David

FIRE NORDISKE DANSE see Emborg, Jens
Laurson

FIRE VARIATIONS see Argento, Dominick

FIREBALLS see Meyer, Krzysztof

FIREBIRD see Stravinsky, Igor

FIRECRACKER, FOR OBOE AND CHAMBER
ORCHESTRA see Daugherty, Michael

FIRECYCLE BETA see Ferneyhough, Brian

FIRESTONE, IDABELLE (1874-1954)
In My Garden, For Solo Voice And
Orchestra
1.1.2.1.2alto sax.tenor sax.
2.2.1.0. timp,vibra,strings,
solo voice
SCHIRM.G perf mat rent   (F153)

FIREWORKS see Stravinsky, Igor

FIRMAMENTUM, FOR ORGAN AND ORCHESTRA
see Viitanen, Harri

FIRSOVA, ELENA (1950-   )
Chamber Concerto No. 1, For Flute And
String Orchestra *Op.19 [12']
string orch,fl solo
SIKORSKI perf mat rent   (F154)
VAAP perf mat rent   (F155)

Chamber Concerto No. 2, For
Violoncello And Orchestra *Op.26
[12']
1.1.1.1. 1.1.1.0. perc,harp,cel,
strings,vcl solo
SIKORSKI perf mat rent   (F156)
VAAP perf mat rent   (F157)

Chamber Concerto No. 3, For Piano And
Orchestra *Op.33 [15']
pic,4horn,trp,trom,perc,strings,
pno solo
VAAP perf mat rent   (F158)

Chamber Music *Op.9 [12']
string orch
VAAP perf mat rent   (F159)

Concerto for Violin and Orchestra,
No. 1, Op. 14 [11']
3.3.3.3. 3.3.3.1. perc,harp,cel,
strings,vln solo

FIRSOVA, ELENA (cont'd.)

SIKORSKI perf mat rent   (F160)
VAAP perf mat rent   (F161)

Concerto for Violin and Orchestra,
   No. 2, Op. 29 [15']
   3.3.3.3. 3.4.3.1. perc,cel,
   strings,vln solo
VAAP perf mat rent   (F162)

Concerto for Violoncello and
   Orchestra, No. 1, Op. 10 [18']
   2.1.1.1. 3.1.0.0. timp,perc,harp,
   cel,strings,vcl solo
SIKORSKI perf mat rent   (F163)
VAAP perf mat rent   (F164)

Five Pieces *Op.6 [12']
   2.2.2.2. 4.3.3.0. perc,strings
VAAP perf mat rent   (F165)

Postlude for Harp and Orchestra, Op.
   18 [5']
   bells,glock,cel,strings,harp solo
SIKORSKI perf mat rent   (F166)
VAAP perf mat rent   (F167)

Stanzas *Op.13 [11']
   3.2.2.2. 4.3.3.1. timp,perc,harp,
   cel,strings
SIKORSKI perf mat rent   (F168)
VAAP perf mat rent   (F169)

Stein, Der, For Solo Voice And
   Orchestra
   see Stone, The, For Solo Voice And
   Orchestra

Stone, The, For Solo Voice And
   Orchestra *Op.28 [18']
   2.2.2.2. 2.4.3.1. perc,harp,cel,
   strings,solo voice
VAAP perf mat rent   (F170)
   "Stein, Der, For Solo Voice And
   Orchestra" SIKORSKI perf mat rent
                                          (F171)

Tristia, For Solo Voice And Chamber
   Orchestra *Op.22 [16']
   1.1.1.1. 2.0.0.0. perc,harp,cel,
   strings,S solo
SIKORSKI perf mat rent   (F172)
VAAP perf mat rent   (F173)

FIRST LANDSCAPE see Boone, Charles N.

FIRST LIGHT see Danielpour, Richard

FIRST MEETING, THE, FOR SOLO VOICE AND
   ORCHESTRA [ARR] see Grieg, Edvard
   Hagerup

FIRST SHOOT, THE [ARR.] see Walton,
   [Sir] William (Turner)

FISCHER, IRWIN (1903-1977)
   Piece Heroique [8']
   2.3.2.2. 4.3.3.1. timp,opt org,
   strings
AM.COMP.AL. perf mat rent   (F174)

Sea-Bird, The, For Solo Voice And
   Orchestra [3']
   3.2.2.2. 4.2.3.1. timp,cym,
   strings,med solo
sc AM.COMP.AL. $4.60   (F175)

FISCHER, JOHANN CASPAR FERDINAND
   (ca. 1665-1746)
   Suite De Danses, For Trumpet And
   String Orchestra
   (Thilde, J.) string orch,trp solo
   [7'10"] sc BILLAUDOT f.s., perf
   mat rent   (F176)

FISCHER, MICHAEL GOTTHARD (1773-1829)
   Concerto for Clarinet, Bassoon and
   Orchestra, Op. 11, in C
MUS. RARA perf mat rent   (F177)

FISCHERKNABE, DER, FOR SOLO VOICE AND
   ORCHESTRA see Liszt, Franz

FIŠER, LUBOŠ (1935-   )
   Labyrinth [9']
   2.2.2.2. 2.2.2.0. timp,strings
SUPRAPHON   (F178)

FISHER, ALFRED (1942-   )
   Elegiac Variations, For Violoncello
   And Orchestra
   1.1.2.2. 2.0.2.0. timp,cel,harp,
   strings,vcl solo
SEESAW   (F179)

Morning - Peniel
   3.3.3.3. 4.3.3.1. harp,pno/cel,
   strings
SEESAW   (F180)

Overture Petillante
   3.2.3.3. 4.3.3.1. timp,perc,
   strings
sc SEESAW $26.00, perf mat rent
                                          (F181)

FISHER, ALFRED (cont'd.)

Peace Variations
   string orch
SEESAW   (F182)

Warrior
   3.2.3.3. 4.3.3.1. 3perc,harp,cel,
   strings
sc SEESAW $33.00, perf mat rent   (F183)

FISHERMAN'S SONG see Zhou, Long

FISHER'S WIDOW, THE [ARR.] see Edwards,
   Clara

FITELBERG, JERZY (1903-1951)
   Concerto for Violin and Orchestra,
   No. 2 [20']
   3.2.2.3. 4.3.2.1. timp,perc,
   strings,vln solo
ESCHIG perf mat rent   (F184)

Golden Horn, The
   string orch
AMP perf mat rent   (F185)

Konzertstück [20']
   2.2.2.2. 4.3.2.1. timp,perc,harp,
   pno,strings
ESCHIG perf mat rent   (F186)

Symphony No. 2 for String Orchestra
   string orch
PEER perf mat rent   (F187)

FIVE AUSTRALIAN LYRICS, FOR SOLO VOICE
   AND ORCHESTRA see Antill, John
   Henry

FIVE CHRISTMAS SONGS, FOR SOLO VOICE
   AND ORCHESTRA [ARR.] see Sibelius,
   Jean

FIVE DAYS AND FIVE NIGHTS: SUITE see
   Shostakovich, Dmitri

FIVE EPISODES see Trimble, Lester
   Albert

FIVE ETUDES, FOR PIANO AND ORCHESTRA
   see Ponse, Luctor

FIVE FOLK TUNES FROM SARNA see Sköld,
   Sven

FIVE FRAGMENTS FOR ORCHESTRA see
   Shostakovich, Dmitri

FIVE INHIBITIONS see Mourant, Walter

FIVE MOVEMENTS, FOR PIANO AND STRING
   ORCHESTRA see Downes, Andrew

FIVE MOVEMENTS FOR ORCHESTRA see
   Geelen, Mathieu

FIVE MYSTICAL SONGS, FOR SOLO VOICE AND
   ORCHESTRA see Vaughan Williams,
   Ralph

FIVE NORDIC MELODIES see Sonninen, Ahti

FIVE OF A KIND, FOR BRASS QUINTET AND
   ORCHESTRA see Schickele, Peter

FIVE ORCHESTRAL SONGS, FOR SOLO VOICE
   AND ORCHESTRA see Karchin, Louis S.

FIVE PIECES see Firsova, Elena

FIVE PIECES FOR CHAMBER ORCHESTRA see
   Eiriksdottir, Karolina

FIVE PIECES FOR ORCHESTRA see
   Shostakovich, Dmitri, Five
   Fragments For Orchestra

FIVE PIECES FOR ORCHESTRA, AFTER
   PAINTINGS OF ANDREW WYETH, FOR SOLO
   VOICE AND ORCHESTRA see Nelson,
   Ronald J. (Ron)

FIVE PIECES FOR ORCHESTRA, OP. 16,
   ORIGINAL VERSION see Schoenberg,
   Arnold

FIVE PRELUDES, FOR VIOLIN AND
   INSTRUMENTAL ENSEMBLE see Ogdon,
   Wilbur L.

FIVE PRELUDES [ARR.] see Shostakovich,
   Dmitri

FIVE PSALMS, FOR SOLO VOICE AND STRING
   ORCHESTRA see Wishart, Peter

FIVE ROMANTIC SONGS ON LOVE, FOR SOLO
   VOICE AND STRING ORCHESTRA see
   Kalabis, Viktor

FIVE SETTINGS OF RUCKERT POEMS, FOR
   SOLO VOICE AND ORCHESTRA see
   Mahler, Gustav

FIVE SHORT PIECES see Handel, George
   Frideric

FIVE SHORT PIECES FOR STRINGS see
   Krenek, Ernst

FIVE SONATAS IN THE FORM OF A SUITE
   [ARR.] see Scarlatti, Domenico

FIVE SONGS, FOR SOLO VOICE AND
   ORCHESTRA see Shifrin, Seymour J.
   see Yannay, Yehuda

FIVE SONGS, FOR SOLO VOICE AND
   ORCHESTRA [ARR] see Wolf, Hugo

FIVE SONGS FOR SOLO VOICE AND ORCHESTRA
   [ARR.] see Kjerulf, Halfdan

FIVE SONGS FROM "THE MOUNTAIN KID", FOR
   SOLO VOICE AND ORCHESTRA [ARR.] see
   Grieg, Edvard Hagerup

FIVE SONGS OF REMEMBRANCE, FOR SOLO
   VOICE AND STRING ORCHESTRA see
   Weigl, [Mrs.] Vally

FIVE SONGS TO POEMS BY IRINA
   RATUSHINKSKAYA, FOR SOLO VOICE AND
   ORCHESTRA see Élias, Brian

FIVE VARIATIONS ON A THEME FROM "THE
   MAGIC FLUTE", FOR FLUTE AND
   ORCHESTRA see Lerstad, Terje B.

FIXED DOUBLES see Butler, Martin

FJELL-LENGT see Kielland, Olav

FJELL-NORIG, FOR SOLO VOICE AND
   ORCHESTRA see Egge, Klaus

FJELL-SUITE, FOR SOLO VOICE, RECORDER
   AND ORCHESTRA [ARR.] see
   Storbekken, Egil

FJELLBEKKEN, FOR RECORDER AND STRING
   ORCHESTRA [ARR.] see Storbekken,
   Egil

FJELLVIND, FOR SOLO VOICE AND ORCHESTRA
   see Groven, Eivind

FLADMOE, ARVID (1915-   )
   Bukkerittet, For Solo Voices And
   Orchestra
   2.2.2.2. 2.2.2.1. timp,perc,
   strings,MezBar soli
   "Reindeer Ride From Peer Gynt, The,
   For Solo Voices And Orchestra"
NORGE   (F188)

Music for Strings [6']
   string orch
NORGE   (F189)

Music for Violoncello and Orchestra
   2.1.2.1. 2.2.0.0. timp,strings,
   vcl solo
NORGE   (F190)

Pa Kannarhaugene
   see Three Songs, For Solo Voice And
   Orchestra, Op. 11

Reindeer Ride From Peer Gynt, The,
   For Solo Voices And Orchestra
   see Bukkerittet, For Solo Voices
   And Orchestra

Ride Batkvelvet
   see Three Songs, For Solo Voice And
   Orchestra, Op. 11

Suite for Orchestra, Op. 13 [10']
   3(pic).2.2.2. 2.2.1.0. timp,perc,
   strings
NORGE   (F191)

Svana Eld
   see Three Songs, For Solo Voice And
   Orchestra, Op. 11

Three Songs, For Solo Voice And
   Orchestra, Op. 11
   2.2.2.2. 0.3.0.0. timp,perc,cel,
   strings,Bar solo NORGE f.s.
   contains: Pa Kannarhaugene; Ride
   Batkvelvet; Svana Eld   (F192)

FLAFF see Meijering, Chiel

FLAGELLANTENZUG see Bleyle, Karl

FLAGWALK WITH "O" see Guy, Barry

FLAHERTY, THOMAS (1950-   )
   Concerto for Flute and Chamber
   Orchestra [16']
   2.2.2.2. 2.0.0.0. timp,harp,pno,
   strings,fl solo
MARGUN MP2091 perf mat rent (F193)

FLÄKA see Torstensson, Klas

FLAMENCO see Goossens, [Sir] Eugene

FLAMENT, EDUOARD (1880-1958)
    Concerto for Piano and Orchestra, No.
        1 [20']
        2.2.2.2. 4.2.0.0. timp,strings,
            pno solo
        BILLAUDOT perf mat rent   (F194)

    Symphony No. 7 [30']
        0.0.4.0.3alto sax. 0.4.3.0.
            5perc,4harp,gtr,2pno,org,
            strings,girl solo
        BILLAUDOT perf mat rent   (F195)

FLAMINIO, IL: SINFONIA see Pergolesi,
    Giovanni Battista

FLANAGAN, WILLIAM (1926-1969)
    Weeping Pleiades, The, For Solo Voice
        And Instrumental Ensemble
        fl,clar,pno,strings,vln solo,Bar
            solo
        PEER perf mat rent   (F196)

FLARES AND DECLAMATIONS see Gould,
    Morton

FLAVIO ANICIO OLIBRIO: RECITATIVO E
    ARIA DI FLAVIO, FOR SOLO VOICE AND
    ORCHESTRA see Porpora, Nicola
    Antonio

FLEA, THE: FOUR PIECES see
    Shostakovich, Dmitri

FLEA DANCE see Mourant, Walter

FLEDERMAUS, DIE: BALLET MUSIC AND
    FINALE see Strauss, Johann, [Jr.]

FLEDERMAUS POLKA see Strauss, Johann,
    [Jr.]

FLEDERMAUS QUADRILLE see Strauss,
    Johann, [Jr.]

FLEM, KJELL (1943-   )
    Ultima Thule
        3.2.3.2. 4.4.3.1. timp,perc,
            2harp,cel&pno,strings
        NORGE   (F197)

FLEMING, CHRISTOPHER LE
    see LE FLEMING, CHRISTOPHER

FLEMING, ROBERT (1921-1976)
    Hymn To War, For Solo Voice And
        String Orchestra
        string orch,T solo
        CAN.MUS.CENT. MV 1600 F598HY (F198)

    Snuff Box
        string orch
        CAN.MUS.CENT. MI 1500 F598S (F199)

    String Thing, A [3']
        string orch
        CAN.MUS.CENT. MI 1500 598ST (F200)

FLENDER, REINHARD DAVID (1953-   )
    Pirkei Tehillim, For Solo Voice And
        Orchestra [20']
        2.2.2.2. 3.2.0.1. timp,perc,
            marimba,harp,strings,Mez solo
        "Three Hebrew Psalms, For Solo
            Voice And Orchestra" PEER MUSIK
            perf mat rent   (F201)

    Three Hebrew Psalms, For Solo Voice
        And Orchestra
        see Pirkei Tehillim, For Solo Voice
        And Orchestra

FLEST see Thommessen, Olav Anton

FLEURS DE FRANCE see Tailleferre,
    Germaine

FLEUVE see Leroux, Philippe

FLEUVES, FOR PIANO AND ORCHESTRA see
    Tremblay, Gilles

FLIEGENDE HOLLÄNDER, DER: DIE FRIST IST
    UM, FOR SOLO VOICE AND ORCHESTRA
    see Wagner, Richard

FLIEGENDE HOLLÄNDER, DER: OVERTURE see
    Wagner, Richard

FLIEGENDE HOLLÄNDER, DER: TRAFT IHR DAS
    SCHIFF, FOR SOLO VOICE AND
    ORCHESTRA see Wagner, Richard

FLIEGENDE HOLLÄNDER, DER: WILLST JENES
    TAGS DU DICH NICHT MEHR ENTSINNEN,
    FOR SOLO VOICE AND ORCHESTRA see
    Wagner, Richard

FLIES, J. BERNHARD (1770- ?)
    Schlafe Mein Prinzchen, For Solo
        Voice And Orchestra, [arr.]
        (Mottl) fl,strings,S solo
        (Wiegenlied formerly attributed
            to Mozart) BREITKOPF-L perf mat

FLIES, J. BERNHARD (cont'd.)

    rent   (F202)

FLIGHT INTO EGYPT see Berlioz, Hector
    (Louis), Enfance Du Christ, L':
    Prelude, Part II, "La Fuite En
    Egypte"

FLIGHT OF THE TRAPEZE see Proto, Frank

FLIGHTS OF COL, THE see Butler, Martin

FLIGHTY see Gentile, Ada

FLIRT EN BLEU see Kochan, Ernst

FLIRTATIOUS JIG, FOR VIOLIN AND STRING
    ORCHESTRA see Cowell, Henry Dixon

FLOCK DESCENDS INTO THE PENTAGONAL
    GARDEN, A see Takemitsu, Toru

FLOHLIED AUS GOETHES "FAUST", FOR SOLO
    VOICE AND ORCHESTRA [ARR.] see
    Beethoven, Ludwig van, Es War
    Einmal Ein Konig, For Solo Voice
    And Orchestra [arr.]

FLORAL VIEW WITH MAIDENS SINGING see
    Heininen, Paavo

FLORENTINER MARSCH see Fucik, Julius

FLORENTZ
    Marches Du Soleil, Les
        LEDUC perf mat rent   (F203)

FLORETE PRATA, FOR SOLO VOICE AND
    ORCHESTRA see Campra, André

FLOSMAN, OLDRICH (1925-   )
    Concerto for Violin and Orchestra,
        No. 2 [26']
        3.2.3.2. 4.2.2.0. timp,perc,
            strings,vln solo
        SUPRAPHON   (F204)

    Symphony-Concerto, For Piano And
        Orchestra
        sc PANTON 2275 f.s.   (F205)

    Symphony No. 2 [26']
        3.3.3.2. 4.3.3.1. timp,perc,
            strings
        SUPRAPHON   (F206)

FLOTHUIS, MARIUS (1914-   )
    Santa Espina, For Solo Voice And
        Orchestra *Op.88 [9']
        DONEMUS perf mat rent   (F207)

FLOTOW, FRIEDRICH VON (1812-1883)
    Martha: Ach So Fromm, For Solo Voice
        And Orchestra
        BREITKOPF-L perf mat rent   (F208)

    Martha: Die Letzte Rose, For Solo
        Voice And Orchestra
        2.2.2.2. 4.2.2.1. timp,harp,
            strings,S solo
        BREITKOPF-L perf mat rent   (F209)

    Martha: Ja Was Nun, Was Nur Tun, For
        Solo Voices And Orchestra [9']
        1+pic.2.2.2. 4.2.3.1. timp,
            strings,AB soli
        BREITKOPF-W perf mat rent   (F210)

    Martha: Schlafe Wohl, For Solo Voices
        And Orchestra [6']
        1+pic.2.2.2. 4.2.3.1. timp,2perc,
            harp,strings,SATB soli
        BREITKOPF-W perf mat rent   (F211)

FLOTTES LEBEN POLKA see Strauss, Eduard

FLOURISHES AND GALOP see Gould, Morton

FLOWER OF THE MOUNTAIN, FOR SOLO VOICE
    AND ORCHESTRA see Albert, Stephen
    Joel

FLOWER SHOWER see Sveinsson, Atli
    Heimir

FLOWER VARIATIONS AND WHEELS see
    Beckwith, John

FLOWERS see Soll, Burkhardt

FLOWING TIDE, THE see Dale, Benjamin
    James

FLUCTUANTE-IMMUABLE see Eloy, Jean-
    Claude

FLUCTUATIONS see Norholm, Ib,
    Fluktuationer see Sigurbjörnsson,
    Thorkell

FLUGSCHRIFTEN WALZER see Strauss,
    Johann, [Jr.]

FLUKTUATIONER see Norholm, Ib

FLUTE FUYANT LE SOL A PERDRE HALEINE,
    UNE, FOR FLUTE AND INSTRUMENTAL
    ENSEMBLE see Saguer, Louis

FLUXASKA see Ekström, Lars

FLUXUS 1 see Antoniou, Theodore

FLUXUS 2, FOR PIANO AND CHAMBER
    ORCHESTRA see Antoniou, Theodore

FLYING DUTCHMAN: OVERTURE see Wagner,
    Richard, Fliegende Hollander, Der:
    Overture

FLYING THEME, THE [ARR.] see Williams,
    John T.

FOCI see Anhalt, István

FOCI I see Rosenman, Leonard

FODI, JOHN (1944-   )
    Concertino for Bassoon and Chamber
        Orchestra
        2.0.2.0. 2.0.0.1. 2vla,2vcl,db,
            bsn solo
        CAN.MUS.CENT. MI 1324 F653CO (F212)

    Concerto Grosso, Op. 74 [5']
        0.1.1.1. 1.1.1.0. kbd,strings
        CAN.MUS.CENT. MI 1200 F653CO (F213)

    Kootenay *Op.76
        1.1.1.1. 2.1.0.0. timp,strings
        CAN.MUS.CENT. MI 1200 F653K (F214)

FODOR, CAREL ANTON (1768-1846)
    Symphony No. 4, Op. 19, in C [17']
        1.2.2.2. 2.2.0.0. timp,strings
        sc DONEMUS f.s., perf mat rent
                                       (F215)

FODOR, GEORGE
    Concerto For Violin And Orchestra In
        D *see THREE CENTURIES OF MUSIC
        IN SCORE, VOL. 5: CONCERTO IV,
        CLASSICAL STRINGS AND WINDS

FOERSTER, CHRISTOPH (1693-1745)
    Symphony in E flat, [arr.]
        (Schneider, M.) 2horn,hpsd,strings
        [6'30"] KALMUS A5428 sc $3.00,
        set $7.00   (F216)

FOLEY, DANIEL (1952-   )
    Athabascan Dances *Op.21 [15']
        2.2.2.2. 4.2.0.0. timp,perc,
            strings
        CAN.MUS.CENT. MI 1100 F663AT (F217)

FOLIA, LA see Hachimura, Yoshio

FOLIART, DAN (1951-   )
    Sonata for String Orchestra [8']
        string orch
        KALMUS A6736 sc $8.00, set $10.00,
        pts $2.00, ea.   (F218)

FOLIE ET MORT D'OPHELIE, FOR SOLO
    VOICES AND ORCHESTRA see Abbott,
    Alain see Louvier, Alain

FOLIES FRANCAISES, LES [ARR.] see
    Couperin, François (le Grand)

FOLK DANCE AND FUGUE NO. 2 see Kenins,
    Talivaldis

FOLK OVERTURE see Mennin, Peter
    (Mennini)

FOLKERAADET see Delius, Frederick

FOLLIES OVERTURE see Barnes, Milton

FOLLOW-THE-LEADER INTO MY SONG see
    Börtz, Daniel

FONGAARD, BJØRN (1919-1981)
    Angelicum *Op.91 [15']
        2.2.2.2. 2.2.0.0. perc,strings
        NORGE   (F219)

    Calisto *Op.76,No.2 [7']
        1.1.1.0. 2.0.2.0. timp,perc,
            strings
        NORGE   (F220)

    Concerto for Accordion and Orchestra,
        Op. 143, No. 3 [20']
        perc,strings,acord solo
        NORGE   (F221)

    Concerto for Alto Saxophone and
        Orchestra, Op. 120, No. 11 [17']
        string orch,alto sax solo
        NORGE   (F222)

    Concerto for Bass Clarinet and String
        Orchestra, Op. 120, No. 10 [18']
        string orch,bass clar solo
        NORGE   (F223)

FONGAARD, BJØRN (cont'd.)

Concerto for Bassoon and String
Orchestra, Op. 120, No. 12 [18']
string orch,bsn solo
NORGE   (F224)

Concerto for Clarinet and Orchestra,
No. 1, Op. 120, No. 8 [18']
perc,strings,clar solo
NORGE   (F225)

Concerto for Clarinet and Orchestra,
No. 2, Op. 120, No. 9 [17']
string orch,clar solo
NORGE   (F226)

Concerto for Double Bass and
Orchestra, Op. 119, No. 12 [20']
1.1.1.0. 1.0.0.0. perc,strings,db
solo
NORGE   (F227)

Concerto for English Horn and
Orchestra, Op. 120, No. 7 [21']
elec org,perc,strings,English
horn solo
NORGE   (F228)

Concerto for Flute and Orchestra, No.
1, Op. 120, No. 2 [18']
3horn,strings,fl solo
NORGE   (F229)

Concerto for Flute and Orchestra, No.
2, Op. 120, No. 3 [21']
elec org,perc,strings,fl solo
NORGE   (F230)

Concerto for Flute and Orchestra, No.
4, Op. 120, No. 4 [18']
elec org,perc,strings,fl solo
NORGE   (F231)

Concerto for Guitar and String
Orchestra, Op. 143, No. 2 [18']
string orch,gtr solo
NORGE   (F232)

Concerto for Harp and Orchestra, Op.
143, No. 1 [21']
perc,strings,harp solo
NORGE   (F233)

Concerto for Horn and Orchestra, No.
1, Op. 121, No. 1 [16']
2.1.0.1. 0.0.0.0. perc,strings,
horn solo
NORGE   (F234)

Concerto for Horn and Orchestra, No.
2, Op. 121, No. 2 [21']
string orch,horn solo
NORGE   (F235)

Concerto for Horn and Orchestra, No.
3, Op. 121, No. 3 [17']
string orch,horn solo
NORGE   (F236)

Concerto for Oboe and Orchestra, No.
1, Op. 120, No. 5
elec org,perc,strings,ob solo
NORGE   (F237)

Concerto for Oboe and Orchestra, No.
2, Op. 120, No. 6 [17']
elec org,perc,strings,ob solo
NORGE   (F238)

Concerto for Organ and Orchestra, No.
1, Op. 122, No. 1 [18']
perc,strings,org solo
NORGE   (F239)

Concerto for Organ and Orchestra, No.
2, Op. 122, No. 2 [17']
perc,strings,org solo
NORGE   (F240)

Concerto for Organ and Orchestra, No.
3, Op. 122, No. 3 [18']
perc,strings,org solo
NORGE   (F241)

Concerto for Organ and Orchestra, No.
4, Op. 122, No. 4 [17']
perc,strings,org solo
NORGE   (F242)

Concerto for Organ and Orchestra, No.
5, Op. 122, No. 5 [18']
perc,strings,org solo
NORGE   (F243)

Concerto for Percussion and
Orchestra, Op. 143, No. 4 [17']
1.1.0.0. 2.0.0.0. strings,perc
solo
NORGE   (F244)

Concerto for Piano and Orchestra, No.
1, Op. 118, No. 1 [20']
elec org,perc,strings,pno solo
NORGE   (F245)

FONGAARD, BJØRN (cont'd.)

Concerto for Piano and Orchestra, No.
2, Op. 118, No. 2 [23']
1.1.0.0. 1.0.0.0. perc,strings,
pno solo
NORGE   (F246)

Concerto for Piano and Orchestra, No.
3, Op. 118, No. 3 [21']
3.1.1.1. 4.0.0.0. timp,perc,
strings,pno solo
NORGE   (F247)

Concerto for Piano and Orchestra, No.
4, Op. 118, No. 4 [18']
2.1.0.1. 2.0.0.0. perc,strings,
pno solo
NORGE   (F248)

Concerto for Piano and Orchestra, No.
5, Op. 118, No. 5 [23']
2.1.0.1. 3.0.0.0. perc,strings,
pno solo
NORGE   (F249)

Concerto for Piano and Orchestra, No.
6, Op. 118, No. 6 [18']
2.2.0.0. 2.0.0.0. strings,pno
solo
NORGE   (F250)

Concerto for Piano and Orchestra, No.
7, Op. 118, No. 7 [15']
1.0.1.1. 2.0.0.0. strings,pno
solo
NORGE   (F251)

Concerto for Piano and Orchestra, No.
8, Op. 118, No. 8 [23']
1.0.1.0. 1.0.0.0. perc,strings,
pno solo
NORGE   (F252)

Concerto for Piano and Orchestra, No.
9, Op. 118, No. 9 [21']
timp,strings,pno solo
NORGE   (F253)

Concerto for Piano and Orchestra, No.
10, Op. 118, No. 10 [24']
1.1.0.0. 1.0.0.0. timp,perc,
strings,pno solo
NORGE   (F254)

Concerto for Piano and Orchestra, No.
11, Op. 118, No. 11 [17']
3.0.0.0. 4.0.0.0. perc,strings,
pno solo
NORGE   (F255)

Concerto for Piano and Orchestra, No.
12, Op. 118, No. 12 [23']
1.1.0.0. 1.0.0.1. perc,strings,
pno solo
NORGE   (F256)

Concerto for Piano and Orchestra, No.
13, Op. 118, No. 13 [20']
1.1.0.0. 1.0.0.0. perc,strings,
pno solo
NORGE   (F257)

Concerto for Piano and Orchestra, No.
14, Op. 118, No. 14 [23']
2.1.0.0. 1.0.0.0. perc,strings,
pno solo
NORGE   (F258)

Concerto for Piano and Orchestra, No.
15, Op. 118, No. 15 [27']
1.1.0.0. 1.0.0.0. perc,strings,
pno solo
NORGE   (F259)

Concerto for Piano and Orchestra, No.
16, Op. 118, No. 16 [20']
1.1.0.0. 1.0.0.0. perc,strings,
pno solo
NORGE   (F260)

Concerto for Piano and Orchestra, No.
17, Op. 118, No. 17 [17']
1.1.0.0. 1.0.0.0. perc,strings,
pno solo
NORGE   (F261)

Concerto for Piano and Orchestra, No.
18, Op. 118, No. 18 [24']
1.1.0.0. 1.0.0.0. strings,pno
solo
NORGE   (F262)

Concerto for Piano and Orchestra, No.
19, Op. 118, No. 19 [22']
1.1.0.0. 1.0.0.0. perc,strings,
pno solo
NORGE   (F263)

Concerto for Piano and Orchestra, No.
20, Op. 118, No. 20 [21']
perc,strings,pno solo
NORGE   (F264)

FONGAARD, BJØRN (cont'd.)

Concerto for Piano and Orchestra, No.
21, Op. 118, No. 21 [20']
perc,strings,pno solo
NORGE   (F265)

Concerto for Piano and Orchestra, No.
22, Op. 118, No. 22 [24']
perc,strings,pno solo
NORGE   (F266)

Concerto for Piano and Orchestra, No.
23, Op. 118, No. 23 [18']
perc,strings,pno solo
NORGE   (F267)

Concerto for Piccolo and Orchestra,
Op. 120, No. 1 [14']
2horn,strings,pic solo
NORGE   (F268)

Concerto for Trombone and String
Orchestra, Op. 121, No. 6 [17']
string orch,trom solo
NORGE   (F269)

Concerto for Trumpet and String
Orchestra, No. 1, Op. 121, No. 4
[18']
string orch,trp solo
NORGE   (F270)

Concerto for Trumpet and String
Orchestra, No. 2, Op. 121, No. 5
[17']
string orch,trp solo
NORGE   (F271)

Concerto for Viola and Orchestra, Op.
119, No. 8 [21']
1.1.1.0. 1.0.0.0. perc,strings,
vla solo
NORGE   (F272)

Concerto for Violin and Orchestra,
No. 1, Op. 119, No. 1 [15']
2.1.0.1. 2.0.0.0. perc,strings,
vln solo
NORGE   (F273)

Concerto for Violin and Orchestra,
No. 2, Op. 119, No. 2 [25']
2.1.0.1. 3.0.0.0. perc,strings,
vln solo
NORGE   (F274)

Concerto for Violin and Orchestra,
No. 3, Op. 119, No. 3 [20']
2.1.0.0. 1.0.0.0. perc,strings,
vln solo
NORGE   (F275)

Concerto for Violin and Orchestra,
No. 4, Op. 119, No. 4 [22']
2.1.0.0. 1.0.0.0. perc,strings,
vln solo
NORGE   (F276)

Concerto for Violin and Orchestra,
No. 5, Op. 119, No. 5 [21']
1.1.0.0. 1.0.0.0. perc,strings,
vln solo
NORGE   (F277)

Concerto for Violin and Orchestra,
No. 6, Op. 119, No. 6 [23']
1.1.0.0. 2.0.0.0. perc,strings,
vln solo
NORGE   (F278)

Concerto for Violin and Orchestra,
No. 7, Op. 119, No. 7 [18']
1.1.1.0. 2.0.0.0. perc,strings,
vln solo
NORGE   (F279)

Concerto for Violoncello and
Orchestra, No. 1, Op. 119, No. 9
[20']
1.1.1.0. 1.0.0.0. perc,strings,
vcl solo
NORGE   (F280)

Concerto for Violoncello and
Orchestra, No. 2, Op. 119, No. 10
[21']
1.1.1.0. 1.0.0.0. perc,strings,
vcl solo
NORGE   (F281)

Concerto for Violoncello and
Orchestra, No. 3, Op. 119, No. 11
[19']
1.1.1.0. 1.0.0.0. perc,strings,
vcl solo
NORGE   (F282)

Fantasy, Op. 69 [5']
string orch
NORGE   (F283)

Francis Of Assisi
see Frans Av Assi'si

FONGAARD, BJØRN (cont'd.)

Frans Av Assi'si *Op.148,No.2 [12']
4.3.3.3. 6.4.3.1. timp,perc,org,
strings
"Francis Of Assisi" NORGE (F284)

Hjemmefronten *Op.148,No.3 [12']
3.3.3.3. 4.4.3.1. timp,perc,harp,
strings
"Home Guard" NORGE (F285)

Home Guard
see Hjemmefronten

Klangbilder *Op.72 [16']
string orch
"Sound Pictures" NORGE (F286)

Legende *Op.68 [9']
1.1.1.1. 2.1.2.0. timp,perc,
strings
NORGE (F287)

Life
see Livet

Livet *Op.107 [29']
2.2.2.2. 4.2.3.0. timp,perc,elec
org,strings,electronic tape
"Life" NORGE (F288)

Mare Tranquillitatis *Op.76,No.1
[11']
1.1.1.0. 2.0.2.0. timp,perc,
strings
NORGE (F289)

Naturen *Op.106 [25']
2.2.2.2. 4.2.3.0. timp,perc,
strings,electronic tape
.NORGE (F290)

Orchestra Antiphonalis *Op.67 [11']
1.0.1.3. 2.2.0.0. timp,perc,
strings
NORGE (F291)

Pflantzenwelt, Die *Op.100 [21']
2.2.2.2. 6.3.3.0. perc,elec org,
strings
NORGE (F292)

Relativity 1: The Lorenz
Transformation *Op.88 [15']
2.2.2.0. 6.2.3.1. timp,perc,
strings
NORGE (F293)

Relativity 2: Gravitation *Op.89
[16']
2.2.2.0. 6.2.3.1. timp,perc,
strings
NORGE (F294)

Relativity 3: Cosmology *Op.90 [16']
2.2.2.2. 6.0.3.1. timp,perc,
strings
NORGE (F295)

Serenade, Op. 55 [28']
string orch
NORGE (F296)

Serenade, Op. 147, No. 1 [14']
1.1.0.0. 2.0.0.0. timp,perc,
strings
NORGE (F297)

Serenade, Op. 147, No. 2 [16']
1.1.0.0. 2.0.0.0. perc,strings
NORGE (F298)

Serenade, Op. 147, No. 3
1.1.0.0. 2.0.0.0. perc,strings
NORGE (F299)

Sinfonia Geo-Paleontologica No. 1
*Op.82 [16']
3.2.2.2. 5.2.3.0. timp,perc,
strings
NORGE (F300)

Sinfonia Geo-Paleontologica No. 2
*Op.83 [15']
3.2.2.2. 6.0.2.0. timp,perc,
strings
NORGE (F301)

Sinfonia Geo-Paleontologica No. 3
*Op.84 [15']
3.2.2.1. 6.2.3.0. timp,perc,
strings
NORGE (F302)

Sinfonia Geo-Paleontologica No. 4
*Op.85 [19']
3.2.3.2. 6.2.3.1. timp,perc,
strings
NORGE (F303)

Sinfonia Geo-Paleontologica No. 5
*Op.86
3.2.2.2. 6.2.3.1. timp,perc,
strings
NORGE (F304)

FONGAARD, BJØRN (cont'd.)

Sinfonietta, No. 1, Op. 27 [20']
2.3.2.2. 4.2.2.1. timp,perc,
NORGE (F305)

Sinfonietta, No. 2, Op. 71 [11']
2.2.2.1. 4.2.2.0. timp,perc,
strings
NORGE (F306)

Sinus Iridum *Op.76,No.5 [8']
1.1.1.0. 2.0.2.0. timp,perc,
strings
NORGE (F307)

Sound Pictures
see Klangbilder

Svalbard *Op.148,No.1 [14']
4.2.3.2. 6.4.3.1. timp,perc,harp,
pno,org,strings
NORGE (F308)

Symphony No. 1, Op. 150, No. 1 [23']
string orch
NORGE (F309)

Symphony No. 2, Op. 150, No. 2 [21']
string orch
NORGE (F310)

Symphony No. 3, Op. 150, No. 3 [24']
string orch
NORGE (F311)

Symphony No. 4, Op. 150, No. 4 [20']
string orch
NORGE (F312)

Symphony No. 5, Op. 150, No. 5 [22']
string orch
NORGE (F313)

Symphony No. 6, Op. 150, No. 6 [21']
string orch
NORGE (F314)

Symphony No. 7, Op. 150, No. 7 [25']
string orch
NORGE (F315)

Titan *Op.76,No.3 [7']
1.1.1.0. 2.0.1.0. timp,perc,
strings
NORGE (F316)

Triton *Op.76,No.4 [6']
1.1.1.0. 2.1.2.0. timp,perc,
strings
NORGE (F317)

Universum *Op.87 [10']
2.1.2.1. 4.2.2.0. perc,strings
NORGE (F318)

Uran 235 *Op.58 [11']
3.2.3.2. 4.2.2.0. timp,perc,
strings
NORGE (F319)

FONTAINE DE JOUVENCE, LA see Auric,
Georges

FONTYN, JACQUELINE (1930-)
Creneaux [10']
2(pic).2(English horn).2(bass
clar).2(contrabsn).opt alto
sax.opt tenor sax. 4.2+opt
trp.3.1. 3perc,harp,opt cel,
strings
PERFORM perf mat rent (F320)

Danceries [10']
2.2.2.2. 2.2.2.0. timp,perc,harp,
strings
SCHIRM.G perf mat rent (F321)

Halo, For Harp And Chamber Orchestra
[16']
1.1.2.0. 2.1.1.0. 2perc,pno,
strings,harp solo
BOTE perf mat rent (F322)

Pour Onze Archets [13']
6vln,2vla,2vcl,db
sc SCHIRM.G 50339930 $20.00, perf
mat rent (F323)

FOOTE, ARTHUR (1853-1937)
Four Character Pieces After The
Rubaiyat Of Omar Khayyam *Op.48
[20']
2.2.2.2. 4.2.3.1. timp,perc,harp,
strings
KALMUS A6479 sc $25.00, set $45.00,
pts $2.00, ea., perf mat rent
(F324)

Irish Folksong
KALMUS A5763 sc $3.00, set $5.00
(F325)

Suite, Op. 36, in D minor [14'30"]
2(pic).2(English horn).2.2.
4.2.3.1. timp,perc,harp,strings
KALMUS A5764 sc $60.00, set $75.00,

FOOTE, ARTHUR (cont'd.)

perf mat rent (F326)

Suite, Op. 63, in E [14'30"]
string orch
KALMUS A5682 sc $12.00, set $10.00
(F327)

FOOTPRINTS OF THE BIRDS see De Vos
Malan, Jacques

FOR A CHANGE, FOR PERCUSSION AND
ORCHESTRA see Norgaard, Per

FOR A FESTAL OCCASION see Bush, Alan
[Dudley]

FOR A STATESMAN see Berners, Lord
(Gerald Tyrwhitt)

FOR GESCHAPEN see Meijering, Chiel

FOR MORE THAN ONE see Rudi, Joran

FOR MRS. TOMOYASU, FOR SOLO VOICE AND
ORCHESTRA see Berkeley, Michael

FOR SAMUEL BECKETT see Feldman, Morton

FOR STACEY see Maestri, Fabio

FOR THE KING'S SAKE see Isolfsson, Pall

FOR THE ORCHESTRA TOO see Lindroth,
Peter

FORBES, SEBASTIAN (1941-)
Essay For Clarinet And Orchestra
[15']
2.2.2.2. 4.3.3.0. timp,4perc,
strings,clar solo
OXFORD perf mat rent (F328)

FORD, CLIFFORD (1947-)
Conte Fantasmagorique
4.4.4.4. 6.4.3.1. timp,2perc,
harp,strings
CAN.MUS.CENT. MI 1100 F699CO (F329)

FORD, RONALD (1959-)
Aria Bravura, For Solo Instrument And
Orchestra [12']
2.2.2.2.2alto sax. 2.1.1.0. perc,
strings, wind-pno solo
DONEMUS perf mat rent (F330)

Building Blocks [12']
2.1.1.2. 4.2.2.0. timp,harp,pno,
strings
DONEMUS perf mat rent (F331)

FOREIGN COMPOSERS IN FRANCE, 1750- 1790
*CC15L
(Viano; Callen; Foster) sc GARLAND
ISBN 0-8240-3845-2 $90.00 "The
Symphony" Vol. D-II (F332)

FORELLE, DIE, FOR SOLO VOICE AND
ORCHESTRA [ARR.] see Schubert,
Franz (Peter)

FOREST SONGS see Bajura, Keith V.A.

FORET, FELICIEN (1890-1978)
Tryptique Hellene, For Oboe And
Orchestra [14'25"]
2.0.2.2. 2.2.3.0. timp,harp,
strings,ob solo
BILLAUDOT perf mat rent (F333)

FORET PAIENNE, LA see Koechlin, Charles

FORGET-ME-NOT see Herbert, Victor

FORGOTTEN RITE, THE see Ireland, John

FORGOTTEN SONGS, FOR SOLO VOICE AND
ORCHESTRA see Lipovsek, Marijan,
Pozabljene Pesmi, For Solo Voice
And Orchestra

FORMA MAGISTRA LUDI, FOR CHAMBER
ORCHESTRA see Pasquotti, Corrado

FORMANT MIRRORS, FOR SOLO VOICE AND
ORCHESTRA see Sandström, Jan

FORMANTS see Niculescu, Stefan

FORMAS PLANAS see Villa Rojo, Jesus

FORMAZIONI see Berio, Luciano see
Kocsar, Miklos

FORME RIFLESSE, LE see Maggi, Dario

FORSAKEN see Waxman, Franz

FORSPIL, FOR VIOLIN AND ORCHESTRA see
Janson, Alfred

FORSPILL TIL ET LYRISK DRAMA see
Jordan, Sverre

FORSYTH, MALCOLM (1936-   )
    African Ode (Symphony No. 3) [16']
        3.2.3.3. 4.2.3.1. timp,2perc,
        harp,cel,strings
        CAN.MUS.CENT. MI 1100 F735AF (F334)

    Atayoskewin [19']
        2.2.2.2. 4.2.3.1. timp,2perc,pno/
        perc,harp,strings
        CAN.MUS.CENT. MI 1100 F735A (F335)

    Concerto for Piano and Orchestra
        [23']
        KERBY 20701 perf mat rent   (F336)

    Concerto for Trumpet and Orchestra
        [19']
        2.2.2.2. 2.3.0.0. timp,perc,
        strings,trp solo
        CAN.MUS.CENT. MI 1331 F735CO (F337)

    Little Suite For Strings
        string orch
        CAN.MUS.CENT. MI 1500 F735LI (F338)

    Serenade for Strings [13']
        string orch
        CAN.MUS.CENT. MI 1500 F735SE (F339)

    Sketches From Natal [14']
        2ob,2horn,strings
        sc KERBY 28138 $47.50, perf mat
        rent   (F340)

    Springtide
        CAN.MUS.CENT. MI 1100 F735S (F341)

    Sun Songs, For Solo Voice And
        Orchestra [19']
        2.2.2(clar in E flat).2. 2.2.0.0.
        timp,2perc,strings,Mez solo
        CAN.MUS.CENT. MV 1400 F735 SU (F342)

    Symphony No. 3
        see African Ode

    Ukuzalwa [13']
        2(pic).2.2.2. 4.2.3.1. timp,
        2perc,harp,strings
        CAN.MUS.CENT. MI 1100 F735UK (F343)

FORSYTH, W.O.
    Romance [7']
        2.2.2.2. 2.0.0.0. timp,harp,
        strings
        sc,pts CAN.MUS.HER. f.s.   (F344)

FORTROLLA SKOG see Tveitt, Geirr

FORTUNATI, GIAN FRANCESCO (1746-1821)
    Sinfonia No. 3 in D [13']
        2.2.0.1. 2.0.0.0. strings
        (Brosche, Gunter) sc,pts DOBLINGER
        DM 852 f.s.   (F345)

FORTUNE TELLER, THE: GYPSY LOVE SONG,
    FOR SOLO VOICE AND ORCHESTRA [ARR.]
    see Herbert, Victor

FORTUNE TELLER, THE: ROMANY LIFE:
    CZARDAS [ARR.] see Herbert, Victor

44TH SONNET OF MICHELANGELO, FOR SOLO
    VOICE AND INSTRUMENTAL ENSEMBLE see
    Svoboda, Tomas

FORTY SECOND STREET see Warren, Harry

FORTY SECOND STREET: MEDLEY [ARR.] see
    Warren, Harry

FORVANDLING see Sønstevold, Gunnar

FORZA DEL DESTINO, LA: PRELUDIO see
    Verdi, Giuseppe

FOSS, LUKAS (1922-   )
    Exeunt
        2.2.2.2. 4.2.3.1. timp,perc,harp,
        pno,elec gtr,strings
        sc PEMBROKE $15.00, perf mat rent
                                      (F346)

    Fanfare [10']
        2.2.2.2. 0.3.3.0. perc,pno,org/
        acord,4vln,2vla,2vcl,2db,
        guirnata, zurna, kaval
        SALABERT perf mat rent   (F347)

    Measure For Measure, For Solo Voice
        And Orchestra (from Suite Salomon
        Rossi) [10']
        0+pic(opt S rec).2(English
        horn).0.2. 0.2.2.0. timp,harp,
        strings,T solo
        sc SALABERT f.s., perf mat rent
                                      (F348)

    Night Music For John Lennon
        sc PEMBROKE $15.00, perf mat rent
                                      (F349)

    Symphony No. 1 [32']
        2+pic.2+English horn.2+bass
        clar.2+contrabsn. 4.3.3.0.
        timp,perc,harp,pno,strings
        SCHIRM.G perf mat rent   (F350)

FOSTER, ARNOLD (1898-1963)
    Suite For Strings On English Folk
        Airs [15']
        string orch
        NOVELLO perf mat rent   (F351)

FOTOMONTAGE see Benguerel, Xavier see
    Bentzon, Jørgen

FOUGSTEDT, NILS-ERIC (1910-1961)
    Romanssi [arr.]
        (Lehtinen, R.) gtr,strings [4']
        FAZER perf mat rent   (F352)

FOULDS, JOHN HERBERT (1880-1939)
    Belle Pierrette, La [5']
        1.1.2.1. 2.2.3.0. perc,strings
        BOOSEY perf mat rent   (F353)

    Darby And Joan, For Violin,
        Violoncello And String Orchestra
        *Op.42,No.2 [5']
        string orch,vln solo,vcl solo
        BOOSEY perf mat rent   (F354)

    Gaelic Dream Song *Op.68 [5']
        2.1.2.2. 2.1.3.0. perc,harp,
        strings
        BOOSEY perf mat rent   (F355)

    Keltic Suite *Op.29 [15']
        2(pic).2.2.2. 2.2.3.1. timp,perc,
        harp,strings
        BOOSEY perf mat rent   (F356)

    Keltic Suite: Keltic Lament *Op.29,
        No.2 [5']
        0.0.2.2. 2.0.1.0. harp,strings
        BOOSEY perf mat rent   (F357)

    Music-Pictures (Group IV) *Op.55
        [10']
        string orch
        BOOSEY perf mat rent   (F358)

    Suite Fantastique *Op.72b [15']
        1+pic.2.2.2. 4.2.3.1. timp,perc,
        strings
        BOOSEY perf mat rent   (F359)

    Suite Francaise *Op.22 [20']
        1+pic.2.2.2. 2.3.3.1. timp,opt
        org,strings
        BOOSEY perf mat rent   (F360)

FOUNTAIN, PRIMOUS (1949-   )
    Manifestation [15']
        3.2.2.2. 4.5.3.1. timp,3perc,pno,
        strings
        sc MARGUN MP2094 $25.00, perf mat
        rent   (F361)

    Ritual Dances Of The Amaks [24']
        3.3.4.2. 4.3.3.0. timp,perc,pno,
        strings
        sc MARGUN MP2096 $40.00, perf mat
        rent   (F362)

FOUR BAGATELLES see Pleskow, Raoul

FOUR CANTOS see Luedeke, Raymond

FOUR CARPATHIAN PASTORALS see Shumeiko,
    Volodymyr

FOUR CHARACTER PIECES AFTER THE
    RUBAIYAT OF OMAR KHAYYAM see Foote,
    Arthur

FOUR DANCES IN ONE MOVEMENT see Ruders,
    Poul

FOUR EARLY AMERICAN TUNES see Adler,
    Samuel Hans

FOUR EARLY SINFONIAS see Bach, Johann
    Christoph Friedrich

FOUR ELEMENTS: RECITATIVO AND ARIA OF
    WEATHER, FOR SOLO VOICE AND
    ORCHESTRA see Mica, Frantisek
    Vaclav

FOUR EPISODES see Bloch, Ernest

FOUR EPITAPHS, FOR SOLO VOICE AND
    STRING ORCHESTRA see Boldemann,
    Laci

FOUR ETUDES see Stravinsky, Igor

FOUR FANTASIES ON AMERICAN FOLK SONGS
    see Townsend, Douglas

FOUR-FOLD WORLD VIEW see Newell, Robert
    M.

FOUR FREEDOMS SYMPHONY, THE see
    Bennett, Robert Russell

FOUR HINDU POEMS, FOR SOLO VOICE AND
    ORCHESTRA see Delage, Maurice,
    Quatre Poemes Hindous, For Solo
    Voice And Orchestra

FOUR HORSEMEN OF THE APOCALYPSE
    OVERTURE see Josephs, Wilfred

FOUR IMAGES see Jaffe, Stephen

FOUR IRISH DANCES see Arnold, Malcolm

FOUR IRISH TALES, FOR PIANO AND
    ORCHESTRA see Cowell, Henry Dixon

FOUR LATE SINFONIAS see Bach, Johann
    Christoph Friedrich

FOUR LATIN LYRICS, FOR SOLO VOICE AND
    ORCHESTRA see Hartzell, Eugene

FOUR LETTERS FROM GRIEG TO FRANTS
    BEYER, FOR SOLO VOICE AND ORCHESTRA
    see Tveitt, Geirr

FOUR LITURGICAL PIECES, FOR SOLO VOICE
    AND ORCHESTRA see Szymanski, Pawel

FOUR MINIATURES see Sköld, Sven, Fyra
    Miniatyrer

FOUR MOTETS FOR ORCHESTRA see Bäck,
    Sven-Erik

FOUR MOTETS FOR STRINGS see Bäck, Sven-
    Erik

FOUR MOVEMENTS FOR STRINGS see
    Krogseth, Gisle

FOUR NOCTURNES, FOR SOLO VOICES AND
    ORCHESTRA see Chavez, Carlos,
    Cuatro Nocturnos, For Solo Voices
    And Orchestra

FOUR NORDIC DANCES see Emborg, Jens
    Laurson, Fire Nordiske Danse

FOUR OHIO PORTRAITS see Schwartz,
    Elliott Schelling

FOUR ORCHESTRAL PIECES see Bartók, Béla

FOUR ORCHESTRAL SONGS, FOR SOLO VOICE
    AND ORCHESTRA see Kohs, Ellis
    Bonoff

FOUR ORCHESTRAL WORKS see Ravel,
    Maurice

FOUR ORDTAK see Kvam, Oddvar S.

FOUR PARABLES, FOR PIANO AND ORCHESTRA
    see Schoenfield, Paul

FOUR PIECES FROM THE SONATE ACCADEMICHE
    see Veracini, Francesco Maria,
    Quattro Pezzi

FOUR POEMS see Rønnes, Robert

FOUR SAINTS: AN OLIO see Thomson,
    Virgil Garnett

FOUR SEASONS, THE see Polgar, Tibor

FOUR SECTIONS, THE see Reich, Steve

FOUR SHORT PIECES see Heiss, John C.

FOUR SKETCHES see Ledenev, Roman

FOUR SLOVENE FOLK SONGS see Golob,
    Jani, Stiri Slovenske Ljudske Pesmi

FOUR SMALL ORCHESTRAL PIECES see
    Bruckner, Anton, Vier
    Orchesterstücke

FOUR SONGS, FOR SOLO VOICE AND
    ORCHESTRA see Constantinides, Dinos
    Demetrios see Nordentoft, Anders

FOUR SONGS, FOR SOLO VOICE AND
    ORCHESTRA, OP. 17 see Dorumsgaard,
    Arne

FOUR SONGS, FOR SOLO VOICE AND STRING
    ORCHESTRA [ARR.] see Gurney, Ivor

FOUR SONGS FOR ANN, FOR SOLO VOICE AND
    ORCHESTRA see Baker, Michael Conway

FOUR SONGS FROM THE OLD TESTAMENT, FOR
    SOLO VOICE AND ORCHESTRA see
    Koppel, Herman David, Fire
    Gammeltestamentlige Sange, For Solo
    Voice And Orchestra

FOUR SONNETS see MacBride, David Huston

FOUR SONNETS, FOR SOLO VOICE AND
    ORCHESTRA see Davis, Curtis W.

FOUR SONNETS FROM THE PORTUGUESE, FOR
    SOLO VOICE AND ORCHESTRA see
    Parmentier, F. Gordon

FOUR SPIRITUALS FOR SOLO VOICE AND
    ORCHESTRA [ARR]
    (Towne, Charles Hanson; Kennedy, John

Brodbin) 2.1.2.1. 2.1.1.0. harp,
strings,med-high solo [8'] BOURNE
perf mat rent   (F363)

FOUR SYMPHONIC MYTHS see Koch, Erland
von, Fyra Symfoniska Myter

FOUR TABLEAUX see Victory, Gerard

FOUR VIOLIN CONCERTOS, PART I see
Viotti, Giovanni Battista

FOUR VIOLIN CONCERTOS, PART II see
Viotti, Giovanni Battista

FOURCHOTTE, ALAIN (1943-   )
Concerto for Clarinet and Orchestra
[17']
2.2.2.2. 2.2.1.1. 2perc,cel,harp,
strings,clar solo
BILLAUDOT perf mat rent   (F364)

FOURMIS, LES: SUITE see Sancan, Pierre

FOWLER, JENNIFER (1939-   )
Arrows Of Saint Sebastian, The [20']
1(pic).1.1.1. 1.1.1.1. pno,2vln,
vla,vcl
UNIVER. perf mat rent   (F365)

Ring Out The Changes [20']
bells, (2 players), str
UNIVER. perf mat rent   (F366)

FOX see Hoyland, Victor

FOX, FREDERICK ALFRED (FRED)
(1931-   )
Beyond Winterlock
3.2.3.2. 4.3.3.1. perc,pno,
strings
SEESAW   (F367)

FOX HUNT, THE see Amram, David Werner

FOXTROT (ON A DUTCH FOLKSONG) see Boer,
Ed de

FRA ALSTAHAUG see Karlsen, Rolf

FRA BARNETS VERDEN see Brustad, Bjarne

FRA CENTO AFFANNI, FOR SOLO VOICE AND
ORCHESTRA see Mozart, Wolfgang
Amadeus

FRA FJORD OG FJAERE [ARR.]
(Tveitt, Geirr) 0.1.0.1. 1.0.0.0.
strings NORGE   (F368)

FRA ST. HALVARDS TID see Lindeman,
Signe

FRA VIRGOLETTE see Schultheiss, Ulrich

FRAGMENT: A DANCE see Schneider, Ernst

FRAGMENT AUS "MNEMOSYNE", FOR SOLO
VOICE AND STRING ORCHESTRA see
Marx, Karl

FRAGMENT DE L'APOCALYPSE see Liadov,
Anatol Konstantinovich

FRAGMENT FROM "CITIES OF THE INTERIOR",
FOR SOLO VOICE AND ORCHESTRA see
Barati, George

FRAGMENTE FÜR ORCHESTER see Wolhauser,
Rene

FRAGMENTS see Richter, Marga

FRAGMENTS D'APOCALYPSE, FOR SOLO VOICES
AND ORCHESTRA see Bancquart, Alain

FRAGMENTS FROM ANTIQUITY, FOR SOLO
VOICE AND ORCHESTRA see Wyner,
Yehudi

FRAGMENTS FROM "SYMPHONY NOSFERATU" see
Van Nostrand, Burr

FRAGMENTS - HEDGEHOGS see Lewis, Peter
Tod

FRAGMENTS POETIQUES see Godard,
Benjamin Louis Paul

FRAGOR, FOR 2 PIANOS AND ORCHESTRA see
Brenet, Therese

FRANCAIX, JEAN (1912-   )
Cinq Pieces, For Violoncello And
String Orchestra
string orch,vcl solo
ESCHIG perf mat rent   (F369)

Concerto for Guitar and String
Orchestra [13']
string orch,gtr solo
ESCHIG perf mat rent   (F370)

Concerto for 2 Harps and Strings
[23']
6vln,2vla,2vcl,db,2harp soli

FRANCAIX, JEAN (cont'd.)

ESCHIG perf mat rent   (F371)

Concerto Pour 15 Instruments
Solistes, Timbales Et Cordes
timp,strings, soli: fl, ob, clar,
bsn, contrabsn, horn, trp,
trom, tuba, harp, string quin
ESCHIG perf mat rent   (F372)

Happy Birthday Alla Francaix [3']
1.1.1.1. 1.1.0.0. strings
ESCHIG perf mat rent   (F373)

Impromptu for Flute and String
Orchestra [8']
string orch,fl solo
ESCHIG perf mat rent   (F374)

Pavan [3']
2.2.2.2. 0.0.0.0. strings
SCHOTTS perf mat rent   (F375)

Pavane Pour Un Genie Vivant [3']
2.1+English horn.1.1. 0.0.0.0.
strings
ESCHIG perf mat rent   (F376)

Pierrot Ou Les Secrets De La Nuit
[35']
2.2.2.2. 2.2.2.1. timp,perc,harp,
strings
ESCHIG perf mat rent   (F377)

Prelude, Sarabande Et Gigue, For
Trumpet And Orchestra [9']
2.2.2.2. 2.1.0.0. timp,perc,
strings,trp solo
ESCHIG perf mat rent   (F378)

Psyche, For Narrator And Orchestra
2.2.2.2. 2.1.0.0. timp,3perc,cel,
harp,strings,narrator
[45'] ESCHIG perf mat rent   (F379)

Theme and Variations for Clarinet and
Strings [7']
6vln,2vla,2vcl,db,clar solo
ESCHIG perf mat rent   (F380)

FRANCE D'OUTRE MER see Tomasi, Henri

FRANCESCA: OVERTURE see Goetz, Hermann

FRANCESCHINI, ROMULUS (1929-   )
White Spirituals, For Solo Voice And
Orchestra [18']
1(pic).1.1+bass clar.1. 2.1.1.0.
strings,high solo
KALMUS A4098 sc $27.00, set $30.00,
pts $2.50, ea., perf mat rent
(F381)

FRANCESCONI, LUCA (1956-   )
Passacaglia [9'20"]
3.3.4.3. 4.3.3.1. perc,harp,pno&
cel,strings
RICORDI-IT 133781 perf mat rent
(F382)

Plot In The Fiction, For Oboe And
Chamber Orchestra [10']
1(pic).0.1(bass clar).1. 1.0.0.0.
perc,pno,strings,ob solo
sc RICORDI-IT 134186 f.s., perf mat
rent   (F383)

Vertige [11']
14vln,4vla,4vcl,2db
RICORDI-IT 133991 perf mat rent
(F384)

FRANCIS OF ASSISI see Fongaard, Bjørn,
Frans Av Assi'si

FRANCK, CESAR (1822-1890)
Djinns, Les, For Piano And Orchestra
ENOCH perf mat rent   (F385)

Eolides, Les
ENOCH perf mat rent   (F386)
min sc KALMUS K01404 $5.00   (F387)

Huit Pieces Breves, Series I, Nos. 1-
4 [arr.] (from L'organiste)
(Busser, Henri) 1.1.1.1. 1.1.0.0.
timp,strings [14'] ENOCH perf mat
rent   (F388)

Huit Pieces Breves, Series II, Nos.
5-8 [Arr.] (from L'organiste)
(Busser, Henri) 1(pic).1(English
horn).1.1. 1.1.0.0. timp,harp,
strings [12'] ENOCH perf mat rent
(F389)

Hulda: Ballet Music
2(pic).2(English horn).2+bass
clar.4. 4.4.3.1. timp,perc,
strings KALMUS A5765 sc $45.00,
set $55.00, perf mat rent   (F390)
KALMUS A5765 sc $45.00, set $55.00,
perf mat rent   (F391)

Prelude, Choral Et Fugue [arr.]
(Pierne, Gabriel) 3.2+English
horn.2+bass clar.4. 4.3.3.1.
sarrusophone,timp,perc,2harp,
strings [20'] ENOCH perf mat rent

FRANCK, CESAR (cont'd.)

(F392)
Symphony in D minor
sc DOVER 253732 $7.95   (F393)
SONZOGNO perf mat rent   (F394)
(Jancsovics) study sc EMB 40084
f.s.   (F395)

Variations Symphoniques, For Piano
And Orchestra
ENOCH perf mat rent   (F396)
study sc UNITED MUS 597-00231 $4.75
(F397)

FRANCO, CESARE
see FRANCK, CESAR

FRANCO, JOHAN (1908-   )
Clodagh, For Solo Voice And Orchestra
[6']
1.2.2.2. 2.2.2.0. timp,perc,harp,
strings,Mez solo
sc AM.COMP.AL. $11.45   (F398)

Concerto Lirico No. 5, For Guitar And
Chamber Orchestra [20']
1.1.1.1. 2.1.1.0. perc,harp,
strings,gtr solo
sc AM.COMP.AL. $32.50, perf mat
rent   (F399)

Introduction And The Virgin Queen's
Dream, For Solo Voice And
Orchestra [10']
2.2.2.3. 2.3.4.0. perc,xylo,
strings,S solo
sc AM.COMP.AL. $18.40, perf mat
rent   (F400)

Nocturne [8']
2.2.3.2. 2.1.1.1. timp,cym,harp,
cel,strings
AM.COMP.AL. perf mat rent   (F401)

Peripetie [12']
4.4.4.4. 2.3.2.1. timp,snare
drum,pno,cel,strings
AM.COMP.AL. perf mat rent   (F402)

Prophecy From "Locksley Hall", For
Solo Voice And Orchestra [4']
1.1.1.1. 1.1.0.0. strings,Mez
solo
AM.COMP.AL. perf mat rent   (F403)

Serenade Concertante, For Piano And
Chamber Orchestra [12']
1.1.1.1. 1.1.1.0. timp,perc,
strings,pno solo
AM.COMP.AL. perf mat rent   (F404)

Symphony No. 4 for Solo Voice and
Orchestra [17']
3.3.3.3. 2.2.3.0. cel,strings,T
solo
sc AM.COMP.AL. $27.55, perf mat
rent   (F405)

FRANCOIS, RENAUD (1943-   )
Automne, For Clarinet And Orchestra
2.1.1.1. 1.1.1.1. pno&cel,3perc,
strings,clar solo
SALABERT perf mat rent   (F406)

Chemins De La Nuit, Les, For
Violoncello And Orchestra [22']
1(pic).1.2(bass clar).1. 2.1.1.0.
2perc,harp,strings,vcl solo
SALABERT perf mat rent   (F407)

Regard Oblique, Un, For 2 Flutes And
Instrumental Ensemble [15']
clar,3trom,2perc,pno,3vln,vla,
vcl,db,2fl soli
SALABERT perf mat rent   (F408)

FRANCS-JUGES, LES: OVERTURE see
Berlioz, Hector (Louis)

FRANDSEN, JOHN (1956-   )
Symphony No. 1 [25']
2+pic.3(English horn).3(clar in E
flat,bass clar).3(contrabsn).
4.3.3.1. timp,2perc,strings
(Dance of the Demons) HANSEN-DEN
perf mat rent   (F409)

FRANK, ANDREW (1946-   )
Chamber Concerto For Clarinet And
Eleven Players [20']
1.1.0.1. 1.1.1.0. perc,pno,vln,
vla,vcl,clar solo
study sc MARGUN MP2086 $45.00, perf
mat rent   (F410)

Sinfonia Concertante for Violin,
Viola and Chamber Orchestra [20']
2.2.2.2. 2.2.1.0. 2perc,harp,
strings,vln solo,vla solo
MARGUN MP2072 perf mat rent   (F411)

FRANK, MARCEL [GUSTAVE] (1909-   )
Concerto for Flute and Orchestra in C
[8']
2.1.4.1. 2.0.0.0. timp,strings,fl
solo

FRANK, MARCEL [GUSTAVE] (cont'd.)

    BOURNE perf mat rent   (F412)

FRANKEL, BENJAMIN (1906-1973)
    Catalogue Of Incidents From Romeo And
      Juliet *Op.42 [20']
      0.1(English horn).2.1. 1.0.0.0.
        timp,perc,harp,strings
      NOVELLO perf mat rent   (F413)

    Concertante Lirico *Op.27 [11']
      string orch
      NOVELLO perf mat rent   (F414)

FRANS AV ASSI'SI see Fongaard, Bjørn

FRANSSENS, JOEP (1955-)
    Echo's [25']
      4.3.0.0. 0.3.0.0. vibra,marimba,
        strings
      DONEMUS perf mat rent   (F415)

FRANZEN, OLOV (1946-)
    Conterso [5']
      4.1.2.0. 0.1.1.0. perc,vln,vcl
      STIM   (F416)

FRANZETTI, CARLOS
    Voyager [15']
      2+pic.2+English horn.2(clar in E
        flat)+bass clar.2(contrabsn).
        4.4.3.1. timp,perc,harp,pno,
        cel,strings
      NEWAM 19016 perf mat rent (F417)

FRANZOSISCHES KONZERT, FOR 2 FLUTES AND
    STRING ORCHESTRA see Koetsier, Jan

FRANZOSISCHES LIEDERBUCH, FOR SOLO
    VOICES AND CHAMBER ORCHESTRA see
    Killmayer, Wilhelm

FRATE 'NNAMORATO, LO: SINFONIA see
    Pergolesi, Giovanni Battista

FRATRES see Pärt, Arvo

FRATRES, FOR 12 VIOLONCELLI see Pärt,
    Arvo

FRATRES, FOR STRINGS AND PERCUSSION see
    Pärt, Arvo

FRATRES, FOR VIOLIN AND INSTRUMENTAL
    ENSEMBLE see Pärt, Arvo

FRAU-STIMME, FOR SOLO VOICE AND
    ORCHESTRA see Rihm, Wolfgang

FRAUEN KAFERIN see Strauss, Johann,
    [Jr.]

FRAUENHERZ see Strauss, Josef

FRAUENWURDE WALZER see Strauss, Josef

FRAZELLE, KENNETH
    Playing The "Miraculous Game"
      [14'30"]
      2+pic.2(English horn).2.2.
        2.2.2.0. timp,perc,strings
      PEER perf mat rent   (F418)

FRECHON, LUCIEN (1921-)
    Concerto for Timpani and Orchestra
      [25']
      2.2.2.2. 2.2.0.0. strings,timp
        solo
      BILLAUDOT perf mat rent   (F419)

FRED, FOR SOLO VOICE AND ORCHESTRA see
    Groven, Eivind

FRED ASTAIRE MUSIC see Brandmüller,
    Theo

FREDDIE THE FOOTBALL, FOR NARRATOR AND
    ORCHESTRA see Hayman, Richard
    Warren Joseph

FREDERICK THE GREAT
    see FRIEDRICH II, KING OF PRUSSIA

FREDERIKA POLKA see Strauss, Johann,
    [Sr.]

FREEDMAN, HARRY (1922-)
    Contrasts: The Web And The Wind [14']
      15strings soli
      CAN.MUS.CENT. MI 1500 F853CO (F420)

    Garland For Terry, A, For Narrator
      And Orchestra [12']
      2(pic).2(English horn).2.2.
        4.2.3.1. timp,2perc,strings,
        narrator
      CAN.MUS.CENT. MV 1400 F853GA (F421)

    Oiseaux Exotiques: Suite
      3.2.2.2. 4.3.3.1. timp,3perc,
        harp,bass gtr,strings
      CAN.MUS.CENT. MI 1100 F853SU (F422)

FREISCHÜTZ, DER: EINST TRÄUMTE MEINER
    SEL'GEN BASE, FOR SOLO VOICE AND
    ORCHESTRA see Weber, Carl Maria von

FREISCHÜTZ, DER: HIER IM IRD'SCHEN
    JAMMERTAL, FOR SOLO VOICE AND
    ORCHESTRA see Weber, Carl Maria von

FREISCHÜTZ, DER: KOMMT EIN SCHLANKER
    BURSCH GEGANGEN, FOR SOLO VOICE AND
    ORCHESTRA see Weber, Carl Maria von

FREISCHÜTZ, DER: NEIN, LÄNGER TRAG ICH
    NICHT DIE QUALEN; DURCH DIE WÄLDER,
    DURCH DIE AUEN, FOR SOLO VOICE AND
    ORCHESTRA see Weber, Carl Maria von

FREISCHÜTZ, DER: SCHELM, HALT FEST, FOR
    SOLO VOICES AND ORCHESTRA see
    Weber, Carl Maria von

FREISCHÜTZ, DER: SCHWEIG', SCHWEIG',
    DAMIT, FOR SOLO VOICE AND ORCHESTRA
    see Weber, Carl Maria von

FREISCHÜTZ, DER: UND OB DIE WOLKE SIE
    VERHULLE, FOR SOLO VOICE AND
    ORCHESTRA see Weber, Carl Maria von

FREISCHUTZ, DER: WIE NAHTE MIR DER
    SCHLUMMER, FOR SOLO VOICE AND
    ORCHESTRA see Weber, Carl Maria von

FREIWILLIGE VOR! MARSCH see Strauss,
    Johann, [Jr.]

FRENCH GAGAKU see Barbaud, Pierre

FRENETTE, CLAUDE (1955-)
    Felure [9']
      2.2.2.2. 2.2.3.0. timp,perc,
        strings
      CAN.MUS.CENT. MI 1100 F878FE (F423)

FRESCOBALDI, GIROLAMO (1583-1643)
    Toccate
      (Malipiero) KALMUS A7293 sc $6.00,
        set $6.00, pts $1.50, ea. (F424)

FRESCOS OF KIEV'S ST. SOFIA see
    Hodziatsky, Vitaliy

FRESKEN see Baur, Jürg

FRESQUE SYMPHONIQUE see Noda, Teruyuki
    see Petric, Ivo

FREUDENTHAL, OTTO (1934-)
    Minne Fran Ashendon [8']
      string orch
      STIM   (F425)

FREUT EUCH DES LEBENS WALZER see
    Strauss, Johann, [Jr.]

FRIBOULET, GEORGES (1910-)
    Suite Sans Fin [11']
      string orch
      BILLAUDOT perf mat rent   (F426)

FRICKER, PETER RACINE (1920-1990)
    Gryphius Songs, For Solo Voice And
      Orchestra
      2.2.2.2. 4.2.3.0. timp,harp,
        strings,high solo
      UNICORN 4.0060.7 perf mat rent
                   (F427)

FRID, GEZA (1904-)
    Toccata, Op. 84 [10']
      3.2.2.3. 4.3.3.1. 8perc,2harp,
        cel,strings
      sc DONEMUS f.s., perf mat rent
                   (F428)

FRID, GRIGORI (1915-)
    Concerto for Viola, Piano and String
      Orchestra, Op. 73 [27']
      string orch,vla solo,pno solo
      VAAP perf mat rent   (F429)

FRIEDE? FRAGEN ZU UNSERE ZEIT, FOR SOLO
    VOICE AND ORCHESTRA see Vogel,
    Wladimir

FRIEDENSPALMEN WALZER see Strauss,
    Josef

FRIEDMAN, STANLEY
    Concerto for Trumpet and Orchestra in
      C
      2.2.0.2. 2.0.0.0. timp,strings,
        trp solo
      sc SEESAW $61.00, perf mat rent
                   (F430)

    Concerto Grosso
      2.2.2.2. 2.2.0.0. timp,strings
      sc SEESAW $49.00, perf mat rent
                   (F431)

FRIEDRICH II, DER GROSSE, KING OF
    PRUSSIA (1712-1786)
    Concerto for Flute and String
      Orchestra, No. 1, in G
      string orch,fl solo
      (Augsbach) BREITKOPF-L perf mat
        rent   (F432)

FRIEDRICH II, DER GROSSE, KING OF
    PRUSSIA (cont'd.)

    Concerto for Flute and String
      Orchestra, No. 3, in C
      KALMUS A7463 sc $15.00, set $7.50,
        pts $1.50, ea.   (F433)

    Concerto for Flute and String
      Orchestra, No. 4, in D
      KALMUS A7464 sc $15.00, set $15.00,
        pts $2.50, ea.   (F434)

    Symphony, No. 4, in A
      (Lenzewski) KALMUS A7413 sc $8.00,
        set $6.25, pts $1.25, ea. (F435)

FRIML, RUDOLF (1879-1972)
    Rose Marie: Selections, [arr.]
      [12'30"]
      (Schoenfeld) WARNER perf mat rent
                   (F436)
    Rudolph Friml Favorites, [arr.] [7']
      (Stone, Gregory) WARNER perf mat
        rent   (F437)

FRISCH HERAN POLKA see Strauss, Johann,
    [Jr.]

FRITSCH, JOHANNES GEORG (1941-)
    Akroasis For Solo Voices And
      Orchestra [21']
      3(pic,alto fl).3(English horn,ob
        d'amore).3+bass clar.2+
        contrabsn.3sax. 4.4.5.1. timp,
        6perc,cel,elec gtr,elec bass,
        harp,pno,org,strings,electronic
        tape,speaking voice&AB soli
      sc FEEDBACK FB 7101 f.s.   (F438)

    Ares Und Aphrodite
      1.0+English horn.0+bass clar.1.
        1.0.1.0. 2perc,strings
      sc FEEDBACK FB 7302 f.s.   (F439)

    Concerto for Trumpet and Orchestra
      [18']
      3.3.3.3. 5.3.3.1. timp,perc,
        marimba,cel,pno,strings,trp
        solo
      sc FEEDBACK FB 7408 f.s.   (F440)

    Filigranfalter, For Solo Voice And
      Strings [17']
      7vln,2vla,2vcl,db,high solo
      sc FEEDBACK FB 7131 f.s.   (F441)

    Hugenotten, Die, For Violin, Zymbal
      And Orchestra [20']
      2.2.2.2. 2.2.2.0. 3perc,strings,
        electronic tape,vln solo,
        zymbal solo
      sc FEEDBACK FB 7813 f.s.   (F442)

    Kreuzgange [15']
      4.3+English horn.3+bass clar.3+
        contrabsn. 4.3.3.1. timp,3perc,
        pno,cel,harp,strings
      sc FEEDBACK FB 8305 f.s.   (F443)

FROG PRINCE, THE, FOR NARRATOR AND
    ORCHESTRA see Bond, Victoria

FROHE JUGEND see Lundkvist, Per

FROHES LEBEN WALZER see Strauss, Josef

FROHLICH, J.F.
    Majgildet
      "May Festival" sc,pts SAMFUNDET
        f.s.   (F444)

    May Festival
      see Majgildet

    Riberhuus March
      sc,pts SAMFUNDET f.s.   (F445)

FROHLICHE MUSIK see Grabner, Hermann

FROHLICHES WANDERN see Vancura, A.

FROISSART OVERTURE see Elgar, [Sir]
    Edward (William)

FROLIC see Rorem, Ned

FROM A SOURCE EVOLVING see Bassett,
    Leslie

FROM ABOVE, FOR SYNTHESIZER AND
    ORCHESTRA see Thommessen, Olav
    Anton

FROM ALTSTAHAUG: SUITE see Karlsen,
    Rolf, Fra Alstahaug

FROM BEHIND THE GLASS see Dolatshahi,
    Dariush

FROM CLIFF TO SEA see Liszt, Franz, Vom
    Fels Zum Meer

FROM DARKNESS SHINES see Ott, David

FROM GITANJALI, FOR SOLO VOICE AND ORCHESTRA see Sohal, Naresh

FROM JEWISH FOLK POETRY, FOR SOLO VOICES AND ORCHESTRA see Shostakovich, Dmitri

FROM KATHLEEN RAINE'S POETRY, FOR SOLO VOICE AND ORCHESTRA [ARR.] see Sommerfeldt, Oistein

FROM LIFE TO GREATER LIFE see Saul, Walter

FROM ROCK AND SEA see Liszt, Franz, Vom Fels Zum Meer

FROM TABUH TABUHAN see Sculthorpe, Peter [Joshua]

FROM THE BOHEMIAN FOREST: IN THE SPINNING ROOM [ARR.] see Dvorák, Antonín

FROM THE CRADLE TO THE GRAVE see Liszt, Franz, Von Der Wiege Bis Zum Grabe

FROM THE DARK TOWER, FOR SOLO VOICE AND ORCHESTRA see Rudd-Moore, Dorothy

FROM THE HEART OF A BELIEVER see Still, William Grant

FROM THE HEARTS OF WOMEN, FOR SOLO VOICE AND STRING ORCHESTRA see Still, William Grant

FROM THE JOURNAL OF A WANDERER see Still, William Grant

FROM THE MATTRESS GRAVE, FOR SOLO VOICE AND ORCHESTRA see Blake, David

FROM THE MIDDLE AGES see Glazunov, Alexander Konstantinovich

FROM THE MORNING LAND see Heuberger, Richard, Aus Dem Morgenlande

FROM THE NORTH see Sibelius, Jean

FROM THE SONG OF SONGS, FOR SOLO VOICE AND ORCHESTRA [ARR.] see Isolfsson, Pall

FROM THE SUPAI FORMATION see Hall, Jeffrey

FROM THE TIME OF ST. HALVARD see Lindeman, Signe, Fra St. Halvards Tid

FROM THESE SHORES see Siegmeister, Elie

FROM WHERE I STAND see Winther, Terje

FRONTISPICE [ARR.] see Ravel, Maurice

FROSCHMAUSEKRIEG, FOR SOLO VOICE AND ORCHESTRA see Willi, Herbert

FROST, DONALD
Concerto for Guitar and Chamber Orchestra, No. 1 [17']
2.2.2.2. 2.0.0.0. strings,gtr solo
PEER perf mat rent (F446)

FROST, ROBERT S. (1942-)
Engravings In Sound
string orch SOUTHERN SO-49 sc $3.00, set $20.00, pts $1.25, ea. (F447)

Pair Of Soks, A
2perc,pno,strings SOUTHERN SO-46 sc $5.00, set $25.00, pts $1.25, ea. (F448)

FRUHLINGS-PHANTASIE, FOR SOLO VOICES AND ORCHESTRA see Gade, Niels Wilhelm

FRUHLINGSMORGEN see Mahler, Gustav

FRUHLINGSNACHT, FOR SOLO VOICE AND ORCHESTRA [ARR.] see Schumann, Robert (Alexander)

FRUHLINGSOUVERTURE see Goetz, Hermann

FRUHLINGSSTIMMEN WALZER see Strauss, Johann, [Jr.]

FRÜHLINGSSTIMMEN WALZER, [ARR.] see Strauss, Johann, [Jr.]

FRUMERIE, (PER) GUNNAR (FREDRIK) DE (1908-1987)
Concertino for Piano and String Orchestra, Op. 78 [12']
string orch,pno solo
GEHRMANS perf mat rent (F449)

Concerto for Piano and Orchestra, No. 2, Op. 17, in A minor [40']
2.2.2.2. 4.2.3.0. timp,2perc, harp,strings,pno solo

FRUMERIE, (PER) GUNNAR (FREDRIK) DE (cont'd.)

STIM (F450)

Concerto for 2 Pianos and Orchestra, Op. 46 [20']
2.2.2.2. 2.2.1.0. timp,2perc, strings,2pno soli
STIM (F451)

Concerto for Trombone and Orchestra, Op. 81 [23']
2.2.2.2. 3.2.2.1. timp,3perc, strings,trom solo
sc GEHRMANS 6533P f.s., perf mat rent (F452)

Longing For Home, For Solo Voice And Orchestra [3']
1.0.1.2. 2.0.0.0. cel,harp, strings,med solo
NORDISKA perf mat rent (F453)

When You Close My Eyes, For Solo Voice And Orchestra [3']
2.2.2.2. 2.2.0.0. cel,harp, strings,med solo
NORDISKA perf mat rent (F454)

FRUSTRATED PLANS: OVERTURE see Cimarosa, Domenico, Trame Deluse, Le: Overture

FRY, GARY D. (1955-)
Challenge, The [5']
3+alto fl.2(English horn).3(bass clar).2.2alto sax.tenor sax.baritone sax. 4.4(flügelhorn).4.1. perc,harp, pno,gtr,elec bass,strings, synclavier
NEWAM 19017 perf mat rent (F455)

FUCHS, ALBERT (1858-1910)
Concerto for Violin and Orchestra, Op. 25, in G minor
KISTNER perf mat rent (F456)

FUCHS, JOHANN JOSEPH
see FUX, JOHANN JOSEPH

FUCHS, ROBERT (1847-1927)
Serenade No. 1, Op. 9, in D
string orch
KISTNER (F457)

Serenade No. 2, Op. 14, in C
string orch
KISTNER perf mat rent (F458)

Serenade No. 3, Op. 21, in E minor
string orch
KISTNER perf mat rent (F459)

Symphony No. 2, Op. 45, in E flat [35']
2.2.2.3. 4.2.3.0. timp,strings
SIMROCK perf mat rent (F460)

FUCIK, JULIUS (1872-1916)
Florentiner Marsch *Op.214 (Hartmann) 1+pic.1.2.1. 2.2.3.0. perc,strings [4'] pno-cond sc,set
KALMUS A6134 $12.00 (F461)

Polka, "The Old Bear With The Sore Head", For Bassoon And Orchestra [4']
BUBONIC perf mat rent (F462)

FUEGO FATUO see Falla, Manuel de

FUGA, SANDRO (1906-)
Concerto for Piano, Strings and Timpani [20'5"]
timp,strings,pno solo
sc CURCI 10544 perf mat rent (F463)

FUGACE see Tykesson, Nils

FUGAL CONCERTO, OP. 40, NO. 2 see Holst, Gustav

FUGATO see Poot, Marcel

FUGE, K.401, [ARR.] see Mozart, Wolfgang Amadeus

FUGE, K.546, [ARR.] see Mozart, Wolfgang Amadeus

FUGEN UBER DEN NAMEN BACH [ARR.] see Schumann, Robert (Alexander)

FUGHETTA A QUATERNI VOCI see Salvesen, Thomas

FUGUE SYMPHONIQUE see Koechlin, Charles

FUJITA, MASANORI (1946-)
Angelus [8']
string orch
ONGAKU perf mat rent (F464)

FUJITA, MASANORI (cont'd.)

Aurora IV, For Piano And Orchestra [16']
3.3.2+bass clar.2+contrabsn. 6.3.3.1. perc,harp,cel,strings, pno solo
sc ONGAKU 493031 f.s., perf mat rent (F465)

FUKUSHI, NORIO (1945-)
Chromosphere, For Percussion And Orchestra [18']
3(pic,alto fl).3.3.3. 4.3.3.1. perc,harp,strings,perc solo
sc ZEN-ON 899280 f.s., perf mat rent (F466)

FULEIHAN, ANIS (1900-1970)
Mediterranean [13']
3.3.4.3. 4.3.3.1. timp,perc,harp, strings
PEER perf mat rent (F467)

FULKERSON, JAMES (1945-)
Concerto (Fierce And Coming From Far Away)
SEESAW (F468)

Stations, Regions And Clouds, For Amplified Trombone And Orchestra [22']
3.3.3.3. 5.3.3.1. timp,2perc, strings,trom solo
MODERN 2174 (F469)

FUNERAL TRIUMPH OF TASSO see Liszt, Franz, Triomphe Funebre Du Tasse, Le

FUNF BRUCHSTUCKE see Ruzicka, Peter

FÜNF FRUHE LIEDER, FOR SOLO VOICE AND ORCHESTRA [ARR.] see Mahler, Gustav

FUNF GEISTLICHE LIEDER, FOR SOLO VOICE AND ORCHESTRA [ARR.] see Bach, Johann Sebastian

FUNF GESANGE, FOR SOLO VOICE AND INSTRUMENTAL ENSEMBLE see Bose, Hans Jürgen

FUNF HAIKU (LO-SHU IV), FOR FLUTE AND STRING ORCHESTRA see Zender, Hans

FUNF IMPROMPTUS see Thurm, Joachim

FUNF ORCHESTERSTUCKE see Ostendorf, Jens-Peter

FUNF SZENEN see Gattermayer, Heinrich

FUNF TAGE UND FUNF NACHTE: SUITE see Shostakovich, Dmitri, Five Days And Five Nights: Suite

FUNF TONBILDER see Reinecke, Carl

FÜNFTE ABGESANGSSZENE see Rihm, Wolfgang

FUNFTE ABGESANGSSZENE, FOR SOLO VOICES AND ORCHESTRA see Rihm, Wolfgang

FUNFTES SEE-BILD "DER TOD DER LIEBENDEN", FOR SOLO VOICE AND ORCHESTRA see Trojahn, Manfred

FÜNFZEHN TANZSÄTZE, [ARR.] see Staden, Johann

FÜNFZEHN VARIATIONEN UBER "WAS WOLLEN WIR AUF DEN ABEND TUN" see Marx, Karl

FÜR ANTON see Roo, Paul de

FUR LUSTIGE LEUT see Strauss, Eduard

FURIES, THE: SUITE see Waxman, Franz

FURRER, BEAT (1954-)
Illuminations, For Solo Voice And Chamber Group [20']
1(pic).0.2.0. 0.0.2.0. 2-3perc, pno,2vcl,db,S solo
UNIVER. perf mat rent (F470)

In Der Stille Des Hauses Wohnt Ein Ton [12']
1.0.1+bass clar.0. 0.1.2.1. 2perc,pno,vln,vla,2vcl,db
UNIVER. perf mat rent (F471)

Risonanze [25']
3(pic,alto fl).0.2+bass clar.2. 2.2.2.1. 3perc,9vln,4vla,5vcl, 5db,electronic equipment
UNIVER. perf mat rent (F472)

Sinfonia for Strings [12']
string orch
UNIVER. perf mat rent (F473)

FURRER, BEAT (cont'd.)

   Tiro Mis Tristes Redes [15']
      2.2.2.2. 2.2.2.0. 2perc,pno,
      strings
      UNIVER. perf mat rent   (F474)

   Tsunamis [12']
      4(pic).3.4.4. 4.2.4.1. 2perc,pno,
      strings
      UNIVER. perf mat rent   (F475)

FÜRST, PAUL WALTER (1926-   )
   Cavillo Et Carillon *Op.72 [15']
      2(pic).2.2.2. 2.2.0.0. timp,perc,
      strings
      DOBLINGER perf mat rent   (F476)

   Concerto for Viola, Violoncello and
     Orchestra, Op. 58
      2(pic).2.2.2. 2.2.1.0. timp,perc,
      strings,vla solo,vcl solo
      DOBLINGER perf mat rent   (F477)

   Concerto for 2 Violas and Woodwinds,
     Op. 28 [14']
      4(pic).3+English horn.2+bass
      clar.basset horn.3+contrabsn.
      0.0.0.0. 2vla soli
      DOBLINGER perf mat rent   (F478)

   Dorian Gray: Suite *Op.35a [20']
      3(pic).2+English horn.2+bass
      clar.2+contrabsn. 4.4.3.1.
      timp,perc,harp,glock,strings
      DOBLINGER perf mat rent   (F479)

   Emotionen, For Viola, Double Bass And
     String Orchestra *Op.57a [14']
      string orch,vla solo,db solo
      DOBLINGER perf mat rent   (F480)

   Kontinuum, For Bassoon And String
     Orchestra *Op.62 [15']
      string orch,bsn solo
      DOBLINGER perf mat rent   (F481)

   Omedeto *Op.54 [10']
      13vla
      DOBLINGER perf mat rent   (F482)

   Orchestron IV *Op.56 [10']
      3(pic).2+English horn.2+bass
      clar.2+contrabsn. 4.4.3.1.
      timp,perc,harp,strings
      study sc DOBLINGER STP 637 f.s.,
      perf mat rent   (F483)

   Sinfonietta, Op. 24 [15']
      2.2.2.2. 3.2.2.0. timp,strings
      study sc DOBLINGER STP 645 f.s.,
      perf mat rent   (F484)

FURST BARIATINSKY MARSCH see Strauss,
   Johann, [Jr.]

FURUENES SANG see Haug, Halvor

FUSEES see Rihm, Wolfgang

FUSIONEN WALZER see Strauss, Eduard

FUSIONS see Bazelon, Irwin Allen see
   Miroglio, Francis

FÜSSL, KARL-HEINZ (1924-   )
   Bilder Der Jahreszeit, For Solo Voice
     And String Orchestra [12'30"]
      string orch,high solo
      sc UNIVER. UE17750 f.s., perf mat
      rent   (F485)

   Cantiunculae Amoris, For Solo Voice
     And String Orchestra [12']
      string orch,T solo
      sc UNIVER. UE16831 f.s., perf mat
      rent   (F486)

FUX, JOHANN JOSEPH (1660-1741)
   Orfeo Ed Euridice: Overture
     string orch
      (Thomas, T. Donley) sc,pts MEDICI
      $10.00   (F487)

   Suite in D minor (from Concentus
     Musico Instrumentalis) [12']
      string orch,hpsd
      (Hockner) KALMUS A5604 sc $7.00,
      set $5.00, pts $1.00, ea. (F488)

FYLGIA, FOR SOLO VOICE AND ORCHESTRA
   see Stenhammar, Wilhelm

FYRA BAGATELLER FOR STRAKAR see Börtz,
   Daniel

FYRA MINIATYRER see Sköld, Sven

FYRA SANGER, FOR SOLO VOICE AND
   ORCHESTRA see Jonsson, Josef
   [Petrus]

FYRA SYMFONISKA MYTER see Koch, Erland
   von

FYRSTE SONGEN, DEN see Kielland, Olav

G

G.A.G.E., FOR NARRATOR AND ORCHESTRA
   see Barab, Seymour

GAATHAUG, MORTEN (1955-   )
   De Profundis, For Solo Voice And
     Orchestra *Op.20 [10']
      2.2.2.2. 4.2.3.1. timp,perc,harp,
      pno,strings,S solo
      NORGE   (G1)

   Gammeldags Julajten, En
     string orch
      "Old Fashioned Christmas Eve, An,
      Op. 11" [4'] NORGE   (G2)

   Old Fashioned Christmas Eve, An, Op.
     11
     see Gammeldags Julajten, En

   Suite Caracteristique [15']
      2.2.2.2. 3.3.3.1. timp,perc,cel,
      harp,strings
      (Op.21-bis) NORSK   (G3)

   Suite Chevaleresque *Op.35
      3.2.2.2. 4.2.3.1. timp,perc,
      strings
      NORGE   (G4)

GABELI, I.
   Works For Symphony Orchestra *CCU
     sc MEZ KNIGA f.s.   (G5)

GABICHVADZE, REVAZ (1913-   )
   Symphony No. 3 [23']
      3.3.3.3. 4.3.3.1. timp,perc,harp,
      cel,pno,strings,cor
      SIKORSKI perf mat rent   (G6)

GABLENZ MARSCH see Strauss, Josef

GABON ZAR SORIGNAK see Arambarri, Jesús

GABRIEL-MARIE
   see MARIE, GABRIEL

GABRIELI, DOMENICO (ca. 1650-1690)
   Sonata No. 9, Op. 11, in C
     org,strings,2trp soli
      INTERNAT. perf mat rent   (G7)

GABRIELI, GIOVANNI (1557-1612)
   Canzona, [arr.]
     (Davies, Peter Maxwell) 1.1.1.1.
     1.0.0.0. strings [4'] sc CHESTER
     JWC557 f.s., perf mat rent   (G8)

   Canzona For Double String Orchestra
     see Canzona Per Doppia Orchestra
     D'archi

   Canzona Per Doppia Orchestra D'archi
     [6']
     string orch
      (Napolitano) "Canzona For Double
      String Orchestra" KALMUS A7343 sc
      $5.00, set $10.00, pts $1.00, ea.
                                     (G9)

   Canzone Quarti Toni [arr.]
     (Fromme) 2.3.3.2. 4.2.3.1. timp,
     strings AMP perf mat rent   (G10)

   Sonata in D, MIN 141
     trp,org,strings
      (XI 5) MUS. RARA 1934B $13.75 (G11)

   Sonata No. 16, [arr.]
     (Fromme) 2.3.3.2. 4.2.3.1. timp,
     strings,horn solo,2trp soli,2trom
     soli AMP perf mat rent   (G12)

GABRIJELCIC, MARIJAN (1940-   )
   Intonacija [11']
      2.2.2.2(contrabsn). 4.4.4.1.
      timp,perc,strings
      DRUSTVO DSS 1055 perf mat rent
                                    (G13)

   Ostinato II, For Solo Voice And
     Orchestra [18']
      timp,strings,Mez solo
      DRUSTVO DSS 1100 perf mat rent
                                    (G14)

   Predigra [12']
      4.2(English horn).2(bass
      clar).2(contrabsn). 6.4.3.1.
      timp,perc,strings
      DRUSTVO DSS 950 perf mat rent (G15)

   Tulminenses [13']
      4(2pic).2(English horn).3(bass
      clar).3(contrabsn). 6.4.4.1.
      timp,perc,strings
      DRUSTVO DSS 903 perf mat rent (G16)

GABRIOLA see Healey, Derek

GADE, NIELS WILHELM (1817-1890)
Aquarelles [arr.] *Op.19
(Hoffmann) string orch [9'] KALMUS
A5839 sc $5.00, set $5.00   (G17)

Capriccio for Violin and Orchestra
[14']
2.2.2.2. 2.1.0.0. perc,strings,
vln solo
RIES   (G18)

Echoes Of Ossian Overture
see Nachklange Von Ossian: Overture

Fruhlings-Phantasie, For Solo Voices
And Orchestra *Op.23
2.2.2.2. 2.2.0.0. timp,pno,
strings,SSTB soli
BREITKOPF-W perf mat rent   (G19)

Holbergiana *Op.61
KALMUS A5810 sc $30.00, set $65.00,
perf mat rent   (G20)

Michelangelo *Op.39
KISTNER perf mat rent   (G21)

Nachklange Von Ossian: Overture
*Op.1
"Echoes Of Ossian Overture" KALMUS
A5692 sc $25.00, set $25.00, perf
mat rent   (G22)

Novelletten In E *Op.58
string orch
BREITKOPF-W perf mat rent   (G23)

Novelletten In F *Op.53
KALMUS A6982 sc $10.00, set $18.00,
pts $3.00, ea., perf mat rent
                                 (G24)

Sommertag Auf Dem Lande *Op.55
2.2.2.2. 3.2.0.0. timp,strings
BREITKOPF-W perf mat rent   (G25)

Symphony No. 1, Op. 5, in C minor
[26']
2+pic.2.2.2. 4.2.3.1. timp,
strings
KALMUS A6960 sc $75.00, set $80.00,
pts $4.00, ea., perf mat rent
                                 (G26)
sc KISTNER f.s., perf mat rent
                                 (G27)

Symphony No. 2, Op. 10, in E [26']
2.2.2.2. 4.2.3.0. timp,strings
BREITKOPF-W perf mat rent   (G28)
KALMUS A7048 sc $65.00, set $60.00,
pts $3.00, ea., perf mat rent
                                 (G29)

Symphony No. 3, Op. 15, in A minor
[26']
2.2.2.2. 4.2.1.0. timp,strings
BREITKOPF-W perf mat rent   (G30)
KALMUS A7043 sc $65.00, set $75.00,
pts $4.00, ea., perf mat rent
                                 (G31)

Symphony No. 4, Op. 20, in B flat
[27']
2.2.2.2. 4.2.0.0. timp,strings
KALMUS A7050 sc $40.00, set $50.00,
pts $3.00, ea., perf mat rent
                                 (G32)
KISTNER perf mat rent   (G33)

Symphony No. 5, Op. 25, in D minor
[25']
3.2.2.2. 4.2.3.0. timp,pno,
strings
BREITKOPF-W perf mat rent   (G34)
KALMUS A6781 sc $75.00, set $60.00,
pts $3.00, ea., perf mat rent
                                 (G35)

Symphony No. 6, Op. 32, in G minor
[24']
3.2.2.2. 4.2.1.0. timp,strings
KALMUS A7256 sc $60.00, set
$100.00, pts $5.00, ea., perf mat
rent   (G36)
KISTNER perf mat rent   (G37)

Symphony No. 7, Op. 45, in F
2.2.2.2. 4.2.3.0. timp,strings
BREITKOPF-W perf mat rent   (G38)
KALMUS A5840 sc $80.00, set $80.00,
perf mat rent   (G39)

Symphony No. 8, Op. 47, in B minor
[30']
2+pic.2.2.2. 4.2.3.0. timp,
strings
KALMUS A7049 sc $65.00, set $80.00,
pts $4.00, ea., perf mat rent
                                 (G40)

GADFLY, THE: SUITE see Shostakovich,
Dmitri

GAELIC DREAM SONG see Foulds, John
Herbert

GAGNON, ALAIN (1938-   )
Enfant Roi, L', For Solo Voice And
Orchestra *Op.33
2.2.2.2. 4.1.0.0. timp,perc,harp,
strings,solo voice
CAN.MUS.CENT. MV 1400 G135 EN (G41)

GAHRICH, WENZEL (1794-1864)
Concertino for Viola and Orchestra,
No. 2
WOLLENWEBER 905   (G42)

GAITE PARISIENNE [ARR.] see Offenbach,
Jacques

GAJANEH: GOPAK see Khachaturian, Aram
Ilyich, Gayane: Hopak

GAJANEH: NUNES VARIATION see
Khachaturian, Aram Ilyich, Gayane:
Noune's Variation

GAJANEH: RUSSISCHER TANZ see
Khachaturian, Aram Ilyich, Gayane:
Russian Dance

GAJANEH: TANZ DER ROSENMADCHEN UND
LESGINKA see Khachaturian, Aram
Ilyich, Gayane: Dance Of The Rose
Maidens And Lesginka

GALA FANFARE see Bach, Jan Morris

GALATEA, FOR SOLO VOICE AND ORCHESTRA
see Lora, Antonio

GALAXIES see Paynter, John

GALDRA LOFTUR see Masson, Askell

GALERIA GOLDONI see Hanuš, Jan

GALUPPI, BALDASSARE (1706-1785)
Concerto No. 5 in E flat [8']
string orch,cont
(Heussner, Horst) sc,pts DOBLINGER
DM 997 f.s.   (G43)

Concerto No. 6 in B flat [8']
string orch,cont
(Heussner, Horst) sc,pts DOBLINGER
DM 998 f.s.   (G44)

Concerto No. 7 in A [8']
string orch,cont
(Heussner, Horst) sc,pts DOBLINGER
DM 999 f.s.   (G45)

Olimpiade, L': Overture
(Lupi) KALMUS A7453 sc $7.00, set
$13.00, pts $1.50, ea.   (G46)

Sinfonia Della Serenata In F
(Bonelli) KALMUS A7387 sc $8.00,
set $10.50, pts $1.50, ea.   (G47)

Sinfonia in D, MIN 4
(Bonelli) KALMUS A7386 sc $7.00,
set $10.50, pts $1.50, ea.   (G48)

Sinfonia in D, MIN 148
string orch,cont
KUNZEL 10198 sc $12.00, kbd pt
$6.00, pts $3.00, ea.   (G49)

Sinfonia, No. 1, in D
(Piccioli) KALMUS A7402 sc $15.00,
set $20.00, pts $1.50, ea., perf
mat rent   (G50)

Sinfonia, No. 2, in D
(Piccioli) KALMUS A7403 sc $15.00,
set $20.00, pts $1.50, ea., perf
mat rent   (G51)

Sinfonia, No. 3, in D
(Piccioli) KALMUS A7404 sc $15.00,
set $20.00, pts $1.50, ea., perf
mat rent   (G52)

GALYNIN, GERMAN (1922-1966)
Concerto for Piano and Orchestra, No.
1 [20']
3.2.2.2. 4.2.3.1. timp,perc,
strings,pno solo
SIKORSKI perf mat rent   (G53)

Suite for String Orchestra
string orch
VAAP perf mat rent   (G54)

GAMBLER, THE see Rybrant, Stig,
Hasardoren

GAMBOL see Goeb, Roger

GAMES, THE see Ištvan, Miloslav

GAMES AROUND THE SIX WITH ELEVEN see
Chiti, Gian Paolo

GAMINO, EL, FOR FLUGELHORN AND
ORCHESTRA see Grove, Richard

GAMLE MAJORS FORUNDERLIGE DROMME, DEN
see Sønstevold, Maj

GAMLE PORTRETTER see Sønstevold, Gunnar

GAMMALSVENSKT, FOR SOLO VOICE AND
ORCHESTRA see Rangström, Ture

GAMMALSWENSKA WIJSOR, FOR SOLO VOICE
AND ORCHESTRA see Koch, Erland von

GAMMEL VISE, EN, FOR SOLO VOICE AND
ORCHESTRA see Jordan, Sverre

GAMMELDAGS JULAJTEN, EN see Gaathaug,
Morten

GAMSTORP, GORAN (1957-   )
Meetings, For Clarinet And Orchestra
[19']
3.3.3.3. 4.3.3.1. alto sax,tenor
sax,timp,2perc,harp,strings,
clar solo
STIM   (G55)

GANGSO, ARVID
Zustand Fur Kleines Orchester [7']
4.2.2.0. 0.0.0.0. timp,perc,pno,
strings
NORGE   (G56)

GANNE, (GUSTAVE) LOUIS (1862-1923)
Saltimbanques, Les: Ballet Music
CHOUDENS perf mat rent   (G57)

Saltimbanques, Les: Overture
1+pic.1.2.1. 2.2.3.0. timp,perc,
strings
CHOUDENS perf mat rent   (G58)

GANSBACHER, JOHANN BAPTIST (1778-1844)
Symphony
see Hoffmeister, Franz Anton,
Symphonies, Two

GARANT, SERGE (1929-1986)
Phrases II, For 2 Orchestras [15']
4.3.3.4. 4.4.3.1. 4perc,pno,cel,
strings
CAN.MUS.CENT. MI 1100 G212PH (G59)

Plages
2.2.2.2. 2.2.0.0. perc,harp,
strings
sc DOBER $35.00, perf mat rent
                                 (G60)

GARBAREK, JAN (1956-   )
Suite For Jazz-Quartet And String
Orchestra
string orch, jazz quar
NORGE   (G61)

GARCIA-ABRÍL, ANTÓN (1933-   )
Cadencias, For Violin And Orchestra
[30']
sc ALPUERTO f.s.   (G62)

Celebidachiana
REAL RM-07-2222   (G63)

Concierto Aguediano, For Guitar And
Orchestra
2(pic).2(English horn).2(bass
clar).2. 0.3.0.0. harp,strings,
gtr solo
sc REAL RM-16-1001 f.s., perf mat
rent   (G64)

Concierto Mudejar, For Guitar And
String Orchestra
string orch,gtr solo
sc REAL RM-16-1004 f.s., perf mat
rent   (G65)

Danza Y Tronio
REAL RM-07-2223 perf mat rent (G66)

Fandango Sobre Un Tema De Boccherini
REAL RM-07-2225 perf mat rent (G67)

Hemeroscopium [23']
2(pic).2+English horn.2+bass
clar.2+contrabsn. 4.2.3.1.
timp,perc,pno&cel,2harp,strings
ALPUERTO   (G68)

GARCÍA-CATURLA, ALEJANDRO (1906-1940)
Bembe [14']
1.1.2.1. 2.1.1.0. perc,harp,
strings
ESCHIG perf mat rent   (G69)

GARCÍA LEOZ, JESUS (1905-1953)
Sonatina
2+pic.2.2.2. 2.1.0.0. harp,
strings
UNION ESP. perf mat rent   (G70)

GARCIA ROMAN, JOSE (1945-   )
Contra Esto Y Aquello [18']
1.1.1.1. 1.0.3.0. perc,2pno,
strings
sc ALPUERTO f.s.   (G71)

O Tempora, For Solo Voices And
Chamber Orchestra [17']
1.1.1.1. 1.1.1.0. perc,org,
strings,3 solo voices
sc ALPUERTO f.s.   (G72)

GARCIN, GERARD (1947-   )
Nacimento [25']
1.1.1.1. 1.0.0.0. vibra,2vln,vla,
vcl,db
SALABERT perf mat rent   (G73)

GARDEN OF LOVE see Sherman, Norman

GARDEN OF PEACE see Kelly, Robert T.

GARDEN OF THE HEART, THE, FOR SOLO
VOICE AND ORCHESTRA see Schafer, R.
Murray

GARDENS OF HIERONYMUS B see Horvit,
Michael M.

GARDUNAK see Larrauri, Anton

GARLAND FOR TERRY, A, FOR NARRATOR AND
ORCHESTRA see Freedman, Harry

GARLICK, ANTONY (1927-   )
Danza Barbara
3.2.3.2. 4.3.3.1. timp,perc,
strings
SEESAW   (G74)

Pasticcio
3.2.2.2. 4.3.3.1. timp,perc,pno,
strings
SEESAW   (G75)

Simple Symphony (Symphony No. 1)
3.2.2.2. 4.3.3.1. timp,perc,
strings
SEESAW   (G76)

Symphony No. 1
see Simple Symphony

Symphony No. 2
3.2.2.2. 4.3.3.1. timp,perc,
strings
SEESAW   (G77)

Symphony No. 3
3.2.3.2. 4.3.3.1. timp,perc,
strings
SEESAW   (G78)

Symphony No. 4
SEESAW   (G79)

Symphony No. 5
2.2.3.2. 4.3.3.1. timp,perc,
strings
sc SEESAW $99.00, perf mat rent
     (G80)

GARTENLAUBE WALZER see Strauss, Johann,
[Jr.]

GARUTI, MARIO (1957-   )
A La Fenetre Recelant [10']
3.3.3.3. 4.3.3.1. timp,3perc,
harp,strings
RICORDI-IT 134190 perf mat rent
     (G81)

GASELLER, FOR PIANO AND ORCHESTRA see
Jacobsen, Julius

GASIENIEC, MIROSLAW
Triptych
fl,clar,3perc,pno,harp,2vln,vla,
vcl
POLSKIE   (G82)

GASSANOV, GOTFRIED (1900-   )
Concerto for Piano and Orchestra, No.
2, in E minor
2.2.2.2. 4.3.3.1. timp,perc,
strings,pno solo
VAAP perf mat rent   (G83)

GASSER, LUIS (1951-   )
Christ's Sermon On The Mount, For
Solo Voice And Chamber Orchestra
[17']
1.1.1.1. 1.0.0.0. pno,strings,T
solo
ALPUERTO   (G84)

GASSER, ULRICH (1950-   )
Baum-Fels-Eiswasser- Und Fischstucke,
For Piano And Orchestra [37']
3.3.2.2. 4.3.3.0. timp,perc,pno,
org,acord,strings,pno solo
RICORDI-GER SY 2377 perf mat rent
     (G85)
Steinstucke II; Vier Kleine Stucke II
[16']
ob,English horn,clar,bass clar,
bsn,contrabsn,5vln,4vla,3vcl,
2db
sc RICORDI-GER SY 2348 f.s., perf
mat rent   (G86)

GASSMANN, REMI
Symphonic Overture
3.3.3.3. 4.4.3.1. timp,perc,
strings
AMP perf mat rent   (G87)

GASTEINER SERENDE, FOR FLUTE AND
ORCHESTRA see Grabner, Hermann

GATES OF HARVARD see Lewis, John Aaron

GATHERING MUSHROOMS, FOR SOLO VOICE AND
ORCHESTRA [ARR.] see Mussorgsky,
Modest Petrovich

GATTERMAYER, HEINRICH (1923-   )
Funf Szenen [26']
string orch
study sc DOBLINGER STP 524 f.s.,
perf mat rent   (G88)

Symphonische Tanzstucke [19']
2(pic).2.2(bass clar).2. 4.3.3.1.
timp,perc,harp,strings
DOBLINGER perf mat rent   (G89)

GAUBERT, PHILIPPE (1879-1941)
Ballade for Viola and Orchestra [6']
2.2.2.2. 2.2.0.0. timp,perc,harp,
strings,vla solo
ESCHIG perf mat rent   (G90)

GAUCHO SUITE see Reesen, Emil

GAUDE MATER ECCLESIA, FOR SOLO VOICE
AND STRING ORCHESTRA see Vivaldi,
Antonio

GAUDIBERT, ERIC (1936-   )
Écharppe d'Iris, L'
3.3.3.3. 4.3.3.1. perc,cel,harp,
strings [11'] study sc GUILYS
f.s., perf mat rent   (G91)

Gemmes, 4 Pièces Pour Orchestre
2.2.2.2. 2.2.1.0. perc,strings
[12'] study sc GUILYS f.s., perf
mat rent   (G92)

GAUSSIN, ALLAIN (1943-   )
Aria [10']
2fl,4clar,2bsn,perc,pno,strings
(may be performed by strings alone)
SALABERT perf mat rent   (G93)

Irisation-Rituel, For Solo Voices,
Flute, And Orchestra [29']
3(pic).3(English horn).3(bass
clar).3(contrabsn). 3.4.3.1.
4perc,pno,strings,fl solo,opt
speaking voice&S solo
SALABERT perf mat rent   (G94)

GAVOTTE EN RONDEAU [ARR.] see Bach,
Johann Sebastian

GAVOTTO STACCATO see Whitney, Maurice
Cary

GAVRILIN, VALERY (1939-   )
Anuta: Suite [30']
0.2.2.2. 3.3.3.1. 3perc,harp,pno,
elec gtr,strings
VAAP perf mat rent   (G95)

Enchanted Forest, The
2fl,2horn,trp,strings
SCHIRM.G perf mat rent   (G96)

GAWAIN'S PASSAGE see Park, James

GAYANE: ADAGIO see Khachaturian, Aram
Ilyich

GAYANE: ARMEN'S VARIATIONS see
Khachaturian, Aram Ilyich

GAYANE: AWAKENING AND DANCE OF AYSHE
see Khachaturian, Aram Ilyich

GAYANE: DANCE OF THE ROSE MAIDENS see
Khachaturian, Aram Ilyich

GAYANE: DANCE OF THE ROSE MAIDENS AND
LESGINKA see Khachaturian, Aram
Ilyich

GAYANE: DANCE OF THE YOUNG KURDS see
Khachaturian, Aram Ilyich

GAYANE: HOPAK see Khachaturian, Aram
Ilyich

GAYANE: LULLABY see Khachaturian, Aram
Ilyich

GAYANE: NOUNE'S VARIATION see
Khachaturian, Aram Ilyich

GAYANE: RUSSIAN DANCE see Khachaturian,
Aram Ilyich

GAYANE: SCENE OF GAYANE AND GUIKO see
Khachaturian, Aram Ilyich

GAYFER, JAMES MCDONALD (1916-   )
Holiday Waltz [4']
2.2.2.2. 2.2.0.0. perc,strings
CAN.MUS.CENT. MI 1200 G286H   (G97)

Tyl [7']
pno,strings
CAN.MUS.CENT. MI 1661 G286T   (G98)

GAYFER, JAMES MCDONALD (cont'd.)

Yukon Summer Suite [14']
3.3.3.3. 4.3.3.1. timp,perc,harp,
strings
CAN.MUS.CENT. MI 1100 G286Y   (G99)

GAZELLE, DIE see Strauss, Josef

GAZELLES, FOR PIANO AND ORCHESTRA see
Jacobsen, Julius, Gaseller, For
Piano And Orchestra

GAZZA LADRA, LA: DI PIACER MI BALZA IL
COR, FOR SOLO VOICE AND ORCHESTRA
see Rossini, Gioacchino

GAZZA LADRA, LA: EBEN, PER MIA MEMORIA,
FOR SOLO VOICES AND ORCHESTRA see
Rossini, Gioacchino

GAZZA LADRA, LA: FORSE UN DI
CONOSCERETE, FOR SOLO VOICES AND
ORCHESTRA see Rossini, Gioacchino

GAZZA LADRA, LA: IDOLO MIO, FOR SOLO
VOICES AND ORCHESTRA see Rossini,
Gioacchino

GAZZA LADRA, LA: IL MIO PIANO E
PREPARATO, FOR SOLO VOICE AND
ORCHESTRA see Rossini, Gioacchino

GAZZA LADRA, LA: OVERTURE see Rossini,
Gioacchino

GAZZA LADRA, LA: SI PER VOI, PUPILLE
AMATE, FOR SOLO VOICE AND ORCHESTRA
see Rossini, Gioacchino

GAZZA LADRA, LA: STRINGHE E FERRI DA
CALZETTE, FOR SOLO VOICE AND
ORCHESTRA see Rossini, Gioacchino

GAZZA LADRA, LA: VIENI FRA QUESTE
BRACCIA, FOR SOLO VOICE AND
ORCHESTRA see Rossini, Gioacchino

GBYSO MUSIC, THE see Antoniou, Theodore

GE, GAN-RU
Chamber Symphony
1.1.1.1. 1.1.1.0. timp,perc,pno,
strings
HONG KONG perf mat rent   (G100)

Three Pieces For Orchestra
2+opt pic+alto fl.2+English
horn.2.2. 4.3.3.1. timp,perc,
harp,strings
HONG KONG perf mat rent   (G101)

GEBAUER, ADOLF
Divertimento for String Orchestra
string orch
sc MOECK $28.00, perf mat rent
   (G102)

GEBILD see Rihm, Wolfgang

GEBROKEN OOR, HET see Bondt, Cornelis
de

GEBURT DES TANZES see Beyer, Frank
Michael

GEDANKEN ÜBER EIN KLAVIERSTÜCK VON
PROKOFJEW, FOR PIANO AND CHAMBER
ORCHESTRA see Zechlin, Ruth

GEDENKBLATTER WALZER see Strauss, Josef

GEDICHTE DER MARIA STUART, FOR SOLO
VOICE AND CHAMBER GROUP [ARR.] see
Schumann, Robert (Alexander)

GEDULDIGE SOKRATES, DER: OVERTURE see
Telemann, Georg Philipp

GEELEN, MATHIEU (1933-   )
Five Movements For Orchestra [14']
variable instrumentation
sc DONEMUS f.s., perf mat rent
   (G103)

GEESE, HEINZ (1930-   )
Bolero, For Guitar And Orchestra [6']
ZIMMER. perf mat rent   (G104)

GEFANGENE, DIE, FOR SOLO VOICE AND
ORCHESTRA see Berlioz, Hector
(Louis), Captive, La, For Solo
Voice And Orchestra

GEFORS, HANS (1952-   )
Christina Suite, For Solo Voices And
Orchestra
2(pic,alto fl).2(English
horn).2(clar in E flat,bass
clar).2(contrabsn). 4.3.3.1.
perc,mand,harp,gtr, electric
bass guitar, 2 synthesizers,
strings, 3 solo voices
NORDISKA perf mat rent   (G105)

Slits [17']
1+pic.2.2.2. 4.2.3.0. perc,
strings

GEFORS, HANS (cont'd.)

   HANSEN-DEN perf mat rent   (G106)

  Twine [20']
    3.3.3.3. 0.3.3.0. timp,3perc,elec
    gtr,synthesizer,strings
    STIM   (G107)

GEGEN DEN STROM see Busch-Orphal,
  Ulrich

GEHEIMNSVOLLE FLOTE, THE, FOR SOLO
  VOICE AND ORCHESTRA see Sjögren,
  (Johan Gustaf) Emil

GEHENNA see Etler, Alvin [Derald]

GEHLHAAR, ROLF (1943-)
  Lamina, For Trombone And Orchestra
    [23']
    2.2.2.2. 3.2.2.1. perc,pno,
    strings,trom solo
    sc FEEDBACK FB 7701 f.s.   (G108)

  Liebeslied, For Solo Voice And
    Orchestra [21']
    2.2.2.2. 3.2.2.0. 3perc,pno,
    strings,A solo
    sc FEEDBACK FB 7403 f.s.   (G109)

  Particles, For Solo Voice And
    Orchestra [17']
    1.0.1+bass clar.0. 1.1.1.0. perc,
    strings without db,synthesizer,
    S/Mez solo
    sc FEEDBACK f.s.   (G110)

  Phase [16']
    3.3.3(bass clar).3(contrabsn).
    4.3.3.1. 3perc,harp,pno,strings
    sc FEEDBACK FB 7202 f.s.   (G111)

  Prototypen 1, 2, 3
    4-16 players
    sc FEEDBACK FB 7312, 7313, 7314
    f.s.   (G112)

  Resonanzen [58']
    4.2.4.2. 4.4.4.0. 4perc,strings
    study sc FEEDBACK FB 7606 f.s.
                                       (G113)
  Tokamak, For Piano And Orchestra
    [22']
    3(pic).3.3+bass clar.3+contrabsn.
    6.3.3.1. 3perc,strings,pno solo
    sc FEEDBACK FB 8207 f.s.   (G114)

GEISHA, FOR SOLO VOICE AND ORCHESTRA
  see Madetoja, Leevi

GEISTERLIEBE: SCHAMANENGESANGE, FOR
  SOLO VOICE AND CHAMBER ORCHESTRA
  [ARR] see Yun, Isang

GEISTLICHE ARIEN, FOR SOLO VOICE AND
  ORCHESTRA see Schubert, Franz
  (Peter)

GEISTLICHES LIED, FOR SOLO VOICE AND
  ORCHESTRA see Castiglioni, Niccolò

GELLER, TIMOTHY (1954-)
  Where Silence Reigns, For Solo Voice
    And Chamber Orchestra [25']
    1(alto fl,pic).0.1(bass clar).0.
    1.1.1.0. 2perc,harp,pno&cel,
    2vln,vla,vcl,db,Bar solo, two
    wine glasses
    study sc MARGUN MP3040 $40.00, perf
    mat rent   (G115)

GELLMAN, STEVEN (1947-)
  Andante for String Orchestra [12']
    string orch
    CAN.MUS.CENT. MZ 1500 G319AN (G116)

  Love's Garden, For Solo Voice And
    Orchestra
    2.2.2.2. 2.2.0.0. timp,3perc,
    harp,strings,S solo
    CAN.MUS.CENT. MV 1400 G319LO (G117)

  Universe Symphony [50']
    4(alto fl).4.4.4. 4.3.3.1. timp,
    3perc,harp,strings,3synthesizer
    CAN.MUS.CENT. MI 1765 G319U (G118)

GEMA JAWA see Van de Vate, Nancy Hayes

GEMEAUX, FOR OBOE, TROMBONE, AND 2
  ORCHESTRAS see Takemitsu, Toru

GEMINI DANCES, FOR 2 VIOLINS AND
  ORCHESTRA see Crawley, Clifford

GEMINIANI, FRANCESCO (1687-1762)
  Concerti Grossi, Op. 3, Nos. 1-3
    min sc KALMUS K01407 $4.50   (G119)

  Concerti Grossi, Op. 3, Nos. 4-6
    min sc KALMUS K01408 $4.50   (G120)

  Concerto Grosso, Op. 2, No. 1, in C
    minor
    string orch,cont,2vln solo,vla

GEMINIANI, FRANCESCO (cont'd.)

    solo,vcl solo
    (Angerer) sc,pts CARUS 40.514 f.s.
                                       (G121)
  Concerto Grosso, Op. 2, No. 2, in C
    minor
    string orch,cont,2vln solo,vla
    solo,vcl solo
    (Angerer) sc,pts CARUS 40.515 f.s.
                                       (G122)
  Concerto Grosso, Op. 2, No. 3, in D
    minor
    string orch,cont,2vln solo,vla
    solo,vcl solo
    (Angerer) sc,pts CARUS 40.516 f.s.
                                       (G123)
  Concerto Grosso, Op. 2, No. 4, in D
    string orch,cont,2vln solo,vla
    solo,vcl solo
    (Angerer) sc,pts CARUS 40.517 f.s.
                                       (G124)
  Concerto Grosso, Op. 2, No. 5, in D
    minor
    string orch,cont,2vln solo,vla
    solo,vcl solo
    (Angerer) sc,pts CARUS 40.518 f.s.
                                       (G125)
  Concerto Grosso, Op. 2, No. 6, in A
    string orch,cont,2vln solo,vla
    solo,vcl solo
    (Angerer) sc,pts CARUS 40.519 f.s.
                                       (G126)
  Concerto Grosso, Op. 3, No. 5, in B
    flat [10']
    string orch,cont,2vln soli,vla
    solo,vcl solo
    (Schering) KAHNT KT 8024 f.s.
                                       (G127)
  Concerto Grosso, Op. 4, No. 1, in D
    string orch,cont,2vln soli,2vla
    soli,vcl solo
    (Angerer) CARUS 40.520   (G128)

  Concerto Grosso, Op. 4, No. 2, in B
    minor
    string orch,cont,2vln soli,2vla
    soli,vcl solo
    (Angerer) CARUS 40.521   (G129)

  Concerto Grosso, Op. 4, No. 3, in E
    minor
    string orch,cont,2vln soli,2vla
    soli,vcl solo
    (Angerer) CARUS 40.522   (G130)

  Concerto Grosso, Op. 4, No. 4, in A
    minor
    string orch,cont,2vln soli,2vla
    soli,vcl solo
    (Angerer) CARUS 40.523   (G131)

  Concerto Grosso, Op. 4, No. 5, in A
    string orch,cont,2vln soli,2vla
    soli,vcl solo
    (Angerer) CARUS 40.524   (G132)

  Concerto Grosso, Op. 4, No. 6, in G
    minor
    string orch,cont,2vln soli,2vla
    soli,vcl solo
    (Angerer) CARUS 40.525   (G133)

  Concerto Grosso, Op. 7, No. 1, in D
    (Platen) KALMUS A7434 sc $12.00,
    set $22.00, pts $2.50, ea., perf
    mat rent   (G134)

GEMMES, 4 PIÈCES POUR ORCHESTRE see
  Gaudibert, Eric

GEMS FROM SPOON RIVER see Thorne,
  Francis Burritt

GENERAL CADWALADER'S GRAND MARCH see
  Johnson, Francis

GENERAL WASHINGTON'S MARCH see
  Revolutionary Garland, A

GENERATEUR 1 ET 2 see Charbonnier,
  Janine

GENERATION OF LEAVES, A, FOR SOLO VOICE
  AND ORCHESTRA see Nielson, Lewis

GENERATIVE CELLS see Baldissera, Livid

GENESIS see Gorecki, Henryk Mikolaj see
  Villa-Lobos, Heitor

GENESIS II see Ott, David

GENEZING VAN DEN BLINDE, FOR NARRATOR
  AND ORCHESTRA see Colaço Osorio-
  Swaab, Reine

GENOVEFA QUADRILLE see Strauss, Josef

GENOVEVA, OP. 81: OVERTURE see
  Schumann, Robert (Alexander)

GENTILE, ADA (1947-)
  Criptografia, For Viola, And
    Orchestra [15']
    2.2.2.2. 2.2.0.0. 2perc,pno,
    strings,vla solo
    RICORDI-IT 134045 perf mat rent
                                       (G135)
  Flighty [8']
    1.1.2.0. 1.1.1.0. perc,hpsd,pno,
    strings
    RICORDI-IT 133440 perf mat rent
                                       (G136)
  Why Not [15']
    2.2.2.2. 2.2.2.0. 2perc,strings
    RICORDI-IT 134131 perf mat rent
                                       (G137)
GENTILUCCI, ARMANDO (1939-)
  Azzurri Abissi, For Clarinet And
    Orchestra [23']
    3.2.0.2. 2.1.1.0. timp,perc,harp,
    strings,clar solo
    RICORDI-IT 134137 perf mat rent
                                       (G138)
  Canti Di Maiakovski, For Solo Voices
    And Instrumental Ensemble [23']
    1.0.1.0. 1.1.1.0. perc,pno,8vln,
    4vla,2vcl,2db,speaking voice&S
    solo
    RICORDI-IT 132506 perf mat rent
                                       (G139)
  Canto Notturno, For Solo Voice And
    Chamber Ensemble [12']
    3.1.2.1. 2.1.1.0. perc,harp,
    strings,S solo
    RICORDI-IT 133640 perf mat rent
                                       (G140)
  Chiarore Dell'utopia, Il, For Solo
    Voice And Orchestra [16']
    3.1.3.1. 2.0.2.1. 1-2perc,harp,
    strings,S solo
    RICORDI-IT 133865 perf mat rent
                                       (G141)
  Coinvolgimento, For 2 Violins, Viola
    And Instrumental Ensemble [19']
    2.1.2.1. 2.0.0.0. 4vln,2vla,2vcl,
    2db,2vln soli,vla solo
    RICORDI-IT 132279 perf mat rent
                                       (G142)
  Dal Fondo Di Uno Specchio [14']
    alto fl,pic,ob,2clar,bass clar,
    horn,perc,harp,pno,4vln,2vla,
    vcl,db
    RICORDI-IT 133757 perf mat rent
                                       (G143)
  In Divenire, For Viola And Orchestra
    [16']
    2.2.3.2. 2.1.1.0. perc,harp,
    strings,vla solo
    RICORDI-IT 132411 perf mat rent
                                       (G144)
  Mensurale [7'30"]
    string orch
    RICORDI-IT 132860 perf mat rent
                                       (G145)
  Nei Quieti Silenzi [11']
    1(pic,alto fl).1.1(bass clar).1.
    1.0.1.0. strings
    RICORDI-IT 133557 perf mat rent
                                       (G146)
  Ramo Di Foglia Verde, For Solo Voices
    And Orchestra [18']
    3.2.3.2. 3.2.2.1. timp,perc,cel,
    harp,strings, B solo, voce
    bianca solo
    RICORDI-IT perf mat rent   (G147)
  Ritorno Di Un Canto Dimenticato, For
    Oboe And Instrumental Ensemble
    [16']
    English horn,clar in A,trom,perc,
    pno,2vla,2vcl,db,ob solo
    RICORDI-IT 133690 perf mat rent
                                       (G148)
  Scontri [13'30"]
    2.2.2.2. 2.2.0.0. perc,org,
    strings
    RICORDI-IT 132434 perf mat rent
                                       (G149)
  Studi Per Un Dies Irae
    3.3.3.2. 4.3.3.0. timp,perc,
    harmonium,strings
    [25'] RICORDI-IT 132028 perf mat
    rent   (G150)
  Tempo Sullo Sfondo, Il [20']
    2.2.2.2. 2.2.1.0. perc,pno,harp,
    strings
    sc RICORDI-IT 132871 $29.50, perf
    mat rent   (G151)
  Voci Dal Silenzio [18']
    3.2.2.2. 2.2.2.0. perc,strings
    RICORDI-IT 133320 perf mat rent
                                       (G152)
GENTLE, INTO THAT NIGHT see Averitt,
  William Earl

GENZMER, HARALD (1909-)
  Cassation for Strings [1130']
    string orch
    study sc PETERS P8654 f.s.   (G153)

  Concerto for 2 Clarinets and String
    Orchestra [12']
    string orch,2clar soli
    PETERS   (G154)

GENZMER, HARALD (cont'd.)

Concerto for 4 Horns and Orchestra
[20']
2.2.2.2. 0.1.1.0. timp,perc,
strings,4horn soli
PETERS   (G155)

Concerto for Piano and Orchestra, No.
3 [27']
2.2.2.2. 3.2.1.0. timp,perc,
strings,pno solo
PETERS   (G156)

Concerto for Trumpet and String
Orchestra, No. 2
string orch,trp solo
[14'] PETERS P8592 perf mat rent
                                (G157)

Concerto for Violoncello, Double Bass
and String Orchestra
string orch,vcl solo,db solo
PETERS   (G158)

Lyrisches Konzert, For Violoncello
And Orchestra [25']
2.2.2.2. 2.2.2.1. strings,vcl
solo
RIES perf mat rent   (G159)

Mistral-Kantate, For Solo Voice And
Orchestra [21']
2.2.2.2. 2.2.2.1. timp,perc,harp,
strings,S solo
PETERS   (G160)

Symphony No. 3 [30']
3.2.3.3. 4.2.2.1. timp,2perc,
strings
sc PETERS 8621 f.s.   (G161)

GEOGRAPHIES see Jaubert, Maurice

GEOMETRAL see Pinho Vargas, Antonio

GEOMETRIE DES TONES see Shchedrin,
Rodion

GEORGE, GRAHAM (1912-   )
Queen's Jig, The
fl,ob,clar,bsn,horn/trom,timp,
pno,strings
CAN.MUS.CENT. MI 1200 G347QU (G162)

Variations for Strings
string orch
CAN.MUS.CENT. MI 1500 G347VA (G163)

GERBER, STEVEN R. (1948-   )
Harmonium, For Solo Voice And
Orchestra [20']
2.2.2.2. 4.2.2.0. timp,perc,harp,
cel/pno,strings,S solo
sc AM.COMP.AL. $21.30   (G164)

GERHARD, FRITZ CHRISTIAN (1911-   )
Fantasy for Violoncello and String
Orchestra [9']
string orch,vcl solo
HANSEN-GER perf mat rent   (G165)

Sinfonia Concertante, For Piano And
Orchestra [18']
perc,strings,pno solo
HANSEN-GER perf mat rent   (G166)

Symphony No. 1 [24']
2.2.2.2. 3.2.3.0. timp,perc,
strings
HANSEN-GER perf mat rent   (G167)

GERHARD, ROBERTO (1896-1970)
Albada, Interludi I Dansa [10']
2(pic).2(English horn).2.2.
2.2.2.1. timp,perc,strings
BOOSEY perf mat rent   (G168)

Ariel [30']
3(pic).3(English horn) 3+bass
clar.2+contrabsn. 4.3.3.1.
timp,perc,strings
BOOSEY perf mat rent   (G169)

Cadiz [9']
2(pic).1+English horn.2.2.
4.2.3.0. 2perc,harp,strings
BOOSEY perf mat rent   (G170)

Cancionero De Pedrell, For Solo Voice
And Instrumental Ensemble [19']
1(pic).1(English horn).1.0.
0.0.0.0. perc,harp,pno,strings,
high solo
sc BOOSEY $36.00, perf mat rent
                                (G171)

Canciones Toreras, For Solo Voice And
Orchestra [9']
2(pic).2(English horn).2.2.
4.2.3.1. 2perc,harp,strings,med
solo
BOOSEY perf mat rent   (G172)

Don Quixote [32']
2+pic.2+English horn.2+bass
clar.2. 4.3.3.1. timp,2perc,
harp,pno 4-hands,strings

GERHARD, ROBERTO (cont'd.)

BOOSEY perf mat rent   (G173)

Don Quixote: Dances [16']
2(pic).2.2(bass clar).2. 4.2.2.0.
timp,2perc,pno,strings
BOOSEY perf mat rent   (G174)

Don Quixote: Symphonic Suite [27']
2(pic).2(English horn).2(bass
clar).2. 4.3.3.0. 2perc,2pno,
strings
BOOSEY perf mat rent   (G175)

Giants And Dwarfs
see Gigantes Y Cabezudos

Gigantes Y Cabezudos [9']
2(pic).2(English horn).2.2.
4.2.3.1. timp,2perc,harp,pno&
cel,strings
"Giants And Dwarfs" BOOSEY perf mat
rent   (G176)

Lamparilla [5']
1+pic.2.2.2. 2.1.1.0. timp,perc,
cel,harp,strings
BOOSEY perf mat rent   (G177)

Seguidillas (from El Barberillo De
Lavapies) [3']
2.2.2.2. 4.2.3.0. timp,perc,harp,
pno&cel,strings
BOOSEY perf mat rent   (G178)

Soirees De Barcelone [18']
2+pic.2+English horn.2+clar in E
flat+bass clar.2+contrabsn.
4.3.3.1. timp,perc,harp,pno,
cel,strings
BOOSEY perf mat rent   (G179)

Tirana (from El Barberillo De
Lavapies) [4']
2.2(English horn).2+bass clar.2.
4.2.3.0. timp,perc,harp,pno&
cel,strings
BOOSEY perf mat rent   (G180)

Viejecita, La [5']
2(pic).2(English horn).2.2.
4.2.2.0. 2perc,harp,strings
BOOSEY perf mat rent   (G181)

GERMAN, [SIR] EDWARD (EDWARD GERMAN
JONES) (1862-1936)
Conqueror, The: Romance And Two
Dances
1(pic).1.2.1. 2.2.2.0. timp,perc,
harp,strings [8'] KALMUS A5766
pno-cond sc $4.00, set $35.00,
perf mat rent   (G182)

Coronation March [6']
2.2.2.2. 2.2.3.0. timp,perc,
strings
KALMUS A7315 sc $12.00, set $30.00,
pts $1.50, ea., perf mat rent
                                (G183)

GERMAN DANCES AND CONTREDANCES see
Mozart, Wolfgang Amadeus

GERMETEN, GUNNAR (1947-   )
Case Janice, The, For Solo Voice And
Orchestra
see Tilfellet Janice, For Solo
Voice And Orchestra

Dance Through The Land Of Shadows,
The [14']
string orch
NORSK perf mat rent   (G184)

Lock Out
1.0.1.1. 2.0.0.0. strings
NORGE   (G185)

Tilfellet Janice, For Solo Voice And
Orchestra [8']
3.2.3.2.sax. 4.2.3.1. timp,perc,
strings,S solo
"Case Janice, The, For Solo Voice
And Orchestra" NORGE   (G186)

GERNSHEIM, FRIEDRICH (1839-1916)
Concerto for Piano and Orchestra, Op.
16
2.2.2.2. 2.2.0.0. perc,strings,
pno solo
RIES perf mat rent   (G187)

GERSHWIN, GEORGE (1898-1937)
Delicious Suite, [arr.] [9']
(Rose, Don) WARNER perf mat rent
                                (G188)
Embraceable You, [arr.] [3'15"]
(Herfurth) WARNER perf mat rent
                                (G189)
Girl Crazy: Overture, [arr.] [6'45"]
(McBride) WARNER perf mat rent
                                (G190)
Girl Crazy: Scenario [10']
2.2+English horn.2+bass clar.2+
contrabsn. 4.3.3.1. timp,perc,
pno,harp,strings

GERSHWIN, GEORGE (cont'd.)

WARNER perf mat rent   (G191)

I Got Rhythm Variations
1.1.2(bass clar).1.2alto
sax.tenor sax.baritone sax.
3.3.3.1. timp,2perc,pno,strings
WARNER perf mat rent   (G192)

Lady Be Good: Overture, [arr.] [7']
(Rose, Don) WARNER perf mat rent
                                (G193)

Love Walked In, Somebody Loves Me,
and The Man I Love, For Solo
Voices And Orchestra [5'18"]
WARNER perf mat rent   (G194)

My One And Only [arr.]
(Esposito, Tony) 2+pic.2.2+bass
clar.2. 4.3.3.1. timp,perc,cel,
harp,strings [10'] WARNER perf
mat rent   (G195)

Of Thee I Sing, [arr.]
see Wintergreen For President,
[arr.]

Of Thee I Sing: Overture, [arr.] [8']
(McBride) WARNER perf mat rent
                                (G196)

135th Street: A La Blue Monday [arr.]
(De Sylva) [20'] WARNER perf mat
rent   (G197)

Overture For A Gershwin Concert,
[arr.]
(Stone, Gregory) WARNER perf mat
rent   (G198)

Someone To Watch Over Me and
Embraceable You, For Solo Voice
And Orchestra, [arr.] [3'52"]
(Leyden, Norman) WARNER perf mat
rent   (G199)

Strike Up The Band [arr.]
(Leyden, Norman) 2+pic.2+English
horn.2+bass clar.2+contrabsn.
4.3.3.1. 4perc,pno,harp,strings
WARNER perf mat rent   (G200)

Tip Toes: Overture, [arr.] [6']
(Rose, Don) WARNER perf mat rent
                                (G201)
Who Cares
WARNER perf mat rent   (G202)

Wintergreen For President, [arr.]
(McBride) WARNER perf mat rent
contains also: Of Thee I Sing,
[arr.]   (G203)

GESANGE DER LIEBE, FOR SOLO VOICE AND
ORCHESTRA see Kelterborn, Rudolf

GESANGE DER SCHIRIN, FOR SOLO VOICE,
VIOLA D'AMORE AND STRING ORCHESTRA
see Muller-Hornbach, Gerhard

GESÄNGE ZUR NACHT, FOR SOLO VOICE AND
CHAMBER ORCHESTRA see Kelterborn,
Rudolf

GESAR LEGEND see Lieberson, Peter

GESCHICHTE VOM FAULEN BAREN, DIE, FOR
NARRATOR, TUBA AND ORCHESTRA see
Lothar, Mark

GESCHICHTEN AUS DEM WIENERWALD WALZER
see Strauss, Johann, [Jr.]

GESCHICHTEN AUS DEM WIENERWALD WALZER,
[ARR.] see Strauss, Johann, [Jr.]

GESCHOPFE DES PROMETHEUS, DIE see
Beethoven, Ludwig van

GESCHOPFE DES PROMETHEUS, DIE: OVERTURE
see Beethoven, Ludwig van

GESPENST VON CANTERVILLE, DAS: SZENEN,
FOR SOLO VOICES AND CHAMBER
ORCHESTRA see Knaifel, Alexander,
Canterville Ghost, The: Scenes, For
Solo Voices And Chamber Orchestra

GESPENSTER, FOR SOLO VOICE AND
ORCHESTRA see Huber, Nicolaus A.

GESTE ET LE SYMBOLE, LE see Sbordoni,
Alessandro

GESTEN see Antoniou, Theodore,
Cheironomiës

GESTOS see Schwartz, Francis

GETHSEMANI, FOR HORN AND ORCHESTRA see
Marc, Edmond

GEUR BLIJFT HANGEN, DE, FOR 3 GUITARS
AND ORCHESTRA see Meijering, Chiel

GEWICKSMANN, VITALI
    Great Patriotic War, The [35']
        sc MUZYKA f.s.   (G204)

GEYSIR see Leifs, Jon

GHEZZO, DINU DUMITRU (1941-   )
    Seven Short Pieces
        1.1.1.1. 1.1.1.0. perc,vln,vla,
        vcl,db
        SEESAW   (G205)

    Thalla, For Piano And Chamber
        Orchestra
        1.1.1.1.sax. 2.2.1.0. strings,pno
        solo
        SEESAW   (G206)

GIAL'EOLIA DI NOTTE see Correggia,
    Enrico

GIANI LUPORINI, GAETANO (1936-   )
    Concerto for Piano and Orchestra
        [22']
        3.3.3.3. 4.3.3.1. timp,3perc,cel,
        harp,strings,pno solo
        SONZOGNO perf mat rent   (G207)

    Kontakion [19']
        2.2.2.2. 2.2.0.0. timp,perc,pno,
        strings
        SONZOGNO perf mat rent   (G208)

GIANNI DI PARIGI: OVERTURE see
    Donizetti, Gaetano

GIANNINA E BERNARDONE: OVERTURE see
    Cimarosa, Domenico

GIANTS AND DWARFS see Gerhard, Roberto,
    Gigantes Y Cabezudos

GIARDINI, FELICE DE' (1716-1796)
    Rondo in G
        (Bonelli) KALMUS A7347 sc $7.00,
        set $7.50, pts $1.50, ea. (G209)

GIARDINO DELLE DELIZIE, IL see
    Schiaffini, Giancarlo

GIBBONS, ORLANDO (1583-1625)
    Wood So Wild, The [arr.]
        (Cruft, Adrian) 2ob,2horn,strings
        [5'] sc JOAD f.s., perf mat rent
                                          (G210)

GIBBS, MICHAEL
    Interviews [11'30"]
        2+pic.2.2+bass clar.2. 4.2+
        2flügelhorn.3.1. timp,perc,pno,
        harp,strings
        NEWAM 19018 perf mat rent (G211)

GIFT OF THE SUN see Vizzutti, Allen

GIGANTES Y CABEZUDOS see Gerhard,
    Roberto

GIL SERRANO, JOSE M. (1908-   )
    Evocacion Goyesca
        2+pic.1.2.1. 2.2.3.0. timp,perc,
        harp,strings
        UNION ESP. perf mat rent   (G212)

    Seguiriyas
        2+pic.1.2.1. 2.2.2.0. timp,perc,
        harp,strings
        UNION ESP. perf mat rent   (G213)

GILBERT, ANTHONY (1934-   )
    Towards Asavari, For Piano And
        Orchestra [19']
        fl&pic,clar in A&clar in E flat,
        bsn,horn,trp,perc,12vln,4vla,
        4vcl,2db,pno solo
        study sc SCHOTT ED 12195 $35.00,
        perf mat rent   (G214)

GILDE, FOR BASSET CLARINET AND
    ORCHESTRA see Rypdal, Terje

GILLET, BRUNO (1936-   )
    Scene [9']
        24strings
        BILLAUDOT perf mat rent   (G215)

    Treize Petits Airs [9']
        3.3.3.3. 4.3.1.0. 3perc,strings
        BILLAUDOT perf mat rent   (G216)

GILLIS, DON E. (1912-1978)
    Bing, Bang, Bong [5'30"]
        2.2.3.2. 4.3.3.1. timp,perc,pno&
        cel,strings
        MILLS perf mat rent   (G217)

    Boogie In Brass (from Pep Rally) [4']
        3.3.3.2. 3.3.3.1. timp,perc,pno,
        strings
        MILLS perf mat rent   (G218)

    Encore Concerto, The [15']
        2(pic),2(English horn).3.2.
        4.3.3.1. timp,perc,strings
        MILLS perf mat rent   (G219)

GILLIS, DON E. (cont'd.)

    Jubilee Festival Overture
        2.2.3.2. 4.3.3.1. perc,pno&cel,
        harp,strings
        MILLS perf mat rent   (G220)

    Procession And Finale [4'30"]
        3.2.3.2. 3.3.3.1. timp,perc,pno,
        strings
        MILLS perf mat rent   (G221)

    Shindig [6']
        2.2.3.2. 3.3.3.1. timp,perc,pno,
        opt banjo,harp,strings
        MILLS perf mat rent   (G222)

    Twinkletoes Ballet [21']
        MILLS perf mat rent   (G223)

GILLYFLOWER, FOR SOLO VOICE AND
    ORCHESTRA see Groven, Eivind, Til
    Min Gyllenlakk, For Solo Voice And
    Orchestra

GILSE, JAN VAN (1881-1944)
    Drie Tanzskizzen, For Piano And
        Orchestra
        2.2.2.1. 2.1.0.0. 3perc,harp,cel,
        6vln,4vla,3vcl,2db,pno solo
        sc DONEMUS f.s., perf mat rent
                                          (G224)

GILTAY, BEREND (1910-1975)
    Koncert Za Groznjan [18']
        2.2.2.2. 2.2.0.0. timp,2perc,
        strings
        sc DONEMUS f.s., perf mat rent
                                          (G225)

GIMENEZ, JERONIMO (1854-1923)
    Torre Del Oro, La, For Solo Voice And
        Orchestra
        1+pic.1+English horn.2.1.
        2.2.3.0. timp,perc,strings,solo
        voice
        UNION ESP. perf mat rent   (G226)

GINASTERA, ALBERTO (1916-1983)
    Concerto for Violoncello and
        Orchestra, Op. 50 [28']
        3(pic).3(English horn).3(bass
        clar).3(contrabsn). 4.3.3.1.
        timp,3perc,cel,harp,strings,vcl
        solo
        BOOSEY perf mat rent   (G227)

    Iubilum *Op.51 [10']
        3.3.3.3. 4.4.4.1. timp,4perc,
        harp,cel,strings
        min sc BOOSEY $17.50, perf mat rent
                                          (G228)

GIOCO DI MINUETTI BALLABILI, UN see
    Boccherini, Luigi

GIOIELLI DELLA MADONNA, I: DANZA DEI
    CAMORRISTI see Wolf-Ferrari,
    Ermanno

GIOIELLI DELLA MADONNA, I: INTERMEZZO
    NO. 2 see Wolf-Ferrari, Ermanno

GIORDANI, TOMMASO (1730-1806)
    Concerto for Keyboard Instrument and
        String Orchestra in C [13']
        string orch without vla,kbd solo
        (Bittner) KALMUS A5616 sc $10.00,
        set $4.00, pts $1.00, ea. (G229)

GIORDANO, UMBERTO (1867-1948)
    Fedora: Amor Ti Vieta, For Solo Voice
        And Orchestra
        KALMUS A6211 sc $3.00, set $12.00,
        pts $.75, ea.   (G230)

GIORNO FELICE, IL: OVERTURE see
    Cimarosa, Domenico

GIOSTRA GENOVESE see Zimmermann, Bernd
    Alois

GIOVANNA D'ARCO: AMAI, MA UN SOLO
    ISTANTE, FOR SOLO VOICES AND
    ORCHESTRA see Verdi, Giuseppe

GIOVANNA D'ARCO: DUNQUE, O CRUDA, E
    GLORIA E TRONO, FOR SOLO VOICE AND
    ORCHESTRA see Verdi, Giuseppe

GIOVANNA D'ARCO: FRANCO SON IO, MA IN
    CORE, FOR SOLO VOICE AND ORCHESTRA
    see Verdi, Giuseppe

GIOVANNA D'ARCO: MARCH see Verdi,
    Giuseppe

GIOVANNA D'ARCO: O FATIDICA FORESTA,
    FOR SOLO VOICE AND ORCHESTRA see
    Verdi, Giuseppe

GIOVANNA D'ARCO: OVERTURE see Verdi,
    Giuseppe

GIOVANNA D'ARCO: QUALE PIU FIDO AMICO,
    FOR SOLO VOICE AND ORCHESTRA see
    Verdi, Giuseppe

GIOVANNA D'ARCO: S' APRE IL CIELO, FOR
    SOLO VOICES AND ORCHESTRA see
    Verdi, Giuseppe

GIOVANNA D'ARCO: SEMPRE ALL' ALBA ED
    ALLA SERA, FOR SOLO VOICE AND
    ORCHESTRA see Verdi, Giuseppe

GIOVANNA D'ARCO: SOTTO UNA QUERCIA
    PARVEMI, FOR SOLO VOICE AND
    ORCHESTRA see Verdi, Giuseppe

GIOVANNA D'ARCO: SPEME AL VECCHIO ERA
    UNA FIGLIA, FOR SOLO VOICE AND
    ORCHESTRA see Verdi, Giuseppe

GIPSY SONGS, FOR SOLO VOICE AND
    ORCHESTRA, [ARR.] see Dvorák,
    Antonín

GIRANDOLA see Weiner-Dillmann, H.

GIRARD, ANTHONY (1959-   )
    Nuit, La, For Trumpet And Strings
        [14']
        12strings,trp solo
        BILLAUDOT perf mat rent   (G231)

GIRAUD, SUZANNE (1958-   )
    Contrees D'un Reve [25']
        2.0.1(clar in E flat)+bass
        clar.0. 0.2.2.0. 2perc,strings
        SALABERT perf mat rent   (G232)

    Terre-Essor [19'30"]
        3(pic).1+English horn.2+bass
        clar.2. 4.2.3.0. timp,2perc,
        harp,pno,strings
        SALABERT perf mat rent   (G233)

GIRL CRAZY: OVERTURE, [ARR.] see
    Gershwin, George

GIRL CRAZY: SCENARIO see Gershwin,
    George

GIRL OF THE MOUNTAIN, FOR VIOLIN AND
    ORCHESTRA see Ju, Xiao-Song

GIRL WITH THE MATCHES see Huang, An-Lun

GIRLANDE VON REZITATIONEN see Artyomov,
    Vyacheslav

GIRO see Salonen, Esa-Pekka

GIROTONDO: A GUARDAR, FOR SOLO VOICE
    AND ORCHESTRA see Vacchi, Fabio

GIROTONDO: SUITE, FOR SOLO VOICES AND
    ORCHESTRA see Vacchi, Fabio

GISLINGE, FREDERIK
    Sorcerer In Bakkeby, The, For
        Narrator And Orchestra
        see Troldmanden I Bakkeby, For
        Narrator And Orchestra

    Troldmanden I Bakkeby, For Narrator
        And Orchestra [30']
        2.2.2.2. 4.2.2.1. 2perc,harp,
        strings,narrator
        "Sorcerer In Bakkeby, The, For
        Narrator And Orchestra" SAMFUNDET
        perf mat rent   (G234)

GITIMALYA "BOUQUET OF SONGS", FOR
    MARIMBA AND ORCHESTRA see
    Takemitsu, Toru

GIUFFRE, JAMES PETER (JIMMY)
    (1921-   )
    Hex [4'30"]
        2.2.0.2. alto sax.tenor sax.
        2.4.2.1. timp,2perc,gtr,strings
        sc MJQ $6.00, perf mat rent (G235)

    Mobiles, For Clarinet And String
        Orchestra [21']
        string orch,clar solo
        sc MJQ $15.95, perf mat rent (G236)

    Piece for Clarinet and String
        Orchestra [18']
        string orch,clar solo
        sc MJQ $15.95, perf mat rent (G237)

    Threshold [10']
        2.1.1.1. 2.0.0.0. strings,vibra
        solo,pno solo,db solo,drums
        solo
        sc,pts MJQ perf mat rent   (G238)

GIULIANI, ANTONIO
    Concerto for 2 Mandolins, Viola and
        Orchestra in E
        2ob/2fl,2horn,strings,2mand soli,
        vla solo
        (Gladd) PLUCKED STR perf mat rent
                                          (G239)

GIULIO CESARE: CARO! BELLA! PIU AMABILE
    BELTA, FOR SOLO VOICES AND
    ORCHESTRA see Handel, George
    Frideric

GIULIO CESARE: PIANGERO, LA SORTE MIA,
FOR SOLO VOICE AND ORCHESTRA see
Handel, George Frideric

GIVE ME YOUR HEART see Templeton, Alec

GJERSTROM, BJORN G. (1939-   )
Camara De Lobos [12']
3.2.2.2. 4.0.3.1. perc,pno,
strings
NORGE   (G240)

Concerto for Oboe and String
Orchestra, Op. 17
string orch,ob solo
NORGE   (G241)

Concerto for Piano and Orchestra, Op.
7 [30']
3.2.2.2. 4.2.3.1. timp,perc,
strings,pno solo
NORGE   (G242)

Overture
3.2.2.2. 4.2.3.1. perc,strings
NORGE   (G243)

GJERSTRÖM, GUNNAR (1891-1951)
Concerto No. 1 for Piano and
Orchestra [28']
2.2.2.2. 3.2.3.0. timp,strings,
pno solo
NORSK perf mat rent   (G244)

GLAD DAY, FOR SOLO VOICE AND
INSTRUMENTAL ENSEMBLE see Martland,
Steve

GLADIATOR MARCH, THE see Sousa, John
Philip

GLANERT, DETLEV (1960-   )
Aufbruch *Op.11 [13']
2.2.2.2. 3.2.3.0. timp,3perc,
strings
sc BOTE f.s., perf mat rent   (G245)

Mahler Skizze *Op.20 [11']
fl,clar,horn,trom,harp,pno&cel,
string quin
BOTE perf mat rent   (G246)

Mitternachtstanz, For Timpani And
String Orchestra *Op.17 [12']
string orch,timp solo
BOTE perf mat rent   (G247)

Norden [11'35"]
1(pic,alto fl).0.1(bass clar).0.
0.0.0.0. timp,pno,strings
sc BOTE f.s., perf mat rent   (G248)

Parke, Die, For Solo Voice And
Orchestra *Op.3 [18']
2(pic).2.2.0. 3.0.0.0. timp,
2perc,harp,pno,cel,strings,S
solo
BOTE perf mat rent   (G249)

Symphony No. 1, Op. 6 [19']
3(pic).2+English horn.2+bass
clar.2+contrabsn. 4.3.3.1.
timp,3perc,strings
BOTE perf mat rent   (G250)

GLANVILLE-HICKS, PEGGY (1912-1990)
Etruscan Concerto, For Piano And
Orchestra
sc PETERS P66125 $22.00, perf mat
rent   (G251)

GLANZEN DER NATUR, DAS, FOR SOLO VOICE
AND ORCHESTRA see Nieder, Fabio

GLASBA FOR ORKESTER see Rojko, Uroš

GLASBA ZA GODALA see Srebotnjak, Alojz
F.

GLASER, WERNER WOLF (1910-   )
Arioso E Toccata II, For Piano And
Orchestra [18']
2.2.0.2. 2.2.0.0. timp,strings,
pno solo
STIM   (G252)

Divertimento No. 2 [17']
1.1.1.1. 1.0.0.0. strings
sc GEHRMANS 6129P f.s., perf mat
rent   (G253)

Tema Con Variazioni [22']
2.2.2.2. 4.2.3.1. timp,perc,
strings
STIM   (G254)

GLASERNER TAG see Pennisi, Francesco

GLASS, LOUIS (1864-1936)
Skovsymfoni
"Woodland Symphony" sc SAMFUNDET
f.s., perf mat rent   (G255)

Summer Life *Op.27 [20']
2.2.2.2. 4.2.3.0. timp,perc,
strings

GLASS, LOUIS (cont'd.)

HANSEN-DEN perf mat rent   (G256)

Woodland Symphony
see Skovsymfoni

GLASS, PHILIP (1937-   )
Akhnaton: Dance [6']
2.2.2+bass clar.2. 2.2.2+bass
trom.1. 3perc,strings without
vln
DUNV perf mat rent   (G257)

Canyon, The [18']
2(pic).2.2+bass clar.2. 4.3.2+
bass trom.1. timp,8perc,strings
DUNV perf mat rent   (G258)

Civil Wars, The: Cologne [28']
2(pic).2.2+bass clar.2. 4.3.2+
bass trom.1. timp,4perc,harp,
strings,opt cor
DUNV perf mat rent   (G259)

Concerto for Violin and Orchestra
[30']
1(pic).2.2+bass clar.2. 4.3.3.1.
timp,5perc,harp,strings,vln
solo
DUNV perf mat rent   (G260)

Light, The [24']
2+pic.2.2+bass clar.2. 4.3.3.1.
timp,4perc,2harp,pno,strings
DUNV perf mat rent   (G261)

GLAZUNOV, ALEXANDER KONSTANTINOVICH
(1865-1936)
Ballade, Op. 78
KALMUS A5767 sc $15.00, set $35.00,
perf mat rent   (G262)

Chant Du Destin, Le *Op.84
KALMUS A5769 sc $20.00, set $60.00,
perf mat rent   (G263)

Concerto for Piano and Orchestra, No.
1, Op. 92, in F minor
KALMUS A5819 sc $40.00, set $70.00,
perf mat rent   (G264)

Concerto for Saxophone and String
Orchestra in E flat
min sc KALMUS K01503 $4.00   (G265)

Concerto for Violin and Orchestra,
Op. 82, in A minor
min sc KALMUS K01409 $7.00   (G266)

Fete Slave, Une *Op.26,No.4
KALMUS A5770 sc $30.00, set $50.00,
perf mat rent   (G267)

From The Middle Ages *Op.79
KALMUS A5601 sc $40.00, perf mat
rent, set $85.00, pts $4.00, ea.
                              (G268)

Idylle Et Reverie Orientale *Op.14
KALMUS A6069 sc $12.00, set $15.00,
perf mat rent   (G269)

Marche Sur Un Theme Russe *Op.76
KALMUS A5768 sc $12.00, set $35.00,
perf mat rent   (G270)

Mazurka Oberek, For Violin And
Orchestra [17']
2.2.2.2. 4.2.3.0. timp,perc,
strings,vln solo
BELAIEFF   (G271)

Ouverture Solennelle *Op.73
KALMUS A6478 sc $25.00, set $40.00,
pts $2.00, ea., perf mat rent (G272)

Reverie for Horn and Orchestra, Op.
24
KALMUS A7039 sc $6.00, set $12.00,
pts $.75, ea.   (G273)

Scenes De Ballet No. 1: Preamble
[3'30"]
2+pic.2.3.2. 4.3.3.1. timp,perc,
strings
KALMUS A1467 sc $8.00, set $20.00,
pts $1.00, ea., perf mat rent
                              (G274)

Scenes De Ballet No. 2: Marionettes
[2'30"]
2+pic.2.3.2. 2.0.0.0. perc,harp,
strings without db
KALMUS A1468 sc $8.00, set $15.00,
pts $1.00, ea., perf mat rent
                              (G275)

Scenes De Ballet No. 3: Mazurka [5']
2+pic.2.3.2. 4.3.3.1. timp,perc,
strings
KALMUS A1469 sc $8.00, set $20.00,
pts $1.00, ea., perf mat rent
                              (G276)

Scenes De Ballet No. 4: Scherzine
[2']
2+pic.2.3.2. 4.0.0.0. timp,perc,
strings
KALMUS A1470 sc $8.00, set $15.00,

GLAZUNOV, ALEXANDER KONSTANTINOVICH
(cont'd.)

pts $1.00, ea., perf mat rent
                              (G277)
Scenes De Ballet No. 5: Pas D'action
[4']
2+pic.2.3.2. 4.3.0.1. timp,harp,
strings
KALMUS A1471 sc $8.00, set $15.00,
pts $1.00, ea., perf mat rent
                              (G278)
Scenes De Ballet No. 6: Danse
Orientale [3']
2+pic.2(English horn).3.2.
4.2.0.0. timp,perc,strings
KALMUS A1472 sc $8.00, set $15.00,
pts $1.00, ea., perf mat rent
                              (G279)
Scenes De Ballet No. 7: Valse [4']
2+pic.2.3.2. 4.2.0.0. timp,perc,
harp,strings
KALMUS A1473 sc $8.00, set $15.00,
pts $1.00, ea., perf mat rent
                              (G280)
Scenes De Ballet No. 8: Polonaise
[5']
2+pic.2.3.2. 4.3.3.1. timp,perc,
strings
KALMUS A1474 sc $8.00, set $20.00,
pts $1.00, ea., perf mat rent
                              (G281)

Seasons, The, Op. 67: Autumn
min sc KALMUS K01478 $5.00   (G282)

Seasons, The, Op. 67: Spring
min sc KALMUS K01476 $5.00   (G283)

Seasons, The, Op. 67: Summer
min sc KALMUS K01477 $5.00   (G284)

Seasons, The, Op. 67: Winter
min sc KALMUS K01479 $5.00   (G285)

Serenade No. 1, Op. 7
KALMUS A6118 sc $10.00, set $18.00,
perf mat rent   (G286)

Serenade No. 2, Op. 11
KALMUS A6119 sc $8.00, set $12.00
                              (G287)
Symphony No. 1, Op. 5, in E
KALMUS A5827 sc $70.00, set $80.00,
perf mat rent   (G288)

Symphony No. 2, Op. 16, in F sharp
minor
KALMUS A5824 sc $70.00, set
$100.00, perf mat rent   (G289)

Symphony No. 3, Op. 33, in D
KALMUS A5826 sc $60.00, set
$125.00, perf mat rent   (G290)

Symphony No. 7, Op. 77, in F
KALMUS A5830 sc $50.00, set
$100.00, perf mat rent   (G291)

Symphony No. 8, Op. 83, in E flat
KALMUS A5817 sc $60.00, set
$125.00, perf mat rent   (G292)

Symphony No. 9 in D minor
*reconstruction
(Judin) 3.3.3.3. 4.3.3.1. timp,
perc,strings [40'] sc BELAIEFF
BEL526 $17.50, perf mat rent
                              (G293)

GLEICHSAM EINE SINFONIE see Pernes,
Thomas

GLICK, SRUL IRVING (1934-   )
Divertimento for String Orchestra
[18']
CAN.MUS.CENT. MI 1500 G559DI (G294)

Fantasy for Violin and Orchestra
[14']
3.3.3.2. 4.3.3.1. timp,2perc,
harp,strings,vln solo
(Vision of Ezekiel, the)
CAN.MUS.CENT. MI 1311 G559FA
                              (G295)
Hatikvah
string orch
CAN.MUS.CENT. MI 1500 G559H (G296)

I Never Saw Another Butterfly, For
Solo Voice And Orchestra [22']
2.2.2.2. 2.2.1.0. 2perc,harp,
strings,med solo
LEEDS perf mat rent   (G297)

Lament And Cantorial Chant, For Viola
And String Orchestra
string orch,vla/sax/clar solo
CAN.MUS.CENT. MI 1612 G559L (G298)

GLIÈRE, REINHOLD MORITZOVICH
(1875-1956)
Concerto for Horn and Orchestra, Op.
91
KALMUS A7254 sc $35.00, set
$100.00, pts $5.00, ea., perf mat
rent   (G299)

GLIÈRE, REINHOLD MORITZOVICH (cont'd.)

Concerto for Violin and Orchestra,
Op. 100, in G minor
*reconstruction
2.2.2.2. 4.2.0.0. timp,perc,harp,
strings,vln solo
(Lyatoshinsky, Boris) VAAP perf mat
rent   (G300)

Concerto for Violoncello and
Orchestra, Op. 87 [38']
3.2.2.2. 4.2.0.0. timp,perc,
strings,vcl solo
SIKORSKI perf mat rent   (G301)
VAAP perf mat rent   (G302)

Symphony No. 1, Op. 8, in E flat
3.2.2.2. 4.2.3.1. timp,perc,
strings
VAAP perf mat rent   (G303)

GLINDEMANN, IB (1934-   )
Concerto for Trumpet and Orchestra,
Op. 1 [15']
2.2.2.2. 4.3.3.1. perc,strings,
trp solo
HANSEN-DEN perf mat rent   (G304)

GLINKA, MIKHAIL IVANOVICH (1804-1857)
Kamarinskaia
min sc KALMUS K01410 $4.00   (G305)

Life For The Tsar, A: Krakowiak
KALMUS A5704 sc $12.00, set $40.00,
perf mat rent   (G306)

Life For The Tsar, A: Overture
min sc KALMUS K01411 $4.00   (G307)

Life For The Tsar, A: Waltz
KALMUS A5703 sc $5.00, set $20.00,
perf mat rent   (G308)

Prince Kholmsky: Incidental Music
[6']
2.1.2.2. 4.2.1.0. timp,strings
VAAP perf mat rent   (G309)

Prince Kholmsky: Overture
(Glazunov; Rimsky-Korsakov) KALMUS
A5598 sc $15.00, set $18.00, perf
mat rent   (G310)

GLINKIANA SUITE see Kazanly, Nikolai

GLOBAL SUITE see Dominique, Carl-Axel

GLOBOKAR, VINKO (1934-   )
Laboratorium Fur 11 Musiker
vln/vla,vcl/db,clar/sax,ob/bsn,
trp/horn,trom/tuba,harp,pno,
2perc, koordinator
PETERS   (G311)

Miserere [50']
3+pic+alto fl.4.4+bass clar+
contrabass clar.3+
2contrabsn.soprano sax.alto
sax.2baritone sax. 4.6.6.2.
perc,elec gtr,pno,14vln,5vla,
9vcl,7db,synthesizer,S&3
speaking voices, actor
RICORDI-FR perf mat rent   (G312)

GLOCKEN-ALPHABET see Holliger, Heinz

GLOCKEN IM NEBEL see Denisov, Edison
Vasilievich

GLORY AND THE GRANDEUR, THE, FOR
PERCUSSION AND ORCHESTRA see Peck,
Russell James

GLUCK, CHRISTOPH WILLIBALD, RITTER VON
(1714-1787)
Alceste: Die Ihr Im Hades Herrscht,
For Solo Voice And Orchestra
see Alceste: Divinites Du Styx, For
Solo Voice And Orchestra

Alceste: Divinites Du Styx, For Solo
Voice And Orchestra
"Alceste: Die Ihr Im Hades
Herrscht, For Solo Voice And
Orchestra" BREITKOPF-L perf mat
rent   (G313)

Alceste: Où Suis-Je? Non, Ce N'est
Point Un Sacrifice, For Solo
Voice And Orchestra
2.2.2.0. 2.0.0.0. strings,S solo
"Alceste: Wo Bin Ich? Nein, Nicht
Ein Opfer Werd Ich's Nennen, For
Solo Voice And Orchestra"
BREITKOPF-L perf mat rent   (G314)

Alceste: Wo Bin Ich? Nein, Nicht Ein
Opfer Werd Ich's Nennen, For Solo
Voice And Orchestra
see Alceste: Où Suis-Je? Non, Ce
N'est Point Un Sacrifice, For
Solo Voice And Orchestra

GLUCK, CHRISTOPH WILLIBALD, RITTER VON
(cont'd.)

Armide: Ach Soll Dies Freie Herz, For
Solo Voice And Orchestra
ob,strings,S solo
BREITKOPF-L perf mat rent   (G315)

Don Juan: Ballet Music, [arr.]
(Haas) 2.2.0.1. 2.2.1.0. strings
BREITKOPF-L perf mat rent   (G316)

Drei Festliche Marsche
(Fischer) "Three Festive Marches"
KALMUS A5607 sc $5.00, set $10.00
(G317)

Iphigenie En Aulide: Overture
min sc KALMUS K01413 $4.00   (G318)

Iphigenie En Tauride: Le Calme Rentre
Dans Mon Coeur, For Solo Voice
And Orchestra
ob,strings,Bar solo
"Iphigenie In Tauris: Die Ruhe
Kehret Mir Zurück, For Solo Voice
And Orchestra" BREITKOPF-L perf
mat rent   (G319)

Iphigenie En Tauride: O Toi Qui
Prolongues Mes Jours, For Solo
Voice And Orchestra
"Iphigenie In Tauris: O Du, Die Mir
Das Leben Gab, For Solo Voice And
Orchestra" BREITKOPF-W perf mat
rent   (G320)
"Iphigenie In Tauris: O Du, Die Mir
Das Leben Gab, For Solo Voice And
Orchestra" BREITKOPF-L perf mat
rent   (G321)
"Iphigenie In Taurus: O Du Mir
Einst, For Solo Voice And
Orchestra" KALMUS A2804 set
$8.00, pts $.75, ea.   (G322)

Iphigenie In Tauris: Die Ruhe Kehret
Mir Zurück, For Solo Voice And
Orchestra
see Iphigenie En Tauride: Le Calme
Rentre Dans Mon Coeur, For Solo
Voice And Orchestra

Iphigenie In Tauris: O Du, Die Mir
Das Leben Gab, For Solo Voice And
Orchestra
see Iphigenie En Tauride: O Toi Qui
Prolongues Mes Jours, For Solo
Voice And Orchestra

Iphigenie In Tauris: Von Jugend Auf
Im Treusten Bunde, For Solo Voice
And Orchestra
bsn,strings,T solo
BREITKOPF-L perf mat rent   (G323)

Iphigenie In Taurus: O Du Mir Einst,
For Solo Voice And Orchestra
see Iphigenie En Tauride: O Toi Qui
Prolongues Mes Jours, For Solo
Voice And Orchestra

Orfeo Ed Euridice: Ballet Des Ombres
Heureuses, For 2 Flutes And
Orchestra [arr.]
(de Reede) "Reigen Seliger Geister,
For 2 Flutes And Orchestra
[arr.]" sc AMADEUS BP 2072 f.s.
(G324)

Orfeo Ed Euridice: Che Faro Senza
Euridice, For Solo Voice And
Orchestra
"Orpheus Und Eurydike: Ach, Ich
Habe Sie Verloren, For Solo Voice
And Orchestra" BREITKOPF-L perf
mat rent   (G325)

Orpheus Und Eurydike: Ach, Ich Habe
Sie Verloren, For Solo Voice And
Orchestra
see Orfeo Ed Euridice: Che Faro
Senza Euridice, For Solo Voice
And Orchestra

Reigen Seliger Geister, For 2 Flutes
And Orchestra [arr.]
see Orfeo Ed Euridice: Ballet Des
Ombres Heureuses, For 2 Flutes
And Orchestra [arr.]

Three Festive Marches
see Drei Festliche Marsche

GLUCKLICH IST, WER VERGISST see
Strauss, Johann, [Jr.]

GNESSIN, MIKHAIL (1883-1957)
Fantasy, Op. 30
1.1.2.1. 1.1.0.0. timp,perc,pno,
hpsd,strings
VAAP perf mat rent   (G326)

GNOMENTANZ see Bleyle, Karl

GO AHEAD see Huber, Nicolaus A.

GO DOWN, MOSES, FOR SOLO VOICE AND
ORCHESTRA [ARR.]
(Burleigh, Harry T.) 2.2.2.2.
4.2.3.1. harp,strings,high solo
COLOMBO perf mat rent   (G327)

GOBEC, RADOVAN (1909-   )
Drazgose [14']
2(pic).2.2.2(contrabsn). 4.3.3.1.
timp,perc,harp,strings
DRUSTVO DSS 927 perf mat rent
(G328)

GODAR, VLADIMIR
Concerto Grosso
hpsd,strings
SLOV.HUD.FOND   (G329)

Meditation for Violin and String
Orchestra
48strings,vln solo
SLOV.HUD.FOND   (G330)

GODARD, BENJAMIN LOUIS PAUL (1849-1895)
Fragments Poetiques
2.1.1.1. 2.0.0.0. harp,strings
[10'30"] KALMUS A5807 sc $12.00,
set $12.00   (G331)

Scenes Ecossaises: Legende Pastorale
*Op.138,No.1
KALMUS A7370 sc $7.00, set $22.00,
pts $1.50, ea., perf mat rent
(G332)

Scenes Ecossaises: Marche Des
Highlanders *Op.138,No.3
KALMUS A7366 sc $12.00, set $28.00,
pts $1.50, ea., perf mat rent
(G333)

Scenes Ecossaises: Serenade *Op.138,
No.2 [3']
1.0.2.2. 2.0.0.0. strings,ob solo
KALMUS A7371 sc $5.00, set $18.00,
pts $1.50, ea.   (G334)

Suite for Flute and Orchestra, Op.
116
KALMUS A4110 sc $15.00, set $22.00,
perf mat rent   (G335)

GODDESS OF RIVER LUO, THE see Du, Ming-
Xin

GODFREY, DANIEL (1949-   )
Concentus [14']
1(alto fl,pic).1(English
horn).1.1. 1.1.1.0. perc,
strings
MARGUN MP3039 perf mat rent (G336)

Rhapsody [10']
3.4.4.3. 3.3.2.3. perc,harp,
strings
sc AM.COMP.AL. $22.90   (G337)

Wild Horses [11']
3.3.3.3. 4.3.3.1. timp,harp,
strings
sc AM.COMP.AL. $63.90, perf mat
rent   (G338)
sc MARGUN MP3053 $30.00, perf mat
rent   (G339)

GODØY, ROLF INGE (1952-   )
Block
see Blokk

Blokk [8']
string orch
"Block" NORGE   (G340)

Fasetter Av En Figur
2.2.2.1. 2.2.2.0. 2perc,harp,
strings
NORGE   (G341)

Teksturer [19']
3.3.3.3. 4.3.3.1. timp,perc,
strings
"Textures" NORGE   (G342)

Textures
see Teksturer

GOEB, ROGER (1914-   )
American Dance No. 1, No. 2 And No. 3
[3']
string orch
sc AM.COMP.AL. $4.60, perf mat rent
(G343)

American Dance No. 4 [3']
2.1.2.1. 2.2.2.0. timp,strings
sc AM.COMP.AL. $6.15, perf mat rent
(G344)

American Dance No. 5 [3']
2.1.2.2. 2.1.1.0. timp,strings
sc AM.COMP.AL. $7.70, perf mat rent
(G345)

Capriccio [8']
3.3.3.2. 4.3.3.1. perc,strings
sc AM.COMP.AL. $16.75, perf mat
rent   (G346)

Concertant II, For Bassoon And String
Orchestra [12']
string orch,bsn solo
sc AM.COMP.AL. $9.15, perf mat rent

GOEB, ROGER (cont'd.)

(G347)

Concertant No. 1 [14']
fl,ob,clar,strings
sc AM.COMP.AL. $15.30   (G348)

Concertant No. 4, For Clarinet And
Chamber Orchestra [16']
timp,perc,pno,strings,clar solo
AM.COMP.AL. perf mat rent   (G349)

Concertino No. 1 [18']
2.2.3.2. 4.3.3.1. timp,strings
sc AM.COMP.AL. $30.10, perf mat
rent   (G350)

Concertino No. 2 [15']
2.2.2.2. 4.2.3.1. timp,perc,pno,
strings
sc AM.COMP.AL. $24.45, perf mat
rent   (G351)

Concerto for Piano and Orchestra
[18']
2.1.2.1. 2.2.0.0. timp,perc,
strings,pno solo
AM.COMP.AL. sc $32.50, pts $9.15,
perf mat rent   (G352)

Concerto for Violin and Orchestra
[19']
2.2.2.2. 3.2.1.0. timp,perc,pno,
strings,vln solo
AM.COMP.AL. sc $22.90, pts $4.60,
perf mat rent   (G353)

Divertissement [8']
string orch
sc AM.COMP.AL. $9.15, perf mat rent
                             (G354)

Essay [8']
3.3.3.2. 4.3.3.1. perc,strings
sc AM.COMP.AL. $11.50, perf mat
rent   (G355)

Fantasy [11']
3.3.3.2. 4.3.3.1. perc,strings
sc AM.COMP.AL. $22.15, perf mat
rent   (G356)

Gambol [5']
2+pic.2+English horn.2.2.
4.3.3.1. timp,perc,strings
sc AM.COMP.AL. $13.75   (G357)

Iowa Concerto [16']
1.1.1.1. 1.1.1.0. timp,perc,
strings
sc AM.COMP.AL. $18.30, perf mat
rent   (G358)

Memorial [8']
3.3.3.2. 4.3.3.1. timp,perc,
strings
sc AM.COMP.AL. $12.25, perf mat
rent   (G359)

Romanza [12']
string orch
sc AM.COMP.AL. $9.15, perf mat rent
                             (G360)

Symphony No. 1 [12']
2.2.2.2. 4.2.3.1. timp,perc,pno,
strings
sc AM.COMP.AL. $16.75, perf mat
rent   (G361)

Symphony No. 2 [10']
2.2.2.2. 4.2.2.1. timp,perc,
strings
sc AM.COMP.AL. $16.75, perf mat
rent   (G362)

Symphony No. 3 [25']
3.3.3.3. 4.3.3.1. timp,perc,cel,
strings
sc AM.COMP.AL. $36.55, perf mat
rent   (G363)

Symphony No. 4 [25']
3.3.3.2. 4.3.3.1. timp,perc,
strings
sc AM.COMP.AL. $30.60, perf mat
rent   (G364)

Symphony No. 5 [24']
3.3.3.2. 4.3.3.1. perc,strings
sc AM.COMP.AL. $33.50, perf mat
rent   (G365)

Symphony No. 6 [23']
3.3.3.3. 4.3.3.1. 3perc,strings
sc AM.COMP.AL. $94.75, perf mat
rent   (G366)

GOEDICKE, ALEXANDER (1877-1957)
Concert Etude, For Trumpet And
Orchestra *Op.49 [6']
2.2.2.2. 4.0.0.0. timp,strings,
trp solo
SIKORSKI perf mat rent   (G367)

Concert Etude For Trumpet And Strings
(Miller) string orch,trp solo [6']
KALMUS A6954 sc $6.00, set $6.00,

GOEDICKE, ALEXANDER (cont'd.)

pts $1.50, ea.   (G368)

Concerto for Horn and Orchestra, Op.
40 [18']
2.2.2.2. 2.0.0.0. timp,strings,
horn solo
SIKORSKI 2137 perf mat rent (G369)
VAAP perf mat rent   (G370)

Concerto for Organ and String
Orchestra, Op. 35, in D
string orch,org solo
VAAP perf mat rent   (G371)

Concerto for Piano and Orchestra, Op.
11
2.2.2.2. 2.1.3.0. timp,perc,
strings,pno solo
VAAP perf mat rent   (G372)

Concerto for Trumpet and Orchestra,
Op. 41 [15']
2.2.2.2. 4.0.0.0. timp,perc,
strings,trp solo
KALMUS A5873 sc $20.00, set $40.00,
perf mat rent   (G373)
SIKORSKI perf mat rent   (G374)
VAAP perf mat rent   (G375)

Dramatic Overture *Op.7
3.2.2.2. 4.3.3.1. timp,harp,
strings
VAAP perf mat rent   (G376)

In War *Op.26
3.2.2.2. 4.2.3.1. timp,perc,xylo,
strings
VAAP perf mat rent   (G377)

Symphony No. 3 in C minor [43']
3.3.3.3. 4.3.3.1. timp,perc,harp,
cel,strings
SIKORSKI perf mat rent   (G378)

GOEHR, ALEXANDER (1932-   )
Concerto, Op. 32 [17']
1.0.2(bass clar).0. 0.2.0.1.
perc,2vln,vla,db
(Concerto For Eleven) study sc
SCHOTT ED 12081 $39.00, perf mat
rent   (G379)

Deux Etudes, Op. 43
3.3.3.3. 4.2.3.1. timp,perc,harp,
cel,glock,strings
sc SCHOTTS $40.00   (G380)

Eve Dreams In Paradise, For Solo
Voice And Orchestra [25']
3(pic,alto fl).2.3.0. 4.2.3.1.
timp,perc,harp,org,strings,ST
soli
SCHOTT perf mat rent   (G381)

Musical Offering, A (J.S.B. 1985)
*Op.46 [25']
1.0.2(bass clar).0. 1.1.1.0.
perc,pno,3vln,2vla,db
study sc SCHOTT ED 12257 $45.00,
perf mat rent   (G382)

Sinfonia, Op. 42 [23']
1(pic).2.0.0. 2.0.0.0. strings
sc SCHOTTS $35.00, perf mat rent
                             (G383)

Symphony With Chaconne [35']
3(pic,alto fl).2+English
horn.3(clar in E flat,bass
clar).2. 4.2.3.1. timp,4perc,
harp,strings
study sc SCHOTT ED 12328 f.s., perf
mat rent   (G384)

GOETZ, HERMANN (1840-1876)
Concerto for Piano and Orchestra, Op.
18, in B flat
sc KISTNER f.s., perf mat rent
                             (G385)

Concerto for Violin and Orchestra,
Op. 22, in G
KISTNER   (G386)

Francesca: Overture
KISTNER perf mat rent   (G387)

Fruhlingsouverture
sc KISTNER f.s.   (G388)

Symphony, Op. 9, in F
KISTNER perf mat rent   (G389)

Widerspenstigen Zahmung, Der:
Overture
KISTNER perf mat rent   (G390)

GOLD DIGGER'S SONG, THE see Warren,
Harry

GOLDBERG, THEO (1921-   )
Canadiana, For Piano And Orchestra
2.2.2.2. 4.2.2.0. timp,perc,harp,
strings,pno solo
CAN.MUS.CENT. MI 1361 G618CA (G391)

GOLDEN AGE, THE: SUITE see
Shostakovich, Dmitri

GOLDEN BIRD, THE, FOR SOLO VOICE AND
ORCHESTRA see Russo, William Joseph

GOLDEN DANCE, THE see Wuorinen, Charles

GOLDEN FISH, THE see Burgon, Geoffrey

GOLDEN GATE, THE see Isolfsson, Pall

GOLDEN GOOSE, THE: SUITE see Holst,
Gustav

GOLDEN HORN, THE see Fitelberg, Jerzy

GOLDEN MOUNTAINS, THE: SUITE see
Shostakovich, Dmitri

GOLDEN SPINNING WHEEL, THE see Dvořák,
Antonín

GOLDEN WINDOWS, THE see Leon, Tania
Justina

GOLDENE BERGE: SUITE see Shostakovich,
Dmitri, Golden Mountains, The:
Suite

GOLDFISCHLEIN POLKA see Strauss, Eduard

GOLDMANN, FRIEDRICH (1941-   )
Ensemble-Konzert
wind quin,trp,trom,2perc,harp,
pno,2vln,vla,vcl,db
sc PETERS $35.00   (G392)

GOLDMARK, KARL (1830-1915)
Cricket On The Hearth, The: Prelude,
Act III
see Heimchen Am Herd, Das: Prelude,
Act III

Heimchen Am Herd, Das: Prelude, Act
III [5'30"]
2(pic).2+English horn.2+bass
clar.2. 4.3.3.1. timp,perc,
strings
"Cricket On The Hearth, The:
Prelude, Act III" KALMUS A5771 sc
$10.00, set $45.00, perf mat rent
                             (G393)

Königin Von Saba, Die: Festlicher-
Einzugs-Marsch
"Queen Of Sheba, The: Entrance
March" KALMUS A5772 sc $15.00,
set $50.00, perf mat rent   (G394)

Königin Von Saba, Die: Overture
"Queen Of Sheba, The: Overture"
KALMUS A5801 sc $5.00, set
$25.00, perf mat rent   (G395)

Queen Of Sheba, The: Entrance March
see Königin Von Saba, Die:
Festlicher-Einzugs-Marsch

Queen Of Sheba, The: Overture
see Königin Von Saba, Die: Overture

Sakuntala Overture *Op.13
SONZOGNO perf mat rent   (G396)

Sappho *Op.44 [13']
3.2+English horn.2+bass clar.2.
4.3.4.1. timp,harp,strings
KALMUS A5773 sc $35.00, set $50.00,
perf mat rent   (G397)

Scherzo, Op. 45, in A
KALMUS A5836 sc $12.00, set $40.00,
perf mat rent   (G398)

Symphony No. 2, Op. 35, in E flat
[30']
2.2.2.2. 4.2.3.1. timp,perc,
strings
KALMUS A5816 sc $25.00, set $80.00,
perf mat rent   (G399)

GOLDONI MUSIK, FOR 3 WOODWINDS AND
ORCHESTRA see Lothar, Mark

GOLDSCHMIDT, BERTHOLD (1903-   )
Chronica [20']
2(pic).2+English horn.2.1.
4.2.3.0. timp,4perc,harp,
strings
BOOSEY perf mat rent   (G400)

Chronica: Suite [14']
2(pic).2+English horn.2.1.
4.2.3.0. timp,4perc,harp,
strings
BOOSEY perf mat rent   (G401)

Ciaconna Sinfonica [11']
1+pic.2(English horn).2(bass
clar).2(contrabsn). 2.2.2.0.
timp,perc,harp,strings
BOOSEY perf mat rent   (G402)

Intrada And Marche Militaire [9']
2(pic).2.2.2. 4.2.3.1. timp,perc,
strings

GOLDSCHMIDT, BERTHOLD (cont'd.)

    BOOSEY perf mat rent   (G403)

GOLDSMITH, JERRY (1929-   )
    Masada
        3(pic).3+English horn.3(bass
            clar).3+contrabsn. 4.4.3.1. timp,
            3perc,pno,harp,strings DUCHESS
            perf mat rent   (G404)

    Star Trek [3'52"]
        3(pic).3(English horn).3(bass
            clar).3(contrabsn). 6.4.4.2.
            timp,perc,harp,pno&cel,pno&elec
            pno,strings
        CPP perf mat rent   (G405)

    Swarm, The
        2+pic.2+English horn.3(bass
            clar).2+contrabsn. 6.3.3.1.
            timp,5perc,pno,harp,strings
        WARNER perf mat rent   (G406)

GOLEM see Kruse, Bjørn Howard

GOLOB, JANI (1948-   )
    Chamber Music, For Instrumental
        Ensemble
        see Komorna Glasba, For
            Instrumental Ensemble

    Chamber Music, For Orchestra
        see Komorna Glasba, For Orchestra

    Elegy for Bugle and String Orchestra
        [5']
        string orch,bugle solo
        DRUSTVO DSS 973 perf mat rent
                                            (G407)
    Four Slovene Folk Songs
        see Stiri Slovenske Ljudske Pesmi

    Komorna Glasba, For Instrumental
        Ensemble [5']
        1.1.1.1. 1.0.0.0. vibra,harp,
            string quar
        "Chamber Music, For Instrumental
            Ensemble" DRUSTVO DSS 896 perf
            mat rent   (G408)

    Komorna Glasba, For Orchestra [5']
        1.1.1.1. 1.0.0.0. vibra,harp,
            strings
        "Chamber Music, For Orchestra"
            DRUSTVO DSS 906 perf mat rent
                                            (G409)
    Koncertantna Glasba, For Wind Quintet
        And Orchestra [19']
        0.0.0.0. 4.3.3.1. timp,perc,harp,
            strings,woodwind quin soli
        "Music Concertant, For Wind Quintet
            And Orchestra" DRUSTVO DSS 1043
            perf mat rent   (G410)

    Music Concertant, For Wind Quintet
        And Orchestra
        see Koncertantna Glasba, For Wind
            Quintet And Orchestra

    Overture [7']
        3(pic).2(English horn).2(bass
            clar).2(contrabsn). 4.3.3.1.
            timp,perc,harp,strings
        DRUSTVO DSS 981 perf mat rent
                                            (G411)
    Stiri Slovenske Ljudske Pesmi [12']
        string orch
        "Four Slovene Folk Songs" min sc
            DRUSTVO DSS 897 f.s., perf mat
            rent   (G412)
    Wheat Has Ripened, For Solo Voice And
        Orchestra
        see Zreilo Je Zito, For Solo Voice
            And Orchestra

    Zreilo Je Zito, For Solo Voice And
        Orchestra [4']
        perc,strings,A solo, ocarina,
            dulcimer
        "Wheat Has Ripened, For Solo Voice
            And Orchestra" DRUSTVO DSS 1081
            perf mat rent   (G413)

GOLONDRINAS, LAS [ARR.] see Chueca,
    Federico

GOLOVIN, ANDREY (1950-   )
    Sinfonia Concertante No. 2 for Viola,
        Piano and Orchestra [22']
        2trp,trom,strings,vla solo,pno
            solo
        SIKORSKI perf mat rent   (G414)

    Symphonie Concertante for Viola,
        Piano and Orchestra [30']
        min sc MUZYKA f.s.   (G415)

GOLUBEV, EVGENI (1910-   )
    Concerto for Violoncello and
        Orchestra, Op. 41 [35']
        3.2.2.2. 3.2.3.1. timp,perc,harp,
            strings,vcl solo
        SIKORSKI perf mat rent   (G416)
        VAAP perf mat rent   (G417)

GOLUBEV, EVGENI (cont'd.)

    Symphony No. 1 [25']
        sc MUZYKA f.s.   (G418)

GOM MIG, GOM MIG see Dorumsgaard, Arne

GOMBAU, GERARDO (1906-1971)
    Escenia Y Danza Charra
        2+pic.1+English horn.2+bass
            clar.2. 2.2.3.1. timp,perc,
            harp,strings
        UNION ESP. perf mat rent   (G419)

GOMEZ SENOSIAIN, RAFAEL (1949-   )
    Sinfonia [8']
        1.1.1.1. 1.1.1.0. strings
        ALPUERTO   (G420)

GOMNES, FREDERICK W.
    Symphony in A minor
        2(pic).2.2.2. 4.2.3.1. timp,perc,
            strings
        NORSK perf mat rent   (G421)

GONG-HU see Yun, Isang

GONG-RING see Harvey, Jonathan

GONZALEZ ACILU, AGUSTIN (1929-   )
    Aschermittwoch, For Solo Voice And
        Chamber Orchestra [10']
        1(pic).0.1.1. 0.1.0.0. perc,pno,
            strings without db,solo voice
        ALPUERTO   (G422)

    Concerto for String Orchestra [18']
        6vln,3vla,2vcl,db
        sc ALPUERTO f.s.   (G423)

GOOD TIMES see Davies, Victor

GOODMAN, DAVID
    Chamber Fantasy [9']
        pic,fl,bass clar,contrabsn,alto
            sax,acord,pno,5vln,3vla,2vcl,
            2db
        sc APNM $13.50, perf mat rent
                                            (G424)
    Dion [6']
        harp,perc,elec pno,3vln,2vla,
            2vcl,db
        sc APNM $9.00, perf mat rent (G425)

GOODWIN, GORDON (1941-   )
    Suite for Trombone and Orchestra
        2.2.2+bass clar.2.baritone sax.
            4.4+flügelhorn.3.1. perc,pno,
            harp,strings,trom solo
        [23'] NEWAM 19019 perf mat rent
                                            (G426)
GOOSSEN, FREDERIC (1927-   )
    Grimmtales [40']
        2.2.2.3. 4.3.3.1. timp,perc,
            strings
        sc AM.COMP.AL. $21.50, perf mat
            rent   (G427)

    Litanies [21']
        2.2.2.2. 4.2.3.0. timp,perc,
            strings
        AM.COMP.AL. perf mat rent   (G428)

    Music for Orchestra [13']
        2.2.2.3. 4.3.3.1. timp,perc,
            strings
        AM.COMP.AL. perf mat rent   (G429)

    Ode, For Solo Voice And Orchestra
        [15']
        2.2.2.2. 4.2.3.0. timp,perc,
            strings,Mez solo
        sc AM.COMP.AL. $10.70, perf mat
            rent   (G430)

    Prospero's Spell [12']
        2.2.2.3. 4.3.3.1. timp,2perc,
            strings
        sc AM.COMP.AL. $79.45, perf mat
            rent   (G431)

    Symphony No. 2 [25']
        2.2.2.2. 4.2.3.1. timp,perc,
            strings
        AM.COMP.AL. perf mat rent   (G432)

GOOSSENS, [SIR] EUGENE (1893-1962)
    By The Tarn *Op.15,No.1 [3']
        strings,opt clar
        KALMUS A3694 sc $3.00, set $6.00,
            pts $1.00, ea.   (G433)

    Flamenco [8']
        3(pic).3(English horn).3(bass
            clar).2+contrabsn. 4.3.3.1.
            2harp,timp,perc,strings
        CHESTER JWC159 perf mat rent (G434)

    Judith: Ballet Music [7'30"]
        3(pic).2+English horn.3(bass
            clar).2+contrabsn. 4.3.3.1.
            timp,perc,cel,harp,strings
        KALMUS A6427 sc $17.00, set $45.00,
            pts $2.00, ea., perf mat rent
                                            (G435)

GOOSSENS, [SIR] EUGENE (cont'd.)

    Kaleidoscope [14']
        2(pic).2(English horn).2.2.
            2.2.1.0. harp,perc,strings
        CHESTER JWC141 perf mat rent (G436)

    Miniature Fantasy *Op.2
        KALMUS A7414 sc $8.00, set $7.50,
            pts $1.50, ea.   (G437)

    Rhythmic Dance
        KALMUS A6956 sc $10.00, set $25.00,
            pts $1.00, ea., perf mat rent
                                            (G438)

    Sinfonietta, Op. 34
        KALMUS A6109 sc $30.00, set $80.00,
            perf mat rent   (G439)

    Twelve Marches
        see Zwölf Marsche

    Variations On "Cadet Roussel" [3']
        2.2.2.1. 2.1.0.0. harp,timp,perc,
            strings
        CHESTER JWC156 perf mat rent (G440)
        KALMUS A4045 sc $10.00, set $18.00,
            pts $1.00, ea.   (G441)

    Zwölf Marsche
        (Steglich) "Twelve Marches" KALMUS
            A5622 sc $7.00, set $17.00, pts
            $1.00, ea.   (G442)

GORDELI, OTAR (1928-   )
    Tribute Of Carols, A [7']
        2.1.2+bass clar.1.2alto sax.tenor
            sax.baritone sax. 2.3.3.1.
            timp,perc,strings
        WARNER perf mat rent   (G443)

    Yuletide Feast, A [6']
        string orch
        WARNER perf mat rent   (G444)

GORDON, PHILIP (1894-1983)
    Three Preludes
        string orch
        BOURNE perf mat rent   (G445)

GORECKI, HENRYK MIKOLAJ (1933-   )
    Genesis *Op.19,No.2 [8']
        fl,fl&pic,trp,mand,2pno,gtr,
            2perc,3vln,3vla
        POLSKIE   (G446)

    Old Polish Music; Three Pieces In The
        Old Style *Op.24 [10']
        0.0.0.0. 5.4.4.0. strings
        POLSKIE   (G447)

    Three Dances
        see Trzy Tance

    Trzy Tance *Op.34 [12']
        2.2.2.2. 4.3.3.1. timp,strings
        "Three Dances" sc POLSKIE f.s.
                                            (G448)

GORIANKA: SUITE see Kazhlayev, Murad

GORLI, SANDRO (1948-   )
    Bambino Perduto, Il [16']
        4.4.4.4. 6.4.4.0. 2perc,cel,
            2harp,strings
        RICORDI-IT 133273 perf mat rent
                                            (G449)

    Due Sorgenti, Le [15']
        2fl,2ob,2horn,strings
        RICORDI-IT 133731 perf mat rent
                                            (G450)

    Silent Stream, The, For Violoncello
        And Orchestra [17']
        2.2.2.2. 2.2.2.0. 2perc,cel,harp,
            pno,pno&hpsd,strings,vcl solo
        sc RICORDI-IT 133066 f.s., perf mat
            rent   (G451)

GORY see Lason, Aleksander

GOSPEL FUSE, FOR SOLO VOICES AND
    ORCHESTRA see Moore, Carman

GOSSAMER see Rimmer, John

GOSSEC, FRANÇOIS JOSEPH (1734-1829)
    Mirzal (Symphonie Concertante in F)
        0.0.1.1. 1.0.0.0. strings
        (Brook, Barry) FRANK perf mat rent
                                            (G452)

    Symphonic Works, Eight *CCU
        (Brook, Barry S.) sc GARLAND
            ISBN 0-8240-3839-8 $90.00 "The
            Symphony" Vol. D-III   (G453)

    Symphonie Concertante in F
        see Mirzal

    Symphony, Op. 3, No. 6, in D
        2ob,strings
        (Brook, Barry) FRANK perf mat rent
                                            (G454)

    Symphony, Op. 5, No. 3, in D
        2fl,2horn,cont,strings
        sc KUNZEL 10148 $28.00, ipa (G455)

GOSSEC, FRANÇOIS JOSEPH (cont'd.)

Symphony, Op. 8, No. 1, in E flat
0.0.2.0. 2.0.0.0. strings
(Brook, Barry) FRANK perf mat rent
(G456)

GOTHLANDIAN RHAPSODY see Myrtelius,
Hugo, Gotlandsk Rapsodi

GOTKOVSKY, IDA (1933-   )
Concerto for Trombone and String
Orchestra [14'30"]
string orch,trom solo
BILLAUDOT perf mat rent   (G457)

Concerto Lyrique, For Clarinet And
String Orchestra [30']
string orch,clar solo
sc BILLAUDOT f.s., perf mat rent
(G458)

Musique En Couleurs [20']
1.1.1.2. 2.2.0.0. timp,perc,harp,
pno,strings
BILLAUDOT perf mat rent   (G459)

Variations Pathetiques, For Alto
Saxophone And String Orchestra
[28']
string orch,alto sax solo
BILLAUDOT perf mat rent   (G460)

GOTLANDSK RAPSODI see Myrtelius, Hugo

GOTSKOSIK, OLEG (1951-   )
Changing Landscape, The [10']
7vln,4vla,3vcl,db
STIM   (G461)

Symphonic Triptych [18']
3.3.3.3. 4.3.3.1. timp,4perc,
harp,pno/cel,strings
STIM   (G462)

GOTT UND DIE BAJADERE, DER, FOR SOLO
VOICE AND ORCHESTRA, [ARR.] see
Schoeck, Othmar

GOTTERDAMMERUNG: FUNERAL MUSIC see
Wagner, Richard, Gotterdammerung:
Trauermusik Beim Tode Siegfrieds

GOTTERDAMMERUNG: TRAUERMUSIK BEIM TODE
SIEGFRIEDS see Wagner, Richard

GÖTTERDÄMMERUNG: TRAUERMUSIK BEIM TODE
SIEGFRIEDS [ARR.] see Wagner,
Richard

GOTTERDAMMERUNG: WALTRAUTE'S SCENE see
Wagner, Richard

GOTTSCHALK, LOUIS MOREAU (1829-1869)
Escenas Campestras, For Solo Voices
And Orchestra [13'30"]
3.2.5(clar in E flat).4.3.4.1.
ophicleide, 3 bombardino,
strings, s, t, b soli
MCA perf mat rent   (G463)

Hymne Portugais, L', For Piano And
Orchestra [9'30"]
3.2.2.2. 2.2.2.1. timp,perc,
strings,pno solo
MCA perf mat rent   (G464)

GOUGEON, DENIS (1951-   )
Choral Des Anges, Le, For Piano And
Orchestra [5']
2.2.2.2. 2.2.0.0. perc,strings,
pno solo
CAN.MUS.CENT. MI 1361 G691C (G465)

Eternite, For Solo Voice And
Orchestra
3.3.3(clar in E flat).2. 2.2.2.1.
2perc,strings,electronic tape,S
solo
CAN.MUS.CENT. MV 1980 G691E (G466)

Fete Sacree, La, For Piccolo, 3
Flutes And String Orchestra
string orch,pic solo,alto fl
solo,2fl soli
CAN.MUS.CENT. MI 1721 G691FE (G467)

Jardin Mysterieux, Le [6']
2.2.2.2. 2.2.2.1. perc,strings
CAN.MUS.CENT. 1100 G691J   (G468)

Musique En Memoire, For Solo Voices
And Orchestra
2.2.2(clar in E flat).0. 1.0.1.0.
2perc,strings,2S
CAN.MUS.CENT. MV 2400 G691M (G469)

GOULD, MORTON (1913-   )
Audubon, No. 1: Apple Waltzes [18']
3(pic).2(English horn).3(bass
clar).2+contrabsn. 4.3.3.1.
timp,perc,pno&cel,harp,strings
SCHIRM.G perf mat rent   (G470)

Audubon, No. 2: Bird Movements [12']
3(pic,alto fl).2(English
horn).3(clar in E flat,bass
clar).2+contrabsn. 0.0.0.1.

GOULD, MORTON (cont'd.)

perc,elec bass
SCHIRM.G perf mat rent   (G471)

Audubon, No. 3: Chorales And Rags
[6']
3(pic).2(English horn).3.2+
contrabsn. 4.3.3.1. perc,pno&
cel,harp,strings
SCHIRM.G perf mat rent   (G472)

Audubon, No. 4: Concerto Grosso [19']
3(pic).2(English horn).3(bass
clar).2(contrabsn). 4.3.3.1.
timp,perc,harp,strings,4vln
soli
SCHIRM.G perf mat rent   (G473)

Audubon, No. 5: Fire Music [4']
2+pic.2+English horn.2+bass
clar.2+contrabsn. 4.3.3.1.
perc,strings,electronic tape,
electric keyboard, wind machine
SCHIRM.G perf mat rent   (G474)

Audubon, No. 6: Indian Attack [3']
3(pic).2(English horn).3(clar in
E flat).2+contrabsn. 4.3.3.3.
timp,perc,strings
SCHIRM.G perf mat rent   (G475)

Audubon, No. 7: Night Music [5']
3(pic).1+English horn.2+bass
clar.3. 0.0.0.0. perc,gtr,harp,
strings,electronic tape
SCHIRM.G perf mat rent   (G476)

Audubon, No. 8: Scherzo [3']
2+pic.2(English horn).1+bass
clar+clar in E flat.1+
contrabsn. 4.3.3.1. timp,pno,
harp,strings
SCHIRM.G perf mat rent   (G477)

Audubon, No. 9: Serenade [8']
2.2.2+bass clar.2. 0.0.0.0. harp,
strings
SCHIRM.G perf mat rent   (G478)

Audubon, No. 10: Tribal Dance [5']
2+pic.2+English horn.2+bass
clar.2+contrabsn. 4.3.3.1.
timp,perc,pno,harp,strings
SCHIRM.G perf mat rent   (G479)

Big City Blues [5']
2(pic).1(English horn).2.1.
4.3.3.1. timp,perc,harp,pno,
strings
SCHIRM.G perf mat rent   (G480)

Burchfield Gallery [27']
2+pic.3(English horn).3(clar in E
flat).3(contrabsn). 4.3.3.1.
timp,3perc,pno,harp,strings
sc SCHIRM.G $35.00, perf mat rent
(G481)

Cafe Rio [3']
4sax,2horn,2trp,trom,perc,harp,
pno,gtr,strings
SCHIRM.G perf mat rent   (G482)

Calypso Souvenir [3']
3.0.2+bass clar.1. 0.3.0.0. perc,
harp,strings
SCHIRM.G perf mat rent   (G483)

Celebration Strut [3']
3(pic).2.3.2. 4.3.3.1. timp,perc,
harp,strings
SCHIRM.G perf mat rent   (G484)

Cheers! A Celebration March [5']
3.3.3.3. 4.4.3.1. timp,3perc,opt
org,strings
sc SCHIRM.G $16.00, perf mat rent
(G485)

Classical Variations On Colonial
Themes [14']
2(pic).2.2.2. 4.2.2.0. timp,2-
3perc,harp,strings
sc SCHIRM.G f.s., perf mat rent
(G486)

Concerto for Flute and Orchestra
[34']
0+pic.3.3.3(contrabsn). 4.3.3.1.
timp,3perc,harp,cel,strings,fl
solo
SCHIRM.G perf mat rent   (G487)

Concerto for Orchestra [18']
3.3.4.3.alto sax.tenor sax.
4.3.3.1. timp,3perc,harp,pno,
strings
SCHIRM.G perf mat rent   (G488)

Concerto for Piano and Orchestra
[20']
1(pic).1.1.1. 2.2.1.0. timp,perc,
strings,pno solo
SCHIRM.G perf mat rent   (G489)

Dance Gallery: Soft Shoe Gavotte [4']
2(pic).2(English horn).3(bass
clar).2. 4.2.2.0. perc,harp,

GOULD, MORTON (cont'd.)

strings
set SCHIRM.G 50457230 $20.00 (G490)

Flares And Declamations [4']
2(pic).2.2.2. 4.2.2.1. timp,2-
3perc,strings
SCHIRM.G perf mat rent   (G491)

Flourishes And Galop [4']
3.3.3.3. 4.3.3.1. timp,perc,harp,
strings
sc SCHIRM.G 50480351 $7.50, perf
mat rent   (G492)

Guajira, For Clarinet And Orchestra
[3']
2.2(English horn).1.2. 2.0.0.0.
perc,harp,strings,clar solo
SCHIRM.G perf mat rent   (G493)

Harvest [12']
vibra,harp,strings
SCHIRM.G perf mat rent   (G494)

Holocaust Suite [21']
2(pic).2(English horn).2(clar in
E flat).2(contrabsn). 4.3.3.1.
timp,2perc,harp,pno,strings
SCHIRM.G perf mat rent   (G495)

Homespun Overture, A [6']
3(pic).2.3(bass clar).2. 4.3.3.1.
timp,2perc,harp,banjo,strings
SCHIRM.G perf mat rent   (G496)

Hoofer Suite [11']
1(pic).1.2.1. 2.2.2.1. timp,perc,
strings
SCHIRM.G perf mat rent   (G497)

Housewarming [9']
3(pic).3(English horn).3(clar in
E flat,bass clar).3(contrabsn).
4.3.3.1. timp,3-4perc,cel,harp,
strings
SCHIRM.G perf mat rent   (G498)

I'm Old Fashioned: Astaire Variations
[35']
3(pic).3.3(bass clar).3. 4.3.3.1.
timp,2perc,pno,harp,strings
SCHIRM.G perf mat rent   (G499)

Lincoln Legend [18']
2(pic).2(English horn).3.2.
4.3.3.1. timp,2perc,harp,
strings
SCHIRM.G perf mat rent   (G500)

Notes Of Remembrance [10']
2(pic).1.2.1. 2.2.2.0. timp,perc,
strings
SCHIRM.G perf mat rent   (G501)

Philharmonic Waltzes [9']
2(pic).2.3(bass
clar).3(contrabsn). 4.3.3.1.
timp,3perc,harp,pno,strings
study sc SCHIRM.G f.s., perf mat
rent   (G502)

Rhythm Gallery, For Narrator And
Orchestra [24']
2(pic).2(English horn).2.2.
3.2.2.1. timp,perc,harp,pno,
strings,narrator
SCHIRM.G perf mat rent   (G503)

Showpiece [19']
3.3.4.3. 6.3.3.1. timp,4perc,
harp,pno&cel,strings
SCHIRM.G perf mat rent   (G504)

Stephen Foster Gallery [30']
3(pic).3(English horn).3(bass
clar).2+contrabsn. 4.4.3.1.
timp,perc,harp,banjo,strings
SCHIRM.G perf mat rent   (G505)

Swanee River In The Style Of Bach
[4']
1.1.2.1. 2.2.1.0. perc,strings
SCHIRM.G perf mat rent   (G506)

Swanee River In The Style Of
Beethoven [4']
1.1.2.1. 2.2.0.0. perc,pno,
strings
SCHIRM.G perf mat rent   (G507)

Swanee River In The Style Of Brahms
[4']
1.1.3.1. 2.2.1.0. perc,pno,
strings
SCHIRM.G perf mat rent   (G508)

Swanee River In The Style Of Debussy
[4']
1.1.3.0. 2.2.1.0. perc,pno,
strings
SCHIRM.G perf mat rent   (G509)

GOULD, MORTON (cont'd.)

Swanee River In The Style Of Gershwin
[4']
1.1.1.0.3sax. 2.2.1.0. perc,pno,
gtr,strings
SCHIRM.G perf mat rent   (G510)

Swanee River In The Style Of J.
Strauss [4']
2.2.2.1. 2.2.1.1. perc,pno,
strings
SCHIRM.G perf mat rent   (G511)

Swanee River In The Style Of Liszt
[4']
2.1.2.1. 2.3.3.1. perc,pno,
strings
SCHIRM.G perf mat rent   (G512)

Swanee River In The Style Of Mozart
[4']
1.1.2.1. 2.2.0.0. strings
SCHIRM.G perf mat rent   (G513)

Swanee River In The Style Of Rimsky-
Korsakov [4']
2.1.2.1. 2.3.3.1. perc,pno,
strings
SCHIRM.G perf mat rent   (G514)

Swanee River In The Style Of
Tchaikovsky [4']
1.1.1.1.3sax. 2.3.2.1. perc,pno,
strings
SCHIRM.G perf mat rent   (G515)

Swanee River In The Style Of Wagner
[4']
1.1.3+bass clar.1.sax. 2.3.2.1.
perc,pno,strings
SCHIRM.G perf mat rent   (G516)

Symphony No. 1 [32']
3.3.3.3. 4.3.3.1. timp,3perc,
harp,strings
SCHIRM.G perf mat rent   (G517)

Symphony No. 2 [31']
3.3.3.3. 4.3.3.1. timp,3perc,
harp,strings
(Symphony On Marching Tunes)
SCHIRM.G perf mat rent   (G518)

Symphony No. 3 [36']
3.2.3.3. 4.3.3.1. timp,3perc,
harp,cel,strings
SCHIRM.G perf mat rent   (G519)

Tap Dance Concerto [16']
2(pic).2.2.2. 4.2.2.0. timp,
strings
sc SCHIRM.G $15.00, perf mat rent
(G520)

Troubadour Music, For 4 Guitars And
Orchestra [24']
2(pic).2(English horn).2.2.
2.2.2.2. 2perc,strings,4gtr
soli
SCHIRM.G perf mat rent   (G521)

Venice [30']
4(pic).3(English horn).4(bass
clar).3(contrabsn). 6.4.5.1.
timp,2perc,2harp,strings
sc SCHIRM.G $20.00, perf mat rent
(G522)

Windjammer: Main Theme, "The Ship"
[4']
2.2.2.2. 4.3.3.1. timp,2perc,
harp,cel,strings
SCHIRM.G perf mat rent   (G523)

Windjammer: Night Watch [3']
2.1(English horn).2.1. 2.0.0.0.
perc,harp,strings
SCHIRM.G perf mat rent   (G524)

World War I: Selections
2(pic).1.2.1. 2.2.2.1. timp,perc,
harp,pno&cel,strings
SCHIRM.G perf mat rent   (G525)

GOUNOD, CHARLES FRANÇOIS (1818-1893)
Colombe, La: Entr'acte
2.1.2.2. 4.0.0.0. perc,harp,
strings
CHOUDENS perf mat rent   (G526)

D'un Coeur Qui T'aime, For Solo
Voices And Orchestra
(Busser) 2horn,strings,SMez soli
LEMOINE perf mat rent   (G527)

Faust: Ballet Music
CHOUDENS perf mat rent   (G528)

Faust: Introduction
CHOUDENS perf mat rent   (G529)

Marche Funebre D'une Marionette [4']
1.1.1.0. 1.1.3.1. timp,perc,
strings
LEMOINE perf mat rent   (G530)
SONZOGNO perf mat rent   (G531)

GOUNOD, CHARLES FRANÇOIS (cont'd.)

Meditation for Violin and Orchestra,
[arr.]
2+pic.2.2.2. 4.0.0.0. harp,strings,
vln solo [4'] KALMUS A7314 sc
$7.00, set $25.00, pts $1.50,
ea., perf mat rent   (G532)

Mireille: Overture [6'45"]
2.2.2.2. 4.2.3.0. timp,perc,
strings
CHOUDENS perf mat rent   (G533)

Philemon Et Baucis: 4 Fragments
Symphoniques
[11'50"] CHOUDENS perf mat rent
(G534)

Queen Of Sheba: Marche Et Cortege
see Reine De Saba, La: Marche Et
Cortege

Reine De Saba, La: Ballet Music
[16'35"]
2(pic).2.2.2. 4.2.3.0. timp,perc,
harp,strings
CHOUDENS perf mat rent   (G535)

Reine De Saba, La: Marche Et Cortege
[5']
2(pic).2.2.2. 4.4.3.1. timp,perc,
strings
"Queen Of Sheba: Marche Et Cortege"
KALMUS A5591 sc $15.00, perf mat
rent, set $30.00, pts $1.50, ea.
(G536)

Romeo Et Juliette: Ballet Music
[19'15"]
2(pic).2.2.2. 4.2+2cornet.3.1.
timp,perc,2harp,strings
CHOUDENS perf mat rent   (G537)

Romeo Et Juliette: Fragments
Symphoniques [11']
2(pic).2.2.2. 4.2.3.0. timp,perc,
harp,strings
CHOUDENS perf mat rent   (G538)

Saltarello [5']
2+pic.2.2.2. 4.2.3.1. timp,perc,
strings
KALMUS A5820 sc $12.00, set $45.00,
perf mat rent   (G539)

Souvenir D'un Bal [arr.]
2fl,strings [1'30"] set KALMUS
A7280 $17.00, and up   (G540)

Symphony No. 1 [25']
2.2.2.2. 2.2.0.0. timp,strings
SONZOGNO perf mat rent   (G541)

Tribut De Zamora, Le: Ballet Music
[26']
2(pic).2.2.2. 4.2.3.1. timp,perc,
harp,strings
CHOUDENS perf mat rent   (G542)

GOUVY, LOUIS (1819-1898)
Serenade No. 2 for Flute and String
Orchestra
string orch,fl solo
RAHTER perf mat rent   (G543)

GOUVY, THEODORE (1819-1898)
Schwedischer Tanz *Op.71
string orch
KISTNER perf mat rent   (G544)

GOYA: SUITE see Menotti, Gian Carlo

GOYA SYMPHONY see Gurlitt, Manfred

GOYESCAS: LA CALESA see Granados,
Enrique

GRABMUSIK: BETRACHT DIES HERZ, FOR SOLO
VOICE AND STRING ORCHESTRA see
Mozart, Wolfgang Amadeus

GRABNER, HERMANN (1886-1969)
Alpenlandische Suite *Op.34
KISTNER   (G545)

Concerto for Flute, Clarinet,
Bassoon, Horn and String
Orchestra, Op. 48
string orch,fl solo,clar solo,bsn
solo,horn solo
KISTNER perf mat rent   (G546)

Frohliche Musik *Op.39
KISTNER perf mat rent   (G547)

Gasteiner Serende, For Flute And
Orchestra
KISTNER perf mat rent   (G548)

Kleine Abendmusik *Op.25 [15']
1.1.1.1. 1.0.0.0. strings
KAHNT perf mat rent   (G549)

Pastorale
KISTNER perf mat rent   (G550)

GRABNER, HERMANN (cont'd.)

Tanze *Op.43
KISTNER perf mat rent   (G551)

Variationen Und Fuge Uber Ein Thema
Von J.S. Bach *Op.14 [30']
2.2.2.2. 4.2.3.0. timp,strings
KAHNT perf mat rent   (G552)

GRABOVSKY, LEONID (1935-   )
Constanti [14']
6perc,4pno,vln solo
VAAP perf mat rent   (G553)

Eve Of St. John Kupalo, The [35']
3.3.3.3. 4.3.3.1. timp,3perc,
harp,pno,strings
VAAP perf mat rent   (G554)
"Johannisnacht, Die" SIKORSKI perf
mat rent   (G555)

Homeomorphia IV [20']
4.4.4.4. 8.4.4.1. perc,2harp,cel,
pno 4-hands,strings
SIKORSKI perf mat rent   (G556)
VAAP perf mat rent   (G557)

Johannisnacht, Die
see Eve Of St. John Kupalo, The

Kleine Kammermusik No. 1
see Small Chamber Music No. 1

Kleine Kammermusik No. 2
see Small Chamber Music No. 2

Kogda, For Solo Voice And
Instrumental Ensemble [18']
clar,perc,pno,12strings,Mez solo
VAAP perf mat rent   (G558)

Misterioso [12']
15 solo strings
SIKORSKI perf mat rent   (G559)
VAAP perf mat rent   (G560)

Small Chamber Music No. 1 [10']
15strings
VAAP perf mat rent   (G561)
"Kleine Kammermusik No. 1" SIKORSKI
perf mat rent   (G562)

Small Chamber Music No. 2 [15']
ob,harp,12strings
VAAP perf mat rent   (G563)
"Kleine Kammermusik No. 2" SIKORSKI
perf mat rent   (G564)

Symphonic Frescos [35']
4.3.4.3.alto sax. 4.4.3.1. timp,
4perc,2harp,pno&cel,strings
VAAP perf mat rent   (G565)

GRACE, PRELUDIUM AND RESPONSE see
McBeth, William Francis

GRADSTEIN, ALFRED (1904-1954)
Concerto for Piano and Orchestra, No.
1 [25']
3.2.2.2.2sax. 4.2.2.0. timp,perc,
harp,cel,strings,pno solo
ESCHIG perf mat rent   (G566)

GRADUS AD PARNASSUM, FOR SOLO VOICE AND
CHAMBER ORCHESTRA see Yttrehus,
Rolv

GRAENER, PAUL (1872-1944)
Waldmusik *Op.60
KISTNER perf mat rent   (G567)

GRAF ODERLAND, FOR SOLO VOICES AND
ORCHESTRA see Jacob, Werner

GRAF VON LUXEMBOURG: LUXEMBOURG WALTZ
see Lehar, Franz

GRAHN, ULF (1942-   )
Ancient Music, For Piano And Chamber
Orchestra
1.1.1.1. 0.0.0.0. perc,strings,
pno solo
SEESAW perf mat rent   (G568)

GRAINGER, PERCY ALDRIDGE (1882-1961)
Colonial Song [6']
2+pic.2.2.2. 4.3.3.1. perc,2harp,
pno,strings
KALMUS A7241 sc $10.00, set $25.00,
pts $1.25, ea., perf mat rent
(G569)

Colonial Songs [7']
2+pic.2.2.2. 2.3.3.1. perc,pno,
2harp,strings
SCHIRM.G perf mat rent   (G570)

Country Gardens
2.2.2.2.2sax. 4.2.3.1. timp,perc,
harp,strings
SCHIRM.G perf mat rent   (G571)

Immovable Do
2+pic.2+English horn.2+bass
clar.2+contrabsn. 4.3.3.1.
timp,perc,strings

GRAINGER, PERCY ALDRIDGE (cont'd.)

SCHIRM.G perf mat rent   (G572)

Irish Tune From County Derby
set KALMUS A6753 $7.00, and up
(G573)

Irish Tune From County Derry, For
Violin And Orchestra [arr.]
(Schmid, Adolf) 1.1.2.1.2sax.
2.2.1.0. timp,strings,vln solo
[5'] SCHIRM.G perf mat rent
(G574)

Jutish Medley
2+pic.2.2+bass clar.2.alto
sax.tenor sax.
4.3.3.0.euphonium. timp,perc,
harp,org,cel,pno 4-hands,
strings
SCHIRM.G perf mat rent   (G575)

Mock Morris
KALMUS A6097 sc $5.00, set $7.00
(G576)

Molly On The Shore
string orch KALMUS A6096 sc $5.00,
set $5.00   (G577)
2(pic).2.2.2. 4.2.3.1. perc,cel,
strings [3'] KALMUS A7251 sc
$12.00, set $25.00, pts $1.25,
ea.   (G578)

Power Of Love, The
2+pic.2.2+bass clar.2.alto
sax.tenor sax.baritone sax.
4.3.3.1. harp,harmonium,org,
strings
SCHIRM.G perf mat rent   (G579)

Power Of Rome And The Christian
Spirit, The
2.0.2+bass clar.0. 3.0.3.0.
strings
SCHIRM.G perf mat rent   (G580)

Shepherd's Hey
KALMUS A6301 sc $5.00, set $12.00
(G581)
KALMUS A6749 sc $6.00, set $25.00,
pts $1.00, ea., perf mat rent
(G582)

Spoon River
1+pic.1.1.1.alto sax.tenor sax.
1.1.3.1. timp,perc,2pno,
harmonium,harp,strings
SCHIRM.G perf mat rent   (G583)

Thanksgiving Song
1+pic.0.2+bass clar.1.alto sax.
1.1.0.0. perc,pno,harmonium/
org,strings
SCHIRM.G perf mat rent   (G584)

GRALBILDER see Hamel, Peter Michael

GRAM, PEDER (1881-1957)
Overture in C
sc,pts SAMFUNDET f.s.   (G585)

Poeme Lyrique
sc,pts SAMFUNDET f.s.   (G586)

Prolog Til Et Drama Af Shakespeare
"Prologue For A Shakespeare Drama"
sc,pts SAMFUNDET f.s.   (G587)

Prologue For A Shakespeare Drama
see Prolog Til Et Drama Af
Shakespeare

Symphony No. 2
sc,pts SAMFUNDET f.s.   (G588)

GRANADOS, ENRIQUE (1867-1916)
Goyescas: La Calesa
3+pic.2+English horn.2+bass
clar.3. 4.3.4.1. timp,perc,pno,
strings
SCHIRM.G perf mat rent   (G589)

Suite Sobre Cantos Gallegos [21']
2(pic).2(English horn).1(bass
clar).2. 2.2.3.1. timp,perc,
harp,strings
UNION ESP. perf mat rent   (G590)

Tiempo Romantico [arr.]
(Ferrer, Rafael) 2.2.2.2. 4.2.0.0.
timp,perc,harp,strings UNION ESP.
perf mat rent   (G591)

GRAND BANKS see Murray, Lyn

GRAND CANYON SUITE see Grofe, Ferde
(Ferdinand Rudolph von)

GRAND DUKE, THE: OVERTURE see Sullivan,
[Sir] Arthur Seymour

GRAND JEU CLASSIQUE, FOR VIOLIN AND
ORCHESTRA see Kelemen, Milko

GRAND PAS CLASSIQUE [ARR.] see Auber,
Daniel-François-Esprit

GRAND PRINCIPE DE VIOLENCE COMMANDAIT A
NOS MOEURS, UN see Lenot, Jacques

GRAND SLAM JAM, FOR PIANO, CLARINET,
TRUMPET AND ORCHESTRA see
Ellington, Edward Kennedy (Duke)

GRAND SOLO FOR GLASS HARMONICA AND
ORCHESTRA IN F see Reicha, Anton

GRAND TRAVERSE, THE, FOR TRUMPET AND
ORCHESTRA see Hilliard, John

GRAND YACHT DESPAIR, LE, FOR SOLO
VOICES AND ORCHESTRA see
Petitgirard, Alain

GRANDE MARCHE HEROIQUE [ARR.] see
Schubert, Franz (Peter)

GRANDE MENACE, LA see Pichaureau,
Claude

GRANDE POLONAISE BRILLANTE, FOR PIANO
AND ORCHESTRA see Chopin, Frédéric

GRANDE SONATA DA CAMERA see Sciarrino,
Salvatore

GRANDE VALSE BRILLANTE, OP. 18 [ARR.]
see Chopin, Frédéric, Valse, Op. 18
[arr.]

GRANDIS, RENATO DE
see DE GRANDIS, RENATO

GRANDMA'S FOOTSTEPS see Tavener, John

GRANT, STEWART (1948-   )
Bhajan, For Violoncello And String
Orchestra [11']
string orch,vcl solo
CAN.MUS.CENT. MI 1613 G763BH (G592)

Chaconne for String Orchestra [5']
string orch
CAN.MUS.CENT. MI 1500 G763CH (G593)

Prairies And Mountains [13']
3.2.2.2. 4.2.3.1. timp,2perc,
strings
CAN.MUS.CENT. MI 1100 G763PR (G594)

Prelude and Fugue for String
Orchestra [8']
string orch
CAN.MUS.CENT. MI 1500 G763PR (G595)

Symphonic Variations [15']
3.2.2.2. 4.2.3.1. timp,2perc,
strings
CAN.MUS.CENT. MI 1100 G763SY (G596)

GRANTHAM, DONALD (1947-   )
Album De Los Duendecitos, El [15']
PRESSER perf mat rent   (G597)

GRANULATIONS see Buck, Ole

GRÄSBECK, GOTTFRID (1927-   )
Concerto for Piano and Orchestra
2.2.2.2. 2.2.3.0. timp,strings,
pno solo
sc SUOMEN f.s.   (G598)

GRASBECK, MANFRED (1955-   )
Symphony No. 3 [45']
2.2.3.2. 4.2.0.0. timp,perc,harp,
strings
sc FAZER f.s., perf mat rent (G599)

GRATIAS AGIMUS, FOR SOLO VOICE AND
ORCHESTRA see Bellini, Vincenzo

GRAUN, CARL HEINRICH (1704-1759)
Overtures, Two
see Agrell, Johan Joachim,
Symphonies, Five

GRAUN, JOHANN GOTTLIEB (1703-1771)
Concerto for Harpsichord and String
Orchestra [5']
string orch,hpsd solo
SUPRAPHON   (G600)

Symphonic Works, Three
see Agrell, Johan Joachim,
Symphonies, Five

GRAUPNER, CHRISTOPH (1683-1760)
Concerto in A, MIN 40
(Noack) KALMUS A7072 sc $8.00, set
$9.00, pts $1.50, ea.   (G601)

Concerto in C minor, MIN 480
(Noack) KALMUS A7073 sc $5.00, set
$9.00, pts $1.50, ea.   (G602)

Concerto in D, MIN 150
string orch,cont, clarino solo
(in this ed, called Concerto No. 2)
KUNZEL 10172 sc $15.00, pts
$3.00, ea.   (G603)

GRAUPNER, CHRISTOPH (cont'd.)

Concerto in F, MIN 169
string orch,rec solo
(Sokoll) CARUS 40.510   (G604)

Concerto, MIN 149
timp,cont,strings, 2clarini soli
KUNZEL 10165 sc $25.00, pts $3.50,
ea., kbd pt $7.00   (G605)

Overture in E
(Noack) KALMUS A7074 sc $10.00, set
$12.00, pts $2.00, ea.   (G606)

Sonata in G, MIN 463
(Hoffman) KALMUS A7023 sc $5.00,
set $5.00, pts $1.00, ea.   (G607)

Symphonies, Four
(Rosenblum; Forsberg; Biermann;
Johnson) ("The Symphony" Vol. C-
II) sc GARLAND ISBN 0-8240-3841-X
$90.00 contains also: Camerloher,
Joseph, Symphonies, Three
(composed with Camerloher,
Placidus von); Endler, Johann
Samuel, Symphonies, Three;
Schetky, Johann Georg Christoff,
Quartetto   (G608)

GRAVE, FOR VIOLONCELLO AND STRING
ORCHESTRA see Lutoslawski, Witold

GREAT AMERICAN BICYCLE RACE, THE see
Knight, Eric

GREAT AMERICAN SYMPHONY see Curtis-
Smith, Curtis O.B.

GREAT ATTRACTOR, THE: CADENZA
ACCOMPAGNATA, FOR VIOLIN AND
ORCHESTRA see Thommessen, Olav
Anton

GREAT GALLOPING GOTTSCHALK, FOR PIANO
AND ORCHESTRA see Elliott, Jack

GREAT LAKES SUITE see Stein, Leon

GREAT ORNAMENTED FUGA CANONICA see Yu,
Julian

GREAT PATRIOTIC WAR, THE see
Gewicksmann, Vitali

GREAT ROMANTIC CELLO CONCERTOS
sc DOVER 245845 $7.95
contains: Dvořák, Antonín, Concerto
for Violoncello and Orchestra,
Op. 104, in B minor; Saint-Saëns,
Camille, Concerto for Violoncello
and Orchestra, No. 1, Op. 33, in
A minor; Schumann, Robert
(Alexander), Concerto for
Violoncello and Orchestra, Op.
129, in A minor   (G609)

GREAT ROMANTIC VIOLIN CONCERTOS
sc DOVER 249891 $9.95
contains: Beethoven, Ludwig van,
Concerto for Violin and
Orchestra, Op. 61, in D;
Mendelssohn-Bartholdy, Felix,
Concerto for Violin and
Orchestra, Op. 64, in E minor;
Tchaikovsky, Piotr Ilyich,
Concerto for Violin and
Orchestra, Op. 35, in D   (G610)

GREAT WHITE ORACLE OF LITTLE PORTUGAL,
THE see Shepherd, Stuart

GREEK RHAPSODY NO. 2 see Hovhaness,
Alan

GREEN, GEORGE C. (1930-   )
Passacaglia
2.2.2.2. 2.2.0.0. perc,strings
SEESAW perf mat rent   (G611)

GREEN, W.
Playful Rondo [arr.]
(Frost, Robert S.) string orch,opt
pno SOUTHERN SO-50 sc $3.00, set
$20.00, pts $1.25, ea.   (G612)

GREEN AIR, FOR SOLO VOICE AND ORCHESTRA
see Lora, Antonio

GREEN BALLOONS: SUITE see Ledenev,
Roman

GREENBURG, LAURA (1942-   )
Concert Music [12']
1.0.1.0. 1.1.0.0. perc,pno,
strings
sc AM.COMP.AL. $34.15, perf mat
rent   (G613)

GREETING OVERTURE see Khachaturian,
Aram Ilyich

GREETINGS FROM AN OLD WORLD see
Lidholm, Ingvar

GREGOR, CESTMÍR (1926-   )
    Concerto for Violin and Orchestra
      [18']
        3.1.3.1. 2.2.1.0. timp,perc,xylo,
        harp,pno,strings,vln solo
      SUPRAPHON   (G614)

    Concerto for Violoncello and
      Orchestra [32']
        3.3.3.2. 4.2.3.1. timp,perc,harp,
        strings,vcl solo
      SUPRAPHON   (G615)

GREGORIAN VARIATIONS see Berkeley,
    Michael

GREGSON, EDWARD
    Concerto for Trombone and Orchestra
      [16']
        2(pic).2.2.2. 2.2.0.0. timp,
        4perc,strings,trom solo
      NOVELLO perf mat rent   (G616)

    Concerto for Tuba and Orchestra [18']
        2.2.2.2. 4.2.3.0. timp,2perc,
        strings,tuba solo
      NOVELLO perf mat rent   (G617)

    Metamorphoses [10']
        4(pic).3.4(bass clar).2. 4.4.3.1.
        timp,5perc,pno,3db
      NOVELLO perf mat rent   (G618)

    Music for Chamber Orchestra [22']
        0.2.0.2. 2.0.0.0. strings
      NOVELLO perf mat rent   (G619)

GREISENGESANG, FOR SOLO VOICE AND
    ORCHESTRA [ARR.] see Schubert,
    Franz (Peter)

GRENOBLE see Stekel, Eric-Paul

GRENSEFESTNING see Kristoffersen,
    Fridthjof

GRETCHEN AM SPINNRAD [ARR.] see
    Schubert, Franz (Peter)

GRÉTRY, ANDRÉ ERNEST MODESTE
    (1741-1813)
    Collected Works. Leipzig, 1884-1936
      (microfiche reprint, $515.00)
      UNIV.MUS.ED.   (G620)

    Neuf Airs d'Operas Comique, For Solo
      Voice And Chamber Orchestra
      [arr.]
        (Petit, J.L.) 2ob,2bsn,2horn,opt
        kbd,strings,S solo sc BOIS f.s.,
        perf mat rent   (G621)

GRIDLOCK see Taub, Bruce J.H.

GRIEBLING
    Queensmere
      set SOUTHERN $27.50   (G622)

GRIECHENLAND see Beyer, Frank Michael

GRIEG, EDVARD HAGERUP (1843-1907)
    Allegro Energico [arr.] (Symphony in
      C minor,Third Movement, [arr.])
        (Bergh, Sverre) 3.2.2.2. 4.2.3.0.
        timp,perc,strings NORGE   (G623)

    Ballade, Op. 24, [arr.]
        (Soderlind, Ragnar) 2.2.2.2.
        4.3.3.1. timp,perc,strings [22']
      NORGE   (G624)

    Bergliot, For Narrator And Orchestra
      *Op.42
      KALMUS A5700 sc $12.00, set $20.00,
        pts $1.00, ea., perf mat rent   (G625)

    Borte, For Solo Voice And Orchestra
      [arr.] *Op.70,No.3
        (Vea, Ketil) 2.1.1.1. 1.1.1.0.
        timp,strings,Mez solo NORGE   (G626)

    First Meeting, The, For Solo Voice
      And Orchestra [arr] *Op.21,No.1
        (Olsen, Sparre) 1.1.2.1. 2.0.0.0.
        strings,med solo [3'] NORSK   (G627)

    Five Songs From "The Mountain Kid",
      For Solo Voice And Orchestra
      [arr.] *Op.67
        (Olsen, Sparre) 2(pic).2.2.2.
        2.1.1.0. pno,strings,med solo
        [17'] NORSK perf mat rent   (G628)

    Hjemad [arr.]
        (Bergh, Sverre) "Homewards [arr.]"
        1.1.2.1. 2.0.0.0. strings NORGE
                                           (G629)
    Homewards [arr.]
      see Hjemad [arr.]

    I Love You [arr.]
        (Gould, Morton) "Ich Liebe Dich
        [arr.]" 2.2.2.2. 4.3.3.1. timp,
        harp,strings [3'] SCHIRM.G perf
        mat rent   (G630)

GRIEG, EDVARD HAGERUP (cont'd.)

    Ich Liebe Dich [arr.]
      see I Love You [arr.]

    In Autumn *Op.11
      KALMUS A5639 sc $20.00, perf mat
        rent, set $45.00, pts $2.00, ea.
                                           (G631)
    It Was A Lovely Evening In Summer,
      For Solo Voice And String
      Orchestra [arr.] *Op.26,No.2
        (Olsen, Sparre) string orch,med
        solo [3'] NORSK perf mat rent
                                           (G632)
    Lys Nat, For Solo Voice And Orchestra
      [arr.] *Op.25,No.5
        (Vea, Ketil) 2.1.1.1. 1.1.1.0.
        timp,strings,Mez solo NORGE
                                           (G633)
    Peer Gynt: Suite No. 1 *Op.46
      SONZOGNO perf mat rent   (G634)

    Peer Gynt: Suite No. 2 *Op.55
      SONZOGNO perf mat rent   (G635)

    Sonata, Op. 7, [arr.]
        (Bergh, Sverre) string orch NORGE
                                           (G636)
    Suite No. 1, Op. 38, [arr.]
        (Sommerfeldt) 2(pic).2(English
        horn).2.2. 4.3.3.1. timp,perc,
        harp,strings [9'] NORSK perf mat
        rent   (G637)

    Symphony
        (Katayev, V.) sc MUZYKA f.s. (G638)

    Symphony in C minor [37']
        2.2.2.2. 2.2.3.0. timp,strings
        study sc PETERS P8500 $16.50 (G639)
      PETERS perf mat rent   (G640)

    Symphony in C minor,Third Movement,
      [arr.]
      see Allegro Energico [arr.]

    Ten Songs To Poems By Vinje, For Solo
      Voice And Orchestra [arr.]
      *Op.33, CC1OL
        (Soderlind, Ragnar) 2.2.2.2.
        4.2.3.1. timp,perc,harp,strings,
        Bar solo NORGE   (G641)

    Til Norge, For Solo Voice And
      Orchestra [arr.] *Op.58,No.2
        (Vea, Ketil) 2.1.1.1. 1.1.1.0.
        timp,strings,Mez solo NORGE
                                           (G642)
    To Spring [arr.]
        (Gould, Morton) 2.2.2.2. 4.3.3.1.
        timp,perc,harp,cel,strings [4']
      SCHIRM.G perf mat rent   (G643)

    Wedding Day At Troldhaugen [arr.]
        (Gould, Morton) 2.2.2.2. 4.3.3.1.
        timp,perc,harp,cel,strings [5']
      SCHIRM.G perf mat rent   (G644)

GRIESBACH, KARL-RUDI (1916-   )
    Ostinati
        2.2.2.2. 2.3.3.0. perc,strings
        sc BREITKOPF-L PB 4074 f.s., perf
        mat rent   (G645)

GRILL, LEO
    Serenade, Op. 3
      KISTNER   (G646)

GRIMM, CARL HUGO (1890-1978)
    Concerto Miniature, For Flute And
      Orchestra
      SOUTHERN rent   (G647)

GRIMM, JULIUS OTTO (1827-1903)
    Suite No. 3, Op. 25, in G minor
        string orch
        [14'] BREITKOPF-W perf mat rent
                                           (G648)
GRIMMTALES see Goossen, Frederic

GRINBLAT, ROMUALD (1930-   )
    Concerto for Piano and Orchestra
      [18']
        3.1.1.1.sax. 2.1.1.0. timp,perc,
        harp,strings,pno solo
      SIKORSKI perf mat rent   (G649)

    Leben Molieres, Das: Suite [18']
        hpsd,6vln,3vla,2vcl,db
      SIKORSKI perf mat rent   (G650)

    Symphony No. 4 [25']
        3.2.4.3. 6.4.4.2. timp,5perc,cel,
        2harp,pno,strings
      SIKORSKI perf mat rent   (G651)
      VAAP perf mat rent   (G652)

GRIPPE, RAGNAR (1951-   )
    Six Pieces For Oboe And String
      Orchestra
        string orch,ob solo
      STIM   (G653)

GRISAILLE see Kolb, Barbara

GRISEY, GERARD (1946-   )
    D'eau Et De Pierre [20']
        1(pic).1(English horn).2.1.
        1.1.2.0. 2perc,2vln,vla,vcl,db
      SALABERT perf mat rent   (G654)

    Derives [27'30"]
        4.3.5.4.sax. 5.4.3.2. 4perc,elec
        gtr,acord,strings
        sc RICORDI-IT 132281 f.s., perf
        mat rent   (G655)

    Epilogue [10']
        4.4.5.2.alto sax.tenor sax.
        4.4.3.1. perc,harp,acord,elec
        gtr,Hamm,strings
        sc RICORDI-FR f.s.   (G656)

    Partiels [22']
        2.1.3.0. 2.0.1.0. 2perc,acord,
        2vln,2vla,vcl,db
        sc RICORDI-IT 132423 f.s., perf mat
        rent   (G657)

GRISONI, RENATO (1922-   )
    Aforismi In Modo Frigio
        string orch
        min sc CURCI 9980 f.s., perf mat
        rent   (G658)

    Suite Trovadorica *Op.27 [18']
        2.2.2.2. 3.2.2.0. perc,harp,
        strings
      SONZOGNO perf mat rent   (G659)

GROBA, ROGELIO (1934-   )
    Malleus Animatus, For Piano And
      String Orchestra
        string orch,pno solo
      ALPUERTO   (G660)

GRODAN OCH VAGEN see Jonsson, Reine

GROFE, FERDE (FERDINAND RUDOLPH VON)
    (1892-1972)
    Death Valley Suite [arr.]
        (Glasser, Albert) 3(pic).3(English
        horn).3(bass clar).3(contrabsn).
        4.3.3.1. timp,3perc,cel,harp,
        strings [17'30"] ROBBINS perf mat
        rent   (G661)

    Grand Canyon Suite [32']
        3(pic).0.3(bass
        clar).3(contrabsn). 4.3.3.1.
        timp,2perc,pno&cel,harp,strings
      ROBBINS perf mat rent   (G662)

    Hudson River Suite [18'30"]
        3(pic).3(English horn).3(bass
        clar).3(contrabsn). 4.3.3.1.
        timp,3perc,cel,pno,harp,strings
      ROBBINS perf mat rent   (G663)

    Mississippi Suite [25']
        3(pic).3(English horn).3(bass
        clar).3(contrabsn). 4.3.3.1.
        timp,2perc,cel,harp,strings
      FEIST perf mat rent   (G664)

    World's Fair Suite [arr.]
        (Marquardt, P.A.) 3(pic).3(English
        horn).3(bass clar).3(contrabsn).
        4.3.3.1. timp,4perc,pno,harp,
        strings [33'30"] ROBBINS perf mat
        rent   (G665)

GROHARJEVE IMPRESIJE see Petric, Ivo

GROHAR'S IMPRESSIONS see Petric, Ivo,
    Groharjeve Impresije

GROLSCH see Grøthe, Anders

GRONDAHL, LAUNY (1886-1960)
    Concerto for Bassoon and Orchestra
      SAMFUNDET perf mat rent   (G666)

    Concerto for Violin and Orchestra
      SAMFUNDET perf mat rent   (G667)

GROOM IS GLOOMY see Mori, Kurodo

GROOT, ROKUS DE (1947-   )
    Promenades, Marches Et Danses [20']
        1.1.1.1. 1.1.1.1. 2perc,harp,pno&
        cel,strings
        sc DONEMUS f.s., perf mat rent
                                           (G668)
GROOTTE, DE see Meijering, Chiel

GROPP, JOHANN-MARIA (1954-   )
    Alla Marcia [16']
        3.3.3.3. 4.3.2.1. timp,perc,
        strings
      PETERS   (G669)

GROS NUAGES GRIS see Tomasi, Henri

GROSS, ROBERT ARTHUR (1914-   )
    Resonants [10']
        3.3.4.2. 4.2.2.1. timp,perc,xylo,
        harp,strings
        sc AM.COMP.AL. $19.10, perf mat

GROSS, ROBERT ARTHUR (cont'd.)

    rent   (G670)

GROSS CONCERTO NO. 2 see "Bach, P.D.Q."
    (Peter Schickele)

GROSS WIEN WALZER see Strauss, Johann,
    [Jr.]

GROSSE FUGE [ARR.] see Beethoven,
    Ludwig van

GRØTHE, ANDERS (1944-   )
    Grolsch
        3.3.3.3. 4.3.3.1. timp,perc,pno,
        harp,strings
    NORGE   (G671)

GROTHE, FRANZ (1908-1982)
    Concerto for Piano and Orchestra,
    [arr.]
      (Alexander, Axel) 2.2.2.1. 4.2.3.0.
      perc,harp,strings,pno solo [10']
      SIKORSKI perf mat rent   (G672)

    Herz, Du Kennst Meine Sehnsucht, For
      Solo Voice And Orchestra [arr.]
      (Friebe, W.) 2.2.2.2. 3.0.0.0.
      timp,drums,glock,vibra,harp,
      strings,S solo [5'] SIKORSKI perf
      mat rent   (G673)

    Ich Traume Nur Von Dem Einen, For
      Solo Voice And Orchestra [arr.]
      (Weninger, L.) 3.2.2.2. 4.2.3.0.
      perc,harp,harmonium,strings,S
      solo [3'] SIKORSKI perf mat rent
                                  (G674)

    Immer, Wenn Ich Glucklich Bin, For
      Solo Voice And Orchestra [arr.]
      (Schroder, F.) 2alto sax,tenor sax,
      2trp,trom,perc,strings,S solo
      [4'] SIKORSKI perf mat rent
                                  (G675)

    Und Jetzt Erklingt Franz Grothe
      [arr.]
      (Rixner, J.) 1.0.2.0.2alto
      sax.2tenor sax. 0.2.1.0. perc,
      pno,gtr,strings [15'] SIKORSKI
      perf mat rent   (G676)

GROTTA DI TROFONIO, LA: SINFONIA see
    Salieri, Antonio

GROTTO DI FINGAL, LA see Mendelssohn-
    Bartholdy, Felix, Hebriden, Die

GROUND see Ruders, Poul

GROUP OF SEVEN, A see Crawley, Clifford

GROV, MAGNE (1938-   )
    Ballade [14']
      harp,pno,strings
    NORGE   (G677)

    Lyrical March And Halling
      see Lyrisk Marsj Og Halling

    Lyrisk Marsj Og Halling [6']
      2.2.2.2. 4.2.3.1. timp,perc,
      strings
      "Lyrical March And Halling" NORGE
                                  (G678)

    Nar Linden Ber Lov, For Violin And
      Orchestra
      2.2.2.2. 2.1.0.0. timp,strings,
      vln solo
    NORGE   (G679)

GROVE, RICHARD (1927-   )
    Gamino, El, For Flugelhorn And
      Orchestra [11'30"]
      3.2.3+bass clar.2.2alto
      sax.2tenor sax.baritone sax.
      4.3.3.1. perc,pno,gtr,strings,
      flügelhorn solo
      "Street Urchin, The, For Flugelhorn
      And Orchestra" NEWAM 19020 perf
      mat rent   (G680)

    Street Urchin, The, For Flugelhorn
      And Orchestra
      see Gamino, El, For Flugelhorn And
      Orchestra

GROVEN, EIVIND (1901-1977)
    A Sa Rodblond, For Solo Voice And
      Orchestra *Op.9,No.1 [2']
      2.1.2.2. 4.1.0.0. harp,strings,
      solo voice
      "Oh, So Sandy, For Solo Voice And
      Orchestra" NORGE   (G681)

    Autumn Song, The, For Solo Voice And
      Orchestra
      see Hostsangen, For Solo Voice And
      Orchestra

    Ballad About Toscana, The, For Solo
      Voice And Orchestra
      see Balladen Om Toscanaland, For
      Solo Voice And Orchestra

GROVEN, EIVIND (cont'd.)

    Balladen Om Toscanaland, For Solo
      Voice And Orchestra *Op.8 [6']
      2.2.2.2. 4.2.2.0. timp,perc,harp,
      strings,solo voice
      "Ballad About Toscana, The, For
      Solo Voice And Orchestra" NORGE
                                  (G682)

    Bryllaup I Skogen *Op.28 [10']
      2.2.2.2. 2.2.2.0. timp,perc,
      strings
      "Wedding In The Wood" NORGE (G683)

    Faldafeykir *Op.53 [14']
      3.2.2.2. 4.2.3.1. timp,perc,pno,
      strings
    NORGE   (G684)

    Fjellvind, For Solo Voice And
      Orchestra *Op.10 [2']
      3.2.2.2. 0.0.0.0. strings,solo
      voice
      "Mountain Wind, For Solo Voice And
      Orchestra" NORGE   (G685)

    Fred, For Solo Voice And Orchestra
      [5']
      3.2.2.2. 3.2.3.0. timp,strings,
      solo voice
      "Peace, For Solo Voice And
      Orchestra" NORGE   (G686)

    Gillyflower, For Solo Voice And
      Orchestra
      see Til Min Gyllenlakk, For Solo
      Voice And Orchestra

    Heath, The, For Solo Voice And
      Orchestra
      see Moen, For Solo Voice And
      Orchestra

    Historical Visions
      see Historiske Syner

    Historiske Syner *Op.25 [3']
      2.2.2.2. 4.2.3.1. timp,perc,harp,
      strings
      "Historical Visions" NORGE (G687)

    Hostsangen, For Solo Voice And
      Orchestra *Op.35 [4']
      2.2.2.2. 4.1.0.1. strings,solo
      voice
      "Autumn Song, The, For Solo Voice
      And Orchestra" NORGE   (G688)

    In The Evening
      see Om Kvelden

    In The Hospital At Night, For Solo
      Voice And Orchestra
      see Pa Hospitalet Om Natten, For
      Solo Voice And Orchestra

    Moderens Korstegn, For Solo Voice And
      And Orchestra *Op.13,No.1 [3']
      1.0.2.0. 0.0.0.0. strings,S solo
      "Mother's Sign Of The Cross, The,
      For Solo Voice And Orchestra"
      NORGE   (G689)

    Moen, For Solo Voice And Orchestra
      [3']
      1.0.1.2. 1.1.0.0. timp,strings,S
      solo
      "Heath, The, For Solo Voice And
      Orchestra" NORGE   (G690)

    Mother's Sign Of The Cross, The, For
      Solo Voice And Orchestra
      see Moderens Korstegn, For Solo
      Voice And And Orchestra

    Mountain Wind, For Solo Voice And
      Orchestra
      see Fjellvind, For Solo Voice And
      Orchestra

    Nesland Church, The, For Solo Voice
      And Orchestra
      see Neslandskyrkja, For Solo Voice
      And Orchestra

    Neslandskyrkja, For Solo Voice And
      Orchestra *Op.11 [3']
      1.0.2.2. 0.0.0.0. strings,S solo
      "Nesland Church, The, For Solo
      Voice And Orchestra" NORGE (G691)

    Oh, So Sandy, For Solo Voice And
      Orchestra
      see A Sa Rodblond, For Solo Voice
      And Orchestra

    Om Kvelden
      "In The Evening" sc,pts MUSIKK f.s.
                                  (G692)

    Pa Hospitalet Om Natten, For Solo
      Voice And Orchestra *Op.13,No.2
      [3']
      2.0.2.0. 0.0.0.0. harp,strings,S
      solo
      "In The Hospital At Night, For Solo
      Voice And Orchestra" NORGE (G693)

GROVEN, EIVIND (cont'd.)

    Peace, For Solo Voice And Orchestra
      see Fred, For Solo Voice And
      Orchestra

    Prayer Of Veronica, The, For Solo
      Voice And Orchestra
      see Veronicas Bon, For Solo Voice
      And Orchestra

    Renaessanse *Op.24a [40']
      2.2.2.2. 4.2.3.1. timp,perc,harp,
      strings
      "Renaissance" NORGE   (G694)

    Renaissance
      see Renaessanse

    Rondo for Flute and Orchestra, Op. 37
      0.0.1.1. 0.1.0.0. strings,fl solo
    NORGE   (G695)

    Symphony No. 1, Op. 26 [30']
      2.2.2.2. 4.2.3.1. timp,perc,
      strings
      (Innover Viddene) NORGE   (G696)

    Til Min Gyllenlakk, For Solo Voice
      And Orchestra *Op.22 [3']
      2.0.1.0. 1.0.0.0. harp,strings,
      solo voice
      "Gillyflower, For Solo Voice And
      Orchestra" NORGE   (G697)

    Veronicas Bon, For Solo Voice And
      Orchestra [4']
      1.1.2.2. 1.0.0.0. timp,strings,S
      solo
      "Prayer Of Veronica, The, For Solo
      Voice And Orchestra" NORGE (G698)

    Wedding In The Wood
      see Bryllaup I Skogen

GRUBER, HEINZ KARL (1943-   )
    Charivari [12']
      2(pic).2.2.2. 2.2.2.1. timp,
      2perc,harp,strings
      BOOSEY perf mat rent   (G699)

    Concerto for Violin and Orchestra
      [25']
      1(pic).1.1+bass clar.1. 1.1.1.1.
      timp,2perc,harp,strings,vln
      solo
      ("...aus schatten duft gewebt")
      BOOSEY perf mat rent   (G700)

    Concerto for Violin and String
      Orchestra, No. 2
      see Nebelsteinmusik, For Violin And
      String Orchestra

    Concerto for Violoncello and Chamber
      Orchestra [21']
      1.1.1.1. 1.1.1.0. perc,pno,
      strings,vcl solo
      BOOSEY perf mat rent   (G701)

    Manhattan Broadcasts [11']
      1.1.2.1. 0.2.2.0. 2perc,cel,gtr,
      pno,strings
      BOOSEY perf mat rent   (G702)

    Nebelsteinmusik, For Violin And
      String Orchestra (Concerto for
      Violin and String Orchestra, No.
      2) [16']
      string orch,vln solo
      BOOSEY perf mat rent   (G703)

    Phantom-Bilder Auf Der Spur Eines
      Verdachtigen Themas [13']
      fl&pic,ob,clar,trp,trom,perc,gtr,
      pno,string quin
      "Photofit Pictures On The Tracks Of
      A Suspect Theme" BOOSEY perf mat
      rent   (G704)

    Photofit Pictures On The Tracks Of A
      Suspect Theme
      see Phantom-Bilder Auf Der Spur
      Eines Verdachtigen Themas

    Revue Fur Kammerorchester *Op.22
      [19']
      1(pic).1.1.1. 1.0.0.0. strings
      study sc DOBLINGER STP 633 f.s.,
      perf mat rent   (G705)

    Rough Music, For Percussion And
      Orchestra [26']
      2(pic).2.2+bass clar.2. 2.2.2.1.
      timp,pno&elec org,elec gtr,
      strings,perc solo
      BOOSEY perf mat rent   (G706)

GRUENBERG, LOUIS (1884-1964)
    Jazz Suite *Op.28 [15']
      3.3.3.3. 4.3.3.1. timp,3perc,cel,
      harp,strings
      MARGUN BP 3031 perf mat rent (G707)

GRUENBERG, LOUIS (cont'd.)

White Lilacs, For Violin And
    Orchestra [arr.]
    (Schuller, Gunther)
    2(pic).2(English horn).3(bass
    clar).1. 2.1.3.1. harp,cel,
    strings,vln solo [8'] GUNMAR
    MP3036 perf mat rent   (G708)

GRUPOS DE CAMERA see Oliver, Angel

GRYPHIUS SONGS, FOR SOLO VOICE AND
    ORCHESTRA see Fricker, Peter Racine

GUAJIRA, FOR CLARINET AND ORCHESTRA see
    Gould, Morton

GUANG LINGSAN see Zhou, Long

GUARNIERI, ADRIANO (1947-   )
    Alia [12']
    2.2.2.2. 2.2.2.0. timp,perc,
    strings
    RICORDI-IT 132741 perf mat rent
                                   (G709)
    Concerto for Violin and Orchestra
    [18']
    4.2.4.2. 4.4.2.0. 3perc,pno,cel,
    strings,vln solo
    RICORDI-IT 134049 perf mat rent
                                   (G710)
    ...Di Sussulti E Di Tremori, For
    Piano And Orchestra [20']
    4.0.4.0. 4.4.2.0. timp,3perc,
    strings,pno solo
    RICORDI-IT 133449 perf mat rent
                                   (G711)
    Excerpts [10']
    6vln,2vla,2vcl,db
    RICORDI-IT 132587 perf mat rent
                                   (G712)
    "...Il Tubare Della Tortora...Non
    Odi?...", For Solo Voice And
    Orchestra [20']
    4.3.4.0. 4.4.2.0. 4perc,pno,cel,
    strings,S solo
    RICORDI-IT 133907 perf mat rent
                                   (G713)
    Pierrot Suite [15']
    2(pic,alto fl).0.1.0. 1.0.0.0.
    4perc,cel,vln,vla,vcl
    RICORDI-IT 133128 perf mat rent
                                   (G714)
    Pierrot Suite II, For Flute And
    Instrumental Ensemble [22']
    1+pic.0+English horn.1.0.
    1.1.1.0. 3perc,pno/cel,2vln,
    vla,vcl,db,fl solo
    RICORDI-IT 133842 perf mat rent
                                   (G715)
    Poesia In Forma Di Rosa [10']
    1+alto fl.0.1.1. 1.1.1.0. perc,
    vibra,harp,vln,vla,vcl
    RICORDI-IT 132991 perf mat rent
                                   (G716)
    Romanze Zur Nacht, For Violoncello
    And Instrumental Ensemble [16']
    2fl,clar,horn,trp,trom,2perc,
    2vln,vla,vcl solo
    RICORDI-IT 133499 perf mat rent
                                   (G717)

GUARNIERI, CAMARGO MOZART (1907-   )
    Choro, For Orchestra [15']
    3.3.2.2. 3.2.3.1. timp,perc,xylo,
    vibra,strings
    AMP perf mat rent   (G718)

GUBAIDULINA, SOFIA (1931-   )
    Antwort Ohne Frage [8']
    SIKORSKI perf mat rent   (G719)

    Concerto for Bassoon and Strings
    [30']
    8vcl,6db,bsn solo
    SIKORSKI perf mat rent   (G720)
    VAAP perf mat rent   (G721)

    Concerto For Symphony Orchestra And
    Jazz Band [15']
    3.3.0.0. 4.3.3.1. 3perc,pno,
    strings,SSS soli, jazz band:
    3sax, 2 horn, 4trp, 4trb,
    2drums, 2elec gtr, harp, elec
    org, cel
    SIKORSKI perf mat rent   (G722)

    Concordanza [15']
    1.1.1.1. 1.0.0.0. perc,strings
    SIKORSKI perf mat rent   (G723)

    Detto II, For Violoncello And
    Instrumental Ensemble [13']
    1.1.1.1. 1.0.0.0. 2perc,cel,2vln,
    vla,vcl,db,vcl solo
    SIKORSKI perf mat rent   (G724)

    Hour Of The Soul, For Percussion,
    Solo Voice And Orchestra [30']
    3.3.3.2.tenor sax. 4.4.4.1.
    3perc,2harp,cel/pno,strings,
    perc solo,Mez solo
    "Stunde Der Seele, For Percussion,
    Solo Voice And Orchestra"
    (revised version of "Percussio di
    Pekarski") SIKORSKI perf mat rent

GUBAIDULINA, SOFIA (cont'd.)

                                   (G725)
    Introitus, For Piano And Chamber
    Orchestra [29']
    1.1.0.1. 0.0.0.0. 10vln,4vla,
    3vcl,db,pno solo
    SIKORSKI perf mat rent   (G726)
    VAAP perf mat rent   (G727)

    Offertorium, For Violin And Orchestra
    [40']
    3.2.3.2. 3.3.3.1. timp,4perc,
    2harp,pno&cel,strings,vln solo
    SIKORSKI perf mat rent   (G728)
    VAAP perf mat rent   (G729)

    Percussio Di Pekarski, For
    Percussion, Solo Voice And
    Orchestra [30']
    3.3.3.2.tenor sax. 4.4.4.1. timp,
    perc,2harp,cel,pno,strings,perc
    solo,Mez solo
    SIKORSKI perf mat rent   (G730)

    Pro Et Contra [43']
    2(pic)+alto fl.2.2+clar in E
    flat+bass clar.2+contrabsn.
    4.3.3.1. timp,5perc,2harp,cel&
    hpsd&pno,strings
    SCHIRM.G perf mat rent   (G731)

    Rubayat, For Solo Voice And Chamber
    Orchestra [16']
    1.1.1.1. 2.1.1.0. 2perc,pno,
    strings,Bar solo
    SIKORSKI perf mat rent   (G732)

    Seven Words, For Violoncello, Bayan
    And Strings [32']
    9vln,3vla,2vcl,db,vcl solo, bayan
    solo
    study sc SIKORSKI f.s., perf mat
    rent   (G733)
    VAAP perf mat rent   (G734)

    Stages, The [20']
    3.3.3.3. 6.4.4.1. timp,5perc,
    harp,cel,hpsd,pno,strings
    VAAP perf mat rent   (G735)
    "Stufen" SIKORSKI perf mat rent
                                   (G736)

    Stimmen...Verstummen [40']
    4.2.4.4. 4.4.3.1. 4perc,2harp,
    cel,org,strings
    SIKORSKI perf mat rent   (G737)

    Stufen
    see Stages, The

    Stunde Der Seele [23']
    3.3.3.2.sax. 4.4.4.1. timp,3perc,
    2harp,cel,pno,strings
    PETERS   (G738)

    Stunde Der Seele, For Percussion,
    Solo Voice And Orchestra
    see Hour Of The Soul, For
    Percussion, Solo Voice And
    Orchestra

GUDMUNDSEN-HOLMGREEN, PELLE (1932-   )
    Chronos
    sc,pts SAMFUNDET f.s.   (G739)

    Concord [14']
    1.1.1(bass clar).1. 2.1.1.0.
    perc,pno,string quar
    HANSEN-DEN perf mat rent   (G740)

    Symphony-Antiphony
    3(pic).3(English horn).3(clar in
    E flat,bass clar).2+contrabsn.
    4.3.3.1. timp,6perc,vibra,mand,
    cel,pno,harp,strings
    HANSEN-DEN perf mat rent   (G741)

    Triptykon, For Percussion And
    Orchestra
    3(pic).3(English horn).2+bass
    clar.2+contrabsn. 4.3.3.1.
    timp,strings,perc solo
    HANSEN-DEN perf mat rent   (G742)

GUERNICA, FOR VIOLA AND ORCHESTRA see
    Steffens, Walter

GUERRERO, FRANCISCO (1951-   )
    Actus [15']
    contrabsn,2trom,6vln,4vla,2vcl,
    2db
    sc ALPUERTO f.s.   (G743)

    Datura Fastuosa [15']
    string orch
    ALPUERTO   (G744)

    Ecce Opus [15']
    4(pic).3+English horn.3+bass
    clar.3+contrabsn. 0.4.4.0.
    perc,cel,pno,strings,4 speaking
    voices
    ALPUERTO   (G745)

GUERRERO, FRANCISCO (cont'd.)

    Xenias Pacatas [10']
    6vln,6vla,6vcl
    ALPUERTO   (G746)

GUEZEC, JEAN-PIERRE (1934-   )
    Concert En Trois Parties [16']
    1.1.1.1. 0.0.0.0. 2perc,pno,2vln,
    vla,vcl,db
    SALABERT perf mat rent   (G747)

    Concerto for Violin and Instrumental
    Ensemble [11']
    1.1.1.1. 1.1.0.0. timp,perc,hpsd,
    2vln,vla,vcl,db,vln solo
    SALABERT perf mat rent   (G748)

    Successif-Simultane, For 12 Solo
    Strings [13']
    7vln,2vla,2vcl,db
    sc SALABERT f.s., perf mat rent
                                   (G749)
    Suite Pour Mondrian [20']
    3(pic).2(English horn).3(clar in
    E flat).2. 2.2.2.1. timp,6perc,
    harp,cel,pno,strings
    SALABERT perf mat rent   (G750)

GUIGNOL ET PANDORE: SUITE see Jolivet,
    Andre

GUILHAUD, GEORGES
    Concertino for Oboe and Orchestra
    [7']
    2.0.2.2. 2.0.3.0. timp,strings,ob
    solo
    BILLAUDOT perf mat rent   (G751)

GUILMANT, FELIX ALEXANDRE (1837-1911)
    Symphony No. 1 for Organ and
    Orchestra, Op. 42
    SONZOGNO perf mat rent   (G752)

GUINAND, JULES
    Saltarelle Et Lied, For Violoncello
    And Instrumental Ensemble [5']
    1.1.1.1. 0.0.0.0. harp,strings,
    vcl solo
    BILLAUDOT perf mat rent   (G753)

GUINJOAN, JOAN (1931-   )
    Magma [15']
    1+pic.0.0+bass clar.1. 2.1.1.0.
    3perc,pno,vln,vla,vcl,db
    sc ALPUERTO f.s.   (G754)

    Music for Violoncello and Orchestra
    [20']
    3.3.3.3. 4.3.3.1. 5perc,harp,pno,
    strings,vcl solo
    SALABERT perf mat rent   (G755)

GUINOT, GEORGES LEONCE
    Concerto De Lourmarin, For Organ And
    String Orchestra [20']
    string orch,org solo
    CHOUDENS perf mat rent   (G756)

GUION, DAVID WENDALL FENTRESS
    (1895-1981)
    Arkansas Traveler
    2.2.2.2.2sax. 4.2.3.1. timp,perc,
    harp,strings SCHIRM.G perf mat
    rent   (G757)

    Cowboy's Meditation, For Solo Voice
    And Orchestra
    1.1.1.1. 1.1.1.0. timp,strings,solo
    voice SCHIRM.G perf mat rent
                                   (G758)
    De Laud's Baptizin' [arr.]
    (Crawford) 2(pic).2.2+bass clar.2.
    4.2.3.1. timp,perc,harp,strings
    SCHIRM.G perf mat rent   (G759)

    Home On The Range [arr.]
    (Schmid, Adolf) 1.1.2.1. 2.2.1.0.
    timp,vibra/bells,pno,harp,strings
    [4'] SCHIRM.G perf mat rent
                                   (G760)
    Mam'selle Marie, For Solo Voice And
    Orchestra
    2.1.2.1.2sax. 0.0.0.0. strings,solo
    voice SCHIRM.G perf mat rent
                                   (G761)
    My Cowboy Love Song [arr.]
    (Agnolucci) 1.1.2.1.4sax. 2.3.2.0.
    perc,gtr/banjo,strings SCHIRM.G
    perf mat rent   (G762)

    Pickaninny Dance [arr.]
    (Schmid, Adolf) 1.1.2.1.2sax.
    2.2.1.0. timp,perc,harp,
    harmonium,strings SCHIRM.G perf
    mat rent   (G763)

    Sheep And Goat
    1.1.2.1.2sax. 2.2.1.0. timp,perc,
    harp,harmonium,strings SCHIRM.G
    perf mat rent   (G764)

    Turkey In The Straw
    1(pic).1.2.1. 2.2.1.0. perc,
    harmonium,strings SCHIRM.G perf
    mat rent   (G765)

GUIRLANDE, LA [ARR.] see Rameau, Jean-
Philippe

GUIRLANDES see Taranu, Cornel

GUIRLANDES, FOR SOLO VOICE AND STRING
ORCHESTRA see Bull, Edvard Hagerup

GULBRANSON, EILIF (1897-1958)
Bonn, For Solo Voice And String
Orchestra [2']
string orch,S solo
"Prayer, For Solo Voice And String
Orchestra" NORGE   (G766)

Prayer, For Solo Voice And String
Orchestra
see Bonn, For Solo Voice And String
Orchestra

GULLIN, PETER (1959-   )
Concerto for Trombone and Orchestra
[45']
3.3.3.3. 4.3.3.1. timp,perc,
strings,trom solo
STIM   (G767)

Manniskans Vag
string orch
STIM   (G768)

GUNZO see Tanaka, Toshimitsu

GUO SHANG see Ye, Xiao-Gang

GUPTA, ROLF (1967-   )
All My Instincts
2.3.2.2.4sax. 2.4.2.1(euphonium).
4perc,pno,acord,synthesizer,
strings
NORGE   (G769)

GURDJIEFF, FOR VIOLIN AND CHAMBER
ORCHESTRA see Sitsky, Larry

GURE SEASKA see Larrauri, Anton

GURIDI BIDAOLA, JESUS (1886-1961)
Homenaje A Walt Disney
2+pic.2+English horn.2.2+
contrabsn. 4.3.3.1. timp,perc,
harp,strings
UNION ESP. perf mat rent   (G770)

GURLITT, MANFRED (1890-1972)
Goya Symphony [30']
3.3.3(bass clar).3(contrabsn).
4.3.3.1. timp,perc,harp,strings
ZEN-ON perf mat rent   (G771)

GURNEY, IVOR (1890-1937)
Four Songs, For Solo Voice And String
Orchestra [arr.]
(Finzi, Gerald) string orch,solo
voice BOOSEY perf mat rent
contains: Orpheus; Sleep; Spring;
Under The Greenwood Tree (G772)

Orpheus
see Four Songs, For Solo Voice And
String Orchestra [arr.]

Sleep
see Four Songs, For Solo Voice And
String Orchestra [arr.]

Spring
see Four Songs, For Solo Voice And
String Orchestra [arr.]

Under The Greenwood Tree
see Four Songs, For Solo Voice And
String Orchestra [arr.]

GURRE see Halvorsen, Johan

GÜRSCHING, ALBRECHT (1934-   )
Ballade for Violin and Orchestra
[10']
2.2.2.2. 4.2.3.1. timp,strings,
vln solo
PEER MUSIK perf mat rent   (G773)

Concerto for Bassoon and Strings
[18'50"]
8vln,3vla,3vcl,db,bsn solo
PEER MUSIK perf mat rent   (G774)

Concerto for Oboe and String
Orchestra [12']
string orch,ob solo
PEER MUSIK perf mat rent   (G775)

Nachtigallentraenen, For Solo Voice
And Orchestra [14']
2.2.2.2. 4.2.3.0. strings,S solo
PEER MUSIK perf mat rent   (G776)

Petite Sinfonie [13']
string orch
PEER MUSIK perf mat rent   (G777)

GUSIKOFF, MICHEL (1895-1978)
American Concerto, For Violin And
Orchestra [arr.]
(Machan, B.; Baron, Maurice) 2+
pic.2+English horn.2+bass clar.2+
contrabsn.2alto sax.opt tenor
sax. 4.3.3.1. timp,perc,harp,
strings,vln solo [14'] SCHIRM.G
perf mat rent   (G778)

GUTIERREZ DEL BARRIO, RAMON
Yaravi [11']
2.3.2.2. 4.2.3.1. timp,perc,cel,
harp,strings
ARGM perf mat rent   (G779)

GUY, BARRY (1947-   )
Anna (Concerto for Double Bass and
Orchestra) [33']
2(pic).2.4(bass
clar).2(contrabsn). 4.4.4.1.
4perc,2harp,pno&cel&Hamm,
strings,db solo
NOVELLO perf mat rent   (G780)

Concerto for Double Bass and
Orchestra
see Anna

Eos, For Double Bass And Orchestra
[23']
4(pic).4.4(bass clar).0. 3.3.3.1.
timp,3perc,harp,strings,db solo
NOVELLO perf mat rent   (G781)

Flagwalk With "O" [20']
6vln,2vla,3vcl,db,hpsd
NOVELLO perf mat rent   (G782)

Play [22']
1.0.1.0. 0.1.1.0. perc,strings,
pno solo
NOVELLO perf mat rent   (G783)

Statements II [20']
1.1.1.1. 1.1.1.0. perc,pno,
strings without db
NOVELLO perf mat rent   (G784)

GUY-ROPARTZ, JOSEPH
see ROPARTZ, JOSEPH GUY (MARIE)

GUYS AND DOLLS: A WOMAN IN LOVE, FOR
SOLO VOICE AND ORCHESTRA see
Loesser, Frank

GUYS AND DOLLS: ADELAIDE'S LAMENT, FOR
SOLO VOICE AND ORCHESTRA see
Loesser, Frank

GUYS AND DOLLS: IF I WERE A BELL, FOR
SOLO VOICE AND ORCHESTRA see
Loesser, Frank

GUYS AND DOLLS: I'VE NEVER BEEN IN LOVE
BEFORE, FOR SOLO VOICE AND
ORCHESTRA see Loesser, Frank

GUYS AND DOLLS: OVERTURE see Loesser,
Frank

GUYS AND DOLLS: SUE ME, FOR SOLO VOICES
AND ORCHESTRA see Loesser, Frank

GWENDOLINE: OVERTURE see Chabrier,
[Alexis-] Emmanuel

GWENDOLINE: PRELUDE, ACT II see
Chabrier, [Alexis-] Emmanuel

GYMNASTIQUE DE L'EPONGE, FOR PIANO AND
INSTRUMENTAL ENSEMBLE see Masson,
Gerard

GYMNOPEDIE NO. 2 [ARR.] see Satie, Erik

GYPSY BARON, THE: OVERTURE, [ARR.] see
Strauss, Johann, [Jr.],
Zigeunerbaron, Der: Overture,
[arr.]

GYPSY LEGEND see Tapia Colman, Simon,
Leyenda Gitana

GYPSY RONDO, [ARR.] see Haydn, [Franz]
Joseph, Rondo All' Ongarese, [arr.]

GYROWETZ, ADALBERT (JIROVEC)
(1763-1850)
Symphonies, Four
(Rice, John A.; Craw, H. Allen)
("The Symphony" Vol. B-XI) sc
GARLAND ISBN 0-8240-3826-6 $90.00
contains also: Dussek, Johann
Ladislaus, Symphonie Concertante
(G785)

H

H.M.S. PINAFORE: A MANY YEARS AGO, FOR
SOLO VOICE AND ORCHESTRA see
Sullivan, [Sir] Arthur Seymour

H.M.S. PINAFORE: FAIR MOON, TO THEE I
SING, FOR SOLO VOICE AND ORCHESTRA
see Sullivan, [Sir] Arthur Seymour

H.M.S. PINAFORE: I'M CALLED LITTLE
BUTTERCUP, FOR SOLO VOICE AND
ORCHESTRA see Sullivan, [Sir]
Arthur Seymour

H.M.S. PINAFORE: KIND CAPTAIN, I'VE
IMPORTANT INFORMATION, FOR SOLO
VOICES AND ORCHESTRA see Sullivan,
[Sir] Arthur Seymour

H.M.S. PINAFORE: NEVER MIND THE WHY AND
WHEREFORE, FOR SOLO VOICES AND
ORCHESTRA see Sullivan, [Sir]
Arthur Seymour

H.M.S. PINAFORE: REFRAIN, AUDACIOUS
TAR, FOR SOLO VOICES AND ORCHESTRA
see Sullivan, [Sir] Arthur Seymour

H.M.S. PINAFORE: SORRY HER LOT, FOR
SOLO VOICE AND ORCHESTRA see
Sullivan, [Sir] Arthur Seymour

H.M.S. PINAFORE: THINGS ARE SELDOM WHAT
THEY SEEM, FOR SOLO VOICES AND
ORCHESTRA see Sullivan, [Sir]
Arthur Seymour

H.M.S. PINAFORE: WHEN I WAS A LAD, FOR
SOLO VOICE AND ORCHESTRA see
Sullivan, [Sir] Arthur Seymour

HAAG, HANNO
Concerto for Trombone and String
Orchestra, Op. 23
string orch,trom solo
MÖSELER M 11.455 sc rent, pts f.s.
(H1)

HAAP see Sivertsen, Kenneth

HAAPALAINEN, VÄINÖ (1916-   )
Lemminkainen Overture [7']
2.2.2.2. 3.2.3.0. timp,perc,
strings
FAZER perf mat rent   (H2)

HAARKLOU, JOHANNES (1847-1925)
Symphony No. 4, Op. 57, in E flat
[41']
2.2.2.2. 4.3.3.1. timp,perc,
strings
NORGE   (H3)

HAAS EN DE SCHILDPAD, DE see Rispens,
Jan

HABANERA see Chabrier, [Alexis-]
Emmanuel

HACHIMURA, YOSHIO (1938-1985)
Folia, La [7']
3(pic).3(English horn).4(bass
clar).3(contrabsn). 4.4.3.1.
perc,2harp,strings
sc ZEN-ON f.s., perf mat rent (H4)

HADDOCK'S EYES, FOR SOLO VOICE AND
INSTRUMENTAL ENSEMBLE see Del
Tredici, David

HADLEY, PATRICK ARTHUR SHELDON
(1899-1973)
One Morning In Spring [5']
2.2.2.2. 2.0.0.0. harp,strings
OXFORD perf mat rent   (H5)

HAEC EST REGINA VIRGINUM, FOR SOLO
VOICE AND ORCHESTRA see
Handel, George Frideric

HAENFLEIN, ROBERT
Wedding On The Moon [3'5"]
2.2.2.1. 2.3.3.1. timp,perc,gtr,
harp,pno,strings
BUSCH HBM 012 perf mat rent (H6)

HAENSEL, FRANZ (1726-1805)
Concerto for 2 Horns and String
Orchestra in F
(Leloir, E.) string orch,2horn soli
[10'10"] sc BILLAUDOT f.s., perf
mat rent   (H7)

HAFRSFJORD, FOR SOLO VOICE AND
ORCHESTRA see Sommerfeldt, Öistein

HAFSTEINSSON, GUDMUNDUR (1953-   )
Concert Cantata, For Solo Voices And
Orchestra [30']
0.0.4.4. 4.0.0.0. timp,perc,harp,
strings,TBarB soli

HAFSTEINSSON, GUDMUNDUR (cont'd.)

ICELAND 035-001 (H8)

HAGEMAN, RICHARD (1882-1966)
At The Well
2.2.2.1. 2.0.0.0. timp,perc,harp,
strings SCHIRM.G perf mat rent
(H9)

HAGERTY, MARK
Chamber Concerto [14']
alto fl,ob,clar,bsn,3perc,pno,
2vln,vla,vcl
sc APNM $12.25, perf mat rent (H10)

HAGERUP BULL, EDVARD
see BULL, EDVARD HAGERUP

HAGSTRÖM, ROBERT (1950-   )
Prelude for Orchestra
STIM (H11)

HAIMONSKINDER QUADRILLE see Strauss,
Johann, [Sr.]

HAJAH, FOR ACCORDION AND ORCHESTRA see
Hosokawa, Toshio

HAJDU, ANDRE (1937-   )
Divertimento for String Orchestra
[8']
string orch
MMB perf mat rent (H12)

HAKÅNSON, KNUT ALGOT (1887-1929)
Slottstappning, For Solo Voice And
Orchestra [5']
2.2.2.2. 4.2.3.1. timp,strings,
med solo
NORDISKA perf mat rent (H13)

HAKON JARL see Hartmann, Johan Peder
Emilius see Smetana, Bedrich

HALD UT, HJARTE, FOR SOLO VOICES AND
ORCHESTRA see Eggen, Arne

HALF HEARD IN THE STILLNESS see Payne,
Anthony

HALFFTER, CRISTOBAL (1930-   )
Antifonia Pascual A La Virgen, For
Solo Voices And Orchestra [15']
1+pic.1.1+bass clar.1. 2.1.0.0.
timp,strings,SA soli
UNION ESP. perf mat rent (H14)

Concerto for Piano and Orchestra
[28']
4(pic).4.4.3+contrabsn. 6.4.4.0.
4perc,harp,cel,strings,pno solo
sc UNIVER. UE19340 f.s., perf mat
rent (H15)

Concerto for Violin and Orchestra
4.3.3.4. 6.4.4.1. perc,strings,
vln solo
sc UNIVER. 17199 $48.00, perf mat
rent (H16)

Concerto for Violin, Viola and
Orchestra [24']
2.2.2.2. 2.2.0.0. 3perc,hpsd&cel,
strings,vln solo,vla solo
UNIVER. perf mat rent (H17)

Concerto for Violoncello and
Orchestra, No. 2 [37']
2.2.2.2. 4.3.3.1. perc,harp,
strings,vcl solo
("No queda mas que el silencio")
UNIVER. perf mat rent (H18)

Dortmunder Variationen [18']
4(pic).4.4(clar in E flat,bass
clar).4(contrabsn). 6.4.4.1.
4perc,strings
UNIVER. perf mat rent (H19)

Dos Movimentos, For Timpani And
String Orchestra [14']
string orch,timp solo
UNION ESP. perf mat rent (H20)

Fantasia Über Einen Klang Von G.F.
Handel, Für Violoncelli-Gruppe
Und Streicher [17']
string orch,4-12vcl soli
sc UNIVER. UE17456 f.s., perf mat
rent (H21)

Parafrasis Uber Die "Fantasia Über
Einen Klang Von G.F. Handel"
[18']
3.4.4.4. 4.4.4.0. strings
UNIVER. perf mat rent (H22)

Preludio A Nemesis [16']
4(pic).3.3(bass
clar).4(contrabsn). 4.4.4.1.
5perc,harp,cel,strings
UNIVER. perf mat rent (H23)

Sinfonia Ricercata, For Organ And
Orchestra [23']
3.3.3.4. 6.4.4.1. strings,org

HALFFTER, CRISTOBAL (cont'd.)

solo
sc UNIVER. UE17753 f.s., perf mat
rent (H24)

Tiento
4.4.4.4. 6.4.4.0. perc,strings
sc UNIVER. 17441 $48.00, perf mat
rent (H25)

Tiento Del Primer Tono Y Batalla
Imperial [10']
4(pic).4(English
horn).4.4(contrabsn). 6.4.4.1.
4perc,strings
UNIVER. perf mat rent (H26)

Tres Poemas De La Lirica Espanola,
For Solo Voice And Orchestra
[25']
4(pic).4.4.4(contrabsn). 6.4.4.0.
4perc,4harp,cel,strings,Bar
solo
UNIVER. perf mat rent (H27)

Versus [36']
4.4.4.4. 4.4.4.0. 4perc,strings
UNIVER. perf mat rent (H28)

HALFFTER, ERNESTO (1905-   )
Cavatina [5']
0.2.2.1.sax. 1.1.1.0. perc,harp,
strings
sc ESCHIG f.s., perf mat rent (H29)

Cojo Enamorado, El [23']
2(pic).1.2.1. 2.2.1.0. timp,perc,
strings
UNION ESP. perf mat rent (H30)

Concerto for Guitar and Orchestra
[30']
4(pic).0.4(bass clar).0. 4.0.0.0.
timp,perc,harp,strings,gtr solo
UNION ESP. perf mat rent (H31)

HALFFTER, RODOLFO (1900-   )
Diferencias Para Orquesta [13'50"]
2(pic).2.2.2. 4.2.2.1. timp,perc,
pno,strings
ALPUERTO (H32)

Dos Ambientes Sonoros *Op.37
2.2.2.2. 4.2.2.1. timp,perc,
strings
UNION ESP. perf mat rent (H33)

Elegia In Memoriam Carlos Chavez [7']
string orch
MEXICANAS perf mat rent (H34)

Obertura Concertante, For Piano And
Orchestra [9'30"]
1.1+English horn.1.2. 0.1.1.0.
timp,strings,pno solo
MEXICANAS perf mat rent (H35)
ALPUERTO (H36)

Tripartita [12'30"]
2+pic.2.2.2+contrabsn. 4.2.3.1.
timp,perc,xylo,pno,strings
MEXICANAS perf mat rent (H37)

HALIER, RONALD (1952-   )
Evviva [12'30"]
3.2.2.2. 2.2.0.0. 3perc,harp,
strings
sc DONEMUS f.s., perf mat rent
(H38)

HALIL, FOR FLUTE AND ORCHESTRA see
Bernstein, Leonard

HALL, JEFFREY (1941-   )
From The Supai Formation
string orch
study sc MOBART $10.00 (H39)

HALL, PAULINE (1890-1969)
Circus Pictures: Small Suite
see Cirkusbilleder: Liten Suite

Cirkusbilleder: Liten Suite [7']
2.2.2.2. 4.2.3.1. timp,perc,harp,
strings
"Circus Pictures: Small Suite"
(alternate scoring: .1110 1110.,
timp, perc, pno, str) NORGE (H40)

Suite From The Incidental Music To
"Julius Caesar" [10']
3.2.2.2. 4.2.3.1. timp,perc,harp,
strings
NORGE (H41)

Tango
2.2.1.1. 2.0.0.0. strings
NORGE (H42)

To Unge Elskende, For Solo Voice And
Orchestra
2.2.2.2. 4.2.3.1. timp,perc,harp,
cel,strings,solo voice
NORGE (H43)

HALL, PAULINE (cont'd.)

Verlaine Suite [23']
3.2.2.2. 4.2.3.1. timp,perc,harp,
cel,strings
(alternate scoring: .1111 2220.,
perc, cel, str) NORGE (H44)

HALLBERG, BENGT (1932-   )
Concerto "Groovy", For Swing Band And
Orchestra [15']
2.2.2.2. 2.2.1.0. timp,perc,
strings, swing band: clar,
vibr, elec gtr, db, drums
STIM (H45)

Lyrisk Ballad, For 2 Pianos And
Orchestra [20']
2.2.2.2. 2.2.1.0. timp,perc,
2harp,strings,2pno soli
STIM (H46)

HALLDORSSON, SKULI (1914-   )
Dimmalimm (Suite No. 1) [17']
2.2.2.2. 4.2.3.1. timp,perc,harp,
strings
ICELAND 023-002 (H47)

Eruption At Heimaey [14']
3.2.2.3. 4.2.3.1. timp,perc,
strings
ICELAND 023-006 (H48)

Lad Of The Harp, For Solo Voice And
Orchestra [9']
2.1.2.1. 2.1.1.0. timp,perc,
strings,solo voice
ICELAND 023-005 (H49)

Patriotic Songs For Trumpet And
String Orchestra
string orch,trp solo
ICELAND 023-014 (H50)

Ravishment (Suite No. 4)
2.2.2.2. 2.2.2.1. timp,perc,
strings
ICELAND 023-020 (H51)

Sog [8']
2.2.2.2. 4.2.3.1. timp,perc,
strings
(River In Iceland) ICELAND 023-009
(H52)

Song Cycle, A, For Solo Voices And
Orchestra
1.1.1.1. 0.0.0.0. strings,SBar
soli
ICELAND 023-010 (H53)

Suite No. 1
see Dimmalimm

Suite No. 2
2.2.2.2. 4.2.3.1. timp,perc,harp,
strings
ICELAND 023-011 (H54)

Suite No. 3
see Sun's Glitter

Suite No. 4
see Ravishment

Sunny Night [9']
3.2.2.2. 4.2.2.1. timp,perc,
strings
ICELAND 023-003 (H55)

Sun's Glitter (Suite No. 3) [12']
3.2.2.2. 4.2.3.1. timp,perc,
strings
ICELAND 023-019 (H56)

Symphony No. 1
3.2.2.2. 4.2.3.1. timp,perc,
strings
(Our World) ICELAND 023-025 (H57)

Three Fugues [5'20"]
2.2.2.2. 0.0.0.0. strings
ICELAND 023-004 (H58)

HALLELUJAH II see Vriend, Jan N.M.

HALLGRIMSSON, HAFLIDI (1941-   )
Daydreams In Numbers
string orch
CHESTER perf mat rent (H59)

Poemi, For Violin And String
Orchestra [20']
string orch,vln solo
CHESTER perf mat rent (H60)

Words In Winter, For Solo Voice And
Orchestra [20']
2.2.2.2. 2.2.2.0. timp,perc,
strings,S solo
CHESTER perf mat rent (H61)

HALLING see Nystedt, Knut

HALLING IN BOOGALOO see Tveit, Sigvald

HALLING MARCH see Oulie, Einar,
  Halling-Marsj

HALLING-MARSJ see Oulie, Einar

HALLMAN, BJORN
  Persefone [10']
    3.2.3.2. 4.3.3.1. timp,2perc,
    harp,strings
    sc GEHRMANS 6115P f.s., perf mat
    rent   (H62)

  Sagan Om Snovit, For Narrator And
    Orchestra [30']
    2.2.2.2. 4.3.3.1. timp,4perc,
    harp,pno,strings,narrator
    "Snow-White, For Narrator And
    Orchestra" sc GEHRMANS 6109P
    f.s., perf mat rent   (H63)

  Snow-White, For Narrator And
    Orchestra
    see Sagan Om Snovit, For Narrator
    And Orchestra

HALLNÄS, EYVIND (1937-   )
  Dialog Av Marionetter, For Solo
    Voices And String Orchestra
    string orch,SBar soli
    STIM   (H64)

  Rhapsody for Orchestra [4']
    2.2.2.2. 2.2.2.0. timp,harp,
    strings
    STIM   (H65)

  Sinfonietta
    2.2.2.2. 2.2.2.0. timp,strings
    STIM   (H66)

HALLNÄS, HILDING (1903-1984)
  Concerto for Violoncello and
    Orchestra
    2.2.2.2. 2.2.0.0. timp,perc,
    strings,vcl solo
    STIM   (H67)

HALMRAST, TOR (1951-   )
  Pyrondus [14']
    2.2.2.1. 3.2.2.0. timp,perc,harp,
    strings,gtr solo,acord solo,bsn
    solo
    NORGE   (H68)

HALO, FOR HARP AND CHAMBER ORCHESTRA
  see Fontyn, Jacqueline

HALVORSEN, JOHAN (1864-1935)
  Chant De La "Veslemøy", For Violin
    And String Orchestra [3']
    string orch,vln solo
    HANSEN-DEN perf mat rent   (H69)

  Gurre *Op.17 [15']
    2(pic).2.2.2. 4.2.3.1. timp,perc,
    harp,strings
    HANSEN-DEN perf mat rent   (H70)

  King, The *Op.19 [17']
    2(pic).2.2.2. 4.2.3.1. timp,perc,
    harp,strings
    HANSEN-DEN perf mat rent   (H71)

  Norwegian Air, For Violin And
    Orchestra [5']
    2(pic).2.2.2. 2.0.0.0. timp,perc,
    strings,vln solo
    HANSEN-DEN perf mat rent   (H72)

  Norwegian Song, For Violin And String
    Orchestra *Op.31 [3']
    string orch,vln solo
    HANSEN-DEN perf mat rent   (H73)

  Tordenskiold *Op.18 [15']
    2(pic).2.2.2. 4.2.3.1. timp,perc,
    strings
    HANSEN-DEN perf mat rent   (H74)

HAMBRAEUS, BENGT (1928-   )
  Litanies [17']
    2(pic).2.2.2. 4.2.3.1. timp,perc,
    strings
    CAN.MUS.CENT. MI 1100 H199LI (H75)

  Quodlibet Re Bach [11']
    0.3.0.1. 2.0.0.0. strings
    CAN.MUS.CENT. MI 1100 H199Q   (H76)

HAMBURG, JEFF (1956-   )
  Concertino for Alto Saxophone and
    Orchestra [21']
    2.2.2.2. 2.2.2.0. 2perc,pno,4vcl,
    db,alto sax solo
    DONEMUS perf mat rent   (H77)

  Partus [16']
    3.3.3.4.soprano sax. 4.3.3.1.
    4perc,1-2harp,pno,strings
    sc DONEMUS f.s., perf mat rent
                                    (H78)

HAMEENNIEMI, EERO (1951-   )
  Dialogue For Piano And Orchestra
    [14']
    2.1.2.2. 2.2.2.0. timp,perc,
    strings,pno solo

HAMEENNIEMI, EERO (cont'd.)
    FAZER perf mat rent   (H79)

  Efisaes, For Piano And Strings [6']
    12strings,pno solo
    sc FAZER f.s., perf mat rent   (H80)

  Symphony
    2.2.3.2. 4.2.2.1. timp,perc,pno,
    strings
    sc FAZER f.s.   (H81)

HAMEL
  Perles De Cristal
    BILLAUDOT f.s.   (H82)

HAMEL, PETER MICHAEL (1947-   )
  Gralbilder [15']
    2+alto fl(pic).2+English horn.2+
    bass clar.0+contrabsn. 2.2.3.1.
    timp,2perc,harp,strings
    BÄREN. BA 7125 perf mat rent   (H83)

  Klangspirale (First Version-1977)
    [15'-18']
    1(alto fl).1(English horn).1(bass
    clar).1. 1.1.1.0. perc,pno,
    strings
    "Spiral Of Sounds [1]" BÄREN.
    BA 6743   (H84)

  Klangspirale (Second Version-1977)
    [15'-18']
    1+alto fl.2+English horn.1+bass
    clar.2. 2.2.2.0. 2perc,3pno,
    strings
    "Spiral Of Sounds [2]" BÄREN. sc
    BA 6743 f.s., perf mat rent,
    study sc BA 6781 f.s.   (H85)

  Lichtung, Die
    see Sinfonie In Sechs Teilen

  Maitreya [12'-15']
    2(alto fl).2+English horn.2+bass
    clar.2+contrabsn. 4.2.4+bass
    trom.0+db tuba. 3perc,strings,
    electronic
    BÄREN. sc BA 6724 f.s., perf mat
    rent, study sc BA 6781 f.s. (H86)

  Semiramis [21']
    2.2.3+basset horn.0+contrabsn.
    2.0.0.0. 3perc,harp,cel,strings
    study sc BÄREN. BA 7089 f.s., perf
    mat rent   (H87)

  Sinfonie In Sechs Teilen [45']
    2+pic+alto fl.2+English horn.2+
    bass clar.2+contrabsn.alto sax.
    4.2.2.1. timp,4perc,harp,pno,
    strings
    "Lichtung, Die" BÄREN. BA 7305
                                    (H88)
  Spiral Of Sounds [1]
    see Klangspirale (First Version-
    1977)

  Spiral Of Sounds [2]
    see Klangspirale (Second Version-
    1977)

  Von Traum Und Tod (from Ein
    Menschentraum) [15'30"]
    2(pic,alto fl).2(English horn).2+
    bass clar.2+contrabsn.
    2.2.3(bass trom).1. timp,3perc,
    harp,pno&cel&elec org,strings,
    electronic equipment
    BÄREN. BA 7131 perf mat rent   (H89)

HAMERIK, EBBE (1898-1951)
  Orkestervariationer
    sc SAMFUNDET f.s., perf mat rent
                                    (H90)

HAMILTON, IAIN (1922-   )
  Alexandrian Sequence, The [24']
    1.1.1.1. 1.1.1.0. 2vln,vla,vcl,db
    PRESSER perf mat rent   (H91)

  Cleopatra, For Solo Voice And
    Orchestra [21']
    2.2.2.2. 4.2.3.0. timp,perc,harp,
    strings,S solo
    PRESSER perf mat rent   (H92)

  Paris De Crepuscule A L'Aube, For
    Solo Voice And Orchestra [25']
    PRESSER perf mat rent   (H93)

  Ricordanza, For Solo Voice And
    Orchestra [25']
    2.2.2.2. 4.2.3.0. timp,perc,harp,
    strings,high solo
    PRESSER perf mat rent   (H94)

  Symphony No. 3 in G [26']
    2.2.2.2. 2.0.0.0. strings
    PRESSER perf mat rent   (H95)

  Symphony No. 4 in B [50']
    3.3.3.3. 4.3.3.1. timp,perc,harp,
    strings
    PRESSER perf mat rent   (H96)

HAMLET see Liszt, Franz see
  Tchaikovsky, Piotr Ilyich

HAMLET AND OPHELIA see MacDowell,
  Edward Alexander

HAMLET [ARR.] see Walton, [Sir] William
  (Turner)

HAMLET, OP. 67BIS see Tchaikovsky,
  Piotr Ilyich

HAMLET: SUITE see Chervinsky, Nikolai
  see Shostakovich, Dmitri

HAMMERTH, JOHAN (1953-   )
  Concerto for Bassoon, Flute, Clarinet
    and String Orchestra [18']
    string orch,fl solo,clar solo,bsn
    solo
    STIM   (H97)

  Concerto for Violin and String
    Orchestra [20']
    string orch,vln solo
    STIM   (H98)

  Utbrott [28']
    3perc,strings
    STIM   (H99)

HAND, COLIN (1929-   )
  Variations And Fugue On A Cheshire
    Souling Song [17']
    2.2.2.2. 2.2.2.0. timp,2perc,
    strings
    NOVELLO perf mat rent   (H100)

HANDEL, GEORGE FRIDERIC (1685-1759)
  Acis And Galatea: As When The Dove,
    For Solo Voice And Orchestra
    "Acis Und Galathea: So Wie Die
    Taube, For Solo Voice And
    Orchestra" BREITKOPF-L perf mat
    rent   (H101)

  Acis And Galathea: I Rage, I Melt, I
    Burn; O Ruddier Than The Cherry,
    For Solo Voice And Orchestra
    fl,hpsd,strings,B solo
    "Acis Und Galathea: O Schmach, O
    Wut; O Rosig Wie Die Pfirsche,
    For Solo Voice And Orchestra"
    BREITKOPF-L perf mat rent (H102)

  Acis And Galathea: 'Tis Done; Heart,
    The Seat Of Soft Delight, For
    Solo Voice And Orchestra
    2fl,hpsd,strings,S solo
    "Acis Und Galathea: So Sei's; Herz,
    Der Liebe Süsser Born, For Solo
    Voice And Orchestra" BREITKOPF-L
    perf mat rent   (H103)

  Acis Und Galathea: O Schmach, O Wut;
    O Rosig Wie Die Pfirsche, For
    Solo Voice And Orchestra
    see Acis And Galathea: I Rage, I
    Melt, I Burn; O Ruddier Than The
    Cherry, For Solo Voice And
    Orchestra

  Acis Und Galathea: So Sei's; Herz,
    Der Liebe Süsser Born, For Solo
    Voice And Orchestra
    see Acis And Galathea: 'Tis Done;
    Heart, The Seat Of Soft Delight,
    For Solo Voice And Orchestra

  Acis Und Galathea: So Wie Die Taube,
    For Solo Voice And Orchestra
    see Acis And Galatea: As When The
    Dove, For Solo Voice And
    Orchestra

  Ah! Crudel, Nel Pianto Mio, For Solo
    Voice And Orchestra
    2ob,bsn,hpsd,strings,S solo
    BREITKOPF-L perf mat rent (H104)

  Alexander Balu: Horch, Er Schlägt Das
    Goldne Spiel, For Solo Voice And
    Orchestra
    see Alexander Balus: Hark! He
    Strikes The Golden Lyre, For Solo
    Voice And Orchestra

  Alexander Balus: Hark! He Strikes The
    Golden Lyre, For Solo Voice And
    Orchestra
    2fl,2bsn,harp,mand,org,strings,S
    solo
    "Alexander Balu: Horch, Er Schlägt
    Das Goldne Spiel, For Solo Voice
    And Orchestra" BREITKOPF-L perf
    mat rent   (H105)

  Amadigi: Pena Tiranna, For Solo Voice
    And Orchestra
    ob,bsn,strings,A solo
    "Amadigi: Qualen Ohne Ende, For
    Solo Voice And Orchestra"
    BREITKOPF-L perf mat rent (H106)

HANDEL, GEORGE FRIDERIC (cont'd.)

Amadigi: Qualen Ohne Ende, For Solo
  Voice And Orchestra
  see Amadigi: Pena Tiranna, For Solo
  Voice And Orchestra

Apollo Und Daphne: Die Freiheit Gab
  Ich Dir Wieder, For Solo Voices
  And Orchestra
  fl,2ob,bsn,hpsd,strings,SB soli
  (Seiffert) BREITKOPF-L perf mat
  rent   (H107)

Ariodante: Bramo Haver Mille Vite,
  For Solo Voices And Orchestra
  (Simpson, Carl) string orch,cont,
  SMez soli [5'] NORRUTH perf mat
  rent   (H108)

Armida Abbandonata, For Solo Voice
  And String Orchestra
  BREITKOPF-L perf mat rent   (H109)

Arrival Of The Queen Of Sheba
  see Solomon: Entrance Of The Queen
  Of Sheba

Atalanta: Overture
  2ob,trp,strings,cont
  sc,pts HANSSLER f.s.   (H110)

Complete Works, Chrysander Edition,
  1858-1894, 1902
  (microfiche reprint, $525.00)
  UNIV.MUS.ED.   (H111)

Concerti A Due Cori, Three
  min sc LEA 140 $2.40
  contains: Concerto Grosso No. 27
  in B flat; Concerto Grosso No.
  28 in F; Concerto Grosso No. 29
  in F   (H112)

Concerti For Oboe And Orchestra, Four
  see Concerti Grossi, Five

Concerti for Organ and Orchestra, Op.
  4, Nos. 1-6
  min sc KALMUS K01363 $7.00 (H113)
  (reprinted from Deutsche
  Handelgesellschaft edition) sc
  DOVER 244628 $6.50 contains also:
  Concerti for Organ and Orchestra,
  Op. 7, Nos. 1-6   (H114)

Concerti for Organ and Orchestra, Op.
  7, Nos. 1-6
  see Concerti for Organ and
  Orchestra, Op. 4, Nos. 1-6

Concerti Grossi, Five
  min sc KALMUS K00778 $5.50
  contains: Concerti For Oboe And
  Orchestra, Four; Concerto
  Grosso In C (Alexander's Feast)
                                 (H115)

Concerti Grossi, Op. 6, Nos. 1-6
  min sc KALMUS K00763 $5.50 (H116)

Concerti Grossi, Op. 6, Nos. 1-12
  min sc KALMUS K01359 $14.25 (H117)

Concerto a Due Cori In B flat, Hwv
  332
  see Concerto Grosso No. 27 in B
  flat

Concerto a Due Cori In F, Hwv 333
  see Concerto Grosso No. 28 in F

Concerto a Due Cori In F, Hwv 334
  see Concerto Grosso No. 29 in F

Concerto for Flute and String
  Orchestra in D, MIN 45
  (Hoffmann) KALMUS A7088 sc $8.00,
  set $12.00, pts $2.00, ea. (H118)

Concerto for 2 Horns and Orchestra,
  [arr.]
  (Leloir, E.) 2ob,2bsn,strings,2horn
  soli [11'30"] BILLAUDOT perf mat
  rent   (H119)

Concerto for Oboe and String
  Orchestra, No. 1, in B flat
  KALMUS A6093 sc $5.00, set $6.00
                                 (H120)

Concerto for Organ and Orchestra, No.
  7, Op. 7, No. 1, in B flat
  (Koopman, Ton) BREITKOPF-W sc
  PB 5211 f.s., pts OB 5211 f.s.
                                 (H121)
  (Williams, Peter) OXFORD perf mat
  rent   (H122)

Concerto for Organ and Orchestra, No.
  8, Op. 7, No. 2, in A
  (Koopman, Ton) BREITKOPF-W sc
  PB 5212 f.s., pts OB 5212 f.s.
                                 (H123)
  (Williams, Peter) OXFORD perf mat
  rent   (H124)

HANDEL, GEORGE FRIDERIC (cont'd.)

Concerto for Organ and Orchestra, No.
  9, Op. 7, No. 3, in B flat
  (Williams, Peter) OXFORD perf mat
  rent   (H125)

Concerto for Organ and Orchestra, No.
  10, Op. 7, No. 4, in D minor
  (Williams, Peter) OXFORD perf mat
  rent   (H126)

Concerto for Organ and Orchestra, No.
  11, Op. 7, No. 5, in G minor
  (Williams, Peter) OXFORD perf mat
  rent   (H127)

Concerto for Organ and Orchestra, No.
  12, Op. 7, No. 6, in B flat
  (Williams, Peter) OXFORD perf mat
  rent   (H128)

Concerto for Organ and Orchestra, No.
  13, in F
  2ob,bsn,strings,org solo
  (Best, Terence) sc OXFORD 31.254
  $15.95, perf mat rent   (H129)

Concerto for Organ and Orchestra, No.
  14, in A
  2ob,bsn,strings,org solo
  (Best, Terence) sc OXFORD 31.255
  $15.95, perf mat rent   (H130)

Concerto for Organ and Orchestra, No.
  17, in D minor [20']
  (Mohr, Wilhelm) org,2ob,hpsd,
  strings BAREN. BA 6722   (H131)

Concerto for Trumpet and String
  Orchestra in G minor, [arr.]
  (Thilde, J.) string orch,hpsd,trp
  solo [9'5"] sc BILLAUDOT f.s.,
  perf mat rent   (H132)

Concerto for 2 Trumpets and String
  Orchestra in A flat, [arr.]
  (Thilde, J.) string orch,2trp soli
  [8'] BILLAUDOT perf mat rent
                                 (H133)

Concerto Grosso In C (Alexander's
  Feast)
  see Concerti Grossi, Five

Concerto Grosso No. 27 in B flat
  (Hudson, Frederick) "Concerto a Due
  Cori In B flat, Hwv 332" study sc
  BAREN. $5.40   (H134)
  see Concerti A Due Cori, Three

Concerto Grosso No. 28 in F
  (Hudson, Frederick) "Concerto a Due
  Cori In F, Hwv 333" study sc
  BAREN. $9.00   (H135)
  see Concerti A Due Cori, Three

Concerto Grosso No. 29 in F
  (Hudson, Frederick) "Concerto a Due
  Cori In F, Hwv 334" study sc
  BAREN. $9.00   (H136)
  see Concerti A Due Cori, Three

Concerto Grosso, Op. 3, No. 2, in B
  flat
  min sc PHILH PH. 128 $4.75 (H137)

Concerto in D, MIN 214 [7']
  0.2.0.1. 4.2.0.0. timp,org,
  strings
  (Court, Robert) UNIV.CR study sc
  P00201 f.s., pts P00202 rent
                                 (H138)

Concerto in F, MIN 1 [12']
  0.2.0.1. 2.0.0.0. hpsd,strings
  (Schering) KAHNT KT 7793 f.s.
                                 (H139)

Concerto in F, MIN 151
  2ob,2horn,bsn,strings,cont
  KUNZEL 10180 sc $12.00, ipa, kbd pt
  $7.00   (H140)

Deidamia: Es Birgt Die Nachtigall,
  For Solo Voice And String
  Orchestra
  see Deidamia: Nasconde l'Usignol'
  In Altri Rami Il Nido, For Solo
  Voice And String Orchestra

Deidamia: Nasconde l'Usignol' In
  Altri Rami Il Nido, For Solo
  Voice And String Orchestra
  string orch,S solo
  "Deidamia: Es Birgt Die Nachtigall,
  For Solo Voice And String
  Orchestra" BREITKOPF-L perf mat
  rent   (H141)

Esther: Turn Not, O Queen, Thy Face
  Away, For Solo Voice And
  Orchestra
  KALMUS A6217 sc $3.00, set $3.75,
  pts $.75, ea.   (H142)

Ezio: Folle È Colui; Nasce Al Bosco,
  For Solo Voice And Orchestra
  ob,bsn,strings,hpsd,B solo

HANDEL, GEORGE FRIDERIC (cont'd.)

  BREITKOPF-L perf mat rent   (H143)

Feuerwerksmusik
  see Royal Fireworks Music

Five Short Pieces
  (Dunhill) string orch [5'] KALMUS
  A7373 sc $5.00, set $7.50, pts
  $1.50, ea.   (H144)

Giulio Cesare: Caro! Bella! Piu
  Amabile Belta, For Solo Voices
  And Orchestra
  (Simpson, Carl) 2ob,bsn,cont,
  strings,SMez soli [5'] NORRUTH
  perf mat rent   (H145)

Giulio Cesare: Piangero, La Sorte
  Mia, For Solo Voice And Orchestra
  (Simpson, Carl) fl,cont,strings,S
  solo [5'] NORRUTH perf mat rent
                                 (H146)

Haec Est Regina Virginum, For Solo
  Voice And String Orchestra [4']
  string orch,org,S solo
  (Gorini, R.) BREITKOPF-W sc PB 5149
  f.s., pts OB 5149 f.s.   (H147)

Jephtha: Farewell, Ye Limpid Springs,
  For Solo Voice And Orchestra
  KALMUS A6229 sc $3.00, set $6.75,
  pts $.75, ea.   (H148)

Joshua: O Had I Jubal's Lyre, For
  Solo Voice And Orchestra
  string orch,T solo
  "Josua: O Hätt' Ich Jubals Harf,
  For Solo Voice And Orchestra"
  BREITKOPF-L perf mat rent   (H149)

Josua: O Hätt' Ich Jubals Harf, For
  Solo Voice And Orchestra
  see Joshua: O Had I Jubal's Lyre,
  For Solo Voice And Orchestra

Lucrezia: O Numi Eterni, For Solo
  Voice And String Orchestra [18']
  string orch,cont,S solo
  (Leppard, Raymond) FABER perf mat
  rent   (H150)

Mirtillo Suite. Excerpts From "Il
  Pastor Fido"
  (Schering) KALMUS A5362 f.s. (H151)

Nun Schweiget Winde, For Solo Voice
  And Orchestra
  see Silete Venti, For Solo Voice
  And Orchestra

Otho: Overture, [arr.]
  see Ottone: Overture, [arr.]

Otto Und Theophano: Ah! Tu Non Sai,
  For Solo Voice And Orchestra
  see Ottone: Ah! Tu Non Sai, For
  Solo Voice And String Orchestra

Ottone: Ah! Tu Non Sai, For Solo
  Voice And String Orchestra
  string orch,A solo
  "Otto Und Theophano: Ah! Tu Non
  Sai, For Solo Voice And
  Orchestra" BREITKOPF-L perf mat
  rent   (H152)

Ottone: Overture, [arr.] [5']
  (Bantock) "Otho: Overture, [arr.]"
  string orch NOVELLO perf mat rent
                                 (H153)

Overturen Und Tanze Aus Den Opern
  "Alezander" Und "Berenice" Und
  Dem Oratorium "Theodora"
  "Overtures And Dances To The Operas
  "Alexander" And "Berenice" And
  The Oratorio "Theodora"" KALMUS
  A7450 sc $15.00, set $12.50, pts
  $2.50, ea.   (H154)

Overtures And Dances To The Operas
  "Alexander" And "Berenice" And
  The Oratorio "Theodora"
  see Overturen Und Tanze Aus Den
  Opern "Alezander" Und "Berenice"
  Und Dem Oratorium "Theodora"

Passacaglia, [arr.] (from Concerto
  For Organ, Op. 7, No. 1)
  (Aslamasjan, S.) string orch [7']
  SIKORSKI perf mat rent   (H155)

Patenza, For Solo Voice And Orchestra
  vcl,hpsd,S solo
  BREITKOPF-L perf mat rent   (H156)

Radamisto: Sommi Dei, For Solo Voice
  And String Orchestra
  string orch,S solo
  BOIS perf mat rent   (H157)

Rinaldo: Overture (First Version)
  [10']
  2ob,strings,cont
  KALMUS A4343 sc $2.00, set $4.00,

HANDEL, GEORGE FRIDERIC (cont'd.)

pts $.75, ea. (H158)

Rinaldo: Sibillar Gli Angui d'Aletto,
For Solo Voice And Orchestra
ob,bsn,2trp,timp,strings,hpsd,B
solo
BREITKOPF-L perf mat rent (H159)

Rinaldo: Suite
2ob,strings [15'] KALMUS A7086 sc
$10.00, set $14.00, pts $2.00,
ea. (H160)

Royal Fireworks Music
MMB perf mat rent (H161)
(Redlich, H.F.) "Feuerwerksmusik"
study sc DEUTSCHER 4208B f.s.
(H162)

see Water Music

Salve Regina for Solo Voice and
Orchestra
(Seiffert) BREITKOPF-L perf mat
rent (H163)

Samson: With Plaintive Notes, For
Solo Voice And Orchestra
KALMUS A6222 sc $4.00, set $5.00,
pts $1.00, ea. (H164)

Saul: Overture
(Prout) 2.2.2.2. 2.0.0.0. strings
[15'] KALMUS A2379 sc $7.50, set
$15.00, pts $1.00, ea., perf mat
rent (H165)

Serse: Frondi Tenere; Ombra Mai Fu,
For Solo Voice And Orchestra,
[arr.]
(Mottl) "Xerxes: Meine Liebliche
Platane; So Schatt'gen Raum, For
Solo Voice And Orchestra"
0.1.2.2. 1.0.0.0. harp,strings,S
solo BREITKOPF-L perf mat rent
(H166)

Serse: Suite
(Hoffmann) "Xerxes: Suite" KALMUS
A7129 sc $10.00, set $10.00, pts
$2.00, ea. (H167)

Silete Venti, For Solo Voice And
Orchestra
"Nun Schweiget Winde, For Solo
Voice And Orchestra" BREITKOPF-L
perf mat rent (H168)

Solomon: Entrance Of The Queen Of
Sheba
"Arrival Of The Queen Of Sheba"
2ob,bsn,strings [4'] OXFORD perf
mat rent (H169)

Solomon: Overture [10']
2ob,strings,cont
(Schering) KALMUS A2383 sc $4.00,
set $7.00, pts $1.00, ea. (H170)

Solomon: Sacred Raptures Cheer My
Heart, For Solo Voice And
Orchestra
KALMUS A6223 sc $3.00, set $5.00,
pts $1.00, ea. (H171)

Sonata for Trumpet and String
Orchestra in F, MIN 1, [arr.]
(Thilde, J.) string orch,trp solo
[9'55"] BILLAUDOT perf mat rent
(H172)

Sonata for Trumpet and String
Orchestra in F, MIN 2, [arr.]
(Jevtic, I.) string orch,trp solo
[9'] BILLAUDOT perf mat rent
(H173)

Sonata for Trumpet and String
Orchestra in G minor, [arr.]
(Thilde, J.) string orch,trp solo
[7'] sc BILLAUDOT f.s., perf mat
rent (H174)

Song Of Jupiter[arr.]
(Anderson, Leroy) 2+pic.2.2.2.4sax.
4.3.3.1. timp,strings [4'] KALMUS
A7317 sc $7.00, set $15.00, pts
$.75, ea. (H175)

Suite for Trumpet and String
Orchestra in D, [arr.]
(Thilde, J.) string orch,trp solo
[10'] BILLAUDOT perf mat rent
(H176)

Suite in F, MIN 124 [11']
string orch,hpsd
(Martini) KALMUS A5609 sc $8.00,
set $5.00, pts $1.00, ea. (H177)

Suite in G minor, MIN 125 [11']
string orch,hpsd
(Martini) KALMUS A5610 sc $8.00,
set $5.00, pts $1.00, ea. (H178)

Tamerlan: Erd' Und Himmel Mag Sich
Wappnen, For Solo Voice And
Orchestra
see Tamerlano: Ciel E Terra Armi Di

HANDEL, GEORGE FRIDERIC (cont'd.)

Sdegno, For Solo Voice And
Orchestra

Tamerlano: Ciel E Terra Armi Di
Sdegno, For Solo Voice And
Orchestra
4ob,2bsn,3trp,timp,hpsd,strings,T
solo
"Tamerlan: Erd' Und Himmel Mag Sich
Wappnen, For Solo Voice And
Orchestra" BREITKOPF-L perf mat
rent (H179)

Theodora: Overture [12']
2ob,strings,cont
(Schering) KALMUS A2384 sc $5.00,
set $7.00, pts $1.00, ea. (H180)
(Schering) KAHNT KT 8938 f.s.
(H181)

Tolomeo: Che Piu Si Tarda Omai, For
Solo Voice And String Orchestra
string orch,T solo
BREITKOPF-L perf mat rent (H182)

Twelve Sinfonias
see Zwolf Sinfonien

Water Music
(reprinted from the Deutsche
Handelgesellschaft edition of
1886) sc DOVER 250709 $4.95
contains also: Royal Fireworks
Music (H183)

Xerxes: Meine Liebliche Platane; So
Schatt'gen Raum, For Solo Voice
And Orchestra
see Serse: Frondi Tenere; Ombra Mai
Fu, For Solo Voice And Orchestra,
[arr.]

Xerxes: Suite
see Serse: Suite

Zwolf Sinfonien
"Twelve Sinfonias" KALMUS A7089 sc
$12.00, set $10.00, pts $2.00,
ea. (H184)

HANDELS ELITE QUADRILLE see Strauss,
Johann, [Jr.]

HANDLER, LEONARD (1946-   )
Concerto for Guitar and Orchestra
[18']
1.1.1.1. 1.0.0.0. strings,gtr
solo
PRESSER perf mat rent (H185)

HANDOSHKIN, IVAN
see KHANDOSHKIN, IVAN

HANDS see Palsson, Pall P.

HANNEMANN, JOHANNES
Symphonische Fantasie Uber B.A.C.H.
KISTNER (H186)

HANNIKÁINEN, ILMARI (1892-1955)
Odotan Jouluvierasta, For Solo Voice
And String Orchestra[arr.]
(Kuusisto, I.) string orch,solo
voice [2'] FAZER perf mat rent
(H187)

HANNIKAINEN, P.J. (1854-1924)
Joulun Kellot, For Solo Voice And
Orchestra [arr.]
(Kuusisto, I.) harp,strings,solo
voice [3'27"] FAZER perf mat rent
(H188)
Kautta Tyynen, Vienon Yon, For Solo
Voice And String Orchestra [arr.]
(Kuusisto, I.) string orch,solo
voice [2'22"] FAZER perf mat rent
(H189)
Tuikkikaa, Oi Joulun Tahtoset, For
Solo Voice And String Orchestra
[arr.]
(Kuusisto, I.) string orch,solo
voice [2'] FAZER perf mat rent
(H190)

HANNIKAINEN, VÄINÖ (1900-1960)
On Maasa Hanget Puhtahat, For Solo
Voice And String Orchestra [arr.]
(Kuusisto, I.) string orch,solo
voice [2'] FAZER perf mat rent
(H191)

HANS CHRISTIAN ANDERSEN: NO TWO PEOPLE,
FOR SOLO VOICES AND ORCHESTRA see
Loesser, Frank

HANS HEILING: AN JENEM TAG, FOR SOLO
VOICE AND ORCHESTRA see Marschner,
Heinrich (August)

HANS OG GRETE see Hauger, Kristian

HANS UND GRETE see Mahler, Gustav

HANSEN, THEODORE CARL (1935-   )
Contrasts, For English Horn And
String Orchestra
string orch,English horn solo
SEESAW (H192)

HANSON, HOWARD (1896-1981)
Merry Mount: Children's Dance
2.2.2+bass clar.2+contrabsn.
4.3.3.0. 5perc,2harp,strings
WARNER perf mat rent (H193)

Merry Mount: Love Duet [5']
2+pic.2.2+bass clar.2+contrabsn.
4.3.3.1. harp,strings
WARNER perf mat rent (H194)

HANUŠ, JAN (1915-   )
Galeria Goldoni *Op.42a [21']
CZECH RADIO (H195)

Notturni Di Praga *Op.75 [27']
CESKY HUD. (H196)

Symphony No. 6, Op. 92 [28']
CESKY HUD. (H197)

Three Essays *Op.86 [22']
CZECH RADIO (H198)

HAPAX see Brenet, Therese

HAPPINESS see Koch, Marten

HAPPY BIRTHDAY ALLA FRANCAIX see
Francaix, Jean

HAPPY DAY, THE: OVERTURE see Cimarosa,
Domenico, Giorno Felice, Il:
Overture

HAPPY GRASSLAND see Qin, Yong Cheng

HAPPY PRINCE, THE, FOR NARRATOR AND
CHAMBER ORCHESTRA see Bach, Jan
Morris

HAPPY VOICES see Del Tredici, David

HAQUINIUS, ALGOT (1886-1966)
Archipelago Isle, For Solo Voice And
Orchestra [3']
1.1.2.1. 2.1.0.0. strings,med
solo
NORDISKA perf mat rent (H199)

Passion Of Our Lord, The, For Solo
Voice And Orchestra [5']
2.2.2.2. 4.2.3.1. timp,perc,
strings,low solo
NORDISKA perf mat rent (H200)

HAR SLET INGEN HAST, DET see Wellejus,
Henning

HARA, HIROSHI (1933-   )
Concerto for Piano and Orchestra
[30']
3(pic).2.2.2. 2.2.3.0. timp,
strings,pno solo
sc ZEN-ON 899443 f.s., perf mat
rent (H201)

Concerto for Violin and Orchestra
[27']
2(pic).2.2.2. 2.2.2.0. timp,perc,
strings,vln solo
sc ZEN-ON 899449 f.s., perf mat
rent (H202)

Serenade No. 1 [20']
string orch
sc ZEN-ON f.s., perf mat rent
(H203)

Serenade No. 2 [23']
string orch
sc ZEN-ON f.s., perf mat rent
(H204)

Serenade No. 3 [20']
string orch
sc ZEN-ON f.s., perf mat rent
(H205)

Sinfonia in F [50']
3(pic).3(English horn).3(bass
clar).3(contrabsn). 4.3.3.1.
timp,perc,strings
sc ZEN-ON 899410 f.s., perf mat
rent (H206)

HARAKKA, FOR SOLO VOICE AND ORCHESTRA
see Heimovalta, Edvin

HARBISON, JOHN (1938-   )
Concerto For Double Brass Choir And
Orchestra [20']
2.2.2.2. 4.3.3.1. timp,strings
SCHIRM.G perf mat rent (H207)

Concerto for Oboe, Clarinet and
String Orchestra [13']
string orch,ob solo,clar solo
AMP perf mat rent (H208)

Concerto for Piano and Orchestra
[20']
2.2.2.2. 2.2.2.1. perc,harp,
strings,pno solo
sc AMP f.s., perf mat rent (H209)

Concerto for Viola and Orchestra
[20']
2(pic).2(English horn).2(bass

HARBISON, JOHN (cont'd.)

clar).2. 2.2.0.0. timp,perc,
harp,cel,strings,vla solo
SCHIRM.G perf mat rent   (H210)

Concerto for Violin and Orchestra
[28']
2.2.2.2. 2.2.2.1. timp,vibra,
harp,pno,strings,vln solo
AMP perf mat rent   (H211)

Diotima [18']
3.2.3.3. 4.3.3.1. timp,perc,harp,
cel,strings
AMP perf mat rent   (H212)

Remembering Gatsby [8']
3(pic).3(English horn).3(bass
clar).2+contrabsn.soprano sax.
4.3.3.1. timp,perc,pno,strings
study sc AMP 50480538 $18.00, perf
mat rent   (H213)

Symphony No. 1 [23']
3(pic,alto fl).3(English
horn).3(bass
clar).3(contrabsn). 4.2.3.1.
timp,6perc,harp,strings
study sc AMP 50480027 $16.00, perf
mat rent   (H214)

Symphony No. 2 [23']
3(pic).2+English horn.2+clar in E
flat+bass clar.2+contrabsn.
4.4.3.1. timp,3perc,harp,pno,
strings
study sc AMP f.s., perf mat rent
                                (H215)

Ulysses' Bow [33']
3(pic).3(English horn).2+clar in
E flat+bass clar.2(contrabsn).
4.2.3.1. timp,4perc,harp,
strings
AMP perf mat rent   (H216)

Ulysses' Raft [47']
3(pic).3(English horn).2+clar in
E flat+bass clar.2(contrabsn).
4.2.3.1. timp,4perc,harp,
strings
AMP perf mat rent   (H217)

HARBOUR NOCTURNE see Pruden, Larry

HARD TERMS, THE, FOR SOLO VOICE AND
ORCHESTRA see Sköld, Yngve

HARD TRIALS, FOR SOLO VOICE AND
ORCHESTRA [ARR.]
(Burleigh, Harry T.) 2.2.1.2.
2.2.2.1. strings,med solo COLOMBO
perf mat rent   (H218)

HARFENSPIELER I, FOR SOLO VOICE AND
ORCHESTRA see Wolf, Hugo

HARFENSPIELER II, FOR SOLO VOICE AND
ORCHESTRA see Wolf, Hugo

HARFENSPIELER III, FOR SOLO VOICE AND
ORCHESTRA see Wolf, Hugo

HARLEM see Ellington, Edward Kennedy
(Duke)

HARLEQUIN, FOR PIANO AND CHAMBER
ORCHESTRA see Zahler, Noel Barry

HARMONICA see Lachenmann, Helmut
Friedrich

HARMONIE CELESTE see Strauss, Johann,
[Sr.]

HARMONIELEHRE see Adams, John

HARMONIUM, FOR SOLO VOICE AND ORCHESTRA
see Gerber, Steven R.

HARMONY see Panufnik, Andrzej

HARMONY OF SILENCE, THE see Lendvay,
Kamillo

HARO see Dusapin, Pascal

HAROLD EN ITALIE see Berlioz, Hector
(Louis)

HARPER, EDWARD JAMES (1941-   )
Concerto for Clarinet and Orchestra
[18']
2.2.2.2. 4.2.3.1. harp,strings,
clar solo
OXFORD perf mat rent   (H219)

Fantasia IV, For Violin, Piano, And
Orchestra
0.2.2.2. 2.2.0.0. strings,vln
solo,pno solo
sc OXFORD 363917-3 $54.95, perf mat
rent   (H220)

HARPER, EDWARD JAMES (cont'd.)

Fantasia V [5']
2.2.2.2. 2.2.0.0. timp,perc,
strings
OXFORD perf mat rent   (H221)

Intrada After Monteverdi, Chamber
Orchestra Version [5']
2.0.2.2. 2.2.0.0. timp,perc,
strings
OXFORD perf mat rent   (H222)

Intrada After Monteverdi, Full
Orchestra Version [5']
3.2.2.2. 4.3.3.1. timp,2perc,pno,
harp,strings
OXFORD perf mat rent   (H223)

HARRIS, MATTHEW
Ancient Greek Melodies [18']
2.2.2.2. 2.2.2.0. timp,3perc,
strings
sc AM.COMP.AL. $44.10, perf mat
rent   (H224)

Illuminations [11']
2.3.3.3. 4.2.3.1. timp,perc,
2harp,cel,pno,strings
sc AM.COMP.AL. $39.40   (H225)

Invitation To The Waltz [7']
string orch
sc AM.COMP.AL. $21.55, perf mat
rent   (H226)

Music for Orchestra [10']
2.3.3.2. 4.3.3.1. timp,5perc,
2harp,cel,pno,strings
sc AM.COMP.AL. $63.10   (H227)

HARRIS, ROSS
Hills Of Time, The [11']
2.2.2.2. 2.2.2.0. timp,strings
sc WAI-TE-ATA f.s.   (H228)

HARRIS, ROY ELLSWORTH (1898-1979)
Canticle Of The Sun, For Solo Voice
And Instrumental Ensemble [37']
fl,English horn,clar,bass clar,
pno,3vln,2vla,vcl,high solo
AMP perf mat rent   (H229)

Dance [5']
2+pic.2+English horn.2+bass
clar.2. 4.3.3.1. timp,perc,
harp,strings
SCHIRM.G perf mat rent   (H230)

Symphony No. 8
2+pic.2+English horn.2+bass
clar.2+contrabsn. 4.3.3.1.
timp,perc,harp,strings
(San Francisco Symphony) SCHIRM.G
perf mat rent   (H231)

HARRIS, RUSSELL G. (1914-   )
Litany, The, For Solo Voices And
Orchestra *Op.19 [12']
4.3.3.2.2sax. 4.2.3.1. timp,perc,
harp,strings,SABar soli
sc AM.COMP.AL. $15.20   (H232)

HARRISON, LOU (1917-   )
At The Tomb Of Charles Ives
trom,2-3harp,tam-tam,strings, 2
psalteries, 2 dulcimers (extra
inst pts: $1.00) PEER sc
60073-851 $6.00, set 60072-852
$25.00   (H233)

Concerto For Piano With Selected
Orchestra [25']
3trom,4perc,2harp,strings,pno
solo
PETERS P67077 perf mat rent.   (H234)

Elegiac Symphony [31']
3(pic).3(English
horn).3.3(contrabsn). 4.3.3.1.
timp,perc,2harp,pno,org,cel,
vibra,strings, tack pno
PEER perf mat rent   (H235)

Pacifika Rondo [25']
fl,pic, niguk piris or sax or
clar, trb, jahla or cel, vibra,
sheng or psaltery, kayageum or
harp or psaltery, hpsd, org,
perc, strings
PEER perf mat rent   (H236)

Suite for Violin and String
Orchestra, [arr.]
(Lewis) string orch,vln solo PEER
perf mat rent   (H237)

Suite for Violin, Piano and Orchestra
[17']
2.1.0.0. 0.0.0.0. harp,cel, tack
piano, tam-tam, 2vcl, db, vln
solo, pno solo
PETERS P67075 perf mat rent   (H238)

HARRISON, LOU (cont'd.)

Symphony No. 3 [30']
3.3.3.3. 4.3.3.1. 3perc,harp,cel,
strings, tackpiano
PETERS P66922 rent   (H239)

HARTIG, HEINZ FRIEDRICH (1907-1969)
Aria And Toccata, For Piano And
Orchestra *Op.30a (from Concerto
For Piano And Orchestra, Op. 30)
[15']
1(pic).1.1.1. 2.2.1.1. timp,
2perc,harp,strings,pno solo
BOTE perf mat rent   (H240)

HARTKE, STEPHEN PAUL (1952-   )
Alvorada
12vln,4vla,4vcl,2db
NORRUTH 4.0090.7 perf mat rent
                                (H241)

Bull Transcended, The [5']
string orch
PEER perf mat rent   (H242)

Infinito, L', For Solo Voice And
Orchestra
2.1.2.2. 2.1.1.0. perc,harp,pno&
cel,8vln,3vla,3vcl,db,S solo
UNICORN 4.0070.7 perf mat rent
                                (H243)

Maltese Cat Blues [16']
2+pic.2+English horn.2+clar in E
flat.3. 4.3.3.1. 4perc,strings
NORRUTH perf mat rent   (H244)

Pacific Rim [10']
2(pic).2+opt English horn.1+clar
in E flat.2. 2+opt 2horn.2.2.0.
perc,strings
NORRUTH perf mat rent   (H245)

Precession [4']
1.0+English horn.1.1. 1.1.0.0.
2perc,pno,vln,vla,vcl,db
NORRUTH perf mat rent   (H246)

Symphony No. 1
3.3.3.2.2alto sax. 4.4.3.1. perc,
strings
UNICORN 4.0010.7 perf mat rent
                                (H247)

Symphony No. 2 [23']
2.2.2.2. 2.2.0.0. perc,cel,harp,
strings
NORRUTH perf mat rent   (H248)

Two Songs For An Uncertain Age, For
Solo Voice And Orchestra [16']
3.3.3.3. 4.3.3.1. timp,2perc,pno,
cel,harp,strings,S solo
NORRUTH perf mat rent   (H249)

HARTLEY, WALTER SINCLAIR (1927-   )
Psalm for Strings
KALMUS A7460 sc $5.00, set $7.50,
pts $1.50, ea.   (H250)

Rhapsody for Saxophone and String
Orchestra
string orch,tenor sax solo
sc,pts DORN $54.00   (H251)

Sinfonia, No. 7 [7'30"]
2(pic).1.2(bass clar).1. 2.2.1.1.
timp,perc,strings
KALMUS A7042 sc $20.00, set $40.00,
pts $2.50, ea., perf mat rent
                                (H252)

Symphony No. 3
sc GALAXY 1.3006 $15.00   (H253)

HARTMANN, CHRISTIAN (1910-   )
Mot Natt
2.2.2.2. 4.2.3.0. perc,harp,
strings
"Night Fall" NORGE   (H254)

Night Fall
see Mot Natt

HARTMANN, EMIL (1836-1898)
Concerto for Violin and Orchestra,
Op. 26
KISTNER perf mat rent   (H255)

Skandinavische Volksmusik *Op.30
[8']
2.2.2.2. 4.2.3.1. timp,perc,harp,
strings
BREITKOPF-W perf mat rent   (H256)

Symphony No. 3 in D [28']
2.2.2.2. 4.2.3.1. timp,strings
HANSEN-DEN perf mat rent   (H257)

HARTMANN, ERICH (1920-   )
Divertimento for Double Bass and
Orchestra [12']
perc,harp,strings,db solo
BOTE perf mat rent   (H258)

HARTMANN, JOHAN PEDER EMILIUS
    (1805-1900)
  Corregio
    sc,pts SAMFUNDET f.s.   (H259)

  Hakon Jarl
    sc,pts SAMFUNDET f.s.   (H260)

  Yrsa
    sc,pts SAMFUNDET f.s.   (H261)

HARTMANN, KARL AMADEUS (1905-1963)
  Sinfonia Tragica [35']
    2.2.2.3. 4.3.3.1. timp,perc,cel,
    harp,strings
    SCHOTTS perf mat rent   (H262)

HARTMANN, PER JOHANNES (1945-   )
  Evocare [23']
    4.5.5.4. 6.4.4.2. timp,perc,harp,
    cel,pno,strings
    NORGE   (H263)

  Sonetto Di Petrarca *Op.26 [11']
    1.1.1.1. 1.1.1.0. strings
    NORGE   (H264)

  Tausenundeineblume, Op. 33
    7(pic).3(English horn).5(bass
    clar).4(contrabsn).
    5.4(cornet).4.1. strings
    NORGE   (H265)

HARTMANN, THOMAS ALEXANDROVICH DE
    (1885-1956)
  Concerto for Violin and Orchestra,
    Op. 66 [29']
    3.2.2.2. 4.3.1.0. timp,perc,harp,
    pno,strings,vln solo
    BOOSEY perf mat rent   (H266)

HARTO see Hidalgo, Manuel

HARTY, [SIR] HAMILTON (1879-1941)
  Concerto for Violin and Orchestra
    KALMUS A6429 sc $50.00, set $50.00,
    pts $3.00, ea., perf mat rent
                                 (H267)
  With The Wild Geese
    KALMUS A7184 sc $30.00, set $75.00,
    pts $3.00, ea., perf mat rent
                                 (H268)

HARTZELL, EUGENE (1932-   )
  Four Latin Lyrics, For Solo Voice And
    Orchestra [20']
    2.2.2.2. 2.2.0.0. harp,strings,T
    solo
    DOBLINGER perf mat rent   (H269)

  Sinfoniettina For Strings [14']
    string orch
    DOBLINGER perf mat rent   (H270)

  Variations for Chamber Orchestra
    [15']
    1.1.1.1. 1.1.1.1. perc,pno,
    strings
    DOBLINGER perf mat rent   (H271)

HARVEST see Gould, Morton

HARVEST SCENES see Chu, Wei

HARVEY, JONATHAN (1939-   )
  Bhakti [50']
    1(pic).1(English horn).1(clar in
    E flat)+bass clar.0. 1.1.1.0.
    perc,harp,pno,3vln,vla,vcl,
    electronic tape
    FABER perf mat rent   (H272)

  Chaccone On "Iam Dulcis Amica" [9']
    2(pic).2(English horn).2(bass
    clar).5. 4.4.4.1. 3perc,
    strings,string quar soli
    NOVELLO perf mat rent   (H273)

  Easter Orisons [19']
    2(pic).2(English horn).2.2.
    2.0.0.0. 1-2perc,11vln,3vla,
    3vcl,db
    sc FABER F0821 f.s., perf mat rent
                                 (H274)
  Gong-Ring [22']
    4perc,cel,harp,strings, ring
    modulator
    FABER perf mat rent   (H275)

  Inner Light 2, For Solo Voices And
    Instrumental Ensemble
    horn,trp,trom,perc,pno,elec org,
    2vln,vla,vcl,synthesizer,SSATB
    soli
    study sc FABER F0559 f.s.   (H276)

  Inner Light 3 [30']
    3.3.3.3. 4.3.3.1. 4perc,pno,cel,
    harp,strings,2Wagner tuba,
    electronic tape
    sc NOVELLO 2853-90 $22.00, perf mat
    rent   (H277)

  Lightness And Weight, For Tuba And
    Orchestra [15']
    2+pic.2+English horn.2+bass
    clar.2+contrabsn. 5.2.3.1.

HARVEY, JONATHAN (cont'd.)
    4perc,harp,strings,tuba solo
    FABER perf mat rent   (H278)

  Madonna Of Winter And Spring [40']
    4.3.3.3. 4.4.3.1. 5perc,harp,pno,
    strings,2synthesizer,electronic
    equipment
    FABER perf mat rent   (H279)

  Persephone Dream
    study sc NOVELLO 2396-90 $15.25
                                 (H280)
  Smiling Immortal [17']
    1.1.1.0. 0.0.0.0. perc,pno,string
    quar,electronic tape
    FABER perf mat rent   (H281)

  Symphony [18']
    2(pic).2.3.2. 4.3.2.1. 3perc,
    timp,harp,cel&pno,strings
    NOVELLO perf mat rent   (H282)

  Whom Ye Adore [15']
    3.3.3.3. 4.4.3.1. 3perc,harp,pno,
    strings
    FABER perf mat rent   (H283)

HASARDOREN see Rybrant, Stig

HASE UND DER IGEL, DER, FOR NARRATOR
    AND ORCHESTRA see Reuter, Fritz

HASEGAWA, YOSHIO (1907-1981)
  Noh [15']
    fl,ob,clar,pno,vibra,strings
    sc ONGAKU 492532 f.s., perf mat
    rent   (H284)

HASELBACH, JOSEF (1936-   )
  Prelude for Orchestra [13']
    3.3.2.2. 4.0.0.0. perc,2harp,
    strings
    HUG GH 11250 perf mat rent   (H285)

  Sinfonietta for Orchestra [16']
    string orch
    sc HUG GH 11301 f.s., perf mat rent
                                 (H286)
HASELBÖCK, MARTIN (1954-   )
  Manilom, For Solo Voices And
    Instrumental Ensemble [19']
    2fl,3vln,3vla,3vcl,3db,SSS soli
    UNIVER. perf mat rent   (H287)

HASQUENOPH, PIERRE (1922-1982)
  Concertino for Trumpet and String
    Orchestra [10']
    string orch,trp solo
    ESCHIG perf mat rent   (H288)

  Concerto De Nuremberg, For Alto
    Saxophone And Strings *Op.43a
    [14']
    7vln,2vla,2vcl,db,alto sax solo
    (completed by Jean-Jacques Werner)
    ESCHIG perf mat rent   (H289)

  Concerto for Flute and String
    Orchestra [20']
    string orch,fl solo
    ESCHIG perf mat rent   (H290)

  Papillon Qui Tapait Du Pied, Le [18']
    min sc CHOUDENS f.s., perf mat rent
                                 (H291)
  Pentamorphoses [18']
    hpsd,11strings
    CHOUDENS perf mat rent   (H292)

  Quatre Poesies For Solo Voice And
    Orchestra
    2.2.2.2. 2.2.1.0. timp,perc,cel,
    pno,strings,S solo
    BILLAUDOT perf mat rent   (H293)

HASSAN: SERENADE, FOR VIOLONCELLO AND
    ORCHESTRA [ARR.] see Delius,
    Frederick

HASSE, JOHANN ADOLPH (1699-1783)
  Clemenza Di Tito, La: Allegro Ma Non
    Troppo From Act III [2']
    2ob,bsn,hpsd,strings, archlute
    SUPRAPHON   (H294)

  Clemenza Di Tito, La: Tardi Savoede
    D'un Tradimento, For Solo Voice
    And Orchestra [3']
    1.0.0.1. 2.0.0.0. hpsd,strings,T
    solo
    SUPRAPHON   (H295)

  Concerto for Flute and String
    Orchestra in F, MIN 3
    (Jeney; Müller; Fodor) EMB f.s. sc
    6235, pts 6236   (H296)

  Concerto for Mandolin and Orchestra
    [5']
    lute,gtr,strings without vla,mand
    solo
    (Neemann) KALMUS A5570 sc $5.00,
    set $10.00, pts $1.25, ea. (H297)

HASSE, JOHANN ADOLPH (cont'd.)

  Pallido Il Sole, For Solo Voice And
    String Orchestra [3']
    string orch,cont,countertenor
    (Blanchard, R.) BOIS perf mat rent
                                 (H298)
HASSENEH see Press, Jacques

HASSENEH: WEDDING DANCE [ARR.] see
    Press, Jacques

HATE-LOVE, FOR VIOLONCELLO AND STRING
    ORCHESTRA see Nordgren, Pehr Henrik

HATIKVAH see Glick, Srul Irving

HATRIK, JURAJ (1941-   )
  Ponorena Hudba, For Solo Voice,
    Violin And Strings
    12strings,vln solo,S solo
    "Submerged Music, For Solo Voice,
    Violin And Strings" SLOV.HUD.FOND
                                 (H299)
  Submerged Music, For Solo Voice,
    Violin And Strings
    see Ponorena Hudba, For Solo Voice,
    Violin And Strings

HAUBENSTOCK-RAMATI, ROMAN (1919-   )
  Beaubourg Musique [18']
    2fl,2trom,4perc,harp,cel,pno,
    hpsd,4vln,2vla,2vcl
    sc UNIVER. UE19476 f.s., perf mat
    rent   (H300)

  Concerto for Harpsichord and
    Orchestra [10']
    2fl,2clar,timp,2perc,harp,cel,
    strings,hpsd solo
    min sc UNIVER. 16976 $15.00, perf
    mat rent   (H301)

  Imaginaire [20']
    4fl,4trom,4perc,harp,cel,pno,
    hpsd,strings without db
    UNIVER. perf mat rent   (H302)

  Music for 12 Instruments [12']
    fl,ob,clar,bsn,horn,trp,trom,
    string quin
    study sc HANSEN-GER f.s.   (H303)

  Nocturnes I
    2fl,4trom,perc,harp,cel,hpsd,pno,
    strings
    study sc UNIVER. $28.00   (H304)

  Nocturnes II
    4fl,4trom,hpsd,harp,cel,pno,
    4perc,16vln,8vla,8vcl
    sc UNIVER. UE 18309 f.s.   (H305)

  Nocturnes III [20']
    4fl,4trom,4perc,harp,cel,pno,
    hpsd,strings without db
    UNIVER. perf mat rent   (H306)

  Sequences, For Violin And Chamber
    Orchestra [13']
    2fl,2perc,harp,cel,pno,2vln,vla,
    vcl,vln solo
    UNIVER. perf mat rent   (H307)

  Symphonien [20']
    4fl,4trom,4perc,cel,harp,pno,
    strings
    HANSEN-GER perf mat rent   (H308)

HAUDEBERT, LUCIEN (1877-1963)
  Voyage En Bretagne [32']
    2.2.2.2. 2.1.3.0. timp,perc,pno,
    strings
    BILLAUDOT perf mat rent   (H309)

HAUFF, WILHELM GOTTLIEB (1755-1807)
  Concerto for Horn and Orchestra in E
    flat [13'30"]
    2ob,2horn,strings,horn solo
    (Leloir, E.) sc BILLAUDOT f.s.,
    perf mat rent   (H310)

HAUFRECHT, HERBERT (1909-   )
  Divertimento for Guitar and Chamber
    Orchestra [13']
    2.2.2.1. 2.2.1.0. perc,strings,
    gtr solo
    sc AM.COMP.AL. $16.75, perf mat
    rent   (H311)

  Suite for String Orchestra [14']
    string orch
    AM.COMP.AL. perf mat rent   (H312)

  Suite On Catskill Mountain Tunes
    [12']
    1.2.2.2. 2.0.0.0. strings
    sc AM.COMP.AL. $36.75, perf mat
    rent   (H313)

  Variations On A Catskill Mountain
    Folksong [4']
    string orch
    sc AM.COMP.AL. $5.40   (H314)

HAUG, HALVOR (1952-   )
Furuenes Sang [11'30"]
    string orch
    NORGE   (H315)

Miniature Concerto, For Horn And
    Orchestra [17']
    2.2.2.2. 2.0.0.0. timp,perc,
    strings,horn solo
    NORGE   (H316)

Poema Patetica [13']
    2.2.2.2. 4.2.3.0. timp,perc,harp,
    strings
    NORGE   (H317)

Sinfonietta [19']
    3.2.2.2. 4.2.3.1. timp,perc,
    strings
    NORSK   (H318)

Stillhet [9']
    string orch
    "Stillness" NORGE   (H319)

Stillness
    see Stillhet

Symfonisk Bilde [10']
    3.3.3.3. 4.3.3.1. timp,perc,pno,
    cel,strings
    "Symphonic Picture" NORGE   (H320)

Symfoniske Konturer [9']
    3.2.2.2. 4.3.3.1. timp,perc,
    strings
    "Symphonic Contours" NORGE   (H321)

Symphonic Contours
    see Symfoniske Konturer

Symphonic Picture
    see Symfonisk Bilde

Symphony No. 1 [29']
    3(pic).3(English horn).3(bass
    clar).3(contrabsn). 4.3.3.1.
    timp,perc,cel,harp,strings
    NORSK   (H322)

Winter Scenery [9']
    2.2.2.2. 4.2.3.0. timp,perc,harp,
    strings
    NORGE   (H323)

HAUGER, KRISTIAN
Hans Og Grete
    pts MUSIKK f.s.   (H324)

Norske Toner
    "Norwegian Folk Tunes" pts MUSIKK
    f.s.   (H325)

Norwegian Folk Tunes
    see Norske Toner

HAUGLAND, GLENN ERIK (1961-   )
Den Som Bygger Pa Stein [5']
    3.3.3.3. 4.3.3.1. timp,perc,harp,
    strings
    NORGE   (H326)

HAUKSSON, THORSTEINN (1948-   )
Ad Astra
    2.2.2.1. 2.1.1.0. perc,harp,
    strings
    ICELAND 041-005   (H327)

Boy And The Glass Violin, The
    3.3.4.4. 4.4.3.1. timp,perc,harp,
    strings
    ICELAND 041-006   (H328)

HAUNTED LANDSCAPE, A see Crumb, George

HAUSEGGER, SIEGMUND VON (1872-1948)
Drei Hymnen An Die Nacht, For Solo
    Voice And Orchestra [15']
    3.3.3.3. 4.3.2.1. timp,perc,harp,
    strings,Bar solo
    KAHNT perf mat rent   (H329)

HAUST see Kielland, Olav

HAUTA-AHO, TEPPO (1941-   )
Fantasy for Trumpet and Orchestra
    [16']
    2.2.3.2. 3.3.3.1. timp,3perc,pno,
    cel,strings,trp solo
    sc SUOMEN f.s.   (H330)

HAUTE VOLEE POLKA see Strauss, Johann,
    [Jr.]

HAUTEURS-LOINTAINS see Lejet, Edith

HAVAMAL, FOR SOLO VOICE AND ORCHESTRA
    see Tveitt, Geirr

HAVANAISE, FOR VIOLIN AND ORCHESTRA see
    Saint-Saëns, Camille

HAVANGSVIT, FOR PIANO AND STRING
    ORCHESTRA see Söderlundh, Lille
    Bror

HAWKINS, JOHN (1944-   )
Two Pieces For Orchestra [8']
    3.3.3(clar in E flat).3. 3.3.3.1.
    timp,4perc,harp,pno&cel,strings
    CAN.MUS.CENT. MI 1100 H393TW (H331)

HAXTON, KENNETH
Chorale, Prelude And Fugue [11']
    2.2.3.2. 4.3.3.1. timp,strings
    AM.COMP.AL. perf mat rent   (H332)

Concerto for Piano and Orchestra, No.
    1 [45']
    2.3.2.2. 4.3.3.1. timp,perc,
    strings,pno solo
    AM.COMP.AL. perf mat rent   (H333)

Elegy [10']
    2.2.2.2. 4.2.3.1. timp,perc,
    strings
    sc AM.COMP.AL. $16.20, perf mat
    rent   (H334)

Fugue [4']
    2.2.2.2. 4.3.3.1. timp,perc,
    strings
    sc AM.COMP.AL. $13.80, perf mat
    rent   (H335)

Involvement [8']
    2.2.3.3. 4.3.3.1. timp,perc,
    strings
    sc AM.COMP.AL. $23.95, perf mat
    rent   (H336)

Largo [9']
    string orch
    sc AM.COMP.AL. $15.45, perf mat
    rent   (H337)

Music for English Horn and String
    Orchestra [7']
    string orch,English horn solo
    sc AM.COMP.AL. $9.95, perf mat rent
                                 (H338)

Rose For Emily, A [7']
    2.2.3.2. 4.2.3.1. timp,perc,
    strings
    sc AM.COMP.AL. $22.20, perf mat
    rent   (H339)

Welty Women [43']
    2.3.3.2. 4.3.3.1. timp,perc,pno,
    strings
    sc AM.COMP.AL. $107.65, perf mat
    rent   (H340)

HAYASHI, HIKARU (1931-   )
Symphony No. 2 [24']
    3(pic).2(English horn).3(bass
    clar).2. 4.3.3.0. perc,strings,
    pno solo
    (Canciones) sc ZEN-ON 899390 f.s.,
    perf mat rent   (H341)

HAYDN, [FRANZ] JOSEPH (1732-1809)
Anima Del Filosofo Ossia Orfeo Et
    Euridice, L': Overture
    0.2.0.2. 2.2.0.0. timp,harp,hpsd,
    strings
    (Wirth, Helmut) BÄREN. BA 4658
                                 (H342)
Arianna A Naxos, For Solo Voice And
    Orchestra
    (Wishart, Peter) 2ob,bsn,2horn,
    strings,Mez solo [20'] STAINER
    HL224 perf mat rent   (H343)

Arianna A Naxos, For Solo Voice And
    Orchestra, [arr.]
    2.2.2.2. 2.2.0.0. timp,strings,
    Mez solo
    (Frank, E.) BREITKOPF-L perf mat
    rent   (H344)

Berenice Che Fai, For Solo Voice And
    Orchestra
    see Zwei Konzertarien

Cassation in E flat, Hob.II: 21
    2horn,strings
    (Abendmusik) KALMUS A5695 sc $5.00,
    set $10.00   (H345)
    (Landon, H.C.R.) sc FABER $15.00,
    perf mat rent   (H346)

Cassation in G, Hob.II: 1 [13']
    fl,ob,hpsd,strings without vla
    (Landon, H.C.R.) sc,pts DOBLINGER
    DM 846 f.s.   (H347)

Chi Vive Amante, For Solo Voice And
    Orchestra
    see Zwei Konzertarien

Circe, La: Lavatevi Presto, For Solo
    Voices And Orchestra
    1.2.0.2. 2.0.0.0. strings,TTB
    soli
    (Landon, H.C.R.) UNIV.CR voc sc
    f.s., study sc f.s., perf mat
    rent   (H348)

Concerti for Harpsichord and
    Orchestra
    (Joseph Haydn Werke, Series XV,

HAYDN, [FRANZ] JOSEPH (cont'd.)

    Vol.2) HENLE pap 5421 $71.50,
    cloth 5422 $79.75   (H349)

Concerti For One Wind Instrument And
    Orchestra
    (Joseph Haydn Werke, Series III,
    Vol.3) HENLE pap 5204 $30.75,
    cloth 5205 $39.00   (H350)

Concerto for Harpsichord and String
    Orchestra in F, Hob.XVIII: 7
    (Weelink) KALMUS A6146 sc $5.00,
    set $5.00   (H351)

Concerto for Horn and Orchestra
    see Sinfonia Concertante for
    Violin, Violoncello, Oboe,
    Bassoon and Orchestra, Op. 84, in
    B flat, Hob.I: 105

Concerto for 2 Horns and Orchestra in
    E flat
    (Winschermann; Buck) 2ob,strings,
    cont,2horn soli [24'] SIKORSKI
    perf mat rent   (H352)

Concerto for Oboe and Orchestra in C
    (Glaetzner, Burkhard) BREITKOPF-L
    sc PB 3112 f.s., pts OB 2834 f.s.
                                 (H353)

Concerto for Organ and Orchestra in
    C, Hob.XVIII: 1 [19']
    2ob,2trp,strings,org solo
    (Hodell) BREITKOPF-W sc PB 5132
    f.s., pts OB 5132 f.s., study sc
    5166 f.s.   (H354)

Concerto for Piano and Orchestra in
    C, Hob.XVIII: 5
    (Heussner) KALMUS A7283 sc $12.00,
    set $7.50, pts $1.50, ea.   (H355)

Concerto for Piano and Orchestra in
    D, Hob.XVIII: 11, [arr.]
    (Pijper, Willem) 1.2.0.2. 2.0.0.0.
    timp,strings (called Op. 21 in
    this ed) sc DONEMUS f.s., perf
    mat rent   (H356)

Concerto for Trumpet and Orchestra in
    E flat, Hob.VIIe: 1
    (McAlister) KALMUS A7278 sc $20.00,
    set $50.00, pts $3.00, ea., perf
    mat rent   (H357)
    (Smithers, Don) BREITKOPF-L sc
    PB 4081 f.s., pts OB 4081 f.s.
                                 (H358)
    (Tarr; Landon) HAYMOZ sc HMP 221
    $22.00, set HMP 222 $32.00, pts
    HMP 222 $2.00, ea.   (H359)
    (Thilde, J.) sc BILLAUDOT f.s.,
    perf mat rent   (H360)

Concerto for Violin and Orchestra in
    A, Hob.VIIa: 3
    0.2.0.0. 2.0.0.0. hpsd,strings,
    vln solo
    (Landon, H.C. Robbins) HAYMOZ sc
    HMP4 $31.00, pts HMP 5 f.s.
                                 (H361)

Concerto for Violin and Orchestra in
    C, Hob.VIIa: 1, [arr.]
    (Klengel, P.) 1.2.0.2. 2.0.0.0.
    strings,vln solo BREITKOPF-L perf
    mat rent   (H362)

Concerto for Violin and Orchestra in
    D [20']
    0.2.0.0. 2.0.0.0. strings,vln
    solo
    (Hob.VIIa:D1) SUPRAPHON   (H363)

Concerto for Violin, Harpsichord and
    String Orchestra in F, Hob.XVIII:
    6
    (Schultz) KALMUS A7396 sc $20.00,
    set $17.50, pts $2.50, ea., perf
    mat rent   (H364)

Concerto for Violoncello and
    Orchestra in C, Hob.VIIb: 1
    (Gerlach, Sonja) BAREN. sc,pts
    BA 4684 f.s., min sc TP 291 f.s.
                                 (H365)

Concerto for Violoncello and
    Orchestra in C, Hob.VIIb: 5
    *reconstruction
    (Popper, David) min sc KALMUS
    K01509 $6.00   (H366)

Concerto for Violoncello and
    Orchestra, Op. 101, in D,
    Hob.VIIb: 2
    (Gerlach, Sonja) BÄREN. BA 4681
                                 (H367)
    (Landon, H.C.R.) UNIV.CR sc f.s.,
    perf mat rent, study sc f.s., pno
    red f.s.   (H368)

Deutsche Tänze, Sechs [arr.]
    2.2.2.0. 0.2.0.0. timp,strings
    HARMONIA 3033 f.s.   (H369)

HAYDN, [FRANZ] JOSEPH (cont'd.)

Divertimento *see also Cassation

Divertimento in C, Hob.II: 11 [17']
  fl,ob,strings
  SUPRAPHON   (H370)

Divertimento in D, Hob.II: 22
  2horn,strings
  (Landon, H.C.R.) sc FABER $15.00,
  perf mat rent   (H371)

Divertimento, Op. 31, No. 1, in G,
  Hob.X: 12
  (Schmid, E.F.) KALMUS A4138 sc
  $10.00, set $12.00   (H372)

Divertimento, Op. 31, No. 3, in G,
  (Egidi) KALMUS A5880 sc $5.00, set
  $8.00   (H373)

Divertimento, Op. 31, No. 5, in G,
  Hob.X: 4
  (Schmid, E.F.) KALMUS A4138 sc
  $10.00, set $12.00   (H374)

English Opera, An: Overture
  *Hob.Ia:3
  2.2.0.2. 2.2.0.0. timp,strings
  (Landon, H.C. Robbins) sc HAYMOZ
  HMP 12 $14.00, perf mat rent   (H375)

Gypsy Rondo, [arr.]
  see Rondo All' Ongarese, [arr.]

Incontro Improvviso, L': Overture
  0.2.0.2. 2.0.0.0. timp,perc,hpsd,
  strings
  (Wirth, Helmut) BÄREN. BA 4665   (H376)

Infedeltà Delusa, L': Overture
  *Hob.Ia:1
  0.2.0.1. 2.0+opt 2trp.0.0. timp,
  strings
  (Landon, H.C. Robbins) HAYMOZ f.s.
  sc HMP 53, pts HMP 54   (H377)

Isola Disabitata, L': Overture
  1.2.0.1. 2.0.0.0. timp,strings
  (Landon, H.C. Robbins) BÄREN.
  BA 4664   (H378)

Jahreszeiten, Die: Schon Eilet Froh
  Der Ackersmann, For Solo Voice
  And Orchestra
  BREITKOPF-L perf mat rent   (H379)

Leichte Satze Aus Sinfonien
  string orch,opt ob,opt horn sc,pts
  TONGER PJT 836 f.s.   (H380)

London Symphonies, Series 1
  see Symphonies Nos. 93-98

London Symphonies, Series 2
  see Symphonies Nos. 99-104

Notturno for 2 Lire Organizzate and
  Orchestra, No. 7, in C, Hob.II:
  31, [arr.] [14']
  (Schmid) 1.1.2.0. 2.0.0.0. strings
  (in this ed called Notturno no.
  1) KALMUS A5657 sc $8.00, set
  $18.00, pts $2.00, ea.   (H381)

Notturno for 2 Lire Organizzate and
  Orchestra, No. 8, in C, Hob.II:
  32, [arr.] [11']
  (Schmid) 0.2.0.0. 2.0.0.0. strings
  (in this ed called Notturno no.
  2) KALMUS A5565 sc $8.00, set
  $12.00, pts $1.25, ea.   (H382)

Orlando Paladino: Overture
  0.2.0.2. 2.0.0.0. timp,hpsd,
  strings
  (Geiringer, Karl) BÄREN. BA 4663   (H383)

Paris Symphonies, Vol. 1
  sc MEZ KNIGA f.s.
  contains: Symphony No. 82 in C;
  Symphony No. 83 in G minor   (H384)

Pescatrici, Le: Overture
  FABER sc F0841 f.s., pts F0856 f.s. (H385)

Ritorno Di Tobia, Il: Overture [7']
  0.2.0.2. 2.2.0.0. timp,strings
  (available in the United States
  only) MMB perf mat rent   (H386)

Rondo All' Ongarese, [arr.] [4']
  (Muller-Berghaus) "Gypsy Rondo,
  [arr.]" 2(pic).2.2.2. 2.2.3.0.
  timp,perc,strings KALMUS A5600
  sc $12.00, perf mat rent, set
  $25.00, pts $1.25, ea.   (H387)

Schöpfung, Die: Auf Starkem Fittiche,
  For Solo Voice And Orchestra
  BREITKOPF-L perf mat rent   (H388)

Schöpfung, Die: Mit Würd Und Hoheit
  Angetan, For Solo Voice And
  Orchestra

HAYDN, [FRANZ] JOSEPH (cont'd.)

BREITKOPF-L perf mat rent   (H389)

Schöpfung, Die: Nun Beut Die Flur,
  For Solo Voice And Orchestra
  BREITKOPF-L perf mat rent   (H390)

Schöpfung, Die: Nun Scheint In Vollem
  Glanz Der Himmel, For Solo Voice
  And Orchestra
  2.2.0.3. 2.2.0.0. timp,strings,B
  solo
  BREITKOPF-L perf mat rent   (H391)

Sinfonia Concertante for Violin,
  Violoncello, Oboe, Bassoon and
  Orchestra, Op. 84, in B flat,
  Hob.I: 105
  min sc KALMUS K00102 $7.00 contains
  also: Concerto for Horn and
  Orchestra   (H392)

Symphonies, Five, Vol. 1
  min sc KALMUS K00401 $11.50
  contains: Symphony No. 7 in C;
  Symphony No. 8 in G; Symphony
  No. 40 in F; Symphony No. 44 in
  E minor; Symphony No. 48 in C   (H393)

Symphonies, Five, Vol. 2
  min sc KALMUS K00109 $11.50
  contains: Symphony No. 73 in D;
  Symphony No. 82 in C; Symphony
  No. 83 in G minor; Symphony No.
  84 in E flat; Symphony No. 86
  in D   (H394)

Symphonies, Four
  min sc KALMUS K00110 $11.50
  contains: Symphony No. 96 in D;
  Symphony No. 97 in C; Symphony
  No. 98 in B flat; Symphony No.
  99 in E flat   (H395)

Symphonies Nos. 1-5
  min sc KALMUS K01367 $5.00   (H396)

Symphonies Nos. 6-8
  min sc KALMUS K01368 $6.00   (H397)

Symphonies Nos. 9-12
  min sc KALMUS K01369 $5.00   (H398)

Symphonies Nos. 13-18
  min sc KALMUS K01370 $5.00   (H399)

Symphonies Nos. 19-22
  min sc KALMUS K01371 $5.00   (H400)

Symphonies Nos. 23-27
  min sc KALMUS K01372 $5.00   (H401)

Symphonies Nos. 28-31
  min sc KALMUS K01373 $5.00   (H402)

Symphonies Nos. 32-35
  min sc KALMUS K01374 $5.00   (H403)

Symphonies Nos. 36-40
  min sc KALMUS K01375 $5.00   (H404)

Symphonies Nos. 41-43
  min sc KALMUS K01376 $5.00   (H405)

Symphonies Nos. 44-46
  min sc KALMUS K01377 $5.75   (H406)

Symphonies Nos. 88-92
  (Haydn Society edition) sc DOVER
  244458 $11.95   (H407)

Symphonies Nos. 93-98
  "London Symphonies, Series 1" sc
  DOVER 249824 $12.95   (H408)

Symphonies Nos. 99-104
  "London Symphonies, Series 2" sc
  DOVER 249832 $12.95   (H409)

Symphonies, Vols. 1-12 *CCU
  (Robbins Landon, H.C.) min sc
  UNIVER. PH00500 $250.00   (H410)

Symphony in B flat
  (Gal, Hans) 2ob,2horn,opt hpsd,
  strings [10'] (Hob.I:B2) BOOSEY
  perf mat rent   (H411)

Symphony No. 1 in D
  SUPRAPHON   (H412)

Symphony No. 7 in C
  see Symphonies, Five, Vol. 1

Symphony No. 8 in G
  see Symphonies, Five, Vol. 1

Symphony No. 34 in D minor
  (Raphael, G.) BREITKOPF-W perf mat
  rent   (H413)

Symphony No. 40 in F
  see Symphonies, Five, Vol. 1

HAYDN, [FRANZ] JOSEPH (cont'd.)

Symphony No. 44 in E minor
  see Symphonies, Five, Vol. 1

Symphony No. 45 in F sharp minor
  min sc KALMUS K00288 $4.00   (H414)
  (Fodor) study sc EMB 40026 f.s.
                                      (H415)

Symphony No. 48 in C
  see Symphonies, Five, Vol. 1

Symphony No. 50 in C
  (Schultz) KALMUS A6717 sc $15.00,
  set $30.00, pts $3.00, ea., perf
  mat rent   (H416)

Symphony No. 51 in B flat
  (Schultz) KALMUS A6720 sc $15.00,
  set $25.00, pts $3.00, ea., perf
  mat rent   (H417)

Symphony No. 52 in C minor
  min sc KALMUS K01379 $3.50   (H418)
  (Schultz) KALMUS A6379 sc $15.00,
  set $20.00, pts $2.00, ea., perf
  mat rent   (H419)

Symphony No. 53 in D
  min sc KALMUS K01380 $4.00   (H420)
  (Schultz) KALMUS A6722 sc $25.00,
  set $35.00, pts $3.50, ea., perf
  mat rent   (H421)

Symphony No. 54 in G
  (Banck) KALMUS A4275 sc $20.00, set
  $22.00, perf mat rent   (H422)
  (Schultz) KALMUS A6723 sc $15.00,
  set $40.00, pts $3.50, ea., perf
  mat rent   (H423)

Symphony No. 55 in E flat
  min sc KALMUS K01381 $3.50   (H424)
  (Schultz) KALMUS A6340 sc $15.00,
  set $30.00, pts $3.50, ea., perf
  mat rent   (H425)

Symphony No. 56 in C
  (Schultz) KALMUS A6724 sc $17.00,
  set $30.00, pts $3.00, ea., perf
  mat rent   (H426)

Symphony No. 57 in D
  min sc KALMUS K01382 $3.50   (H427)
  (Schultz) KALMUS A6725 sc $15.00,
  set $30.00, pts $3.00, ea., perf
  mat rent   (H428)

Symphony No. 58 in F
  KALMUS A6761 sc $8.00, set $25.00,
  pts $2.50, ea., perf mat rent
                                      (H429)

Symphony No. 59 in A
  KALMUS A6760 sc $10.00, set $20.00,
  pts $2.00, ea., perf mat rent
                                      (H430)

Symphony No. 60 in C
  KALMUS A7224 sc $12.00, set $35.00,
  pts $3.50, ea., perf mat rent
                                      (H431)

Symphony No. 61 in D
  KALMUS A7225 sc $15.00, set $38.00,
  pts $3.50, ea., perf mat rent
                                      (H432)

Symphony No. 63 in C
  min sc KALMUS K01383 $3.50   (H433)

Symphony No. 65 in A
  KALMUS A6759 sc $10.00, set $20.00,
  pts $2.00, ea., perf mat rent
                                      (H434)

Symphony No. 73 in D
  see Symphonies, Five, Vol. 2

Symphony No. 80 in D minor
  min sc KALMUS K01384 $4.00   (H435)

Symphony No. 82 in C
  KALMUS A7053 sc $25.00, set $40.00,
  pts $3.00, ea., perf mat rent
                                      (H436)
  (Held) sc PETERS P10502 f.s. (H437)
  see Paris Symphonies, Vol. 1
  see Symphonies, Five, Vol. 2

Symphony No. 83 in G minor
  study sc EMB 40025 f.s.   (H438)
  KALMUS A7054 sc $20.00, set $35.00,
  pts $3.00, ea., perf mat rent
                                      (H439)
  (Fodor) study sc EMB 40025 f.s.
                                      (H440)
  see Paris Symphonies, Vol. 1
  see Symphonies, Five, Vol. 2

Symphony No. 84 in E flat
  KALMUS A7055 sc $20.00, set $35.00,
  pts $3.00, ea., perf mat rent
                                      (H441)
  min sc KALMUS K01385 $3.50   (H442)
  see Symphonies, Five, Vol. 2

Symphony No. 85 in B flat
  KALMUS A7056 sc $20.00, set $35.00,
  pts $3.00, ea., perf mat rent
                                      (H443)

HAYDN, [FRANZ] JOSEPH (cont'd.)

(Jancsovics) study sc EMB 40017
f.s.   (H444)

Symphony No. 86 in D
KALMUS A7057 sc $20.00, set $45.00,
pts $3.50, ea., perf mat rent
                                    (H445)
min sc KALMUS K01386 $5.00   (H446)
see Symphonies, Five, Vol. 2

Symphony No. 87 in A
min sc KALMUS K01387 $4.00   (H447)
KALMUS A7058 sc $20.00, set $35.00,
pts $3.00, ea., perf mat rent
                                    (H448)
Symphony No. 88 in G
KALMUS A7059 sc $20.00, set $45.00,
pts $3.00, ea., perf mat rent
                                    (H449)
(Druian) set SCHIRM.G 50347310
$17.50   (H450)
(Jancsovics) study sc EMB 40010
f.s.   (H451)

Symphony No. 89 in F
KALMUS A7060 sc $20.00, set $35.00,
pts $3.00, ea., perf mat rent
                                    (H452)
Symphony No. 90 in C
KALMUS 7061 sc $20.00, set $50.00,
pts $4.00, ea., perf mat rent
                                    (H453)
Symphony No. 91 in E flat
KALMUS A7062 sc $20.00, set $35.00,
pts $3.00, ea., perf mat rent
                                    (H454)
Symphony No. 92 in G
KALMUS A7063 sc $25.00, set $45.00,
pts $3.00, ea., perf mat rent
                                    (H455)
Symphony No. 93 in D
min sc KALMUS K01388 $4.50   (H456)

Symphony No. 94 in G
(Fodor) study sc EMB 40024 f.s.
                                    (H457)
Symphony No. 95 in C minor
min sc KALMUS K01389 $4.50   (H458)

Symphony No. 96 in D
(Fodor) study sc EMB 40031 f.s.
                                    (H459)
(Newstone, Harry) min sc EULENBURG
EU00481 $4.50   (H460)
see Symphonies, Four

Symphony No. 97 in C
see Symphonies, Four

Symphony No. 98 in B flat
see Symphonies, Four

Symphony No. 99 in E flat
see Symphonies, Four

Symphony No. 100 in G
(Fodor) study sc EMB 40030 f.s.
                                    (H461)
Symphony No. 101 in D
(Fodor) study sc EMB 40027 f.s.
                                    (H462)
Symphony No. 102 in B flat
min sc KALMUS K00252 $4.00   (H463)

Symphony No. 103 in E flat
(Fodor) study sc EMB 40029 f.s.
                                    (H464)
Symphony No. 104 in D
(Fodor) study sc EMB 40028 f.s.
                                    (H465)

Two Concert Arias
see Zwei Konzertarien

Two Pastorales, For Solo Voice And
Orchestra
(Biba) 2horn,strings,S solo [6']
KALMUS A7281 sc $8.00, set
$12.00, pts $1.50, ea.   (H466)

Vera Costanza, La: Overture
*Hob.Ia:15
(Hoffmann) KALMUS A7085 sc $10.00,
set $20.00, pts $2.00, ea., perf
mat rent   (H467)

Zwei Konzertarien
(Orel) BREITKOPF-L perf mat rent
contains: Berenice Che Fai, For
Solo Voice And Orchestra,
"Szene Der Berenice"; Chi Vive
Amante, For Solo Voice And
Orchestra, "Arie Der Errisena"
                                    (H468)
Zwei Konzertarien
"Two Concert Arias" KALMUS A6426 sc
$15.00, set $30.00, pts $2.00,
ea.   (H469)

HAYDN, [JOHANN] MICHAEL (1737-1806)
Adagio Et Allegro Molto, For Horn,
Trombone And Orchestra
(Janetsky-Meek) 2ob,2horn,strings,
horn solo,trom solo [16'10"] sc
BILLAUDOT f.s., perf mat rent

HAYDN, [JOHANN] MICHAEL (cont'd.)
                                    (H470)
Concertino for Bassoon and Orchestra
in F, Perger 52, No. 2 [10']
2ob,2horn,strings,bsn solo
(Rainer, Werner) sc,pts DOBLINGER
DB 878 f.s.   (H471)

Concertino for 2 Horns and Orchestra
in D
2ob,strings,2horn soli
(Muranyi, Robert Arpad) SCHOTTS sc
CON 207 $20.00, set CON 207-50
$48.00   (H472)

Concertino for Piccolo Trumpet and
String Orchestra in D [12']
string orch,trp solo
(Rainer, Werner) sc,pts DOBLINGER
DM 896 f.s.   (H473)

Marcia Mit Posthorn
2fl,strings, 2cornetto
postiglione
(Rainer, Werner) sc,pts DOBLINGER
DM 940 f.s.   (H474)

Sechs Deutsche Tanze, Pe 72
1.2.0.1. 2.0.0.0. drums,strings
without vla
(Rainer, Werner) sc,pts DOBLINGER
DM 937 f.s.   (H475)

Symphony for String Orchestra
string orch
SONZOGNO perf mat rent   (H476)

Symphony in D minor, MIN 121
(Vécsey) min sc EMB 2937 f.s.
                                    (H477)
Symphony, Op. 1, No. 3, in C
BREITKOPF-W perf mat rent   (H478)
KALMUS A5803 sc $15.00, set $35.00,
perf mat rent   (H479)

HAYMAN, RICHARD WARREN JOSEPH
(1920-   )
Freddie The Football, For Narrator
And Orchestra [12']
3.3.3.3. 4.3.3.1. timp,3perc,
harp,pno,strings,narrator
PRESSER perf mat rent   (H480)

HAYS, DORIS ERNESTINE (1941-   )
Southern Voices [18']
4(pic).3(English horn).3(bass
clar).3(contrabsn). 4.3.3.1.
timp,2perc,pno,strings,opt S
solo
sc PETERS P66912 $25.00, perf mat
rent   (H481)

HAZON, ROBERTO (1930-   )
Canti D'amore, For Solo Voice And
Orchestra [20']
2.2.2.2. 4.2.3.1. timp,perc,harp,
strings,solo voice
SONZOGNO perf mat rent   (H482)

Canti Sacri, For Solo Voice And
Orchestra [22']
2.2.2.2. 2.2.0.0. harp,strings,
solo voice
SONZOGNO perf mat rent   (H483)

Canti Spirituali Di Ragazzi D'oggi,
For Solo Voice And Orchestra
[21']
1.2.0.1. 2.0.0.0. perc,org,pno,
strings,S solo
SONZOGNO perf mat rent   (H484)

Concerto Di Ariele, For Oboe And
Orchestra [20']
2.0.2.2. 2.0.0.0. perc,strings,ob
solo
SONZOGNO perf mat rent   (H485)

Elegy [7']
3.2.2.2. 2.2.0.0. timp,strings
SONZOGNO perf mat rent   (H486)

Figlia Di Iorio, La: Suite, For Solo
Voice And Orchestra [42']
3.2.2.2. 4.3.3.1. timp,perc,pno&
cel,harp,strings,S solo
SONZOGNO perf mat rent   (H487)

Promessi Sposi, I: Suite [22']
3.3.3.3. 4.3.3.1. timp,perc,xylo,
vibra,cel,pno,harp,strings
SONZOGNO perf mat rent   (H488)

HE AND THEY, FOR VIOLIN AND ORCHESTRA
see Enriquez, Manuel, El Y Ellos,
For Violin And Orchestra

HEALEY, DEREK (1936-   )
Gabriola *Op.70 [21']
2.2.2.2. 2.2.1.0. 3perc,pno,
strings
CAN.MUS.CENT. MI 1100 H434GA (H489)

HEARD, ALAN (1942-   )
Concerto Grosso for String Quartet
and String Orchestra [16']
string orch,string quar soli
CAN.MUS.CENT. MI 1710 H435C (H490)

Variations for Orchestra
sc BERANDOL BER 1782 $7.00   (H491)

HEART ON THE WALL, FOR SOLO VOICE AND
ORCHESTRA see Owens, Robert

HEARTBEAT see Blake, Howard

HEATH, DAVE
Out Of The Cool, For Saxophone And
Orchestra [6']
2(pic).2.2(bass clar).2. 4.0.0.0.
strings,sax solo
CHESTER perf mat rent   (H492)

HEATH, THE, FOR SOLO VOICE AND
ORCHESTRA see Groven, Eivind, Moen,
For Solo Voice And Orchestra

HEAVENS DECLARE, THE [ARR.] see
Marcello, Benedetto

HEBRIDEN, DIE see Mendelssohn-
Bartholdy, Felix

HEDDA see Mortensen, Finn

HEDDA GABLER see Søderlind, Ragnar

HEDSTROM, ÅSE (1950-   )
Faser [9']
3.3.3.3. 4.3.3.1. timp,perc,harp,
pno,cel,strings
"Phases" NORGE   (H493)

Phases
see Faser

Saisir [12']
2.1.2.1. 2.2.2.1. 2perc,harp,
strings
NORGE   (H494)

Utdrivelsen [15']
4.4.3.3. 5.4.3.1. timp,3perc,
strings
NORGE   (H495)

HEDWALL, LENNART (1932-   )
Arstidsstycken, For Solo Voice And
String Orchestra [8']
string orch,solo voice
NORDISKA perf mat rent   (H496)

Sagan
STIM   (H497)

HEEGAARD, LARS
Hymner, For Solo Voice And Orchestra
[15']
1.1.1.1. 1.1.0.0. perc,harp,
strings,B solo
SAMFUNDET perf mat rent   (H498)

Letter To My Son [10']
3.2.2.4. 2.2.2.0. perc,pno,
strings
SAMFUNDET perf mat rent   (H499)

HEGDAL, MAGNE (1944-   )
Concerto No. 2 [18']
1.1.1.1. 1.1.1.1. perc,pno,
strings
NORGE   (H500)

Sinfonia [7']
3.3.3.3. 4.2.3.1. timp,perc,harp,
strings
NORGE   (H501)

Ubung, For 2 Pianos And Orchestra
[14']
2.2.2.2. 4.2.3.1. timp,perc,
strings,2pno soli
NORGE   (H502)

HEIDEN, BERNHARD (1910-   )
Concerto for Recorder and Orchestra
[19']
0.2.0.1. 2.0.0.0. strings,rec
solo
NORRUTH perf mat rent   (H503)

Concerto for Tuba and Orchestra [17']
3.2.2.2. 4.2.3.0. perc,strings,
tuba solo
PEER perf mat rent   (H504)

Recitative And Aria, For Violoncello
And Orchestra [9']
2(pic).2.2(bass clar).2. 3.2.1.0.
timp,perc,strings,vcl solo
PEER perf mat rent   (H505)

Triptych, For Solo Voice And
Orchestra [10']
2+pic.2+English horn.2+bass
clar.2+contrabsn. 4.3.2+bass
trom.1. timp,3perc,harp,
strings,Bar solo

HEIDEN, BERNHARD (cont'd.)

    AMP perf mat rent   (H506)

HEIDER, WERNER (1930-   )
  Divertimento [8']
    2.1.1.1. 2.0.0.0. strings,vibra
     solo,pno solo,db solo,drums
     solo
    sc MJQ $7.95, perf mat rent (H507)

  Rock-Art
    3(pic).3.3(bass
     clar).3(contrabsn). 4.3.3.1.
     4perc,pno,strings
    study sc PETERS P8521 f.s., perf
     mat rent   (H508)

HEIFETZ, ROBIN
  Kalpa
    string orch
    SEESAW   (H509)

HEILNER, IRWIN (1908-   )
  Chinese Songs, For Solo Voice And
    Orchestra [7']
    1.1.1.1. 1.1.1.0. perc,pno,
     strings,med solo
    sc AM.COMP.AL. $19.15, perf mat
     rent   (H510)

  Suite for Orchestra [15']
    2.2.2.2.alto sax. 2.2.2.0. timp,
     perc,2harp,strings
    AM.COMP.AL. perf mat rent   (H511)

  Traveler, The, For Solo Voice And
    Orchestra [3']
    2.2.2.2. 2.0.0.0. perc,harp,
     strings,med solo
    AM.COMP.AL. perf mat rent   (H512)

HEIM see Kielland, Olav

HEIMCHEN AM HERD, DAS: PRELUDE, ACT III
  see Goldmark, Karl

HEIMERL, CHR.
  Arabeske
    BOHM perf mat rent   (H513)

HEIMISCHE KLANGE WALZER see Strauss,
  Eduard

HEIMOVALTA, EDVIN
  Harakka, For Solo Voice And Orchestra
    [3']
    2.2.2.2. 3.2.0.0. perc,harp,
     strings,solo voice
    FAZER perf mat rent   (H514)

HEINICHEN, JOHANN DAVID (1683-1729)
  Concerto, MIN 195
    2fl,2horn,strings
    (Janetzky) sc,pts KUNZEL 10214 f.s.
               (H515)

  Pastorale Per La Notte Della
    Nativitate Christi
    MUS. RARA perf mat rent   (H516)

HEININEN, PAAVO (1938-   )
  Concerto for Violoncello and
    Orchestra [29']
    2.2.2.2. 2.2.2.0. 2perc,harp,cel,
     strings,vcl solo
    sc SUOMEN f.s.   (H517)

  Floral View With Maidens Singing
    *Op.47 [14']
    string orch
    sc FAZER f.s., perf mat rent (H518)

HEINIO, MIKKO (1948-   )
  Possible Worlds [34']
    3.3.3.3. 4.3.3.1. timp,3perc,
     harp,pno&cel,strings
    sc SUOMEN f.s.   (H519)

  Vuelo De Alambre, For Solo Voice And
    Orchestra [28']
    3.3.3.3. 4.3.3.1. timp,3perc,
     harp,pno,cel,strings,S solo
    sc SUOMEN f.s.   (H520)

HEINTZE, GUSTAF (1879-1946)
  Concert Piece for Piano and Orchestra
    [17']
    2.2.2.2. 2.0.0.0. strings,pno
     solo
    STIM   (H521)

  Concerto for Piano and Orchestra, No.
    1, Op. 15, in F minor [30']
    2.2.2.2. 2.2.3.0. timp,strings,
     pno solo
    STIM   (H522)

  Concerto for Piano and Orchestra, No.
    2, Op. 21, in E minor [25']
    3.2.2.2. 4.2.3.0. timp,strings,
     pno solo
    STIM   (H523)

  Concerto for 2 Pianos and Orchestra
    in A minor [25']
    3.2.2.2. 4.2.2.1. timp,strings,

HEINTZE, GUSTAF (cont'd.)

    2pno soli
    STIM   (H524)

HEINZELMANNCHEN, DIE, FOR SOLO VOICE
  AND ORCHESTRA see Pfitzner, Hans

HEISS, JOHN C. (1938-   )
  Four Short Pieces
    2.2.2.2. 2.0.0.0. strings
    MEDIA 4611 $12.00   (H525)

  Inventions, Contours And Colors [8']
    1.0.1.1. 1.1.1.1. vln,vla,vcl,db
    BOOSEY perf mat rent   (H526)

HEITERE SUITE see Reznicek, Emil
  Nikolaus von

HEKSTER, WALTER (1937-   )
  Concerto for Clarinet and Orchestra
    [12']
    2.2.1.1.alto sax. 0.3.0.0. timp,
     3perc,harp,strings,clar solo
    sc DONEMUS f.s., perf mat rent
               (H527)
  Concerto for Oboe and Orchestra [12']
    2.1.2.1.alto sax. 3.0.0.0. perc,
     harp,strings,ob solo
    DONEMUS perf mat rent   (H528)

  Concerto for Violoncello and
    Orchestra [14']
    2.2.2.1. 0.0.3.0. perc,harp,
     strings,vcl solo
    DONEMUS perf mat rent   (H529)

HEKTOGRAF POLKA see Strauss, Eduard

HELDENLEBEN, EIN [ARR.] see Strauss,
  Richard

HELGASON, HALLGRIMUR (1914-   )
  Concertino for Flute, Clarinet and
    String Orchestra
    string orch,fl solo,clar solo
    ICELAND 007-004   (H530)

  Nocturne for Flute, Clarinet and
    String Orchestra [11']
    string orch,fl solo,clar solo
    ICELAND 007-003   (H531)

  Rhapsody, Op. 47 [25']
    2.2.2.2. 4.3.3.1. timp,strings
    ICELAND 007-005   (H532)

  Sacred Theme, A [24'45"]
    2.2.2.2. 4.3.3.1. timp,perc,
     strings
    ICELAND 007-008   (H533)

  Symphony
    2.2.2.2. 4.3.3.1. timp,perc,
     strings
    ICELAND 007-009   (H534)

HELGELAND see Vea, Ketil

HELLAN, ARNE (1953-   )
  Dream Sequences
    2.1.2.1. 2.1.1.0. timp,perc,
     strings
    NORGE   (H535)

  Music for Orchestra [8']
    2.2.2.2. 4.2.3.1. timp,perc,
     strings
    NORGE   (H536)

HELLERMANN, WILLIAM (1939-   )
  Anyway... [15']
    2.2.2.2. 4.2.2.0. perc,harp,pno,
     strings
    AM.COMP.AL. perf mat rent   (H537)

HELLO see Russo, William Joseph

HELLO FROM THE NORTH see McConnell, Rob

HELLO WORLD, FOR NARRATOR AND ORCHESTRA
  see Mayer, William Robert

HELMSCHROTT, ROBERT M. (1938-   )
  Entelechiae (Sinfonia No. 2) [24']
    2+pic.2+English horn.2+bass
     clar.2. 4.2.3.1. timp,perc,
     harp,pno,strings,S solo
    ORLANDO perf mat rent   (H538)

  Influentiae (Sinfonia No. 1) [16'30"]
    2+pic.2+English horn.2+bass
     clar.2. 4.3.3.1. timp,perc,
     harp,pno,strings,speaking voice
    ORLANDO perf mat rent   (H539)

  Sinfonia No. 1
    see Influentiae

  Sinfonia No. 2
    see Entelechiae

HELMUS, MENNO (1962-   )
  Collage [16']
    1.2.2.1. 1.1.1.1. 2perc,harp,
     2pno,2vln,vla,vcl,db
    sc DONEMUS f.s., perf mat rent
               (H540)

HELPS, ROBERT (1928-   )
  Concerto for Piano and Orchestra, No.
    2 [14']
    2+pic.2+English horn.2+bass
     clar.2+contrabsn. 4.3.3.1.
     timp,perc,harp,strings,pno solo
    AMP perf mat rent   (H541)

  Symphony No. 1 [22']
    2(pic).2+English horn.2+bass
     clar.2+contrabsn. 4.2.3.1.
     timp,perc,strings
    AMP perf mat rent   (H542)

HELSTED (1816-1900)
  Fete Des Fleurs A Genzano, La [arr.]
    [11']
    (Stirn, D.) 2.2.2.2. 4.2.3.1. timp,
     perc,harp,strings BOIS perf mat
     rent   (H543)

HELVETIA, THE LAND OF MOUNTAINS AND ITS
  PEOPLE see Bloch, Ernest

HELY-HUTCHINSON, (CHRISTIAN) VICTOR
  (1901-1947)
  Symphony
    PATERSON perf mat rent   (H544)

HEMEL, OSCAR VAN (1892-1981)
  Balletsuite
    2.2.2.2. 2.2.0.0. timp,strings
    sc DONEMUS f.s., perf mat rent
               (H545)

  Divertimento [13']
    3.3.3.3. 4.3.3.1. timp,perc,harp,
     pno,strings
    sc DONEMUS f.s., perf mat rent
               (H546)

  Mei Plaisant, De [3']
    2.2.2.2. 4.3.3.0. timp,perc,harp,
     cel,strings
    sc DONEMUS f.s., perf mat rent
               (H547)

  Moments Symphoniques [18']
    3.3.3.2. 4.3.3.1. timp,2perc,
     harp,pno,cel,strings
    sc DONEMUS f.s., perf mat rent
               (H548)

HEMEROSCOPIUM see Garcia-Abril, Antón

HEMINGWAY: SYMPHONIC SUITE see Waxman,
  Franz

HEMSOBORNA see Nilsson, Bo

HENDERSON, RUTH WATSON (1932-   )
  Suite for Strings
    string orch
    CAN.MUS.CENT. MI 1500 H497SU (H549)

HENGEVELD, GERARD (1910-   )
  Concertino for Piano and Orchestra
    BROEKMANS 803 perf mat rent (H550)

HENKEMANS, HANS (1913-   )
  Riflessioni [17']
    8vln,4vla,3vcl,db
    DONEMUS perf mat rent   (H551)

HENNEMAN, IG (1945-   )
  Big Marble [6']
    2.2.2.2. 2.2.1.1. 2perc,harp,cel,
     pno,strings
    sc DONEMUS f.s., perf mat rent
               (H552)

HENRIC VAN VELDEKE, FOR SOLO VOICES AND
  ORCHESTRA see Strategier, Herman

HENZE, HANS WERNER (1926-   )
  An Eine Aolsharfe, For Guitar And
    Instrumental Ensemble [18']
    alto fl,bass fl,ob d'amore,
     English horn,bass clar,bsn,
     perc,harp,2vla,vla d'amore,
     2vcl,vla da gamba,db,gtr solo
    SCHOTTS perf mat rent   (H553)

  Fandango Sopra Un Basso Del Padre
    Soler [12']
    3(pic,alto fl).3.3(bass
     clar).3(contrabsn). 4.3.3.1.
     timp,perc,2harp,pno&cel,strings
    SCHOTTS perf mat rent   (H554)

  Kleine Elegien Fur Alte Instrumente
    [17']
    3rec,2trom,timp,perc,lute,harp,
     org,vln,vla,vcl, zink, zither
    (Parrot, Andrew) SCHOTTS perf mat
     rent   (H555)

  Konzertstück for Violoncello and
    Instrumental Ensemble [5']
    1.1.1.1. 1.1.1.1. perc,pno,harp,
     cel,db,vcl solo
    SCHOTTS perf mat rent   (H556)

HENZE, HANS WERNER (cont'd.)

Miracle De La Rose, Le, For Clarinet
And Instrumental Ensemble
1.1.0.1. 1.1.1.0. perc,pno&cel,
2vln,vla,vcl,db,clar solo
sc SCHOTTS $48.00   (H557)

Sieben Liebeslieder, For Violoncello
And Orchestra [30']
3(pic).3.3.3(contrabsn). 4.3.3.1.
timp,3perc,cel,harp,pno,
strings,vcl solo
SCHOTTS perf mat rent   (H558)

Spielmusiken (from Pollicino)
SCHOTTS sc CON 194 $25.00,
CON 194-50 $89.00   (H559)

Symphony No. 7
4.4.5.4. 4.6.5.1. timp,perc,cel,
harp,pno,strings
sc SCHOTTS $59.00   (H560)

Telemanniana
sc SCHOTTS $29.50   (H561)

HEPPENER, ROBERT (1925-   )
Boog [27']
4.3.4.3. 6.4.3.1. 5perc,pno,
strings
sc DONEMUS f.s., perf mat rent
                                (H562)

HERACLITEAN FIRE, FOR STRING QUARTET
AND STRING ORCHESTRA see Edwards,
George

HERALDIQUES, FOR TRUMPET AND STRING
ORCHESTRA see Tisne, Antoine

HERBECK, JOHANN FRANZ VON (1831-1877)
Tanz-Momente [14']
2+pic.2.2.2. 2.2.0.0. timp,
strings
DOBLINGER perf mat rent   (H563)

HERBERT, VICTOR (1859-1924)
Air De Ballet
see Three Compositions For String
Orchestra

Babes In Toyland: March Of The Toys,
[arr.] [4'30"]
(Campbell-Watson) WARNER perf mat
rent   (H564)

Forget-Me-Not
see Three Compositions For String
Orchestra

Fortune Teller, The: Gypsy Love Song,
For Solo Voice And Orchestra
[arr.]
(Leyden, Norman) 2.1+English
horn.2.2. 3.0.3.0. xylo,tamb,
harp,strings,Bar solo WARNER perf
mat rent   (H565)

Fortune Teller, The: Romany Life:
Czardas [arr.]
(Leyden, Norman) 2.2.2.2. 4.3.3.1.
timp,2perc,harp,strings,vln solo
[3'] WARNER perf mat rent (H566)

Irish Rhapsody
KALMUS A4271 sc $20.00, set $45.00,
perf mat rent   (H567)

Natoma: Grand Fantasia
3(pic).2+English horn.2+bass
clar.2+contrabsn. 4.3.3.1.
timp,perc,harp,strings
SCHIRM.G perf mat rent   (H568)

Natoma: Prelude To Act III
2+pic.2+English horn.2+bass
clar.2+contrabsn. 4.3.3.1.
timp,perc,harp,strings
SCHIRM.G perf mat rent   (H569)

Naughty Marietta: Ah! Sweet Mystery
Of Life, For Solo Voices And
Orchestra, [arr.]
(Leyden, Norman) 2.2.2.2. 2.3.3.0.
timp,perc,harp,strings,ST soli
[3'] WARNER perf mat rent (H570)

Naughty Marietta: I'm Falling In Love
With Someone, For Solo Voice And
Orchestra, [arr.]
(Leyden, Norman) 2.2.2.2. 4.3.3.1.
2perc,harp,strings,T solo [3']
WARNER perf mat rent   (H571)

Suite Romantique *Op.31
KALMUS A6334 sc $30.00, set $50.00,
pts $2.00, ea., perf mat rent
                                (H572)

Sunset
see Three Compositions For String
Orchestra

Three Compositions For String
Orchestra
string orch,triangle KALMUS A7312
sc $7.00, set $12.00, pts $2.50,

HERBERT, VICTOR (cont'd.)

ea. [10']
contains: Air De Ballet; Forget-
Me-Not; Sunset   (H573)

HERBSTABEND "SONNE VERLISCHT UND WOLKEN
WANDERN", FOR SOLO VOICE AND
ORCHESTRA see Sibelius, Jean

HERBSTBILDER see Prokofiev, Serge,
Autumnal Sketch

HERBSTLIED, FOR 2 VIOLINS AND CHAMBER
ORCHESTRA see Martinov, Vladimir

HERBSTROSEN WALZER see Strauss, Josef

HEREIN, FOR VIOLIN AND CHAMBER
ORCHESTRA see Martinov, Vladimir

HERETIC HYMN see Norholm, Ib

HERITAGE, FOR ORCHESTRA AND JAZZ-ROCK
TRIO see Kompanek, Rudolph

HERITIER DE PAIMPOL, L' see Bochsa,
Robert-Nicolas-Charles

HERMANN UND DOROTHEA: OVERTURE see
Schumann, Robert (Alexander)

HERMANNSSCHLACHT, DIE see Vierling,
Georg

HERMANS, NICO (1919-1988)
Concerto for Viola and String
Orchestra [21']
string orch,vla solo
DONEMUS perf mat rent   (H574)

Coup De Couperin [12']
3.2.2.2. 4.3.3.0. timp,perc,harp,
strings
DONEMUS perf mat rent   (H575)

Ode, For English Horn And String
Orchestra [13']
string orch,English horn solo
DONEMUS perf mat rent   (H576)

HERMINIE, FOR SOLO VOICE AND ORCHESTRA
see Berlioz, Hector (Louis)

HERMSEN, PIETER (1961-   )
Concerto for Violin and Orchestra
[23']
3.2.2.3. 4.2.3.1. timp,3-4perc,
harp,pno,strings,vln solo
DONEMUS perf mat rent   (H577)

HEROIDE FUNEBRE see Liszt, Franz

HERO'S MONUMENT see Chu, Wei

HERO'S SONG see Dvorák, Antonín

HERR OLUF, FOR SOLO VOICE AND ORCHESTRA
see Loewe, Carl Gottfried

HERRMANN, BERNARD (1911-1975)
Citizen Kane Overture [2'45"]
2.2.3(bass clar).2. 4.3.3.1.
timp,2perc,harp,cel,strings
BOURNE perf mat rent   (H578)

Devil And Daniel Webster, The: Suite
[21']
2.2.3(bass clar).3(contrabsn).
4.3.3.1. timp,4perc,pno,harp,
org,strings
BOURNE perf mat rent   (H579)

Psycho: Suite [14'30"]
string orch
CPP perf mat rent   (H580)

Salammbo's Aria (from Citizen Kane)
[5'45"]
2.2.2.2. 4.3.3.1. timp,harp,
strings
BOURNE perf mat rent   (H581)

HERSCHEL, WILLIAM (1738-1822)
Symphonies, Three
(Murray; Platt; Divalli; Schwarz)
("The Symphony" Vol. E-III) sc
GARLAND ISBN 0-8240-3824-X $90.00
contains also: Smethergell,
William, Overtures, Four; Wesley,
Samuel, Symphonic Works, Two;
Wesley, Samuel Sebastian,
Symphony   (H582)

HERTEL, JOHANN WILHELM (1727-1789)
Concerto for Keyboard Instrument and
Orchestra in E flat
(Hertel, Romana) sc A-R ED $27.95,
perf mat rent contains also:
Concerto for Keyboard Instrument
and Orchestra in F minor   (H583)

Concerto for Keyboard Instrument and
Orchestra in F minor
see Concerto for Keyboard
Instrument and Orchestra in E

HERTEL, JOHANN WILHELM (cont'd.)

flat

HERTEL, THOMAS (1951-   )
Hölderin-Report, For Solo Voice And
Orchestra
1.1.1.1. 1.1.1.0. perc,strings,
speaking voice
sc DEUTSCHER 1126 f.s., perf mat
rent   (H584)

HERVELOIS, CAIX D'
see CAIX D'HERVELOIS, LOUIS DE

HERVIG, RICHARD B. (1917-   )
Music For A Concert [8']
2+pic.2+English horn.2.2.
4.3.3.1. timp,perc,pno,harp,
strings
AM.COMP.AL. perf mat rent   (H585)

HERZ, DU KENNST MEINE SEHNSUCHT, FOR
SOLO VOICE AND ORCHESTRA [ARR.] see
Grothe, Franz

HERZEL POLKA see Strauss, Johann, [Jr.]

HESELTINE, PHILIP ("PETER WARLOCK")
(1894-1930)
Serenade
KALMUS A6166 sc $5.00, set $5.00
                                (H586)

Six Italian Dances [5']
string orch
KALMUS A7461 sc $7.00, set $7.50,
pts $1.50, ea.   (H587)

HESPERUS POLKA see Strauss, Johann,
[Jr.]

HESS, ERNST (1912-1968)
Concerto Da Camera, For Violoncello
And Orchestra *Op.63 [20']
1.0.1.1. 1.0.0.0. strings,vcl
solo
BÄREN. BA 6278   (H588)

HESS, WILLY (1906-   )
Sommernacht, For Solo Voice And
Chamber Orchestra *Op.73
sc AMADEUS BP 2696 f.s.   (H589)

HESSELBERG, EYVIND (1898-   )
Allegretto Giocoso [5']
3.2.2.2. 4.3.3.1. timp,perc,harp,
strings
NORGE   (H590)

Chorale
see Koral

Koral [10']
2.2.2.2. 2.2.3.1. timp,pno,
strings
"Chorale" NORGE   (H591)

Scherzino, For Bassoon And Orchestra
[4']
2.2.2.1. 0.0.0.0. strings,bsn
solo
NORGE   (H592)

Scherzo Notturno [6']
3.2.3.2. 4.2.1.1. timp,perc,harp,
cel,strings
NORGE   (H593)

HESSENBERG, KURT (1908-   )
Concertino for Bassoon and Orchestra,
Op. 106 [14']
1.1.2.0. 1.0.0.0. strings,bsn
solo
HANSEN-GER perf mat rent   (H594)

Sinfonietta, Op. 73 [13']
string orch
HANSEN-GER perf mat rent   (H595)

Spielmusik *Op.61 [11']
string orch
HANSEN-GER perf mat rent   (H596)

Symphony No. 3, Op. 62 [23']
2.2.2.2. 3.2.0.0. perc,strings
HANSEN-GER perf mat rent   (H597)

Variationen-Suite *Op.86
0.1.1.1. 1.0.0.0. strings
BREITKOPF-W perf mat rent   (H598)

HETEROGENEO, FOR SOLO VOICES AND
ORCHESTRA see Pablo, Luis de

HETEROPHONY, FOR TWO PIANOS AND
ORCHESTRA see Nishimura, Akira

HETU, JACQUES (1938-   )
Antinomie [8']
2.2.2.2. 2.2.0.0. timp,perc,
strings
DOBER   (H599)

Concerto for Trumpet and Orchestra,
Op. 43
0.1.1.1. 0.0.0.0. strings,trp

HETU, JACQUES (cont'd.)

    solo
    CAN.MUS.CENT. MI 1331 H591CO (H600)

    Images De La Revolution *Op.44 [19']
      4(pic).3(English horn).3(bass
      clar).3(contrabsn). 4.3.3.1.
      timp,4perc,strings
    CAN.MUS.CENT. MI 1100 H591IM (H601)

    Poem, Op. 47
      string orch
    CAN.MUS.CENT. MI 1500 H591PO (H602)

    Symphonie Concertante for Wind
      Quintet and String Orchestra, Op.
      40 [25']
      string orch,wind quin soli
    CAN.MUS.CENT. MI 1726 H591SY (H603)

    Symphony No. 3, Op. 18
    sc BERANDOL BER 1763 $20.00 (H604)

HEUBERGER, RICHARD (1850-1914)
    Aus Dem Morgenlande *Op.25 [11']
      2.2.2.2. 2.2.0.0. timp,perc,harp,
      strings
      "From The Morning Land" SIMROCK
      perf mat rent   (H605)

    From The Morning Land
      see Aus Dem Morgenlande

    Nachtmusik *Op.7
      string orch
      KISTNER   (H606)

    Variationen Uber Ein Thema Von Franz
      Schubert *Op.11
      KISTNER perf mat rent   (H607)

HEURE DES TRACES, L' see Dufourt,
    Hugues

HEURE GALANTE, L' [ARR.] see Scarlatti,
    Domenico

HEURES ANTIQUES: AU BOIS SACRE see Le
    Boucher, Maurice Georges Eugene

HEURES ANTIQUES: LA DANSE DES FAUVES
    see Le Boucher, Maurice Georges
    Eugene

HEWITT-JONES, TONY (1926-   )
    Fanfare And Procession [5']
      ROBERTON 95427   (H608)

HEX see Giuffre, James Peter (Jimmy)

HEXEN, FOR BASSOON AND STRING ORCHESTRA
    see Aguila, Miguel Del

HEYN, VOLKER (1938-   )
    Dukurrahsch Mongkhohr [19']
      2(2pic).2+English horn.3(sax)+
      bass clar.2+contrabsn. 4.4.4.1.
      3perc,2pno,strings,electronic
      tape
    sc BREITKOPF-W PB 5150 f.s. (H609)

    Eezy Comma [19']
      4.3+English horn.4.4.3sax.
      6.6.4.2. 3perc,2harp,3pno,
      strings
      BREITKOPF-W perf mat rent (H610)

    Ferro Canto
      BREITKOPF-W perf mat rent (H611)

    K'mon Siggebeybe, For Violoncello And
      Instrumental Ensemble [20']
      1(pic).1(English horn).1(bass
      clar,sax).0. 0.1.1.0. vln,vla,
      vcl,db,vcl solo
      BREITKOPF-W perf mat rent (H612)

    Tem [15']
      2(pic,alto fl).2+English
      horn.2(2sax,bass clar).1+
      contrabsn. 0.2.2.1. 2perc,pno,
      8vln,4vcl,2db
      sc BREITKOPF-W f.s., perf mat rent
                                 (H613)

HIBBARD, WILLIAM (1939-   )
    Concerto for Viola and Orchestra
      [23']
      1+alto fl.1+English horn.1+bass
      clar.1. 0.2.2+bass trom.0.
      3perc,harp,pno,strings,vla solo
      AMP perf mat rent   (H614)

    Processionals [12']
      2+pic.2.2+clar in A.2. 4.2.3.1.
      strings
      AMP perf mat rent   (H615)

    Stabiles [8']
      fl,alto fl,clar,bass clar,trp,
      trom,vibra,harp,pno,vln,vla,
      vcl,db
      AMP perf mat rent   (H616)

HIDALGO, MANUEL (1956-   )
    Al Componer, For Viola, Violoncello,
      Double Bass And Orchestra [30']
      4.0.4(2bass clar).2(2contrabsn).
      0.2.2.0. perc,harp,mand,cel,
      strings,vla solo,vcl solo,db
      solo
      BREITKOPF-W perf mat rent (H617)

    Alegrias, For Piano And Chamber
      Orchestra [13']
      2.0.2.0. 0.1.1.0. 2perc,harp,
      2vln,2vla,2vcl,2db,AA soli,pno
      solo
      study sc BREITKOPF-W PB 5404 f.s.,
      perf mat rent   (H618)

    Harto [21'30"]
      2(2pic)+alto fl.2(English
      horn).4.2+contrabsn. 4.3.3.1.
      perc,harp,pno&cel,strings
      study sc BREITKOPF-W PB 5119 f.s.,
      perf mat rent   (H619)

    Inercia Y La Mierda, La [15'43"]
      3clar,3timp,2vln,2vla,2vcl
      BREITKOPF-W perf mat rent (H620)

    Music for String Quartet and String
      Orchestra [15']
      string orch,string quar soli
      BREITKOPF-W perf mat rent (H621)

HIDAS, FRIGYES (1928-   )
    Ballade for Violoncello and Orchestra
      sc EMB 10256 f.s., perf mat rent
                                 (H622)

    Baroque Concerto For Trombone And
      String Orchestra
      string orch,trom solo
      sc EMB 12805 f.s., perf mat rent
                                 (H623)

    Szechenyi Concerto
      sc EMB 10281 f.s., perf mat rent
                                 (H624)

HIDDEN WALLS OF TIME see Hunt, Michael

HIEROPHONIE II see Taira, Yoshihisa

HIEROPHONIE III see Taira, Yoshihisa

HIGH SCHOOL CADETS MARCH see Sousa,
    John Philip

HIGHLAND EXPRESS, THE, FOR NARRATOR AND
    ORCHESTRA see Wilby, Philip

HIGO, ICHIRO (1940-   )
    Prologo Per Leggenda E Sinfonia [30']
      3(pic,alto fl).3(English
      horn).3(bass
      clar).3(contrabsn). 6.4.3.1.
      perc,harp,cel,pno 4-hands,
      strings
      sc ZEN-ON 899330 f.s., perf mat
      rent   (H625)

HILDRING I SPEIL, FOR SOLO VOICE AND
    ORCHESTRA [ARR.] see Sommerfeldt,
    Oistein

HILL, ALFRED (1870-1960)
    Concerto for Viola and Orchestra
      [16']
      1.1.2.1. 2.0.0.0. timp,triangle,
      strings,vla solo
      SOUTHRN PUB perf mat rent (H626)

HILLBORG, ANDERS (1954-   )
    Celestial Mechanics [16']
      perc,strings
      NORDISKA perf mat rent   (H627)

    Worlds [12']
      perc,elec gtr,strings, 2 amp.
      piano, 2 amp. harp
      NORDISKA perf mat rent   (H628)

HILLER, WILFRIED (1941-   )
    Jose Mit Der Zauberfiedel, Der, For
      Narrator, Violin And Orchestra
      [45']
      1(pic).0.1.0. 1.1.1.1. timp,perc,
      harp,pno,strings,vln solo,
      narrator
      SCHOTTS perf mat rent   (H629)

HILLIARD, JOHN
    Grand Traverse, The, For Trumpet And
      Orchestra [20']
      2.2.3.2. 2.3.3.1. harp,strings,
      trp/flügelhorn solo
      AM.COMP.AL. sc $28.20, pts $3.10
                                 (H630)

HILLS OF TIME, THE see Harris, Ross

HIMMELHOCH JAUCHZEND- ZUM TODE BETRUBT
    see Ruders, Poul

HIMMELSKA FAGELN, DEN, FOR PIANO AND
    STRING ORCHESTRA see Karkoff,
    Ingvar

HIMNO NACIONAL MEXICANO see Chavez,
    Carlos

HINDEMITH, PAUL (1895-1963)
    Lustige Sinfonietta In D Minor, Op. 4
      2.3.3.1. 2.2.0.0. timp,perc,
      strings
      sc SCHOTTS $39.50   (H631)

    Mathis Der Maler: Sinfonie
      2.2.2.2. 4.2.3.1. timp,perc,
      min sc EULENBURG $8.75   (H632)

    Ragtime [4']
      3.2.3.2. 4.2.3.1. timp,perc,
      strings
      SCHOTTS perf mat rent   (H633)

    Schwanendreher, Der, For Viola And
      Orchestra
      min sc EULENBURG EU01816 f.s.
                                 (H634)

    Symphonic Metamorphosis On Themes By
      Carl Maria von Weber
      3.3.3.3. 4.2.3.1. timp,perc,
      strings
      min sc EULENBURG $8.75   (H635)

HINTER DEN COULISSEN QUADRILLE see
    Strauss, Johann, [Jr.]

HIPPOLYTE SUITE see Rieti, Vittorio

HIRAYOSHI, TAKEKUNI (1936-   )
    Concerto for Guitar and Orchestra
      JAPAN 8201   (H636)

HIRCHMANN
    Petite Boheme, La: Ballet Music
      [5'30"]
      CHOUDENS perf mat rent   (H637)

    Petite Boheme, La: Overture
      CHOUDENS perf mat rent   (H638)

HIREATH, FOR VIOLONCELLO AND ORCHESTRA
    see Rands, Bernard

HIRT AUF DEM FELSEN, DER, FOR SOLO
    VOICE AND ORCHESTRA [ARR.] see
    Schubert, Franz (Peter)

HIS EXCELLENCY MARCH see Fillmore,
    Henry

HISTOIRE VERITABLE DE L'EXECRABLE COUNT
    DRACULA see Mendelssohn, Vladimir

HISTORICAL VISIONS see Groven, Eivind,
    Historiske Syner

HISTORIEN OM MALINCHE see Johansen,
    Svend Aaquist

HISTORISKE SYNER see Groven, Eivind

HIT see Moore, Carman

HIVELY, WELLS (1902-1969)
    Adolescent, The [30']
      2.2.2.2. 4.2.3.1. timp,perc,harp,
      strings
      AM.COMP.AL. perf mat rent (H639)

    Priscilla Variations, For Piano And
      Chamber Orchestra [5']
      2.1.2.1. 2.2.1.0. timp,strings,
      pno solo
      AM.COMP.AL. perf mat rent (H640)

HIVER DANS L'AME, FOR SOLO VOICE AND
    ORCHESTRA see Prevost, Andre

HJELLEMO, OLE (1873-1938)
    Andante Con Moto [6']
      2.2.2.2. 2.0.0.0. timp,strings
      NORGE   (H641)

HJEMAD [ARR.] see Grieg, Edvard Hagerup

HJEMMEFRONTEN see Fongaard, Bjørn

HLOBIL, EMIL (1901-   )
    Symphony No. 7 [18']
      3.3.3.3. 4.3.3.1. timp,perc,xylo,
      harp,strings
      SUPRAPHON   (H642)

HO, LIU TING
    Night Party [2']
      3.1.2.2. 2.2.3.1. timp,perc,
      strings
      HONG KONG perf mat rent   (H643)

    Sum Che Tak Ma [3']
      3.1.2.1. 2.2.1.0. strings
      HONG KONG perf mat rent   (H644)

HO MOR FAER LOFOTFOLKET SITT HEIM, FOR
    SOLO VOICE AND STRING ORCHESTRA see
    Eggen, Arne

HOAG, CHARLES K.
    After-Intermission Overture, An
      2.2.2.2. 4.3.3.1. timp,perc,pno,
      strings
      SCHIRM.G perf mat rent   (H645)

HOANG HON, FOR SOLO VOICE AND ORCHESTRA
see Dao, Nguyen Thien

HOBSON, BRUCE (1943-   )
Three, For 2 Trumpets And Orchestra
[22']
3.3.3.0. 3.0.2.1. 2perc,strings
without vla,2trp soli
sc APNM $25.00, perf mat rent
(H646)

HOBSONS CHOICE see Arnold, Malcolm

HOCH, PETER (1937-   )
Interludien
ZIMMER.   (H647)

HOCH ÖSTERREICH MARSCH see Strauss,
Johann, [Jr.]

HOCHQUELLE POLKA, DIE see Strauss,
Eduard

HOCHZEIT DES FIGARO, DIE: ALLES IST
RICHTIG; ACH, ÖFFNET EURE AUGEN,
FOR SOLO VOICE AND ORCHESTRA see
Mozart, Wolfgang Amadeus, Nozze Di
Figaro, Le: Tutto E Disposto, For
Solo Voice And Orchestra

HOCHZEIT DES FIGARO, DIE: DER PROZESS
SCHON GEWONNEN; ICH SOLL EIN GLÜCK
ENTBEHREN, FOR SOLO VOICE AND
ORCHESTRA see Mozart, Wolfgang
Amadeus, Nozze Di Figaro, Le: Hai
Gia Vinta La Causa; Vedro Mentr' Io
Sospiro, For Solo Voice And
Orchestra

HOCHZEIT DES FIGARO, DIE: ENDLICH NAHT
SICH DIE STUNDE, FOR SOLO VOICE AND
ORCHESTRA see Mozart, Wolfgang
Amadeus, Nozze Di Figaro, Le:
Giunse Alfin Il Momento, For Solo
Voice And Orchestra

HOCHZEIT DES FIGARO, DIE: EUCH HOLDE
FRAUEN, FOR SOLO VOICE AND
ORCHESTRA see Mozart, Wolfgang
Amadeus, Nozze Di Figaro, Le: Voi
Che Sapete, For Solo Voice And
Orchestra

HOCHZEIT DES FIGARO, DIE: HÖR' MEIN
FLEHN, FOR SOLO VOICE AND ORCHESTRA
see Mozart, Wolfgang Amadeus, Nozze
Di Figaro, Le: Porgi Amor, For Solo
Voice And Orchestra

HOCHZEIT DES FIGARO, DIE: ICH WEISS
NICHT, WO ICH BIN, FOR SOLO VOICE
AND ORCHESTRA see Mozart, Wolfgang
Amadeus, Nozze Di Figaro, Le: Non
So Piu Cosa Son, For Solo Voice And
Orchestra

HOCHZEIT DES FIGARO, DIE: NUN VERGISS
LEISES FLEHN, FOR SOLO VOICE AND
ORCHESTRA see Mozart, Wolfgang
Amadeus, Nozze Di Figaro, Le: Non
Piu Andrai, For Solo Voice And
Orchestra

HOCHZEIT DES FIGARO, DIE: SO LANG HAB
ICH GESCHMACHTET, FOR SOLO VOICES
AND ORCHESTRA see Mozart, Wolfgang
Amadeus, Nozze Di Figaro, Le:
Crudel! Perche Finora, For Solo
Voices And Orchestra

HOCHZEIT DES FIGARO, DIE: SÜSSE RACHE,
JA SÜSSE RACHE, FOR SOLO VOICE AND
ORCHESTRA see Mozart, Wolfgang
Amadeus, Nozze Di Figaro, Le: La
Vendetta, For Solo Voice And
Orchestra

HOCHZEIT DES FIGARO, DIE: WENN DIE
SANFTEN ABENDWINDE, FOR SOLO VOICES
AND ORCHESTRA see Mozart, Wolfgang
Amadeus, Nozze Di Figaro, Le:
Sull'aria! Che Soave Zeffiretto,
For Solo Voices And Orchestra

HOCHZEIT DES FIGARO, DIE: WILL DER HERR
GRAF EIN TÄNZCHEN NUN WAGEN, FOR
SOLO VOICE AND ORCHESTRA see
Mozart, Wolfgang Amadeus, Nozze Di
Figaro, Le: Se Vuol Ballare, For
Solo Voice And Orchestra

HOCHZEIT DES FIGARO, DIE: WOHIN FLOHEN
DIE WONNESTUNDEN, FOR SOLO VOICE
AND ORCHESTRA see Mozart, Wolfgang
Amadeus, Nozze Di Figaro, Le: Dove
Sono, For Solo Voice And Orchestra

HOCHZEITSKLANGE WALZER see Strauss,
Josef

HOCHZEITSMENUETTE see Mozart, Leopold

HODDINOTT, ALUN (1929-   )
Contemplation Upon Flowers, A, For
Solo Voice And Orchestra *Op.90
[15']
2.1.2.1. 2.1.0.0. perc,strings,S

HODDINOTT, ALUN (cont'd.)

solo
OXFORD perf mat rent   (H648)

Doubles *Op.106 [20']
ob,hpsd,strings
OXFORD perf mat rent   (H649)

Lanternes Des Mortes [15']
2.2.2.2. 4.2.3.0. timp,perc,harp,
strings
sc OXFORD f.s., perf mat rent   (H650)

Scenes And Interludes, For Trumpet,
Harpsichord And String Orchestra
[20']
string orch,trp solo,hpsd solo
study sc UNIV.CR P00601 f.s., perf
mat rent   (H651)

Symphony No. 6, Op. 116 [24']
3(pic).2+English horn.2+bass
clar.2+contrabsn. 4.3.3.1.
timp,2perc,harp,strings
study sc UNIV.CR P01017 f.s., perf
mat rent   (H652)

Trumpet Major, The: Four Scenes [20']
2.2.2.2. 2.2.2.0. perc,strings
OXFORD perf mat rent   (H653)

Variations for Orchestra, Op. 31
[10']
2.1.2.1. 2.2.1.0. timp,perc,pno,
strings
NOVELLO perf mat rent   (H654)

Welsh Nursery Tunes [5'30"]
2.1+opt ob.2.1+opt bsn. 2.2.3.0.
perc,opt cel,opt harp,strings
study sc OXFORD f.s., perf mat rent
(H655)

HODEIR, ANDRE (1921-   )
Around The Blues [9']
0.0.0+clar in E flat.1. 2.0.0.0.
strings,vibra solo,pno solo,db
solo,drums solo
sc MJQ $6.95, perf mat rent   (H656)

Details [15']
2.1(English horn)+English
horn.2.2. 4.3.2.1. 2perc,harp,
strings,vibra solo,db solo,
drums solo
sc,pts MJQ rent   (H657)

HODKINSON, SYDNEY P. (1934-   )
Bumberboom [15']
3(pic,alto fl).2+English
horn.3(clar in E flat,bass
clar).2+contrabsn. 4.3.3.1.
timp,3perc,harp,strings
AMP perf mat rent   (H658)

Chansons De Jadis: Six Songs Of
Loneliness, For Solo Voice And
Orchestra [30']
2.2.2.2. 2.2.0.0. 2perc,strings,
solo voice
MERION perf mat rent   (H659)

Dynamics [5']
2.2.2.2. 4.2.3.1. perc,pno,
strings
sc AM.COMP.AL. $14.50   (H660)

Edge Of The Olde One, The, For
English Horn And Orchestra [25']
2perc,strings, electric English
horn solo
MERION perf mat rent   (H661)

Laments [8']
1.1.1.1. 0.0.0.0. strings
sc AM.COMP.AL. $13.80   (H662)

Symphony No. 1 [22']
3.3.3.3.alto sax. 4.3.3.1. timp,
3perc,elec gtr,harp,pno,strings
(Fresco) JOBERT   (H663)

Symphony No. 5 [22']
1.2.1.2. 2.0.0.0. opt perc,pno,
strings
(Sinfonia Concertante) MERION perf
mat rent   (H664)

HODZIATSKY, VITALIY (1936-   )
Frescos Of Kiev's St. Sofia [14']
fl,clar,2perc,cel,pno,strings
VAAP perf mat rent   (H665)

HOEBERG, GEORG (1872-1950)
Legende *Op.15 [5']
string orch
HANSEN-DEN perf mat rent   (H666)

HOELLER, KARL
see HÖLLER, KARL

HOEMSNES, BJØRN KORSAN (1954-   )
Andantino
string orch
NORGE   (H667)

HOEMSNES, BJØRN KORSAN (cont'd.)

Audiane, For Solo Voice And Orchestra
0.2.0.0. 2.0.0.0. hpsd,strings,
female solo
NORGE   (H668)

Intrada Sinfonia [9']
2.2.2.2. 4.2.2.0. timp,perc,
strings
NORGE   (H669)

HOENDERDOS, MARGRIET (1952-   )
Hunker, Schor & Hasselaar [12']
2.2.3.2. 4.4.3.1. timp,strings
sc DONEMUS f.s., perf mat rent (H670)

Nieuwe Verlaat, Het [10']
3.1.4.2. 2.2.3.0. harp,gtr,pno,
2vln,vla,2vcl,db
DONEMUS perf mat rent   (H671)

HOÉRÉE, ARTHUR (1897-1986)
Famille De Charles IV, La [8']
2.2.2.2. 2.2.2.0. timp,perc,cel,
strings
BILLAUDOT perf mat rent   (H672)

HOFBALL QUADRILLE see Strauss, Johann,
[Jr.]

HOFBALLTANZE see Strauss, Johann, [Jr.]

HOFFDING, FINN (1899-   )
Celebration Of May-Day
2+pic.2.2.2. 4.2.3.1. timp,perc&
cel,strings
[11'] HANSEN-DEN perf mat rent
(H673)

Det Er Ganske Vist
"It's Perfectly True" sc,pts
SAMFUNDET f.s.   (H674)

Evolution
sc,pts SAMFUNDET f.s.   (H675)

It's Perfectly True
see Det Er Ganske Vist

Sinfonia Concertante
sc SAMFUNDET f.s., perf mat rent
(H676)
Symphony No. 3
sc SAMFUNDET f.s., perf mat rent
(H677)

HOFFMAN, JOEL
Chamber Symphony
sc GALAXY 1.2938 f.s., perf mat
rent   (H678)

HOFFMANN, ERNST THEODOR AMADEUS
(1776-1822)
Undine: Overture [5']
2.2.2.2. 4.2.3.0. timp,strings
DOBLINGER perf mat rent   (H679)

HOFFMANN, GEORG MELCHIOR
Meine Seele Rühmt Und Preist, For
Solo Voice And Orchestra
fl,ob,strings,hpsd,vln solo,T
solo
(formerly attributed to J.S. Bach)
sc,pts BREITKOPF-L EB 7189 KIA
rent   (H680)

Schlage Doch, Gewünschte Stunde, For
Solo Voice And Orchestra
bells,strings,org,hpsd,A solo
(formerly attributed to J.S. Bach)
sc BREITKOPF-L EB 7053 KIA f.s.,
perf mat rent   (H681)

HOFFMEISTER, FRANZ ANTON (1754-1812)
Concerto for Clarinet, Bassoon and
Orchestra
2ob,2horn,strings,clar solo,bsn
solo
sc KUNZEL 10179 $25.00, perf mat
rent   (H682)

Concerto for Flute and Orchestra in
G, MIN 154
2ob,2horn,strings without vcl,fl
solo
INTERNAT. perf mat rent   (H683)

Concerto for Flute and Orchestra, No.
4, in D [25'30"]
2ob,2horn,strings,fl solo
(Paubon, P.) BILLAUDOT perf mat
rent   (H684)

Concerto for Flute and Orchestra, No.
8, in D [22'30"]
2fl,2horn,strings,fl solo
(Paubon, P.) BILLAUDOT perf mat
rent   (H685)

Concerto for Flute and Orchestra, No.
23, in G [29'42"]
2ob,2horn,strings,fl solo
(Paubon, P.) BILLAUDOT perf mat
rent   (H686)

HOFFMEISTER, FRANZ ANTON (cont'd.)

Concerto for Flute and Orchestra, No. 34, in G [22'10"]
2ob,2horn,strings,fl solo
(Paubon, P.) BILLAUDOT perf mat rent
(H687)

Concerto for 2 Flutes and Orchestra, Op. 64, in D
(Mueller) sc KUNZEL 10203 $28.00, perf mat rent
(H688)

Concerto for Viola and Orchestra in D, MIN 1
(Mlynarczyk) 2ob,2horn,strings,vla solo [16'] KALMUS A6409 pno-cond sc $8.00, set $18.00, pts $2.00, ea.
(H689)

Concerto for Viola and Orchestra in D, MIN 153
2ob,2horn,strings,vla solo
sc KUNZEL 10185 $20.00, perf mat rent
(H690)

Symphonies, Two
(Hickman, Roger; Hermann-Schneider, Hildegard) ("The Symphony" Vol. B-V) sc GARLAND
ISBN 0-8240-3842-8 $90.00
contains also: Eybler, Joseph, Symphony; Gansbacher, Johann Baptist, Symphony
(H691)

HÖFFNER, PAUL MARX (1895-1949)
Altdeutsche Suite
KISTNER perf mat rent
(H692)

Concerto for Oboe and String Orchestra
string orch,ob solo
KISTNER perf mat rent
(H693)

Concerto for Piano and Orchestra, Op. 45
KISTNER perf mat rent
(H694)

Drei Volkstanze
KISTNER
(H695)

Kammerkonzert *Op.49
KISTNER perf mat rent
(H696)

Serenade for String Orchestra
string orch
KISTNER perf mat rent
(H697)

Sinfonie Der Grossen Stadt
KISTNER perf mat rent
(H698)

HOFMAN
Konzertstück for Flute and Orchestra
SOUTHERN rent
(H699)

HOFMANN, HEINRICH
Huldigungsmarsch *Op.128 [12']
1+pic.2.2.2. 4.3.3.0. timp,2perc, strings
BREITKOPF-W perf mat rent
(H700)

HOFMANN, LEOPOLD (1738-1793)
Symphonies, Four
see Asplmayr, Franz, Symphonies, Three

HOFMANN, WOLFGANG (1922-)
Concertino for Trombone and String Orchestra [17']
string orch,trom solo
PETERS
(H701)

HOGENHAVEN, KNUD
Danse Triomphale
sc,pts SAMFUNDET f.s.
(H702)

Lamento
sc,pts SAMFUNDET f.s.
(H703)

HOGENHUIS, JELLE (1954-)
Variaties '85 [10']
2.2.2.2. 4.2.2.0. timp,2perc, strings
sc DONEMUS f.s., perf mat rent
(H704)

HOGFJELL see Nystedt, Knut

HOJSGAARD, ERIK (1954-)
Concerto for Piano and Orchestra [22']
0.0.3.0. 4.3.0.0. perc,strings, pno solo
SAMFUNDET perf mat rent
(H705)

Concerto for Violoncello and Orchestra
2(pic).2(English horn).2(clar in E flat,bass clar).2. 2.2.2.0. timp,4perc,cel,mand,harp, strings,vcl solo
HANSEN-DEN perf mat rent
(H706)

HOLBERGIANA see Gade, Niels Wilhelm

HOLBROOKE, JOSEPH (1878-1958)
Three Blind Mice *Op.37,No.1 [20']
2+pic.2+English horn.2.2+ contrabsn. 4.2.3.1. timp,perc, harp,strings
KALMUS A6773 sc $20.00, set $45.00, pts $2.00, ea., perf mat rent
(H707)

HÖLDERIN-REPORT, FOR SOLO VOICE AND ORCHESTRA see Hertel, Thomas

HOLDERLIN-LIEDER, ZYKLUS I, FOR SOLO VOICE AND ORCHESTRA see Killmayer, Wilhelm

HOLDERLIN-LIEDER, ZYKLUS II, FOR SOLO VOICE AND ORCHESTRA see Killmayer, Wilhelm

HOLENIA, H.
Valse Estatico *Op.39,No.1
string orch
KRENN
(H708)

Waltz, Op. 27, No. 6, in E flat
2.2.2.2. 4.2.3.0. perc,harp, strings
KRENN
(H709)

HOLEWA, HANS (1905-)
Concertino No. 7 for Harpsichord and Chamber Orchestra [14']
0.1.1.1. 1.1.1.0. strings,hpsd solo
STIM
(H710)

Concerto for Piano and Orchestra, No. 1 [17']
2.2.2.2. 4.2.3.1. timp,perc,harp, strings,pno solo
STIM
(H711)

Concerto for Piano and Orchestra, No. 3 [20']
4.4.4.4. 4.3.3.1. timp,perc, 2harp,strings,pno solo
STIM
(H712)

Concerto for 2 Pianos and String Orchestra [17']
string orch,2pno soli
STIM
(H713)

Symphony No. 6
STIM
(H714)

HOLIDAY see Stempnevsky, Stanislav

HOLIDAY SUITE, FOR ORCHESTRA see Pentland, Barbara

HOLIDAY SUITE, FOR STRING ORCHESTRA see Pentland, Barbara

HOLIDAY WALTZ see Gayfer, James McDonald

HOLLAND, JACK
Oh Jericho [2'45"]
3.3.4.3. 4.3.4.1. timp,perc,pno, org,elec gtr,strings, ram's horn
BOURNE perf mat rent
(H715)

Peanuts
(Tawfik, Jean; Logan, Harold)
3.3.3.3. 4.3.3.1. perc,org,elec gtr,strings [2'45"] BOURNE perf mat rent
(H716)

HOLLANDER, BENOIT (1853-1942)
Concerto for Violin and Orchestra [20']
3(pic).2.2.2. 2.2.0.0. timp, strings,vln solo
CHESTER JWC166B perf mat rent
(H717)

HÖLLANDER, GUSTAV
Andante Cantabile, Op. 60a
2.2.2.2. 2.2.0.0. timp,strings
ZIMMER.
(H718)

HÖLLER, KARL (1907-)
Concerto for Organ and Chamber Orchestra, Op. 15 [28']
0.0.0.0. 2.2.2.1. timp,vcl,db,org solo
LEUCKART perf mat rent
(H719)

Symphony No. 2, Op. 65 [34']
3.2.2.3. 4.2.3.1. timp,perc,harp, strings
(Huldigung an Mozart) SIKORSKI perf mat rent
(H720)

HÖLLER, YORK (1944-)
Concerto for Piano and Orchestra [18']
2(pic).2.2(bass clar).2(contrabsn). 4.3.3.0. 3perc,harp,cel,strings,pno solo
BOOSEY perf mat rent
(H721)

Dreamplay, For Solo Voice And Orchestra
see Traumspiel, For Solo Voice And

HÖLLER, YORK (cont'd.)

Orchestra

Improvisations Sur Le Nom De Pierre Boulez [4']
1.1.2(bass clar).1. 2.0.0.0. 2perc,harp,pno,2vln,vla,vcl,db
BOOSEY perf mat rent
(H722)

Magische Klanggestalt [11']
3(pic).3(English horn).3(bass clar).3(contrabsn). 4.3.3.1. 4perc,pno&cel,pno&elec org, harp,strings
BOOSEY perf mat rent
(H723)

Schwarze Halbinseln [23']
3(3pic).3(English horn).3(bass clar).3(contrabsn). 4.3.3.1. timp,perc,harp,pno&cel,strings, electronic tape
study sc BREITKOPF-W f.s., perf mat rent
(H724)

Traumspiel, For Solo Voice And Orchestra [25']
3(pic).3(English horn).3(bass clar).2+contrabsn. 4.3.3.1. timp,5perc,harp,pno&cel,elec org,strings,electronic tape,opt synthesizer,S solo
"Dreamplay, For Solo Voice And Orchestra" BOOSEY perf mat rent
(H725)

HOLLIGER, HEINZ (1939-)
Ad Marginem [7']
2fl,2clar,2vln,2vla,2vcl,db, electronic tape
SCHOTTS perf mat rent
(H726)

Bruchstucke [4']
3(pic,alto fl).2(English horn).2(bass clar).2. 2.1.1.0. timp,perc,harp,pno,2vln,2vla, 2vcl,db
SCHOTTS perf mat rent
(H727)

Engfuhrung [9']
0+alto fl.0+ob d'amore+English horn.2.1. 2.0.0.0. 2vln,2vla, 2vcl,db
SCHOTTS perf mat rent
(H728)

Ferne Klang, Der [6']
2.0+ob d'amore+English horn.2.1. 1.0.0.0. vln,2vla,vcl, electronic tape
SCHOTTS perf mat rent
(H729)

Glocken-Alphabet [5']
1+alto fl.0+English horn.1+bass clar.1. 1.1.1.0. perc,vln,vla, 2vcl
SCHOTTS perf mat rent
(H730)

Tonscherben [12']
4(pic,alto fl).4(English horn).4(clar in E flat,bass clar).3(contrabsn). 4.3.3.1. timp,4perc,harp,pno,strings
study sc SCHOTTS ED 7624 f.s., perf mat rent
(H731)

Turm-Musik, For Flute And Orchestra [25']
2(pic,alto fl).2(English horn,ob d'amore).2(bass clar).2. 2.2.1.0. timp,perc,harp,pno, 2vln,2vla,2vcl,db,electronic tape,fl solo
study sc SCHOTTS ED 7680 f.s., perf mat rent
(H732)

Zwei Liszt-Transkriptionen [12']
4(pic).3.6.3. 5.4.4.1. timp,perc, harp,strings
sc SCHOTTS ED 7732 f.s., perf mat rent
(H733)

HOLLOWANGELS see Kievman, Carson

HOLLOWAY, ROBIN (1943-)
Adagio And Rondo, For Horn And Orchestra *Op.43b [17']
2(pic).2(English horn).2.2. 2.2.0.0. timp,harp,strings,horn solo
BOOSEY perf mat rent
(H734)

Aria, Op. 44
1(alto fl,pic).1(English horn).1.1. 1.1.1.0. perc,pno, 2vln,vla,vcl,db
sc BOOSEY f.s.
(H735)

Ballade for Harp and Orchestra, Op. 61 [20']
2.1+English horn.1+bass clar.2. 2.0.0.0. strings,harp solo
BOOSEY perf mat rent
(H736)

Clarissa Symphony, For Solo Voices And Orchestra *Op.30a [45']
3(pic,alto fl).3(English horn).3(clar in E flat,bass

HOLLOWAY, ROBIN (cont'd.)

    clar).3(contrabsn). 4.3(trp in
    D).3.1. perc,harp,pno,cel,
    strings,ST soli
    BOOSEY perf mat rent   (H737)

Concertino No. 1, Op. 2 [20']
    1(pic).1.1.1. 1.1.1.0. strings
    BOOSEY perf mat rent   (H738)

Concertino No. 4, Op. 53
    see Showpiece

Concerto for Bassoon and Orchestra,
    Op. 63 [17']
    1.2.2.0. 2.0.0.0. strings,bsn
    solo
    BOOSEY perf mat rent   (H739)

Concerto for Orchestra, No. 2, Op. 40
    [30']
    3(pic,alto fl).2+English
    horn.3(clar in E flat,bass
    clar).3(contrabsn).sax.
    4.3.3.1. timp,4perc,harp,pno&
    cel,strings
    BOOSEY perf mat rent   (H740)

Concerto for Viola and Orchestra, Op.
    56 [20']
    2.1+English horn.1.1. 2.1.1.0.
    cel,strings,vla solo
    BOOSEY perf mat rent   (H741)

Divertimento No. 1, Op. 11 [20']
    2(pic).1+English horn.1.2.sax.
    2.2.1.0. timp,perc,pno,strings
    BOOSEY perf mat rent   (H742)

Idyll *Op.42
    1.2.2.2. 2.0.0.0. strings
    sc BOOSEY $13.00   (H743)

Idyll No. 2 *Op.54 [20']
    1(pic).2(English horn).0.2.
    2.0.0.0. strings
    BOOSEY perf mat rent   (H744)

Inquietus *Op.66 [10']
    1.1+English horn.1.1. 1.0.0.0.
    harp,strings
    BOOSEY perf mat rent   (H745)

Ode *Op.45 [14']
    2ob,2horn,strings
    sc BOOSEY $12.00, perf mat rent
                                       (H746)

Panorama [9']
    3(pic).2+English horn.2+bass
    clar.2+contrabsn. 4.3.3.1.
    timp,3perc,pno&cel,2harp,
    strings
    BOOSEY perf mat rent   (H747)

Romanza, For Oboe And String
    Orchestra *Op.59 [15']
    string orch,ob solo
    BOOSEY perf mat rent   (H748)

Seascape And Harvest *Op.55 [25']
    3(pic,alto fl).3(English
    horn).3(clar in E flat,bass
    clar).3(contrabsn). 4.4.3.1.
    4perc,harp,cel,strings
    BOOSEY perf mat rent   (H749)

Serenade, Op. 64, in G [12']
    string orch
    BOOSEY perf mat rent   (H750)

Serenata Notturna, For Four Horns And
    Orchestra *Op.52 [10']
    2trp,strings,4horn soli
    BOOSEY perf mat rent   (H751)

Showpiece (Concertino No. 4, Op. 53)
    [8']
    1(pic).1.1.1. 1.1.1.0. perc,pno,
    2vln,vla,vcl,db
    (the number of string players may
    be increased) study sc BOOSEY
    f.s., perf mat rent   (H752)

Sonata for Horn and Orchestra, Op.
    43a [12']
    2(pic).2(English horn).2.2.
    2.2.0.0. harp,strings,horn solo
    BOOSEY perf mat rent   (H753)

HOLM, KRISTIN (1965-   )
IS Per Orchestra *Op.6 [8']
    3.3.3.3. 4.3.3.1. 4perc,harp,pno,
    strings
    NORGE   (H754)

Lux Aeterna *Op.5 [3'50"]
    1.1.1.1. 1.1.1.1. 2perc,harp,pno,
    strings
    NORGE   (H755)

HOLM, MOGENS WINKEL (1936-   )
Aiolos [20']
    4(2pic).2+English horn.2(2clar in
    E flat)+bass clar.1+contrabsn.
    4.2.2.0. pno,perc,harp,strings

HOLM, MOGENS WINKEL (cont'd.)

    sc HANSEN-DEN f.s.   (H756)

Concerto Piccolo
    sc SAMFUNDET f.s., perf mat rent
                                       (H757)

Cries [12']
    2.2.2.2. 2.2.2.0. harp,strings
    SAMFUNDET perf mat rent   (H758)

Ricercare for Oboe and Orchestra, Op.
    26 [8']
    1+pic.0.0.0. 0.1.1.0. mand,gtr,
    pno,hpsd,3vln,3vla,vcl,db,ob
    solo
    HANSEN-DEN perf mat rent   (H759)

HOLM, PEDER (1926-   )
Pezzo Concertante
    sc,pts SAMFUNDET f.s.   (H760)

Three Orchestral Pieces
    see Tre Orkesterstykker

Tre Orkesterstykker
    "Three Orchestral Pieces" sc,pts
    SAMFUNDET f.s.   (H761)

HOLMAN, BILL (1927-   )
Concerto Duo For Trombone, Guitar And
    Orchestra [31']
    3+pic.2+English horn.3.0.2alto
    sax.2tenor sax.baritone sax.
    4.4+flügelhorn.3.1. perc,pno,
    harp,strings,trom solo,gtr solo
    NEWAM 19022 perf mat rent   (H762)

Concerto for Saxophone and Orchestra
    [25'30"]
    2+pic.2(English horn).3.2.
    4.4(flügelhorn).3.1. perc,pno,
    pno,harp,strings,tenor sax solo
    NEWAM 19023 perf mat rent   (H763)

HOLMAN, DEREK
Homage To Handel [17']
    string orch,opt hpsd
    CAN.MUS.CENT. MI 1500 H747H (H764)

HOLMBERG, PETER (1948-   )
Concertino, Op. 14 [12']
    wind quin,strings
    STIM   (H765)

HOLMBOE, VAGN (1909-   )
Chamber Symphony For Oboe, Viola And
    Orchestra *Op.67 [15']
    1.1.1.1. 4.0.0.0. strings,ob
    solo,vla solo
    HANSEN-DEN perf mat rent   (H766)

Chamber Symphony No. 1 *Op.53 [19']
    1.1.1.1. 1.1.0.0. timp,strings
    HANSEN-DEN perf mat rent   (H767)

Concertino for Violin, Viola and
    String Orchestra, Op. 22 [10']
    string orch,vln solo,vla solo
    HANSEN-DEN perf mat rent   (H768)

Concerto for Flute and Orchestra, Op.
    126 [25']
    0+pic.2(English horn).2.2.
    4.2.0.0. timp,perc,strings,fl
    solo
    HANSEN-DEN perf mat rent   (H769)

Concerto for Flute and Orchestra, Op.
    147 [20']
    0.2.2.2. 4.2.0.0. vibra,cel,
    strings,fl solo
    HANSEN-DEN perf mat rent   (H770)

Concerto for Oboe and Orchestra, Op.
    37 [20']
    2.0.2.2. 2.2.0.0. timp,perc,
    strings,ob solo
    HANSEN-DEN perf mat rent   (H771)

Concerto for Recorder and Orchestra,
    Op. 122 [17']
    cel,perc,strings,rec solo
    HANSEN-DEN perf mat rent   (H772)

Concerto for Trombone and Orchestra,
    Op. 52 [20']
    1+2pic.2.2.2. 4.3.0.0. timp,perc,
    strings,trom solo
    HANSEN-DEN perf mat rent   (H773)

Concerto for Trumpet and Orchestra,
    Op. 44 [15']
    2horn,strings,trp solo
    HANSEN-DEN perf mat rent   (H774)

Concerto for Tuba and Orchestra, Op.
    127 [17']
    2.2.2.2. 4.2.0.0. timp,perc,
    strings,tuba solo
    HANSEN-DEN perf mat rent   (H775)

Concerto for Viola and Orchestra, Op.
    31 [20']
    2.2.2.2. 2.2.0.0. timp,strings,
    vla solo

HOLMBOE, VAGN (cont'd.)

    HANSEN-DEN perf mat rent   (H776)

Concerto for Violin and Orchestra,
    Op. 139 [25']
    2+pic.2+English horn.2+bass
    clar.2+contrabsn. 4.3.0.0.
    timp,5perc,cel,strings,vln solo
    HANSEN-DEN perf mat rent   (H777)

Concerto for Violin, Viola and
    Orchestra, Op. 39 [20']
    2.2.2.2. 3.3.0.0. timp,2perc,
    strings,vln solo,vla solo
    HANSEN-DEN perf mat rent   (H778)

Concerto for Violoncello and
    Orchestra, Op. 120 [23']
    2+pic.2+English horn.2+bass
    clar.2+contrabsn. 4.3.0.0.
    timp,cel,perc,strings,vcl solo
    HANSEN-DEN perf mat rent   (H779)

Concerto Giocondo E Severo *Op.132
    [15']
    2+pic.2+English horn.2+bass
    clar.2+contrabsn. 4.3.3.1.
    timp,perc,strings
    HANSEN-DEN perf mat rent   (H780)

Concerto No. 8 [17']
    2.2.2.2. 2.2.2.0. timp,strings
    (Sinfonia Concertante) HANSEN-DEN
    perf mat rent   (H781)

Concerto No. 10 [15']
    2(pic).2.2.2. 2.2.0.0. timp,perc,
    strings
    (Wood, Brass & Gut) HANSEN-DEN
    perf mat rent   (H782)

Diafora *Op.118 [18']
    string orch HANSEN-DEN perf mat
    rent   (H783)

Divertimento for String Orchestra
    [15']
    string orch HANSEN-DEN perf mat
    rent   (H784)

Epitaph *Op.68 [25']
    3(pic).3(English horn).2+bass
    clar.2+contrabsn. 4.3.3.1.
    timp,3perc,strings
    HANSEN-DEN perf mat rent   (H785)

Fanfare [5']
    2+pic.3.2+bass clar.0. 4.4.3.1.
    timp,perc,strings
    HANSEN-DEN perf mat rent   (H786)

Intermezzo Concertante, For Tuba And
    String Orchestra [8']
    string orch,tuba solo
    HANSEN-DEN perf mat rent   (H787)

Kairos
    string orch HANSEN-DEN perf mat
    rent
    contains: Sinfonia No. 1, Op. 73;
    Sinfonia No. 2, Op. 73;
    Sinfonia No. 3, Op. 73;
    Sinfonia No. 4, Op. 73 (H788)

Louisiana Concerto *Op.131 [19']
    string orch HANSEN-DEN perf mat
    rent   (H789)

Prelude To A Dolphin *Op.166 [12']
    1.1.1.1. 2.1.0.0. 2perc,string
    quin
    HANSEN-DEN perf mat rent   (H790)

Prelude To A Living Stone *Op.172c
    [22']
    1.1.1.1. 2.1.0.0. 2perc,strings
    HANSEN-DEN perf mat rent   (H791)

Prelude To A Maple Tree *Op.168
    [10']
    1.1.1.1. 2.1.0.0. 3perc,string
    quin
    HANSEN-DEN perf mat rent   (H792)

Prelude To A Pine Tree *Op.164 [8']
    1.1.1.1. 2.1.0.0. timp,perc,pno,
    string quin
    HANSEN-DEN perf mat rent   (H793)

Prelude To A Willow Tree *Op.170
    [6']
    1.1.1.1. 2.1.0.0. timp,perc,cel,
    strings
    HANSEN-DEN perf mat rent   (H794)

Prelude To The Pollution Of Nature
    *Op.180 [9']
    1.1.1.1. 2.1.0.0. timp,perc,2vln,
    vla,vcl,db
    HANSEN-DEN perf mat rent   (H795)

Prelude To The Seagulls And The
    Cormorants *Op.174 [7']
    1.1.1.1. 2.1.0.0. 2perc,strings
    HANSEN-DEN perf mat rent   (H796)

HOLMBOE, VAGN (cont'd.)

Sinfonia No. 1, Op. 73
see Kairos

Sinfonia No. 2, Op. 73
see Kairos

Sinfonia No. 3, Op. 73
see Kairos

Sinfonia No. 4, Op. 73
see Kairos

Symphony No. 5, Op. 35 [30']
1+2pic.2.2.2. 4.3.3.1. timp,
3perc,strings
HANSEN-DEN perf mat rent   (H797)

Symphony No. 6, Op. 43 [35']
1+2pic.2+English horn.2+bass
clar.2+contrabsn. 4.3.3.1.
timp,3perc,strings
HANSEN-DEN perf mat rent   (H798)

Symphony No. 7, Op. 50 [24']
1+2pic.2(English horn).2.2.
4.3.3.1. timp,3perc,strings
HANSEN-DEN perf mat rent   (H799)

Symphony No. 8, Op. 56 [35']
3(pic).3(English horn).3(bass
clar).2+contrabsn. 4.3.3.1.
timp,3perc,strings
(Sinfonia Boreale) HANSEN-DEN perf
mat rent   (H800)

Symphony No. 11, Op. 144 [25']
2+pic.2+English horn.2+bass
clar.2+contrabsn. 4.3.3.1.
timp,perc,cel,strings
HANSEN-DEN perf mat rent   (H801)

Symphony No. 12, Op. 175 [22']
3(pic).2+English horn.2+bass
clar.2+contrabsn. 4.3.3.1.
timp,3perc,harp,strings
HANSEN-DEN perf mat rent   (H802)

Tempo Variabile-Symphonic
Metamorphoses *Op.108 [16']
3(pic).2+English horn.2+bass
clar.2+contrabsn. 4.3.3.1.
timp,perc,cel,strings
HANSEN-DEN perf mat rent   (H803)

Wee Wee Man, The, For Solo Voice And
Orchestra [5']
1.2.0.2. 4.0.0.0. strings,T solo
HANSEN-DEN perf mat rent   (H804)

HOLMES, AUGUSTA (MARY ANNE) (1847-1903)
Irlande
2(pic).2(English horn).1.4.
4.1.3.1. timp,perc,2harp,
strings
LEMOINE perf mat rent   (H805)

Pologne
2(pic).1.1.1. 4.5(cornet).3.1.
timp,perc,2harp,strings
LEMOINE perf mat rent   (H806)

HOLOCAUST SUITE see Gould, Morton

HOLST, GUSTAV (1874-1934)
Beni Mora *Op.29,No.1
sc CURWEN 046-00046 $19.50   (H807)

Brook Green Suite
see Collected Facsimile Edition,
Vol. 2: Works For Small Orchestra

Collected Facsimile Edition, Vol. 2:
Works For Small Orchestra
fac ed,sc FABER $90.00
contains: Brook Green Suite;
Double Concerto, Op. 49; Fugal
Concerto, Op. 40, No. 2; Lyric
Movement; St. Paul's Suite, Op.
29, No. 2   (H80B)

Concerto for 2 Violins and Orchestra,
Op. 49 [14']
2.2.2.2. 2.2.0.0. timp,strings,
2vln soli
study sc FABER C90841 f.s., perf
mat rent   (H809)

Double Concerto, Op. 49
see Collected Facsimile Edition,
Vol. 2: Works For Small Orchestra

Egdon Heath *Op.47
2.3.2.3. 4.3.3.1. strings
sc FABER F0844 f.s.   (H810)

Elegy "In Memoriam William Morris"
[10']
2.2.2.2. 4.3.3.1. timp,opt 2perc,
strings
FABER perf mat rent   (H811)

Fugal Concerto, Op. 40, No. 2
see Collected Facsimile Edition,
Vol. 2: Works For Small Orchestra

HOLST, GUSTAV (cont'd.)

Golden Goose, The: Suite [30']
3.3.2.2. 2.2.3.1. timp,2perc,
strings
(alternate scoring: piano and
strings) OXFORD perf mat rent
                                (H812)

Invocation, For Violoncello And
Orchestra [10']
2.2.2.2. 2.1.0.0. perc,harp,
strings,vcl solo
sc FABER 023-00319 $15.75, perf mat
rent   (H813)

Lure, The
3.3.3.3. 4.3.3.1. timp,perc,cel,
harp,strings
sc FABER 023-00340 $19.50, perf mat
rent   (H814)

Lyric Movement
see Collected Facsimile Edition,
Vol. 2: Works For Small Orchestra

Mystic Trumpeter, The, For Solo Voice
And Orchestra *Op.18 [20']
3.3.3.3. 4.3.3.1. timp,3perc,
harp,opt cel,strings,S solo
sc FABER f.s., perf mat rent (H815)

Song Of The Night, A, For Violin And
Orchestra *Op.19,No.1 [8']
2.1+English horn.2.2. 2.1.0.0.
timp,strings,vln solo
sc FABER F0887 f.s., perf mat rent
                                (H816)

St. Paul's Suite, Op. 29, No. 2
see Collected Facsimile Edition,
Vol. 2: Works For Small Orchestra

Suite De Ballet *Op.10 [18']
3.2.2.2. 4.2.3.1. timp,perc,harp,
strings
NOVELLO perf mat rent   (H817)

Walt Whitman Overture *Op.7 [7']
2.2.2.2. 4.3.3.1. timp,perc,
strings
FABER perf mat rent   (H818)

HOLST, IMOGEN (1907-1984)
Variations On "Loth To Depart", For
String Quartet And Orchestra
[12']
OXFORD perf mat rent   (H819)

HOLSTEIN, JEAN-PAUL (1939-   )
Tombeau d'Andre Jolivet, Le [13'20"]
string orch
BILLAUDOT perf mat rent   (H820)

HOLSZKY, ADRIANA
Spiegelung, For Flute, Violin And
Orchestra [30']
BREITKOPF-W perf mat rent   (H821)

HOLT, PATRICIA BLOMFIELD (1910-   )
Legend Of The North Woods
1.2.1.1. 2.1.0.0. timp,perc,
strings
CAN.MUS.CENT. MI 1100 H758L   (H822)

Songs Of My Country, For Solo Voice
And Instrumental Ensemble
horn,harp,strings,male solo
CAN.MUS.CENT. MV 1300 H758SO (H823)

HOLT, SIMON (1958-   )
Ballad Of The Black Sorrow, For Solo
Voices And Chamber Orchestra
[13']
1(pic).1.2(clar in A,clar in E
flat,bass clar).1(contrabsn).
1.2.1.0. harp,strings,
SSMezTBarB soli
sc UNIVER. UE18785 $75.00, perf mat
rent   (H824)

Syrensong [15']
3(pic,alto fl).2(English horn).2+
bass clar.1+contrabsn. 4.3.2.1.
2perc,2harp,pno,strings
sc UNIVER. UE18523 $65.00, perf mat
rent   (H825)

Wyrdchanging, For Solo Voice And
Chamber Orchestra [17']
2(pic,alto fl).1.1+bass clar.0.
1.0.0.0. perc,3vln,vla,2vcl,db,
Mez solo
UNIVER. perf mat rent   (H826)

HOLTEN, BO (1948-   )
Caccia [20']
3(pic,alto fl).3(English
horn).3(bass
clar).3(contrabsn). 4.3.3.1.
4perc,strings
HANSEN-DEN perf mat rent   (H827)

Concerto for Clarinet and Orchestra
[28']
3(alto fl).2+English horn.3(bass
clar).3(contrabsn). 4.3.3.1.
strings,clar solo

HOLTEN, BO (cont'd.)

HANSEN-DEN perf mat rent   (H828)

Plainsongs, For Trumpet And Orchestra
[45']
3.2+English horn.3.3. 4.3.3.1.
3perc,strings,trp solo
HANSEN-DEN perf mat rent   (H829)

Sinfonia Concertante For Violoncello
And Orchestra [40']
3(pic).3(English horn).3(clar in
E flat,bass clar).3(contrabsn).
4.3.3.1. 3perc,strings,vcl solo
HANSEN-DEN perf mat rent   (H830)

Songs Of Dusk, For Solo Voice,
Bassoon And Orchestra
see Tusmorkets Viser, For Solo
Voice, Bassoon And Orchestra

Tusmorkets Viser, For Solo Voice,
Bassoon And Orchestra [25']
2(pic).2(English horn).2(bass
clar).2(contrabsn). 4.1.0.0.
perc,strings,bsn solo,S solo
"Songs Of Dusk, For Solo Voice,
Bassoon And Orchestra" HANSEN-DEN
perf mat rent   (H831)

HOLZBAUER, IGNAZ JAKOB (1711-1783)
Symphonic Works, Three
(Agee, Richard J.) ("The Symphony"
Vol. C-IV) sc GARLAND
ISBN 0-8240-3834-7 $90.00
contains also: Fils, [Johann]
Anton, Symphonies, Two; Stamitz,
Carl, Symphonic Works, Three
                                (H832)

HOLZER, GERHARD (1932-   )
Chaka, For Solo Voice And Orchestra
1.1.2.1. 1.0.1.1. strings,S solo
PETERS   (H833)

HOMAGE see Cooper, Paul

HOMAGE: BARTOK, BIRD, DUKE see Baker,
David N.

HOMAGE TO HANDEL see Holman, Derek

HOMAGE TO INGOLFUR see Thorarinsson,
Jón

HOME GUARD see Fongaard, Bjørn,
Hjemmefronten

HOME ON THE RANGE [ARR.] see Guion,
David Wendall Fentress

HOME ROAD, THE, FOR SOLO VOICE AND
ORCHESTRA [ARR.] see Carpenter,
John Alden

HOMENAJE A FALLA see Nin-Culmell,
Joaquin

HOMENAJE A JOAN PRATS see Mestres-
Quadreny, Josep Maria

HOMENAJE A LA TEMPRANICA see Rodrigo,
Joaquin

HOMENAJE A MANOLO HUGUE, FOR SOLO VOICE
AND ORCHESTRA see Montsalvatge,
Xavier

HOMENAJE A WALT DISNEY see Guridi
Bidaola, Jesus

HOMEOMORPHIA IV see Grabovsky, Leonid

HOMESPUN OVERTURE, A see Gould, Morton

HOMEWARDS [ARR.] see Grieg, Edvard
Hagerup, Hjemad [arr.]

HOMILIUS, GOTTFRIED AUGUST (1714-1785)
Was Suchet Ihr: Die Hölle Flieht, For
Solo Voice And Orchestra
2horn,strings,B solo
BREITKOPF-L perf mat rent   (H834)

HOMMAGE A... see Cecconi, Monic

HOMMAGE A COMENIUS, FOR SOLO VOICES AND
ORCHESTRA see Milhaud, Darius

HOMMAGE A ERASME DE ROTTERDAM see
Tansman, Alexandre

HOMMAGE A GHIRLANDAIO, FOR VIOLONCELLO
AND ORCHESTRA see Ancelin, Pierre

HOMMAGE A HAYDN
(Miller) 2(pic).2(English horn).2.2.
2.2.0.0. timp,perc,strings [8']
(contains: Dukas, Prelude Elegiaque
[arr.]; Ravel, Menuet sur le Nom
d'Haydn [arr.]; Debussy, Hommage a
Haydn [arr.]) KALMUS A7331 sc
$8.00, set $25.00, pts $1.50, ea.
perf mat rent   (H835)

HOMMAGE A JACQUES IBERT, FOR ALTO
SAXOPHONE AND ORCHESTRA see Lacour,
Guy

HOMMAGE A JOHANNES see Petric, Ivo

HOMMAGE A JOHANNES BRAHMS see Meyer,
Krzysztof

HOMMAGE A KANDINSKY see Petitgirard,
Alain

HOMMAGE A MAURICE EMMANUEL see
Desportes, Yvonne

HOMMAGE A MAURICE RAVEL see Decoust,
Michel

HOMMAGE A MILHAUD see Andriessen,
Jurriaan

HOMMAGE A PIERRE see Denisov, Edison
Vasilievich

HOMMAGE A RABELAIS see DuBois, Pierre-
Max

HOMMAGE A RAVEL see Reibel, Guy

HOMMAGE A WEBERN see Alcazar, Miguel

HOMMES SUR LA TERRE, LES, FOR SOLO
VOICES AND ORCHESTRA see Brenet,
Therese

HOMO LUDENS see Masseus, Jan

HOMS, JOAQUIN (1906-   )
Dos Soliloquios Para Orquesta [11']
ALPUERTO   (H836)

Musica Para 11 [9']
1(pic).1.1.0. 1.1.0.0. perc,pno,
strings
ALPUERTO   (H837)

Presencias [25'50"]
1+pic.1+English horn.1+bass
clar.1. 1.1.1.1. perc,harp,
strings
ALPUERTO   (H838)

HONEGGER, ARTHUR (1892-1955)
Appel De La Montagne, L' [28']
3.3.2.3. 4.3.3.1. timp,perc,cel,
pno,strings
SALABERT perf mat rent   (H839)

Mort Passe, La [3']
1.1.1.1. 1.0.0.0. harp,perc,4vln,
2vla,2vcl,db
CHESTER JWC166A perf mat rent
                                  (H840)
Napoleon [25']
2(pic).2.2.2. 4.3.3.1. timp,perc,
strings
SALABERT perf mat rent   (H841)

Nocturne
min sc BOOSEY 993 $12.00   (H842)

Pacific 231
min sc EULENBURG EU01397 $5.00
                                  (H843)
Roue Ouverture, La [4'30"]
2.0.2.2. 0.0.0.0. strings
SALABERT perf mat rent   (H844)

Symphony No. 5
min sc EULENBURG EU01519 $8.75
                                  (H845)
HONOR, HONOR, FOR SOLO VOICE AND STRING
ORCHESTRA see Erb, Donald

HONOR SONG, FOR VIOLONCELLO AND
ORCHESTRA see Amram, David Werner

HOOFER SUITE see Gould, Morton

HOOK, JAMES (1746-1827)
Concerto for Clarinet and Orchestra
(Meecham, Paul) (in the US
available from Boosey) study sc
WEINBERGER W200 $10.00, perf mat
rent   (H846)

Concerto, Op. 20, No. 2
(Langley) 2fl,2horn,kbd,strings
[15'] sc OXFORD 77.602 $19.95,
perf mat rent   (H847)

HOOPER, LES
Fantasy for Saxophone and Orchestra
[15'20"]
3(pic).0.3(clar in E flat,bass
clar,contrabass
clar).2(contrabsn). 4.4.3.1.
timp,perc,pno,gtr,harp,strings,
fender-rhodes, sop sax solo
NEWAM 19024 perf mat rent   (H848)

Visitor, The, For Violin And
Orchestra [19'30"]
2.1.3+bass clar.1. 4.4.3+bass
trom.0. perc,pno,harp,gtr,
strings,vln solo

HOOPER, LES (cont'd.)

NEWAM 19025 perf mat rent   (H849)

HOOPS [ARR.] see Poulenc, Francis

HOOVER, KATHERINE
Summer Night [7']
fl,horn,strings
PRESSER perf mat rent   (H850)

HOP see Dusapin, Pascal

HOPE see Sivertsen, Kenneth, Haap

HOPKIN-EVANS, T. (1879-1940)
Introduction And Allegro For
Orchestra
2.2.2.2. 4.2.3.1. timp,perc,harp,
strings
UNIV.CR perf mat rent   (H851)

HOPKINS, JOHN (1949-1990)
Blue Yonder [12']
5.5.1.1. 0.2.2.0. timp,4perc,pno,
strings
SCHIRM.G perf mat rent   (H852)

Downstream [10']
string orch
SCHIRM.G perf mat rent   (H853)

Im Zauberkreis Der Nacht [26']
3(pic,alto fl).3(English
horn).3(bass
clar).3(contrabsn). 4.3.3.1.
timp,3perc,harp,strings
SCHIRM.G perf mat rent   (H854)

Magic Mountain, The, For Piano And
Orchestra [30']
3(pic,alto fl).3(English
horn).3(bass
clar).3(contrabsn). 4.3.3.0.
timp,2perc,harp,strings,pno
solo
SCHIRM.G perf mat rent   (H855)

Ra [5']
winds,perc,pno,strings, flexible
scoring
SCHIRM.G perf mat rent   (H856)

Soltice [18']
3(pic,alto fl).3(English
horn).3(bass clar).2. 4.3.3.0.
timp,3perc,harp,strings
SCHIRM.G perf mat rent   (H857)

HORACES, LES: OVERTURE see Salieri,
Antonio

HORBAN, WALTER (1941-   )
Australis, For Flute And String
Orchestra [8']
string orch,fl solo
NORRUTH perf mat rent   (H858)

HORIZON, THE see Ye, Xiao-Gang

HORIZONS '76, FOR SOLO VOICE AND
ORCHESTRA see Anderson, Thomas
Jefferson

HORIZONS COURBES, FOR 9-16
INSTRUMENTALISTS see Miroglio,
Francis

HORNEMANN, CHRISTIAN EMIL (1841-1906)
Aladdin
sc,pts SAMFUNDET f.s.   (H859)

HORNISSE, DIE: SUITE see Shostakovich,
Dmitri, Gadfly, The: Suite

HOROS see Xenakis, Yannis (Iannis)

HOROVITZ, JOSEPH (1926-   )
Concertino Classico, For 2 Trumpets
And Orchestra
timp,strings,2trp soli
NOVELLO perf mat rent   (H860)

Concerto for Bassoon and Orchestra,
[arr.] [16']
0.2.0.1. 2.0.0.0. strings,bsn solo
(arr from Euphonium Concerto)
NOVELLO perf mat rent   (H861)

HORST DU MEINE VIOLINE, FOR VIOLIN AND
ORCHESTRA see Mahr, Herman Carl
(Curley)

HORVATH, JOSEF MARIA (1931-   )
Passacaglia for String Orchestra
[16']
string orch
study sc DOBLINGER STP 609 f.s.,
perf mat rent   (H862)

Sothis I [15']
1(pic).1(English horn).1+bass
clar.1. 1.1.1.0. 2vln,vla,vcl,
db
DOBLINGER perf mat rent   (H863)

HORVIT, MICHAEL M. (1932-   )
Gardens Of Hieronymus B
SHAWNEE perf mat rent   (H864)

HORWOOD, MICHAEL (1947-   )
Amusement Park Suite [15']
3.2.2.2. 4.2.2.1. timp,2perc,
strings
CAN.MUS.CENT. MI 1100 H824AM (H865)

Symphony No. 1 [16']
2.2.2.2. 2.2.0.0. timp,perc,
strings
CAN.MUS.CENT. MI 1100 H824SY (H866)

HOSOKAWA, TOSHIO (1955-   )
Hajah, For Accordion And Orchestra
[13']
2pic,fl,3ob,perc,cel,harp,
strings,acord solo
ONGAKU perf mat rent   (H867)

Jenseits Der Zeit, For Violin And
String Orchestra [26']
string orch,vln solo
sc ZEN-ON f.s., perf mat rent
                                  (H868)
Pass Into Silence [17']
2(pic,alto fl).2.2(bass clar).2.
4.3.2.1. perc,cel,harp,strings
ONGAKU perf mat rent   (H869)

Prelude for Orchestra [7']
3(pic,alto fl).3.3.3. 4.3.2.1.
perc,cel,harp,strings
ONGAKU perf mat rent   (H870)

HOST, FOR SOLO VOICE AND STRING
ORCHESTRA see Eggen, Arne

HOSTSANGEN, FOR SOLO VOICE AND
ORCHESTRA see Groven, Eivind

HOUDY, PIERICK (1929-   )
Anao [13']
2.2.0.0. 2.0.0.0. timp,strings
CAN.MUS.CENT. MI 1200 H863AN (H871)

Concerto for String Quartet and
String Orchestra
string orch,string quar soli
CAN.MUS.CENT. MI 1717 H836CO (H872)

HOUR OF SILENCE, THE see Tanaka,
Satoshi

HOUR OF THE SOUL, FOR PERCUSSION, SOLO
VOICE AND ORCHESTRA see
Gubaidulina, Sofia

HOUSEWARMING see Gould, Morton

HOUSTON FANFARE see Wilson, Olly

HOVHANESS, ALAN (1911-   )
Greek Rhapsody No. 2 [12']
3.2.2.2. 4.3.3.1. timp,strings
PETERS P66837 perf mat rent (H873)

Majnun Symphony (Symphony No. 24, Op.
273) [25']
trp,strings,SATB,T solo
sc AMP $27.50   (H874)

Mount St. Helens Symphony (Symphony
No. 50) [25']
3.2.2.2. 4.3.3.1. timp,4perc,
harp,strings
PETERS P66020 perf mat rent (H875)

Symphony No. 10, Op. 184
sc PETERS P6251 $20.00   (H876)

Symphony No. 24, Op. 273
see Majnun Symphony

Symphony No. 26 [35']
3.2.2.2. 3.4.3.1. timp,perc,harp,
strings
PEER perf mat rent   (H877)

Symphony No. 50
see Mount St. Helens Symphony

HOVLAND, EGIL (1924-   )
August, For Solo Voice And Orchestra
*Op.34,No.4
0.0.2.2. 1.0.0.0. strings,solo
voice
NORGE   (H878)

Concert Overture *Op.39b [6']
3.3.3.3. 4.3.3.1. timp,perc,
strings
NORGE   (H879)

Concerto for Piano and Orchestra, Op.
91 [29']
0.0.3.3. 4.2.3.1. timp,perc,cel,
strings,pno solo
NORGE   (H880)

Concerto for Piccolo and String
Orchestra, Op. 117 [22']
string orch,pic solo
NORGE   (H881)

HOVLAND, EGIL (cont'd.)

Danses De La Mort *Op.127 [30']
  3.3.3.3. 4.3.3.1. timp,perc,
  2harp,hpsd,strings
  NORGE   (H882)

Festival Overture
  see Festouverture

Festouverture *Op.18 [7']
  3.2.2.2. 4.2.3.1. timp,perc,
  strings
  "Festival Overture" NORGE   (H883)

I Want To Go Home, For Solo Voice And
  Orchestra
  see Jeg Vil Hjem, For Solo Voice
  And Orchestra

Jeg Vil Hjem, For Solo Voice And
  Orchestra *Op.34,No.6
  cel,strings,solo voice
  "I Want To Go Home, For Solo Voice
  And Orchestra" NORGE   (H884)

Lilja, For Solo Voice And Orchestra
  *Op.61 [16']
  3.3.2.2. 2.1.1.0. perc,pno,
  strings,narrator
  NORGE   (H885)

Most Beautiful Rose, The, For Solo
  Voices And Orchestra
  see Vakresterosen, Den, For Solo
  Voices And Orchestra

Rorate, For Solo Voices And Orchestra
  *Op.55 [24']
  1(pic).1.0.0. 0.0.0.0. 4perc,
  strings,electronic tape,SSSS
  soli
  NORSK perf mat rent   (H886)

Suite for Flute and String Orchestra,
  Op. 31 [20']
  string orch,fl solo
  NORGE   (H887)

Symphony No. 1, Op. 20 [27']
  3.3.3.3. 4.3.3.1. timp,perc,harp,
  cel,strings
  NORGE   (H888)

Symphony No. 2, Op. 24 [16']
  3.2.2.2. 4.3.3.1. timp,perc,harp,
  strings
  NORGE   (H889)

Symphony No. 3, Op. 30 [19']
  1.1.1.2. 4.3.3.1. perc,pno,
  strings,narrator,cor
  NORGE   (H890)

Tombeau De Bach *Op.95 [19']
  4(pic).4(English horn).4(bass
  clar).4(contrabsn). 4.3.4.1.
  timp,2perc,cel,2harp,strings
  NORSK perf mat rent   (H891)

Vakresterosen, Den, For Solo Voices
  And Orchestra [20']
  1(alto fl).2(English horn).1.0.
  1.1.0.0. 2perc,org,pno,cel,
  strings,narrator&SSSS soli
  "Most Beautiful Rose, The, For Solo
  Voices And Orchestra" NORSK perf
  mat rent   (H892)

HOW TO SUCCEED IN BUSINESS WITHOUT
  REALLY TRYING: I BELIEVE IN YOU,
  FOR SOLO VOICES AND ORCHESTRA see
  Loesser, Frank

HOWARTH, ELGAR (1935-   )
  Concerto for Trombone and Orchestra
  [17']
  2.2.2.2. 4.2.0.0. timp,perc,
  strings,trom solo
  CHESTER perf mat rent   (H893)

Concerto for Trumpet and Orchestra
  [19']
  2(pic).2(English horn).2(clar in
  E flat,bass clar).2. 2.0.1.0.
  timp,3perc,strings,trp solo
  CHESTER perf mat rent   (H894)

HOWE, MARY (1882-1964)
  Berceuse for Solo Voice and Orchestra
  2.2.2.0. 0.0.0.0. triangle,harp,
  strings,solo voice
  SCHIRM.G perf mat rent   (H895)

Dirge
  2.2.2.2. 4.3.3.1. timp,perc,
  strings
  SCHIRM.G perf mat rent   (H896)

Little Elegy
  1.1.1.0. 0.0.0.0. harp,strings
  SCHIRM.G perf mat rent   (H897)

Little Rose, For Solo Voice And
  String Orchestra
  string orch,solo voice

HOWE, MARY (cont'd.)

  SCHIRM.G perf mat rent   (H898)

O Mistress Mine
  string orch
  SCHIRM.G perf mat rent   (H899)

Sand
  1(pic).1.1.1. 0.0.0.0. perc,
  strings
  SCHIRM.G perf mat rent   (H900)

Spring Pastoral
  1.1.1.1. 1.1.0.0. strings
  SCHIRM.G perf mat rent   (H901)

To The Unknown Soldier
  2.2+English horn.2.2. 4.2.3.0.
  timp,perc,harp,strings
  SCHIRM.G perf mat rent   (H902)

When I Died In Berners Street
  2.2.2.2. 4.0.0.0. timp,xylo,
  strings
  SCHIRM.G perf mat rent   (H903)

HOWELLS, HERBERT NORMAN (1892-1983)
  Concerto for String Orchestra
  study sc NOVELLO 2949-90 $19.00
                                    (H904)

Fantasy for Violoncello and Orchestra
  [20']
  2+pic.2+English horn.2.2.
  4.3.3.1. timp,2perc,harp,
  strings,vcl solo
  NOVELLO perf mat rent   (H905)

Merry Eye [9']
  3(pic).0.2.2. 3.0.0.0. timp,
  2perc,pno,strings
  NOVELLO perf mat rent   (H906)

Puck's Minuet *Op.20,No.1 [3'30"]
  2.0.2+bass clar.1. 0.0.0.0. timp,
  perc,pno,strings
  KALMUS A6131 sc $10.00, set $12.00
                                    (H907)
  CURWEN perf mat rent   (H908)

HOYLAND, VICTOR (1945-   )
  Fox [17']
  2(pic,alto fl).0.1(bass clar).0.
  0.0.0.0. vibra,harp,pno,2vln,
  vla,vcl,db
  UNIVER. perf mat rent   (H909)

In Transit, For Two Orchestras [16']
  3(pic,alto fl).2+English
  horn.3(bass clar).2+contrabsn.
  4.4.3.1. 4perc,2harp,cel,pno,
  strings
  sc UNIVER. UE18503 $75.00, perf mat
  rent   (H910)

Of Fantasy, Of Dreams And Ceremonies
  [19']
  7vln,3vla,2vcl,db
  UNIVER. perf mat rent   (H911)

Serenade [12']
  2(pic).0.2.0. 0.1.1.0. vibra,
  harp,pno&cel,3vcl,2db
  sc UNIVER. UE16404 $37.50, perf mat
  rent   (H912)

HRABOVSKY, LEONID
  see Grabovsky, Leonid

HRUŠOVSKY, IVAN (1927-   )
  Hudba K V.Hloznikovi
  "Music To V.Hloznik" SLOV.HUD.FOND
                                    (H913)

Music To V.Hloznik
  see Hudba K V.Hloznikovi

HSIEN, HSING-HAI (1905-1945)
  China Rhapsody
  3.2+English horn.2.3. 2.2.1.1.
  timp,perc,xylo,strings
  HONG KONG perf mat rent   (H914)

Yellow River, The, For Piano And
  Orchestra [arr.]
  (Liu Shi-Kun) 3.1.2.2. 3.2.1.0.
  timp,harp,strings, bamboo flute,
  pipa, piano solo [19'] HONG KONG
  perf mat rent   (H915)

HSIN, HU-KUANG
  Ka Ta Mei Ling [22']
  3.2.2.2. 4.3.3.1. timp,perc,pno,
  strings
  HONG KONG perf mat rent   (H916)

HUAN, CHIN
  White-Haired Girl, The: Suite *see
  Chu, Wei

HUANG, AN-LUN
  Girl With The Matches
  3.2.2.2. 4.2.3.1. timp,perc,harp,
  strings
  HONG KONG perf mat rent   (H917)

HUBA, VOLODYMYR (1938-   )
  Autumn Music (Sinfonietta No. 1)
  [12']
  1.1.1.1. 1.1.1.0. perc,harp,pno&
  org&hpsd,strings
  VAAP perf mat rent   (H918)

Obelisks [14']
  3trp,trom,timp,org,strings
  VAAP perf mat rent   (H919)

Sinfonietta No. 1
  see Autumn Music

HUBAY, JENÖ (1858-1937)
  Fantasy On "Carmen" By Bizet, For
  Violin And Orchestra
  CHOUDENS perf mat rent   (H920)

Scenes De La Csarda, For Violin And
  Orchestra
  KISTNER perf mat rent   (H921)

HUBEAU, JEAN (1917-   )
  Quatre Chansons De Paul Fort, No. 1:
  Il Faut Nous Aimer, For Solo
  Voice And Orchestra [1'30"]
  2.2.2.2. 4.3.3.0. timp,perc,harp,
  strings,med solo
  BILLAUDOT perf mat rent   (H922)

Quatre Chansons De Paul Fort, No. 2:
  Chanson De Fol, For Solo Voice
  And Orchestra [1'30"]
  2.1.1.1. 2.2.0.0. timp,perc,harp,
  strings,med solo
  BILLAUDOT perf mat rent   (H923)

Quatre Chansons De Paul Fort, No. 3:
  Le Diable Dans La Nuit, For Solo
  Voice And Orchestra [1'10"]
  2.2.2.2. 2.2.0.0. timp,perc,harp,
  strings,med solo
  BILLAUDOT perf mat rent   (H924)

Quatre Chansons De Paul Fort, No. 4:
  La Ronde Autour Du Monde, For
  Solo Voice And Orchestra [1'30"]
  2.2.2.2. 4.3.3.0. timp,perc,
  strings,med solo
  BILLAUDOT perf mat rent   (H925)

HUBER, HANS (1852-1921)
  Simplicius, Der: Einleitung
  KISTNER perf mat rent   (H926)

HUBER, KLAUS (1924-   )
  Drei Kleine Stucke Fur Orchester [9']
  2(alto fl).2.2.2. 2.1.2.0. timp,
  perc,strings
  RICORDI-GER SY 3016 perf mat rent
                                    (H927)
  Ich Singe Ein Land, Das Bald Geboren
  Wird [14']
  2.1.2.0. 1.1.0.0. 2perc,pno,2vln,
  vla,2vcl,db,electronic tape
  RICORDI-GER SY 2452 perf mat rent
                                    (H928)
  Seht Den Boden Blutgetrankt [5']
  1.1.1.1. 1.1.1.0. perc,pno,2vln,
  vla,vcl,db
  RICORDI-GER SY 2424 perf mat rent
                                    (H929)

HUBER, NICOLAUS A. (1939-   )
  Air Mit Sphinxes [16']
  1.1.1.1. 1.1.1.0. 2perc,harp,
  2vln,vla,vcl,db
  BREITKOPF-W perf mat rent   (H930)

Gespenster, For Solo Voice And
  Orchestra [17']
  3(pic,alto fl).3(English horn,
  Heckelphone).3(bass
  clar).3(contrabsn). 4.4.4.0.
  timp,perc,harp,pno,cel,strings,
  electronic tape,solo voice
  BREITKOPF-W perf mat rent   (H931)

Go Ahead
  BREITKOPF-W perf mat rent   (H932)

Nocturnes [22']
  2(2pic).2.2.2(contrabsn).
  2.3.2.0. timp,3perc,harp,pno,
  cel,strings
  study sc BREITKOPF-W PB 5164 f.s.,
  perf mat rent   (H933)

Vier Stucke [17']
  3(pic).3.3(clar in E
  flat).3(contrabsn). 4.3.3.0.
  timp,3perc,harp,cel,strings,
  electronic tape
  BREITKOPF-W perf mat rent   (H934)

HÜBLER, KLAUS-K. (1955-   )
  Arie Dissolute, For Viola And
  Instrumental Ensemble [12']
  2(pic,alto fl).0.1.0. 0.2.1.0.
  perc,2vln,2vcl,vla solo
  BREITKOPF-W perf mat rent   (H935)

Epiphyt, For Flute And Chamber
  Orchestra [13']
  2.1.3.2. 0.2.1.0. perc,harp,3vln,
  2vla,3vcl,db,fl solo

HÜBLER, KLAUS-K. (cont'd.)

    BREITKOPF-W perf mat rent   (H936)

HUCKLEBERRY FINN OVERTURE see De
    Lamarter, Eric see Waxman, Franz

HUDBA K V.HLOZNIKOVI see Hrušovsky,
    Ivan

HUDBA PRE J.S. see Benes, Juraj

HUDSON RIVER SUITE see Grofe, Ferde
    (Ferdinand Rudolph von)

HUDSON VALLEY SUITE see Starer, Robert

HUGENOTTEN, DIE, FOR VIOLIN, ZYMBAL AND
    ORCHESTRA see Fritsch, Johannes
    Georg

HUGH THE DROVER: HUGH'S SONG OF THE
    ROAD FOR SOLO VOICE AND ORCHESTRA
    see Vaughan Williams, Ralph

HUGUENOTS, LES: A FAU TOURANE see
    Meyerbeer, Giacomo

HUIT PIECES BREVES, SERIES I, NOS. 1-4
    [ARR.] see Franck, Cesar

HUIT PIECES BREVES, SERIES II, NOS. 5-8
    [ARR.] see Franck, Cesar

HUIT STELES DE VICTOR SEGALEN, FOR SOLO
    VOICE AND CHAMBER ORCHESTRA see
    Tansman, Alexandre

HUKVARI, JENO (1935-   )
    Symphony in A [15']
      3.2.3.3. 4.4.3.1. timp,perc,
      vibra,cel,strings
      NORGE   (H937)

HULDA: BALLET MUSIC see Franck, Cesar

HULDIGUNGEN WALZER see Strauss, Eduard

HULDIGUNGSMARSCH see Hofmann, Heinrich
    see Liszt, Franz

HULTER TIL BULTER, FOR PERCUSSION AND
    ORCHESTRA see Rypdal, Terje

HULTQVIST, ANDERS (1955-   )
    Aire Claro, L' [16']
      3.3.3.3. 4.3.3.1. timp,4perc,
      strings
      STIM   (H938)

    Time [14']
      19strings soli
      STIM   (H939)

    Time And The Bell [14']
      3.3.3.3. 4.3.3.1. timp,4perc,pno,
      strings
      STIM   (H940)

HUMMEL, BERTOLD (1925-   )
    Concerto for Percussion and
      Orchestra, Op. 70 [32']
      3(pic).3.3.2. 4.3.3.1. timp,perc,
      harp,strings,perc solo
      SCHOTTS perf mat rent   (H941)

HUMMEL, JOHANN NEPOMUK (1778-1837)
    Acht Variationen Und Coda Uber "O Du
      Lieber Augustin"
      (Stein) "Eight Variations And Coda
      On "O Du Lieber Augustin"" KALMUS
      A7432 sc $10.00, set $30.00, pts
      $2.50, ea.   (H942)

    Concerto for Piano and Orchestra, Op.
      89, in B minor [20']
      1.2.2.2. 4.2.0.0. timp,strings,
      pno solo
      KALMUS A5539 set $40.00, pts $2.00,
      ea., perf mat rent   (H943)

    Concerto for Piano and Orchestra, Op.
      113
      (Sachs, Joel) sc A-R ED
      ISBN 0-89579-135-8 f.s.   (H944)

    Concerto for Trumpet and Orchestra
      (Ritter, Eugene W.) min sc KALMUS
      K01511 $11.50   (H945)

    Eight Variations And Coda On "O Du
      Lieber Augustin"
      see Acht Variationen Und Coda Uber
      "O Du Lieber Augustin"

    Fantasy for Viola and Orchestra
      orch,vla solo
      MUS. RARA perf mat rent   (H946)

    Potpourri, For Viola And Orchestra
      *Op.94
      MUS. RARA 1919 perf mat rent (H947)

HUMORESKA, FOR HORN AND STRING
    ORCHESTRA see Bozic, Darijan

HUMORESKE see Andersen, Karl August see
    Humperdinck, Engelbert see Spalder,
    Frithjof

HUMORESQUE see Thorne, Francis Burritt

HUMORESQUE, FOR VIOLIN AND ORCHESTRA,
    [ARR.] see Dvorák, Antonín

HUMORISTICA see Lindgren, Olof

HUMPERDINCK, ENGELBERT (1854-1921)
    Humoreske
      KALMUS A5874 sc $10.00, set $18.00,
      perf mat rent   (H948)

    Königskinder: Prelude, Act II [3'30"]
      3(pic).2.2.2+contrabsn. 4.2.3.1.
      timp,perc,strings
      KALMUS A5896 sc $8.00, set $22.00,
      perf mat rent   (H949)

    Königskinder: Prelude, Act III [9']
      3(pic).2+English horn.2+bass
      clar.2+contrabsn. 4.2.3.1.
      timp,perc,harp,strings
      KALMUS A5897 sc $8.00, set $22.00,
      perf mat rent   (H950)

    Love Scene From "The Merchant Of
      Venice" [7']
      2.1.2.2. 2.0.0.0. timp,harp,
      strings
      KALMUS A6108 sc $5.00, set $15.00,
      perf mat rent   (H951)

    Marketenderin, Die: Overture [10']
      3.3.2.2. 4.3.3.0. timp,perc,
      strings
      SCHOTTS perf mat rent   (H952)

HUMPHRIES, JOHN (ca. 1707-1730)
    Concerti Grossi, Op. 2, Twelve *see
      THREE CENTURIES OF MUSIC IN
      SCORE, VOL. 3: CONCERTO II,
      ENGLAND

150 DAVIDS SALME see Maehlum, Svein

HUNDRED FOLK TUNES FROM HARDANGER, A,
    NOS. 16-30 see Tveitt, Geirr

HUNDRED FOLK TUNES FROM HARDANGER, A,
    NOS. 46-60 see Tveitt, Geirr

HUNDRED FOLK TUNES FROM HARDANGER, A,
    NOS. 61-75 see Tveitt, Geirr

HUNDSNES, SVEIN (1951-   )
    Concerto for Chamber Orchestra
      1.1.1.1. 1.0.0.0. strings
      NORGE   (H953)

    Concerto for Guitar and Chamber
      Orchestra [23']
      2fl,strings,gtr solo
      NORGE   (H954)

    Jeux Jeunesse
      3.3.3.3. 6.4.3.1. perc,strings
      NORGE   (H955)

    Konsertfantasi No. 2: Masterswinger
      3(pic).3(English horn).3(bass
      clar).3(contrabsn). 4.4.3.1.
      timp,perc,strings
      NORGE   (H956)

    Konsertfantasi No. 3: Danza
      3(pic).2.3(bass
      clar).3(contrabsn). 4.4.3.1.
      perc,harp,strings, clavinet(el)
      NORGE   (H957)

    Sinfonietta Romantica [11'30"]
      2.2.2.2. 4.3.3.1. timp,perc,
      strings
      NORGE   (H958)

    Symfonisk Rendez-Vous
      3.3(English horn).3(bass
      clar).3(contrabsn). 4.2.3.1.
      perc,gtr,strings, clavinet(el)
      NORGE   (H959)

    Symphony No. 1 [29']
      2.2.2.2. 4.3.3.1. timp,perc,
      strings
      NORGE   (H960)

HUNFELD, XANDER (1949-   )
    Course Of Nature [8']
      3.3.3.0. 4.3.3.1. 3perc,strings
      DONEMUS perf mat rent   (H961)

    In Retrospectieve Zin [7']
      2.2.2.2. 2.2.0.0. 3perc,harp,
      strings
      DONEMUS perf mat rent   (H962)

    Phenomena: I. Course II. Cycle [15']
      3.3.3.3. 4.3.3.1. 3perc,harp,
      strings
      sc DONEMUS f.s., perf mat rent
                                   (H963)

HUNG HU, FOR VIOLIN AND ORCHESTRA see
    E, Ke Jian

HUNGARIA see Liszt, Franz

HUNGARIAN DANCE NO. 4 [ARR.] see
    Brahms, Johannes, Ungarischer Tanz
    No. 4 [arr.]

HUNGARIAN DANCE NO. 8 [ARR.] see
    Brahms, Johannes, Ungarischer Tanz
    No. 8 [arr.]

HUNGARIAN DANCE NO. 9 [ARR.] see
    Brahms, Johannes, Ungarischer Tanz
    No. 9 [arr.]

HUNGARIAN DANCES NOS. 1 AND 3 [ARR.]
    see Brahms, Johannes, Ungarische
    Tanze Nos. 1 And 3 [arr.]

HUNGARIAN FANTASY, FOR FLUTE AND
    ORCHESTRA, [ARR.] see Doppler,
    Franz, Fantaisie Pastorale
    Hongroise, For Flute And Orchestra,
    [Arr.]

HUNGARIAN MARCH see Liszt, Franz

HUNGARIAN MARCH IN C [ARR.] see
    Schubert, Franz (Peter)

HUNGARIAN MARCH, TO THE ASSAULT see
    Liszt, Franz, Ungarischer
    Sturmmarsch

HUNGARIAN NATIONAL ANTHEM see Erkel,
    Franz (Ferenc)

HUNGARIAN RHAPSODIES NOS. 1-9 [ARR.]
    see Liszt, Franz, Rhapsodies
    Hongroises Nos. 1-9 [arr.]

HUNGARIAN RHAPSODY NO. 13 [ARR.] see
    Liszt, Franz, Rhapsodie Hongroise
    No. 13 [arr.]

HUNGARIAN STORM MARCH see Liszt, Franz,
    Ungarischer Sturmmarsch

HUNGARIAN TUNES, FOR VIOLIN AND
    ORCHESTRA see Eshpai, Andrey Y.

HUNKER, SCHOR & HASSELAAR see
    Hoenderdos, Margriet

HUNNENSCHLACHT see Liszt, Franz

HUNT, MICHAEL (1945-   )
    Asymptopia I [7']
      3(pic).2.2.1. 2.2.3.1. perc,pno,
      strings
      MMB perf mat rent   (H964)

    Asymptopia II [8']
      3(pic).2.2.1. 2.2.3.1. perc,pno,
      strings
      MMB perf mat rent   (H965)

    Con Cordes [7']
      string orch
      MMB perf mat rent   (H966)

    Emerald Reflections [12']
      2(pic).1+English horn.2.2.
      4.2.3.1. 2perc,strings
      MMB perf mat rent   (H967)

    Hidden Walls Of Time [28']
      3perc,strings
      MMB perf mat rent   (H968)

    Lento, For String Orchestra [9']
      string orch
      MMB perf mat rent   (H969)

    Theme In Two Moods [4']
      2.2.2.2. 4.2.3.1. perc,pno,
      strings
      MMB perf mat rent   (H970)

HUNT, THE [ARR.] see Tchaikovsky, Piotr
    Ilyich

HUREL, PHILIPPE (1955-   )
    Diamants Imaginaires [12']
      2+2pic+alto fl.1.2+bass
      clar.1.alto sax.2.1.1.0.
      2perc,harp,elec org,strings,
      synthesizer
      BILLAUDOT perf mat rent   (H971)

    Memento Pour Marc [16']
      3.2.2.2. 4.3.3.1. 2perc,2harp,
      pno,strings
      BILLAUDOT perf mat rent   (H972)

    Memoire Vive [22']
      3.3.4.4. 4.3.3.1. 3perc,cel,
      2harp,pno,strings
      BILLAUDOT perf mat rent   (H973)

    Pour l'image [12']
      1.1.1.0.alto sax. 1.1.1.0. 2perc,
      string quin
      BILLAUDOT perf mat rent   (H974)

HUREL, PHILIPPE (cont'd.)

Trames [11']
6vln,2vla,2vcl,db
BILLAUDOT perf mat rent   (H975)

HURNÍK, ILJA (1922-   )
Concerto for Piano and Orchestra
[16']
CESKÝ HUD.   (H976)

Nouveau Clavecin, Le, For Harpsichord
And String Orchestra [15']
string orch,hpsd solo
SUPRAPHON   (H977)

Things, The [18']
CESKÝ HUD.   (H978)

HURQUALIA, FOR TIMPANI, PERCUSSION AND
ORCHESTRA see Scelsi, Giacinto

HURST, GEORGE (1926-   )
Sinfonia in D
2.2.2.2. 2.2.2.1. timp,strings
AMP perf mat rent   (H979)

HURUM, ALF (1882-1972)
Bendik Og Arolilja *Op.20 [16']
3.2.2.2. 4.2.3.1. timp,perc,harp,
strings
NORGE   (H980)

Eksotisk Suite *Op.9 [20']
3.2.2.2. 4.2.3.1. timp,perc,harp,
cel,strings
"Exotic Suite" NORGE   (H981)

Eventyrland *Op.16 [26']
3.2.2.3. 4.2.3.1. timp,perc,harp,
strings
"Fairyland" NORGE   (H982)

Exotic Suite
see Eksotisk Suite

Fairyland
see Eventyrland

Symphony
3.2.2.2. 4.2.3.1. timp,perc,
strings
NORGE   (H983)

HURUM, HELGE (1936-   )
Concentus Ad Libitum, For Jazz
Quintet And Orchestra [23']
2.2.3.2. 4.4.3.1. timp,perc,
strings, Quintet: sop sax, trp,
double bass, perc, pno
NORGE   (H984)

HUS FOR ORKESTER see Mostad, Jon

HUSA, KAREL (1921-   )
Concerto for Orchestra [25']
3.3.3.3. 4.4.3.1. timp,perc,harp,
pno,strings
AMP   (H985)

Concerto for Organ and Orchestra
[22']
3trp,timp,2perc,strings,org solo
AMP perf mat rent   (H986)

Concerto for Trumpet and Orchestra
[20']
2(pic).2.2(bass
clar).2(contrabsn). 2.2.0.0.
timp,3perc,harp,strings,trp
solo
AMP perf mat rent   (H987)

Monodrama (Portrait Of An Artist)
[23']
3.3.3.3. 4.3.3.1. timp,perc,harp,
strings
sc AMP $35.00   (H988)

Pastorale
string orch
sc,pts AMP $16.00   (H989)

Reflections (Symphony No. 2) [20']
2.2.2.2. 2.2.0.0. timp,perc,harp,
strings
AMP   (H990)

Steadfast Tin Soldier, The, For
Narrator And Orchestra [26']
2.2.2.2. 2.2.0.0. timp,perc,harp,
strings,narrator
AMP   (H991)

Symphonic Suite [19']
3.3.3.3. 4.3.3.1. timp,perc,harp,
pno,strings
AMP   (H992)

Symphony No. 2
see Reflections

Trojan Women, The: Suite [20']
2.2.2.2. 2.2.1.0. timp,perc,harp,
pno,strings
study sc AMP f.s., perf mat rent

HUSA, KAREL (cont'd.)

                                 (H993)
HUSITSKA. OVERTURE see Dvorák, Antonín

HUSZAR, LAJOS
Musica Concertante
sc EMB 10221 f.s.   (H994)

Scherzo E Adagio *Op.8
sc EMB 12071 f.s.   (H995)

HUTCHINSON, HELY
see HELY-HUTCHINSON, (CHRISTIAN)
VICTOR

HUZELLA, ELEK (1915-1971)
Meditation
sc EMB 10222 f.s., perf mat rent
                                 (H996)
HVOSLEF, KETIL (1939)
Air [3']
3.2.2.2. 4.2.3.1. timp,perc,
strings
NORGE   (H997)

Antigone [21']
4(pic).4.4(bass
clar).4(contrabsn). 4.4.3.1.
timp,3perc,harp,pno,strings
NORSK   (H998)

Compleanno, Il, For Orchestra And Two
Sextets [17']
2(pic).2.2(bass clar).2. 3.3.3.0.
timp,perc,harp,pno,strings,
sextets: fl, ob, 2vln, 2vcl or
vcl & db soli
NORSK   (H999)

Concertino for Orchestra [10']
2(pic).2.1(bass clar)+clar in E
flat.2. 2.2.1.0. timp,2perc,
strings
NORSK perf mat rent   (H1000)

Concertino for Piano and Orchestra
[8']
3.2.2.2. 0.2.0.0. strings,pno
solo
NORGE   (H1001)

Concerto for Bassoon and String
Orchestra [14']
string orch,bsn solo
NORGE   (H1002)

Concerto for Double Bass and
Orchestra [21']
3.3.2.2. 2.2.0.0. timp,perc,
strings,db solo
sc NORSK f.s., perf mat rent
                                 (H1003)
Concerto for Flute, Guitar and String
Orchestra [20']
string orch,fl solo,gtr solo
NORGE   (H1004)

Concerto for Trumpet and Orchestra
[17']
3.2.2.2. 0.0.0.0. timp,perc,
strings,trp solo
NORGE   (H1005)

Concerto for Violin and Orchestra
[36'20"]
3.3.3.3. 3.3.3.0. timp,perc,pno,
strings,vln solo
NORGE   (H1006)

Mi-Fi-Li [17']
3(pic).3(English horn).3(bass
clar).2. 4.2.0.0. timp,perc,
strings
NORSK perf mat rent   (H1007)

Trio For Thirteen: Acotral, For Solo
Voices And Orchestra
fl,ob,clar,bsn,perc,2vln,vla,vcl,
SMezTB soli
NORGE   (H1008)

Variations for Chamber Orchestra
[12']
1.1.1.1. 1.1.0.0. strings
NORSK   (H1009)

HY VONG 14 see Ton That, Tiet

HYDRA see Stalheim, Jostein

HYLA, LEON (LEE) (1952-   )
Also Norway [10']
alto fl,ob,bass clar,tenor sax,
horn,trom,2perc,pno,2vln,vla,db
sc APNM $12.25, perf mat rent
                                 (H1010)
Pre-Pulse Suspended [14']
1(alto fl).0.1+bass clar.1.
1.0.1.0. pno,2vln,vla,vcl,db
sc APNM $16.25, perf mat rent
                                 (H1011)
HYMN see Birgisson, Snorri Sigfus

HYMN FOR FOURTEEN STRINGS see Stout,
Alan

HYMN TO PAN see Eastwood, Thomas

HYMN TO THE OCEAN, FOR SOLO VOICE AND
ORCHESTRA see Tveitt, Geirr, Hymne
Til Havet, For Solo Voice And
Orchestra

HYMN TO WAR, FOR SOLO VOICE AND STRING
ORCHESTRA see Fleming, Robert

HYMNE, FOR SOLO VOICE AND ORCHESTRA see
Strand, Ragnvald

HYMNE A LA VIE see Martinon, Jean

HYMNE PORTUGAIS, L', FOR PIANO AND
ORCHESTRA see Gottschalk, Louis
Moreau

HYMNE TIL HAVET, FOR SOLO VOICE AND
ORCHESTRA see Tveitt, Geirr

HYMNEN AN DIE NACHT see Rubin, Marcel

HYMNER, FOR SOLO VOICE AND ORCHESTRA
see Heegaard, Lars

HYMNISK DANS see Thoresen, Lasse

HYMNKUS, FOR SOLO VOICE AND ORCHESTRA
see Cage, John

HYMNOS, FOR ORGAN AND ORCHESTRA see
Scelsi, Giacinto

HYMNUS see Klengel, Julius see
Silvestrov, Valentin

HYPOTHESEN WALZER see Strauss, Eduard

I

I DE TUNGE TIDER: OUVERTURE see Strom, Alf Gotlin

I DET FJERNE see Solås, Eyvind

I DON'T KNOW WHY YOU THINK ABOUT ME, FOR SOLO VOICE AND CHAMBER ORCHESTRA see Revueltas, Silvestre, No Se Por Que Piensas Tu, For Solo Voice And Chamber Orchestra

I GOT RHYTHM VARIATIONS see Gershwin, George

I HAVE FOUND MY HANDSOME LOVER BACK, FOR SOLO VOICE AND ORCHESTRA see Søderlind, Ragnar, Eg Hev Funne Min Floysne Lokkar Att I Mitt Svarmerus, For Solo Voice And Orchestra

I HEAR THE WATER DREAMING, FOR FLUTE AND ORCHESTRA see Takemitsu, Toru

I-JURA PIRAMA see Prado, José-Antonio (Almeida)

I KNOW STARLIGHT, FOR SOLO VOICE AND ORCHESTRA see Lockwood, Normand

I LOVE YOU [ARR.] see Grieg, Edvard Hagerup

I NEVER SAW ANOTHER BUTTERFLY, FOR SOLO VOICE AND ORCHESTRA see Glick, Srul Irving

I STOOD ON DE RIBBER, FOR SOLO VOICE AND ORCHESTRA [ARR.]
   (Burleigh, Harry T.) 2.2.2.2. 2.0.0.0. harp,strings,high solo
   COLOMBO perf mat rent   (I1)

I TVERASAL-HYTTA see Kielland, Olav

I WANT TO BE READY, FOR SOLO VOICE AND ORCHESTRA [ARR.]
   (Burleigh, Harry T.) 1.2.1.0. 2.1.1.0. timp,strings,med solo
   COLOMBO perf mat rent   (I2)

I WANT TO GO HOME, FOR SOLO VOICE AND ORCHESTRA see Hovland, Egil, Jeg Vil Hjem, For Solo Voice And Orchestra

IAM MANET ULTIMA SPES see Schibler, Armin

IANNACCONE, ANTHONY (1943-   )
   Divertimento for Orchestra [11']
      3.2.3.2. 4.3.3.1. timp,perc,harp, pno&cel,strings
      sc TENUTO 496-00001 $9.50, perf mat rent   (I3)

IARA, FOR SOLO VOICE AND ORCHESTRA see Villa-Lobos, Heitor

IBARRONDO, FELIX (1943-   )
   Abyssal, For 2 Guitars And Instrumental Ensemble [18']
      1.1.1.0. 0.0.0.0. 2pno,strings, 2gtr soli
      sc BILLAUDOT f.s., perf mat rent   (I4)

   Alucinacion [13']
      7vln,2vla,2vcl,db
      ALPUERTO   (I5)

   Au Bord D'abimes [14'20"]
      1+pic.1.1.1. 1.1.2.0. perc, marimba,pno,harp,strings
      sc ALPUERTO f.s.   (I6)

   Sous L'emprise D'une Ombre [18'15"]
      1.1.2.1. 1.2.2.0. perc,pno,3vln, vla,vcl,db
      sc ALPUERTO f.s.   (I7)

ICE-NINE, FOR PIANO AND CHAMBER ORCHESTRA see Wegner, August Martin

ICE PALACE, THE: SUITE [ARR.] see Bohren, Geir

ICELAND OVERTURE see Leifs, Jon

ICELANDIC DANCES see Leifs, Jon

ICELANDIC FOLK SONG see Sandby, Herman

ICELANDIC FOLK SONGS, FOR SOLO VOICE AND ORCHESTRA see Asgeirsson, Jon

ICH BIN WENIG - GEMEINSAM SIND WIR STARK: SUITE see Polovinkin, Leonid

ICH GING MIT LUST DURCH EINEN GRUNEN WALD see Mahler, Gustav

ICH LIEBE DICH, FOR SOLO VOICE AND ORCHESTRA [ARR.] see Stolz, Robert

ICH LIEBE DICH [ARR.] see Grieg, Edvard Hagerup, I Love You [arr.]

ICH LIEBE DICH, GELIEBTER, FOR SOLO VOICE AND ORCHESTRA see Kühnl, Claus

ICH LIEBE JESUM IN DER NOT see Bach, Johann Sebastian

ICH MÖCHTE WOHL DER KAISER SEIN, FOR SOLO VOICE AND ORCHESTRA see Mozart, Wolfgang Amadeus

ICH SINGE EIN LAND, DAS BALD GEBOREN WIRD see Huber, Klaus

ICH STEH AN DEINER KRIPPEN HIER see Bach, Johann Sebastian

ICH TRAUME NUR VON DEM EINEN, FOR SOLO VOICE AND ORCHESTRA [ARR.] see Grothe, Franz

ICHIBA, KOSUKE (1910-   )
   Symphony [23']
      2(pic).2(English horn).2.2. 4.2.3.1. timp,2perc,strings
      sc JAPAN 8401 f.s.   (I8)

ICHIYANAGI, TOSHI (1933-   )
   Circulating Scenery, For Violin And Orchestra (Concerto for Violin and Orchestra) [26']
      3.3.3.3. 4.3.2.1. perc,cel,pno, strings,vln solo
      sc SCHOTT,J $35.00   (I9)

   Concerto for Violin and Orchestra see Circulating Scenery, For Violin And Orchestra

   Engen, For Koto And Orchestra [22']
      2.3(English horn).2.2. 4.2.3.0. perc,pno&cel,harp,strings, koto solo
      ZEN-ON perf mat rent   (I10)

   In Recollection Of Space Image, For Piano And Orchestra [14']
      SCHOTT,J   (I11)

   Interspace
      string orch
      study sc SCHOTT,J SJ 1047 f.s., perf mat rent   (I12)

ICHTHYS see Nystedt, Knut

ICONOGRAPHY NO. 2, FOR HORN AND CHAMBER ORCHESTRA see Durko, Zsolt

ID see Wallin, Rolf

IDEALE, DIE see Liszt, Franz

IDEALE [ARR.] see Tosti, Francesco Paolo

IDEES FIXES, LES see Kagel, Mauricio

IDOMENEO: BALLETTMUSIK see Mozart, Wolfgang Amadeus

IDOMENEO: EUCH, IHR EINSAMEN SCHATTEN; ZEPHIRETTEN LEICHT GEFIEDERT, FOR SOLO VOICE AND ORCHESTRA see Mozart, Wolfgang Amadeus, Idomeneo: Solitudini Amiche; Zeffiretti Lusinghieri, For Solo Voice And Orchestra

IDOMENEO: OVERTURE see Mozart, Wolfgang Amadeus

IDOMENEO: SE IL PADRE PERDEI, FOR SOLO VOICE AND ORCHESTRA see Mozart, Wolfgang Amadeus

IDOMENEO: SOLITUDINI AMICHE; ZEFFIRETTI LUSINGHIERI, FOR SOLO VOICE AND ORCHESTRA see Mozart, Wolfgang Amadeus

IDOMENEO: TORNA LA PACE, FOR SOLO VOICE AND ORCHESTRA see Mozart, Wolfgang Amadeus

IDOMENEUS CONCERTO, FOR OBOE AND STRINGS see Righini, Vincenzo

IDYLL see Holloway, Robin

IDYLL NO. 2 see Holloway, Robin

IDYLLE ET REVERIE ORIENTALE see Glazunov, Alexander Konstantinovich

IDYLLEN see Bose, Hans Jürgen

IDYLLEN WALZER see Strauss, Johann, [Jr.]

IDYLLES D'APOCALYPSE, FOR ORGAN AND CHAMBER ORCHESTRA see Norholm, Ib

IF I COULD TURN YOU ON, FOR SOLO VOICE AND CHAMBER ORCHESTRA see Lloyd, Jonathan

IF WE LIFT AS ONE see Åm, Magnar

IF YOU SHOULD GO, FOR SOLO VOICE AND ORCHESTRA see Still, William Grant

IFIGENIA IN TAURIDE: OVERTURE see Traetta, Tommaso (Michele Francesco Saverio)

IFUKUBE, AKIRA (1914-   )
   Sinfonia Tapkaara [28']
      2.2.2.2. 4.3.3.1. timp,perc,harp, strings
      JAPAN 8101 f.s.   (I13)

IK HEB TENEN see Meijering, Chiel

IKAROS see Bäck, Sven-Erik

IKARUS: SUITE see Slonimsky, Sergey

IKEBE, SHIN-ICHIRO (1943-   )
   Concerto for Piano and Orchestra, No. 2 [15']
      3(pic).3(English horn).2(bass clar).2(contrabsn). 4.4.3.1. perc,2harp,cel,strings,pno solo ("Tu m'...") sc ZEN-ON 899448 f.s., perf mat rent   (I14)

   Concerto for Violin and Orchestra [20']
      3(pic).2(English horn).4(bass clar).3(contrabsn). 4.2.3.1. perc,pno&cel,strings,vln solo
      ONGAKU perf mat rent   (I15)

   Imagine [3']
      2.2.2.2. 4.2.3.0. timp,perc,harp, strings
      ZEN-ON perf mat rent   (I16)

   Petite Symphonie [8']
      2(pic).2.2.2.alto sax. 4.2.2.0. timp,perc,strings
      ONGAKU perf mat rent   (I17)

   Symphony No. 3 [22']
      3(pic).3(English horn).3(bass clar).3(contrabsn). 4.3.3.1. perc,pno&cel,harp,strings (Ego Phano) sc ZEN-ON 899340 f.s., perf mat rent   (I18)

IKKE ENHVER SOM SIGER TIL MIG, FOR SOLO VOICE AND ORCHESTRA see Eggen, Arne

"...IL TUBARE DELLA TORTORA...NON ODI?...", FOR SOLO VOICE AND ORCHESTRA see Guarnieri, Adriano

ILE, L' see Eckhardt-Gramatte, Sophie Carmen

ILLUMINATIONS see Cherney, Brian see Harris, Matthew

ILLUMINATIONS, FOR SOLO VOICE AND CHAMBER GROUP see Furrer, Beat

ILLUSTRASJONER see Lunde, Ivar

ILLUSTRATIONEN WALZER see Strauss, Johann, [Jr.]

ILLUSTRATIONS see Lunde, Ivar, Illustrasjoner

IM ABENDROT, FOR SOLO VOICE AND ORCHESTRA, [ARR.] see Schubert, Franz (Peter)

IM FREIEN see Killmayer, Wilhelm

IM JANUAR AM NIL see Barlow, Klarens

IM KRAPFENWALDL see Strauss, Johann, [Jr.]

I'M OLD FASHIONED: ASTAIRE VARIATIONS see Gould, Morton

IM WALD see Ciurlionis, Mikolajus, In The Forest

IM ZAUBERKREIS DER NACHT see Hopkins, John

IM ZIRKUS see Khachaturian, Karen, At The Circus

IMAGE see Tailleferre, Germaine

IMAGE POUR ORCHESTRE see Otaka, Atsutada

IMAGES see Debussy, Claude see Plante, Daniel

IMAGES, FOR TWO PIANOS AND ORCHESTRA see Zwilich, Ellen Taaffe

IMAGES DE LA REVOLUTION see Hetu, Jacques

IMAGES FROM A TWISTED DREAM see Ellis, David Graham

IMAGES, NO. 1: GIGUES see Debussy, Claude

IMAGES, NO. 2: IBERIA see Debussy, Claude

IMAGES, NO. 3: RONDES DE PRINTEMPS see Debussy, Claude

IMAGES OF BIRTH see Carl, Robert

IMAGES POUR UN JOUR D'ETE, FOR 2 PIANOS AND ORCHESTRA see Casterede, Jacques

IMAGES ROMANES see Carles, Marc

IMAGINAIRE see Haubenstock-Ramati, Roman

IMAGINAIRES, LES see Tabachnik, Michel

IMAGINARY LANDSCAPE, AN see Birtwistle, Harrison

IMAGINATIONEN II, FOR ALTO SAXOPHONE AND ORCHESTRA see Einfeld(t), Dieter

IMAGINE see Ikebe, Shin-Ichiro

IMBRIE, ANDREW WELSH (1921-   )
    Concerto for Flute and Orchestra
    SHAWNEE perf mat rent   (I19)

IMMAGINARIO see Sary, Laszlo

IMMER HEITERER WALZER see Strauss, Johann, [Jr.]

IMMER, WENN ICH GLUCKLICH BIN, FOR SOLO VOICE AND ORCHESTRA [ARR.] see Grothe, Franz

IMMOBILE, FOR PIANO AND ORCHESTRA see Volkonsky, Andrei

IMMOVABLE DO see Grainger, Percy Aldridge

IMMUREMENT OF ANTIGONE, THE, FOR SOLO VOICE AND ORCHESTRA see Tavener, John

IMPRESARIO: ICH BIN DIE ERSTE SANGERIN, FOR SOLO VOICES AND ORCHESTRA see Mozart, Wolfgang Amadeus, Schauspieldirektor, Der: Ich Bin Die Erste Sangerin, For Solo Voices And Orchestra

IMPRESION, FOR SOLO VOICE AND CHAMBER ORCHESTRA see Alis, Roman

IMPRESSION see Yun, Isang

IMPRESSION, FOR VIOLIN AND ORCHESTRA see Andersson, Gert Ove

IMPRESSIONI DAL VERO, II see Malipiero, Gian Francesco

IMPRESSIONS DE VOYAGE: MUNICH see Charpentier, Gustave

IMPROMPTUS IN F, FOR FLUTE AND ORCHESTRA see Durko, Zsolt

IMPROMPTUS SYMPHONIQUES see Lemeland, Aubert

IMPROVISACION Y CANON see Arteaga, Angel

IMPROVISATION, FOR TROMBONE AND ORCHESTRA see Landowski, Marcel

IMPROVISATION AND SCHERZO, FOR FLUTE AND CHAMBER ORCHESTRA see Susskind, Walter

IMPROVISATION ON A NAME see Archer, Violet

IMPROVISATION ON "DIVINUM MYSTERIUM" see Stevens, Halsey

IMPROVISATIONS FOR ORCHESTRA AND JAZZ SOLOISTS see Austin, Larry

IMPROVISATIONS SUR LE NOM DE PIERRE BOULEZ see Höller, York

IMPULSIONI, FOR OBOE AND CHAMBER ORCHESTRA see Lang, Istvan

IMPULSOS see Aponte-Ledee, Rafael see Bernaola, Carmelo

IN A HAPPY MOOD see Rybrant, Stig, Pa Gott Humor

IN A SUMMER GARDEN see Delius, Frederick

IN APPREHENSION OF SPRING see Stallcop, Glenn

IN AUTUMN see Grieg, Edvard Hagerup

IN BETWEEN, FOR VIOLONCELLO AND ORCHESTRA see Norgaard, Per

IN CAMERA see Osborne, Nigel

IN COMMEMORATION see Borishansky, Elliot

IN CONCORDIAM, FOR VIOLIN AND ORCHESTRA see Albert, Stephen Joel

IN DEN SPINNSTUBEN [ARR.] see Dvorák, Antonín, From The Bohemian Forest: In The Spinning Room [arr.]

IN DER STILLE DES HAUSES WOHNT EIN TON see Furrer, Beat

IN DIR IST FREUDE, [ARR.] see Bach, Johann Sebastian

IN DIVENIRE, FOR VIOLA AND ORCHESTRA see Gentilucci, Armando

IN DULCI JUBILO see Busch, Richard

IN GEDANKEN AN DEN STERBENDEN WALD see Krebs, Joachim

IN HEINRICH'S SHOES see London, Edwin

IN JUST SPRING see Adler, Samuel Hans

IN LIEB ENTBRANNT POLKA see Strauss, Eduard

IN LIEBESLUST, FOR SOLO VOICE AND ORCHESTRA [ARR.] see Liszt, Franz

IN MEMORIA DI... see Börtz, Daniel

IN MEMORIA DI VALENTINO BUCCHI see Vlad, Roman

IN MEMORIAM see Arambarri, Jesús see Schnittke, Alfred see Sibelius, Jean see Thomas, Andrew

IN MEMORIAM ALBAN BERG see Strömholm, Folke

IN MEMORIAM IGOR STRAVINSKY see Smirnov, Dmitri

IN MEMORIAM JOSEF BERG see Ištvan, Miloslav

IN MEMORIAM MALCOLM X, FOR SOLO VOICE AND ORCHESTRA see Anderson, Thomas Jefferson

IN MEMORIAM: PEDRO DE FREITAS BRANCO see Cassuto, Alvaro

IN MEMORIAM RAINER WERNER FASSBINDER see Krebs, Joachim

IN MEMORIAM RUDI DUTSCHKE see Krebs, Joachim

IN MEMORY OF A SUMMER DAY, FOR SOLO VOICE AND ORCHESTRA see Del Tredici, David

IN MY GARDEN, FOR SOLO VOICE AND ORCHESTRA see Firestone, Idabelle

IN NATIVITATE DOMINI, FOR SOLO VOICE AND ORCHESTRA see Bettinelli, Bruno

IN NATURE'S REALM see Dvorák, Antonín, Amid Nature

IN NOMINE DOMINI see Di Lotti, Silvana

IN PRAISE OF FOLLY see Walker, George Theophilus

IN PRAISE OF KRISHNA, FOR SOLO VOICE AND ORCHESTRA see Blake, David

IN QUANTO A L'OPUS 61, FOR PIANO AND INSTRUMENTAL ENSEMBLE see Rosse, Francois

IN RECOLLECTION OF SPACE IMAGE, FOR PIANO AND ORCHESTRA see Ichiyanagi, Toshi

IN RETROSPECTIEVE ZIN see Hunfeld, Xander

IN SLEEP, IN THUNDER, FOR SOLO VOICE AND INSTRUMENTAL ENSEMBLE see Carter, Elliott Cook, Jr.

IN SPRING, FOR FLUTE AND CHAMBER ORCHESTRA see Vassilenko, Sergey

IN TEMPORIS VERNALIS see Weis, Flemming

IN THE BEGINNING see Saxton, Robert

IN THE CATARACT OF THE GANGES MARCH see Johnson, Francis

IN THE COTSWOLDS see Downes, Andrew

IN THE DARK TIME see Matthews, David

IN THE DISTANCE see Solås, Eyvind, I Det Fjerne

IN THE EVENING see Groven, Eivind, Om Kvelden

IN THE FOREST see Ciurlionis, Mikolajus

IN THE HOSPITAL AT NIGHT, FOR SOLO VOICE AND ORCHESTRA see Groven, Eivind, Pa Hospitalet Om Natten, For Solo Voice And Orchestra

IN THE LATE WIND OF DEATH see Parker, Michael

IN THE MEANTIME see Sandström, Sven-David

IN THE MOUNTAINS see Björnsson, Arni

IN THE SOUTH see Elgar, [Sir] Edward (William)

IN TRANSIT, FOR TWO ORCHESTRAS see Hoyland, Victor

IN WAR see Goedicke, Alexander

IN WILDNESS IS THE PRESERVATION OF THE WORLD see Fennelly, Brian

IN YOUR MEDIUM, FOR SOLO VOICE AND ORCHESTRA see Pennycook, Bruce

INCANDESCENCES, FOR SOLO VOICES AND ORCHESTRA see Zbar, Michel

INCANTATION OF TIME, FOR 2 NARRATORS AND ORCHESTRA see Ištvan, Miloslav

INCARDONA, FEDERICO (1959-   )
    Des Freundes Umnachtung [18'30"]
    3.3.5.3. 5.3.3.1. 5perc,2harp,
    pno,strings
    RICORDI-IT 134024 perf mat rent
                                    (I20)

INCIDENCES, FOR PIANO AND ORCHESTRA see Mefano, Paul

INCONNUE, L', POLKA see Strauss, Johann, [Jr.]

INCONTRI see Moss, Piotr

INCONTRO IMPROVVISO, L': OVERTURE see Haydn, [Franz] Joseph

INDES GALANTES, LES: SUITE NO. 2 see Rameau, Jean-Philippe

INDIGO MARSCH see Strauss, Johann, [Jr.]

INDIGO QUADRILLE see Strauss, Johann, [Jr.]

INDIGO UND DIE VIERZIG RAUBER: BALLETTMUSIK see Strauss, Johann, [Jr.]

INDISCHES MARCHEN, EIN , FOR SOLO VOICES AND ORCHESTRA see Steffens, Walter

INDRA DHANUSH see Sohal, Naresh

INDRI. CAVE CANEM see Sandström, Jan

INDY, VINCENT D' (1851-1931)
    Andante for Horn and String Orchestra
    (Leloir, E.) string orch,horn solo
    [2'10"] sc BILLAUDOT f.s., perf
    mat rent   (I21)

    Fantasy for Oboe and Orchestra, Op. 31
    KALMUS A5701 sc $12.00, set $45.00,
    perf mat rent   (I22)

INDY, VINCENT D' (cont'd.)

Fervaal: Prelude, Act I
KALMUS A6968 sc $3.00, set $12.00,
pts $.75, ea.   (I23)

Fervaal: Prelude, Act III
KALMUS A6791 sc $15.00, set $30.00,
pts $1.00, ea., perf mat rent
                                     (I24)

Medee *Op.47
KALMUS A6794 sc $25.00, set $60.00,
pts $3.00, ea., perf mat rent
                                     (I25)

Souvenirs *Op.62
KALMUS A6139 sc $30.00, set $50.00,
perf mat rent   (I26)

Symphony No. 2, Op. 57, in B flat
KALMUS A5571 sc $75.00, perf mat
rent, set $125.00, pts $5.00, ea.
                                     (I27)

Wallenstein: La Mort De Wallenstein
"Wallenstein's Death" KALMUS A5720
sc $30.00, set $50.00, perf mat
rent   (I28)

Wallenstein: Le Camp De Wallenstein
"Wallenstein's Camp" KALMUS A5718
sc $30.00, set $50.00, perf mat
rent   (I29)

Wallenstein: Max Et Thecla
KALMUS A5719 sc $20.00, set $25.00,
perf mat rent   (I30)

Wallenstein's Camp
see Wallenstein: Le Camp De
Wallenstein

Wallenstein's Death
see Wallenstein: La Mort De
Wallenstein

INERCIA Y LA MIERDA, LA see Hidalgo,
Manuel

INFEDELTÀ DELUSA, L': OVERTURE see
Haydn, [Franz] Joseph

INFELICE!, FOR SOLO VOICE AND ORCHESTRA
see Mendelssohn-Bartholdy, Felix

INFERENCE see Decoust, Michel

INFERNAL MACHINE, THE see Rouse,
Christopher

INFERNO see Soler, Josep

INFINITESIMAL FRAGMENTS OF ETERNITY see
Sveinsson, Atli Heimir

INFINITO, L', FOR SOLO VOICE AND
ORCHESTRA see Hartke, Stephen Paul

INFINITY see Kelemen, Milko

INFLUENTIAE see Helmschrott, Robert M.

INGLORIOUS FOURTH, FOR SOLO VOICE AND
CHAMBER ORCHESTRA see Lister,
Rodney

INITIATION see Wilson, Richard (Edward)

INNER AND OUTER STRINGS, FOR STRING
QUARTET AND STRING ORCHESTRA see
Mayer, William Robert

INNER LIGHT 2, FOR SOLO VOICES AND
INSTRUMENTAL ENSEMBLE see Harvey,
Jonathan

INNER LIGHT 3 see Harvey, Jonathan

INNER VOICES see Ung, Chinary

INO, FOR SOLO VOICE AND ORCHESTRA see
Telemann, Georg Philipp

INQUIETUS see Holloway, Robin

INRI see Arnestad, Finn

INSTANT MUSIC, FOR FLUTE AND ORCHESTRA
see Schwertsik, Kurt

INSTANTANES see Jarrell, Michael

INSTANTANES, FOR CHAMBER ORCHESTRA see
Manoury, Philippe

INSTANTANES 1 ET 2, FOR CLARINET AND
STRING ORCHESTRA see DuBois,
Pierre-Max

INSTANTANES I see Manoury, Philippe

INSTANTANES II see Manoury, Philippe

INSTANTANES III see Manoury, Philippe

INSTANTANES, VERSION "ETUDE" see
Manoury, Philippe

INSTANTS see Lancen, Serge

INSTANTS ECLATES see Darasse, Xavier

INSTANTS PASSES see Darasse, Xavier

INSTRUMENTAL MUSIC OF FAITH, BOOK 1
*CC14L
(McCoy, Floyd) SOUTHERN $3.50   (I31)

INSTRUMENTAL MUSIC OF FAITH, BOOK 2
*CC14L
(McCoy, Floyd) SOUTHERN $4.50   (I32)

INTERFACES see Marietan, Pierre

INTERFERENCES see Mefano, Paul

INTERLUDE see Lutoslawski, Witold

INTERLUDES DE LA MAGICIENNE DE LA MER,
FOR SOLO VOICE AND ORCHESTRA see Le
Flem, Paul

INTERLUDIEN see Hoch, Peter

INTERMEDES, LES see Jaubert, Maurice

INTERMEDIO, FOR SOLO VOICE AND STRING
ORCHESTRA see Wyner, Yehudi

INTERMEZZO AND GAVOTTE CAPRICE see
Björkander, Nils

INTERMEZZO CONCERTANTE, FOR TUBA AND
STRING ORCHESTRA see Holmboe, Vagn

INTERMEZZO DIATONIC see Shumeiko,
Volodymyr

INTERMEZZO IN MODO CLASSICO see
Mussorgsky, Modest Petrovich

INTERMITTENZE see Rietmann, Carlo
Marcello

INTERNATIONAL RHAPSODY see Søderlind,
Ragnar

INTERPLAY see Kraft, William see Smith,
William Overton

INTERPLAY I see Adomian, Lan

INTERPLAY II see Adomian, Lan

INTERRUPTIONS see Tanenbaum, Elias

INTERSPACE see Ichiyanagi, Toshi

INTERVIEWS see Gibbs, Michael

INTO ECLIPSE, FOR SOLO VOICE AND
ORCHESTRA see Albert, Stephen Joel

INTO FLIGHT FROM see Samuel, Gerhard

INTO THE LABYRINTH, FOR SOLO VOICE AND
ORCHESTRA see Davies, Peter Maxwell

INTO THE SUN see Brown, Christopher
(Roland)

INTONACIJA see Gabrijelcic, Marijan

INTONAZIONE - QUASI UNA FANTASIA see
Skouen, Synne

INTRADA see Brevik, Tor see Carlstedt,
Jan see Ferenczy, Oto see
Sommerfeldt, Øistein

INTRADA AFTER MONTEVERDI, CHAMBER
ORCHESTRA VERSION see Harper,
Edward James

INTRADA AFTER MONTEVERDI, FULL
ORCHESTRA VERSION see Harper,
Edward James

INTRADA AND MARCHE MILITAIRE see
Goldschmidt, Berthold

INTRADA FOR ORCHESTRA see Leitermeyer,
Fritz

INTRADA IN C see Vejvanovsky, Pavel
Josef

INTRADA NO. 2 see Vea, Ketil

INTRADA SINFONIA see Hoemsnes, Bjørn
Korsan

INTRADA SINFONICA see Baden, Conrad

INTRATA see Bergh, Sverre

INTRECCIO see Wittinger, Robert

INTRODUCTION AND ALLEGRO FOR ORCHESTRA
see Hopkin-Evans, T.

INTRODUCTION AND ALLEGRO FOR STRING
QUARTET AND STRING ORCHESTRA see
Elgar, [Sir] Edward (William)

INTRODUCTION AND KRAKOWIAK, FOR VIOLIN
AND ORCHESTRA see Zarzycki,
Alexander

INTRODUCTION AND SEQUENCES see
Mihelcic, Pavle, Introdukcija In
Sekvence

INTRODUCTION AND THE VIRGIN QUEEN'S
DREAM, FOR SOLO VOICE AND ORCHESTRA
see Franco, Johan

INTRODUCTION ET MARCHE FUNEBRE see
Milhaud, Darius

INTRODUCTION, GRAVE AND ALLEGRO see
Lobanov, Vassily

INTRODUCTION, ROMANCE ET ALLEGRO, FOR
BASS TROMBONE AND ORCHESTRA see
Lantier, Pierre

INTRODUCTION, THEME AND VARIATIONS, FOR
CLARINET AND ORCHESTRA see
Rosenman, Leonard

INTRODUCTION, VARIATION ET RONDEAU, FOR
WOODWIND QUARTET AND ORCHESTRA see
Vaubourgoin, Marc

INTRODUCTION, VARIATIONS AND RONDO, FOR
ALTO SAXOPHONE AND STRING ORCHESTRA
see Bentzon, Jørgen

INTRODUKCIJA IN SEKVENCE see Mihelcic,
Pavle

INTRODUKTION UND TRAUERMARSCH see
Milhaud, Darius, Introduction Et
Marche Funebre

INTRODUKTION UND VARIATIONEN UBER EIN
SCHWEDISCHES LIED see Crusell,
Bernhard Henrik

INTRODUZIONE ALL'OSCURO see Sciarrino,
Salvatore

INTRODUZIONE, ARIA, PRESTO [ARR.] see
Marcello, Benedetto

INTRODUZIONE E ALLEGRO APPASSIONATO,
FOR PIANO AND ORCHESTRA, OP. 92 see
Schumann, Robert (Alexander),
Konzertstück for Piano and
Orchestra, Op. 92

INTRODUZIONE E SCHERZO see Trexler,
Georg

INTRODUZZIONE E ALLEGRO, FOR
HARPSICHORD AND STRING ORCHESTRA
see Eklund, Hans

INTROIT see Matthews, David see Wilson,
Thomas

INTROIT, FOR VIOLIN AND ORCHESTRA see
Finzi, Gerald

INTROITUS, FOR PIANO AND CHAMBER
ORCHESTRA see Gubaidulina, Sofia

INTRUSUS see Phillips, Mark

INTURBATO MARE IRATO, FOR SOLO VOICE
AND STRING ORCHESTRA see Vivaldi,
Antonio

INVENCE see Martinu, Bohuslav (Jan)

INVENTION A SEIZE VOIX see Tabachnik,
Michel

INVENTIONEN see Stendel, Wolfgang

INVENTIONS see Martinu, Bohuslav (Jan),
Invence

INVENTIONS, CONTOURS AND COLORS see
Heiss, John C.

INVINCIBLE BUNBURY, THE see Cohen,
Jerome D.

INVISIBLE MOSAIC II see Kernis, Aaron
Jay

INVISIBLE MOSAIC III see Kernis, Aaron
Jay

INVITATION TO THE DANCE [ARR.] see
Weber, Carl Maria von, Aufforderung
Zum Tanz [arr.]

INVITATION TO THE WALTZ see Harris,
Matthew

INVITATION TO THE WORLD see Schipizky,
Frederick

INVITO ALLA DANZA [ARR.] see Weber,
Carl Maria von, Aufforderung Zum
Tanz [arr.]

INVOCACION, FOR SOLO VOICE AND
ORCHESTRA see Alis, Roman

INVOCATION, FOR ALTO SAXOPHONE AND
ORCHESTRA see Cosma, Edgar

INVOCATION, FOR VIOLONCELLO AND
ORCHESTRA see Holst, Gustav

INVOCATION AND DANCE, FOR VIOLIN AND
ORCHESTRA see Brott, Alexander

INVOCATIONS see Schifrin, Lalo (Boris)

INVOCAZIONE see Jansson, Johannes

INVOLVEMENT see Haxton, Kenneth

IO see Saariaho, Kaija

IO TI LASCIO, OH CARA, ADDIO, FOR SOLO
VOICE AND STRING ORCHESTRA see
Mozart, Wolfgang Amadeus

IOANNIDES, YANNIS (1930-   )
Metaplasis A [8']
2+pic.2.2.2. 3.3.3.0. 12vln,4vla,
3vcl,3db
sc BREITKOPF-W f.s., perf mat rent
(I33)

IOLANTHE: NONE SHALL PART US, FOR SOLO
VOICES AND ORCHESTRA see Sullivan,
[Sir] Arthur Seymour

IOLANTHE: OVERTURE see Sullivan, [Sir]
Arthur Seymour

IOLANTHE: WHEN ALL NIGHT LONG A CHAP
REMAINS, FOR SOLO VOICE AND
ORCHESTRA see Sullivan, [Sir]
Arthur Seymour

IOWA CONCERTO see Goeb, Roger

IPHIGENIE EN AULIDE: OVERTURE see
Gluck, Christoph Willibald, Ritter
von

IPHIGENIE EN TAURIDE: LE CALME RENTRE
DANS MON COEUR, FOR SOLO VOICE AND
ORCHESTRA see Gluck, Christoph
Willibald, Ritter von

IPHIGENIE EN TAURIDE: O TOI QUI
PROLONGUES MES JOURS, FOR SOLO
VOICE AND ORCHESTRA see Gluck,
Christoph Willibald, Ritter von

IPHIGENIE IN TAURIS: DIE RUHE KEHRET
MIR ZURÜCK, FOR SOLO VOICE AND
ORCHESTRA see Gluck, Christoph
Willibald, Ritter von, Iphigenie En
Tauride: Le Calme Rentre Dans Mon
Coeur, For Solo Voice And Orchestra

IPHIGENIE IN TAURIS: O DU, DIE MIR DAS
LEBEN GAB, FOR SOLO VOICE AND
ORCHESTRA see Gluck, Christoph
Willibald, Ritter von, Iphigenie En
Tauride: O Toi Qui Prolongues Mes
Jours, For Solo Voice And Orchestra

IPHIGENIE IN TAURIS: VON JUGEND AUF IM
TREUSTEN BUNDE, FOR SOLO VOICE AND
ORCHESTRA see Gluck, Christoph
Willibald, Ritter von

IPHIGENIE IN TAURUS: O DU MIR EINST,
FOR SOLO VOICE AND ORCHESTRA see
Gluck, Christoph Willibald, Ritter
von, Iphigenie En Tauride: O Toi
Qui Prolongues Mes Jours, For Solo
Voice And Orchestra

IPPOLITOV-IVANOV, MIKHAIL MIKHAILOVICH
(1859-1935)
Armenian Rhapsody   *Op.48 [12']
2.2.2.2. 4.2.0.0. timp,perc,
strings,vln solo
KALMUS A6115 sc $10.00, set $20.00
(I34)
Caucasian Sketches, Series II *Op.42
KALMUS 5669 sc $40.00, ipr, set
$80.00, pts $3.00, ea.   (I35)

Turkish March *Op.55
KALMUS A7353 sc $15.00, set $35.00,
pts $1.50, ea., perf mat rent
(I36)

IRATO see Wagemans, Peter-Jan

IRDISCHE KLANGE see Schwertsik, Kurt

IRDISCHEN KLANGE, DER: FUNF NATURSTUCKE
see Schwertsik, Kurt

"IRE IN ORBEM" see Angerer, Paul

IRELAND, JOHN (1879-1962)
Forgotten Rite, The
see Symphonic Rhapsody

Legend, For Piano And Orchestra [15']
2.2.2.2. 4.0.2.0. timp,perc,
strings,pno solo
AMP perf mat rent   (I37)

IRELAND, JOHN (cont'd.)

Mai Dun
see Symphonic Rhapsody

Symphonic Rhapsody
study sc STAINER B646 f.s. contains
also: Mai Dun; Forgotten Rite,
The   (I38)

Tritons, The [12']
2(pic).2.2+bass clar.2. 4.2.3.1.
timp,perc,strings
BOOSEY perf mat rent   (I39)

IRIS POLKA see Strauss, Eduard

IRISATION-RITUEL, FOR SOLO VOICES,
FLUTE, AND ORCHESTRA see Gaussin,
Allain

IRISH FOLK SONG SUITE see Erickson,
Frank William

IRISH FOLKSONG see Foote, Arthur

IRISH RHAPSODY see Herbert, Victor

IRISH TUNE FROM COUNTY DERBY see
Grainger, Percy Aldridge

IRISH TUNE FROM COUNTY DERRY, FOR
VIOLIN AND ORCHESTRA [ARR.] see
Grainger, Percy Aldridge

IRLANDE see Holmes, Augusta (Mary Anne)

IROLD'S YOUTH see Kox, Hans

IRRFAHRT UM'S GLUCK, DIE: OVERTURE see
Suppe, Franz von

IS PER ORCHESTRA see Holm, Kristin

ISABELLA see Nielsen, Ludolf

ISABELLA: OVERTURE see Suppe, Franz von

ISERNA see Plompen, Peter

ISHII, MAKI (1936-   )
Afro-Concerto, For Percussion And
Orchestra *Op.50
2.2.2.3. 4.2.3.1. strings,4perc
soli
study sc MOECK $58.00   (I40)

Translucent Vision *Op..44 [16']
2(pic).2.3(soprano clar in E
flat,bass clar).2+contrabsn.
4.2.3.1. perc,harp,pno&cel,
strings
ONGAKU perf mat rent   (I41)

ISHIJIMA, MASAHIRO (1960-   )
Ode For Violin And Orchestra [9'32"]
2(pic).2.2.2. 4.2.3.0. perc,gtr,
cel,2harp,strings,vln solo
sc ZEN-ON 899370 f.s., perf mat
rent   (I42)

ISHIKETA, MAREO (1916-   )
Symphonic Revelation, For Solo Voice
And Orchestra [40']
3(pic).3(English horn).3(clar in
E flat,bass clar).3(contrabsn.
4.3.3.1. timp,perc,vibra,
marimba,cel,harp,strings,S solo
sc ZEN-ON f.s., perf mat rent (I43)

ISLAMEY [ARR.] see Balakirev, Mily
Alexeyevich

ISLAND IN THE SKERRIES, FOR SOLO VOICE
AND ORCHESTRA see Tveitt, Geirr,
Skjaergaardso, For Solo Voice And
Orchestra

ISLAND OF EVERLASTING YOUTH, THE see
Balassa, Sándor

ISLAND PRELUDES, FOR OBOE AND STRING
ORCHESTRA see Tower, Joan

ISLAND RHYTHMS see Tower, Joan

ISLANDS see Cunningham, Michael Gerald

ISOCHRONISMS NO. 2 see Read, Thomas
Lawrence

ISOLA DISABITATA, L': OVERTURE see
Haydn, [Franz] Joseph

ISOLFSSON, PALL (1893-   )
Festival Overture
2.2.2.2. 3.2.2.1. timp,perc,
strings
ICELAND 019-024   (I44)

For The King's Sake
1.1.1.1. 3.1.0.0. timp,perc,
strings
ICELAND 019-017   (I45)

ISOLFSSON, PALL (cont'd.)

From The Song Of Songs, For Solo
Voice And Orchestra [arr.]
(Sveinsson, Atli Heimir) 2.2.2.2.
2.2.2.0. timp,perc,harp,cel,
strings,solo voice ICELAND
019-006   (I46)

Golden Gate, The
1.0.2.1. 0.3.0.0. timp,strings
ICELAND 019-003   (I47)

Mary
string orch
ICELAND 019-016   (I48)

Passacaglia
2.2.2.2. 4.3.3.1. timp,perc,
strings
ICELAND 019-002   (I49)

ISON I see Niculescu, Stefan

ISRAEL see Adomian, Lan

ISRAEL-MEYER, PIERRE (1933-1979)
Anna La Bonne, For Solo Voice And
Orchestra [11']
2perc,pno/harmonium,strings,A
solo
"Mädchen Anna, Das, For Solo Voice
And Orchestra" BILLAUDOT perf mat
rent   (I50)

Concerto Da Camera [10']
min sc CHOUDENS f.s., perf mat rent
(I51)
Mädchen Anna, Das, For Solo Voice And
Orchestra
see Anna La Bonne, For Solo Voice
And Orchestra

Tombeau D'Alban Berg, Le [10']
string orch
ESCHIG perf mat rent   (I52)

ISSIPILE: SO CHE RIDUCE A PIANGERE, FOR
SOLO VOICE AND ORCHESTRA see Bioni,
Antonio

ISTI MIRANT STELLE see Weir, Judith

IŠTVAN, MILOSLAV (1928-1990)
Games, The [18']
CESKY HUD.   (I53)

In Memoriam Josef Berg [8']
CESKY HUD.   (I54)

Incantation Of Time, For 2 Narrators
And Orchestra
0.0.0.0.3sax. 4.3.3.1. perc,elec
gtr,pno,strings,2 narrators
SUPRAPHON   (I55)

IT WAS A LOVELY EVENING IN SUMMER, FOR
SOLO VOICE AND STRING ORCHESTRA
[ARR.] see Grieg, Edvard Hagerup

ITALIA see Casella, Alfredo

ITALIAN ARIAS, FOR SOLO VOICE AND
ORCHESTRA see Reicha, Anton

ITALIAN VIOLIN CONCERTOS FROM FONDS
BLANCHETON, PART I *CCU
(Hirshberg, Jehoash) sc A-R ED
ISBN 0-89579-171-4 f.s.   (I56)

ITALIAN VIOLIN CONCERTOS FROM FONDS
BLANCHETON, PART II *CCU
(Hirshberg, Jehoash) sc A-R ED
ISBN 0-89579-172-2 f.s.   (I57)

ITALIANA IN ALGERI, L': AH, COME IL COR
DI GIUBILO, FOR SOLO VOICE AND
ORCHESTRA see Rossini, Gioacchino

ITALIANA IN ALGERI, L': AI CAPRICCI
DELLA SORTE, FOR SOLO VOICES AND
ORCHESTRA see Rossini, Gioacchino

ITALIANA IN ALGERI, L': GIA D' INSOLITO
ADORE, FOR SOLO VOICE AND ORCHESTRA
see Rossini, Gioacchino

ITALIANA IN ALGERI, L': IO PRESENTO DI
MIA MAN, FOR SOLO VOICES AND
ORCHESTRA see Rossini, Gioacchino

ITALIANA IN ALGERI, L': LANGUIR PER UNA
BELLA, FOR SOLO VOICE AND ORCHESTRA
see Rossini, Gioacchino

ITALIANA IN ALGERI, L': LE FEMMINE
D'ITALIA, FOR SOLO VOICE AND
ORCHESTRA see Rossini, Gioacchino

ITALIANA IN ALGERI, L': OVERTURE see
Rossini, Gioacchino

ITALIANA IN ALGERI, L': PAPPATACI CHE
MAI SENTO, FOR SOLO VOICES AND
ORCHESTRA see Rossini, Gioacchino

ITALIANA IN ALGERI, L': PENSA ALLA PATRIA, FOR SOLO VOICE AND ORCHESTRA see Rossini, Gioacchino

ITALIANA IN ALGERI, L': PER LUI CHE ADORO, FOR SOLO VOICE AND ORCHESTRA see Rossini, Gioacchino

ITALIANA IN ALGERI, L': SE INCLINASSI A PRENDER MOGLIE, FOR SOLO VOICES AND ORCHESTRA see Rossini, Gioacchino

ITALIANS IN VIENNA
    (Williams; Toscani; Hettrick; Lazarevich) sc GARLAND ISBN 0-8240-3830-4 $90.00 "The Symphony" Vol. B-II contains: Caldara, Antonio, Introduzioni, Six And Sinfonia; Conti, Francesco, Sinfonie, Nine; Salieri, Antonio, Symphonies, Three And Overture   (I58)

ITALIENISCHE SERENADE [ARR.] see Wolf, Hugo

ITHAKA, FOR SOLO VOICE AND ORCHESTRA see Stenhammar, Wilhelm

I'TIPFERL POLKA see Strauss, Johann, [Jr.]

ITO, YASUHIDE (1960-   )
    Concerto for Alto Saxophone and Orchestra [12']
        3.2.2.2. 4.2.2.1. perc,strings, alto sax solo
        LEMOINE perf mat rent   (I59)

IT'S PERFECTLY TRUE see Hoffding, Finn, Det Er Ganske Vist

IUBILUM see Ginastera, Alberto

IVAN IV: PRELUDE see Bizet, Georges

IVAN THE TERRIBLE: SUITE [ARR.] see Prokofiev, Serge

IVANCIC, AMANDUS (fl. 1750)
    Symphonies, Two
        (Pokorn; Biondi; Powley; Wright; Inwood) ("The Symphony" Vol. B-XIV) sc GARLAND ISBN 0-8240-3957-6 $90.00 contains also: Zimmermann, Anton, Symphony; Druschetzky, Georg, Symphonies, Two; Neubauer, Franz Christoph, Symphony; Süssmayr, Franz Xavier, Symphony   (I60)

IVANHOE see Bondon, Jacques

IVES, CHARLES (1874-1954)
    Charlie Rutlage [arr.]
        (Singleton, Kenneth) pic,clar in E flat,English horn,bsn,trp,trom, tuba,drums,pno,strings,opt solo voice (may be performed as an accompanied song by substituting baritone voice for eng h and trp) set AMP 50243300 $35.00   (I61)

    Chromâtimemelôdtune [6']
        reconstruction
        0.1.1.1. 1.1.1.1. pno,3vln,vla, vcl,db
        (Schuller, Gunther) sc MJQ $6.95, perf mat rent   (I62)

    Decoration Day [9']
        2+opt pic.2+English horn.2+clar in E flat.2. 4.2+opt trp.3.1. timp,perc,strings
        (Sinclair, James) sc PEER $27.50, perf mat rent   (I63)

    Overture And March "1776"
        (Sinclair, James) 2(pic).1.1.0. 0.0+2cornet.1.0. perc,pno,strings [3'] study sc MERION 446-41025 $6.00, perf mat rent   (I64)

    Ragtime Dance No. 1 [arr.]
        (Sinclair, James B.) PEER MUSIK perf mat rent   (I65)

    Ragtime Dance No. 2 [arr.]
        (Sinclair, James B.) PEER MUSIK perf mat rent   (I66)

    Ragtime Dance No. 3 [arr.]
        (Sinclair, James B.) PEER MUSIK perf mat rent   (I67)

    Ragtime Dance No. 4 [arr.]
        (Sinclair, James B.) PEER MUSIK perf mat rent   (I68)

    Symphony No. 2,Finale [11']
        3(pic).2.2.3(contrabsn). 4.2.3.1. timp,perc,strings
        PEER perf mat rent   (I69)

IVES, CHARLES (cont'd.)

    Unanswered Question, The
        (Echols, Paul; Zahler, Noel) 4fl, trp,strings [6'] sc PEER MUSIK 61552-851 $20.00   (I70)

IWAN GROSNY [ARR.] see Prokofiev, Serge, Ivan The Terrible: Suite [arr.]

IZAHT: PRELUDE see Villa-Lobos, Heitor

IZCOVICH, EZEQUIEL (1959-   )
    Pieges [11']
        2.2.2.2. 2.2.1.0. 3perc,strings
        SALABERT perf mat rent   (I71)

IZEYL see Pierne, Gabriel

IZEYL SUITE [ARR.] see Pierne, Gabriel

IZKOR, FOR ENGLISH HORN, PIANO AND ORCHESTRA see Ashkenazy, Benjamin

J

J. FUCIK: REPORT WRITTEN WITH A ROPE see Tausinger, Jan

JACCHINI, GIUSEPPE MARIA
    (ca. 1663-1727)
    Concerto, Op. 4, No. 2, in G [5']
        string orch,hpsd,vcl solo
        (Townsend) PETERS sc P66108S $10.00, kbd pt 66108C $2.00, pts 66108B, P $1.50, ea.   (J1)

    Concerto, Op. 4, No. 9, in F [5']
        string orch,hpsd,vcl solo
        (Townsend) PETERS sc P66109S $10.00, kbd pt P66109C $2.00, pts 66109B, P $1.50, ea.   (J2)

JACK AND JILL AT BUNKER HILL, FOR NARRATOR AND ORCHESTRA see Peck, Russell James

JACOB, [DOM] CLEMENT (1906-1977)
    Deux Preludes [3'20"]
        pno/org,strings
        BILLAUDOT perf mat rent   (J3)

JACOB, GORDON (1895-1984)
    Concerto for Flute and String Orchestra, No. 2 [15']
        string orch,fl solo
        BOOSEY perf mat rent   (J4)

    Concerto for Oboe and String Orchestra, No. 1
        KALMUS A6788 sc $17.00, set $14.00, pts $2.00, ea.   (J5)

    Concerto for Viola and String Orchestra, No. 2 [17']
        string orch,vla solo
        SIMROCK perf mat rent   (J6)

    Festal March [7']
        3.2.2.2. 4.3.3.1. timp,2perc, harp,strings
        STAINER HL123 perf mat rent   (J7)

    Mini-Concerto For Clarinet And String Orchestra [13']
        string orch,clar solo
        BOOSEY perf mat rent   (J8)

    Prelude And Toccata [12']
        3(pic).2+English horn.2+bass clar.2. 4.3.3.0. timp,2-5perc, 2harp,strings
        STAINER HL131 perf mat rent   (J9)

    Sinfonietta No. 1
        KALMUS A6073 sc $30.00, set $35.00, perf mat rent   (J10)

    Suite for Tuba and Orchestra [18']
        perc,strings,tuba solo
        BOOSEY perf mat rent   (J11)

    Suite, No. 1, in F
        KALMUS A6789 sc $20.00, set $18.00, pts $1.25, ea., perf mat rent   (J12)

JACOB, MAXIME
    see JACOB, [DOM] CLEMENT

JACOB, WERNER (1938-   )
    Graf Oderland, For Solo Voices And Orchestra [18']
        3(pic,alto fl,bass fl).3(English horn).3(bass clar).3(contrabsn).tenor sax. 0.0.0.0. 3perc,2harp,pno,cel, strings,SBar soli
        BREITKOPF-W perf mat rent   (J13)

JACOB'S LADDERS see Kernis, Aaron Jay

JACOBSEN, JULIUS
    Butterflies
        see Papillons

    Gaseller, For Piano And Orchestra [2'20"]
        2(pic).1.2.1. 2.2.1.0. timp,perc, gtr,strings,pno solo
        "Gazelles, For Piano And Orchestra" BUSCH DM 025 perf mat rent   (J14)

    Gazelles, For Piano And Orchestra see Gaseller, For Piano And Orchestra

    Papillons [2'50"]
        horn,perc,cel,harp,gtr,strings, 3fl soli
        "Butterflies" BUSCH DM 042 perf mat rent   (J15)

JACOBSON, MAURICE (1896-1976)
Lament [5']
string orch
CURWEN perf mat rent   (J16)

Symphonic Suite For Strings [17']
string orch
CURWEN perf mat rent   (J17)

JAEGERMARCH see Tworek, Wandy

JAFFE, STEPHEN (1954-   )
Four Images [19']
MERION perf mat rent   (J18)

JAGD, DIE [ARR] see Mendelssohn-
Bartholdy, Felix

JAGDOUVERTURE see Schlemm, Gustav Adolf

JAHN, THOMAS (1940-   )
Tango Habanera, For Violin, And
Orchestra [16']
1(pic,alto fl).1(English
horn).1(bass clar).1.alto sax.
0.1.0.0. perc,harp,pno,gtr,db,
vln solo
SCHIRM.G perf mat rent   (J19)

JAHR WIE EIN LEBEN, EIN: SUITE see
Shostakovich, Dmitri, Year Is Like
A Lifetime, A: Suite

JAHRESZEITEN, DIE: SCHON EILET FROH DER
ACKERSMANN, FOR SOLO VOICE AND
ORCHESTRA see Haydn, [Franz] Joseph

JAHRMARKT VON SOROTSCHINZI, DER: SCHÖNE
CHIWRIA, FOR SOLO VOICE AND
ORCHESTRA see Mussorgsky, Modest
Petrovich

JAHRMARKT VON SOROTSCHINZI, DER: WAS
SOLL DEIN WEINEN, LIEBSTER?, FOR
SOLO VOICE AND ORCHESTRA see
Mussorgsky, Modest Petrovich

JALAS, JUSSI (1908-   )
Kiirastulen Lauluja, For Solo Voice
And Orchestra [15']
2.2.2.2. 4.3.3.0. timp,perc,harp,
strings,solo voice
FAZER perf mat rent   (J20)

JALKANEN, PEKKA
Serf Of Viro, The, For Two Violins
And String Orchestra
string orch,2vln soli
sc FAZER $33.50   (J21)

JALONS see Xenakis, Yannis (Iannis)

JAMAICAN RUMBA see Benjamin, Arthur

JAMAICAN SONG see Benjamin, Arthur

JAMES, PHILIP (1890-1975)
Sinfonietta
SHAWNEE perf mat rent   (J22)

JANÁCEK, LEOŠ (1854-1928)
Adagio
min sc UNIVER. 16789 $12.50   (J23)

Concerto for Violin and Orchestra
*reconstruction
(Faltus, Leos; Stedron, Milos)
3(pic,alto fl).2(English
horn).3(clar in E flat)+bass
clar.2+contrabsn. 4.4.3.1. timp,
perc,harp,cel,strings,vln solo
[12'] BÄREN. BA 7324   (J24)

Fiddler's Child
KALMUS A7036 sc $15.00, set $60.00,
pts $3.50, ea., perf mat rent
(J25)
Jealousy
see Zarlivost

Kosakentanz
see Zwei Tänze

Lachian Dances Nos. 1-6
KALMUS A6364 sc $35.00, set
$100.00, pts $5.00, ea., perf mat
rent   (J26)

Lachian Dances Nos. 1 And 2 [8']
2(pic).2+English horn.2+bass
clar.2. 4.2.3.0. timp,perc,
harp,strings, lyre
KALMUS A4657 sc $20.00, set $60.00,
pts $3.00, ea., perf mat rent
(J27)
Lachian Dances Nos. 3 And 4 [6']
2.2.2.2. 3.2.2.0. timp,perc,
strings
KALMUS A6387 sc $12.00, set $35.00,
pts $2.00, ea., perf mat rent
(J28)
Lachian Dances Nos. 5 And 6 [4']
2.2.2.2. 3.2.3.0. timp,harp,
strings, lyre
KALMUS A6388 sc $10.00, set $30.00,
pts $2.00, ea., perf mat rent

JANÁCEK, LEOŠ (cont'd.)
(J29)
Pilky [3']
2.2.2.2. 3.2.3.0. timp,strings
SUPRAPHON   (J30)

Schluck Und Jau [7']
4.3.4.3. 4.3.3.1. timp,perc,harp,
strings,vla d'amore solo
SUPRAPHON   (J31)

Serbischer Kolo
see Zwei Tänze

Suite for String Orchestra
KALMUS A6363 sc $10.00, set $15.00,
pts $3.00, ea., perf mat rent
(J32)
Suite, Op. 3
min sc UNIVER. PH00480 $19.00 (J33)

Zarlivost
"Jealousy" min sc UNIVER. 16787
$21.00   (J34)

Zwei Tänze
(Burghauser, Jarmil) 2.2.2.2.
3.2.3.0. timp,triangle,strings sc
BÄREN. BA 6171 f.s.
contains: Kosakentanz; Serbischer
Kolo   (J35)

JANSON, ALFRED (1937-   )
Forspil, For Violin And Orchestra
(Prelude for Violin and
Orchestra) [23']
3.3.3.3. 6.3.3.1. timp,perc,pno,
strings,vln solo
sc HANSEN-NY $74.00   (J36)
HANSEN-DEN perf mat rent   (J37)

Mellomspill For Orkester
2.3.3.3. 4.3.3.1. perc,acord,
strings
NORGE   (J38)

Nasjonalsang, For Trumpet, Trombone
And Orchestra
see National Anthem, For Trumpet,
Trombone And Orchestra

National Anthem, For Trumpet,
Trombone And Orchestra [25']
2.2.2.2. 4.3.3.0. perc,strings,
electronic tape,trp solo,trom
solo
"Nasjonalsang, For Trumpet,
Trombone And Orchestra" NORGE
(J39)
Prelude for Violin and Orchestra
see Forspil, For Violin And
Orchestra

JANSSEN, GUUS (1951-   )
Bruuks [13']
1.0.2.0.soprano sax. 0.1.1.0.
perc,harp,pno,vln,vcl,db
DONEMUS perf mat rent   (J40)

Deviäties [12']
2.0.0.0. 2.0.0.0. 2perc,9vln,db
DONEMUS rent   (J41)

Keer [15']
3.2.3.3. 6.3.3.1. timp,3perc,
2harp,strings
sc DONEMUS f.s., perf mat rent
(J42)
Ut Re Mi Sol La [14']
fl,ob,basset horn,bsn,horn,2vln,
vla,vcl,db,pno
DONEMUS perf mat rent   (J43)

JANSSON, JOHANNES (1950-   )
Corpo In Luce, For Piano And
Orchestra
2.2.2.2. 4.2.1.0. timp,perc,
strings,pno solo
[30'] STIM   (J44)

Invocazione
1.1.1.1. 1.0.0.0. pno,strings
STIM   (J45)

New Life, The
see Nya Livet, Det

Nimbus, For Solo Voice And Orchestra
STIM   (J46)

Nya Livet, Det [22']
2.2.2.2. 2.2.1.0. timp,strings
"New Life, The" STIM   (J47)

Sogno, Il [30']
1.2.1.1. 2.0.0.0. harp,strings
STIM   (J48)

JANUS see Ostergaard, Edvin see
Wigglesworth, Frank

JANUS, FOR VIOLIN, PIANO, AND
INSTRUMENTAL ENSEMBLE see Stranz,
Ulrich

JARANA, LA see Navarro, Tadeo

JARDIN DE LOS SENDEROS QUE SE BIFURCAN,
EL, FOR PIANO AND ORCHESTRA see
Asturias, Rodrigo

JARDIN MYSTERIEUX, LE see Gougeon,
Denis

JARNNATTEN see Ekström, Lars

JARRELL, MICHAEL (1958-   )
Congruences, For Flute, Oboe And
Instrumental Ensemble [14']
1.1.2(bass clar).2(contrabsn).
1.1.1.0. 2perc,synthesizer,
strings,fl solo,ob solo
LEMOINE perf mat rent   (J49)

Conversions, For Harp And String
Orchestra [12']
string orch,harp solo
LEMOINE perf mat rent   (J50)

Essaims-Cribles, For Bass Clarinet
And Instrumental Ensemble [17']
2(alto fl).0.2(bass clar).0.
1.0.1.0. perc,harp,pno&cel&org,
vla,vcl,db,bass clar solo
LEMOINE perf mat rent   (J51)

Instantanes [13']
3.3(English horn).3.3(contrabsn).
4.3.3.1. 4perc,pno&cel,harp,
strings
LEMOINE perf mat rent   (J52)

Shatten, Das Band, Das Uns An Die
Erde Bindet, Der [20']
0+2alto fl.2.4(2bass
clar).3(contrabsn). 4.2.3.2.
perc,harp,pno,strings
LEMOINE perf mat rent   (J53)

Trace-Ecart, For Solo Voices And
Orchestra [22']
1(pic,alto fl).1(English
horn).1(bass
clar).1(contrabsn). 2.1.1.0.
3perc,pno&cel&org,harp,strings,
SA soli
sc LEMOINE $30.25, perf mat rent
(J54)
JARVLEPP, JAN (1953-   )
Concerto for Violoncello and
Orchestra
4(rec).0.4(rec).0. 4.2.2.0.
3perc,strings,vcl solo
CAN.MUS.CENT. MI 1313 J38C   (J55)

Fanfare [3']
3.3.3.3. 4.0.3.1. 3perc,org,harp,
strings,4trp, or 12 natural
trumpets
CAN.MUS.CENT. MI 1431 J38FA   (J56)

JASPURE see Lejet, Edith

JAUBERT, MAURICE (1900-1940)
Concert Flamand [15'35"]
2.1.3.2. 0.2.2.1. timp,perc,harp,
strings
BILLAUDOT perf mat rent   (J57)

Geographies [10'35"]
3.3.3.3. 4.3.3.1. timp,perc,harp,
strings
BILLAUDOT perf mat rent   (J58)

Intermedes, Les [10'15"]
string orch
BILLAUDOT perf mat rent   (J59)

Jeanne D'arc, For Solo Voice And
Orchestra [26'40"]
3.3.3.3. 0.2.2.1. timp,3perc,
harp,pno,strings without db,S
solo
BILLAUDOT perf mat rent   (J60)

Sonata A Due, For Violin, Violoncello
And String Orchestra [18']
string orch,vln solo,vcl solo
BILLAUDOT perf mat rent   (J61)

Suite Francaise [12'20"]
1.1.1.1. 0.1.1.0. perc,harp,pno,
strings
BILLAUDOT perf mat rent   (J62)

JAWS I: SUITE [ARR.] see Williams, John
T.

JAYHAWKS, THE see Mechem, Kirke Lewis

JAZWINSKI, BARBARA
Concerto for Violoncello and Chamber
Orchestra [18']
1.1.1.1. 1.1.1.0. 2perc,pno,
strings,vcl solo
sc AM.COMP.AL. $70.15, perf mat
rent   (J63)

Stryga [32']
3.2+English horn.2+bass clar.2+
contrabsn. 6.3.2.1. perc,pno,

JAZWINSKI, BARBARA (cont'd.)

strings
sc AM.COMP.AL. $41.90   (J64)

JAZZ OSTINATO see Lewis, John Aaron

JAZZ SINFONIE see Trozjuk, Bogdan

JAZZ SUITE see Gruenberg, Louis

JAZZ SYMPHONY, A, 1925 VERSION see
Antheil, George

JAZZ SYMPHONY, A, 1955 VERSION see
Antheil, George

JE MANGE, TU MANGES see Pablo, Luis de

JE, QUI, D'AUTRE, FOR SOLO VOICES AND
ORCHESTRA see Decoust, Michel

JE TE VEUX [ARR.] see Satie, Erik

JEALOUSY see Janácek, Leoš, Zarlivost

JEANNA see Knaifel, Alexander

JEANNE D'ARC, FOR SOLO VOICE AND
ORCHESTRA see Jaubert, Maurice see
Riondy, Lucien

JEANNE D'ARC, FOR SOLO VOICES AND
CHAMBER GROUP see Finnissy, Michael

JEANNE D'ARC: MARCHE see Verdi,
Giovanna, Giovanna D'Arco: March

JEANNE D'ARC: OUVERTURE see Verdi,
Giuseppe, Giovanna D'Arco: Overture

JEG SYNES AT VERDEN SKINNER, FOR SOLO
VOICE AND ORCHESTRA see Wiklund,
Adolf

JEG VAELGER MIG APRIL see Bangert, Emil

JEG VIL HJEM, FOR SOLO VOICE AND
ORCHESTRA see Hovland, Egil

JENEY, ZOLTAN (1943-   )
Alef. Hommage À Schönberg
sc EMB 10147 f.s.   (J65)

Something Like
25strings
sc EMB $12.25   (J66)

Something Round
25strings
sc EMB 12600 f.s., perf mat rent
(J67)

Sostenuto, For Orchestra
sc EMB 12474 f.s.   (J68)

JENKINS, GORDON HILL (1910-1984)
Concerto for Clarinet and Orchestra
[15'30"]
2.2.3.2. 4.3.3.1. timp,perc,harp,
strings,clar solo
MCA perf mat rent   (J69)

JENNER, GUSTAV (1865-1920)
Serenade [40']
2.2.2.2. 2.2.0.0. timp,strings
(Heussner, Horst) sc BÄREN. BA 6726
f.s.   (J70)

JENNI, DONALD MARTIN (1937-   )
Chopiniana
3(pic),2(English horn).2.2.
2.1.0.0. perc,harp,pno,strings
AMP perf mat rent   (J71)

JENSEITS DER ZEIT, FOR VIOLIN AND
STRING ORCHESTRA see Hosokawa,
Toshio

JENSEN, LUDWIG IRGENS (1894-1969)
Altar, For Solo Voice And String
Orchestra [3']
string orch,solo voice
NORGE   (J72)

Canto d'Omaggio [9']
3.2.2.2. 4.3.3.1. timp,perc,harp,
org,strings
NORGE   (J73)

Leaning On The Fence, For Solo Voice
And Orchestra
see Lutad Mot Gardet, For Solo
Voice And Orchestra

Lutad Mot Gardet, For Solo Voice And
Orchestra [3']
2.1.1.1. 2.0.0.0. cel,strings,
solo voice
"Leaning On The Fence, For Solo
Voice And Orchestra" NORGE (J74)

Rondo Maritale [13']
3.2.3.3. 4.3.3.1. timp,perc,harp,
cel,strings
NORGE   (J75)

JENSEN, LUDWIG IRGENS (cont'd.)

Symphony in D minor [27']
3.2.3.3. 4.3.3.1. timp,perc,harp,
cel,strings
NORGE   (J76)

JEPHTHA: FAREWELL, YE LIMPID SPRINGS,
FOR SOLO VOICE AND ORCHESTRA see
Handel, George Frideric

JEREB, E.
Concerto for Trumpet and Orchestra
sc EMB 13070 f.s., perf mat rent
(J77)

JERMOLAYEV, MIKHAIL (1952-   )
Concerto for Viola and Orchestra, Op.
8 [28']
1.0.0.0.tenor sax. 3.2.0.1.
4perc,cel/pno,strings,vla solo
SIKORSKI perf mat rent   (J78)

JERUSALEM see Parry, [Sir] Charles
Hubert Hastings

JESIEN, FOR SOLO VOICE AND ORCHESTRA
see Lutoslawski, Witold

JESSONDA: OVERTURE see Spohr, Ludwig
(Louis)

JETHS, WILLEM (1959-   )
Concerto for Alto Saxophone and
String Orchestra [15']
string orch,alto sax solo
DONEMUS perf mat rent   (J79)

Procurans Odium [7']
2.2.3.0. 4.2.3.1. timp,3perc,
harp,strings
DONEMUS perf mat rent   (J80)

JETZT HAST DU DIE MACHT, PROLET, FOR
SOLO VOICE AND STRINGS see Eisler,
Hanns

JEU DE BACH, FOR OBOE, TRUMPET AND
STRING ORCHESTRA see Beecroft,
Norma

JEU DE VALEURS ET D'INTENSITÉS see
Schweizer, Klaus

JEUNE PATRE BRETON, LE, FOR SOLO VOICE
AND ORCHESTRA see Berlioz, Hector
(Louis)

JEUX see Debussy, Claude see Lauba,
Christian

JEUX, FOR PIANO AND ORCHESTRA see
Vieru, Anatol

JEUX DES MASQUES, FOR SOLO VOICE,
HARPSICHORD AND ORCHESTRA see
D'amico, Matteo

JEUX JEUNESSE see Hundsnes, Svein

JEVERUD, JOHAN (1962-   )
Terrèst Mekanik
STIM   (J81)

JEVTIC, IVAN (1947-   )
Concerto for Flute and String
Orchestra [16'30"]
string orch,pno,fl solo
sc BILLAUDOT f.s., perf mat rent
(J82)
Concerto for Trumpet and Orchestra,
No. 2 [19']
2.2.2.2. 4.3.3.1. timp,2perc,cel,
harp,strings,trp solo
BILLAUDOT perf mat rent   (J83)

Vers Byzance, For Viola And String
Orchestra [20']
string orch,vla solo
BILLAUDOT perf mat rent   (J84)

JEWELS OF THE MADONNA: DANCE OF THE
CAMORRISTS see Wolf-Ferrari,
Ermanno, Gioielli Della Madonna, I:
Danza Dei Camorristi

JEWELS OF THE MADONNA: INTERMEZZO NO. 2
see Wolf-Ferrari, Ermanno, Gioielli
Della Madonna, I: Intermezzo No. 2

JIEDNA see Vea, Ketil

JIMMACK THE POSTIE see Davies, Peter
Maxwell

JINGLE-JANGLE, FOR VIBRAPHONE AND
STRING ORCHESTRA see McBride,
Robert Guyn

JIRÁK, KAREL BOLESLAV (1891-1972)
Symphonic Variations *Op.40 [21']
3.3.3.3. 4.4.3.1. timp,perc,harp,
strings
SUPRAPHON   (J85)

JIROVEC, VOJTECH MATEJ
see GYROWETZ, ADALBERT

JO GJENDE [ARR.] see Johansen, David
Monrad

JOACHIM, JOSEPH (1831-1907)
Notturno for Violin and Orchestra,
Op. 12 [11'30"]
2.2.2.2. 2.0.0.0. strings,vln
solo
SIMROCK perf mat rent   (J86)

Szene Der Marfa, For Solo Voice And
Orchestra *Op.14 [10']
2.2.2.2. 4.2.0.0. timp,strings,
Mez solo
SIMROCK perf mat rent   (J87)

JOAN VON ZARISSA: SUITE, FOR SOLO
VOICES AND ORCHESTRA see Egk,
Werner

JOCHUM, OTTO (1898-   )
Wanderschaft *Op.58
string orch
sc,pts BOHM f.s.   (J88)

JODELET: SIX LITTLE PIECES see Reiser,
Reinhardt

JOHANNESSEN, PER BERGE (1950-   )
Sinfonietta [11']
3.2.3.2. 4.3.3.1. timp,strings
NORGE   (J89)

JOHANNIS KAFERLN WALZER see Strauss,
Johann, [Jr.]

JOHANNISNACHT, DIE see Grabovsky,
Leonid, Eve Of St. John Kupalo, The

JOHANNSSON, MAGNUS BL. (1925-   )
Adagio
perc,cel,strings
ICELAND 018-006   (J90)

Points [15'35"]
1.1.1.1. 1.0.0.0. perc,harp,pno,
strings,electronic tape
ICELAND 018-002   (J91)

JOHANSEN, BERTIL PALMAR (1954-   )
Concerto for Violin and Orchestra,
No. 1 [20']
2.3.2.3. 3.2.2.0. timp,perc,harp,
strings,vln solo
NORGE   (J92)

Pictures Of Medea, For Recorder And
Chamber Orchestra [18'30"]
2horn,perc,strings,electronic
tape,rec solo
NORGE   (J93)

Utspill [6']
2.1.2.1. 2.2.1.0. timp,strings
NORGE   (J94)

JOHANSEN, DAVID MONRAD (1888-1974)
Jo Gjende [arr.]
(Bergh, Sverre) 1.1.2.1. 2.0.0.0.
strings NORGE   (J95)

JOHANSEN, SVEND AAQUIST
Historien Om Malinche [30']
3.3.3.2. 4.2.2.1. 2perc,pno,
strings, actor
"Story Of Malinche, The" SAMFUNDET
perf mat rent   (J96)

Story Of Malinche, The
see Historien Om Malinche

JOHANSON, SVEN-ERIC (1919-   )
Serenade [9'25"]
fl,ob,clar,horn,strings
BUSCH perf mat rent   (J97)

JOHN COME KISSE ME NOW [ARR.] see Byrd,
William

JOHNNY REITET WESTWARTS, FOR NARRATOR
AND ORCHESTRA see Ostendorf, Jens-
Peter

JOHNSEN, HALLVARD (1916-   )
Bergmannen, For Solo Voice And
Orchestra *Op.81
4.3.2.3. 4.3.2.1. timp,perc,
strings,narrator
"Miner, The, For Solo Voice And
Orchestra" NORGE   (J98)

Concerto for Flute and String
Orchestra, Op. 25 [14']
string orch,fl solo
NORGE   (J99)

Concerto for Trumpet and Orchestra,
Op. 50 [14']
2.2.2.2. 2.0.0.1. timp,2perc,pno,
strings,trp solo
NORSK perf mat rent   (J100)

JOHNSEN, HALLVARD (cont'd.)

Concerto for Violin and Orchestra,
No. 2, Op. 51 [17']
2.2.2.2. 2.0.1.1. timp,perc,
strings,vln solo
NORGE   (J101)

Concerto for Violoncello and
Orchestra, Op. 73 [18']
2.2.2.2. 4.2.0.0. timp,perc,
strings,vcl solo
NORGE   (J102)

Miner, The, For Solo Voice And
Orchestra
see Bergmannen, For Solo Voice And
Orchestra

Ouverture Festoso *Op.55 [11']
2.2.2.2. 4.3.3.1. perc,strings
NORGE   (J103)

Suite, Op. 20 [16']
1.1.1.1. 0.0.0.0. strings
NORGE   (J104)

Symphony No. 1, Op. 17 [28']
2.2.3.2. 4.2.3.0. timp,perc,
strings
NORGE   (J105)

Symphony No. 2, Op. 22 [18']
2.2.2.2. 4.2.2.1. timp,perc,harp,
strings
NORGE   (J106)

Symphony No. 3, Op. 26 [20']
2.2.2.2. 4.2.3.1. timp,perc,
strings
NORGE   (J107)

Symphony No. 4, Op. 29 [19']
3.2.2.2. 4.3.3.1. timp,perc,cel,
strings
NORGE   (J108)

Symphony No. 5, Op. 32 [18']
2.2.2.2. 4.3.3.1. timp,perc,
strings
NORGE   (J109)

Symphony No. 6, Op. 35 [21']
3.2.2.2. 4.3.3.1. timp,perc,cel,
strings
NORGE   (J110)

Symphony No. 7, Op. 38 [31']
3.2.2.2. 4.3.3.1. timp,perc,cel,
strings
NORGE   (J111)

Symphony No. 8, Op. 42 [21']
3.2.2.2. 4.3.3.1. timp,perc,
strings
NORGE   (J112)

Symphony No. 9, Op. 53 [30']
2.2.2.2. 4.3.2.1. timp,perc,
strings
NORGE   (J113)

Symphony No. 10, Op. 59 [24']
2.2.2.2. 4.2.3.1. timp,perc,cel,
strings
NORGE   (J114)

Symphony No. 11, Op. 70 [26']
2.2.2.2. 4.2.2.1. timp,perc,
strings
NORGE   (J115)

Symphony No. 12, Op. 72 [21']
2.2.2.2. 4.2.2.1. timp,perc,
strings
NORGE   (J116)

Symphony No. 13, Op. 90
2.3.2.2. 4.3.2.1. timp,perc,
strings
NORGE   (J117)

Symphony No. 14, Op. 97
2.2.2.2. 4.2.3.1. timp,perc,
strings
NORGE   (J118)

Symphony No. 15, Op. 103
2.2.2.3. 4.3.2.1. timp,perc,
strings
NORGE   (J119)

Symphony No. 16, Op. 104
1.1.1.1. 2.1.1.1. timp,perc,
strings
NORGE   (J120)

Symphony No. 17, Op. 107
2.2.2.2. 4.3.2.1. timp,perc,
strings
NORGE   (J121)

JOHNSEN, KJELL (1945-   )
Symphony
2.2.2.2. 4.2.3.1. timp,perc,harp,
pno,strings,opt electronic tape
NORGE   (J122)

JOHNSON, A. PAUL (1955-   )
Cento [40']
3.3.4.3.sax. 6.3.3.1. 4perc,pno,
strings
sc AM.COMP.AL. $120.25   (J123)

JOHNSON, FRANCIS (1792-1844)
Buffalo City Guard Parade March
(Nightingale) 2+pic.2.2.2. 4.2.3.1.
timp,perc,strings [3'] KALMUS
A7220 sc $8.00, set $18.00, pts
$1.00, ea.   (J124)

General Cadwalader's Grand March
(Nightingale) 2+pic.2.2.2. 4.2.3.1.
timp,perc,strings [3'] KALMUS
A7218 sc $5.00, set $15.00, pts
$.75, ea.   (J125)

In The Cataract Of The Ganges March
(Nightingale) 2+pic.2.2.2. 4.2.3.1.
timp,perc,strings [3'] KALMUS
7221 sc $8.00, set $18.00, pts
$1.00, ea.   (J126)

Philadelphia Grays Quickstep
(Nightingale) 2+pic.2.2.2. 4.2.3.1.
timp,perc,strings [4'] KALMUS
A7219 sc $8.00, set $18.00, pts
$1.00, ea.   (J127)

JOHNSON, J.J. (1924-   )
Rondeau For Quartet And Orchestra
[18']
1.1.2.1. 2.0.0.0. strings,vibra
solo,pno solo,db solo,drums solo
sc,pts MJQ rent   (J128)

JOHNSON, JAMES P. (1891-1955)
Yamekraw [arr.]
(Still, William Grant)
1.0.2.0.2alto sax.2tenor sax.
0.2.1.0. drums,banjo,strings sc
STILL $14.20   (J129)

JOHNSON, JOHN ROSAMOND (1873-1954)
Lift Every Voice And Sing [arr.]
(Still, William Grant) fl,pno,
strings sc STILL $3.70   (J130)

JOHNSON, ROBERT SHERLAW (1932-   )
Concerto for Clarinet and Orchestra
[28']
2(pic).2.2.3. 4.3.3.0. timp,
3perc,strings,clar solo
OXFORD perf mat rent   (J131)

Concerto for Piano and Orchestra
[25']
2.2.2.2. 4.3.3.1. timp,2perc,
strings,pno solo
OXFORD perf mat rent   (J132)

Sinfonietta Concertante [15']
1.1.1.1. 1.1.1.0. perc,pno,string
quin
OXFORD perf mat rent   (J133)

JOHNSTON, DONALD O. (1929-   )
Montage [8']
2.2.2.2. 4.3.3.1. timp,perc,harp,
strings
KALMUS A7397 sc $30.00, set $75.00,
pts $3.00, ea., perf mat rent
                                 (J134)

JOI, AMOR & CORTEZIA see Adler, Samuel
Hans

JOKINEN, ERKKI (1941-   )
Concerto for Accordion and Chamber
Orchestra [15'15"]
fl,clar,perc,4vln,2vla,2vcl,db,
acord solo
PAN F   (J135)

JOLAS, BETSY (1926-   )
D'un Opera De Poupee En Sept Musiques
[19']
fl,clar,horn,perc,elec gtr,pno,
2Ondes Martenot, 4electric kbd,
vln, vcl, electronic equipment
SALABERT perf mat rent   (J136)

Points d'Or, For Saxophone And
Instrumental Ensemble
2clar,bass clar,2trp,2trom,2perc,
pno,2vla,2vcl,db,sax solo
RICORDI-FR perf mat rent   (J137)

Tales Of Summer Sea
HEUGEL HE 33657 perf mat rent
                                 (J138)

JOLESVEINANE see Tveitt, Geirr

JOLIE FILLE DE PERTH, LA: SCENES
BOHEMIENNES see Bizet, Georges

JOLIVET, ANDRE (1905-1974)
Choral Et Fugato [10']
3.3.3.3.sax. 4.3.3.1. 3perc,cel,
pno,strings
BILLAUDOT perf mat rent   (J139)

Cosmogonie [8']
3.3.3.3. 4.3.3.1. perc,cel,2harp,
strings
ESCHIG perf mat rent   (J140)

Danse Incantatoire [8']
3.3.3.3. 4.3.3.1. timp,6perc,
2harp,pno,2Ondes Martenot,
strings
BILLAUDOT perf mat rent   (J141)

Guignol Et Pandore: Suite [18']
3.3.3.3. 4.4.3.1. timp,3perc,
2harp,cel,pno,strings
sc ESCHIG f.s., perf mat rent
                                 (J142)

Poemes Pour L'enfant, For Solo Voice
And Instrumental Ensemble [22']
1.1.1.1. 0.1.0.0. pno,harp,2vln,
vla,vcl,S/Mez solo
sc BILLAUDOT f.s., perf mat rent
                                 (J143)

Quatre Melodies Sur Des Poesies
Anciennes, For Solo Voice And
Orchestra [8']
1.1.2.1. 0.2.2.0. 2perc,pno,
string quin,S/Mez solo
BILLAUDOT perf mat rent   (J144)

Sarabande Sur Le Nom D'Erik Satie
3.3.3.3.2sax. 4.3.3.1. cel,
strings
BILLAUDOT perf mat rent   (J145)

Suite Francaise [18']
2.2.2.2. 2.2.2.1. timp,perc,harp,
strings
min sc BILLAUDOT f.s., perf mat
rent   (J146)

Trois Chants Des Hommes, For Solo
Voice And Orchestra [30']
3.3.3.3. 4.3.3.1. timp,3perc,
2harp,pno,strings,Bar solo
BILLAUDOT perf mat rent   (J147)

JOLLY GOOD FELLOW see Kroll, William

JOLSTERSLATT see Søderlind, Ragnar

JOMMELLI, NICCOLO (1714-1774)
Achille A Syros: Air d'Ulysse, For
Solo Voice And Orchestra
see Achille In Sciro: Aria
d'Ulisse, For Solo Voice And
Orchestra

Achille A Syros: Duo Achille Et
Ulysse, For Solo Voices And
Orchestra
see Achille In Sciro: Duo Achille E
Ulisse, For Solo Voices And
Orchestra

Achille A Syros: Recit Et Air
d'Achille, For Solo Voice And
Orchestra
see Achille In Sciro: Recitativo E
Aria d'Achille, For Solo Voice
And Orchestra

Achille In Sciro: Aria d'Ulisse, For
Solo Voice And Orchestra
(Blanchard, R.) "Achille A Syros:
Air d'Ulysse, For Solo Voice And
Orchestra" 2ob,2horn,hpsd,
strings,countertenor [6'] BOIS
perf mat rent   (J148)

Achille In Sciro: Duo Achille E
Ulisse, For Solo Voices And
Orchestra
(Blanchard, R.) "Achille A Syros:
Duo Achille Et Ulysse, For Solo
Voices And Orchestra" 2ob,2horn,
2trp,hpsd,strings,T&countertenor
[5'] BOIS perf mat rent   (J149)

Achille In Sciro: Overture [6']
0.2.0.0. 2.2.0.0. strings
(Blanchard, R.) BOIS perf mat rent
                                 (J150)

Achille In Sciro: Recitativo E Aria
d'Achille, For Solo Voice And
Orchestra
(Blanchard, R.) "Achille A Syros:
Recit Et Air d'Achille, For Solo
Voice And Orchestra" 2ob,2horn,
hpsd,strings,T solo [11'] BOIS
perf mat rent   (J151)

Cantata, "E Quando Sara Mai Che Alle
Mie Pene", For Solo Voice And
String Orchestra [arr.]
(Chiti, G.P.) string orch,cont,S
solo [14'] SONZOGNO perf mat rent
                                 (J152)

Cantata, "Gia La Notte Si Avvicina",
For Solo Voice And String
Orchestra, [arr.]

JOMMELLI, NICCOLO (cont'd.)

(Chiti, G.P.) string orch,cont,med
female solo [14'] SONZOGNO perf
mat rent   (J153)

Ciaccona [12']
2ob,2horn,strings
BSE 143 perf mat rent   (J154)

JONATHAN SWIFT see Victory, Gerard

JONCHAIES see Xenakis, Yannis (Iannis)

JONES, LLIFON HUGHES
see HUGHES-JONES, LLIFON

JONES, ROBERT WILLIAM (1932-   )
Concertino for Strings
string orch
SHAWNEE perf mat rent   (J155)

JONSOKBALET see Tveitt, Geirr

JONSOKKVELDEN see Tveitt, Geirr

JONSOKNATT, FOR SOLO VOICES AND
ORCHESTRA see Tveitt, Geirr

JONSSON, JOSEF [PETRUS] (1887-1969)
Blir Vackert Dar Du Gar, Det, For
Solo Voice And Orchestra [3']
2.1.2.2. 1.0.0.0. strings,med
solo
NORDISKA perf mat rent   (J156)

Fiddler's Journey To His Last Resting
Place, The [15']
2.1(English horn).2.2. 2.2.1.0.
timp,perc,harp,strings
NORDISKA perf mat rent   (J157)

Fyra Sanger, For Solo Voice And
Orchestra *Op.47 [9']
2.2+English horn.2.2. 0.2.1.0.
timp,perc,strings,med solo
NORDISKA perf mat rent   (J158)

Omkring Tiggarn Fran Loussa, For
Narrator And Orchestra [10']
2.2.2.2. 2.2.1.0. timp,harp,pno,
strings,narrator
NORDISKA perf mat rent   (J159)

Sista Sangen, Den, For Solo Voice And
Orchestra *Op.29,No.1 [2']
2.2.2.2. 2.2.0.0. timp,harp,
strings,solo voice
NORDISKA perf mat rent   (J160)

Som Ett Silversmycke, For Solo Voice
And Orchestra *Op.26,No.2 [4']
2.1.2.2. 2.0.0.0. strings,solo
voice
NORDISKA perf mat rent   (J161)

Under Haggarna, For Solo Voice And
Orchestra [3']
2.1.2.1. 2.0.0.0. harp,strings,
high solo
NORDISKA perf mat rent   (J162)

Va A' En Operaaria?, For Solo Voice
And Orchestra [3']
1.1.2.1. 2.2.1.1. timp,perc,
strings,solo voice
NORDISKA perf mat rent   (J163)

JONSSON, REINE (1960-   )
Bortburen [8']
string orch
STIM   (J164)

Dar Den Stora Tigern Ljuger
3.3.3.3. 4.3.3.1. timp,2perc,
harp,strings
STIM   (J165)

Grodan Och Vagen [20']
5fl,5clar,5perc,2string quin
STIM   (J166)

JOPLIN, SCOTT (1868-1917)
Entertainer, The [arr.]
(Fraser, Donald) string orch
FENTONE   (J167)

Seven Scott Joplin Rags [arr.]
(Zinn, William) string orch
EXCELSIOR sc 494-00580 $10.00,
pts 494-00581-00585 $4.00, ea.
(J168)

JORD, FOR SOLO VOICE AND ORCHESTRA see
Strand, Ragnvald

JORDAN, SVERRE (1889-1972)
An Magrit *Op.72a [7']
3.3.2.2. 4.2.3.0. timp,perc,
strings
NORGE   (J169)

Av "Tue Bentsons Viser", For Solo
Voice And Orchestra *Op.44 [10']
3.2.2.2. 4.2.2.0. timp,perc,
2harp,cel,strings,T solo
"Tue Bentsons Songs, For Solo Voice

JORDAN, SVERRE (cont'd.)

And Orchestra" NORGE   (J170)

By The Sea, For Solo Voice And
Orchestra
see Ved Havet, For Solo Voice And
Orchestra

Christ Complains, For Solo Voice And
Orchestra
see Christus Klagt, For Solo Voice
And Orchestra

Christus Klagt, For Solo Voice And
Orchestra *Op.7,No.1 [4']
2.2.2.2. 2.0.0.0. strings,T/Bar
solo
"Christ Complains, For Solo Voice
And Orchestra" NORGE   (J171)

Concerto for Horn and Orchestra, Op.
63, in C [15']
2.2.2.2. 3.2.2.0. timp,perc,
strings,horn solo
NORGE   (J172)

Concerto for Piano and Orchestra, No.
1, Op. 45, in E minor [30']
3.2.2.2. 4.2.2.1. timp,perc,
strings,pno solo
NORGE   (J173)

Concerto for Piano and Orchestra, No.
2, Op. 77, in F [17']
3.2.2.2. 4.2.2.0. timp,perc,
strings,pno solo
NORGE   (J174)

Concerto for Violin and Orchestra,
Op. 82, in G minor [23']
2.2.2.2. 4.2.2.0. timp,perc,
strings,vln solo
NORGE   (J175)

Der Synger Ingen Fugle, For Solo
Voice And Orchestra *Op.33,No.3
[2']
2.2.2.1. 2.0.0.0. strings,S/T
solo
"There Are No Birds Singing, For
Solo Voice And Orchestra" NORGE
(J176)

Eftersommer, For Solo Voice And
Orchestra *Op.73,No.4 [3']
2.2.2.2. 2.0.0.0. harp,strings,
solo voice
"Late Summer, For Solo Voice And
Orchestra" NORGE   (J177)

Feberdigte, For Solo Voice And
Orchestra *Op.13 [20']
3.2.2.2. 2.2.2.1. timp,perc,harp,
strings,narrator
"Fever Poems, For Solo Voice And
Orchestra" NORGE   (J178)

Festforspill *Op.46 [5']
3.2.2.2. 4.2.3.1. timp,perc,harp,
strings
"Festival Overture" NORGE   (J179)

Festival Overture
see Festforspill

Fever Poems, For Solo Voice And
Orchestra
see Feberdigte, For Solo Voice And
Orchestra

Forspill Til Et Lyrisk Drama *Op.75
[7']
3.2.2.2. 4.2.3.1. timp,perc,cel,
strings
"Overture To A Lyrical Drama" NORGE
(J180)

Gammel Vise, En, For Solo Voice And
Orchestra *Op.41,No.4 [3']
2.2.2.2. 2.0.0.0. harp,strings,
solo voice
"Old Tune, An, For Solo Voice And
Orchestra" NORGE   (J181)

Jutta Comes To Folkungarna, For Solo
Voice And Orchestra
see Jutta Kommer Til Folkungarna,
For Solo Voice And Orchestra

Jutta Kommer Til Folkungarna, For
Solo Voice And Orchestra *Op.18,
No.3 [2']
1.1.2.1. 2.0.0.0. harp,strings,S
solo
"Jutta Comes To Folkungarna, For
Solo Voice And Orchestra" NORGE
(J182)

Kindesgebet, For Solo Voice And
Orchestra *Op.69,No.2 [2']
2.0.0.1. 2.0.0.0. harp,strings,S
solo
NORGE   (J183)

Landscape, For Solo Voice And
Orchestra
see Landskab, For Solo Voice And
Orchestra

JORDAN, SVERRE (cont'd.)

Landskab, For Solo Voice And
Orchestra *Op.33,No.1 [2']
2.1.2.1. 2.0.0.0. harp,strings,
Mez/Bar solo
"Landscape, For Solo Voice And
Orchestra" NORGE   (J184)

Late Summer, For Solo Voice And
Orchestra
see Eftersommer, For Solo Voice And
Orchestra

Norsk Rapsodi, Op. 53, In D [11']
3.2.2.2. 4.2.3.1. timp,perc,
strings
NORGE   (J185)

Old Tune, An, For Solo Voice And
Orchestra
see Gammel Vise, En, For Solo Voice
And Orchestra

Ouverture Til Et Romantisk Lystspill
Av Shakespeare *Op.42 [7']
3.2.2.2. 4.3.3.0. timp,perc,harp,
strings
"Overture To A Romantic Play By
Shakespeare" NORGE   (J186)

Overture To A Lyrical Drama
see Forspill Til Et Lyrisk Drama

Overture To A Romantic Play By
Shakespeare
see Ouverture Til Et Romantisk
Lystspill Av Shakespeare

Serenade, Op. 68, in A [22']
string orch
NORGE   (J187)

Sing My Chords, For Solo Voice And
Orchestra
see Syng Mine Strengjer, For Solo
Voice And Orchestra

Spring Song, For Solo Voice And
Orchestra
see Varvisa, For Solo Voice And
Orchestra

Syng Mine Strengjer, For Solo Voice
And Orchestra *Op.41,No.3 [2']
2.2.2.2. 2.2.0.0. harp,strings,
solo voice
"Sing My Chords, For Solo Voice And
Orchestra" NORGE   (J188)

There Are No Birds Singing, For Solo
Voice And Orchestra
see Der Synger Ingen Fugle, For
Solo Voice And Orchestra

Thirteen Years, For Solo Voice And
Orchestra
see Tretton Ar, For Solo Voice And
Orchestra

Three Nocturnal Scenes
see Tre Nattlige Scener

Tre Nattlige Scener *Op.66 [11']
2.1.2.1. 2.2.1.0. timp,perc,harp,
strings
"Three Nocturnal Scenes" NORGE
(J189)

Tretton Ar, For Solo Voice And
Orchestra *Op.54,No.1 [2']
2fl,2clar,harp,cel,strings,S solo
"Thirteen Years, For Solo Voice And
Orchestra" NORGE   (J190)

Tue Bentsons Songs, For Solo Voice
And Orchestra
see Av "Tue Bentsons Viser", For
Solo Voice And Orchestra

Varvisa, For Solo Voice And Orchestra
*Op.21,No.4 [3']
2.2.2.2. 2.2.2.0. timp,harp,
strings,solo voice
"Spring Song, For Solo Voice And
Orchestra" NORGE   (J191)

Ved Havet, For Solo Voice And
Orchestra *Op.73,No.1 [2']
2.2.2.2. 4.2.3.0. timp,perc,
strings,S/T solo
"By The Sea, For Solo Voice And
Orchestra" NORGE   (J192)

JORDEN AR MANNISKANS HEM see
Dorumsgaard, Arne

JORGENSEN, AXEL (1881-1947)
Romance for Trombone and Orchestra
[4']
2.2.2.2. 4.2.2.1. timp,strings,
trom solo
HANSEN-DEN perf mat rent   (J193)

JØRGENSEN, ERIK
  Confrontations
    see Konfrontationer

  Konfrontationer [15']
      3.3.3.3. 4.3.3.1. 4perc,strings
      "Confrontations" sc SAMFUNDET f.s.,
      perf mat rent   (J194)

  Modello Per Archi
    sc,pts SAMFUNDET f.s.   (J195)

JOSE MIT DER ZAUBERFIEDEL, DER, FOR
  NARRATOR, VIOLIN AND ORCHESTRA see
  Hiller, Wilfried

JOSEPH, I.
  Regina Coeli, For Solo Voice And
    String Orchestra
      string orch,cont,opt bsn,S solo
    KUNZEL 10154 sc $20.00, pts $3.80,
    ea.   (J196)

JOSEPHS, WILFRED (1927-   )
  Caen Wood
    NOVELLO perf mat rent   (J197)

  Circadian Rhythms *Op.137
    NOVELLO perf mat rent   (J198)

  Concerto for Clarinet and Orchestra,
    Op. 95 [23']
      2(pic).0.0.2(contrabsn). 2.0.0.0.
      perc,harp,cel,strings,clar solo
    sc NOVELLO $13.75, perf mat rent
                                         (J199)

  Encore (On A Theme Of Scott Joplin)
    [5']
      1.1.1.1. 1.0.0.0. strings,gtr
      solo,harp solo,hpsd solo
    NOVELLO perf mat rent   (J200)

  Four Horsemen Of The Apocalypse
    Overture *Op.86 [13']
      4(pic).4(English horn).4(bass
      clar).4(contrabsn). 4.5.4.1.
      4perc,timp,strings
    NOVELLO perf mat rent   (J201)

  Philippa Variations [11']
      3(pic).3(English horn).3(bass
      clar).3. 3.3.3.0. 3perc,harp/
      pno,strings
    NOVELLO perf mat rent   (J202)

  Saratoga Concerto, For Guitar And
    Orchestra [26']
      1.1.1.1. 1.0.0.0. harp,hpsd,
      strings,gtr solo
    NOVELLO perf mat rent   (J203)

  Symphony No. 6, Op. 83 [31']
      3(pic).3(English horn).3(bass
      clar).3(contrabsn). 4.3.3.1.
      4perc,timp,strings,SATB,SBar
      soli
    NOVELLO perf mat rent   (J204)

JOSHUA: O HAD I JUBAL'S LYRE, FOR SOLO
  VOICE AND ORCHESTRA see Handel,
  George Frideric

JOSUA: O HÄTT' ICH JUBALS HARF, FOR
  SOLO VOICE AND ORCHESTRA see
  Handel, George Frideric, Joshua: O
  Had I Jubal's Lyre, For Solo Voice
  And Orchestra

JOUARD, PAUL E. (1928-   )
  Victorian Suite
    SHAWNEE perf mat rent   (J205)

JOUBERT, JOHN (1927-   )
  Deploration *Op.92 [18']
      3(pic).3(English horn).3(bass
      clar).3(contrabsn). 4.4.3.1.
      timp,3perc,harp,strings
    NOVELLO perf mat rent   (J206)

  Temps Perdu *Op.99
      string orch
    sc NOVELLO $41.75   (J207)

  Threnos [10']
      hpsd,12strings soli
    NOVELLO perf mat rent   (J208)

JOULU TULLUT ON, FOR SOLO VOICE AND
  ORCHESTRA see Merikanto, Oskar

JOULUN KELLOT, FOR SOLO VOICE AND
  ORCHESTRA [ARR.] see Hannikainen,
  P.J.

JOUR DE FETE see Olthuis, Kees

JOURNEY see Thorarinsson, Leifur

JOURNEY INTO SUNRISE, FOR 5 SAXOPHONES
  AND ORCHESTRA see Kulesha, Gary

JOURNEY THROUGH see Rickley, James

JOURNEYS see Van de Vate, Nancy Hayes

JOURS DE SILENCE, FOR SOLO VOICE AND
  ORCHESTRA see Zender, Hans

JOUSTING see Norgaard, Per, Turnering

JOUVIN, PIERRE (1921-   )
  Concerto for Guitar and Orchestra
      2.2.2.2. 2.2.2.0. timp,perc,
      strings,gtr solo
    BILLAUDOT perf mat rent   (J209)

  Symphony No. 2 [38']
      3.2.2.2. 4.3.3.0. timp,2perc,cel,
      harp,strings
    BILLAUDOT perf mat rent   (J210)

JOY see Lunde, Ivar

JOYEUSE MARCHE see Chabrier, [Alexis-]
  Emmanuel

JOYFUL, JOYFUL, WE ADORE THEE
  (Kirkland, Camp) 1.1.0.1. 1.3.3.1.
    baritone horn,perc,org,pno,strings
    sc,pts BROADMAN 4573-49 $30.00
                                         (J211)

JOYFUL NOISE, A see Stock, David
  Frederick

JOYFUL YOUTH see Lundkvist, Per, Frohe
  Jugend

JU, XIAO-SONG
  Girl Of The Mountain, For Violin And
    Orchestra [12']
      3.2.2.2. 4.2.3.1. timp,perc,harp,
      cel,strings,vln solo
    HONG KONG perf mat rent   (J212)

  Mountain And The Folk Style, The
      3.2.2+bass clar.2+contrabsn.
      4.3.3.1. timp,perc,harp,strings
    HONG KONG perf mat rent   (J213)

  Mountain Song, For Violoncello And
    Orchestra [10']
      3.2.2.2. 4.3.3.0. timp,perc,xylo,
      harp,cel,strings,vcl solo
    HONG KONG perf mat rent   (J214)

  String Symphony [21']
      timp,perc,xylo,harp,pno,strings
    HONG KONG perf mat rent   (J215)

JUBEL OUVERTURE see Weber, Carl Maria
  von

JUBEL QUADRILLE see Strauss, Johann,
  [Sr.]

JUBILAEUS MUSICUS "AD HONOREM
  UNIVERSITATIS SANCTAE MARIAE" see
  Orrego-Salas, Juan A.

JUBILEE FESTIVAL OVERTURE see Gillis,
  Don E.

JUBILEE MUSIC see Schuller, Gunther

JUBILEE OVERTURE see Reinecke, Carl see
  Weber, Carl Maria von, Jubel
  Ouverture

JUBILEE SUITE see McCabe, John

JUBILO see Sierra

JUDITH: BALLET MUSIC see Goossens,
  [Sir] Eugene

JUEGOS see Bernaola, Carmelo

JUGENDGEDENKEN "ICH WILL SPIEGELN MICH
  IN JENEN TAGEN", FOR SOLO VOICE AND
  ORCHESTRA see Schoeck, Othmar

JUGENDZEIT see Killmayer, Wilhelm

JUGLARES see Rodrigo, Joaquín

JUILLIARD SERENADE see Maderna, Bruno

JULEMUSIKK FOR STRYKERE see Rypdal,
  Terje

JULEPARTITA see Karlsen, Kjell Mørk

JULEREISA see Tveitt, Geirr

JULIE: OVERTURE see Spontini, Gaspare

JULIUS CAESAR see Kurka, Robert Frank

JULIUS CAESAR, OP. 128: OVERTURE see
  Schumann, Robert (Alexander)

JUNCTURES see Kalbfleisch, Rodger

JUNCTURES FOR ORCHESTRA see Bazelon,
  Irwin Allen

JUNE 28, 1982- HOTEL JEROME see
  Lieberman, David

JUNG, HELGE (1943-   )
  Concerto for Flute and Orchestra, Op.
    31
      2.2.2.2. 4.2.0.0. timp,perc,
      strings,fl solo
    sc PETERS $25.00   (J216)

  Concerto for Organ and Orchestra, Op.
    38
      perc,strings,org solo
    sc PETERS $40.00   (J217)

JUNGLE DANCE see Steiner, Max(imillian
  Raoul Walter)

JUOZAPAITIS, JURGIS (1942-   )
  Rex [22']
      3.2.2.2. 4.3.3.1. timp,2perc,
      strings
    SIKORSKI perf mat rent   (J218)

  Symphony No. 3
    see Zodiac, The

  Zodiac, The (Symphony No. 3)
    sc MEZ KNIGA f.s.   (J219)

JURGUTIS, V.
  Concerto for Violin and Chamber
    Orchestra
    sc MEZ KNIGA f.s.   (J220)

JURISTEN-BALL POLKA see Strauss,
  Johann, [Jr.]

JURISTS, MARCH see Tchaikovsky, Piotr
  Ilyich

JUROVSKY, VLADIMIR (1915-   )
  Eugenie Grandet *Op.60 [35']
      3.3.3.3. 4.3.3.1. timp,perc,harp,
      cel,strings
    SIKORSKI perf mat rent   (J221)

JUTISH MEDLEY see Grainger, Percy
  Aldridge

JUTTA COMES TO FOLKUNGARNA, FOR SOLO
  VOICE AND ORCHESTRA see Jordan,
  Sverre, Jutta Kommer Til
  Folkungarna, For Solo Voice And
  Orchestra

JUTTA KOMMER TIL FOLKUNGARNA, FOR SOLO
  VOICE AND ORCHESTRA see Jordan,
  Sverre

JUTTA KOMMER TILL FOLKUNGARNA, FOR SOLO
  VOICE AND ORCHESTRA see Nordqvist,
  Gustaf

JUXBRUDER WALZER see Strauss, Johann,
  [Jr.]

JUZELIUNAS, JULIUS (1916-   )
  Concerto for Organ, Violin and String
    Orchestra
      string orch,org solo,vln solo
    VAAP perf mat rent   (J222)

JYOTIR, BRILLIANCE see Buhr, Glenn

K

"K" CHOREOGRAPHISCHE SZENEN see Kont, Paul

(K)EIN SOMMERNACHTSTRAUM see Schnittke, Alfred, Not A Midsummer Night's Dream

KA TA MEI LING see Hsin, Hu-Kuang

KABALEVSKY, DMITRI BORISOVICH (1904-1987)
Cedre Et Le Palmier, Le [7']
2.2.2.2. 4.2.2.0. timp,harp, strings
KALMUS A7267 sc $15.00, set $25.00, pts $1.25, ea., perf mat rent
(K1)

Comedians, The *Op.26
min sc KALMUS K00377 $8.75   (K2)

Concerto for Flute and Orchestra, Op. 48, [arr.]
(Duchemin, Andre-Gilles) 1.1.2.1. 2.1.1.0. timp,perc,xylo,strings, fl solo [16'] VAAP perf mat rent
(K3)

Concerto for Piano and Orchestra, No. 3, Op. 50, in D
min sc KALMUS K00534 $3.50   (K4)

Concerto for Piano and Orchestra, No. 4, Op. 99 [12']
drums,strings,pno solo
SIKORSKI perf mat rent   (K5)

Concerto for Violoncello and Orchestra, No. 2, Op. 77
sc SIKORSKI 2138-K $25.75, perf mat rent
(K6)

Poem Of Struggle *Op.12
3(pic).3(English horn).3(bass clar).3(contrabsn). 4.3.3.1. timp,perc,strings
KALMUS A5774 sc $25.00, set $50.00, perf mat rent
(K7)

Symphony No. 1, Op. 18
min sc KALMUS K01485 $8.50   (K8)

KABIOSILE, FOR PIANO AND ORCHESTRA see Leon, Tania Justina

KADDISH, FOR SOLO VOICE AND STRING ORCHESTRA see Stein, Leon

KADOSA, PAL (1903-1983)
Suite For Youth
min sc EMB 4554 f.s.   (K9)

KAGEL, MAURICIO (1931-   )
Brief, Ein, For Solo Voice And Orchestra [9']
1.1.3(bass clar).0. 4.0.0.0. timp,2perc,2pno,strings,Mez solo
study sc PETERS P8638 f.s.   (K10)

Idees Fixes, Les
2.1(English horn).2(bass clar).2. 2.2.2.1. 3perc,harp,cel,pno, strings
PETERS   (K11)

Musik Fur Tasteninstrumenten Und Orchester [26']
2.0.2.2. 2.2.2.0. timp,2perc, 2pno,elec org,strings
PETERS   (K12)

Quodlibet, For Solo Voice And Orchestra [18']
4.2.3.2. 2.2.2.1. 2perc,cel,pno, elec org,vcl,db,female solo
PETERS   (K13)

Szenario
string orch,electronic tape [14'] study sc PETERS P8532 f.s., perf mat rent
(K14)

Tantz-Schul
2.1.2.1.tenor sax. 2.1.1.1. 3perc,gtr,harp,cel,hpsd,strings
PETERS   (K15)

KAHN, ERICH ITOR (1905-1956)
Suite Concertante, For Violin And Orchestra
MERION perf mat rent   (K16)

Symphonies Bretonnes, Les
MERION perf mat rent   (K17)

KAHOWEZ, GÜNTER (1940-   )
Prolationen II *Op.54 [10']
3(pic).2+English horn.2+bass clar.2+contrabsn. 4.3.3.1. perc,harp,strings

KAHOWEZ, GÜNTER (cont'd.)
DOBLINGER perf mat rent   (K18)

Serenade, Op. 24b [18']
1(pic).1.1.1. 1.1.1.0. perc,harp, pno,strings
study sc DOBLINGER STP 517 f.s., perf mat rent
(K19)

KAHRS, SVEN LYDER (1959-   )
Passioni Di Corrispondenza [15']
3.3.3.1.sax. 4.2.3.1. 2Wagner tuba,2flügelhorn,timp,perc, harp,pno,strings
NORGE   (K20)

KAINTUCK' see Still, William Grant

KAIPAINEN, JOUNI
Cinq Poemes De Rene Char, For Solo Voice And Orchestra *Op.12a [13']
1(pic).1+English horn.1(bass clar).0. 0.1.0.0. timp,2perc, harp,pno,strings,solo voice
HANSEN-FIN perf mat rent   (K21)

Symphony, Op. 20 [25']
2+2pic(alto fl).3(English horn).2+clar in E flat+bass clar.3(contrabsn). 4.4.3.1. timp,4perc,harp,pno,cel,strings
HANSEN-FIN perf mat rent   (K22)

KAIROS see Holmboe, Vagn

KAISER-WALZER [ARR.] see Strauss, Johann, [Jr.]

KAISER WILHELM POLONAISE see Strauss, Johann, [Jr.]

KAISERMARSCH see Wagner, Richard

KAKUDU QUADRILLE see Strauss, Josef

KALABIS, VIKTOR (1923-   )
Concerto for Harpsichord and String Orchestra [25']
string orch,hpsd solo
SUPRAPHON   (K23)

Concerto for Trumpet and Orchestra, Op. 36 [18']
2.2.2.2. 4.2.3.1. timp,perc,cel, strings,trp solo
SUPRAPHON   (K24)

Five Romantic Songs On Love, For Solo Voice And String Orchestra
string orch,T solo
SUPRAPHON   (K25)

Symphony No. 4, Op. 34 [24']
3.3.3.3. 4.3.3.1. timp,perc, strings
SUPRAPHON   (K26)

KALBFLEISCH, RODGER
Eruptions (Symphony No. 1) [20']
2+pic.2.2+bass clar.2+contrabsn. 4.3.3.1. perc,harp,pno,strings
MMB perf mat rent   (K27)

Junctures (Symphony No. 2) [10']
2.2.2.2. 3.2.2.0. perc,pno, strings,tape recorder
MMB perf mat rent   (K28)

Symphony No. 1
see Eruptions

Symphony No. 2
see Junctures

KALEIDOSCOPE see Dennison, Sam see Goossens, [Sir] Eugene see McKay, Neil see Tanenbaum, Elias

KALEIDOSCOPE, FOR SOLO VOICE AND ORCHESTRA see Constantinides, Dinos Demetrios

KALIF STORCH, FOR NARRATOR AND ORCHESTRA see Linder, Torsten

KALINNIKOV, VASSILI SERGEIEVICH (1866-1901)
Intermezzo No. 1 in F sharp minor [4']
2.2.2.2. 2.2.1.0. timp,strings
KALMUS A6083 sc $10.00, set $15.00, perf mat rent
(K29)

Intermezzo No. 2 in G [5']
2.2.2.2. 2.2.1.0. timp,perc, strings
KALMUS A6084 sc $10.00, set $15.00, perf mat rent
(K30)

KALIVODA, JAN KRTITEL
see KALLIWODA, JOHANN WENZEL

KALLAUSCH, KURT (1926-   )
Mittagswelt, For Solo Voice And Orchestra
2.2.2.2. 4.2.3.0. timp,perc,pno, strings,S solo
BREITKOPF-L perf mat rent   (K31)

KALLAVESI see Ahvenainen, Veikko

KALLIWODA, JOHANN WENZEL (1801-1866)
Concertino for Flute, Oboe and Orchestra
orch,fl solo,ob solo
MUS. RARA perf mat rent   (K32)

Symphonies, Two
see Knecht, Justin Heinrich, Symphony

Symphonies, Two *see Knecht, Justin Heinrich, Symphony

KALLOS, SANDOR (1935-   )
Concerto for Flute and Chamber Orchestra [25']
hpsd,strings without vln,fl solo
SIKORSKI perf mat rent   (K33)

Concerto for Violoncello and Orchestra, No. 2 [18']
1.0.1.2. 3.2.0.0. perc,hpsd, strings without vln,vcl solo
SIKORSKI perf mat rent   (K34)

KALLSTENIUS, EDVIN (1881-1967)
Berceuse [4']
0.0.1.1. 1.1.0.0. perc,pno, strings
NORDISKA perf mat rent   (K35)

Sinfonia Concertante for Piano and Orchestra, Op. 12, in C [28']
2.2.2.2. 4.2.2.1. timp,strings, pno solo
STIM   (K36)

Swedish National Anthem [3']
2.2.2.2. 4.2.3.1. perc,pno, strings
NORDISKA perf mat rent   (K37)

KALPA see Heifetz, Robin

KALSON, ROMUALD (1936-   )
Concerto for Clarinet, Harpsichord and Chamber Orchestra [18']
VAAP perf mat rent   (K38)

KALSONS, R.
Concerto for Violin and Orchestra
sc MEZ KNIGA f.s.   (K39)

KALTE ZEITEN see Koch-Raphael, Erwin

KAMARINSKAIA see Glinka, Mikhail Ivanovich

KAMINSKI, HEINRICH (1886-1946)
Spiel Vom König Aphelius, Das: Sinfonischer Epilog [9']
3.2.3.3. 4.4.3.0. timp,perc,cel, harp,strings
BÄREN. BA 2200A perf mat rent (K40)

KAMMEL, ANTONIN
Symphonies, Two
see Laube, Antonin, Symphony

KAMMERKONSERT, FOR VIOLIN AND STRING ORCHESTRA see Eklund, Hans

KAMMERKONZERT see Höffner, Paul Marx see Steffen, Wolfgang

KAMMERKONZERT, FOR HARPSICHORD OR PIANO AND STRING ORCHESTRA see Bialas, Günter

KAMMERKONZERT, FOR PIANO, VIOLIN AND WINDS see Berg, Alban

KAMMERKONZERT FOR VIOLIN AND STRING ORCHESTRA see Vogel, Ernst

KAMMERKONZERT "SOUVENIR" see Stuppner, Hubert

KAMMERSINFONIE see Bruns, Victor see Engel, Paul see Tchaikovsky, Boris, Chamber Symphony

KAMMERSINFONIE I see Yun, Isang

KAMMERSINFONIE II see Yun, Isang

KAMMERSYMPHONIE see Karetnikov, Nikolai see Lauermann, Herbert see Stuppner, Hubert

KAMMERVARIATIONEN see Ekimovsky, Viktor, Chamber Variations

KAMPTALER DIVERTIMENTO, FOR FLUTE, CLARINET, TRUMPET, HORN AND ORCHESTRA see Kubizek, Augustin

KANACH, SHARON (1957-   )
Offrande, For Solo Voice And
    Orchestra
    PRESSER perf mat rent   (K41)

KANCHELI, GIYA (1935-   )
Largo And Adagio [16']
    timp,pno,strings
    SIKORSKI perf mat rent   (K42)
    VAAP perf mat rent   (K43)

Symphony No. 1 [19']
    3.3.3.2. 4.4.3.1. timp,perc,cel,
        pno,strings
    SIKORSKI perf mat rent   (K44)
    VAAP perf mat rent   (K45)

Symphony No. 2 [21']
    4.3.3.3. 4.4.3.1. timp,perc,harp,
        pno,strings
    SIKORSKI perf mat rent   (K46)
    (Canticle) VAAP perf mat rent   (K47)

Symphony No. 3 [22']
    4.2.3.2. 4.4.3.1. timp,perc,pno,
        strings,med solo
    SIKORSKI perf mat rent   (K48)
    VAAP perf mat rent   (K49)

Symphony No. 4 [23']
    4.2.3.3. 4.4.3.1. timp,perc,cel,
        harp,strings
    SIKORSKI perf mat rent   (K50)
    (In memoriam Michelangelo) VAAP
        perf mat rent   (K51)

Symphony No. 5 [20']
    4.3.3.3. 4.4.3.1. timp,perc,harp,
        hpsd,strings
    sc MEZ KNIGA $20.00   (K52)
    SIKORSKI perf mat rent   (K53)

Symphony No. 6 [25']
    4.3.3.3. 4.4.3.1. timp,perc,harp,
        hpsd,pno,strings
    VAAP perf mat rent   (K54)

Vom Winde Beweint [44']
    4.3.3.3. 4.4.3.1. timp,4-5perc,
        harp, spinet, pno, bass gtr,
        strings, vla solo
    SIKORSKI perf mat rent   (K55)

KANGAROO KAPER see Creston, Paul

KANGRO, RAIMO (1949-   )
Concerto for 2 Pianos and Chamber
    Orchestra [19']
    perc,strings,2pno soli
    SIKORSKI perf mat rent   (K56)
    VAAP perf mat rent   (K57)

KANSANLAULU, FOR SOLO VOICE AND
    ORCHESTRA [ARR.] see Merikanto,
    Oskar

KANTSCHELI, GIJA
Symphony No. 6
    3.3.3.3. 4.4.3.1. timp,perc,harp,
        hpsd,pno,strings
    sc PETERS $25.00   (K58)

KANTUSER, BOZIDAR (1921-   )
Symphony No. 4
    3(pic).3.3.3(contrabsn). 4.4.3.1.
        timp,perc,harp,strings
    DRUSTVO DSS 1113 perf mat rent
                                       (K59)

KAPER, BRONISLAW (1902-1983)
Confetti [2'30"]
    3(pic).3(English horn).3(clar in
        E flat).3. 4.3.3.1. timp,2perc,
        cel,pno,harp,strings
    ROBBINS perf mat rent   (K60)

KAPR, JAN (1914-1988)
Campanae Pragenses (Symphony No. 8)
    [53']
    2+pic.2.2+bass clar.2+contrabsn.
        4.3.3.1. timp,4perc,hpsd,pno,
        harp,strings,SATB,SB soli.
        electronic equipment
    [Lat/Czech] BAREN. BA 6765 perf mat
        rent   (K61)

Symphony No. 8
    see Campanae Pragenses

KAPRIZIOSE BEGEGNUNG see Müller-Marc,
    Raymund

KARABITS, IVAN (1945-   )
Concerto for Orchestra [11']
    3.3.3.3. 4.3.3.1. timp,4perc,cel,
        2harp,strings
    VAAP perf mat rent   (K62)

KARABOTASAT CUTINTAPATA see Valcarcel,
    Edgar

KARAM, FREDERICK (1926-   )
Stay 'N See [6']
    2(pic).1.1.1.2alto sax.2tenor
        sax.baritone sax. 4.4.3+bass
        trom.1. perc,pno,harp,strings
    NEWAM 19002 perf mat rent   (K63)

KARAYEV, FARADZH (1943-   )
Schatten Von Kobistan, Die: Suite
    see Spirits Of Kobystan, The: Suite

Serenade for Orchestra [25']
    4.3.3.2+contrabsn. 4.4.3.0. timp,
        vibra,bells,cel,hpsd,pno,
        strings
    VAAP perf mat rent   (K64)

1791. Serenade For Small Orchestra
    [22']
    2.2.2.2. 2.2.1.0. 2perc,cel,hpsd,
        pno,strings
    SIKORSKI perf mat rent   (K65)

Spirits Of Kobystan, The: Suite [28']
    4.3.3.3. 4.4.3.1. timp,perc,
        2harp,pno,strings
    VAAP perf mat rent   (K66)
    "Schatten Von Kobistan, Die: Suite"
    SIKORSKI perf mat rent   (K67)

KARAYEV, KARA (1918-1982)
Concerto for Violin and Orchestra
    [23']
    3.3.3.3. 4.3.3.1. timp,perc,
        2harp,pno,strings,vln solo
    SIKORSKI perf mat rent   (K68)

Don Quixote [18']
    3.3.2.3. 4.3.3.1. timp,perc,
        2harp,cel,pno,strings
    SIKORSKI perf mat rent   (K69)

Seven Beauties: Suite [33']
    3.3.3.3. 4.3.3.1. timp,perc,harp,
        cel,pno,strings
    VAAP perf mat rent   (K70)
    "Sieben Schonen, Die: Suite"
    SIKORSKI perf mat rent   (K71)

Sieben Schonen, Die: Suite
    see Seven Beauties: Suite

Symphony No. 3 [25']
    2.2.0.2. 2.0.0.0. hpsd,pno,
        strings
    SIKORSKI perf mat rent   (K72)

KARCHIN, LOUIS S. (1951-   )
Five Orchestral Songs, For Solo Voice
    And Orchestra [18']
    2+pic.2.2(bass clar).2+contrabsn.
        4.2.2.1. perc,strings,S solo
    sc AM.COMP.AL. $36.35   (K73)

Songs Of John Keats, For Solo Voice
    And Orchestra [10']
    2.2.2.3. 1.1.0.0. perc,harp,
        strings,S solo
    sc AM.COMP.AL. $42.45   (K74)

KAREL, RUDOLF (1880-1945)
Slavonic Dance Melody No. 1 In C
    *Op.16,No.1
    3.2.2.2. 4.2.3.1. timp,perc,
        strings
    SIMROCK perf mat rent   (K75)

Slavonic Dance Melody No. 2 In G
    *Op.16,No.2
    3.2.2.2. 4.2.3.1. timp,perc,harp,
        strings
    SIMROCK perf mat rent   (K76)

KARENNA, FOR SOLO VOICE, HARP, AND
    STRING ORCHESTRA see Patriquin,
    Donald

KARETNIKOV, NIKOLAI (1930-   )
Kammersymphonie *Op.21
    sc PETERS f.s.   (K77)

Symphony No. 3 [20']
    3.0.2.3.tenor sax. 4.3.3.1. timp,
        perc,harp,pno,strings
    VAAP perf mat rent   (K78)

Symphony No. 4, Op. 17 [26']
    4.2.4.3.tenor sax. 6.4.4.1. timp,
        perc,2harp,pno,strings
    SIKORSKI perf mat rent   (K79)

KARG-ELERT, SIGFRID (1877-1933)
Suite in A minor [15']
    2(pic).2(English horn).2.2.
        4.2.3.1. timp,perc,harp,strings
    (based on melodies from Bizet's
        "Jeux d'Enfants") KALMUS A5814 sc
        $30.00, set $40.00, perf mat rent
                                       (K80)

KARKOFF, INGVAR (1958-   )
Celestial Bird, The, For Piano And
    String Orchestra
    see Himmelska Fageln, Den, For
    Piano And String Orchestra

Himmelska Fageln, Den, For Piano And
    String Orchestra [15']
    string orch,pno solo
    "Celestial Bird, The, For Piano And
        String Orchestra" STIM   (K81)

KARKOFF, INGVAR (cont'd.)

Nostalgia [13']
    2.2.2.2. 2.0.0.0. perc,strings
    STIM   (K82)

Ora [20']
    3.3.3.3. 0.3.3.0. harp,cel,
        strings
    STIM   (K83)

KARKOFF, MAURICE (1927-   )
Dolorous Symphony [17']
    string orch
    sc GEHRMANS 6511P f.s., perf mat
        rent   (K84)

Musical Contrasts
    sc,pts NORDISKA f.s.   (K85)

Symphony No. 10, Op. 158 [17']
    3.2.2.2. 4.3.2.1. timp,perc,
        strings
    STIM perf mat rent   (K86)

Tre Colori *Op.142 [5']
    string orch
    GEHRMANS sc 6040P f.s., pts 6040S
        f.s.   (K87)

KARLINS, M. WILLIAM (1932-   )
Catena [14']
    ob,clar,trp,trom,pno,strings
    sc AM.COMP.AL. $28.95   (K88)

Catena III, For Horn And Orchestra
    [20']
    2(pic).2.2.2.alto sax+tenor sax.
        3.3.2+bass trom.1. timp,perc,
        strings,horn solo
    sc AM.COMP.AL. $40.90   (K89)

Concerto for Alto Saxophone and
    Orchestra [21']
    2.2.2.2. 2.2.2.0. timp,perc,
        strings,alto sax solo
    sc AM.COMP.AL. $38.15   (K90)

Symphony No. 1 [19']
    2.2.2.2. 2.2.0.0. timp,perc,
        strings
    sc AM.COMP.AL. $30.50, perf mat
        rent   (K91)

KARLSEN, KJELL MØRK (1947-   )
Christmas Partita
    see Julepartita

Concerto for Bassoon, Strings and
    Percussion, Op. 76b
    perc,strings,bsn solo
    [17'] NORGE   (K92)

Concerto for Chamber Orchestra, Op.
    60
    fl,timp,strings
    NORGE   (K93)

Concerto for Piano and String
    Orchestra, Op. 90 [21']
    string orch,pno solo
    NORGE   (K94)

Concerto for Trombone and String
    Orchestra, Op. 83 [20']
    string orch,trom solo
    NORGE   (K95)

Julepartita *Op.64 [11']
    1.1.1.1. 1.0.0.0. perc,harp,
        strings
    "Christmas Partita" NORGE   (K96)

Symphony No. 3, Op. 78 [19']
    3.2.2.2. 4.2.0.0. timp,perc,
        strings
    (Is-Slottet) NORGE   (K97)

Symphony No. 4, Op. 87b [24']
    2.2.2.2. 4.3.3.1. timp,3perc,pno,
        org,strings
    (Liturgical Symphony) NORGE   (K98)

Vikinghymne, Op. 59b [12'30"]
    2.2.2.2. 4.6.3.1. timp,perc,
        strings
    NORGE   (K99)

KARLSEN, ROLF (1911-1982)
Fra Alstahaug
    string orch
    "From Altstahaug: Suite" NORGE
                                       (K100)

From Altstahaug: Suite
    see Fra Alstahaug

Suite for Orchestra
    1.1.2.1. 2.2.2.0. timp,harp,
        strings
    NORGE   (K101)

KARNEVAL see Christensen, Bernhard

KARNEVAL I PARIS see Svendsen, Johan
    (Severin)

KARPMAN, LAURA (1959-   )
  Six Of One, A Dozen Of The Other [9']
    2.3.3.2. 0.2.2.1. perc,pno,
    strings
    sc AM.COMP.AL. $76.80   (K102)

  Switching Stations [13']
    2.2.2.2. 2.1.1.0. 2perc,pno,
    strings
    NORRUTH perf mat rent   (K103)

  Theme and Variations for Piano and
    Orchestra [14']
    2(pic).1+English horn.1+bass
    clar.1. 1.0.0.0. perc,strings,
    pno solo
    NORRUTH perf mat rent   (K104)

KARST SUITE, THE see Srebotnjak, Alojz
  F., Kraska Suita

KASACHOK see Dargomyzhsky, Alexander
  Sergeyevich

KASANLI, NIKOLAI
  see KAZANLY, NIKOLAI

KASKI, HEINO (1885-1957)
  Mokit Nukkuu Lumiset, For Solo Voice
    And Orchestra [arr.]
    (Kuusisto, I.) harp,strings,solo
    voice [4'] FAZER perf mat rent
                                   (K105)

KAST see Rehnqvist, Karin

KATADRONE see Tremblay, Gilles

KATERINA ISMAILOWA: SUITE see
  Shostakovich, Dmitri, Lady Macbeth
  Of Mtzensk: Suite

KATHARSIS see Lier, Bertus van

KATHCHEN VON HEILBRONN: OVERTURE see
  Pfitzner, Hans

KATZER, GEORG (1935-   )
  Concerto for Violin and Chamber
    Orchestra
    sc,solo pt PETERS $25.00   (K106)

KAUDER, HUGO (1888-1972)
  Concerto for Piano and String
    Orchestra
    string orch,pno solo
    sc SEESAW $11.00, perf mat rent
                                   (K107)
  Kleines Konzert, For Piano And String
    Orchestra
    string orch,pno solo
    sc SEESAW $11.00, perf mat rent
                                   (K108)

KAUFMAN, FREDRICK
  American Symphony No. 5 [22']
    2.2.4.2. 4.3.3.1.baritone horn.
    timp,perc,harp,strings
    AM.COMP.AL. perf mat rent   (K109)

  Concerto for Clarinet and String
    Orchestra [15']
    string orch,clar solo
    sc AM.COMP.AL. $28.95, perf mat
    rent   (K110)

  Concerto for Violoncello and String
    Orchestra [15']
    string orch,vcl solo
    PRESSER perf mat rent   (K111)

  Symphony For Strings And Percussion
    [14']
    perc,strings
    AM.COMP.AL. perf mat rent   (K112)

  When The Twain Meet [17']
    2.2.2.2. 2.2.0.0. timp,strings
    AM.COMP.AL. perf mat rent   (K113)

KAUFMANN, ARMIN (1902-1980)
  Kuckuckssinfonie [20']
    1(pic).2.2.2. 2.0.0.0. strings
    DOBLINGER perf mat rent   (K114)

KAUFMANN, SERGE (1930-   )
  Souvenance [9'30"]
    fl,harp,strings
    BILLAUDOT perf mat rent   (K115)

KAUTTA TYYNEN, VIENON YON, FOR SOLO
  VOICE AND STRING ORCHESTRA [ARR.]
  see Hannikainen, P.J.

KAWAI, MANABU (1944-   )
  Ode For Piano And Orchestra [15']
    3(pic).2.3(bass clar).2. 4.3.3.0.
    perc,2harp,cel,strings,pno solo
    sc ZEN-ON 899230 f.s., perf mat
    rent   (K116)

KAY, HERSHY (1919-1981)
  Pat-A-Pan [4']
    3(pic).2+English horn.2+bass
    clar.3. 4.3.3.1. timp,perc,
    harp,cel,strings
    BOOSEY perf mat rent   (K117)

KAY, HERSHY (cont'd.)

  Stars And Stripes: Pas De Deux [6']
    2(pic).2.2(clar in E flat)+bass
    clar.2. 4.4(cornet).2.1.
    euphonium,perc,harp,strings
    BOOSEY perf mat rent   (K118)

KAY, ULYSSES SIMPSON (1917-   )
  Brief Elegy, For Oboe And String
    Orchestra [5']
    string orch,ob solo
    DUCHESS perf mat rent   (K119)

  Chariots
    3.3.3.3. 4.3.3.1. timp,perc,harp,
    strings
    sc PEMBROKE $15.00, perf mat rent
                                   (K120)

  Fantasy Variations [15']
    2.2.2.2. 4.3.3.1. timp,perc,
    strings
    study sc DUCHESS f.s., perf mat
    rent   (K121)

  Markings [18']
    3(pic).3(English horn).3(bass
    clar).3(contrabsn). 4.3.3.1.
    timp,perc,strings
    study sc DUCHESS f.s., perf mat
    rent   (K122)

  Scherzi Musicale [17']
    1.1.1.1. 1.0.0.0. strings
    study sc DUCHESS f.s., perf mat
    rent   (K123)

  Short Overture, A [7']
    2(pic).2.2.2. 2.2.2.0. timp,
    2perc,strings
    study sc DUCHESS f.s., perf mat
    rent   (K124)

  Six Dances For String Orchestra [18']
    string orch
    DUCHESS perf mat rent   (K125)

  Suite for Orchestra [17']
    3.3.3.3. 4.3.3.1. perc,pno,
    strings
    study sc AMP f.s., perf mat rent
                                   (K126)

  Theater Set [15']
    3.3.3.3. 4.3.3.1. timp,perc,harp,
    strings
    study sc DUCHESS f.s., perf mat
    rent   (K127)

  Umbrian Scene [12']
    2(pic).2.2.2. 4.3.3.1. timp,perc,
    harp,strings
    study sc DUCHESS f.s., perf mat
    rent   (K128)

KAYSER, LEIF (1919-   )
  King Christian Stood
    see Kong Kristian Stod

  Kong Kristian Stod
    "King Christian Stood" sc SAMFUNDET
    f.s., perf mat rent   (K129)

  Symphony No. 1 [12']
    2(pic).2.2.2. 4.2.3.1. timp,perc,
    strings
    HANSEN-DEN perf mat rent   (K130)

KAZANLY, NIKOLAI (1869-1916)
  Glinkiana Suite
    2.2.2.2. 4.0.0.0. timp,harp,
    strings
    VAAP perf mat rent   (K131)

KAZHLAYEV, MURAD (1931-   )
  Gorianka: Suite [16']
    3.2.3.3. 4.4.4.1. timp,perc,harp,
    strings
    VAAP perf mat rent   (K132)
    "Studenten" SIKORSKI perf mat rent
                                   (K133)

  Studenten
    see Gorianka: Suite

KEATS, DONALD HOWARD (1929-   )
  Symphony No. 2 [20']
    2+pic.2+English horn.2+bass
    clar.2+contrabsn. 4.3.3.1.
    timp,perc,cel,strings
    (Elegiac Symphony) sc BOOSEY
    $20.00, perf mat rent   (K134)

KEAY, NIGEL
  Diffractions [9']
    1.1.1.1. 1.1.1.0. perc,pno,
    strings
    sc WAI-TE-ATA f.s.   (K135)

KEENING, THE see Macmillan, James

KEER see Janssen, Guus

KEHTOLAULU see Lindberg, Valter

KEIN FIRMÁMENT see Rihm, Wolfgang

KEINTATE I, FOR SOLO VOICE AND
  INSTRUMENTAL ENSEMBLE see Cerha,
  Friedrich

KEINTATE II, FOR SOLO VOICE AND
  INSTRUMENTAL ENSEMBLE see Cerha,
  Friedrich

KEIR'S KICK see Lloyd, Jonathan

KEIZER, HENK (1948-   )
  Canto Continuo [arr.]
    3.2.2.1. 4.4.3.0. timp,2perc,
    strings [10'] sc DONEMUS f.s.,
    perf mat rent   (K136)

  Elegy [14']
    3.2.3.2. 2.3.3.0. 4perc,pno&cel,
    strings
    DONEMUS perf mat rent   (K137)

  Litanie [19']
    2.2.2.2. 2.1.0.0. 4perc,pno,vcl,
    db/vcl
    DONEMUS perf mat rent   (K138)

  Organum [14']
    variable instrumentation sc DONEMUS
    f.s., perf mat rent   (K139)

KEJSARN AV PORTUGALLIEN see Söderlundh,
  Lille Bror

KEKOSMESTHAI see Brustad, Karsten

KELEMEN, MILKO (1924-   )
  Antiphonie, For Organ And Orchestra
    [18']
    4trp,3trom,tuba,timp,2perc,harp,
    pno/hpsd,strings,org solo
    SIKORSKI perf mat rent   (K140)

  Archetypon [20']
    4.4.4.4. 6.4.3.2. timp,3perc,
    harp,pno/hpsd,strings
    SIKORSKI perf mat rent   (K141)

  Drammatico, For Violoncello And
    Orchestra [23']
    3.1.3.0. 0.3.3.0. timp,2perc,
    harp,cel&hpsd&pno&elec org,
    12vln,6vla,4db,vcl solo
    SIKORSKI perf mat rent   (K142)

  Grand Jeu Classique, For Violin And
    Orchestra [21']
    3.0.3.0. 2.1.1.0. timp,2perc,
    harp,pno&cel&hpsd&elec org,
    8vla,4db,vln solo
    study sc SIKORSKI f.s., perf mat
    rent   (K143)

  Infinity [13']
    3.3.3.3. 4.3.3.1. perc,strings
    sc PETERS P8477 f.s., perf mat rent
                                   (K144)

  Love Song [7']
    string orch
    sc PETERS P8623 f.s., perf mat rent
                                   (K145)

  Phantasms, For Viola And Orchestra
    [25']
    2.2.2.1. 2.2.2.0. timp,2perc,
    harp,cel&hpsd&pno,strings
    without vla,vla solo
    SIKORSKI perf mat rent   (K146)

KELER-BELA (ADALBERT PAUL VON KELER)
  (1820-1882)
  Annoncier Polka *Op.14 [5']
    2.2.2.2. 4.3.3.0. timp,perc,
    strings
    ORLANDO perf mat rent   (K147)

KELLAWAY, ROGER (1939-   )
  Dialogues Of The Mind And Heart, For
    Jazz Trio And Orchestra [25']
    3+pic.1.3.2+contrabsn.2alto
    sax.2tenor sax.baritone sax.
    4.4.3+bass trom.1. perc,pno,
    harp,2gtr,strings, jazz trio:
    pno, rhythm bass, drums
    NEWAM 19026 perf mat rent   (K148)

KELLER, HOMER (1915-   )
  Sonorities [12']
    3.3.2.2. 4.3.3.1. timp,perc,harp,
    pno,strings
    AM.COMP.AL.   (K149)

KELLY, BRYAN (1934-   )
  Concertante Dances [19']
    1.1.1.1. 0.0.0.0. strings
    NOVELLO perf mat rent   (K150)

  Concerto for Guitar and Orchestra
    [20']
    2(pic).2.2.2. 2.2.0.0. strings,
    gtr solo
    NOVELLO perf mat rent   (K151)

  Sinfonia Concertante [15']
    2(pic).2.2.2. 4.2.3.1. timp,
    2perc,pno,strings
    NOVELLO perf mat rent   (K152)

KELLY, ROBERT T. (1916-   )
Concertino, Op. 54 [12']
2.2.2.2. 2.2.0.0. perc,strings
sc AM.COMP.AL. $16.50, perf mat
rent   (K153)

Concerto for Viola and Orchestra, Op.
53 [22']
2.2.2.2. 2.2.2.0. timp,perc,
strings,vla solo
AM.COMP.AL. sc $32.50, pts $4.10,
perf mat rent   (K154)

Concerto for Violin, Viola and
Chamber Orchestra, Op. 57 [22']
2.2.2.2. 2.0.0.0. strings,vln
solo,vla solo
AM.COMP.AL. sc $33.50, pts $9.95,
perf mat rent   (K155)

Fantasy for Harp and String
Orchestra, Op. 62 [16']
string orch,harp solo
sc AM.COMP.AL. $57.20, perf mat
rent   (K156)

Garden Of Peace *Op.56 [9']
string orch
sc AM.COMP.AL. $7.70, perf mat rent
(K157)

Patterns, For Solo Voice And
Orchestra [15']
1.1.1.1. 1.1.1.0. perc,strings,S
solo
sc AM.COMP.AL. $16.75, perf mat
rent   (K158)

Rural Songs, For Solo Voice And
Orchestra *Op.58 [21']
2.2.2.2. 2.0.0.0. timp,perc,
strings,S solo
sc AM.COMP.AL. $25.85   (K159)

Shenandoah Variations *Op.59 [8']
string orch
AM.COMP.AL. perf mat rent   (K160)

KELTERBORN, RUDOLF (1931-   )
Espansioni (Symphony No. 3) [15']
3(alto fl,pic).3(English
horn).3.2+contrabsn. 4.3.4.0.
timp/2perc,harp,strings,Bar
solo,electronic tape
study sc BÄREN. BA 6712 f.s. (K161)

Gesange Der Liebe, For Solo Voice And
Orchestra
3(pic).2(English horn).3(bass
clar).2(contrabsn). 3.3.3.0.
timp,3perc,harp,strings,Bar
solo
BÄREN. BA 7302   (K162)

Gesänge Zur Nacht, For Solo Voice And
Chamber Orchestra [16']
1(pic).0.2(bass clar).0. 1.1.1.0.
perc,harp,pno,strings,S solo
study sc BÄREN. BA 6764 f.s. (K163)

Monolog Der Ophelia, For Solo Voice
And Orchestra [15']
1(pic).2(English
horn).3.1(contrabsn). 2.2.2.0.
3perc,harp,pno,strings,S solo
BÄREN. BA 7153   (K164)

Music for Double Bass and Orchestra
[18']
2(pic).1.2(bass clar).1. 2.2.1.0.
timp,2perc,harp,strings,db solo
BÄREN. BA 7301   (K165)

Musica Luminosa [10']
2.2.2.2. 2.2.0.0. timp&perc,
strings
sc BÄREN. BA 7134 $12.50   (K166)

Nuovi Canti, For Flute And Chamber
Orchestra [12']
.0.2.1.0. 2.0.0.0. strings,fl solo
BÄREN. BA 6279 perf mat rent (K167)

Relations. Ballet For Solo Voice And
Orchestra [22']
2(pic).2.2.1(contrabsn). 2.2.2.0.
2-3perc,harp,strings,S solo
BÄREN. BA 6298   (K168)

Symphony No. 3
see Espansioni

Symphony No. 4 [19']
4(pic).3(English horn).3+clar in
E flat.3(contrabsn). 4.4.3.1.
timp,3perc,harp,strings
BÄREN. BA 7159   (K169)

Szene [8']
.12vcl
BÄREN. BA 6745 perf mat rent (K170)

Tableaux Encadrés [13']
.7vln,3vla,2vcl,db
BÄREN. BA 6706 perf mat rent (K171)

KELTIC SUITE see Foulds, John Herbert

KELTIC SUITE: KELTIC LAMENT see Foulds,
John Herbert

KENINS, TALIVALDIS (1919-   )
Canzona Sonata, For Viola And String
Orchestra [11']
string orch,vla solo
CAN.MUS.CENT. MI 1612 K33C   (K172)

Concerto for Flute, Guitar and
Orchestra
perc,strings,fl solo,gtr solo
CAN.MUS.CENT. MI 1450 K33C   (K173)

Concerto for Violin, Piano and
Orchestra [16']
2.2.2.2. 2.0.0.0. timp,perc,
strings,vln solo,pno solo
CAN.MUS.CENT. MI 1418 K33D   (K174)

Folk Dance And Fugue No. 2 [7']
2.2.2.2. 4.3.3.1. timp,2perc,
harp,strings
CAN.MUS.CENT. MI 1100 K33F2 (K175)

Little Concerto, For Piano And
Chamber Orchestra [12']
1.1.1.1. 0.1.1.1. timp,2perc,
strings,pno solo
CAN.MUS.CENT. MI 1361 K33LI (K176)

Songs To The Almighty, For Solo Voice
And Orchestra [11']
1.1.1.1. 2.2.1.0. timp,perc,
strings,Mez solo
CAN.MUS.CENT. MV 1400 K33S   (K177)

Symphony No. 4
sc BERANDOL BER 1815 $20.00   (K178)

Symphony No. 8 for Organ and
Orchestra [25']
2.2.2.2. 4.2.3.0. timp,2perc,
strings,org solo
CAN.MUS.CENT. MI 1364 K33S   (K179)

KENNAN, KENT WHEELER (1913-   )
Campo Dei Fiori, II, For Trumpet And
Orchestra [2'30"]
2(pic).2.2.2. 2.0.0.0. timp,perc,
pno,strings,trp solo
KALMUS A6423 sc $10.00, set $25.00,
pts $1.50, ea., perf mat rent
(K180)

Elegy for Oboe and Orchestra [4']
2.0.2.2. 3.0.0.0. timp,perc,
strings,ob solo
KALMUS A2626 sc $8.00, set $15.00,
pts $1.00, ea.   (K181)

Notturno for Viola and Orchestra [4']
2.2.2.2. 2.2.0.0. timp,perc,pno,
strings,vla solo
KALMUS A6727 sc $5.00, set $17.00,
pts $1.00, ea.   (K182)

KENNINGAR see Stucky, Steven Edward

KENNST DU MICH? WALZER see Strauss,
Johann, [Jr.]

KEQROPS, FOR PIANO AND ORCHESTRA see
Xenakis, Yannis (Iannis)

KERKERBALLADE, DE, FOR NARRATOR AND
ORCHESTRA see Zagwijn, Henri

KERNIS, AARON JAY (1960-   )
America(N) (Day)Dreams, For Solo
Voice And Orchestra [18']
1(pic).0.1(bass clar).0. 1.1.0.0.
perc,harp,pno,strings,Mez solo
AMP perf mat rent   (K183)

Dream Of The Morning Sky, For Solo
Voice And Orchestra [24']
3(pic).3(English horn).3(bass
clar).3+contrabsn. 4.3.2+bass
trom.1. perc,pno&cel,harp,
strings,S solo
sc AMP $37.85, perf mat rent (K184)

Invisible Mosaic II [18']
1(pic).1.1.1. 1.1.1.1. 2perc,
harp,pno,strings
AMP perf mat rent   (K185)

Invisible Mosaic III [15']
3(pic).3(English horn).3(clar in
E flat,bass clar).3(contrabsn).
4.3.3.1. timp,4perc,harp,pno&
cel,strings
AMP perf mat rent   (K186)

Jacob's Ladders [5']
1(pic).1.1(bass clar).0. 1.1.1.0.
perc,pno,vln,vla,vcl
N.LIGHT perf mat rent   (K187)

Mirror Of Heat And Light [16']
3(pic).3+English horn.5.2+
contrabsn. 4.3.2+bass trom.1.
perc,harp,pno,strings
sc AMP $49.75, perf mat rent (K188)

KERNIS, AARON JAY (cont'd.)

Morning Songs, For Solo Voice And
Orchestra [15']
1(pic,alto fl).0.2(bass clar).1.
1.0.0.0. perc,harp,strings,Bar
solo
AMP perf mat rent   (K189)

Symphony In Waves [30']
1.2.1.2. 3.1.0.0. perc,pno,
strings
AMP perf mat rent   (K190)

KERSTENS, HUUB (1947-   )
Concerto for Piano and Orchestra
[17']
1.1.1.1. 1.1.1.0. perc,strings,
pno solo
DONEMUS perf mat rent   (K191)

Megaliet, De *Op.18b [12']
string orch
DONEMUS perf mat rent   (K192)

Vision Der Wirklichkeit, For Solo
Voice And Orchestra *Op.23
[18'30"]
1.1.1.1. 1.1.1.1. 4perc,harp,pno,
strings,Bar solo
DONEMUS perf mat rent   (K193)

KESAILLAN, VALSSI, FOR SOLO VOICE AND
ORCHESTRA [ARR.] see Merikanto,
Oskar

KESAYO, FOR SOLO VOICE AND ORCHESTRA
[ARR.] see Kilpinen, Yrjö

KETTING, OTTO (1935-   )
Alleman [18']
2.1.2.1.alto sax. 2.2.2.0. harp,
pno,drums,strings
DONEMUS perf mat rent   (K194)

KEULEN, GEERT VAN (1943-   )
Armonia [9']
string orch
DONEMUS perf mat rent   (K195)

Sinfonia [14']
3.3.3.3. 4.3.3.1. 4perc,harp,
strings
sc DONEMUS f.s., perf mat rent
(K196)

Terze [14']
2.2.2.2. 2.2.1.0. 2perc,pno,
strings
sc DONEMUS f.s., perf mat rent
(K197)

KEURIS, TRISTAN (1946-   )
Seven Pieces, For Bass Clarinet And
Orchestra [17']
2.2.2.2. 2.0.0.0. 3perc,harp,
10vla,8vcl,4db,bass clar solo
sc DONEMUS f.s., perf mat rent
(K198)

Variations for Strings [10']
7vln,2vla,2vcl,db
DONEMUS perf mat rent   (K199)

KEVATLINNUILLE ETELASSA, FOR SOLO VOICE
AND ORCHESTRA [ARR.] see Merikanto,
Oskar

KEYBOARD CONCERTOS, NOS 38, 39 see
Bach, Carl Philipp Emanuel

KEYES, NELSON (1928-   )
Concerto Grosso [15']
string orch,2vln,vla,vcl,db soli
MMB perf mat rent   (K200)

KEYS TO THE CITY, FOR PIANO AND
ORCHESTRA see Picker, Tobias

KHACHATURIAN, ARAM ILYICH (1903-1978)
Ballad About The Motherland, For Solo
Voice And Orchestra [8']
2.2.2.2. 4.3.3.1. timp,perc,harp,
strings,B solo
VAAP perf mat rent   (K201)

Battle Of Stalingrad, The [29']
3.3.4.2. 4.4.3.1. timp,perc,harp,
pno,strings
VAAP perf mat rent   (K202)

Concert Rhapsody, For Piano And
Orchestra
min sc SIKORSKI 034-35964 $12.25
(K203)

Concerto for Flute and Orchestra,
[arr.]
(Sebon, K.H.) 3.3.2.2. 4.3.3.1.
timp,perc,harp,strings,fl solo
[35'] (arrangement of the violin
concerto) SIKORSKI perf mat rent
(K204)

Concerto for Violin and Orchestra
min sc KALMUS K01480 $8.75   (K205)
(Collected Works, Vol. 17) sc
MUZYKA f.s. contains:
Concerto-Rhapsody, For Violin And
Orchestra   (K206)
study sc SIKORSKI 2212 $28.25, perf

KHACHATURIAN, ARAM ILYICH (cont'd.)

mat rent   (K207)

Concerto-Rhapsody, For Violin And
    Orchestra
    see Concerto for Violin and
    Orchestra

Drei Konzertarien, For Solo Voice And
    Orchestra
    see Three Concert Arias, For Solo
    Voice And Orchestra

Gajaneh: Gopak
    see Gayane: Hopak

Gajaneh: Nunes Variation
    see Gayane: Noune's Variation

Gajaneh: Russischer Tanz
    see Gayane: Russian Dance

Gajaneh: Tanz Der Rosenmadchen Und
    Lesginka
    see Gayane: Dance Of The Rose
    Maidens And Lesginka

Gayane: Adagio [4']
    timp,harp,strings
    VAAP perf mat rent   (K208)

Gayane: Armen's Variations
    3.3.3.2. 4.2.3.1. timp,perc,harp,
    strings
    VAAP perf mat rent   (K209)

Gayane: Awakening And Dance Of Ayshe
    3.3.3.2. 4.3.3.1. timp,perc,cel,
    harp,strings
    VAAP perf mat rent   (K210)

Gayane: Dance Of The Rose Maidens
    [2']
    3.3.2.2. 4.3+cornet.3.0. timp,
    perc,strings
    VAAP perf mat rent   (K211)

Gayane: Dance Of The Rose Maidens And
    Lesginka [6']
    3.3.2.2. 4.3.3.1. timp,perc,harp,
    strings
    "Gajaneh: Tanz Der Rosenmadchen Und
    Lesginka" SIKORSKI perf mat rent
                                          (K212)
Gayane: Dance Of The Young Kurds [3']
    3.3.2.3. 4.3.3.1. timp,perc,pno,
    harp,strings
    VAAP perf mat rent   (K213)

Gayane: Hopak [3']
    3.3.2.2. 4.3.3.1. timp,perc,pno,
    strings
    "Gajaneh: Gopak" SIKORSKI perf mat
    rent   (K214)

Gayane: Lullaby [5']
    3.3.2.2. 4.0.2.0. timp,perc,harp,
    cel,strings
    VAAP perf mat rent   (K215)

Gayane: Noune's Variation [2']
    2.2+English horn.3.2. 4.3.3.1.
    timp,perc,harp,strings
    "Gajaneh: Nunes Variation" SIKORSKI
    perf mat rent   (K216)

Gayane: Russian Dance [5']
    2.2.2.2. 2.2.2.1. timp,perc,harp,
    strings
    "Gajaneh: Russischer Tanz" SIKORSKI
    perf mat rent   (K217)

Gayane: Scene Of Gayane And Guiko
    3.3.3.2. 4.3.3.1. timp,perc,cel,
    harp,strings
    VAAP perf mat rent   (K218)

Greeting Overture
    see Ode In Memory Of Lenin

Lermontov: Suite [23']
    3.3.3.2. 4.3.3.1. timp,perc,harp,
    strings
    SIKORSKI perf mat rent   (K219)
    VAAP perf mat rent   (K220)

Ode In Memory Of Lenin
    (Collected Works, Vol. 3) sc MUZYKA
    f.s. contains also: Greeting
    Overture   (K221)

Spartacus: Adagio [9']
    3.3.3.2. 4.3.3.1. timp,perc,harp,
    pno,strings
    SIKORSKI perf mat rent   (K222)

Spartacus: Scene 9
    3.3.3.2.alto sax. 4.3.3.1. timp,
    perc,cel,harp,pno,strings
    VAAP perf mat rent   (K223)

Spartacus: Scene 3
    3.3.3.2. 4.4.3.1. timp,perc,harp,
    pno,strings
    VAAP perf mat rent   (K224)

KHACHATURIAN, ARAM ILYICH (cont'd.)

Spartacus: Suite No. 4 [19']
    3.3.3.2.alto sax. 4.3.3.1. timp,
    perc,2harp,cel,pno,strings
    SIKORSKI perf mat rent   (K225)

Suites From Music To Plays
    (Collected Works, Vol. 4) sc MUZYKA
    f.s.   (K226)

Symphony No. 2
    KALMUS A5729 sc $75.00, set
    $225.00, perf mat rent   (K227)

Three Concert Arias, For Solo Voice
    And Orchestra [25']
    2.2.2.2. 4.2.3.1. timp,perc,harp,
    strings,S solo
    VAAP perf mat rent   (K228)
    "Drei Konzertarien, For Solo Voice
    And Orchestra" SIKORSKI perf mat
    rent   (K229)

Triumphal Poem [20']
    3.3.3.2. 4.3.3.1. timp,perc,harp,
    strings
    VAAP perf mat rent   (K230)

Welcoming Overture
    3.3.3.2. 4.4.3.1. timp,perc,harp,
    pno,strings
    VAAP perf mat rent   (K231)

Widow Of Valencia, The: Suite [25']
    2.2.2.2. 4.3.3.1. timp,perc,harp,
    cel,strings
    "Witwe Aus Valencia, Die: Suite"
    SIKORSKI perf mat rent   (K232)

Witwe Aus Valencia, Die: Suite
    see Widow Of Valencia, The: Suite

KHACHATURIAN, KAREN (1920-   )
At The Circus [14']
    3.2.2.2. 4.4.3.1. timp,perc,gtr,
    harp,strings
    VAAP perf mat rent   (K233)
    "Im Zirkus" SIKORSKI perf mat rent
                                          (K234)

Concerto for Violoncello and
    Orchestra [25']
    3.3.3.2. 4.2.3.1. timp,tam-tam,
    strings,vcl solo
    VAAP perf mat rent   (K235)

Im Zirkus
    see At The Circus

Symphony No. 1, Op. 12 [33']
    3.3.3.3. 4.3.3.1. timp,perc,harp,
    strings
    VAAP perf mat rent   (K236)

Symphony No. 2 [14']
    3(pic).3(English
    horn).3.3(contrabsn). 4.3.3.1.
    timp,perc,cel,harp,pno,strings
    SIKORSKI perf mat rent   (K237)
    VAAP perf mat rent   (K238)

Symphony No. 3 [25']
    3(pic).3(English
    horn).3.3(contrabsn). 4.3.3.1.
    timp,perc,harp,cel,pno,strings
    SIKORSKI perf mat rent   (K239)
    VAAP perf mat rent   (K240)

KHANDOSHKIN, IVAN (1747-1804)
Concerto for Viola and Orchestra in
    C, [arr.]
    (Borissowski, W.) 2.2.2.2. 2.0.0.0.
    timp,perc,harp,strings,vla solo
    [25'] SIKORSKI perf mat rent
                                          (K241)
KHOLMINOV, ALEXANDER NICOLAYEVICH
    (1925-   )
Concerto for Flute and String
    Orchestra [20']
    string orch,fl solo
    VAAP perf mat rent   (K242)

KHOVANTCHINA: FURCHTERLICH IST DIESER
    LIEBE QUAL, FOR SOLO VOICE AND
    ORCHESTRA [ARR] see Mussorgsky,
    Modest Petrovich

KHOVANTCHINA: HÖRET MICH AN, GEHEIME
    MÄCHTE, FOR SOLO VOICES AND
    ORCHESTRA see Mussorgsky, Modest
    Petrovich, Khovantchina: Ye Powers
    Concealed From Us, For Solo Voices
    And Orchestra

KHOVANTCHINA: OVERTURE, [ARR.] see
    Mussorgsky, Modest Petrovich

KHOVANTCHINA: YE POWERS CONCEALED FROM
    US, FOR SOLO VOICES AND ORCHESTRA
    see Mussorgsky, Modest Petrovich

KHRENNIKOV, TIKHON (1913-   )
Concerto for Piano and Orchestra, No.
    2, Op. 21 [15']
    3.3.3.3. 4.3.3.1. timp,perc,harp,
    strings,pno solo

KHRENNIKOV, TIKHON (cont'd.)

SIKORSKI perf mat rent   (K243)

Concerto for Piano and Orchestra, No.
    3, Op. 28 [18']
    3.3.3.3. 4.3.3.3. timp,4perc,
    2cel,2harp,strings,pno solo
    SIKORSKI perf mat rent   (K244)
    VAAP perf mat rent   (K245)

Concerto for Violin and Orchestra,
    No. 2, Op. 23 [17']
    3.2.3.3. 4.3.3.1. timp,perc,cel,
    harp,strings,vln solo
    SIKORSKI perf mat rent   (K246)
    VAAP perf mat rent   (K247)

Concerto for Violoncello and
    Orchestra, Op. 16 [14']
    3.2.3.2. 4.3.3.0. timp,perc,harp,
    cel&pno,strings,vcl solo
    SIKORSKI perf mat rent   (K248)
    VAAP perf mat rent   (K249)

Symphony No. 1, Op. 4 [20']
    3.2.2.2. 4.2.2.1. timp,perc,cel,
    strings
    SIKORSKI perf mat rent   (K250)
    VAAP perf mat rent   (K251)

Symphony No. 3, Op. 22 [16']
    3.3.3.3. 4.3.3.1. timp,perc,harp,
    strings
    SIKORSKI perf mat rent   (K252)
    VAAP perf mat rent   (K253)

KIDNAPPED see Knight, Eric

KIEL, FRIEDRICH (1821-1885)
Waltz, Op. 73
    string orch sc,pts WOLLENWEBER
    WW 104B f.s.   (K254)

KIELLAND, OLAV (1901-   )
Arabesco [4']
    2.1.2.1. 2.3.2.0. timp,perc,pno/
    harp,strings
    NORGE   (K255)

Concerto for Piano and Orchestra, Op.
    27 [25']
    2.3.3.2. 4.2.0.0. timp,strings,
    pno solo
    NORGE   (K256)

Concerto for Violin and Orchestra,
    Op. 7 [33']
    1.2.0.1. 2.2.0.0. timp,strings,
    vln solo
    NORGE   (K257)

Dagen Vaknar
    see Mot Blasnohogdom, For Solo
    Voice And Orchestra

Ferdamann
    see Six Songs, For Solo Voice And
    Orchestra, Op. 17

Fjell-Lengt
    see Mot Blasnohogdom, For Solo
    Voice And Orchestra

Fyrste Songen, Den
    see Six Songs, For Solo Voice And
    Orchestra, Op. 17

Haust
    see Six Songs, For Solo Voice And
    Orchestra, Op. 17

Heim
    see Six Songs, For Solo Voice And
    Orchestra, Op. 17

I Tverasal-Hytta
    see Mot Blasnohogdom, For Solo
    Voice And Orchestra

Melodia Per Strumenti A Corda *Op.15
    [6']
    string orch
    NORGE   (K258)

Mot Blasnohogdom, For Solo Voice And
    Orchestra *Op.14
    2.2.2.2. 4.2.0.0. timp,harp,
    strings,high solo NORGE f.s.
    contains: Dagen Vaknar; Fjell-
    Lengt; I Tverasal-Hytta   (K259)

Musica Incidentale Per "Brand"
    d'Ibsen *Op.9 [45']
    1.1.2.1. 2.2.2.1. timp,strings
    NORGE   (K260)

Overtura Solenne *Op.25 [10']
    3.2.2.2. 4.3.3.1. timp,perc,
    strings
    NORGE   (K261)

Overtura Tragica All' "Brand" d'Ibsen
    *Op.8 [13']
    2.2.2.2. 4.2.3.1. timp,perc,
    strings

KIELLAND, OLAV (cont'd.)

NORGE   (K262)

Sinfonia No. 1, Op. 3 [25']
    2.2.2.2. 4.2.3.1. timp,perc,
    strings
NORGE   (K263)

Sinfonia No. 2, Op. 21 [35']
    2.2.2.2. 4.2.3.1. timp,perc,
    strings
NORGE   (K264)

Sinfonia No. 3, Op. 23 [26']
    3.3.2.2. 4.3.3.1. timp,perc,
    strings
NORGE   (K265)

Sinfonia No. 4, Op. 26 [30']
    3.3.3.2. 4.2.3.1. timp,perc,
    strings
NORGE   (K266)

Six Songs, For Solo Voice And
    Orchestra, Op. 17
    2.2.3.2. 4.2.0.0. timp,perc,harp,
    strings,solo voice NORGE f.s.
    contains: Ferdamann; Fyrste
    Songen, Den; Haust; Heim; Te
    Kjaerasten Min; Til Telemork
                                         (K267)
Suite, Op. 5 [23']
    2.2.2.2. 4.2.3.1. timp,perc,
    strings
NORGE   (K268)

Te Kjaerasten Min
    see Six Songs, For Solo Voice And
    Orchestra, Op. 17

Til Telemork
    see Six Songs, For Solo Voice And
    Orchestra, Op. 17

KIEVMAN, CARSON (1949-   )
    California Mystery Park: Overture
    AMP perf mat rent   (K269)

Hollowangels [17']
    2.2.3.3. 3.2.2.1. timp,perc,harp,
    pno&cel,elec gtr,strings
    sc AMP $40.00   (K270)

KIIRASTULEN LAULUJA, FOR SOLO VOICE AND
    ORCHESTRA see Jalas, Jussi

KILAR, WOJCIECH (1932-   )
    Orawa
    string orch
    sc PETERS P8629 f.s., perf mat rent
                                         (K271)
POLSKIE   (K272)

KILLMAYER, WILHELM (1927-   )
    Antiphone, For Solo Voice And
    Orchestra [8']
    3(pic,alto fl).2.3(bass clar).2.
    2.4.3.1. timp,perc,cel,pno,
    strings,Bar solo
    SCHOTTS perf mat rent   (K273)

Fin Al Punto
    sc SCHOTTS ED 7144 f.s.   (K274)

Franzosisches Liederbuch, For Solo
    Voices And Chamber Orchestra
    [30']
    2fl,trp,4perc,2vln,vla,vcl,db,SBar
    soli sc SCHOTTS ED 7239 f.s.
                                         (K275)
Holderlin-Lieder, Zyklus I, For Solo
    Voice And Orchestra [45']
    2(pic).2.2(clar in E flat,bass
    clar).2(contrabsn). 2.0+
    cornet.2.0. timp,perc,cel,harp,
    strings,T solo
    SCHOTTS perf mat rent   (K276)

Holderlin-Lieder, Zyklus II, For Solo
    Voice And Orchestra [45']
    2(pic,alto fl,S rec).2(English
    horn).2(bass
    clar).2(contrabsn). 4.0+
    cornet.2.0. timp,perc,harp,
    strings,T solo
    SCHOTTS perf mat rent   (K277)

Im Freien
    2.2.2.2. 2.3.3.0. timp,perc,cel,
    harp,strings
    sc SCHOTTS 71 A7067 $17.50, perf
    mat rent   (K278)

Jugendzeit [13']
    sc SCHOTTS 71 A6904 $13.00, perf
    mat rent   (K279)

Saraband [17']
    string orch sc SCHOTTS 71 A6944
    $21.00, perf mat rent   (K280)

Sostenuto, For Violoncello And String
    Orchestra [8']
    string orch,vcl solo
    SCHOTTS perf mat rent   (K281)

KILLMAYER, WILHELM (cont'd.)

Uberstehen Und Hoffen [10']
    sc SCHOTTS 71 A6905 $10.00, perf
    mat rent   (K282)

Verschüttete Zeichen
    4.3.3.3. 4.3.3.1. timp,perc,cel,
    harp,strings
    sc SCHOTTS 71 A7066 $21.00, perf
    mat rent   (K283)

KILPINEN, YRJÖ (1892-1959)
    Kesayo, For Solo Voice And Orchestra
    [arr.] *Op.23,No.3
    (Fougstedt, N.E.) 0.1.2.0. 2.0.0.0.
    strings,solo voice [2'] FAZER
    perf mat rent   (K284)

Lauluja Kantelettaren Runoihnin, For
    Solo Voice And Orchestra *Op.100
    2.2.2.2. 4.2.3.1. timp,perc,harp,
    strings,solo voice
    FAZER perf mat rent   (K285)

Mondschein-Ode, For Solo Voice And
    Orchestra *Op.62,No.7
    2clar,2bsn,3horn,harp,vla,vcl,db,
    A solo
    BREITKOPF-L perf mat rent   (K286)

KIND OF BLUE see Turnage, Mark-Anthony

KINDERMANN, ERNST
    Filmball (Walzer)
    2.2.2.2. 4.2.2.0. timp,perc,harp,
    strings
    ZIMMER.   (K287)

KINDERSPIELE POLKA see Strauss, Johann,
    [Jr.]

KINDERSTUBE, FOR SOLO VOICE AND
    ORCHESTRA [ARR.] see Mussorgsky,
    Modest Petrovich, Nursery, The, For
    Solo Voice And Orchestra [arr.]

KINDERSUITE see Denisov, Edison
    Vasilievich, Children's Suite

KINDERTOTENLIED, FOR SOLO VOICES AND
    ORCHESTRA see Sciarrino, Salvatore

KINDERTOTENLIEDER, FOR SOLO VOICE AND
    ORCHESTRA see Mahler, Gustav

KINDESGEBET, FOR SOLO VOICE AND
    ORCHESTRA see Jordan, Sverre

KINDSCHER, LUDWIG (1836-1903)
    Lieder Des Monches Eliland, For Solo
    Voice And Orchestra [25']
    0.1.2.2. 2.0.0.0. strings,med
    solo
    (Mottl) KAHNT perf mat rent (K288)

KINESIS see Koykkar, Joseph

KINETICS see Lindberg, Magnus

KING, HAROLD C. (1895-1984)
    Serenade for String Orchestra [16']
    string orch sc DONEMUS f.s., perf
    mat rent   (K289)

KING, JOHN
    Orchestravariations [20']
    2.2.2.3. 4.0.3.0. strings
    sc AM.COMP.AL. $32.50   (K290)

Sinfonietta [16']
    2.2.2.2. 2.2.0.0. timp,perc,
    2harp,strings
    sc AM.COMP.AL. $35.50   (K291)

KING, THE see Halvorsen, Johan

KING CHRISTIAN II: SUITE see Sibelius,
    Jean

KING CHRISTIAN STOOD see Kayser, Leif,
    Kong Kristian Stod

KING LEAR OVERTURE see Berlioz, Hector
    (Louis)

KING MATTHIAS see Bravnicar, Matija,
    Kralj Matjaz

KING OLAV: DAY IS BRIGHTENING, FOR SOLO
    VOICE AND ORCHESTRA see Eggen,
    Arne, Kong Olav: Dag Er Pa Himlen
    Komin, For Solo Voice And Orchestra

KING, QUEEN AND ACE, FOR HARP AND
    ORCHESTRA see Norgaard, Per

KING'S CONTEST, THE, FOR SOLO VOICES
    AND ORCHESTRA see Mechem, Kirke
    Lewis

KING'S ROW see Korngold, Erich Wolfgang

KINGSLEY, GERSHON GARY (1925-   )
    Concerto Moogo [13']
    2.2.2.2. 4.4.3.1. timp,perc,
    strings, 4 moog synthesizers
    BOURNE perf mat rent   (K292)

Popcorn [3']
    2.2.2.2. 4.2.2.1. timp,perc,harp,
    strings
    BOURNE perf mat rent   (K293)

KINKELDER, DOLF DE (1953-   )
    Cartastraccia, For Saxophone And
    Orchestra [8']
    1.2.1.0. 1.1.1.0. harp,marimba&
    vibra,pno&cel,2vln,vla,vcl,db,
    soprano sax solo
    DONEMUS perf mat rent   (K294)

Verloedering 3, De, For Marimba And
    Orchestra [9']
    3.3.3.3. 4.3.3.1. 3perc,strings,
    marimba solo
    DONEMUS perf mat rent   (K295)

KIRCHEN SUITE see Zipp, Friedrich

KIRCHNER, LEON (1919-   )
    Concerto for Violin, Violoncello and
    Instrumental Ensemble [19']
    1.1.1.1+contrabsn. 1.2.2.0. timp,
    3perc,cel,vln solo,vcl solo
    sc AMP $30.00, perf mat rent (K296)

Lily, For Solo Voice And Instrumental
    Ensemble [22']
    woodwind quin,perc,pno,cel,vln,
    vla,vcl,electronic tape,S solo
    AMP perf mat rent   (K297)

Music for Flute and Orchestra [13']
    3.3.3.3. 4.3.3.1. timp,5perc,
    pno-cel-fender, harp, str, fl
    solo
    AMP perf mat rent   (K298)

Music For Twelve [10']
    1.1.1.1. 1.1.1.0. pno,vln,vla,
    vcl,db
    AMP perf mat rent   (K299)

KIRCHNER, VOLKER DAVID (1942-   )
    Bildnisse I [17']
    2.3.2.2. 2.2.2.0. strings
    sc SCHOTTS ED 7145 $24.50   (K300)

Bildnisse II [12']
    2.3.2.2. 2.2.2.0. harp,pno,
    strings
    sc SCHOTTS ED 7251 $19.50   (K301)

Nachtstuck, For Viola And Orchestra
    study sc SCHOTTS $19.50   (K302)

KISIELEWSKI, STEFAN (1911-   )
    Symphony In A Square [22']
    4.3.3.6. 4.3.3.1. perc,strings
    POLSKIE   (K303)

KITAZUME, MICHIO (1948-   )
    Sky, The [6']
    2(pic).2.2.2. 4.2.3.0. perc,cel,
    harp,strings
    ONGAKU perf mat rent   (K304)

KITTL, JAN BEDRICH (1806-1868)
    Symphony, Op. 9, in E flat [22']
    2.2.2.2. 4.2.1.0. timp,strings
    (La Caccia) sc SUPRAPHON f.s.   (K305)

KITZKE, JEROME P.
    Snow Crazy Copybook, The [14']
    2.2.2.2. 2.2.0.0. perc,cel,elec
    pno,strings
    sc AM.COMP.AL. $34.10, perf mat
    rent   (K306)

KIVA, OLEH (1947-   )
    Chamber Cantata No. 1, For Solo Voice
    And Chamber Orchestra [15']
    2fl,2horn,2perc,harp,hpsd,pno,
    3vln,2vla,vcl,db,S solo
    VAAP perf mat rent   (K307)

Chamber Cantata No. 2, For Solo Voice
    And Orchestra [16']
    2.1.1.1. 2.1.1.0. 2perc,harp,cel,
    pno,strings,S solo
    VAAP perf mat rent   (K308)

Chamber Cantata No. 3, For Solo Voice
    And Chamber Orchestra [18']
    fl,ob,clar,perc,harp,cel,pno,
    4vln,2vla,vcl,db,S solo
    VAAP perf mat rent   (K309)

Chamber Cantata No. 4, For Solo
    Voices And Chamber Orchestra
    [16']
    fl,8vln,2vla,2vcl,db,SBar soli
    VAAP perf mat rent   (K310)

Three Poems, For Solo Voice And
    Chamber Orchestra [12']
    fl,ob,clar,perc,harp,cel,pno,
    4vln,2vla,vcl,db,Bar solo

KIVA, OLEH (cont'd.)

VAAP perf mat rent (K311)

KJAERNES, BJORN MORTEN
Relations For Orchestra [9']
2.2.2.2. 4.3.3.1. timp,2perc,
strings
NORGE (K312)

KJELDAAS, ARNLJOT (1916-)
Concerto for Harpsichord and
Orchestra, Op. 70 [28']
1.1.2.1. 2.1.0.0. timp,perc,
strings,hpsd solo
NORGE (K313)

Romance for Violin and Orchestra, Op.
4 [4']
1.1.2.2. 2.0.1.0. timp,perc,
strings,vln solo
NORGE (K314)

KJELLSBY, ERLING (1901-1976)
Chaconne And Fugue On A Norwegian
Folk Tune
see Chaconne Og Fuga Over Et Norsk
Folketonetema

Chaconne Og Fuga Over Et Norsk
Folketonetema [8']
2.2.2.2. 4.2.3.1. timp,perc,
strings
"Chaconne And Fugue On A Norwegian
Folk Tune" NORGE (K315)

Einsam Mann, For Solo Voice And
Orchestra [3']
2.2.2.2. 4.1.3.0. timp,perc,harp,
strings,solo voice
"Lonesome Man, For Solo Voice And
Orchestra" NORGE (K316)

Lonesome Man, For Solo Voice And
Orchestra
see Einsam Mann, For Solo Voice And
Orchestra

KJERTEGN [ARR.] see Cleve, Cissi

KJERULF, HALFDAN (1815-1868)
Five Songs For Solo Voice And
Orchestra [arr.]
(Olsen, Sparre) 1.1.2.0. 0.1.0.0.
strings,high solo [18'] NORSK
perf mat rent (K317)

KLAGELIED, THE MEMORY OF IGOR
STRAVINSKY see Antoniou, Theodore,
Threnos

KLANG see Castagnoli, Giulio see
Wagemans, Peter-Jan

KLANGBESCHREIBUNG I, FUR DREI
ORCHESTERGRUPPEN see Rihm, Wolfgang

KLANGBESCHREIBUNG III see Rihm,
Wolfgang

KLANGBILDER see Fongaard, Bjørn

KLANGMINUTEN see Schweizer, Klaus

KLANGSPIRALE (FIRST VERSION-1977) see
Hamel, Peter Michael

KLANGSPIRALE (SECOND VERSION-1977) see
Hamel, Peter Michael

KLARINETTEN KLARINA, FOR SOLO VOICE,
CLARINET AND ORCHESTRA see Kvam,
Oddvar S.

KLASICNA SIMFONIJA see Lovec, Vladimir

KLASICNI KONCERT, FOR PIANO AND
ORCHESTRA see Rojko, Uros

KLEBE, GISELHER (1925-)
Concerto for Clarinet and Orchestra,
Op. 92 [25']
1+pic.2.2.2. 4.2.3.1. timp,2perc,
harp,strings,clar solo
BÄREN. BA 7164 (K318)

Lied Fur Orchester *Op.94 [15']
1+pic.1+English horn.1+bass
clar.2. 2.2.0.0. perc,harp,
strings
BÄREN. perf mat rent (K319)

Notturno, Op. 97 [15']
1.2.1+basset horn.2. 2.2.0.0.
timp,strings
BÄREN. BA 7309 (K320)

Orchesterstücke *Op.82a (from Der
Jungste Tag) [20']
3(alto fl,pic).2+English
horn.3(bass clar).2. 4.3.3.1.
timp,2perc,pno,harp,strings,opt
org
BÄREN. BA 7132 perf mat rent (K321)

KLEBE, GISELHER (cont'd.)

Symphony No. 5, Op. 75 [30']
3(pic).2+English horn.2+bass
clar.2+contrabsn. 4.4.4.0+db
tuba. timp,4perc,harp,pno 4-
hands,14strings
BÄREN. BA 6727 perf mat rent (K322)

Tomba Di Igor Strawinsky, La *Op.81
[20']
ob&ob d'amore&English horn,pno,
strings
BÄREN. BA 6760 perf mat rent (K323)

KLEFISCH, WALTER (1910-)
Rondo Über Ein Savoyardisches
Volkslied [4']
string orch
TISCHER perf mat rent (K324)

KLEIBERG, STÅLE (1958-)
Stilla, For Solo Voice And Orchestra
[7']
2.3.2.2. 4.0.2.0. perc,cel,pno,
harp,strings,S solo
NORGE (K325)

Understrommer, For Bassoon And String
Orchestra [11']
string orch,bsn solo
NORGE (K326)

KLEIN, IMMANUEL (1960-)
Couleurs Printanières *Op.3 [7'30"]
3.2.3.3. 4.2.3.1. timp,2perc,
harp,pno,strings
DONEMUS perf mat rent (K327)

KLEIN, JOSEF
Concerto for Violin and Orchestra
KRENN (K328)

KLEIN, LEONARD
Muff.1 [15']
1.1.1.1. 1.1.1.0. timp,6vln,3vla,
3vcl,db
sc APNM $28.50, perf mat rent
(K329)

KLEIN, LOTHAR (1932-)
Concerto Sacro, For Viola And
Orchestra [15']
2.2.2.2. 2.2.0.0. perc,harp,hpsd,
strings,vla solo
CAN.MUS.CENT. MI 1312 K64CON (K330)

Espana, For Violoncello And Orchestra
PRESSER perf mat rent (K331)

Landscape With Pipers
pic,English horn,bass clar,pno/
harp,7vln,2vla,2vcl,db
CAN.MUS.CENT. MI 1200 K64L (K332)

Story Of Celeste, The, For Narrator
And Orchestra
2.2.2.1. 2.3.2.1. 2perc,cel,
strings,narrator
SCHIRM.G perf mat rent (K333)

Symphonic Fanfares [8']
3.3.3(clar in E flat).3. 4.3.3.1.
3perc,harp,pno/hpsd,strings
CAN.MUS.CENT. MI 1100 K64S (K334)

Symphony No. 3 [15']
(Symphonic Etudes) PRESSER perf mat
rent (K335)

KLEIN, RICHARD RUDOLF (1921-)
Concertino for Recorder and String
Orchestra
string orch,rec solo
sc,pts MÖSELER M 11.454 f.s. (K336)

KLEINE ABENDMUSIK see Grabner, Hermann

KLEINE CHRONIK POLKA see Strauss,
Eduard

KLEINE ELEGIEN FUR ALTE INSTRUMENTE see
Henze, Hans Werner

KLEINE FRITZ AN SEINE JUNGEN FREUNDE,
DER, "ACH, WENN ICH NUR EIN
LIEBCHEN HÄTTE", FOR SOLO VOICE AND
ORCHESTRA, [ARR.] see Weber, Carl
Maria von

KLEINE KAMMERMUSIK NO. 1 see Grabovsky,
Leonid, Small Chamber Music No. 1

KLEINE KAMMERMUSIK NO. 2 see Grabovsky,
Leonid, Small Chamber Music No. 2

KLEINE LACHMUSIK, EINE see Schroder,
Wolfgang

KLEINE NACHTMUSIK, EINE see Mozart,
Wolfgang Amadeus

KLEINE POPMUSIK, EINE see Korn, Peter
Jona

KLEINE SUITE see Sekles, Bernhard

KLEINE SUITE FOR 3 BASSOONS AND
ORCHESTRA [ARR.] see Weissenborn,
Julius

KLEINE SUITE IN D see Telemann, Georg
Philipp

KLEINE SYMPHONIE see Egk, Werner

KLEINES ERLEBNIS see Müller-Marc,
Raymund

KLEINES KONZERT, FOR ORGAN, HARPSICHORD
AND CHAMBER ORCHESTRA see Krenek,
Ernst

KLEINES KONZERT, FOR PIANO AND STRING
ORCHESTRA see Kauder, Hugo

KLEIO see Stalheim, Jostein

KLEIST-OUVERTURE see Wetz, Richard

KLENAU, PAUL VON (1883-1946)
Rembrandt van Rijn: Lied Des
Cornelis, For Solo Voice And
Orchestra [arr]
(Walter, Fried) 2.1.2.2. 2.0.0.0.
harp,strings,T solo [5'] BOTE
perf mat rent (K337)

KLENGEL, JULIUS (1859-1933)
Hymnus *Op.57 [9']
12vcl
BREITKOPF-L perf mat rent (K338)

KLERKX, WIM (1956-)
Twee Scenes: Monoloog- Pas De Quatre
[13']
2.2.2.2. 4.2.3.1. 2perc,strings
sc DONEMUS f.s., perf mat rent
(K339)

KLETZKI, PAUL (KLECKI) (1900-1973)
Concerto for Violin and Orchestra,
Op. 19, in G
2.2.2.3. 4.2.0.0. timp,perc,
strings,vln solo
SIMROCK perf mat rent (K340)

Sinfonietta, Op. 7
string orch
SIMROCK perf mat rent (K341)

Symphony No. 2, Op. 18, in G minor
4.3.3.3. 6.3.0.0. timp,perc,harp,
strings,A/Bar solo
SIMROCK perf mat rent (K342)

Variations, Op. 20
3.3.3.3. 4.3.3.1. timp,perc,harp,
cel,strings
SIMROCK perf mat rent (K343)

KLEYNJANS
Concerto for Guitar and Orchestra,
No. 1, in G
LEDUC AL 27167-27168 perf mat rent
(K344)

KLEYNJANS, FRANCIS (1951-)
Concerto for Guitar and String
Orchestra, Op. 80, No. 2, in D
[11']
string orch,gtr solo
LEMOINE perf mat rent (K345)

Concerto for 2 Guitars and String
Orchestra, Op. 101, in D minor
[18']
string orch,2gtr soli
LEMOINE perf mat rent (K346)

KLI ZEMER, FOR CLARINET AND ORCHESTRA
see Starer, Robert

KLIC NARAVE see Srebotnjak, Alojz F.

KLIMA TIS APUSSIAS, FOR SOLO VOICE AND
CHAMBER ORCHESTRA see Antoniou,
Theodore

KLING' LEISE MEIN LIED, FOR SOLO VOICE
AND ORCHESTRA [ARR.] see Liszt,
Franz

KLOPSTOCKS MORGENGESANG AM
SCHÖPFUNGSFESTE "NOCH KOMMT SIE
NICHT, DIE SONNE", FOR SOLO VOICES
AND ORCHESTRA see Bach, Carl
Philipp Emanuel

KLUGERE GIEBT NACH, DER: POLKA see
Strauss, Johann, [Jr.]

KLUGHARDT, AUGUST (1847-1902)
Concerto for Violoncello and
Orchestra, Op. 59
KISTNER perf mat rent (K347)

KLUSÁK, JAN (1934-)
Sonata for Violin and Winds [13']
1.2.2.2. 2.1.1.0. vln solo
SUPRAPHON (K348)

KLUSSMANN, ERNST GERNOT (1901-   )
    Symphony No. 3, Op. 20
        KISTNER perf mat rent   (K349)

K'MON SIGGEBEYBE, FOR VIOLONCELLO AND
    INSTRUMENTAL ENSEMBLE see Heyn,
    Volker

KNAB
    Landliche Tanze
        string orch
        sc,pts BOHM f.s.   (K350)

KNAIFEL, ALEXANDER (1943-   )
    Canterville Ghost, The: Scenes [45']
        1.1.2.1. 1.1.1.1. timp,4perc,pno&
            cel,org,string quin
        VAAP perf mat rent   (K351)

    Canterville Ghost, The: Scenes, For
        Solo Voices And Chamber Orchestra
        [45']
        1.1.2.1. 1.1.1.1. timp,4perc,pno&
            cel,org,string quin,SB soli
        "Gespenst Von Canterville, Das:
            Szenen, For Solo Voices And
            Chamber Orchestra" SIKORSKI perf
            mat rent   (K352)

    Da! [15']
        pic,rec,ob,clar in E flat,soprano
            sax,cornet,cym,cel,hpsd,vln,
            vla,vcl,db,electronic tape, opt
            flexaton
        SIKORSKI perf mat rent   (K353)
        VAAP perf mat rent   (K354)

    Gespenst Von Canterville, Das:
        Szenen, For Solo Voices And
        Chamber Orchestra
        see Canterville Ghost, The: Scenes,
            For Solo Voices And Chamber
            Orchestra

    Jeanna [80']
        .4.4.4.4. 4rec, 4sax, 14.4.4.2.,
            perc, strings
        SIKORSKI perf mat rent   (K355)
        VAAP perf mat rent   (K356)

    Litany [35']
        3.0.0.0. 0.3.0.1. timp,perc,harp,
            pno,mand,gtr,bass gtr,6vln,
            3vla,6vcl,3db
        SIKORSKI perf mat rent   (K357)

    Medea: Suite [30']
        0.0.0.1. 4.4.4.4.1. timp,4perc,
            2harp,strings
        SIKORSKI perf mat rent   (K358)
        VAAP perf mat rent   (K359)

KNALL UND FALL POLKA see Strauss,
    Eduard

KNAPIK, EUGENIUSZ (1951-   )
    Corale, Interludio E Aria [16']
        fl,hpsd,6vln,2vla,2vcl,db
        POLSKIE   (K360)

KNECHT, JUSTIN HEINRICH (1752-1817)
    Symphony
        (Hohnen; Klusen; Fenske) sc GARLAND
            ISBN 0-8240-3843-6 $90.00
            contains also: Wilms, Johann
            Wilhelm, Symphony; Kalliwoda,
            Johann Wenzel, Symphonies, Two
                                         (K361)

KNIGHT, ERIC
    American Overture [6']
        2+pic.2+English horn.2+bass
            clar.2+contrabsn. 4.4.3.1.
            timp,3perc,pno,harp,strings
        SCHIRM.G perf mat rent   (K362)

    Canadian Tribute [10']
        2(pic).2.2.2. 4.4.3.1. timp,
            6perc,pno,harp,strings
        SCHIRM.G perf mat rent   (K363)

    Great American Bicycle Race, The [6']
        2+pic.2+English horn.2+bass
            clar.2+contrabsn. 4.4.2+bass
            trom.1. timp,2perc,harp,strings
        SCHIRM.G perf mat rent   (K364)

    Kidnapped [7']
        2.2.2.2. 4.3.2+bass trom.0. timp,
            2perc,harp,strings
        SCHIRM.G perf mat rent   (K365)

    Reel Chaplin, The [20']
        3.3.3.3. 4.4.3.1. timp,3perc,
            harp,pno,strings
        BOURNE perf mat rent   (K366)

    Symphony In Four American Idioms, A
        [24']
        2+pic.2+English horn.2+bass
            clar.2+contrabsn. 4.4.3.1.
            timp,3perc,harp,pno,strings
        SCHIRM.G perf mat rent   (K367)

    Three Musical Elements [12']
        3(pic).2.3(bass clar).2. 4.3.2+
            bass trom.1. 3perc,harp,pno,

KNIGHT, ERIC (cont'd.)
        strings
        SCHIRM.G perf mat rent   (K368)

KNIPPER, LEV KONSTANTINOVICH
    (1898-1974)
    Concerto for Violin and Orchestra
        2.1.3.1. 3.0.0.1. timp,strings,
            vln solo
        VAAP perf mat rent   (K369)

    Symphony No. 4, Op. 41
        3.2.2.2. 4.2.3.1. timp,perc,
            strings
        VAAP perf mat rent   (K370)

    Youth Overture
        3.2.2.2. 4.3.3.1. timp,perc,
            strings
        VAAP perf mat rent   (K371)

KNUSSEN, OLIVER (1952-   )
    Coursing (Étude No. 1, Op. 17) [6']
        1.1.1.1. 1.1.1.0. perc,pno,vln,
            vla,vcl,db
        sc FABER 023-00354 $16.75, perf mat
            rent   (K372)

    Étude No. 1, Op. 17
        see Coursing

    Music For A Puppet Court *Op.11 [9']
        2.2.2.2. 2.0.0.0. 2-3perc,gtr,
            harp,cel,strings
        sc FABER f.s., perf mat rent (K373)

    Songs And A Sea Interlude, For Solo
        Voice And Orchestra (from Where
        The Wild Things Are) [17']
        3.2.3.2. 4.0.3.0. 4perc,harp,pno,
            strings,S solo
        study sc FABER 023-00308 $33.50,
            perf mat rent   (K374)

    Symphony No. 2, Op. 7 for Solo Voice
        and Orchestra [17']
        2.2.2.2. 2.0.0.0. opt perc,
            strings,S solo
        study sc FABER 023-00339 $19.50,
            perf mat rent   (K375)

KNUTSEN, TORBJORN (1904-1987)
    Air for Viola and String Orchestra
        [2']
        string orch,vla/vcl solo
        NORGE   (K376)

    Concerto for Clarinet and String
        Orchestra
        string orch,clar solo
        NORGE   (K377)

    Concerto for Oboe and String
        Orchestra [20']
        string orch,ob solo
        NORGE   (K378)

    Romance [6']
        string orch
        sc,pts MUSIKK f.s.   (K379)

KO WO KIKU see Schafer, R. Murray

KOAN, UN see Leroux, Maurice

KOANGA: CLOSING SCENE, FOR SOLO VOICES
    AND ORCHESTRA [ARR.] see Delius,
    Frederick

KOANGA: INTERMEZZO [ARR.] see Delius,
    Frederick

KOBAYASHI, AKIRA (1960-   )
    Asterion, For Piano And Orchestra
        [10']
        3(pic).3.3(bass
            clar).3(contrabsn). 4.3.3.1.
            perc,2harp,cel,strings,pno solo
        sc ZEN-ON 899453 f.s., perf mat
            rent   (K380)

KOCH, ERLAND VON (1910-   )
    Arioso E Furioso
        string orch
        sc,pts NORSK f.s.   (K381)

    Cantilena E Marcia Populaire No. 1
        [5']
        string orch
        GEHRMANS sc 6134P f.s., pts 6134S
            f.s.   (K382)

    Concerto for Guitar and Orchestra
        [20']
        1.1.1.1. 0.0.0.0. strings,gtr
            solo
        sc GEHRMANS 6153P f.s., perf mat
            rent   (K383)

    Concerto for Piano and Orchestra, No.
        2 [23']
        2.2.2.2. 2.2.1.0. timp,perc,
            strings,pno solo
        PEER MUSIK perf mat rent   (K384)

KOCH, ERLAND VON (cont'd.)
    Concerto for Piano and Orchestra, No.
        3
        2(pic).2.2(bass clar).2.alto sax.
            4.2.3.1. timp,perc,strings,pno
            solo
        AMP perf mat rent   (K385)

    Concerto for Tuba and String
        Orchestra [14']
        string orch,tuba solo
        sc GEHRMANS 6026P f.s., perf mat
            rent   (K386)

    Concerto Lirico [17']
        string orch
        PEER MUSIK perf mat rent   (K387)

    Dance No. 1, For Violin And Orchestra
        [4']
        fl,clar,pno,strings,vln solo
        NORDISKA perf mat rent   (K388)

    Dance No. 3, For Violin And Orchestra
        [4']
        fl,clar,pno,strings,vln/vcl solo
        NORDISKA perf mat rent   (K389)

    Dance No. 4 [5']
        fl,clar,pno,strings
        NORDISKA perf mat rent   (K390)

    Dance No. 5 [4']
        fl,clar,pno,strings
        NORDISKA perf mat rent   (K391)

    Fantasia Melodica, For Guitar And
        String Orchestra [9']
        string orch,gtr solo
        PEER MUSIK perf mat rent   (K392)

    Four Symphonic Myths
        see Fyra Symfoniska Myter

    Fyra Symfoniska Myter [25']
        3.3.3.3. 4.3.3.1. timp,4perc,
            harp,strings
        "Four Symphonic Myths" sc GEHRMANS
            6132P f.s., perf mat rent (K393)

    Gammalswenska Wijsor, For Solo Voice
        And Orchestra [25']
        2.2.2.2. 2.2.1.0. timp,strings,
            low solo
        NORDISKA perf mat rent   (K394)

    Lapponica (Symphony No. 5) [25']
        3.3.3.3. 4.3.3.1. timp,4perc,
            strings
        sc GEHRMANS 6131P f.s., perf mat
            rent   (K395)

    Midvinterblot; Sommarsolstand
        3.3.3.3. 4.3.3.1. timp,3perc,harp,
            strings [20'] STIM   (K396)

    Rhythmic String Bagatelles [arr.]
        see Rytmiska Strakbagateller [arr.]

    Rytmiska Strakbagateller [arr.]
        (Kallberg, Ernst) "Rhythmic String
            Bagatelles [arr.]" string orch
            [10'] GEHRMANS sc 6029P f.s., pts
            6029S f.s.   (K397)

    Scandinavian Dance
        see Scandinavische Tanze

    Scandinavische Tanze
        2.2.2.2. 2.2.1.0. timp,perc,
            strings
        "Scandinavian Dance" PEER MUSIK
            perf mat rent   (K398)

    Sicilienne [3']
        1.0.1.0. 2.2.1.0. perc,strings
        NORDISKA perf mat rent   (K399)

    Symphony No. 5
        see Lapponica

    Trombonia, For Trombone And String
        Orchestra
        string orch,trom solo
        STIM   (K400)

KOCH, FRIEDRICH E. (1862-1927)
    Deutsche Rhapsodie, For Violin And
        Orchestra *Op.31 [19']
        2.2.2.2. 4.2.0.0. timp,harp,
            strings,vln solo
        KAHNT perf mat rent   (K401)

KOCH, MARTEN (1882-1940)
    Happiness [2']
        string orch
        NORDISKA perf mat rent   (K402)

KOCH-RAPHAEL, ERWIN (1949-   )
    Concerto for Piano and Orchestra, No.
        1, Op. 38 [31']
        3(pic).3(English horn).3(bass
            clar).3(contrabsn). 4.3.3.1.
            timp,perc,cel,strings,pno solo
        BOTE perf mat rent   (K403)

KOCH-RAPHAEL, ERWIN (cont'd.)

Kalte Zeiten *Op.34 [9']
1(pic).0.2(bass
clar).2(contrabsn).2.1.1.1.
timp,perc,pno&cel,string quin
BOTE perf mat rent (K404)

Petites Aventures Au Bord De La Mer
*Op.33 [15']
1(pic).1.1(bass
clar).1(contrabsn). 1.0.0.0.
strings
BOTE perf mat rent (K405)

KOCHAN, ERNST
Canzonetta, For Oboe And String
Orchestra
string orch,ob solo
TONOS (K406)

Flirt En Bleu
2.1.2.0. 2.0.0.0. perc,gtr,
strings
TONOS (K407)

Revue Marsch
2.1.2.1. 4.3.3.0. perc,strings
TONOS (K408)

Serenade D'Antoinette, For Flute And
String Orchestra
string orch,fl solo
TONOS (K409)

Valse Caprice
2.1.2.1. 4.0.0.0. perc,strings
TONOS (K410)

KOCHAN, GÜNTER (1930-   )
Concerto for Violoncello and
Orchestra, No. 2
orch,vcl solo
sc PETERS P5357 f.s., perf mat rent
(K411)
Symphony No. 3
sc PETERS 9598 $52.00 (K412)

KOCSAR, MIKLOS (1933-   )
Capricorn Concerto, For Flute And
Chamber Orchestra
sc EMB 10240 f.s. (K413)

Cinque Movimenti, For Clarinet And
Orchestra
hpsd,opt cimbalom,strings,clar
solo
sc EMB 8745 f.s. (K414)

Concertino In Memoriam Z.H., For Horn
And Chamber Orchestra
sc EMB 10276 f.s., perf mat rent
(K415)
Episodi, For Oboe And String
Orchestra
string orch,ob solo
sc EMB 12842 f.s., perf mat rent
(K416)
Formazioni
sc EMB 13694 f.s., perf mat rent
(K417)
Metamorphoses
sc EMB 10239 f.s. (K418)

Sequenze
string orch sc EMB 12302 f.s.
(K419)
Variations
sc EMB 10251 f.s. (K420)

KODÁLY, ZOLTÁN (1882-1967)
Minuetto Serio
KALMUS A6406 sc $10.00, set $20.00,
pts $1.00, ea., perf mat rent
(K421)

KOECHLIN, CHARLES (1867-1950)
Automne, L' *Op.30 [51']
4.4.4.3.sax. 6.4.3.2. timp,perc,
cel,2harp,pno,2vla d'amore,
strings
ESCHIG perf mat rent (K422)

Buisson Ardent, Le *Op.171,Op.203
[36']
4.3.4.3.2sax. 4.4.4.1. timp,perc,
Ondes Martenot,org,2harp,pno,
strings
ESCHIG perf mat rent (K423)

Cite Nouvelle, La *Op.170 [32']
4.3.4.3.sax. 4.4.3.1. timp,perc,
cel,2harp,pno,strings
ESCHIG perf mat rent (K424)

Confidences d'Un Joueur De
Clarinette, Les: Grande Valse Du
Bal A La Fete d'Eckerswir, For
Clarinet And Orchestra [2'45"]
fl,4horn,strings,clar solo
BILLAUDOT perf mat rent (K425)

Confidences d'Un Joueur De
Clarinette, Les: Nocturne, For
Viola And Orchestra [4'35"]
fl,clar,4horn,strings,vla solo
BILLAUDOT perf mat rent (K426)

KOECHLIN, CHARLES (cont'd.)

Deux Poemes Symphoniques *Op.43
4.4.4.4. 6.4.4.2. timp,perc,cel,
2harp,pno,strings ESCHIG perf mat
rent
contains: Soleil Et Danses Dans
La Foret; Vers La Plage
Lointaine Nocturne (K427)

Docteur Fabricius, Le *Op.202 [30']
4.4.5.4.2sax. 5.4.4.2. timp,perc,
cel,2harp,pno,org,Ondes
Martenot,strings, 4 saxhorn
ESCHIG perf mat rent (K428)

En Mer, La Nuit, Version A *Op.27
[17']
3.3.3.3. 4.3.3.0. timp,perc,harp,
strings
ESCHIG perf mat rent (K429)

En Mer, La Nuit, Version B *Op.27
[17']
4.4.4.4.2sax. 6.4.3.2. timp,perc,
harp,strings
ESCHIG perf mat rent (K430)

Etudes Antiques, Op. 46, No. 1: Les
Temples [8']
3.3.3.2. 4.2.3.1. timp,perc,
2harp,strings
ESCHIG perf mat rent (K431)

Etudes Antiques, Op. 46, No. 2: Le
Soir Au Bord Du Lac [8']
3.3.4.2. 4.2.3.0. timp,perc,cel,
2harp,pno,strings
ESCHIG perf mat rent (K432)

Etudes Antiques, Op. 46, No. 3:
Cortege D'Amphitrite [8']
4.4.4.2. 4.2.3.0. timp,perc,cel,
2harp,pno,strings
ESCHIG perf mat rent (K433)

Etudes Antiques, Op. 46, No. 4:
Epitaphe D'une Jeune Femme [8']
3.4.4.2. 4.2.3.0. timp,perc,
2harp,pno,strings
ESCHIG perf mat rent (K434)

Etudes Antiques, Op. 46, No. 5: La
Joie Paienne [17']
4.4.4.5. 6.4.4.2. timp,perc,cel,
2harp,pno,strings
ESCHIG perf mat rent (K435)

Foret Paienne, La *Op.45 [30']
4.3.3.3. 4.4.4.3.1. timp,perc,harp,
pno,strings
ESCHIG perf mat rent (K436)

Fugue Symphonique *Op.121 [12']
4.3.3.3. 4.4.3.1. timp,perc,
2harp,pno,strings
ESCHIG perf mat rent (K437)

Loi De La Jungle, La *Op.175 [5']
4.3.4.3.2sax. 4.4.4.1. bugle,
timp,perc,strings
min sc ESCHIG $17.95, perf mat rent
(K438)

Meditation De Purun Baght, La
*Op.159
3.3.3.3. 6.4.4.1. timp,perc,
2harp,pno,org,strings
min sc ESCHIG $21.50, perf mat rent
(K439)

Nuits De Walpurgis Classique, La
*Op.38 [14']
4.3.3.5. 5.4.3.1. timp,perc,cel,
hpsd,2harp,lute,pno,strings
ESCHIG perf mat rent (K440)

Poem, For Horn And Orchestra, Op. 70
Bis [16']
3.3.3.3. 3.3.3.1. timp,perc,harp,
strings,horn solo
ESCHIG perf mat rent (K441)

Quatre Sonatines Francaises, Op. 60
Bis [30']
2.2.2.2. 2.2.0.0. timp,perc,cel,
harp,pno,strings
ESCHIG perf mat rent (K442)

Seven Stars Symphony, The *Op.132
[45']
3.3.3.3.alto sax. 4.2.3.0. timp,
perc,cel,pno,harp,strings
ESCHIG perf mat rent (K443)

Soleil Et Danses Dans La Foret
see Deux Poemes Symphoniques

Sonatina No. 1, Op. 194, No. 1
[10'15"]
ob d'amore/soprano sax,2fl,clar,
hpsd, string sextet
study sc ESCHIG f.s., perf mat rent
(K444)

Sonatina No. 2, Op. 194, No. 2
ob d'amore/soprano sax,2fl,clar,
hpsd, string sextet
study sc ESCHIG f.s., perf mat rent

KOECHLIN, CHARLES (cont'd.)

(K445)
Symphonie D'Hymnes [40']
4.4.4.4.6sax. 6.5.5.2. timp,perc,
2harp,cel,pno,org,Ondes
Martenot,strings,cor
ESCHIG perf mat rent (K446)

Symphony No.1, Op.57bis [40']
3.3.3.3. 4.4.3.1. timp,perc,
2harp,pno,strings
(after String Quartet No. 2) ESCHIG
perf mat rent (K447)

Symphony No. 2, Op. 196 [44']
4.4.4.4.2sax. 6.4.3.1. timp,perc,
cel,2harp,pno,Ondes Martenot,
opt org,strings
ESCHIG perf mat rent (K448)

Vers La Plage Lointaine Nocturne
see Deux Poemes Symphoniques

Victoire De La Vie *Op.167
1.1.1.1. 1.1.0.0. timp,perc,pno,
2vln,vla,vcl
ESCHIG perf mat rent (K449)

KOERING, RENE (1940-   )
A. De Mahler, For Solo Voices And
Orchestra [15']
1.1.1.0. 2.1.1.0. 2perc,pno,
strings,SA soli
BILLAUDOT perf mat rent (K450)

Deux Lieder, For Piano And Orchestra
*Op.31 [15']
3.3.3.3. 4.3.0.0. strings,pno
solo
SALABERT perf mat rent (K451)

Lecture Trois De Mahler, For Solo
Voices And String Orchestra
string orch,S&narrator
BILLAUDOT perf mat rent (K452)

Messe D'avila, For Solo Voices And
Orchestra [60']
3.3(English horn).3(contrabass
clar).3(contrabsn). 6.3.3.1.
timp,4perc,strings,Mez/Bar solo
SALABERT perf mat rent (K453)

Paralleles-Distorsion, For Clarinet,
Violin, Double Bass, Piano, And
Instrumental Ensemble [31']
1.1+English horn.0.0+contrabsn.
1.2.2.0. timp,2perc,harp,
strings,clar solo,vln solo,db
solo,pno solo
BILLAUDOT perf mat rent (K454)

Portrait I, For Solo Voice And
Orchestra
1.1.1.1. 2.1.1.0. 2perc,pno,
strings,S solo
SALABERT perf mat rent (K455)

Portrait II
1(alto fl).1(English horn).1(bass
clar).1. 2.1.1.0. 2perc,strings
SALABERT perf mat rent (K456)

R. De Mahler, For Solo Voice,
Violoncello And Orchestra [20']
3.3.3.3. 6.4.3.1. timp,4perc,
2harp,2pno,strings,vcl solo,S
solo
BILLAUDOT perf mat rent (K457)

Trente-Quatre Mesures Pour Un
Portrait De T [18']
English horn,2clar,2bsn,2horn,
3perc,strings,string quar soli
SALABERT perf mat rent (K458)

KOETSIER, JAN (1911-   )
Burg-Serenade *Op.109 [30']
2.2.0.2. 2.2.2.0. timp,perc,harp,
strings
sc DONEMUS f.s., perf mat rent
(K459)
Concertino for Trombone and String
Orchestra, Op. 91 [15']
string orch,trom solo
sc DONEMUS f.s., perf mat rent
(K460)
Concerto for 4 Horns and Orchestra,
Op. 95 [18']
2.2.2.2. 0.2.0.0. timp,2perc,
strings,4horn soli
DONEMUS perf mat rent (K461)

Duo Concertante, For Violoncello,
Bassoon And Orchestra, No.2
*Op.92 [15']
0.2.0.0. 2.0.0.0. strings,vcl
solo,bsn solo
DONEMUS perf mat rent (K462)

Fantasy for Harp and Orchestra, Op.
113 [10']
1.1.1.1. 1.1.0.0. perc,strings,
harp solo
DONEMUS perf mat rent (K463)

KOETSIER, JAN (cont'd.)

Franzosisches Konzert, For 2 Flutes
    And String Orchestra *Op.98
    [12']
    string orch,2fl soli
    DONEMUS perf mat rent   (K464)

Symphony No. 1
    3.3.3.3. 4.2.3.1. timp,4perc,
    harp,strings
    sc DONEMUS f.s., perf mat rent
                                   (K465)

Tanzsuite *Op.103b [15']
    2.2.2.2. 2.2.0.0. timp,2perc,
    harp,strings
    DONEMUS perf mat rent   (K466)

Vor-Und Nachspiel, For 4 Horns And
    Orchestra *Op.114a [10']
    2.2.2.2. 0.1.0.0. strings,4horn
    soli
    DONEMUS perf mat rent   (K467)

KOGDA, FOR SOLO VOICE AND INSTRUMENTAL
    ENSEMBLE see Grabovsky, Leonid

KOGOJ, MARIJ (1895-1956)
    Andante for Violin and Orchestra [8']
    2.2.2.2. 2.2.2.0. timp,harp,
    strings,vln solo
    (Srebotnjak, Alojz) DRUSTVO
    DSS 1045 perf mat rent   (K468)

Bagatelle [13']
    0.2.2.2. 2.2.0.0. timp,harp,
    strings
    (Srebotnjak, Alojz) "Bagatelles"
    DRUSTVO DSS 1044 perf mat rent
                                   (K469)

Bagatelles
    see Bagatelle

Sest Skladb, For String Orchestra
    [23']
    string orch
    (Srebotnjak, Alojz) "Six Pieces For
    String Orchestra" DRUSTVO
    DSS 1105 perf mat rent   (K470)

Six Pieces For String Orchestra
    see Sest Skladb, For String
    Orchestra

KÖHLER, WOLFGANG (1923-   )
    Concertino, Op. 17
    timp,strings
    sc,pts MERSEBURGER EM 2052 f.s.
                                   (K471)

KOHS, ELLIS BONOFF (1916-   )
    Amerika: Orchestra Suite [15']
    MERION perf mat rent   (K472)

Concerto for Violin and Orchestra
    [17']
    3.3.3.3.sax. 4.3.3.1. timp,perc,
    harp,strings,vln solo
    AM.COMP.AL. perf mat rent   (K473)

Four Orchestral Songs, For Solo Voice
    And Orchestra [12']
    2(pic).2(English horn).2.2.
    2.2.2.1. perc,harp,strings,T
    solo
    sc AM.COMP.AL. $13.00, perf mat
    rent   (K474)

KOIMETERION (HOMMAGE A ANDRÉ JOLIVET)
    see Bleuse, Marc

KOJIBA, TOMIKO
    Requiem "Hiroshima" [12']
    string orch
    ONGAKU perf mat rent   (K475)

KOKAI, REZSÖ (1906-1962)
    Recruiting Suite
    sc EMB 959 f.s.   (K476)

KOKAJI, KUNITAKA (1955-   )
    Miroir III
    AMPHION perf mat rent   (K477)

KOKKONEN, JOONAS (1921-   )
    Metamorphosis
    12strings,hpsd
    study sc SCHIRM.G $30.00   (K478)

Music for String Orchestra
    string orch
    sc FAZER $26.00   (K479)

Paesaggio, Il [8']
    1.1.1.1. 1.0.0.0. strings
    sc SUOMEN f.s.   (K480)

KOL NIDREI MEMORIAL see Zinn, William

KOLAR, VICTOR (1888-1957)
    Americana
    2+pic.2+English horn.2.2+
    contrabsn. 4.3.3.1. timp,perc,
    harp,strings
    SCHIRM.G perf mat rent   (K481)

KOLB, BARBARA (1939-   )
    Enchanted Loom, The [18']
    3(pic).2+English horn.2+bass
    clar.2+contrabsn. 4.3.3.1.
    timp,3perc,harp,strings
    BOOSEY perf mat rent   (K482)

Grisaille
    3.3.4.3. 4.3.3.1. perc,strings
    min sc BOOSEY 975 $12.00, perf mat
    rent   (K483)

Yet That Things Go Round [14']
    2(pic).2.2(bass clar).2. 2.2.1.0.
    timp,2perc,pno,strings
    BOOSEY perf mat rent   (K484)

KOLBERG, KÅRE (1936-   )
    Suoni [12']
    1.0.1.0. 0.1.1.0. timp,perc,pno,
    cel,strings
    NORGE   (K485)

KOLLBOTTEN see Lindeman, Signe

KOLLOQUIUM, FOR TROMBONE, PERCUSSION
    AND ORCHESTRA see Ebenhöh, Horst

KOLODUB, LEVKO (1930-   )
    Symphony No. 3 [23']
    5perc,cel,harp,hpsd,pno,8vln,
    3vla,3vcl,2db
    VAAP perf mat rent   (K486)

KOM HAVSVINDAR, KOM see Søderlind,
    Ragnar

KOMIVES, JANOS (1932-   )
    Ritournelles Du Chat Abgral, Les, For
    Clarinet And Orchestra [12']
    2fl,2bsn,2horn,strings,clar solo
    sc BILLAUDOT $33.75, perf mat rent
                                   (K487)

KOMM SUSSER TOD see Bach, Johann
    Sebastian

KOMMET HER, IHR FRECHEN SUNDER, FOR
    SOLO VOICE AND STRING ORCHESTRA see
    Mozart, Wolfgang Amadeus

KOMMT WIEDER AUS DER FINSTREN GRUFT see
    Bach, Johann Sebastian

KOMODO DRAGONS see Meijering, Chiel

KOMORNA GLASBA, FOR INSTRUMENTAL
    ENSEMBLE see Golob, Jani

KOMORNA GLASBA, FOR ORCHESTRA see
    Golob, Jani

KOMPANEK, RUDOLPH (1943-   )
    Heritage, For Orchestra And Jazz-Rock
    Trio [70']
    3.3.2.2. 4.3.3.1. timp,perc,harp,
    strings, jazz-rock trio: pno,
    db, drm
    MCA perf mat rent   (K488)

KONCERT ZA GROZNJAN see Giltay, Berend

KONCERTANTNA GLASBA see Bozic, Darijan

KONCERTANTNA GLASBA, FOR WIND QUINTET
    AND ORCHESTRA see Golob, Jani

KONCERTANTNE EPIZODE see Srebotnjak,
    Alojz F.

KONCERTNA HUDBA see Bázlik, Miroslav

KONFLIKTER see Andersson, Gert Ove

KONFRONTATIONER see Jørgensen, Erik

KONG KRISTIAN STOD see Kayser, Leif

KONG OLAV: DAG ER PA HIMLEN KOMIN, FOR
    SOLO VOICE AND ORCHESTRA see Eggen,
    Arne

KONG VALEMON, FOR SOLO VOICE AND
    ORCHESTRA see Kverndokk, Gisle

KÖNIG ENZIO: OVERTURE see Wagner,
    Richard

KONIG STEPHAN OVERTURE see Beethoven,
    Ludwig van

KONIGIN ELISABETH: ARIE DES DUDLEY, FOR
    SOLO VOICE AND ORCHESTRA see
    Walter, Fried

KÖNIGIN VON SABA, DIE: FESTLICHER-
    EINZUGS-MARSCH see Goldmark, Karl

KÖNIGIN VON SABA, DIE: OVERTURE see
    Goldmark, Karl

KÖNIGLICHE SCHÄFER, DER: DEIN BIN ICH,
    FOR SOLO VOICE AND ORCHESTRA see
    Mozart, Wolfgang Amadeus, Re
    Pastore, Il: L'Amero Saro Costante,
    For Solo Voice And Orchestra

KÖNIGSKINDER: PRELUDE, ACT II see
    Humperdinck, Engelbert

KÖNIGSKINDER: PRELUDE, ACT III see
    Humperdinck, Engelbert

KÖNIGSLIEDER WALZER see Strauss,
    Johann, [Jr.]

KONIGSMARSCH see Strauss, Richard

KONSERT OUVERTURE see Kvam, Oddvar S.

KONSERTANTE MUZIEK II, FOR VIOLIN,
    VIOLA AND WINDS see Beurden,
    Bernard van

KONSERTFANTASI NO. 2: MASTERSWINGER see
    Hundsnes, Svein

KONSERTFANTASI NO. 3: DANZA see
    Hundsnes, Svein

KONT, PAUL (1920-   )
    Concertino for Flute and String
    Orchestra [12']
    string orch,fl solo
    DOBLINGER perf mat rent   (K489)

Concertino for Organ and String
    Orchestra [12']
    string orch,org solo
    DOBLINGER perf mat rent   (K490)

Concerto for Brass and Strings [14']
    0.0.0.0. 4.2.3.1. 12vln,8vla
    (Vom Manne Und Vom Weibe) study sc
    DOBLINGER STP 222 f.s., perf mat
    rent   (K491)

Concerto for Percussion and Orchestra
    [10']
    3(pic).3.3.3. 3.3.3.1. org,
    strings,3perc soli
    DOBLINGER perf mat rent   (K492)

"K" Choreographische Szenen [23']
    string orch
    DOBLINGER perf mat rent   (K493)

Mediterrane Harmonien, For Double
    Bass And Orchestra [19']
    1+pic.1+English horn.1+bass
    clar.1+contrabsn. 1.1.1.1.
    strings,db solo
    DOBLINGER perf mat rent   (K494)

Roma (from Il Ballo Del Mondo) [25']
    3(pic).3(English horn).3(bass
    clar).3(contrabsn). 4.2.3.1.
    timp,perc,harp,cel,strings
    DOBLINGER perf mat rent   (K495)

Romanische Tanze [22']
    0.2(English horn).0.0. 2.0.0.0.
    strings
    DOBLINGER perf mat rent   (K496)

Serenade for String Orchestra [16']
    string orch
    DOBLINGER perf mat rent   (K497)

Sinfonia Und Sinfonina [12']
    2(pic).2+English horn.2(clar in
    A).2. 2.2.2.1. timp,perc,
    strings
    DOBLINGER perf mat rent   (K498)

Strohkoffer, For Violin And Chamber
    Orchestra [arr.] [6']
    (Cerha, Friedrich) fl&pic,2clar,
    2horn,baritone horn,acord,pno,
    strings,vln solo DOBLINGER perf
    mat rent   (K499)

Symphony No. 5 [12']
    2.2(English horn).2+bass clar.2+
    contrabsn. 4.2.3.1. strings
    DOBLINGER perf mat rent   (K500)

KONTAKION see Giani Luporini, Gaetano

KONTAKTION see Lidholm, Ingvar

KONTINUUM, FOR BASSOON AND STRING
    ORCHESTRA see Fürst, Paul Walter

KONTRAPUNKT IV see Schedl, Gerhard

KONTRASTE, KONFLIKTE see Meyer, Ernst
    Hermann

KONTRASTER FOR SYMFONIORKESTER OG
    JAZZGRUPPE see Bjorklund, Terje

KONTRETÄNZE, ZWÖLF, WOO. 14 see
    Beethoven, Ludwig van

KONZERT-ALLEGRO MIT INTRODUKTION, FOR
    PIANO AND ORCHESTRA, OP. 134 see
    Schumann, Robert (Alexander)

KONZERT SERENADE, FOR CLARINET AND
    INSTRUMENTAL ENSEMBLE see
    Pavlyenko, Sergei

KONZERTANTE DIVERTIMENTI, FOR PIANO AND
ORCHESTRA see Vogt, Hans

KONZERTANTE FANTASIE, FOR ORGAN AND
STRING ORCHESTRA see Baur, Jürg

KONZERTANTE FANTASIE, FOR VIOLA AND
STRING ORCHESTRA see Eröd, Ivan

KONZERTANTE MUSIK see Brunner, Adolf
see Werner, Fritz

KONZERTOUVERTURE see Schweinitz,
Wolfgang von

KONZERTOUVERTURE IN C MINOR see
Strauss, Richard

KONZERTSATZ, FOR ACCORDION AND STRING
ORCHESTRA see Maros, Miklos

KONZERTSATZ, FOR HORN AND ORCHESTRA, K.
370B see Mozart, Wolfgang Amadeus

KONZERTSATZ, FOR HORN AND ORCHESTRA, K.
494A see Mozart, Wolfgang Amadeus

KONZERTSATZ, FOR HORN AND ORCHESTRA, K.
494B see Mozart, Wolfgang Amadeus

KONZERTSATZ FOR PIANO AND ORCHESTRA IN
D MINOR see Schumann, Robert
(Alexander)

KONZERTSTUCKE FOR CLARINET, BASSET HORN
AND STRING ORCHESTRA, OP. 113 AND
OP. 114 see Mendelssohn-Bartholdy,
Felix

KOOTENAY see Fodi, John

KOPELENT, MAREK (1932-   )
Agnus Dei for Solo Voice and Chamber
Orchestra [20']
1(pic).0.1.0. 0.0.1.0. 2perc,pno&
harmonium,vln,vla,vcl,S solo
BREITKOPF-W perf mat rent   (K501)

Concertino for English Horn and
Orchestra [16']
4(pic,alto fl).0.3+bass clar.0.
0.1.3.0. opt glock,6vln,2vla,
2vcl,db,English horn solo
(alternate scoring for brass:
1.1.2.0.) BREITKOPF-W perf mat
rent   (K502)

Pozdraveni [10']
3(3pic).3(English horn).3.3.
4.2.3.1. perc,harp,org,strings
BREITKOPF-W perf mat rent   (K503)

Symphony [32']
3(3pic,alto fl).3.3(bass
clar).3(contrabsn).
4.3(flügelhorn,cornet).3.1.
perc,harp,pno&cel,strings
BREITKOPF-W perf mat rent   (K504)

KOPLON see Stefansson, Fjölnir

KOPPEL, HERMAN DAVID (1908-   )
Concertino for Violin, Viola,
Violoncello and Orchestra, Op.
110 [15']
2.2.2.2. 2.0.0.0. strings,vln
solo,vla solo,vcl solo
SAMFUNDET perf mat rent   (K505)

Concertino No. 2
sc,pts SAMFUNDET f.s.   (K506)

Concerto for Clarinet and Orchestra,
Op. 35 [23']
2.1.0.2. 1.0.0.0. timp,strings,
clar solo
HANSEN-DEN perf mat rent   (K507)

Concerto for Violoncello and
Orchestra, Op. 56 [27']
2(pic).2.2.2. 2.2.0.0. timp,cel,
strings,vcl solo
HANSEN-DEN perf mat rent   (K508)

Fest-Ouverture
sc,pts SAMFUNDET f.s.   (K509)

Fire Gammeltestamentlige Sange, For
Solo Voice And Orchestra [10']
2.2.2.2. 4.2.2.1. perc,pno,
strings,S solo
"Four Songs From The Old Testament,
For Solo Voice And Orchestra"
SAMFUNDET perf mat rent   (K510)

Four Songs From The Old Testament,
For Solo Voice And Orchestra
see Fire Gammeltestamentlige Sange,
For Solo Voice And Orchestra

To Bibelske Sange, For Solo Voice And
Orchestra *Op.59 [6']
2.2.2.2. 2.2.0.0. timp,harp,cel,
strings,S solo
"Two Biblical Songs, For Solo Voice
And Orchestra" SAMFUNDET perf mat

KOPPEL, HERMAN DAVID (cont'd.)

rent   (K511)

Two Biblical Songs, For Solo Voice
And Orchestra
see To Bibelske Sange, For Solo
Voice And Orchestra

KORAL see Hesselberg, Eyvind

KORF, ANTHONY (1951-   )
Symphony In The Twilight [27']
4.2.3(bass clar,contrabass
clar).1. 4.2.2(bass trom).1.
timp,perc,harp,pno&cel,strings
sc AM.COMP.AL. $80.00, perf mat
rent   (K512)

Symphony No. 2 [27']
2.2.2.2. 2.2.2.0. timp,perc,
strings,synthesizer
(Blue Note) sc AM.COMP.AL. $133.30,
perf mat rent   (K513)

KORÍNEK, MILOŠLAV (1925-   )
Recollect In February
see Rozpomienka Na Februar

Rozpomienka Na Februar
"Recollect In February" string orch
SLOV.HUD.FOND   (K514)

KORK see Sønstevold, Gunnar

KORN, PETER JONA (1922-   )
Beckmesser Variationen Über Themen
Aus Richard Wagners
"Meistersinger von Nurnberg"
*Op.64
study sc SCHUBERTH,J f.s.   (K515)

Concerto for Alto Saxophone and
Orchestra, Op. 31 [17']
2.2.2.2. 4.2.3.0. timp,perc,
strings,alto sax solo
HANSEN-GER perf mat rent   (K516)

Kleine Popmusik, Eine *Op.50 [16']
3(pic).3(English
horn).3.3(contrabsn). 4.3.3.1.
4perc,harp,cel,strings
LEUCKART perf mat rent   (K517)

Morgenmusik, For Trumpet And String
Orchestra *Op.54 [16']
string orch,trp solo
LEUCKART perf mat rent   (K518)

Toccata, Op. 42a [8']
2(pic).2.2.2. 3.2.3.1. timp,
3perc,strings
LEUCKART perf mat rent   (K519)

KORNDORF, NICOLAI (1947-   )
Confessions [21']
1.1.1.1. 1.1.1.0. perc,vln,vla,
vcl,db,electronic tape
SIKORSKI perf mat rent   (K520)
VAAP perf mat rent   (K521)

Sempre Tutti [24']
4.3.3.3. 8.5.4.2. 11perc,bass
gtr,strings
SIKORSKI perf mat rent   (K522)

Symphony No. 1 [30']
3.3.3.3. 6.3.3.1. timp,perc,pno/
cel,strings
SIKORSKI perf mat rent   (K523)

KORNGOLD, ERICH WOLFGANG (1897-1957)
Adventures Of Robin Hood: Symphonic
Suite [17'30"]
WARNER perf mat rent   (K524)

Baby Serenade *Op.24 [17']
2(pic).1.2.1.alto sax.tenor sax.
1.3.1.0. timp,perc,banjo,harp,
pno,strings
SCHOTTS perf mat rent   (K525)

King's Row [4']
3.2+English horn.2+bass clar.2+
contrabsn. 4.3.3.1. timp,3perc,
pno,cel,2harp,strings
WARNER perf mat rent   (K526)

Schauspiel-Ouverture *Op.4
KALMUS A7169 sc $25.00, set $50.00,
pts $2.00, ea., perf mat rent   (K527)

Schneemann, Der: Overture [5']
2(pic).2.2.2. 4.2.3.0. timp,perc,
harp,strings
KALMUS A5892 sc $10.00, set $25.00,
perf mat rent   (K528)

Tomorrow (from the film Constant
Nymph)
WARNER perf mat rent   (K529)

KOROLYOV, ANATOLI (1949-   )
Uber Gras, Steine, Wasser [14']
3.3.3.3. 4.3.3.1. 4perc,harp,
strings
SIKORSKI perf mat rent   (K530)

KORSAR, DER; OPERNFRAGMENT see
Schumann, Robert (Alexander)

KORTE, KARL (1928-   )
Symphony No. 3
3.3.4.3. 4.3.3.1. timp,4perc,
harp,pno,strings
sc SEESAW $82.00, perf mat rent   (K531)

KORTEKANGAS, OLLI (1955-   )
Okologie 2 [19'15"]
3.3.3.3. 4.4.3.1. timp,3perc,
harp,pno,strings
sc SUOMEN f.s.   (K532)

KOSA, GYÖRGY (1897-   )
Todesfuge, For Solo Voice And Chamber
Orchestra
[Ger/Hung] orch,S solo sc EMB 12015
f.s.   (K533)

KOSAKENTANZ see Janácek, Leoš

KOSBRO see Baker, David N.

KOSKENLASKIAN MORSIAMET, FOR SOLO VOICE
AND ORCHESTRA see Sibelius, Jean

KOSKOM see Dao, Nguyen Thien

KOSMA, JOSEPH (1905-1969)
Burlesque, For Flute, Bassoon And
Orchestra [10']
1.2.2.1. 2.2.2.0. timp,perc,harp,
strings,fl solo,bsn solo
ESCHIG perf mat rent   (K534)

KOSMOIGRAMM see Terzakis, Dimitri

KOSTER, TITUS (1955-   )
Stijl [7']
1.1.1.1.2sax. 1.1.1.1. marimba,
harp,pno,2vln,vla,vcl,db
DONEMUS perf mat rent   (K535)

KOTILAINEN, OTTO (1868-1936)
Kun Joulu On, For Solo Voice And
Orchestra [arr.]
(Kuusisto, I.) 2fl,strings,solo
voice [2'] FAZER perf mat rent   (K536)

Varpunen Jouluaamuna, For Solo Voice
And Orchestra [arr.]
(Godzinsky, George De) 2.0.1.1.
1.0.0.0. perc,harp,strings,solo
voice FAZER perf mat rent   (K537)
(Kuusisto, I.) harp,strings,solo
voice [4'] FAZER perf mat rent   (K538)

KOTKO, SEMYON
Suite for Orchestra
3.3.3.3. 4.3.3.0. timp,perc,harp,
strings
VAAP perf mat rent   (K539)

KOTONSKI, WLODZIMIERZ (1925-   )
Terra Incognita
3.3.3.3. 4.3.3.1. perc,harp,cel,
strings
study sc MOECK 5298 f.s.   (K540)

KOTZ see Vries, Klaas de

KOUNTZ, G.
American Ode, An
1.1.1.1. 1.1.1.0. timp,perc,
strings
WARNER perf mat rent   (K541)

Wondrous Story, A [10']
1.1.2.1. 2.2.1.0. timp,strings
WARNER perf mat rent   (K542)

KOWALSKI, JÚLIUS (1912-   )
Concertino for Viola and Chamber
Orchestra
SLOV.HUD.FOND   (K543)

KOX, HANS (1930-   )
Irold's Youth [15']
2.2.2.2. 4.3.3.1. timp,2perc,
strings
DONEMUS perf mat rent   (K544)

Musica Reservata, for symphonic band
and symphony orchestra [16']
4.4.9.3.3sax. 8.6.6.3. cornet,
2bugle,timp,3-4perc,strings
sc DONEMUS f.s., perf mat rent   (K545)

Notturno E Danza [10']
pno,strings,vln solo,vla/clar
solo,vcl solo
sc DONEMUS f.s., perf mat rent   (K546)

Sinfonia Concertante for 4 Saxophones
and Orchestra [16']
1.2.0.2. 2.2.0.0. timp,strings,
4sax soli
DONEMUS perf mat rent   (K547)

KOX, HANS (cont'd.)

Songe Du Vergier, Le, For Violoncello
And Orchestra [8']
2.0.0.0. 2.0.0.0. vibra,strings,
vcl solo
DONEMUS perf mat rent   (K548)

Symphony No. 3 [40']
3.3.3.3. 6.4.3.1. timp,perc,
strings
DONEMUS perf mat rent   (K549)

KOYKKAR, JOSEPH
Chamber Symphony
ob,clar,bsn,horn,strings
SEESAW perf mat rent   (K550)

Kinesis
3.2.4.2. 4.3.3.1. perc,strings
SEESAW   (K551)

**KOZELUCH, JOHANN ANTON (JAN
EVANGELISTA) (1738-1814)**
Alexander In India, For Solo Voice
And Orchestra [5']
0.2.0.2. 2.0.0.0. strings,T solo
SUPRAPHON   (K552)

KRAFT see Lindberg, Magnus

KRAFT, WILLIAM (1923-   )
American Carnival Overture [5']
2+pic.2+English horn.2+bass
clar.2. 4.2.3.1. timp,perc,
harp,pno&cel,strings
NEW MUSIC WEST perf mat rent (K553)

Concerto for Timpani and Orchestra
[23'10"]
2(pic).2(English horn).2.2.
4.3.3.1. perc,pno&cel,harp,
strings,timp solo
NEW MUSIC WEST perf mat rent (K554)

Concerto for Tuba and Orchestra [18']
3(pic).2+English horn.2+bass
clar.3(contrabsn). 4.3.3.0.
timp,perc,pno&cel,harp,strings,
tuba solo
NEW MUSIC WEST perf mat rent (K555)

Contextures II: The Final Beast, For
Solo Voices And Chamber Orchestra
[21']
fl&alto fl,clar&bass clar,horn,
perc,harmonium&cel,elec gtr,
vla,vcl,vla da gamba, vielle,
rebec, krumhorn, hurdy gurdy,
lute-medieval harp, recorders,
hand bells, (st)
NEW MUSIC WEST perf mat rent (K556)

Double Play, For Violin, Piano And
Chamber Orchestra [17']
1.2(English horn).1(bass clar).2.
2.1.0.0. perc,strings,vln solo,
pno solo
NEW MUSIC WEST perf mat rent (K557)

Fire And Ice Suite [22']
2(pic).3(English horn).2.2.
4.3.3.1. timp,perc,harp,pno&
cel,strings
NEW MUSIC WEST perf mat rent (K558)

Interplay [17']
3(pic).3(English horn).3(bass
clar).3(contrabsn). 4.3.3.1.
timp,perc,pno&cel,harp,strings,
6 offstage crotale players
NEW MUSIC WEST perf mat rent (K559)

Settlers Suite [15']
1.1.1.1. 2.2.2.0. timp,perc,pno,
strings
NEW MUSIC WEST perf mat rent (K560)

Triangles, For Percussion And
Instrumental Ensemble [18']
1(pic).1(English horn).1.1.
1.1.1.0. vln,vla,vcl,perc solo
NEW MUSIC WEST perf mat rent (K561)

KRAK, EGON
Suita Z Goldbergovskych Variacii
"Suite From Goldberg Variations"
SLOV.HUD.FOND   (K562)

Suite From Goldberg Variations
see Suita Z Goldbergovskych
Variacii

KRAKOWIAK, FOR PIANO AND ORCHESTRA see
Chopin, Frédéric

KRALJ MATJAZ see Bravnicar, Matija

KRAMAR, FRANTISEK
see KROMMER, FRANZ

KRAMAR-KROMMER
see KROMMER, FRANZ

KRAMER, JONATHAN (1942-   )
Moments In And Out Of Time [29']
3(pic).2+English horn.3(clar in E
flat,bass clar).3(contrabsn).
4.3.2+bass trom.1. timp,3perc,
harp,pno,strings
SCHIRM.G perf mat rent   (K563)

KRASKA SUITA see Srebotnjak, Alojz F.

KRATOCHWIL, HEINZ (1932-   )
Adagio, Op. 110 [7']
string orch
DOBLINGER perf mat rent   (K564)

Concerto for Percussion and Chamber
Orchestra, Op. 107 [13']
fl,tenor sax,trp,strings,perc
solo
DOBLINGER perf mat rent   (K565)

Concerto for Violin, Viola,
Violoncello and Orchestra [20']
2(pic).2(English horn).2(bass
clar).2(contrabsn).tenor sax.
3.3.2.1. timp,perc,strings,vln
solo,vla solo,vcl solo
DOBLINGER perf mat rent   (K566)

KRATZSCHMAR, WILFRIED (1944-   )
Wettermaschine, Die
2.2.2.2. 2.2.2.0. timp,perc,harp,
strings
sc PETERS $30.00   (K567)

KRAUZE, ZYGMUNT (1938-   )
Arabesque, For Piano And Chamber
Group [13']
1.1.1.1. 1.0.1.0. 4vln,4vla,2vcl,
db,pno solo
UNIVER. perf mat rent   (K568)

Concerto for Violin and Orchestra
2.2.2.2. 2.2.1.0. 2elec gtr,
strings,vln solo
sc UNIVER. $40.00   (K569)

Fete Galante Et Pastorale [18']
2clar,2acord,elec org,vibra,2pno,
hpsd,elec gtr,16vln,8vcl,2db, 2
melodikas, 4 players for folk-
violinen, fifes, dudelsack,
hurdy-gurdy
UNIVER. perf mat rent   (K570)

Piece for Orchestra, No. 3 [12']
2.2.2.2. 2.2.2.0. strings
AMPHION perf mat rent   (K571)

Suite De Danses Et De Chansons, For
Harpsichord And Orchestra
3.3.3.3. 0.0.0.0. 2acord,2mand,
strings,hpsd solo [13'] sc
UNIVER. $40.00   (K572)

Tableau Vivant [15']
1.1.2.1. 1.1.1.0. pno,2vln,2vla,
vcl,db
UNIVER. perf mat rent   (K573)

KRCEK, JAROSLAV (1939-   )
Concerto for Violin and Orchestra
CESKY HUD.   (K574)

Music for Orchestra
CZECH RADIO   (K575)

Symphony No. 1
CESKY HUD.   (K576)

KREBS, JOACHIM (1952-   )
In Gedanken An Den Sterbenden Wald
[4']
2+pic.2+English horn.2+bass
clar.3(contrabsn). 4.3.3.1.
timp,perc,pno,harp,strings
PEER MUSIK perf mat rent   (K577)

In Memoriam Rainer Werner Fassbinder
[10']
3(pic).2+English horn.2+bass
clar.2+contrabsn. 4.3.3.1.
timp,perc,pno/cel,harp,strings
PEER MUSIK perf mat rent   (K578)

In Memoriam Rudi Dutschke [9']
2+pic.3(English horn).2(clar in E
flat)+bass clar.2+contrabsn.
4.3.3.1. timp,perc,harp,strings
PEER MUSIK perf mat rent   (K579)

Musik Fur Kleines Orchester [25']
1(pic,alto fl).1(English
horn).1(bass
clar).1(contrabsn). 1.1.1.0.
timp,perc,pno/cel,strings
PEER MUSIK perf mat rent   (K580)

Traumkraut, For Solo Voices And
Chamber Orchestra [23']
2(pic,alto fl).1+English
horn.1(bass clar).1+contrabsn.
2.0.0.0. perc,2vln,2vcl,ABar
soli
PEER MUSIK perf mat rent   (K581)

KREISLER, FRITZ (1875-1962)
Caprice Viennois, For Violin And
Orchestra [arr.]
(McAlister) 0.2.2.2. 2.0.0.0. timp,
harp,strings,vln solo [4'30"]
KALMUS A6314 sc $5.00, set $15.00
(K582)

Chanson Louis XIII And Pavane, For
Violin And Orchestra [arr.]
(McAlister) 0.1+English horn.0.2.
2.0.0.0. strings,vln solo [3']
KALMUS A6319 sc $5.00, set $10.00
(K583)

Chasse, La, For Violin And Orchestra
[arr.]
(McAlister) 0.2.2.2. 2.0.0.0. timp,
strings,vln solo [2'] KALMUS
A6321 sc $3.00, set $8.00 (K584)

Liebesfreud, For Violin And Orchestra
[arr.]
(McAlister) 0.0.2.2. 2.0.0.0.
strings,vln solo [3'] KALMUS
A6316 sc $7.00, set $12.00 (K585)

Liebeslied, For Violin And Orchestra
[arr.]
(McAlister) 0.1+English horn.2.2.
2.2.0.0. strings,vln solo [4']
KALMUS A6317 sc $7.00, set $12.00
(K586)

Praeludium And Allegro, For Violin
And Orchestra [arr.]
(McAlister) 0.2.2.2. 2.0.0.0. timp,
strings,vln solo [5'30"] KALMUS
A6322 sc $8.00, set $12.00 (K587)

Schon Rosmarin, For Violin And
Orchestra [arr.]
(McAlister) 0.1.1.2. 2.0.0.0.
strings,vln solo [2'30"] KALMUS
A6318 sc $5.00, set $12.00 (K588)

Sicilienne And Rigaudon, For Violin
And Orchestra [arr.]
(McAlister) 0.1+English horn.0.2.
2.0.0.0. strings,vln solo [4']
KALMUS A6320 sc $7.00, set $10.00
(K589)

Tambourin Chinois, For Violin And
Orchestra [arr.]
(McAlister) 0.2(English horn).2.2.
2.2.0.0. timp,perc,harp,strings,
vln solo [4'] KALMUS A6315 sc
$10.00, set $15.00   (K590)

KREMSER KONZERT, FOR ORGAN AND STRING
ORCHESTRA see Planyavsky, Peter

KREMSKI, ALAIN (1940-   )
Retour Au Principe [45']
string orch, cloches anciennes
d'Iran
BOIS perf mat rent   (K591)

KRENEK, ERNST (1900-1991)
Acht Lieder Aus Dem "Reisebuch", For
Solo Voice And Orchestra *Op.62
[17']
2(pic).2.2.2. 4.1.1.0. 2perc,
harp,strings,solo
sc UNIVER. 16669 f.s.   (K592)

Auf- Und Ablehnung *Op.220 [18']
2(pic).2.3.2(contrabsn). 4.4.3.1.
5perc,cel,harp,pno,strings
BÄREN. BA 6707 perf mat rent (K593)

Concerto for Organ and Orchestra, Op.
235 [25']
2(pic).2(English horn).2(bass
clar).2. 4.2.2.1. timp,perc,
harp,strings,org solo
BÄREN. BA 7124 perf mat rent (K594)

Concerto for Organ and String
Orchestra, Op. 230 [10']
string orch,org solo
sc UNIVER. 17066 f.s.   (K595)
min sc PHILH PH. 492 $13.00 (K596)

Concerto for Violin, Piano and
Chamber Orchestra [20']
1.1.1.1. 2.1.1.0. strings,vln
solo,pno solo
sc UNIVER. 16859 f.s.   (K597)

Concerto for Violoncello and
Orchestra, No. 2, Op. 236 [20']
2(pic).2.2(bass clar).2. 4.2.2.0.
2-3perc,harp,strings,vcl solo
BÄREN. BA 7126 perf mat rent (K598)

Dissembler, The, For Solo Voice And
Chamber Orchestra *Op.229 [20']
1(pic).1(English horn).1.1.
1.1.1.0. 4perc,cel,harp,pno,
strings
BÄREN. BA 6759 perf mat rent (K599)

Divertimento for Orchestra [7']
study sc RONGWEN 28 $9.50   (K600)
study sc BROUDE BR. $12.50 (K601)

KRENEK, ERNST (cont'd.)

Five Short Pieces For Strings
*Op.116 [10']
study sc,pts BÄREN. BA 6154 f.s.
(K602)

Kleines Konzert, For Organ,
Harpsichord And Chamber Orchestra
*Op.88 [10']
fl,clar,strings,org solo,hpsd
solo
sc UNIVER. 17080 f.s. (K603)

KRETSCHMER, EDMUND (1830-1908)
Fabrice-Marsch *Op.44 [7']
2.2.2.2. 4.2.3.1. timp,3perc,
strings
BREITKOPF-W perf mat rent (K604)

KREUDER, PETER (1905-1981)
Traummusik [5']
2.2.2.2.alto sax. 4.4.4.0. perc,
harp,strings
(composed with Schutz, Dirk)
SIKORSKI perf mat rent (K605)

KREUSSER, GEORG ANTON (1746-1810)
Symphonies, Two *see Richter, Franz
Xaver, Symphonies, Five
see Richter, Franz Xaver,
Symphonies, Five

KREUTZER, KONRADIN (1780-1849)
Nachtlager In Granada, Das: Ein
Schütz Bin Ich, For Solo Voice
And Orchestra
BREITKOPF-L perf mat rent (K606)

KREUZGANGE see Fritsch, Johannes Georg

KRI see Vuori, Harri

KRICKA, JAROSLAV (1882-1969)
Scherzo Idyllic
SIMROCK perf mat rent (K607)

KRIEGER, ARMANDO (1940-)
Piedra Negra Sobre Una Piedra Blanca,
For Solo Voice And Chamber
Orchestra
1.1.1.1. 1.0.0.0. perc,pno,
strings,S solo
TONOS (K608)

Radiante America, For Solo Voices And
Orchestra
1.1.1.1. 2.2.2.0. 3perc,harp,pno,
strings,ST soli
TONOS (K609)

KRIEGER, ARTHUR
Remnants [15']
2.2.3.3. 6.3.2.1. perc,pno,
strings
sc AM.COMP.AL. $27.50, perf mat
rent (K610)

Riverside Variations [10']
2.2.2.2. 4.2.2.1. timp,3perc,
harp,pno,strings
sc AM.COMP.AL. $46.25, perf mat
rent (K611)

KRIEGERS LIEBCHEN POLKA see Strauss,
Johann, [Jr.]

KRIESBERG, MATTHIAS (1953-)
Parte Sin Novedad, For Solo Voice And
Orchestra [20']
2.2.2.2. 2.1.1.0. 2perc,strings,
Mez solo
sc APNM $30.00, perf mat rent
(K612)

Short Symphony [11']
2(pic)+alto fl.2+English horn.2+
bass clar.2+contrabsn. 4.3.2+
bass trom.1. timp,perc,harp,
strings
AMP perf mat rent (K613)

KRISTALLWELT, TEIL III see Obst,
Michael

KRISTENSEN, KUNO KJAERBYE
Tavli [10']
3.2.2.2. 2.2.2.0. 2timp,6perc,
strings
SAMFUNDET perf mat rent (K614)

KRISTINSSON, SIGURSVEINN D.
Suite in G minor
3.3.2.2. 4.3.3.1. timp,perc,
strings
ICELAND 021-009 (K615)

KRISTOFFERSEN, FRIDTHJOF (1894-1962)
Border Fort
see Grensefestning

Caprice Norvegien, Nr. 1, 2 Og 3
2.2.2.2. 4.3.3.1. timp,perc,harp,
strings
NORGE (K616)

KRISTOFFERSEN, FRIDTHJOF (cont'd.)

Fanarapsodi
2.2.2.2. 4.2.3.0. timp,cel,
strings
"Rhapsody From Fana" NORGE (K617)

Grensefestning
2.2.2.2. 4.2.3.0. timp,perc,harp,
strings
"Border Fort" NORGE (K618)

Mai-Fest
1.1.1.1. 2.2.2.0. timp,perc,pno,
strings
"May Feast" NORGE (K619)

May Feast
see Mai-Fest

Ostlandsskisse Nr. 2
2.3.3.3. 4.2.3.0. timp,perc,harp,
strings
"Sketch From Eastern Norway No. 2"
NORGE (K620)

Rhapsody From Fana
see Fanarapsodi

Sketch From Eastern Norway No. 2
see Ostlandsskisse Nr. 2

Suite
3.2.2.2. 4.2.3.1. timp,perc,harp,
strings
NORGE (K621)

KRIVINKA, GUSTAV (1928-)
Concerto Grosso No. 2 for String
Quartet and Chamber Orchestra
study sc PANTON 1822 f.s. (K622)

KROGSETH, GISLE (1952-)
Fantasy for Guitar and Orchestra
[8'50']
3.2.2.2. 4.2.3.1. timp,perc,harp,
strings,gtr solo
NORGE (K623)

Four Movements For Strings (Partita,
Op. 6)
string orch
NORGE (K624)

Partita, Op. 6
see Four Movements For Strings

KROKODILSLIEDER, FOR SOLO VOICE AND
CHAMBER ORCHESTRA see Eröd, Ivan

KROL, BERNHARD (1920-)
Concertino Sereno, For Violin, Double
Bass And Orchestra *Op.50 [18']
2.2.2.2. 4.2.3.1. hpsd,harp,pno,
gtr,mand,vln solo,db solo
BENJ perf mat rent (K625)

Concerto Barocco, For Horn And
Orchestra *Op.86 [23']
2(pic).2+English horn.0.2+
contrabsn. 0.3.3.0. timp,
strings without vln,horn solo
BOTE perf mat rent (K626)

Consolazione Concerto, For English
Horn And String Orchestra *Op.70
string orch,English horn solo
[17'] BOTE perf mat rent (K627)

Sinfonische Etude *Op.109 [20']
2.2+English horn.2+bass clar.3.
4.2.3.1. timp,3perc,harp,cel,
strings
BOTE perf mat rent (K628)

KROLL, WILLIAM (1901-1980)
Arabesque
2+pic.1.2.1. 2.2.2.1. strings
SCHIRM.G perf mat rent (K629)

Jolly Good Fellow
2.1.2.1. 2.2.2.1. timp,strings
SCHIRM.G perf mat rent (K630)

Little March
2.1.2.1. 2.2.2.1. timp,perc,
strings
SCHIRM.G perf mat rent (K631)

KROMMER, FRANZ (1759-1831)
Concertino for 2 Clarinets and
Orchestra
MUS. RARA perf mat rent (K632)

Concertino for Flute, Oboe and String
Orchestra
string orch,fl solo,ob solo
(Muller, Hermann) sc,solo pt KUNZEL
$35.00, perf mat rent (K633)

Concerto For Clarinet And Orchestra,
Op. 52, In E-Flat *see THREE
CENTURIES OF MUSIC IN SCORE, VOL.
5: CONCERTO IV, CLASSICAL STRINGS
AND WINDS

KROMMER, FRANZ (cont'd.)

Concerto for Clarinet and Orchestra,
Op. 86, in E minor
MUS. RARA 2054 perf mat rent (K634)

Concerto for 2 Clarinets and
Orchestra, Op. 35, in E flat
MUS. RARA 1249 perf mat rent (K635)

Concerto for 2 Clarinets and
Orchestra, Op. 91, in B flat
MUS. RARA 2158 perf mat rent (K636)

Concerto for Oboe and Orchestra, Op.
37, in F [20']
1.2.0.0. 2.2.0.0. timp,strings,ob
solo
SUPRAPHON (K637)

Concerto for Oboe and Orchestra, Op.
65, in C
MUS. RARA 2153 perf mat rent (K638)

KRONINGSMARSJ see Svendsen, Johan
(Severin)

KRONUNGSLIEDER WALZER see Strauss,
Josef

KRONUNGSMARSCH see Strauss, Johann,
[Jr.]

KROPATSCHEK, H.
Fanfare
BOHM perf mat rent (K639)

KROPFREITER, AUGUSTINUS FRANZ
(1936-)
Altdorfer-Passion, For Solo Voices
And Instrumental Ensemble [47']
1(pic).1(English horn).1.1.
1.0.0.0. organ positive, 2vla,
2vcl, db, abar soli
DOBLINGER sc 08 820 f.s., pts
08 821 f.s. (K640)

Concertino for Guitar and String
Orchestra [18']
string orch,gtr solo
DOBLINGER perf mat rent (K641)

Concerto for Clarinet and Chamber
Orchestra [20']
DOBLINGER perf mat rent (K642)

Concerto for Organ and Orchestra
[30']
2(pic).2(English horn).2(clar in
E flat).2. 4.3.3.0. perc,
strings,org solo
(Leipziger Konzert) DOBLINGER perf
mat rent (K643)

Concerto for String Orchestra [25']
string orch
DOBLINGER perf mat rent (K644)

Concerto for Violin, Viola,
Violoncello and String Orchestra
[18']
string orch,vln solo,vla solo,vcl
solo
DOBLINGER perf mat rent (K645)

Symphony for String Orchestra [20']
string orch
DOBLINGER perf mat rent (K646)

Symphony No. 1 [38']
2(pic).2(English horn).2.2.
4.3.3.1. timp,perc,harp,strings
DOBLINGER perf mat rent (K647)

KRUMELUR see Lundkvist, Per

KRUSE, BJØRN HOWARD (1946-)
Exit [9']
2.2.2.2.sax. 4.4.3.1. perc,pno,
strings
NORGE (K648)

Golem [10']
2.3.2.3. 4.3.3.1. perc,harp,elec
gtr,bass gtr,strings
NORGE (K649)

KRUSH, JAY
Concerto for Brass Quintet and
Orchestra
2(alto fl).2(English
horn).2.2.4sax. 4.3.3.0. timp,
perc,pno,elec org,elec gtr,elec
bass,harp,strings,trp solo,trp/
flügelhorn solo,horn solo,trom
solo,tuba solo
UNICORN 3.9998.7 perf mat rent
(K650)

KRUYF, TON DE (1937-)
Adagio for Orchestra [9']
3.3.3.3. 4.3.3.1. 3perc,harp,pno,
strings
(in memoriam wolfgang fortner) sc
DONEMUS f.s., perf mat rent
(K651)

KRUYF, TON DE (cont'd.)

Canti E Capricci, For Violoncello And
Orch [24']
1.2.0.1. 2.0.0.0. strings,vcl
solo
DONEMUS perf mat rent   (K652)

KRYSTALLER, FOR ALTO FLUTE AND
ORCHESTRA see Rypdal, Terje

KUBELIK, JAN (1880-1940)
Concerto for Violin and Orchestra,
No. 6 [36']
3.3.3.3. 4.2.3.1. timp,2perc,
harp,cel,strings,vln solo
PETERS perf mat rent   (K653)

KUBELIK, RAFAEL (1914-   )
Symphonische Peripetie, For Organ And
Orchestra [20']
3.3.3.3.sax. 4.3.3.1. timp,perc,
cel,strings,org solo
PETERS   (K654)

KUBIK, GAIL (1914-1984)
Symphony No. 3 [15']
2+pic.2+English horn.2+bass
clar.2+contrabsn. 4.3.3.1.
timp,3perc,pno&cel,strings
SCHIRM.G perf mat rent   (K655)

KUBIK, LADISLAV
Concerto for Violin and Orchestra
sc PANTON 2352 f.s.   (K656)

KUBINSKY, R.
Fastnachtstraum, For Saxophone And
Orchestra
KRENN   (K657)

KUBIZEK, AUGUSTIN (1918-   )
Es Liegt Ein Schloss In Osterreich,
For Clarinet And Chamber
Orchestra *Op.43b [11']
2ob,bsn,2horn,strings,clar solo
DOBLINGER perf mat rent   (K658)

Kamptaler Divertimento, For Flute,
Clarinet, Trumpet, Horn And
Orchestra *Op.43 [18']
1(pic).2.1.2. 2.1.3.0. timp,perc,
strings,fl solo,clar solo,trp
solo,horn solo
DOBLINGER perf mat rent   (K659)

KUBLA KHAN, FOR SOLO VOICE AND CHAMBER
ORCHESTRA see McKay, Neil

KUBO, MAYAKO (1947-   )
Concerto for Piano and Orchestra
[26'30"]
3(3pic).2.2.2(contrabsn).
2.3.2.1. 3perc,harp,gtr,
strings,pno solo
study sc BREITKOPF-W PB 5175 f.s.,
perf mat rent   (K660)

KUCERA, VÁCLAV (1929-   )
Avanti [9']
CZECH RADIO   (K661)

Operand [11']
CESKY HUD.   (K662)

Salut [10']
SUPRAPHON   (K663)

KUCHARZYK, HENRY (1953-   )
Chromatics
1.1.1.1. 1.1.1.1. 2perc,pno,
synthesizer,strings
CAN.MUS.CENT. MI 1200 K95C   (K664)

Collisions
2.2.2.2. 4.2.2.1. timp,2perc,pno&
synthesizer,harp,strings
CAN.MUS.CENT. MI 1100 K95CO   (K665)

KUCKUCKSSINFONIE see Kaufmann, Armin

KUHLAU, FRIEDRICH (1786-1832)
Romances, Two, For Alto Flute And
String Orchestra, In A And D
[arr.]
(Bodensohn) string orch,alto fl/fl/
vln solo [5'] pts BODENS 71 f.s.
(K666)

KÜHNL, CLAUS (1957-   )
Ich Liebe Dich, Geliebter, For Solo
Voice And Orchestra [8']
3(pic).2+English horn.2+bass
clar.2+contrabsn. 3.2.2.0.
timp,2perc,harp,cel,strings,S
solo
BREITKOPF-W perf mat rent   (K667)

Music for Double Bass, Harp and
Orchestra [30']
2(alto fl)+pic.1.2+bass clar.0+
contrabsn. 2.2.2.0. timp,perc,
cel,strings,db solo,harp solo
BREITKOPF-W perf mat rent   (K668)

KÜHNL, CLAUS (cont'd.)

Reflexionen [21']
12vln,3vla,3vcl,2db
study sc BREITKOPF-W PB 5104 f.s.
(K669)

Vorspruch Und Gesang Des Einhorns,
For Doublebass And Orchestra
[16']
2(pic,alto fl).1+English horn.1+
bass clar.1+contrabsn. 3.2.0.0.
timp,4perc,harp,cel,strings,db
solo
BREITKOPF-W perf mat rent   (K670)

KULESHA, GARY (1953-   )
Celebration Overture
2.2.2.2. 2.2.0.0. perc,strings
CAN.MUS.CENT. MI 1100 K96C   (K671)

Celebration Overture, version for
large orchestra [10']
2.2.2.2. 4.2.3.1. timp,2perc,
strings
CAN.MUS.CENT. MI 1100 K96C   (K672)

Dreams [21']
2(pic).2.2.2. 4.2.3.1. 3perc,
strings
CAN.MUS.CENT. MI 1100 K96DR   (K673)

Dreams, version for small orchestra
[21']
2(pic).2.2.2. 2.2.1.0. 2perc,
strings
CAN.MUS.CENT. MI 1200 K96DR   (K674)

Journey Into Sunrise, For 5
Saxophones And Orchestra [6']
2.2.2.2. 4.2.3.1. timp,2perc,
strings,soprano sax solo,alto
sax solo,tenor sax solo,
baritone sax solo,bass sax solo
CAN.MUS.CENT. MI 1426 K96JO   (K675)

Lifesongs, For Solo Voice And String
Orchestra [20']
string orch,A solo
CAN.MUS.CENT. MV 1600 K96L   (K676)

Nocturne for Chamber Orchestra [12']
1(alto fl).1.1.1. 1.1.0.1. perc,
strings
CAN.MUS.CENT. MI 1200 K96N   (K677)

Second Essay For Orchestra
2.2.2.2. 4.2.3.1. timp,3perc,pno&
cel,strings
CAN.MUS.CENT. MI 1100 K96S   (K678)

Serenade for String Orchestra
string orch
CAN.MUS.CENT. MI 1500 K96S   (K679)

Snake, For Solo Voice And Chamber
Orchestra [15']
fl,bsn,horn,perc,pno,2vln,vla,
vcl,db,Bar solo
CAN.MUS.CENT. MV 1375 K96SN   (K680)

KUN JOULU ON, FOR SOLO VOICE AND
ORCHESTRA [ARR.] see Kotilainen,
Otto

KUN PAIVA PAISTAA, FOR SOLO VOICE AND
ORCHESTRA [ARR.] see Merikanto,
Oskar

KUNST, JOS (1936-   )
One Way [17']
2.1.3.2. 2.1.1.0. perc,4vln,2vla,
3vcl,2db
PETERS   (K681)

KUNST DER FUGE, DIE [ARR] see Bach,
Johann Sebastian

KUNSTLER CAPRICE see Strauss, Josef

KUNSTLER QUADRILLE see Strauss, Johann,
[Jr.]

KUNSTLERFESTZUG see Liszt, Franz

KUNSTLERLEBEN WALZER see Strauss,
Johann, [Jr.]

KUNZ, ALFRED (1929-   )
Dana's Piece [5']
1.1.1.1. 2.2.1.1. perc,strings
CAN.MUS.CENT. MI 1200 K96DA   (K682)

Saturday Night Barn Dance: Boy's
Night Out [5']
1(pic).1.1.1. 2.2.1.1. timp,perc,
strings
CAN.MUS.CENT. MI 1200 K96SA   (K683)

Singende Vogel Der Ewigkeit, Der, For
Flute And String Orchestra
string orch,fl solo
"Singing Bird Of Eternity, The, For
Flute And String Orchestra"
CAN.MUS.CENT. MI 1621 K96SI
(K684)

KUNZ, ALFRED (cont'd.)

Singing Bird Of Eternity, The, For
Flute And String Orchestra
see Singende Vogel Der Ewigkeit,
Der, For Flute And String
Orchestra

KUNZEN, FRIEDRICH (1761-1817)
Symphony in G minor [15']
0.2.0.2. 2.0.0.0. strings
(Fendler, Edvard) BOOSEY perf mat
rent   (K685)

KUPFERMAN, MEYER (1926-   )
Little Symphony [22']
1(pic).2.0.2. 2.0.0.0. strings
WEINTRB perf mat rent   (K686)

Symphony No. 4 [26']
2(pic).2(English horn).2(bass
clar).2. 4.3.3.0. timp,perc,
harp,strings
WEINTRB perf mat rent   (K687)

KUPKOVIC, LADISLAV (1936-   )
Schwetzinger Divertimento [25']
string orch
sc UNIVER. UE17265 f.s., perf mat
rent   (K688)

KUPREVICIUS, GREDRIUS-ANTANAS
(1944-   )
Sinfonia [22']
2.2.2.2. 4.3.3.0. timp,drums,
bells,harp,2gtr,synthesizer,
fender-orgel, strings
SIKORSKI perf mat rent   (K689)

KURKA, ROBERT FRANK (1921-1957)
Ballade for Horn and String
Orchestra, Op. 36
string orch,horn solo
WEINTRB perf mat rent   (K690)

Concertino for 2 Pianos and
Orchestra, Op. 31
trp,strings,2pno soli
[15'] WEINTRB perf mat rent   (K691)

Concerto for Marimba and Orchestra,
Op. 34 [20']
2(pic).2.2.2. 2.2.1.0. timp,snare
drum,strings,marimba solo
WEINTRB perf mat rent   (K692)

Concerto for Violin and Orchestra,
Op. 8 [15']
2.2.2.2. 2.0.0.0. strings,vln
solo
WEINTRB perf mat rent   (K693)

Julius Caesar *Op.28 [9']
2+pic.2.2.2. 4.2.2.1. timp,
strings
WEINTRB perf mat rent   (K694)

Music for Orchestra, Op. 11
2(pic).3.3(bass
clar).3(contrabsn). 4.3.3.1.
timp,perc,harp,cel,strings
WEINTRB perf mat rent   (K695)

Serenade [20']
1+pic.2.2.2. 2.2.0.0. timp,
strings
WEINTRB perf mat rent   (K696)

Symphony No. 2, Op. 24 [22']
2+pic.2+English horn.2+bass
clar.2+contrabsn. 4.3.3.1.
timp,3perc,strings
WEINTRB perf mat rent   (K697)

KUSAWA see Ware, Peter

KUSS, DER: OVERTURE see Smetana,
Bedrich

KUSS MICH HEUTE BEI MUSIK, FOR SOLO
VOICE AND ORCHESTRA see Pauspertl,
K.

KUTZER, ERNST (1918-   )
Zu Regensburg Auf Der Kirchturmspitz
*Op.39
string orch
BOHM f.s.   (K698)

KUULA, TOIVO (1883-1918)
Aamulaulu, For Solo Voice And String
Orchestra [arr.] *Op.2,No.3
(Koskimies, Eero) string orch,solo
voice [2'] FAZER perf mat rent
(K699)

KUUSISTO, TANELI (1905-1988)
Oi Saavu, Rauhan Juhla, For Solo
Voice And Orchestra [arr.]
(Kuusisto, I.) harp,strings,solo
voice [3'] FAZER perf mat rent
(K700)

KUVIA SUOMESTA see Raasted, Niels Otto

KVALLSFLANOREN see Lunden-Welden,
Gunnar

KVAM, ODDVAR S. (1927-   )
Afterwards Everything Is Too Late,
For Solo Voice And Orchestra
see Att Doda Ett Barn, For Solo
Voice And Orchestra

Att Doda Ett Barn, For Solo Voice And
Orchestra *Op.44 [21']
3.3.3.3. 4.3.2.1. timp,perc,
strings,narrator
"Afterwards Everything Is Too Late,
For Solo Voice And Orchestra"
NORGE   (K701)

Clarinet Clarina, The, For Solo
Voice, Clarinet And Orchestra
see Klarinetten Klarina, For Solo
Voice, Clarinet And Orchestra

Colours, For Harmonica And String
Orchestra *Op.81 [21']
string orch,harmonica solo
NORGE   (K702)

Dagens Nyheter, For Solo Voice And
Chamber Orchestra *Op.54 [18']
"Today's News, For Solo Voice And
Chamber Orchestra" sc MUSIKK
f.s., perf mat rent   (K703)

Elegy for English Horn and Orchestra,
Op. 8 [7']
timp,strings,English horn solo
NORGE   (K704)

Four Ordtak *Op.40a
1.1.1.1. 2.1.1.0. timp,2perc,
strings
NORGE   (K705)

Klarinetten Klarina, For Solo Voice,
Clarinet And Orchestra *Op.34
[11']
2.2.1.2. 2.0.1.1. timp,perc,
strings,clar solo,narrator
"Clarinet Clarina, The, For Solo
Voice, Clarinet And Orchestra"
NORGE   (K706)

Konsert Ouverture *Op.17 [10']
2.2.1.2. 4.4.4.1. timp,perc,harp,
strings
NORGE   (K707)

Ostinato Festoso *Op.37 [8']
3.3.3.3. 4.3.3.0. timp,perc,harp,
strings
NORGE   (K708)

Phoenix, For Violoncello And
Orchestra *Op.78 [18'30"]
2.2.2.2. 4.2.3.0. timp,3perc,
harp,strings,vcl solo
NORGE   (K709)

Prolog *Op.13 [7']
2.2.2.2. 4.3.3.1. timp,perc,
strings
NORGE   (K710)

Suffragette, For Piano And Orchestra
*Op.29 [21']
2.2.2.2. 4.3.2.0. timp,perc,
strings,pno solo
NORGE   (K711)

Symphony No. 1, Op. 23
see Tre Kontraster For Orkester

Today's News, For Solo Voice And
Chamber Orchestra
see Dagens Nyheter, For Solo Voice
And Chamber Orchestra

Tre Kontraster For Orkester (Symphony
No. 1, Op. 23) [18']
2.2.2.2. 4.4.4.0. timp,perc,harp,
strings
NORGE   (K712)

Vibrasjoner *Op.38 [12']
3.3.3.3. 4.3.2.1. perc,harp,
strings
"Vibrations" NORGE   (K713)

Vibrations
see Vibrasjoner

KVANDAL, JOHAN (1919-   )
Cantata for Solo Voice and Orchestra,
Op. 10 [8']
3.2.2.2. 4.2.0.0. timp,perc,
strings,S/T solo
NORGE   (K714)

Che Cosa E Questa Amore, For Solo
Voice And Orchestra *Op.49
1.2.0.2. 2.0.0.0. strings,S solo
NORSK perf mat rent   (K715)

Concerto for Chamber Orchestra, Op.
55
sc NORSK $23.75, perf mat rent
                                   (K716)

KVANDAL, JOHAN (cont'd.)

Concerto for Oboe and String
Orchestra, Op. 46
string orch,ob solo
NORSK perf mat rent   (K717)

Concerto for Organ and String
Orchestra, Op. 62 [15']
string orch,org solo
NORSK perf mat rent   (K718)

Concerto for Violin and Orchestra,
Op. 52 [31']
2(pic).2.2.2. 4.3.3.1. timp,
3perc,cel,strings,vln solo
NORSK perf mat rent   (K719)

Legend, For Bassoon And String
Orchestra *Op.61 [7']
string orch,bsn solo NORSK perf mat
rent   (K720)

Norsk Utsyn *Op.67 [15']
2.2.2.2. 4.3.3.0. timp,perc,
strings
NORGE   (K721)

Poem for Violin and String Orchestra
[6']
string orch,vln solo
NORSK perf mat rent   (K722)

Skipper Worse Suite *Op.28 [17']
2.2.2.2. 2.3.2.0. timp,perc,cel,
strings
study sc NORSK f.s.   (K723)

Symphony No. 1, Op. 18 [32']
1(pic).2(English horn).2.2.
4.2.0.0. timp,perc,strings
NORSK perf mat rent   (K724)

Triptychon *Op.53
3.2.2.2. 4.3.3.1. timp,perc,
strings
sc NORSK $19.75, perf mat rent
                                   (K725)

Visions Norvegiennes *Op.76 [15']
2.2.2.2. 4.3.3.0. timp,perc,
strings
NORSK perf mat rent   (K726)

KVEITA, FOR NARRATOR AND CHAMBER
ORCHESTRA see Berg, Olav

KVELDINGSETER, FOR SOLO VOICE AND
ORCHESTRA [ARR.] see Sommerfeldt,
Oistein

KVERNDOKK, GISLE (1967-   )
Kong Valemon, For Solo Voice And
Orchestra
2.2.2.2. 4.2.3.1. timp,perc,harp,
strings,S solo
(Version B) NORGE   (K727)

Puls
4.3.3.3. 6.4.3.1. timp,perc,harp,
pno&cel,strings
NORGE   (K728)

KVINTEKVAESA see Vea, Ketil

KYU NO KYOKU see Miki, Minoru

L

LA MOTTE, DIETER DE
see MOTTE, DIETHER DE LA

LA PRESLE, JACQUES (PAUL GABRIEL) DE
(1888-1969)
Concerto for Piano and Orchestra in D
[22']
3.3.2.2. 4.2.3.1. timp,3perc,
harp,cel,strings,pno solo
BILLAUDOT perf mat rent   (L1)

LABOR! see Sermila, Jarmo

LABORATORIUM FUR 11 MUSIKER see
Globokar, Vinko

LABYRINTH see Fišer, Luboš see Rypdal,
Terje see Svoboda, Tomas

LABYRINTH I see Bose, Hans Jürgen

LABYRINTH: SUITE see Schnittke, Alfred

LAC DES CYGNES, LE: SELECTION [ARR.]
see Tchaikovsky, Piotr Ilyich, Swan
Lake: Selection [arr.]

LAC DES CYGNES: PAS DE DEUX, "LE CYGNE
BLANC" [ARR.] see Tchaikovsky,
Piotr Ilyich, Swan Lake: Pas De
Deux, "White Swan" [arr.]

LAC DES CYGNES: PAS DE DEUX, "LE CYGNE
NOIR" [ARR.] see Tchaikovsky, Piotr
Ilyich, Swan Lake: Pas De Deux,
"Black Swan" [arr.]

LACHENMANN, HELMUT FRIEDRICH
(1935-   )
Accanto, For Clarinet And Orchestra
study sc BREITKOPF-W PB 5109 f.s.
                                   (L2)

Ausklang, For Piano And Orchestra
[50']
4(pic,alto fl).3.3+bass clar.3+
contrabsn. 4.3.3.1. 4perc,harp,
strings,pno solo
study sc BREITKOPF-W PB 5168 f.s.,
perf mat rent   (L3)

Harmonica [31']
4(pic).4.3+bass clar.3+contrabsn.
4.4.3+bass trom.0+db tuba.
8perc,harp,pno,elec org,cel,
strings,tuba solo
study sc BREITKOPF-W PB 5117 f.s.
                                   (L4)

Mouvement
2.0.2(bass clar).0. 0.2.0.0.
timp,perc,2vla,2vcl,db
BREITKOPF-W perf mat rent   (L5)

Staub [23']
3(pic).2.2.2+contrabsn. 4.2.3.0.
3perc,strings
study sc BREITKOPF-W PB 5177 f.s.,
perf mat rent   (L6)

Tableau [8']
BREITKOPF-W perf mat rent   (L7)

Tanzsuite Mit Deutschlandlied
study sc BREITKOPF-W PB 5114 f.s.
                                   (L8)

LACHIAN DANCES NOS. 1-6 see Janácek,
Leos

LACHIAN DANCES NOS. 1 AND 2 see
Janácek, Leos

LACHIAN DANCES NOS. 3 AND 4 see
Janácek, Leos

LACHIAN DANCES NOS. 5 AND 6 see
Janácek, Leos

LACHNER, FRANZ (1803-1890)
Ball Suite *Op.170
KISTNER perf mat rent   (L9)

LACHRIMAE see Sorensen, Bent

LACOME, PAUL (-JEAN-JACQUES)
(1838-1920)
Suite Africaine
2.2.2.2. 4.2.3.0. timp,perc,harp,
strings
BILLAUDOT perf mat rent   (L10)

LACOUR, GUY (1932-   )
Hommage A Jacques Ibert, For Alto
Saxophone And Orchestra [13']
1.1.2.1. 0.1.0.0. timp,perc,
strings,alto sax solo
BILLAUDOT perf mat rent   (L11)

LACRIMOSA see Penderecki, Krzysztof

LAD OF THE HARP, FOR SOLO VOICE AND
    ORCHESTRA see Halldorsson, Skuli

LADERMAN, EZRA (1924-   )
    Concerto for Flute and Orchestra
        [29']
        3(pic).2+English horn.2+bass
        clar.2+contrabsn. 4.2.3.0.
        timp,3perc,harp,strings,fl solo
        SCHIRM.G perf mat rent   (L12)

    Concerto for Flute, Bassoon and
        Orchestra [30']
        2+pic.2+English horn.2+bass
        clar.1+contrabsn. 4.2.3(bass
        trom).0. timp,2perc,harp,
        strings,fl solo,bsn solo
        SCHIRM.G perf mat rent   (L13)

    Concerto for Orchestra [35']
        3(pic).2+English horn.2+bass
        clar.2+contrabsn. 4.3.3.1.
        timp,perc,strings
        (A Play Within A Play) SCHIRM.G
        perf mat rent   (L14)

    Concerto For Orchestra, Chamber
        Orchestra Version [20']
        2.2.2.2. 2.2.1.0. 2perc,strings
        SCHIRM.G perf mat rent   (L15)

    Concerto for Piano and Orchestra
        [26']
        2.2.2.2. 4.3.4.0. timp,2perc,
        strings,pno solo
        SCHIRM.G perf mat rent   (L16)

    Concerto for Piano and Orchestra, No.
        2
        2.2.2.2. 4.2.2.0. timp,3perc,
        strings,pno solo
        SCHIRM.G perf mat rent   (L17)

    Concerto for String Quartet and
        Orchestra [25']
        2+pic.2.2.2+contrabsn. 4.2.3.0.
        timp,strings,string quar soli
        SCHIRM.G perf mat rent   (L18)

    Concerto for Viola and Chamber
        Orchestra [32']
        1(pic).2.1.2. 2.0.0.0. pno,
        strings,vla solo
        SCHIRM.G perf mat rent   (L19)

    Concerto for Violin and Orchestra
        [27']
        2+pic.2.2+bass clar.2+contrabsn.
        4.2.3.0. timp,perc,strings,vln
        solo
        SCHIRM.G perf mat rent   (L20)

    Concerto for Violin, Violoncello and
        Orchestra [40']
        2.2.2.2. 4.2.3.0. timp,3perc,
        harp,strings,vln solo,vcl solo
        SCHIRM.G perf mat rent   (L21)

    Concerto for Violoncello and
        Orchestra [28']
        2+pic.2.2.2. 4.2.3.1. timp,3perc,
        strings,vcl solo
        SCHIRM.G perf mat rent   (L22)

    Pentimento [28']
        3(pic).2+English horn.2+clar in E
        flat+bass clar.2+contrabsn.
        4.3.3.1. timp,3perc,pno&cel,
        strings
        SCHIRM.G perf mat rent   (L23)

    Sanctuary [23']
        3(pic).2+English horn.2+bass
        clar.2+contrabsn. 4.3.3.1.
        timp,3perc,harp,strings
        SCHIRM.G perf mat rent   (L24)

    Sonore [25']
        2+pic+alto fl.2+English horn.2+
        clar in E flat+bass clar.2+
        contrabsn. 4.3.2+bass trom.1.
        timp,4perc,strings
        SCHIRM.G perf mat rent   (L25)

    Summer Solstice [17']
        2.2.2.2. 4.2.3.1. timp,3perc,cel,
        vibra,strings
        SCHIRM.G perf mat rent   (L26)

    Symphonie Concertante [30']
        2.2.2.2. 4.2.2.0. timp,4perc,
        strings,pic solo,English horn
        solo,clar solo,trp solo,trom
        solo
        SCHIRM.G perf mat rent   (L27)

    Symphony No. 1 [30']
        2+pic.2+English horn.2(clar in E
        flat)+bass clar.2+contrabsn.
        4.3.4.1. timp,5perc,harp,
        strings
        SCHIRM.G perf mat rent   (L28)

    Symphony No. 2 [24']
        3.3.3.3(contrabsn). 4.3.3.2.
        timp,perc,harp,org,cel,strings

LADERMAN, EZRA (cont'd.)

    (Luther) SCHIRM.G perf mat rent
                                    (L29)
    Symphony No. 3 [45']
        3.3.3.3. 4.3.3.1. timp,harp,org,
        strings
        (Jerusalem) SCHIRM.G perf mat rent
                                    (L30)
    Symphony No. 4 [28']
        2+pic.2+English horn.2+bass
        clar.2+contrabsn. 6.4.4.1.
        timp,3perc,strings
        SCHIRM.G perf mat rent   (L31)

    Symphony No. 5 [40']
        3+pic.3+English horn.3+bass
        clar.3+contrabsn. 4.4.3.1.
        timp,strings
        (Isaiah) SCHIRM.G perf mat rent
                                    (L32)
    Symphony No. 6 [38']
        2+pic.2+English horn.2+bass
        clar.2+contrabsn.tenor sax.
        4.3.3.1. timp,4perc,cel,harp,
        strings,S solo
        SCHIRM.G perf mat rent   (L33)

    Symphony No. 7 [40']
        3(pic).3(English horn).3(bass
        clar).2+contrabsn. 4.3.3.1.
        timp,3perc,strings
        SCHIRM.G perf mat rent   (L34)

    Visions "Columbus" [25']
        3(pic).2+English horn.2(bass
        clar).2+contrabsn.tenor sax.
        4.3(piccolo trp).3.1. timp,
        perc,2harp,pno,cel,Ondes
        Martenot,synthesizer,strings
        SCHIRM.G perf mat rent   (L35)

LADINA see Lorenzini, Danilo

LADY BE GOOD: OVERTURE, [ARR.] see
    Gershwin, George

LADY MACBETH OF MTZENSK: SUITE see
    Shostakovich, Dmitri

LADY OF SHALOTT, THE see Bliss, [Sir]
    Arthur (Drummond)

LADY RADNOR'S SUITE see Parry, [Sir]
    Charles Hubert Hastings

LAETI see Sigurbjörnsson, Thorkell

LAGANA, RUGGERO (1956-   )
    A L'allemande [11']
        pic,fl,clar,bass clar,vibra,cel,
        pno,2vln,vla,vcl
        SONZOGNO perf mat rent   (L36)

LAJOVIC, ALEKSANDER (1920-   )
    Estro Melodico, L' [27']
        string orch
        DRUSTVO DSS 1048 perf mat rent
                                    (L37)
    Ludi Contrapunctici [11']
        2(pic).2(English horn).2(bass
        clar).2(contrabsn). 4.3.3.1.
        timp,strings
        DRUSTVO DSS 979 perf mat rent (L38)

    Musica Ad Morem Maiorum [25']
        string orch
        DRUSTVO DSS 978 perf mat rent (L39)

LAJTHA, LASZLO (1891-1963)
    Variations, Op. 44
        sc EMB 10278 f.s., perf mat rent
                                    (L40)
LALANDE, MICHEL RICHARD DE
    see DÉLALANDE, MICHEL-RICHARD

LALO, EDOUARD (1823-1892)
    Arlequin [3']
        2+pic.2.2.2. 2.2.3.0. timp,perc,
        strings
        KALMUS A6790 sc $10.00, set $15.00,
        pts $1.00, ea.   (L41)

    Deux Aubades [9']
        1.1.1.1. 1.0.0.0. strings
        KALMUS A6102 sc $10.00, set $10.00
                                    (L42)
    Rhapsody
        KALMUS A7368 sc $25.00, set $65.00,
        pts $2.50, ea., perf mat rent
                                    (L43)
    Scherzo
        KALMUS A5576 sc $12.00, perf mat
        rent, set $25.00, pts $1.00, ea.
                                    (L44)
    Suite En Blanc [arr.]
        (Lifar, Serge) 2.2.2.4. 4.4.3.1.
        timp,perc,2harp,strings [43']
        BOIS perf mat rent   (L45)

LALONDE, ALAIN (1951-   )
    Air-Metal
        4.3.3.3. 4.3.3.1. 3perc,strings
        CAN.MUS.CENT. MI 1100 L 212A (L46)

LALONDE, ALAIN (cont'd.)

    Dans L'univers, L'amour
        2.2.3.3. 2.2.2.1. 2perc,strings,
        electronic tape
        CAN.MUS.CENT. MI 9400 L212DA (L47)

LAMAN, WIM (1946-   )
    Confronti, For Horn And Orchestra
        [14'15"]
        2.0.3.0.3sax. 8.2.2.1. perc,
        strings,horn solo
        sc DONEMUS f.s., perf mat rent
                                    (L48)
    Pancabana [17']
        fl&pic,ob,basset horn,bsn,horn,
        harmonium,pno,2vln,vla,vcl,db
        DONEMUS perf mat rent   (L49)

LAMB, PETER (1925-   )
    Concertino for Flute and Chamber
        Orchestra [10']
        2.2.2.2. 2.0.0.0. strings,fl solo
        BOOSEY perf mat rent   (L50)

LAMBERT, CONSTANT (1905-1951)
    Pomona [20']
        2.1.2.1. 2.2.1.0. timp,triangle,
        strings
        OXFORD perf mat rent   (L51)

    Romeo And Juliet [30']
        1.1.2.1. 2.2.1.0. timp,perc,
        strings
        OXFORD perf mat rent   (L52)

LAMBIJ, TON (1954-   )
    Scenes, For Violoncello And Orchestra
        [21']
        2.2.2.2. 2.2.0.0. timp,strings,
        vcl solo
        DONEMUS perf mat rent   (L53)

LAMBTON QUAY MARCH see Pruden, Larry

LAMENT see Bridge, Frank see Jacobson,
    Maurice see Pentland, Barbara

LAMENT AND CANTORIAL CHANT, FOR VIOLA
    AND STRING ORCHESTRA see Glick,
    Srul Irving

LAMENT FOR STRINGS see Sculthorpe,
    Peter [Joshua]

LAMENT IN MEMORY OF LORD MOUNTBATTEN OF
    BURMA see Williamson, Malcolm

LAMENTATIONES JEREMIAE PROPHETAE, FOR
    SOLO VOICES AND ORCHESTRA see
    Zelenka, Jan Dismas

LAMENTATIONS see Dorff, Daniel Jay

LAMENTO see Dallinger, Fridolin see
    Eklund, Hans see Hogenhaven, Knud
    see Srebotnjak, Alojz F.

LAMENTO "ACH, DASS ICH WASSERS GNUG
    HÄTTE", FOR SOLO VOICE AND
    ORCHESTRA see Bach, Johann
    Christoph

LAMENTO DI ORLANDO, FOR SOLO VOICE AND
    ORCHESTRA see Bialas, Günter

LAMENTS see Hodkinson, Sydney P.

LAMINA, FOR TROMBONE AND ORCHESTRA see
    Gehlhaar, Rolf

LAMPARILLA see Gerhard, Roberto

LAMPERSBERG, GERHARD (1928-   )
    Ahnung, For Violin And Orchestra
        [15']
        1.1.1.1.alto sax. 1.1.1.1. 2perc,
        cel,harmonium,pno,strings,vln
        solo
        UNIVER. perf mat rent   (L54)

    Dornroschen, For Solo Voices And
        Chamber Group [35']
        1(pic).0.1.0. 1.1.1.0. 2perc,
        string quin,SSAATBar&speaking
        voice
        UNIVER. perf mat rent   (L55)

    Pfeffer Und Salz, For Solo Voice And
        Instrumental Ensemble [12']
        clar,sax,horn,trp,trom,perc,cel&
        harmonium&pno,2vln,vla,vcl,db,
        speaking voice
        UNIVER. perf mat rent   (L56)

    Verwirrung, For Violoncello And
        Orchestra [15']
        1.1.1.1.alto sax. 1.1.1.1. perc,
        cel,harmonium,pno,strings
        without vcl,vcl solo
        UNIVER. perf mat rent   (L57)

LAMPUGNANI, GIOVANNI BATTISTA
(ca. 1708-ca. 1788)
Sinfonie, Five
see Martini, [Padre] Giovanni
Battista, Sinfonie, Four

Sinfonie, Five *see Martini, [Padre]
Giovanni Battista, Sinfonie, Four

LANCEN, SERGE (1922-)
Concert, For Violin, Double Bass And
String Orchestra [16']
string orch,vln solo,db solo
BILLAUDOT perf mat rent   (L58)

Concerto for Violin and Orchestra
[26']
2.2.2.2. 2.2.0.0. timp,perc,
strings,vln solo
BILLAUDOT perf mat rent   (L59)

Concerto Rapsodie, For Piano And
Orchestra [14'30"]
2.1.2.1. 2.2.2.1. timp,perc,
strings,pno solo
BILLAUDOT perf mat rent   (L60)

Fantaisie Creole, For Piano And
Orchestra [24']
2.1.2.1. 2.2.2.0. timp,2perc,
strings,pno solo
BILLAUDOT perf mat rent   (L61)

Instants [16']
timp,2perc,strings
BILLAUDOT perf mat rent   (L62)

Triptyque [25']
3.3.3.3. 4.3.3.1. timp,2perc,pno,
strings
BILLAUDOT perf mat rent   (L63)

LANCINO, THIERRY
Profondeurs De Champ, For Bass
Clarinet And Instrumental
Ensemble [16']
1(pic).1.1(clar in E flat,bass
clar).1.tenor sax. 1.1.1.1.
timp,2perc,pno,harp,2vln,vla,
vcl,db,electronic equipment
AMPHION perf mat rent   (L64)

LAND BEAUTIFUL, THE see Chan, Ka Nin

LANDES FARBEN see Strauss, Johann,
[Sr.]

LANDLER see Rihm, Wolfgang

LANDLER-FANTASIE see Bialas, Günter

LANDLER TOPOGRAPHIEN see Zimmermann,
Walter

LÄNDLICHE SUITE see Provazník, Anatol

LANDLICHE TANZE see Knab

LANDOWSKI, MARCEL (1915-)
Au Bout Du Chagrin Une Fenetre
Ouverte, For Trumpet And
Orchestra [24']
2.0.2.2. 2.0.1.0. perc,pno,
strings,electronic tape,trp
solo
SALABERT perf mat rent   (L65)

Aux Mendiants Du Ciel, For Solo Voice
And Orchestra [9']
CHOUDENS perf mat rent   (L66)

Chant De Solitude, For Solo Voices
And Orchestra [10']
CHOUDENS perf mat rent   (L67)

Enfant Appelle, Un, For Solo Voice,
Violoncello And Orchestra [23']
3.2.2.2. 4.2.2.1. perc,harp,pno,
strings,vcl solo,S solo
SALABERT perf mat rent   (L68)

Fantome De L'opera, Le: Suite [55']
3.2.2+bass clar.2+contrabsn.
4.4.3.1. 3perc,pno,org,harp,
strings,electronic tape
SALABERT perf mat rent   (L69)

Femme Sans Passe, La [11']
CHOUDENS perf mat rent   (L70)

Improvisation, For Trombone And
Orchestra [11'30"]
2.2.2.2. 2.2.0.0. timp,perc,
strings,trom solo
SALABERT perf mat rent   (L71)

Prison, La, For Solo Voice,
Violoncello And String Orchestra
[30']
string orch,pno,vcl solo,S solo
study sc SALABERT f.s., perf mat
rent   (L72)

Quatre Preludes Pour L'opera Des
Bastilles, For Violin And String
Orchestra [20']

LANDOWSKI, MARCEL (cont'd.)
string orch,opt timp,vln solo
SALABERT perf mat rent   (L73)

Rire De Nils Halerius, Le: Ballet Des
Jeux Du Monde [20']
CHOUDENS perf mat rent   (L74)

Symphonie De Montsegur, La, For Solo
Voice And Orchestra [35']
2+pic.2+ob d'amore.2(bass
clar).2+contrabsn. 4.4.3.1.
perc,gtr,Ondes Martenot,
strings,synthesizer,SBar soli
SALABERT perf mat rent   (L75)

Symphony No. 4
3.3(ob d'amore).3(bass
clar).3(contrabsn). 4.4.3.1.
perc,harp,pno,strings
SALABERT perf mat rent   (L76)

LANDSCAPE see Matthews, Colin

LANDSCAPE, FOR SOLO VOICE AND ORCHESTRA
see Jordan, Sverre, Landskab, For
Solo Voice And Orchestra

LANDSCAPE IN THOUGHTS see Vacek, Miloš

LANDSCAPE OF NORTHERN SHENSI, FOR
HARMONICA AND ORCHESTRA see Du,
Ming-Xin

LANDSCAPE; OPEN; QUIET see Berge,
Håkon, Landskap; Apent; Stille

LANDSCAPE WITH PIPERS see Klein, Lothar

LANDSCAPE WITH TRAVELER see Swafford,
Jan

LANDSCAPES see Revueltas, Silvestre,
Paisajes

LANDSCHAFT DER VERGANGENHEIT see Brass,
Nikolaus

LANDSKAB, FOR SOLO VOICE AND ORCHESTRA
see Jordan, Sverre

LANDSKAP; APENT; STILLE see Berge,
Håkon

LANG, DAVID (1957-)
Eating Living Monkeys [8']
3(pic).3(English horn).3(bass
clar).3. 4.3.3.1. 4perc,harp,
pno,strings
sc GUNMAR MP4032 $20.00, perf mat
rent   (L77)

LANG, ISTVAN (1933-)
Concerto for Clarinet, Harp and
Orchestra
sc EMB 10246 f.s.   (L78)

Egloga
sc EMB 10253 f.s.   (L79)

Impulsioni, For Oboe And Chamber
Orchestra
sc EMB 10100 f.s.   (L80)

Symphony No. 2
sc EMB 10207 f.s.   (L81)

Symphony No. 3
sc EMB 10269 f.s., perf mat rent
                               (L82)
Symphony No. 4
sc EMB 10270 f.s., perf mat rent
                               (L83)
LANG, JOHANN GEORG (1724-1794)
Symphonies,Three
see Agrell, Johan Joachim,
Symphonies, Five

LANG, PHILIP JOSEPH (1911-)
Pow Wow [4']
3(pic).3(English
horn).3.3(contrabsn). 4.4.3.1.
timp,5perc,strings
MARKS   (L84)

LANGELEIKEN see Tveitt, Geirr

LANGLAIS, JEAN (1907-1991)
Concerto for Organ and Orchestra, No.
3
min sc UNIVER. PH00504 $17.50 (L85)

LÅNGSTRÖM, OLLE (1952-)
Symphony No. 2 [34']
0.0.0.0. 4.3.3.1. timp,perc,harp,
strings,org
STIM   (L86)

LANKESTER, MICHAEL
Make Your Own Orchestra [16']
2.2.2.2. 3.2.0.1. perc,harp,
strings, bamboo flute, drinking
straw, hosepipe in F, bottles,
broomstick bass
MMB perf mat rent   (L87)

LANKESTER, MICHAEL (cont'd.)
Seven Nursery Rhymes [20']
2(pic).2.2(bass clar).2. 2.1.1.0.
timp,2perc,harp,strings
MMB perf mat rent   (L88)

Time Machine, The, For Narrator And
Orchestra [7']
1(pic).1.1.1. 2.1.1.0. perc,
strings,narrator
MMB perf mat rent   (L89)

Two Christmas Carols
1+alto fl.2.1+bass clar.2. 4.2.3.0.
2perc,harp,strings [6']
(contains: Dormi, Il Mio Bimbo;
Stille Nacht) MMB perf mat rent
                               (L90)
LANTERNES DES MORTES see Hoddinott,
Alun

LANTIER, PIERRE (1910-)
Concert En 3 Parties, For Trumpet And
Orchestra [9']
2.2.1.1. 1.0.0.0. timp,strings,
trp solo
LEMOINE perf mat rent   (L91)

Introduction, Romance Et Allegro, For
Bass Trombone And Orchestra [8']
1.1.1.1. 1.1.0.0. timp,perc,cel,
strings,bass trom/vcl solo
LEMOINE perf mat rent   (L92)

LANZA, ALCIDES E. (1929-)
Bour-Drones [13']
13strings
CAN.MUS.CENT. MI 1500 L297B0 (L93)

Eideses II [10']
2horn,2trom,tuba,3perc,3vcl,2db
BOOSEY perf mat rent   (L94)

Transformaciones
1.0.1(bass clar).1. 1.0.0.0.
strings
min sc PEER MUSIK 61480-851 $8.00
                               (L95)
LAPARRA, RAOUL (1876-1943)
Dimanche Basque, Un [20']
CHOUDENS perf mat rent   (L96)

LAPHAM, CLAUDE
Concerto for Saxophone and Orchestra
[28']
2.2.2.2. 4.2.3.1. timp,perc,harp,
strings,sax solo
MCA perf mat rent   (L97)

LAPORTE, ANDRE (1931-)
Schloss, Das: Suite No. 1 [17']
4(pic,alto fl).4(English
horn).4(clar in E flat,bass
clar).3(contrabsn). 4.4.3.1.
timp,3perc,harp,pno,cel,strings
BREITKOPF-W perf mat rent   (L98)

Schloss, Das: Suite No. 2 [12']
4(pic,alto fl).4(English
horn).4(clar in E flat,bass
clar).3(contrabsn). 4.4.3.1.
timp,3perc,harp,pno,cel,strings
BREITKOPF-W perf mat rent   (L99)

Schloss-Sinfonie [26']
4(pic,alto fl).4(English
horn).4(clar in E flat,bass
clar).3(contrabsn). 4.4.3.1.
timp,3perc,harp,pno,cel,strings
BREITKOPF-W perf mat rent   (L100)

LAPPISH OVERTURE see Strömholm, Folke,
Samisk Ouverture

LAPPONICA see Koch, Erland von

LARCH TREES see Arnold, Malcolm

LARCHET, JOHN F.
Two Characteristic Pieces [6']
4.3.2(bass clar).1. 0.0.0.0.
xylo,strings
NOVELLO perf mat rent   (L101)

LAREDO [ARR.] see Williams, Clifton

LARGHETTO, FOR HORN AND ORCHESTRA see
Chabrier, [Alexis-] Emmanuel

LARGHETTO FOR STRINGS see Pluister,
Simon

LARGO AND ADAGIO see Kancheli, Giya

LARGO AND ALLEGRO, FOR FLUTE AND STRING
ORCHESTRA see Tchaikovsky, Piotr
Ilyich

LARGO DESOLATO see Bischof, Rainer

LARGO NOSTALGICO see Breimo, Bjørn

LARGO-SINFONIE see Shut, Vladislav

LARMES DE JACQUELINE, LES, FOR
    VIOLONCELLO AND STRING ORCHESTRA,
    OP. 76, NO. 2 [ARR.] see Offenbach,
    Jacques

LARMES DES ROCHERS, LES see Cerchio,
    Bruno

LARRAURI, ANTON (1932-   )
    Aldatza, For Solo Voice And Chamber
        Orchestra [16']
        1.1.1.1. 1.0.0.0. bells,strings,
            Bar solo
        ALPUERTO   (L102)

    Aldatza, For Solo Voice And Orchestra
        [17']
        2.2.2.2. 2.2.2.1. timp,perc,
            strings,Mez solo
        ALPUERTO   (L103)

    Ari-Ta-Ari [12']
        2(pic).2.2.2. 4.3.3.1. timp,perc,
            strings
        ALPUERTO   (L104)

    Contingencias [22']
        2.1+English horn.2.2. 2.2.2.0.
            timp,6perc,pno,strings
        ALPUERTO   (L105)

    De Profundis [8']
        fl,ob,clar,bsn,strings
        ALPUERTO   (L106)

    Dedalo [15']
        2+pic.2+English horn.2+bass
            clar.2+contrabsn. 4.2.3.1.
            perc,pno,cel,xylo,harp,strings
        ALPUERTO   (L107)

    Dialogos, For Piano And Orchestra
        [30']
        2.2.2.2. 4.3.3.1. 5perc,strings,
            pno solo
        ALPUERTO   (L108)

    Gardunak [15']
        2+pic.2.2.2. 4.4.3.1. timp,perc,
            strings
        ALPUERTO   (L109)

    Gure Seaska [15']
        2+pic.2.2.2. 4.3.3.1. timp,perc,
            strings
        ALPUERTO   (L110)

    Maritxu [8'30"]
        2+pic.2.2.2. 3.3.2.1. timp,perc,
            strings
        ALPUERTO   (L111)

    Soinua, For Solo Voice And Orchestra
        [11']
        1.1.2.1. 2.2.2.1. perc,harp,
            strings,T solo
        ALPUERTO   (L112)

LARSEN, EILERT LINDORFF
    see LINDORFF-LARSEN, EILERT

LARSSON, LARS-ERIK (1908-1986)
    Musica Permutatio *Op.66 [10']
        2.2.2.2. 4.2.3.1. timp,perc,
            strings
        sc GEHRMANS 6091P f.s., perf mat
            rent   (L113)

LASON, ALEKSANDER (1951-   )
    Gory
        "Mountains, The" (co-edition with
            Tonos) POLSKIE   (L114)

    Mountains, The
        see Gory

    Symphony No. 2
        4.3.3.3. 4.4.4.1. perc,pno,
            strings
        TONOS   (L115)

LATE SUMMER, FOR SOLO VOICE AND
    ORCHESTRA see Jordan, Sverre,
    Eftersommer, For Solo Voice And
    Orchestra

LATHAM, WILLIAM PETERS (1917-   )
    Concertino for Alto Saxophone and
        Orchestra
        sc,pts DORN $80.00   (L116)

    Sisyphus 1971, For Alto Saxophone And
        Instrumental Ensemble [6'40"]
        elec pno,strings,alto sax solo
        BILLAUDOT perf mat rent   (L117)

LATIN SUITE see Lorentzen, Bent

LAUBA, CHRISTIAN (1952-   )
    Jeux [21']
        fl,4sax,horn,trp,trom,perc,pno,
            strings
        BILLAUDOT perf mat rent   (L118)

LAUBE, ANTONIN (1718-1784)
    Symphony
        (Rutova; Pilkova; Peskova) ("The
            Symphony" Vol. B-XIII) sc GARLAND
            ISBN 0-8240-3851-7 $90.00
            contains also: Barta, Josef,
            Symphonies, Two; Kammel, Antonin,
            Symphonies, Two; Mysliveczek,
            Joseph, Symphonies, Three; Mašek,
            Vincenc, Symphony   (L119)

LAUBER, ANNE (1943-   )
    Concerto for String Quartet and
        Orchestra
        2.2.2.2. 4.2.3.0. timp,perc,
            strings,string quar soli
        CAN.MUS.CENT. MI 1417 L366CO (L120)

    Ouverture Canadienne [9']
        2(pic).2.2.2. 4.2.3.0. timp,
            2perc,strings
        CAN.MUS.CENT. MI 1100 L3660U (L121)

    Three Moods, For Doublebass And
        Orchestra [25']
        2.2.2.2. 4.2.2.0. timp,perc,
            strings,db solo
        CAN.MUS.CENT. MI 1314 L366TH (L122)

LAUDATE DOMINUM, FOR SOLO VOICE AND
    STRING ORCHESTRA see Campra, André

LAUDATE PUERI, FOR SOLO VOICE AND
    ORCHESTRA see Fiocco, Joseph-Hector
    see Zelenka, Jan Dismas

LAUDES I see Stroe, Aurel

LAUDES II see Stroe, Aurel

LAUDI, FOR SOLO VOICES AND ORCHESTRA
    see Stout, Alan

LAUERMANN, HERBERT (1955-   )
    Caccia [9']
        2.2.2.2. 3.2.1.0. timp,glock,
            harp,strings
        DOBLINGER perf mat rent   (L123)

    Ehepaar, Das, For Solo Voices And
        Instrumental Ensemble [37']
        1(pic).0.1.1. 0.1.1.0. mand,gtr,
            harp,xylorimba,3perc,pno,vla,
            db,S&speaking voice
        DOBLINGER perf mat rent   (L124)

    Kammersymphonie [20']
        1(pic).1.1.1. 2.0.0.0. 2vln,vla,
            vcl,db
        DOBLINGER perf mat rent   (L125)

    Phantasy On Me [17']
        2(pic).2+English horn.2+bass
            clar.2+contrabsn. 4.2.3.1.
            timp,perc,harp,pno,strings
        study sc DOBLINGER STP 607 f.s.,
            perf mat rent   (L126)

LAUFER, BEATRICE (1923-   )
    Orchestral Trilogy [20']
        2(pic).1.2.2. 2.3.2.1. timp,
            2perc,strings
        MCA perf mat rent   (L127)

LAULUJA KANTELETTAREN RUNOIHNIN, FOR
    SOLO VOICE AND ORCHESTRA see
    Kilpinen, Yrjö

LAURIE LEE SONGS, FOR SOLO VOICE AND
    ORCHESTRA see Wood, Hugh Bradshaw

LAUT UND TRAUT POLKA see Strauss,
    Eduard

LAVAGNE, ANDRE (1913-   )
    Poeme D'Adonis [20'30"]
        2.2.2.2. 2.2.1.0. timp,perc,pno,
            cel,harp,strings
        BILLAUDOT perf mat rent   (L128)

    Vision De La Quatrieme Eglogue
        [8'40"]
        9vln,4vla,4vcl,2db
        BILLAUDOT perf mat rent   (L129)

LAVENDA, RICHARD (1955-   )
    Star-Shadow [18']
        3(pic).2+English horn.2+bass
            clar.2+contrabsn. 4.2.3.0.
            timp,3perc,harp,strings
        NORRUTH perf mat rent   (L130)

LAVINIA: OVERTURE see Barraud, Henry

LAVRANSDATTERS VISE see Tveitt, Geirr

LAWRENCE, CHARLES
    What Makes Me Believe You? [arr.]
        (Still, William Grant) 2.1(English
            horn).1.0.3sax. 2.2.0.0. vibra,
            cym,banjo,pno,strings sc STILL
            $5.50   (L131)

LAZARO, JOSE
    Concerto No. 2 for Guitar and String
        Orchestra
        string orch,gtr solo
        sc ALPUERTO f.s.   (L132)

LAZAROF, HENRI (1932-   )
    Chamber Symphony [18']
        1(alto fl).2(English horn).0.2.
            2.0.0.0. strings
        study sc PRESSER 446-41033 $15.00,
            perf mat rent   (L133)

    Concertante For 16 Strings And 2
        French Horns
        2horn,16strings
        sc MERION $20.00, perf mat rent
                                        (L134)

    Concerto for Orchestra, No. 2 [22']
        4.4.4.4. 4.6.3.1. timp,perc,harp,
            pno,strings
        ("Icarus") sc MERION 446-41050
            $15.00, perf mat rent   (L135)

    Concerto for Violin and Orchestra
        [25']
        2.2.2.2. 2.2.0.0. perc,harp,pno&
            cel,strings,vln solo
        sc MERION $25.00, perf mat rent
                                        (L136)

    Poema [11']
        3.3.3.3. 4.3.3.1. timp,perc,harp,
            pno&cel,strings
        sc MERION 146-40012 $12.00, perf
            mat rent   (L137)

    Tableaux
        sc MERION 446-41058 $20.00, perf
            mat rent   (L138)

LAZARUS, DANIEL (1898-1964)
    Concerto for Piano and Orchestra
        [26']
        2.2.2.2. 2.2.0.0. timp,strings,
            pno solo
        ESCHIG perf mat rent   (L139)

    Suite Concertante [16'30"]
        2fl,bass clar,trp,perc,strings
        BILLAUDOT perf mat rent   (L140)

LAZZARI, SILVIO (1857-1944)
    Symphony in E flat [45']
        3.3.3.3. 4.3.3.1. timp,perc,harp,
            strings
        ESCHIG perf mat rent   (L141)

LE BARON, ANNE (1953-   )
    Strange Attractors [13']
        2(pic).2(English horn).2(clar in
            E flat).2(contrabsn). 4.3.3.1.
            timp,3perc,harp,strings
        NORRUTH perf mat rent   (L142)

    Three Movements [11']
        perc,strings
        sc AM.COMP.AL. $11.45, perf mat
            rent   (L143)

LE BOUCHER, MAURICE GEORGES EUGENE
    (1882-1964)
    Ballade for Clarinet and Orchestra in
        D minor [10']
        2.2.0.2. 2.0.0.0. timp,harp,
            strings,clar solo
        sc BILLAUDOT f.s., perf mat rent
                                        (L144)

    Heures Antiques: Au Bois Sacre
        [4'40"]
        2.2.2.2. 2.0.0.0. timp,harp,
            strings
        BILLAUDOT perf mat rent   (L145)

    Heures Antiques: La Danse Des Fauves
        [8'40"]
        3.2.2.2. 4.3.3.1. timp,perc,harp,
            strings
        BILLAUDOT perf mat rent   (L146)

LE DUC, SIMON (ca. 1745-1777)
    Orchestral Trios, Op. 2, Nos. 2-3,
        and Trio-Divertimento, Op. 5, No.
        3
        2vln, bass
        ("The Symphony", Vol. D-IV) sc
            GARLAND $90.00 contains also: Le
            Duc, Simon, Symphony No. 2 in D
            (Brook, Barry S.) (2fl,2horn,
            strings); Le Duc, Simon, Sinfonia
            Concertante for 2 Violins and
            Orchestra in G (2.2.0.2. 2.0.0.0.
            strings,2vln soli); Saint-
            Georges, Joseph Boulogne de,
            Symphony, Op. 11, No. 1, in G
            (Hudson, Bryant T.) (2ob,2horn,
            strings); Saint-Georges, Joseph
            Boulogne de, Sinfonia Concertante
            for 2 Violins and Orchestra, Op.
            6, No. 1, in C (Braun, Melanie)
            (2ob,2horn,strings,2vln soli/vln,
            vcl soli); Saint-Georges, Joseph
            Boulogne de, Sinfonia Concertante
            for 2 Violins, Viola and
            Orchestra, Op. 10, No. 2, in A
            (Braun, Melanie) (2ob,2horn,
            strings,2vln soli,vla solo)

LE DUC, SIMON (cont'd.)
(L147)
Sinfonia Concertante for 2 Violins
and Orchestra in G
see Le Duc, Simon, Orchestral
Trios, Op. 2, Nos. 2-3, and Trio-
Divertimento, Op. 5, No. 3

Symphony in E flat
2fl,2horn,strings
(Brook, Barry) FRANK perf mat rent
(L148)
Symphony No. 2 in D
see Le Duc, Simon, Orchestral
Trios, Op. 2, Nos. 2-3, and Trio-
Divertimento, Op. 5, No. 3

LE FANU, NICOLA
see LEFANU, NICOLA

LE FLEM, PAUL (1881-1984)
Interludes De La Magicienne De La
Mer, For Solo Voice And Orchestra
[10']
3(pic).3(English horn).3(bass
clar).2.alto sax. 4.3.3.1.
timp,perc,harp,cel,pno,strings,
solo voice
LEMOINE perf mat rent   (L149)

Konzertstück for Violin and Orchestra
[14'30"]
2.3.3.2.alto sax. 4.2.2.1. timp,
perc,strings,vln solo
BILLAUDOT perf mat rent   (L150)

Magicienne De La Mer, La [10']
3.3.3.2.sax. 4.3.3.1. timp,perc,
harp,cel,pno,strings
ESCHIG perf mat rent   (L151)

LE FLEMING, CHRISTOPHER (KAYE)
(1908-1985)
Southwark Festival Overture [9']
2.2.2.2. 4.2.3.1. timp,perc,
strings
CHESTER perf mat rent   (L152)

LE ROUX, MAURICE (1923-   )
Crin Blanc: Suite [14']
CHOUDENS perf mat rent   (L153)

Musique Pour Un Petit Prince [10']
CHOUDENS perf mat rent   (L154)

LE SIEGE, ANNETTE
Sapphire Seesaw
3.3.3.3. 4.3.3.1. timp,3perc,
strings
sc SEESAW $82.00. perf mat rent
(L155)
Star Gazers And Other Pilgrims
3.2.2.2. 4.2.2.1. timp,3perc,
strings
SEESAW   (L156)

LEADEN ECHO AND THE GOLDEN ECHO, THE,
FOR SOLO VOICE AND ORCHESTRA see
Parris, Robert

LEANDA see Rapf, Kurt

LEANDRE ET HERO, FOR SOLO VOICE AND
INSTRUMENTAL ENSEMBLE see
Clérambault, Louis-Nicolas

LEANING ON THE FENCE, FOR SOLO VOICE
AND ORCHESTRA see Jensen, Ludwig
Irgens, Lutad Mot Gardet, For Solo
Voice And Orchestra

LEB WOHL see Suslin, Viktor, Farewell

LEBEN, EIN TANZ, DAS [ARR.] see
Strauss, Johann, [Sr.]

LEBEN IST DOCH SCHON WALZER, DAS see
Strauss, Eduard

LEBEN MOLIERES, DAS: SUITE see
Grinblat, Romuald

LEBENDIG BEGRABEN, FOR SOLO VOICE AND
ORCHESTRA see Schoeck, Othmar

LEBENSWECKER WALZER see Strauss,
Johann, [Jr.]

LEBIC, LOJZE (1934-   )
November Songs, For Solo Voice And
Orchestra
see Novemberske Pesmi, For Solo
Voice And Orchestra

Novemberske Pesmi, For Solo Voice And
Orchestra [30']
3(pic).2.3(bass
clar).2(contrabsn). 4.3.3.1.
3perc,harp,pno&cel,strings,solo
voice
"November Songs, For Solo Voice And
Orchestra" DRUSTVO ED.DSS 1011
f.s., perf mat rent   (L157)

LECLAIR, JEAN MARIE (1697-1764)
Concerto for Violin and Orchestra,
Op. 10, No. 3, in D [20']
string orch,cont,vln solo
(Blanchard, Roger) sc BOIS f.s.,
perf mat rent   (L158)

Concerto for Violin and String
Orchestra, Op. 10, No. 4, in F
string orch,cont,vln solo
sc BOIS f.s., perf mat rent (L159)

Concerto for Violin and String
Orchestra, Op. 10, No. 5, in E
minor [16']
string orch,cont,vln solo
(Blanchard, Roger) sc BOIS f.s.,
perf mat rent   (L160)

LECLERC, SOPHIE (1964-   )
Cassandre [11'40"]
2perc,harp,2string quin
BILLAUDOT perf mat rent   (L161)

Syzygies [9']
3.3.3.3. 4.3.3.0. 3perc,harp,pno&
cel,strings
BILLAUDOT perf mat rent   (L162)

LECOCQ, CHARLES (1832-1918)
Mademoiselle Angot Suite [arr.]
(Mohaupt, Richard) 2.2.2.2.
4.2.3.1. perc,harp,pno,strings
[15'] AMP perf mat rent   (L163)

Mam'zelle Angot: Ballet Suite [arr.]
(Jacob, Gordon) 3(pic).2(English
horn).2.2. 4.2.3.1. timp,2perc,
harp,strings [24'] BOOSEY perf
mat rent   (L164)

LECTURE TROIS DE MAHLER, FOR SOLO
VOICES AND STRING ORCHESTRA see
Koering, Rene

LECUONA, ERNESTO (1896-1963)
Malaguena [arr.]
2.2.2.2. 4.3.3.1. timp,perc,harp,
cel,strings
(Gould, Morton) SCHIRM.G perf mat
rent   (L165)

LECUONA, MARGARITA
Tabu
3(pic).3(English horn).3(bass
clar).2.alto sax.tenor
sax.baritone sax. 4.3.3.1.
timp,perc,harp,strings
PEER perf mat rent   (L166)

LEDENEV, ROMAN (1930-   )
Four Sketches [11']
1.1.2.1. 1.0.0.0. perc,hpsd/cel/
pno,harp,string quin
"Vier Skizzen" SIKORSKI perf mat
rent   (L167)

Green Balloons: Suite [30']
3.3.3.3.2alto sax.tenor sax.
4.4.4.1. timp,perc,cel,2harp,
pno,strings
VAAP perf mat rent   (L168)

Sieben Stimmungsbilder *Op.18 [5']
1.1.1.1. 1.1.0.0. pno,string quin
SIKORSKI perf mat rent   (L169)

Ten Sketches *Op.17 [11']
1.1.1.1. 1.0.0.0. perc,string
quin
"Zehn Skizzen" SIKORSKI perf mat
rent   (L170)

Vier Skizzen
see Four Sketches

Zehn Skizzen
see Ten Sketches

LEE, EUGENE (1942-   )
Chamber Symphony [15']
1(pic).1(English horn).1(bass
clar).1. 1.2.1.0. 4perc,pno,
2vln,vla,vcl,db
sc APNM $18.00, perf mat rent
(L171)
Transience [12']
1.0.1.1. 1.1.1.0. 2perc,pno,vln,
vcl
sc APNM $9.50, perf mat rent (L172)

LEE, NOEL (1924-   )
Caprices On The Name Schoenberg, For
Piano And Orchestra [23']
2+pic.2(English horn).2(bass
clar)+clar in E flat.2.
4.2.2.1. timp,4perc,harp,
strings,pno solo
NORRUTH perf mat rent   (L173)

Triptyque, For Violin, Piano And
Orchestra [20']
2(pic).2(English horn).1+clar in
E flat+bass clar.2. 3.2.1.1.
timp,4perc,cel,harp,strings,vln
solo,pno solo

LEE, NOEL (cont'd.)
NORRUTH perf mat rent   (L174)

LEE, THOMAS OBOE (1945-   )
Concerto for Harp and Orchestra [19']
1(pic).1.2.0. 2.2.0.0. 2perc,
strings,harp solo
MARGUN BP 4015 perf mat rent (L175)

Phantasia For Elvira Shatayev, For
Solo Voice And Orchestra [20']
0+pic.2.1.2. 2.1(flügelhorn).2.1.
2perc,harp,pno,strings,S solo
MARGUN BP 4014 perf mat rent (L176)

LEE, WILLIAM FRANKLIN (1929-   )
Concerto Grosso for Brass Quintet and
Orchestra [12']
3.3.3.3. 3.1.2.0. timp,perc,harp,
strings,brass quin soli
PEER perf mat rent   (L177)

LEEF, YINAM (1953-   )
Fanfares And Whispers, For Trumpet
And String Orchestra [9']
string orch,trp solo
PRESSER perf mat rent   (L178)

LEES, BENJAMIN (1924-   )
Concerto for Chamber Orchestra
min sc BOOSEY 817 $15.00   (L179)

Concerto for Piano and Orchestra, No.
2
min sc BOOSEY 1108 $23.00   (L180)

Concerto for Piano, Violoncello and
Orchestra [20']
2(pic).2.2.2(contrabsn). 4.3.3.1.
timp,perc,strings,pno solo,vcl
solo
BOOSEY perf mat rent   (L181)

Mobiles [20']
2(pic).2.2(bass
clar).2(contrabsn). 2.2.0.0.
timp,perc,harp,cel,strings
BOOSEY perf mat rent   (L182)

Portrait Of Rodin [17']
3(2pic).3.3(bass
clar).3(contrabsn). 4.3.3.1.
timp,perc,harp,cel,strings
BOOSEY perf mat rent   (L183)

Symphony No. 4 for Solo Voice, Violin
and Orchestra [60']
3(pic).3.3.3(contrabsn). 4.3.3.1.
timp,perc,harp,cel,strings,vln
solo,Mez solo
(Memorial Candles) BOOSEY perf mat
rent   (L184)

LEEUW, TON DE (1926-   )
Alba [32']
0.2.0.0. 2.0.0.0. 14vln,4vla,
4vcl,2db
sc DONEMUS f.s., perf mat rent
(L185)
Concerto for 2 Guitars and Strings
[16']
12strings,2gtr solo
DONEMUS perf mat rent   (L186)

Resonances [38']
4.4.4.4. 4.4.3.1. perc,harp,pno,
strings
DONEMUS perf mat rent   (L187)

LEFANU, NICOLA (1947-   )
Collana [11']
1(pic).0.1(bass clar).0. 0.0.0.0.
perc,strings without vla
NOVELLO perf mat rent   (L188)

Columbia Falls [20']
2(pic).2.3.2(contrabsn). 0.0.0.0.
4perc,harp,strings
NOVELLO perf mat rent   (L189)

Farne [20']
2.2.2.2. 2.3.3.1. timp,4perc,
strings
NOVELLO perf mat rent   (L190)

Old Woman Of Beare, The, For Solo
Voice And Instrumental Ensemble
1.1.1.1. 1.1.1.0. 2perc,harp,vln,
vla,vcl,S solo
sc NOVELLO 2940-90 $22.00   (L191)

Prelude No. 2 [10']
1.1.1.1. 2.0.0.0. strings
NOVELLO perf mat rent   (L192)

LEFEBVRE, CLAUDE (1931-   )
Etwas Weiter [12']
1.1.1+clar in E flat+bass
clar.1.alto sax. 2.2.2.0.
3perc,elec gtr,pno,2vln,vla,
vcl,db
SALABERT perf mat rent   (L193)

LEGEND see Still, William Grant

LEGEND, FOR BASSOON AND STRING
ORCHESTRA see Kvandal, Johan

LEGEND, FOR PIANO AND ORCHESTRA see
Ireland, John

LEGEND OF THE NORTH WOODS see Holt,
Patricia Blomfield

LEGEND OF THE YELLOW CRANE see Shih,
Yun-Kang

LEGENDE see Fongaard, Bjørn see
Hoeberg, Georg

LEGENDE, FOR VIOLIN AND ORCHESTRA see
Delius, Frederick see Wieniawski,
Henryk

LEGENDE [ARR.] see Cleve, Cissi

LEGENDE EPIQUE, FOR PIANO AND ORCHESTRA
see Poot, Marcel

LEGENDE VON DER HEILIGEN ELISABETH,
DIE: GEBET DER HEILIGEN ELISABETH,
FOR SOLO VOICE AND ORCHESTRA see
Liszt, Franz

LEGENDE VON DER HEILIGEN ELISABETH,
DIE: OUVERTURE UND MARSCH DER
KREUZRITTER see Liszt, Franz

LEGENDES [ARR.] see Liszt, Franz

LEGENDS see Barnes, Milton

LEGG, JAMES
Ariel [4']
2(pic).2.2(bass clar).2. 4.2.3.1.
timp,2perc,harp,strings
AMP perf mat rent   (L194)

LEGG IKKJE DITT LIV I MI HAND see
Søderlind, Ragnar

LEGGENDA see Danielsson, Harry

LEGIDO, JESUS (1943-   )
Bucolica [9']
1.1.2.1. 0.0.0.0. timp,perc,harp,
2pno,string quin
ALPUERTO   (L195)

Exotica [14']
fl,clar,bsn,2trom,2perc,pno,vln,
vla,vcl
ALPUERTO   (L196)

Praviada [17']
2.2.2.2. 2.2.1.0. timp,string
quin
ALPUERTO   (L197)

Saudades, For Solo Voice And Chamber
Orchestra [12']
1.1.1.1. 0.0.0.0. perc,harp,pno,
string quar,Bar solo
ALPUERTO   (L198)

LEGRAND, HERVE
Music for Violin, Vibraphone and
String Orchestra
string orch,vln solo,vibra solo
SCHIRM.G perf mat rent   (L199)

LEGRAND, MICHEL (1932-   )
Summer Of '42: Theme, [arr.] [3'25"]
(Muller, Frederick) WARNER perf mat
rent   (L200)

LEGRENZI, GIOVANNI (1626-1690)
Sonata A Tre "La Raspona" [arr.]
(Gandolfi) KALMUS A7374 sc $7.00,
set $9.00, pts $1.50, ea.   (L201)

LEGUAY, JEAN-PIERRE (1939-   )
Souffle [24']
2.1(English horn).2(bass clar).0.
1.2.1.1. 2vln,vla,vcl,db
LEMOINE perf mat rent   (L202)

LEGUERNEY, JACQUES (1897-   )
Solitude, La, For Solo Voice And
Orchestra
2(pic).2(English horn).2(bass
clar).2(sarrusophone). 4.3.2.1.
timp,perc,harp,cel,strings,med
solo
SALABERT perf mat rent   (L203)

LEHAR, FRANZ (1870-1948)
Ballsirenen (from Die Lustige Witwe)
2+pic.2.2.2. 4.2.3.0. timp,perc,
harp,strings [8'] KALMUS A6977
pno-cond sc $3.00, set $20.00,
pts $1.00, ea., perf mat rent (L204)

Elfentanz
KALMUS A7443 pno-cond sc $3.00, set
$30.00, pts $1.50, ea., perf mat
rent   (L205)

LEHAR, FRANZ (cont'd.)
Graf Von Luxembourg: Luxembourg Waltz
(Higgs) 2(pic).2.2.2. 2.2.3.0.
timp,perc,harp,strings [7']
KALMUS A6391 pno-cond sc $5.00,
set $30.00, pts $1.50, ea., perf
mat rent   (L206)

Lustige Witwe, Die: Paraphrase [arr.]
(Gould, Morton) "Merry Widow, The:
Paraphrase [arr.]"
2(pic).2(English horn).2.2.
4.3.3.1. timp,perc,harp,cel,
strings [10'] SCHIRM.G perf mat
rent   (L207)

Merry Widow, The: Paraphrase [arr.]
see Lustige Witwe, Die: Paraphrase
[arr.]

Vision, Eine [5']
2+pic.2.2.2. 4.2.3.1. timp,perc,
harp,strings
DOBLINGER perf mat rent   (L208)
KALMUS A5717 sc $15.00, set $45.00,
perf mat rent   (L209)

LEHELLET see Szöllösy, Andras

LEICHTE SATZE AUS SINFONIEN see Haydn,
[Franz] Joseph

LEICHTE TANZE UND CHARAKTERSTUCKE *CCU
(Lemacher; Mies) string orch,opt fl,
opt horn,opt hpsd sc,pts TONGER
f.s. contains works by Haydn,
Keiser, Dittersdorf, Gluck, Lanner
(L210)

LEICHTES BLUT see Strauss, Johann,
[Jr.]

LEICHTLING, ALAN (1947-   )
Capriccio
1.2.1.2. 2.0.0.0. timp,perc,cel,
strings
SEESAW   (L211)

Concerto for Tuba, 2 Harps and
Strings
tuba,2harp,strings
SEESAW   (L212)

Concerto for Violin, Violoncello,
Piano and Orchestra
3.3.4.3. 4.3.3.1. timp,perc,harp,
strings,vln solo,vcl solo,pno
solo
SEESAW   (L213)

Eleven Songs "Shropshire", For Solo
Voice And Orchestra
1.1.3.2. 2.2.2.0. perc,harp,pno,
strings,Bar solo
SEESAW perf mat rent   (L214)

Fantasy Piece V
3.3.3.3. 4.3.3.1. timp,perc,harp,
cel,strings
SEESAW   (L215)

Symphony No. 3
3.3.3.3. 4.3.3.1. timp,perc,harp,
strings
SEESAW perf mat rent   (L216)

LEIFS, JON (1899-1968)
Consolation *Op.66
string orch
ICELAND 033-013   (L217)

Elegy, Op. 53
string orch
ICELAND 033-025   (L218)

Geysir *Op.51
3.3.3.3. 4.4.3.1. timp,perc,
strings
ICELAND 033-019   (L219)

Iceland Overture *Op.9 [15']
2.2.2.2. 2.2.0.0. timp,perc,
strings,opt cor
ICELAND 033-009   (L220)

Icelandic Dances *Op.11
1.1.2.1. 2.2.1.0. strings
ICELAND 033-022   (L221)

Music To Galdra-Loftr *Op.6 [6']
2.1.2.1. 2.1.1.0. timp,strings
ICELAND 033-017   (L222)

Overture, Op. 41
3.3.3.2. 4.3.3.1. timp,perc,
strings
ICELAND 033-016   (L223)

Reflections From The North *Op.40
[20']
string orch
ICELAND 033-015   (L224)

Saga Symphony *Op.26 [70']
2.2.2.2. 2.2.2.1. timp,perc,
strings, 6 luren

LEIFS, JON (cont'd.)
ICELAND 033-018   (L225)

Three Images *Op.44 [12']
2.1.3.2. 4.4.3.1. timp,perc,
strings
ICELAND 033-012   (L226)

Trilogia Piccola *Op.1
3.3.3.3. 4.3.3.1. timp,perc,
strings
ICELAND 033-023   (L227)

LEIGH, MITCH (1928-   )
Man Of La Mancha: Orchestral
Synthesis [arr.]
(Hayman, Richard) 3.3.3.3. 4.4.3.1.
timp,perc,strings [15'] FOX,S
perf mat rent   (L228)

LEIGH, WALTER (1908-1942)
Concertino for Harpsichord and String
Orchestra
KALMUS A6965 sc $8.00, set $5.00,
pts $1.25, ea.   (L229)

Music for String Orchestra
set KALMUS A6965 $10.00, and up
(L230)

LEIGHTON, KENNETH (1929-1988)
Festive Overture [8']
2.1.2.1. 2.2.1.0. timp,2perc,
strings
NOVELLO perf mat rent   (L231)

LEIPZIGER TAG, FOR PIANO AND STRING
ORCHESTRA see Bentzon, Niels Viggo

LEITARTICKEL, DIE, WALZER see Strauss,
Johann, [Jr.]

LEITERMEYER, FRITZ (1925-   )
Drei Studien For 12 Violoncellos
*Op.40b [12']
12vcl
DOBLINGER perf mat rent   (L232)

Drei Studien, For Orchestra *Op.85
[14']
2+pic.2(English horn).2(bass
clar).2(contrabsn). 4.4.3.1.
timp,perc,harp,strings
DOBLINGER perf mat rent   (L233)

Intrada For Orchestra *Op.67a [14']
2.2.2.2. 4.4.4.1. timp,strings
DOBLINGER perf mat rent   (L234)

Mutationen In Honorem J.S.B. *Op.82
[17']
2+pic.2+English horn.2+bass
clar.2+contrabsn. 4.4.3.1.
timp,harp,strings
DOBLINGER perf mat rent   (L235)

Notturno for Double Bass and String
Orchestra, Op. 66 [8']
string orch,db solo
DOBLINGER perf mat rent   (L236)

Pezzo Per Archi *Op.88 [15']
string orch
DOBLINGER perf mat rent   (L237)

Virtuoso, For Violin And Orchestra
*Op.81 [6']
1+pic.2.2.2. 4.2.0.0. timp,
strings,vln solo
DOBLINGER perf mat rent   (L238)

LEITNER, ERNST LUDWIG (1943-   )
Concerto [23']
org,perc,cel,strings
DOBLINGER perf mat rent   (L239)

LEJET, EDITH (1941-   )
Hauteurs-Lointains
string orch
BILLAUDOT perf mat rent   (L240)

Jaspure [20']
24strings
BILLAUDOT perf mat rent   (L241)

Plages [5']
2.2.3.2. 2.2.2.0. 3perc,hpsd,
strings
BILLAUDOT perf mat rent   (L242)

LEKEU, GUILLAUME (1870-1894)
Barberine, For Solo Voice And
Orchestra, [Arr.]
(Levinas, Michael) 0.0.1(bass
clar).1. 1.0.1.0. perc,pno,2vln,
vla,vcl,db,S solo [5'] SALABERT
perf mat rent   (L243)

Nocturne for Solo Voice and String
Orchestra, [arr.]
string orch,pno,Mez solo [4']
KALMUS A4245 sc $3.00, set $5.00,
pts $1.00, ea.   (L244)

LELIAH see Minard, Robin

LEMAIRE, JEAN (1927-)
Choral Et Variations, For 4
Saxophones And String Orchestra
[12']
string orch,4sax soli
BILLAUDOT perf mat rent (L245)

LEMELAND, AUBERT (1932-)
Concerto for Flute, Oboe and String
Orchestra, Op. 110 [17']
string orch,fl solo,ob solo
BILLAUDOT perf mat rent (L246)

Concerto for 2 String Orchestras, Op.
8 [17']
string orch
sc BILLAUDOT f.s., perf mat rent
(L247)

Concerto for Violin and Orchestra,
Op. 116 [25']
3.3.3.2. 4.3.3.1. timp,vibra,pno,
strings,vln solo
BILLAUDOT perf mat rent (L248)

Etat d'Horizon 3 [10']
2.2.1.1. 1.0.0.0. strings
sc BILLAUDOT f.s., perf mat rent
(L249)

Impromptus Symphoniques *Op.21 [12']
2.2.2.2. 2.2.1.0. timp,perc,
strings
sc BILLAUDOT f.s., perf mat rent
(L250)

Sinfonietta for String Orchestra [9']
string orch
BILLAUDOT perf mat rent (L251)

Symphony No. 1, Op. 32 [26']
4.4.3.3. 4.3.3.1. timp,perc,
strings
BILLAUDOT perf mat rent (L252)

Symphony No. 3, Op. 97 [18']
2.2.2.2. 2.2.0.0. strings
BILLAUDOT perf mat rent (L253)

Ultramarine Nocturne [11']
3.3.3.3. 4.3.3.1. timp,perc,
strings
sc BILLAUDOT f.s., perf mat rent
(L254)

LEMMINKAINEN OVERTURE see Haapalainen,
Väinö

LENDVAY, KAMILLO (1928-)
Concerto for Violin and Orchestra,
No. 1
sc EMB 10062 f.s., perf mat rent
(L255)

Concerto for Violin and Orchestra,
No. 2
sc EMB 13424 f.s., perf mat rent
(L256)

Harmony Of Silence, The
sc EMB 10279 f.s., perf mat rent
(L257)

Mauthausen
sc EMB 3941 f.s. (L258)

Metamorphosis Of A Piece For Cimbalom
sc EMB 10259 f.s. (L259)

Tragic Overture
sc EMB 3492 f.s. (L260)

LENGSEL see Lunde, Ivar

LENNON, JOHN ANTHONY (1950-)
Symphonic Rhapsody, For Alto
Saxophone And Orchestra [20']
2(pic).2.2(bass
clar).2(contrabsn). 4.2.2.1.
3perc,harp,pno,strings,alto sax
solo
PETERS P67098 perf mat rent (L261)

LENORE see Duparc, Henri

LENOT, JACQUES (1945-)
Allegories D'exil I: Exergue, For
Violoncello And Instrumental
Ensemble [12']
1.1.2.1. 1.1.1.0. perc,harp,pno,
3vln,vla,vcl,db,vcl solo
SALABERT perf mat rent (L262)

Allegories D'exil IV: Dolcezze Ignote
All'estasi [17']
2.2.3.1. 2.2.2.1. perc,harp,pno,
3vln,2vla,2vcl,db
SALABERT perf mat rent (L263)

Allegories D'exil X: Epilogue [15']
3.3.3.3. 3.3.3.1. 2perc,harp,pno,
strings
SALABERT perf mat rent (L264)

Aux Rives Ulterieures, For Violin And
Instrumental Ensemble [9']
1.1.1.1. 1.0.0.0. 2vln,vla,vcl,
db,vln solo
SALABERT perf mat rent (L265)

LENOT, JACQUES (cont'd.)
Celui Qui Est Couronne, For Solo
Voice And Instrumental Ensemble
[17']
2.2.2.1. 2.1.1.1. 2perc,2pno,
2vln,2vla,2vcl,db,countertenor
SALABERT perf mat rent (L266)

Concerto for Instrumental Ensemble
[23']
1(pic).1(English horn).1.0.
0.2.1.0. timp,vibra,marimba,
pno,2vln,vcl
SALABERT perf mat rent (L267)

Dans Le Tumulte Des Flots II, For
Violin And Instrumental Ensemble
[20']
2.2.3.2. 2.2.2.1. 3perc,harp,cel,
2pno,db,vln solo, 2 string
trios
SALABERT perf mat rent (L268)

Diaphaneis [11']
perc,strings
BILLAUDOT perf mat rent (L269)

Enclaves, For Violoncello And
Orchestra [20']
3.3.3.3. 3.3.3.1. harp,pno,
strings,vcl solo
sc SALABERT f.s., perf mat rent
(L270)

Grand Principe De Violence Commandait
A Nos Moeurs, Un [20']
1+pic.1+English horn.0+clar in E
flat+bass clar.2. 2.0.0.0.
harp,cel,pno,vln,vla,vcl
SALABERT perf mat rent (L271)

Nuit D'ete: Cinq Interludes, For
Violoncello And Orchestra [50']
2.1(English horn).2.2. 3.0.0.0.
harp,strings,vcl solo
SALABERT perf mat rent (L272)

Nuit d'Ete II, For Violoncello And
Instrumental Ensemble [45']
1.1(English horn).1.1.
1.1.1.0(opt tuba). perc,pno,
org/harmonium,2vln,vla,vcl,db,
vcl solo
SALABERT perf mat rent (L273)

Parmi Les Hierarchies Des Anges, For
Viola And Orchestra [21']
3(alto fl).3(English horn).3(bass
clar).3(contrabsn). 4.3.2.1.
3perc,org,12vcl,vla solo
SALABERT perf mat rent (L274)

Pour Memoire I, For Piano And
Orchestra [23']
4(pic,alto fl).4(English
horn).4(clar in E flat)+bass
clar.4(contrabsn). 6.4.4.1.
timp,3perc,2harp,cel,strings,
pno solo
SALABERT perf mat rent (L275)

Pour Memoire II, For Solo Voice And
Orchestra [23']
4(pic,alto fl).4(English
horn).4(clar in E flat)+bass
clar.4(contrabsn). 6.4.4.1.
timp,3perc,2harp,cel,pno,
strings,S solo
SALABERT perf mat rent (L276)

Pour Memoire III, For String
Orchestra [15']
string orch
SALABERT perf mat rent (L277)

Pour Memoire IV, For Solo Voices And
Orchestra [23']
4(pic,alto fl).4(English
horn).4(clar in E flat)+bass
clar.4(contrabsn). 6.4.4.1.
timp,3perc,2harp,cel,strings,
SATB soli
SALABERT perf mat rent (L278)

Utopia Parafrasi [15']
1(pic,alto fl,bass fl).1(English
horn).1(clar in E flat,clar in
A,bass clar).1(contrabsn).
2.1.1.0. perc,opt cel,pno,2vln,
vla,vcl,db
SALABERT perf mat rent (L279)

Variations for Orchestra [18']
3.3.3.3. 3.3.3.0. strings
SALABERT perf mat rent (L280)

Vent Du Soir Ramene Sa Depouille Vers
La Greve, Le (from L'esprit Des
Lieux, Book 2) [5'30]
2.1.3.1. 2.1.1.0. harp,pno,cel,
2vln,vla,vcl,db
SALABERT perf mat rent (L281)

LENTO, FOR STRING ORCHESTRA see Hunt,
Michael

LENTO DOLOROSO see Rivier, Jean

LENZ-FRAGMENTE, FOR SOLO VOICE AND
ORCHESTRA see Rihm, Wolfgang

LEO, LEONARDO (ORTENSIO SALVATORE DE)
(1694-1744)
Emira: Sinfonia
(Pastore) KALMUS A7355 sc $7.00,
set $12.00, pts $1.50, ea. (L282)

Morte Di Abel, La: Sinfonia
(Pastore) KALMUS A7309 sc $7.00,
set $12.00, pts $1.50, ea. (L283)

Santa Genoviefa: Sinfonia
(Pastore) KALMUS A7308 sc $7.00,
set $12.00, pts $1.50, ea. (L284)

Sinfonia Concertante for Violoncello
and String Orchestra, [excerpt]
(Blanchard, R.) string orch,hpsd,
vcl solo (Larghetto) BOIS perf
mat rent (L285)

LEON, TANIA JUSTINA (1944-)
Bata [12']
2(pic).2(English horn).2(bass
clar).2. 2.2.2.1. perc,harp,
pno,cel,strings
PEER perf mat rent (L286)

Concerto Criollo, For Piano And
Orchestra [20']
2.2.2.2. 4.4.3.0. timp,perc,
strings,pno solo
PEER perf mat rent (L287)

Golden Windows, The [30']
1(pic,alto fl).1(English
horn).0.0. 0.1.0.0. perc,hpsd,
pno,strings
PEER perf mat rent (L288)

Kabiosile, For Piano And Orchestra
[8']
2(pic).2(English horn).2(bass
clar).2(contrabsn). 4.2.3.0.
timp,2perc,strings,pno solo
PEER perf mat rent (L289)

Tones [18']
2.2.1.0. 1.0.1.1. timp,perc,pno,
strings
PEER perf mat rent (L290)

LEONCAVALLO, RUGGIERO (1858-1919)
Pagliacci, I: Silvio, A Quest' Ora,
For Solo Voices And Orchestra
KALMUS A3557 sc $10.00, set $40.00,
pts $2.00, ea. (L291)

Tarantelle [4']
2+pic.2.2.2. 4.2.3.1. timp,perc,
harp,strings
KALMUS A7459 sc $15.00, set $40.00,
pts $1.50, ea., perf mat rent
(L292)

LEONIDES, LES see Matsumoto, Hinoharu

LEONORA OSSIA L'AMORE CONIUGALE:
OVERTURE see Paer, Ferdinando

LEONORE OVERTURE NO. 1 see Beethoven,
Ludwig van

LEONORE OVERTURE NO. 2 see Beethoven,
Ludwig van

LEONORE OVERTURE NO. 3 see Beethoven,
Ludwig van

LEOPOLD, BOHUSLAV (1888-1956)
Ballet Suite
2.2.2.2. 4.2.3.1. timp,perc,
strings
SUPRAPHON (L293)

Danse Basque, La [4']
1.1.2.1.sax. 1.2.1.0. timp,
harmonium,strings
SUPRAPHON (L294)

LEOPOLDSTADTER POLKA see Strauss,
Johann, [Jr.]

LEPA VIDA: SUITE see Ukmar, Vilko

LEPNUR, HUGO
Concerto for Clarinet, Bassoon and
Orchestra, Op. 34 [18']
1.1.1.1. 3.3.1.0. perc,harp,
strings,clar solo,bsn solo
VAAP perf mat rent (L295)

Concerto for Organ and Orchestra
0.0.0.0. 4.2.3.1. timp,strings,
org solo
VAAP perf mat rent (L296)

LERDAHL, FRED (1943-)
Beyond The Realm Of Bird, For Solo
Voice And Orchestra
2.2.2.2. 1.1.1.0. 2perc,pno,harp,
strings,S solo
sc BOELKE-BOM f.s. (L297)

LERMONTOV: SUITE see Khachaturian, Aram
  Ilyich

LEROUX, MAURICE (1923-   )
  Koan, Un [14']
    1.2.3(bass clar).2. 2.2.2.0.
    2perc,pno,org,harp,strings
    SALABERT perf mat rent   (L298)

LEROUX, PHILIPPE (1959-   )
  Corps De Louange, Un [14']
    3.2.2.3. 2.2.2.1. 3perc,harp,pno,
    strings
    BILLAUDOT perf mat rent   (L299)

  Fleuve [30']
    fl,ob,clar,bass clar,horn,trp,
    trom,perc,synthesizer,2vln,vla,
    vcl,db
    BILLAUDOT perf mat rent   (L300)

LERSTAD, TERJE B. (1955-   )
  Canzona, Op. 119c [12']
    4(pic).0.2(bass clar,A rec).0.
    0.3.0.1. timp,perc,pno,strings
    NORGE   (L301)

  Concertino for Contrabassoon and
    Chamber Orchestra, Op. 113a [14']
    1.1.1.0. 0.0.0.0. timp,perc,
    strings,contrabsn solo
    NORGE   (L302)

  Concertino, Op. 159 [14']
    timp,pno,strings
    NORGE   (L303)

  Concerto for Clarinet and Orchestra,
    No. 1, Op. 20 [18']
    3(pic).1(English horn).2(bass
    clar).2(contrabsn). 0.0.3.0.
    timp,perc,strings,clar solo
    NORGE   (L304)

  Concerto for Clarinet and Orchestra,
    No. 2, Op. 27 [15']
    0.2.0.0. 0.0.0.0. gong,strings,
    clar solo
    NORGE   (L305)

  Concerto for Clarinet and Orchestra,
    No. 3 [17'30"]
    2(pic).2(English horn).0.2.
    2.0.0.0. timp,strings,clar solo
    NORGE   (L306)

  Concerto for Saxophone and Orchestra,
    No. 1, Op. 104, in C minor [24']
    4+rec.2.2.3. 4.3.4.0. timp,perc,
    strings,tenor sax solo
    NORGE   (L307)

  Concerto for Strings, Op. 29 [22']
    13strings soli
    NORGE   (L308)

  De Profundis, For Solo Voice And
    Orchestra *Op.139 [12']
    clar,strings,electronic tape,A
    solo
    NORGE   (L309)

  Extase Perdu, L', Op. 148 [20'30"]
    2(pic).2(English horn).2(bass
    clar).2(contrabsn). 3.2.2.0.
    timp,perc,pno,strings
    NORGE   (L310)

  Five Variations On A Theme From "The
    Magic Flute", For Flute And
    Orchestra *Op.174,No.2 [9']
    1.1.1.2. 1.1.1.0. 2perc,2vln,vla,
    vcl,T solo,fl solo
    NORGE   (L311)

  Symfoniske Fragmenter Fra Andre Akt
    Av Operaen, Op. 185b [24']
    2.2.2.2. 2.1.3.1. 4perc,pno,
    synthesizer,strings
    NORGE   (L312)

  Symfoniske Fragmenter Fra Forste Akt
    Av Operaen, Op185a [23'30"]
    2.2.2.2. 2.1.3.1. 4perc,
    synthesizer,strings
    NORGE   (L313)

  Symphony No. 1, Op. 45, in B flat
    [30']
    3(pic).3(English horn).3(bass
    clar).3(contrabsn). 4.3.3.1.
    timp,perc,pno,strings
    NORGE   (L314)

  Symphony No. 2, Op. 70 [25']
    2(pic).2.2.3(contrabsn). 2.2.0.0.
    timp,perc,strings
    (Hommage A Tsjaikovsky) NORGE
                                 (L315)

  Symphony No. 3, Op. 78 [48'30"]
    3(pic).3(English horn).3(bass
    clar).3(contrabsn).
    4.2(cornet).3.1. timp,perc,
    harp,strings
    (Lokrisk Symfoni) NORGE   (L316)

LERSTAD, TERJE B. (cont'd.)

  Symphony No. 4, Op. 119 [38'30"]
    4(pic).2(English horn).3(bass
    clar).3(contrabsn). 4.2.2.1.
    timp,perc,pno,strings
    NORGE   (L317)

  Three Pieces, Op. 21 [9'30"]
    2.2(English horn).2(bass
    clar).3(contrabsn). 2.2.0.0.
    timp,strings
    NORGE   (L318)

LESSARD, JOHN AYRES (1920-   )
  Concerto For Winds And Strings [15']
    fl,clar,bsn,strings,string quar
    soli
    sc AM.COMP.AL. $27.50, perf mat
    rent   (L319)

  Concerto For Winds And Strings,
    Version 2 [15']
    0.2.0.1. 1.0.0.0. strings,string
    quar soli
    sc AM.COMP.AL. $27.50, perf mat
    rent   (L320)

  Don Quixote And The Sheep, For Solo
    Voices And Orchestra [23']
    2.1.2.2. 2.2.2.0. perc,harp,
    strings,db soli
    AM.COMP.AL. sc $45.63, pts $19.00
                                 (L321)

  Little Concert [12']
    2+pic.2.2+bass clar.2. 4.2.2.0.
    timp,strings
    sc AM.COMP.AL. $60.60   (L322)

  Pastimes And An Alleluia [15']
    2.1.1.1. 2.2.2.0. perc,harp,pno&
    cel,strings,electronic
    equipment
    sc AM.COMP.AL. $23.25   (L323)

  Sinfonietta Concertante [15']
    2.0.2.0. 2.2.1.0. strings
    sc AM.COMP.AL. $16.75   (L324)

LESSICO see Manzoni, Giacomo

LET MAN LIVE see Thorarinsson, Jón

LET ME KEEP MY UNREST see Solås,
  Eyvind, Ta Ikke Denne Uro Fra Meg

LET MY SONG FILL YOUR HEART, FOR SOLO
  VOICE AND ORCHESTRA see Charles,
  Ernest

LET US SLEEP NOW see Turnage, Mark-
  Anthony

LETHE, FOR SOLO VOICE AND ORCHESTRA see
  Pfitzner, Hans

LETTER FROM MOZART see Colgrass,
  Michael (Charles)

LETTER TO MY SON see Heegaard, Lars

LETTERS FROM MIGNON, FOR SOLO VOICE AND
  ORCHESTRA see Schafer, R. Murray

LETTRE DE ROXANA A DECEBAL HORMUZ see
  Longtin, Michel

LEVI, PAUL ALAN (1941-   )
  Spring Sestina, For Solo Voice And
    Chamber Group [11']
    fl,ob,clar,bsn,vibra,pno,vln,vla,
    vcl,db,S solo
    MARGUN MP4021 perf mat rent (L325)

  Transformations Of The Heart [12']
    2.2.2.2. 2.2.2.0. 2perc,harp,
    strings
    sc AM.COMP.AL. $80.35, perf mat
    rent   (L326)

LEVIATHAN see Cowie, Edward

LEVIEV, MILCHO
  Sympho-Jazz Sketches, For Jazz
    Quintet And Orchestra [30'45"]
    3+pic.1+English horn.3+bass
    clar.2+contrabsn.soprano
    sax.3alto sax.2tenor
    sax.baritone sax. 4.4.3+bass
    trom.1. timp,perc,cel/hpsd,
    harp,gtr/banjo,strings,fender-
    rhodes, jazz quintet soli: pno,
    bass, drums, 2woodwinds
    NEWAM 19027 perf mat rent   (L327)

LEVINAS, MICHAEL (1949-   )
  Arcade II, For Viola And Instrumental
    Ensemble [10']
    timp,pno,4vla,4vcl,2db,vla solo
    SALABERT perf mat rent   (L328)

  Arcade III: Le Choeur Des Arches
    [10']
    perc,pno,4vla,4vcl,2db,electronic
    tape
    SALABERT perf mat rent   (L329)

LEVINAS, MICHAEL (cont'd.)

  Cloche Felee, La [10']
    3(pic).3.3(clar in E
    flat).3(contrabsn). 4.3.3.1.
    3perc,pno,strings,synthesizer
    SALABERT perf mat rent   (L330)

  Musiques Et Musiques
    4.3.4.4. 5.4.4.1. timp,2perc,
    strings,electronic equipment
    BILLAUDOT perf mat rent   (L331)

  Orateur Muet, L'
    fl,2clar,2perc,pno,strings,
    electronic tape
    SALABERT perf mat rent   (L332)

  Orchestre [8']
    3(pic).2.2.2+contrabsn. 4.2.3.1.
    3perc,2ondes Martenot,strings
    SALABERT perf mat rent   (L333)

  Ouverture Pour Une Fete Etrange [16']
    8fl,4clar,2bass clar,4bsn,
    2contrabsn,12horn,8trp,6trom,
    2bass trom,2tuba,4perc,elec
    org,strings,electronic
    equipment
    SALABERT perf mat rent   (L334)

  Reminiscence Du Jardin Feerique
    [3'20"]
    3(pic).0.2.2+contrabsn. 4.0.2.1.
    timp,3perc,pno,strings
    SALABERT perf mat rent   (L335)

LEVINSON, GERALD (1951-   )
  Anahata (Symphony No. 1) [32']
    MERION perf mat rent   (L336)

  Symphony No. 1
    see Anahata

LEVITIN, YURI (1912-   )
  Don-Elegie [arr.]
    (Diernhammer, C.) 1.1.4.1. 0.0.0.0.
    timp,perc,2mand,strings [5']
    SIKORSKI perf mat rent   (L337)

  Symphony for Solo Voice and Chamber
    Orchestra
    1.1.1.0. 1.0.0.0. timp,strings,
    Mez solo
    VAAP perf mat rent   (L338)

LEVY, MICHEL MAURICE (1883-1965)
  Largo for String Orchestra [7']
    string orch
    BILLAUDOT perf mat rent   (L339)

LEWIN, FRANK (1925-   )
  Concerto On Silesian Tunes, For Viola
    And Chamber Orchestra [20']
    2.2.2.2. 2.0.0.0. timp,perc,harp,
    cel,strings,vla solo
    AM.COMP.AL. perf mat rent   (L340)

  Evocation [18']
    2.2.2.2. 4.2.0.0. timp,perc,
    strings
    AM.COMP.AL. perf mat rent   (L341)

LEWIS, JAMES (1938-   )
  ...the errant note to seize, for
    chamber orchestra [9']
    2.3(English horn).3(bass clar).2.
    2.2.2.1. perc,harp,pno&cel,
    strings
    GUNMAR MP4023 perf mat rent (L342)

  ... the errant note to seize, for
    orchestra [9']
    2.2(English horn).3(bass clar).2.
    4.2.3.1. timp,perc,pno&cel,
    strings
    GUNMAR MP4023A perf mat rent (L343)

LEWIS, JOHN AARON (1920-   )
  Concert Piece [20']
    3.2.2.2. 4.3.2.1. perc,harp,
    strings,vibra solo,pno solo,db
    solo,drums solo
    sc,pts MJQ rent   (L344)

  England's Carol [7']
    1.1.1.1. 0.0.0.0. harp,strings,
    vibra solo,pno solo,db solo,
    drums solo
    sc MJQ $7.95, perf mat rent (L345)

  Fanfare (Salute To Basie) [5']
    3.3.2+bass clar.2+contrabsn.
    4.4.3.1. timp,perc,vibra,bells,
    harp,strings
    sc MJQ $6.95, perf mat rent (L346)

  Gates Of Harvard [12']
    2alto sax.2tenor sax,bass sax,
    4trp,4trom,perc,string quar,pno
    solo,db solo,drums solo
    sc MJQ $14.95, perf mat rent (L347)

  Jazz Ostinato [6']
    2+pic.2+English horn.2+bass
    clar.2+contrabsn. 4.4.3.1.

LEWIS, JOHN AARON (cont'd.)

    timp,perc,cel,bells,harp,
    strings,vibra solo,pno solo,db
    solo,drums solo
    sc MJQ $6.95, perf mat rent   (L348)

    Na Dubrovacki Nacim [20']
    strings,vibra solo,pno solo,gtr
    solo,drums solo
    sc,pts MJQ rent   (L349)

    Original Sin [24']
    2.2.1+bass clar.1+contrabsn.
    2.1.1.0. timp,perc,strings
    sc,pts MJQ rent   (L350)

    Queen's Fancy, The [5']
    1.1.1.1. 2.3.2.1. timp,harp,
    strings,vibra solo,pno solo,db
    solo,drums solo
    sc,pts MJQ rent   (L351)

    Spiritual, The [7']
    2+pic.2+English horn.2+bass
    clar.2+contrabsn. 4.4.3.1.
    timp,perc,cel,bells,harp,
    strings,vibra solo,pno solo,db
    solo,drums solo
    sc MJQ $6.95, perf mat rent (L352)

LEWIS, PETER TOD (1932-1982)
    Fragments - Hedgehogs [15']
    2.3.4.2. 2.2.3.1. perc,pno,
    strings,electronic tape
    sc AM.COMP.AL. $18.30, perf mat
    rent   (L353)

LEWIS, ROBERT HALL (1926-)
    Destini [15']
    PRESSER perf mat rent   (L354)

LEWISOHN STADIUM FANFARE see Menotti,
Gian Carlo

LEYENDA GITANA see Tapia Colman, Simon

LEYENDECKER, ULRICH (1946-)
    Cancion Ultima, For Solo Voice And
    Orchestra [16']
    3.3.3.3.alto sax. 4.3.3.1. timp,
    3perc,harp,pno/cel,elec gtr,
    strings,A solo
    SIKORSKI perf mat rent   (L355)

    Con Espressione [12']
    3.3.3.3. 4.3.3.1. timp,5perc,
    harp,pno,mand,elec gtr,strings
    SIKORSKI perf mat rent   (L356)

    Concerto for Piano and Orchestra
    [18']
    3.2.3.3.alto sax. 4.3.3.1. timp,
    3perc,harp,strings,pno solo
    study sc SIKORSKI f.s., perf mat
    rent   (L357)

    Concerto for Violoncello and
    Orchestra [20']
    3.2.3.3.alto sax. 4.2.3.1. timp,
    2perc,harp,pno,strings,vcl solo
    study sc SIKORSKI f.s., perf mat
    rent   (L358)

    Impromptu [8']
    2.0.3.2.alto sax. 3.1.2.1. timp,
    perc,harp,pno,strings
    SIKORSKI perf mat rent   (L359)

    Symphony No. 1 [15']
    3.3.3.3.alto sax. 4.3.3.1. timp,
    3perc,harp,pno,strings
    SIKORSKI perf mat rent   (L360)

    Symphony No. 2 [26']
    4.3.4.3.alto sax. 4.3.3.1. timp,
    3-4perc,2harp,cel,pno,strings
    SIKORSKI perf mat rent   (L361)

    Versunken In Die Nacht, For Solo
    Voice And Chamber Orchestra [10']
    1.1.1.1. 1.0.0.0. perc,strings,S
    solo
    SIKORSKI perf mat rent   (L362)

    Verwandlung [12']
    3.0.2.0.sax. 2.1.1.1. timp,2perc,
    harp,pno,strings
    SIKORSKI perf mat rent   (L363)

LI, HUAN-CHIH
    Spring Festival [5']
    3.2.2.2. 4.2.3.1. timp,perc,
    strings
    HONG KONG perf mat rent   (L364)

LIADOV, ANATOL KONSTANTINOVICH
(1855-1914)
    Danse De l'Amazone *Op.65 [4']
    3(pic).3(English horn).3.2.
    4.3.3.1. timp,perc,strings
    KALMUS A5775 sc $8.00, set $25.00,
    perf mat rent   (L365)

LIADOV, ANATOL KONSTANTINOVICH
(cont'd.)

    Fragment De l'Apocalypse *Op.66
    KALMUS A6107 sc $12.00, set $25.00,
    perf mat rent   (L366)

    Musical Snuff Box, The [arr.]
    (Lawrence) 2.2.2.1. 2.1.1.0. perc,
    pno&cel,harp,strings SCHIRM.G
    perf mat rent   (L367)

    Nenie *Op.67
    KALMUS A6092 sc $4.00, set $11.00
       (L368)

    Scherzo, Op. 16
    3.2.2.2. 4.2.3.0. timp,strings
    VAAP perf mat rent   (L369)

LIAISON, FOR VIOLONCELLO, PIANO AND
ORCHESTRA see Liebermann, Rolf

LIATOSHINSKY, BORIS (1895-1968)
    Lyric Poem, Op. 66 [10']
    3.3.3.3. 4.4.3.1. timp,3perc,cel,
    harp,strings
    SIKORSKI perf mat rent   (L370)
    VAAP perf mat rent   (L371)

    Symphony No. 2 [30']
    3.3.3.3. 4.3.3.1. timp,3perc,
    harp,strings
    VAAP perf mat rent   (L372)

    Symphony No. 3 [45']
    3.3.3.3. 4.3.3.1. timp,3perc,
    2harp,strings
    VAAP perf mat rent   (L373)

    Symphony No. 4, Op. 63 [26']
    3.3.3.3. 4.4.3.1. timp,3perc,cel,
    2harp,strings
    SIKORSKI perf mat rent   (L374)
    VAAP perf mat rent   (L375)

    Symphony No. 5, Op. 67 [33']
    3.3.3.3. 6.4.3.1. timp,3perc,
    harp,pno,strings
    SIKORSKI perf mat rent   (L376)
    (Slavic) VAAP perf mat rent   (L377)

LIBBEY, DEE
    Essence And Distractions [8']
    3.2.3.2. 4.3.2.1. timp,perc,harp,
    pno,strings
    BOURNE perf mat rent   (L378)

LIBELLEN WALZER see Strauss, Johann,
[Jr.]

LIBERA ME, FOR SOLO VOICE AND ORCHESTRA
see Donizetti, Gaetano

LIBERTY FANFARE see Williams, John T.

LICE DES NUITS, LA see Cuniot, Laurent

LICHENS I see Xenakis, Yannis (Iannis)

LICHTUNG, DIE see Hamel, Peter Michael,
Sinfonie In Sechs Teilen

LICKS & BRAINS II, FOR 4 SAXOPHONES AND
ORCHESTRA see Torstensson, Klas

LIDHOLM, INGVAR (1921-)
    Greetings From An Old World [16']
    2.2.2.2. 2.2.2.0. timp,perc,pno,
    strings
    sc NORDISKA f.s., perf mat rent
       (L379)

    Kontaktion [17']
    3.3.3.3. 4.3.3.1. timp,perc,harp,
    strings
    sc NORDISKA f.s., perf mat rent
       (L380)

    Motus - Colores [12']
    2.2.3.2. 2.2.2.1. perc,harp,elec
    gtr,cel,strings, electric
    mandolin
    SUECIA perf mat rent   (L381)

    Mutanza [12']
    2.2.1.2.alto sax. 2.2.1.0. 4perc,
    cel,strings
    study sc UNIVER. UE13175 $12.00,
    perf mat rent   (L382)

LIDICE see Martinu, Bohuslav (Jan)

LIE, HARALD (1902-1942)
    Elegy for Solo Voice and Orchestra,
    Op. 3 [9']
    2.2.3.2. 4.2.0.0. harp,strings,
    Bar solo
    NORGE   (L383)

    Symphony No. 2, Op. 5 [35']
    2.2.2.2. 4.3.3.1. timp,harp,
    strings
    NORGE   (L384)

LIE, SIGURD (1871-1904)
    Two Songs [arr.]
    (Halvorsen) string orch KALMUS
    A4583 sc $3.00, set $3.00   (L385)

LIEB UND WEIN POLKA see Strauss, Josef

LIEBERMAN, DAVID
    June 28, 1982 - Hotel Jerome [8']
    3.3.2.2. 4.2.2.1. 2perc,harp,
    strings
    sc AM.COMP.AL. $49.90, perf mat
    rent   (L386)

LIEBERMAN, GLENN
    Beards Of A Father [12']
    1.1.2.1. 1.1.0.0. perc,pno,
    strings
    sc AM.COMP.AL. $13.80, perf mat
    rent   (L387)

    Lighted Stones, For Piano And String
    Orchestra [23']
    string orch,pno solo
    sc AM.COMP.AL. $19.10   (L388)

LIEBERMANN, ROLF (1910-)
    Liaison, For Violoncello, Piano And
    Orchestra
    study sc UNIVER. UE 18381 f.s.
       (L389)

LIEBERSON, PETER (1946-)
    Concerto For Four Groups Of
    Instruments [9']
    fl,ob,clar,bsn,harp,pno,2vln,vla,
    vcl,db
    AMP perf mat rent   (L390)

    Concerto for Piano and Orchestra
    [45']
    3(pic).2+English horn.2+bass
    clar(contrabass clar).2+
    contrabsn. 4.3.3.1. timp,6perc,
    harp,cel,strings,pno solo
    AMP perf mat rent   (L391)

    Concerto for Violoncello and
    Instrumental Ensemble [13']
    fl,ob,bass clar,trp,mand,drums,
    harp,pno,2vln,vla,db,vcl solo
    AMP perf mat rent   (L392)

    Drala [17']
    3(pic,alto fl).2.3(clar in E
    flat).2+contrabsn. 4.3.3.1.
    timp,6perc,harp,pno,strings
    AMP perf mat rent   (L393)

    Gesar Legend [18']
    4(pic).2(English horn).3(bass
    clar).3+contrabsn. 4.3.3.1.
    timp,4perc,harp,pno&cel,strings
    AMP perf mat rent   (L394)

    Three Songs, For Solo Voice And
    Chamber Orchestra [10']
    1.1.1.1. 1.1.1.0. pno,harp,2vln,
    vla,vcl,S solo
    AMP perf mat rent   (L395)

LIEBES LIED, FOR SOLO VOICE AND
ORCHESTRA see Banfield, Raffaello
de

LIEBES MANNDEL, WO IST'S BANDEL, FOR
SOLO VOICES AND STRING ORCHESTRA
see Mozart, Wolfgang Amadeus

LIEBES ROCK see Thorne, Francis Burritt

LIEBESFREUD, FOR VIOLIN AND ORCHESTRA
[ARR.] see Kreisler, Fritz

LIEBESLIED, FOR SOLO VOICE AND
ORCHESTRA see Gehlhaar, Rolf

LIEBESLIED, FOR VIOLIN AND ORCHESTRA
[ARR.] see Kreisler, Fritz

LIEBESPROBE ODER DIE REKRUTIERUNG, DIE
see Mozart, Wolfgang Amadeus

LIEBESTRAUM (NOTTURNO NO. 3) [ARR.] see
Liszt, Franz

LIEBESZAUBER POLKA see Strauss, Eduard

LIED AM HERDE, FOR SOLO VOICE AND
ORCHESTRA see Distler, Hugo

LIED AUS DER FERNE, FOR SOLO VOICE AND
ORCHESTRA see Boehmer, Konrad

LIED DES VÖLLIG ARGLOSEN, DAS, FOR SOLO
VOICE AND ORCHESTRA see Trexler,
Georg

LIED FUR ORCHESTER see Klebe, Giselher

LIED IN FALL, FOR VIOLONCELLO AND
ORCHESTRA see Abrahamsen, Hans

LIED OHNE WORTE [ARR.] see Valen,
Fartein

LIED VON DER ERDE, DAS, FOR SOLO VOICES AND ORCHESTRA see Mahler, Gustav

LIEDER DES MONCHES ELILAND, FOR SOLO VOICE AND ORCHESTRA see Kindscher, Ludwig

LIEDER EINES FAHRENDEN GESELLEN, FOR SOLO VOICE AND ORCHESTRA see Mahler, Gustav

LIEDER MIT ORCHESTERBEGLEITUNG I see Wolf, Hugo

LIEDER MIT ORCHESTERBEGLEITUNG II see Wolf, Hugo

LIEDER OHNE WORTE, OP.30, NO.1; OP.38, NO.2; OP.53, NO.4; OP.85, NO.3 [ARR.] see Mendelssohn-Bartholdy, Felix

LIEDER OHNE WORTE, VOL. 1 [ARR.] see Mendelssohn-Bartholdy, Felix

LIEDER OHNE WORTE, VOL. 2 [ARR.] see Mendelssohn-Bartholdy, Felix

LIEDER QUADRILLE see Strauss, Johann, [Jr.]

LIEDER UND PAVANEN, FOR SOLO VOICE AND ORCHESTRA see Müller-Siemens, Detlev

LIEDER UND TANZE DES TODES, FOR SOLO VOICE AND ORCHESTRA [ARR] see Mussorgsky, Modest Petrovich, Songs And Dances Of Death, For Solo Voice And Orchestra [arr]

LIEDER UND TÄNZE DES TODES: DER FELDHERR, FOR SOLO VOICE AND ORCHESTRA, [ARR.] see Mussorgsky, Modest Petrovich, Songs And Dances Of Death: The Field Marshal, For Solo Voice And Orchestra, [arr.]

LIEDER UND TÄNZE DES TODES: STÄNDCHEN, FOR SOLO VOICE AND ORCHESTRA, [ARR.] see Mussorgsky, Modest Petrovich, Songs And Dances Of Death: Serenade, For Solo Voice And Orchestra, [arr.]

LIEDER UND TÄNZE DES TODES: TREPAK, FOR SOLO VOICE AND ORCHESTRA, [ARR.] see Mussorgsky, Modest Petrovich, Songs And Dances Of Death: Trepak, For Solo Voice And Orchestra, [arr.]

LIEDER UND TÄNZE DES TODES: WIEGENLIED, FOR SOLO VOICE AND ORCHESTRA, [ARR.] see Mussorgsky, Modest Petrovich, Songs And Dances Of Death: Berceuse, For Solo Voice And Orchestra, [arr.]

LIER, BERTUS VAN (1906-1972)
Dijk, De, For Narrator And Orchestra [30']
2.2.2.2. 2.3.2.1. timp,perc,harp, pno,strings,narrator
sc DONEMUS f.s., perf mat rent
(L396)

Katharsis [26']
3.3.4.3. 4.4.3.2.4Wagner tuba. timp,perc,strings
sc DONEMUS f.s., perf mat rent
(L397)

Variaties En Thema
3.2.2.2. 4.2.3.0. timp,perc, strings
sc DONEMUS f.s., perf mat rent
(L398)

LIERRE see Decoust, Michel

LIEUTENANT KIJE see Prokofiev, Serge

LIEUWEN, PETER (1953-)
Angelfire [16']
2(pic).1+English horn.2.2. 4.2.3.1. timp,3perc,pno&cel, harp,strings
NORRUTH perf mat rent
(L399)

LIFE see Fongaard, Bjørn, Livet

LIFE FOR THE TSAR, A: KRAKOWIAK see Glinka, Mikhail Ivanovich

LIFE FOR THE TSAR, A: OVERTURE see Glinka, Mikhail Ivanovich

LIFE FOR THE TSAR, A: WALTZ see Glinka, Mikhail Ivanovich

LIFE STORY see Maconchy, Elizabeth

LIFE'S DANCE see Delius, Frederick

LIFESONGS, FOR SOLO VOICE AND STRING ORCHESTRA see Kulesha, Gary

LIFT EVERY VOICE AND SING [ARR.] see Johnson, John Rosamond

LIGETI, GYÖRGY (1923-)
Concerto for Piano and Orchestra [22']
1(pic).1.1.1. 1.1.1.0. perc, strings,pno solo
sc SCHOTTS $75.00, perf mat rent
(L400)

Concerto for Violoncello and Orchestra [16']
1.1.2.1. 1.1.1.0. harp,strings, vcl solo
study sc PETERS P5936 f.s.
(L401)

LIGHT, THE see Glass, Philip

LIGHT IN THE WILDERNESS, THE: EXCERPTS see Brubeck, David (Dave) Warren

LIGHT SHINES IN THE DARKNESS, THE see Mostad, Jon

LIGHTED STONES, FOR PIANO AND STRING ORCHESTRA see Lieberman, Glenn

LIGHTNESS AND WEIGHT, FOR TUBA AND ORCHESTRA see Harvey, Jonathan

LILBURN, DOUGLAS (1915-)
Suite for Orchestra [23']
2.2.2.2. 4.2.3.0. timp,strings
sc WAI-TE-ATA f.s.
(L402)

Three Poems Of The Sea, For Narrator And String Orchestra [12']
string orch,narrator
sc WAI-TE-ATA f.s.
(L403)

LILJA, BERNHARD (1895-)
Autumn Lyrics, For Solo Voice And Orchestra [3']
2.1.2.2. 2.0.0.0. harp,strings, high solo/med solo
NORDISKA perf mat rent
(L404)

LILJA, FOR SOLO VOICE AND ORCHESTRA see Hovland, Egil

LILJEFORS, RUBEN (1871-1936)
Silent Songs, The, For Solo Voice And Orchestra [10']
3.3.3.3. 4.2.3.0. harp,strings, high solo/med solo
NORDISKA perf mat rent
(L405)

LILLEBJERKA, SIGMUND (1931-)
Adagio for String Orchestra [5']
string orch
NORGE
(L406)

Epigram
0.2.0.0. 2.0.0.0. strings
NORGE
(L407)

Symphony No. 2
2.2.2.2. 4.2.3.0. timp,strings
NORGE
(L408)

LILY, FOR SOLO VOICE AND INSTRUMENTAL ENSEMBLE see Kirchner, Leon

LIMITES, FOR HORN AND ORCHESTRA see Barboteau, G.

LIMPID BROOK, THE: SUITE see Shostakovich, Dmitri

LINCOLN LEGEND see Gould, Morton

LINCOLN'S GETTYSBURG ADDRESS, FOR SOLO VOICE AND ORCHESTRA see Adomian, Lan

LINDA CHAMOUNIX: AL BEN DESTIN CHE ATTENDEVI, FOR SOLO VOICES AND ORCHESTRA see Donizetti, Gaetano

LINDA DI CHAMOUNIX: AH! DIMMI...DIMMI, IO T' AMO, FOR SOLO VOICES AND ORCHESTRA see Donizetti, Gaetano

LINDA DI CHAMOUNIX: BUONA GENTE, FOR SOLO VOICE AND ORCHESTRA see Donizetti, Gaetano

LINDA DI CHAMOUNIX: CARI LUOGHI OV' IO PASSAI, FOR SOLO VOICE AND ORCHESTRA see Donizetti, Gaetano

LINDA DI CHAMOUNIX: CIEL, CHE DITE? LINDA E MORTA, FOR SOLO VOICES AND ORCHESTRA see Donizetti, Gaetano

LINDA DI CHAMOUNIX: DA QUEL DI CHE T' INCONTRAI, FOR SOLO VOICES AND ORCHESTRA see Donizetti, Gaetano

LINDA DI CHAMOUNIX: DI TUE PENE SPARVE IL SOGNO, FOR SOLO VOICES AND ORCHESTRA see Donizetti, Gaetano

LINDA DI CHAMOUNIX: E LA VOCE CHE PRIMIERA, FOR SOLO VOICE AND ORCHESTRA see Donizetti, Gaetano

LINDA DI CHAMOUNIX: ELLA E UN GIGLIO DI PURO CANDORE, FOR SOLO VOICE AND ORCHESTRA see Donizetti, Gaetano

LINDA DI CHAMOUNIX: IO VI DICO CHE PARTIATE, FOR SOLO VOICES AND ORCHESTRA see Donizetti, Gaetano

LINDA DI CHAMOUNIX: OVERTURE see Donizetti, Gaetano

LINDA DI CHAMOUNIX: QUELLA PIETA SI PROVVIDA, FOR SOLO VOICES AND ORCHESTRA see Donizetti, Gaetano

LINDA DI CHAMOUNIX: SE TANTO IN IRA AGLI UOMINI, FOR SOLO VOICE AND ORCHESTRA see Donizetti, Gaetano

LINDBERG, MAGNUS (1958-)
Kinetics [16']
2+pic.2+English horn.2(clar in E flat)+bass clar.2+ contrabsn.alto sax. 4.3.3.1. timp,3perc,harp,pno,strings, synthesizer
HANSEN-FIN perf mat rent
(L409)

Kraft [27']
4(pic)+alto fl.3+English horn.3(clar in E flat)+bass clar.3+contrabsn.alto sax. 4.4.4.1. 4perc,2harp,pno&cel, strings
HANSEN-DEN perf mat rent
(L410)

Marea [13']
2(pic).1+English horn.1+bass clar.1+contrabsn. 2.1.1.1. timp,perc,pno,strings
HANSEN-DEN perf mat rent
(L411)

Ritratto [12']
2(pic).1.2(bass clar).1. 2.0.0.0. perc,pno,3vln,2vla,2vcl,db
RICORDI-IT 133834 perf mat rent
(L412)

Tendenza [15']
2.3.2.0.alto sax. 1.1.1.1. 2perc, harp,pno,2vln,vla,vcl,db
sc SUOMEN f.s.
(L413)

LINDBERG, OSKAR [FREDRIK] (1887-1955)
Summer Evening, For Solo Voice And Orchestra [8']
2.2.2.2. 4.0.0.0. strings,high solo
NORDISKA perf mat rent
(L414)

Two Sacred Songs, For Solo Voice And Orchestra [7']
2.1.2.1. 2.2.1.0. timp,strings, low solo
NORDISKA perf mat rent
(L415)

Two Songs, For Solo Voice And Orchestra [7']
1.1.2.2. 4.0.0.0. harp,strings, high solo
NORDISKA perf mat rent
(L416)

Yearning Is My Share Of Heritage, For Solo Voice And Orchestra [4']
2.2.2.2. 2.0.0.0. harp,strings, med solo
NORDISKA perf mat rent
(L417)

LINDBERG, VALTER
Kehtolaulu
string orch
sc,pts FAZER f.s.
(L418)

LINDEMAN, SIGNE (1895-1974)
Fra St. Halvards Tid [16']
string orch
"From The Time Of St. Halvard"
NORGE
(L419)

From The Time Of St. Halvard see Fra St. Halvards Tid

Kollbotten [5']
2.1.2.1. 4.2.3.0. timp,perc, strings
NORGE
(L420)

LINDER, TORSTEN (1968-)
Kalif Storch, For Narrator And Orchestra *Op.3 [25']
2.2.2.2. 2.0.0.0. timp,perc, strings,narrator
SIKORSKI perf mat rent
(L421)

LINDGREN, KURT (1937-)
Variationer Över Ett Lockrop, For Solo Voice And Orchestra [20']
fl,trp,timp,pno,strings,S solo
NORDISKA perf mat rent
(L422)

LINDGREN, OLOF (1934-)
Humoristica
STIM
(L423)

LINDGREN, PÄR (1952-   )
Meander, For Percussion And Orchestra
4.4.5.3. 4.4.4.1. timp,perc,
2harp,2pno,strings,2perc soli
STIM   (L424)

Sanger Av Ljus
STIM   (L425)

LINDGREN, STEFAN (1960-   )
Concerto for Chamber Orchestra
1.1.1.1. 1.0.0.0. pno,6vln,2vla,
2vcl,db
STIM   (L426)

Concerto for Piano and String
Orchestra, No. 3 [21']
string orch,pno solo
STIM   (L427)

LINDNER, AUGUST (1820-1878)
Concerto for Violoncello and
Orchestra, Op. 34
KISTNER perf mat rent   (L428)

LINDORFF-LARSEN, EILERT (1902-   )
Poem for Horn and Orchestra [6']
1.1.2.1. 0.0.0.0. strings,horn
solo
HANSEN-DEN perf mat rent   (L429)

LINDPAINTER, PETER JOSEPH (1791-1856)
Andante, Variationen Und Bolero, For
Flute And Orchestra *Op.62
(Forster) sc KUNZEL 10178 f.s.,
perf mat rent   (L430)

Fantasy for Flute and Orchestra, Op.
123, in A
(Forster) sc KUNZEL 10182 f.s.,
perf mat rent   (L431)

LINDROTH, PETER (1950-   )
For The Orchestra Too [30']
2.2.2.2. 2.2.2.1. 3perc,strings
STIM   (L432)

LINEAIRE I, FOR SAXOPHONE AND ORCHESTRA
see Weber, Alain

LINEK, JIRI IGNATZ (1725-1791)
Sinfonia Pastoralis [13']
2ob,2trp,strings
sc SUPRAPHON MVH 36 f.s.   (L433)

LINK, HELMUT
Concertino for Trumpet and Orchestra,
Op. 21 [22']
2.2.2.2. 2.2.0.0. timp,strings,
trp solo
RIES   (L434)

Concerto for Piano and Orchestra, Op.
22 [24']
2(pic).2(English horn).2.2.
2.2.3.0. timp,perc,strings,pno
solo
RIES   (L435)

Concerto for Violin and Orchestra,
Op. 14, in E minor [31']
2(pic).2(English horn).2(bass
clar).2. 4.2.3.0. timp,2perc,
harp,strings,vln solo
RIES perf mat rent   (L436)

LINKOLA, JUKKA (1955-   )
Concerto for Trumpet and Orchestra
[25']
2.2.2.2. 3.2.2.1. timp,2perc,
harp,pno,strings,trp solo
sc SUOMEN f.s.   (L437)

Crossings [33']
3.3.3.3. 4.2.2.1. timp,3perc,
2harp,pno,cel,strings
sc SUOMEN f.s.   (L438)

Snow Queen, The [45']
1.1.1.1. 1.1.1.0. 2perc,harp,pno,
strings
sc SUOMEN f.s.   (L439)

LINNETT, ANNE
Symphony No. 1 [13']
2(alto fl)+pic.2+English horn.2+
bass clar.2+contrabsn. 4.4.3.1.
timp,perc,harp,strings,AAA soli
(Spring Capricious) HANSEN-DEN perf
mat rent   (L440)

LIONGATE, FOR FLUTE AND CHAMBER
ORCHESTRA see Sigurbjörnsson,
Thorkell

LIPKIN, MALCOLM (1932-   )
Sinfonia Di Roma [28']
2+pic.2.2+bass clar.2. 4.3.3.1.
timp,perc,strings
CHESTER JWC-A perf mat rent   (L441)

LIPOVSEK, MARIJAN (1910-   )
Antichaos [8']
2.2.2(bass clar).2. 4.3.3.1.
timp,perc,harp,strings
DRUSTVO DSS 901 perf mat rent

LIPOVSEK, MARIJAN (cont'd.)

                                  (L442)
Forgotten Songs, For Solo Voice And
Orchestra
see Pozabljene Pesmi, For Solo
Voice And Orchestra

Pozabljene Pesmi, For Solo Voice And
Orchestra [16']
2.2.2.2. 2.0.0.0. timp,2perc,
harp,strings,solo voice
"Forgotten Songs, For Solo Voice
And Orchestra" DRUSTVO
ED.DSS 1010 f.s., perf mat rent
                                  (L443)
Shine, Little Sun, For Solo Voice And
Orchestra
see Soncece, Sij, For Solo Voice
And Orchestra

Soncece, Sij, For Solo Voice And
Orchestra [31']
2.2.2.2. 2.0.0.0. timp,perc,
vibra,harp,cel,strings,S solo
"Shine, Little Sun, For Solo Voice
And Orchestra" DRUSTVO DSS 1101
perf mat rent   (L444)

LIPTAK, DAVID (1949-   )
Beginnings [10']
1.2.1.2. 2.1.1.0. perc,pno,
strings
sc AM.COMP.AL. $41.95, perf mat
rent   (L445)

Ellipsis [13']
string orch
sc AM.COMP.AL. $10.30   (L446)

LIRICA Y RITMICA see Sanjuan, Pedro

LIRIO AZUL, EL see Rodrigo, Joaquín

LISTEN TO THE INCENSE see Schafer, R.
Murray, Ko Wo Kiku

LISTER, RODNEY (1951-   )
Inglorious Fourth, For Solo Voice And
Chamber Orchestra [15']
1+pic.1(English horn).2.2.
1.1.0.0. perc,harp,strings,Mez
solo
GUNMAR MP 4033 perf mat rent   (L447)

LISZT, FRANZ (1811-1886)
Annees De Pelerinage: Sposalizio, Il
Penseroso [arr.]
(Kasanli) 2(pic).1+English horn.2+
bass clar.2. 4.2.3.1. timp,perc,
harp,strings [8'] KALMUS A6311 sc
$5.00, set $22.00, pts $1.00,
ea., perf mat rent   (L448)

Battle Of The Huns
see Hunnenschlacht

Bird Sermon Of St. Francis Of Assisi
[arr.]
see St. Francois D'assise: La
Predication Aux Oiseaux [arr.]

Bist Du! Mild Wie Ein Lufthauch, For
Solo Voice And Orchestra [arr.]
(D'albert; Mottl) 2.2.2.2. 4.0.0.0.
harp,strings,high solo [5'] KAHNT
perf mat rent   (L449)

Ce Qu'on Entend Sur La Montagne
"What One Hears On The Mountain"
min sc KALMUS K09328 $9.25 (L450)

Christus: Einzug In Jerusalem [18']
3.2.2.2. 4.2.2.1. perc,harp,
strings
KAHNT perf mat rent   (L451)

Christus: Hirtengesang [13']
3.3.2.2. 4.3.3.1. timp,perc,harp,
org,strings
KAHNT perf mat rent   (L452)

Christus: Overture [10']
3.3.2.2. 4.3.3.1. timp,perc,org,
harp,strings
KAHNT perf mat rent   (L453)

Concerti for Piano and Orchestra
(reprint of Breitkopf and Hartel
edition) sc DOVER 252213 $6.95
                                  (L454)
Concerto Pathetique, For Piano And
Orchestra
3.2.2.2. 2.2.3.0. timp,perc,harp,
strings,pno solo [14'] SONZOGNO
perf mat rent   (L455)

Concerto Pathetique, For Piano And
Orchestra In E Minor [arr]
(Reuss, E.) 3.2.2.2. 2.2.3.0. timp,
perc,harp,strings,pno solo [17']
BREITKOPF-W perf mat rent (L456)

Csardas Macabre [arr.]
(Darvas) min sc EMB 2736 f.s.
                                  (L457)

LISZT, FRANZ (cont'd.)

Dance Macabre, For Piano And
Orchestra
(Mezo) study sc EMB 40048 f.s.
                                  (L458)
Drei Zigeuner, Die, For Solo Voice
And Orchestra [6']
2.2.2.2. 4.0.3.0. timp,strings,
vln solo,med solo
KAHNT perf mat rent   (L459)

Enfant, Si J'etais Roi, For Solo
Voice And Orchestra [arr.]
(D'albert) "Mein Kind, War' Ich
Konig, For Solo Voice And
Orchestra [arr.]" 2.2.2.2.
4.2.3.1. timp,strings,high solo
[5'] KAHNT perf mat rent   (L460)

Es Muss Ein Wunderbares Sein, For
Solo Voice And Orchestra [arr.]
(D'albert; Mottl) 0.1.2.1. 4.0.0.0.
strings,med solo [5'] KAHNT perf
mat rent   (L461)

Es War Ein Konig In Thule, For Solo
Voice And Orchestra
2.1.2.2. 2.2.0.0. timp,strings,med
solo [4'] KAHNT perf mat rent
                                  (L462)
Fantasie Uber Ungarische
Volksmelodien, For Piano And
Orchestra
min sc EULENBURG EU01298 $6.50
                                  (L463)
Festklange
min sc KALMUS K09335 $9.25   (L464)

Feux Follets [arr.]
(Weiner) "Will O' The Wisp [arr.]"
KALMUS A6989 sc $15.00, set
$40.00, pts $2.00, ea., perf mat
rent   (L465)

Fischerknabe, Der, For Solo Voice And
Orchestra [6']
2.2.2.2. 2.0.0.0. strings,high
solo
KAHNT perf mat rent   (L466)

From Cliff To Sea
see Vom Fels Zum Meer

From Rock And Sea
see Vom Fels Zum Meer

From The Cradle To The Grave
see Von Der Wiege Bis Zum Grabe

Funeral Triumph Of Tasso
see Triomphe Funebre Du Tasse, Le

Hamlet
min sc KALMUS K09338 $4.50   (L467)

Heroide Funebre
min sc KALMUS K09336 $5.00   (L468)
SONZOGNO perf mat rent   (L469)

Huldigungsmarsch
"March Of Homage" min sc KALMUS
K09353 $3.50   (L470)

Hungaria
min sc KALMUS K09337 $7.00   (L471)
KALMUS A6480 sc $35.00, set $70.00,
pts $3.00, ea., perf mat rent
                                  (L472)
Hungarian March
see Vom Fels Zum Meer

Hungarian March, To The Assault
see Ungarischer Sturmmarsch

Hungarian Rhapsodies Nos. 1-9 [arr.]
see Rhapsodies Hongroises Nos. 1-9
[arr.]

Hungarian Rhapsody No. 13 [arr.]
see Rhapsodie Hongroise No. 13
[arr.]

Hungarian Storm March
see Ungarischer Sturmmarsch

Hunnenschlacht
"Battle Of The Huns" min sc KALMUS
K09339 $5.00   (L473)

Ideale, Die
min sc KALMUS K09340 $6.00   (L474)
KALMUS A6638 sc $40.00, set $90.00,
pts $4.00, ea., perf mat rent
                                  (L475)
In Liebeslust, For Solo Voice And
Orchestra [arr.]
(Mottl) 2.2.2.2. 4.2.0.0. strings,
high solo [3'] KAHNT perf mat
rent   (L476)

Kling' Leise Mein Lied, For Solo
Voice And Orchestra [arr.]
(Mottl) 2.2.2.2. 2.0.0.0. harp,
strings,high solo [4'] KAHNT perf
mat rent   (L477)

LISZT, FRANZ (cont'd.)

Kunstlerfestzug [12']
 3.2.2.2. 4.2.3.1. timp,perc,harp,
  strings
 KAHNT perf mat rent   (L478)

Legende Von Der Heiligen Elisabeth,
 Die: Gebet Der Heiligen
 Elisabeth, For Solo Voice And
 Orchestra [5']
 3.2.2.2. 4.2.2.1. timp,strings,S
  solo
 KAHNT perf mat rent   (L479)

Legende Von Der Heiligen Elisabeth,
 Die: Ouverture Und Marsch Der
 Kreuzritter [14']
 3.2.2.2. 4.2.2.1. timp,perc,
  strings
 KAHNT perf mat rent   (L480)

Legendes [arr.]
 (Schnapp) study sc EMB 40051 f.s.
          (L481)

Liebestraum (Notturno No. 3) [arr.]
 "Reve d'Amour [arr.]" 2.2.2.2.
  2.2.1.0. harmonium,perc,strings
 BOIS perf mat rent   (L482)

Loreley, Die, For Solo Voice And
 Orchestra [5']
 2.2.2.2. 2.1.2.1. timp,strings,
  solo voice
 KAHNT perf mat rent   (L483)

Lugubre Gondola No. 2, La [arr.]
 (Adams, John) 2.2(English
  horn).2(bass clar).2. 3.0.0.0.
  timp,harp,strings [9'] HENDON
  perf mat rent   (L484)

Malediction, For Piano And String
 Orchestra
 min sc KALMUS K09349 $4.00   (L485)

March Of Homage
 see Huldigungsmarsch

Mazeppa
 min sc KALMUS K09334 $7.00   (L486)

Mazurka Brillante [arr.]
 (Muller-Berghaus) 2+pic.2.2.2.
  4.2.3.0. timp,perc,harp,strings
  [5'] KALMUS A5776 sc $15.00, set
  $30.00, perf mat rent   (L487)

Mein Kind, War' Ich Konig, For Solo
 Voice And Orchestra [arr.]
 see Enfant, Si J'etais Roi, For
  Solo Voice And Orchestra [arr.]

Mephisto Waltz No. 1
 (Sulyok) sc KUNZEL 10100 $16.00,
  perf mat rent   (L488)

Mephisto Waltz No. 2
 min sc KALMUS K09342 $5.00   (L489)
 (Sulyok) sc KUNZEL 10101 $18.00,
  perf mat rent   (L490)

Mephisto Waltzes
 (Sulyok) study sc EMB 40064 f.s.
          (L491)

Mignons Lied, For Solo Voice And
 Orchestra [6']
 2.2.2.2. 2.2.3.0. timp,harp,
  strings,solo voice
 KAHNT perf mat rent   (L492)

Nacht, Die
 see Trois Odes Funebres: La Nuit

Nachtliche Zug, Der (from Two
 Episodes From Lenau's Faust)
 [15']
 3(pic).2+English horn.2.2.
  4.2.3.1. timp,bells,harp,
  strings
 "Nocturnal Procession" KALMUS A6125
  sc $20.00, set $50.00, perf mat
  rent   (L493)

Nocturnal Procession
 see Nachtliche Zug, Der

O Komm Im Traum, For Solo Voice And
 Orchestra [arr.]
 see Oh! Quand Je Dors, For Solo
  Voice And Orchestra [arr.]

Oh! Quand Je Dors, For Solo Voice And
 Orchestra [arr.]
 (D'albert; Mottl) "O Komm Im Traum,
  For Solo Voice And Orchestra
  [arr.]" 2.2.2.2. 4.0.0.0. harp,
  strings,high solo [8'] KAHNT perf
  mat rent   (L494)

Orpheus
 min sc KALMUS K09332 $4.00   (L495)

Preludes, Les
 study sc BREITKOPF-W PB 2360 f.s.
          (L496)

LISZT, FRANZ (cont'd.)

 min sc EMB 3017 f.s.   (L497)
 min sc KALMUS K09331 $5.75   (L498)

Prometheus
 min sc KALMUS K09333 $5.00   (L499)

Rakoczy-Marsch [12']
 2+pic.2.2.2. 4.2.3.1. timp,3perc,
  strings
 BREITKOPF-W perf mat rent   (L500)
 KALMUS A6420 sc $30.00, set $45.00,
  pts $2.00, ea., perf mat rent
          (L501)

Reve d'Amour [arr.]
 see Liebestraum (Notturno No. 3)
  [arr.]

Rhapsodie Espagnole, For Piano And
 Orchestra [arr.]
 (Busoni) KISTNER perf mat rent
          (L502)

Rhapsodie Hongroise No. 13 [arr.]
 (Hutschenruyter) "Hungarian
  Rhapsody No. 13 [arr.]" 3.2.2.2.
  4.3.3.1. timp,perc,harp,strings
  [11'] KALMUS A6485 pno-cond sc
  $3.00, set $25.00, pts $1.00,
  ea., perf mat rent   (L503)

Rhapsodies Hongroises Nos. 1-9 [arr.]
 "Hungarian Rhapsodies Nos. 1-9
  [arr.]" min sc KALMUS K09373
  $7.00   (L504)

Sonetto 104 Del Petrarca, For Solo
 Voice And Orchestra [arr.]
 (Busoni) "Sonnet No. 104, For Solo
  Voice And Orchestra [arr.]"
  2.2.2.2. 2.0.3.0. timp,harp,
  strings,T solo [7'] KALMUS A6797
  sc $10.00, set $18.00, pts $1.00,
  ea.   (L505)

Song And Hymn (Two Patriotic
 Melodies) [9'30"]
 2.2.2.2. 4.2.2.1. timp,harp,
  strings
 KALMUS A6138 sc $15.00, set $20.00,
  pts $1.00, ea., perf mat rent
          (L506)

Sonnenhymnus Des Heiligen Franziskus
 Von Assisi, For Solo Voice And
 Orchestra [29']
 2.2.2.2. 4.0.3.1. timp,org,
  strings,med solo
 KAHNT perf mat rent   (L507)

Sonnet No. 104, For Solo Voice And
 Orchestra [arr.]
 see Sonetto 104 Del Petrarca, For
  Solo Voice And Orchestra [arr.]

Sospiro, Un [arr.]
 2.2.2.2. 2.2.3.0. timp,perc,harp,
  strings BOIS perf mat rent (L508)

St. Francois D'assise: La Predication
 Aux Oiseaux [arr.]
 (Mottl) "Bird Sermon Of St. Francis
  Of Assisi [arr.]" 2.2.2.2.
  4.2.3.1. timp,2harp,strings [10']
  KALMUS A6310 sc $12.00, set
  $22.00, pts $1.00, ea., perf mat
  rent   (L509)

Tasso, Lamento E Trionfo
 min sc KALMUS K09329 $6.00   (L510)
 (Balla, G.) study sc EMB 40069
  $5.50   (L511)

Totentanz, For Piano And Orchestra
 min sc KALMUS K09348 $4.50   (L512)

Triomphe Funebre Du Tasse, Le
 KALMUS A6419 sc $15.00, set $40.00,
  pts $2.00, ea., perf mat rent
          (L513)
 "Funeral Triumph Of Tasso" min sc
  KALMUS K09330 $4.00   (L514)

Trois Odes Funebres: La Nuit
 "Nacht, Die" min sc KALMUS K09356
  $3.50   (L515)

Two Episodes From Lenau's Faust: Der
 Nachtliche Zug; Der Tanz In Der
 Dorfschenke
 "Two Episodes From Lenau's Faust:
  Nightly March; Dance In The
  Village Inn" min sc KALMUS K09341
  $5.00   (L516)

Two Episodes From Lenau's Faust:
 Nightly March; Dance In The
 Village Inn
 see Two Episodes From Lenau's
  Faust: Der Nachtliche Zug; Der
  Tanz In Der Dorfschenke

Two Movements For Strings
 see Zwei Satze Für Streicher

LISZT, FRANZ (cont'd.)

Ungarischer Sturmmarsch
 "Hungarian March, To The Assault"
  min sc KALMUS K09355 $3.50 (L517)
 "Hungarian Storm March" KALMUS
  A7028 sc $20.00, set $20.00, pts
  $1.00, ea.   (L518)

Vatergruft, Die, For Solo Voice And
 Orchestra [5']
 2.2.2.2. 2.3.2.1. timp,strings,
  low solo
 KAHNT perf mat rent   (L519)

Vom Fels Zum Meer
 "From Cliff To Sea" KALMUS A5777 sc
  $10.00, set $30.00, perf mat rent
          (L520)
 "From Rock And Sea" min sc KALMUS
  K09354 $5.00 contains also:
  Hungarian March   (L521)

Von Der Wiege Bis Zum Grabe
 "From The Cradle To The Grave"
  KALMUS min sc K09343 $3.50, sc
  A6798 $10.00, set $40.00, pts
  $2.00, ea., perf mat rent   (L522)

What One Hears On The Mountain
 see Ce Qu'on Entend Sur La Montagne

Wieder Mocht' Ich Dir Begegnen, For
 Solo Voice And Orchestra [arr.]
 (D'albert; Mottl) 2.2.2.2. 2.0.0.0.
  harp,strings,med solo [4'] KAHNT
  perf mat rent   (L523)

Wiegenlied [arr.]
 (Adams, John) 2.1.2.0. 0.0.0.0.
  harp,strings [4'] HENDON perf mat
  rent   (L524)

Wienen, Klagen [arr.]
 (Weiner) KALMUS A6779 sc $20.00,
  set $40.00, pts $2.00, ea., perf
  mat rent   (L525)

Will O' The Wisp [arr.]
 see Feux Follets [arr.]

Zwei Satze Für Streicher
 "Two Movements For Strings" string
  orch sc,pts AMADEUS BP 2685 f.s.
          (L526)

LIT DE NEIGE, FOR SOLO VOICE AND
 INSTRUMENTAL ENSEMBLE see
 Boucourechliev, André

LITANEI AUF DAS FEST ALLERSEELEN, FOR
 SOLO VOICE AND ORCHESTRA, [ARR.]
 see Schubert, Franz (Peter)

LITANIA see Buczynski, Pawel

LITANIE see Keizer, Henk

LITANIES see Goossen, Frederic see
 Hambraeus, Bengt

LITANY see Knaifel, Alexander

LITANY, THE, FOR SOLO VOICES AND
 ORCHESTRA see Harris, Russell G.

LITANY OF THE VICTIMS OF WAR see Marez
 Oyens, Tera de

LITEN SUITE FOR STRYKEORKESTER see
 Albertsen, Per Hjort

LITI KJERSTI: LITTLE BIRD, A, FOR SOLO
 VOICE AND ORCHESTRA see Eggen,
 Arne, Liti Kjersti: Og Det Var
 Litin Smafugl, For Solo Voice And
 Orchestra

LITI KJERSTI: OG DET VAR LITIN SMAFUGL,
 FOR SOLO VOICE AND ORCHESTRA see
 Eggen, Arne

LITI KJERSTI SUITE see Eggen, Arne

LITI KJERSTI SUITE: SYMFONISK
 MELLOMSPILL see Eggen, Arne

LITI KJERSTI SUITE: SYMPHONIC
 INTERMEZZO see Eggen, Arne, Liti
 Kjersti Suite: Symfonisk
 Mellomspill

LITIOS: LA FONTE, DEL SENTIRE, FOR
 FLUTE AND ORCHESTRA see Soccio,
 Giuseppe

LITTLE, DAVID (1952-)
 Shunyata [18']
 2.2.2.2. 0.0.0.0. perc,pno,
  strings
 sc DONEMUS f.s., perf mat rent
          (L527)

LITTLE CONCERT see Lessard, John Ayres

LITTLE CONCERTO, FOR PIANO AND CHAMBER
 ORCHESTRA see Kenins, Talivaldis

LITTLE CONCERTO FOR VIOLIN see Warren, B.

LITTLE ELEGIES see Body, Jack

LITTLE ELEGY see Howe, Mary

LITTLE HUMPBACK HORSE, THE: SUITE NO. 2 see Shchedrin, Rodion

LITTLE INDIAN; LITTLE DANCER see Carpenter, John Alden

LITTLE MARCH see Kroll, William

LITTLE MUSIC, FOR CLARINET AND CHAMBER ORCHESTRA see Speight, John A.

LITTLE RED SCHOOLHOUSE see Ewazen, Eric

LITTLE ROSE, FOR SOLO VOICE AND STRING ORCHESTRA see Howe, Mary

LITTLE SERENADE see Adomian, Lan

LITTLE SERENADE, A see Vea, Ketil

LITTLE SUITE see Björnsson, Arni see Denisov, Edison Vasilievich see Lundvik, H. see Nielsen, Carl see Sekles, Bernhard, Kleine Suite

LITTLE SUITE, FOR 2 VIOLINS AND CHAMBER ORCHESTRA see Biggs, John

LITTLE SUITE FOR STRINGS see Forsyth, Malcolm

LITTLE SUITE IN D see Telemann, Georg Philipp, Kleine Suite In D

LITTLE SUITE NO. 1 see Matthews, Colin

LITTLE SUITE NO. 2 see Matthews, Colin

LITTLE SYMPHONY see Chapple, Brian see Kupferman, Meyer see Maconchy, Elizabeth

LITURGY see Chance, Nancy Laird

LIU, DUN-NAN
    Mountain And The Forest, The, For Piano And Orchestra
        3.2.2.2. 4.3.3.1. timp,perc, strings,pno solo
        HONG KONG perf mat rent   (L528)

LIVET see Fongaard, Bjørn

LIVRE D'HEURES, FOR SOLO VOICES AND ORCHESTRA see Canat, Anne Edith

LIVRE POUR ORCHESTRA see Asturias, Rodrigo

LLAMA DEL AMOR VIVA see Espla, Oscar

LLOYD, JONATHAN (1948-   )
    Cantique [10']
        2(pic,alto fl).2(English horn).2(clar in E flat,bass clar).0. 2.2(trp in D).2.0. 4perc,pno,cel,glock,vibra,4vln, 4vla,2vcl,db
        BOOSEY perf mat rent   (L529)

    Concerto for Viola and Orchestra [25']
        2(pic,alto fl).2(English horn).2(clar in E flat,bass clar).1.soprano sax.alto sax. 2.1.1.0. 4perc,harp,mand&elec gtr,strings,vla solo
        BOOSEY perf mat rent   (L530)

    Everything Returns, For Solo Voice And Orchestra [15']
        2(pic)+alto fl.2+English horn.3(clar in E flat,bass clar).2+contrabsn. 4.3.3.1. 4perc,2harp,elec gtr,bass gtr, strings,S solo
        BOOSEY perf mat rent   (L531)

    Fantasy for Violin and Orchestra [7']
        2.2.2.2.soprano sax. 2.0+ cornet.1.0. 4perc,2harp,cel, hpsd&elec org,2elec gtr, strings,vln solo
        BOOSEY perf mat rent   (L532)

    If I Could Turn You On, For Solo Voice And Chamber Orchestra [9']
        2(pic,alto fl).2(English horn).1+ bass clar.0+contrabsn.alto sax. 2.1.1.0. perc,harp,elec org& cel,elec gtr,4vln,2vla,2vcl,db, electronic tape,S solo
        BOOSEY perf mat rent   (L533)

    Keir's Kick [5']
        string orch
        BOOSEY perf mat rent   (L534)

LLOYD, JONATHAN (cont'd.)
    Rhapsody for Violoncello and Orchestra [13']
        3(alto fl).2+English horn.3(clar in E flat,bass clar).2+ contrabsn. 4.3(trp in D).3.1. timp,2perc,cel&pno&hpsd,harp, gtr,strings,vcl solo,opt wom cor
        BOOSEY perf mat rent   (L535)

    Symphony No. 1 [28']
        2(pic,alto fl).2(English horn).2(bass clar).2(contrabsn). 2.2(opt trp in D).0.0. timp,strings
        BOOSEY perf mat rent   (L536)

    Symphony No. 2 [22']
        3(pic,alto fl).3(English horn).3(bass clar).3(contrabsn).opt alto sax. 4.3(opt trp in D).3.1. timp,2perc,cel,harp,strings, 4 recorders off-stage
        BOOSEY perf mat rent   (L537)

    Symphony No. 3 [28']
        1(pic,alto fl).1(English horn).2(bass clar).1(contrabsn). 2.0.0.0. 6vln,2vla,2vcl,db
        BOOSEY perf mat rent   (L538)

    Symphony No. 4 [30']
        3(pic)+alto fl.3(English horn).3(clar in E flat)+bass clar.4(contrabsn).4sax. 6.4.3.1. timp,5perc,cel,mand, gtr,harp,strings
        BOOSEY perf mat rent   (L539)

    Three Dances [15']
        1.0+English horn.1.1. 1.0.0.0. strings
        BOOSEY perf mat rent   (L540)

    Waiting For Gozo
        1(pic).1(English horn).2(bass clar).1(contrabsn). 1.1.1.0. 2vln,vla,vcl,db
        sc BOOSEY $15.00   (L541)

    Won't It Ever Be Morning [17']
        0+alto fl(pic).1(English horn).0+ clar in E flat(bass clar).1.alto sax. 2.1.1.0. perc,pno&harmonium,elec gtr, 2vln,vla,vcl
        BOOSEY perf mat rent   (L542)

LO see Scherchen, Tona

LO-SHU III, FOR FLUTE AND INSTRUMENTAL ENSEMBLE see Zender, Hans

LOA, FOR DOUBLEBASS AND STRING ORCHESTRA see Estevez, Francisco

LOB DER FRAUEN see Strauss, Johann, [Jr.]

LOBANOV, VASSILY (1947-   )
    Concerto for Violoncello and Orchestra [31']
        3.3.3.3. 4.3.3.1. timp,perc,cel, harp,pno,strings,vcl solo
        VAAP perf mat rent   (L543)

    Introduction, Grave And Allegro
        2.2.2.1. 2.2.3.0. timp,perc,pno, strings
        SCHIRM.G perf mat rent   (L544)

LOBGESANG, FOR SOLO VOICE AND ORCHESTRA see Schütz, Heinrich

LOCANDIERA, LA: OVERTURE see Salieri, Antonio

LOCATELLI, PIETRO (1695-1764)
    Concerto Grosso, Op. 1, No. 9, in D (Bonelli) KALMUS A7349 sc $10.00, set $17.50, pts $2.50, ea., perf mat rent   (L545)

    Concerto Grosso, Op. 1, No. 11, in C minor
        (Géczy) EMB f.s. sc 6775, pts 7039   (L546)

    Concerto, Op. 44, No. 2, [arr.]
        (Philippot, Michel) string orch, cont [10'] SALABERT perf mat rent   (L547)

LOCK OUT see Germeten, Gunnar

LOCKE, MATTHEW (1630-1677)
    Suite in B flat
        (Tilmouth, Michael) string orch, cont STAINER sc H294 f.s., pts AC37 f.s.   (L548)

    Suite in C
        string orch,cont
        (Tilmouth, Michael) STAINER sc H293

LOCKE, MATTHEW (cont'd.)
        f.s., pts AC36 f.s.   (L549)

LOCKLAIR, DAN STEVEN (1949-   )
    Dances For Orchestra [12'55"]
        (Three original dances by Claude Gervaise, each reelaborated and followed by a commentary in the spirit of the dance) sc KERBY DL 1 $80.00, perf mat rent (L550)

    Prism Of Life [19']
        sc KERBY 28241 $55.00, perf mat rent   (L551)

LOCKVOGEL see Strauss, Johann, [Jr.]

LOCKWOOD, NORMAND (1906-   )
    Concerto for 2 Harps and Chamber Orchestra [30']
        2.1.1.1. 2.1.1.0. perc,marimba, cel,strings,2harp soli
        sc AM.COMP.AL. $57.15   (L552)

    I Know Starlight, For Solo Voice And Orchestra [3']
        2.1.1.1. 2.0.0.0. timp,strings,S solo
        sc AM.COMP.AL. $4.60, perf mat rent   (L553)

    Mary, Who Stood In Sorrow, For Solo Voice And Orchestra [10']
        2.1.1.1. 2.1.1.0. timp,perc,harp, strings,S solo
        AM.COMP.AL. perf mat rent   (L554)

    Psalm No. 23 for Solo Voice and Orchestra [6']
        2.1.2.1. 2.2.2.1. timp,strings,S solo
        AM.COMP.AL. perf mat rent   (L555)

    Symphony for String Orchestra [14']
        string orch
        sc AM.COMP.AL. $11.45, perf mat rent   (L556)

LOCUS SOLUS see Marco, Tomas

LOEFFLER, CHARLES MARTIN (1861-1935)
    Devil's Round, The
        see Villanelle Du Diable

    Mort De Tinagiles, La, For Viola d'Amore And Orchestra *Op.6
        KALMUS A5885 sc $40.00, set $85.00, perf mat rent   (L557)

    Pagan Poem, A *Op.14
        KALMUS A5885 sc $40.00, set $60.00, perf mat rent   (L558)

    Villanelle Du Diable *Op.9
        "Devil's Round, The" KALMUS A5888 sc $30.00, set $55.00, perf mat rent   (L559)

LOEILLET, JEAN-BAPTISTE (JOHN, OF LONDON) (1680-1730)
    Concerto for 2 Trumpets and String Orchestra in D, [arr.]
        (Thilde, J.) string orch,2trp soli [6'45"] sc BILLAUDOT f.s., perf mat rent   (L560)

LOESSER, FRANK (1910-1969)
    Evening With Frank Loesser, An, Part I [arr.] *CCU
        (Martin, J.) 2.2.2.2. 4.3.3.1. timp,perc,xylo,strings FRANK perf mat rent   (L561)

    Evening With Frank Loesser, An, Part II [Arr.] *CCU
        (Martin, J.) 2.2.2.2. 4.3.3.1. timp,perc,xylo,strings FRANK perf mat rent   (L562)

    Guys And Dolls: A Woman In Love, For Solo Voice And Orchestra
        2.2.2.2. 4.3.3.1. timp,perc, strings,male solo
        FRANK perf mat rent   (L563)

    Guys And Dolls: Adelaide's Lament, For Solo Voice And Orchestra
        1.0.3+bass clar.0.alto sax.tenor sax.baritone sax. 1.3.1.0. perc,strings,female solo
        FRANK perf mat rent   (L564)

    Guys And Dolls: If I Were A Bell, For Solo Voice And Orchestra
        2.2.2.1. 4.3.3.0. perc,strings, female solo
        FRANK perf mat rent   (L565)

    Guys And Dolls: I've Never Been In Love Before, For Solo Voice And Orchestra
        2.2.2.2. 4.3.3.1. perc,strings, male solo
        FRANK perf mat rent   (L566)

LOESSER, FRANK (cont'd.)

Guys And Dolls: Overture
2alto sax/clar,2tenor sax,
baritone sax,horn,3trp,trom,
perc,strings
FRANK perf mat rent   (L567)

Guys And Dolls: Sue Me, For Solo
Voices And Orchestra
0.1.3+bass clar.0.2alto sax.tenor
sax.baritone sax. 1.3.1.0.
perc,strings,female solo&male
solo
FRANK perf mat rent   (L568)

Hans Christian Andersen: No Two
People, For Solo Voices And
Orchestra
2.2.2.2. 2.0.0.0. strings,male
solo&female solo
FRANK perf mat rent   (L569)

How To Succeed In Business Without
Really Trying: I Believe In You,
For Solo Voices And Orchestra
2.2.2.2. 4.3.3.1. perc,strings,
male solo&female solo
FRANK perf mat rent   (L570)

Most Happy Fella, The: Big D, For
Solo Voices And Orchestra
1.1(English horn).2(bass clar).1.
3.2.2.0. timp,perc,harp,
strings,male solo&female solo
FRANK perf mat rent   (L571)

Most Happy Fella, The: Happy To Make
Your Acquaintance, For Solo
Voices And Orchestra
0.1(English horn).2.1. 3.2.2.0.
perc,harp,cel,strings,male
solo&female solo
FRANK perf mat rent   (L572)

Most Happy Fella, The: Mama, Mama,
For Solo Voice And Orchestra
2.2.2.2. 4.3.3.1. timp,perc,
strings,Bar/B solo
FRANK perf mat rent   (L573)

Most Happy Fella, The: My Heart Is So
Full Of You, For Solo Voices And
Orchestra
1.1.2.1. 3.2.2.0. timp,perc,harp,
cel,acord,strings,male solo&
female solo
FRANK perf mat rent   (L574)

Most Happy Fella, The: Overture
1.1.2.1. 3.2.2.0. timp,perc,harp,
acord,strings
FRANK perf mat rent   (L575)

Most Happy Fella, The: Somebody,
Somewhere, For Solo Voice And
Orchestra
1.1(English horn).2.1. 3.2.2.0.
timp,cel,harp,strings,female
solo
FRANK perf mat rent   (L576)

Where's Charley: My Darling, My
Darling, For Solo Voices And
Orchestra
2.2.2.2. 4.3.3.1. timp,perc,
strings,male solo&female solo
FRANK perf mat rent   (L577)

Where's Charley: Once In Love With
Amy, For Solo Voice And Orchestra
2.2.2.1. 4.3.3.1. perc,cel,
strings,male solo
FRANK perf mat rent   (L578)

LOEVENDIE, THEO (1930-   )
Naima: Intermezzo [7'30"]
3.3.3.3.alto sax. 4.4.0.1. timp,
perc,harp,pno&cel,strings
DONEMUS perf mat rent   (L579)

Naima: Music For A Strange Wedding
[10']
3.3.3.3.alto sax. 4.4.0.1. timp,
3perc,harp,pno&cel,strings
DONEMUS perf mat rent   (L580)

Naima: Suite [26']
3.3.3.3.alto sax. 4.4.0.1. perc,
harp,pno&cel,strings
DONEMUS perf mat rent   (L581)

LOEWE, CARL GOTTFRIED (1796-1869)
Archibald Douglas, For Solo Voice And
Orchestra
3.4.4.3. 6.3.3.1. timp,drums,
harp,strings,Bar/Mez solo
BREITKOPF-L perf mat rent   (L582)

Archibald Douglas [arr.]
(Siebert, Friedrich) sc KUNZEL
10166 f.s., perf mat rent   (L583)

Herr Oluf, For Solo Voice And
Orchestra
3.2.3.3. 4.2.3.1. harp,strings,

LOEWE, CARL GOTTFRIED (cont'd.)

Bar/Mez solo
BREITKOPF-L perf mat rent   (L584)

Nächtliche Heerschau, Die, For Solo
Voice And Orchestra, [arr.]
*Op.23
(Pijper, Willem) 2.2.2.3. 4.2.3.0.
timp,3perc,strings sc DONEMUS
perf mat rent   (L585)

Odins Meeresritt, For Solo Voice And
Orchestra
3.2.2.2. 2.2.4.5. timp,perc,
strings,Bar/Mez solo
BREITKOPF-L perf mat rent   (L586)

LOEWE, KARL
see LOEWE, CARL GOTTFRIED

LOHENGRIN, FOR SOLO VOICES AND
ORCHESTRA see Sciarrino, Salvatore

LOHENGRIN: DAS SÜSSE LIED VERHALLT, FOR
SOLO VOICES AND ORCHESTRA see
Wagner, Richard

LOHENGRIN: EINSAM IN TRÜBEN TAGEN, FOR
SOLO VOICE AND ORCHESTRA see
Wagner, Richard

LOHENGRIN: ELSA'S PROCESSION TO THE
CATHEDRAL, [ARR.] see Wagner,
Richard, Lohengrin: Feierlicher Zug
Zum Münster, [arr.]

LOHENGRIN: ERHEBE DICH, GENOSSIN MEINER
SCHMACH, FOR SOLO VOICES AND
ORCHESTRA see Wagner, Richard

LOHENGRIN: EUCH LÜFTEN, DIE MEINE
KLAGEN, FOR SOLO VOICE AND
ORCHESTRA see Wagner, Richard

LOHENGRIN: FEIERLICHER ZUG ZUM MÜNSTER,
[ARR.] see Wagner, Richard

LOHENGRIN: HÖCHSTES VERTRAUN, FOR SOLO
VOICE AND ORCHESTRA see Wagner,
Richard

LOHENGRIN: NUN SEI BEDANKT, MEIN LIEBER
SCHWAN, FOR SOLO VOICE AND
ORCHESTRA see Wagner, Richard

LOI DE LA JUNGLE, LA see Koechlin,
Charles

LOMBARDI, I: LA MIA LETIZIA, FOR SOLO
VOICE AND ORCHESTRA see Verdi,
Giuseppe

LOMBARDO, MARIO (1931-   )
Spectrum [12']
PRESSER perf mat rent   (L587)

LOMBARDO, ROBERT M. (1932-   )
Aphorisms [8']
2.2.2.2. 2.2.2.1. perc,harp,
strings
sc AM.COMP.AL. $11.45, perf mat
rent   (L588)

Mesto, For Bassoon And String
Orchestra [9']
string orch,bsn solo
sc AM.COMP.AL. $5.40   (L589)

Sicilian Lyric [10']
2.2.2.2. 2.2.2.1. timp,perc,harp,
pno,strings
sc AM.COMP.AL. $19.10   (L590)

Threnody [9']
string orch
sc AM.COMP.AL. $5.40, perf mat rent
(L591)

LONDON, EDWIN (1929-   )
In Heinrich's Shoes [30']
1(pic,alto fl).1(English
horn).1(clar in A,bass
clar).0.soprano sax. 1.2.2.0.
2-3perc,strings
PETERS P67190 perf mat rent (L592)

LONDON, POUL
Serenade for Trombone and Orchestra
[5']
HANSEN-DEN perf mat rent   (L593)

LONDON SERENADE see Rands, Bernard

LONDON SYMPHONIES, SERIES 1 see Haydn,
[Franz] Joseph, Symphonies Nos. 93-
98

LONDON SYMPHONIES, SERIES 2 see Haydn,
[Franz] Joseph, Symphonies Nos. 99-
104

LONE SAILOR, THE see Vacek, Miloš

LONELY CHILD, FOR SOLO VOICE AND
CHAMBER ORCHESTRA see Vivier,
Claude

LONELY FIELD, THE, FOR SOLO VOICE AND
ORCHESTRA [ARR.] see Brahms,
Johannes, Feldeinsamkeit, For Solo
Voice And Orchestra [arr.]

LONELY ONES, THE see Cazden, Norman

LONESOME MAN, FOR SOLO VOICE AND
ORCHESTRA see Kjellsby, Erling,
Einsam Mann, For Solo Voice And
Orchestra

LONG MARCH SYMPHONY see Ding, Shan-De

LONG PEACE MARCH see Wolff, Christian

LONG SONG, FOR CLARINET AND
INSTRUMENTAL ENSEMBLE see Taranu,
Cornel

LONGING see Lunde, Ivar, Lengsel

LONGING FOR HOME, FOR SOLO VOICE AND
ORCHESTRA see Frumerie, (Per)
Gunnar (Fredrik) de

LONGTIN, MICHEL (1946-   )
Lettre De Roxana A Decebal Hormuz
2.2.2.2. 2.2.2.0. 2perc,strings
CAN.MUS.CENT. MI 1100 L857LE (L594)

Route De Pelerins Reclus, La [15']
3.4.3.3. 4.3.3.1. timp,3perc,
harp,strings
CAN.MUS.CENT. MI 1100 L857R (L595)

LOOKING AT ORPHEUS LOOKING see Samuel,
Gerhard

LOOS, ARMIN (1904-1971)
Two Orchestra Pieces
sc APNM $11.50   (L596)

LORA, ANTONIO (1899-1965)
Galatea, For Solo Voice And Orchestra
[6']
2.2.2.2. 4.3.3.1. timp,triangle,
strings,med solo
sc AM.COMP.AL. $9.15   (L597)

Green Air, For Solo Voice And
Orchestra [9']
1.1.1.1. 1.1.1.0. timp,strings,S
solo
sc AM.COMP.AL. $15.30   (L598)

LORD BYRON: FIVE TENOR SOLOS, FOR SOLO
VOICE AND ORCHESTRA see Thomson,
Virgil Garnett

LORD'S PRAYER, THE, FOR SOLO VOICE AND
ORCHESTRA [ARR.] see Malotte,
Albert Hay

LORELEI-RHEINKLANGE see Strauss,
Johann, [Sr.]

LORELEY, DIE, FOR SOLO VOICE AND
ORCHESTRA see Liszt, Franz

LORELEY, DIE: EINLEITUNG see Bruch, Max

LORELEY: DANZA DELLE ONDINE see
Catalani, Alfredo

LORENTZEN, BENT (1935-   )
Concerto for Oboe and Orchestra
1.0+English horn.1.1. 2.1.1.0.
perc,cel,strings,ob solo
sc HANSEN-NY $33.00, perf mat rent
(L599)
Concerto for Piano and Orchestra
[21']
2.2.2.2(contrabsn). 2.2.2.1.
timp,3perc,strings,pno solo
HANSEN-DEN perf mat rent   (L600)

Concerto for Violoncello and
Orchestra [25']
0+alto fl.0+English horn.0+basset
horn.1. 1.0.0.0. timp,2perc,
harp,strings,vcl solo
HANSEN-DEN perf mat rent   (L601)

Deep [22']
3.2+English horn.2+bass clar.2+
contrabsn. 4.2+bass trp.3.1.
timp,4perc,cel,harp,pno,strings
HANSEN-DEN perf mat rent   (L602)

Latin Suite [11']
2.2.2.2. 2.2.2.0. timp,3perc,
strings
HANSEN-DEN perf mat rent   (L603)

Partita Populare [12']
string orch HANSEN-DEN perf mat
rent   (L604)

LORENZACCIO: ARIA DI MARA, FOR SOLO
VOICE AND ORCHESTRA see Bussotti,
Sylvano

LORENZACCIO SYMPHONY I, FOR SOLO VOICE
AND ORCHESTRA see Bussotti, Sylvano

LORENZACCIO SYMPHONY II see Bussotti, Sylvano

LORENZINI, DANILO (1952-)
Fantasia Sinfonica, Sul Corale
"Liebster Jesu Wir Sind Hier" Di
J.S. Bach [18']
2.2.2.2. 2.2.0.0. timp,strings
SONZOGNO perf mat rent   (L605)

Ladina [10']
2.2.2.2. 4.2.3.0. timp,cel,harp,
strings
SONZOGNO perf mat rent   (L606)

LORENZO FERNANDEZ, OSCAR
see FERNANDEZ, OSCAR LORENZO

LORIN, MICHEL (1937-)
Ballade for Vibraphone and Orchestra
[7']
1.1.1.0. 0.4.4.0. timp,harp,pno,
gtr,strings,vibra solo
BILLAUDOT perf mat rent   (L607)

LORTZING, (GUSTAV) ALBERT (1801-1851)
Theme and Variations for Trumpet and
Orchestra [7'30"]
2.2.2.2. 2.2.0.1. strings,trp
solo
BOTE perf mat rent   (L608)

Undine: Ich War In Meinen Jungen
Jahren, For Solo Voice And
Orchestra
1.2.0.2. 0.0.0.0. strings,B solo
BREITKOPF-L perf mat rent   (L609)

Undine: Overture
KALMUS A5778 sc $15.00, set $45.00,
perf mat rent   (L610)

Undine: So Wisse, Dass In Allen
Elementen, For Solo Voice And
Orchestra
BREITKOPF-L perf mat rent   (L611)

Undine: Vater, Mutter, Schwestern,
Brüder, For Solo Voice And
Orchestra
BREITKOPF-L perf mat rent   (L612)

Undine: Was Seh Ich?, For Solo Voices
And Orchestra
2.0.2.2. 2.0.0.0. strings,TB soli
BREITKOPF-L perf mat rent   (L613)

Waffenschmied, Der: Auch Ich War Ein
Jüngling, For Solo Voice And
Orchestra
BREITKOPF-L perf mat rent   (L614)

Waffenschmied, Der: Du Bist Ein
Arbeitsamer Mensch, For Solo
Voices And Orchestra
2.0.2.2. 2.0.0.0. strings,TB soli
BREITKOPF-L perf mat rent   (L615)

Waffenschmied, Der: Er Schläft, Wir
Alle Sind In Angst, For Solo
Voice And Orchestra
BREITKOPF-L perf mat rent   (L616)

Waffenschmied, Der: Ihr Wisst, Dass
Er Euch Liebt, For Solo Voices
And Orchestra
2.0.2.2. 4.0.0.0. strings,SBar
soli
BREITKOPF-L perf mat rent   (L617)

Waffenschmied, Der: Man Wird Ja
Einmal Nur Geboren, For Solo
Voice And Orchestra
2.0.2.2. 2.0.0.0. strings,T solo
BREITKOPF-W perf mat rent   (L618)
BREITKOPF-L perf mat rent   (L619)

Waffenschmied, Der: Welt, Du Kannst
Mir Nicht Gefallen, For Solo
Voice And Orchestra
2.2.0.2. 2.0.0.0. strings,A solo
BREITKOPF-W perf mat rent   (L620)
BREITKOPF-L perf mat rent   (L621)

Waffenschmied, Der: Wir Armen, Armen
Mädchen, For Solo Voice And
Orchestra
2.2.0.2. 2.0.0.0. strings,S solo
BREITKOPF-L perf mat rent   (L622)

Wildschutz, Der: Auf Des Lebens
Raschen Wogen, For Solo Voice And
Orchestra
2.2.2.2. 2.2.0.0. timp,strings,S
solo
BREITKOPF-W perf mat rent   (L623)
BREITKOPF-L perf mat rent   (L624)

Wildschütz, Der: Fünftausend Taler,
For Solo Voice And Orchestra
BREITKOPF-L perf mat rent   (L625)

Wildschütz, Der: Heiterkeit Und
Fröhlichkeit, For Solo Voice And
Orchestra
2.2.2.2. 4.2.3.0. timp,strings,

LORTZING, (GUSTAV) ALBERT (cont'd.)

Bar solo
BREITKOPF-L perf mat rent   (L626)

Wildschutz, Der: Ihr Weib? Mein
Teures Weib!, For Solo Voices And
Orchestra [8']
2.0.2.2. 2.0.0.0. strings,ST soli
BREITKOPF-W perf mat rent   (L627)

Wildschütz, Der: Lass Er Doch Hören,
For Solo Voices And Orchestra
2.2.0.2. 4.0.0.0. strings,SB soli
BREITKOPF-L perf mat rent   (L628)

Zar Und Zimmermann: Darf Eine Niedre
Magd Es Wagen, For Solo Voices
And Orchestra
2.0.2.2. 4.0.0.0. strings,ST soli
BREITKOPF-L perf mat rent   (L629)

Zar Und Zimmermann: Die Eifersucht
Ist Eine Plage, For Solo Voice
And Orchestra
BREITKOPF-L perf mat rent   (L630)

Zar Und Zimmermann: Holzschuhtanz
[6']
2(pic).2.2.2. 4.2.3.0. timp,perc,
strings
BREITKOPF-W perf mat rent   (L631)

Zar Und Zimmermann: Lebe Wohl, Mein
Flandrisch Mädchen, For Solo
Voice And Orchestra
BREITKOPF-L perf mat rent   (L632)

Zar Und Zimmermann: O Sancta
Justitia, For Solo Voice And
Orchestra
BREITKOPF-L perf mat rent   (L633)

Zar Und Zimmermann: Sonst Spielt Ich
Mit Zepter, For Solo Voice And
Orchestra
BREITKOPF-L perf mat rent   (L634)

LOSH, WERNER J.
Coronach [9']
3(pic).2(English
horn).2.3(contrabsn). 4.4.3.1.
timp,perc,pno,strings
MCA perf mat rent   (L635)

LOST HOUR, THE: THEME see Applebaum,
Stanley

LOTHAR, MARK (1902-1985)
Geschichte Vom Faulen Baren, Die, For
Narrator, Tuba And Orchestra
[26']
2.2.2.2. 2.1.1.0. timp,perc,harp,
pno,cel,strings,tuba solo,
narrator
SIKORSKI perf mat rent   (L636)

Goldoni Musik, For 3 Woodwinds And
Orchestra *Op.89 [20']
2(pic).1.1.1. 2.0.0.0. 2perc,
hpsd,strings,fl solo,clar solo,
bsn solo
BOTE perf mat rent   (L637)

LOTTA CONTINUA see Martland, Steve

LOU SALOME: SUITE II see Sinopoli,
Giuseppe

LOUCHEUR, RAYMOND (1899-1979)
Concerto for Violoncello and
Orchestra [21']
2.2.2.2. 2.2.2.1. timp,2perc,
harp,strings,vcl solo
SALABERT perf mat rent   (L638)

Defile [9']
3.3.3.3. 4.2.3.1. 2cornet,timp,
perc,2harp,pno,cel,strings
SALABERT perf mat rent   (L639)

Symphony No. 3 [21']
3(pic).3(English horn).2+bass
clar.2+contrabsn. 4.3.3.1.
3perc,harp,strings
SALABERT perf mat rent   (L640)

LOUIE, ALEXINA (1949-)
Music For A Celebration [5']
2.2.2.2. 2.2.1.0. timp,perc,
strings
CAN.MUS.CENT. MI 1100 L888MU (L641)

Music For A Thousand Autumns [17']
2(pic).1.1.1. 0.0.0.0. 2perc,pno,
vln,vla,vcl,db
CAN.MUS.CENT. MI 1200 L888M (L642)

Ringing Earth, The [6']
3(alto fl).3.3.3. 4.3.3.1. timp,
3perc,harp,strings
CAN.MUS.CENT. MI 1100 L888RI (L643)

Winter Music, For Viola And
Instrumental Ensemble [17']
1.1.1.1. 1.0.0.0. 2perc,harp,vln,

LOUIE, ALEXINA (cont'd.)

vcl,db,vla solo
CAN.MUS.CENT. MI 1312 L888^OWI
        (L644)

LOUISCHEN POLKA see Strauss, Johann,
[Jr.]

LOUISIANA CONCERTO see Holmboe, Vagn

LOUVIER, ALAIN (1945-)
Concerto for Orchestra
LEDUC perf mat rent   (L645)

Folie Et Mort D'ophelie, For Solo
Voices And Orchestra [20']
2.2.2.2. 2.2.2.0. timp,perc,
strings,SBar soli
BILLAUDOT perf mat rent   (L646)

Poemes De Ronsard, For Solo Voice And
Chamber Orchestra
LEDUC AL 27158-27159 perf mat rent
        (L647)

Psudr [4']
2.2.3.1. 1.1.1.0. 3perc,hpsd,vln,
vla,2vcl,db
BILLAUDOT perf mat rent   (L648)

LOVE 200, FOR ROCK BAND AND ORCHESTRA
see Sculthorpe, Peter [Joshua]

LOVE FOR SALE, FOR SOLO VOICE AND
ORCHESTRA see Porter, Cole

LOVE IN THE ASYLUM, FOR SOLO VOICE AND
ORCHESTRA see Plante, Daniel

LOVE OF THREE ORANGES: SUITE see
Prokofiev, Serge

LOVE SCENE FROM "THE MERCHANT OF
VENICE" see Humperdinck, Engelbert

LOVE SIGN [ARR.] see Cleve, Cissi,
Kjertegn [arr.]

LOVE SONG see Kelemen, Milko

LOVE SONGS AND DANCES see Cooper, Paul

LOVE SPELLS, FOR SOLO VOICE AND
ORCHESTRA see Bennett, Richard
Rodney

LOVE WALKED IN, SOMEBODY LOVES ME, AND
THE MAN I LOVE, FOR SOLO VOICES AND
ORCHESTRA see Gershwin, George

LOVEC, VLADIMIR (1922-)
Classical Symphony
see Klasicna Simfonija

Klasicna Simfonija
2(pic).2.2.2. 4.2.3.1. timp,
strings
"Classical Symphony" DRUSTVO
DSS 899 perf mat rent   (L649)

LOVENDUSKY, JAMES
Metathesis [15']
2(pic,alto fl).2(English
horn).2(bass clar).2. 4.2.2.0.
perc,strings
sc AM.COMP.AL. $33.50   (L650)

LOVER, THE see Sibelius, Jean,
Rakastava

LOVE'S GARDEN, FOR SOLO VOICE AND
ORCHESTRA see Gellman, Steven

LOWRY LIEDER, FOR SOLO VOICE AND
ORCHESTRA see Rihm, Wolfgang

LU, YEN (1930-)
Music for Chamber Orchestra
fl,ob,bass clar,timp,4perc,harp,
cel,strings
SEESAW   (L651)

LUBETSKY, RONALD
Monumentum [27']
4.4.4.4. 4.4.4.1. timp,perc,
2harp,pno&cel,strings
sc AM.COMP.AL. $59.40, perf mat
rent   (L652)

Surfaces [10']
4.2.3.2. 4.2.2.0. perc,harp,cel,
strings
sc AM.COMP.AL. $9.60, perf mat rent
        (L653)

LUCAS, CLARENCE
Macbeth
3.2.2.2. 4.2.3.1. timp,perc,
strings
sc,pts CAN.MUS.HER. f.s.   (L654)

LUCAS, LEIGHTON (1903-1982)
Concert Champêtre, For Violin And
Orchestra [17']
2(pic).2(English horn).2.2.
2.0.0.0. harp,timp,strings,vln
solo
CHESTER JWC196A perf mat rent

LUCAS, LEIGHTON (cont'd.)
                                    (L655)
LUCE ETERNA, LA, FOR SOLO VOICE AND
  ORCHESTRA see Thorne, Francis
  Burritt

LUCIA SILLA: OVERTURE see Mozart,
  Wolfgang Amadeus

LUCIFER POLKA see Strauss, Johann,
  [Jr.]

LUCIFER'S DANCE see Stockhausen,
  Karlheinz, Luzifers Tanz

LUCIS CREATOR see Rogers, Rodney

LUCKY, ŠTEPÁN (1919-   )
  Nenia, For Violin And Orchestra
    2.2.2.2. 3.2.2.0. timp,perc,
    vibra,harp,strings,vln solo
    SUPRAPHON   (L656)

LUCREZIA: O NUMI ETERNI, FOR SOLO VOICE
  AND STRING ORCHESTRA see Handel,
  George Frideric

LUCTUS ET GAUDIUM, FOR TROMBONE AND
  STRING ORCHESTRA see Angerer, Paul

LUDI CONTRAPUNCTICI see Lajovic,
  Aleksander

LUDWIG, NORBERT (1902-1960)
  Blue Scarecrow, The [arr.]
    (Carroll) 3.3.3.2. 4.3.3.0. timp,
    perc,xylo,harp,strings [5'] MCA
    perf mat rent   (L657)

LUDWIG, THOMAS (1952-   )
  Symphony No. 1 [22']
    3(pic).2+English horn.2+bass
    clar.2. 4.3.2(bass trom).1.
    timp,5perc,pno,strings
    (Age Of Victory) AMP perf mat rent
                                    (L658)

LUDZUWEIT, GÜNTER
  Concerto for Flute and Orchestra
    2trp,3trom,tuba,timp,harp,
    strings,fl solo
    ZIMMER.   (L659)

LUEDEKE, RAYMOND (1944-   )
  Chamber Symphony No. 1 [17']
    2.1.3.2. 1.1.0.1. perc,strings
    sc AM.COMP.AL. $45.75, perf mat
    rent   (L660)
    CAN.MUS.CENT. MI 1100 L948CH (L661)

  Clockworks [8']
    2.2.2.2. 4.2.3.1. timp,3perc,
    harp,strings
    CAN.MUS.CENT. MI 1100 L948CL (L662)

  Concerto for 4 Saxophones and
    Orchestra [23']
    2.2.2.2. 4.2.3.1. timp,strings,
    4sax soli
    AM.COMP.AL. sc $48.25, pts $49.55
                                    (L663)
    CAN.MUS.CENT. MI 1425 L948CO (L664)

  Fanfare [3']
    3.3.3(clar in E flat).3. 6.0.3.1.
    timp,3perc,harp,pno,org,
    strings, 12 herald trumpets
    CAN.MUS.CENT. MI 1100 L948FA (L665)

  Four Cantos [16']
    2.2.2.2. 4.2.3.1. perc,strings
    sc AM.COMP.AL. $14.50   (L666)
    CAN.MUS.CENT. MI 1100 L948FO (L667)

  Moon In The Labyrinth, The [25']
    string orch
    sc AM.COMP.AL. $25.25, perf mat
    rent   (L668)

  Shadow Music [17']
    2.2.2.2. 4.2.3.1. timp,3perc,
    strings
    CAN.MUS.CENT. MI 1100 L948SH (L669)

  Tales Of The Netsilik, For Solo Voice
    And Orchestra [41']
    2(pic).2(English horn).2(bass
    clar).2(contrabsn). 4.2.3.1.
    timp,2perc,pno,cel,harp,
    strings,narrator
    CAN.MUS.CENT. MV 1400 L948TA (L670)

  Transparency Of Time, The, For Piano
    And Orchestra [17']
    2.2.2.2. 4.2.3.1. timp,2perc,
    harp,strings,pno solo
    CAN.MUS.CENT. MI 1361 L 948TR
                                    (L671)
LUENING, OTTO (1900-   )
  Elegy For The Lonesome Ones, For
    Clarinet And String Orchestra
    [6']
    string orch,clar solo
    sc AM.COMP.AL. $4.60   (L672)

LUENING, OTTO (cont'd.)
  Potawatomi Legends [18']
    1.1.1.1. 1.1.1.0. perc,pno 4-
    hands,strings
    sc AM.COMP.AL. $22.60   (L673)

  Short Symphony [12']
    2.2.2.2. 4.3.3.0. perc,strings
    sc AM.COMP.AL. $11.45, perf mat
    rent   (L674)

  Sonority Forms [14']
    4.2.3.2. 4.3.3.1. perc,harp,pno,
    strings
    sc AM.COMP.AL. $26.70, perf mat
    rent   (L675)

  Symphonic Fantasia No. 1 [18']
    3.3.2.3. 4.3.3.1. perc,harp,pno,
    org,cel,strings
    sc AM.COMP.AL. $15.30   (L676)

  Symphonic Fantasia No. 2 [17']
    3.3.3.3. 4.3.3.1. timp,perc,harp,
    pno,strings
    sc AM.COMP.AL. $18.30, perf mat
    rent   (L677)

  Symphonic Fantasia No. 3 [3']
    2.2.2.2. 1.1.1.1. perc,pno,
    strings
    AM.COMP.AL. perf mat rent   (L678)

  Symphonic Fantasia No. 4 [9']
    2.2.2.2. 1.1.1.1. perc,pno,
    strings
    sc AM.COMP.AL. $13.80   (L679)

  Symphonic Fantasia No.5 [6']
    4.3.3.3. 4.3.3.1. 2perc,harp,pno,
    strings
    sc AM.COMP.AL. $41.95, perf mat
    rent   (L680)

  Symphonic Fantasia No.6 [13']
    4.3.3.3. 4.3.3.1. 2perc,pno,
    strings
    sc AM.COMP.AL. $53.80, perf mat
    rent   (L681)

  Symphonic Fantasia No.7 [6']
    2.2.2.2. 2.2.0.0. timp,perc,
    strings
    sc AM.COMP.AL. $36.90, perf mat
    rent   (L682)

  Symphonic Fantasia No.8 [5']
    2.2.2.2. 2.2.0.0. timp,perc,pno,
    strings
    sc AM.COMP.AL. $23.05, perf mat
    rent   (L683)

  Symphonic Fantasia No.9 [12']
    2.2.2.2. 1.1.1.1. timp,perc,
    strings
    sc AM.COMP.AL. $65.00, perf mat
    rent   (L684)

  Symphonic Interlude No. 3
    3(pic).2+English horn.2.2+
    contrabsn. 4.3.3.1. timp,perc,
    strings
    sc JOSHUA 981 $8.50   (L685)

  Symphonic Interlude No.4 [8']
    2.2.2.2. 1.1.1.1. perc,harp,cel,
    strings
    sc AM.COMP.AL. $34.15, perf mat
    rent   (L686)

  Symphonic Interlude No. 5 [6']
    3.2.2.2. 4.3.3.1. timp,perc,harp,
    strings
    PETERS P67166 perf mat rent (L687)

  Wisconsin Suite
    2(pic).2.2.2. 2.2.2.0. timp,perc,
    pno,strings sc JOSHUA 1001 $12.95
                                    (L688)

  Wisconsin Symphony, A [30']
    3.3.3.3.tenor sax. 4.3.3.1. timp,
    perc,harp,pno,strings
    sc AM.COMP.AL. $48.80, perf mat
    rent   (L689)

LUETZOW-HOLM, OLE (1954-   )
  Sounding [12']
    1.1.1.1. 1.1.1.0. perc,harp,3vln,
    2vla,2vcl,db
    STIM   (L690)

LUFTIG UND DUFTIG POLKA see Strauss,
  Eduard

LUG see Martin, Frederick

LUGUBRE GONDOLA NO. 2, LA [ARR.] see
  Liszt, Franz

LUIGINI, ALEXANDRE (1850-1906)
  Ballet Egyptien: Suites Nos. 1 And 2
    *Op.12
    4(pic).1.2.1. 4.2.3.1. timp,perc,
    harp,strings
    LEMOINE perf mat rent   (L691)

LUIGINI, ALEXANDRE (cont'd.)
  Romance for Horn and Orchestra, Op.
    48 [5']
    2.2.2.2. 0.0.0.0. timp,harp,
    strings,horn solo
    (Leloir, E.) sc BILLAUDOT f.s.,
    perf mat rent   (L692)

LUISA MILLER: DALL' AULE RAGGIANTI DI
  VANO SPLENDORE, FOR SOLO VOICES AND
  ORCHESTRA see Verdi, Giuseppe

LUISA MILLER: IL MIO SANGUE, LA VITA
  DAREI, FOR SOLO VOICE AND ORCHESTRA
  see Verdi, Giuseppe

LUISA MILLER: L'ALTO RETAGGIO NON HO
  BRAMATO, FOR SOLO VOICES AND
  ORCHESTRA see Verdi, Giuseppe

LUISA MILLER: PRESENTARTI ALLA
  DUCHESSA, FOR SOLO VOICES AND
  ORCHESTRA see Verdi, Giuseppe

LUISA MILLER: SACRA LA SCELTA E D' UN
  CONSORTE, FOR SOLO VOICE AND
  ORCHESTRA see Verdi, Giuseppe

LUISA MILLER: SOTTO IL MIO PIE IL SUOL
  VACILLA, FOR SOLO VOICES AND
  ORCHESTRA see Verdi, Giuseppe

LUISA MILLER: TU PUNISCIMI, O SIGNORE,
  FOR SOLO VOICE AND ORCHESTRA see
  Verdi, Giuseppe

LUKAS, ZDENEK (1928-   )
  Verba Laudata, For Solo Voice And
    Chamber Orchestra
    strings,pno,S solo
    SUPRAPHON   (L693)

LUKASZEWSKI, WOJCIECH (1936-   )
  Episodes [12']
    3.2.2.3. 4.2.3.1. perc,strings
    POLSKIE   (L694)

LULLABY see Spalder, Frithjof,
  Vuggevise

LULLABY, FOR SOLO VOICE AND ORCHESTRA
  see Tveitt, Geirr, Voggesong, For
  Solo Voice And Orchestra

LULLABY FOR THE EARTH see Werle, Lars-
  Johan, Vaggsang For Jorden

LULLABY OF BROADWAY, [ARR.] see Warren,
  Harry

LULLY, JEAN-BAPTISTE (LULLI)
  (1632-1687)
  Armide Et Renaud: Three Instrumental
    Pieces
    (Hockner) string orch,hpsd [4']
    KALMUS A6469 sc $4.00, set $5.00,
    pts $.75, ea., perf mat rent
                                    (L695)

  Ballet Des Muses [arr.]
    (Husa, Karel) opt 2fl,opt 2ob,hpsd,
    strings [18'] AMP   (L696)

  Sinfonies Pour Les Pastres
    string orch
    (Petit, J.L.) [15'] BILLAUDOT
    597-00321 sc $3.50, pts f.s.
                                    (L697)
  Six Pieces For String Orchestra
    (Brown) string orch [10'] KALMUS
    A5706 sc $5.00, set $5.00 (L698)

LUMBYE, HANS CHRISTIAN (1810-1874)
  Danse: Suite No. 1
    sc,pts SAMFUNDET f.s.   (L699)

LUMIERES DE GUANG-LING see Chen, Qigang

LUMIERES ET FORMES ANIMEES, FOR
  ORCHESTRA see Bondon, Jacques

LUMIERES ET FORMES ANIMEES, FOR STRING
  ORCHESTRA see Bondon, Jacques

LUMINA see Ferrari, Giorgio see Malec,
  Ivo see Wilson, Olly

LUNA, FOR ALTO FLUTE AND ORCHESTRA see
  Bois, Rob du

LUNA, PABLO (1880-1942)
  Nino Judio, El, For Solo Voice And
    Orchestra [6']
    2.1.2.1. 2.2.2.0. timp,perc,harp,
    strings,solo voice
    UNION ESP. perf mat rent   (L700)

LUND, SIGNE (1868-1950)
  Armestic Chimes *Op.52
    2.2.2.3. 4.2.3.1. timp,perc,harp,
    cel,strings
    NORGE   (L701)

  Selfdependence, For Solo Voice And
    Orchestra *Op.54
    2.2.2.2. 4.2.3.0. timp,perc,harp,

LUND, SIGNE (cont'd.)

    strings,solo voice
    NORGE   (L702)

LUNDBORG, (CHARLES) ERIK (1948-)
  Concerto for Piano and Orchestra
    [16']
      2.2.2.2. 4.2.3.1. timp,perc,harp,
      strings,pno solo
      sc AM.COMP.AL. $59.40, perf mat
      rent   (L703)

  Passacaglia [13']
    1.1.1.1. 2.1.1.1. perc,2vln,vla,
    vcl,db
    sc APNM $17.25, perf mat rent
          (L704)

  Scherzo [12']
    3.3.3.3. 4.2.3.1. timp,2perc,
    harp,pno&cel,strings
    AM.COMP.AL. perf mat rent (L705)

LUNDE, IVAR (1944-)
  Aiga *Op.36 [11']
    2.2.2.2. 4.3.2.1. timp,perc,
    strings
    NORGE   (L706)

  Concertino for Flute, Oboe,
    Harpsichord and String Orchestra,
    Op. 21 [11']
    string orch,fl solo,ob solo,hpsd
    solo
    (revised version) NORGE (L707)

  Concertino for Violin, Oboe and
    String Orchestra, Op. 21 [10']
    string orch,vln solo,ob solo
    NORGE   (L708)

  Erindringer, For Solo Voice Abd
    String Orchestra *Op.68b [11']
    string orch,T solo
    "Memories, For Solo Voice And
    String Orchestra" NORGE (L709)

  Illustrasjoner *Op.12 [8']
    string orch
    "Illustrations" NORGE   (L710)

  Illustrations
    see Illustrasjoner

  Joy *Op.84 [7']
    2+pic.2+English horn.2.2.
    4.2.3.1. timp,perc,harp,strings
    NORSK perf mat rent   (L711)

  Lengsel *Op.16 [8']
    string orch
    "Longing" NORGE   (L712)

  Longing
    see Lengsel

  Memories, For Solo Voice And String
    Orchestra
    see Erindringer, For Solo Voice Abd
    String Orchestra

  Nordic Suite *Op.43 [28']
    3.3.3.2. 4.4.3.1. timp,perc,
    strings
    NORGE   (L713)

  Renee, For Violin And String
    Orchestra *Op.17 [6']
    string orch,vln solo
    NORGE   (L714)

  Seks Norske Danser *Op.82 [12'] .
    3.2.3.2. 4.3.3.1. timp,perc,harp,
    strings
    "Six Norwegian Dances" NORGE (L715)

  Six Norwegian Dances
    see Seks Norske Danser

  Symphony No. 1, Op. 57 [21']
    3.3.3.2. 4.4.3.1. timp,perc,harp,
    strings
    NORGE   (L716)

  Symphony No. 3, Op. 83 [40']
    2.2.2.2. 4.2.3.1. timp,perc,cel&
    pno,strings
    NORGE   (L717)
    NORGE   (L718)

LUNDE, JOHAN BACKER
  see BACKER-LUNDE, JOHAN

LUNDEN-WELDEN, GUNNAR
  Calling All Tourists [3']
    1.1.2.1. 2.2.1.0. perc,acord,
    pno-cond sc,pts BUSCH HBM 005 f.s.
          (L719)

  Kvallsflanoren [3'25"]
    2.1.2.1. 2.2.1.0. cel,pno,gtr,
    drums,strings
    "Saunterer, The" sc,pts BUSCH
    HBM 006 f.s.   (L720)

LUNDEN-WELDEN, GUNNAR (cont'd.)

  Saunterer, The
    see Kvallsflanoren

LUNDKVIST, PER (1916-)
  Frohe Jugend [10'35"]
    1.1.2.1. 2.2.1.0. perc,strings
    "Joyful Youth" pno-cond sc,pts
    BUSCH DM 030 f.s.   (L721)

  Joyful Youth
    see Frohe Jugend

  Krumelur [3'40"]
    1.1.2.1. 2.2.1.0. perc,strings
    "Wag, The" pno-cond sc,pts BUSCH
    DM 034 f.s.   (L722)

  Wag, The
    see Krumelur

LUNDQVIST, GUNNAR (1948-)
  Passacaglia, Op. 10 [2']
    string orch
    perf sc GEHRMANS 6090 f.s. (L723)

LUNDSTEN, RALPH (1936-)
  Pompata [arr.] (from Paradissymfonin,
    Op. 180)
    (Lundqvist, Gunnar) [7'30"]
    GEHRMANS sc 6031P f.s., pts 6013S
    f.s.   (L724)

  Summer Saga, A [arr.]
    (Genetay, Claude) 1.1.1.1. 2.0.0.0.
    strings [17'] sc GEHRMANS 6349P
    f.s., perf mat rent   (L725)

LUNDVIK, H.
  Little Suite [10']
    string orch
    NORDISKA perf mat rent   (L726)

LURE, THE see Holst, Gustav

LURE OF THE FALLEN SERAPHIM see Buhr,
  Glenn

LUST'GER RATH POLKA see Strauss,
  Johann, [Jr.]

LUSTIG IM KREISE POLKA see Strauss,
  Eduard

LUSTIGE G'SCHICHTEN WALZER see Strauss,
  Eduard

LUSTIGE KREIG, DER, QUADRILLE see
  Strauss, Johann, [Jr.]

LUSTIGE SINFONIETTA IN D MINOR, OP. 4
  see Hindemith, Paul

LUSTIGE SUITE IN C see Telemann, Georg
  Philipp, Bouffonne, La

LUSTIGE WEIBER VON WINDSOR, DIE: ALS
  BUBLEIN KLEIN, FOR SOLO VOICE AND
  ORCHESTRA see Nicolai, Otto
.
LUSTIGE WEIBER VON WINDSOR, DIE: GOTT
  GRUSS EUCH SIR!, FOR SOLO VOICES
  AND ORCHESTRA see Nicolai, Otto

LUSTIGE WEIBER VON WINDSOR, DIE: HORCH,
  DIE LERCHE SINGT IM HAIN!, FOR SOLO
  VOICE AND ORCHESTRA see Nicolai,
  Otto

LUSTIGE WEIBER VON WINDSOR, DIE: NEIN,
  DAS IST WIRKLICH DOCH ZU KECK, FOR
  SOLO VOICE AND ORCHESTRA see
  Nicolai, Otto

LUSTIGE WEIBER VON WINDSOR, DIE: NUN
  EILT HERBEI, FOR SOLO VOICE AND
  ORCHESTRA see Nicolai, Otto

LUSTIGE WEIBER VON WINDSOR, DIE: WOHL
  DENN, GEFASST IST DER ENTSCHLUSS,
  FOR SOLO VOICE AND ORCHESTRA see
  Nicolai, Otto

LUSTIGE WITWE, DIE: PARAPHRASE [ARR.]
  see Lehar, Franz

LUSTSPIEL-OVERTURE see Busoni,
  Ferruccio Benvenuto

LUSTSPIEL OVERTURE, EINE see Reznicek,
  Emil Nikolaus von

LUTAD MOT GARDET, FOR SOLO VOICE AND
  ORCHESTRA see Jensen, Ludwig Irgens

LUTOSLAWSKI, WITOLD (1913-1994)
  Autumn, For Solo Voice And Orchestra
    see Jesien, For Solo Voice And
    Orchestra

  Chain 1
    1(pic,alto fl).1(English
    horn).1.1. 1.1.1.0. perc,hpsd,
    2vln,vla,vcl,db
    sc CHESTER CH 55633 f.s., perf mat

LUTOSLAWSKI, WITOLD (cont'd.)

    rent   (L727)

  Chain 2, For Violin And Orchestra
    [18']
    2(pic).2(English horn).2(bass
    clar).2. 0.2.2.0. perc,pno&cel,
    strings,vln solo
    CHESTER CH697   (L728)

  Chain 3 [10']
    3(pic).3.3(bass clar).3. 4.3.3.1.
    timp,4perc,2harp,pno,cel,
    strings
    CHESTER CH746 perf mat rent (L729)

  Concerto for Oboe, Harp and Orchestra
    [20']
    2perc,strings,ob solo,harp solo
    CHESTER perf mat rent   (L730)

  Concerto for Piano and Orchestra
    [27']
    3(pic).3.3(bass
    clar).3(contrabsn). 2.4.3.1.
    perc,harp,strings,pno solo
    CHESTER perf mat rent   (L731)

  Grave, For Violoncello And String
    Orchestra [7']
    string orch
    sc CHESTER f.s.   (L732)

  Interlude [5']
    0+pic.1(English horn).2.1.
    0.1.1.0. perc,harp,pno&cel,
    4vln,2vla,2vcl,db
    CHESTER perf mat rent   (L733)

  Jesien, For Solo Voice And Orchestra
    [5']
    2.1.2.1. 0.1.0.0. strings,Mez
    solo
    "Autumn, For Solo Voice And
    Orchestra" CHESTER perf mat rent
          (L734)

  Partita for Violin and Orchestra
    [15']
    2(pic).0.2(bass
    clar).2(contrabsn). 0.2.2.0.
    perc,harp,cel,pno,strings,vln
    solo
    CHESTER perf mat rent   (L735)

  Prelude For Guildhall School Of
    Music: Worldes Blis Ne Last No
    Throwe [2']
    2.2.2.2. 2.2.2.1. timp,perc,harp,
    strings
    CHESTER perf mat rent   (L736)

  Slides [4']
    1.1.1.1. 1.0.0.0. perc,pno&cel,
    vln,vla,vcl,db
    CHESTER perf mat rent   (L737)

  Spring, For Solo Voice And Orchestra
    see Wiosna, For Solo Voice And
    Orchestra

  Symphony No. 3
    3.3.3.3. 4.4.4.1. timp,perc,
    2harp,pno 4-hands,cel,strings
    sc CHESTER CH 55613 $59.75, perf
    mat rent   (L738)

  Two Children's Songs, For Solo Voice
    And String Orchestra
    string orch,solo voice
    POLSKIE   (L739)

  Variations On A Theme Of Paganini,
    For Piano And Orchestra [9']
    2(pic).2.2.2(contrabsn). 4.3.3.1.
    timp,perc,harp,strings,pno solo
    CHESTER CH487 perf mat rent (L740)

  Wiosna, For Solo Voice And Orchestra
    [5']
    2.1.2.1. 0.0.0.0. strings,Mez
    solo
    "Spring, For Solo Voice And
    Orchestra" CHESTER perf mat rent
          (L741)

LUTYENS, ELISABETH (1906-1983)
  Cascando, For Solo Voice, Violin, And
    String Orchestra *Op.117
    string orch,vln solo,A solo
    UNIVER.   (L742)

LUV see Oliver, Stephen

LUX AETERNA see Holm, Kristin

LUX COELESTIS see Rovsing Olsen, Poul

LUZIFERS TANZ see Stockhausen,
  Karlheinz

LYBBERT, DONALD (1923-)
  Concert Overture [10']
    3.2.3.2. 4.3.3.1. timp,perc,xylo,
    pno,strings
    sc AM.COMP.AL. $38.15   (L743)

LYKKEN I MIN SJAL, FOR SOLO VOICE AND ORCHESTRA see Wiklund, Adolf

LYRIC DANCES see Dello Joio, Norman

LYRIC FOR STRINGS see Walker, George Theophilus

LYRIC III, FOR VIOLONCELLO AND ORCHESTRA see Buczynski, Walter

LYRIC MOVEMENT see Holst, Gustav

LYRIC POEM, OP. 66 see Liatoshinsky, Boris

LYRIC V, FOR OBOE AND STRING ORCHESTRA see Buczynski, Walter

LYRIC VARIATIONS, FOR TUBA AND STRING ORCHESTRA see Brown, Jonathan Bruce

LYRIC VARIATIONS NO.5 see Thorne, Francis Burritt

LYRICA see Urbanner, Erich

LYRICAL MARCH AND HALLING see Grov, Magne, Lyrisk Marsj Og Halling

LYRIKOS, FOR SOLO VOICE AND ORCHESTRA see Crockett, Donald

LYRISCHE ABWEICHUNGEN, FOR 10 VIOLONCELLI AND ORCHESTRA see Ekimovsky, Viktor

LYRISCHES INTERMEZZO, FOR SOLO VOICES AND ORCHESTRA see Togni, Camillo

LYRISCHES KONZERT, FOR VIOLONCELLO AND ORCHESTRA see Genzmer, Harald

LYRISK BALLAD, FOR 2 PIANOS AND ORCHESTRA see Hallberg, Bengt

LYRISK MARSJ OG HALLING see Grov, Magne

LYS NAT, FOR SOLO VOICE AND ORCHESTRA [ARR.] see Grieg, Edvard Hagerup

LYSTSPILOUVERTURE see Tarp, Svend Erik

M

MA, KO
Shanbei Suite [7']
3.1.2.1. 1.1.1.1. perc,strings
HONG KONG perf mat rent   (M1)

White-Haired Girl, The: Suite *see Chu, Wei

MA CHE VI FECE, FOR SOLO VOICE AND ORCHESTRA see Mozart, Wolfgang Amadeus

MA ELAN, FOR SOLO VOICE AND ORCHESTRA [ARR.] see Merikanto, Oskar

MA MERE L'OYE see Ravel, Maurice

MA MERE L'OYE: CINQ PIECES ENFANTINES see Ravel, Maurice

MA MERE L'OYE: PRELUDE ET DANSE DU ROUET see Ravel, Maurice

MA VLAST: SARKA see Smetana, Bedrich, My Country, No. 3: Sarka

MAASZ, GERHARD (1906-1984)
Da Lachen Ja Die Huhner, For Solo Voice And Orchestra [24']
2.1.2.1. 1.2.1.0. perc,strings, speaking voice
RIES perf mat rent   (M2)

MCALISTER, CLARK (1946-   )
Barcarolle [8']
2(pic).1+English horn.2.2. 2.2.0.0. timp,perc,strings
KALMUS A7131 sc $15.00, set $25.00, pts $1.50, ea., perf mat rent   (M3)

Nightwatch, For Viola And Orchestra [10']
2+pic.1+English horn.2+bass clar.2+contrabsn. 4.2.3.1. timp,perc,vla solo
KALMUS A5868 sc $15.00, set $22.00, perf mat rent   (M4)

MACBETH see Lucas, Clarence see Strauss, Richard

MCBETH, WILLIAM FRANCIS (1933-   )
Badlands
SOUTHERN rent   (M5)

Grace, Preludium And Response
SOUTHERN rent   (M6)

Symphony No. 3
SOUTHERN rent   (M7)

Symphony No. 4
SOUTHERN rent   (M8)

MACBETH AND THE WITCHES, FOR PIANO AND ORCHESTRA see Smetana, Bedrich

MACBETH: FANFARE AND MARCH [ARR.] see Walton, [Sir] William (Turner)

MACBRIDE, DAVID HUSTON (1951-   )
Dance Interlude [6']
2.2.2.2. 4.4.3.0. 4perc,strings
sc AM.COMP.AL. $29.80, perf mat rent   (M9)

Elegies, For Harp And String Orchestra [12']
string orch,harp solo
AM.COMP.AL. sc $9.60, pts $4.10, perf mat rent   (M10)

Four Sonnets [20']
2.1.2.1.alto sax. 1.2.1.0. perc, cel,strings
sc AM.COMP.AL. $32.50, perf mat rent   (M11)

Measuring The Future [14']
3(pic).3.3.3. 4.3.2+bass trom.1. timp,perc,strings
sc AM.COMP.AL. $24.45   (M12)

Parallax [20']
3.3.3.2. 4.3.3.1. perc,harp,pno, cel,strings
sc AM.COMP.AL. $28.20, perf mat rent   (M13)

Produce [10']
2.3.2.3. 2.2.2.1. timp,perc,xylo, harp,strings
sc AM.COMP.AL. $13.80   (M14)

See What Happens [17']
2.2.2.2. 3.3.3.0. perc,harp,cel, strings
sc AM.COMP.AL. $20.60   (M15)

MACBRIDE, DAVID HUSTON (cont'd.)
1010 [14']
2.2.2.2. 1.2.1.0. 2perc,strings
sc AM.COMP.AL. $58.05   (M16)

MCBRIDE, ROBERT GUYN (1911-   )
Jingle-Jangle, For Vibraphone And String Orchestra [4']
string orch,vibra solo
sc AM.COMP.AL. $8.80, perf mat rent   (M17)

Variation On An Unknown Theme [3']
string orch
sc AM.COMP.AL. $3.85, perf mat rent   (M18)

Wise-Apple Five, For Clarinet And String Orchestra [5']
string orch,clar solo
AM.COMP.AL. sc $9.15, pts $1.20   (M19)

MCCABE, JOHN (1939-   )
Basse Danse [15']
3(pic).3.3(bass clar).3(contrabsn). 4.3.3.1. 2perc,timp,pno&cel,harp,strings
NOVELLO perf mat rent   (M20)

Chagall Windows, The [31']
3(pic).3.(English horn).2(bass clar).2(contrabsn). 4.4.3.1. timp,4perc,harp,pno&cel,strings
NOVELLO perf mat rent   (M21)

Concertino for Piano 4-Hands and Orchestra [12']
2.2.2.1. 2.2.2.0. timp,perc, vibra,strings,pno 4-hands soli
NOVELLO perf mat rent   (M22)

Concerto for Clarinet and Orchestra [13']
2.1.1.1. 2.0.0.0. timp,harp, strings,clar solo
NOVELLO perf mat rent   (M23)

Concerto for Orchestra [24']
3.3.3.3. 4.3.3.1. timp,perc,pno/ cel,harp,strings
sc NOVELLO $54.50   (M24)

Concerto for Violin and Orchestra, No. 2 [38']
3.3(English horn).3.3. 4.3.3.1. timp,3perc,cel,harp,strings,vln solo
NOVELLO perf mat rent   (M25)

Jubilee Suite [12']
3(pic).3.3.3. 4.3.3.1. timp, 3perc,cel,strings
NOVELLO perf mat rent   (M26)

Mary, Queen Of Scots: Suite No. 1 [19']
2.2.2.2. 4.2.3.1. timp,2perc, harp,cel,strings
NOVELLO perf mat rent   (M27)

Mary, Queen Of Scots: Suite No. 2 [22']
1+opt fl.1+opt ob.1+opt clar.1+ opt bsn. 2+opt 2horn.2+opt trp.1+opt 2trom.0+opt tuba. timp,2perc,cel,harp,strings
NOVELLO perf mat rent   (M28)

Sam: Orchestral Version [3']
2(pic).0.2.0. 0.1.0.0. perc, strings
NOVELLO perf mat rent   (M29)

Shadow Of Light [23']
3(pic).3.3.2. 4.3.3.1. timp, 3perc,harp,strings
NOVELLO perf mat rent   (M30)

Symphony No. 3 [24']
3(pic).3.3.3(contrabsn). 4.3.3.1. timp,3perc,harp,pno&cel,strings
NOVELLO perf mat rent   (M31)

Tuning
NOVELLO perf mat rent   (M32)

MCCONNELL, ROB
Hello From The North [9']
3+pic.1.3.2+contrabsn.soprano sax.2alto sax.2tenor sax.baritone sax. 4.4.4.0. timp,perc,pno,harp,3gtr, strings, fender-rhodes
NEWAM 19029 perf mat rent   (M33)

MACDOWELL, EDWARD ALEXANDER (1861-1908)
Hamlet And Ophelia *Op.22
KALMUS A6436 sc $20.00, set $40.00, pts $2.00, ea., perf mat rent   (M34)

Poet's Dream, The [arr.] *Op.31,No.6
(Jungnickel) 2.2+English horn.2.2. 2.2.1.0. timp,harp,strings [3']
KALMUS A5779 sc $4.00, set $15.00, perf mat rent   (M35)

MACDOWELL, EDWARD ALEXANDER (cont'd.)

Saracens, The: Two Fragments [3']
    2+pic.2.2.2. 4.2.3.1. timp,perc,
    strings
    KALMUS A6448 sc $15.00, set $25.00,
    pts $1.00, ea., perf mat rent
                                        (M36)

Scotch Poem [arr.] *Op.31,No.2
    (Jungnickel) 2.2.2.2. 4.2.3.1.
    timp,perc,harp,strings [3']
    KALMUS A5798 sc $8.00, set
    $25.00, perf mat rent   (M37)

To A Wild Rose, For Harp And
    Orchestra [arr.]
    2.2.2.2. 4.2.3.1. perc,cel,strings,
    harp solo SCHIRM.G perf mat rent
                                        (M38)

MACEDONIAN DANCES see Srebotnjak, Alojz
    F., Makedonski Plesi

MCGUIRE, JOHN (1942-   )
    Cadence Music
    2.2.2.2. 2.0.0.0. perc,harp,pno,
    2vln,2vla,db
    BREITKOPF-W perf mat rent   (M39)

MÁCHA, OTMAR (1922-   )
    Concerto for Violin, Piano and
    Orchestra [18']
    CESKY HUD.   (M40)

    Slovak Rhapsody [7']
    SUPRAPHON   (M41)

MACHAUT A MA MANIERE see Birtwistle,
    Harrison

MACHAVARIANI, ALEXEI (1913-   )
    Concerto for Violin and Orchestra
    [27']
    3.3.4.2. 4.3.3.1. timp,perc,harp,
    strings,vln solo
    SIKORSKI perf mat rent   (M42)
    VAAP perf mat rent   (M43)

    Othello: Suite No. 1 [30']
    3.3.4.3.3sax. 4.3.3.1. timp,perc,
    2harp,cel,pno,strings
    SIKORSKI perf mat rent   (M44)

    Othello: Suite No. 2 [28']
    3.3.4.3.3sax. 4.3.3.1. timp,perc,
    2harp,cel,pno,strings
    SIKORSKI perf mat rent   (M45)

MACHE, FRANCOIS BERNARD (1935-   )
    Synergies [7'20"]
    2.1.2.2. 2.2.1.0. 2perc,harp,
    2vln,vla,2vcl,db,electronic
    equipment
    BILLAUDOT perf mat rent   (M46)

MACHOVER, TOD (1953-   )
    Nature's Breath [20']
    1.1.1.1. 1.0.0.0. harp,vibra,
    marimba,2vln,vla,vcl,db
    RICORDI-FR perf mat rent   (M47)

MACHT, ROBERT
    Concerto for Percussion and Orchestra
    [10'15"]
    2.2.2(clar in A).2(contrabsn).
    2.2.1.0. strings,perc solo
    PEER perf mat rent   (M48)

MACIE see Durieux, Frederic

MCINTOSH, DIANA
    Margins Of Reality [13']
    string orch
    CAN.MUS.CENT. MI 1500 M152MA   (M49)

MCINTYRE, PAUL (1931-   )
    Matins For The Vigil Of Assumption
    [15']
    3(pic).3(English horn).4(bass
    clar,clar in E flat).3.alto
    sax. 4.2.3.1. 3perc,strings
    CAN.MUS.CENT. MI 1100 M1525MA   (M50)

    Song Of Autumn
    string orch
    CAN.MUS.CENT. MI 1500 M1525SO   (M51)

MCKAY, GEORGE FREDERICK (1899-1970)
    Sinfonietta in D
    GALAXY pno-cond sc $2.25, set
    $12.00, and up   (M52)

MCKAY, NEIL (1924-   )
    Dance Overture
    SHAWNEE perf mat rent   (M53)

    Kaleidoscope
    SHAWNEE perf mat rent   (M54)

    Kubla Khan, For Solo Voice And
    Chamber Orchestra
    fl,perc,pno,strings,S solo
    SHAWNEE perf mat rent   (M55)

MACKEY, STEVEN (1956-   )
    Big Bang And Beyond, The [17']
    2(pic).1+English horn.2(bass
    clar).2(contrabsn). 2.2.2.1.
    timp,3perc,harp,pno,strings
    MARGUN BP 5026 perf mat rent   (M56)

    Square Holes, Round Pegs [11']
    2.2.2.2. 2.2.0.0. timp,perc,harp,
    pno,strings
    sc MARGUN MP5041 $50.00, perf mat
    rent   (M57)

MCLEAN, EDWIN
    Big City Ballads, For 3 Saxophones
    And Orchestra [14']
    2.2.3.2. 4.2.3.1. timp,3perc,
    strings,3sax soli
    sc AM.COMP.AL. $58.95   (M58)

    Big Variations [8']
    2.0.2.0. 1.1.1.0. xylo,strings
    sc AM.COMP.AL. $12.65, perf mat
    rent   (M59)

MCLENNAN, JOHN STEWART (1915-   )
    Triptych [14']
    2.3.2.3. 4.3.3.1. timp,strings
    sc MARGUN $25.15, perf mat rent
                                        (M60)

MACMILLAN, JAMES (1959-   )
    Cumnock Orcadian, The [8']
    0.1.0.4. 0.2.1.0. pno,6-12vln,1-
    2vcl
    UNIVER. perf mat rent   (M61)

    Keening, The [25']
    3.3.3.3. 4.3.3.1. timp,3perc,cel&
    pno,strings
    UNIVER. perf mat rent   (M62)

    Tryst [30']
    2.2.2.2. 2.2.0.0. timp,strings
    sc UNIVER. UE19238 $95.00, perf mat
    rent   (M63)

MACONCHY, ELIZABETH (1907-   )
    Ariadne, For Solo Voice And Orchestra
    [20']
    2(pic).2(English horn).2.2.
    2.2.0.0. harp,timp,strings,S
    solo
    CHESTER JWC 415 perf mat rent   (M64)

    Concertino for Clarinet and Orchestra
    [10']
    1.1.1.1. 2.1.0.0. timp,strings,
    clar solo
    CHESTER perf mat rent   (M65)

    Concertino for Clarinet and String
    Orchestra [14']
    string orch,clar solo
    CHESTER perf mat rent   (M66)

    Epyllion, For Violoncello And Strings
    [14']
    10vln,2vla,db,vcl solo
    CHESTER JWC 419 perf mat rent   (M67)

    Life Story
    string orch
    CHESTER perf mat rent   (M68)

    Little Symphony [18']
    3(pic).3(English horn).3(bass
    clar).3. 4.3.3.1. timp,2perc,
    strings
    CHESTER   (M69)

    Music for Strings [18']
    string orch
    CHESTER perf mat rent   (M70)

    Romance for Viola and Orchestra [12']
    1.1.1.1. 1.0.0.0. string quin,vla
    solo
    CHESTER JWC577 perf mat rent   (M71)

    Serenata Concertante, For Violin And
    Orchestra [20']
    2(pic).2(English horn).2(bass
    clar).2. 4.3.3.1. timp,perc,
    harp,strings,vln solo
    CHESTER perf mat rent   (M72)

    Sinfonietta [16']
    3(pic).2+English horn.2+bass
    clar.2+contrabsn. 4.3.3.1.
    timp,2perc,strings
    CHESTER JWC453 perf mat rent   (M73)

    Three Settings Of Poems By Gerard
    Manley Hopkins, For Solo Voice
    And Orchestra [12']
    1.1(English horn).1.1. 2.1.0.0.
    strings,S solo
    CHESTER JWC 416-18 perf mat rent
                                        (M74)

    Variazioni Concertanti [18']
    strings,ob solo,clar solo,horn
    solo,bsn solo
    CHESTER perf mat rent   (M75)

MCTEE, CINDY (1953-   )
    On Wings Of Infinite Night [9']
    3.3.2+bass clar.2+contrabsn.
    4.3.3.1. timp,perc,harp,pno
    NORRUTH perf mat rent   (M76)

MAD SCENE, FOR SOLO VOICES AND
    ORCHESTRA see Parris, Robert

MADAMA BUTTERFLY: ADDIO, FIORITO ASIL,
    FOR SOLO VOICE AND ORCHESTRA see
    Puccini, Giacomo

MADAMA BUTTERFLY: BUTTERFLY ENTRANCE,
    FOR SOLO VOICE AND ORCHESTRA see
    Puccini, Giacomo, Madama Butterfly:
    Spira Sul Mare, For Solo Voice And
    Orchestra

MADAMA BUTTERFLY: BUTTERFLY'S DEATH,
    FOR SOLO VOICE AND ORCHESTRA see
    Puccini, Giacomo, Madama Butterfly:
    Tu, Tu Piccolo Iddio, For Solo
    Voice And Orchestra

MADAMA BUTTERFLY: DUETTO D'AMORE, FOR
    SOLO VOICES AND ORCHESTRA see
    Puccini, Giacomo

MADAMA BUTTERFLY: FLOWER DUET, FOR SOLO
    VOICES AND ORCHESTRA see Puccini,
    Giacomo, Madama Butterfly: Tutti I
    Fior, For Solo Voices And Orchestra

MADAMA BUTTERFLY: SPIRA SUL MARE, FOR
    SOLO VOICE AND ORCHESTRA see
    Puccini, Giacomo

MADAMA BUTTERFLY: TU, TU PICCOLO IDDIO,
    FOR SOLO VOICE AND ORCHESTRA see
    Puccini, Giacomo

MADAMA BUTTERFLY: TUTTI I FIOR, FOR
    SOLO VOICES AND ORCHESTRA see
    Puccini, Giacomo

MÄDCHEN ANNA, DAS, FOR SOLO VOICE AND
    ORCHESTRA see Israel-Meyer, Pierre,
    Anna La Bonne, For Solo Voice And
    Orchestra

MÄDCHENLAUNE POLKA see Strauss, Eduard

MADEMOISELLE ANGOT SUITE [ARR.] see
    Lecocq, Charles

MADERNA, BRUNO (1920-1973)
    Ausstrahlung, For Solo Voice And
    Orchestra [35']
    4(2pic).4.7.3. 4.5.4.1. perc,cel,
    2harp,strings,electronic tape,
    female solo
    RICORDI-IT 131908 perf mat rent
                                        (M77)

    Concerto for Oboe and Orchestra, No.
    3 [15']
    4(pic).3(English horn).3(bass
    clar).3. 4.5.4.1. perc,2harp,
    cel,strings,ob solo
    SALABERT perf mat rent   (M78)

    Juilliard Serenade [25']
    3.2.3.1. 1.1.1.0. xylo,marimba,
    cel,2pno,harp,vln,vla,vcl,db,
    electronic tape
    RICORDI-IT 131884 perf mat rent
                                        (M79)

MADETOJA, LEEVI (1887-1947)
    Arkihuolesi Heita, For Solo Voice And
    Orchestra [arr.]
    (Kuusisto, I.) harp,strings,solo
    voice [2'] FAZER perf mat rent
                                        (M80)

    Enkelien Joululaulu, For Solo Voice
    And Orchestra [arr.]
    (Kuusisto, I.) 2fl,strings,solo
    voice [2'24"] FAZER perf mat rent
                                        (M81)

    Far, Hvor Flyver Svanerne Hen?, For
    Solo Voice And Orchestra *Op.44,
    No.2 [3']
    2.2.2.2. 3.3.0.0. timp,harp,
    strings,S solo
    HANSEN-DEN perf mat rent   (M82)

    Geisha, For Solo Voice And Orchestra
    *Op.9,No.5 [2']
    2.2.2.2. 4.2.0.0. timp,perc,
    strings,solo voice
    FAZER perf mat rent   (M83)

    Yiain Laulu, For Solo Voice And
    Orchestra
    see Yiais Sang, For Solo Voice And
    Orchestra

    Yiais Sang, For Solo Voice And
    Orchestra *Op.58
    2.2.2.2. 1.2.0.0. harp,strings,
    solo voice
    ([7']) FAZER perf mat rent contains
    also: Yiain Laulu, For Solo Voice
    And Orchestra   (M84)

MADETOJA, LEEVI (cont'd.)

Yrtit Tummat, For Solo Voice And
Orchestra [arr.] *Op.9,No.1
(Koskimies, Eero) 1.2.2.2. 3.2.1.0.
timp,strings,solo voice [3']
FAZER perf mat rent   (M85)

MADGE, GEOFFREY (1941-   )
Concerto for Piano and Instrumental
Ensemble [23']
1.1.1.1. 1.1.0.0. vln,vla,vcl,db,
pno solo
sc,pts DONEMUS f.s.   (M86)

MADI see Pagh-Paan, Younghi

MADONA see Villa-Lobos, Heitor

MADONNA OF WINTER AND SPRING see
Harvey, Jonathan

MADSEN, TRYGVE (1940-   )
Brudemarsj
2.1.2.0. 0.0.0.0. strings
"Wedding March" NORGE   (M87)

Concerto for Clarinet and Orchestra,
Op. 40 [22']
timp,strings,clar solo
sc MUSIKK f.s., perf mat rent   (M88)

Concerto For Euphonium And Orchestra,
Op. 55
2.2.2.2. 0.0.0.0. strings,
euphonium solo
NORGE   (M89)

Concerto for Horn and Orchestra, Op.
45 [20']
2.2.2.2. 0.0.0.0. timp,strings,
horn solo
sc MUSIKK f.s., perf mat rent   (M90)

Concerto for Tuba and Orchestra, Op.
35 [20']
2.2.2.2. 0.0.0.0. timp,perc,
strings,tuba solo
MUSIKK perf mat rent   (M91)

Festival Ouverture *Op.53
2.2.2.2. 4.3.3.1. timp,perc,
strings
NORGE   (M92)

Med Bratsj Og Dram
2.2.2.2. 3.2.2.1. timp,perc,
strings
NORGE   (M93)

Sieben Schleier Der Salome, Die, For
Solo Voice And Chamber Orchestra
*Op.37
ob,strings,S solo
[Ger] NORGE   (M94)

Symphony No. 1, Op. 54
3.3.3.3. 4.3.3.1. timp,perc,
2harp,strings
NORGE   (M95)

Wedding March
see Brudemarsj

MAEGAARD, JAN (1926-   )
Chamber Concerto No. 2
sc,pts SAMFUNDET f.s.   (M96)

MAEHLUM, SVEIN (1943-   )
150 Davids Salme *Op.9 [7']
3.3.4.1. 3.3.2.1. timp,perc,harp,
strings
NORGE   (M97)

MAESTRAZGO see Dubedout, Bertrand

MAESTRI, FABIO (1956-   )
For Stacey [12']
fl,2ob,bass clar,2perc,vibra,
hpsd,pno,vln,2vla,vcl
RICORDI-IT 133124 perf mat rent
                                (M98)

MAGABUNDA, FOR SOLO VOICE AND ORCHESTRA
see Schwantner, Joseph

MAGANINI, QUINTO (1897-1974)
Romanesca, La
string orch,harp/lute/gtr/pno
solo
sc,pts MUSICUS f.s.   (M99)

MAGDALENA: SUITE NO. 1 see Villa-Lobos,
Heitor

MAGDALENA: SUITE NO. 2 see Villa-Lobos,
Heitor

MAGGI, DARIO (1944-   )
Forme Riflesse, Le
2.2.2.2. 2.2.0.0. perc,strings
RICORDI-IT 133151 perf mat rent
                                (M100)
Progetto Trakl [17']
3.3.3.3. 4.4.3.1. 6perc,hpsd,cel,
pno,2harp,strings
RICORDI-IT 134037 perf mat rent

MAGGI, DARIO (cont'd.)
                                (M101)
Selva, For Piano And Instrumental
Ensemble [16'30"]
1(pic).1.1(bass clar).0. 1.1.1.0.
2perc,vln,vla,vcl,pno solo
RICORDI-IT 133728 perf mat rent
                                (M102)

MAGIC MOUNTAIN, THE, FOR PIANO AND
ORCHESTRA see Hopkins, John

MAGICIENNE DE LA MER, LA see Le Flem,
Paul

MAGIQUE- CIRCONSTANCIELLE, FOR SOLO
VOICES AND ORCHESTRA see Bancquart,
Alain

MAGISCHE KLANGGESTALT see Höller, York

MAGMA see Guinjoan, Joan see Nordheim,
Arne see Rihm, Wolfgang

MAGNALIA DEI, FOR SPEAKING VOICE AND
ORCHESTRA see Bresgen, Cesar

MAGNARD, ALBERIC (1865-1914)
Suite Dans Le Style Ancien *Op.2
[20']
2.2.2.2. 2.1.0.0. timp,perc,
strings
KALMUS A7378 sc $25.00, set $40.00,
pts $2.50, ea., perf mat rent
                                (M103)
Symphony No. 3, Op. 11
KALMUS A6531 sc $60.00, set
$100.00, pts $5.00, ea., perf mat
rent   (M104)

MAGNETIQUES, FOR VIOLIN AND ORCHESTRA
see Miroglio, Francis

MAGNIFICAT: FECIT POTENTIAM, FOR SOLO
VOICE AND ORCHESTRA see Bach, Carl
Philipp Emanuel

MAHLER, GUSTAV (1860-1911)
Ablosung Im Sommer
see Fünf Fruhe Lieder, For Solo
Voice And Orchestra [arr.]

Des Knaben Wunderhorn: Lied Des
Verfolgten Im Turm, For Solo
Voice And Orchestra
KALMUS A5661 sc $10.00, set $25.00,
pts $1.50, ea., perf mat rent
                                (M105)
Des Knaben Wunderhorn: Lieder, Vol. I
"Youth's Magic Horn, The, Vol. I"
min sc KALMUS K00524 $5.00 (M106)

Des Knaben Wunderhorn: Lieder, Vol.
II
"Youth's Magic Horn, The, Vol. II"
min sc KALMUS K00525 $7.00 (M107)

Des Knaben Wunderhorn: Lob Des Hohen
Verstandes, For Solo Voice And
Orchestra
KALMUS A5660 sc $5.00, set $20.00,
pts $1.00, ea., perf mat rent
                                (M108)
Des Knaben Wunderhorn:
Rheinlegendchen, For Solo Voice
And Orchestra
KALMUS A5663 sc $5.00, set $10.00,
pts $1.00, ea.   (M109)

Des Knaben Wunderhorn: Trost Im
Ungluck, For Solo Voice And
Orchestra
KALMUS A5664 sc $7.00, set $20.00,
pts $1.00, ea., perf mat rent
                                (M110)
Des Knaben Wunderhorn: Two Songs, For
Solo Voice And Orchestra
see Seven Songs

Des Knaben Wunderhorn: Verlorne Muh',
For Solo Voice And Orchestra
KALMUS A5665 sc $5.00, set $15.00,
pts $1.00, ea.   (M111)

Des Knaben Wunderhorn: Wer Hat Dies
Liedlein Erdacht? For Solo Voice
And Orchestra
KALMUS A5666 sc $4.00, set $15.00,
pts $1.00, ea.   (M112)

Erinnerung
see Fünf Fruhe Lieder, For Solo
Voice And Orchestra [arr.]
see Sechs Fruhe Lieder, For Solo
Voice And Orchestra [arr.]

Five Settings Of Ruckert Poems, For
Solo Voice And Orchestra
see Seven Songs

Fruhlingsmorgen
see Sechs Fruhe Lieder, For Solo
Voice And Orchestra [arr.]

MAHLER, GUSTAV (cont'd.)
Fünf Fruhe Lieder, For Solo Voice And
Orchestra [arr.]
(Berio, Luciano) 2(pic).1+English
horn.2+bass clar.2+contrabsn.
3.2.1.1. timp,perc,harp,strings,
male solo sc UNIVER. UE18651
$29.50, perf mat rent duration:
13 min.
contains: Ablosung Im Sommer;
Erinnerung; Nicht Wiedersehen;
Um Schlimme Kinder Artig Zu
Machen; Zu Strassburg Auf Der
Schanz   (M113)

Hans Und Grete
see Sechs Fruhe Lieder, For Solo
Voice And Orchestra [arr.]

Ich Ging Mit Lust Durch Einen Grunen
Wald
see Sechs Fruhe Lieder, For Solo
Voice And Orchestra [arr.]

Kindertotenlieder, For Solo Voice And
Orchestra
KAHNT f.s.   (M114)
(Ballstaedt, Andreas; Doge, Klaus)
min sc EULENBURG EU01060 $6.50
                                (M115)
Lied Von Der Erde, Das, For Solo
Voices And Orchestra
sc KUNZEL 10017 $23.00   (M116)
"Song Of The Earth, The, For Solo
Voices And Orchestra" KALMUS
A6358 sc $50.00, set $125.00, pts
$5.00, ea., perf mat rent (M117)

Lieder Eines Fahrenden Gesellen, For
Solo Voice And Orchestra
min sc PHILH PH. 251 $5.00 (M118)
"Songs Of A Wayfarer, For Solo
Voice And Orchestra" min sc
KALMUS K00111 $5.00   (M119)
"Songs Of A Wayfarer, For Solo
Voice And Orchestra" AMP perf mat
rent   (M120)

Nicht Wiedersehen
see Fünf Fruhe Lieder, For Solo
Voice And Orchestra [arr.]

Phantasie
see Sechs Fruhe Lieder, For Solo
Voice And Orchestra [arr.]

Scheiden Und Meiden
see Sechs Fruhe Lieder, For Solo
Voice And Orchestra [arr.]

Sechs Fruhe Lieder, For Solo Voice
And Orchestra [arr.]
(Berio, Luciano) 2+pic.2+English
horn.2+bass clar.2+contrabsn.
4.4.3.1. timp,2perc,harp,cel,
strings,Bar solo UNIVER. perf mat
rent duration: 22 min.
contains: Erinnerung;
Fruhlingsmorgen; Hans Und
Grete; Ich Ging Mit Lust Durch
Einen Grunen Wald; Phantasie;
Scheiden Und Meiden   (M121)

Seven Songs
min sc KALMUS K01391 $5.00
contains: Des Knaben Wunderhorn:
Two Songs, For Solo Voice And
Orchestra; Five Settings Of
Ruckert Poems, For Solo Voice
And Orchestra   (M122)

Sieben Lieder Aus Letzter Zeit: Der
Tamboursg'sell, For Solo Voice
And Orchestra
KAHNT perf mat rent   (M123)

Sieben Lieder Aus Letzter Zeit:
Blicke Mir Nicht In Die Lieder,
For Solo Voice And Orchestra
KAHNT perf mat rent   (M124)

Sieben Lieder Aus Letzter Zeit: Ich
Atmet' Einen Linden Duft, For
Solo Voice And Orchestra
KAHNT perf mat rent   (M125)

Sieben Lieder Aus Letzter Zeit: Ich
Bin Der Welt Abhanden Gekommen,
For Solo Voice And Orchestra
KAHNT perf mat rent   (M126)

Sieben Lieder Aus Letzter Zeit:
Liebst Du Um Schonheit? For Solo
Voice And Orchestra
KALMUS A5667 sc $4.00, set $12.00,
pts $.75, ea.   (M127)
KAHNT perf mat rent   (M128)

Sieben Lieder Aus Letzter Zeit:
Revelge, For Solo Voice And
Orchestra
KALMUS A5662 sc $12.00, set $33.00,
pts $1.50, ea., perf mat rent
                                (M129)
KAHNT perf mat rent   (M130)

MAHLER, GUSTAV (cont'd.)

Sieben Lieder Aus Letzter Zeit: Um
Mitternacht, For Solo Voice And
Orchestra
KAHNT perf mat rent   (M131)

Song Of The Earth, The, For Solo
Voices And Orchestra
see Lied Von Der Erde, Das, For
Solo Voices And Orchestra

Songs Of A Wayfarer, For Solo Voice
And Orchestra
see Lieder Eines Fahrenden
Gesellen, For Solo Voice And
Orchestra

Symphonies Nos. 1-2
sc DOVER 254739 $14.95   (M132)

Symphonisches Praeludium [arr.]
(Gursching, A.) 3.2.2.3. 4.2.3.1.
timp,perc,harp,strings [10']
study sc SIKORSKI 1431 $38.00,
perf mat rent   (M133)

Symphony No. 2 in C minor
fac ed,sc FABER $195.00   (M134)

Symphony No. 5 in C sharp minor,
Fourth Movement
harp,strings
(Adagietto) sc CURCI 10517 f.s.,
perf mat rent   (M135)

Symphony No. 6 in A minor
min sc KALMUS K01475 $20.00   (M136)

Symphony No. 7 in E minor
(set price: $250.00) KALMUS A5680
sc $90.00, pts $10.00, ea., perf
mat rent   (M137)

Symphony No. 8 in E flat
(complete set: $250.00, perf mat
rent) sc KALMUS A6070 $85.00
                              (M138)
pts KALMUS A6070 $6.00, ea.   (M139)
min sc KALMUS K01528 $9.25   (M140)

Symphony No. 9 in D
KALMUS A7160 sc $75.00, set
$150.00, pts $6.00, ea., perf mat
rent   (M141)

Symphony No. 10 *reconstruction
(Carpenter, Clinton) 4+pic.3+
English horn.3+bass
clar.4(contrabsn). 4.4.3.1. timp,
2harp,strings AMP perf mat rent
                              (M142)
(Mazzetti, N.) 4+pic.3+English
horn.3+bass clar.4(contrabsn).
4.4.4.1. timp,perc,2harp,strings
[80'] AMP perf mat rent   (M143)

Totenfeier
3.3.3.3. 4.3.3.1. timp,perc,harp,
strings
sc UNIVER. UE13827 $49.00   (M144)

Um Schlimme Kinder Artig Zu Machen
see Fünf Fruhe Lieder, For Solo
Voice And Orchestra [arr.]

Youth's Magic Horn, The, Vol. I
see Des Knaben Wunderhorn: Lieder,
Vol. I

Youth's Magic Horn, The, Vol. II
see Des Knaben Wunderhorn: Lieder,
Vol. II

Zu Strassburg Auf Der Schanz
see Fünf Fruhe Lieder, For Solo
Voice And Orchestra [arr.]

MAHLER-MOMENT see Schnebel, Dieter

MAHLER SKIZZE see Glanert, Detlev

MAHR, HERMAN CARL (CURLEY) (1901-1964)
Horst Du Meine Violine, For Violin
And Orchestra
KRENN f.s.   (M145)

MAI DUN see Ireland, John

MAI-FEST see Kristoffersen, Fridthjof

MAI-SAU, FOR VIOLIN AND STRINGS see
Dao, Nguyen Thien

MAID OF PSKOV, THE: BERCEUSE, [ARR.]
see Rimsky-Korsakov, Nikolai

MAIDEN ON THE MOOR, FOR SOLO VOICE AND
CHAMBER ORCHESTRA see Schickele,
Peter

MAIGUASHCA, MESIAS (1938-   )
Ecos I [18']
4+pic.3.3+bass clar.0. 1.2.4.0.
3perc,strings,electronic tape,
2 performers for 32 sonorous

MAIGUASHCA, MESIAS (cont'd.)

objects
SALABERT perf mat rent   (M146)

Ecos II
0+2pic.0.2(clar in A).0. 1.1.1.0.
perc,2vln,2vla,2vcl, 2
performers for sonorous objects
SALABERT perf mat rent   (M147)

F Melodies [23'15"]
2(pic).1.2(clar in E flat)+bass
clar.0. 1.1.2.1. 4perc,strings,
electronic tape
SALABERT perf mat rent   (M148)

Monodias E Interludios [20']
4(pic,alto fl).2.2(bass clar).1+
contrabsn. 0.2.2.1. 2perc,pno,
strings,synthesizer
SALABERT perf mat rent   (M149)

MAIGULL [ARR.] see Thommessen, Reidar

MAILCOACH IS ROLLING, THE see Wellejus,
Henning

MAILMAN, MARTIN (1932-   )
Concerto for Violin and Orchestra
[17']
2.2.2.2. 4.2.1.1. timp,3perc,
harp,strings,vln solo
BOOSEY perf mat rent   (M150)

Symphony No. 2 [24']
2+pic.2+English horn.2+bass
clar.2. 4.2.3.1. timp,4perc,
harp,pno,strings
BOOSEY perf mat rent   (M151)

Symphony No. 3 [25']
2+pic.2+English horn.2+bass
clar.2+contrabsn. 4.2.3.1.
timp,5perc,harp,pno,strings
BOOSEY perf mat rent   (M152)

MAINGUENEAU, LOUIS (1884-1950)
Cantabile Expressivo, For Violoncello
And Orchestra [2'30"]
2.1.2.2. 2.1.0.0. timp,harp,
strings,vcl solo
BILLAUDOT perf mat rent   (M153)

MAIONE, RINO
Musikstuck *Op.32
2.2.2.2. 2.2.0.0. timp,perc,harp,
pno,strings
sc CURCI 1011 perf mat rent   (M154)

MAITRE PATHELIN: JE PENSE A VOUS, FOR
SOLO VOICE AND ORCHESTRA see Bazin,
François-Emanuel-Joseph

MAITREYA see Hamel, Peter Michael

MAJGILDET see Frohlich, J.F.

MAJNUN SYMPHONY see Hovhaness, Alan

MAJOR BARBARA [ARR.] see Walton, [Sir]
William (Turner)

MAJORELLE, PHILIPPE (1941-   )
Fantasy for Flute and String
Orchestra [5'10"]
string orch,fl solo
BILLAUDOT perf mat rent   (M155)

MAKE YOUR OWN ORCHESTRA see Lankester,
Michael

MAKEDONSKI PLESI see Srebotnjak, Alojz
F.

MALAGUENA [ARR.] see Lecuona, Ernesto

MALCOLM'S PRISON ARIA, FOR SOLO VOICE
AND ORCHESTRA see Davis, Anthony

MALEC, IVO (1925-   )
Aquatheme [17']
3(pic).1.1(bass
clar).1(contrabsn). 2.2.2.1.
2perc,harp,pno,strings
sc BREITKOPF-W f.s., perf mat rent
                              (M156)
Arco-22 [21']
22strings
sc SALABERT f.s., perf mat rent
                              (M157)
Lumina [14']
7vln,2vla,2vcl,db,electronic tape
sc SALABERT f.s., perf mat rent
                              (M158)
Opera-Bus, Chapitre IV: Les Clowns,
For Solo Voice And Instrumental
Ensemble [7']
1.1.2.0. 1.1.1.0. 3perc,harp,pno,
2vln,vla,vcl,db,T solo
BILLAUDOT perf mat rent   (M159)

Opera-Bus, Chapitre VII: Ressources,
For Solo Voice And Instrumental
Ensemble [10']
1.1.2.0. 1.1.1.0. 3perc,harp,pno,

MALEC, IVO (cont'd.)

2vln,vla,vcl,db,solo voice
BILLAUDOT perf mat rent   (M160)

Ottava Bassa, For Doublebass And
Orchestra [40']
3(pic).3.3+bass clar.2+contrabsn.
5.4.3+bass trom.1. timp,5perc,
harp,pno,elec org,strings,db
solo
SALABERT perf mat rent   (M161)

Tehrana [18']
3(pic).3.3(bass
clar).3(contrabsn). 4.4.3.1.
timp,4perc,harp,pno,cel,elec
org,strings
SALABERT perf mat rent   (M162)

MALEDICTION, FOR PIANO AND STRING
ORCHESTRA see Liszt, Franz

MALIBU-SINFONIE see Anders, Christian

MALIPIERO, GIAN FRANCESCO (1882-1973)
Cimarosiana, La
KALMUS A5687 sc $20.00, set $20.00,
perf mat rent   (M163)

Impressioni Dal Vero, II
KALMUS A6088 sc $25.00, set $80.00,
perf mat rent   (M164)

Omaggio A Belmonte [8']
3.2.2.2. 4.2.0.0. perc,cel,xylo,
pno,harp,strings
RICORDI-IT 131926 perf mat rent
                              (M165)

MALLEUS ANIMATUS, FOR PIANO AND STRING
ORCHESTRA see Groba, Rogelio

MALOTTE, ALBERT HAY (1895-1964)
Lord's Prayer, The, For Solo Voice
And Orchestra [arr.]
(Sopkin) 1.0.2.1.2alto sax.tenor
sax. 0.2.1.0. timp,perc,pno,org,
strings,solo voice SCHIRM.G perf
mat rent   (M166)

MALTESE CAT BLUES see Hartke, Stephen
Paul

MAMIYA, MICHIO (1929-   )
Tableaux, For Solo Voices And
Orchestra [22']
3(pic).3.3(bass clar,clar in E
flat).3(contrabsn). 4.3.3.0.
perc,harp,pno,strings,ΤΤΤΤΤΤΤΤ
soli
sc ZEN-ON 899360 f.s., perf mat
rent   (M167)

MAMLOK, URSULA (1928-   )
Concerto for String Orchestra [29']
string orch
sc AM.COMP.AL. $26.00, perf mat
rent   (M168)

One Piece For Five Woodwinds And
Strings [1']
1.1.1.1. 1.0.0.0. strings
sc AM.COMP.AL. $9.55, perf mat rent
                              (M169)

MAM'SELLE MARIE, FOR SOLO VOICE AND
ORCHESTRA see Guion, David Wendall
Fentress

MAM'ZELLE ANGOT: BALLET SUITE [ARR.]
see Lecocq, Charles

MAN JIANG HONG see Zhang, Xiao-Fu

MAN LEBT NUR EINMAL WALZER see Strauss,
Johann, [Jr.]

MAN OF LA MANCHA: ORCHESTRAL SYNTHESIS
[ARR.] see Leigh, Mitch

MAN WITH A HOE, THE: SINFONIA see
Ultan, Lloyd

MANCINI, HENRY (1924-   )
Piece For Jazz Bassoon And Orchestra
[19'45"]
3.2+English horn.3+bass clar.3.
4.4(flügelhorn).3.1. perc,elec
bass,pno/synthesizer,strings,
fender-rhodes, bassoon solo
NEWAM 19028 perf mat rent   (M170)

Thorn Birds, The: Suite
[11'] WARNER perf mat rent   (M171)

MANDINA AMABILE, FOR SOLO VOICES AND
ORCHESTRA see Mozart, Wolfgang
Amadeus

MANDUELL, JOHN (1928-   )
Double Concerto For Two Solo
Instruments And Orchestra
NOVELLO perf mat rent   (M172)

MANEN, CHRISTIAN
  Concerto for Piano and Orchestra
    [24']
    CHOUDENS perf mat rent   (M173)

MANEN, JOAN (1883-1971)
  Romanza Mistica
    string orch
    UNION ESP. perf mat rent   (M174)

MANESOLV [ARR.] see Cleve, Cissi

MANFRED see Tchaikovsky, Piotr Ilyich

MANFRED, OP. 115: OVERTURE see
  Schumann, Robert (Alexander)

MANFREDINI, FRANCESCO (1680-1748)
  Concerto for 2 Trumpets and String
    Orchestra, MIN 196
    string orch,cont,2trp soli
    sc,pts KUNZEL 10218 f.s.   (M176)

  Concerto Grosso, Op. 3, No. 9, in D
    (Bonelli) KALMUS A7348 sc $8.00,
    set $7.50, pts $1.50, ea.   (M177)

  Concerto Grosso, Op. 3, No. 11, in C
    minor
    (Upmeyer, W.) KALMUS A5707 sc
    $5.00, set $7.00   (M178)

  Concerto Grosso, Op. 3, No. 12, in C
    SONZOGNO perf mat rent   (M179)

MANGROVE see Sculthorpe, Peter [Joshua]

MANHATTAN ABSTRACTION see Ruders, Poul

MANHATTAN BEACH MARCH see Sousa, John
  Philip

MANHATTAN BROADCASTS see Gruber, Heinz
  Karl

MANHATTAN PLAZA PAINTING see Pehrson,
  Joseph Ralph

MANIFESTATION see Fountain, Primous

MANIFESTO see Sermila, Jarmo

MANILOM, FOR SOLO VOICES AND
  INSTRUMENTAL ENSEMBLE see
  Haselböck, Martin

MANINYAS, FOR VIOLIN AND ORCHESTRA see
  Edwards, Ross

MANKELL, HENNING (1868-1930)
  Concerto for Piano and Orchestra, Op.
    30 [31']
    2.2.2.2. 4.2.0.0. timp,strings,
    pno solo
    STIM   (M180)

MANN, JOHANN CHRISTOPH (1726-1782)
  Symphony
    see Dittersdorf, Karl Ditters von,
    Symphonies, Six

MANNEKE, DAAN (1939-   )
  Babel [17']
    DONEMUS perf mat rent   (M181)

  Organum II [10']
    1.1.2.1. 1.1.1.0. strings
    sc DONEMUS f.s., perf mat rent
                                     (M182)
  Prelude From Chamber Music [2']
    fl,ob,clar,bsn,horn,2vln,vla,vcl,
    db,pno
    DONEMUS perf mat rent   (M183)

  Sinfonia [7'30"]
    fl,ob,clar,bsn,horn,2vln,vla,vcl,
    db,pno
    DONEMUS perf mat rent   (M184)

  Stages III [12']
    variable instrumentation sc DONEMUS
    f.s., perf mat rent   (M185)

MANNHEIM SYMPHONISTS (18TH CENTURY); A
  COLLECTION OF TWENTY-FOUR
  ORCHESTRAL WORKS *CC24U
  sc BROUDE BR. $55.00 2 vols.   (M186)

MANNINO, FRANCO (1924-   )
  Cinque Romanze, For Viola And
    Orchestra
    2(pic).2.2.2. 2.0.0.0. 2mand,
    strings,vla solo
    sc CURCI 9974 perf mat rent (M187)

  Concerto for 6 Violins, 2 Pianos and
    Orchestra [30']
    1+pic.0.2+bass clar.2+contrabsn.
    4.2.1.0. timp,2perc,strings,
    6vln soli,2pno soli

MANNINO, FRANCO (cont'd.)
    sc BSE BSM 2 f.s., perf mat rent
                                     (M188)
  Molto Vibrato, For Violin And
    Orchestra [4'30"]
    clar,horn,harp,strings,vln solo
    sc CURCI 10217 perf mat rent (M189)

  Nirvana [12']
    3+pic.2+English horn.3+bass
    clar.2+contrabsn. 4.3.3.1.
    timp,perc,cel,pno,strings
    sc BSE 1024 f.s., perf mat rent
                                     (M190)
  Sons Enchantes
    fl,strings, alphorn
    sc CURCI 10044 perf mat rent (M191)

  Symphony No. 3, Op. 177
    string orch
    COSTALL C.3669 f.s.   (M192)

  Symphony No. 5, Op. 237 [28']
    1(pic).1(English horn).2.2.
    2.2.0.0. timp,perc,strings
    (Rideau Lake) sc CURCI 10605 f.s.,
    perf mat rent   (M193)

  Symphony No. 6, Op. 262 [31']
    4.3.3.0. 4.3.3.1. timp,perc,harp,
    pno,cel,strings,opt mix cor
    RICORDI-IT 134208 perf mat rent
                                     (M194)
  Tropical Dances, For 20 Violoncellos
    [30']
    20vcl
    BSE BSM 12 perf mat rent   (M195)

  Tropical Dances, For Orchestra [30']
    2+pic.2+English horn.3+bass
    clar.0. 4.3.3.1. perc,strings
    BSE BSM 13 perf mat rent   (M196)

MANNISKANS VAG see Gullin, Peter

MANON: ADIEU, NOTRE PETITE TABLE, FOR
  SOLO VOICE AND ORCHESTRA see
  Massenet, Jules

MANON: AH! DES GRIEUX, FOR SOLO VOICES
  AND ORCHESTRA see Massenet, Jules

MANON: MINUET AND GAVOTTE [ARR.] see
  Massenet, Jules

MANON: OUI, C'EST MOI, FOR SOLO VOICES
  AND ORCHESTRA see Massenet, Jules

MANON LESCAUT: DONNA NON VIDI MAI, FOR
  SOLO VOICE AND ORCHESTRA see
  Puccini, Giacomo

MANON LESCAUT: IN QUELLE TRINE MORBIDE,
  FOR SOLO VOICE AND ORCHESTRA see
  Puccini, Giacomo

MANON LESCAUT: PRELUDE, ACT II see
  Puccini, Giacomo

MANOURY, PHILIPPE
  Aleph, For Solo Voices And Orchestra
    [65']
    2.2.2+bass clar.0. 3.3.2.1.
    2perc,harp,pno,8vln,4vla,4vcl,
    3db,synthesizer,SATB soli
    AMPHION perf mat rent   (M197)

  Instantanes, For Chamber Orchestra
    [30'-40']
    1.1.1+bass clar.0. 1.2.1.0.
    2vibra,marimba,harp,Hamm,pno,
    2vln,2vcl
    AMPHION perf mat rent   (M198)

  Instantanes I [30']
    1.1.1+bass clar.0. 1.2.1.0.
    2vibra,marimba,harp,pno,Hamm,
    2vln,2vcl
    AMPHION perf mat rent   (M199)

  Instantanes II [10']
    2.1.1.0. 0.0.0.0. xylo,vibra,
    2gtr,pno,2vln,2vla,3vcl,2db
    (version "etude") AMPHION perf mat
    rent   (M200)

  Instantanes III [5']
    2.1.2+bass clar.1. 0.0.0.0.
    2perc,harp,pno,2vln,vla,vcl,db
    (version "baden-baden") AMPHION
    perf mat rent   (M201)

  Instantanes, Version "Etude" [30'-
    40']
    2.1.1.0. 0.0.0.0. xylo,vibra,
    2gtr,pno,2vln,2vla,3vcl,2db
    AMPHION perf mat rent   (M202)

  Numero Cinq, For Piano And
    Instrumental Ensemble [25']
    1.1+English horn.0.1. 1.2.1.0.
    2vln,vla,vcl,pno solo
    RIDEAU perf mat rent   (M203)

MANOURY, PHILIPPE (cont'd.)
  Puzzle, For Solo Voice And Orchestra
    [20']
    1.1+English horn.1+bass clar.0.
    1.1.1.0. perc,cel,harp,pno,
    Hamm,strings,S/Mez solo
    RIDEAU perf mat rent   (M204)

MANQUE DE CHANCE, FOR SOLO VOICE AND
  ORCHESTRA see Charpentier, Jacques

MANSURIAN, TIGRAN (1939-   )
  Concerto for Violin and String
    Orchestra [18']
    10vln,4vla,3vcl,db,vln solo
    SIKORSKI perf mat rent   (M205)
    VAAP perf mat rent   (M206)

  Concerto for Violin, Violoncello and
    String Orchestra [27']
    10vln,4vla,3vcl,db,vln solo,vcl
    solo
    SIKORSKI perf mat rent   (M207)
    VAAP perf mat rent   (M208)

  Concerto for Violoncello and
    Orchestra, No. 1 [14']
    3.3.3.2. 4.3.3.1. timp,perc,harp,
    pno,strings,vcl solo
    SIKORSKI perf mat rent   (M209)
    VAAP perf mat rent   (M210)

  Concerto for Violoncello and String
    Orchestra, No. 2 [25']
    10vln,4vla,3vcl,db,vcl solo
    SIKORSKI perf mat rent   (M211)
    VAAP perf mat rent   (M212)

  Nachtmusik
    3.3.3.3. 4.3.3.1. timp,perc,cel,
    harp,pno,strings
    RICORDI-IT 133343 perf mat rent
                                     (M213)
    SIKORSKI perf mat rent   (M214)
    VAAP perf mat rent   (M215)

  Preludes For Orchestra [14']
    3.3.2.2. 4.3.3.0. timp,perc,harp,
    cel,pno,gtr,strings
    SIKORSKI perf mat rent   (M216)
    VAAP perf mat rent   (M217)

  Tovem [10']
    1.1.1.1. 1.1.1.0. cym,bass drum,
    pno,string quin
    SIKORSKI perf mat rent   (M218)
    VAAP perf mat rent   (M219)

MANTERO, AJMONE (1943-   )
  Aube Des Bleuets [12'42"]
    4.4.6.5. 4.4.3.1. timp,3perc,cel,
    2harp,strings
    RICORDI-IT 133656 perf mat rent
                                     (M220)
  Musica Per Bruno [22']
    3.3.3.3. 4.3.3.0. timp,perc,
    vibra,bells,strings
    RICORDI-IT 132336 perf mat rent
                                     (M221)

MANZONI, GIACOMO (1932-   )
  Dedica, For Flute, Solo Voice And
    Orchestra [18']
    4.4.4.4. 6.4.4.2. timp,5perc,
    2harp,strings,fl solo,B solo
    (opt instrumental group: 1.1.1.1.
    2.2.2.0., 2perc, str) RICORDI-IT
    134112 perf mat rent   (M222)

  Lessico [14']
    24 or 52 strings
    RICORDI-IT 132762 perf mat rent
                                     (M223)
  Masse: Omaggio A Edgard Varese, For
    Piano And Orchestra [20']
    4.4.3.4. 4.3.3.1. timp,2perc,
    strings,pno solo
    RICORDI-IT 132600 perf mat rent
                                     (M224)
  Modulor [25']
    5.4.5.4. 6.4.4.1. 4perc,strings
    RICORDI-IT 132962 perf mat rent
                                     (M225)
  Nuovo Incontro, For Violin And String
    Orchestra [16']
    string orch,vln solo
    RICORDI-IT 133737 perf mat rent
                                     (M226)
  Ode [18']
    4.3.3.3. 4.3.3.1. timp,perc,
    strings
    sc RICORDI-IT 031-35862 $56.25,
    perf mat rent   (M227)
  Opus 50, (Daunium) [9'30"]
    1(pic).1.1.1. 1.0.0.0. perc,2vln,
    vla,vcl,db
    sc RICORDI-IT 133805 f.s., perf mat
    rent   (M228)
  Scene Sinfoniche Per Il Doktor
    Faustus [16']
    3.3.4.3. 4.4.3.1. timp,5perc,cel,
    pno,Ondes Martenot,elec org,
    harp,strings
    RICORDI-IT 133790 perf mat rent

MANZONI, GIACOMO (cont'd.)
(M229)
MAPS, FOR VIOLIN AND ORCHESTRA see
Davis, Anthony

MAQAMAT, FOR SOLO VOICE AND CHAMBER
ORCHESTRA see Szekely, Endre

MARAIS, MARIN (1656-1728)
Ariane Et Bacchus: Suite [4']
string orch,opt pno
(Brown) KALMUS A5615 sc $5.00, set
$5.00, pts $1.00, ea.   (M230)

MARC, EDMOND
Gethsemani, For Horn And Orchestra
[5']
2.2.2.2. 3.0.0.0. timp,perc,harp,
strings,horn solo
BILLAUDOT perf mat rent   (M231)

MARCELLO, ALESSANDRO
(ca. 1684-ca. 1750)
Concerto, [arr.]
(Jevtic, I.) strings,hpsd,trp solo
[9'] BILLAUDOT perf mat rent
(M232)

MARCELLO, BENEDETTO (1686-1739)
Concerti, Twelve, [arr.]
string orch,cont
(Waxman, Franz) FIDELIO perf mat
rent   (M233)

Concerto Grosso, Op. 1, No. 4, in F
(Bonelli) KALMUS A7437 sc $10.00,
set $12.00, pts $1.50, ea. (M234)

Heavens Declare, The [arr.] (Psalm
No. 19, [arr.])
(Smith, Kile) 2.2.2.2. 4.3.3.1.
timp,perc,strings [4'] KALMUS
A4099 sc $5.00, set $22.00 (M235)

Introduzione, Aria, Presto [arr.]
(Bonelli) string orch [9'] KALMUS
A7350 sc $8.00, set $7.50, pts
$1.50, ea.   (M236)

Presto, Adagio, Allegro Vivace [arr.]
(from Sonata No. 8 For Cembalo)
(Bonelli) string orch [10'] KALMUS
A7342 sc $8.00, set $7.50, pts
$1.50, ea.   (M237)

Psalm No. 19, [arr.]
see Heavens Declare, The [arr.]

Sonata for Violoncello and String
Orchestra in F
(Toscano) KALMUS A7341 sc $5.00,
set $9.00, pts $1.50, ea. (M238)

Suite for Trombone and String
Orchestra, [arr.]
(Thilde, J.) string orch,trom solo
[6'30"] BILLAUDOT perf mat rent
(M239)
MARCH OF FRIENDSHIP see Vacek, Miloš

MARCH OF HOMAGE see Bliss, [Sir] Arthur
(Drummond) see Liszt, Franz,
Huldigungsmarsch

MARCH TO BATTLE, FOR SOLO VOICE AND
ORCHESTRA see Berenholtz, Jim

MARCH TO TONALITY see Del Tredici,
David

MARCHAND DE SABLE QUI PASSE, LE see
Roussel, Albert (Charles Paul)

MARCHE ECOSSAISE [ARR.] see Debussy,
Claude

MARCHE ECOSSAISE SUR UN THEME POPULAIRE
see Debussy, Claude

MARCHE FUNEBRE see Bizet, Georges see
Cherubini, Luigi see Suk, Josef

MARCHE FUNEBRE D'UNE MARIONETTE see
Gounod, Charles François

MARCHE SUR UN THEME RUSSE see Glazunov,
Alexander Konstantinovich

MARCHEN AUS DEM ORIENT WALZER see
Strauss, Johann, [Jr.]

MARCHEN AUS DER HEIMAT WALZER see
Strauss, Eduard

MARCHENBILDER see Abrahamsen, Hans

MARCHES DU SOLEIL, LES see Florentz

MARCHES POUR LA POMPE FUNEBRE DE
GENERAL HOCHE see Cherubini, Luigi

MARCIA E FANDANGO [ARR.] see Scarlatti,
Domenico

MARCIA LUGUBRE see Mayr, [Johann] Simon

MARCIA MIT POSTHORN see Haydn, [Johann]
Michael

MARCO, TOMAS (1942-   )
Autodafe, For Piano And Instrumental
Ensemble [15']
1.1.2+bass clar.1. 0.2.1.0.
3perc,org,3vln,vcl,2db
sc ALPUERTO f.s.   (M240)

Concerto Austral, For Oboe And
Orchestra [20']
2+pic.2(English horn).2(bass
clar).2(contrabsn). 4.3.3.1.
timp,2perc,harp,pno,strings,ob
solo
SALABERT perf mat rent   (M241)

Concerto for Violoncello and
Orchestra [20']
2.1+English horn.2+bass
clar.2.soprano sax.alto
sax.tenor sax.baritone sax.
4.3.3.1. timp,perc,pno,harp,
strings,vcl solo
sc ALPUERTO f.s.   (M242)

Concierto Del Alma, For Violin And
String Orchestra [22']
string orch,vln solo
SALABERT perf mat rent   (M243)

Escorial [18']
2.2+English horn.2+bass clar.2+
contrabsn.alto sax.tenor
sax.baritone sax.bass sax.
4.3.3.1. timp,perc,strings
ALPUERTO   (M244)

Locus Solus
1.1.1.1. 0.1.1.0. pno,vln,vla,
vcl,db
ALPUERTO   (M245)

Mysteria [15']
2.2.2.2. 0.2.0.0. timp,perc,harp,
cel,strings
SALABERT perf mat rent   (M246)

Quasi Un Requiem, For String Quartet
And String Orchestra [17']
string orch,string quar soli
sc ALPUERTO f.s.   (M247)

Sinfonia No. 3 [25']
2.2.2.2. 2.2.2.0. timp,2perc,
harp,pno,strings
SALABERT EAS18369P perf mat rent
(M248)
Symphony No. 1 [17']
1.1+English horn.2.1+contrabsn.
3.1.3.0. timp,perc,elec org,
strings
ALPUERTO   (M249)

Tauromaquia, For Piano Four Hands And
Instrumental Ensemble [11']
1(pic).1.1.1. 1.1.1.0. perc,vln,
vcl,pno 4-hands soli
ALPUERTO   (M250)

Vitral "Musica Celestial No. 1", For
Organ And Orchestra [14']
string orch,org solo
SALABERT perf mat rent   (M251)

MARCUSSEN, KJELL (1952-   )
Esperanza For Sinfonietta
1.1.1.0. 1.1.1.0. perc,harp,pno,
2vln,vla,vcl,db
NORGE   (M252)

Morning Glory
2.3.2.2. 4.3.3.1. timp,perc,harp,
elec gtr,strings,synthesizer
NORGE   (M253)

MARE NOSTRO: INTERMEZZO NOTTURNO see
Ferrero, Lorenzo

MARE TRANQUILLITATIS see Fongaard,
Bjørn

MAREA see Lindberg, Magnus

MARESCOTTI, ANDRÉ FRANÇOIS (1902-   )
Ballade for Violin and Orchestra
JOBERT   (M254)

MAREZ OYENS, TERA DE (1932-   )
Canzone Per Sonar [9']
variable instrumentation sc DONEMUS
f.s., perf mat rent   (M255)

Litany Of The Victims Of War [9']
2.2.2.2. 4.3.3.1. timp,3perc,
strings
sc DONEMUS f.s., perf mat rent
(M256)
Starmobile [8']
combine the groups: recorders,
brass, perc, strings, voices sc
DONEMUS f.s., perf mat rent
(M257)

MAREZ OYENS, TERA DE (cont'd.)
Symmetrical Memories, For Violoncello
And Orchestra [10']
3.3.2.2. 4.3.3.1. timp,4perc,
harp,strings,vcl solo
DONEMUS perf mat rent   (M258)

MARGINALIA see Takemitsu, Toru

MARGINS OF REALITY see Mcintosh, Diana

MARGUERITE AU ROUET [ARR.] see
Schubert, Franz (Peter), Gretchen
Am Spinnrad [arr.]

MARI, PIERETTE (1929-   )
Concerto for Guitar and Orchestra
[18']
perc,strings,gtr solo
sc BILLAUDOT f.s., perf mat rent
(M259)
MARIA DI ROHAN: OVERTURE see Donizetti,
Gaetano

MARIAGE SECRET: AIR DE GERONIMO, FOR
SOLO VOICE AND ORCHESTRA see
Cimarosa, Domenico, Matrimonio
Segreto, Il: Aria Di Geronimo, For
Solo Voice And Orchestra

MARIAGE SECRET: OVERTURE see Cimarosa,
Domenico, Matrimonio Segreto, Il:
Overture

MARIE, JEAN ÉTIENNE (1917-   )
Ecce Ancella Domini [15']
32strings
BILLAUDOT perf mat rent   (M260)

MARIE TAGLIONI POLKA see Strauss,
Johann, [Jr.]

MARIENKLANGE WALZER see Strauss, Josef

MARIETAN, PIERRE (1935-   )
Interfaces
strings,electronic tape,vcl solo
BILLAUDOT perf mat rent   (M261)

MARIISCHE SUITE see Rakov, Nikolai

MARILYN SUITE, FOR SOLO VOICES AND
ORCHESTRA see Ferrero, Lorenzo

MARIN see Borup-Jorgensen, Axel

MARINO FALIERO: OVERTURE see Donizetti,
Gaetano

MARIONETTE'S DANCE SUITE see Farkas,
Ferenc see Rosenberg, Hilding

MARISCHAL, LOUIS (1928-   )
Concerto for Flute, Harp and
Orchestra [13'30"]
2.2.3.0. 2.2.3.0. timp,3perc,
strings,fl solo,harp solo
BILLAUDOT perf mat rent   (M262)

Douze Emotions Sonores [16']
3.3.3.3. 4.4.4.1. timp,2perc,
2harp,cel,strings
BILLAUDOT perf mat rent   (M263)

Quatre Caprices [14'30"]
3.3.3.3. 4.4.3.1. timp,3perc,
harp,strings
BILLAUDOT perf mat rent   (M264)

Trois Pieces, For Harp And Chamber
Orchestra [9'50"]
2.2.2.0. 1.0.0.0. strings,harp
solo
BILLAUDOT perf mat rent   (M265)

MARITXU see Larrauri, Anton

MARKETENDERIN, DIE: OVERTURE see
Humperdinck, Engelbert

MARKEVITCH, IGOR (1912-1983)
Cantique d'Amour [9']
2+pic.1+English horn.2+bass
clar.2+contrabsn. 4.2.3.1.
timp,3perc,cel,pno,strings
sc BOOSEY $15.00, perf mat rent
(M266)
MARKINGS see Kay, Ulysses Simpson

MARLBORIAN CONCERTO, FOR 2 HORNS AND
STRING ORCHESTRA see Moyse, Louis

MAROS, MIKLOS (1943-   )
Concerto for Harpsichord and Chamber
Orchestra [13']
1.1.1.1. 1.1.0.0. harp,strings,
hpsd solo
STIM   (M267)

Konzertsatz, For Accordion And String
Orchestra [6']
string orch,acord solo
STIM   (M268)

MAROS, MIKLOS (cont'd.)

Sinfonia Concertante for Violin,
Violoncello, Double Bass and
String Orchestra [17']
string orch,vln solo,vcl solo,db
solo
STIM   (M269)

Sinfonietta [14']
1.1.1.1. 2.2.1.1. perc,pno,
strings
STIM perf mat rent   (M270)

MAROS, RUDOLF (1917-1982)
Ricercare
min sc EMB 3616 f.s.   (M271)

Two Dirges, For Solo Voice And
Chamber Orchestra
min sc EMB 4557 f.s.   (M272)

MAROUF: BALLET MUSIC see Rabaud, Henri

MARRIAGE BY TRICKERY: OVERTURE see
Cimarosa, Domenico, Matrimonio Per
Raggiro, Il: Overture

MARSCH- FANTASIE see Bialas, Günter

MARSCH IN D, K. 215 see Mozart,
Wolfgang Amadeus

MARSCH IN D, K. 237 see Mozart,
Wolfgang Amadeus

MARSCH IN D, K. 249 see Mozart,
Wolfgang Amadeus

MARSCHE, DREI, K. 408 see Mozart,
Wolfgang Amadeus

MARSCHNER, HEINRICH (AUGUST)
(1795-1861)
Hans Heiling: An Jenem Tag, For Solo
Voice And Orchestra
2.2.2.2. 4.0.0.0. strings,Bar
solo
BREITKOPF-L perf mat rent   (M273)

MARSH, ROGER (1949-   )
Music for Instrumental Ensemble [10']
2.1.2.1. 1.1.2.1. 2perc,2pno,
strings without db,4 solo
voices
NOVELLO perf mat rent   (M274)

Serenade [15']
8vln,3vla,3vcl,db solo
NOVELLO perf mat rent   (M275)

Still [12']
3(pic).3.3(bass
clar).3(contrabsn). 4.3.2.1.
4perc,3harp,strings
NOVELLO perf mat rent   (M276)

MARTELLI, HENRI (1895-1980)
Bas Reliefs Assyriens *Op.27 [13']
3.3.4.3. 4.3.3.1. timp,perc,
2harp,strings
study sc ESCHIG f.s., perf mat rent
(M277)
Concerto for Violin and Orchestra,
No. 1, Op. 44 [25']
1.1.1.1. 1.0.0.0. timp,strings,
vln solo
ESCHIG perf mat rent   (M278)

Concerto for Violin and Orchestra,
No. 2, Op. 84 [14']
1.0.1.1. 0.0.0.0. strings,vln
solo
ESCHIG perf mat rent   (M279)

Danse Adagio Et Fugato *Op.5 [9']
1.1.1.1. 2.1.0.0. timp,perc,
strings
ESCHIG perf mat rent   (M280)

Fantaisie Sur Un Theme Malgache, For
Piano And Orchestra *Op.63 [19']
3.3.3.3.alto sax. 4.3.3.1. timp,
3perc,cel,strings,pno solo
BILLAUDOT perf mat rent   (M281)

Ouverture Pour Un Conte De Boccace
*Op.52 [13']
3.3.3.3. 4.3.3.1. timp,perc,
strings
study sc ESCHIG f.s., perf mat rent
(M282)
Radeau De La Meduse, Le *Op.91 [7']
2.2.2.2. 2.2.2.0. timp,perc,
strings
BILLAUDOT perf mat rent   (M283)

Rhapsody for Violoncello and
Orchestra, Op. 101 [15'30"]
2.3.2.2. 4.3.3.0. timp,perc,
strings,vcl solo
BILLAUDOT perf mat rent   (M284)

Suite No. 3, Op. 104 [12'40"]
2.2.2.2. 2.2.2.0. timp,perc,
strings

MARTELLI, HENRI (cont'd.)

BILLAUDOT perf mat rent   (M285)

Symphony No. 1, Op. 94 [20']
string orch
ESCHIG perf mat rent   (M286)

Variations, Op. 94 [7']
string orch
ESCHIG perf mat rent   (M287)

MARTHA: ACH SO FROMM, FOR SOLO VOICE
AND ORCHESTRA see Flotow, Friedrich
von

MARTHA: DIE LETZTE ROSE, FOR SOLO VOICE
AND ORCHESTRA see Flotow, Friedrich
von

MARTHA: JA WAS NUN, WAS NUR TUN, FOR
SOLO VOICES AND ORCHESTRA see
Flotow, Friedrich von

MARTHA: SCHLAFE WOHL, FOR SOLO VOICES
AND ORCHESTRA see Flotow, Friedrich
von

MARTI, HEINZ (1934-   )
Passacaglia for Orchestra [13']
2.2.2.2. 2.1.0.0. perc,strings
sc HUG GH 11324A f.s., perf mat
rent   (M288)

Passacaglia for String Orchestra
[13']
string orch
sc HUG GH 11324B f.s., perf mat
rent   (M289)

MARTIN, FREDERICK (1958-   )
Concerto for Clarinet and
Instrumental Ensemble [14']
fl,bsn,horn,trom,perc,harp,2vln,
vla,vcl,clar solo
BILLAUDOT perf mat rent   (M290)

Concerto for Violin and Instrumental
Ensemble, Op. 21 [14']
1.1.1.1.baritone sax. 1.1.1.0.
timp,2perc,harp,pno,2vln,vla,
vcl,db,vln solo
BILLAUDOT perf mat rent   (M291)

Lug [15']
2.2.2.2. 4.2.3.1. 2perc,pno,harp,
strings
BILLAUDOT perf mat rent   (M292)

MARTINEZ, MARIANNE DE (1744-1812)
Concerto for Piano and Orchestra
FURORE FUE 2503 perf mat rent   (M293)

MARTINI, [PADRE] GIOVANNI BATTISTA
(1706-1784)
Concerto for Flute and String
Orchestra in G
string orch,hpsd,fl solo
(Homolya) SCHOTTS sc CON 201
$20.00, set CON 201-70 $43.00
(M294)
Concerto for Harpsichord and String
Orchestra in G, MIN 1
(Desderi) KALMUS A7339 sc $8.00,
set $16.00, pts $2.50, ea. (M295)

Concerto for Violoncello and
Orchestra, MIN 197
2trp,strings,cont,vcl solo
sc,pts KUNZEL 10229 f.s.   (M296)

Concerto for Violoncello and String
Orchestra in D
string orch,cont,vcl solo
(Kolos) SCHOTTS sc CON 208 $15.00,
set CON 208-70 $48.00   (M297)

Sinfonia A Quattro [7']
string orch
(Desderi) KALMUS A7337 sc $7.00,
set $7.50, pts $1.50, ea. (M298)

Sinfonie, Four
(Brofsky; Vitali; Girardi; Johnson;
Almeida; Facoetti; Froom) ("The
Symphony" Vol. A-IV) sc GARLAND
ISBN 0-8240-3829-0 $90.00
contains also: Lampugnani,
Giovanni Battista, Sinfonie,
Five; Anfossi, Pasquale,
Sinfonie, Two; Boccherini, Luigi,
Sinfonie, Six; Mayr, [Johann]
Simon, Sinfonia; Donizetti,
Gaetano, Sinfonia   (M299)

MARTINI, GIOVANNI
see MARTINI, JEAN PAUL EGIDE

MARTINO, DONALD JAMES (1931-   )
Concerto for Alto Saxophone and
Orchestra [20']
1.2.1.2. 3.1.1.0. 2perc,pno,
strings,alto sax solo
DANTALIAN DSE107 perf mat rent
(M300)

MARTINON, JEAN (1910-1976)
Concerto Lyrique, For String Quartet
And Orchestra *Op.38 [21']
2.1.2.1. 2.1.0.0. harp,strings,
string quar soli
BILLAUDOT perf mat rent   (M301)

Hymne A La Vie (Symphony No. 2, Op.
37) [23']
3.3.4.3.alto sax.tenor sax.
4.4.3.1. timp,4perc,2harp,opt
Ondes Martenot,strings
BILLAUDOT perf mat rent   (M302)

Symphony No. 2, Op. 37
see Hymne A La Vie

Vigintour *Op.58 [16']
2.1.1+bass clar.1+contrabsn.
0.1.1.0. perc,pno&cel,4vln,
2vla,2vcl,db
BILLAUDOT perf mat rent   (M303)

MARTINOV, VLADIMIR (1946-   )
Herbstlied, For 2 Violins And Chamber
Orchestra [20']
bells,vibra,cel,strings,2vln soli
SIKORSKI perf mat rent   (M304)

Herein, For Violin And Chamber
Orchestra [15']
wood blocks,cel,strings,vln solo
SIKORSKI perf mat rent   (M305)

MARTINU, BOHUSLAV (JAN) (1890-1959)
Concertino for Piano, Violin,
Violoncello and String Orchestra
KALMUS A7207 sc $20.00, set $27.00,
pts $3.00, ea., perf mat rent
(M306)
Concerto for Flute and Orchestra,
[arr.] (from Sonata No. 1 For
Flute)
(Wilson, Ransom) 2(pic).2(English
horn).2(bass clar).2. 0.2.1.0.
timp,2perc,harp,strings,fl solo
[15'] AMP perf mat rent   (M307)

Concerto for Piano and Orchestra, No.
3
study sc PANTON 2272 f.s.   (M308)

Concerto for Violin and Orchestra,
No. 1, in E [24']
2.2.2.2. 4.2.3.0. timp,3perc,
strings,vln solo
BÄREN. BA 6720 perf mat rent (M309)

Concerto for Violin and Orchestra,
No. 2 [27']
2.2.2.2. 4.3.3.1. timp,perc,
strings,vln solo
KALMUS A7205 sc $40.00, set $60.00,
pts $3.00, ea., perf mat rent
(M310)
min sc SUPRAPHON f.s.   (M311)

Concerto for Violin, Violoncello,
Piano and String Orchestra, No. 1
[21']
string orch,vln solo,vcl solo,pno
solo
ESCHIG perf mat rent   (M312)

Divertimento - Serenade No. 4
KALMUS A6695 sc $12.00, set $20.00,
pts $2.00, ea., perf mat rent
(M313)

Dream About The Past
see Sen O Minulosti

Invence
"Inventions" KALMUS A7431 sc
$35.00, set $60.00, pts $2.50,
ea., perf mat rent   (M314)

Inventions
see Invence

Lidice
KALMUS A7206 sc $6.00, set $18.00,
pts $.75, ea.   (M315)

Overture [8']
2.2.2.2. 4.2.0.0. timp,perc,
strings
study sc ESCHIG f.s., perf mat rent
(M316)
Parables, The
KALMUS A7027 sc $35.00, set $90.00,
pts $4.00, ea., perf mat rent
(M317)

Sen O Minulosti
"Dream About The Past" study sc
PANTON 2273 f.s.   (M318)

Serenade No. 1 [7']
clar,horn,strings
SUPRAPHON   (M319)

Serenade No. 3 [7']
ob,clar,strings
SUPRAPHON   (M320)

MARTINU, BOHUSLAV (JAN) (cont'd.)

Thunderbolt P-47 [9']
3.3.3.3. 4.3.3.1. timp,perc,
strings
study sc ESCHIG f.s., perf mat rent
(M321)

MARTLAND, STEVE (1958-)
American Invention [22']
2fl,2bass clar,horn,2pno,perc,
bass gtr,synthesizer,2vln,vla,
vcl
sc SCHOTT ED 12281 $39.00, perf mat
rent (M322)

Glad Day, For Solo Voice And
Instrumental Ensemble [13']
tenor sax,bass clar,horn,trp,
trom,perc,bass gtr,synthesizer,
2vln,vla,vcl,solo voice
SCHOTT perf mat rent (M323)

Lotta Continua [20']
2+pic.2.2(clar in A).2.alto sax.
2.2.2.0.flügelhorn. 5perc,pno,
elec gtr,strings
sc SCHOTT MIS 30 f.s., perf mat
rent (M324)

Orc, For Horn And Orchestra [20']
1(pic).1.1.1. 0.1.1.0. perc,pno,
synthesizer,strings,horn solo
SCHOTT perf mat rent (M325)

MARTUCCI, GIUSEPPE (1856-1909)
Sinfonia, Op. 75, in D minor
KISTNER perf mat rent (M326)

MARTYRE DE SAINT SEBASTIAN, LE: SUITE
see Debussy, Claude

MARTYRS, LES: OVERTURE see Donizetti,
Gaetano

MARTYRS, THE see Ye, Xiao-Gang, Guo
Shang

MARX, KARL (1897-1985)
Fragment Aus "Mnemosyne", For Solo
Voice And String Orchestra
*Op.70,No.1 [6']
string orch,S solo
BÄREN. BA 6276 perf mat rent (M327)

Fünfzehn Variationen Uber "Was Wollen
Wir Auf Den Abend Tun"
KISTNER perf mat rent (M328)

MARY see Isolfsson, Pall

MARY, QUEEN OF SCOTS: SUITE NO. 1 see
McCabe, John

MARY, QUEEN OF SCOTS: SUITE NO. 2 see
McCabe, John

MARY, WHO STOOD IN SORROW, FOR SOLO
VOICE AND ORCHESTRA see Lockwood,
Normand

MARZVEILCHEN POLKA see Strauss, Eduard

MASADA see Goldsmith, Jerry

MASCAGNI, PIETRO (1863-1945)
A Giacomo Leopardi, For Solo Voice
And Orchestra [48']
2(pic).2(English horn).2(bass
clar).2. 4.3.3.1. timp,perc,
harp,strings,S solo
sc CURCI 10196 perf mat rent (M329)

Amico Fritz, L': Duet And Suzel's
Lament "Non Mi Resta Che Il
Pianto Ed Il Dolore", For Solo
Voices And Orchestra
KALMUS A4878 sc $12.00, set $20.00,
pts $1.00, ea., perf mat rent
(M330)
Amico Fritz, L': Ed Anche Beppe Amo;
O Amore, For Solo Voice And
Orchestra
KALMUS A4877 sc $10.00, set $20.00,
pts $1.00, ea., perf mat rent
(M331)
Amico Fritz, L': Il Padrone Fra Poco
Sara Desto, For Solo Voices And
Orchestra
KALMUS A4873 sc $12.00, set $35.00,
pts $2.00, ea., perf mat rent
(M332)
Amico Fritz, L': Laceri Miseri, For
Solo Voice And Orchestra
KALMUS A4871 sc $6.00, set $15.00,
pts $.75, ea., perf mat rent
(M333)
Amico Fritz, L': O Pallida Che Un
Giorno Mi Guardasti, For Solo
Voice And Orchestra
KALMUS A4876 sc $5.00, set $18.00,
pts $1.00, ea., perf mat rent
(M334)
Amico Fritz, L': Per Voi, For Solo
Voice And Orchestra
KALMUS A4872 sc $4.00, set $15.00,
pts $.75, ea., perf mat rent

MASCAGNI, PIETRO (cont'd.)
(M335)
Amico Fritz, L': Son Pochi Fiori, For
Solo Voice And Orchestra
KALMUS A4870 sc $5.00, set $15.00,
pts $1.00, ea., perf mat rent
(M336)

MASCOTTE, LA: BALLET MUSIC see Audran,
Edmond

MAŠEK, VINCENC
Symphony
see Laube, Antonin, Symphony

MASKARADE: MAGDALONE'S DANCE SCENE, FOR
SOLO VOICES AND ORCHESTRA see
Nielsen, Carl

MASKARADE: OVERTURE see Nielsen, Carl

MASKENBALL QUADRILLE see Strauss,
Johann, [Jr.]

MASKENZUG POLKA see Strauss, Johann,
[Jr.]

MASQUE see Casken, John see Schelle,
Michael

MASS: THREE MEDITATIONS, FOR
VIOLONCELLO AND ORCHESTRA see
Bernstein, Leonard

MASS: TWO MEDITATIONS see Bernstein,
Leonard

MASSE: OMAGGIO A EDGARD VARESE, FOR
PIANO AND ORCHESTRA see Manzoni,
Giacomo

MASSENET, JULES (1842-1912)
Cantique
2fl,strings [3'] KALMUS A5732 sc
$3.00, set $5.00 (M337)

Cid, Le: Aragonaise [arr.] *see
Tchaikovsky, Piotr Ilyich, Chant
Sans Paroles [arr.]

Cid, Le: Overture [8'30"]
1+pic.1+English horn.2.2. 4.2+
2cornet.3.1. timp,perc,harp,
strings
KALMUS A6996 sc $10.00, set $25.00,
pts $1.00, ea., perf mat rent
(M338)

Cigale, La: Suite
2+pic.2+English horn.2.2. 4.3.3.1.
timp,perc,cel,2harp,strings [15']
KALMUS A5838 sc $30.00, set
$80.00, perf mat rent (M339)

Crepuscule
string orch,fl solo,vln solo,vcl
solo [3'] KALMUS A5804 sc $2.00,
set $5.00 (M340)

Dernier Sommeil De La Vierge, Le, For
Cello And String Orchestra
string orch,vcl solo [4'30"] set
KALMUS A4094 $7.00, and up (M341)

Erynnies, Les
KALMUS A5821 sc $50.00, set $80.00,
perf mat rent (M342)

Manon: Adieu, Notre Petite Table, For
Solo Voice And Orchestra
KALMUS A4348 sc $3.00, set $15.00,
pts $1.00, ea., perf mat rent
(M343)
Manon: Ah! Des Grieux, For Solo
Voices And Orchestra
KALMUS A4222 sc $6.00, set $18.00,
pts $1.00, ea., perf mat rent
(M344)
Manon: Minuet And Gavotte [arr.]
(Tobani) 1.2.2.2. 2.2.1.0. timp,
triangle,strings [4'] KALMUS
A5731 pno-cond sc $3.00, set
$13.00 (M345)

Manon: Oui, C'est Moi, For Solo
Voices And Orchestra
KALMUS A4221 sc $6.00, set $15.00,
pts $1.00, ea., perf mat rent
(M346)
Parade Militaire [3']
1+pic.2.2.2. 4.2.3.0. perc,
strings
KALMUS A6998 sc $10.00, set $20.00,
pts $1.00, ea., perf mat rent
(M347)
Roman d'Arlequin, Le [9']
1+pic.2.2.2. 2.2.0.0. timp,
strings
KALMUS A6181 sc $15.00, set $15.00,
perf mat rent (M348)

Sarabande Du XVIe Siecle [4']
1.1.0.1. 0.2.0.0. snare drum,
strings
"Spanish Sarabande From The 16th
Century" KALMUS A6105 sc $3.00,
set $11.00 (M349)

MASSENET, JULES (cont'd.)

Simple Phrase, For Violoncello And
Orchestra
0.0.2.2. 4.0.0.0. timp,harp,
strings,vcl solo [2'30"] KALMUS
A5837 sc $5.00, set $10.00 (M350)

Spanish Sarabande From The 16th
Century
see Sarabande Du XVIe Siecle

Suite No. 1, Op. 13
KALMUS A5833 sc $40.00, set $80.00,
perf mat rent (M351)

Valse Tres Lente
1.1.1.1. 0.0.0.0. strings [6']
KALMUS A7471 sc $7.00, set
$12.00, pts $1.50, ea. (M352)

MASSEUS, JAN (1913-)
Homo Ludens *Op.65 [15']
2.2.2.2. 2.2.0.0. timp,2perc,
strings
sc DONEMUS f.s., perf mat rent
(M353)

Skriabinade *Op.60 [30']
3.3.3.3. 4.2.2.1. timp,2-3perc,
cel,strings
DONEMUS perf mat rent (M354)

MASSON, ASKELL (1953-)
Concerto for Clarinet and Orchestra
[18']
2.2.2.2. 4.2.3.1. timp,3perc,
harp,cel,pno,strings,clar solo
ICELAND 003-015 (M355)

Concerto for Marimba and Orchestra
[27']
2.2.2.2. 4.2.3.2. timp,perc,
strings,marimba solo
ICELAND 003-035 (M356)

Concerto for Piano and Orchestra
2.2.2.2. 4.2.3.1. timp,3perc,
harp,cel,strings,pno solo
ICELAND 003-032 (M357)

Concerto for Trombone and Orchestra
[24']
2.2.2.2. 6.3.3.2. timp,perc,cel,
strings,trom solo
ICELAND 003-041 (M358)

Concerto for Viola and Orchestra
[14'15"]
2.2.2.2. 2.2.3.1. timp,3perc,pno&
cel,strings,vla solo
ICELAND 003-022 (M359)

Galdra Loftur
ICELAND 003-014 (M360)

Impromptu [13']
2.2.2.2. 4.4.4.2. timp,3perc,cel,
strings
ICELAND 003-034 (M361)

Konzertstück for Percussion and
Orchestra [10']
2.2.2.2. 6.2.3.1. timp,3perc,
strings,snare drum solo
ICELAND 003-018 (M362)

Okto November [11']
string orch
ICELAND 003-019 (M363)

MASSON, GERARD (1936-)
Alto-Septuor [25']
alto fl,ob d'amore,clar,bass
clar,bsn,horn,2trp,trom,tuba,
harp,pno,2vln,vla,vcl,
electronic tape
SALABERT perf mat rent (M364)

Alto Tambour, For 2 Violas And String
Orchestra [23']
string orch,2vla soli
SALABERT perf mat rent (M365)

Bleu Loin [25']
7vln,2vla,2vcl,db
SALABERT perf mat rent (M366)

Dans Le Deuil Des Vagues II [18']
4+pic.0+4English horn.2+2clar in
A+bass clar.3+contrabsn.alto
sax.tenor sax. 6.4.3.2+db tuba.
2harp,2cel,strings
SALABERT perf mat rent (M367)

Gymnastique De L'eponge, For Piano
And Instrumental Ensemble [28']
ob,English horn,clar,bass clar,
bsn,2vln,vla,vcl,db,pno solo
SALABERT perf mat rent (M368)

Offs [31']
2+2alto fl.2+2English horn.0+
2clar in A+bass clar+contrabass
clar.3+contrabsn. 4.3+bass
trp.3+bass trom.1. 4perc,cel,
strings

MASSON, GERARD (cont'd.)

SALABERT perf mat rent   (M369)

Ouest II, For Solo Voice And
    Instrumental Ensemble [25']
    fl,English horn,clar in A,bass
    clar,bsn,trp,trom,pno,harp,
    2vln,vla,vcl,Mez solo
SALABERT perf mat rent   (M370)

W3a6m4, For Violin, Viola And
    Orchestra [21']
    1+alto fl.1+English horn.1+
    contrabass clar.1. 2.0.0.1.
    strings,vln solo,vla solo
SALABERT perf mat rent   (M371)

MATEJ, JOZKA (JOSEF) (1922-   )
Concerto for Bass Trombone and
    Orchestra [22']
SUPRAPHON   (M372)

Concerto for Trumpet, Horn, Trombone
    and Chamber Orchestra [18']
PANTON   (M373)

Concerto for Violoncello and
    Orchestra [20']
SUPRAPHON   (M374)

Symphony No. 4 [24']
SUPRAPHON   (M375)

Symphony No. 5 [26']
CESKY HUD.   (M376)

Three Dances From The Beskydy Area
    [38']
CZECH RADIO   (M377)

MATHER, BRUCE (1939-   )
Dialogue Pour Trio Basso Et Orchestre
    2(pic).2.2.2. 4.2.2.1. 3perc,
    violins, vla solo, vcl solo, db
    solo
CAN.MUS.CENT. MI 1417 M427DI (M378)

Scherzo for Orchestra [16']
    2.2.2.2. 2.2.0.0. pno,perc,
    strings
CAN.MUS.CENT. MI 1100 M427SC (M379)

Scherzo, Version For 18 Instruments
    [16']
    2(pic).1.1.1. 1.1.0.0. perc,pno,
    strings
CAN.MUS.CENT. MI 1200 M427SC (M380)

MATHIAS, WILLIAM (1934-1992)
Carnival Of Wales [26']
    3.2.2.3. 4.3.3.1. timp,perc,harp,
    cel,strings
OXFORD perf mat rent   (M381)

Concerto for Horn and Orchestra [20']
    timp,strings,horn solo
OXFORD perf mat rent   (M382)

Concerto for Organ and Orchestra, Op.
    91
    2.2.2.2. 4.6.3.0. timp,perc,cel,
    harp,strings,org solo
sc OXFORD $79.95, perf mat rent
                                (M383)
Elegy For A Prince, For Solo Voice
    And Orchestra *Op.59 [15']
    2.2.2.2+contrabsn. 4.2.3.0. timp,
    2perc,cel,pno,strings,Bar solo
OXFORD perf mat rent   (M384)

National Anthems: Welsh; English
    2trp,timp,perc,strings
OXFORD perf mat rent   (M385)

Reflections On A Theme Of Tomkins
    [17']
    fl,ob,org,hpsd,strings
OXFORD perf mat rent   (M386)

Requiescat
    2.2.2.2. 4.2.3.0. timp,perc,cel,
    harp,strings
sc OXFORD $14.00, perf mat rent
                                (M387)
Songs Of William Blake, For Solo
    Voice And Orchestra *Op.82 [24']
    cel,harp,pno,strings,Mez solo
sc OXFORD 365676-0 $49.95, perf mat
    rent   (M388)
Symphony No. 2, Op. 90 [30']
    3.2.2.3. 4.3.3.1. timp,perc,harp,
    pno,cel,strings
    (Summer Music) OXFORD perf mat rent
                                (M389)
MATHIEU, RODOLPHE (1890-1962)
Trois Preludes [7'5"]
    3.2.2.2. 2.2.0.0. timp,perc,harp,
    strings
sc,pts CAN.MUS.HER. f.s.   (M390)

MATHIS DER MALER: SINFONIE see
    Hindemith, Paul

MATI, FOR SOLO VOICE AND STRING
    ORCHESTRA see Srebotnjak, Alojz F.

MATICIC, JANEZ (1926-   )
Concerto for Violin and Orchestra
    [16']
    2(pic).2(English horn).2(bass
    clar).2. 4.3.3.1. perc,harp,
    cel,pno,hpsd,strings,vln solo
DRUSTVO DSS 952 perf mat rent
                                (M391)
MATIN DES MAGICIENS, LE see Adomian,
    Lan

MATINS FOR THE VIGIL OF ASSUMPTION see
    McIntyre, Paul

MATRIMONIO PER RAGGIRO, IL: OVERTURE
    see Cimarosa, Domenico

MATRIMONIO SEGRETO, IL: ARIA DI
    GERONIMO, FOR SOLO VOICE AND
    ORCHESTRA see Cimarosa, Domenico

MATRIMONIO SEGRETO, IL: BRILLAR MI
    SENTO IL CORE, FOR SOLO VOICE AND
    ORCHESTRA see Cimarosa, Domenico

MATRIMONIO SEGRETO, IL: CARA NON
    DUBITAR, FOR SOLO VOICES AND
    ORCHESTRA see Cimarosa, Domenico

MATRIMONIO SEGRETO, IL: COSA FARETE?,
    FOR SOLO VOICES AND ORCHESTRA see
    Cimarosa, Domenico

MATRIMONIO SEGRETO, IL: E VERO CHE IN
    CASA, FOR SOLO VOICE AND ORCHESTRA
    see Cimarosa, Domenico

MATRIMONIO SEGRETO, IL: IL PARLAR DI
    CAROLINA, FOR SOLO VOICES AND
    ORCHESTRA see Cimarosa, Domenico

MATRIMONIO SEGRETO, IL: IO TI LASCIO,
    PERCHE UNITI, FOR SOLO VOICES AND
    ORCHESTRA see Cimarosa, Domenico

MATRIMONIO SEGRETO, IL: LE FACCIO UN
    INCHINO, FOR SOLO VOICES AND
    ORCHESTRA see Cimarosa, Domenico

MATRIMONIO SEGRETO, IL: OVERTURE see
    Cimarosa, Domenico

MATRIMONIO SEGRETO, IL: PERDONATE
    SIGNOR MIO, FOR SOLO VOICE AND
    ORCHESTRA see Cimarosa, Domenico

MATRIMONIO SEGRETO, IL: PRIA CHE SPUNTI
    IN CIEL L'AURORA, FOR SOLO VOICE
    AND ORCHESTRA see Cimarosa,
    Domenico

MATRIMONIO SEGRETO, IL: SE FIATO IN
    CORPO AVETE, FOR SOLO VOICE AND
    ORCHESTRA see Cimarosa, Domenico

MATRIMONIO SEGRETO, IL: SE NON
    VENDICATA, FOR SOLO VOICE AND
    ORCHESTRA see Cimarosa, Domenico

MATRIMONIO SEGRETO, IL: SENTO IN PETTO
    UN FREDDO GELO, FOR SOLO VOICES AND
    ORCHESTRA see Cimarosa, Domenico

MATRIMONIO SEGRETO, IL: SENTO OHIME!
    CHE MI VIEN MALE, FOR SOLO VOICES
    AND ORCHESTRA see Cimarosa,
    Domenico

MATRIMONIO SEGRETO, IL: SENZA TANTE
    CERIMONIE, FOR SOLO VOICE AND
    ORCHESTRA see Cimarosa, Domenico

MATRIMONIO SEGRETO, IL: SIGNOR, DEH!
    CONCEDETE, FOR SOLO VOICES AND
    ORCHESTRA see Cimarosa, Domenico

MATRIMONIO SEGRETO, IL: SON LUNATICO,
    BILIOSO, FOR SOLO VOICE AND
    ORCHESTRA see Cimarosa, Domenico

MATRIMONIO SEGRETO, IL: UDITE TUTTI,
    UDITE, FOR SOLO VOICE AND ORCHESTRA
    see Cimarosa, Domenico

MATSUMOTO, HINOHARU (1945-   )
Leonides, Les [22']
    2+alto fl.2+English horn.2+bass
    clar.2+contrabsn. 6.6.6.1.
    perc,strings
    (for 3 orchestral groups) sc ZEN-ON
    899310 f.s., perf mat rent (M392)

MATSUMURA, TEIZO (1929-   )
Concerto for Violoncello and
    Orchestra [27']
    3(pic).3(English
    horn).3.3(contrabsn). 4.4.3.1.
    timp,perc,harp,pno,cel,strings,
    vcl solo
ZEN-ON perf mat rent   (M393)

MATSUMURA, TEIZO (cont'd.)

Offrande Orchestrale [13']
    3(pic,alto fl).3(ob
    d'amore).3(bass
    clar).3(contrabsn). 4.3.3.1.
    perc,harp,pno,strings
ZEN-ON perf mat rent   (M394)

Pneuma [10']
    string orch
ZEN-ON perf mat rent   (M395)

MATSUSHITA, ISAO (1951-   )
Alabaster [13']
sc JAPAN 8301 f.s.   (M396)

MATTAPAN RAG [ARR.] see Carriker, Rob

MATTHEWS, COLIN (1946-   )
Canonic Overture: Arms Racing
    *Op.24a [5']
    2.2.2.2. 2.2.0.0. timp,strings
FABER perf mat rent   (M397)

Concerto for Violoncello and
    Orchestra, Op. 27
    3.2.4.2. 4.2.3.1. timp,4perc,
    harp,pno&cel,strings,vcl solo
sc FABER 023-00361 $34.25   (M398)

Divertimento
    string orch
    study sc FABER 023-00310 $22.25
                                (M399)
Landscape (Sonata No. 5 for
    Orchestra) Op.17
    3.3.4.3. 4.3.3.1. timp,4perc,
    2harp,strings
sc FABER 023-00344 $28.00, perf mat
    rent   (M400)
Little Suite No. 1 *Op.18a [6']
    1.1.2.1. 1.1.0.0. strings
FABER perf mat rent   (M401)

Little Suite No. 2 *Op.18b [6']
    1.1+English horn.2+bass clar.1.
    1.1.0.0. perc,strings
FABER perf mat rent   (M402)

Monody [20']
    3.2.4.3. 4.2.3.1. timp,3perc,
    harp,pno,strings
sc FABER f.s., perf mat rent (M403)

Sonata No. 4 [24']
    3.3.3.3. 4.2.3.1. 4perc,harp,
    timp,strings
NOVELLO perf mat rent   (M404)

Sonata No. 5 for Orchestra
    see Landscape

Toccata Meccanica *Op.24b [10']
    2.2.2.2. 4.2.3.0. timp,perc,
    strings
sc FABER $30.00, perf mat rent
                                (M405)
MATTHEWS, DAVID (1943-   )
Chaconne, Op. 43 [21']
    3.3.3.0.3sax. 4.3.3.1. timp,
    3perc,harp,cel,strings
sc FABER f.s., perf mat rent (M406)

Concerto for Violin and Orchestra,
    Op. 31 [24']
    2.2.2.2.sax. 4.2.2.1. timp,2perc,
    pno&cel,harp,strings,vln solo
FABER perf mat rent   (M407)

In The Dark Time *Op.38 [25']
    3.3.4.3. 4.4.3.1. timp,4perc,
    harp,pno&cel,gtr,strings
FABER perf mat rent   (M408)

Introit *Op.28
    2trp,strings
sc FABER 023-00314 $11.25   (M409)

September Music *Op.24 [10']
    2.1+English horn.2.2(contrabsn).
    4.0.0.0. harp,cel,strings
BOOSEY perf mat rent   (M410)

Serenade, Op. 29 [17']
    1(pic,alto fl).2(English
    horn).0.2. 2.0.0.0. strings
sc BOOSEY $22.00, perf mat rent
                                (M411)
Symphony No. 2, Op. 17 [30']
    3(pic).3(English horn).3(bass
    clar).3(contrabsn). 4.3.3.1.
    timp,3perc,cel,harp,strings
sc FABER F0810 f.s., perf mat rent
                                (M412)
Symphony No. 3, Op. 37 [20']
    3(pic).3(English horn).3(clar in
    E flat,bass clar).3(contrabsn).
    4.4.3.1. timp,2perc,harp,
    strings
sc FABER $24.00, perf mat rent
                                (M413)
Three Songs, For Solo Voice And
    Orchestra [18']
    3.3.4.3. 4.3.3.1. timp,3perc,

MATTHEWS, DAVID (cont'd.)

    harp,strings,S solo
    FABER perf mat rent   (M414)

    Variations On Bach's Chorale "Die
      Nacht Ist Kommen" [18']
      string orch
    FABER perf mat rent   (M415)

MAU VA HOA see Dao, Nguyen Thien

MAUGUE, JULES MARIE (1869- ?)
    Pastorale for Oboe and Orchestra
      [4'10"]
      1.1.1.0. 2.0.0.0. strings,ob solo
    BILLAUDOT perf mat rent   (M416)

MAURERISCHE TRAUERMUSIK see Mozart,
    Wolfgang Amadeus

MAURICE, PAULE (1910-1967)
    Concerto Giocoso, For Piano And
      Orchestra
      1.1.1.1. 2.1.0.0. timp,perc,cel,
      strings,pno solo
    LEMOINE perf mat rent   (M417)

MAUTHAUSEN see Lendvay, Kamillo

MAVES, DAVID (1937-   )
    Concerto for Organ and Chamber
      Orchestra [7']
      0.2.0.1. 0.1.0.0. hpsd,strings,
      org solo
    MMB perf mat rent   (M418)

    Concerto for 2 Pianos and Orchestra
      [15']
      2+pic.2+English horn.2+bass
      clar.2. 4.3.3.1. timp,perc,
      strings,2pno soli
    MMB perf mat rent   (M419)

    Overture To An Opera [8']
      2+pic.2.2+bass clar.2+contrabsn.
      4.3.3.1. timp,perc,cel,strings
    MMB perf mat rent   (M420)

    Symphony No. 2 [17']
      2+pic.2+English horn.2+bass
      clar.2+contrabsn. 4.3.3.1.
      timp,perc,harp,strings
    MMB perf mat rent   (M421)

MAW, NICHOLAS (1935-   )
    Odyssey [70']
      3.3.3.3. 6.4.3.1. 3perc,harp,cel,
      strings
    FABER perf mat rent   (M422)

    Sonata Notturna, For Violoncello And
      String Orchestra [15']
      string orch,vcl solo
    FABER perf mat rent   (M423)

    Spring Music [15']
      2.2.2.2. 4.3.3.1. timp,harp,
      strings
    sc FABER F0815 f.s., perf mat rent
                     (M424)

MAXING TANZE WALZER see Strauss,
    Johann, [Jr.]

MAXWELL DAVIES, PETER
    see DAVIES, PETER MAXWELL

MAY see Burian, Emil František

MAY DAY PRELUDE see Burgon, Geoffrey

MAY FEAST see Kristoffersen, Fridthjof,
    Mai-Fest

MAY FESTIVAL see Frohlich, J.F.,
    Majgildet

MAY GOLD [ARR.] see Thommessen, Reidar,
    Maigull [arr.]

MAY 1973 see Dolatshahi, Dariush

MAY SONG see Elgar, [Sir] Edward
    (William)

MAY SONG IT FLOURISH, FOR SOLO VOICES
    AND ORCHESTRA see Roosevelt,
    [Joseph] Willard

MAY SYMPHONY see Vacek, Miloš

MAYER, WILLIAM ROBERT (1925-   )
    Hello World, For Narrator And
      Orchestra [26']
      2.2.2.2. 3.2.2.0. perc,pno,
      strings,narrator
    BOOSEY perf mat rent   (M425)

    Inner And Outer Strings, For String
      Quartet And String Orchestra
      string orch,string quar soli
    sc BOELKE-BOM $15.00   (M426)

MAYR, [JOHANN] SIMON (1763-1845)
    Concerto for Bassoon and Orchestra
      [15']
      2ob,2horn,strings,bsn solo
    sc BSE 32 f.s., perf mat rent
                     (M427)
    Concerto for Piano and Orchestra in C
      [25']
      2ob,2horn,strings,pno solo
    BSE 30 perf mat rent   (M428)

    Concerto for Piccolo, Flute,
      Clarinet, Basset Horn and
      Orchestra [20']
      0.2.0.1. 1.2.0.0. timp,strings,
      pic solo,fl solo,clar solo,
      basset horn solo
    BSE 34 perf mat rent   (M429)

    Marcia Lugubre
      2.2.2.2.basset horn. 4.3.1.0.
      timp,drums,vcl,db
      [10'] sc BSE 137 f.s., perf mat
      rent   (M430)

    Sinfonia *see Martini, [Padre]
      Giovanni Battista, Sinfonie, Four
      see Martini, [Padre] Giovanni
      Battista, Sinfonie, Four

MAYUZUMI, TOSHIRO (1929-   )
    Bugaku
      sc PETERS P6445 $27.50   (M431)

MAZELLIER, JULES (1879-1959)
    Poeme Romantique, For Violin And
      Orchestra [16'30"]
      2.2.2.2. 2.2.3.1. timp,harp,
      strings,vln solo
    BILLAUDOT perf mat rent   (M432)

MAZEPPA see Liszt, Franz

MAZEPPA: THE BATTLE OF POLTAVA see
    Tchaikovsky, Piotr Ilyich

MAZURKA BRILLANTE [ARR.] see Liszt,
    Franz

MAZURKA OBEREK, FOR VIOLIN AND
    ORCHESTRA see Glazunov, Alexander
    Konstantinovich

MCKONKEY'S FERRY see Antheil, George

ME KAYMME JOULUN VIETTOHON, FOR SOLO
    VOICE AND ORCHESTRA [ARR.] see
    Turunen, Martti (Johannes)

MEALE, RICHARD (1932-   )
    Variations for Orchestra [13']
      2.2.2.2. 2.2.2.0. timp,perc,
      strings
    UNIVER. perf mat rent   (M433)

MEANDER, FOR PERCUSSION AND ORCHESTRA
    see Lindgren, Pär

MEANDRES, FOR OBOE AND STRING ORCHESTRA
    see Damase, Jean-Michel

MEASURE FOR MEASURE, FOR SOLO VOICE AND
    ORCHESTRA see Foss, Lukas

MEASURING THE FUTURE see MacBride,
    David Huston

MECHANICAL DOLL, THE see Reed, Alfred

MECHEM, KIRKE LEWIS (1925-   )
    Jayhawks, The *Op.43 [8']
      3.2.3.2. 4.3.3.1. timp,2perc,pno,
      strings
    SCHIRM.G perf mat rent   (M434)

    King's Contest, The, For Solo Voices
      And Orchestra [26']
      3.3.3.3. 4.3.3.1. timp,4perc,
      harp,strings,MezTBarB soli,
      alternate scoring: 1.1.1.1.
      1.0.0.0. perc, pno, 2vln, vla,
      vcl, db
    SCHIRM.G perf mat rent   (M435)

MED BRATSJ OG DRAM see Madsen, Trygve

MEDEA see Barber, Samuel

MEDEA, FOR SOLO VOICE AND ORCHESTRA see
    Caltabiano, Ronald

MEDEA-SPIEL see Rihm, Wolfgang

MEDEA: SUITE see Knaifel, Alexander

MEDEE see Indy, Vincent d'

MEDEE: OVERTURE see Cherubini, Luigi

MEDEK, TILO (1940-   )
    Concerto for Marimba and Orchestra
      [31']
      3.3.3.3. 4.1.1.1. timp,strings,
      marimba solo
    study sc HANSEN-GER f.s., perf mat
    rent   (M436)

MEDEK, TILO (cont'd.)

    Concerto for Violoncello and
      Orchestra [34']
      3.3.3.3. 4.1.1.1. timp,strings,
      vcl solo
    HANSEN-GER perf mat rent   (M437)

    Nachtgedanken
      string orch
      sc MOECK 5311 f.s., perf mat rent
                     (M438)

    Zögernde Lied, Das [8']
      3.3.3.3. 4.0.0.0. flügelhorn,
      mand,strings
    HANSEN-GER perf mat rent   (M439)

MEDINS, YAKOV (1885-1937)
    Concerto for Organ, Timpani, 2 Harps
      and String Orchestra
      timp,2harp,org,strings
    VAAP perf mat rent   (M440)

MEDITATION AND THREE DANCES, FOR VIOLA
    AND STRING ORCHESTRA see Coulthard,
    Jean

MEDITATION DE PURUN BAGHT, LA see
    Koechlin, Charles

MEDITATION ON "L" see Palsson, Pall P.

MEDITATION ON THE PASSION CHORALE see
    Cruft, Adrian

MEDITATION POETIQUE, FOR VIOLIN AND
    ORCHESTRA see El-Khoury, Bechara

MEDITATION SYMPHONIQUE NO. 3 see Ciry,
    Michel

MEDITERRANE HARMONIEN, FOR DOUBLE BASS
    AND ORCHESTRA see Kont, Paul

MEDITERRANEAN see Fuleihan, Anis

MEDTNER, NIKOLAI KARLOVICH (1880-1951)
    Concerto for Piano and Orchestra, No.
      1, Op. 33 [37']
      2.2.2.2. 4.2.3.1. timp,strings,
      pno solo
    BOOSEY perf mat rent   (M441)

MEER, DAS, FOR ORGAN AND ORCHESTRA see
    Ciurlionis, Mikolajus, Sea, The,
    For Organ And Orchestra

MEETINGS, FOR CLARINET AND ORCHESTRA
    see Gamstorp, Goran

MEFANO, PAUL (1937-   )
    Estampes Japonaises, For Solo Voice
      And Instrumental Ensemble [10']
      2fl,2clar,harp,pno,cel,strings,S
      solo
    SALABERT perf mat rent   (M442)

    Incidences, For Piano And Orchestra
      [15']
      3(pic).3(English horn).3(bass
      clar).3. 4.3.3.0. timp,3perc,
      harp,strings,pno solo
    SALABERT perf mat rent   (M443)

    Interferences [6'15"]
      1.1.1.1. 1.0.0.0. perc,3vln,vla,
      vcl
    sc HEUGEL $22.25   (M444)

    Signe-Oubli [9']
      0+pic.1+English horn.0+clar in E
      flat+bass clar.0+contrabsn.
      1.1.1+bass trom.0+db tuba.
      perc,Hamm,elec gtr,2vln,2vla,
      2vcl,2db
    SALABERT perf mat rent   (M445)

    Variations Libres [1'50"]
      string orch
    SALABERT perf mat rent   (M446)

    Voyager
      2(alto fl).0+English horn.0.0+
      contrabsn.tenor sax.baritone
      sax. 1.2.0.0. 3perc,pno,strings
    SALABERT perf mat rent   (M447)

MEFISTOFELE: AVE, SIGNOR, FOR SOLO
    VOICE AND ORCHESTRA see Boito,
    Arrigo

MEFISTOFELE: DAI CAMPI, DAI PRATI, FOR
    SOLO VOICE AND ORCHESTRA see Boito,
    Arrigo

MEFISTOFELE: EPILOGUE- THE DEATH OF
    FAUST, FOR SOLO VOICE AND ORCHESTRA
    see Boito, Arrigo

MEFISTOFELE: LA LUNA IMMOBILE, FOR SOLO
    VOICES AND ORCHESTRA see Boito,
    Arrigo

MEFISTOFELE: LONTANO, LONTANO, FOR SOLO
    VOICES AND ORCHESTRA see Boito,
    Arrigo

MEFISTOFELE: SON LO SPIRITO, FOR SOLO
VOICE AND ORCHESTRA see Boito,
Arrigo

MEFISTOFELE: SPUNTA L'AURORA PALLIDA,
FOR SOLO VOICE AND ORCHESTRA see
Boito, Arrigo

MEFISTOFELE: STRANO FIGLIO DEL CAOS,
FOR SOLO VOICES AND ORCHESTRA see
Boito, Arrigo

MEFISTOFELE: SU CAMMINA, CAMMINA, FOR
SOLO VOICES AND ORCHESTRA see
Boito, Arrigo

MEGALIET, DE see Kerstens, Huub

MÉHUL, ÉTIENNE-NICOLAS (1763-1817)
Symphony No. 1 in G minor
(Charlton, David) sc A-R ED
ISBN 0-89579-174-9 f.s., ipa
(M448)

MEI PLAISANT, DE see Hemel, Oscar van

MEIJERING, CHIEL (1954-   )
Ahnung Des Endes [60']
3.3.3.3. 8.4.3.1. 4perc,2harp,
pno&cel,strings
sc DONEMUS f.s., perf mat rent
(M449)

Flaff [17']
2.2.2.2. 4.2.3.1. 4perc,harp,
strings
sc DONEMUS f.s., perf mat rent
(M450)

For Geschapen [8']
3.2.2.2.alto sax. 2.2.1.0. 2vln,
vla,vcl,db
DONEMUS perf mat rent   (M451)

Geur Blijft Hangen, De, For 3 Guitars
And Orchestra [30']
3.3.3.3. 4.4.3.1. 5perc,2harp,
strings,3gtr soli
sc DONEMUS f.s., perf mat rent
(M452)

Grootte, De [9']
string orch
DONEMUS perf mat rent   (M453)

Ik Heb Tenen [10'30"]
3.3.3.3. 4.3.3.1. timp,3perc,pno&
cel,strings
sc DONEMUS f.s., perf mat rent
(M454)

Komodo Dragons [14']
6rec,3hpsd,org,3vla da gamba
sc DONEMUS f.s., perf mat rent
(M455)

Mogadon [11']
2.2.2.2. 4.2.3.1. perc,harp,pno,
strings
DONEMUS perf mat rent   (M456)

Neigingen, For Violin And Orchestra
[18']
2.2.2.2. 4.2.3.1. timp,3-4perc,
harp,pno&cel,strings,vln solo
DONEMUS perf mat rent   (M457)

Neo Geo, For Bassoon And Orchestra
[12']
2.2.2.2. 2.2.3.0. strings,bsn
solo
DONEMUS perf mat rent   (M458)

Neusgaten Van Sophia Loren, De [14']
1.1.1.1. 1.1.0.0. perc,pno&cel,
vln,vla,vcl,db
DONEMUS perf mat rent   (M459)

Onderwerping, For Alto Saxophone And
Orchestra [18']
3.3.3.3. 8.4.3.1. timp,perc,
2harp,pno&cel,strings,alto sax
solo
DONEMUS perf mat rent   (M460)

Poedel In Pyama [10']
2.2.2.2. 2.0.0.1. 4perc,vln,vcl
DONEMUS perf mat rent   (M461)

Zip [13']
2clar,alto sax,opt perc,pno,4vln,
2vcl,2db
sc DONEMUS f.s., perf mat rent
(M462)

MEIN KIND, WAR' ICH KONIG, FOR SOLO
VOICE AND ORCHESTRA [ARR.] see
Liszt, Franz, Enfant, Si J'etais
Roi, For Solo Voice And Orchestra
[arr.]

MEIN LEBENSLAUF IST LIEB UND LUST see
Strauss, Josef

MEIN TOD, REQUIEM IN MEMORIAM JANE S.,
FOR SOLO VOICE AND ORCHESTRA see
Rihm, Wolfgang

MEIN WAGNER see Ostendorf, Jens-Peter

MEINE LIEDER, MEINE SÄNGER, FOR SOLO
VOICE AND ORCHESTRA, [ARR.] see
Weber, Carl Maria von

MEINE SEELE RÜHMT UND PREIST, FOR SOLO
VOICE AND ORCHESTRA see Hoffmann,
Georg Melchior

MEINER ALLERLIEBSTEN SCHÖNEN, FOR SOLO
VOICE AND ORCHESTRA see Bach,
Johann Christian

MEISTERSINGER, DIE: FESTIVAL PRELUDE,
[ARR.] see Wagner, Richard

MEISTERSINGER, DIE: FESTIVAL PRELUDE
FOR BRASS SEXTET AND ORCHESTRA
[ARR.] see Wagner, Richard

MEKEEL, JOYCE (1931-   )
Vigil [10']
6.2.4.2. 4.2.1.1. timp,2perc,
harp,pno,strings
GUNMAR MP5039 perf mat rent (M463)

MELANCOLIA see Denhoff, Michael

MELARTIN, ERKKI (1875-1937)
Songs From Ladoga *Op.153 [13']
2.0.2.0. 2.1.1.0. timp,pno,cel,
strings
FAZER perf mat rent   (M464)

Yon Keskella Tahtonen Loisti, For
Solo Voice And String Orchestra
[arr.]
(Kuusisto, I.) string orch,solo
voice [2'] FAZER perf mat rent
(M465)

MELCHERS, H. MELCHER
Concerto for Piano and Orchestra, No.
1, Op. 18 [30']
2.2.2.0. 4.0.0.0. timp,strings,
pno solo
STIM   (M466)

MELEE FANTASQUE see Bliss, [Sir] Arthur
(Drummond)

MELLNÄS, ARNE (1933-   )
Capriccio [11']
2.1.2.1. 2.2.2.0. 2perc,strings
sc GEHRMANS 6010P f.s., perf mat
rent   (M467)

Symphony No. 1 [26']
3.3.3.3. 4.3.3.1. timp,4perc,
harp,cel,strings
(Ikaros) REIMERS   (M468)

Transparence [14']
4.4.4.4. 4.4.4.0. perc,harp,cel,
strings
SUECIA perf mat rent   (M469)

MELLOM SPEIL, FOR VIOLIN AND STRING
ORCHESTRA see Berge, Sigurd

MELLOMSPILL FOR ORKESTER see Janson,
Alfred

MELODI, FOR SOLO VOICE AND ORCHESTRA
[ARR.] see Danielsson, Harry

MELODIA PER STRUMENTI A CORDA see
Kielland, Olav

MELODIE, ACCORDI E FRAMMENTI see
Vandor, Ivan

MELODIE, ACCORDI E FRAMMENTI, PARTE II
see Vandor, Ivan

MELODIE CONCERTANTE, FOR VIOLONCELLO
AND ORCHESTRA see Sauguet, Henri

MELODIE DES SONS DU TEMPS see Mitrea-
Celarianu, Mihai

MELODIEN QUADRILLE see Strauss, Johann,
[Jr.]

MELODIES see Fetras, Oscar

MELODIES: SECHS LIEDER FOR SOLO VOICE
AND ORCHESTRA [ARR] see Offenbach,
Jacques

MELODY, FOR VIOLONCELLO AND ORCHESTRA
see Sköld, Sven

MELOS, FOR SOLO VOICE AND ORCHESTRA see
Cardi, Mauro

MELTING VOICE, THE see Crockett, Donald

MELTING VOICES see Crockett, Donald

MELZER, FRITZ (1915-   )
Concerto for Bass Clarinet and
Orchestra [17']
2.2.0.1. 2.1.0.0. timp,perc,
strings,bass clar solo
SIKORSKI perf mat rent   (M470)

MEMENTO, FOR 2 PIANOS AND ORCHESTRA see
Colgrass, Michael (Charles)

MEMENTO POUR MARC see Hurel, Philippe

MEMNON, FOR SOLO VOICE AND ORCHESTRA,
[ARR.] see Schubert, Franz (Peter)

MEMOIRE VIVE see Hurel, Philippe

MEMOIRES-MIROIRS, FOR HARPSICHORD AND
STRINGS see Peixinho, Jorge

MEMORIA see Baggiani, Guido

MEMORIA 2 see Vustin, Alexander

MEMORIA 2 see Vustin, Alexander

MEMORIAL see Goeb, Roger

MEMORIE E VARIANTI see Pennisi,
Francesco

MEMORIES, FOR SOLO VOICE AND STRING
ORCHESTRA see Lunde, Ivar,
Erindringer, For Solo Voice Abd
String Orchestra

MEMORIES OVERTURE [6']
(Arnaud, Leo) WARNER perf mat rent
(M471)

MEN OF GOODWILL see Britten, [Sir]
Benjamin

MENDELSSOHN, VLADIMIR (1949-   )
Histoire Veritable De l'Execrable
Count Dracula [20']
4.1.4.1. 6.4.3.1. perc,2harp,pno,
cel&synthesizer,strings
DONEMUS perf mat rent   (M472)

MENDELSSOHN-BARTHOLDY, FELIX
(1809-1847)
Adagio *see Mendelssohn-Bartholdy,
Felix, Lieder Ohne Worte, Vol. 1
[arr.] *see Mendelssohn-
Bartholdy, Felix, Lieder Ohne
Worte, Vol. 2 [arr.]

Athalia: Kriegsmarsch Der Priester
BREITKOPF-W perf mat rent (M473)

Capriccio Brillant, For Piano And
Orchestra *Op.22
SONZOGNO perf mat rent   (M474)

Capriccio Brillant, For Piano And
Orchestra *Op.22
min sc KALMUS K01188 $5.00 contains
also: Rondo Brillant, For Piano
And Orchestra, Op.29   (M475)

Concerto for Piano and Orchestra, No.
1, Op. 25, in G minor
sc,pts BREITKOPF-W PB-OB 5128 f.s.
(M476)
Concerto for Piano and Orchestra, No.
2, Op. 40, in D minor
sc,pts BREITKOPF-W PB-OB 5129 f.s.
(M477)
Concerto for Violin and Orchestra,
Op. 64, in E minor
SONZOGNO perf mat rent   (M478)
(Darvas) study sc EMB 40049 f.s.
(M479)
*see GREAT ROMANTIC VIOLIN
CONCERTOS

Cornelius March *Op.108 [4']
0.2.2.2. 2.2.3.0. timp,strings
KALMUS A5623 sc $3.00, perf mat
rent, set $15.00, pts $1.00, ea.
(M480)
Elias: Hore Israel, For Solo Voice
And Orchestra [5']
2.2.2.2. 2.2.0.0. strings,S solo
BREITKOPF-W perf mat rent (M481)

Folksong *see Mendelssohn-Bartholdy,
Felix, Lieder Ohne Worte, Vol. 1
[arr.]

Grotto Di Fingal, La
see Hebriden, Die

Hebriden, Die *Op.26
"Grotto Di Fingal, La" SONZOGNO
perf mat rent   (M482)

Hunting Song *see Mendelssohn-
Bartholdy, Felix, Lieder Ohne
Worte, Vol. 2 [arr.]

Infelice!, For Solo Voice And
Orchestra *Op.94 [10']
2.2.2.2. 2.2.0.0. strings,S solo
BREITKOPF-W perf mat rent (M483)
"Unglücksel'ge! Er Ist Auf Immer
Mir Entflo'n, For Solo Voice And
Orchestra" BREITKOPF-L perf mat
rent   (M484)

Jagd, Die [arr]
(Mefano, Paul) 2.2.2.2. 2.2.0.0.
timp,strings [5'] SALABERT perf
mat rent   (M485)

MENDELSSOHN-BARTHOLDY, FELIX (cont'd.)

Konzertstück for Clarinet, Basset
    Horn and Orchestra, Op. 113, in F
    minor
    (Meyer, Sabine; Meyer, Wolfgang;
    Wehle, Reiner) 2.2.0.2. 2.2.0.0.
    timp,strings,clar solo,basset
    horn solo, or 2 clar soli [8']
    BREITKOPF-W sc PB 5191 f.s., pts
    OB 5191 f.s.   (M486)

Konzertstucke For Clarinet, Basset
    Horn And String Orchestra, Op.
    113 and Op. 114
    (Schottstadt, Rainer) string orch,
    clar solo,basset horn solo/2clar
    soli sc PETERS P8595A f.s., perf
    mat rent   (M487)

Lieder Ohne Worte, Op.30, No.1;
    Op.38, No.2; Op.53, No.4; Op.85,
    No.3 [arr.]
    (Angerer, Paul) trom,strings [11']
    DÖBLINGER perf mat rent   (M488)

Lieder Ohne Worte, Vol. 1 [arr.]
    (Burger) "Songs Without Words, Vol.
    1 [arr.]" string orch [6']
    (contains Folksong; Adagio;
    Springsong; Venetian Gondoliers)
    KALMUS A7467 sc $7.00, set $7.50,
    pts $1.50, ea.   (M489)

Lieder Ohne Worte, Vol. 2 [arr.]
    (Burger) "Songs Without Words, Vol.
    2 [arr.]" string orch [8']
    (contains Hunting Song; Moderato;
    Sorrowful Song; Adagio) KALMUS
    A7468 sc $7.00, set $7.50, pts
    $1.50, ea.   (M490)

Midsummer Night's Dream: Overture
    sc MUZYKA f.s.   (M491)

Moderato *see Mendelssohn-Bartholdy,
    Felix, Lieder Ohne Worte, Vol. 2
    [arr.]

Rondo Brillant, For Piano And
    Orchestra *Op.29
    sc KUNZEL 10070 f.s.   (M492)

Rondo Brillant, For Piano And
    Orchestra
    see Capriccio Brillant, For Piano
    And Orchestra

Ruy Blas Overture *Op.95
    SONZOGNO perf mat rent   (M493)

Sinfonia No. 1 in C [10']
    string orch
    SCHIRM.G perf mat rent   (M494)

Sinfonia No. 8 in D
    string orch
    (Freudenthal) KALMUS 6762 sc
    $15.00, set $20.00, pts $4.00,
    ea., perf mat rent   (M495)

Sinfonia No. 9 in C
    SONZOGNO perf mat rent   (M496)

Sinfonia No. 10 in B minor [10']
    string orch
    SCHIRM.G perf mat rent   (M497)

Sinfonia No. 12 in G minor [18']
    string orch
    SCHIRM.G perf mat rent   (M498)

Songs Without Words, Vol. 1 [arr.]
    see Lieder Ohne Worte, Vol. 1
    [arr.]

Songs Without Words, Vol. 2 [arr.]
    see Lieder Ohne Worte, Vol. 2
    [arr.]

Sorrowful Song *see Mendelssohn-
    Bartholdy, Felix, Lieder Ohne
    Worte, Vol. 2 [arr.]

Springsong *see Mendelssohn-
    Bartholdy, Felix, Lieder Ohne
    Worte, Vol. 1 [arr.]

Symphony No. 4, Op. 90, in A
    (Druian) set SCHIRM.G 50347520
    $17.50   (M499)

Symphony No. 5, Op. 107, in D minor
    SONZOGNO perf mat rent   (M500)

Unglücksel'ge! Er Ist Auf Immer Mir
    Entfloh'n, For Solo Voice And
    Orchestra
    see Infelice!, For Solo Voice And
    Orchestra

Venetian Gondoliers *see
    Mendelssohn-Bartholdy, Felix,
    Lieder Ohne Worte, Vol. 1 [arr.]

MENGAL, MARTIN JOSEPH (1784-1851)
    Solo for Horn and Orchestra [9'30"]
    1.2.2.2. 2.0.0.0. strings,horn
    solo
    sc BILLAUDOT f.s., perf mat rent
                                    (M501)

MENGELBERG, KAREL (1902-1984)
    Bergen, De [14']
    2.2.2.2. 2.2.0.0. timp,strings
    sc DONEMUS f.s., perf mat rent
                                    (M502)

Parfait Amour [16']
    2.2.2.2. 4.2.3.1. timp,2-3perc,
    harp,strings
    sc DONEMUS f.s., perf mat rent
                                    (M503)

Signalen [10']
    3.3.3.3.alto sax. 4.3.3.1. timp,
    3perc,2harp,strings
    sc DONEMUS f.s., perf mat rent
                                    (M504)

MENGELBERG, KURT RUDOLF (1892-1959)
    Ballade Van Den Boer, For Narrator
    And Orchestra [12']
    2.3.3.2. 4.2.3.1. timp,cel,harp,
    strings,narrator
    sc DONEMUS perf mat rent   (M505)

MENNIN, PETER (MENNINI) (1923-1983)
    Concertino for Flute and Orchestra
    [11']
    timp,snare drum,strings,fl solo
    FISCHER,C perf mat rent   (M506)

Concerto for Flute and Orchestra
    [22']
    2(pic).2+English horn.2+bass
    clar.2+contrabsn. 4.3.3.1.
    timp,3perc,strings,fl solo
    FISCHER,C perf mat rent   (M507)
    SCHIRM.G perf mat rent   (M508)

Fantasia For String Orchestra [11']
    string orch
    FISCHER,C perf mat rent   (M509)

Folk Overture [8']
    2(pic).2.2.2. 4.3.3.1. timp,perc,
    strings
    FISCHER,C perf mat rent   (M510)

Sinfonia for Chamber Orchestra [5']
    2(pic).2.2.2. 2.2.1.0. pno,
    strings
    FISCHER,C perf mat rent   (M511)

Symphony No. 1 [56']
    2+pic.2+English horn.2+bass
    clar.2. 4.3.3.1. timp,3perc,
    strings
    FISCHER,C perf mat rent   (M512)

Symphony No. 3 [23']
    3(pic).2.2.2. 4.3.3.1. timp,
    3perc,strings
    FISCHER,C perf mat rent   (M513)

Symphony No. 9 [20']
    3(pic).2+English horn.2+bass
    clar.2+contrabsn. 4.4.3.1.
    timp,3perc,strings
    FISCHER,C perf mat rent   (M514)
    (Sinfonia Capricciosa) SCHIRM.G
    perf mat rent   (M515)

MENOTTI, GIAN CARLO (1911-   )
    Barcarolle (from Sebastian)
    1(pic).1.2(bass clar).1. 2.2.0.0.
    timp,perc,harp,strings
    COLOMBO perf mat rent   (M516)

Concerto for Double Bass and
    Orchestra [23']
    2+pic.2.2+bass clar.2. 4.2.3.1.
    timp,perc,harp,strings,db solo
    SCHIRM.G perf mat rent   (M517)

Goya: Suite [25']
    2+pic.2+English horn.2+bass
    clar.2. 4.3.3.1. timp,perc,
    harp,strings
    SCHIRM.G perf mat rent   (M518)

Lewisohn Stadium Fanfare
    0.0.0.0. 4.3.3.1. timp,perc,
    strings
    SCHIRM.G perf mat rent   (M519)

Symphony No. 1 in A minor [30']
    2+pic.2+English horn.2+bass
    clar.2+contrabsn. 4.2.3.1.
    timp,perc,harp,pno,strings
    (The Halcyon) SCHIRM.G perf mat
    rent   (M520)

MENSURALE see Gentilucci, Armando

MENTRE TI LASCIO, O FIGLIA, FOR SOLO
    VOICE AND ORCHESTRA see Mozart,
    Wolfgang Amadeus

MENUET FROM A SERENATA [ARR.] see Bach,
    Johann Sebastian, Menuette Aus
    Einer Serenata [arr.]

MENUET POMPEUX [ARR.] see Chabrier,
    [Alexis-] Emmanuel

MENUETTE, ZWOLF, WOO. 12 see Beethoven,
    Ludwig van

MENUETTE AUS EINER SERENATA [ARR.] see
    Bach, Johann Sebastian

MEPHISTO see Dewanger, Anton

MEPHISTO WALTZ NO. 1 see Liszt, Franz

MEPHISTO WALTZ NO. 2 see Liszt, Franz

MEPHISTO WALTZES see Liszt, Franz

MEPHISTOPHELES' SONG OF THE FLEA, FOR
    SOLO VOICE AND ORCHESTRA [ARR.] see
    Beethoven, Ludwig van, Es War
    Einmal Ein Konig, For Solo Voice
    And Orchestra [arr.]

MER, LA see Debussy, Claude

MER, LA, FOR SOLO VOICE AND ORCHESTRA
    see Borodin, Alexander Porfirievich

MERANGER, PAUL (1936-   )
    Concerto for Saxophone and
    Instrumental Ensemble, Op. 20
    [14']
    opt harp,strings,sax solo
    BILLAUDOT perf mat rent   (M521)

Concerto 25, For Guitar And Chamber
    Orchestra [20']
    ●1.1.1.1. 0.0.0.0. strings,gtr
    solo
    BILLAUDOT perf mat rent   (M522)

MERCADANTE, G. SAVERIO (1795-1870)
    Concerto for Clarinet and Orchestra
    in E flat [25']
    2.2.2.2. 2.2.1.0. strings,clar
    solo
    sc BSE 1262 f.s., perf mat rent
                                    (M523)

Concerto for Flute and Orchestra in D
    [25']
    2ob,2horn,strings,fl solo
    sc BSE 43 f.s., perf mat rent
                                    (M524)

Concerto for Flute and Orchestra in E
    [27']
    2.2.2.2. 2.2.1.0. timp,strings,fl
    solo
    sc BSE 45 f.s., perf mat rent
                                    (M525)

Concerto for Horn and Chamber
    Orchestra in D minor
    1.2.0.1. 2.0.0.0. strings,horn solo
    sc CURCI 10101 perf mat rent
                                    (M526)

Concertone For Flute, Two Clarinets,
    Horn And Orchestra In F
    0.2.0.2. 2.0.1.0. strings,fl
    solo,2clar soli,horn solo
    BSE 106 perf mat rent   (M527)

Concertone For Two Flutes, Two
    Clarinets, Horn And Orchestra In
    F [16']
    0.2.0.2. 2.0.0.0. strings,2fl
    soli,2clar soli,horn solo
    BSE 49 perf mat rent   (M528)

Danza, La [20']
    2+pic.2.2.2. 0.2.3.1. timp,
    strings
    sc BSE 1260 f.s., perf mat rent
                                    (M529)

Omaggio A Bellini [9']
    2+pic.2.2.2. 4.2.3.1. timp,perc,
    harp,strings
    BSE 61 perf mat rent   (M530)

Overture in C [8']
    2.2.2.2. 2.2.1.0. timp,perc,
    strings
    BSE 37 perf mat rent   (M531)

Overture in D [10']
    2.2.2.2. 2.2.1.0. timp,strings
    sc BSE 36 f.s., perf mat rent
                                    (M532)

Sinfonia in D [25']
    2.2.2.2. 2.2.0.0. strings
    BSE 35 perf mat rent   (M533)

Sinfonia Sullo Stabat Di Rossini
    [15']
    2.2.2.2. 4.2.3.1. timp,perc,
    strings
    sc BSE 1261 f.s., perf mat rent
                                    (M534)

Variations for Flute and String
    Orchestra [10']
    string orch,fl solo
    sc BSE 41 f.s., perf mat rent
                                    (M535)

Variations for Horn and Orchestra
    [10']
    2ob,2horn,strings,horn solo
    sc BSE 39 f.s., perf mat rent
                                    (M536)

MERCADANTE, G. SAVERIO (cont'd.)

Variations for Violin and String
Orchestra [10']
string orch,vln solo
BSE 142 perf mat rent   (M537)

MERE, FOR SOLO VOICES AND ORCHESTRA see
Bienvenu, Lily

MERE TRES DOUCE see Tomasi, Henri

MERELLA, FOR SOLO VOICE AND ORCHESTRA
[ARR.] see Merikanto, Oskar

MERIKANTO, OSKAR (1868-1924)
Annina, For Solo Voice And Orchestra
[arr.]
(Koskimies, Eero) 2.0.2.0. 2.0.0.0.
strings,solo voice [4'] FAZER
perf mat rent   (M538)

Joulu Tullut On, For Solo Voice And
Orchestra [2']
fl,harp,strings,solo voice
FAZER perf mat rent   (M539)

Kansanlaulu, For Solo Voice And
Orchestra [arr.]
(Fougstedt, N-E) 0.1.2.0. 2.0.0.0.
harp,strings,solo voice [3']
FAZER perf mat rent   (M540)

Kesaillan, Valssi, For Solo Voice And
Orchestra [arr.]
(Panula, Jorma) 2.4.1.0. 2.2.2.0.
perc,harp,strings,solo voice [4']
FAZER perf mat rent   (M541)

Kevatlinnuille Etelassa, For Solo
Voice And Orchestra [arr.]
(Panula, Jorma) fl,strings,solo
voice [2'] FAZER perf mat rent
(M542)

Kun Paiva Paistaa, For Solo Voice And
Orchestra [arr.] *Op.24,No.1
(Panula, Jorma) 1.1.0.0. 2.1.1.0.
perc,harp,strings,solo voice [2']
FAZER perf mat rent   (M543)

Ma Elan, For Solo Voice And Orchestra
[arr.]
(Koskimies Eero) 1.1.2.1. 2.0.0.0.
harp,strings,solo voice [2']
FAZER perf mat rent   (M544)

Merella, For Solo Voice And Orchestra
[arr.]
(Koskimies, Eero) 2.2.2.2. 2.2.1.0.
timp,perc,strings,solo voice [4']
FAZER perf mat rent   (M545)

Myrskylintu, For Solo Voice And
Orchestra [arr.]
(Simila, M.) 1.1.1.1. 2.1.1.1.
perc,harp,strings,solo voice
[2'30"] FAZER perf mat rent
(M546)

Onnelliset, For Solo Voice And
Orchestra [arr.]
(Panula, Jorma) harp,strings,solo
voice [3'] FAZER perf mat rent
(M547)

Valse Lengte, For Solo Voice And
Orchestra [arr.]
(Fougstedt, N-E) 2.2.2.2. 4.0.0.0.
perc,strings,solo voice [2']
FAZER perf mat rent   (M548)

MERILAINEN, USKO (1930-   )
"...But This Is A Landscape, Monsieur
Dali!" [11']
3.2.3.3. 4.3.3.1. timp,4perc,
strings
sc SUOMEN f.s.   (M549)

Visions And Whispers, For Flute And
Orchestra [18']
3.2.3.3. 4.3.3.1. timp,3perc,
harp,hpsd,strings,fl solo
sc SUOMEN f.s.   (M550)

MERLE, JOHN
see ISAAC, MERLE JOHN

MERLET, MICHEL (1939-   )
Concert In Quarto, For Violin And
String Orchestra [20']
string orch,vln solo
BILLAUDOT perf mat rent   (M551)

Concerto for Piano and Orchestra
CHOUDENS perf mat rent   (M552)

Psalmos *Op.28 [6']
string orch
BILLAUDOT perf mat rent   (M553)

Triptyque Symphonique [17']
2.2.2.2. 3.3.3.1. timp,3perc,
harp,strings
BILLAUDOT perf mat rent   (M554)

MERMAID SUITE see Du, Ming-Xin

MERMAID SUITE: CORAL DANCE [ARR.] see
Du, Ming-Xin

MERMAID SUITE: DANCE OF GINSENG [ARR.]
see Du, Ming-Xin

MERMAID SUITE: DANCE OF THE SEAWEED
[ARR.] see Du, Ming-Xin

MERMAID SUITE: DANCE OF TWENTY-FOUR
MERMAIDS [ARR.] see Du, Ming-Xin

MERMAID SUITE: MASS DANCE AT THE
WEDDING [ARR.] see Du, Ming-Xin

MERMAID SUITE: STRAW HATS FLOWER DANCE
[ARR.] see Du, Ming-Xin

MEROPE: BALLET MUSIC see Broschi,
Riccardo

MERRY EYE see Howells, Herbert Norman

MERRY MOUNT: CHILDREN'S DANCE see
Hanson, Howard

MERRY MOUNT: LOVE DUET see Hanson,
Howard

MERRY POVERTY: FUCIK, FOR SOLO VOICE
AND ORCHESTRA see Branzovsky,
Vaclav

MERRY WIDOW, THE: PARAPHRASE [ARR.] see
Lehar, Franz, Lustige Witwe, Die:
Paraphrase [arr.]

MERRYMAN, MARJORIE
River Song, The [10']
2.2.2.2. 2.2.2.0. 2perc,strings
sc APNM $6.75, perf mat rent (M555)

MERSSON, BORIS (1921-   )
Fantasy for Alto Saxophone and
Orchestra
sc KUNZEL 10206 $20.00, perf mat
rent   (M556)

MESCHWITZ, FRIEDER (1936-1983)
Rotkehlehen, Das, For Narrator And
Orchestra [25']
2ob,2horn,pno,5vln,2vla,2vcl,db,
narrator
HANSEN-GER perf mat rent   (M557)

MESSAGER, ANDRE (1853-1929)
Aventure De La Guimard, Une: Danses
Anciennes [11']
2.2.2.2. 4.2.0.0. timp,perc,harp,
strings
CHOUDENS perf mat rent   (M558)

Basoche, La: Passepied
2.2.2.2. 4.2.0.0. timp,strings
CHOUDENS perf mat rent   (M559)

Deux Pigeons, Les: Suite [22']
1+pic.2.2.2. 4.0+2cornet.3.1.
timp,perc,harp,strings
ENOCH perf mat rent   (M560)

MESSE D'AVILA, FOR SOLO VOICES AND
ORCHESTRA see Koering, Rene

MESSE DES PAUVRES [ARR.] see Satie,
Erik

MESSENGER RNA see Becker, Frank

MESTO, FOR BASSOON AND STRING ORCHESTRA
see Lombardo, Robert M.

MESTRES-QUADRENY, JOSEP MARIA
(1929-   )
Homenaje A Joan Prats [18']
1.0.1.0. 1.2.2.1. perc,string
quar,electronic equipment, 6
actors
ALPUERTO   (M561)

Quadre [8']
fl,ob,clar,perc,pno,strings
ALPUERTO   (M562)

MESTRINO, NICOLO
Concerto For Violin And Orchestra No.
4 In D *see THREE CENTURIES OF
MUSIC IN SCORE, VOL. 6: CONCERTO
V. LATE CLASSICAL STRINGS AND
WINDS

METABOLAI see Stroppa, Marco

METALAYI 2 see Ducol, Bruno

METALAYI NO. 3, FOR PIANO AND ORCHESTRA
see Ducol, Bruno

METAMORFOSIS DE CONCIERTO, FOR GUITAR
AND ORCHESTRA see Montsalvatge,
Xavier

METAMORPHOSE see Voss, Friedrich see
Zimmermann, Bernd Alois

METAMORPHOSE DU CRI see Desilets,
Richard

METAMORPHOSEN see Vogel, Ernst see
Zechlin, Ruth

METAMORPHOSEN, FOR VIOLIN, PIANO, WINDS
AND PERCUSSION see Pflüger, Hans
Georg

METAMORPHOSES see Gregson, Edward see
Kocsar, Miklos

METAMORPHOSI PER ARCHI see Carlstedt,
Jan

METAMORPHOSIS see Kokkonen, Joonas

METAMORPHOSIS, FOR PIANO AND ORCHESTRA
see Saul, Walter

METAMORPHOSIS OF A PIECE FOR CIMBALOM
see Lendvay, Kamillo

METAMUSIC see Vostrák, Zbynek

METANOIA see Thomas, Andrew

METAPHONIA see Shibata, Minao

METAPLASIS A see Ioannides, Yannis

METASINFONIA, FOR ORGAN AND ORCHESTRA
see Panufnik, Andrzej

METATHESIS see Lovendusky, James

METRUM, FOR 4 SAXOPHONES AND ORCHESTRA
see Wagenaar, Diderek

METRUM, FOR TIMPANI AND ORCHESTRA see
Wüsthoff, Klaus

METZLER, FRIEDRICH (1910-1979)
Concerto for Violoncello and
Orchestra [21']
3(pic).2(opt English horn).2.2.
4.2.3.1. timp,2perc,harp,
strings,vcl solo
RIES perf mat rent   (M563)

MEYER, AUBREY (1947-   )
Chorus [27']
2(pic).2(English horn).2(clar in
E flat,bass
clar).2(contrabsn).alto sax.
4.2(piccolo trp).3.1. timp,
3perc,harp,pno&cel,strings
CHESTER perf mat rent   (M564)

MEYER, ERNST HERMANN (1905-   )
Kontraste, Konflikte
sc PETERS f.s.   (M565)

MEYER, KRZYSZTOF (1943-   )
Concerto Da Camera, For Harp,
Violoncello And String Orchestra
*Op.64 [24']
9vln,3vla,2vcl,db,harp solo,vcl
solo
SIKORSKI perf mat rent   (M566)

Concerto for Flute and Orchestra, Op.
61 [20']
3.3.3.3. 3.3.3.0. 3perc,harp,cel,
pno,strings,fl solo
SIKORSKI perf mat rent   (M567)

Fireballs *Op.37 [16']
4horn,4trp,3trom,tuba,perc,
strings
sc POLSKIE f.s.   (M568)

Hommage A Johannes Brahms *Op.59
[13']
3.2.3.3. 4.2.2.0. timp,perc,pno,
strings
study sc SIKORSKI f.s., perf mat
rent   (M569)

Musica Incrostata *Op.70 [18']
4.3.3.3. 4.3.3.0. 4perc,harp,cel,
strings
SIKORSKI perf mat rent   (M570)

Symphony No. 6, Op. 57 [46']
4.3.3.3. 3.4.3.1. perc,harp,
strings
(Polish Symphony) POLSKIE   (M571)

Symphony, Op. 41, in D [28']
2.2.0.2. 2.0.0.0. timp,strings
(In Mozartean Style) POLSKIE (M572)

MEYER-HELMUND, ERIK (1861-1932)
Fantasy for Violin and Orchestra, Op.
44 [10']
2.2.2.2. 2.1.0.0. timp,harp,
strings,vln solo
RAHTER perf mat rent   (M573)

MEYERBEER, GIACOMO (1791-1864)
Huguenots, Les: A Fau Tourane
KALMUS A6247 set $17.00, pts $1.00,
ea.   (M574)

MEYERBEER, GIACOMO (cont'd.)

Prophet, Der: Ach Mein Sohn, For Solo
  Voice And Orchestra
  see Prophete, Le: Ah, Mon Fils, For
  Solo Voice And Orchestra

Prophet, Der: O Gebt, For Solo Voice
  And Orchestra
  see Prophete, Le: Romance De La
  Mendiante, For Solo Voice And
  Orchestra

Prophete, Le: Ah, Mon Fils, For Solo
  Voice And Orchestra
  "Prophet, Der: Ach Mein Sohn, For
  Solo Voice And Orchestra"
  BREITKOPF-L perf mat rent (M575)

Prophete, Le: Romance De La
  Mendiante, For Solo Voice And
  Orchestra
  "Prophet, Der: O Gebt, For Solo
  Voice And Orchestra" BREITKOPF-L
  perf mat rent   (M576)

MEYEROWITZ, JAN (1913-   )
  Mulatto, Il: Suite [20']
    2.2.2.2. 4.2.3.1. timp,perc,harp,
    strings
    SONZOGNO perf mat rent   (M577)

  Sei Canti, For Solo Voice And
    Orchestra [16']
    2.2.2.2. 4.0.0.0. timp,perc,pno,
    harp,strings,solo voice
    SONZOGNO perf mat rent   (M578)

MI-FI-LI see Hvoslef, Ketil

MIA SPERANZA ADORATA, FOR SOLO VOICE
  AND ORCHESTRA see Mozart, Wolfgang
  Amadeus

MIAMI, JOE
  see BALLARD, LOUIS WAYNE

MIASKOVSKY, NIKOLAI YAKOVLEVICH
  (1881-1950)
  Military March No. 1 [4']
    1.1.2.1. 2.2.1.0. perc,strings
    set KALMUS A5781 $15.00, perf mat
    rent   (M579)

  Overture in G [5']
    3.3.2.2. 4.2.3.1. timp,perc,
    strings
    SIKORSKI perf mat rent   (M580)

  Overture, Op. 76, in C minor [14']
    3.3.3.3. 4.3.3.1. timp,perc,
    strings
    (Ouverture pathetique) SIKORSKI
    perf mat rent   (M581)

  Symphonic Poem *Op.14
    3.3.3.3. 6.3.3.1. timp,perc,
    2harp,strings
    VAAP perf mat rent   (M582)

  Symphony No. 1, Op. 3, in C minor
    (N5780) KALMUS sc $50.00, set
    $100.00, perf mat rent   (M583)

  Symphony No. 21, Op. 51, in F sharp
    minor
    KALMUS A5668 sc $18.00, perf mat
    rent, set $50.00, pts $2.00, ea.
                               (M584)

MICA, FRANTISEK VACLAV (1694-1744)
  Four Elements: Recitativo And Aria Of
    Weather, For Solo Voice And
    Orchestra [4']
    1.2.0.1. 0.0.0.0. hpsd,strings,S
    solo
    SUPRAPHON   (M585)

  On Seven Planets: Mara's Aria, For
    Solo Voices And Orchestra [6']
    horn,trp,timp,hpsd,strings,SB
    soli
    SUPRAPHON   (M586)

  Origine Di Jaromeriz In Moravia, L':
    Duet Of Bimbalca And Aidalacco,
    For Solo Voices And Orchestra
    [9']
    hpsd,strings,SB soli
    SUPRAPHON   (M587)

  Origine Di Jaromeriz In Moravia, L':
    Hedvika's Aria, For Solo Voice
    And Orchestra [7']
    2ob,bsn,hpsd,strings,S solo
    SUPRAPHON   (M588)

  Origine Di Jaromeriz In Moravia, L':
    Operosa Terni Colossi Moles, For
    Solo Voice And Orchestra
    2ob,bsn,hpsd,strings,A solo
    [6'] SUPRAPHON   (M589)

  Origine Di Jaromeriz In Moravia, L':
    Recitativo Ed Aria Di Gualterus,
    For Solo Voice And Orchestra [6']
    2ob,bsn,hpsd,strings,T solo

MICA, FRANTISEK VACLAV (cont'd.)

  SUPRAPHON   (M590)

  Sinfonia Nel Giorni Natalizio [6']
    hpsd,strings
    SUPRAPHON   (M591)

MICHAEL'S JOURNEY ROUND THE EARTH, FOR
  TRUMPET AND ORCHESTRA see
  Stockhausen, Karlheinz, Michaels
  Reise Um Die Erde, For Trumpet And
  Orchestra

MICHAELS REISE UM DIE ERDE, FOR TRUMPET
  AND ORCHESTRA see Stockhausen,
  Karlheinz

MICHANS, CARLOS (1950-   )
  Episodes [13']
    1.1.2.1. 1.0.0.0. 5perc,harp,pno,
    2vln,vla,vcl,db
    sc DONEMUS f.s., perf mat rent
                               (M592)

  Sinfonia Concertante for 2 Violins
    and String Orchestra [30']
    string orch,2vln soli
    DONEMUS perf mat rent   (M593)

MICHELANGELO see Gade, Niels Wilhelm

MICKYMAUSPARADE see Streicher, F.

MICROSYMPHONY see Vine, Carl

MIDDAY WITCH see Dvořák, Antonín

MIDI, FOR 2 PIANOS AND ORCHESTRA see
  Tomasson, Jonas

MIDSUMMER EVENING, THE see Tveitt,
  Geirr, Jonsokkvelden

MIDSUMMER FIRE, THE see Tveitt, Geirr,
  Jonsokbalet

MIDSUMMER NIGHT, FOR SOLO VOICES AND
  ORCHESTRA see Tveitt, Geirr,
  Jonsoknatt, For Solo Voices And
  Orchestra

MIDSUMMER NIGHT'S DREAM, A: INCIDENTAL
  MUSIC, VOL.1 see Purcell, Henry

MIDSUMMER NIGHT'S DREAM, A: INCIDENTAL
  MUSIC, VOL.2 see Purcell, Henry

MIDSUMMER NIGHT'S DREAM: OVERTURE see
  Mendelssohn-Bartholdy, Felix

MIDVINTERBLOT; SOMMARSOLSTAND see Koch,
  Erland von

MIEDO see Rodrigo, Joaquín

MIEG, PETER (1906-   )
  Concerto for Piano, Violin and
    Orchestra
    1.1.1.1. 2.1.0.0. timp,strings,
    pno solo,vcl solo
    sc AMADEUS $56.00   (M594)

  Concerto in D flat for Piano 4-Hands
    and String Orchestra
    string orch,pno 4-hands soli
    sc AMADEUS BP 405 f.s., perf mat
    rent   (M595)

MIEREANU, COSTIN (1943-   )
  Couleurs Du Temps, Version No. 1
    [10']
    string orch
    SALABERT perf mat rent   (M596)

  Cuivres Celestes [20']
    0.0.0.0. 1.2.1.1. 2perc,strings
    SALABERT perf mat rent   (M597)

  Cuivres Do-Re [17'30"]
    0.0.0.0. 1.2.1.1. 2perc,3gtr,pno,
    strings
    SALABERT perf mat rent   (M598)

  Donum Sacrum Brancusi, For Solo Voice
    And Orchestra [14']
    1+2pic.0.2.1. 4.3.4.0. 4perc,
    harp,elec org,strings,S solo
    SALABERT perf mat rent   (M599)

  Doppel Konzert, For Saxophone,
    Percussion And Chamber Orchestra
    [17']
    2.2.2+bass clar.2. 2.1.1.0.
    2perc,pno,strings,sax solo,perc
    solo
    SALABERT EAS18334P perf mat rent
                               (M600)

  Enlacements Infinis, For Solo Voice
    And Instrumental Ensemble [14']
    1(pic,alto fl).0.2(clar in E
    flat,bass clar).0. 1.1.1.0.
    2perc,pno&cel,vln,vcl,S solo
    SALABERT perf mat rent   (M601)

MIEREANU, COSTIN (cont'd.)

  Espace Au-Dela Du Dernier [11']
    1(pic,alto fl).0.1(clar in E
    flat,bass clar).0. 2.2.2.0.
    perc,pno,strings
    SALABERT perf mat rent   (M602)

  Espace II [15']
    1-2pno,strings,electronic tape
    SALABERT perf mat rent   (M603)

  Finis Coronat Opus, For Piano And
    Orchestra [21']
    1+pic+alto fl.1+English
    horn.1.2.tenor sax. 0.4.4.0.
    4perc,2elec gtr,strings,pno
    solo
    SALABERT perf mat rent   (M604)

  Miroirs Celestes [18']
    3(pic,alto fl).3(English
    horn).3(clar in E flat,bass
    clar).3(contrabsn). 4.3.3.1.
    5perc,harp,pno&cel&glock,
    strings
    SALABERT perf mat rent   (M605)

  Monostructures I [10']
    4horn,4trp,4trom,strings
    SALABERT perf mat rent   (M606)

  Monostructures II [6']
    4horn,4trp,4trom,strings,
    electronic equipment
    SALABERT perf mat rent   (M607)

  Rosario [24'30"]
    5(pic,alto fl).3(English
    horn).3(bass
    clar).3(contrabsn).2alto
    sax.opt tenor sax. 6.4.4.2.
    6perc,strings
    SALABERT perf mat rent   (M608)

  Rosenzeit [21'30"]
    3(pic).3(English horn).3(bass
    clar).3(contrabsn). 5.4.3.1.
    timp,3perc,harp,pno&cel&strings
    SALABERT perf mat rent   (M609)

  Sempre Azzuro [15']
    7vln,2vla,2vcl,db
    SALABERT perf mat rent   (M610)

  Voyage D'hiver II [13']
    4(pic).3(English horn).4(bass
    clar,contrabass
    clar).3(contrabsn). 4.3.3.1.
    5perc,harp,cel,pno,org,strings
    SALABERT perf mat rent   (M611)

MIGHTY FORTRESS IS OUR GOD, A [ARR.]
  see Bach, Johann Sebastian, Feste
  Burg Ist Unser Gott, Ein' [arr.]

MIGNON (FIRST VERSION), FOR SOLO VOICE
  AND ORCHESTRA see Wolf, Hugo

MIGNON (SECOND VERSION), FOR SOLO VOICE
  AND ORCHESTRA see Wolf, Hugo

MIGNONS LIED, FOR SOLO VOICE AND
  ORCHESTRA see Liszt, Franz

MIHALOVICI, MARCEL (1898-   )
  Concerto for Violin and Orchestra,
    Op. 33 [18']
    2.2.2.2. 0.2.1.1. pno,vcl,db,vln
    solo
    study sc ESCHIG f.s., perf mat rent
                               (M612)

  Prelude And Invention *Op.42 [13']
    string orch
    min sc ESCHIG f.s., perf mat rent
                               (M613)

MIHALY, ANDRAS (1917-   )
  Concerto for Violin, Piano and
    Orchestra
    sc EMB 10171 f.s.   (M614)

  Musica Per 15
    sc EMB 7762 f.s.   (M615)

  Three Movements, For Chamber
    Orchestra
    sc EMB 10091 f.s.   (M616)

MIHELCIC, PAVLE (1937-   )
  Introduction And Sequences
    see Introdukcija In Sekvence

  Introdukcija In Sekvence [11']
    3(pic).2.1(bass
    clar).2(contrabsn). 4.3.3.0.
    perc,harp,strings
    "Introduction And Sequences"
    DRUSTVO DSS 999 perf mat rent
                               (M617)

  Prizori Iz Bele Krajine [12']
    3(alto fl).2.2(bass clar).2.
    4.3.3.1. perc,org,strings
    "Scenes From Bela Krajina" DRUSTVO
    DSS 1028 perf mat rent   (M618)

MIHELCIC, PAVLE (cont'd.)

Scenes From Bela Krajina
see Prizori Iz Bele Krajine

Slike, Ki Izginjajo [14']
3.2(English horn).2(bass
clar).2(contrabsn). 4.3.3.1.
perc,cel,strings
"Vanishing Pictures" DRUSTVO
DSS 1082 perf mat rent   (M619)

Vanishing Pictures
see Slike, Ki Izginjajo

MIKADO, THE: SUN WHOSE RAYS ARE ALL
ABLAZE, FOR SOLO VOICE AND
ORCHESTRA see Sullivan, [Sir]
Arthur Seymour

MIKI, MINORU (1930-   )
Kyu No Kyoku [33']
3(pic).3(English horn).3(soprano
clar in E flat,bass
clar).3(contrabsn). 4.3.3.1.
perc,strings, nohkan, 4-6
shakuhachi, 2-4 shamisen, 1-2
biwa, 2-3 koto, 2-3 bass-koto,
Japanese perc.
"Symphony For Two Worlds" ONGAKU
perf mat rent   (M620)

Shunju No Fu [20']
3(pic).3(English horn,ob
d'amore).3(soprano clar in E
flat).3(contrabsn). 4.3.3.1.
perc,harp,strings
"Symphony From Life" ONGAKU perf
mat rent   (M621)

Symphony For Two Worlds
see Kyu No Kyoku

Symphony From Life [20']
3(pic).3(English horn,ob
d'amore).3(soprano clar in E
flat).3(contrabsn). 4.3.3.1.
perc,harp,strings
FABER perf mat rent   (M622)
see Shunju No Fu

MILBURN, ELLSWORTH (1938-   )
Armies Of The Night, The [3']
3.3.3.3. 4.3.3.1. timp,perc,harp,
pno,strings
MMB perf mat rent   (M623)

Chiaroscuro [14']
1(pic).2.2.1. 2.1.0.0. timp,perc,
harp,pno&cel,strings
MMB perf mat rent   (M624)

Salus...Esto [12']
3(pic).2.2.1. 4.4.3.1. timp,perc,
harp,pno,strings
MMB perf mat rent   (M625)

Voussoirs [15']
3(pic,alto fl).2+English
horn.3(clar in E flat,bass
clar).3(contrabsn). 4.3.3.1.
timp,perc,pno&cel,strings
MMB perf mat rent   (M626)

MILCHSTRASSENMUSIK see Mitrea-
Celarianu, Mihai

MILHAUD, DARIUS (1892-1974)
Album De Madame Bovary [14']
2(pic).1(English horn).2.1.
2.2.1.0. timp,perc,harp,strings
ENOCH perf mat rent   (M627)

Bells, The *Op.259 [23']
3.1.2.1. 2.2.1.0. perc,pno,
strings
"Cloches, Les" ESCHIG perf mat rent
(M628)
Chamber Concerto For 11 Instruments
*Op.389 [15']
1.1.1.1. 1.0.0.0. pno,2vln,vla,
vcl,db
ESCHIG perf mat rent   (M629)

Cloches, Les
see Bells, The

Hommage A Comenius, For Solo Voices
And Orchestra *Op.421 [17']
2.2.2.2. 2.2.2.1. timp,perc,harp,
strings,SBar soli
ESCHIG perf mat rent   (M630)

Introduction Et Marche Funebre [5']
2.2.2.2. 2.2.2.0. timp,perc,
strings
"Introduktion Und Trauermarsch"
SIKORSKI perf mat rent   (M631)

Introduktion Und Trauermarsch
see Introduction Et Marche Funebre

Music For San Francisco *Op.436
[11']
2.2.2.2. 2.2.2.0. perc,strings
ESCHIG perf mat rent   (M632)

MILHAUD, DARIUS (cont'd.)

Musique Pour Ars Nova [12']
fl,clar,bass clar,bsn,horn,trp,
trom,2perc,pno,harp,vln,vcl
sc ESCHIG $31.00   (M633)

Ode Pour Jerusalem *Op.440 [13']
2.2.2.2. 2.2.3.1. timp,perc,
strings
ESCHIG perf mat rent   (M634)

Prends Cette Rose, For Solo Voices
And Orchestra [4']
2.2.2.2. 2.2.2.0. timp,perc,harp,
strings,ST soli
BOOSEY perf mat rent   (M635)

Stanford Serenade, For Oboe And
Instrumental Ensemble *Op.430
[12']
fl,clar,bsn,trp,perc,harp,2vln,
vla,vcl,db,ob solo
ESCHIG perf mat rent   (M636)

Suite for Ondes Martenot and String
Orchestra [10']
string orch,Ondes Martenot/pno
solo
BILLAUDOT perf mat rent   (M637)

Suite, Op. 431, in G [18']
2.2.2.3. 4.3.3.1. timp,perc,harp,
strings
ESCHIG perf mat rent   (M638)

Symphonie Pour L'Univers Claudelien
*Op.427 [25']
2.2.3.3. 4.3.3.1. timp,perc,cel,
harp,strings
ESCHIG perf mat rent   (M639)

Trois Elegies De Francis Jammes, For
Solo Voices And String Orchestra
[12']
string orch,ST soli
BOOSEY perf mat rent   (M640)

Trois Valses [4']
2(pic).1.2.1. 2.2.1.0. timp,perc,
harp,strings
ENOCH perf mat rent   (M641)

MILITARY MARCH NO. 1 see Miaskovsky,
Nikolai Yakovlevich

MILLE E UNA NOTTE see De Sabata, Victor

MILLER, EDWARD JAY (1930-   )
Mists And Waters, For Solo Voice And
Orchestra [12']
1.1.1.1. 1.0.0.0. perc,harp,
strings,S solo
sc AM.COMP.AL. $17.65   (M642)

MILLER, FRANZ R. (1926-   )
Danza
BOHM perf mat rent   (M643)

MILLER, MICHAEL R. (1932-   )
Before Alline [8']
2.2.2.2. 2.2.1.0. timp,perc,
strings
CAN.MUS.CENT. MI 1100 M469BE (M644)

MILLION D'OISEAUX D'OR see Nigg, Serge

MILLIONS D'ARLEQUIN, LES: BERCEUSE see
Drigo, Riccardo

MILLIONS D'ARLEQUIN, LES: DIE GUTE FEE
see Drigo, Riccardo

MILLIONS D'ARLEQUIN, LES: DRAMATISCHE
SZENE see Drigo, Riccardo

MILLIONS D'ARLEQUIN, LES: FLIEGENTANZ
see Drigo, Riccardo

MILLIONS D'ARLEQUIN, LES: GALOPP see
Drigo, Riccardo

MILLIONS D'ARLEQUIN, LES: HARLEKIN UND
DIE LERCHEN see Drigo, Riccardo

MILLIONS D'ARLEQUIN, LES:
LERCHENBALLETT see Drigo, Riccardo

MILLIONS D'ARLEQUIN, LES:
MASKENGESELLSCHAFT see Drigo,
Riccardo

MILLIONS D'ARLEQUIN, LES: PIERROT UND
PIERRETTE see Drigo, Riccardo

MILLIONS D'ARLEQUIN, LES: PIZZICATO see
Drigo, Riccardo

MILLIONS D'ARLEQUIN, LES: POLONAISE see
Drigo, Riccardo

MILLIONS D'ARLEQUIN, LES: SERENADE see
Drigo, Riccardo

MILLIONS D'ARLEQUIN, LES: TANZ DER
FREUNDE see Drigo, Riccardo

MILLIONS D'ARLEQUIN, LES: UNTERREDUNG
see Drigo, Riccardo

MILLIONS D'ARLEQUIN, LES: VALSE DES
ALOUETTES see Drigo, Riccardo

MILLIONS D'ARLEQUIN, LES: VORSPIEL see
Drigo, Riccardo

MILLS, CHARLES BORROMEO (1914-1982)
Concertino for Oboe and String
Orchestra [12']
string orch,ob solo
sc AM.COMP.AL. $12.10   (M645)

Symphony No. 5 [16']
string orch
sc AM.COMP.AL. $16.75   (M646)

MILNER, ANTHONY (1925-   )
Chamber Symphony [15']
1.2.1.2. 2.0.0.0. strings
NOVELLO perf mat rent   (M647)

Symphony No. 1, Op. 28
3.3.3.3. 4.3.3.1. timp,perc,
2harp,strings
study sc NOVELLO 2972-90 $45.50,
perf mat rent   (M648)

Variations for Orchestra
2.2.2.3. 4.3.3.1. timp,perc,
strings
sc UNIVER. UE 12895 f.s.   (M649)

MIN KLODE MI SJEL see Åm, Magnar

MIN STAMFAR HADE EN STOR POKAL, FOR
SOLO VOICE AND ORCHESTRA see
Stenhammar, Wilhelm

MINAMI, HIROAKI (1934-   )
Orion, For Synthesizer And Orchestra
[24']
3(pic).3(English horn).3(bass
clar).3(contrabsn). 4.3.3.1.
timp,perc,harp,cel,synthesizer,
strings
sc ZEN-ON 899441 f.s., perf mat
rent   (M650)

MINARD, ROBIN (1953-   )
Au Lieu Des Fleurs [15']
1(pic).1(English horn).1+bass
clar.0.soprano sax.alto
sax.tenor sax. 1.2.0.0. 3perc,
pno,vln,vla,vcl,db
CAN.MUS.CENT. MI 1200 M663A (M651)

Leliah [15']
2.2.3(clar in E flat).2. 4.3.4.0.
2perc,strings
CAN.MUS.CENT. MI 1100 M663L (M652)

MIND OF WINTER, A, FOR SOLO VOICE AND
ORCHESTRA see Benjamin, George

MINDIA: ELEGY see Taktakishvili, Otar

MINDIA: MARCH see Taktakishvili, Otar

MINER, THE, FOR SOLO VOICE AND
ORCHESTRA see Johnsen, Hallvard,
Bergmannen, For Solo Voice And
Orchestra

MINI-CONCERTO FOR CLARINET AND STRING
ORCHESTRA see Jacob, Gordon

MINIATURE CONCERTO, FOR HORN AND
ORCHESTRA see Haug, Halvor

MINIATURE FANTASY see Goossens, [Sir]
Eugene

MINIATURE OVERTURE see Blumenfeld,
Harold see Still, William Grant

MINIATURE SUITE see Coates, Eric

MINKUS, LÉON (FYODOROVICH) [ALOIS;
LOUIS] (1826-1917)
Don Quixote: Pas De Deux [arr.]
(Stirn, D.) 3.2.2.2. 4.2.3.1. timp,
perc,harp,strings [12'] BOIS perf
mat rent   (M653)

Paquita: Pas De Trois [arr.]
(Stirn, D.) 2.2.2.2. 2.2.2.1. timp,
perc,strings [13'] BOIS perf mat
rent   (M654)

MINNA VON BARNHELM: OVERTURE see Bruns,
Victor

MINNE FRAN ASHENDON see Freudenthal,
Otto

MINNELIEDER, FOR SOLO VOICE AND
ORCHESTRA see Schafer, R. Murray

MINNESANGER WALZER see Strauss, Johann, [Sr.]

MINNEWATER: THOUSANDS OF CANONS see Sorensen, Bent

MINTZER, ROBERT
Then And Now, For Saxophone And Orchestra [13'30"]
2.1.4.3+contrabsn. 4.4.4.0. timp, perc,elec bass,pno,harp, strings,tenor sax solo
NEWAM 19030 perf mat rent (M655)

MINUET AND TRIO see Wallace, William

MINUETO Y RONDO see Arambarri, Jesús

MINUETTO SERIO see Kodály, Zoltán

MIRACLE DE LA ROSE, LE, FOR CLARINET AND INSTRUMENTAL ENSEMBLE see Henze, Hans Werner

MIRAGE see Chatman, Stephen

MIRAGES see Conyngham, Barry see Dolatshahi, Dariush

MIREILLE: OVERTURE see Gounod, Charles François

MIRIGLIANO, ROSARIO (1950-)
Largo for Orchestra [10']
2.2.2.0. 2.2.0.0. perc,strings
RICORDI-IT 134144 perf mat rent (M656)

MIROGLIO, FRANCIS (1924-)
Deltas [22']
3.3.3.3. 4.3.3.1. timp,5perc, 2harp,elec org,strings
SALABERT perf mat rent (M657)

Fusions [28']
3.3.3.3. 4.3.3.1. timp,3perc, 2harp,pno,strings
SALABERT perf mat rent (M658)

Horizons Courbes, For 9-16 Instrumentalists [18']
1(alto fl).1(English horn).1(bass clar).0. 1.0.1.0. perc,vln,vcl, db,opt vln,opt harp,opt gtr,opt hpsd,opt marimba,opt pno, opt sitar
SALABERT perf mat rent (M659)

Magnetiques, For Violin And Orchestra [20']
3.3.3.3. 4.3.3.1. timp,3perc, 2harp,pno,strings,vln solo
SALABERT perf mat rent (M660)

Strates Eclatees [20']
1.1.1.2. 2.1.1.0. 2perc,strings
PETERS (M661)

MIROIR, LE, FOR SOLO VOICE AND ORCHESTRA see Boucourechliev, André

MIROIR FUGACE see Evangelista, Jose

MIROIR III see Kokaji, Kunitaka

MIROIRS CELESTES see Miereanu, Costin

MIRROR see Asheim, Nils Henrik

MIRROR OF HEAT AND LIGHT see Kernis, Aaron Jay

MIRRORS, FOR PIANO AND ORCHESTRA see Parmentier, F. Gordon

MIRTILLO SUITE. EXCERPTS FROM "IL PASTOR FIDO" see Handel, George Frideric

MIRZAL see Gossec, François Joseph

MIRZOYAN, EDVARD (1921-)
Symphony for String Orchestra and Timpani [20']
timp,strings
SIKORSKI perf mat rent (M662)

MIRZOYEV, M.
Concert Works, For Symphony Orchestra
*CCU
sc MEZ KNIGA f.s. (M663)

MISCHIEVOUS CHASTUSHKI see Shchedrin, Rodion, Concerto for Orchestra, No. 1

MISERA, DOVE SON, FOR SOLO VOICE AND ORCHESTRA see Mozart, Wolfgang Amadeus

MISERERE see Globokar, Vinko

MISERO ME! MISERO PARGOLETTO, FOR SOLO VOICE AND ORCHESTRA see Mozart, Wolfgang Amadeus

MISERO! O SOGNO, FOR SOLO VOICE AND ORCHESTRA see Mozart, Wolfgang Amadeus

MISS HELYETT: VALSE CELEBRE see Audran, Edmond

MISSISSIPPI SUITE see Grofe, Ferde (Ferdinand Rudolph von)

MIST see Sigurbjörnsson, Thorkell

MR. ROBERTS: MINI-SUITE see Waxman, Franz

MR. SKEFFINGTON: SUITE see Waxman, Franz

MISTERIOSO see Grabovsky, Leonid

MISTRAL see Reynolds, Roger

MISTRAL-KANTATE, FOR SOLO VOICE AND ORCHESTRA see Genzmer, Harald

MISTRESS OF SEVEN ROBBERS, THE: SUITE see Vacek, Miloš

MISTS AND WATERS, FOR SOLO VOICE AND ORCHESTRA see Miller, Edward Jay

MIT DAMPF POLKA see Strauss, Eduard

MIT DER FEDER POLKA see Strauss, Eduard

MIT DER STRIEMUNG POLKA see Strauss, Eduard

MIT MÄDELN SICH VERTRAGEN, FOR SOLO VOICE AND ORCHESTRA see Beethoven, Ludwig van

MITREA-CELARIANU, MIHAI (1935-)
Ain Mi [14']
2(pic).2(English horn).2.2. 2.2.3.1. 6cornet,3-4perc,Hamm, strings
SALABERT perf mat rent (M664)

Melodie Des Sons Du Temps [12']
pic,rec,fl,clar,bass clar,bugle, trp,trom,perc,Hamm,pno,hpsd,vla da gamba,2vln,2vla,vcl,db
SALABERT perf mat rent (M665)

Milchstrassenmusik [21']
1(pic).1.1(bass clar).1(contrabsn). 2.1.1.0+opt tuba. 3perc,pno&elec org&cel, 2vln,vla,vcl,db
SALABERT perf mat rent (M666)

MITRIDATE: OVERTURE see Mozart, Wolfgang Amadeus

MITTAGSWELT, FOR SOLO VOICE AND ORCHESTRA see Kallausch, Kurt

MITTE DES JAHRHUNDERTS: PRÄLUDIUM, FOR SOLO VOICE AND ORCHESTRA see Eisler, Hanns

MITTERNACHTSTANZ, FOR TIMPANI AND STRING ORCHESTRA see Glanert, Detlev

MIXTURAS see Bernaola, Carmelo

MIYOSHI, AKIRA (1933-)
Duel, For Solo Voice And Orchestra [15']
2(pic).2.2.2. 2.2.3.0. perc,pno& cel,harp,strings,S solo
sc ONGAKU 493564 f.s., perf mat rent (M667)

En Passant For Violin And Orchestra [15']
2(pic).2.2.2. 4.2.3.0. perc,harp, cel,strings,vln solo
sc ZEN-ON 899380 f.s., perf mat rent (M668)

En Soi Lointain [20']
3(pic,alto fl).3.3.3(contrabsn). 4.4.4.0. perc,cel,2harp,pno, strings
ZEN-ON perf mat rent (M669)

MIZUNO, SHUKO (1934-)
Symphonic Metamorphoses. The First Part, Metamorphoses Of Tutti
JAPAN 8101 (M670)

MLADA: FINALE see Borodin, Alexander Porfirievich

MLADA: NIGHT ON MOUNT TRIGLAV see Rimsky-Korsakov, Nikolai

MOBBERLEY, JAMES
Aquaria [9']
4(2pic).2.2.2. 4.4.3.1. perc, harp,pno,strings
MMB perf mat rent (M671)

MOBBERLEY, JAMES (cont'd.)

Synthesis [13']
3(alto fl,pic).2(English horn).2+ bass clar.2(contrabsn). 4.4.3.1. timp,perc,harp,cel, strings
MMB perf mat rent (M672)

MOBIEL see Brozak, Daniel

MOBILE see Bjelik, Martin see Neikrug, Marc E.

MOBILE CONCERTANTE see Benker, Heinz

MOBILE-IMMOBILE see Tessier, Roger

MOBILES see Lees, Benjamin

MOBILES, FOR CLARINET AND STRING ORCHESTRA see Giuffre, James Peter (Jimmy)

MOCK MORRIS see Grainger, Percy Aldridge

MOD DODEN see Børresen, Hakon

MODELL see Stiebler, Ernstalbrecht

MODELLO PER ARCHI see Jørgensen, Erik

MODERENS KORSTEGN, FOR SOLO VOICE AND AND ORCHESTRA see Groven, Eivind

MODERN SKETCHES FOR HARP see Wurtzler, Aristid Von

MODI see Vogel, Ernst

MODINHAS E CANCOES, FIRST SUITE, NO. 1: CANCAO DO MARINHEIRO, FOR SOLO VOICE AND ORCHESTRA see Villa-Lobos, Heitor

MODINHAS E CANCOES, FIRST SUITE, NO. 2: LUNDU DA MARQUEZA DE SANTOS, FOR SOLO VOICE AND ORCHESTRA see Villa-Lobos, Heitor

MODINHAS E CANCOES, FIRST SUITE, NO. 3: REMEIRO DE SAO-FRANCISCO, FOR SOLO VOICE AND ORCHESTRA see Villa-Lobos, Heitor

MODINHAS E CANCOES, FIRST SUITE, NO. 4: NHAPOPE, FOR SOLO VOICE AND ORCHESTRA see Villa-Lobos, Heitor

MODINHAS E CANCOES, FIRST SUITE, NO. 5: EVOCACAO, FOR SOLO VOICE AND ORCHESTRA see Villa-Lobos, Heitor

MODINHAS E CANCOES, SECOND SUITE, NO. 1: POBRE PEREGRINO, FOR SOLO VOICE AND ORCHESTRA see Villa-Lobos, Heitor

MODINHAS E CANCOES, SECOND SUITE, NO.3: NESTA RUA, FOR SOLO VOICE AND ORCHESTRA see Villa-Lobos, Heitor

MODINHAS E CANCOES, SECOND SUITE, NO. 4: MANDA TIRO, TIRO LA, FOR SOLO VOICE AND ORCHESTRA see Villa-Lobos, Heitor

MODULAR MELLIPHONY see Newell, Robert M.

MODULES see Powell, Mel

MODULOR see Manzoni, Giacomo

MODULOS I see Pablo, Luis de

MOEL BRYN DIVISIONS see Boyle, Rory

MOEN, FOR SOLO VOICE AND ORCHESTRA see Groven, Eivind

MOESCHINGER, ALBERT (1897-)
Concert Pour Une Ballerine, For Alto Saxophone And Chamber Orchestra [10']
pno,vibra,cel,strings,alto sax solo
BILLAUDOT perf mat rent (M673)

MOEVS, ROBERT WALTER (1921-)
Concerto for Piano, Percussion and Orchestra [18']
3.3.3.3. 4.3.3.1. harp,strings, pno solo,perc solo
RICORDI-IT 132752 perf mat rent (M674)

Symphonic Piece No. 1 [10']
PRESSER perf mat rent (M675)

Symphonic Piece No. 2 [7']
PRESSER perf mat rent (M676)

Symphonic Piece No. 3 [9']
PRESSER perf mat rent (M677)

MOEVS, ROBERT WALTER (cont'd.)

Symphonic Piece No. 5 [10']
    PRESSER perf mat rent   (M678)

MOGADON see Meijering, Chiel

MOHAUPT, RICHARD (1904-1957)
Much Ado About Nothing [5'30"]
    WARNER perf mat rent   (M679)

MOHLER, PHILIPP (1908-1982)
Traumer Und Vaganten, For Solo Voice
    And Orchestra *Op.46 [20']
    2.2.2.2. 4.3.3.1. timp,perc,harp,
    strings,Bar solo
    SIKORSKI perf mat rent   (M680)

MOHR, GERHARD (1901-1979)
Finnische Polka
    2.1.2.1. 3.0.0.0. perc,acord,
    strings
    TONOS   (M681)

MOIRA see Vogel, Ernst

MOIS DE MAI, LE, FOR SOLO VOICE AND
    ORCHESTRA see Arrieu, Claude

MOJAVE, FOR NARRATOR AND ORCHESTRA see
    Cansler, Larry

MOKIT NUKKUU LUMISET, FOR SOLO VOICE
    AND ORCHESTRA [ARR.] see Kaski,
    Heino

MOLDAU KLANGE WALZER see Strauss,
    Johann, [Sr.]

MOLIQUE, (WILHELM) BERNHARD (1802-1869)
Concerto for Flute and Orchestra
    [20'50"]
    2.2.2.2. 2.2.0.0. timp,strings,fl
    solo
    sc BILLAUDOT $51.25, perf mat rent
                                         (M682)

MOLLY ON THE SHORE see Grainger, Percy
    Aldridge

MOLTER, JOHANN MELCHIOR (1695-1765)
Concerto for Flute and Orchestra in
    D, [arr.]
    (Bodensohn, E.) 2ob,2horn,strings,
    fl solo [12'] sc,pts BODENS E 62
    f.s.   (M683)

Concerto for Flute and String
    Orchestra, No. 2, in D [14']
    string orch,fl solo
    (Bodensohn, E.) (with cadenzas)
    BODENS 74 f.s.   (M684)

MOLTO VIBRATO, FOR VIOLIN AND ORCHESTRA
    see Mannino, Franco

MOMENTAUFNAHMEN, FOR SOLO VOICE AND
    CHAMBER ORCHESTRA see Stahmer,
    Klaus H.

MOMENTI MUSICALI, DUE [ARR.] see
    Schubert, Franz (Peter)

MOMENTS 1977 see Beerman, Burton

MOMENTS IN AND OUT OF TIME see Kramer,
    Jonathan

MOMENTS MUSICAUX see Block, Hans Volker

MOMENTS MUSICAUX, FOR ALTO SAXOPHONE
    AND STRING ORCHESTRA see DuBois,
    Pierre-Max

MOMENTS SYMPHONIQUES see Hemel, Oscar
    van

MOMENTUM JUBILO see Cordero, Roque

MONADE III, FOR VIOLIN AND ORCHESTRA
    see Pepin, Clermont

MONDE SENSIBLE, LE, FOR FLUTE, PIANO,
    AND INSTRUMENTAL ENSEMBLE see
    Renosto, Paolo

MONDES, PER UNA GRANDE ORCHESTRA E UNA
    PICCOLA ORCHESTRA see Tabachnik,
    Michel

MONDSCHEIN, FOR SOLO VOICE AND
    ORCHESTRA see Trexler, Georg

MONDSCHEIN-ODE, FOR SOLO VOICE AND
    ORCHESTRA see Kilpinen, Yrjö

MONETA'S MOURN see Edwards, George

MONN, GEORG MATTHIAS (1717-1750)
Concerto for Violoncello and String
    Orchestra in G minor
    (Nagy) EMB f.s. sc 7114, pts 7175
                                         (M685)

Symphonies, Five
    see Dittersdorf, Karl Ditters von,
    Symphonies, Six

MONNET, MARC (1947-   )
Aiuto
    6vln,6vcl
    SALABERT perf mat rent   (M686)

Du Soleil Et De La Lune, For Solo
    Voices And Instrumental Ensemble
    [24']
    3(pic).0.3.3. 0.0.0.0. perc,gtr,
    pno,hpsd,3vcl,3db,S&speaking
    voice
    RICORDI-IT perf mat rent   (M687)

Musik Ohne Renaissance Pour 18
    Instruments De La Renaissance
    [9']
    SALABERT perf mat rent   (M688)

Musik Ohne Renaissance Pour 18
    Instruments Modernes [9']
    0.1.4(clar in A,bass clar,basset
    horn).3. 0.1.3.0. vln,2vla,
    2vcl,db
    SALABERT perf mat rent   (M689)

Scene, La [10']
    2pic,bass clar,bsn,contrabsn,
    trom,2perc,pno,harp,Hamm,cel,
    2vla,2vcl,db
    RICORDI-FR perf mat rent   (M690)

Siecle, Pierre, Tombeau [9']
    1.1.1.1. 1.0.0.0. 2vln,2vla,vcl,
    db
    SALABERT perf mat rent   (M691)

MONODIA, FOR PIANO AND ORCHESTRA see
    Silvestrov, Valentin

MONODIAS E INTERLUDIOS see Maiguashca,
    Mesias

MONODRAM, FOR VIOLONCELLO AND ORCHESTRA
    see Rihm, Wolfgang

MONODRAMA, FOR PERCUSSION AND ORCHESTRA
    see Ruders, Poul

MONODRAMA (PORTRAIT OF AN ARTIST) see
    Husa, Karel

MONODY see Matthews, Colin

MONOLOG, FOR VIOLA AND STRING ORCHESTRA
    see Schnittke, Alfred

MONOLOG DER OPHELIA, FOR SOLO VOICE AND
    ORCHESTRA see Kelterborn, Rudolf

MONOLOGI see Srebotnjak, Alojz F.

MONOLOGUE FOR STRINGS see Dickinson,
    Peter

MONOMANIA E POLICROMIA see Andriessen,
    Jurriaan

MONOSTRUCTURES I see Miereanu, Costin

MONOSTRUCTURES II see Miereanu, Costin

MONRAD JOHANSEN, DAVID
    see JOHANSEN, DAVID MONRAD

MONTAGE see Johnston, Donald O. see
    Roxburgh, Edwin

MONTAGUE, STEPHEN (1943-   )
At The White Edge Of Phrygia
    UNITED MUS   (M692)

MONTE GELBOE, FOR SOLO VOICE AND
    ORCHESTRA see Orbon, Julian

MONTEVERDI, CLAUDIO (ca. 1567-1643)
Orfeo: Toccata And Ritornello [arr.]
    (Samuel, Gerhard) 4(pic).0.0.0.
    0.4.3.0. timp,hpsd,2harp,strings
    [6'] MMB perf mat rent   (M693)

MONTS DE L'ETOILE, LES, FOR SOLO VOICE
    AND ORCHESTRA see Bondon, Jacques

MONTSALVAT see Street, Tison

MONTSALVATGE, XAVIER (1912-   )
Concierto Breve, For Piano And
    Orchestra [24']
    2+pic.2+English horn.2+bass
    clar.2+contrabsn. 4.2.2.0.
    timp,perc,strings,pno solo
    UNION ESP. perf mat rent   (M694)

Concierto Del Albayzin, For
    Harpsichord And Orchestra [30']
    1+pic.2.2.1. 2.1.0.0. harp,
    strings,hpsd solo
    UNION ESP. perf mat rent   (M695)

Desintegracion Morfologica De La
    Chacona De J.S. Bach [22']
    2+pic.2.2+bass clar.2+contrabsn.
    4.2.3.0. timp,3perc,2xylo,
    strings
    min sc UNION ESP. f.s., perf mat
    rent   (M696)

MONTSALVATGE, XAVIER (cont'd.)

Fanfarria Para La Alegria Por La Paz
    [4']
    2+pic.2.2(bass clar).2. 4.3.3.0.
    timp,perc,strings
    UNION ESP. perf mat rent   (M697)

Homenaje A Manolo Hugue, For Solo
    Voice And Orchestra [16']
    2+pic.2+English horn.2+bass
    clar.2. 4.3.3.0. timp,harp,
    strings,S solo
    UNION ESP. perf mat rent   (M698)

Metamorfosis De Concierto, For Guitar
    And Orchestra [18']
    2+pic.2.2+bass clar.2. 2.2.1.0.
    timp,perc,harp,strings,gtr solo
    UNION ESP. perf mat rent   (M699)

Reflexus [6']
    2+pic.2.2+bass clar.2. 4.3.3.0.
    perc,strings
    UNION ESP. perf mat rent   (M700)

Serenade A Lydia De Cadaques [10']
    1+pic.2.2.1. 2.2.1.0. timp,perc,
    harp,strings
    UNION ESP. perf mat rent   (M701)

MONUMENTAL THOUGHTS ...MARTTI TALVELA
    IN MEMORIAM see Segerstam, Leif

MONUMENTS, FOR PIANO AND ORCHESTRA see
    Conyngham, Barry

MONUMENTUM see Lubetsky, Ronald

MONUMENTUM A LUIGI DALLAPICCOLA, FOR
    SOLO VOICE AND ORCHESTRA see
    Zanettovich, Daniele

MONUMENTUM FÜR KARL PRANTI see Cerha,
    Friedrich

MONUMENTUM PRO CAECILIA, FOR
    HARPSICHORD AND STRING ORCHESTRA
    see Samama, Leo

MOOD PIECE, FOR HARP AND STRING
    ORCHESTRA see Valenti, Michael

MOON IN THE LABYRINTH, THE see Luedeke,
    Raymond

MOON, SEA AND STARS, THE: NOCTURNES,
    FOR SOLO VOICE AND CHAMBER
    ORCHESTRA see Cowie, Edward

MOON SILVER [ARR.] see Cleve, Cissi,
    Manesolv [arr.]

MOORE, CARMAN (1936-   )
Gospel Fuse, For Solo Voices And
    Orchestra [23']
    3(pic).3(English
    horn).3.3(contrabsn).soprano
    sax. 4.3.3.1. timp,4perc,elec
    org,harp,pno,elec bass,strings,
    SSAA soli
    PEER perf mat rent   (M702)

Hit [23']
    2+pic.2+English horn.2+bass
    clar.2. 4.3.3.1. timp,perc,
    strings
    PEER perf mat rent   (M703)

Tone Roads To HK: Four Movements For
    A Fashionable Five-Toed Dragon,
    For Jazz Ensemble And Orchestra
    [55']
    2(pic,alto fl).2(English
    horn).1.1. 2.2.1.1. perc,harp,
    strings, jazz ensemble: gtel,
    db, kbd, drm, sax
    PEER perf mat rent   (M704)

Wildfires And Field Songs [21']
    4(pic).5(English horn).4(bass
    clar).4(contrabsn).alto sax.
    4.4.4.1. timp,perc,harp,strings
    PEER perf mat rent   (M705)

MOORE, DOROTHY RUDD
    see RUDD-MOORE, DOROTHY

MORALITETER see Norholm, Ib

MORANCON, GUY (1927-   )
Musique, For Organ And String
    Orchestra [24']
    string orch,org solo
    BILLAUDOT perf mat rent   (M706)

MORCEAU DE CONCERT, FOR VIOLIN AND
    ORCHESTRA see Saint-Saëns, Camille

MORCEAU DE CONCOURS, FOR FLUTE AND
    STRING ORCHESTRA see Faure,
    Gabriel-Urbain

MORDUR VALGARDSSON see Thorarinsson,
    Leifur

MORDVIN LULLABY [ARR.] see Seiber, Matyas György

MOREAUX LYRIQUES, FOR OBOE AND ORCHESTRA see Castiglioni, Niccolò

MOREL, JORGE (1931-   )
Southern Suite, For Guitar And Chamber Orchestra
see Suite Del Sur, For Guitar And Chamber Orchestra

Suite Del Sur, For Guitar And Chamber Orchestra [22']
2.1.0.0. 2.0.0.0. perc,strings, gtr solo
"Southern Suite, For Guitar And Chamber Orchestra" PEER perf mat rent   (M707)

MORENE see Bjorklund, Terje

MORGAN, DAVID (1933-   )
Concerto for Violin and Orchestra [26']
3.2.3(clar in E flat).2. 4.4.3.1. timp,perc,cel,harp,strings,vln solo
CAN.MUS.CENT. MI 1311 M847VI (M708)

Concerto for Violoncello and Orchestra
3.3.2(clar in E flat,bass clar).3. 4.3.3.1. timp,4perc, pno&cel,harp,strings,vcl solo
CAN.MUS.CENT. MI 1313 M847CO (M709)

Contrasts [22']
2.2.2.2. 2.2.1.0. timp,perc,harp, strings
CAN.MUS.CENT. MI 1100 M847CO (M710)

Sinfonia Da Requiem [30']
3.3.3(clar in E flat).3.soprano sax. 4.4.4.1. timp,6perc,pno& cel,harp,strings
CAN.MUS.CENT. MI 1100 M847SI (M711)

Sonata for Chamber Orchestra
2.2.3(clar in E flat).2. 2.0.0.0. strings
CAN.MUS.CENT. MI 1200 M847SO (M712)

MORGANA see Burt, Francis

MORGENMUSIK, FOR TRUMPET AND STRING ORCHESTRA see Korn, Peter Jona

MORGON, FOR SOLO VOICE AND ORCHESTRA see Braein, Edvard Fliflet

MORI, KURODO (1950-   )
En Attendant [7'30"]
6vln,2vla,2vcl,db
JAPAN 8204 f.s.   (M713)

Groom Is Gloomy [14']
3(pic).3(English horn).3.3(contrabsn). 4.3.3.1. timp,perc,cel,harp,pno,strings
sc ZEN-ON 899180 f.s., perf mat rent   (M714)

MÖRIKE-LIEDER, ZWÖLF, FOR SOLO VOICE AND ORCHESTRA see Wolf, Hugo

MORNING see Ames, William T.

MORNING, FOR SOLO VOICE AND ORCHESTRA see Braein, Edvard Fliflet, Morgon, For Solo Voice And Orchestra

MORNING [ARR.]
(Pethel, Stan) sc,pts BROADMAN 4186-13 $12.95   (M715)

MORNING GLORY see Marcussen, Kjell

MORNING - PENIEL see Fisher, Alfred

MORNING SONGS, FOR SOLO VOICE AND ORCHESTRA see Kernis, Aaron Jay

MORT DE CHENIER, LA see Cools, Eugène

MORT DE CLEOPATRE, LA, FOR SOLO VOICE AND ORCHESTRA see Berlioz, Hector (Louis)

MORT DE TINAGILES, LA, FOR VIOLA D'AMORE AND ORCHESTRA see Loeffler, Charles Martin

MORT D'OPHELIE, LA, FOR SOLO VOICE AND ORCHESTRA [ARR.] see Berlioz, Hector (Louis)

MORT DU SILENCE see Tomasi, Henri

MORT D'UN SAMOURAI, LA see Delage, Maurice

MORT PASSE, LA see Honegger, Arthur

MORTARI, VIRGILIO (1902-   )
Concerto Per Mstislav Rostropovic, For Violoncello And Orchestra [25']
2.2.2.2. 2.2.0.0. timp,perc, strings,vcl solo
RICORDI-IT 131630 perf mat rent   (M716)

Rapsodia Elegiaca, For Doublebass And Orchestra [18']
2.2.2.2. 2.0.0.0. perc,strings,db solo
RICORDI-IT 132684 perf mat rent   (M717)

MORTE DI ABEL, LA: SINFONIA see Leo, Leonardo (Ortensio Salvatore de)

MORTENSEN, FINN (1922-   )
Hedda *Op.42 [10']
3(pic).3(English horn).2+bass clar.2+contrabsn. 4.3.3.1. timp,perc,strings
study sc NORSK f.s., perf mat rent   (M718)

Tone Colors *Op.24 [6']
3.3.3.3. 5.3.3.1. strings
NORGE   (M719)

MOSAICS see Wilson, Thomas

MOSCA, LUCA (1957-   )
Concerto for Piano and Orchestra [30']
2.2.2.2. 2.2.0.0. timp,perc, vibra,cel,4vln,3vla,2vcl,db,pno solo
RICORDI-IT 133154 perf mat rent   (M720)

MOSCHELES, IGNAZ (1794-1870)
Concertante, For Flute, Oboe And Orchestra In F
2.2.2.2. 2.2.0.0. timp,strings,fl solo,ob solo
sc KUNZEL 10162 f.s., perf mat rent   (M721)
MUS. RARA 2101 perf mat rent (M722)

Concertino for Flute, Oboe and Orchestra
(Wojciechowski; Molich) 2.2.2.2. 2.2.0.0. timp,strings,fl solo,ob solo [13'] PETERS P8593 perf mat rent   (M723)

MOSE: AH! SE PUOI COSI, FOR SOLO VOICES AND ORCHESTRA see Rossini, Gioacchino

MOSE: CELESTE MAN PLACATA, FOR SOLO VOICES AND ORCHESTRA see Rossini, Gioacchino

MOSE: PARLAR, SPIEGAR, FOR SOLO VOICES AND ORCHESTRA see Rossini, Gioacchino

MOSE: QUAL' ORRIBILE SCIAGURA, FOR SOLO VOICE AND ORCHESTRA see Rossini, Gioacchino

MOSE: QUALE ASSALTO, FOR SOLO VOICES AND ORCHESTRA see Rossini, Gioacchino

MOSE: TUTTO SORRIDE, FOR SOLO VOICES AND ORCHESTRA see Rossini, Gioacchino

MOSER, ROLAND OLIVIER (1943-   )
Ding [5'30"]
2(pic).2(English horn).2(bass clar).2(contrabsn). 2.2.2.1. perc,mand,gtr,8vln,6vla,6vcl, 4db
HUG GH 11300 perf mat rent (M724)

Rand [16']
1.1.3.0. 4.0.3.1. perc,2harp, 2vln,6vla,3db
HUG GH 11336 perf mat rent (M725)

Wal [26']
4.4.4.4.5sax. 4.4.4.4+db tuba. perc,strings
HUG GH 11335 perf mat rent (M726)

MOSES, FOR PIANO AND ORCHESTRA see Finko, David

MOSONYI, M.
Concerto for Piano and Orchestra
(Váczi) min sc EMB 4261 f.s.   (M727)

MOSS, LAWRENCE KENNETH (1927-   )
Symphonies, For Brass Quintet And Orchestra
2.1.1.1. 0.0.0.0. 3perc,pno, strings,brass quin soli
SEESAW perf mat rent   (M728)

MOSS, PIOTR (1949-   )
Incontri [20']
3.3.3.3. 4.3.3.0. perc,harp, strings
BILLAUDOT perf mat rent   (M729)

MOSSOLOV, ALEXANDER (1900-1973)
Advertisements, For Solo Voice And Orchestra [arr.]
(Denisov, Edison) 1.1.1.1. 1.1.1.0. 2perc,harp,pno,vln,vla,vcl,db, solo voice [4'] VAAP perf mat rent   (M730)
(Denisov, Edison) "Vier Zeitungsannoncen, For Solo Voice And Orchestra [arr.]" 1.1.1.1. 1.1.1.0. 2perc,harp,pno,vln,vla, vcl,db,solo voice SIKORSKI perf mat rent   (M731)

Vier Zeitungsannoncen, For Solo Voice And Orchestra [arr.]
see Advertisements, For Solo Voice And Orchestra [arr.]

MOST BEAUTIFUL ROSE, THE, FOR SOLO VOICES AND ORCHESTRA see Hovland, Egil, Vakresterosen, Den, For Solo Voices And Orchestra

MOST BEAUTIFUL ROSE, THE [ARR.] see Thommessen, Reidar, Vakreste Rose, Den [arr.]

MOST HAPPY FELLA, THE: BIG D, FOR SOLO VOICES AND ORCHESTRA see Loesser, Frank

MOST HAPPY FELLA, THE: HAPPY TO MAKE YOUR ACQUAINTANCE, FOR SOLO VOICES AND ORCHESTRA see Loesser, Frank

MOST HAPPY FELLA, THE: MAMA, MAMA, FOR SOLO VOICE AND ORCHESTRA see Loesser, Frank

MOST HAPPY FELLA, THE: MY HEART IS SO FULL OF YOU, FOR SOLO VOICES AND ORCHESTRA see Loesser, Frank

MOST HAPPY FELLA, THE: OVERTURE see Loesser, Frank

MOST HAPPY FELLA, THE: SOMEBODY, SOMEWHERE, FOR SOLO VOICE AND ORCHESTRA see Loesser, Frank

MOSTAD, JON (1942-   )
Fanfares And Arabesques [13']
4.4.4.4. 4.4.3.1. timp,4perc, harp,pno,strings
NORGE   (M732)

Hus For Orkester [26']
4.4.4.4. 4.4.3.1. timp,perc,harp, cel,strings
NORGE   (M733)

Light Shines In The Darkness, The [12']
4.4.4.4. 4.4.3.1. timp,perc,harp, pno,cel,strings
NORGE   (M734)

Mot Likevekt [12']
3.3.3.2. 4.3.3.1. timp,perc,harp, pno/cel,strings
"Towards Balance" NORGE (M735)

Nocturne [9']
4.4.4.4. 4.4.3.1. timp,4perc, harp,pno&cel,strings
NORGE   (M736)

Prelude [6']
2.2.2.2. 4.2.3.1. perc,strings
NORGE   (M737)

Sang For Orkester [8']
3.3.3.3. 4.3.3.1. timp,perc,harp, cel,strings
"Song For Orchestra" NORGE (M738)

Song For Orchestra
see Sang For Orkester

Towards Balance
see Mot Likevekt

MOSZUMANSKA-NAZAR, KRYSTYNA (1924-   )
Rhapsody No. 2
3.3.3.3. 4.4.3.1. perc,harp,pno, strings
POLSKIE   (M739)

MOT BLASNOHOGDOM, FOR SOLO VOICE AND ORCHESTRA see Kielland, Olav

MOT EN FANFARE see Berg, Olav

MOT EN LENGSEL, FOR PIANO AND ORCHESTRA see Sommerfeldt, Öistein

MOT EN VERDEN AV LYS, FOR SOLO VOICE AND ORCHESTRA see Sommerfeldt, Öistein

MOT LIKEVEKT see Mostad, Jon

MOT NATT see Hartmann, Christian

MOTHER, FOR SOLO VOICE AND STRING ORCHESTRA see Srebotnjak, Alojz F., Mati, For Solo Voice And String Orchestra

MOTHER, THE: PRELUDE TO THE SEVENTH PICTURE see Nielsen, Carl

MOTHER AND CHILD see Still, William Grant

MOTHER'S SIGN OF THE CROSS, THE, FOR SOLO VOICE AND ORCHESTRA see Groven, Eivind, Moderens Korstegn, For Solo Voice And And Orchestra

MOTIONLESS MOVE see Evangelista, Jose

MOTLEY LEAFLETS see Sörenson, Torsten Napoleon, Brokiga Blad

MOTO DI GIOIA, UN, FOR SOLO VOICE AND ORCHESTRA see Mozart, Wolfgang Amadeus

MOTTE, DIETHER DE LA (1928-   )
Concerto Avventuroso [15'-21']
    .1.1.1. 2.1.0.0. strings
    BÄREN. BA 6294 perf mat rent (M740)

Tafel-Musik
    7woodwinds,2trom,6strings
    BÄREN. BA 6281 perf mat rent (M741)

MOTUS see Wimberger, Gerhard

MOTUS - COLORES see Lidholm, Ingvar

MOUNT OLYMPUS see Bajura, Keith V.A.

MOUNT ST. HELENS SYMPHONY see Hovhaness, Alan

MOUNTAIN AND THE FOLK STYLE, THE see Ju, Xiao-Song

MOUNTAIN AND THE FOREST, THE, FOR PIANO AND ORCHESTRA see Liu, Dun-Nan

MOUNTAIN SONG, FOR VIOLONCELLO AND ORCHESTRA see Ju, Xiao-Song

MOUNTAIN VILLAGE see Edwards, Ross

MOUNTAIN VILLAGE IN A CLEARING MIST see Edwards, Ross

MOUNTAIN WIND, FOR SOLO VOICE AND ORCHESTRA see Groven, Eivind, Fjellvind, For Solo Voice And Orchestra

MOUNTAINEERINGS see Björklund, Staffan

MOUNTAINOUS NORWAY, FOR SOLO VOICE AND ORCHESTRA see Egge, Klaus, Fjell-Norig, For Solo Voice And Orchestra

MOUNTAINS, THE see Lason, Aleksander, Gory see Nystedt, Knut, Hogfjell

MOUQUET, JULES (1867-1946)
Au Village *Op.11 [7']
    2.2.2.2. 4.1.0.0. timp,pno 4-hands,strings
    LEMOINE perf mat rent (M742)

MOURANT, WALTER (1910-   )
Fantasy
see Waltzing Mannequins

Five Inhibitions [8']
    3.2.2.2. 4.3.3.1. timp,perc,harp, strings
    sc AM.COMP.AL. $16.50 (M743)

Flea Dance [14']
    2.2.2.2. 4.3.3.0. perc,harp, strings
    sc AM.COMP.AL. $7.50, perf mat rent (M744)

Song Of The Caribbean [9']
    2.2.2.2. 4.3.3.1. timp,perc,harp, cel,strings
    sc AM.COMP.AL. $10.30, perf mat rent (M745)

Spring Idyll, For Flute And String Orchestra [4']
    string orch,fl solo
    AM.COMP.AL. sc $1.60, pts $.80, perf mat rent (M746)

Three Acts (from Punch And Judy) [8']
    2.2.2.2. 4.3.3.1. timp,perc,pno, strings
    sc AM.COMP.AL. $49.50, perf mat rent (M747)

Waltzing Mannequins (Fantasy) [4']
    string orch
    sc AM.COMP.AL. $4.60, perf mat rent (M748)

MOURAVIEFF, LEON (1905-   )
Easter Triptychon, For Violoncello And Chamber Orchestra
see Oster-Triptychon, For Violoncello And Chamber Orchestra

Oster-Triptychon, For Violoncello And Chamber Orchestra
    "Easter Triptychon, For Violoncello And Chamber Orchestra" 2clar, 2bsn,strings,vcl solo sc BELAIEFF f.s., perf mat rent (M749)

Pieta
    1.1.1.1. 0.0.0.0. strings [20']
    study sc BELAIEFF f.s., perf mat rent (M750)

MOURET, JEAN JOSEPH (1682-1738)
Andromede Et Persee, For Solo Voice And String Orchestra [15']
    string orch,cont,S solo
    sc BILLAUDOT f.s., perf mat rent (M751)

Regina Coeli, For Solo Voice And String Orchesta
    (Durand, H.A.) string orch,hpsd,vla da gamba,S solo [10'] COSTALL C.3397 perf mat rent (M752)

Venite Exultemus, For Solo Voice And String Orchestra
    (Durand, H.A.) string orch,hpsd, cont,S solo [7'] COSTALL C.3409 perf mat rent (M753)

MOURNFUL-TRIUMPHAL PRELUDE see Shostakovich, Dmitri

MOURNING SONG, FOR SOLO VOICE AND STRING ORCHESTRA see Rangström, Ture

MOUSSORGSKY, MODEST PETROVITCH see MUSSORGSKY, MODEST PETROVICH

MOUVEMENT see Lachenmann, Helmut Friedrich

MOUVEMENT CONCERTANT, FOR DOUBLE BASS AND ORCHESTRA see Arnestad, Finn

MOVEMENT, FOR STRING ORCHESTRA see Cowell, Henry Dixon

MOVEMENT FROM "SUITE FOR CHAMBER ORCHESTRA" see Strang, Gerald

MOVEMENTS see Dollarhide, Theodore

MOVEMENTS FOR STRINGS see Rajna, Thomas

MOVEMENTS ON A MOVING LINE see Rasmussen, Karl Aage

MOVERS AND SHAKERS see Wuorinen, Charles

MOVIMENTI see Bull, Edvard Hagerup

MOVIMENTO see Einaudi, Ludovico see Ferrero, Lorenzo

MOYLAN, WILLIAM (1956-   )
Concerto for Bass Trombone and Orchestra
    2.2.2.2. 4.1.1.1. perc,strings, bass trom solo
    SEESAW (M754)

Two Movements For String Orchestra
    string orch
    SEESAW (M755)

MOYSE, LOUIS
Divertimento
    2.2.2.2. 2.0.0.0. timp,2vcl,db
    MCGIN-MARX perf mat rent (M756)

Marlborian Concerto, For 2 Horns And String Orchestra
    string orch,2horn soli
    MCGIN-MARX perf mat rent (M757)

MOYZES, ALEXANDER (1906-1984)
Concerto for Violin and Orchestra, Op. 53 [30']
    3.3.3.3. 4.2.0.0. timp,perc,harp, cel,strings,vln solo
    SIKORSKI perf mat rent (M758)

MOZ-ART A LA HAYDN, FOR 2 VIOLINS AND STRING ORCHESTRA see Schnittke, Alfred

MOZART, LEOPOLD (1719-1787)
Concerto for Horn and String Orchestra in E flat [11'30"]
    string orch,horn solo
    (Leloir) BILLAUDOT perf mat rent (M759)

Concerto for Trumpet and Orchestra in D
    (Thilde, J.) 2horn,hpsd,strings,trp solo sc BILLAUDOT f.s., perf mat rent (M760)

MOZART, LEOPOLD (cont'd.)

Hochzeitsmenuette
    opt 2horn,hpsd/pno,strings without vla BOHM f.s. (M761)

Musikalische Schlittenfahrt, Die
    (Ruegge, Raimund) 2.2.2.2. 2.2.0.0. timp,strings, 5 sleigh bells sc, pts KUNZEL 10222 f.s. (M762)

Serenade in D
    2ob,2horn,trom,timp,strings, 2clarini
    (Weinmann) sc KUNZEL 10137 $29.00, perf mat rent (M763)

Sinfonia Pastorale
    horn,strings
    KUNZEL 10159 sc $12.00, solo pt $5.00, pts $3.00, ea. (M764)

Symphonies, Three
see Asplmayr, Franz, Symphonies, Three

MOZART, WOLFGANG AMADEUS (1756-1791)
A Berenice; Sol Nascente, For Solo Voice And Orchestra *K.70 [7']
    .0.2.0.0. 2.0.0.0. strings,S solo
    BÄREN. BA 4801 perf mat rent (M765)
    BREITKOPF-L perf mat rent (M766)

A Questo Seno Deh Vieni, For Solo Voice And Orchestra *K.374
    .0.2.0.0. 2.0.0.0. strings,S solo
    BÄREN. BA 4819 perf mat rent (M767)
    BREITKOPF-L perf mat rent (M768)

Abendempfindung, For Solo Voice And Orchestra, [arr.] *K.523
    (Mottl) 1.1.1.1. 2.0.0.0. strings,S solo BREITKOPF-L perf mat rent (M769)

Adagio And Fuge In C Minor, K.546
    sc,pts BREITKOPF-W PB-OB 5130 f.s. (M770)

Adagio for English Horn and String Orchestra, K. 580a *reconstruction
    (Cowart, Robert) string orch without vla,English horn solo [5'] NORRUTH perf mat rent (M771)

Adagio for Violin and Orchestra in E, K. 261
    KALMUS A7446 sc $5.00, set $15.00, pts $1.50, ea. (M772)
    see Mozart Violin Concerti, The

Ah Lo Previdi, For Solo Voice And Orchestra *K.272
    .0.2.0.0. 2.0.0.0. strings,S solo
    BÄREN. BA 4812 perf mat rent (M773)
    BREITKOPF-L perf mat rent (M774)

Ah Se In Ciel, Benigne Stelle, For Solo Voice And Orchestra *K.538
    .0.2.0.2. 2.0.0.0. strings,S solo
    BÄREN. BA 4833 perf mat rent (M775)
    BREITKOPF-L perf mat rent (M776)

Al Desio, Di Chi T'Adora, For Solo Voice And Orchestra *K.577
    2basset horn,2horn,2bsn,strings,S solo
    BREITKOPF-L perf mat rent (M777)

Alcandro, Lo Confesso, For Solo Voice And Orchestra *K.294
    .2.0.2.2. 2.0.0.0. strings,S solo
    BÄREN. BA 4813 perf mat rent (M778)
    BÄREN. BA 4830 perf mat rent (M779)

Alcandro, Lo Confesso (I), For Solo Voice And Orchestra *K.294
    BREITKOPF-L perf mat rent (M780)

Alcandro, Lo Confesso (II), For Solo Voice And Orchestra *K.512
    BREITKOPF-L perf mat rent (M781)

Alma Grande E Nobil Core, For Solo Voice And Orchestra *K.578
    .0.2.0.2. 2.0.0.0. strings,S solo
    BÄREN. BA 4836 perf mat rent (M782)
    BREITKOPF-L perf mat rent (M783)

Andante Cantabile Et Rondo, For Trumpet And String Orchestra [arr.]
    (Thilde, J.) string orch,trp solo [9'40"] BILLAUDOT perf mat rent (M784)

Andante for Flute and Orchestra in C, K. 315
see Concerti for Flute and Orchestra, Nos. 1-2
see Concerto for Flute and Orchestra, No. 1, in G, K. 313

Bacio Di Mano, Un, For Solo Voice And Orchestra *K.541
    .1.2.0.2. 2.0.0.0. strings,B solo
    BÄREN. BA 4835 perf mat rent (M785)
    BREITKOPF-L perf mat rent (M786)

MOZART, WOLFGANG AMADEUS (cont'd.)

Basta, Vincesti, For Solo Voice And
Orchestra *K.486a
.2.0.0.2. 2.0.0.0. strings,S solo
BÄREN. BA 4815 perf mat rent (M787)
BREITKOPF-L perf mat rent (M788)

Bella Mia Fiamma, For Solo Voice And
Orchestra *K.528
.1.2.0.2. 2.0.0.0. strings,B solo
BÄREN. BA 4832 perf mat rent (M789)
sc,pts BREITKOPF-L rent (M790)

Cara, Se Le Mie Pene, For Solo Voice
And Orchestra *K.6
BREITKOPF-L perf mat rent (M791)

Cassations Nos. 1-2, K. 63, K. 99
min sc KALMUS K00954 $5.50 contains
also: Serenades, Nos.1-3, K. 100,
K. 101, K. 185 (M792)

Chi Sà, Chi Sà, Qual Sia, For Solo
Voice And Orchestra *K.582
.0.0.2.2. 2.0.0.0. strings,S solo
BÄREN. BA 4837 perf mat rent (M793)
BREITKOPF-L perf mat rent (M794)

Ch'Io Mi Scordi Di Te, For Solo Voice
And Orchestra *K.505 [8']
0.0.2.2. 2.0.0.0. pno,strings,S
solo
BÄREN. BA 4827 perf mat rent (M795)
BREITKOPF-L perf mat rent (M796)

Clarice Cara Mia Sposa, For Solo
Voice And Orchestra *K.256
.0.2.0.0. 2.0.0.0. strings,T solo
BÄREN. BA 4811 perf mat rent (M797)
BREITKOPF-L perf mat rent (M798)

Clemenza Di Tito, La: Deh, Per Questo
Istante Solo, For Solo Voice And
Orchestra
1.2.0.2. 2.0.0.0. strings,Mez
solo
"Titus: Lass Es Einmal Nur
Geschehen, For Solo Voice And
Orchestra" BREITKOPF-L perf mat
rent (M799)

Clemenza Di Tito, La: Ecco Il Punto;
Non Piu Di Fiori, For Solo Voice
And Orchestra
1.2.1.2. 2.0.0.0. strings,A solo
"Titus: Jetzt, Vitellia! Schlägt
Die Stunde; Nie Soll Mit Rosen,
For Solo Voice And Orchestra"
BREITKOPF-L perf mat rent (M800)

Clemenza Di Tito, La: Overture
2.2.2+basset horn.2. 1.2.0.0.
timp,strings,cont
(Giegling, Franz) BÄREN. BA 4554
(M801)

Clemenza Di Tito, La: Parto, Ma Tu
Ben Mio, For Solo Voice And
Orchestra
BREITKOPF-L perf mat rent (M802)

Con Ossequio, Con Rispetto, For Solo
Voice And Orchestra *K.210
.0.2.0.0. 2.0.0.0. strings,T solo
BÄREN. BA 4808 perf mat rent (M803)
BREITKOPF-L perf mat rent (M804)

Concerti for Flute and Orchestra,
Nos. 1-2
min sc KALMUS K00967 $5.50 contains
also: Andante for Flute and
Orchestra in C, K. 315 (M805)

Concerti For Flute, For Oboe And For
Bassoon
(Giegling, Franz) sc BÄREN. $75.00
(M806)

Concerti for Horn and Orchestra, Nos.
1-4
min sc KALMUS 00091 $10.50 (M807)

Concerti for Piano and Orchestra, No.
9, No. 11, No. 12
min sc KALMUS K00973 $5.50 (M808)

Concerti for Piano and Orchestra,
Nos. 1-3
min sc KALMUS K00970 $5.50 (M809)

Concerti for Piano and Orchestra,
Nos. 4-6
min sc KALMUS K00971 $5.50 (M810)

Concerti for Piano and Orchestra,
Nos. 11-16
(reprint of Breitkopf and Hartel)
sc DOVER 254682 $10.95 (M811)

Concerti for Piano and Orchestra,
Nos. 13-14
min sc KALMUS K00974 $5.50 (M812)

Concerti for Piano and Orchestra,
Nos. 15-16
min sc KALMUS K00975 $5.50 (M813)

MOZART, WOLFGANG AMADEUS (cont'd.)

Concerti for Piano and Orchestra,
Nos. 17-18
min sc KALMUS K00976 $5.50 (M814)

Concerti for Piano and Orchestra,
Nos. 19-20
min sc KALMUS K00977 $5.50 (M815)

Concerti for Piano and Orchestra,
Nos. 21-22
min sc KALMUS K00978 $5.50 (M816)

Concerti for Piano and Orchestra,
Nos. 23-24
min sc KALMUS K00979 $5.50 (M817)

Concerti for Piano and Orchestra,
Nos. 25-26
min sc KALMUS K00980 $5.50 (M818)

Concerti for Piano and Orchestra,
Nos. 27-28
min sc KALMUS K00981 $5.50 (M819)

Concerti for Violin and Orchestra
(Mahling, Christoph-Hellmut)
"Violinkonzerte Und Einzelsatze"
sc BÄREN. f.s. (M820)

Concerti for Violin and Orchestra,
Nos. 1-4
min sc KALMUS K00964 $5.50 (M821)

Concerti for Violin and Orchestra,
Nos. 1-5
(reprint of Breitkopf and Hartel
edition) sc DOVER 251691 $8.95
contains also: Symphonie
Concertante for Violin, Viola and
Orchestra in E flat, K. 364
(M822)
see Mozart Violin Concerti, The

Concerti For Wind Instruments *CC10L
sc DOVER 252280 $11.95 reprint of
Breitkopf and Hartel editions
(M823)

Concerto for Bassoon and Orchestra in
B flat, K. 191
BROUDE BR. set $22.50, pts $2.50,
ea. (M824)
min sc KALMUS K00966 $5.50 contains
also: Concerto for Flute, Harp
and Orchestra in C, K. 299 (M825)
(Giegling, Franz) BÄREN. sc,pts
BA 4868 f.s., min sc TP 253 f.s.
(M826)

Concerto for Bassoon and Orchestra in
B flat, MIN 174
(Allard, M.) 2ob,2horn,strings,bsn
solo [18'] sc BILLAUDOT f.s.,
perf mat rent (M827)

Concerto for Clarinet and Orchestra
in A, K. 622
(Burmeister) sc PETERS P9820 f.s.
(M828)

Concerto for Flute and Orchestra, K.
622, [arr.]
(Muller, A.E.; Forster, D.H.) 2ob,
2bsn,2horn,strings,fl solo sc,pts
KUNZEL 10207 f.s. (M829)

Concerto for Flute and Orchestra, No.
1, in G, K. 313
sc,pts BÄREN. BA 4854 f.s. contains
also: Andante for Flute and
Orchestra in C, K. 315 (M830)

Concerto for Flute and Orchestra, No.
2, in D, K. 314
sc,pts BÄREN. BA 4855 f.s. (M831)

Concerto for Flute, Harp and
Orchestra in C, K. 299
SONZOGNO perf mat rent (M832)
(Giegling, Franz) study sc BÄREN.
$6.30 (M833)
see Concerto for Bassoon and
Orchestra in B flat, K. 191

Concerto for Oboe and Orchestra in C,
K. 314
sc,pts BÄREN. BA 4856 f.s. (M834)
SONZOGNO perf mat rent (M835)

Concerto for Piano and Orchestra, No.
3, in D, K. 40
KALMUS A4125 sc $12.00, set $10.00
(M836)

Concerto for Piano and Orchestra, No.
8, in C, K. 246
min sc KALMUS K00972 $5.50 contains
also: Concerto for 3 Pianos and
Orchestra, No. 7, in F, K. 242
(M837)

Concerto for Piano and Orchestra, No.
15, in B flat, K. 450
(Flothuis, Marius) sc BÄREN. $6.30
(M838)

Concerto for Piano and Orchestra, No.
16, in D, K. 451
(Flothuis, Marius) sc BÄREN. $8.70
(M839)

MOZART, WOLFGANG AMADEUS (cont'd.)

Concerto for Piano and Orchestra, No.
19, in F, K. 459
(Elvers, Rudolf) fac ed BÄREN.
$72.00 (M840)

Concerto for Piano and Orchestra, No.
20, in D minor, K. 466
(Darvas) study sc EMB 40070 f.s.
(M841)

Concerto for Piano and Orchestra, No.
21, in C, K. 467
(reproduction of autograph at the
pierpont morgan library) sc DOVER
249689 $9.95 (M842)

Concerto for Piano and Orchestra, No.
25, in C, K. 503
(Darvas) study sc EMB 40082 f.s.
(M843)

Concerto for Piano and Orchestra, No.
27, in B flat, K. 595
(Rehm, Wolfgang) BÄREN. sc,pts
BA 4872 f.s., min sc TP 91 f.s.
(M844)

Concerto for 2 Pianos and Orchestra,
No. 10, in E flat, K. 365
min sc KALMUS K00270 $5.00 (M845)

Concerto for 3 Pianos and Orchestra,
No. 7, in F, K. 242
sc KUNZEL 10050 $18.00 (M846)
see Concerto for Piano and
Orchestra, No. 8, in C, K. 246

Concerto for Viola and Orchestra,
[arr.]
(Tertis) 2.0.0.2. 2.0.0.0. strings,
vla solo [25'] (arr of the clar
concerto) CHESTER perf mat rent
(M847)

Concerto for Violin and Orchestra,
No. 1, in B flat, K. 207
(Mahling, Christoph-Hellmut) BÄREN.
sc,pts BA 4863 f.s., min sc
TP 270 f.s. (M848)

Concerto for Violin and Orchestra,
No. 2, in D, K. 211
(Mahling, Christoph-Hellmut) BÄREN.
sc,pts BA 4864 f.s., min sc
TP 271 f.s. (M849)

Concerto for Violin and Orchestra,
No. 3, in G, K. 216
(Mahling, Christoph-Hellmut) BÄREN.
sc,pts BA 4865 f.s., min sc
TP 272 f.s. (M850)

Concerto for Violin and Orchestra,
No. 4, in D, K. 218
(Mahling, Christoph-Hellmut) BÄREN.
sc,pts BA 4866 f.s., min sc
TP 273 f.s. (M851)

Concerto for Violin and Orchestra,
No. 7, in D, K. 271a
KALMUS A4104 sc $15.00, set $25.00,
perf mat rent (M852)

Concerto in D for Violoncello and
Orchestra, [arr.]
(Szell, Georg) 2ob,2horn,strings,
vcl solo SCHIRM.G perf mat rent
(M853)

Conservati Fedele, For Solo Voice And
Orchestra *K.23
.strings,S solo
BÄREN. BA 4797 perf mat rent (M854)
BREITKOPF-L perf mat rent (M855)

Cosi Dunque Tradisci, For Solo Voice
And Orchestra *K.432
.2.2.0.2. 2.0.0.0. strings,B solo
BÄREN. BA 4825 perf mat rent (M856)
BREITKOPF-L perf mat rent (M857)

Cosi Fan Tutte: Ah Guarda, Sorella,
For Solo Voices And Orchestra
KALMUS A6248 sc $3.00, set $8.00,
pts $.75, ea. (M858)

Cosi Fan Tutte: Der Odem Der Liebe,
For Solo Voice And Orchestra
see Cosi Fan Tutte: Un' Aura
Amorosa, For Solo Voice And
Orchestra

Cosi Fan Tutte: Donne Mie, La Fate A
Tanti, For Solo Voice And
Orchestra
2.2.0.2. 2.2.0.0. timp,strings,
Bar solo
"Cosi Fan Tutte: Mädchen, So Treibt
Ihr's Mit Allen, For Solo Voice
And Orchestra" BREITKOPF-L perf
mat rent (M859)

Cosi Fan Tutte: E Amore Un
Ladroncello, For Solo Voice And
Orchestra [4']
1.2.2.2. 2.0.0.0. strings,Mez/A
solo
"Cosi Fan Tutte: Ein Loser Dieb Ist
Amor, For Solo Voice And

MOZART, WOLFGANG AMADEUS (cont'd.)

Orchestra" BREITKOPF-W perf mat
rent   (M860)

Cosi Fan Tutte: Ein Loser Dieb Ist
Amor, For Solo Voice And
Orchestra
see Cosi Fan Tutte: E Amore Un
Ladroncello, For Solo Voice And
Orchestra

Cosi Fan Tutte: Mädchen, So Treibt
Ihr's Mit Allen, For Solo Voice
And Orchestra
see Cosi Fan Tutte: Donne Mie, La
Fate A Tanti, For Solo Voice And
Orchestra

Cosi Fan Tutte: Schon Ein Mädchen Von
Fünfzehn Jahren, For Solo Voice
And Orchestra
see Cosi Fan Tutte: Una Donna A
Quindici Anni, For Solo Voice And
Orchestra

Cosi Fan Tutte: Un' Aura Amorosa, For
Solo Voice And Orchestra
"Cosi Fan Tutte: Der Odem Der
Liebe, For Solo Voice And
Orchestra" BREITKOPF-L perf mat
rent   (M861)

Cosi Fan Tutte: Una Donna A Quindici
Anni, For Solo Voice And
Orchestra [5']
BREITKOPF-W perf mat rent   (M862)
"Cosi Fan Tutte: Schon Ein Mädchen
Von Fünfzehn Jahren, For Solo
Voice And Orchestra" BREITKOPF-L
perf mat rent   (M863)

Die Ihr Des Unermesslichen Weltalls
Schöpfer, For Solo Voice And
Orchestra, [arr.] *K.619
(Liebeskind) 2.2.2.2. 2.2.0.0.
timp,strings,S/T solo BREITKOPF-L
perf mat rent   (M864)

Dite Almeno, For Solo Voices And
Orchestra *K.479
0.2.2.2. 2.0.0.0. strings,STBB
soli
BÄREN. BA 4828 perf mat rent (M865)
BREITKOPF-L perf mat rent   (M866)

Divertimenti, Six
min sc KALMUS K00960 $5.50
contains: Divertimento, K. 251;
Divertimento, K. 252;
Divertimento, K. 253;
Divertimento, K. 287;
Divertimento, K. 289;
Divertimento, K. 334   (M867)

Divertimenti, Ten
min sc KALMUS K00959 $5.50
contains: Divertimento, K. 113;
Divertimento, K. 131;
Divertimento, K. 166;
Divertimento, K. 186;
Divertimento, K. 187;
Divertimento, K. 188;
Divertimento, K. 205;
Divertimento, K. 213;
Divertimento, K. 240;
Divertimento, K. 247   (M868)

Divertimenti, K. 136-138
(Fussl, Karl Heinz) BAREN. sc,pts
BA 4857 f.s., min sc TP 278 f.s.
                                 (M869)

Divertimento, K. 113
see Divertimenti, Ten

Divertimento, K. 131
see Divertimenti, Ten

Divertimento, K. 166
see Divertimenti, Ten

Divertimento, K. 186
see Divertimenti, Ten

Divertimento, K. 187
see Divertimenti, Ten

Divertimento, K. 188
see Divertimenti, Ten

Divertimento, K. 205
see Divertimenti, Ten

Divertimento, K. 213
see Divertimenti, Ten

Divertimento, K. 240
see Divertimenti, Ten

Divertimento, K. 247
see Divertimenti, Ten

Divertimento, K. 251
see Divertimenti, Six

MOZART, WOLFGANG AMADEUS (cont'd.)

Divertimento, K. 252
see Divertimenti, Six

Divertimento, K. 253
see Divertimenti, Six

Divertimento, K. 287
see Divertimenti, Six

Divertimento, K. 289
see Divertimenti, Six

Divertimento, K. 334
see Divertimenti, Six

Don Giovanni: Auf Denn Zum Feste, For
Solo Voice And Orchestra
see Don Giovanni: Finch' Han Dal
Vino, For Solo Voice And
Orchestra

Don Giovanni: Auf Zu Dem Feste, For
Solo Voice And Orchestra
see Don Giovanni: Finch' Han Dal
Vino, For Solo Voice And
Orchestra

Don Giovanni: Batti, Batti, O Bel
Masetto, For Solo Voice And
Orchestra
"Don Giovanni: Schmäle, Tobe,
Lieber Junge, For Solo Voice And
Orchestra" BREITKOPF-L perf mat
rent   (M870)

Don Giovanni: Dalla Sua Pace, For
Solo Voice And Orchestra [3']
1.2.0.2. 2.0.0.0. strings,T solo
"Don Giovanni: Nur Ihrem Frieden,
For Solo Voice And Orchestra"
BREITKOPF-W perf mat rent (M871)

Don Giovanni: Deh Vieni Alla
Finestra, For Solo Voice And
Orchestra
mand,strings,Bar solo
"Don Giovanni: Feinsliebchen, Komm
Ans Fenster, For Solo Voice And
Orchestra" BREITKOPF-L perf mat
rent   (M872)

Don Giovanni: Don Ottavio,
Entsetzlich; Du Kennst Nun Den
Frevier, For Solo Voice And
Orchestra
see Don Giovanni: Don Ottavio, Son
Morta; Or Sai Chi L'onore, For
Solo Voice And Orchestra

Don Giovanni: Don Ottavio, Son Morta;
Or Sai Chi L'onore, For Solo
Voice And Orchestra [8']
2.2.0.2. 2.2.0.0. strings,S solo
"Don Giovanni: Don Ottavio,
Entsetzlich; Du Kennst Nun Den
Frevier, For Solo Voice And
Orchestra" BREITKOPF-W perf mat
rent   (M873)

Don Giovanni: Feinsliebchen, Komm Ans
Fenster, For Solo Voice And
Orchestra
see Don Giovanni: Deh Vieni Alla
Finestra, For Solo Voice And
Orchestra

Don Giovanni: Finch' Han Dal Vino,
For Solo Voice And Orchestra [5']
2.2.2.2. 2.0.0.0. strings,Bar
solo
"Don Giovanni: Auf Denn Zum Feste,
For Solo Voice And Orchestra"
BREITKOPF-L perf mat rent (M874)
"Don Giovanni: Auf Zu Dem Feste,
For Solo Voice And Orchestra"
BREITKOPF-W perf mat rent (M875)

Don Giovanni: In Quali Eccessi; Mi
Tradi Quell'alma Ingrata, For
Solo Voice And Orchestra [10']
1.2.2.2. 2.0.3.0. strings,S solo
"Don Giovanni: In Welche Frevel;
Mich Verriet Der Undankbare, For
Solo Voice And Orchestra"
BREITKOPF-W perf mat rent (M876)

Don Giovanni: In Welche Frevel; Mich
Verriet Der Undankbare, For Solo
Voice And Orchestra
see Don Giovanni: In Quali Eccessi;
Mi Tradi Quell'alma Ingrata, For
Solo Voice And Orchestra

Don Giovanni: La Ci Darem La Mano,
For Solo Voices And Orchestra
"Don Giovanni: Reich Mir Die Hand,
Mein Leben, For Solo Voices And
Orchestra" BREITKOPF-L perf mat
rent   (M877)

Don Giovanni: Madamina! Il Catalogo,
For Solo Voice And Orchestra
"Don Giovanni: Schöne Donna! Dieses
Kleine Register, For Solo Voice

MOZART, WOLFGANG AMADEUS (cont'd.)

And Orchestra" BREITKOPF-L perf
mat rent   (M878)

Don Giovanni: Nur Ihrem Frieden, For
Solo Voice And Orchestra
see Don Giovanni: Dalla Sua Pace,
For Solo Voice And Orchestra

Don Giovanni: Overture
KALMUS A6417 sc $10.00, set $22.00,
pts $1.25, ea., perf mat rent
                                 (M879)
(Plath, Wolgang) BÄREN. BA 4550
                                 (M880)

Don Giovanni: Reich Mir Die Hand,
Mein Leben, For Solo Voices And
Orchestra
see Don Giovanni: La Ci Darem La
Mano, For Solo Voices And
Orchestra

Don Giovanni: Schmäle, Tobe, Lieber
Junge, For Solo Voice And
Orchestra
see Don Giovanni: Batti, Batti, O
Bel Masetto, For Solo Voice And
Orchestra

Don Giovanni: Schöne Donna! Dieses
Kleine Register, For Solo Voice
And Orchestra
see Don Giovanni: Madamina! Il
Catalogo, For Solo Voice And
Orchestra

Don Giovanni: Vedrai Carino, For Solo
Voice And Orchestra
"Don Giovanni: Wenn Du Fein Fromm
Bist, For Solo Voice And
Orchestra" BREITKOPF-L perf mat
rent   (M881)

Don Giovanni: Wenn Du Fein Fromm
Bist, For Solo Voice And
Orchestra
see Don Giovanni: Vedrai Carino,
For Solo Voice And Orchestra

Entführung Aus Dem Serail, Die: Durch
Zärtlichkeit, For Solo Voice And
Orchestra
string orch,S solo
BREITKOPF-L perf mat rent   (M882)

Entfuhrung Aus Dem Serail, Die:
Frisch Zum Kampfe! Frisch Zum
Streite!, For Solo Voice And
Orchestra [3']
0.2.0.0. 2.2.0.0. timp,strings,T
solo
BREITKOPF-W perf mat rent   (M883)

Entfuhrung Aus Dem Serail, Die: Ha!
Wie Will Ich Triumphieren, For
Solo Voice And Orchestra [5']
0+pic.2.2.2. 2.0.0.0. strings,B
solo
BREITKOPF-W perf mat rent   (M884)
BREITKOPF-L perf mat rent   (M885)

Entfuhrung Aus Dem Serail, Die: Ich
Baue Ganz Auf Deine Starke, For
Solo Voice And Orchestra [5']
2.0.2.2. 2.0.0.0. strings,T solo
BREITKOPF-W perf mat rent   (M886)

Entfuhrung Aus Dem Serail, Die:
Martern Aller Arten, For Solo
Voice And Orchestra
BREITKOPF-L perf mat rent   (M887)

Entfuhrung Aus Dem Serail, Die:
Overture
(Busoni) "Seraglio, Il: Overture"
KALMUS A6443 sc $10.00, set
$15.00, pts $1.00, ea.   (M888)
(Croll, Gerhard) BÄREN. BA 4591
                                 (M889)

Entfuhrung Aus Dem Serail, Die:
Welche Wonne, Welche Lust, For
Solo Voice And Orchestra
2.0.0.2. 2.0.0.0. strings,S solo
[4'] BREITKOPF-W perf mat rent
                                 (M890)

Entfuhrung Aus Dem Serail, Die: Wenn
Der Freude Tranen Fliessen, For
Solo Voice And Orchestra [5']
0.2.2.2. 2.0.0.0. strings,T solo
BREITKOPF-W perf mat rent   (M891)

Ergo Interest; Quaere Superna, For
Solo Voice And Orchestra *K.143
BREITKOPF-L perf mat rent   (M892)

Exsultate, Jubilate, For Solo Voice
And Orchestra *K.165
(Klengel, P.) 2ob,2horn,strings,
org,S solo sc,pts BREITKOPF-L
EB 5232 KlA rent   (M893)

Exultate Jubilate: Alleluja, For Solo
Voice And Orchestra [arr.]
2.2.2.2. 4.2.2.0. timp,strings,solo
voice SCHIRM.G perf mat rent

MOZART, WOLFGANG AMADEUS (cont'd.)

(M894)
Fantasie, K.608, [arr.]
see Zwei Fugen Und Eine Fantasie

Finalmusik In G, K. 63 [15']
2ob,2horn,strings
BREITKOPF-L perf mat rent   (M895)

Finta Giardiniera, La: Overture
2ob,2horn,timp,strings
(Angermuller, Rudolph; Berke,
Dietrich) BÄREN. BA 4578   (M896)

Finta Semplice, La: Ella Vuole Ed Io
Torrei, For Solo Voice And String
Orchestra
string orch,solo voice INTERNAT.
perf mat rent   (M897)

Finta Semplice, La: Overture [12']
2.2.0.2. 2.0.0.0. strings
BREITKOPF-W perf mat rent   (M898)
(Angermuller, Rudolph; Rehm,
Wolfgang) BÄREN. BA 4594   (M899)

Finta Semplice, La: Sono In Amore,
For Solo Voice And Orchestra
2fl,strings,S solo
BREITKOPF-L perf mat rent   (M900)

Fra Cento Affanni, For Solo Voice And
Orchestra *K.88
0.2.0.0. 2.2.0.0. strings,S solo
BÄREN. BA 4802 perf mat rent (M901)
BREITKOPF-L perf mat rent   (M902)

Fuge, K.401, [arr.]
see Zwei Fugen Und Eine Fantasie

Fuge, K.546, [arr.]
see Zwei Fugen Und Eine Fantasie

German Dances And Contredances
min sc KALMUS K00963 $5.50   (M903)

Grabmusik: Betracht Dies Herz, For
Solo Voice And String Orchestra
string orch,S solo
(Giegling, Franz) BÄREN. BA 4785
(M904)
Hochzeit Des Figaro, Die: Alles Ist
Richtig; Ach, Öffnet Eure Augen,
For Solo Voice And Orchestra
see Nozze Di Figaro, Le: Tutto E
Disposto, For Solo Voice And
Orchestra

Hochzeit Des Figaro, Die: Der Prozess
Schon Gewonnen; Ich Soll Ein
Glück Entbehren, For Solo Voice
And Orchestra
see Nozze Di Figaro, Le: Hai Gia
Vinta La Causa; Vedro Mentr' Io
Sospiro, For Solo Voice And
Orchestra

Hochzeit Des Figaro, Die: Endlich
Naht Sich Die Stunde, For Solo
Voice And Orchestra
see Nozze Di Figaro, Le: Giunse
Alfin Il Momento, For Solo Voice
And Orchestra

Hochzeit Des Figaro, Die: Euch Holde
Frauen, For Solo Voice And
Orchestra
see Nozze Di Figaro, Le: Voi Che
Sapete, For Solo Voice And
Orchestra

Hochzeit Des Figaro, Die: Hör' Mein
Flehn, For Solo Voice And
Orchestra
see Nozze Di Figaro, Le: Porgi
Amor, For Solo Voice And
Orchestra

Hochzeit Des Figaro, Die: Ich Weiss
Nicht, Wo Ich Bin, For Solo Voice
And Orchestra
see Nozze Di Figaro, Le: Non So Piu
Cosa Son, For Solo Voice And
Orchestra

Hochzeit Des Figaro, Die: Nun Vergiss
Leises Flehn, For Solo Voice And
Orchestra
see Nozze Di Figaro, Le: Non Piu
Andrai, For Solo Voice And
Orchestra

Hochzeit Des Figaro, Die: So Lang Hab
Ich Geschmachtet, For Solo Voices
And Orchestra
see Nozze Di Figaro, Le: Crudel!
Perche Finora, For Solo Voices
And Orchestra

Hochzeit Des Figaro, Die: Süsse
Rache, Ja Süsse Rache, For Solo
Voice And Orchestra
see Nozze Di Figaro, Le: La
Vendetta, For Solo Voice And
Orchestra

MOZART, WOLFGANG AMADEUS (cont'd.)

Hochzeit Des Figaro, Die: Wenn Die
Sanften Abendwinde, For Solo
Voices And Orchestra
see Nozze Di Figaro, Le: Sull'aria!
Che Soave Zeffiretto, For Solo
Voices And Orchestra

Hochzeit Des Figaro, Die: Will Der
Herr Graf Ein Tänzchen Nun Wagen,
For Solo Voice And Orchestra
see Nozze Di Figaro, Le: Se Vuol
Ballare, For Solo Voice And
Orchestra

Hochzeit Des Figaro, Die: Wohin
Flohen Die Wonnestunden, For Solo
Voice And Orchestra
see Nozze Di Figaro, Le: Dove Sono,
For Solo Voice And Orchestra

Ich Möchte Wohl Der Kaiser Sein, For
Solo Voice And Orchestra *K.539
0(pic).2.0.2. 2.0.0.0. perc,
strings,Bar solo
BÄREN. BA 4834 perf mat rent (M905)

Idomeneo: Ballettmusik *K.367 [25']
2.2.2.2. 2.2.0.0. timp,strings
BREITKOPF-W perf mat rent   (M906)
(Heartz, Daniel) BÄREN. BA 4768
perf mat rent   (M907)

Idomeneo: Euch, Ihr Einsamen
Schatten; Zephiretten Leicht
Gefiedert, For Solo Voice And
Orchestra
see Idomeneo: Solitudini Amiche;
Zeffiretti Lusinghieri, For Solo
Voice And Orchestra

Idomeneo: Overture
(Heartz, Daniel) BÄREN. BA 4562
(M908)
Idomeneo: Se Il Padre Perdei, For
Solo Voice And Orchestra
KALMUS A4548 sc $4.00, set $9.00,
pts $1.00, ea.   (M909)

Idomeneo: Solitudini Amiche;
Zeffiretti Lusinghieri, For Solo
Voice And Orchestra
"Idomeneo: Euch, Ihr Einsamen
Schatten; Zephiretten Leicht
Gefiedert, For Solo Voice And
Orchestra" BREITKOPF-L perf mat
rent   (M910)

Idomeneo: Torna La Pace, For Solo
Voice And Orchestra
KALMUS 5009 sc $5.00, set $11.00,
pts $1.00, ea.   (M911)

Impresario: Ich Bin Die Erste
Sangerin, For Solo Voices And
Orchestra
see Schauspieldirektor, Der: Ich
Bin Die Erste Sangerin, For Solo
Voices And Orchestra

Io Ti Lascio, Oh Cara, Addio, For
Solo Voice And String Orchestra
*K. Anh.245
string orch,B solo
BÄREN. BA 4840 perf mat rent (M912)

Kleine Nachtmusik, Eine *K.525
FENTONE   (M913)
(Darvas) study sc EMB 40021 f.s.
(M914)
Kommet Her, Ihr Frechen Sunder, For
Solo Voice And String Orchestra
*K.146 [3']
string orch,org,S solo
BREITKOPF-W perf mat rent   (M915)
BREITKOPF-L perf mat rent   (M916)

Königliche Schäfer, Der: Dein Bin
Ich, For Solo Voice And Orchestra
see Re Pastore, Il: L'Amero Saro
Costante, For Solo Voice And
Orchestra

Konzertsatz, For Horn And Orchestra,
K. 370b *reconstruction
(Collorafi) SHAWNEE perf mat rent
(M917)
(Jeurissen, H.) 2ob,2horn,strings,
horn solo [8'] SIKORSKI perf mat
rent   (M918)

Konzertsatz, For Horn And Orchestra,
K. 494a *reconstruction
(Jeurissen, H.) 2ob,2horn,strings,
horn solo [10'] SIKORSKI perf mat
rent   (M919)

Konzertsatz, For Horn And Orchestra,
K. 494b
(Collorafi) SHAWNEE perf mat rent
(M920)
Liebes Manndel, Wo Ist's Bandel, For
Solo Voices And String Orchestra
*K.441
string orch,STB soli

MOZART, WOLFGANG AMADEUS (cont'd.)

BÄREN. BA 4794 perf mat rent (M921)

Liebesprobe Oder Die Rekrutierung,
Die
BREITKOPF-L perf mat rent   (M922)

Lucia Silla: Overture
0.2.0.0. 2.2.0.0. timp,strings,
cont
(Hansell, Kathleen Kuzmick) BÄREN.
BA 4590   (M923)

Ma Che Vi Fece, For Solo Voice And
Orchestra *K.368
.2.0.0.2. 2.0.0.0. strings,S solo
BÄREN. BA 4817 perf mat rent (M924)
BREITKOPF-L perf mat rent   (M925)

Mandina Amabile, For Solo Voices And
Orchestra *K.480
2.2.2.2. 2.0.0.0. strings,STB
soli
BÄREN. BA 4829 perf mat rent (M926)
BREITKOPF-L perf mat rent   (M927)

Marsch In D, K. 215 [5']
0.2.0.0. 2.2.0.0. strings
BREITKOPF-W perf mat rent   (M928)

Marsch In D, K. 237 [4']
2.0.2.2. 2.2.0.0. strings
BREITKOPF-W perf mat rent   (M929)

Marsch In D, K. 249
sc,pts BREITKOPF-W PB-OB 5131 f.s.
(M930)
KALMUS A6338 sc $2.00, set $12.00,
pts $1.00, ea.   (M931)

Marsche, Drei, K. 408
KALMUS A6337 sc $5.00, set $15.00,
pts $1.00, ea.   (M932)

Maurerische Trauermusik *K.477
sc,pts BREITKOPF-W PB-OB 5147 f.s.
(M933)
(Landon, H.C.R.) KALMUS A7330 sc
$6.00, set $10.00, pts $.75, ea.
(M934)
Mentre Ti Lascio, O Figlia, For Solo
Voice And Orchestra *K.513
.1.0.2.2. 2.0.0.0. strings,B solo
BÄREN. BA 4831 perf mat rent (M935)
BREITKOPF-L perf mat rent   (M936)

Mia Speranza Adorata, For Solo Voice
And Orchestra *K.416
0.2.0.2. 2.0.0.0. strings,S solo
BÄREN. BA 4821 perf mat rent (M937)
BREITKOPF-L perf mat rent   (M938)

Minuet, K. 409
see Symphony No. 34 in C, K. 338

Misera, Dove Son, For Solo Voice And
Orchestra *K.369
.2.0.0.0. 2.0.0.0. strings,S solo
BÄREN. BA 4818 perf mat rent (M939)
BREITKOPF-L perf mat rent   (M940)

Misero Me! Misero Pargoletto, For
Solo Voice And Orchestra *K.77
.0.2.0.2. 2.0.0.0. strings,S solo
BÄREN. BA 4803 perf mat rent (M941)
sc,pts BREITKOPF-L rent   (M942)

Misero! O Sogno, For Solo Voice And
Orchestra *K.431
2.0.2.2. 2.0.0.0. strings,T solo
BÄREN. BA 4826 perf mat rent (M943)
BREITKOPF-L perf mat rent   (M944)

Mitridate: Overture
KALMUS A4108 sc $3.00, set $11.00
(M945)
Moto Di Gioia, Un, For Solo Voice And
Orchestra *K.579
KALMUS A 3587 sc $4.00, set $8.00,
pts $.75, ea.   (M946)
BREITKOPF-L perf mat rent   (M947)

Mozart Violin Concerti, The
(Banat, Gabriel) fac ed RAVEN
$145.00
contains: Adagio for Violin and
Orchestra in E, K. 261;
Concerti for Violin and
Orchestra, Nos. 1-5; Rondo for
Violin and Orchestra in B flat,
K. 269   (M948)

Nehmt Meinen Dank, For Solo Voice And
Orchestra *K.383
.1.1.0.1. 0.0.0.0. strings,S solo
BÄREN. BA 4793 perf mat rent (M949)
BREITKOPF-L perf mat rent   (M950)

No, No, Che Non Sei Capace, For Solo
Voice And Orchestra *K.419
0.2.0.0. 2.2.0.0. timp,strings,S
solo
BÄREN. BA 4823 perf mat rent (M951)
BREITKOPF-L perf mat rent   (M952)

MOZART, WOLFGANG AMADEUS (cont'd.)

Non Curo l'Affetto, For Solo Voice
And Orchestra *K.74b
 .2.0.0.0. 2.0.0.0. strings,S solo
BÄREN. BA 4806 perf mat rent (M953)
BREITKOPF-L perf mat rent   (M954)

Non Piu! Tutto Ascoltai, For Solo
Voice And Orchestra *K.490
BREITKOPF-L perf mat rent   (M955)

Nozze Di Figaro, Le: Crudel! Perche
Finora, For Solo Voices And
Orchestra
"Hochzeit Des Figaro, Die: So Lang
Hab Ich Geschmachtet, For Solo
Voices And Orchestra" BREITKOPF-L
perf mat rent   (M956)

Nozze Di Figaro, Le: Dove Sono, For
Solo Voice And Orchestra
0.2.0.2. 2.0.0.0. strings,S solo
[4'] BREITKOPF-W perf mat rent
                             (M957)
"Hochzeit Des Figaro, Die: Wohin
Flohen Die Wonnestunden, For Solo
Voice And Orchestra" BREITKOPF-L
perf mat rent   (M958)

Nozze Di Figaro, Le: Giunse Alfin Il
Momento, For Solo Voice And
Orchestra
"Hochzeit Des Figaro, Die: Endlich
Naht Sich Die Stunde, For Solo
Voice And Orchestra" BREITKOPF-L
perf mat rent   (M959)

Nozze Di Figaro, Le: Hai Gia Vinta La
Causa; Vedro Mentr' Io Sospiro,
For Solo Voice And Orchestra
BREITKOPF-W perf mat rent   (M960)
"Hochzeit Des Figaro, Die: Der
Prozess Schon Gewonnen; Ich Soll
Ein Glück Entbehren, For Solo
Voice And Orchestra" BREITKOPF-L
perf mat rent   (M961)

Nozze Di Figaro, Le: La Vendetta, For
Solo Voice And Orchestra
"Hochzeit Des Figaro, Die: Süsse
Rache, Ja Süsse Rache, For Solo
Voice And Orchestra" BREITKOPF-L
perf mat rent   (M962)

Nozze Di Figaro, Le: Non Piu Andrai,
For Solo Voice And Orchestra
"Hochzeit Des Figaro, Die: Nun
Vergiss Leises Flehn, For Solo
Voice And Orchestra" BREITKOPF-L
perf mat rent   (M963)

Nozze Di Figaro, Le: Non So Piu Cosa
Son, For Solo Voice And Orchestra
"Hochzeit Des Figaro, Die: Ich
Weiss Nicht, Wo Ich Bin, For Solo
Voice And Orchestra" BREITKOPF-L
perf mat rent   (M964)

Nozze Di Figaro, Le: Overture
(Finscher, Ludwig) BÄREN. BA 4565
                             (M965)
Nozze Di Figaro, Le: Porgi Amor, For
Solo Voice And Orchestra
"Hochzeit Des Figaro, Die: Hör'
Mein Flehn, For Solo Voice And
Orchestra" BREITKOPF-L perf mat
rent   (M966)

Nozze Di Figaro, Le: Se Vuol Ballare,
For Solo Voice And Orchestra
"Hochzeit Des Figaro, Die: Will Der
Herr Graf Ein Tänzchen Nun Wagen,
For Solo Voice And Orchestra"
BREITKOPF-L perf mat rent   (M967)

Nozze Di Figaro, Le: Sull'aria! Che
Soave Zeffiretto, For Solo Voices
And Orchestra
"Hochzeit Des Figaro, Die: Wenn Die
Sanften Abendwinde, For Solo
Voices And Orchestra" BREITKOPF-L
perf mat rent   (M968)

Nozze Di Figaro, Le: Tutto E
Disposto, For Solo Voice And
Orchestra
"Hochzeit Des Figaro, Die: Alles
Ist Richtig; Ach, Öffnet Eure
Augen, For Solo Voice And
Orchestra" BREITKOPF-L perf mat
rent   (M969)

Nozze Di Figaro, Le: Voi Che Sapete,
For Solo Voice And Orchestra
"Hochzeit Des Figaro, Die: Euch
Holde Frauen, For Solo Voice And
Orchestra" BREITKOPF-L perf mat
rent   (M970)

O Temerario Arbace, For Solo Voice
And Orchestra *K.79
 .0.2.0.2. 2.0.0.0. strings,S solo
BÄREN. BA 4799 perf mat rent (M971)
BREITKOPF-L perf mat rent   (M972)

MOZART, WOLFGANG AMADEUS (cont'd.)

Ombra Felice, For Solo Voice And
Orchestra *K.255
 .0.2.0.0. 2.0.0.0. strings,A solo
BÄREN. BA 4810 perf mat rent (M973)
BREITKOPF-L perf mat rent   (M974)

Or Che Il Dover, For Solo Voice And
Orchestra *K.36
0.2.0.2. 2.2.0.0. timp,strings,T
solo
BÄREN. BA 4800 perf mat rent (M975)
BREITKOPF-L perf mat rent   (M976)

Pantalon Und Colombine *K.446,
reconstruction
(Beyer, Franz) sc KUNZEL 10113
f.s., perf mat rent   (M977)

Per Pietà, Bell' Idol Mio, For Solo
Voice And Orchestra *K.78
0.2.0.0. 2.0.0.0. strings,solo
voice
BÄREN. BA 4798 perf mat rent (M978)
BREITKOPF-L perf mat rent   (M979)

Per Pietà, Non Ricercate, For Solo
Voice And Orchestra *K.420
 .0.0.2.2. 2.0.0.0. strings,T solo
BÄREN. BA 4824 perf mat rent (M980)
BREITKOPF-L perf mat rent   (M981)

Per Questa Bella Mano, For Solo Voice
And Orchestra *K.612
 .1.2.0.2. 2.0.0.0. strings,B solo
BÄREN. BA 4839 perf mat rent (M982)
BREITKOPF-L perf mat rent   (M983)

Petits Riens, Les *K. Anh.10
2.2.2.2. 2.2.0.0. timp,strings
(Heckmann, Harald) BÄREN. BA 4841
perf mat rent   (M984)

Popoli Di Tessaglia! Io Non Chiedo,
Eterni Dei, For Solo Voice And
Orchestra *K.316
 .0.1.0.1. 2.0.0.0. strings,S solo
BÄREN. BA 4816 perf mat rent (M985)
BREITKOPF-L perf mat rent   (M986)

Re Pastore, Il: L'Amero Saro
Costante, For Solo Voice And
Orchestra
"Königliche Schäfer, Der: Dein Bin
Ich, For Solo Voice And
Orchestra" sc,pts BREITKOPF-L
rent   (M987)

Rivolgete A Lui Lo Sguardo, For Solo
Voice And Orchestra *K.584
BREITKOPF-L perf mat rent   (M988)

Rondo for Trumpet and String
Orchestra, [arr.]
(Thilde, J.) string orch,hpsd,trp
solo [8'] sc BILLAUDOT f.s., perf
mat rent   (M989)

Rondo for Violin and Orchestra in B
flat, K. 269
see Mozart Violin Concerti, The

Schauspieldirektor, Der: Bester
Jüngling! Mit Entzücken, For Solo
Voice And Orchestra
0.0.2.2. 2.0.0.0. strings,S solo
BREITKOPF-L perf mat rent (M990)

Schauspieldirektor, Der: Ich Bin Die
Erste Sangerin, For Solo Voices
And Orchestra
"Impresario: Ich Bin Die Erste
Sangerin, For Solo Voices And
Orchestra" KALMUS A6251 sc $6.00,
set $12.00, pts $1.00, ea. (M991)

Schauspieldirektor, Der: Liebes
Mandel, Wo Ist's Bandel, For Solo
Voices And Orchestra, [arr.]
2.2.0.2. 2.0.0.0. strings,STB
soli
(Seidelmann) BREITKOPF-L perf mat
rent   (M992)

Schauspieldirektor, Der: Männer
Suchen Stets Zu Naschen, For Solo
Voice And Orchestra
2ob,2horn,strings,S solo
BREITKOPF-L perf mat rent   (M993)

Schon Lacht Der Holde Fruhling, For
Solo Voice And Orchestra *K.580
(Seidelman) KALMUS A7051 sc $8.00,
set $12.00, pts $1.25, ea. (M994)
(Seidelmann) BREITKOPF-L sc PB 4010
f.s., pts OB 4010 f.s.   (M995)

Se Al Labbro Mio Non Credi, For Solo
Voice And Orchestra *K.295
 .2.2.0.2. 2.0.0.0. strings,T solo
BÄREN. BA 4814 perf mat rent (M996)
BREITKOPF-L perf mat rent   (M997)

MOZART, WOLFGANG AMADEUS (cont'd.)

Se Ardire E Speranza, For Solo Voice
And Orchestra *K.82
 .2.0.0.0. 2.0.0.0. strings,S solo
BÄREN. BA 4804 perf mat rent (M998)
BREITKOPF-L perf mat rent   (M999)

Se Tutti I Mali Miei, For Solo
Voice And Orchestra *K.83
 .0.2.0.0. 2.0.0.0. strings,S solo
BÄREN. BA 4805 perf mat rent
                             (M1000)
BREITKOPF-L perf mat rent   (M1001)

Seraglio, Il: Overture
see Entfuhrung Aus Dem Serail, Die:
Overture

Serenade No. 8 in D, K. 286
KALMUS A3666 sc $12.00, ipr, set
$65.00, pts $3.50, ea.   (M1002)

Serenades, Nos.1-3, K. 100, K. 101,
K. 185
see Cassations Nos. 1-2, K. 63, K.
99

Serenades Nos. 4-6
min sc KALMUS K00955 $5.50 (M1003)

Si Mostra La Sorte, For Solo Voice
And Orchestra *K.209
 .0.2.0.0. 2.0.0.0. strings,T solo
BÄREN. BA 4807 perf mat rent
                             (M1004)
BREITKOPF-L perf mat rent   (M1005)

Sinfonia Concertante for Violin,
Viola and Orchestra in E flat, K.
364
(Mahling, Christoph-Hellmut) sc
BÄREN. $6.90   (M1006)

Sinfonia Concertante in E flat, K.
297b *reconstruction
(Levin, Robert D.) 2ob,2horn,
strings,fl solo,ob solo,horn
solo,bsn solo [26'] BÄREN.
BA 7137   (M1007)

Small Orchestral Works, K. Anh. 1,
Nos. 9 & 10, K. 102, 120, 163,
291
min sc KALMUS K0091 $5.50   (M1008)

Sogno Di Scipione, Il: Overture
(Lederer, Josef Horst) BÄREN.
BA 4577   (M1009)

Sonatas For Organ And Orchestra,
Twelve
(contains K.67, 68, 144, 145, 212,
224, 245, 274, 278, 328, 329,
336) min sc KALMUS K00989 $5.50
                             (M1010)
Sposo Deluso, Lo: Overture [6']
2.2.0.2. 2.2.0.0. timp,strings
BREITKOPF-W perf mat rent   (M1011)

Sylphe Des Friedens, Der, For Solo
Voice And Orchestra, [arr.]
*K.152
(Mottl) 0.1.2.2. 2.0.0.0. strings,S
solo BREITKOPF-L perf mat rent
                             (M1012)
Symphonie Concertante for Violin,
Viola and Orchestra in E flat, K.
364
see Concerti for Violin and
Orchestra, Nos. 1-5

Symphonie Concertante in A, K. 320e
*reconstruction
(Wilby, Philip) 2ob,2horn,strings,
vln solo,vla solo,vcl solo [12']
CHESTER perf mat rent   (M1013)

Symphonies, K. 75, 76, 81, 95, 96, 97
min sc KALMUS K00990 $5.50   (M1014)

Symphonies Nos. 1-8
min sc KALMUS K00948 $6.00   (M1015)

Symphonies Nos. 9-16
min sc KALMUS K00949 $8.00   (M1016)

Symphonies Nos. 17-21
min sc KALMUS K00950 $6.00   (M1017)

Symphonies Nos. 22-26
min sc KALMUS K00951 $5.75   (M1018)

Symphonies Nos. 27-31
min sc KALMUS K00952 $6.00   (M1019)

Symphonies Nos. 32-34, 37
min sc KALMUS K00953 $6.00   (M1020)

Symphonies, Vol. 1 *CC32U
sc RICORDI-IT $42.00 contains: 32
symphonies, K.16-183   (M1021)

Symphonies, Vol. 1
(Allroggen, Gerhard) sc BÄREN. f.s.
                             (M1022)

MOZART, WOLFGANG AMADEUS (cont'd.)

Symphonies, Vol. 2
(contains: 17 symphonies, K.184-
551) sc RICORDI-IT $42.00 (M1023)
(Allroggen, Gerhard) (1770-1772) sc
BÄREN. $76.00 (M1024)

Symphony in B flat, K. Anh. 216
(in this edition called Symphony
No. 54) KALMUS A4146 sc $5.00,
set $18.00, perf mat rent (M1025)

Symphony in C, K. 96
KALMUS A6158 sc $5.00, set $10.00
(M1026)

Symphony in D, K. 81
KALMUS A6156 sc $5.00, set $9.00
(M1027)

Symphony in D, K. 95
KALMUS A6157 sc $5.00, set $10.00
(M1028)

Symphony in D, K. 97
KALMUS A6159 sc $5.00, set $10.00
(M1029)

Symphony in D, K. 141a
(Fischer) (Overture to Il Sogno di
Scipione, K. 126, K. 161, K. 163)
KALMUS A7400 sc $12.00, set
$25.00, pts $2.50, ea., perf mat
rent (M1030)

Symphony in D, K. 196, K. 121
(Beck) (Overture to La Finta
Giardiniera, K. 196 and K. 121
(207a)) KALMUS A7287 sc $10.00,
set $20.00, pts $2.50, ea., perf
mat rent (M1031)

Symphony in E minor, K. 16a [14']
0.2.0.2. 2.0.0.0. strings
(Plath, Wolfgang) (Odense Symphony)
BÄREN. BA 4845 perf mat rent
(M1032)

Symphony in F, K. 76
KALMUS A6155 sc $5.00, set $10.00
(M1033)

Symphony No. 15 in G, K. 124
BREITKOPF-W perf mat rent (M1034)

Symphony No. 16 in C, K. 128
(Beck) KALMUS A7327 sc $7.00, set
$22.00, pts $2.50, ea., perf mat
rent (M1035)

Symphony No. 17 in G, K. 129
(Beck) KALMUS A7292 sc $7.00, set
$20.00, pts $2.50, ea., perf mat
rent (M1036)

Symphony No. 18 in F, K. 130
(Beck) KALMUS A7291 sc $10.00, set
$25.00, pts $2.50, ea., perf mat
rent (M1037)

Symphony No. 19 in E flat, K. 132
(Fischer) KALMUS A7399 sc $15.00,
set $25.00, pts $2.50, ea., perf
mat rent (M1038)

Symphony No. 20 in D, K. 133
(Beck) KALMUS A7290 sc $12.00, set
$25.00, pts $2.50, ea., perf mat
rent (M1039)

Symphony No. 21 in A, K. 134
(Fischer) KALMUS A7398 sc $12.00,
set $22.50, pts $2.50, ea., perf
mat rent (M1040)

Symphony No. 29 in A, K. 201
(Darvas) study sc EMB 40012 f.s.
(M1041)

Symphony No. 30 in D, K. 202
(Beck) KALMUS A7395 sc $12.00, set
$27.50, pts $2.50, ea., perf mat
rent (M1042)

Symphony No. 31 in D, K. 297
(Beck) KALMUS A7289 sc $32.00, set
$60.00, pts $3.50, ea., perf mat
rent (M1043)

Symphony No. 33 in B flat, K. 319
(Darvas) study sc EMB 40050 f.s.
(M1044)

Symphony No. 34 in C, K. 338
(Redlich, Hans) min sc EULENBURG
EU00542 $6.00 contains also:
Minuet, K. 409 (M1045)

Symphony No. 35 in D, K. 385
(Landon, H.C.R.) study sc FABER
$12.50 (M1046)

Symphony No. 36 in C, K. 425
(Darvas) study sc EMB 40037 f.s.
(M1047)

Symphony No. 38 in D, K. 504
(Darvas) study sc EMB 40014 f.s.
(M1048)

Symphony No. 39 in E flat, K. 543
(Darvas) study sc EMB 40018 f.s.
(M1049)

MOZART, WOLFGANG AMADEUS (cont'd.)

Symphony No. 40 in G minor, K. 550
(Darvas) study sc EMB 40013 f.s.
(M1050)

Symphony No. 41 in C, K. 551
(Darvas) study sc EMB 40016 f.s.
(M1051)
(Haan, Stefan De) min sc EULENBURG
EU00401 $6.00 (M1052)

Tanze Und Marsche
(Flothuis, Marius) sc BÄREN.
$108.00 (M1053)

Titus: Jetzt, Vitellia! Schlägt Die
Stunde; Nie Soll Mit Rosen, For
Solo Voice And Orchestra
see Clemenza Di Tito, La: Ecco Il
Punto; Non Piu Di Fiori, For Solo
Voice And Orchestra

Titus: Lass Es Einmal Nur Geschehen,
For Solo Voice And Orchestra
see Clemenza Di Tito, La: Deh, Per
Questo Istante Solo, For Solo
Voice And Orchestra

Va, Dal Furor Portata, For Solo Voice
And Orchestra *K.21
0.2.0.2. 2.0.0.0. strings,T solo
BÄREN. BA 4796 perf mat rent
(M1054)
BREITKOPF-L perf mat rent (M1055)

Vado, Ma Dove, For Solo Voice And
Orchestra *K.583
0.0.2.2. 2.0.0.0. strings,S solo
BÄREN. BA 4838 perf mat rent
(M1056)
BREITKOPF-L perf mat rent (M1057)

Violinkonzerte Und Einzelsatze
see Concerti for Violin and
Orchestra

Voi Avete Un Cor Fedele, For Solo
Voice And Orchestra *K.217
0.2.0.0. 2.0.0.0. strings,S solo
BÄREN. BA 4809 perf mat rent
(M1058)
BREITKOPF-L perf mat rent (M1059)

Vorrei Spiegarvi, Oh Dio, For Solo
Voice And Orchestra *K.418
0.2.0.2. 2.0.0.0. strings,S solo
BÄREN. BA 4822 perf mat rent
(M1060)
BREITKOPF-L perf mat rent (M1061)

Zaïde: Ruhe Sanft, For Solo Voice And
Orchestra
BREITKOPF-L perf mat rent (M1062)

Zauberflöte, Die: Ach, Ich Fühl's, Es
Ist Verschwunden, For Solo Voice
And Orchestra
BREITKOPF-L perf mat rent (M1063)

Zauberflöte, Die: Bei Männern, For
Solo Voices And Orchestra
BREITKOPF-L perf mat rent (M1064)

Zauberflöte, Die: Der Hölle Rache,
For Solo Voice And Orchestra
2.2.0.2. 2.2.0.0. timp,strings,S
solo
BREITKOPF-L perf mat rent (M1065)

Zauberflöte, Die: Der Vogelfänger Bin
Ich Ja, For Solo Voice And
Orchestra
BREITKOPF-L perf mat rent (M1066)

Zauberflöte, Die: Dies Bildnis Ist
Bezaubernd Schön, For Solo Voice
And Orchestra
BREITKOPF-L perf mat rent (M1067)

Zauberflöte, Die: Ein Mädchen Oder
Weibchen, For Solo Voice And
Orchestra
BREITKOPF-L perf mat rent (M1068)

Zauberflöte, Die: In Diesen Heil'gen
Hallen, For Solo Voice And
Orchestra
BREITKOPF-L perf mat rent (M1069)

Zauberflöte, Die: O Zitt're Nicht,
For Solo Voice And Orchestra
BREITKOPF-L perf mat rent (M1070)

Zauberflote, Die: Overture
2.2.2.2. 1.2.3.0. timp,glock,
strings
(Gruber, Gernot; Orel, Alfred)
BÄREN. BA 4553 (M1071)

Zauberflöte, Die: Pa-Pa-Pa-
Papapagena, For Solo Voices And
Orchestra
BREITKOPF-L perf mat rent (M1072)

MOZART, WOLFGANG AMADEUS (cont'd.)

Zwei Fugen Und Eine Fantasie
(Hoffmann) string orch KALMUS A7096
sc $10.00, set $10.00, pts $2.00,
ea.
contains: Fantasie, K.608,
[arr.]; Fuge, K.401, [arr.];
Fuge, K.546, [arr.] (M1073)

MOZART VARIATIONEN, FOR TRUMPET AND
ORCHESTRA see Etti, Karl

MOZART VIOLIN CONCERTI, THE see Mozart,
Wolfgang Amadeus

MU, FOR CLARINET AND CHAMBER ORCHESTRA
see Smith, William Overton

MUCH ADO see Sigurbjörnsson, Thorkell

MUCH ADO ABOUT NOTHING see Mohaupt,
Richard

MUCZYNSKI, ROBERT STANLEY (1929-   )
Cavalcade *Op.39
SHAWNEE perf mat rent (M1074)

Serenade For Summer
SHAWNEE perf mat rent (M1075)

MUFF.1 see Klein, Leonard

MUGUNG-DONG see Yun, Isang

MULATTO, IL: SUITE see Meyerowitz, Jan

MULDER, HERMAN (1894-   )
Suite, Op. 30
4.3.3.3. 4.2.3.0. timp,harp,
strings
sc DONEMUS f.s., perf mat rent
(M1076)

MULDOWNEY, DOMINIC (1952-   )
Concerto for Piano and Orchestra
[25']
2(pic).2.2+bass clar.2+
contrabsn.alto sax. 4.3.3.1.
2perc,strings,pno solo
sc UNIVER. UE17637 $45.00, perf mat
rent (M1077)

Concerto for Saxophone and Orchestra
[20']
1(pic,alto fl).1(English
horn).1(bass
clar).1(contrabsn). 1.1.1.0.
perc,pno,strings,alto sax solo
sc UNIVER. UE 17671 $62.50, perf
mat rent (M1078)

Driftwood To The Flow [15']
18 strings
NOVELLO perf mat rent (M1079)

Music At Chartres [12']
2(pic).1.2.0. 0.2.1.0. 2perc,pno,
claves,strings
NOVELLO perf mat rent (M1080)

Perspectives [15']
2.2.2.2. 4.2.2.1. 2perc,timp,
strings
NOVELLO perf mat rent (M1081)

Sinfonietta [18']
1(pic).1.1(bass
clar).1(contrabsn). 1.1.1.0.
perc,pno,2vln,vla,vcl,db
UNIVER. perf mat rent (M1082)

MULLENBACH, ALEXANDER (1949-   )
Reflexe II [17']
3+pic.2+English horn.3+clar in E
flat+bass clar.2+contrabsn.
4.4.3.1. timp,perc,harp,cel,
pno,strings
DOBLINGER perf mat rent (M1083)

Stimmen Der Nacht, For Solo Voice And
Orchestra [23']
3(pic).2+English horn.3(clar in E
flat)+bass clar.2+contrabsn.
4.3.3.1. timp,perc,harp,cel,
pno,strings,S solo
DOBLINGER perf mat rent (M1084)

MÜLLER, KARL FRANZ (1922-   )
Drei Griechische Tanze
2.2.2.2. 4.2.3.0. timp,perc,harp,
strings
KRENN (M1085)

MULLER-HORNBACH, GERHARD (1951-   )
Gesange Der Schirin, For Solo Voice,
Viola d'Amore And String
Orchestra [20']
21strings,vla d'amore solo,S solo
study sc BREITKOPF-W PB5163 f.s.,
perf mat rent (M1086)

Passacaglia No. 1 [15']
2.2.2.3(contrabsn). 4.2.3.0.
strings
sc BREITKOPF-W f.s., perf mat rent
(M1087)

MULLER-HORNBACH, GERHARD (cont'd.)

Passacaglia No. 2 [15']
  1.1.0+bass clar.1. 1.1.2.0. 2vln,
  vla,vcl,db
  sc BREITKOPF-W f.s., perf mat rent
                                    (M1088)

Wandlungen In D [10']
  4(pic,alto fl).4(English
  horn).4(clar in E flat,bass
  clar).4. 5.4.4.1. 2perc,strings
  sc BREITKOPF-W f.s., perf mat rent
                                    (M1089)

MÜLLER-MARC, RAYMUND
Kapriziose Begegnung
  (Mohr, Gerhard) 2.1.2.1. 2.0.0.0.
  perc,acord,strings TONOS (M1090)

Kleines Erlebnis
  (Mohr, Gerhard) 2.1.2.1. 2.0.0.0.
  perc,acord,strings TONOS (M1091)

Spielerei
  (Mohr, Gerhard) 2.1.2.1. 2.0.0.0.
  perc,acord,strings TONOS (M1092)

MÜLLER-MEDEK, TILO
see MEDEK, TILO

MÜLLER-SIEMENS, DETLEV (1957-   )
Concerto for Viola and Orchestra
  [18']
  2(pic).4.2.2.alto sax. 4.3.2.1.
  perc,pno,6vln,4vcl,4db,vla solo
  SCHOTTS perf mat rent   (M1093)

Lieder Und Pavanen, For Solo Voice
  And Orchestra [35']
  3(pic).3.3(bass
  clar).3(contrabsn). 4.3(trp in
  D).3.1. strings,T solo
  SCHOTTS   (M1094)

Under Moonlight I
  sc ARS VIVA $13.50   (M1095)
  sc ARS VIVA $13.50   (M1096)

MÜLLER-ZÜRICH, PAUL (1898-   )
Dorisches Stuck, For Violoncello And
  String Orchestra [5']
  string orch,vcl solo
  HUG GH 10300 perf mat rent (M1097)

MÜLLICH, HERMANN (1943-   )
Dualismen
  string orch
  sc,pts RIES f.s.   (M1098)

MUNCH-MUSIK see Schmidt, Christfried

MUNICH SYMPHONY see Einem, Gottfried
von

MUNNHARPELAT [ARR.] see Storbekken,
Egil

MURA DELLA CITTA DI DITE see Dufourt,
Hugues

MURAIL, TRISTAN (1947-   )
De Terre Et De Ciel [15']
  4(pic,alto fl).4(English
  horn).4(bass
  clar).4(contrabsn). 4.4.4.1.
  4perc,2harp,pno,strings
  SALABERT perf mat rent   (M1099)

Derive Des Continents, La, For Viola
  And String Orchestra [18']
  string orch,vla solo
  RIDEAU perf mat rent   (M1100)

Desintegrations [22']
  2.1.2.1. 1.1.1.0. 2perc,pno,2vln,
  vla,vcl,db,electronic tape
  SALABERT perf mat rent   (M1101)

Sables [16']
  RIDEAU perf mat rent   (M1102)

Sillages [18']
  4(pic,alto fl).3(English
  horn).4(bass
  clar).3(contrabsn). 4.4.3.1.
  4perc,harp,cel,pno,strings
  SALABERT perf mat rent   (M1103)

Time And Again [18']
  3(pic).3.4.2(contrabsn). 4.3.3.1.
  4perc,pno,strings,synthesizer
  SALABERT EAS18343P perf mat rent
                                    (M1104)

MURRAY, LYN (1909-1989)
American Overture [4'30"]
  3+pic.2+English horn.3.2+
  contrabsn. 4.3.3.1. timp,perc,
  strings
  NEWAM 19000 perf mat rent (M1105)

Grand Banks [5']
  3+pic.2.3.2+contrabsn. 4.3.3.1.
  timp,perc,strings
  NEWAM 19031 perf mat rent (M1106)

MURTO, MATTI (1947-   )
Fantasies For Strings [10'30"]
  string orch
  sc FAZER f.s., perf mat rent
                                    (M1107)

MUSAIQUES, FOR PERCUSSION AND ORCHESTRA
see Reibel, Guy

MUSE ET LE POETE, LA, FOR VIOLIN, CELLO
AND ORCHESTRA see Saint-Saëns,
Camille

MUSE QUI EST LA GRACE, LA, FOR SOLO
VOICES AND ORCHESTRA see Cecconi,
Monic

MUSEN QUADRILLE see Strauss, Johann,
[Sr.]

MUSEUM MUSIC, FOR HARPSICHORD AND
STRINGS see Vieru, Anatol

MUSGRAVE, THEA (1928-   )
Peripeteia [15']
  study sc NOVELLO 2839-90 $16.00,
  perf mat rent   (M1108)

Soliloquy II, For Guitar And
  Orchestra [10']
  1(pic).2.0.1. 0.0.0.0. strings,
  gtr solo
  CHESTER perf mat rent   (M1109)

Theme And Interludes [11']
  2.1.3.1. 2.2.1.0. 6perc,strings
  NOVELLO perf mat rent   (M1110)

MUSIC, FOR VIOLA AND ORCHESTRA see
Stranz, Ulrich, Auguri

MUSIC AT CHARTRES see Muldowney,
Dominic

MUSIC BOX see Ballou, Philip

MUSIC CONCERTANT see Bozic, Darijan,
Koncertantna Glasba

MUSIC CONCERTANT, FOR WIND QUINTET AND
ORCHESTRA see Golob, Jani,
Koncertantna Glasba, For Wind
Quintet And Orchestra

MUSIC FOR A CELEBRATION see Louie,
Alexina

MUSIC FOR A CONCERT see Hervig, Richard
B.

MUSIC FOR A LARGE ENSEMBLE see Reich,
Steve

MUSIC FOR A POETIC READING see
Siekmann, Frank H.

MUSIC FOR A PUPPET COURT see Knussen,
Oliver

MUSIC FOR A THOUSAND AUTUMNS see Louie,
Alexina

MUSIC FOR CARLOW see Blackford, Richard

MUSIC FOR CHUANG TZU see De Vos Malan,
Jacques

MUSIC FOR EIGHTEEN MUSICIANS see Reich,
Steve

MUSIC FOR FILMS, VOL. 1 see
Shostakovich, Dmitri

MUSIC FOR FILMS, VOL. 2 see
Shostakovich, Dmitri

MUSIC FOR J.S. see Benes, Juraj, Hudba
Pre J.S.

MUSIC FOR JAPAN see Sculthorpe, Peter
[Joshua]

MUSIC FOR ORCHESTRA see Rojko, Uroš,
Glasba For Orkester

MUSIC FOR ORCHESTRA I
  (Kallmann, Helmut) CAN.MUS.HER.
  ISBN 0-919883-09-5 f.s.
  contains: Couture, Guillaume,
  Reverie; Dessane, Antoine,
  Overture; Forsyth, W.O.,
  Romance; Lucas, Clarence,
  Macbeth; MacMillan, [Sir] Ernest
  Campbell, Overture; Mathieu,
  Rodolphe, Trois Preludes; Vezina,
  Joseph, Ton Sourire   (M1111)

MUSIC FOR PSYCHOPATHS see Björklund,
Staffan

MUSIC FOR SAN FRANCISCO see Milhaud,
Darius

MUSIC FOR STRINGS see Srebotnjak, Alojz
F., Glasba Za Godala

MUSIC FOR SYMPHONY ORCHESTRA AND JAZZ
ENSEMBLE see Bartles, Alfred H.

MUSIC FOR THE THEATER see Shostakovich,
Dmitri

MUSIC FOR THE TOWN OF KOTHEN see
Shchedrin, Rodion

MUSIC FOR TWELVE see Kirchner, Leon

MUSIC FROM THE FIFTH STRING see Wright,
Maurice

MUSIC FROM THE 1920'S: THE MEMORIES
OVERTURE see Waxman, Franz

MUSIC OF FALLING LEAVES see Buczynski,
Pawel, Fallende Blatter

MUSIC OF THE CANVAS see Ott, David

MUSIC-PICTURES (GROUP IV) see Foulds,
John Herbert

MUSIC: THE INSIDE STORY, FOR NARRATOR
AND ORCHESTRA see Peck, Russell
James

MUSIC TO CELEBRATE THE RESURRECTION OF
CHRIST see Saxton, Robert

MUSIC TO GALDRA-LOFTR see Leifs, Jon

MUSIC TO V.HLOZNIK see Hrušovsky, Ivan,
Hudba K V.Hloznikovi

MUSICA AD MOREM MAIORUM see Lajovic,
Aleksander

MUSICA CONCERTANTE see Bergamo, Petar
see Huszar, Lajos

MUSICA CONCERTANTE, FOR DOUBLE BASS AND
ORCHESTRA see Szalonek, Witold

MUSICA CONQUISITA PRO FIDICINA ET
CORDARUM SONUS, FOR HARP AND STRING
ORCHESTRA see Angerer, Paul

MUSICA DA CAMERA NO.4, FOR PIANO AND
ORCHESTRA see Eklund, Hans

MUSICA DA CAMERA NO. 6, FOR OBOE AND
ORCHESTRA see Eklund, Hans

MUSICA DA CONCERTO, FOR HARPSICHORD AND
CHAMBER ORCHESTRA see Bonifacio,
Mauro

MUSICA DA CONCERTO NO. 7, FOR GUITAR
AND STRINGS see Testi, Flavio

MUSICA DE DON QUIJOTE see Arteaga,
Angel

MUSICA DOLOROSA see Vasks, Peteris

MUSICA DOMESTICA see Bujarski, Zbigniew

MUSICA EXANIMATA, FOR VIOLONCELLO AND
CHAMBER ORCHESTRA see Angerer, Paul

MUSICA FRANCESCANA, FOR SOLO VOICE AND
ORCHESTRA see Ferrari, Giorgio

MUSICA GIOCOSA see Farkas, Ferenc

MUSICA HUMANA see Dello Joio, Justin

MUSICA INCIDENTALE PER "BRAND" D'IBSEN
see Kielland, Olav

MUSICA INCROSTATA see Meyer, Krzysztof

MUSICA LEGGIERA I see Ostendorf, Jens-
Peter

MUSICA LUMINOSA see Kelterborn, Rudolf

MUSICA NOTTURNA see Szekely, Endre

MUSICA PARA 11 see Homs, Joaquin

MUSICA PARA UN FESTIVAL see Arteaga,
Angel

MUSICA PARA UN FESTIVAL EN SEVILLA see
Alis, Roman

MUSICA PARA UN JARDIN see Rodrigo,
Joaquín

MUSICA PARA UN POEMA A LA ALHAMBRA see
Rodrigo, Joaquín

MUSICA PER 15 see Mihaly, Andras

MUSICA PER BRUNO see Mantero, Ajmone

MUSICA PERMUTATIO see Larsson, Lars-
Erik

MUSICA POETICA see Vacek, Miloš

MUSICA RESERVATA, FOR SYMPHONIC BAND AND SYMPHONY ORCHESTRA see Kox, Hans

MUSICA SACRA see Tcherepnin, Alexander

MUSICA TONALIS see Bjelinski, Bruno

MUSICAL CONTRASTS see Karkoff, Maurice

MUSICAL OFFERING, A (J.S.B. 1985) see Goehr, Alexander

MUSICAL OFFERING [ARR.] see Bach, Johann Sebastian, Musikalisches Opfer [arr.]

MUSICAL SNUFF BOX, THE [ARR.] see Liadov, Anatol Konstantinovich

MUSICAL TOAST, A see Bernstein, Leonard

MUSICAL WORKS. LEIPZIG, 1905-1906 see Cornelius, Peter

MUSICAMERA see Nobre, Marlos

MUSICK'S HANDMAID: FIRST SUITE [ARR.] (Cruft, Adrian) string orch [10'] (contains 7 movements by John Blow and anonymous composers) sc JOAD f.s., perf mat rent (M1112)

MUSICK'S HANDMAID: SECOND SUITE [ARR.] (Cruft, Adrian) string orch [7'] (contains 5 movements by Henry Purcell and anonymous composers) sc JOAD f.s., perf mat rent (M1113)

MUSICK'S HANDMAID: THIRD SUITE [ARR.] (Cruft, Adrian) string orch [8'] (contains 8 movements by Matthew Locke and Henry Purcell) sc JOAD f.s., perf mat rent (M1114)

MUSICK'S HANDMAID: FOURTH SUITE [ARR.] (Cruft, Adrian) string orch [9'] (contains 8 movements by anonymous composers) sc JOAD f.s., perf mat rent (M1115)

MUSIK DER FRUHE see Nunes, Emmanuel

MUSIK FÖR EN SJUK VARLD see Ericsson, Hans-Ola

MUSIK FUR DIE STADT KOTHEN see Shchedrin, Rodion, Music For The Town Of Kothen

MUSIK FÜR JOHANNA see Evensen, Bernt Kasberg

MUSIK FUR KLEINES ORCHESTER see Krebs, Joachim

MUSIK FUR TASTENINSTRUMENTEN UND ORCHESTER see Kagel, Mauricio

MUSIK OHNE FILM see Ostendorf, Jens-Peter

MUSIK OHNE RENAISSANCE POUR 18 INSTRUMENTS DE LA RENAISSANCE see Monnet, Marc

MUSIK OHNE RENAISSANCE POUR 18 INSTRUMENTS MODERNES see Monnet, Marc

MUSIK UBER DREI ALTDEUTSCHE VOLKSLIEDER see Blum, Robert

MUSIKALISCHE SCHLITTENFAHRT, DIE see Mozart, Leopold

MUSIKALISCHES OPFER [ARR.] see Bach, Johann Sebastian

MUSIKALISCHES OPFER: RICERCARE A 3 UND 8 KANONS [ARR] see Bach, Johann Sebastian

MUSIKANTISK OUVERTURE see Weis, Flemming

MUSIKK TIL EN BY VED HAVET see Solås, Eyvind

MUSIKSTUCK see Maione, Rino

MUSIQUE, FOR ORGAN AND STRING ORCHESTRA see Morancon, Guy

MUSIQUE CONCERTANTE see Ponse, Luctor

MUSIQUE CONCERTANTE, FOR 2 HARPSICHORDS AND CHAMBER ORCHESTRA see Wanek, Friedrich K.

MUSIQUE EN COULEURS see Gotkovsky, Ida

MUSIQUE EN MEMOIRE, FOR SOLO VOICES AND ORCHESTRA see Gougeon, Denis

MUSIQUE POUR ARS NOVA see Milhaud, Darius

MUSIQUE POUR CELEBRER LA MEMOIRE DES GRANDS HOMMES see Reicha, Anton

MUSIQUE POUR FAIRE PLAISIR [ARR.] see Poulenc, Francis

MUSIQUE POUR HAMLET see Cools, Eugène

MUSIQUE POUR LES SOUPERS DU ROI UBU see Zimmermann, Bernd Alois

MUSIQUE POUR UN PETIT PRINCE see Le Roux, Maurice

MUSIQUES ET MUSIQUES see Levinas, Michael

MUSIQUETTES III, FOR ACCORDION AND STRING ORCHESTRA see Strietman, Willem

MUSSORGSKY, MODEST PETROVICH (1839-1881) Berceuse Du Paysan, For Solo Voice And Orchestra [arr] (Rimsky-Korsakov, N.) 2.2.2.2. 2.0.0.0. strings,Mez solo [6'] BREITKOPF-W perf mat rent (M1116)

Bilder Einer Ausstellung [arr.] see Pictures At An Exhibition [arr.]

Boris Godunov: Death Of Boris, For Solo Voice And Orchestra "Boris Godunov: Leb Wohl, Mein Sohn, For Solo Voice And Orchestra" BREITKOPF-L perf mat rent (M1117)

Boris Godunov: Die Höchste Macht Ist Mein, For Solo Voice And Orchestra see Boris Godunov: Monologue Of Boris, For Solo Voice And Orchestra

Boris Godunov: Gestattet Ihr, Dem Enscheinbaren Knechte Gottes, For Solo Voices And Orchestra see Boris Godunov: May A Humble Slave Of God, For Solo Voices And Orchestra

Boris Godunov: Hört, Was Einst In Der Stadt Kasan Geschehen, For Solo Voice And Orchestra see Boris Godunov: Varlaam's Song, For Solo Voice And Orchestra

Boris Godunov: Leb Wohl, Mein Sohn, For Solo Voice And Orchestra see Boris Godunov: Death Of Boris, For Solo Voice And Orchestra

Boris Godunov: May A Humble Slave Of God, For Solo Voices And Orchestra 3.2.3.2. 4.3.3.1. timp,2harp, strings,BMez soli "Boris Godunov: Gestattet Ihr, Dem Enscheinbaren Knechte Gottes, For Solo Voices And Orchestra" BREITKOPF-L perf mat rent (M1118)

Boris Godunov: Monologue Of Boris, For Solo Voice And Orchestra "Boris Godunov: Die Höchste Macht Ist Mein, For Solo Voice And Orchestra" BREITKOPF-L perf mat rent (M1119)

Boris Godunov: Varlaam's Song, For Solo Voice And Orchestra "Boris Godunov: Hört, Was Einst In Der Stadt Kasan Geschehen, For Solo Voice And Orchestra" BREITKOPF-L perf mat rent (M1120)

Chanson De Mephistopheles, For Solo Voice And Orchestra [arr.] (Stravinsky) KALMUS A6951 sc $8.00, set $15.00, pts $1.00, ea. (M1121)

Chanson De Mephistopheles Dans Le Cave d'Auerbach, For Solo Voice And Orchestra [arr.] (Stravinsky, Igor) 3.2.2.2. 4.2.3.1. timp,strings,Bar/B solo [3'] BOOSEY perf mat rent (M1122)

Chowanschtschina: Vorspiel [arr.] see Khovantchina: Overture, [arr.]

Chowansjtsjina: Prélude, [arr.] see Khovantchina: Overture, [arr.]

Fair At Sorotchinsk, The: Gopak [arr] (Liadov, A.C.) 2+pic.2.2.2. 4.2.3.1. timp,2perc,strings [3'] BREITKOPF-W perf mat rent (M1123)

MUSSORGSKY, MODEST PETROVICH (cont'd.)

Gathering Mushrooms, For Solo Voice And Orchestra [arr.] (Rimsky-Korsakov) 2.2.2.1+ contrabsn. 4.0.0.0. timp,perc, strings,solo voice KALMUS A4647 sc $5.00, set $11.00, pts $.75, ea. (M1124)

Intermezzo *see RUSSIAN SYMPHONIC MUSIC, VOL. 4

Intermezzo In Modo Classico [9'] 2.2.2.2. 4.2.3.1. timp,perc, strings SIKORSKI perf mat rent (M1125)

Jahrmarkt Von Sorotschinzi, Der: Schöne Chiwria, For Solo Voice And Orchestra (from Fair At Sorotchinsk, The) 2.2.2.2. 4.2.3.0. perc,strings, Mez solo BREITKOPF-L perf mat rent (M1126)

Jahrmarkt Von Sorotschinzi, Der: Was Soll Dein Weinen, Liebster?, For Solo Voice And Orchestra (from Fair At Sorotchinsk, The) 3.2.2.2. 4.3.1.1. perc,harp, strings,S solo BREITKOPF-L perf mat rent (M1127)

Khovantchina: Furchterlich Ist Dieser Liebe Qual, For Solo Voice And Orchestra [arr] (Borg, K.) 2.2(English horn).2.2. 2.0.0.0. timp,opt perc,strings, Mez solo [5'] BREITKOPF-W perf mat rent (M1128)

Khovantchina: Höret Mich An, Geheime Mächte, For Solo Voices And Orchestra see Khovantchina: Ye Powers Concealed From Us, For Solo Voices And Orchestra

Khovantchina: Overture, [arr.] (Blomhert, Bastiaan) "Chowansjtsjina: Prélude, [arr.]" 3.2.2.2. 4.0.0.0. 3perc,harp, strings [6'] sc DONEMUS f.s., perf mat rent (M1129) (Shostakovich, D.) "Chowanschtschina: Vorspiel [arr.]" 3.3.3.3. 4.0.0.0. timp, perc,2harp,cel,pno,strings [5'] SIKORSKI perf mat rent (M1130)

Khovantchina: Ye Powers Concealed From Us, For Solo Voices And Orchestra 3.2.2.2. 4.2.3.0. timp,drums, harp,strings,AT/MezT soli "Khovantchina: Höret Mich An, Geheime Mächte, For Solo Voices And Orchestra" BREITKOPF-L perf mat rent (M1131)

Kinderstube, For Solo Voice And Orchestra [arr.] see Nursery, The, For Solo Voice And Orchestra [arr.]

Lieder Und Tanze Des Todes, For Solo Voice And Orchestra [arr] see Songs And Dances Of Death, For Solo Voice And Orchestra [arr]

Lieder Und Tänze Des Todes: Der Feldherr, For Solo Voice And Orchestra, [arr.] see Songs And Dances Of Death: The Field Marshal, For Solo Voice And Orchestra, [arr.]

Lieder Und Tänze Des Todes: Ständchen, For Solo Voice And Orchestra, [arr.] see Songs And Dances Of Death: Serenade, For Solo Voice And Orchestra, [arr.]

Lieder Und Tänze Des Todes: Trepak, For Solo Voice And Orchestra, [arr.] see Songs And Dances Of Death: Trepak, For Solo Voice And Orchestra, [arr.]

Lieder Und Tänze Des Todes: Wiegenlied, For Solo Voice And Orchestra, [arr.] see Songs And Dances Of Death: Berceuse, For Solo Voice And Orchestra, [arr.]

Nacht Auf Dem Kahlen Berge, Eine see Night On Bald Mountain

Night On Bald Mountain [17'] 3.2.2.2. 4.2+2cornet.3.1. timp, perc,strings "Nacht Auf Dem Kahlen Berge, Eine"

MUSSORGSKY, MODEST PETROVICH (cont'd.)

SIKORSKI perf mat rent   (M1132)
(Kirkor; McAlister) KALMUS A5799 sc
$50.00, set $75.00, perf mat rent
(M1133)
*see RUSSIAN SYMPHONIC MUSIC,
VOL. 4

Nursery, The, For Solo Voice And
Orchestra [arr.]
(Shchedrin, R.) "Kinderstube, For
Solo Voice And Orchestra [arr.]"
3.3.2.2. 4.3.3.1. timp,2perc,
harp,cel,strings [21'] SIKORSKI
perf mat rent   (M1134)
(Shchedrin, Rodion) 3.3.2.2.
4.3.3.1. perc,cel,harp,strings,S
solo [19'] VAAP perf mat rent
(M1135)

Nursery, The [arr.]
(Denisov, Edison) 2.2.2.2. 4.3.3.1.
perc,cel,harp,strings VAAP perf
mat rent   (M1136)

Pictures At An Exhibition, For Piano
And Orchestra [arr.]
(Leonard, Lawrence)
3(pic).2(English horn).2(bass
clar).2(contrabsn). 4.3.3.1.
timp,3perc,strings,pno solo [29']
BOOSEY perf mat rent   (M1137)

Pictures At An Exhibition [arr.]
(Gortschakow, S.) "Bilder Einer
Ausstellung [arr.]" 3.3.4.3.
4.3.3.2. timp,perc,harp,cel,
strings [31'] SIKORSKI perf mat
rent   (M1138)
(Ravel, Maurice) study sc EMB 40104
f.s.   (M1139)

Roi Saul, Le, For Solo Voice And
Orchestra [arr]
(Glazunov, A.) 2.2.2.2. 4.2.3.0.
timp,strings,T solo [6']
BREITKOPF-W perf mat rent (M1140)

Scherzo *see RUSSIAN SYMPHONIC
MUSIC, VOL. 4

Scherzo in B flat [6']
2.2.2.2. 2.2.3.0. timp,strings
SIKORSKI perf mat rent   (M1141)

Scherzo in B flat, [arr.]
(Rimsky-Korsakov, N.) 2.2.2.2.
2.2.3.0. timp,strings [8']
BREITKOPF-W perf mat rent (M1142)

Seizure Of Karse, The *see RUSSIAN
SYMPHONIC MUSIC, VOL. 4

Songs And Dances Of Death, For Solo
Voice And Orchestra [arr]
(Borg, K.) "Lieder Und Tanze Des
Todes, For Solo Voice And
Orchestra [arr]" 2(pic).2+English
horn.2+bass clar.1+contrabsn.
4.2.3.1. timp,perc,xylo,strings,B
solo BREITKOPF-W perf mat rent
(M1143)
(Keulen, Geert Van) fl,ob,English
horn,clar,bass clar,bsn,
contrabsn,2horn,vcl,db,low solo
[18'] sc,pts DONEMUS f.s. (M1144)
(Shostakovich, D.) KALMUS A7118 sc
$22.00, set $60.00, pts $3.00,
ea., perf mat rent   (M1145)

Songs And Dances Of Death [arr.]
(Denisov, Edison) 2.2.2+bass
clar.0.alto sax. 4.3.3.1. perc,
cel,harp,strings VAAP perf mat
rent   (M1146)

Songs And Dances Of Death: Berceuse,
For Solo Voice And Orchestra,
[arr.]
(Glasunow) "Lieder Und Tänze Des
Todes: Wiegenlied, For Solo Voice
And Orchestra, [arr.]" 2.2.2.2.
2.2.0.0. timp,strings,Bar solo
BREITKOPF-L perf mat rent (M1147)

Songs And Dances Of Death: Serenade,
For Solo Voice And Orchestra,
[arr.]
(Liabounow) "Lieder Und Tänze Des
Todes: Ständchen, For Solo Voice
And Orchestra, [arr.]" 2.2.2.2.
2.2.0.0. timp,drums,xylo,harp,
strings,Bar solo BREITKOPF-L perf
mat rent   (M1148)

Songs And Dances Of Death: The Field
Marshal, For Solo Voice And
Orchestra, [arr.]
(Liabounow) "Lieder Und Tänze Des
Todes: Der Feldherr, For Solo
Voice And Orchestra, [arr.]"
3.2.2.2. 4.2.3.1. timp,perc,xylo,
strings,Bar solo BREITKOPF-L perf
mat rent   (M1149)

MUSSORGSKY, MODEST PETROVICH (cont'd.)

Songs And Dances Of Death: Trepak,
For Solo Voice And Orchestra,
[arr.]
(Rimski-Korsakow) "Lieder Und Tänze
Des Todes: Trepak, For Solo Voice
And Orchestra, [arr.]" 2.2.2.2.
2.2.3.0. timp,strings,Bar solo
BREITKOPF-L perf mat rent (M1150)

Sunless [arr.]
(Denisov, Edison) 2.2.2+bass
clar.0.alto sax. 4.3.3.1. perc,
cel,harp,strings VAAP perf mat
rent   (M1151)

To The Little Star, For Solo Voice
And Orchestra
2.2.2.2. 4.2.3.0. timp,harp,
strings,solo voice KALMUS A1862
sc $2.50, set $15.00, pts $.75,
ea., perf mat rent   (M1152)

MUT, MAN-CHUNG
Ambush On All Sides, For Pipa And
Orchestra [23']
3.2.2.2. 3.2.2.0. timp,perc,pno,
strings, pipa solo
HONG KONG perf mat rent   (M1153)

Princess Chang Ping, For Violin And
Orchestra
3.2.2.2. 4.2.3.1. timp,perc,cel,
pno,strings,vln solo
HONG KONG perf mat rent   (M1154)

MUTANZA see Lidholm, Ingvar

MUTATIONEN IN HONOREM J.S.B. see
Leitermeyer, Fritz

MUTATIONS see Bottje, Will Gay

MUTAZIONE I see Vosträk, Zbynek

MUTAZIONI see Denhoff, Michael

MUTAZIONI, FOR 2 PIANOS AND ORCHESTRA
see Wieslander, Ingvar

MÜTHEL, JOHANN GOTTFRIED (1728-1788)
Concerto For Harpsichord And String
Orchestra In D Minor *see THREE
CENTURIES OF MUSIC IN SCORE, VOL.
4: CONCERTO III, KEYBOARD

MUTUMISHI see Smith, Leo

MXPZKL see Tiensuu, Jukka

MXYZPTLK, FOR 2 FLUTES AND CHAMBER
ORCHESTRA see Daugherty, Michael

MY BLUES see Ferrero, Lorenzo

MY COUNTRY, NO. 1: VYSEHRAD see
Smetana, Bedrich

MY COUNTRY, NO. 2: THE MOLDAU see
Smetana, Bedrich

MY COUNTRY, NO. 3: SARKA see Smetana,
Bedrich

MY COUNTRY, NO. 4: FROM BOHEMIA'S
MEADOWS AND FORESTS see Smetana,
Bedrich

MY COUNTRY, NO. 5: TABOR see Smetana,
Bedrich

MY COUNTRY NO. 6: BLANIK see Smetana,
Bedrich

MY COWBOY LOVE SONG [ARR.] see Guion,
David Wendall Fentress

MY LITTLE MULE see Antonini, Alfredo

MY LOVE'S AN ARBUTUS see Boswell,
Robert

MY ONE AND ONLY [ARR.] see Gershwin,
George

MY ROCK see Ferrero, Lorenzo

MY WEARY HEART, FOR SOLO VOICE AND
ORCHESTRA see Eggen, Arne, Hald Ut,
Hjarte, For Solo Voices And
Orchestra

MYCIELSKI, ZYGMUNT (1907-   )
Symphony No. 5
3(pic).2+English horn.3.2+
contrabsn. 4.4.4.1. perc,harp,
pno,strings
sc POLSKIE f.s.   (M1155)

MYRIAD see Perlongo, Daniel James

MYRRHA, FOR SOLO VOICES AND ORCHESTRA
see Ravel, Maurice

MYRSKYLINTU, FOR SOLO VOICE AND
ORCHESTRA [ARR.] see Merikanto,
Oskar

MYRTELIUS, HUGO
Gothlandian Rhapsody
see Gotlandsk Rapsodi

Gotlandsk Rapsodi [12']
2.2.2.2. 2.2.3.1. timp,perc,
strings
"Gothlandian Rhapsody" BUSCH DM 029
perf mat rent   (M1156)

Sverige I Toner [16']
2.2.2.2. 2.2.3.1. timp,perc,
strings
"Sweden In Tunes" BUSCH HBM 007
perf mat rent   (M1157)

Sweden In Tunes
see Sverige I Toner

MYRTHEN-KRANZE WALZER see Strauss,
Johann, [Jr.]

MYRTHENBLUTHEN WALZER see Strauss,
Johann, [Jr.]

MYRTHENSTRAUSSCHEN WALZER see Strauss,
Eduard

MYSLIVECZEK, JOSEPH (1737-1781)
Sinfonia in D, MIN 153
2ob,2horn,strings
sc KUNZEL 10157 $12.00, ipa (M1158)

Sinfonia, Op. 1, No. 1, in D [8']
2ob,2horn,strings
SUPRAPHON   (M1159)

Sinfonia, Op. 1, No. 2, in G [10']
2ob,2horn,strings
SUPRAPHON   (M1160)

Sinfonia, Op. 1, No. 3, in C [9']
2ob,2horn,strings
SUPRAPHON   (M1161)

Sinfonia, Op. 1, No. 4, in F [12']
2ob,2horn,strings
SUPRAPHON   (M1162)

Sinfonia, Op. 1, No. 5, in G minor
[8']
2ob,2horn,strings
SUPRAPHON   (M1163)

Sinfonia, Op. 1, No. 6, in D [7']
2ob,2horn,strings
SUPRAPHON   (M1164)

Symphonies, Three
see Laube, Antonin, Symphony

Tre Notturni, For Solo Voices And
Orchestra [10']
2clar,2horn,strings,SS soli
SUPRAPHON   (M1165)

MYSTERIA see Marco, Tomas

MYSTERIENSONATE see Beyer, Frank
Michael

MYSTIC TRUMPETER, THE see Converse,
Frederick Shepherd

MYSTIC TRUMPETER, THE, FOR SOLO VOICE
AND ORCHESTRA see Holst, Gustav

MYTHOS see Solås, Eyvind

N

NA DUBROVACKI NACIM see Lewis, John
Aaron

NABUCCO: ANCH' IO DISCHIUSO UN GIORNO,
FOR SOLO VOICE AND ORCHESTRA see
Verdi, Giuseppe

NABUCCO: DONNA CHI SEI? FOR SOLO VOICES
AND ORCHESTRA see Verdi, Giuseppe

NABUCCO: OH, DISCHIUSO E IL FIRMAMENTO,
FOR SOLO VOICE AND ORCHESTRA see
Verdi, Giuseppe

NABUCCO: PRODE GUERRIER!... D'AMORE,
FOR SOLO VOICES AND ORCHESTRA see
Verdi, Giuseppe

NABUCCO: TU SUL LABBRO DE' VEGGENTI,
FOR SOLO VOICE AND ORCHESTRA see
Verdi, Giuseppe

NACH KURZER POST POLKA see Strauss,
Eduard

NACHKLANGE see Beck, Conrad

NACHKLANGE VON OSSIAN: OVERTURE see
Gade, Niels Wilhelm

NACHRUF see Nordheim, Arne

NACHT, DIE see Liszt, Franz, Trois Odes
Funebres: La Nuit

NACHT AUF DEM KAHLEN BERGE, EINE see
Mussorgsky, Modest Petrovich, Night
On Bald Mountain

NACHT IN VENEDIG, EINE: SELECTION see
Strauss, Johann, [Jr.]

NACHT UND TRÄUME, FOR SOLO VOICE AND
ORCHESTRA, [ARR.] see Schubert,
Franz (Peter)

NACHT UND TROMPETEN see Abrahamsen,
Hans

NACHTANZ see Egk, Werner

NACHTBLAU, FOR CLARINET AND STRING
ORCHESTRA see Renosto, Paolo

NACHTFALTER WALZER see Strauss, Johann,
[Jr.]

NACHTGEDANKEN see Medek, Tilo

NACHTGESANG, FOR SOLO VOICE AND
ORCHESTRA see Cerha, Friedrich

NACHTIGALL POLKA see Strauss, Johann,
[Jr.]

NACHTIGALLENTRAENEN, FOR SOLO VOICE AND
ORCHESTRA see Gürsching, Albrecht

NACHTLAGER IN GRANADA, DAS: EIN SCHÜTZ
BIN ICH, FOR SOLO VOICE AND
ORCHESTRA see Kreutzer, Konradin

NÄCHTLICHE HEERSCHAU, DIE, FOR SOLO
VOICE AND ORCHESTRA, [ARR.] see
Loewe, Carl Gottfried

NACHTLICHE ZUG, DER see Liszt, Franz

NACHTLIEDER, FOR SOLO VOICE AND
ORCHESTRA see Neikrug, Marc E.

NACHTMUSIK see Heuberger, Richard see
Mansurian, Tigran

NACHTMUSIK, FOR GUITAR AND ORCHESTRA
see Weiss, Harald

NACHTMUSIK- TRAUERMUSIK- FINALMUSIK see
Wimberger, Gerhard

NACHTSCHATTEN see Strauss, Josef

NACHTSTUCK see Bjelik, Martin

NACHTSTUCK, FOR VIOLA AND ORCHESTRA see
Kirchner, Volker David

NACHTWANDLUNG AUF FRAGMENTE VON GEORG
TRAKL, FOR SOLO VOICE AND
INSTRUMENTAL ENSEMBLE see Trojahn,
Manfred

NACIMENTO see Garcin, Gerard

NADELSON, ANDREW
Tapestry [10']
1(pic).1.1(bass clar).1. 1.1.1.0.
2vln,vla,vcl,db
sc APNM $13.00, perf mat rent   (N1)

NADERMANN, FRANCOIS-JOSEPH (1773-1835)
Concerto for Harp and Orchestra, No.
2
2.0.2.2. 2.2.0.0. strings,harp
solo
COSTALL C.3654 perf mat rent   (N2)

NAENIA see Vantus, Istvan

NAGRAS see Termos, Paul

NAIMA: INTERMEZZO see Loevendie, Theo

NAIMA: MUSIC FOR A STRANGE WEDDING see
Loevendie, Theo

NAIMA: SUITE see Loevendie, Theo

NAJADEN QUADRILLE see Strauss, Johann,
[Sr.]

NAKED MASKS see Consoli, Marc-Antonio

NAMENSFEIER OVERTURE see Beethoven,
Ludwig van

NAPOLEON see Honegger, Arthur

NAPOLI, JACOPO (1911-   )
Barone Avaro, Il: Preludio [5'5"]
2.2.2.2. 4.3.3.1. timp,perc,pno,
strings
CURCI perf mat rent   (N3)

Chaconne [8'30"]
string orch
sc CURCI 10350 perf mat rent   (N4)

NAPRAVNIK, EDUARD (1839-1916)
National Dances: Casatschiok *Op.20,
No.2 [7']
2.2.2.2. 4.2.3.1. timp,perc,
strings
RAHTER perf mat rent   (N5)

Russian Fantasy, For Piano And
Orchestra *Op.39
2.2.2.2. 2.2.3.0. timp,perc,
strings,pno solo
RAHTER perf mat rent   (N6)

Symphony No. 3, Op. 18
3.2.2.2. 4.2.3.1. timp,perc,harp,
strings
(The Demon) RAHTER perf mat rent
(N7)

NAR LINDEN BER LOV, FOR VIOLIN AND
ORCHESTRA see Grov, Magne

NARCISSUS, FOR SOLO VOICE AND ORCHESTRA
[ARR.] see Sibelius, Jean

NARDINI, PIETRO (1722-1793)
Adagio in E flat
(Bonelli) set KALMUS A7338 $13.00,
and up   (N8)

Concerto for Violin and String
Orchestra in G, MIN 361
(Nagy; Ney) EMB f.s. sc 5985, pts
5986   (N9)

NARRATION II, FOR SAXOPHONE AND
ORCHESTRA see Vieru, Anatol

NASH, PETER PAUL (1950-   )
Etudes For Orchestra, No. 1: On The
Beach [7']
3.3.3.3. 4.3.3.1. 2perc,pno,harp,
strings
FABER perf mat rent   (N10)

Etudes For Orchestra, No. 2: The
Empty Beach [7']
3.3.3.3. 4.3.3.1. 3perc,pno,harp,
strings
FABER perf mat rent   (N11)

Etudes For Orchestra, No. 3: Parting
[6']
3.3.3.3. 4.3.3.1. 2perc,pno,harp,
strings
FABER perf mat rent   (N12)

NASJONALSANG, FOR TRUMPET, TROMBONE AND
ORCHESTRA see Janson, Alfred,
National Anthem, For Trumpet,
Trombone And Orchestra

NATIONAL ANTHEM, FOR TRUMPET, TROMBONE
AND ORCHESTRA see Janson, Alfred

NATIONAL ANTHEM, "GOD SAVE THE QUEEN"
see Walton, [Sir] William (Turner)

NATIONAL ANTHEMS: WELSH; ENGLISH see
Mathias, William

NATIONAL DANCES: CASATSCHIOK see
Napravnik, Eduard

NATIONAL FENCIBLES MARCH see Sousa,
John Philip

NATOMA: GRAND FANTASIA see Herbert,
Victor

NATOMA: PRELUDE TO ACT III see Herbert,
Victor

NATTEN see Schierbeck, Poul

NATTJAKT, FOR SOLO VOICE AND ORCHESTRA
see Werle, Lars-Johan

NATTSTEN see Schuback, Peter

NATTSTYKKE see Skouen, Synne

NATURA RENOVATUR see Scelsi, Giacinto

NATURE MORTE - STILL ALIVE see Rihm,
Wolfgang

NATUREN see Fongaard, Bjørn

NATURE'S BREATH see Machover, Tod

NAUDOT, JACQUES-CHRISTOPHE
(ca. 1700-1762)
Concerto for Flute and String
Orchestra, Op. 11, No. 4
string orch,fl solo
(Petit, J.L.) [13'] BILLAUDOT
597-00365 sc $5.50, pts f.s.
(N13)

NAUDOT, JEAN JACQUES
see NAUDOT, JACQUES-CHRISTOPHE

NAUFRAGIO DE KLEONICOS see Villa-Lobos,
Heitor

NAUGHTY LIMERICKS see Shchedrin,
Rodion, Concerto for Orchestra, No.
1

NAUGHTY MARIETTA: AH! SWEET MYSTERY OF
LIFE, FOR SOLO VOICES AND
ORCHESTRA, [ARR.] see Herbert,
Victor

NAUGHTY MARIETTA: I'M FALLING IN LOVE
WITH SOMEONE, FOR SOLO VOICE AND
ORCHESTRA, [ARR.] see Herbert,
Victor

NAVARRA, FOR TWO VIOLINS AND ORCHESTRA
see Sarasate, Pablo de

NAVARRO, TADEO
Jarana, La
1+pic.1.2.1. 2.1.2.0. timp,harp,
strings
UNION ESP. perf mat rent   (N14)

NAVEL OF THE SUN, THE see Nishimura,
Akira

NE PROCIAS ME, FOR SOLO VOICE, HORN AND
ORCHESTRA see Donizetti, Gaetano

NEBELSTEINMUSIK, FOR VIOLIN AND STRING
ORCHESTRA see Gruber, Heinz Karl

NEGRI, GINO (1919-   )
Concerto Per Contrabbasso Ladro E
Orchestra [10']
2.2.0.2. 2.0.0.0. perc,hpsd,
strings,db solo
SONZOGNO perf mat rent   (N15)

NEHMT MEINEN DANK, FOR SOLO VOICE AND
ORCHESTRA see Mozart, Wolfgang
Amadeus

NEI QUIETI SILENZI see Gentilucci,
Armando

NEIGE see Durey, Louis

NEIGINGEN, FOR VIOLIN AND ORCHESTRA see
Meijering, Chiel

NEIKRUG, MARC E. (1946-   )
Chetro Ketl [15']
1.2(English horn).2.2. 2.2.0.0.
perc,strings
HANSEN-NY perf mat rent   (N16)

Concertino for Flute and Orchestra
[20']
3(pic).3.3(bass
clar).3(contrabsn). 4.3.2.1.
timp,3perc,harp,pno&cel,
strings,fl solo
HANSEN-NY perf mat rent   (N17)

Concerto for String Quartet and
Orchestra [15']
1.2.1.2. 2.1.0.0. perc,strings,
string quar soli
HANSEN-NY perf mat rent   (N18)

Concerto for Viola and Orchestra
3(pic).3(English horn).3(bass
clar).3. 4.3.3.1. timp,pno,
2harp,7perc,strings,vla solo
HANSEN-NY perf mat rent   (N19)

NEIKRUG, MARC E. (cont'd.)

   Concerto for Violin and Orchestra
     [21']
     3(pic).3.3(clar in E
      flat).3(contrabsn). 4.3.3.1.
      timp,3perc,harp,pno&cel,
      strings,vln solo
     HANSEN-NY perf mat rent   (N20)

   Eternity's Sunrise
     4.4.4.4. 4.3.3.1. timp,perc,harp,
      pno,cel,strings
     sc HANSEN-NY $25.75, perf mat rent
                          (N21)

   Mobile [17']
     2.1.3(bass clar).0. 0.0.0.0.
      2perc,pno,strings
     HANSEN-NY perf mat rent   (N22)

   Nachtlieder, For Solo Voice And
     Orchestra [18']
     3(pic,alto fl).2(English
      horn).2(bass
      clar).3(contrabsn). 4.2.2.1.
      timp,3perc,harp,pno&cel,
      strings,S solo
     HANSEN-NY perf mat rent   (N23)

NEITHER FROM NOR TOWARDS see Elmsly,
   John

NEKROLOG see Pärt, Arvo

NEL FUGGIR DEL TEMPO, FOR SOLO VOICES
   AND ORCHESTRA see Arrigo, Girolamo

NEL TEMPO E NELLA RAGIONE see
   Pernaiachi, Gianfranco

NELHYBEL, VACLAV (1919-   )
   Concerto Spirituoso No.4, For Solo
     Voice, String Quartet And
     Orchestra
     2(pic).1.2+bass clar.0. 2.2.2.0.
      3perc,strings,string quar soli,
      solo voice
     sc EUR.AM.MUS. 01381FS f.s., perf
      mat rent   (N24)

   Etude Symphonic [12']
     3.3.4.3. 4.3.3.1. timp,4perc,pno,
      strings
     sc GENERAL 1004 $8.50   (N25)

NELSON, RONALD J. (RON) (1929-   )
   All Praise To Music [2']
     2+pic.2.2.2. 4.3.3.1. timp,3perc,
      harp,strings
     BOOSEY perf mat rent   (N26)

   Five Pieces For Orchestra, After
     Paintings Of Andrew Wyeth, For
     Solo Voice And Orchestra [22']
     3.3.3.3. 4.3.3.1. timp,perc,harp,
      pno,strings,Bar solo
     min sc BOOSEY 926 $23.00   (N27)

NEMTIN, ALEXANDER (1936-   )
   Nuances
     2+pic.2(English horn).3(bass
      clar).2. 4.2.3.0. timp,perc,
      cel,harp,pno,strings
     VAAP perf mat rent   (N28)

NENIA, FOR VIOLIN AND ORCHESTRA see
   Lucky, Štepán

NENIE see Liadov, Anatol
   Konstantinovich

NEO GEO, FOR BASSOON AND ORCHESTRA see
   Meijering, Chiel

NEON see Bauer, Ross

NERUDA, JOHANN BAPTIST (JAN KRTITEL)
   (ca. 1707-1780)
   Concerto for Trumpet and Orchestra in
     E flat, MIN 144
     orch,trp solo
     MUS. RARA perf mat rent   (N29)

NESLAND CHURCH, THE, FOR SOLO VOICE AND
   ORCHESTRA see Groven, Eivind,
   Neslandskyrkja, For Solo Voice And
   Orchestra

NESLANDSKYRKJA, FOR SOLO VOICE AND
   ORCHESTRA see Groven, Eivind

NEUBAUER, FRANZ CHRISTOPH (1760-1795)
   Symphony
     see Ivancic, Amandus, Symphonies,
     Two

NEUE BABYLON, DAS: SUITE see
   Shostakovich, Dmitri, New Babylon:
   Suite

NEUE MELODIEN QUADRILLE see Strauss,
   Johann, [Jr.]

NEUE WELT POLKA, EINE see Strauss,
   Eduard

NEUES LEBEN POLKA see Strauss, Johann,
   [Jr.]

NEUF AIRS D'OPERAS COMIQUE, FOR SOLO
   VOICE AND CHAMBER ORCHESTRA [ARR.]
   see Grétry, André Ernest Modeste

NEUSGATEN VAN SOPHIA LOREN, DE see
   Meijering, Chiel

NEUTRON SONATA see Boogaard, Bernard
   van den

NEVANLINNA, TAPIO (1954-   )
   Zoom
     2.2.2.2. 2.2.0.0. 3perc,harp,pno,
      strings
     sc SUOMEN f.s.   (N30)

NEW BABYLON: SUITE see Shostakovich,
   Dmitri

NEW CARNIVAL OF VENICE, A, FOR 4
   TROMBETTES AND ORCHESTRA see
   Stevens, Thomas

NEW CHINA SUITE see Ding, Shan-De

NEW CONSONANCE, THE see Tcherepnin,
   Ivan Alexandrovitch

NEW ENGLAND AUTUMN see Coolidge, Peggy
   Stuart

NEW GENERATION FROM THE GRASSLAND, FOR
   VIOLIN AND ORCHESTRA see Wu, Ju
   Jiang

NEW LIFE, THE see Jansson, Johannes,
   Nya Livet, Det

NEW MOON, THE: LOVER, COME BACK TO ME,
   FOR SOLO VOICE AND ORCHESTRA,
   [ARR.] see Romberg, Sigmund

NEW MOON, THE: ONE KISS, [ARR.] see
   Romberg, Sigmund

NEW MOON, THE: SELECTIONS, [ARR.] see
   Romberg, Sigmund

NEW MOON, THE: SOFTLY, AS IN A MORNING
   SUNRISE, FOR SOLO VOICE AND
   ORCHESTRA, [ARR.] see Romberg,
   Sigmund

NEW MOON, THE: STOUTHEARTED MEN, [ARR.]
   see Romberg, Sigmund

NEW MOON, THE: WANTING YOU, FOR SOLO
   VOICES AND ORCHESTRA, [ARR.] see
   Romberg, Sigmund

NEW MORNING FOR THE WORLD: "DAYBREAK OF
   FREEDOM", FOR SOLO VOICE AND
   ORCHESTRA see Schwantner, Joseph

NEW ORLEANS CONCERTO, FOR PIANO AND
   ORCHESTRA see Dickerson, Roger
   Donald

NEW WORLD A' COMIN', FOR PIANO AND
   ORCHESTRA [ARR.] see Ellington,
   Edward Kennedy (Duke)

NEW YORK OVERTURE, A see Smith, Larry
   Alan

NEW YORK SKYLINE MELODY see Villa-
   Lobos, Heitor

NEWA POLKA see Strauss, Johann, [Jr.]

NEWE AUSERLESENE LIEBLICHE BRANDEN see
   Brade, William

NEWELL, ROBERT M. (1940-   )
   Concerto for Piano and Orchestra
     [15']
     1.1.1.1. 2.1.0.0. 2perc,gtr,
      strings,pno solo
     sc AM.COMP.AL. $61.55, perf mat
      rent   (N31)

   Edifice In Memoriam [5']
     2.1.2.2. 2.2.2+bass trom.0. perc,
      pno,strings without vla
     sc AM.COMP.AL. $7.65, perf mat rent
                          (N32)

   Four-Fold World View [13']
     2(pic).2.2.2.tenor sax. 4.4.3.1.
      perc,harp,strings
     sc AM.COMP.AL. $21.35, perf mat
      rent   (N33)

   Modular Melliphony [20']
     4(pic).2.2.2. 4.3.3.1. perc,
      strings
     sc AM.COMP.AL. $33.50, perf mat
      rent   (N34)

   Viola-Mobile, For Viola And Chamber
     Orchestra [15']
     1.1.1.1. 2.2.1.1. perc,strings,
      vla solo
     sc AM.COMP.AL. $16.10, perf mat

NEWELL, ROBERT M. (cont'd.)

     rent   (N35)

NEWMAN, ANTHONY JOSEPH (1941-   )
   Concerto for Violin and Orchestra
     [40']
     2+pic.2.2+bass clar.2+contrabsn.
      2.2.3.0. perc,strings,vln solo
     SCHIRM.G perf mat rent   (N36)

NEWTON, JAMES
   Psalm No. 91 for Solo Voice, Piano
     and Orchestra [15'10"]
     2.2+English horn.2.2. 3.2.2.0.
      timp,perc,harp,strings,pno
      solo,S solo
     NEWAM 19032 perf mat rent   (N37)

NEWTON-VARIAZIONI, FOR CHAMBER
   ORCHESTRA see Chailly, Luciano

NEWTON-VARIAZIONI, FOR INSTRUMENTAL
   ENSEMBLE see Chailly, Luciano

NGUYEN THIEN DAO
   see DAO, NGUYEN THIEN

NGUYEN VAN TY, L.
   Fêtes Du Têt, For Piano And Orchestra
     study sc LÉMOINE $1.75   (N38)

NICE AND EASY, FOR VIOLIN AND ORCHESTRA
   see Wang, Li-San

NICHELMANN, CHRISTOPH (1717-1762)
   Clavier Concertos, Two
     (Lee, Douglas A.) sc A-R ED
      ISBN 0-89579-095-5 f.s.
      contains: Concerto for Keyboard
       Instrument and Orchestra in A;
       Concerto for Keyboard
       Instrument and Orchestra in E
                           (N39)
   Concerto for Keyboard Instrument and
     Orchestra in A
     see Clavier Concertos, Two

   Concerto for Keyboard Instrument and
     Orchestra in E
     see Clavier Concertos, Two

NICHOLSON, GEORGE (1949-   )
   Blisworth Tunnel Blues, For Solo
     Voice And Chamber Orchestra [25']
     2.2.3.1. 2.0.1.0. 2perc,harp,pno,
      2vln,vla,vcl,db,S solo
     SCHOTT perf mat rent   (N40)

   Convergence Of The Twain, The
     study sc SCHOTT ED 12095 $39.00,
      perf mat rent   (N41)

   Sea Change [15']
     9vln,2vla,2vcl,db
     SCHOTT perf mat rent   (N42)

NICHT WIEDERSEHEN see Mahler, Gustav

NICKLEBY, NICHOLAS: SUITE [ARR] see
   Berners, Lord (Gerald Tyrwhitt)

NICODE, JEAN LOUIS (1853-1919)
   Symphonische Variationen *Op.27
     2.2.2.2. 4.2.3.0. timp,drums,
      strings
     BREITKOPF-L perf mat rent   (N43)

NICOLAI, OTTO (1810-1849)
   Fest Overture *Op.31 [5']
     2.2.2.2. 2.2.3.0. timp,org,
      strings
     KALMUS A5782 sc $12.00, set $15.00,
      perf mat rent   (N44)

   Lustige Weiber Von Windsor, Die: Als
     Büblein Klein, For Solo Voice And
     Orchestra
     BREITKOPF-L perf mat rent   (N45)

   Lustige Weiber Von Windsor, Die: Gott
     Grüss Euch Sir!, For Solo Voices
     And Orchestra
     2.2.2.2. 4.2.0.0. timp,strings,
      BBar soli
     BREITKOPF-L perf mat rent   (N46)

   Lustige Weiber Von Windsor, Die:
     Horch, Die Lerche Singt Im Hain!,
     For Solo Voice And Orchestra
     BREITKOPF-L perf mat rent   (N47)

   Lustige Weiber Von Windsor, Die:
     Nein, Das Ist Wirklich Doch Zu
     Keck, For Solo Voice And
     Orchestra
     BREITKOPF-L perf mat rent   (N48)

   Lustige Weiber Von Windsor, Die: Nun
     Eilt Herbei, For Solo Voice And
     Orchestra
     BREITKOPF-L perf mat rent   (N49)

   Lustige Weiber Von Windsor, Die: Wohl
     Denn, Gefasst Ist Der Entschluss,
     For Solo Voice And Orchestra

NICOLAI, OTTO (cont'd.)

2.2.2.2. 2.0.0.0. strings,S solo
BREITKOPF-L perf mat rent   (N50)

Overture On The Chorale "Von Himmel Hoch"
see Weihnachtsouverture Uber Den Chorale "Vom Himmel Hoch"

Weihnachtsouverture Uber Den Chorale "Vom Himmel Hoch"
"Overture On The Chorale "Von Himmel Hoch"" KALMUS A6328 sc $25.00, set $40.00   (N51)

NICULESCU, STEFAN (1927-   )
Cantos, For Saxophone And Orchestra [25']
3.0.0.0. 4.3.3.1. 3perc,strings, sax solo
SALABERT perf mat rent   (N52)

Formants [12']
9vln,4vla,3vcl,db
sc SALABERT f.s., perf mat rent   (N53)

Ison I
1.1.3.1(contrabsn). 1.1.1.1. 2vln,vla,vcl,db
(strings may be doubled) sc
SALABERT f.s., perf mat rent   (N54)

Sincronie II [12']
1.1.1.1. 1.1.0.0. perc,cel, strings
(Omaggio a Enescu e Bartok)
SALABERT perf mat rent   (N55)

Symphony No. 2 [25']
3(pic).3(English horn).3(clar in E flat,bass clar).4(contrabsn). 4.3.3.1. 4perc,harp,cel,elec org,strings
SALABERT EAS18351P perf mat rent   (N56)

NIDUR, FOR DOUBLE BASS AND ORCHESTRA
see Sigurbjörnsson, Thorkell

NIEDER, FABIO (1957-   )
Glanzen Der Natur, Das, For Solo Voice And Orchestra [13']
3.2.3.4. 2.2.2.0. timp,perc,cel, hpsd,harp,strings,solo voice
SONZOGNO perf mat rent   (N57)

Tristans Klage [9']
1.1.2.0. 2.1.0.0. strings
SONZOGNO perf mat rent   (N58)

Zwei Sentimentale-Ironische Lieder, For Solo Voice And Orchestra [3']
1.1.2.2.sax. 1.2.1.0. timp,perc, vibra,gtr,mand,harp,strings,S solo
SONZOGNO perf mat rent   (N59)

NIELAND, H.
Paraphrase On The Song "Nearer My God To Thee"
sc,pts BROEKMANS f.s.   (N60)

NIELSEN, CARL (1865-1931)
Ableblomst, For Solo Voice And Orchestra, [arr.] [5']
(Bentzon) "Apple Blossom, For Solo Voice And Orchestra, [arr.]"
2.2.2.2. 2.0.0.0. timp,bells, strings,S solo HANSEN-DEN perf mat rent   (N61)

Aladdin: Seven Pieces [25']
2(pic).2(English horn).2.2. 4.2.3.1. timp,perc,cel,strings
KALMUS A6380 sc $35.00, set $50.00, pts $2.00, ea., perf mat rent   (N62)

Apple Blossom, For Solo Voice And Orchestra, [arr.]
see Ableblomst, For Solo Voice And Orchestra, [arr.]

At The Bier Of A Young Artist [5']
string orch
HANSEN-DEN perf mat rent   (N63)
set KALMUS A6494 $10.00, and up, perf mat rent   (N64)

Bohemian-Danish Folk Song
string orch [8'] HANSEN-DEN perf mat rent   (N65)
KALMUS A6796 sc $5.00, set $6.00, pts $1.25, ea.   (N66)

Concerto for Clarinet and Orchestra, Op. 57
min sc KALMUS K01508 $6.00   (N67)

Little Suite *Op.1
min sc KALMUS K01506 $6.00   (N68)

Maskarade: Magdalone's Dance Scene, For Solo Voices And Orchestra [8']
3(pic).2.2.2. 4.3.0.0. timp, strings,MezTBarB soli

NIELSEN, CARL (cont'd.)

HANSEN-DEN perf mat rent   (N69)

Maskarade: Overture
KALMUS A6302 sc $12.00, set $40.00, perf mat rent, pts $2.00, ea.   (N70)

Mother, The: Prelude To The Seventh Picture
KALMUS A6488 sc $3.00, set $12.00, pts $.75, ea.   (N71)

Rhapsodisk Overture
KALMUS A6381 sc $15.00, set $22.00, pts $1.00, ea., perf mat rent   (N72)

Romance for Violin and Orchestra, Op. 2
(Sitt) KALMUS A6481 sc $5.00, set $10.00, pts $1.00, ea.   (N73)

Symphony No. 1, Op. 7, in G minor
KALMUS A5606 sc $60.00, perf mat rent, set $70.00, pts $3.00, ea.   (N74)
min sc KALMUS K01512 $11.50   (N75)

Symphony No. 2, Op. 16
min sc KALMUS K01507 $11.50   (N76)

Symphony No. 3, Op. 27
KALMUS A5726 sc $60.00, set $100.00, perf mat rent, pts $4.00, ea.   (N77)
study sc KAHNT KT 7039 f.s., perf mat rent   (N78)

Symphony No. 5, Op. 50
KALMUS A5659 sc $50.00, perf mat rent, set $125.00, pts $5.00, ea.   (N79)

Symphony No. 5, Op. 50, Revised [37']
2+pic.2.2.2+contrabsn. 4.3.3.1. timp,perc,cel,strings
(Tuxen) KALMUS A5671 sc $60.00, perf mat rent, set $125.00, pts $5.00, ea.   (N80)

Symphony No. 6
KALMUS A5727 sc $40.00, set $100.00, perf mat rent, pts $5.00, ea.   (N81)

NIELSEN, LUDOLF (1876-1939)
Isabella
sc SAMFUNDET f.s., perf mat rent   (N82)

NIELSEN, LUDVIG (1906-   )
Concerto for Organ and Orchestra, No. 2, Op. 56 [20']
2.2.2.2. 3.2.2.0. timp,strings, org solo
study sc NORSK f.s.   (N83)

Passacaglia, Op. 23b [10']
2.2.2.2. 3.2.2.0. timp,perc,cel, strings
NORGE   (N84)

NIELSEN, SVEND (1937-   )
Concerto for Violin and Orchestra [25']
2(pic).2.2(bass clar).2. 2.2.3.0. 2perc,strings,vln solo
HANSEN-DEN perf mat rent   (N85)

Dyveke Sange, For Solo Voice And Orchestra [20']
2.2.2.2. 2.2.0.0. timp,perc, strings,S solo
HANSEN-DEN perf mat rent   (N86)

Fastes De l'Imaginaire, Les [15']
3.3.3.3. 4.4.3.1. timp,perc, vibra,marimba,2harp,pno,cel, strings
BILLAUDOT perf mat rent   (N87)

Nocturne [15']
7vln soli,2vla soli,2vcl soli,db solo
HANSEN-DEN perf mat rent   (N88)

Stratocumulus (Symphony,Second Movement) [18']
3(pic,alto fl).3.3.2. 4.3.3.1. timp,perc,strings
HANSEN-DEN perf mat rent   (N89)

Symphony [25']
3(pic,alto fl).3.3.2. 4.3.3.1. timp,perc,strings
sc HANSEN-DEN f.s., perf mat rent   (N90)

Symphony,Second Movement
see Stratocumulus

NIELSEN, TAGE (1929-   )
Passacaglia [10']
3.3.3.3. 4.3.3.1. 4perc,harp,pno, strings
SAMFUNDET perf mat rent   (N91)

NIELSON, LEWIS
Ballad Of Reading Gaol, The, For Solo Voice And Chamber Orchestra [19']
fl,clar,2bsn,trom,perc,pno,vla, 2vcl,Mez/S solo
AM.COMP.AL. sc $26.75, pts $32.95   (N92)

Concerto for Viola and Orchestra [20']
2(pic).1+English horn.2(bass clar).1. 4.2.4.0. perc,harp, strings,vla solo
sc AM.COMP.AL. $21.35   (N93)

Fantasy for Percussion and Chamber Orchestra [19']
1.1.1.1. 1.1.1.0. strings,perc solo
sc AM.COMP.AL. $70.00, perf mat rent   (N94)

Generation Of Leaves, A, For Solo Voice And Orchestra [14']
2.0+English horn.1.0. 1.2.0+bass trom.0. perc,strings,Mez solo
sc AM.COMP.AL. $23.00, perf mat rent   (N95)

NIEMANN, WALTER (1876-1953)
Alte Niederdeutsche Volkstanze [13']
1.1.1.1. 2.2.0.0. timp,perc, strings
KAHNT perf mat rent   (N96)

Pompeji [14']
2fl,strings
KAHNT perf mat rent   (N97)

NIEUWE VERLAAT, HET see Hoenderdos, Margriet

NIGG, SERGE (1924-   )
Concerto for Viola and Orchestra [20']
2.2.2.2. 3.2.3.0. timp,perc,harp, strings,vla solo
BILLAUDOT perf mat rent   (N98)

Du Clair Au Sombre, For Solo Voice And Chamber Orchestra [20'25"]
1.1.1.1. 2.1.1.0. timp,2perc, harp,cel,strings,S solo
BILLAUDOT perf mat rent   (N99)

Fastes De L'imaginaire [15']
3.3.3.3. 4.4.3.1. timp,3perc, 2harp,cel,pno,strings
BILLAUDOT perf mat rent   (N100)

Million d'Oiseaux d'Or [12'30"]
sc JOBERT 576-00239 $55.00, perf mat rent   (N101)

Poem for Orchestra [20']
3.3.3.3. 4.4.3.1. timp,2perc, 2harp,pno,cel,strings
BILLAUDOT perf mat rent   (N102)

NIGHT see Schierbeck, Poul, Natten

NIGHT, FOR SOLO VOICE AND STRING ORCHESTRA [ARR.] see Purcell, Henry

NIGHT AND DAY see Ansink, Caroline

NIGHT AND DAY, [ARR.] see Porter, Cole

NIGHT CLOUDS see Börtz, Daniel

NIGHT CONJURE-VERSE, FOR SOLO VOICES AND INSTRUMENTAL ENSEMBLE see Del Tredici, David

NIGHT CREATURE see Ellington, Edward Kennedy (Duke)

NIGHT DANCES see Turnage, Mark-Anthony

NIGHT DANCES, FOR CLARINET, DANCER AND ORCHESTRA see Beerman, Burton

NIGHT FALL see Hartmann, Christian, Mot Natt

NIGHT HOURS, FOR WOODWIND QUINTET AND ORCHESTRA see Eben, Petr

NIGHT IN VENICE, A: SELECTION see Strauss, Johann, [Jr.], Nacht In Venedig, Eine: Selection

NIGHT JOURNEY see Adolphe, Bruce

NIGHT MUSIC see Swanson, Howard

NIGHT MUSIC FOR JOHN LENNON see Foss, Lukas

NIGHT ON BALD MOUNTAIN see Mussorgsky, Modest Petrovich

NIGHT PARTY see Ho, Liu Ting

NIGHT PICTURES see Boyle, Rory

NIGHT PIECES see Regner, Hermann

NIGHT SHADOW, THE see Rieti, Vittorio,
Sonnambula, La

NIGHT UNTO NIGHT see Waxman, Franz

NIGHT WALTZ, FOR GUITAR AND ORCHESTRA
see Applebaum, Edward

NIGHTBIRD, FOR SAXOPHONE AND ORCHESTRA
see Colombier, Michel, Oiseau De
Nuit, For Saxophone And Orchestra

NIGHTMOODS see Waxman, Franz

NIGHTRIDE see Waxman, Franz

NIGHTRIDE AND SUNRISE see Sibelius,
Jean

NIGHTSONGS, FOR FLUTE AND ORCHESTRA see
Peaslee, Richard

NIGHTWATCH, FOR VIOLA AND ORCHESTRA see
McAlister, Clark

NIIMI, TOKUHIDE (1947-   )
Symphony No. 2 [36']
    3(pic).3.3.3(contrabsn). 3.3.3.0.
    timp,perc,harp,pno&cel,strings
    sc ZEN-ON 899430 f.s., perf mat
    rent   (N103)

NIKIPROWETZKY, TOLIA (1916-   )
Concerto for Trumpet and Orchestra
    [22']
    2.2.2.2. 2.0.0.0. strings,trp
    solo
    BILLAUDOT perf mat rent   (N104)

NIKOLAYEVA, TATIANA (1924-1993)
Concerto for Piano and Orchestra, No.
    1, Op. 10 [25']
    3.2.2.2. 4.2.3.1. timp,perc,harp,
    strings,pno solo
    VAAP perf mat rent   (N105)

NILFLUTHEN WALZER see Strauss, Josef

NILO, CALLE
Bellman-Soiree [10']
    1.1.2.1. 2.2.1.0. perc,elec org,
    opt acord,strings
    pno-cond sc,pts BUSCH HBM 024 f.s.
                                  (N106)

NILSSON, ANDERS (1954-   )
Aurora [11']
    11strings soli
    STIM   (N107)

Concerto for Organ and Orchestra
    [27']
    4.4.4.4. 6.4.4.1. timp,3perc,
    harp,cel,strings,org solo
    STIM   (N108)

NILSSON, BO (1937-   )
Bombi Bitt
    2fl,clar,pno,strings
    NORDISKA perf mat rent   (N109)

Drei Szenen [6']
    1.1.3.1. 1.1.1.0. 2perc,harp,pno&
    cel,2vln,vla,vcl
    SUECIA   (N110)

Hemsoborna
    fl,pno,strings
    NORDISKA perf mat rent   (N111)

Röda Rummet [15']
    2.2.2.0. 2.2.0.0. pno,perc,
    strings
    NORDISKA perf mat rent   (N112)

Taqsim-Caprice-Maqam
    2.2.0.2. 2.2.0.1. perc,pno,bass
    gtr,strings,electronic tape
    NORDISKA perf mat rent   (N113)

Three Laponian Folktunes, For
    Narrator And Orchestra
    perc,strings,narrator
    NORDISKA perf mat rent   (N114)

Vier Prologen [16']
    3pic,4trp,timp,perc,pno,strings
    NORDISKA perf mat rent   (N115)

NILSSON, TORSTEN (1920-   )
Concerto for Piano and String
    Orchestra, Op. 63 [25']
    string orch,pno solo
    sc REIMERS $33.50   (N116)

NIMBUS, FOR SOLO VOICE AND ORCHESTRA
see Jansson, Johannes

NIMMONS, PHIL (1923-   )
Concerto for Trumpet and Orchestra
    2(pic).2(English horn).2(bass
    clar).2. 4.2.3.1. timp,perc,
    harp,strings,trp solo
    CAN.MUS.CENT. MI 1331 N713CO (N117)

NIMMONS, PHIL (cont'd.)
Plateaus [14']
    2.2.2.2. 2.2.0.0. strings
    CAN.MUS.CENT. MI 1100 N713PL (N118)

NIMRUD see Sandström, Sven-David

NIN-CULMELL, JOAQUIN (1908-   )
Homenaje A Falla
    2.2.2.2. 2.2.0.0. strings
    ESCHIG perf mat rent   (N119)

Six Chansons Populaires Sephardiques,
    For Solo Voice And Orchestra
    [11']
    2.2.2.2. 4.2.2.0. timp,perc,
    strings,solo voice
    ESCHIG perf mat rent   (N120)

NINA, O LA PAZZA PER AMORE: OVERTURE
see Paisiello, Giovanni

NINE ORCHESTRAL INTERLUDES see Sitsky,
Larry

NINE PIECES [ARR.] see Purcell, Henry

NINE POEMS OF HEINE, FOR SOLO VOICE AND
ORCHESTRA see Blake, David

NINE SLOVAK SKETCHES see Susskind,
Walter

NINO JUDIO, EL, FOR SOLO VOICE AND
ORCHESTRA see Luna, Pablo

NIRVANA see Mannino, Franco

NISHIMURA, AKIRA (1953-   )
Heterophony, For Two Pianos And
    Orchestra [20']
    3(pic).3(English horn,ob
    d'amore).3(clar in E
    flat).3(contrabsn).soprano sax.
    4.4(trp in D).3.1. perc,harp,
    strings,2pno soli
    sc ZEN-ON 899442 f.s., perf mat
    rent   (N121)

Navel Of The Sun, The [20']
    3(pic).3(English horn).3(clar in
    E flat).3(contrabsn).soprano
    sax. 4.3.3.0. perc,harp,pno,
    strings, hichiriki solo
    sc ZEN-ON f.s., perf mat rent
                                 (N122)

Nostalgia [13'30"]
    3.1+English horn.3.2. 4.3.0.0.
    perc,harp,pno,strings sc ONGAKU
    576-00414 $18.75, perf mat rent
                                 (N123)

NISI DOMINUS, FOR SOLO VOICE AND STRING
ORCHESTRA see Vivaldi, Antonio

NIVERD, RAYMOND (1922-   )
Concerto for Piccolo and String
    Orchestra [8'30"]
    string orch,pic solo
    BILLAUDOT perf mat rent   (N124)

NIXIE, THE see Tveitt, Geirr, Nykken

NO LONGER THAN TEN (10) MINUTES see
Schafer, R. Murray

NO, NO, CHE NON SEI CAPACE, FOR SOLO
VOICE AND ORCHESTRA see Mozart,
Wolfgang Amadeus

NO, NON TURBATI!, FOR SOLO VOICE AND
STRING ORCHESTRA see Beethoven,
Ludwig van

NO SE POR QUE PIENSAS TU, FOR SOLO
VOICE AND CHAMBER ORCHESTRA see
Revueltas, Silvestre

NO SPRETTE LAUVET, FOR SOLO VOICE AND
ORCHESTRA see Eggen, Arne

NOAH'S ARK, FOR NARRATOR AND ORCHESTRA
see Weiner, Stanley, Arche Noah,
For Narrator And Orchestra

NOBODY KNOWS THE TROUBLE I'VE SEEN, FOR
SOLO VOICE AND ORCHESTRA [ARR.]
(Burleigh, Harry T.) 1.1.1.1.
    1.1.1.0. timp,strings,high solo
    COLOMBO perf mat rent   (N125)

NOBRE, MARLOS (1939-   )
Musicamera
    1.1.1.1. 0.0.0.0. strings
    TONOS   (N126)

NOCES DE VENUS, LES: SUITE [ARR.] see
Campra, André

NOCHE BUENA DEL DIABLO see Espla, Oscar

NOCHES EN LOS JARDINES DE ESPANA, FOR
PIANO AND CHAMBER ORCHESTRA see
Falla, Manuel de

NOCTURNAL PROCESSION see Liszt, Franz,
Nachtliche Zug, Der

NOCTURNE AND SCHERZO FOR 2 PIANOS AND
STRING ORCHESTRA see Ames, William
T.

NOCTURNE SYMPHONIQUE see Busoni,
Ferruccio Benvenuto

NOCTURNES see Debussy, Claude see
Huber, Nicolaus A.

NOCTURNES, FOR SOLO VOICE AND ORCHESTRA
see Vustin, Alexander

NOCTURNES I see Haubenstock-Ramati,
Roman

NOCTURNES II see Haubenstock-Ramati,
Roman

NOCTURNES III see Haubenstock-Ramati,
Roman

NODA, TERUYUKI (1940-   )
Fresque Symphonique [17']
    3(pic).3.3.3(contrabsn). 4.4.3.1.
    timp,perc,harp,cel&pno,strings
    (banda: 4 trp, 4 trb) sc ZEN-ON
    f.s., perf mat rent   (N127)

Symphony No. 2 [27']
    3(pic).3.3.3(contrabsn). 4.4.3.1.
    timp,perc,strings
    sc ZEN-ON 899290 f.s., perf mat
    rent   (N128)

NOEL [ARR.] see Tchaikovsky, Piotr
Ilyich

NOELANI'S ARIA, FOR SOLO VOICE AND
ORCHESTRA see Barati, George

NOH see Hasegawa, Yoshio

NON CURO L'AFFETTO, FOR SOLO VOICE AND
ORCHESTRA see Mozart, Wolfgang
Amadeus

NON IN PRATIS AUT IN HORTIS, FOR SOLO
VOICE AND STRING ORCHESTRA see
Vivaldi, Antonio

NON PAPA, JACOBUS CLEMENS
see CLEMENS, JACOBUS

NON PIU! TUTTO ASCOLTAI, FOR SOLO VOICE
AND ORCHESTRA see Mozart, Wolfgang
Amadeus

NONO, LUIGI (1924-1990)
A Carlo Scarpa Architetto, Ai Suoi
    Infiniti Possibili [7']
    4.0.3.3. 4.3.4.0. timp,bells,
    triangle,cel,harp,strings
    sc RICORDI-IT 133838 f.s., perf mat
    rent   (N129)

Variazioni Canoniche, Sulla Serie
    Dell', Op. 41 Di Arnold
    Schoenberg [10']
    2.2.3.1.soprano sax. 2.1.1.0.
    timp,perc,harp,pno,4vln,4vla,
    2vcl,2db
    sc RICORDI-IT 133874 f.s., perf mat
    rent   (N130)

NOOMENA see Xenakis, Yannis (Iannis)

NOON DANCES see Riley, Dennis

NOON WITCH, THE see Dvorák, Antonín,
Midday Witch

NORA, FOR 2 VIOLINS AND STRING
ORCHESTRA see Ferrari, Giorgio

NORBY, ERIK (1936-   )
Rainbow Snake, The [17']
    3(pic,alto fl)+pic.3+English
    horn.3+bass clar.3+contrabsn.
    6.4.4.1. timp,perc,pno,harp,
    strings
    sc HANSEN-DEN f.s., perf mat rent
                                 (N131)
Rainbow Snake, The: Reduced Orchestra
    Version [17']
    3(pic,alto fl).3(English
    horn).3(bass
    clar).3(contrabsn). 5.3.3.1.
    timp,perc,pno,harp,strings
    HANSEN-DEN perf mat rent   (N132)

NORD UND SUD POLKA see Strauss, Johann,
[Jr.]

NORDAL, JON (1926-   )
Adagio for Flute, Harp, Piano and
    String Orchestra [10']
    string orch,fl solo,harp solo,pno
    solo
    ICELAND 012-008   (N133)

NORDAL, JON (cont'd.)

Choralis [12']
    3.2.2+bass clar.2+contrabsn.
    4.3.2.1. timp,3perc,cel,harp,
    pno,strings
    HANSEN-DEN perf mat rent   (N134)

Concerto for Orchestra
    1.1.2.1. 1.1.1.0. timp,strings
    ICELAND 012-020   (N135)

Concerto for Piano and Orchestra
    [12']
    2.2.3.2. 2.2.2.0. timp,perc,
    strings,pno solo
    ICELAND 012-007   (N136)

Concerto for Violoncello and
    Orchestra [20']
    2.2.3.2. 3.3.0.0. timp,perc,harp,
    pno,cel,strings,vcl solo
    ICELAND 012-019   (N137)
    HANSEN-DEN perf mat rent   (N138)

Concerto Lirico, For Harp And String
    Orchestra [20'25"]
    string orch,harp solo
    ICELAND 012-001   (N139)

Dedication
    2.1.2.1. 3.2.1.0. timp,perc,harp,
    cel,strings
    ICELAND 012-016   (N140)

Epitafion [11'45"]
    1.1.1.1. 0.0.0.0. perc,pno,
    strings
    ICELAND 012-002   (N141)

Play Of Fragments, A [12']
    2.2.3.2. 2.2.2.0. timp,perc,harp,
    strings
    ICELAND 012-006   (N142)

Reverie [14'40"]
    3.2.2.2. 3.3.2.1. timp,2perc,
    harp,pno,strings
    ICELAND 012-005   (N143)

Sinfonietta Seriosa [24']
    2.2.3.2. 2.2.2.1. timp,perc,
    strings
    ICELAND 012-014   (N144)

Stepping Stones [11'30"]
    3.2.2.2. 2.2.1.1. timp,perc,pno,
    cel,strings
    ICELAND 012-003   (N145)

Twin Song, For Violin, Viola And
    Orchestra [17']
    perc,pno,strings,vln solo,vla
    solo
    ICELAND 012-012   (N146)

Winternight [11']
    2.2.3.2. 2.3.3.0. timp,perc,harp,
    pno,cel,strings
    ICELAND 012-009   (N147)

NORDEN see Glanert, Detlev

NORDEN, FOR SOLO VOICE AND ORCHESTRA
    [ARR.] see Sibelius, Jean

NORDENSTEN, FRANK TVEOR (1955-   )
    XPO *Op.72a [2'30"]
    2.1.1.1. 1.0.0.0. pno 4-hands,
    strings
    NORGE   (N148)

NORDENTOFT, ANDERS
    Born [10']
    3(pic).3(English horn).3(bass
    clar).3. 4.3.3.1. 3perc,harp,
    pno,strings
    HANSEN-DEN perf mat rent   (N149)

Cirkus
    1(pic).0.0.1.sax. 0.1.1.1. perc,
    strings
    HANSEN-DEN perf mat rent   (N150)

Con Fuoco [12']
    3clar,3trp,3perc,2pno,3db
    SAMFUNDET perf mat rent   (N151)

Entgegen
    1.1.1(bass clar).1. 1.1.1.0.
    perc,pno,string quin
    HANSEN-DEN perf mat rent   (N152)

Four Songs, For Solo Voice And
    Orchestra [20']
    1(pic).1.2(bass
    clar).2(contrabsn). 2.1.0.0.
    perc,harp,strings,Mez solo
    HANSEN-DEN perf mat rent   (N153)

NORDGREN, PEHR HENRIK (1944-   )
    Concerto for Viola and Chamber
    Orchestra, Op. 68 [31']
    strings,hpsd,vla solo
    sc SUOMEN f.s.   (N154)

NORDGREN, PEHR HENRIK (cont'd.)

Elegy For Vilho Lampi *Op.65 [15']
    3.2.3.2. 4.4.3.1. perc,harp,pno,
    strings
    sc SUOMEN f.s.   (N155)

Fate Nostalgia
    clar,pno,vln,12vcl
    sc SUOMEN f.s.   (N156)

Hate-Love, For Violoncello And String
    Orchestra *Op.71
    string orch,vcl solo
    sc SUOMEN f.s.   (N157)

Symphony No. 2, Op. 74 [27']
    3.2.3.3. 4.3.3.1. timp,4perc,
    harp,pno,strings
    sc SUOMEN f.s.   (N158)

Transe-Choral *Op.67 [33']
    9vln,3vla,2vcl,db
    sc SUOMEN f.s.   (N159)

NORDHEIM, ARNE (1931-   )
    Be Not Afeard, For Solo Voices And
    Orchestra [8']
    2(pic).1+English horn.1(clar in E
    flat)+bass clar.1+contrabsn.
    1.1.1.0. timp,3perc,cel,harp,
    pno,strings,electronic tape,
    SBar soli
    HANSEN-DEN perf mat rent   (N160)

Boomerang, For Oboe And Chamber
    Orchestra [17']
    2horn,hpsd,strings,ob solo
    HANSEN-DEN perf mat rent   (N161)

Magma [23']
    0+4pic.4.1+clar in E flat+2bass
    clar.2+2contrabsn. 4.4.4.1.
    timp,6perc,harp,pno,cel,org,
    strings
    HANSEN-DEN perf mat rent   (N162)

Nachruf
    string orch
    sc HANSEN-DEN f.s., perf mat rent
                                    (N163)

Spur, For Accordion And Orchestra
    [25']
    0+2pic.1+English horn.1+bass
    clar.1+contrabsn. 1.1.1.1.
    perc,cel,harp,strings,acord
    solo
    sc HANSEN-DEN f.s., perf mat rent
                                    (N164)

Tempest, The: Suite, For Solo Voices
    And Orchestra [40']
    2(pic).1+English horn.1+bass
    clar.1+contrabsn. 1.1.1.0.
    timp,3perc,harp,cel,elec pno,
    strings,electronic tape,SBar
    soli
    HANSEN-DEN perf mat rent   (N165)

Tempora Noctis, For Solo Voices And
    Orchestra [30']
    1+pic.1+English horn.1+bass
    clar.1+contrabsn. 1.1.1.1.
    timp,perc,harp,cel,pno,strings,
    electronic tape,SS soli
    HANSEN-DEN perf mat rent   (N166)

Tenebrae, For Violoncello And
    Orchestra [25']
    1+pic.1+English horn.1+bass
    clar.1+contrabsn. 2.4.1.1.
    timp,perc,cel,harp,pno,strings,
    vcl solo
    HANSEN-DEN perf mat rent   (N167)

Tractatus, For Flute And Orchestra
    [13']
    English horn,bass clar,contrabsn,
    2perc,harp,pno,cel,string quin,
    fl solo
    HANSEN-DEN perf mat rent   (N168)

Varder
    3.3.3.4. 4.4.3.1. timp,perc,org,
    strings, emulator
    NORGE   (N169)

NORDIC RHAPSODY see Sandby, Herman

NORDIC SUITE see Lunde, Ivar

NORDIC SUMMER PASTORAL see Borup-
    Jorgensen, Axel, Nordisk
    Sommerpastorale

NORDISK SOMMERPASTORALE see Borup-
    Jorgensen, Axel

NORDISKE FOLKETONER see Børresen, Hakon

NORDLICH DER ALPEN see Rebensburg,
    Thomas

NORDQVIST, GUSTAF (1886-1949)
    Bishop Thomas' Song Of Freedom, For
    Solo Voice And Orchestra [3']
    2.2.2.2. 4.2.3.1. timp,harp,
    strings,high solo
    NORDISKA perf mat rent   (N170)

Dryaden, For Solo Voice And Orchestra
    [8']
    2.1.1.1. 1.1.1.0. timp,harp,
    strings,high solo
    NORDISKA perf mat rent   (N171)

Facklor I Stormen, For Solo Voice And
    Orchestra [2']
    2.2.2.1. 2.2.1.0. timp,strings,
    med solo
    NORDISKA perf mat rent   (N172)

Jutta Kommer Till Folkungarna, For
    Solo Voice And Orchestra [4']
    2.2.2.2. 2.0.0.0. timp,harp,cel,
    strings,med solo
    NORDISKA perf mat rent   (N173)

Till Havs, For Solo Voice And
    Orchestra [3']
    2.2.2.2. 2.2.3.1. timp,perc,
    strings,solo voice
    NORDISKA perf mat rent   (N174)

NORDRAAK, RIKARD (1842-1866)
    Three Songs, For Solo Voice And
    Orchestra [arr.]
    (Olsen, Sparre) 1.1.1.0. 0.1.1.0.
    strings,high solo [11'] NORSK
    perf mat rent   (N175)

NORDREN, PEHR HENRIK (1944-   )
    Concerto for Violin and String
    Orchestra, Op. 53 [21']
    string orch,vln solo
    sc FAZER f.s., perf mat rent (N176)

Concerto for Violoncello and String
    Orchestra, Op. 50 [22']
    string orch,vcl solo
    sc FAZER f.s., perf mat rent (N177)

NORDSEEBILDER WALZER see Strauss,
    Johann, [Jr.]

NORDSTERN QUADRILLE see Strauss,
    Johann, [Jr.]

NORGAARD, PER (1932-   )
    Braending [10']
    2.0.2.0. 2.2.0.0. vibra,acord,
    pno,2vln,2vcl
    HANSEN-DEN perf mat rent   (N178)

Burn [12']
    3(pic).2+English horn.2(clar in E
    flat)+bass clar.2+contrabsn.
    4.3.3.0. timp,3perc,harp,pno,
    strings
    HANSEN-DEN perf mat rent   (N179)

Concerto for Strings [22']
    string orch
    HANSEN-DEN perf mat rent   (N180)

Concerto for Violin and Orchestra
    [35']
    2(pic).2(English horn).2(clar in
    E flat,bass clar).2(contrabsn).
    4.3.3.0. timp,3perc,strings,vln
    solo
    (Helle Nacht) HANSEN-DEN perf mat
    rent   (N181)

For A Change, For Percussion And
    Orchestra [22']
    2(pic).2.2.2. 4.3.3.0. strings,
    perc solo
    HANSEN-DEN perf mat rent   (N182)

In Between, For Violoncello And
    Orchestra [29']
    2(pic,alto fl).2+English
    horn.2(clar in E flat)+bass
    clar.2+contrabsn. 4.3.3.1.
    3perc,harp,pno,strings,vcl solo
    HANSEN-DEN perf mat rent   (N183)

Jousting
    see Turnering

King, Queen And Ace, For Harp And
    Orchestra [15']
    1(pic,alto fl).1(English
    horn).1(clar in E flat,bass
    clar).1(contrabsn). 1.1(cornet,
    piccolo trp).1.0. perc,strings,
    harp solo
    HANSEN-DEN perf mat rent   (N184)

Pastorale [8']
    string orch
    HANSEN-DEN perf mat rent   (N185)

Remembering Child, For Viola And
    Orchestra
    1(pic,alto fl).2(English
    horn).1(clar in E flat,bass
    clar).2(contrabsn). 2.1.0.0.

NORGAARD, PER (cont'd.)

    perc,pno,strings,vla solo
    HANSEN-DEN perf mat rent   (N186)

   Symphony No. 4 [22']
    2+pic.2(English horn).2(clar in E
    flat,bass clar).2. 4.3.3.1.
    5perc,harp,pno,strings
    (Indischer Roosen- Gaarten Und
    Chineesischer Hexen-See) HANSEN-
    DEN perf mat rent   (N187)

   Towards Freedom? [10']
    1+pic.2.2.2. 4.2.2.0. timp,perc,
    strings
    HANSEN-DEN perf mat rent   (N188)

   Turnering [10']
    2(pic).1.2.1. 2.2.0.0. perc,cel/
    vibra,pno,strings
    "Jousting" (trombones may be
    substituted for horns) HANSEN-DEN
    perf mat rent   (N189)

NORHOLM, IB (1931-)
   Fluctuations
   see Fluktuationer

   Fluktuationer
    "Fluctuations" sc SAMFUNDET f.s.,
    perf mat rent   (N190)

   Heretic Hymn *Op.62 [12']
    3(pic).3(English horn).3(bass
    clar).2+contrabsn. 4.3.3.0.
    timp,4perc,cel,strings
    HANSEN-DEN perf mat rent   (N191)

   Idylles d'Apocalypse, For Organ And
    Chamber Orchestra
    2.2.2.2. 2.2.2.1. strings,org
    solo
    sc HANSEN-DEN $27.25, perf mat rent
       (N192)
   Moraliteter (Symphony No. 6, Op. 85)
    [34']
    2.2.2.2. 4.3.3.1. timp,4-5perc,
    cel,strings,MezBar&2 speaking
    voices
    SAMFUNDET perf mat rent   (N193)

   Relief I And II
    sc SAMFUNDET f.s., perf mat rent
       (N194)
   Sandskornets Topologi *Op.102 [15']
    string orch
    "Topology Of Grains Of Sand"
    HANSEN-DEN perf mat rent   (N195)

   Symphony No. 6, Op. 85
   see Moraliteter

   Symphony No. 7, Op. 88 [22']
    3(pic).3(English horn).3(clar in
    E flat,bass clar).3(contrabsn).
    4.4.3.1. 7perc,harp,cel,strings
    (Ecliptic Instincts) HANSEN-DEN
    perf mat rent   (N196)

   Topology Of Grains Of Sand
   see Sandskornets Topologi

NORMAN OVERTURE, A see Williams, Julius
   P.

NORMANNERNE see Børresen, Hakon

NORMANS, THE see Børresen, Hakon,
   Normannerne

NORODOM SIHANOUK
   Cambodian Suite [6'15"]
    3.3.2.2. 4.2.4.0. timp,perc,
    strings
    (Kostelanetz) LUDWIG perf mat rent
       (N197)

NORSE LEGEND see Bridge, Frank

NORSK LANDSKAP see Taube, Lillian
   Gulowna

NORSK RAPSODI NR. 2 see Strand,
   Ragnvald

NORSK RAPSODI, OP. 53, IN D see Jordan,
   Sverre

NORSK SOMMERNATT see Willock, Einar

NORSK UTSYN see Kvandal, Johan

NORSKE TONER see Hauger, Kristian

NORTH, ALEX (1910-)
   Streetcar Named Desire, A
    WARNER perf mat rent   (N198)

NORTH COUNTRY SKETCHES see Delius,
   Frederick

NORWEGIAN AIR, FOR VIOLIN AND ORCHESTRA
   see Halvorsen, Johan

NORWEGIAN FOLK TUNES see Hauger,
   Kristian, Norske Toner

NORWEGIAN RHAPSODY see Eggen, Erik

NORWEGIAN RHAPSODY NO. 1 see Svendsen,
   Johan (Severin)

NORWEGIAN RHAPSODY NO. 2 see Svendsen,
   Johan (Severin)

NORWEGIAN SONG, FOR VIOLIN AND STRING
   ORCHESTRA see Halvorsen, Johan

NORWEGIAN SUITE NO. 1 see Tveitt, Geirr

NORWEGIAN SUITE NO. 2 see Tveitt, Geirr

NORWEGIAN SUMMER NIGHT see Willock,
   Einar, Norsk Sommernatt

NOSTALGHIA, FOR VIOLIN AND STRING
   ORCHESTRA see Takemitsu, Toru

NOSTALGIA see Karkoff, Ingvar see
   Nishimura, Akira

NOSTALGIC FILM THEMES see Waxman, Franz

NOSTOS see Uppström, Tore

NOT A MIDSUMMER NIGHT'S DREAM see
   Schnittke, Alfred

NOT WAVING BUT DROWNING, FOR SOLO VOICE
   AND ORCHESTRA see Berg, Christopher

NOTATIONS I-IV see Boulez, Pierre

NOTCH see Zuidam, Rob

NOTES see Eiriksdottir, Karolina

NOTES FROM THE UNDERGROUND see Davis,
   Anthony

NOTES OF REMEMBRANCE see Gould, Morton

NOTRE-DAME MUSIK see Beyer, Frank
   Michael

NOTTURNI DI PRAGA see Hanuš, Jan

NOTTURNI, OP.79, NO.3 see Eder, Helmut

NOTTURNI TRASOGNATI, FOR ALTO FLUTE AND
   CHAMBER ORCHESTRA see Trojahn,
   Manfred

NOTTURNO E DANZA see Albertsen, Per
   Hjort see Kox, Hans

NOTTURNO IV see Tomasson, Jonas

NOTTURNO PATETICO see Adomian, Lan

NOUVEAU CLAVECIN, LE, FOR HARPSICHORD
   AND STRING ORCHESTRA see Hurník,
   Ilja

NOVA, JACQUELINE
   Doce Moviles Para Conjunto De Camera
    [9']
    6vln,2vla,2vcl,db,pno
    "Twelve Mobiles For Chamber
    Ensemble" PAN AM perf mat rent
       (N199)
   Twelve Mobiles For Chamber Ensemble
   see Doce Moviles Para Conjunto De
   Camera

NOVA TEMPESTA, LA see Ruge, Filippo

NOVÁK, MILAN (1927-)
   Dve Fanfary
    "Two Fanfares" SLOV.HUD.FOND (N200)

   Two Fanfares
   see Dve Fanfary

NOVELETTE, OP. 52, NO. 1, IN A see
   Coleridge-Taylor, Samuel

NOVELETTE, OP. 52, NO. 2, IN C see
   Coleridge-Taylor, Samuel

NOVELETTE, OP 52, NO.3, IN A MINOR see
   Coleridge-Taylor, Samuel

NOVELETTE, OP 52, NO. 4, IN D see
   Coleridge-Taylor, Samuel

NOVELLETTEN IN E see Gade, Niels
   Wilhelm

NOVELLETTEN IN F see Gade, Niels
   Wilhelm

NOVEMBER SONGS, FOR SOLO VOICE AND
   ORCHESTRA see Lebic, Lojze,
   Novemberske Pesmi, For Solo Voice
   And Orchestra

NOVEMBERSKE PESMI, FOR SOLO VOICE AND
   ORCHESTRA see Lebic, Lojze

NOW YOU SEE IT, FOR SOLO VOICE AND
   ORCHESTRA see Babbitt, Milton Byron

NOWAK, ALISON (1911-)
   Blend [17']
    3.2.2.1. 2.2.1.1. 2perc,strings
    AM.COMP.AL. perf mat rent   (N201)

   Quid Pro Quo [15']
    3.3(English horn).3(bass clar).3.
    4.3.3.1. timp,strings
    sc AM.COMP.AL. $28.70, perf mat
    rent   (N202)

NOZAWA, KAZUYO (1945-)
   Tempi Adorni, For Solo Voice And
    Orchestra [12']
    1.2.2.0. 2.0.0.0. perc,hpsd&cel,
    pno,harp,strings,S solo
    SONZOGNO perf mat rent   (N203)

NOZZE DI FIGARO, LE: CRUDEL! PERCHE
   FINORA, FOR SOLO VOICES AND
   ORCHESTRA see Mozart, Wolfgang
   Amadeus

NOZZE DI FIGARO, LE: DOVE SONO, FOR
   SOLO VOICE AND ORCHESTRA see
   Mozart, Wolfgang Amadeus

NOZZE DI FIGARO, LE: GIUNSE ALFIN IL
   MOMENTO, FOR SOLO VOICE AND
   ORCHESTRA see Mozart, Wolfgang
   Amadeus

NOZZE DI FIGARO, LE: HAI GIA VINTA LA
   CAUSA: VEDRO MENTR' IO SOSPIRO, FOR
   SOLO VOICE AND ORCHESTRA see
   Mozart, Wolfgang Amadeus

NOZZE DI FIGARO, LE: LA VENDETTA, FOR
   SOLO VOICE AND ORCHESTRA see
   Mozart, Wolfgang Amadeus

NOZZE DI FIGARO, LE: NON PIU ANDRAI,
   FOR SOLO VOICE AND ORCHESTRA see
   Mozart, Wolfgang Amadeus

NOZZE DI FIGARO, LE: NON SO PIU COSA
   SON, FOR SOLO VOICE AND ORCHESTRA
   see Mozart, Wolfgang Amadeus

NOZZE DI FIGARO, LE: OVERTURE see
   Mozart, Wolfgang Amadeus

NOZZE DI FIGARO, LE: PORGI AMOR, FOR
   SOLO VOICE AND ORCHESTRA see
   Mozart, Wolfgang Amadeus

NOZZE DI FIGARO, LE: SE VUOL BALLARE,
   FOR SOLO VOICE AND ORCHESTRA see
   Mozart, Wolfgang Amadeus

NOZZE DI FIGARO, LE: SULL'ARIA! CHE
   SOAVE ZEFFIRETTO, FOR SOLO VOICES
   AND ORCHESTRA see Mozart, Wolfgang
   Amadeus

NOZZE DI FIGARO, LE: TUTTO E DISPOSTO,
   FOR SOLO VOICE AND ORCHESTRA see
   Mozart, Wolfgang Amadeus

NOZZE DI FIGARO, LE: VOI CHE SAPETE,
   FOR SOLO VOICE AND ORCHESTRA see
   Mozart, Wolfgang Amadeus

NOZZE ISTRIANE: PRELUDIO see Smareglia,
   Antonio

NUANCES see Nemtin, Alexander

NUBE-MUSICA, FOR SOLO VOICE AND CHAMBER
   ORCHESTRA see Alonso, Miguel

NUIT, LA, FOR TRUMPET AND STRINGS see
   Girard, Anthony

NUIT, LA, FOR VIOLIN AND STRING
   ORCHESTRA see Sciortino, Patrice

NUIT D'ETE: CINQ INTERLUDES, FOR
   VIOLONCELLO AND ORCHESTRA see
   Lenot, Jacques

NUIT D'ETE II, FOR VIOLONCELLO AND
   INSTRUMENTAL ENSEMBLE see Lenot,
   Jacques

NUITS, LES see Carraud, Gaston

NUITS DANS LES JARDINS D'ESPAGNE, FOR
   PIANO AND CHAMBER ORCHESTRA see
   Falla, Manuel de, Noches En Los
   Jardines De Espana, For Piano And
   Chamber Orchestra

NUITS DE WALPURGIS CLASSIQUE, LA see
   Koechlin, Charles

NUITS D'ETE, LES, FOR SOLO VOICE AND
   ORCHESTRA see Berlioz, Hector
   (Louis)

NUITS D'ETE, LES: L'ILE INCONNUE, FOR
   SOLO VOICE AND ORCHESTRA [ARR] see
   Berlioz, Hector (Louis)

NUITS D'ETE, LES: SUR LES LAGUNES, FOR SOLO VOICE AND ORCHESTRA [ARR] see Berlioz, Hector (Louis)

NUITS D'ETE, LES: VILLANELLE, FOR SOLO VOICE AND ORCHESTRA [ARR] see Berlioz, Hector (Louis)

NULLA IN MUNDO PAX SINCERE, FOR SOLO VOICE AND STRING ORCHESTRA see Vivaldi, Antonio

NUMERO CINQ, FOR PIANO AND INSTRUMENTAL ENSEMBLE see Manoury, Philippe

NUN SCHWEIGET WINDE, FOR SOLO VOICE AND ORCHESTRA see Handel, George Frideric, Silete Venti, For Solo Voice And Orchestra

NUNES, EMMANUEL (1941-   )
    Musik Der Fruhe [40']
        1.1.3.0. 1.1.4.0. 2vln,2vla,2vcl, db
    RICORDI-GER SY 3026 perf mat rent
                                    (N204)
    Ruf
    JOBERT   (N205)

    Tif'ereth For 6 Solo Instruments And Orchestra [80']
        4.4.4.2+contrabsn. 6.4.4.0.
        6perc,strings,vln solo,ob solo, trom solo,horn solo,db solo, perc solo
    RICORDI-GER SY 3022 perf mat rent
                                    (N206)
    Wandlungen [29']
        2.2.3.1. 1.1.1.0. 3perc,bells, cel,harp,3vln,2vla,2vcl,db,opt electronic equipment
    sc RICORDI-GER SY 3025 f.s., perf mat rent   (N207)

NUN'S STORY, THE: SUITE see Waxman, Franz

NUOVI CANTI, FOR FLUTE AND CHAMBER ORCHESTRA see Kelterborn, Rudolf

NUOVO INCONTRO, FOR VIOLIN AND STRING ORCHESTRA see Manzoni, Giacomo

NURSERY, THE, FOR SOLO VOICE AND ORCHESTRA [ARR.] see Mussorgsky, Modest Petrovich

NURSERY, THE [ARR.] see Mussorgsky, Modest Petrovich

NURYMOV, CHARY (1941-   )
    Destan Concerto [16']
        fl,ob,perc,pno,strings
    VAAP perf mat rent   (N208)

NUTCRACKER: GRAND PAS DE DEUX [ARR.] see Tchaikovsky, Piotr Ilyich

NUTCRACKER: PAS DE DEUX see Tchaikovsky, Piotr Ilyich

NUTCRACKER: SUITE see Tchaikovsky, Piotr Ilyich

NUVOLE, LE see Testoni, Giampaolo

NYA LIVET, DET see Jansson, Johannes

NYKKEN see Tveitt, Geirr

NYMPHEAS see Powers, Anthony

NYSTEDT, KNUT (1915-   )
    Collocations *Op.53 [9']
        3.2.2.2. 4.3.3.0. timp,perc,cel, strings
    NORGE   (N209)

    Concertino for English Horn, Clarinet and String Orchestra, Op. 29 [19']
        string orch,English horn solo, clar solo
    NORSK perf mat rent   (N210)

    Concerto for Horn and Orchestra, Op. 114 [17']
        3.2.2.2. 3.3.3.0. timp,perc,cel, strings,horn solo
    NORGE   (N211)

    Exsultate *Op.74b [10']
        3.2.2.2. 4.3.3.0. timp,perc, strings
    NORSK perf mat rent   (N212)

    Fest-Ouverture *Op.25 [9']
        3.2.2.2. 4.3.3.1. timp,perc, strings
    "Festival Overture" NORGE   (N213)

    Festival Overture
    see Fest-Ouverture

NYSTEDT, KNUT (cont'd.)

    Halling *Op.16
        1.1.1.0. 0.2.1.0. perc,pno, harmonium,strings
    pts MUSIKK f.s.   (N214)

    Hogfjell *Op.8 [21']
        2.2.1.1. 2.2.2.0. timp,perc, strings
    "Mountains, The" NORGE   (N215)

    Ichthys *Op.76 [12']
        3.2.3.3. 4.3.3.0. timp,perc,cel, org,strings
    sc NORSK f.s., perf mat rent   (N216)

    Mountains, The
    see Hogfjell

    Sinfonia Del Mare *Op.97 [14']
        5.3.4.4. 6.4.3.1. timp,perc,pno, strings
    sc NORSK f.s., perf mat rent   (N217)

    Symphony, Op. 13
        2.1.2.1. 2.2.2.0. timp,strings
    NORGE   (N218)

NYSTROEM, GÖSTA (1890-1966)
    Three Love Songs, For Solo Voice And Orchestra [10']
        1.1.2.1. 2.1.0.0. timp,harp,cel, strings,med solo
    NORDISKA perf mat rent   (N219)

O

O DU LIEBE MEINER LIEBE see Bach, Johann Sebastian

O DU LIEBER AUGUSTIN see Zipp, Friedrich

O DU LIEBER AUGUSTIN, FOR STRING ORCHESTRA see Zipp, Friedrich

O JESU AMANTISSIME, FOR SOLO VOICES AND ORCHESTRA see Campra, André

O KOMM IM TRAUM, FOR SOLO VOICE AND ORCHESTRA [ARR.] see Liszt, Franz, Oh! Quand Je Dors, For Solo Voice And Orchestra [arr.]

O MENSCH, BEWEIN SEIN SUNDE GROSS [ARR.] see Bach, Johann Sebastian

O MIE PORPORE PIU BELLE, FOR SOLO VOICE AND STRING ORCHESTRA see Vivaldi, Antonio

O MISTRESS MINE see Howe, Mary

O PAPAGAIO DO MOLEQUE see Villa-Lobos, Heitor

O QUI COELI TERRAEQUE SERENITAS, FOR SOLO VOICE AND STRING ORCHESTRA see Vivaldi, Antonio

O TEMERARIO ARBACE, FOR SOLO VOICE AND ORCHESTRA see Mozart, Wolfgang Amadeus

O TEMPORA, FOR SOLO VOICES AND CHAMBER ORCHESTRA see Garcia Roman, Jose

O TIEMPO TUS PIRAMIDES see Essl, Karl Heinz

O WELCH EIN LEBEN, FOR SOLO VOICE AND ORCHESTRA see Beethoven, Ludwig van

OAK, THE see Sommerfeldt, Öistein, Elka

OBELISKS see Huba, Volodymyr

OBERON: OZEAN, DU UNGEHEUER, FOR SOLO VOICE AND ORCHESTRA see Weber, Carl Maria von

OBERSON, RENÉ (1945-   )
    Ceng-Men [20']
    study sc GUILYS f.s., perf mat rent
                                    (01)

OBERTURA CONCERTANTE, FOR PIANO AND ORCHESTRA see Halffter, Rodolfo

OBERTURA see Server, Juan Pons

OBJECTIVE, BURMA: SUITE see Waxman, Franz

OBOE AND ORCHESTRA see Feldman, Morton

OBST, MICHAEL (1955-   )
    Kristallwelt, Teil III
        1.1.1+bass clar.1. 1.2.1.0.
        2perc,pno,cel,elec org/ synthesizer,3vln,2vla,2vcl,db, electronic equipment
    BREITKOPF-W perf mat rent   (02)

OCCASIONAL OVERTURE see Britten, [Sir] Benjamin

OCEANA: OVERTURE see Smareglia, Antonio

OCEANSIDE STOMP, THE see Proto, Frank

OCTAVE STUDY, FOR VIOLIN AND ORCHESTRA [ARR.] see Paganini, Niccolo

OCTOBER see Shostakovich, Dmitri

ODA A MANUEL DE FALLA, FOR HARPSICHORD AND ORCHESTRA see Blanquer, Amando

ODE see Holloway, Robin see Manzoni, Giacomo

ODE, FOR ENGLISH HORN AND STRING ORCHESTRA see Hermans, Nico

ODE, FOR SOLO VOICE AND ORCHESTRA see Goossen, Frederic

ODE AU SILENCE see Vieru, Anatol

ODE FOR PIANO AND ORCHESTRA see Kawai, Manabu

ODE FOR VIOLIN AND ORCHESTRA see Ishijima, Masahiro

ODE II see Bon, Andre

ODE IN MEMORY OF LENIN see Khachaturian, Aram Ilyich

ODE POUR JERUSALEM see Milhaud, Darius

ODE TO LIFE see Adams, Leslie

ODE TO THE NIGHTINGALE, FOR SOLO VOICE AND CHAMBER ORCHESTRA see Silvestrov, Valentin

ODE TO THE VIOLA, FOR VIOLA AND CHAMBER ORCHESTRA see Wyman, Dann Coriot

ODEON TANZE WALZER see Strauss, Johann, [Sr.]

ODINS MEERESRITT, FOR SOLO VOICE AND ORCHESTRA see Loewe, Carl Gottfried

ODOTAN JOULUVIERASTA, FOR SOLO VOICE AND STRING ORCHESTRA[ARR.] see Hannikainen, Ilmari

ODYSSEUS, FOR SOLO VOICE AND ORCHESTRA see Chance, Nancy Laird

ODYSSEY see Maw, Nicholas

OF FANTASY, OF DREAMS AND CEREMONIES see Hoyland, Victor

OF QUEENS' GARDENS see Barry, Gerald

OF THEE I SING, [ARR.] see Gershwin, George

OF THEE I SING: OVERTURE, [ARR.] see Gershwin, George

OFFENBACH, JACQUES (1819-1880)
A Spasso Con La Figlia Del Tamburo Maggiore, For Solo Voice And Orchestra [arr.]
(Negri, G.) 2.2.2.2. 2.2.0.0. timp, perc,strings,solo voice [35']
SONZOGNO perf mat rent   (03)

Barbe-Bleue: Overture [arr.]
(Hoffmann, Fritz) "Bluebeard: Overture [arr.]" KALMUS A5783 sc $12.00, set $25.00, perf mat rent
(04)

Barcarolle *see Melodies: Sechs Lieder For Solo Voice And Orchestra [arr.]

Barcarolle From Tales Of Hoffman, [arr.] *see TWELVE POP HITS FROM THE CLASSICS, VOL. 1

Bluebeard: Overture [arr.]
see Barbe-Bleue: Overture [arr.]

Gaite Parisienne [arr.]
(Rosenthal, M.) 2.2.2.2. 2.3.3.1. timp,perc,harp,strings [44'] sc BOIS f.s., perf mat rent   (05)

Hiver, L' *see Melodies: Sechs Lieder For Solo Voice And Orchestra [arr.]

Jalousie *see Melodies: Sechs Lieder For Solo Voice And Orchestra [arr.]

Larmes De Jacqueline, Les, For Violoncello And String Orchestra, Op. 76, No. 2 [arr.]
(Thomas-Mifune, Werner) string orch,vcl solo sc,pts KUNZEL $21.00   (06)

Melodies: Sechs Lieder For Solo Voice And Orchestra [arr]
(Smola, Emmerich) "Six Songs For Solo Voice And Orchestra [arr]" 2.2.2.1. 2.1.0.0. timp,perc, strings,high solo [12'] (contains: Barcarolle; Jalousie; L'Hiver; Sur La Greve; Le Sergent Recruteur; Serenade Du Torero) BOTE perf mat rent   (07)

Offenbach Waltz, For Cornet And Orchestra [arr.]
(Almeida, Antonio De) 3(pic).2.2.2. 4.2.3.1. timp,perc,strings,cornet solo [6'] BELWIN perf mat rent   (08)

Orphee Aux Enfers: Suite [arr.]
(Negri, G.) 1.1.1.1. 1.1.1.0. perc, strings [35'] SONZOGNO perf mat rent   (09)

Perichole, La: Overture [arr.]
(Zorzor, Stefan) 2.2.2.2. 4.3.3.0. timp,perc,harp,pno,strings ORLANDO perf mat rent   (010)

Princesse De Trebizonde, La: Overture [arr.]
(Hoffmann, Fritz) KALMUS A5784 sc

OFFENBACH, JACQUES (cont'd.)

$15.00, set $40.00, perf mat rent   (011)

Sechs Fabeln Nach Jean De La Fontaine, For Solo Voice And Orchestra [arr]
(Stamm, Peter) "Six Fables After Jean De La Fontaine, For Solo Voice And Orchestra [arr]" 2(pic).1.2.1. 2.2.1.0. timp,perc, harp,strings,solo voice [23'] BOTE perf mat rent   (012)

Serenade Du Torero *see Melodies: Sechs Lieder For Solo Voice And Orchestra [arr.]

Sergent Recruteur, Le *see Melodies: Sechs Lieder For Solo Voice And Orchestra [arr.]

Six Fables After Jean De La Fontaine, For Solo Voice And Orchestra [arr]
see Sechs Fabeln Nach Jean De La Fontaine, For Solo Voice And Orchestra [arr]

Six Songs For Solo Voice And Orchestra [arr]
see Melodies: Sechs Lieder For Solo Voice And Orchestra [arr]

Sur La Greve *see Melodies: Sechs Lieder For Solo Voice And Orchestra [arr.]

Vie Parisienne, La: Overture [arr.]
(Dorati, Antal) 2(pic).2.2.2.3sax. 4.2.2.0. timp,perc,strings [12'] MILLS perf mat rent   (013)

Vie Parisienne, La: Quadrille [4'20"]
1.1.2.0.alto sax. 1.3.3.0. perc, strings
pno-cond sc,pts BILLAUDOT f.s.   (014)

Vier Impressionen, For Violoncello And Orchestra [arr.]
(Geese, H.) 1.1.2.1. 2.0.0.0. perc, harp,strings,vcl solo [21'] SIKORSKI perf mat rent   (015)

OFFENBACH WALTZ, FOR CORNET AND ORCHESTRA [ARR.] see Offenbach, Jacques

OFFERTORIUM, FOR VIOLIN AND ORCHESTRA see Gubaidulina, Sofia

OFFRANDE, FOR SOLO VOICE AND ORCHESTRA see Kanach, Sharon

OFFRANDE ORCHESTRALE see Matsumura, Teizo

OFFS see Masson, Gerard

OFFSHORE see Finnissy, Michael

OFRENDA A FALLA, FOR ENGLISH HORN AND STRING ORCHESTRA see Arambarri, Jesús

OFSTAD, KOLBJORN (1917-   )
Divertimento for Strings [8']
string orch
NORGE   (016)

OGANESIAN, EDGAR (1930-   )
Blue Nocturne [37']
3.3.5.3.alto sax. 4.4.3.1. timp, perc,harp,cel,pno,strings
SIKORSKI perf mat rent   (017)

Concerto for Alto Saxophone and Orchestra [20']
clar,2alto sax,2tenor sax, baritone sax,4trp,4trom,perc, harp,pno,gtr,strings,alto sax solo
SIKORSKI perf mat rent   (018)

OGDON, WILBUR L. (1921-   )
Capriccio And Five Comments [12']
3.2.3.3. 4.2.2.1. 3perc,harp,cel, strings
sc APNM $7.25, perf mat rent   (019)

Five Preludes, For Violin And Instrumental Ensemble [9']
sc APNM $6.50, perf mat rent   (020)

OGERMAN, CLAUS
Symphonic Dances [21'40"]
3(pic,alto fl).3(English horn).3+ bass clar.3(contrabsn).tenor sax. 4.3(flügelhorn).3.1. timp, perc,harp,pno,cel,strings
NEWAM 19033 perf mat rent   (021)

OGGETTO, L' see Schultheiss, Ulrich

OGURA, ROH (1916-   )
Composition In F Sharp [20']
JAPAN 8801   (022)

OH DIDN'T IT RAIN, FOR SOLO VOICE AND ORCHESTRA [ARR.]
(Burleigh, Harry T.) 1.1.2.0. 2.1.1.0. timp,strings,low solo
COLOMBO perf mat rent   (023)

OH JERICHO see Holland, Jack

OH LOIS! see Daugherty, Michael

OH! QUAND JE DORS, FOR SOLO VOICE AND ORCHESTRA [ARR.] see Liszt, Franz

OH, SO SANDY, FOR SOLO VOICE AND ORCHESTRA see Groven, Eivind, A Sa Rodblond, For Solo Voice And Orchestra

OHANA, MAURICE (1914-   )
Concerto for Piano and Orchestra [26'30"]
3(pic).2+English horn.3+bass clar.2+contrabsn. 4.3.3.1. timp,3perc,harp,strings,pno solo
JOBERT   (024)

Paso Doble [8']
2.2.2.2. 4.2.3.1. timp,perc,harp, pno,strings
BILLAUDOT perf mat rent   (025)

Promethee [28']
1.2.1.1. 2.2.1.0. perc,pno, strings without vla
BILLAUDOT perf mat rent   (026)

Representations De Tanit, Les [27']
2.2.2.2. 4.2.2.1. timp,perc,harp, pno,strings
BILLAUDOT perf mat rent   (027)

OHOI see Scelsi, Giacinto

OI SAAVU, RAUHAN JUHLA, FOR SOLO VOICE AND ORCHESTRA [ARR.] see Kuusisto, Taneli

OISEAU DE FEU, L' see Stravinsky, Igor, Firebird

OISEAU DE NUIT, FOR SAXOPHONE AND ORCHESTRA see Colombier, Michel

OISEAUX EXOTIQUES: SUITE see Freedman, Harry

OKAMOTO, MASAMI (1932-   )
Allegro Alla Tala, For Violoncello And Orchestra [9']
2+pic+alto fl.2+English horn.2+ bass clar.2+contrabsn. 4.3.3.1. timp,perc,strings,vcl solo
sc JAPAN 8417 f.s.   (028)

Spring Has Come [2'30"]
2+pic.2+English horn.2+bass clar.2+contrabsn. 4.3.2+bass trom.1. timp,perc,strings
JAPAN 8223 f.s.   (029)

OKOLOGIE 2 see Kortekangas, Olli

OKTO NOVEMBER see Masson, Askell

OLAFSSON, KJARTAN (1958-   )
Rugged Cliff, The, For Solo Voices And Orchestra
1.1.1.1. 1.1.1.0. timp,perc,pno, strings,TB soli
ICELAND 049-001   (030)

Symphonic Poem
1.1.1.1. 2.1.1.0. timp,perc, strings
ICELAND 049-003   (031)

OLAFUR LILJUROS see Vidar, Jorunn

OLAH, TIBERIU (1928-   )
Colonne Infinie [9']
3(pic).2(English horn).2(bass clar).2(contrabsn). 4.4.3.1. timp,6perc,cel,harp,pno,strings
SALABERT perf mat rent   (032)

Perspective [12']
1.1(English horn).1(bass clar).0. 1.1.1.0. 3perc,vln,vla,vcl,db
sc SALABERT f.s., perf mat rent   (033)

Porte Du Baiser, La [7']
3+2pic.3(English horn).3(bass clar).3+contrabsn. 4.4.4.1. 5perc,strings
SALABERT perf mat rent   (034)

Table Du Silence, La
4.4.4.4. 4.3.4.1. 5perc,strings
SALABERT perf mat rent   (035)

OLAH, TIBERIU (cont'd.)

Translations [12'30"]
    string orch
    SALABERT perf mat rent   (036)

OLAN, DAVID
    Symphony [22']
        2.2.2.2. 4.2.3.1. timp,perc,harp,
        pno,strings
    sc AM.COMP.AL. $139.30   (037)

OLAV KYRRE, FOR SOLO VOICE AND
    ORCHESTRA see Tveitt, Geirr

OLAV LILJEKRANS: FRAGMENT FROM ACT III
    see Eggen, Arne

OLAV LILJEKRANS: MIN MODERS ARVESOLV,
    FOR SOLO VOICE AND ORCHESTRA see
    Eggen, Arne

OLAV LILJEKRANS: MY MOTHER'S SILVER,
    FOR SOLO VOICE AND ORCHESTRA see
    Eggen, Arne, Olav Liljekrans: Min
    Moders Arvesolv, For Solo Voice And
    Orchestra

OLAV LILJEKRANS: OLAVS FORTELLING, FOR
    SOLO VOICE AND ORCHESTRA see Eggen,
    Arne

OLAV LILJEKRANS: OLAVS MONOLOG OG ARIE,
    FOR SOLO VOICE AND ORCHESTRA see
    Eggen, Arne

OLAV LILJEKRANS: OLAV'S MONOLOGUE AND
    ARIA, FOR SOLO VOICE AND ORCHESTRA
    see Eggen, Arne, Olav Liljekrans:
    Olavs Monolog Og Arie, For Solo
    Voice And Orchestra

OLAV LILJEKRANS: OLAV'S STORY, FOR SOLO
    VOICE AND ORCHESTRA see Eggen,
    Arne, Olav Liljekrans: Olavs
    Fortelling, For Solo Voice And
    Orchestra

OLAVIDE, GONZALO DE (1934-   )
    Sine Die
        3(pic).3(English horn).3(bass
        clar).2+contrabsn. 4.3.3.1.
        3perc,2harp,cel,pno,strings
    SALABERT perf mat rent   (038)

OLD CALIFORNIA see Still, William Grant

OLD ENGLISH SUITE see Bantock, [Sir]
    Granville

OLD FASHIONED CHRISTMAS EVE, AN, OP. 11
    see Gaathaug, Morten, Gammeldags
    Julajten, En

OLD NETHERLANDS DANCES see Röntgen,
    Julius

OLD POLISH MUSIC; THREE PIECES IN THE
    OLD STYLE see Gorecki, Henryk
    Mikolaj

OLD PORTRAITS see Sønstevold, Gunnar,
    Gamle Portretter

OLD SWEDISH FOLK TUNE, FOR SOLO VOICE
    AND ORCHESTRA see Törnquist, F.

OLD-TIME POLKA see Rieti, Vittorio

OLD TUNE, AN, FOR SOLO VOICE AND
    ORCHESTRA see Jordan, Sverre,
    Gammel Vise, En, For Solo Voice And
    Orchestra

OLD WOMAN OF BEARE, THE, FOR SOLO VOICE
    AND INSTRUMENTAL ENSEMBLE see
    LeFanu, Nicola

OLDBERG, ARNE (1874-1962)
    Paolo And Francesca
        3(pic).2+English horn.2+bass
        clar.2+contrabsn. 4.3.2.1.
        timp,perc,harp,cel,org,strings
    SCHIRM.G perf mat rent   (039)

OLDRICH AND BOZENA OVERTURE see
    Smetana, Bedrich

OLGA, DANASOVA
    Largo for String Orchestra
        string orch
    SLOV.HUD.FOND   (040)

OLIMPIADE, L': OVERTURE see Galuppi,
    Baldassare

OLIMPIADE, L': SINFONIA see Pergolesi,
    Giovanni Battista

OLIVE, VIVIENNE (1950-   )
    Music for 2 Saxophones and Orchestra
    FURORE FUE 2502 perf mat rent (041)

    Tomba Di Bruno, For Flute And
        Orchestra
    FURORE FUE 2501 perf mat rent (042)

OLIVER, ANGEL (1937-   )
    Grupos De Camera [18'30"]
        ob,clar,bsn,trp,1-2perc,pno,
        strings
    ALPUERTO   (043)

    Riflessi [9'30"]
        3.0.2+bass clar.2+contrabsn.
        4.2.3.0. timp,perc,harp,cel,
        pno,gtr,strings
    ALPUERTO   (044)

OLIVER, HAROLD (1942-   )
    Concerto for Piano and Orchestra
        [25']
    sc APNM $25.00, perf mat rent (045)

    Concerto for Violin and String
        Orchestra [21']
        string orch,vln solo
    sc APNM $10.50, perf mat rent (046)

OLIVER, STEPHEN (1950-   )
    Boy And The Dolphin, The [15']
        flexible instrumentation NOVELLO
        perf mat rent   (047)

    Luv [12']
        3(pic).3.3(bass clar).3. 4.4.3.1.
        3perc,timp,strings
    NOVELLO perf mat rent   (048)

    Symphony [20']
        2.2.2.2. 2.2.0.0. timp,strings
    NOVELLO perf mat rent   (049)

OLIVERO, BETTY (1954-   )
    Batnun, For Double Bass And Chamber
        Orchestra [14']
        2.2.2.1. 0.0.0.0. 2perc,harp,pno,
        pno&cel,strings,db solo
    RICORDI-IT 134009 perf mat rent
                                      (050)

OLSEN, OLE (1817-1909)
    Svein Uraed: Suite
        string orch
    NORSK perf mat rent   (051)

OLSEN, OTTO
    Rhapsodie Danoise *Op.6 [15']
        2(pic).2.2.2. 4.2.3.1. timp,perc,
        harp,strings
    HANSEN-DEN perf mat rent   (052)

OLSEN, POUL ROVSING
    see ROVSING OLSEN, POUL

OLSEN, SPARRE (1903-1984)
    Air for Oboe and String Orchestra
        string orch,ob solo
    NORSK perf mat rent   (053)

    Andante Funebre *Op.60,No.2
        string orch sc LYCHE 867 f.s. (054)

    Music for Orchestra, Op. 38 [12']
        2.2.2.2. 4.2.2.1. timp,perc,
        strings
    NORGE   (055)

    Symphonic Fantasy No.3 *Op.56
        2.2.2.2. 2.3.3.1. timp,strings
    NORSK perf mat rent   (056)

    Two Edda Kvad, For Solo Voice And
        Orchestra *Op.8 [4']
        2.2.2.2. 1.1.0.0. timp,strings,S
        solo
    NORSK perf mat rent   (057)

OLSON, BYRON
    Theme and Variations for Piano and
        Orchestra [21']
        4.1(English horn).3.2. 4.4.3+bass
        trom.1. timp,perc,cel,harp,
        strings,pno solo
    NEWAM 19001 perf mat rent   (058)

OLTHUIS, KEES (1940-   )
    Jour De Fete [18']
        3.3.4.3. 4.3.3.1. timp,4perc,
        2harp,strings
    sc DONEMUS f.s., perf mat rent
                                      (059)

    Theseusfantasie [18']
        3.3.4.3. 4.3.3.1. timp,4perc,
        2harp,strings
    DONEMUS perf mat rent   (060)

    Tours De Carte [18']
        2.2.2.2. 2.2.0.0. timp,perc,
        strings
    sc DONEMUS f.s., perf mat rent
                                      (061)

OLYMPIC FLAME see Vacek, Miloš

OLYMPICS OVERTURE see Ward-Steinman,
    David

OLYMPIQUES, LES, FOR SOLO VOICE AND
    STRING ORCHESTRA see Williamson,
    Malcolm

OLYMPISK HYMNE see Børresen, Hakon

OM KVELDEN see Groven, Eivind

OMAGGI see Blank, William

OMAGGIO A BELLINI see Mercadante, G.
    Saverio

OMAGGIO A BELMONTE see Malipiero, Gian
    Francesco

OMAGGIO A CARPACCIO see Tessier, Roger

OMAGGIO A STRAVINSKY see Bettinelli,
    Bruno

OMBRA FELICE, FOR SOLO VOICE AND
    ORCHESTRA see Mozart, Wolfgang
    Amadeus

OMBRE RIFLESSE, LE, FOR PIANO AND
    ORCHESTRA see Sbordoni, Alessandro

OMBRES see Ferrero, Lorenzo

OMEDETO see Fürst, Paul Walter

OMKRING TIGGARN FRAN LOUSSA, FOR
    NARRATOR AND ORCHESTRA see Jonsson,
    Josef [Petrus]

OMPHALE'S SPINNING WHEEL see Saint-
    Saëns, Camille, Rouet D'Omphale, Le

ON A DREAM, FOR VIOLA AND ORCHESTRA see
    Samuel, Gerhard

ON ALL FOURS see Turnage, Mark-Anthony

ON GAZING AT AN OLD PAINTING, FOR SOLO
    VOICE AND ORCHESTRA see Wolf, Hugo,
    Auf Ein Altes Bild "In Gruner
    Landschaft", For Solo Voice And
    Orchestra

ON GREEN MOUNTAIN see Shapero, Harold
    Samuel

ON HANGET KORKEAT NIETOKSET, FOR SOLO
    VOICE AND ORCHESTRA [ARR.] see
    Sibelius, Jean

ON HEARING THE FIRST CUCKOO IN SPRING
    see Delius, Frederick

ON MAASA HANGET PUHTAHAT, FOR SOLO
    VOICE AND STRING ORCHESTRA [ARR.]
    see Hannikainen, Väinö

ON PARADE MARCH see Sousa, John Philip

ON SEVEN PLANETS: MARA'S ARIA, FOR SOLO
    VOICES AND ORCHESTRA see Mica,
    Frantisek Vaclav

ON THE DEATH OF A YOUNG PRINCESS see
    Ravel, Maurice, Pavane Pour Une
    Infante Defunte

ON THE SHOULDERS OF GIANTS see Stock,
    David Frederick

ON WINGS OF INFINITE NIGHT see McTee,
    Cindy

ONDERWERPING, FOR ALTO SAXOPHONE AND
    ORCHESTRA see Meijering, Chiel

1.41 see Tomasson, Jonas

ONE HEART, ONE MIND see Strauss,
    Johann, [Jr.], Ein Herz Ein Sinn

135TH STREET: A LA BLUE MONDAY [ARR.]
    see Gershwin, George

ONE MORNING IN SPRING see Hadley,
    Patrick Arthur Sheldon

ONE PEARL, FOR SOLO VOICE AND ORCHESTRA
    see Bauld, Alison

ONE PIECE FOR FIVE WOODWINDS AND
    STRINGS see Mamlok, Ursula

ONE WAY see Kunst, Jos

ONEMO see Cline, Thornton

ONLY TIME, THE, FOR SOLO VOICE AND
    STRING ORCHESTRA see Rangström,
    Ture

ONNELLISET, FOR SOLO VOICE AND
    ORCHESTRA [ARR.] see Merikanto,
    Oskar

ONWARD, YE PEOPLES see Sibelius, Jean

ONZE CONVERGENCES see Arma, Paul (Pál)
    (Imre Weisshaus)

OPEN FIELD, THE see Tann, Hilary

OPENING see Asheim, Nils Henrik

OPENING FANFARE FOR THE WEDDING OF
    PRINCE CHARLES AND LADY DIANA
    SPENCER see Willcocks, David
    Valentine

OPENING STATEMENT see Weisberg, Arthur

OPERA-BUS, CHAPITRE I: PROLOGUE see
    Bayle, Francois

OPERA-BUS, CHAPITRE IV: LES CLOWNS, FOR
    SOLO VOICE AND INSTRUMENTAL
    ENSEMBLE see Malec, Ivo

OPERA-BUS, CHAPITRE V: LA MUSIQUE A
    L'ENVERS see Ferrari, Luc

OPERA-BUS, CHAPITRE VII: RESSOURCES,
    FOR SOLO VOICE AND INSTRUMENTAL
    ENSEMBLE see Malec, Ivo

OPERA-BUS, CHAPITRES II, III, VI see
    Canton, Edouardo

OPERA STRUMENTALE see Balakauskas,
    Osvaldas

OPERAND see Kucera, Václav

OPERATION MAMBO see Templeton, Alec

OPRITCHNIK: DANCE see Tchaikovsky,
    Piotr Ilyich

OPUS 35 see Testi, Flavio

OPUS 50, (DAUNIUM) see Manzoni, Giacomo

OPUS INCERTUM see Raxach, Enrique

OPUS NEWER PADUANEN: FIVE DANCES see
    Simpson, Thomas, Opus Newer
    Paduanen: Funf Tanzsatze

OPUS NEWER PADUANEN: FUNF TANZSATZE see
    Simpson, Thomas

OPVARMING see Sønstevold, Gunnar

OR CHE IL DOVER, FOR SOLO VOICE AND
    ORCHESTRA see Mozart, Wolfgang
    Amadeus

ORA see Karkoff, Ingvar

ORACLE see Brott, Alexander

ORAGE, L'. OVERTURE see Tchaikovsky,
    Piotr Ilyich

ORATEUR MUET, L' see Levinas, Michael

ORAWA see Kilar, Wojciech

ORBÁN, GYORGY
    Serenade No. 1
        sc EMB 13087 f.s., perf mat rent
                                        (062)
    Serenade No. 2
        sc EMB 13243 f.s., perf mat rent
                                        (063)
    Triple-Sextet
        sc EMB 13088 f.s., perf mat rent
                                        (064)

ØRBECK, ANNE MARIE (1911-   )
    Pastorale And Allegro, For Flute And
        String Orchestra [10']
        string orch,fl solo
        NORSK perf mat rent   (065)

    So Rodde Dei Fjordan, For Solo Voice
        And Orchestra [3']
        2.2.0.2. 2.0.0.0. perc,harp,
            strings,solo voice
        "Then They Rowed On The Fjord, For
            Solo Voice And Orchestra" NORGE
                                        (066)
    Symphony [32']
        3.2.2.2. 4.2.3.1. timp,perc,harp,
            strings
        NORGE   (067)

    Then They Rowed On The Fjord, For
        Solo Voice And Orchestra
        see So Rodde Dei Fjordan, For Solo
        Voice And Orchestra

    Vill-Guri, For Solo Voice And
        Orchestra [2']
        1.0.2.2. 2.0.0.0. timp,harp,cel,
            strings,solo voice
        NORGE   (068)

ORBES DE FEU see Tisne, Antoine

ORBON, JULIAN (1925-   )
    Monte Gelboe, For Solo Voice And
        Orchestra
        2.2.2(bass clar).2. 4.3.0.0.
            timp,perc,harp,cel,hpsd,
            strings,narrator&T solo
        PEER perf mat rent   (069)

ORC, FOR HORN AND ORCHESTRA see
    Martland, Steve

ORCHESTERDIVERTIMENTO IN C-JONISCH see
    Wolter, Detlef

ORCHESTERDIVERTIMENTO IN ES-LYDISCH see
    Wolter, Detlef

ORCHESTERSTUCK see Rihm, Wolfgang

ORCHESTERSTUCKE see Bischof, Rainer see
    Klebe, Giselher

ORCHESTERSUITE IN ZEHN SATZEN see
    Schultze, Norbert

ORCHESTRA ANTIPHONALIS see Fongaard,
    Bjørn

ORCHESTRAL COMPOSITIONS see Peiko,
    Nikolai

ORCHESTRAL PIECE NO. 2 see Persen,
    John, Orkesterverk II

ORCHESTRAL TRILOGY see Laufer, Beatrice

ORCHESTRAL TRIOS, OP. 2, NOS. 2-3, AND
    TRIO-DIVERTIMENTO, OP. 5, NO. 3 see
    Le Duc, Simon

ORCHESTRAVARIATIONS see King, John

ORCHESTRE see Levinas, Michael

ORCHESTRON IV see Fürst, Paul Walter

ORDRE SANS ORDRE (SANS DESORDRE), FOR
    GUITAR AND CHAMBER ORCHESTRA see
    Steven, Donald

ORE, CECILIE (1954-   )
    Porphyre [10']
        2.2.2.2. 4.2.2.0. 2perc,strings
        NORSK perf mat rent   (070)

    Strata
        13strings
        NORGE   (071)

OREST: SUITE see Erkanian, Edvand

OREVERK FOR ORKESTER see Persen, John

ORFEO see Brophy, Gerard

ORFEO ED EURIDICE: BALLET DES OMBRES
    HEUREUSES, FOR 2 FLUTES AND
    ORCHESTRA [ARR.] see Gluck,
    Christoph Willibald, Ritter von

ORFEO ED EURIDICE: CHE FARO SENZA
    EURIDICE, FOR SOLO VOICE AND
    ORCHESTRA see Gluck, Christoph
    Willibald, Ritter von

ORFEO ED EURIDICE: OVERTURE see Fux,
    Johann Joseph

ORFEO: TOCCATA AND RITORNELLO [ARR.]
    see Monteverdi, Claudio

ORGANOFONIJA see Ramovs, Primoz

ORGANUM see Keizer, Henk

ORGANUM II see Manneke, Daan

ORGEL-SINFONIE see Eder, Helmut

ORGIA see Tomasson, Jonas

ORIENT ET OCCIDENT see Saint-Saëns,
    Camille

ORIENTAL TALE see Szervanszky, Endre

ORIGINAL SIN see Lewis, John Aaron

ORIGINE DI JAROMERIZ IN MORAVIA, L':
    DUET OF BIMBALCA AND AIDALACCO, FOR
    SOLO VOICES AND ORCHESTRA see Mica,
    Frantisek Vaclav

ORIGINE DI JAROMERIZ IN MORAVIA, L':
    HEDVIKA'S ARIA, FOR SOLO VOICE AND
    ORCHESTRA see Mica, Frantisek
    Vaclav

ORIGINE DI JAROMERIZ IN MORAVIA, L':
    OPEROSA TERNI COLOSSI MOLES, FOR
    SOLO VOICE AND ORCHESTRA see Mica,
    Frantisek Vaclav

ORIGINE DI JAROMERIZ IN MORAVIA, L':
    RECITATIVO ED ARIA DI GUALTERUS,
    FOR SOLO VOICE AND ORCHESTRA see
    Mica, Frantisek Vaclav

ORION, FOR SYNTHESIZER AND ORCHESTRA
    see Minami, Hiroaki

ORION AND PLEIADES, FOR VIOLONCELLO AND
    ORCHESTRA see Takemitsu, Toru

ORION OVER FARNE see Casken, John

ORKESTERVARIATIONER see Hamerik, Ebbe

ORKESTERVERK II see Persen, John

ORKESTMOZAIEK see Rossem, Andries van

ORKESTSTUK see Riedstra, Tom

ORKESTSUITE DE 7 PLANETEN see Delft,
    Marc van

ORKESTVARIATIES, CHACONNE EN FANTASIE
    see Delft, Marc van

ORKNEY WEDDING WITH SUNRISE, AN see
    Davies, Peter Maxwell

ORLANDO PALADINO: OVERTURE see Haydn,
    [Franz] Joseph

ORLANDO'S MUSIC see Swayne, Giles

ORLINSKI, HEINZ BERNHARD
    Evoe, For Harpsichord, Flute,
        Violoncello And String Orchestra
        [10']
        string orch,hpsd solo,fl solo,vcl
            solo
        HUG GH 11016 perf mat rent   (072)

ORNAMENTI NO. 2 see Durko, Zsolt

ORNAMENTI NO. 1 see Durko, Zsolt

OROITALDI see Pablo, Luis de

ORPHEE AUX ENFERS: SUITE [ARR.] see
    Offenbach, Jacques

ORPHEUS see Gurney, Ivor see Liszt,
    Franz

ORPHEUS' GARDEN, FOR DOUBLEBASS AND
    STRINGS see Sharman, Rodney

ORPHEUS QUADRILLE see Strauss, Johann,
    [Sr.]

ORPHEUS TIMES LIGHT, FOR SOLO VOICE AND
    CHAMBER ORCHESTRA see Serebrier,
    Jose

ORPHEUS UND EURYDIKE: ACH, ICH HABE SIE
    VERLOREN, FOR SOLO VOICE AND
    ORCHESTRA see Gluck, Christoph
    Willibald, Ritter von, Orfeo Ed
    Euridice: Che Faro Senza Euridice,
    For Solo Voice And Orchestra

ORPHIKA see Takahashi, Yuji

ORREGO-SALAS, JUAN A. (1919-   )
    Ash Wednesday, For Solo Voice And
        String Orchestra *Op.88 [12']
        string orch,Mez solo
        NORRUTH perf mat rent   (073)

    Cantata De Navidad, For Solo Voice
        And Orchestra *Op.13 [19']
        1.1.1.1. 2.1.0.0. timp,perc,
            strings,S solo
        NORRUTH perf mat rent   (074)

    Concerto for Oboe and String
        Orchestra, Op. 77 [17']
        string orch,ob solo
        NORRUTH perf mat rent   (075)

    Concerto for Piano and Orchestra, No.
        1, Op. 28 [13']
        3.3.3.3. 4.2.3.1. timp,2perc,
            strings,pno solo
        NORRUTH perf mat rent   (076)

    Concerto for Piano and Orchestra, No.
        2, Op. 93 [30']
        2+pic.2+English horn.2+bass
            clar.2. 4.3.3.1. timp,2perc,
            harp,strings,pno solo
        NORRUTH perf mat rent   (077)

    Concerto for Violin and Orchestra,
        Op. 86 [20']
        2+pic.2+English horn.2+bass
            clar.2. 4.2.3.1. timp,3perc,
            cel,harp,strings,vln solo
        NORRUTH perf mat rent   (078)

    Concerto for Violin, Violoncello,
        Piano and Orchestra, Op. 52 [37']
        3.2.2.2. 4.2.2.0. timp,3perc,
            strings,vln solo,vcl solo,pno
            solo
        NORRUTH perf mat rent   (079)

    Concierto De Camara *Op.34 [18']
        1.1.1.1. 2.0.0.0. harp,strings
        NORRUTH perf mat rent   (080)

    Escenas De Cortes Y Pastores *Op.19
        [20']
        2.2.2.2. 4.2.3.0. timp,2perc,pno,
            harp,strings
        NORRUTH perf mat rent   (081)

ORREGO-SALAS, JUAN A. (cont'd.)

Fanfare For Large Orchestra *Op.97
[2']
3.3.3.2. 4.3.3.1. 2perc,strings
NORRUTH perf mat rent   (082)

Jubilaeus Musicus "Ad Honorem
Universitatis Sanctae Mariae"
*Op.45 [15']
2.2.2.2. 4.3.3.1. timp,harp,
strings
NORRUTH perf mat rent   (083)

Palabras De Don Quijote, For Solo
Voice And Orchestra *Op.66 [17']
1.1.1.1. 2.0.0.0. perc,hpsd,gtr,
harp,2vln,2vla,2vcl,db,Bar solo
NORRUTH perf mat rent   (084)

Quattro Liriche Brevi, For Alto
Saxophone And Chamber Orchestra
1.1.1+bass clar.0. 1.1.0.0. perc,
strings,alto sax solo
PEER MUSIK perf mat rent   (085)

Riley's Merriment *Op.94 [9']
3.2.3.2.alto sax. 4.3.3.1. 3perc,
pno,strings
NORRUTH perf mat rent   (086)

Serenata Concertante *Op.40 [18']
3.3.2.2. 4.2.3.1. timp,2perc,
harp,strings
NORRUTH perf mat rent   (087)

Symphony No. 1, Op. 26 [22']
3.3.2.3. 4.4.3.1. timp,3perc,pno,
harp,strings
NORRUTH perf mat rent   (088)

Symphony No. 2, Op. 39 [35']
3.3.3.3. 4.3.3.1. timp,3perc,pno,
harp,strings
NORRUTH perf mat rent   (089)

Symphony No. 3, Op. 50 [24']
3.3.3.3. 4.2.3.1. timp,3perc,
harp,strings
NORRUTH perf mat rent   (090)

Symphony No. 4, Op. 59 [22']
3.3.3.3. 4.3.3.1. timp,harp,
strings, offstage: 2 horn, trp
(Of The Distant Answer) NORRUTH
perf mat rent   (091)

Tangos *Op.82 [8']
1.0.1.0. 0.1.1.0. perc,gtr,acord,
pno,vln,vcl,db
NORRUTH perf mat rent   (092)

Tumbler's Prayer, The *Op.48 [21']
3.2.2.2. 2.2.1.0. timp,3perc,cel,
harp,strings
NORRUTH perf mat rent   (093)

Umbral Del Sueno *Op.30 [28']
2.2.2.2. 3.2.2.1. timp,2perc,pno,
cel,harp,strings
NORRUTH perf mat rent   (094)

Variaciones Serenas *Op.69 [14']
string orch
NORRUTH perf mat rent   (095)

ORTHEL, LEON (1905-1985)
Concerto for Violoncello and
Orchestra, No. 2, Op. 95 [23']
3.2.3.2. 4.2.3.1. timp,2perc,
strings,vcl solo
DONEMUS perf mat rent   (096)

ORTIZ, WILLIAM
Antillas [15']
1.1.1.1. 1.0.0.0. perc,pno,
strings
sc AM.COMP.AL. $21.25   (097)

Resonancia Esferica [18']
2.2.2.2.sax. 4.2.3.1. perc,
strings
AM.COMP.AL. perf mat rent   (098)

ORTOLANI, RIZ
Cristoforo Columbo [14']
2.2.2.2. 4.4.3.1. timp,perc,harp,
org,strings
WARNER perf mat rent   (099)

OSBORNE, NIGEL (1948-   )
Alba, For Solo Voice And Chamber
Orchestra [17']
1(alto fl).1.1(bass clar).0.
1.1.1.0. perc,harp,2vln,vla,
vcl,db,electronic tape,Mez solo
sc UNIVER. UE17694 f.s., perf
rent   (0100)

Concerto for Flute and Chamber
Orchestra [16']
2ob,2horn,10vln,3vla,2vcl,db,fl
solo
sc UNIVER. UE 16420 $35.00   (0101)

OSBORNE, NIGEL (cont'd.)

Esquisse I [7']
6vln,2vla,2vcl,db
UNIVER. perf mat rent   (0102)

Esquisse II [10']
6vln,2vla,2vcl,db
UNIVER. perf mat rent   (0103)

In Camera [19']
1.1.1.1. 1.1.1.0. gtr,2vln,vla,
vcl,db
UNIVER. perf mat rent   (0104)

Sinfonia
4.3.4.3. 6.4.4.1. 4perc,harp,
strings
sc UNIVER. $20.00   (0105)

Sinfonia No. 2 [19']
4(pic,alto fl).4(English
horn).4(bass clar).4+contrabsn.
4.4.4.1. perc,harp,cel,pno,
strings
UNIVER. perf mat rent   (0106)

Stone Garden [15']
1(pic,bass fl).1.1(clar in E
flat,bass clar).1(contrabsn).
1.1.1.0. perc,harp,string quin
UNIVER. perf mat rent   (0107)

Zansa [20']
1.1(English horn).1.1. 1.1.1.0.
perc,pno,2vln,vla,vcl,db
UNIVER. perf mat rent   (0108)

OSIECK, HANS (1910-   )
Acht Korte Karakterschetsen [13']
2.2.2.2. 2.2.0.0. timp,perc,harp,
strings
sc DONEMUS f.s., perf mat rent
(0109)

OSORIO SWAAB, REINE COLAÇO
see COLAÇO OSORIO-SWAAB, REINE

OSTACOLI see Eliasson, Anders

OSTENDORF, JENS-PETER (1944-   )
Funf Orchesterstucke [17']
3.2.2.2. 4.3.3.1. 3perc,acord,
pno/cel,elec gtr,elec pno/elec
org/synthesizer,bass gtr,drums,
strings, elec vln, opt 2
cassette recorders, opt men cor
SIKORSKI perf mat rent   (0110)

Johnny Reitet Westwarts, For Narrator
And Orchestra [21']
3.3.3.3. 3.4.3.0. timp,3perc,pno,
harmonica,strings
SIKORSKI perf mat rent   (0111)

Mein Wagner [15']
3.3.3.3. 4.3.4.1. timp,2perc,
strings, opt speaking voice or
electronic tape
SIKORSKI perf mat rent   (0112)

Musica Leggiera I [6']
3.3.1.3.2sax. 4.3.3.1. 2-4perc,
kbd,elec gtr,2bass gtr,strings
SIKORSKI perf mat rent   (0113)

Musik Ohne Film [20']
string orch
study sc SIKORSKI f.s., perf mat
rent   (0114)

Varia Iter [15']
3.3.3.3. 4.3.3.1. timp,3perc,kbd,
strings
SIKORSKI perf mat rent   (0115)

Vorwarts Zur Unzeit [15']
2.1.2.1. 1.1.1.0. timp,perc,pno/
cel,elec gtr,bass gtr,strings,
electronic tape
SIKORSKI perf mat rent   (0116)

William Ratcliff
1+pic+alto fl.1+English horn.0+
bass clar.0+contrabsn.alto sax.
0.3.2.0. 2perc,harp,pno,strings
[20'] study sc SIKORSKI f.s., perf
mat rent   (0117)

Zeitlupenklang [12'-15']
variable instrumentation; 25
players minimum
perf sc SIKORSKI f.s.   (0118)

OSTER-TRIPTYCHON, FOR VIOLONCELLO AND
CHAMBER ORCHESTRA see Mouravieff,
Leon

OSTERC, SLAVKO (1895-1941)
Ouverture Classique [6']
2(pic).1(English horn).2.2.
4.3.3.1. timp,strings
DRUSTVO DSS 1070 perf mat rent
(0119)

Saloma [20']
1(pic).1(English horn).1(bass
clar).1. 2.1.0.1. perc,string

OSTERC, SLAVKO (cont'd.)

quin
DRUSTVO DSS 928 perf mat rent
(0120)

OSTERGAARD, EDVIN (1959-   )
Janus [16']
4horn,2trom,strings
NORGE   (0121)

OSTINATI see Griesbach, Karl-Rudi

OSTINATO FESTOSO see Kvam, Oddvar S.

OSTINATO II, FOR SOLO VOICE AND
ORCHESTRA see Gabrijelcic, Marijan

OSTLANDSSKISSE NR. 2 see Kristoffersen,
Fridthjof

OTAKA, ATSUTADA (1944-   )
Image Pour Orchestre [10']
3(pic).3.3.3(contrabsn). 4.3.3.0.
timp,perc,harp,pno&cel,strings
sc ZEN-ON 899190 f.s., perf mat
rent   (0122)

OTERO, FRANCISCO (1941-   )
Cancion Desesperada, For Solo Voices
And Chamber Orchestra [15']
1+pic.0.2.0+contrabsn. 0.2.2.1.
perc,pno,harp,gtr,strings,3
solo voices
sc ALPUERTO f.s.   (0123)

Endecha Para Una Encordadura [15']
bsn,tenor sax,trp,trom,2gtr,4vln,
2vla,2vcl,db
sc ALPUERTO f.s.   (0124)

OTHELLO see Bortkiewicz, Sergei
Eduardovich

OTHELLO OVERTURE see Dvorák, Antonín

OTHELLO: SUITE NO. 1 see Machavariani,
Alexei

OTHELLO: SUITE NO. 2 see Machavariani,
Alexei

OTHER DREAMS, OTHER DREAMERS see
Dollarhide, Theodore

"...OTHER ECHOES INHABIT THE GARDEN",
FOR OBOE AND ORCHESTRA see Bose,
Hans Jürgen

OTHO: OVERTURE, [ARR.] see Handel,
George Frideric, Ottone: Overture,
[arr.]

OTRAR see Serkebayev, Almas

OTT, DAVID (1947-   )
Celebration At Vanderburgh [13']
2+pic.2+English horn.2+bass
clar.2. 4.3.3.1. timp,3perc,
harp,strings
MMB perf mat rent   (0125)

Commemoration And Celebration
Overture [10']
2.2.2+bass clar.2. 4.3.3.1. timp,
3perc,strings
MMB perf mat rent   (0126)

Concerto for Alto Flute and Strings
[20']
6vln,2vla,2vcl,opt db,alto fl
solo
MMB perf mat rent   (0127)

Concerto for Percussion and Orchestra
[23']
2+pic(alto fl).2(English horn).2+
bass clar.2(contrabsn).
4.3.3.1. timp,perc,harp,pno,
strings,perc solo
MMB perf mat rent   (0128)

Concerto for Piano and Orchestra in B
flat [25']
2(pic).2(English horn).2+bass
clar.2. 4.3.3.1. timp,perc,
strings,pno solo
MMB perf mat rent   (0129)

Concerto for Saxophone and Orchestra
[19']
2(pic,alto fl).2(English
horn).2.2. 2.1.1.0. timp,2perc,
pno,harp,strings,sax solo
MMB perf mat rent   (0130)

Concerto for Viola and Orchestra
[22']
2+pic.2.2.2+contrabsn. 4.3.3.1.
timp,2perc,harp,strings,vla
solo
MMB perf mat rent   (0131)

Concerto for 2 Violoncelli and
Orchestra [19']
2+pic.2.2.2+contrabsn. 4.3.3.1.
timp,2perc,harp,strings,2vcl

OTT, DAVID (cont'd.)

    soli
    (winds may be reduced to 1.1.1.1.
    2.1.1.0.) MMB perf mat rent
    (0132)

    Concerto for Violoncello and
    Orchestra [30']
    2(pic).2.2.2. 2.2.3.0. timp,perc,
    pno,harp,strings,vcl solo
    MMB perf mat rent   (0133)

    Dodecacelli [16']
    12vcl
    MMB perf mat rent   (0134)

    From Darkness Shines [15']
    2+pic.2.2+bass clar.2. 4.3.3.1.
    timp,perc,harp,pno,strings
    MMB perf mat rent   (0135)

    Genesis II [7']
    2+pic.2.2+bass clar.2. 4.3.3.1.
    timp,perc,pno,strings
    MMB perf mat rent   (0136)

    Music Of The Canvas [20']
    3.2(English horn).3.3. 4.3.3.1.
    timp,3perc,harp,strings
    MMB perf mat rent   (0137)

    Symphony for String Orchestra [15']
    string orch
    MMB perf mat rent   (0138)

    Symphony No. 1 [18']
    2.2.2.2. 2.2.2.0. timp,perc,harp,
    strings
    (Short Symphony) MMB perf mat rent
    (0139)

    Symphony No. 2 [35']
    3.2(English horn).3.3. 4.3.3.1.
    timp,3perc,harp,strings
    MMB perf mat rent   (0140)

    Vertical Shrines [32']
    2+pic.2.2+bass clar.2+contrabsn.
    4.4.3.1. timp,3perc,pno,harp,
    strings
    MMB perf mat rent   (0141)

    Visions [24']
    1.1.2.1. 2.1.1.0. timp,perc,pno,
    harp,strings
    MMB perf mat rent   (0142)

    Water Garden, The [12']
    2+pic.3.2.2+contrabsn. 4.3.3.1.
    timp,perc,harp,pno&cel,strings
    MMB perf mat rent   (0143)

OTTAVA BASSA, FOR DOUBLEBASS AND
ORCHESTRA see Malec, Ivo

OTTE, HANS (1926-   )
    Ensemble For Strings [15']
    string orch
    PETERS   (0144)

OTTO MESI IN DUE ORE: OVERTURE see
Donizetti, Gaetano

OTTO UND THEOPHANO: AH! TU NON SAI, FOR
SOLO VOICE AND ORCHESTRA see
Handel, George Frideric, Ottone:
Ah! Tu Non Sai, For Solo Voice And
String Orchestra

OTTONE: AH! TU NON SAI, FOR SOLO VOICE
AND STRING ORCHESTRA see Handel,
George Frideric

OTTONE: OVERTURE, [ARR.] see Handel,
George Frideric

OUEST II, FOR SOLO VOICE AND
INSTRUMENTAL ENSEMBLE see Masson,
Gerard

OUI see Desilets, Richard

OULIE, EINAR (1890-1957)
    Eventyr, Et *Op.21 [10']
    string orch
    "Fairy Tale, A" NORGE   (0145)

    Fairy Tale, A
    see Eventyr, Et

    Halling March
    see Halling-Marsj

    Halling-Marsj *Op.6 [3']
    2.2.2.2. 4.2.3.1. timp,perc,
    strings
    "Halling March" NORGE   (0146)

    Symphony No. 1, Op. 19 [26']
    2.3.2.3. 4.3.3.1. timp,perc,
    strings
    NORGE   (0147)

    Symphony No. 2, Op. 29 [24']
    2.2.2.2. 2.2.2.0. timp,perc,harp,
    strings
    NORGE   (0148)

OUR FLIRTATION MARCH see Sousa, John
Philip

OUT ISLAND see Park, James

OUT OF SHADOWS AND SOLITUDE see
Richter, Marga

OUT OF THE COOL, FOR SAXOPHONE AND
ORCHESTRA see Heath, Dave

OUT OF THE DARKNESS see Rudhyar, Dane
(Daniel Chennevière)

OUT OF THE SILENCE see Still, William
Grant

OUT OF THE WAY OF THE PEOPLE see
Brubeck, David (Dave) Warren

OUT OF TIME see Samuel, Gerhard

OUT, OUT, THAT IS NORSEMEN'S YEARNING,
FOR SOLO VOICE AND ORCHESTRA see
Eggen, Arne, Ut, Ja Ut, Det Var
Nordmanns Traa, For Solo Voice And
Orchestra

OUVERTURA MONUMENTALE see Saeverud,
Harald

OUVERTURE BRILLANTE see Rapf, Kurt

OUVERTURE CANADIENNE see Lauber, Anne

OUVERTURE CLASSIQUE see Osterc, Slavko

OUVERTURE CONCERTANTE see Stolarczyk,
Willy

OUVERTURE DE CONCERT [ARR.] see Alkan,
Charles-Henri Valentin

OUVERTURE DES NATIONS ANCIENS ET
MODERNES see Telemann, Georg
Philipp

OUVERTURE D'UN OPERA COMIQUE INACHEVE
see Saint-Saëns, Camille

OUVERTURE FANTAISIE see El-Khoury,
Bechara

OUVERTURE FESTIVO see Brustad, Bjarne

OUVERTURE FESTOSO see Johnsen, Hallvard

OUVERTURE IN D see Endler, Johann
Samuel, Suite in D see Telemann,
Georg Philipp

OUVERTURE IN D, MIN72 see Telemann,
Georg Philipp

OUVERTURE IN D, MIN73 see Telemann,
Georg Philipp

OUVERTURE IN F SHARP MINOR see
Telemann, Georg Philipp

OUVERTURE IN G MINOR see Telemann,
Georg Philipp

OUVERTURE: NORD I FJELLOM [ARR.] see
Storbekken, Egil

OUVERTURE POUR LES ACHARIENS see
Ancelin, Pierre

OUVERTURE POUR UN CONTE DE BOCCACE see
Martelli, Henri

OUVERTURE POUR UN DRAME LYRIQUE see
Aliprandi, Paul

OUVERTURE POUR UN OPERA INTERDIT see
Barraud, Henry

OUVERTURE POUR UNE FETE ETRANGE see
Levinas, Michael

OUVERTURE RUSSE see Prokofiev, Serge

OUVERTURE SOLENNELLE see Glazunov,
Alexander Konstantinovich

OUVERTURE SYMPHONIQUE see Cools, Eugène

OUVERTURE TIL ET ROMANTISK LYSTSPILL AV
SHAKESPEARE see Jordan, Sverre

OUVERTURE ZUM 1. MAI see Polovinkin,
Leonid

OVANIN, NIKOLA LEONARD (1911-   )
    Suite for Flute and Orchestra
    strings,bells,fl solo
    UNICORN 1.0105.7 perf mat rent
    (0149)

OVCHINNIKOV, VIACHESLAV (1936-   )
    Festival (Symphony No. 1)
    3.3.3.3. 4.3.3.1. timp,perc,2harp,
    strings [24'] sc VAAP f.s. (0150)

OVCHINNIKOV, VIACHESLAV (cont'd.)

    Symphony No. 1
    see Festival

    Symphony No. 2 [48']
    sc MUZYKA f.s.   (0151)

OVER THE PLAINS see Antheil, George

OVER THE WAVES [ARR.] see Rosas,
Juventino, Sobre Las Olas [arr.]

OVER TIME see Rea, John

OVERTON, HALL (1920-1972)
    Rhythms, For Violin And Chamber
    Orchestra [12']
    1.1.1.1. 1.1.0.0. perc,pno,
    strings,vln solo
    AM.COMP.AL. perf mat rent (0152)

    Sonorities [7']
    2.2.2.2. 2.4.2.1. timp,perc,
    vibra,strings
    sc MJQ $6.95, perf mat rent (0153)

OVERTURA ALLA VITA see Yngwe, Jan

OVERTURA GIOIA see Baden, Conrad

OVERTURA SOLENNE see Kielland, Olav

OVERTURA TRAGICA ALL' "BRAND" D'IBSEN
see Kielland, Olav

OVERTURE 1812 see Tchaikovsky, Piotr
Ilyich

OVERTURE AND CONCLUSION IN E MINOR see
Telemann, Georg Philipp, Tafelmusik
I, No. 1

OVERTURE AND MARCH"1776" see Ives,
Charles

OVERTURE CHAMPETRE see Schultz, Svend
S.

OVERTURE FOR A GERSHWIN CONCERT, [ARR.]
see Gershwin, George

OVERTURE FOR A HAPPY OCCASION see
Blank, Allan see Sculthorpe, Peter
[Joshua]

OVERTURE FOR LIGHT ORCHESTRA see
Berkeley, [Sir] Lennox

OVERTURE FOR ST. CERE see Downes,
Andrew

OVERTURE IN D, TO "THE CAMBRIDGE ODE"
[ARR.] see Boyce, William

OVERTURE IN ENGLAND, THE, 1800-1840
(Temperly, Nicholas; Greenbaum,
Matthew) sc GARLAND
ISBN 0-8240-3844-4 $90.00 "The
Symphony" Vol. E-VI
contains: Bennett, [Sir] William
Sterndale, Overtures, Two;
Bishop, [Sir] Henry (Rowley),
Overtures, Two; MacFarren, [Sir]
George Alexander, Overture;
Potter, Philip Cipriani Hambly,
Overture; Thomson, John,
Overtures, Two   (0154)

OVERTURE IN FRANCE, THE, 1790-1810
(Charlton; La France; Murphy) sc
GARLAND ISBN 0-8240-3836-3 $90.00
"The Symphony" Vol. D-VII
contains: Boieldieu, François-
Adrien, Overture; Catel, Charles
Simon, Overture; Kreutzer,
Rodolphe, Overture; Méhul,
Étienne-Nicolas, Overture;
Rebeyrol, Pierre, Overture;
Widerkehr, Jacques, Symphonie
Concertante   (0155)

OVERTURE "LA BELLA VENEZIANA" see Poné,
Gundaris

OVERTURE "LA PUTAIN" see Telemann,
Georg Philipp, Putain, La

OVERTURE, NEW YEAR'S EVE see Björnsson,
Arni

OVERTURE, ODE FOR HIS MAJESTY'S
BIRTHDAY, 1772 see Boyce, William

OVERTURE, ODE FOR THE NEW YEAR, 1770
see Boyce, William

OVERTURE ON HEBREW THEMES see
Prokofiev, Serge

OVERTURE ON RUSSIAN AND KIRGHIZ FOLK
THEMES see Shostakovich, Dmitri

OVERTURE ON RUSSIAN THEMES see Rimsky-
Korsakov, Nikolai

OVERTURE ON THE CHORALE "VON HIMMEL
  HOCH" see Nicolai, Otto,
  Weihnachtsouverture Uber Den
  Chorale "Vom Himmel Hoch"

OVERTURE ON THE DANISH NATIONAL ANTHEM
  see Tchaikovsky, Piotr Ilyich

OVERTURE PETILLANTE see Fisher, Alfred

OVERTURE, SCHERZO UND FINALE, OP. 52
  see Schumann, Robert (Alexander)

OVERTURE SU TEMA DI I. PIZZETTI see
  Bellisario, Angelo

OVERTURE TO A CARNIVAL see Proto, Frank

OVERTURE TO A COMEDY see Tarp, Svend
  Erik, Lystspilouverture

OVERTURE TO A LEGACY see Tull, Fisher
  Aubrey

OVERTURE TO A LYRICAL DRAMA see Jordan,
  Sverre, Forspill Til Et Lyrisk
  Drama

OVERTURE TO A ROMANTIC PLAY BY
  SHAKESPEARE see Jordan, Sverre,
  Ouverture Til Et Romantisk
  Lystspill Av Shakespeare

OVERTURE TO AN OPERA see Maves, David

OVERTURE TO AN UNFINISHED COMIC OPERA
  see Saint-Saëns, Camille, Ouverture
  D'un Opera Comique Inacheve

OVERTURE TO THE IMAGINARY INVALID see
  Corigliano, John

OVERTURE TO WILLIAM SHAKESPEARE'S
  TWELFTH NIGHT, AN see Bunge, Sas

OVERTUREN UND TANZE AUS DEN OPERN
  "ALEZANDER" UND "BERENICE" UND DEM
  ORATORIUM "THEODORA" see Handel,
  George Frideric

OVERTURES see Boyce, William

OVERTURES, FIVE see Berlioz, Hector
  (Louis)

OVERTURES, FOUR see Bach, Johann
  Sebastian, Suites Nos. 1-4, BWV
  1066- 1069 see Smethergell, William

OVERTURES, FOUR see Beethoven, Ludwig
  van

OVERTURES, FOUR see Beethoven, Ludwig
  van

OVERTURES, FOUR, VOL. 1 see Rossini,
  Gioacchino

OVERTURES, FOUR, VOL. 2 see Rossini,
  Gioacchino

OVERTURES, FOUR see Cherubini, Luigi

OVERTURES, SIX see Beethoven, Ludwig
  van

OVERTURES, TWO see Graun, Carl Heinrich

OVERTURES AND DANCES TO THE OPERAS
  "ALEXANDER" AND "BERENICE" AND THE
  ORATORIO "THEODORA" see Handel,
  George Frideric, Overturen Und
  Tanze Aus Den Opern "Alezander" Und
  "Berenice" Und Dem Oratorium
  "Theodora"

OVERTURES, VOL. 1 see Beethoven, Ludwig
  van

OVERTURES, VOL. 2 see Beethoven, Ludwig
  van

OWENS, ROBERT (1925-   )
  Fields Of Wonder, For Solo Voice And
    String Orchestra [22']
    string orch,T solo
    ORLANDO   (O156)

  Heart On The Wall, For Solo Voice And
    Orchestra [16']
    1.1.2.1. 3.3.0.0. strings,S solo
    ORLANDO perf mat rent   (O157)

OWL AND THE PUSSYCAT, THE, FOR NARRATOR
  AND ORCHESTRA see Surinach, Carlos

OXFORD SUITE see Cruft, Adrian

OYENS, TERA DE MARZ
  see MAREZ OYENS, TERA DE

OZI, ETIENNE (1754-1813)
  Concerto for Bassoon and Orchestra,
    No. 5
    (Ouzounoff, A.) 0.2.0.0. 2.0.0.0.
    strings,bsn solo [18'] SALABERT

OZI, ETIENNE (cont'd.)

    perf mat rent   (O158)

  Symphonie Concertante No. 2, Op. 7
    (Ouzounoff, A.) 0.2.0.0. 2.0.0.0.
    strings,ob/clar solo,bsn solo
    SALABERT perf mat rent   (O159)

  Symphonie Concertante No. 3, Op. 10
    (Ouzounoff, A.) 0.2.0.0. 2.0.0.0.
    strings,ob/clar solo,bsn solo
    [20'] SALABERT perf mat rent
                                   (O160)

P

PA BLUSSUMVOLLUM, FOR SOLO VOICE AND
  ORCHESTRA [ARR.] see Storbekken,
  Egil

PA BOTNEN AV ALT see Søderlind, Ragnar

PA GOTT HUMOR see Rybrant, Stig

PA HOSPITALET OM NATTEN, FOR SOLO VOICE
  AND ORCHESTRA see Groven, Eivind

PA KANNARHAUGENE see Fladmoe, Arvid

PA VALASJOEN, FOR SOLO VOICE AND
  CHAMBER ORCHESTRA see Baden, Conrad

PAA HVAELVET, FOR SOLO VOICE AND
  ORCHESTRA see Tveitt, Geirr

PAA VIDDERNE, FOR NARRATOR AND
  ORCHESTRA see Delius, Frederick

PAA VIDDERNE, FOR ORCHESTRA see Delius,
  Frederick

PAAP, WOUTER (1908-1981)
  Declamatorium "De Drukkunst", For
    Narrator And Orchestra [17']
    2.2.2.1. 2.1.0.0. timp,harp,
    14vln,3vla,4vcl,3db,narrator
    sc DONEMUS f.s.   (P1)

PABLO, LUIS DE (1930-   )
  Heterogeneo, For Solo Voices And
    Orchestra [25']
    4(pic).4.4.4. 4.4.4.2. timp,Hamm,
    2pno,2harp,2cel,2xylo,strings,2
    speaking voices
    SALABERT perf mat rent   (P2)

  Je Mange, Tu Manges [20']
    2.2.2.2. 2.2.0.0. timp,strings,
    opt electronic tape
    SALABERT perf mat rent   (P3)

  Modulos I
    3clar,2xylo,2pno,string quar
    TONOS   (P4)

  Oroitaldi [20']
    3.3.3.2+contrabsn. 5.4.3.1.
    3perc,pno,cel,strings
    SALABERT perf mat rent   (P5)

  Parafrasis [12']
    2.2.2.2. 2.2.2.0. 4vln,2vla,2vcl,
    2db
    SALABERT perf mat rent   (P6)

  Quasi Una Fantasia [25']
    4.4.4.4. 4.3.3.1. timp,4perc,
    2harp,pno,Hamm,strings,6strings
    soli
    SALABERT perf mat rent   (P7)

PACCAGNINI, ANGELO (1930-   )
  Quattro Studi [14']
    1.1.1.1. 1.1.1.0. strings
    SONZOGNO perf mat rent   (P8)

PACHELBEL, JOHANN (1653-1706)
  Chaconne, [arr.]
    (Muller-Hartmann) KALMUS A5708 sc
    $5.00, set $5.00   (P9)

  Partita in G [6'30"]
    string orch,hpsd
    (Seiffert) KALMUS A5581 sc $4.00,
    set $5.00, pts $1.00, ea.   (P10)

PACHMUTOVA, ALEXANDRA (1929-   )
  Concerto for Trumpet and Orchestra
    [19']
    3.2.2.2. 4.2.3.1. timp,perc,harp,
    strings,trp solo
    SIKORSKI perf mat rent   (P11)

PACIFIC 231 see Honegger, Arthur

PACIFIC RIM see Hartke, Stephen Paul

PACIFIC SUITE see Baker, Michael Conway

PACIFIKA RONDO see Harrison, Lou

PACINI, GIOVANNI (1796-1867)
  Sinfonia Dante [30']
    2+pic.2.2.2. 4.2.3.1. timp,perc,
    harp,pno,strings
    BSE 86 perf mat rent   (P12)

PADDINGTON BEAR'S FIRST CONCERT, FOR
  NARRATOR AND ORCHESTRA see
  Chappell, Herbert

PADE, STEEN (1956-)
　　Arcus [20']
　　　　2.2.2.2. 2.2.2.0. perc,harp,
　　　　　strings
　　　　SAMFUNDET perf mat rent　　　　(P13)

　　Symphony [8']
　　　　3(pic).3.3(clar in E
　　　　　flat).3(contrabsn). 4.3.3.0.
　　　　　2perc,pno,strings
　　　　HANSEN-DEN perf mat rent　　　　(P14)

PAEAN see Antoniou, Theodore

PAER, FERDINANDO (1771-1839)
　　Concerto for Organ and Orchestra
　　　[25']
　　　　2.2.2.2. 4.2.0.0. timp,strings,
　　　　　org solo
　　　　BSE 158 perf mat rent　　　　(P15)

　　Leonora Ossia L'amore Coniugale:
　　　Overture
　　　　2.2.2.2. 2.2.0.0. timp,strings
　　　(Maag, Peter) BÄREN. BA 6768　(P16)

PAESAGGI CON L'UNICORNO, FOR PIANO AND
　　ORCHESTRA see Taglietti, Gabrio

PAESAGGIO, IL see Kokkonen, Joonas

PAESE SENZ' ALBA, IL, FOR SOLO VOICE
　　AND ORCHESTRA see Sciarrino,
　　Salvatore

PAGAN POEM, A see Loeffler, Charles
　　Martin

PAGANINI, NICCOLO (1782-1840)
　　Caprice No. 13, For Violin And
　　　Orchestra [arr.]
　　　(Kreisler; McAlister) 0.1.2.2.
　　　　2.0.0.0. strings,vln solo [3']
　　　　KALMUS A7164 sc $3.00, set
　　　　$10.00, pts $1.00, ea.　　　(P17)

　　Caprice No. 20, For Violin And
　　　Orchestra [arr.]
　　　(Kreisler; McAlister) 0.0.2.2.
　　　　2.0.0.0. vln solo [2'30"] KALMUS
　　　　A7165 sc $3.00, set $10.00, pts
　　　　$1.00, ea.　　　　　　　　(P18)

　　Caprice No. 24, For Violin And
　　　Orchestra [arr.]
　　　(Kreisler; McAlister) 0.1+English
　　　　horn.2.2. 2.0.0.0. harp,strings,
　　　　vln solo [5'] KALMUS A7166 sc
　　　　$5.00, set $15.00, pts $1.25, ea.
　　　　　　　　　　　　　　　　(P19)

　　Caprices, Five, For Violin And String
　　　Orchestra [arr.]
　　　(Denisov, Edison) SIKORSKI perf mat
　　　　rent　　　　　　　　　　　(P20)
　　　(Denisov, Edison) string orch,vln
　　　　solo [15'] VAAP perf mat rent (P21)

　　Concerto for Violin and Orchestra,
　　　No. 3, in E [30']
　　　　2+pic.2.2.2. 2.2.3.1. timp,perc,
　　　　　strings,vln solo
　　　　BSE 101 perf mat rent　　　(P22)
　　　　IISM　　　　　　　　　　　(P23)

　　Concerto for Violin and Orchestra,
　　　No. 4, in D minor [30']
　　　　2+pic.2.2.2. 2.2.3.1. timp,perc,
　　　　　strings,vln solo
　　　　BSE 110 perf mat rent　　　(P24)

　　Einleitung Und Thema Mit Variationen,
　　　For Violin And String Orchestra
　　　string orch,vln solo ZIMMER. perf
　　　　mat rent　　　　　　　　　(P25)

　　Octave Study, For Violin And
　　　Orchestra [arr.] (from Caprices
　　　Nos. 17 And 23)
　　　(Nachez) 2.2.2.2. 2.0.0.0. timp,
　　　　strings,vln solo [3'30"] KALMUS
　　　　A5578 sc $5.00, set $15.00, perf
　　　　mat rent　　　　　　　　　(P26)

　　Streghe, Le, For Violin And Orchestra
　　　*Op.8
　　　　2.2.2.1. 2.2.3.0. timp,perc,
　　　　　strings,vln solo [10'] LEMOINE
　　　　perf mat rent　　　　　　　(P27)

　　Tarantelle for Violin and Orchestra,
　　　[arr.]
　　　(Bulatoff) 1.0.2.1. 2.0.1.0.
　　　　strings,vln solo sc CURCI 10113
　　　　perf mat rent　　　　　　　(P28)

　　Variations On A Theme By Rossini, For
　　　Violoncello And String Orchestra
　　　[arr.]
　　　see Variazioni Di Bravura Sopra I
　　　　Temi Del "Mose" Di Rossini, For
　　　　Violoncello And String Orchestra
　　　　[arr.]

　　Variations On A Theme From Rossini's
　　　"Moses", For Violoncello And
　　　String Orchestra [arr.]

PAGANINI, NICCOLO (cont'd.)
　　see Variazioni Di Bravura Sopra I
　　　Temi Del "Mose" Di Rossini, For
　　　Violoncello And String Orchestra
　　　[arr.]

　　Variazioni Di Bravura Sopra I Temi
　　　Del "Mose" Di Rossini, For
　　　Violoncello And String Orchestra
　　　[arr.]
　　　(Thomas-Mifune) "Variations On A
　　　　Theme By Rossini, For Violoncello
　　　　And String Orchestra [arr.]"
　　　　string orch,vcl solo sc,pts
　　　　KUNZEL GM 1177 f.s.　　　(P29)
　　　(Tortelier, Paul) "Variations On A
　　　　Theme From Rossini's "Moses", For
　　　　Violoncello And String Orchestra
　　　　[arr.]" string orch,vcl solo
　　　　[10'] CHESTER perf mat rent (P30)

PAGES OF SOLITARY DELIGHTS, FOR SOLO
　　VOICE AND ORCHESTRA see Steven,
　　Donald

PAGH-PAAN, YOUNGHI (1945-)
　　Madi [20']
　　　　2fl,2clar,bass clar,horn,3vla,
　　　　　2vcl,db
　　　　sc RICORDI-GER SY 2380 f.s., perf
　　　　mat rent　　　　　　　　　(P31)

　　Sori [15']
　　　　3(pic).3(English horn).2+bass
　　　　　clar.3(contrabsn). 4.3.3.1.
　　　　　timp,3perc,strings
　　　　sc RICORDI-GER SY 2344 f.s., perf
　　　　mat rent　　　　　　　　　(P32)

PAGINA see Wendelboe, Jens

PAGLIACCI, I: SILVIO, A QUEST' ORA, FOR
　　SOLO VOICES AND ORCHESTRA see
　　Leoncavallo, Ruggiero

PAHLMAN, EMIL (1837-1890)
　　Finnish Folk Tunes
　　　　3.3.4.2. 2.3.2.0. timp,2perc,
　　　　　strings
　　　　FAZER perf mat rent　　　　(P33)

PAIR OF SOKS, A see Frost, Robert S.

PAISAJES see Revueltas, Silvestre

PAISIELLO, GIOVANNI (1740-1816)
　　Barbiere Di Siviglia, Il: Ah Rosina!
　　　Voi Lindoro? For Solo Voices And
　　　Orchestra
　　　　KALMUS A4888 sc $9.00, set $11.00,
　　　　pts $2.00, ea., perf mat rent
　　　　　　　　　　　　　　　　(P34)
　　Barbiere Di Siviglia, Il: Diamo Allo
　　　Noia Il Bando, For Solo Voices
　　　And Orchestra
　　　　KALMUS A4880 sc $9.00, set $11.00,
　　　　pts $2.00, ea., perf mat rent
　　　　　　　　　　　　　　　　(P35)
　　Barbiere Di Siviglia, Il: Gia Riede
　　　Primavera, For Solo Voice And
　　　Orchestra
　　　　KALMUS A4891 sc $10.00, set $15.00,
　　　　pts $2.00, ea., perf mat rent
　　　　　　　　　　　　　　　　(P36)
　　Barbiere Di Siviglia, Il: Giusto
　　　Ciel, Che Conoscete, For Solo
　　　Voice And Orchestra
　　　　KALMUS A4889 sc $5.00, set $8.00,
　　　　pts $.75, ea.　　　　　　　(P37)
　　Barbiere Di Siviglia, Il: La
　　　Calumnia, Mio Signor, For Solo
　　　Voice And Orchestra
　　　　KALMUS A4886 sc $5.00, set $13.00,
　　　　pts $1.00, ea., perf mat rent
　　　　　　　　　　　　　　　　(P38)
　　Barbiere Di Siviglia, Il: Lode Al
　　　Ciel, For Solo Voices And
　　　Orchestra
　　　　KALMUS A4882 sc $9.00, set $15.00,
　　　　pts $2.00, ea., perf mat rent
　　　　　　　　　　　　　　　　(P39)
　　Barbiere Di Siviglia, Il: Ma Dov' Eri
　　　Tu, Stordito, For Solo Voices And
　　　Orchestra
　　　　KALMUS A4885 sc $9.00, set $11.00,
　　　　pts $2.00, ea., perf mat rent
　　　　　　　　　　　　　　　　(P40)
　　Barbiere Di Siviglia, Il: Non
　　　Dubitar, O Figaro, For Solo
　　　Voices And Orchestra
　　　　KALMUS A4884 sc $5.00, set $6.00,
　　　　pts $1.00, ea.　　　　　　(P41)
　　Barbiere Di Siviglia, Il: Oh Che
　　　Umore, For Solo Voices And
　　　Orchestra
　　　　KALMUS A4890 sc $5.00, set $11.00,
　　　　pts $1.00, ea., perf mat rent
　　　　　　　　　　　　　　　　(P42)
　　Barbiere Di Siviglia, Il: Saper
　　　Bramate, For Solo Voice And
　　　Orchestra
　　　　KALMUS A4883 sc $7.00, set $10.00,
　　　　pts $1.00, ea.　　　　　　(P43)

PAISIELLO, GIOVANNI (cont'd.)
　　Barbiere Di Siviglia, Il: Scorsi Gia
　　　Molti Paesi, For Solo Voice And
　　　Orchestra
　　　　KALMUS A4881 sc $7.00, set $9.00,
　　　　pts $1.00, ea.　　　　　　(P44)

　　Barbiere Di Siviglia, Il: Veramente
　　　Ha Torto, E Vero, For Solo Voice
　　　And Orchestra
　　　　KALMUS K A4887 sc $6.00, set $9.00,
　　　　pts $1.00, ea.　　　　　　(P45)

　　Barbiere Di Siviglia, Il: Vuoi Tu,
　　　Rosina, For Solo Voice And
　　　Orchestra
　　　　KALMUS 4892 sc $3.00, set $6.00,
　　　　pts $.75, ea.　　　　　　　(P46)

　　Concerto for Harpsichord and
　　　Orchestra, No. 3, in A [15']
　　　　2horn,strings,hpsd solo
　　　　sc BSE 52 f.s., perf mat rent (P47)

　　Concerto for Harpsichord and
　　　Orchestra, No. 4, in G minor
　　　[25']
　　　　2horn,strings,hpsd solo
　　　　sc BSE 54 f.s., perf mat rent (P48)

　　Concerto for Harpsichord and
　　　Orchestra, No. 5, in D [17']
　　　　2horn,strings,hpsd solo
　　　　sc BSE 56 f.s., perf mat rent (P49)

　　Concerto for Harpsichord and
　　　Orchestra, No. 6, in B flat [17']
　　　　2horn,strings,hpsd
　　　　sc BSE 58 f.s., perf mat rent (P50)

　　Concerto for Harpsichord and
　　　Orchestra, No. 7, in A
　　　　2horn,strings,hpsd solo
　　　　sc BSE 60 f.s., perf mat rent (P51)

　　Concerto for Harpsichord and
　　　Orchestra, No. 8, in C [20']
　　　　2fl,2ob,2horn,strings,hpsd solo
　　　　BSE 62 perf mat rent　　　(P52)

　　Nina, O La Pazza Per Amore: Overture
　　　(Piccioli) KALMUS A7412 sc $10.00,
　　　　set $19.50, pts $1.50, ea., perf
　　　　mat rent　　　　　　　　　(P53)

　　Sinfonia In Tre Tempi
　　　(Piccioli) KALMUS A7415 sc $15.00,
　　　　set $22.00, pts $2.50, ea., perf
　　　　mat rent　　　　　　　　　(P54)

PAIX DU PARNASSE, LA [ARR.] see
　　Couperin, François (le Grand)

PAJAMA GAME: A NEW TOWN IS A BLUE TOWN,
　　FOR SOLO VOICE AND ORCHESTRA see
　　Adler, Richard

PAJAMA GAME: ENTR'ACTE see Adler,
　　Richard

PAJAMA GAME: HERNANDO'S HIDEAWAY, FOR
　　SOLO VOICE AND ORCHESTRA see Adler,
　　Richard

PAJAMA GAME: HEY THERE, FOR SOLO VOICE
　　AND ORCHESTRA see Adler, Richard

PAJAMA GAME: OVERTURE see Adler,
　　Richard

PAJAMA GAME: SMALL TOWN, FOR SOLO
　　VOICES AND ORCHESTRA see Adler,
　　Richard

PAJAMA GAME: THERE ONCE WAS A MAN, FOR
　　SOLO VOICES AND ORCHESTRA see
　　Adler, Richard

PAKHMUTOVA, ALEXANDRA (1929-)
　　Russian Suite
　　　　3.2.2.2. 4.3.3.1. timp,perc,pno,
　　　　　harp,strings
　　　　VAAP perf mat rent　　　　(P55)

PAKKANEN, FOR SOLO VOICE AND ORCHESTRA
　　see Palmgren, Selim

PALABRAS DE DON QUIJOTE, FOR SOLO VOICE
　　AND ORCHESTRA see Orrego-Salas,
　　Juan A.

PÁLENÍCEK, JOSEF (1914-)
　　Concerto for Piano and Orchestra, No.
　　　3 [20']
　　　　1.1.1.1. 1.1.0.0. timp,perc,
　　　　　strings,pno solo
　　　　SUPRAPHON　　　　　　　　(P56)

PALESTER, ROMAN (1907-)
　　Symphony No. 5, Op. 57
　　　　4.3.4.3.sax. 6.4.4.1. perc,2harp,
　　　　　pno,cel,mand,gtr,strings
　　　　POLSKIE　　　　　　　　　(P57)

PALESTRA DI UN DIAVOLO, LA, FOR VIOLIN AND ORCHESTRA see Schuback, Peter

PALESTRINA, GIOVANNI PIERLUIGI DA (1525-1594)
Tenebrae Factae Sunt [arr.]
(Schreck) 2+pic.2.2.2. 4.2.3.1.
timp,perc,harp,strings [3']
KALMUS A5590 sc $3.00, set
$15.00, perf mat rent   (P58)

PALETTE see Carlsen, Philip

PALIASHVILI, SACHARI (1871-1933)
Daissi: Suite [17']
3.3.2.2. 4.2.3.1. timp,perc,harp,
strings
SIKORSKI perf mat rent   (P59)
VAAP perf mat rent   (P60)

PALIMPSEST see Xenakis, Yannis (Iannis)

PALINDROME EN CHACONNE II see Capdenat,
Philippe

PALINTROPOS, FOR PIANO AND ORCHESTRA
see Tavener, John

PALLASZ, EDWARD (1936-   )
Three Kashubian Folk Tales
see Trzy Bajki Kaszubskie

Trzy Bajki Kaszubskie [8']
2(pic).2(English horn).2(bass
clar).2. 4.2.2.0. 3perc,cel,
pno,harp,strings
"Three Kashubian Folk Tales" sc
POLSKIE f.s.   (P61)

PALLIDO IL SOLE, FOR SOLO VOICE AND
STRING ORCHESTRA see Hasse, Johann
Adolph

PALLILOS Y PANDERETAS see Rodrigo,
Joaquín

PALM COURT MUSIC see Berkeley, [Sir]
Lennox

PALMGREN, SELIM (1878-1951)
Pakkanen, For Solo Voice And
Orchestra *Op.97 [6']
2.2.2.2. 4.2.3.1. timp,perc,
strings,S solo
FAZER perf mat rent   (P62)

PALMIRA REGINA DI PERSIA: OVERTURE see
Salieri, Antonio

PALOMA, LA, FOR SOLO VOICE AND
ORCHESTRA [ARR.] see Yradier,
Sebastian

PALSSON, PALL P. (1928-   )
Braiding Game [25'10"]
2.3.3.3. 3.2.3.1. timp,perc,harp,
pno,cel,strings
ICELAND 020-021   (P63)

Concerto for Bassoon and Orchestra
[24']
2.1.2.1. 3.0.0.0. timp,perc,
strings,bsn solo
ICELAND 020-004   (P64)

Concerto for Clarinet and Orchestra
[27'40"]
2.2.2.2. 3.2.1.0. timp,perc,
strings,clar solo
ICELAND 020-023   (P65)

Few Autumn Leaves, A [13']
3.3.3.3. 3.3.3.1. timp,perc,harp,
cel,strings
ICELAND 020-018   (P66)

Hands
string orch
ICELAND 020-32   (P67)

Meditation On "L" [17'30"]
2.2.2.3. 4.3.3.1. timp,perc,harp,
strings
ICELAND 020-005   (P68)

PAMPA, FOR CLARINET AND ORCHESTRA see
Alandia, Edgar

PAN, FOR SOLO VOICE AND ORCHESTRA see
Rangström, Ture

PAN TWARDOWSKI: DANCE DES MONTAGNARDS
see Rocycki, Ludomir

PANACEA KLANGE WALZER see Strauss,
Johann, [Jr.]

PANCABANA see Laman, Wim

PANDORA: ESSAY see Segerstam, Leif

PANDORA: SKETCHES see Segerstam, Leif

PANIQUE see Delerue, Georges

PANNI, MARCELLO (1940-   )
Capriccio for Piano and Chamber
Orchestra [8']
1.1.1+bass clar.1. 1.1.1.0. perc,
2vln,vla,db,pno solo
SALABERT perf mat rent   (P69)

PANORAMA see Holloway, Robin see Tate,
Phyllis

PANTALON UND COLOMBINE see Mozart,
Wolfgang Amadeus

PANTOMIME see Adomian, Lan

PANUFNIK, ANDRZEJ (1914-1991)
Arbor Cosmica [40']
6vln,3vla,2vcl,db
BOOSEY perf mat rent   (P70)

Concertino for Percussion and String
Orchestra [15']
string orch,2perc soli
sc BOOSEY $24.00, perf mat rent
(P71)

Concerto Festivo [15']
3(pic).2+English horn.2+bass
clar.2+contrabsn. 4.3.3.1.
timp,2-3perc,strings
BOOSEY perf mat rent   (P72)

Concerto for Bassoon and Orchestra
[24']
1.0.2.0. 0.0.0.0. strings,bsn
solo
BOOSEY perf mat rent   (P73)

Divertimento for Strings, [arr.]
[15']
string orch
(Janiewicz) BOOSEY perf mat rent
(P74)

Harmony [17']
2.2.2.2. 0.0.0.0. strings
BOOSEY perf mat rent   (P75)

Metasinfonia, For Organ And Orchestra
[25']
timp,strings,org solo
BOOSEY perf mat rent   (P76)

Procession For Peace, A [7']
3(pic).2+English horn.2+bass
clar.2+contrabsn. 4.3.3.1.
timp,2perc,strings
BOOSEY perf mat rent   (P77)

Sinfonia Votiva [25']
2+pic.2+English horn.2+bass
clar.2+contrabsn. 4.3.3.1.
5perc,1-2harp,strings
sc BOOSEY $20.00, perf mat rent
(P78)

Symphony No. 10 [20']
3.2.3(bass clar).2+contrabsn.
6.3.3.1. 2perc,pno,harp,strings
BOOSEY perf mat rent   (P79)

PAOLO AND FRANCESCA see Oldberg, Arne

PAPAGENO VARIATIONS, FOR DOUBLEBASS AND
STRING ORCHESTRA see Barnes, Milton

PAPILLON, LE, FOR FLUTE AND ORCHESTRA
see Rose, David

PAPILLON QUI TAPAIT DU PIED, LE see
Hasquenoph, Pierre

PAPILLONS see Jacobsen, Julius

PAPINEAU-COUTURE, JEAN (1916-   )
Clair-Obscur, For Contrabassoon,
Doublebass And Orchestra
3.3.3.0. 4.3.3.1. timp,perc,harp,
strings,contrabsn solo,db solo
CAN.MUS.CENT. MI 1450 P217CL (P80)

PAPPACODA POLKA see Strauss, Johann,
[Jr.]

PAQUITA: PAS DE TROIS [ARR.] see
Minkus, Léon (Fyodorovich) [Alois;
Louis]

PARA NINOS see Adomian, Lan

PARABLES, THE see Martinu, Bohuslav
(Jan)

PARABOLE, FOR FLUTE, VIOLONCELLO, PIANO
AND STRING ORCHESTRA see Ferrari,
Giorgio

PARADE MILITAIRE see Massenet, Jules

PARADE QUADRILLE see Strauss, Josef

PARAFRASIS see Pablo, Luis de

PARAFRASIS UBER DIE "FANTASIA ÜBER
EINEN KLANG VON G.F. HANDEL" see
Halffter, Cristobal

PARALLAX see MacBride, David Huston

PARALLEL MOVEMENTS see Sary, Laszlo

PARALLELES-DISTORSION, FOR CLARINET,
VIOLIN, DOUBLE BASS, PIANO, AND
INSTRUMENTAL ENSEMBLE see Koering,
Rene

PARAPHRASE ON THE SONG "NEARER MY GOD
TO THEE" see Nieland, H.

PARCHMAN, GEN LOUIS (1929-   )
Concerto for 2 Pianos and Orchestra,
No. 2
3.3.3.3. 4.3.2.1. timp,3perc,
strings,2pno soli
SEESAW perf mat rent   (P81)

PARCOURS, FOR FLUTE AND STRING
ORCHESTRA see Petit, Pierre

PARCOURS PLURIEL see Durieux, Frederic

PARENTHESES see Aperghis, Georges

PARFAIT AMOUR see Mengelberg, Karel

PARINAMA see Bahk, Junsang

PARIS see Delius, Frederick

PARIS DE CREPUSCULE A L'AUBE, FOR SOLO
VOICE AND ORCHESTRA see Hamilton,
Iain

PARIS SYMPHONIES, VOL. 1 see Haydn,
[Franz] Joseph

PARISIAN IN NEW YORK, A see Trenet,
Charles

PARK, JAMES
Fantasy for String Orchestra
see Out Island

Fantasy No. 2 for String Orchestra
[15']
string orch
sc AM.COMP.AL. $16.20, perf mat
rent   (P82)

Gawain's Passage [14']
2(pic).2(English horn).0.2.
2.2.0.0. timp,perc,strings
sc AM.COMP.AL. $11.85   (P83)

Out Island (Fantasy for String
Orchestra) [10']
string orch
sc AM.COMP.AL. $13.80, perf mat
rent   (P84)

Rondo Con Fantasia Concertante [16']
fl,ob,bsn,strings
sc AM.COMP.AL. $14.50   (P85)

PARKE, DIE, FOR SOLO VOICE AND
ORCHESTRA see Glanert, Detlev

PARKER, MICHAEL (1948-   )
Concerto for Percussion and
Orchestra, Op. 36
2.2.2.2. 4.2.3.1. timp,strings,
perc solo
("...and a roll on the gong")
CAN.MUS.CENT. MI 1340 P242AN
(P86)

In The Late Wind Of Death *Op.35
[17']
2.2.2.2. 4.3.3.1. timp,2perc,
harp,strings
CAN.MUS.CENT. MI 1100 P242IN (P87)

PARMENTIER, F. GORDON
Concerto for Piano and Orchestra
see Mirrors, For Piano And
Orchestra

Double Entendre [10']
2.2.2.2. 4.3.2.0. perc,harp,
strings
AM.COMP.AL. perf mat rent   (P88)

Four Sonnets From The Portuguese, For
Solo Voice And Orchestra [14']
2.2.2.0. 2.2.2.0. timp,perc,harp,
strings,S/T solo
AM.COMP.AL. perf mat rent   (P89)

Mirrors, For Piano And Orchestra
(Concerto for Piano and
Orchestra) [20']
2.2.2.2. 0.2.2.0. timp,strings,
pno solo
AM.COMP.AL. perf mat rent   (P90)

Symphony No. 3 [33']
2.2.2.3. 4.3.3.0. timp,perc,harp,
cel,strings
AM.COMP.AL. perf mat rent   (P91)

PARMI LES HIERARCHIES DES ANGES, FOR
VIOLA AND ORCHESTRA see Lenot,
Jacques

PARODOS see Börtz, Daniel

PAROLES ET L'AIR, LES see Delas, Jose
Luis de

PARRIS, ROBERT (1924-   )
Chamber Music For Orchestra [24']
2+pic.2.2+bass clar.2+contrabsn.
4.3.2+bass trom.1. perc,harp,
cel,strings
AM.COMP.AL. perf mat rent   (P92)

Concerto for Piano and Chamber
Orchestra [20']
1.1.1.1. 2.1.0.0. strings,pno
solo
AM.COMP.AL. perf mat rent   (P93)

Leaden Echo And The Golden Echo, The,
For Solo Voice And Orchestra
[17']
3+pic.2.2(clar in A).2. 2.2.2.0.
timp,strings,Bar solo
sc AM.COMP.AL. $19.90   (P94)

Mad Scene, For Solo Voices And
Orchestra [14']
1.1.1.1. 1.1.0.0. perc,string
quar,SBar soli
AM.COMP.AL. sc $19.80, pts $10.65
(P95)

Symphonic Variations [25']
3.2.3.3. 4.4.3.1. timp,4perc,
harp,cel,pno,strings
sc AM.COMP.AL. $124.80, perf mat
rent   (P96)

Unquiet Heart, The, For Violin And
Orchestra [10']
3.2.2.2. 4.2.3.1. perc,harp,pno&
cel,strings,vln solo
AM.COMP.AL. sc $9.95, pts $3.10
(P97)

PARRY, [SIR] CHARLES HUBERT HASTINGS
(1848-1918)
English Suite, An [14']
string orch
KALMUS A4279 sc $15.00, set $20.00,
perf mat rent   (P98)

Jerusalem [4']
2.2.2.2. 4.2.3.1. timp,strings
ROBERTON perf mat rent   (P99)

Lady Radnor's Suite (Suite in F)
[12']
string orch
KALMUS A4278 sc $10.00, set $10.00
(P100)

Suite in F
see Lady Radnor's Suite

Symphonic Fantasia [55']
2.3.3.3. 4.1.3.1. timp,2harp,
strings
CURWEN perf mat rent   (P101)

Symphonic Variations [12']
2.2.2.2. 4.2.3.1. timp,strings
KALMUS A5886 sc $30.00, set $45.00,
perf mat rent   (P102)

Symphony No. 2 [40']
2.2.2.2. 2.2.3.0. timp,strings
(Cambridge) KALMUS A7466 sc $75.00,
set $100.00, pts $5.00, ea., perf
mat rent   (P103)

Symphony No. 3 in C [31'30"]
2.2.2.2. 4.2.3.0. timp,strings
KALMUS A6356 sc $50.00, set
$100.00, pts $5.00, ea., perf mat
rent   (P104)

PARSIFAL: GOOD FRIDAY SPELL see Wagner,
Richard, Parsifal:
Karfreitagszauber

PARSIFAL: KARFREITAGSZAUBER see Wagner,
Richard

PARSIFAL: MARCH OF THE GRAIL KNIGHTS
see Wagner, Richard

PARSIFAL: SYMPHONIC FRAGMENTS [ARR.]
see Wagner, Richard

PARSIFAL: TITUREL, DER FROMME HELD, FOR
SOLO VOICE AND ORCHESTRA see
Wagner, Richard

PÄRT, ARVO (1935-   )
Arbos [7']
1.1.1.1. 1.1.1.0. triangle,vln,
vla,vcl,db
UNIVER. perf mat rent   (P105)

Cantus In Memory Of Benjamin Britten
string orch,bells
sc UNIVER. 17498 $17.00, perf mat
rent   (P106)

Collage On B-A-C-H [8']
ob,hpsd,pno,strings
SIKORSKI perf mat rent   (P107)
VAAP perf mat rent   (P108)

PÄRT, ARVO (cont'd.)

Dreiklangskonzert, For Violin,
Violoncello And Chamber Orchestra
[22']
fl,bsn,strings,vln solo,vcl solo
sc UNIVER. UE17416 f.s., perf mat
rent   (P109)

Festina Lente [9']
clar,bass clar,harp,strings
UNIVER. perf mat rent   (P110)

Fratres [9']
1.1.1.1. 1.0.0.0. perc,strings
UNIVER. perf mat rent   (P111)

Fratres, For 12 Violoncelli [7']
12vcl
UNIVER. perf mat rent   (P112)

Fratres, For Strings And Percussion
[9']
perc,strings
UNIVER. perf mat rent   (P113)

Fratres, For Violin And Instrumental
Ensemble [9']
1.1.1.1. 1.0.0.0. perc,strings,
vln solo
UNIVER. perf mat rent   (P114)

Nekrolog *Op.5 [12']
3.3.3.3. 4.4.3.1. timp,perc,pno,
strings
BELAIEFF   (P115)

Perpetuum Mobile *Op.10 [5'30"]
3.2+English horn.4.3. 4.4.3.1.
6perc,strings
sc UNIVER. UE13560 $17.50, perf mat
rent   (P116)

Pro Et Contra, For Violoncello And
Orchestra [7']
1.1.1.1.alto sax. 1.1.1.0. timp,
perc,pno,strings,vcl solo
SIKORSKI perf mat rent   (P117)
VAAP perf mat rent   (P118)

Symphony No. 1
1.1.1.1. 2.1.1.0. timp,perc,
strings
SIKORSKI perf mat rent   (P119)
VAAP perf mat rent   (P120)

Symphony No. 2 [14']
3.3.4.3. 6.4.4.0. timp,perc,harp,
pno,strings
SIKORSKI perf mat rent   (P121)
VAAP perf mat rent   (P122)

Tabula Rasa, For 2 Violins And String
Orchestra
string orch,prepared pno,2vln
soli
sc UNIVER. 17249 $33.00   (P123)

Wenn Bach Bienen Gezuchtet Hatte
wind quin,pno,strings
sc UNIVER. UE 18646 f.s.   (P124)

PARTE SIN NOVEDAD, FOR SOLO VOICE AND
ORCHESTRA see Kriesberg, Matthias

PARTENOPE, LA: OVERTURE see Sarro,
Domenico (Sarri)

PARTENZA DI TISIAS, LA, FOR VIOLA AND
ORCHESTRA see Pennisi, Francesco

PARTICLES, FOR SOLO VOICE AND ORCHESTRA
see Gehlhaar, Rolf

PARTIELS see Grisey, Gerard

PARTITA ARGENTEA, FOR SOLO VOICES AND
INSTRUMENTAL ENSEMBLE see
Strategier, Herman

PARTITA IN BAROCCO, FOR SOLO VOICE AND
CHAMBER ORCHESTRA see Zarins,
Margeris

PARTITA POPULARE see Lorentzen, Bent

PARTUS see Hamburg, Jeff

PARVIAINEN, JARMO (1928-   )
Betlehem, For Solo Voice And String
Orchestra [3']
string orch,solo voice
FAZER perf mat rent   (P125)

PARWEZ, AKMAL (1948-   )
Punjab, Land Of Five Rivers
alto fl,ob,clar,bsn,tenor sax,
timp,perc,harp,strings
sc SEESAW $27.00, perf mat rent
(P126)

PAS A PAS see Csemiczky, M.

PAS DE QUATRE [ARR.] see Pugni, Cesare

PASATIERI, THOMAS (1945-   )
Three Sisters [14']
2(pic).2(English horn).2(bass
clar).2(contrabsn). 4.2.3.1.
timp,perc,harp,strings
SCHIRM.G perf mat rent   (P127)

PASCULLI, ANTONIO (1842-1924)
Api, Le, For Oboe And String
Orchestra [arr.]
(Zani, G.) string orch,ob solo [4']
SONZOGNO perf mat rent   (P128)

Concerto Per Oboe E Orchestra, Su
Temi Dell'opera "I Vespri
Siciliani" Di G. Verdi [arr.]
(Zani, G.) 2.0.2.2. 2.0.0.0. timp,
strings,ob solo [15'] SONZOGNO
perf mat rent   (P129)

Concerto Per Oboe E Orchestra, Su
Temi Dell'opera "La Favorita" Di
G. Donizetti [arr.]
(Zani, G.) 2.2.2.2. 2.2.0.0. timp,
perc,strings,ob solo [13']
SONZOGNO perf mat rent   (P130)

PASO DOBLE see Ohana, Maurice

PASQUOTTI, CORRADO (1954-   )
Architesto, L', For Solo Voice And
Orchestra (Cantata No. 1 for Solo
Voice and Orchestra) [20']
3.2.2.2. 2.2.1.0. timp,2perc,
vibra,cel,harp,pno,strings,Bar
solo
RICORDI-IT 133706 perf mat rent
(P131)

Cantata No. 1 for Solo Voice and
Orchestra
see Architesto, L', For Solo Voice
And Orchestra

Forma Magistra Ludi, For Chamber
Orchestra [10']
fl,2ob,2horn,pno,8vln,2vla,2vcl,
db
RICORDI-IT 133197 perf mat rent
(P132)

Poiesis [9']
2.2.2.2. 2.2.0.0. timp,perc,pno,
strings
SONZOGNO perf mat rent   (P133)

PASS INTO SILENCE see Hosokawa, Toshio

PASSACAGLIA AND PERPETUUM MOBILE, FOR
ACCORDION AND CHAMBER ORCHESTRA see
Serebrier, Jose

PASSAGE see Booren, Jo van den see
Spahlinger, Mathias

PASSAGE, FOR SOLO VOICE AND STRING
ORCHESTRA see Tisne, Antoine

PASSAGE, LE see Engel, Paul

PASSAGES see Ducol, Bruno

PASSAGES, FOR SOLO VOICE AND ORCHESTRA
see Rinehart, John see Zwilich,
Ellen Taaffe

PASSELETH TAPESTRY see Wilson, Thomas

PASSIM see Rihm, Wolfgang

PASSING FANCIES see Silverman, Faye-
Ellen

PASSION see Döhl, Friedhelm

PASSION CHORALE, THE [ARR.] see Bach,
Johann Sebastian

PASSION DE JEANNE D'ARC, LA see Booren,
Jo van den

PASSION OF OUR LORD, THE, FOR SOLO
VOICE AND ORCHESTRA see Haquinius,
Algot

PASSION OF ST. CECILIA, THE, FOR PIANO
AND ORCHESTRA see Shatin, Judith

PASSION SELON SADE, LA: SOLO see
Bussotti, Sylvano

PASSIONE AMOROSE, FOR 2 DOUBLE BASSES
AND ORCHESTRA see Bottesini,
Giovani

PASSIONI DI CORRISPONDENZA see Kahrs,
Sven Lyder

PASSO DEL DIAVOLO see Eisma, Will

PASTEL II see Tabachnik, Michel

PASTICCIO see Garlick, Antony

PASTIMES AND AN ALLELUIA see Lessard,
John Ayres

PASTORAL INVENTION, FOR VIOLIN AND
ORCHESTRA see Rojko, Uroš,
Pastoralna Invencija, For Violin
And Orchestra

PASTORAL MORNING, FOR OBOE AND STRING
ORCHESTRA see Weeks

PASTORAL SYMPHONY IN D see Rosetti,
Francesco Antonio

PASTORALE AND ALLEGRO, FOR FLUTE AND
STRING ORCHESTRA see Ørbeck, Anne
Marie

PASTORALE CEVENOLE, FOR CLARINET AND
STRING ORCHESTRA see Cahuzac, Louis

PASTORALE D'AUTOMNE see Sandby, Herman

PASTORALE DE NOEL see Renault, Andre

PASTORALE E RONDO see Sugar, Rezsö

PASTORALE LAMENT, FOR HORN AND STRING
ORCHESTRA see Whear, Paul William

PASTORALE OG FUGE see Baden, Conrad

PASTORALE PER LA NOTTE DELLA NATIVITATE
CHRISTI see Heinichen, Johann David

PASTORALNA INVENCIJA, FOR VIOLIN AND
ORCHESTRA see Rojko, Uroš

PASTORALS see Buck, Ole

PASTORELA, FOR VIOLIN AND ORCHESTRA see
Still, William Grant

PASTORELLA SINFONIA, OP. 2, NO. 5, IN C
see Falb, Remigius

PAT-A-PAN see Kay, Hershy

PATACHICH, IVAN (1922-   )
Capriccio
sc EMB 3473 f.s.   (P134)

Sinfonietta Savariensis
sc EMB 10113 f.s.   (P135)

PATENZA, FOR SOLO VOICE AND ORCHESTRA
see Handel, George Frideric

PATH OF GLORY, THE, FOR SOLO VOICE AND
ORCHESTRA see Still, William Grant

PATLAYENKO, EDUARD (1936-   )
Renaissance Suite *Op.23 [20']
3.1.0.1.sax. 2.0.0.0. timp,glock,
vibra,marimba,hpsd,harp,strings
SIKORSKI perf mat rent   (P136)
VAAP perf mat rent   (P137)

PATRICK, ANDRE (1934-   )
Rhapsody for Clarinet and Orchestra,
No. 1 [8']
2.2.2.2. 2.2.2.0. timp,2pno,harp,
strings,clar solo
BILLAUDOT perf mat rent   (P138)

PATRIOTIC SONGS FOR TRUMPET AND STRING
ORCHESTRA see Halldorsson, Skuli

PATRIQUIN, DONALD
Karenna, For Solo Voice, Harp, And
String Orchestra [17']
string orch,harp,S solo
CAN.MUS.CENT. MV 1306 P314K (P139)

PATTERNS see Still, William Grant

PATTERNS, FOR SOLO VOICE AND ORCHESTRA
see Kelly, Robert T.

PATTERSON, MICHAEL
Campo Traviesa [9'30"]
2+pic.1.2.0.soprano sax.alto
sax.tenor sax.baritone sax.
4.3.4.1. timp,perc,harp,pno,
cel,strings
NEWAM 19034 perf mat rent   (P140)

PATTERSON, PAUL (1947-   )
Concerto for Orchestra, Op. 45 [20']
3.3.3.3. 4.3.3.1. timp,4perc,
strings
study sc UNIVER. UE17342 f.s., perf
mat rent   (P141)

Europhony *Op.55 [15']
2ob,2horn,strings
UNIVER. perf mat rent   (P142)

Propositions, For Harmonica And
String Orchestra *Op.61 [17']
string orch,harmonica solo
UNIVER. perf mat rent   (P143)

Sinfonia, Op. 46
string orch
sc UNIVER. UE 17633 f.s.   (P144)

PATTERSON, PAUL (cont'd.)

Sonors *Op.17
sc,pts WEINBERGER f.s.   (P145)

Upside-Down-Under Variations *Op.56
[5']
2(pic).2.2(clar in E flat).2.
4.3.3.1. timp,2perc,strings
UNIVER. perf mat rent   (P146)

PAUER, JIRÍ (1919-   )
Symphony for Strings
string orch
study sc PANTON 2274 f.s.   (P147)

PAUL BUNYAN: OVERTURE see Britten,
[Sir] Benjamin

PAULINE POLKA see Strauss, Josef

PAULSON, GUSTAF (1898-1966)
Concerto for Piano and Orchestra, No.
2, Op. 115 [21']
2.2.2.2. 2.2.1.0. timp,2perc,
strings,pno solo
STIM   (P148)

PAULUS, STEPHEN HARRISON (1949-   )
Concerto for Orchestra
3.3.3.3. 4.4.3.1. timp,perc,harp,
strings
study sc EUR.AM.MUS. EA00512 f.s.,
perf mat rent   (P149)

Spectra
EUR.AM.MUS. perf mat rent   (P150)

PAUSPERTL, K.
Kuss Mich Heute Bei Musik, For Solo
Voice And Orchestra
KRENN   (P151)

PAVANA [ARR.] see Dumont, Henri

PAVANA E GAGLIARDA [ARR.] see Farina,
Carlo

PAVANA E RONDO, FOR HORN AND ORCHESTRA
see Piaquadio, Peter

PAVANE, OP. 50 see Faure, Gabriel-
Urbain

PAVANE POUR UN GENIE VIVANT see
Francaix, Jean

PAVANE POUR UNE INFANTE DEFUNTE see
Ravel, Maurice

PAVANE POUR UNE INFANTE DEFUNTE [ARR.]
see Ravel, Maurice

PAVLYENKO, SERGEI (1952-   )
Concerto for Flute and Orchestra
[13']
2.2.2.2. 4.3.3.1. timp,perc,harp,
cel,strings,fl solo
SIKORSKI perf mat rent   (P152)

Concerto for Oboe and String
Orchestra [30']
6vln,3vla,3vcl,db,ob solo
SIKORSKI perf mat rent   (P153)

Konzert Serenade, For Clarinet And
Instrumental Ensemble [15']
8vln,4vla,4vcl,db,clar solo
SIKORSKI perf mat rent   (P154)

Symphony No. 3 [15']
1.1.1.1. 1.1.1.0. timp,2perc,cel,
pno,harp,strings
SIKORSKI perf mat rent   (P155)
VAAP perf mat rent   (P156)

PAYNE, ANTHONY (1936-   )
Concerto for Orchestra [21']
2.2.2.2. 2.2.0.0. timp&perc,
strings
study sc CHESTER JWC359 f.s., perf
mat rent   (P157)

Contrapuncti, For String Quartet And
String Orchestra [18']
string orch,string quar soli
CHESTER perf mat rent   (P158)

Half Heard In The Stillness [10']
2.2.2.3. 4.3.3.1. timp,perc,
strings
CHESTER perf mat rent   (P159)

Song Of The Clouds, For Oboe And
Orchestra [25']
2horn,perc,strings,ob solo
CHESTER perf mat rent   (P160)

Songs And Dances [18']
string orch
CHESTER perf mat rent   (P161)

Spirit's Harvest, The [25']
3(pic).2+English horn.2(bass
clar)+clar in E flat.2.
4.3.3.1. timp,2perc,harp,

PAYNE, ANTHONY (cont'd.)
strings
CHESTER perf mat rent   (P162)

Spring's Shining Wake [15']
1.1.2.1. 2.0.0.0. perc,6vln,3vla,
3vcl,2db
CHESTER perf mat rent   (P163)

Suite From A Forgotten Ballet [25']
2.2.2.2. 4.2.3.1. timp,harp,
strings
CHESTER perf mat rent   (P164)

Time's Arrow [25']
3(pic).2+English horn.3(bass
clar).2+contrabsn. 6.4.3.1.
timp,perc,harp,strings
CHESTER perf mat rent   (P165)

PAYNTER, JOHN (1931-   )
Galaxies [15']
2.2.2.2. 4.4.3.1. timp,perc,harp,
pno,strings
UNIVER. perf mat rent   (P166)

PAYSAGES MEDITERRANEES see Wal-Berg

PAYSANNA see Champagne, Claude

PEACE, FOR SOLO VOICE AND ORCHESTRA see
Groven, Eivind, Fred, For Solo
Voice And Orchestra

PEACE OVERTURE see Peck, Russell James

PEACE VARIATIONS see Fisher, Alfred

PEANUTS see Holland, Jack

PEASANT A ROGUE, THE: OVERTURE see
Dvorák, Antonín, Roguish Peasant,
The: Overture

PEASLEE, RICHARD (1930-   )
Afterlight [14'20"]
2.2.2.2. 4.3.3.1. timp,perc,pno,
harp,strings
NEWAM 19035 perf mat rent   (P167)

Nightsongs, For Flute And Orchestra
[10']
harp,strings,flügelhorn/trp solo
MARGUN MM61A sc $8.00, set $25.00
                                    (P168)

PECK, RUSSELL JAMES (1945-   )
Amber Waves, For Brass Quartet And
Orchestra [11']
1.2.2.2. 2.2.0.0. timp,perc,
strings,brass quar soli
PECK perf mat rent   (P169)

Classical Romance [11']
3(pic).2+English horn.2+bass
clar.2+contrabsn. 4.3.3.1.
timp,3perc,strings
PECK perf mat rent   (P170)

Glory And The Grandeur, The, For
Percussion And Orchestra [12']
3(pic).2+bass clar.2+contrabsn.
4.3.3.1. timp,harp,strings,
3perc soli
PECK perf mat rent   (P171)

Jack And Jill At Bunker Hill, For
Narrator And Orchestra [12']
3(pic).2+English horn.2+bass
clar.2+contrabsn. 4.3.3.1.
timp,3perc,harp,strings,
narrator
(alternative scoring: 1+pic.2.2.2.
2.2.1.0. timp, perc, strings,
narrator) PECK perf mat rent
                                    (P172)

Music: The Inside Story, For Narrator
And Orchestra [12']
2.2.2.2. 4.2.3.1. timp,2perc,
strings,narrator
(brass may be reduced to 2.2.0.0.)
PECK perf mat rent   (P173)

Peace Overture [11']
3(pic).2+English horn.2+bass
clar.2+contrabsn. 4.3.3.1.
timp,4perc,pno,strings
PECK perf mat rent   (P174)

Phoenix, The, For Trumpet And
Orchestra [19']
3(pic).2.2.2+opt contrabsn.
4.2.3.1. timp,3perc,strings,trp
solo
PECK perf mat rent   (P175)

Revolutionary Action, For Narrator
And Orchestra [4']
3(pic).2+English horn.2+bass
clar.2+contrabsn. 4.3.3.1.
timp,3perc,harp,strings,
narrator
PECK perf mat rent   (P176)

PECK, RUSSELL JAMES (cont'd.)

Signs Of Life [12']
    string orch
    PECK perf mat rent   (P177)

Thrill Of The Orchestra, The, For
    Narrator And Orchestra [13']
    3(pic).2+English horn.2+bass
    clar.2+opt contrabsn. 4.3.3.1.
    timp,3perc,strings,narrator
    PECK perf mat rent   (P178)

Upward Stream, The, For Saxophone And
    Orchestra [20']
    3(pic).2.2.2. 4.3.3.1. timp,
    2perc,strings,tenor sax solo
    PECK perf mat rent   (P179)

Who Killed Cock Robin, For Narrator
    And Orchestra [17']
    3(pic).3.2+clar in E flat.2+
    contrabsn. 4.3.3.1. timp,2perc,
    harp,pno,strings,narrator
    (winds may be reduced to 1+pic.2.1+
    clref.1+cnbsn.4.2.2.1.) PECK perf
    mat rent   (P180)

PEDERSEN, GUNNER MOLLER
    Sinfonia No. 1
    sc,pts SAMFUNDET f.s.   (P181)

PEDINI, CARLO (1956-   )
    Cantico Dei Cantici [10']
    2.2.2.2. 2.2.0.0. timp,strings
    SONZOGNO perf mat rent   (P182)

Concerto for Violin and Orchestra
    [25']
    4.3.3.3. 4.3.3.1. timp,4perc,cel,
    strings,vln solo
    RICORDI-IT 133354 perf mat rent
                                      (P183)

PEER GYNT: SUITE NO. 1 see Grieg,
    Edvard Hagerup

PEER GYNT: SUITE NO. 2 see Grieg,
    Edvard Hagerup

PEHRSON, JOSEPH RALPH (1950-   )
    Manhattan Plaza Painting
    2.2.2.2. 4.3.3.1. timp,perc,harp,
    strings
    sc SEESAW $33.00, perf mat rent
                                      (P184)
    Regions
    3.3.3.3. 4.3.3.1. timp,3perc,pno,
    harp,strings
    SEESAW   (P185)

PEIKO, NIKOLAI (1916-   )
    Capriccio
    see Orchestral Compositions

    Elegy
    see Orchestral Compositions

    Orchestral Compositions
    sc MUZYKA f.s.
    contains: Capriccio; Elegy;
    Sinfonietta   (P186)

    Sinfonietta
    see Orchestral Compositions

    Symphony No. 5
    3.2.3.2. 4.2.2.1. timp,perc,pno,
    cel,harp,strings
    VAAP perf mat rent   (P187)

    Yakutian Suite
    2.2.2.2. 4.3.3.1. perc,pno,harp,
    strings
    VAAP perf mat rent   (P188)

PEIXINHO, JORGE (1940-   )
    Memoires-Miroirs, For Harpsichord And
    Strings [23']
    6vln,2vla,2vcl,2db, hpsd or clav
    solo
    SALABERT perf mat rent   (P189)

    Voix, For Solo Voice And Chamber
    Orchestra
    2.2.2.2. 2.2.2.0. perc,harp,
    strings,Mez solo
    ALPUERTO   (P190)

PELE see Winslow, Walter

PELLEAS UND MELISANDE see Schoenberg,
    Arnold

PEMBERTON VALLEY, THE see Turner,
    Robert [Comrie]

PEN, THE, FOR PERCUSSION AND STRING
    ORCHESTRA see Wallin, Peter

PENALARA see Fernandez Alvez, Gabriel

PENDERECKI, KRZYSZTOF (1933-   )
    Concerto for Viola and Orchestra
    [18']
    2(pic).2.2.2(contrabsn). 2.2.2.0.
    timp,perc,cel,strings,vla solo,

PENDERECKI, KRZYSZTOF (cont'd.)

    alternate scoring: timp, perc,
    str, vla solo
    study sc SCHOTTS ED 7573 $29.50,
    perf mat rent   (P191)

    Concerto for Violoncello and
    Orchestra, No. 2
    3.2.3.2. 4.2.3.1. timp,perc,cel,
    strings,vcl solo
    study sc SCHOTTS ED 7566 f.s., perf
    mat rent   (P192)

    Lacrimosa [6']
    2.2.2.3. 5.3.3.1. timp,perc,
    strings
    sc SCHOTTS 71 A7075 $12.00, perf
    mat rent   (P193)

    Passacaglia [15']
    2+pic.2+English horn.4.3.
    5.4.4.1. timp,perc,strings
    SCHOTTS perf mat rent   (P194)

    Symphony No. 2
    3.3.3.3. 5.3.3.1. timp,perc,cel,
    strings
    sc SCHOTTS $35.00   (P195)

    Three Pieces In Baroque Style
    string orch
    SCHOTTS sc CONO241 $15.00, set
    CONO241-70 $39.00   (P196)

PENELOPE see Faure, Gabriel-Urbain

PENELOPE'S KNEES, FOR ALTO SAXOPHONE,
    DOUBLEBASS AND CHAMBER GROUP see
    Spratlan, Lewis

PENHERSKI, ZBIGNIEW (1935-   )
    String Play [15']
    string orch
    sc POLSKIE f.s.   (P197)

PENNISI, FRANCESCO (1934-   )
    Andante Sostenuto [7'30"]
    2.2.2.2. 2.2.0.0. 2perc,pno&cel,
    12vln,4vla,4vcl,2db
    RICORDI-IT 132580 perf mat rent
                                      (P198)
    Arioso Mobile, For Flute And
    Orchestra [10']
    2.2.3.2. 2.0.0.0. 2perc,pno,cel,
    harp,6vla,6vcl,2db,fl solo
    RICORDI-IT 133279 perf mat rent
                                      (P199)
    Arrivo Dell' Unicorno, L', For Harp
    And Instrumental Ensemble [8']
    fl,ob,clar,bass clar,horn,perc,
    pno&cel,harp,6vln,3vla,3vcl,
    2db,harp solo
    RICORDI-IT 133862 perf mat rent
                                      (P200)
    Capricci E Cadenze, For Harpsichord
    And Orchestra [10']
    3.2.3.2. 2.2.0.0. 2perc,harp,pno,
    12vln,6vla,6vcl,3db,hpsd solo
    RICORDI-IT 133027 perf mat rent
                                      (P201)
    Due Canzoni Natalizie Etnee [4'30"]
    fl,clar,bass clar,horn,perc,harp,
    2vln,vla,vcl,db
    RICORDI-IT 133725 perf mat rent
                                      (P202)
    Eclisse A Fleri, For 2 Flutes And
    Orchestra [13']
    2.1.3.2. 2.1.1.0. 4perc,pno,harp,
    strings,alto fl solo,bass fl
    solo
    RICORDI-IT 134079 perf mat rent
                                      (P203)
    Era La Notte, For Solo Voice,
    Harpsichord And Orchestra [9']
    2.1.2.1. 2.0.0.0. 2perc,harp,
    strings,S solo,hpsd solo
    RICORDI-IT 133442 perf mat rent
                                      (P204)
    Fantasy for Violoncello and Orchestra
    [7']
    2.0.2.0. 2.1.1.0. 2perc,gtr,harp,
    pno,strings,vcl solo
    RICORDI-IT 132576 perf mat rent
                                      (P205)
    Glaserner Tag [7'30"]
    3.3.3.3. 3.3.0.0. perc,harp,pno&
    cel,strings
    RICORDI-IT 132771 perf mat rent
                                      (P206)
    Memorie E Varianti [15']
    4.4.4.4. 4.3.3.1. 2perc,cel,harp,
    pno,strings
    RICORDI-IT 133160 perf mat rent
                                      (P207)
    Partenza Di Tisias, La, For Viola And
    Orchestra [14'38"]
    4.3.3.3. 2.2.2.0. perc,harp,pno&
    cel,strings,vla solo
    RICORDI-IT 133050 perf mat rent
                                      (P208)
    Postilla Per Aldo Clementi For Harp
    And Instrumental Ensemble [1'40"]
    1.1.2.1. 1.0.0.0. 2perc,harp,cel,
    6vln,3vla,3vcl,2db,harp solo
    (Appendice a "L' Arrivo

PENNISI, FRANCESCO (cont'd.)

    dell'Unicorno") RICORDI-IT 134424
    perf mat rent   (P209)

PENNPLAY see Davidovsky, Mario

PENNYCOOK, BRUCE (1949-   )
    In Your Medium, For Solo Voice And
    Orchestra [52']
    3.2.3.2. 4.3.2.1. 3perc,pno,
    strings,S solo
    CAN.MUS.CENT. MV 1400 P416IN (P210)

PENTAMORPHOSES see Hasquenoph, Pierre

PENTATHLON, FOR 5 VIOLAS AND ORCHESTRA
    see Eisma, Will

PENTATON IN MEMORIAM R.M. see Vajda, J.

PENTECOST MUSIC see Swayne, Giles

PENTHESILEA see Draeseke, Felix see
    Wolf, Hugo

PENTHODE see Carter, Elliott Cook, Jr.

PENTIMENTO see Laderman, Ezra

PENTLAND, BARBARA (1912-   )
    Holiday Suite, For Orchestra [9']
    1.1.1.1. 1.1.1.0. perc,strings
    CAN.MUS.CENT. MI 1200 P419HO (P211)

    Holiday Suite, For String Orchestra
    [9']
    string orch
    CAN.MUS.CENT. MI 1500 P419HO (P212)

    Lament
    2.2.2.2. 4.2.3.0. timp,perc,harp,
    strings
    CAN.MUS.CENT. MI 1100 P419LA (P213)

PEPERMINT-GET see Severac, Deodat de

PEPIN, CLERMONT (1926-   )
    Adagio for Strings [4']
    string orch
    CAN.MUS.CENT. MI 1500 P422A (P214)

    Monade III, For Violin And Orchestra
    [11']
    3.2.2.2. 2.2.2.0. perc,harp,pno,
    strings,vln solo
    CAN.MUS.CENT. MI 1311 P422M3 (P215)

    Quasers (Symphony No. 3)
    4(alto fl).3.3.3. 4.3.3.1. timp,
    4perc,harp,pno,opt Ondes
    Martenot,strings
    CAN.MUS.CENT. MI 1100 P422QU (P216)

    Ronde Villageoise (from L'oiseau-
    Phenix) [5']
    string orch
    CAN.MUS.CENT. MI 1500 P422RO (P217)

    Symphony No. 3
    see Quasers

    Trois Miniatures [4']
    string orch
    CAN.MUS.CENT. MI 1500 P422T (P218)

PEPPING, ERNST (1901-1981)
    Serenade
    KALMUS A6990 sc $60.00, set $50.00,
    pts $3.00, ea., perf mat rent
                                      (P219)
    Variations for Orchestra
    KALMUS A6991 sc $35.00, set $40.00,
    pts $2.00, ea., perf mat rent
                                      (P220)

PEPUSCH, JOHN CHRISTOPHER (1667-1752)
    Concerto for 2 Flutes and String
    Orchestra in C, [arr.]
    (Bodensohn) [13'] sc,pts BODENS
    E 67 f.s.   (P221)

PER ORCHESTRA see Chiiti, Gian Paolo

PER PIETÀ, BELL' IDOL MIO, FOR SOLO
    VOICE AND ORCHESTRA see Mozart,
    Wolfgang Amadeus

PER PIETÀ, NON RICERCATE, FOR SOLO
    VOICE AND ORCHESTRA see Mozart,
    Wolfgang Amadeus

PER QUESTA BELLA MANO, FOR SOLO VOICE
    AND ORCHESTRA see Mozart, Wolfgang
    Amadeus

PER VIE D'ACQUA see Einaudi, Ludovico

PERCEVAL ET BLANCHEFLEUR, FOR SOLO
    VOICE AND ORCHESTRA see Voorn, Joop

PERCUSSIO DI PEKARSKI, FOR PERCUSSION,
    SOLO VOICE AND ORCHESTRA see
    Gubaidulina, Sofia

PERERA, RONALD CHRISTOPHER (1941-   )
Chanteys [13']
2.3.3.3. 4.3.3.1. timp,perc,cel,
harp,acord,strings
study sc SCHIRM.EC $10.00, perf mat
rent   (P222)

PERGAMENT, MOSES (1893-1977)
Concerto for Piano and Orchestra
[27']
2.2.2.2. 4.2.0.0. timp,perc,
strings,pno solo
STIM   (P223)

PERGOLESI, GIOVANNI BATTISTA
(1710-1736)
Adriano In Siria: Sinfonia [6']
2ob,2horn,strings
sc BSE 1185 f.s., perf mat rent
(P224)

Aria Di Farnaspe, For Solo Voice And
String Orchestra [9']
string orch,hpsd,T solo
(Blanchard, R.) BOIS perf mat rent
(P225)

Concerto for Flute and String
Orchestra in D, MIN 633 [12']
string orch without vla,fl solo
INTERNAT. perf mat rent   (P226)

Concerto for Flute and String
Orchestra in G, MIN 634 [10']
string orch without vla,fl solo
INTERNAT. perf mat rent   (P227)

Concerto for 2 Harpsichords and
String Orchestra in C [20']
string orch,2hpsd soli
sc BSE 118 f.s., perf mat rent
(P228)

Concerto for Trumpet and String
Orchestra in G, [arr.]
(Thilde, J.) string orch,trp solo
[12'15"] BILLAUDOT perf mat rent (P229)

Flaminio, Il: Sinfonia [6']
2ob,2horn,strings
sc BSE 1213 f.s., perf mat rent
(P230)

Frate 'Nnamorato, Lo: Sinfonia [6']
string orch
sc BSE 1187 f.s., perf mat rent
(P231)

Olimpiade, L': Sinfonia [6']
2ob,2horn,2trp,strings
sc BSE 1188 f.s., perf mat rent
(P232)

Prigioniero Superbo, Il: Sinfonia
[6']
2ob,2horn,strings
sc BSE 1184 f.s., perf mat rent
(P233)

Salustia: Sinfonia [6']
2ob,2horn,2trp,strings
sc BSE 1192 f.s., perf mat rent
(P234)

Salve Regina for Solo Voice and
String Orchestra
(Darvas) string orch,A solo EMB
f.s. sc 6682, pts 7602   (P235)

Serva Padrona, La: A Serpina
Penserete, For Solo Voice And
Orchestra
KALMUS A4899 sc $5.00, set $3.50,
pts $.75, ea.   (P236)

Serva Padrona, La: Contento Tu Sarai,
For Solo Voices And Orchestra
KALMUS A4902 sc $5.00, set $5.00,
pts $1.00, ea.   (P237)

Serva Padrona, La: La Conosco A
Quegli Occhietti, For Solo Voices
And Orchestra
KALMUS A4898 sc $6.00, set $6.00,
pts $1.00, ea.   (P238)

Serva Padrona, La: Per Te Ho Io Nel
Core, For Solo Voices And
Orchestra
KALMUS A4901 sc $6.00, set $6.00,
pts $1.00, ea.   (P239)

Serva Padrona, La: Sempre In
Contrasti, For Solo Voice And
Orchestra
KALMUS A4896 sc $6.00, set $8.00,
pts $1.00, ea.   (P240)

Serva Padrona, La: Son Imbrogliato Io
Gia, For Solo Voice And Orchestra
KALMUS A4900 sc $5.00, set $6.00,
pts $1.00, ea.   (P241)

Serva Padrona, La: Stizzoso, Mio
Stizzoso, For Solo Voice And
Orchestra
KALMUS A4897 sc $4.00, set $5.00,
pts $1.00, ea.   (P242)

Sinfonia in B flat [10']
string orch
BSE 147 perf mat rent   (P243)

PERGOLESI, GIOVANNI BATTISTA (cont'd.)
Sinfonia in F, MIN 635 [10']
string orch
sc BSE 1190 f.s., perf mat rent
(P244)

Stabat Mater for Solo Voices and
String Orchestra
org,strings,SA soli
KUNZEL 10173 sc $12.00, pts $4.00,
ea., kbd pt $12.00   (P245)

PERI, LA see Dukas, Paul

PERICHOLE, LA: OVERTURE [ARR.] see
Offenbach, Jacques

PERIODICAL SYMPHONIES, TWO see Pleyel,
Ignace Joseph

PERIPETEIA see Musgrave, Thea

PERIPETIE see Franco, Johan

PERLE, GEORGE (1915-   )
Serenade No. 2
1.1.1.1.sax. 0.1.0.0. perc,pno,
vln,vla,vcl
study sc PRESSER 416-41080 perf mat
rent   (P246)

Serenade No. 3 for Piano and Chamber
Orchestra
1.1.1.1.sax. 1.0.0.0. perc,vln,
vla,vcl,pno solo
sc GALAXY 1.3008 $18.50   (P247)

Short Symphony, A
3.3.2.3. 4.2.3.1. timp,perc,harp,
cel,strings
sc BOELKE-BOM $30.00   (P248)

PERLES DE CRISTAL see Hamel

PERLONGO, DANIEL JAMES (1942-   )
Concertino [12']
1.1.1.1. 1.1.1.0. harp,pno,
strings
sc AM.COMP.AL. $23.65   (P249)

Ephemeron [15']
4.3.3.3. 4.4.3.1. timp,perc,harp,
strings
sc AM.COMP.AL. $57.90   (P250)

Myriad [9']
4.3.3.3. 4.4.3.1. timp,perc,
2harp,cel,strings
sc AM.COMP.AL. $18.30, perf mat
rent   (P251)

Variations [10']
2.2.2.2. 2.1.1.0. harp,pno,
strings
sc AM.COMP.AL. $12.25   (P252)

Voyage [14']
2.2.2.2. 2.1.1.0. pno,harp,
strings
AM.COMP.AL. perf mat rent   (P253)

PERNAIACHI, GIANFRANCO (1951-   )
Aeon [15']
2.2.2.2. 0.0.0.0. perc,strings
sc SONZOGNO f.s., perf mat rent
(P254)

Aforismi II [14']
2.2.2.2. 2.2.0.0. perc,harp,pno,
strings
sc SONZOGNO f.s., perf mat rent
(P255)

Elogio De La Sombra [14']
string orch
sc SONZOGNO f.s., perf mat rent
(P256)

Nel Tempo E Nella Ragione [11']
2.2.2.2. 2.2.0.0. timp,perc,harp,
pno,strings
sc SONZOGNO f.s., perf mat rent
(P257)

PERNES, THOMAS (1956-   )
Concerto for Harp, Double Bass and
Orchestra [15']
2gtr,pno,8vla,6vcl,3db,harp solo,
db solo
DOBLINGER perf mat rent   (P258)

Concerto for Violin and Orchestra
[19']
0.1.4.3. 6.0.0.0. strings,vln
solo
UNIVER. perf mat rent   (P259)

Gleichsam Eine Sinfonie [39']
3(pic).2+English horn.2+bass
clar.2(contrabsn). 2.3.4.1.
timp,4perc,strings
DOBLINGER perf mat rent   (P260)

PEROSI, [DON] LORENZO (1872-1956)
Tema Variato [15']
2.2.2.2. 4.3.3.1. timp,strings
KAHNT perf mat rent   (P261)

PERPETUO see Constant, Marius

PERPETUUM MOBILE see Pärt, Arvo

PERRY, JULIA (1924-1979)
Concerto In Two Uninterrupted Speeds,
For Piano And Orchestra
2.2.3.2. 4.2.3.0. timp,perc,
strings,pno solo
PEER perf mat rent   (P262)

Symphony No. 4
3(pic).2.2+bass clar.2.tenor sax.
4.2.3.0. baritone horn,perc,
harp,pno,cel,strings
PEER perf mat rent   (P263)

PERSEFONE see Hallman, Bjorn

PERSEIDES, LES see Tabachnik, Michel

PERSEN, JOHN (1941-   )
Alternating Notes For Orchestra
see Dreietoner For Orkester

CSV: Konkurransemusikk [10']
3.3.3.3. 5.3.3.1. timp,perc,
strings
NORGE   (P264)

Dreietoner For Orkester [12']
2.2.2.2. 2.2.1.0. timp,harp,
strings
"Alternating Notes For Orchestra"
NORGE   (P265)

Ear Piece For Orchestra
see Oreverk For Orkester

Orchestral Piece No. 2
see Orkesterverk II

Oreverk For Orkester [12']
"Ear Piece For Orchestra" NORGE
(P266)

Orkesterverk II [14']
2.2.2.2. 3.3.3.0. timp,perc,
strings
"Orchestral Piece No. 2" NORGE
(P267)

Under Kors Og Krone: Amarxia
3.3.3.3. 5.3.3.1. timp,3perc,
harp,strings
NORGE   (P268)

PERSEPHONE DREAM see Harvey, Jonathan

PERSISTENCIAS, FOR GUITAR AND ORCHESTRA
see Balada, Leonardo

PERSPECTIVE see Olah, Tiberiu see
Yuasa, Joji

PERSPECTIVES see Muldowney, Dominic

PERSPECTIVES, FOR CHAMBER ORCHESTRA see
Rosen, Robert

PERTI, GIACOMO ANTONIO (1661-1756)
Sinfonia Avanti La Serenata
(Peress, Maurice) 2trp,strings,cont
sc,pts SCHIRM.G 50480103 $20.00
(P269)

PESCATRICI, LE: OVERTURE see Haydn,
[Franz] Joseph

PESEM ZIVLJENJA, FOR SOLO VOICE AND
ORCHESTRA see Petric, Ivo

PESSON, GERARD (1958-   )
Chants Faez, Les, For Piano And
Chamber Orchestra [9'30"]
1(pic).1.1.1. 1.1.1.0. perc,vln,
vla,vcl,pno solo
SALABERT perf mat rent   (P270)

PESTALOZZA, A. (1851-1934)
Ciribiribin, For Solo Voice And
Orchestra
2.2.2.2. 2.2.0.0. timp,perc,
strings,med solo
SONZOGNO perf mat rent   (P271)

PESTHER CSARDAS see Strauss, Johann,
[Jr.]

PETENERAS, FOR VIOLIN AND ORCHESTRA see
Sarasate, Pablo de

PETER AND THE WOLF, FOR NARRATOR AND
ORCHESTRA see Prokofiev, Serge

PETER SCHMOLL: OVERTURE see Weber, Carl
Maria von

PETIT, JEAN ARMAND (1886-1973)
Reves Et Realites, For Solo Voice And
Orchestra [17']
2.2.2.2. 4.3.2.1. perc,strings,
solo voice
BILLAUDOT perf mat rent   (P272)

PETIT, PIERRE (1922-)
Parcours, For Flute And String
Orchestra [8']
string orch,fl solo
ESCHIG perf mat rent   (P273)

PETIT AIR, FOR SOLO VOICE AND ORCHESTRA
see Elos, E. Giuseppe

PETIT RIEN, UN see Zimmermann, Bernd
Alois

PETIT VILLAGE, FOR SOLO VOICE AND
ORCHESTRA see Vellones, Pierre

PETITE BOHEME, LA: BALLET MUSIC see
Hirchmann

PETITE BOHEME, LA: OVERTURE see
Hirchmann

PETITE CONCERTO, FOR GUITAR AND
ORCHESTRA see Carulli, Ferdinando

PETITE SINFONIE see Gürsching, Albrecht

PETITE SUITE see Absil, Jean see
Castiglioni, Niccolò

PETITE SUITE [ARR.] see Debussy, Claude

PETITE SUITE FOR ORCHESTRA see Delius,
Frederick

PETITE SYMPHONIE see Ikebe, Shin-Ichiro

PETITE SYMPHONIE IN G MINOR [ARR.] see
Schubert, Franz (Peter)

PETITES AVENTURES AU BORD DE LA MER see
Koch-Raphael, Erwin

PETITGIRARD, ALAIN (1940-)
Grand Yacht Despair, Le, For Solo
Voices And Orchestra
2.2.2.2. 2.2.2.1. timp,3perc,
harp,cel,strings,BarB soli
BILLAUDOT perf mat rent   (P274)

Hommage A Kandinsky [19']
1.1.1.1. 1.1.1.0. 2perc,pno,harp,
strings
BILLAUDOT perf mat rent   (P275)

PETITS RIENS, LES see Mozart, Wolfgang
Amadeus

PETRIC, IVO (1931-)
Concerto for Orchestra [20']
3(pic).3(English horn).3(bass
clar).3(contrabsn). 3.3.3.1.
perc,harp,pno&cel,strings
DRUSTVO DSS 1053 perf mat rent
(P276)
Fresque Symphonique
sc PETERS f.s.   (P277)

Groharjeve Impresije [18']
1(pic,alto fl).1(English
horn).1(soprano clar in E flat,
bass clar).1(contrabsn).
3.3.3.1. perc,harp,pno&cel,
strings
"Grohar's Impressions" (this
edition is available from Drustvo
only in Yugoslavia; available in
other countries from Edition
Peters) DRUSTVO DSS 975 perf mat
rent   (P278)

Grohar's Impressions
see Groharjeve Impresije

Hommage A Johannes [21']
1(pic).1(English horn).1(soprano
clar in E flat,bass
clar).1(contrabsn). 3.3.3.0.
perc,harp,pno&cel,strings
DRUSTVO DSS 942 perf mat rent
(P279)
Pesem Zivljenja, For Solo Voice And
Orchestra [30']
2(pic,alto fl).1(English
horn).1(soprano clar in E flat,
bass clar).1(contrabsn).
3.3.3.1. 3perc,harp,pno&cel,
strings,Mez solo
"The Song Of Life, For Solo Voice
And Orchestra" DRUSTVO
ED.DSS 1003 f.s., perf mat rent
(P280)
The Song Of Life, For Solo Voice And
Orchestra
see Pesem Zivljenja, For Solo Voice
And Orchestra

Toccata Concertante, For Percussion
And Orchestra [16']
1(pic).1(English horn).1(soprano
clar in E flat,bass
clar).1(contrabsn). 3.3.3.0.
harp,pno&cel,strings,perc solo
DRUSTVO DSS 923 perf mat rent
(P281)

PETRINI, FRANCESCO (1744-1819)
Symphony for Harp and Orchestra, Op.
26, No. 2
fl,2horn,strings,harp solo
COSTALL C.3642 perf mat rent (P282)

Symphony for Harp and Orchestra, Op.
26, No. 3
fl,2horn,strings,harp solo
COSTALL C.3643 perf mat rent (P283)

PETROUCHKA see Stravinsky, Igor

PETROV, ANDREI P. (1930-)
Concerto for Violin and Orchestra
[18']
3.3.3.2. 4.2.3.1. timp,perc,cel,
harp,strings,vln solo
SIKORSKI perf mat rent   (P284)
VAAP perf mat rent   (P285)

Poem In Memory Of The Battle Of
Leningrad [15']
4trp,timp,perc,org,2pno,hpsd,
strings
SIKORSKI perf mat rent   (P286)
VAAP perf mat rent   (P287)

PETROVICS, EMIL (1930-)
Cantata No. 1
see Egyedül Az Erdöben, For Solo
Voice And Chamber Orchestra

Cantata No. 3
see Fanni Hagyományai, For Solo
Voice And Chamber Orchestra

Cantata No. 5
see Törökországi Levelek, For Solo
Voice And Chamber Orchestra

Egyedül Az Erdöben, For Solo Voice
And Chamber Orchestra (Cantata
No. 1)
sc EMB 10214 f.s.   (P288)

Fanni Hagyományai, For Solo Voice And
Chamber Orchestra (Cantata No. 3)
sc EMB 10233 f.s.   (P289)

Törökországi Levelek, For Solo Voice
And Chamber Orchestra (Cantata
No. 5)
sc EMB 10249 f.s.   (P290)

PETRZELKA, VILÉM (1889-1967)
Concerto for Violin and Orchestra,
Op. 40
2.2.2.2. 4.3.3.1. timp,perc,harp,
strings,vln solo
SUPRAPHON   (P291)

PETTERSSON, ALLAN (1911-1980)
Concerto for Viola and Orchestra
2.2.2.1. 4.2.3.0. timp,strings,
vla solo
NORDISKA perf mat rent   (P292)

Concerto No. 1 for String Orchestra
[21']
string orch
NORDISKA perf mat rent   (P293)

Concerto No. 2 for String Orchestra
[22']
string orch
NORDISKA perf mat rent   (P294)

Eight Barefoot Songs, For Solo Voice
And Orchestra [30']
1.1.2.2. 4.2.2.0. perc,strings,
low solo
NORDISKA perf mat rent   (P295)

Symphonic Movement [11']
3.2.3.3. 4.3.3.1. timp,perc,
strings
NORDISKA perf mat rent   (P296)

Symphony No. 2 [42']
2.2.2.2. 2.2.2.0. timp,perc,cel,
strings
NORDISKA perf mat rent   (P297)

Symphony No. 3 [40']
3.3.3.3. 4.3.3.1. timp,perc,
strings
NORDISKA perf mat rent   (P298)

Symphony No. 4 [38']
3.3.3.3. 4.3.3.1. timp,perc,cel,
strings
NORDISKA perf mat rent   (P299)

Symphony No. 5 [42']
2.2.2.3. 4.3.3.1. timp,perc,
strings
sc NORDISKA $32.50, perf mat rent
(P300)

Symphony No. 6 [59']
3.2.3.3. 4.3.3.1. timp,perc,
strings
sc NORDISKA $39.50, perf mat rent
(P301)

PETTERSSON, ALLAN (cont'd.)

Symphony No. 8 [45']
2+pic.2.2+bass clar.2+contrabsn.
4.3.3.1. timp,perc,strings
study sc NORDISKA f.s., perf mat
rent   (P302)

PEUPLIERS see Cornilios, Nicos

PEZZO, FOR VIOLIN AND ORCHESTRA see
Tardos, Bela

PEZZO CAPRICCIOSO, FOR VIOLONCELLO AND
ORCHESTRA see Tchaikovsky, Piotr
Ilyich

PEZZO CAPRICCIOSO, FOR VIOLONCELLO AND
STRING ORCHESTRA [ARR.] see
Tchaikovsky, Piotr Ilyich

PEZZO CONCERTANTE see Holm, Peder

PEZZO ORCHESTRALE see Berge, Sigurd

PEZZO PER ARCHI see Leitermeyer, Fritz

PEZZO PER ORCHESTRA see Berg, Olav

PEZZO SERENO see Eder, Helmut

PFEFFER UND SALZ, FOR SOLO VOICE AND
INSTRUMENTAL ENSEMBLE see
Lampersberg, Gerhard

PFEIFFER, FRANZ ANTON (1754-1787)
Concerto for Oboe, Bassoon and
Orchestra [14']
2ob,2horn,strings,ob solo,bsn
solo
SUPRAPHON   (P303)

PFITZNER, HANS (1869-1949)
Christelflein, Das, Op.20: Overture
"Christmas Elf, The, Op.20:
Overture" KALMUS A5877 sc $25.00,
set $35.00, perf mat rent   (P304)

Christmas Elf, The, Op.20: Overture
see Christelflein, Das, Op.20:
Overture

Concerto for Piano and Orchestra, Op.
31
min sc EULENBURG EU01820 $10.00
(P305)
Heinzelmannchen, Die, For Solo Voice
And Orchestra *Op.14 [7']
2+pic.2+English horn.2+bass
clar.2+contrabsn. 4.3.3.1.
timp,perc,harp,strings,B solo
KALMUS A6437 sc $12.00, set $36.00,
pts $1.75, ea., perf mat rent
(P306)
Kathchen Von Heilbronn: Overture
KALMUS A6459 sc $17.00, set $40.00,
pts $2.00, ea., perf mat rent
(P307)
Lethe, For Solo Voice And Orchestra
*Op.37 [5']
1.1.3.2. 0.0.3.1. perc,harp,
strings,Bar solo
BOOSEY perf mat rent   (P308)

Scherzo, Op. 1 [12']
2+pic.2.2.2. 2.2.0.0. timp,
strings
KALMUS A6104 sc $8.00, set $15.00,
perf mat rent   (P309)

Symphony, Op. 36a, in C sharp minor
min sc EULENBURG EU01521 $10.00
(P310)
Willkommen Und Abschied, For Solo
Voice And Orchestra *Op.29,No.3
[4']
2.2.3(bass clar).2+contrabsn.
6.2.3.1. timp,perc,harp,
strings,Bar solo
BOOSEY perf mat rent   (P311)

PFLANTZENWELT, DIE see Fongaard, Bjørn

PFLÜGER, HANS GEORG (1944-)
Concerto for Horn and Orchestra [15']
3(pic).3.3.3(contrabsn). 4.3.3.1.
timp,perc,strings,horn solo
BOTE perf mat rent   (P312)

Concerto for Violin, Violoncello and
Orchestra [30']
2(pic).2.2.2(contrabsn). 3.3.2.0.
timp,perc,strings,vln solo,vcl
solo
BOTE perf mat rent   (P313)

Metamorphosen, For Violin, Piano,
Winds And Percussion [18']
2(pic).2(English horn).3(bass
clar).2(contrabsn). 2.1.1.0.
timp,perc,vln solo,pno solo
BOTE perf mat rent   (P314)

PHANOMENE WALZER see Strauss, Johann,
[Jr.]

PHANTASIA FOR ELVIRA SHATAYEV, FOR SOLO VOICE AND ORCHESTRA see Lee, Thomas Oboe

PHANTASIE see Mahler, Gustav

PHANTASIE UBER "LA CI DAREM LA MANO" AUS DON GIOVANNI VON W. A. MOZART, FOR CLARINET AND ORCHESTRA see Danzi, Franz

PHANTASMATA see Rouse, Christopher

PHANTASMS, FOR VIOLA AND ORCHESTRA see Kelemen, Milko

PHANTASY ON ME see Lauermann, Herbert

PHANTOM-BILDER AUF DER SPUR EINES VERDACHTIGEN THEMAS see Gruber, Heinz Karl

PHANTOM CHAPEL see Still, William Grant

PHASE see Gehlhaar, Rolf

PHASES see Bruynèl, Ton see Hedstrom, Åse, Faser see Risset, Jean Claude

PHENOMENA, FOR SOLO VOICE AND CHAMBER ORCHESTRA see Bazelon, Irwin Allen

PHENOMENA: I. COURSE II. CYCLE see Hunfeld, Xander

PHILADELPHIA GRAYS QUICKSTEP see Johnson, Francis

PHILEMON ET BAUCIS: 4 FRAGMENTS SYMPHONIQUES see Gounod, Charles François

PHILHARMONIC CONCERTO see Arnold, Malcolm

PHILHARMONIC OVERTURE see Farkas, Ferenc

PHILHARMONIC WALTZES see Gould, Morton

PHILIAPAIDEIA see Becker, Frank

PHILIBA, NICOLE (1937-   )
Symphony [24']
2.2.2.2. 4.3.3.1. timp,3perc, harp,cel,strings
BILLAUDOT perf mat rent   (P315)

PHILIPPA VARIATIONS see Josephs, Wilfred

PHILIPPE, PIERRE
Fille Qui Chante, La, For Solo Voice And Orchestra [1'45"]
2.2.2.2. 2.0.0.0. perc,pno, strings,S solo
BILLAUDOT perf mat rent   (P316)

PHILIPPOT, MICHEL PAUL (1925-   )
Carres Magiques [16']
1.1.1.1. 2.1.1.0. timp,perc,harp, strings
(Hommage a Evariste Gallois)
SALABERT perf mat rent   (P317)

Composition IV [17'30"]
2.2+English horn.2+bass clar.2+ contrabsn. 4.3.3.1. timp,perc, harp,strings
SALABERT perf mat rent   (P318)

Concerto Pour Alto Et-Ou Violon [20']
2(pic).2+English horn.2(bass clar).2. 4.2.2.1. timp,perc, strings,vln/vla solo, or vln, vla soli
SALABERT perf mat rent   (P319)

Esquisse A La Memoir De Maurice Ravel [3'30"]
string orch
SALABERT perf mat rent   (P320)

Passacaglia [6'30"]
2.2.2.0. 0.1.1.0. harp,vln,vla, vcl
BILLAUDOT perf mat rent   (P321)

PHILLIPS, MARK (1952-   )
Intrusus [18']
1(pic).1.1.1. 1.1.1.1. timp, 3perc,pno&cel,strings
MMB perf mat rent   (P322)

Turning [12']
3+pic.2+English horn.3(bass clar).2+contrabsn. 4.4.3.1. timp,5perc,pno&cel,harp,strings
MMB perf mat rent   (P323)

PHILLIPS, PETER (1930-   )
Concerto Grosso [24']
1.1.1+bass clar.0. 0.1.1.0. 3vln, 2vla,2vcl
sc,pts MJQ rent   (P324)

PHILLIPS, STU
Battlestar Galactica: Suite
3(pic).2(English horn).3(clar in E flat,bass clar).3(contrabsn). 6.4.3.1. timp,3perc,cel,org, strings,synthesizer [10'] DUCHESS perf mat rent   (P325)

PHILOMELEN WALZER see Strauss, Johann, [Sr.]

PHLEGRA see Xenakis, Yannis (Iannis)

PHOENIX, FOR VIOLONCELLO AND ORCHESTRA see Kvam, Oddvar S.

PHOENIX, THE, FOR TRUMPET AND ORCHESTRA see Peck, Russell James

PHONIC DESIGN A see Tosi, Daniel

PHONIC DESIGN B see Tosi, Daniel

PHOTOFIT PICTURES ON THE TRACKS OF A SUSPECT THEME see Gruber, Heinz Karl, Phantom-Bilder Auf Der Spur Eines Verdachtigen Themas

PHRASES II, FOR 2 ORCHESTRAS see Garant, Serge

PHRENOLOGIE see Auriol, Hubert

PIANISSIMO see Schnittke, Alfred

PIANO AND ORCHESTRA see De Vos Malan, Jacques

PIANO CONCERTANT, FOR PIANO AND ORCHESTRA see Evangelista, Jose

PIANO PERSONNAGE, FOR PIANO AND INSTRUMENTAL ENSEMBLE see Constant, Marius

PIANO-PIANO see Barreau, Gisele

PIAQUADIO, PETER
Pavana E Rondo, For Horn And Orchestra
SHAWNEE perf mat rent   (P326)

PIAZZOLLA, ASTOR (1921-1992)
Concerto For Bandoneon And Orchestra [21'40"]
pno,timp,perc,harp,strings, Bandoneon solo
sc CURCI 10367 f.s., perf mat rent   (P327)

Tres Tangos, For Bandoneon And Orchestra [17'30"]
pno,timp,perc,harp,strings, Bandoneon solo
sc CURCI 10372 f.s., perf mat rent   (P328)

PICADORE MARCH, THE see Sousa, John Philip

PICCINNI, NICCOLO (1728-1800)
Atys: Overture [8']
2.2.2.2. 2.2.0.0. timp,strings
BSE 98 perf mat rent   (P329)

Didon: Overture
(Piccioli) KALMUS A7310 sc $15.00, set $40.00, pts $2.50, ea., perf mat rent   (P330)

PICCOLA DIVERTIMENTO see Szunyogh, Balázs

PICCOLA SINFONIA see Abe, Komei

PICCOLA SUITE see Scarlatti, Alessandro

PICCOLO CONCERTO, FOR PICCOLO AND ORCHESTRA see Schudel, Thomas

PICHAUREAU, CLAUDE
Eau Et Le Feu, L' [11']
3(pic,alto fl).2.1+clar in A.3. 4.3.3.1. timp,4perc,cel,harp, strings
RIDEAU perf mat rent   (P331)

Grande Menace, La [14'45"]
2+pic.2+English horn.1+clar in A.2+contrabsn. 4.3.3.1. timp, 4perc,cel,harp,strings
RIDEAU perf mat rent   (P332)

PICHL, WENZEL (VACLAV) (1741-1805)
Symphonies, Three
see Asplmayr, Franz, Symphonies, Three

Symphony No. 4 in E flat
2ob,2horn,strings
sc KUNZEL 10199 $20.00, ipa (P333)

PICKANINNY DANCE [ARR.] see Guion, David Wendall Fentress

PICKER, TOBIAS (1954-   )
Concerto for Piano and Orchestra, No. 2
see Keys To The City, For Piano And Orchestra

Keys To The City, For Piano And Orchestra (Concerto for Piano and Orchestra, No. 2)
2.2.2.2. 4.2.3.1. timp,perc, strings,pno solo
study sc HELICON EA00535 f.s., perf mat rent   (P334)

PICTURES AT AN EXHIBITION, FOR PIANO AND ORCHESTRA [ARR.] see Mussorgsky, Modest Petrovich

PICTURES AT AN EXHIBITION [ARR.] see Mussorgsky, Modest Petrovich

PICTURES FROM A JOURNEY see Tveitt, Geirr, Reisebilleder

PICTURES OF MEDEA, FOR RECORDER AND CHAMBER ORCHESTRA see Johansen, Bertil Palmar

PIECE FOR ELEVEN PLAYERS see Roens, Steve

PIECE FOR JAZZ BASSOON AND ORCHESTRA see Mancini, Henry

PIECE HEROIQUE see Fischer, Irwin

PIECE I see Stefansson, Finnur Torfi

PIECE II see Stefansson, Finnur Torfi

PIECE IN THREE PARTS, FOR PIANO AND SIXTEEN INSTRUMENTS see Wolpe, Stefan

PIED PIPER, THE see Borkovec, Pavel

PIED PIPER FANTASY, FOR FLUTE AND ORCHESTRA see Corigliano, John

PIED PIPER OF HAMLIN, FOR NARRATOR AND ORCHESTRA see Templeton, Alec

PIED PIPER SUITE see Weigl, Karl

PIEDRA NEGRA SOBRE UNA PIEDRA BLANCA, FOR SOLO VOICE AND CHAMBER ORCHESTRA see Krieger, Armando

PIEGES see Izcovich, Ezequiel

PIEPER, RENE (1955-   )
Concerto for Alto Saxophone and Orchestra [23']
2.2.3.2. 4.2.3.1. 2perc,harp, strings,alto sax solo
DONEMUS perf mat rent   (P335)

PIERNE, GABRIEL (1863-1937)
Bouton D'Or: Suite [11'30"]
2.1.2.1. 2.2.3.0. timp,perc, strings
CHOUDENS perf mat rent   (P336)

Children's Crusade, The: Prelude, Part II
see Croisade Des Enfants, La: Prelude, Part II

Croisade Des Enfants, La: Prelude, Part II
"Children's Crusade, The: Prelude, Part II" 2+pic.2+English horn.2+ bass clar.2+ contrabsn(sarrusophone). 4.3.3.1. timp,perc,2harp,strings [5'] KALMUS A7026 sc $5.00, set $20.00, pts $1.00, ea., perf mat rent   (P337)

Izeyl
KALMUS A6439 sc $15.00, set $25.00, pts $1.00, ea., perf mat rent   (P338)

Izeyl Suite [arr.]
(Mouton) 1(pic).1.2.2. 2.2.1.0. timp,perc,strings [12'] KALMUS A6143 pno-cond sc $5.00, set $30.00, perf mat rent   (P339)

Ramuntcho: Basque Rhapsody (from Suite No. 2) [9']
2.2.2.2. 4.2.3.0. sarrusophone, timp,perc,2harp,strings
ENOCH perf mat rent   (P340)

Ramuntcho: Overture (from Suite No. 1) [7']
2+pic.2.2.2. 4.2.3.0. sarrusophone,timp,2perc,harp, strings
ENOCH perf mat rent   (P341)

Ramuntcho: Suite No. 1 [17']
2+pic.2.2.2. 4.2.3.0. sarrusophone,timp,perc,2harp, strings

PIERNE, GABRIEL (cont'd.)

ENOCH perf mat rent   (P342)

Ramuntcho: Suite No. 2 [14']
2.2.2.2. 4.2.3.1. sarrusophone,
timp,perc,2harp,strings
ENOCH perf mat rent   (P343)
KALMUS A5884 sc $10.00, set $25.00,
perf mat rent   (P344)

Solo De Concert, For Bassoon And
Orchestra *Op.35 [9']
2.2.2.2. 2.0.0.0. timp,strings,
bsn solo
KALMUS A7264 sc $12.00, set $22.00,
pts $1.50, ea., perf mat rent
(P345)

PIERNE, PAUL (1874-1952)
Concertino for Alto Saxophone and
Orchestra [15'50"]
1.1.2.2. 2.2.0.0. timp,strings,
alto sax solo
BILLAUDOT perf mat rent   (P346)

PIERRE-IDYLL see Eötvös, Pèter

PIERROT OF THE MINUTE, THE see Bantock,
[Sir] Granville

PIERROT OU LES SECRETS DE LA NUIT see
Francaix, Jean

PIERROT SUITE see Guarnieri, Adriano

PIERROT SUITE II, FOR FLUTE AND
INSTRUMENTAL ENSEMBLE see
Guarnieri, Adriano

PIERSON, TOM
Eye In The Pyramid, The [12']
1(pic).1.1.1+contrabsn.5soprano
sax. 4.4.3+bass trom.1. timp,
perc,2pno,harp,strings
NEWAM 19036 perf mat rent   (P347)

PIETA see Mouravieff, Leon

PIETA, FOR SOLO VOICE AND STRING
ORCHESTRA see Søderlind, Ragnar

PIETA D'AVIGNON, LA see Dandelot,
Georges

PIEZAS CARACTERISTICAS see Albéniz,
Isaac

PILEMONSTERET: SUITE see Andersen, Karl
August

PILEN; SKRIVET PA VANDRING EN TIDIG
VARDAG, FOR SOLO VOICE AND
ORCHESTRA see Danielsson, Harry

PILGER QUADRILLE, DIE see Strauss,
Eduard

PILHOFER, HERB
Three Pieces For Jazz Quartet And
Orchestra [14']
2+pic.2+English horn.2+bass
clar.2+contrabsn. 4.3.3.1.
timp,3perc,harp,strings,gtr
solo,pno solo,db solo,drums
solo
sc,pts MJQ rent   (P348)

PILKY see Janácek, Leoš

PILLNEY, KARL HERMANN (1896-   )
Divertimento for Orchestra [14']
2.2.2.2. 4.2.3.0. timp,perc,harp,
pno,strings
TISCHER perf mat rent   (P349)

PINHO VARGAS, ANTONIO
Geometral [17']
2.1.2.1.alto sax. 2.1.2.0. vibra,
marimba,cel,pno,2vln,vla,vcl,db
sc DONEMUS f.s., perf mat rent
(P350)

PINKHAM, DANIEL (1923-   )
Nocturne [10']
string orch
sc AM.COMP.AL. $9.55   (P351)

Symphony No. 3 [25']
3.3.3.2. 4.3.3.1. timp,perc,harp,
cel,strings
PETERS P6663 perf mat rent   (P352)

PINOCCHIO: SUITE NO. 1 see Bjelinski,
Bruno

PINOCCHIO: SUITE NO. 2 see Bjelinski,
Bruno

PIONEER, THE: SUITE see Waxman, Franz

PIONEER DANCES FOR CHAMBER ORCHESTRA
see Coolidge, Peggy Stuart

PIONEER DANCES FOR STRING ORCHESTRA see
Coolidge, Peggy Stuart

PIPER AT THE GATES OF DAWN, THE see
Stearns, Peter Pindar

PIPOLO, GUIDO (1936-   )
Ricercare for English Horn and String
Orchestra [16']
string orch,English horn solo
SONZOGNO perf mat rent   (P353)

PIQUE DAME: ARIA OF LISA, FOR SOLO
VOICE AND ORCHESTRA see
Tchaikovsky, Piotr Ilyich, Queen Of
Spades, The: Aria Of Lisa, For Solo
Voice And Orchestra

PIQUE DAME: HERMAN'S ARIA, FOR SOLO
VOICE AND ORCHESTRA see
Tchaikovsky, Piotr Ilyich, Queen Of
Spades, The: Herman's Aria, For
Solo Voice And Orchestra

PIQUE DAME: ROMANCE OF PAULINE, FOR
SOLO VOICE AND ORCHESTRA see
Tchaikovsky, Piotr Ilyich, Queen Of
Spades, The: Romance Of Pauline,
For Solo Voice And Orchestra

PIRATA, IL: CEDO AL DESTIN ORRIBLE, FOR
SOLO VOICES AND ORCHESTRA see
Bellini, Vincenzo

PIRATA, IL: COL SORRISO D'INNOCENZA,
FOR SOLO VOICE AND ORCHESTRA see
Bellini, Vincenzo

PIRATA, IL: LO SOGNAI FERITO, ESANGUE,
FOR SOLO VOICE AND ORCHESTRA see
Bellini, Vincenzo

PIRATA, IL: NEL FUROR DELLA TEMPESTE,
FOR SOLO VOICE AND ORCHESTRA see
Bellini, Vincenzo

PIRATA, IL: SI, VINCEMMO, E IL PREGIO
IO SENTO, FOR SOLO VOICE AND
ORCHESTRA see Bellini, Vincenzo

PIRATA, IL: TU M' APRISTI IN COR
FERITA, FOR SOLO VOICES AND
ORCHESTRA see Bellini, Vincenzo

PIRATA, IL: TU SCIAGURATO! AH! FUGGI,
FOR SOLO VOICES AND ORCHESTRA see
Bellini, Vincenzo

PIRATA, IL: TU VEDRAI LA SVENTURATA,
FOR SOLO VOICE AND ORCHESTRA see
Bellini, Vincenzo

PIRATA CAUTIVO, EL see Espla, Oscar

PIRCKMAYER, GEORG (1918-1977)
Bericht Vom Menschen [33']
3(pic).2+English horn.2+bass
clar.2+contrabsn. 4.4.3.1.
timp,perc,harp,org,strings
DOBLINGER perf mat rent   (P354)

PIRIOU, ADOLPHE (1878-1964)
Divertissement No. 1 for String
Orchestra [13']
string orch
BILLAUDOT perf mat rent   (P355)

Symphony No. 2, Op. 56 [20']
2.3.3.3. 4.3.2.0. timp,2perc,cel,
pno,strings
(par les landes fleuries) BILLAUDOT
perf mat rent   (P356)

PIRKEI TEHILLIM, FOR SOLO VOICE AND
ORCHESTRA see Flender, Reinhard
David

PIRUMOV, ALEXANDER
Symphony Of Hymns [30']
string orch
sc MUZYKA f.s.   (P357)

PISANELLA, LA: SUITE see Pizzetti,
Ildebrando

PISEN LASKY [ARR.] see Suk, Josef

PISENDEL, JOHANN GEORG (1687-1755)
Concerto for 2 Oboes and Orchestra in
E flat
MUS. RARA perf mat rent   (P358)

PISHNY-FLOYD, MONTE KEENE (1941-   )
Theme and Variations [15']
3.3.2.3. 4.2.3.1. timp,perc,pno&
cel,strings
CAN.MUS.CENT. MI 1100 677TH (P359)

Variations On Themes Of Stravinsky
[18']
2.2.2(clar in E flat).2.sax.
4.2.3.1. timp,perc,pno,strings
CAN.MUS.CENT. MI 1100 P677VA (P360)

PISK, PAUL AMADEUS (1893-1990)
Divertimento [20']
2.2.2.2. 3.2.0.0. timp,perc,
strings
AM.COMP.AL. perf mat rent   (P361)

PISK, PAUL AMADEUS (cont'd.)

Three Ceremonial Rites [14']
2.2.2.2. 2.2.1.0. timp,perc,harp,
strings
AM.COMP.AL. perf mat rent   (P362)

Three Psalms, For Solo Voice And
Orchestra *Op.21 [18']
2.2.2.2. 2.2.0.0. perc,strings,
Bar solo
sc AM.COMP.AL. $19.15   (P363)

PISTON, WALTER (1894-1976)
Bicentennial Fanfare
2+pic.3.3.3. 4.3.3.1. timp,4perc,
strings
AMP perf mat rent   (P364)

Concerto for String Quartet, Winds
and Percussion [12']
3.3.3.2. 2.2.2.0. timp,perc,2vln,
vla,vcl
study sc AMP f.s., perf mat rent
(P365)

PITCHIPOI, FOR SOLO VOICES AND
ORCHESTRA see Ultan, Lloyd

PITFIELD, THOMAS BARON (1903-   )
Bucolics [13']
ROBERTON 95428   (P366)

Epitaph [6'30"]
string orch
ROBERTON 95418   (P367)

PITTORI FIAMMINGHI: PRELUDIO, ACT I see
Smareglia, Antonio

PITTORI FIAMMINGHI: PRELUDIO, ACT II
see Smareglia, Antonio

PITTORI FIAMMINGHI: PRELUDIO, ACT III
see Smareglia, Antonio

PIZZETTI, ILDEBRANDO (1880-1968)
Pisanella, La: Suite [25']
2(pic).2.2.2. 4.2.0.0. timp,perc,
2harp,pno,cel,strings
KALMUS A6386 sc $40.00, set $70.00,
pts $3.00, ea., perf mat rent
(P368)

PLACE IN THE SUN, A: SYMPHONIC SCENARIO
see Waxman, Franz

PLAGES see Garant, Serge see Lejet,
Edith

PLAGGE, WOLFGANG (1960-   )
Fugue, Op. 7b [6']
2.3.2.3. 4.2.2.0. timp,perc,
strings
NORGE   (P369)

PLAINSONGS, FOR TRUMPET AND ORCHESTRA
see Holten, Bo

PLAKIDIS, PETR (1947-   )
Concerto for 2 Oboes and String
Orchestra [11']
string orch,2ob soli
SIKORSKI perf mat rent   (P370)
VAAP perf mat rent   (P371)

PLANET FOR THE TAKING see Baker,
Michael Conway

PLANTE, DANIEL
Images [7']
1.2.1.2. 2.1.0.0. 2perc,12vln,
4vla,4vcl,2db
sc APNM $3.50, perf mat rent (P372)

Love In The Asylum, For Solo Voice
And Orchestra [7']
fl&alto fl,ob d'amore,3perc,
3harp,cel,hpsd,2vla,vcl,S solo
sc APNM $15.00, perf mat rent
(P373)

PLANYAVSKY, PETER (1947-   )
Kremser Konzert, For Organ And String
Orchestra [18']
string orch,org solo
DOBLINGER perf mat rent   (P374)

PLAPPERMOULCHEN POLKA see Strauss,
Josef

PLATEAUS see Nimmons, Phil

PLATEE: SUITE NO. 1 see Rameau, Jean-
Philippe

PLATÉE: SUITE NO. 2 see Rameau, Jean-
Philippe

PLATZ, ROBERT (1951-   )
Schwelle [63']
4(2pic).4(English horn).4(bass
clar).4(contrabsn). 4.4.3.1.
6perc,2harp,pno,strings,
electronic tape
sc BREITKOPF-W f.s., perf mat rent
(P375)

PLAY see Guy, Barry

PLAY OF FRAGMENTS, A see Nordal, Jon

PLAY US CHASTITY ON YOUR VIOLIN, FOR
VIOLIN AND INSTRUMENTAL ENSEMBLE
see Schelle, Michael

PLAYERS' FAIRYTALE, THE: SUITE NO. 1
see Vacek, Miloš

PLAYERS' FAIRYTALE, THE: SUITE NO. 2
see Vacek, Miloš

PLAYFUL RONDO [ARR.] see Green, W.

PLAYHOUSE MUSIC see Turner, Robert
[Comrie]

PLAYING THE "MIRACULOUS GAME" see
Frazelle, Kenneth

PLEIADES see Roizenblat, A.

PLESKOW, RAOUL (1931-   )
Consort For Strings [10']
string orch
sc AM.COMP.AL. $43.65, perf mat
rent   (P376)

Epitaphium [8']
string orch
sc AM.COMP.AL. $7.10   (P377)

Epitaphium: Stefan Wolpe In Memoriam
[7']
2.2.2.2. 3.2.0.1. strings
sc AM.COMP.AL. $21.90   (P378)

Four Bagatelles [6']
2.2.2.2. 4.0.0.0. strings
(2 horns and 2 trumpets may be
substituted for 4 horns) sc
AM.COMP.AL. $13.80   (P379)

Music for Orchestra [15']
3.2.2.2. 2.2.1.1. perc,pno,
strings
sc AM.COMP.AL. $30.10, perf mat
rent   (P380)

Preludium No.1 [6']
3.2.2.2. 2.2.2.0. timp,strings
sc AM.COMP.AL. $33.25, perf mat
rent   (P381)

Preludium No.2 [5']
2.2.2.2. 2.2.2.0. timp,strings
sc AM.COMP.AL. $34.15, perf mat
rent   (P382)

Six Epigrams [10']
2+pic.2.2.2. 4.2.2.0. timp,perc,
pno,strings
sc AM.COMP.AL. $20.30   (P383)

Suite [15']
2.2.2.2. 2.1.0.1. perc,2pno,
strings
sc AM.COMP.AL. $28.95, perf mat
rent   (P384)

Three Epigrams [8']
string orch
sc AM.COMP.AL. $11.70   (P385)

Villanelle, Dirge And Song, For Solo
Voice And Orchestra [10']
3.2.2.2. 2.2.0.0. pno,strings,
high solo
sc AM.COMP.AL. $25.10   (P386)

PLEYEL, IGNACE JOSEPH (1757-1831)
Concerto for Clarinet and Orchestra
in C, Benton 1090
2ob,2horn,strings,clar solo
MUS. RARA 1164 perf mat rent (P387)

Concerto for Viola and Orchestra, Op.
31, in D, Benton 105
(Herrmann) KALMUS A6433 pno-cond sc
$10.00, set $20.00, pts $2.00,
ea., perf mat rent   (P388)

Concerto for Violoncello and
Orchestra in C
2ob,2horn,strings,vcl solo
sc KUNZEL 10212 $22.00   (P389)

Periodical Symphonies, Two
(Smith, Raymond R.) sc A-R ED
ISBN 0-89579-113-7 f.s.
contains: Symphonie Periodique
No.1; Symphonie Periodique
No.14   (P390)

Symphonie Periodique No.1
see Periodical Symphonies, Two

Symphonie Periodique No.14
see Periodical Symphonies, Two

Symphony in D, MIN 205 [20']
2ob,2horn,strings
(Riessberger, Helmut) pts DOBLINGER
DM 895 f.s.   (P391)

PLOMPEN, PETER (1944-   )
Iserna [10']
4.2.3.3.2alto sax. 4.2.3.1.
12vln,6vla,6vcl,4db
sc DONEMUS f.s., perf mat rent
(P392)

PLOT IN THE FICTION, FOR OBOE AND
CHAMBER ORCHESTRA see Francesconi,
Luca

PLUISTER, SIMON (1913-   )
Larghetto For Strings [5'25"]
string orch
DONEMUS perf mat rent   (P393)

Rhapsody In Beer-Tonality [11']
3.2.2.2. 4.3.3.0. timp,5perc,
strings
DONEMUS perf mat rent   (P394)

Three Cascades [10']
3.2.2.2. 4.3.3.0. timp,3perc,
harp,strings
DONEMUS perf mat rent   (P395)

PLURIEL see Bayle, Francois

PLURIELS see Dollarhide, Theodore

PLUS CA CHANGE see Barkin, Elaine R.

PLUS QUE LENT, LA [ARR.] see Debussy,
Claude

PNEUMA see Matsumura, Teizo

PODGAITS, EFREM (1949-   )
Concerto for Harpsichord and Strings
[17']
strings,hpsd solo
VAAP perf mat rent   (P396)

POEDEL IN PYAMA see Meijering, Chiel

POEM, FOR HORN AND ORCHESTRA, OP. 70
BIS see Koechlin, Charles

POEM IN MEMORIAM BORIS LYATOSHINSKY see
Silvestrov, Valentin

POEM IN MEMORY OF THE BATTLE OF
LENINGRAD see Petrov, Andrei P.

POEM OF FALLEN HEROES, FOR SOLO VOICE
AND ORCHESTRA see Vacek, Miloš

POEM OF ROLAND, FOR VIOLIN AND CHAMBER
ORCHESTRA see Whear, Paul William

POEM OF SEVEN STRINGS, A see
Asgeirsson, Jon

POEM OF STRUGGLE see Kabalevsky, Dmitri
Borisovich

POEM SYMPHONIQUE see Svete, Tomaz

POEMA see Lazarof, Henri

POEMA DE ITABIRA, FOR SOLO VOICE AND
ORCHESTRA see Villa-Lobos, Heitor

POEMA DE PALAVRAS, FOR SOLO VOICE AND
ORCHESTRA see Villa-Lobos, Heitor

POEMA ELEGIACO see Serebrier, Jose

POEMA PATETICA see Haug, Halvor

POEMA SINFONICO PARA CUERDAS see Saxe,
Serge

POEME D'ADONIS see Lavagne, Andre

POEME DE LA FORET see Roussel, Albert
(Charles Paul)

POEME DE L'EXTASE see Scriabin,
Alexander

POEME LYRIQUE see Gram, Peder

POEME LYRIQUE, FOR SOLO VOICE AND
INSTRUMENTAL ENSEMBLE see Chen,
Qigang

POEME ROMANTIQUE, FOR VIOLIN AND
ORCHESTRA see Mazellier, Jules

POEME ROUMAIN see Enesco, Georges
(Enescu)

POEME SYMPHONIQUE see Roger-Ducasse,
Jean-Jules Aimable

POEME SYMPHONIQUE NO. 3 see El-Khoury,
Bechara

POEMES DE RONSARD, FOR SOLO VOICE AND
CHAMBER ORCHESTRA see Louvier,
Alain

POEMES POUR L'ENFANT, FOR SOLO VOICE
AND INSTRUMENTAL ENSEMBLE see
Jolivet, Andre

POEMETTO (NELL'ALI DEI VIVI PENSIERI)
see Vacchi, Fabio

POEMI, FOR VIOLIN AND STRING ORCHESTRA
see Hallgrimsson, Haflidi

POEMS, FOR ALTO SAXOPHONE AND ORCHESTRA
see Strobl, Otto

POEMS OF SOLITARY DELIGHTS, FOR
NARRATOR AND ORCHESTRA see Body,
Jack

POESIA DI DE PISIS, FOR SOLO VOICE AND
INSTRUMENTAL ENSEMBLE see Bussotti,
Sylvano

POESIA IN FORMA DI ROSA see Guarnieri,
Adriano

POET SPEAKS, THE [ARR.] see Schumann,
Robert (Alexander)

POET'S DREAM, THE [ARR.] see MacDowell,
Edward Alexander

POEZJE, FOR SOLO VOICE AND CHAMBER
ORCHESTRA see Serocki, Kazimierz

POGLIETTI, ALESSANDRO (? -1683)
Balletti In C
3trp,trom/trp,bsn,strings,cont
MUS. RARA 1709 $20.00   (P397)

POHJANMIES, JUHANI
Talvi-Iltana, For Solo Voice And
String Orchestra [arr.]
(Kuusisto, I.) string orch,solo
voice [2'] FAZER perf mat rent
(P398)

POIESIS see Pasquotti, Corrado

POINTING see Bredemeyer, Reiner

POINTS see Johannsson, Magnus Bl.

POINTS D'OR, FOR SAXOPHONE AND
INSTRUMENTAL ENSEMBLE see Jolas,
Betsy

POKORNY, FRANZ XAVER (1729-1794)
Concerto for 2 Horns and Orchestra in
F, MIN 1 [13'14"]
2fl,strings without db,2horn soli
INTERNAT. perf mat rent   (P399)

Symphonies, Three *see SEVEN
SYMPHONIES FROM THE COURT OF
THURN UND TAXIS

POLARIS see Søderlind, Ragnar

POLDMAA, A.
Sea Maiden, The: Suite
sc MEZ KNIGA f.s.   (P400)

POLGAR, TIBOR (1907-   )
Concertino for Trumpet and Orchestra
[14']
2.2.2.2. 4.0.0.0. timp,3perc,
harp,cel,strings,trp solo
CAN.MUS.CENT. MI 1331 P765CO (P401)

Concerto Romantico, For Harp And
Orchestra [14']
2.2.2.2. 3.2.1.0. timp,perc,cel,
strings,harp solo
CAN.MUS.CENT. MI 1316 P765CON
(P402)

Four Seasons, The
2.2.2.2. 4.0.3.1. timp,perc,harp,
cel,strings
CAN.MUS.CENT. MI 1100 P765FO (P403)

POLICHINELLE [ARR.] see Rachmaninoff,
Sergey Vassilievich

POLIPTIH see Ramovs, Primoz

POLISH CONCERTO see Telemann, Georg
Philipp, Concerto Polonois

POLISH SUITE see Zarzycki, Alexander

POLITOPHONIE see Bartholomée, Pierre

POLKA, "THE OLD BEAR WITH THE SORE
HEAD", FOR BASSOON AND ORCHESTRA
see Fucik, Julius

POLOGNE see Holmes, Augusta (Mary Anne)

POLONIA see Wagner, Richard

POLOVINKIN, LEONID (1894-1949)
Dance Of The Rat
1.1.1.0. 0.2+2cornet.1.0. perc,
strings
VAAP perf mat rent   (P404)

Ich Bin Wenig - Gemeinsam Sind Wir
Stark: Suite [25']
2.1.1.1. 2.2.1.0. timp,perc,harp,
strings
SIKORSKI perf mat rent   (P405)

POLOVINKIN, LEONID (cont'd.)

Ouverture Zum 1. Mai [14']
    4.2.2.3. 4.3.2.2. timp,perc,
    2harp,strings
    SIKORSKI perf mat rent   (P406)

Telescope II [18']
    3.2.2.2. 4.3.3.1. timp,perc,harp,
    strings
    SIKORSKI perf mat rent   (P407)
    VAAP perf mat rent   (P408)

POLYDIAPHONIE see Arma, Paul (Pál)
    (Imre Weisshaus)

POLYDRAMA, FOR VIOLONCELLO AND
    ORCHESTRA see Ruders, Poul

POLYEUCTE see Dukas, Paul

POLYMORPHIE see Decoust, Michel

POLYPHONIE 4 see Baumgartner, Jean-Paul

POLYTEMPI NO. 4, FOR PIANO AND
    ORCHESTRA see Dragostinov, Stefan

POMONA see Lambert, Constant

POMP AND CIRCUMSTANCE MARCH NO. 3 IN C
    MINOR see Elgar, [Sir] Edward
    (William)

POMP AND CIRCUMSTANCE MARCH NO. 4 IN G
    see Elgar, [Sir] Edward (William)

POMPATA [ARR.] see Lundsten, Ralph

POMPEJI see Niemann, Walter

PONCE, MANUEL MARIA (1882-1948)
    Estrellita [arr.]
    (Gould, Morton) harp,strings
    SCHIRM.G perf mat rent   (P409)

PONCHIELLI, AMILCARE (1834-1886)
    Scena Campestre (Sinfonia in A) [28']
    2+pic.2.2.2. 2.2.3.1. timp,perc,
    harp,org,strings
    sc BSE 117 f.s., perf mat rent
                                    (P410)

    Sinfonia in A
    see Scena Campestre

PONCTUATION FRANCAISE, FOR SOLO VOICE
    AND CHAMBER ORCHESTRA see Tansman,
    Alexandre

PONÉ, GUNDARIS (1932-   )
    Overture "La Bella Veneziana" [10']
    2.2.2.2. 2.2.2.0. timp,strings
    sc AM.COMP.AL. $70.15   (P411)

PONJEE, TED (1953-   )
    Square World, The, For Alto Saxophone
    And Orchestra [15']
    2.2.2.2. 2.1.1.0. 2perc,strings,
    alto sax solo
    DONEMUS perf mat rent   (P412)

PONORENA HUDBA, FOR SOLO VOICE, VIOLIN
    AND STRINGS see Hatrik, Juraj

PONSE, LUCTOR (1914-   )
    Concerto for Harp and Orchestra [25']
    3.3.3.3. 4.2.4.0. timp,5perc,
    strings,harp solo
    DONEMUS perf mat rent   (P413)

    Concerto for 2 Pianos and Orchestra,
    Op. 33 [24']
    1.1.2.1.alto sax.tenor sax.
    1.1.1.0. 4perc,harp,strings,pno
    solo (second version, 1975) sc
    DONEMUS f.s., perf mat rent
                                    (P414)

    Deux Caprices, For Flute And
    Orchestra [10'30"]
    1.2.3.2. 3.2.2.0. perc,harp,
    strings,fl solo
    DONEMUS perf mat rent   (P415)

    Five Etudes, For Piano And Orchestra
    [15'30"]
    2.2.3.3. 3.2.3.1. 3perc,harp,
    strings,pno solo
    sc DONEMUS f.s., perf mat rent
                                    (P416)

    Musique Concertante [22']
    2.2.3.2. 2.2.2.0. 5-6perc,harp,
    pno,strings
    sc DONEMUS f.s., perf mat rent
                                    (P417)

    Suite for Piano and Orchestra, Op.
    31, No. 3a [13']
    2.2.3.3. 4.3.3.1. 6perc,strings,
    pno solo
    DONEMUS perf mat rent   (P418)

    Symphony No. 3 [24']
    3.3.4.3. 4.3.3.1. perc,harp,pno,
    strings
    DONEMUS perf mat rent   (P419)

POOT, MARCEL (1901-   )
    Ballade for String Quartet and
    Orchestra [11']
    2.2.2.2. 4.2.2.0. timp,strings,
    string quar soli
    study sc ESCHIG f.s., perf mat rent
                                    (P420)

    Ballade for Violin and Orchestra
    [13']
    2.2.2.2. 2.0.0.0. timp,strings,
    vln solo
    ESCHIG perf mat rent   (P421)

    Fantaisie Rhythmique [5']
    1.1.2.1. 2.2.1.0. timp,perc,cel,
    strings
    ESCHIG perf mat rent   (P422)

    Fete A Theleme [6']
    1.1.2.1. 2.2.1.0. timp,perc,
    strings
    ESCHIG perf mat rent   (P423)

    Fugato [7']
    3.3.3.3. 4.3.3.1. strings
    ESCHIG perf mat rent   (P424)

    Legende Epique, For Piano And
    Orchestra [15']
    2.2.2.2. 4.2.3.1. timp,perc,cel,
    strings,pno solo
    study sc ESCHIG f.s., perf mat rent
                                    (P425)

POP CONCERT CONCERTO, FOR PIANO AND
    ORCHESTRA see Claflin, [Alan] Avery

POP PARTITA see Thorne, Francis Burritt

POPCORN see Kingsley, Gershon Gary

POPLARS see Caltabiano, Ronald

POPOLI DI TESSAGLIA! IO NON CHIEDO,
    ETERNI DEI, FOR SOLO VOICE AND
    ORCHESTRA see Mozart, Wolfgang
    Amadeus

POPPER, DAVID (1843-1913)
    Spinnlied, For Violoncello And
    Orchestra [arr.] *Op.55,No.1
    (Suslin, Viktor) 2.2.2.2. 2.0.0.0.
    timp,perc,strings,vcl solo [5']
    SIKORSKI perf mat rent   (P426)

PORCELIJN, DAVID (1947-   )
    Sinfonia Concertante for Viola,
    Double Bass and Orchestra, Op. 2
    [30']
    3.3.3.3. 4.2.3.1. timp,2perc,
    harp,strings,vla solo,db solo
    DONEMUS perf mat rent   (P427)

    Symphonisch Requiem *Op.1 [33']
    4.4.6.4.2alto sax. 4.4.3.1. timp,
    2perc,harp,strings
    DONEMUS perf mat rent   (P428)

PORPHYRE see Ore, Cecilie

PORPORA, NICOLA ANTONIO (1686-1768)
    Adelaide: Sinfonia [3'30"]
    0.2.0.1. 2.2.0.0. strings
    (Blanchard, R.) BOIS perf mat rent
                                    (P429)

    Concerto for Flute and String
    Orchestra in D [10']
    string orch,fl solo
    BSE 129 perf mat rent   (P430)

    Concerto for Violoncello and String
    Orchestra
    string orch without vla,vcl solo
    KUNZEL 10211 sc $15.00, pts $2.70,
    ea.   (P431)

    Flavio Anicio Olibrio: Recitativo E
    Aria Di Flavio, For Solo Voice
    And Orchestra [2'30"]
    trp,strings,cont,countertenor
    (Blanchard, R.) BOIS perf mat rent
                                    (P432)

    Sinfonia in D [8']
    2ob,2horn,strings
    BSE 130 perf mat rent   (P433)

PORT ESSINGTON, FOR STRING TRIO AND
    STRING ORCHESTRA see Sculthorpe,
    Peter [Joshua]

PORTE DU BAISER, LA see Olah, Tiberiu

PORTER, COLE (1892-1964)
    Anything Goes [6']
    1(pic).1(English horn).2.0.alto
    sax.tenor sax.baritone sax.
    0.3.1.0. 2perc,pno,strings
    WARNER perf mat rent   (P434)

    Love For Sale, For Solo Voice And
    Orchestra [3']
    (Leyden, Norman) WARNER perf mat
    rent   (P435)

    Night And Day, [arr.] [4']
    (Herfurth) WARNER perf mat rent
                                    (P436)

PORTER, QUINCY (1897-1966)
    Desolate City, The, For Solo Voice
    And Orchestra [13']
    3.2.2.2. 4.3.3.0. timp,perc,
    strings,Bar solo
    sc AM.COMP.AL. $9.60, perf mat rent
                                    (P437)

    Twelve Songs For Solo Helen, For
    Voice And Orchestra [12']
    1.1.1.1. 0.0.0.0. perc,strings,S
    solo
    sc AM.COMP.AL. $18.40, perf mat
    rent   (P438)

PORTRAIT I, FOR SOLO VOICE AND
    ORCHESTRA see Koering, Rene

PORTRAIT II see Koering, Rene

PORTRAIT OF RODIN see Lees, Benjamin

POSEIDON see Berg, Olav see Prado,
    José-Antonio (Almeida)

POSSESSED: SUITE see Waxman, Franz

POSSIBLE SELECTIONS, FOR FLUTE AND
    ORCHESTRA see Slettholm, Yngve

POSSIBLE WORLDS see Heinio, Mikko

POSTILLA PER ALDO CLEMENTI FOR HARP AND
    INSTRUMENTAL ENSEMBLE see Pennisi,
    Francesco

POSTILLON D'AMOUR see Strauss, Johann,
    [Jr.]

POSTILLON DE LONGJUMEAU, LE: MES AMIS
    ÉCOUTEZ L'HISTOIRE, FOR SOLO VOICE
    AND ORCHESTRA see Adam, Adolphe-
    Charles

POSTLUDE: POUR L'EPILOGUE D'UNE MONDE
    see Bull, Edvard Hagerup

POSTLUDIUM FOR PIANO AND ORCHESTRA see
    Silvestrov, Valentin

POTAWATOMI LEGENDS see Luening, Otto

POTPOURRI, FOR VIOLA AND ORCHESTRA see
    Hummel, Johann Nepomuk

POTTER'S WHEEL, FOR 2 PIANOS AND STRING
    ORCHESTRA see Shakidi, Tolib

POULENC, FRANCIS (1899-1963)
    Animaux Modeles, Les: Suite [21']
    3.3.4.4. 4.3.3.1. timp,perc,cel,
    2harp,strings
    study sc ESCHIG f.s., perf mat rent
                                    (P439)

    Biches, Les: Suite [15'30"]
    3.3.3.3. 4.3.4.0. timp,perc,harp,
    cel,strings
    sc HEUGEL 597-00023 $39.75   (P440)

    Chansons Villageoises, For Solo Voice
    And Orchestra [10']
    2.2.2.2. 2.1.0.0. timp,perc,cel,
    harp,strings
    ESCHIG perf mat rent   (P441)

    Hoops [arr.]
    (Lucas) 1.1.1.1. 2.1.1.0. timp&
    perc,strings,opt pno [20'] (brass
    may be reduced to 0100) CHESTER
    JWC264 perf mat rent   (P442)

    Musique Pour Faire Plaisir [arr.]
    (Francaix, Jean) 2.2.2.2. 2.1.1.0.
    timp,perc,cel,harp,strings [10']
    ESCHIG perf mat rent   (P443)

    Overture, [arr.]
    (Françaix) 2.2.2.2. 2.2.2.1. timp&
    perc,harp,strings [5'] CHESTER
    JWC260A perf mat rent   (P444)

    Sonata for Flute and Orchestra,
    [arr.] [14']
    (Berkeley) 1.2.2.2. 2.0.0.0. timp,
    strings,fl solo CHESTER JWC 467
    perf mat rent   (P445)

POUR L'IMAGE see Hurel, Philippe

POUR "MARGUERITE INFANTE" see Bibalo,
    Antonio

POUR MEMOIRE I, FOR PIANO AND ORCHESTRA
    see Lenot, Jacques

POUR MEMOIRE II, FOR SOLO VOICE AND
    ORCHESTRA see Lenot, Jacques

POUR MEMOIRE III, FOR STRING ORCHESTRA
    see Lenot, Jacques

POUR MEMOIRE IV, FOR SOLO VOICES AND
    ORCHESTRA see Lenot, Jacques

POUR ONZE ARCHETS see Fontyn,
    Jacqueline

POUR UN LIVRE A VENISE see Sinopoli, Giuseppe

POUR UN POEME INCONNU, FOR PIANO AND ORCHESTRA see Brenet, Therese

POURSUIVANT, LE, FOR SOLO VOICE AND INSTRUMENTAL ENSEMBLE see Depraz, Raymond

POW WOW see Lang, Philip Joseph

POWELL, MEL (1923-   )
    Duplicates, For 2 Pianos And
        Orchestra [32']
        2(alto fl)+pic.2+English horn.2+
        clar in E flat+bass clar.2+
        contrabsn. 4.3.3.1. 3perc,
        2harp,strings,2pno soli
        SCHIRM.G perf mat rent   (P446)

    Modules [14']
        1.1.1.1. 2.1.1.0. 2perc,vln,vla,
        vcl,db
        sc SCHIRM.G 50488483 $15.00, perf
        mat rent   (P447)

POWER OF LOVE, THE see Grainger, Percy Aldridge

POWER OF ROME AND THE CHRISTIAN SPIRIT, THE see Grainger, Percy Aldridge

POWERS, ANTHONY (1953-   )
    Aurora [14']
        clar,strings
        OXFORD perf mat rent   (P448)

    Chamber Concerto
        1(alto fl).1(English horn).1(bass
        clar).1. 1.1.1.0. marimba&
        vibra,pno,2vln,vla,vcl,db
        sc OXFORD $33.00   (P449)

    Darkness To Day, For Clarinet And
        String Orchestra [28']
        string orch,clar solo
        study sc OXFORD f.s., perf mat rent
                                    (P450)

    Music for Strings
        string orch,2vln soli,string quar
        soli
        sc OXFORD $39.00, perf mat rent
                                    (P451)

    Nympheas [14']
        2(alto fl,pic).0.1.0. 0.0.0.0.
        vibra&glock,harp,pno,gtr,2vln,
        vla,vcl,db
        sc OXFORD 358296-1 $27.00   (P452)

    Stone, Water, Stars
        3.3.3.3. 4.3.3.1. timp,perc,
        2harp,pno,strings
        sc OXFORD 366589-1 $59.95, perf mat
        rent   (P453)

    Venexiana II, For Solo Voices And
        Orchestra [18']
        3.0.3.0. 0.2.2.0. 2perc,pno,
        strings,2 high soli
        OXFORD perf mat rent   (P454)

    Vespers [14']
        string orch
        OXFORD perf mat rent   (P455)

POWHATAN'S DAUGHTER MARCH see Sousa, John Philip

POZABLJENE PESMI, FOR SOLO VOICE AND ORCHESTRA see Lipovsek, Marijan

POZDRAVENI see Kopelent, Marek

PRADO, JOSÉ-ANTONIO (ALMEIDA)
    (1943-   )
    Chronik Eines Sommertages, For
        Clarinet And String Orchestra
        string orch,clar solo
        TONOS   (P456)

    Concerto for Piano and Orchestra
        3.2.2.2. 4.3.3.1. timp,3perc,
        harp,cel,strings,pno solo
        TONOS perf mat rent   (P457)

    I-Jura Pirama
        2+pic.2+English horn.2.2+
        contrabsn. 4.3.3.1. timp,perc,
        pno&cel,harp,strings
        TONOS perf mat rent   (P458)

    Poseidon
        marimba,vibra,strings
        TONOS perf mat rent   (P459)

    Sao Paulo
        2+pic.2.2.2+contrabsn. 4.3.3.1.
        timp,4perc,pno,strings
        TONOS perf mat rent   (P460)

    Sinfonia Unicamp
        2+pic.2+English horn.2.2.
        2.3.3.1. timp,perc,cel,pno,
        strings
        TONOS perf mat rent   (P461)

PRAEFIXUM see Bus, Jan

PRAELUDIUM AND ALLEGRO, FOR VIOLIN AND ORCHESTRA [ARR.] see Kreisler, Fritz

PRAIRIE LIGHT see Welcher, Dan Edward

PRAIRIE SKETCHES see Robinovitch, Sid

PRAIRIES AND MOUNTAINS see Grant, Stewart

PRAJNA-NAYA SYMPHONY see Takahashi, Yutaka

PRALUDIUM UND MEDITATION, FOR VIOLONCELLO AND ORCHESTRA see Blendinger, Herbert

PRANAM I, FOR SOLO VOICE AND INSTRUMENTAL ENSEMBLE see Scelsi, Giacinto

PRAVDA LOVE see Ekström, Lars

PRAVIADA see Legido, Jesus

PRAYER, FOR SOLO VOICE AND STRING ORCHESTRA see Gulbranson, Eilif, Bonn, For Solo Voice And String Orchestra

PRAYER OF VERONICA, THE, FOR SOLO VOICE AND ORCHESTRA see Groven, Eivind, Veronicas Bon, For Solo Voice And Orchestra

PRE-PULSE SUSPENDED see Hyla, Leon (Lee)

PREACHERS OF CRIMETHEUS see "Bach, P.D.Q." (Peter Schickele)

PRECESSION see Hartke, Stephen Paul

PRECIPICES OF ZEALAND see Werner, Sven Erik, Sjellandske Afgrunde

PREDIGRA see Gabrijelcic, Marijan

PREGUE NO. 1 IN D see Rice, Thomas N.

PREKMURSKA SUITA see Svete, Tomaz

PRELUDE A L'APRES-MIDI D'UN FAUNE see Debussy, Claude

PRELUDE A L'APRES-MIDI D'UN FAUNE [ARR.] see Debussy, Claude

PRELUDE A L'INFINI see Arseneault, Raynald

PRELUDE AND ALLEGRO see Watson, Anthony

PRELUDE AND CHORALE ON "NUN KOMM DER HEIDEN HEILAND" see Eder, Helmut

PRELUDE AND FANTASY, FOR ALTO SAXOPHONE AND ORCHESTRA see Rokeach, Martin

PRELUDE AND FANTASY [ARR.] see Byrd, William

PRELUDE AND INVENTION see Mihalovici, Marcel

PRELUDE AND PASSACAGLIA see Weber, Ben Brian

PRELUDE AND RONDO see Backer-Lunde, Johan see Dolatshahi, Dariush

PRELUDE AND TOCCATA see Jacob, Gordon

PRELUDE, ARIA AND WALTZ see Berger, Arthur Victor

PRELUDE, BARCAROLLE, VALSE A LA MANIERE DE CHOPIN see Alix, René

PRELUDE, CHORAL ET FUGUE [ARR.] see Franck, Cesar

PRELUDE DE LA PORTE HEROIQUE DU CIEL [ARR.] see Satie, Erik

PRELUDE DU TE DEUM see Charpentier, Marc-Antoine

PRELUDE ET DANSE, FOR OBOE AND STRING ORCHESTRA see Delerue, Georges

PRELUDE ET INVENTION see Bozza, Eugène

PRELUDE FOR A MARITIME NATION see Bedford, David

PRELUDE FOR GUILDHALL SCHOOL OF MUSIC: WORLDES BLIS NE LAST NO THROWE see Lutoslawski, Witold

PRELUDE FROM CHAMBER MUSIC see Manneke, Daan

PRELUDE, FUGUE AND CHORALE see Austin, John

PRELUDE PASTORAL see Chabrier, [Alexis-] Emmanuel

PRELUDE POUR LA MORT DE TINTAGILES see Cools, Eugène

PRELUDE POUR REBECCA see Aliprandi, Paul

PRELUDE, SARABANDE ET GIGUE, FOR TRUMPET AND ORCHESTRA see Francaix, Jean

PRELUDE, THEME AND VARIATIONS, FOR HORN AND ORCHESTRA [ARR.] see Rossini, Gioacchino

PRELUDE, THEME ET VARIATIONS, FOR HORN AND STRING ORCHESTRA [ARR.] see Rossini, Gioacchino

PRELUDE, THEME ET VARIATIONS IN E, FOR HORN AND ORCHESTRA [ARR.] see Rossini, Gioacchino

PRELUDE TO A DOLPHIN see Holmboe, Vagn

PRELUDE TO A DRAMA see Schreker, Franz, Vorspiel Zu Einem Drama

PRELUDE TO A LIVING STONE see Holmboe, Vagn

PRELUDE TO A MAPLE TREE see Holmboe, Vagn

PRELUDE TO A PINE TREE see Holmboe, Vagn

PRELUDE TO A WILLOW TREE see Holmboe, Vagn

PRELUDE TO KULLERVO, FOR TUBA AND ORCHESTRA see Wuorinen, Charles

PRELUDE TO THE POLLUTION OF NATURE see Holmboe, Vagn

PRELUDE TO THE SEAGULLS AND THE CORMORANTS see Holmboe, Vagn

PRELUDE UND KONZERTARIE, FOR SOLO VOICE AND ORCHESTRA see Blacher, Boris

PRELUDES, FIVE see Still, William Grant

PRELUDES, LES see Liszt, Franz

PRELUDES: AFRICAN DANCER; GAMIN see Still, William Grant

PRELUDES AND FUGUES FROM OP. 87 [ARR.] see Shostakovich, Dmitri

PRELUDES FOR ORCHESTRA see Mansurian, Tigran

PRELUDES FROM OP. 34 [ARR.] see Shostakovich, Dmitri

PRELUDIO A NEMESIS see Halffter, Cristobal

PRELUDIO CLASSICO, FOR VIOLIN AND ORCHESTRA see Szeryng, Henryk

PRELUDIO, CORALE E FUGA see Respighi, Ottorino

PRELUDIO FESTIVO see Tarp, Svend Erik

PRELUDIO FUNEBRE see Donizetti, Gaetano

PRELUDIO, NOTTURNO E SCHERZO DIABOLICO see Weiner, Leo

PRELUDIO PATETICO see Tarp, Svend Erik

PRELUDIO SINFONICO see Puccini, Giacomo

PRELUDIUM FESTIVUM see Debie, Rick

PRELUDIUM NO.1 see Pleskow, Raoul

PRELUDIUM NO.2 see Pleskow, Raoul

PRENDS CETTE ROSE, FOR SOLO VOICES AND ORCHESTRA see Milhaud, Darius

PRESENCIAS see Homs, Joaquin

PRESENTASJON OUVERTURE see Albertsen, Per Hjort

PRESIDENTIAL POLONAISE see Sousa, John Philip

PRESLE, JACQUES DE LA see LA PRESLE, JACQUES (PAUL GABRIEL) DE

PRESS, JACQUES (1903-   )
    Hasseneh [20']
        2+pic.2(English horn).2+clar in E
        flat.2+contrabsn. 4.3.3.1.
        timp,perc,strings
        WEINTRB perf mat rent   (P462)

    Hasseneh: Wedding Dance [arr.]
        (Warner, Ken) 1.1.1.1. 0.0.0.0.
        acord,pno,strings [3'] WEINTRB
        perf mat rent   (P463)

PRESTO, ADAGIO, ALLEGRO VIVACE [ARR.]
    see Marcello, Benedetto

PRESTO, OP. 4 see Sibelius, Jean

PREUSSISCHES MARCHEN: CONCORDIA WALZER
    [ARR] see Blacher, Boris

PREVIN, ANDRE (1929-   )
    Concerto for Piano and Orchestra
        [28']
        3(pic).2+English horn.3(clar in E
        flat,bass
        clar).3(contrabsn).alto sax.
        4.3.3.1. timp,4perc,harp,
        strings,pno solo
        HANSEN-NY perf mat rent   (P464)

    Principals
        sc HANSEN-NY f.s., perf mat rent
                                      (P465)
    Reflections, For English Horn,
        Violoncello And Orchestra [12']
        2(pic).2.2(bass clar).2. 4.2.2.0.
        timp,perc,harp,strings,English
        horn solo,vcl solo
        sc HANSEN-NY $31.25, perf mat rent
                                      (P466)

PREVOST, ANDRE (1934-   )
    Cantate Pour Cordes [28']
        string orch
        CAN.MUS.CENT. MI 1500 P944CA (P467)

    Cosmophonie [22']
        1.1.1.1. 2.2.1.1. 3perc,cel,2vln,
        vla,vcl,db
        CAN.MUS.CENT. MI 1200 P944   (P468)

    Hiver Dans L'ame, For Solo Voice And
        Orchestra [27']
        2.2.2.2. 2.2.1.0. timp,2perc,cel,
        strings,Bar solo
        CAN.MUS.CENT. MV 1400 P944H (P469)

    Scherzo for String Orchestra
        string orch
        sc DOBER $25.00, perf mat rent
                                      (P470)

PRIEGNITZ, HANS (1913-   )
    Wie Einst Lili Marleen [15']
        3.3.3.2.sax. 4.2.3.1. timp,perc,
        harp,cel,pno,strings
        SIKORSKI perf mat rent   (P471)

PRIERE DANS L'ARCHE, FOR SOLO VOICE AND
    CHAMBER ORCHESTRA see Yannatos,
    James D.

PRIETO, CLAUDIO
    Concerto No. 1 [15']
        2.2.2.2. 2.2.0.0. perc,hpsd,6vln,
        2vla,vcl,db.
        sc ALPUERTO f.s.   (P472)

PRIGIONIERO SUPERBO, IL: SINFONIA see
    Pergolesi, Giovanni Battista

PRIGOZHIN, LUCIAN (1926-   )
    Sinfonia Concertante for Violin and
        Orchestra [22']
        3.3.3.3. 4.3.3.1. timp,perc,
        strings,vln solo
        SIKORSKI perf mat rent   (P473)

PRIMA SINFONIA see Akutagawa, Yasushi

PRIMAVERA see Riisager, Knudage

PRIMAVERA, FOR VIOLIN AND ORCHESTRA see
    Devillers, Jean Baptiste

PRIMEVAL HUM, THE see Sigurbjörnsson,
    Thorkell

PRIMO AMORE PIACER DEL CIEL, FOR SOLO
    VOICE AND ORCHESTRA see Beethoven,
    Ludwig van

PRIMOSCH, JAMES (1956-   )
    Cloud Of Unknowing, The, For Solo
        Voice And Chamber Orchestra [37']
        1(pic).1.1(bass
        clar).1(contrabsn). 1.1.1.0.
        3perc,pno&cel,4vln,2vla,2vcl,
        db,S solo
        study sc MARGUN MP6074 $40.00, perf
        mat rent   (P474)

    Dappled Things [7']
        2.2.2.2. 4.2.2.0. 4perc,pno&cel,
        strings
        study sc MARGUN MP6042 $15.00, perf
        mat rent   (P475)

PRIN, YVES (1933-   )
    Actions Simultanees [14']
        bass clar,contrabsn,horn,tuba,
        3perc,pno,strings
        RIDEAU perf mat rent   (P476)

    Au Souffle D'une Voix, For Solo
        Voices And Orchestra [22']
        0.0.0.0. 4.4.4.1. 6perc,org,pno&
        cel&hpsd,strings,electronic
        tape,SB soli
        RIDEAU perf mat rent   (P477)

PRINCE CHOCOLAT see Einem, Gottfried
    von

PRINCE IGOR: MARCH see Borodin,
    Alexander Porfirievich

PRINCE IGOR: POLOVTSIAN DANCES see
    Borodin, Alexander Porfirievich

PRINCE KHOLMSKY: INCIDENTAL MUSIC see
    Glinka, Mikhail Ivanovich

PRINCE KHOLMSKY: OVERTURE see Glinka,
    Mikhail Ivanovich

PRINCE METHUSALEM: O LOVELY MAY see
    Strauss, Johann, [Jr.], Prinz
    Methusalem: O Schöner Mai

PRINCESS CHANG PING, FOR VIOLIN AND
    ORCHESTRA see Mut, Man-Chung

PRINCESS IDA: I AM A MAIDEN COLD, FOR
    SOLO VOICES AND ORCHESTRA see
    Sullivan, [Sir] Arthur Seymour

PRINCESS IN THE GARDEN, THE see
    Applebaum, Edward

PRINCESSE DE TREBIZONDE, LA: OVERTURE
    [ARR.] see Offenbach, Jacques

PRINCESSE DE TREBIZONDE, LA: QUADRILLE
    see Strauss, Johann, [Jr.]

PRINCESSE ENDORMIE, LA, FOR SOLO VOICE
    AND ORCHESTRA [ARR.] see Borodin,
    Alexander Porfirievich, Sleeping
    Princess, For Solo Voice And
    Orchestra [arr.]

PRINCIPALS see Previn, Andre

PRINTEMPS see Debussy, Claude

PRINZ METHUSALEM: O SCHÖNER MAI see
    Strauss, Johann, [Jr.]

PRINZ METHUSALEM: OVERTURE see Strauss,
    Johann, [Jr.]

PRINZ METHUSALEM: SELECTIONS see
    Strauss, Johann, [Jr.]

PRISCILLA VARIATIONS, FOR PIANO AND
    CHAMBER ORCHESTRA see Hively, Wells

PRISM see Druckman, Jacob Raphael

PRISM OF LIFE see Locklair, Dan Steven

PRISMA see Travlos, Michael

PRISMA, FOR PIANO AND ORCHESTRA see
    Boogaard, Bernard van den

PRISMATIC VARIATIONS see Erb, Donald

PRISMES see Tanaka, Karen

PRISON, LA, FOR SOLO VOICE, VIOLONCELLO
    AND STRING ORCHESTRA see Landowski,
    Marcel

PRISONERS, THE, FOR SOLO VOICE AND
    ORCHESTRA see Rangström, Ture

PRISONNIERE, LA: OVERTURE see
    Cherubini, Luigi

PRIZORI IZ BELE KRAJINE see Mihelcic,
    Pavle

PRO DEFUNCTIS see Tarp, Svend Erik

PRO ET CONTRA see Gubaidulina, Sofia

PRO ET CONTRA, FOR VIOLONCELLO AND
    ORCHESTRA see Pärt, Arvo

PRO FISTULIS ET FIDIBUS see Riisager,
    Knudage

PRO VARSOVIA see Boguslawski, Edward

PROCENCA, FOR SOLO VOICE, GUITAR, AND
    ORCHESTRA see Buller, John

PROCESION DEL ROCIO, LA see Turina,
    Joaquin

PROCESO see Cruz de Castro, Carlos

PROCESSION AND FINALE see Gillis, Don
    E.

PROCESSION FOR PEACE, A see Panufnik,
    Andrzej

PROCESSIONALS see Hibbard, William

PROCESSIONS see Trojahn, Manfred

PROCLAMATION [ARR.] see Copland, Aaron

PROCTER, LELAND (1914-   )
    Seascape [18']
        3.3.3.3. 4.2.3.1. timp,perc,harp,
        strings
        AM.COMP.AL. perf mat rent   (P478)

    Suite for String Orchestra [23']
        string orch
        AM.COMP.AL. perf mat rent   (P479)

PROCURANS ODIUM see Jeths, Willem

PRODROMIDES, JEAN
    Crossways
        CHOUDENS perf mat rent   (P480)

PRODUCE see MacBride, David Huston

PROFONDEURS DE CHAMP, FOR BASS CLARINET
    AND INSTRUMENTAL ENSEMBLE see
    Lancino, Thierry

PROGETTO TRAKL see Maggi, Dario

PROHASKA, MILJENKO
    Concertino For Jazz Quartet And
        Strings [14']
        string orch,vibra solo,pno solo,
        db solo,drums solo
        sc,pts MJQ rent   (P481)

    Concerto for Orchestra, No. 2 [11']
        1.1.2.0.alto sax.2tenor sax.bass
        sax. 3.2.1.1. vibra,drums,perc,
        gtr,strings,alto sax solo,trp
        solo,pno solo
        sc,pts MJQ rent   (P482)

PROJECTION: FLOWER, BIRD, WIND, MOON,
    FOR 8 KOTOS AND ORCHESTRA see
    Yuasa, Joji

PROKOFIEV, SERGE (1891-1953)
    Amour Des Trois Oranges, L': Suite
        see Love Of Three Oranges: Suite

    Andante, Op. 50b, [arr.] (from String
        Quartet No. 1)
        string orch [9'] BOOSEY perf mat
        rent   (P483)

    Autumn Nocturne
        see Autumnal Sketch

    Autumnal Sketch *Op.8 [6']
        2.2.3.2. 4.1.0.0. harp,strings
        2.2.2+bass clar.2. 4.1.0.0. harp,
        strings [7'] BOOSEY perf mat rent
                                      (P484)
        "Herbstbilder" SIKORSKI perf mat
        rent   (P485)
        (Malcolm) "Autumn Nocturne" 2.2.2+
        bass clar.2. 4.1.0.0. harp,
        strings [6'] KALMUS A6983 sc
        $12.00, set $20.00, pts $1.00,
        ea., perf mat rent   (P486)

    Cinderella: Suite No. 2 *Op.108
        KALMUS A7052 sc $80.00, set
        $150.00, pts $7.00, ea., perf mat
        rent   (P487)

    Concertino for Violoncello and
        Orchestra, Op. 132
        KALMUS A7253 sc $25.00, set $80.00,
        pts $3.50, ea., perf mat rent
                                      (P488)
        min sc SIKORSKI 034-35918 $13.75
                                      (P489)
    Concerto for Piano and Orchestra, No.
        2, Op. 16, in G minor
        KALMUS A6459 sc $60.00, set $75.00,
        pts $3.50, ea., perf mat rent
                                      (P490)
    Concerto for Piano and Orchestra, No.
        4, Op. 53, in B flat
        KALMUS A7119 sc $35.00, set $45.00,
        pts $3.00, ea., perf mat rent
                                      (P491)
    Divertimento, Op. 43
        min sc BOOSEY 968 $16.00   (P492)
        KALMUS A5608 sc $30.00, perf mat
        rent, set $65.00, pts $3.00, ea.
                                      (P493)

    Dreams
        see Reves

    Herbstbilder
        see Autumnal Sketch

PROKOFIEV, SERGE (cont'd.)

Ivan The Terrible: Suite [arr.]
(Haletzki; Madjera) "Iwan Grosny
[arr.]" 2.2.2.2. 4.3.3.1. timp,
perc,strings [20'] SIKORSKI perf
mat rent   (P494)

Iwan Grosny [arr.]
see Ivan The Terrible: Suite [arr.]

Lieutenant Kije *Op.60
VAAP perf mat rent   (P495)

Love Of Three Oranges: Suite *Op.33a
"Amour Des Trois Oranges, L':
Suite" min sc BOOSEY 967 $25.00
                                  (P496)

Ouverture Russe (from Op.72)
min sc BOOSEY 991 $23.00   (P497)

Overture On Hebrew Themes *Op.34a
[9']
2.2.2.2. 2.2.0.0. perc,pno,
strings
BOOSEY perf mat rent   (P498)

Peter And The Wolf, For Narrator And
Orchestra
min sc EULENBURG EU01393 $7.50
                                  (P499)

Puschkiniana [arr.]
see Pushkin Suite [arr.]

Pushkin Suite [arr.] *Op.70-71
(Rozhdestvensky, Gennadi)
2.3.3.2.2sax. 4.2.3.1. timp,perc,
pno/hpsd,harp,strings [18'] VAAP
perf mat rent   (P500)
(Rozhdestvensky, Gennadi)
"Puschkiniana [arr.]" SIKORSKI
perf mat rent   (P501)

Reves *Op.6 [12']
2+pic.2+English horn.2+bass
clar.2+contrabsn. 6.3.3.1.
timp,perc,2harp,strings
"Dreams" BOOSEY perf mat rent
                                  (P502)

Simeon Kotko: Suite *Op.81a [37']
3.3.3.3. 4.3.3.1. timp,perc,
2harp,cel,strings
SIKORSKI perf mat rent   (P503)

Sinfonietta, Op. 5, Op. 48
min sc BOOSEY 990 $16.00   (P504)
KALMUS A6182 sc $35.00, set
$100.00, perf mat rent   (P505)

Sonata for Clarinet and Orchestra,
Op. 94, [arr.]
(Kennan, Kent) LUDWIG perf mat rent
                                  (P506)

Steinerne Blume, Die: Suite
see Tale Of The Stone Flower: Suite

Steinerne Blume, Die:
Zigeunerfantasie
see Tale Of The Stone Flower: Gypsy
Fantasy

Summer Night Suite *Op.123
3.3.3.3. 4.3.3.1. timp,perc,harp,
strings
SIKORSKI perf mat rent   (P507)
VAAP perf mat rent   (P508)

Symphony No. 2, Op. 40
min sc BOOSEY 1111 $21.00   (P509)
KALMUS A5697 sc $30.00, set
$155.00, pts $6.00, ea., perf mat
rent   (P510)

Symphony No. 3, Op. 44
KALMUS A5698 sc $30.00, set
$150.00, pts $7.00, ea., perf mat
rent   (P511)

Symphony No. 4, Op. 47, Op. 112
KALMUS A5699 sc $35.00, set
$150.00, pts $6.00, ea., perf mat
rent   (P512)

Symphony No. 5, Op. 100
min sc PETERS 5715 $18.25   (P513)
min sc SIKORSKI 034-27663 $40.25
                                  (P514)

Symphony No. 6, Op. 111
min sc SIKORSKI 034-27662 $38.25 (P515)

Symphony No. 7, Op. 131
min sc SIKORSKI 034-27661 $36.25
                                  (P516)

Tale Of The Stone Flower: Gypsy
Fantasy [8']
3.3.4.3. 4.3.3.1. timp,perc,harp,
pno,strings
"Steinerne Blume, Die:
Zigeunerfantasie" SIKORSKI perf
mat rent   (P517)

Tale Of The Stone Flower: Suite [25']
3.3.4.3. 4.3.3.1. timp,perc,harp,
pno,strings
"Steinerne Blume, Die: Suite"
SIKORSKI perf mat rent   (P518)

PROKOFIEV, SERGE (cont'd.)

Visions Fugitives [arr.] *Op.22
(Adomian, Lan) 2.2.2.2. 2.2.2.0.
timp,perc,pno,strings [18']
SCHIRM.G perf mat rent   (P519)
(Susskind, Walter) 3(pic).3(English
horn).3(clar in E flat,bass
clar).3(contrabsn).alto sax.
4.3.3.1. timp,3perc,harp,cel,
strings [20'] BOOSEY perf mat
rent   (P520)

PROLATIONEN II see Kahowez, Günter

PROLIFERATION III, FOR BASS CLARINET
AND INSTRUMENTAL ENSEMBLE see
Vandenbogaerde, Fernand

PROLOG see Kvam, Oddvar S.

PROLOG TIL ET DRAMA AF SHAKESPEARE see
Gram, Peder

PROLOGO E FANTASIA see Walton, [Sir]
William (Turner)

PROLOGO PER LEGGENDA E SINFONIA see
Higo, Ichiro

PROLOGUE see Verhoff, Carlos H.

PROLOGUE AND VARIATIONS see Zwilich,
Ellen Taaffe

PROLOGUE FOR A SHAKESPEARE DRAMA see
Gram, Peder, Prolog Til Et Drama Af
Shakespeare

PROLOGUE POUR UN MARCO POLO, FOR SOLO
VOICES AND INSTRUMENTAL ENSEMBLE
see Vivier, Claude

PROLOGUE TO QUIPU see Smit, Sytze

PROMENADE DANS ROME see Rousseau,
Marcel (Samuel-Rousseau)

PROMENADE OVERTURE see Corigliano, John

PROMENADE QUADRILLE see Strauss,
Johann, [Jr.]

PROMENADEN see Schwaen, Kurt

PROMENADES, MARCHES ET DANSES see
Groot, Rokus de

PROMESSI SPOSI, I: SUITE see Hazon,
Roberto

PROMETHEE see Ohana, Maurice

PROMETHEUS see Liszt, Franz

PROMETHEUS, FOR SOLO VOICE AND
ORCHESTRA see Wolf, Hugo

PROMOTIONEN WALZER see Strauss, Johann,
[Jr.]

PROPHECY FROM "LOCKSLEY HALL", FOR SOLO
VOICE AND ORCHESTRA see Franco,
Johan

PROPHET, DER: ACH MEIN SOHN, FOR SOLO
VOICE AND ORCHESTRA see Meyerbeer,
Giacomo, Prophete, Le: Ah, Mon
Fils, For Solo Voice And Orchestra

PROPHET, DER: O GEBT, FOR SOLO VOICE
AND ORCHESTRA see Meyerbeer,
Giacomo, Prophete, Le: Romance De
La Mendiante, For Solo Voice And
Orchestra

PROPHETE, LE: AH, MON FILS, FOR SOLO
VOICE AND ORCHESTRA see Meyerbeer,
Giacomo

PROPHETE, LE: ROMANCE DE LA MENDIANTE,
FOR SOLO VOICE AND ORCHESTRA see
Meyerbeer, Giacomo

PROPOSITIONS, FOR HARMONICA AND STRING
ORCHESTRA see Patterson, Paul

PROSPECT: 1983 see Weisgall, Hugo

PROSPERO'S ISLAND see Cruft, Adrian

PROSPERO'S SPELL see Goossen, Frederic

PROTECTING VEIL, THE, FOR VIOLONCELLO
AND STRING ORCHESTRA see Tavener,
John

PROTO, FRANK (1941-   )
Carmen Fantasy, A, For Trumpet And
Orchestra
LIBEN   (P521)

Concerto for Double Bass and
Orchestra, No. 2
LIBEN   (P522)

PROTO, FRANK (cont'd.)

Dialogue For Synclavier And Orchestra
LIBEN   (P523)

Early Evening [5']
3(pic).2.2.2. 4.3.3.1. timp,
3perc,harp,pno,cel,elec bass,
strings
(orchestra may be reduced to:
2.2.2.2. 2.2.1.0., timp, 2 perc,
pno, dbel, str) LIBEN   (P524)

Fanfare For A Festive Occasion [1']
3+pic.3.3+bass clar.2. 4.4.3.1.
timp,4perc,harp,strings
LIBEN   (P525)

Fantasy for Double Bass and Orchestra
LIBEN   (P526)

Flight Of The Trapeze [9']
3+pic.3+English horn.3+bass
clar.3+contrabsn. 4.3.3.1.
timp,4perc,harp,pno&cel,elec
bass,strings
LIBEN   (P527)

Oceanside Stomp, The [4']
3+pic.2.2.2. 4.3.3.1. timp,3perc,
harp,pno,elec bass,strings
LIBEN   (P528)

Overture To A Carnival [5']
2(pic).2(English horn).2.2.
4.3.3.1. timp,3perc,harp,pno,
elec bass,strings
(orchestra may be reduced to:
2.2.2.2. 3.3.2.1., timp, 2perc
pno, dbel, str) LIBEN   (P529)

Rhapsody for Clarinet and Orchestra
LIBEN   (P530)

Sea Beach Revisited, The, For
Synclavier And Orchestra
LIBEN   (P531)

Southern Breeze [4']
2(pic).2.2.2. 4.3.3.1. timp,2-
3perc,harp,pno,elec bass,
strings
LIBEN   (P532)

PROTOTYPEN 1, 2, 3 see Gehlhaar, Rolf

PROVAZNÍK, ANATOL (1887-1950)
Ländliche Suite *Op.53
2(pic).1.2.1. 2.2.1.0. timp,perc,
cel,strings
sc UNIVER. 10734 f.s.   (P533)

PRÖVE, BERNFRIED (1963-   )
Brennend, For Solo Voice And
Orchestra [20']
3(pic).3.3.3(contrabsn). 4.3.3.1.
timp,perc,cel,pno,strings,Mez
solo
MODERN 2256   (P534)

PROXIMITY OF MARS, THE see Sharman,
Rodney

PROYECCION DE LA VERICAL see Cruz de
Castro, Carlos

PROZESS see Bose, Hans Jürgen

PRUDEN, LARRY
Dances Of Brittany
string orch
sc WAI-TE-ATA f.s.   (P535)

Harbour Nocturne [8']
2.0.2.0. 1.1.0.0. perc,pno,
strings
sc WAI-TE-ATA f.s.   (P536)

Lambton Quay March [9']
3.2.2.2. 4.3.3.1. timp,perc,harp,
strings
sc WAI-TE-ATA f.s.   (P537)

Taranaki Overture [11']
2.2.2.2. 4.3.3.0. timp,perc,pno,
strings
sc WAI-TE-ATA f.s.   (P538)

PRÜFUNG DES KÜSSENS, FOR SOLO VOICE AND
ORCHESTRA see Beethoven, Ludwig van

PRYTZ, HOLGER
Symphony No. 2, Op. 34 [30']
2.2.2.2. 2.2.2.1. timp,perc,harp,
pno,strings,T solo
NORGE   (P539)

PRZYBYLSKI, BRONISLAW KAZIMIERZ
(1941-   )
Sinfonia Polacca [16'30"]
3.3.3.3. 4.3.3.1. perc,strings
sc POLSKIE f.s.   (P540)

PSALM FOR SOLO VOICE AND ORCHESTRA see
Eggen, Arne, Ikke Enhver Som Siger
Til Mig, For Solo Voice And

Orchestra

PSALM FOR STRINGS see Hartley, Walter Sinclair

PSALM NO. 19, [ARR.] see Marcello, Benedetto, Heavens Declare, The [arr.]

PSALM NO. 23 FOR SOLO VOICE AND ORCHESTRA see Lockwood, Normand

PSALM NO. 91 FOR SOLO VOICE, PIANO AND ORCHESTRA see Newton, James

PSALM NO. 126 FOR SOLO VOICE AND STRING ORCHESTRA, RV 608 see Vivaldi, Antonio, Nisi Dominus, For Solo Voice And String Orchestra

PSALMOS see Merlet, Michel

PSUDR see Louvier, Alain

PSYCHE, FOR NARRATOR AND ORCHESTRA see Francaix, Jean

PSYCHO: SUITE see Herrmann, Bernard

PUBLICISTEN, DIE, WALZER see Strauss, Johann, [Jr.]

PUCCINI, GIACOMO (1858-1924)
  Edgar: Preludio
    (Spada) study sc ELKAN-V 466-00028
    $7.50   (P541)

  Madama Butterfly: Addio, Fiorito
    Asil, For Solo Voice And
    Orchestra
    KALMUS A5633 sc $3.00, perf mat
    rent, set $15.00, pts $.75, ea.
                                       (P542)
  Madama Butterfly: Butterfly Entrance,
    For Solo Voice And Orchestra
    see Madama Butterfly: Spira Sul
    Mare, For Solo Voice And
    Orchestra

  Madama Butterfly: Butterfly's Death,
    For Solo Voice And Orchestra
    see Madama Butterfly: Tu, Tu
    Piccolo Iddio, For Solo Voice And
    Orchestra

  Madama Butterfly: Duetto d'Amore, For
    Solo Voices And Orchestra
    KALMUS A5629 sc $20.00, perf mat
    rent, set $50.00, pts $2.00, ea.
                                       (P543)
  Madama Butterfly: Flower Duet, For
    Solo Voices And Orchestra
    see Madama Butterfly: Tutti I Fior,
    For Solo Voices And Orchestra

  Madama Butterfly: Spira Sul Mare, For
    Solo Voice And Orchestra
    "Madama Butterfly: Butterfly
    Entrance, For Solo Voice And
    Orchestra" KALMUS A 5628 sc
    $5.00, perf mat rent, set $25.00,
    pts $1.25, ea.   (P544)

  Madama Butterfly: Tu, Tu Piccolo
    Iddio, For Solo Voice And
    Orchestra
    "Madama Butterfly: Butterfly's
    Death, For Solo Voice And
    Orchestra" KALMUS A5634 sc $5.00,
    perf mat rent, set $30.00, pts
    $1.25, ea.   (P545)

  Madama Butterfly: Tutti I Fior, For
    Solo Voices And Orchestra
    "Madama Butterfly: Flower Duet, For
    Solo Voices And Orchestra" KALMUS
    A5632 sc $20.00, perf mat rent,
    set $50.00, pts $2.00, ea. (P546)

  Manon Lescaut: Donna Non Vidi Mai,
    For Solo Voice And Orchestra
    KALMUS A6271 sc $5.00, set $23.00,
    pts $1.00, ea.   (P547)

  Manon Lescaut: In Quelle Trine
    Morbide, For Solo Voice And
    Orchestra
    KALMUS A6270 sc $7.00, set $20.00,
    pts $1.00, ea.   (P548)

  Manon Lescaut: Prelude, Act II
    2.2+English horn.2.3. 4.0.0.0.
    timp,harp,strings
    (Spada, Pietro) sc BSE $14.25
                                       (P549)
  Preludio Sinfonico
    (Wojciechowski) sc PETERS P8625
    f.s.   (P550)

  Villi, Le: Se Come Voi, For Solo
    Voice And Orchestra
    KALMUS A6269 set $20.00, pts $1.00,
    ea.   (P551)

PUCK'S MINUET see Howells, Herbert Norman

PUGNANI, GAETANO (1731-1798)
  Sinfonie, Six
    see Brioschi, Antonio, Symphonies, Three

PUGNI, CESARE (1802-1870)
  Pas De Quatre [arr.]
    (Stirn, D.) 2.1.2.1. 2.0.0.0. timp,
    perc,harp,strings [19'] BOIS perf
    mat rent   (P552)

PUIG-ROGET, HENRIETTE
  see ROGET, HENRIETTE

PULAU DEWATA [ARR] see Vivier, Claude

PULS see Kverndokk, Gisle

PUNJAB, LAND OF FIVE RIVERS see Parwez, Akmal

PUPAZZETTI see Casella, Alfredo

PUPAZZI, OP. 36, NOS. 2 AND 5 see Schmitt, Florent

PURCELL, HENRY (1658 or 59-1695)
  Abdelazar: Suite, [arr.] [16']
    (Cooper; Hayward) string orch
    NOVELLO perf mat rent   (P553)

  Abdelazar: Incidental Music
    (Hogwood, Christopher) FABER sc
    F0811 f.s., pts F0812 f.s. (P554)

  Abdelazar: Spielmusik
    (Hockner) KALMUS A6476 sc $8.00,
    set $12.00, pts $2.00, ea., perf
    mat rent   (P555)

  Amphitryon: Suite, [arr.] [12']
    (Cooper) string orch NOVELLO perf
    mat rent   (P556)

  Behold, I Bring You Glad Tidings: Two
    Pieces
    (Hockner) "Christmas Music" set
    KALMUS A6783 $7.00, and up (P557)

  Chaconne in G minor, [arr.]
    (Binney; McAlister) string orch
    [6'] KALMUS A4147 sc $5.00, set
    $5.00   (P558)

  Christmas Music
    see Behold, I Bring You Glad
    Tidings: Two Pieces

  Concerto for Horn and String
    Orchestra in D, [arr.]
    (Leloir, E.) string orch,horn solo
    [10'] BILLAUDOT perf mat rent
                                       (P559)
  Dido And Aeneas: Suite, [arr.] [12']
    strings,pno
    (Shaw) NOVELLO perf mat rent (P560)
    (Wienandt, Elwyn) string orch (gr.
    II) SOUTHERN SO-47 sc $3.00, set
    $20.00, pts $1.25, ea.   (P561)

  Double Dealer, The
    FABER sc F0813 f.s., pts F0814 f.s.
                                       (P562)
  Fairy Queen, The: Two Suites
    string orch sc,pts KUNZEL 10181
    f.s.   (P563)

  Midsummer Night's Dream, A:
    Incidental Music, Vol.1 [18']
    (Höckner, Hilmar) "Spielmusik Zum
    Sommernachtstraum, Heft 1" string
    orch,cont,opt winds sc,pts BAREN.
    HM 50 f.s.   (P564)

  Midsummer Night's Dream, A:
    Incidental Music, Vol.2 [15']
    (Höckner, Hilmar) "Spielmusik Zum
    Sommernachtstraum, Heft 2" string
    orch,cont,opt winds sc,pts BAREN.
    HM 58 f.s.   (P565)

  Night, For Solo Voice And String
    Orchestra [arr.]
    (Just) string orch,high solo [8']
    KALMUS 7021 sc $5.00, set $5.00,
    pts $1.00, ea.   (P566)

  Nine Pieces [arr.] (from Incidental
    Music To "Distressed Innocence"
    And "Amphitryon")
    (Hockner) string orch [15'] KALMUS
    A5711 sc $8.00, set $5.00   (P567)

  Set Of Act Tunes And Dances [arr.]
    (Bliss, Arthur) string orch [9']
    CURWEN perf mat rent   (P568)

  Sonata for Trumpet and String
    Orchestra, MIN 198 (from Timon Of
    Athens)
    string orch,cont,trp solo
    sc,pts KUNZEL 10216 f.s.   (P569)

PURCELL, HENRY (cont'd.)
  Spielmusik Zum Sommernachtstraum,
    Heft 1
    see Midsummer Night's Dream, A:
    Incidental Music, Vol.1

  Spielmusik Zum Sommernachtstraum,
    Heft 2
    see Midsummer Night's Dream, A:
    Incidental Music, Vol.2

  Three Overtures, [arr.] [9']
    (Cooper; Hayward) 2trp,timp,strings
    NOVELLO perf mat rent   (P570)

  Three Overtures For Trumpets, Drums
    And Strings
    2trp,timp,strings
    KALMUS A4038 sc $10.00, perf mat
    rent, set $16.00, pts $2.00, ea.
                                       (P571)
  Trumpet Tune And Air, For Trumpet And
    Orchestra [arr.]
    (Woodgate, Leslie) 2.2.2.2.
    4.0.3.1. timp,perc,org,strings,
    trp solo [4'] BOOSEY perf mat
    rent   (P572)

PUREBL, J.
  Concerto for Clarinet and Orchestra
    in A
    MUS. RARA perf mat rent   (P573)

PURITANI, I: AH, PER SEMPRE IO TI
  PERDEI, FOR SOLO VOICE AND
  ORCHESTRA see Bellini, Vincenzo

PURITANI, I: CINTA DI FIORI, FOR SOLO
  VOICE AND ORCHESTRA see Bellini,
  Vincenzo

PURITANI, I: IL RIVAL SALVAR TU DEI,
  FOR SOLO VOICES AND ORCHESTRA see
  Bellini, Vincenzo

PURITANI, I: NEL MIRATI UN SOLO
  ISTANTE, FOR SOLO VOICES AND
  ORCHESTRA see Bellini, Vincenzo

PURITANI, I: SAI COM'ARDE IN PETTO MIO,
  FOR SOLO VOICES AND ORCHESTRA see
  Bellini, Vincenzo

PURO, FOR CLARINET AND ORCHESTRA see
  Tiensuu, Jukka

PURPLE see Torke, Michael

PUSCHKINIANA [ARR.] see Prokofiev,
  Serge, Pushkin Suite [arr.]

PUSHKIN SUITE [ARR.] see Prokofiev,
  Serge

PUTAIN, LA see Telemann, Georg Philipp

PÜTZ, EDUARD (1911-   )
  Concerto Giocoso, For Piano And
    Orchestra
    2.2.2.2. 4.2.3.1. timp,perc,harp,
    strings,pno solo
    TONOS perf mat rent   (P574)

  Concerto Grosso
    string orch, jazz combo
    TONOS   (P575)

  Pyrenaen Suite, For Piano And
    Orchestra
    2.2.2.2. 4.2.3.1. timp,perc,harp,
    strings,pno solo
    TONOS perf mat rent   (P576)

  Tagebuchblatter Aus Frankreich
    2.2.2.2. 4.2.3.0. timp,perc,harp,
    strings
    TONOS perf mat rent   (P577)

PUZZLE, FOR SOLO VOICE AND ORCHESTRA
  see Manoury, Philippe

PYRENAEN SUITE, FOR PIANO AND ORCHESTRA
  see Pütz, Eduard

PYRONDUS see Halmrast, Tor

PYTALEV, F.
  Symphony No. 3
    sc MEZ KNIGA f.s.   (P578)

Q

QARRTSILUNI see Riisager, Knudage

QIN, YONG CHENG
  Happy Grassland [6']
    2.2.2.2. 4.2.3.1. timp,perc,pno,
    strings
    HONG KONG perf mat rent   (Q1)

QUADRE see Mestres-Quadreny, Josep
  Maria

QUADRI see Smith, William Overton

QUADRILLE SUR DES AIRS FRANCAISE see
  Strauss, Johann, [Jr.]

QUADRUPLUM see Bettinelli, Bruno

QUAINT EVENTS, FOR SOLO VOICE AND
  ORCHESTRA see Del Tredici, David

QUANDO INCISE SU QUEL MARMO, FOR SOLO
  VOICE AND ORCHESTRA see Bellini,
  Vincenzo

QUANTUM MECHANICS, LESSON I: ECSTATIC
  STATES see Rudhyar, Dane (Daniel
  Chennevière)

QUANTZ, JOHANN JOACHIM (1697-1773)
  Concerto for Flute and String
    Orchestra in C [14']
    string orch,cont,fl solo
    (Sonntag) KALMUS A7406 sc $15.00,
    set $17.50, pts $2.50, ea., perf
    mat rent   (Q2)

  Concerto for Horn and String
    Orchestra in E flat
    string orch,cont,horn solo
    (Delius, N.) sc,pts KUNZEL 10227
    f.s.   (Q3)

QUARANTA, FELICE (1910-   )
  San Miguel, For Solo Voice And
    Orchestra [14']
    1.1.1.1. 2.1.1.0. timp,perc,pno,
    harp,strings,Bar solo
    RICORDI-IT 132101 perf mat rent
                                     (Q4)

QUARTESSENCE see Thorne, Francis
  Burritt

QUARTETTO see Schetky, Johann Georg
  Christoff

QUASERS see Pepin, Clermont

QUASI PASSACAGLIA see Breimo, Bjørn

QUASI UN PASADOBLE see Balada, Leonardo

QUASI UN REQUIEM, FOR STRING QUARTET
  AND STRING ORCHESTRA see Marco,
  Tomas

QUASI UNA FANTASIA see Pablo, Luis de

QUASI UNA SONATA, FOR VIOLIN AND
  CHAMBER ORCHESTRA see Schnittke,
  Alfred

QUATERNI II, FOR VIOLIN, HORN, PIANO
  AND ORCHESTRA see Vlijmen, Jan van

QUATRAIN, FOR VIOLIN, CLARINET,
  VIOLONCELLO, PIANO AND ORCHESTRA
  see Takemitsu, Toru

QUATRE CAPRICES see Marischal, Louis

QUATRE CHANSONS DE PAUL FORT, NO. 1: IL
  FAUT NOUS AIMER, FOR SOLO VOICE AND
  ORCHESTRA see Hubeau, Jean

QUATRE CHANSONS DE PAUL FORT, NO. 2:
  CHANSON DE FOL, FOR SOLO VOICE AND
  ORCHESTRA see Hubeau, Jean

QUATRE CHANSONS DE PAUL FORT, NO. 3: LE
  DIABLE DANS LA NUIT, FOR SOLO VOICE
  AND ORCHESTRA see Hubeau, Jean

QUATRE CHANSONS DE PAUL FORT, NO. 4: LA
  RONDE AUTOUR DU MONDE, FOR SOLO
  VOICE AND ORCHESTRA see Hubeau,
  Jean

QUATRE CHANSONS FRANÇAISES, FOR SOLO
  VOICE AND ORCHESTRA see Britten,
  [Sir] Benjamin

QUATRE MELODIES DE FRANCIS CARCO, FOR
  SOLO VOICE AND ORCHESTRA see
  Tomasi, Henri

QUATRE MELODIES SUR DES POESIES
  ANCIENNES, FOR SOLO VOICE AND
  ORCHESTRA see Jolivet, Andre

QUATRE MOUVEMENTS, FOR ORCHESTRA see
  Tansman, Alexandre

QUATRE POEMES HINDOUS, FOR SOLO VOICE
  AND ORCHESTRA see Delage, Maurice

QUATRE POESIES FOR SOLO VOICE AND
  ORCHESTRA see Hasquenoph, Pierre

QUATRE PRELUDES POUR L'OPERA DES
  BASTILLES, FOR VIOLIN AND STRING
  ORCHESTRA see Landowski, Marcel

QUATRE SONATINES FRANCAISES, OP. 60 BIS
  see Koechlin, Charles

QUATTRO DIALOGHI, FOR TWO PERCUSSION
  SOLOISTS AND ORCHESTRA see Durko,
  Zsolt

QUATTRO LIRICHE BREVI, FOR ALTO
  SAXOPHONE AND CHAMBER ORCHESTRA see
  Orrego-Salas, Juan A.

QUATTRO PEZZI see Scelsi, Giacinto see
  Theorin, Hakan see Veracini,
  Francesco Maria

QUATTRO STAGIONI, LE see Vivaldi,
  Antonio

QUATTRO STUDI see Paccagnini, Angelo
  see Vavolo, Marco

QUEEN OF SHEBA, THE: ENTRANCE MARCH see
  Goldmark, Karl, Königin Von Saba,
  Die: Festlicher-Einzugs-Marsch

QUEEN OF SHEBA, THE: OVERTURE see
  Goldmark, Karl, Königin Von Saba,
  Die: Overture

QUEEN OF SHEBA: MARCHE ET CORTEGE see
  Gounod, Charles François, Reine De
  Saba, La: Marche Et Cortege

QUEEN OF SPADES, THE: ARIA OF LISA, FOR
  SOLO VOICE AND ORCHESTRA see
  Tchaikovsky, Piotr Ilyich

QUEEN OF SPADES, THE: HERMAN'S ARIA,
  FOR SOLO VOICE AND ORCHESTRA see
  Tchaikovsky, Piotr Ilyich

QUEEN OF SPADES, THE: ROMANCE OF
  PAULINE, FOR SOLO VOICE AND
  ORCHESTRA see Tchaikovsky, Piotr
  Ilyich

QUEEN'S FANCY, THE see Lewis, John
  Aaron

QUEEN'S JIG, THE see George, Graham

QUEENSMERE see Griebling

QUELLE, ERNST AUGUST (1931-   )
  Boyfriends-Girlfriends [5']
    2.2.1+bass clar.0. 3.3.3.0. perc,
    pno,gtr,strings
    ZIMMER.   (Q5)

QUELLEN I see Busch-Orphal, Ulrich

QUELLEN II see Busch-Orphal, Ulrich

QUELLEN III see Busch-Orphal, Ulrich

QUERELA PACIS see Dorati, Antal

QUERFURTH, F.
  Concerto for Trumpet and Orchestra
    MUS. RARA perf mat rent   (Q6)

QUEUE LEU LEU see DuBois, Pierre-Max

"QUICQUAM", FOR DOUBLE BASS AND STRINGS
  see Angerer, Paul

QUID PRO QUO see Nowak, Alison

QUILTER, ROGER (1877-1953)
  Three English Dances *Op.11 [10']
    2.1.2.2. 2.2.0.0. timp,perc,
    strings
    BOOSEY perf mat rent   (Q7)

  Three English Dances [arr.] *Op.11
    (Fletcher) 2(pic).2.2.2.sax.
    2.2.3.1. timp,perc,strings
    [7'30"] KALMUS A7451 pno-cond sc
    $8.00, set $50.00, pts $2.50,
    ea., perf mat rent   (Q8)

QUINTEMENTO see Cable, Howard

QUINTUPLE FORM III see Weis, Flemming,
  Femdelt Form III

QUIPU see Smit, Sytze

QUO VADIS MUSICA-SYMFONIE see Sporck,
  Jo

QUO VADIS: SUITE see Rozsa, Miklos

QUODLIBET see Castiglioni, Niccolò see
  Schickele, Peter

QUODLIBET, FOR SOLO VOICE AND ORCHESTRA
  see Kagel, Mauricio

QUODLIBET RE BACH see Hambraeus, Bengt

R

R. DE MAHLER, FOR SOLO VOICE,
VIOLONCELLO AND ORCHESTRA see
Koering, Rene

RA see Hopkins, John

RAASTED, NIELS OTTO (1888-1966)
Kuvia Suomesta
sc,pts SAMFUNDET f.s.   (R1)

Sinfonia Da Chiesa
sc,pts SAMFUNDET f.s.   (R2)

RAATS, JAAN (1932-   )
Concerto for Chamber Orchestra, Op.
16 [12']
string orch
SIKORSKI perf mat rent   (R3)

Concerto for Piano and Chamber
Orchestra, Op. 41 [18']
2ob,2horn,strings,pno solo
SIKORSKI perf mat rent   (R4)

Concerto for Violin, Strings and
Piano, Op. 21 [16']
strings,pno,vln solo
SIKORSKI perf mat rent   (R5)

Symphony No. 3, Op. 10 [19']
3.0.3.3.alto sax. 2.2.3.1. timp,
perc,strings
SIKORSKI perf mat rent   (R6)

Symphony No. 5 [38']
2.0.2.2. 3.4.3.1. timp,perc,pno,
strings
SIKORSKI perf mat rent   (R7)

Symphony No. 7, Op. 47 [21']
3.3.3.3. 3.4.3.1. timp,perc,pno,
strings
SIKORSKI perf mat rent   (R8)
VAAP perf mat rent   (R9)

RABAUD, HENRI (1873-1949)
Deuxieme Poeme Lyrique Sur Le Livre
De Job, For Solo Voice And
Orchestra [16']
CHOUDENS perf mat rent   (R10)

Divertissement Sur Des Chansons
Russes *Op.2 [15']
2.2.2.2. 4.2.3.0. timp,cym,harp,
strings
ENOCH perf mat rent   (R11)

Marouf: Ballet Music [15']
CHOUDENS perf mat rent   (R12)

Symphony No. 2, Op. 5, in E minor
[41']
2(pic).2.2.2. 4.2.3.1. timp,cym,
harp,strings
ENOCH perf mat rent   (R13)

RABELAISIANA, FOR SOLO VOICE AND
ORCHESTRA see Rota, Nino

RABINOWITCH, ALEXANDRE
Belle Musique No. 3, La [20']
3.3.3.3. 4.3.3.1. timp,perc,pno&
cel,harp,strings
BELAIEFF   (R14)

RACCONTO DI MONSIEUR B., IL see
Battistelli, Giorgio

RACCORDS see Taranu, Cornel

RACHMANINOFF, SERGEY VASSILIEVICH
(1873-1943)
Aleko: Suite [20']
3.3.2.2. 4.2.3.1. timp,perc,harp,
strings
SIKORSKI perf mat rent   (R15)

Concerto for Piano and Orchestra, No.
4, Op. 40, in G minor
sc KALMUS A7016 $60.00   (R16)

Polichinelle [arr.] *Op.3,No.4
(Jacquet) 1(pic).1.2.1. 2.2.1.0.
timp,perc,harp,strings [3']
KALMUS A5752 pno-cond sc $5.00,
set $15.00, perf mat rent   (R17)

Prelude, Op. 3, No. 2, in C sharp
minor, [arr.]
(Schmid, Adolf) 2.2.2.2. 2.2.3.0.
timp,perc,harp,strings [4']
BOOSEY perf mat rent   (R18)

Prelude, Op. 23, No. 5, in G minor,
[arr.]
(Rubbra, Edmund) 2.2.2.2. 4.2.3.1.
timp,perc,harp,strings [4']
BOOSEY perf mat rent   (R19)

RACHMANINOFF, SERGEY VASSILIEVICH
(cont'd.)

Romanze Und Scherzo
string orch WOLLENWEBER 999 f.s.
(R20)

Scherzo
(Lamm; Malcolm) 2.2.2.2. 2.2.0.0.
timp,strings [5'] KALMUS A6782 sc
$10.00, set $20.00, pts $1.50,
ea., perf mat rent   (R21)

Symphony in D minor
(Lamm) KALMUS 7238 sc $30.00, set
$75.00, pts $3.50, ea., perf mat
rent   (R22)

Symphony No. 1, Op. 13
study sc SIKORSKI f.s., perf mat
rent   (R23)

RACINE FRICKER, PETER
see FRICKER, PETER RACINE

RADAMISTO: SOMMI DEI, FOR SOLO VOICE
AND STRING ORCHESTRA see Handel,
George Frideric

RADEAU DE LA MEDUSE, LE see Martelli,
Henri

RADIANCE, FOR PIANO AND INSTRUMENTAL
ENSEMBLE see Taira, Yoshihisa

RADIANTE AMERICA, FOR SOLO VOICES AND
ORCHESTRA see Krieger, Armando

RADULESCU, HORATIO (1942-   )
Everlasting Longings [13']
24strings
BILLAUDOT perf mat rent   (R24)

RAFF, JOSEPH JOACHIM (1822-1882)
Concerto for Piano and Orchestra, Op.
185
sc KISTNER f.s., perf mat rent
(R25)
Concerto for Violin and Orchestra,
Op. 161
(Wilhelmy) KISTNER perf mat rent
(R26)
Dame Kobold: Overture [8']
2.2.2.2. 4.2.0.0. timp,strings
BOTE perf mat rent   (R27)

Symphony No. 3, Op. 153
sc KISTNER f.s., perf mat rent
(R28)
Symphony No. 7, Op. 201 [45']
2.2.2.2. 4.2.3.0. timp,perc,
strings
(In den Alpen) RIES perf mat rent
(R29)
Symphony No. 8, Op. 205
KISTNER perf mat rent   (R30)

Symphony No. 9, Op. 208
KISTNER perf mat rent   (R31)

Ungrischer, For Violin And Orchestra,
Op. 203
KISTNER perf mat rent   (R32)

RAGA, FOR OBOE AND ORCHESTRA see Berge,
Sigurd

RAGOMANIA see Bolcom, William Elden

RAGTIME see Hindemith, Paul

RAGTIME CAPRICE, FOR PIANO AND
ORCHESTRA see Turok, Paul Harris

RAGTIME DANCE NO. 1 [ARR.] see Ives,
Charles

RAGTIME DANCE NO. 2 [ARR.] see Ives,
Charles

RAGTIME DANCE NO. 3 [ARR.] see Ives,
Charles

RAGTIME DANCE NO. 4 [ARR.] see Ives,
Charles

RAGUE, LOUIS CHARLES (1760-1793)
Symphony, Op. 10, No. 1, in D minor
1.2.0.0. 2.0.0.0. strings
(Brooks, Barry) FRANK perf mat rent
(R33)
Symphony, Op. 10, No. 2, in F
0.2.0.0. 2.0.0.0. strings
(Brook, Barry) FRANK perf mat rent
(R34)

RAICES see Enriquez, Manuel

RAIDERS OF THE LOST ARK: THE RAIDERS
MARCH see Williams, John T.

RAIN COMING see Takemitsu, Toru

RAIN DOWN DEATH see Becker, John Joseph

RAINBOW RISING see Erickson, Robert

RAINBOW SNAKE, THE see Norby, Erik

RAINBOW SNAKE, THE: REDUCED ORCHESTRA
VERSION see Norby, Erik

RAISES HISPANICAS see Benguerel, Xavier

RAITIO, PENTTI (1930-   )
Concerto for Flute and Orchestra
[20']
0.0.0.0. 2.2.2.0. timp,perc,
strings,fl solo
sc SUOMEN f.s.   (R35)

RAJNA, THOMAS (1928-   )
Cantilenas And Interludes [24']
2(pic).2(English horn).2.2.
2.0.0.0. strings
BOOSEY perf mat rent   (R36)

Concerto for Piano and Orchestra, No.
1 [26']
1+pic.2.2.2. 2.0.0.0. timp,
strings,pno solo
BOOSEY perf mat rent   (R37)

Concerto for Piano and Orchestra, No.
2 [35']
2+pic.2.2.2. 4.3.3.1. timp,perc,
strings,pno solo
BOOSEY perf mat rent   (R38)

Movements For Strings [15']
string orch
BOOSEY perf mat rent   (R39)

Suite for Strings [24']
string orch
BOOSEY perf mat rent   (R40)

RAJTER, L'UDOVÍT (1906-   )
Suite Miniature
SLOV.HUD.FOND   (R41)

RAKASTAVA see Sibelius, Jean

RAKOCZY-MARSCH see Liszt, Franz

RAKOV, NIKOLAI (1908-   )
Concerto for Violin and Orchestra
[29']
2.2.2.2. 4.2.0.0. timp,perc,harp,
strings,vln solo
SIKORSKI perf mat rent   (R42)

Dance Suite
1.1.1.1. 2.1.1.0. timp,perc,pno,
strings
VAAP perf mat rent   (R43)

Mariische Suite [12']
3.2.2.2. 4.3.3.1. timp,perc,harp,
strings
VAAP perf mat rent   (R44)

Symphony [34']
2.2.2.2. 4.2.3.1. timp,perc,
strings
SIKORSKI perf mat rent   (R45)

RAMEAU, JEAN-PHILIPPE (1683-1764)
Acante Et Cephise: Suite
(Petit, J.L.) string orch [12'] sc,
pts BOIS f.s.   (R46)

Castor Et Pollux: Suite
(Gevaert) 2(pic).2.0.2. 0.0.0.0.
perc,strings [25'] KALMUS A5787
sc $20.00, set $30.00, perf mat
rent   (R47)

Collected Works. Paris, 1895-1913
(microfiche reprint, $285.00)
UNIV.MUS.ED.   (R48)

Concert No. 6 [arr.]
(Mottl) 2(pic).2.2.2. 2.0.0.0.
perc,strings [13'] KALMUS A7237
sc $12.00, set $35.00, pts $2.50,
ea., perf mat rent   (R49)

Dardanus: Suite [arr.]
(Leppard, Raymond) 2.2.0.2.
2.0.0.0. 1-2perc,hpsd,strings
[25'] FABER perf mat rent   (R50)
(Vaubourgoin, M.) 2.2.0.2. 0.0.0.0.
strings [15'] BILLAUDOT perf mat
rent   (R51)

Guirlande, La [arr.]
(Vaubourgoin, M.) 2.4.0.4. 0.0.0.0.
strings [9'] BILLAUDOT perf mat
rent   (R52)

Indes Galantes, Les: Suite No. 2
(Dukas, Paul) sc DURAND f.s.   (R53)

Platee: Suite No. 1 [16']
2fl,2ob,2bsn,strings
(Marty) sc DURAND f.s.   (R54)

Platée: Suite No. 2 [7']
2ob,2bsn,strings
(Airs de Ballet) DURAND 576-00282
sc $7.75, set $18.00, pts $2.50,
ea.   (R55)

RAMEAU, JEAN-PHILIPPE (cont'd.)

Suite for Strings, [arr.]
(Temple Savage) string orch [15']
BOOSEY perf mat rent   (R56)

Zais: Overture [6']
2.2.0.2. 0.0.0.0. perc,cont,
strings
(d'Indy) KALMUS A6095 sc $5.00, set
$10.00   (R57)
(d'Indy) DURAND sc $13.25, set
$26.50, pts $2.00, ea.   (R58)

Zoroastre: Suite [arr.]
(Gervais, F.) 2.2.0.2. 2.0.0.0.
strings [10'] BILLAUDOT perf mat
rent   (R59)

RAMESSES THE GREAT see El-Dabh, Halim

RAMINSH, IMANT (1943-   )
And The Great Day That Dawns [18']
3.2.3.2. 2.2.0.0. timp,glock,
strings
CAN.MUS.CENT. MI 1100 R137A   (R60)

Suite On Five Latvian Folk Songs
[12']
1.1.1.1. 1.0.0.0. timp,strings
CAN.MUS.CENT. MI 1200 R137SU   (R61)

Three Spanish Lyrics, For Solo Voice
And Orchestra [8']
2.2.2.2. 2.2.2.0. timp,harp,
strings,S solo
CAN.MUS.CENT. MV 1400 R137TH   (R62)

RAMIREZ, LUIS ANTONIO (1923-   )
Three Tributes
see Tres Homenajes

Tres Homenajes
string orch
"Three Tributes" PEER perf mat rent
(R63)
Tres Piezas Breves
horn,2trp,trom,perc,pno,strings
sc SEESAW $13.00, perf mat rent
(R64)
RAMO DI FOGLIA VERDE, FOR SOLO VOICES
AND ORCHESTRA see Gentilucci,
Armando

RAMOVS, PRIMOZ (1921-   )
Concerto A Becco, For Recorder And
Chamber Orchestra [12']
2horn,strings,rec solo
DRUSTVO DSS 951 perf mat rent (R65)

Concerto for Double Bass and
Orchestra [19']
2.2.2.2. 3.3.3.0. timp,perc,
strings,db solo
DRUSTVO DSS 794 perf mat rent (R66)

Concerto for Organ and Orchestra
[18']
0.0.0.0. 4.4.3.1. perc,strings,
org solo
DRUSTVO DSS 1056 perf mat rent
(R67)
Concerto for 2 Pianos and Orchestra
[16']
2(pic).2(English horn).2(bass
clar).2(contrabsn). 4.3.3.1.
timp,perc,strings,2pno soli
DRUSTVO DSS 1022 perf mat rent
(R68)
Concerto for Recorder, Flute and
Orchestra [16']
0.2(English horn).2(bass
clar).2(contrabsn). 3.3.3.0.
perc,strings,rec solo,fl solo
DRUSTVO DSS 1104 perf mat rent
(R69)
Concerto for Violin, Viola and
Orchestra
study sc GERIG BG 1336 f.s.   (R70)

Duo Concertante, For Flute, Harp And
Orchestra [15']
perc,strings,fl solo,harp solo
DRUSTVO DSS 945 perf mat rent (R71)

Finale [8']
2.2.2.2. 3.2.3.0. timp,strings
DRUSTVO DSS 943 perf mat rent (R72)

Organofonija [14']
2(pic).2(English horn).2(bass
clar).2(contrabsn). 4.3.3.1.
timp,perc,org,strings
DRUSTVO DSS 1030 perf mat rent
(R73)
Poliptih [14']
2(pic,rec).2(English horn).2(bass
clar).2(contrabsn). 4.2.3.1.
timp,perc,strings
DRUSTVO DSS 919 perf mat rent (R74)

RAMUNTCHO: BASQUE RHAPSODY see Pierne,
Gabriel

RAMUNTCHO: OVERTURE see Pierne, Gabriel

RAMUNTCHO: SUITE NO. 1 see Pierne,
Gabriel

RAMUNTCHO: SUITE NO. 2 see Pierne,
Gabriel

RAN, SHULAMIT (1949-   )
Concerto for Orchestra [25']
PRESSER perf mat rent   (R75)

RANCIGAJ, LJUBO (1936-   )
Concertino for Piano and Orchestra
[18']
2(pic).2(English horn).2(bass
clar).2(contrabsn). 4.3.3.1.
timp,perc,strings,pno solo
DRUSTVO DSS 1014 perf mat rent
(R76)

Concerto for Orchestra [23']
2(pic).2(English horn).2(bass
clar).2(contrabsn). 4.3.3.1.
timp,perc,harp,pno,cel,strings
DRUSTVO DSS 1065 perf mat rent
(R77)
RAND see Moser, Roland Olivier

RANDS, BERNARD (1935-   )
"...Body And Shadow..." [20']
UNIVER. perf mat rent   (R78)

Canti Del Sole, For Solo Voice And
Orchestra [28']
2(pic,alto fl).2.2(clar in E
flat,bass clar).2. 3.3.3.0.
3perc,2harp,cel,pno,elec org,
strings,T solo
UNIVER. perf mat rent   (R79)

Canti Lunatici, For Solo Voice And
Orchestra [29']
2(pic,alto fl).2.2(clar in E
flat,bass clar).2. 2.2.2.0.
2perc,2harp,cel,pno,strings,S
solo
sc UNIVER. UE16471 $28.00, perf mat
rent   (R80)

Ceremonial 1 [12']
2+2pic.2+English horn.2+bass
clar.2+contrabsn. 4.3.3.1.
timp,3perc,2harp,cel,pno,elec
org,strings
UNIVER. perf mat rent   (R81)

Ceremonial 2 [15']
3.2+English horn.2+bass clar.1+
contrabsn. 4.3.3.1. timp,3perc,
harp,cel,pno,elec org,strings
UNIVER. perf mat rent   (R82)

Etendre
fl,clar,horn,trp,trom,elec org,
perc,cel,pno,vln,vla,vcl
sc UNIVER. $19.00   (R83)

Hireath, For Violoncello And
Orchestra [26']
3.3.4.3. 4.3.3.1. timp,4perc,
2harp,pno,elec org,strings,vcl
solo
UNIVER. perf mat rent   (R84)

London Serenade [15']
2.2.2.2. 1.1.1.0. perc,harp,9vln,
3vla,2vcl,db
UNIVER. perf mat rent   (R85)

Tambourin, Le. Suites 1 And 2 [20']
2+pic.2+English horn.3+bass
clar.2+contrabsn. 4.3.3.1.
timp,4perc,2harp,cel,pno,elec
org,strings
sc UNIVER. UE17930 f.s., perf mat
rent   (R86)

RANGSTRÖM, TURE (1884-1947)
Bishop Thomas' Song Of Freedom, For
Solo Voice And Orchestra [5']
2.2.2.2. 4.3.0.1. timp,perc,
strings,med solo
NORDISKA perf mat rent   (R87)

Dying Tree, The, For Solo Voice And
Orchestra [3']
2.2.2.2. 2.2.0.0. timp,perc,
strings,med solo
NORDISKA perf mat rent   (R88)

Gammalsvenskt, For Solo Voice And
Orchestra [3']
2.0.2.2. 2.2.1.0. timp,perc,
strings,med solo
NORDISKA perf mat rent   (R89)

Mourning Song, For Solo Voice And
String Orchestra [5']
string orch,med solo
NORDISKA perf mat rent   (R90)

Only Time, The, For Solo Voice And
String Orchestra [3']
string orch,med solo
NORDISKA perf mat rent   (R91)

RANGSTRÖM, TURE (cont'd.)
Pan, For Solo Voice And Orchestra
[5']
2.1.2.1. 2.0.0.0. harp,strings,
med solo
NORDISKA perf mat rent   (R92)

Prisoners, The, For Solo Voice And
Orchestra [5']
2.0.2.0. 4.0.0.0. harp,strings,
med solo
NORDISKA perf mat rent   (R93)

Spelar, Det, For Solo Voice And
Orchestra [3']
2.2.2.2. 2.2.0.0. timp,strings,
med solo
NORDISKA perf mat rent   (R94)

Summernight, The, For Solo Voice And
Orchestra [3']
2.0.0.0. 2.0.0.0. perc,strings,
med solo
NORDISKA perf mat rent   (R95)

Villemo, For Solo Voice And Orchestra
[2']
0.0.1.1. 0.0.0.0. strings,med
solo
NORDISKA perf mat rent   (R96)

Words Of Her, The, For Solo Voice And
Orchestra [4']
2.1.2.1. 2.0.0.0. timp,strings,
med solo
NORDISKA perf mat rent   (R97)

RANKI, GYÖRGY (1907-   )
Circus, The
sc EMB 10126 f.s.   (R98)

Concertino For Cimbalom And Orchestra
sc EMB 10228 f.s.   (R99)

Divertimento for Clarinet and String
Orchestra
string orch,clar solo
sc EMB 13035 f.s., perf mat rent
(R100)
Sword Dance
sc EMB 205 f.s.   (R101)

Symphony No. 1
sc EMB 10232 f.s.   (R102)

Symphony No. 2
sc EMB 10265 f.s.   (R103)

Two Wonder Oxen
sc EMB 10211 f.s.   (R104)

RANTA, MICHAEL (1942-   )
Transits I [25']
4perc,gtr,9strings
sc FEEDBACK FB 7712 f.s.   (R105)

RAPF, KURT (1922-   )
Concerto Estivo [12']
1.1.1.1. 0.1.0.0. strings
DOBLINGER perf mat rent   (R106)

Concerto for Flute and String
Orchestra [20']
string orch,opt perc,fl solo
DOBLINGER perf mat rent   (R107)

Concerto for Orchestra [21']
2+pic.3(English horn).3(bass
clar).3(contrabsn). 4.3.3.1.
timp,perc,harp,cel,strings
DOBLINGER perf mat rent   (R108)

Concerto for Organ and Orchestra
[23']
2(pic).2(English
horn).2.2(contrabsn). 4.3.3.1.
timp,perc,strings,org solo
DOBLINGER perf mat rent   (R109)

Concerto for Organ and String
Orchestra [14'30"]
string orch,org solo
DOBLINGER perf mat rent   (R110)

Concerto for Piano and Orchestra
[17']
2(pic).2(English
horn).2.2(contrabsn).2soprano
sax. 4.3.3.1. timp,perc,harp,
strings,pno solo
DOBLINGER perf mat rent   (R111)

Concerto for Violin and Winds [20']
2(pic).1+English horn.0+clar in E
flat+clar in A+bass clar.1+
contrabsn. 2.1.1.0. vln solo
(Hommage a Alban Berg) DOBLINGER
perf mat rent   (R112)

Concerto for Violin, Piano and
Orchestra [21']
2.2.2.2. 3.2.0.1. timp,perc,
strings,vln solo,pno solo
DOBLINGER perf mat rent   (R113)

RAPF, KURT (cont'd.)

Concerto for Violin, Violoncello and
    Orchestra [25']
    2(pic).2(English horn).2(bass
        clar).2(contrabsn). 4.3.3.1.
        timp,perc,harp,cel,strings,vln
        solo,vcl solo
    DOBLINGER perf mat rent   (R114)

Concerto No. 6 for Chamber Orchestra
    [12'30"]
    1(pic).1(English horn).1.1.
        1.2.2.0. timp,perc,harp,cel,
        pno,vln,db
    (Fantasies) DOBLINGER perf mat rent
                                     (R115)

Leanda [14']
    2+pic.3(English horn).2(bass
        clar).3(contrabsn). 4.3.3.1.
        timp,perc,harp,strings
    DOBLINGER perf mat rent   (R116)

Ouverture Brillante [7']
    2(pic).2(English horn).2(bass
        clar,clar in E flat).2.
        2.2.0.0. timp,perc,harp,strings
    DOBLINGER perf mat rent   (R117)

Schone Und Das Tier, Die, For
    Narrator And Orchestra [26']
    English horn,clar&bass clar,
        contrabsn,perc,strings,narrator
    DOBLINGER perf mat rent   (R118)

Symphony No. 1 [23']
    3(pic).3(English horn).2+bass
        clar.2+contrabsn. 4.3.3.1.
        timp,perc,cel,harp,strings
    DOBLINGER perf mat rent   (R119)

Symphony No. 2 [25']
    3(pic,alto fl).3(English
        horn).3(bass
        clar).3(contrabsn). 4.3.3.1.
        timp,perc,harp,cel,gtr,opt org,
        strings
    DOBLINGER perf mat rent   (R120)

Vier Orchesterstucke [15']
    2(pic).2(English horn).2+bass
        clar.2+contrabsn. 4.3.3.1.
        timp,perc,harp,strings
    DOBLINGER perf mat rent   (R121)

RAPHAEL, GÜNTHER (1903-1960)
Acht Gedichte Von Hermann Hesse, For
    Solo Voice And Orchestra *Op.72
    BREITKOPF-L perf mat rent   (R122)

RAPHLING, SAM (1910-1988)
Concerto for Trumpet and String
    Orchestra [8']
    string orch,trp in C solo
    BOURNE perf mat rent   (R123)

Suite for Strings
    string orch
    study sc PRESSER 456-40005 $3.00
                                     (R124)

Ticker-Tape Parade [5']
    2+pic.2(English horn).2.2.
        4.3.3.1. timp,perc,strings
    WEINTRB perf mat rent   (R125)

RAPSODIA DEL PLATA see Stefani, Daniel

RAPSODIA E DANZA, FOR 2 FLUTES AND
    ORCHESTRA see Roos, Robert de

RAPSODIA ELEGIACA, FOR DOUBLEBASS AND
    ORCHESTRA see Mortari, Virgilio

RAPSODIA ESPANOLA, FOR PIANO AND
    ORCHESTRA [ARR] see Albéniz, Isaac

RAPSODIE BRETONNE see Saint-Saëns,
    Camille

RAPSODIE ESPAGNOLE see Ravel, Maurice

RAPSODIE HEBRAIQUE see Tansman,
    Alexandre

RAPSODIE POLONAISE see Tansman,
    Alexandre

RAPSODIE VIENNOISE see Schmitt, Florent

RASKATOV, ALEXANDER (1953-   )
Concerto for Piano and Chamber
    Orchestra [24']
    0.0.2.2. 2.0.1.0. elec gtr,bass
        gtr,strings,electronic tape,pno
        solo
    VAAP perf mat rent   (R126)

RASMUSSEN, KARL AAGE (1947-   )
Contrafactum, For Violoncello And
    Orchestra [30']
    3(pic).2+English horn.2+bass
        clar.3(contrabsn). 4.3.3.1.
        3perc,strings,vcl solo
    HANSEN-DEN perf mat rent   (R127)

RASMUSSEN, KARL AAGE (cont'd.)

Movements On A Moving Line [20']
    1(pic).1.1.1. 1.1.1(bass trom).0.
        perc,pno,2vln,vla,vcl,db
    HANSEN-DEN perf mat rent   (R128)

Symphony: "Anfang Und Ende" [40']
    2(rec)+pic.2+English horn.2+bass
        clar.2+contrabsn. 4.3.3.1.
        perc,cel,2pno,harp,strings
    HANSEN-DEN perf mat rent   (R129)

Symphony In Time, A [32']
    2+pic.2+English horn.2+clar in E
        flat+bass clar.2+contrabsn.
        4.3.3.1. timp,3perc,harp,pno,
        hpsd&org&cel,strings
    HANSEN-DEN perf mat rent   (R130)

RATHAUS, KAROL (1895-1954)
Sweet Music
    2.2.2.2. 4.0.0.0. triangle,harp,
        strings
    AMP perf mat rent   (R131)

RATHAUSBALL TANZE WALZER see Strauss,
    Johann, [Jr.]

RATHBURN, ELDON (1916-   )
Train To Mariposa, The [7']
    2.2.2.2. 4.3.3.1. timp,2perc,
        harp,pno&cel,strings
    CAN.MUS.CENT. MI 1100 R234TR   (R132)

RATIU, HORIA (1951-   )
Convergences [12']
    4(pic).2+English horn.3(bass
        clar).2(contrabsn). 4.3.3.1.
        4perc,cel,pno,strings
    SALABERT perf mat rent   (R133)

RATTENFÄNGER, DER, FOR SOLO VOICE AND
    ORCHESTRA see Wolf, Hugo

RAUB DER EUROPA, DER, FOR SOLO VOICE
    AND ORCHESTRA see Terzakis, Dimitri

RAUM, ELIZABETH (1945-   )
Adventures Of Ian The Oboe, The, For
    Oboe And Chamber Orchestra
    1.1.1.1. 1.1.0.0. strings,ob
        solo,opt narrator
    CAN.MUS.CENT. MV 1343 R246A   (R134)

Evolution [10']
    1.1.1.1. 1.1.0.0. strings
    CAN.MUS.CENT. MI 1200 R246E   (R135)

Robot From Orion, The, For Narrator
    And Instrumental Ensemble [20']
    1.1.1.1. 1.1.0.0. opt pno,2vln,
        vla,vcl,db,narrator
    CAN.MUS.CENT. MV 1300 R246RO   (R136)

Suite For Sir Gawain And The Green
    Knight [17']
    1(pic).1.1.1. 1.1.0.0. strings
    CAN.MUS.CENT. MI 1200 R246SU   (R137)

RAUSCH, CARLOS
Sonorities [6']
    3.0.1.0.alto sax.tenor sax.
        1.3.0.1. timp,perc,xylo,strings
    sc AM.COMP.AL. $9.60   (R138)

RAUTAVAARA, EINOJUHANI (1928-   )
Concerto for Piano and Orchestra, No.
    2
    1.1.2.2. 3.4.0.0. timp,2perc,
        strings,pno solo
    PAN F   (R139)

Finnish Myth, A
    string orch
    sc FAZER $17.25   (R140)

Symphony No. 5 [31']
    3.3.3.3. 4.4.4.1. timp,3perc,
        strings
    PAN F   (R141)

Three Cantos, For String Orchestra
    [21'28"]
    string orch
    sc FAZER f.s., perf mat rent   (R142)

RAVEL, MAURICE (1875-1937)
Alcyone, For Solo Voices And
    Orchestra [23']
    2+pic.2+English horn.2.2.
        4.2.3.1. timp,perc,harp,
        strings,SMezT soli
    SALABERT perf mat rent   (R143)

Alyssa, For Solo Voices And Orchestra
    [28']
    2+pic.2+English horn.2.2.
        4.2.3.1. timp,perc,harp,
        strings,STBar soli
    SALABERT perf mat rent   (R144)

Barque Sur l'Ocean, Une [arr.]
    study sc ESCHIG 032-35757 $42.00
                                     (R145)
    (Nieweg) 2+pic.2+English horn.2+

RAVEL, MAURICE (cont'd.)

    bass clar.2. 4.2.3.1. timp,perc,
        2harp,cel,strings [7'] KALMUS
        A6453 sc $15.00, set $70.00, pts
        $3.50, ea., perf mat rent   (R146)

Bolero
    sc MUZYKA f.s.   (R147)
    (Jancsovics) study sc EMB 40102
        f.s.   (R148)

Daphnis Et Chloe
    sc DOVER 258262 $13.95   (R149)

Daphnis Et Chloe: Suite No. 1
    (McAlister) KALMUS A6082 sc $30.00,
        set $100.00, perf mat rent (R150)

Four Orchestral Works
    sc DOVER 259625 f.s.
        contains: Ma Mere L'oye; Pavane
        Pour Une Infante Defunte;
        Rapsodie Espagnole; Valses
        Nobles Et Setimentales   (R151)

Frontispice [arr.]
    (Boulez, Pierre) 1+pic.1+English
        horn.1+bass clar.2. 2.2.2.1.
        perc,harp,cel,pno,3vln,2vla,2vcl,
        db [1'30"] UNIVER. perf mat rent
                                     (R152)

Ma Mere L'Oye
    (Jancsovics) study sc EMB 40103
        f.s.   (R153)
    see Four Orchestral Works

Ma Mere L'Oye: Cing Pieces Enfantines
    (Bradbur) KALMUS A6392 sc $20.00,
        set $35.00, pts $2.00, ea., perf
        mat rent   (R154)

Ma Mere L'Oye: Prelude Et Danse Du
    Rouet
    (Nieweg) KALMUS A6393 sc $10.00,
        set $30.00, pts $2.00, ea., perf
        mat rent   (R155)

Myrrha, For Solo Voices And Orchestra
    [22']
    2+pic.2+English horn.2.2.
        4.2.3.0. timp,perc,strings,
        STBar soli
    SALABERT perf mat rent   (R156)

On The Death Of A Young Princess
    see Pavane Pour Une Infante Defunte

Pavane Pour Une Infante Defunte
    "On The Death Of A Young Princess"
    KALMUS A4152 sc $5.00, set $11.00
                                     (R157)
    see Four Orchestral Works

Pavane Pour Une Infante Defunte
    [arr.]
    (Jancsovics) study sc EMB 40105
        f.s.   (R158)
    (Walther, D.) 1.1.1.1. 1.0.0.0.
        harp,strings [7'] ESCHIG perf mat
        rent   (R159)

Rapsodie Espagnole
    (Bradbur) KALMUS A3434 sc $35.00,
        set $100.00, pts $4.00, ea., perf
        mat rent   (R160)
    see Four Orchestral Works

Sheherazade, For Solo Voice And
    Orchestra
    (Nieweg) KALMUS A7250 sc $20.00,
        set $60.00, pts $2.50, ea., perf
        mat rent   (R161)

Valses Nobles Et Sentimentales
    (Nieweg) KALMUS A6450 sc $25.00,
        set $80.00, pts $4.00, ea., perf
        mat rent   (R162)

Valses Nobles Et Setimentales
    see Four Orchestral Works

RAVISHMENT see Halldorsson, Skuli

RAWSTHORNE, ALAN (1905-1971)
Concertante Pastorale [10']
    fl,horn,strings
    OXFORD perf mat rent   (R163)

RAXACH, ENRIQUE (1932-   )
Calles Y Suenos [13']
    2.1.3.1. 1.1.1.0. 3perc,harp,gtr,
        2pno,3vln,2vla,3vcl,db
    sc DONEMUS f.s., perf mat rent
                                     (R164)

Opus Incertum [18']
    2.2.2.2. 2.2.1.0. perc,pno,
        strings
    DONEMUS perf mat rent   (R165)

RAZ DE SEIN see Baudrier, Yves

RAZZI, FAUSTO (1932-   )
Music No. 9 [12']
   2.2.2.2. 2.2.2.0. 14vln,4vla,
   4vcl,2db
   RICORDI-IT 132776 perf mat rent
                                    (R166)

RE PASTORE, IL: L'AMERO SARO COSTANTE,
   FOR SOLO VOICE AND ORCHESTRA see
   Mozart, Wolfgang Amadeus

REA, JOHN (1944-   )
Over Time [10']
   2.2.2.2. 4.2.3.1. timp,2perc,
   strings
   CAN.MUS.CENT. MI 1100 R2810V (R167)

READ, THOMAS LAWRENCE (1938-   )
Adventura [15']
   3.2.2.2. 4.3.3.1. timp,3perc,
   strings
   sc AM.COMP.AL. $81.15, perf mat
   rent   (R168)

   Isochronisms No: 2 [10']
   string orch
   sc AM.COMP.AL. $11.45   (R169)

   Symphonic Episodes [11']
   3.2.2.2. 4.3.3.1. timp,3perc,
   strings
   sc AM.COMP.AL. $43.65   (R170)

   Symphony For Orchestra With Piano
   Obbligato [15']
   2.2.2.2. 4.3.3.0. timp,2perc,pno,
   strings
   AM.COMP.AL. perf mat rent   (R171)

REAR WINDOW: SUITE see Waxman, Franz

REBAMBARAMBA, LA: SUITE see Roldan,
   Amadeo

REBEL, MEEUWIS (1957-   )
Deuteronomium, For Solo Voices And
   Instrumental Ensemble [45']
   1.1.1.1. 2.1.1.0. perc,pno,2vln,
   vla,vcl,SS soli sc DONEMUS f.s.,
   perf mat rent   (R172)

REBENSBURG, THOMAS (1958-   )
Nordlich Der Alpen [9']
   2.1.1.1. 3.1.2.0. timp,perc,opt
   harp,opt cel,pno,strings
   LEUCKART perf mat rent   (R173)

REBILD see Schröder, Walther

RECHBERGER, HERMAN (1947-   )
Consort Music 4 [12']
   2.2.2.2. 2.2.2.0. 2perc,strings
   sc JASE $22.00   (R174)

   Consort Music 5 [15']
   2.2.2.2. 3.3.3.1. timp,perc,harp,
   cel,strings
   JASE   (R175)

   Venezia, For Solo Voices And
   Orchestra [27']
   4(pic, alto fl,
   ocarina).4(english horn).4(bass
   clar).4(contrabsn). 6.4.4.1.
   4perc, harp, mand, gtr, acord,
   cel or hpsd, strings,
   electronic tape, countertenor+
   ttdb soli
   sc SUOMEN f.s.   (R176)

RECITATIVE AND ARIA, FOR VIOLONCELLO
   AND ORCHESTRA see Heiden, Bernhard

RECITATIVES AND ARIAS, FOR PIANO AND
   ORCHESTRA see Ruders, Poul

RECITS EPIQUES DU TEMPS DE LA GUERRE
   see Tisne, Antoine

RECOLLECT IN FEBRUARY see Korínek,
   Milošlav, Rozpomienka Na Februar

RECRUITING SUITE see Kokai, Rezsö

RECURRENCES see Conyngham, Barry

RED AND BLACK, FOR PIANO AND ORCHESTRA
   see Bauer, Jerzy, Czerwone I
   Czarne, For Piano And Orchestra

RED EARTH see Finnissy, Michael

RED LADY, THE see Chu, Wei

RED RIVER, THE see Zhang, Xiao-Fu, Man
   Jiang Hong

REDEL, MARTIN CHRISTOPH (1947-   )
Bruckner Essay *Op.31
   3(pic).3(English horn).3(bass
   clar).2+contrabsn. 4.3.3.1.
   timp,2perc,harp,strings
   study sc BOTE 037-35917 $48.00
                                    (R177)
Rhapsody for Viola and Orchestra, Op.
   36
   2.2.2(bass clar).2. 2.2.2.0.

REDEL, MARTIN CHRISTOPH (cont'd.)
   timp,perc,harp,strings,vla solo
   [16'] BOTE perf mat rent   (R178)

   Szenen, For Flute And Chamber
   Orchestra *Op.26a [13']
   ob,horn,perc,pno,strings,fl solo
   BOTE perf mat rent   (R179)

   Traumtanz, For Percussion And String
   Orchestra *Op.30 [15']
   string orch,perc solo
   BOTE perf mat rent   (R180)

REDJEPOV, REDJEP (1944-   )
Concerto for Oboe and Chamber
   Orchestra [13']
   perc,harp,strings,ob solo
   VAAP perf mat rent   (R181)

REED
Siciliano Notturno
   string orch MARKS 00008382 $16.00
                                    (R182)

REED, ALFRED (1921-   )
By The Lagoon [4']
   2.1.2.1. 2.2.1.0. perc,harp,
   strings
   KALMUS A7193 sc $5.00, set $10.00,
   pts $.75, ea.   (R183)

   Country Night [3'30"]
   2.1+English horn.2.2. 2.0.0.0.
   harp,strings
   KALMUS A7192 sc $3.00, set $10.00,
   pts $.75, ea.   (R184)

   Fashion Show [2'30"]
   2.1.2.1. 2.2.1.0. perc,harp,
   strings
   KALMUS A7191 sc $5.00, set $10.00,
   pts $1.00, ea.   (R185)

   Mechanical Doll, The [2'30"]
   2(pic).1.2.1. 2.2.1.0. perc,harp,
   strings
   KALMUS A7194 sc $7.00, set $10.00,
   pts $1.00, ea.   (R186)

   Strings 'N' Things [2']
   2.1.2.1. 2.2.1.0. perc,harp/pno,
   strings
   KALMUS A7190 sc $5.00, set $10.00,
   pts $1.00, ea.   (R187)

REEL CHAPLIN, THE see Knight, Eric

REEL WORLD, THE, FOR OBOE AND ORCHESTRA
   see Emmer, Huib

REESEN, EMIL
Gaucho Suite
   sc,pts SAMFUNDET f.s.   (R188)

   Schubert Variations
   sc SAMFUNDET f.s., perf mat rent
                                    (R189)
REFLECTION, FOR SOLO VOICE AND
   ORCHESTRA see Burritt, Lloyd

REFLECTIONS see Husa, Karel see Vantus,
   Istvan

REFLECTIONS, FOR ENGLISH HORN,
   VIOLONCELLO AND ORCHESTRA see
   Previn, Andre

REFLECTIONS FROM THE NORTH see Leifs,
   Jon

REFLECTIONS OF NARZISS AND GOLDMUND see
   Saxton, Robert

REFLECTIONS ON A LOST DREAM, FOR VIOLIN
   AND STRING ORCHESTRA see Baker,
   Michael Conway

REFLECTIONS ON A THEME OF TOMKINS see
   Mathias, William

REFLECTIONS ON A THEME OF WILLIAM
   WALTON see Bennett, Richard Rodney

REFLECTIONS ON A TRADITION see Ultan,
   Lloyd

REFLETS D'ALLEMAGNE: SUITE DE VALSES
   see Schmitt, Florent

REFLEX see Renosto, Paolo

REFLEXE II see Mullenbach, Alexander

REFLEXIONEN see Kühnl, Claus see
   Zechlin, Ruth

REFLEXUS see Montsalvatge, Xavier

REFRACTION-RETRACJA see Dembski,
   Stephen

REFRAINS see Amy, Gilbert

REFRAINS, FOR VIOLIN AND ORCHESTRA see
   Durko, Zsolt

REFUGE, FOR SOLO VOICE AND ORCHESTRA
   see Ágústsson, Herbert Hriberschek

REGARD OBLIQUE, UN, FOR 2 FLUTES AND
   INSTRUMENTAL ENSEMBLE see Francois,
   Renaud

REGER, MAX (1873-1916)
Christmas
   see Weihnachten, For String
   Orchestra

   Concerto for Violin and Orchestra,
   Op. 123 [16']
   3.3.0.2. 3.2.0.0. timp,strings,
   vln solo
   (Concerto in Olden Style) KALMUS
   A6335 sc $35.00, set $35.00, pts
   $2.00, ea., perf mat rent   (R190)

   Weihnachten, For String Orchestra
   *Op.145,No.3c
   "Christmas" set KALMUS A6163
   $10.00, and up   (R191)

REGIMENTER GEHN, FOR SOLO VOICE AND
   ORCHESTRA see Eisler, Hanns

REGINA COELI, FOR SOLO VOICE AND STRING
   ORCHESTA see Mouret, Jean Joseph

REGINA COELI, FOR SOLO VOICE AND STRING
   ORCHESTRA see Joseph, I.

REGIONS see Pehrson, Joseph Ralph

REGIONS INCONNUES, LES see Bertotto,
   Daniele

REGNER, HERMANN (1928-   )
Night Pieces [11']
   string orch
   MMB perf mat rent   (R192)

REHNQVIST, KARIN (1957-   )
Kast [10']
   string orch
   STIM   (R193)

   Strak [10']
   string orch
   STIM   (R194)

   Taromirs Tid [11']
   11strings,fl/vln,clar/vla
   "Time Of Taromir" STIM   (R195)

   Time Of Taromir
   see Taromirs Tid

REIBEL, GUY (1936-   )
Etudes De Flux [12']
   4(pic).4(English horn).4(bass
   clar).4(contrabsn). 4.4.3.1.
   4perc,pno,strings
   SALABERT perf mat rent   (R196)

   Hommage A Ravel [3']
   7vln,2vla,2vcl,db
   SALABERT perf mat rent   (R197)

   Musaiques, For Percussion And
   Orchestra [24']
   4(pic).3+English horn.4(bass
   clar).3+contrabsn. 4.4.3.1.
   4perc,pno,strings,perc solo,2
   solo voices
   SALABERT perf mat rent   (R198)

   Zoom [12']
   2.1+English horn.2.2. 2.2.1.1.
   2perc,harp,strings
   SALABERT perf mat rent   (R199)

REICH, STEVE (1936-   )
Eight Lines [17']
   2(pic).0.2(bass clar).0. 0.0.0.0.
   2pno,strings
   sc HENDON $40.00, perf mat rent
                                    (R200)
   Four Sections, The [25']
   4(pic).4.4(bass
   clar).4(contrabsn). 4.4.4.1.
   perc,2synthesizer,2pno,strings
   HENDON perf mat rent   (R201)

   Music For A Large Ensemble [15']
   1.0.2.0.2sax. 0.4.0.0. perc,4pno,
   2vln,2vla,2vcl,2db, 2 female
   voices
   HENDON perf mat rent   (R202)

   Music For Eighteen Musicians [58']
   2clar,4pno,3marimba,2xylo,
   metallophone,vln,vcl, 4 female
   voices
   HENDON perf mat rent   (R203)

   Tehillim, For Solo Voices And
   Orchestra
   3+pic.2+English horn.4.1.
   0.0.0.0. 6perc,2elec org,
   strings, 4 female voices

REICH, STEVE (cont'd.)

[30'] HENDON perf mat rent   (R204)

Three Movements [15']
3(pic).2+English horn.2+bass
clar.3(contrabsn). 4.3.3.1.
perc,harp,2pno,strings
HENDON perf mat rent   (R205)

Variations
3.3.0.0. 0.3.3.1. 2pno,3elec org,
strings
[21'] min sc HENDON $50.00, perf
mat rent   (R206)

REICHA, ANTON (1770-1836)
Basta! Ti Credo!
see Italian Arias, For Solo Voice
And Orchestra

Cagliostro: Overture
2.2.2.2. 4.0.3.0. timp,strings
CESKY HUD. perf mat rent   (R207)

Concertante, For Flute, Violin, And
Orchestra
0.2.0.0. 2.0.0.0. strings,fl
solo,vln solo
CESKY HUD. perf mat rent   (R208)

Concerto for Piano and Orchestra in E
flat [23']
1.2.0.0. 2.0.0.0. strings,pno
solo
(Krupka, Hanus) CESKY HUD. perf mat
rent   (R209)

Donne, Donne, Chi Vi Crede
see Italian Arias, For Solo Voice
And Orchestra

Grand Solo For Glass Harmonica And
Orchestra In F [10']
1.1.0.2. 2.0.0.0. strings, glass
harmonica solo
CESKY HUD. perf mat rent   (R210)

Italian Arias, For Solo Voice And
Orchestra
0.2.0.0. 2.0.0.0. strings,high solo
CESKY HUD. perf mat rent
duration: 11 minutes
contains: Basta! Ti Credo!;
Donne, Donne, Chi Vi Crede   (R211)

Musique Pour Celebrer La Memoire Des
Grands Hommes [25']
3(pic).6.6.6. 6.6.0.0. perc,3db
CESKY HUD. perf mat rent   (R212)

Overture in C, MIN 193 [10']
1.1.0.2. 2.2.0.0. timp,strings
CESKY HUD. perf mat rent   (R213)

Overture in D, MIN 190 [23']
2.2.2.2. 2.2.0.0. timp,strings
CESKY HUD. perf mat rent   (R214)

Overture in D, MIN 192 [12']
1.2.0.2. 2.2.0.0. timp,strings
CESKY HUD. perf mat rent   (R215)

Overture in E flat, MIN 191 [11']
1.2.0.2. 2.2.0.0. timp,strings
CESKY HUD. perf mat rent   (R216)

Overture in E minor, MIN 189
2.2.2.2. 4.0.3.0. timp,strings
CESKY HUD. perf mat rent   (R217)

Overture, Op. 24, in C [9']
1.2.0.2. 2.2.0.0. timp,strings
(Smetacek, Vaclav) CESKY HUD. perf
mat rent   (R218)

Sappho: Overture
2.2.2.2. 4.0.3.0. timp,strings
CESKY HUD. perf mat rent   (R219)

Symphonic Movements From The Turn Of
The Century
1.2.0.2. 2.2.0.0. timp,strings
(Ondracek, Stanislav; Smetacek,
Vaclav) (compiled from symphonic
fragments) CESKY HUD. perf mat
rent   (R220)

Symphonies, Two
see Witt, Friedrich, Symphony

Symphony in C minor [28']
1.2.0.2. 2.0.0.0. timp,strings
CESKY HUD. perf mat rent   (R221)

Symphony in D [28']
1.2.0.2. 2.2.0.0. timp,strings
CESKY HUD. perf mat rent   (R222)

Symphony in F [30']
1.2.2.2. 2.0.0.0. timp,strings
CESKY HUD. perf mat rent   (R223)

Symphony in F minor [31']
2.2.2.3. 2.2.0.0. timp,strings
CESKY HUD. perf mat rent   (R224)

REICHA, ANTON (cont'd.)

Symphony in G, MIN 194 [20']
reconstruction
1.2.0.2. 2.0.0.0. timp,strings
(Novenko, Michal) CESKY HUD. perf
mat rent   (R225)

Symphony, Op. 41, in E flat [22']
1.2.0.2. 2.2.0.0. strings
SUPRAPHON   (R226)

Variations for Bassoon and String
Orchestra [8']
string orch,bsn solo
CESKY HUD. perf mat rent   (R227)

Variations On A Russian Theme, For
Violoncello And String Orchestra
[10']
string orch,vcl solo
CESKY HUD. perf mat rent   (R228)

Variations On A Theme By Dittersdorf,
For Violoncello And Orchestra
[10']
1.2.0.0. 2.0.0.0. strings,vcl
solo
CESKY HUD. perf mat rent   (R229)

REICHA, JOSEPH (1746-1795)
Concerto for Flute and Orchestra, MIN
133
2ob,2horn,strings,fl solo
(Anspacher) sc,pts AMADEUS BP 2053
f.s.   (R230)

Concerto for 2 Horns and Orchestra
[18']
2ob,strings,2horn soli
SUPRAPHON   (R231)

REICHARDT, JOHANN FRIEDRICH (1752-1814)
Concerto for Violin and String
Orchestra in E flat, MIN 477
(Lungershausen) KALMUS A6343 sc
$6.00, set $9.00, pts $1.50, ea.,
perf mat rent   (R232)

REIGEN SELIGER GEISTER, FOR 2 FLUTES
AND ORCHESTRA [ARR.] see Gluck,
Christoph Willibald, Ritter von,
Orfeo Ed Euridice: Ballet Des
Ombres Heureuses, For 2 Flutes And
Orchestra [arr.]

REIMANN, ARIBERT (1936-   )
Apokalyptisches Fragment, Ein, For
Solo Voice, Piano And Orchestra
Orchestra [25']
2(pic).3.3.2. 2.0.0.0. timp,perc,
harp,strings,pno solo,Mez solo
SCHOTTS perf mat rent   (R233)

Drei Lieder Nach Gedichten Von Edgar
Allan Poe, For Solo Voice And
Orchestra
2.2.2.2. 2.1.1.0. 2harp,strings,S
solo
sc SCHOTTS $52.00   (R234)

Sieben Fragmente In Memoriam Robert
Schumann [11']
3.2.3.3. 4.4.2.1. harp,strings
SCHOTTS perf mat rent   (R235)

REINDEER RIDE FROM PEER GYNT, THE, FOR
SOLO VOICES AND ORCHESTRA see
Fladmoe, Arvid, Bukkerittet, For
Solo Voices And Orchestra

REINE DE SABA, LA: BALLET MUSIC see
Gounod, Charles François

REINE DE SABA, LA: MARCHE ET CORTEGE
see Gounod, Charles François

REINECKE, CARL (1824-1910)
Ballade for Flute and Orchestra, Op.
288
KALMUS A6641 pno-cond sc $5.00, set
$20.00, pts $1.00, ea., perf mat
rent   (R236)

Concerto for Flute and Orchestra, Op.
283, in D
KALMUS A6128 sc $45.00, set $50.00,
perf mat rent   (R237)

Dame Kobold Overture *Op.51 [8']
2.2.2.2. 2.2.0.0. timp,strings
BREITKOPF-W perf mat rent   (R238)
KALMUS A6137 sc $25.00, set $30.00,
perf mat rent   (R239)

Fest Overture *Op.148 [7']
2.2.2.2. 4.2.3.1. timp,strings
KALMUS A5788 sc $30.00, set $60.00,
perf mat rent   (R240)

Funf Tonbilder [20']
2.2.2.2. 4.2.3.0. timp,perc,
strings
KALMUS A7470 sc $15.00, set $50.00,
pts $2.50, ea., perf mat rent
(R241)

REINECKE, CARL (cont'd.)

Jubilee Overture *Op.166 [9']
2+pic.2.2(basset horn).2.
4.2.3.0. timp,strings
KALMUS A7266 sc $30.00, set $50.00,
pts $2.50, ea., perf mat rent
(R242)

Notturno for Horn and Orchestra, Op.
112 [6']
2.1.2.2. 2.0.0.0. timp,strings,
horn solo
KALMUS A6644 sc $8.00, set $12.00,
pts $.75, ea.   (R243)

Serenade, Op. 242, in G minor
KALMUS A7020 sc $10.00, set $15.00,
pts $3.00, ea.   (R244)

Symphony No. 3, Op. 227, in G minor
[33']
2.2.2.2. 4.2.3.0. timp,strings
KALMUS A7469 sc $40.00, set
$100.00, pts $5.00, ea., perf mat
rent   (R245)

REISE, JAY (1950-   )
Symphony No. 3 [18']
MERION perf mat rent   (R246)

REISEBILLEDER see Tveitt, Geirr

REISER, REINHARDT (1674-1739)
Jodelet: Six Little Pieces
string orch,hpsd [8'] KALMUS A6471
sc $4.00, set $5.00, pts $1.00,
ea., perf mat rent   (R247)

REISSIGER, KARL GOTTLIEB (1798-1859)
Concertino for Flute and Orchestra,
Op. 60, in D
(Foerster) sc KUNZEL 10142 $21.00,
ipa   (R248)

REITERMARSCH see Strauss, Johann, [Jr.]

REJOUISSANCE see Eröd, Ivan

REKASIUS, ANTANAS (1928-   )
Concerto for Saxophone, Percussion
and Strings [7']
perc,bells,vibra,harp,pno,9vln,
3vla,3vcl,db,sax solo
SIKORSKI perf mat rent   (R249)

RELATIONS. BALLET FOR SOLO VOICE AND
ORCHESTRA see Kelterborn, Rudolf

RELATIONS FOR ORCHESTRA see Kjaernes,
Bjorn Morten

RELATIVIDADES see Bernaola, Carmelo

RELATIVITY 1: THE LORENZ TRANSFORMATION
see Fongaard, Bjørn

RELATIVITY 2: GRAVITATION see Fongaard,
Bjørn

RELATIVITY 3: COSMOLOGY see Fongaard,
Bjørn

RELIEF see Bjelik, Martin

RELIEF I AND II see Norholm, Ib

RELIEFS IRRADIANTS DE NEW YORK see
Tisne, Antoine

REMBRANDT VAN RIJN: LIED DES CORNELIS,
FOR SOLO VOICE AND ORCHESTRA [ARR]
see Klenau, Paul von

REMEMBERING CHILD, FOR VIOLA AND
ORCHESTRA see Norgaard, Per

REMEMBERING GATSBY see Harbison, John

REMEMBERING ROME see Eaton, John C.

REMEMBERING TOMMY, FOR VIOLIN,
VIOLONCELLO AND ORCHESTRA see
Rorem, Ned

REMEMBRANCE see Carter, Elliott Cook,
Jr.

REMINISCENCE DU JARDIN FEERIQUE see
Levinas, Michael

REMINISCENCES see Sivic, Pavle see
Waxman, Franz

REMINISCENTIE IV see Voortman, Roland

REMINISCENZE, AGGIUNTE, VARIANTI see
Vandor, Ivan

REMNANTS see Krieger, Arthur

RENAESSANSE see Groven, Eivind

RENAISSANCE see Groven, Eivind,
Renaessanse

RENAISSANCE SUITE see Patlayenko,
Eduard see Rollin, Robert Leon

RENAULT, ANDRE
Pastorale De Noel [3'20"]
2.2.2.2. 2.2.0.0. timp,perc,harp,
strings
BILLAUDOT perf mat rent   (R250)

RENCONTRES, FOR FLUTE AND STRINGS see
Chiiti, Gian Paolo

RENDERING [ARR.] see Schubert, Franz
(Peter)

RENDEZ-VOUS DE CHASSE, LE, FOR 4 HORNS
AND ORCHESTRA see Rossini,
Gioacchino

RENDEZVOUS, LES [ARR.] see Auber,
Daniel-François-Esprit

RENEE, FOR VIOLIN AND STRING ORCHESTRA
see Lunde, Ivar

RENOSTO, PAOLO (1935-1988)
Albero Dei Vivi, L'
2.2.2.2. 1.1.0.0. perc,strings
TONOS perf mat rent   (R251)

Concerto for Harp and Orchestra [25']
3.4.4.3. 4.3.3.1. timp,3perc,pno,
glock,strings,harp solo
RICORDI-IT 134039 perf mat rent
(R252)
Concerto for Violin and Orchestra
[18']
2.2.2.2. 2.2.0.0. timp,perc,
14vln,4vla,4vcl,2db,vln solo
RICORDI-IT 133056 perf mat rent
(R253)
Monde Sensible, Le, For Flute, Piano,
And Instrumental Ensemble [9']
ob,clar,bsn,horn,trom,timp,2vln,
vla,vcl,db,fl solo,pno solo
sc RICORDI-IT 133017 f.s., perf mat
rent   (R254)

Nachtblau, For Clarinet And String
Orchestra [15']
string orch,clar solo
RICORDI-IT 132375 perf mat rent
(R255)
Reflex [11']
clar,bass clar,horn,trp,trom,
2vln,vla,2vcl,db
RICORDI-IT 133661 perf mat rent
(R256)
Soli
2.2.2.2. 2.2.0.0. timp,perc,
strings
TONOS perf mat rent   (R257)

Suite for String Orchestra [11']
string orch
RICORDI-IT 134041 perf mat rent
(R258)

REPONS see Boulez, Pierre

REPRESENTATIONS DE TANIT, LES see
Ohana, Maurice

REQUIEM FOR SOLO ALLISON, FOR VOICE AND
STRING ORCHESTRA see Weigl, [Mrs.]
Vally

REQUIEM FOR SURVIVORS see Samuel,
Gerhard

REQUIEM FÜR RIKKE, FOR SOLO VOICE AND
ORCHESTRA see Cerha, Friedrich

REQUIEM "HIROSHIMA" see Kojiba, Tomiko

REQUIEM: INGEMISCO, FOR SOLO VOICE AND
ORCHESTRA see Verdi, Giuseppe

REQUIES see Berio, Luciano

REQUIESCAT see Mathias, William

RESONANCES see Leeuw, Ton de

RESONANCIA ESFERICA see Ortiz, William

RESONANTS see Gross, Robert Arthur

RESONANZEN see Gehlhaar, Rolf

RESPIGHI, OTTORINO (1879-1936)
Fantasia Slava, For Piano And
Orchestra [13']
3.2.2.2. 4.2.0.0. timp,perc,
strings,pno solo
sc RICORDI-IT 134178 f.s., perf mat
rent   (R259)

Preludio, Corale E Fuga [19']
3.3.3.3. 4.4.3.1. timp,perc,
2harp,strings
RICORDI-IT 134226 perf mat rent
(R260)
Rossiniana
KALMUS A3907 sc $35.00, set $75.00,
perf mat rent   (R261)

RESPIGHI, OTTORINO (cont'd.)

Rossiniana: Tarantella
(Gammon) 3.2.0.0. 1.3.3.0. perc,
pno,strings [7'] RAHTER perf mat
rent   (R262)

RESPONSO, HOMMAGE NO. 2 see Sarmientos,
Jorge

RESURGENCE, FOR HARPSICHORD AND STRING
ORCHESTRA see Tamba, Akira

RESURRECTION see Roussel, Albert
(Charles Paul)

RESURRECTION SYMPHONIES see Ball,
Michael

RETOUR AU PRINCIPE see Kremski, Alain

RETOUR-WINDUNGEN see Xenakis, Yannis
(Iannis)

RETRATS CATALANS, FOR GUITAR AND
ORCHESTRA see Brouwer, Leo

RETTFERDIGHETENS SOL see Thoresen,
Lasse

RETURN OF THE ANDREAN RIDER, THE see
Valcarcel, Edgar, Karabotasat
Cutintapata

RETURN OF THE JEDI: SUITE see Williams,
John T.

RETURN OF THE LOFOTEN PEOPLE, THE, FOR
SOLO VOICE AND STRING ORCHESTRA see
Eggen, Arne, Ho Mor Faer
Lofotfolket Sitt Heim, For Solo
Voice And String Orchestra

RETZEL, FRANK (1948-   )
Chansonnier [7']
sc APNM $6.00, perf mat rent (R263)

Tapestries [18']
3+pic.0.3.3+contrabsn.alto
sax.tenor sax.baritone sax.
4.0.0.0. 6perc,pno,cel,strings
sc APNM $16.00, perf mat rent
(R264)
REUTER, FRITZ (1896-1963)
Hase Und Der Igel, Der, For Narrator
And Orchestra
2.2.2.2. 4.2.1.0. timp,perc,
strings,pno,speaking voice
sc,pts BREITKOPF-L perf mat rent
(R265)
Serenade for Violin and Orchestra
[6']
2.1.2.1. 2.2.0.0. strings,vln
solo
KAHNT perf mat rent   (R266)

REVE D'AMOUR [ARR.] see Liszt, Franz,
Liebestraum (Notturno No. 3) [arr.]

REVEALED TIME, FOR VIOLA AND ORCHESTRA
see Yuasa, Joji

REVEIL DE FLORE, LE: APPARITION
D'AURORE, SCÈNE ET VALSE see Drigo,
Riccardo

REVEIL DE FLORE, LE: GALOPP see Drigo,
Riccardo

REVEIL DE FLORE, LE: MARCHE BACCHANALE
see Drigo, Riccardo

REVEIL DE FLORE, LE: NOCTURNE see
Drigo, Riccardo

REVEIL DE FLORE, LE: SCÈNE ET PAS
D'ENSEMBLE see Drigo, Riccardo

REVEIL DE FLORE, LE: VARIATION DE FLORE
see Drigo, Riccardo

REVEL see Anderson, Beth

REVELATION see Anderson, Beth

REVELATIONS see Thorne, Nicholas C.K.

REVERBERACIONES see Alis, Roman

REVERDY, MICHELE (1943-   )
Cercle Du Vent, Le [16']
2(pic).2(English horn).4(clar in
E flat,bass clar).0. 2.2.1.0.
3perc,strings
SALABERT perf mat rent   (R267)

Corro Infrangible, El [15']
1.1.1+bass clar.1. 1.1.1.0. vln,
vla,vcl,db
SALABERT perf mat rent   (R268)

REVERIE [ARR.] see Debussy, Claude

REVERIE DU PAUVRE [ARR.] see Satie,
Erik

REVERSIBILITE, FOR SOLO VOICE AND
ORCHESTRA see Aliprandi, Paul

REVES see Prokofiev, Serge

REVES ET REALITES, FOR SOLO VOICE AND
ORCHESTRA see Petit, Jean Armand

REVOLUTIONARY ACTION, FOR NARRATOR AND
ORCHESTRA see Peck, Russell James

REVOLUTIONARY GARLAND, A
(Kingman, Daniel) 2(pic).2.2.2.
2.2.0.0. timp,perc,strings KALMUS
A7223 sc $15.00, set $30.00, pts
$2.00, ea. [8']
contains: General Washington's
March; St. Patrick's Day In The
Morning; Soldier's Joy; York
Fusiliers   (R269)

REVOLVING WHEEL see Rowe, Robert

REVUE FUR KAMMERORCHESTER see Gruber,
Heinz Karl

REVUE MARSCH see Kochan, Ernst

REVUELTAS, SILVESTRE (1899-1940)
I Don't Know Why You Think About Me,
For Solo Voice And Chamber
Orchestra
see No Se Por Que Piensas Tu, For
Solo Voice And Chamber Orchestra

Landscapes
see Paisajes

No Se Por Que Piensas Tu, For Solo
Voice And Chamber Orchestra
0.0.1+bass clar.1. 0.2.2.0.
banjo,4vln,db,Bar solo
"I Don't Know Why You Think About
Me, For Solo Voice And Chamber
Orchestra" PEER perf mat rent
(R270)
Paisajes [20']
1.0.1.1. 1.2.1.1. timp,perc,pno,
strings
"Landscapes" PEER perf mat rent
(R271)
Seven Songs, For Solo Voice And
Chamber Orchestra
see Siete Canciones, For Solo Voice
And Chamber Orchestra

Siete Canciones, For Solo Voice And
Chamber Orchestra
1.0.3.1. 1.2.1.1. tamb,strings,
Mez solo
"Seven Songs, For Solo Voice And
Chamber Orchestra" PEER perf mat
rent   (R272)

REVUTSKY, LEV (1889-1977)
Concerto for Piano and Orchestra
3.2.2.2. 4.2.3.1. timp,2perc,
strings,pno solo
VAAP perf mat rent   (R273)

Symphony No. 2
3.3.3.2. 4.3.3.1. timp,3perc,cel,
harp,strings
VAAP perf mat rent   (R274)

REX see Juozapaitis, Jurgis

REYNOLDS, ROGER (1934-   )
Archipelago [33']
2(pic).2(English horn).3(clar in
E flat,bass clar).2(contrabsn).
2.3.2.1. 3perc,harp,pno,hpsd,
3vln,2vla,2vcl,2db,electronic
tape
sc PETERS P66956 f.s., perf mat
rent   (R275)

Dream Of The Infinite Rooms, The, For
Violoncello And Orchestra [20']
2.2.2(bass clar).2. 2.2.2.0.
2perc,strings,electronic tape,
vcl solo
PETERS P67168 perf mat rent (R276)

Mistral [19']
0.0.0.0. 2.2.2.0. hpsd,2vln,2vcl,
2db
PETERS P 67038 perf mat rent (R277)

Symphony [20']
3(pic,alto fl).3(English
horn).3(clar in E flat,bass
clar).3(contrabsn). 4.3.3.1.
perc,xylo,vibra,pno,harp,
strings,electronic tape
(Vertigo) PETERS P67198 perf mat
rent   (R278)

Transfigured Wind II, For Flute And
Orchestra [35']
2(pic).2.2.2. 2.2.2.1. 2perc,pno,
strings,electronic tape,fl solo
PETERS P67002B perf mat rent (R279)

REYNOLDS, ROGER (cont'd.)

Transfigured Wind III, For Flute And
Orchestra [35']
0.1.2(clar in E flat).1. 1.1.1.0.
2perc,pno,vla,vcl,db,electronic
tape,fl solo
PETERS P67002C perf mat rent (R280)

Whispers Out Of Time
string orch
sc PETERS P67261 f.s., perf mat
rent   (R281)

REZNICEK, EMIL NIKOLAUS VON (1860-1945)
Heitere Suite
KISTNER perf mat rent   (R282)

Lustspiel Overture, Eine
2(pic).2.2.2. 4.2.0.0. timp,strings
[12'] KALMUS A4652 sc $20.00, set
$35.00, perf mat rent   (R283)

Suite in E minor
3(pic).2.2.2. 4.2.3.1. timp,perc,
strings [25'] KALMUS A5259 sc
$50.00, set $65.00, perf mat rent
                              (R284)

Symphonische Suite
KISTNER perf mat rent   (R285)

Tanz Symphonie
3(pic).2+English horn.2+bass
clar.2+contrabsn. 4.3.3.1. timp,
perc,cel,harp,strings KALMUS
A5183 sc $40.00, set $125.00,
perf mat rent   (R286)

RHAPSODIC DANCE NO. 1: THE BAMBOULA see
Coleridge-Taylor, Samuel

RHAPSODIC FANTASY, FOR PERCUSSION AND
ORCHESTRA see Colgrass, Michael
(Charles)

RHAPSODIC VARIATIONS NO. 3, FOR OBOE
AND STRING ORCHESTRA see Thorne,
Francis Burritt

RHAPSODIE DANOISE see Olsen, Otto

RHAPSODIE ESPAGNOLE, FOR PIANO AND
ORCHESTRA [ARR.] see Liszt, Franz

RHAPSODIE HONGROISE NO. 13 [ARR.] see
Liszt, Franz

RHAPSODIE POUR UN JOUR DE FETE, FOR
GUITAR AND ORCHESTRA see Casterede,
Jacques

RHAPSODIES HONGROISES NOS. 1-9 [ARR.]
see Liszt, Franz

RHAPSODISK OVERTURE see Nielsen, Carl

RHAPSODY FROM FANA see Kristoffersen,
Fridthjof, Fanarapsodi

RHAPSODY IN BEER-TONALITY see Pluister,
Simon

RHEINBERGER, JOSEF (1839-1901)
Concerto for Organ and Orchestra, No.
1, Op. 137, in F
CARUS 50.137   (R287)

Concerto for Organ and Orchestra, No.
2, Op. 177, in G minor
CARUS 50.177   (R288)

Suite, Op. 149
CARUS 50.149   (R289)

Wallenstein
KISTNER perf mat rent   (R290)

RHODES, PHILLIP (1940-   )
Visions Of Remembrance, For Solo
Voices And Chamber Orchestra
[22']
1.1(English horn).1.0. 1.1.1.0.
vln,vla,vcl,pno,SMez soli
PETERS P66860 perf mat rent (R291)

RHYTHM GALLERY, FOR NARRATOR AND
ORCHESTRA see Gould, Morton

RHYTHMIC DANCE see Goossens, [Sir]
Eugene

RHYTHMIC STRING BAGATELLES [ARR.] see
Koch, Erland von, Rytmiska
Strakbagatelleri [arr.]

RHYTHMICANA see Cowell, Henry Dixon

RHYTHMS, FOR VIOLIN AND CHAMBER
ORCHESTRA see Overton, Hall

RIBARI, ANTAL (1924-   )
Symphony No. 4
(Elegiac) sc EMB 12893 f.s., perf
mat rent   (R292)

RIBERHUUS MARCH see Frohlich, J.F.

RICCIOTTI, CARLO (1681-1756)
Concertino No. 1 in G [12']
(Hinnenthal, Johann Philipp) string
orch,cont BAREN. BA 6059   (R293)

Concertino No. 2 in G [12']
(Hinnenthal, Johann Philipp) string
orch,cont sc,pts BAREN. HM 82
f.s.   (R294)

Concertino No. 3 in A [10']
(Hinnenthal, Johann Philipp) string
orch,cont BAREN. BA 6057   (R295)

Concertino No. 4 in F minor [10']
(Hinnenthal, Johann Philipp) string
orch,cont sc,pts BAREN. HM 144
f.s.   (R296)

Concertino No. 5 in B flat [13']
(Hinnenthal, Johann Philipp) string
orch,cont BAREN. BA 6054   (R297)

Concertino No. 6 in E flat [8']
(Hinnenthal, Johann Philipp) string
orch,cont BAREN. BA 6058   (R298)

RICE, THOMAS N. (1933-   )
Corona, La, For Solo Voices And
Chamber Orchestra
fl,clar,trom,perc,hpsd,strings,
narrator&T solo
SEESAW perf mat rent   (R299)

Fantasy And Fugue, For Woodwind
Quintet And String Orchestra
string orch,woodwind quin soli
SEESAW   (R300)

Pregue No. 1 In D
string orch
sc SEESAW $9.00, perf mat rent
                            (R301)

Tempest
string orch
sc SEESAW $33.00, perf mat rent
                            (R302)

RICERCARI NOTTURNI, FOR SAXOPHONE AND
ORCHESTRA see Skrowaczewski,
Stanislaw

RICERCATA see Spinner, Leopold

RICHARD, ANDRE (1944-   )
Echanges [17'30"]
2.2.2.2. 4.2.3.0. 3-4perc,pno&
cel,harp,strings
RICORDI-IT 134315 perf mat rent
                            (R303)

RICHARD III see Smetana, Bedrich

RICHARD III [ARR.] see Walton, [Sir]
William (Turner)

RICHTER, FRANZ XAVER (1709-1789)
Concerto for Trumpet and String
Orchestra in D, MIN 106
(Thilde, J.) string orch,trp solo
[13'45"] BILLAUDOT perf mat rent
                            (R304)

Drei Sinfonien *CC3U
(Hoffmann) KALMUS A7112 sc $10.00,
set $15.00, pts $3.00, ea. (R305)

Symphonies, Five
(Boer; Klenk; Berrett) ("The
Symphony" Vol. C-XIV) sc GARLAND
ISBN 0-8240-3856-8 $90.00
contains also: Eichner, Ernst,
Symphony; Kreusser, Georg Anton,
Symphonies, Two; Romberg,
Andreas, Symphony; Romberg,
Bernhard Heinrich, Symphony
                            (R306)

RICHTER, MARGA (1926-   )
Bird Of Yearning [27']
2.2.2.2. 4.2.2.0. timp,perc,cel,
harp,pno,strings
(alternate wind scoring: 2121 2110)
FISCHER,C perf mat rent   (R307)

Blackberry Vines And Winter Fruit
[13']
3.2.2.2. 4.2.3.1. timp,perc,cel,
harp,strings
study sc FISCHER,C 05073 f.s., perf
mat rent   (R308)

Duesseldorf Concerto [20']
string orch,fl solo,vla solo,perc
solo,harp solo
SCHIRM.G perf mat rent   (R309)

Fragments [6']
2.2.2.2. 2.1.1.1. timp,perc,cel,
harp,strings
FISCHER,C perf mat rent   (R310)

Out Of Shadows And Solitude [16']
3.3.3.3. 4.3.3.1. timp,perc,cel,
harp,strings
FISCHER,C perf mat rent   (R311)

RICHTER, MARGA (cont'd.)

Spectral Chimes-Enshrouded Hills, For
Three Orchestral Quintets And
Orchestra [25']
2.2.2.2. 2.2.2.0. timp,perc,harp,
strings,wind quin soli,brass
quin soli,string quin soli
FISCHER,C perf mat rent   (R312)

RICKLEY, JAMES
Journey Through
2.2.2.2. 4.2.3.1. timp,strings
SEESAW perf mat rent   (R313)

To Come To A Place
1.2.1.2. 2.1.0.0. perc,pno,
strings
sc SEESAW $22.00, perf mat rent
                            (R314)

RICKY-TICKY SERENADE see Shulman, Alan
M.

RICORDANZA, FOR SOLO VOICE AND
ORCHESTRA see Hamilton, Iain

RIDE BATKVELVET see Fladmoe, Arvid

RIDE TO DUBNO, THE see Waxman, Franz

RIEDSTRA, TOM (1957-   )
Orkeststuk [9']
3.3.3.3. 4.3.3.1. 3perc,pno,
strings
DONEMUS perf mat rent   (R315)

RIEGGER, WALLINGFORD (1885-1961)
Variations for Violin and Orchestra,
Op. 71
3.2.2.3. 4.2.3.1. timp,perc,harp,
strings,vln solo
sc AMP $14.00, perf mat rent (R316)

RIENZI: OVERTURE see Wagner, Richard

RIEPEL, JOSEPH (1709-1782)
Symphony *see SEVEN SYMPHONIES FROM
THE COURT OF THURN UND TAXIS

RIES, FERDINAND (1784-1838)
Concerto for Violin and Orchestra,
Op. 24, in E minor [18']
1.2.0.2. 2.0.0.0. strings,vln
solo
RIES   (R317)

Symphony No. 3, Op. 90 [30']
1.0.2.2. 2.2.1.0. timp,strings
RIES perf mat rent   (R318)

RIETI, VITTORIO (1898-   )
Concerto for Violin and Orchestra
2.2.2.2. 2.2.2.0. perc,strings,
vln solo
CURCI perf mat rent   (R319)

Conundrum
3+pic.2.2.2. 4.3.3.1. timp,perc,
harp,strings, alternate
scoring:2.1.2.1. 2.1.1.0.,
timp, perc, pno, str
AMP perf mat rent   (R320)

Don Perlimplin: Prologue
2.2.2.2. 4.2.2.0. timp,perc,
strings
AMP perf mat rent   (R321)

Hippolyte Suite
4.2+English horn.3+bass clar.2+
contrabsn. 4.4.3.1. timp,perc,
strings
min sc ESCHIG f.s., perf mat rent
                            (R322)

Night Shadow, The
see Sonnambula, La

Old-Time Polka
2.0.2.1. 0.1.0.0. timp,perc,
strings
CURCI perf mat rent   (R323)

Sonnambula, La
2(pic).2.2.2. 4.2.3.0. timp,perc,
strings
"Night Shadow, The" sc AMP $22.00
                            (R324)

Tarantelle
2.0.2.1. 0.1.0.0. timp,perc,
strings
CURCI perf mat rent   (R325)

RIETMANN, CARLO MARCELLO
Intermittenze [13']
2(pic).2(English horn).2.2.
2.3.3.1. timp,perc,harp,strings
sc CURCI 10225 perf mat rent (R326)

RIFLESSI see Oliver, Angel

RIFLESSIONI see Henkemans, Hans

RIFLESSIONI, FOR VIOLONCELLO AND
ORCHESTRA see Szekely, Endre

RIGHINI, VINCENZO (1756-1812)
Idomeneus Concerto, For Oboe And Strings
opt 2ob,opt 2horn,strings,ob solo
(Heussner, Horst) DOBLINGER DM 888
sc $11.40, set $14.80 (R327)

RIGOLETTO: QUEL VECCHIO, FOR SOLO VOICES AND ORCHESTRA see Verdi, Giuseppe

RIHM, WOLFGANG (1952-)
Abgewandt [7']
1(pic).0+English horn.0+bass clar.0+contrabsn. 1.0.0.0. pno, 2vln,vla,vcl,db
UNIVER. perf mat rent (R328)

Abkehr [8']
0+5pic.4.5.3+contrabsn. 4.3.3.1. timp,2perc,2harp,strings
UNIVER. perf mat rent (R329)

Aufzeichnung: Dammerung Und Umriss [12']
3+2pic.3+English horn.3+2bass clar.3+contrabsn. 4.4.4.1. 6perc,2harp,pno,strings
UNIVER. perf mat rent (R330)

Blick [17']
3.3.3.3. 3.3.3.1. timp,4perc, harp,pno,2vln,vla,3vcl,2db
UNIVER. perf mat rent (R331)

Brahmsliebewalzer *see Rihm, Wolfgang, Drei Walzer

Bruchstuck "Die Vorzeichen"
2+2pic.4.2+2bass clar.2+ 2contrabsn. 4.4.4.0. 4perc, harp,strings
[7'] UNIVER. perf mat rent (R332)

Chiffre III [6']
0.0+English horn.0+bass clar.1(contrabsn). 1.0+bass trp.1.0. 2perc,pno,2vcl,db
sc UNIVER. UE17865 f.s., perf mat rent (R333)

Chiffre V [11']
1(pic).1(English horn).1(bass clar).1(contrabsn). 1.1+bass trp.1.0. 2perc,2vln,vla,2vcl,db
UNIVER. perf mat rent (R334)

Chiffre VII [11']
1.1.1.1. 1.1+bass trp.1.0. 2perc, pno,2vln,vla,2vcl,db
UNIVER. perf mat rent (R335)

Chiffre-Zyklus [80']
1(pic).1(English horn).1(bass clar).1(contrabsn). 1.1+bass trp.1.0. 2perc,pno,2vln,vla, 2vcl,db
UNIVER. perf mat rent (R336)

Compresenze [15']
3+2pic.2+English horn.3+2bass clar.2+contrabsn. 4.5.3.1. 6perc,harp,pno,strings
UNIVER. perf mat rent (R337)

Concerto for Viola and Orchestra
3.3.1.0. 4.2.2.0. timp,perc,harp, strings,vla solo
sc UNIVER. $15.50 (R338)

Dammerung [5']
3+2pic.2.3+bass clar.3+contrabsn. 4.4.4.1. 4perc,strings
UNIVER. perf mat rent (R339)

Danse [5']
2+2pic.2.1+bass clar.1+contrabsn. 4.2.3.1. timp,2harp,strings
UNIVER. perf mat rent (R340)

Drangender Walzer *see Rihm, Wolfgang, Drei Walzer

Drei Walzer [17']
2.2.2.2. 4.2.3.0. timp,perc, strings
(contains: Sehnsuchtswalzer; Brahmsliebewalzer; Drangender Walzer) UNIVER. perf mat rent (R341)

Dritte Abgesangsszene, For Solo Voice And Orchestra
min sc UNIVER. 17238 $22.00, perf mat rent (R342)

Engel, For Solo Voices And Instrumental Ensemble [12']
English horn,tenor sax,bass clar, contrabsn,2trp,2trom,2perc, harp,pno,2vln,2vla,2vcl,2db, 2 male soli
UNIVER. perf mat rent (R343)

Erste Abgesangsszene
min sc UNIVER. 17086 $7.00, perf mat rent (R344)

RIHM, WOLFGANG (cont'd.)
Erster Doppelgesang, For Viola, Violoncello And Orchestra [15']
2.2.2.2. 2.1.1.0. timp,perc,harp, strings,vla solo,vcl solo
sc UNIVER. UE17240 f.s., perf mat rent (R345)

Frau-Stimme, For Solo Voice And Orchestra [15']
4(4pic).0.4.0. 4.4.4.0. 7perc, 2harp,pno&elec org&cel,2vln, 6vcl,2db,S solo
UNIVER. perf mat rent (R346)

Fünfte Abgesangsszene
min sc UNIVER. 17150 $24.00, perf mat rent (R347)

Funfte Abgesangsszene, For Solo Voices And Orchestra [12']
3.3.3.3. 4.2.3.1. timp,2perc, strings,MezBar soli
UNIVER. perf mat rent (R348)

Fusees [4']
0+pic.0+2English horn.2+bass clar.1+contrabsn. 2.0.0.0. 2perc,pno,vla,vcl,db
UNIVER. perf mat rent (R349)

Gebild [8']
trp,2perc,11vln,4vla,3vcl,2db
sc UNIVER. UE17791 f.s., perf mat rent (R350)

Kein Firmament [35']
bass clar,contrabsn,horn,trp, trom,2perc,pno,2vln,vla,2vcl,db
UNIVER. perf mat rent (R351)

Klangbeschreibung I, Fur Drei Orchestergruppen [30']
5(pic).3.4+bass clar+contrabass clar.0+contrabsn. 4.5.4.1. 6perc,pno,2harp,strings
UNIVER. perf mat rent (R352)

Klangbeschreibung III [45']
2+2pic.3(English horn).3+bass clar.2+contrabsn. 4.4.4.1. 6perc,2harp,cel/elec org,pno, strings
UNIVER. perf mat rent (R353)

Landler [10']
6vln,3vla,3vcl,db
sc UNIVER. UE17148 f.s., perf mat rent (R354)

Lenz-Fragmente, For Solo Voice And Orchestra [10']
3.2+English horn.0+bass clar.2. 0.1.2.1. perc,harp,12vln,6vcl, 4db,solo voice
sc UNIVER. UE17429 f.s., perf mat rent (R355)

Lowry Lieder, For Solo Voice And Orchestra [25']
3.3.3.3. 4.3.3.1. timp,2perc, harp,strings,solo voice
UNIVER. perf mat rent (R356)

Magma [15']
4(pic).3+English horn.3+bass clar.3+contrabsn. 4.4.4.1. 4perc,harp,pno,org,strings
UNIVER. perf mat rent (R357)

Medea-Spiel [20']
English horn,tenor sax,bass clar, contrabsn,2trp,2trom,2perc, harp,pno,6vln,4vcl,2db
UNIVER. perf mat rent (R358)

Mein Tod. Requiem In Memoriam Jane S., For Solo Voice And Orchestra [35']
3(pic).2+English horn.2+bass clar.2+contrabsn. 4.3.3.1. timp,2perc,harp,strings,S solo
UNIVER. perf mat rent (R359)

Monodram, For Violoncello And Orchestra
3.3.3.3. 4.3.3.1. timp,perc,harp, pno,strings,vcl solo
sc UNIVER. $25.00 (R360)

Nature Morte - Still Alive [9']
6vln,3vla,3vcl,db
sc UNIVER. UE17192 f.s., perf mat rent (R361)

Orchesterstuck [15']
2.2.2.2. 4.2.3.1. timp,2perc, strings
UNIVER. perf mat rent (R362)

Passim [10']
2+pic.2+English horn.2+bass clar.2+contrabsn. 4.3.3.1. timp,2perc,strings
UNIVER. perf mat rent (R363)

RIHM, WOLFGANG (cont'd.)
Schattenstuck [18']
3.2+English horn.3.3. 4.2.3.1. timp,2perc,pno,strings
UNIVER. perf mat rent (R364)

Schwarzer Und Roter Tanz [16']
3(3pic).3(English horn).3(2bass clar).3(contrabsn). 4.3.3.1. timp,6perc,harp,pno,strings
UNIVER. perf mat rent (R365)

Schwebende Begegnung [10']
0+4pic.3.3.0. 4.3.4.0. 5perc, harp,pno,4vla,3db
UNIVER. perf mat rent (R366)

Sehnsuchtswalzer *see Rihm, Wolfgang, Drei Walzer

Silence To Be Beaten [14']
1.1.1.1. 1.1.1.0. 2perc,1-2pno, 2vln,vla,vcl,db
sc UNIVER. UE17862 f.s., perf mat rent (R367)

Splitter [12']
4(4pic).2+2English horn.4(clar in E flat,bass clar).4(contrabsn). 4.4.4.0. 6perc,2harp,2pno,2vln
UNIVER. perf mat rent (R368)

Spur [10']
3.2+English horn.2+bass clar.2+ contrabsn. 3.3.3.0. timp,2perc, harp,cel,pno,strings
UNIVER. perf mat rent (R369)

Symphony No. 1, Op. 3
study sc UNIVER. UE 17832 f.s. (R370)

Tutuguri I [13']
1(pic).2.2.0+contrabsn. 2.1.1.0. timp,2perc,harp,pno,strings
UNIVER. perf mat rent (R371)

Tutuguri II [10']
3.3.3.3. 4.3.3.1. timp,3perc, harp,pno,strings
UNIVER. perf mat rent (R372)

Tutuguri III [10']
1.2.2.0+contrabsn. 2.1.1.0. 6perc,harp,pno,strings
UNIVER. perf mat rent (R373)

Tutuguri IV [15']
3.3.3(bass clar).2+contrabsn. 4.3.3.1. timp,3perc,pno,strings
UNIVER. perf mat rent (R374)

Umriss [6']
3+2pic.2+English horn.3+2bass clar.2+contrabsn. 4.4.4.1. 6perc,2harp,pno,strings
UNIVER. perf mat rent (R375)

Unbenannt I [18']
3+2pic.3+2English horn.3+2bass clar.3+2contrabsn. 6.4.4.2. timp,4perc,2harp,pno,org,2vln, 12vla,10vcl,8db
UNIVER. perf mat rent (R376)

Unbenannt II [20']
0+5pic.5.5.5(contrabsn). 6.6.4.2. timp,6perc,2harp,pno,strings
UNIVER. perf mat rent (R377)

Vierte Abgesangsszene, For Solo Voice And Orchestra [20']
3.3.3.3. 4.2.3.1. timp,2perc, harp,pno&cel,strings,med solo
sc UNIVER. UE17280 f.s., perf mat rent (R378)

Vorgefuhle [8']
2(pic).2(English horn).3(bass clar).3(contrabsn). 4.2.2.1. timp,2perc,cel,pno,strings
UNIVER. perf mat rent (R379)

Was Aber, For Solo Voices And Orchestra [8']
2.0.2.0. 2.2.2.0. timp,2perc, harp,cel,pno,org,strings, 2 female soli
UNIVER. perf mat rent (R380)

Wofli-Lieder, For Solo Voice And Orchestra [10']
2.2.2.2. 4.2.3.1. timp,perc,harp, pno,strings,Bar solo
UNIVER. perf mat rent (R381)

Zeichen I Fur Zwei Solisten Und Zwei Orchestergruppen [16']
5(pic).3.4.0+contrabsn. 4.5.4.1. 5perc,4vcl,4db,fl solo,clar solo
UNIVER. perf mat rent (R382)

Zweite Abgesangsszene, For Solo Voice And Orchestra
min sc UNIVER. 17198 $31.00, perf

RIHM, WOLFGANG (cont'd.)

mat rent (R383)

Zweiter Doppelgesang, For Clarinet, Violoncello And Orchestra [15']
0.2(English horn).0.2(contrabsn).
2.0.0.0. strings,clar solo,vcl solo
sc UNIVER. UE17835 f.s., perf mat rent (R384)

RIISAGER, KNUDAGE (1897-1974)
Archaeopteryx
sc,pts SAMFUNDET f.s. (R385)

Primavera *Op.31
KALMUS A7044 sc $12.00, set $20.00, pts $1.00, ea., perf mat rent (R386)

Pro Fistulis Et Fidibus
sc,pts SAMFUNDET f.s. (R387)

Qarrtsiluni *Op.36
"Silence" KALMUS A6767 sc $12.00, set $28.00, pts $1.25, ea., perf mat rent (R388)

Silence
see Qarrtsiluni

Summer Rhapsody
KALMUS A6766 sc $15.00, set $30.00, pts $1.50, ea., perf mat rent (R389)

Three Danish Songs From The 16th Century
see Tre Dansk Peblingeviser

Three Danish Street Songs [8']
2+pic.2(English horn).2(clar in E flat).2(contrabsn). 4.3.3.1. timp,perc,strings
KALMUS A7040 sc $10.00, set $22.00, pts $1.00, ea., perf mat rent (R390)

Tre Dansk Peblingeviser
"Three Danish Songs From The 16th Century" sc,pts SAMFUNDET f.s. (R391)

Variations for Strings [12']
string orch HANSEN-DEN perf mat rent (R392)

Variations On A Theme Of C.M. Bellman *Op.45
KALMUS A7041 sc $25.00, set $15.00, pts $1.00, ea., perf mat rent (R393)

RILEY, DENNIS (1943-)
Noon Dances [19']
1(pic).1.1.1. 1.1.0.0. perc,harp, strings
PETERS P67061 perf mat rent (R394)

Seven Songs, For Solo Voice And Orchestra [15']
2(pic).2.2(bass clar).2(contrabsn). 2.0.0.0. 2perc,harp,strings,S solo
PETERS P67055 perf mat rent (R395)

Symphony [35']
3(pic,alto fl).3.3.3. 4.3.3.1. timp,3perc,harp,pno,strings
PETERS P67060 perf mat rent (R396)

RILEY'S MERRIMENT see Orrego-Salas, Juan A.

RIMA see Sigurbjörnsson, Thorkell

RIME DE MICHELANGELO, FOR SOLO VOICE AND CHAMBER ORCHESTRA see Taranu, Cornel

RIMED WOOD, FOR SOLO VOICE AND ORCHESTRA see Tveitt, Geirr, Rimet Skog, For Solo Voice And Orchestra

RIMET SKOG, FOR SOLO VOICE AND ORCHESTRA see Tveitt, Geirr

RIMMER, JOHN
Gossamer [10']
string orch
sc WAI-TE-ATA f.s. (R397)

RIMSKY-KORSAKOV, NIKOLAI (1844-1908)
Antchar, For Solo Voice And Orchestra *Op.49,No.1 [3']
2.2.2.2. 2.2.3.0. timp,strings,B solo
BELAIEFF (R398)

At The Tomb *Op.61
KALMUS A5829 sc $4.00, set $18.00 (R399)

Capriccio Espagnol *Op.34
SONZOGNO perf mat rent (R400)

Concerto for Piano and Orchestra, Op. 30, in C sharp minor
SONZOGNO perf mat rent (R401)

RIMSKY-KORSAKOV, NIKOLAI (cont'd.)
Concerto for Trombone and Orchestra, [arr.]
(Leloir, E.) 3.2.2.2. 4.2.3.1. timp,perc,strings,trom solo [10'15"] sc BILLAUDOT f.s., perf mat rent (R402)

Conte Feerique
"Russian Fairy Tale" KALMUS A5593 sc $30.00, perf mat rent, set $50.00, pts $2.00, ea. (R403)

Deutlich Liegt Vor Mir
see Tsar's Bride, The: Aria Of Martha, For Solo Voice And Orchestra

Fantaisie De Concert, For Violin And Orchestra *Op.33
"Fantasy On Russian Themes, For Violin And Orchestra" KALMUS A6795 sc $20.00, set $20.00, pts $1.00, ea., perf mat rent (R404)

Fantasy On Russian Themes, For Violin And Orchestra
see Fantaisie De Concert, For Violin And Orchestra

Fantasy On Serbian Themes *Op.6
KALMUS A5828 sc $20.00, set $25.00, perf mat rent (R405)

Maid Of Pskov, The: Berceuse, [arr.]
(Wood) 2.0.2.2. 3.0.0.0. harp, strings,opt glock [5'] CHESTER JWC571 perf mat rent (R406)

Mlada: Night On Mount Triglav
KALMUS A6173 sc $50.00, set $175.00, perf mat rent (R407)

Overture On Russian Themes *Op.28
sc MEZ KNIGA f.s. (R408)

Russian Fairy Tale
see Conte Feerique

Sadko: Musical Pictures [11']
3.2.2.2. 4.2.3.1. timp,perc, 3harp,strings
VAAP perf mat rent (R409)

Scheherazade *Op.35
(reprint of Belaieff edition) sc DOVER 247341 $9.95 (R410)
SONZOGNO perf mat rent (R411)

Schneeflöckchen: Zu Dem Donner Eine Wolke Sprach, For Solo Voice And Orchestra
0.0.1.1. 3.0.0.0. timp,tamb,harp, strings,T solo
BREITKOPF-L perf mat rent (R412)

Serenade for Violoncello and Orchestra, Op. 37 [4']
2.2.2.2. 2.0.0.0. timp,strings, vcl solo
SIKORSKI perf mat rent (R413)

Symphony No. 1, Op. 1
KALMUS A7035 sc $40.00, set $60.00, pts $3.00, ea., perf mat rent (R414)

Tsar Saltan: Flight Of The Bumblebee, For Double Bass And String Orchestra [arr.]
(Girard, A.) "Vol Du Bourdon, Le, For Double Bass And String Orchestra [arr.]" string orch,db solo [2'] BILLAUDOT perf mat rent (R415)

Tsar's Bride, The: Aria Of Martha, For Solo Voice And Orchestra
"Deutlich Liegt Vor Mir" KALMUS A4619 sc $5.00, set $15.00, pts $1.00, perf mat rent (R416)

Vol Du Bourdon, Le, For Double Bass And String Orchestra [arr.]
see Tsar Saltan: Flight Of The Bumblebee, For Double Bass And String Orchestra [arr.]

RINALDO DI CAPUA (ca. 1710-ca. 1770)
Zingara, La: Aria Di Tagliaborse, For Solo Voice And String Orchestra [4']
string orch,T solo
(Blanchard, R.) BOIS perf mat rent (R417)

RINALDO: OVERTURE (FIRST VERSION) see Handel, George Frideric

RINALDO: SIBILLAR GLI ANGUI D'ALETTO, FOR SOLO VOICE AND ORCHESTRA see Handel, George Frideric

RINALDO: SUITE see Handel, George Frideric

RINEHART, JOHN (1937-)
Passages, For Solo Voice And Orchestra [10']
3.2.2.2. 4.2.3.1. timp,perc,harp, pno,strings,electronic tape,S solo
sc AM.COMP.AL. $20.55 (R418)

Totentanz, For Piano And Orchestra [14']
3(pic).2.2.2(contrabsn). 4.2.2+ bass trom.1. timp,perc,strings, pno solo
sc AM.COMP.AL. $26.80 (R419)

RING OF ETERNITY, THE see Saxton, Robert

RING OUT THE CHANGES see Fowler, Jennifer

RING ROUND THE MOON see Farquhar, David

RINGED BY THE FLAT HORIZON see Benjamin, George

RINGING EARTH, THE see Louie, Alexina

RIONDY, LUCIEN (1919-)
Jeanne D'arc, For Solo Voice And Orchestra [20']
3.2.2.2. 4.3.3.1. timp,2perc, strings,Mez solo
BILLAUDOT perf mat rent (R420)

RIRE DE NILS HALERIUS, LE: BALLET DES JEUX DU MONDE see Landowski, Marcel

RISONANZE see Furrer, Beat

RISPENS, JAN (1944-)
Haas En De Schildpad, De [8'16"]
1.1.1.1. 1.0.0.0. marimba,vibra, 2pno,2vln,vla,vcl,db
DONEMUS perf mat rent (R421)

RISSET, JEAN CLAUDE (1938-)
Phases [25']
3(pic,alto fl).2+English horn.2+ bass clar.2+contrabsn. 4.3.3.0+ db tuba. timp,3perc,2harp,pno& cel,strings
SALABERT perf mat rent (R422)

RITCHIE, ANTHONY
Concertino for Piano and String Orchestra [19']
string orch,pno solo
sc WAI-TE-ATA f.s. (R423)

RITE OF SPRING see Stravinsky, Igor, Sacre Du Printemps, Le

RITORNELL, FOR PIANO AND ORCHESTRA see Wolter, Detlef

RITORNO DI TOBIA, IL: OVERTURE see Haydn, [Franz] Joseph

RITORNO DI UN CANTO DIMENTICATO, FOR OBOE AND INSTRUMENTAL ENSEMBLE see Gentilucci, Armando

RITOURNELLES DU CHAT ABGRAL, LES, FOR CLARINET AND ORCHESTRA see Komives, Janos

RITRATTO see Lindberg, Magnus

RITTER PASMAN: WALZER see Strauss, Johann, [Jr.]

RITUAL see Schnittke, Alfred

RITUAL DANCE see Corigliano, John

RITUAL DANCES OF THE AMAKS see Fountain, Primous

RITUALS FOR ORCHESTRA see Bell, Elizabeth

RIVER SONG, THE see Merryman, Marjorie

RIVERING WATERS see Albert, Stephen Joel

RIVERRUN see Albert, Stephen Joel see Engstrom, Torbjorn

RIVERRUN, FOR PIANO AND ORCHESTRA see Takemitsu, Toru

RIVERSIDE VARIATIONS see Krieger, Arthur

RIVERSONG see Siegmeister, Elie

RIVIER, JEAN (1896-)
Climats [20']
cel,vibra,xylo,pno,strings
SALABERT perf mat rent (R424)

Lento Doloroso [7'30"]
string orch
SALABERT perf mat rent (R425)

RIVIER, JEAN (cont'd.)

Symphony No. 8 [19']
string orch
sc SALABERT f.s., perf mat rent
(R426)

RIVIERE, LA see Dusapin, Pascal

RIVIERE, PABLO (1951-   )
Suerte De Varas [13']
1.1.1.1. 1.1.1.0. perc,harp,org,
strings
sc ALPUERTO f.s.   (R427)

RIVOLGETE A LUI LO SGUARDO, FOR SOLO
VOICE AND ORCHESTRA see Mozart,
Wolfgang Amadeus

ROBBER'S CHRISTMAS EVE, THE, FOR
NARRATOR AND ORCHESTRA see
Stolarczyk, Willy, Roverens
Juleaften, For Narrator And
Orchestra

ROBERT BRUCE: OVERTURE see Rossini,
Gioacchino

ROBINOVITCH, SID (1942-   )
Prairie Sketches [26']
1.1.1.1. 0.0.0.0. strings
CAN.MUS.CENT. MI 1200 R656PR (R428)

ROBOT FROM ORION, THE, FOR NARRATOR AND
INSTRUMENTAL ENSEMBLE see Raum,
Elizabeth

ROCCISANO, JOE
Synthesis, For Saxophone And
Orchestra [28']
3+2pic+2alto fl.2+English horn.3+
bass clar.2.5soprano sax.2alto
sax.2tenor sax.baritone sax.
4.4.3+bass trom.0. perc,2pno,
harp,strings,tenor sax solo
NEWAM 19037 perf mat rent   (R429)

ROCHBERG, A. GEORGE (1918-   )
Concerto for Oboe and Orchestra [20']
PRESSER perf mat rent   (R430)

Symphony No. 1, Original Version
[60']
3.3.3.3. 4.3.3.1. timp,perc,
strings
PRESSER perf mat rent   (R431)

Symphony No. 5 [25']
4.2.1.3. 4.4.3.1. timp,perc,harp,
pno&cel,strings
PRESSER perf mat rent   (R432)

Symphony No. 6 [35']
4.4.5.4. 4.4.3.1. timp,3perc,
2harp,cel,strings
PRESSER perf mat rent   (R433)

Time Span
PRESSER perf mat rent   (R434)

ROCK-ART see Heider, Werner

ROCK RHAPSODY see Dorff, Daniel Jay

ROCKIN' RONDO see Stock, David
Frederick

ROCYCKI, LUDOMIR (1884-1952)
Pan Twardowski: Dance Des Montagnards
[8']
2+pic.2+English horn.2+bass
clar.2+contrabsn. 4.3.3.1.
timp,perc,strings
HANSEN-DEN perf mat rent   (R435)

RÖDA RUMMET see Nilsson, Bo

RODRIGO, JOAQUÍN (1902-   )
A La Busca Del Mas Alla [17']
3.3.2.2. 4.3.2.1. perc,cel,harp,
strings
SCHOTTS perf mat rent   (R436)

Absence De Dulcinee, L', For Solo
Voices And Orchestra [15']
3.2.2.3. 4.3.3.1. timp,harp,
strings, B solo, 4Women's
voices soli
study sc ESCHIG f.s., perf mat rent
(R437)

Canconeta, For Violin And String
Orchestra
string orch,vln solo
SCHOTTS sc CON 209 $9.95, set
CON 209-70 $22.00   (R438)

Concierto Como Un Divertimento, For
Violoncello And Orchestra [21']
2(pic).2.2.0. 1.2.0.0. xylo,cel,
strings,vcl solo
SCHOTTS perf mat rent   (R439)

Concierto De Aranjuez, For Guitar And
Orchestra
2(pic).2.2.2. 2.2.0.0. strings,
gtr solo
min sc SCHOTTS ST07242-SC $10.00

RODRIGO, JOAQUÍN (cont'd.)
(R440)
Concierto De Aranjuez, For Harp And
Orchestra [20']
2(pic).2(English horn).2.2.
2.2.0.0. strings,harp solo
study sc SCHOTTS $10.00, perf mat
rent   (R441)

Concierto Heroico, For Piano And
Orchestra [30']
2(pic).2.2.2. 4.2.3.0. timp,perc,
strings,pno solo
AMP perf mat rent   (R442)

Concierto Madrigal, For 2 Guitars And
Orchestra [30']
2.1.1.1. 1.1.0.0. strings,2gtr
soli
SCHOTTS perf mat rent   (R443)

Concierto Para Una Fiesta, For Guitar
And Orchestra [27']
2.2.1.1. 1.1.0.0. perc,strings,
gtr solo
SCHOTTS perf mat rent   (R444)

Cuatre Cancons En Lengua Catalana,
For Solo Voice And Orchestra
[12']
2(pic).1.1.1. 2.2.0.0. timp,perc,
2harp,strings,solo voice
SCHOTTS perf mat rent   (R445)

Dos Berceuses [5']
1.2.1.0. 1.1.0.0. glock,cel,harp,
strings
SCHOTTS perf mat rent   (R446)

Dos Danzas Espanolas [9']
2(pic).2.2.2. 2.2.0.0. strings
SCHOTTS perf mat rent   (R447)

Duermete, Nino, For Solo Voices And
Orchestra [3']
ob,English horn,strings,SBar soli
SCHOTTS perf mat rent   (R448)

Homenaje A La Tempranica [4']
2.1.1.1. 2.2.0.0. timp,perc,harp,
strings
SCHOTTS perf mat rent   (R449)

Juglares [5']
3(pic).2(English horn).2.2.
4.3.3.1. timp,perc,harp,strings
SCHOTTS perf mat rent   (R450)

Lirio Azul, El [16']
2+pic.2+English horn.2+bass
clar.2+contrabsn. 4.3.3.1.
timp,perc,harp,strings
UNION ESP. perf mat rent   (R451)

Miedo [15']
2.1.1.1. 2.1.1.0. timp,perc,cel,
harp,strings
SCHOTTS perf mat rent   (R452)

Musica Para Un Jardin [12']
2.2.1.0. 1.1.0.0. perc,cel,harp,
strings
SCHOTTS perf mat rent   (R453)

Musica Para Un Poema A La Alhambra
[8']
3.3.2.2. 4.3.3.1. timp,perc,harp,
strings
SCHOTTS perf mat rent   (R454)

Pallilos Y Panderetas [12']
2(pic).2.2.2. 2.2.0.0. timp,perc,
strings
SCHOTTS perf mat rent   (R455)

Rosaliana, For Solo Voice And Chamber
Orchestra [12']
1.1.1.0. 1.0.0.0. drums,strings,S
solo
SCHOTTS perf mat rent   (R456)

Tres Viejos Aires De Danza [8']
1.1.1.1. 2.0.0.0. strings
SCHOTTS perf mat rent   (R457)

Triptic De Mosen Cinto, For Solo
Voice And Orchestra [12']
2.2.1.1. 2.2.0.0. perc,cel,harp,
strings,solo voice
SCHOTTS perf mat rent   (R458)

RODRIGUEZ, ROBERT XAVIER (1946-   )
Estampie
sc GALAXY 1.3058 $20.00   (R459)

ROENS, STEVE
Piece For Eleven Players [10']
fl,ob,clar,bass clar,horn,trp,
pno,vln,vla,vcl,db
sc APNM $8.00, perf mat rent (R460)

ROGER-DUCASSE, JEAN-JULES AIMABLE
(1873-1954)
Poeme Symphonique (Saraband)
KALMUS A6123 sc $12.00, set $50.00,
perf mat rent   (R461)

Saraband
see Poeme Symphonique

ROGERS, RODNEY (1953-   )
Lucis Creator [20']
AMP perf mat rent   (R462)

ROGET, HENRIETTE (1910-   )
Symphonie Pour Rire [13'40"]
2.2.2.2. 2.2.0.0. timp,2perc,
strings
BILLAUDOT perf mat rent   (R463)

ROGUISH PEASANT, THE: OVERTURE see
Dvořák, Antonín

ROI MALGRE LUI, LE: DANSE SLAVE see
Chabrier, [Alexis-] Emmanuel

ROI MALGRE LUI, LE: FETE POLONAISE see
Chabrier, [Alexis-] Emmanuel

ROI SAUL, LE, FOR SOLO VOICE AND
ORCHESTRA [ARR] see Mussorgsky,
Modest Petrovich

ROIKJER, KJELL (1901-   )
Concerto for Xylophone and Orchestra,
Op. 34 [14']
2.2.2.2. 3.2.1.0. timp,perc,
strings,xylo solo
HANSEN-DEN perf mat rent   (R464)

ROIS MAGES, LES, FOR SOLO VOICES AND
ORCHESTRA see Brenet, Therese

ROIZEMBLAT, ALAIN (1934-   )
Concerto for Violin and String
Orchestra [20']
string orch,vln solo
(Apparitions) BILLAUDOT perf mat
rent   (R465)

ROIZENBLAT, A.
Concerto for Violin and Orchestra
[17']
CHOUDENS perf mat rent   (R466)

Enneades, For Bassoon And Orchestra
[25']
CHOUDENS perf mat rent   (R467)

Pleiades [17']
CHOUDENS perf mat rent   (R468)

ROJKO, UROŠ (1954-   )
Classical Concerto, For Piano And
Orchestra
see Klasicni Koncert, For Piano And
Orchestra

"8 - 80" [14']
perc,strings
DRUSTVO DSS 971 perf mat rent
(R469)

Glasba For Orkester [12']
2(pic).2(English horn).2(bass
clar).2(contrabsn). 4.3.3.1.
timp,perc,harp,pno,strings
"Music For Orchestra" DRUSTVO
DSS 997 perf mat rent   (R470)

Klasicni Koncert, For Piano And
Orchestra [30']
2(pic).2(English horn).2(bass
clar).2(contrabsn). 4.2.3.1.
timp,perc,harp,strings,pno solo
"Classical Concerto, For Piano And
Orchestra" DRUSTVO DSS 1080 perf
mat rent   (R471)

Music For Orchestra
see Glasba For Orkester

Pastoral Invention, For Violin And
Orchestra
see Pastoralna Invencija, For
Violin And Orchestra

Pastoralna Invencija, For Violin And
Orchestra [6']
2.2.2.2. 2.0.0.0. timp,perc,
strings,vln solo
"Pastoral Invention, For Violin And
Orchestra" DRUSTVO DSS 921 perf
mat rent   (R472)

Tongenesis [18']
2.2.2.3. 4.2.3.1. 3perc,strings
RICORDI-IT 134158 perf mat rent
(R473)

ROKEACH, MARTIN
Prelude And Fantasy, For Alto
Saxophone And Orchestra
sc,pts DORN $90.00   (R474)

ROKKOMBORRE see Søderlind, Ragnar

ROLDAN, AMADEO (1900-1939)
Rebambaramba, La: Suite [25']
3.3.3.3. 4.3.3.1. timp,perc,pno,
strings
ESCHIG perf mat rent   (R475)

ROLLA, ALESSANDRO (1757-1841)
Concerto for Basset Horn and
Orchestra in F
2ob,2horn,strings,basset horn
solo
KNEUSSLIN perf mat rent   (R476)

Concerto For Viola And Orchestra, Op.
3 In E-Flat *see THREE CENTURIES
OF MUSIC IN SCORE, VOL. 6:
CONCERTO V, LATE CLASSICAL
STRINGS AND WINDS

ROLLIN, ROBERT LEON (1947-   )
Concerto for Wind Quintet and
Orchestra
4.4.4.4. 4.5.4.1. perc,strings,
wind quin soli
sc SEESAW $66.00, perf mat rent
(R477)
Concerto Pastorale, For Horn And
Orchestra
2.2.2.2. 2.2.0.0. 2perc,strings,
horn solo
SEESAW   (R478)

Renaissance Suite
SEESAW perf mat rent   (R479)

Song Of Deborah, For Solo Voice And
Chamber Orchestra
soprano sax,alto sax,2trp,trom,
tuba,timp,perc,strings,S solo
sc SEESAW $17.00, perf mat rent
(R480)

Three Western Images
1.1.1.1. 2.1.2.1. perc,pno,
strings
SEESAW   (R481)

ROMA see Kont, Paul

ROMAN, JOHAN HELMICH (1694-1758)
Concerto for Oboe d'Amore and String
Orchestra, [arr.]
(Gillblad, Per-Olof) string orch,
hpsd,ob d'amore solo [16'] sc
GEHRMANS 6149P f.s., perf mat
rent   (R482)

Drottningholmsmusiken [arr.]
(Genetay, Claude) 2.2.0.1. 2.2.0.0.
timp,hpsd,strings [57'] sc
GEHRMANS 6540P f.s., perf mat
rent   (R483)

Drottningholmsmusiken: Suite No.
1[arr.]
(Genetay, Claude) 2.2.0.2. 2.2.0.0.
timp,hpsd,strings [20'] sc
GEHRMANS 6323P f.s., perf mat
rent   (R484)

Drottningholmsmusiken: Suite No. 2
[arr.]
(Genetay, Claude) 2.2.0.1. 2.2.0.0.
timp,hpsd,strings [17'] sc
GEHRMANS 6324P f.s., perf mat
rent   (R485)

Drottningholmsmusiken: Suite No. 3
[arr.]
(Genetay, Claude) 1.2.0.1. 2.2.0.0.
timp,hpsd,strings [20'] sc
GEHRMANS 6325P f.s., perf mat
rent   (R486)

Drottningholmsmusiken: Suites Nos. 1,
2, 3 [arr.]
(Genetay, Claude) sc GEHRMANS 6323R
f.s.   (R487)

Sinfonia Da Chiesa
(Ohrwall, Anders) opt 2ob,strings
[3'30"] GEHRMANS sc 6187P f.s.,
pts 6187S f.s.   (R488)

ROMAN D'ARLEQUIN, LE see Massenet,
Jules

ROMANCE FOR A MUMMY, A: FOUR FRAGMENTS
see Tcherepnin, Nikolay
Nikolayevich

ROMANCE OF THE ROSE, THE see Berkeley,
Michael

ROMANCES, TWO, FOR ALTO FLUTE AND
STRING ORCHESTRA, IN A AND D [ARR.]
see Kuhlau, Friedrich

ROMANCES FOR JAZZ SOLOIST AND ORCHESTRA
see Williams, Patrick M.

ROMANESCA, LA see Maganini, Quinto

ROMANIS, GEORGE
Concerto for Guitar and Orchestra
[30'10"]
3(pic).0.2(bass clar).1. 4.4.4.0+
opt tuba. 3perc,pno,strings,gtr
solo
NEWAM 19038 perf mat rent   (R489)

ROMANISCHE TANZE see Kont, Paul

ROMANSSI [ARR.] see Fougstedt, Nils-
Eric

ROMANTIC CONCERTO, FOR PIANO AND
ORCHESTRA see Schneider, Ernst

ROMANTIC MESSAGES see Shut, Vladislav

ROMANTIC READING see Vidovszky, Laszlo

ROMANTISCHE BOTSCHAFTEN see Shut,
Vladislav, Romantic Messages

ROMANTISCHE OUVERTURE see Thuille,
Ludwig (Wilhelm Andreas Maria)

ROMANTISCHES CONCERTINO, FOR PIANO AND
ORCHESTRA see Sirowy, Josef

ROMANZA see Goeb, Roger

ROMANZA, FOR OBOE AND STRING ORCHESTRA
see Holloway, Robin

ROMANZA MISTICA see Manen, Joan

ROMANZE UND SCHERZO see Rachmaninoff,
Sergey Vassilievich

ROMANZE ZUR NACHT, FOR VIOLONCELLO AND
INSTRUMENTAL ENSEMBLE see
Guarnieri, Adriano

ROMBERG, ANDREAS (1767-1821)
Symphony *see Richter, Franz Xaver,
Symphonies, Five
see Richter, Franz Xaver,
Symphonies, Five

ROMBERG, BERNHARD HEINRICH (1767-1841)
Concertino for 2 Violoncelli and
Orchestra, MIN 199
(Thomas-Mifune) sc KUNZEL 10217
f.s., perf mat rent   (R490)

Symphony *see Richter, Franz Xaver,
Symphonies, Five
see Richter, Franz Xaver,
Symphonies, Five

ROMBERG, SIGMUND (1887-1951)
Desert Song, The, For Solo Voice And
Orchestra, [arr.]
(Leyden, Norman) WARNER perf mat
rent   (R491)

Desert Song, The: One Alone, For Solo
Voice And Orchestra, [arr.]
(Leyden, Norman) WARNER perf mat
rent   (R492)

Desert Song, The: Selections, [arr.]
[14'30"]
(Schoenfeld) WARNER perf mat rent
(R493)

New Moon, The: Lover, Come Back To
Me, For Solo Voice And Orchestra,
[arr.]
(Leyden, Norman) WARNER perf mat
rent   (R494)

New Moon, The: One Kiss, [arr.]
string orch
(Leyden, Norman) WARNER perf mat
rent   (R495)

New Moon, The: Selections, [arr.]
(Paul) WARNER perf mat rent   (R496)

New Moon, The: Softly, As In A
Morning Sunrise, For Solo Voice
And Orchestra, [arr.]
(Leyden, Norman) WARNER perf mat
rent   (R497)

New Moon, The: Stouthearted Men,
[arr.]
(Campbell-Watson) WARNER perf mat
rent   (R498)

New Moon, The: Wanting You, For Solo
Voices And Orchestra, [arr.]
(Leyden, Norman) WARNER perf mat
rent   (R499)

Student Prince, The: Selections,
[arr.] [12'30"]
(Campbell-Watson) WARNER perf mat
rent   (R500)
(Paul) WARNER perf mat rent   (R501)

Student Prince, The: Serenade, For
Solo Voice And Orchestra, [arr.]
(Leyden, Norman) WARNER perf mat
rent   (R502)

ROMEO AND JULIET see Lambert, Constant
see Tchaikovsky, Piotr Ilyich

ROMEO AND JULIET. OVERTURE-FANTASY see
Tchaikovsky, Piotr Ilyich

ROMEO ET JULIETTE: BALLET MUSIC see
Gounod, Charles François

ROMEO ET JULIETTE: FRAGMENTS
SYMPHONIQUES see Gounod, Charles
François

ROMEO ET JULIETTE: GRANDE FÊTE CHEZ
CAPULET see Berlioz, Hector (Louis)

ROMEO ET JULIETTE: LA REINE MAB,
SCHERZO see Berlioz, Hector (Louis)

ROMEO ET JULIETTE: SCENE D'AMOUR see
Berlioz, Hector (Louis)

ROMEO UND JULIA: GROSSES FEST BEI
CAPULET see Berlioz, Hector
(Louis), Romeo Et Juliette: Grande
Fête Chez Capulet

ROMEO UND JULIA: KÖNIGIN MAB see
Berlioz, Hector (Louis), Romeo Et
Juliette: La Reine Mab, Scherzo

ROMEO UND JULIA: LIEBESSZENE see
Berlioz, Hector (Louis), Romeo Et
Juliette: Scene d'Amour

RONDE DES SAISONS, FOR SOLO VOICE AND
STRING ORCHESTRA see Eastwood,
Thomas

RONDE VILLAGEOISE see Pepin, Clermont

RONDEAU FOR QUARTET AND ORCHESTRA see
Johnson, J.J.

RONDO ALL' ONGARESE, [ARR.] see Haydn,
[Franz] Joseph

RONDO BRILLANT, FOR PIANO AND ORCHESTRA
see Mendelssohn-Bartholdy, Felix

RONDO BRILLANT, FOR PIANO AND ORCHESTRA
see Mendelssohn-Bartholdy, Felix

RONDO CAPRICCIOSO, FOR VIOLIN AND
ORCHESTRA see Vellones, Pierre

RONDO CON FANTASIA CONCERTANTE see
Park, James

RONDO FANTASTICO see Sanjuan, Pedro

RONDO INFINITO see Sinding, Christian

RONDO MARITALE see Jensen, Ludwig
Irgens

RONDO ÜBER EIN SAVOYARDISCHES VOLKSLIED
see Klefisch, Walter

RØNNES, ROBERT (1959-   )
Concerto for Bass Trombone and
Orchestra
timp,strings,bass trom/tuba solo
NORGE   (R503)

Four Poems
2.2.1.2. 3.2.3.0. cel/harp,perc,
strings
NORGE   (R504)

Romance for Violin and String
Orchestra [10']
string orch,vln solo
NORGE   (R505)

RÖNTGEN, JULIUS (1855-1932)
Concerto for Violin, Viola,
Violoncello and String Orchestra
string orch,vln solo,vla solo,vcl
solo
DONEMUS perf mat rent   (R506)

Old Netherlands Dances *Op.46 [9']
2.2.0.2. 4.2.0.0. timp,perc,harp,
strings
KALMUS A7316 sc $20.00, set $20.00,
pts $1.00, ea., perf mat rent
(R507)

Zwei Konzerte, For Piano And
Orchestra
2.2.2.2. 3.2.0.0. timp,perc,
strings,pno solo
DONEMUS   (R508)

ROO, PAUL DE (1957-   )
Für Anton [12']
4.3.3.3. 4.4.3.1. 4perc,strings
DONEMUS perf mat rent   (R509)

ROOF OF HEAVEN, THE, FOR SOLO VOICE AND
ORCHESTRA see Cowie, Edward

ROOS, ROBERT DE (1907-1976)
Adam In Ballingschap, For Narrator
And Orchestra [30']
2.0.0.0. 2.0.0.0. strings,
narrator
sc DONEMUS f.s., perf mat rent
(R510)

Rapsodia E Danza, For 2 Flutes And
Orchestra [14']
1.2.2.3. 2.2.2.0. timp,perc,
strings,2fl soli
sc DONEMUS f.s., perf mat rent
(R511)

Wiegenlied, Das, For Narrator And
Orchestra
3.2.3.1. 4.3.3.0. timp,perc,
strings,narrator
sc DONEMUS f.s., perf mat rent
(R512)

ROOSENDAEL, JAN ROKUS VAN (1960-)
Anabasis [16']
3.3.3.3. 4.3.3.1. perc,harp,cel,
pno,strings
DONEMUS perf mat rent   (R513)

Facetten, For Solo Voice And
Orchestra [15']
pic,fl,clar,bass clar,pno,
strings,S solo
sc DONEMUS f.s., perf mat rent
(R514)

Sinfonia for Strings [13']
string orch
DONEMUS perf mat rent   (R515)

Tala [20']
3.3.3.3. 4.3.3.1. 6perc,harp,pno,
strings
sc DONEMUS f.s., perf mat rent
(R516)

ROOSEVELT, [JOSEPH] WILLARD (1918-)
Amistad [14']
2.2.2.2. 4.2.3.1. perc,pno,
strings
sc AM.COMP.AL. $19.85, perf mat
rent   (R517)

Concerto for Piano and Orchestra
[15']
2.2.2.0. 2.1.1.0. perc,strings,
pno solo
sc AM.COMP.AL.   (R518)

May Song It Flourish, For Solo Voices
And Orchestra [14']
1.1.1.1. 2.1.1.0. perc,strings,
SMezBar soli
sc AM.COMP.AL. $18.25, perf mat
rent   (R519)

Suite [16']
ob,bsn,strings
sc AM.COMP.AL. $21.35   (R520)

ROPARTZ, JOSEPH GUY (MARIE) (1864-1955)
Bourrees Bourbonnaises [3'15"]
fl,ob,perc,strings
sc DURAND f.s.   (R521)

RORATE, FOR SOLO VOICES AND ORCHESTRA
see Hovland, Egil

ROREM, NED (1923-)
After Long Silence, For Solo Voice,
Oboe And String Orchestra [24']
string orch,S solo,ob solo
BOOSEY perf mat rent   (R522)

Air Music
min sc BOOSEY 815 $15.00   (R523)

Concerto for Piano and Orchestra, No.
2 [20']
2(pic).2.2.2. 2.1.0.0. timp,perc,
harp,strings,pno solo
PEER perf mat rent   (R524)

Frolic [2'15"]
3.3.3.2. 4.4.3.1. timp,2-3perc,
pno,strings
BOOSEY perf mat rent   (R525)

Remembering Tommy, For Violin,
Violoncello And Orchestra [28']
2(pic).2(English horn).2.2.
2.2.2.0. timp,perc,harp,
strings,vln solo,vcl solo
BOOSEY perf mat rent   (R526)

Six Irish Poems, For Solo Voice And
Orchestra [18']
2.2.2.2. 2.0.0.0. perc,harp,
strings,med solo
PEER perf mat rent   (R527)

Symphony for Strings [23']
string orch
min sc BOOSEY $19.00, perf mat rent
(R528)

ROSA MYSTICA, FOR SOLO VOICE AND
ORCHESTRA see Einem, Gottfried von

ROSALIANA, FOR SOLO VOICE AND CHAMBER
ORCHESTRA see Rodrigo, Joaquín

ROSARIO see Miereanu, Costin

ROSAS, JUVENTINO (1868-1894)
Over The Waves [arr.]
see Sobre Las Olas [arr.]

Sobre Las Olas [arr.]
"Over The Waves [arr.]" 1.1.2.1.
2.2.1.0. perc,strings [7'30"]
KALMUS A6948 set $15.00, pts
$1.00, ea.   (R529)

ROSE, DAVID (1919-1990)
Betty, For Trombone And Orchestra
[4']
2.2.3+bass clar.2. 4.3.3.1. timp,
perc,pno/harp,strings,trom/ob
solo
NEWAM 19039 perf mat rent   (R530)

Papillon, Le, For Flute And Orchestra
[14'40"]
2+pic.2.3+bass clar.1. 4.4.4.0.
timp,perc,pno,harp,strings,fl
solo
NEWAM 19040 perf mat rent   (R531)

ROSE, DIE, "ES LOCKTE SCHÖNE WÄRME",
FOR SOLO VOICE AND ORCHESTRA,
[ARR.] see Schubert, Franz (Peter)

ROSE FOR EMILY, A see Haxton, Kenneth

ROSE MARIE: SELECTIONS, [ARR.] see
Friml, Rudolf

ROSELL, LARS-ERIK (1944-)
Concerto for Organ and Orchestra
3.3.3.3. 5.4.3.1. timp,2perc,
harp,strings,org solo
STIM   (R532)

ROSEMAN, RONALD
Concertino for English Horn and
String Orchestra [14']
string orch,English horn solo
AM.COMP.AL. sc $16.50, pts $3.85,
perf mat rent   (R533)

Fantasy for Bassoon and String
Orchestra [9']
string orch,bsn solo
sc AM.COMP.AL. $7.35, perf mat rent
(R534)

ROSEMARY [ARR.] see Bridge, Frank

ROSEMARY - THAT'S FOR REMEMBRANCE see
Elgar, [Sir] Edward (William)

ROSEN, JEROME (1921-)
Scenes From "Calisto And Melibea",
For Solo Voices And Orchestra
[20']
1.1.1. 1.1.1.0. perc,pno,2vln,
vla,2vcl,3 solo voices
sc AM.COMP.AL. $59.30   (R535)

ROSEN, ROBERT (1956-)
Perspectives, For Chamber Orchestra
2.2.2.0. 0.0.0.0. perc,pno,
strings
CAN.MUS.CENT. MI 1100 R813P   (R536)

"...Sans Bruit..." [9']
2.2.2.2. 2.2.1.1. timp,perc,opt
harp,strings
CAN.MUS.CENT. MI 1100 R813SA   (R537)

ROSEN OHNE DORNE WALZER see Strauss,
Johann, [Sr.]

ROSENBERG, HILDING (1892-1985)
Marionettes: Dance Suite [11']
2.2.2.2. 2.2.0.0. timp,perc,
strings
NORDISKA perf mat rent   (R538)

Sinfonia Da Chiesa No. 1 [20']
1.1.1.1. 2.0.0.0. timp,perc,org,
strings
NORDISKA perf mat rent   (R539)

Symphony No. 8 [18']
2.2.2.2. 4.3.3.1. timp,perc,cel,
harp,strings
NORDISKA perf mat rent   (R540)

ROSENKAVALIER, DER, OP. 59: CLOSING
DUET-IST EIN TRAUM, FOR SOLO VOICES
AND ORCHESTRA see Strauss, Richard

ROSENKAVALIER, DER, OP. 59: ENTRY OF
THE ROSENKAVALIER- MIR EST DIE
EHRE, FOR SOLO VOICES AND ORCHESTRA
see Strauss, Richard

ROSENKAVALIER, DER, OP. 59: MONOLOGUE
OF THE MARSCHALLIN- KANN ICH MICH
AUCH AN EIN MADEL ERINNERN, FOR
SOLO VOICE AND ORCHESTRA see
Strauss, Richard

ROSENKAVALIER, DER, OP. 59: SUITE
[ARR.] see Strauss, Richard

ROSENKAVALIER, DER, OP. 59: TRIO-HAB'S
MIR GELOBT, FOR SOLO VOICES AND
ORCHESTRA see Strauss, Richard

ROSENKAVALIER, DER, OP. 59: WALTZES
[ARR.] see Strauss, Richard

ROSENMAN, LEONARD (1924-)
Chamber Music No. 2, For Solo Voice
And Instrumental Ensemble [22']
alto fl,English horn,clar,bass
clar,alto sax,harp,pno,vln,vla,
vcl,db,electronic tape,S solo
PEER perf mat rent   (R541)

Foci I [22']
2(pic).2(English horn).2(bass
clar).2(contrabsn). 2.2(trp in
C).1.0. perc,strings
SCHIRM.G perf mat rent   (R542)

Introduction, Theme And Variations,
For Clarinet And Orchestra [17']
1.2.0.1. 2.0.0.0. strings,clar
solo
(Michaels, Jost) SIKORSKI perf mat
rent   (R543)

Stabat Mater: Inflammatus, For Solo
Voice And Orchestra
2.2.2.2. 4.2.2.0. timp,strings,T
solo
SCHIRM.G perf mat rent   (R544)

ROSENMÜLLER, JOHANN (ca. 1620-1684)
Suites In C And In D Minor (from
Studentmusik) [20']
string orch,hpsd
(Hamel) KALMUS A5574 sc $8.00, set
$12.00, pts $2.00, ea.   (R545)

ROSENTHAL, MANUEL (1904-)
Temple De Memoire, Le, For Solo Voice
And Orchestra
JOBERT   (R546)

ROSENZEIT see Miereanu, Costin

ROSETTI, FRANCESCO ANTONIO (1746-1792)
Concerto for Clarinet and Orchestra
in E flat
sc KUNZEL 10045 $20.00, ipa   (R547)

Concerto for Flute and Orchestra, No.
2, in F
sc KUNZEL 10196 $18.00, ipa   (R548)

Concerto for Horn and Orchestra in D
minor, MIN 130
(Krol) DOBLINGER sc $19.00, set
$34.00, pts $5.00, ea.   (R549)

Concerto for 2 Horns and Orchestra in
E flat, MIN 637
2ob,2horn,strings,2horn soli
INTERNAT. perf mat rent   (R550)

Concerto for Oboe and Orchestra in G,
MIN 200
2fl,2bsn,2horn,strings,ob solo
sc,pts KUNZEL 10129 f.s.   (R551)

Notturno in D [12']
fl,2horn,strings
sc SUPRAPHON MAB I-32 f.s.   (R552)

Pastoral Symphony In D
(Schultz) KALMUS A6424 sc $10.00,
set $12.00, pts $1.00, ea. (R553)

ROSING-SCHOW, NIELS
Twofold [12']
3.2.2.2. 4.3.3.0. 3perc,pno,
strings
SAMFUNDET perf mat rent   (R554)

ROSS, WALTER BEGHTOL (1936-)
Concerto for Wind Quintet and String
Orchestra [22']
1.1.1.1. 1.0.0.0. strings
BOOSEY perf mat rent   (R555)

ROSSE, FRANCOIS (1945-)
Bachflussigkeit [19']
rec,ob,English horn,clar,bsn,sax,
horn,trom,perc,harp,hpsd,acord,
gtr,vcl,db
BILLAUDOT perf mat rent   (R556)

In Quanto A L'opus 61, For Piano And
Instrumental Ensemble [13']
2fl,clar,bass clar,2perc,2harp,
2vla,2db,pno solo
BILLAUDOT perf mat rent   (R557)

Triangle Pour Un Souffle, For Alto
Saxophone And String Orchestra
[11']
string orch,alto sax solo
sc BILLAUDOT f.s., perf mat rent
(R558)

ROSSELLINI, RENZO (1908-1982)
Cio Che Dicono I Fiori, For Solo
Voices And Orchestra [12']
2.2.2.2. 2.2.1.0. cel,vibra,harp,
strings,SSSMez soli

ROSSELLINI, RENZO (cont'd.)

RICORDI-IT 131707 perf mat rent
(R559)

ROSSEM, ANDRIES VAN (1957-   )
Escape [8']
    1.1.1.0. 1.1.1.0. marimba,2vln,
        vla,vcl,db
    DONEMUS perf mat rent   (R560)

Orkestmozaiek [11']
    2.2.2.2. 2.2.1.0. 3perc,pno,harp,
        strings
    sc DONEMUS f.s., perf mat rent
(R561)

ROSSINI, GIOACCHINO (1792-1868)
Barbier Von Sevilla, Der: Die
    Verleumdung, For Solo Voice And
    Orchestra
    see Barbiere Di Siviglia, Il: La
        Calunnia, For Solo Voice And
        Orchestra

Barbier Von Sevilla, Der: Frag Ich
    Mein Beklommen Herz, For Solo
    Voice And Orchestra
    see Barbiere Di Siviglia, Il: Una
        Voce Poco Fa, For Solo Voice And
        Orchestra

Barbier Von Sevilla, Der: Glück Und
    Huld, Mein Herr, Zum Grusse, For
    Solo Voices And Orchestra
    0.0.2.2. 2.0.0.0. strings,TB soli
    BREITKOPF-L perf mat rent   (R562)

Barbier Von Sevilla, Der: Ich Bin Das
    Faktotum, For Solo Voice And
    Orchestra
    see Barbiere Di Siviglia, Il: Largo
        Al Factotum, For Solo Voice And
        Orchestra

Barbiere Di Siviglia, Il: La
    Calunnia, For Solo Voice And
    Orchestra
    "Barbier Von Sevilla, Der: Die
    Verleumdung, For Solo Voice And
    Orchestra" BREITKOPF-L perf mat
    rent   (R563)

Barbiere Di Siviglia, Il: Largo Al
    Factotum, For Solo Voice And
    Orchestra
    "Barbier Von Sevilla, Der: Ich Bin
    Das Faktotum, For Solo Voice And
    Orchestra" BREITKOPF-L perf mat
    rent   (R564)

Barbiere Di Siviglia, Il: Overture
    2.2.2.2. 2.2.1.0. timp,perc,strings
    (original Italian edition) KALMUS
    A5640 sc $10.00, set $35.00, perf
    mat rent   (R565)

Barbiere Di Siviglia, Il: Una Voce
    Poco Fa, For Solo Voice And
    Orchestra
    "Barbier Von Sevilla, Der: Frag Ich
    Mein Beklommen Herz, For Solo
    Voice And Orchestra" BREITKOPF-L
    perf mat rent   (R566)

Cambiale Di Matrimonio, La: Anch' Io
    Son Giovane, For Solo Voice And
    Orchestra
    KALMUS A4910 sc $3.50, set $3.50,
    pts $.75, ea.   (R567)

Cambiale Di Matrimonio, La: Chi Mai
    Trova Il Dritto, Il Fondo, For
    Solo Voice And Orchestra
    KALMUS A4906 sc $7.00, set $10.00,
    pts $1.00, ea.   (R568)

Cambiale Di Matrimonio, La: Darei Per
    Si Bel Fondo, For Solo Voices And
    Orchestra
    KALMUS A4908 sc $6.00, set $7.00,
    pts $.75, ea.   (R569)

Cambiale Di Matrimonio, La: Dite,
    Presto, Dove Sta, For Solo Voices
    And Orchestra
    KALMUS A4911 sc $12.00, set $13.00,
    pts $1.00, ea., perf mat rent
(R570)

Cambiale Di Matrimonio, La: Grazie...
    Grazie, For Solo Voice And
    Orchestra
    KALMUS A4907 sc $7.00, set $10.00,
    pts $1.00, ea.   (R571)

Cambiale Di Matrimonio, La: Non C'e
    Il Vecchio Sussurrone, For Solo
    Voices And Orchestra
    KALMUS A4904 sc $5.00, set $7.00,
    pts $.75, ea.   (R572)

Cambiale Di Matrimonio, La: Portero
    Cosi Il Cappello, For Solo Voices
    And Orchestra
    KALMUS A4913 sc $6.00, set $7.50,
    pts $.75, ea.   (R573)

ROSSINI, GIOACCHINO (cont'd.)

Cambiale Di Matrimonio, La: Qual Ira,
    Oh Ciel, V'accende, For Solo
    Voices And Orchestra
    KALMUS A4914 sc $3.00, set $6.50,
    pts $.75, ea.   (R574)

Cambiale Di Matrimonio, La: Quell'
    Amabile Visino, For Solo Voices
    And Orchestra
    KALMUS A4909 sc $9.00, set $10.00,
    pts $1.00, ea.   (R575)

Cambiale Di Matrimonio, La: Tornami A
    Dir Che M' Ami, For Solo Voices
    And Orchestra
    KALMUS A4905 sc $9.00, set $10.00,
    pts $1.00, ea.   (R576)

Cambiale Di Matrimonio, La: Vorrei
    Spiegarvi Il Giubilo, For Solo
    Voice And Orchestra
    KALMUS A4912 sc $9.00, set $10.00,
    pts $1.00, ea.   (R577)

Cenerentola, La: Overture
    see Overtures, Four, Vol. 1

Comte Ory, Le: A La Faveur De Cette
    Nuit Obscure, For Solo Voices And
    Orchestra
    KALMUS A4965 sc $15.00, set $31.00,
    pts $1.75, ea., perf mat rent
(R578)

Comte Ory, Le: Ah Quel Respect,
    Madame, For Solo Voices And
    Orchestra
    KALMUS A4962 sc $9.00, set $25.00,
    pts $1.25, ea., perf mat rent
(R579)

Comte Ory, Le: Une Dame De Haut
    Parage, For Solo Voices And
    Orchestra
    KALMUS A4959 sc $9.00, set $22.00,
    pts $1.25, ea., perf mat rent
(R580)

Danza, La, For Solo Voice And
    Orchestra [arr.]
    2(pic).0.2.2. 4.2.3.0. timp,tamb,
    strings,solo voice [4'] KALMUS
    A3012 sc $4.00, set $12.00, pts
    $.75, ea.   (R581)

Eduardo E Cristina: Overture
    (Gorgni) KALMUS A7303 sc $20.00,
    set $30.00, pts $1.50, ea., perf
    mat rent   (R582)

Ermione: Overture [10']
    2+pic.2.2.2. 4.2.3.0. timp,perc,
    strings
    sc BSE 64 f.s., perf mat rent
(R583)

Gazza Ladra, La: Di Piacer Mi Balza
    Il Cor, For Solo Voice And
    Orchestra
    KALMUS A4917 sc $8.00, set $12.00,
    pts $1.00, ea.   (R584)

Gazza Ladra, La: Eben, Per Mia
    Memoria, For Solo Voices And
    Orchestra
    KALMUS A4927 sc $10.00, set $25.00,
    pts $2.00, ea., perf mat rent
(R585)

Gazza Ladra, La: Forse Un Di
    Conoscerete, For Solo Voices And
    Orchestra
    KALMUS A4925 sc $4.00, set $12.00,
    pts $1.00, ea.   (R586)

Gazza Ladra, La: Idolo Mio, For Solo
    Voices And Orchestra
    KALMUS A4922 sc $7.00, set $12.00,
    pts $1.00, ea.   (R587)

Gazza Ladra, La: Il Mio Piano E
    Preparato, For Solo Voice And
    Orchestra
    KALMUS A4923 sc $7.00, set $12.00,
    pts $1.00, ea.   (R588)

Gazza Ladra, La: Overture
    "Thieving Magpie, The: Overture" 1+
    pic.2.2.2. 4.2.1.0. timp,perc,
    strings (original Italian
    edition) KALMUS A5641 sc $18.00,
    set $35.00, perf mat rent   (R589)
    see Overtures, Four, Vol. 2

Gazza Ladra, La: Si Per Voi, Pupille
    Amate, For Solo Voice And
    Orchestra
    KALMUS A4926 sc $5.00, set $15.00,
    pts $1.00, ea.   (R590)

Gazza Ladra, La: Stringhe E Ferri Da
    Calzette, For Solo Voice And
    Orchestra
    KALMUS A4918 sc $4.00, set $7.00,
    pts $.75, ea.   (R591)

Gazza Ladra, La: Vieni Fra Queste
    Braccia, For Solo Voice And
    Orchestra

ROSSINI, GIOACCHINO (cont'd.)

    KALMUS A4920 sc $6.00, set $15.00,
    pts $1.00, ea.   (R592)

Italiana In Algeri, L': Ah, Come Il
    Cor Di Giubilo, For Solo Voice
    And Orchestra
    KALMUS A4948 sc $8.00, set $12.00,
    pts $.75, ea., perf mat rent
(R593)

Italiana In Algeri, L': Ai Capricci
    Della Sorte, For Solo Voices And
    Orchestra
    KALMUS A4945 sc $10.00, set $20.00,
    pts $2.00, ea., perf mat rent
(R594)

Italiana In Algeri, L': Gia D'
    Insolito Adore, For Solo Voice
    And Orchestra
    KALMUS A4946 sc $5.00, set $12.00,
    pts $.75, ea., perf mat rent
(R595)

Italiana In Algeri, L': Io Presento
    Di Mia Man, For Solo Voices And
    Orchestra
    KALMUS A4951 sc $25.00, set $35.00,
    pts $3.00, ea., perf mat rent
(R596)

Italiana In Algeri, L': Languir Per
    Una Bella, For Solo Voice And
    Orchestra
    KALMUS A4942 sc $5.00, set $19.00,
    pts $1.00, ea., perf mat rent
(R597)

Italiana In Algeri, L': Le Femmine
    D'italia, For Solo Voice And
    Orchestra
    KALMUS A4952 sc $3.00, set $8.00,
    pts $.75, ea.   (R598)

Italiana In Algeri, L': Overture
    2.2.2.2. 2.2.1.0. timp,perc,strings
    (original Italian edition) KALMUS
    A5202 sc $25.00, set $40.00, perf
    mat rent   (R599)
    see Overtures, Four, Vol. 2

Italiana In Algeri, L': Pappataci Che
    Mai Sento, For Solo Voices And
    Orchestra
    KALMUS A4953 sc $9.00, set $15.00,
    pts $1.00, ea., perf mat rent
(R600)

Italiana In Algeri, L': Pensa Alla
    Patria, For Solo Voice And
    Orchestra
    KALMUS A4955 sc $12.00, set $20.00,
    pts $2.00, ea., perf mat rent
(R601)

Italiana In Algeri, L': Per Lui Che
    Adoro, For Solo Voice And
    Orchestra
    KALMUS A4950 sc $8.00, set $15.00,
    pts $1.00, ea., perf mat rent
(R602)

Italiana In Algeri, L': Se Inclinassi
    A Prender Moglie, For Solo Voices
    And Orchestra
    KALMUS A4943 sc $9.00, set $19.00,
    pts $1.00, ea., perf mat rent
(R603)

Mose: Ah! Se Puoi Cosi, For Solo
    Voices And Orchestra
    KALMUS A4970 set $40.00, pts $2.50,
    ea., perf mat rent   (R604)

Mose: Celeste Man Placata, For Solo
    Voices And Orchestra
    KALMUS A4975 set $40.00, pts $2.50,
    ea., perf mat rent   (R605)

Mose: Parlar, Spiegar, For Solo
    Voices And Orchestra
    KALMUS A4976 set $25.00, pts $2.00,
    ea., perf mat rent   (R606)

Mose: Qual' Orribile Sciagura, For
    Solo Voice And Orchestra
    KALMUS A4982 set $25.00, pts $2.00,
    ea., perf mat rent   (R607)

Mose: Quale Assalto, For Solo Voices
    And Orchestra
    KALMUS A4981 set $20.00, pts $1.00,
    ea., perf mat rent   (R608)

Mose: Tutto Sorride, For Solo Voices
    And Orchestra
    KALMUS A4972 set $12.00, pts $.75,
    ea., perf mat rent   (R609)

Overtures, Four, Vol. 1
    min sc KALMUS K00088 $9.25
    contains: Cenerentola, La:
        Overture; Scala Di Seta, La:
        Overture; Semiramide: Overture;
        Tancredi: Overture   (R610)

Overtures, Four, Vol. 2
    min sc KALMUS K00089 $11.50
    contains: Gazza Ladra, La:
        Overture; Italiana In Algeri,
        L': Overture; Siege De
        Corinthe, Le: Overture; Turco
        In Italia, Il: Overture   (R611)

ROSSINI, GIOACCHINO (cont'd.)

Prelude, Theme And Variations, For Horn And Orchestra [arr.] (McAlister) 1.2.2.2. 0.0.0.0. strings,horn solo [10'] KALMUS A6955 sc $15.00, set $25.00, pts $2.00, ea., perf mat rent (R612)

Prelude, Theme Et Variations, For Horn And String Orchestra [arr.] (Benzi, R.) string orch,horn/English horn solo LEMOINE perf mat rent (R613)

Prelude, Theme Et Variations In E, For Horn And Orchestra [arr.] (Leloir, E.) 2.2.2.2. 0.0.0.0. strings,horn solo [10'30"] BILLAUDOT perf mat rent (R614)

Rendez-Vous De Chasse, Le, For 4 Horns And Orchestra (Leloir, E.) 3.2.2.2. 0.2.3.0. timp,strings,4horn soli [5'15"] BILLAUDOT perf mat rent (R615)

Robert Bruce: Overture 2.2.2.2. 4.4.2.1. timp,perc, strings (Niedermeyer, A.L.) [7'] (Overture to an opera adapted by Niedermeyer from several of Rossini's operas) KALMUS A3438 sc $10.00, set $25.00, perf mat rent (R616)

Scala Di Seta, La: Overture see Overtures, Four, Vol. 1

Semiramide: Overture see Overtures, Four, Vol. 1

Siege De Corinthe, Le: Overture see Overtures, Four, Vol. 2

Signor Bruschino, Il: Ah Donate Il Caro Sposo, For Solo Voice And Orchestra KALMUS A4936 sc $9.00, set $12.00, pts $1.00, ea., perf mat rent (R617)

Signor Bruschino, Il: Ah Se Il Colpo Arrivo A Fare, For Solo Voices And Orchestra KALMUS A4933 sc $9.00, set $14.00, pts $1.00, ea., perf mat rent (R618)

Signor Bruschino, Il: Deh! Tu M'assisti Amore, For Solo Voice And Orchestra KALMUS A4930 sc $3.00, set $9.00, pts $1.00, ea. (R619)

Signor Bruschino, Il: E Bel Nodo, Che Due Cori, For Solo Voices And Orchestra KALMUS A4938 sc $12.00, set $12.00, pts $1.00, ea., perf mat rent (R620)

Signor Bruschino, Il: Ebben, Ragion Dovere, For Solo Voices And Orchestra KALMUS A 4939 sc $4.00, set $12.00, pts $1.00, ea., perf mat rent (R621)

Signor Bruschino, Il: Ho La Testa, O E Andata Via? For Solo Voice And Orchestra KALMUS A4937 sc $12.00, set $18.00, pts $2.00, ea., perf mat rent (R622)

Signor Bruschino, Il: Marianna! Voi Signore? For Solo Voices And Orchestra KALMUS A4931 sc $5.00, set $8.00, pts $.75, ea. (R623)

Signor Bruschino, Il: Nel Teatro Del Gran Mondo, For Solo Voice And Orchestra KALMUS A4934 sc $6.00, set $12.00, pts $1.00, ea., perf mat rent (R624)

Signor Bruschino, Il: Per Un Figlio Gia Pentito, For Solo Voices And Orchestra KALMUS A4935 sc $20.00, set $15.00, pts $2.00, ea., perf mat rent (R625)

Signor Bruschino, Il: Quanto E Dolce A Un' Alma Amante, For Solo Voices And Orchestra KALMUS A4932 sc $5.00, set $14.00, pts $1.00, ea., perf mat rent (R626)

Sonata, No. 1, [arr.] (Wright, Carla) string orch (gr. V) SOUTHERN SO-44 sc $7.50, set $37.50, pts $2.50, ea. (R627)

Sonata No. 1 in G string orch (Lebermann) SCHOTTS sc CON 126 $15.00, set CON 126-70 $38.00 (R628)

ROSSINI, GIOACCHINO (cont'd.)

Sonata No. 2 in A string orch (Lebermann) SCHOTTS sc CON 127 $15.00, set CON 127-70 $38.00 (R629)

Tancredi: Overture BREITKOPF-W perf mat rent (R630) see Overtures, Four, Vol. 1

Thieving Magpie, The: Overture see Gazza Ladra, La: Overture

Turco In Italia, Il: Overture "Turk In Italy, The: Overture" min sc KALMUS K01419 $5.00 (R631) see Overtures, Four, Vol. 2

Turk In Italy, The: Overture see Turco In Italia, Il: Overture

Variazioni A Piu Strumenti Obbligati [6'] 1.0.2.1. 2.0.0.0. strings,clar solo,string quar soli KALMUS A4277 sc $15.00, set $15.00, perf mat rent (R632)

ROSSINI IN PARIS, FOR CLARINET AND ORCHESTRA see Argento, Dominick

ROSSINIANA see Respighi, Ottorino

ROSSINIANA: TARANTELLA see Respighi, Ottorino

RÖSSLER, FRANZ ANTON see ROSETTI, FRANCESCO ANTONIO

ROSSO see Bussotti, Sylvano

ROTA, NINO (1911-1979) Balli [10'] 2.2.2.2. 2.1.0.0. strings RICORDI-IT perf mat rent (R633)

Castel Del Monte, For Horn And Orchestra [10'] 2.2.2.2. 2.2.0.0. timp,cel, handbells,harp,strings,horn solo RICORDI-IT perf mat rent (R634)

Concerto for Bassoon and Orchestra sc BERBEN 576-00390 $23.75 (R635)

Concerto for Piano and Orchestra in C 2.2.2.2. 4.2.0.0. timp,strings, pno solo RICORDI-IT perf mat rent (R636)

Concerto for Piano and Orchestra in E [35'] 3.2.2.2. 3.3.0.0. timp,strings, pno solo RICORDI-IT perf mat rent (R637)

Concerto for Trombone and Orchestra [14'] 1.1.2.2. 2.0.0.0. timp,strings, trom solo sc RICORDI-IT 131532 f.s., perf mat rent (R638)

Concerto for Violoncello and Orchestra, No. 1 [30'] 2.2.2.2. 4.2.3.1. timp,strings, vcl solo RICORDI-IT perf mat rent (R639)

Concerto for Violoncello and Orchestra, No. 2 [28'] 2.2.2.2. 2.2.0.0. timp,strings, vcl solo RICORDI-IT perf mat rent (R640)

Rabelaisiana, For Solo Voice And Orchestra [18'] 2.2.3.1. 4.2.3.1. timp,perc,cel, harp,strings,S solo RICORDI-IT 133220 perf mat rent (R641)

Sinfonia No. 2 in F [20'] 2.2.2.2. 0.2.3.0. timp,strings (Anni di Pellegrinaggio) RICORDI-IT perf mat rent (R642)

Sinfonia Sopra Una Canzone D'amore [30'] 3.3.3.2. 4.3.3.1. timp,perc, strings RICORDI-IT 133091 perf mat rent (R643)

Strada, La: Suite 3.3.3.2. 4.3.3.1. timp,perc,cel, harp,pno,strings, sistro RICORDI-IT 134427 perf mat rent (R644)

ROTATIONS, FOR PIANO AND ORCHESTRA see Swerts, Piet

ROTKEHLEHEN, DAS, FOR NARRATOR AND ORCHESTRA see Meschwitz, Frieder

RÖTTGERING, MARTIN ALMAR (1926-) Runen Sage, De, For Piano And Orchestra 2.2.2.2. 4.2.0.0. timp,perc, strings,pno solo sc DONEMUS f.s., perf mat rent (R645)

ROUE OUVERTURE, LA see Honegger, Arthur

ROUET D'OMPHALE, LE see Saint-Saëns, Camille

ROUGERON, PHILIPPE (1928-) Divertissement for String Orchestra [13'15"] string orch BILLAUDOT perf mat rent (R646)

ROUGH MUSIC, FOR PERCUSSION AND ORCHESTRA see Gruber, Heinz Karl

ROUMANIAN RHAPSODY NO. 1 FOR VIOLIN AND ORCHESTRA see Waxman, Franz

ROUSE, CHRISTOPHER (1949-) Alloeidea [32'] 2.2.2.2. 6.4.3.1. timp,perc,harp, strings sc AM.COMP.AL. $44.65 (R647)

Infernal Machine, The 3.3.4.3. 4.3.3.1. perc,cel,harp, strings sc HELICON $20.00 (R648)

Phantasmata 3.3.4.3. 5.4.4.1. perc,harp,cel, pno,strings study sc HELICON EA00567 $35.00, perf mat rent (R649)

ROUSSAKIS, NICOLAS (1943-) Fire And Earth And Water And Air [21'] 3.3.3.3. 4.4.2.1. perc,pno, strings AM.COMP.AL. perf mat rent (R650)

ROUSSEAU, MARCEL (SAMUEL-ROUSSEAU) (1882-1955) Promenade Dans Rome [40'] CHOUDENS perf mat rent (R651)

ROUSSEL, ALBERT (CHARLES PAUL) (1869-1937) Evocations, Op. 15: La Villa Rose KALMUS A6398 sc $25.00, set $70.00, pts $3.00, ea., perf mat rent (R652)

Evocations, Op. 15: Les Dieux Dans L'ombre Des Cavernes KALMUS A6397 sc $20.00, set $55.00, pts $2.00, ea., perf mat rent (R653)

Festin De L'araignee, Le *Op.17 KALMUS A7246 sc $30.00, set $70.00, pts $3.50, ea., perf mat rent (R654)

Marchand De Sable Qui Passe, Le "Sand Vendor Passing By, The" KALMUS A4273 sc $12.00, set $10.00 (R655)

Poeme De La Foret (Symphony No. 1, Op. 7, in D minor) KALMUS A5681 sc $60.00, set $125.00, perf mat rent (R656)

Resurrection [15'] 3.3.3.2. 4.3.3.1. timp,harp, strings SALABERT perf mat rent (R657)

Sand Vendor Passing By, The see Marchand De Sable Qui Passe, Le

Symphony No. 1, Op. 7, in D minor see Poeme De La Foret

ROUT FOR SOLO VOICE AND ORCHESTRA see Bliss, [Sir] Arthur (Drummond)

ROUTE DE PELERINS RECLUS, LA see Longtin, Michel

ROUX, MAURICE LE see LE ROUX, MAURICE

ROVERENS JULEAFTEN, FOR NARRATOR AND ORCHESTRA see Stolarczyk, Willy

ROVICS, HOWARD (1936-) Affirmation [8'] ob,2horn,timp,strings sc AM.COMP.AL. $10.70, perf mat rent (R658)

Concerto for Piano and Chamber Orchestra [14'] 1.1.1.1. 2.1.1.0. perc,strings, pno solo sc AM.COMP.AL. $25.90 (R659)

ROVSING OLSEN, POUL (1922-   )
Concerto for Piano and Orchestra
sc,pts SAMFUNDET f.s.   (R660)

Lux Coelestis *Op.82 [10']
3(pic).3.3.3. 4.3.2.1. timp,perc,
cel,pno,harp,strings
HANSEN-DEN perf mat rent   (R661)

Sinfonia No. 1
sc,pts SAMFUNDET f.s.   (R662)

Variations Symphoniques
sc,pts SAMFUNDET f.s.   (R663)

ROWE, ROBERT (1954-   )
Revolving Wheel [10'30"]
1.1.1.1.alto sax. 1.1.0.0. perc,
pno,harp,2vln,vla,vcl,db
DONEMUS perf mat rent   (R664)

ROWLAND, DAVID (1939-   )
Scenes From The Painted Bird [15']
3.3.3.3. 4.3.3.1. timp,3perc,
harp,cel,strings
sc DONEMUS f.s., perf mat rent
(R665)

ROXBURGH, EDWIN
Montage
UNITED MUS   (R666)

Saturn
UNITED MUS   (R667)

Serenade
string orch
UNITED MUS   (R668)

Seven Tableaux, For Trumpet And
Orchestra
UNITED MUS   (R669)

Tamesis
UNITED MUS   (R670)

ROYAL FIREWATER MUSICK see "Bach,
P.D.Q." (Peter Schickele)

ROYAL FIREWORKS MUSIC see Handel,
George Frideric

ROYAL FUSILIERS' ARRIVAL AT QUEBEC
[ARR] see Voyer De Poligny
D'Argenson, Charles

ROYAUME ENCHANTE, LE see Tcherepnin,
Nikolay Nikolayevich

ROYER, PANCRACE (1705-1755)
Zaide: Suite [arr.]
(Boulay, L.) 1.1.0.1. 1.1.0.0.
timp,hpsd,strings [17'10"]
BILLAUDOT perf mat rent   (R671)

ROZPOMIENKA NA FEBRUAR see Korínek,
Miloslav

ROZSA, MIKLOS (1907-   )
Ben Hur: Suite [16']
3(pic).2(English horn).3(clar in
E flat,bass clar).3(contrabsn).
4.3.3.2. timp,3perc,pno&cel,
2harp,strings
ROBBINS perf mat rent   (R672)

El Cid: Suite [11']
3(pic).2.3(bass
clar).2(contrabsn). 4.3.3.1.
timp,2perc,pno,harp,strings
ROBBINS perf mat rent   (R673)

Quo Vadis: Suite [19'30"]
3(pic).3(English horn).3(bass
clar).3(contrabsn). 4.3.3.1.
timp,3perc,pno&cel,harp,strings
ROBBINS perf mat rent   (R674)

RUBAYAT, FOR SOLO VOICE AND CHAMBER
ORCHESTRA see Gubaidulina, Sofia

RUBIN, MARCEL (1905-   )
Ballade for Orchestra [12']
2+pic.2+English horn.2+bass
clar.2+contrabsn. 4.3.3.1.
timp,perc,strings
DOBLINGER perf mat rent   (R675)

Hymnen An Die Nacht [29']
2+pic.2.2.2. 4.3.3.1. timp,perc,
cel,strings
DOBLINGER perf mat rent   (R676)

Stadt, Die, For Solo Voice And
Orchestra [29']
2+pic.2.2.2. 4.2.3.1. timp,perc,
strings,speaking voice
DOBLINGER perf mat rent   (R677)

Symphony No. 7 [29']
2+pic.2+English horn.2+bass
clar.2+contrabsn. 4.3.3.1.
timp,perc,cel,strings
study sc DOBLINGER STP 500 f.s.,
perf mat rent   (R678)

RUBIN, MARCEL (cont'd.)

Symphony No. 8 [30']
3(pic,alto fl).2+English horn.2+
bass clar.2+contrabsn. 4.3.3.1.
timp,perc,strings
DOBLINGER perf mat rent   (R679)

Symphony No. 9 [28']
2+pic.2+English horn.2+bass
clar.2+contrabsn. 4.3.3.1.
timp,perc,strings
(Angelus Silesius) DOBLINGER perf
mat rent   (R680)

Symphony No. 10 [33']
2+pic.2+English horn.2+bass
clar.2+contrabsn. 4.3.3.1.
timp,perc,strings
(Hommage a Chartres) DOBLINGER perf
mat rent   (R681)

Triptychon Fur Schutz, Bach Und
Handel [18']
2+pic.2.2.2. 4.3.3.1. timp,perc,
strings
DOBLINGER perf mat rent   (R682)

RUBINSTEIN, ANTON (1829-1894)
Concerto for Piano and Orchestra, No.
3, Op. 45 [26']
2.2.2.2. 2.2.0.0. timp,strings,
pno solo
BOTE perf mat rent   (R683)

Concerto for Piano and Orchestra, No.
5, Op. 94, in E flat [28']
2.2.2.2. 2.2.0.0. timp,strings,
pno solo
KALMUS A5791 sc $80.00, set $35.00,
perf mat rent   (R684)

Concerto for Violoncello and
Orchestra, Op. 65
KALMUS A7465 sc $60.00, set $45.00,
pts $2.50, ea., perf mat rent
(R685)

Don Quixote *Op.87 [25']
3.2.2.2. 4.2.3.0. timp,strings
SIMROCK perf mat rent   (R686)

Dumka [arr.] *Op.93,No.3
(Muller-Berghaus) 2(pic).2.2.2.
4.0.0.0. timp,perc,harp,strings
[4'] KALMUS A5790 sc $12.00, set
$18.00, perf mat rent   (R687)

Ivan The Terrible *see RUSSIAN
SYMPHONIC MUSIC, VOL. 3

Symphony No. 1 [50']
3.2.2.2. 4.2.3.0. timp,strings
KAHNT perf mat rent   (R688)

Valse Caprice [arr.]
(Muller-Berghaus) KALMUS A5792 sc
$20.00, set $32.00, perf mat rent
(R689)

RUDA see Villa-Lobos, Heitor

RUDD-MOORE, DOROTHY (1940-   )
From The Dark Tower, For Solo Voice
And Orchestra [22']
2.3.3.2. 4.3.3.1. timp,cel,
strings,Mez solo
sc AM.COMP.AL. $19.15, perf mat
rent   (R690)

Weary Blues, For Solo Voice And
Orchestra [5']
2.2+English horn.2+bass clar.2.
2.0.0.0. timp,pno,strings,Bar
solo
sc AM.COMP.AL. $9.95   (R691)

RUDERS, POUL (1949-   )
Capriccio Pian' E Forte [14']
3.3.3.3. 4.3.3.1. timp,perc,harp,
pno,strings
HANSEN-DEN 310 f.s.   (R692)

Concerto for Clarinet and 2
Orchestras [20']
2(pic).2(English horn).2(bass
clar).2(contrabsn). 2.2.2.0.
4perc,strings,clar solo
HANSEN-DEN perf mat rent   (R693)

Concerto for Violin and Orchestra
[20']
harp,hpsd,vln solo
HANSEN-DEN perf mat rent   (R694)

Corpus Cum Figuris [20']
1(pic).1(English horn).2(bass
clar).2(contrabsn). 1.1.1.0.
2perc,harp,pno,2vln,2vla,2vcl,
db
HANSEN-DEN perf mat rent   (R695)

Dramaphonia, For Piano And Orchestra
[15']
1(pic).1.1(bass clar,clar in E
flat).1(contrabsn). 1.1(piccolo
trp).1.0. perc,vln,vcl,db,pno
solo

RUDERS, POUL (cont'd.)

HANSEN-DEN perf mat rent   (R696)

Four Dances In One Movement [18']
1(pic).1(English horn).1.1.
1.1.1.0. perc,pno,string quin
HANSEN-DEN perf mat rent   (R697)

Ground [10']
2.2.2.2. 2.2.1.0. timp,perc,pno,
strings
HANSEN-DEN perf mat rent   (R698)

Himmelhoch Jauchzend- Zum Tode
Betrubt (Symphony) [33']
4(pic,alto fl).4(English
horn).4.4(contrabsn).sax.
6.4.4.1. timp,4perc,harp,pno,
strings,synthesizer
HANSEN-DEN perf mat rent   (R699)

Manhattan Abstraction [20']
4.4.4.3. 6.4.6.3.1. timp,5perc,
harp,pno,strings
HANSEN-DEN perf mat rent   (R700)

Monodrama, For Percussion And
Orchestra [32']
0.3.3(clar in E flat).2+
contrabsn. 4.0.3.1. 8vcl,6db,
perc solo
HANSEN-DEN perf mat rent   (R701)

Pavan [12']
2.0.2.2. 2.2.0.0. perc,harp,cel,
Hamm,pno,elec gtr,strings
sc SAMFUNDET f.s., perf mat rent
(R702)

Polydrama, For Violoncello And
Orchestra [25']
3(pic).3(ob d'amore).3(clar in E
flat).2+contrabsn. 4.2.2.0.
2perc,harp,pno,strings,vcl solo
HANSEN-DEN perf mat rent   (R703)

Recitatives And Arias, For Piano And
Orchestra [20']
1(pic,alto fl).1(English
horn).1(bass clar).1.
1.1.1(bass trom).0. timp,perc,
harp,strings,pno solo
HANSEN-DEN perf mat rent   (R704)

Symphony
see Himmelhoch Jauchzend- Zum Tode
Betrubt

Thus Saw Saint John [11']
3(pic).3(English horn).3(clar in
E flat).2+contrabsn. 4.3.2.1.
3perc,cel,harp,pno 4-hands,
strings
HANSEN-DEN perf mat rent   (R705)

Tundra
2.2.2.2. 4.2.3.0. timp,strings
[4'30"] HANSEN-DEN perf mat rent
(R706)

RUDHYAR, DANE (DANIEL CHENNEVIÈRE)
(1895-   )
Cosmic Cycle [23']
3.3.3.2. 4.3.3.1. timp,perc,harp,
cel,pno,strings
sc AM.COMP.AL. $38.10   (R707)

Dialogues [25']
2.2.2.2. 2.1.1.0. timp,pno,
strings
sc AM.COMP.AL. $26.70   (R708)

Encounter, For Piano And Orchestra
[21']
2.1+English horn.2(bass clar).2.
2.2.2.1. timp,gong,cym,strings,
pno solo
sc AM.COMP.AL. $25.90, perf mat
rent   (R709)

Out Of The Darkness [23']
2.2.2.2. 3.2.2.1. timp,perc,pno,
strings
sc AM.COMP.AL. $32.50   (R710)

Quantum Mechanics, Lesson I: Ecstatic
States [30']
3.3.3.3. 4.3.3.1. 4perc,harp,pno,
strings
sc AM.COMP.AL. $103.90, perf mat
rent   (R711)

Three Poems Of Youth [32']
2.2.2.2. 4.2.3.1. timp,3perc,
harp,pno,strings
sc AM.COMP.AL. $93.75, perf mat
rent   (R712)

Three Poems Of Youth, No.1: Yearning
[11']
2.2.2.2. 4.2.3.1. timp,3perc,pno,
strings
sc AM.COMP.AL. $40.20   (R713)

Trois Chansons De Bilitis, For Solo
Voice And Chamber Orchestra [15']
1.1.1.1. 1.1.1.0. vibra,cel,pno,

RUDHYAR, DANE (DANIEL CHENNEVIÈRE)
    (cont'd.)

        harp,2vln,vla,vcl,db,low female
        solo
    AM.COMP.AL. sc $13.70, pts $21.45,
        perf mat rent   (R714)

    Warrior, The, For Piano And Orchestra
        [9']
        2.2+English horn.2.2. 4.3.2.1.
        timp,perc,strings,pno solo
    sc AM.COMP.AL. $12.40   (R715)

    When Quiet Implodes [16']
        1.2.1.2. 2.1.0.0. perc,pno,cel,
        strings
    AM.COMP.AL. perf mat rent   (R716)

RUDI, JORAN (1954-   )
    For More Than One
        string orch
    NORGE   (R717)

RUDOLPH FRIML FAVORITES, [ARR.] see
    Friml, Rudolf

RUF see Nunes, Emmanuel

RUGE, FILIPPO (1735-1775)
    Nova Tempesta, La (Symphony in D)
        2horn,strings
        (Brook, Barry) FRANK perf mat rent
                                         (R718)

    Symphony in D
        see Nova Tempesta, La

    Symphony, Op. 1, No. 6, in D
        2horn,strings
        (Brook, Barry) FRANK perf mat rent
                                         (R719)
RUGGED CLIFF, THE, FOR SOLO VOICES AND
    ORCHESTRA see Olafsson, Kjartan

RUGGLES, CARL SPRAGUE (1876-1971)
    Vox Clamans In Deserto, For Solo
        Voice And Chamber Orchestra
        (Smith, Hale) 1.1.1.1. 1.2.0.0.
        pno,2vln,vla,2vcl,db,Mez solo sc
        PRESSER 416-41111 $10.00, perf
        mat rent   (R720)

RUINEN VON ATHEN OVERTURE see
    Beethoven, Ludwig van

RUISENOR, EL see Dalby, Martin

RUISSEAU SUR L'ESCALIER, LE, FOR
    VIOLONCELLO AND INSTRUMENTAL
    ENSEMBLE see Donatoni, Franco

RUITER, WIM DE (1943-   )
    Concerto for Accordion and Orchestra
        [21']
        2.2.2.2. 2.2.1.0. 2perc,strings,
        acord solo
    DONEMUS perf mat rent   (R721)

    Concerto for Piano and Orchestra
        [32']
        3.3.3.2. 4.3.2.1. 3-4perc,
        strings,pno solo
    sc DONEMUS f.s., perf mat rent   (R722)
RUIZ PIPÓ, ANTONIO (1934-   )
    Tablas, For Guitar And Orchestra
        [20']
        2.2(English horn).2.2. 4.2.3.0.
        timp,perc,cel,strings,gtr solo
    UNION ESP. perf mat rent   (R723)

RULE, BRITANNIA see Arne, Thomas
    Augustine see Wagner, Richard

RULE, BRITANNIA [ARR] see Arne, Thomas
    Augustine

RULON, C. BRYAN
    Three Poems Of Youth, No. 2: Rite Of
        Love [12']
        2.2.2.2. 4.2.3.1. timp,2perc,
        harp,pno,strings
    sc AM.COMP.AL. $30.85   (R724)

    Three Poems Of Youth, No. 3: Threnody
        [9']
        2.2.2.2. 4.2.3.1. timp,2perc,pno,
        strings
    sc AM.COMP.AL. $36.00   (R725)

RUMANIAN DANCE see Bartók, Béla

RUMANIAN RHAPSODY NO. 1 IN A see
    Enesco, Georges (Enescu)

RUMANIAN RHAPSODY NO. 2 IN D see
    Enesco, Georges (Enescu)

RUMPELSTILZCHEN, FOR NARRATOR AND
    ORCHESTRA see Soring, Wolfgang

RUMPUS see Wooldridge, Clifford

RUNEN SAGE, DE, FOR PIANO AND ORCHESTRA
    see Röttgering, Martin Almar

RUPTURAS see Villa Rojo, Jesus

RURAL SONGS, FOR SOLO VOICE AND
    ORCHESTRA see Kelly, Robert T.

RUSSIAN FAIRY TALE see Rimsky-Korsakov,
    Nikolai, Conte Feerique

RUSSIAN FANTASY, FOR PIANO AND
    ORCHESTRA see Napravnik, Eduard

RUSSIAN PIECES, SET 1 see Dodgson,
    Stephen

RUSSIAN PIECES, SET 2 see Dodgson,
    Stephen

RUSSIAN SUITE see Pakhmutova, Alexandra

RUSSIAN SYMPHONIC MUSIC, VOL. 3
    sc MUZYKA f.s.
    contains: Dargomyzhsky, Alexander
        Sergeyevich, Baba Yaga;
        Dargomyzhsky, Alexander
        Sergeyevich, Chukhon Fantasy;
        Dargomyzhsky, Alexander
        Sergeyevich, Ukrainian Cossack
        Dance; Rubinstein, Anton, Ivan
        The Terrible   (R726)

RUSSIAN SYMPHONIC MUSIC, VOL. 4
    sc MUZYKA f.s.
    contains: Mussorgsky, Modest
        Petrovich, Intermezzo;
        Mussorgsky, Modest Petrovich,
        Night On Bald Mountain;
        Mussorgsky, Modest Petrovich,
        Scherzo; Mussorgsky, Modest
        Petrovich, Seizure Of Karse, The;
        Serov, Alexander, Dance Of The
        Zaporozh Cossacks   (R727)

RUSSISCHE TANZE see Bortkiewicz, Sergei
    Eduardovich

RUSSISCHER MARSCH FANTASIE see Strauss,
    Johann, [Jr.]

RUSSISCHES KONZERT, FOR PIANO AND
    ORCHESTRA see Sidelnikov, Leonid

RUSSO, WILLIAM JOSEPH (1928-   )
    Carousel Suite, For Narrator And
        Chamber Group *Op.63 [34']
        0.1(English horn).1.1.sax.
        1.1.2.0. perc,pno,vln,vla,vcl,
        db,narrator
    GUNMAR MP6060 perf mat rent (R728)

    Golden Bird, The, For Solo Voice And
        Orchestra *Op.77 [44']
        1.2.1.1. 2.1.1.0. 2perc,pno,
        strings,SBar&narrator
    GUNMAR MP6065 perf mat rent (R729)

    Hello *Op.79 [15']
        1.1.1.1. 2.1.1.0. perc,mand,pno,
        strings
    GUNMAR MP6066 perf mat rent (R730)

    Music for Alto Saxophone and
        Orchestra, Op. 9 [9']
        perc,gtr,pno,strings,alto sax
        solo
    GUNMAR MP6068 perf mat rent (R731)

    Street Music
        3(pic).2.2.2. 4.2.3.1. timp,perc,
        strings,harmonica solo,pno
        solo,vln solo
    sc PEER 61265-861 $25.00. perf mat
        rent   (R732)

    Suite for Violin and Strings, Op. 46
        [14']
        6vln,2vla,2vcl,db,vln solo
    GUNMAR MP6069 perf mat rent (R733)

    Symphony No. 1, Op. 15 [18']
        3(pic).2.3(bass clar).2. 4.3.3.1.
        timp,2perc,strings
    GUNMAR MP6070 perf mat rent (R734)

    Symphony No. 2, Op. 32
        see Titans

    Titans (Symphony No. 2, Op. 32) [20']
        4.4(English horn).4(bass
        clar).4(contrabsn). 4.5.4.1.
        timp,2perc,harp,pno,strings
    sc PEER 61380-856 $30.00, perf mat
        rent   (R735)

    Variations On An American Theme
        *Op.40 [14']
        3(pic).2.2.2. 2+opt 2horn.3.3.1.
        timp,2perc,pno,strings
    GUNMAR MP6072 perf mat rent (R736)

RUTH see Waxman, Franz

RUTTER, JOHN
    Suite Antique, For Flute And String
        Orchestra [14']
        hpsd,strings,fl solo
    OXFORD perf mat rent   (R737)

RUY BLAS OVERTURE see Mendelssohn-
    Bartholdy, Felix

RUYNEMAN, DANIEL (1886-1963)
    Weise Von Liebe Und Tod Des Kornets
        Cristoph Rilke, Die, For Narrator
        And Orchestra [50']
        3.3.4.3. 3.2.3.1. timp,perc,harp,
        cel,strings,narrator
    sc DONEMUS f.s., perf mat rent
                                         (R738)
RUZICKA, PETER (1948-   )
    Abbruche [14']
        3.3.3.3. 4.3.3.1. timp,perc,harp,
        pno/cel,org/hpsd,elec gtr,
        strings
    study sc SIKORSKI f.s., perf mat
        rent   (R739)

    Annaherung Und Stille, For Piano And
        Strings [14']
        22vln,8vla,6vcl,6db,pno solo
    study sc SIKORSKI f.s., perf mat
        rent   (R740)

    "...Den Impuls Zum Weitersprechen
        Erst Empfinge", For Viola And
        Orchestra [14']
        2+alto fl.2+English horn.3.3.
        4.2.3.1. timp,2perc,harp,
        strings,vla solo
    sc UNIVER. UE17493 $31.00, perf mat
        rent   (R741)

    "...Der Die Gesange Zerschlug", For
        Solo Voice And Chamber Orchestra
        [20']
        1.0.1.0. 0.1.0.0. perc,harp,pno,
        strings,Bar solo
    SIKORSKI perf mat rent   (R742)

    Funf Bruchstucke [10']
        3.2.3.3. 4.3.3.1. timp,4perc,
        harp,cel/pno,strings
    study sc SIKORSKI f.s., perf mat
        rent   (R743)

    Satyagraha [10']
        3.2.3.3. 4.4.3.1. timp,4perc,
        strings
    study sc SIKORSKI f.s., perf mat
        rent   (R744)

RYBRANT, STIG
    Gambler, The
        see Hasardoren

    Hasardoren [7'40"]
        2(pic).2.2.2. 2.2.1.0. timp,perc,
        strings
    "Gambler, The" BUSCH HBM 031 perf
        mat rent   (R745)

    In A Happy Mood
        see Pa Gott Humor

    Pa Gott Humor [9'45"]
        2.2.2.2. 2.2.3.0. timp,perc,harp,
        strings
    "In A Happy Mood" BUSCH perf mat
        rent   (R746)

RYPDAL, TERJE (1947-   )
    Bla Folket, Det *Op.40 [22']
        2.1.0.1. 2.2.0.0. 2kbd,strings
    NORGE   (R747)

    Capriccio for String Orchestra
        string orch
    NORGE   (R748)

    Christmas Music For Strings
        see Julemusikk For Strykere

    Concerto for Piano and Orchestra
        [32']
        4.2.4.4. 6.4.4.1. timp,perc,
        strings,pno solo
    NORGE   (R749)

    Crystals, For Alto Flute And
        Orchestra
        see Krystaller, For Alto Flute And
        Orchestra

    Gilde, For Basset Clarinet And
        Orchestra [37']
    NORGE   (R750)

    Hulter Til Bulter, For Percussion And
        Orchestra
        2.2.2.4. 6.4.4.1. pno,
        synthesizer,perc solo
    NORGE   (R751)

    Julemusikk For Strykere [10']
        string orch,electronic tape
    "Christmas Music For Strings" NORGE
                                         (R752)

    Krystaller, For Alto Flute And
        Orchestra [22']
        bsn,harp,hpsd,strings,alto fl
        solo
    "Crystals, For Alto Flute And
        Orchestra" NORGE   (R753)

RYPDAL, TERJE (cont'd.)

Labyrinth [45']
    1(pic).1(English horn).1(bass
        clar).4(contrabsn).
    4.1(cornet).2.1. perc,pno,kbd,
        strings
    NORGE   (R754)

Shadows, For Oboe And Orchestra [16']
    4trom,perc,strings,ob solo
    NORGE   (R755)

Symphony No. 1 [44']
    1.1.1.1. 1.0.0.0. timp,perc,hpsd,
        harp,strings
    NORGE   (R756)

Symphony No. 2 [52']
    4.2.3.3. 6.5.4.2. timp,perc,elec
        gtr,elec bass,kbd,org,strings
    NORGE   (R757)

Symphony No. 4 [20']
    3.2.3.2. 5.4.2.0. perc,harp,elec
        pno,strings
    NORGE   (R758)

Symphony No. 4, Op. 35 [11']
    3.3.3.2. 5.4.2.0. perc,harp,elec
        pno,strings
    NORGE   (R759)

Telegram [18']
    1.1.1.1. 1.0.0.0. perc,kbd,
        strings
    NORGE   (R760)

Tumulter, For Percussion And
    Orchestra [14']
    1.2.2.1.soprano sax.baritone sax.
    1.1.4.2. Hamm,pno,strings,perc
        solo
    NORGE   (R761)

Undisonus, For Violin And Orchestra
    [19']
    4.0.3.2. 6.0.4.1. harp,strings,
        vln solo
    NORGE   (R762)

RYTMISKA STRAKBAGATELLER [ARR.] see
    Koch, Erland von

S

SAARIAHO, KAIJA (1952-   )
Du Cristal [18']
    4(pic,alto fl).3.3(clar in E
        flat)+bass clar(contrabass
        clar).2(contrabsn). 4.2.2.1.
        timp,4perc,harp,pno,strings,
        synthesizer
    HANSEN-FIN perf mat rent   (S1)

Io [18']
    2(pic,alto fl)+bass fl.0.0.0.
        2.0.1.1. 2perc,pno&cel,harp,
        2vln,vla,vcl,db
    HANSEN-DEN perf mat rent   (S2)

Verblendungen [14']
    1+alto
        fl(pic).1.1.1(contrabsn).sax.
        4.1.1.1. 2perc,harp,pno,
        strings,electronic tape
    HANSEN-DEN perf mat rent   (S3)

SAAT UND ERNTE POLKA see Strauss,
    Eduard

SABBAT DE SORCIERE, LE see Bajura,
    Keith V.A.

SABLES see Murail, Tristan

SACCHINI, ANTONIO (MARIA GASPARO
    GIOACCHINO) (1730-1786)
Sinfonia in D [14']
    2ob,2horn,strings
    BSE 136 perf mat rent   (S4)

Symphonies, Two
    see Brioschi, Antonio, Symphonies,
    Three

SACKMAN, NICHOLAS (1950-   )
Alap [20']
    2(pic)+alto fl.1.1+clar in E
        flat+bass clar.1+contrabsn.
        3.2(piccolo trp).2.1. timp,
        3perc,strings
    SCHOTT perf mat rent   (S5)

SACRE DU PRINTEMPS, LE see Stravinsky,
    Igor

SACRE DU PRINTEMPS, LE: DANSE SACRALE
    see Stravinsky, Igor

SACRED SELECTIONS FOR THE INSTRUMENTAL
    CHOIR *CC13L
    (McCoy, Floyd) SOUTHERN $3.50   (S6)

SACRED THEME, A see Helgason,
    Hallgrimur

SADHANA, FOR VIOLONCELLO AND ORCHESTRA
    see Creston, Paul

SADKO: MUSICAL PICTURES see Rimsky-
    Korsakov, Nikolai

SADLER, HELMUT (1921-   )
Toccatina Quasi Una Rhapsodia [10']
    1+pic.1+English horn.2.1+
        contrabsn. 4.2.3.0. timp,perc,
        strings
    BREITKOPF-W perf mat rent   (S7)

SADO see Shakidi, Tolib

SAEGUSA, SHIGEAKI (1942-   )
Symphony
    JAPAN 8402   (S8)

SAEVERUD, HARALD (1897-   )
Cinquanta Variazione Piccole *Op.9
    [5']
    2.2.2.1. 1.0.0.0. timp,strings
    NORSK perf mat rent   (S9)

Concerto for Bassoon and Orchestra,
    Op. 44 [19'30"]
    2.2.2.0. 2.2.0.0. timp,perc,
        strings,bsn solo
    sc MUSIKK f.s., perf mat rent   (S10)

Emperor And Galilean
    2.2.2.2. 2.2.1.0. timp,perc,harp,
        strings
    NORGE   (S11)

Ouvertura Monumentale *Op.53 [11']
    3.2.3.3. 4.3.2.1. timp,perc,harp,
        pno,cel,strings
    NORGE   (S12)

Symphony No. 4, Op. 11 [25']
    3.2.2.3. 4.3.3.1. timp,perc,harp,
        cel,pno,strings
    NORGE   (S13)

SAEVERUD, HARALD (cont'd.)

Symphony No. 9, Op. 45 [27']
    3.2(English horn).3.3. 4.3.3.1.
        timp,perc,harp,pno,strings
    MUSIKK perf mat rent   (S14)

Vade Mors *Op.38 [10']
    3.2.2.3. 4.4.3.1. timp,perc,
        strings
    NORGE   (S15)

SAGA, EN see Sibelius, Jean

SAGA SYMPHONY see Leifs, Jon

SAGAN see Hedwall, Lennart

SAGAN OM SNOVIT, FOR NARRATOR AND
    ORCHESTRA see Hallman, Bjorn

SAGUER, LOUIS (1907-   )
Flute Fuyant Le Sol A Perdre Haleine,
    Une, For Flute And Instrumental
    Ensemble [22']
    4perc,harp,strings,fl solo
    BILLAUDOT perf mat rent   (S16)

SAIKYO see Shimoyama, Hifumi

SAILING see Amdahl, Magne, Seiling

SAINT-GEORGES, CHEVALIER DE
    see SAINT-GEORGES, JOSEPH BOULOGNE DE

SAINT-GEORGES, JOSEPH BOULOGNE DE
    (1739-1799)
Ernestine: Duo, For Solo Voices And
    Orchestra [5']
    2ob,2bsn,2horn,strings,SS soli
    PEER perf mat rent   (S17)

Sinfonia Concertante for 2 Violins
    and Orchestra, Op. 6, No. 1, in C
    see Le Duc, Simon, Orchestral
    Trios, Op. 2, Nos. 2-3, and Trio-
    Divertimento, Op. 5, No. 3

Sinfonia Concertante for 2 Violins,
    Viola and Orchestra, Op. 10, No.
    2, in A
    see Le Duc, Simon, Orchestral
    Trios, Op. 2, Nos. 2-3, and Trio-
    Divertimento, Op. 5, No. 3

Symphony No. 1 in G [16']
    2ob,2horn,strings
    (Lerma, Dominique Rene De) PEER
    perf mat rent   (S18)

Symphony, Op. 11, No. 1, in G
    see Le Duc, Simon, Orchestral
    Trios, Op. 2, Nos. 2-3, and Trio-
    Divertimento, Op. 5, No. 3

SAINT KENTIGERN SUITE see Wilson,
    Thomas

ST. PATRICK'S DAY IN THE MORNING see
    Revolutionary Garland, A

SAINT-SAËNS, CAMILLE (1835-1921)
Allegro Appassionato, For Piano And
    Orchestra *Op.70
    KALMUS A4106 sc $12.00, set $15.00,
        perf mat rent   (S19)

Andromaque: Overture
    KALMUS A7268 sc $20.00, set $25.00,
        pts $1.25, ea., perf mat rent
                                    (S20)

Carnaval Des Animaux, Le
    "Carnival Of The Animals" sc KUNZEL
    10076 $17.00   (S21)

Carnival Of The Animals
    see Carnaval Des Animaux, Le

Concerto for Piano and Orchestra, No.
    4, Op. 44, in C minor
    min sc KALMUS K01394 $11.50   (S22)

Concerto for Piano and Orchestra, No.
    5, Op. 103, in F
    min sc KALMUS K01393 $11.50   (S23)

Concerto for Violin and Orchestra,
    No. 3, Op. 61, in B minor
    min sc KALMUS K01392 $8.00   (S24)

Concerto for Violoncello and
    Orchestra, No. 1, Op. 33, in A
    minor
    min sc KALMUS K01395 $8.75   (S25)
    *see GREAT ROMANTIC CELLO
    CONCERTOS

Havanaise, For Violin And Orchestra
    study sc DURAND $14.25   (S26)

Morceau De Concert, For Violin And
    Orchestra *Op.62
    KALMUS A5685 sc $20.00, set $15.00,
        perf mat rent   (S27)

SAINT-SAËNS, CAMILLE (cont'd.)

Muse Et Le Poete, La, For Violin,
Cello And Orchestra *Op.132
KALMUS A6994 sc $25.00, set $40.00,
pts $2.00, ea., perf mat rent
(S28)

Omphale's Spinning Wheel
see Rouet D'Omphale, Le

Orient Et Occident *Op.25
KALMUS A6777 sc $15.00, set $45.00,
pts $2.00, ea., perf mat rent
(S29)

Ouverture D'un Opera Comique Inacheve
"Overture To An Unfinished Comic
Opera" KALMUS A6746 sc $8.00, set
$18.00, pts $1.00, ea., perf mat
rent   (S30)

Overture To An Unfinished Comic Opera
see Ouverture D'un Opera Comique
Inacheve

Rapsodie Bretonne
KALMUS A6460 sc $12.00, set $40.00,
pts $2.00, perf mat rent   (S31)

Rouet D'Omphale, Le
"Omphale's Spinning Wheel" min sc
KALMUS K005538 $3.50   (S32)

Serenade
CHOUDENS perf mat rent   (S33)

Serenade for Orchestra [5']
2.0+English horn.2.0. 2.0.0.0.
harp/pno,strings
KALMUS A6993 sc $5.00, set $12.00,
pts $1.00, ea.   (S34)

Spartacus Overture [18']
2.2.2.2. 2.2.3.0. timp,perc,harp,
strings
sc BSE 576-00354 $30.00, perf mat
rent   (S35)

Suite in D [22']
2.2+English horn.2.2. 2.2.0.0.
timp,strings
sc BSE 65 f.s., perf mat rent   (S36)

Suite, Op. 49
KALMUS A5825 sc $20.00, set $35.00,
perf mat rent   (S37)

Timbre D'Argent, Le: Overture
2.2.2.2. 4.2.3.0. timp,perc,harp,
strings
CHOUDENS perf mat rent   (S38)

Timbre D'Argent, Le: Valse Venitienne
2.2.2.2. 4.2.3.0. timp,perc,harp,
strings
CHOUDENS perf mat rent   (S39)

SAISIR see Hedstrom, Åse

SAISON EN ENFER, UNE see Barraud, Henry

SAISON QUADRILLE see Strauss, Johann,
[Sr.]

SAISONS, LES see Barlow, Fred

SAJSAYHUAMAN see Alandia, Edgar

SAKUNTALA, FOR SOLO VOICE AND ORCHESTRA
see Delius, Frederick

SAKUNTALA OVERTURE see Goldmark, Karl

SALAMBO: ZWEI ORCHESTERSTÜCKE see
Tiessen, Heinz

SALAMINE: OVERTURE see Emmanuel,
Maurice

SALAMMBO: SUITE see Arends, H.

SALAMMBO'S ARIA see Herrmann, Bernard

SALAS, JUAN ORREGO
see ORREGO-SALAS, JUAN

SALIERI, ANTONIO (1750-1825)
Cifra, La: Overture [8']
2.2.2.2. 2.2.0.0. timp,strings
BSE perf mat rent   (S40)

Contredanse
(Fendler, Edvard) string orch [5']
BOOSEY perf mat rent   (S41)

Danaides, Les: Overture
2.2.2.2. 0.2.3.0. timp,strings
sc BSE 1177 f.s., perf mat rent
(S42)

Falstaff, Ossia Le Tre Burle:
Overture [8']
2.2.2.2. 4.2.0.0. timp,strings
BSE 114 perf mat rent   (S43)

Fiera Di Venezia, La: Sinfonia [4']
2.2.0.1. 2.0.0.0. strings
(McAlister) KALMUS A5994 sc $6.00,

SALIERI, ANTONIO (cont'd.)
set $12.00   (S44)

Grotta Di Trofonio, La: Sinfonia [7']
2.2.0.2. 0.2.0.0. strings
PETERS   (S45)

Horaces, Les: Overture [8']
2.2.2.2. 2.2.3.0. timp,strings
BSE 67 perf mat rent   (S46)

Locandiera, La: Overture [10']
2.2.2.2. 2.2.0.0. timp,strings
BSE 162 perf mat rent   (S47)

Palmira Regina Di Persia: Overture
[8']
2.2.2.2. 2.2.0.0. timp,strings
sc BSE 68 f.s., perf mat rent   (S48)

Scuola Di Gelosi, La: Overture
(McAlister) 2ob,2horn,strings [4']
KALMUS A5736 sc $8.00, set $10.00
(S49)

Semiramide: Overture [8']
2.2.2.2. 2.2.0.0. timp,strings
BSE 164 perf mat rent   (S50)

Sinfonia in D, MIN 2 [18']
2.2.2.2. 2.2.0.0. timp,strings
(giorno onomastico) sc BSE 70 f.s.,
perf mat rent   (S51)

Sinfonia in D, MIN 3 [15']
2ob,2horn,strings
(veneziana) sc BSE 69 f.s., perf
mat rent   (S52)

Talismano, Il: Overture [8']
2.2.2.2. 2.2.0.0. timp,strings
BSE 165 perf mat rent   (S53)

SALLINEN, AULIS (1935-   )
Chamber Music 1 *Op.38 [13']
string orch
study sc NOVELLO $12.25, perf mat
rent   (S54)

Chamber Music 2 *Op.41 [14']
alto fl,strings
NOVELLO perf mat rent   (S55)
sc NOVELLO 2939-90 $16.00   (S56)

Chamber Music 3, For Violoncello And
String Orchestra *Op.58
string orch,vcl solo
NOVELLO perf mat rent   (S57)

Concerto for Chamber Orchestra [22']
1(pic).1.1+bass clar.1. 1.0.0.0.
strings
sc NOVELLO 2948-90 $37.50, perf mat
rent   (S58)

Concerto for Violoncello and
Orchestra, Op. 44 [22']
2(pic).2.2(bass clar).2. 4.2.2.0.
timp,2perc,harp,cel,strings,vcl
solo
NOVELLO perf mat rent   (S59)

Shadows
3.3.3.3. 4.3.3.0. timp,perc,harp,
pno,strings
sc NOVELLO $20.75   (S60)

Symphony No. 1 [16']
3(pic).3.3(bass
clar).3(contrabsn). 4.3.3.0.
4perc,harp,strings
sc NOVELLO 2883-90 $20.75, perf mat
rent   (S61)

Symphony No. 2, Op. 29 [17']
2(pic).2.2(bass
clar).2(contrabsn). 4.3.2.1.
harp,strings,perc solo
sc NOVELLO $40.25, perf mat rent
(S62)

Symphony No. 5, Op. 57
study sc NOVELLO $41.00, perf mat
rent   (S63)

Variations for Orchestra [12']
2.2.2.2. 2.2.2.0. marimba,strings
sc NOVELLO $20.75, perf mat rent
(S64)

SALM see Cresswell, Lyell

SALMENHAARA, ERKKI (1941-   )
Concerto for Violoncello and
Orchestra [20']
2.2.2.2. 4.2.3.0. timp,perc,
strings,vcl solo
sc SUOMEN f.s.   (S65)

Poem for Violin and String Orchestra
string orch,vln solo
sc FAZER $15.00   (S66)

SALOMA see Osterc, Slavko

SALOME: DANCES see Davies, Peter
Maxwell

SALOME FANTASY [ARR.] see Strauss,
Richard

SALONEN, ESA-PEKKA (1958-   )
Concerto for Alto Saxophone and
Orchestra [18']
3(pic).3(English horn).3(bass
clar).3. 4.3.3.1. 4perc,pno&
cel,harp,strings,alto sax solo
HANSEN-DEN perf mat rent   (S67)

Giro [7']
2.2(English horn).2.2. 4.2.2.0.
perc,pno,strings
HANSEN-DEN perf mat rent   (S68)

SALTARELLE ET LIED, FOR VIOLONCELLO AND
INSTRUMENTAL ENSEMBLE see Guinand,
Jules

SALTIMBANQUES, LES: BALLET MUSIC see
Ganne, (Gustave) Louis

SALTIMBANQUES, LES: OVERTURE see Ganne,
(Gustave) Louis

SALUS...ESTO see Milburn, Ellsworth

SALUSTIA: SINFONIA see Pergolesi,
Giovanni Battista

SALUT see Kucera, Václav

SALUT D'AMOUR [ARR.] see Elgar, [Sir]
Edward (William)

SALVA, TADEAS (1937-   )
Symfonia Pastoralis In E, For English
Horn And Orchestra
trp,timp,org,strings,English horn
solo
SLOV.HUD.FOND   (S69)

SALVESEN, THOMAS (1915-   )
Fughetta A Quaterni Voci *Op.18
2.2.1.1. 2.0.0.0. 2vln,vla,2vcl,
db
NORGE   (S70)

SALZEDO, LEONARD (LOPES)
Witch Boy, The: Square Dance [arr.]
(Dexter, Harry) 2.1.2.1. 2.3.0.0.
perc,harp,strings [4'] CHESTER
perf mat rent   (S71)

Witch Boy, The: Suite [19']
2(pic).2.2.2. 4.3.3.1. timp,perc,
harp,pno,strings
CHESTER perf mat rent   (S72)

Witch Boy, The: Three Dances [12']
2(pic).2.2.2. 4.3.3.1. timp,perc,
harp,pno,strings
CHESTER perf mat rent   (S73)

SAM: ORCHESTRAL VERSION see McCabe,
John

SAMAMA, LEO (1951-   )
Afterthoughts *Op.22 [12']
2.2.2.2. 2.2.0.0. 2perc,strings
DONEMUS perf mat rent   (S74)

Against Odds *Op.35 [13']
2.2.2.2. 4.2.3.1. 4perc,strings
sc DONEMUS f.s., perf mat rent
(S75)

Concertino for Strings, Op. 29 [12']
string orch
DONEMUS perf mat rent   (S76)

Monumentum Pro Caecilia, For
Harpsichord And String Orchestra
*Op.23 [15']
string orch,hpsd solo
DONEMUS perf mat rent   (S77)

San Yueh *Op.26 [9']
2.2.2.2. 4.2.3.1. 5perc,harp,
strings
DONEMUS perf mat rent   (S78)

Zefiro *Op.34 [19']
2ob,2horn,strings
sc DONEMUS f.s., perf mat rent
(S79)

SAMBA CLASSICO, FOR SOLO VOICE AND
ORCHESTRA see Villa-Lobos, Heitor

SAMINSKY, LAZARE (1882-1959)
Symphony No. 3, Op. 30
sc UNIVER. 8644 f.s.   (S80)

SAMISK OUVERTURE see Strömholm, Folke

SAMKOPF, KJELL (1952-   )
Overture [11']
3.2.3.2. 4.3.3.0. timp,perc,
strings
NORGE   (S81)

SAMMARTINI, GIOVANNI BATTISTA
(1701-1775)
Concertino in G, J-C 83
(Jenkins) KALMUS A6342 sc $5.00,
set $5.00, pts $1.00, ea., perf

SAMMARTINI, GIOVANNI BATTISTA (cont'd.)

   mat rent   (S82)

  Concerto, For Oboe And String
    Orchestra [arr.]
    (Jenkins, N.) string orch,hpsd,ob/
    fl solo SCHIRM.G perf mat rent
                  (S83)

  Sinfonia in C, J-C 2
    (Torrefranca) KALMUS A7455 sc
    $7.00, set $18.00, pts $1.50,
    ea., perf mat rent   (S84)

  Sinfonia in C, J-C 4
    (Bonelli) KALMUS A7442 sc $7.00,
    set $12.00, pts $1.50, ea. (S85)

  Sinfonia in F, J-C 32
    (Jenkins) KALMUS A6341 sc $4.00,
    set $5.00, pts $1.00, ea., perf
    mat rent   (S86)

  Symphonies, Ten
    (Churgin, Bathia) sc GARLAND
    ISBN 0-8240-3853-3 $90.00 "The
    Symphony" Vol. A-II   (S87)

SAMMARTINI, GIUSEPPE
  (ca. 1693-ca. 1770)
  Aria, [arr.] (from Sonata, Op. 3, No.
    9)
    (Gui) string orch sc UNIVER. 8508
    f.s.   (S88)

  Concerti Grossi, Op. 2, Nos. 1, 2, 3,
    5 *see THREE CENTURIES OF MUSIC
    IN SCORE, VOL. 2: CONCERTO I,
    ITALY

  Concerti, Op. 9. Four *see THREE
    CENTURIES OF MUSIC IN SCORE, VOL.
    2: CONCERTO I, ITALY

  Concerto for Recorder and String
    Orchestra in F, MIN 204
    string orch,S rec solo
    (Michel) sc,pts AMADEUS BP 2414
    f.s.   (S89)

SAMORI, AURELIO (1946-)
  Variations for Orchestra [15'30"]
    2.2.2.2. 2.2.0.0. perc,14vln,
    6vla,4vcl,2db
    RICORDI-IT 134211 perf mat rent
                  (S90)

SAMSON: WITH PLAINTIVE NOTES, FOR SOLO
  VOICE AND ORCHESTRA see Handel,
  George Frideric

SÄMTLICHE KONZERTE see Brahms,
  Johannes, Complete Concerti

SAMTLICHE SYMPHONIEN see Brahms,
  Johannes, Symphonies, Nos. 1-4

SAMUEL, GERHARD (1924-)
  Agam [24']
    2.2.2.2(contrabsn). 2.2.3.1.
    timp,2perc,harp,strings
    MMB perf mat rent   (S91)

  And Marsyas, For Solo Voice And
    Instrumental Ensemble [22']
    fl,ob,clar,2perc,pno,harp,vln,
    vla,vcl,Mez solo
    MMB perf mat rent   (S92)

  Apollo & Hyacinth [13']
    1(pic).1.1.1. 1.0.0.0. 2perc,pno,
    harp,2vln,vla,vcl,db
    MMB perf mat rent   (S93)

  As Imperceptibly As Grief, For
    Percussion And Orchestra [14']
    2(pic,alto fl).2.2(bass
    clar).2(contrabsn). 2.0.0.0.
    timp,strings,3perc soli
    MMB perf mat rent   (S94)

  Beyond McBean, For Violin And Chamber
    Orchestra [12']
    1.1.1.1. 1.1.1.0. 2perc,hpsd,
    harp,vla,vcl,db,vln solo
    MMB perf mat rent   (S95)

  Chamber Concerto In The Shape Of A
    Summer, For Flute And Chamber
    Orchestra [16']
    3perc,strings,fl solo
    MMB perf mat rent   (S96)

  Cold When The Drum Sounds For Dawn
    [16']
    1(pic,alto fl).2(English
    horn).0.1. 2.0.0.0. 2perc,hpsd,
    cel,strings
    MMB perf mat rent   (S97)

  Concerto for Violin, Viola and
    Orchestra [28']
    3(pic).3(English horn).3(bass
    clar).3(contrabsn). 4.2.3.1.
    timp,2perc,strings,vln solo,vla
    solo
    MMB perf mat rent   (S98)

SAMUEL, GERHARD (cont'd.)
  Into Flight From [13']
    3(pic).3.3.3. 4.3.3.1. timp,
    4perc,strings, elec kbd
    MMB perf mat rent   (S99)

  Looking At Orpheus Looking [16']
    4.4.4.4. 4.4.3.1. 3perc,elec org,
    harp,strings, elec hpsd
    MMB perf mat rent   (S100)

  On A Dream, For Viola And Orchestra
    [20']
    1.2.1.2. 2.0.0.0. perc,strings,
    vla solo
    MMB perf mat rent   (S101)

  Out Of Time [16']
    3(pic,alto fl).3(English
    horn).3(clar in E flat,bass
    clar).3(contrabsn).alto sax.
    4.3.3.1. timp,4perc,2harp,
    strings
    MMB perf mat rent   (S102)

  Requiem For Survivors [18']
    4(pic).4.4(bass
    clar).4(contrabsn).tenor sax.
    0.4.3.1. timp,5perc,harp,
    strings
    MMB perf mat rent   (S103)

  Sun-Like, For Solo Voice And
    Instrumental Ensemble [18']
    soprano sax,alto sax,tenor sax,
    perc,pno,cel,2vln,vla,vcl,Mez
    solo
    MMB perf mat rent   (S104)

  Three Minor Desperations, For Solo
    Voice And Orchestra [17']
    1.2.2.1. 1.1.1.1. 3perc,harp,
    strings,Mez solo
    MMB perf mat rent   (S105)

  Traumbild, For Solo Voices And
    Orchestra [20']
    1(pic).1.1.1. 1.1.1.0. 2perc,cel,
    strings,ST soli
    MMB perf mat rent   (S106)

  Twelve On Death And No, For Solo
    Voice And Orchestra [10']
    1(pic).1.1.1. 1.1.1.0. timp,perc,
    strings,T solo
    MMB perf mat rent   (S107)

SAMUEL-ROUSSEAU
  see ROUSSEAU, MARCEL

SAN MIGUEL, FOR SOLO VOICE AND
  ORCHESTRA see Quaranta, Felice

SAN YUEH see Samama, Leo

SANCAN, PIERRE (1916-)
  Fourmis, Les: Suite [30']
    2(pic).2+English horn.2+bass
    clar.2+contrabsn. 3.4.2.1.
    perc,pno,Ondes Martenot,2harp,
    strings
    RIDEAU perf mat rent   (S108)

  Rhapsody for Trumpet and Orchestra
    [10']
    2(pic).2.2.2. 0.2.0.1. timp,perc,
    strings,trp solo
    RIDEAU perf mat rent   (S109)

SANCTORUM MERITIS, FOR SOLO VOICE AND
  STRING ORCHESTRA see Vivaldi,
  Antonio

SANCTUARY see Laderman, Ezra

SAND see Howe, Mary

SAND VENDOR PASSING BY, THE see
  Roussel, Albert (Charles Paul),
  Marchand De Sable Qui Passe, Le

SANDBY, HERMAN (1881-1965)
  Icelandic Folk Song [3']
    harp,strings
    HANSEN-DEN perf mat rent   (S110)

  Nordic Rhapsody [16']
    2.2+English horn.2.2. 4.2.3.1.
    timp,strings
    HANSEN-DEN perf mat rent   (S111)

  Pastorale d'Automne [6']
    3(pic).2(English horn).3(bass
    clar).2+contrabsn. 4.3.3.1.
    timp,cel,harp,strings
    HANSEN-DEN perf mat rent   (S112)

  Valravnen [3']
    harp,strings
    HANSEN-DEN perf mat rent   (S113)

SANDI, LUIS (1905-)
  Bonampak: Suite
    3(pic).2.2.0. 3.3.2.1. timp,perc,
    strings
    min sc PEER MUSIK 61343-856 $8.00,
    perf mat rent   (S114)

  Sinfonia Minima
    string orch
    LIGA   (S115)

SANDPOINT RAG see Schuller, Gunther

SANDSKORNETS TOPOLOGI see Norholm, Ib

SANDSTRÖM, JAN (1954-)
  Acintyas [13']
    string orch
    NORDISKA perf mat rent   (S116)

  Concerto for Trumpet and Orchestra
    [23']
    3.2.2.3. 2.2.1.0. perc,strings,
    trp solo
    NORDISKA perf mat rent   (S117)

  Formant Mirrors, For Solo Voice And
    Orchestra [12']
    fl&alto fl,clar&bass clar,
    strings,S solo
    STIM   (S118)

  Indri. Cave Canem [8']
    3.2.2.3. 4.3.3.1. timp,4perc,pno/
    xylo,strings
    STIM   (S119)

SANDSTRÖM, SVEN-DAVID (1942-)
  A Day - The Days [35']
    4.4.4.4. 4.4.4.0. timp,4perc,
    harp,pno,strings
    STIM   (S120)

  Agitato, For Piano And Orchestra
    [17']
    2.2.2.2. 2.2.2.1. timp,perc,harp,
    strings,pno solo
    NORDISKA perf mat rent   (S121)

  And All The Flavours Around [11']
    fl,clar,vln,pno, and variable
    symphonic instrumentation
    NORDISKA perf mat rent   (S122)

  Concerto for Alto Saxophone and
    Orchestra [23']
    2.2.2.2. 4.2.2.0. timp,perc,harp,
    strings,alto sax solo
    NORDISKA perf mat rent   (S123)

  Concerto for Flute and Orchestra
    [18']
    0.1.1.1. 1.1.1.0. timp,strings,fl
    solo
    NORDISKA perf mat rent   (S124)

  Culminations [13']
    2.2.2.2. 2.2.2.0. perc,harp,pno,
    strings
    sc NORDISKA $57.75, perf mat rent
                  (S125)

  In The Meantime [10']
    1.1.2.1. 1.1.1.0. perc,2pno,harp,
    timp,strings
    NORDISKA perf mat rent   (S126)

  Nimrud [26']
    2.2.2.2. 3.3.3.0. pno,harp,
    strings
    NORDISKA perf mat rent   (S127)

  Overture [6']
    3.3.3.2. 4.3.4.1. timp,perc,
    strings
    NORDISKA perf mat rent   (S128)

  Sounds From 14 Strings [7']
    string orch
    NORDISKA perf mat rent   (S129)

  Through And Through [20']
    4.4.4.4. 6.4.4.1. timp,perc,
    strings
    sc NORDISKA f.s., perf mat rent
                  (S130)

SANG FOR ORKESTER see Mostad, Jon

SANG VIENNOIS [ARR.] see Strauss,
  Johann, [Sr.]

SANGER AV LJUS see Lindgren, Pär

SANJUAN, PEDRO (1886-1976)
  Castilla [23']
    3.3.3.3.sax. 4.3.3.1. timp,perc,
    cel,2harp,strings
    ESCHIG perf mat rent   (S131)

  Danse Rituelle [15']
    3.3.3.3. 4.3.3.1. perc,harp,
    strings
    ESCHIG perf mat rent   (S132)

  Lirica Y Ritmica
    3.3.3.3. 4.3.3.1. perc,harp,
    strings

SANJUAN, PEDRO (cont'd.)

ESCHIG perf mat rent   (S133)

Rondo Fantastico [5']
3.3.2.2. 4.3.3.1. timp,perc,
strings
ESCHIG perf mat rent   (S134)

Sons De Castilla [23']
2.1.1.1. 0.2.2.0. pno,strings
ESCHIG perf mat rent   (S135)

SANKEY, STUART
Concerto for Double Bass and
Orchestra [28']
INTERNAT. perf mat rent   (S136)

"...SANS BRUIT..." see Rosen, Robert

SANTA CLAUS OVERTURE see Shelley, Harry
Rowe see Smith, Leland C.

SANTA ESPINA, FOR SOLO VOICE AND
ORCHESTRA see Flothuis, Marius

SANTA GENOVIEFA: SINFONIA see Leo,
Leonardo (Ortensio Salvatore de)

SANTANA see Sitsky, Larry

SANTIAGO, RODRIGO DE (1907-   )
Coordenadas Informales [10'15"]
fl,ob,clar,bsn,horn,strings
sc ALPUERTO f.s.   (S137)

SAO PAULO see Prado, José-Antonio
(Almeida)

SAPPHIRE SEESAW see Le Siege, Annette

SAPPHO see Goldmark, Karl

SAPPHO: LYRICAL FRAGMENTS, FOR SOLO
VOICES AND STRING ORCHESTRA see
Tavener, John

SAPPHO: OVERTURE see Reicha, Anton

SARABANDE AND CHACONNE [ARR.] see
Couperin, Louis

SARABANDE DU XVIE SIECLE see Massenet,
Jules

SARABANDE SUR LE NOM D'ERIK SATIE see
Jolivet, Andre

SARACENS, THE: TWO FRAGMENTS see
MacDowell, Edward Alexander

SARAI, TIBOR (1919-   )
Epitaffio In Memoriam Szabó Ferenc
sc EMB 10197 f.s.   (S138)

Notturno
sc EMB 10236 f.s.   (S139)

SARASATE, PABLO DE (1844-1908)
Fantasy On "Carmen" By Bizet, For
Violin And Orchestra
CHOUDENS perf mat rent   (S140)

Navarra, For Two Violins And
Orchestra *Op.33
KALMUS A6793 sc $15.00, set $20.00,
pts $1.00, ea., perf mat rent
(S141)
Peteneras, For Violin And Orchestra
*Op.35
2.2.2.2. 2.2.3.0. timp,perc,
strings,vln solo
SIMROCK perf mat rent   (S142)

Zapateado, For Violoncello And String
Orchestra [arr.]
(Thomas-Mifune) string orch,vcl
solo sc,pts KUNZEL GM 1182 f.s.
(S143)

SARATOGA CONCERTO, FOR GUITAR AND
ORCHESTRA see Josephs, Wilfred

SARATOGA VICTORY MARCH see Brillon De
Jouy, Anne Louise D'Hardancourt

SARDANA see Balada, Leonardo

SAREK, FOR VIOLIN AND STRING ORCHESTRA
see Bjorklund, Terje

SARMIENTOS, JORGE (1931-   )
Diferencias, For Violoncello And
Orchestra [20']
3(pic).3(English horn).3(bass
clar).3(contrabsn). 4.4.4.1.
perc,strings,vcl solo
PEER perf mat rent   (S144)

Responso, Hommage No. 2
3+pic.3+English horn.4.2+
contrabsn. 4.4.3.1. timp,perc,
2harp,pno,cel,strings
TONOS   (S145)

SARON, THOMAS
Music for Flute and Chamber Orchestra
[8']
clar,trp,perc,pno,strings,fl solo
RIES   (S146)

SARRO, DOMENICO (SARRI) (1679-1744)
Partenope, La: Overture [2'30"]
2ob,strings
(Blanchard, R.) BOIS perf mat rent
(S147)

Sonata in A minor
fl,hpsd,strings
(Meylan, R.) sc,pts LEUCKART AM 36
f.s.   (S148)

SARY, LASZLO (1940-   )
Concerto Classico
sc EMB 12547 f.s.   (S149)

Diana's Farewell
8vln,8vla
sc EMB 8762 f.s.   (S150)

Immaginario
sc EMB 10152 f.s.   (S151)

Music for 24 Strings and 24 Winds
24strings,24winds
sc EMB 10231 f.s.   (S152)

Parallel Movements
sc EMB 13000 f.s., perf mat rent
(S153)

SATANELLA POLKA see Strauss, Johann,
[Jr.]

SATIE, ERIK (1866-1925)
Aventures De Mercure [arr.]
(Birtwistle, Harrison) 1(pic,alto
fl).1(English horn).1(bass
clar).1(contrabsn). 1.1.1.0.
perc,pno,string quin [17']
UNIVER. perf mat rent   (S154)

Belle Excentrique, La [13']
1.1.1.1. 1.1.1.0. perc,pno,
strings
ESCHIG perf mat rent   (S155)

Carnet De Croquis [arr.]
(Caby, Robert) 2.2.1+clar in A.2.
0.0.0.0. perc,strings SALABERT
perf mat rent   (S156)

Deux Sketches Montmartrois [arr.]
(Caby, Robert) 1.0.1.1. 0.1.1.1.
perc,strings SALABERT perf mat
rent   (S157)

Gymnopedie No. 2 [arr.]
(Gagneux, Renaud) 2.0.2.2. 4.0.0.0.
harp,strings [4'] SALABERT perf
mat rent   (S158)

Je Te Veux [arr.]
(Benzi, Roberto) 2.2.2.2. 4.3.3.1.
timp,perc,harp,cel,strings [5']
SALABERT perf mat rent   (S159)

Messe Des Pauvres [arr.]
(Constant, Marius) 1.0.1+bass
clar.1. 1.1.1.0. 2perc,pno,harp,
vln,vcl [8'] SALABERT perf mat
rent   (S160)

Prelude De La Porte Heroique Du Ciel
[arr.]
(Manuel, R.) 3.2+English horn.2.3.
4.3.2.1. timp,cym,2harp,cel,
strings [4'] SALABERT perf mat
rent   (S161)

Reverie Du Pauvre [arr.]
(Caby, Robert) string orch [4']
SALABERT perf mat rent   (S162)

Socrate, For Solo Voice And Orchestra
[25']
1.2.1.1. 1.1.0.0. timp,harp,
strings,solo voice
study sc ESCHIG f.s., perf mat rent
(S163)

Sports Et Divertissements [arr.]
(Miereanu, Costin; Ratiu, Horia)
3(pic).1.2(clar in E flat,bass
clar).1.alto sax.tenor sax.
2.2.2.0. perc,cel,2gtr,acord,
harp,strings, saxhorn, saw,
spinet [25'] sc SALABERT f.s.,
perf mat rent   (S164)

Tendrement [3']
1.1.2.1. 2.2(cornet).2.0. perc,
strings
SALABERT perf mat rent   (S165)

Trois Petites Pieces Montees [3']
1.1.1.1. 1.2.1.0. perc,strings
study sc ESCHIG f.s., perf mat rent
(S166)

SATIRES, FOR SOLO VOICE AND ORCHESTRA
[ARR.] see Shostakovich, Dmitri

SATIRO, FOR PIANO AND ORCHESTRA see
Becker, John Joseph

SATO, KIMI (1949-   )
Bleu Du Ciel, Le [11']
7vln,2vla,2vcl,db
sc JAPAN 8009 f.s.   (S167)

SATO, TOSHINAO (1936-   )
Three Compositions For Orchestra
[23']
3(pic).3(English horn).3(bass
clar).3(contrabsn). 4.3.3.1.
timp,perc,harp,pno,strings
sc ZEN-ON 899460 f.s., perf mat
rent   (S168)

SATOH, SHIN (1938-   )
Concerto for Orchestra
JAPAN 8901 perf mat rent   (S169)

Concerto for Piano and Orchestra
[20']
3(pic).2.2.2(contrabsn). 4.3.3.1.
timp,perc,harp,strings,pno solo
sc ZEN-ON f.s., perf mat rent
(S170)

Symphony No. 3 [20']
4(pic).4(English horn).4(clar in
E flat).4(contrabsn). 4.4.4.1.
perc,strings
sc ZEN-ON 899220 f.s., perf mat
rent   (S171)

SATURDAY NIGHT BARN DANCE: BOY'S NIGHT
OUT see Kunz, Alfred

SATURN see Roxburgh, Edwin

SATYAGRAHA see Ruzicka, Peter

SAUDADES, FOR SOLO VOICE AND CHAMBER
ORCHESTRA see Legido, Jesus

SAUGUET, HENRI (1901-1989)
Melodie Concertante, For Violoncello
And Orchestra [25']
2.2.2.2. 2.2.1.0. timp,perc,harp,
strings,vcl solo
SIKORSKI perf mat rent   (S172)

Sonata D'Eglise, For Organ And String
Orchestra [26']
string orch,org solo
study sc ESCHIG f.s., perf mat rent
(S173)

SAUL, WALTER (1954-   )
From Life To Greater Life [10']
2(pic).2(English
horn).2.2(contrabsn). 4.3.3.1.
timp&triangle,harp,strings
MMB perf mat rent   (S174)

Metamorphosis, For Piano And
Orchestra [20']
3(pic).3.3.2+contrabsn. 4.3.3.1.
timp,perc,harp,pno solo
MMB perf mat rent   (S175)

SAUL: OVERTURE see Handel, George
Frideric

SAUNTERER, THE see Lunden-Welden,
Gunnar, Kvallsflanoren

SAVERY, FINN (1933-   )
Shunting In A Peaceful Morning
20strings
SAMFUNDET perf mat rent   (S176)

SAXE, SERGE
Poema Sinfonico Para Cuerdas
string orch
"Symphonic Poem For Strings" sc
PEER MUSIK 60923-766 $6.00 (S177)

Symphonic Poem For Strings
see Poema Sinfonico Para Cuerdas

SAXTON, ROBERT (1953-   )
Birthday Music For RRB [2']
string orch
CHESTER perf mat rent   (S178)

Choruses To Apollo [9']
2.2+English horn.2.1.alto sax.
4.2.1.1. 3perc,cel,pno,2harp,
strings
CHESTER perf mat rent   (S179)

Circles Of Light [19']
1.1.1.1. 1.1.1.0. perc,pno,string
quar,db
CHESTER CH709 perf mat rent   (S180)

Concerto for Orchestra [17']
3(alto fl).3(English horn).3(bass
clar).3(contrabsn). 4.3.3.1.
timp,perc,harp,cel,2harp,strings
CHESTER perf mat rent   (S181)

Concerto for Viola and Orchestra
[17']
2(pic).2(English horn).2(bass
clar).2(contrabsn). 2.2.0.0.
perc,pno,strings,vla solo

SAXTON, ROBERT (cont'd.)

CHESTER perf mat rent   (S182)

Concerto for Violin and Orchestra
[22']
2(pic).2.2.2. 4.3.3.1. timp,
2perc,strings,vln solo
CHESTER perf mat rent   (S183)

Elijah's Violin [21']
1(pic).2(English horn).0.2.
2.0.0.0. 7vln,2vla,2vcl,db
CHESTER perf mat rent   (S184)

In The Beginning [17']
2(pic).2(English horn).2(clar in
E flat,bass clar).2(contrabsn).
4.3.3.1. timp,2perc,strings
CHESTER perf mat rent   (S185)

Music To Celebrate The Resurrection
Of Christ [10']
2.2.2.2. 1.1.1.0. timp,2perc,
8vln,3vla,3vcl,2db
CHESTER perf mat rent   (S186)

Reflections Of Narziss And Goldmund
[12']
1(alto fl).1.1.0.alto sax.
1.1.1.0. harp,pno&cel,2vla,vcl,
db
sc CHESTER JWC443 f.s., perf mat
rent   (S187)

Ring Of Eternity, The [14']
2(pic).2(English horn).2(clar in
E flat).2. 2.2.0.0. perc,pno&
cel,strings
CHESTER perf mat rent   (S188)

Traumstadt [13']
2.2.2.2. 2.2.1.0. perc,2vln,vla,
vcl,db
CHESTER perf mat rent   (S189)

Variation On "Sumer Is A' Cumin In"
[6']
2.2.2.2. 2.2.0.0. timp,harp,
strings
CHESTER perf mat rent   (S190)

SAYGUN, AHMED ADNAN (1907-   )
Concerto for Violin and Orchestra
[32']
2.2.2.2. 4.3.3.0. timp,perc,harp,
strings,vln solo
PEER perf mat rent   (S191)

SAYONARA: KATSUMI see Waxman, Franz

SBORDONI, ALESSANDRO (1948-   )
Geste Et Le Symbole, Le [9']
2.2.2.2. 2.2.0.0. 2perc,strings
RICORDI-IT 133335 perf mat rent
(S192)
Ombre Riflesse, Le, For Piano And
Orchestra
4.4.4.4. 4.3.3.1. timp,bass drum,
vibra,strings,pno solo
RICORDI-IT 134064 perf mat rent
(S193)

SCALA DI SETA, LA: OVERTURE see
Rossini, Gioacchino

SCANDINAVIAN DANCE see Koch, Erland
von, Scandinavische Tanze

SCANDINAVISCHE TANZE see Koch, Erland
von

SCARLATTI, ALESSANDRO (1660-1725)
Concerto Grosso in F minor [9']
strings,hpsd
(Schering) KAHNT KT 8991 f.s.
(S194)
Concerto Grosso, No. 1, in F minor
(Schering) KALMUS A7417 sc $6.00,
set $9.00, pts $1.50, ea.   (S195)
Concerto Grosso, No. 3, in F
(Napolitano) KALMUS A7438 sc $7.00,
set $10.00, pts $1.50, ea. (S196)
Duetto (Musique De Scene) [2']
2ob,hpsd,strings
(Blanchard, R.) BOIS perf mat rent
(S197)
Piccola Suite
(Napolitano) set KALMUS A7439
$20.00, and up   (S198)
Serenade for Solo Voice and String
Orchestra [18']
string orch,cont,T/S solo
(Blanchard, R.) sc BOIS f.s., perf
mat rent   (S199)
Sonate A 4, Two *see THREE CENTURIES
OF MUSIC IN SCORE, VOL. 2:
CONCERTO I, ITALY

Su Le Sponde Del Tebro, For Solo
Voice And Orchestra
(Paumgartner) trp,strings without
vla,solo voice [18'] KALMUS A7318

SCARLATTI, ALESSANDRO (cont'd.)
sc $7.00, set $7.50, pts $1.50,
ea.   (S200)

SCARLATTI, DOMENICO (1685-1757)
Concertino for Oboe and String
Orchestra in G
(Thilde, J.) string orch,ob solo
[7'10"] BILLAUDOT perf mat rent
(S201)
Concerto for Oboe and String
Orchestra in C
(Thilde, J.) string orch,ob solo
[7'35"] BILLAUDOT perf mat rent
(S202)
Five Sonatas In The Form Of A Suite
[arr.]
(Bonelli) string orch [13'] KALMUS
A7441 sc $10.00, set $12.50, pts
$2.50, ea.   (S203)
Heure Galante, L' [arr.]
(Ward, Lionel) 2.2.2.2. 2.1.1.0.
strings [10'] BOOSEY perf mat
rent   (S204)
Marcia E Fandango [arr.]
(McAlister) 2(2pic).1+2English
horn.2.2. 2.2.0.0. timp,perc,
strings [7'] (in this edition,
Sonatas nos. 1 and 2) KALMUS
A6178 sc $12.00, set $20.00, perf
mat rent   (S205)
Pastorale, [arr.]
(McAlister) 2(pic).2+English
horn.2.2. 2.2.0.0. timp,perc,
strings [5'] (in this edition,
Sonata no. 3) KALMUS A6179 sc
$10.00, set $18.00, perf mat rent
(S206)
Scherzo, Pastorale E Capriccio [arr.]
(McAlister) 2(pic).2.2.2. 2.2.0.0.
timp,perc,strings [9'30"] (in
this edition, Sonatas nos. 4-6)
KALMUS A6180 sc $15.00, set
$18.00, perf mat rent   (S207)
Sonatas Nos. 380, 423, 518, 401, 69
[arr.]
(Jevtic, I.) string orch,piccolo
trp solo [16'] BILLAUDOT perf mat
rent   (S208)
Three Pieces [arr.]
(Roland-Manuel) 2.2.2.2. 2.2.0.0.
timp,harp,strings [11'] KALMUS
A6136 sc $10.00, set $18.00, perf
mat rent   (S209)
Toccata, Bourree Et Gigue [arr.]
(Casella) KALMUS A3896 sc $12.00,
set $30.00, perf mat rent   (S210)

SCARLATTI, FRANCESCO ANTONIO NICOLA
(ca. 1666-1741)
Tolomeo E Alessandro: Sinfonia [3']
string orch,hpsd
(Blanchard, R.) BOIS perf mat rent
(S211)

SCATOLA see Birnstein, Renate M.

SCELSI, GIACINTO (1905-1988)
Aion, For Timpani, Percussion And
Orchestra [19']
0.2+English horn.2+bass clar.2+
contrabsn. 6.3.4.4. harp,4vcl,
4db,timp solo,6perc soli
SALABERT perf mat rent   (S212)
Anagamin [6']
12strings
SALABERT perf mat rent   (S213)
Anahit, For Violin And Instrumental
Ensemble
2+bass fl.0+English horn.1+bass
clar.0.tenor sax. 2.1.2.0. 2vla,
2vcl,2db,vln solo SALABERT perf
mat rent   (S214)
Chukrum [14']
string orch
SALABERT perf mat rent   (S215)
Hurqualia, For Timpani, Percussion
And Orchestra [6']
2+pic.2.2+bass clar.2. 4.3.2.1+db
tuba. strings without vln,timp
solo,4perc soli, additional
amplified instruments: ob, eng
h, e-flat clar, horn, ten-sax,
vla, db, 2trp, trb, saw
SALABERT perf mat rent   (S216)
Hymnos, For Organ And Orchestra [10']
2+pic.2+English horn.2+bass
clar.3. 6.4.4.2. timp,2perc,
strings,org solo
SALABERT perf mat rent   (S217)
Natura Renovatur [10'30"]
11strings
SALABERT perf mat rent   (S218)

SCELSI, GIACINTO (cont'd.)
Ohoi [7']
16strings
SALABERT perf mat rent   (S219)
Pranam I, For Solo Voice And
Instrumental Ensemble [7'30"]
1.0+English horn.1.1.alto sax.
1.1.1.0. 2vln,vla,vcl,
electronic tape,solo voice
SALABERT perf mat rent   (S220)
Quattro Pezzi [13'30"]
0+alto fl.1+English horn.2+bass
clar.1.sax. 4.3.2.1. timp,perc,
2vla,2vcl,db
SALABERT 018-03467 perf mat rent
(S221)

SCENA CAMPESTRE see Ponchielli,
Amilcare

SCENE see Gillet, Bruno

SCENE, FOR VIOLONCELLO AND STRING
ORCHESTRA see Takemitsu, Toru

SCENE, LA see Monnet, Marc

SCENE SINFONICHE PER IL DOKTOR FAUSTUS
see Manzoni, Giacomo

SCENES, FOR VIOLONCELLO AND ORCHESTRA
see Lambij, Ton

SCENES AND INTERLUDES, FOR TRUMPET,
HARPSICHORD AND STRING ORCHESTRA
see Hoddinott, Alun

SCENES AT THE FAIR see Shleg, L.

SCENES DE BALLET NO. 1: PREAMBLE see
Glazunov, Alexander Konstantinovich

SCENES DE BALLET NO. 2: MARIONETTES see
Glazunov, Alexander Konstantinovich

SCENES DE BALLET NO. 3: MAZURKA see
Glazunov, Alexander Konstantinovich

SCENES DE BALLET NO. 4: SCHERZINE see
Glazunov, Alexander Konstantinovich

SCENES DE BALLET NO. 5: PAS D'ACTION
see Glazunov, Alexander
Konstantinovich

SCENES DE BALLET NO. 6: DANSE ORIENTALE
see Glazunov, Alexander
Konstantinovich

SCENES DE BALLET NO. 7: VALSE see
Glazunov, Alexander Konstantinovich

SCENES DE BALLET NO. 8: POLONAISE see
Glazunov, Alexander Konstantinovich

SCENES DE LA CSARDA, FOR VIOLIN AND
ORCHESTRA see Hubay, Jenö

SCENES ECOSSAISES: LEGENDE PASTORALE
see Godard, Benjamin Louis Paul

SCENES ECOSSAISES: MARCHE DES
HIGHLANDERS see Godard, Benjamin
Louis Paul

SCENES ECOSSAISES: SERENADE see Godard,
Benjamin Louis Paul

SCENES FROM BELA KRAJINA see Mihelcic,
Pavle, Prizori Iz Bele Krajina

SCENES FROM "CALISTO AND MELIBEA", FOR
SOLO VOICES AND ORCHESTRA see
Rosen, Jerome

SCENES FROM INDIAN LIFE see Ballard,
Louis Wayne

SCENES FROM RIMBAUD see Blumenfeld,
Harold

SCENES FROM SHIR HA-SHIRIM, FOR SOLO
VOICES AND CHAMBER ORCHESTRA see
Davidovsky, Mario

SCENES FROM THE EAST [ARR.] see
Schumann, Robert (Alexander),
Bilder Aus Osten [arr.]

SCENES FROM THE PAINTED BIRD see
Rowland, David

SCENES HISTORIQUES, SUITE NO. 1:
ALL'OVERTURA see Sibelius, Jean

SCENES HISTORIQUES, SUITE NO. 1:
FESTIVO see Sibelius, Jean

SCENES HISTORIQUES, SUITE NO. 1: SCENA
see Sibelius, Jean

SCENES HISTORIQUES, SUITE NO. 2: AT THE
DRAW BRIDGE see Sibelius, Jean

SCENES HISTORIQUES, SUITE NO. 2: LOVE SONG see Sibelius, Jean

SCENES HISTORIQUES, SUITE NO. 2: THE CHASE see Sibelius, Jean

SCHACHT, THEODOR VON (1748-1823)
Symphonies, Two *see SEVEN SYMPHONIES FROM THE COURT OF THURN UND TAXIS

SCHAFE KONNEN SICHER WEIDEN [ARR.] see Bach, Johann Sebastian

SCHAFER, M.
see SCHAFER, R. MURRAY

SCHAFER, R. MURRAY (1933-   )
Canzoni For Prisoners
sc BERANDOL BER 1671 $18.00   (S222)

Concerto for Flute and Orchestra
2.2.2.2. 4.2.2.1. perc,harp,pno& cel,strings,fl solo
study sc ARCANA $30.00, perf mat rent   (S223)

Concerto for Harp and Orchestra
3.2.2.2. 4.2.2.1. perc,pno&cel, strings,harp solo
study sc ARCANA $30.00, perf mat rent   (S224)

Dream Rainbow Dream Thunder [12']
3.3.3.3. 4.3.3.1. perc,harp,pno& cel,strings
study sc ARCANA $15.00, perf mat rent   (S225)

Garden Of The Heart, The, For Solo Voice And Orchestra [24']
3.2.2.2. 4.2.1.1. 2perc,strings, Mez solo
sc ARCANA $25.00, perf mat rent   (S226)

Ko Wo Kiku [30']
3.3.3.3. 4.3.3.1. perc,harp,pno& cel,strings
"Listen To The Incense" study sc ARCANA $30.00, perf mat rent   (S227)

Letters From Mignon, For Solo Voice And Orchestra [25']
3.3.3.3. 4.2.2.0. perc,harp,pno, strings,Mez solo
study sc ARCANA $30.00, perf mat rent   (S228)

Listen To The Incense
see Ko Wo Kiku

Minnelieder, For Solo Voice And Orchestra
3.3.3.2. 4.2.2.0. perc,harp, strings,Mez solo
ARCANA perf mat rent   (S229)

No Longer Than Ten (10) Minutes
sc BERANDOL BER 1672 $20.00 (S230)

Untitled Composition No.2 [3'15"]
1+2pic.2+English horn.2+bass clar.2+contrabsn. 3.4.3.1. timp,perc,harp,pno&cel,strings
sc BERANDOL BER 1673 $6.50   (S231)

SCHAFFRATH, CHRISTOPH (1709-1763)
Concerto for Harpsichord and String Orchestra in B flat
(Louwenaar, Karyl) (Collegium Musicum Series of Yale University) sc A-R ED
ISBN 0-89579-100-5 $17.95 (S232)

SCHAT, PETER (1935-   )
Entelechie II, For Solo Voice And Instrumental Ensemble *Op.13
fl,clar,trp,perc,harp,pno,vibra, vln,vla,vcl,Mez solo
sc DONEMUS f.s., perf mat rent   (S233)

Serenade, Op. 31 [12']
string orch
DONEMUS perf mat rent   (S234)

Symphony No. 2, Op. 30 [40']
4.4.4.3.4sax. 4.3.3.2. 5perc, 2harp,strings
DONEMUS perf mat rent   (S235)

Symposion: De Trein, For Solo Voices And Orchestra [45']
3.3.4.3.3sax. 4.3.3.2. 2marimba, perc,2harp,strings,TBarBarBarB soli
DONEMUS perf mat rent   (S236)

SCHATTEN VON KOBISTAN, DIE: SUITE see Karayev, Faradzh, Spirits Of Kobystan, The: Suite

SCHATTENSTUCK see Rihm, Wolfgang

SCHAUSPIEL-OUVERTURE see Korngold, Erich Wolfgang

SCHAUSPIELDIREKTOR, DER: BESTER JÜNGLING! MIT ENTZÜCKEN, FOR SOLO VOICE AND ORCHESTRA see Mozart, Wolfgang Amadeus

SCHAUSPIELDIREKTOR, DER: ICH BIN DIE ERSTE SÄNGERIN, FOR SOLO VOICES AND ORCHESTRA see Mozart, Wolfgang Amadeus

SCHAUSPIELDIREKTOR, DER: LIEBES MANDEL, WO IST'S BANDEL, FOR SOLO VOICES AND ORCHESTRA, [ARR.] see Mozart, Wolfgang Amadeus

SCHAUSPIELDIREKTOR, DER: MÄNNER SUCHEN STETS ZU NASCHEN, FOR SOLO VOICE AND ORCHESTRA see Mozart, Wolfgang Amadeus

SCHECHTER, BORIS (1900-1961)
Turkmenien
3.2.2.2. 4.2.3.1. timp,perc, strings
VAAP perf mat rent   (S237)

SCHEDL, GERHARD (1957-   )
Concerto for Viola and Orchestra [22']
2(pic).2.2.2. 4.2.2.0. timp,perc, strings,vla solo
DOBLINGER perf mat rent   (S238)

Concerto for Violin, Violoncello, Strings and Harpsichord [17']
3vln,3vla,3vcl,db,hpsd,vln solo, vcl solo
(über die Sinfonia bWV 795 von J.S. Bach) DOBLINGER perf mat rent   (S239)

Drei Miniaturen [4']
3(pic).2+English horn.2+bass clar.2+contrabsn. 4.3.3.1. timp,perc,harp,cel,strings
DOBLINGER perf mat rent   (S240)

Kontrapunkt IV [5']
3.3.3.3. 4.3.3.1. timp,perc,harp, pno,cel,strings,electronic tape
DOBLINGER perf mat rent   (S241)

"...So Zu Licht Und Lust Geboren...", For Solo Voice And Orchestra [15']
2(pic).2+ob d'amore.0.2. 4.0.0.0. timp,perc,harp,cel,pno,strings, Bar solo
study sc DOBLINGER STR 616 f.s., perf mat rent   (S242)

Symphony [30']
3(pic).3.3(bass clar).3(contrabsn). 4.3.3.1. timp,perc,harp,strings
DOBLINGER perf mat rent   (S243)

Symphony No. 2 [10']
0.3.2+bass clar.3. 4.4.3.1. timp, perc,harp,pno,10vla,9vcl,6db
study sc DOBLINGER STP 629 f.s., perf mat rent   (S244)

Tango [9']
2.2.2.2.alto sax. 4.2.3.0. timp, perc,strings
study sc DOBLINGER STP 523 f.s., perf mat rent   (S245)

SCHEHERAZADE see Rimsky-Korsakov, Nikolai

SCHEIDEN UND MEIDEN see Mahler, Gustav

SCHEIN, JOHANN HERMANN (1586-1630)
Banchetto Musicale: Suite No. 7 [8']
string orch
(Prufer) set KALMUS A7409 $20.00 and up   (S246)

Banchetto Musicale: Suite No. 8 [8']
string orch
(Prufer) set KALMUS A7410 $20.00, and up   (S247)

Banchetto Musicale: Suite No. 14 [6']
string orch
(Prufer) set KALMUS A7411 $20.00, and up   (S248)

Canzone No. 26 [5']
string orch
(Prufer) set KALMUS A7416 $20.00, and up   (S249)

Venuskranzlein: Intradas And Gagliards
string orch [6'] KALMUS A6470 sc $4.00, set $5.00, pts $1.00, ea., perf mat rent   (S250)

SCHEIN UND SEIN, FOR SOLO VOICE AND ORCHESTRA see Finke, Fidelio Friedrich (Fritz)

SCHELLE, MICHAEL (1950-   )
Big Night, The [15']
2+pic.2(English horn).2+bass clar.2. 4.2.2.1. timp,3perc, pno,harp,strings,opt cor
NORRUTH perf mat rent   (S251)

Concerto for 2 Pianos and Orchestra [28']
2+pic.2.2.2. 4.2.2.1. timp,3perc, harp,strings,2pno soli
NORRUTH perf mat rent   (S252)

Masque [20']
1(pic).2.1.2. 2.0.0.0. perc,pno, strings
sc NORRUTH perf mat rent   (S253)

Play Us Chastity On Your Violin, For Violin And Instrumental Ensemble [19']
1.1.1.1. 1.1.1.0. perc,pno,harp, vcl,db,vln solo
NORRUTH perf mat rent   (S254)

Swashbuckler [18']
2+pic.2.2.2. 4.4.3.1. timp,3perc, harp,strings
NORRUTH perf mat rent   (S255)

SCHERCHEN, TONA (1938-   )
Lo [20']
trom,6vln,3vla,2vcl,db
BOOSEY perf mat rent   (S256)

SCHERZETTO, FOR VIOLIN AND STRING ORCHESTRA see Cruft, Adrian

SCHERZETTO, FOR VIOLONCELLO AND ORCHESTRA [ARR.] see Bridge, Frank

SCHERZI see Taylor, Timothy

SCHERZI MUSICALE see Kay, Ulysses Simpson

SCHERZI MUSICALI see Brings, Allen Stephen

SCHERZINO, FOR BASSOON AND ORCHESTRA see Hesselberg, Eyvind

SCHERZO CAPRICCIOSO see Dvořák, Antonín

SCHERZO E ADAGIO see Huszar, Lajos

SCHERZO FANTASQUE see Coppola, Piero

SCHERZO IDYLLIC see Kricka, Jaroslav

SCHERZO NOTTURNO see Hesselberg, Eyvind

SCHERZO, PASTORALE E CAPRICCIO [ARR.] see Scarlatti, Domenico

SCHERZO UND FINALE see Wolf, Hugo

SCHERZO, VERSION FOR 18 INSTRUMENTS see Mather, Bruce

SCHETKY, JOHANN GEORG CHRISTOFF (1740-1824)
Quartetto
see Graupner, Christoph, Symphonies, Four

SCHIAFFINI, GIANCARLO
Giardino Delle Delizie, Il [12']
0.1.1.1. 1.1.1.1. perc,2vln,vla, vcl,db
sc RICORDI-IT 031-35850 $19.50, perf mat rent   (S257)

SCHIBLER, ARMIN (1920-   )
Concerto for Trumpet and Orchestra, Op. 68
sc KUNZEL GM 862 $36.00, perf mat rent   (S258)

Iam Manet Ultima Spes *Op.92
string orch
sc KUNZEL 10089 $17.00, perf mat rent   (S259)

Trauermusik
fl,clar,bsn,perc,strings,opt speaking voice
sc KUNZEL 10094 $14.00, ipa (S260)

SCHICKE, KARL
Symphony No. 2, Op. 26
2.2.2.2. 4.3.3.1. timp,perc, strings
min sc UNIVER. $29.00   (S261)

SCHICKELE, PETER (1935-   )
see "BACH, P.D.Q."

see also "BACH, P.D.Q."

Bach Portrait, For Narrator And Orchestra [15']
(restricted to Peter Schickele's personal appearances) PRESSER perf mat rent   (S262)

SCHICKELE, PETER (cont'd.)

Chenoo Who Stayed To Dinner, The, For
  Narrator And Orchestra [24']
  2.2.2.2. 3.2.2.1. 2perc,strings,
  narrator
  PRESSER perf mat rent   (S263)

Five Of A Kind, For Brass Quintet And
  Orchestra [23']
  2.2.2.2. 4.2.2.0. timp,3perc,
  strings,2trp,horn,trom,tuba
  soli
  PRESSER perf mat rent   (S264)

Maiden On The Moor, For Solo Voice
  And Chamber Orchestra [8']
  ob,2horn,perc,strings,
  countertenor/A solo
  PRESSER perf mat rent   (S265)

Quodlibet [10']
  (restricted to Peter Schickele's
  personal appearances) PRESSER
  perf mat rent   (S266)

Three Girls, Three Women, For Solo
  Voice And Orchestra [20']
  2.2.2.2. 3.2.1.1. 2perc,cel,harp,
  strings,male solo
  ELKAN-V perf mat rent   (S267)

SCHIERBECK, POUL (1888-1949)
  Adrienne Lecouvreur
  sc,pts SAMFUNDET f.s.   (S268)

  Fest-Musik
  sc,pts SAMFUNDET f.s.   (S269)

  Fete Galante
  sc SAMFUNDET f.s., perf mat rent
                                 (S270)

  Natten
  "Night" sc SAMFUNDET f.s., perf mat
  rent   (S271)

  Night
  see Natten

SCHIFRIN, LALO (BORIS) (1932-   )
  Capriccio for Clarinet and String
  Orchestra [10']
  string orch,clar solo
  AMP perf mat rent   (S272)

  Concerto for Piano and Orchestra
  [23']
  2(alto fl)+pic.2+English horn.2+
  bass clar.2+contrabsn. 4.3.3.0.
  perc,2harp,strings,pno solo
  sc,pts MJQ rent   (S273)

  Dialogues For Jazz Quintet And
  Orchestra
  2.2.1.2. 2.3.2.0. timp,perc,
  strings, jazz quintet
  AMP perf mat rent   (S274)

  Invocations
  2+pic.2+English horn.2(clar in E
  flat)+bass clar.2+contrabsn.
  4.4.4(bass trom).1. 6perc,pno,
  2harp,cel,strings
  AMP perf mat rent   (S275)

SCHIPIZKY, FREDERICK (1952-   )
  Invitation To The World
  2.2.3.3. 4.4.3.1. timp,3perc,
  strings
  CAN.MUS.CENT. MI 1100 S336I   (S276)

  Symphony No. 1
  3.3.3(clar in E flat).3. 4.3.3.1.
  timp,3perc,harp,strings
  CAN.MUS.CENT. MI 1100 S336SY (S277)

  Symphony No. 2 [24']
  2.2.2.2. 2+opt horn.2.0.0. timp,
  strings
  CAN.MUS.CENT. MI 1100 S336S2 (S278)

SCHLAFE MEIN PRINZCHEN, FOR SOLO VOICE
  AND ORCHESTRA, [ARR.] see Flies, J.
  Bernhard

SCHLAFENDE PRINZESSIN, DIE, FOR SOLO
  VOICE AND ORCHESTRA[ARR.] see
  Borodin, Alexander Porfirievich,
  Sleeping Princess, For Solo Voice
  And Orchestra [arr.]

SCHLAGE DOCH, GEWÜNSCHTE STUNDE, FOR
  SOLO VOICE AND ORCHESTRA see
  Hoffmann, Georg Melchior

SCHLAGSTUCK 3 FÜR SCHLAGZEUGE UND
  ORCHESTER see Bredemeyer, Reiner

SCHLEIER DER PIERRETTE, DER, OP. 18:
  HOCHZEITSWALZER see Dohnányi, Ernst
  von

SCHLEIER DER PIERRETTE, DER, OP. 18:
  LUSTIGER TRAUERMARSCH see Dohnányi,
  Ernst von

SCHLEIER DER PIERRETTE, DER, OP. 18:
  MENUETT see Dohnányi, Ernst von

SCHLEIER DER PIERRETTE, DER, OP. 18:
  PIERRETTENS WAHNSINNSTANZ see
  Dohnányi, Ernst von

SCHLEIER DER PIERRETTE, DER, OP. 18:
  PIERROTS LIEBESKLAGE see Dohnányi,
  Ernst von

SCHLEIER DER PIERRETTE, DER, OP. 18:
  WALZER-REIGEN see Dohnányi, Ernst
  von

SCHLEMM, GUSTAV ADOLF (1902-   )
  Beschwingtes Vorspiel
  2.2.2.2. 4.2.3.0. timp,perc,harp,
  strings
  TONOS perf mat rent   (S279)

  Concerto for Violoncello and
  Orchestra
  2.2.2.2. 3.2.0.0. timp,strings,
  vcl solo
  TONOS   (S280)

  Jagdouverture
  2.1.2.1. 4.2.1.0. timp,perc,
  strings
  TONOS   (S281)

SCHLOSS, DAS: SUITE NO. 1 see Laporte,
  Andre

SCHLOSS, DAS: SUITE NO. 2 see Laporte,
  Andre

SCHLOSS-SINFONIE see Laporte, Andre

SCHLUCK UND JAU see Janácek, Leoš

SCHMIDT, CHRISTFRIED (1932-   )
  Munch-Musik
  3.3.3.3. 4.4.3.1. timp,perc,
  strings
  sc DEUTSCHER 1735 f.s.   (S282)

SCHMIDT, OLE (1928-   )
  Concerto for Guitar and Orchestra
  [14']
  1.1(English horn).0+bass clar.0.
  0.0.0.0. perc,harp,strings,gtr
  solo
  HANSEN-DEN perf mat rent   (S283)

  Concerto for Tuba and Orchestra [15']
  2.2.2.2. 4.0.0.0. timp,perc,8vcl,
  6db,tuba solo
  HANSEN-DEN perf mat rent   (S284)

  Concerto for Violin and Orchestra
  [20']
  2gtr,mand,2harp,hpsd,6perc,vln
  solo,SATB
  HANSEN-DEN perf mat rent   (S285)

SCHMIDT, WILLIAM JOSEPH (1926-   )
  Concerto for Trumpet and Orchestra
  WESTERN AV248 $200.00   (S286)

SCHMIERER, JOHANN ABRAHAM (1661-1719)
  Zodiacus [6']
  string orch,hpsd
  KALMUS A7122 sc $5.00, set $5.00,
  pts $1.00, ea.   (S287)

SCHMITT, FLORENT (1870-1958)
  Chant Elegiaque, For Cello And
  Orchestra *Op.24
  KALMUS A7185 sc $10.00, set $22.00,
  pts $1.00, ea., perf mat rent
                                 (S288)

  Pupazzi, Op. 36, Nos. 2 And 5
  string orch [5'] KALMUS A5875 sc
  $5.00, set $5.00   (S289)

  Rapsodie Viennoise *Op.53,No.1
  3.3.2.3. 4.2.3.1. timp,perc,
  2harp,strings
  KALMUS A6440 sc $20.00, set $50.00,
  pts $2.00, ea., perf mat rent
                                 (S290)
  study sc DURAND 597-00445 $5.50
                                 (S291)

  Reflets D'allemagne: Suite De Valses
  KALMUS A6967 sc $22.00, set $40.00,
  pts $2.00, ea., perf mat rent
                                 (S292)

  Tragedie De Salome, La *Op.50
  KALMUS A6355 sc $50.00, set
  $100.00, pts $4.00, ea., perf mat
  rent   (S293)

SCHMITT, JOSEPH (1734-1791)
  Concerto for 2 Flutes and Orchestra
  in G [18']
  2ob,2horn,strings,2fl soli
  (Bodensohn, E.) (with cadenzas) sc,
  pts BODENS E 61 f.s.   (S294)

SCHMITT, MEINRAD (1935-   )
  Concerto for Harp and String
  Orchestra [15']
  string orch,harp solo
  BOTE perf mat rent   (S295)

SCHNABEL, ARTUR (1882-1951)
  Rhapsody
  2+pic.2+English horn.2+bass
  clar.2+contrabsn. 4.1.2.1.
  perc,pno,strings
  sc APNM $17.00, perf mat rent
                                 (S296)

  Symphony No. 2
  2(pic).3(English horn).3(bass
  clar).3(contrabsn). 4.3.3.1.
  perc,strings
  sc APNM $50.00, perf mat rent
                                 (S297)

  Symphony No. 3
  2(2pic).2(English horn).3+bass
  clar.2+contrabsn. 4.4.3.1.
  perc,pno,strings
  sc APNM $28.00, perf mat rent
                                 (S298)

SCHNEBEL, DIETER (1930-   )
  Mahler-Moment [3']
  string orch
  SCHOTTS perf mat rent   (S299)

  Sinfonie-Stucke [10']
  3(pic,alto fl).3.3.3(contrabsn).
  4.3.3.1. timp,perc,harp,
  strings, lotos flute
  SCHOTTS perf mat rent   (S300)

SCHNEEFLOCKCHEN: VORSPIEL see
  Tchaikovsky, Piotr Ilyich, Snow
  Maiden, The: Prelude

SCHNEEFLÖCKCHEN: ZU DEM DONNER EINE
  WOLKE SPRACH, FOR SOLO VOICE AND
  ORCHESTRA see Rimsky-Korsakov,
  Nikolai

SCHNEEMANN, DER: OVERTURE see Korngold,
  Erich Wolfgang

SCHNEESTERNCHEN POLKA see Strauss,
  Eduard

SCHNEESTURM, DER see Sviridov, Georgy,
  Snowstorm

SCHNEIDER, ERNST (1939-   )
  Fragment: A Dance [20']
  2(pic).2.2.2. 4.2.3.1. timp,perc,
  strings
  CAN.MUS.CENT. MI 1100 S358FR (S301)

  Romantic Concerto, For Piano And
  Orchestra [20']
  2(pic).2.2.2. 4.2.3.1. timp,perc,
  strings,pno solo
  CAN.MUS.CENT. MI 1361 S358RO (S302)

SCHNEIDER, GARY M.
  Concerto For Jazz Clarinet And String
  Orchestra [11']
  string orch,clar solo
  sc AM.COMP.AL. $15.55, perf mat
  rent   (S303)

  Nocturne for Bassoon and String
  Orchestra [5']
  string orch,bsn solo
  sc AM.COMP.AL. $13.80, perf mat
  rent   (S304)

  Sheva [7']
  1.1.1.1. 2.1.0.0. timp,harp,
  strings
  sc AM.COMP.AL. $12.10   (S305)

SCHNELL, JOHANN JAKOB (1687-1754)
  Concerto for Flute and String
  Orchestra in A [14']
  string orch,hpsd,fl solo
  (Bodensohn, E.F.W.) (with cadenzas)
  sc,pts BODENS E 58 f.s.   (S306)

SCHNITTKE, ALFRED (1934-   )
  Concerto for Piano 4-Hands and
  Chamber Orchestra [15']
  1.1.1.1. 1.1.1.1. 2perc,strings,
  pno 4-hands soli
  UNIVER. perf mat rent   (S307)
  SIKORSKI perf mat rent   (S308)

  Concerto for Piano and String
  Orchestra [28']
  string orch,pno solo
  SIKORSKI perf mat rent   (S309)
  VAAP perf mat rent   (S310)

  Concerto for Viola and Orchestra
  [35']
  3(pic,alto fl).3(English
  horn).3(clar in E flat,bass
  clar).3(contrabsn). 4.4.4.1.
  timp,perc,harp,cel,hpsd,pno,
  8vla,8vcl,8db,vla solo
  SIKORSKI perf mat rent   (S311)
  VAAP perf mat rent   (S312)

  Concerto for Violin and Chamber
  Orchestra, No. 2 [20']
  1.1.1. 1.1.1.0. timp,2perc,pno,
  strings,vln solo
  VAAP perf mat rent   (S313)

SCHNITTKE, ALFRED (cont'd.)

Concerto for Violin and Chamber
    Orchestra, No. 3 [28']
    2.2.3.2. 2.1.1.0. strings,vln
    solo
    min sc UNIVER. PH. 496 $29.00, perf
    mat rent   (S314)
    study sc VAAP f.s., perf mat rent
                                    (S315)
Concerto for Violin and Orchestra,
    No. 1 [40']
    3.2.3.2. 4.2.0.0. timp,perc,cel,
    harp,pno,strings,vln solo
    SIKORSKI perf mat rent   (S316)
    VAAP perf mat rent   (S317)
Concerto for Violin and Orchestra,
    No. 4 [34']
    3.2+English horn.2+bass clar.2+
    contrabsn.alto sax. 4.4.4.1.
    timp,6perc,harp,cel,hpsd,
    prepared pno,strings,vln solo
    min sc UNIVER. PH. 525 f.s., perf
    mat rent   (S318)
    SIKORSKI perf mat rent   (S319)
    sc VAAP f.s., perf mat rent   (S320)
Concerto for Violoncello and
    Orchestra [40']
    3.3.3.3. 4.4.4.1. timp,perc,harp,
    cel,pno,strings,vcl solo
    study sc SIKORSKI f.s., perf mat
    rent   (S321)
    VAAP perf mat rent   (S322)
Concerto Grosso No. 1 [25']
    hpsd,prepared pno,strings,2vln
    soli
    min sc UNIVER. PH. 488 f.s., perf
    mat rent   (S323)
    SIKORSKI perf mat rent   (S324)
    study sc VAAP f.s., perf mat rent
                                    (S325)
Concerto Grosso No. 2 for Violin,
    Violoncello and Orchestra [35']
    3.3.3.3. 4.4.4.1. timp,4perc,cel,
    hpsd,pno,elec gtr,bass gtr,
    strings,vln solo,vcl solo
    SIKORSKI perf mat rent   (S326)
Concerto Grosso No. 3 for 2 Violins
    and Chamber Orchestra [17']
    bells,hpsd&cel&pno,strings,2vln
    soli
    SIKORSKI perf mat rent   (S327)
    VAAP perf mat rent   (S328)
Concerto Grosso No. 4 [40']
    3.3.3.3. 4.4.4.1. 6perc,harp,cel,
    hpsd,pno,strings
    SIKORSKI perf mat rent   (S329)
In Memoriam [27']
    3.3.3.3. 4.4.4.1. timp,perc,harp,
    cel,hpsd,2pno,org,elec gtr,
    strings
    VAAP perf mat rent   (S330)
(K)Ein Sommernachtstraum
    see Not A Midsummer Night's Dream
Labyrinth: Suite [35']
    3perc,hpsd,cel,strings
    SIKORSKI perf mat rent   (S331)
    VAAP perf mat rent   (S332)
Monolog, For Viola And String
    Orchestra [15']
    string orch,vla solo
    SIKORSKI perf mat rent   (S333)
Moz-Art A La Haydn, For 2 Violins And
    String Orchestra [8']
    string orch,2vln soli
    SIKORSKI perf mat rent   (S334)
    VAAP perf mat rent   (S335)
Music for Piano and Chamber Orchestra
    [25']
    1.1.1.0. 1.1.0.0. timp,perc,
    strings,pno solo
    VAAP perf mat rent   (S336)
Not A Midsummer Night's Dream [15']
    4(pic).4.4(bass clar).2. 4.4.4.1.
    timp,4-5perc,cel,hpsd,pno,harp,
    strings
    VAAP perf mat rent   (S337)
    "(K)Ein Sommernachtstraum" UNIVER.
    perf mat rent   (S338)
    "(K)Ein Sommernachtstraum" SIKORSKI
    perf mat rent   (S339)
Passacaglia [20']
    4.4.4.4. 6.4.4.1. timp,4perc,
    2harp,hpsd,pno,strings
    UNIVER. perf mat rent   (S340)
    VAAP perf mat rent   (S341)
Pianissimo [9']
    2.1.1.1. 1.1.1.1. timp,4perc,
    harp,cel,hpsd,2pno,elec gtr,
    strings
    sc VAAP f.s., perf mat rent   (S342)

SCHNITTKE, ALFRED (cont'd.)

Quasi Una Sonata, For Violin And
    Chamber Orchestra [21']
    2.2.2.2. 2.0.0.0. hpsd&pno,9vln,
    3vla,3vcl,db,vln solo
    UNIVER. perf mat rent   (S343)
    SIKORSKI perf mat rent   (S344)
Ritual [8']
    3.3.3.3. 4.4.4.1. perc,harp,cel,
    hpsd,pno,org,elec gtr,bass gtr,
    strings
    SIKORSKI perf mat rent   (S345)
Symphony No. 1 [60']
    4.4.4.4.3sax. 4.4.4.1. timp,perc,
    2harp,cel,hpsd,pno,org,elec
    gtr,strings,electronic tape
    SIKORSKI perf mat rent   (S346)
    VAAP perf mat rent   (S347)
Symphony No. 2 [55']
    4.4.4.4. 4.4.4.1. timp,6perc,
    2harp,cel,hpsd,pno,org,elec
    gtr,bass gtr,cor
    min sc UNIVER. 17188 $62.00, perf
    mat rent   (S348)
    (St. Florian) sc VAAP f.s., perf
    mat rent   (S349)
Symphony No. 3 [60']
    4.4.4.4. 6.4.4.1. timp,6perc,
    2harp,cel,hpsd,pno,org,elec
    gtr,bass gtr,strings
    VAAP perf mat rent   (S350)
Symphony No. 4 [41']
    1.1.1.1. 1.1.1.0. bells,glock,
    vibra,gong,cel,hpsd,pno,
    strings,SATB soli
    SIKORSKI perf mat rent   (S351)
    VAAP perf mat rent   (S352)
Vier Aphorismen [10']
    1.1.2.1. 2.1.1.0. 3perc,cel,hpsd,
    pno,strings
    SIKORSKI perf mat rent   (S353)

SCHOBER, BRIAN (1951-   )
Bucolics [23']
    2(pic).2(English horn).2(bass
    clar).0.soprano sax. 2.4.3.1.
    3perc,pno,cel,harp,strings
    SALABERT perf mat rent   (S354)
Divertissements [15']
    2.0.2.0. 2.2.0.0. 2perc,harp,pno,
    strings without db
    sc AM.COMP.AL. $63.10   (S355)

SCHOECK, OTHMAR (1886-1957)
Auf Meines Kindes Tod "Von Fern Die
    Uhren Schlagen", For Solo Voice
    And Orchestra *Op.20,No.8
    (Brun) BREITKOPF-L perf mat rent
                                    (S356)
Consolation [arr] *Op.29,No.1
    (David, K.H.) 1.1.1.2. 2.0.3.0.
    timp,harp,strings [7'] BREITKOPF-
    W perf mat rent   (S357)
Drei Zigeuner, Die. "Drei Zigeuner
    Fand Ich Einmal", For Solo Voice
    And Orchestra
    (Brun) BREITKOPF-L perf mat rent
                                    (S358)
Elegy for Solo Voice and Orchestra,
    Op. 36
    BREITKOPF-L perf mat rent   (S359)
Gott Und Die Bajadere, Der, For Solo
    Voice And Orchestra, [arr.]
    *Op.34
    (David, K.H.) 3.3.3.3. 4.3.3.1.
    timp,perc,harp,cel,org,strings,B
    solo BREITKOPF-L perf mat rent
                                    (S360)
Jugendgedenken "Ich Will Spiegeln
    Mich In Jenen Tagen", For Solo
    Voice And Orchestra *Op.24,No.10
    BREITKOPF-L perf mat rent   (S361)
Lebendig Begraben, For Solo Voice And
    Orchestra *Op.40
    2.2.3.3. 4.2.3.1. timp,perc,xylo,
    cel,harp,org,pno,strings,Mez/
    Bar solo
    BREITKOPF-L perf mat rent   (S362)
Serenade, Op. 1 [10']
    1.1.1.1. 1.0.0.0. strings
    HUG GH 4156 perf mat rent   (S363)

SCHOENBERG, ARNOLD (1874-1951)
Chamber Symphony No. 1, Op. 9
    KALMUS A6396 sc $20.00, set $40.00,
    pts $3.00, ea., perf mat rent
                                    (S364)
Five Pieces For Orchestra, Op. 16,
    Original Version
    KALMUS A6447 sc $20.00, set $70.00,
    pts $2.00, ea., perf mat rent
                                    (S365)

SCHOENBERG, ARNOLD (cont'd.)

Pelleas Und Melisande *Op.5
    KALMUS A6152 sc $55.00, set
    $150.00, perf mat rent   (S366)
Three Pieces, For Chamber Orchestra
    1.1.1.1. 1.0.0.0. org/harmonium,
    cel,strings
    sc UNIVER. 15166 f.s.   (S367)

SCHOENDLINGER, ANTON (1919-   )
Concerto for Organ and String
    Orchestra
    string orch,org solo
    BREITKOPF-L perf mat rent   (S368)

SCHOENFIELD, PAUL
Four Parables, For Piano And
    Orchestra [25']
    3(pic).2+English horn.3(clar in E
    flat,bass clar).2+contrabsn.
    4.3.3.1. timp,perc,strings,
    synthesizer,pno solo
    SCHIRM.G perf mat rent   (S369)

SCHOLLUM, ROBERT (1913-1987)
Concerto for Violin and Orchestra,
    No. 3, Op. 115 [31']
    2+pic.2+English horn.2+bass
    clar.2+contrabsn.alto sax.
    4.2.3.1. perc,harp,strings,vln
    solo
    DOBLINGER perf mat rent   (S370)
Epitaph Für Hingerichtete *Op.99
    (from Markus-Passion) [5']
    2+pic.2+English horn.2+bass
    clar.2+contrabsn. 4.3.4.1.
    timp,perc,pno,strings
    DOBLINGER perf mat rent   (S371)
Konzertstück, Op. 127 for Orchestra
    [10']
    2+pic.2+English horn.2+bass
    clar.2+contrabsn.alto sax.
    4.4.3.1. timp,perc,harp,strings
    DOBLINGER perf mat rent   (S372)
Symphony No. 5, Op. 77 [12']
    1.1.1.1. 0.0.0.0. perc,pno,
    strings
    (Venezianische Ergebnisse) study sc
    DOBLINGER STP 283 f.s., perf mat
    rent   (S373)
Symphony No. 6, Op. 110 [30']
    2+pic.2+English horn.2+clar in E
    flat+bass clar.2+contrabsn.
    4.4.4.1. timp,perc,cel,pno,
    strings,electronic tape
    DOBLINGER perf mat rent   (S374)
Symphony No. 7, Op. 137 [15']
    string orch
    study sc DOBLINGER STP 626 f.s.,
    perf mat rent   (S375)

SCHON LACHT DER HOLDE FRUHLING, FOR
    SOLO VOICE AND ORCHESTRA see
    Mozart, Wolfgang Amadeus

SCHON ROSMARIN, FOR VIOLIN AND
    ORCHESTRA [ARR.] see Kreisler,
    Fritz

SCHONE UND DAS TIER, DIE, FOR NARRATOR
    AND ORCHESTRA see Rapf, Kurt

SCHÖNHERR, MAX (1903-   )
Tarantella, La, For Solo Voice And
    Orchestra
    KRENN   (S376)
Ungarland
    2.2.2.2. 4.2.3.0. perc,strings
    KRENN f.s.   (S377)
Warum Fragt Mein Herz, For Solo Voice
    And Orchestra
    KRENN   (S378)

SCHOONENBEEK, KEES (1947-   )
Symphony No. 1 [20']
    3.2.3.2. 4.4.3.1. 3perc,strings
    DONEMUS perf mat rent   (S379)
Tournee, For Alto Saxophone And
    Orchestra [19']
    2.2.3.2. 3.4.3.1. timp,3-4perc,
    strings,alto sax solo
    DONEMUS perf mat rent   (S380)

SCHÖPFUNG, DIE: AUF STARKEM FITTICHE,
    FOR SOLO VOICE AND ORCHESTRA see
    Haydn, [Franz] Joseph

SCHÖPFUNG, DIE: MIT WÜRD UND HOHEIT
    ANGETAN, FOR SOLO VOICE AND
    ORCHESTRA see Haydn, [Franz] Joseph

SCHÖPFUNG, DIE: NUN BEUT DIE FLUR, FOR
    SOLO VOICE AND ORCHESTRA see Haydn,
    [Franz] Joseph

SCHÖPFUNG, DIE: NUN SCHEINT IN VOLLEM
    GLANZ DER HIMMEL, FOR SOLO VOICE
    AND ORCHESTRA see Haydn, [Franz]
    Joseph

SCHOSTAKOWITSCH, DMITRI
    see SHOSTAKOVICH, DMITRI

SCHREKER, FRANZ (1878-1934)
    Ekkehard *Op.12 [8']
        2.2+English horn.2+bass clar.2+
        contrabsn. 4.3.3.1. timp,perc,
        harp,opt org,strings
        KALMUS A5882 sc $20.00, set $25.00,
        perf mat rent   (S381)

    Prelude To A Drama
        see Vorspiel Zu Einem Drama

    Valse Lente [5']
        2fl,ob,clar in A,bsn,glock,
        triangle,harp,strings
        sc UNIVER. UE18541 $12.50, perf mat
        rent   (S382)

    Vorspiel Zu Einem Drama
        "Prelude To A Drama" KALMUS A7249
        sc $40.00, set $100.00, pts
        $3.50, ea., perf mat rent (S383)

SCHRÖDER, WALTHER (1895-   )
    Rebild [14']
        2+pic.2+English horn.2.2.
        4.2.3.1. timp,perc,cel,harp,
        strings
        HANSEN-DEN perf mat rent   (S384)

SCHRODER, WOLFGANG
    Kleine Lachmusik, Eine
        string orch
        sc,pts MOSELER M 12.427 f.s. (S385)

SCHRÖTER, JOHANN SAMUEL (1752-1788)
    Concerti, Six *see THREE CENTURIES
        OF MUSIC IN SCORE, VOL. 4:
        CONCERTO III, KEYBOARD

SCHUBACK, PETER (1947-   )
    Canti Di Euridici [9']
        5.4.4.4. 6.4.4.1. strings
        STIM   (S386)

    Canto Di Spettro, For Violoncello And
        Orchestra
        STIM   (S387)

    Nattsten [15']
        2.2.2.2. 2.2.2.1. timp,perc,
        strings
        STIM   (S388)

    Palestra Di Un Diavolo, La, For
        Violin And Orchestra
        STIM   (S389)

SCHUBERT, FRANZ (1808-1878)
    Abeille, L', For Violoncello And
        String Orchestra [arr.]
        (Thomas-Mifune) "Biene, Die, For
        Violoncello And String Orchestra
        [arr.]" string orch,vcl solo sc,
        pts KUNZEL GM 1180 f.s.   (S390)

    Biene, Die, For Violoncello And
        String Orchestra [arr.]
        see Abeille, L', For Violoncello
        And String Orchestra [arr.]

SCHUBERT, FRANZ (PETER) (1797-1828)
    Ach Um Deine Feuchten Schwingen
        see Suleika II, For Solo Voice And
        Orchestra[arr.]

    Allmacht, Die, "Gross Ist Jehova",
        For Solo Voice And Orchestra,
        [arr.] *Op.79,No.2
        (Mottl) 2.2.2.2. 4.3.3.1. timp,
        harp,strings,S solo BREITKOPF-L
        perf mat rent   (S391)

    An Die Musik, For Solo Voice And
        Orchestra, [arr.] *Op.88,No.4
        (Reger) 1.1.1.1. 2.0.0.0. timp,
        strings,S/T solo BREITKOPF-L perf
        mat rent   (S392)

    Arpeggione-Sonate, For Violoncello
        And Orchestra [arr.] *D.821
        (Spengel, Julius) 1.1.2.2. 2.0.0.0.
        strings,vcl solo [12']
        (originally for arpeggione and
        piano) DOBLINGER perf mat rent (S393)

    Arpeggione-Sonate, For Violoncello
        And String Orchestra, [arr.]
        *D.821
        (Klug, Heinrich) string orch,vcl
        solo [22'] BAREN. BA 6087 (S394)

    Auguste Iam Coelestium, D.488
        see Geistliche Arien, For Solo
        Voice And Orchestra

    Delphine "Ach, Was Soll Ich
        Beginnen", For Solo Voice And
        Orchestra, [arr.] *Op.124,No.2

SCHUBERT, FRANZ (PETER) (cont'd.)
        (Mottl) 2.2.2.2. 4.0.3.0. timp,
        strings,S solo BREITKOPF-L perf
        mat rent   (S395)

    Dem Unendlichen, For Solo Voice And
        Orchestra, [arr.] *D.291
        (Mottl) 3.2.2.2. 4.2.3.1. timp,
        2harp,strings,A/B solo BREITKOPF-
        L perf mat rent   (S396)

    Du Bist Die Ruh, For Solo Voice And
        Orchestra, [arr.] *Op.59,No.3
        (Reger) 2.1.2.2. 2.0.0.0. timp,
        strings,S solo BREITKOPF-L perf
        mat rent   (S397)

    Fantasy for Piano and Orchestra, Op.
        15, in C, [arr.]
        (Liszt, Franz) "Wanderer Fantasy
        For Piano and Orchestra [arr.]"
        2.2.2.2. 2.2.3.0. timp,strings,
        pno solo [20'] SONZOGNO perf mat
        rent   (S398)

    Fantasy for Piano and Orchestra, Op.
        103, in F minor, [arr.]
        (Kabalevsky, Dmitri) 3.2.2.2.
        4.2.3.1. timp,strings,pno solo
        [17'] SIKORSKI perf mat rent
                                         (S399)
        (Kabalevsky, Dmitri) 3.2.2.2.
        4.2.3.1. timp,strings,pno solo
        [17'] VAAP perf mat rent   (S400)

    Fantasy, Op. 103, in F minor, [arr.]
        (Mottl) 2+pic.2.2.2. 4.2.3.0. timp,
        perc,harp,strings [18'] KALMUS
        A5822 sc $20.00, set $45.00, perf
        mat rent   (S401)

    Forelle, Die, For Solo Voice And
        Orchestra [arr.]
        (Britten) "Trout, The, For Solo
        Voice And Orchestra [arr.]"
        2clar,strings,solo voice [4']
        BOOSEY perf mat rent   (S402)

    Geistliche Arien, For Solo Voice And
        Orchestra
        (Pfannhauser) 2.2.2.2. 2.2.0.0.
        org,strings,high solo pts
        DOBLINGER OKM 4-1, 2 f.s.
        contains: Auguste Iam Coelestium,
        D.488; Salve Regina, D. 27;
        Salve Regina, D. 106; Salve
        Regina, D. 223; Salve Regina,
        D. 676; Totus In Corde Langueo,
        D.136   (S403)

    Grande Marche Heroique [arr.]
        (Liszt) 2+pic.2.2.2. 4.2.3.1. timp,
        perc,strings [4'] KALMUS A5794 sc
        $20.00, set $30.00, perf mat rent
                                         (S404)

    Greisengesang, For Solo Voice And
        Orchestra [arr.] *Op.60,No.1
        (Reger) "Song Of Old Age, A, For
        Solo Voice And Orchestra[arr.]"
        KALMUS A7536 sc $5.00, set $8.00,
        pts $.75, ea.   (S405)

    Gretchen Am Spinnrad [arr.]
        (Offenbach, J.) "Marguerite Au
        Rouet [arr.]" 1.1.2.1. 2.1.0.0.
        timp,strings [4'40"] BILLAUDOT
        perf mat rent   (S406)

    Hirt Auf Dem Felsen, Der, For Solo
        Voice And Orchestra [arr.]
        (Reinecke, Carl) 2.2.1.2. 2.0.0.0.
        strings,clar solo,high solo [17']
        KAHNT perf mat rent   (S407)

    Hungarian March In C [arr.] (from
        Divertissement A l'Hongroise)
        (Liszt) 2.2.2.2. 4.2.3.1. timp,
        perc,strings [4'] KALMUS A5793 sc
        $12.00, set $25.00, perf mat rent
                                         (S408)

    Im Abendrot, For Solo Voice And
        Orchestra, [arr.]
        (Reger) 1.1.2.2. 2.0.0.0. timp,
        strings,A solo BREITKOPF-L perf
        mat rent   (S409)

    Litanei Auf Das Fest Allerseelen, For
        Solo Voice And Orchestra, [arr.]
        (Reger) 1.1.2.0. 2.0.0.0. timp,
        strings,A solo BREITKOPF-L perf
        mat rent   (S410)

    Marguerite Au Rouet [arr.]
        see Gretchen Am Spinnrad [arr.]

    Memnon, For Solo Voice And Orchestra,
        [arr.] *D.541
        (Reger) 2.0.2.2. 2.0.0.0. timp,
        strings,A solo BREITKOPF-L perf
        mat rent   (S411)

    Momenti Musicali, Due [arr.]
        (Mannino, Franco) 2.2.2+bass
        clar.2. 2.2.0.0. timp,strings
        [8'] sc BSE 1194 f.s., perf mat

SCHUBERT, FRANZ (PETER) (cont'd.)
        rent   (S412)

    Nacht Und Träume, For Solo Voice And
        Orchestra, [arr.] *Op.43,No.2
        (Reger) fl,clar,3harp,timp,strings,
        A solo BREITKOPF-L perf mat rent
                                         (S413)

    Overture in B flat, D. 470
        BREITKOPF-L perf mat rent   (S414)

    Overture in D, D. 26
        KALMUS A3867 sc $8.00, perf mat
        rent, set $25.00, pts $2.00, ea.
                                         (S415)

    Petite Symphonie In G Minor [arr.]
        (Sonatina, Op. 137, No. 3,
        [arr.])
        (Dikj, Jan van) 2.2.3.0. 1.2.0.0.
        strings [13'] DONEMUS perf mat
        rent   (S416)

    Polonaise for Violin and Orchestra
        [5']
        0.2.0.2. 2.0.0.0. strings,vln
        solo
        KALMUS A6405 sc $5.00, set $8.00,
        pts $.75, ea.   (S417)

    Rendering [arr.]
        (Berio, Luciano) 2.2.2.2. 2.2.3.0.
        timp,cel,strings [25'] UNIVER.
        perf mat rent   (S418)

    Rose, Die, "Es Lockte Schöne Wärme",
        For Solo Voice And Orchestra,
        [arr.] *Op.73
        (Mottl) 2.2.2.2. 2.0.0.0. strings,S
        solo BREITKOPF-L perf mat rent
                                         (S419)

    Salve Regina, D. 27
        see Geistliche Arien, For Solo
        Voice And Orchestra

    Salve Regina, D. 106
        see Geistliche Arien, For Solo
        Voice And Orchestra

    Salve Regina, D. 223
        see Geistliche Arien, For Solo
        Voice And Orchestra

    Salve Regina, D. 676
        string orch,S solo BREITKOPF-L perf
        mat rent   (S420)
        see Geistliche Arien, For Solo
        Voice And Orchestra

    Sonatina, Op. 137, No. 3, [arr.]
        see Petite Symphonie In G Minor
        [arr.]

    Song Of Old Age, A, For Solo Voice
        And Orchestra[arr.]
        see Greisengesang, For Solo Voice
        And Orchestra [arr.]

    Ständchen "Leise Flehen Meine
        Lieder", For Solo Voice And
        Orchestra, [arr.]
        (Mottl) 2.1.2.0. 2.0.0.0. harp,
        strings,T solo BREITKOPF-L perf
        mat rent   (S421)

    Suleika I, For Solo Voice And
        Orchestra[arr.] *Op.14,No.1
        (Mottl) "Was Bedeutet Die
        Bewegung?" 2.2.2.2. 2.0.0.0.
        strings,solo voice KALMUS A5834
        sc $4.00, set $15.00, pts $1.00,
        ea., perf mat rent   (S422)
        (Mottl) "Was Bedeutet Die
        Bewegung?" 2.2.2.2. 2.0.0.0.
        strings,S solo BREITKOPF-L perf
        mat rent   (S423)

    Suleika II, For Solo Voice And
        Orchestra[arr.] *Op.31
        (Mottl) "Ach Um Deine Feuchten
        Schwingen" 2.2.2.2. 2.0.0.0.
        strings,S solo KALMUS A5835 sc
        $5.00, set $15.00, pts $1.00,
        ea., perf mat rent   (S424)
        (Mottl) "Ach Um Deine Feuchten
        Schwingen" 2.2.2.2. 2.0.0.0.
        strings,S solo BREITKOPF-L perf
        mat rent   (S425)

    Symphonic Fragments, Three: D. 615,
        D. 708a, D. 936a
        (Gulke, Peter) sc PETERS P9351
        f.s., perf mat rent   (S426)

    Symphony in E, D. 729
        *reconstruction
        (Newbould, Brian) 2.2.2.2. 4.2.3.1.
        perc,strings [38'] BOIS perf mat
        rent   (S427)

    Symphony No. 1 in D, D. 82
        sc BAREN. BA 5601 f.s.   (S428)

    Symphony No. 2 in B flat, D. 125
        sc BAREN. BA 5602 f.s.   (S429)

SCHUBERT, FRANZ (PETER) (cont'd.)

Symphony No. 3 in D, D. 200
sc BAREN. BA 5603 f.s.   (S430)

Symphony No. 8 in B minor, D. 759
(Gulkel, P.) BREITKOPF-W sc PB 5207
f.s., pts OB 5207 f.s.   (S431)
(Reichenberger, Teresa) min sc
EULENBURG EU00403 $5.75   (S432)

Symphony No. 8 in B minor, D. 759,
Scherzo *reconstruction
(Hollard, Florian) 2.2.2.2.
2.1.3.0. perc,strings [8'] sc
BOIS f.s., perf mat rent   (S433)

Symphony No. 8 in B minor, D. 759,
Scherzo,Finale *reconstruction
(Abraham, Gerald) 2.2.2.2. 2.2.3.0.
timp,strings [17'] OXFORD perf
mat rent   (S434)

Teufel Als Hydraulicus, Der: Overture
KALMUS A5694 sc $5.00, set $12.00
(S435)

Thekla, For Solo Voice And Orchestra,
[arr.] *Op.88,No.2
(Mottl) 2.2.2.2. 2.0.0.0. harp,
strings,S solo BREITKOPF-L perf
mat rent   (S436)

Tod Und Das Mädchen, Der, For Solo
Voice And Orchestra, [arr.]
*Op.7,No.3
(Mottl) 0.1.2.2. 1.0.0.0. timp,
strings,A solo BREITKOPF-L perf
mat rent   (S437)

Totus In Corde Lanqueo, D.136
see Geistliche Arien, For Solo
Voice And Orchestra

Trout, The, For Solo Voice And
Orchestra [arr.]
see Forelle, Die, For Solo Voice
And Orchestra [arr.]

Unfinished Symphony *see Symphony
No. 8 In B Minor, D. 759

Wanderer Fantasy For Piano And
Orchestra [arr.]
see Fantasy for Piano and
Orchestra, Op. 15, in C, [arr.]

Was Bedeutet Die Bewegung?
see Suleika I, For Solo Voice And
Orchestra[arr.]

Wiegenlied "Schlafe, Holder Süsser
Knabe", For Solo Voice And
Orchestra, [arr.] *Op.98,No.2
(Mottl) fl,clar,strings,S solo
BREITKOPF-L perf mat rent (S438)

SCHUBERT, MANFRED (1937-   )
Divertimento
sc DEUTSCHER 1679 f.s.   (S439)

SCHUBERT VARIATIONS see Reesen, Emil

SCHUDEL, THOMAS (1937-   )
Piccolo Concerto, For Piccolo And
Orchestra
perc,strings,pic solo
CAN.MUS.CENT. MI 1621 S384PI (S440)

SCHUETZ, HEINRICH
see SCHÜTZ, HEINRICH

SCHULLER, GUNTHER (1925-   )
Chamber Symphony [14']
1+pic.2(English horn).2(bass
clar).2(contrabsn). 1.1.1.1.
harp,strings
AMP perf mat rent   (S441)

Chimeric Images [15']
fl,clar,bsn,horn,trp,harp,pno&
cel,vln,vla,vcl,db
sc MARGUN MP7159 $28.00, perf mat
rent   (S442)

Concertino For Jazz Quartet And
Orchestra [19']
2.1.2.1. 2.3.2.0. timp,perc,
strings,vibra solo,pno solo,db
solo,drums solo
sc MJQ $9.50, perf mat rent (S443)

Concerto Festiva, For Brass Quintet
And Orchestra [20']
3(pic).2+English horn.2+bass
clar.3+contrabsn. 4.3.3.1.
perc,pno&cel,harp,strings,horn,
2trp,trom,tuba soli
AMP perf mat rent   (S444)

Concerto for Alto Saxophone and
Orchestra [29']
2.2.3.2. 4.3.3.1. perc,cel,harp,
strings,alto sax solo
AMP perf mat rent   (S445)

SCHULLER, GUNTHER (cont'd.)

Concerto for Bassoon and Orchestra
[22']
2+pic.2+English horn.2+bass
clar.3(contrabsn).soprano sax.
4.3.3.1. timp,4perc,harp,pno&
cel,strings,bsn solo
(Eine Kleine Fagottmusik) AMP perf
mat rent   (S446)

Concerto for Contrabassoon and
Orchestra [23']
3+pic.3+English horn.2+bass
clar(contrabass
clar).3(contrabsn). 4.4.4.1.
timp,perc,cel&pno,harp,strings,
contrabsn solo
AMP perf mat rent   (S447)

Concerto for Flute and Orchestra
[16']
2(pic,alto fl).2+English
horn.2(clar in E flat,bass
clar).3(contrabsn). 4.3.3.1.
timp,5perc,harp,elec pno/cel,
strings,fl solo
AMP perf mat rent   (S448)

Concerto for Horn and Orchestra, No.
2 [24']
3(pic,alto fl).2+English horn.2+
bass clar.2+contrabsn. 4.4.4.1.
7perc,cel,harp,pno,strings,horn
solo
AMP perf mat rent   (S449)

Concerto for Orchestra, No. 2
4.4.4.4. 4.4.4.1. perc,harp,cel,
pno,opt org,strings
sc AMP 066-35623 $35.00, perf mat
rent   (S450)

Concerto for Piano and Orchestra, No.
2 [30']
2+pic.2+English horn.2+bass clar+
contrabass clar.3. 4.3.4.1.
timp,perc,harp,strings,pno solo
AMP perf mat rent   (S451)

Concerto For Piano Three Hands [25']
2(pic).2(English horn).2(clar in
E flat).2. 2.2.1.0. timp,2perc,
harp,strings,2pno soli
AMP perf mat rent   (S452)

Concerto for Trumpet and Chamber
Orchestra [15']
2.2(English horn).2.2. 4.3.1.0.
timp,perc,harp,pno,strings,trp
solo
AMP perf mat rent   (S453)

Concerto for Viola and Orchestra
[20']
3(pic).3(English horn).2+bass
clar.3(contrabsn). 4.3.3.1.
timp,perc,harp,pno&cel,strings,
vla solo
AMP perf mat rent   (S454)

Concerto for Violin and Orchestra
[25']
4(pic).3(English horn).4(bass
clar).3(contrabsn).alto sax.
4.4.4.1. timp,5-6perc,cel,
2harp,pno,strings,vln solo
AMP perf mat rent   (S455)

Concerto for Violoncello and
Orchestra [18']
3.3.3.3. 4.3.3.1. timp,3perc,
harp,pno&cel,strings,vcl solo
MARGUN BP 7132 perf mat rent (S456)

Concerto Quaternio [20']
1+pic+alto fl.2+English horn.2+
clar in E flat+bass clar.3.
4.3.3.1.baritone horn. timp,
4perc,hpsd,cel,pno,strings,
SMezT soli
AMP perf mat rent   (S457)

Deai [28']
3+pic.3+English horn.3+bass clar+
contrabass clar.3+contrabsn.
5.5.4.1. perc,2harp,cel,pno,
strings
AMP perf mat rent   (S458)

Farbenspiel [25']
3+pic.2+English horn.2+bass
clar.4. 4.4.4.1. timp,5perc,
harp,pno,strings
AMP perf mat rent   (S459)

Jubilee Music [24']
3(pic).2+English horn.2+bass
clar.2+contrabsn. 4.3.3.1.
timp,perc,pno&cel,harp,strings
AMP perf mat rent   (S460)

Sandpoint Rag [3']
1.1.1.1. 1.1.1.1. drums,pno,2vln,
vla,vcl,db
MARGUN MP7147 sc $8.00, set $30.00,

SCHULLER, GUNTHER (cont'd.)

pts $22.00   (S461)

Three Nocturnes [15']
3(pic).3(English horn).3(bass
clar).3(contrabsn). 4.3.3.1.
timp,4perc,cel,harp,pno,strings
AMP perf mat rent   (S462)

Trial, The, For Piano And Chamber
Orchestra [20']
1.1(English horn).3.0. 0.1.1.0.
drums,harp,2vln,vla,vcl,db,pno
solo
(piano solo improvised: co-
conceived with Ran Blake) MARGUN
MP7164 perf mat rent   (S463)

Variants [18']
2.1.2+bass clar.2+contrabsn.
4.3.3.1. timp,3perc,harp,
strings,vibra solo,pno solo,db
solo,drums solo
sc MJQ $9.50, perf mat rent (S464)

SCHULTHEISS, ULRICH (1956-   )
Akrostichon [11']
3.3.3.3. 4.3.3.1. timp,perc,harp,
strings
PETERS   (S465)

Down East (Sinfonia No. 1)
string orch
sc PETERS P8637 f.s., perf mat rent
(S466)

Fra Virgolette [10'30"]
3.3.3.3. 4.3.3.1. perc,harp,
strings
PETERS   (S467)

Oggetto, L' [13']
3.3.3.3. 4.3.3.1. timp,perc,harp,
strings
PETERS   (S468)

Sinfonia No. 1
see Down East

SCHULTZ, SVEND S. (1913-   )
Coffee House, The: Overture [15']
2+pic.2.2.2. 4.3.2.1. timp,perc,
cel,harp,strings
HANSEN-DEN perf mat rent   (S469)

Overture Champetre [12']
2+pic.2(English horn).2.2.
4.3.2.1. timp,4perc,harp,
strings
HANSEN-DEN perf mat rent   (S470)

Storstroem Bridge, The
see Storstromsbroen

Storstromsbroen
"Storstroem Bridge, The" sc,pts
SAMFUNDET f.s.   (S471)

SCHULTZE, NORBERT (1911-   )
Orchestersuite In Zehn Satzen [40']
2.2.2.2. 3.3.3.1. timp,perc,harp,
pno,strings
SIKORSKI perf mat rent   (S472)

SCHUMAN, WILLIAM HOWARD (1910-1992)
American Hymn [27']
sc MERION 446-41044 $20.00, perf
mat rent   (S473)

Showcase [5']
MERION perf mat rent   (S474)

SCHUMANN, CLARA (WIECK) (1819-1896)
Concerto for Piano and Orchestra, Op.
7, in A minor [28']
2.2.2.2. 2.2.1.0. perc,strings,
pno solo
RIES   (S475)
(Klassen, J.) study sc BREITKOPF-W
PB 5183 f.s., perf mat rent
(S476)

SCHUMANN, ROBERT (ALEXANDER)
(1810-1856)
Bilder Aus Osten [arr.] *Op.66
(Reinecke) "Scenes From The East
[arr.]" 2.2.2.2. 2.2.0.0. timp,
perc,strings [22'] KALMUS A6140
sc $45.00, set $75.00, perf mat
rent   (S477)

Braut Von Messina, Die, Op. 100:
Overture
see Overture, Scherzo Und Finale,
Op. 52

Carnaval [arr.]
(Konstaninov, K.) 2+pic.2.2.2.
4.2.3.1. timp,perc,harp,cel,
strings [25'] BOOSEY perf mat
rent   (S478)
(Ravel, Maurice) 2+pic.2.2.2.
2.2.0.0. timp,perc,harp,strings
SALABERT perf mat rent   (S479)

SCHUMANN, ROBERT (ALEXANDER) (cont'd.)

Concerto for Piano and Orchestra, Op.
54, in A minor
min sc EULENBURG 556 f.s.			(S480)
SONZOGNO perf mat rent			(S481)

Concerto For Violoncello And
Orchestra, Op. 129, In A Minor
*see GREAT ROMANTIC CELLO
CONCERTOS
see Fantasy for Violin and
Orchestra, Op. 131

Concerto for Violoncello and
Orchestra, Op. 129, in A minor,
[arr.]
(Shostakovich, D.) 2.2.2.2.
4.2.0.0. timp,strings,vcl solo
[21'] SIKORSKI perf mat rent	(S482)
(Shostakovich, Dmitri) 2.2.2.2.
4.2.0.0. timp,harp,strings,vcl
solo [24'] VAAP perf mat rent
(S483)

Fantasy for Violin and Orchestra, Op.
131
min sc KALMUS K01101 $5.50 contains
also: Concerto for Violoncello
and Orchestra, Op. 129, in A
minor			(S484)

Faust-Szenen: Overture
see Hermann Und Dorothea: Overture

Fest-Ouverture, Op. 123
see Manfred, Op. 115: Overture

Fruhlingsnacht, For Solo Voice And
Orchestra [arr.]
(Britten) "Spring Night, For Solo
Voice And Orchestra [arr.]"
1.1.2.1. 2.2.1.0. perc,harp/pno,
strings,solo voice [1'30'] BOOSEY
perf mat rent			(S485)

Fugen Uber Den Namen BACH [aRR.]
*Op.60,Nos.1-4
(Angerer, Paul) string orch [20']
sc,pts DOBLINGER 74 007 f.s.
(S486)

Gedichte Der Maria Stuart, For Solo
Voice And Chamber Group [arr.]
*Op.135
(Reimann, Aribert) 2.0+English
horn.1.2. 1.0.0.0. 4vla,3vcl,2db,
Mez solo [9'] SCHOTTS perf mat
rent			(S487)

Genoveva, Op. 81: Overture
see Overture, Scherzo Und Finale,
Op. 52

Hermann Und Dorothea: Overture
min sc KALMUS K01100 $5.00 contains
also: Faust-Szenen: Overture
(S488)

Introduzione E Allegro Appassionato,
For Piano And Orchestra, Op. 92
see Konzertstück for Piano and
Orchestra, Op. 92

Julius Caesar, Op. 128: Overture
KALMUS A5795 sc $15.00, set $45.00,
perf mat rent			(S489)
see Manfred, Op. 115: Overture

Konzert-Allegro Mit Introduktion, For
Piano And Orchestra, Op. 134
SONZOGNO perf mat rent			(S490)
see Konzertstück for Piano and
Orchestra, Op. 92, in G

Konzertsatz For Piano And Orchestra
In D Minor
(De Beenhouwer, Jozef; Draheim,
Joachim) 2.2.2.2. 2.2.0.0. timp,
strings,pno solo [8'] study sc
BREITKOPF-W PB 5181 f.s., perf
mat rent			(S491)

Konzertstück for Piano and Orchestra,
Op. 92
"Introduzione E Allegro
Appassionato, For Piano And
Orchestra, Op. 92" SONZOGNO perf
mat rent			(S492)

Konzertstück for Piano and Orchestra,
Op. 92, in G
min sc KALMUS K01104 $5.50 contains
also: Konzert-Allegro Mit
Introduktion, For Piano And
Orchestra, Op. 134			(S493)

Korsar, Der; Opernfragment
(Draheim, Joachim) sc BREITKOPF-W
f.s.			(S494)

Manfred, Op. 115: Overture
min sc KALMUS K01099 $5.50 contains
also: Julius Caesar, Op. 128:
Overture; Fest-Ouverture, Op. 123
(S495)

SCHUMANN, ROBERT (ALEXANDER) (cont'd.)

Overture, Scherzo Und Finale, Op. 52
min sc KALMUS K01098 $5.50 contains
also: Genoveva, Op. 81: Overture;
Braut Von Messina, Die, Op. 100:
Overture			(S496)

Poet Speaks, The [arr.]
(Vinter, Gilbert) clar,harp,strings
[16'] BOOSEY perf mat rent (S497)

Scenes From The East [arr.]
see Bilder Aus Osten [arr.]

Spring Night, For Solo Voice And
Orchestra [arr.]
see Fruhlingsnacht, For Solo Voice
And Orchestra [arr.]

Suite No. 1
(Suben) 1.1.1.1. 2.1.1.0. perc,
harp,strings [6'] KALMUS A7479 sc
$20.00, set $20.00, pts $1.50,
ea., perf mat rent			(S498)

Symphonies Nos. 1-4
min sc KALMUS K00424 $20.00	(S499)

Symphony No. 2, Op. 61, in C
(Druian) set SCHIRM.G 50347570
$17.50			(S500)

SCHÜTZ, HEINRICH (1585-1672)
Lobgesang, For Solo Voice And
Orchestra
2fl,opt 2trp,opt timp,org,strings,
S/T solo BREITKOPF-L perf mat
rent			(S501)

SCHWAEN, KURT (1909-   )
Promenaden
sc PETERS 4979 f.s.			(S502)

SCHWALBEN WALZER, DIE see Strauss,
Johann, [Sr.]

SCHWANENDREHER, DER, FOR VIOLA AND
ORCHESTRA see Hindemith, Paul

SCHWANENGESANG, FOR VIOLONCELLO AND
CHAMBER ORCHESTRA see Eder, Helmut

SCHWANTNER, JOSEPH (1943-   )
Canticle Of The Evening Bells, For
Flute And Orchestra [20']
0.1(English horn).1.1. 1.1.1.0.
perc,pno,vln,vla,vcl,db,fl solo
sc PETERS P66678 $25.00, perf mat
rent			(S503)

Distant Runes And Incantations, For
Piano And Orchestra [15']
2(pic).2(English horn).2(bass
clar).2. 2.2.0.0. 2perc,cel,
strings,pno solo
sc HELICON EA00541 $25.00, perf mat
rent			(S504)

Magabunda, For Solo Voice And
Orchestra
4.3.3.3. 4.3.3.1. pno&cel,harp,
timp,perc,strings,S solo
sc HELICON EA00516 $35.00	(S505)

New Morning For The World: "Daybreak
Of Freedom", For Solo Voice And
Orchestra
3.3.3.3. 4.0.0.0. timp,perc,cel,
pno,strings,speaking voice
sc HELICON $25.00			(S506)

Sudden Rainbow, A
3.3.3.3. 3.3.3.1. timp,harp,pno&
cel,strings
study sc HELICON EA00558 f.s., perf
mat rent			(S507)

SCHWARTZ, ARTHUR (1901-1984)
Dancing In The Dark, [arr.] [4'45"]
(Herfurth) WARNER perf mat rent
(S508)
SCHWARTZ, ELLIOTT SCHELLING (1936-   )
Celebrations - Reflections [15']
2(pic).2.2(bass clar).2. 4.2.2.1.
timp,perc,pno,cel,strings
sc NORRUTH perf mat rent	(S509)

Chamber Concerto No.1, For Double
Bass And Chamber Orchestra [11']
1.1.1.1. 1.0.0.0. perc,pno,
strings,db solo
NORRUTH perf mat rent			(S510)

Chamber Concerto No.3, For Piano And
Chamber Orchestra [15']
1.2.1.2. 2.0.0.0. perc,strings,
pno solo
NORRUTH perf mat rent			(S511)

Chamber Concerto No. 4, For Saxophone
And Instrumental Ensemble [12']
clar,clar&bass clar,trp,trom,
3perc,vln,vla,vcl,sax solo
sc MARGUN BP 7138 $8.50, perf mat
rent			(S512)

SCHWARTZ, ELLIOTT SCHELLING (cont'd.)

Dream Overture [9']
2.2.2.2. 4.2.2.1. timp,perc,pno,
strings,electronic equipment
sc AM.COMP.AL. $12.10			(S513)

Four Ohio Portraits [17']
2(pic).1(English horn).2(bass
clar).1(contrabsn). 2.1.0.0.
perc,pno,strings
sc NORRUTH perf mat rent	(S514)

Zebra [9']
2fl,pic,opt ob,2clar,2bsn,2horn,
2trp,2trom,opt tuba,perc,
strings,electronic tape
NORRUTH perf mat rent			(S515)

SCHWARTZ, FRANCIS (1940-   )
Gestos [20']
2+pic.2.2.2. 4.2.3.1. timp,perc,
strings
SALABERT perf mat rent			(S516)

Tropical Trek Of Tristan Trimble, The
[8']
1.1.1.1. 0.1.1.1. timp,gong,
strings
PEER perf mat rent			(S517)

SCHWARZE HALBINSELN see Höller, York

SCHWARZER UND ROTER TANZ see Rihm,
Wolfgang

SCHWARZERDE, FOR SOLO VOICE AND
ORCHESTRA see Eröd, Ivan

SCHWATZERIN, DIE see Strauss, Josef

SCHWEBENDE BEGEGNUNG see Rihm, Wolfgang

SCHWEDISCHER TANZ see Gouvy, Theodore

SCHWEINITZ, WOLFGANG VON (1953-   )
Brucke, Die, For Solo Voices And
Orchestra *Op.15 [12']
1.1.1.1. 1.1.1.0. timp,perc,harp,
strings,TBar soli
SIKORSKI perf mat rent			(S518)

Concerto for Piano and Orchestra, Op.
18 [16']
3.3.3.3. 3.3.3.1. timp,2perc,
strings,pno solo
SIKORSKI perf mat rent			(S519)

Konzertouverture *Op.19 [8']
2+pic.3.2+bass clar.2+contrabsn.
4.3.3.1. timp,2perc,strings
BOOSEY perf mat rent			(S520)

Symphony No. 2, Op. 8 [27']
3.3.4.2.sax. 3.2.2.1. timp,5perc,
harp,pno,strings
SIKORSKI perf mat rent			(S521)

SCHWEIZER, KLAUS (1939-   )
Jeu De Valeurs Et d'Intensités
[12'30"]
0.0.0.0. 0.3.3.0. marimba&vibra,
cel,harp,strings
BÄREN. BA 6295 perf mat rent (S522)

Klangminuten [12']
2+pic.3.3.3. 5.3.2.0+db tuba.
strings
BÄREN. BA 6737 perf mat rent (S523)

SCHWELLE see Platz, Robert

SCHWERTSIK, KURT (1935-   )
Alphorn Concerto "In The Celtic
Manner" *Op.27 [17']
0.1.0.2.alto sax.tenor sax.
2.0.2.0. timp,perc,strings
without vln,vla
BOOSEY perf mat rent			(S524)

Concerto for Guitar and Orchestra,
Op. 35 [17']
2.0.0.2. 0.0.0.0. 3perc,harp,cel,
strings,gtr solo
BOOSEY perf mat rent			(S525)

Concerto for Timpani and Orchestra,
Op. 51 [20']
1+pic.1+English horn.1+clar in E
flat+bass clar.2. 2.2.2.1.
strings,timp/tom-tom solo
BOOSEY perf mat rent			(S526)

Empfindsames Konzert, Ein, For Double
Bass And Orchestra *Op.56 [16']
2(pic).1.1+bass clar.1+contrabsn.
0.0.1.1. strings,db solo
BOOSEY perf mat rent			(S527)

Fanferlieschen Schonefusschen:
Verwandlungsmusik [21']
3.0.0+bass clar.0. 0.3.0.1. perc,
pno,vln,4vcl,db
BOOSEY perf mat rent			(S528)

SCHWERTSIK, KURT (cont'd.)

Instant Music, For Flute And
Orchestra *Op.40 [15']
0+pic.2.2+bass clar.2. 3.2.2.1.
strings,fl solo
sc BOOSEY $21.00, perf mat rent
(S529)

Irdische Klange *Op.37 [15']
4(pic).3+English horn.2+clar in E
flat+bass clar.3+contrabsn.
4.4.4.1. timp,perc,harp,pno,
strings
BOOSEY perf mat rent   (S530)

Irdischen Klange, Der: Funf
Naturstucke *Op.45 [16']
3.2.2+bass clar.2+contrabsn.
3.3.3.1. timp,5perc,harp,
strings
BOOSEY perf mat rent   (S531)

Starckdeutsche Lieder Und Tanze, For
Solo Voice And Orchestra *Op.44
[28']
2(pic).1+English horn.2+bass
clar.2+contrabsn.alto sax.
1.2.2.1. timp,perc,pno&cel,elec
gtr,strings,Bar solo
BOOSEY perf mat rent   (S532)

Tag- Und Nachtweisen *Op.34 [14']
3.3.0.3. 0.3.3.0. perc,org,
strings
BOOSEY perf mat rent   (S533)

Wiener Chronik 1848 *Op.28 [52']
1+pic.2.2+clar in E flat+bass
clar.2. 4.2.3.1. timp,perc,
harp,cel,strings
BOOSEY perf mat rent   (S534)

SCHWETZINGER DIVERTIMENTO see Kupkovic,
Ladislav

SCHWEYK IM ZEITEN WELTKRIEG: IN DEN
HOHEREN REGIONEN NO. 1, FOR SOLO
VOICES AND STRINGS see Eisler,
Hanns

SCHWEYK IM ZEITEN WELTKRIEG: IN DEN
HOHEREN REGIONEN NO. 2, FOR SOLO
VOICES AND STRINGS see Eisler,
Hanns

SCHWEYK IM ZEITEN WELTKRIEG: IN DEN
HOHEREN REGIONEN NO. 3, FOR SOLO
VOICES AND STRINGS see Eisler,
Hanns

SCHWUNGRADER WALZER see Strauss,
Johann, [Jr.]

SCIARRINO, SALVATORE (1947-   )
Aka Aka To I, II, III, For Solo Voice
And Instrumental Ensemble [5']
fl,horn,trp,4perc,elec org,2vln,
2vcl,female solo
RICORDI-IT 131636 perf mat rent
(S535)

Allegoria Della Notte, For Violin And
Orchestra [16'40"]
2.2.2.2. 2.2.2.1. timp,perc,cel,
harp,strings,vln solo
RICORDI-IT 133745 perf mat rent
(S536)

Attraverso I Cancelli
fl,ob,clar in A,bass clar,bsn,
horn,trom,timp,cel,strings
sc RICORDI-IT 031-35827 $19.00
(S537)

Autoritratto Nella Notte [15']
2.0.2.2. 2.2.2.0. perc,12vln,
4vla,4vcl,2db
RICORDI-IT 133504 perf mat rent
(S538)

Che Sai Guardiano Delle Notte, For
Clarinet And Orchestra [12']
2.1.0+bass clar.1. 2.2.2.0. timp,
cel,strings,clar solo
sc RICORDI-IT 031-35828 $33.50,
perf mat rent   (S539)

Clair De Lune, For Piano And
Orchestra *Op.25 [5']
2.2.2.2. 2.2.0.0. timp,6vln,2vla,
2vcl,2db,pno solo
sc RICORDI-IT 132426 f.s., perf mat
rent   (S540)

Da A Da Da [8']
6.6.6.4. 6.4.4.2. 7perc,2pno,
2harp,strings
RICORDI-IT 131769 perf mat rent
(S541)

Efebo Con Radio, For Solo Voice And
Orchestra [15']
2.2.2.2. 2.2.1.0. timp,perc,cel,
harp,strings,solo voice
RICORDI-IT 133243 perf mat rent
(S542)

Grande Sonata Da Camera [10']
2.1.2.1. 2.2.2.0. 2perc,cel,pno,
harp,2vln,2vla,2vcl,db
sc RICORDI-IT 131954 f.s., perf mat
rent   (S543)

SCIARRINO, SALVATORE (cont'd.)

Introduzione All'oscuro [16']
1.1.1.1. 1.1.1.0. string quin
RICORDI-IT 133209 perf mat rent
(S544)

Kindertotenlied, For Solo Voices And
Orchestra [4']
2.0.0.2. 2.2.2.0. perc,strings,ST
soli
RICORDI-IT 132849 perf mat rent
(S545)

Lohengrin, For Solo Voices And
Orchestra [45']
2.1.2.2. 1.1.1.0. perc,strings,4
solo voices
RICORDI-IT 133753 perf mat rent
(S546)

Paese Senz' Alba, Il, For Solo Voice
And Orchestra
(contains also: Paese Senza
Tramonto, Il) sc RICORDI-IT
031-35919 $118.50, perf mat rent
(S547)

Romance for Viola d'Amore and
Orchestra [15']
3.3.3.3. 4.4.4.0. timp,perc,cel,
harp,2pno,strings,vla d'amore
solo
RICORDI-IT 132127 perf mat rent
(S548)

Rondo for Flute and Orchestra
2ob,2horn,6vln,2vla,2vcl,db,fl
solo
sc RICORDI-IT 132083 $27.00, perf
mat rent   (S549)

Sonata da Camera [10']
1.1.1.1. 1.1.1.0. timp,perc,cel,
pno,harp,strings
RICORDI-IT 131924 perf mat rent
(S550)

Variations for Violoncello and
Orchestra [17']
3.3.3.3. 4.3.3.1. perc,cel,pno,
harp,strings,vcl solo
sc RICORDI-IT 132227 f.s., perf mat
rent   (S551)

SCINTILLA PRISCA, FOR VIOLONCELLO AND
ORCHESTRA see Fennelly, Brian

SCIORTINO, PATRICE (1922-   )
Nuit, La, For Violin And String
Orchestra [15']
string orch,vln solo
CHOUDENS perf mat rent   (S552)

Soleil De Papier, Le [16']
string orch
CHOUDENS perf mat rent   (S553)

Symphony No. 1 [22']
CHOUDENS perf mat rent   (S554)

SCIOSTAKOVIC, DMITRI
see SHOSTAKOVICH, DMITRI

SCONTRI see Gentilucci, Armando

SCORDATURA 14 see Tosi, Daniel

SCOTCH POEM [ARR.] see MacDowell,
Edward Alexander

SCRIABIN, ALEXANDER (1872-1915)
Concerto for Piano and Orchestra, Op.
20, in F sharp minor
VAAP perf mat rent   (S555)

Divin Poeme, Le *See Symphony No. 3

Poem No. 2, [arr.]
(Maganini) 1+pic.2.2.2. 2.2.2.0.
timp,strings [3'] KALMUS A5806
pno-cond sc $2.00, set $12.00
(S556)

Poeme De L'Extase *Op.54,
reconstruction
(Ahronovitch, Yuri) 4.4.4.4.
8.5.3.1. timp,perc,2harp,cel,org,
strings [24'] BELAIEFF (S557)

Symphony No. 1, Op. 26
min sc KALMUS K01481 $14.25 (S558)

Symphony No. 2, Op. 29
min sc KALMUS K01482 $14.25 (S559)

Symphony No. 3, Op. 43
min sc KALMUS K01483 $20.00 (S560)

Symphony No. 3, Op. 43
*reconstruction
(Ahronovitch, Yuri) 4.4.4.4.
8.5.3.1. timp,harp,strings [48']
BELAIEFF   (S561)

Three Preludes, Op. 11, Nos. 4, 5,
15, For Cello And String
Orchestra[arr.]
(Hartmann) string orch,vcl/vln solo
[6'30"] KALMUS A7269 pno-cond sc
$3.00, set $9.00, pts $1.50, ea.
(S562)

SCROOGE: THE STINGIEST MAN IN TOWN see
Speilman

SCULTHORPE, PETER [JOSHUA] (1929-   )
Concerto for Piano and Orchestra
[23']
0.2.0.3. 2.2.3.1. 3perc,strings,
pno solo
FABER perf mat rent   (S563)

Earth Cry [12']
3.2.3.2+contrabsn. 4.4.3.1. timp,
perc,strings
FABER perf mat rent   (S564)

From Tabuh Tabuhan [6']
2perc,strings
FABER perf mat rent   (S565)

Lament For Strings [11']
string orch sc FABER F0553 f.s.,
perf mat rent   (S566)

Love 200, For Rock Band And Orchestra
[20']
2.2.2.3. 4.3.3.1. timp,3perc,
strings, rock band: 2 singers,
woodwinds, keyboard, bass
guitar, drums
FABER perf mat rent   (S567)

Mangrove [17']
0.0.0.0. 4.2.3.1. 3perc,strings
sc FABER F0631 f.s., perf mat rent
(S568)

Music For Japan [12']
3.3.3.3. 4.4.3.1. timp,3perc,
strings
sc FABER F0535 $16.00, perf mat
rent   (S569)

Overture For A Happy Occasion [4']
2.2.2.2. 2.2.2.1. timp,perc,harp,
strings
FABER perf mat rent   (S570)

Port Essington, For String Trio And
String Orchestra
string orch, string trio soli
sc FABER F0579 f.s., perf mat rent
(S571)

Small Town [6']
ob,2trp,timp,2perc,harp,strings
sc FABER F0274 $9.00, perf mat rent
(S572)

SCUOLA DI GELOSI, LA: OVERTURE see
Salieri, Antonio

SE AL LABBRO MIO NON CREDI, FOR SOLO
VOICE AND ORCHESTRA see Mozart,
Wolfgang Amadeus

SE ARDIRE E SPERANZA, FOR SOLO VOICE
AND ORCHESTRA see Mozart, Wolfgang
Amadeus

SE TUTTI I MALI MIEI, FOR SOLO VOICE
AND ORCHESTRA see Mozart, Wolfgang
Amadeus

SEA, THE, FOR ORGAN AND ORCHESTRA see
Ciurlionis, Mikolajus

SEA AND SKY see Finnissy, Michael

SEA BEACH REVISITED, THE, FOR
SYNCLAVIER AND ORCHESTRA see Proto,
Frank

SEA-BIRD, THE, FOR SOLO VOICE AND
ORCHESTRA see Fischer, Irwin

SEA CHANGE see Nicholson, George

SEA CHANGES, FOR SOLO VOICE AND CHAMBER
ORCHESTRA see Eckert, Michael

SEA MAIDEN, THE: SUITE see Poldmaa, A.

SEA PICTURES, FOR SOLO VOICE AND
ORCHESTRA see Elgar, [Sir] Edward
(William)

SEA SKETCHES see Williams, Grace

SEA WINDS see Wigglesworth, Frank

SEAGULL, THE: SUITE see Shchedrin,
Rodion

SEARLE, HUMPHREY (1915-1982)
Contemplations, For Solo Voice And
Chamber Orchestra *Op.66 [20']
2.2.2.2. 2.2.0.0. timp,perc,
strings,Mez solo
FABER perf mat rent   (S573)

SEASCAPE see Brooks, Richard James see
Procter, Leland

SEASCAPE AND HARVEST see Holloway,
Robin

SEASONGS see Sigurbjörnsson, Thorkell

SEASONS, THE see Soproni, Jozsef

SEASONS, THE, FOR PIANO AND ORCHESTRA
[ARR.] see Tchaikovsky, Piotr
Ilyich

SEASONS, THE, OP. 67: AUTUMN see
Glazunov, Alexander Konstantinovich

SEASONS, THE, OP. 67: SPRING see
Glazunov, Alexander Konstantinovich

SEASONS, THE, OP. 67: SUMMER see
Glazunov, Alexander Konstantinovich

SEASONS, THE, OP. 67: WINTER see
Glazunov, Alexander Konstantinovich

SECHS BILDER FUR ORCHESTER see
Einfeld(t), Dieter

SECHS DEUTSCHE TANZE, PE 72 see Haydn,
[Johann] Michael

SECHS FABELN NACH JEAN DE LA FONTAINE,
FOR SOLO VOICE AND ORCHESTRA [ARR]
see Offenbach, Jacques

SECHS FRUHE LIEDER, FOR SOLO VOICE AND
ORCHESTRA [ARR.] see Mahler, Gustav

SECHS GEDICHTE VON MARINA ZWETAJEWA,
FOR SOLO VOICE AND ORCHESTRA see
Shostakovich, Dmitri, Six Poems By
Marina Tsvetayeva, For Solo Voice
And Chamber Orchestra

SECHS ROMANZEN NACH GEDICHTEN VON
RALEIGH, BURNS UND SHAKESPEARE, FOR
SOLO VOICE AND CHAMBER ORCHESTRA
see Shostakovich, Dmitri, Six
Romances On Poems By Raleigh,
Burns, And Shakespeare, For Solo
Voice And Chamber Orchestra

SECHS ROMANZEN NACH VERSEN JAPANISCHER
DICHTER, FOR SOLO VOICE AND
ORCHESTRA see Shostakovich, Dmitri,
Six Romances On Words By Japanese
Poets, For Solo Voice And Orchestra

SECHSZEHN LIEDER: NOS. 1-8, FOR SOLO
VOICE AND ORCHESTRA, [ARR.] see
Wolf, Hugo

SECHSZEHN LIEDER: NOS. 9-16, FOR SOLO
VOICE AND ORCHESTRA, [ARR.] see
Wolf, Hugo

SECO DE ARPE, MANUEL (1958-   )
Claro-Oscuro, For Solo Voices And
Chamber Orchestra [15']
1.1.1.1. 1.1.1.0. pno,strings,3
solo voices
sc ALPUERTO f.s.   (S574)

Sinestesia [7']
fl,ob,clar,bsn,horn,perc,strings
ALPUERTO   (S575)

SECOND CREATION, THE: AN ORCHESTRAL
DRAMA FOR TRUMPETS see Thommessen,
Olav Anton

SECOND ESSAY FOR ORCHESTRA see Kulesha,
Gary

SECOND LANDSCAPE see Boone, Charles N.

SECRET THEATRE see Birtwistle, Harrison

SECUNDEN POLKA see Strauss, Johann,
[Jr.]

SEDEM MINIATUR see Vremsak, Samo

SEDERUNT PRINCIPES see Weir, Judith

SEE WHAT HAPPENS see MacBride, David
Huston

SEECADET QUADRILLE see Strauss, Eduard

SEGERSTAM, LEIF (1944-   )
Monumental Thoughts ...Martti Talvela
In Memoriam [13']
3.3.3.3. 4.4.3.1. timp,5perc,
harp,pno,strings
sc SUOMEN f.s.   (S576)

Pandora: Essay [40']
3(pic).2+English horn.2+bass
clar.2+contrabsn. 4.3.3.1.
timp,perc,cel,harp,strings
SCHIRM.G perf mat rent   (S577)

Pandora: Sketches [20']
3(pic).2+English horn.2+bass
clar.2+contrabsn. 4.3.3.1.
timp,perc,harp,cel,strings
SCHIRM.G perf mat rent   (S578)

Six Songs Of Experience, For Solo
Voice And Orchestra [28']
2(pic).1+English horn.0+bass
clar.1+contrabsn. 2.3.3.1.

SEGERSTAM, LEIF (cont'd.)

timp,2perc,2pno,cel,harp,
strings,5vln soli,S solo
SCHIRM.G perf mat rent   (S579)

Symphony No. 10 [26']
2.1.2.1. 2.2.1.0. timp,2-3perc,
pno,strings,horn solo
sc SUOMEN f.s.   (S580)

Symphony No. 14 [30']
2.2.2.2. 4.3.3.1. timp,4perc,
harp,pno,strings
(Moments of Peace) sc SUOMEN f.s.
(S581)

Thoughts 1988 [15']
2.2.2.2. 4.3.3.1. timp,5perc,
harp,pno,strings
sc SUOMEN f.s.   (S582)

Thoughts 1989 [24']
2.2.2.2. 4.3.3.1. timp,5perc,
harp,pno,strings
sc SUOMEN f.s.   (S583)

SEGUIDILLAS see Albéniz, Isaac see
Gerhard, Roberto

SEGUIRIYAS see Gil Serrano, Jose M.

SEHT DEN BODEN BLUTGETRANKT see Huber,
Klaus

SEI CANTI, FOR SOLO VOICE AND ORCHESTRA
see Meyerowitz, Jan

SEI PRELUDI see Cusatelli, Alessandro

SEIBER, MATYAS GYÖRGY (1905-1960)
Mordvin Lullaby [arr.]
(Docker, Robert) harp/pno,strings
[3'] CURWEN perf mat rent   (S584)

Transylvanian Rhapsody [9']
2(pic).2.2.2. 4.2.3.1. timp,perc,
harp,strings
BOOSEY perf mat rent   (S585)

SEILING see Amdahl, Magne

SEKLES, BERNHARD (1872-1934)
Kleine Suite *Op.21
"Little Suite" KALMUS A7408 sc
$35.00, set $90.00, pts $3.50,
ea., perf mat rent   (S586)

Little Suite
see Kleine Suite

Serenade, Op. 14
KALMUS A7170 sc $25.00, set $30.00,
pts $3.00, ea., perf mat rent
(S587)

SEKS NORSKE DANSER see Lunde, Ivar

SELBSTPORTRAIT see Shchedrin, Rodion,
Self-Portrait

SELECTED WORKS, VOL. 6: SYMPHONIES see
Spohr, Ludwig (Louis)

SELECTED WORKS, VOL. 7: CONCERTOS see
Spohr, Ludwig (Louis)

SELF-PORTRAIT see Shchedrin, Rodion

SELFDEPENDENCE, FOR SOLO VOICE AND
ORCHESTRA see Lund, Signe

SELKIRK MUSIC see Crawford, Paul

SELVA, FOR PIANO AND INSTRUMENTAL
ENSEMBLE see Maggi, Dario

SEMENOFF, IVAN (1917-1972)
Concerto for Violin and Orchestra
[23']
CHOUDENS perf mat rent   (S588)

Concerto for Violin, Piano and
Orchestra
2.2.2.2. 2.2.2.0. timp,strings,vln
solo,pno solo BILLAUDOT perf mat
rent   (S589)

Contagion, La, For Solo Voice And
Orchestra [33']
2.2.2.2. 2.2.2.0. timp,2perc,
harp,strings,SBar soli
BILLAUDOT perf mat rent   (S590)

SEMIRAMIDE: OVERTURE see Rossini,
Gioacchino see Salieri, Antonio

SEMIRAMIS see Hamel, Peter Michael

SEMPER FIDELIS MARCH see Sousa, John
Philip

SEMPRE AZZURO see Miereanu, Costin

SEMPRE TUTTI see Korndorf, Nicolai

SEN O MINULOSTI see Martinu, Bohuslav
(Jan)

SENJA SUITE see Brevik, Tor

SENSE OF ABSENCE, FOR SOLO VOICE AND
CHAMBER ORCHESTRA see Antoniou,
Theodore, Klima Tis Apussias, For
Solo Voice And Chamber Orchestra

SENSTIUS, KAI
Concertino for Flute and Orchestra
sc SAMFUNDET f.s., perf mat rent
(S591)

SEPTEMBER MUSIC see Matthews, David

SEQUENCES, FOR VIOLIN AND CHAMBER
ORCHESTRA see Haubenstock-Ramati,
Roman

SEQUENCES, FOR VIOLIN AND ORCHESTRA see
Sigurbjörnsson, Thorkell

SEQUENZE see Kocsar, Miklos

SEQUOIA see Tower, Joan

SERAGLIO, IL: OVERTURE see Mozart,
Wolfgang Amadeus, Entfuhrung Aus
Dem Serail, Die: Overture

SERALE, FOR SOLO VOICE AND ORCHESTRA
see Banfield, Raffaello de

SERBISCHER KOLO see Janácek, Leoš

SEREBRIER, JOSE (1938-   )
Dorothy And Carmine, For Flute And
String Orchestra [7']
string orch,fl solo
PEER perf mat rent   (S592)

Orpheus Times Light, For Solo Voice
And Chamber Orchestra
2(pic).1.0.0. 2.2.2.1. timp,perc,
harp,pno/cel,strings,S solo
PEER perf mat rent   (S593)

Passacaglia And Perpetuum Mobile, For
Accordion And Chamber Orchestra
2horn,trp,bass trom,perc,strings,
acord solo
PEER perf mat rent   (S594)

Poema Elegiaco
2+pic.2+English horn.2+bass
clar.2+contrabsn.alto sax.
4.3.3.1. timp,perc,pno,strings
sc PEER MUSIK 60922-856 $10.00,
perf mat rent   (S595)

SERENADE A LYDIA DE CADAQUES see
Montsalvatge, Xavier

SERENADE AND AUBADE see Williamson,
Malcolm

SERENADE CONCERTANTE, FOR PIANO AND
CHAMBER ORCHESTRA see Franco, Johan

SERENADE CONCERTANTE, FOR VIOLIN AND
ORCHESTRA see Delannoy, Marcel

SERENADE D'ANTOINETTE, FOR FLUTE AND
STRING ORCHESTRA see Kochan, Ernst

SERENADE FOR A SUMMER EVENING see
Wuensch, Gerhard

SERENADE FOR MARGUERITA see Smith,
Larry Alan

SERENADE FOR NIKOLAI RUBINSTEIN'S
SAINT'S DAY see Tchaikovsky, Piotr
Ilyich

SERENADE FOR SUMMER see Muczynski,
Robert Stanley

SERENADE, HYMN AND TOCCATA [ARR.] see
Berlioz, Hector (Louis)

SERENADE LYRIQUE see Elgar, [Sir]
Edward (William)

SERENADE MAURESQUE see Elgar, [Sir]
Edward (William)

SERENADE MELANCOLIQUE, FOR VIOLIN AND
ORCHESTRA see Tchaikovsky, Piotr
Ilyich

SERENADE NACH SCHWEDISCHEN VOLKSLIEDERN
see Bruch, Max

SERENADE, OP. 48, IN C see Tchaikovsky,
Piotr Ilyich

SERENADE POUR UN INSECTE see Volkonsky,
Andrei

SERENADE VENITIENNE, FOR SOLO VOICE AND
ORCHESTRA see Tomasi, Henri

SERENADES, NOS.1-3, K. 100, K. 101, K. 185 see Mozart, Wolfgang Amadeus

SERENADES NOS. 4-6 see Mozart, Wolfgang Amadeus

SERENATA see Walker, George Theophilus

SERENATA CONCERTANTE see Orrego-Salas, Juan A.

SERENATA CONCERTANTE, FOR VIOLIN AND ORCHESTRA see Maconchy, Elizabeth

SERENATA NOTTURNA, FOR FOUR HORNS AND ORCHESTRA see Holloway, Robin

SERENATA ROMANTICA see Walter, Fried

SERENATA ROMANTICA NO. 2 see Bolzoni, Giovanni

SERENITA NOTTURNA see Erdmann, Dietrich

SERF OF VIRO, THE, FOR TWO VIOLINS AND STRING ORCHESTRA see Jalkanen, Pekka

SERIAL SET IN FOUR see Coakley, Donald

SERIEUX S'ABSTENIR see DuBois, Pierre-Max

SERKEBAYEV, ALMAS (1948-   )
    Otrar [12']
        perc,strings
        VAAP perf mat rent   (S596)

SERMILA, JARMO (1939-   )
    Circle Of The Moon, A, For Oboe And Orchestra [14']
        2horn,perc,harp,strings,ob solo
        sc JASE $20.00   (S597)

    Labor! [13']
        2.2.2.2. 2.2.2.0. 3perc,strings
        sc JASE $22.00   (S598)

    Manifesto [13']
        2.2.2.2. 4.3.3.0. 2perc,strings
        sc JASE $22.00   (S599)

    Transformations [14']
        string orch
        sc SUOMEN f.s.   (S600)

SEROCKI, KAZIMIERZ (1922-1981)
    Poezje, For Solo Voice And Chamber Orchestra
        fl,alto fl&pic,clar,bass clar, alto sax,2perc,cel,pno,2harp, 6vln,3vla,3vcl,S solo
        [11'] sc POLSKIE f.s.   (S601)

SEROV, ALEXANDER
    Dance Of The Zaporozh Cossacks *see RUSSIAN SYMPHONIC MUSIC, VOL. 4

SERSE: FRONDI TENERE; OMBRA MAI FU, FOR SOLO VOICE AND ORCHESTRA, [ARR.] see Handel, George Frideric

SERSE: SUITE see Handel, George Frideric

SERVA PADRONA, LA: A SERPINA PENSERETE, FOR SOLO VOICE AND ORCHESTRA see Pergolesi, Giovanni Battista

SERVA PADRONA, LA: CONTENTO TU SARAI, FOR SOLO VOICES AND ORCHESTRA see Pergolesi, Giovanni Battista

SERVA PADRONA, LA: LA CONOSCO A QUEGLI OCCHIETTI, FOR SOLO VOICES AND ORCHESTRA see Pergolesi, Giovanni Battista

SERVA PADRONA, LA: PER TE HO IO NEL CORE, FOR SOLO VOICES AND ORCHESTRA see Pergolesi, Giovanni Battista

SERVA PADRONA, LA: SEMPRE IN CONTRASTI, FOR SOLO VOICE AND ORCHESTRA see Pergolesi, Giovanni Battista

SERVA PADRONA, LA: SON IMBROGLIATO IO GIA, FOR SOLO VOICE AND ORCHESTRA see Pergolesi, Giovanni Battista

SERVA PADRONA, LA: STIZZOSO, MIO STIZZOSO, FOR SOLO VOICE AND ORCHESTRA see Pergolesi, Giovanni Battista

SERVER, JUAN PONS
    Obertura
        sc PILES f.s.   (S602)

SESSIONS, ROGER (1896-   )
    Concerto for Orchestra [15']
        sc MERION 446-41042 $35.00, perf mat rent   (S603)

SESSIONS, ROGER (cont'd.)

    Symphony No. 9
        3.3.4.3. 4.4.3.1. timp,perc,pno, harp,strings
        sc MERION 446-41047 $65.00, perf mat rent   (S604)

SEST SKLADB, FOR STRING ORCHESTRA see Kogoj, Marij

ŠESTÁK, ZDENĚK (1925-   )
    Concerto for String Orchestra [20']
        string orch
        SUPRAPHON   (S605)

SET OF ACT TUNES AND DANCES [ARR.] see Purcell, Henry

SETE VEZES, FOR SOLO VOICE AND ORCHESTRA see Villa-Lobos, Heitor

SETTLERS SUITE see Kraft, William

SEUIL DEPLOYE see Durieux, Frederic

SEVEN BEAUTIES: SUITE see Karayev, Kara

SEVEN MIKROPHONAE see Yavelow, Christopher Johnson

SEVEN MINIATURES see Bibik, Valentin see Vremsak, Samo, Sedem Miniatur

SEVEN NURSERY RHYMES see Lankester, Michael

SEVEN PIECES, FOR BASS CLARINET AND ORCHESTRA see Keuris, Tristan

SEVEN RITUALS see Silsbee, Ann

SEVEN SCOTT JOPLIN RAGS [ARR.] see Joplin, Scott

SEVEN SHORT PIECES see Ghezzo, Dinu Dumitru

SEVEN SONGS, FOR SOLO VOICE AND CHAMBER ORCHESTRA see Revueltas, Silvestre, Siete Canciones, For Solo Voice And Chamber Orchestra

SEVEN SONGS, FOR SOLO VOICE AND ORCHESTRA see Riley, Dennis

SEVEN SONGS see Mahler, Gustav

SEVEN STARS SYMPHONY, THE see Koechlin, Charles

SEVEN SYMPHONIES FROM THE COURT OF THURN UND TAXIS
    (Emmerig, Thomas; Angerer, Hugo) sc GARLAND ISBN 0-8240-3855-X $90.00 "The Symphony" Vol. C-VII contains: Pokorny, Franz Xaver, Symphonies, Three; Riepel, Joseph, Symphony; Schacht, Theodor von, Symphonies, Two; Touchemoulin, Joseph, Symphony
                                            (S606)

SEVEN TABLEAUX, FOR TRUMPET AND ORCHESTRA see Roxburgh, Edwin

SEVEN TEXTURAL SETTINGS OF JAPANESE POETRY, FOR SOLO VOICE AND CHAMBER ORCHESTRA see Udow, Michael William

SEVEN WORDS, FOR VIOLONCELLO, BAYAN AND STRINGS see Gubaidulina, Sofia

1791. SERENADE FOR SMALL ORCHESTRA see Karayev, Faradzh

1712 OVERTURE see "Bach, P.D.Q." (Peter Schickele)

SEVENTEENTH OF NOVEMBER see Vacek, Miloš

SEVERAC, DEODAT DE (1872-1921)
    Pepermint-Get
        3.2.2.2. 2.2.3.0. timp,perc, strings
        SALABERT perf mat rent   (S607)

SEVERN RHAPSODY, A see Finzi, Gerald

SEYMER, WILLIAM (1890-1964)
    Solitude [4']
        1.1.2.0. 2.2.1.0. pno,strings
        NORDISKA perf mat rent   (S608)

SHAAR see Xenakis, Yannis (Iannis)

SHADES OF AUTUMN see Turner, Robert [Comrie]

SHADOW MUSIC see Luedeke, Raymond

SHADOW OF LIGHT see McCabe, John

SHADOW WALTZ [ARR.] see Warren, Harry

SHADOWLAND see Sorensen, Bent

SHADOWS see Sallinen, Aulis

SHADOWS, FOR OBOE AND ORCHESTRA see Rypdal, Terje

SHADOWS AND LIGHT see Siegmeister, Elie

SHAKER LOOPS see Adams, John

SHAKIDI, TOLIB (1946-   )
    Concerto for Piano and Orchestra
        3.2+English horn.2.2. 4.3.3.1. timp,5perc,pno,strings,pno solo
        VAAP perf mat rent   (S609)

    Potter's Wheel, For 2 Pianos And String Orchestra [16']
        string orch,2pno soli
        VAAP perf mat rent   (S610)

    Sado [10']
        3.3.3.2. 4.4.3.1. timp,perc,harp, pno,strings
        VAAP perf mat rent   (S611)

SHANBEI SUITE see Ma, Ko

SHANTY POTPOURRI see Danczak, Jul

SHAPERO, HAROLD SAMUEL (1920-   )
    On Green Mountain [12']
        2(pic).2.2.2.alto sax.tenor sax. 2.3.3.1. timp,perc,vibra,elec gtr,bass gtr,harp,pno,strings
        PEER perf mat rent   (S612)

SHAPEY, RALPH (1921-   )
    Concerto for Violin, Violoncello and Orchestra [32']
        PRESSER perf mat rent   (S613)

    Symphonie Concertante [30']
        PRESSER perf mat rent   (S614)

SHARMAN, RODNEY (1958-   )
    Chiaroscuro [11']
        3.2.3(clar in E flat).2. 3.2.3.1. perc,2harp,2pno,strings
        CAN.MUS.CENT. MI 1100 S531C   (S615)

    Concerto for Flute and Chamber Orchestra
        1.1.1.1. 0.0.0.0. timp,perc, strings,fl solo
        CAN.MUS.CENT. MI 1321 S531CO (S616)

    Fandance
        1.1.1.1. 1.1.0.0. perc,pno&cel, strings
        CAN.MUS.CENT. MI 1200 S531FA (S617)

    Orpheus' Garden, For Doublebass And Strings
        6vln,2vla,2vcl,db solo
        CAN.MUS.CENT. MI 1614 S5310R (S618)

    Proximity Of Mars, The
        2.0.0.0. 2.2.2.0. perc,harp,pno, vln,vcl
        CAN.MUS.CENT. MI 1200 S531PR (S619)

SHATIN, JUDITH (1949-   )
    Arche, For Viola And Chamber Orchestra [15']
        2.1.1.1. 0.1.2.1. perc,harp, strings,vla solo
        sc AM.COMP.AL. $33.50, perf mat rent   (S620)

    Aura [17']
        2.2.2.2. 4.2.3.1. perc,strings
        sc AM.COMP.AL. $42.65, perf mat rent   (S621)

    Passion Of St. Cecelia, The, For Piano And Orchestra [20']
        2.2.2.2. 4.2.2.1. 2perc,strings, pno solo
        sc AM.COMP.AL. $75.15, perf mat rent   (S622)

SHATTEN, DAS BAND, DAS UNS AN DIE ERDE BINDET, DER see Jarrell, Michael

SHCHEDRIN, RODION (1932-   )
    Anna Karenina: Romantic Music For Orchestra [27']
        4.3.3.3. 4.3.3.1. timp,4perc,cel, harp,pno,strings
        SIKORSKI perf mat rent   (S623)
        VAAP perf mat rent   (S624)

    Bells Ringing
        see Concerto for Orchestra, No. 2

    Bucklige Pferdchen, Das: Suite No. 2
        see Little Humpback Horse, The: Suite No. 2

    Chimes, The
        see Concerto for Orchestra, No. 2

SHCHEDRIN, RODION (cont'd.)

Concerto for Orchestra, No. 1 [8']
3.3.3.3. 4.4.4.0. timp,perc,harp,
pno,strings
"Mischievous Chastushki" sc MUZYKA
f.s.   (S625)
"Naughty Limericks" KALMUS 7351 sc
$50.00, set $150.00, pts $5.00,
ea., perf mat rent   (S626)
"Naughty Limericks" SIKORSKI perf
mat rent   (S627)

Concerto for Orchestra, No. 2 [10']
4.2.4.2. 4.4.4.0. timp,perc,cel,
pno,strings
"Bells Ringing" SIKORSKI perf mat
rent   (S628)
"Bells Ringing" VAAP perf mat rent
(S629)
"Chimes, The" 4.2.4.2. 4.4.4.0.
timp,perc,cel,pno,strings [10']
KALMUS A7344 sc $25.00, set
$75.00, pts $2.50, ea., perf mat
rent   (S630)

Concerto for Piano and Orchestra, No.
1 [23']
3.3.3.2. 4.3.3.1. timp,perc,harp,
strings,pno solo
VAAP perf mat rent   (S631)

Concerto for Piano and Orchestra, No.
2 [24']
3.2.2.2. 4.3.3.0. timp,perc,
strings,pno solo
SIKORSKI perf mat rent   (S632)
VAAP perf mat rent   (S633)

Concerto for Piano and Orchestra, No.
3 [22']
3(pic).2.3.2. 4.3.2.1. timp,
2perc,cel,harp,strings,pno solo
SIKORSKI perf mat rent   (S634)
VAAP perf mat rent   (S635)

Geometrie Des Tones [15']
1.1.1.1. 1.1.1.0. 2perc,harp,cel,
hpsd,synthesizer,string quin
sc UNIVER. UE19049 f.s., perf mat
rent   (S636)

Little Humpback Horse, The: Suite No.
2 [50']
3.3.3.3. 4.3.3.1. timp,perc,cel,
2harp,pno,strings
VAAP perf mat rent   (S637)
"Bucklige Pferdchen, Das: Suite No.
2" SIKORSKI perf mat rent   (S638)

Mischievous Chastushki
see Concerto for Orchestra, No. 1

Music For The Town Of Kothen [18']
2ob,2bsn,hpsd,strings
"Musik Fur Die Stadt Kothen"
SIKORSKI perf mat rent   (S639)

Musik Fur Die Stadt Kothen
see Music For The Town Of Kothen

Naughty Limericks
see Concerto for Orchestra, No. 1

Seagull, The: Suite [20']
3.3.3.3. 4.3.3.1. timp,3perc,
harp,cel,hpsd,strings
sc SCHIRM.G 50488728 $15.00, perf
mat rent   (S640)
SIKORSKI perf mat rent   (S641)

Selbstportrait
see Self-Portrait

Self-Portrait [19']
3(alto fl,pic).3(English
horn).3.3. 4.3.3.1. timp,4perc,
harp,pno&cel,strings
SIKORSKI perf mat rent   (S642)
VAAP perf mat rent   (S643)
"Selbstportrait" sc UNIVER.
UE 18320 f.s.   (S644)

Solemn Overture
3.2.3.3. 4.0.0.0. timp,4perc,
2harp,strings
VAAP perf mat rent   (S645)

Symphonic Festive Fanfares [5']
3.2.2.2. 4.3.3.1. timp,perc,
strings
VAAP perf mat rent   (S646)

Symphony No. 1
3.3.3.3. 4.3.3.1. timp,perc,
2harp,pno&cel,strings
SIKORSKI perf mat rent   (S647)
[30'] VAAP perf mat rent   (S648)

SHEEP AND GOAT see Guion, David Wendall
Fentress

SHEEP MAY SAFELY GRAZE [ARR.] see Bach,
Johann Sebastian, Schafe Konnen
Sicher Weiden [arr.]

SHEHERAZADE, FOR SOLO VOICE AND
ORCHESTRA see Ravel, Maurice

SHELLEY, HARRY ROWE (1858-1947)
Santa Claus Overture [8']
2.2.2.2. 4.2.3.1. timp,perc,
strings
KALMUS A7430 sc $20.00, set $35.00,
pts $1.50, ea., perf mat rent
(S649)

SHELTERING SKY see Manen, Willem van

SHENANDOAH, A see Cooper, Paul

SHENANDOAH VARIATIONS see Kelly, Robert
T.

SHEPHERD, STUART
Great White Oracle Of Little
Portugal, The [17']
2.2(English horn).2.2. 4.3.3.1.
2perc,strings
CAN.MUS.CENT. MI 1100 S548GR (S650)

SHEPHERD'S HEY see Grainger, Percy
Aldridge

SHERIFF, NOAM (1935-   )
Concerto for Violin and Orchestra
[20']
3.3.3.2. 4.3.3.1. timp,5perc,
harp,strings,vln solo
PETERS   (S651)

Davids Vision [18']
3.3.3.3. 4.3.3.1. timp,3perc,
harp,strings
PETERS   (S652)

SHERLAW-JOHNSON, ROBERT
see JOHNSON, ROBERT SHERLAW

SHERMAN, NORMAN (1926-   )
Garden Of Love
0.0.0.0. 1.1.1.0. perc,strings
CAN.MUS.CENT. MI 1200 S553GA (S653)

SHEVA see Schneider, Gary M.

SHIBATA, MINAO (1916-   )
Metaphonia [14']
3.3.3.3. 4.4.3.1. timp,perc,
strings
sc ZEN-ON 899300 f.s., perf mat
rent   (S654)

SHIFRIN, SEYMOUR J. (1926-1979)
Five Songs, For Solo Voice And
Orchestra [17']
sc APNM $15.00, perf mat rent
(S655)

SHIH, YUN-KANG
Legend Of The Yellow Crane
3.2.2.2. 4.3.3.1. timp,perc,harp,
cel,strings
HONG KONG perf mat rent   (S656)

SHIMOYAMA, HIFUMI (1930-   )
Chromophony
see Saikyo

Saikyo [14'30"]
"Chromophony" JAPAN 8711   (S657)

Wave, For Violoncello And Orchestra
perc,harp,pno,strings,vcl solo
JAPAN 8401   (S658)

SHIN'ANIM SHA'ANANIM, FOR SOLO VOICE,
VIOLONCELLO AND INSTRUMENTAL
ENSEMBLE see Amy, Gilbert

SHINDIG see Gillis, Don E.

SHINE, LITTLE SUN, FOR SOLO VOICE AND
ORCHESTRA see Lipovsek, Marijan,
Soncece, Sij, For Solo Voice And
Orchestra

SHISHAKOV, YURI (1925-   )
Concerto for Balalaika and Orchestra
fl,ob,strings, 9 Russian
instruments
VAAP perf mat rent   (S659)

SHLEG, L.
Scenes At The Fair
sc MEZ KNIGA f.s.   (S660)

SHORT OVERTURE, A see Kay, Ulysses
Simpson

SHORT RIDE IN A FAST MACHINE see Adams,
John

SHORT SUITE FOR ORCHESTRA see Wuorinen,
Charles

SHORT SYMPHONY see Kriesberg, Matthias
see Luening, Otto see Swanson,
Howard

SHORT SYMPHONY, A see Perle, George

SHOSTAKOVICH, DMITRI (1906-1975)
Aus Jiddischer Volkspoesie, For Solo
Voices And Orchestra
see From Jewish Folk Poetry, For
Solo Voices And Orchestra

Ballet Suite No.1 [20']
2.1.2.1. 3.2.2.1. timp,perc,cel,
pno,strings
SIKORSKI perf mat rent   (S661)

Ballet Suite No. 2 [12']
2.1.2.1. 3.2.2.1. timp,perc,cel,
pno,strings
SIKORSKI perf mat rent   (S662)

Ballet Suite No. 3 [20']
2.1.2.1. 3.2.2.1. timp,perc,cel,
pno,strings
SIKORSKI perf mat rent   (S663)

Ballet Suite No. 4 [16']
3.3.3.3. 4.3.3.1. timp,perc,harp,
cel,strings
SIKORSKI perf mat rent   (S664)

Bolt, The: Suite
see Suites From Ballets

Chamber Symphony, Op. 110a [arr.]
(from String Quartet No. 8, Op.
110)
(Barshai, R.) string orch SIKORSKI
perf mat rent   (S665)
(Barshai, R.) string orch [19']
VAAP perf mat rent   (S666)

Chamber Symphony, Op. 118a [arr.]
(from String Quartet No. 10, Op.
118)
(Barshai, R.) string orch SIKORSKI
perf mat rent   (S667)
(Barshai, R.) string orch [22']
VAAP perf mat rent   (S668)

Concerto for Piano and Orchestra, No.
1, Op. 35, in C minor
min sc KALMUS K01462 $6.00   (S669)
(Collected Works, Vol. 12) sc
MUZYKA f.s. contains also:
Concerto for Piano and Orchestra,
No. 2, Op. 102, in F   (S670)
study sc SIKORSKI 6210 $28.00, perf
mat rent   (S671)

Concerto for Piano and Orchestra, No.
2, Op. 102, in F
study sc SIKORSKI f.s., perf mat
rent   (S672)
see Concerto for Piano and
Orchestra, No. 1, Op. 35, in C
minor

Concerto for Violin and Orchestra,
No. 1, Op. 77, in A minor
KALMUS A6184 sc $50.00, set
$150.00, perf mat rent   (S673)
study sc SIKORSKI f.s., perf mat
rent   (S674)

Concerto for Violin and Orchestra,
No. 2, Op. 129, in C sharp minor
[28']
3.2.2.3. 4.0.0.0. timp,perc,
strings,vln solo
sc SIKORSKI 2163-K $25.75, perf mat
rent   (S675)
VAAP perf mat rent   (S676)

Concerto for Violoncello and
Orchestra, No. 1, Op. 107, in E
flat
KALMUS A5865 sc $30.00, set $60.00,
perf mat rent   (S677)
min sc KALMUS K01484 $8.75   (S678)
min sc SIKORSKI 034-35020 $15.50
(S679)
(Collected Works, Vol. 16) sc
MUZYKA f.s. contains also:
Concerto for Violoncello and
Orchestra, No. 2, Op. 126, in G
minor   (S680)

Concerto for Violoncello and
Orchestra, No. 2, Op. 126, in G
minor
study sc SIKORSKI f.s., perf mat
rent   (S681)
see Concerto for Violoncello and
Orchestra, No. 1, Op. 107, in E
flat

Drei Romanzen Nach Gedichten Von A.
Puschkin, For Solo Voice And
Chamber Orchestra
see Three Songs On Poems Of
Pushkin, For Solo Voice And
Chamber Orchestra

Eight British And American Folk Songs
1.3.2.2. 4.1.0.0. timp,perc,harp,
strings
VAAP perf mat rent   (S682)

SHOSTAKOVICH, DMITRI (cont'd.)

Five Days And Five Nights: Suite
  *Op.111a
    3.3.3.3. 4.3.3.1. timp,perc,harp,
    pno,strings
  VAAP perf mat rent   (S683)
  "Funf Tage Und Funf Nachte: Suite"
  SIKORSKI perf mat rent   (S684)

Five Fragments For Orchestra *Op.42
  [11']
    2.1+English horn.2+bass clar.2+
    contrabsn. 2.1.1.1. perc,harp,
    strings
  sc SIKORSKI 2311 $29.00, perf mat
    rent   (S685)
  "Five Pieces For Orchestra" VAAP
    perf mat rent   (S686)

Five Pieces For Orchestra
  see Five Fragments For Orchestra

Five Preludes [arr.]
  (Adomian, Lan) 3.3.3.2. 4.3.3.1.
    timp,perc,strings SCHIRM.G perf
    mat rent   (S687)

Flea, The: Four Pieces *Op.19 [20']
    2.0.1.0.sax. 1.2.1.1. perc,pno,
    strings, flexaton, band
  "Wanze, Die: Vier Stucke" SIKORSKI
    perf mat rent   (S688)

From Jewish Folk Poetry, For Solo
  Voices And Orchestra *Op.79a
  [23']
    2.2.3.3. 4.0.0.0. timp,perc,harp,
    strings,SAT soli
  "Aus Jiddischer Volkspoesie, For
    Solo Voices And Orchestra"
  SIKORSKI perf mat rent   (S689)

Funf Tage Und Funf Nachte: Suite
  see Five Days And Five Nights:
  Suite

Gadfly, The: Suite *Op.97a [40']
    3.3.3.3. 4.4.3.1. timp,perc,harp,
    cel,pno,strings
  "Hornisse, Die: Suite" SIKORSKI
    perf mat rent   (S690)

Golden Age, The: Suite
  see Suites From Ballets

Golden Mountains, The: Suite *Op.30a
  [14']
    3.3.3.3.soprano sax.alto
    sax.tenor sax. 8.4.4.2. timp,
    perc,gtr,2harp,org,strings
  VAAP perf mat rent   (S691)
  "Goldene Berge: Suite" SIKORSKI
    perf mat rent   (S692)

Goldene Berge: Suite
  see Golden Mountains, The: Suite

Hamlet: Suite *Op.116a [42']
    3.2.2.2. 4.3.3.1. timp,perc,cel,
    harp,hpsd,pno,strings
  SIKORSKI perf mat rent   (S693)
  VAAP perf mat rent   (S694)

Hornisse, Die: Suite
  see Gadfly, The: Suite

Jahr Wie Ein Leben, Ein: Suite
  see Year Is Like A Lifetime, A:
  Suite

Katerina Ismailowa: Suite
  see Lady Macbeth Of Mtzensk: Suite

Lady Macbeth Of Mtzensk: Suite
  *Op.29,Op.114 [24']
    3.3.4.3. 4.3.3.1. timp,perc,
    2harp,strings,band
  "Katerina Ismailowa: Suite"
  SIKORSKI perf mat rent   (S695)

Limpid Brook, The: Suite
  see Suites From Ballets

Mournful-Triumphal Prelude *Op.130
  [2']
    3.3.3.3. 4.3.3.1. timp,perc,
    strings, stage band
  VAAP perf mat rent   (S696)
  "Triumphales Trauerpraludium"
  SIKORSKI perf mat rent   (S697)

Music For Films, Vol. 1
  (Collected Works, Vol. 41, contains
    music for films produced before
    1944) sc MUZYKA f.s.   (S698)

Music For Films, Vol. 2
  (Collected Works, Vol. 42, contains
    music for films produced after
    1944) sc MUZYKA f.s.   (S699)

Music For The Theater
  (Collected Works, Vol. 27) sc
    MUZYKA f.s.   (S700)

SHOSTAKOVICH, DMITRI (cont'd.)

Neue Babylon, Das: Suite
  see New Babylon: Suite

New Babylon: Suite *Op.18a [40']
    1.1.1.1. 2.1.1.1. timp,perc,harp,
    strings
  VAAP perf mat rent   (S701)
  "Neue Babylon, Das: Suite" SIKORSKI
    perf mat rent   (S702)

October *Op.131 [20']
    3.3.3.3. 4.3.3.1. timp,perc,
    strings
  SIKORSKI perf mat rent   (S703)
  VAAP perf mat rent   (S704)

Overture On Russian And Kirghiz Folk
  Themes *Op.115
  min sc KALMUS K01461 $6.00   (S705)

Preludes And Fugues From Op. 87
  [arr.]
  (Scharitsch, L.) 2.3.3.3. 4.3.3.1.
    timp,drums,harp,pno,strings [15']
    (contains nos. 4 and 6) SIKORSKI
    perf mat rent   (S706)

Preludes From Op. 34 [arr.]
  (Boer, E. De) 3.2.2.3. 2.2.2.1.
    timp,perc,cel,strings [14']
    (contains: nos. 1, 6, 8, 10, 13-
    16, 19, 22) SIKORSKI perf mat
    rent   (S707)

Satires, For Solo Voice And Orchestra
  [arr.] *Op.109
  (Tischenko, Boris) 2.2.2.2.
    2.2.1.0. timp,perc,harp,pno,
    strings SIKORSKI perf mat rent
                                (S708)
  (Tishchenko, Boris) 2.2.2.2.
    2.2.1.0. timp,perc,harp,pno,
    strings,Mez solo [12'] VAAP perf
    mat rent   (S709)

Sechs Gedichte Von Marina Zwetajewa,
  For Solo Voice And Orchestra
  see Six Poems By Marina Tsvetayeva,
  For Solo Voice And Chamber
  Orchestra

Sechs Romanzen Nach Gedichten Von
  Raleigh, Burns Und Shakespeare,
  For Solo Voice And Chamber
  Orchestra
  see Six Romances On Poems By
  Raleigh, Burns, And Shakespeare,
  For Solo Voice And Chamber
  Orchestra

Sechs Romanzen Nach Versen
  Japanischer Dichter, For Solo
  Voice And Orchestra
  see Six Romances On Words By
  Japanese Poets, For Solo Voice
  And Orchestra

Sinfonietta, [arr.] (from String
  Quartet No. 8, Op. 110)
  (Stassewitsch, A.) timp,strings
  [20'] SIKORSKI perf mat rent
                                (S710)

Six Poems By Marina Tsvetayeva, For
  Solo Voice And Chamber Orchestra
  *Op.143a [20']
    2.0.0.2. 2.0.0.0. timp,perc,cel,
    strings,A solo
  VAAP perf mat rent   (S711)
  "Sechs Gedichte Von Marina
    Zwetajewa, For Solo Voice And
    Orchestra" SIKORSKI perf mat rent
                                (S712)

Six Romances On Poems By Raleigh,
  Burns, And Shakespeare, For Solo
  Voice And Chamber Orchestra
  *Op.62,Op.140 [25']
    1.0.0.1. 2.0.0.0. timp,perc,
    strings,B solo
  VAAP perf mat rent   (S713)
  "Sechs Romanzen Nach Gedichten Von
    Raleigh, Burns Und Shakespeare,
    For Solo Voice And Chamber
    Orchestra" SIKORSKI perf mat rent
                                (S714)

Six Romances On Words By Japanese
  Poets, For Solo Voice And
  Orchestra *Op.21 [26']
    3.2.4.2. 4.3.3.1. timp,perc,
    2harp,strings,T solo
  VAAP perf mat rent   (S715)
  "Sechs Romanzen Nach Versen
    Japanischer Dichter, For Solo
    Voice And Orchestra" SIKORSKI
    perf mat rent   (S716)

Suite Nach Gedichten Von Michelangelo
  Buonarroti, For Solo Voice And
  Orchestra
  see Suite On Poems Of Michelangelo,
  For Solo Voice And Orchestra

Suite On Poems Of Michelangelo, For
  Solo Voice And Orchestra
  *Op.145a [45']

SHOSTAKOVICH, DMITRI (cont'd.)

    2(pic).2.2.2(contrabsn). 4.2.3.1.
    timp,perc,cel,harp,pno,strings,
    B solo
  VAAP perf mat rent   (S717)
  "Suite Nach Gedichten Von
    Michelangelo Buonarroti, For Solo
    Voice And Orchestra" study sc
    SIKORSKI 2278 $32.00, perf mat
    rent   (S718)

Suites From Ballets
  sc MUZYKA f.s. Collected Works,
    Vol. 26
  contains: Bolt, The: Suite;
    Golden Age, The: Suite; Limpid
    Brook, The: Suite   (S719)

Symphony for Strings, [arr.] (from
  Quartet No. 8, Op. 110)
  (Drew, Lucas) string orch [22']
  KALMUS A5843 sc $12.00, set
    $15.00   (S720)

Symphony No. 1, Op. 10, in F minor
  [30']
    3(pic).2.2.2. 4.3.3.1. timp,perc,
    pno,strings
  (Collected Works, Vol. 1) sc MUZYKA
    f.s. contains also: Symphony No.
    2, Op. 14, in B   (S721)
  study sc SIKORSKI f.s., perf mat
    rent   (S722)
  min sc VAAP f.s., perf mat rent
                                (S723)

Symphony No. 2, Op. 14, in B
  min sc KALMUS K01457 $7.00   (S724)
  sc SIKORSKI 2225 f.s., perf mat
    rent   (S725)
  see Symphony No. 1, Op. 10, in F
    minor

Symphony No. 3, Op. 20, in E flat
  min sc KALMUS K01464 $8.75   (S726)
  SIKORSKI perf mat rent   (S727)

Symphony No. 4, Op. 43, in C minor
  sc SIKORSKI 2218 $42.25, perf mat
    rent   (S728)

Symphony No. 4, Op. 43, in C minor,
  [arr.]
  (Taynton, Jesse) 4.4.4.4. 7.4.3.2.
    timp,perc,cel,2harp,strings [60']
    (alternate scoring for brass:
    6.4.4.1.) MCA perf mat rent
                                (S729)

Symphony No. 5, Op. 47, in D minor
  study sc MCA 00123411 $15.00 (S730)
  study sc SIKORSKI f.s., perf mat
    rent   (S731)

Symphony No. 6, Op. 53-54, in B minor
  study sc SIKORSKI f.s., perf mat
    rent   (S732)

Symphony No. 6, Op. 54, in B minor
  min sc KALMUS K01458 $11.50   (S733)

Symphony No. 7, Op. 60, in C
  min sc KALMUS K01390 $14.25   (S734)
  sc SIKORSKI 2229 $38.25, perf mat
    rent   (S735)

Symphony No. 8, Op. 65, in C minor
  min sc KALMUS K01459 $11.50   (S736)
  SIKORSKI perf mat rent   (S737)

Symphony No. 9, Op. 70, in E flat
  study sc MCA 00123412 $15.00 (S738)
  study sc SIKORSKI f.s., perf mat
    rent   (S739)

Symphony No. 10, Op. 93, in D minor
  study sc MCA 00123527 $15.00 (S740)
  sc SIKORSKI 2219 $29.25, perf mat
    rent   (S741)

Symphony No. 11, Op. 103, in G minor
  min sc KALMUS K01460 $14.00   (S742)
  study sc MCA 00123413 $25.00 (S743)
  sc SIKORSKI 2217 $36.25, perf mat
    rent   (S744)

Symphony No. 12, Op. 112, in D minor
  sc KUNZEL 10031 $22.00   (S745)

Three Songs On Poems Of Pushkin, For
  Solo Voice And Chamber Orchestra
  *Op.46a [7']
    clar,harp,strings,B solo
  "Drei Romanzen Nach Gedichten Von
    A. Puschkin, For Solo Voice And
    Chamber Orchestra" SIKORSKI perf
    mat rent   (S746)

Triumphales Trauerpraludium
  see Mournful-Triumphal Prelude

Two Fables Of Krylov, For Solo Voice
  And Orchestra *Op.4 [8']
    3.2.2.3. 4.3.3.1. timp,perc,harp,
    cel,strings,Mez solo
  "Zwei Fabeln Von Krylow, For Solo
    Voice And Orchestra" SIKORSKI

SHOSTAKOVICH, DMITRI (cont'd.)

    perf mat rent   (S747)

    Two Pieces For String Orchestra
      *Op.11 [11']
      string orch
      "Zwei Stucke For String Orchestra"
      study sc SIKORSKI f.s., perf mat
      rent   (S748)

    Wanze, Die: Vier Stucke
      see Flea, The: Four Pieces

    Year Is Like A Lifetime, A: Suite
      *Op.120a [35']
      3.2.2.2. 4.3.3.1. timp,perc,
      strings
      "Jahr Wie Ein Leben, Ein: Suite"
      SIKORSKI perf mat rent   (S749)

    Zwei Fabeln Von Krylow, For Solo
      Voice And Orchestra
      see Two Fables Of Krylov, For Solo
      Voice And Orchestra

    Zwei Stucke For String Orchestra
      see Two Pieces For String Orchestra

SHOUJOUIAN, PETROS (1957-   )
    Rhapsody for Violoncello and
      Orchestra
      1.1.1.1. 0.0.0.0. timp,strings,
      vcl solo
      CAN.MUS.CENT. MI 1313 S559R (S750)

    Trois Miniatures [15']
      string orch
      CAN.MUS.CENT. MI 1500 S559T (S751)

SHOULD, S. 365, A CHORALE PRELUDE FOR
    THE NEW YEAR see "Bach, P.D.Q."
    (Peter Schickele)

SHOWCASE see Schuman, William Howard

SHOWPIECE see Gould, Morton see
    Holloway, Robin

SHROPSHIRE LAD, A see Butterworth,
    George Sainton Kaye

SHULMAN, ALAN M. (1915-   )
    Ricky-Ticky Serenade
      SHAWNEE perf mat rent   (S752)

SHUMEIKO, VOLODYMYR (1949-   )
    Four Carpathian Pastorals
      1.1.1.1. 1.0.0.0. pno,strings
      VAAP perf mat rent   (S753)

    Intermezzo Diatonic
      string orch
      VAAP perf mat rent   (S754)

SHUNJU NO FU see Miki, Minoru

SHUNTING IN A PEACEFUL MORNING see
    Savery, Finn

SHUNYATA see Little, David

SHUT, VLADISLAV (1941-   )
    Largo-Sinfonie [28']
      1.1.1.1. 1.1.1.0. timp,2perc,org/
      pno/hpsd/cel,strings
      SIKORSKI perf mat rent   (S755)

    Romantic Messages [15']
      fl,bsn,pno,strings
      VAAP perf mat rent   (S756)
      "Romantische Botschaften" SIKORSKI
      perf mat rent   (S757)

    Romantische Botschaften
      see Romantic Messages

    Sinfonia Da Camera No. 3 [18']
      fl,ob,perc,marimba,vibra,strings
      SIKORSKI perf mat rent   (S758)
      VAAP perf mat rent   (S759)

SHYLOCK: INCIDENTAL MUSIC, FOR SOLO
    VOICE AND ORCHESTRA see Faure,
    Gabriel-Urbain

SI J'ETAIS DOMENICO, FOR HARPSICHORD
    AND STRING ORCHESTRA see
    Brandmüller, Theo

SI MOSTRA LA SORTE, FOR SOLO VOICE AND
    ORCHESTRA see Mozart, Wolfgang
    Amadeus

SI PER TE, GRAN NUME ETERNO, FOR SOLO
    VOICE AND ORCHESTRA see Bellini,
    Vincenzo

SIBELIUS, JEAN (1865-1957)
    Andante Festivo *Op.117a
      KALMUS A5702 sc $3.00, set $4.50
                                    (S760)

    Belshazzar's Feast: Suite
      KALMUS A5624 sc $8.00, set $12.00,
      pts $1.00, ea.   (S761)

SIBELIUS, JEAN (cont'd.)

    Canzonetta *Op.62a [8']
      string orch
      BROUDE BR. sc $5.00, set $7.50, pts
      $1.50, ea.   (S762)
      KALMUS A5674 sc $4.00, set $6.25
                                    (S763)

    Dance Intermezzo *Op.45,No.2 [4']
      2.2.2.2. 4.2.0.0. timp,perc,harp,
      strings
      KALMUS A5721 sc $10.00, set $15.00,
      perf mat rent   (S764)

    Des Fährmanns Bräute, For Solo Voice
      And Orchestra
      see Koskenlaskian Morsiamet, For
      Solo Voice And Orchestra

    Dryad, The *Op.45,No.1
      KALMUS A4151 sc $10.00, set $25.00,
      perf mat rent   (S765)

    En Etsi Valtaa Loistoa, For Solo
      Voice And String Orchestra [arr.]
      *Op.1,No.4
      (Sandberg, Sven) string orch,solo
      voice [3'] FAZER perf mat rent
                                    (S766)

    Five Christmas Songs, For Solo Voice
      And Orchestra [arr.] *Op.1
      (Kuusisto, I.) 2fl,strings,solo
      voice [13'] FAZER perf mat rent
                                    (S767)

    From The North
      (Bauer; Schmid) 2.2.2.2.2sax.
      4.2.3.1. timp,perc,harp,strings
      [3'] KALMUS A5751 pno-cond sc
      $3.00, set $16.00, perf mat rent
                                    (S768)

    Herbstabend "Sonne Verlischt Und
      Wolken Wandern", For Solo Voice
      And Orchestra *Op.38,No.1
      BREITKOPF-L perf mat rent   (S769)

    Impromptu, [arr.] (from Impromptus,
      Op. 5, Nos. 5 And 6)
      (Reinisch, Frank) string orch [6']
      (arranged by the composer)
      BREITKOPF-W sc PB 5127 f.s., pts
      OB 5127 f.s.   (S770)

    In Memoriam *Op.59
      KALMUS A6071 sc $15.00, set $60.00,
      perf mat rent   (S771)

    King Christian II: Suite *Op.27
      KALMUS A4342 sc $25.00, set $65.00,
      perf mat rent   (S772)

    Koskenlaskian Morsiamet, For Solo
      Voice And Orchestra *Op.33
      "Des Fährmanns Bräute, For Solo
      Voice And Orchestra" BREITKOPF-L
      perf mat rent   (S773)

    Lover, The
      see Rakastava

    Narcissus, For Solo Voice And
      Orchestra [arr.]
      (Sandberg, Sven) 2.2.2.2. 2.2.0.0.
      harp,strings,solo voice [3']
      FAZER perf mat rent   (S774)

    Nightride And Sunrise *Op.55
      KALMUS A5691 sc $20.00, set $55.00,
      perf mat rent   (S775)

    Norden, For Solo Voice And Orchestra
      [arr.] *Op.90,No.1
      (Parmet, Simon) 2.2.2.2. 4.0.0.0.
      strings,solo voice [3'] FAZER
      perf mat rent   (S776)

    On Hanget Korkeat Nietokset, For Solo
      Voice And Orchestra [arr.]
      *Op.1,No.5
      (Kuusisto, I.) 2.2.2.2. 4.2.3.0.
      timp,perc,harp,strings,solo voice
      [3'] FAZER perf mat rent   (S777)

    Onward, Ye Peoples
      GALAXY pno-cond sc $4.00, set
      $5.00, and up   (S778)

    Polonaise, Op. 40, No. 10, [arr.]
      (Tiger, K.) 1.1.2.1. 2.2.1.0. perc,
      strings [2'] FAZER perf mat rent
                                    (S779)

    Presto, Op. 4 [7']
      string orch
      FAZER perf mat rent   (S780)

    Rakastava *Op.14 [10']
      timp,strings
      "Lover, The" sc,pts FAZER f.s.
                                    (S781)

    Romance, Op. 42, in C [5']
      string orch
      BROUDE BR. sc $5.00, set $6.25, pts
      $1.25, ea.   (S782)

    Saga, En
      min sc KALMUS K01420 $4.00 (S783)

SIBELIUS, JEAN (cont'd.)

    Scenes Historiques, Suite No. 1:
      All'overtura *Op.25,No.1
      KALMUS A6368 sc $8.00, set $20.00,
      pts $1.00, ea., perf mat rent
                                    (S784)

    Scenes Historiques, Suite No. 1:
      Festivo *Op.25,No.3
      KALMUS A6370 sc $10.00, set $20.00,
      pts $1.00, ea., perf mat rent
                                    (S785)

    Scenes Historiques, Suite No. 1:
      Scena *Op.25,No.2
      KALMUS A6369 sc $8.00, set $20.00,
      pts $1.00, perf mat rent   (S786)

    Scenes Historiques, Suite No. 2: At
      The Draw Bridge *Op.66,No.3
      KALMUS A7313 sc $8.00, set $25.00,
      pts $1.50, ea., perf mat rent
                                    (S787)

    Scenes Historiques, Suite No. 2: Love
      Song *Op.66,No.2
      KALMUS A7311 sc $5.00, set $19.00,
      pts $1.00, ea., perf mat rent
                                    (S788)

    Scenes Historiques, Suite No. 2: The
      Chase *Op.66,No.1
      KALMUS A7311 sc $8.00, set $25.00,
      pts $1.50, ea., perf mat rent
                                    (S789)

    Serenade for Violin and Orchestra,
      No. 1, Op. 69a, in D
      KALMUS A5675 sc $10.00, set $20.00,
      perf mat rent   (S790)

    Serenade for Violin and Orchestra,
      No. 2, Op. 69b, in G minor
      KALMUS A5677 sc $15.00, set $35.00,
      perf mat rent   (S791)

    Suite Caracteristique *Op.100 [5']
      harp,strings
      HANSEN-DEN perf mat rent   (S792)

    Swanwhite: Suite *Op.54
      KALMUS A5899 sc $20.00, set $50.00,
      perf mat rent   (S793)

    Symphony No. 4, Op. 63, in A minor
      KALMUS A6353 sc $25.00, set $80.00,
      pts $4.00, ea., perf mat rent
                                    (S794)

    Symphony No. 6, Op. 104
      KALMUS A5730 sc $35.00, set
      $110.00, perf mat rent   (S795)

    Valse Romantique *Op.62b
      KALMUS A5676 sc $10.00, set $18.00,
      perf mat rent   (S796)

SICILIAN LYRIC see Lombardo, Robert M.

SICILIANO NOTTURNO see Reed

SICILIENNE see Koch, Erland von

SICILIENNE AND RIGAUDON, FOR VIOLIN AND
    ORCHESTRA [ARR.] see Kreisler,
    Fritz

SICILIENNE [ARR.] see Faure, Gabriel-
    Urbain

SIDELNIKOV, LEONID (1931-   )
    Russisches Konzert, For Piano And
      Orchestra [16']
      4.2.2.2. 4.4.3.1. timp,perc,
      strings,pno solo
      SIKORSKI perf mat rent   (S797)

    Solemn Overture [7']
      sc MUZYKA f.s.   (S798)

SIDERALES see Brenet, Therese see
    Tisne, Antoine

SIEBEN FELD- WALD- UND WIESENSTUCKE see
    Stranz, Ulrich

SIEBEN FRAGMENTE IN MEMORIAM ROBERT
    SCHUMANN see Reimann, Aribert

SIEBEN LIEBESLIEDER, FOR VIOLONCELLO
    AND ORCHESTRA see Henze, Hans
    Werner

SIEBEN LIEDER AUS LETZER ZEIT: DER
    TAMBOURSG'SELL, FOR SOLO VOICE AND
    ORCHESTRA see Mahler, Gustav

SIEBEN LIEDER AUS LETZTER ZEIT: BLICKE
    MIR NICHT IN DIE LIEDER, FOR SOLO
    VOICE AND ORCHESTRA see Mahler,
    Gustav

SIEBEN LIEDER AUS LETZTER ZEIT: ICH
    ATMET' EINEN LINDEN DUFT, FOR SOLO
    VOICE AND ORCHESTRA see Mahler,
    Gustav

SIEBEN LIEDER AUS LETZTER ZEIT: ICH BIN
    DER WELT ABHANDEN GEKOMMEN, FOR
    SOLO VOICE AND ORCHESTRA see
    Mahler, Gustav

SIEBEN LIEDER AUS LETZTER ZEIT: LIEBST DU UM SCHONHEIT? FOR SOLO VOICE AND ORCHESTRA see Mahler, Gustav

SIEBEN LIEDER AUS LETZTER ZEIT: REVELGE, FOR SOLO VOICE AND ORCHESTRA see Mahler, Gustav

SIEBEN LIEDER AUS LETZTER ZEIT: UM MITTERNACHT, FOR SOLO VOICE AND ORCHESTRA see Mahler, Gustav

SIEBEN SCHLEIER DER SALOME, DIE, FOR SOLO VOICE AND CHAMBER ORCHESTRA see Madsen, Trygve

SIEBEN SCHONEN, DIE: SUITE see Karayev, Kara, Seven Beauties: Suite

SIEBEN SKIZZEN IN FORM EINER ALTEN SUITE, FOR VIOLONCELLO AND CHAMBER ORCHESTRA see Erbse, Heimo

SIEBEN STIMMUNGSBILDER see Ledenev, Roman

SIEBEN TODSUNDEN, DIE see Dallinger, Fridolin

SIECLE, PIERRE, TOMBEAU see Monnet, Marc

SIECZYNSKI, RUDOLF
   Vienna, My City Of Dreams, For Solo
     Voice And Orchestra, [arr.]
     (Schoenfeld) WARNER perf mat rent
                (S799)

SIEGE DE CORINTHE, LE: OVERTURE see Rossini, Gioacchino

SIEGFRIED'S DEATH AND FUNERAL MUSIC [ARR.] see Wagner, Richard, Götterdämmerung: Trauermusik Beim Tode Siegfrieds [arr.]

SIEGMEISTER, ELIE (1909-   )
   Concerto for Violin and Orchestra
     [31']
     2(pic).2(English horn).2(bass
      clar).2(contrabsn). 3.2.3.0.
      timp,3perc,harp,pno,strings,vln
      solo
     FISCHER,C   (S800)

   Concerto for Violin, Piano and
     Orchestra [20']
     2(pic).2(English horn).2(bass
      clar).2(contrabsn). 4.3.3.1.
      4perc,strings,vln solo,pno solo
     (An Entertainment) FISCHER,C (S801)

   Fables From The Dark Wood [27']
     2(pic).2(English
      horn).2.2(contrabsn). 3.2.2.1.
      timp,2perc,harp,pno,strings
     FISCHER,C   (S802)

   Fantasies In Line And Color [21']
     3(2pic).3(English horn).3(clar in
      E flat,bass clar).3(contrabsn).
      4.3.3.1. timp,4perc,harp,pno,
      cel,strings
     FISCHER,C   (S803)

   From These Shores [14']
     2(pic).2.2(clar in E flat,bass
      clar).2. 4.3.3.0. timp,3perc,
      harp,pno,strings
     FISCHER,C   (S804)

   Riversong [6']
     2(pic).2(English horn).2(bass
      clar).2. 2.2.1.1. timp,perc,
      strings
     FISCHER,C   (S805)

   Shadows And Light [16']
     2(pic).2(English horn).2(clar in
      E flat,bass clar).2(contrabsn).
      4.3.3.1. timp,3perc,harp,pno,
      cel,strings
     FISCHER,C   (S806)

   Symphony No. 6 [28']
     3(pic).2+English horn.2(clar in E
      flat)+bass clar.2(contrabsn).
      4.3.3.1. timp,4perc,harp,pno,
      strings
     FISCHER,C   (S807)

   Theater Set
     2.2.3.2. 4.3.3.1. timp,perc,harp,
      pno,strings
     study sc FISCHER,C $18.00, perf mat
      rent   (S808)

SIEKMANN, FRANK H. (1925-   )
   Music For A Poetic Reading
     1.1.1.1. 1.1.1.0. perc,strings,
      narrator
     set SEESAW $22.00   (S809)

SIERRA
   Jubilo [8']
     2+pic.2+English horn.2+bass
      clar.2(contrabsn). 4.3.3.1.
      timp,perc,harp,strings
     SALABERT EAS18370P perf mat rent
                (S810)

SIETE CANCIONES, FOR SOLO VOICE AND CHAMBER ORCHESTRA see Revueltas, Silvestre

SIGNAL FOR CHAMBER ORCHESTRA AND MAGNETIC TAPE see Berge, Håkon

SIGNALEN see Mengelberg, Karel

SIGNALS AND ECHOES, FOR CLARINET AND ORCHESTRA see Straesser, Joep

SIGNE-OUBLI see Mefano, Paul

SIGNOR BRUSCHINO, IL: AH DONATE IL CARO SPOSO, FOR SOLO VOICE AND ORCHESTRA see Rossini, Gioacchino

SIGNOR BRUSCHINO, IL: AH SE IL COLPO ARRIVO A FARE, FOR SOLO VOICES AND ORCHESTRA see Rossini, Gioacchino

SIGNOR BRUSCHINO, IL: DEH! TU M'ASSISTI AMORE, FOR SOLO VOICE AND ORCHESTRA see Rossini, Gioacchino

SIGNOR BRUSCHINO, IL: E BEL NODO, CHE DUE CORI, FOR SOLO VOICES AND ORCHESTRA see Rossini, Gioacchino

SIGNOR BRUSCHINO, IL: EBBEN, RAGION DOVERE, FOR SOLO VOICES AND ORCHESTRA see Rossini, Gioacchino

SIGNOR BRUSCHINO, IL: HO LA TESTA, O E ANDATA VIA? FOR SOLO VOICE AND ORCHESTRA see Rossini, Gioacchino

SIGNOR BRUSCHINO, IL: MARIANNA! VOI SIGNORE? FOR SOLO VOICES AND ORCHESTRA see Rossini, Gioacchino

SIGNOR BRUSCHINO, IL: NEL TEATRO DEL GRAN MONDO, FOR SOLO VOICE AND ORCHESTRA see Rossini, Gioacchino

SIGNOR BRUSCHINO, IL: PER UN FIGLIO GIA PENTITO, FOR SOLO VOICES AND ORCHESTRA see Rossini, Gioacchino

SIGNOR BRUSCHINO, IL: QUANTO E DOLCE A UN' ALMA AMANTE, FOR SOLO VOICES AND ORCHESTRA see Rossini, Gioacchino

SIGNS OF LIFE see Peck, Russell James

SIGURBJORNSSON, HRODMAR INGI
   (1958-   )
   As The Beast Dies, For Solo Voice And
     Chamber Orchestra [21']
     1.1.1.1. 2.1.1.1. perc,pno,
      strings,A solo
     ICELAND 052-004   (S811)

   Skref [13']
     1.1.1.1. 1.1.1.0. perc,pno,
      strings
     ICELAND 052-001   (S812)

SIGURBJÖRNSSON, THORKELL (1938-   )
   Albumblatt [10']
     2.2.2.2. 3.2.2.1. timp,perc,
      strings
     ICELAND 022-027   (S813)

   Bukolla, For Clarinet And Orchestra
     [16'30"]
     2.2.2.2. 4.2.2.1. perc,harp,
      strings,clar solo
     ICELAND 022-007   (S814)

   Bull Man, The [24'10"]
     0.1.3.2. 1.1.0.1. timp,perc,pno,
      hpsd,strings, langspil
     ICELAND 022-028   (S815)

   Cadenza And Dance, For Violin And
     Orchestra [10']
     1.1.1.1. 3.2.1.1. timp,2perc,pno,
      strings,vln solo
     ICELAND 022-025   (S816)

   Caprice, For Piano And Chamber
     Orchestra [7'35"]
     2.2.2.2. 1.1.1.1. timp,perc,gtr,
      strings,pno solo
     ICELAND 022-032   (S817)

   Columbine, For Flute And String
     Orchestra
     string orch,fl solo
     ICELAND 022-084   (S818)

   Commotion [12']
     3.2.2.2. 3.2.2.1. perc,harp,pno,
      cel,strings,electronic tape
     ICELAND 022-029   (S819)

SIGURBJÖRNSSON, THORKELL (cont'd.)

   Concerto for Violin, Violoncello,
     Piano and Orchestra
     2.2.2.2. 1.1.1.1. perc,strings,
      vln solo,vcl solo,pno solo
     ICELAND 022-104   (S820)

   Diaphony [15']
     2.2.2.2. 2.2.2.1. 2perc,strings
     sc APNM $12.50, perf mat rent
                (S821)

   Euridice, For Flute And Orchestra
     [15']
     0.0.2+bass clar.2+contrabsn.
      3.3.2.1. timp,2perc,elec gtr,
      strings,fl solo
     sc APNM $8.00, perf mat rent (S822)

   Fluctuations [5']
     2.2.2.2. 2.2.2.0. 3perc,harp,pno,
      strings
     ICELAND 022-030   (S823)

   Laeti [20']
     3(pic).2(bass clar).2. 3.2.2.1.
      timp,perc,pno&cel,harp,strings,
      electronic tape
     sc APNM $10.00, perf mat rent
                (S824)

   Liongate, For Flute And Chamber
     Orchestra
     perc,strings,fl solo
     ICELAND 022-105   (S825)

   Mist [11'30"]
     2.1.2.2. 2.1.0.0. harp,pno,
      strings
     ICELAND 022-001   (S826)

   Much Ado [6'50"]
     2.2.2.2. 2.2.2.0. perc,pno,
      strings
     ICELAND 022-037   (S827)

   Nidur, For Double Bass And Orchestra
     [18']
     2.2.2.2. 4.2.0.0. 2perc,strings,
      db solo
     sc APNM $15.75, perf mat rent
                (S828)

   Primeval Hum, The [12']
     3.3.3.2. 4.3.2.1. timp,2perc,pno,
      strings
     ICELAND 022-031   (S829)

   Rima [9'20"]
     2.2.2.2. 3.2.2.0. timp,perc,cel,
      strings
     ICELAND 022-033   (S830)

   Seasongs [19']
     2.2.2.2. 4.3.2.1. timp,2perc,
      synthesizer,strings
     ICELAND 022-026   (S831)

   Sequences, For Violin And Orchestra
     2.1.3.2. 1.1.1.1. timp,perc,pno,
      cel,strings,vln solo
     ICELAND 022-082   (S832)

   Ulisse Ritorna, For Violoncello And
     Orchestra [18']
     2.2.2.2. 2.2.0.1. 2perc,strings,
      vcl solo
     sc APNM $15.25, perf mat rent
                (S833)

   Wiblo [15'30"]
     horn,pno,strings
     ICELAND 022-020   (S834)

SIHANOUK, NORODOM
see NORODOM SIHANOUK

SIKORSKI, KAZIMIERZ (1895-1986)
   Symphony No. 4 [35']
     3.3.3.3. 4.3.3.1. perc,strings
     POLSKIE   (S835)

   Symphony No. 5 [31']
     3.3.4.3. 4.3.3.1. perc,strings
     sc,fac ed POLSKIE f.s.   (S836)

SIKORSKI, TOMASZ (1939-   )
   Strings In The Earth
     see Struny W Ziemi

   Struny W Ziemi
     string orch
     "Strings In The Earth" sc POLSKIE
      f.s.   (S837)

SILENCE see Riisager, Knudage, Qarrtsiluni

SILENCE TO BE BEATEN see Rihm, Wolfgang

SILENCES see Trojahn, Manfred

SILENE, FOR BASSOON AND INSTRUMENTAL ENSEMBLE see Ancelin, Pierre

SILENT SONGS, THE, FOR SOLO VOICE AND ORCHESTRA see Liljefors, Ruben

SILENT STREAM, THE, FOR VIOLONCELLO AND
ORCHESTRA see Gorli, Sandro

SILETE VENTI, FOR SOLO VOICE AND
ORCHESTRA see Handel, George
Frideric

SILHOUETTE see Wilson, Richard (Edward)

SILHOUETTE OF TARA, [ARR.] see Steiner,
Max(imillian Raoul Walter)

SILK RHAPSODY see Damase, Jean-Michel

SILLAGES see Murail, Tristan

SILSBEE, ANN (1930-   )
Seven Rituals [23']
3.3.4.3. 4.3.3.1. timp,perc,pno,
strings
sc AM.COMP.AL. $28.20   (S838)

SILVANA: OVERTURE see Weber, Carl Maria
von

SILVER CHALICE, THE: SUITE see Waxman,
Franz

SILVER LADDERS see Tower, Joan

SILVER PLATED BRONZE, FOR DOUBLEBASS
AND ORCHESTRA see Eisma, Will

SILVERMAN, FAYE-ELLEN (1947-   )
Adhesions
3.3.3.3. 4.3.3.1. timp,2perc,
2harp,pno,strings
sc SEESAW $55.00, perf mat rent
(S839)
Candlelight, For Piano And Orchestra
3.3.3.3. 4.3.3.1. timp,2perc,
harp,strings,pno solo
sc SEESAW $39.00, perf mat rent
(S840)
Passing Fancies
1.1.1.1. 1.1.1.0. perc,2vln,vla,
vcl,db
sc SEESAW $30.00, perf mat rent
(S841)
Winds And Sines
3.3.3.3. 4.2.2.1. perc,harp,pno,
strings
SEESAW   (S842)

SILVESTRI, CONSTANTIN (1913-   )
Bihor Dances [5']
2.2.2.2. 2.2.2.0. timp,harp/pno,
strings
NOVELLO perf mat rent   (S843)

Three Sketches [8']
string orch
NOVELLO perf mat rent   (S844)

SILVESTROV, VALENTIN (1937-   )
Cantata for Solo Voice and Chamber
Orchestra [10']
1.1.0.0. 2.0.0.0. 2perc,harp,
hpsd,4vla,2vcl,2db,S solo
SIKORSKI perf mat rent   (S845)
VAAP perf mat rent   (S846)

Hymnus [10']
4fl,4trp,bells,harp,cel,pno,6vln,
6db
SIKORSKI perf mat rent   (S847)
VAAP perf mat rent   (S848)

Meditation for Violoncello and
Chamber Orchestra [33']
1.2.0.1. 2.0.0.0. bells,cel,hpsd/
pno,10vln,4vla,3vcl,2db,vcl
solo
SIKORSKI perf mat rent   (S849)
VAAP perf mat rent   (S850)

Monodia, For Piano And Orchestra
[20']
2.1.1.1. 2.1.1.1. 2perc,harp,cel,
strings,pno solo
SIKORSKI perf mat rent   (S851)
VAAP perf mat rent   (S852)

Ode To The Nightingale, For Solo
Voice And Chamber Orchestra
1.1.1.0. 1.1.1.1. perc,harp,pno,
strings,S solo
SIKORSKI perf mat rent   (S853)
VAAP perf mat rent   (S854)

Poem In Memoriam Boris Lyatoshinsky
[19']
0.0.0.0. 2.2.2.1. 4perc,2harp,
cel,pno,10vla,8vcl
SIKORSKI perf mat rent   (S855)
VAAP perf mat rent   (S856)

Postludium For Piano And Orchestra
2.2.2.2. 2.1.2.1. 2perc,harp,
strings,pno solo
VAAP perf mat rent   (S857)

Serenade for 2 Violins and Strings
[15']
8vln,4vla,3vcl,2db,2vln soli
SIKORSKI perf mat rent   (S858)

SILVESTROV, VALENTIN (cont'd.)

VAAP perf mat rent   (S859)

Spectres [15']
2.0.1.1. 1.1.1.0. 2perc,harp,pno,
elec org,strings
SIKORSKI perf mat rent   (S860)
VAAP perf mat rent   (S861)

Symphony No. 1 [18']
3.3.3.3. 4.3.3.1. 3perc,2harp,
pno&cel,strings
SIKORSKI perf mat rent   (S862)
VAAP perf mat rent   (S863)

Symphony No. 2 [24']
fl,2perc,pno,strings
SIKORSKI perf mat rent   (S864)
VAAP perf mat rent   (S865)

Symphony No. 3
4.4.4.4. 4.4.3.1. 4perc,2harp,
pno&cel,strings
SIKORSKI perf mat rent   (S866)
(Eschatophony) VAAP perf mat rent
(S867)

Symphony No. 4 [30']
0.0.0.0. 4.2.3.1. strings
SIKORSKI perf mat rent   (S868)
VAAP perf mat rent   (S869)

Symphony No. 5
3.3.3.3. 4.3.3.1. 4perc,cel,
2harp,pno,strings
SIKORSKI perf mat rent   (S870)
VAAP perf mat rent   (S871)

Symphony No. 6 [23']
2.2.2.2. 4.2.3.1. 3perc,2harp,
cel,pno,strings,Bar/B solo
(Exegi monumentum) SIKORSKI perf
mat rent   (S872)

ŠIMAI, PAVOL (1930-   )
Concerto for Violoncello and String
Orchestra [31']
string orch,vcl solo
STIM   (S873)

SIMARD SUITE, FOR VIBRAPHONE, MARIMBA
AND ORCHESTRA see DuBois, Pierre-
Max

SIMEON KOTKO: SUITE see Prokofiev,
Serge

SIMFONICNE METAMORFOZE see Strmcnik,
Maksimiljan

SIMILIS GRECO I see Bujarski, Zbigniew

SIMON BOCCANEGRA: CHI IL VARCO T'APRIA?
FOR SOLO VOICES AND ORCHESTRA see
Verdi, Giuseppe

SIMON BOCCANEGRA: COME IN QUEST' ORA
BRUNA, FOR SOLO VOICE AND ORCHESTRA
see Verdi, Giuseppe

SIMON BOCCANEGRA: FIGLIA! A TAL NOME
PALPITO, FOR SOLO VOICES AND
ORCHESTRA see Verdi, Giuseppe

SIMON BOCCANEGRA: PRELUDIO see Verdi,
Giuseppe

SIMON BOCCANEGRA: SENTO AVVAMPAR NELL'
ANIMA FURENTE, FOR SOLO VOICE AND
ORCHESTRA see Verdi, Giuseppe

SIMON BOCCANEGRA: T'INGANNI... MA TU
PIANGEVI, FOR SOLO VOICES AND
ORCHESTRA see Verdi, Giuseppe

SIMONETTI, GIOVANNI PAOLO
Concerto for Recorder and String
Orchestra, Op. 4, in D minor
string orch,cont,A rec solo
(Michel) sc,pts AMADEUS BP 579 f.s.
(S874)

SIMONIS, JEAN-MARIE (1931-   )
Cantilene, For Violin And Orchestra
*Op.39 [16']
2+pic.3.2+bass clar.2. 4.3.3.1.
2perc,pno,cel,harp,strings,vln
solo
sc CBDM f.s.   (S875)

SIMONS, NETTY (1923-   )
Big Sur [20']
3.3.3.3. 4.3.3.1. timp,perc,
2harp,strings
MERION perf mat rent   (S876)

SIMPLE PHRASE, FOR VIOLONCELLO AND
ORCHESTRA see Massenet, Jules

SIMPLE SYMPHONY see Garlick, Antony

SIMPLICIUS, DER: EINLEITUNG see Huber,
Hans

SIMPSON, ROBERT
Symphony No. 7 [28']
2.2.2.2. 2.2.0.0. timp,strings
FABER perf mat rent   (S877)

Symphony No. 8 [45']
3.3.3.3. 4.4.4.2. timp,perc,
strings
FABER perf mat rent   (S878)

Symphony No. 9 [55']
2+pic.2+English horn.2.2+
contrabsn.4.3.3.1. timp,
strings
FABER perf mat rent   (S879)

SIMPSON, THOMAS (fl. ca. 1610-   )
Opus Newer Paduanen: Five Dances
see Opus Newer Paduanen: Funf
Tanzsatze

Opus Newer Paduanen: Funf Tanzsatze
"Opus Newer Paduanen: Five Dances"
KALMUS A6473 sc $4.00, set $5.00,
pts $1.00, ea., perf mat rent
(S880)

SIMS, EZRA (1928-   )
Three Songs, For Solo Voice And
Orchestra [8']
2.2.2.2. 2.2.0.0. glock,vibra,
pno,strings,T solo
sc AM.COMP.AL. $28.30   (S881)

Yr Obedt Servt II [12']
2.0.2.2. 2.0.2.0. marimba,strings
sc AM.COMP.AL. $16.50, perf mat
rent   (S882)

SIMULACRUM see Anhalt, István

SINCRONIE II see Niculescu, Stefan

SINDING, CHRISTIAN (1856-1941)
Rondo Infinito *Op.42
KALMUS A6395 sc $22.00, set $50.00,
pts $2.00, ea., perf mat rent
(S883)

SINE DIE see Olavide, Gonzalo De

SINESTESIA see Seco De Arpe, Manuel

SINFONIA see Donizetti, Gaetano see
Mayr, [Johann] Simon

SINFONIA A GRAND' ORCHESTRA see Asioli,
Bonifazio

SINFONIA A QUATTRO see Martini, [Padre]
Giovanni Battista

SINFONIA AVANTI LA SERENATA see Perti,
Giacomo Antonio

SINFONIA B-A-C-H see Szalonek, Witold

SINFONIA BREVE see Takacs, Jenö

SINFONIA BREVE IN D see Bellini,
Vincenzo

SINFONIA BREVIS see Einfeld(t), Dieter

SINFONIA BUFFA see Bentzon, Jørgen

SINFONIA CON GIARDINO see Castiglioni,
Niccolò

SINFONIA CONCERTANTE, FOR PIANO AND
ORCHESTRA see Gerhard, Fritz
Christian

SINFONIA CONCERTANTE FOR VIOLONCELLO
AND ORCHESTRA see Holten, Bo

SINFONIA DA CAMERA NO. 3 see Shut,
Vladislav

SINFONIA DA CAMERA, OP.46 see
Engelmann, Hans Ulrich

SINFONIA DA CHIESA see Raasted, Niels
Otto see Roman, Johan Helmich

SINFONIA DA CHIESA NO. 1 see Rosenberg,
Hilding

SINFONIA DA REQUIEM see Morgan, David

SINFONIA DANTE see Pacini, Giovanni

SINFONIA DEL MARE see Nystedt, Knut

SINFONIA DELLA SERENATA IN F see
Galuppi, Baldassare

SINFONIA DI ROMA see Lipkin, Malcolm

SINFONIA FROM RV719 see Vivaldi,
Antonio

SINFONIA GEO-PALEONTOLOGICA NO. 1 see
Fongaard, Bjørn

SINFONIA GEO-PALEONTOLOGICA NO. 2 see
Fongaard, Bjørn

SINFONIA GEO-PALEONTOLOGICA NO. 3 see Fongaard, Bjørn

SINFONIA GEO-PALEONTOLOGICA NO. 4 see Fongaard, Bjørn

SINFONIA GEO-PALEONTOLOGICA NO. 5 see Fongaard, Bjørn

SINFONIA HUMANA see Bull, Edvard Hagerup

SINFONIA IN QUATTRO TEMPI see Vacchi, Fabio

SINFONIA IN TRE TEMPI see Paisiello, Giovanni

SINFONIA LIRICO NO. 4 see Tubin, Eduard

SINFONIA MELODICA IN C see Telemann, Georg Philipp

SINFONIA MINIMA see Sandi, Luis

SINFONIA MINIMALE see Søderlind, Ragnar

SINFONIA NEL GIORNI NATALIZIO see Mica, Frantisek Vaclav

SINFONIA ON THE BIRTHDAY OF FREDERICK THE GREAT see Bach, Wilhelm Friedemann

SINFONIA OR CONCERTO, RV146 see Vivaldi, Antonio

SINFONIA PASTORALE see Mozart, Leopold see Tartini, Giuseppe

SINFONIA PASTORALIS see Linek, Jiri Ignatz

SINFONIA PICCOLA see Suolahti, Heikki

SINFONIA POLACCA see Przybylski, Bronislaw Kazimierz

SINFONIA PROSODICA see Zimmermann, Bernd Alois

SINFONIA RICERCATA, FOR ORGAN AND ORCHESTRA see Halffter, Cristobal

SINFONIA ROBUSTA see Tishchenko, Boris

SINFONIA SACRA see Escudero, Francisco

SINFONIA SOPRA I MIGLIORI MOTIVI DI BELLINI see Donizetti, Gaetano

SINFONIA SOPRA UN DISCANTO AQUILEIESE see Zanettovich, Daniele

SINFONIA SOPRA UNA CANZONE D'AMORE see Rota, Nino

SINFONIA SULLO STABAT DI ROSSINI see Mercadante, G. Saverio

SINFONIA SUPER TENOR ACQUILEIENSIS see Zanettovich, Daniele

SINFONIA TAPKAARA see Ifukube, Akira

SINFONIA TRAGICA see Hartmann, Karl Amadeus

SINFONIA UMANA, FOR VIOLONCELLO AND ORCHESTRA see Brandström, Christer

SINFONIA UND SINFONINA see Kont, Paul

SINFONIA UNICAMP see Prado, José-Antonio (Almeida)

SINFONIA VOTIVA see Panufnik, Andrzej

SINFONIAS, THREE see Bach, Johann Sebastian

SINFONIAS FOR STRING ORCHESTRA, FIVE see Zach, Johann (Jan)

SINFONIAS NOS. 1 AND 2 see Vivaldi, Antonio

SINFONIE, FIVE see Lampugnani, Giovanni Battista

SINFONIE, FOUR see Martini, [Padre] Giovanni Battista

SINFONIE, SIX see Boccherini, Luigi see Pugnani, Gaetano

SINFONIE, TWO see Anfossi, Pasquale

SINFONIE CAPRICIEUSE see Berwald, Franz (Adolf)

SINFONIE DER GROSSEN STADT see Höffner, Paul Marx

SINFONIE "DONA NOBIS PACEM" see Vogt, Hans

SINFONIE EINER STADT see Baur, Jürg

SINFONIE IN SECHS TEILEN see Hamel, Peter Michael

SINFONIE IN VIER FRAGMENTEN see Butzko, Yuri

SINFONIE NAIVE see Berwald, Franz (Adolf)

SINFONIE SÉRIEUSE see Berwald, Franz (Adolf)

SINFONIE SINGULIERE see Berwald, Franz (Adolf)

SINFONIE-STUCKE see Schnebel, Dieter

SINFONIEN UND RITORNELL see Bach, Johann Sebastian

SINFONIES POUR LES PASTRES see Lully, Jean-Baptiste (Lulli)

SINFONIETTA ACCADEMICA see Davies, Peter Maxwell

SINFONIETTA CONCERTANTE see Johnson, Robert Sherlaw see Lessard, John Ayres

SINFONIETTA CONCERTANTE, FOR FLUTE, HARP AND ORCHESTRA see Wissmer, Pierre

SINFONIETTA ON ESTONIAN THEMES see Tubin, Eduard

SINFONIETTA ON JEWISH THEMES see Vainberg, Moysey Samuilovitch

SINFONIETTA ROMANTICA see Hundsnes, Svein

SINFONIETTA SAVARIENSIS see Patachich, Ivan

SINFONIETTA SERIOSA see Nordal, Jon

SINFONIETTINA FOR STRINGS see Hartzell, Eugene

SINFONISCHE ETUDE see Krol, Bernhard

SINFONISCHE METAMORPHOSEN UBER GESUALDO see Baur, Jürg

SINFONISCHER FESTMARSCH see Thuille, Ludwig (Wilhelm Andreas Maria)

SINFONISCHER PROLOG ZU "TIRIEL" see Smirnov, Dmitri

SING MY CHORDS, FOR SOLO VOICE AND ORCHESTRA see Jordan, Sverre, Syng Mine Strengjer, For Solo Voice And Orchestra

SINGENDE VOGEL DER EWIGKEIT, DER, FOR FLUTE AND STRING ORCHESTRA see Kunz, Alfred

SINGIER, JEAN MARC (1954-   )
Blocs En Vrac De Bric Et De Broc [6']
1.1(English horn).1+bass clar.1.
1.1.0+bass trom.0. 2perc,vla,
vcl,db
SALABERT perf mat rent   (S884)

SINGING BIRD OF ETERNITY, THE, FOR FLUTE AND STRING ORCHESTRA see Kunz, Alfred, Singende Vogel Der Ewigkeit, Der, For Flute And String Orchestra

SINGLETON, ALVIN
Yellow Rose Petal, A
2.2.2.0. 2.2.1.0. perc,cel,
strings
sc EUR.AM.MUS. EA00563 $20.00, perf mat rent   (S885)

SINIGAGLIA, LEONE (1868-1944)
Baruffe Chiozzotte, Le: Overture *Op.32
KALMUS A6421 sc $15.00, set $40.00, pts $2.00, ea., perf mat rent   (S886)
Danze Piemontesi, No. 1 *Op.31,No.1
KALMUS A7477 sc $10.00, set $30.00, pts $1.50, ea., perf mat rent   (S887)
Danze Piemontesi, No. 2 *Op.31,No.2
KALMUS A7478 sc $25.00, set $60.00, pts $2.50, ea., perf mat rent   (S888)
Two Character Pieces
see Zwei Charakterstucke

Zwei Charakterstucke *Op.35 [6']
string orch
"Two Character Pieces" KALMUS A6422

SINIGAGLIA, LEONE (cont'd.)

sc $5.00, set $10.00, pts $2.00, ea., perf mat rent   (S889)

SINKIANG DANCE NO. 1, FOR VIOLIN AND ORCHESTRA see Du, Ming-Xin

SINKIANG DANCE NO. 2, FOR ORCHESTRA see Ding, Shan-De

SINKIANG DANCE NO. 2, FOR VIOLIN AND ORCHESTRA see Du, Ming-Xin

SINKIANG DANCE NO. 3, FOR VIOLIN AND ORCHESTRA see Du, Ming-Xin

SINKIANG DANCE NO. 4, FOR VIOLIN AND ORCHESTRA see Du, Ming-Xin

SINKIANG DANCE NO. 5, FOR VIOLIN AND ORCHESTRA see Du, Ming-Xin

SINKIANG DANCE NO. 6, FOR VIOLIN AND ORCHESTRA see Du, Ming-Xin

SINKIANG DANCE NO. 7, FOR VIOLIN AND ORCHESTRA see Du, Ming-Xin

SINKIANG DANCE NO. 8, FOR VIOLIN AND ORCHESTRA see Du, Ming-Xin

SINKIANG DANCE NO. 9, FOR VIOLIN AND ORCHESTRA see Du, Ming-Xin

SINKIANG DANCE NO. 10, FOR VIOLIN AND ORCHESTRA see Du, Ming-Xin

SINOPOLI, GIUSEPPE (1946-   )
Concerto for Piano and Orchestra [20']
8.5.4.4. 6.4.3.1. timp,perc,cel, hpsd,harp,strings,pno solo
RICORDI-IT 132319 perf mat rent   (S890)
Lou Salome: Suite II
3.3.6.4.4sax. 6.5.5.2. timp,perc, harmonium,cel,2pno,org,acord, strings
RICORDI-IT 133996 perf mat rent   (S891)
Pour Un Livre A Venise [11']
4.4.2.2. 2.2.3.1. vibra,cel, bells,pno,harp,2vln,vla,vcl,db
(transcription of "Mottetti a 6" by Costanzo Porta) RICORDI-IT 132343 perf mat rent   (S892)

Souvenirs A La Memoire: Drei Stucke [12']
1(alto fl)+pic.1.1+bass clar.1. 1.1.1.0. perc,cel,pno,strings
RICORDI-IT 132188 perf mat rent   (S893)

Tombeau D'armor II [14'20"]
4.4.5.4. 6.4.3.1. timp,perc,2pno& 2cel,2harp,strings
sc RICORDI-IT 132590 f.s., perf mat rent   (S894)

Tombeau D'armor III, For Violoncello And Orchestra [21']
3.3.4.3. 4.4.3.1. timp,4perc, harp,cel,pno,strings,vcl solo
RICORDI-IT 132824 perf mat rent   (S895)

SINUS see Berge, Sigurd

SINUS IRIDUM see Fongaard, Bjørn

SIOHAN, ROBERT (1894-   )
Concert, For Violin And Orchestra [10']
2.2.2.2. 4.3.2.1. timp,perc, strings,vln solo
SALABERT perf mat rent   (S896)

SIR EGLAMORE *see TWO SONGS WITHOUT WORDS [arr.]

SIROWY, JOSEF
Romantisches Concertino, For Piano And Orchestra
(Sandauer) KRENN   (S897)

SISTA SANGEN, DEN, FOR SOLO VOICE AND ORCHESTRA see Jonsson, Josef [Petrus]

SISYPHUS 1971, FOR ALTO SAXOPHONE AND INSTRUMENTAL ENSEMBLE see Latham, William Peters

SITSKY, LARRY (1934-   )
Apparitions [8']
2.1.2.0. 2.2.2.1. timp,perc,pno 4-hands,strings
BOOSEY perf mat rent   (S898)

Concerto for Guitar and Orchestra
2.0.2.1. 2.2.2.0. timp,perc,pno, strings,gtr solo
sc SEESAW $55.00, perf mat rent   (S899)

SITSKY, LARRY (cont'd.)

Concerto for Wind Quintet and
    Orchestra
    1.1.1.1. 0.3.3.1. 3perc,harp,
    strings,wind quin soli
    sc SEESAW $44.00, perf mat rent
                                    (S900)

Fantasy No. 3
    trp,strings
    sc SEESAW $9.00, perf mat rent
                                    (S901)

Gurdjieff, For Violin And Chamber
    Orchestra
    1.0.1.0. 0.1.0.0. perc,strings,
    vln solo
    sc SEESAW $37.00, perf mat rent
                                    (S902)

Nine Orchestral Interludes
    3.3.3.3. 4.3.3.1. perc,harp,pno,
    strings
    SEESAW perf mat rent   (S903)

Santana
    clar,strings
    sc SEESAW $35.00, perf mat rent
                                    (S904)

Songs And Dances From Golem
    3.3.3.3. 4.3.3.1. perc,harp,pno,
    strings
    sc SEESAW $55.00, perf mat rent
                                    (S905)

SIVERTSEN, KENNETH (1961-   )
Dragning, For Clarinet And String
    Orchestra [12']
    string orch,clar solo
    NORGE   (S906)

Haap
    1.2(English horn).3(bass
    clar).1(contrabsn). 3.2.3(bass
    trom).0. timp,perc,gtr,strings,
    S solo
    "Hope" NORGE   (S907)

Hope
    see Haap

Timeglaset Og Morgonstjerna [35']
    2.3.3.2. 3.2.4.1. timp,4perc,
    harp,pno&cel,strings,electronic
    tape
    NORGE   (S908)

SIVIC, PAVLE (1908-   )
Ballade for Trombone and Orchestra
    [8']
    perc,strings,trom solo
    DRUSTVO DSS 1042 perf mat rent
                                    (S909)

Concerto for Organ and Orchestra
    [14']
    2(pic).2.2.2(contrabsn). 4.3.3.1.
    timp,perc,strings,org solo
    DRUSTVO DSS 1025 perf mat rent
                                    (S910)

Concerto for Violoncello and
    Orchestra [16']
    2(pic).2.2.2(contrabsn). 4.3.3.1.
    timp,perc,vibra,xylo,harp,pno,
    cel,strings,vcl solo
    DRUSTVO DSS 1066 perf mat rent
                                    (S911)

Reminiscences [16']
    2.2.2.2. 4.4.4.1. timp,perc,harp,
    pno,strings
    DRUSTVO DSS 924 perf mat rent
                                    (S912)

Tri Koncertne Arije, For Solo Voice
    And Orchestra [12']
    2.2.2.2. 2.0.0.0. timp,perc,
    strings,T solo
    DRUSTVO ED.DSS 977 f.s., perf mat
    rent   (S913)

SIX BLUEGRASS HITS *CC6U
    (Zinn, William) string orch EXCELSIOR
    sc 494-01267 $10.00, pts
    494-01268-01272 $4.00, ea.   (S914)

SIX CHANSONS DE BILITIS, FOR SOLO VOICE
    AND ORCHESTRA see Dandelot, Georges

SIX CHANSONS POPULAIRES SEPHARDIQUES,
    FOR SOLO VOICE AND ORCHESTRA see
    Nin-Culmell, Joaquin

SIX DANCES FOR STRING ORCHESTRA see
    Kay, Ulysses Simpson

SIX DESIGNS, FOR SOLO VOICE AND
    ORCHESTRA see Tanenbaum, Elias

SIX EPIGRAMS see Pleskow, Raoul

SIX ETUDES POUR ORCHESTRE see Tansman,
    Alexandre

SIX FABLES AFTER JEAN DE LA FONTAINE,
    FOR SOLO VOICE AND ORCHESTRA [ARR]
    see Offenbach, Jacques, Sechs
    Fabeln Nach Jean De La Fontaine,
    For Solo Voice And Orchestra [arr]

SIX HEURES A PERDRE see Dutilleux,
    Henri

SIX IRISH POEMS, FOR SOLO VOICE AND
    ORCHESTRA see Rorem, Ned

SIX ITALIAN DANCES see Heseltine,
    Philip ("Peter Warlock")

SIX MELODIES POPULAIRES CORSES, FOR
    SOLO VOICE AND ORCHESTRA see
    Tomasi, Henri

SIX MOUVEMENTS POUR ORCHESTRE A CORDES
    see Tansman, Alexandre

SIX NORWEGIAN DANCES see Lunde, Ivar,
    Seks Norske Danser

SIX OF ONE, A DOZEN OF THE OTHER see
    Karpman, Laura

SIX OGDEN NASH SONGS, FOR SOLO VOICE
    AND ORCHESTRA see Susskind, Walter

SIX PIECES FOR OBOE AND STRING
    ORCHESTRA see Grippe, Ragnar

SIX PIECES FOR STRING ORCHESTRA see
    Kogoj, Marij, Sest Skladb, For
    String Orchestra see Lully, Jean-
    Baptiste (Lulli)

SIX POEMS BY MARINA TSVETAYEVA, FOR
    SOLO VOICE AND CHAMBER ORCHESTRA
    see Shostakovich, Dmitri

SIX PORTRAITS FOR ORCHESTRA see
    Einfeld(t), Dieter, Sechs Bilder
    Fur Orchester

SIX PRELUDES EN FORME DE SUITE, FOR
    VIOLIN AND CHAMBER ORCHESTRA see
    DuBois, Pierre-Max

SIX ROMANCES ON POEMS BY RALEIGH,
    BURNS, AND SHAKESPEARE, FOR SOLO
    VOICE AND CHAMBER ORCHESTRA see
    Shostakovich, Dmitri

SIX ROMANCES ON WORDS BY JAPANESE
    POETS, FOR SOLO VOICE AND ORCHESTRA
    see Shostakovich, Dmitri

SIX SELECTED SYMPHONIES see Abel, Carl
    Friedrich

SIX SIGNIFICANT LANDSCAPES, FOR SOLO
    VOICE AND CHAMBER ORCHESTRA see
    Blank, Allan

SIX SONGS, FOR SOLO VOICE AND
    ORCHESTRA, OP. 17 see Kielland,
    Olav

SIX SONGS FOR SOLO VOICE AND ORCHESTRA
    [ARR] see Offenbach, Jacques,
    Melodies: Sechs Lieder For Solo
    Voice And Orchestra [arr]

SIX SONGS OF EXPERIENCE, FOR SOLO VOICE
    AND ORCHESTRA see Segerstam, Leif

SIX STUDIES IN ENGLISH FOLK SONG, FOR
    ENGLISH HORN AND STRING ORCHESTRA
    [ARR.] see Vaughan Williams, Ralph

SIX SYMPHONIES, PART I see Wanhal,
    Johann Baptist (Jan Krtitel)

SIX SYMPHONIES, PART II see Wanhal,
    Johann Baptist (Jan Krtitel)

SIXTEEN HAIKU OF SEFERIS, FOR SOLO
    VOICES AND ORCHESTRA see Tavener,
    John

SJELLANDSKE AFGRUNDE see Werner, Sven
    Erik

SJÖBERG, JOHAN MAGNUS (1953-   )
Amen II [20']
    1.1.1.0. 1.1.1.0. perc,pno/cel,
    vln,vla,vcl
    STIM   (S915)

SJÖBLOM, HEIMER (1910-   )
Suite Of Yesterday *Op.21 [15']
    1.1.1.1. 1.0.0.0. strings
    STIM   (S916)

SJÖGREN, (JOHAN GUSTAF) EMIL
    (1853-1918)
Alt Vandrer Maanen, For Solo Voice
    And Orchestra [4']
    2.1.2.1. 2.0.0.0. timp,strings,
    med solo
    NORDISKA perf mat rent   (S917)

Geheimnsvolle Flote, The, For Solo
    Voice And Orchestra [3']
    1.2.2.2. 2.0.0.0. harp,strings,
    med solo
    NORDISKA perf mat rent   (S918)

SKALKOTTAS, NIKOS (1904-1949)
Concertino for Oboe and Chamber
    Orchestra, [arr.]
    (Schuller, Gunther) 2.1(English
    horn).1+bass clar.1. 2.1.1.1.
    harp,strings,ob solo [11'] MARGUN
    MM065 perf mat rent   (S919)

SKANDINAVISCHE VOLKSMUSIK see Hartmann,
    Emil

SKERL, DANE (1931-   )
Concerto for Violin and Orchestra
    [16']
    1(pic).1.1(alto clar in E flat,
    bass clar).1. 2.1.1.1. timp,
    perc,xylo,harp,cel,strings,vln
    solo
    DRUSTVO DSS 1071 perf mat rent
                                    (S920)

Three Symphonic Sketches
    see Tri Simfonicne Skice

Tri Simfonicne Skice [12']
    2(pic).2(English horn).2(bass
    clar).2(contrabsn). 4.4.3.1.
    timp,perc,harp,cel,strings
    "Three Symphonic Sketches" DRUSTVO
    DSS 1020 perf mat rent   (S921)

SKERPLA II see Tomasson, Jonas

SKETCH FROM EASTERN NORWAY NO. 2 see
    Kristoffersen, Fridthjof,
    Ostlandsskisse Nr. 2

SKETCHES FROM NATAL see Forsyth,
    Malcolm

SKINNER, J. SCOTT
Cradle Song [arr.]
    (Dalby, M.) NOVELLO perf mat rent
                                    (S922)

SKIPPER WORSE SUITE see Kvandal, Johan

SKJAERGAARDSO, FOR SOLO VOICE AND
    ORCHESTRA see Tveitt, Geirr

SKOGENS OYNE see Solås, Eyvind

SKÖLD, SVEN (1899-1956)
At Rivers, On Mountains And In
    Valleys
    see Vid Alvom, Pa Berg Och I Dalom

Burlesk [4'45"]
    2.2.2.2. 2.2.3.0. timp,perc,cel,
    strings
    BUSCH DM 027 perf mat rent   (S923)

Canzonetta, For Violin And Orchestra
    [3']
    1.1.1.1. 1.0.0.0. pno,strings,vln
    solo
    NORDISKA perf mat rent   (S924)

Five Folk Tunes From Sarna [5']
    1.1.1.1. 1.0.0.0. pno,strings
    NORDISKA perf mat rent   (S925)

Four Miniatures
    see Fyra Miniatyrer

Fyra Miniatyrer [8'15"]
    1.1.2.1. 2.2.1.0. perc,opt pno,
    strings
    "Four Miniatures" BUSCH DM 064 perf
    mat rent   (S926)

Melody, For Violoncello And Orchestra
    [4']
    fl,clar,strings,vcl solo
    NORDISKA perf mat rent   (S927)

Sommar, For Violin And Orchestra [5']
    1.0.2.1. 0.0.0.0. strings,vln
    solo
    NORDISKA perf mat rent   (S928)

Valse Romantique [4']
    1.1.1.1. 1.0.0.0. pno,strings
    NORDISKA perf mat rent   (S929)

Vid Alvom, Pa Berg Och I Dalom [25']
    1.1.2.1. 2.2.1.0. timp,perc,pno,
    strings
    "At Rivers, On Mountains And In
    Valleys" BUSCH HBM 003 perf mat
    rent   (S930)

SKÖLD, YNGVE (1899-   )
Hard Terms, The, For Solo Voice And
    Orchestra [6']
    2.1.2.2. 2.2.0.0. timp,strings,
    med solo
    NORDISKA perf mat rent   (S931)

Suite No. 1 for String Orchestra
    [18']
    string orch
    BUSCH perf mat rent   (S932)

SKOLION see Antoniou, Theodore

SKORYK, MYROSLAV (1938-   )
  Concerto for Orchestra
    3.3.3.2. 4.3.3.1. timp,3perc,
    harp,pno,strings
    (Carpathian) VAAP perf mat rent
                                        (S933)
  Concerto for Violin and Orchestra
    [16']
    3.3.3.2. 4.3.3.1. timp,perc,pno,
    strings,vln solo
    SIKORSKI perf mat rent   (S934)
    VAAP perf mat rent   (S935)
  Concerto for Violoncello and
    Orchestra [24']
    3.3.3.2. 4.3.3.1. timp,perc,mand,
    strings,vcl solo
    VAAP perf mat rent   (S936)
  Partita No. 1
    string orch
    VAAP perf mat rent   (S937)
  Partita No. 2
    1.1.1.1. 0.0.0.0. timp,2perc,
    strings
    VAAP perf mat rent   (S938)

SKOUEN, SYNNE (1950-   )
  Canto Delle Balene [4'30"]
    2.2.2.2. 4.2.2.1. timp,perc,harp,
    strings,electronic tape
    NORGE   (S939)
  Intonazione - Quasi Una Fantasia [7']
    2.2.2.2. 4.2.2.1. timp,perc,harp,
    strings,electronic tape
    NORGE   (S940)
  Nattstykke
    2.2.2.2. 4.3.3.1. timp,3perc,
    harp,strings
    NORGE   (S941)
  Tombeau Til Minona [6']
    3.3.3.3. 4.3.3.1. timp,perc,
    strings
    NORGE   (S942)
  Tre Haner Galer, For Solo Voices And
    Orchestra
    2.2.2.2. 4.2.1.1. timp,3perc,
    harp,strings,SSAA soli
    NORGE   (S943)

SKOVSYMFONI see Glass, Louis

SKREF see Sigurbjornsson, Hrodmar Ingi

SKRIABINADE see Masseus, Jan

SKROUP, FRANTISEK (1801-1862)
  Chrudimska Overture [7']
    2.2.2.2. 4.2.3.1. timp,strings
    SUPRAPHON   (S944)

SKROWACZEWSKI, STANISLAW (1923-   )
  Concerto for Clarinet and Orchestra
    3.0.0+bass clar.2(contrabsn).
    2.0.3.0. timp,perc,hpsd,cel,
    strings,clar solo
    EUR.AM.MUS.   (S945)
  Concerto for Orchestra [32']
    4.4.4.4. 4.4.3.1. timp,perc,harp,
    pno&cel,strings
    BOELKE-BOM   (S946)
  Concerto for Violin and Orchestra
    [20']
    3.2.3.3. 3.0.3.1. timp,perc,harp,
    hpsd,cel,strings without vln,
    vln solo
    BOELKE-BOM   (S947)
  Ricercari Notturni, For Saxophone And
    Orchestra [25']
    3(pic).0.0.2. 2.2.3.1. timp,3perc,
    hpsd,strings,sax/clar solo
    EUR.AM.MUS.   (S948)

SKY, THE see Kitazume, Michio

SLATE FOR CONCERTANTE GROUP AND
  ORCHESTRA see Torke, Michael

SLATTESTEV TIL JOL see Tveitt, Geirr

SLAVICKY, KLEMENT (1910-   )
  Sinfonietta No. 3 [25']
    3.3.3.2. 4.3.3.1. perc,xylo,
    vibra,strings
    SUPRAPHON   (S949)

SLAVONIC DANCE MELODY NO. 1 IN C see
  Karel, Rudolf

SLAVONIC DANCE MELODY NO. 2 IN G see
  Karel, Rudolf

SLAVONIC DANCES, OP. 46 see Dvorák,
  Antonín

SLAVONIC DANCES, OP. 46, BOOK I, NOS.
  1-4 see Dvorák, Antonín

SLAVONIC DANCES, OP. 46, BOOK II, NOS.
  5-8 see Dvorák, Antonín

SLAVONIC DANCES, OP. 72, BOOK I, NOS.
  9-12 see Dvorák, Antonín

SLAVONIC DANCES, OP. 72, BOOK II, NOS.
  13-16 see Dvorák, Antonín

SLAVONIC RHAPSODY, OP. 45, NO. 1, IN D
  see Dvorák, Antonín

SLAVONIC RHAPSODY, OP. 45, NO. 2, IN G
  MINOR see Dvorák, Antonín

SLAVONIC RHAPSODY, OP. 45, NO. 3, IN A
  FLAT see Dvorák, Antonín

SLEEP see Gurney, Ivor

SLEEP LITTLE CHILD JESUS, FOR SOLO
  VOICE AND ORCHESTRA see Eggen,
  Arne, Sov Barn Jesus Lille, For
  Solo Voice And Orchestra

SLEEPING BEAUTY, THE: ENTR'ACTE, FOR
  VIOLIN AND ORCHESTRA [ARR.] see
  Tchaikovsky, Piotr Ilyich

SLEEPING BEAUTY, THE: PAS DE DEUX see
  Tchaikovsky, Piotr Ilyich

SLEEPING BEAUTY, THE: PAS DE DEUX, ACT
  III [ARR.] see Tchaikovsky, Piotr
  Ilyich

SLEEPING BEAUTY, THE: PAS DE DEUX,
  "BLUEBIRD" [ARR.] see Tchaikovsky,
  Piotr Ilyich

SLEEPING BEAUTY, THE: POLACCA see
  Tchaikovsky, Piotr Ilyich

SLEEPING BEAUTY, THE: TWO PIECES see
  Tchaikovsky, Piotr Ilyich

SLEEPING BEAUTY, THE: VARIATION
  D'AURORE [ARR.] see Tchaikovsky,
  Piotr Ilyich

SLEEPING PRINCESS, FOR SOLO VOICE AND
  ORCHESTRA [ARR.] see Borodin,
  Alexander Porfirievich

SLETTHOLM, YNGVE (1955-   )
  Possible Selections, For Flute And
    Orchestra [24'30"]
    4.2.2.2. 3.3.3.1. timp,4perc,
    strings,fl solo
    NORGE   (S950)

SLIDES see Lutoslawski, Witold

SLIKE, KI IZGINJAJO see Mihelcic, Pavle

SLIMÁCEK, JAN
  Dramatic Picture
    sc PANTON 2417 f.s.   (S951)

SLITS see Gefors, Hans

SLONIMSKY, SERGEY (1932-   )
  Concerto Buffo [12']
    fl,trp,perc,pno,strings
    SIKORSKI perf mat rent   (S952)
    VAAP perf mat rent   (S953)
  Concerto For 3 Guitars, Solo
    Instruments And Orchestra [27']
    3.1.1.1. 2.2.3.1. opt flügelhorn,
    timp,perc,strings, soli: 3 elec
    gtr, sax, pno, traps
    SIKORSKI perf mat rent   (S954)
    VAAP perf mat rent   (S955)
  Dramatic Song [10']
    3.2.2.2. 4.2.3.1. timp,perc,cel,
    harp,strings
    VAAP perf mat rent   (S956)
    "Dramatisches Lied" SIKORSKI perf
    mat rent   (S957)
  Dramatisches Lied
    see Dramatic Song
  Ikarus: Suite [28']
    3.3.3.3.alto sax. 4.4.3.1. timp,
    perc,2harp,gtr,cel,pno,org,
    strings
    SIKORSKI perf mat rent   (S958)
    VAAP perf mat rent   (S959)
  Symphonic Motet [12']
    3.2.2.3. 4.2.4.1. timp,4perc,
    2harp,pno,strings
    SIKORSKI perf mat rent   (S960)
    VAAP perf mat rent   (S961)
  Symphony No. 2 [33']
    3.2.3.3. 4.3.3.1. timp,3perc,
    2harp,pno&cel,strings
    SIKORSKI perf mat rent   (S962)
    VAAP perf mat rent   (S963)

SLONIMSKY, SERGEY (cont'd.)
  Symphony No. 4 [30']
    3.2.2.2. 4.3.3.1. timp,perc,harp,
    pno,strings
    VAAP perf mat rent   (S964)

SLOTTSTAPPNING, FOR SOLO VOICE AND
  ORCHESTRA see Hakånson, Knut Algot

SLOVAK RHAPSODY see Mácha, Otmar

SLOVANKA QUADRILLE see Strauss, Johann,
  [Jr.]

SLOVENE DANCES see Svara, Danilo,
  Slovenski Plesi

SLOVENE FOLK DANCES see Srebotnjak,
  Alojz F., Slovenski Ljudski Plesi

SLOVENICA see Srebotnjak, Alojz F.

SLOVENSKI LJUDSKI PLESI see Srebotnjak,
  Alojz F.

SLOVENSKI PLESI see Svara, Danilo

SMALL CHAMBER MUSIC NO. 1 see
  Grabovsky, Leonid

SMALL CHAMBER MUSIC NO. 2 see
  Grabovsky, Leonid

SMALL IS BEAUTIFUL see Castiglioni,
  Niccolò

SMALL ORCHESTRAL WORKS, K. ANH. 1, NOS.
  9 & 10, K. 102, 120, 163, 291 see
  Mozart, Wolfgang Amadeus

SMALL SUITE FOR STRING ORCHESTRA see
  Albertsen, Per Hjort, Liten Suite
  For Strykeorkester

SMALL TOWN see Sculthorpe, Peter
  [Joshua]

SMALLEY, ROGER (1943-   )
  Konzertstück for Violin and Orchestra
    [22']
    2.2.2.2. 2.2.2.1. 2perc,harp,cel,
    strings,vln solo
    FABER perf mat rent   (S965)
  Symphony [38']
    3.3.3.3. 4.4.3.1. timp,5perc,
    2harp,pno&cel,elec org,strings
    sc FABER f.s., perf mat rent (S966)

SMAREGLIA, ANTONIO (1854-1929)
  Nozze Istriane: Preludio [5']
    2.2.2.2. 4.3.3.0. timp,strings
    SONZOGNO perf mat rent   (S967)
  Oceana: Overture [11']
    3.3.3.3. 4.3.3.1. timp,perc,harp,
    strings
    SONZOGNO perf mat rent   (S968)
  Pittori Fiamminghi: Preludio, Act I
    [6']
    3.2.3.2. 4.2.3.1. timp,perc,harp,
    strings
    SONZOGNO perf mat rent   (S969)
  Pittori Fiamminghi: Preludio, Act II
    [4']
    2.2.2.2. 4.0.0.0. strings
    SONZOGNO perf mat rent   (S970)
  Pittori Fiamminghi: Preludio, Act III
    [3'30"]
    3.2.3.2. 4.2.3.1. timp,perc,harp,
    strings
    SONZOGNO perf mat rent   (S971)
  Vassallo, Il: Danze Ungheresi [11']
    3.2.3.2. 4.2.3.1. timp,perc,
    strings
    SONZOGNO perf mat rent   (S972)

SMEDEN OG BAGEREN, FOR SOLO VOICE AND
  CHAMBER ORCHESTRA see Arnestad,
  Finn

SMETANA, BEDRICH (1824-1884)
  Bartered Bride, The: Dearest Son, For
    Solo Voice And Orchestra
    KALMUS A4994 sc $3.00, set $8.00,
    pts $.75, ea.   (S973)
  Bartered Bride, The: Gladly Will I Be
    Believing, For Solo Voice And
    Orchestra
    KALMUS A4987 sc $4.00, set $9.00,
    pts $.75, ea.   (S974)
  Bartered Bride, The: Ha, That Hit
    Like A Lightning Blast, For Solo
    Voices And Orchestra
    KALMUS A5000 sc $8.00, set $15.00,
    pts $.75, ea., perf mat rent
                                (S975)

SMETANA, BEDRICH (cont'd.)

Bartered Bride, The: He Would Have
  Come Here, For Solo Voices And
  Orchestra
  KALMUS A4990 sc $7.00, set $15.00,
    pts $1.00, ea., perf mat rent
                                    (S976)
Bartered Bride, The: Here She Comes
  Without Suspicion, For Solo
  Voices And Orchestra
  KALMUS A4991 sc $7.00, set $12.00,
    pts $1.00, ea., perf mat rent
                                    (S977)
Bartered Bride, The: He's Blessed, So
  Blessed Who Loves And Can
  Believe, For Solo Voices And
  Orchestra
  KALMUS A5004 sc $4.00, set $12.00,
    pts $1.00, ea.   (S978)
Bartered Bride, The: I Know A Girl So
  Sweet And Dear, For Solo Voices
  And Orchestra
  KALMUS A4995 sc $9.00, set $15.00,
    pts $1.00, ea., perf mat rent
                                    (S979)
Bartered Bride, The: It Is
  Succeeding, For Solo Voice And
  Orchestra
  KALMUS A4997 sc $5.00, set $10.00,
    pts $.75, ea.   (S980)
Bartered Bride, The: Just One Word
  Will Be Enough, For Solo Voices
  And Orchestra
  KALMUS A4996 sc $12.00, set $22.00,
    pts $2.00, ea., perf mat rent
                                    (S981)
Bartered Bride, The: My Dearest Love,
  I Beg You Please, For Solo Voices
  And Orchestra
  KALMUS A5003 sc $4.00, set $9.00,
    pts $.75, ea.   (S982)
Bartered Bride, The: Oh, I Feel So
  Queasy, For Solo Voice And
  Orchestra
  KALMUS A3020 sc $4.00, set $8.00,
    pts $.75, ea.   (S983)
Bartered Bride, The: Overture
  BROUDE BR. set $47.50, pts $2.50,
    ea.   (S984)
Bartered Bride, The: So Now All Is
  Decided, For Solo Voices And
  Orchestra
  KALMUS A4989 sc $8.00, set $15.00,
    pts $1.00, ea., perf mat rent
                                    (S985)
Bartered Bride, The: The World Is
  Dead And Blacker Than Night, For
  Solo Voice And Orchestra
  KALMUS A5002 sc $4.00, set $10.00,
    pts $1.00, ea.   (S986)
Bartered Bride, The: There's No Need
  To Worry, For Solo Voices And
  Orchestra
  KALMUS A4999 sc $5.00, set $10.00,
    pts $2.00, ea.   (S987)
Bartered Bride, The: With My Mother
  Hope Was Ended, For Solo Voices
  And Orchestra
  KALMUS A4988 sc $5.00, set $10.00,
    pts $1.00, ea.   (S988)
Betty's Polka [3']
  2.2.3.3. 2.2.0.0. timp,perc,
    strings
  SUPRAPHON   (S989)
Dve Vdovy: Ballet Music
  see Two Widows, The: Ballet Music
Hakon Jarl
  KALMUS A5705 sc $30.00, set $50.00,
    perf mat rent   (S990)
Hubicka: Overture *see Kiss, The:
  Overture
Kuss, Der: Overture
  KALMUS A5653 sc $12.00, perf mat
    rent, set $22.00, pts $1.00, ea.
                                    (S991)
Ma Vlast: Sarka
  see My Country, No. 3: Sarka
Macbeth And The Witches, For Piano
  And Orchestra [15']
  reconstruction
  2+pic.2.2(bass
    clar).2(contrabsn). 4.2.3.1.
    timp,3perc,strings,pno solo
  (Burghauser, Jarmil) sc SUPRAPHON
    f.s.   (S992)
My Country, No. 1: Vysehrad
  SONZOGNO perf mat rent   (S993)
  (Jancsovics) study sc EMB 40106
    f.s.   (S994)

SMETANA, BEDRICH (cont'd.)

My Country, No. 2: The Moldau
  SONZOGNO perf mat rent   (S995)
  (Jancsovics) study sc EMB 40076
    f.s.   (S996)
My Country, No. 3: Sarka
  SONZOGNO perf mat rent   (S997)
  "Ma Vlast: Sarka" BREITKOPF·L perf
    mat rent   (S998)
  (Jancsovics) study sc EMB 40107
    f.s.   (S999)
My Country, No. 4: From Bohemia's
  Meadows And Forests
  SONZOGNO perf mat rent   (S1000)
  (Jancsovics) study sc EMB 40108
    f.s.   (S1001)
My Country, No. 5: Tabor
  SONZOGNO perf mat rent   (S1002)
  (Jancsovics) study sc EMB 40109
    f.s.   (S1003)
My Country No. 6: Blanik
  SONZOGNO perf mat rent   (S1004)
  (Jancsovics) study sc EMB 40110
    f.s.   (S1005)
Oldrich And Bozena Overture [3']
  2clar,trp,timp,strings
  KALMUS A6111 sc $5.00, set $9.00
                                    (S1006)
Richard III [20']
  3.2.2.2. 4.2.2.1. timp,perc,harp,
    strings
  KALMUS A4107 sc $30.00, set $45.00,
    perf mat rent   (S1007)
  SIMROCK perf mat rent   (S1008)
Three Czech Dances [arr.]
  (Susskind, Walter) 3(pic).3(English
    horn).3(bass clar).2+contrabsn.
    4.2.3.1. timp,3perc,harp,strings
    [14'] NORRUTH perf mat rent
                                    (S1009)
Triumph-Symphonie [36']
  2+pic.2.2.2. 4.2.3.0. timp,3perc,
    strings
  sc SUPRAPHON f.s.   (S1010)
Two Widows, The: Ballet Music
  "Dve Vdovy: Ballet Music" KALMUS
    A5797 sc $10.00, set $20.00, perf
    mat rent   (S1011)
Wallenstein's Camp
  KALMUS A6087 sc $35.00, set $45.00,
    perf mat rent   (S1012)

SMETHERGELL, WILLIAM (ca. 1745-1825)
Overtures, Four
  see Herschel, William, Symphonies,
    Three
Overtures, Four *see Herschel,
  William, Symphonies, Three

SMILING IMMORTAL see Harvey, Jonathan

SMIRNOV, DMITRI (1948-   )
Concerto for Alto Saxophone, Piano,
  Double Bass and Chamber Orchestra
  [18']
  perc,strings,alto sax solo,pno
    solo,db solo
  SIKORSKI perf mat rent   (S1013)
Concerto for Piano and String
  Orchestra, No. 2 [15']
  10vln,4vla,3vcl,2db,pno solo
  SIKORSKI perf mat rent   (S1014)
Eternal Calm, For Solo Voice And
  Chamber Orchestra [10']
  timp,perc,org,7vln,3vla,2vcl,db,
    solo voice
  "Ewige Zuflucht, For Solo Voice And
    Chamber Orchestra" SIKORSKI perf
    mat rent   (S1015)
Ewige Zuflucht, For Solo Voice And
  Chamber Orchestra
  see Eternal Calm, For Solo Voice
    And Chamber Orchestra
In Memoriam Igor Stravinsky [12']
  1.1.1.1. 1.1.1.1. timp/glock,vln,
    vla,vcl,db
  SIKORSKI perf mat rent   (S1016)
  VAAP perf mat rent   (S1017)
Pastorale [12']
  2.2.2.2. 4.2.3.1. timp,perc,
    strings
  SIKORSKI perf mat rent   (S1018)
  VAAP perf mat rent   (S1019)
Sinfonischer Prolog Zu "Tiriel" [11']
  3.3.3.3. 4.3.3.1. timp,harp,cel,
    strings
  SIKORSKI perf mat rent   (S1020)

SMIRNOV, DMITRI (cont'd.)

Symphony No. 1 [26']
  3.3.3.3. 4.3.3.1. timp,perc,harp,
    cel,pno,strings
  SIKORSKI perf mat rent   (S1021)
  (The Seasons) VAAP perf mat rent
                                    (S1022)
Symphony No. 2 [26']
  2.1.1.1.alto sax. 1.1.1.1. timp,
    5perc,harp,cel/pno,org,gtr/elec
    gtr,bass gtr,strings,cor
  SIKORSKI perf mat rent   (S1023)
  VAAP perf mat rent   (S1024)

SMIT, SYTZE (1944-   )
Prologue To Quipu [10']
  1.1.1.0. 1.1.1.0. pno,2vln,vla,
    vcl,db
  sc DONEMUS f.s., perf mat rent
                                    (S1025)
Quipu [21']
  1.1.1.0. 1.1.1.0. pno,strings
  DONEMUS f.s.   (S1026)

SMITH, JOHN CHRISTOPHER (1712-1795)
Fairies, The: Overture
  opt 2ob,opt trp,strings [7'] OXFORD
    perf mat rent   (S1027)

SMITH, JOHN STAFFORD (1750-1836)
Star-Spangled Banner, The [arr.]
  (Zaninelli) PRESSER 116-40025 sc
    $3.00, set $25.00, pts $1.00, ea.
                                    (S1028)

SMITH, JOLYON BRETTINGHAM
see BRETTINGHAM SMITH, JOLYON

SMITH, LARRY ALAN (1955-   )
Concerto for Piano and Orchestra
  [17']
  MERION perf mat rent   (S1029)
Concerto for Viola and Orchestra
  MERION perf mat rent   (S1030)
Crucifixus, For Solo Voice And
  Orchestra [16']
  MERION perf mat rent   (S1031)
New York Overture, A *Op.13 [5'30"]
  3.3.3.3. 4.3.3.1. timp,3perc,
    strings
  BOURNE perf mat rent   (S1032)
Serenade For Marguerita [8']
  string orch
  MERION perf mat rent   (S1033)
Symphony No. 1 [29']
  MERION perf mat rent   (S1034)
Symphony No. 2 [17']
  MERION perf mat rent   (S1035)

SMITH, LELAND C. (1925-   )
Arabesque, For Saxophone And Chamber
  Orchestra [9']
  1+pic.0.1.0. 1.1.1.0. vibra,2vln,
    vcl,tenor sax/bsn solo
  AM.COMP.AL. perf mat rent   (S1036)
Santa Claus: Overture [7']
  3.3.3.3. 4.3.3.0. timp,perc,
    strings
  AM.COMP.AL. perf mat rent   (S1037)

SMITH, LEO
Mutumishi [12']
  any instruments
  sc AM.COMP.AL. $3.85   (S1038)

SMITH, WILLIAM OVERTON (1926-   )
Concerto For Jazz Soloist And
  Orchestra (Variants) [18']
  2.1.2(bass clar).2. 2.2.2.1.
    timp,perc,harp,strings,clar&
    soprano clar in E flat solo,db
    solo,drums solo
  sc,pts MJQ rent   (S1039)
Ecco! [6']
  2+alto fl.2+English horn.2+bass
    clar.3. 4.3.3.1. perc,pno,harp,
    strings,clar solo
  sc MJQ $8.95, perf mat rent   (S1040)
Elegy [15']
  6vln,2vla,2vcl,db,clar solo
  sc MJQ $9.95, perf mat rent   (S1041)
Interplay [14']
  2.1.2.2. 2.3.1.1. timp,perc,cel,
    gtr,strings,vibra solo,pno
    solo,db solo,drums solo
  sc MJQ $7.95, perf mat rent   (S1042)
Mu, For Clarinet And Chamber
  Orchestra [12']
  alto sax,tenor sax,bass sax,horn,
    2trp,tuba,gtr,db,drums,vln,vcl,
    clar solo
  sc,pts MJQ rent   (S1043)

SMITH, WILLIAM OVERTON (cont'd.)

Quadri [18']
3(pic).3.3(bass
clar).3(contrabsn). 4.3.2+bass
trom.1. timp,2perc,harp,
strings,vibra solo,pno solo,db
solo,drums solo
sc MJQ $8.95, perf mat rent (S1044)

Theona [15']
2.2.2.2. 4.3.3.1. 3perc,strings,
clar solo,trp solo,pno solo,db
solo,drums solo
sc,pts MJQ rent (S1045)

SMORBLOMSTER, FOR SOLO VOICE AND
ORCHESTRA see Tveitt, Geirr

SMULTRONVISA, FOR SOLO VOICE AND
CHAMBER ORCHESTRA see Werle, Lars-
Johan

SMYTH, ETHEL (MARY) (1858-1944)
Concerto for Violin, Horn and
Orchestra [26']
2.2.2.2. 2.1.0.0. timp,perc,harp,
strings,vln solo,horn solo
CURWEN perf mat rent (S1046)

SNAKE, FOR SOLO VOICE AND CHAMBER
ORCHESTRA see Kulesha, Gary

SNAPSHOTS see Charles, Jon

SNELHEID, DE see Andriessen, Louis

SNJO, FOR SOLO VOICE AND STRING
ORCHESTRA see Eggen, Arne

SNOSTORM, FOR SOLO VOICE AND ORCHESTRA
see Tveitt, Geirr

SNOW, FOR SOLO VOICE AND STRING
ORCHESTRA see Eggen, Arne, Snjo,
For Solo Voice And String Orchestra

SNOW CRAZY COPYBOOK, THE see Kitzke,
Jerome P.

SNOW MAIDEN, THE see Tchaikovsky, Piotr
Ilyich

SNOW MAIDEN, THE: PRELUDE see
Tchaikovsky, Piotr Ilyich

SNOW QUEEN, THE see Linkola, Jukka

SNOW-WHITE, FOR NARRATOR AND ORCHESTRA
see Hallman, Bjorn, Sagan Om
Snovit, For Narrator And Orchestra

SNOWFLAKES [ARR.] see Dunayevszky,
Isaak O.

SNOWMAN, THE, FOR SOLO VOICES AND
ORCHESTRA see Blake, Howard

SNOWSTORM see Sviridov, Georgy

SNOWSTORM, FOR SOLO VOICE AND ORCHESTRA
see Tveitt, Geirr, Snostorm, For
Solo Voice And Orchestra

SNUFF BOX see Fleming, Robert

SO RODDE DEI FJORDAN, FOR SOLO VOICE
AND ORCHESTRA see Ørbeck, Anne
Marie

"...SO ZU LICHT UND LUST GEBOREN...",
FOR SOLO VOICE AND ORCHESTRA see
Schedl, Gerhard

SOBRE LAS OLAS [ARR.] see Rosas,
Juventino

SOCCIO, GIUSEPPE (1950-)
Litios: La Fonte, Del Sentire, For
Flute And Orchestra [20']
4.3.4.3. 5.4.4.1. 3perc,strings,
fl solo
RICORDI-IT 133945 perf mat rent
(S1047)

SOCRATE, FOR SOLO VOICE AND ORCHESTRA
see Satie, Erik

SÖDERBERG, HANS (1937-)
Concerto for Orchestra
horn,perc,pno,strings
STIM (S1048)

Tabula Rasa
string orch
STIM (S1049)

SØDERLIND, RAGNAR (1945-)
Amor Et Labor *Op.27 [10']
3(pic).1+English horn.2.1+
contrabsn. 4.3.3.1. 3perc,harp,
pno,strings
NORSK perf mat rent (S1050)

Come Ocean Winds, Come
see Kom Havsvindar, Kom

SØDERLIND, RAGNAR (cont'd.)
Concerto for Violin and Orchestra,
Op. 46
3.3.3.3. 4.3.3.1. timp,2perc,
harp,cel,strings,vln solo
NORGE (S1051)

Ecstasy *Op.45 [6'30"]
string orch
NORGE (S1052)

Eg Hev Funne Min Floysne Lokkar Att I
Mitt Svarmerus, For Solo Voice
And Orchestra *Op.35c [10']
2.2.2.2. 4.3.3.1. timp,perc,harp,
strings,S solo
"I Have Found My Handsome Lover
Back, For Solo Voice And
Orchestra" NORGE (S1053)

Fantasia Borealis *Op.14 [11']
3.2.2.2. 4.2.3.1. timp,perc,
strings
NORGE (S1054)

Hedda Gabler *Op.26 [30']
3.3.3.3. 4.4.3.1. timp,perc,harp,
pno/cel,strings
NORGE (S1055)

I Have Found My Handsome Lover Back,
For Solo Voice And Orchestra
see Eg Hev Funne Min Floysne Lokkar
Att I Mitt Svarmerus, For Solo
Voice And Orchestra

International Rhapsody *Op.17 [10']
2.2.2.2. 4.4.3.1. timp,perc,
strings
(alternate scoring: .1110 2220.,
perc, str) NORGE (S1056)

Jolsterslatt *Op.2 [3']
3.2.2.2. 4.3.3.1. timp,perc,
strings
NORGE (S1057)

Kom Havsvindar, Kom *Op.33 [6']
2.2.2.2. 4.2.3.1. timp,perc,harp,
pno/cel,strings
"Come Ocean Winds, Come" NORGE
(S1058)

Legg Ikkje Ditt Liv I Mi Hand
see Two Songs To Poems By Ase Marie
Nesse, For Solo Voice And
Orchestra

Pa Botnen Av Alt
see Two Songs To Poems By Ase Marie
Nesse, For Solo Voice And
Orchestra

Pieta, For Solo Voice And String
Orchestra *Op.5 [6']
string orch,Mez solo
NORGE (S1059)

Polaris *Op.11 [14']
3.3.3.3. 6.4.3.1. timp,perc,
2harp,strings
NORGE (S1060)

Prelude, Op. 4 [9']
3.3.3.3. 4.3.3.1. timp,perc,harp,
pno/cel,strings
NORGE (S1061)

Rokkomborre *Op.8 [8']
3(pic).2.2+bass clar.2. 4.3.3.1.
timp,perc,harp,cel,strings
NORSK perf mat rent (S1062)

Sinfonia Minimale *Op.16 [7']
2.0.2.0. 1.0.0.0. strings
NORGE (S1063)

Symphony No. 1, Op. 23 [27']
4.3.4.3. 5.3.3.1. timp,perc,harp,
strings
NORGE (S1064)

Symphony No. 2, Op. 30 [15']
2+pic.2+English horn.2+bass
clar.2+contrabsn. 4.4.3.1.
timp,4perc,cel&pno,harp,strings
sc NORSK $32.50, perf mat rent
(S1065)

Two Pieces From The Desert, For Oboe
And Orchestra *Op.21b [11']
2.0.3.0. 3.0.0.0. timp,perc,harp,
strings,ob solo
NORGE (S1066)

Two Songs To Poems By Ase Marie
Nesse, For Solo Voice And
Orchestra *Op.39b
2.2.2.2. 4.2.3.0. timp,perc,harp,
strings,solo voice NORGE f.s.
contains: Legg Ikkje Ditt Liv I
Mi Hand; Pa Botnen Av Alt
(S1067)

SÖDERLUNDH, LILLE BROR (1912-1957)
Bollelaten [3']
2fl,2clar,strings
NORDISKA perf mat rent (S1068)

Dalasvit [8']
string orch
sc,pts BUSCH f.s. (S1069)

Dance From Klockrikemusiken [4']
2fl,2clar,strings
NORDISKA perf mat rent (S1070)

Emperor Of Portugallia, The
see Kejsarn Av Portugallien

Havangsvit, For Piano And String
Orchestra [11']
string orch,pno solo
STIM (S1071)

Kejsarn Av Portugallien [20']
2.2.2.2. 3.3.2.0. timp,perc,harp,
hpsd,strings
"Emperor Of Portugallia, The" BUSCH
HBM 075 perf mat rent (S1072)

SÖDERMAN, [JOHAN] AUGUST (1832-1876)
Burlesk [3']
2.2.2.2. 2.2.3.0. timp,perc,harp,
strings
BUSCH DM 026 perf mat rent (S1073)

SÖDERSTEN, GUNNO (1920-)
Concerto for Organ and String
Orchestra, No. 3
string orch,org solo
STIM (S1074)

SOETEMAN, IMAN (1935-)
Symphony in C [37']
2.2.2.3. 2.2.3.1. timp,2perc,
strings
sc DONEMUS f.s., perf mat rent
(S1075)

SOFIEN QUADRILLE see Strauss, Josef

SOG see Halldorsson, Skuli

SOGNI, FOR SOLO VOICE AND ORCHESTRA see
Ferritto, John E.

SOGNO, IL see Jansson, Johannes

SOGNO DI SCIPIONE, IL: OVERTURE see
Mozart, Wolfgang Amadeus

SOHAL, NARESH (1939-)
Dhyan 1 [16']
1(pic).1.1.1. 1.1.1.0. 3perc,
harp,pno,strings,vcl solo
NOVELLO perf mat rent (S1076)

From Gitanjali, For Solo Voice And
Orchestra
NOVELLO perf mat rent (S1077)

Indra Dhanush [16']
3(pic).3.3(bass
clar).3(contrabsn). 4.4.3.1.
4perc,pno,cel,2harp,strings
NOVELLO perf mat rent (S1078)

Tandava Nritya
NOVELLO perf mat rent (S1079)

SOINUA, FOR SOLO VOICE AND ORCHESTRA
see Larrauri, Anton

SOIREES DE BARCELONE see Gerhard,
Roberto

SOIREES IMAGINAIRES see Eröd, Ivan

SOKOLA, MILOS (1913-1976)
Variational Symphony
sc PANTON 2276 f.s. (S1080)

SOLARIUM see Arrigo, Girolamo

SOLÅS, EYVIND (1937-)
Concerto for Piano and Orchestra
[28'35"]
2.2.2.2. 2.3.2.0. timp,perc,harp,
strings,pno solo
NORGE (S1081)

Eyes Of The Forest, The
see Skogens Oyne

I Det Fjerne [8']
2.2.3.2. 3.2.2.0. perc,harp,pno,
org,strings
"In The Distance" NORGE (S1082)

In The Distance
see I Det Fjerne

Let Me Keep My Unrest
see Ta Ikke Denne Uro Fra Meg

Musikk Til En By Ved Havet
2.2.2.2. 2.2.2.1. timp,perc,
strings
NORGE (S1083)

SOLÅS, EYVIND (cont'd.)

Mythos
  2.2.3.2. 4.3.3.1. timp,perc,harp,
    strings
  NORGE   (S1084)

Serenade [3']
  2.2.3.2. 3.2.2.0. perc,pno,
    strings
  NORGE   (S1085)

Skogens Oyne [18']
  string orch
  "Eyes Of The Forest, The" NORGE
                                     (S1086)

Ta Ikke Denne Uro Fra Meg [18']
  2.2.3.2. 3.2.2.0. perc,harp,pno,
    strings
  "Let Me Keep My Unrest" NORGE
                                     (S1087)

SOLBERG, LEIF (1914-   )
Symphony No. 1 [22']
  2.2.2.2. 4.2.3.1. timp,harp,
    strings
  NORGE   (S1088)

SOLDATENGRUSS POLKA see Strauss, Eduard

SOLDIER'S JOY see Revolutionary
  Garland, A

SOLEDADES see Adrian

SOLEIL DE PAPIER, LE see Sciortino,
  Patrice

SOLEIL ET DANSES DANS LA FORET see
  Koechlin, Charles

SOLEMN ENTRANCE see Strauss, Richard,
  Feierlicher Einzug

SOLEMN OVERTURE see Shchedrin, Rodion
  see Sidelnikov, Leonid

SOLER, [PADRE] ANTONIO (1729-1783)
Sonatas, Three [arr.]
  (Halffter, R.) 2.2.2.2. 2.2.0.0.
    timp,perc,strings [12'] UNION
  ESP. perf mat rent   (S1089)

SOLER, JOSEP (1935-   )
Concerto for Piano and Orchestra
  [30']
  1.2.1.0. 1.0.0.0. cel,strings,pno
    solo
  PEER perf mat rent   (S1090)

Danae
  string orch
  PEER perf mat rent   (S1091)

Inferno
  1.2.2+bass clar.1. 0.0.2.0. perc,
    strings
  PEER perf mat rent   (S1092)

Sinfonia
  2.2.2.2. 5.3.3.1. perc,2harp,
    strings
  SEESAW perf mat rent   (S1093)

SOLFAGER, FOR SOLO VOICE AND ORCHESTRA
  see Eggen, Arne

SOLGLOTT [ARR.] see Cleve, Cissi

SOLI see Renosto, Paolo

SOLILOQUY, FOR CLARINET AND ORCHESTRA
  see Corigliano, John

SOLILOQUY, FOR SOLO VOICE AND ORCHESTRA
  see Brown, Christopher (Roland)

SOLILOQUY II, FOR GUITAR AND ORCHESTRA
  see Musgrave, Thea

SOLITAIRE: SARABAND AND POLKA see
  Arnold, Malcolm

SOLITARY SEAMAN, A see Vacek, Miloš

SOLITUDE see Seymer, William

SOLITUDE, LA, FOR SOLO VOICE AND
  ORCHESTRA see Leguerney, Jacques

SOLITUDINE DEL GIORNO MARTEDI see
  Bilucaglia, Claudio

SOLJEVALSEN see Cleve, Cissi

SOLJEVALSEN [ARR.] see Cleve, Cissi

SOLL, BURKHARDT (1944-   )
Flowers [25']
  1.1.2.1. 1.1.1.1. 2perc,harp,pno,
    2vln,vla,vcl,db
  sc DONEMUS f.s., perf mat rent
                                     (S1094)
SOLL EIN SCHUH NICHT DRÜCKEN, FOR SOLO
  VOICE AND ORCHESTRA see Beethoven,
  Ludwig van

SOLLBERGER, HARVEY (1938-   )
Three Or Four Things I Know About The
  Oboe, For Oboe And Orchestra
  1.0.1.1. 0.1.1.1. perc,harp,pno,
    vla,vcl,db,ob solo
  study sc MCGIN-MARX f.s., perf mat
    rent   (S1095)

SOLO DE CONCERT, FOR BASSOON AND
  ORCHESTRA see Pierne, Gabriel

SOLOMON: ENTRANCE OF THE QUEEN OF SHEBA
  see Handel, George Frideric

SOLOMON: OVERTURE see Handel, George
  Frideric

SOLOMON: SACRED RAPTURES CHEER MY
  HEART, FOR SOLO VOICE AND ORCHESTRA
  see Handel, George Frideric

SOLOPPGANG [ARR.] see Cleve, Cissi

SOLTICE see Hopkins, John

SOM ETT SILVERSMYCKE, FOR SOLO VOICE
  AND ORCHESTRA see Jonsson, Josef
  [Petrus]

SOMEONE TO WATCH OVER ME AND
  EMBRACEABLE YOU, FOR SOLO VOICE AND
  ORCHESTRA, [ARR.] see Gershwin,
  George

SOMERS, HARRY STEWART (1925-   )
Concertante, For Violin, Strings And
  Percussion [22']
  perc,strings,vln solo
  CAN.MUS.CENT. MI 1311 S694C (S1096)

Elegy
  3.1.1.0. 1.1.0.0. 2perc,strings
  CAN.MUS.CENT. MI 1200 S694EL
                                     (S1097)
Elegy, Transformation, Jubilation
  4.4.4.4. 6.4.3.1. timp,3perc,
    strings
  CAN.MUS.CENT. MI 1100 S694EL
                                     (S1098)

SOMETHING LIKE see Jeney, Zoltan

SOMETHING ROUND see Jeney, Zoltan

SOMETIMES I FEEL LIKE A MOTHERLESS
  CHILD, FOR SOLO VOICE AND ORCHESTRA
  [ARR.]
  (Burleigh, Harry T.) 1.0.1.0.
    0.0.0.0. strings,med solo COLOMBO
    perf mat rent   (S1099)
  (Burleigh, Harry T.) 1.1.2.1.
    2.0.0.0. strings,low solo COLOMBO
    perf mat rent   (S1100)

SOMIS, GIOVANNI BATTISTA (1686-1763)
Concerto in B flat
  string orch,cont,vln solo
  (Bertotto, D.) RICORDI-IT sc 134250
    f.s., pts 134251 f.s.   (S1101)

Concerto in F
  string orch,cont,vln solo
  (Ferrari, G.) RICORDI-IT sc 134238
    f.s., pts 134249 f.s.   (S1102)

Concerto in G
  string orch,cont,vln solo
  (Di Lotti, S.) RICORDI-IT sc 134252
    f.s., pts 134253 f.s.   (S1103)

SOMMAR, FOR VIOLIN AND ORCHESTRA see
  Sköld, Sven

SOMMER, VLADIMÍR (1921-   )
Bajaja The Prince [18']
  CZECH RADIO   (S1104)

Concerto for Violoncello and
  Orchestra [30']
  CESKY HUD.   (S1105)

SOMMERFELDT, ÖISTEIN (1919-   )
Elka *Op.63 [10']
  3.2.2.2. 4.3.3.1. timp,perc,
    strings
  "Oak, The" study sc NORSK f.s.,
    perf mat rent   (S1106)

From Kathleen Raine's Poetry, For
  Solo Voice And Orchestra [arr.]
  *Op.55
  (Kruse, Bjorn) 1.1.1.0. 0.0.0.0.
    vibra,perc,harp,strings,S solo
  NORGE   (S1107)

Hafrsfjord, For Solo Voice And
  Orchestra *Op.30 [15']
  3.2.2.2. 4.3.3.1. perc,pno,cel,
    strings,narrator
  NORGE   (S1108)

Hildring I Speil, For Solo Voice And
  Orchestra [arr.] *Op.49b
  (Kruse, Bjorn) 1.1.1.0. 0.0.0.0.
    vibra,harp,strings,S solo NORGE
                                     (S1109)

SOMMERFELDT, ÖISTEIN (cont'd.)

Intrada *Op.57 [7']
  2.2.2.2. 4.3.3.1. timp,perc,
    strings
  NORGE   (S1110)

Kveldingseter, For Solo Voice And
  Orchestra [arr.]
  (Kruse, Bjorn) 1.0.1.0. 0.0.0.0.
    vibra,harp,strings,S solo NORGE
                                     (S1111)
Mot En Lengsel, For Piano And
  Orchestra *Op.50 [12']
  2+pic.2.2.2. 4.0.0.0. timp,perc,
    strings,pno solo
  "Towards A Yearning, For Piano And
    Orchestra" NORSK perf mat rent
                                     (S1112)
Mot En Verden Av Lys, For Solo Voice
  And Orchestra *Op.34b [7']
  2+pic.2.2.2. 3.2.2.0. perc,harp,
    cel,pno,strings,Bar solo
  NORSK perf mat rent   (S1113)

Oak, The
  see Elka

Suite No. 1, Op. 38 [9']
  2(pic).2(English horn).2.2.
    4.3.3.1. timp,perc,harp,strings
  NORSK perf mat rent   (S1114)

Three Lyrical Pictures, For Solo
  Voice And Orchestra *Op.33b [8']
  2.2.2.2. 3.3.0.0. timp,harp,
    strings,high solo
  NORSK perf mat rent   (S1115)

Towards A Yearning, For Piano And
  Orchestra
  see Mot En Lengsel, For Piano And
    Orchestra

SOMMERNACHT, FOR SOLO VOICE AND CHAMBER
  ORCHESTRA see Hess, Willy

SOMMERTAG AUF DEM LANDE see Gade, Niels
  Wilhelm

SOMNIA, FOR SOLO VOICE AND ORCHESTRA
  see Elias, Brian

SON ET LUMIERE see Stucky, Steven
  Edward

SONANCE-RESONANCE: WELCHE TONE? see
  Anhalt, István

SONANS see Eiriksdottir, Karolina

SONANTE FOR STRING ORCHESTRA see
  Chavez, Carlos

SONATA À 6 IN B FLAT see Biber,
  Heinrich Ignaz Franz von

SONATA A DUE, FOR VIOLIN, VIOLONCELLO
  AND STRING ORCHESTRA see Jaubert,
  Maurice

SONATA A TRE "LA RASPONA" [ARR.] see
  Legrenzi, Giovanni

SONATA ALLA MARCIA see Blake, David

SONATA BREVIS FOR CHAMBER ORCHESTRA see
  Urbanner, Erich

SONATA D'EGLISE, FOR ORGAN AND STRING
  ORCHESTRA see Sauguet, Henri

SONATA, "IL TRILLO DEL DIAVOLO" FOR
  VIOLIN AND ORCHESTRA, [ARR.] see
  Tartini, Giuseppe

SONATA NOTTURNA, FOR VIOLONCELLO AND
  STRING ORCHESTRA see Maw, Nicholas

SONATA-RICERCAR, FOR VIOLIN AND CHAMBER
  ORCHESTRA see Butzko, Yuri

SONATA-RICERCAR, FOR VIOLONCELLO AND
  CHAMBER ORCHESTRA see Butzko, Yuri

SONATAS, THREE [ARR.] see Soler,
  [Padre] Antonio

SONATAS FOR ORGAN AND ORCHESTRA, TWELVE
  see Mozart, Wolfgang Amadeus

SONATAS NOS. 380, 423, 518, 401, 69
  [ARR.] see Scarlatti, Domenico

SONATAS, TWO see Boyce, William

SONCECE, SIJ, FOR SOLO VOICE AND
  ORCHESTRA see Lipovsek, Marijan

SONETTO 104 DEL PETRARCA, FOR SOLO
  VOICE AND ORCHESTRA [ARR.] see
  Liszt, Franz

SONETTO DI MICHELANGELO see Valen,
  Fartein

SONETTO DI PETRARCA see Hartmann, Per Johannes

SONG AND HYMN (TWO PATRIOTIC MELODIES) see Liszt, Franz

SONG AT DUSK, A see Still, William Grant

SONG BEFORE SUNRISE, A see Delius, Frederick

SONG CYCLE, A, FOR SOLO VOICES AND ORCHESTRA see Halldorsson, Skuli

SONG CYCLE ON POEMS BY PABLO NERUDA, FOR SOLO VOICE AND CHAMBER ORCHESTRA see Wood, Hugh Bradshaw

SONG FOR ORCHESTRA see Mostad, Jon, Sang For Orkester

SONG FOR THE LONELY see Still, William Grant

SONG FOR THE LONELY, FOR SOLO VOICE AND ORCHESTRA see Still, William Grant

SONG FOR THE VALIANT, FOR SOLO VOICE AND ORCHESTRA see Still, William Grant

SONG OF AUTUMN see McIntyre, Paul

SONG OF DEBORAH, FOR SOLO VOICE AND CHAMBER ORCHESTRA see Rollin, Robert Leon

SONG OF JUPITER[ARR.] see Handel, George Frideric

SONG OF KRISTIN LAVRANSDATTER see Tveitt, Geirr, Lavransdatters Vise

SONG OF LOVE [ARR.] see Suk, Josef, Pisen Lasky [arr.]

SONG OF OLD AGE, A, FOR SOLO VOICE AND ORCHESTRA[ARR.] see Schubert, Franz (Peter), Greisengesang, For Solo Voice And Orchestra [arr.]

SONG OF SOLOMON, THE, FOR SOLO VOICE AND ORCHESTRA see Chatman, Stephen

SONG OF SONGS, FOR SOLO VOICES AND ORCHESTRA see Blaustein, Susan

SONG OF THE CARIBBEAN see Mourant, Walter

SONG OF THE CLOUDS, FOR OBOE AND ORCHESTRA see Payne, Anthony

SONG OF THE EARTH, THE, FOR SOLO VOICES AND ORCHESTRA see Mahler, Gustav, Lied Von Der Erde, Das, For Solo Voices And Orchestra

SONG OF THE NIGHT, A, FOR VIOLIN AND ORCHESTRA see Holst, Gustav

SONG WITHOUT WORDS [ARR.] see Tchaikovsky, Piotr Ilyich, Chant Sans Paroles [arr.]

SONGE DU VERGIER, LE, FOR VIOLONCELLO AND ORCHESTRA see Kox, Hans

SONGS AND A SEA INTERLUDE, FOR SOLO VOICE AND ORCHESTRA see Knussen, Oliver

SONGS AND DANCES see Payne, Anthony

SONGS AND DANCES FROM GOLEM see Sitsky, Larry

SONGS AND DANCES OF DEATH, FOR SOLO VOICE AND ORCHESTRA [ARR] see Mussorgsky, Modest Petrovich

SONGS AND DANCES OF DEATH [ARR.] see Mussorgsky, Modest Petrovich

SONGS AND DANCES OF DEATH: BERCEUSE, FOR SOLO VOICE AND ORCHESTRA, [ARR.] see Mussorgsky, Modest Petrovich

SONGS AND DANCES OF DEATH: SERENADE, FOR SOLO VOICE AND ORCHESTRA, [ARR.] see Mussorgsky, Modest Petrovich

SONGS AND DANCES OF DEATH: THE FIELD MARSHAL, FOR SOLO VOICE AND ORCHESTRA, [ARR.] see Mussorgsky, Modest Petrovich

SONGS AND DANCES OF DEATH: TREPAK, FOR SOLO VOICE AND ORCHESTRA, [ARR.] see Mussorgsky, Modest Petrovich

SONGS AND PLACES see Birgisson, Snorri Sigfus

SONGS FOR PATRICIA, SOLO VOICE AND STRING ORCHESTRA see Swanson, Howard

SONGS FROM LADOGA see Melartin, Erkki

SONGS OF A WAYFARER, FOR SOLO VOICE AND ORCHESTRA see Mahler, Gustav, Lieder Eines Fahrenden Gesellen, For Solo Voice And Orchestra

SONGS OF AWAKENING LOVE, FOR SOLO VOICE AND ORCHESTRA see Berkeley, Michael

SONGS OF DARKNESS, POWER AND RADIANCE, FOR TROMBONE AND ORCHESTRA see Thorne, Nicholas C.K.

SONGS OF DESPAIR, FOR SOLO VOICE AND CHAMBER ORCHESTRA see Eaton, John C.

SONGS OF DUSK, FOR SOLO VOICE, BASSOON AND ORCHESTRA see Holten, Bo, Tusmorkets Viser, For Solo Voice, Bassoon And Orchestra

SONGS OF INNOCENCE, FOR SOLO VOICE AND ORCHESTRA see Bezanson, Philip

SONGS OF JOHN KEATS, FOR SOLO VOICE AND ORCHESTRA see Karchin, Louis S.

SONGS OF LAUGHTER, LOVE AND TEARS, FOR SOLO VOICE AND STRING ORCHESTRA see Biggs, John

SONGS OF MY COUNTRY, FOR SOLO VOICE AND INSTRUMENTAL ENSEMBLE see Holt, Patricia Blomfield

SONGS OF REMEMBRANCE, FOR SOLO VOICE AND ORCHESTRA see Dello Joio, Norman

SONGS OF SEPARATION, FOR SOLO VOICE AND ORCHESTRA see Still, William Grant

SONGS OF THE PEOPLE OF MARREE IN MOUNTAINS AND MEADS, THE see Eshpai, Andrey Y.

SONGS OF THE SEA [ARR.] see Stanford, Charles Villiers

SONGS OF THE SOUTHWEST, FOR SOLO VOICE AND ORCHESTRA see Waldrop, Gideon William

SONGS OF WILLIAM BLAKE, FOR SOLO VOICE AND ORCHESTRA see Mathias, William

SONGS TO POEMS BY ARNULF OVERLAND, FOR SOLO VOICE AND ORCHESTRA see Tveitt, Geirr

SONGS TO POEMS BY ASLAUG VAA, FOR SOLO VOICE AND ORCHESTRA see Tveitt, Geirr

SONGS TO POEMS BY KNUT HORVEI, FOR SOLO VOICE AND ORCHESTRA see Tveitt, Geirr

SONGS TO POEMS BY OLAV H. HAUGE, FOR SOLO VOICE AND ORCHESTRA see Tveitt, Geirr

SONGS TO THE ALMIGHTY, FOR SOLO VOICE AND ORCHESTRA see Kenins, Talivaldis

SONGS WITH ORCHESTRA, PART I, FOR SOLO VOICE AND ORCHESTRA see Delius, Frederick

SONGS WITHOUT WORDS, VOL. 1 [ARR.] see Mendelssohn-Bartholdy, Felix, Lieder Ohne Worte, Vol. 1 [arr.]

SONGS WITHOUT WORDS, VOL. 2 [ARR.] see Mendelssohn-Bartholdy, Felix, Lieder Ohne Worte, Vol. 2 [arr.]

SONIC LANDSCAPE see Trimble, Lester Albert

SONNAMBULA, LA see Rieti, Vittorio

SONNAMBULA, LA: AH! NON CREDEA MIRATI, FOR SOLO VOICE AND ORCHESTRA see Bellini, Vincenzo

SONNAMBULA, LA: SON GELOSO DEL ZEFFIRO ERRANTE, FOR SOLO VOICES AND ORCHESTRA see Bellini, Vincenzo

SONNAMBULA, LA: TUTTO E SCIOLTO, FOR SOLO VOICE AND ORCHESTRA see Bellini, Vincenzo

SONNENHYMNUS DES HEILIGEN FRANZISKUS VON ASSISI, FOR SOLO VOICE AND ORCHESTRA see Liszt, Franz

SONNENSTRUKTUR see Fahres, Michael

SONNET see Decoust, Michel

SONNET NO. 104, FOR SOLO VOICE AND ORCHESTRA [ARR.] see Liszt, Franz, Sonetto 104 Del Petrarca, For Solo Voice And Orchestra [arr.]

SONNET SEQUENCE, FOR SOLO VOICE AND STRING ORCHESTRA see Bennett, Richard Rodney

SONNETS AFTER E.B. BROWNING, FOR SOLO VOICE AND ORCHESTRA see Balazs, Frederic

SONNETS FROM SHAKESPEARE, FOR SOLO VOICE AND CHAMBER ORCHESTRA see Whear, Paul William

SONNETS TO ORPHEUS, FOR VIOLONCELLO AND ORCHESTRA see Bennett, Richard Rodney

SONNINEN, AHTI (1914-)
Cantate Cantica Socii (from Piae Cantiones)
sc,pts FAZER f.s. (S1116)

Five Nordic Melodies [13'40"]
string orch
sc,pts FAZER f.s. (S1117)

SONOMORPHIE III see Taira, Yoshihisa

SONORALIA, OPUS 2 see Arias, Emmanuel

SONORALIA, OPUS 3 see Arias, Emmanuel

SONORE see Laderman, Ezra

SONORITIES see Keller, Homer see Overton, Hall see Rausch, Carlos

SONORITY FORMS see Luening, Otto

SONORS see Patterson, Paul

SONS DE CASTILLA see Sanjuan, Pedro

SONS ENCHANTES see Mannino, Franco

SØNSTEVOLD, GUNNAR (1912-1991)
Change
see Forvandling

Concerto for Flute, Bassoon and Orchestra [21']
2.3.3.3. 4.3.3.1. timp,perc,harp, cel,strings,fl solo,bsn solo
NORGE (S1118)

Concerto for Oboe, Harp and Orchestra [28']
3.2.3.3. 4.3.3.1. timp,perc,pno, strings,ob solo,harp solo
NORGE (S1119)

Concerto for Saxophone and Orchestra [21']
2.2.2.2. 4.3.3.1. timp,perc, strings,sax solo
NORGE (S1120)

Forvandling
3.3.3.3. 4.3.3.1. timp,perc,harp, pno,strings
"Change" NORGE (S1121)

Gamle Portretter [19']
2.1.2.1. 2.2.2.0. timp,perc,harp, pno,cel,strings
"Old Portraits" NORGE (S1122)

Kork
2.2.2.2. 4.4.3.1. timp,perc,harp, elec bass,strings
NORGE (S1123)

Old Portraits
see Gamle Portretter

Opvarming [10']
3.3.4.3. 5.4.4.1. timp,perc,pno/ cel,strings
"Warmup" NORGE (S1124)

Sinfonietta, Op. 1, No. 12 [23']
2.2.2.2. 4.3.3.1. timp,perc, strings
NORGE (S1125)

Warmup
see Opvarming

SØNSTEVOLD, MAJ (1917-)
Fest-Ouverture [6']
2.2.2.2. 4.4.3.1. timp,perc,harp, cel,strings
"Festival Overture" NORGE (S1126)

SØNSTEVOLD, MAJ (cont'd.)

Festival Overture
see Fest-Ouverture

Gamle Majors Forunderlige Dromme, Den
[8']
2.2.2.2. 2.2.2.0. timp,perc,harp,
pno,cel,strings
"Strange Dreams Of The Old Major,
The" NORGE　　　　　　　(S1127)

Sorlandssomer [10']
1.1.2.1. 1.0.0.0. perc,harp,pno/
cel,acord,strings
NORGE　　　　　　　　　(S1128)

Strange Dreams Of The Old Major, The
see Gamle Majors Forunderlige
Dromme, Den

SOPRONI, JOZSEF (1930-　　)
Concerto Da Camera
sc EMB 7423 f.s.　　　　(S1129)

Concerto for Violin and Orchestra
sc EMB 13349 f.s., perf mat rent
　　　　　　　　　　　(S1130)

Seasons, The (Symphony No. 2)
sc EMB 10242 f.s.　　　　(S1131)

Symphony No. 2
see Seasons, The

Symphony No. 3
sc EMB 10271 f.s., perf mat rent
　　　　　　　　　　　(S1132)

SORCERER IN BAKKEBY, THE, FOR NARRATOR
AND ORCHESTRA see Gislinge,
Frederik, Troldmanden I Bakkeby,
For Narrator And Orchestra

SORENSEN, BENT (1958-　　)
Lachrimae [13']
3(pic,alto fl).2(English
horn).2(contrabsn).
2.2(piccolo trp).2.0. timp,
4perc,harp,pno,cel,strings
HANSEN-DEN perf mat rent　(S1133)

Minnewater: Thousands Of Canons [12']
2(pic,alto fl).1.1(clar in E
flat,bass clar).0. 2.1.1.0.
2perc,strings,opt electronic
tape
HANSEN-DEN perf mat rent　(S1134)

Shadowland [19']
HANSEN-DEN perf mat rent　(S1135)

SÖRENSON, TORSTEN NAPOLEON (1908-　　)
Brokiga Blad [21']
string orch
"Motley Leaflets" sc GEHRMANS 6178P
f.s., perf mat rent　　(S1136)

Motley Leaflets
see Brokiga Blad

SORGENBRECHER WALZER see Strauss,
Johann, [Sr.]

SORI see Pagh-Paan, Younghi

SORING, WOLFGANG (1943-　　)
Bremer Stadtmusikanten, Die, For
Narrator And Orchestra [40']
3.2.2.2. 3.2.2.1. 3perc,pno,
strings,narrator
SIKORSKI perf mat rent　　(S1137)

Concerto for Bassoon and String
Orchestra [15']
opt perc,strings,bsn solo
SIKORSKI perf mat rent　　(S1138)

Concerto for Violin and Orchestra
[20']
2.2.2.2. 2.2.0.0. timp,2perc,
harp,strings,vln solo
SIKORSKI perf mat rent　　(S1139)

Rumpelstilzchen, For Narrator And
Orchestra [35']
3.2.2.2. 3.2.1.1. timp,perc,harp,
strings,narrator
SIKORSKI perf mat rent　　(S1140)

SORLANDSSOMER see Sønstevold, Maj

SORRY WRONG NUMBER see Waxman, Franz

SOSPENSO see Bauer, Ross

SOSPIRI see Elgar, [Sir] Edward
(William)

SOSPIRO, UN [ARR.] see Liszt, Franz

SOSTENUTO, FOR ORCHESTRA see Jeney,
Zoltan

SOSTENUTO, FOR VIOLONCELLO AND STRING
ORCHESTRA see Killmayer, Wilhelm

SOTHIS I see Horvath, Josef Maria

SOUFFLE see Leguay, Jean-Pierre

SOUND BARRIER, THE see Arnold, Malcolm

SOUND OFF MARCH see Sousa, John Philip

SOUND PICTURES see Fongaard, Bjørn,
Klangbilder

SOUNDING see Luetzow-Holm, Ole

SOUNDINGS see Sveinsson, Atli Heimir

SOUNDS, FOR ORGAN AND ORCHESTRA see
Akutagawa, Yasushi

SOUNDS FROM 14 STRINGS see Sandström,
Sven-David

SOUNDS FROM THE WEST SHORE see Bottje,
Will Gay

SOUS L'EMPRISE D'UNE OMBRE see
Ibarrondo, Felix

SOUSA, JOHN PHILIP (1854-1932)
Beau Ideal March, The [3']
1.1.2.1. 2.2.1.0. perc,strings
set KALMUS A4056 $12.00　(S1141)

Belle Of Chicago March, The [3']
1.1.2.2. 2.2.3.0. drums,strings
set KALMUS A5864 $12.00　(S1142)

Crusader March, The [3']
1.1.2.1. 2.2.1.0. perc,strings
set KALMUS A4058 $12.00　(S1143)

Directorate March, The [3']
2.2.2.1. 2.2.1.0. perc,strings
set KALMUS A5863 $12.00　(S1144)

Gladiator March, The [3']
1+pic.1.2.1. 4.2.3.1. perc,
strings
set KALMUS A5842 $12.00　(S1145)

High School Cadets March [3']
1(pic).2.2.1. 2.2.1.0. perc,
strings
set KALMUS A5849 $15.00　(S1146)

Manhattan Beach March [3']
2.2.2.2. 2.2.1.1. perc,strings
set KALMUS A5844 $12.00　(S1147)

National Fencibles March [3']
1.1.2.2. 2.2.1.1. perc,strings
set KALMUS A5845 $12.00　(S1148)

On Parade March [3']
0+pic.1.2.1. 2.2.1.0. perc,
strings
set KALMUS A5850 $12.00　(S1149)

Our Flirtation March [3']
1.1.2.1. 2.2.1.0. perc,strings
set KALMUS A4082 $12.00　(S1150)

Picadore March, The
1+pic.1.2.2. 2.2.1.0. perc,
strings
[3'] set KALMUS A5848 $12.00
　　　　　　　　　　　(S1151)

Powhatan's Daughter March
2.2.2.2. 2.2.3.1. perc,strings
[3'] set KALMUS A2381 $12.00
　　　　　　　　　　　(S1152)

Presidential Polonaise
1.2.2.1. 2.2.1.0. perc,strings
[3'] set KALMUS A4096 $12.00
　　　　　　　　　　　(S1153)

Semper Fidelis March
1+2pic.2.2.2. 2.2.1.1. perc,
strings
[3'] set KALMUS A5846 $12.00
　　　　　　　　　　　(S1154)

Sound Off March [3']
1.1.2.1. 2.2.1.0. perc,strings
set KALMUS A4136 $12.00　(S1155)

Stars And Stripes Forever March, The,
For Pianos And Orchestra [arr.]
(Gould, Morton) 2+pic.2+English
horn.3.3(contrabsn). 4.3.3.1.
timp,perc,strings, 3 or more
piano soli [5'] SCHIRM.G perf mat
rent　　　　　　　　(S1156)

Thunderer March, The [3']
1+pic.2.2.2. 2.2.1.0. perc,
strings
set KALMUS A5847 $12.00　(S1157)

SOUTHAM, ANN (1937-　　)
Throughways: Improvising Music
fl,clar,bsn,soprano sax,alto sax,
tenor sax,baritone sax,trp,
trom,perc,elec gtr,pno,vln,vcl,
elec bass
CAN.MUS.CENT. MI 1200 S726TH
　　　　　　　　　　　(S1158)

SOUTHERN BREEZE see Proto, Frank

SOUTHERN ECHOES see Dello Joio, Norman

SOUTHERN SEA, THE see Du, Ming-Xin

SOUTHERN SUITE, FOR GUITAR AND CHAMBER
ORCHESTRA see Morel, Jorge, Suite
Del Sur, For Guitar And Chamber
Orchestra

SOUTHERN VOICES see Hays, Doris
Ernestine

SOUTHWARK FESTIVAL OVERTURE see Le
Fleming, Christopher (Kaye)

SOUVENANCE see Kaufmann, Serge

SOUVENIR DE BADE POLKA see Strauss,
Eduard

SOUVENIR DE BUDAPEST see Booren, Jo van
den

SOUVENIR DE FLORENCE [ARR.] see
Tchaikovsky, Piotr Ilyich

SOUVENIR DE HAPSAL: RUINES D'UN CHATEAU
[ARR.] see Tchaikovsky, Piotr
Ilyich

SOUVENIR DE HAPSAL: RUINS OF A CASTLE
[ARR.] see Tchaikovsky, Piotr
Ilyich, Souvenir De Hapsal: Ruines
d'Un Chateau [arr.]

SOUVENIR DE MOSCOU, FOR VIOLIN AND
ORCHESTRA [ARR.] see Wieniawski,
Henryk

SOUVENIR D'UN BAL [ARR.] see Gounod,
Charles François

SOUVENIRS see Indy, Vincent d'

SOUVENIRS A LA MEMOIRE: DREI STUCKE see
Sinopoli, Giuseppe

SOV BARN JESUS LILLE, FOR SOLO VOICE
AND ORCHESTRA see Eggen, Arne

SOWERBY, LEO (1895-1968)
Comes Autumn Time [10']
2+pic.2.2+bass clar.2. 4.3.3.1.
timp,perc,harp,cel,strings
SCHIRM.G perf mat rent　(S1159)

SPAHLINGER, MATHIAS (1944-　　)
Passage [50']
4.4.4.4. 4.4.4.1. 6perc,elec gtr,
2harp,2pno,strings
BREITKOPF-W perf mat rent　(S1160)

SPALDER, FRITHJOF (1896-　　)
Humoreske [5']
1.1.1.0. 1.1.1.0. pno,strings
NORGE　　　　　　　　(S1161)

Lullaby
see Vuggevise

Prelude [5']
2.2.2.2. 4.2.3.1. timp,strings
NORGE　　　　　　　　(S1162)

Vuggevise [6']
1.1.1.0. 1.1.1.0. harp,pno,
strings
"Lullaby" NORGE　　　　(S1163)

SPANISCHE IMPRESSIONEN, FOR GUITAR AND
ORCHESTRA, [ARR.] see Behrend,
Siegfried

SPANISCHES KONZERT, FOR GUITAR AND
ORCHESTRA see Behrend, Siegfried

SPANISCHES LIEDERBUCH: VIER LIEDER, FOR
SOLO VOICE AND ORCHESTRA see Wolf,
Hugo

SPANISCHES LIEDERBUCH: ZWEI LIEDER, FOR
SOLO VOICE AND ORCHESTRA see Wolf,
Hugo

SPANISH LADY SUITE, [ARR.] see Elgar,
[Sir] Edward (William)

SPANISH SARABANDE FROM THE 16TH CENTURY
see Massenet, Jules, Sarabande Du
XVIe Siecle

SPANNHEIMER, FRANZ ERASMUS (1946-　　)
Bagatellen [15']
string orch
ZIMMER.　　　　　　　(S1164)

SPARKSKRAPS see Anhalt, Istvan

SPARROW, THE, FOR SOLO VOICE AND
ORCHESTRA see Eggen, Arne, Sporven,
For Solo Voice And Orchestra

SPARTACUS: ADAGIO see Khachaturian, Aram Ilyich

SPARTACUS OVERTURE see Saint-Saëns, Camille

SPARTACUS: SCENE 9 see Khachaturian, Aram Ilyich

SPARTACUS: SCENE 3 see Khachaturian, Aram Ilyich

SPARTACUS: SUITE NO. 4 see Khachaturian, Aram Ilyich

SPASSOV, BOLJIDAR
Symphony
3.3.3.3. 4.3.3.1. timp,perc,cel, harp,strings
sc PETERS $30.00   (S1165)

SPEAK TO ME, MY LOVE, FOR SOLO VOICE AND ORCHESTRA see Bridge, Frank

SPECTRA see Dembski, Stephen see Paulus, Stephen Harrison

SPECTRAL CHIMES-ENSHROUDED HILLS, FOR THREE ORCHESTRAL QUINTETS AND ORCHESTRA see Richter, Marga

SPECTRES see Silvestrov, Valentin

SPECTRUM see Lombardo, Mario

SPECULUM AMORIS see Dimitrakopoulos, Apostolo

SPEIGHT, JOHN A. (1945-)
Concertino for Piano and Orchestra [9'30"]
2fl,horn,strings,pno solo
ICELAND 011-009   (S1166)

Concerto for Clarinet and Orchestra [12']
2.2.2.2. 4.3.3.1. timp,3perc, strings,clar solo
(Melodious Birds Sing Madrigals)
ICELAND 011- 014   (S1167)

Concerto for Guitar and Orchestra
3.3.3.0. 4.2.3.0. timp,perc, strings,gtr solo
ICELAND 011-031   (S1168)

Emperor And The Nightingale, The
1.1.2.0. 2.1.1.0. 4perc,cel, strings
ICELAND 011-132   (S1169)

Little Music, For Clarinet And Chamber Orchestra [9']
2fl,2clar,strings,clar solo
ICELAND 011-013   (S1170)

Symphony
3.3.3.3. 6.3.3.1. timp,perc,harp, pno,strings
ICELAND 011-022   (S1171)

Vistula
2.2.2+bass clar.2. 4.2.2.1. timp, 2perc,harp,strings
ICELAND 011-010   (S1172)

SPEILMAN
Scrooge: The Stingiest Man In Town [3']
0.0.0.1. 2.2.0.0. 3perc,pno, strings
WARNER perf mat rent   (S1173)

SPELAR, DET, FOR SOLO VOICE AND ORCHESTRA see Rangström, Ture

SPERGER, JOHANN M. (1750-1812)
Concerto for Double Bass and Orchestra [30']
2fl,2ob,2horn,strings,cont,db solo
SIKORSKI perf mat rent   (S1174)

Concerto for Horn and Orchestra, MIN 175
(Leloir, E.) 2ob,2horn,timp, strings,horn solo [16'40"] sc BILLAUDOT f.s., perf mat rent   (S1175)

Romance for Double Bass and Orchestra in D
2ob,2horn,strings,db solo
(Malaric, Rudolf) sc,pts DOBLINGER KRM 39 f.s.   (S1176)

SPIEGELUNG, FOR FLUTE, VIOLIN AND ORCHESTRA see Holszky, Adriana

SPIEL VOM KÖNIG APHELIUS, DAS: SINFONISCHER EPILOG see Kaminski, Heinrich

SPIELEREI see Müller-Marc, Raymund

SPIELMUSIK see Hessenberg, Kurt

SPIELMUSIK ZUM SOMMERNACHTSTRAUM, HEFT 1 see Purcell, Henry, Midsummer Night's Dream, A: Incidental Music, Vol.1

SPIELMUSIK ZUM SOMMERNACHTSTRAUM, HEFT 2 see Purcell, Henry, Midsummer Night's Dream, A: Incidental Music, Vol.2

SPIELMUSIKEN see Henze, Hans Werner

SPIELWERK, FOR SOLO VOICE, SAXOPHONE AND THREE ENSEMBLES see Zimmermann, Walter

SPINNER, LEOPOLD (1906-   )
Chamber Symphony *Op.28 [11']
0+alto fl.1.1+bass clar.1.tenor sax. 1.1.0.0. harp,string quar
BOOSEY perf mat rent   (S1177)

Concerto for Orchestra, Op. 12 [8']
1+pic.1+English horn.1+bass clar.0. 1.1.1.1. perc,harp,cel, strings
BOOSEY perf mat rent   (S1178)

Overture, Op. 5 [6']
3(pic).3(English horn).3(bass clar).0. 3.3.3.0. timp,perc, harp,cel,strings
BOOSEY perf mat rent   (S1179)

Passacaglia [14']
2(pic).0.1+bass clar.1+contrabsn. 2.1.0.0. pno,vln,vcl
BOOSEY perf mat rent   (S1180)

Ricercata *Op.21 [16']
1+alto fl.1+English horn.1+bass clar.0. 1.1.1.1. harp,cel,6vln, 3vla,3vcl
BOOSEY perf mat rent   (S1181)

SPINNERIN, DIE see Strauss, Josef

SPINNLIED, FOR VIOLONCELLO AND ORCHESTRA [ARR.] see Popper, David

SPIRAL OF SOUNDS [1] see Hamel, Peter Michael, Klangspirale (First Version-1977)

SPIRAL OF SOUNDS [2] see Hamel, Peter Michael, Klangspirale (Second Version-1977)

SPIRALEN WALZER see Strauss, Johann, [Jr.]

SPIRALES INSOLITES see Bousch, François

SPIRIT FLOWER, A, FOR SOLO VOICE AND ORCHESTRA see Campbell-Tipton, Louis

SPIRIT OF ST. LOUIS, THE see Waxman, Franz

SPIRIT'S HARVEST, THE see Payne, Anthony

SPIRITS OF KOBYSTAN, THE: SUITE see Karayev, Faradzh

SPIRITS OF THE NIGHT see Bazelon, Irwin Allen

SPIRITUAL, FOR VIOLIN AND STRING ORCHESTRA see Werner, Jean-Jacques

SPIRITUAL, THE see Lewis, John Aaron

SPIRITUAL CYCLE, FOR SOLO VOICE AND ORCHESTRA see Tillis, Frederick C.

SPIRITUAL FANTASY NO. 6, FOR TRUMPET AND ORCHESTRA see Tillis, Frederick C.

SPIRITUALS: A MEDLEY see Still, William Grant

SPIRITUALS IN SUNSHINE AND SHADOW see Coolidge, Peggy Stuart

SPITZMUELLER, ALEXANDER (1894-1962)
Concerto for Piano and Orchestra, No. 1, Op. 15 [16']
2.2.2.2. 4.3.3.1. timp,strings, pno solo
BOOSEY perf mat rent   (S1182)

SPLENDEURS OUBLIEES see Succari, Dia

SPLITTER see Rihm, Wolfgang

SPLITTING see Campana, Jose Luis

SPOHR, LUDWIG (LOUIS) (1784-1859)
Concertante For Violin, Violoncello And Orchestra, WoO. 11
see Selected Works, Vol. 7: Concertos

Concerto for Clarinet and Orchestra, No. 3, in F minor
BREITKOPF-W perf mat rent   (S1183)

Concerto for Clarinet and Orchestra, No. 4, in E minor
BREITKOPF-W perf mat rent   (S1184)

Concerto for Violin and Orchestra in A, MIN 30
(Gothel) KALMUS A4062 sc $30.00, set $40.00, pts $3.00, ea., perf mat rent   (S1185)

Concerto for Violin and Orchestra, No. 7, Op. 38, in E minor
BREITKOPF-W perf mat rent   (S1186)

Concerto For Violin And Orchestra, Op. 62
see Selected Works, Vol. 7: Concertos

Concerto For Violin And Orchestra, Op. 79
see Selected Works, Vol. 7: Concertos

Concerto for 2 Violins and Orchestra, Op. 88, in B minor [25']
2.0.2.2. 4.0.0.0. strings,2vln soli
SIMROCK perf mat rent   (S1187)

Faust: Overture
KALMUS A5649 sc $5.00, set $20.00, perf mat rent   (S1188)

Jessonda: Overture
KALMUS A7377 sc $8.00, set $30.00, pts $1.50, ea., perf mat rent   (S1189)

Selected Works, Vol. 6: Symphonies
sc GARLAND ISBN 0-8240-1505-3 $115.00
contains: Symphony No. 1, Op. 20, in E flat; Symphony No. 2, Op. 49, in D minor; Symphony No. 5, Op. 102, in C minor   (S1190)

Selected Works, Vol. 7: Concertos
sc GARLAND ISBN 0-8240-1506-1 $70.00
contains: Concertante For Violin, Violoncello And Orchestra, WoO. 11; Concerto For Violin And Orchestra, Op. 62; Concerto For Violin And Orchestra, Op. 79   (S1191)

Symphony No. 1, Op. 20, in E flat
see Selected Works, Vol. 6: Symphonies

Symphony No. 2, Op. 49, in D minor
see Selected Works, Vol. 6: Symphonies

Symphony No. 3, Op. 78, in C minor
(Heussner) KALMUS A7022 sc $70.00, set $90.00, pts $5.00, ea., perf mat rent   (S1192)

Symphony No. 5, Op. 102, in C minor
see Selected Works, Vol. 6: Symphonies

Symphony No. 9, Op. 143 [30']
2.2.2.2. 4.2.3.1. timp,strings
(The Seasons) KALMUS A5818 sc $60.00, set $75.00, perf mat rent   (S1193)

SPONTINI, GASPARE (1774-1851)
Eroismo Ridicolo, L': Overture
(Negrotti) 1.2.1.1. 2.0.0.0. timp, strings [4'30"] KALMUS A7304 sc $20.00, set $19.00, pts $1.50, ea., perf mat rent   (S1194)

Julie: Overture
2.2.2.2. 2.0.0.0. timp,strings
(Tozzi, L.) sc BSE 597-00466 $5.00   (S1195)

Vestale, La: Sinfonia [arr.]
(Clemandh) 3.2.2.2. 4.2.3.0. timp, strings [7'30"] BILLAUDOT perf mat rent   (S1196)

SPOON RIVER see Grainger, Percy Aldridge

SPORCK, JO (1953-   )
Quo Vadis Musica-Symfonie *Op.33 [21']
2.2.2.2. 2.2.2.0. 2perc,strings
sc DONEMUS f.s., perf mat rent   (S1197)

SPORTS ET DIVERTISSEMENTS [ARR.] see Satie, Erik

SPORVEN, FOR SOLO VOICE AND ORCHESTRA
see Eggen, Arne

SPOSO DELUSO, LO: OVERTURE see Mozart,
Wolfgang Amadeus

SPRATLAN, LEWIS (1940-   )
Penelope's Knees, For Alto Saxophone,
Doublebass And Chamber Group
[23']
1(pic).0.1(bass clar).0. 1.1.1.1.
perc,pno,2vln,vla,vcl,alto sax
solo,db solo
sc MARGUN MP7153 $45.00, perf mat
rent   (S1198)

SPRING see Gurney, Ivor

SPRING FESTIVAL see Li, Huan-Chih

SPRING, FOR SOLO VOICE AND ORCHESTRA
see Lutoslawski, Witold, Wiosna,
For Solo Voice And Orchestra

SPRING HAS COME see Okamoto, Masami

SPRING IDYLL, FOR FLUTE AND STRING
ORCHESTRA see Mourant, Walter

SPRING MORNING see Delius, Frederick

SPRING MUSIC see Maw, Nicholas

SPRING NIGHT, FOR SOLO VOICE AND
ORCHESTRA [ARR.] see Schumann,
Robert (Alexander), Fruhlingsnacht,
For Solo Voice And Orchestra [arr.]

SPRING PASTORAL see Howe, Mary

SPRING SESTINA, FOR SOLO VOICE AND
CHAMBER GROUP see Levi, Paul Alan

SPRING SONG, FOR SOLO VOICE AND
ORCHESTRA see Jordan, Sverre,
Varvisa, For Solo Voice And
Orchestra

SPRING SONGS see Dychko, Liudmyla,
Vesnyanky

SPRING TIDE, FOR SOLO VOICE AND
ORCHESTRA see Eggen, Arne, No
Sprette Lauvet, For Solo Voice And
Orchestra

SPRING WINGS, FOR PIANO, SAXOPHONE AND
ORCHESTRA see Williams, Patrick M.

SPRING YEARNING [ARR.] see Cleve,
Cissi, Varlengsel [arr.]

SPRING'S SHINING WAKE see Payne,
Anthony

SPRINGTIDE see Forsyth, Malcolm

SPRINGTIME MUSIC see Brons, Carel

SPRONGL, NORBERT (1892-1983)
Concerto for Violin and Orchestra,
No. 2, Op. 155 [23']
2.2.2.2. 4.3.0.0. timp,strings,
vln solo
DOBLINGER perf mat rent   (S1199)

SPUR see Rihm, Wolfgang

SPUR, FOR ACCORDION AND ORCHESTRA see
Nordheim, Arne

SQUARE HOLES, ROUND PEGS see Mackey,
Steven

SQUARE OF SUNLIGHT see Trefousse, Roger

SQUARE WORLD, THE, FOR ALTO SAXOPHONE
AND ORCHESTRA see Ponjee, Ted

SREBOTNJAK, ALOJZ F. (1931-   )
Balade [16']
3.3.2(bass clar).2(contrabsn).
4.4.4.0. timp,perc,harp,strings
"Ballads" DRUSTVO DSS 935 perf mat
rent   (S1200)

Ballads
see Balade

Concerto for Violin and Orchestra
[19']
2(pic).2.2(bass clar).2. 2.3.2.1.
timp,perc,harp,strings,vln solo
DRUSTVO DSS 937 perf mat rent
(S1201)

Episodes Concertantes
see Koncertantne Epizode

Glasba Za Godala [13']
string orch
"Music For Strings" DRUSTVO
DSS 1023 perf mat rent   (S1202)

Karst Suite, The
see Kraska Suita

SREBOTNJAK, ALOJZ F. (cont'd.)

Klic Narave [22']
2.2.2.2. 4.2.2.0. timp,perc,
strings
DRUSTVO DSS 994 perf mat rent
(S1203)

Koncertantne Epizode [19']
1.1.1.1. 4.4.4.1. harp,strings
"Episodes Concertantes" DRUSTVO
DSS 1067 perf mat rent   (S1204)

Kraska Suita [21']
2.2.2.2. 4.3.3.1. timp,perc,pno,
strings
"Karst Suite, The" DRUSTVO DSS 940
perf mat rent   (S1205)

Lamento [13']
1.1.1.1. 1.1.1.0. perc,string
quin
DRUSTVO DSS 1068 perf mat rent
(S1206)

Macedonian Dances
see Makedonski Plesi

Makedonski Plesi [10']
string orch
"Macedonian Dances" DRUSTVO
DSS 1050 perf mat rent   (S1207)

Mati, For Solo Voice And String
Orchestra [12']
string orch,solo voice
"Mother, For Solo Voice And String
Orchestra" DRUSTVO ED.DSS 74
f.s., perf mat rent   (S1208)

Monologi [15']
fl,ob,horn,timp,strings
DRUSTVO DSS 150 perf mat rent
(S1209)

Mother, For Solo Voice And String
Orchestra
see Mati, For Solo Voice And String
Orchestra

Music For Strings
see Glasba Za Godala

Sinfonietta [13']
2.1.1.1. 2.2.0.0. strings
DRUSTVO DSS 1021 perf mat rent
(S1210)

Slovene Folk Dances
see Slovenski Ljudski Plesi

Slovenica [17']
0.0.0.0. 4.4.4.0. perc,cel,harp,
strings
min sc DRUSTVO DSS 936 f.s., perf
mat rent   (S1211)

Slovenski Ljudski Plesi [11']
string orch
"Slovene Folk Dances" DRUSTVO
DSS 1051 perf mat rent   (S1212)

Trobenta In Vrag: Suita [22']
2(pic).2.2.2. 2.3.1.1. timp,perc,
strings
"Trumpet And The Devil, The: Suite"
DRUSTVO DSS 1069 perf mat rent
(S1213)

Trumpet And The Devil, The: Suite
see Trobenta In Vrag: Suita

ST. FRANCOIS D'ASSISE: LA PREDICATION
AUX OISEAUX [ARR.] see Liszt, Franz

ST. PAUL'S SUITE, OP. 29, NO. 2 see
Holst, Gustav

STABAT MATER, FOR SOLO VOICE AND STRING
ORCHESTRA, RV 621 see Vivaldi,
Antonio

STABAT MATER: INFLAMMATUS, FOR SOLO
VOICE AND ORCHESTRA see Rosenman,
Leonard

STABILES see Hibbard, William

STACHOWSKI, MAREK (1936-   )
Divertimento for String Orchestra
[13']
string orch
POLSKIE   (S1214)

STADEN, JOHANN (1581-1634)
Fünfzehn Tanzsätze, [arr.] (from
Venus-Kränzlein 1610) [13']
(Sannwald, Karl) string orch sc,pts
NAGELS NMA 119 f.s.   (S1215)

STADLMAIR, HANS (1929-   )
Concerto Capriccioso, For 2 Flutes
And Orchestra
perc,strings,2fl soli
HIEBER MH 1007 perf mat rent
(S1216)

STADT, DIE see Eisenmann, Will

STADT, DIE, FOR SOLO VOICE AND
ORCHESTRA see Rubin, Marcel

STADT UND LAND POLKA see Strauss,
Johann, [Jr.]

STAGES, THE see Gubaidulina, Sofia

STAGES III see Manneke, Daan

STAHMER, KLAUS H. (1941-   )
Momentaufnahmen, For Solo Voice And
Chamber Orchestra [32']
1(pic,bass fl).0.1.0.sax.
0.0.1.0. 1-2perc,gtr,pno/hpsd,
vln,vla,vcl,db,speaking voice
study sc BREITKOPF-W PB 5402 f.s.,
perf mat rent   (S1217)

STALDER, JOSEF DOMINIK XAVER
(1725-1765)
Concerto for Recorder and String
Orchestra, MIN 135
string orch,A rec/fl solo
(Diethelm) sc,pts AMADEUS BP 2087
f.s.   (S1218)

STALHEIM, JOSTEIN (1960-   )
Hydra
1.1.1.1. 1.0.0.0. perc,2vln,vla,
vcl,db
NORGE   (S1219)

Kleio [10']
string orch
NORGE   (S1220)

STALLAERT, ALPHONSE (1920-   )
Symphonie De Requiem: Les Ames
Maudites [30']
3.3.3.3.sax. 4.4.3.1. timp,3perc,
2harp,pno,strings
BILLAUDOT perf mat rent   (S1221)

STALLCOP, GLENN
City Music: Song And Dance [30']
2.2.2.2. 4.3.3.1. timp,perc,harp,
strings
sc AM.COMP.AL. $50.25   (S1222)

Concerto for Double Bass and String
Orchestra [23']
string orch,db solo
AM.COMP.AL. sc $25.15, pts $6.50,
perf mat rent   (S1223)

Couplet For A Desert Summer [14']
1.2.1.2. 2.0.0.0. perc,pno,
strings
sc AM.COMP.AL. $22.60, perf mat
rent   (S1224)

In Apprehension Of Spring [4']
2.2.2.2. 4.3.3.1. timp,perc,
strings
AM.COMP.AL. perf mat rent   (S1225)

STALVEY, DORRANCE (1930-   )
Celebration Sequent I [13']
1(pic,alto fl).1(English
horn).2(clar in E flat,bass
clar).1. 1.1.1.0. 2perc,pno,
harp,vln,vla,vcl,db
sc SALABERT f.s., perf mat rent
(S1226)

STAMITZ, ANTON (1754-ca. 1809)
Concerto for Viola and Orchestra in B
flat
MUS. RARA 2055 perf mat rent
(S1227)

STAMITZ, CARL (1745-1801)
Concerto for Basset Horn and
Orchestra, MIN 134
2ob,2horn,strings,basset horn/
clar solo
(Hess) sc,pts AMADEUS BP 2458 f.s.
(S1228)
Concerto for Clarinet and Orchestra
in E flat, MIN 145
orch,clar solo
MUS. RARA perf mat rent   (S1229)

Concerto for Clarinet and Orchestra
in F, MIN 364
(Balassa) EMB f.s. sc 6223, pts
6224   (S1230)

Concerto for Clarinet, Violin and
Orchestra, No. 4
2ob,2horn,strings,clar solo,vln
solo
(Balassa) EMB f.s. sc 6044, pts
6045   (S1231)

Concerto for Flute and Orchestra in D
[14']
(Sonntag) 2horn,strings,fl solo
SIKORSKI perf mat rent   (S1232)

Concerto for Flute and String
Orchestra, Op. 29, in G
SONZOGNO perf mat rent   (S1233)

Concerto for Oboe, Bassoon and
Orchestra in D
MUS. RARA perf mat rent   (S1234)

STAMITZ, CARL (cont'd.)

Concerto for Trumpet and String Orchestra in B flat, MIN 176 (Thilde, J.) string orch,trp solo [15'] sc BILLAUDOT f.s., perf mat rent (S1235)

Concerto For Viola And Orchestra, Op. 1, In D *see THREE CENTURIES OF MUSIC IN SCORE, VOL. 5: CONCERTO IV, CLASSICAL STRINGS AND WINDS

Concerto for Violoncello and Orchestra, No. 1, in G (Upmeyer) KALMUS A6352 sc $15.00, set $20.00, pts $2.00, ea., perf mat rent (S1236)

Concerto for Violoncello and Orchestra, No. 2, in A (Upmeyer) KALMUS A5612 sc $20.00, perf mat rent, set $20.00, pts $2.00, ea. (S1237)

Concerto for Violoncello and Orchestra, No. 3, in C (Upmeyer) KALMUS A6334 sc $15.00, set $20.00, pts $2.00, ea. (S1238)

Sinfonia in E flat (Lenzewski) KALMUS A5614 sc $10.00, perf mat rent, set $18.00, pts $2.00, ea. (S1239)

Symphonic Works, Three see Holzbauer, Ignaz Jakob, Symphonic Works, Three

STAMITZ, JOHANN WENZEL ANTON (1717-1757)
Concerto for Flute and String Orchestra in D, MIN 135 string orch,fl solo (Anspacher) sc,pts AMADEUS BP 2452 f.s. (S1240)

Concerto for Harpsichord and Orchestra, MIN 157 2fl,2ob,opt 2horn,strings,hpsd/ pno/org solo (Walter, Rudolf) sc,pts DOBLINGER DM 877 f.s. (S1241)

Drei Mannheimer Sinfonien *CCU (Hoffmann) KALMUS A7114 sc $8.00, set $15.00, pts $3.00, ea. (S1242)

Largo for Viola and String Orchestra, [arr.] (Zani, G.) string orch,vla solo [7'] SONZOGNO perf mat rent (S1243)

Symphony in E flat, MIN 158 [19'] 2ob,2horn,hpsd,strings SUPRAPHON (S1244)

STANDCHEN see Winderstein, Hans

STÄNDCHEN "LEISE FLEHEN MEINE LIEDER", FOR SOLO VOICE AND ORCHESTRA, [ARR.] see Schubert, Franz (Peter)

STANFORD, CHARLES VILLIERS (1852-1924)
Elegiac Ode [24'] 2.2.2.2+contrabsn. 4.2.3.1. timp, perc,harp,strings BOOSEY perf mat rent (S1245)

Songs Of The Sea [arr.] (Dunhill, Thomas) 1+pic.1.2.1. 2.2.2.0. timp,perc,strings [17'] BOOSEY perf mat rent (S1246)

Veiled Prophet, The: Ballet Music, For Solo Voice And Orchestra [20'] 2+pic.2.2.2. 4.2.3.1. timp,perc, harp,strings,S solo BOOSEY perf mat rent (S1247)

Veiled Prophet, The: Overture [8'] 2.2.2.2. 4.2.3.0. timp,perc, strings BOOSEY perf mat rent (S1248)

STANFORD SERENADE, FOR OBOE AND INSTRUMENTAL ENSEMBLE see Milhaud, Darius

STANGBERG, ALLAN
Romance for Viola and Orchestra [5'35"] 1.1.2.1. 2.0.0.0. strings,vla solo (alternate scoring: sorch, vla solo) BUSCH perf mat rent (S1249)

STANKOVICH, EVGENY (1942-   )
Chamber Symphony No. 1 1.0.1.0. 0.0.1.0. timp,2perc, harp,pno,vln solo VAAP perf mat rent (S1250)

STANKOVICH, EVGENY (cont'd.)

Chamber Symphony No. 2 2.1.1.1. 0.0.0.0. 2perc,pno, strings VAAP perf mat rent (S1251)

Chamber Symphony No. 3 7vln,2vla,2vcl,db,fl solo VAAP perf mat rent (S1252)

Sinfonietta 2.2.2.2. 4.2.2.1. 4perc,harp,pno& cel,strings VAAP perf mat rent (S1253)

Symphony No. 1 15strings (Sinfonia larga) VAAP perf mat rent (S1254)

Symphony No. 2 4.3.3.3. 4.4.3.1. 5perc,cel,harp, pno,strings (Heroic) VAAP perf mat rent (S1255)

Symphony No. 3 [33'] 3(pic).2+English horn.3(bass clar).2+contrabsn. 4.3.3.1. 5perc,2harp,pno,strings,Bar solo,mix cor (Self-Assertion) VAAP perf mat rent (S1256)

Symphony No. 4 16strings (Sinfonia lirica) VAAP perf mat rent (S1257)

Symphony Of Pastorals, For Violin And Orchestra 3.3.3.3. 4.3.3.1. timp,3perc,cel, harp,pno,strings,vln solo VAAP perf mat rent (S1258)

STANLEY, JOHN (1713-1786)
Concerti, Op. 2, Nos. 1-6 string orch,kbd (Caldwell, John) OXFORD 367684-2 $39.95 (S1259)

Concerti, Op. 10, Nos. 1-6 string orch,kbd (Gifford, Gerald) sc OXFORD 30.019 $19.95, perf mat rent (S1260)

Concertino for Violin and String Orchestra, [arr.] (Finch, Ronald) string orch,vln solo [9'] OXFORD 367709-1 sc $8.95, pts $2.00, ea. (S1261)

Suite No. 1, [arr.] (from Trumpet Voluntaries) (Fladmoe, Arvid) string orch NORGE (S1262)

STANZAS see Firsova, Elena

STAR EYE, FOR SOLO VOICE AND ORCHESTRA see Stenhammar, Wilhelm

STAR GAZERS AND OTHER PILGRIMS see Le Siege, Annette

STAR ISLE see Takemitsu, Toru

STAR-SHADOW see Lavenda, Richard

STAR SOUND see Stockhausen, Karlheinz, Sternklang

STAR-SPANGLED BANNER, THE [ARR.] see Smith, John Stafford

STAR TREK see Goldsmith, Jerry

STAR WARS: SYMPHONIC SUITE see Williams, John T.

STARCKDEUTSCHE LIEDER UND TANZE, FOR SOLO VOICE AND ORCHESTRA see Schwertsik, Kurt

STARER, ROBERT (1924-   )
Concerto for Violoncello and Orchestra [25'] 2(pic).2.2.2. 4.0.0.0. timp,perc, strings,vcl solo MMB perf mat rent (S1263)

Dances From Arimintha (Divertimento) SHAWNEE perf mat rent (S1264)

Divertimento see Dances From Arimintha

Elegy for Violin and String Orchestra [5'] string orch,vln/clar solo MMB perf mat rent (S1265)

Hudson Valley Suite 2.2.2.2. 4.2.2.1. timp,perc, strings study sc MCA 00123581 $15.00 (S1266)

STARER, ROBERT (cont'd.)

Kli Zemer, For Clarinet And Orchestra [24'] 2(pic).2(English horn).2.2. 2.2.2.0. timp,perc,strings,clar solo MMB perf mat rent (S1267)

STARFIRES, FOR SOLO VOICES AND ORCHESTRA see Blumenfeld, Harold

STARLIGHT EXPRESS, THE: INCIDENTAL MUSIC see Elgar, [Sir] Edward (William)

STARMOBILE see Marez Oyens, Tera de

STARS AND STRIPES FOREVER MARCH, THE, FOR PIANOS AND ORCHESTRA [ARR.] see Sousa, John Philip

STARS AND STRIPES: PAS DE DEUX see Kay, Hershy

STATEMENTS II see Guy, Barry

STATIONS, REGIONS AND CLOUDS, FOR AMPLIFIED TROMBONE AND ORCHESTRA see Fulkerson, James

STAUB see Lachenmann, Helmut Friedrich

STAY 'N SEE see Karam, Frederick

STEADFAST TIN SOLDIER, THE, FOR NARRATOR AND ORCHESTRA see Husa, Karel

STEARNS, PETER PINDAR (1931-   )
Becoming Perfectly One [8'] 2.1.2.1. 2.1.0.0. timp,perc,harp, strings sc AM.COMP.AL. $10.70 (S1268)

Piper At The Gates Of Dawn, The [18'] 2(pic).1+English horn.2+bass clar.2. 3.3.2+bass trom.0. rec, perc,harp,strings sc AM.COMP.AL. $22.15 (S1269)

Symphony No. 7 [26'] 2.2.2.2. 4.3.3.1. timp,perc,harp, strings sc AM.COMP.AL. $44.95 (S1270)

STEEL, CHRISTOPHER [CHARLES] (1939-   )
Symphony No. 5, Op. 73 NOVELLO perf mat rent (S1271)

STEFANI, DANIEL (1949-   )
Rapsodia Del Plata [20'] 2.2.2.2. 2.2.0.0. timp,perc, strings ALPUERTO (S1272)

STEFANSSON, FINNUR TORFI (1947-   )
Piece I 2.3.2.2. 4.2.2.1. timp,perc, strings ICELAND 057-001 (S1273)

Piece II [15'] 3.2.2.2. 3.4.2.1. timp,3perc,pno, strings ICELAND 057-014 (S1274)

STEFANSSON, FJÖLNIR (1930-   )
Koplon [14'] 1.1+English horn.1+bass clar.0. 1.1.1.0. 2perc,harp,strings ICELAND 004-009 (S1275)

Time And Water, For Solo Voice And Orchestra [3'15"] 1.1.1.1. 2.1.0.0. 12vln,4vla, 4vcl,S solo ICELAND 004-001 (S1276)

STEFFAN, JOSEPH ANTON (1726-1797)
Concerto for Piano and Orchestra in B flat (Picton, Howard) sc A-R ED ISBN 0-89579-133-1 f.s. (S1277)

STEFFEN, WOLFGANG (1923-   )
Concerto for Flute and Orchestra, Op. 49 [25'] 2.2.2.2. 4.3.3.1. perc,strings,fl solo BOTE perf mat rent (S1278)

Kammerkonzert *Op.48 [13'] 1.1.1(bass clar).1. 1.0.0.0. perc,pno,strings BOTE perf mat rent (S1279)

STEFFENS, WALTER (1934-   )
Guernica, For Viola And Orchestra *Op.32 [17'] 3(pic).3(English horn).3(bass clar).3(contrabsn). 4.3.3.1. timp,perc,cel,harp,strings,vla solo sc HANSEN-DEN $12.00 (S1280)

STEFFENS, WALTER (cont'd.)

   HANSEN-GER perf mat rent   (S1281)

   Indisches Marchen, Ein , For Solo
     Voices And Orchestra *Op.1b
     [35']
     1.1.1.1. 1.0.0.0. 2harp,strings,
     ABar soli
     sc BREITKOPF-W f.s., perf mat rent
                           (S1282)
   Tarec: Versuch Eines Abschieds [11']
     3(pic).2.2.3(contrabsn). 2.1.1.0.
     strings
     PEER MUSIK perf mat rent   (S1283)

STEIN, DER, FOR SOLO VOICE AND
   ORCHESTRA see Firsova, Elena,
   Stone, The, For Solo Voice And
   Orchestra

STEIN, LEON (1910-   )
   Aria Hebraique [4']
     string orch
     sc AM.COMP.AL. $5.40   (S1284)

   Concerto for Violoncello and
     Orchestra [30']
     2.2.2.2. 4.2.3.0. timp,perc,
     strings,vcl solo
     AM.COMP.AL. perf mat rent   (S1285)

   Festive Overture [9'30"]
     3.2.2.2. 4.3.3.1. timp,perc,
     strings
     MCA perf mat rent   (S1286)

   Great Lakes Suite [11']
     1.1.2.1. 2.2.1.0. timp,strings
     MCA perf mat rent   (S1287)

   Kaddish, For Solo Voice And String
     Orchestra
     string orch,T solo
     sc AM.COMP.AL. $5.75   (S1288)

   Symphonic Movement [12']
     3.2.4.2. 4.3.3.1. timp,strings
     AM.COMP.AL. perf mat rent   (S1289)

   Symphony No. 4 [30']
     3.3.3.3. 4.3.3.1. timp,perc,
     strings
     AM.COMP.AL. perf mat rent   (S1290)

   Then Shall The Dust Return [20']
     3.3.3.3. 4.3.3.1. perc,harp,
     strings
     sc AM.COMP.AL. $27.50, perf mat
     rent   (S1291)

STEINBERG, MAXIMILIAN (1883-1946)
   Symphony No. 1, Op. 3 [40']
     3.2.2.2. 4.2.3.1. timp,perc,
     strings
     BELAIEFF   (S1292)

   Vier Lieder, For Solo Voice And
     Orchestra *Op.14 [16']
     2(pic).1+English horn.2.1.
     2.0.0.0. perc,harp,cel,strings,
     S/T solo
     BREITKOPF-W perf mat rent   (S1293)

STEINER, MAX(IMILIAN RAOUL WALTER)
   (1888-1971)
   Casablanca: Suite
     WARNER perf mat rent   (S1294)

   Jungle Dance (from King Kong) [8'45"]
     2.1.3.1. 2.3.3.1. timp,perc,harp,
     pno,strings
     BOURNE perf mat rent   (S1295)

   Silhouette Of Tara, [arr.] [4']
     (Hastings) WARNER perf mat rent
                           (S1296)

   Summer Place, A [5']
     2.2.2+bass clar.0. 4.0.0.0.
     2perc,pno,cel,harp,gtr,strings
     WARNER perf mat rent   (S1297)

   Tara, [arr.]
     (Campbell- Watson) WARNER perf mat
     rent   (S1298)

   Theme From King Kong [4'5"]
     1.1.3.1. 1.3.4.1. timp,harp,pno,
     strings
     BOURNE perf mat rent   (S1299)

STEINERNE BLUME, DIE: SUITE see
   Prokofiev, Serge, Tale Of The Stone
   Flower: Suite

STEINERNE BLUME, DIE: ZIGEUNERFANTASIE
   see Prokofiev, Serge, Tale Of The
   Stone Flower: Gypsy Fantasy

STEINKE, GREG A. (1942-   )
   Three Sonnets, For Solo Voice And
     Chamber Orchestra
     fl,strings,S solo
     SEESAW   (S1300)

STEINSTUCKE II; VIER KLEINE STUCKE II
   see Gasser, Ulrich

STEKEL, ERIC-PAUL (1898-   )
   Concerto for Violin and Orchestra
     PATERSON perf mat rent   (S1301)

   Grenoble
     PATERSON perf mat rent   (S1302)

   Symphony No. 1
     PATERSON perf mat rent   (S1303)

   Symphony No. 2
     PATERSON perf mat rent   (S1304)

   Symphony No. 4
     PATERSON perf mat rent   (S1305)

STELE IN MEMORIAM IGOR STRAVINSKY see
   Tansman, Alexandre

STEMPNEVSKY, STANISLAV
   Holiday [18']
     sc MUZYKA f.s.   (S1306)

STENBERG, JOHANNES
   Minuet, [arr.]
     (Orbeck) sc,pts MUSIKK f.s. (S1307)

STENDEL, WOLFGANG
   Inventionen
     2.2.3.1. 2.2.3.1. timp,perc,pno,
     cel,harp,strings
     sc PETERS $25.00   (S1308)

STENHAMMAR, WILHELM (1871-1927)
   Adagio for Solo Voice and Orchestra
     [4']
     2clar,strings,med solo
     NORDISKA perf mat rent   (S1309)

   Concerto for Piano and Orchestra, No.
     1, Op. 1 [48']
     2.2.2.2. 4.2.3.0. timp,strings,
     pno solo
     STIM   (S1310)

   Fylgia, For Solo Voice And Orchestra
     [3']
     2.2.2.2. 4.0.0.0. harp,strings,
     med-high solo
     NORDISKA perf mat rent   (S1311)

   Ithaka, For Solo Voice And Orchestra
     [13']
     2.2.3.3. 4.3.3.1. timp,harp,
     strings,low solo
     NORDISKA perf mat rent   (S1312)

   Min Stamfar Hade En Stor Pokal, For
     Solo Voice And Orchestra [3']
     2.2.2.2. 2.0.0.0. strings,med
     solo
     NORDISKA perf mat rent   (S1313)

   Star Eye, For Solo Voice And
     Orchestra [3']
     0.1.2.0. 0.0.0.0. strings,med
     solo
     NORDISKA perf mat rent   (S1314)

STEPHEN FOSTER GALLERY see Gould,
   Morton

STEPPING STONES see Nordal, Jon

STEPTOE, ROGER
   Concerto for Oboe and Orchestra [23']
     string orch,ob solo
     STAINER HL261 perf mat rent (S1315)

   Concerto for Tuba and String
     Orchestra
     string orch,tuba solo
     STAINER 3.3184 perf mat rent
                           (S1316)
   Elegy On The Death And Burial Of Cock
     Robin, For Solo Voice And Strings
     [7'30"]
     11 solo strings, solo
     countertenor
     STAINER HL278 perf mat rent (S1317)

   Sinfonia Concertante for Violin,
     Viola, Violoncello and String
     Orchestra [18']
     string orch,vln solo,vla solo,vcl
     solo
     STAINER sc AC42 f.s., pts AC43 f.s.
                           (S1318)
   Two Miniatures
     string orch
     sc,pts STAINER H277 f.s.   (S1319)

STERNDALE BENNETT, WILLIAM
   see BENNETT, [SIR] WILLIAM STERNDALE

STERNKLANG see Stockhausen, Karlheinz

STEUERMANN, EDWARD (1892-1964)
   Suite for Chamber Orchestra
     sc APNM perf mat rent   (S1320)

STEUERMANN, EDWARD (cont'd.)

   Variations for Orchestra [10']
     sc APNM $7.50, perf mat rent
                           (S1321)
STEVEN, DONALD (1945-   )
   Ordre Sans Ordre (Sans Desordre), For
     Guitar And Chamber Orchestra
     [20']
     1.1.1.1. 0.0.0.0. 2perc,hpsd,
     harp,strings,gtr solo
     CAN.MUS.CENT. MI 1315 S8430 (S1322)

   Pages Of Solitary Delights, For Solo
     Voice And Orchestra [11']
     2(alto fl).2.2.2. 2.2.3.0. 2perc,
     harp,cel/synthesizer,strings,A
     solo
     CAN.MUS.CENT. MV 1400 S843P (S1323)

STEVENS, HALSEY (1908-1989)
   Improvisation On "Divinum Mysterium"
     [3']
     string orch
     PEER perf mat rent   (S1324)

STEVENS, THOMAS (1938-   )
   New Carnival Of Venice, A, For 4
     Trombettes And Orchestra
     LEDUC AL 27343-27344 perf mat rent
                          (S1325)
STIEBLER, ERNSTALBRECHT (1934-   )
   Modell [14'40"]
     string orch
     MODERN 1706   (S1326)

STIERKAMPFMUSIK, FOR GUITAR AND
   ORCHESTRA, [ARR.] see Behrend,
   Siegfried

STIJL see Koster, Titus

STILL see Marsh, Roger

STILL, WILLIAM GRANT (1895-1978)
   Africa [30']
     3(pic).2+English horn.4.2.
     4.3.3.1. timp,perc,harp,pno,
     cel,strings
     sc STILL $12.50   (S1327)

   Alnados De Espana, Los [12']
     3(pic).2+English horn.3.2.
     4.3.3.1. timp,perc,harp,cel,
     strings
     sc STILL $12.50   (S1328)

   American Scene, The [50']
     3(pic).2+English
     horn.3.2(contrabsn). 4.3.3.1.
     timp,perc,harp,cel,strings
     sc STILL $25.00   (S1329)

   Archaic Ritual [20']
     3(pic).2+English
     horn.3.2(contrabsn). 4.3.3.1.
     timp,perc,harp,cel,strings
     sc STILL $14.30   (S1330)

   Black Bottom [10']
     3(pic).1.3.2. 2.3.2.1. timp,perc,
     strings
     sc STILL $8.90   (S1331)

   Black Man Dances, The [10']
     1.1.1.0.3sax. 1.2.1.1. bells,
     drums,pno,gtr,strings
     sc STILL $20.60   (S1332)

   Black Pierrot, A (from Songs Of
     Separation)
     2.2.2.2. 3.1.2.1. harp,cel,strings
     [3'] sc STILL $5.50   (S1333)

   Blues, The (from Lenox Avenue)
     [3'30"]
     1.1.3.2.4sax. 2.2.1.0. drums,
     strings,vln solo
     sc STILL $2.60   (S1334)

   Boy's Dance From "Miss Sally's Party"
     see Three Dances

   Can'tcha Line 'Em [5']
     1.1.2.1. 2.2.1.0. perc,strings
     sc STILL $3.50   (S1335)

   Choreographic Prelude
     2(pic).2.2.2. 3.2.2.1. timp,perc,
     harp,strings
     (alternate scoring: fl, pno, str)
     sc STILL $2.60   (S1336)

   Dance Before The Hut From "Sahdji"
     see Three Dances

   Ebon Chronicle [9']
     3(pic).2+English
     horn.4.3(contrabsn). 4.3.3.1.
     timp,perc,harp,strings
     sc STILL $8.90   (S1337)

   Entrance Of Les Porteuses (from La
     Guiablesse)
     string orch
     sc STILL $5.30   (S1338)

STILL, WILLIAM GRANT (cont'd.)

Fanfare For American War Heroes [1']
3(pic).2+English horn.3.2.
4.3.3.1. timp,cym,harp,strings
sc STILL $5.30   (S1339)

From The Heart Of A Believer [10']
3(pic).2+English
horn.3.3(contrabsn). 4.3.3.1.
timp,perc,cel,strings
sc STILL $22.40   (S1340)

From The Hearts Of Women, For Solo
Voice And String Orchestra [9']
strings,harp,S solo
sc STILL $13.60   (S1341)

From The Journal Of A Wanderer [20']
3(pic).3+English
horn.4.2(contrabsn). 4.3.3.1.
timp,perc,harp,cel,strings
sc STILL $25.00   (S1342)

If You Should Go, For Solo Voice And
Orchestra (from Songs Of
Separation)
3(pic).2+English horn.3.2. 4.0.3.1.
timp,cym,harp,cel,strings,S solo
[3'] sc STILL $5.30   (S1343)

Kaintuck' [13']
3(pic).2+English horn.4.2.
4.3.3.1. timp,perc,strings
sc STILL $13.60   (S1344)

Legend
3(pic).2+English horn.3.2.
4.3.3.1. timp,perc,harp,cel,
strings
sc STILL $4.40   (S1345)

Miniature Overture [2']
3.2+English horn.3.2. 4.3.3.1.
timp,perc,harp,strings
sc STILL $2.60   (S1346)

Mother And Child (from Suite For
Violin And Piano)
string orch sc STILL $1.70 (S1347)

Old California [10']
3(pic).2+English horn.3.3.
4.3.3.1. timp,perc,harp,strings
sc STILL $7.90   (S1348)

Out Of The Silence (from Seven
Traceries)
opt fl,pno,strings sc STILL $2.80
                                  (S1349)

Pastorela, For Violin And Orchestra
[11']
3(pic).2+English horn.3.2.
4.3.3.1. timp,chimes,cym,harp,
strings,vln solo
sc STILL $9.80   (S1350)

Path Of Glory, The, For Solo Voice
And Orchestra [15']
3.2+English horn.3.2. 4.3.3.1.
timp,perc,strings,Bar solo
sc STILL $17.20   (S1351)

Patterns [15']
2(pic).2+English horn.2.2.
2.0.0.0. strings
sc STILL $4.60   (S1352)

Phantom Chapel (from Bells)
string orch,pno,vcl solo sc STILL
$1.70   (S1353)

Preludes, Five
fl,pno,strings
sc STILL $10.70   (S1354)

Preludes: African Dancer; Gamin [12']
fl,pno,strings
sc STILL $6.40   (S1355)

Serenade for Violin and String
Orchestra [8']
string orch,pno,vln solo
(alternate scoring: fl, clar, harp,
str) sc STILL $7.10   (S1356)

Song At Dusk, A [9']
3(pic).2+English horn.3.2.
4.3.3.1. timp,perc,harp,cel,
strings
sc STILL $8.00   (S1357)

Song For The Lonely
2.2.2.2. 3.1.2.1. harp,cel,strings
[4'] (alternate scoring: sorch,
pno) sc STILL $6.20   (S1358)

Song For The Lonely, For Solo Voice
And Orchestra [4']
2.2.2.2. 3.1.2.1. harp,cel,
strings,Mez solo
sc STILL $6.20   (S1359)

Song For The Valiant, For Solo Voice
And Orchestra [3']
0.0.0.0. 4.0.3.1. harp,strings,

STILL, WILLIAM GRANT (cont'd.)

high solo
sc STILL $10.70   (S1360)

Songs Of Separation, For Solo Voice
And Orchestra
2(pic).2+English horn.3.2. 4.3.3.1.
timp,chimes,cym,harp,cel,strings,
Mez solo [12'] sc STILL $8.90
                                  (S1361)

Spirituals: A Medley
1.0.2.1. 0.0.0.0. harp,pno,
strings
sc STILL $14.30   (S1362)

Suite for Violin and Orchestra [15']
2(pic).2+English
horn.3.2(contrabsn). 4.3.3.1.
timp,perc,harp,cel,strings,vln
solo
sc STILL $15.20   (S1363)

Summerland (from Three Visions)
1.1.2.1. 2.2.1.0. drums,strings sc
STILL $5.30   (S1364)

Symphony No. 4 [27']
3(pic).2+English
horn.3.2(contrabsn). 4.3.3.1.
timp,perc,harp,cel,strings
(Autochthonous Symphony, The) sc
STILL $14.75   (S1365)

Symphony No. 5 [25']
3(pic).2+English horn.3.2.
4.3.3.1. timp,perc,harp,cel,
strings
(Western Hemisphere, The) sc STILL
$10.70   (S1366)

Three Dances From La Guiablesse
3(pic).2+English horn.3.2.
4.3.3.1. timp,perc,harp,strings
sc STILL $6.20   (S1367)

Three Dances
2(pic).2.2.2. 3.2.2.0. timp,perc,
pno,strings sc STILL $5.30 [8']
contains: Boy's Dance From "Miss
Sally's Party"; Dance Before
The Hut From "Sahdji"; Tribal
Dance   (S1368)

Three Negro Songs [10']
3(pic).2(English horn).3.2.
4.3.3.1. timp,perc,harp,strings
sc STILL $8.20   (S1369)

Threnody: In Memory Of Jean Sibelius
[4']
2.2.2.2. 3.2.2.1. timp,perc,harp,
strings
sc STILL $3.50   (S1370)

Tribal Dance
see Three Dances

STILL LIFE WITH BELL see Crockett,
Donald

STILL MOVEMENT see Birtwistle, Harrison

STILL WATERS see Davis, Anthony

STILLA, FOR SOLO VOICE AND ORCHESTRA
see Kleiberg, Ståle

STILLHET see Haug, Halvor

STILLNESS see Haug, Halvor, Stillhet

STIMMEN, DIE, FOR SOLO VOICE AND
ORCHESTRA see Dorati, Antal

STIMMEN AUS DEM PUBLIKUM see Strauss,
Eduard

STIMMEN DER NACHT, FOR SOLO VOICE AND
ORCHESTRA see Mullenbach, Alexander

STIMMEN...VERSTUMMEN see Gubaidulina,
Sofia

STIRI SLOVENSKE LJUDSKE PESMI see
Golob, Jani

STIRN, D. (1915-   )
Arlequin [20']
2.2.2.2. 4.2.3.1. timp,perc,harp/
pno,strings
BOIS perf mat rent   (S1371)

Faust For Fun [35']
2.2.2.2. 4.2.3.1. timp,perc,xylo,
harp,cel,strings
BOIS perf mat rent   (S1372)

STOCK, DAVID FREDERICK (1939-   )
American Accents [9']
2(pic).1+English horn.1+bass
clar.2. 2.2.0.0. perc,strings
sc AM.COMP.AL. $28.95, perf mat
rent   (S1373)

STOCK, DAVID FREDERICK (cont'd.)

Back To Bass-Ics [4']
string orch
sc AM.COMP.AL. $9.95   (S1374)

Divertimento [8']
3.2.2.2. 4.3.3.1. timp,perc,harp,
strings
sc AM.COMP.AL. $20.60, perf mat
rent   (S1375)

Fast Break [6']
3.3.3.3. 3.3.3.1. timp,3perc,
strings
sc AM.COMP.AL. $57.20, perf mat
rent   (S1376)

Joyful Noise, A [20']
3.3.3.3. 4.4.3.1. timp,perc,
2harp,2kbd,elec gtr,strings
sc AM.COMP.AL. $59.25   (S1377)

On The Shoulders Of Giants [24']
4.3.3.3. 4.4.4.1. timp,4perc,
harp,pno,strings
sc AM.COMP.AL. $173.40   (S1378)

Rockin' Rondo [6']
3.3.3.3. 4.3.3.1. timp,3perc,
strings
sc AM.COMP.AL. $57.15, perf mat
rent   (S1379)

Symphony In One Movement [15']
3.3.3.3. 4.4.3.1. timp,perc,
strings
sc AM.COMP.AL. $28.20, perf mat
rent   (S1380)

Tekiah, For Trumpet And Orchestra
[20']
1.1.1.1. 1.1.1.0. perc,harp,pno,
strings,trp solo
AM.COMP.AL. perf mat rent   (S1381)

STOCKHAUSEN, KARLHEINZ (1928-   )
Lucifer's Dance
see Luzifers Tanz

Luzifers Tanz [55']
"Lucifer's Dance" STOCKHAUS (S1382)

Michael's Journey Round The Earth,
For Trumpet And Orchestra
see Michaels Reise Um Die Erde, For
Trumpet And Orchestra

Michaels Reise Um Die Erde, For
Trumpet And Orchestra [48']
"Michael's Journey Round The Earth,
For Trumpet And Orchestra"
STOCKHAUS   (S1383)

Star Sound
see Sternklang

Sternklang *No.34 [150']
"Star Sound" sc STOCKHAUS f.s.
                                 (S1384)

STOESSEL, ALBERT (1894-1943)
Suite Antique, For 2 Violins And
Chamber Orchestra [10']
1.1.1.1. 0.0.0.0. strings,2vln
soli
SCHIRM.G perf mat rent   (S1385)

STOKER, RICHARD (1938-   )
Chorale For Strings
string orch
FENTONE   (S1386)

STOLARCZYK, WILLY
Ouverture Concertante *Op.16 [15']
2.1.1.1. 1.1.1.1. strings,vln
solo,trp solo,pno solo,perc
solo
SAMFUNDET perf mat rent   (S1387)

Robber's Christmas Eve, The, For
Narrator And Orchestra
see Roverens Juleaften, For
Narrator And Orchestra

Roverens Juleaften, For Narrator And
Orchestra [23']
2.1.2.0. 1.2.0.0. timp,2perc,
harmonium,pno,cel,strings,
narrator
"Robber's Christmas Eve, The, For
Narrator And Orchestra" SAMFUNDET
perf mat rent   (S1388)

STOLZ, ROBERT (1880-1975)
Ich Liebe Dich, For Solo Voice And
Orchestra [arr.]
(Michalski, C.) 2.2.2.2. 4.2.3.0.
perc,harp,gtr,strings,solo voice
[5'] SIKORSKI perf mat rent   (S1389)

Vor Meinem Vaterhaus Steht Eine
Linde, For Solo Voice And
Orchestra [arr.]
(Michalski, C.) 2.3.2.2. 4.2.3.0.
perc,harp,strings,solo voice [4']
SIKORSKI perf mat rent   (S1390)

STOLZ, ROBERT (cont'd.)

Weine Nicht, Bricht Eine Schone Frau
   Dir Das Herz, For Solo Voice And
   Orchestra [arr.]
   (Michalski, C.) 2.2.2.2. 4.2.3.0.
   perc,harp,gtr,strings,solo voice
   [5'] SIKORSKI perf mat rent
                              (S1391)

STÖLZEL, GOTTFRIED HEINRICH (1690-1749)
   Aus Der Tiefe Rufe Ich, Herr, Zu Dir,
      For Solo Voice And String
      Orchestra
      (Adrio, Adam) string orch,cont,B
      solo sc,pts MERSEBURGER EM 916
      f.s.   (S1392)

   Concertino in E minor, MIN 177
      (Thilde, J.) string orch,trp solo
      [6'5"] sc BILLAUDOT f.s., perf
      mat rent   (S1393)

   Concerto in B flat, MIN 179
      (Thilde, J.) string orch,trp solo
      [9'25"] sc BILLAUDOT f.s., perf
      mat rent   (S1394)

   Concerto in C minor, MIN 180
      (Thilde, J.) string orch,trp solo
      [11'15"] sc BILLAUDOT f.s., perf
      mat rent   (S1395)

   Concerto in F, MIN 178
      (Thilde, J.) string orch,2trp soli
      [7'35"] sc BILLAUDOT f.s., perf
      mat rent   (S1396)

   Sonata in D, MIN 181
      (Thilde, J.) string orch,trp solo
      [7'5"] sc BILLAUDOT f.s., perf
      mat rent   (S1397)

STONE, THE, FOR SOLO VOICE AND
   ORCHESTRA see Firsova, Elena

STONE AND EARTH, FOR SOLO VOICE AND
   STRING ORCHESTRA see Cohen, Edward

STONE GARDEN see Osborne, Nigel

STONE LITANY: "RUNES FROM A HOUSE OF
   THE DEAD", FOR SOLO VOICE AND
   ORCHESTRA see Davies, Peter Maxwell

STONE, WATER, STARS see Powers, Anthony

STOOP, HENK (1943-   )
   Symphony No. 1 [15']
      3.3.2.3. 4.3.3.1. timp,4perc,
      2harp,strings
      DONEMUS perf mat rent   (S1398)

STORBEKKEN, EGIL (1911-   )
   Buffers-Visa, For Solo Voice And
      Orchestra [arr.]
      (Brevik, Tor) 1.1.1.1. 2.0.0.0.
      strings,solo voice NORGE   (S1399)

   Femund [arr.]
      (Groven, Eivind) 1.1.2.1. 2.2.2.0.
      timp,strings NORGE   (S1400)

   Fjell-Suite, For Solo Voice, Recorder
      And Orchestra [arr.]
      (Brevik, Tor) 1.1.2.1. 2.0.0.0.
      perc,strings,rec solo,solo voice
      NORGE   (S1401)

   Fjellbekken, For Recorder And String
      Orchestra [arr.]
      (Brevik, Tor) string orch,rec solo
      NORGE   (S1402)

   Munnharpelat [arr.]
      (Brevik, Tor) 1.1.1.1. 0.0.0.0.
      strings NORGE   (S1403)

   Ouverture: Nord I Fjellom [arr.]
      (Brevik, Tor) 1.1.1.1. 2.0.0.0.
      strings NORGE   (S1404)

   Pa Blussumvollum, For Solo Voice And
      Orchestra [arr.]
      (Brevik, Tor) 1.1.1.1. 0.0.0.0.
      strings,solo voice NORGE   (S1405)

   Trolldans: Grautmarsj [arr.]
      (Brevik, Tor) 1.1.1.1. 1.0.0.0.
      strings NORGE   (S1406)

   Varnattstone, For Recorder And String
      Orchestra [arr.]
      (Brevik, Tor) string orch,rec solo
      NORGE   (S1407)

STORIA DELLA MILLE E UNA NOTTE, UNA see
   Coppoolse, David

STORM, THE, OVERTURE see Tchaikovsky,
   Piotr Ilyich, Orage, L'. Overture

STÖRRLE, HEINZ (1932-   )
   Concerto for Brass Quintet and
      Orchestra [24'40"]
      2.2.2.2. 2.2.2.0. perc,strings,
      brass quin soli

STÖRRLE, HEINZ (cont'd.)

   ORLANDO   (S1408)

STORSTROEM BRIDGE, THE see Schultz,
   Svend S., Storstromsbroen

STORSTROMSBROEN see Schultz, Svend S.

STORY OF CELESTE, THE, FOR NARRATOR AND
   ORCHESTRA see Klein, Lothar

STORY OF MALINCHE, THE see Johansen,
   Svend Aaquist, Historien Om
   Malinche

STOUT, ALAN (1932-   )
   Crux Fidelis, For Solo Voice And
      Orchestra *Op.68,No.11 [5']
      2.0+English horn.2.2. 4.0.0.0.
      perc,1-2harp,cel/org,strings,
      Mez solo
      sc AM.COMP.AL. $6.90   (S1409)

   Elegiac Suite, For Solo Voice And
      String Orchestra [11']
      string orch,S solo
      NORDISKA perf mat rent   (S1410)

   Hymn For Fourteen Strings [5']
      string orch
      sc AM.COMP.AL. $10.70, perf mat
      rent   (S1411)

   Laudi, For Solo Voices And Orchestra
      [20']
      1.1.1.0. 1.2.0.0. perc,cel,pno,
      harp,2vln,2vla,2vcl,db,SBar
      soli
      sc AM.COMP.AL. $14.45   (S1412)

   Two Finnish Songs, For Solo Voice And
      Orchestra *Op.53 [9']
      3.2.3.2. 4.3.3.1. timp,perc,
      2harp,strings,S solo
      sc AM.COMP.AL. $16.90, perf mat
      rent   (S1413)

   Two Hymns, For Solo Voice And
      Orchestra [9']
      2.2.2.1. 1.1.1.0. timp,perc,harp,
      pno,strings,T solo
      sc AM.COMP.AL. $13.00   (S1414)

STRADA, LA: SUITE see Rota, Nino

STRADELLA, ALESSANDRO (1645-1682)
   Concerto Grosso, No. 2, in D
      (Bonelli) KALMUS A7440 sc $7.00,
      set $12.00, pts $1.50, ea.
                                  (S1415)

STRAESSER, JOEP (1934-   )
   Signals And Echoes, For Clarinet And
      Orchestra [12']
      1.1.1.0. 1.1.0.0. perc,pno,vln,
      vla,vcl,db,bass clar solo
      sc DONEMUS f.s., perf mat rent
                                  (S1416)

   Uber Erich M.: Tableaux Vivants [27']
      3.3.3.3. 4.3.3.1. timp,2perc,pno,
      strings
      sc DONEMUS f.s., perf mat rent
                                  (S1417)

   Winter Concerto, For Saxophone And
      Orchestra [18']
      2.2.2.2. 2.2.2.0. 3perc,harp,
      strings,soprano sax solo
      DONEMUS perf mat rent   (S1418)

STRAHLENDE STERNE, FOR SOLO VOICE AND
   ORCHESTRA see Bartos, A.

STRAK see Rehnqvist, Karin

STRAND, RAGNVALD (1910-   )
   Earth, For Solo Voice And Orchestra
      see Jord, For Solo Voice And
      Orchestra

   Hymne, For Solo Voice And Orchestra
      1.1.2.1. 2.2.1.0. pno,strings,Bar
      solo
      NORGE   (S1419)

   Jord, For Solo Voice And Orchestra
      1.1.2.1. 2.2.1.0. pno,strings,
      narrator
      "Earth, For Solo Voice And
      Orchestra" NORGE   (S1420)

   Norsk Rapsodi Nr. 2
      2.2.2.2. 4.3.3.0. timp,perc,
      strings
      NORGE   (S1421)

STRANG, GERALD (1908-   )
   Movement From "Suite For Chamber
      Orchestra"
      2.2.2.2. 2.0.2.0. strings
      AM.COMP.AL. perf mat rent   (S1422)

   Symphony No. 1 [25']
      3.3.3.3. 4.3.3.0. timp,perc,harp,
      strings
      AM.COMP.AL. perf mat rent   (S1423)

STRANG, GERALD (cont'd.)

   Symphony No. 2 [30']
      3.3.3.3. 4.3.3.1. timp,perc,
      strings
      AM.COMP.AL. perf mat rent   (S1424)

STRANGE ATTRACTORS see Le Baron, Anne

STRANGE DREAMS OF THE OLD MAJOR, THE
   see Sønstevold, Maj, Gamle Majors
   Forunderlige Dromme, Den

STRANIERA, LA: AH! SE NON M' AMI PIU,
   FOR SOLO VOICE AND ORCHESTRA see
   Bellini, Vincenzo

STRANIERA, LA: IO LA VIDI, FOR SOLO
   VOICES AND ORCHESTRA see Bellini,
   Vincenzo

STRANIERA, LA: SERBA, SERBA I TUOI
   SEGRETI, FOR SOLO VOICES AND
   ORCHESTRA see Bellini, Vincenzo

STRANIERA, LA: SI LI SCIOGLIETE, O
   GIUDICI, FOR SOLO VOICE AND
   ORCHESTRA see Bellini, Vincenzo

STRANIERA, LA: SI! SULLA SALMA DEL
   FRATELLO, FOR SOLO VOICES AND
   ORCHESTRA see Bellini, Vincenzo

STRANIERA, LA: SVENTURATO IL COR CHE
   FIDA, FOR SOLO VOICE AND ORCHESTRA
   see Bellini, Vincenzo

STRANZ, ULRICH (1946-   )
   Auguri [20']
      0.2.0.0. 2.0.0.0. 9vln,3vla,3vcl,
      2db,vla solo
      "Music, For Viola And Orchestra"
      BÄREN. BA 6794 perf mat rent
                                  (S1425)

   Déjà Vu, For Oboe D'Amore And Chamber
      Orchestra [20']
      0.0.1.0. 0.1.0.0. 2perc,harp,
      strings,ob d'amore solo study sc
      BÄREN. BA 6292 f.s.   (S1426)

   Janus, For Violin, Piano, And
      Instrumental Ensemble [17']
      2(pic).1+English horn.2+bass
      clar.1+contrabsn. 2.1.1.0. vln
      solo,pno solo
      BÄREN. BA 7171   (S1427)

   Music, For Viola And Orchestra
      see Auguri

   Music for Piano and Orchestra [20']
      2(pic).2(English horn).2(bass
      clar).2(contrabsn). 3.2.2.0+db
      tuba. timp,4perc,harp,cel,
      strings,pno solo
      BÄREN. BA 6758 perf mat rent
                                  (S1428)

   Sieben Feld- Wald- Und Wiesenstucke
      [15']
      7vln,2vla,2vcl,db
      BÄREN. BA 7149   (S1429)

   Szenen I, II, III [20']
      2(pic).2(English horn).2(bass
      clar).2(contrabsn). 3.2.2.1.
      timp,2perc,harp,cel,pno,strings
      BÄREN. BA 6785 perf mat rent
                                  (S1430)

   Tachys [18']
      2+pic.2+English horn.2+bass
      clar.2+contrabsn. 3.3.3.1.
      timp,4perc,harp,cel,strings,
      Aeolian harp
      BÄREN. BA 6293 perf mat rent
                                  (S1431)

   Zeitbiegung [22']
      2(pic).2+English horn.2+bass
      clar.2+contrabsn. 4.3.2.0+db
      tuba. timp,3perc,harp,pno,3db
      BÄREN. BA 6734 perf mat rent
                                  (S1432)

STRATA see Ore, Cecilie

STRATEGIER, HERMAN (1912-1988)
   Henric Van Veldeke, For Solo Voices
      And Orchestra
      2.2.2.2. 4.3.3.0. timp,perc,harp,
      cel,strings,Bar&narrator
      sc DONEMUS f.s., perf mat rent
                                  (S1433)

   Partita Argentea, For Solo Voices And
      Instrumental Ensemble [15']
      S rec,fl,clar,trp,perc,pno 4-
      hands,3vln,vcl,3 solo voices
      DONEMUS perf mat rent   (S1434)

STRATES ECLATEES see Miroglio, Francis

STRATHCLYDE CONCERTO NO. 1, FOR OBOE
   AND ORCHESTRA see Davies, Peter
   Maxwell

STRATHCLYDE CONCERTO NO. 2, FOR
   VIOLONCELLO AND ORCHESTRA see
   Davies, Peter Maxwell

STRATIFICATIONS see Abrahamsen, Hans

STRATOCUMULUS see Nielsen, Svend

STRATUS, VERSION I see Taira, Yoshihisa

STRATUS, VERSION II see Taira, Yoshihisa

STRAUS, OSCAR (1870-1954)
Chocolate Soldier, The: Selections (Lampe) 1.1.2.1. 2.2.1.0. perc, strings set KALMUS A6718 $20.00 (S1435)

Chocolate Soldier, The: Waltzes (Danmark) 1.1.2.1. 2.2.1.0. perc, strings [7'] KALMUS A4148 pno-cond sc $3.00, set $25.00, perf mat rent (S1436)

Waltz Dream: Waltzes 2(pic).2.2.2. 4.2.2.0. timp,perc, harp,strings set KALMUS A6719 $21.00 (S1437)

STRAUSS, EDUARD (1835-1916)
Abonnenten Walzer *Op.116 1+pic.2.1+clar in D.2. 4.2.3.0. timp,perc,harp,strings set KALMUS A5903 $23.00, perf mat rent (S1438)

Akademische-Burger Walzer *Op.68 1+pic.2.2.2. 4.2.3.1. timp,perc, harp,strings set KALMUS A5904 $25.00, perf mat rent (S1439)

Angot Quadrille *Op.110 1+pic.2.2.2. 4.2.3.0. timp,perc, harp,strings set KALMUS A5905 $13.00 (S1440)

Augensprache *Op.119 1+pic.2.1+clar in D.2. 4.2.3.0. timp,harp,strings set KALMUS A5906 $10.00 (S1441)

Aula-Lieder Walzer *Op.113 1+pic.2.1+clar in E flat.2. 4.2.3.0. timp,perc,strings set KALMUS A5907 $23.00 (S1442)

Aus Dem Rechtsleben Walzer *Op.126 1+pic.2.2.2. 4.2.3.0. timp,perc, harp,strings set KALMUS A5902 $24.00, perf mat rent (S1443)

Aus Der Studienzeit Walzer *Op.141 1+pic.2.2.2. 4.2.3.0. timp,perc, harp,strings set KALMUS A5908 $22.00, perf mat rent (S1444)

Aus Lieb' Zu Ihr Polka *Op.135 1+pic.2.1+clar in D.2. 4.2.3.0. timp,perc,harp,strings set KALMUS A5909 $13.00 (S1445)

Ausser Rand Und Band Polka *Op.168 1+pic.1.1+clar in D.2. 4.2.3.0. timp,perc,strings set KALMUS A5910 $15.00 (S1446)

Ball Promessen Walzer *Op.82 1+pic.2.2.2. 4.2.3.0. timp,perc, harp,strings set KALMUS A5912 $25.00, perf mat rent (S1447)

Ballchronik Walzer *Op.167 1+pic.1.2.2. 4.2.3.0. timp,perc, harp,strings set KALMUS A5911 $25.00, perf mat rent (S1448)

Bessere Zeiten Walzer *Op.130 1+pic.2.1+clar in D.2. 4.2.3.0. timp,perc,strings set KALMUS A5914 $23.00, perf mat rent (S1449)

Boccaccio Quadrille *Op.180 1+pic.1.2.2. 4.3.3.0. perc,strings set KALMUS A5913 $20.00, perf mat rent (S1450)

Bruder Studio Polka *Op.78 2(pic).2.1+clar in D.2. 4.2.3.0. timp,perc,strings set KALMUS A5915 $15.00, perf mat rent (S1451)

Colombine Polka *Op.89 1+pic.2.1+clar in E flat.2. 4.2.3.0. timp,harp,strings set KALMUS A5916 $15.00, perf mat rent (S1452)

Consequenzen Walzer *Op.143 1+pic.2.1+clar in E flat.2. 4.2.3.0. timp,perc,harp,strings set KALMUS A5917 $15.00, perf mat rent (S1453)

Deutsche Herzen Walzer *Op.65 1+pic.2.1+clar in D.2. 4.2.3.1. timp,perc,harp,strings set KALMUS 5918 $30.00, perf mat rent (S1454)

Doctrinen Walzer *Op.79 1+pic.2.2.2. 4.2.3.0. timp,perc, harp,strings set KALMUS A5919

STRAUSS, EDUARD (cont'd.)
$25.00, perf mat rent (S1455)

Ehret Die Frauen Walzer *Op.80 1+pic.2.1+clar in D.2. 4.2.3.0. timp,perc,strings set KALMUS A5920 $20.00, perf mat rent (S1456)

En Miniatur Polka *Op.181 1+pic.1.1+clar in D.1. 4.2.3.0. timp,perc,harp,strings set KALMUS A5922 $14.00, perf mat rent (S1457)

Fantasie Über Neure Deutsche Lieder *Op.133 2.1.2.2. 4.2.3.1. timp,perc,harp, strings set KALMUS A5923 $25.00, perf mat rent (S1458)

Fatinitza Quadrille *Op.136 1+pic.2.2.2. 4.3.3.0. timp,perc, harp,strings set KALMUS A5924 $15.00, perf mat rent (S1459)

Fidele Bursche Walzer *Op.124 1+pic.2.2.2. 4.2.3.0. timp,perc, harp,strings set KALMUS A5925 $25.00, perf mat rent (S1460)

Flottes Leben Polka *Op.115 1+pic.2.2.2. 4.2.3.0. timp,perc, strings set KALMUS A5926 $15.00, perf mat rent (S1461)

Fur Lustige Leut *Op.255 1+pic.1.2.2. 4.2.3.0. timp,perc, harp,strings set KALMUS A5927 $15.00, perf mat rent (S1462)

Fusionen Walzer *Op.74 1+pic.2.2.2. 4.2.3.0. timp,perc, harp,strings set KALMUS A5928 $23.00, perf mat rent (S1463)

Goldfischlein Polka *Op.77 1+pic.2.2.2. 4.2.3.0. perc,harp, strings set KALMUS A5929 $14.00, perf mat rent (S1464)

Heimische Klange Walzer *Op.252 1+pic.1.2.1. 4.2.3.0. timp,perc, harp,strings set KALMUS A5931 $22.00, perf mat rent (S1465)

Hektograf Polka *Op.186 1+pic.1.2.2. 4.2.2.0. timp,perc, strings set KALMUS A5930 $13.00, perf mat rent (S1466)

Hochquelle Polka, Die *Op.114 1+pic.2.1+clar in E flat.2. 4.2.3.0. timp,perc,harp,strings set KALMUS A5932 $15.00, perf mat rent (S1467)

Huldigungen Walzer *Op.88 1+pic.2.2.2. 4.2.3.1. timp,perc, harp,strings set KALMUS A5933 $30.00, perf mat rent (S1468)

Hypothesen Walzer *Op.72 1+pic.2.2.2. 4.2.3.0. timp,perc, harp,strings set KALMUS A5934 $25.00, perf mat rent (S1469)

In Lieb Entbrannt Polka *Op.117 1+pic.2.1+clar in E flat.2. 4.2.3.0. timp,perc,strings set KALMUS A5935 $14.00, perf mat rent (S1470)

Iris Polka *Op.9 1+pic.2.1+clar in D.2. 4.2.1.0. timp,perc,strings set KALMUS A5936 $13.00 (S1471)

Kleine Chronik Polka *Op.128 1+pic.2.2.2. 4.2.3.0. timp,perc, strings set KALMUS A5937 $15.00, perf mat rent (S1472)

Knall Und Fall Polka *Op.132 1+pic.2.1+clar in D.2. 4.2.3.0. timp,perc,strings set KALMUS A5938 $15.00, perf mat rent (S1473)

Laut Und Traut Polka *Op.106 1+pic.2.1+clar in D.2. 4.2.3.0. timp,perc,harp,strings set KALMUS A5939 $15.00, perf mat rent (S1474)

Leben Ist Doch Schon Walzer, Das *Op.150 1+pic.1.2.2. 4.2.3.0. timp,perc, harp,strings set KALMUS A5940 $23.00, perf mat rent (S1475)

Liebeszauber Polka *Op.84 1+pic.2.1+clar in E flat.2. 4.2.3.0. timp,perc,harp,strings set KALMUS A5941 $15.00, perf mat rent (S1476)

STRAUSS, EDUARD (cont'd.)
Luftig Und Duftig Polka *Op.206 1+pic.1.1+clar in D.2. 4.2.3.0. timp,perc,strings set KALMUS A5944 $15.00, perf mat rent (S1477)

Lustig Im Kreise Polka *Op.93 1+pic.2.2.2. 4.2.3.0. timp,perc, harp,strings set KALMUS A5943 $15.00, perf mat rent (S1478)

Lustige G'schichten Walzer *Op.227 1+pic.1.1+clar in D.2. 4.2.3.0. timp,perc,harp,strings set KALMUS A5942 $23.00, perf mat rent (S1479)

Mädchenlaune Polka *Op.99 1+pic.2.2.2. 4.2.3.0. perc,harp, strings set KALMUS A5945 $14.00 (S1480)

Marchen Aus Der Heimat Walzer *Op.155 1+pic.2.2.2. 4.2.3.0. timp,perc, harp,strings set KALMUS A5946 $25.00, perf mat rent (S1481)

Marzveilchen Polka *Op.129 1+pic.2.1+clar in D.2. 4.2.3.0. timp,perc,harp,strings set KALMUS A5947 $15.00, perf mat rent (S1482)

Mit Dampf Polka *Op.70 1+pic.2.1+clar in E flat.2. 4.2.3.0. timp,perc,strings set KALMUS A5948 $15.00, perf mat rent (S1483)

Mit Der Feder Polka *Op.69 1+pic.2.1+clar in E flat.2. 4.2.3.0. timp,perc,harp,strings set KALMUS A5949 $15.00, perf mat rent (S1484)

Mit Der Striemung Polka *Op.174 1+pic.2.2.2. 4.2.3.0. timp,perc, strings set KALMUS A5950 $15.00, perf mat rent (S1485)

Myrthenstrausschen Walzer *Op.87 1+pic.2.1+clar in D.2. 4.2.3.0. timp,perc,harp,strings set KALMUS A5951 $25.00, perf mat rent (S1486)

Nach Kurzer Post Polka *Op.100 1+pic.2.1+clar in D.2. 2.2.3.0. timp,perc,strings set KALMUS A5952 $12.00 (S1487)

Neue Welt Polka, Eine *Op.86 1+pic.2.1+clar in D.2. 4.2.3.0. timp,perc,strings set KALMUS A5921 $15.00, perf mat rent (S1488)

Pilger Quadrille, Die *Op.91 1+pic.2.2.2. 4.2.3.0. timp,perc, harp,strings set KALMUS A5953 $15.00, perf mat rent (S1489)

Saat Und Ernte Polka *Op.159 1+pic.1.1+clar in D.2. 4.2.3.0. timp,perc,strings set KALMUS A5954 $14.00 (S1490)

Schneesternchen Polka *Op.157 1+pic.1.2.0. 2.2.3.0. timp,perc, harp,strings set KALMUS A5955 $10.00 (S1491)

Seecadet Quadrille *Op.151 1+pic.2.2.2. 4.2.3.0. timp,perc, strings set KALMUS A5957 $14.00 (S1492)

Soldatengruss Polka *Op.85 1+pic.2.1+clar in E flat.2. 4.2.3.0. timp,perc,strings set KALMUS A5958 $14.00 (S1493)

Souvenir De Bade Polka *Op.146 1+pic.2.1+clar in D.2. 4.2.3.0. timp,perc,harp,strings set KALMUS A5959 $15.00, perf mat rent (S1494)

Stimmen Aus Dem Publikum *Op.104 1+pic.2.2.2. 4.2.3.0. timp,perc, harp,strings set KALMUS A5960 $23.00, perf mat rent (S1495)

Studentenball-Tanze Walzer *Op.101 1+pic.2.1+clar in D.2. 4.2.3.0. timp,perc,harp,strings set KALMUS A5961 $14.00 (S1496)

Teufels Quadrille *Op.163 1+pic.1.2.2. 4.2.3.0. timp,perc, strings set KALMUS A5962 $18.00, perf mat rent (S1497)

Thauperle Polka *Op.42 1+pic.1.2.2. 4.4.3.1. timp,perc, harp,strings set KALMUS A5963 $14.00 (S1498)

Theorien Walzer *Op.111 1+pic.2.1+clar in D.2. 4.2.3.0. timp,perc,harp,strings set KALMUS

STRAUSS, EDUARD (cont'd.)

    A5964 $15.00, perf mat rent
                      (S1499)
Tour Un Retour Polka *Op.125
  1+pic.2.2.2. 4.2.3.0. timp,perc,
  harp,strings set KALMUS A5965
  $13.00   (S1500)
Träumerin Polka, Die *Op.208
  1+pic.1.1+clar in D.2. 4.2.3.0.
  timp,perc,harp,strings set KALMUS
  A5966 $13.00   (S1501)
Traumgebilde Walzer *Op.170
  1+pic.1.1+clar in D.2. 4.2.3.0.
  timp,perc,harp,strings set KALMUS
  A5967 $23.00, perf mat rent
                      (S1502)
Treuliebchen Polka *Op.152
  1+pic.2.2.2. 4.2.3.0. timp,perc,
  strings set KALMUS A5968 $13.00
                      (S1503)
Unter Der Enns Polka *Op.121
  1+pic.2.1+clar in D.2. 4.2.3.0.
  timp,perc,strings set KALMUS
  A5969 $13.00   (S1504)
Verdichte Walzer *Op.137
  1+pic.2.2.2. 4.2.3.0. timp,perc,
  harp,strings set KALMUS A5970
  $14.00   (S1505)

STRAUSS, JOHANN, [SR.] (1804-1849)
Adepten Walzer, Die *Op.216
  1+pic.1.1+clar in E flat.1.
  2.2.1.0. timp,strings set KALMUS
  A5971 $12.00   (S1506)
Almacks Quadrille *Op.243
  1+pic.1.2.2. 2.2.1.0. timp,strings
  set KALMUS A5972 $11.00   (S1507)
Charivari Quadrille *Op.196
  1+pic.1.1+clar in E flat.1.
  2.2.1.0. timp,strings set KALMUS
  A5974 $12.00   (S1508)
Concordia Tanze *Op.184
  1.1.2.1. 2.2.1.0. timp,strings set
  KALMUS A5976 $17.00, perf mat
  rent   (S1509)
Damen Souvenir Polka *Op.236
  1+pic.1.2.1. 2.2.1.0. timp,strings
  set KALMUS A5977 $12.00   (S1510)
Epionen Tanze *Op.190
  2.1.2.1. 2.2.1.0. timp,strings set
  KALMUS A5978 $17.00, perf mat
  rent   (S1511)
Ferdinand Quadrille *Op.151
  1+pic.1.2.1. 2.2.1.0. timp,strings
  set KALMUS A5979 $12.00   (S1512)
Fest Quadrille *Op.165
  1+pic.1.2.1. 2.2.1.0. timp,strings
  set KALMUS A5980 $12.00   (S1513)
Frederika Polka *Op.239
  2.1.2.1. 2.2.1.0. timp,strings set
  KALMUS A5981 $12.00   (S1514)
Haimonskinder Quadrille *Op.169
  1+pic.1.2.1. 2.2.1.0. timp,strings
  set KALMUS A5982 $12.00   (S1515)
Harmonie Celeste
  (Sibert, A.) 2.2.2.2. 4.3.3.0.
  timp,perc,harp,strings [7'30"]
  BILLAUDOT perf mat rent   (S1516)
Jubel Quadrille *Op.130
  1+pic.1.2.1. 2.2.1.0. timp,perc,
  strings set KALMUS A5983 $14.00
                      (S1517)
Landes Farben *Op.232
  1+pic.1.1+clar in E flat.1.
  2.2.1.0. timp,strings set KALMUS
  A5985 $12.00   (S1518)
Leben, Ein Tanz, Das [arr.]
  (Waldenmaier, A.P.) 2.2.2.2.
  4.2.3.0. timp,perc,strings [6']
  ORLANDO perf mat rent   (S1519)
Lorelei-Rheinklange *Op.154
  1(pic).1.2.1. 2.2.1.0. timp,strings
  set KALMUS A5986 $10.00   (S1520)
Minnesanger Walzer *Op.141
  1(pic).1.2.1. 2.2.1.0. timp,strings
  set KALMUS A5987 $17.00, perf mat
  rent   (S1521)
Moldau Klange Walzer *Op.186
  2.1.1+clar in E flat.1. 2.2.1.0.
  timp,strings set KALMUS A5988
  $17.00, perf mat rent   (S1522)
Musen Quadrille *Op.174
  1+pic.1.2.1. 2.2.1.0. timp,strings
  set KALMUS A5989 $15.00, perf mat
  rent   (S1523)

STRAUSS, JOHANN, [SR.] (cont'd.)
Najaden Quadrille *Op.206
  1+pic.1.2.1. 2.2.1.0. timp,perc,
  set KALMUS A5990 $12.00   (S1524)
Odeon Tanze Walzer *Op.172
  2(pic).1.2.1. 2.2.1.0. timp,perc,
  strings set KALMUS A5991 $13.00
                      (S1525)
Orpheus Quadrille *Op.162
  1+pic.1.2.1. 2.2.1.0. timp,perc,
  strings set KALMUS A5992 $16.00,
  perf mat rent   (S1526)
Philomelen Walzer *Op.82
  1.1.2.1. 2.2.1.0. timp,strings set
  KALMUS A5993 $17.00, perf mat
  rent   (S1527)
Rosen Ohne Dorne Walzer *Op.166
  1(pic).1.2.1. 2.2.1.0. timp,strings
  set KALMUS A5995 $18.00, perf mat
  rent   (S1528)
Saison Quadrille *Op.148
  1+pic.1.2.1. 2.2.1.0. timp,strings
  set KALMUS A5996 $12.00   (S1529)
Sang Viennois [arr.]
  (Silbert, A.) 2.2.2.2. 4.2.3.0.
  timp,perc,harp,strings [6']
  BILLAUDOT perf mat rent   (S1530)
Schwalben Walzer, Die *Op.208
  1+pic.1.2.1. 2.2.1.0. timp,strings
  set KALMUS A5997 $20.00, perf mat
  rent   (S1531)
Sorgenbrecher Walzer *Op.230
  1+pic.1.2.2. 2.2.1.0. timp,strings
  set KALMUS A5998 $24.00, perf mat
  rent   (S1532)
Wiener Carnevals Quadrille *Op.124
  1+pic.1.2.1. 2.2.1.0. timp,strings
  set KALMUS A5999 $12.00   (S1533)

STRAUSS, JOHANN, [JR.] (1825-1899)
Afrikanerin Quadrille, Die *Op.299
  1+pic.2.2.2. 4.2.3.1. timp,perc,
  strings KALMUS A6501 $15.00,
  perf mat rent   (S1534)
Albion Polka *Op.102
  (Durr, Johannes Martin) 1+
  pic.2.2.2. 4.4.1.0. timp,perc,
  strings DOBLINGER sc JSGA 1 6-14
  f.s., pts DM 1013 f.s.   (S1535)
Alexandrine Polka *Op.198
  1+pic.2.2.2. 4.2.1.1. timp,perc,
  strings set KALMUS A6502 $20.00,
  perf mat rent   (S1536)
An Der Moldau Polka *Op.366
  1+pic.1.2.2. 4.2.3.0. timp,perc,
  strings set KALMUS A6503 $13.00
                      (S1537)
An Der Wolga Polka *Op.425
  1.1.2.1. 2.2.1.0. perc,strings set
  KALMUS A6504 $12.00   (S1538)
Armen Ball Polka *Op.176
  1+pic.1.1+clar in D.1. 4.2.1.0.
  timp,perc,strings set KALMUS
  A6506 $10.00   (S1539)
Artist's Life
  see Kunstlerleben Walzer
Auf Zum Tanze *Op.436
  1+pic.1.2.2. 4.2.3.0. timp,perc,
  strings set KALMUS A6508 $14.00
                      (S1540)
Aus Den Bergen Walzer *Op.292
  1+pic.1.1+clar in E flat.2.
  4.2.1.1. timp,perc,strings set
  KALMUS A 6509 $13.00   (S1541)
Autograph Waltzes
  1+pic.1.2.1. 2.2.1.0. timp,perc,
  strings set KALMUS A6510 $13.00
                      (S1542)
Bal Champetre Quadrille *Op.303
  1+pic.1.2.2. 4.2.3.1. timp,perc,
  strings set KALMUS A6511 $13.00
                      (S1543)
Ball Geschichten Walzer *Op.150
  1+pic.2.2.2. 4.2.1.0. timp,perc,
  set KALMUS $20.00, perf mat rent
                      (S1544)
Ballstrausschen Polka *Op.380
  1+pic.2.2.2. 4.2.3.0. timp,perc,
  harp,strings set KALMUS A6513
  $14.00   (S1545)
Banditen Galopp Polka *Op.378
  1+pic.2.2.2. 4.2.3.0. timp,perc,
  strings set KALMUS A6514 $15.00,
  perf mat rent   (S1546)
Bauern Polka *Op.276
  1+pic.2.2.2. 4.2.1.0. timp,perc,
  strings,solo voice set KALMUS
  A6515 $15.00, perf mat rent

STRAUSS, JOHANN, [JR.] (cont'd.)
                      (S1547)
Beau Monde Quadrille, Le *Op.199
  1+pic.2.2.2. 4.2.1.1. timp,perc,
  strings,solo voice set KALMUS
  A6516 $14.00   (S1548)
Bei Uns Z'Haus *Op.361
  1+pic.2.2.2. 4.2.3.0. timp,perc,
  strings set KALMUS A6517 $25.00,
  perf mat rent   (S1549)
Berceuse, La *Op.194
  1+pic.2.2.2. 4.2.1.1. timp,perc,
  harp,strings set KALMUS A6518
  $13.00   (S1550)
Bijoux Polka *Op.242
  1+pic.2.1+clar in D.2. 4.2.1.0.
  timp,strings set KALMUS A6519
  $15.00, perf mat rent   (S1551)
Bitte Schön Polka *Op.372
  1+pic.2.2.2. 4.2.3.0. timp,perc,
  strings set KALMUS A6520 $14.00
                      (S1552)
Bluette Polka *Op.271
  1+pic.2.2.2. 4.2.1.0. timp,perc,
  strings set KALMUS A6521 $12.00
                      (S1553)
Blumenfest Polka *Op.111
  (Durr, Johannes Martin) 1+
  pic.2.2.2. 4.2.1.0. timp,perc,
  strings DOBLINGER sc JSGA 1 7-6
  f.s., pts DM 1011 f.s.   (S1554)
Brautschau Polka *Op.417
  1+pic.2.2.2. 4.2.3.0. timp,perc,
  strings set KALMUS A6522 $14.00
                      (S1555)
Burgersinn Walzer *Op.295
  1+pic.1.2.1. 4.2.1.1. timp,perc,
  strings set KALMUS A6523 $20.00,
  perf mat rent   (S1556)
Burgerweisen Walzer *Op.306
  (Racek, Fritz) 1+pic.2.2.2.
  4.2.1.1. timp,perc,harp,strings
  sc,pts DOBLINGER DM 880 f.s.
                      (S1557)
Burschenwanderung Polka *Op.389
  1+pic.1.2.1. 4.2.3.0. timp,perc,
  strings set KALMUS A6524 $12.00
                      (S1558)
Cagliostro Quadrille *Op.369
  1+pic.1.2.2. 4.2.3.0. timp,perc,
  strings set KALMUS A6526 $13.00
                      (S1559)
Camelien Polka *Op.248
  1+pic.2.2.2. 4.2.1.0. timp,perc,
  strings set KALMUS A6527 $12.00
                      (S1560)
  (Fuhrer, Rudolf) 1+pic.2.2.2.
  4.2.1.0. timp,perc,strings
  DOBLINGER sc JSGA 1 f.s., pts
  DM 1017 f.s.   (S1561)
Carneval In Rom: Ballettmusik
  (Schonherr) KALMUS A7456 pno-cond
  sc $7.00, set $50.00, pts $2.50,
  ea., perf mat rent   (S1562)
Carneval-Spektakel Quadrille *Op.152
  1+pic.1.1+clar in D.2. 4.2.1.1.
  timp,perc,strings set KALMUS
  A6530 $22.00, perf mat rent
                      (S1563)
Carnevals-Botschafter Walzer *Op.270
  1+pic.2.1+clar in E flat.2.
  4.2.1.0. timp,perc,strings set
  KALMUS A6529 $25.00, perf mat
  rent   (S1564)
Centennial Waltz
  1.0.2.0. 2.2.1.0. perc,strings set
  KALMUS A6531 $14.00   (S1565)
Champagne Party [arr.]
  (Stirn, D.) 2.2.2.2. 4.2.2.1. timp,
  perc,strings [31'] BOIS perf mat
  rent   (S1566)
Chansonnettes Quadrille *Op.259
  1+pic.2.2.2. 4.2.1.1. timp,perc,
  strings set KALMUS A6532 $22.00,
  perf mat rent   (S1567)
Colonnen Walzer *Op.262
  1+pic.2.2.2. 4.2.1.0. timp,strings
  set KALMUS A6533 $20.00, perf mat
  rent   (S1568)
Concurrenzen Walzer *Op.267
  1+pic.2.2.2. 4.2.1.0. timp,perc,
  strings set KALMUS A6534 $20.00,
  perf mat rent   (S1569)
Controversen Walzer *Op.191
  1+pic.2.2.2. 4.2.1.1. timp,perc,
  strings set KALMUS A6535 $25.00,
  perf mat rent   (S1570)
Cotillon Polka
  1+pic.2.2.2. 4.2.3.0. timp,perc,
  harp,harmonium,strings set KALMUS

STRAUSS, JOHANN, [JR.] (cont'd.)

A6536 $20.00, perf mat rent
                      (S1571)

Cycloiden Walzer *Op.207
  1+pic.2.1+clar in E flat.2.
  4.2.1.1. timp,perc,strings set
  KALMUS A6537 $22.00, perf mat
  rent   (S1572)

Cytheren Quadrille *Op.6
  1+pic.1.1+clar in E flat.2.
  2.2.1.0. timp,perc,strings set
  KALMUS A6538 $10.00   (S1573)

Demi Fortune Polka *Op.186
  1+pic.2.1+clar in E flat.2.
  4.2.1.0. timp,perc,strings set
  KALMUS A6539 $12.00   (S1574)

Demolirer Polka *Op.269
  1+pic.2.2.2. 4.2.1.0. timp,perc,
  strings set KALMUS A6540 $15.00,
  perf mat rent   (S1575)

Deutschmeister Jubiläums Marsch
  *Op.470
  (Dürr, J.M.) 1+pic.2.2.2. 4.2.3.0.
  perc,strings sc,pts DOBLINGER
  DM 1005 f.s.   (S1576)

Diabolin Polka *Op.244
  1+pic.2.2.2. 4.2.1.0. timp,perc,
  strings set KALMUS A6541 $15.00,
  perf mat rent   (S1577)

Dinorah Quadrille *Op.224
  1+pic.1.2.2. 4.2.1.1. timp,perc,
  strings set KALMUS A6542 $12.00
                    (S1578)

Ein Herz Ein Sinn *Op.323
  "One Heart, One Mind" 1+pic.2.2.2.
  4.3.3.1. timp,perc,harp,strings
  set KALMUS A6543 $20.00, perf mat
  rent   (S1579)
  (Racek, Fritz) 1+pic.2.2.2.
  4.3.3.1. timp,perc,harp,strings
  sc,pts DOBLINGER DM 868 f.s.
                    (S1580)

Elisen Polka *Op.151
  1+pic.1.2.1. 4.2.1.0. timp,strings
  set KALMUS A6544 $13.00 (S1581)

Entweder Oder Polka *Op.403
  1+pic.1.2.2. 4.2.3.0. timp,perc,
  strings set KALMUS A6545 $14.00
                    (S1582)

Erinnerung An Covent Garden Walzer
  *Op.329
  1+pic.2.2.2. 4.2.3.1. timp,perc,
  strings set KALMUS A6546 $23.00,
  perf mat rent   (S1583)

Ersten Curen Walzer, Die *Op.261
  1+pic.2.2.2. 4.2.1.0. timp,perc,
  strings set KALMUS A6547 $22.00,
  perf mat rent   (S1584)

Extravaganten Walzer, Die *Op.205
  1+pic.2.2.2. 4.2.1.1. timp,perc,
  harp,strings set KALMUS A6549
  $27.00, perf mat rent (S1585)

Fata Morgana *Op.330
  1+pic.2.2.2. 4.3.3.0. timp,perc,
  harp,strings set KALMUS A6550
  $17.00, perf mat rent (S1586)
  sc UNIVER. 17095 $15.00 (S1587)

Feemarchen Walzer *Op.312
  1+pic.2.2.2. 4.2.1.0. timp,perc,
  harp,strings set KALMUS 6551
  $22.00, perf mat rent (S1588)

Festival Quadrille *Op.341
  1+pic.2.2.2. 4.3.3.0. timp,perc,
  strings set KALMUS A6552 $15.00,
  perf mat rent   (S1589)

Feuilleton Walzer *Op.293
  (Racek, Fritz) 1+pic.2.2.2.
  4.2.1.1. timp,perc,strings sc,pts
  DOBLINGER DM 858 f.s. (S1590)

Figaro Polka *Op.320
  (Racek, Fritz) 1+pic.2.2.2.
  4.2.1.0. timp,perc,strings sc,pts
  DOBLINGER DM 867 f.s. (S1591)

Fledermaus, Die: Ballet Music And
  Finale
  (Schonherr) 2.2.2.2. 4.2.3.0. timp,
  perc,harp,strings [10'] KALMUS
  A7457 pno-cond sc $10.00, set
  $60.00, pts $2.50, ea., perf mat
  rent   (S1592)

Fledermaus Polka *Op.362
  (Fuhrer, Rudolf H.) 1+pic.2.2.2.
  4.2.3.0. timp,perc,strings
  DOBLINGER sc JSGA 1 23-7 f.s.,
  pts DM 1020 f.s.   (S1593)

Fledermaus Quadrille *Op.363
  (Fuhrer, Rudolf H.) 1+pic.2.2.2.
  4.2.3.0. timp,perc,strings

STRAUSS, JOHANN, [JR.] (cont'd.)

DOBLINGER sc JSGA 1 23-8 f.s.,
  pts DM 1021 f.s.   (S1594)

Flugschriften Walzer *Op.300
  1+pic.1.2.2. 4.2.2.0. timp,perc,
  harp,strings set KALMUS A6553
  $12.00   (S1595)

Frauen Kaferin *Op.99
  1+pic.1.1+clar in D.1. 4.2.1.0.
  timp,strings set KALMUS A6554
  $20.00, perf mat rent (S1596)

Freiwillige Vor! Marsch *Op.1
  1+pic.1.2.2. 4.2.3.0. timp,perc,
  strings KALMUS   (S1597)

Freut Euch Des Lebens Walzer *Op.340
  1+pic.2.2.2. 4.2.3.1. timp,harp,
  strings set KALMUS A6556 $28.00,
  perf mat rent   (S1598)
  (Racek, Fritz) 1+pic.2.0.0.
  4.2.3.1. timp,perc,harp,strings
  DOBLINGER sc JSGA 1 12-11 $22.40,
  pts DM 1014 f.s.   (S1599)

Frisch Heran Polka *Op.386
  1+pic.1.2.2. 4.2.3.0. timp,perc,
  strings set KALMUS A6557 $13.00
                    (S1600)

Fruhlingsstimmen Walzer *Op.410
  SONZOGNO perf mat rent (S1601)

Frühlingsstimmen Walzer, [arr.]
  (Zinn, William) "Voices Of Spring,
  [arr.]" string orch EXCELSIOR
  494-00443 $8.00   (S1602)

Furst Bariatinsky Marsch *Op.212
  1+pic.1.1+clar in E flat.2.
  4.2.1.1. perc,strings set KALMUS
  A6558 $12.00   (S1603)

Gartenlaube Walzer *Op.461
  (Durr, Johannes Martin)
  2(pic).2.2.2. 4.2.3.0. timp,perc,
  harp,strings DOBLINGER sc
  JSGA 1 29-17 f.s., pts DM 1016
  f.s.   (S1604)

Geschichten Aus Dem Wienerwald Walzer
  min sc MUZYKA f.s.   (S1605)

Geschichten Aus Dem Wienerwald
  Walzer, [arr.]
  (Zinn, William) "Tales From The
  Vienna Woods, [arr.]" string orch
  EXCELSIOR 494-00447 $8.00 (S1606)

Glucklich Ist, Wer Vergisst *Op.368
  1+pic.1.1+clar in D.2. 4.2.3.0.
  timp,perc,strings set KALMUS
  A6560 $14.00   (S1607)

Gross Wien Walzer *Op.440
  2(pic).2.2.2. 4.2.3.0. timp,perc,
  harp,strings set KALMUS A6561
  $25.00, perf mat rent (S1608)

Gypsy Baron, The: Overture, [arr.]
  see Zigeunerbaron, Der: Overture,
  [arr.]

Handels Elite Quadrille *Op.166
  1+pic.1.2.1. 4.2.1.1. timp,perc,
  strings set KALMUS A6562 $12.00
                    (S1609)

Haute Volee Polka *Op.155
  1+pic.1.1+clar in E flat.1.
  4.2.1.0. timp,perc,strings set
  KALMUS A6563 $12.00   (S1610)

Herzel Polka *Op.188
  1+pic.1.2.2. 4.2.3.0. timp,perc,
  strings set KALMUS A6564 $14.00
                    (S1611)

Hesperus Polka *Op.249
  1+pic.2.2.2. 4.2.1.0. timp,strings
  set KALMUS A6565 $12.00 (S1612)

Hinter Den Coulissen Quadrille
  (composed with Strauss, Josef)
  1+pic.2.2.2. 4.2.1.1. timp,perc,
  strings set KALMUS A6657 $13.00
                    (S1613)

Hoch Österreich Marsch *Op.371
  1+pic.2.1+clar in E flat.2.
  4.2.3.0. perc,strings set KALMUS
  A6566 $14.00   (S1614)

Hofball Quadrille *Op.116
  1+pic.1.2.1. 4.2.1.0. timp,perc,
  strings set KALMUS A6567 $12.00 (S1615)

Hofballtanze *Op.298
  1+pic.2.1+clar in E flat.2.
  4.3.2.1. timp,perc,harp,strings
  set KALMUS A6568 $22.00, perf mat
  rent   (S1616)

Idyllen Walzer *Op.95
  1+pic.1.1+clar in E flat.1.
  4.2.1.0. timp,perc,strings set
  KALMUS A6569 $20.00, perf mat

STRAUSS, JOHANN, [JR.] (cont'd.)

rent   (S1617)

Illustrationen Walzer *Op.331
  1+pic.2.1+clar in E flat.2.
  4.2.3.0. timp,perc,strings set
  KALMUS A6570 $28.00, perf mat
  rent   (S1618)
  sc UNIVER. 17076 $13.50 (S1619)

Im Krapfenwaldl *Op.336
  (Racek, Fritz) 1+pic.2.2.2.
  4.2.3.0. timp,perc,strings
  DOBLINGER sc JSGA 1 21-7 f.s.,
  pts DM 1019 f.s.   (S1620)

Immer Heiterer Walzer *Op.235
  1+pic.2.1+clar in D.2. 4.2.1.0.
  timp,strings set KALMUS A6571
  $12.00   (S1621)

Inconnue, L' Polka *Op.182
  1+pic.2.2.2. 4.2.1.0. timp,perc,
  strings set KALMUS A6595 $15.00
                    (S1622)

Indigo Marsch *Op.349
  1+pic.2.1+clar in E flat.2.
  4.2.3.1. perc,strings set KALMUS
  A6574 $13.00   (S1623)

Indigo Quadrille *Op.334
  1+pic.2.2.2. 4.2.3.0. timp,perc,
  strings set KALMUS A6575 $15.00,
  perf mat rent   (S1624)

Indigo Und Die Vierzig Rauber:
  Ballettmusik
  (Schonherr) KALMUS A7474 pno-cond
  sc $7.00, set $50.00, pts $2.50,
  ea., perf mat rent   (S1625)

I'Tipferl Polka *Op.377
  1+pic.2.2.2. 4.2.3.0. timp,perc,
  strings set KALMUS A6577 $15.00,
  perf mat rent   (S1626)

Johannis Kaferln Walzer *Op.82
  1+pic.2.2.2. 4.2.1.0. timp,perc,
  strings,solo voice set KALMUS
  A6578 $27.00, perf mat rent
                    (S1627)

Juristen-Ball Polka *Op.280
  1+pic.1.1+clar in D.1. 4.2.1.0.
  timp,perc,strings set KALMUS
  A6579 $15.00   (S1628)

Juxbruder Walzer *Op.208
  1+pic.2.2.2. 4.2.1.1. timp,perc,
  strings set KALMUS A6580 $20.00,
  perf mat rent   (S1629)

Kaiser-Walzer [arr.] *Op.437
  (Furst, Paul Walter) 13vla
  DOBLINGER   (S1630)

Kaiser Wilhelm Polonaise *Op.352
  1+pic.2.2.2. 4.2.3.0. timp,perc,
  strings set KALMUS A6581 $22.00,
  perf mat rent   (S1631)

Kennst Du Mich? Walzer *Op.381
  1+pic.1.2.2. 4.2.2.0. timp,perc,
  harp,strings set KALMUS A6582
  $25.00, perf mat rent (S1632)

Kinderspiele Polka *Op.304
  1+pic.2.2.2. 4.2.1.1. timp,perc,
  strings set KALMUS A 6583 $28.00,
  perf mat rent   (S1633)
  (Racek, Fritz) 1+pic.2.2.2.
  4.2.1.0. timp,perc,strings sc,pts
  DOBLINGER DM 951 f.s. (S1634)

Klugere Giebt Nach, Der: Polka
  *Op.401
  1+pic.1.2.2. 4.2.3.0. timp,perc,
  strings set KALMUS A6584 $18.00,
  perf mat rent   (S1635)

Königslieder Walzer *Op.334
  1+pic.2.2.2. 4.2.3.0. timp,perc,
  harp,strings set KALMUS A6585
  $22.00, perf mat rent (S1636)
  (Racek, Fritz) 1+pic.2.2.2.
  4.2.3.0. timp,perc,harp,strings
  DOBLINGER sc JSGA 1 21-5 f.s.,
  pts DM 1022 f.s.   (S1637)

Kriegers Liebchen Polka *Op.379
  1+pic.1.2.2. 2.2.1.0. perc,strings
  set KALMUS A6586 $12.00 (S1638)

Kronungsmarsch *Op.183
  1+pic.2.1+clar in E flat.2.
  4.2.1.1. perc,strings set KALMUS
  A6587 $15.00   (S1639)

Kunstler Quadrille *Op.201
  1+pic.2.2.2. 4.2.1.1. timp,perc,
  strings set KALMUS A6588 $18.00,
  perf mat rent   (S1640)

Kunstlerleben Walzer
  "Artist's Life" min sc KALMUS
  K01422 $4.00   (S1641)

STRAUSS, JOHANN, [JR.] (cont'd.)

Lebenswecker Walzer *Op.232
1+pic.2.2.2. 4.2.1.0. timp,harp,
strings set KALMUS A6589 $15.00
(S1642)

Leichtes Blut *Op.319
1+pic.2.2.2.3sax. 4.2.3.0. timp,
perc,harmonium,strings set KALMUS
A6590 $18.00, perf mat rent
(S1643)

Leitartickel, Die, Walzer *Op.273
1+pic.2.2.2. 4.2.1.1. timp,perc,
harp,strings set KALMUS A6591
$22.00, perf mat rent
(S1644)

Leopoldstadter Polka *Op.168
1+pic.2.2.2. 4.2.1.0. timp,perc,
strings set KALMUS 6592 $14.00
(S1645)

Libellen Walzer *Op.180
1+pic.2.1+clar in D.2. 4.2.1.0.
timp,perc,strings set KALMUS
A6593 $18.00, perf mat rent
(S1646)

Lieder Quadrille *Op.275
1+pic.2.2.2. 4.2.3.0. timp,perc,
strings set KALMUS A6594 $16.00,
perf mat rent
(S1647)

Lob Der Frauen *Op.315
1.2.2.2. 2.2.1.0. drums,strings set
KALMUS A6596 $12.00   (S1648)

Lockvogel *Op.118
1+pic.1.2.2. 4.2.1.0. timp,strings
set KALMUS A6597 $18.00, perf mat
rent   (S1649)

Louischen Polka *Op.339
(Racek, Fritz) 1+pic.2.2.2.
4.2.3.1. timp,perc,strings
DOBLINGER sc JSGA 1 21-10 f.s.,
pts DM 1018 f.s.   (S1650)

Lucifer Polka *Op.266
1+pic.2.2.2. 4.2.0.0. timp,perc,
strings set KALMUS A659B $14.00
(S1651)

Lust'ger Rath Polka *Op.350
1+pic.2.2.2. 4.2.3.0. timp,perc,
pno,strings set KALMUS A6599
$18.00   (S1652)

Lustige Kreig, Der, Quadrille
*Op.402
1+pic.2.2.2. 4.2.3.0. timp,perc,
strings set KALMUS A6600 $18.00,
perf mat rent   (S1653)

Man Lebt Nur Einmal Walzer *Op.167
1+pic.2.2.2. 4.2.1.1. timp,perc,
strings set KALMUS A6601 $20.00,
perf mat rent   (S1654)

Marchen Aus Dem Orient Walzer
*Op.444
1+pic.2.2.2. 4.2.3.0. timp,perc,
harp,strings set KALMUS A6602
$22.00, perf mat rent   (S1655)

Marie Taglioni Polka *Op.173
1+pic.1.2.2. 4.0.1.0. timp,perc,
strings set KALMUS A6603 $12.00
(S1656)

Maskenball Quadrille *Op.272
(Fuhrer, Rudolf H.) 1+pic.2.2.2.
4.2.3.0. timp,perc,strings
DOBLINGER sc JSGA 1 17-2 f.s.,
pts DM 1023 f.s.   (S1657)

Maskenzug Polka *Op.240
1+pic.2.1+clar in E flat.2.
2.2.1.0. timp,perc,strings set
KALMUS A6604 $14.00   (S1658)

Maxing Tanze Walzer *Op.79
1+pic.2.2.2. 4.2.1.0. timp,perc,
strings set KALMUS A6605 $16.00,
perf mat rent   (S1659)

Melodien Quadrille *Op.112
1+pic.2.1+clar in E flat.2.
4.2.1.1. timp,perc,strings set
KALMUS A6607 $15.00   (S1660)

Myrthen-Kranze Walzer *Op.154
1+pic.2.2.2. 4.2.1.1. timp,perc,
harp,strings set KALMUS A6609
$21.00, perf mat rent   (S1661)

Myrthenbluthen Walzer *Op.395
1+pic.2.2.2. 4.2.3.0. timp,perc,
harp,strings set KALMUS A6608
$20.00, perf mat rent   (S1662)

Nacht In Venedig, Eine: Selection
(Moses) "Night In Venice, A:
Selection" 1.1.2.1. 2.2.1.0.
perc,drums,strings set KALMUS A6613
$20.00, perf mat rent   (S1663)

Nachtfalter Walzer *Op.157
1+pic.1.2.2. 4.2.1.1. timp,strings
set KALMUS A6610 $17.00, perf mat
rent   (S1664)

STRAUSS, JOHANN, [JR.] (cont'd.)

Nachtigall Polka *Op.222
(Fuhrer, Rudolf H.) 1+pic.2.2.2.
4.2.1.0. perc,strings
DOBLINGER sc JSGA 1 13-13 f.s.,
pts DM 1024 f.s.   (S1665)

Neue Melodien Quadrille *Op.254
1+pic.2.2.2. 4.2.1.0. timp,perc,
strings set KALMUS A6611 $15.00
(S1666)

Neues Leben Polka *Op.278
1+pic.2.1+clar in E flat.2.
4.2.1.0. timp,perc,strings set
KALMUS A6612 $16.00   (S1667)

Newa Polka *Op.288
(Durr, Johannes Martin) 1+
pic.2.2.2. 4.2.1.1. timp,perc,
strings DOBLINGER sc JSGA 1 17-18
f.s., pts DM 1007 f.s.   (S1668)

Night In Venice, A: Selection
see Nacht In Venedig, Eine:
Selection

Nord Und Sud Polka *Op.405
1+pic.2.2.2. 4.2.3.0. timp,perc,
strings set KALMUS A6616 $13.00
(S1669)

Nordseebilder Walzer *Op.390
1+pic.2.2.2. 4.2.3.0. timp,perc,
harp,strings set KALMUS A6614
$20.00, perf mat rent   (S1670)

Nordstern Quadrille *Op.153
1+pic.2.2.2. 4.2.1.0. timp,perc,
strings set KALMUS A6615 $18.00,
perf mat rent   (S1671)

One Heart, One Mind
see Ein Herz Ein Sinn

Panacea Klange Walzer *Op.161
1+pic.2.1+clar in E flat.2.
4.2.1.1. timp,perc,strings set
KALMUS A6617 $20.00, perf mat
rent   (S1672)

Pappacoda Polka *Op.412
2(pic).2.2.2. 4.2.3.0. timp,perc,
strings set KALMUS A6618 $14.00
(S1673)

Pesther Csardas *Op.23
(Durr, Johannes Martin) 1+
pic.2.2.2. 2.2.1.0. timp,strings
DOBLINGER sc JSGA 1 2-6 f.s., pts
DM 1012 f.s.   (S1674)

Phanomene Walzer *Op.193
1+pic.2.2.2. 4.2.1.1. timp,perc,
harp,strings set KALMUS A6620
$20.00, perf mat rent   (S1675)

Postillon d'Amour *Op.317
(Racek, Fritz) 1+pic.2.2.2.
4.2.1.0. timp,perc,strings sc,pts
DOBLINGER DM 899 f.s.   (S1676)

Prince Methusalem: O Lovely May
see Prinz Methusalem: O Schöner Mai

Princesse De Trebizonde, La,
Quadrille *Op.40
1+pic.2.2.2. 4.2.3.0. timp,perc,
strings set KALMUS A6624 $18.00,
perf mat rent   (S1677)

Prinz Methusalem: O Schöner Mai
"Prince Methusalem: O Lovely May"
1+pic.2.2.2. 2.3.3.0. timp,perc,
strings set KALMUS A6622 $13.00
(S1678)

Prinz Methusalem: Overture
1.1.2.1. 2.2.1.0. drums,org,strings
set KALMUS A6621 $24.00   (S1679)

Prinz Methusalem: Selections
1.1.2.1. 2.2.1.0. perc,strings set
KALMUS A6623 $15.00   (S1680)

Promenade Quadrille *Op.98
1+pic.1.2.1. 4.2.1.0. timp,perc,
strings set KALMUS A6625 $11.00
(S1681)

Promotionen Walzer *Op.221
1+pic.2.2.2. 4.2.1.0. timp,perc,
harp,strings set KALMUS A6626
$21.00, perf mat rent   (S1682)

Publicisten, Die, Walzer *Op.321
1+pic.2.1+clar in D.2. 4.2.3.1.
timp,perc,strings set KALMUS
A6627 $24.00, perf mat rent
(S1683)

Quadrille Sur Des Airs Francaise
*Op.290
1+pic.2.2.2. 4.2.3.0. timp,perc,
strings set KALMUS A6628 $14.00
(S1684)

Rathausball Tanze Walzer *Op.438
2.2.2.2. 4.2.3.0. timp,perc,harp,
strings set KALMUS A6629 $23.00,
perf mat rent   (S1685)

STRAUSS, JOHANN, [JR.] (cont'd.)

Reitermarsch *Op.428
(Fuhrer, Rudolf H.) 1+pic.2.2.2.
4.2.3.0. perc,strings DOBLINGER
sc JSGA 1 27-6 f.s., pts DM 1025
f.s.   (S1686)

Ritter Pasman: Walzer
2(pic).2.2.2. 4.2.3.0. timp,perc,
harp,strings set KALMUS A5956
$24.00   (S1687)

Russischer Marsch Fantasie *Op.353
1+pic.2.2.2. 4.2.3.0. timp,perc,
harp,strings set KALMUS A6630
$15.00   (S1688)

Satanella Polka *Op.124
1+pic.2.2.2. 4.2.1.0. timp,strings
set KALMUS A6633 $10.00   (S1689)

Schwungrader Walzer *Op.223
(Durr, Johannes Martin) 1+
pic.2.2.2. 4.2.1.1. timp,perc,
strings DOBLINGER sc JSGA 1 13-14
f.s., pts DM 1006 f.s.   (S1690)

Secunden Polka *Op.258
1+pic.2.1+clar in E flat.2.
4.2.1.1. timp,perc,strings set
KALMUS A6634 $16.00   (S1691)
(Fuhrer, Rudolf H.) 1+pic.2.2.2.
4.2.1.1. timp,perc,strings
DOBLINGER sc JSGA 1 16-2 f.s.,
pts DM 1026 f.s.   (S1692)

Slovanka Quadrille *Op.338
1+pic.2.2.2. 4.2.3.1. timp,perc,
harp,strings set KALMUS A6636
$15.00   (S1693)

Spiralen Walzer *Op.209
1+pic.2.2.2. 4.2.1.1. timp,perc,
harp,strings set KALMUS A6637
$20.00, perf mat rent   (S1694)

Stadt Und Land Polka *Op.332
1+pic.2.2.2. 4.3.3.0. timp,perc,
strings set KALMUS A6640 $15.00
(S1695)
(Racek, Fritz) 1+pic.2.2.2.
4.3.3.0. timp,perc,strings sc,pts
DOBLINGER DM 857 f.s.   (S1696)

Sturmisch In Lieb Und Tanze *Op.393
1+pic.1.2.2. 4.2.3.0. timp,perc,
strings set KALMUS A6642 $14.00
(S1697)

Sympathie Polka *Op.246
1+pic.1.2.2. 4.2.1.0. timp,perc,
strings set KALMUS A6643 $12.00
(S1698)

Tales From The Vienna Woods, [arr.]
see Geschichten Aus Dem Wienerwald
Walzer, [arr.]

Tandelei. Polka-Mazurka *Op.310
(Racek, Fritz) 1+pic.2.2.2.
4.2.1.0. timp,perc,strings sc,pts
DOBLINGER DM 881 f.s.   (S1699)

Telegramme Walzer *Op.318
1+pic.2.2.2. 4.2.1.0. timp,strings
set KALMUS A6646 $23.00, perf mat
rent   (S1700)

Telegraphische Depeschen Walzer
*Op.195
1+pic.2.1+clar in E flat.2.
4.2.1.0. timp,perc,strings set
KALMUS A6645 $23.00, perf mat
rent   (S1701)
(Durr, Johannes Martin) 1+
pic.2.2.2. 4.4.1.1. timp,perc,
strings DOBLINGER sc JSGA 1 12-2
f.s., pts DM 1015 f.s.   (S1702)

Tritsch-Tratsch Polka *Op.214
SONZOGNO perf mat rent   (S1703)

Unter Donner Und Blitz *Op.324
SONZOGNO perf mat rent   (S1704)

Vaterlandischer Marsch (composed with
Strauss, Josef)
1+pic.2.1+clar in E flat.2.
2.4.1.0. perc,strings set KALMUS
A6659 $12.00   (S1705)

Verbruderungs Marsch *Op.287
(Durr, Johannes Martin) 1+
pic.2.2.2. 4.2.3.1. perc,strings
DOBLINGER sc JSGA 1 17-1 f.s.,
pts DM 1008 f.s.   (S1706)

Vergnugungszug [arr.] *Op.281
(Shostakovich, D.) 2.2.2.2.
4.2.3.0. timp,perc,strings [2']
SIKORSKI perf mat rent   (S1707)

Vibrationen Walzer *Op.204
1+pic.2.1+clar in E flat.2.
4.2.1.1. timp,perc,harp,strings
set KALMUS A6648 $23.00, perf mat
rent   (S1708)

STRAUSS, JOHANN, [JR.] (cont'd.)

Voices Of Spring, [arr.]
see Frühlingsstimmen Walzer, [arr.]

Von Der Börse *Op.337
sc UNIVER. 17100 $15.00 (S1709)

Wahlstimmen Walzer *Op.250
1+pic.2.2.2. 4.2.1.0. timp,perc,
harp,strings set KALMUS A6649
$15.00 (S1710)

Wahrsagerin, Die *Op.420
string orch KRENN (S1711)

Was Sich Liebt Neckt Sich *Op.399
1+pic.1.2.1. 4.2.3.0. timp,perc,
strings set KALMUS A6651 $14.00
(S1712)

Wein, Weib Und Gesang *Op.333
(Racek, F.) 2(pic).2.2.2. 4.2.3.0.
timp,perc,harp,strings sc,pts
DOBLINGER DM 1009 f.s. (S1713)

Where The Citrons Bloom
see Wo Die Zitronen Bluh'n

Wien, Mein Sinn Walzer *Op.192
1+pic.2.2.2. 4.2.1.1. timp,perc,
strings set KALMUS A6655 $20.00,
perf mat rent (S1714)

Wiener Bonbons Walzer *Op.307
1+pic.2.2.2. 4.2.3.0. timp,perc,
strings set KALMUS A6653 $23.00,
perf mat rent (S1715)

Wiener Chronik Walzer *Op.268
1+pic.2.2.2. 4.2.1.0. timp,perc,
strings set KALMUS A6654 $17.00,
perf mat rent (S1716)

Wiener Frauen Walzer *Op.423
(Durr, Johannes Martin)
2(pic).2.2.2. 4.2.3.0. timp,perc,
strings DOBLINGER sc JSGA 1 27-1
f.s., pts DM 1010 f.s. (S1717)

Windsor Klange Walzer *Op.104
1+pic.1.1+clar in E flat.1.
4.2.1.0. timp,harp,strings set
KALMUS A6656 $17.00, perf mat
rent (S1718)

Wo Die Zitronen Bluh'n *Op.364
"Where The Citrons Bloom"
2(pic).2.1+clar in D.2. 4.2.3.0.
timp,perc,harp,strings set KALMUS
A6652 $14.00 (S1719)

Zeitlose, Die. Polka *Op.302
(Racek, Fritz) 1+pic.2.2.2.
4.2.1.0. timp,perc,strings sc,pts
DOBLINGER DM 870 f.s. (S1720)

Zigeunerbaron, Der: Overture, [arr.]
(Zinn, William) "Gypsy Baron, The:
Overture, [arr.]" string orch
EXCELSIOR 494-00448 $8.00 (S1721)

STRAUSS, JOSEF (1827-1870)
Abendstern *Op.160
1+pic.1.1+clar in D.1. 4.2.1.1.
timp,perc,strings set KALMUS
A6660 $10.00 (S1722)

Actionen Walzer *Op.174
1+pic.2.2.2. 4.2.2.0. timp,perc,
strings set KALMUS A6661 $13.00
(S1723)

Amazonen Quadrille *Op.118
1+pic.2.2.2. 4.2.1.0. timp,perc,
strings set KALMUS A6662 $22.00,
perf mat rent (S1724)

Auf Ferienreisen *Op.133
2.2.2.2. 4.2.3.0. perc,strings [2']
set KALMUS A2114 $13.00 (S1725)

Aus Der Ferne *Op.270
1+pic.2.2.2. 4.3.3.0. timp,perc,
harp,strings set KALMUS A6664
$20.00, perf mat rent (S1726)

Blaubart Quadrille *Op.206
1+pic.2.1+clar in D.2. 4.2.1.0.
timp,perc,strings set KALMUS
A6665 $13.00 (S1727)

Brennende Liebe *Op.129
1+pic.2.2.2. 4.2.1.0. timp,perc,
harp,strings set KALMUS A6666
$13.00 (S1728)

Chatterbox Polka
see Plappermoulchen Polka

Consortien Walzer *Op.260
1+pic.2.2.2. 4.4.3.1. timp,perc,
strings set KALMUS A6667 $22.00,
perf mat rent (S1729)

Crispino Quadrille *Op.224
1+pic.2.1+clar in D.2. 4.4.3.1.
timp,perc,strings set KALMUS

STRAUSS, JOSEF (cont'd.)

A6668 $16.00 (S1730)

Debaradeurs Quadrille *Op.97
1+pic.2.2.2. 4.2.1.0. timp,perc,
strings set KALMUS A6669 $12.00
(S1731)

Deutsche Grusse Walzer *Op.191
1+pic.2.2.2. 4.2.1.1. perc,harp,
strings set KALMUS A6671 $20.00,
perf mat rent (S1732)

Disputationen Walzer *Op.243
1+pic.2.1+clar in E flat.2.
4.4.3.1. timp,perc,harp,strings
set KALMUS A6672 $26.00, perf mat
rent (S1733)

Dithyrambe *Op.236
1.2.2.2. 2.2.1.0. timp,perc,strings
set KALMUS A6673 $11.00 (S1734)

Elfen Polka *Op.74
1+pic.2.1+clar in E flat.2.
4.2.1.0. timp,perc,harp,strings
set KALMUS A6674 $11.00 (S1735)

Ernst Und Humor Walzer *Op.254
1+pic.2.1+clar in E flat.2.
4.4.3.1. timp,perc,harp,strings
set KALMUS A6675 $27.00, perf mat
rent (S1736)

Ersten Und Die Letzten, Die *Op.1
(Mailer, Franz; Fuhrer, Rudolf) 1+
pic.1.2.1. 3.2.3.0. timp,perc,
strings DOBLINGER perf mat rent
(S1737)

Frauenherz *Op.166
1.1.2.1. 2.2.1.0. drums,strings set
KALMUS A6677 $12.00 (S1738)

Frauenwurde Walzer *Op.277
1+pic.2.1+clar in E flat.2.
4.3.3.1. timp,perc,harp,strings
set KALMUS A6678 $25.00, perf mat
rent (S1739)

Friedenspalmen Walzer *Op.207
1+pic.2.1+clar in E flat.2.
4.2.1.0. timp,perc,harp,strings
set KALMUS A6679 $20.00, perf mat
rent (S1740)

Frohes Leben Walzer *Op.272
1+pic.2.2.2. 4.4.3.1. timp,perc,
harp,strings set KALMUS A6680
$25.00, perf mat rent (S1741)

Gablenz Marsch *Op.159
1+pic.2.1+clar in E flat.2.
4.2.1.0. timp,perc,strings set
KALMUS A6681 $12.00 (S1742)

Gazelle, Die *Op.155
1+pic.1.2.2. 4.2.1.0. timp,perc,
strings set KALMUS A6682 $12.00
(S1743)

Gedenkblatter Walzer *Op.178
1+pic.2.1+clar in E flat.2.
4.2.1.1. timp,perc,harp,strings
set KALMUS A6683 $22.00, perf mat
rent (S1744)

Genovefa Quadrille *Op.246
1+pic.2.1+clar in E flat.2.
4.4.3.1. timp,perc,harp,strings
set KALMUS A6684 $25.00, perf mat
rent (S1745)

Herbstrosen Walzer *Op.232
1+pic.2.2.2. 4.2.1.1. timp,perc,
harp,strings set KALMUS A6685
$22.00, perf mat rent (S1746)

Hochzeitsklange Walzer *Op.242
1+pic.2.1+clar in E flat.2.
4.4.3.1. timp,perc,harp,strings
set KALMUS A6686 $25.00, perf mat
rent (S1747)

Kakudu Quadrille *Op.276
1+pic.2.2.2. 4.3.3.1. timp,perc,
strings set KALMUS A6689 $15.00
(S1748)

Kronungslieder Walzer *Op.226
1+pic.2.2.2. 4.2.1.0. timp,perc,
harp,strings set KALMUS A6690
$25.00, perf mat rent (S1749)

Kunstler Caprice *Op.135
1+pic.2.2.2. 4.2.1.0. timp,perc,
strings set KALMUS A6691 $15.00
(S1750)

Lieb Und Wein Polka *Op.122
1+pic.2.1+clar in D.2. 4.2.1.0.
timp,perc,harp,strings set KALMUS
A6692 $12.00 (S1751)

Marienklange Walzer *Op.214
1+pic.2.1+clar in D.2. 4.2.1.0.
timp,perc,harp,strings set KALMUS
6693 $20.00, perf mat rent
(S1752)

STRAUSS, JOSEF (cont'd.)

Mein Lebenslauf Ist Lieb Und Lust
*Op.263
1+pic.2.2.2. 4.4.3.1. timp,perc,
harp,strings set KALMUS A6694
$20.00, perf mat rent (S1753)

Nachtschatten *Op.229
1+pic.2.2.2. 4.4.3.1. timp,perc,
harp,strings set KALMUS A6696
$15.00 (S1754)

Nilfluthen Walzer *Op.275
1+pic.2.1+clar in E flat.2.
4.4.3.1. timp,perc,harp,strings
set KALMUS A6697 $15.00 (S1755)

Parade Quadrille *Op.45
1+pic.2.1+clar in D.2. 4.2.1.1.
timp,perc,harp,strings set KALMUS
A6699 $14.00 (S1756)

Pauline Polka
1+pic.2.1+clar in D.2. 4.2.1.0.
timp,perc,harp,strings set KALMUS
A6700 $15.00 (S1757)

Plappermoulchen Polka *Op.245
"Chatterbox Polka" 1+pic.2.2.2.
4.3.3.1. timp,perc,harmonium,
strings,vln solo set KALMUS A6701
$20.00, perf mat rent (S1758)

Schwatzerin, Die *Op.144
1+pic.2.1+clar in D.2. 4.2.1.0.
timp,perc,strings set KALMUS
A6702 $12.00 (S1759)

Sofien Quadrille *Op.137
1+pic.2.2.2. 4.2.1.0. timp,perc,
strings set KALMUS A6703 $12.00
(S1760)

Spinnerin, Die *Op.192
1+pic.2.1+clar in D.2. 4.2.1.0.
timp,perc,strings set KALMUS
A6704 $15.00 (S1761)

Studententraume Walzer *Op.222
1+pic.2.1+clar in E flat.2.
4.2.1.0. timp,perc,harp,strings
set KALMUS A6705 $22.00, perf mat
rent (S1762)

Tanz Prioritaten Walzer *Op.280
1+pic.2.2+clar in D.2. 4.3.3.1.
timp,perc,harp,strings set KALMUS
A6706 $35.00, perf mat rent
(S1763)

Tanzadressen Walzer *Op.234
1+pic.2.2.2. 4.4.3.1. timp,perc,
harp,strings set KALMUS A6706
$25.00, perf mat rent (S1764)

Theatre Quadrille *Op.213
1+pic.2.2.2. 4.2.1.0. timp,perc,
strings set KALMUS A6708 $12.00
(S1765)

Transactionen *Op.184
1+pic.2.1+clar in D.2. 4.2.1.0.
timp,perc,harp,strings set KALMUS
A6709 $20.00, perf mat rent
(S1766)

Verliebte Augen *Op.185
1+pic.2.1+clar in E flat.2.
4.2.1.0. timp,perc,strings set
KALMUS A6710 $12.00 (S1767)

Victoria Polka *Op.228
1+pic.2.2.2. 4.2.1.0. timp,perc,
strings set KALMUS A6711 $12.00
(S1768)

Vorwarts *Op.127
1+pic.2.2.2. 4.2.1.0. timp,perc,
strings set KALMUS A6713 $12.00
(S1769)

Wallonen Marsch [arr.] *Op.41
(Waldenmaier, A.P.) 2.2.2.2.
4.3.3.0. timp,perc,strings [4']
ORLANDO perf mat rent (S1770)

Wiener Fresken Walzer *Op.249
1+pic.2.2.2. 4.4.3.1. timp,perc,
harp,strings set KALMUS A6714
$24.00 (S1771)

Wiener Kinder Walzer *Op.61
1+pic.2.1+clar in E flat.2.
4.2.1.1. timp,strings set KALMUS
A6715 $20.00 (S1772)

Wiener Stimmen Walzer *Op.239
1+pic.1.2.2. 4.4.3.1. timp,perc,
harp,strings set KALMUS A6716
$15.00 (S1773)

STRAUSS, RICHARD (1864-1949)
Alpensinfonie, Eine [arr.] *Op.64
(Lessing, G.E.) 3(pic).3(English
horn).4(bass clar).3(contrabsn).
6(4Wagner tuba).4.3.1. timp,
3perc,2harp,cel,org,strings
LEUCKART perf mat rent (S1774)

STRAUSS, RICHARD (cont'd.)

Divertimento, Op. 86
min sc KALMUS K01522 $11.50 (S1775)

Feierlicher Einzug
"Solemn Entrance" KALMUS A6130 sc
$5.00, set $15.00, perf mat rent
(S1776)

Festliches Praeludium *Op.61
KALMUS A7195 sc $20.00, set $75.00,
pts $2.00, ea., perf mat rent
(S1777)

Feuersnot: Love Scene
see Feuersnot, Op. 50: Liebesszene

Feuersnot, Op. 50: Liebesszene
"Feuersnot: Love Scene" KALMUS
A5728 sc $12.00, set $30.00, perf
mat rent (S1778)

Heldenleben, Ein [arr.] *Op.40
(Lessing, G.E.) 3(pic).3(English
horn).4(bass clar).3(contrabsn).
6.4.3.2. timp,4perc,harp,strings
LEUCKART perf mat rent (S1779)

Konigsmarsch
KALMUS A6132 sc $8.00, set $30.00,
perf mat rent (S1780)

Konzertouverture In C Minor [13']
2.2.2.2. 4.2.3.1. timp,strings
SCHOTTS perf mat rent (S1781)

Macbeth *Op.23
min sc KALMUS K01514 $8.50 (S1782)

Romance for Violoncello and Orchestra
in F [12']
2.2.2.2. 2.0.0.0. strings,vcl
solo
SCHOTTS perf mat rent (S1783)

Rosenkavalier, Der, Op. 59: Closing
Duet-Ist Ein Traum, For Solo
Voices And Orchestra
KALMUS A 6308 sc $5.00, set $15.00,
pts $1.00, ea., perf mat rent
(S1784)

Rosenkavalier, Der, Op. 59: Entry Of
The Rosenkavalier- Mir Est Die
Ehre, For Solo Voices And
Orchestra
KALMUS A6306 sc $8.00, set $25.00,
pts $2.00, ea., perf mat rent
(S1785)

Rosenkavalier, Der, Op. 59: Monologue
Of The Marschallin- Kann Ich Mich
Auch An Ein Madel Erinnern, For
Solo Voice And Orchestra
KALMUS A6305 sc $4.00, set $15.00,
pts $1.00, ea., perf mat rent
(S1786)

Rosenkavalier, Der, Op. 59: Suite
[arr.]
(Naumbat) 2.2.2.2. 4.2.3.0.
euphonium,timp,perc,strings [20']
KALMUS A6389 pno-cond sc $8.00,
set $40.00, pts $2.00, ea., perf
mat rent (S1787)

Rosenkavalier, Der, Op. 59: Trio-
Hab's Mir Gelobt, For Solo Voices
And Orchestra
KALMUS A6307 sc $3.00, set $15.00,
pts $1.00, ea., perf mat rent
(S1788)

Rosenkavalier, Der, Op. 59: Waltzes
[arr.]
(Singer; Doebber) 2(pic).2.2.2.
4.2.3.0. timp,perc,harp,strings
[8'] KALMUS A6394 pno-cond sc
$5.00, set $22.00, pts $1.00,
ea., perf mat rent (S1789)

Salome Fantasy [arr.]
(Doebber) 2(pic).2(English
horn).2.2+contrabsn. 4.3.3.1.
timp,perc,harp,strings [10']
KALMUS A7276 sc $35.00, set
$60.00, pts $2.50, ea., perf mat
rent (S1790)

Solemn Entrance
see Feierlicher Einzug

Symphony For Strings[arr.] (from
String Quartet, Op. 2)
(Drew) string orch [30'] KALMUS
A6350 sc $18.00, set $17.00, pts
$3.50, ea., perf mat rent (S1791)

Symphony, Op. 12, in F minor
min sc KALMUS K01486 $23.00 (S1792)

STRAVINSKY, IGOR (1882-1971)
Capriccio for Piano and Orchestra
min sc KALMUS K01524 $14.25 (S1793)

Capriccio For Piano And Orchestra
(1929 Version) [18']
2+pic.2+English horn.2+bass
clar.2. 4.2.3.1. timp,string
quar,pno solo
KALMUS A5627 sc $40.00, perf mat

STRAVINSKY, IGOR (cont'd.)

rent, set $75.00, pts $2.50, ea.
(S1794)

Concerto for Violin and Orchestra in
D
min sc EULENBURG EU01815 f.s.
(S1795)

Faune Et La Bergere, Le, For Solo
Voice And Orchestra *Op.2
min sc KALMUS K01518 $6.00 (S1796)

Firebird
sc DOVER 255352 $8.95 (S1797)
"Oiseau De Feu, L'" fac ed MINKOFF
f.s. (S1798)

Fireworks
min sc EULENBURG EU01396 $4.95
(S1799)

Four Etudes *CCU
min sc KALMUS K01490 $6.00 (S1800)

Oiseau De Feu, L'
see Firebird

Petrouchka
min sc KALMUS K00079 $11.50 (S1801)
sc DOVER 256804 $8.95 (S1802)

Rite Of Spring
see Sacre Du Printemps, Le

Sacre Du Printemps, Le
"Rite Of Spring" sc DOVER 258572
$8.95 (S1803)

Sacre Du Printemps, Le: Danse Sacrale
[4'30"]
3(pic)+alto fl.4+English horn.3+
clar in E flat+bass clar.4+
contrabsn. 8.4.4.2. timp,perc,
strings
min sc BOOSEY 936 $6.50 (S1804)

Suite No. 2
min sc KALMUS K01488 $4.00 (S1805)

Symphony in C
min sc EULENBURG EU01511 $11.75
(S1806)

Symphony In Three Movements
min sc EULENBURG EU00574 $9.75
(S1807)

Symphony No. 1, Op. 13, in E flat
min sc KALMUS K01487 $14.25 (S1808)

STREET, TISON (1943-   )
Adagio for Oboe and String Orchestra
in E flat [15']
string orch,ob solo
AMP perf mat rent (S1809)

Montsalvat [10']
2.2.2+clar in A.2. 2.2.2(bass
trom).0. timp,perc,harp,strings
AMP perf mat rent (S1810)

Variations On A Ground, For Organ And
Orchestra [28']
2+pic.2(English horn).2(bass
clar).2+contrabsn. 0.3.3.1.
timp,3perc,strings,org solo
AMP perf mat rent (S1811)

STREET MUSIC see Russo, William Joseph

STREET URCHIN, THE, FOR FLUGELHORN AND
ORCHESTRA see Grove, Richard,
Gamino, El, For Flugelhorn And
Orchestra

STREETCAR NAMED DESIRE, A see North,
Alex

STREGHE, LE, FOR VIOLIN AND ORCHESTRA
see Paganini, Niccolo

STREICHER, F.
Mickymausparade
1.2.2.1. 4.2.3.0. perc,xylo,harp,
strings
KRENN f.s. (S1812)

STREICHERFANTASIEN ZU EINEM MOTIV VON
J.S. BACH see Beyer, Frank Michael

STRIETMAN, WILLEM (1918-   )
Musiquettes III, For Accordion And
String Orchestra [13']
string orch,acord solo
DONEMUS perf mat rent (S1813)

Toamna, For Pan-Flute And Orchestra
[10']
2.2.2.2.alto sax. 2.1.1.0. 2perc,
harp,cel,14vla,4vcl,db,
pan-flute solo
sc DONEMUS f.s., perf mat rent
(S1814)

STRIKE UP THE BAND [ARR.] see Gershwin,
George

STRING PIECE see Boone, Charles N.

STRING PLAY see Penherski, Zbigniew

STRING SYMPHONY see Bäck, Sven-Erik see
Ju, Xiao-Song

STRING THING, A see Fleming, Robert

STRINGENDO see Eder de Lastra, Erich

STRINGS FOR GUITAR AND STRINGS see
Constant, Marius

STRINGS FOR HARPSICHORD AND STRINGS see
Constant, Marius

STRINGS IN THE EARTH see Sikorski,
Tomasz, Struny W Ziemi

STRINGS 'N' THINGS see Reed, Alfred

STRMCNIK, MAKSIMILJAN (1948-   )
Simfonicne Metamorfoze [25']
2(pic).2(English horn).2(bass
clar).2(contrabsn). 4.3.3.1.
timp,perc,harp,pno,cel,org,
strings
"Symphonic Metamorphoses" DRUSTVO
DSS 1077 perf mat rent (S1815)

Symphonic Metamorphoses
see Simfonicne Metamorfoze

STROBL, OTTO (1927-   )
Concerto for Bass Trombone and
Orchestra [20']
1.2.2.1. 2.2.0.0. timp,strings,
bass trom solo
DOBLINGER perf mat rent (S1816)

Poems, For Alto Saxophone And
Orchestra [12']
strings,harp,alto sax solo
DOBLINGER perf mat rent (S1817)

STROE, AUREL (1932-   )
Arcades [9']
3pic,2fl,clar in E flat,2clar,
2contrabsn,4sax,2db tuba,2perc,
2vibra,2cel,org,elec org,Ondes
Martenot,pno,harp,strings, 6
Saxhorns, Ondioline
SALABERT perf mat rent (S1818)

Canto I [7']
3(pic).2.3+bass clar.1+
contrabsn.tenor sax. 2.3.2.2.
2elec org,strings
SALABERT perf mat rent (S1819)

Canto II [9']
3(pic).2.3.1+contrabsn. 3.3.3.2.
2Ondes Martenot,elec org,
strings
SALABERT perf mat rent (S1820)

Concerto for Clarinet and Orchestra
[25']
3trp,3trom,3perc,strings,clar
solo
SALABERT perf mat rent (S1821)

Laudes I [9']
28strings
SALABERT perf mat rent (S1822)

Laudes II [10']
2+2pic.2.3.2+contrabsn. 0.0.4.2.
3perc,2elec org,2Ondes
Martenot,strings
SALABERT perf mat rent (S1823)

STROHKOFFER, FOR VIOLIN AND CHAMBER
ORCHESTRA [ARR.] see Kont, Paul

STROM, ALF GOTLIN (1922-   )
Aftenvinden
1.0.2.0. 0.1.1.0. pno,strings
NORGE (S1824)

I De Tunge Tider: Ouverture
2.1.2.2. 2.3.2.1. timp,strings
NORGE (S1825)

Meditation
string orch
NORGE (S1826)

STROMAN, SCOTT
Earth's Sketches, For Solo Voice,
Violin And Strings [20']
strings,vln solo,solo voice
STAINER AC46 f.s. (S1827)

STRÖMHOLM, FOLKE (1941-   )
Concertino for Piano and String
Orchestra, Op. 1 [14']
string orch,pno solo
NORGE (S1828)

Concerto for Piano and Orchestra, Op.
12 [9']
1.0.1.1. 1.1.1.0. strings,pno
solo
NORGE (S1829)

STRÖMHOLM, FOLKE (cont'd.)

In Memoriam Alban Berg *Op.9b [6']
2.2.2.2. 2.2.2.1. timp,strings
NORGE   (S1830)

Lappish Overture
see Samisk Ouverture

Samisk Ouverture *Op.20 [10']
1.1.1.1. 2.1.1.0. perc,strings
"Lappish Overture" NORGE   (S1831)

Syntaks, For Solo Voice And Orchestra
*Op.14 [18']
2.2.2.2. 4.3.3.1. timp,perc,harp,
strings,B solo
"Syntax, For Solo Voice And
Orchestra" NORGE   (S1832)

Syntax, For Solo Voice And Orchestra
see Syntaks, For Solo Voice And
Orchestra

STROPHES see Casanova, André

STROPPA, MARCO (1959-   )
Metabolai [10'15"]
2.2.2.2. 2.2.0.0. timp,pno,
strings
RICORDI-IT 133531 perf mat rent
(S1833)

STROUSE, CHARLES LOUIS (1928-   )
Ditto [3']
2.2.2.2. 2.2.2.0. timp,perc,harp,
pno,strings
MCA perf mat rent   (S1834)

STRUCTURE II, FOR VIOLIN AND ORCHESTRA
see Ágústsson, Herbert Hriberschek

STRUNY W ZIEMI see Sikorski, Tomasz

STRUT see Daugherty, Michael

STRUTTURE see Bettinelli, Bruno

STRYCHNINE LADY, THE see Christou, Jani

STRYGA see Jazwinski, Barbara

STUCKY, STEVEN EDWARD (1949-   )
Concerto for Orchestra [28']
3(pic,alto fl).3(English
horn).3(bass
clar).3(contrabsn). 4.4.3.1.
timp,3perc,harp,pno&cel,strings
MERION perf mat rent   (S1835)

Concerto for Violin, Oboe and Chamber
Orchestra [18']
perc,pno,strings,vln solo,ob&ob
d'amore solo
MERION perf mat rent   (S1836)

Dreamwaltzes [15']
3(2pic).3(English horn).3(bass
clar).2+contrabsn. 4.4.3.1.
timp,3perc,harp,pno&cel,strings
MERION perf mat rent   (S1837)

Kenningar (Symphony No. 4) [21']
3.3.3.3. 4.4.3.1. 5perc,harp,pno,
cel,strings
sc MERION $24.45, perf mat rent
(S1838)
Son Et Lumiere
MERION perf mat rent   (S1839)

Symphony No. 4
see Kenningar

Transparent Things: In Memoriam VN
[8']
3.2.2.2. 4.3.3.1. 3perc,pno,cel,
strings
sc MERION $21.35, perf mat rent
(S1840)
STUDENT PRINCE, THE: SELECTIONS, [ARR.]
see Romberg, Sigmund

STUDENT PRINCE, THE: SERENADE, FOR SOLO
VOICE AND ORCHESTRA, [ARR.] see
Romberg, Sigmund

STUDENTEN see Kazhlayev, Murad,
Gorianka: Suite

STUDENTENBALL-TANZE WALZER see Strauss,
Eduard

STUDENTENTRAUME WALZER see Strauss,
Josef

STUDI PER UN DIES IRAE see Gentilucci,
Armando

STUDIE OVER EIN SALMETONE FRA LUSTER
see Åm, Magnar

STUDIEN see Eröd, Ivan

STUDY OF SHADE, A see Szymanski, Pawel

STUDY ON A NORWEGIAN HYMN see Åm,
Magnar, Studie Over Ein Salmetone
Fra Luster

STUFEN see Gubaidulina, Sofia, Stages,
The

STUHEC, IGOR (1932-   )
Ction [6']
1.0.1.0. 1.1.1.0. perc,harp,pno,
vln,vcl,db
DRUSTVO DSS 694 perf mat rent
(S1841)
Entuziazmi Gama [14']
3(pic).2(English horn).2(soprano
clar in E flat,bass
clar).2(contrabsn). 4.3.3.1.
timp,perc,harp,pno,hpsd,cel,
strings
DRUSTVO DSS 905 perf mat rent
(S1842)
STUNDE DER SEELE see Gubaidulina, Sofia

STUNDE DER SEELE, FOR PERCUSSION, SOLO
VOICE AND ORCHESTRA see
Gubaidulina, Sofia, Hour Of The
Soul, For Percussion, Solo Voice
And Orchestra

STUPPNER, HUBERT (1944-   )
Capriccio Viennese, For Violin And
Orchestra [18']
2.2.2.2. 4.2.2.0. 2perc,harp,cel,
strings,vln solo
RICORDI-GER SY 2439 perf mat rent
(S1843)
Concerto for Piano and Orchestra, No.
1 [25']
2.2.2.2. 4.2.2.0. 2perc,harp,cel,
strings,pno solo
RICORDI-GER SY 2426 perf mat rent
(S1844)
Concerto for Piano and Orchestra, No.
2 [28']
2.2.2.2. 4.2.2.1. timp,2perc,
harp,cel,strings,pno solo
RICORDI-GER SY 3015 perf mat rent
(S1845)
Kammerkonzert "Souvenir" [25']
2.2.2.2. 2.0.0.0. 2perc,cel,harp,
strings
RICORDI-GER SY 2387 perf mat rent
(S1846)
Kammersymphonie [23']
2.2.2.2. 2.2.0.0. perc,harp,
strings
RICORDI-GER SY 3027 perf mat rent
(S1847)
Symphony No. 1 [35']
4.4.4+bass clar.3+contrabsn.
8.6.4.3. timp,3-4perc,harp,cel,
strings
RICORDI-GER SY 3001 perf mat rent
(S1848)
Tanz-Suite III [20']
1.1.1.1. 1.1.1.0. perc,harp,
strings
RICORDI-GER SY 3003 perf mat rent
(S1849)
Valse-Caprice [15']
3.3.3.3. 4.3.2.1. timp,3perc,cel,
harp,strings
RICORDI-GER SY 2454 perf mat rent
(S1850)
STURM, DER see Weingartner, (Paul)
Felix von

STURM, DER, FOR SOLO VOICE AND
ORCHESTRA see Banfield, Raffaello
de

STURMISCH IN LIEB UND TANZE see
Strauss, Johann, [Jr.]

STURZENEGGER, RICHARD (1905-1976)
Drei Gesänge Davids, For Violin And
String Orchestra
"Three Songs Of David, For Violin
And String Orchestra" sc KUNZEL
10110 $33.00   (S1851)

Three Songs Of David, For Violin And
String Orchestra
see Drei Gesänge Davids, For Violin
And String Orchestra

STYR, FOR PIANO AND CHAMBER ORCHESTRA
see Thorarinsson, Leifur

SU, CONG (1957-   )
Anbruch Des Tages, Der [11']
2.2.2.2. 4.2.3.1. timp,perc,
strings
PETERS   (S1852)

Concert Overture [14']
2.2.2.2. 4.2.3.1. 3perc,harp,
strings
PETERS   (S1853)

SU FRAMMENTI DI PEIRE VIDAL, FOR SOLO
VOICE AND ORCHESTRA see Togni,
Camillo

SU LE SPONDE DEL TEBRO, FOR SOLO VOICE
AND ORCHESTRA see Scarlatti,
Alessandro

SUBEN, JOEL ERIC (1946-   )
Academic Overture [5']
3.2.2.2. 2.3.0.0. timp,perc,
strings
sc AM.COMP.AL. $44.40, perf mat
rent   (S1854)
Concerto for Piano and Orchestra
[17']
3(pic,alto fl).2+English horn.2+
bass clar.2+contrabsn.alto sax.
4.3.3.1. 3perc,harp,strings
sc APNM $39.50, perf mat rent
(S1855)
Fantasia Su Un Soggetto Cavato [4']
1.0.1.1.alto sax. 1.1.1.1. perc,
harp,pno,strings
sc AM.COMP.AL. $13.80   (S1856)
Serenade [9']
alto fl,English horn,bass clar,
horn,trom,tuba,perc,harp,pno,
vla,vcl,db
sc APNM $19.75, perf mat rent
(S1857)
Traeume Auf Dicterhoehe, For Horn And
String Orchestra [6']
string orch,horn solo
sc APNM $7.75, perf mat rent
(S1858)
Verses Of Mourning [8']
2.2.2.2. 2.2.1.1. timp,perc,pno,
strings
sc AM.COMP.AL. $16.75   (S1859)

SUBLIMATIONEN see Ekimovsky, Viktor

SUBMERGED MUSIC, FOR SOLO VOICE, VIOLIN
AND STRINGS see Hatrik, Juraj,
Ponorena Hudba, For Solo Voice,
Violin And Strings

SUBSIDENCES INTO SILENCE see Vantus,
Istvan

SUCCARI, DIA
Etincelle Du Silex, L'
JOBERT   (S1860)

Splendeurs Oubliees
JOBERT   (S1861)

SUCCESSIF-SIMULTANE, FOR 12 SOLO
STRINGS see Guezec, Jean-Pierre

SUCH A DAY OF SWEETNESS, FOR SOLO VOICE
AND ORCHESTRA see Vlijmen, Jan van

SUDDEN RAINBOW, A see Schwantner,
Joseph

SUDER, JOSEPH (1892-1980)
Suite Alter Art
string orch
"Suite In Old Style" sc,pts AMADEUS
BP 417 f.s.   (S1862)

Suite In Old Style
see Suite Alter Art

SUERTE DE VARAS see Riviere, Pablo

SUFFOLK PUNCH see Wood, Gareth

SUFFRAGETTE, FOR PIANO AND ORCHESTRA
see Kvam, Oddvar S.

SUGAR, REZSÖ (1919-   )
Pastorale E Rondo
3.2.2.2. 4.2.3.0. timp,perc,pno,
strings
sc EMB 8873 f.s.   (S1863)

SUITA DRAMMATICA see Bohác, Josef

SUITA Z GOLDBERGOVSKYCH VARIACII see
Krak, Egon

SUITE A JEAN HURE see Casella, Alfredo

SUITE AFRICAINE see Lacome, Paul (-
Jean-Jacques)

SUITE ALTER ART see Suder, Joseph

SUITE ANTIQUE, FOR 2 VIOLINS AND
CHAMBER ORCHESTRA see Stoessel,
Albert

SUITE ANTIQUE, FOR FLUTE AND STRING
ORCHESTRA see Rutter, John

SUITE BRETONNE see Brucken-Fock, Gerard
H.G. von

SUITE CARACTERISTIQUE see Gaathaug,
Morten see Sibelius, Jean

SUITE CHEVALERESQUE see Gaathaug,
Morten

SUITE CONCERTANTE, FOR OBOE AND CHAMBER ORCHESTRA see Damase, Jean-Michel

SUITE CONCERTANTE, FOR SAXOPHONE AND STRING ORCHESTRA see Dakin, Charles

SUITE CONCERTANTE, FOR VIOLIN AND ORCHESTRA see Kahn, Erich Itor

SUITE CONCERTANTE, FOR WOODWIND QUINTET, PERCUSSION AND ORCHESTRA see DuBois, Pierre-Max

SUITE DANS LE STYLE ANCIEN see Magnard, Alberic

SUITE DE BALLET see Holst, Gustav

SUITE DE DANSES, FOR TRUMPET AND STRING ORCHESTRA see Fischer, Johann Caspar Ferdinand

SUITE DE DANSES ET DE CHANSONS, FOR HARPSICHORD AND ORCHESTRA see Krauze, Zygmunt

SUITE DEL SUR, FOR GUITAR AND CHAMBER ORCHESTRA see Morel, Jorge

SUITE EN BLANC [ARR.] see Lalo, Edouard

SUITE ESPANOLA [ARR.] see Albéniz, Isaac

SUITE FANTASTIQUE see Foulds, John Herbert

SUITE FOR BAMBOO FLUTE ENSEMBLE AND STRING ORCHESTRA see Bonsel, Adriaan

SUITE FOR JAZZ-QUARTET AND STRING ORCHESTRA see Garbarek, Jan

SUITE FOR ORCHESTRA: SONGS OF HOME see Broadbent, Alan

SUITE FOR SIR GAWAIN AND THE GREEN KNIGHT see Raum, Elizabeth

SUITE FOR STRINGS ON ENGLISH FOLK AIRS see Foster, Arnold

SUITE FOR YOUTH see Kadosa, Pal

SUITE FRANCAISE see Charpentier, Raymond see Foulds, John Herbert see Jaubert, Maurice see Jolivet, Andre

SUITE FROM A FORGOTTEN BALLET see Payne, Anthony

SUITE FROM GOLDBERG VARIATIONS see Krak, Egon, Suita Z Goldbergovskych Variacii

SUITE FROM THE INCIDENTAL MUSIC TO "JULIUS CAESAR" see Hall, Pauline

SUITE FROM WALTZES, OP. 39 [ARR.] see Brahms, Johannes

SUITE I GAMLE DANSERYTMER see Arnestad, Finn

SUITE IN OLD DANCE RHYTHMS see Arnestad, Finn, Suite I Gamle Danserytmer

SUITE IN OLD STYLE see Suder, Joseph, Suite Alter Art

SUITE MINIATURE see Rajter, L'udovít

SUITE MODERNE see Adler, James R.

SUITE NACH GEDICHTEN VON MICHELANGELO BUONARROTI, FOR SOLO VOICE AND ORCHESTRA see Shostakovich, Dmitri, Suite On Poems Of Michelangelo, For Solo Voice And Orchestra

SUITE NOSTALGIQUE see Felderhof, Jan

SUITE OF AIRS AND GRACES see Dillon, Shaun

SUITE OF DANCES [ARR.] see Arne, Thomas Augustine

SUITE OF EARLY CANADIAN DANCES [ARR] (Coles, Graham) string orch CAN.MUS.CENT. MI 1500 C693SU
(S1864)

SUITE OF SEVEN PIECES [ARR.] see Farnaby, Giles

SUITE OF YESTERDAY see Sjöblom, Heimer

SUITE ON CATSKILL MOUNTAIN TUNES see Haufrecht, Herbert

SUITE ON EARLY KEYBOARD MUSIC [ARR.] (Cruft, Adrian) string orch [5'] (contains 4 movements by Orlando

Gibbons, Edmund Hooper and anonymous composers) sc JOAD f.s. perf mat rent
(S1865)

SUITE ON ESTONIAN DANCE TUNES, FOR VIOLIN AND ORCHESTRA see Tubin, Eduard

SUITE ON ESTONIAN THEMES see Tubin, Eduard

SUITE ON FIVE LATVIAN FOLK SONGS see Raminsh, Imant

SUITE ON HUNGARIAN FOLK THEMES see Weiner, Leo, Suite, Op. 18

SUITE ON POEMS OF MICHELANGELO, FOR SOLO VOICE AND ORCHESTRA see Shostakovich, Dmitri

SUITE PASTORALE see Chabrier, [Alexis-] Emmanuel

SUITE POUR LES DIXIEMES JEUX see Bondon, Jacques

SUITE POUR MONDRIAN see Guezec, Jean-Pierre

SUITE ROMANTIQUE see Herbert, Victor

SUITE SAHARIENNE see Tomasi, Henri

SUITE SANS FIN see Friboulet, Georges

SUITE SOBRE CANTOS GALLEGOS see Granados, Enrique

SUITE SYMPHONIQUE see Bitsch, Marcel

SUITE SYMPHONIQUE IN E FLAT see Chadwick, George Whitefield

SUITE SYMPHONIQUE NO. 1 see Baumgartner, Jean-Paul

SUITE, TABLEAUX, FOR WIND QUINTET AND STRING ORCHESTRA see Dondeyne, Desire

SUITE TROVADORICA see Grisoni, Renato

SUITES FROM BALLETS see Shostakovich, Dmitri

SUITES FROM MUSIC TO PLAYS see Khachaturian, Aram Ilyich

SUITES IN C AND IN D MINOR see Rosenmüller, Johann

SUITES NOS. 1-4, BWV 1066- 1069 see Bach, Johann Sebastian

SUK, JOSEF (1874-1935)
  Marche Funebre [7']
    string orch
    SUPRAPHON
(S1866)

  Pisen Lasky [arr.] *Op.7
    (Leopold, B.) "Song Of Love [arr.]"
    3.3.3.3. 4.2.3.1. perc,harmonium,
    strings [6'] SUPRAPHON   (S1867)
    (Macha, O.) "Song Of Love [arr.]"
    3.3.3.2. 4.2.3.1. timp,perc,harp,
    strings [6'] SUPRAPHON   (S1868)

  Song Of Love [arr.]
    see Pisen Lasky [arr.]

  Symphonie Asrael *Op.27
    BREITKOPF-L perf mat rent   (S1869)

SULEIKA I, FOR SOLO VOICE AND ORCHESTRA[ARR.] see Schubert, Franz (Peter)

SULEIKA II, FOR SOLO VOICE AND ORCHESTRA[ARR.] see Schubert, Franz (Peter)

SULLIVAN, [SIR] ARTHUR SEYMOUR (1842-1900)
  Concerto for Violoncello and Orchestra
    study sc WEINBERGER f.s., perf mat rent
(S1870)

  Di Ballo: Overture [10']
    2(pic).2.2.2. 4.2.3.1. timp,perc,
    org,strings
    KALMUS A5688 sc $35.00, set $70.00,
    perf mat rent   (S1871)

  Grand Duke, The: Overture [5'30"]
    3(pic).2.2.2. 4.3.3.1. timp,perc,
    strings
    KALMUS A5672 sc $15.00, set $30.00,
    perf mat rent   (S1872)

  H.M.S. Pinafore: A Many Years Ago,
    For Solo Voice And Orchestra
    KALMUS A4867 sc $2.50, set $7.00,
    pts $.75, ea.   (S1873)

SULLIVAN, [SIR] ARTHUR SEYMOUR (cont'd.)

  H.M.S. Pinafore: Fair Moon, To Thee I
    Sing, For Solo Voice And Orchestra
    KALMUS A4860 sc $2.00, set $7.50,
    pts $.75, ea.   (S1874)

  H.M.S. Pinafore: I'm Called Little
    Buttercup, For Solo Voice And Orchestra
    KALMUS A4847 sc $3.00, set $6.00,
    pts $.75, ea.   (S1875)

  H.M.S. Pinafore: Kind Captain, I've
    Important Information, For Solo
    Voices And Orchestra
    KALMUS A4864 sc $2.00, set $3.00,
    pts $.75, ea.   (S1876)

  H.M.S. Pinafore: Never Mind The Why
    And Wherefore, For Solo Voices
    And Orchestra
    KALMUS A4863 sc $2.50, set $8.00,
    pts $.75, ea.   (S1877)

  H.M.S. Pinafore: Refrain, Audacious
    Tar, For Solo Voices And Orchestra
    KALMUS A4858 sc $2.00, set $5.50,
    pts $.75, ea.   (S1878)

  H.M.S. Pinafore: Sorry Her Lot, For
    Solo Voice And Orchestra
    KALMUS A4851 sc $2.50, set $8.00,
    pts $.75, ea.   (S1879)

  H.M.S. Pinafore: Things Are Seldom
    What They Seem, For Solo Voices
    And Orchestra
    KALMUS A4861 sc $2.00, set $7.00,
    pts $.75, ea.   (S1880)

  H.M.S. Pinafore: When I Was A Lad,
    For Solo Voice And Orchestra
    KALMUS A4855 sc $3.00, set $9.00,
    pts $.75, ea.   (S1881)

  Iolanthe: None Shall Part Us, For
    Solo Voices And Orchestra
    KALMUS A6277 sc $3.00, set $10.00,
    pts $.75, ea.   (S1882)

  Iolanthe: Overture
    2.2.2.2. 2.2.2.0. timp,perc,
    strings
    KALMUS A5465 sc $8.00, set $35.00,
    perf mat rent   (S1883)

  Iolanthe: When All Night Long A Chap
    Remains, For Solo Voice And Orchestra
    KALMUS A6276 sc $3.00, set $10.00,
    pts $.75, ea.   (S1884)

  Mikado, The: Sun Whose Rays Are All
    Ablaze, For Solo Voice And Orchestra
    KALMUS A6280 sc $3.00, set $6.00,
    pts $.75, ea.   (S1885)

  Princess Ida: I Am A Maiden Cold, For
    Solo Voices And Orchestra
    KALMUS A6278 set $12.00, pts $.75,
    ea.   (S1886)

  Tempest, The: Three Dances [12']
    2.2.2.2. 2.0.3.0. timp,perc,
    strings
    KALMUS A6094 sc $25.00, set $35.00,
    perf mat rent   (S1887)

  Thespis: Overture [9']
    2(pic).2.2.2. 2.2.3.0. timp,perc,
    strings
    KALMUS A5673 sc $30.00, set $50.00,
    perf mat rent   (S1888)

SUM CHE TAK MA see Ho, Liu Ting

SUM IN MEDIO TEMPESTATUM, FOR SOLO VOICE AND STRING ORCHESTRA see Vivaldi, Antonio

SUMERA, LEPO (1950-   )
  Symphony No. 1 [24']
    2(pic).2.2.2. 4.3.3.1. 3perc,cel,
    harp,strings
    VAAP perf mat rent   (S1889)

  Symphony No. 2 [18']
    2.2.2.2. 4.3.3.1. timp,perc,
    2harp,strings
    VAAP perf mat rent   (S1890)

  Symphony No. 3 [23']
    2.2.2.2. 4.3.3.0. perc,harp,pno,
    strings
    SIKORSKI perf mat rent   (S1891)

SUMERKEI see Bäck, Sven-Erik

SUMMARY see Szabo, Ferenc

SUMMER ELEGI, FOR FLUTE AND STRING ORCHESTRA see Börtz, Daniel

SUMMER EVENING, FOR SOLO VOICE AND ORCHESTRA see Lindberg, Oskar [Fredrik]

SUMMER FANFARE see Corigliano, John

SUMMER LIFE see Glass, Louis

SUMMER NIGHT see Hoover, Katherine

SUMMER NIGHT ON THE RIVER see Delius, Frederick

SUMMER NIGHT SUITE see Prokofiev, Serge

SUMMER NIGHTS, FOR SOLO VOICE AND ORCHESTRA see Boyd, Anne see Delius, Frederick

SUMMER OF '42: THEME, [ARR.] see Legrand, Michel

SUMMER OLYMPIC FANFARE see Williams, John T.

SUMMER PLACE, A see Steiner, Max(imilian Raoul Walter)

SUMMER RHAPSODY see Riisager, Knudage

SUMMER RITES AT NOON, FOR 2 ORCHESTRAS [ARR.] see Escher, Rudolf George

SUMMER SAGA, A [ARR.] see Lundsten, Ralph

SUMMER SOLSTICE see Laderman, Ezra

SUMMERLAND see Still, William Grant

SUMMERLAND FANTASY see Verrall, John Weedon

SUMMERNIGHT, THE, FOR SOLO VOICE AND ORCHESTRA see Rangström, Ture

SUN AND MOON DANCE AND BLOW TRUMPETS, THE see Crockett, Donald

SUN-LIKE, FOR SOLO VOICE AND INSTRUMENTAL ENSEMBLE see Samuel, Gerhard

SUN OF JUSTICE, THE see Thoresen, Lasse, Rettferdighetens Sol

SUN RISE [ARR.] see Cleve, Cissi, Soloppgang [arr.]

SUN SONGS, FOR SOLO VOICE AND ORCHESTRA see Forsyth, Malcolm

SUNFAIR, FOR SOLO VOICE AND ORCHESTRA see Eggen, Arne, Solfager, For Solo Voice And Orchestra

SUNLESS [ARR.] see Mussorgsky, Modest Petrovich

SUNNUNTAI, FOR SOLO VOICE AND ORCHESTRA [ARR.] see Turunen, Martti (Johannes)

SUNNY NIGHT see Halldorsson, Skuli

SUN'S GLITTER see Halldorsson, Skuli

SUN'S HEAT, FOR SOLO VOICE AND INSTRUMENTAL ENSEMBLE see Albert, Stephen Joel

SUNSET see Herbert, Victor

SUNSTUDY see Wilby, Philip

SUNYATA see Tamba, Akira

SUOLAHTI, HEIKKI (1920-1936)
  Sinfonia Piccola [25']
    2(pic).2(English horn).2.2.
    4.3.3.1. timp,perc,harp,strings
    BOOSEY perf mat rent   (S1892)

SUONI see Kolberg, Kåre

SUPERMAN: SYMPHONIC SUITE, [ARR.] see Williams, John

SUPPE, FRANZ VON (1819-1895)
  Bella Fiame Del Mio Core, For Solo
    Voice And Orchestra [arr.]
    (Waldenmaier, A.P.) 2.2.2.2.
    4.2.3.0. timp,perc,strings,S solo
    [4'] ORLANDO perf mat rent
                                  (S1893)
  Boccaccio: Menuett Und Tarantella
    [arr.]
    (Schonherr) 2.2.2.2. 4.2.3.0. timp,
    perc,harp,strings [10'] KALMUS
    A7473 pno-cond sc $7.00, set
    $50.00, pts $2.50, ea., perf mat
    rent   (S1894)

SUPPE, FRANZ VON (cont'd.)

  Fatinitza: Marziale [arr.]
    (Schonherr) 2.2.2.2. 4.2.3.0. timp,
    harp,strings [4'] KALMUS A7472
    pno-cond sc $7.00, set $50.00,
    pts $2.50, ea., perf mat rent
                                  (S1895)
  Irrfahrt Um's Gluck, Die: Overture
    [7'30"]
    1+pic.2.2.2. 4.2.3.1. timp,perc,
    strings
    KALMUS A4340 sc $20.00, set $40.00,
    perf mat rent   (S1896)

  Isabella: Overture
    KALMUS A6461 sc $15.00, set $40.00,
    pts $2.00, ea., perf mat rent
                                  (S1897)
  Tantalusqualen: Overture [6'30"]
    1+pic.2.2.2. 4.2.3.0. perc,
    strings
    KALMUS A6336 sc $15.00, set $35.00,
    pts $2.00, ea., perf mat rent
                                  (S1898)

SUPPLIANTES D'ESCHYLE see Xenakis, Yannis (Iannis)

SURFACES see Lubetsky, Ronald

SURINACH, CARLOS (1915-   )
  Blood Wedding
    see Bodas De Sangre

  Bodas De Sangre [45']
    1(pic).1(English horn).2(bass
    clar).1. 1.2.1.0. timp,perc,
    pno,strings
    "Blood Wedding" AMP perf mat rent
                                  (S1899)
  Concerto for Harp and Orchestra [22']
    2(pic).1.2(bass clar).1. 2.2.2.0.
    timp,perc,strings,harp solo
    sc AMP $30.00, perf mat rent
                                  (S1900)
  Concerto for Violin and Orchestra
    2.1.2.1. 2.2.2.0. timp,perc,harp,
    strings,vln solo
    sc AMP 066-35677 $28.00, perf mat
    rent   (S1901)

  Owl And The Pussycat, The, For
    Narrator And Orchestra [23']
    2(pic).1(English horn).2.1.
    2.2.2.0. timp,2perc,harp,
    strings,narrator, Hohner
    clavinet: alternate scoring:
    1(pic) 0. 2(bsclr) 1. 1.2.1.0.,
    , 2perc, harp, str, nar
    AMP perf mat rent   (S1902)

  Symphony No. 2 [28']
    3.3.3.2. 4.3.3.1. timp,3perc,
    strings
    ESCHIG perf mat rent   (S1903)

SUSLIN, VIKTOR (1942-   )
  Concerto for Piano and Orchestra
    [38']
    3.2.2.2. 4.2.2.0. timp,strings,
    pno solo
    SIKORSKI perf mat rent   (S1904)
    VAAP perf mat rent   (S1905)

  Concerto for Violin and Chamber
    Orchestra [13']
    1.1.1. 1.0.0.0. timp,perc,harp,
    pno,strings,vln solo
    SIKORSKI perf mat rent   (S1906)
    VAAP perf mat rent   (S1907)

  Etudes For Strings [18']
    20vln,4vcl
    SIKORSKI perf mat rent   (S1908)
    VAAP perf mat rent   (S1909)

  Farewell [25']
    3.3.3.3. 6.3.3.1. timp,2perc,
    harp,cel,pno,bass gtr,strings
    VAAP perf mat rent   (S1910)
    "Leb Wohl" SIKORSKI perf mat rent
                                  (S1911)

  Leb Wohl
    see Farewell

SUSPICION: SUITE see Waxman, Franz

SUSSKIND, WALTER (1913-1980)
  Capriccio Concertante [17']
    2+2pic.3+English horn.3+bass
    clar.3+contrabsn. 4.3.3.1.
    timp,4perc,cel&pno,harp,
    strings,electronic tape
    NORRUTH perf mat rent   (S1912)

  Improvisation And Scherzo, For Flute
    And Chamber Orchestra [14']
    3perc,cel&pno,harp,strings,fl
    solo
    NORRUTH perf mat rent   (S1913)

  Nine Slovak Sketches [15']
    3(pic).3(English horn).3(bass
    clar).3(contrabsn). 4.3.3.1.
    timp,4perc,cel,harp,strings
    NORRUTH perf mat rent   (S1914)

SUSSKIND, WALTER (cont'd.)

  Passacaglia for Timpani and Orchestra
    [12']
    1+pic.1+English horn.1+bass
    clar.1+contrabsn. 0.0.0.0.
    3perc,cel&pno,harp,strings,timp
    solo
    NORRUTH perf mat rent   (S1915)

  Six Ogden Nash Songs, For Solo Voice
    And Orchestra [16']
    1+pic.1+English horn.1+bass
    clar.1+contrabsn. 4.3.3.1.
    timp,3perc,cel,harp,strings,T
    solo
    NORRUTH perf mat rent   (S1916)

SÜSSMAYR, FRANZ XAVIER (1766-1803)
  Symphony
    see Ivancic, Amandus, Symphonies,
    Two

SUTER, HERMANN (1870-1916)
  Concerto, Op. 23, in A [40']
    2.3.2.2. 3.2.0.0. timp,triangle,
    harp,strings
    HUG GH 6292 perf mat rent   (S1917)

  Symphony, Op. 17, in D minor [40']
    3.3.4.3. 6.4.3.1. timp,perc,
    strings
    HUG GH 5655   (S1918)

SUZUKI, TERUAKI (1958-   )
  Concerto for Violin and Orchestra
    [20']
    3(pic).2.3(bass clar).2. 4.2.2.1.
    perc,2harp,pno,cel,strings,vln
    solo
    sc ZEN-ON 899350 f.s., perf mat
    rent   (S1919)

SVALBARD see Fongaard, Bjørn

SVANA ELD see Fladmoe, Arvid

SVARA, DANILO (1902-1981)
  Slovene Dances
    see Slovenski Plesi

  Slovenski Plesi [20']
    2(pic).2(English horn).2(bass
    clar).2. 4.3.3.1. timp,perc,
    harp,strings
    "Slovene Dances" DRUSTVO DSS 953
    perf mat rent   (S1920)

  Symphony No. 3 [29']
    2(pic).2(English horn).2(bass
    clar).2. 4.3.3.1. timp,perc,
    harp,strings
    DRUSTVO DSS 944 perf mat rent
                                  (S1921)
  Trois Morphoses, For Horn And Chamber
    Orchestra [10']
    1.1.1.1. 0.1.0.0. string quin,
    horn solo
    DRUSTVO DSS 536 perf mat rent
                                  (S1922)

SVARTE KROSSAR see Tveitt, Geirr

SVEIN URAED: SUITE see Olsen, Ole

SVEINSSON, ATLI HEIMIR (1938-   )
  Concerto for Flute and Orchestra
    [18']
    3.1+English horn.1+bass clar+alto
    sax.1+contrabsn. 2.2.2.0. elec
    org,harp,pno,7perc,strings,fl
    solo
    HANSEN-DEN perf mat rent   (S1923)

  Dreamboat, For Violin And Chamber
    Orchestra
    hpsd,strings,vln solo
    ICELAND 002-077   (S1924)

  Exploration, For Viola And Orchestra
    [19'10"]
    3.3.3.3. 4.3.3.1. timp,4perc,
    harp,cel,elec org,gtr,strings,
    vla solo
    ICELAND 002-002   (S1925)

  Flower Shower [25'45"]
    2.1+English horn.1+bass clar.1+
    contrabsn. 3.2.1.1. 3perc,pno,
    harp,strings,electronic tape
    ICELAND 002-022   (S1926)

  Infinitesimal Fragments Of Eternity
    [15']
    1.1.1.1. 2.1.0.0. pno,strings
    HANSEN-DEN perf mat rent   (S1927)

  Soundings
    1.1.1.1. 0.0.0.0. 2perc,harp,pno,
    cel,strings
    ICELAND 002-012   (S1928)

  Tautophony [14']
    2.2.2.2.alto sax. 2.2.2.1. timp,
    5perc,harp,pno,hpsd,strings
    ICELAND 002-013   (S1929)

SVEINSSON, ATLI HEIMIR (cont'd.)

Tengsl
    2+pic.2+English horn.2.2.
      4.2.2.1. 4perc,2pno,cel,hpsd,
      harp,strings
    ICELAND 002-001B   (S1930)

Trobar Clus, For Bassoon And
    Orchestra [17']
    3(pic).3(English horn).3(bass
      clar).3(contrabsn). 4.5.3.1.
      3perc,harp,pno,strings,bsn solo
    HANSEN-DEN perf mat rent   (S1931)

SVENDSEN, JOHAN (SEVERIN) (1840-1911)
Carnival In Paris
    see Karneval I Paris

Concerto for Violin and Orchestra,
    Op. 6, in A [30']
    sc KISTNER f.s., perf mat rent
                                  (S1932)

Concerto for Violoncello and
    Orchestra, Op. 7, in D
    2.2.2.2. 2.2.0.0. timp,strings,
      vcl solo
    KISTNER perf mat rent   (S1933)

Coronation March
    see Kroningsmarsj

Karneval I Paris *Op.9 [12']
    3.2.2.2. 4.2.3.1. timp,perc,
      strings
    "Carnival In Paris" KISTNER perf
      mat rent   (S1934)

Kroningsmarsj *Op.13
    2.2.2.2. 4.3.3.1. timp,perc,
      strings
    "Coronation March" KISTNER perf mat
      rent   (S1935)

Norwegian Rhapsody No. 1 *Op.17
    KALMUS A6365 sc $15.00, set $20.00,
      pts $1.00, ea., perf mat rent
                                  (S1936)
Norwegian Rhapsody No. 2 *Op.19
    KALMUS A6366 sc $20.00, set $36.00,
      pts $2.00, ea., perf mat rent
                                  (S1937)

Symphony No. 1, Op. 4 [30']
    2.2.2.2. 4.2.3.0. timp,strings
    KISTNER perf mat rent   (S1938)

Symphony No. 2, Op. 15 [32']
    2.2.2.2. 4.2.3.0. timp,strings
    KISTNER perf mat rent   (S1939)

Two Old Swedish Folk Songs
    string orch [7'] KALMUS A5831 sc
      $4.00, set $5.00   (S1940)

SVERIGE I TONER see Myrtelius, Hugo

SVETE, TOMAZ (1956-   )
Poem Symphonique [10']
    2(pic).2.2.0. 2.1.0.0. timp,perc,
      harp,pno,strings
    DRUSTVO DSS 1074 perf mat rent
                                  (S1941)

Prekmurska Suita [17']
    string orch
    DRUSTVO DSS 1073 perf mat rent
                                  (S1942)

Sinfonietta [17']
    2(pic).2.2.2. 2.2.0.0. timp,perc,
      strings
    DRUSTVO DSS 1075 perf mat rent
                                  (S1943)

SVIRIDOV, GEORGY (1915-   )
Schneesturm, Der
    see Snowstorm

Snowstorm [27']
    3(pic).3(English
      horn).2.3(contrabsn). 4.3.3.1.
      timp,perc,cel,2harp,pno,strings
    VAAP perf mat rent   (S1944)
    "Schneesturm, Der" SIKORSKI perf
      mat rent   (S1945)

SVOBODA, TOMAS (1939-   )
Christmas Concertino, For Harp And
    Chamber Orchestra *Op.34 [13']
    2.2.2.2. 2.0.0.0. strings,harp
      solo
    STANGLAND perf mat rent   (S1946)

Concerto for Chamber Orchestra, Op.
    125 [23']
    1.1.1.1. 0.0.0.0. perc,harp,
      strings,S solo
    sc STANGLAND f.s., perf mat rent
                                  (S1947)
Concerto for Piano and Orchestra, No.
    2, Op. 134
    3.2.2.2. 4.3.3.1. timp,4perc,
      strings,pno solo
    STANGLAND   (S1948)

Dance Suite *Op.128 [23']
    3.2.2.2. 4.2.3.1. timp,2perc,
      strings
    STANGLAND perf mat rent   (S1949)

SVOBODA, TOMAS (cont'd.)

Ex Libris *Op.113 [6'30"]
    3.2.3.3. 4.3.4.1. timp,perc,
      strings
    STANGLAND perf mat rent   (S1950)

44th Sonnet Of Michelangelo, For Solo
    Voice And Instrumental Ensemble
    *Op.51 [8']
    1.1.2.0. 1.1.0.0. pno,string
      quar,A solo
    STANGLAND perf mat rent   (S1951)

Labyrinth *Op.72 [11']
    2.1.1.1. 1.1.1.0. perc,pno,vln,
      vla,vcl,db,electronic tape
      (electronic tape for rent) sc
    STANGLAND rent   (S1952)

Serenade, Op. 115 [6'30"]
    3.2.2.2. 4.3.3.1. timp,perc,
      strings
    STANGLAND perf mat rent   (S1953)

Symphony No. 1, Op. 20 [36']
    3.2.3.2. 4.3.4.1. timp,perc,pno,
      strings
    STANGLAND perf mat rent   (S1954)

Symphony No. 2, Op. 41 [28']
    4.2.3.2. 4.3.4.1. timp,4perc,pno,
      strings
    sc STANGLAND f.s.   (S1955)

SWAFFORD, JAN (1946-   )
After Spring Rain [19']
    3.2.3.2. 4.3.3.1. perc,harp,
      strings
    PEER perf mat rent   (S1956)

Landscape With Traveler [17']
    2(pic).3.3.3(contrabsn). 4.4.3.1.
      perc,strings
    PEER perf mat rent   (S1957)

SWALLOWS, THE [ARR.] see Chueca,
    Federico, Golondrinas, Las [arr.]

SWAN LAKE: PAS DE DEUX, "BLACK SWAN"
    [ARR.] see Tchaikovsky, Piotr
    Ilyich

SWAN LAKE: PAS DE DEUX, "WHITE SWAN"
    [ARR.] see Tchaikovsky, Piotr
    Ilyich

SWAN LAKE: SELECTION [ARR.] see
    Tchaikovsky, Piotr Ilyich

SWAN LAKE: VALSE BLUETTE see
    Tchaikovsky, Piotr Ilyich

SWANEE RIVER IN THE STYLE OF BACH see
    Gould, Morton

SWANEE RIVER IN THE STYLE OF BEETHOVEN
    see Gould, Morton

SWANEE RIVER IN THE STYLE OF BRAHMS see
    Gould, Morton

SWANEE RIVER IN THE STYLE OF DEBUSSY
    see Gould, Morton

SWANEE RIVER IN THE STYLE OF GERSHWIN
    see Gould, Morton

SWANEE RIVER IN THE STYLE OF J. STRAUSS
    see Gould, Morton

SWANEE RIVER IN THE STYLE OF LISZT see
    Gould, Morton

SWANEE RIVER IN THE STYLE OF MOZART see
    Gould, Morton

SWANEE RIVER IN THE STYLE OF RIMSKY-
    KORSAKOV see Gould, Morton

SWANEE RIVER IN THE STYLE OF
    TCHAIKOVSKY see Gould, Morton

SWANEE RIVER IN THE STYLE OF WAGNER see
    Gould, Morton

SWANSON, HOWARD (1909-1978)
Concerto for Orchestra
    2.2.0.2. 4.2.3.1. strings
    WEINTRB perf mat rent   (S1958)

Fantasy Piece For Saxophone And
    String Orchestra
    string orch,sax/clar solo
    WEINTRB perf mat rent   (S1959)

Music for Strings [10']
    string orch
    WEINTRB perf mat rent   (S1960)

Night Music [9']
    1.1.1.1. 1.0.0.0. strings
    WEINTRB perf mat rent   (S1961)

SWANSON, HOWARD (cont'd.)

Short Symphony [11']
    2(pic).2.2.2. 2.2.1.0. timp,
      strings
    WEINTRB perf mat rent   (S1962)

Songs For Patricia, Solo Voice And
    String Orchestra
    string orch,S solo
    WEINTRB perf mat rent   (S1963)

Symphony No. 1
    2(pic).2.2.1. 4.2.2.1. timp,perc,
      strings
    WEINTRB perf mat rent   (S1964)

Symphony No. 3
    3(pic).3(English horn).3(bass
      clar).2(contrabsn). 4.3.3.1.
      perc,strings
    WEINTRB perf mat rent   (S1965)

SWANWHITE: SUITE see Sibelius, Jean

SWARM, THE see Goldsmith, Jerry

SWASHBUCKLER see Schelle, Michael

SWAYNE, GILES (1946-   )
Orlando's Music [20']
    3(pic).0.2(bass
      clar).3(contrabsn). 4.3.0.0.
      pno&cel,strings
    NOVELLO perf mat rent   (S1966)

Pentecost Music [30']
    4(pic).3(English horn).4(bass
      clar).3(contrabsn).alto sax+
      tenor sax. 6.4.3.1. 5perc,harp,
      pno&cel,strings
    NOVELLO perf mat rent   (S1967)

Serenade [10']
    2.0.2.2. 2.2.0.0. 2perc,pno,
      strings
    NOVELLO perf mat rent   (S1968)

SWEDEN IN TUNES see Myrtelius, Hugo,
    Sverige I Toner

SWEDISH NATIONAL ANTHEM see
    Kallstenius, Edvin

SWEENEY TODD: SUITE see Arnold, Malcolm

SWEET MUSIC see Rathaus, Karol

SWEET SONG OF LONG AGO, FOR SOLO VOICE
    AND ORCHESTRA [ARR.] see Charles,
    Ernest

SWERTS, PIET
Rotations, For Piano And Orchestra
    [13'30"]
    2(pic).2.2.1+contrabsn. 3.2.2.1.
      4perc,strings,pno solo
    sc CBDM f.s.   (S1969)

SWIATEO, FOR SOLO VOICES AND ORCHESTRA
    see Bregent, Michel

SWING LOW, SWEET CHARIOT, FOR SOLO
    VOICE AND ORCHESTRA [ARR.]
    (Burleigh, Harry T.) 2.1.1.2.
      4.0.0.0. harp,strings,high solo
    COLOMBO perf mat rent   (S1970)

SWITCHING STATIONS see Karpman, Laura

SWORD DANCE see Ranki, György

SYBILLE, FOR FLUTE AND ORCHESTRA see
    Dimitriev, Georgi

SYLPHE DES FRIEDENS, DER, FOR SOLO
    VOICE AND ORCHESTRA, [ARR.] see
    Mozart, Wolfgang Amadeus

SYLPHIDES, LES [ARR.] see Chopin,
    Frédéric

SYLVIAN JOULULAULU, FOR SOLO VOICE AND
    ORCHESTRA [ARR.] see Collan, Karl

SYLVIANO, R.
Casanova [12']
    CHOUDENS perf mat rent   (S1971)

SYMBOLON see Zwilich, Ellen Taaffe

SYMBOLUM, FOR ORGAN AND ORCHESTRA see
    Bose, Hans Jürgen

SYMFONIA PASTORALIS IN E, FOR ENGLISH
    HORN AND ORCHESTRA see Salva,
    Tadeas

SYMFONIE DER DUINEN see Boogaard,
    Bernard van den

SYMFONIE - HET LEGER see Douw, Andre

SYMFONIE IN E KLEINE TERTS see Bunge,
    Sas

SYMFONISK BILDE see Haug, Halvor

SYMFONISK FORSPILL see Albertsen, Per Hjort see Braein, Edvard Fliflet

SYMFONISK RENDEZ-VOUS see Hundsnes, Svein

SYMFONISKE FRAGMENTER FRA ANDRE AKT AV OPERAEN, OP. 185B see Lerstad, Terje B.

SYMFONISKE FRAGMENTER FRA FORSTE AKT AV OPERAEN, OP185A see Lerstad, Terje B.

SYMFONISKE KONTURER see Haug, Halvor

SYMMETRICAL MEMORIES, FOR VIOLONCELLO AND ORCHESTRA see Marez Oyens, Tera de

SYMPATHIE POLKA see Strauss, Johann, [Jr.]

SYMPHO-JAZZ SKETCHES, FOR JAZZ QUINTET AND ORCHESTRA see Leviev, Milcho

SYMPHONIA 1 ET 2 [ARR.] see Dumont, Henri

SYMPHONIA TRAGICA see Draeseke, Felix

SYMPHONIC BALLAD see Tsuchida, Eisuke

SYMPHONIC BALLADE see Yamamoto, Naozumi

SYMPHONIC CONTOURS see Haug, Halvor, Symfoniske Konturer

SYMPHONIC DANCES see Ogerman, Claus

SYMPHONIC EPISODES see Read, Thomas Lawrence

SYMPHONIC ETUDES see Falik, Yuri

SYMPHONIC FANFARES see Klein, Lothar

SYMPHONIC FANTASIA see Parry, [Sir] Charles Hubert Hastings

SYMPHONIC FANTASIA NO. 1 see Luening, Otto

SYMPHONIC FANTASIA NO. 2 see Luening, Otto

SYMPHONIC FANTASIA NO. 3 see Luening, Otto

SYMPHONIC FANTASIA NO. 4 see Luening, Otto

SYMPHONIC FANTASIA NO.5 see Luening, Otto

SYMPHONIC FANTASIA NO.6 see Luening, Otto

SYMPHONIC FANTASIA NO.7 see Luening, Otto

SYMPHONIC FANTASIA NO.8 see Luening, Otto

SYMPHONIC FANTASIA NO.9 see Luening, Otto

SYMPHONIC FANTASY, FOR ORGAN AND ORCHESTRA see Brons, Carel

SYMPHONIC FANTASY, FOR TWO PIANOS AND ORCHESTRA see Bentzon, Niels Viggo

SYMPHONIC FANTASY NO.3 see Olsen, Sparre

SYMPHONIC FESTIVE FANFARES see Shchedrin, Rodion

SYMPHONIC FRAGMENTS, THREE: D. 615, D. 708A, D. 936A see Schubert, Franz (Peter)

SYMPHONIC FRESCOS see Grabovsky, Leonid

SYMPHONIC INTERLUDE NO. 3 see Luening, Otto

SYMPHONIC INTERLUDE NO.4 see Luening, Otto

SYMPHONIC INTERLUDE NO. 5 see Luening, Otto

SYMPHONIC METAMORPHOSES see Strmcnik, Maksimiljan, Simfonicne Metamorfoze

SYMPHONIC METAMORPHOSES. THE FIRST PART, METAMORPHOSES OF TUTTI see Mizuno, Shuko

SYMPHONIC METAMORPHOSIS ON THEMES BY CARL MARIA VON WEBER see Hindemith, Paul

SYMPHONIC MOTET see Slonimsky, Sergey

SYMPHONIC MOVEMENT see Pettersson, Allan see Stein, Leon

SYMPHONIC MOVEMENTS see Brandon, Seymour (Sy)

SYMPHONIC MOVEMENTS FROM THE TURN OF THE CENTURY see Reicha, Anton

SYMPHONIC OVERTURE see Gassmann, Remi

SYMPHONIC PICTURE see Haug, Halvor, Symfonisk Bilde

SYMPHONIC PIECE NO. 1 see Moevs, Robert Walter

SYMPHONIC PIECE NO. 2 see Moevs, Robert Walter

SYMPHONIC PIECE NO. 3 see Moevs, Robert Walter

SYMPHONIC PIECE NO. 5 see Moevs, Robert Walter

SYMPHONIC POEM see Miaskovsky, Nikolai Yakovlevich see Olafsson, Kjartan

SYMPHONIC POEM FOR STRINGS see Saxe, Serge, Poema Sinfonico Para Cuerdas

SYMPHONIC PRELUDE see Albertsen, Per Hjort, Symfonisk Forspill see Braein, Edvard Fliflet, Symfonisk Forspill

SYMPHONIC RACE, A see Wallin, Peter

SYMPHONIC REVELATION, FOR SOLO VOICE AND ORCHESTRA see Ishiketa, Mareo

SYMPHONIC RHAPSODY see Ireland, John

SYMPHONIC RHAPSODY, FOR ALTO SAXOPHONE AND ORCHESTRA see Lennon, John Anthony

SYMPHONIC SKETCHES see Chadwick, George Whitefield

SYMPHONIC STUDY, "MACHINES" see Arnold, Malcolm

SYMPHONIC SUITE see Husa, Karel

SYMPHONIC SUITE FOR STRINGS see Jacobson, Maurice

SYMPHONIC TRIO see Bentzon, Jørgen

SYMPHONIC TRIPTYCH see Gotskosik, Oleg

SYMPHONIC VARIATIONS see Dvorák, Antonín see Grant, Stewart see Jirák, Karel Boleslav see Parris, Robert see Parry, [Sir] Charles Hubert Hastings see Wallace, William

SYMPHONIC WORKS, EIGHT see Gossec, François Joseph

SYMPHONIC WORKS, THREE see Danzi, Franz see Graun, Johann Gottlieb see Holzbauer, Ignaz Jakob see Stamitz, Carl

SYMPHONIC WORKS, TWO see Wesley, Samuel

SYMPHONIE ASRAEL see Suk, Josef

SYMPHONIE CONCERTANTE see Campagnoli, Bartolommeo see Dussek, Johann Ladislaus

SYMPHONIE CONCERTANTE, THE
(Foster; Parcell; Carlson; Viano; Vasseur) sc GARLAND
ISBN 0-8240-3835-5 $90.00 "The Symphony" Vol. D-V
contains: Barrière, Étienne, Symphonie Concertante; Bertheaume, Isadore, Symphonie Concertante; Bréval, Jean Baptiste, Symphonies Concertantes, Two; Cambini, Giovanni Giuseppe, Symphonies Concertantes, Three; Davaux, Jean Baptiste, Symphonies Concertantes, Three   (S1972)

SYMPHONIE DA CAMERA see Bozza, Eugène

SYMPHONIE DE MONTSEGUR, LA, FOR SOLO VOICE AND ORCHESTRA see Landowski, Marcel

SYMPHONIE DE REQUIEM: LES AMES MAUDITES see Stallaert, Alphonse

SYMPHONIE DES SOUPERS DU ROI see Delalande, Michel-Richard

SYMPHONIE D'HYMNES see Koechlin, Charles

SYMPHONIE DRAMATIQUE see Dewanger, Anton

SYMPHONIE FANTASTIQUE see Berlioz, Hector (Louis)

SYMPHONIE LATINE see Bondon, Jacques

SYMPHONIE NORMANDE see Thierac, Jacques

SYMPHONIE PERIODIQUE NO.1 see Pleyel, Ignace Joseph

SYMPHONIE PERIODIQUE NO.14 see Pleyel, Ignace Joseph

SYMPHONIE POUR LES TEMPS NOUVEAUX see Duclos, Pierre

SYMPHONIE POUR L'UNIVERS CLAUDELIEN see Milhaud, Darius

SYMPHONIE POUR POUVOIR, FOR SOLO VOICE AND ORCHESTRA see Dao, Nguyen Thien

SYMPHONIE POUR RIRE see Roget, Henriette

SYMPHONIE SERENADE see DuBois, Pierre-Max

SYMPHONIEN see Haubenstock-Ramati, Roman

SYMPHONIES, FIVE see Agrell, Johan Joachim see Monn, Georg Matthias see Richter, Franz Xaver

SYMPHONIES, FIVE, VOL. 1 see Haydn, [Franz] Joseph

SYMPHONIES, FIVE, VOL. 2 see Haydn, [Franz] Joseph

SYMPHONIES, FOR BRASS QUINTET AND ORCHESTRA see Moss, Lawrence Kenneth

SYMPHONIES, FOUR see Graupner, Christoph see Gyrowetz, Adalbert (Jirovec) see Hofmann, Leopold

SYMPHONIES, FOUR see Haydn, [Franz] Joseph

SYMPHONIES, SIX see Abel, Carl Friedrich see Dittersdorf, Karl Ditters von

SYMPHONIES, TEN see Sammartini, Giovanni Battista

SYMPHONIES, THREE see Asplmayr, Franz see Brioschi, Antonio see Camerloher, Joseph see Endler, Johann Samuel see Herschel, William see Lang, Johann Georg see Mozart, Leopold see Mysliveczek, Joseph see Pichl, Wenzel (Vaclav)

SYMPHONIES, TWO see Barta, Josef see Druschetzky, Georg see Fils, [Johann] Anton see Hoffmeister, Franz Anton see Ivancic, Amandus see Kalliwoda, Johann Wenzel see Kammel, Antonin see Kreusser, Georg Anton see Reicha, Anton see Sacchini, Antonio (Maria Gasparo Gioacchino)

SYMPHONIES BRETONNES, LES see Kahn, Erich Itor

SYMPHONIES, K. 75, 76, 81, 95, 96, 97 see Mozart, Wolfgang Amadeus

SYMPHONIES NOS. 1-2 see Brahms, Johannes see Mahler, Gustav

SYMPHONIES NOS. 1-4 see Beethoven, Ludwig van see Brahms, Johannes see Schumann, Robert (Alexander)

SYMPHONIES NOS. 1-5 see Haydn, [Franz] Joseph

SYMPHONIES NOS. 1-8 see Mozart, Wolfgang Amadeus

SYMPHONIES NOS. 1-9, VOLS. 1 AND 2 see Beethoven, Ludwig van

SYMPHONIES NOS. 3-4 see Brahms, Johannes

SYMPHONIES NOS.5-7 see Beethoven, Ludwig van

SYMPHONIES, NOS.6-8 see Beethoven, Ludwig van see Haydn, [Franz] Joseph

SYMPHONIES NOS.8-9 see Beethoven,
Ludwig van

SYMPHONIES NOS. 9-12 see Haydn, [Franz]
Joseph

SYMPHONIES NOS. 9-16 see Mozart,
Wolfgang Amadeus

SYMPHONIES NOS. 13-18 see Haydn,
[Franz] Joseph

SYMPHONIES NOS. 17-21 see Mozart,
Wolfgang Amadeus

SYMPHONIES NOS. 19-22 see Haydn,
[Franz] Joseph

SYMPHONIES NOS. 22-26 see Mozart,
Wolfgang Amadeus

SYMPHONIES NOS. 23-27 see Haydn,
[Franz] Joseph

SYMPHONIES NOS. 27-31 see Mozart,
Wolfgang Amadeus

SYMPHONIES NOS. 28-31 see Haydn,
[Franz] Joseph

SYMPHONIES NOS. 32-34, 37 see Mozart,
Wolfgang Amadeus

SYMPHONIES NOS. 32-35 see Haydn,
[Franz] Joseph

SYMPHONIES NOS. 36-40 see Haydn,
[Franz] Joseph

SYMPHONIES NOS. 41-43 see Haydn,
[Franz] Joseph

SYMPHONIES NOS. 44-46 see Haydn,
[Franz] Joseph

SYMPHONIES NOS. 88-92 see Haydn,
[Franz] Joseph

SYMPHONIES NOS. 93-98 see Haydn,
[Franz] Joseph

SYMPHONIES NOS. 99-104 see Haydn,
[Franz] Joseph

SYMPHONIES, VOL. 1 see Mozart, Wolfgang
Amadeus see Mozart, Wolfgang
Amadeus

SYMPHONIES, VOL. 2 see Engel, Jan see
Mozart, Wolfgang Amadeus

SYMPHONIES, VOLS. 1-12 see Haydn,
[Franz] Joseph

SYMPHONISCH GEDICHT, FOR SOLO VOICE AND
ORCHESTRA see Delft, Marc van

SYMPHONISCH REQUIEM see Porcelijn,
David

SYMPHONISCHE ADAPTATIONEN DES
QUINTETTS, KV 614 VON MOZART see
Dessau, Paul

SYMPHONISCHE FANTASIE UBER B.A.C.H. see
Hannemann, Johannes

SYMPHONISCHE MUSIK see Werner, Fritz

SYMPHONISCHE PERIPETIE, FOR ORGAN AND
ORCHESTRA see Kubelik, Rafael

SYMPHONISCHE SUITE see Reznicek, Emil
Nikolaus von

SYMPHONISCHE SZENE see Eröd, Ivan

SYMPHONISCHE TANZSTUCKE see
Gattermayer, Heinrich

SYMPHONISCHE VARIATIONEN see Nicode,
Jean Louis

SYMPHONISCHE VARIATIONEN UND FUGE UBER
"IN DULCI JUBILO" see Zimmermann,
Bernd Alois

SYMPHONISCHER MARSCH see Dallinger,
Fridolin

SYMPHONISCHES PRAELUDIUM [ARR.] see
Mahler, Gustav

SYMPHONY see Chelleri, Fortunato see
Eichner, Ernst see Eybler, Joseph
see Gansbacher, Johann Baptist see
Mann, Johann Christoph see
Neubauer, Franz Christoph see
Romberg, Andreas see Romberg,
Bernhard Heinrich see Süssmayr,
Franz Xaver see Wesley, Samuel
Sebastian see Zimmermann, Anton

SYMPHONY AND OVERTURE IN GREAT BRITAIN,
THE *CCU
(Platt; Kirakowska; Johnson;

McIntosh) sc GARLAND
ISBN 0-8240-3840-1 $90.00 "The
Symphony" Vol. E-I   (S1973)

SYMPHONY: "ANFANG UND ENDE" see
Rasmussen, Karl Aage

SYMPHONY-ANTIPHONY see Gudmundsen-
Holmgreen, Pelle

SYMPHONY AT MANNHEIM, THE
(Wolf, Eugene K.; Wolf, Jean K.) sc
GARLAND ISBN 0-8240-3849-5 $90.00
"The Symphony" Vol. C-III
contains: Cannabich, Christian,
Symphonies, Four; Stamitz, Johann
Wenzel Anton, Symphonies, Five
(S1974)

SYMPHONY-CONCERTO, FOR PIANO AND
ORCHESTRA see Flosman, Oldrich

SYMPHONY FOR ORCHESTRA WITH PIANO
OBBLIGATO see Read, Thomas Lawrence

SYMPHONY FOR STRINGS AND PERCUSSION see
Kaufman, Fredrick

SYMPHONY FOR STRINGS[ARR.] see Strauss,
Richard

SYMPHONY FOR 12 MUSICIANS see Bedford,
David

SYMPHONY FOR 21 PLAYERS see Delnooz,
Henri

SYMPHONY FOR TWO WORLDS see Miki,
Minoru, Kyu No Kyoku

SYMPHONY FROM LIFE see Miki, Minoru see
Miki, Minoru, Shunju No Fu

SYMPHONY FROM SILENCE see Thorne,
Nicholas C.K.

SYMPHONY IN A SQUARE see Kisielewski,
Stefan

SYMPHONY IN CROATIA, THE; THE SYMPHONY
IN THE NEW WORLD
(Kos; Zupanovic; Mattos; Dennison) sc
GARLAND ISBN 0-8240-3847-9 $90.00
"The Symphony" Vol. F-VIII
contains: Bajamonti, Julije,
Symphony; Heinrich, Anton Philip,
Symphony; Nunes-Garcia, Jose
Mauricio, Symphonies, Two;
Sorkocevic, Luka, Symphonies, Two
(S1975)

SYMPHONY IN DENMARK, THE
(Hatting, Carsten E.; Krabbe, Niels;
Schiødt, Nanna) sc GARLAND $90.00
"The Symphony", Vol. F-VI
contains: Croubelis, Simoni dall,
Sinfonia Concertante in B flat
(fl,2clar,bsn,2horn,strings);
Croubelis, Simoni dall, Symphony
Dans Le Gout Asiatique (Symphony
in D) (2fl,2ob,2horn,strings);
Gerson, Georg, Symphony in E
flat, MIN 139 (2.2.2.2. 2.2.0.0.
timp,strings); Hartmann, Johan
Peder Emilius, Symphony, Op. 17,
in G minor (2.2.2.2. 4.2.3.0.
timp,strings); Hartmann, Johann
Ernst, Symphony in D, MIN 136
(2ob,2horn,strings); Schall,
Claus Nielsen, Symphony in B
flat, MIN 137 (2.2.2.2. 2.0.0.0.
strings); Weyse, Christoph Ernst
Friedrich, Symphony in E flat,
MIN 138 (2.2.0.2. 2.2.0.0. timp,
strings)   (S1976)

SYMPHONY IN DRESDEN, THE *CC10L
(Ottenberg, Hans-Gunter; Pilkova,
Zdenka) sc GARLAND
ISBN 0-8240-3850-9 $90.00 "the
symphony" vol. C-X   (S1977)

SYMPHONY IN FOUR AMERICAN IDIOMS, A see
Knight, Eric

SYMPHONY IN FRANCE, THE, 1730-1790
*CC17L
(Rice, John A.; Castonguay, Gerald)
sc GARLAND ISBN 0-8240-3846-0
$90.00 "The Symphony" Vol. D-I
(S1978)

SYMPHONY IN HUNGARY, THE; THE SYMPHONY
IN BOHEMIA
(Somorjay; Altner; Novak; Hennigova-
Dubova) sc GARLAND
ISBN 0-8240-3848-7 $90.00 "The
Symphony" Vol. B-XII
contains: Brixi, Franz Xaver,
Symphonies, Two; Dussek, Franz,
Symphonies, Four; Notvotny,
Ferenc, Symphonies, Two;
Wranitzky, Anton, Symphony
(S1979)

SYMPHONY IN NAPLES, THE, 1800-1840
(Longyear, Rey M.) sc GARLAND
ISBN 0-8240-3831-2 $90.00 "The
Symphony" Vol. A-VII
contains: Florimo, Francesco,

Sinfonie, Two; Mercadante, G.
Saverio, Sinfonie, Four; Tritto,
Domenico, Sinfonia   (S1980)

SYMPHONY IN ONE MOVEMENT see Brooks,
Richard James see Stock, David
Frederick

SYMPHONY IN PORTUGAL, THE; THE SYMPHONY
IN SPAIN
(Salzmann; Sousa; Bochmann; Lopez-
Calo; Trillo) sc GARLAND
ISBN 0-8240-3837-1 $90.00 "The
Symphony" Vol. F-V
contains: Bomtempo, João Domingos,
Symphony; Leal Moreira, Antonio,
Symphony; Pons, Jose, Symphonies,
Three   (S1981)

SYMPHONY IN SWEDEN, THE, PART 2 *CC16L
sc GARLAND ISBN 0-8240-3827-4 $90.00
"The Symphony" Vol. F-III (S1982)

SYMPHONY IN THE TWILIGHT see Korf,
Anthony

SYMPHONY IN THREE MOVEMENTS see
Stravinsky, Igor

SYMPHONY IN TIME, A see Rasmussen, Karl
Aage

SYMPHONY IN TWO MOVEMENTS see
Applebaum, Allyson Brown see
Cooper, Paul

SYMPHONY IN WAVES see Kernis, Aaron Jay

SYMPHONY NO.1, OP.57BIS see Koechlin,
Charles

SYMPHONY NO. 1, ORIGINAL VERSION see
Rochberg, A. George

SYMPHONY NO. 3, OP. 43 see Scriabin,
Alexander

SYMPHONY NO. 5, OP. 50, REVISED see
Nielsen, Carl

SYMPHONY OF DUNES see Boogaard, Bernard
van den, Symfonie Der Duinen

SYMPHONY OF HYMNS see Pirumov,
Alexander

SYMPHONY OF PASTORALS, FOR VIOLIN AND
ORCHESTRA see Stankovich, Evgeny

SYMPHONY WITH CHACONNE see Goehr,
Alexander

SYMPOSION: DE TREIN, FOR SOLO VOICES
AND ORCHESTRA see Schat, Peter

SYNAPHAI, FOR PIANO AND ORCHESTRA see
Xenakis, Yannis (Iannis)

SYNERGIES see Mache, Francois Bernard

SYNG MINE STRENGJER, FOR SOLO VOICE AND
ORCHESTRA see Jordan, Sverre

SYNOPSIS see Decoust, Michel

SYNTAKS, FOR SOLO VOICE AND ORCHESTRA
see Strömholm, Folke

SYNTAX, FOR SOLO VOICE AND ORCHESTRA
see Strömholm, Folke, Syntaks, For
Solo Voice And Orchestra

SYNTHESE see Burgers, Simon

SYNTHESIS see Mobberley, James

SYNTHESIS, FOR SAXOPHONE AND ORCHESTRA
see Roccisano, Joe

SYRENSONG see Holt, Simon

SYRINGA, FOR SOLO VOICES AND
INSTRUMENTAL ENSEMBLE see Carter,
Elliott Cook, Jr.

SYVINKI, ESKO (1943-   )
Concerto for Accordion and Orchestra
[21']
2.2.2.2. 0.0.0.0. 2perc,strings,
acord solo
sc SUOMEN f.s.   (S1983)

SYZYGIES see Leclerc, Sophie

SZABO, FERENC (1902-1969)
Summary
sc EMB 708 f.s.   (S1984)

SZALONEK, WITOLD (1927-   )
Musica Concertante, For Double Bass
And Orchestra [27']
3.3.3.3. 4.3.3.0. perc,harp,pno,
strings,db solo
sc POLSKIE f.s.   (S1985)

SZALONEK, WITOLD (cont'd.)

Sinfonia B-A-C-H
fl,clar,pno,strings
SEESAW   (S1986)

SZALOWSKI, ANTONI (1907-1973)
Allegretto, For Bassoon And Orchestra
[4']
2.1.2.1. 3.3.3.0. timp,2perc,
harp,cel,strings,bsn solo
BILLAUDOT perf mat rent   (S1987)

Concerto for Oboe, Clarinet, Bassoon
and Orchestra [20']
0.0.0.0. 4.3.2.1. timp,harp,
strings,ob solo,clar solo,bsn
solo
BILLAUDOT perf mat rent   (S1988)

SZE, MAN-TSUEN
Festival Overture [11']
3.2.2.2. 4.3.3.1. timp,perc,harp,
strings
HONG KONG perf mat rent   (S1989)

SZECHENYI CONCERTO see Hidas, Frigyes

SZEKELY, ENDRE (1912-   )
Cantata for Solo Voice and Chamber
Orchestra
[Ger] sc EMB 10177 f.s.   (S1990)

Maqamat, For Solo Voice And Chamber
Orchestra
sc EMB 10151 f.s.   (S1991)

Musica Notturna
pno,5winds,5strings
sc EMB 10068 f.s.   (S1992)

Riflessioni, For Violoncello And
Orchestra
sc EMB 10234 f.s.   (S1993)

SZENARIO see Kagel, Mauricio

SZENE see Kelterborn, Rudolf

SZENE DER MARFA, FOR SOLO VOICE AND
ORCHESTRA see Joachim, Joseph

SZENEN, FOR FLUTE AND CHAMBER ORCHESTRA
see Redel, Martin Christoph

SZENEN I, II, III see Stranz, Ulrich

SZERVANSZKY, ENDRE (1911-   )
Concerto In Memoriam József Attila
sc EMB 2081 f.s.   (S1994)

Oriental Tale
sc EMB 526 f.s.   (S1995)

SZERYNG, HENRYK (1918-1988)
Preludio Classico, For Violin And
Orchestra [3'30"]
2.2.0.0. 2.0.0.0. timp,strings,
vln solo
(alternate wind scoring: 2.2.1.1.
4.0.0.0.) BILLAUDOT perf mat rent
(S1996)
SZOKOLAY, SANDOR (1931-   )
Concerto for Orchestra [35']
3(pic).3(English horn).3(bass
clar).3(contrabsn). 4.4.3.1.
5perc,harp,cel,strings
sc UNIVER. UE17871 f.s., perf mat
rent   (S1997)

Rhapsody for Chamber Orchestra
sc EMB 10266 f.s., perf mat rent
(S1998)
SZÖLLÖSY, ANDRAS (1921-   )
Canto D'Antunno
sc EMB 13403 f.s., perf mat rent
(S1999)
Concerto No. 5
see Lehellet

Lehellet (Concerto No. 5)
sc EMB 10219 f.s.   (S2000)

Tristia
string orch
sc EMB 12785 f.s., perf mat rent
(S2001)
SZÖNYI, ERZSEBET (ELIZABETH)
(1924-   )
Divertimento No. 2
sc EMB 714 f.s.   (S2002)

Three Ideas In Four Movements, For
Piano And Chamber Orchestra
sc EMB 12207 f.s.   (S2003)

SZUNYOGH, BALÁZS
Piccola Divertimento
string orch
sc EMB 12764 f.s., perf mat rent
(S2004)
SZYMANOWSKI, KAROL (1882-1937)
Concerto for Violin and Orchestra,
No. 1, Op. 35
study sc UNIVER. UE 17402 $27.00
(S2005)

SZYMANSKI, PAWEL (1954-   )
Four Liturgical Pieces, For Solo
Voice And Orchestra [22']
pic,2ob,trom,3perc,pno,9vla,6vcl,
S solo
CHESTER perf mat rent   (S2006)

Partita No. 3 for Harpsichord and
Orchestra [14']
3(pic).0.3.0.soprano sax.2alto
sax. 0.3.3.1. perc,elec gtr,
strings without vla,hpsd solo
CHESTER perf mat rent   (S2007)

Partita No. 4 [13']
2(pic).2.2.2. 4.2.3.1. 2perc,
strings
CHESTER perf mat rent   (S2008)

Study Of Shade, A [11']
2.2.3.2. 2.2.2.0. 2vibra,pno,
strings
CHESTER perf mat rent   (S2009)

Through The Looking Glass I [13']
1.1.1.0. 1.0.0.0. 5perc,cel,pno,
hpsd,harp,3mand,gtr,2vln,vla,
vcl,db
CHESTER perf mat rent   (S2010)

T

TA DEN SPRINGAR see Berge, Sigurd

TA IKKE DENNE URO FRA MEG see Solås,
Eyvind

TABACHNIK, MICHEL (1942-   )
Arch, L', For Solo Voice And Chamber
Orchestra [25']
alto fl,ob&English horn,bass
clar,bass trom,2perc,harp,
strings,S solo
SALABERT perf mat rent   (T1)

Imaginaires, Les [8']
4.4.4.4. 8.5.4.2. 4tam-tam,4bass
drum,strings
RICORDI-IT 132285 perf mat rent
(T2)
Invention A Seize Voix [17'30"]
1.0+English horn+ob d'amore.0+
bass clar(contrabass clar).0+
contrabsn.basset horn. 1.1.1.1.
2vibra,2marimba,tam-tam,tubular
bells,org,2pno,harp,2vln,4vcl,
2db,electronic equipment
RICORDI-IT 132024 perf mat rent
(T3)
Mondes, Per Una Grande Orchestra E
Una Piccola Orchestra [40']
4.4.5.4. 6.5.4.1. timp,5perc,
2pno,2cel,org,hpsd,2harp,
strings
RICORDI-IT 131913 perf mat rent
(T4)
Pastel II
1(pic).1(English horn).2(bass
clar).1. 0.1.2.0. 4perc,pno,
cel,2harp,strings
NOVELLO perf mat rent   (T5)

Perseides, Les
3.3.3.3. 4.3.3.1. 2perc,pno,
2harp,strings
RICORDI-IT 132494 perf mat rent
(T6)
TABLAS, FOR GUITAR AND ORCHESTRA see
Ruiz Pipó, Antonio

TABLE DU SILENCE, LA see Olah, Tiberiu

TABLEAU see Lachenmann, Helmut
Friedrich

TABLEAU VIVANT see Krauze, Zygmunt

TABLEAUX see Lazarof, Henri

TABLEAUX, FOR SOLO VOICES AND ORCHESTRA
see Mamiya, Michio

TABLEAUX ENCADRÉS see Kelterborn,
Rudolf

TABLEAUX SYMPHONIQUES see Fanelli,
Ernest

TABU see Lecuona, Margarita

TABULA RASA see Söderberg, Hans

TABULA RASA, FOR 2 VIOLINS AND STRING
ORCHESTRA see Pärt, Arvo

TACHYS see Stranz, Ulrich

TADA, EIICHI (1950-   )
Symphony No. 2 [45']
4(alto fl,pic).4.4(clar in E
flat,bass clar).4(contrabsn).
6.4.4.1. timp,perc,cel&pno,
2harp,strings
sc ZEN-ON 899400 f.s., perf mat
rent   (T7)

TAFEL-MUSIK see Motte, Diether de la

TAFELMUSIK I, NO. 1 see Telemann, Georg
Philipp

TAFELMUSIK I, NO. 3 see Telemann, Georg
Philipp

TAG- UND NACHTWEISEN see Schwertsik,
Kurt

TAGEBUCHBLATTER AUS FRANKREICH see
Pütz, Eduard

TAGLIETTI, GABRIO (1955-   )
Paesaggi Con L'unicorno, For Piano
And Orchestra [11']
2.0.2(bass clar).0. 2.0.0.0.
2perc,2vln,vla,vcl,db,pno solo
RICORDI-IT 133486 perf mat rent
(T8)
TAI CHI see Chan, Ka Nin

TAILLEFERRE, GERMAINE (1892-1983)
Ballade for Piano and Orchestra [15']
2+pic.2+English horn.2.2.
4.3.3.1. 2harp,cel,timp,perc,
strings,pno solo
CHESTER JWC308B perf mat rent   (T9)

Concerto Pour Voix Elevee [14']
2.2.2.2. 2.1.0.0. perc,harp,
strings,high solo
LEMOINE perf mat rent   (T10)

Fleurs De France
1.1.1.1. 2.1.1.0. timp,drums,
harp,cel,hpsd,strings
LEMOINE perf mat rent   (T11)

Image [3']
1.0.1.0. 0.0.0.0. harp,cel,
strings
CHESTER JWC308A perf mat rent (T12)

Partita for Flute, Oboe, Clarinet and
Strings [15']
fl,ob,clar,strings
SIKORSKI perf mat rent   (T13)

Sinfonietta [9']
trp,timp,strings
LEMOINE perf mat rent   (T14)

TAIRA, YOSHIHISA
Chromophonie [27']
RIDEAU perf mat rent   (T15)

Clea [14']
7vln,2vla,2vcl,db
RIDEAU perf mat rent   (T16)

Hierophonie II [16']
3fl,4perc,pno,harp,4vla,2db
RIDEAU perf mat rent   (T17)

Hierophonie III [14']
2(pic,alto fl).2(English
horn).2.2. 4.3.3.1. timp,3perc,
harp,strings
RIDEAU perf mat rent   (T18)

Radiance, For Piano And Instrumental
Ensemble [11']
fl,ob,clar,horn,trp,perc,harp,
strings,pno solo
RIDEAU perf mat rent   (T19)

Sonomorphie III [15'50"]
RIDEAU perf mat rent   (T20)

Stratus, Version I [11']
12vln,4vla,4vcl,2db
RIDEAU perf mat rent   (T21)

Stratus, Version II [11']
fl,harp,strings
RIDEAU perf mat rent   (T22)

TAKACS, JENÖ (1902-   )
Partita for Guitar and String
Orchestra, Op. 55b [20']
string orch,gtr/hpsd solo
DOBLINGER perf mat rent   (T23)

Sinfonia Breve *Op.108 [17']
2.2.2.2. 2.1.0.0. timp,strings
DOBLINGER perf mat rent   (T24)

TAKAHASHI, YUJI (1938-   )
Orphika [12']
3.3.3.3. 4.4.4.1. strings
PETERS   (T25)

TAKAHASHI, YUTAKA (1953-   )
Prajna-Naya Symphony
JAPAN 8301   (T26)

TAKE CARE OF THIS HOUSE, FOR SOLO VOICE
AND ORCHESTRA see Bernstein,
Leonard

TAKEMITSU, TORU (1930-   )
Arc, Part I, For Piano And Orchestra
[15']
3.3.3.3. 4.4.3.1. 4perc,harp,cel,
elec gtr,strings,pno solo
SALABERT perf mat rent   (T27)

Arc, Part II, For Piano And Orchestra
[15']
3.3.3.3. 4.4.3.1. 4perc,harp,cel,
elec gtr,strings,pno solo
SALABERT perf mat rent   (T28)

Arc For Strings [6']
12vln,8vcl
SALABERT perf mat rent   (T29)

Autumn, For Biwa, Shakuhachi, And
Orchestra [18']
3(pic,alto fl,bass fl).2(English
horn).3(bass clar,contrabass
clar).2(contrabsn). 3.4.3.0.
4perc,cel,2harp,strings,biwa
solo,shakuhachi solo
SALABERT perf mat rent   (T30)

TAKEMITSU, TORU (cont'd.)

Cassiopeia, For Percussion And
Orchestra [20']
4(pic,alto fl).3(English
horn).4(clar in E flat,bass
clar).2+contrabsn. 4.2+
cornet.2+bass trom.1. 4perc,
2harp,cel,elec gtr,strings,perc
solo
SALABERT perf mat rent   (T31)

Corona [15']
18vln,4vcl
SALABERT perf mat rent   (T32)

Dream-Window [15']
4(pic,alto fl).3(English
horn).4(bass
clar).3(contrabsn). 4.3.3.0.
timp,4perc,2harp,cel,gtr,
strings
study sc SCHOTT,J SJ 1044 $45.00,
perf mat rent   (T33)

Dreamtime [14']
3.3.3.3. 4.3.3.1. perc,2harp,cel,
strings
sc SCHOTT,J $32.00   (T34)

Far Calls, Coming, Far, For Violin
And Orchestra
3.3.4.3. 4.3.2.1. timp,perc,
2harp,cel,strings,vln solo
sc SCHOTT,J 73 1005 $32.00, perf
mat rent   (T35)

Flock Descends Into The Pentagonal
Garden, A [15']
3(pic,alto fl).3(English
horn).3(clar in E flat,bass
clar).2(contrabsn). 4.2.3.0.
3perc,2harp,cel,strings
SALABERT perf mat rent   (T36)

Gemeaux, For Oboe, Trombone, And 2
Orchestras [37']
4(pic,alto fl).2(English
horn).4(clar in E flat,bass
clar,contrabass
clar).4(contrabsn). 6.4.4.0.
timp,6perc,2harp,mand,gtr,cel,
pno,strings,ob solo,trom solo
SCHOTT,J perf mat rent   (T37)

Gitimalya "Bouquet Of Songs", For
Marimba And Orchestra [16']
1(pic,bass fl).1+English horn.1+
clar in E flat+bass clar.1+
contrabsn. 3.2.2+bass trom.0.
4perc,2harp,pno,cel,gtr,10vla,
8vcl,6db,marimba solo
SALABERT perf mat rent   (T38)

I Hear The Water Dreaming, For Flute
And Orchestra [14']
2(pic,alto fl).2(English
horn).2(bass
clar).2(contrabsn). 2.3.2.0.
perc,cel,2harp,strings,fl solo
study sc SCHOTT,J SJ 1052 f.s.,
perf mat rent   (T39)

Marginalia [12']
3(pic).3(English horn).3(bass
clar).3(contrabsn). 4.3.3.1. 4-
5perc,2harp,cel,pno,strings
SALABERT perf mat rent   (T40)

Nostalghia, For Violin And String
Orchestra [11']
string orch,vln solo
study sc SCHOTT,J SJ 1045 $19.50,
perf mat rent   (T41)

Orion And Pleiades, For Violoncello
And Orchestra [25']
3.3.3.3. 4.3.3.1. perc,2harp,cel,
strings,vcl solo
sc SCHOTT,J $49.00   (T42)

Quatrain, For Violin, Clarinet,
Violoncello, Piano And Orchestra
[19']
3(pic,alto fl).2(English
horn).4(clar in E flat,bass
clar,contrabass
clar).3(contrabsn). 3.4.3.1.
5perc,2harp,cel,strings,vln
solo,clar solo,vcl solo,pno
solo
SALABERT perf mat rent   (T43)

Rain Coming
sc SCHOTT,J $16.00   (T44)

Requiem [9']
string orch
sc SALABERT f.s., perf mat rent
(T45)
Riverrun, For Piano And Orchestra
[15']
3.3.4.3. 4.3.3.0. perc,cel/harp,
strings,pno solo
sc SCHOTT,J $49.00   (T46)

TAKEMITSU, TORU (cont'd.)

Scene, For Violoncello And String
Orchestra [6']
string orch,vcl solo
SCHOTT,J perf mat rent   (T47)

Star Isle [7']
3.3.3.3. 4.3.3.1. perc,cel,2harp,
strings
sc SCHOTT,J $15.00   (T48)

Textures, For Piano And Orchestra
[6']
3+pic+alto fl.1+English
horn.2(clar in E flat)+bass
clar.2(contrabsn). 3.3.6.1.
6perc,harp,gtr,cel,strings,pno
solo
SALABERT perf mat rent   (T49)

To The Edge Of A Dream, For Guitar
And Orchestra [15']
3.3.3.3. 4.2.3.0. perc,cel,2harp,
strings,gtr solo
sc SCHOTT,J $29.00   (T50)

Toward The Rainbow, Palma, For Oboe
d'Amore, Guitar And Orchestra
[15']
SCHOTT,J   (T51)

Toward The Sea II, For Alto Flute,
Harp And String Orchestra [14']
string orch,alto fl solo,harp
solo
SCHOTT,J   (T52)

Twill By Twilight [12']
4.3.4.3. 4.4.3.1. perc,cel,2harp,
strings
study sc SCHOTT,J SJ 1053 f.s.,
perf mat rent   (T53)

Vers, L'arc-En-Ciel, Palma, For Oboe
D'amore, Guitar And Orchestra
[15']
3(pic,alto fl).3(English
horn).3(clar in E flat,bass
clar).3(contrabsn). 4.3.3.0.
4perc,2harp,cel,strings,ob
d'amore solo,gtr solo
sc SCHOTT,J $35.00, perf mat rent
(T54)

Way A Lone II, A [14']
string orch
sc SCHOTT,J $12.00   (T55)

Winter [6']
2.2.2.2. 4.2.3.1. 6perc,harp,
strings
SALABERT perf mat rent   (T56)

TAKTAKISHVILI, OTAR (1924-   )
Concerto for Piano and Orchestra, No.
2
SIKORSKI perf mat rent   (T57)

Concerto for Piano and Orchestra, No.
4 [30']
2+pic.2+English horn.2+bass
clar.2+contrabsn. 4.4.3.1.
timp,perc,strings,pno solo
VAAP perf mat rent   (T58)

Concerto for Violin and Orchestra
[30']
3.3.3.3. 4.0.0.1. timp,perc,harp,
cel,strings,vln solo
SIKORSKI perf mat rent   (T59)

Concerto for Violoncello and
Orchestra [30']
3.3.3.3. 4.3.3.1. timp,perc,harp,
cel,pno,strings,vcl solo
SIKORSKI perf mat rent   (T60)

Festtag In Kartli [8']
2.1.2.2. 2.2.1.0. timp,xylo,harp,
pno,strings
SIKORSKI perf mat rent   (T61)

Mindia: Elegy [5']
2.2.2.2. 4.0.0.0. glock,harp,cel,
strings
SIKORSKI perf mat rent   (T62)

Mindia: March [5']
2.2.3.2. 4.4.3.1. timp,drums,
xylo,harp,strings
SIKORSKI perf mat rent   (T63)

Symphony No. 2 [35']
3.3.3.2. 4.3.3.1. timp,perc,harp,
strings
SIKORSKI perf mat rent   (T64)

TALA see Roosendael, Jan Rokus van

TALE OF PETER RABBIT, THE, FOR NARRATOR
AND ORCHESTRA see Zaninelli, Luigi

TALE OF THE STONE FLOWER: GYPSY FANTASY
see Prokofiev, Serge

TALE OF THE STONE FLOWER: SUITE see
Prokofiev, Serge

TALES FROM THE VIENNA WOODS, [ARR.] see
Strauss, Johann, [Jr.], Geschichten
Aus Dem Wienerwald Walzer, [arr.]

TALES OF SUMMER SEA see Jolas, Betsy

TALES OF THE NETSILIK, FOR SOLO VOICE
AND ORCHESTRA see Luedeke, Raymond

TALISMANO, IL: OVERTURE see Salieri,
Antonio

TALVI-ILTANA, FOR SOLO VOICE AND STRING
ORCHESTRA [ARR.] see Pohjanmies,
Juhani

TAMARA see Balakirev, Mily Alexeyevich

TAMAYANA see Adomian, Lan

TAMBA, AKIRA (1932-   )
Complex Simple, For 2 Ondes Martinot
And Instrumental Ensemble [11']
1(pic).0.1.0. 1.1.1.0. 4perc,vln,
vla,vcl,db,2Ondes Martenot
RIDEAU perf mat rent   (T65)

Concerto Da Camera, For Flute And
String Orchestra [14']
string orch,fl solo
RIDEAU perf mat rent   (T66)

Resurgence, For Harpsichord And
String Orchestra [20']
7vln,2vla,2vcl,db,pno solo
RIDEAU perf mat rent   (T67)

Sunyata [28']
2(pic).2.2+bass clar.1+contrabsn.
3.2.2.1. 2perc,strings
RIDEAU perf mat rent   (T68)

TAMBERG, EINO (1930-   )
Concerto for Trumpet and Orchestra,
Op. 42
2.2.2.2. 2.1.0.0. timp,perc,pno,
strings,trp solo
SIKORSKI perf mat rent   (T69)
VAAP perf mat rent   (T70)

TAMBOURIN see Durufle, Maurice

TAMBOURIN, LE. SUITES 1 AND 2 see
Rands, Bernard

TAMBOURIN CHINOIS, FOR VIOLIN AND
ORCHESTRA [ARR.] see Kreisler,
Fritz

TAMBURLAINE see Cruft, Adrian

TAMBURO PICCOLO see Berge, Sigurd

TAMERLAN: ERD' UND HIMMEL MAG SICH
WAPPNEN, FOR SOLO VOICE AND
ORCHESTRA see Handel, George
Frideric, Tamerlano: Ciel E Terra
Armi Di Sdegno, For Solo Voice And
Orchestra

TAMERLANO: CIEL E TERRA ARMI DI SDEGNO,
FOR SOLO VOICE AND ORCHESTRA see
Handel, George Frideric

TAMESIS see Roxburgh, Edwin

TAMIAMI, CORY
see SCHMIDT, WILLIAM

TANAKA, KAREN (1961-   )
Anamorphose, For Piano And Chamber
Orchestra [16']
2(pic).1(English horn).1(bass
clar).1(contrabsn). 2.2.2.0.
timp,perc,2harp,strings,pno
solo
CHESTER perf mat rent   (T71)

Aubade [10']
3(pic,alto fl).3(English
horn).3.3. 4.3.3.1. 5perc,cel,
2harp,strings
CHESTER perf mat rent   (T72)

Prismes [10']
2+pic.3.3(bass
clar).3(contrabsn). 4.4.3.0.
4perc,cel,2harp,pno,strings
CHESTER perf mat rent   (T73)

TANAKA, SATOSHI (1956-   )
Hour Of Silence, The
JAPAN 8501   (T74)

TANAKA, TOSHIMITSU (1930-   )
Gunzo [17'15"]
2+pic.3(English horn).3(bass
clar).2+contrabsn. 4.3.2.1.
timp,perc,strings
JAPAN f.s.   (T75)

TANCREDI: OVERTURE see Rossini,
Gioacchino

TANDAVA NRITYA see Sohal, Naresh

TANDELEI. POLKA-MAZURKA see Strauss,
Johann, [Jr.]

TANENBAUM, ELIAS (1924-   )
Birthday Waves [1']
2.2.2.2. 4.3.3.1. perc,strings
sc AM.COMP.AL. $6.50   (T76)

Cygnology, For Solo Voice And
Orchestra [16']
fl,clar,pno,strings,S solo
sc AM.COMP.AL. $23.00   (T77)

Interruptions [12']
2.3.3.3. 4.3.3.1. timp,perc,
strings,electronic tape, jazz
ensemble
sc AM.COMP.AL. $17.55   (T78)

Kaleidoscope [18']
string orch,electronic tape
sc AM.COMP.AL. $61.35, perf mat
rent   (T79)

Six Designs, For Solo Voice And
Orchestra [30']
2.2.3.3. 4.3.3.1. perc,harp,
strings,S solo
sc AM.COMP.AL. $56.60   (T80)

Waves, For Guitar And Orchestra [20']
2.2+English horn.2+bass clar.2+
contrabsn. 4.3.3.1. perc,harp,
strings,gtr solo
sc AM.COMP.AL. $25.15, perf mat
rent   (T81)

TANGO see Hall, Pauline see Schedl,
Gerhard

TANGO HABANERA, FOR VIOLIN, AND
ORCHESTRA see Jahn, Thomas

TANGOS see Orrego-Salas, Juan A.

TANN, HILARY
Open Field, The [10']
2+pic.2.2.2. 4.3.3.1. timp,3perc,
strings
OXFORD perf mat rent   (T82)

TANNHÄUSER: ALLMÄCHTIGE JUNGFRAU, FOR
SOLO VOICE AND ORCHESTRA see
Wagner, Richard

TANNHÄUSER: DICH, TEURE HALLE, FOR SOLO
VOICE AND ORCHESTRA see Wagner,
Richard

TANNHÄUSER: O DU MEIN HOLDER
ABENDSTERN, FOR SOLO VOICE AND
ORCHESTRA see Wagner, Richard

TANNHÄUSER: OVERTURE see Wagner,
Richard

TANNHAUSER: OVERTURE AND VENUSBERG
MUSIC see Wagner, Richard

TANNHAUSER: WIE TODESAHNUNG, FOR SOLO
VOICE AND ORCHESTRA see Wagner,
Richard

TANSMAN, ALEXANDRE (1897-1986)
Capriccio for Orchestra [15']
3.2.2.2. 4.2.3.1. timp,perc,cel,
harp,pno,strings
ESCHIG perf mat rent   (T83)

Concertino for Flute and Orchestra
[15']
pno,strings,fl solo
ESCHIG perf mat rent   (T84)

Concertino for Guitar and Orchestra
[20']
2.2.2.2. 2.2.0.0. timp,cel,
strings,gtr solo
ESCHIG perf mat rent   (T85)

Concerto for Viola and Orchestra
[20']
2.2.2.2. 4.3.0.0. timp,perc,pno,
strings,vla solo
ESCHIG perf mat rent   (T86)

Concerto for Violin and Orchestra
[25']
2.2.2.2. 4.3.3.1. timp,perc,cel,
pno,strings,vln solo
ESCHIG perf mat rent   (T87)

Concerto for Violoncello and
Orchestra [25']
3.2.2.2. 4.3.0.0. perc,cel,pno,
strings,vcl solo
ESCHIG perf mat rent   (T88)

Deux Images De La Bible
2.2.2.2. 4.3.3.1. timp,perc,cel,
pno,strings

TANSMAN, ALEXANDRE (cont'd.)

ESCHIG perf mat rent   (T89)

Diptych [15']
2.1.1.0. 2.0.0.0. perc,cel,pno,
strings
ESCHIG perf mat rent   (T90)

Divertimento for Chamber Orchestra
[15']
1.1.1.1. 1.1.0.0. cel,xylo,pno,
strings
study sc ESCHIG f.s., perf mat rent
(T91)

Dix Commandements, Les [16']
2.2.2.2. 4.3.3.1. timp,perc,pno,
strings
study sc ESCHIG f.s., perf mat rent
(T92)

Due Intermezzi, For Orchestra [8']
2.2.2.2. 4.3.3.1. timp,perc,cel,
pno,strings
ESCHIG perf mat rent   (T93)

Elegie In Memory Of Darius Milhaud
[13']
2.2.2.2. 4.3.3.1. timp,perc,cel,
pno,strings
study sc ESCHIG f.s., perf mat rent
(T94)

Fantasy for Piano and Orchestra [16']
2.2.2.2. 2.2.2.2. timp,strings,
pno solo
ESCHIG perf mat rent   (T95)

Fantasy for Violoncello and Orchestra
[18']
2.2.2.2. 2.2.2.0. timp,perc,cel,
pno,strings,vcl solo
ESCHIG perf mat rent   (T96)

Hommage A Erasme De Rotterdam [15']
2.2.2.2. 4.3.3.1. timp,perc,cel,
pno,strings
study sc ESCHIG f.s., perf mat rent
(T97)

Huit Steles De Victor Segalen, For
Solo Voice And Chamber Orchestra
[16']
1.1.1.1. 1.0.0.0. timp,perc,cel,
strings,S solo
ESCHIG perf mat rent   (T98)

Partita No. 2 for Piano and Chamber
Orchestra [15']
3.2.2.2. 2.1.0.0. timp,perc,
strings,pno solo
ESCHIG perf mat rent   (T99)

Ponctuation Francaise, For Solo Voice
And Chamber Orchestra [15']
2.2.2.2. 2.2.0.0. timp,perc,pno,
strings,solo voice
ESCHIG perf mat rent   (T100)

Quatre Mouvements, For Orchestra
[22']
2.2.2.2. 4.3.3.1. timp,perc,cel,
pno,strings
study sc ESCHIG f.s., perf mat rent
(T101)

Rapsodie Hebraique [8']
3.3.3.2.sax. 4.3.3.1. timp,perc,
cel,pno,strings
ESCHIG perf mat rent   (T102)

Rapsodie Polonaise [12']
3.3.3.2.sax. 4.3.3.1. timp,perc,
cel,pno,strings
ESCHIG perf mat rent   (T103)

Serenade No. 3 for Orchestra [11']
3.2.2.2. 4.3.3.1. timp,perc,cel,
pno,strings
ESCHIG perf mat rent   (T104)

Sinfonietta No. 2 [16']
1.1.0. 1.0.0.0. timp,perc,pno,
strings
sc ESCHIG f.s., perf mat rent
(T105)

Six Etudes Pour Orchestre [25']
3.3.2.2. 4.3.3.1. timp,perc,cel,
pno,harp,strings
study sc ESCHIG f.s., perf mat rent
(T106)

Six Mouvements Pour Orchestre A
Cordes [25']
string orch
sc ESCHIG f.s., perf mat rent
(T107)

Stele In Memoriam Igor Stravinsky
[18']
2.2.2.2. 4.3.3.1. timp,perc,cel,
pno,strings
study sc ESCHIG f.s., perf mat rent
(T108)

Suite Concertante for Oboe and
Chamber Orchestra [16']
2.0.2.2. 2.0.0.0. timp,perc,cel,
pno,strings,ob solo
ESCHIG perf mat rent   (T109)

TANSMAN, ALEXANDRE (cont'd.)

Symphony No. 3 for Piano, Violin,
Viola, Violoncello and Orchestra
[25']
3.3.3.2.sax. 4.3.3.1. timp,perc,
cel,strings,pno solo,vln solo,
vla solo,vcl solo
ESCHIG perf mat rent   (T110)

Symphony No. 4 [24']
3.2.2.2. 4.3.3.1. timp,perc,pno,
strings
ESCHIG perf mat rent   (T111)

Symphony No. 6 [23']
3.2.3.2. 4.3.3.1. timp,perc,pno,
strings,cor
(In Memoriam) study sc ESCHIG f.s.,
perf mat rent   (T112)

Symphony No. 7 [25']
3.2.2.2. 4.3.3.1. timp,perc,pno,
strings
ESCHIG perf mat rent   (T113)

Variations On A Theme Of Frescobaldi
[16']
string orch
ESCHIG perf mat rent   (T114)

TANTALUSQUALEN: OVERTURE see Suppe,
Franz von

TANTERL, H.
Almzauber Idylle, For Trumpet And
Orchestra
4horn,strings,trp solo
KRENN f.s.   (T115)

TANTO FOCO, FOR SOLO VOICE AND STRING
ORCHESTRA see Ziani, Marc Antonio

TANTZ-SCHUL see Kagel, Mauricio

TANZ-MOMENTE see Herbeck, Johann Franz
von

TANZ PRIORITATEN WALZER see Strauss,
Josef

TANZ-SUITE III see Stuppner, Hubert

TANZ SYMPHONIE see Reznicek, Emil
Nikolaus von

TANZADRESSEN WALZER see Strauss, Josef

TANZE see Grabner, Hermann

TANZE UND MARSCHE see Mozart, Wolfgang
Amadeus

TANZREIHEN see Eder, Helmut

TANZSPIEL see Zwilich, Ellen Taaffe

TANZSUITE see Koetsier, Jan

TANZSUITE MIT DEUTSCHLANDLIED see
Lachenmann, Helmut Friedrich

TAP DANCE CONCERTO see Gould, Morton

TAPESTRIES see Retzel, Frank

TAPESTRY see Cory, Eleanor see
Nadelson, Andrew

TAPIA COLMAN, SIMON
Gypsy Legend
see Leyenda Gitana

Leyenda Gitana
2+pic.2+English horn.2+bass
clar.2+contrabsn. 4.3.3.1.
timp,perc,pno,strings
"Gypsy Legend" sc PEER MUSIK
60689-856 $20.00, perf mat rent
(T116)

TAPIS POUR CORDES see Yun, Isang

TAQSIM-CAPRICE-MAQAM see Nilsson, Bo

TARA, [ARR.] see Steiner, Max(imillian
Raoul Walter)

TARANAKI OVERTURE see Pruden, Larry

TARANTELLA, LA, FOR SOLO VOICE AND
ORCHESTRA see Schönherr, Max

TARANU, CORNEL (1934-   )
Epitaphe Pour Enesco [6']
timp,harp,strings
SALABERT perf mat rent   (T117)

Guirlandes [16']
1.1.1.1. 1.1.1.0. 4perc,harp,pno&
cel,strings
SALABERT perf mat rent   (T118)

Long Song, For Clarinet And
Instrumental Ensemble [10']
pno,12strings,clar solo
SALABERT perf mat rent   (T119)

TARANU, CORNEL (cont'd.)

Raccords [9']
1.1.1.0. 1.1.0.0. perc,harp,pno,
strings
SALABERT perf mat rent   (T120)

Rime De Michelangelo, For Solo Voice
And Chamber Orchestra [9']
1.0.1.0. 1.1.1.0. perc,pno,vln,
vla,vcl,db,Bar solo
SALABERT perf mat rent   (T121)

TARAS BULBA: THE RIDE TO DUBNO see
Waxman, Franz

TARDOS, BELA (1910-1966)
Pezzo, For Violin And Orchestra
sc EMB 10274 f.s., perf mat rent
(T122)

TAREC: VERSUCH EINES ABSCHIEDS see
Steffens, Walter

TARIVERDIYEV, MIKAEL (1931-   )
Concerto for Violin and Orchestra
[31']
2.2.2.2. 2.2.2.0. timp,perc,harp,
hpsd,strings,vln solo
SIKORSKI perf mat rent   (T123)

TARNOPOLSKY, VLADIMIR (1955-   )
Concerto for Violoncello and
Orchestra [20']
3.3.3.3. 4.3.3.1. 2perc,harp,pno/
cel,strings,vcl solo
SIKORSKI perf mat rent   (T124)

TAROMIRS TID see Rehnqvist, Karin

TARP, SVEND ERIK (1908-   )
Burlesque Overture [4']
1.2.2.1. 2.2.2.0. timp,perc,pno,
strings
HANSEN-DEN perf mat rent   (T125)

Concertino for Flute and Orchestra
sc,pts SAMFUNDET f.s.   (T126)

Lystspilouverture
"Overture To A Comedy" sc,pts
SAMFUNDET f.s.   (T127)

Overture To A Comedy
see Lystspilouverture

Preludio Festivo [3']
2.1.2.1. 2.2.1.0. timp,strings
HANSEN-DEN perf mat rent   (T128)

Preludio Patetico [3']
2.2.2.2. 2.2.1.0. perc,strings
HANSEN-DEN perf mat rent   (T129)

Pro Defunctis [5']
2.2.2.2. 4.3.3.1. timp,perc,
strings
HANSEN-DEN perf mat rent   (T130)

Symphony in E flat
sc,pts SAMFUNDET f.s.   (T131)

Symphony No. 3
sc,pts SAMFUNDET f.s.   (T132)

TARTINI, GIUSEPPE (1692-1770)
Andante E Presto In D [arr.]
string orch [6'] KALMUS A7323 sc
$5.00, set $7.50, pts $1.50, ea.
(T133)

Concerto for Flute and String
Orchestra
string orch,fl/vln solo
fac ed AUTOGR $20.00   (T134)

Concerto for Trumpet and String
Orchestra in C, MIN 182, [arr.]
(Thilde, J.) string orch,hpsd,trp
solo [13'5"] sc BILLAUDOT f.s.,
perf mat rent   (T135)

Concerto for Trumpet and String
Orchestra in D, [arr.]
(Jevtic, I.) string orch,trp solo
[8'] BILLAUDOT perf mat rent
(T136)

Concerto for Violin and Orchestra in
D, Dounias 28 [20']
0.0.0.0. 2.2.0.0. timp,strings,
vln solo
(Bonelli) (in this edition listed
as No. 57) KALMUS A7325 sc
$12.00, set $20.00, pts $1.50,
ea., perf mat rent   (T137)

Concerto for Violin and String
Orchestra in A
min sc KALMUS K01423 $4.00   (T138)

Concerto for Violin and String
Orchestra in D minor, MIN 183
string orch,vln solo
(Pente) BENJ perf mat rent   (T139)

Concerto for Violin and String
Orchestra in E, MIN 119
string orch,vln solo

TARTINI, GIUSEPPE (cont'd.)

(Ney) EMB f.s. sc 6126, pts 6127
(T140)

Concerto for Violin and String
Orchestra in G minor [20']
string orch,hpsd,vln solo
BREITKOPF-W perf mat rent   (T141)

Concerto for Violoncello and String
Orchestra in A, MIN 35
(Leyden) KALMUS A6619 sc $3.00, set
$5.00, pts $1.25, ea., perf mat
rent   (T142)

Concerto for Violoncello and String
Orchestra in A, No. 87
(Ravanello) KALMUS A7324 sc $10.00,
set $13.00, pts $1.50, ea.   (T143)

Concerto in F, No. 58 [12']
2ob,2horn,strings
(Bonelli) KALMUS A7307 sc $7.00,
set $12.00, pts $1.50, ea.   (T144)

Devil's Trill, The, [arr.]
see Sonata, "Il Trillo Del Diavolo"
For Violin And Orchestra, [arr.]

Sinfonia Pastorale
(Schering) pno,strings [13'] KAHNT
KT 8891 f.s.   (T145)

Sonata, "Il Trillo Del Diavolo" For
Violin And Orchestra, [arr.] [8']
(Becker) "Devil's Trill, The,
[arr.]" 0.2.2.2. 2.0.0.0. timp,
strings,vln solo KALMUS A 5651 sc
$12.00, perf mat rent, set
$25.00, pts $2.00, ea.   (T146)

Variations On A Theme Of Corelli, For
Violin And Orchestra [arr.]
(Kreisler; McAlister) 0.2.2.2.
2.0.0.0. strings,vln solo [3'30"]
KALMUS A6323 sc $5.00, set $12.00
(T147)

TASSO, LAMENTO E TRIONFO see Liszt,
Franz

TATE, BRIAN
Brixham Overture
sc BERANDOL BER 1799 $7.00   (T148)

TATE, PHYLLIS (1912-1987)
Panorama [12']
string orch
OXFORD perf mat rent   (T149)

TATGENHORST, JOHN (1938-   )
Esprit [9'30"]
5.1.3.1.alto sax.2tenor
sax.baritone sax. 4.4.4.1.
timp,perc,pno,harp,elec bass,
gtr,strings
NEWAM 19041 perf mat rent   (T150)

TAUB, BRUCE J.H. (1948-   )
Ballet [30']
2.0.2.2. 0.2.2.1. perc,2pno,
strings
sc AM.COMP.AL. $42.65   (T151)

Chromatic Fantasy [11']
2+pic+alto fl.2+English horn.2+
clar in E flat+bass clar.1+
contrabsn.3sax. 4.4.3.1+
baritone horn. pno&cel,timp,
3perc,strings
PETERS P66975A perf mat rent (T152)

Gridlock [12']
3.3.3.3. 4.3.3.1. timp,3perc,
harp,pno,strings
sc AM.COMP.AL. $107.55   (T153)

TAUBO, LILLIAN GULOWNA
Norsk Landskap
2.2.2.1. 0.0.0.0. strings
NORGE   (T154)

TAURIELLO, ANTONIO (1931-   )
Music for Trumpet and String
Orchestra
string orch,trp solo
min sc PEER MUSIK 60815-766 $3.00
(T155)

TAUROMAQUIA, FOR PIANO FOUR HANDS AND
INSTRUMENTAL ENSEMBLE see Marco,
Tomas

TAUSENUNDEINEBLUME, OP. 33 see
Hartmann, Per Johannes

TAUSINGER, JAN (1921-1980)
J. Fucik: Report Written With A Rope
[10']
1.0.1.0. 1.2.1.0. tam-tam,cym,
hpsd,pno,xylo,vibra,strings
SUPRAPHON   (T156)

TAUSKY, VILEM (1910-   )
Coventry [8']
string orch
CHESTER JWC-A perf mat rent   (T157)

TAUTENHAHN, GUNTHER (1938-   )
Concept, Three
3.3.3.3. 3.6.3.1. timp,perc,pno,
harp,strings
SEESAW   (T158)

Concerto for Violin and Orchestra
3.3.3.3. 4.3.3.1. timp,2perc,
harp,strings,vln solo
SEESAW   (T159)

TAUTOPHONY see Sveinsson, Atli Heimir

TAVENER, JOHN (1944-   )
Akhmatova: Requiem, For Solo Voices
And Orchestra [56']
3horn,3trp,3trom,timp,5perc,cel,
strings,SB soli
CHESTER perf mat rent   (T160)

Eis Thanaton, For Solo Voices And
Orchestra
2bass trom,timp,harp,7vln,3vla,
6vcl,2db,SB soli
CHESTER perf mat rent   (T161)

Grandma's Footsteps [15']
ob,bsn,horn,2string quar, 5
musical boxes
CHESTER JWC310 perf mat rent (T162)

Immurement Of Antigone, The, For Solo
Voice And Orchestra [19']
0+2alto fl.0.0.0+2contrabsn.
4.3.2.0. harp,cel,2timp,8perc,
strings,Mez solo
CHESTER JWC 525 perf mat rent
(T163)
Palintropos, For Piano And Orchestra
[24']
0.0.0.0. 2.2.2.0. harp,cel,timp,
perc,strings,pno solo
CHESTER JWC510 perf mat rent (T164)

Protecting Veil, The, For Violoncello
And String Orchestra [30']
string orch,vcl solo
CHESTER perf mat rent   (T165)

Sappho: Lyrical Fragments, For Solo
Voices And String Orchestra [15']
string orch,SS soli
CHESTER perf mat rent   (T166)

Sixteen Haiku Of Seferis, For Solo
Voices And Orchestra [20']
timp,perc,strings,ST soli
CHESTER perf mat rent   (T167)

Towards The Son [18']
0.2.0.2. 0.2.2.0. timp,perc,
strings without vln, 4 bowed
psalteries, optional 3 treble
voices
CHESTER perf mat rent   (T168)

TAVLI see Kristensen, Kuno Kjaerbye

TAYLOR, CLIFFORD OLIVER (1923-1987)
Commencement Suite: Processional, For
String Orchestra [15']
string orch
sc AM.COMP.AL. $11.45, perf mat
rent   (T169)

Concerto for Clarinet and Orchestra
[15']
2+pic.2+English horn.2.2+
contrabsn. 4.2.2+bass trom.0.
timp,harp,strings,clar solo
sc AM.COMP.AL. $53.50   (T170)

Concerto No. 2 [10']
string orch,vln solo,vla solo
sc AM.COMP.AL. $9.15   (T171)

Concerto No. 3 [14']
string orch,vln solo,vla solo
sc AM.COMP.AL. $15.30   (T172)

Symphony No. 3 [23']
3.3.4.2. 4.2.3.1. perc,harp,cel,
strings
sc AM.COMP.AL. $59.40   (T173)

TAYLOR, DEAN
Concerto for Orchestra, Piano and
Percussion [40']
sc APNM $30.00, perf mat rent
(T174)
TAYLOR, TIMOTHY (1955-   )
Scherzi [11']
2(pic).2.2.2. 4.2.3.1. timp,
3perc,harp,strings
study sc UNIV.CR P66617 f.s., perf
mat rent   (T175)

TCHAIKOVSKY, ALEXANDER (1946-   )
Battleship Potemkin, The: Suite [24']
3(pic,alto fl).3(English
horn).3(bass
clar).3(contrabsn). 4.4.4.1.
timp,5perc,harp,pno,org,
strings,electronic tape
VAAP perf mat rent   (T176)

TCHAIKOVSKY, ALEXANDER (cont'd.)

Concerto for Bassoon and Orchestra
horn,trp,cel,harp,pno,strings,bsn
solo
VAAP perf mat rent   (T177)

Concerto for Violoncello and
Orchestra [27']
2.2.2.2. 4.3.2.0. perc,harp,cel,
strings,vcl solo
SIKORSKI perf mat rent   (T178)
VAAP perf mat rent   (T179)

Symphony
3(pic,alto fl).3(English
horn).3(bass
clar).3(contrabsn). 4.4.4.1.
timp,5perc,harp,pno,strings
VAAP perf mat rent   (T180)

TCHAIKOVSKY, BORIS (1925-   )
Chamber Symphony [25']
2ob,2horn,hpsd,strings
"Kammersinfonie" SIKORSKI perf mat
rent   (T181)

Concerto for Clarinet and Chamber
Orchestra [11']
3trp,timp,strings,clar solo
SIKORSKI perf mat rent   (T182)

Concerto for Piano and Chamber
Orchestra [26']
2horn,drums,strings,pno solo
SIKORSKI perf mat rent   (T183)

Concerto for Violin and Orchestra
[20']
0.0.0.0. 4.4.3.1. timp,strings,
vln solo
SIKORSKI perf mat rent   (T184)

Concerto for Violoncello and
Orchestra [33']
3fl,3trp,3trom,timp,perc,harp,
strings,vcl solo
SIKORSKI perf mat rent   (T185)

Kammersinfonie
see Chamber Symphony

Symphony No. 2 [50']
4.4.4.4. 4.4.4.0. timp,perc,cel,
harp,strings
SIKORSKI perf mat rent   (T186)
VAAP perf mat rent   (T187)

Teenager [31']
4.0.4.3. 4.4.3.0. timp,bells,S
rec,vla d'amore,cel,pno,strings
VAAP perf mat rent   (T188)

Theme and Variations [19']
4.4.4.4. 6.4.4.1. timp,perc,cel,
harp,strings
SIKORSKI perf mat rent   (T189)
VAAP perf mat rent   (T190)

Tierkreiszeichen, Die, For Solo
Voice, Harpsichord And Strings
[23']
hpsd,14vln,6vla,4vcl,2db,S solo
SIKORSKI perf mat rent   (T191)

TCHAIKOVSKY, PIOTR ILYICH (1840-1893)
Andante Cantabile, [arr.] (from
String Quartet No. 1, Op. 11)
(McAlister) string orch [8'] KALMUS
A6351 sc $3.00, set $7.50, pts
$1.50, ea., perf mat rent (T192)

Andante Cantabile for Violoncello and
String Orchestra, [arr.] (from
String Quartet No. 1, Op. 11)
(Tchaikovsky, P.I.) string orch,vcl
solo WOLLENWEBER 10 f.s.   (T193)

Autumn Song [arr.] *Op.37,No.10
(Tobani) 1.2.2.2. 2.2.3.0. timp,
perc,harmonium,strings [4']
KALMUS A5749 pno-cond sc $2.00,
set $14.00   (T194)

Barcarolle, [arr.] *Op.37,No.6
(Tobani) 1.2.2.2. 2.2.1.0. timp,
perc,strings [3'] KALMUS A5747
pno-cond sc $2.00, set $12.00
(T195)
Belle Au Bois Dormant, La: Pas De
Deux
see Sleeping Beauty, The: Pas De
Deux

Belle Au Bois Dormant, La: Pas De
Deux, Act III [arr.]
see Sleeping Beauty, The: Pas De
Deux, Act III [arr.]

Belle Au Bois Dormant, La: Pas De
Deux, "L'Oiseau Bleu" [arr.]
see Sleeping Beauty, The: Pas De
Deux, "Bluebird" [arr.]

TCHAIKOVSKY, PIOTR ILYICH (cont'd.)

Capriccio Italien
see Romeo And Juliet. Overture-
Fantasy
see Works For Orchestra, Vol. 2

Casse-Noisette: Grand Pas De Deux
[arr.]
see Nutcracker: Grand Pas De Deux
[arr.]

Casse-Noisette: Pas De Deux
see Nutcracker: Pas De Deux

Chant d'Alouette [arr.] *Op.37,No.3
(Tobani) 2.2.2.2. 4.2.3.0. timp,
perc,harmonium,strings [3']
KALMUS A5746 pno-cond sc $2.00,
set $15.00, perf mat rent (T196)

Chant Sans Paroles [arr.] *Op.2,No.3
(Kretschmer) "Song Without Words
[arr.]" 1.2.2.2. 2.2.1.0. timp,
perc,strings (also contains: Le
Cid: Aragonaise [arr.] by
Massenet) KALMUS A4128 pno-cond
sc $3.00, set $15.00, perf mat
rent   (T197)

Children's Album [arr.]
(Rogal-Levitsky) 2.2.2.1. 2.2.1.0.
perc,acord,mand,balalaika,strings
VAAP perf mat rent   (T198)

Concerto for Piano and Orchestra, No.
1, Op. 23, in B flat minor
VAAP perf mat rent   (T199)

Concerto for Piano and Orchestra, No.
2, Op. 44, in G
min sc KALMUS K00591 $8.75   (T200)

Concerto for Piano and Orchestra, No.
3, in E flat,First Movement
min sc KALMUS K00593 $7.00   (T201)

Concerto for Piano and Orchestra, No.
3, in E flat, [excerpt]
(Andante and Finale) min sc KALMUS
K00597 $8.75   (T202)

Concerto for Violin and Orchestra,
Op. 35, in D
VAAP perf mat rent   (T203)
*see GREAT ROMANTIC VIOLIN
CONCERTOS

Dance Suite [arr.]
(Tchemberdzhi, Nikolas) 3.3.2.2.
4.3.3.1. timp,perc,harp,strings
VAAP perf mat rent   (T204)

Elegy in G
string orch [7'] KALMUS A7262 sc
$5.00, set $7.00, pts $1.50, ea.
(T205)
Elegy In Honour Of Ivan Samarin
min sc KALMUS K00582 $4.50 contains
also: Jurists, March   (T206)

Eugene Onegin: Aria Of Lenski, For
Solo Voice And Orchestra
BREITKOPF-W 61 03125 $5.25   (T207)

Eugene Onegin: Aria Of Prince Gremin,
For Solo Voice And Orchestra
BREITKOPF-W 61 03126 $5.25   (T208)

Eugene Onegin: Triquet's Song, For
Solo Voice And Orchestra
KALMUS A3800 sc $5.00, set $10.00,
pts $.75, ea.   (T209)

Fatum
see Works For Orchestra, Vol. 2

Hamlet *Op.67 [21']
3.3.2.2. 4.4.3.1. timp,perc,
strings
RAHTER perf mat rent   (T210)
see Works For Orchestra, Vol. 1

Hamlet, Op. 67bis
(Andreae) 2.2.2.2. 2.0.3.0. timp,
perc,strings [5'] sc BELAIEFF
BEL514 f.s., perf mat rent (T211)

Hunt, The [arr.] *Op.37,No.9
(Tobani) 1.2.2.2. 2.2.1.0. timp,
perc,strings [4'] KALMUS A5748
pno-cond sc $2.00, set $12.00
(T212)
Jurists, March
see Elegy In Honour Of Ivan Samarin

Lac Des Cygnes, Le: Selection [arr.]
see Swan Lake: Selection [arr.]

Lac Des Cygnes: Pas De Deux, "Le
Cygne Blanc" [arr.]
see Swan Lake: Pas De Deux, "White
Swan" [arr.]

TCHAIKOVSKY, PIOTR ILYICH (cont'd.)

Lac Des Cygnes: Pas De Deux, "Le Cygne Noir" [arr.]
see Swan Lake: Pas De Deux, "Black Swan" [arr.]

Largo And Allegro, For Flute And String Orchestra
string orch,fl solo WOLLENWEBER 906 f.s.　　　(T213)

Manfred
(Russian Symphonic Music, Vol. 17)
sc MUZYKA f.s.　　　(T214)

Mazeppa: The Battle Of Poltava [7']
3.3.2.2. 4.4.3.1. timp,perc, strings
RAHTER perf mat rent　　　(T215)

Nocturne for Violoncello and Orchestra, Op. 19, No. 4 [5']
2.2.2.2. 2.0.0.0. strings,vcl solo
2.2.2.2. 2.0.0.0. strings,vcl solo
sc,pts WOLLENWEBER WW 901A f.s.　　　(T216)
SIKORSKI perf mat rent　　　(T217)

Nocturne for Violoncello and String Orchestra, Op. 19, No. 4, [arr.]
string orch,vcl solo sc,pts WOLLENWEBER WW 901B f.s.　　　(T218)

Noel [arr.] *Op.37,No.12
(Tobani) 1.2.2.2. 2.2.1.0. timp, perc,harmonium,strings [5']
KALMUS A5750 pno-cond sc $2.00, set $15.00, perf mat rent　(T219)

Nutcracker: Grand Pas De Deux [arr.]
(Stirn, D.) "Casse-Noisette: Grand Pas De Deux [arr.]" 3.3.3.2. 4.2.3.1. timp,2harp,strings [11']
BOIS perf mat rent　　　(T220)

Nutcracker: Pas De Deux
"Casse-Noisette: Pas De Deux" 3.3.3.2. 4.3.3.1. timp,harp, strings [10'] SALABERT perf mat rent　　　(T221)

Nutcracker: Suite
sc DOVER 253791 $5.95　　　(T222)

Opritchnik: Dance [12']
2+pic.2.2.2. 4.2.3.1. timp,3perc, strings
BREITKOPF-W perf mat rent　(T223)

Orage, L'. Overture *Op.76
"Storm, The. Overture" min sc KALMUS K00570 $8.50　　　(T224)

Overture 1812 *Op.49
sc MEZ KNIGA f.s.　　　(T225)
see Works For Orchestra, Vol. 2

Overture in C minor
min sc KALMUS K00572 $6.00　(T226)

Overture in F [12']
2.2.2.2. 4.2.3.0. timp,strings min sc KALMUS K00571 $11.50　(T227)
(Andreae) (second version, 1866) sc BELAIEFF BEL515 f.s., perf mat rent　　　(T228)

Overture On The Danish National Anthem *Op.15
3.2.2.2. 4.2.3.1. timp,perc, strings
min sc KALMUS K00573 $6.50　(T229)
VAAP perf mat rent　　　(T230)

Pathetique Symphony, [arr.] *see TWELVE POP HITS FROM THE CLASSICS, VOL. 2

Pezzo Capriccioso, For Violoncello And Orchestra *Op.62
KALMUS A6149 sc $8.00, set $16.00, perf mat rent　　　(T231)

Pezzo Capriccioso, For Violoncello And String Orchestra [arr.] *Op.62
(Suslin, Viktor) string orch,vcl solo SIKORSKI perf mat rent　　　(T232)

Piano Concerto No. 1, [arr.] *see TWELVE POP HITS FROM THE CLASSICS, VOL. 2

Pique Dame: Aria Of Lisa, For Solo Voice And Orchestra
see Queen Of Spades, The: Aria Of Lisa, For Solo Voice And Orchestra

Pique Dame: Herman's Aria, For Solo Voice And Orchestra
see Queen Of Spades, The: Herman's Aria, For Solo Voice And Orchestra

Pique Dame: Romance Of Pauline, For Solo Voice And Orchestra
see Queen Of Spades, The: Romance Of Pauline, For Solo Voice And Orchestra

Queen Of Spades, The: Aria Of Lisa, For Solo Voice And Orchestra
"Pique Dame: Aria Of Lisa, For Solo Voice And Orchestra" BREITKOPF-W 61 03074 $5.25　　　(T233)

Queen Of Spades, The: Herman's Aria, For Solo Voice And Orchestra
3.2.2.2. 4.2.3.1. timp,strings,T solo
"Pique Dame: Herman's Aria, For Solo Voice And Orchestra" VAAP perf mat rent　　　(T234)

Queen Of Spades, The: Romance Of Pauline, For Solo Voice And Orchestra
"Pique Dame: Romance Of Pauline, For Solo Voice And Orchestra" BREITKOPF-W 61 03075 $5.25 (T235)

Romeo and Juliet
see Works For Orchestra, Vol. 1

Romeo And Juliet, [arr.] *see TWELVE POP HITS FROM THE CLASSICS, VOL. 1

Romeo And Juliet. Overture-Fantasy
sc DOVER 252175 $7.95 contains also: Capriccio Italien　　(T236)
SONZOGNO perf mat rent　　(T237)
(Darvas) study sc EMB 40072 f.s.　　　(T238)

Schneeflockchen: Vorspiel
see Snow Maiden, The: Prelude

Seasons, The, For Piano And Orchestra [arr.]
(Gould, Morton) 1.1.2.1. 4.2.2.0. perc,harp,strings,pno solo [35']
SCHIRM.G perf mat rent　　(T239)

Serenade For Nikolai Rubinstein's Saint's Day
min sc KALMUS K00576 $6.00 contains also: Tempete, La: Fantasy, Op. 18　　　(T240)

Serenade Melancolique, For Violin And Orchestra
min sc KALMUS K00594 $4.50 contains also: Valse Scherzo, For Violin And Orchestra　　　(T241)

Serenade, Op. 48, in C
(Darvas) study sc EMB 40052 f.s.　　　(T242)
see Works For Orchestra, Vol. 2

Sleeping Beauty, The: Entr'acte, For Violin And Orchestra [arr.]
(Stravinsky, Igor) 2.2.2.2. 4.2+ 2cornet.3.1. timp,strings,vln solo [5'] BOOSEY perf mat rent (T243)

Sleeping Beauty, The: Pas De Deux
"Belle Au Bois Dormant, La: Pas De Deux" 3.3.2.2. 4.2.3.1. timp, 2harp,pno,strings [10'] SALABERT perf mat rent　　　(T244)

Sleeping Beauty, The: Pas De Deux, Act III [arr.]
(Stirn, D.) "Belle Au Bois Dormant, La: Pas De Deux, Act III [arr.]" 3.3.2.2. 4.2.3.1. timp,harp, strings [11'] BOIS perf mat rent　　　(T245)

Sleeping Beauty, The: Pas De Deux, "Bluebird" [arr.]
(Stirn, D.) "Belle Au Bois Dormant, La: Pas De Deux, "L'Oiseau Bleu" [arr.]" 3.3.2.2. 4.2.3.1. timp, perc,strings [8'] BOIS perf mat rent　　　(T246)

Sleeping Beauty, The: Polacca
KALMUS A6283 sc $14.00, set $40.00, pts $2.00, ea., perf mat rent　　　(T247)

Sleeping Beauty, The: Two Pieces
(Stravinsky, Igor) min sc BOOSEY 959 $11.00　　　(T248)

Sleeping Beauty, The: Variation D'Aurore [arr.]
(Stravinsky, Igor) 1.2.1.1. 4.2.3.1. strings [5'] BOOSEY perf mat rent　　　(T249)

Snow Maiden, The
sc MEZ KNIGA f.s.　　　(T250)

Snow Maiden, The: Prelude *Op.12 [9']
3.3.2.2. 4.2.3.1. timp,perc,harp, strings

"Schneeflockchen: Vorspiel" SIKORSKI perf mat rent　　(T251)

Song Without Words [arr.]
see Chant Sans Paroles [arr.]

Souvenir De Florence [arr.]
string orch sc,pts MUSICUS f.s.　　　(T252)

Souvenir De Hapsal: Ruines d'Un Chateau [arr.] *Op.2,No.1
(Vladimirov) "Souvenir De Hapsal: Ruins Of A Castle [arr.]" 3(pic).2+English horn.2.2. 4.4.3.1. timp,perc,harp,strings [3'] KALMUS A6160 sc $5.00, set $12.00　　　(T253)

Souvenir De Hapsal: Ruins Of A Castle [arr.]
see Souvenir De Hapsal: Ruines d'Un Chateau [arr.]

Storm, The. Overture
see Orage, L'. Overture

Suite No. 1, Op. 43
(Russian Symphonic Music, Vol. 18)
sc MUZYKA f.s. contains also: Suite No. 2, Op. 53　　　(T254)

Suite No. 2, Op. 53 [36']
3.2.2.2. 4.2.3.1. timp,perc, strings
VAAP perf mat rent　　　(T255)
see Suite No. 1, Op. 43

Suite No. 3, Op. 55
(Russian Symphonic Music, Vol. 19)
sc MUZYKA f.s. contains also: Suite No. 4, Op. 61　　　(T256)

Suite No. 4, Op. 61
see Suite No. 3, Op. 55

Swan Lake: Pas De Deux, "Black Swan" [arr.]
(Stirn, D.) "Lac Des Cygnes: Pas De Deux, "Le Cygne Noir" [arr.]" 3.2.2.2. 4.2.3.1. timp,perc,harp, strings [11'] BOIS perf mat rent　　　(T257)

Swan Lake: Pas De Deux, "White Swan" [arr.]
(Stirn, D.) "Lac Des Cygnes: Pas De Deux, "Le Cygne Blanc" [arr.]" 2(pic).2.2.2. 4.2(cornet).3.1. timp,perc,harp,strings [13'] BOIS perf mat rent　　　(T258)

Swan Lake: Selection [arr.]
(Wal-Berg) "Lac Des Cygnes, Le: Selection [arr.]" [5'10"] CHOUDENS perf mat rent　　(T259)

Swan Lake: Valse Bluette [6']
2.1.1.1. 4.0.0.0. perc,harp, strings
VAAP perf mat rent　　　(T260)

Symphony No. 1, Op. 13, in G minor [41']
3.2.2.2. 4.2.3.1. timp,perc, strings
(Russian Symphonic Music, Vol. 14)
sc MUZYKA f.s. contains also: Symphony No. 2, Op. 17, in C minor　　　(T261)
VAAP perf mat rent　　　(T262)

Symphony No. 2, Op. 17, in C minor
(Bessel edition) KALMUS A5725 sc $60.00, set $110.00, perf mat rent　　　(T263)
(second version) sc VAAP f.s.　　　(T264)
see Symphony No. 1, Op. 13, in G minor

Symphony No. 3, Op. 29, in D
study sc BREITKOPF-W PB 3625 f.s.　　　(T265)
(Russian Symphonic Music, Vol. 15)
sc MUZYKA f.s. contains also: Symphony No. 4, Op. 36, in F minor　　　(T266)

Symphony No. 4, Op. 36, in F minor
(German edition) KALMUS A6150 sc $50.00, set $110.00, perf mat rent　　　(T267)
see Symphony No. 3, Op. 29, in D

Symphony No. 5, [arr.] *see TWELVE POP HITS FROM THE CLASSICS, VOL. 1

Symphony No. 5, Op. 64, in E minor
(German edition) KALMUS A6151 sc $60.00, set $110.00, perf mat rent　　　(T268)
min sc UNIVER. PH00063 $10.75　　　(T269)
(Russian Symphonic Music, Vol. 16)

TCHAIKOVSKY, PIOTR ILYICH (cont'd.)

sc MUZYKA f.s. contains also:
Symphony No. 6, Op. 74, in B
minor   (T270)

Symphony No. 6, Op. 74, in B minor
see Symphony No. 5, Op. 64, in E
minor

Symphony No. 7 in E flat
*reconstruction
min sc SIKORSKI 034-27846 $44.00
(T271)

Tempest, The
see Works For Orchestra, Vol. 1

Tempete, La: Fantasy, Op. 18
see Serenade For Nikolai
Rubinstein's Saint's Day

Troika [arr.] *Op.37,No.11
(Baron) 0+pic.1.2.1. 2.2.1.0. timp,
perc,strings [3'] KALMUS A5841
pno-cond sc $2.00, set $15.00,
perf mat rent   (T272)

Valse Scherzo, For Violin And
Orchestra
see Serenade Melancolique, For
Violin And Orchestra

Voyevode
see Works For Orchestra, Vol. 2

Works For Orchestra, Vol. 1
sc MUZYKA f.s. Russian Symphonic
Music, Vol. 20
contains: Hamlet; Romeo and
Juliet; Tempest, The   (T273)

Works For Orchestra, Vol. 2
sc MUZYKA f.s. Russian Symphonic
Music, Vol. 21
contains: Capriccio Italien;
Fatum; Overture 1812; Serenade,
Op. 48, In C; Voyevode   (T274)

TCHEREPNIN, ALEXANDER (1899-1977)
Concerto for Piano and Orchestra, No.
1, Op. 12, in F [16']
2.2.2.2. 4.2.3.1. timp,strings,
pno solo
BELAIEFF perf mat rent   (T275)

Musica Sacra (from String Quartet,
Op. 36)
(Redel, Kurt) string orch [9']
SCHOTTS perf mat rent   (T276)

Symphony No. 3, Op. 83 [26']
3.3.3.3. 4.3.3.1. timp,perc,harp,
strings
BELAIEFF perf mat rent   (T277)

Symphony, Op. 42, in E [20']
2.2.2.2. 4.2.3.1. timp,perc,
strings
study sc DURAND 597-00472 $5.75
(T278)

TCHEREPNIN, IVAN ALEXANDROVITCH
(1943-   )
New Consonance, The [20']
string orch
BELAIEFF   (T279)

TCHEREPNIN, NIKOLAY NIKOLAYEVICH
(1873-1945)
Romance For A Mummy, A: Four
Fragments [12']
1+pic.2.2.2. 2.2(cornet).3.0+
sousaphone. harp,cel,org/
harmonium,timp,perc,strings
(Goossens, Albert) CHESTER JWC321
perf mat rent   (T280)

Royaume Enchante, Le *Op.39
4.3.3.2. 4.3.2.0. timp,perc,cel,
2harp,pno,strings
VAAP perf mat rent   (T281)

TE KJAERASTEN MIN see Kielland, Olav

TEA FOR TWO, [ARR.] see Youmans,
Vincent Millie

TEAR, THE, FOR SAXOPHONE AND ORCHESTRA
see Dominello, Larry

TECHNOPHRENIA see Baker, Michael Conway

TECUM PRINCIPIUM, FOR SOLO VOICE AND
ORCHESTRA see Bellini, Vincenzo

TEENAGER see Tchaikovsky, Boris

TEGENBEWEGING see Verbey, Theo

TEHILLIM, FOR SOLO VOICES AND ORCHESTRA
see Reich, Steve

TEHRANA see Malec, Ivo

TEILE DICH NACHT, FOR SOLO VOICE AND
CHAMBER ORCHESTRA see Yun, Isang

TEKIAH, FOR TRUMPET AND ORCHESTRA see
Stock, David Frederick

TEKIATOT see Weisgall, Hugo

TEKSTURER see Godøy, Rolf Inge

TELEGRAM see Rypdal, Terje

TELEGRAMME WALZER see Strauss, Johann,
[Jr.]

TELEGRAPHISCHE DEPESCHEN WALZER see
Strauss, Johann, [Jr.]

TELEMANN, GEORG PHILIPP (1681-1767)
Album D'enfants [arr.] *Op.39
(Rogal-Levitsky) "Album For The
Young [arr.]" 2+pic.1(English
horn).2.1.alto sax. 2.2.1.0.
timp,perc,harp,balalaika,mand,
acord,strings [35'] KALMUS A6758
sc $40.00, set $90.00, pts $6.00,
ea., perf mat rent   (T282)

Album For The Young [arr.]
see Album D'enfants [arr.]

Alles Redet Jetzt Und Singet, For
Solo Voices And Orchestra
(Menke, W.) KALMUS A7120 sc $15.00,
set $20.00, pts $2.00, ea., perf
mat rent   (T283)

Bouffonne, La
(Hoffmann) "Lustige Suite In C"
KALMUS A6434 sc $8.00, set
$10.00, pts $2.00, ea., perf_mat
rent   (T284)

Concert Suite
(Hoffmann) fl,strings,cont [19']
KALMUS A6414 sc $8.00, set
$12.00, pts $2.00, ea.   (T285)

Concerto Grosso in A, MIN 69 [12']
2fl,bsn,strings,hpsd
BREITKOPF-L sc PB 4058 f.s., pts
OB 4058 f.s.   (T286)

Concerto in A, MIN 1
see Tafelmusik I, No. 3

Concerto in A, MIN 186
(Thilde, J.) string orch,trp solo
[15'40"] sc BILLAUDOT f.s., perf
mat rent   (T287)

Concerto in A minor, MIN 50
(Stein) KALMUS A6416 sc $8.00, set
$8.00, pts $1.25, ea.   (T288)

Concerto in B flat, MIN 39
(Hoffmann) KALMUS A6371 sc $8.00,
set $8.00, pts $1.25, ea. (T289)

Concerto in B flat, MIN 833
hpsd,strings,2trp soli
INTERNAT. perf mat rent   (T290)

Concerto in B minor, MIN 208
string orch,hpsd,fl solo
(Malina, Janos; Spanyi, Miklos)
SCHOTTS sc $9.95, pts f.s. (T291)

Concerto in C, MIN 448
(Hoffmann) KALMUS A6764 sc $8.00,
set $9.00, pts $1.50, ea. (T292)

Concerto in C minor, MIN 71
strings,cont,hpsd,vln solo
BREITKOPF-L sc PB 4062 f.s., pts
OB 4062 f.s.   (T293)

Concerto in C minor, MIN 209
string orch,cont,ob solo,vln solo
(Fechner, Manfred) sc PETERS f.s.
(T294)

Concerto in D, MIN 127
string orch,hpsd,fl solo
(Hinnenthal, J.P.) sc,pts LEUCKART
AM 4A f.s.   (T295)

Concerto in D, MIN 142
string orch,hpsd,ob solo
MUS. RARA 1941B $16.25   (T296)

Concerto in D, MIN 143
string orch,hpsd,trp solo
MUS. RARA 1848B $13.75   (T297)

Concerto in D, MIN 185
(Thilde, J.) string orch,hpsd,trp
solo [8'30"] sc BILLAUDOT f.s.,
perf mat rent   (T298)

Concerto in E flat, MIN 835
(Leloir, E.) string orch,2horn soli
[7'] BILLAUDOT perf mat rent
(T299)

Concerto in E, MIN 202
string orch,cont,fl solo
sc,pts KUNZEL 10219 f.s.   (T300)

TELEMANN, GEORG PHILIPP (cont'd.)
Concerto in E minor, MIN 51
KALMUS A6333 sc $8.00, set $14.00,
pts $3.00, ea.   (T301)

Concerto in E minor, MIN 184
(Thilde, J.) string orch,trp solo
[11'] sc BILLAUDOT f.s., perf mat
rent   (T302)

Concerto in F, MIN 816 [12']
string orch,cont,fl solo
(Ruetz) KALMUS A6413 sc $5.00, set
$6.00, pts $1.00, ea.   (T303)

Concerto in F sharp minor, MIN 836
[12']
string orch,cont,vln solo
(Pietsch) sc,pts SIKORSKI 1251 f.s.
(T304)

Concerto in G, MIN 201
string orch,cont,fl solo
sc,pts KUNZEL 10220 f.s.   (T305)

Concerto in G minor, MIN 834
(Thilde, J.) string orch,2trp soli
[8'20"] sc BILLAUDOT f.s., perf
mat rent   (T306)

Concerto, MIN 183, [arr.]
(Thilde, J.) string orch,harp solo,
vcl solo [8'] BILLAUDOT perf mat
rent   (T307)

Concerto Polonois
(Ochlewski- Gabrys) "Polish
Concerto" POLSKIE   (T308)

Geduldige Sokrates, Der: Overture
[12']
2ob,bsn,hpsd,strings
(Baselt, Bernd) BÄREN. BA 6553
(T309)

Ino, For Solo Voice And Orchestra
BREITKOPF-L perf mat rent (T310)

Kleine Suite In D (Suite in D, No.
16)
(Hockner) "Little Suite In D"
KALMUS A7065 sc $5.00, set $6.00,
pts $1.25, ea.   (T311)

Little Suite In D
see Kleine Suite In D

Lustige Suite In C
see Bouffonne, La

Ouverture Des Nations Anciens Et
Modernes
(Noack) KALMUS A6377 sc $8.00, set
$7.50, pts $1.50, ea., perf mat
rent   (T312)

Ouverture In D
(Noack) KALMUS A6374 sc $8.00, set
$12.00, pts $1.25, ea.   (T313)

Ouverture In D, MIN72 (Suite in D,
No. 22)
opt 2ob,opt bsn,3trp,timp,
strings,hpsd
(TWV55, D22) BREITKOPF-L sc PB 4060
f.s., pts OB 4060 f.s.   (T314)

Ouverture In D, MIN73 (Suite in D,
No. 18)
opt 2ob,bsn,2trp,timp,strings,
hpsd
(TWV55, D18) BREITKOPF-L sc PB 4061
f.s., pts OB 4061 f.s.   (T315)

Ouverture In F Sharp Minor
(Noack) KALMUS A6375 sc $6.00, set
$10.00, pts $2.00, ea., perf mat
rent   (T316)

Ouverture In G Minor
(Noack) KALMUS A6373 sc $8.00, set
$10.00, pts $1.25, ea.   (T317)

Overture And Conclusion In E Minor
see Tafelmusik I, No. 1

Overture "La Putain"
see Putain, La

Polish Concerto
see Concerto Polonois

Putain, La
(Noack) "Overture "La Putain""
KALMUS A6378 sc $8.00, set
$12.00, pts $2.50, ea., perf mat
rent   (T318)

Sinfonia Melodica In C
(Oberdorfer) KALMUS A5655 sc $5.00,
set $7.00   (T319)

Sonata in G minor, MIN 187
(Thilde, J.) string orch,trp solo
[10'15"] BILLAUDOT perf mat rent
(T320)

TELEMANN, GEORG PHILIPP (cont'd.)

Suite in D, No. 6
(Hoffmann) KALMUS A7107 sc $10.00.
set $14.00, pts $2.00, ea. (T321)

Suite in D, No. 16
see Kleine Suite In D

Suite in D, No. 18
see Ouverture In D, MIN73

Suite in D, No. 22
see Ouverture In D, MIN72

Tafelmusik I, No. 1
(Hinnenthal) "Overture And
Conclusion In E Minor" KALMUS
A6411 sc $14.00, set $14.00, pts
$2.00, ea.   (T322)

Tafelmusik I, No. 3 (Concerto in A,
MIN 1)
(Hinnenthal) KALMUS A6412 sc
$14.00, set $14.00, pts $2.00,
ea.   (T323)

Wasser-Ouverture In C
(Noack) "Water Music" KALMUS A6376
sc $10.00, set $17.00, pts $2.50,
ea.   (T324)

Water Music
see Wasser-Ouverture In C

TELEMANNIANA see Henze, Hans Werner

TELESCOPE II see Polovinkin, Leonid

TELFER, NANCY
Child's Christmas In Wales, A, For
Narrator And Orchestra [27']
2.2.0.0. 0.0.0.0. 2perc,strings,
narrator
CAN.MUS.CENT. MV 1300 T271C (T325)

Dance No. 1 [7']
string orch
CAN.MUS.CENT. MI 1500 T271D (T326)

Dance No. 2 [6']
2.3.2.2. 4.3.3.1. timp,perc,
strings
CAN.MUS.CENT. MI 1100 T271D2 (T327)

TEM see Heyn, Volker

TEMA see Donatoni, Franco

TEMA CON VARIAZIONI see Glaser, Werner
Wolf

TEMA VARIATO see Perosi, [Don] Lorenzo

TEML, JIRI (1935-   )
Concerto for Violin and Orchestra
sc PANTON 2194 f.s.   (T328)

TEMPEST see Rice, Thomas N.

TEMPEST, THE see Bajura, Keith V.A. see
Tchaikovsky, Piotr Ilyich

TEMPEST, THE: SUITE see Chihara, Paul
Seiko

TEMPEST, THE: SUITE, FOR SOLO VOICES
AND ORCHESTRA see Nordheim, Arne

TEMPEST, THE: THREE DANCES see
Sullivan, [Sir] Arthur Seymour

TEMPETE, LA: FANTASY, OP. 18 see
Tchaikovsky, Piotr Ilyich

TEMPI ADORNI, FOR SOLO VOICE AND
ORCHESTRA see Nozawa, Kazuyo

TEMPI INQUIETI, FOR PIANO, PERCUSSION
AND ORCHESTRA see Zinsstag, Gérard

TEMPLE DE MEMOIRE, LE, FOR SOLO VOICE
AND ORCHESTRA see Rosenthal, Manuel

TEMPLETON, ALEC (1910-1963)
Ballade De Ballet
SHAWNEE perf mat rent   (T329)

Give Me Your Heart
SHAWNEE perf mat rent   (T330)

Operation Mambo
SHAWNEE perf mat rent   (T331)

Pied Piper Of Hamlin, For Narrator
And Orchestra
(Jouard, Paul) SHAWNEE perf mat
rent   (T332)

Waltz Antique
SHAWNEE perf mat rent   (T333)

TEMPO CONSTANTE see Artyomov,
Vyacheslav

TEMPO DI MARCIA, VERSION I see Adomian,
Lan

TEMPO DI MARCIA, VERSION II see
Adomian, Lan

TEMPO SULLO SFONDO, IL see Gentilucci,
Armando

TEMPO VARIABILE-SYMPHONIC METAMORPHOSES
see Holmboe, Vagn

TEMPORA NOCTIS, FOR SOLO VOICES AND
ORCHESTRA see Nordheim, Arne

TEMPS PERDU see Joubert, John

TEN DO GU, FOR PERCUSSION AND ORCHESTRA
see Dao, Nguyen Thien

TEN HAVE, WILLEM
see HAVE, WILLEM TEN

TEN SKETCHES see Ledenev, Roman

TEN SONGS TO POEMS BY VINJE, FOR SOLO
VOICE AND ORCHESTRA [ARR.] see
Grieg, Edvard Hagerup

1010 see MacBride, David Huston

TENDENZA see Lindberg, Magnus

TENDREMENT see Satie, Erik

TENEBRAE, FOR VIOLONCELLO AND ORCHESTRA
see Nordheim, Arne

TENEBRAE FACTAE SUNT, FOR SOLO VOICE
AND STRING ORCHESTRA see
Charpentier, Marc-Antoine

TENEBRAE FACTAE SUNT [ARR.] see
Palestrina, Giovanni Pierluigi da

TENGSL see Sveinsson, Atli Heimir

TENTH MUSE, THE, FOR SOLO VOICE AND
ORCHESTRA see Crockett, Donald

TER-OSIPOV, YURI (1933-   )
Concerto for Violin and Orchestra,
No. 1 [20']
VAAP perf mat rent   (T334)

TER VELDHUIS, JACOB
see VELDHUIS, JACOB TER

TERLEZKI, VLADIMIR (1931-   )
Rhapsody for Violin and Orchestra
[15']
2.1.1.0.5sax. 3.4.4.1. timp,perc,
harp,pno,gtr,strings,vln solo
SIKORSKI perf mat rent   (T335)

TERMOS, PAUL (1942-   )
Concerto for Alto Saxophone and
Chamber Orchestra [15']
2.2.2.2. 0.0.0.0. 16vln,6vla,
4vcl,2db,alto sax solo
sc DONEMUS f.s., perf mat rent
(T336)

Nagras [15']
2.2.2.2. 4.3.3.1. opt 4Wagner
tuba,2perc,strings
sc DONEMUS f.s., perf mat rent
(T337)

TERRA INCOGNITA see Kotonski,
Wlodzimierz

TERRE-ESSOR see Giraud, Suzanne

TERREST MEKANIK see Jeverud, Johan

TERTERIAN, AVET (1929-   )
Symphony No. 2 [23']
3.3.3.4. 4.3.3.1. timp,perc,
2harp,pno,strings,cor
SIKORSKI perf mat rent   (T338)
VAAP perf mat rent   (T339)

Symphony No. 3 [26']
3(pic).3(English
horn).4.3(contrabsn). 6.3.3.1.
timp,perc,2pno,strings, 3
zurnas, 2 duduks
SIKORSKI perf mat rent   (T340)
VAAP perf mat rent   (T341)

Symphony No. 4 [30']
3.3(English horn).4.3(contrabsn).
4.4.3.1. timp,perc,cel,hpsd,
pno, organella, strings
SIKORSKI perf mat rent   (T342)
VAAP perf mat rent   (T343)

Symphony No. 5 [30']
3.2.3.2. 6.4.3.1. timp,perc,hpsd,
2gtr,strings,electronic tape,
kyamancha
SIKORSKI perf mat rent   (T344)
VAAP perf mat rent   (T345)

Symphony No. 6 [34']
1.2.2.0. 1.0.0.0. perc,hpsd,
strings,cor

TERTERIAN, AVET (cont'd.)

VAAP perf mat rent   (T346)

TERZAKIS, DIMITRI (1938-   )
Kosmoigramm [13']
2.2.3.3. 4.2.2.1. timp,3perc,
harp,strings
BÄREN. BA 6297 perf mat rent (T347)

Raub Der Europa, Der, For Solo Voice
And Orchestra [15']
1.1.1.1. 1.0.0.0. vibra,2vln,vla,
vcl,S solo
BREITKOPF-W perf mat rent   (T348)

TERZE see Keulen, Geert van

TERZIAN, ALICIA (1934-   )
Carmen Criaturalis, For Horn And
Instrumental Ensemble [8']
timp,cym,vibra,strings,horn solo
SALABERT perf mat rent   (T349)

TESERAC see Black, Charles

TESSIER, ROGER (1939-   )
Coalescence, For Clarinet And
Orchestra [18'30"]
2.2.2.2. 4.2.2.1. 4perc,harp,elec
gtr,strings,clar solo
SALABERT perf mat rent   (T350)

Mobile-Immobile [12'30"]
1+pic.1+English horn.1+bass
clar.1. 1.1.1.0. 2perc,harp,
pno&cel,Ondes Martenot,vln,vla,
vcl,db
SALABERT perf mat rent   (T351)

Omaggio A Carpaccio [14']
4fl,4rec,4trom,2vln,vla,vcl
SALABERT perf mat rent   (T352)

TESTI, FLAVIO (1923-   )
Musica Da Concerto No. 7, For Guitar
And Strings *Op.40 [15']
8vln,3vla,2vcl,db,gtr solo
RICORDI-IT 133524 perf mat rent
(T353)

Opus 35 [17']
2.2.2.2. 0.2.1.0. timp,strings
without vla
RICORDI-IT 132743 perf mat rent
(T354)

TESTONI, GIAMPAOLO (1957-   )
Alice Nel Paese Delle Meraviglie:
Wonderland Variations [7']
2.2.2.2. 2.2.1.0. timp,2perc,
harp,pno&cel,strings
RICORDI-IT 133810 perf mat rent
(T355)

Nuvole, Le *Op.5 [10']
2fl,ob,clar,bsn,pno,cel,harp,
2vln,vla,vcl,db
RICORDI-IT 133286 perf mat rent
(T356)

Sinfonia, Op. 15 [21']
3.2.3.3. 4.3.3.1. timp,perc,cel,
pno,harp,strings
RICORDI-IT 133679 perf mat rent
(T357)

TEUBER, FRED
Three Scoops
string orch
sc,pts GALAXY $20.00   (T358)

TEUFEL ALS HYDRAULICUS, DER: OVERTURE
see Schubert, Franz (Peter)

TEUFELS QUADRILLE see Strauss, Eduard

TEXAS TWILIGHT see Constant, Marius

TEXTURE see Verhoff, Carlos H.

TEXTURES see Godøy, Rolf Inge,
Teksturer

TEXTURES, FOR PIANO AND ORCHESTRA see
Takemitsu, Toru

T'FILAT SHALOM, FOR VIOLIN AND
ORCHESTRA see Adaskin, Murray

THALIA see Bon, Maarten

THALLA, FOR PIANO AND CHAMBER ORCHESTRA
see Ghezzo, Dinu Dumitru

THALLEIN see Xenakis, Yannis (Iannis)

THAN MONG, FOR VIOLONCELLO AND
ORCHESTRA see Dao, Nguyen Thien

THANKSGIVING SONG see Grainger, Percy
Aldridge

THAUPERLE POLKA see Strauss, Eduard

THAW see Thommessen, Olav Anton,
Varlosning

...THE ERRANT NOTE TO SEIZE, FOR
CHAMBER ORCHESTRA see Lewis, James

... THE ERRANT NOTE TO SEIZE, FOR ORCHESTRA see Lewis, James

THE SONG OF LIFE, FOR SOLO VOICE AND ORCHESTRA see Petric, Ivo, Pesem Zivljenja, For Solo Voice And Orchestra

THEATER SET see Kay, Ulysses Simpson see Siegmeister, Elie

THEATRE OF MEMORY, THE see Buller, John

THEATRE QUADRILLE see Strauss, Josef

THEKLA, FOR SOLO VOICE AND ORCHESTRA, [ARR.] see Schubert, Franz (Peter)

THEL, FOR FLUTE AND ORCHESTRA see Crosse, Gordon

THEMA 44 (AD HONOREM J. HAYDN) see Ferrero, Lorenzo

THEME AND INTERLUDES see Musgrave, Thea

THEME FROM KING KONG see Steiner, Max(imillian Raoul Walter)

THEME IN TWO MOODS see Hunt, Michael

THEN AND NOW, FOR SAXOPHONE AND ORCHESTRA see Mintzer, Robert

THEN SHALL THE DUST RETURN see Stein, Leon

THEN THEY ROWED ON THE FJORD, FOR SOLO VOICE AND ORCHESTRA see Ørbeck, Anne Marie, So Rodde Dei Fjordan, For Solo Voice And Orchestra

THEODORA: OVERTURE see Handel, George Frideric

THEODORAKIS, MIKIS (1925-)
Symphony No. 1
3.3.3.2. 4.3.3.1. timp,perc,pno, strings
sc DEUTSCHER 1736 f.s. (T359)

Symphony No. 7 [60']
3.2.2.3. 4.4.3.1. timp,4perc,pno/ cel,strings,SATB soli,cor
(Der Fruhling) SIKORSKI perf mat rent (T360)

THEONA see Smith, William Overton

THEORIEN WALZER see Strauss, Eduard

THEORIN, HAKAN (1959-)
Aria
fl,clar,strings
STIM (T361)

Episodi [16']
wind quin,strings
STIM (T362)

Quattro Pezzi
3.3.3.3. 4.3.3.1. timp,7perc, harp,strings
STIM (T363)

THERE ARE NO BIRDS SINGING, FOR SOLO VOICE AND ORCHESTRA see Jordan, Sverre, Der Synger Ingen Fugle, For Solo Voice And Orchestra

THESEUSFANTASIE see Olthuis, Kees

THESPIS: OVERTURE see Sullivan, [Sir] Arthur Seymour

THIERAC, JACQUES
Deux Essais Symphoniques [16'20"]
2.2.2.2.soprano sax. 4.4.3.1. timp,4perc,2harp,cel,strings
BILLAUDOT perf mat rent (T364)

Symphonie Normande [30']
3.3.3.3. 4.2.3.1. timp,3perc,pno, harp,cel,strings
BILLAUDOT perf mat rent (T365)

THIEVING MAGPIE, THE: OVERTURE see Rossini, Gioacchino, Gazza Ladra, La: Overture

THILMAN, JOHANNES PAUL (1906-1973)
Concertino for Piano Left-Hand and Orchestra, Op. 65
2.2.2.2. 2.2.0.0. timp,strings, pno left-hand solo
BREITKOPF-L perf mat rent (T366)

Music for String Orchestra
string orch without db
BREITKOPF-L sc PB 3911 f.s., pts OB 2941 f.s. (T367)

THINGS, THE see Hurnik, Ilja

THINGS TO COME: MUSIC, [ARR.] see Bliss, [Sir] Arthur (Drummond)

THIRIET, MAURICE (1906-1972)
Vautrin [5'32"]
2.1.2.2. 4.2.2.1. timp,perc,harp, cel,strings
BILLAUDOT perf mat rent (T368)

THIRTEEN YEARS, FOR SOLO VOICE AND ORCHESTRA see Jordan, Sverre, Tretton Ar, For Solo Voice And Orchestra

THOMAS, ANDREW (1939-)
In Memoriam [12']
fl,horn,perc,harp,strings
sc AM.COMP.AL. $24.55 (T369)

Metanoia [28']
1.1.1.1. 1.1.1.0. perc,harp, strings
sc AM.COMP.AL. $162.10 (T370)

Twelve Points Of The Modified Mercalli Scale, The, For Solo Voice And Orchestra [20']
2.2.2.2. 2.2.2.0. perc,harp,pno, strings,electronic tape,S solo
sc AM.COMP.AL. $55.05 (T371)

THOMAS, FOR TAPE AND 19 INSTRUMENTS see Bank, Jacques

THOMMESSEN, OLAV ANTON (1946-)
As Many As
see Flest

Beyond Neon; Postcommercial Sound Sculptures For Horn And Orchestra *Op.41
3(pic).3(English horn).3(bass clar).3(contrabsn). 4.2.3.1. timp,perc,harp,org,cel,strings, horn solo
HANSEN-DEN (T372)

Eclat Approchant, L' [10']
1.1.1.1. 1.0.0.0. pno,hpsd, strings,synthesizer
NORGE (T373)

Flest [7']
1.0.1.0. 0.1.0.0. timp,pno, strings
"As Many As" NORGE (T374)

From Above, For Synthesizer And Orchestra [14']
2.2.2.2. 4.2.3.0. timp,2perc, harp,strings,synthesizer
NORGE (T375)

Great Attractor, The: Cadenza Accompagnata, For Violin And Orchestra [8']
2.1.2.2. 4.2.3.0. timp,2perc, harp,strings without vln,vln solo
NORGE (T376)

Second Creation, The: An Orchestral Drama For Trumpets [28']
3.4.3.3. 4.4.3.1. timp,4perc, 2harp,org,strings
NORGE (T377)

Thaw
see Varlosning

Threat Towards The Light, The [9']
2.1.2.1. 2.1.2.1. timp,2perc, strings
NORGE (T378)

Vadstena Ouverture [8']
1.1.1.1. 1.2.0.0. perc,strings
NORGE (T379)

Varlosning [8']
fl,5horn,perc,strings
"Thaw" NORGE (T380)

THOMMESSEN, REIDAR (1889-1986)
Maigull [arr.]
(Soderling, Ragnar) "May Gold [arr.]" 2.2.2.2. 4.2.3.0. timp, perc,harp,strings [4'] NORGE (T381)

May Gold [arr.]
see Maigull [arr.]

Most Beautiful Rose, The [arr.]
see Vakreste Rose, Den [arr.]

Vakreste Rose, Den [arr.]
(Soderlind, Ragnar) "Most Beautiful Rose, The [arr.]" fl,bsn,perc, harp,strings [3'] NORGE (T382)

THOMSON, VIRGIL GARNETT (1896-1989)
Concerto for Flute and Orchestra
sc KALMUS A7018 $15.00 (T383)

THOMSON, VIRGIL GARNETT (cont'd.)

Eleven Portraits For Orchestra
2.2+English horn.2+bass clar.2. 4.2.3.0. 2perc,harp,strings [14'] (orchestrated by the composer, Scott Wheeler and Rodney Lister)
BOOSEY perf mat rent (T384)

Filling Station: Suite [20']
2(pic).2(English horn).2.2. 4.3.3.1. timp,perc,pno,strings (reduced scoring: 2222 2210, 2 perc, pno, strings) BOOSEY perf mat rent (T385)

Four Saints: An Olio [20']
2(pic).2(English horn).2(clar in A).2. 2.1.1.0. 2perc,glock, acord,2vln,vla,vcl,db
SCHIRM.G perf mat rent (T386)

Lord Byron: Five Tenor Solos, For Solo Voice And Orchestra [10']
2(pic).2(English horn).2(bass clar).2. 4.2.3.1. timp,perc, strings,T solo
PEER perf mat rent (T387)

THORARINSSON, JÓN (1917-)
Homage To Ingolfur
2.2.2.2. 4.3.3.1. timp,perc, strings
ICELAND 013-016 (T388)

Let Man Live [23']
1.1.1.0. 1.1.1.0. timp,perc, strings
ICELAND 013-013 (T389)

THORARINSSON, LEIFUR (1934-)
Autumn Play
3.3.3.3. 4.3.3.1. timp,3perc, harp,cel,strings
ICELAND 017-036 (T390)

Concerto for Oboe and Orchestra [21'30"]
3.2.2.3. 4.3.3.0. timp,perc,harp, strings,ob solo
ICELAND 017-031 (T391)

Concerto for Violin and Orchestra [20'35"]
2.2.2.2. 4.3.3.0. timp,perc,harp, pno,strings,vln solo
ICELAND 017-018 (T392)

Dream About "The House", A, For Harp And String Orchestra [5'45"]
string orch,harp solo
ICELAND 017-004 (T393)

Journey [15']
2.2.2.2. 4.3.3.1. timp,perc,harp, strings
ICELAND 017-042 (T394)

Mordur Valgardsson
3.3.3.3. 4.3.3.1. timp,perc, strings
ICELAND 017-035 (T395)

Styr, For Piano And Chamber Orchestra [12'25"]
1.1.1.1. 2.0.0.0. cel,strings,pno solo
ICELAND 017-041 (T396)

To Damascus
2.2.2.2. 4.3.3.1. timp,perc,harp, strings
ICELAND 017-039 (T397)

THORDARSON, HILMAR (1960-)
Concerto for Violin and Orchestra
1.1.1.1. 1.1.1.1. perc,strings, vln solo
ICELAND 067-001 (T398)

THOREAU FANTASY NO. 2 see Fennelly, Brian

THORESEN, LASSE (1949-)
Concerto for 2 Violoncelli and Orchestra [28']
2.2.2.2. 4.3.3.1. timp,3perc, harp,pno,strings,2vcl soli
NORGE (T399)

Hymnisk Dans [16']
3.2.3.3. 4.2.3.0. timp,perc,harp, strings,synthesizer
NORGE (T400)

Rettferdighetens Sol
3(pic).3(English horn).3(bass clar).3(contrabsn). 4.3.3.1. timp,perc,cel,pno,strings
"Sun Of Justice, The" [16'] NORGE (T401)

Sun Of Justice, The
see Rettferdighetens Sol

THORESEN, LASSE (cont'd.)

Transition [4']
    string orch
    NORGE   (T402)

THORKELSDOTTIR, MIST (1960-   )
    David, For Solo Voice And Orchestra
    1.1.1.1. 1.1.1.0. strings,Bar
        solo
    ICELAND 048-001   (T403)

Fantasea
    2.2.2.2. 2.2.1.1. timp,perc,
        strings
    ICELAND 048-009   (T404)

THORKILDSEN, JOHN (1883-1947)
    Concerto for Piano and Orchestra in G
    [15']
    2.2.2.2. 2.2.0.0. timp,strings,
        pno solo
    NORGE   (T405)

THORN BIRDS, THE: SUITE see Mancini,
    Henry

THORNE, FRANCIS BURRITT (1922-   )
    Concerto Concertante [18']
    0.2.0.2. 2.2.2+bass trom.0. perc,
        harp,strings,fl solo,clar solo,
        vln solo,vcl solo
    sc AM.COMP.AL. $34.45   (T406)

Concerto for Viola, Double Bass and
    Orchestra [20']
    2.2.2.2. 4.2.2.0. timp,2perc,
        strings,vla solo,db solo
    sc AM.COMP.AL. $86.20, perf mat
        rent   (T407)

Concerto for Violin and Orchestra
    [23']
    2.2.2.2. 2.2.2.0. 2perc,strings,
        vln solo
    AMP perf mat rent   (T408)

Divertimento No. 1 for Flute and
    String Orchestra [17']
    string orch,fl solo
    AMP perf mat rent   (T409)

Divertimento No. 2 for Bassoon and
    String Orchestra [17']
    string orch,bsn solo
    AMP perf mat rent   (T410)

Eternal Light, The, For Solo Voice
    And Orchestra
    see Luce Eterna, La, For Solo Voice
        And Orchestra

Fanfare, Fugue And Fast Four, For 3
    Trumpets And Orchestra [11']
    2.2.2.2. 3.0.3.0. timp,3perc,elec
        gtr,strings,3trp soli
    sc AM.COMP.AL. $44.40, perf mat
        rent   (T411)
    sc JOSHUA 1056 $8.50   (T412)

Fantasy for String Orchestra [9']
    string orch
    sc AM.COMP.AL. $34.15, perf mat
        rent   (T413)

Gems From Spoon River [8']
    3.2.2.2. 4.2.3.1. timp,2perc,
        banjo,strings, tack piano
    sc AM.COMP.AL. $33.25   (T414)

Humoresque [9']
    2.2.2.2. 4.2.3.1. timp,2perc,
        harp,pno,strings
    sc AM.COMP.AL. $49.50, perf mat
        rent   (T415)

Liebes Rock [12']
    0.0.0.0. 4.3.3.1. timp,perc,harp,
        pno,elec gtr,elec bass,strings
    AM.COMP.AL. perf mat rent   (T416)

Luce Eterna, La, For Solo Voice And
    Orchestra [21']
    2.2.2.2. 4.2.3.1. timp,perc,harp,
        strings,S/T solo
    "Eternal Light, The, For Solo Voice
        And Orchestra" AMP perf mat rent (T417)

Lyric Variations No.5 [20']
    2.2.2.2. 4.2.3.1. timp,2perc,
        harp,pno,strings
    sc AM.COMP.AL. $110.95, perf mat
        rent   (T418)

Pop Partita [17']
    2.2.2.2. 4.3.3.1. timp,2perc,pno,
        strings
    sc AM.COMP.AL. $84.40, perf mat
        rent   (T419)

Quartessence [21']
    0.0.0.3. 4.3.2+bass trom.0. perc,
        strings,vibra solo,pno solo,db
        solo,drums solo
    sc MJQ $14.95, perf mat rent   (T420)

THORNE, FRANCIS BURRITT (cont'd.)

Rhapsodic Variations No. 3, For Oboe
    And String Orchestra [15']
    string orch,ob solo
    sc AM.COMP.AL. $36.90, perf mat
        rent   (T421)

Symphony No. 3 [25']
    timp,harp,pno,strings
    (Self-portrait) AMP perf mat rent (T422)

Symphony No. 4
    2.2.2.2. 4.1.3.1. 2perc,harp,
        strings,trp solo, tack piano
    [30'] (Waterloo Bridge) AM.COMP.AL.
        perf mat rent   (T423)

Symphony No. 5 [22']
    2+pic.2+English horn.2+bass
        clar.2+contrabsn. 4.3.2+bass
        trom.1. timp,3perc,pno,harp,
        strings
    AMP perf mat rent   (T424)

THORNE, NICHOLAS C.K. (1953-   )
    Chaconne: Passion Of The Heart
    *Op.18 [17']
    1(alto fl,pic).2(English
        horn).1.2. 2.1.0.0. timp,pno,
        12vln,4vla,4vcl,2db
    MARGUN MM 76 perf mat rent   (T425)

Eight Movements For Orchestra *Op.22
    [14']
    2.2.2.2. 4.2.2.1. timp,2perc,pno,
        strings
    AMP perf mat rent   (T426)

Revelations [18']
    2.2.2.2. 4.2.1.0. timp,3perc,pno,
        strings
    N.LIGHT perf mat rent   (T427)

Songs Of Darkness, Power And
    Radiance, For Trombone And
    Orchestra [18']
    2(pic).2(English horn).2.2.
        2.2.0.0. timp,perc,pno,strings,
        trom solo
    N.LIGHT perf mat rent   (T428)

Symphony From Silence *Op.17 [33']
    4(alto fl,pic).3.3.3. 4.3.3.1.
        timp,2perc,pno,strings
    MARGUN BP 7134 perf mat rent   (T429)

Symphony No. 2 [25']
    3(pic).2+English horn.2+bass
        clar.2+contrabsn. 4.3.3.1.
        timp,3perc,pno&cel,strings
    (A Symphony Of Light) N.LIGHT perf
        mat rent   (T430)

Three Tales For Eleven Players
    *Op.11 [36']
    fl&pic&alto fl,ob,English horn,
        clar,clar&bass clar,horn,perc,
        pno,vln,vcl,db
    MARGUN BP 7098 perf mat rent   (T431)

Voices Of Spring, The *Op.6 [6']
    3.2.2.2. 4.2.2.1. timp,pno,
        strings
    N.LIGHT perf mat rent   (T432)

THOUGHT, THE see Borgström, Hjalmar

THOUGHTS 1988 see Segerstam, Leif

THOUGHTS 1989 see Segerstam, Leif

THREAT TOWARDS THE LIGHT, THE see
    Thommessen, Olav Anton

THREE, FOR 2 TRUMPETS AND ORCHESTRA see
    Hobson, Bruce

THREE ACTS see Mourant, Walter

THREE ANECDOTES, FOR PERCUSSION AND
    CHAMBER ORCHESTRA see Balada,
    Leonardo

THREE AUTUMN SONGS, FOR SOLO VOICE AND
    ORCHESTRA see Burritt, Lloyd

THREE BAVARIAN DANCES see Elgar, [Sir]
    Edward (William)

THREE BLACK KINGS see Ellington, Edward
    Kennedy (Duke)

THREE BLACK KINGS, CONCERTO GROSSO
    VERSION [ARR.] see Ellington,
    Edward Kennedy (Duke)

THREE BLIND MICE see Holbrooke, Joseph

THREE CANTOS, FOR STRING ORCHESTRA see
    Rautavaara, Einojuhani

THREE CASCADES see Pluister, Simon

THREE CENTURIES OF MUSIC IN SCORE,
    VOL.1: SYMPHONIES AND OVERTURES
    sc GARLAND ISBN 0-8240-0928-2 $55.00
    contains works by: Gaetano
        Brunetti, Anton Filtz, Francois
        Joseph Gossec, Johann Gottlieb
        Graun, Leopold Kozeluch, Ignaz
        Pleyel, Johann Baptist Vanhal
                                      (T433)

THREE CENTURIES OF MUSIC IN SCORE, VOL.
    2: CONCERTO I, ITALY
    sc GARLAND ISBN 0-8240-0829-0 $75.00
    contains: Bianchi, Giovanni,
        Concerti Grossi, Op.2, Six;
        Sammartini, Giuseppe, Concerti
        Grossi, Op.2, Nos. 1, 2, 3, 5;
        Sammartini, Giuseppe, Concerti,
        Op.9, Four; Scarlatti,
        Alessandro, Sonate A4, Two (T434)

THREE CENTURIES OF MUSIC IN SCORE, VOL.
    3: CONCERTO II, ENGLAND
    sc GARLAND ISBN 0-8240-0930-4 $75.00
    contains: Alcock, John, Concerti
        Grossi, Six; Festing, Michael
        Christian, Concerti, Eight;
        Humphries, John, Concerti Grossi,
        Op. 2, Twelve   (T435)

THREE CENTURIES OF MUSIC IN SCORE, VOL.
    4: CONCERTO III, KEYBOARD
    sc GARLAND ISBN 0-8240-0931-2 $65.00
    contains: Bach, Wilhelm Friedrich
        Ernst, Concerto For 2
        Harpsichords And String Orchestra
        In E Flat; Bach, Wilhelm
        Friedrich Ernst, Concerto For
        Harpsichord And String Orchestra
        In G Minor; Müthel, Johann
        Gottfried, Concerto For
        Harpsichord And String Orchestra
        In D Minor; Schröter, Johann
        Samuel, Concerti, Six   (T436)

THREE CENTURIES OF MUSIC IN SCORE,
    VOL.5: CONCERTO IV, CLASSICAL
    STRINGS AND WINDS
    sc GARLAND ISBN 0-8240-0932-0 $65.00
    contains: Amon, Johann Andreas,
        Concerto for Viola and Orchestra,
        Op. 10, in G; Boccherini, Luigi,
        Concerto for Violoncello and
        Orchestra in D; Fodor, George,
        Concerto for Violin and Orchestra
        in D; Krommer, Franz, Concerto
        for Clarinet and Orchestra, Op.
        52, in E flat; Stamitz, Carl,
        Concerto for Viola and Orchestra,
        Op. 1, in D   (T437)

THREE CENTURIES OF MUSIC IN SCORE,
    VOL.6: CONCERTO V, LATE CLASSICAL
    STRINGS AND WINDS
    sc GARLAND ISBN 0-8240-0933-9 $65.00
    contains: Auber, Daniel-François-
        Esprit, Concerto for Violin and
        Orchestra in D; Cambini, Giovanni
        Giuseppe, Symphonie Concertante
        No. 4 in D; Mestrino, Nicolo,
        Concerto for Violin and
        Orchestra, No. 4, in D; Rolla,
        Alessandro, Concerto for Viola
        and Orchestra, Op. 3, in E flat;
        Winter, Peter von, Concerto for
        Oboe and Orchestra   (T438)

THREE CENTURIES OF MUSIC IN SCORE, VOL.
    13: AMERICAN CLASSICAL MUSIC
    *CC10L
    sc GARLAND ISBN 0-8240-0940-1 $60.00
    contains works by Johannes Herbst,
        Peter Wolle, Francis F. Hagen,
        Johann Friedrich Peter, Anton
        Philip Heinrich   (T439)

THREE CEREMONIAL RITES see Pisk, Paul
    Amadeus

THREE COMPOSITIONS FOR ORCHESTRA see
    Sato, Toshinao

THREE COMPOSITIONS FOR STRING ORCHESTRA
    see Herbert, Victor

THREE CONCERT ARIAS, FOR SOLO VOICE AND
    ORCHESTRA see Khachaturian, Aram
    Ilyich

THREE CZECH DANCES [ARR.] see Smetana,
    Bedrich

THREE DANCES see Gorecki, Henryk
    Mikolaj, Trzy Tance see Lloyd,
    Jonathan

THREE DANCES FOR STRINGS see Berger,
    Jean

THREE DANCES FROM LA GUIABLESSE see
    Still, William Grant

THREE DANCES FROM THE BESKYDY AREA see
    Matej, Jozka (Josef)

THREE DANCES see Still, William Grant

THREE DANISH SONGS FROM THE 16TH CENTURY see Riisager, Knudage, Tre Dansk Peblingeviser

THREE DANISH STREET SONGS see Riisager, Knudage

THREE DIALOGUE MOTETS, FOR VIOLONCELLO AND STRING ORCHESTRA see Bäck, Sven-Erik

THREE ENGLISH DANCES see Quilter, Roger

THREE ENGLISH DANCES [ARR.] see Quilter, Roger

THREE EPIGRAMS see Pleskow, Raoul

THREE EPISODES see Tull, Fisher Aubrey

THREE ESSAYS see Hanuš, Jan

THREE FANTASIES see Balassa, Sándor

THREE FESTIVE MARCHES see Gluck, Christoph Willibald, Ritter von, Drei Festliche Marsche

THREE FUGUES see Halldorsson, Skuli

THREE GIRLS, THREE WOMEN, FOR SOLO VOICE AND ORCHESTRA see Schickele, Peter

THREE HALLUCINATIONS see Corigliano, John

THREE HEBREW PSALMS, FOR SOLO VOICE AND ORCHESTRA see Flender, Reinhard David, Pirkei Tehillim, For Solo Voice And Orchestra

THREE IDEAS IN FOUR MOVEMENTS, FOR PIANO AND CHAMBER ORCHESTRA see Szönyi, Erzsebet (Elizabeth)

THREE IMAGES see Leifs, Jon

THREE ISRAELI CHASSIDIC SONGS, FOR SOLO VOICE AND STRING ORCHESTRA[ARR] (Barnes, Milton) string orch,opt pno, high solo CAN.MUS.CENT.
MV 1600 B261T   (T440)

THREE KASHUBIAN FOLK TALES see Pallasz, Edward, Trzy Bajki Kaszubskie

THREE LAPONIAN FOLKTUNES, FOR NARRATOR AND ORCHESTRA see Nilsson, Bo

THREE LATIN AMERICAN SKETCHES see Copland, Aaron

THREE LITTLE PIECES FOR STRINGS see Bush, Geoffrey

THREE LOVE SONGS, FOR SOLO VOICE AND ORCHESTRA see Nystroem, Gösta

THREE LYRICAL PICTURES, FOR SOLO VOICE AND ORCHESTRA see Sommerfeldt, Öistein

THREE MINOR DESPERATIONS, FOR SOLO VOICE AND ORCHESTRA see Samuel, Gerhard

THREE MOODS, FOR DOUBLEBASS AND ORCHESTRA see Lauber, Anne

THREE MOVEMENTS see Le Baron, Anne see Reich, Steve

THREE MOVEMENTS, FOR CHAMBER ORCHESTRA see Mihaly, Andras

THREE MOVEMENTS, FOR PERCUSSION AND ORCHESTRA see Watanabe, Urato

THREE MOVEMENTS FOR ORCHESTRA see Dix, Robert

THREE MOVEMENTS FOR ORCHESTRA-II see Dix, Robert

THREE MUSICAL ELEMENTS see Knight, Eric

THREE MYSTICAL SONGS, FOR SOLO VOICE AND STRING ORCHESTRA see Tremain, Ronald

THREE NEGRO SONGS see Still, William Grant

THREE NOCTURNAL PIECES see Dam, Herman Van

THREE NOCTURNAL SCENES see Jordan, Sverre, Tre Nattlige Scener

THREE NOCTURNES see Schuller, Gunther

THREE OR FOUR THINGS I KNOW ABOUT THE OBOE, FOR OBOE AND ORCHESTRA see Sollberger, Harvey

THREE ORCHESTRAL PIECES see Berners, Lord (Gerald Tyrwhitt) see Holm, Peder, Tre Orkesterstykker

THREE ORCHESTRAL WORKS see Brahms, Johannes

THREE ORCHESTRAL WORKS see Debussy, Claude

THREE OVERTURES, [ARR.] see Purcell, Henry

THREE OVERTURES FOR TRUMPETS, DRUMS AND STRINGS see Purcell, Henry

THREE PARODIES, FOR TRUMPET AND CHAMBER ORCHESTRA see Wienhorst, Richard

THREE PIECES, FOR CHAMBER ORCHESTRA see Schoenberg, Arnold

THREE PIECES see Buxtehude, Dietrich

THREE PIECES [ARR.] see Scarlatti, Domenico

THREE PIECES FOR GUITAR AND STRING ORCHESTRA see Armstrong, John

THREE PIECES FOR HANSSON, FOR DOUBLE BASS AND STRING ORCHESTRA see Wallin, Peter

THREE PIECES FOR JAZZ QUARTET AND ORCHESTRA see Pilhofer, Herb

THREE PIECES FOR ORCHESTRA see Ge, Gan-Ru

THREE PIECES FOR SMALL ORCHESTRA see Delius, Frederick

THREE PIECES FOR STRING ORCHESTRA see Brustad, Karsten

THREE PIECES IN BAROQUE STYLE see Penderecki, Krzysztof

THREE PIECES, OP. 10 see Elgar, [Sir] Edward (William)

THREE PIECES, OP. 10: MAZURKA see Elgar, [Sir] Edward (William)

THREE PIECES, OP. 21 see Lerstad, Terje B.

THREE POEMS, FOR SOLO VOICE AND CHAMBER ORCHESTRA see Kiva, Oleh

THREE POEMS BY WALT WHITMAN, FOR NARRATOR AND ORCHESTRA see Fetler, Paul

THREE POEMS OF THE SEA, FOR NARRATOR AND STRING ORCHESTRA see Lilburn, Douglas

THREE POEMS OF YOUTH see Rudhyar, Dane (Daniel Chennevière)

THREE POEMS OF YOUTH, NO.1: YEARNING see Rudhyar, Dane (Daniel Chennevière)

THREE POEMS OF YOUTH, NO. 2: RITE OF LOVE see Rulon, C. Bryan

THREE POEMS OF YOUTH, NO. 3: THRENODY see Rulon, C. Bryan

THREE PORTRAITS see Wigglesworth, Frank

THREE PRELUDES see Gordon, Philip

THREE PRELUDES, OP. 11, NOS. 4, 5, 15, FOR CELLO AND STRING ORCHESTRA[ARR.] see Scriabin, Alexander

THREE PSALMS, FOR SOLO VOICE AND ORCHESTRA see Pisk, Paul Amadeus

THREE ROSES, FOR SOLO VOICE AND ORCHESTRA see Wiklund, Adolf

THREE SCOOPS see Teuber, Fred

THREE SETTINGS OF POEMS BY GERARD MANLEY HOPKINS, FOR SOLO VOICE AND ORCHESTRA see Maconchy, Elizabeth

THREE SISTERS see Pasatieri, Thomas see Walton, [Sir] William (Turner)

THREE SKETCHES see Silvestri, Constantin

THREE SONGS, FOR SOLO VOICE AND CHAMBER ORCHESTRA see Lieberson, Peter

THREE SONGS, FOR SOLO VOICE AND INSTRUMENTAL ENSEMBLE see Zahler, Noel Barry

THREE SONGS, FOR SOLO VOICE AND ORCHESTRA see Delius, Frederick see Elgar, [Sir] Edward (William) see Matthews, David see Sims, Ezra

THREE SONGS, FOR SOLO VOICE AND ORCHESTRA [ARR.] see Nordraak, Rikard

THREE SONGS, FOR SOLO VOICE AND ORCHESTRA, OP. 11 see Fladmoe, Arvid

THREE SONGS, FOR SOLO VOICE AND ORCHESTRA, OP. 17 see Alnaes, Eyvind

THREE SONGS, FOR SOLO VOICE AND ORCHESTRA, OP. 26, NO. 2, OP. 30, NO. 2, OP.31, NO. 3 see Alnaes, Eyvind

THREE SONGS OF DAVID, FOR VIOLIN AND STRING ORCHESTRA see Sturzenegger, Richard, Drei Gesänge Davids, For Violin And String Orchestra

THREE SONGS ON POEMS OF PUSHKIN, FOR SOLO VOICE AND CHAMBER ORCHESTRA see Shostakovich, Dmitri

THREE SONNETS, FOR SOLO VOICE AND CHAMBER ORCHESTRA see Steinke, Greg A.

THREE SPANISH LYRICS, FOR SOLO VOICE AND ORCHESTRA see Raminsh, Imant

THREE SPIRITUAL SONGS, FOR SOLO VOICE AND ORCHESTRA see Ágústsson, Herbert Hriberschek

THREE SYMPHONIC SKETCHES see Skerl, Dane, Tri Simfonicne Skice

THREE SYMPHONIC SPIRITUALS, FOR SOLO VOICE AND ORCHESTRA see Tillis, Frederick C.

THREE TALES FOR ELEVEN PLAYERS see Thorne, Nicholas C.K.

THREE TEXTURES, FOR VIOLONCELLO AND STRING ORCHESTRA see Allik, Kristi

THREE TRADITIONAL SCOTTISH SONGS see Williams, [John] Gerrard

THREE TRIBUTES see Ramirez, Luis Antonio, Tres Homenajes

THREE WESTERN IMAGES see Rollin, Robert Leon

THRENODY see Crawley, Clifford see Lombardo, Robert M. see Turok, Paul Harris

THRENODY: IN MEMORY OF JEAN SIBELIUS see Still, William Grant

THRENOS see Antoniou, Theodore see Joubert, John

THRESHOLD see Giuffre, James Peter (Jimmy)

THRILL OF THE ORCHESTRA, THE, FOR NARRATOR AND ORCHESTRA see Peck, Russell James

THROUGH AND THROUGH see Sandström, Sven-David

THROUGH LONG, LONG, YEARS, FOR SOLO VOICE AND ORCHESTRA see Delius, Frederick

THROUGH THE LIONS' GATE see Baker, Michael Conway

THROUGH THE LOOKING GLASS I see Szymanski, Pawel

THROUGHWAYS: IMPROVISING MUSIC see Southam, Ann

THUILLE, LUDWIG (WILHELM ANDREAS MARIA) (1861-1907)
Romantische Ouverture *Op.16
sc KISTNER f.s., perf mat rent
(T441)
Sinfonischer Festmarsch *Op.38
KISTNER perf mat rent   (T442)

THUNDERBOLT P-47 see Martinu, Bohuslav (Jan)

THUNDERER MARCH, THE see Sousa, John Philip

THURM, JOACHIM (1927-   )
Concerto for Trumpet and Orchestra
[15']
3.2.2.2. 3.0.0.1. timp,perc,
strings,trp solo
BREITKOPF-L perf mat rent   (T443)

Funf Impromptus
3.2.3.2. 4.2.3.0. timp,perc,
strings
sc PETERS $25.00   (T444)

THUS SAW SAINT JOHN see Ruders, Poul

THYBO, LEIF (1922-   )
Concerto for Trombone, Timpani and
String Orchestra [30']
trom,timp,strings
EGTVED MF410   (T445)

Concerto for Trumpet, Trombone and
String Orchestra [30']
trp,trom,strings
EGTVED MF411   (T446)

TIBI SOLI PECCARI, FOR SOLO VOICE,
BASSET HORN AND STRING ORCHESTRA
see Donizetti, Gaetano

TICKER-TAPE PARADE see Raphling, Sam

TIEMPO ROMANTICO [ARR.] see Granados,
Enrique

TIENSUU, JUKKA (1948-   )
MXPZKL [10']
3.3.3.2. 4.3.3.1. timp,3perc,pno,
strings
sc SUOMEN f.s.   (T447)

Puro, For Clarinet And Orchestra
[18']
2.2.2.0. 2.2.2.0. perc,strings,
clar solo
sc SUOMEN f.s.   (T448)

TIENTO see Halffter, Cristobal

TIENTO DEL PRIMER TONO Y BATALLA
IMPERIAL see Halffter, Cristobal

TIERKREISZEICHEN, DIE, FOR SOLO VOICE,
HARPSICHORD AND STRINGS see
Tchaikovsky, Boris

TIERSOT, (JEAN BAPTISTE ELISEE) JULIEN
(1857-1936)
Danses Populaires Francaises [19']
2(pic).1(English horn).1.1.
1.1.3.0. timp,perc,harp,strings
LEMOINE perf mat rent   (T449)

TIESSEN, HEINZ (1887-1971)
Salambo: Zwei Orchesterstücke [13']
2.2.2.3. 4.2.3.1. timp,perc,harp,
strings
TISCHER perf mat rent   (T450)

TIF'ERETH FOR 6 SOLO INSTRUMENTS AND
ORCHESTRA see Nunes, Emmanuel

TIKKA, KARI (1946-   )
Concerto for Violoncello and
Orchestra
sc SUOMEN f.s.   (T451)

TIL EN GAMMEL KIRKE, FOR SOLO VOICE AND
ORCHESTRA see Eggen, Arne

TIL MIN GYLLENLAKK, FOR SOLO VOICE AND
ORCHESTRA see Groven, Eivind

TIL NORGE, FOR SOLO VOICE AND ORCHESTRA
[ARR.] see Grieg, Edvard Hagerup

TIL TELEMORK see Kielland, Olav

TILFELLET JANICE, FOR SOLO VOICE AND
ORCHESTRA see Germeten, Gunnar

TILL EULENSPIEGEL see Falik, Yuri

TILL HAVS, FOR SOLO VOICE AND ORCHESTRA
see Nordqvist, Gustaf

TILLIS, FREDERICK C. (1930-   )
Concerto for Flute, Violoncello,
Piano and Chamber Orchestra [21']
horn,trp,perc,strings,fl solo,vcl
solo,pno solo
AM.COMP.AL. sc $36.55, pts $16.75
(T452)
Concerto For Jazz Trio And Orchestra
[18']
2.2.2.2. 4.3.3.1. timp,perc,
strings,pno solo,perc solo,db
solo
AM.COMP.AL. sc $28.20, pts $6.15
(T453)
Spiritual Cycle, For Solo Voice And
Orchestra [15']
2.2.2.2. 4.3.3.1. timp,perc,
strings,S solo
sc AM.COMP.AL. $32.20, perf mat
rent   (T454)

TILLIS, FREDERICK C. (cont'd.)
Spiritual Fantasy No. 6, For Trumpet
And Orchestra [7']
2.2.0.2. 2.2.0.0. timp,perc,
strings,trp solo
AM.COMP.AL. sc $16.50, pts $4.60
(T455)
Three Symphonic Spirituals, For Solo
Voice And Orchestra [14']
2.2.2.2. 2.2.2.1. timp,perc,cel,
strings,med solo
sc AM.COMP.AL. $18.40   (T456)

TIM FINNIGAN'S WAKE see Vogt, Hans

TIMBRE D'ARGENT, LE: OVERTURE see
Saint-Saëns, Camille

TIMBRE D'ARGENT, LE: VALSE VENITIENNE
see Saint-Saëns, Camille

TIME see Hultqvist, Anders

TIME AND AGAIN see Murail, Tristan

TIME AND THE BELL see Hultqvist, Anders

TIME AND WATER, FOR SOLO VOICE AND
ORCHESTRA see Stefansson, Fjölnir

TIME MACHINE, THE, FOR NARRATOR AND
ORCHESTRA see Lankester, Michael

TIME OF TAROMIR see Rehnqvist, Karin,
Taromirs Tid

TIME SPAN see Rochberg, A. George

TIME SUSPENDED see Andriessen, Jurriaan

TIMEGLASET OG MORGONSTJERNA see
Sivertsen, Kenneth

TIME'S ARROW see Payne, Anthony

TIMES WILL CHANGE, THE see Wright,
Maurice

TING TANG THE ELEPHANT, FOR NARRATOR
AND ORCHESTRA see Coombes, Douglas

TING TANG THE ELEPHANT, FOR NARRATOR
AND CHAMBER ORCHESTRA see Coombes,
Douglas

TIP TOES: OVERTURE, [ARR.] see
Gershwin, George

TIPEI, SEVER (1943-   )
Undulating Michigamme, For Solo Voice
And Orchestra [28']
3.3.3.3. 4.3.3.2. perc,2harp,org,
2pno,strings,S solo
sc AM.COMP.AL. $38.00   (T457)

TIPPETT, [SIR] MICHAEL (1905-   )
Concerto for Violin, Viola,
Violoncello and Orchestra [32']
1(pic,alto fl).2+English horn.2+
bass clar.1+contrabsn. 4.2.2.0.
timp,perc,harp,strings,vln
solo,vla solo,vcl solo
min sc SCHOTTS 11860 f.s.   (T458)

Fantasia Concertante On A Theme Of
Corelli
string orch
min sc EULENBURG $7.75   (T459)

Water Out Of Sunlight
(Bowen, Meirion) string orch [23']
SCHOTT perf mat rent   (T460)

TIRANA see Gerhard, Roberto

TIRCUIT, HEUWELL (ANDREW) (1931-   )
Concerto for Brass Quintet and
Orchestra [18']
2.2.2.2. 2.0.0.0. perc,harp,pno,
strings,brass quin soli
AMP perf mat rent   (T461)

Concerto for Percussion and Orchestra
[23']
2+pic.2+English horn.2.0+
contrabsn. 4.3.2.1. timp,3perc,
harp,strings,perc solo
study sc AMP f.s., perf mat rent
(T462)
Concerto No. 4
see Fantasias

Fantasias (Concerto No. 4) [12']
2+pic.2+English horn.2+bass
clar.2. 4.3.3.1. timp,perc,pno,
strings
AMP perf mat rent   (T463)

TIRO MIS TRISTES REDES see Furrer, Beat

TISCHHAUSER, FRANZ (1921-   )
Beggar's Concerto, The, For Clarinet
And String Orchestra
sc AMADEUS BP 2094 f.s.   (T464)

TISHCHENKO, BORIS (1939-   )
Concerto for Flute, Piano and String
Orchestra, Op. 54 [23']
string orch,fl solo,pno solo
SIKORSKI perf mat rent   (T465)
VAAP perf mat rent   (T466)

Concerto for Harp and Orchestra, Op.
69 [26']
2.2.2.2. 3.2.0.0. 2perc,2harp,
pno,strings,harp solo,S solo
SIKORSKI perf mat rent   (T467)
VAAP perf mat rent   (T468)

Concerto for Violin and Orchestra,
No. 2 [60']
3.2.4.2. 6.2.4.1. perc,2harp,
2pno,strings,vln solo
VAAP perf mat rent   (T469)

Concerto for Violin and Orchestra,
Op. 9-29 [30']
3.3.4.3. 4.3.3.1. timp,perc,
2harp,cel,pno,strings,vln solo
SIKORSKI perf mat rent   (T470)

Concerto for Violoncello and
Orchestra, No. 1, [arr.]
(Shostakovich, Dmitri) 2.2.2.2.
1.0.0.0. timp,cel,strings,vcl
solo [29'] VAAP perf mat rent
(T471)
Concerto for Violoncello and
Orchestra, No. 1, Op. 23 [25']
0.3.3.3. 2.3.3.1. timp,perc,org,
vcl solo
SIKORSKI perf mat rent   (T472)
VAAP perf mat rent   (T473)

Concerto for Violoncello and
Orchestra, No. 2, Op. 44, No. 2
[40']
2perc,strings,vcl solo
SIKORSKI perf mat rent   (T474)
VAAP perf mat rent   (T475)

Sinfonia Robusta [14']
4.3.4.3. 6.3.4.1. timp,perc,
strings
SIKORSKI perf mat rent   (T476)
VAAP perf mat rent   (T477)

Symphony No. 2 [46']
2+pic.3+English horn.3+clar in E
flat.3+contrabsn. 6.4.4.2.
timp,perc,strings,mix cor
(Marina) VAAP perf mat rent   (T478)

Symphony No. 3 [31']
2.2.2.1. 1.1.1.0. timp,perc,pno,
vln,vla,vcl,db,SBar soli
SIKORSKI perf mat rent   (T479)
VAAP perf mat rent   (T480)

Symphony No. 5 [50']
3.3.4.3. 6.3.4.1. timp,5perc,
strings
SIKORSKI perf mat rent   (T481)
VAAP perf mat rent   (T482)

TISNE, ANTOINE (1932-   )
A Une Ombre
fl,clar,horn,trp,trom,perc,pno,
8vln,3vla,3vcl,db
sc BILLAUDOT 514-00955S $16.00,
perf mat rent   (T483)

Alcaphante Pour Flutes, For Flute And
Orchestra [23']
horn,pno,strings,speaking voice,
fl solo
BILLAUDOT perf mat rent   (T484)

Arches De Lumiere [7']
2.2.2.2. 2.2.1.0. perc,harp,
strings
sc BILLAUDOT f.s., perf mat rent
(T485)
Caracteres [17']
1.1.1.1. 1.0.0.0. 2perc,2vln,vla,
vcl,db
sc BILLAUDOT f.s., perf mat rent
(T486)
Chant Pour Une Autre Galaxie [25']
timp,org,strings
BILLAUDOT perf mat rent   (T487)

Concerto for Flute and String
Orchestra [35']
string orch,fl solo
sc BILLAUDOT f.s., perf mat rent
(T488)
Concerto for Ondes Martenot and
Orchestra [25']
CHOUDENS perf mat rent   (T489)

Concerto for Piano and Orchestra, No.
1 [18']
perc,strings,pno solo
sc BILLAUDOT f.s., perf mat rent
(T490)
Concerto for Violin and Orchestra
[40']
2.2.2.2. 2.2.2.1. perc,harp,
strings,vln solo
BILLAUDOT perf mat rent   (T491)

TISNE, ANTOINE (cont'd.)

Cosmogonies [21']
3.3.3.3. 3.3.3.0. perc,harp,pno,
strings
BILLAUDOT perf mat rent   (T492)

Elegy for Double Bass and String
Orchestra [10']
string orch,db solo
BILLAUDOT perf mat rent   (T493)

Etude I d'Apres Goya [12']
2.2.2.2. 4.2.2.1. timp,perc,
vibra,marimba,xylo,harp,cel,
strings
sc BILLAUDOT f.s., perf mat rent
(T494)

Heraldiques, For Trumpet And String
Orchestra [6']
string orch,trp solo
BILLAUDOT perf mat rent   (T495)

Orbes De Feu [13']
2.2.2.2. 2.2.2.0. perc,2harp,
strings
BILLAUDOT perf mat rent   (T496)

Passage, For Solo Voice And String
Orchestra [21']
string orch,S solo
BILLAUDOT perf mat rent   (T497)

Recits Epiques Du Temps De La Guerre
[21']
1.0.2.0. 1.1.1.0. timp,6perc,pno,
2vla,2vcl,db
BILLAUDOT perf mat rent   (T498)

Reliefs Irradiants De New York [30']
3.3.3.3. 4.4.3.1. timp,perc,harp,
strings
BILLAUDOT perf mat rent   (T499)

Siderales [15']
perc,strings
BILLAUDOT perf mat rent   (T500)

Symphony No. 1 [15']
3.3.3.3. 4.3.3.1. timp,perc,harp,
pno,strings
BILLAUDOT perf mat rent   (T501)

Symphony No. 2 [25']
2.2.2.2. 2.2.2.1. timp,perc,harp,
strings
BILLAUDOT perf mat rent   (T502)

Voix, For Horn And String Orchestra
[20']
string orch,horn solo
BILLAUDOT perf mat rent   (T503)

TITAN see Fongaard, Bjørn

TITANIA IN LOVE see Trojan, Václav

TITANS see Russo, William Joseph

TITLE DIVINE, FOR SOLO VOICE AND
ORCHESTRA see Burgon, Geoffrey

TITUS: JETZT, VITELLIA! SCHLÄGT DIE
STUNDE; NIE SOLL MIT ROSEN, FOR
SOLO VOICE AND ORCHESTRA see
Mozart, Wolfgang Amadeus, Clemenza
Di Tito, La: Ecco Il Punto; Non Piu
Di Fiori, For Solo Voice And
Orchestra

TITUS: LASS ES EINMAL NUR GESCHEHEN,
FOR SOLO VOICE AND ORCHESTRA see
Mozart, Wolfgang Amadeus, Clemenza
Di Tito, La: Deh, Per Questo
Istante Solo, For Solo Voice And
Orchestra

TO A CHILD DANCING IN THE WIND, FOR
SOLO VOICE AND ORCHESTRA see
Cacioppo, Curt

TO A WILD ROSE, FOR HARP AND ORCHESTRA
[ARR.] see MacDowell, Edward
Alexander

TO AN OLD CHURCH, FOR SOLO VOICE AND
ORCHESTRA see Eggen, Arne, Til En
Gammel Kirke, For Solo Voice And
Orchestra

TO BIBELSKE SANGE, FOR SOLO VOICE AND
ORCHESTRA see Koppel, Herman David

TO COME TO A PLACE see Rickley, James

TO DAMASCUS see Thorarinsson, Leifur

TO EMILY see Weigl, [Mrs.] Vally

TO HAVE AND HAVE NOT: OVERTURE see
Waxman, Franz

TO MY KAMENICE AND LIPOU see Vacek,
Miloš

TO NORSKE DANSER see Andersen, Karl
August

TO PLAY TO DAY, FOR SOLO VOICES AND
ORCHESTRA see Christiansen, Henning

TO SPRING [ARR.] see Grieg, Edvard
Hagerup

TO THE EDGE OF A DREAM, FOR GUITAR AND
ORCHESTRA see Takemitsu, Toru

TO THE LITTLE STAR, FOR SOLO VOICE AND
ORCHESTRA see Mussorgsky, Modest
Petrovich

TO THE UNKNOWN SOLDIER see Howe, Mary

TO UNGE ELSKENDE, FOR SOLO VOICE AND
ORCHESTRA see Hall, Pauline

TOAMNA, FOR PAN-FLUTE AND ORCHESTRA see
Strietman, Willem

TOCCAMENTO see Barkauskas, Vytautas

TOCCATA, BOURREE ET GIGUE [ARR.] see
Scarlatti, Domenico

TOCCATA CONCERTANTE, FOR PERCUSSION AND
ORCHESTRA see Petric, Ivo

TOCCATA MECCANICA see Matthews, Colin

TOCCATE see Frescobaldi, Girolamo

TOCCATINA IN D see Williams, Julius P.

TOCCATINA QUASI UNA RHAPSODIA see
Sadler, Helmut

TOCH, ERNST (1887-1964)
Intermezzo [4'30"]
2.2.2.2. 2.2.0.0. 2perc,harp/pno,
strings
KALMUS A7257 sc $8.00, set $25.00,
pts $1.50, ea., perf mat rent
(T504)

TOD DER GELIEBTEN, DER, FOR SOLO VOICE
AND ORCHESTRA see Banfield,
Raffaello de

TOD UND DAS MÄDCHEN, DER, FOR SOLO
VOICE AND ORCHESTRA, [ARR.] see
Schubert, Franz (Peter)

TODAY'S NEWS, FOR SOLO VOICE AND
CHAMBER ORCHESTRA see Kvam, Oddvar
S., Dagens Nyheter, For Solo Voice
And Chamber Orchestra

TODESFUGE, FOR SOLO VOICE AND CHAMBER
ORCHESTRA see Kosa, György

TOEBOSCH, LOUIS (1916-   )
Concerto for Organ and Orchestra, Op.
125 [15']
2.2.2.2. 2.2.2.0. strings,elec
org solo
DONEMUS perf mat rent   (T505)

TOFFT, ALFRED (1865-1931)
Vifadanka
sc SAMFUNDET f.s., perf mat rent
(T506)

TOGNI, CAMILLO (1922-   )
Lyrisches Intermezzo, For Solo Voices
And Orchestra [3'30"]
3(pic).0.3.3.3sax. 3.0.0.0.
glock,vibra,harp,cel,12vln,
4vla,3vcl,2db,ATBar soli
RICORDI-IT 134072 perf mat rent
(T507)
Su Frammenti Di Peire Vidal, For Solo
Voice And Orchestra [9']
3.0.3.3.2sax. 3.0.0.0. glock,
vibra,harp,cel,12vln,4vla,3vcl,
2db,S solo
RICORDI-IT 133456 perf mat rent
(T508)

TOKAMAK, FOR PIANO AND ORCHESTRA see
Gehlhaar, Rolf

TOLOMEO: CHE PIU SI TARDA OMAI, FOR
SOLO VOICE AND STRING ORCHESTRA see
Handel, George Frideric

TOLOMEO E ALESSANDRO: SINFONIA see
Scarlatti, Francesco Antonio Nicola

TOLV MASKER, DE see Emborg, Jens
Laurson

TOMASEK, VACLAV JAN KRTITEL (1774-1850)
Concerto for Piano and Orchestra, Op.
18 [26']
1.2.2.2. 2.0.0.0. timp,strings,
pno solo, 2 clarini
SUPRAPHON   (T509)

TOMASI, HENRI (1901-1971)
Boite De Nuit
1.1(English horn).2(bass
clar).1.alto sax. 1.1.1.1.
timp,perc,harp,strings
LEMOINE perf mat rent   (T510)

TOMASI, HENRI (cont'd.)

Caravanes [14']
1(pic).1(English horn).1.1.
2.1.1.0. timp,perc,harp,strings
LEMOINE perf mat rent   (T511)

C'Etait Un Baiser, For Solo Voice And
Orchestra [3']
1.1.1.0.sax. 0.1.1.1. perc,harp,
pno,strings,solo voice
LEMOINE perf mat rent   (T512)

Chanson De Marin, For Solo Voice And
Orchestra [5']
1.1.0+bass clar.1.sax. 0.1.1.0.
perc,harp,strings,solo voice
LEMOINE perf mat rent   (T513)

Chant De La Fee Des Iles, For Solo
Voice And Orchestra
1.1.1.1. 1.1.0.0. perc,cel,harp,
strings,solo voice
LEMOINE perf mat rent   (T514)

Chants Laotiens, For Solo Voice And
Orchestra [18']
1(pic).1(English horn).2(bass
clar).1(contrabsn). 2.1.0.0.
timp,2perc,harp,strings,solo
voice
LEMOINE perf mat rent   (T515)

Clairieres Dans Le Ciel, For Solo
Voice And Orchestra [6']
3.2(English horn).2.3. 4.3.3.1.
timp,2harp,cel,strings,solo
voice
LEMOINE perf mat rent   (T516)

Concerto for Guitar and Orchestra
2.2(English horn).2.2. 3.3.0.0.
timp,perc,strings,gtr solo
LEDUC AL 27605-27606 perf mat rent
(T517)

Danses De Reve
3(pic).3(English horn).2.3.
4.3.3.1. timp,perc,2harp,cel,
strings
LEMOINE perf mat rent   (T518)

Danseuses De Degas, For Harp And
String Orchestra [2'20"]
string orch,harp
CHOUDENS perf mat rent   (T519)

Deux Melodies De Paul Fort, For Solo
Voice And Orchestra [9']
3.2(English horn).1.3. 4.3.3.1.
timp,perc,2harp,cel,strings,
solo voice
LEMOINE perf mat rent   (T520)

Dolores
1(pic).1(English horn).1.1.
2.2.3.0. timp,perc,harp,strings
LEMOINE perf mat rent   (T521)

Enfances De La Fontaine, For Solo
Voice And Orchestra
1.1.1.1. 0.1.0.0. perc,harp,
strings,solo voice
LEMOINE perf mat rent   (T522)

France D'Outre Mer
2(pic).1.1.2(contrabsn).alto
sax.tenor sax. 1.1.1.1. timp,
perc,harp,strings
LEMOINE perf mat rent   (T523)

Gros Nuages Gris [6']
1.1(English horn).1.1. 1.0.0.0.
timp,harp,strings
LEMOINE perf mat rent   (T524)

Mere Tres Douce [6']
1.1.1.1. 1.0.0.0. timp,harp,
strings
LEMOINE perf mat rent   (T525)

Mort Du Silence
1.1.1.0.sax. 0.1.0.0. perc,harp,
cel,strings
LEMOINE perf mat rent   (T526)

Quatre Melodies De Francis Carco, For
Solo Voice And Orchestra [10']
1(pic).1.1.1.alto sax. 2.1.2.0.
timp,perc,harp,strings,solo
voice
LEMOINE perf mat rent   (T527)

Serenade Venitienne, For Solo Voice
And Orchestra [3']
1(pic).1.1.0.sax. 0.1.0.0. harp,
strings,solo voice
LEMOINE perf mat rent   (T528)

Six Melodies Populaires Corses, For
Solo Voice And Orchestra [15']
2.1.1.2. 4.2.3.1. timp,perc,harp,
cel,strings,solo voice
LEMOINE perf mat rent   (T529)

TOMASI, HENRI (cont'd.)

Suite Saharienne [12']
0.1(English horn).1(bass
clar).1.sax. 0.1.1.1. perc,
harp,pno,strings
LEMOINE perf mat rent   (T530)

Trois Chansons Ecossaises, For Solo
Voice And Instrumental Ensemble
[11']
3clar,strings,solo voice
LEMOINE perf mat rent   (T531)

TOMASSON, JONAS (1946-   )

Another Symphony [21']
3.3.3.3. 4.4.3.0. strings
ICELAND 014-031   (T532)

Cantata No. 3 for Solo Voice and
Orchestra [7']
0.4(English horn).0.1. 1.0.1.0.
6vln,4vla,4vcl,2db,S solo
ICELAND 014-001   (T533)

Concerto for Violin and Orchestra
perc,4vln,4vla,4vcl,2db,vln solo
ICELAND 014-016   (T534)

Concerto Trittico
ICELAND 014-037   (T535)

Eleven Meditations On Settlement
[15']
1.3.1.3. 2.2.2.0. perc,strings
ICELAND 014-011   (T536)

Midi, For 2 Pianos And Orchestra
3.3.2.2. 4.3.3.1. perc,strings,
2pno soli
ICELAND 014-039   (T537)

Notturno IV
2.2.2.2. 4.2.3.1. timp,perc,
strings
ICELAND 014-028   (T538)

1.41 [8'35"]
3.2.3.2. 4.4.3.1. strings
ICELAND 014-003   (T539)

Orgia
1+alto fl.1.3.3. 3.2.3.1. perc,
strings
ICELAND 014-013   (T540)

Skerpla II [6'30"]
2.2.2.2. 4.2.3.1. strings
ICELAND 014-029   (T541)

Symphony for Viola and Chamber
Orchestra [12']
1.1.1.1. 1.1.1.1. strings,vla
solo
ICELAND 014-017   (T542)

TOMBA DI BRUNO, FOR FLUTE AND ORCHESTRA
see Olive, Vivienne

TOMBA DI IGOR STRAWINSKY, LA see Klebe,
Giselher

TOMBEAU see Döhl, Friedhelm

TOMBEAU D'ALBAN BERG, LE see Israel-
Meyer, Pierre

TOMBEAU D'ANDRE JOLIVET, LE see
Holstein, Jean-Paul

TOMBEAU D'ARMOR II see Sinopoli,
Giuseppe

TOMBEAU D'ARMOR III, FOR VIOLONCELLO
AND ORCHESTRA see Sinopoli,
Giuseppe

TOMBEAU DE BACH see Hovland, Egil

TOMBEAU DE PHILIPPE D'ORLEANS, LE see
Duhamel

TOMBEAU DE RAINER MARIA RILKE, LE, FOR
SOLO VOICE AND ORCHESTRA see
Bailly, Jean Guy

TOMBEAU D'EDGAR POE, LE see Argento,
Dominick

TOMBEAU TIL MINONA see Skouen, Synne

TOMORROW see Korngold, Erich Wolfgang

TON IMAGE CHARMANTE, FOR SOLO VOICE AND
ORCHESTRA see Denisov, Edison
Vasilievich

TON SOURIRE see Vezina, Joseph

TON THAT, TIET (1933-   )

Concerto for Violoncello and
Orchestra [26'30"]
2.2.2.2. 2.2.2.0. timp,2perc,
strings,vcl solo
BILLAUDOT perf mat rent   (T543)

TON THAT, TIET (cont'd.)

Hy Vong 14 [15']
English horn,hpsd,7vln,2vla,2vcl,
db
SALABERT perf mat rent   (T544)

Vang Bong Thoi Xua, For Solo Voice
And Instrumental Ensemble
1.1.1.1. 1.1.1.0. 4perc,pno&cel,
2vln,vla,2vcl,S solo
(Reflets Du Temps Passe) SALABERT
perf mat rent   (T545)

Vision I, For Violoncello And
Instrumental Ensemble [11'20"]
2.2.2.2. 1.1.1.0. perc,pno,vcl
solo
BILLAUDOT perf mat rent   (T546)

Vo-Vi [16']
24strings
BILLAUDOT perf mat rent   (T547)

TONE COLORS see Mortensen, Finn

TONE ROADS TO HK: FOUR MOVEMENTS FOR A
FASHIONABLE FIVE-TOED DRAGON, FOR
JAZZ ENSEMBLE AND ORCHESTRA see
Moore, Carman

TONEN, FOR SOLO VOICE AND ORCHESTRA see
Tveitt, Geirr

TONES see Leon, Tania Justina

TONGENESIS see Rojko, Uroš

TONSCHERBEN see Holliger, Heinz

TOOVEY, ANDREW (1962-   )

Ate [12']
0+pic(alto fl).1(English
horn).1(bass
clar).1(contrabsn). 1.1.1.0.
2perc,harp,pno,2vln,vla,vcl,db
BOOSEY perf mat rent   (T548)

Black Light [10']
1(pic).1(English horn).1(bass
clar).1+contrabsn. 1.1.1.0.
2perc,harp,pno,strings
BOOSEY perf mat rent   (T549)

TOPOLOGY OF GRAINS OF SAND see Norholm,
Ib, Sandskornets Topologi

TORCH, THE, FOR SOLO VOICE AND
ORCHESTRA see Elgar, [Sir] Edward
(William)

TORD FOLESON, FOR SOLO VOICE AND
ORCHESTRA see Tveitt, Geirr

TORDENSKIOLD see Halvorsen, Johan

TORDENSKIOLDIANA see Albertsen, Per
Hjort

TORELLI, GIUSEPPE (1658-1709)

Concertino in D, MIN 576 [6']
string orch,hpsd,trp solo
INTERNAT. perf mat rent   (T550)

Concerto, Op. 8, No. 6, in G minor
(Schering) KAHNT KT 8871 f.s. (T551)

TORKE, MICHAEL

Adjustable Wrench [11']
0.1.2.1. 1.2.1.0. marimba,pno,
synthesizer,vln,vla,vcl,db
HENDON perf mat rent   (T552)

Ash [16']
1.2.1.2. 3.1.0.0. timp,
synthesizer,strings
HENDON perf mat rent   (T553)

Black & White [24']
3(pic).2+English horn.2+bass
clar.3. 4.3.3.1. timp,3perc,
pno&cel,harp,synthesizer,
strings
HENDON perf mat rent   (T554)

Bright Blue Music [12']
3(2pic).2.2.2. 4.3.3.1. timp,
4perc,pno,strings
sc HENDON $19.00, perf mat rent
(T555)

Copper, For Brass Quintet And
Orchestra [12']
2+pic.2+English horn.2.2.
4.2.3.1. timp,3perc,pno,harp,
strings,brass quin soli
HENDON perf mat rent   (T556)

Ecstatic Orange [12']
2+pic.2.2.2. 4.2+piccolo trp(trp
in C).3.1. timp,3perc,pno,
strings
HENDON perf mat rent   (T557)

Purple [7']
3(pic).2+English horn.2+bass
clar.2. 4.3.3.1. timp,3perc,

TORKE, MICHAEL (cont'd.)

pno,harp,strings
HENDON perf mat rent   (T558)

Slate For Concertante Group And
Orchestra [32']
2.2.2.2. 4.3.1.0. timp,strings,
concertante group: 3 kbd, xylo,
marimba
HENDON perf mat rent   (T559)

Verdant Music [23']
3(2pic).2+English horn.2+bass
clar.2. 4.3.3.1. timp,3perc,
pno,strings
HENDON perf mat rent   (T560)

TORNA A SORRENTO, FOR SOLO VOICE AND
ORCHESTRA see Curtis, Ernesto de

TÖRNQUIST, F.

Old Swedish Folk Tune, For Solo Voice
And Orchestra [3']
clar,strings,med solo
NORDISKA perf mat rent   (T561)

TÖRÖKORSZÁGI LEVELEK, FOR SOLO VOICE
AND CHAMBER ORCHESTRA see
Petrovics, Emil

TORRE DEL ORO, LA, FOR SOLO VOICE AND
ORCHESTRA see Gimenez, Jeronimo

TORRENGA, BENNO (1953-   )

Feest [9']
3.3.3.3. 4.2.3.1. timp,perc,
strings
sc DONEMUS f.s., perf mat rent
(T562)

TORSTENSSON, KLAS (1951-   )

Fläka [14']
0.0.2.0.sax. 1.1.1.0. perc,pno,
2vln,vla,vcl,db
DONEMUS perf mat rent   (T563)

Licks & Brains II, For 4 Saxophones
And Orchestra [30']
2.2.3.2. 2.2.3.0. 4perc,bass gtr,
elec pno,strings,4sax soli
DONEMUS perf mat rent   (T564)

TORTELIER, PAUL (1914-1990)

Concerto for Piano and Orchestra
[24']
2(pic).2(English horn).2.2.
4.3.3.1. timp,perc,strings,pno
solo
CHESTER JWC491 perf mat rent (T565)

Valse No. 1 "Alla Maud", For 2
Violoncelli And String Orchestra
[6']
string orch,2vcl soli
COSTALL C.3668 perf mat rent (T566)

TOSI, DANIEL

Phonic Design A [20']
1.1.1.1. 1.1.1+bass trom.0. tenor
sax/bass clar,xylo,marimba,
7vln,2vla,2vcl,db
SALABERT perf mat rent   (T567)

Phonic Design B [20']
3.3.3.3. 3.3.3.3. 6perc,strings
(may be played simultaneously with
Phonic Design A) SALABERT perf
mat rent   (T568)

Scordatura 14 [16']
9-14strings,opt electronic tape
SALABERT perf mat rent   (T569)

TOSTI, FRANCESCO PAOLO (1846-1916)

Ideale [arr.]
(Tavan) 1.1.1.0. 0.0.0.0. strings
set KALMUS A7458 $20.00, and up
(T570)

TOTENFEIER see Mahler, Gustav

TOTENTANZ, FOR PIANO AND ORCHESTRA see
Liszt, Franz see Rinehart, John

TOTUS IN CORDE LANQUEO, D.136 see
Schubert, Franz (Peter)

TOUCHEMOULIN, JOSEPH (1727-1801)

Symphony *see SEVEN SYMPHONIES FROM
THE COURT OF THURN UND TAXIS

TOUR UN RETOUR POLKA see Strauss,
Eduard

TOURNAMENTS see Corigliano, John

TOURNEE, FOR ALTO SAXOPHONE AND
ORCHESTRA see Schoonenbeek, Kees

TOURNEMIRE, CHARLES (1870-1939)

Poem for Organ and Orchestra, Op. 38
[10']
3.3.3.3. 4.3.3.1. timp,2harp,
strings,org solo
ESCHIG perf mat rent   (T571)

TOURNEMIRE, CHARLES (cont'd.)

Symphony No. 1, Op. 18
    4.3.2.2. 4.4.3.1. timp,perc,
    2harp,strings
    ESCHIG perf mat rent   (T572)

Symphony No. 2, Op. 36 [46']
    4.4.3.3. 6.3.3.1. timp,2harp,
    strings
    ESCHIG perf mat rent   (T573)

Symphony No. 3, Op. 43 [28']
    4.3.3.4. 5.3.3.1. timp,perc,cel,
    2harp,org,strings
    ESCHIG perf mat rent   (T574)

Symphony No. 4, Op. 44
    3.3.2.4. 4.3.3.1. timp,perc,
    2harp,org,strings
    ESCHIG perf mat rent   (T575)

Symphony No. 5, Op. 47 [35']
    3.3.3.4. 4.4.3.1. timp,perc,
    2harp,strings
    ESCHIG perf mat rent   (T576)

TOURNIER, FRANZ
Concertino for Trumpet and String
    Orchestra [13'30"]
    string orch,trp solo
    RIDEAU perf mat rent   (T577)

Concerto for Piano and Orchestra
    [24'20"]
    2.2.2.2. 2.2.2.0. timp,strings,
    pno solo
    RIDEAU perf mat rent   (T578)

TOURS DE CARTE see Olthuis, Kees

TOUSSAINT: SONG OF THE COMMON WIND, FOR
    SOLO VOICE AND ORCHESTRA see Blake,
    David

TOUSSAINT: SUITE, FOR SOLO VOICES AND
    ORCHESTRA see Blake, David

TOUT A COUP ET COMME PAR JEU, FOR FLUTE
    AND ORCHESTRA see Coral, Giampaolo

TOVEM see Mansurian, Tigran

TOWARD THE RAINBOW, PALMA, FOR OBOE
    D'AMORE, GUITAR AND ORCHESTRA see
    Takemitsu, Toru

TOWARD THE SEA II, FOR ALTO FLUTE, HARP
    AND STRING ORCHESTRA see Takemitsu,
    Toru

TOWARDS A YEARNING, FOR PIANO AND
    ORCHESTRA see Sommerfeldt, Oistein,
    Mot En Lengsel, For Piano And
    Orchestra

TOWARDS AQUARIUS see Buller, John

TOWARDS ASAVARI, FOR PIANO AND
    ORCHESTRA see Gilbert, Anthony

TOWARDS BALANCE see Mostad, Jon, Mot
    Likevekt

TOWARDS DEATH see Børresen, Hakon, Mod
    Doden

TOWARDS FREEDOM? see Norgaard, Per

TOWARDS THE SON see Tavener, John

TOWER, JOAN (1938-   )
Amazon II [14']
    2(pic).2.2.2. 2.2.1.1. 3perc,
    harp,pno/cel,strings
    AMP perf mat rent   (T579)

Concerto for Clarinet and Orchestra
    [19']
    2(pic).2.2.2. 4.2.2.1. 2perc,
    harp,pno,cel,strings,clar/
    basset horn solo
    AMP perf mat rent   (T580)

Concerto for Flute and Orchestra
    [15']
    1(pic).1.1(bass clar).1. 0.1.1.0.
    2perc,strings,fl solo
    AMP   (T581)

Concerto for Piano and Orchestra
    [21']
    2(pic).1.2(bass clar).1. 2.2.1.0.
    2perc,strings,pno solo
    (homage to Beethoven) AMP perf mat
    rent   (T582)

Island Preludes, For Oboe And String
    Orchestra [10']
    string orch,ob solo
    AMP perf mat rent   (T583)

Island Rhythms [8']
    2(pic).2.2.2. 2.2.1.1. timp,
    2perc,strings
    AMP perf mat rent   (T584)

TOWER, JOAN (cont'd.)

Music for Violoncello and Orchestra
    [19']
    2(pic).2.2.2. 2.2.1.0. timp,
    2perc,harp,strings,vcl solo
    AMP perf mat rent   (T585)

Sequoia [16']
    2(pic).2.2.2. 4.2.3.1. 4perc,
    harp,pno,cel,strings
    AMP perf mat rent   (T586)

Silver Ladders [22']
    2+pic.2+English horn.2+bass
    clar.2+contrabsn. 4.3.3.1.
    timp,4perc,harp,pno/cel,strings
    sc AMP 50481139 $30.00, perf mat
    rent   (T587)

TOWNSEND, DOUGLAS (1921-   )
Four Fantasies On American Folk Songs
    [14']
    2(pic).2(English horn).2.2.
    4.2.3.1. timp,pno,opt harp,
    strings
    PETERS P604A perf mat rent   (T588)

TRACCE see Edlund, Lars

TRACE, FOR FLUTE AND INSTRUMENTAL
    ENSEMBLE see Boone, Charles N.

TRACE-ECART, FOR SOLO VOICES AND
    ORCHESTRA see Jarrell, Michael

TRACEES see Xenakis, Yannis (Iannis)

TRACI AMANTI, I: OVERTURE see Cimarosa,
    Domenico

TRACI AMANTI, I: OVERTURE [ARR.] see
    Cimarosa, Domenico

TRACTATUS, FOR FLUTE AND ORCHESTRA see
    Nordheim, Arne

TRAD-SENS CONCERTIO, FOR PIANO AND
    ORCHESTRA see Bregent, Michel

TRADITIONAL HORNPIPE SUITE [ARR.]
    (Cruft, Adrian) 2.1.2.1. 2.1.1.0.
    perc,strings [8'] sc JOAD f.s.
    perf mat rent   (T589)

TRAENE, DIE, FOR SAXOPHONE AND
    ORCHESTRA see Dominello, Larry,
    Tear, The, For Saxophone And
    Orchestra

TRAETTA, TOMMASO (MICHELE FRANCESCO
    SAVERIO) (1727-1779)
Aria Di Sammete "Se d'Amor Se Di
    Contento", For Solo Voice And
    String Orchestra [6']
    string orch,cont,countertenor/Mez
    solo
    (Blanchard, R.) BOIS perf mat rent
            (T590)
Ifigenia In Tauride: Overture
    (Sulyok) sc EMB 8942 f.s.   (T591)

Overture in D [12']
    2ob,2horn,strings
    sc BSE 127 f.s., perf mat rent
            (T592)
Overture in F [12']
    2ob,2horn,strings
    sc BSE 135 f.s., perf mat rent
            (T593)
Sinfonia in D
    (Bonelli) KALMUS A7305 sc $7.00,
    set $12.00, pts $1.50, ea. (T594)

TRAEUME AUF DICTERHOEHE, FOR HORN AND
    STRING ORCHESTRA see Suben, Joel
    Eric

TRAGEDIE DE SALOME, LA see Schmitt,
    Florent

TRAGIC OVERTURE see Dvorák, Antonín see
    Lendvay, Kamillo

TRAGISCHE OUVERTURE see Brahms,
    Johannes

TRAIN, THE see Waggoner, Andrew

TRAIN TO MARIPOSA, THE see Rathburn,
    Eldon

TRAME DELUSE, LE: OVERTURE see
    Cimarosa, Domenico

TRAMES see Hurel, Philippe

TRANS ACTIONS see Cunningham, Michael
    Gerald

TRANSACTIONEN see Strauss, Josef

TRANSE-CHORAL see Nordgren, Pehr Henrik

TRANSFIGURATION, THE see Bedford, David

TRANSFIGURED NOTES see Babbitt, Milton
    Byron

TRANSFIGURED WIND II, FOR FLUTE AND
    ORCHESTRA see Reynolds, Roger

TRANSFIGURED WIND III, FOR FLUTE AND
    ORCHESTRA see Reynolds, Roger

TRANSFORMACIONES see Lanza, Alcides E.

TRANSFORMATIONS see Sermila, Jarmo

TRANSFORMATIONS OF THE HEART see Levi,
    Paul Alan

TRANSFORMED PRELUDE, THE, FOR PIANO AND
    ORCHESTRA see Warfield, Gerald
    Alexander

TRANSIENCE see Lee, Eugene

TRANSIR: EPITAPH POUR RENE CHAR see
    Trojahn, Manfred

TRANSITION see Thoresen, Lasse

TRANSITS I see Ranta, Michael

TRANSLATIONS see Olah, Tiberiu

TRANSLUCENT VISION see Ishii, Maki

TRANSPARENCE see Mellnäs, Arne

TRANSPARENCY OF TIME, THE, FOR PIANO
    AND ORCHESTRA see Luedeke, Raymond

TRANSPARENT THINGS: IN MEMORIAM VN see
    Stucky, Steven Edward

TRANSYLVANIAN RHAPSODY see Seiber,
    Matyas György

TRASFORMAZIONI SINFONICHE, FOR PIANO
    AND ORCHESTRA see Westergaard,
    Svend

TRAUERMUSIK see Schibler, Armin

TRAUMBILD, FOR SOLO VOICES AND
    ORCHESTRA see Samuel, Gerhard

TRAUME, FOR VIOLIN AND ORCHESTRA [ARR]
    see Wagner, Richard

TRAUMER UND VAGANTEN, FOR SOLO VOICE
    AND ORCHESTRA see Mohler, Philipp

TRÄUMERIN POLKA, DIE see Strauss,
    Eduard

TRAUMGEBILDE WALZER see Strauss, Eduard

TRAUMKRAUT, FOR SOLO VOICES AND CHAMBER
    ORCHESTRA see Krebs, Joachim

TRAUMMUSIK see Kreuder, Peter

TRAUMSPIEL, FOR SOLO VOICE AND
    ORCHESTRA see Höller, York

TRAUMSTADT see Saxton, Robert

TRAUMTANZ, FOR PERCUSSION AND STRING
    ORCHESTRA see Redel, Martin
    Christoph

TRAVELER, THE, FOR SOLO VOICE AND
    ORCHESTRA see Heilner, Irwin

TRAVELS, FOR TRUMPET AND ORCHESTRA see
    Amram, David Werner

TRAVIATA, LA: PRELUDE, ACT III see
    Verdi, Giuseppe

TRAVLOS, MICHAEL (1950-   )
Eniwetock
    3(pic).3.3(bass
    clar).3(contrabsn). 4.3.3.1.
    timp,3perc,harp,cel,strings
    TONOS perf mat rent   (T595)

Prisma
    3(pic,alto fl).3(English
    horn).3(bass
    clar).3(contrabsn). 4.3.3.1.
    timp,3perc,harp,cel,org,strings
    TONOS   (T596)

TRE COLORI see Karkoff, Maurice

TRE DANSK PEBLINGEVISER see Riisager,
    Knudage

TRE HANER GALER, FOR SOLO VOICES AND
    ORCHESTRA see Skouen, Synne

TRE KONTRASTER FOR ORKESTER see Kvam,
    Oddvar S.

TRE NATTLIGE SCENER see Jordan, Sverre

TRE NOTTURNI, FOR SOLO VOICES AND
ORCHESTRA see Mysliveczek, Joseph

TRE ORKESTERSTYKKER see Holm, Peder

TRE PEZZI PAZZI, FOR SOLO VOICE AND
ORCHESTRA see Albin, Roger

TRE POESIE DI MONTALE, FOR SOLO VOICE
AND ORCHESTRA see Vlad, Roman

TRE SCALINI see Dusapin, Pascal

TREASURE TRAIL, THE FOR NARRATOR AND
ORCHESTRA see Coombes, Douglas

TREDE, YNGRE JAN (1903-   )
Concerto for Viola and Orchestra
[21']
1(pic).1.2.2. 2.0.0.0. timp,
strings,vla solo
HANSEN-DEN perf mat rent   (T597)

TREESTONE, FOR SOLO VOICES AND CHAMBER
ORCHESTRA see Albert, Stephen Joel

TREFOUSSE, ROGER
Square Of Sunlight [10']
string orch
sc AM.COMP.AL. $24.85   (T598)

TREIZE PETITS AIRS see Gillet, Bruno

TREMAIN, RONALD (1923-   )
Symphony for Strings [15']
string orch
CAN.MUS.CENT. MI 1500 T789SY (T599)

Three Mystical Songs, For Solo Voice
And String Orchestra [9']
string orch,Mez solo
sc WAI-TE-ATA f.s.   (T600)

War Of The Newts [15']
0.0.1.1. 2.2.2.0. perc,vln,vcl,db
CAN.MUS.CENT. MI 1200 T789 WA
                              (T601)
TREMATE, EMPI, TREMATE, FOR SOLO VOICES
AND ORCHESTRA, OP. 116 see
Beethoven, Ludwig van

TREMBLAY, GILLES (1932-   )
Compostelle I [18']
2.0.1.0. 1.0.2.0. 4perc,2harp,
3vln,3db
sc SALABERT f.s., perf mat rent
                              (T602)
Envoi, For Piano And Instrumental
Ensemble [30']
2.0.1+bass clar.0. 1.2.2.0.
3perc,2vln,db,pno solo
SALABERT perf mat rent   (T603)

Fleuves, For Piano And Orchestra
[17']
4.4.4.4. 5.4.3.1. 4perc,harp,
strings,pno solo
SALABERT perf mat rent   (T604)

Katadrone [20']
2(pic).2.2.2. 4.4.4.1. 3perc,
strings
SALABERT perf mat rent   (T605)

Vers [24']
2.0.1.0. 1.1.0.0. 3perc,3vcl,db
(Champs III) sc SALABERT f.s., perf
mat rent   (T606)

Vers Le Soleil, For Piano And Chamber
Orchestra [16']
2.1.1.1. 2.1.2.0. 3perc,7vln,
2vla,2vcl,db,pno solo
sc SALABERT f.s., perf mat rent
                              (T607)
TRENET, CHARLES
Parisian In New York, A [17']
2.2.2.2. 3.3.4.0. timp,perc,cel,
gtr,harp,pno,strings
AMP perf mat rent   (T608)

TRENTE-QUATRE MESURES POUR UN PORTRAIT
DE T see Koering, Rene

TRES DANZAS CONCERTANTES, FOR GUITAR
AND STRING ORCHESTRA see Brouwer,
Leo

TRES HOMENAJES see Ramirez, Luis
Antonio

TRES PIEZAS [ARR.] see Cabanilles, Juan
Bautista José

TRES PIEZAS BREVES see Ramirez, Luis
Antonio

TRES POEMAS DE LA LIRICA ESPANOLA, FOR
SOLO VOICE AND ORCHESTRA see
Halffter, Cristobal

TRES RETRATOS see Bresgen, Cesar

TRES TANGOS, FOR BANDONEON AND
ORCHESTRA see Piazzolla, Astor

TRES VIEJOS AIRES DE DANZA see Rodrigo,
Joaquín

TRESSES, FOR SOLO VOICE AND CHAMBER
ORCHESTRA see Balassa, Sándor

TRETTON AR, FOR SOLO VOICE AND
ORCHESTRA see Jordan, Sverre

TREULIEBCHEN POLKA see Strauss, Eduard

TREXLER, GEORG (1903-1979)
Drei Gesänge, For Solo Voice And
Orchestra
1.2.2.2. 2.0.0.0. timp,triangle,
strings,S solo BREITKOPF-L perf
mat rent
contains: Lied Des Völlig
Arglosen, Das, For Solo Voice
And Orchestra; Mondschein, For
Solo Voice And Orchestra; Und
So Wird Kommen Ein Sommertag,
For Solo Voice And Orchestra
                              (T609)

Introduzione E Scherzo [12']
2.2.2.2. 2.2.3.0. timp,perc,harp,
strings
BREITKOPF-L perf mat rent   (T610)

Lied Des Völlig Arglosen, Das, For
Solo Voice And Orchestra
see Drei Gesänge, For Solo Voice
And Orchestra

Mondschein, For Solo Voice And
Orchestra
see Drei Gesänge, For Solo Voice
And Orchestra

Und So Wird Kommen Ein Sommertag, For
Solo Voice And Orchestra
see Drei Gesänge, For Solo Voice
And Orchestra

TRI KONCERTNE ARIJE, FOR SOLO VOICE AND
ORCHESTRA see Sivic, Pavle

TRI SIMFONICNE SKICE see Skerl, Dane

TRIAL, THE, FOR PIANO AND CHAMBER
ORCHESTRA see Schuller, Gunther

TRIAL OF PROMETHEUS, THE see Burgon,
Geoffrey

TRIANGLE POUR UN SOUFFLE, FOR ALTO
SAXOPHONE AND STRING ORCHESTRA see
Rosse, Francois

TRIANGLES, FOR PERCUSSION AND
INSTRUMENTAL ENSEMBLE see Kraft,
William

TRIBAL DANCE see Still, William Grant

TRIBUT DE ZAMORA, LE: BALLET MUSIC see
Gounod, Charles François

TRIBUTE OF CAROLS, A see Gordeli, Otar

TRIDIMENSIONAL see Fernandez Alvez,
Gabriel

TRIEB 1 see Campana, Jose Luis

TRIEB 2, FOR 4 PERCUSSION AND ORCHESTRA
see Campana, Jose Luis

TRILOGIA PICCOLA see Leifs, Jon

TRILOGY see Banks, Don

TRIMBLE, LESTER ALBERT (1923-   )
Five Episodes [11']
3.3.3.3. 4.3.3.1. timp,perc,
2harp,strings
DUCHESS perf mat rent   (T611)

Sonic Landscape [10']
3.3.3.2. 4.2.3.1. timp,3perc,
strings
DUCHESS perf mat rent   (T612)

Symphony No. 2 [28']
4(pic).4(English horn).4(bass
clar).5(contrabsn).alto sax.
4.3.3.1. timp,5perc,harp,cel,
pno,strings
DUCHESS perf mat rent   (T613)

TRINITA SINFONICA see Akutagawa,
Yasushi

TRIO CONCERTANTE, FOR VIOLIN, VIOLA,
VIOLONCELLO AND STRING ORCHESTRA
see Coignet, Antoine

TRIO FOR THIRTEEN: ACOTRAL, FOR SOLO
VOICES AND ORCHESTRA see Hvoslef,
Ketil

TRIOMPHE DE BACCHUS see Debussy, Claude

TRIOMPHE FUNEBRE DU TASSE, LE see
Liszt, Franz

TRIPARTITA see Halffter, Rodolfo

TRIPLE CONCERTO, FOR TRUMPET, HORN,
TROMBONE AND STRING ORCHESTRA see
Biggs, John

TRIPLE PLAY see Austin, John

TRIPLE-SEXTET see Orbán, Gyorgy

TRIPTIC DE MOSEN CINTO, FOR SOLO VOICE
AND ORCHESTRA see Rodrigo, Joaquín

TRIPTIH, FOR SOLO VOICE AND ORCHESTRA
see Ciglic, Zvonimir

TRIPTYCH see Brown, Christopher
(Roland) see Clarke, F.R.C. see
Gasieniec, Miroslaw see McLennan,
John Stewart

TRIPTYCH, FOR SOLO VOICE AND ORCHESTRA
see Heiden, Bernhard

TRIPTYCH, FOR VIOLA AND CHAMBER
ORCHESTRA see Bibik, Valentin

TRIPTYCHON see Butting, Max see Cerha,
Friedrich see Kvandal, Johan

TRIPTYCHON FUR SCHUTZ, BACH UND HANDEL
see Rubin, Marcel

TRIPTYKON, FOR PERCUSSION AND ORCHESTRA
see Gudmundsen-Holmgreen, Pelle

TRIPTYQUE see Lancen, Serge

TRIPTYQUE, FOR BASSOON AND ORCHESTRA
see Bereau, J.S.

TRIPTYQUE, FOR VIOLIN, PIANO AND
ORCHESTRA see Lee, Noel

TRIPTYQUE SYMPHONIQUE see Merlet,
Michel

TRISTAN UND ISOLDE: ERFUHREST DU MEINE
SCHMACH, FOR SOLO VOICE AND
ORCHESTRA see Wagner, Richard

TRISTAN UND ISOLDE: FANTASY, FOR VIOLIN
AND ORCHESTRA, [ARR.] see Wagner,
Richard

TRISTAN UND ISOLDE: KING MARK'S
MONOLOGUE, FOR SOLO VOICE AND
ORCHESTRA see Wagner, Richard

TRISTAN UND ISOLDE: LIEBESTOD, "MILD
UND LEISE", FOR SOLO VOICE AND
ORCHESTRA see Wagner, Richard

TRISTAN UND ISOLDE: PRELUDE AND
LIEBESTOD see Wagner, Richard

TRISTAN UND ISOLDE: PRELUDE AND LOVE
DEATH see Wagner, Richard, Tristan
Und Isolde: Prelude And Liebestod

TRISTANS KLAGE see Nieder, Fabio

TRISTIA see Szöllösy, Andras

TRISTIA, FOR SOLO VOICE AND CHAMBER
ORCHESTRA see Firsova, Elena

TRITON see Fongaard, Bjørn

TRITONS, THE see Ireland, John

TRITSCH-TRATSCH POLKA see Strauss,
Johann, [Jr.]

TRIUMPH OF NEPTUNE, THE: SUITE see
Berners, Lord (Gerald Tyrwhitt)

TRIUMPH OF NEPTUNE, THE: SUITE, [ARR.]
see Berners, Lord (Gerald Tyrwhitt)

TRIUMPH-SYMPHONIE see Smetana, Bedrich

TRIUMPHAL POEM see Khachaturian, Aram
Ilyich

TRIUMPHALES TRAUERPRALUDIUM see
Shostakovich, Dmitri, Mournful-
Triumphal Prelude

TRIVIUM, FOR SOLO VOICE AND STRING
ORCHESTRA see Chiti, Gian Paolo

TRNECKA, BOHUMIL
Fantasy for 4 Horns and Orchestra
SLOV.HUD.FOND   (T614)

TROBAR CLUS, FOR BASSOON AND ORCHESTRA
see Sveinsson, Atli Heimir

TROBENTA IN VRAG: SUITA see Srebotnjak, Alojz F.

TROICA see Bottari, G.

TROIKA [ARR.] see Tchaikovsky, Piotr Ilyich

TROILUS AND CRESSIDA: SUITE [ARR.] see Walton, [Sir] William (Turner)

TROIS AIRS POUR UN OPERA IMAGINAIRE, FOR SOLO VOICE AND INSTRUMENTAL ENSEMBLE see Vivier, Claude

TROIS BALLADES DE FRANCOIS VILLON, FOR SOLO VOICE AND ORCHESTRA see Debussy, Claude

TROIS CHANSONS DE BILITIS, FOR SOLO VOICE AND CHAMBER ORCHESTRA see Rudhyar, Dane (Daniel Chennevière)

TROIS CHANSONS ECOSSAISES, FOR SOLO VOICE AND INSTRUMENTAL ENSEMBLE see Tomasi, Henri

TROIS CHANTS DES HOMMES, FOR SOLO VOICE AND ORCHESTRA see Jolivet, Andre

TROIS DANSES see Durufle, Maurice

TROIS ELEGIES DE FRANCIS JAMMES, FOR SOLO VOICES AND STRING ORCHESTRA see Milhaud, Darius

TROIS IMAGES see Bitsch, Marcel

TROIS IMAGES CONCERTANTES, FOR BASSOON AND ORCHESTRA see Bondon, Jacques

TROIS INTERLUDES see Damase, Jean-Michel

TROIS JOLIS TAMBOURS, FOR SOLO VOICE AND ORCHESTRA see Arrieu, Claude

TROIS LITANIES, FOR SOLO VOICES AND STRING ORCHESTRA see Durante, Francesco

TROIS MINIATURES see Pepin, Clermont
  see Shoujouian, Petros

TROIS MORCEAUX RAPSODIQUES see Bull, Edvard Hagerup

TROIS MORPHOSES, FOR HORN AND CHAMBER ORCHESTRA see Svara, Danilo

TROIS ODES FUNEBRES: LA NUIT see Liszt, Franz

TROIS PETITES PIECES MONTEES see Satie, Erik

TROIS PIECES, FOR HARP AND CHAMBER ORCHESTRA see Marischal, Louis

TROIS PRÉLUDES see Borstlap, John see Mathieu, Rodolphe

TROIS SERENADES see DuBois, Pierre-Max

TROIS VALSES see Milhaud, Darius

TROIS VALSES ROMANTIQUES see Chabrier, [Alexis-] Emmanuel

TROIS VISIONS DE GENEVIEVE, FOR SOLO VOICE AND STRINGS see Vacchi, Fabio

TROJAHN, MANFRED (1949-   )
  Abschied [12']
    0.0+English horn.2+bass clar.2+
      contrabsn. 4.0.3.0+db tuba.
      perc,harp,6vla,6vcl,5-6db
    BÄREN. BA 6763 perf mat rent (T615)

  Autunno, L' [12']
    1+alto fl.1+English horn.1+bass
      clar.1+contrabsn. 2.2.2.0. cel,
      harp,strings
    BÄREN. BA 7168   (T616)

  Berceuse for Strings [10']
    8vln,3vla,3vcl,db
    BÄREN. BA 7150   (T617)

  Chants Noirs (from Une Campagne Noire
    De Soleil) [21']
    1(pic).1.0+bass clar(clar in E
      flat).0. 0.0.0.0. 2perc,pno,
      string quin
    BÄREN. BA 7145   (T618)

  Cinq Epigraphes [14']
    3(bass fl,alto fl,pic).2+English
      horn.3+bass clar.2+contrabsn.
      4.4.3.1. timp,6perc,harp,cel,
      strings
    BÄREN. BA 7173   (T619)

  Concerto for Flute and Orchestra
    [20']
    2(pic).2+English horn.2(soprano

TROJAHN, MANFRED (cont'd.)
    clar in E flat,tenor sax)+bass
      clar.2+contrabsn. 2.2.2.1.
      timp,2perc,8vln,3vla,3vcl,db,fl
      solo
    BÄREN. BA 7127 perf mat rent (T620)

  Conduct (Second Version) [15']
    perc,11strings
    BÄREN. BA 6749 perf mat rent (T621)

  Funftes See-Bild "Der Tod Der
    Liebenden", For Solo Voice And
    Orchestra [15']
    3(pic,bass fl,alto fl).2+English
      horn.3(soprano clar in E flat)+
      bass clar.3(contrabsn).
      4.4.3.1. timp,3perc,harp,
      strings,Mez solo
    BÄREN. BA 7122 perf mat rent (T622)

  Nachtwandlung Auf Fragmente Von Georg
    Trakl, For Solo Voice And
    Instrumental Ensemble
    1.1.1+bass clar.0+contrabsn.
      1.1.1.0. harp,cel,4vcl,Mez solo
    BÄREN. BA 7156 perf mat rent (T623)

  Notturni Trasognati, For Alto Flute
    And Chamber Orchestra [14']
    0.0+English horn.1+bass clar.1.
      2.1.1.0. perc,cel,harp,strings,
      alto fl solo
    study sc BÄREN. BA 6728 f.s. (T624)

  Processions (from Une Campagne Noire
    De Soleil) [22']
    1(pic)+alto fl(bass fl).1(English
      horn).1(clar in E flat)+bass
      clar.1(contrabsn). 2.2.1.0.
      2perc,cel,strings
    BÄREN. BA 7147   (T625)

  Silences (from Une Campagne Noire De
    Soleil) [20']
    1(pic,alto fl,bass fl).1.1+bass
      clar.1(contrabsn). 2.2.1.0.
      2perc,cel,strings
    BÄREN. BA 7142 perf mat rent (T626)

  Symphony No. 2 [32']
    3(pic,alto fl).2+English
      horn.3(soprano clar in E flat)+
      bass clar.2+contrabsn. 4.3.3.0+db
      tuba. timp,3perc,harp,strings
    study sc BÄREN. BA 6757 f.s.
                           (T627)

  Symphony No. 3 [21']
    3.2.2.2. 4.3.3.0. timp,3perc,
      harp,cel,strings
    BÄREN. BA 7148 perf mat rent (T628)

  Transir: Epitaph Pour Rene Char [18']
    3(pic).3(English horn).2+bass
      clar.2+contrabsn. 4.4.3.1.
      timp,3perc,harp,strings
    BÄREN. BA 7311   (T629)

  Variations for Orchestra [22']
    3(pic,alto fl).2+English
      horn.2(clar in E flat)+bass
      clar.2+contrabsn. 4.4.3.1.
      timp,2-3perc,harp,cel,strings
    BÄREN. BA 7172   (T630)

  Viertes See-Bild "Das Schwarze
    Wasser", For Solo Voice And
    Orchestra [10']
    0+2pic.0+English horn.3+bass
      clar.0+contrabsn. 1.1.0.0.
      perc,harp,4vln,2vla,2vcl,db,Mez
      solo
    BÄREN. BA 7121 perf mat rent (T631)

TROJAN, VÁCLAV (1907-1983)
  Bayaya, For Solo Voice And Orchestra
    [22']
    3.3.3.3. 4.4.3.1. timp,perc,harp,
      pno,bagpipe,mand,strings,T solo
    SUPRAPHON   (T632)

  Titania In Love (from
    Midsummernight's Dream) [3']
    2.1.2.3.soprano sax. 4.2.3.1.
      timp,perc,harp,strings
    SUPRAPHON   (T633)

TROJAN WOMEN, THE: SUITE see Husa, Karel

TROJANS, THE: HAIL, ALL HAIL TO THE QUEEN see Berlioz, Hector (Louis)

TROLDMANDEN I BAKKEBY, FOR NARRATOR AND ORCHESTRA see Gislinge, Frederik

TROLLDANS: GRAUTMARSJ [ARR.] see Storbekken, Egil

TROMBA LONTANA see Adams, John

TROMBONE, FOR SOLO VOICE AND ORCHESTRA see Tveitt, Geirr, Basun, For Solo Voice And Orchestra

TROMBONIA, FOR TROMBONE AND STRING ORCHESTRA see Koch, Erland von

TROPES AND ECHOES, FOR CLARINET AND CHAMBER ORCHESTRA see Fennelly, Brian

TROPICAL DANCES, FOR 20 VIOLONCELLOS see Mannino, Franco

TROPICAL DANCES, FOR ORCHESTRA see Mannino, Franco

TROPICAL TREK OF TRISTAN TRIMBLE, THE see Schwartz, Francis

TROPISMES, FOR VIOLIN AND ORCHESTRA see Zbar, Michel

TROUBADOUR MUSIC, FOR 4 GUITARS AND ORCHESTRA see Gould, Morton

TROUT, THE, FOR SOLO VOICE AND ORCHESTRA [ARR.] see Schubert, Franz (Peter), Forelle, Die, For Solo Voice And Orchestra [arr.]

TROYENS, LES: CHASSE ET ORAGE see Berlioz, Hector (Louis)

TROZJUK, BOGDAN (1931-   )
  Jazz Sinfonie [21']
    2.1.1.1.5sax. 4.4.4.1. timp,perc,
      harp,pno,strings
    SIKORSKI perf mat rent   (T634)

TRUHLAR
  Concerto for Guitar and Orchestra
    1.1.2.1. 0.1.1.0. timp,strings,
      gtr solo
    BILLAUDOT perf mat rent   (T635)

TRUMPET AND THE DEVIL, THE: SUITE see Srebotnjak, Alojz F., Trobenta In Vrag: Suita

TRUMPET MAJOR, THE: FOUR SCENES see Hoddinott, Alun

TRUMPET TUNE AND AIR, FOR TRUMPET AND ORCHESTRA [ARR.] see Purcell, Henry

TRUMPET TUNE [ARR.] see Clarke, Jeremiah

TRYPTIQUE HELLENE, FOR OBOE AND ORCHESTRA see Foret, Felicien

TRYST see Macmillan, James

TRYTHALL, GILBERT (1930-   )
  Dionysia *Op.11
    2.2.2.2. 2.1.0.0. strings
    BOURNE perf mat rent   (T636)

TRZY BAJKI KASZUBSKIE see Pallasz, Edward

TRZY TANCE see Gorecki, Henryk Mikolaj

TSANKAWI see Ware, Peter

TSAR SALTAN: FLIGHT OF THE BUMBLEBEE, FOR DOUBLE BASS AND STRING ORCHESTRA [ARR.] see Rimsky-Korsakov, Nikolai

TSAR'S BRIDE, THE: ARIA OF MARTHA, FOR SOLO VOICE AND ORCHESTRA see Rimsky-Korsakov, Nikolai

TSCHAIKIN, NIKOLAJ see Chaikin, Nikolai

TSCHAIKOWSKY, PJOTR ILJITSCH see TCHAIKOVSKY, PIOTR ILYICH

TSCHALAJEW, SCHIRWANI see Chalaiev, Shirvani

TSCHERWINSKI, NIKOLAJ see Chervinsky, Nikolai

TSONTAKIS, GEORGE
  Fantasia Habanera [13']
    3.3.3.3. 4.2.3.0. timp,3perc,pno&
      cel,strings
    AM.COMP.AL. perf mat rent (T637)

TSUCHIDA, EISUKE (1963-   )
  Symphonic Ballad [18']
    3(pic).3(English horn).3(bass
      clar).3(contrabsn). 4.3.3.1.
      timp,perc,2harp,cel,pno,strings
    sc ZEN-ON 899458 f.s., perf mat
      rent   (T638)

TSUNAMIS see Furrer, Beat

TUBA MIRUM. MOZART PARAPHRASE, FOR TROMBONE AND ORCHESTRA see Etti, Karl

TUBIN, EDUARD (1905-1982)
  Ballade for Violin and Orchestra [7']
    2.2.2.2. 2.0.0.0. timp,perc,harp,
    strings,vln solo
    NORDISKA perf mat rent   (T639)

  Concerto for Violin and Orchestra,
    No. 1 [30']
    2.2.2.2. 4.3.3.1. timp,harp,
    strings,vln solo
    NORDISKA perf mat rent   (T640)

  Estonian Folk Dances [5']
    1.1.2.1. 2.2.1.0. timp,perc,harp,
    pno,strings
    NORDISKA perf mat rent   (T641)

  Music for Strings [15']
    string orch
    NORDISKA perf mat rent   (T642)

  Sinfonia Lirico No. 4 [35']
    3(pic).2(English horn).3(bass
    clar).2. 4.3.3.0. timp,harp,
    strings
    NORDISKA perf mat rent   (T643)

  Sinfonietta On Estonian Themes
    2.2.2.2. 2.2.1.0. timp,harp,
    strings
    NORDISKA perf mat rent   (T644)

  Suite On Estonian Dance Tunes, For
    Violin And Orchestra [17']
    3.3.3.2. 3.0.0.0. timp,2perc,
    harp,cel,strings,vln solo
    NORDISKA perf mat rent   (T645)

  Suite On Estonian Themes
    2.2.2.2. 4.2.3.1. timp,perc,harp,
    strings
    NORDISKA perf mat rent   (T646)

  Symphony No. 1 in C minor
    2.2.2.2. 4.2.3.1. timp,perc,harp,
    strings
    NORDISKA perf mat rent   (T647)

  Symphony No. 2 [35']
    3.3.2.2. 4.3.3.1. timp,perc,harp,
    pno,strings
    (The Legendary) NORDISKA perf mat
    rent   (T648)

  Symphony No. 3 in D minor [36']
    3.3.2.2. 4.3.3.1. timp,perc,harp,
    strings
    NORDISKA perf mat rent   (T649)

  Symphony No. 6 [33']
    3.3.3.3.tenor sax. 4.3.3.1. timp,
    4perc,pno,strings
    NORDISKA perf mat rent   (T650)

  Symphony No. 7 [24']
    2.2.2.2. 2.2.0.0. strings
    NORDISKA perf mat rent   (T651)

  Symphony No. 8 [26']
    3.3.3.3. 4.3.3.1. timp,perc,cel,
    strings
    NORDISKA perf mat rent   (T652)

  Symphony No. 9 [22']
    2.2.2.2. 4.2.3.0. timp,strings
    (Sinfonia Semplice) NORDISKA perf
    mat rent   (T653)

  Symphony No. 10 [27']
    3.3.2.2. 4.2.3.1. timp,strings
    NORDISKA perf mat rent   (T654)

  Symphony No. 11
    3.3.3.3. 4.3.3.1. timp,strings
    (The unfinished) NORDISKA perf mat
    rent   (T655)

  Valse Triste [4']
    1.1.2.1. 2.1.0.0. timp,harp,
    strings
    NORDISKA perf mat rent   (T656)

  Wooing Songs, The, For Solo Voice And
    Orchestra
    3.3.3.3. 4.3.3.1. timp,perc,
    strings,Bar solo
    NORDISKA perf mat rent   (T657)

  Ylermi, For Solo Voice And Orchestra
    3.3.3.3. 4.3.3.1. timp,strings,
    Bar solo
    NORDISKA perf mat rent   (T658)

TUE BENTSONS SONGS, FOR SOLO VOICE AND
  ORCHESTRA see Jordan, Sverre, Av
  "Tue Bentsons Viser", For Solo
  Voice And Orchestra

TUIKKIKAA, OI JOULUN TAHTOSET, FOR SOLO
  VOICE AND STRING ORCHESTRA [ARR.]
  see Hannikainen, P.J.

TULL, FISHER AUBREY (1934-   )
  Allen's Landing [25']
    2.1.2.1. 2.2.1.1. timp,perc,pno,
    strings
    BOOSEY perf mat rent   (T659)

  Fanfare For Orchestra And Antiphonal
    Brass
    SOUTHERN A-33 sc $7.50, set $37.50,
    pts $2.25, ea.   (T660)

  Overture To A Legacy [11']
    2(pic,alto fl).1.2+bass clar.1.
    2.1.0.0. 2perc,strings
    BOOSEY perf mat rent   (T661)

  Three Episodes [14']
    2+pic.2+English horn.2+bass
    clar.2+contrabsn. 4.3.3.1.
    timp,perc,harp,strings
    BOOSEY perf mat rent   (T662)

TULMINENSES see Gabrijelcic, Marijan

TUMA, FRANZ IGNAZ ANTON (1704-1774)
  Symphony No. 6 [10']
    org,strings
    SUPRAPHON   (T663)

  Symphony No. 7 [10']
    hpsd,strings
    SUPRAPHON   (T664)

  Symphony No. 8 [9']
    hpsd,strings
    SUPRAPHON   (T665)

TUMBLER'S PRAYER, THE see Orrego-Salas,
  Juan A.

TUMULTER, FOR PERCUSSION AND ORCHESTRA
  see Rypdal, Terje

TUNDER, FRANZ (1614-1667)
  Ach Herr, Lass Deine Lieben Engelein,
    For Solo Voice And String
    Orchestra
    BREITKOPF-L perf mat rent   (T666)

TUNDRA see Ruders, Poul

TUNE, THE, FOR SOLO VOICE AND ORCHESTRA
  see Tveitt, Geirr, Tonen, For Solo
  Voice And Orchestra

TUNING see McCabe, John

TURANDOT: OVERTURE AND MARCH see Weber,
  Carl Maria von

TURANDOT: SUITE see Busoni, Ferruccio
  Benvenuto

TURANDOT: VERZWEIFLUNG UND ERGEBUNG see
  Busoni, Ferruccio Benvenuto

TURBULENCE, STILLNESS AND SALUTATION
  see Wallach, Joelle

TURCHI, GUIDO (1916-   )
  Adagio for Orchestra [12'35"]
    2.3.3.2. 4.2.3.1. timp,harp,
    strings
    sc RICORDI-IT 133898 f.s., perf mat
    rent   (T667)

  Dedalo II [14']
    3.3.3.3. 4.3.3.1. timp,perc,pno,
    harp,strings
    sc RICORDI-IT 131975 f.s., perf mat
    rent   (T668)

TURCO IN ITALIA, IL: OVERTURE see
  Rossini, Gioacchino

TURFAN FRAGMENTS, THE see Feldman,
  Morton

TURINA, JOAQUIN (1882-1949)
  Procesion Del Rocio, La [8']
    2+pic.2+English horn.2+bass
    clar.2+contrabsn. 4.3.3.1.
    timp,perc,harp,strings
    KALMUS A6751 sc $15.00, set $28.00,
    pts $1.00, ea., perf mat rent   (T669)

TURINA DE SANTOS, JOSE LUIS (1952-   )
  Crucifixus [13']
    pno,8vln,6vla,4vcl,2db
    sc ALPUERTO f.s.   (T670)

TURK IN ITALY, THE: OVERTURE see
  Rossini, Gioacchino, Turco In
  Italia, Il: Overture

TURKEY IN THE STRAW see Guion, David
  Wendall Fentress

TURKISH MARCH see Ippolitov-Ivanov,
  Mikhail Mikhailovich

TURKISH MARCH [ARR.] see Beethoven,
  Ludwig van

TURKMENIEN see Schechter, Boris

TURM-MUSIK, FOR FLUTE AND ORCHESTRA see
  Holliger, Heinz

TURNAGE, MARK-ANTHONY (1960-   )
  Ekaya [7']
    3(pic).3.3.3.soprano sax.
    0.0.0.0. 2perc,pno,harp,strings
    SCHOTT perf mat rent   (T671)

  Kind Of Blue [10']
    2.3.2.2. 2.2.0.0. 12vln,4vla,
    4vcl,2db
    study sc SCHOTT MIS 34 f.s., perf
    mat rent   (T672)

  Let Us Sleep Now [11']
    1(alto fl).0.1(bass clar).0.
    1.1.0.0. perc,cel,harp,8vln,
    2vla
    SCHOTT perf mat rent   (T673)

  Night Dances [14']
    2(pic).0.2.1. 2.1.0.0. 2perc,
    strings,cel solo,ob solo,trp
    solo,harp solo, off-stage
    quintet: 2vln, vla, 2vcl
    study sc SCHOTT ED 12309 $75.00,
    perf mat rent   (T674)

  On All Fours [12']
    1(bass fl).1(English horn).1(bass
    clar).1.alto sax(soprano sax).
    0.1.1.0. perc,pno,strings
    study sc SCHOTT ED 12280 $35.00,
    perf mat rent   (T675)

TURNER, ROBERT [COMRIE] (1920-   )
  Concerto for Viola and Orchestra
    [30']
    2(pic).2(English horn).2(bass
    clar).2. 2.2.2.0. timp,perc,
    harp,cel,strings,vla solo
    CAN.MUS.CENT. MI 1312 T951CO (T676)

  Encounters I-IX [6']
    fl,harp,strings
    CAN.MUS.CENT. MI 1400 T951E (T677)

  Pemberton Valley, The [20']
    1.1.2(bass clar).1. 2.2.1.0.
    timp,perc,strings
    CAN.MUS.CENT. MI 1100 T951PE (T678)

  Playhouse Music [9']
    2.2.2.2. 2.2.1.0. timp,3perc,pno&
    cel,harp,strings
    CAN.MUS.CENT. MI 1100 T951PL (T679)

  Shades Of Autumn [14']
    3.3.3(clar in E flat).3. 4.3.3.1.
    timp,3perc,harp,pno&cel,strings
    CAN.MUS.CENT. MI 1100 T951SH (T680)

TURNERING see Norgaard, Per

TURNING see Phillips, Mark

TUROK, PAUL HARRIS (1929-   )
  Antoniana *Op.47
    1.1.1.1. 2.1.1.0. timp,pno,
    strings
    [20'] SCHIRM.G perf mat rent (T681)

  Canzona Concertante No. 1, Op. 57,
    For English Horn And Orchestra
    [13']
    2+pic.2.2+bass clar.2+contrabsn.
    4.3.3.1. timp,perc,harp/cel,
    strings,English horn solo
    SCHIRM.G perf mat rent   (T682)

  Canzona Concertante No. 2, Op. 63,
    For Trombone And Orchestra [12']
    2.2.2.2. 4.2.2.1. timp,2perc,
    strings,trom solo
    SCHIRM.G perf mat rent   (T683)

  Canzona Concertante No. 3, Op. 64
    [13']
    fl,ob,trp,strings
    SCHIRM.G perf mat rent   (T684)

  Concerto for Violin and Orchestra
    3.3.3.2. 4.2.3.1. timp,2perc,
    harp,strings,vln solo
    sc SEESAW $82.00, perf mat rent
                                        (T685)

  Danza Viva [4']
    2+pic.2+English horn.2+bass
    clar.2+contrabsn. 4.3.3.1.
    timp,3perc,harp,pno,strings
    SCHIRM.G perf mat rent   (T686)

  Ragtime Caprice, For Piano And
    Orchestra [10']
    2(pic).2.2+bass clar.2. 2.2.2.1.
    timp,perc,harp,strings,pno solo
    SCHIRM.G perf mat rent   (T687)

  Threnody [10']
    string orch
    SCHIRM.G perf mat rent   (T688)

TUROK, PAUL HARRIS (cont'd.)

Ultima Thule *Op.60 [13']
    3(pic).2+English horn.2+bass
    clar.2+contrabsn. 4.3.3.1.
    timp,perc,harp,strings
    SCHIRM.G perf mat rent   (T689)

TURTLE, THE, FOR SOLO VOICE AND
ORCHESTRA see Tveitt, Geirr

TURUNEN, MARTTI (JOHANNES) (1902-1979)
Me Kaymme Joulun Viettohon, For Solo
    Voice And Orchestra [arr.]
    (Kuusisto, I.) harp,strings,solo
    voice [3'] FAZER perf mat rent
                                  (T690)

Sunnuntai, For Solo Voice And
    Orchestra [arr.]
    (Godzinsky, G.) 2.0.2.1. 2.0.0.0.
    harp,strings,solo voice [2']
    FAZER perf mat rent   (T691)

TUSMORKETS VISER, FOR SOLO VOICE,
BASSOON AND ORCHESTRA see Holten,
Bo

TUTUGURI I see Rihm, Wolfgang

TUTUGURI II see Rihm, Wolfgang

TUTUGURI III see Rihm, Wolfgang

TUTUGURI IV see Rihm, Wolfgang

TVA FOLKMELODIER see Alfvén, Hugo

TVEIT, SIGVALD (1945-   )
Halling In Boogaloo
    3.1.2.0. 2.4.4.0. perc,harp,2gtr,
    2vln,vla,vcl,elec bass, willow
    flute
    NORGE   (T692)

TVEITT, GEIRR (1908-1981)
Astrup Suite
    1.1.2.1. 2.2.1.0. timp,perc,pno,
    strings
    NORGE   (T693)

Basun, For Solo Voice And Orchestra
    [11']
    3.3.3.3. 4.3.3.1. timp,perc,pno,
    strings,solo voice
    "Trombone, For Solo Voice And
    Orchestra" NORGE   (T694)

Birgingu [18']
    3.3.3.3. 4.3.3.1. timp,perc,harp,
    strings
    NORGE   (T695)

Buttercup, For Solo Voice And
    Orchestra
    see Smorblomster, For Solo Voice
    And Orchestra

Christmas Journey, The
    see Julereisa

Concerto for Harp and Orchestra, No.
    2, Op. 170 [21']
    3.2.3.2. 4.3.3.1. timp,perc,cel,
    strings,harp solo
    NORGE   (T696)

Concerto for Piano and Orchestra, No.
    1, Op. 1 [25']
    1.1.2.1. 2.1.1.0. timp,strings,
    pno solo
    NORGE   (T697)

Concerto for Piano and Orchestra, No.
    5, Op. 156 [28']
    2.2.2.2. 4.3.3.1. timp,perc,harp,
    strings,pno solo
    NORGE   (T698)

Des Iles, For Solo Voice And
    Orchestra [6']
    1.1.1.1. 1.0.1.0. harp,strings,T
    solo
    NORGE   (T699)

Fortrolla Skog
    see Songs To Poems By Olav H.
    Hauge, For Solo Voice And
    Orchestra

Four Letters From Grieg To Frants
    Beyer, For Solo Voice And
    Orchestra
    3(pic).3(English horn).3(bass
    clar).3(contrabsn). 4.3.3.1.
    timp,perc,harp,strings,T solo
    [Norw] [22'] NORGE   (T700)

Havamal, For Solo Voice And Orchestra
    [20']
    ob,horn,gtr,strings,solo voice
    NORGE   (T701)

Hundred Folk Tunes From Hardanger, A,
    Nos. 16-30
    2(pic).2(English
    horn).2(contrabsn). 4.3.3.1.

TVEITT, GEIRR (cont'd.)

    timp,3perc,cel,harp,strings
    HANSEN-DEN perf mat rent   (T702)

Hundred Folk Tunes From Hardanger, A,
    Nos. 46-60
    3(pic).2+English horn.2+bass
    clar.2+contrabsn. 4.3.3.1.
    timp,perc,pno&cel,harp,strings
    HANSEN-DEN perf mat rent   (T703)

Hundred Folk Tunes From Hardanger, A,
    Nos. 61-75
    3(pic).2+English horn.2+bass
    clar+clar in E flat.2+
    contrabsn. 4.3.3.1. timp,3perc,
    cel&pno,harp,strings
    HANSEN-DEN perf mat rent   (T704)

Hymn To The Ocean, For Solo Voice And
    Orchestra
    see Hymne Til Havet, For Solo Voice
    And Orchestra

Hymne Til Havet, For Solo Voice And
    Orchestra
    2.2.2.2. 3.0.3.0. timp,perc,
    strings,solo voice
    "Hymn To The Ocean, For Solo Voice
    And Orchestra" NORGE   (T705)

Island In The Skerries, For Solo
    Voice And Orchestra
    see Skjaergaardso, For Solo Voice
    And Orchestra

Jolesveinane
    see Two Christmas Tunes From
    Hardanger

Jonsokbalet [4']
    2.1.2.1. 2.2.0.0. perc,cel,
    strings
    "Midsummer Fire, The" NORGE (T706)

Jonsokkvelden
    ob,horn,strings
    "Midsummer Evening, The" NORGE
                                  (T707)

Jonsoknatt, For Solo Voices And
    Orchestra [45']
    fl,clar,pno,strings,STBar&
    narrator
    "Midsummer Night, For Solo Voices
    And Orchestra" NORGE   (T708)

Julereisa [3']
    2.2.2.2. 3.3.3.0. timp,strings
    "Christmas Journey, The" NORGE
                                  (T709)

Langeleiken
    see Songs To Poems By Olav H.
    Hauge, For Solo Voice And
    Orchestra

Lavransdatters Vise [3']
    1.0.1.0. 2.0.0.0. vibra,strings
    "Song Of Kristin Lavransdatter"
    NORGE   (T710)

Lullaby, For Solo Voice And Orchestra
    see Voggesong, For Solo Voice And
    Orchestra

Midsummer Evening, The
    see Jonsokkvelden

Midsummer Fire, The
    see Jonsokbalet

Midsummer Night, For Solo Voices And
    Orchestra
    see Jonsoknatt, For Solo Voices And
    Orchestra

Nixie, The
    see Nykken

Norwegian Suite No. 1
    string orch
    sc,pts NORSK f.s.   (T711)

Norwegian Suite No. 2
    string orch
    sc,pts NORSK f.s.   (T712)

Nykken [14']
    3.2.2.2. 4.3.3.1. timp,perc,harp,
    pno/cel,strings
    "Nixie, The" NORGE   (T713)

Olav Kyrre, For Solo Voice And
    Orchestra *Op.166,No.1
    2.0.2.1. 3.1.1.0. pno,strings,S
    solo
    NORGE   (T714)

Paa Hvalvet, For Solo Voice And
    Orchestra [4']
    3.3.3.3. 4.3.3.1. timp,strings,
    solo voice
    NORGE   (T715)

TVEITT, GEIRR (cont'd.)

Pictures From A Journey
    see Reisebilleder

Reisebilleder [24']
    2.1.2.1. 2.2.2.0. timp,perc,
    strings
    "Pictures From A Journey" NORGE
                                  (T716)

Rimed Wood, For Solo Voice And
    Orchestra
    see Rimet Skog, For Solo Voice And
    Orchestra

Rimet Skog, For Solo Voice And
    Orchestra [7']
    2.2.2.2. 4.2.3.1. timp,strings,
    solo voice
    "Rimed Wood, For Solo Voice And
    Orchestra" NORGE   (T717)

Skjaergaardso, For Solo Voice And
    Orchestra [5']
    3.3.3.3. 4.0.3.1. timp,perc,
    strings,B solo
    "Island In The Skerries, For Solo
    Voice And Orchestra" NORGE (T718)

Slattestev Til Jol
    see Two Christmas Tunes From
    Hardanger

Smorblomster, For Solo Voice And
    Orchestra
    2.0.2.0. 4.0.0.0. harp,strings,S/
    T solo
    "Buttercup, For Solo Voice And
    Orchestra" (alternate scoring:
    .2121 2120., str, sop-ten solo)
    NORGE   (T719)

Snostorm, For Solo Voice And
    Orchestra
    2.1.2.1. 2.2.2.0. timp,pno,
    strings,Bar solo
    "Snowstorm, For Solo Voice And
    Orchestra" NORGE   (T720)

Snowstorm, For Solo Voice And
    Orchestra
    see Snostorm, For Solo Voice And
    Orchestra

Song Of Kristin Lavransdatter
    see Lavransdatters Vise

Songs To Poems By Arnulf Overland,
    For Solo Voice And Orchestra
    *CC10L
    2.1.2.1. 2.2.2.0. timp,perc,pno,
    strings,T solo NORGE   (T721)

Songs To Poems By Aslaug Vaa, For
    Solo Voice And Orchestra *CC11L
    1.1.1.1. 1.0.0.0. vibra,strings
    NORGE   (T722)

Songs To Poems By Knut Horvei, For
    Solo Voice And Orchestra
    *Op.249, CC8L
    2.1.2.1. 2.2.2.0. timp,perc,pno,
    strings,Bar solo NORGE   (T723)

Songs To Poems By Olav H. Hauge, For
    Solo Voice And Orchestra *Op.243
    2.1.1.2. 4.0.3.1. timp,perc,pno,
    hpsd,cel,strings,solo voice NORGE
    f.s.
    contains: Fortrolla Skog;
    Langeleiken; Svarte Krossar
                                  (T724)

Svarte Krossar
    see Songs To Poems By Olav H.
    Hauge, For Solo Voice And
    Orchestra

Tonen, For Solo Voice And Orchestra
    [3']
    1.1.2.3. 4.1.1.0. perc,strings,
    solo voice
    "Tune, The, For Solo Voice And
    Orchestra" NORGE   (T725)

Tord Foleson, For Solo Voice And
    Orchestra *Op.166,No.2
    2.0.2.1. 3.1.1.0. pno,strings,Bar
    solo
    NORGE   (T726)

Trombone, For Solo Voice And
    Orchestra
    see Basun, For Solo Voice And
    Orchestra

Tune, The, For Solo Voice And
    Orchestra
    see Tonen, For Solo Voice And
    Orchestra

Turtle, The, For Solo Voice And
    Orchestra
    3.2.2.2. 4.3.3.1. timp,perc,harp,
    pno,cel,strings,S/T solo
    NORGE   (T727)

TVEITT, GEIRR (cont'd.)

Two Christmas Tunes From Hardanger
1.1.2.1. 2.2.2.0. perc,strings
NORGE f.s.
contains: Jolesveinane;
Slattestev Til Jol   (T728)

Utsyn [4']
1.1.2.1. 1.1.1.0. pno,strings
"View" NORGE   (T729)

Variationer Over En Folkevise Fra
Hardanger, For 2 Pianos And
Orchestra [25']
2.2.2.2. 4.2.2.0. timp,perc,
strings,2pno soli
"Variations On A Folk Tune From
Hardanger, For 2 Pianos And
Orchestra" NORGE   (T730)

Variations On A Folk Tune From
Hardanger, For 2 Pianos And
Orchestra
see Variationer Over En Folkevise
Fra Hardanger, For 2 Pianos And
Orchestra

View
see Utsyn

Voggesong, For Solo Voice And
Orchestra [5']
2.2.2.2. 3.3.3.0. timp,perc,pno,
strings,B solo
"Lullaby, For Solo Voice And
Orchestra" NORGE   (T731)

TVERS GJENNOM ALT DETTE see Åm, Magnar

TWEE SCENES: MONOLOOG- PAS DE QUATRE
see Klerkx, Wim

TWELVE MARCHES see Goossens, [Sir]
Eugene, Zwölf Marsche

TWELVE MASKS, THE see Emborg, Jens
Laurson, Tolv Masker, De

TWELVE MINUETS see Eybler, Joseph,
Zwölf Menuette

TWELVE MINUETS see Beethoven, Ludwig
van, Menuette, Zwolf, WoO. 12

TWELVE MOBILES FOR CHAMBER ENSEMBLE see
Nova, Jacqueline, Doce Moviles Para
Conjunto De Camera

TWELVE ON DEATH AND NO, FOR SOLO VOICE
AND ORCHESTRA see Samuel, Gerhard

TWELVE POINTS OF THE MODIFIED MERCALLI
SCALE, THE, FOR SOLO VOICE AND
ORCHESTRA see Thomas, Andrew

TWELVE POP HITS FROM THE CLASSICS, VOL.
1
(Zinn, William) string orch set
EXCELSIOR 494-00534 $18.00
contains: Borodin, Alexander
Porfirievich, Quartet No. 2,
[arr.]; Brahms, Johannes,
Symphony No. 3, [arr.]; Chopin,
Frédéric, Polonaise In A Flat,
[arr.]; Offenbach, Jacques,
Barcarolle From Tales Of Hoffman,
[arr.]; Tchaikovsky, Piotr
Ilyich, Romeo And Juliet, [arr.];
Tchaikovsky, Piotr Ilyich,
Symphony No. 5, [arr.]   (T732)

TWELVE POP HITS FROM THE CLASSICS, VOL.
2
(Zinn, William) string orch set
EXCELSIOR 494-00535 $18.00
contains: Borodin, Alexander
Porfirievich, Polovetzian Dances,
[arr.]; Chopin, Frédéric,
Fantasie Impromptu, [arr.];
Debussy, Claude, Clair De Lune,
[arr.]; Debussy, Claude, Reverie,
[arr.]; Tchaikovsky, Piotr
Ilyich, Pathetique Symphony,
[arr.]; Tchaikovsky, Piotr
Ilyich, Piano Concerto No. 1,
[arr.]   (T733)

TWELVE SINFONIAS see Handel, George
Frideric, Zwolf Sinfonien

TWELVE SONGS FOR SOLO HELEN, FOR VOICE
AND ORCHESTRA see Porter, Quincy

TWILL BY TWILIGHT see Takemitsu, Toru

TWIN SONG, FOR VIOLIN, VIOLA AND
ORCHESTRA see Nordal, Jon

TWINE see Gefors, Hans

TWINKLETOES BALLET see Gillis, Don E.

TWO ARIAS, FOR SOLO VOICE AND ORCHESTRA
see Beethoven, Ludwig van, Zwei
Arien, For Solo Voice And Orchestra

TWO BIBLICAL SONGS, FOR SOLO VOICE AND
ORCHESTRA see Koppel, Herman David,
To Bibelske Sange, For Solo Voice
And Orchestra

TWO CHARACTER PIECES see Sinigaglia,
Leone, Zwei Charakterstucke

TWO CHARACTERISTIC PIECES see Larchet,
John F.

TWO CHILDREN'S SONGS, FOR SOLO VOICE
AND STRING ORCHESTRA see
Lutoslawski, Witold

TWO CHRISTMAS CAROLS see Lankester,
Michael

TWO CHRISTMAS TUNES FROM HARDANGER see
Tveitt, Geirr

TWO CONCERT ARIAS see Haydn, [Franz]
Joseph, Zwei Konzertarien

TWO DANCES see Zielinska, Lidia

TWO DIRGES, FOR SOLO VOICE AND CHAMBER
ORCHESTRA see Maros, Rudolf

TWO EDDA KVAD, FOR SOLO VOICE AND
ORCHESTRA see Olsen, Sparre

TWO ENTR'ACTES: ROSEMARY; CANZONETTA
see Bridge, Frank

TWO EPISODES FROM LENAU'S FAUST: DER
NACHTLICHE ZUG; DER TANZ IN DER
DORFSCHENKE see Liszt, Franz

TWO EPISODES FROM LENAU'S FAUST:
NIGHTLY MARCH; DANCE IN THE VILLAGE
INN see Liszt, Franz, Two Episodes
From Lenau's Faust: Der Nachtliche
Zug; Der Tanz In Der Dorfschenke

TWO FABLES OF KRYLOV, FOR SOLO VOICE
AND ORCHESTRA see Shostakovich,
Dmitri

TWO FANFARES see Novák, Milan, Dve
Fanfary

TWO FINNISH SONGS, FOR SOLO VOICE AND
ORCHESTRA see Stout, Alan

TWO FOLK SONGS [ARR.]
(Wells, Dorothy) string orch,opt pno
(gr. I) SOUTHERN SO-45 sc $3.00,
set $16.00, pts $1.25, ea.   (T734)

TWO HYMNS, FOR SOLO VOICE AND ORCHESTRA
see Stout, Alan

TWO IMAGES see Ágústsson, Herbert
Hriberschek

TWO INTERMEZZI see Bridge, Frank

TWO JAMAICAN PIECES see Benjamin,
Arthur

TWO MILTON SONNETS, FOR SOLO VOICE AND
ORCHESTRA see Finzi, Gerald

TWO MINIATURES see Steptoe, Roger

TWO MRS. CARROLLS, THE see Waxman,
Franz

TWO MOVEMENTS see Anderson, Ruth

TWO MOVEMENTS FOR STRING ORCHESTRA see
Moylan, William

TWO MOVEMENTS FOR STRINGS see Liszt,
Franz, Zwei Satze Für Streicher

TWO NORWEGIAN DANCES see Andersen, Karl
August, To Norske Danser

TWO OLD SWEDISH FOLK SONGS see
Svendsen, Johan (Severin)

TWO ORCHESTRA PIECES see Loos, Armin

TWO ORCHESTRAL PIECES see Albertsen,
Per Hjort

TWO PASTORALES, FOR SOLO VOICE AND
ORCHESTRA see Haydn, [Franz] Joseph

TWO PATRIOTIC MELODIES: SONG AND HYMN
[ARR.]
(Liszt, Franz) 2.2.2.2. 4.2.2.1.
timp,harp,strings KALMUS A6138 sc
$15.00, set $20.00, perf mat rent
contains: Egressy, B., Szozat
[arr.]; Erkel, Franz (Ferenc),
Hymnus [arr.]   (T735)

TWO PIECES see Anderson, Ruth

TWO PIECES FOR CELLO AND ORCHESTRAL see
Cui, César Antonovich, Deux
Morceaux, For Cello And Orchestra

TWO PIECES FOR ORCHESTRA see Hawkins,
John

TWO PIECES FOR SMALL ORCHESTRA see
Delius, Frederick

TWO PIECES FOR STRING ORCHESTRA see
Shostakovich, Dmitri

TWO PIECES FROM THE DESERT, FOR OBOE
AND ORCHESTRA see Søderlind, Ragnar

TWO ROMANCES FOR VIOLIN AND ORCHESTRA
[ARR.] see Björnsson, Arni

TWO SACRED SONGS, FOR SOLO VOICE AND
ORCHESTRA see Lindberg, Oskar
[Fredrik]

TWO SONGS, FOR SOLO VOICE AND ORCHESTRA
see Bridge, Frank see Lindberg,
Oskar [Fredrik]

TWO SONGS [ARR.] see Lie, Sigurd

TWO SONGS FOR AN UNCERTAIN AGE, FOR
SOLO VOICE AND ORCHESTRA see
Hartke, Stephen Paul

TWO SONGS TO POEMS BY ASE MARIE NESSE,
FOR SOLO VOICE AND ORCHESTRA see
Søderlind, Ragnar

TWO SONGS WITHOUT WORDS [ARR.]
(Cruft, Adrian) 2.2.2.2. 2.2.2.0.
timp,perc,strings [6'] (contains:
Barbara Allen; Sir Eglamore) sc
JOAD f.s., perf mat rent   (T736)

TWO SPINNING SONGS, FOR SOLO VOICE AND
CHAMBER ORCHESTRA see Vass, Lajos

TWO STUDIES see Bliss, [Sir] Arthur
(Drummond)

TWO WALTZES, OP. 54 see Dvořák, Antonín

TWO WIDOWS, THE: BALLET MUSIC see
Smetana, Bedrich

TWO WONDER OXEN see Ranki, György

TWOFOLD see Rosing-Schow, Niels

TWOREK, WANDY
Jaegermarch [4']
1.0.1.0. 0.2.1.0. perc,strings
without vla
HANSEN-DEN perf mat rent   (T737)

TY, L. NGUYEN VAN
see NGUYEN VAN TY, L.

TYKESSON, NILS (1957-   )
Anacrusi [13']
3.3.3.3. 4.3.3.1. timp,4perc,
harp,cel,strings
STIM   (T738)

Fugace
string orch
STIM   (T739)

TYL see Gayfer, James McDonald

U

U(H)R-TONE see Brandmüller, Theo

UBER ERICH M.: TABLEAUX VIVANTS see Straesser, Joep

UBER GRAS, STEINE, WASSER see Korolyov, Anatoli

UBER NACHT, FOR SOLO VOICE AND ORCHESTRA [ARR.] see Wolf, Hugo

UBERSCHREITEN see Dillon, James

UBERSTEHEN UND HOFFEN see Killmayer, Wilhelm

UBUNG, FOR 2 PIANOS AND ORCHESTRA see Hegdal, Magne

UDOW, MICHAEL WILLIAM (1949-   )
  Seven Textural Settings Of Japanese
    Poetry, For Solo Voice And
    Chamber Orchestra [10']
    2fl,bass clar,2trp,2perc,6vln,
    4vcl,female solo
    AM.COMP.AL. sc $10.70, pts $24.45
                                      (U1)

UHL, ALFRED (1909-   )
  Wer Einsam Ist, Der Hat Es Gut:
    Ouverture A [5']
    2(pic).2.2+bass clar.2. 4.3.3.1.
    timp,perc,strings
    DOBLINGER perf mat rent   (U2)

UKMAR, VILKO (1905-   )
  Concertino for Violin and Orchestra
    [16']
    1.1.1(bass clar).1. 0.0.0.0.
    strings,vln solo
    DRUSTVO DSS 941 perf mat rent   (U3)

  Lepa Vida: Suite [30']
    2(pic).2.2(bass clar).2. 4.3.3.1.
    timp,perc,harp,strings
    DRUSTVO DSS 934 perf mat rent   (U4)

UKUZALWA see Forsyth, Malcolm

ULFRSTAD, MARIUS MOARITZ (1890-1968)
  Concerto for Piano and Orchestra
    2.2.2.2. 4.3.3.1. timp,perc,
    strings,pno solo
    NORGE   (U5)

ULISSE RITORNA, FOR VIOLONCELLO AND
  ORCHESTRA see Sigurbjörnsson,
  Thorkell

ULLMAN, BO (1929-   )
  Addio, L' [10']
    2.2.3.2. 2.2.2.0. 2perc,harp,cel,
    strings
    STIM   (U6)

  Canti Commentati [12'30"]
    string orch
    STIM   (U7)

  Capricci Del Dolore, I [15']
    2.2.3.2. 2.2.2.1. perc,strings
    STIM perf mat rent   (U8)

  Epitaffio Agitato
    STIM   (U9)

ULRICH, JÜRGEN (1939-   )
  Wundersame Reise, For Two Horns And
    String Orchestra [18']
    string orch,2horn soli
    HANSEN-GER perf mat rent   (U10)

ULTAN, LLOYD (1929-   )
  Concerto for Organ and Chamber
    Orchestra [27']
    1.2.2.0. 0.0.0.0. timp,strings,
    org solo
    AM.COMP.AL. sc $36.55, pts $7.70,
    perf mat rent   (U11)

  Concerto for Violin and Orchestra
    [38']
    3.3.3.3. 4.3.3.1. timp,perc,cel,
    harp,pno,strings,vln solo
    AM.COMP.AL. sc $56.40, pts $4.10,
    perf mat rent   (U12)

  Man With A Hoe, The: Sinfonia [6']
    4.3.3.2. 4.3.3.1. timp,perc,harp,
    strings
    AM.COMP.AL. perf mat rent   (U13)

  Pitchipoi, For Solo Voices And
    Orchestra [35']
    2.2.2.2. 2.2.0.0. timp,perc,pno,
    strings,vla solo,MezBar soli
    sc AM.COMP.AL. $39.55   (U14)

ULTAN, LLOYD (cont'd.)

  Reflections On A Tradition [11']
    1.2.1.1. 2.0.0.0. strings
    sc AM.COMP.AL. $50.35   (U15)

  Wanaki Win [11']
    3.2.3.2. 4.3.3.1. timp,perc,pno,
    strings
    sc AM.COMP.AL. $16.75, perf mat
    rent   (U16)

ULTIMA THULE see Flem, Kjell see Turok,
  Paul Harris

ULTRAMARINE NOCTURNE see Lemeland,
  Aubert

ULYSSES' BOW see Harbison, John

ULYSSES' RAFT see Harbison, John

UM SCHLIMME KINDER ARTIG ZU MACHEN see
  Mahler, Gustav

UMBRAL DEL SUENO see Orrego-Salas, Juan
  A.

UMBRIAN SCENE see Kay, Ulysses Simpson

UMRISS see Rihm, Wolfgang

UN POCO GIOCOSO, FOR TUBA AND CHAMBER
  ORCHESTRA see Becker, Günther

UNA VIDA see Adomian, Lan

UNANSWERED QUESTION, THE see Ives,
  Charles

UNBEFANGENHEIT, FOR SOLO VOICE AND
  ORCHESTRA, [ARR.] see Weber, Carl
  Maria von

UNBENANNT I see Rihm, Wolfgang

UNBENANNT II see Rihm, Wolfgang

UND DIE WELT WAR DAZWISCHEN..., FOR
  SOLO VOICE AND ORCHESTRA see
  Chalaiev, Shirvani

UND ES BLEIBT UNS UNSER ZWEIFEL see
  Evensen, Bernt Kasberg

UND JETZT ERKLINGT FRANZ GROTHE [ARR.]
  see Grothe, Franz

UND SO WIRD KOMMEN EIN SOMMERTAG, FOR
  SOLO VOICE AND ORCHESTRA see
  Trexler, Georg

UNDER HAGGARNA, FOR SOLO VOICE AND
  ORCHESTRA see Jonsson, Josef
  [Petrus]

UNDER KORS OG KRONE: AMARXIA see
  Persen, John

UNDER MOONLIGHT I see Müller-Siemens,
  Detlev

UNDER THE DOUBLE EAGLE MARCH see
  Wagner, Josef

UNDER THE GREENWOOD TREE see Gurney,
  Ivor

UNDER THE STARS, FOR VIOLIN AND STRING
  ORCHESTRA see Wieslander, Ingvar,
  Unter Den Sternen, For Violin And
  String Orchestra

UNDERSTROMMER, FOR BASSOON AND STRING
  ORCHESTRA see Kleiberg, Ståle

UNDICI TRACCE see Bonifacio, Mauro

UNDINE: ICH WAR IN MEINEN JUNGEN
  JAHREN, FOR SOLO VOICE AND
  ORCHESTRA see Lortzing, (Gustav)
  Albert

UNDINE: OVERTURE see Hoffmann, Ernst
  Theodor Amadeus see Lortzing,
  (Gustav) Albert

UNDINE: SO WISSE, DASS IN ALLEN
  ELEMENTEN, FOR SOLO VOICE AND
  ORCHESTRA see Lortzing, (Gustav)
  Albert

UNDINE: VATER, MUTTER, SCHWESTERN,
  BRÜDER, FOR SOLO VOICE AND
  ORCHESTRA see Lortzing, (Gustav)
  Albert

UNDINE: WAS SEH ICH?, FOR SOLO VOICES
  AND ORCHESTRA see Lortzing,
  (Gustav) Albert

UNDISONUS, FOR VIOLIN AND ORCHESTRA see
  Rypdal, Terje

UNDULATING MICHIGAMME, FOR SOLO VOICE
  AND ORCHESTRA see Tipei, Sever

UNENDLICHE, DAS, FOR SOLO VOICES AND
  ORCHESTRA see Febel, Reinhard

UNG, CHINARY (1942-   )
  Inner Voices
    4(pic,alto fl).3.4(clar in E
    flat,bass clar).3. 4.2.3.1.
    timp,3perc,2harp,pno,cel,
    strings
    PETERS P67146 perf mat rent   (U17)

UNGARISCHE TANZE NOS. 1 AND 3 [ARR.]
  see Brahms, Johannes

UNGARISCHE TANZE NOS.8 AND 9 [ARR.] see
  Brahms, Johannes

UNGARISCHER STURMMARSCH see Liszt,
  Franz

UNGARISCHER TANZ NO. 4 [ARR.] see
  Brahms, Johannes

UNGARISCHER TANZ NO. 8 [ARR.] see
  Brahms, Johannes

UNGARISCHER TANZ NO. 9 [ARR.] see
  Brahms, Johannes

UNGARLAND see Schönherr, Max

UNGDOM see Danielsson, Harry

UNGDOM OG GALSKAB see Dupuy, Edouard

UNGLÜCKSEL'GE! ER IST AUF IMMER MIR
  ENTFLOH'N, FOR SOLO VOICE AND
  ORCHESTRA see Mendelssohn-
  Bartholdy, Felix, Infelice!, For
  Solo Voice And Orchestra

UNGRISCHER, FOR VIOLIN AND ORCHESTRA,
  OP. 203 see Raff, Joseph Joachim

UNIVERSE SYMPHONY see Gellman, Steven

UNIVERSUM see Fongaard, Bjørn

UNQUIET HEART, THE, FOR VIOLIN AND
  ORCHESTRA see Parris, Robert

UNTER DEN STERNEN, FOR VIOLIN AND
  STRING ORCHESTRA see Wieslander,
  Ingvar

UNTER DER ENNS POLKA see Strauss,
  Eduard

UNTER DONNER UND BLITZ see Strauss,
  Johann, [Jr.]

UNTITLED COMPOSITION NO.2 see Schafer,
  R. Murray

UP AND DOWN MAN, THE see Blake, Howard

UPPSTRÖM, TORE (1937-   )
  Nostos
    3.2.3.3. 4.3.3.1. timp,perc,pno,
    strings
    STIM   (U18)

UPSIDE-DOWN-UNDER VARIATIONS see
  Patterson, Paul

UPWARD STREAM, THE, FOR SAXOPHONE AND
  ORCHESTRA see Peck, Russell James

URAN 235 see Fongaard, Bjørn

URATA, KENJIRO (1941-   )
  Symphony [40']
    3(pic,alto fl).3(English
    horn).3(clar in E flat,bass
    clar).4(contrabsn). 6.4.4.1.
    timp,perc,harp,pno&cel,strings
    sc ZEN-ON 899240 f.s., perf mat
    rent   (U19)

URAY, ERNST LUDWIG (1906-   )
  Concerto for Trumpet and Orchestra
    [11']
    2(pic).2.2.2. 3.2.2.1. timp,perc,
    pno,strings,trp solo
    DOBLINGER perf mat rent   (U20)

URBANNER, ERICH (1936-   )
  Concerto for Flute, Clarinet and
    Orchestra [20']
    2(alto fl,pic).2(English horn).1+
    bass clar.2. 2.2.2.0. perc,
    harp,pno,strings,fl solo,clar
    solo
    study sc DOBLINGER STP 540 f.s.,
    perf mat rent   (U21)

  Concerto for Piano and Orchestra
    [18']
    1(pic).1+bass clar.0. 1.0.1.0.
    2vln,vla,vcl,db,pno solo
    DOBLINGER perf mat rent   (U22)

URBANNER, ERICH (cont'd.)

Concerto for Violoncello and
    Orchestra [22']
    2(pic).1+English horn.1+bass
    clar.2. 2.1.1.0. timp,perc,
    strings,vcl solo
    DOBLINGER perf mat rent   (U23)

Lyrica [8']
    1(pic).0.1.0. 1.0.1.0. 2perc,
    harp,cel,pno&hpsd,vln,db
    DOBLINGER perf mat rent   (U24)

Sinfonia Concertante [18']
    2ob,2horn,strings
    DOBLINGER perf mat rent   (U25)

Sinfonietta [16']
    1.1.1.1. 2.1.1.0. strings
    study sc DOBLINGER STP 512 f.s.,
    perf mat rent   (U26)

Sonata Brevis For Chamber Orchestra
    [7']
    2ob,2horn,strings
    DOBLINGER perf mat rent   (U27)

USGNOL IN VATTA A UN FIL, L' see
    Vacchi, Fabio

USPENSKY, VLADISLAV (1937-   )
    Dedication To Courage, For Solo Voice
    And Orchestra [10']
    3.2.2.3. 4.2.3.1. timp,perc,
    strings,S solo
    VAAP perf mat rent   (U28)

USSACHEVSKY, VLADIMIR (1911-1990)
    Celebration [8']
    string orch
    sc AM.COMP.AL. $13.80   (U29)

Divertimento [13']
    1.1.1.0. 1.1.1.0. timp,perc,
    strings,electronic tape
    sc AM.COMP.AL. $24.65   (U30)

USTVOLSKAYA, GALINA (1919-   )
    Concerto for Piano and Orchestra
    [20']
    timp,strings,pno solo
    SIKORSKI perf mat rent   (U31)
    VAAP perf mat rent   (U32)

UT AV TAKA see Winther, Terje

UT, JA UT, DET VAR NORDMANNS TRAA, FOR
    SOLO VOICE AND ORCHESTRA see Eggen,
    Arne

UT RE MI SOL LA see Janssen, Guus

UTBROTT see Hammerth, Johan

UTDRIVELSEN see Hedstrom, Åse

UTOPIA PARAFRASI see Lenot, Jacques

UTSPILL see Johansen, Bertil Palmar

UTSYN see Tveitt, Geirr

V

VA A' EN OPERAARIA?, FOR SOLO VOICE AND
    ORCHESTRA see Jonsson, Josef
    [Petrus]

VA, DAL FUROR PORTATA, FOR SOLO VOICE
    AND ORCHESTRA see Mozart, Wolfgang
    Amadeus

VACCHI, FABIO (1949-   )
    Ballade for Solo Voice and Chamber
    Orchestra [15']
    fl,ob,bass clar,horn,trp,cel,
    harp,tubular bells,vibra,vln,
    vla,vcl,db,S solo
    sc RICORDI-IT 031-35866 $27.75,
    perf mat rent   (V1)

Cerchio E Gli Inganni, Il [15']
    1.1.1.1. 1.1.1.0. perc,gtr,pno,
    strings
    RICORDI-IT 133359 perf mat rent
                                     (V2)

Concerto for Piano and Orchestra
    [15']
    2.2.2.2. 2.2.0.0. 2perc,strings,
    pno solo
    RICORDI-IT 133549 perf mat rent
                                     (V3)

Girotondo: A Guardar, For Solo Voice
    And Orchestra [10'40"]
    1.1+English horn.1.0. 1.1.0.0.
    cel,vibra,6vln,2vla,vcl,db,S
    solo
    RICORDI-IT 133264 perf mat rent
                                     (V4)

Girotondo: Suite, For Solo Voices And
    Orchestra [35']
    1.1.1.0. 1.1.0.0. 2perc,cel,6vln,
    2vla,2vcl,db,SMezT soli
    RICORDI-IT 133674 perf mat rent
                                     (V5)

Poemetto (Nell'ali Dei Vivi Pensieri)
    [20'10"]
    3.3.3.3.alto sax. 4.3.3.1. 3perc,
    harp,cel,strings
    RICORDI-IT 133926 perf mat rent
                                     (V6)

Scherzo for Solo Voice and Chamber
    Orchestra [6']
    1.1.1.1. 1.1.1.0. xylorimba,harp,
    org,pno,vln,vla,vcl,S solo
    RICORDI-IT 132949 perf mat rent
                                     (V7)

Sinfonia In Quattro Tempi [20']
    3.3.3.3.alto sax. 4.3.2.1. timp,
    xylorimba,tubular bells,glock,
    org&cel,2harp,strings
    RICORDI-IT 132471 perf mat rent
                                     (V8)

Trois Visions De Genevieve, For Solo
    Voice And Strings [27']
    6vln,2vla,2vcl,db, voce bianca
    RICORDI-IT 133262 perf mat rent
                                     (V9)

Usgnol In Vatta A Un Fil, L' [10']
    1(pic).1.1.1. 1.0.0.0. 4perc,
    harp,strings
    sc RICORDI-IT 134020 f.s., perf mat
    rent   (V10)

VACEK, MILOŠ (1928-   )
    Burlesque, For Violin And Orchestra
    [6']
    CESKY HUD.   (V11)

Dances In Old Style [17']
    CESKY HUD.   (V12)

Festive Prologue [12']
    CESKY HUD.   (V13)

Landscape In Thoughts [5']
    CESKY HUD.   (V14)

Lone Sailor, The [17']
    CESKY HUD.   (V15)

March Of Friendship [5']
    CESKY HUD.   (V16)

May Symphony [35']
    CESKY HUD.   (V17)

Mistress Of Seven Robbers, The: Suite
    [25'] CESKY HUD.   (V18)

Musica Poetica [13']
    string orch PANTON   (V19)

Olympic Flame [11']
    CESKY HUD.   (V20)

Players' Fairytale, The: Suite No. 1
    [22'] CESKY HUD.   (V21)

Players' Fairytale, The: Suite No. 2
    [22'] CESKY HUD.   (V22)

VACEK, MILOŠ (cont'd.)

Poem Of Fallen Heroes, For Solo Voice
    And Orchestra [17']
    CZECH RADIO   (V23)

Seventeenth Of November [14']
    CESKY HUD.   (V24)

Solitary Seaman, A
    study sc PANTON 2192 f.s.   (V25)

To My Kamenice And Lipou [20']
    CESKY HUD.   (V26)

World's Conscience [12']
    CESKY HUD.   (V27)

VADE MORS see Saeverud, Harald

VADO, MA DOVE, FOR SOLO VOICE AND
    ORCHESTRA see Mozart, Wolfgang
    Amadeus

VADSTENA OUVERTURE see Thommessen, Olav
    Anton

VAGANZA see Casken, John

VAGGSANG FOR JORDEN see Werle, Lars-
    Johan

VAGUES see Burgan, Patrick

VAINBERG, MOYSEY SAMUILOVITCH
    (1919-   )
    Concerto for Trumpet and Orchestra,
    Op. 94 [24']
    3.3.3.3. 4.0.0.0. timp,perc,harp,
    cel,strings,trp solo
    SIKORSKI perf mat rent   (V28)

Fantasy for Violoncello and
    Orchestra, Op. 52 [20']
    1.0.0.0. 3.1.0.0. strings,vcl
    solo
    SIKORSKI perf mat rent   (V29)

Sinfonietta On Jewish Themes *Op.41
    3.2.3.2. 4.3.3.1. timp,perc,
    strings
    VAAP perf mat rent   (V30)

Symphony No. 10, Op. 98 [32']
    string orch
    SIKORSKI perf mat rent   (V31)

Symphony No. 12, Op. 114 [60']
    3.3.4.3. 4.4.3.1. timp,cym,
    marimba,harp,cel,strings
    sc MEZ KNIGA f.s.   (V32)
    SIKORSKI perf mat rent   (V33)

Wenn Die Kraniche Ziehen, For Piano
    And Orchestra [arr.]
    (Haletzki, P.) 2.2.2.2. 4.3.3.0.
    timp,strings,pno solo [5']
    SIKORSKI perf mat rent   (V34)

VAINYUNAS, STASYS (1909-   )
    Concerto for Organ and String
    Orchestra, Op. 18
    string orch,org solo
    VAAP perf mat rent   (V35)

VAJDA, J.
    Farewell
    sc EMB 10262 f.s., perf mat rent
                                     (V36)

Pentaton In Memoriam R.M.
    sc EMB 12662 f.s., perf mat rent
                                     (V37)

VAKRESTE ROSE, DEN [ARR.] see
    Thommessen, Reidar

VAKRESTEROSEN, DEN, FOR SOLO VOICES AND
    ORCHESTRA see Hovland, Egil

VALCARCEL, EDGAR (1932-   )
    Karabotasat Cutintapata
    4.4.4.4. 4.4.4.1. 6perc,strings
    "Return Of The Andrean Rider, The"
    TONOS   (V38)

Return Of The Andrean Rider, The
    see Karabotasat Cutintapata

VÁLEK, JIRÍ (1923-   )
    Symphony No. 10 for Violin, Piano and
    Orchestra [24']
    3.3.2.2. 4.3.3.1. timp,perc,
    strings,vln solo,pno solo
    SUPRAPHON   (V39)

Symphony No. 12
    study sc PANTON 2193 f.s.   (V40)

VALEN, FARTEIN (1887-1952)
    Lied Ohne Worte [arr.]
    (Bergh, Sverre) 1.1.2.1. 2.0.0.0.
    strings NORGE   (V41)

Sonetto Di Michelangelo *Op.17,No.1
    [5']
    2.2.2.2. 1.0.0.0. strings
    NORSK perf mat rent   (V42)

VALENCIANAS see Chavarri, Eduardo López

VALENTI, MICHAEL (1943-   )
Carolina Seasons [10']
3.3.3.3. 4.3.3.1. timp,perc,pno,
harp,strings
AMP perf mat rent   (V43)

Mood Piece, For Harp And String
Orchestra [5']
string orch,harp solo
AMP perf mat rent   (V44)

VALKYRIE, THE: WOTAN'S FAREWELL AND
MAGIC FIRE MUSIC see Wagner,
Richard, Walkure, Die: Wotans
Abschied Und Feuerzauber

VALLEY-SLEEPER, THE CHILDREN, THE
SNAKES AND THE GIANT, THE see
Bedford, David

VALLS GORINA
Fantasies En Forma De Concert, For
Flute And Orchestra
CLIVIS 20E 099   (V45)

VALRAVNEN see Sandby, Herman

VALSE see Vellones, Pierre

VALSE CAPRICE see Kochan, Ernst see
Stuppner, Hubert

VALSE CAPRICE [ARR.] see Rubinstein,
Anton

VALSE ESTATICO see Holenia, H.

VALSE LENGTE, FOR SOLO VOICE AND
ORCHESTRA [ARR.] see Merikanto,
Oskar

VALSE LENTE see Schreker, Franz

VALSE LYRIQUE see Cleve, Cissi

VALSE NO. 1 "ALLA MAUD", FOR 2
VIOLONCELLI AND STRING ORCHESTRA
see Tortelier, Paul

VALSE, OP. 18 [ARR.] see Chopin,
Frédéric

VALSE, OP. 34, NO. 1 [ARR.] see Chopin,
Frédéric

VALSE, OP. 34, NO. 2 [ARR.] see Chopin,
Frédéric

VALSE, OP. 64, NO. 1 [ARR.] see Chopin,
Frédéric

VALSE, OP. 70, NO. 1 [ARR.] see Chopin,
Frédéric

VALSE ROMANTIQUE see Sibelius, Jean see
Sköld, Sven

VALSE SCHERZO, FOR VIOLIN AND ORCHESTRA
see Tchaikovsky, Piotr Ilyich

VALSE TRES LENTE see Massenet, Jules

VALSE TRISTE see Tubin, Eduard

VALSES NOBLES ET SENTIMENTALES see
Ravel, Maurice

VALSES NOBLES ET SETIMENTALES see
Ravel, Maurice

VAN DE VATE, NANCY HAYES (1930-   )
Adagio [7']
2.2.2.2. 2.2.2.1. timp,strings
sc AM.COMP.AL. $9.15, perf mat rent
(V46)
Concertpiece, For Violoncello And
Chamber Orchestra [7']
perc,cel,pno,strings,vcl solo
sc AM.COMP.AL. $13.75, perf mat
rent   (V47)

Dark Nebulae [11']
3.2.2.2. 4.2.2.0. timp,perc,harp,
cel,pno,strings
sc AM.COMP.AL. $15.25, perf mat
rent   (V48)

Gema Jawa [10']
string orch
sc AM.COMP.AL. $10.30, perf mat
rent   (V49)

Journeys [16']
2+pic.2.2.2. 4.3.3.1. timp,perc,
harp,cel,pno,strings
sc AM.COMP.AL. $24.10, perf mat
rent   (V50)

Variations [10']
1.1.1.1. 0.0.0.0. strings
sc AM.COMP.AL. $10.70   (V51)

VAN DIJK, JAN
see DIJK, JAN VAN

VAN LIER, BERTUS
see LIER, BERTUS VAN

VAN NOSTRAND, BURR (1945-   )
Fragments From "Symphony Nosferatu"
[18']
3.2.3.3.2sax. 4.4.3.1. perc,kbd,
harp,elec gtr,strings
sc AM.COMP.AL. $46.50   (V52)

VAN ROOSENDAEL, JAN ROKUS
see ROOSENDAEL, JAN ROKUS VAN

VAN TY, L. NGUYEN
see NGUYEN VAN TY, L.

VANCURA, A.
Frohliches Wandern
2.2.2.2. 4.2.3.0. perc,strings
KRENN   (V53)

VANDENBOGAERDE, FERNAND (1946-   )
Proliferation III, For Bass Clarinet
And Instrumental Ensemble
[14'30"]
1.0.1.1. 1.1.1.0. vln,vcl,bass
clar solo,electronic equipment
BILLAUDOT perf mat rent   (V54)

VANDOR, IVAN (1932-   )
Melodie, Accordi E Frammenti [13']
2.2.2.2. 2.2.1.0. 3perc,pno,8vln,
4vla,2vcl,2db
sc RICORDI-IT 132767 f.s., perf mat
rent   (V55)

Melodie, Accordi E Frammenti, Parte
II [11'45"]
2.2.2.2. 4.2.3.1. perc,pno,
strings
RICORDI-IT 133138 perf mat rent
(V56)

Reminiscenze, Aggiunte, Varianti
[15']
4(pic).3(English horn).3(bass
clar).3(contrabsn). 4.3.3.1.
4perc,pno,cel,harp,strings
RICORDI-IT 132994 perf mat rent
(V57)

VANESSA: ANATOL'S ARIA, FOR SOLO VOICE
AND ORCHESTRA see Barber, Samuel

VANESSA: DO NOT UTTER A WORD, FOR SOLO
VOICE AND ORCHESTRA see Barber,
Samuel

VANESSA: MUST WINTER COME SO SOON, FOR
SOLO VOICE AND ORCHESTRA see
Barber, Samuel

VANG BONG THOI XUA, FOR SOLO VOICE AND
INSTRUMENTAL ENSEMBLE see Ton That,
Tiet

VANGELIS
Chariots Of Fire: Suite, [arr.] [7']
(Rose, Don) WARNER perf mat rent
(V58)

VANHAL, JOHANN BAPTIST
see WANHAL, JOHANN BAPTIST

VANHALL, JAN KRTITEL
see WANHAL, JOHANN BAPTIST

VANISHING PICTURES see Mihelcic, Pavle,
Slike, Ki Izginjajo

VANTUS, ISTVAN
Egloga
sc EMB 12560 f.s.   (V59)

Naenia
string orch
sc EMB 12126 f.s.   (V60)

Notturno
sc EMB 13293 f.s., perf mat rent
(V61)

Reflections
sc EMB 8274 f.s.   (V62)

Subsidences Into Silence
string orch
sc EMB 12833 f.s., perf mat rent
(V63)

VAR EN GANG, DET see Degen, Johannes

VAR INTE RADD FOR MORKRET see
Dorumsgaard, Arne

VAR STILLA HJARTA see Dorumsgaard, Arne

VARDER see Nordheim, Arne

VARESE, EDGARD (1883-1965)
Deserts [13'-23']
2.0.2.0. 2.3.3.2. timp,perc,pno,
electronic tape
study sc COLFRANC COL.4 $18.00,
perf mat rent   (V64)

VARIA ITER see Ostendorf, Jens-Peter

VARIACIONES [ARR.] see Albéniz, Isaac

VARIACIONES SERENAS see Orrego-Salas,
Juan A.

VARIANTI, FOR BASSOON AND STRINGS see
Bianchera, Silvia

VARIANTS see Schuller, Gunther

VARIANTS FOR ORCHESTRA see Cooper, Paul

VARIANTS ON A BACH CHORALE see Dello
Joio, Norman

VARIANTS ON AN IRISH HYMN TUNE see
Beck, John Ness

VARIATIES '85 see Hogenhuis, Jelle

VARIATIES EN THEMA see Lier, Bertus van

VARIATIES OVER EEN FRANS VOLKSLIED see
Bunge, Sas

VARIATION AJOUTEE, LA see Amy, Gilbert

VARIATION ON AN UNKNOWN THEME see
McBride, Robert Guyn

VARIATION ON "SUMER IS A' CUMIN IN" see
Saxton, Robert

VARIATIONAL SYMPHONY see Sokola, Milos

VARIATIONEN-SUITE see Hessenberg, Kurt

VARIATIONEN UBER DAS ALTE ADVENTLIED "O
HEILAND, REISS DIE HIMMEL AUF" see
Eder, Helmut

VARIATIONEN UBER EIN THEMA VON FRANZ
SCHUBERT see Heuberger, Richard

VARIATIONEN ÜBER EIN THEMA VON JOSEPH
HAYDN see Brahms, Johannes

VARIATIONEN UND FUGE UBER EIN MENUETT
VON PADEREWSKI see Etti, Karl

VARIATIONEN UND FUGE UBER EIN THEMA VON
J.S. BACH see Grabner, Hermann

VARIATIONEN UND FUGE UBER EIN THEMA VON
JOSEPH HAYDN see Etti, Karl

VARIATIONER OVER EN FOLKEVISE FRA
HARDANGER, FOR 2 PIANOS AND
ORCHESTRA see Tveitt, Geirr

VARIATIONER ÖVER ETT LOCKROP, FOR SOLO
VOICE AND ORCHESTRA see Lindgren,
Kurt

VARIATIONS A TREIZE see Barraud, Henry

VARIATIONS AND FUGUE ON A CHESHIRE
SOULING SONG see Hand, Colin

VARIATIONS AND SOLILOQUIES see Di
Domenica, Robert

VARIATIONS CHROMATIQUES [ARR.] see
Bizet, Georges

VARIATIONS LIBRES see Mefano, Paul

VARIATIONS MONEGASQUES see Damase,
Jean-Michel

VARIATIONS OF A HYMN see Brown, Rayner

VARIATIONS ON A CANADIAN FOLK SONG, FOR
2 PIANOS AND ORCHESTRA see Chatman,
Stephen

VARIATIONS ON A CATSKILL MOUNTAIN
FOLKSONG see Haufrecht, Herbert

VARIATIONS ON A FOLK TUNE FROM
HARDANGER, FOR 2 PIANOS AND
ORCHESTRA see Tveitt, Geirr,
Variationer Over En Folkevise Fra
Hardanger, For 2 Pianos And
Orchestra

VARIATIONS ON A GROUND, FOR ORGAN AND
ORCHESTRA see Street, Tison

VARIATIONS ON A MEMORY see Finney, Ross
Lee

VARIATIONS ON A MOZART RONDO see Coles,
Graham

VARIATIONS ON A RHYME SONG see
Björnsson, Arni

VARIATIONS ON A RUSSIAN THEME, FOR
VIOLONCELLO AND STRING ORCHESTRA
see Reicha, Anton

VARIATIONS ON A SYMPHONIC LANDSCAPE see Bernstein, David

VARIATIONS ON A THEME BY DITTERSDORF, FOR VIOLONCELLO AND ORCHESTRA see Reicha, Anton

VARIATIONS ON A THEME BY GUNTHER SCHULLER, FOR TUBA AND CHAMBER ORCHESTRA see Di Domenica, Robert

VARIATIONS ON A THEME BY ROSSINI, FOR VIOLONCELLO AND STRING ORCHESTRA [ARR.] see Paganini, Niccolo, Variazioni Di Bravura Sopra I Temi Del "Mose" Di Rossini, For Violoncello And String Orchestra [arr.]

VARIATIONS ON A THEME FROM ROSSINI'S "MOSES", FOR VIOLONCELLO AND STRING ORCHESTRA [ARR.] see Paganini, Niccolo, Variazioni Di Bravura Sopra I Temi Del "Mose" Di Rossini, For Violoncello And String Orchestra [arr.]

VARIATIONS ON A THEME OF C.M. BELLMAN see Riisager, Knudage

VARIATIONS ON A THEME OF CORELLI, FOR VIOLIN AND ORCHESTRA [ARR.] see Tartini, Giuseppe

VARIATIONS ON A THEME OF FRESCOBALDI see Tansman, Alexandre

VARIATIONS ON A THEME OF GILBERT BECAUD see Damase, Jean-Michel

VARIATIONS ON A THEME OF HAYDN see Brahms, Johannes, Variationen Über Ein Thema Von Joseph Haydn

VARIATIONS ON A THEME OF HAYDN "TOD IST EIN LANGER SCHLAF", FOR VIOLONCELLO AND ORCHESTRA see Denisov, Edison Vasilievich

VARIATIONS ON A THEME OF KODALY [20']
2+pic.2+English horn.2+bass clar.2+
contrabsn. 4.3.3.1. timp,perc,
harp,pno,strings
(variations by Dorati, Serly, Partos,
Frid, Veress) sc BOOSEY $25.00,
perf mat rent   (V65)

VARIATIONS ON A THEME OF PAGANINI, FOR PIANO AND ORCHESTRA see Lutoslawski, Witold

VARIATIONS ON A THEME OF ROSSINI, FOR FLUTE AND ORCHESTRA, [ARR.] see Chopin, Frédéric

VARIATIONS ON A THEME OF SHOSTAKOVICH, FOR PIANO AND ORCHESTRA see Biggs, John

VARIATIONS ON AN AMERICAN THEME see Russo, William Joseph

VARIATIONS ON BACH'S CHORALE "DIE NACHT IST KOMMEN" see Matthews, David

VARIATIONS ON "CADET ROUSSEL" see Goossens, [Sir] Eugene

VARIATIONS ON "LA CI DAREM LA MANO", FOR PIANO AND ORCHESTRA see Chopin, Frédéric

VARIATIONS ON "LOTH TO DEPART", FOR STRING QUARTET AND ORCHESTRA see Holst, Imogen

VARIATIONS ON "SELLENGER'S ROUND" [13']
string orch
(variations by Britten, Berkeley,
Oldham, Searle, Tippett, Walton)
BOOSEY perf mat rent   (V66)

VARIATIONS ON THEMES OF STRAVINSKY see Pishny-Floyd, Monte Keene

VARIATIONS PATHETIQUES, FOR ALTO SAXOPHONE AND STRING ORCHESTRA see Gotkovsky, Ida

VARIATIONS POUR QUATORZE INSTRUMENTS see Aperghis, Georges

VARIATIONS SYMPHONIQUES see Rovsing Olsen, Poul

VARIATIONS SYMPHONIQUES, FOR PIANO AND ORCHESTRA see Franck, Cesar

VARIAZIONI A PIU STRUMENTI OBBLIGATI see Rossini, Gioacchino

VARIAZIONI CANONICHE, SULLA SERIE DELL', OP. 41 DI ARNOLD SCHOENBERG see Nono, Luigi

VARIAZIONI CONCERTANTI see Maconchy, Elizabeth

VARIAZIONI DI BRAVURA SOPRA I TEMI DEL "MOSE" DI ROSSINI, FOR VIOLONCELLO AND STRING ORCHESTRA [ARR.] see Paganini, Niccolo

VARIAZIONI SENZA TEMA, FOR PIANO AND ORCHESTRA see Bentzon, Niels Viggo

VARIAZIONI SINFONICHE see Westergaard, Svend

VARLENGSEL [ARR.] see Cleve, Cissi

VARLOSNING see Thommessen, Olav Anton

VARNATTSTONE, FOR RECORDER AND STRING ORCHESTRA [ARR.] see Storbekken, Egil

VARPUNEN JOULUAAMUNA, FOR SOLO VOICE AND ORCHESTRA [ARR.] see Kotilainen, Otto

VARVISA, FOR SOLO VOICE AND ORCHESTRA see Jordan, Sverre

VASCA DA BAGNO see Andersson, Magnus F.

VASKS, PETERIS (1946-   )
Botschaft, Die [14']
4perc,2pno,strings
SIKORSKI perf mat rent   (V67)

Cantabile [9']
string orch
sc MEZ KNIGA f.s.   (V68)
SIKORSKI perf mat rent   (V69)

Musica Dolorosa [15']
string orch
SIKORSKI perf mat rent   (V70)
VAAP perf mat rent   (V71)

VASS, LAJOS (1927-   )
Two Spinning Songs, For Solo Voice And Chamber Orchestra
min sc EMB 2824 f.s.   (V72)

VASSALLO, IL: DANZE UNGHERESI see Smareglia, Antonio

VASSILENKO, SERGEY (1872-1956)
Concerto for Harp and Orchestra, Op. 126
2.2.2.2. 4.2.3.1. timp,perc,
strings,harp solo
VAAP perf mat rent   (V73)

Concerto for Horn and Orchestra, Op. 136 [13']
2.2.2.2. 0.2.3.0. timp,perc,harp,
cel,strings,horn solo
SIKORSKI perf mat rent   (V74)

Concerto for Piano and Orchestra, Op. 128, in F sharp minor
3.2.3.2. 4.3.3.1. timp,perc,
strings,pno solo
VAAP perf mat rent   (V75)

In Spring, For Flute And Chamber Orchestra *Op.138 [16']
2clar,bsn,perc,harp/pno,strings,
fl solo
VAAP perf mat rent   (V76)

VAST I "THE SEA" see Conyngham, Barry

VAST II "THE COAST" see Conyngham, Barry

VAST III "THE CENTRE" see Conyngham, Barry

VAST IV "THE CITIES" see Conyngham, Barry

VASZY, VIKTOR (1903-   )
Suite No. 2
sc EMB 3929 f.s.   (V77)

VATER UNSER IM HIMMELREICH, CHORALE [ARR.] see Buxtehude, Dietrich

VATERGRUFT, DIE, FOR SOLO VOICE AND ORCHESTRA see Liszt, Franz

VATERLANDISCHER MARSCH see Strauss, Johann, [Jr.]

VAUBOURGOIN, MARC (1907-1985)
Concerto for Piano and Orchestra [26']
3.3.3.3. 4.3.3.0. timp,2perc,
harp,cel,strings,pno solo
BILLAUDOT perf mat rent   (V78)

Concerto for Trumpet and Orchestra [22']
2.2.2.2. 2.2.2.0. timp,2perc,
harp,strings,trp solo
BILLAUDOT perf mat rent   (V79)

VAUBOURGOIN, MARC (cont'd.)

Introduction, Variation Et Rondeau, For Woodwind Quartet And Orchestra [12'30"]
1.1.1.1. 4.3.3.0. timp,2perc,
harp,strings,fl solo,ob solo,
clar solo,bsn solo
BILLAUDOT perf mat rent   (V80)

VAUCLAIN, [ANDRE] CONSTANT (1908-   )
Serenade
2+pic.2.2.2. 4.3.3.0. timp,
strings
PEER perf mat rent   (V81)

VAUGHAN WILLIAMS, RALPH (1872-1958)
Charterhouse Suite, The, [arr.]
(Brown, James) 1+pic.1.1.1.
1.1.0.0. timp,perc,strings [18']
STAINER HL214 perf mat rent (V82)

Down Ampney, "Come Down, O Love Divine" [arr.]
(Wedge, James) 2.2.2.2. 2.0.0.0.
strings [5'] OXFORD perf mat rent
(V83)

Fantasia On Sussex Folksongs, For Cello And Orchestra [11'15"]
2.1.2.2. 1.1.0.0. timp,strings,
vcl solo
(Lloyd Webber, Julian) OXFORD perf
mat rent   (V84)

Five Mystical Songs, For Solo Voice And Orchestra
2.2.2.2. 4.2.3.1. timp,harp,
strings,Bar solo KALMUS A6124 sc
$35.00, set $60.00, perf mat rent
(V85)

Hugh The Drover: Hugh's Song Of The Road For Solo Voice And Orchestra [4']
2.2.2.2. 4.2.0.0. timp,perc,harp,
strings,T solo
CURWEN perf mat rent   (V86)

Six Studies In English Folk Song, For English Horn And String Orchestra [arr.]
(Stanton, Robert) string orch,
English horn/sax solo STAINER
H176 f.s.   (V87)

Wasps, The: Suite [20']
2(pic).2.2.2. 4.2.3.0. timp,perc,
harp,strings
KALMUS A5714 sc $40.00, set $70.00,
perf mat rent   (V88)

VAUTRIN see Thiriet, Maurice

VAVOLO, MARCO (1939-   )
Quattro Studi [12']
2.2.2.2. 2.2.0.0. timp,cel,pno,
strings
SONZOGNO perf mat rent   (V89)

VEA, KETIL (1932-   )
Aribla [10']
3.3.2.2. 4.3.3.1. timp,perc,pno,
strings
NORGE   (V90)

Concerto For Flute, Narrator And Chamber Orchestra [20']
1(pic).2.2.2. 2.1.1.0. timp,
2perc,pno,strings,narrator,fl
solo
NORSK perf mat rent   (V91)

Concerto for Piano and Orchestra, No. 1
2.2.3.2. 2.2.2.0. timp,perc,
strings,pno solo
NORGE   (V92)

Concerto for Trumpet, Horn and Orchestra
3.2.2.2. 4.3.3.1. timp,perc,
strings,trp solo,horn solo
NORGE   (V93)

Concerto for Violin and Orchestra [24']
2.2.2.2. 2.2.2.0. timp,perc,
strings,vln solo
NORSK perf mat rent   (V94)

Dei Gamle Fjell
3.2.2.2. 4.3.3.1. timp,perc,
strings
NORGE   (V95)

Helgeland [10']
2.2(English horn).2.2. 2.2.2.0.
timp,perc,opt pno,strings
NORSK perf mat rent   (V96)

Intrada No. 2
3.2.2.2. 4.3.3.1. timp,perc,pno,
strings
NORGE   (V97)

VEA, KETIL (cont'd.)

Jiedna [17']
  3(pic).2.3.2. 4.3.3.1. timp,
  3perc,strings,S solo
  NORSK perf mat rent   (V98)

Kvintekvaesa
  3.2.2.2.sax. 4.3.3.1. timp,perc,
  pno,strings
  NORGE   (V99)

Little Serenade, A
  string orch
  NORGE   (V100)

Overture
  2.1.2.2. 2.3.2.0. timp,perc,
  strings
  NORGE   (V101)

Serenade [15']
  2.2.1.1. 2.2.2.0. timp,perc,
  strings,vln solo,vla solo,clar
  solo,pno solo
  NORGE   (V102)

VED HAVET, FOR SOLO VOICE AND ORCHESTRA
  see Jordan, Sverre

VEERHOFF, CARLOS H. (1926-   )
  Symphony No. 1, Op. 9
  sc BOTE 037-35809 $60.25   (V103)

VEIL OF PIERRETTE, THE, OP. 18: JOLLY
  FUNERAL MARCH see Dohnányi, Ernst
  von, Schleier Der Pierrette, Der,
  Op. 18: Lustiger Trauermarsch

VEIL OF PIERRETTE, THE, OP. 18: MENUETT
  see Dohnányi, Ernst von, Schleier
  Der Pierrette, Der, Op. 18: Menuett

VEIL OF PIERRETTE, THE, OP. 18:
  PIERRETTE'S DANCE OF MADNESS see
  Dohnányi, Ernst von, Schleier Der
  Pierrette, Der, Op. 18: Pierrettens
  Wahnsinnstanz

VEIL OF PIERRETTE, THE, OP. 18:
  PIERROT'S COMPLAINT OF LOVE see
  Dohnányi, Ernst von, Schleier Der
  Pierrette, Der, Op. 18: Pierrots
  Liebesklage

VEIL OF PIERRETTE, THE, OP. 18: WALTZ
  see Dohnányi, Ernst von, Schleier
  Der Pierrette, Der, Op. 18: Walzer-
  Reigen

VEIL OF PIERRETTE, THE, OP. 18: WEDDING
  MARCH see Dohnányi, Ernst von,
  Schleier Der Pierrette, Der, Op.
  18: Hochzeitswalzer

VEILED PROPHET, THE: BALLET MUSIC, FOR
  SOLO VOICE AND ORCHESTRA see
  Stanford, Charles Villiers

VEILED PROPHET, THE: OVERTURE see
  Stanford, Charles Villiers

VEJVANOVSKY, PAVEL JOSEF (1640-1693)
  Composizioni Per Orchestra I
  sc SUPRAPHON MAB 47 f.s.   (V104)

  Composizioni Per Orchestra II
  sc SUPRAPHON MAB 48 f.s.   (V105)

  Composizioni Per Orchestra III
  sc SUPRAPHON MAB 49 f.s.   (V106)

  Intrada In C
  2trp,strings,cont
  (Wetzlar) sc,pts MERSEBURGER
  EM 1341 f.s.   (V107)

VELDEN EN WEGEN see Dormolen, Jan
  Willem van

VELDHUIS, JACOB TER (1951-   )
  Symphony No. 1 [20']
  3.2.2.2. 4.2.3.1. 5perc,elec org&
  pno&cel,strings,synthesizer
  sc DONEMUS f.s., perf mat rent
                               (V108)
  Symphony No. 2, Op. 30 [26']
  4horn,perc,harp,strings,
  synthesizer
  DONEMUS perf mat rent   (V109)

VELLONES, PIERRE (1889-1939)
  A Mon Fils, For Solo Voice And
  Orchestra [5']
  1.1.1.1. 1.0.0.0. perc,2harp,cel,
  strings,solo voice
  LEMOINE perf mat rent   (V110)

  Au Pays Du Tendre [26']
  2(pic).2(English horn).2(bass
  clar).3(contrabsn). 4.2.3.1.
  timp,perc,2harp,cel,strings
  LEMOINE perf mat rent   (V111)

VELLONES, PIERRE (cont'd.)

  Cavaliers Andalous [4']
  1.1.1.1. 3.1.1.0. timp,perc,harp/
  pno,strings
  LEMOINE perf mat rent   (V112)

  Cinq Poemes, For Solo Voice And
  Orchestra
  1.2(English horn).1.1. 1.1.1.0.
  timp,perc,harp,strings,solo
  voice
  LEMOINE perf mat rent   (V113)

  Danse Indienne [11']
  1.1.1.1. 0.0.0.0. perc,harp,
  strings
  LEMOINE perf mat rent   (V114)

  Petit Village, For Solo Voice And
  Orchestra *Op.78 [8']
  2(pic).2(English horn).1.1.
  1.1.1.0. timp,perc,harp,
  strings,solo voice
  LEMOINE perf mat rent   (V115)

  Rondo Capriccioso, For Violin And
  Orchestra
  3(pic).3(English horn).3(bass
  clar).4(contrabsn). 4.3.3.1.
  timp,perc,2harp,strings,vln
  solo
  LEMOINE perf mat rent   (V116)

  Valse *Op.104
  1.0.1.0.2alto sax. 0.1.1.0. perc,
  pno,strings
  LEMOINE perf mat rent   (V117)

VELOCITY see Andriessen, Louis,
  Snelheid, De

VENEXIANA II, FOR SOLO VOICES AND
  ORCHESTRA see Powers, Anthony

VENEZIA, FOR SOLO VOICES AND ORCHESTRA
  see Rechberger, Herman

VENEZIANISCHE SCHATTEN see Brandmüller,
  Theo

VENICE see Gould, Morton

VENITE EXULTAMUS see Werle, Floyd
  Edwards

VENITE EXULTEMUS, FOR SOLO VOICE AND
  STRING ORCHESTRA see Mouret, Jean
  Joseph

VENT DU SOIR RAMENE SA DEPOUILLE VERS
  LA GREVE, LE see Lenot, Jacques

VENUS FLYTRAP see Chapple, Brian

VENUSKRANZLEIN: INTRADAS AND GAGLIARDS
  see Schein, Johann Hermann

VERA COSTANZA, LA: OVERTURE see Haydn,
  [Franz] Joseph

VERACINI, FRANCESCO MARIA (1690-1768)
  Aria Schiavona
  set KALMUS A7306 $16.00, and up
                               (V118)

  Four Pieces From The Sonate
  Accademiche
  see Quattro Pezzi

  Quattro Pezzi (from Sonate
  Academiche)
  "Four Pieces From The Sonate
  Accademiche" KALMUS A7326 sc
  $8.00, set $12.50, pts $2.50, ea.
                               (V119)

VERBA LAUDATA, FOR SOLO VOICE AND
  CHAMBER ORCHESTRA see Lukas, Zdenek

VERBEY, THEO (1959-   )
  Aura [42']
  1.2.3.1. 2.1.3.1. vln,2vla,3vcl,
  db
  DONEMUS perf mat rent   (V120)

  Contrary Motion
  see Tegenbeweging

  Expulsie: Parts III-IV [11']
  1.1.3.1. 1.2.1.1. 2perc,harp,pno,
  strings
  sc DONEMUS f.s., perf mat rent
                               (V121)

  Tegenbeweging [11']
  4.3.4.3. 4.3.0.1. timp,5perc,
  2harp,pno&cel,strings
  "Contrary Motion" DONEMUS perf mat
  rent   (V122)

VERBLENDUNGEN see Saariaho, Kaija

VERBRUDERUNGS MARSCH see Strauss,
  Johann, [Jr.]

VERDANT MUSIC see Torke, Michael

VERDI, GIUSEPPE (1813-1901)
  Aida: Marcia
  "Aida: Triumphal March" (original
  version) KALMUS A4009 sc $25.00,
  set $75.00, perf mat rent   (V123)

  Aïda: Sinfonia 1872
  (Spada, P.) sc BSE 597-00612 $15.75
                               (V124)

  Aida: Triumphal March
  see Aida: Marcia

  Aroldo: Ah Da Me Fuggi, Involati, For
  Solo Voices And Orchestra
  KALMUS A5021 sc $10.00, set $25.00,
  pts $3.00, ea., perf mat rent
                               (V125)
  Aroldo: Ah! Dagli Scanni Eterei, For
  Solo Voices And Orchestra
  KALMUS A5013 sc $15.00, set $40.00,
  pts $2.50, ea., perf mat rent
                               (V126)
  Aroldo: Dite Che Il Fallo A Tergere,
  For Solo Voices And Orchestra
  KALMUS A5011 sc $12.00, set $30.00,
  pts $2.00, ea., perf mat rent
                               (V127)
  Aroldo: Era Vero?...Ah No... E
  Impossible, For Solo Voices And
  Orchestra
  KALMUS A5014 sc $15.00, set $35.00,
  pts $2.00, ea., perf mat rent
                               (V128)
  Aroldo: Mina, Pensai Che Un Angelo,
  For Solo Voice And Orchestra
  KALMUS A5016 sc $8.00, set $20.00,
  pts $1.00, ea., perf mat rent
                               (V129)
  Aroldo: Opposto E Il Calle, Che In
  Avvenire, For Solo Voices And
  Orchestra
  KALMUS A5017 sc $8.00, set $30.00,
  pts $2.00, ea., perf mat rent
                               (V130)
  Aroldo: Salvami Tu, Gran Dio, For
  Solo Voice And Orchestra
  KALMUS A5009 sc $3.00, set $10.00,
  pts $.75, ea.   (V131)
  Aroldo: Sotto Il Sol Di Siria
  Ardente, For Solo Voice And
  Orchestra
  KALMUS A5010 sc $9.00, set $30.00,
  pts $2.00, ea., perf mat rent
                               (V132)
  Attila: Oh! Nel Fuggente Nuvolo, For
  Solo Voice And Orchestra
  KALMUS A6297 sc $4.00, set $6.00,
  pts $.75, ea.   (V133)

  Battaglia Di Legnano, La: Ah! D'un
  Consorte, O Perfidi, For Solo
  Voices And Orchestra
  KALMUS A5098 sc $15.00, set $45.00,
  pts $2.00, ea., perf mat rent
                               (V134)
  Battaglia Di Legnano, La: Ah!
  M'abbraccia...D' Esultanza, For
  Solo Voice And Orchestra
  KALMUS A5088 sc $5.00, set $20.00,
  pts $1.00, ea., perf mat rent
                               (V135)
  Battaglia Di Legnano, La: Ben Vi
  Scorgo Nel Sembiante, For Solo
  Voices And Orchestra
  KALMUS A 5093 sc $6.00, set $20.00,
  pts $1.00, ea., perf mat rent
                               (V136)
  Battaglia Di Legnano, La: Digli Ch' E
  Sangue Italico, For Solo Voices
  And Orchestra
  KALMUS A5096 sc $8.00, set $20.00,
  pts $1.00, ea., perf mat rent
                               (V137)
  Battaglia Di Legnano, La: La Pia
  Materna Mano, For Solo Voice And
  Orchestra
  KALMUS A5087 sc $3.00, set $18.00,
  pts $1.00, ea.   (V138)
  Battaglia Di Legnano, La: Quante
  Volte Come In Dono, For Solo
  Voice And Orchestra
  KALMUS A5091 sc $10.00, set $35.00,
  pts $2.00, ea., perf mat rent
                               (V139)
  Battaglia Di Legnano, La: Se Al Nuovo
  Di Pugnando, For Solo Voice And
  Orchestra
  KALMUS A5097 sc $12.00, set $35.00,
  pts $2.00, ea., perf mat rent
                               (V140)
  Don Carlos: A Mezza Notte, Ai Giardin
  Della Regina, For Solo Voices And
  Orchestra
  KALMUS A5033 sc $12.00, set $35.00,
  pts $2.00, ea., perf mat rent
                               (V141)
  Don Carlos: Giustizia, Giustizia,
  Sire! For Solo Voices And
  Orchestra
  KALMUS A5036 sc $10.00, set $35.00,
  pts $2.00, ea., perf mat rent
                               (V142)

VERDI, GIUSEPPE (cont'd.)

Don Carlos: Il Grand' Inquisitor! For
  Solo Voices And Orchestra
  KALMUS A5035 sc $6.00, set $22.00,
  pts $1.00, ea., perf mat rent
                                    (V143)
Don Carlos: Io Vengo A Domandar
  Grazia Alla Mia Regina, For Solo
  Voices And Orchestra
  KALMUS A5030 sc $9.00, set $22.00,
  pts $1.00, ea., perf mat rent
                                    (V144)
Don Carlos: La Regina! Una Canzone
  Qui Lieta, For Solo Voices And
  Orchestra
  KALMUS 5029 sc $7.00, set $22.00,
  pts $2.00, ea., perf mat rent
                                    (V145)
Don Carlos: Non Pianger, Mia
  Compagna, For Solo Voice And
  Orchestra
  KALMUS A5031 sc $3.00, set $10.00,
  pts $.75, ea., perf mat rent
                                    (V146)
Don Carlos: O Mio Rodrigo, For Solo
  Voices And Orchestra
  KALMUS A5026 sc $12.00, set $35.00,
  pts $2.00, ea., perf mat rent
                                    (V147)
Don Carlos: Presso All Mia Persona,
  For Solo Voices And Orchestra
  KALMUS A5032 sc $12.00, set $35.00,
  pts $2.00, ea., perf mat rent
                                    (V148)
Don Carlos: Tu Che Le Vanita, For
  Solo Voice And Orchestra
  KALMUS A5037 sc $7.00, set $25.00,
  pts $1.00, ea., perf mat rent
                                    (V149)
Don Carlos: Un Detto, Un Sol, For
  Solo Voices And Orchestra
  KALMUS A5038 sc $9.00, set $35.00,
  pts $2.00, ea., perf mat rent
                                    (V150)
Ernani: Come Rugiada Al Cespite, For
  Solo Voice And Orchestra
  KALMUS A5040 sc $8.00, set $20.00,
  pts $1.00, ea., perf mat rent
                                    (V151)
Ernani: Esci...A Te, For Solo Voices
  And Orchestra
  KALMUS A5047 sc $15.00, set $35.00,
  pts $2.00, ea., perf mat rent
                                    (V152)
Ernani: Lo Vedremo, Veglio Audace,
  For Solo Voice And Orchestra
  KALMUS A5046 sc $5.00, set $20.00,
  pts $1.00, ea., perf mat rent
                                    (V153)
Ernani: Oh De' Verd' Anni Miei, For
  Solo Voice And Orchestra
  KALMUS A5048 sc $3.00, set $12.00,
  pts $.75, ea.   (V154)
Ernani: Oro, Quant Oro, For Solo
  Voices And Orchestra
  KALMUS A5045 sc $15.00, set $35.00,
  pts $2.00, ea., perf mat rent
                                    (V155)
Ernani: Qui Mi Trasse Amor Possente,
  For Solo Voices And Orchestra
  KALMUS A5041 sc $6.00, set $20.00,
  pts $1.00, ea., perf mat rent
                                    (V156)
Ernani: Solingo, Errante, Misero, For
  Solo Voices And Orchestra
  KALMUS A5052 sc $15.00, set $40.00,
  pts $2.00, ea., perf mat rent
                                    (V157)
Forza Del Destino, La: Preludio
  3.2.2.2. 4.2.3.1. timp,perc,strings
  (St. Petersburg version, 1862)
  study sc BSE 597-00497 $8.50
                                    (V158)
Giovanna D'arco: Amai, Ma Un Solo
  Istante, For Solo Voices And
  Orchestra
  KALMUS A5065 sc $12.00, set $30.00,
  pts $2.00, ea., perf mat rent
                                    (V159)
Giovanna D'arco: Dunque, O Cruda, E
  Gloria E Trono, For Solo Voices
  And Orchestra
  KALMUS A5061 sc $20.00, set $30.00,
  sc $2.00, perf mat rent
                                    (V160)
Giovanna D'arco: Franco Son Io, Ma In
  Core, For Solo Voice And
  Orchestra
  KALMUS A5059 sc $12.00, set $22.00,
  pts $1.00, ea., perf mat rent
                                    (V161)
Giovanna D'Arco: March
  2+pic.2.2.2. 4.2.3.0. timp,perc,
  strings
  "Jeanne D'Arc: Marche" CHOUDENS
  perf mat rent   (V162)
Giovanna D'arco: O Fatidica Foresta,
  For Solo Voice And Orchestra
  KALMUS A5060 sc $4.00, set $11.00,
  pts $.75, ea., perf mat rent
                                    (V163)

VERDI, GIUSEPPE (cont'd.)

Giovanna D'Arco: Overture
  1+pic.2.2.2. 4.2.3.1. timp,perc,
  strings
  "Jeanne D'Arc: Ouverture" CHOUDENS
  perf mat rent   (V164)
Giovanna D'arco: Quale Piu Fido
  Amico, For Solo Voice And
  Orchestra
  KALMUS A5067 sc $3.00, set $4.00,
  pts $.75, ea., perf mat rent
                                    (V165)
Giovanna D'arco: S' Apre Il Cielo,
  For Solo Voices And Orchestra
  KALMUS A5069 sc $6.00, set $14.00,
  pts $.75, ea., perf mat rent
                                    (V166)
Giovanna D'arco: Sempre All' Alba Ed
  Alla Sera, For Solo Voice And
  Orchestra
  KALMUS A5056 sc $5.00, set $15.00,
  pts $.75, ea., perf mat rent
                                    (V167)
Giovanna D'arco: Sotto Una Quercia
  Parvemi, For Solo Voice And
  Orchestra
  KALMUS A5055 sc $18.00, set $30.00,
  pts $2.00, ea., perf mat rent
                                    (V168)
Giovanna D'arco: Speme Al Vecchio Era
  Una Figlia, For Solo Voice And
  Orchestra
  KALMUS A5063 sc $3.00, set $6.00,
  pts $.75, ea., perf mat rent
                                    (V169)
Jeanne D'Arc: Marche
  see Giovanna D'Arco: March

Jeanne D'Arc: Ouverture
  see Giovanna D'Arco: Overture

Lombardi, I: La Mia Letizia, For Solo
  Voice And Orchestra
  KALMUS A6296 sc $15.00, set $35.00,
  pts $2.00, ea., perf mat rent
                                    (V170)
Luisa Miller: Dall' Aule Raggianti Di
  Vano Splendore, For Solo Voices
  And Orchestra
  KALMUS A5105 sc $7.00, set $18.00,
  pts $1.00, ea., perf mat rent
                                    (V171)
Luisa Miller: Il Mio Sangue, La Vita
  Darei, For Solo Voice And
  Orchestra
  KALMUS A5103 sc $5.00, set $18.00,
  pts $1.00, ea., perf mat rent
                                    (V172)
Luisa Miller: L'alto Retaggio Non Ho
  Bramato, For Solo Voices And
  Orchestra
  KALMUS A5109 sc $9.00, set $18.00,
  pts $1.00, ea., perf mat rent
                                    (V173)
Luisa Miller: Presentarti Alla
  Duchessa, For Solo Voices And
  Orchestra
  KALMUS A5110 sc $6.00, set $15.00,
  pts $1.00, ea., perf mat rent
                                    (V174)
Luisa Miller: Sacra La Scelta E D' Un
  Consorte, For Solo Voice And
  Orchestra
  KALMUS A5102 sc $11.00, set $30.00,
  pts $2.00, ea., perf mat rent
                                    (V175)
Luisa Miller: Sotto Il Mio Pie Il
  Suol Vacilla, For Solo Voices And
  Orchestra
  KALMUS A5112 sc $12.00, set $35.00,
  pts $2.00, ea., perf mat rent
                                    (V176)
Luisa Miller: Tu Puniscimi, O
  Signore, For Solo Voice And
  Orchestra
  KALMUS A5108 sc $12.00, set $30.00,
  pts $2.00, ea., perf mat rent
                                    (V177)
Nabucco: Anch' Io Dischiuso Un
  Giorno, For Solo Voice And
  Orchestra
  KALMUS A5118 sc $12.00, set $40.00,
  pts $2.00, ea., perf mat rent
                                    (V178)
Nabucco: Donna Chi Sei? For Solo
  Voices And Orchestra
  KALMUS A5123 sc $18.00, set $35.00,
  pts $2.00, ea., perf mat rent
                                    (V179)
Nabucco: Oh, Dischiuso E Il
  Firmamento, For Solo Voice And
  Orchestra
  KALMUS A5126 sc $3.00, set $18.00,
  pts $1.00, ea.   (V180)
Nabucco: Prode Guerrier!... D'amore,
  For Solo Voices And Orchestra
  KALMUS A5115 sc $9.00, set $20.00,
  pts $1.00, ea., perf mat rent
                                    (V181)
Nabucco: Tu Sul Labbro De' Veggenti,
  For Solo Voice And Orchestra
  KALMUS A5119 sc $3.00, set $12.00,
  pts $2.00, ea.   (V182)

VERDI, GIUSEPPE (cont'd.)

Requiem: Ingemisco, For Solo Voice
  And Orchestra
  KALMUS A6295 sc $3.00, set $15.00,
  pts $.75, ea.   (V183)
Rigoletto: Quel Vecchio, For Solo
  Voices And Orchestra
  KALMUS A4553 sc $6.00, set $8.00,
  pts $1.00, ea., perf mat rent
                                    (V184)
Simon Boccanegra: Chi Il Varco
  T'apria? For Solo Voices And
  Orchestra
  KALMUS A5135 sc $9.00, set $20.00,
  pts $1.00, ea., perf mat rent
                                    (V185)
Simon Boccanegra: Come In Quest' Ora
  Bruna, For Solo Voice And
  Orchestra
  KALMUS A5129 sc $4.00, set $15.00,
  pts $1.00, ea., perf mat rent
                                    (V186)
Simon Boccanegra: Figlia! A Tal Nome
  Palpito, For Solo Voices And
  Orchestra
  KALMUS A5130 sc $12.00, set $20.00,
  pts $1.00, ea., perf mat rent
                                    (V187)
Simon Boccanegra: Preludio
  (Spada, P.) sc BSE 597-00498 $5.00
                                    (V188)
Simon Boccanegra: Sento Avvampar
  Nell' Anima Furente, For Solo
  Voice And Orchestra
  KALMUS A5133 sc $5.00, set $15.00,
  pts $1.00, ea., perf mat rent
                                    (V189)
Simon Boccanegra: T'inganni... Ma Tu
  Piangevi, For Solo Voices And
  Orchestra
  KALMUS A5136 sc $12.00, set $20.00,
  pts $2.00, ea., perf mat rent
                                    (V190)
Symphony for Strings in E minor,
  [arr.]
  (Drew) string orch [25'] KALMUS
  A4543 sc $25.00, set $25.00,
  $5.00, ea., perf mat rent (V191)
Traviata, La: Prelude, Act III
  CHOUDENS perf mat rent   (V192)
Vespri Siciliani, I: D' Ira Fremo
  All' Aspetto Tremendo, For Solo
  Voices And Orchestra
  KALMUS A5072 sc $3.00, set $6.00,
  pts $.75, ea.   (V193)
Vespri Siciliani, I: Deh! Tu Calma, O
  Dio Possente, For Solo Voice And
  Orchestra
  KALMUS A5071 sc $5.00, set $22.00,
  pts $1.00, ea., perf mat rent
                                    (V194)
Vespri Siciliani, I: Giorno Di
  Pianto, Di Fier Dolore, For Solo
  Voice And Orchestra
  KALMUS A5079 sc $7.00, set $22.00,
  pts $1.00, ea., perf mat rent
                                    (V195)
Vespri Siciliani, I: In Braccio Alle
  Dovizie, For Solo Voice And
  Orchestra
  KALMUS A5076 sc $4.00, set $15.00,
  pts $1.00, ea.   (V196)
Vespri Siciliani, I: Merce, Dilette
  Amiche, For Solo Voice And
  Orchestra
  KALMUS A5083 sc $6.00, set $25.00,
  pts $1.00, ea., perf mat rent
                                    (V197)
Vespri Siciliani, I: Overture
  min sc KALMUS K01434 $4.00 (V198)
Vespri Siciliani, I: Qual E Il Tuo
  Nome, For Solo Voices And
  Orchestra
  KALMUS A5073 sc $10.00, set $35.00,
  pts $2.00, ea., perf mat rent
                                    (V199)
Vespri Siciliani, I: Quale, O Prode,
  Al Tuo Coraggio, For Solo Voices
  And Orchestra
  KALMUS A5074 sc $4.00, set $15.00,
  pts $1.00, ea.   (V200)
Vespri Siciliani, I: Quando Al Mio
  Sen Per Te Parlava, For Solo
  Voices And Orchestra
  KALMUS A5077 sc $12.00, set $40.00,
  pts $3.00, ea., perf mat rent
                                    (V201)
Vespri Siciliani, I: Sorte Fatal! O
  Fier Cimento, For Solo Voices And
  Orchestra
  KALMUS A5084 sc $12.00, set $40.00,
  pts $2.00, ea., perf mat rent
                                    (V202)
Vespri Siciliani, I: Vogli Il Guardo
  A Me Sereno, For Solo Voices And
  Orchestra
  KALMUS A5080 sc $10.00, set $35.00,
  pts $2.00, ea., perf mat rent

VERDI, GIUSEPPE (cont'd.)
(V203)

VERDICHTE WALZER see Strauss, Eduard

VERGNUGUNGSZUG [ARR.] see Strauss, Johann, [Jr.]

VERHOFF, CARLOS H. (1926-)
Prologue [9']
3.3.3.3.sax. 4.4.3.1. timp,perc, harp,pno,strings
sc PETERS P5961 $16.50 (V204)

Texture [11']
string orch
sc PETERS P8149 $27.50 (V205)

VERITA NELL'INGNANNO, LA: NICOMEDES' ARIA, FOR SOLO VOICE AND ORCHESTRA see Caldara, Antonio

VERLAINE SUITE see Hall, Pauline

VERLIEBTE AUGEN see Strauss, Josef

VERLIEBTE SERENADE, FOR SOLO VOICE AND ORCHESTRA see Bartos, A.

VERLOEDERING 3, DE, FOR MARIMBA AND ORCHESTRA see Kinkelder, Dolf de

VERONICAS BON, FOR SOLO VOICE AND ORCHESTRA see Groven, Eivind

VERRALL, JOHN WEEDON (1908-)
Divertimento
string orch
HIGHGATE sc $3.50, pts $.75, ea. (V206)

Rhapsody for Horn and String Orchestra [14']
string orch,horn solo
AM.COMP.AL. sc $12.25, pts $1.60 (V207)

Summerland Fantasy [8']
3.2+English horn.2+bass clar.3. 4.3.3.1. timp,perc,harp,strings
sc AM.COMP.AL. $17.25, perf mat rent (V208)

Winters Tale, A [6']
2.2.2.2. 4.2.2.1. timp,perc, strings
AM.COMP.AL. perf mat rent (V209)

VERS see Tremblay, Gilles

VERS BYZANCE, FOR VIOLA AND STRING ORCHESTRA see Jevtic, Ivan

VERS LA PLAGE LOINTAINE NOCTURNE see Koechlin, Charles

VERS, L'ARC-EN-CIEL, PALMA, FOR OBOE D'AMORE, GUITAR AND ORCHESTRA see Takemitsu, Toru

VERS LE SOLEIL, FOR PIANO AND CHAMBER ORCHESTRA see Tremblay, Gilles

VERSCHÜTTETE ZEICHEN see Killmayer, Wilhelm

VERSES OF MOURNING see Suben, Joel Eric

VERSUNKEN IN DIE NACHT, FOR SOLO VOICE AND CHAMBER ORCHESTRA see Leyendecker, Ulrich

VERSUS see Halffter, Cristobal

VERTICAL SHRINES see Ott, David

VERTIGE see Francesconi, Luca

VERWANDLUNG see Leyendecker, Ulrich

VERWIRRUNG, FOR VIOLONCELLO AND ORCHESTRA see Lampersberg, Gerhard

VESNYANKY see Dychko, Liudmyla

VESPERGESANG [ARR.] see Bortniansky, Dimitri Stepanovich

VESPERS see Powers, Anthony

VESPRI SICILIANI, I: D' IRA FREMO ALL' ASPETTO TREMENDO, FOR SOLO VOICES AND ORCHESTRA see Verdi, Giuseppe

VESPRI SICILIANI, I: DEH! TU CALMA, O DIO POSSENTE, FOR SOLO VOICE AND ORCHESTRA see Verdi, Giuseppe

VESPRI SICILIANI, I: GIORNO DI PIANTO, DI FIER DOLORE, FOR SOLO VOICE AND ORCHESTRA see Verdi, Giuseppe

VESPRI SICILIANI, I: IN BRACCIO ALLE DOVIZIE, FOR SOLO VOICE AND ORCHESTRA see Verdi, Giuseppe

VESPRI SICILIANI, I: MERCE, DILETTE AMICHE, FOR SOLO VOICE AND ORCHESTRA see Verdi, Giuseppe

VESPRI SICILIANI, I: OVERTURE see Verdi, Giuseppe

VESPRI SICILIANI, I: QUAL E IL TUO NOME, FOR SOLO VOICES AND ORCHESTRA see Verdi, Giuseppe

VESPRI SICILIANI, I: QUALE, O PRODE, AL TUO CORAGGIO, FOR SOLO VOICES AND ORCHESTRA see Verdi, Giuseppe

VESPRI SICILIANI, I: QUANDO AL MIO SEN PER TE PARLAVA, FOR SOLO VOICES AND ORCHESTRA see Verdi, Giuseppe

VESPRI SICILIANI, I: SORTE FATAL! O FIER CIMENTO, FOR SOLO VOICES AND ORCHESTRA see Verdi, Giuseppe

VESPRI SICILIANI, I: VOGLI IL GUARDO A ME SERENO, FOR SOLO VOICES AND ORCHESTRA see Verdi, Giuseppe

VESTALE, LA: SINFONIA [ARR.] see Spontini, Gaspare

VESTAS FEUER: SCENE, FOR SOLO VOICES AND ORCHESTRA see Beethoven, Ludwig van

VESTAS FEUER: SCENE, FOR SOLO VOICES AND ORCHESTRA [ARR.] see Beethoven, Ludwig van

VEUILLEZ AGREGER LES SENTIMENTS MES PLUS DISTINCTS, FOR HARPSICHORD AND STRING ORCHESTRA see Dion, Denis

VEZINA, JOSEPH
Ton Sourire [9']
3.2.2.2. 4.4.3.1. timp,perc, strings
sc,pts CAN.MUS.HER. f.s. (V210)

VIANELLO, RICCARDO (1944-)
Eclissi [7']
2.2.2.2.sax. 1.1.1.1. timp,perc, harp,strings
SONZOGNO perf mat rent (V211)

VIBRASJONER see Kvam, Oddvar S.

VIBRATIONEN WALZER see Strauss, Johann, [Jr.]

VIBRATIONS see Kvam, Oddvar S., Vibrasjoner

VIBRATIONS, FOR HARPE CELTIQUE AND STRING ORCHESTRA see Brenet, Therese

VICTOIRE DE LA VIE see Koechlin, Charles

VICTORIA GENNEM SKOVEN, FOR SOLO VOICE AND ORCHESTRA see Colding-Jorgensen, Henrik

VICTORIA POLKA see Strauss, Josef

VICTORIA THROUGH THE FOREST, FOR SOLO VOICE AND ORCHESTRA see Colding-Jorgensen, Henrik, Victoria Gennem Skoven, For Solo Voice And Orchestra

VICTORIAN SUITE see Jouard, Paul E.

VICTORY, GERARD (1921-)
Concerto for Harp and Orchestra [16']
1.2.0.2. 2.0.0.0. strings,harp solo
NOVELLO perf mat rent (V212)

Four Tableaux [25']
3(pic).2.3(bass clar).3.alto sax. 4.3.3.1. timp,3perc,pno,cel, harp,strings
NOVELLO perf mat rent (V213)

Jonathan Swift
3(pic).3(English horn).3(bass clar).3(contrabsn). 4.4.3.1. timp,3perc,harp,cel,hpsd, strings
NOVELLO perf mat rent (V214)

VID ALVOM, PA BERG OCH I DALOM see Sköld, Sven

VIDA BREVE, LA: INTERLUDE AND SPANISH DANCE [ARR.] see Falla, Manuel de

VIDAR, JORUNN (1918-)
Concerto for Piano and Orchestra
2horn,trom,xylo,strings,pno solo
ICELAND 015-001 (V215)

Olafur Liljuros [26'30"]
2.2.2.2. 3.2.2.0. timp,perc,pno, strings

VIDAR, JORUNN (cont'd.)
ICELAND 015-003 (V216)

VIDOVSZKY, LASZLO (1944-)
Romantic Reading
sc EMB 12679 f.s., perf mat rent (V217)

VIE PARISIENNE, LA: OVERTURE [ARR.] see Offenbach, Jacques

VIE PARISIENNE, LA: QUADRILLE see Offenbach, Jacques

VIEJECITA, LA see Gerhard, Roberto

VIENNA, MY CITY OF DREAMS, FOR SOLO VOICE AND ORCHESTRA, [ARR.] see Sieczynski, Rudolf

VIER APHORISMEN see Schnittke, Alfred

VIER ERNSTE GESÄNGE, FOR SOLO VOICE AND ORCHESTRA, [ARR.] see Brahms, Johannes

VIER ERNSTE GESANGE [ARR.] see Brahms, Johannes

VIER IMPRESSIONEN, FOR VIOLONCELLO AND ORCHESTRA [ARR.] see Offenbach, Jacques

VIER LIEDER, FOR SOLO VOICE AND ORCHESTRA see Steinberg, Maximilian

VIER ORCHESTERSTÜCKE see Bruckner, Anton and see Rapf, Kurt

VIER PROLOGEN see Nilsson, Bo

VIER SKIZZEN see Ledenev, Roman, Four Sketches

VIER STIMMUNGSBILDER see Fielitz, Alexander von

VIER STUCKE see Huber, Nicolaus A.

VIER TEMPERAMENTEN, DE see Delft, Marc van

VIER ZEITUNGSANNONCEN, FOR SOLO VOICE AND ORCHESTRA [ARR.] see Mossolov, Alexander, Advertisements, For Solo Voice And Orchestra [arr.]

VIERLING, GEORG (1820-1901)
Hermannsschlacht, Die *Op.31 [12']
2.2.2.2. 4.2.3.0. timp,strings
BREITKOPF-W perf mat rent (V218)

VIERNE, LOUIS (1870-1937)
Djinns, For Solo Voice And Orchestra *Op.35 [18']
3(pic).2(English horn).3(bass clar).2(contrabsn). 4.3.3.1. timp,perc,harp,cel,strings,solo voice
LEMOINE perf mat rent (V219)

Eros, For Solo Voice And Orchestra [11']
2.3(English horn).2.3. 4.3.3.0. timp,harp,strings,solo voice
LEMOINE perf mat rent (V220)

VIERTE ABGESANGSSZENE, FOR SOLO VOICE AND ORCHESTRA see Rihm, Wolfgang

VIERTES SEE-BILD "DAS SCHWARZE WASSER", FOR SOLO VOICE AND ORCHESTRA see Trojahn, Manfred

VIERU, ANATOL (1926-)
Concerto for Violoncello and Orchestra [14']
2.2.2.2. 2.2.1.0. 2perc,cel,pno, strings,vcl solo
SALABERT perf mat rent (V221)

Ecran [15']
3.2.2+bass clar.2+contrabsn. 4.3.3.1. 3perc,strings
SALABERT perf mat rent (V222)

Jeux, For Piano And Orchestra [17']
1+pic.1.1+bass clar.0.3sax. 0.3.3.0. 3perc,bells,marimba, strings,pno solo
SALABERT perf mat rent (V223)

Museum Music, For Harpsichord And Strings [12']
7vln,2vla,2vcl,db, hpsd. or elec. hpsd solo
(these performers also play 2 light Japanese bells, maracas, musical doll) SALABERT perf mat rent (V224)

Narration II, For Saxophone And Orchestra [22']
2(pic).1.1.1. 2.2.0.0. 2perc, 2gtr/synthesizer,strings,sax solo
SALABERT perf mat rent (V225)

VIERU, ANATOL (cont'd.)

Ode Au Silence [18']
3fl,3trp,3trom,5perc,strings,
electronic tape
SALABERT perf mat rent   (V226)

VIEUXTEMPS, HENRI (1820-1881)
Tarantelle for Violin and Orchestra,
Op. 22 [4'30"]
2.2.2.2. 2.2.0.0. timp,perc,
strings,vln solo
BOTE perf mat rent   (V227)

Yankee Doodle, For Violin And String
Orchestra *Op.17 [4']
string orch,vln/vcl solo
KALMUS A7313 pno-cond sc $5.00, set
$12.00, pts $1.50, ea.   (V228)

VIEW see Tveitt, Geirr, Utsyn

VIFADANKA see Tofft, Alfred

VIGIL see Mekeel, Joyce

VIGINTOUR see Martinon, Jean

VIITANEN, HARRI (1954-   )
Firmamentum, For Organ And Orchestra
[40']
2.2.2.2. 2.2.2.3. timp,2perc,
strings,org solo
FAZER perf mat rent   (V229)

VIKINGHYMNE, OP. 59B see Karlsen, Kjell
Mørk

VILL-GURI, FOR SOLO VOICE AND ORCHESTRA
see Ørbeck, Anne Marie

VILLA-LOBOS, HEITOR (1887-1959)
Alvorada Na Floresta Tropical [12']
3.3.3.3. 4.3.4.1. timp,perc,cel,
harp,pno,strings
"Dawn In A Tropical Forest" study
sc ESCHIG f.s., perf mat rent
(V230)
Cancoes Tipicas Brasileiras, For Solo
Voice And Orchestra
2.1+English horn.1.2. 3.0.0.0.
timp,perc,harp,pno,strings,solo
voice
ESCHIG perf mat rent   (V231)

Canide-Ioune-Sabath, For Solo Voice
And Orchestra (from Tres Poemas
Indigenas)
2.2.2.3.alto sax. 3.2.2.0. timp,
perc,harp,pno,strings,Mez solo
ESCHIG perf mat rent   (V232)

Choros No. 11, For Piano And
Orchestra
4.3.4.3.soprano sax.alto sax.
4.4.4.1. timp,perc,2harp,
strings,pno solo
[65'] ESCHIG perf mat rent   (V233)

Choros No. 12 [40']
5.4.4.4.2sax. 8.4.4.1. timp,perc,
cel,harp,pno,strings
study sc ESCHIG f.s., perf mat rent
(V234)
Concerto for Piano and Orchestra, No.
1 [38']
3.3.3.3. 4.3.4.1. timp,perc,harp,
strings,pno solo
ESCHIG perf mat rent   (V235)

Concerto for Piano and Orchestra, No.
2 [30']
3.3.3.3. 4.2.4.1. timp,perc,harp,
strings,pno solo
ESCHIG perf mat rent   (V236)

Concerto for Piano and Orchestra, No.
3 [30']
3.3.3.3. 4.2.2.1. timp,perc,cel,
harp,strings,pno solo
ESCHIG perf mat rent   (V237)

Concerto for Piano and Orchestra, No.
4 [30']
3.3.3.3. 4.2.2.1. timp,perc,
strings,pno solo
ESCHIG perf mat rent   (V238)

Concerto for Piano and Orchestra, No.
5 [20']
3.3.3.3. 4.2.3.1. timp,perc,cel,
harp,strings,pno solo
ESCHIG perf mat rent   (V239)

Concerto for Violoncello and
Orchestra, No. 1 [22']
3.2.2.2. 4.3.3.1. timp,harp,
strings,vcl solo
ESCHIG perf mat rent   (V240)

Concerto for Violoncello and
Orchestra, No. 2 [20']
3.3.3.3. 4.2.3.1. timp,perc,cel,
harp,strings,vcl solo
ESCHIG perf mat rent   (V241)

VILLA-LOBOS, HEITOR (cont'd.)

Danca Dos Mosquitos [8']
3.3.3.3. 4.4.4.1. timp,perc,cel,
harp,pno,strings
ESCHIG perf mat rent   (V242)

Danca Frenetica [8']
3.3.3.3. 4.4.3.1. timp,perc,cel,
harp,strings
ESCHIG perf mat rent   (V243)

Dawn In A Tropical Forest
see Alvorada Na Floresta Tropical

Descobrimento Do Brasil: Suite No. 1
[12']
3.3.3.3.alto sax. 4.3.3.1. timp,
perc,pno,cel,harp,strings
ESCHIG perf mat rent   (V244)

Descobrimento Do Brasil: Suite No. 2
[14']
3.3.3.3.alto sax. 4.3.3.1. timp,
perc,cel,harp,pno,strings
ESCHIG perf mat rent   (V245)

Descobrimento Do Brasil: Suite No. 3
[15']
4.3.3.3.alto sax. 4.4.4.1. timp,
perc,cel,harp,pno,strings
ESCHIG perf mat rent   (V246)

Eu Te Amo, For Solo Voice And
Orchestra [3']
3.3.3.3. 4.2.2.1. timp,perc,cel,
harp,strings,solo voice
ESCHIG perf mat rent   (V247)

Fantasia Concertante, For Orchestra
Of Violoncellos [24']
32vcl, (minimum)
ESCHIG perf mat rent   (V248)

Genesis [20']
3.3.3.3. 4.2.3.1. timp,perc,cel,
harp,pno,strings
study sc ESCHIG f.s., perf mat rent
(V249)
Iara, For Solo Voice And Orchestra
(from Tres Poemas Indigenas)
2.2.2.3.alto sax. 3.2.2.0. timp,
cel,harp,pno,strings,Mez solo
ESCHIG perf mat rent   (V250)

Izaht: Prelude [3']
3.3.3.3. 4.3.3.1. timp,perc,
2harp,strings
ESCHIG perf mat rent   (V251)

Madona [14']
5.4.4.4. 6.4.4.1. timp,perc,cel,
2harp,pno,strings
ESCHIG perf mat rent   (V252)

Magdalena: Suite No. 1 [8']
1.1.1.1.alto sax. 2.2.2.1. timp,
perc,cel,harp,strings
ESCHIG perf mat rent   (V253)

Magdalena: Suite No. 2 [8']
1.1.1.2.alto sax. 4.2.2.1. timp,
perc,cel,harp,pno,strings
ESCHIG perf mat rent   (V254)

Modinhas E Cancoes, First Suite, No.
1: Cancao Do Marinheiro, For Solo
Voice And Orchestra
1.2.2.2.alto sax. 2.1.1.1. harp,
strings,solo voice
[3'] ESCHIG perf mat rent   (V255)

Modinhas E Cancoes, First Suite, No.
2: Lundu Da Marqueza De Santos,
For Solo Voice And Orchestra [3']
1.1.1.2. 2.0.0.0. timp,harp,
strings,solo voice
ESCHIG perf mat rent   (V256)

Modinhas E Cancoes, First Suite, No.
3: Remeiro De Sao-Francisco, For
Solo Voice And Orchestra [3']
2.3.2.3. 4.0.2.1. timp,harp,
strings,solo voice
ESCHIG perf mat rent   (V257)

Modinhas E Cancoes, First Suite, No.
4: Nhapope, For Solo Voice And
Orchestra [3']
1.1.2.2. 2.1.0.0. harp,strings,
solo voice
ESCHIG perf mat rent   (V258)

Modinhas E Cancoes, First Suite, No.
5: Evocacao, For Solo Voice And
Orchestra
3.3.3.2. 3.1.2.1. timp,cel,harp,
strings,solo voice
ESCHIG perf mat rent   (V259)

Modinhas E Cancoes, Second Suite, No.
1: Pobre Peregrino, For Solo
Voice And Orchestra
2.2.3.3. 4.2.2.1. timp,perc,harp,
strings,solo voice
ESCHIG perf mat rent   (V260)

VILLA-LOBOS, HEITOR (cont'd.)

Modinhas E Cancoes, Second Suite,
No.3: Nesta Rua, For Solo Voice
And Orchestra [2']
2.2.2.2. 2.0.0.0. harp,strings,
solo voice
ESCHIG perf mat rent   (V261)

Modinhas E Cancoes, Second Suite, No.
4: Manda Tiro, Tiro La, For Solo
Voice And Orchestra [2']
2.2.2.2. 2.0.0.0. timp,harp,
strings,solo voice
ESCHIG perf mat rent   (V262)

Naufragio De Kleonicos [12']
3.3.3.3. 4.3.4.1. timp,perc,harp,
strings
ESCHIG perf mat rent   (V263)

New York Skyline Melody [6']
2.2.1.1.sax. 3.1.1.0. timp,perc,
cel,harp,strings
study sc ESCHIG f.s., perf mat rent
(V264)
O Papagaio Do Moleque [14']
3.3.3.3.sax. 4.4.4.1. timp,perc,
cel,2harp,pno,strings
study sc ESCHIG f.s., perf mat rent
(V265)
Poema De Itabira, For Solo Voice And
Orchestra [15']
3.3.3.3. 4.2.4.1. timp,perc,cel,
harp,pno,strings,solo voice
ESCHIG perf mat rent   (V266)

Poema De Palavras, For Solo Voice And
Orchestra [3']
2.2.3.2. 3.1.2.1. timp,cel,harp,
strings,solo voice
ESCHIG perf mat rent   (V267)

Ruda
4.3.3.3.soprano sax. 4.4.4.1.
timp,perc,cel,2harp,pno,strings
[40'] ESCHIG perf mat rent   (V268)

Samba Classico, For Solo Voice And
Orchestra [4']
2.2.3.2. 4.3.4.1. timp,perc,harp,
strings,solo voice
ESCHIG perf mat rent   (V269)

Sete Vezes, For Solo Voice And
Orchestra [2']
2.1.3.3. 2.3.2.1. timp,harp,
strings,solo voice
ESCHIG perf mat rent   (V270)

Suite for Piano and Orchestra [25']
3.2.2.2. 2.2.2.1. timp,strings,
pno solo
ESCHIG perf mat rent   (V271)

Suite No. 1 for Chamber Orchestra
[18']
2.2.2.2. 2.2.2.1. timp,strings
ESCHIG perf mat rent   (V272)

Suite No. 2 for Chamber Orchestra
[18']
2.2.2.2. 2.2.2.1. timp,strings
ESCHIG perf mat rent   (V273)

Symphony No. 1 [22']
4.3.3.3. 4.4.3.1. timp,perc,cel,
2harp,strings
(O Imprevisto) ESCHIG perf mat rent
(V274)
Symphony No. 8 [22']
4.3.3.3. 4.4.4.1. timp,perc,cel,
pno,2harp,strings
ESCHIG perf mat rent   (V275)

Symphony No. 9 [20']
3.3.3.3. 4.4.4.1. timp,perc,cel,
harp,strings
ESCHIG perf mat rent   (V276)

Symphony No. 10 [70']
4.3.4.3. 4.4.4.1. timp,perc,cel,
2harp,pno,strings,TBarB soli,
mix cor
(Sinfonia Amerindia) ESCHIG perf
mat rent   (V277)

Symphony No. 11 [22']
4.3.3.3. 4.4.3.1. timp,perc,cel,
2harp,pno,strings
ESCHIG perf mat rent   (V278)

Symphony No. 12 [20']
3.3.3.3. 4.4.4.1. timp,perc,cel,
harp,strings
ESCHIG perf mat rent   (V279)

VILLA ROJO, JESUS (1940-   )
Concerto Grosso No. 1 [15']
ob,clar,bsn,strings
sc ALPUERTO f.s.   (V280)

Formas Planas [18']
4vln,3vla,3vcl,2db
sc ALPUERTO f.s.   (V281)

VILLA ROJO, JESUS (cont'd.)

Rupturas [16']
2+alto fl.2+English horn.2+bass
clar.2+contrabsn. 6.3.3.1.
strings
ALPUERTO (V282)

VILLAGE ROMEO AND JULIET, A: WALTZ
[ARR.] see Delius, Frederick

VILLANELLE, FOR HORN AND ORCHESTRA
[ARR.] see Dukas, Paul

VILLANELLE, DIRGE AND SONG, FOR SOLO
VOICE AND ORCHESTRA see Pleskow,
Raoul

VILLANELLE DU DIABLE see Loeffler,
Charles Martin

VILLEMO, FOR SOLO VOICE AND ORCHESTRA
see Rangström, Ture

VILLI, LE: SE COME VOI, FOR SOLO VOICE
AND ORCHESTRA see Puccini, Giacomo

VINCI, ALBERT (1937-)
Concerto for Bassoon and Orchestra
[12']
pno,strings,bsn solo
KALMUS A6141 sc $12.00, set $10.00
(V283)
Dance Suite [15']
1.1.1.1. 1.2.1.0. perc,strings
KALMUS A4144 sc $35.00, set $30.00,
perf mat rent (V284)

VINCI, LEONARDO (1690-1730)
Didone Abbandonata [7']
2trp,hpsd,strings
SUPRAPHON (V285)

VINCZE, IMRE (1926-1969)
Symphony No. 3
sc EMB 5198 f.s. (V286)

VINE, CARL (1954-)
Concerto for Percussion and Orchestra
[10']
2.2.2.2. 4.2.3.0. strings,perc
solo
CHESTER perf mat rent (V287)

Microsymphony [12']
2.2.2.2. 4.2.3.1. 2perc,pno,
strings
CHESTER perf mat rent (V288)

Symphony No. 2 [20']
2+pic.2+English horn.2+bass
clar.2+contrabsn. 4.3.3.1.
timp,3perc,harp,strings
CHESTER perf mat rent (V289)

VINGT-QUATRE VIOLONS DU ROY, LES
*CC24U
(Paillard, J.F.) hpsd,strings COSTALL
C.3460 f.s. contains 17th century
French dances (V290)

VINTER, GILBERT (1909-1969)
Dance Of The Marionettes [12']
2.1.2.1. 0.0.0.0. strings
BOOSEY perf mat rent (V291)

VIOLA-MOBILE, FOR VIOLA AND CHAMBER
ORCHESTRA see Newell, Robert M.

VIOLIN AND ORCHESTRA see Feldman,
Morton

VIOLINKONZERTE UND EINZELSATZE see
Mozart, Wolfgang Amadeus, Concerti
for Violin and Orchestra

VIOTTI, GIOVANNI BATTISTA (1755-1824)
Concerto for Violin and Orchestra,
No. 7, in B flat
see Four Violin Concertos, Part I

Concerto for Violin and Orchestra,
No. 13, in A
see Four Violin Concertos, Part I

Concerto for Violin and Orchestra,
No. 18, in E minor
see Four Violin Concertos, Part II

Concerto for Violin and Orchestra,
No. 27, in C
see Four Violin Concertos, Part II

Four Violin Concertos, Part I
(White, Chappell) sc A-R ED
ISBN 0-89579-075-0 f.s.
contains: Concerto for Violin and
Orchestra, No. 7, in B flat;
Concerto for Violin and
Orchestra, No. 13, in A (V292)

Four Violin Concertos, Part II
(White, Chappell) sc A-R ED
ISBN 0-89579-075-0 f.s.
contains: Concerto for Violin and
Orchestra, No. 18, in E minor;

VIOTTI, GIOVANNI BATTISTA (cont'd.)

Concerto for Violin and
Orchestra, No. 27, in C (V293)

VIOZZI, GIULIO (1912-)
Concerto for Trombone and Orchestra
[17']
2.2.2.2. 2.2.1.0. timp,strings,
trom solo
SONZOGNO perf mat rent (V294)

VIRTUOSO, FOR VIOLIN AND ORCHESTRA see
Leitermeyer, Fritz

VISION, EINE see Lehar, Franz

VISION DE LA QUATRIEME EGLOGUE see
Lavagne, Andre

VISION DER WIRKLICHKEIT, FOR SOLO VOICE
AND ORCHESTRA see Kerstens, Huub

VISION I, FOR VIOLONCELLO AND
INSTRUMENTAL ENSEMBLE see Ton That,
Tiet

VISION OF COLOURS see Ajdic, Alojz,
Vizija Barv

VISION OF DAYS PAST see Firat, Ertugrul

VISION OF PIERS THE PLOUGHMAN see
Berkeley, Michael

VISIONNAIRE, LA [ARR.] see Couperin,
François (le Grand)

VISIONS see Ott, David see Wallin,
Peter

VISIONS AND WHISPERS, FOR FLUTE AND
ORCHESTRA see Merilainen, Usko

VISIONS "COLUMBUS" see Laderman, Ezra

VISIONS CONCERTANTES, FOR GUITAR AND
STRINGS see Chaynes, Charles

VISIONS FUGITIVES [ARR.] see Prokofiev,
Serge

VISIONS LITURGIQUES see DuBois, Pierre-
Max

VISIONS NORVEGIENNES see Kvandal, Johan

VISIONS OF REMEMBRANCE, FOR SOLO VOICES
AND CHAMBER ORCHESTRA see Rhodes,
Phillip

VISIONS PROPHETIQUES DE CASSANDRE, LES,
FOR SOLO VOICES AND ORCHESTRA see
Brenet, Therese

VISITOR, THE, FOR VIOLIN AND ORCHESTRA
see Hooper, Les

VISTULA see Speight, John A.

VITALI, TOMMASO ANTONIO (ca. 1665- ?)
Ciaccona, For Violin And String
Orchestra [arr.]
(Respighi) string orch,org,vln solo
KALMUS A6091 sc $10.00, set $7.00
(V295)
Ciacconna, For Violin And Orchestra,
[arr.]
(Diepenbrock, Alphons) 2.3.0.0.
0.0.2.0. timp,strings,vln solo
[12'] sc DONEMUS f.s., perf mat
rent (V296)

VITRAIL see Desenclos, Alfred

VITRAIL POUR UN TEMPS DE GUERRE see
Charpentier, Jacques

VITRAL "MUSICA CELESTIAL NO. 1", FOR
ORGAN AND ORCHESTRA see Marco,
Tomas

VITTORIA, MARIO (1911-1984)
Concerto for Oboe and Orchestra
[13'30"]
2.2.2.2. 2.2.1.0. timp,perc,
strings,ob solo
BILLAUDOT perf mat rent (V297)

VITTORIA, V.
Concertino for Strings [15']
string orch
CHOUDENS perf mat rent (V298)

VIVALDI, ANTONIO (1678-1741)
Cetra, La, Op. 9, Vol. 1
(Malipiero) sc RICORDI-IT PR 1237
$17.00 (V299)

Cetra, La, Op. 9, Vol. 2
(Malipiero) sc RICORDI-IT PR 1238
$17.75 (V300)

Clarae Stellae, Scintillate, For Solo
Voice And String Orchestra *RV
625

VIVALDI, ANTONIO (cont'd.)

string orch,A solo
(Everett, P.) RICORDI-IT sc PR 1292
f.s., pts 134925 f.s. (V301)

Concerti, Five
min sc KALMUS K00063 $7.00
contains: Concerto, RV 212a, Op.
35, No. 19, in D, P. 165, F.I
no. 136; Concerto, RV 522, Op.
3, No. 8, in A minor, P. 2, F.I
no. 177; Concerto, RV 565, Op.
3, No. 11, in D minor, P. 250,
F.IV no. 11; Concerto, RV 578,
Op. 3, No. 2, in G minor, P.
326, F.IV no. 8; Concerto, RV
580, Op. 3, No. 10, in B minor,
P. 148, F.IV no. 10 (V302)

Concerto for Violoncello and
Orchestra in E minor, [arr.]
(from Sonata, Op. 14, No. 5)
[12']
(Bazelaire) string orch,vcl solo
KALMUS A5617 sc $3.00, set $6.00,
pts $1.00, ea. (V303)

Concerto in A *reconstruction
(Kipnis, Igor) string orch,hpsd
solo [10'] OXFORD sc 93.007
$18.95, kbd pt 93.006 $9.95, pts
$3.00, ea. (V304)

Concerto in C, MIN 168
(Rougeron) string orch,2fl soli
LEDUC sc AL 26322 f.s., pts
AL 26323 f.s. (V305)

Concerto in D, MIN 188, [arr.]
(Thilde, J.) string orch,trp solo
[10'35"] sc BILLAUDOT f.s., perf
mat rent (V306)

Concerto in F, [arr.]
(Thilde, J.) string orch,hpsd,trp
solo [7'30"] BILLAUDOT perf mat
rent (V307)

Concerto in G, [arr.]
(Jevtic, I.) string orch,trp solo
[7'30"] BILLAUDOT perf mat rent
(V308)

Concerto, MIN 736, [arr.]
(Stevens, Thomas) string orch,4trp
soli [9'] INTERNAT. perf mat rent
(V309)

Concerto, RV 129, Op. 54, No. 1, in D
minor, P. 86, F.XI no. 10
(Fodor) EMB f.s. sc 6538, pts 6539
(V310)

Concerto, RV 151, Op. 51, No. 4, in
G, P. 143, F.XI no. 11
min sc KALMUS K01444 $4.00 (V311)

Concerto, RV 198a, Op. 9, No. 11, in
C minor, P. 416, F.I no. 58
min sc KALMUS K01441 $4.00 (V312)

Concerto, RV 208a, Op. 7, No. 11, P.
151, F.I no. 206
min sc KALMUS K01438 $4.00 (V313)

Concerto, RV 212a, Op. 35, No. 19, in
D, P. 165, F.I no. 136
see Concerti, Five

Concerto, RV 214, Op. 7, No. 12, in
D, P. 152, F.I no. 207
min sc KALMUS K01439 $4.00 (V314)

Concerto, RV 230, Op. 3, No. 9, in D,
P. 147, F.I no. 178
(Upmeyer) KALMUS A6358 sc $7.00,
set $9.00, pts $1.50, ea., perf
mat rent (V315)

Concerto, RV 256, in E flat, F.I no.
231
study sc EMB 40035 f.s. (V316)

Concerto, RV 269, Op. 8, No. 1, in E,
P. 241, F.I no. 22
see Quattro Stagioni, Le

Concerto, RV 293, Op. 8, No. 3, in F,
P. 257, F.I no. 24
see Quattro Stagioni, Le

Concerto, RV 297, Op. 8, No. 4, in F
minor, P. 442, F.I no. 25
see Quattro Stagioni, Le

Concerto, RV 300, Op. 9, No. 10, in
G, P. 103, F.I no. 49
min sc KALMUS K01440 $4.00 (V317)

Concerto, RV 315, Op. 8, No. 2, in G
minor, P. 336, F.I no. 23
see Quattro Stagioni, Le

Concerto, RV 324, Op. 6, No. 1, in G
minor, P. 329, F.I no. 192,
[arr.]
(Chavez, Carlos) 3.3.3.3. 4.3.3.1.
timp,2perc,pno,strings [14']

VIVALDI, ANTONIO (cont'd.)

CARLAN perf mat rent (V318)

Concerto, RV 326, Op. 7, No. 3, in G minor, P. 332, F.I no. 199 (Fechner) sc PETERS 9833 $23.75 (V319)

Concerto, RV 340, in A, P. 228, F.I no. 141 (Landshoff) sc PETERS P4206 f.s. (V320)

Concerto, RV 356, Op. 3, No. 6, in A minor, P. 1, F.I no. 176 (Einstein) KALMUS A6185 sc $8.00, set $6.00 (V321) (Eller) sc,pts PETERS 3794A $6.00 (V322)

Concerto, RV 369, Op. 33, No. 4, in B flat, P. 356, F.I no. 65 string orch,cont,vln solo (Heller) PETERS P9464 (V323)

Concerto, RV 399, Op. 26, No. 8, in C, P. 33, F.III no. 6 (Mariassy; Pejtsik) sc EMB 12048 f.s., perf mat rent (V324)

Concerto, RV 400, Op. 26, No. 1, in C, P. 30, F.III no. 3 KUNZEL 10176 sc $12.00, pts $3.00, ea., solo pt $12.00 (V325)

Concerto, RV 413, Op. 26, No. 16, in G, P. 120, F.III no. 12 (Fodor) EMB f.s. sc 6423, pts 6424 (V326)

Concerto, RV 445, Op. 44, No. 26, in A minor, P. 83, F.VI no. 9 (Nagy) EMB f.s. sc 5569, pts 5570 (V327)

Concerto, RV 447, Op. 39, No. 1, in C, P. 41, F.VII no. 6 (Lampert) EMB f.s. sc 6468, pts 6469 (V328)

Concerto, RV 451, Op. 39, No. 4, in C, P. 44, F.VII no. 4 (Károlyi) EMB f.s. sc 6629, pts 6630 (V329)

Concerto, RV 480, Op. 40, No. 4, in C minor, P. 432, F.VIII no. 14 (Allard, Maurice) sc BILLAUDOT $17.75 (V330)

Concerto, RV 484, Op. 45, No. 2, in E minor, P. 137, F.VIII no. 6 BILLAUDOT perf mat rent (V331)

Concerto, RV 485, Op. 45, No. 5, in F, P. 318, F.VIII no. 8 (Balla) EMB f.s. sc 7004, pts 7061 (V332)

Concerto, RV 488, Op. 40, No. 7, in F, P. 299, F.VIII no. 19 sc BILLAUDOT f.s., perf mat rent (V333)

Concerto, RV 497, Op. 45, No. 6, in A minor, P. 72, F.VIII no. 7 (Hara; Nagy) EMB f.s. sc 6074, pts 6075 (V334)

Concerto, RV 501, Op. 45, No. 8, in B flat, P. 401, F.VIII no. 1 (Allard, M.) (La Notte) sc BILLAUDOT f.s., perf mat rent (V335)

Concerto, RV 503, Op. 40, No. 3, in B flat, P. 387, F.VIII no. 35 sc BILLAUDOT f.s., perf mat rent (V336)

Concerto, RV 509, Op. 21, No. 4, in C minor, P. 436, F.I no. 12 KALMUS A7299 sc $15.00, set $12.00, pts $1.50, ea. (V337)

Concerto, RV 522, Op. 3, No. 8, in A minor, P. 2, F.I no. 177 see Concerti, Five

Concerto, RV 524, Op. 21, No. 5, in B flat, P. 390, F.I no. 40 (Berlász) EMB f.s. sc 6481, pts 6482 (V338)

Concerto, RV 534, Op. 53, No. 1, in C, P. 85, F.VII no. 3 (Nagy) EMB f.s. sc 5660, pts 5661 (V339)

Concerto, RV 537, Op. 46, No. 1, in C, P. 75, F.IX no. 1 MUS. RARA perf mat rent (V340)

Concerto, RV 549, Op. 3, No. 1, in D, P. 146, F.IV no. 7 (Upmeyer) KALMUS A6359 sc $10.00, set $10.00, pts $1.50, ea., perf mat rent (V341)

Concerto, RV 550, Op. 3, No. 4, in E minor, P. 97, F.I no. 174 (Upmeyer) KALMUS A6360 sc $8.00, set $10.00, pts $1.50, ea., perf mat rent (V342)

Concerto, RV 550, Op. 3, No. 4, in E minor, P. 97, F.I no. 174, [arr.] (Hashimoto, Eiji) string orch,4hpsd sc ZEN-ON f.s., perf mat rent (V343)

Concerto, RV 551, Op. 23, No. 1, in F, P. 278, F.I no. 34 (Bonelli) KALMUS A7321 sc $10.00, set $12.00, pts $1.50, ea. (V344) (Károlyi) EMB f.s. sc 6465, pts 6466 (V345)

Concerto, RV 565, Op. 3, No. 11, in D minor, P. 250, F.IV no. 11 SCHOTTS sc CON 165 $9.00, set CON 165BS $21.00 (V346) sc,pts TONGER f.s. (V347) see Concerti, Five

Concerto, RV 567, Op. 3, No. 7, in F, P. 249, F.IV no. 9 (Upmeyer) KALMUS A6361 sc $8.00, set $10.00, pts $1.50, ea., perf mat rent (V348)

Concerto, RV 578, Op. 3, No. 2, in G minor, P. 326, F.IV no. 8 see Concerti, Five

Concerto, RV 580, Op. 3, No. 10, in B minor, P. 148, F.IV no. 10 (Upmeyer) KALMUS A6362 sc $10.00, set $16.00, pts $2.00, ea., perf mat rent (V349) see Concerti, Five

Concerto, RV 761, in C minor, F.I no. 239 string orch,cont,vln solo (Everett, Paul; Talbot, Michael) sc RICORDI-IT f.s. (V350)

Concerto, RV 763, in A, F.I no. 240 (Everett, Paul; Talbot, Michael) string orch,cont,vln solo (L'Ottavina) sc RICORDI-IT f.s. (V351)

Concerto, RV 765, in F string orch,cont,2vln solo (Everett, Paul; Talbot, Michael) sc RICORDI-IT PR 1248 $24.25 (V352)

Farnace: Al Vezzeggiar D'un Volto, For Solo Voice And String Orchestra string orch,S solo SONZOGNO perf mat rent (V353)

Farnace: Combattono Quest'alma, For Solo Voice And Orchestra [6'] ob,strings,Mez solo (Prato, G.) SONZOGNO perf mat rent (V354)

Farnace: Da Quel Ferro Che Ha Svenato, For Solo Voice And String Orchestra [5'] string orch,S/Mez solo (Prato, G.) SONZOGNO perf mat rent (V355)

Farnace: Forse, O Caro, In Questi Accenti, For Solo Voice And Orchestra [8'] ob,strings,Mez solo (Prato, G.) SONZOGNO perf mat rent (V356)

Farnace: Gelido In Ogni Vena, For Solo Voice And Orchestra [10'] ob,strings,S/Mez/T solo (Prato, G.) SONZOGNO perf mat rent (V357)

Farnace: Lascia Di Sospirar, For Solo Voice And String Orchestra [4'] string orch,S solo (Prato, G.) SONZOGNO perf mat rent (V358)

Farnace: Nell'intimo Del Petto, For Solo Voice And Orchestra [4'] 2ob,strings,S solo (Prato, G.) SONZOGNO perf mat rent (V359)

Farnace: Ricordati Che Sei, For Solo Voice And String Orchestra [4'] string orch,Mez/T solo (Prato, G.) SONZOGNO perf mat rent (V360)

Farnace: Roma Invitta, Ma Clemente, For Solo Voice And String Orchestra [4'30"] string orch,A/Mez solo (Prato, G.) SONZOGNO perf mat rent (V361)

Farnace: Sinfonia [6'] string orch (Prato, G.) SONZOGNO perf mat rent (V362)

Farnace: Sorge L'irato Nembo, For Solo Voices And Orchestra [6'] 2ob,strings,AMez soli (Prato, G.) SONZOGNO perf mat rent (V363)

Filiae Maestae Jerusalem, For Solo Voice And String Orchestra *RV 638 string orch,A solo

VIVALDI, ANTONIO (cont'd.)

(Talbot, Michael) sc RICORDI-IT f.s. (V364)

Gaude Mater Ecclesia, For Solo Voice And String Orchestra *RV 613 string orch,S solo (Arnold, Denis) sc RICORDI-IT f.s. (V365)

Inturbato Mare Irato, For Solo Voice And String Orchestra *RV 627 string orch,S solo (Talbot, M.) RICORDI-IT sc PR 1290 f.s., pts 134928 f.s. (V366)

Largo, [arr.] (from Concerto For Lute And Strings, Rv 93) (Drew) string orch [4'] set KALMUS A7279 $22.00, and up (V367)

Nisi Dominus, For Solo Voice And String Orchestra (Psalm No. 126 for Solo Voice and String Orchestra, RV 608) string orch,cont,A solo (Degrada) RICORDI-IT sc 131676 $5.50, pts 131677-I-VI $2.50, ea., kbd pt 131677-VII $4.50 (V368)

Non In Pratis Aut In Hortis, For Solo Voice And String Orchestra *RV 641 string orch,A solo (Talbot, Michael) sc RICORDI-IT f.s. (V369)

Nulla In Mundo Pax Sincere, For Solo Voice And String Orchestra *RV 630 string orch,S solo (Everett, P.) RICORDI-IT sc PR 1294 f.s., pts 134911 f.s. (V370)

O Mie Porpore Piu Belle, For Solo Voice And String Orchestra *RV 685 string orch,A solo (Delgrada, F.) RICORDI-IT sc PR 1289 f.s., pts 134710 f.s. (V371)

O Qui Coeli Terraeque Serenitas, For Solo Voice And String Orchestra *RV 631 string orch,S solo (Everett, P.) RICORDI-IT sc PR 1293 f.s., pts 134929 f.s. (V372)

Psalm No. 126 for Solo Voice and String Orchestra, RV 608 see Nisi Dominus, For Solo Voice And String Orchestra

Quattro Stagioni, Le study sc EMB 40039 f.s. contains: Concerto, RV 269, Op. 8, No. 1, in E, P. 241, F.I no. 22; Concerto, RV 293, Op. 8, No. 3, in F, P. 257, F.I no. 24; Concerto, RV 297, Op. 8, No. 4, in F minor, P. 442, F.I no. 25; Concerto, RV 315, Op. 8, No. 2, in G minor, P. 336, F.I no. 23 (V373)

Sanctorum Meritis, For Solo Voice And String Orchestra *RV 620 string orch,S solo (Arnold, Denis) sc RICORDI-IT f.s. (V374)

Sinfonia From RV719 see Sinfonias Nos. 1 And 2

Sinfonia Or Concerto, RV146 see Sinfonias Nos. 1 And 2

Sinfonias Nos. 1 And 2 (Landshoff) string orch,cont KALMUS A7380 sc $8.00, set $12.50, pts $2.50, ea. contains: Sinfonia From RV719; Sinfonia Or Concerto, RV146 (V375)

Stabat Mater, For Solo Voice And String Orchestra, RV 621 string orch,cont,A solo (Malipiero) RICORDI-IT sc 131563 $7.00, pts 131564-I-V $2.50, ea., kbd pt 131564-VI $4.25 (V376)

Sum In Medio Tempestatum, For Solo Voice And String Orchestra *RV 632 string orch,S solo (Talbot, M.) RICORDI-IT sc PR 1295 f.s., pts 134912 f.s. (V377)

Vos Aurae Per Montes, For Solo Voice And String Orchestra *RV 634 string orch,S solo (Talbot, M.) RICORDI-IT sc PR 1291 f.s., pts 134930 f.s. (V378)

VIVALDIANA see Doolittle, Quentin

VIVAX see Deák, Csaba

VIVIER, CLAUDE (1948-1983)
Bouchara, For Solo Voice And
Instrumental Ensemble [15']
1.1.1.1. 1.0.0.0. perc,2vln,vla,
vcl,db,electronic tape,S solo
SALABERT perf mat rent   (V379)

Lonely Child, For Solo Voice And
Chamber Orchestra [19']
1+pic.2.2.2. 2.0.0.0. perc,
strings,S solo
SALABERT perf mat rent   (V380)

Prologue Pour Un Marco Polo, For Solo
Voices And Instrumental Ensemble
[21']
3clar,clar in E flat,2bass clar,
2perc,7vln,3vla,2vcl,db,SATBarB
soli
SALABERT perf mat rent   (V381)

Pulau Dewata [arr]
(Rea, John) 1.0.1.0. 1.1.0.0.
3perc,harp,vln,2vcl,2db
CAN.MUS.CENT. MI 1200 V862PU
(V382)

Trois Airs Pour Un Opera Imaginaire,
For Solo Voice And Instrumental
Ensemble [15']
1+pic.0.2+bass clar.0. 1.0.0.0.
perc,2vln,vla,db,S solo
SALABERT perf mat rent   (V383)

Wo Bist Du Licht?, For Solo Voice And
Instrumental Ensemble [23']
perc,strings,electronic tape,Mez
solo
SALABERT perf mat rent   (V384)

Zipangu [19']
string orch
DOBER   (V385)

VIZIJA BARV see Ajdic, Alojz

VIZZUTTI, ALLEN
Gift Of The Sun [12'5"]
3+pic.1.2.2.soprano sax.alto
sax.3tenor sax.baritone sax.
4.3.3.1. perc,pno,cel,harp,elec
bass,strings
NEWAM 19042 perf mat rent   (V386)

VLAD, ROMAN (1919-   )
In Memoria Di Valentino Bucchi [16']
1.1.1.1. 1.0.1.0. timp,pno,
strings
sc BSE BSM 7 f.s., perf mat rent
(V387)
Tre Poesie Di Montale, For Solo Voice
And Orchestra [10']
2.2.2.2. 2.2.0.0. perc,harp,
strings,Bar solo
sc RICORDI-IT 133080 f.s., perf mat
rent   (V388)

VLIJMEN, JAN VAN (1935-   )
Quaterni II, For Violin, Horn, Piano
And Orchestra [31']
3.3.5.5. 4.3.4.1. 2harp,4perc,
mand,strings,vln,horn,pno soli
sc DONEMUS f.s., perf mat rent
(V389)
Such A Day Of Sweetness, For Solo
Voice And Orchestra [20']
3.3.5.3. 4.4.3.1. 2harp,cel,
tubular bells,marimba,cimbalom,
2mand,strings,S solo
DONEMUS perf mat rent   (V390)

VO-VI see Ton That, Tiet

VOCALISE, FOR SOLO VOICE AND CHAMBER
ORCHESTRA see Baker, Michael Conway

VOCALISE, FOR SOLO VOICE AND ORCHESTRA
see Chenoweth, Wilbur

VOCI, FOR VIOLA AND TWO INSTRUMENTAL
GROUPS see Berio, Luciano

VOCI DAL SILENZIO see Gentilucci,
Armando

VODICKA, VACLAV (1720-1774)
Sinfonia [8']
hpsd,strings
SUPRAPHON   (V391)

VOGEL, ERNST (1926-   )
Concerto for Organ and Orchestra
[25']
2+pic.2+English horn.2.2+
contrabsn. 4.2.3.1. timp,perc,
strings,org solo
DOBLINGER perf mat rent   (V392)

Kammerkonzert For Violin And String
Orchestra [17'50"]
string orch,vln solo
DOBLINGER perf mat rent   (V393)

VOGEL, ERNST (cont'd.)
Metamorphosen [36']
2+pic.2+English horn.2+bass
clar.2+contrabsn. 4.2.3.1.
timp,perc,strings
DOBLINGER perf mat rent   (V394)

Modi [16']
2+pic.2.2.2+contrabsn. 4.2.3.1.
timp,perc,strings
DOBLINGER perf mat rent   (V395)

Moira [18']
string orch
study sc DOBLINGER STP 414 f.s.,
perf mat rent   (V396)

Music for Double Bass and Orchestra
[12']
1+pic.1+English horn.1.1+
contrabsn. 2.1.1.0. timp,perc,
harp,strings without db,db solo
DOBLINGER perf mat rent   (V397)

Symphony No. 2 [18']
2+pic.2(English
horn).2.2(contrabsn). 4.2.3.1.
timp,perc,strings
DOBLINGER perf mat rent   (V398)

VOGEL, ROGER CRAIG (1947-   )
Concertino for Horn and String
Orchestra
string orch,horn solo
DORN $85.00   (V399)

VOGEL, WLADIMIR (1896-1984)
Concertino for Flute and String
Orchestra
string orch,fl solo
KUNZEL GM 917 sc,pts $21.00, pts
$3.00, ea.   (V400)

Friede? Fragen Zu Unsere Zeit, For
Solo Voice And Orchestra [7']
2trp,2trom,strings,Bar solo
BOTE perf mat rent   (V401)

Zwei Etüden
sc BOTE f.s.   (V402)

VOGGESONG, FOR SOLO VOICE AND ORCHESTRA
see Tveitt, Geirr

VOGLER, [ABBE] GEORG JOSEPH (1749-1814)
Symphony
(Boer; Alexander; Garner) ("The
Symphony" Vol. C-V) sc GARLAND
ISBN 08240-3832-0 $90.00 contains
also: Danzi, Franz, Symphonic
Works, Three; Campagnoli,
Bartolommeo, Symphonie
Concertante   (V403)

VOGT, HANS (1911-   )
Apreslude [23']
3(pic).3(English horn).3(bass
clar).3(contrabsn). 2.3.3.1.
timp,4perc,harp,pno&cel,
strings,opt Mez solo
BOTE perf mat rent   (V404)

Concerto for Violin and Orchestra
[22']
2(pic).2(English horn).2(bass
clar).2(contrabsn). 2.3.2.0.
timp,perc,harp,pno&cel,strings,
vln solo
sc BOTE f.s., perf mat rent   (V405)

Konzertante Divertimenti, For Piano
And Orchestra [18']
1+pic.1+English horn.2.2.
2.1.1.0. timp,perc,strings
without vln,pno solo
BÄREN. BA 7138 perf mat rent   (V406)

Sinfonie "Dona Nobis Pacem" [16']
3(pic,alto fl).3+English horn.3+
bass clar.3+contrabsn.sax.
3.3.3.1. timp,4perc,harp,pno,
cel,strings
sc BOTE f.s., perf mat rent   (V407)

Tim Finnigan's Wake [11']
string orch,ob/vln solo
BOTE perf mat rent   (V408)

VOI AVETE UN COR FEDELE, FOR SOLO VOICE
AND ORCHESTRA see Mozart, Wolfgang
Amadeus

VOICE, THE see Coolidge, Peggy Stuart

VOICES, THE, FOR SOLO VOICE AND
ORCHESTRA see Dorati, Antal,
Stimmen, Die, For Solo Voice And
Orchestra

VOICES OF SPRING, THE see Thorne,
Nicholas C.K.

VOICES OF SPRING, [ARR.] see Strauss,
Johann, [Jr.], Frühlingsstimmen
Walzer, [arr.]

VOIX, FOR HORN AND STRING ORCHESTRA see
Tisne, Antoine

VOIX, FOR SOLO VOICE AND CHAMBER
ORCHESTRA see Peixinho, Jorge

VOIX DANS LE DESERT, UNE, FOR SOLO
VOICE AND ORCHESTRA see Elgar,
[Sir] Edward (William)

VOIX RECONNUE, LA, FOR SOLO VOICES AND
ORCHESTRA see Blumenfeld, Harold

VOL DU BOURDON, LE, FOR DOUBLE BASS AND
STRING ORCHESTRA [ARR.] see Rimsky-
Korsakov, Nikolai, Tsar Saltan:
Flight Of The Bumblebee, For Double
Bass And String Orchestra [arr.]

VOLKMANN, JOACHIM (1931-   )
Alle Meine Entchen, For Solo Voice
And String Orchestra (from
Hanschen Steht Im Walde)
string orch,hpsd,strings,solo voice
[3'] BREITKOPF-W perf mat rent
(V409)

VOLKONSKY, ANDREI (1933-   )
Concerto Itinerant, For Solo Voice,
Flute, Violin, And Instrumental
Ensemble [8']
6perc,harp,strings,fl solo,vln
solo,S solo
SALABERT perf mat rent   (V410)

Immobile, For Piano And Orchestra
[15']
1.1.2+bass clar.1. 1.4.3.0. timp,
vln,vla,vcl,db,pno solo
SALABERT perf mat rent   (V411)

Serenade Pour Un Insecte [8']
1.1.1.1. 1.1.1.1. timp,perc,harp,
mand,gtr,strings
BELAIEFF   (V412)

VOM FELS ZUM MEER see Liszt, Franz

VOM WINDE BEWEINT see Kancheli, Giya

VOMÁCKA, BOLESLAV (1887-1965)
Youth [22']
3.3.4.3. 6.4.3.1. timp,perc,
strings
SUPRAPHON   (V413)

VON DER BÖRSE see Strauss, Johann,
[Jr.]

VON DER WIEGE BIS ZUM GRABE see Liszt,
Franz

VON GOTT WILL ICH NICHT LASSEN, CHORALE
[ARR.] see Buxtehude, Dietrich

VON TRAUM UND TOD see Hamel, Peter
Michael

VOORN, JOOP (1932-   )
Perceval Et Blanchefleur, For Solo
Voice And Orchestra [22']
1.2.2.2. 2.1.1.0. harp,2vln,vla,
vcl,db,T solo
DONEMUS f.s.   (V414)

VOORTMAN, ROLAND (1953-   )
Reminiscentie IV [12']
string orch
DONEMUS perf mat rent   (V415)

Zechum [10']
0.2.0.0. 2.0.0.0. strings
DONEMUS perf mat rent   (V416)

VOR MEINEM VATERHAUS STEHT EINE LINDE,
FOR SOLO VOICE AND ORCHESTRA [ARR.]
see Stolz, Robert

VOR-UND NACHSPIEL, FOR 4 HORNS AND
ORCHESTRA see Koetsier, Jan

VORGEFUHLE see Rihm, Wolfgang

VORÍŠEK, JAN HUGO
see WORZISCHEK, JAN HUGO

VORREI SPIEGARVI, OH DIO, FOR SOLO
VOICE AND ORCHESTRA see Mozart,
Wolfgang Amadeus

VORSPIEL ZU EINEM DRAMA see Schreker,
Franz

VORSPRUCH UND GESANG DES EINHORNS, FOR
DOUBLEBASS AND ORCHESTRA see Kühnl,
Claus

VORWARTS see Strauss, Josef

VORWARTS ZUR UNZEIT see Ostendorf,
Jens-Peter

VOS AURAE PER MONTES, FOR SOLO VOICE
AND STRING ORCHESTRA see Vivaldi,
Antonio

VOSS, FRIEDRICH (1930-   )
   Metamorphose
      study sc BREITKOPF-W PB 5107 f.s.
                                          (V417)

VOSTRÁK, ZBYNEK (1920-1985)
   Metamusic *Op.43 [25']
      4.4.4.4. 6.4.5.1. 3perc,3harp,
         strings
      sc SUPRAPHON f.s.   (V418)

   Mutazione I *Op.47 [14']
      1.1.1.1. 1.0.0.0. perc,cel,
         strings,electronic tape
      SONZOGNO perf mat rent   (V419)

VOUSSOIRS see Milburn, Ellsworth

VOX CLAMANS IN DESERTO, FOR SOLO VOICE
   AND CHAMBER ORCHESTRA see Ruggles,
   Carl Sprague

VOX LUCIS, FOR SOLO VOICE, OBOE AND
   ORCHESTRA see Eröd, Ivan

VOYAGE see Perlongo, Daniel James

VOYAGE D'HIVER II see Miereanu, Costin

VOYAGE EN BRETAGNE see Haudebert,
   Lucien

VOYAGE EN CHINE: OVERTURE see Bazin,
   François-Emanuel-Joseph

VOYAGER see Franzetti, Carlos see
   Mefano, Paul

VOYER DE POLIGNY D'ARGENSON, CHARLES
   Royal Fusiliers' Arrival At Quebec
      [arr]
      (McIntyre, Paul) .2.2.2.2.
         4.2(corn-flu).3.1. timp, perc,
         strings CAN.MUS.CENT.
         MI 1100 M1525RO   (V420)

VOYEVODE see Tchaikovsky, Piotr Ilyich

VRANICKY, PAVEL
   see WRANITZKY, PAUL

VREMSAK, SAMO (1930-   )
   Concerto for Organ and String
      Orchestra [20']
      string orch,org solo
      DRUSTVO DSS 1079 perf mat rent
                                          (V421)

   Sedem Miniatur [13']
      string orch
      "Seven Miniatures" DRUSTVO DSS 998
         perf mat rent   (V422)

   Seven Miniatures
      see Sedem Miniatur

VRIEND, JAN N.M. (1938-   )
   Hallelujah II [13']
      2.2.3.2. 2.2.3.0. 4perc,2vln,vla,
         vcl,db
      sc DONEMUS f.s., perf mat rent
                                          (V423)

VRIES, KLAAS DE (1944-   )
   Discantus [7']
      3.3.3.3. 4.3.3.1. timp,3-4perc,
         pno,strings
      sc DONEMUS f.s., perf mat rent
                                          (V424)

   Kotz [12']
      1(pic).1.1.1. 1.1.1.0. pno,vln,
         vla,vcl
      sc,pts DONEMUS f.s.   (V425)

VUELO DE ALAMBRE, FOR SOLO VOICE AND
   ORCHESTRA see Heinio, Mikko

VUGGEVISE see Spalder, Frithjof

VUORI, HARRI (1957-   )
   KRI [15']
      2.2.3.2. 4.2.3.1. timp,perc,harp,
         acord/cel/pno,strings
      sc SUOMEN f.s.   (V426)

VUSTIN, ALEXANDER (1943-   )
   Memoria 2 [14']
      6perc,cel,pno,strings
      VAAP perf mat rent   (V427)

   Memoria 2
      SIKORSKI perf mat rent   (V428)

   Nocturnes, For Solo Voice And
      Orchestra [12']
      0.1.1.0. 0.1.0.0. perc,2harp,pno/
         bells,elec org,vln,db,opt
         electronic tape,solo voice
      SIKORSKI perf mat rent   (V429)
      VAAP perf mat rent   (V430)

W

W3A6M4, FOR VIOLIN, VIOLA AND ORCHESTRA
   see Masson, Gerard

WAARG see Xenakis, Yannis (Iannis)

WACHET AUF, RUFT UNS DIE STIMME [ARR.]
   see Bach, Johann Sebastian

WACHTELSCHLAG, DER, "HORCH WIE SCHALLTS
   DORTEN", FOR SOLO VOICE AND
   ORCHESTRA, [ARR.] see Beethoven,
   Ludwig van

WAFFENSCHMIED, DER: AUCH ICH WAR EIN
   JÜNGLING, FOR SOLO VOICE AND
   ORCHESTRA see Lortzing, (Gustav)
   Albert

WAFFENSCHMIED, DER: DU BIST EIN
   ARBEITSAMER MENSCH, FOR SOLO VOICES
   AND ORCHESTRA see Lortzing,
   (Gustav) Albert

WAFFENSCHMIED, DER: ER SCHLÄFT, WIR
   ALLE SIND IN ANGST, FOR SOLO VOICE
   AND ORCHESTRA see Lortzing,
   (Gustav) Albert

WAFFENSCHMIED, DER: IHR WISST, DASS ER
   EUCH LIEBT, FOR SOLO VOICES AND
   ORCHESTRA see Lortzing, (Gustav)
   Albert

WAFFENSCHMIED, DER: MAN WIRD JA EINMAL
   NUR GEBOREN, FOR SOLO VOICE AND
   ORCHESTRA see Lortzing, (Gustav)
   Albert

WAFFENSCHMIED, DER: WELT, DU KANNST MIR
   NICHT GEFALLEN, FOR SOLO VOICE AND
   ORCHESTRA see Lortzing, (Gustav)
   Albert

WAFFENSCHMIED, DER: WIR ARMEN, ARMEN
   MADCHEN, FOR SOLO VOICE AND
   ORCHESTRA see Lortzing, (Gustav)
   Albert

WAG, THE see Lundkvist, Per, Krumelur

WAGEMANS, PETER-JAN (1952-   )
   Irato *Op.20b [15']
      3.3.3.3. 4.3.3.1. timp,2-3perc,
         harp,strings
      DONEMUS   (W1)

   Klang *Op.24 [20']
      4.4.4.4. 2.4.4.1. 4Wagner tuba,
         4perc,pno&cel,bass gtr,strings
      sc DONEMUS f.s., perf mat rent   (W2)

WAGENAAR, DIDEREK (1946-   )
   Metrum, For 4 Saxophones And
      Orchestra [18']
      4.4.4.4. 4.4.4.1. Hamm,2pno,
         strings,4alto sax soli
      DONEMUS perf mat rent   (W3)

WAGENAAR, JOHAN (1862-1941)
   Cyrano De Bergerac *Op.23
      KALMUS A5887 sc $30.00, set $50.00,
         perf mat rent   (W4)

WAGENSEIL, GEORG CHRISTOPH (1715-1777)
   Concerto for Horn and String
      Orchestra in E flat
      (Leloir, E.) string orch,horn solo
         [12'] sc BILLAUDOT f.s., perf mat
         rent   (W5)

   Concerto for Organ and String
      Orchestra, No. 1, in C
      string orch,org solo
      (Scholz, Rudolf) sc,pts DOBLINGER
         DM 581 f.s.   (W6)

   Concerto for Organ and String
      Orchestra, No. 2, in A
      string orch,org solo
      (Scholz, Rudolf) sc,pts DOBLINGER
         DM 582 f.s.   (W7)

   Concerto for Organ and String
      Orchestra, No. 3, in C
      string orch,org solo
      (Scholz, Rudolf) sc,pts DOBLINGER
         DM 583 f.s.   (W8)

   Concerto for Organ and String
      Orchestra, No. 4, in E flat
      string orch,org solo
      (Scholz, Rudolf) sc,pts DOBLINGER
         DM 584 f.s.   (W9)

   Concerto for Organ and String
      Orchestra, No. 5, in B flat
      string orch,org solo
      (Scholz, Rudolf) sc,pts DOBLINGER
         DM 585 f.s.   (W10)

WAGENSEIL, GEORG CHRISTOPH (cont'd.)

   Concerto for Organ and String
      Orchestra, No. 6, in G
      string orch,org solo
      (Scholz, Rudolf) sc,pts DOBLINGER
         DM 1110 f.s.   (W11)

   Concerto for Trombone and Orchestra
      in E flat [13']
      2ob,2horn,strings,trom solo
      SUPRAPHON   (W12)

WAGGONER, ANDREW
   Train, The [11']
      3.2.3.3. 3.4.3.1. timp,2perc,pno,
         strings
      sc AM.COMP.AL. $72.65, perf mat
         rent   (W13)

WAGNER, JOSEF (1856-1908)
   Under The Double Eagle March
      (Brooks) 1(pic).1.2.1.2sax.
         2.2.1.0. drums,strings pno-cond
      sc,set KALMUS A6153 $9.00   (W14)

WAGNER, PAUL
   Concertino for Bassoon and String
      Orchestra
      string orch,bsn solo
      DORN $55.00   (W15)

WAGNER, RICHARD (1813-1883)
   Album Suite For Mathilde Wesendonk
      [arr.]
      (Muller-Berghaus) 3.2+English
         horn.2+bass clar.2. 4.3.3.1.
         timp,harp,strings [10'] KALMUS
         A4272 sc $15.00, set $30.00, perf
         mat rent   (W16)

   Albumblatt, Ein, For Violin And
      Orchestra [arr.]
      (Wilhelmj) 1.0.2.2. 2.0.0.0.
         strings,vln solo [3'] KALMUS
         A4344 sc $8.00, set $9.00   (W17)

   Faust Overture
      min sc KALMUS K01456 $3.50   (W18)

   Feen, Die: Overture
      KALMUS A6407 sc $10.00, set $35.00,
         pts $2.00, ea., perf mat rent
                                          (W19)
   Fliegende Holländer, Der: Die Frist
      Ist Um, For Solo Voice And
      Orchestra
      BREITKOPF-L perf mat rent   (W20)

   Fliegende Hollander, Der: Overture
      "Flying Dutchman: Overture"
      (original version) KALMUS A5716
         sc $20.00, set $50.00, perf mat
         rent   (W21)

   Fliegende Holländer, Der: Traft Ihr
      Das Schiff, For Solo Voice And
      Orchestra
      BREITKOPF-L perf mat rent   (W22)

   Fliegende Holländer, Der: Willst
      Jenes Tags Du Dich Nicht Mehr
      Entsinnen, For Solo Voice And
      Orchestra
      BREITKOPF-L perf mat rent   (W23)

   Flying Dutchman: Overture
      see Fliegende Hollander, Der:
      Overture

   Gotterdammerung: Funeral Music
      see Gotterdammerung: Trauermusik
      Beim Tode Siegfrieds

   Gotterdammerung: Trauermusik Beim
      Tode Siegfrieds
      "Gotterdammerung: Funeral Music"
      min sc KALMUS K01455 $4.00 (W24)

   Götterdämmerung: Trauermusik Beim
      Tode Siegfrieds [arr.]
      (Stasny) "Siegfried's Death And
         Funeral Music [arr.]"
      2(pic).2.2.2. 4.2.3.1. timp,perc,
         harp,strings [8'] KALMUS A5894 sc
         $12.00, set $30.00, perf mat rent
                                          (W25)
   Gotterdammerung: Waltraute's Scene
      KALMUS A3958 sc $12.00, set $40.00,
         pts $2.00, ea., perf mat rent
                                          (W26)

   Kaisermarsch [12']
      3.3.3.3. 4.3.3.1. timp,perc,
         strings
      min sc KALMUS K01430 $4.00   (W27)
      PETERS   (W28)

   König Enzio: Overture
      (Mottl) KALMUS A4158 sc $15.00,
         perf mat rent, set $35.00, pts
         $2.00, ea.   (W29)
      (Mottl, F.) BREITKOPF-W perf mat
         rent   (W30)

WAGNER, RICHARD (cont'd.)

Lohengrin: Das Süsse Lied Verhallt,
For Solo Voices And Orchestra
3.3.3.3. 4.3.3.1. timp,strings,ST
soli
BREITKOPF-L perf mat rent   (W31)

Lohengrin: Einsam In Trüben Tagen,
For Solo Voice And Orchestra
BREITKOPF-L perf mat rent   (W32)

Lohengrin: Elsa's Procession To The
Cathedral, [arr.]
see Lohengrin: Feierlicher Zug Zum
Münster, [arr.]

Lohengrin: Erhebe Dich, Genossin
Meiner Schmach, For Solo Voices
And Orchestra
3.3.3.3. 4.3.3.1. timp,drums,
strings,MezBar soli
BREITKOPF-L perf mat rent   (W33)

Lohengrin: Euch Lüften, Die Meine
Klagen, For Solo Voice And
Orchestra
3.3.3.3. 2.0.0.0. S solo
BREITKOPF-L perf mat rent   (W34)

Lohengrin: Feierlicher Zug Zum
Münster, [arr.] [4'30"]
(Campbell- Watson) "Lohengrin:
Elsa's Procession To The
Cathedral, [arr.]" WARNER perf
mat rent   (W35)

Lohengrin: Höchstes Vertraun, For
Solo Voice And Orchestra
2.3.3.3. 4.3.3.1. timp,strings,T
solo
BREITKOPF-L perf mat rent   (W36)

Lohengrin: Nun Sei Bedankt, Mein
Lieber Schwan, For Solo Voice And
Orchestra
3.3.2.2. 0.0.0.0. strings,T solo
BREITKOPF-L perf mat rent   (W37)

Meistersinger, Die: Festival Prelude,
[arr.] [8'30"]
(Krone, Max T.) WARNER perf mat
rent   (W38)

Meistersinger, Die: Festival Prelude
For Brass Sextet And Orchestra
[arr.]
(Krone, Max) 2+pic.2.2.2. 4.4.3.1.
timp,2perc,harp,strings,2horn,
2trp,2trom soli [9'] WARNER perf
mat rent   (W39)

Parsifal: Good Friday Spell
see Parsifal: Karfreitagszauber

Parsifal: Karfreitagszauber
"Parsifal: Good Friday Spell" min
sc KALMUS K01453 $4.00   (W40)

Parsifal: March Of The Grail Knights
(Kistler) 3.2.2.2+contrabsn.
4.3.3.1. timp,perc,strings [4']
KALMUS A7444 sc $10.00, set
$40.00, pts $1.50, ea., perf mat
rent   (W41)

Parsifal: Symphonic Fragments [arr.]
(Foss, Lukas) 3.3.3+bass clar.3+
contrabsn. 4.3.3.1. timp,perc,
2harp,strings [30'] SCHIRM.G perf
mat rent   (W42)

Parsifal: Titurel, Der Fromme Held,
For Solo Voice And Orchestra
KALMUS A3937 sc $6.00, set $12.00,
pts $.75, ea., perf mat rent
                                 (W43)

Polonia
(Mottl) KALMUS A5650 sc $25.00,
perf mat rent, set $50.00, pts
$2.00, ea.   (W44)

Rienzi: Overture [12']
3.2.2.3. 4.4.3.1. timp,perc,
strings
(original version) KALMUS A5713 sc
$25.00, set $50.00, perf mat rent
                                 (W45)
SCHOTTS perf mat rent   (W46)

Rule Britannia
BREITKOPF-W perf mat rent   (W47)

Siegfried's Death And Funeral Music
[arr.]
see Götterdämmerung: Trauermusik
Beim Tode Siegfrieds [arr.]

Symphony in E *reconstruction
(Mottl, Felix) 2.2.2.2. 4.2.2.0.
timp,strings [18'] SCHOTTS perf
mat rent   (W48)

Tannhäuser: Allmächtige Jungfrau, For
Solo Voice And Orchestra
BREITKOPF-L perf mat rent   (W49)

WAGNER, RICHARD (cont'd.)

Tannhäuser: Dich, Teure Halle, For
Solo Voice And Orchestra
BREITKOPF-L perf mat rent   (W50)

Tannhäuser: O Du Mein Holder
Abendstern, For Solo Voice And
Orchestra
BREITKOPF-L perf mat rent   (W51)

Tannhäuser: Overture
(original version) KALMUS A5715 sc
$15.00, set $50.00, perf mat rent
                                 (W52)

Tannhauser: Overture And Venusberg
Music
2+pic.2.2.2. 4.3.3.1. timp,perc,
strings [25'] KALMUS A7429 sc
$30.00, set $60.00, pts $2.50,
ea., perf mat rent   (W53)

Tannhauser: Wie Todesahnung, For Solo
Voice And Orchestra [5']
2.2.1.2. 0.0.3.1. harp,strings,
Bar solo
BREITKOPF-W perf mat rent   (W54)

Traume, For Violin And Orchestra
[arr]
0.0.2.2. 2.0.0.0. strings without
db,vln solo [5'] BREITKOPF-W perf
mat rent   (W55)

Tristan Und Isolde: Erfuhrest Du
Meine Schmach, For Solo Voice And
Orchestra [14']
3(pic).2+English horn.2+bass
clar.3. 4.3.3.1. timp,strings,S
solo
BREITKOPF-W perf mat rent   (W56)

Tristan Und Isolde: Fantasy, For
Violin And Orchestra, [arr.]
[10'55"]
(Waxman, Franz) FIDELIO perf mat
rent   (W57)

Tristan Und Isolde: King Mark's
Monologue, For Solo Voice And
Orchestra
KALMUS A3934 sc $5.00, set $10.00,
pts $1.00, ea.   (W58)

Tristan Und Isolde: Liebestod, "Mild
Und Leise", For Solo Voice And
Orchestra
3.3.3.3. 4.3.3.1. timp,harp,
strings,S solo
BREITKOPF-L perf mat rent   (W59)

Tristan Und Isolde: Prelude And
Liebestod
"Tristan Und Isolde: Prelude And
Love Death" min sc KALMUS K00048
$4.00   (W60)

Tristan Und Isolde: Prelude And Love
Death
see Tristan Und Isolde: Prelude And
Liebestod

Valkyrie, The: Wotan's Farewell And
Magic Fire Music
see Walkure, Die: Wotans Abschied
Und Feuerzauber

Walkure, Die: Sieglinde's Narrative,
For Solo Voice And Orchestra
KALMUS A3944 sc $5.00, set $16.00,
pts $1.00, ea., perf mat rent
                                 (W61)

Walkure, Die: War Es So Schmalich,
For Solo Voices And Orchestra
KALMUS A3952 sc $10.00, set $40.00,
pts $2.50, ea., perf mat rent
                                 (W62)

Walkure, Die: Wotans Abschied Und
Feuerzauber
"Valkyrie, The: Wotan's Farewell
And Magic Fire Music" min sc
KALMUS K01454 $4.50   (W63)

Wesendonk Lieder, For Solo Voice And
Orchestra [arr.]
(Henze, Hans Werner) sc SCHOTTS
$39.00   (W64)

WAGNER, SIEGFRIED (1869-1930)
Barenhauter, Die: Overture [9']
2+pic.2.2.2. 4.2.3.1. timp,perc,
strings
KALMUS A6975 sc $20.00, set $40.00,
pts $2.00, ea., perf mat rent
                                 (W65)

WAHLSTIMMEN WALZER see Strauss, Johann,
[Jr.]

WAHRSAGERIN, DIE see Strauss, Johann,
[Jr.]

WAITING FOR GOZO see Lloyd, Jonathan

WAL see Moser, Roland Olivier

WAL-BERG
Paysages Mediterranees [11']
2.2.2.2. 4.3.3.1. timp,perc,cel,
harp,strings
MARBOT perf mat rent   (W66)

Rhapsody for Flute and Orchestra
[13'30"]
2.2.2.2. 3.3.2.1. timp,2perc,
harp,strings,fl solo
BILLAUDOT perf mat rent   (W67)

WALDMUSIK see Bialas, Günter see
Graener, Paul

WALDROP, GIDEON WILLIAM (1919-   )
Songs Of The Southwest, For Solo
Voice And Orchestra [15']
1.1(English horn).1.1. 2.1.1.0.
timp,perc,harp,strings,Bar solo
BOOSEY perf mat rent   (W68)

WALDTEUFEL, EMILE (1837-1915)
Espana Waltz *Op.236 [7']
1+pic.1.2.1. 2.2.3.0. ophicleide,
timp,perc,strings
KALMUS A6398 set $15.00, pts $1.00,
ea.   (W69)

WALKER, GEORGE THEOPHILUS (1922-   )
Address For Orchestra [19']
3+pic.3+English horn.3+bass
clar.2+contrabsn. 4.2.3.1.
timp,3perc,harp,strings
MMB perf mat rent   (W70)

Address: Passacaglia [6'30"]
4(pic).4(English horn).4(clar in
A,bass clar).3(contrabsn).
4.2.3.1. timp,5perc,harp,
strings
MCA perf mat rent   (W71)

Concerto for Violoncello and
Orchestra [20']
2+pic+alto fl.2+English horn.2+
bass clar.2+contrabsn. 4.4.3.1.
timp,4perc,harp,strings,vcl
solo
MMB perf mat rent   (W72)

Dialogus, For Violoncello And
Orchestra [13']
2+pic+alto fl.0.2+bass clar.2+
contrabsn. 4.4.3.1. perc,harp,
pno&cel,strings,vcl solo
MMB perf mat rent   (W73)

Eastman Overture [8']
2+pic.2+English horn.2+bass
clar.2+contrabsn. 4.4.3.1.
timp,4perc,harp,strings
MMB perf mat rent   (W74)

In Praise Of Folly [8']
2+pic+alto fl.2+English horn.2+
bass clar.2+contrabsn. 4.2.3.1.
timp,perc,harp,strings
MMB perf mat rent   (W75)

Lyric For Strings
string orch
MMB 841 perf mat rent   (W76)

Poem for Violin and Orchestra [18']
1(pic).2.1.1. 2.1.1.1. timp,
2perc,harp,strings,vln solo
MMB perf mat rent   (W77)

Serenata [14']
2(pic).2.2.2. 2.2.1.0. timp,
3perc,pno,strings
MMB perf mat rent   (W78)

Sinfonia [12']
2+pic.2+English horn.2+bass
clar.2+contrabsn. 4.4.3.1.
timp,perc,harp,pno&hpsd,strings
MMB perf mat rent   (W79)

WALKER, GWYNETH (1947-   )
Essay For Orchestra [8'30"]
2.2.2.2. 4.2.3.0. 3perc,strings
WALKER MUS. PRO. sc $200.00, pts
rent   (W80)

WALKER, ROBERT (1946-   )
Pavan [20']
string orch,vln solo
NOVELLO perf mat rent   (W81)

WALKURE, DIE: SIEGLINDE'S NARRATIVE,
FOR SOLO VOICE AND ORCHESTRA see
Wagner, Richard

WALKURE, DIE: WAR ES SO SCHMALICH, FOR
SOLO VOICES AND ORCHESTRA see
Wagner, Richard

WALKURE, DIE: WOTANS ABSCHIED UND
FEUERZAUBER see Wagner, Richard

WALLACE, WILLIAM (1933-   )
Ceremonies
sc BERANDOL BER 1723 $20.00   (W82)

Concerto Variations
2.2.2.2. 3.2.1.0. timp,perc,
strings
CAN.MUS.CENT. MI 1100 W195C   (W83)

Dance Suite
2(pic).2.2.2. 2.2.0.0. timp,perc,
harp,strings
CAN.MUS.CENT. MI 1100 W195DA (W84)

Epilogue [5']
string orch
CAN.MUS.CENT. MI 1500 W195EP (W85)

Minuet And Trio
2.2.0.2. 2.2.0.0. timp,strings
CAN.MUS.CENT. MI 1100 W195MI (W86)

Symphonic Variations [10']
1(pic).1.1.1. 2.2.1.0. perc,kbd&
synthesizer,strings
CAN.MUS.CENT. MI 1200 W195SY (W87)

WALLACH, JOELLE
Turbulence, Stillness And Salutation
[16']
1(pic).1(English horn).1+bass
clar.1. 2.1.1.0. timp,perc,
harp,strings
sc AM.COMP.AL. $20.60   (W88)

WALLENSTEIN see Rheinberger, Josef

WALLENSTEIN: LA MORT DE WALLENSTEIN see
Indy, Vincent d'

WALLENSTEIN: LE CAMP DE WALLENSTEIN see
Indy, Vincent d'

WALLENSTEIN: MAX ET THECLA see Indy,
Vincent d'

WALLENSTEIN SUITE see Weinberger,
Jaromir

WALLENSTEIN'S CAMP see Indy, Vincent
d', Wallenstein: Le Camp De
Wallenstein see Smetana, Bedrich

WALLENSTEIN'S DEATH see Indy, Vincent
d', Wallenstein: La Mort De
Wallenstein

WALLIN, PETER (1964-   )
Pen, The, For Percussion And String
Orchestra
string orch,4perc soli
STIM   (W89)

Symphonic Race, A
3.2.0.0. 4.3.2.1. timp,perc,
strings
STIM   (W90)

Symphony No. 1
3.2.3.2. 4.3.2.1. timp,4perc,
strings,opt electronic tape
(The Visitor) STIM   (W91)

Three Pieces For Hansson, For Double
Bass And String Orchestra [7']
string orch,db solo
STIM   (W92)

Visions [11']
2.2.2.2. 4.3.2.1. timp,3perc,
strings
STIM   (W93)

WALLIN, ROLF (1957-   )
Concert Piece for Trumpet and String
Orchestra
string orch,trp solo
NORGE   (W94)

Concertino for Trombone and String
Orchestra [11']
string orch,trom solo
NORGE   (W95)

Concerto for Timpani and Orchestra
[17']
3.3.3.3. 4.4.3.1. perc,harp,pno/
cel,strings,timp solo
NORGE   (W96)

ID [15'10"]
3(pic).3(English horn).3(bass
clar).3. 4.3.3.1. timp,perc,
harp,strings
NORGE   (W97)

WALLONEN MARSCH [ARR.] see Strauss,
Josef

WALLS HAVE EARS, THE see Aperghis,
Georges, Wande Haben Ohren, Die

WALLVIK, EINAR (1911-   )
Impromptu for Organ and Orchestra
[4']
2.2.2.2. 2.2.0.0. timp,perc,
strings,org solo
STIM   (W98)

WALLY, LA: EBBEN? NE ANDRO LONTANA, FOR
SOLO VOICE AND ORCHESTRA see
Catalani, Alfredo

WALLY, LA: M' HAI SALVATO, FOR SOLO
VOICE AND ORCHESTRA see Catalani,
Alfredo

WALLY, LA: NE MAI DUNQUE AVRO PACE, FOR
SOLO VOICE AND ORCHESTRA see
Catalani, Alfredo

WALLY, LA: T' AMO BEN IO, FOR SOLO
VOICE AND ORCHESTRA see Catalani,
Alfredo

WALT WHITMAN OVERTURE see Holst, Gustav

WALTER, FRIED (1907-   )
Andreas Wolfius: Monolog Des Wolfius,
For Solo Voice And Orchestra [7']
1+pic.2.2.2. 4.3.3.1. timp,perc,
harp,strings,Bar solo
BOTE perf mat rent   (W99)

Concerto for Trumpet and Orchestra
[16']
2.2.2.2. 4.0.3.0. timp,perc,gtr,
elec bass,strings,trp solo
ZIMMER.   (W100)

Epigramme
perc,harmonica,gtr,strings
TONOS   (W101)

Konigin Elisabeth: Arie Des Dudley,
For Solo Voice And Orchestra
[2'30"]
2.2.2.2. 4.3.3.0. timp,harp,
strings,T solo
BOTE perf mat rent   (W102)

Serenata Romantica
string orch
TONOS   (W103)

WALTON, [SIR] WILLIAM (TURNER)
(1902-1983)
As You Like It, For Solo Voice And
Orchestra [arr.]
(Palmer, Christopher) 3.2.2.2.
4.2.2.0. 3perc,2harp,hpsd,
strings,S solo OXFORD perf mat
rent   (W104)

First Shoot, The [arr.] (from Follow
The Sun)
(Palmer, Christopher)
3(pic).2(English horn).3(bass
clar).2. 4.3.3.1. timp,3perc,pno,
strings [10'] OXFORD perf mat
rent   (W105)

Hamlet [arr.]
(Palmer, Christopher) 3.3.3.3.
4.3.6.1. timp,4perc,pno,cel,
strings,speaking voice OXFORD
perf mat rent   (W106)

Macbeth: Fanfare And March [arr.]
(Palmer, Christopher) 4.4.2.2.
4.3.3.1. timp,perc,pno,strings
OXFORD perf mat rent   (W107)

Major Barbara [arr.]
(Palmer, Christopher) 3.3.3.3.
4.3.3.1. timp,4-5perc,2harp,pno&
cel,strings OXFORD perf mat rent
(W108)

National Anthem, "God Save The Queen"
3.3.3.3. 4.3.3.1. timp,perc,harp,
strings OXFORD perf mat rent
(W109)

Prologo E Fantasia [6']
3(pic).3(English horn).3(bass
clar).3(contrabsn). 4.3.3.1.
timp,perc,pno,harp,strings
study sc OXFORD 77.033 $11.50, perf
mat rent   (W110)

Richard III [arr.]
(Palmer, Christopher) 3.3.3.2.
4.4.3.1. timp,4perc,2harp,hpsd,
org,strings,opt speaking voice
OXFORD perf mat rent   (W111)

Three Sisters
3(pic).2.2.2. 4.3.3.1. timp,4perc,
pno,harp,strings OXFORD perf mat
rent   (W112)

Troilus And Cressida: Suite [arr.]
(Palmer, Christopher) 2+pic.2+
English horn.2+bass clar.2+
contrabsn. 4.4.3.1. timp,2perc,
cel,2harp,strings [34'] OXFORD
perf mat rent   (W113)

WALTZ ANTIQUE see Templeton, Alec

WALTZ DREAM: WALTZES see Straus, Oscar

WALTZ IN TWO, FOR NARRATOR AND
ORCHESTRA see Applebaum, Edward

WALTZING MANNEQUINS see Mourant, Walter

WANAKI WIN see Ultan, Lloyd

WAND OF YOUTH SUITE NO. 1 see Elgar,
[Sir] Edward (William)

WAND OF YOUTH SUITE NO. 2 see Elgar,
[Sir] Edward (William)

WANDE HABEN OHREN, DIE see Aperghis,
Georges

WANDERER FANTASY FOR PIANO AND
ORCHESTRA [ARR.] see Schubert,
Franz (Peter), Fantasy for Piano
and Orchestra, Op. 15, in C, [arr.]

WANDERSCHAFT see Jochum, Otto

WANDLUNGEN see Nunes, Emmanuel

WANDLUNGEN IN D see Muller-Hornbach,
Gerhard

WANEK, FRIEDRICH K. (1929-   )
Due Sonetti, For Solo Voice And
String Orchestra [12']
8vln,2vla,2vcl,db,Mez solo
SCHOTTS perf mat rent   (W114)

Musique Concertante, For 2
Harpsichords And Chamber
Orchestra [18']
1.1.1.1. 1.1.0.0. strings,2hpsd
soli
SCHOTTS perf mat rent   (W115)

WANG, JIAN-ZHONG
Concerto for Piano and Orchestra
2(pic).2.2.2. 4.2.3.1. timp,perc,
strings,pno solo
HONG KONG perf mat rent   (W116)

WANG, LI-SAN
Nice And Easy, For Violin And
Orchestra
2.2.2.2. 4.3.3.1. glock,harp,
strings,vln solo
HONG KONG perf mat rent   (W117)

WANG, XI-LIN
Yunnan Scenes [29']
3.2+English horn.2+bass clar.2.
4.3.3.1. timp,perc,vibra,harp,
cel,pno,strings
HONG KONG perf mat rent   (W118)

WANHAL, JOHANN BAPTIST (JAN KRTITEL)
(1739-1813)
Concerto for Bassoon and Orchestra in
C, MIN 206 [17']
BUBONIC perf mat rent   (W119)

Concerto for 2 Bassoons and Orchestra
in F
MUS. RARA 2133 perf mat rent (W120)

Concerto for 2 Bassoons and Orchestra
in F, MIN 207 [23']
BUBONIC perf mat rent   (W121)

Concerto for Double Bass and
Orchestra in D, MIN 158
(Malaric, Rudolf) 2ob,2horn,
strings,db solo [22'] DOBLINGER
perf mat rent   (W122)

Concerto for Piano and Orchestra in
D, MIN 203
sc,pts KUNZEL 10046 f.s.   (W123)

Concerto for Piano and Orchestra, Op.
14, in D
(Gmur, Hanspeter) sc KUNZEL $30.40,
perf mat rent   (W124)

Concerto for Violin, Harpsichord and
String Orchestra in C [29']
string orch,vln solo,hpsd solo
(Strauss, John; Strauss, Virginia)
sc,pts DOBLINGER DM 1107 f.s.
(W125)

Six Symphonies, Part I
(Bryan, Paul) sc A-R ED
ISBN 0-89579-200-1 f.s., ipa
contains: Symphony in D minor;
Symphony in F; Symphony in G
minor   (W126)

Six Symphonies, Part II
(Bryan, Paul) sc A-R ED
ISBN 0-89579-200-X f.s., ipa
contains: Symphony in A; Symphony
in D; Symphony in E minor
(W127)

Symphony in A
see Six Symphonies, Part II

WANHAL, JOHANN BAPTIST (JAN KRTITEL) (cont'd.)

Symphony in C, MIN 123 [25']
1.2.0.0+opt bsn. 2.2.0.0.
strings,timp,cont
(McAllster) (Periodical Overture
No. 42) KALMUS A5638 sc $12.00,
perf mat rent, set $40.00, pts
$3.00, ea. (W128)

Symphony in D
see Six Symphonies, Part II

Symphony in D minor
see Six Symphonies, Part I

Symphony in E minor
see Six Symphonies, Part II

Symphony in F
see Six Symphonies, Part I

Symphony in G minor
see Six Symphonies, Part I

WANSKI, JAN (1762-ca. 1800)
Symphony in D
2fl,2horn,strings
(Dabrowski) POLSKIE (W129)

WANZE, DIE: VIER STUCKE see
Shostakovich, Dmitri, Flea, The:
Four Pieces

WAR OF THE NEWTS see Tremain, Ronald

WARD, ROBERT EUGENE (1917-)
Dialogues, For Violin, Violoncello
And Orchestra
3.2.2.3. 4.3.3.1. timp,perc,
strings,vln solo,vcl solo
HIGHGATE perf mat rent (W130)

WARD-STEINMAN, DAVID (1936-)
And In These Times: Season's
Greetings [5']
MERION perf mat rent (W131)

Chroma [19']
MERION perf mat rent (W132)

Concerto Grosso [17']
3sax,3trp,3trom,tuba,pno,drums,
6vln,2vla,2vcl,db,alto sax
solo,bass sax solo,trp solo,
trom solo
sc,pts MJQ rent (W133)

Elegy For Astronauts [11']
MERION perf mat rent (W134)

Olympics Overture [6']
MERION perf mat rent (W135)

Winging It [13']
MERION perf mat rent (W136)

WARE, PETER (1951-)
Aishihik, For Piano And Orchestra
[14']
3.2.2.3. 4.2.3.1. timp,2perc,
strings,pno solo
CAN.MUS.CENT. MI 1361 W271A (W137)

Baca Location No. 1 [20']
1.1.1.1. 2.2.1.1. timp,strings
CAN.MUS.CENT. MI 1200 W271B (W138)

Fire From Within, The [12']
3(pic).3(English horn).2.2.
4.2.3.1. timp,3perc,strings
CAN.MUS.CENT. MI 1100 W271FI (W139)

Kusawa
3.3.3.2. 4.2.3.1. 4perc,harp,
strings
CAN.MUS.CENT. MI 1100 W271K (W140)

Tsankawi [7']
3.2.2.2. 4.2.3.1. 5perc,strings
CAN.MUS.CENT. MI 1100 W271T (W141)

WARFIELD, GERALD ALEXANDER (1940-)
Transformed Prelude, The, For Piano
And Orchestra [6']
2.2.2.1. 4.2.2.0. perc,strings,
pno solo
AM.COMP.AL. perf mat rent (W142)

WARLOCK, PETER
see HESELTINE, PHILIP

WARMUP see Sønstevold, Gunnar,
Opvarming

WARREN, B.
Little Concerto For Violin
sc WISCAS f.s., perf mat rent
(W143)
Symphony, No. 1
sc WISCAS f.s., perf mat rent
(W144)
Symphony, No. 2
sc WISCAS f.s., perf mat rent
(W145)

WARREN, B. (cont'd.)

Symphony, No. 3
sc WISCAS f.s., perf mat rent
(W146)
WARREN, HARRY (1893-1981)
Forty Second Street
2+pic.2+English horn.2+bass clar.2+
contrabsn. 4.4.3.1. timp,perc,
pno,harp,gtr,elec bass,strings
WARNER perf mat rent (W147)

Forty Second Street: Medley [arr.]
(Gold, Marty) 2+pic.1+English
horn.2+bass clar.2+contrabsn.
4.4.3.1. timp,perc,harp,strings
[6'] WARNER perf mat rent (W148)

Gold Digger's Song, The
2+pic.2.2+bass clar.2. 4.4.3.1.
timp,perc,harp,gtr,elec gtr,
strings WARNER perf mat rent
(W149)
Lullaby Of Broadway, [arr.]
(Nero, Peter) 2+pic.2.2+bass
clar.2. 4.3.3.1. timp,perc,harp,
elec bass,strings WARNER perf mat
rent (W150)

Shadow Waltz [arr.]
(Rose, Don) 2+pic.1+English horn.2+
bass clar.2. 4.3.3.1. timp,perc,
harp,strings WARNER perf mat rent
(W151)
WARRIOR see Fisher, Alfred

WARRIOR, THE, FOR PIANO AND ORCHESTRA
see Rudhyar, Dane (Daniel
Chennevière)

WARUM FRAGT MEIN HERZ, FOR SOLO VOICE
AND ORCHESTRA see Schönherr, Max

WAS ABER, FOR SOLO VOICES AND ORCHESTRA
see Rihm, Wolfgang

WAS BEDEUTET DIE BEWEGUNG? see
Schubert, Franz (Peter), Suleika I,
For Solo Voice And Orchestra[arr.]

WAS SICH LIEBT NECKT SICH see Strauss,
Johann, [Jr.]

WAS SUCHET IHR: DIE HÖLLE FLIEHT, FOR
SOLO VOICE AND ORCHESTRA see
Homilius, Gottfried August

WASHINGTON SQUARE: SUITE see Baker,
Michael Conway

WASPS, THE: SUITE see Vaughan Williams,
Ralph

WASSER-OUVERTURE IN C see Telemann,
Georg Philipp

WATANABE, URATO (1909-)
Three Movements, For Percussion And
Orchestra
3(pic).3(English horn).2.2.
4.2.3.1. timp,perc,harp,cel,
strings,perc solo
sc ZEN-ON 899440 f.s., perf mat
rent (W152)

WATER COLORS, FOR SOLO VOICE AND
ORCHESTRA see Carpenter, John Alden

WATER GARDEN, THE see Ott, David

WATER GOBLIN, THE see Dvořák, Antonín,
Watersprite

WATER MUSIC see Crosse, Gordon see
Handel, George Frideric see
Telemann, Georg Philipp, Wasser-
Ouverture In C

WATER OUT OF SUNLIGHT see Tippett,
[Sir] Michael

WATERSPRITE see Dvořák, Antonín

WATKINS, MICHAEL BLAKE (1948-)
Clouds And Eclipses [10']
string orch,gtr solo
NOVELLO perf mat rent (W153)

Concerto for Horn and String
Orchestra [18']
harp,strings,horn solo
NOVELLO perf mat rent (W154)

Dreams [20']
3(pic).3(English horn).3(bass
clar).3(contrabsn). 4.3.3.1.
3perc,timp,pno&cel,harp,strings
NOVELLO perf mat rent (W155)

Etalage [23']
3(pic).3(English horn).3.3.
4.3.3.1. timp,3perc,harp,
strings
NOVELLO perf mat rent (W156)

WATSON, ANTHONY
Prelude And Allegro [10']
string orch
sc WAI-TE-ATA f.s. (W157)

WATSON, WALTER ROBERT (1933-)
Concerto for Guitar and Chamber
Orchestra [12']
1.1.1(clar in A).0. 1.0.0.0.
timp,perc,pno,strings,gtr solo
LUDWIG perf mat rent (W158)

WAVE, FOR VIOLONCELLO AND ORCHESTRA see
Shimoyama, Hifumi

WAVERLY OVERTURE see Berlioz, Hector
(Louis)

WAVES, FOR GUITAR AND ORCHESTRA see
Tanenbaum, Elias

WAXMAN, FRANZ (1906-1967)
Adagio [3'48"]
string orch
FIDELIO (W159)

Anne Of The Indes Overture [5']
FIDELIO (W160)

Athaneal The Trumpeter, For Trumpet
And Orchestra [6'45"]
FIDELIO (W161)

Botany Bay: Suite [9'35"]
FIDELIO (W162)

Bride Of Frankenstein, The: Dance
Macabre [6']
2.2.2.2. 3.3.0.0. timp,3perc,
harp,elec org,strings
FIDELIO (W163)

Bride Of Frankenstein, The: Suite
[12'22"]
3(pic).2+English horn.2+bass
clar.2+contrabsn.2alto
sax.tenor sax. 4.3.3.1. timp,
4perc,harp,pno,elec org,strings
FIDELIO (W164)

Cafe Waltzes [7']
2.1.2.2. 3.4.3.1. timp,3perc,
harp,strings
FIDELIO (W165)

Captains Courageous: Suite [6'59"]
3.2.3.2. 4.3.3.1. timp,5perc,pno,
harp,strings
FIDELIO (W166)

Charm Bracelet, The [6'8"]
chamber orch FIDELIO (W167)

Classic Film Themes [10']
(contains themes from The
Philadelphia Story, A Place In
The Sun, This Is My Love,
Sayonara) FIDELIO (W168)

Classic Love Themes [8'30"]
3.3.3.3.tenor sax. 4.3.3.1. timp,
3perc,mand,harp,cel,strings
(contains themes from Peyton Place,
Elephant Walk, The Lost Command)
FIDELIO (W169)

Come Back, Little Sheba [5'12"]
2.1.2+bass clar.1. 3.3.3.0. timp,
2perc,pno,harp,strings
FIDELIO (W170)

Dance Macabre (from The Bride Of
Frankenstein) [6'57"]
FIDELIO (W171)

Demetrius And The Gladiators: Suite
[13'7"]
FIDELIO (W172)

Destination Tokyo [10']
3(pic,alto fl).2(English
horn).3(bass clar).2. 6.4.3.1.
timp,4perc,harp,gtr,pno,strings
FIDELIO (W173)

Dusk: A Setting For Orchestra [7'44"]
FIDELIO (W174)

Forsaken [3'48"]
3(alto fl).2(English horn).4(bass
clar).2(contrabsn). 4.3.3.1.
timp,4perc,2harp,pno,strings
FIDELIO (W175)

Furies, The: Suite [7']
FIDELIO (W176)

Hemingway: Symphonic Suite [16'54"]
FIDELIO (W177)

Huckleberry Finn Overture [5']
FIDELIO (W178)

Mr. Roberts: Mini-Suite [3'20"]
FIDELIO (W179)

WAXMAN, FRANZ (cont'd.)

Mr. Skeffington: Suite [5'4"]
FIDELIO   (W180)

Music From The 1920's: The Memories
Overture [6'15"]
2.2.2+bass clar.2. 4.3.3.1. timp,
3perc,harp,pno/cel,strings
FIDELIO   (W181)

Night Unto Night [7'20"]
2.2.5.2. 4.4.4.0. timp,2perc,
2harp,pno/cel,strings
FIDELIO   (W182)

Nightmoods [12'50"]
3(pic).2(English horn).4(bass
clar).3(contrabsn). 4.3.3.1.
timp,3perc,harp,pno,strings
FIDELIO   (W183)

Nightride [7'22"]
3(pic).0+English
horn.0.2(contrabsn).3sax.
4.3.3.1. timp,3perc,harp,pno/
cel,strings
FIDELIO   (W184)

Nostalgic Film Themes [9'53"]
(contains themes from Suspicion, My
Geisha, Beloved Infidel, Prince
Valiant) FIDELIO   (W185)

Nun's Story, The: Suite [13'30"]
FIDELIO   (W186)

Objective, Burma: Suite [14'22"]
FIDELIO   (W187)

Passacaglia [7']
FIDELIO   (W188)

Pioneer, The: Suite [7'30"]
FIDELIO   (W189)

Place In The Sun, A: Symphonic
Scenario [13'17"]
2(pic).2.3(bass
clar).2(contrabsn).alto sax.
4.3.3.1. timp,3perc,pno/cel,
harp,strings
FIDELIO   (W190)

Possessed: Suite [13'11"]
FIDELIO   (W191)

Rear Window: Suite [8']
2.1.3.1. 3.3.3.0. 2perc,harp,pno,
strings
FIDELIO   (W192)

Reminiscences [6']
FIDELIO   (W193)

Rhapsody for Piano and Orchestra
[12'20"]
FIDELIO   (W194)

Ride To Dubno, The [4'55"]
FIDELIO   (W195)

Roumanian Rhapsody No. 1 For Violin
And Orchestra [12']
2+pic.1+English horn.3.2.
4.4.1.1. timp,2perc,2harp,
strings,vln solo
(based on the Enesco Suite) FIDELIO
                                     (W196)

Ruth [24'10"]
FIDELIO   (W197)

Sayonara: Katsumi [3'22"]
2(alto fl)+pic.2.2+bass clar.2.
3.2.0.0. timp,3perc,2harp,pno/
cel,strings
FIDELIO   (W198)

Silver Chalice, The: Suite [16'11"]
FIDELIO   (W199)

Sinfonietta [12'38"]
timp,strings
FIDELIO perf mat rent   (W200)

Sorry Wrong Number [6'58"]
2(pic).2(English
horn).1.2(contrabsn). 4.3.3.1.
timp,3perc,harp,pno/cel,strings
FIDELIO   (W201)

Spirit Of St. Louis, The [30']
FIDELIO   (W202)

Suspicion: Suite [12'4"]
FIDELIO   (W203)

Taras Bulba: The Ride To Dubno
[4'55"]
3(pic).0.3(bass clar).2+
contrabsn.2sax. 4.4.4.1. timp,
4perc,harp,pno,strings
FIDELIO   (W204)

WAXMAN, FRANZ (cont'd.)

To Have And Have Not: Overture
[2'40"]
FIDELIO   (W205)

Two Mrs. Carrolls, The [4'24"]
FIDELIO   (W206)

WAY A LONE II, A see Takemitsu, Toru

WAY TO OLYMPUS, THE see Artyomov,
Vyacheslav

WAYANG V, FOR PIANO AND ORCHESTRA see
Davis, Anthony

WE STROLLED, FOR SOLO VOICE AND
ORCHESTRA [ARR.] see Brahms,
Johannes, Wir Wandelten, For Solo
Voice And Orchestra [arr.]

WEARY BLUES, FOR SOLO VOICE AND
ORCHESTRA see Rudd-Moore, Dorothy

WEBER, ALAIN (1930-   )
Lineaire I, For Saxophone And
Orchestra [20']
2.2.2.2. 2.2.1.0. 2perc,harp,
strings,sax solo
BILLAUDOT perf mat rent   (W207)

WEBER, BEN BRIAN (1916-1979)
Concerto for Piano and Orchestra, Op.
52 [25']
3.3.3.3. 4.2.3.1. timp,perc,
strings,pno solo
sc AM.COMP.AL. $46.35, perf mat
rent   (W208)

Enchanted Midnight, The *Op.60 [6']
2.3.3.3. 4.3.3.1. timp,perc,harp,
cel,strings
sc AM.COMP.AL. $9.15, perf mat rent
                                     (W209)

Prelude And Passacaglia *Op.42 [12']
2.2.2.2. 4.2.3.1. timp,perc,harp,
pno,cel,strings
sc AM.COMP.AL. $20.60, perf mat
rent   (W210)

WEBER, CARL MARIA VON (1786-1826)
Abu Hassan: Overture
min sc KALMUS K01448 $4.00   (W211)

Aufforderung Zum Tanz [arr.]
(Berlioz) "Invitation To The Dance
[arr.]" min sc KALMUS K01238
$5.50   (W212)
(Zani, G.) "Invito Alla Danza
[arr.]" 2.2.2.2. 2.2.0.0. timp,
perc,harp,strings [9'] SONZOGNO
perf mat rent   (W213)

Concerti for Clarinet and Orchestra,
Nos. 1-2
min sc KALMUS K00101 $6.00 contains
also: Concertino for Clarinet and
Orchestra, Op. 26, in E flat;
Concerto for Bassoon and
Orchestra, Op. 75, in F   (W214)

Concertino for Clarinet and
Orchestra, Op. 26, in E flat
see Concerti for Clarinet and
Orchestra, Nos. 1-2

Concertino for Oboe and Orchestra in
C
sc,pts MUS. RARA 1969B f.s.   (W215)

Concerto for Bassoon and Orchestra,
Op. 75, in F
MUS. RARA 1056 perf mat rent (W216)
(Allard, M.) sc BILLAUDOT f.s.,
perf mat rent   (W217)
see Concerti for Clarinet and
Orchestra, Nos. 1-2

Concerto for Clarinet and Orchestra,
No. 2, Op. 74, in E flat
SONZOGNO perf mat rent   (W218)

Concerto for Piano and Orchestra, No.
2, Op. 32, in E flat
BREITKOPF-L perf mat rent   (W219)

Drei Pintos, Die: Entr'acte
(Mahler) 2.2.2.2. 4.2.1.1. timp,
triangle,strings [3'] KALMUS
A5605 sc $5.00, set $20.00, perf
mat rent   (W220)

Euryanthe: Glocklein Im Tale, For
Solo Voice And Orchestra [4']
2.2.2.2. 2.0.0.0. strings,2vcl
soli,S solo
BREITKOPF-W perf mat rent   (W221)

Freischütz, Der: Einst Träumte Meiner
Sel'gen Base, For Solo Voice And
Orchestra
2.0.2.2. 2.0.0.0. strings,S solo
BREITKOPF-L perf mat rent   (W222)

WEBER, CARL MARIA VON (cont'd.)

Freischütz, Der: Hier Im Ird'schen
Jammertal, For Solo Voice And
Orchestra
2.2.0.2. 0.0.0.0. strings,B solo
BREITKOPF-L perf mat rent   (W223)

Freischütz, Der: Kommt Ein Schlanker
Bursch Gegangen, For Solo Voice
And Orchestra
BREITKOPF-L perf mat rent   (W224)

Freischütz, Der: Nein, Länger Trag
Ich Nicht Die Qualen; Durch Die
Wälder, Durch Die Auen, For Solo
Voice And Orchestra
BREITKOPF-L perf mat rent   (W225)

Freischütz, Der: Schelm, Halt Fest,
For Solo Voices And Orchestra
2.0.2.2. 2.0.0.0. strings,SS soli
BREITKOPF-L perf mat rent   (W226)

Freischütz, Der: Schweig', Schweig',
Damit, For Solo Voice And
Orchestra
4.2.2.2. 4.2.3.0. timp,strings,B
solo
BREITKOPF-L perf mat rent   (W227)

Freischütz, Der: Und Ob Die Wolke Sie
Verhülle, For Solo Voice And
Orchestra
BREITKOPF-L perf mat rent   (W228)

Freischütz, Der: Wie Nahte Mir Der
Schlummer, For Solo Voice And
Orchestra
BREITKOPF-L perf mat rent   (W229)

Invitation To The Dance [arr.]
see Aufforderung Zum Tanz [arr.]

Invito Alla Danza [arr.]
see Aufforderung Zum Tanz [arr.]

Jubel Ouverture
"Jubilee Overture" min sc KALMUS
K01449 $3.50   (W230)

Jubilee Overture
see Jubel Ouverture

Kleine Fritz An Seine Jungen Freunde,
Der, "Ach, Wenn Ich Nur Ein
Liebchen Hätte", For Solo Voice
And Orchestra, [arr.] *Op.15,
No.3
(Mottl) fl,2harp,strings,S solo
BREITKOPF-L perf mat rent (W231)

Meine Lieder, Meine Sänger, For Solo
Voice And Orchestra, [arr.]
*Op.15,No.1
(Mottl) 0.1.2.2. 2.0.0.0. strings,S
solo BREITKOPF-L perf mat rent
                                     (W232)

Oberon: Ozean, Du Ungeheuer, For Solo
Voice And Orchestra
BREITKOPF-L perf mat rent   (W233)

Peter Schmoll: Overture
min sc KALMUS K01446 $4.00   (W234)

Silvana: Overture
KALMUS A4276 sc $12.00, set $20.00
                                     (W235)

Turandot: Overture And March
KALMUS A5599 sc $15.00, set $20.00,
perf mat rent   (W236)

Unbefangenheit, For Solo Voice And
Orchestra, [arr.] *Op.30,No.3
(Mottl) 2.2.2.2. 2.0.0.0. strings
sc BREITKOPF-L PB 957 f.s., perf
mat rent   (W237)

WEBERN, ANTON VON (1883-1945)
Passacaglia, Op. 1, [arr.]
(Pousseur, Henri) I(pic).1.1.1.
1.0.1.0. perc,vibra,synthesizer,
vln,vla,vcl,db [15'] UNIVER. perf
mat rent   (W238)

WECKMANN, MATTHIAS (1619-1674)
Wie Liegt Die Stadt So Wueste, For
Solo Voices And String Orchestra
string orch,org,SB soli KALMUS
A4027 sc $6.00, set $7.00, pts
$.75. ea.   (W239)

WEDDING ALBUM, THE, VOL. 1 *CC7U
(Zinn, William) string orch EXCELSIOR
set 494-00536 $18.00, pts
494-00536P $4.00 arr.   (W240)

WEDDING ALBUM, THE, VOL. 2 *CC7U
(Zinn, William) string orch EXCELSIOR
set 494-00537 $18.00, pts
494-00537P $4.00 arr.   (W241)

WEDDING DAY AT TROLDHAUGEN [ARR.] see
Grieg, Edvard Hagerup

WEDDING IN THE WOOD see Groven, Eivind,
Bryllaup I Skogen

WEDDING MARCH see Madsen, Trygve,
Brudemarsj

WEDDING ON THE MOON see Haenflein,
Robert

WEE WEE MAN, THE, FOR SOLO VOICE AND
ORCHESTRA see Holmboe, Vagn

WEEKS
Pastoral Morning, For Oboe And String
Orchestra
string orch,ob solo
sc,pts MUSICUS f.s.   (W242)

WEEPING PLEIADES, THE, FOR SOLO VOICE
AND INSTRUMENTAL ENSEMBLE see
Flanagan, William

WEG ZUM OLYMP, DER see Artyomov,
Vyacheslav, Way To Olympus, The

WEGNER, AUGUST MARTIN (1941-   )
Ice-Nine, For Piano And Chamber
Orchestra
fl,clar,bass clar,horn,trp,trom,
strings,pno solo
SEESAW   (W243)

WEIGL, KARL (1881-1949)
Concerto for Violoncello and
Orchestra [20']
2.2.2.2. 4.2.0.0. timp,perc,
strings,vcl solo
DUCHESS perf mat rent   (W244)

Pied Piper Suite [14']
1.1.1.1. 1.0.0.0. perc,pno,
strings
AM.COMP.AL. perf mat rent   (W245)

WEIGL, [MRS.] VALLY (1889-1982)
Adagio [5']
string orch
sc AM.COMP.AL. $1.95   (W246)

Andante [4']
string orch
sc AM.COMP.AL. $4.60   (W247)

Five Songs Of Remembrance, For Solo
Voice And String Orchestra [11']
string orch,S solo
sc AM.COMP.AL. $9.15   (W248)

Requiem For Solo Allison, For Voice
And String Orchestra [7']
string orch,S solo
sc AM.COMP.AL. $1.95   (W249)

To Emily [5']
string orch
sc AM.COMP.AL. $1.95   (W250)

WEIHE DES HAUSES, DIE see Beethoven,
Ludwig van

WEIHNACHTEN see Weinberger, Jaromir

WEIHNACHTEN, FOR STRING ORCHESTRA see
Reger, Max

WEIHNACHTSOUVERTURE UBER DEN CHORALE
"VOM HIMMEL HOCH" see Nicolai, Otto

WEILL, KURT (1900-1950)
Concerto for Violin and Winds, Op. 12
2.1.2.2. 2.1.0.0. perc,db,vln
solo
sc UNIVER. 8340 $44.00   (W251)

WEIN, WEIB UND GESANG see Strauss,
Johann, [Jr.]

WEINBERGER, JAROMIR (1896-1967)
Bohemian Songs And Dances, No. 1
2.2.2.2. 4.2.3.0. perc,harp,cel,
strings,vln solo
AMP perf mat rent   (W252)

Bohemian Songs And Dances, No. 2
2.2.2.2. 4.2.3.0. timp,perc,harp,
cel,strings
AMP perf mat rent   (W253)

Bohemian Songs And Dances, No. 3
2.2.2.2. 4.2.3.0. timp,perc,harp,
cel,strings
AMP perf mat rent   (W254)

Bohemian Songs And Dances, No. 4
2.2.2.2. 4.2.3.0. timp,perc,harp,
cel,strings
AMP perf mat rent   (W255)

Bohemian Songs And Dances, No. 5
2.2.2.2. 4.2.3.0. timp,perc,harp,
cel,strings
AMP perf mat rent   (W256)

Bohemian Songs And Dances, No. 6
2.2.2.2. 4.2.3.0. timp,perc,harp,
strings

WEINBERGER, JAROMIR (cont'd.)

AMP perf mat rent   (W257)

Wallenstein Suite
2+pic.2.2.2. 4.3.2.1. timp,perc,
harp,cel,strings
AMP perf mat rent   (W258)

Weihnachten [20']
3.3.3.3. 4.3.3.1. timp,perc,cel,
2harp,pno,org,strings
AMP perf mat rent   (W259)

WEINE NICHT, BRICHT EINE SCHONE FRAU
DIR DAS HERZ, FOR SOLO VOICE AND
ORCHESTRA [ARR.] see Stolz, Robert

WEINER, LEO (1885-1960)
Carnival Humoresque
see Fasching

Divertimento, No. 1, Op. 20
KALMUS A2280 sc $10.00, set $12.00,
pts $2.00, ea.   (W260)

Divertimento, No. 2, Op. 24
KALMUS A4132 sc $10.00, set $15.00,
pts $3.00, ea.   (W261)

Fasching *Op.5
"Carnival Humoresque" KALMUS A6531
sc $10.00, set $40.00, pts $3.00,
ea., perf mat rent   (W262)

Preludio, Notturno E Scherzo
Diabolico *Op.31
min sc EMB 3715 f.s.   (W263)

Serenade, Op. 3, in F minor
KALMUS A6997 sc $20.00, set $50.00,
pts $4.00, ea., perf mat rent
                           (W264)

Suite On Hungarian Folk Themes
see Suite, Op. 18

Suite, Op. 18 [30']
2(pic).2(English horn).2.2.
4.2.3.1. timp,perc,cel,harp,
strings
"Suite On Hungarian Folk Themes"
KALMUS A5530 sc $50.00, set
$90.00, pts $5.00, ea., perf mat
rent   (W265)

WEINER, STANLEY (1925-   )
Arche Noah, For Narrator And
Orchestra [26']
2.2.2.2. 2.2.2.1. timp,perc,harp,
cel,strings,narrator
"Noah's Ark, For Narrator And
Orchestra" study sc SIKORSKI 1254
$48.00, perf mat rent   (W266)

Ballade And Allegro, For 2 Violins
And String Orchestra *Op.88
[16']
string orch,2vln soli
SIKORSKI perf mat rent   (W267)

Concerto for Piano and String
Orchestra, Op. 86 [22']
string orch,pno solo
SIKORSKI perf mat rent   (W268)

Concerto for Trumpet and Orchestra,
Op. 46 [18'50"]
2.2.2.2. 2.2.2.0. timp,perc,
strings,trp solo
BILLAUDOT perf mat rent   (W269)

Concerto for Violin, Viola and
Orchestra, Op. 110 [27']
2.2.0.2. 2.0.0.0. timp,strings,
vln solo,vla solo
SIKORSKI perf mat rent   (W270)

Concerto for 2 Violins and Orchestra,
Op. 27 [23']
1.2.0.2. 2.0.0.0. strings,2vln
soli
BILLAUDOT perf mat rent   (W271)

Noah's Ark, For Narrator And
Orchestra
see Arche Noah, For Narrator And
Orchestra

Rhapsody for 2 Trumpets and String
Orchestra, Op. 102 [9']
string orch,2trp soli
SIKORSKI perf mat rent   (W272)

Symphony No. 3, Op. 93 [29']
3.2.3.2. 4.3.3.1. timp,perc,pno,
strings
SIKORSKI perf mat rent   (W273)

WEINER-DILLMANN, H.
Girandola
2.2.2.2. 4.2.3.0. perc,cel,harp,
strings
KRENN f.s.   (W274)

WEINGARDEN, LOUIS (1943-   )
Concerto for Piano and Orchestra
[29']
3(pic).2+English horn.2+bass
clar.2+contrabsn. 4.3.3.1.
5perc,2harp,cel,mand,gtr,
strings,pno solo
BOOSEY perf mat rent   (W275)

WEINGARTNER, (PAUL) FELIX VON
(1863-1942)
Dame Kobold: Walzer [7']
2.2.2.2. 4.2.3.0. timp,perc,harp,
strings
sc UNIVER. 5825 f.s.   (W276)

Sturm, Der *Op.65 [30']
2.2.2.2. 4.2.3.0. timp,perc,
2harp,org,strings
sc UNIVER. 7281 f.s.   (W277)

WEINZWEIG, JOHN (1913-   )
Divertimento No. 10 for Piano and
String Orchestra [15']
string orch,pno solo
CAN.MUS.CENT. MI 1661 W4245D10
                           (W278)

WEIR, JUDITH (1954-   )
Isti Mirant Stelle
2.2.2.2. 2.2.0.0. strings
sc NOVELLO $18.25   (W279)

Sederunt Principes [30']
1.1.2.1. 1.1.1.0. perc,harp,pno,
3vln,2vla,vcl,db
CHESTER perf mat rent   (W280)

Wunderhorn [12']
4(pic).3.4.4. 6.6.3.1. timp,
2perc,harp,strings
NOVELLO perf mat rent   (W281)

WEIS, FLEMMING (1898-   )
Chaconne [14']
2.2.2.2. 2.2.2.0. timp,strings
SAMFUNDET perf mat rent   (W282)

Femdelt Form III
"Quintuple Form III" sc,pts
SAMFUNDET f.s.   (W283)

In Temporis Vernalis [6']
2+pic.2.2.2. 4.2.3.1. timp,perc,
strings
HANSEN-DEN perf mat rent   (W284)

Musikantisk Ouverture [5']
string orch
HANSEN-DEN perf mat rent   (W285)

Quintuple Form III
see Femdelt Form III

WEISBERG, ARTHUR
Opening Statement [19']
2.2.3.3. 4.3.3.1. perc,harp,pno,
strings
sc AM.COMP.AL. $25.60   (W286)

WEISE VON LIEBE UND TOD DES KORNETS
CRISTOPH RILKE, DIE, FOR NARRATOR
AND ORCHESTRA see Ruyneman, Daniel

WEISGALL, HUGO (1912-   )
Prospect: 1983 [14']
PRESSER perf mat rent   (W287)

Tekiatot [8']
PRESSER perf mat rent   (W288)

WEISS, HARALD (1949-   )
Nachtmusik, For Guitar And Orchestra
perc, guitar choir, strings, gtr
solo
SCHOTTS sc CON 180 $20.00, set
CON 180-50 $43.00   (W289)

WEISSENBORN, JULIUS (1837-1888)
Kleine Suite For 3 Bassoons And
Orchestra [arr.]
(Geese, H.) 2.1.2.0. 3.2.3.0. timp,
perc,strings,3bsn soli/1bsn solo
[15'] SIKORSKI perf mat rent
                           (W290)

WELCHER, DAN EDWARD (1948-   )
Prairie Light [14']
PRESSER perf mat rent   (W291)

WELCOMING OVERTURE see Khachaturian,
Aram Ilyich

WELIN, KARL-ERIK (1934-1992)
Concertino for Clarinet, Violin,
Piano and Orchestra [11']
2.1.0.1. 2.0.0.0. timp,strings,
clar solo,vln solo,pno solo
STIM   (W292)

Symphony No. 1 [19']
4.1.0.1. 2.1.1.1. timp,perc,
strings
STIM   (W293)

WELLEJUS, HENNING (1919-   )
Har Slet Ingen Hast, Det
sc,pts SAMFUNDET f.s.   (W294)

Mailcoach Is Rolling, The [4']
2.2.2.2. 2.2.1.0. timp,strings
HANSEN-DEN perf mat rent   (W295)

Passacaglia, Op. 19 [9']
2.2.2.2. 4.3.3.1. timp,perc,
strings
HANSEN-DEN perf mat rent   (W296)

WELLESZ, EGON (1885-1974)
Symphony No. 2, Op. 65
3.3.3.2. 4.3.3.1. timp,perc,
strings
DOBLINGER perf mat rent   (W297)

WELLINGTON'S DEFEAT see Wright, Maurice

WELLINGTONS SIEG see Beethoven, Ludwig van

WELLINGTON'S VICTORY OR THE BATTLE OF
VITTORIA see Beethoven, Ludwig van,
Wellingtons Sieg

WELSH NURSERY TUNES see Hoddinott, Alun

WELTY WOMEN see Haxton, Kenneth

WENDELBOE, JENS (1956-   )
Pagina
2(pic).2.2.2. 4.3.3.1. timp,perc,
strings
NORGE   (W298)

WENN BACH BIENEN GEZUCHTET HATTE see
Pärt, Arvo

WENN DIE KRANICHE ZIEHEN, FOR PIANO AND
ORCHESTRA [ARR.] see Vainberg,
Moysey Samuilovitch

WENN DU ZU DEN BLUMEN GEHST, FOR SOLO
VOICE AND ORCHESTRA see Wolf, Hugo

WENN NACH DER STÜRME TOBEN, FOR SOLO
VOICE AND ORCHESTRA see Bach,
Johann Christian

WER EINSAM IST, DER HAT ES GUT:
OUVERTURE A see Uhl, Alfred

WER SEIN HOLDES LIEB VERLOREN, FOR SOLO
VOICE AND ORCHESTRA see Wolf, Hugo

WERKE FUR STREICHER UND BASSO CONTINUO
see Bach, Johann Sebastian

WERLE, FLOYD EDWARDS (1929-   )
Concerto for Trumpet and Orchestra,
No. 1 [20']
2.2.2.2. 4.4.3.1. timp,perc,
strings,trp solo
BOURNE perf mat rent   (W299)

Concerto for Trumpet and Orchestra,
No. 2 [20']
3.3.3.2. 4.3.3.1. timp,perc,
strings,trp solo
BOURNE perf mat rent   (W300)

Concerto for Trumpet and Orchestra,
No. 3 [23']
2.2.2.2. 4.3.3.1. timp,perc,
strings,trp solo
BOURNE perf mat rent   (W301)

Venite Exultamus [9']
3.3.3.2. 4.3.3.1. timp,perc,
strings
BOURNE perf mat rent   (W302)

WERLE, LARS-JOHAN (1926-   )
Lullaby For The Earth
see Vaggsang For Jorden

Nattjakt, For Solo Voice And
Orchestra [6']
2.2.2.2. 2.2.2.0. timp,perc,
strings,S solo
NORDISKA perf mat rent   (W303)

Smultronvisa, For Solo Voice And
Chamber Orchestra [2']
fl,strings,solo voice
NORDISKA perf mat rent   (W304)

Vaggsang For Jorden [20']
3.3.3.3. 4.3.3.1. timp,perc,harp,
pno,strings
"Lullaby For The Earth" NORDISKA
perf mat rent   (W305)

WERNER, FRITZ (1898-1977)
Concerto for Horn and String
Orchestra, Op. 54 [15']
string orch,horn solo
sc BILLAUDOT f.s., perf mat rent
(W306)
Concerto for Piano and Orchestra, Op.
12, in A minor [25']
2.2.2.2. 2.2.0.0. timp,strings,
pno solo

WERNER, FRITZ (cont'd.)

VIEWEG perf mat rent   (W307)

Konzertante Musik *Op.23 [19']
fl,ob,horn,strings
VIEWEG perf mat rent   (W308)

Symphonische Musik *Op.45 [23']
string orch
VIEWEG perf mat rent   (W309)

WERNER, JEAN-JACQUES (1935-   )
Aleph. Sinfonia Sacra [14']
3.3.3.3. 4.3.2.1. harp,strings
BILLAUDOT perf mat rent   (W310)

Alpha Es Et O [8']
4.3.4.2. 2.2.2.1. timp,perc,harp,
strings
BILLAUDOT perf mat rent   (W311)

Divertimento [16']
1.1.1.1. 1.1.1.0. perc,hpsd/harp,
pno,string quin
BILLAUDOT perf mat rent   (W312)

Spiritual, For Violin And String
Orchestra [8']
string orch,vln solo
BILLAUDOT perf mat rent   (W313)

WERNER, SVEN ERIK
Precipices Of Zealand
see Sjellandske Afgrunde

Sjellandske Afgrunde [20']
3.3.3.3. 4.3.3.1. harp,perc,pno,
cel,mand,strings
"Precipices Of Zealand" SAMFUNDET
perf mat rent   (W314)

WERNICK, RICHARD F. (1934-   )
Concerto for Viola and Orchestra
[20']
PRESSER perf mat rent   (W315)

Concerto for Violin and Orchestra
[23']
PRESSER perf mat rent   (W316)

WERTHEIM, R.
Divertimento
BROEKMANS 304 perf mat rent (W317)

WESENDONK LIEDER, FOR SOLO VOICE AND
ORCHESTRA [ARR.] see Wagner,
Richard

WESLEY, SAMUEL (1766-1837)
Symphonic Works, Two
see Herschel, William, Symphonies,
Three

Symphonic Works, Two *see Herschel,
William, Symphonies, Three

WESLEY, SAMUEL SEBASTIAN (1810-1876)
Symphony *see Herschel, William,
Symphonies, Three
see Herschel, William, Symphonies,
Three

WESSMAN, HARRI (1949-   )
Concerto for Trumpet and Orchestra
[18']
1.1.1.1. 1.1.0.0. perc,strings,
trp solo
sc SUOMEN f.s.   (W318)

Serenade for Piano and String
Orchestra [5']
string orch,pno solo
sc,pts FAZER f.s.   (W319)

WEST SIDE STORY: A BOY LIKE THAT, FOR
SOLO VOICES AND ORCHESTRA see
Bernstein, Leonard

WEST SIDE STORY: BALCONY SCENE
"TONIGHT", FOR SOLO VOICES AND
ORCHESTRA see Bernstein, Leonard

WEST SIDE STORY: BALLET SEQUENCE see
Bernstein, Leonard

WEST SIDE STORY: DANCE SEQUENCE see
Bernstein, Leonard

WEST SIDE STORY: FINALE, FOR SOLO
VOICES AND ORCHESTRA see Bernstein,
Leonard

WEST SIDE STORY: I FEEL PRETTY, FOR
SOLO VOICE AND ORCHESTRA see
Bernstein, Leonard

WEST SIDE STORY: MARIA, FOR SOLO VOICE
AND ORCHESTRA see Bernstein,
Leonard

WEST SIDE STORY: ONE HAND, ONE HEART,
FOR SOLO VOICES AND ORCHESTRA see
Bernstein, Leonard

WEST SIDE STORY: OVERTURE see
Bernstein, Leonard

WEST SIDE STORY: PROLOGUE see
Bernstein, Leonard

WEST SIDE STORY: SOMETHING'S COMING,
FOR SOLO VOICE AND ORCHESTRA see
Bernstein, Leonard

WEST SIDE STORY: SOMEWHERE, FOR SOLO
VOICES AND ORCHESTRA see Bernstein,
Leonard

WESTENWIND, DE, FOR NARRATOR AND
ORCHESTRA see Badings, Henk

WESTERGAARD, SVEND (1922-   )
Trasformazioni Sinfoniche, For Piano
And Orchestra *Op.32
2.2.2.2. 4.3.3.1. timp,perc,
strings,pno solo
sc HANSEN-DEN $58.00, perf mat rent
(W320)
Variazioni Sinfoniche *Op.25 [18']
string orch
SAMFUNDET perf mat rent   (W321)

WETTERMASCHINE, DIE see Kratzschmar,
Wilfried

WETZ, RICHARD (1875-1935)
Concerto for Violin and Orchestra,
Op. 57
KISTNER perf mat rent   (W322)

Kleist-Ouverture *Op.16
KISTNER perf mat rent   (W323)

Symphony No. 2, Op. 47
KISTNER   (W324)

WHAT MAKES ME BELIEVE YOU? [ARR.] see
Lawrence, Charles

WHAT ONE HEARS ON THE MOUNTAIN see
Liszt, Franz, Ce Qu'on Entend Sur
La Montagne

WHEAR, PAUL WILLIAM (1925-   )
Appalachian Folk Tale, An, For
Narrator And Orchestra [23']
2.2.2.2. 2.2.2.0. timp,perc,
strings,narrator,opt harp
LUDWIG perf mat rent   (W325)

Pastorale Lament, For Horn And String
Orchestra [9']
string orch,horn solo
LUDWIG perf mat rent   (W326)

Poem Of Roland, For Violin And
Chamber Orchestra [10']
2.2.2.2. 2.2.0.0. perc,harp,
strings,vln solo
LUDWIG perf mat rent   (W327)

Sonnets From Shakespeare, For Solo
Voice And Chamber Orchestra [12']
2.2.2.2. 2.2.0.0. perc,harp,
strings,Bar solo
LUDWIG perf mat rent   (W328)

Symphony No. 3 [25']
2.2.2.2. 3.2.1.0. timp,perc,harp,
strings
LUDWIG perf mat rent   (W329)

WHEAT HAS RIPENED, FOR SOLO VOICE AND
ORCHESTRA see Golob, Jani, Zreilo
Je Zito, For Solo Voice And
Orchestra

WHEN I DIED IN BERNERS STREET see Howe,
Mary

WHEN QUIET IMPLODES see Rudhyar, Dane
(Daniel Chennevière)

WHEN THE TWAIN MEET see Kaufman,
Fredrick

WHEN THE WILLOW NODS see Becker, John
Joseph

WHEN YOU CLOSE MY EYES, FOR SOLO VOICE
AND ORCHESTRA see Frumerie, (Per)
Gunnar (Fredrik) de

WHERE SILENCE REIGNS, FOR SOLO VOICE
AND CHAMBER ORCHESTRA see Geller,
Timothy

WHERE THE CITRONS BLOOM see Strauss,
Johann, [Jr.], Wo Die Zitronen
Bluh'n

WHERE'S CHARLEY: MY DARLING, MY
DARLING, FOR SOLO VOICES AND
ORCHESTRA see Loesser, Frank

WHERE'S CHARLEY: ONCE IN LOVE WITH AMY,
FOR SOLO VOICE AND ORCHESTRA see
Loesser, Frank

WHISPERS OUT OF TIME see Reynolds, Roger

WHITE, DAVID ASHLEY
Elm Is Scattering, The, For Oboe And Orchestra
SHAWNEE perf mat rent   (W330)

WHITE-HAIRED GIRL, THE: SUITE see Chu, Wei

WHITE LILACS, FOR VIOLIN AND ORCHESTRA [ARR.] see Gruenberg, Louis

WHITE SPIRITUALS, FOR SOLO VOICE AND ORCHESTRA see Franceschini, Romulus

WHITNEY, MAURICE CARY (1909-   )
Deidre Overture (An Irish Legend) [5']
WARNER perf mat rent   (W331)

Gavotto Staccato
2.2.2.2. 4.2.3.1. timp,drums,pno, strings
BOURNE perf mat rent   (W332)

WHO CARES see Gershwin, George

WHO KILLED COCK ROBIN, FOR NARRATOR AND ORCHESTRA see Peck, Russell James

WHOM YE ADORE see Harvey, Jonathan

WHY NOT see Gentile, Ada

WHY REACH FOR THE MOON see Antonini, Alfredo

WHY THE DUCK HAS A SHORT TAIL, FOR NARRATOR AND ORCHESTRA see Ballard, Louis Wayne

WIBLO see Sigurbjörnsson, Thorkell

WIDERHALL see Engel, Paul

WIDERSPENSTIGEN ZAHMUNG, DER: OVERTURE see Goetz, Hermann

WIDOW OF VALENCIA, THE: SUITE see Khachaturian, Aram Ilyich

WIE BIST DU DENN, O GOTT, IN ZORN ENTBRANNT, FOR SOLO VOICE AND ORCHESTRA see Bach, Johann Christoph

WIE EINST LILI MARLEEN see Priegnitz, Hans

WIE LIEGT DIE STADT SO WUESTE, FOR SOLO VOICES AND STRING ORCHESTRA see Weckmann, Matthias

WIEDER MOCHT' ICH DIR BEGEGNEN, FOR SOLO VOICE AND ORCHESTRA [ARR.] see Liszt, Franz

WIEGENLIED, DAS, FOR NARRATOR AND ORCHESTRA see Roos, Robert de

WIEGENLIED [ARR.] see Liszt, Franz

WIEGENLIED "SCHLAFE, HOLDER SÜSSER KNABE", FOR SOLO VOICE AND ORCHESTRA, [ARR.] see Schubert, Franz (Peter)

WIEN, MEIN SINN WALZER see Strauss, Johann, [Jr.]

WIENEN, KLAGEN [ARR.] see Liszt, Franz

WIENER BONBONS WALZER see Strauss, Johann, [Jr.]

WIENER CARNEVALS QUADRILLE see Strauss, Johann, [Sr.]

WIENER CHRONIK 1848 see Schwertsik, Kurt

WIENER CHRONIK WALZER see Strauss, Johann, [Jr.]

WIENER FRAUEN WALZER see Strauss, Johann, [Jr.]

WIENER FRESKEN WALZER see Strauss, Josef

WIENER KINDER WALZER see Strauss, Josef

WIENER STIMMEN WALZER see Strauss, Josef

WIENHORST, RICHARD (1920-   )
Canticle, For Percussion And Chamber Orchestra [11']
1(pic).0.1.1. 1.1.0.0. 2vln,2vla, 2vcl,db,perc solo
sc AM.COMP.AL. $6.90, perf mat rent
(W333)

WIENHORST, RICHARD (cont'd.)

Three Parodies, For Trumpet And Chamber Orchestra [6']
1.1.1.1. 1.1.0.0. timp,perc,xylo, strings,trp solo
sc AM.COMP.AL. $14.90, perf mat rent   (W334)

WIENIAWSKI, HENRYK (1835-1880)
Legende, For Violin And Orchestra *Op.17
SCHIRM.G perf mat rent   (W335)

Souvenir De Moscou, For Violin And Orchestra [arr.] *Op.6
(Nitschke, Manfred) 2.2.2.2. 3.2.0.0. perc,harp,strings,vln solo [10'] SIKORSKI perf mat rent
(W336)

WIESLANDER, INGVAR (1917-1963)
Berceuse [3']
string orch
sc,pts BUSCH HBM 001 f.s.   (W337)

Mutazioni, For 2 Pianos And Orchestra [21']
2.2.2.2. 4.2.3.0. timp,2perc, strings,2pno soli
STIM   (W338)

Under The Stars, For Violin And String Orchestra
see Unter Den Sternen, For Violin And String Orchestra

Unter Den Sternen, For Violin And String Orchestra [4'15']
string orch,vln solo
"Under The Stars, For Violin And String Orchestra" sc,pts BUSCH HBM 002 f.s.   (W339)

WIGGLESWORTH, FRANK (1918-   )
Aurora [14']
string orch
sc AM.COMP.AL. $13.80   (W340)

Janus [10']
3.2.3.2. 4.4.2.1. 3perc,strings
sc AM.COMP.AL. $45.30, perf mat rent   (W341)

Sea Winds [15']
string orch
sc AM.COMP.AL. $11.45, perf mat rent   (W342)

Three Portraits [15']
string orch
sc AM.COMP.AL. $11.45, perf mat rent   (W343)

WIJS, KEES DE (1934-   )
Wilhelmus Van Nassouwe
2.2.2.2. 4.3.3.1. strings
sc DONEMUS f.s., perf mat rent
(W344)

WIKLUND, ADOLF (1879-1950)
Jeg Synes At Verden Skinner, For Solo Voice And Orchestra [3']
2.1.2.1. 2.0.0.0. timp,strings, med solo
NORDISKA perf mat rent   (W345)

Lykken I Min Sjal, For Solo Voice And Orchestra [3']
2.2.2.2. 4.0.0.0. harp,strings, med solo
NORDISKA perf mat rent   (W346)

Three Roses, For Solo Voice And Orchestra [4']
2.2.2.2. 2.2.1.0. timp,harp, strings,med solo
NORDISKA perf mat rent   (W347)

WILBY, PHILIP (1949-   )
Highland Express, The, For Narrator And Orchestra [13']
2(pic).2.2.2. 4.2.3.1. 3perc, strings,narrator
(variable instrumentation; may be performed by string orchestra with synthesizer) CHESTER perf mat rent   (W348)

Sunstudy [12']
2+pic.2+English horn.2+clar in E flat.2+contrabsn. 4.4.3.1. timp,4perc,pno&opt org,strings
CHESTER perf mat rent   (W349)

Wings Of Morning, The [12']
2ob,2horn,strings
CHESTER perf mat rent   (W350)

WILD DOVE , THE see Dvorák, Antonín, Wood Dove

WILD HORSES see Godfrey, Daniel

WILDBOY see Crosse, Gordon

WILDER, ALEC (1907-1980)
Carl Sandburg Suite [16']
2(pic).2(English horn).2.2. 2.2.2.0. 2perc,harp,strings
sc AMP f.s., perf mat rent   (W351)

WILDFIRES AND FIELD SONGS see Moore, Carman

WILDSCHUTZ, DER: AUF DES LEBENS RASCHEN WOGEN, FOR SOLO VOICE AND ORCHESTRA see Lortzing, (Gustav) Albert

WILDSCHÜTZ, DER: FÜNFTAUSEND TALER, FOR SOLO VOICE AND ORCHESTRA see Lortzing, (Gustav) Albert

WILDSCHÜTZ, DER: HEITERKEIT UND FRÖHLICHKEIT, FOR SOLO VOICE AND ORCHESTRA see Lortzing, (Gustav) Albert

WILDSCHUTZ, DER: IHR WEIB? MEIN TEURES WEIB!, FOR SOLO VOICES AND ORCHESTRA see Lortzing, (Gustav) Albert

WILDSCHÜTZ, DER: LASS ER DOCH HÖREN, FOR SOLO VOICES AND ORCHESTRA see Lortzing, (Gustav) Albert

WILHELMUS VAN NASSOUWE see Wijs, Kees de

WILL O' THE WISP [ARR.] see Liszt, Franz, Feux Follets [arr.]

WILLCOCKS, DAVID VALENTINE (1919-   )
Opening Fanfare For The Wedding Of Prince Charles And Lady Diana Spencer
3.2.2.3. 4.3+opt 6trp.3.1. timp, perc,opt org,strings
OXFORD perf mat rent   (W352)

WILLCOCKS, JONATHAN
Concert Overture - Australia [12']
3.3.3.3. 4.3.3.1. timp,5perc, harp,strings
OXFORD perf mat rent   (W353)

WILLEN, NIKLAS (1961-   )
Concerto for Bassoon and Orchestra [12']
2.2.2.2. 2.1.1.0. perc,harp,6vln, 4vla,4vcl,2db,bsn solo
STIM   (W354)

WILLI, HERBERT (1956-   )
Aurora-Giove [13']
1+pic.1+English horn.2(clar in E flat)+bass clar.1+ contrabsn.alto sax. 2.2.2.1. timp,perc,harp,strings
DOBLINGER perf mat rent   (W355)

Combattimento Di Cecco E La Sua Compagnia, Il, For Violoncello And String Orchestra [15']
string orch,vcl solo
DOBLINGER perf mat rent   (W356)

Froschmausekrieg, For Solo Voice And Orchestra [14']
2(pic).1+English horn.1+bass clar.1.soprano sax. 2.2.2.1. timp,perc,harp,pno,strings, electronic tape,solo voice
DOBLINGER perf mat rent   (W357)

WILLIAM RATCLIFF see Ostendorf, Jens-Peter

WILLIAMS, CLIFTON (1923-1976)
Laredo [arr.]
(Astwood, Michael) 2+pic.2.3+bass clar.2. 4.3.3.1. timp,perc, strings (gr. IV) SOUTHERN A-34 sc $7.50, set $50.00, pts $2.50, ea.
(W358)

WILLIAMS, DAVID
Elegy for Alto Saxophone and Orchestra
4perc,strings,alto sax solo
sc,pts DORN $85.00   (W359)

WILLIAMS, [JOHN] GERRARD (1888-1947)
Three Traditional Scottish Songs [6']
2.0.2.0. 0.2.0.0. perc,strings (winds and percussion are optional)
KALMUS A7375 sc $7.00, set $18.00, pts $1.50, ea., perf mat rent   (W360)

WILLIAMS, GRACE (1906-1977)
Sea Sketches [17']
string orch
OXFORD perf mat rent   (W361)

WILLIAMS, GRAHAM (1940-   )
Symphony No. 1 [20']
2.2(English horn).2(clar in E flat,bass clar).2. 4.3.3.1. timp,perc,strings
CHESTER JWC440 perf mat rent (W362)

WILLIAMS, JOHN
Superman: Symphonic Suite, [arr.]
[11']
(Tatgenhorst) WARNER perf mat rent
(W363)

WILLIAMS, JOHN T. (1932-   )
Adventure On Earth [arr.] (from E.T.
The Extra-Terrestrial)
(Spencer, Herb) 3(pic).2(English
horn).2.3(contrabsn). 5.3.3.1.
timp,4perc,pno,2harp,strings
[15'] MCA perf mat rent   (W364)

Concerto for Tuba and Orchestra
WARNER perf mat rent   (W365)

Cowboy's Overture, The
[4'30"] WARNER perf mat rent (W366)

Empire Strikes Back, The: Symphonic
Suite [20']
WARNER perf mat rent   (W367)

Flying Theme, The [arr.] (from E.T.
The Extra-Terrestrial)
(Spencer, Herb) 3.2.2.3. 5.3.3.1.
timp,perc,harp,pno&cel,strings
MCA perf mat rent   (W368)

Jaws I: Suite [arr.]
(Cacavas, John) 3(pic).1.2.1.
4.3.3.1. opt 2alto sax,opt tenor
sax,timp,2perc,opt pno,strings
[7'30"] MCA perf mat rent   (W369)

Liberty Fanfare [5']
2+pic.2+English horn.2.0.
6.6.3.1. timp,perc,pno&cel,
harp,opt org,strings
WARNER perf mat rent   (W370)

Raiders Of The Lost Ark: The Raiders
March [5'12"]
3(pic).3(English horn).3(bass
clar).3(contrabsn). 4.4.4.1.
timp,perc,harp,pno&cel,strings
CPP perf mat rent   (W371)

Return Of The Jedi: Suite
[20'] WARNER perf mat rent   (W372)

Star Wars: Symphonic Suite [30']
WARNER perf mat rent   (W373)

Summer Olympic Fanfare [5']
2+pic.0.3.2+contrabsn. 6.6.0.1.
timp,2perc,org,pno,harp,strings
WARNER perf mat rent   (W374)

WILLIAMS, JULIUS P.
Norman Overture, A [17']
2.2.2.2. 4.3.3.1. timp,perc,
strings
MMB perf mat rent   (W375)

Toccatina In D [4']
string orch
MMB perf mat rent   (W376)

WILLIAMS, PATRICK M. (1939-   )
Romances For Jazz Soloist And
Orchestra [12'10"]
2.2.2.2. 4.2.2.1. timp,perc,
synthesizer,harp,strings,
flügelhorn/tenor sax solo
NEWAM 19044 perf mat rent   (W377)

Spring Wings, For Piano, Saxophone
And Orchestra [16']
2+pic.2+English horn.2+bass
clar.2+contrabsn. 4.4.3+bass
trom.1. timp,perc,cel,harp,
strings,pno solo,baritone sax
solo
NEWAM 19043 perf mat rent   (W378)

WILLIAMS, RALPH VAUGHAN
see VAUGHAN WILLIAMS, [SIR] RALPH

WILLIAMSBURG SAMPLER, A see Corigliano,
John

WILLIAMSON, MALCOLM (1931-   )
Au Tombeau Du Martyr Juif Inconnu,
For Harp And String Orchestra
[17']
string orch,harp solo
sc BOIS f.s., perf mat rent (W379)

Concerto for Organ and Orchestra
[20'] (in the US available from
Boosey) study sc WEINBERGER W202
$20.00   (W380)

Lament In Memory Of Lord Mountbatten
Of Burma
study sc WEINBERGER f.s., perf mat
rent   (W381)

Olympiques, Les, For Solo Voice And
String Orchestra [31']
string orch,Mez/Bar solo
BOIS perf mat rent   (W382)

WILLIAMSON, MALCOLM (cont'd.)

Serenade And Aubade [10']
1.1.1.1. 1.0.0.0. harp,strings
min sc WEINBERGER f.s., perf mat
rent   (W383)

Symphony No. 5
study sc WEINBERGER f.s., perf mat
rent   (W384)

WILLINGHAM, LAWRENCE
Count Ugolino, For Solo Voice And
Chamber Orchestra *Op.12 [24']
ob,timp,perc,3vla,6vcl,Bar solo
sc AM.COMP.AL. $15.30   (W385)

WILLKOMMEN UND ABSCHIED, FOR SOLO VOICE
AND ORCHESTRA see Pfitzner, Hans

WILLOCK, EINAR
Cassation, Op. 5, in C minor [38']
2.2.2.3. 2.0.0.0. timp,strings
NORGE   (W386)

Norsk Sommernatt [45']
2.2.2.2. 2.2.2.1. timp,harp,pno,
strings
"Norwegian Summer Night" NORGE
   (W387)

Norwegian Summer Night
see Norsk Sommernatt

WILMS, JOHANN WILHELM (1772-1847)
Symphony *see Knecht, Justin
Heinrich, Symphony
see Knecht, Justin Heinrich,
Symphony

WILSON, OLLY (1937-   )
Houston Fanfare [2']
3.2.2.2. 4.3.3.1. timp,4perc,
harp,pno,strings
sc GUNMAR MP8012 $15.00, perf mat
rent   (W388)

Lumina [11']
3.2.2.2. 4.3.3.0. timp,2perc,
harp,pno,strings
GUNMAR MP8010 perf mat rent   (W389)

Sinfonia [23']
2(bass fl).2(English horn).2(bass
clar).2(contrabsn). 4.3.3.1.
timp,4perc,harp,pno,strings
MARGUN BP 8008 perf mat rent (W390)

WILSON, RANSOM
Carmen Fantasy, For Flute And
Orchestra [11']
2.2.2.2. 2.2.2.0. timp,perc,harp,
strings,fl solo
PRESSER perf mat rent   (W391)

WILSON, RICHARD (EDWARD) (1941-   )
Articulations [20']
3(pic,alto fl).3(English
horn).3(clar in E flat,bass
clar).3(contrabsn). 4.4.3.1.
timp,perc,cel,harp,strings
PEER perf mat rent   (W392)

Concerto for Bassoon and Chamber
Orchestra [19']
1(pic).1(English horn).1(bass
clar).0+contrabsn. 2.2.1.0.
marimba,harp,strings,bsn solo
PEER perf mat rent   (W393)

Concerto for Bassoon and Orchestra
[18']
1(pic).1(English horn).1(bass
clar).0+contrabsn. 2.2.1.0.
perc,harp,strings,bsn solo
BOOSEY perf mat rent   (W394)

Concerto for Violin and Chamber
Orchestra [26']
2ob,2horn,timp,strings,vln solo
PEER perf mat rent   (W395)

Concerto for Violin and Orchestra
[26']
0.2.0.0. 2.0.0.0. timp,perc,
strings,vln solo
BOOSEY perf mat rent   (W396)

Initiation [13'30"]
3(pic).3(English horn).3(clar in
E flat).3(contrabsn). 4.3.3.1.
timp,perc,pno,strings
PEER perf mat rent   (W397)

Silhouette [5']
2.2.2.2. 4.2.3.0. timp,strings
PEER perf mat rent   (W398)

Suite [11'30"]
1.1(English horn).3(clar in E
flat).1(contrabsn). 2.2.1.0.
marimba,harp,strings
PEER perf mat rent   (W399)

Symphony No. 1 [25']
2(alto fl)+pic.2+English horn.2+
bass clar.2+contrabsn. 4.2.3.1.

WILSON, RICHARD (EDWARD) (cont'd.)

timp,3perc,harp,strings
BOOSEY perf mat rent   (W400)
PEER perf mat rent   (W401)

Symphony No. 2 [28']
2(pic).2.2.2. 4.2.0.0. timp,perc,
strings
PEER perf mat rent   (W402)

WILSON, THOMAS (1927-   )
Concerto for Piano and Orchestra
[28']
QUEEN   (W403)

Concerto for Viola and Orchestra
[25']
QUEEN   (W404)

Introit [25']
2.2.2.2. 4.2.3.0. timp,2perc,
harp,pno,cel,strings
QUEEN   (W405)

Mosaics [20']
fl,hpsd,synthesizer,strings
QUEEN   (W406)

Passeleth Tapestry [29']
QUEEN   (W407)

Saint Kentigern Suite [18']
string orch
QUEEN   (W408)

WIMBERGER, GERHARD (1923-   )
Ausstrahlungen W.A. Mozart'scher
Themen [15']
2.2.2.2. 2.2.0.0. timp,drums,
strings
BÄREN. BA 6766 perf mat rent (W409)

Concerto A Dodici ("Viaggi") [16']
1(pic,alto fl).0.1.1. 1.1.1.0.
perc,pno,vln,vla,vcl,db
BÄREN. BA 6736 perf mat rent (W410)

Concerto for Piano and Orchestra, No.
2 [27']
2(pic).2.2.2+contrabsn. 3.2.2.0.
timp,2perc,gtr,harp,strings,pno
solo
BÄREN. BA 6800 perf mat rent (W411)

Motus [17']
3.2+English horn.3(bass clar).2+
contrabsn. 4.3.3.0+db tuba.
timp,3perc,cel,harp,strings
study sc BÄREN. BA 6733 f.s. (W412)

Nachtmusik- Trauermusik- Finalmusik
[18']
2(pic).1+English horn.2+bass
clar.1+contrabsn. 2.2.3.0.
timp,2perc,synthesizer,strings
BÄREN. BA 7312   (W413)

WINBECK, HEINZ (1946-   )
Denk Ich An Haydn [21']
3(pic,alto fl).3.3(bass
clar).3(contrabsn). 4.3.3.1.
timp,2perc,harp,cel,strings
BÄREN. BA 6799 perf mat rent (W414)

Symphony No. 1 [41']
4.4.3+bass clar.3+contrabsn.tenor
sax. 6.4.4.1. timp,5perc,
harmonium,cel,strings
BÄREN. BA 7129   (W415)

Symphony No. 2 [50']
4(pic,alto fl).2+English horn+ob
d'amore.3(clar in E flat)+2bass
clar.3+contrabsn.alto sax.
6.4.4.1. timp,6perc,elec org,
harmonium,cel,strings without
vla
BÄREN. BA 7170   (W416)

Symphony No. 3 [60']
4(pic,alto fl).4.4(clar in E
flat)+bass clar.3+
contrabsn.alto sax. 6.4.4.2.
timp,perc,harp,elec org&cel&
pno,A&speaking voice
study sc BÄREN. BA 7307 f.s. (W417)

WINDERSTEIN, HANS (1856-1925)
Standchen *Op.11 [7']
2.2.2.2. 4.0.0.0. perc,harp,
strings
BREITKOPF-W perf mat rent   (W418)

WINDJAMMER: MAIN THEME, "THE SHIP" see
Gould, Morton

WINDJAMMER: NIGHT WATCH see Gould,
Morton

WINDOWS see Wollo, Erik

WINDS AND SINES see Silverman, Faye-
Ellen

WINDSONGS, FOR PIANO AND ORCHESTRA see Zupko, Ramon

WINDSOR KLANGE WALZER see Strauss, Johann, [Jr.]

WINE ROSES, FOR SOLO VOICE AND ORCHESTRA see Delius, Frederick

WINGING IT see Ward-Steinman, David

WINGS OF MORNING, THE see Wilby, Philip

WINHAM, GODFREY (1934-1975)
    Composition For Orchestra [15']
        2.2.2.2. 2.2.0.0. strings
        sc APNM $20.00, perf mat rent
                                        (W419)
    Sonata for Orchestra [30']
        (unfinished work) sc APNM $15.25,
        perf mat rent   (W420)

WINSLOW, WALTER
    Concert Aria, For Solo Voice And
        Orchestra [20']
        fl,clar,horn,perc,harp,strings,S
        solo
        sc AM.COMP.AL. $25.85   (W421)
    Concerto for Piano and Orchestra
        [32']
        3.3.3.3. 4.2.2.1. timp,perc,harp,
        strings,pno solo
        sc AM.COMP.AL. $36.55, perf mat
        rent   (W422)
    Pele [9']
        3.2.4.2. 4.3.3.1. perc,strings
        sc AM.COMP.AL. $15.30, perf mat
        rent   (W423)

WINTER see Takemitsu, Toru

WINTER, PETER VON (1754-1825)
    Concerto For Oboe And Orchestra *see
        THREE CENTURIES OF MUSIC IN
        SCORE, VOL. 6: CONCERTO V, LATE
        CLASSICAL STRINGS AND WINDS

WINTER CONCERTO, FOR SAXOPHONE AND
    ORCHESTRA see Straesser, Joep

WINTER MUSIC see Boyle, Rory

WINTER MUSIC, FOR VIOLA AND
    INSTRUMENTAL ENSEMBLE see Louie,
    Alexina

WINTER SCENERY see Haug, Halvor

WINTERGREEN FOR PRESIDENT, [ARR.] see
    Gershwin, George

WINTERNIGHT see Nordal, Jon

WINTERS TALE, A see Verrall, John
    Weedon

WINTHER, TERJE
    From Where I Stand [10']
        1.1.1.1. 2.1.1.0. 2perc,strings,
        synthesizer
        NORGE   (W424)
    Ut Av Taka [11']
        5.0.2.0. 2.2.1.0. strings,
        electronic tape
        NORGE   (W425)

WIOSNA, FOR SOLO VOICE AND ORCHESTRA
    see Lutoslawski, Witold

WIR WANDELTEN, FOR SOLO VOICE AND
    ORCHESTRA [ARR.] see Brahms,
    Johannes

WISCONSIN SUITE see Luening, Otto

WISCONSIN SYMPHONY, A see Luening, Otto

WISE, BRUCE (1929-   )
    Variations [11']
        4.3.3.3. 4.2.3.1. 3perc,harp,cel,
        strings
        sc AM.COMP.AL. $36.75   (W426)

WISE-APPLE FIVE, FOR CLARINET AND
    STRING ORCHESTRA see McBride,
    Robert Guyn

WISHART, PETER (1921-1984)
    Concerto for Violin and Orchestra,
        No. 1 [17']
        0.2+English horn.0.2. 0.2.3.0.
        vln solo
        STAINER HL249 perf mat rent (W427)
    Five Psalms, For Solo Voice And
        String Orchestra [10'30"]
        string orch,Bar solo
        STAINER HL236 perf mat rent (W428)

WISSE, JAN (1921-   )
    Concerto for 2 Pianos and Chamber
        Orchestra [18']
        2.2.2.2. 0.1.0.1. 2perc,6vln,2db,
        2pno soli
        sc DONEMUS f.s., perf mat rent
                                        (W429)

WISSMER, PIERRE (1915-   )
    Sinfonietta Concertante, For Flute,
        Harp And Orchestra [24']
        2.2.2.2. 4.2.3.0. timp,2perc,
        strings,fl solo,harp solo
        AMPHION perf mat rent   (W430)

WITCH BOY, THE: SQUARE DANCE [ARR.] see
    Salzedo, Leonard (Lopes)

WITCH BOY, THE: SUITE see Salzedo,
    Leonard (Lopes)

WITCH BOY, THE: THREE DANCES see
    Salzedo, Leonard (Lopes)

WITCHES, FOR BASSOON AND STRING
    ORCHESTRA see Aguila, Miguel Del,
    Hexen, For Bassoon And String
    Orchestra

WITH THE WILD GEESE see Harty, [Sir]
    Hamilton

WITT, FRIEDRICH (1770-1837)
    Concerto for Flute and Orchestra in G
        (Hess) sc AMADEUS BP 2675 f.s.,
        perf mat rent   (W431)
    Symphony
        (Fisher, Stephen C.; Coeyman,
        Barbara) ("The Symphony" Vol. B-
        IX) sc GARLAND ISBN 0-8240-3838-X
        $90.00 contains also: Reicha,
        Anton, Symphonies, Two; Eberl,
        Anton (Franz Josef), Symphony
                                        (W432)
    Symphony in C
        (Stein) ("Jena Symphony"; formerly
        attributed to Beethoven) KALMUS
        A6121 sc $20.00, set $40.00, perf
        mat rent   (W433)

WITTENBERG, ALEXANDER
    Doende Fjarilen, Den, For English
        Horn, Saxophone And Orchestra
        (composed with Arnryd, Thore)
        [5'30"]
        2.0.2.1. 2.0.0.0. harp,strings,
        English horn solo,alto sax solo
        "Dying Butterfly, The, For English
        Horn, Saxophone And Orchestra"
        BUSCH HBM 008 perf mat rent
                                        (W434)
    Dying Butterfly, The, For English
        Horn, Saxophone And Orchestra
        see Doende Fjarilen, Den, For
        English Horn, Saxophone And
        Orchestra

WITTINGER, ROBERT (1945-   )
    Intreccio *Op.40
        2.2.2.2. 2.2.2.0. perc,harp,pno,
        strings
        sc MOECK 5287 f.s., perf mat rent
                                        (W435)

WITWE AUS VALENCIA, DIE: SUITE see
    Khachaturian, Aram Ilyich, Widow Of
    Valencia, The: Suite

WO BIST DU LICHT?, FOR SOLO VOICE AND
    INSTRUMENTAL ENSEMBLE see Vivier,
    Claude

WO DIE ZITRONEN BLUH'N see Strauss,
    Johann, [Jr.]

WOFLI-LIEDER, FOR SOLO VOICE AND
    ORCHESTRA see Rihm, Wolfgang

WOHLFART, KARL (1874-1943)
    Dawn At The Sea, For Solo Voice And
        Orchestra [4']
        2.2.2.2. 4.2.3.0. timp,strings,
        med solo
        NORDISKA perf mat rent   (W436)

WOLF, DANIEL (1894-1962)
    Dream World, For Solo Voice And
        Orchestra [arr]
        (Cacavas, John) 2.2.3.2. 4.3.3.0.
        timp,perc,harp,strings,Bar solo
        [6'] BOURNE perf mat rent   (W437)

WOLF, HUGO (1860-1903)
    Anakreons Grab, For Solo Voice And
        Orchestra
        see Lieder Mit Orchesterbegleitung
        I
    Auf Ein Altes Bild "In Gruner
        Landschaft", For Solo Voice And
        Orchestra
        "On Gazing At An Old Painting, For
        Solo Voice And Orchestra" KALMUS
        A4631 sc $3.00, set $4.50, pts
        $.75, ea.   (W438)

WOLF, HUGO (cont'd.)
    Corregidor, Der: Vorspiel [6']
        2+pic.2(English horn).2.2.
        4.3.3.1. timp,strings
        "Corregidor: Overture" KALMUS A5579
        sc $8.00, set $22.00, perf mat
        rent   (W439)
    Corregidor: Overture
        see Corregidor, Der: Vorspiel
    Five Songs, For Solo Voice And
        Orchestra [arr]
        (Topilow) LUDWIG perf mat rent
                                        (W440)
    Harfenspieler I, For Solo Voice And
        Orchestra
        see Lieder Mit Orchesterbegleitung
        I
    Harfenspieler II, For Solo Voice And
        Orchestra
        see Lieder Mit Orchesterbegleitung
        I
    Harfenspieler III, For Solo Voice And
        Orchestra
        see Lieder Mit Orchesterbegleitung
        I
    Italienische Serenade [arr.]
        (Drew) string orch [6'] KALMUS
        A7297 sc $8.00, set $7.50, pts
        $1.50, ea.   (W441)
    Lieder Mit Orchesterbegleitung I
        (Jancik, Hans) sc MUSIKWISS. f.s.
        Gesamtausgabe Vol. VIII
        contains: Anakreons Grab, For
        Solo Voice And Orchestra;
        Harfenspieler I, For Solo Voice
        And Orchestra; Harfenspieler
        II, For Solo Voice And
        Orchestra; Harfenspieler III,
        For Solo Voice And Orchestra;
        Mignon (First Version), For
        Solo Voice And Orchestra;
        Mignon (Second Version), For
        Solo Voice And Orchestra;
        Prometheus, For Solo Voice And
        Orchestra; Rattenfänger, Der,
        For Solo Voice And Orchestra
                                        (W442)
    Lieder Mit Orchesterbegleitung II
        (Jancik, Hans) sc MUSIKWISS. f.s.
        Gesamtausgabe Vol.IX
        contains: Mörike-Lieder, Zwölf,
        For Solo Voice And Orchestra;
        Spanisches Liederbuch: Vier
        Lieder, For Solo Voice And
        Orchestra   (W443)
    Mignon (First Version), For Solo
        Voice And Orchestra
        see Lieder Mit Orchesterbegleitung
        I
    Mignon (Second Version), For Solo
        Voice And Orchestra
        see Lieder Mit Orchesterbegleitung
        I
    Mörike-Lieder, Zwölf, For Solo Voice
        And Orchestra
        see Lieder Mit Orchesterbegleitung
        II
    On Gazing At An Old Painting, For
        Solo Voice And Orchestra
        see Auf Ein Altes Bild "In Gruner
        Landschaft", For Solo Voice And
        Orchestra
    Penthesilea
        (Haas) KALMUS A6663 sc $50.00, set
        $80.00, pts $3.00, ea., perf mat
        rent   (W444)
    Prometheus, For Solo Voice And
        Orchestra
        see Lieder Mit Orchesterbegleitung
        I
    Rattenfanger, Der, For Solo Voice And
        Orchestra
        KALMUS A6122 sc $12.00, set $15.00,
        perf mat rent   (W445)
        see Lieder Mit Orchesterbegleitung
        I
    Scherzo Und Finale
        (Schultz) KALMUS A6647 sc $25.00,
        set $45.00, pts $2.00, ea., perf
        mat rent   (W446)
    Sechszehn Lieder: Nos. 1-8, For Solo
        Voice And Orchestra, [arr.]
        *CC8L
        (Wolf; Raphael) 2.3.2.2. 4.2.3.0.
        timp,harp/pno,strings,S&A&T soli
        BREITKOPF-L perf mat rent   (W447)
    Sechszehn Lieder: Nos. 9-16, For Solo
        Voice And Orchestra, [arr.]
        *CC8L

WOLF, HUGO (cont'd.)

(Wolf; Raphael) 2.2.2.2. 2.1.1.0.
drums,harp/pno,strings,S&T soli
BREITKOPF-L perf mat rent (W448)

Spanisches Liederbuch: Vier Lieder,
For Solo Voice And Orchestra
see Lieder Mit Orchesterbegleitung
II

Spanisches Liederbuch: Zwei Lieder,
For Solo Voice And Orchestra
(Haas) 2.2.2.2. 4.0.0.0. harp,
strings,T solo BREITKOPF-L perf
mat rent
contains: Wenn Du Zu Den Blumen
Gehst, For Solo Voice And
Orchestra; Wer Sein Holdes Lieb
Verloren, For Solo Voice And
Orchestra (W449)

Uber Nacht, For Solo Voice And
Orchestra [arr.]
(Pohle) KALMUS A6357 sc $3.00, set
$15.00, pts $.75, ea. (W450)

Wenn Du Zu Den Blumen Gehst, For Solo
Voice And Orchestra
see Spanisches Liederbuch: Zwei
Lieder, For Solo Voice And
Orchestra

Wer Sein Holdes Lieb Verloren, For
Solo Voice And Orchestra
see Spanisches Liederbuch: Zwei
Lieder, For Solo Voice And
Orchestra

WOLF-FERRARI, ERMANNO (1876-1948)
Amore Medico, L': Overture
KALMUS A7196 sc $15.00, set $30.00,
pts $1.25, ea., perf mat rent
(W451)
Chamber Symphony In B Flat *Op.8
[20']
1.1.1.1. 1.0.0.0. pno,strings
KALMUS A5573 sc $30.00, set
$40.00, perf mat rent (W452)

Gioielli Della Madonna, I: Danza Dei
Camorristi
"Jewels Of The Madonna: Dance Of
The Camorrists" KALMUS A6650 pno-
cond sc $5.00, set $25.00, pts
$1.00, ea., perf mat rent (W453)

Gioielli Della Madonna, I: Intermezzo
No. 2
"Jewels Of The Madonna: Intermezzo
No. 2" KALMUS A6112 sc $8.00, set
$25.00, perf mat rent (W454)

Jewels Of The Madonna: Dance Of The
Camorrists
see Gioielli Della Madonna, I:
Danza Dei Camorristi

Jewels Of The Madonna: Intermezzo No.
2
see Gioielli Della Madonna, I:
Intermezzo No. 2

WOLFE, JACQUES (1896-1973)
De Glory Road [arr.]
1.1.2.1. 2.2.1.0. timp,perc,strings
SCHIRM.G perf mat rent (W455)

WOLFF, CHRISTIAN (1934-   )
Exercise No. 24 [5']
1.1.1.1. 2.1.0.0. perc,pno,
strings
(J. C.'S Bread And Roses) PETERS
P67135 perf mat rent (W456)

Exercise No. 25 [5']
2.2.2(bass clar).2. 2.2.2.1.
2perc,harp,strings
(Liyashizwa) PETERS P67136 perf mat
rent (W457)

Long Peace March [20']
1(pic).1.1(bass
clar).1(contrabsn).alto sax.
1.0.1.0. perc,vla,vcl,db
PETERS P67181 perf mat rent (W458)

WOLFF, JEAN-CLAUDE (1946-   )
Symphony No. 2 for Violin and
Orchestra
2+pic.3.3.3. 4.3.3.1. 3perc,harp,
strings,vln solo
TONOS (W459)

WOLHAUSER, RENE (1954-   )
Fragmente Für Orchester
[10'] study sc GUILYS f.s., perf
mat rent (W460)

WOLKEN, DIE, FOR SOLO VOICE AND
ORCHESTRA see Zechlin, Ruth

WOLLO, ERIK (1961-   )
Windows [12']
1.1.1.1. 1.1.1.0. 2perc,2vln,vla,
vcl,db
NORGE (W461)

WOLPE, STEFAN (1902-1972)
Chamber Piece No.1 [8'30"]
pic,fl,ob,English horn,clar,bsn,
horn,trp,trom,2vln,vla,vcl,db
sc PEER 60160-851 $20.00, perf mat
rent (W462)

Chamber Piece No. 2
1.1.1.1. 1.1.1.0. perc,pno,vln,
vla,vcl,db
study sc PEER 61642-851 $14.00,
perf mat rent (W463)

Piece In Three Parts, For Piano And
Sixteen Instruments
2.1.1.0.baritone sax. 2.2.0.1.
harp,elec gtr,perc,vln,vla,vcl,
pno solo
PEER perf mat rent (W464)

Symphony No. 1
3+pic.3+English horn.3+bass
clar.3+contrabsn. 4.3.3.1.
timp,perc,strings
PEER perf mat rent (W465)

WOLTER, DETLEF (1933-   )
Adagio [14']
string orch
LEUCKART perf mat rent (W466)

Cassation No. 2 [11']
2(pic).2.2.2(contrabsn). 2.2.0.0.
timp,2perc,strings
LEUCKART perf mat rent (W467)

Cassation No. 3 In B-Lydisch [5']
2.2.2.2. 3.2.3.0. timp,perc,harp,
strings
KAHNT perf mat rent (W468)

Concertant-Tanzerische Musik In D-
Mixolydisch [10']
string orch
KAHNT perf mat rent (W469)

Orchesterdivertimento In C-Jonisch
[15']
2.2.2.2. 3.3.3.1. timp,perc,pno,
strings
KAHNT perf mat rent (W470)

Orchesterdivertimento In Es-Lydisch
[22']
2.2.2.2. 2.2.0.0. perc,strings
KAHNT perf mat rent (W471)

Ritornell, For Piano And Orchestra
[12']
2.2.0.2. 2.2.0.0. timp,perc,
strings,pno solo
KAHNT perf mat rent (W472)

WONDROUS STORY, A see Kountz, G.

WON'T IT EVER BE MORNING see Lloyd,
Jonathan

WOOD, GARETH (1950-   )
Suffolk Punch [6']
2+pic.2.2.2. 4.2.3.1. timp,4perc,
strings
BOOSEY perf mat rent (W473)

WOOD, HUGH BRADSHAW (1932-   )
Concerto for Violoncello and
Orchestra, Op. 12 [20']
3(pic,alto fl).3(English
horn).3(bass
clar).3(contrabsn). 4.3.3.1.
timp,4perc,2harp,strings,vcl
solo
sc CHESTER JWC 386 f.s., perf mat
rent (W474)

Laurie Lee Songs, For Solo Voice And
Orchestra [20']
2(pic).2(English horn).2(bass
clar).2. 2.0.1.0. perc,harp,
strings,S solo
CHESTER perf mat rent (W475)

Song Cycle On Poems By Pablo Neruda,
For Solo Voice And Chamber
Orchestra *Op.19 [25']
3(pic,alto fl).3(English
horn).3(bass clar).0. 1.1.1.0.
harp,pno&cel,perc,string quar,db,
high solo CHESTER JWC 364 perf
mat rent (W476)

Symphony [44']
4(pic,alto fl).3(English
horn).3(bass clar,clar in E
flat).3(contrabsn). 6.4.4.2.
timp,4perc,2harp,pno&cel,
strings
CHESTER perf mat rent (W477)

WOOD DOVE see Dvořák, Antonín

WOOD SO WILD, THE [ARR.] see Gibbons,
Orlando

WOODARD, JAMES (1929-   )
Ballad For A Summer's Day [8']
string orch
MMB perf mat rent (W478)

WOODCOCK, ROBERT
Concerto No. 2 for Recorder and
String Orchestra [7']
string orch,cont,rec solo
FABER perf mat rent (W479)

WOODLAND SYMPHONY see Glass, Louis,
Skovsymfoni

WOODLAND VALLEY SKETCHES see Cazden,
Norman

WOOING SONGS, THE, FOR SOLO VOICE AND
ORCHESTRA see Tubin, Eduard

WOOLDRIDGE, CLIFFORD
Rumpus [6']
2.1.2.1. 4.3.3.0. timp,perc,harp,
strings
AMP perf mat rent (W480)

WOOLLEN, RUSSELL (1923-   )
Suite for Flute and String Orchestra
[18']
string orch,fl solo
AM.COMP.AL. sc $13.80, pts $3.10,
perf mat rent (W481)

Symphony No. 2, Op. 86 [30']
2+pic.3.3.3. 4.3.3.1. timp,perc,
harp,pno,strings
sc AM.COMP.AL. $45.70 (W482)

WORDS IN WINTER, FOR SOLO VOICE AND
ORCHESTRA see Hallgrimsson, Haflidi

WORDS OF HER, THE, FOR SOLO VOICE AND
ORCHESTRA see Rangström, Ture

WORDS OVERHEARD, FOR SOLO VOICE AND
CHAMBER ORCHESTRA see Birtwistle,
Harrison

WORKS FOR ORCHESTRA, VOL. 1 see
Tchaikovsky, Piotr Ilyich

WORKS FOR ORCHESTRA, VOL. 2 see
Tchaikovsky, Piotr Ilyich

WORKS FOR SYMPHONY ORCHESTRA see
Gabeli, I.

WORLD AGAIN, THE, FOR SOLO VOICE AND
ORCHESTRA see Burgon, Geoffrey

WORLD WAR I: SELECTIONS see Gould,
Morton

WORLDES BLIS see Davies, Peter Maxwell

WORLDS see Hillborg, Anders

WORLD'S CONSCIENCE see Vacek, Miloš

WORLD'S FAIR MARCH, THE see Antonini,
Alfredo

WORLD'S FAIR SUITE [ARR.] see Grofe,
Ferde (Ferdinand Rudolph von)

WORZISCHEK, JOHANN HUGO (1791-1825)
Sinfonia in D [27']
2.2.2.2. 2.2.0.0. timp,strings
KALMUS A7271 sc $30.00, set $75.00,
pts $5.00, ea., perf mat rent
(W483)
WOUND-DRESSER, THE, FOR SOLO VOICE AND
ORCHESTRA see Adams, John

WOYRSCH, FELIX VON (1860-1944)
Symphony, Op. 52, in C minor [30']
3.3.3.3. 4.3.3.1. timp,harp,
strings
KAHNT perf mat rent (W484)

WRANITZKY, PAUL (1756-1808)
Symphony in C, MIN 120
(Bónis) sc EMB 7744 f.s. (W485)

WREN, THE, FOR SOLO VOICE AND
ORCHESTRA, [ARR.] see Benedict,
[Sir] Julius, Capinera, La, For
Solo Voice And Orchestra [arr.]

WRIGHT, MAURICE (1949-   )
Music From The Fifth String [9']
2.2.2.2. 4.3.3.1. timp,perc,pno,
strings
sc APNM $8.25, perf mat rent (W486)

Times Will Change, The [15']
2.2.2.2. 4.3.3.1. perc,pno,
strings
sc APNM $10.50, perf mat rent
(W487)

WRIGHT, MAURICE (cont'd.)

Wellington's Defeat [11']
2.2.2.2. 4.4.3.1. timp,perc,
strings
sc AM.COMP.AL. $18.30, perf mat
rent   (W488)

WU, JU JIANG
New Generation From The Grassland,
For Violin And Orchestra
(composed with Situ, Hua Chang)
3.2+English horn.2.2. 4.2.2.1.
timp,perc,harp,strings,vln solo
HONG KONG perf mat rent   (W489)

WU-YU see Yu, Julian

WUENSCH, GERHARD (1925-   )
Serenade For A Summer Evening [12']
1.2.1.1. 2.1.0.0. timp,strings
CAN.MUS.CENT. MI 1200 W959S (W490)

WUNDERHORN see Weir, Judith

WUNDERSAME REISE, FOR TWO HORNS AND
STRING ORCHESTRA see Ulrich, Jürgen

WUORINEN, CHARLES (1938-   )
Bamboula Beach [6']
3(pic).3.3(bass
clar).3(contrabsn). 4.3.3.1.
timp,2perc,pno,strings
PETERS P67025 perf mat rent (W491)

Bamboula Squared [17']
3.2.3.2. 4.2.3.1. timp,2perc,pno,
strings,electronic tape
PETERS P67013 perf mat rent (W492)

Concertino for Orchestra [16']
2(pic).2.4(bass clar,contrabass
clar).2(contrabsn). 4.0.0.0.
strings,db solo
(version for 15 solo instruments
available) PETERS P67017 perf mat
rent   (W493)

Concerto for Piano and Orchestra, No.
3 [27']
3.2.3.2. 4.2.3.1. timp,3perc,
harp,strings,pno solo
PETERS P66978 perf mat rent (W494)

Crossfire [11']
3.2.3(clar in E flat,bass
clar).2. 4.3.3.1. timp,2perc,
pno,strings
sc PETERS P67066 $20.00, perf mat
rent   (W495)

Fanfare For The Houston Symphony [1']
3.3.3.3. 4.3.3.1. xylo,bass drum,
snare drum,strings
PETERS P67116 perf mat rent (W496)

Galliard [14']
2(pic).2.2.2. 2.2.1.0. pno,
strings
PETERS P67179 perf mat rent (W497)

Golden Dance, The [21']
3.3.3.3. 4.3.3.1. timp,perc,harp,
pno&cel,strings
PETERS P67143 perf mat rent (W498)

Movers And Shakers [27']
3.3.3.3. 4.3.3.1. timp,perc,harp,
pno,strings
sc PETERS P67016 $35.00, perf mat
rent   (W499)

Prelude To Kullervo, For Tuba And
Orchestra [6']
3.2.2.2. 4.3.3.0. timp,perc,pno,
strings,tuba solo
PETERS P67089 perf mat rent (W500)

Rhapsody for Violin and Orchestra
[20']
3.3.3.2. 4.3.3.1. timp,2perc,pno,
harp,strings,vln solo
PETERS P67018 perf mat rent (W501)

Short Suite For Orchestra [15']
2(pic).2.2.2. 4.2.2.1. timp,xylo,
strings
PETERS P66927 $39.50   (W502)

WURTZLER, ARISTID VON
Modern Sketches For Harp
string orch,harp solo
PEER perf mat rent   (W503)

WUSTE HAT ZWOLF DING', DIE, FOR SOLO
VOICE AND ORCHESTRA see Zender,
Hans

WÜSTHOFF, KLAUS
Concertino for Clarinet and String
Orchestra [16']
string orch,clar solo
sc PETERS P8557 f.s., perf mat rent
(W504)

WÜSTHOFF, KLAUS (cont'd.)

Concierto De Samba, For 3 Guitars And
Orchestra [16'30"]
2.2.2.2. 4.3.3.0. timp,2perc,
harp,strings,3gtr soli
ZIMMER.   (W505)

Metrum, For Timpani And Orchestra
[6']
3.2.2.2. 4.3.3.0. 2perc,strings,
timp soli, (2 players)
sc LITOLFF,H P8522 f.s., perf mat
rent   (W506)

WYMAN, DANN CORIOT (1923-   )
Ode To The Viola, For Viola And
Chamber Orchestra
pno,strings,vla solo
sc SEESAW $26.00, perf mat rent
(W507)

WYNER, YEHUDI (1929-   )
Fragments From Antiquity, For Solo
Voice And Orchestra [20']
2.2.3.2. 4.2.2.1. perc,marimba,
harp,strings,S solo
sc AM.COMP.AL. $35.00   (W508)

Intermedio, For Solo Voice And String
Orchestra [16']
string orch,S solo
sc AM.COMP.AL. $15.40, perf mat
rent   (W509)

WYRDCHANGING, FOR SOLO VOICE AND
CHAMBER ORCHESTRA see Holt, Simon

X

X see Zuidam, Rob

XENAKIS, YANNIS (IANNIS) (1922-   )
A L'ile De Goree, For Harpsichord And
Instrumental Ensemble [14']
1(pic).1.1.1. 1.1.1.0. 2vln,vla,
vcl,db,hpsd solo
SALABERT perf mat rent   (X1)

Ais, For Solo Voice And Orchestra
[17']
4(pic).4(English
horn).4(contrabsn).4.4.4.1.
perc,pno,strings,Bar solo
study sc SALABERT $27.00, perf mat
rent   (X2)

Alax [12'30"]
3fl,3clar,6horn,3trom,3perc,3vln,
6vcl
SALABERT perf mat rent   (X3)

Antikhthon [23']
3+pic.3.3.3+contrabsn. 4.3.3.1.
timp,perc,strings
study sc SALABERT $41.00, perf mat
rent   (X4)

Aroura
12strings
study sc SALABERT $22.00   (X5)

Ata [16']
4.4.4.4. 4.4.4.0. perc,strings
SALABERT perf mat rent   (X6)

Duel
0+2pic.2.2+clar in E flat+2bass
clar.2+contrabsn. 0.4.2.0.
perc,4vln,8vcl,4db
SALABERT perf mat rent   (X7)

Echange, For Clarinet And
Instrumental Ensemble [14']
1.1.1.1. 1.1.1.1. 2vln,vla,vcl,
db,clar solo
SALABERT perf mat rent   (X8)

Empreintes [12']
2+pic.3+English horn.2+clar in E
flat+bass clar.2+contrabsn.
4.4.4.1. strings
study sc SALABERT $41.00, perf mat
rent   (X9)

Epicycle, For Violoncello, And
Instrumental Ensemble [12']
1.1.1.1. 1.1.1.1. 2vln,vla,db,vcl
solo
SALABERT perf mat rent   (X10)

Eridanos [11']
2horn,2trp,2trom,strings
sc SALABERT f.s., perf mat rent
(X11)

Erikhthon, For Piano And Orchestra
[14']
3+pic.3.3+bass clar.3+contrabsn.
4.4.4.1. strings,pno solo
study sc SALABERT $49.00, perf mat
rent   (X12)

Horos [16']
4.4.4.4. 4.4.4.0. perc,strings
SALABERT EAS18414P perf mat rent
(X13)

Jalons [15']
1(pic).1.1+bass
clar.1(contrabsn). 1.1.1.1.
harp,2vln,vla,vcl,db
SALABERT perf mat rent   (X14)

Jonchaies [17']
2+2pic.4+2English horn.2+clar in
E flat+bass clar.2+2contrabsn.
6.6.4.1. timp,4perc,strings
study sc SALABERT $49.00, perf mat
rent   (X15)

Keqrops, For Piano And Orchestra
[17']
4.4.4(bass clar).3(contrabsn).
4.4.4.1. timp,perc,harp,
strings,pno solo
SALABERT EAS18362P perf mat rent
(X16)

Lichens I [16']
4(pic).4(English
horn).4.4(contrabsn). 4.4.4+
2bass trom.1. timp,4perc,
strings
SALABERT perf mat rent   (X17)

Noomena [17']
3+pic.3+English horn.3+clar in E
flat+bass clar.3+contrabsn.
6.5.4.1. strings
sc SALABERT f.s., perf mat rent
(X18)

XENAKIS, YANNIS (IANNIS) (cont'd.)

Palimpsest [11']
0.1(English horn).1(bass clar).1.
1.0.0.0. perc,pno,string quin
sc SALABERT f.s., perf mat rent
(X19)

Phlegra [14']
1(pic).1.1(bass clar).1. 1.1.1.0.
vln,vla,vcl,db
sc SALABERT f.s., perf mat rent
(X20)

Retour-Windungen
12vcl
study sc SALABERT $18.25   (X21)

Shaar [14']
string orch
SALABERT perf mat rent   (X22)

Suppliantes D'Eschyle [10']
2trp,2trom,strings
sc SALABERT f.s., perf mat rent
(X23)

Synaphai, For Piano And Orchestra
[14']
3.3.3.3. 4.4.4.1. perc,strings,
pno solo
study sc SALABERT $41.00, perf mat
rent   (X24)

Thallein [17']
1(pic).1.1.1. 1.1.1.0. perc,pno,
2vln,vla,vcl,db
SALABERT perf mat rent   (X25)

Tracees [5'30"]
4.4.4.4. 4.4.4.1. perc,pno,
strings
SALABERT perf mat rent   (X26)

Waarg [16']
1(pic).1.1.1. 1.1.1.1. 2vln,vla,
vcl,db
SALABERT perf mat rent   (X27)

XENIAS PACATAS see Guerrero, Francisco

XERXES: MEINE LIEBLICHE PLATANE; SO
SCHATT'GEN RAUM, FOR SOLO VOICE AND
ORCHESTRA see Handel, George
Frideric, Serse: Frondi Tenere;
Ombra Mai Fu, For Solo Voice And
Orchestra, [arr.]

XERXES: SUITE see Handel, George
Frideric, Serse: Suite

XI JIANG YUE see Ye, Xiao-Gang

XIN YUE see Ye, Xiao-Gang

XOCHICUICATL, FOR SOLO VOICE AND
INSTRUMENTAL ENSEMBLE see Zumaque,
Francisco

XPO see Nordensten, Frank Tveor

Y

YAGLING, VICTORIA
Concerto for Violoncello and
Orchestra, No. 2 [23']
3.2.2.3. 4.0.3.1. timp,perc,cel,
harp,strings,vcl solo
VAAP perf mat rent   (Y1)

YAKUTIAN SUITE see Peiko, Nikolai

YAMAMOTO, NAOZUMI (1932-   )
Symphonic Ballade
JAPAN 8502   (Y2)

YAMEKRAW [ARR.] see Johnson, James P.

YANKEE DOODLE, FOR VIOLIN AND STRING
ORCHESTRA see Vieuxtemps, Henri

YANNATOS, JAMES D. (1929-   )
Priere Dans l'Arche, For Solo Voice
And Chamber Orchestra [9']
1.1.1.1. 1.1.1.0. 2vln,vla,vcl,
db,S solo
AM.COMP.AL. sc $18.40, pts $20.70
(Y3)

YANNAY, YEHUDA (1937-   )
Concertino for Violin and Chamber
Orchestra [11']
1.1.1.1.alto sax. 2.0.0.0. perc,
strings,vln solo
AM.COMP.AL. sc $18.30, pts $3.50,
perf mat rent   (Y4)

Five Songs, For Solo Voice And
Orchestra [15']
2.2.2.2. 2.2.2.1. perc,harp,pno,
strings,T solo
sc AM.COMP.AL. $21.45, perf mat
rent   (Y5)

YARAVI see Gutierrez Del Barrio, Ramon

YARRAGEH, FOR PERCUSSION AND ORCHESTRA
see Edwards, Ross

YASURAOKA, AKIO (1958-   )
Symphony [28']
3(pic).3(English horn).3(bass
clar).3(contrabsn). 4.3.3.1.
perc,harp,pno&cel,strings
sc ZEN-ON 899320 f.s., perf mat
rent   (Y6)

YAVELOW, CHRISTOPHER JOHNSON
(1950-   )
And Then We Saw A Sea Lion, For
Marimba And Orchestra [12']
2.2.2.2. 2.2.2.0. strings,marimba
solo
sc AM.COMP.AL. $15.30, perf mat
rent   (Y7)

Axis [22']
4.4.4.4. 4.4.4.2. timp,perc,
vibra,marimba,harp,cel,pno,
strings
sc AM.COMP.AL. $27.50   (Y8)

Overture [1']
1+opt fl.1+opt ob.2.0. 0.2.2.0.
perc,strings
sc AM.COMP.AL. $1.95   (Y9)

Seven Mikrophonae [4']
2.2.2.2. 2.2.2.0. perc,strings
sc AM.COMP.AL. $12.10, perf mat
rent   (Y10)

YE, XIAO-GANG
Concerto for Violin and Orchestra,
No. 1, Op. 16 [5']
3.2.2.2+contrabsn. 4.3.3.1. timp,
perc,strings,vln solo
HONG KONG perf mat rent   (Y11)

Crescent Moon
see Xin Yue

Distinguish, For Violin And Orchestra
3.2.2.2. 4.3.3.1. timp,perc,xylo,
glock,harp,cel,strings,vln solo
HONG KONG perf mat rent   (Y12)

Guo Shang [16']
2.2.2.2. 4.3.3.1. timp,perc,harp,
pno,strings, pipa solo, xiao
solo
"Martyrs, The" HONG KONG perf mat
rent   (Y13)

Horizon, The *Op.21 [15']
1.1.1.1. 1.1.1.1. perc,pno,
strings
HONG KONG perf mat rent   (Y14)

Martyrs, The
see Guo Shang

YE, XIAO-GANG (cont'd.)

Xi Jiang Yue *Op.18 [16']
1.1.1.0. 0.1.0.0. timp,perc,harp,
pno,strings
HONG KONG perf mat rent   (Y15)

Xin Yue *Op.17 [16']
3.2.2.2. 4.3.3.1. timp,perc,
zheng solo
"Crescent Moon" HONG KONG perf mat
rent   (Y16)

YEAR IS LIKE A LIFETIME, A: SUITE see
Shostakovich, Dmitri

YEARNING IS MY SHARE OF HERITAGE, FOR
SOLO VOICE AND ORCHESTRA see
Lindberg, Oskar [Fredrik]

YELLOW CRANE HOUSE, THE see Chen, Pei-
Xun

YELLOW LEAVES, FOR SOLO VOICE AND
STRING ORCHESTRA see Eggen, Arne,
Det Gulnar Lauvet, For Solo Voice
And String Orchestra

YELLOW RIVER, THE, FOR PIANO AND
ORCHESTRA [ARR.] see Hsien, Hsing-
Hai

YELLOW ROSE PETAL, A see Singleton,
Alvin

YET THAT THINGS GO ROUND see Kolb,
Barbara

YIAIN LAULU, FOR SOLO VOICE AND
ORCHESTRA see Madetoja, Leevi

YIAIS SANG, FOR SOLO VOICE AND
ORCHESTRA see Madetoja, Leevi

YIAN SHI, FOR VIOLA AND ORCHESTRA see
Chen, Yi

YIN FIRE see De Vos Malan, Jacques

YLERMI, FOR SOLO VOICE AND ORCHESTRA
see Tubin, Eduard

YNGWE, JAN (1953-   )
Overtura Alla Vita
2.2.2.2. 4.3.3.1. timp,3perc,pno,
strings
STIM   (Y17)

YON KESKELLA TAHTONEN LOISTI, FOR SOLO
VOICE AND STRING ORCHESTRA [ARR.]
see Melartin, Erkki

YORK FUSILIERS see Revolutionary
Garland, A

YOUMANS, VINCENT MILLIE (1898-1946)
Tea For Two, [arr.] [3'45"]
(Herfurth) WARNER perf mat rent
(Y18)

YOUNG APOLLO, FOR PIANO, STRING QUARTET
AND STRING ORCHESTRA see Britten,
[Sir] Benjamin

YOUNG APOLLO, THE see Crosse, Gordon

YOUNG BRETON SHEPHERD, THE, FOR SOLO
VOICE AND ORCHESTRA see Berlioz,
Hector (Louis), Jeune Patre Breton,
Le, For Solo Voice And Orchestra

YOUTH see Vomácka, Boleslav

YOUTH AND FOLLY see Dupuy, Edouard,
Ungdom Og Galskab

YOUTH OVERTURE see Knipper, Lev
Konstantinovich

YOUTH SYMPHONY see Du, Ming-Xin

YOUTH WALTZ see Du, Ming-Xin

YOUTH'S MAGIC HORN, THE, VOL. I see
Mahler, Gustav, Des Knaben
Wunderhorn: Lieder, Vol. I

YOUTH'S MAGIC HORN, THE, VOL. II see
Mahler, Gustav, Des Knaben
Wunderhorn: Lieder, Vol. II

YR OBEDT SERVT II see Sims, Ezra

YRADIER, SEBASTIAN (1809-1865)
Paloma, La, For Solo Voice And
Orchestra [arr.]
(Geese, H.) 2.1.2.1. 3.2.3.0. timp,
3perc,harp,2mand,gtr,bass gtr,
strings,solo voice [7'] SIKORSKI
perf mat rent   (Y19)

YRSA see Hartmann, Johan Peder Emilius

YRTIT TUMMAT, FOR SOLO VOICE AND
ORCHESTRA [ARR.] see Madetoja,
Leevi

YSAYE, EUGENE (1858-1931)
    Concerto for Violin and Orchestra,
      Op. 9
        2+pic.2+English horn.2.2.
        4.3.3.1. timp,strings,vln solo
      SCHIRM.G perf mat rent   (Y20)

    Cygne, Le *Op.15
        4.2+English horn.2+bass clar.2.
        4.3.3.1. timp,2harp,strings
      SCHIRM.G perf mat rent   (Y21)

YTTREHUS, ROLV (1926-   )
    Gradus Ad Parnassum, For Solo Voice
      And Chamber Orchestra [32']
        1.1.1.1. 1.2.1.0. perc,pno,vln,
        vla,vcl,db,electronic tape
      AM.COMP.AL. sc $59.70, pts $108.70,
      perf mat rent   (Y22)

YU, JULIAN (1957-   )
    Great Ornamented Fuga Canonica
      [9'55"]
        2.2.2.2. 4.2.2.1. 3perc,harp,pno,
        strings
      UNIVER. perf mat rent   (Y23)

    Wu-Yu [10'36"]
        3.2.3.2. 4.2.3.1. 2perc,harp,pno,
        strings
      UNIVER. perf mat rent   (Y24)

YUASA, JOJI (1929-   )
    Dirge By Bach, A [3']
        3(pic).3(English horn).3(bass
        clar).3(contrabsn). 4.3.3.1.
        perc,harp,pno&cel,strings
      ZEN-ON perf mat rent   (Y25)

    Perspective [14']
      SCHOTT,J   (Y26)

    Projection: Flower, Bird, Wind, Moon,
      For 8 Kotos And Orchestra
      [13'30"]
        3(pic,alto fl).3(English
        horn).4(clar in E flat,bass
        clar).3(contrabsn). 4.4.3.1.
        perc,harp,pno&cel,strings, 8
        kotos
      ZEN-ON perf mat rent   (Y27)

    Revealed Time, For Viola And
      Orchestra [16']
        3(pic).2(English horn).3(clar in
        E flat,bass clar).2(contrabsn).
        4.3.3.0. timp,3perc,harp,pno&
        cel,strings,vla solo
      SCHOTT,J perf mat rent   (Y28)

YUEN, MAO
    Dance Of The Yao People [9']
        3.2.2.2. 4.2.3.1. timp,cym,
        strings
      HONG KONG perf mat rent   (Y29)

YUGOSLAV RHAPSODY see Bendl, Karel

YUKON SUMMER SUITE see Gayfer, James
    McDonald

YULETIDE FEAST, A see Gordeli, Otar

YUN, ISANG (1917-   )
    Concerto for Violin and Orchestra,
      No. 2 [33']
        2(pic).2.2.2. 4.2.2.1. timp,
        2perc,harp,strings,vln solo
      sc BOTE f.s., perf mat rent   (Y30)

    Duetto Concertante, For Oboe,
      Violoncello And String Orchestra
      [18']
        string orch,ob solo&English horn
        solo,vcl solo
      BOTE perf mat rent   (Y31)

    Geisterliebe: Schamanengesange, For
      Solo Voice And Chamber Orchestra
      [arr]
        (Koch-Raphael, Erwin) 2(pic,alto
        fl).2(English
        horn).0.2(contrabsn). 2.0.1.0.
        timp,perc,strings,A solo [9']
      BOTE perf mat rent   (Y32)

    Gong-Hu [18']
        harp,strings
      sc BOTE f.s., perf mat rent   (Y33)

    Impression [13']
        2(pic,alto fl).2.1(bass clar).1.
        1.1.1.0. 2perc,harp,strings
      sc BOTE f.s., perf mat rent   (Y34)

    Kammersinfonie I [24']
        2ob,2horn,strings
      sc BOTE f.s., perf mat rent   (Y35)

    Kammersinfonie II [33']
        1(pic).1.1+bass clar.1. 2.1.1.0.
        2perc,harp,pno,strings
      BOTE perf mat rent   (Y36)

YUN, ISANG (cont'd.)

    Mugung-Dong [12']
        3.3.3.3. 4.3.3.1. timp,2perc,4-
        6db
      sc BOTE f.s., perf mat rent   (Y37)

    Symphony No. 1 [45']
        4(pic).4(English horn).4(bass
        clar).4(contrabsn). 6.4.3.1.
        timp,3perc,harp,strings
      study sc BOTE f.s., perf mat rent
                                          (Y38)

    Symphony No. 2 [25']
        2(pic).2.1(bass clar).2. 4.2.2.1.
        timp,2perc,strings
      sc BOTE f.s., perf mat rent   (Y39)

    Symphony No. 3 [24']
        2(pic).2.2(bass
        clar).2(contrabsn). 4.3.2.1.
        timp,2perc,harp,strings
      sc BOTE f.s., perf mat rent   (Y40)

    Symphony No. 4 [33']
        3(pic,alto fl).3(English
        horn).3(bass
        clar).3(contrabsn). 5.3.3.1.
        timp,3perc,strings
      study sc BOTE f.s., perf mat rent
                                          (Y41)

    Symphony No. 5 [56']
        3(pic,alto fl).2(English
        horn).2(bass
        clar).2(contrabsn). 4.2.3.1.
        timp,4perc,2harp,cel,strings,
        Bar solo
      BOTE perf mat rent   (Y42)

    Tapis Pour Cordes [8']
        string orch
      sc BOTE f.s., perf mat rent   (Y43)

    Teile Dich Nacht, For Solo Voice And
      Chamber Orchestra
        fl,ob,clar,bsn,horn,perc,harp,
        2vln,vla,vcl,db,S solo
      sc BOTE 037-35801 $36.25   (Y44)

YUNNAN SCENES see Wang, Xi-Lin

Z

ZACH, JOHANN (JAN) (1699-1773)
    Sinfonia No. 1 in A
      see Sinfonias For String Orchestra,
      Five

    Sinfonia No. 2 in A
      see Sinfonias For String Orchestra,
      Five

    Sinfonia No. 3 in A
      see Sinfonias For String Orchestra,
      Five

    Sinfonia No. 4 in B flat
      see Sinfonias For String Orchestra,
      Five

    Sinfonia No. 5 in B flat
      see Sinfonias For String Orchestra,
      Five

    Sinfonias For String Orchestra, Five
      (Racek, Jan; Pohanka, Jaroslav) sc,
      pts SUPRAPHON MAB 43 f.s.
        contains: Sinfonia No. 1 in A;
        Sinfonia No. 2 in A; Sinfonia
        No. 3 in A; Sinfonia No. 4 in B
        flat; Sinfonia No. 5 in B flat
                                          (Z1)

ZACHOW, FRIEDRICH WILHELM (1663-1712)
    Fantasy in D
      (Lenzewski) set KALMUS A7418
      $22.00, and up   (Z2)

ZAFRED, MARIO (1922-1987)
    Concerto for String Orchestra [16']
        string orch
      RICORDI-IT 131837 perf mat rent
                                          (Z3)

ZAGARE, LE see Bellisario, Angelo

ZAGWIJN, HENRI (1878-1954)
    Kerkerballade, De, For Narrator And
      Orchestra [60']
        4.3.3.3. 4.3.3.1. timp,perc,
        2harp,gtr,mand,cel,strings,
        narrator
      sc DONEMUS f.s., perf mat rent (Z4)

ZAHLER, NOEL BARRY (1951-   )
    Harlequin, For Piano And Chamber
      Orchestra [8']
        1.1.1.1. 1.1.1.0. timp,strings,
        pno solo
      AMP perf mat rent   (Z5)

    Three Songs, For Solo Voice And
      Instrumental Ensemble [13']
        1.1.1.0. 1.1.0.0. 3perc,harp,vln,
        vla,vcl,Mez solo
      sc APNM $7.50, perf mat rent   (Z6)

ZAHORTSEV, VOLODOMYR (1944-   )
    Chamber Cantata No. 2, For Solo Voice
      And Chamber Orchestra
      VAAP perf mat rent   (Z7)

    Chamber Concerto No. 1
      VAAP perf mat rent   (Z8)

    Chamber Concerto No. 3
        fl,perc,harp,pno,strings
      VAAP perf mat rent   (Z9)

    Symphony
        fl,alto sax,perc,strings
      VAAP perf mat rent   (Z10)

    Symphony No. 2
      VAAP perf mat rent   (Z11)

    Symphony No. 3
      VAAP perf mat rent   (Z12)

ZAIDE, FOR SOLO VOICE AND ORCHESTRA see
    Berlioz, Hector (Louis)

ZAÏDE: RUHE SANFT, FOR SOLO VOICE AND
    ORCHESTRA see Mozart, Wolfgang
    Amadeus

ZAIDE: SUITE [ARR.] see Royer, Pancrace

ZAIS: OVERTURE see Rameau, Jean-
    Philippe

ZANETTOVICH, DANIELE (1950-   )
    Monumentum A Luigi Dallapiccola, For
      Solo Voice And Orchestra [22']
        3.3.2.3.sax. 4.4.3.1. timp,perc,
        hpsd,cel,pno,harp,vcl,db,Bar
        solo
      SONZOGNO perf mat rent   (Z13)

    Sinfonia Sopra Un Discanto Aquileiese
      [11']
        2.0.0.2. 0.2.0.0. timp,strings
      SONZOGNO perf mat rent   (Z14)

ZANETTOVICH, DANIELE (cont'd.)

Sinfonia Super Tenor Acquileiensis
[19']
2.2.2.1. 4.4.3.1. timp,perc,
strings
SONZOGNO perf mat rent   (Z15)

ZANINELLI, LUIGI (1932-   )
Canto Lirico, For Trumpet And
Orchestra
SHAWNEE perf mat rent   (Z16)

Tale Of Peter Rabbit, The, For
Narrator And Orchestra
SHAWNEE perf mat rent   (Z17)

ZANSA see Osborne, Nigel

ZAPATEADO, FOR VIOLONCELLO AND STRING
ORCHESTRA [ARR.] see Sarasate,
Pablo de

ZAR UND ZIMMERMANN: DARF EINE NIEDRE
MAGD ES WAGEN, FOR SOLO VOICES AND
ORCHESTRA see Lortzing, (Gustav)
Albert

ZAR UND ZIMMERMANN: DIE EIFERSUCHT IST
EINE PLAGE, FOR SOLO VOICE AND
ORCHESTRA see Lortzing, (Gustav)
Albert

ZAR UND ZIMMERMANN: HOLZSCHUHTANZ see
Lortzing, (Gustav) Albert

ZAR UND ZIMMERMANN: LEBE WOHL, MEIN
FLANDRISCH MADCHEN, FOR SOLO VOICE
AND ORCHESTRA see Lortzing,
(Gustav) Albert

ZAR UND ZIMMERMANN: O SANCTA JUSTITIA,
FOR SOLO VOICE AND ORCHESTRA see
Lortzing, (Gustav) Albert

ZAR UND ZIMMERMANN: SONST SPIELT ICH
MIT ZEPTER, FOR SOLO VOICE AND
ORCHESTRA see Lortzing, (Gustav)
Albert

ZARINS, MARGERIS (1910-   )
Partita In Barocco, For Solo Voice
And Chamber Orchestra [10']
2.2.0.2.sax. 0.0.0.0. perc,harp,
pno,gtr,strings,Mez solo
SIKORSKI perf mat rent   (Z18)

ZARLIVOST see Janácek, Leoš

ZARZYCKI, ALEXANDER (1834-1895)
Introduction And Krakowiak, For
Violin And Orchestra *Op.35
2.2.2.2. 2.2.0.0. timp,perc,
strings,vln solo
SIMROCK perf mat rent   (Z19)

Mazurka for Violin and Orchestra, No.
2
2horn,trp,timp,strings,vln solo
SIMROCK perf mat rent   (Z20)

Polish Suite *Op.37
3.2.2.2. 2.2.3.0. timp,perc,
strings
SIMROCK perf mat rent   (Z21)

ZAUBERFLÖTE, DIE: ACH, ICH FÜHL'S, ES
IST VERSCHWUNDEN, FOR SOLO VOICE
AND ORCHESTRA see Mozart, Wolfgang
Amadeus

ZAUBERFLÖTE, DIE: BEI MÄNNERN, FOR SOLO
VOICES AND ORCHESTRA see Mozart,
Wolfgang Amadeus

ZAUBERFLÖTE, DIE: DER HÖLLE RACHE, FOR
SOLO VOICE AND ORCHESTRA see
Mozart, Wolfgang Amadeus

ZAUBERFLÖTE, DIE: DER VOGELFÄNGER BIN
ICH JA, FOR SOLO VOICE AND
ORCHESTRA see Mozart, Wolfgang
Amadeus

ZAUBERFLÖTE, DIE: DIES BILDNIS IST
BEZAUBERND SCHÖN, FOR SOLO VOICE
AND ORCHESTRA see Mozart, Wolfgang
Amadeus

ZAUBERFLÖTE, DIE: EIN MÄDCHEN ODER
WEIBCHEN, FOR SOLO VOICE AND
ORCHESTRA see Mozart, Wolfgang
Amadeus

ZAUBERFLÖTE, DIE: IN DIESEN HEIL'GEN
HALLEN, FOR SOLO VOICE AND
ORCHESTRA see Mozart, Wolfgang
Amadeus

ZAUBERFLÖTE, DIE: O ZITT'RE NICHT, FOR
SOLO VOICE AND ORCHESTRA see
Mozart, Wolfgang Amadeus

ZAUBERFLOTE, DIE: OVERTURE see Mozart,
Wolfgang Amadeus

ZAUBERFLÖTE, DIE: PA-PA-PA-PAPAPAGENA,
FOR SOLO VOICES AND ORCHESTRA see
Mozart, Wolfgang Amadeus

ZBAR, MICHEL (1942-   )
Apex II [7']
7vln,2vla,2vcl,db
RIDEAU perf mat rent   (Z22)

Ceremonial Nocturne
2+pic+alto fl.2+English horn.2+
bass clar.2+contrabsn. 4.3.3.1.
4perc,2harp,pno&hpsd,cel,
strings
SALABERT perf mat rent   (Z23)

Incandescences, For Solo Voices And
Orchestra [11']
RIDEAU perf mat rent   (Z24)

Tropismes, For Violin And Orchestra
[17']
3.3.3.3. 4.3.3.1. 6perc,harp,pno&
cel,strings,vln solo
BILLAUDOT perf mat rent   (Z25)

ZBINDEN, JULIEN-FRANÇOIS (1917-   )
Concerto Grosso for Violin and
Chamber Orchestra [15']
study sc GUILYS f.s., perf mat rent
(Z26)

ZEBRA see Schwartz, Elliott Schelling

ZECHLIN, RUTH (1926-   )
Briefe
3.2.2.2. 2.2.2.0. timp,perc,harp,
cel,strings
sc PETERS 5531 f.s.   (Z27)

Concerto for Organ and Orchestra, No.
1
2trp,timp,perc,strings,org solo
sc PETERS f.s.   (Z28)

Gedanken Über Ein Klavierstück Von
Prokofjew, For Piano And Chamber
Orchestra [10']
1.1.1.1. 0.1.0.0. perc,vln,vla,
vcl,db,pno solo
sc BREITKOPF-L PB 4044 f.s., ipr
(Z29)

Metamorphosen
3.3.2.3. 4.4.4.1. timp,perc,
strings
sc PETERS f.s.   (Z30)

Reflexionen
14strings
sc PETERS $30.00   (Z31)

Wolken, Die, For Solo Voice And
Orchestra
1.1.0.0. 0.1.0.0. harp,perc,
strings,S solo
BREITKOPF-L perf mat rent   (Z32)

ZECHUM see Voortman, Roland

ZEFIRO see Samama, Leo

ZEHN SKIZZEN see Ledenev, Roman, Ten
Sketches

ZEICHEN I FUR ZWEI SOLISTEN UND ZWEI
ORCHESTERGRUPPEN see Rihm, Wolfgang

ZEIT-ENDEN see Brandmüller, Theo

ZEITBIEGUNG see Stranz, Ulrich

ZEITLOSE, DIE. POLKA see Strauss,
Johann, [Jr.]

ZEITLUPENKLANG see Ostendorf, Jens-
Peter

ZELENKA, JAN DISMAS (1679-1745)
Capriccio No. 1 [13']
0.2.0.1. 2.0.0.0. hpsd,strings
SUPRAPHON   (Z33)

Capriccio No. 2 [9']
0.2.0.1. 2.0.0.0. hpsd,strings
SUPRAPHON   (Z34)

Capriccio No. 3 [11']
0.2.0.1. 2.0.0.0. hpsd,strings
SUPRAPHON   (Z35)

Capriccio No. 4 [19']
0.2.0.1. 2.0.0.0. hpsd,strings
SUPRAPHON   (Z36)

Capriccio No. 5 [14']
0.2.0.1. 2.0.0.0. hpsd,strings
SUPRAPHON   (Z37)

Lamentationes Jeremiae Prophetae, For
Solo Voices And Orchestra [53']
2.2.0.1. 0.0.0.0. org,strings,ATB
soli
sc SUPRAPHON MAB I^9I-4 f.s.   (Z38)

Laudate Pueri, For Solo Voice And
Orchestra
trp,org,strings,T solo

ZELENKA, JAN DISMAS (cont'd.)

sc,pts DEUTSCHER 9519 f.s.   (Z39)

ZELJENKA, ILJA (1932-   )
Concerto for Violin and String
Orchestra
string orch,vln solo
SLOV.HUD.FOND   (Z40)

Elegy for Violin and String Orchestra
string orch,vln solo
SLOV.HUD.FOND   (Z41)

Symphony No. 5
SLOV.HUD.FOND   (Z42)

ZELTER, CARL FRIEDRICH (1758-1832)
Concerto for Viola and Orchestra in E
flat, MIN 1
(Mlynarczyk) KALMUS A6431 pno-cond
sc $7.50, set $18.00, pts $2.00,
ea.   (Z43)

ZENDER, HANS (1936-   )
Concerto for Flute and Orchestra
[27']
2.2.2.0. 2.2.2.1. harp,pno,
strings,fl solo
(Loshu V) UNIVER. perf mat rent
(Z44)

Dialog Mit Haydn [21']
4(2pic).4.4.4(contrabsn).
5.3.3.1. timp,3perc,harp,2pno,
strings
BOTE perf mat rent   (Z45)

Funf Haiku (Lo-Shu IV), For Flute And
String Orchestra [14']
string orch,fl solo
BOTE perf mat rent   (Z46)

Jours De Silence, For Solo Voice And
Orchestra [15']
4(pic).4.3.2+contrabsn. 4.3.3.1.
4perc,strings,Bar solo
sc UNIVER. UE19017 f.s., perf mat
rent   (Z47)

Lo-Shu III, For Flute And
Instrumental Ensemble [20']
2.2.2(bass clar).0. 1.2.2.1.
2perc,2pno,2gtr,3vln,3vcl,fl
solo
BOTE perf mat rent   (Z48)

Wuste Hat Zwolf Ding', Die, For Solo
Voice And Orchestra [10']
0+alto fl.1+English horn.1+bass
clar.1(contrabsn). 2.2.2.0.
4perc,harp,pno,elec org,
strings,A solo
UNIVER. perf mat rent   (Z49)

ZENTNER, JOHANNES (1903-   )
Concerto for Violin and String
Orchestra [21']
string orch,vln solo
HUG GH 1109 perf mat rent   (Z50)

Sinfonietta for String Orchestra
[19']
string orch
HUG GH 11017 perf mat rent   (Z51)

ZEPHYR WITH OUTSTRETCHED WINGS, FOR
VIOLIN AND ORCHESTRA see Endo,
Masao

ZHANG, XIAO-FU
Man Jiang Hong
3.2+English horn.2+bass clar.2+
contrabsn. 4.3.3.1. timp,perc,
xylo,harp,strings
"Red River, The" HONG KONG perf mat
rent   (Z52)

Red River, The
see Man Jiang Hong

ZHOU, LONG
Fisherman's Song [10']
3.2+English horn.2+bass clar.2+
contrabsn. 4.3.3.1. timp,perc,
harp,pno,strings
HONG KONG perf mat rent   (Z53)

Guang Lingsan [25']
3.2+English horn.2+bass clar.2+
contrabsn. 4.3.3.1. timp,perc,
harp,pno,strings
HONG KONG perf mat rent   (Z54)

ZIANI, MARC ANTONIO (1653-1715)
Tanto Foco, For Solo Voice And String
Orchestra [2'30"]
string orch,S solo
(Fagotto, V.) BILLAUDOT perf mat
rent   (Z55)

ZICK-ZACK see Andersson, Gert Ove

ZIELINSKA, LIDIA
Two Dances [13']
string orch
sc APNM $11.25, perf mat rent (Z56)

ZIG-ZAG see Andersson, Gert Ove, Zick-Zack

ZIGEUNERBARON, DER: OVERTURE, [ARR.]
see Strauss, Johann, [Jr.]

ZIGEUNERLIEDER [ARR.] see Brahms, Johannes

ZIINO, OTTAVIO (1909-)
Adagio for String Orchestra [10'45"]
string orch
sc CURCI 10264 perf mat rent (Z57)

Concerto for Orchestra
3.3.3.2. 4.3.3.1. timp,perc,harp,
cel,pno,strings
CARISCH (Z58)

Concerto for Piano and Orchestra
[15'10"]
2(pic).2(English horn).2.2.
2.2.1.0. timp,perc,vibra,xylo,
harp,strings,pno solo
sc CURCI 10110 perf mat rent (Z59)

Concerto for Violin and Orchestra
2(pic).2(English horn).2(bass
clar).2. 4.3.3.1. timp,perc,
xylo,glock,pno,strings,vln solo
sc CURCI 10448 perf mat rent (Z60)

Due Studi [13'25"]
2.2.2.2. 2.2.1.0. perc,vibra,
xylo,cel,harp,pno,strings
sc CURCI 10075 perf mat rent (Z61)

ZIMMERMANN, ANTON (1741-1781)
Symphony
see Ivancic, Amandus, Symphonies,
Two

ZIMMERMANN, BERND ALOIS (1918-1970)
Concerto for Orchestra [17']
3.3.3.3(contrabsn). 4.3.3.1.
timp,perc,pno,strings
SCHOTTS perf mat rent (Z62)

Dialoge, For 2 Pianos And Orchestra
sc SCHOTTS $45.00 (Z63)

Giostra Genovese [14']
3(pic).3.0.3. 0.3.3.1. timp,perc,
2gtr,harp,4db
BÄREN. BA 3572 perf mat rent (Z64)

Metamorphose [25']
1(pic).1(English horn).1.1.alto
sax. 1.1.0.0. timp,3perc,elec
gtr,pno&hpsd&elec org,harp,
4vln,2vla,2vcl,db
SCHOTTS perf mat rent (Z65)

Musique Pour Les Soupers Du Roi Ubu
[18']
3(pic).3(English horn).3(bass
clar).3(contrabsn).tenor sax.
4.3.3.1. timp,2perc,harp,pno&cel,
org,2gtr&mand&elec gtr,4db,
combo: clar, cornet, elec gtr,
elec db study sc BÄREN. BA 4180
f.s. (Z66)

Petit Rien, Un [6']
3fl,perc,gtr,cel,hpsd,3vln,2vla,
vcl,db
SCHOTTS perf mat rent (Z67)

Sinfonia Prosodica [40']
3(pic).3(English
horn).2.3(contrabsn). 4.3.3.1.
timp,perc,2harp,strings
SCHOTTS perf mat rent (Z68)

Symphonische Variationen Und Fuge
Uber "In Dulci Jubilo" [35']
2(pic).2(English horn).2.2.
4.3.3.1. timp,perc,cel,harp,
strings
SCHOTTS perf mat rent (Z69)

ZIMMERMANN, WALTER (1949-)
Landler Topographien [41']
fl,pic,alto fl,clar,clar in E
flat,bass clar,alto sax,tenor
sax,baritone sax,perc,cel,hpsd,
pno,gtr,cimbalom,harp,strings
BOOSEY perf mat rent (Z70)

Spielwerk, For Solo Voice, Saxophone
And Three Ensembles [35']
6.0.6(3bass clar).0. 6.0.0.0.
3perc,3harp,6vln,6vla,6vcl,3db,
tenor sax solo,Mez solo
BOOSEY perf mat rent (Z71)

ZINGARA, LA: ARIA DI TAGLIABORSE, FOR
SOLO VOICE AND STRING ORCHESTRA see
Rinaldo di Capua

ZINGARELLI, NICOLA ANTONIO (1752-1837)
Sinfonia, No. 7, Op. 22, No. 3, in C
(Malone) KALMUS A7322 sc $8.00, set
$22.00, pts $1.50, ea., perf mat
rent (Z72)

ZINN, WILLIAM
Kol Nidrei Memorial
string orch
set EXCELSIOR 494-01346 $10.00
(Z73)

ZINSSTAG, GÉRARD (1941-)
Anaphores, For Piano And Orchestra
[16']
2.2.2.2. 2.2.2.0. harp,marimba,
strings,pno solo
SALABERT perf mat rent (Z74)

Eden...Jeden, For Solo Voices And
Instrumental Ensemble [20']
2.0.2.0. 1.1.1.0. 2perc,pno,cel,
elec gtr,2vcl,electronic tape,
Mez&A/Bar soli
SALABERT perf mat rent (Z75)

Tempi Inquieti, For Piano, Percussion
And Orchestra [25']
4(pic).4.4(bass
clar).4(contrabsn). 4.4.4.1.
4perc,harp,cel,elec gtr,strings
SALABERT perf mat rent (Z76)

ZIP see Meijering, Chiel

ZIPANGU see Vivier, Claude

ZIPP, FRIEDRICH (1914-)
Kirchen Suite
string orch,opt winds
sc,pts MERSEBURGER EM 2002 f.s.
(Z77)

O Du Lieber Augustin
1.2.0.1. 2.0.0.0. strings
sc,pts MERSEBURGER EM 2035A f.s.
(Z78)

O Du Lieber Augustin, For String
Orchestra
string orch
sc,pts MERSEBURGER EM 2035 f.s.
(Z79)

Suite for Flute and String Orchestra,
Op. 35 [15']
string orch,fl solo
study sc PETERS P5841 f.s. (Z80)

ZODIAC, THE see Juozapaitis, Jurgis

ZODIACUS see Schmierer, Johann Abraham

ZÖGERNDE LIED, DAS see Medek, Tilo

ZOOM see Nevanlinna, Tapio see Reibel,
Guy

ZOROASTRE: SUITE [ARR.] see Rameau,
Jean-Philippe

ZREILO JE ZITO, FOR SOLO VOICE AND
ORCHESTRA see Golob, Jani

ZU REGENSBURG AUF DER KIRCHTURMSPITZ
see Kutzer, Ernst

ZU STRASSBURG AUF DER SCHANZ see
Mahler, Gustav

ZUIDAM, ROB (1964-)
Notch [10']
1.1.1.1. 1.1.0.0. 2perc,pno,vln,
vla,vcl,db
sc DONEMUS f.s., perf mat rent
(Z81)

X [13']
2.3.3.3. 4.3.3.1. 2perc,harp,
strings
sc DONEMUS f.s., perf mat rent
(Z82)

ZUMAQUE, FRANCISCO (1945-)
Xochicuicatl, For Solo Voice And
Instrumental Ensemble [20']
fl,clar,pno/cel,perc,strings,S
solo
PEER perf mat rent (Z83)

ZUPKO, RAMON (1932-)
Windsongs, For Piano And Orchestra
3.3.3.3. 4.3.3.1. timp,perc,harp,
strings,pno solo
sc PETERS P66863 $27.50, perf mat
rent (Z84)

ZUR, MENACHEM (1942-)
Chamber Symphony
1.1.1.1. 1.1.1.0. 3perc,harp,
strings
SEESAW (Z85)

ZUSTAND FUR KLEINES ORCHESTER see
Gangso, Arvid

ZWEI ARIEN, FOR SOLO VOICE AND
ORCHESTRA see Beethoven, Ludwig van
see Beethoven, Ludwig van

ZWEI ARIEN ZU IGNAZ UMLAUFS SINGSPIEL
"DIE SCHÖNE SCHUSTERIN" see
Beethoven, Ludwig van

ZWEI CHARAKTERSTUCKE see Sinigaglia,
Leone

ZWEI ETÜDEN see Vogel, Wladimir

ZWEI FABELN VON KRYLOW, FOR SOLO VOICE
AND ORCHESTRA see Shostakovich,
Dmitri, Two Fables Of Krylov, For
Solo Voice And Orchestra

ZWEI FUGEN UND EINE FANTASIE see
Mozart, Wolfgang Amadeus

ZWEI KONZERTARIEN see Haydn, [Franz]
Joseph see Haydn, [Franz] Joseph

ZWEI KONZERTE, FOR PIANO AND ORCHESTRA
see Röntgen, Julius

ZWEI LISZT-TRANSKRIPTIONEN see
Holliger, Heinz

ZWEI SATZE FÜR STREICHER see Liszt,
Franz

ZWEI SENTIMENTALE-IRONISCHE LIEDER, FOR
SOLO VOICE AND ORCHESTRA see
Nieder, Fabio

ZWEI STUCKE FOR STRING ORCHESTRA see
Shostakovich, Dmitri, Two Pieces
For String Orchestra

ZWEI TÄNZE see Janácek, Leoš

ZWEI WELTLICHE ARIEN, FOR SOLO VOICE
AND ORCHESTRA see Bach, Johann
Christian

ZWEIHUNDERTFUNFZIG JAHRE see
Castiglioni, Niccolò

ZWEITE ABGESANGSSZENE, FOR SOLO VOICE
AND ORCHESTRA see Rihm, Wolfgang

ZWEITER DOPPELGESANG, FOR CLARINET,
VIOLONCELLO AND ORCHESTRA see Rihm,
Wolfgang

ZWILICH, ELLEN TAAFFE (1939-)
Celebration [11']
4.3.3.3. 4.3.3.1. timp,3perc,
harp,pno&cel,strings
MERION perf mat rent (Z86)

Concerto for Piano and Orchestra
[24']
3.3.3.3. 4.3.3.1. timp,3perc,
strings,pno solo
study sc MERION 440-40015 $35.00,
perf mat rent (Z87)

Concerto for Trombone and Orchestra
[20']
3.3.3.3. 6.3.3.1. timp,3perc,pno,
strings,trom solo
MERION perf mat rent (Z88)

Concerto Grosso
1.2(English horn).0.1. 2.0.0.0.
hpsd,strings
sc MOBART $25.00 (Z89)

Images, For Two Pianos And Orchestra
[18']
1+pic.1+English horn.1+bass
clar.1+contrabsn. 2.1.1.1.
perc,strings,2pno soli
MERION perf mat rent (Z90)

Passages, For Solo Voice And
Orchestra [25']
2.2(English horn).2(bass
clar).2(contrabsn). 3.1.1.0.
perc,strings,S solo
[Eng] MARGUN perf mat rent (Z91)

Prologue And Variations
string orch
sc MERION 446-41048 $15.00, perf
mat rent (Z92)

Symbolon [16']
4.3.4.3. 4.3.3.1. timp,3perc,
harp,strings
sc MERION $30.00, perf mat rent
(Z93)

Symphony No. 1 [18']
2(pic).1+English horn.2(bass
clar).2(contrabsn). 4.2.3.1.
timp,3perc,harp,pno,strings
sc MARGUN MM 58 $25.00, perf mat
rent (Z94)

Symphony No. 2 [24']
3.3.3.3. 4.3.3.1. timp,3perc,pno,
strings
(Cello Symphony) sc MERION $30.00,
perf mat rent (Z95)

ZWILICH, ELLEN TAAFFE (cont'd.)

Tanzspiel [28']
    3.3.3.4. 4.2.2.1. timp,2perc,pno,
      strings
    MERION perf mat rent   (Z96)

ZWÖLF MARSCHE see Goossens, [Sir]
    Eugene

ZWÖLF MENUETTE see Eybler, Joseph

ZWOLF SINFONIEN see Handel, George
    Frideric

ZYTOVICH, VLADIMIR (1931-   )
    Abenteuer Des Braven Soldaten
      Schwejk, Die, For Narrator And
      Orchestra [13']
        2.2.2.2. 4.2.1.1. timp,perc,pno,
          strings,narrator
    SIKORSKI perf mat rent   (Z97)

    Concerto for Viola and Chamber
      Orchestra [20']
        1.2.0.1. 0.1.0.0. perc,strings,
          vla solo
    SIKORSKI perf mat rent   (Z98)
    VAAP perf mat rent   (Z99)

EDUCATIONAL
ORCHESTRAL MUSIC

A-HUNTING WE WILL GO [ARR.]
(Richardson, Clive) 2.1.2.1.3sax.
2.2.3.0. timp,strings (med easy)
set KALMUS A6051 $27.00, and up (1)

A LA MANIERE DE STRAVINSKY see Cauvin,
A.

ACCOLAY, J.B. (1845-1910)
Concerto for Violin and Orchestra,
No. 1, in A minor
(Klotman) SOUTHERN $24.00 (2)

ADAGIETTO see Korn, Peter Jona

ADAGIO [ARR.] see Bach, Johann
Sebastian

ADAGIO CANTABILE [ARR.] see Beethoven,
Ludwig van

ADAGIO FAVORITO [ARR.] see Mozart,
Wolfgang Amadeus

ADIOS AMIGOS [ARR.] see Chase, Bruce

ADLER, SAMUEL HANS (1928-)
Little Bit Of...Time...Space, A
string orch sets LUDWIG CSO-14
$20.00, and up (3)

ADORATION [ARR.] see Borowski, Felix

ADVENTURES IN STRINGS *CC17L
(Bornoff, George; Budesheim, Charles)
string orch sc,pts FISCHER,C
04407-04412 f.s. (4)

AFTERNOON WALTZ see Goldsmith, Owen

AFTON WATER [ARR.] see Folk-Songs For
Strings, Set 1

AHRENDT, KARL (1904-)
Pastorale for Strings
string orch sets LUDWIG CSO-15
$20.00, and up (5)

AIDA: BALLET MUSIC [ARR.] see Verdi,
Giuseppe

AIR AND RONDO [ARR.] see Purcell, Henry

AIR AND VARIATION [ARR.] see Mozart,
Wolfgang Amadeus

AIR CON VARIAZIONI [ARR.] see Handel,
George Frideric

AIR DITHYRAMBIQUE, FOR TRUMPET AND
ORCHESTRA see Devogel, Jacques

AIR ON THE G STRING [ARR.] see Bach,
Johann Sebastian

ALBÉNIZ, ISAAC (1860-1909)
Sevilla [arr.]
(Cheucle) 3(pic).3(English
horn).2.2.alto sax.baritone sax.
2.2.3.0. saxhorn, timp, drums,
strings LEMOINE perf mat rent (6)

Tango [arr.] (from Op. 165, No. 2)
(Siennicki, Edmund) string orch
(gr. III) set HIGHLAND $29.00 (7)

ALBERT, EUGÈNE FRANCIS CHARLES D'
(1864-1932)
Sultan's Polka, The [arr.]
(Benoy) 2.2.2.1. 2.2.3.0. timp,
perc,pno,strings [3'] (med,
alternate scoring: string orch)
OXFORD 77.030 sc $12.00, set
$42.50, pts $2.50, ea. (8)

ALBERT, THOMAS RUSSELL (1948-)
Suite From "The Gift"
string orch [5'0"] (gr. III)
CONCERT W J-158 $22.50 (9)

ALBUM POUR LA JEUNESSE: PETITE SUITE
NO. 1 [ARR.] see Schumann, Robert
(Alexander)

ALBUMS (VOL. 1-6)
(Anderson, Kenneth) string orch sc,
pts BOSWORTH f.s. (10)

ALCESTE: OVERTURE, [ARR.] see Gluck,
Christoph Willibald, Ritter von

ALEXANDER'S RAGTIME BAND [ARR.] see
Berlin, Irving

ALL SOULS' DAY [ARR.] see Strauss,
Richard, Allerseelen [arr.]

ALLEGRETTO ANIMOSO see Grier, Jon

ALLEGRETTO [ARR.] see Haydn, [Franz]
Joseph see Schubert, Franz (Peter)

ALLEGRETTO QUASI ANDANTINO [ARR.] see
Grieg, Edvard Hagerup

ALLEGRO see Metcalf, Leon V. see Riley,
Dennis

ALLEGRO [ARR.] see Dittersdorf, Karl
Ditters von see Handel, George
Frideric see Mozart, Wolfgang
Amadeus see Senaille, Jean Baptiste

ALLEGRO BRILLANT [ARR.] see Have,
Willem ten

ALLEGRO MODERATO [ARR.] see Handel,
George Frideric

ALLEGRO SPIRITOSO [ARR.] see Senaille,
Jean Baptiste

ALLEMANDE [ARR.] see Beethoven, Ludwig
van

ALLEN, ROBERT (1928-)
Home For The Holidays [arr.]
(Chase, Bruce) string orch JENSON
502-08040 $30.00 (11)

ALLERSEELEN [ARR.] see Strauss, Richard

ALLEY CAT [ARR.] see Bjorn, Frank

ALPHA BETA ALPHA see Frost, Robert S.

ALPINE HOLIDAY see Bauernschmidt,
Robert see Scott, Richard

ALSHIN, HARRY
Three Chinese Scenes
string orch,pno,opt perc [3'30"]
(gr. III) set KENDOR 9922 $23.00,
and up (12)

ALSO SPRACH WHATSHISNAME see Petrone,
John

ÅM, MAGNAR (1952-)
Mirror It
2.0.2.0. 0.0.0.0. timp,perc,
strings
NORGE (13)

AMAZING GRACE [ARR.]
(Spring, Glenn) string orch, fl or
vln or ob or voice (gr. II) BELWIN
BSO 00066 $40.00 (14)

AMELLER, ANDRÉ (CHARLES-GABRIEL)
(1912-)
Aquilon Suite
1.1.2.1. 1.2.2.0. 2perc,opt 2harp,
strings [20'30"] sc,pts BILLAUDOT
f.s. (15)

AMERICA OUR HERITAGE see Steele, Helen

AMERICA! PATRIOTIC THEMES [ARR.]
(Christensen, James) (gr. III) set
HIGHLAND $28.00, and up (16)

AMERICA TAKES NOTE! see Feldstein, Saul
(Sandy)

AMERICAN FOLK BALLAD see Woodard, James

AMERICAN FRONTIER, THE [ARR.]
(Custer) LEONARD-US 08720627 $50.00 (17)

AMERICAN IN PARIS, AN [ARR.] see
Gershwin, George

AMERICAN PATROL [ARR.] see Meacham

AMERICANA
(Zaninelli, Luigi) 2.2.3.2. 4.4.3.1.
perc,harp/pno,strings [8'] (gr. IV)
CONCERT W J-160 $45.00 (18)

AMOUR MALADE, L': SUITE [ARR.] see
Lully, Jean-Baptiste (Lulli)

ANCHORS AWEIGH [ARR.]
(Chase) string orch [2'] (med easy)
LEONARD-US $25.00 (19)

ANDANTE GRAZIOSO see McLeod, James
(Red)

ANDANTINO AND ALLEGRETTO [ARR.] see
Schubert, Franz (Peter)

ANDANTINO AND CON SPIRITO [ARR.] see
Arne, Thomas Augustine

ANDANTINO [ARR.] see Diabelli, Anton

ANDANTINO CANTABILE see McLeod, James
(Red)

ANDERSON, GERALD
Essentials For Strings
string orch,pno KJOS 74 sc $14.95,
pts $5.95, ea. (20)

Merry Go Rondo
string orch (gr. II) KJOS set
SO-73B $22.00, sc SO-73F $3.00 (21)

ANDERSON, KENNETH (1903-)
Sinfonietta
1.1.2.1. 2.2.1.0. perc,strings
(easy) sc,pts BOSWORTH f.s. (22)

Sinfonietta No. 2
1.1.1.0. 0.1.0.0. pno,strings
(easy) sc,pts BOSWORTH f.s. (23)

Theme For A Ceremony
string orch,opt 2clar/2trp,opt pno
(easy) sc,pts BOSWORTH f.s. (24)

ANDERSON, LEROY (1908-1975)
Chicken Reel
2.2.2.2.opt 2alto sax.opt tenor
sax. 4.3.3.1. timp,perc,strings
(med easy) KALMUS pno-cond sc
$4.50, set $38.00, and up (25)

First Day Of Spring, The
2.2.2.2.3sax. 4.3.3.1. timp,strings
(med easy) KALMUS A6044 pno-cond
sc $1.00, set $17.00, and up (26)

Horse And Buggy
2+pic.2.2.2.2alto sax.tenor sax.
4.3.3.1. perc,strings (med easy)
set KALMUS A6001 $17.00, and up (27)

Jazz Pizzicato, [arr.]
(Applebaum, Samuel) string orch
BELWIN sc $3.00, set $15.00 (28)

Leroy Anderson For Strings [arr.]
(Zinn) string orch BELWIN
EL 03450-55 sc $17.50, pts $5.50,
ea. (29)

Magic Of Leroy Anderson, The [arr.]
(Cerulli, Bob) CPP CO158B7X $45.00 (30)

Pirate Dance
2+pic.2.2.2.3sax. 4.3.3.1. perc,
strings (med easy) KALMUS A6036
pno-cond sc $4.00, set $37.50,
and up (31)

Pyramid Dance, From "Goldilocks"
2+pic.2.2.2.opt 2alto sax.opt tenor
sax. 4.3.3.1. perc,strings (med
easy) KALMUS A6010 pno-cond sc
$3.00, set $15.50, and up (32)

Saraband
2+pic.2.2.2. 4.3.3.1. perc,strings
(med easy) set KALMUS A6048
$30.00, and up (33)

Summer Skies
2.2.2.2.3sax. 4.3.3.1. bells,
strings (med easy) KALMUS A6049
pno-cond sc $2.00, set $18.00,
and up (34)

ANDRIESSEN, JURRIAAN (1925-)
Tritogno
4.2.2.1. 2.2.1.0. timp,perc,1-
2harp,harp/pno,strings [12']
DONEMUS perf mat rent (35)

ANGELS, SHEPHERDS, CHRISTMAS, KINGS
(Siennicki, Edmund) string orch (gr.
III) set HIGHLAND $20.00, and up
contains: First Noel, The; God Rest
Ye Merry Gentlemen; Hark, The
Herald Angels Sing; In Dulci
Jubilo; Touching Grace, We
Princes Three (36)

ANGELS WE HAVE HEARD ON HIGH [ARR.]
(Ward, Norman) string orch,opt perc,
opt pno set FIDDLE $16.00 (37)

ANGELUS AND BOHEMIAN FESTIVAL [ARR.]
see Massenet, Jules

ANNEN POLKA [ARR.] see Strauss, Johann,
[Jr.]

ANNIE'S SONG [ARR.] see Deutschendorf,
Henry John (John Denver)

ANNIVERSARY OVERTURE see Arnold,
Malcolm

ANTHONY GELL SUITE see Walker, G.

ANYTHING FOR YOU [ARR.] see Estefan,
G.M.

APACHE PASS see Chase, Bruce

APOGEES see Smith

APRON STRINGS see Niehaus, Leonard

AQUILON SUITE see Ameller, André
(Charles-Gabriel)

ARBRE DE NOEL, L' [ARR.] see Liszt,
Franz

AREL, BÜLENT (1919-1990)
  Masques
    2.2.2.2. 0.0.0.0. strings [12']
    (med) sc AM.COMP.AL. $10.30, perf
    mat rent   (38)

ARIA AND FUGHETTA [ARR.] see Karg-
  Elert, Sigfrid

ARIOSO AND FURIOSO see Koch, Erland von

ARIOSO [ARR.] see Bach, Johann
  Sebastian, Adagio [arr.] see Bach,
  Wilhelm Friedemann

ARKANSAS TRAVELER [ARR.]
  (Duncan, Craig) string orch (gr. III)
    KJOS sc SO-54F $5.00, set SO-54B
    $18.00   (39)
  (Muller, J. Frederick) sets LUDWIG
    BGS-108 $20.00, and up   (40)

ARLEN, HAROLD (1905-   )
  Over The Rainbow [arr.]
    (Cerulli, Bob) string orch (easy)
      CPP T87850B4 $25.00   (41)
    (Rothrock, Carson) string orch set
      MUSICIANS PUB SO-206 $15.00, and
      up   (42)
    (Rothrock, Carson) MUSICIANS PUB
      SOS-605 $30.00   (43)
    (Sayre) (med easy) CPP T87850B6
      $55.00   (44)

ARLESIENNE, L': SUITE NO. 1, ADAGIETTO
  [ARR.] see Bizet, Georges

ARNE, THOMAS AUGUSTINE (1710-1778)
  Andantino And Con Spirito [arr.]
    (Benoy) set STAINER f.s.   (45)

  Jig [arr.] *see TWO COUNTRY DANCES

ARNOLD
  Gitans Quittent Le Village, Les *see
    SIX PIECES FACILES

  Sapin De Noel, Le *see SIX PIECES
    FACILES

ARNOLD, ALAN
  Candy Cane Polka
    string orch,opt perc,opt pno set
      FIDDLE $16.00   (46)

  Icicles
    string orch,opt perc,opt pno set
      FIDDLE $16.00   (47)

ARNOLD, MALCOLM (1921-   )
  Anniversary Overture *Op.99
    2.2.2.2. 4.2.3.0. timp,perc,strings
    [4'] sc FABER f.s., perf mat rent (48)

  Toy Symphony *Op.62
    strings,pno, twelve toy instruments
      sc,pts PATERSON f.s.   (49)

ARTHUR'S THEME [ARR.] see Bacharach,
  Burt F.

ASIA MINOR see Shapiro, Marsha Chusmir

ASSONANCES see Meylan, Raymond

AT END OF DAY [ARR.]
  (Feldstein, Sandy) string orch,opt
    pno,opt perc (gr. I) ALFRED 3215
    $25.00 [3']
    contains: Barnby, [Sir] Joseph, Now
    The Day Is Over[arr.]; Brahms,
    Johannes, Lullaby [arr.]   (50)

ATONALYSE I see Breuer, Karl Günther

AU BAL MASQUE see Joubert, Claude-Henry

AUSSIE HOEDOWN see Hultgren, Ralph

AUSTRALIAN RECOLLECTIONS see
  Bauernschmidt, Robert

AUTON, JOHN
  Up And Back A Double
    string orch [3'30"] (easy) OXFORD
    27.415 sc $11.95, pts $3.00, ea.
                                       (51)

AUTUMN: ALLEGRO, [ARR.] see Vivaldi,
  Antonio, Concerto, Op. 8, No. 3,
  [arr.]

AUTUMN [ARR.] see Vivaldi, Antonio,
  Concerto, Op. 8, No. 3, [arr.]

AVE MARIA [ARR.] see Schubert, Franz
  (Peter)

AVEC VIVACITE see DuBois, Pierre-Max

AVENTURE DE BABAR, UNE: SUITE NO. 1
  [ARR.] see Vellones, Pierre

AVENTURE DE BABAR, UNE: SUITE NO. 2
  [ARR.] see Vellones, Pierre

AWAY IN A MANGER [ARR.]
  (Hermann, Ralph) string orch set
    LAKES $16.00, and up
    see Kirkpatrick   (52)

AY, AY, AY [ARR.]
  (Clebanoff, Herman) string orch
    DORABET D-146 f.s.   (53)

BACH, JOHANN CHRISTIAN (1735-1782)
  Rondo, [arr.]
    (McLeod, James) string orch,opt pno
    [4'25"] (gr. II) set KENDOR 9436
    $24.00, and up   (54)

  Sinfonia, Op. 18, No. 1, [arr.]
    (Dackow, Sandra) string orch (med)
      LUDWIG f.s.   (55)

BACH, JOHANN SEBASTIAN (1685-1750)
  Adagio [arr.] (from Cantata No. 156)
    (Wieloszynski, Stephen) "Arioso
    [arr.]" string orch,vln/vcl solo
    [3'10"] (gr. III) set KENDOR 8158
    $19.00, and up   (56)

  Air, [arr.] (from Peasant Cantata)
    (Jurey) set BELWIN CO169 $20.00   (57)

  Air On The G String [arr.]
    (Riggio, Donald) string orch (gr.
    III) JENSON 502-01010 $24.00   (58)

  Arioso [arr.]
    see Adagio [arr.]

  Bach Chamber Suite [arr.]
    (Applebaum, Samuel) string orch set
      BELWIN BS055 $25.00   (59)

  Bach Double Concerto In D Minor
    [arr.]
    see Concerto for 2 Violins and
      Orchestra in D minor, [arr.]

  Bach Suite, A [arr.]
    (Isaac) set BELWIN CO179 $35.00
                                       (60)
    (Leidig, Vernon) string orch (gr.
      II) set HIGHLAND $29.00   (61)

  Bourree, [arr.] (from Sonata No. 2
    for Violin)
    (Isaac) string orch set BELWIN
    BS048 $20.00   (62)

  Brandenburg Concerto No. 1 [arr.]
    (Leidig, Vernon) string orch (gr.
    II) set HIGHLAND $29.00   (63)

  Brandenburg Concerto No. 2: Allegro
    [arr.]
    (Hermann, Ralph) string orch set
    LAKES $20.00, and up   (64)

  Brandenburg Concerto No. 2 [arr.]
    (Isaac, Merle J.) string orch (gr.
    III) set HIGHLAND $20.00, and up   (65)

  Brandenburg Concerto No. 4, First
    Movement [arr.]
    (Leidig, Vernon) string orch (gr.
    II) set HIGHLAND $29.00   (66)

  Chorale No. 31, [arr.] (from Petit
    Livre D'Orgue)
    3rec,ob,bsn,trp,trom,strings sc,pts
    LEMOINE f.s.   (67)

  Chorale Prelude, "In Deepest Need",
    [arr.]
    (Garden, Edward) 1.1.1.1. 1.1.0.0.
    strings (med diff) sc,pts
    BOSWORTH f.s.   (68)

  Christmas Cantata: Overture [arr.]
    (Gaul) string orch CPP V0140B4X sc
    $2.00, pts $1.00, ea.   (69)

  Come Let Us To The Bagpipes Sound
    [arr.]
    (Applebaum, Samuel; Ployhar, James)
    set BELWIN C000170 $20.00   (70)

  Concerto for 2 Violins and Orchestra
    in D minor, [arr.]
    (Zinn, William) "Bach Double
    Concerto In D Minor"
    string orch EXCELSIOR sc
    494-01304 $7.50, pts 494-01305-09
    $2.50, ea.   (71)

  Concerto in D, BWV 1054, [arr.]
    (Isaac) string orch (gr. III) set
    HIGHLAND $20.00, and up   (72)

  Concerto In D Minor [arr.] (from
    Clavier Concerto No. 3)
    (Isaac, Merle J.) string orch (gr.

BACH, JOHANN SEBASTIAN (cont'd.)

    III) set HIGHLAND $20.00, and up
                                       (73)

  Fantasia And Fugue [arr.]
    (Zinn, William) string orch
    EXCELSIOR sc 494-01316 $7.00, pts
    494-01317-21 $2.50, ea.   (74)

  Four Bach Dances [arr.] *CC4U
    (Cechvala, Al) string orch (gr. II)
    CONCERT W J-163 $22.00 [6']   (75)

  Fugue in C, [arr.]
    (Metcalf) string orch set BELWIN
    BS051 $20.00   (76)

  Fugue in E minor, BWV 945, [arr.]
    (Rougeron) flexible instrumentation
    sc,pts LEDUC AL 27225 f.s.   (77)

  Fugue in G minor, [arr.] (from Sonata
    For Solo Violin)
    (Levenson) (gr. IV) KJOS set
    O-1059B $38.00, sc O-1059F $3.00
                                       (78)

  Fugue No. 7, [arr.] (from The Well-
    Tempered Clavichord)
    (Errante, Belisario) string orch
    [2'30"] (gr. III) set MOSAIC M110
    $15.00, and up   (79)

  Fugue No. 23, [arr.] (from The Well-
    Tempered Clavichord)
    (Errante, Belisario) (gr. IV)
    MOSAIC M160   (80)

  Fugues, Two [arr.]
    (Rougeron) sc,pts BILLAUDOT f.s.
                                       (81)

  Gavotte And Musette [arr.] (from
    English Suite No. 3)
    (Cechvala) string orch set BELWIN
      BS047 $20.00   (82)
    (Dasch) string orch FITZSIMONS F556
      set $12.00, sc $3.00, pts $2.00,
      ea.   (83)

  Gavottes Nos. 1 And 2 [arr.] (from
    Suite No. 3)
    (Lacour, Guy) 2.2+opt English
    horn.2+opt bass clar.0.2alto
    sax.opt tenor sax.opt baritone
    sax. 2.2.1.1. perc,gtr,opt acord,
    pno/harp/elec org,strings sc,pts
    BILLAUDOT f.s. contains also:
    Gluck, Christoph Willibald,
    Ritter von, Iphigenie En Tauride:
    Choeur Des Pretresses [arr.]   (84)

  Hymn And Finale [arr.]
    (Gordon, Philip) [2'30"] PRESSER
    116-40021 sc $1.50, set $15.00,
    pts $.75, ea.   (85)

  Jesu, Joy Of Man's Desiring [arr.]
    (Isaac) (med easy) set WYNN
      4275-5275 $26.00, and up   (86)
    (Wieloszynski, Stephen) string
      orch,kbd,vln/fl/ob solo [3'] (gr.
      I) set KENDOR 8325 $19.00, and up
                                       (87)

  *see THREE CHRISTMAS CLASSICS

  Menuetts 1 & 2 And Gigue [arr.]
    (Levenson) string orch (gr. III)
    KJOS set SO-58B $30.00, sc SO-58F
    $5.00   (88)

  Minuet, MIN 159, [arr.]
    (Applebaum, Samuel; Ployhar, James)
    set BELWIN C000168 $20.00   (89)

  My Heart Ever Faithful [arr.]
    (Isaac) string orch set BELWIN
    BS049 $20.00   (90)

  Passacaglia And Fugue In C Minor
    [arr.]
    (Zinn, William) string orch
    EXCELSIOR sc 494-01310 $7.50, pts
    484-01311-15 $2.50, ea.   (91)

  Passacaglia, [arr.] (from Suite No. 1
    In C)
    (Applebaum, Samuel; Ployhar, James)
    1.1.2.1.2sax. 2.2.1.1. perc,
    strings BELWIN   (92)

  Passepied, [arr.]
    (Applebaum, Samuel; Ployhar, James)
    set BELWIN C000171 $20.00   (93)

  Petite Suite Sur Un Choral [arr.]
    (Voirpy, C.) 3rec,2fl,2clar,2gtr,
    strings sc,pts LEMOINE f.s.   (94)

  Prelude and Fugue in D minor, [arr.]
    (Demarest, Clifford) (gr. III)
      WARNER 575-12056 $30.00   (95)
    (Frost) string orch (gr. IV) LAKES
      $24.00   (96)

  Prelude, MIN 160, [arr.]
    (Metcalf) string orch set BELWIN
    BS050 $20.00   (97)

BACH, JOHANN SEBASTIAN (cont'd.)

Rondo, [arr.] (from Suite No. 2 in B Minor)
(Applebaum, Samuel; Ployhar, James) 1.1.2.1.2sax. 2.2.1.1. perc, strings set BELWIN C000172 $20.00 (98)

(Clebanoff) string orch [2'30"] DORABET sc $2.00, set $16.00, and up, pts $1.25, ea. (99)

Sarabande [arr.]
see Sicilienne [arr.]

Sheep May Safely Graze [arr.] *see THREE CHRISTMAS CLASSICS

Sicilienne [arr.] (from Sonata, Bwv 1031)
(Wystraete) flexible instrumentation sc,pts LEDUC AL 27356 f.s. contains also: Sarabande [arr.] (from Suite No. 2, Bwv 1067) (100)

Sinfonia, MIN 140, [arr.]
(Farago, Frank) string orch BELWIN sc $2.00, set $12.00 (101)

Two Bach Minuets, [arr.]
(Wieloszynski, Stephen) string orch,pno [3'40"] (gr. II) sets KENDOR $14.00, and up (102)

Two Pieces From Peasants' Cantata [arr.] *see BAROQUE SUITE NO. 2

BACH, WILHELM FRIEDEMANN (1710-1784)
Arioso [arr.]
(Track) string orch (gr. III) KJOS set WSO-4B $18.00, sc WSO-4F $3.00 (103)

BACH CHAMBER SUITE [ARR.] see Bach, Johann Sebastian

BACH DOUBLE CONCERTO IN D MINOR [ARR.] see Bach, Johann Sebastian, Concerto for 2 Violins and Orchestra in D minor, [arr.]

BACH SUITE, A [ARR.] see Bach, Johann Sebastian

BACHARACH, BURT F. (1928-   )
Arthur's Theme [arr.]
(Reilly, Jim) (gr. II) WARNER 575-40070 $30.00 (104)

That's What Friends Are For [arr.]
(Curnow, James) string orch (gr. III) JENSON 502-20030 $24.00 (105)

Walk On By [arr.]
(Jennings) string orch [2'30"] (med easy) LEONARD-US $30.00 (106)

BAGLEY, E.E.
National Emblem March [arr.]
(McLeod, James) string orch,opt pno [2'55"] (gr. III) set KENDOR $18.00, and up (107)

BAGPIPE SOUNDS
(Adams, D.) string orch set ADAM 8612 $10.00 (108)

BAHN FREI POLKA [ARR.] see Strauss, Eduard

BAILE EN LA CALLE see Scott, Richard

BAKKE, RUTH (1947-   )
Brumlebuff II
5fl,2clar,timp,perc,3vln,3vcl NORGE (109)

BALLAD SINGER, THE see Bottje, Will Gay

BALLERINA GIRL [ARR.] see Richie, Lionel

BALLET SCENES see Quagenti, Samuel

BALLET SUITE NO. 1: POLKA, WALTZ, GALOP [ARR.] see Shostakovich, Dmitri

BALLETTO see Werdin, Eberhard

BAMBA, LA [ARR.]
(Chase, Bruce) string orch (gr. III) JENSON 502-12010 $30.00 (110)

BAMBINO see Westera, A.

BANCHIERI, ADRIANO (1568-1634)
Sinfonia, [arr.]
(Kohut, Daniel) (gr. II, also contains Galliard [arr.] by Paul Peurl) WARNER 575-10022 $30.00 (111)

BARBARA ANN [ARR.] see Fassert, Fred

BARBER OF SEVILLE: OVERTURE [ARR.] see Rossini, Gioacchino

BARNBY, [SIR] JOSEPH (1838-1896)
Now The Day Is Over[arr.] *see AT END OF DAY [arr.]

BARNES, JAMES
Yorkshire Ballad
2+opt pic.2.2+bass clar.2. 2.3.3.1. timp,perc,strings [3'40"] (gr. III) SOUTHERN A-31 sc $5.00, set $35.00, pts $1.25, ea. (112)

BARNYARD BASH see Chase, Bruce

BAROQUE BAGATELLE, A see Goldsmith, Owen

BAROQUE BOUREE see Fletcher, Gary

BAROQUE SUITE NO. 1
(Isaac, Merle J.) string orch (gr. III) set HIGHLAND $24.00, and up contains: Grétry, André Ernest Modeste, Tambourin [arr.]; Handel, George Frideric, Menuetto From Alcina [arr.]; Mouret, Jean Joseph, Rondeau [arr.]; Senaille, Jean Baptiste, Allegro Spiritoso [arr.] (113)

BAROQUE SUITE NO. 2
(Isaac, Merle J.) string orch (gr. III) set HIGHLAND $31.00 contains: Bach, Johann Sebastian, Two Pieces From Peasants' Cantata [arr.]; Handel, George Frideric, Menuetto From The Royal Fireworks [arr.]; Purcell, Henry, Trumpet Tune [arr.]; Vivaldi, Antonio, Autumn [arr.] (114)

BART, LIONEL
Oliver: Oom-Pah-Pah [arr.]
sc,pts CHESTER CH 55665 $16.50 (115)

BARTÓK, BÉLA (1881-1945)
Bela Bartok For Orchestra [arr.]
(McKay, George; Weeks, Norman) (gr. II) WARNER 575-10007 $30.00 (116)

Moods [arr.]
(Applebaum, Samuel) string orch BELWIN BSO11 sc $3.50, set $15.00 (117)

Music For Children, Vol. 2 [arr.] *CC10U
(McAlister) 1(pic).1.1.1. 1.1.1.0. perc,strings KALMUS A6325 sc $25.00, set $25.00, perf mat rent (118)

Ten Pieces For Children [arr.] *CC10U
(Weiner) string orch, optional third violin KALMUS A6145 sc $5.00, set $6.00 (119)

Two Pieces [arr.]
(Frost, Robert) string orch set LAKES $17.50, and up (120)

BARTOVSKY, JOSEF (1884-1964)
Skola Pro Smyccovy Orchestr
string orch SUPRAPHON f.s. (121)

BATTLE HYMN OF THE REPUBLIC [ARR.]
(Schoenfeld, William; Ringwald, Roy) (med easy) SHAWNEE set $10.00, pts $1.50, ea. (122)

BAUERNSCHMIDT, ROBERT
Alpine Holiday
string orch (med easy) sets WYNN 6301-7301 $18.00, and up (123)

Australian Recollections
(med) set WYNN 4310 $26.00, and up (124)

Beseda
(med) set WYNN 4309 $28.00, and up (125)

Fantasia For Orchestra, On A Theme By Tartini
[3'30"] (med diff) set SHAWNEE J-116 $14.00 (126)

Gypsy Carnival
(med easy) set WYNN 4312 $28.00, and up (127)

BAUMANN, HERBERT (1925-   )
Variationen Uber Ein Thema Von Handel
string orch sc,pts BAREN. BA 8112 f.s. (128)

BEAL, JOSEPH CARLETON (1900-   )
Jingle Bell Rock [arr.] (composed with Boothe, James R.)
(Chase) string orch (easy) LEONARD-US 04621144 $22.50 (129)
(Lowden) string orch LEONARD-US 04849392 $20.00 (130)

BEARD
Concertino in D minor, [arr.]
(Bauernschmidt) string orch (med) set WYNN 6082-7082 $24.00, and up (131)

BEAVER VALLEY see Chase, Bruce

BEBE ROSE see DuBois, Pierre-Max

BEDFORD, DAVID (1937-   )
Ocean Star A Dreaming Song
2.2.2.1. 2.2.0.0. 3perc,strings [11'] UNIVER. perf mat rent (132)

BEECHER, KIRK
Two Pieces For Young Strings
string orch [4'15"] (med easy) set SHAWNEE J-95 $10.00 (133)

BEETHOVEN, LUDWIG VAN (1770-1827)
Adagio Cantabile [arr.] (from Sonata Pathetique)
(Heilmann, Francis) 2fl,2clar,2alto sax,2trp,trom,perc,pno,strings [2'55"] (med easy) set HEILNN $27.00, and up (134)
(Heilmann, Francis) string orch, perc,pno [2'55"] (med easy) set HEILNN $21.00, and up (135)
(McLeod, James) string orch,opt pno [3'30"] (gr. II) set KENDOR 8865 $23.00, and up (136)

Allemande [arr.]
see Beginning Beethoven

Beethoven's Greatest Hits
(Wielosznski, Stephen I Sorch, Opt Pno) (gr. III) KENDOR 9792 f.s. [6'50]
contains: Für Elise [arr.]; Minuet In G [arr.]; Symphony No. 9, Op. 125, Theme From Fourth Movement [arr.] (137)

Beginning Beethoven
(Wieloszynski, Stephen) string orch,opt pno (gr. I) set KENDOR $23.00, and up [2'10]
contains: Allemande [arr.]; Russian Air, Op. 107, No. 3 [arr.]; Russian Theme, Op. 107, No. 7 [arr.] (138)

Best Of Beethoven, The [arr.]
(Paradise, Paul) string orch BELWIN sc EL 03588 $17.50, pts EL 03589-03593 $5.50, ea. (139)

Concerto For Violin And Orchestra, Op. 61: Themes, [arr.]
(Frost, Robert S.) string orch,opt pno [2'15"] (gr. II) sets KENDOR $16.00, and up (140)

Contradance [arr.]
(Bauernschmidt, Robert) 2.2.2.2. 2.2.2.1. timp,perc,strings [3'] (med) set SHAWNEE J-94 $25.00 (141)

Deux Hymnes [arr.]
(Voirby, C.) 2rec,2fl,2clar,2gtr, strings sc,pts LEMOINE f.s. (142)

Four Country Dances [arr.]
(Alshin, Harry A.) string orch [3'15"] (gr. III) set KENDOR 9823 $24.00, and up (143)

From A Sonata [arr.] (from Op. 14, No. 1)
(Myers, Theldon) string orch (med easy) set LAKES $24.00, and up (144)

Für Elise [arr.]
see Beethoven's Greatest Hits

German Dance [arr.]
(Jurey, Edward) (easy) BELWIN CO 00200 $35.00 (145)

Hymne A La Joie [arr.]
(Lacour, Guy) 2.2+opt English horn.2+opt bass clar.0.2alto sax.opt tenor sax.opt baritone sax. 2.2.1.1. perc,gtr,opt acord, pno/harp/elec org,strings sc,pts BILLAUDOT f.s. contains also: Beethoven, Ludwig van, Menuet Du Sextuor, Op. 71 [arr.]; Charpentier, Marc-Antoine, Te Deum [arr.]; Schubert, Franz (Peter), Serenade [arr.] (146)

Menuet Du Sextuor, Op. 71 [arr.]
*see Beethoven, Ludwig Van, Hymne A La Joie [arr.]
see Beethoven, Ludwig van, Hymne A La Joie [arr.]

Minuet And Trio *see THREE CLASSICAL PIECES

Minuet In G [arr.]
see Beethoven's Greatest Hits

Romance [arr.]
(Lacour, Guy) 2.2+opt English horn.2+opt bass clar.0.2alto sax.opt tenor sax.opt baritone sax. 2.2.1.1. perc,gtr,opt acord,

BEETHOVEN, LUDWIG VAN (cont'd.)

pno/harp/elec org,strings sc,pts
BILLAUDOT f.s. contains also:
Diabelli, Anton, Andantino
[arr.]; Schubert, Franz (Peter),
Ave Maria [arr.]   (147)

Russian Air, Op. 107, No. 3 [arr.]
see Beginning Beethoven

Russian Theme, Op. 107, No. 7 [arr.]
see Beginning Beethoven

Sonatina in G, [arr.]
(Applebaum, Samuel; Ployhar, James)
BELWIN C000182 sc $4.00, set
$25.00   (148)

Symphony No. 5, Op. 67,Finale, [arr.]
(Leidig) (gr. III) set HIGHLAND
$28.00, and up   (149)

Symphony No. 9, Op. 125, [excerpt],
[arr.]
(Caponegro, John) string orch,opt
pno [2'] (gr. I, Ode to Joy) sets
KENDOR $14.00, and up   (150)
(Case) string orch ("Ode To Joy")
LAKES   (151)
(Heilmann, Francis) 2fl,2clar,2alto
sax,2trp,trom,perc,pno,strings
[1'55"] (easy, Ode To Joy) set
HEILNN $27.00, and up   (152)
(Heilmann, Francis) string orch,
perc,pno [1'55"] (easy, Ode To
Joy) set HEILNN $21.00, and up   (153)

*see also Beethoven, Ludwig Van,
Hymne A La Joie [arr.]

Symphony No. 9, Op. 125, Theme From
Fourth Movement [arr.]
see Beethoven's Greatest Hits

BEETHOVEN'S GREATEST HITS see
Beethoven, Ludwig van

BEGINNING BEETHOVEN see Beethoven,
Ludwig van

BEGINNING BRAHMS [ARR.] see Brahms,
Johannes

BELA BARTOK FOR ORCHESTRA [ARR.] see
Bartók, Béla

BELINDA'S RIGADOON [ARR.] see Newton,
E.

BELL ANTHEM, THE [ARR.] see Purcell,
Henry

BELLS, SCHOOL ORCHESTRA VERSION see
Still, William Grant

BENCRISCUTTO, FRANK PETER ANTHONY
(1928-   )
Lindbergh Jubilee
[6'40"] (gr. V) KJOS set WO-11B
$40.00, sc WO-11F $5.00   (154)

BENDER, MITCHELL
Chanukah Happening
string orch (gr. II) LAKES $16.00
                                    (155)

BENNETT, RICHARD RODNEY (1936-   )
Serenade
2.2.2.1. 2.2.1.0. timp,3perc,pno,
strings [14'] NOVELLO sc
09.0550.10.00 f.s., pts
09.0550.10.25 f.s.   (156)

BENOY, A.W.
Overture For Christmas, An
2.2.2.2. 2.2.3.1. timp,perc,strings
[5'] OXFORD sc 361992-X $15.00,
set 380088-8 $28.00   (157)

BERGE, SIGURD (1929-   )
Juvenes
string orch [10'] NORGE   (158)

BERGER, JEAN (1909-   )
Suite for Strings
string orch (gr. IV) set KJOS GS01B
$15.00   (159)

BERLIN, IRVING (1888-1989)
Alexander's Ragtime Band [arr.]
see Two By Berlin

Play A Simple Melody [arr.]
see Two By Berlin

Two By Berlin
(Siennicki, Edmund) (gr. III) set
HIGHLAND $39.00
contains: Alexander's Ragtime
Band [arr.]; Play A Simple
Melody [arr.]   (160)

BERLIOZ, HECTOR (LOUIS) (1803-1869)
Damnation Of Faust, The: Hungarian
March [arr.]
(Cobb, Ian) 2.2.2.1. 2.3.2.0. timp,
3perc,opt pno,strings [5'] sc,pts
NOVELLO 09.0540.02 f.s.   (161)

Hungarian March, [arr.]
(Rokos, K.W.) 2.2.3.2. 2.2.2.0.
timp,opt perc,strings (med diff)
sc,pts BOSWORTH f.s.   (162)

March To The Scaffold [arr.]
(Leidig, Vernon) DORABET D-132 f.s.
                                    (163)

BERNARD, FELIX (1897-1949)
Winter Wonderland [arr.]
(Curnow; Lavender) JENSON 593-20010
$45.00   (164)

BERNIE, BEN (1891-1948)
Sweet Georgia Brown [arr.] (composed
with Casey, Kenneth; Pinkard,
Maceo)
(Chase) string orch [2'] (med easy)
LEONARD-US $25.00   (165)

BERRY, CHUCK (1926-   )
Surfin' U.S.A. [arr.]
(Jennings) string orch [2'] (med
easy) LEONARD-US $25.00   (166)

BERTINI, HENRI(-JÉRÔME) (1798-1876)
Bertini Etude, The, [arr.]
(Wieloszynski, Stephen) string
orch,opt pno [2'] (gr. II) sets
KENDOR $16.00, and up   (167)

BERTINI ETUDE, THE, [ARR.] see Bertini,
Henri(-Jérôme)

BESEDA see Bauernschmidt, Robert

BEST OF BEETHOVEN, THE [ARR.] see
Beethoven, Ludwig van

BEST OF BILLY JOEL, THE [ARR.] see
Joel, William Martin (Billy)

BEST OF HAYDN, THE see Haydn, [Franz]
Joseph

BEST OF MOZART, THE [ARR.] see Mozart,
Wolfgang Amadeus

BEST OF SCHUBERT, THE [ARR.] see
Schubert, Franz (Peter)

BEST OF THE BEATLES, THE [ARR.]
(Custer) LEONARD-US 08720625 $45.00
                                    (168)

BEURDEN, BERNARD VAN (1933-   )
Three Minutes Concerto
MOLENAAR   (169)

BIEDERMANN-KLIMESCH, GRETL
Frohlicher Anfang, Vol. 5:
Orchesterschule Für Verschiedene
Instrumente (composed with
Reiter, Albert)
DOBLINGER 04-096 f.s.   (170)

BIEHL, E.
Evening Prayer, An [arr.] *see TWO
PIECES FOR STRING ORCHESTRA

BIGELOW, F.E.
Our Director [arr.]
(McLeod, James) string orch,opt pno
[2'25"] (gr. III) set KENDOR 9855
$24.00, and up   (171)

BILL BAILEY [ARR.]
(Christensen, James) 2(pic).2.2.2.
4.4.3.1. timp,perc,harp,banjo,
strings [3'10"] (gr. V) sc,pts
KENDOR $50.00   (172)
(Leidig, Vernon) (gr. I) set HIGHLAND
$31.00   (173)

BISHOP, STEPHEN
Separate Lives [arr.]
(Whitney) (easy) CPP 1544SB7X
$40.00   (174)

BIZET, GEORGES (1838-1875)
Arlesienne, L': Suite No. 1,
Adagietto [arr.]
string orch FITZSIMONS F0550 set
$12.00, sc $3.00, pts $2.00, ea.
                                    (175)
Arlesienne, L': Suite No. 1, March Of
The Three Kings [arr.] *see
CHRISTMAS CLASSICS

Carmen: Changing Of The Guard, [arr.]
(Carlin, Sidney) 1.1.2.1.alto
sax.tenor sax. 2.2.2.0. timp,
perc,pno,strings [2'30"] set
CARLIN $26.00, and up   (176)

Carmen: Habanera [arr.]
MIDDLE CMK 209 f.s.   (177)
(Ma, H.T.) string orch sc,pts
ZURFLUH $18.75   (178)

BIZET, GEORGES (cont'd.)

Carmen: Prelude, Act IV, [arr.]
(Carlin, Sidney) 1.1.2.1.alto
sax.tenor sax. 2.2.2.0. timp,
perc,pno,strings [2'30"] set
CARLIN $26.00, and up   (179)

Carmen: Seguidilla, [arr.]
(Carlin, Sidney) 1.1.2.1.alto
sax.tenor sax. 2.2.2.0. timp,
perc,pno,strings [2'] set CARLIN
$26.00, and up   (180)

Carmen Suite [arr.]
(Leidig, Vernon) string orch (gr.
II) set HIGHLAND $29.00   (181)

Carmen: The Toreador Song [arr.]
(Frost, Robert) string orch,opt pno
[2'20"] (gr. II) sets KENDOR
$20.00, and up   (182)

Habanera [arr.]
(Siennicki, Edmund) string orch
(gr. III) set HIGHLAND $29.00
                                    (183)

BJORN, FRANK
Alley Cat [arr.]
(Caponegro, John) string orch,opt
perc,opt pno [2'5"] (gr. I) sets
KENDOR $14.00, and up   (184)

BLACK AND WHITE RAG [ARR.] see
Botsford, George

BLACK IS THE COLOR [ARR.]
(Clebanoff, Herman) string orch
DORABET D-147 f.s.   (185)
(Myers, Theldon) string orch set
LAKES $17.50, and up   (186)

BLADES AND ICE see Ward, Norman

BLAKE, HOWARD (1938-   )
Nursery Rhyme Overture
2.1.2.1. 2.1.1.0. 2perc,harp,
strings [8'] sc FABER f.s., perf
mat rent   (187)

Snowman, The: Walking In The Air
[arr.]
sc,pts CHESTER CH 55740 $16.50
                                    (188)

BLESSED ARE THEY [ARR.] see Brahms,
Johannes

BLUE GRASS BALL see Chase, Bruce

BLUE JEAN JACKET see Siennicki, Edmund
John

BLUE MOUNTAIN PASS see Elledge, Chuck

BLUE RIDGE BOOGIE see Chase, Bruce

BLUE TAIL FLY, THE
(Davis, Albert O.) sets LUDWIG
BGS-111 $20.00, and up   (189)

BLUEBELLS OF SCOTLAND, THE [ARR.] see
Folk-Songs For Strings, Set 3

BLUEBERRY JAM see Fletcher, Gary

BLUEGRASS BINGO see Chase, Bruce

BLUEGRASS CAMP MEETING [ARR.]
(McCleod, James) string orch [2'30"]
(gr. III) KJOS set GSO-3B $25.00,
sc GSO-3F $3.00   (190)

BLUEGRASS COUNTRY see Nunez, Carold

BOBBY SHAFTOE [ARR.] see Folk-Songs For
Strings, Set 3

BOCCHERINI, LUIGI (1743-1805)
Minuet, [arr.]
(Wystraete) flexible
instrumentation sc,pts LEDUC
AL 27213 f.s.   (191)

BOCK, JERRY (1928-   )
Fiddler On The Roof: Overture [arr.]
(Lang) LEONARD-US 04500190 $45.00
                                    (192)

If I Were A Rich Man [arr.]
(Rosenhaus) string orch (med easy)
LEONARD-US 04849334 $16.00   (193)

Sunrise, Sunset [arr.]
(Chase) string orch (easy) LEONARD-
US 04622222 $18.00   (194)

BOHEMIAN DANCE [ARR.] see Dvořák,
Antonín see Friml, Rudolf

BOHEMIAN SUITE see Nelhybel, Vaclav

BOHM, CARL
Perpetual Motion [arr.]
(Isaac) FITZSIMONS F0504 set
$30.00, sc $6.50, pts $3.00, ea.
                                    (195)

BOHM, CARL (cont'd.)

Saraband, [arr.]
(Errante) 2.2.3.1. 2.4.2.1. timp,
perc,strings [4'50"] (gr. III)
SHAWNEE J-149 $35.00   (196)

Spanish Dance [arr.]
sc,pts LENGNICK f.s.   (197)

Still As The Night [arr.]
sc,pts LENGNICK f.s.   (198)

BÖHM, GEORG (1661-1733)
Presto Pizzicato [arr.]
(Myers, Theldon) string orch (gr.
III) set LAKES $17.50, and up
(199)

BOLZONI, GIOVANNI (1841-1919)
Minuetto [arr.]
(Dasch) string orch FITZSIMONS
F0559 set $12.00, sc $3.00, pts
$2.00, ea.   (200)

BONAVISTA HARBOUR see Coakley, Donald

BOOGIE BASS NO. 1 see Isaac, Merle John

BOREL-CLERC, CHARLES (1879-1959)
Sorella, La [arr.]
(Isaac) (gr. III) set HIGHLAND
$28.00, and up   (201)

BORODIN, ALEXANDER PORFIRIEVICH
(1833-1887)
On The Steppes Of Central Asia [arr.]
(Leidig, Vernon) (gr. III) set
HIGHLAND $28.00, and up   (202)

Petite Suite: Intermezzo [arr.]
(Reibold) FITZSIMONS F0502 set
$25.00, sc $6.50, pts $2.00, ea.
(203)

Prince Igor: Polovtsian Dance, [arr.]
(Frost, Robert S.) string orch,opt
pno [2'30"] (gr. I/gr. II) sets
KENDOR $14.00, and up   (204)

String Quartet No. 2: Nocturne [arr.]
(Chase, Bruce) string orch (med
diff) set LAKES $20.00, and up
(205)
(Farago, Frank) string orch BELWIN
sc $2.00, set $15.00   (206)
(Isaac, Merle J.) string orch (gr.
III) set HIGHLAND $29.00   (207)

Symphony No. 2,First Movement, [arr.]
(Leidig, Vernon) (gr. III) set
HIGHLAND $37.00   (208)

BOROGYIN, A.P.
see BORODIN, ALEXANDER PORFIREVICH

BOROWSKI, FELIX (1872-1956)
Adoration [arr.]
(Isaac, Merle J.) string orch (gr.
III) set HIGHLAND $20.00, and up
(209)

BOSSLER, KURT (1911-1976)
Concertino For 3 Recorders And String
Orchestra
string orch,3rec soli SIKORSKI sc
414P $17.00, solo pt 414 $2.25,
pts $2.75, ea.   (210)

BOTANY BICENTENARY [ARR.]
(Hultgren, Ralph) string orch set
LAKES $30.00, and up   (211)

BOTSFORD, GEORGE (1874-1949)
Black And White Rag [arr.]
(McLeod, James) string orch,opt pno
[3'45"] (gr. II) sets KENDOR
$20.00, and up   (212)

BOTTJE, WILL GAY (1925-   )
Ballad Singer, The
2.1.3.1. 3.3.3.1. timp,perc,strings
[8'] (med) sc AM.COMP.AL. $8.80,
perf mat rent   (213)

BOUNCE A ROUND see Siennicki, Edmund
John

BOURDON, ROSARIO
Christmas-Tide
(med easy) SHAWNEE set $10.00, pts
$.50, ea.   (214)

BOURGEOIS GENTILHOMME, LE: OVERTURE
[ARR.] see Lully, Jean-Baptiste
(Lulli)

BOW TIES see Niehaus, Leonard

BOWIN' AND SCRAPIN' see Siennicki,
Edmund John

BOWLES, RICHARD W.
Happy Hobo, The
string orch FITZSIMONS F0557 set
$12.00, sc $3.00, pts $2.00, ea.
(215)

BOWS AND ARROWS see Niehaus, Leonard

BOYCE, WILLIAM (1711-1779)
Boyce Suite, A [arr.]
(Benoy, A.W.) 2.2.2.1. 2.2.2.0.
timp,perc,strings OXFORD sc
362215-7 $15.00, pts 380110-8
$38.00   (216)

BOYCE SUITE, A [ARR.] see Boyce,
William

BOYSEN, ANDREW
Casus Belli
(gr. VI) KJOS set O-1058B $40.00,
sc O-1058F $3.00   (217)

BRAHMS, JOHANNES (1833-1897)
Beginning Brahms [arr.]
(Wieloszynski, Stephen) string
orch,opt pno [5'20"] (gr. II) set
KENDOR 8917 $24.00, and up   (218)

Blessed Are They [arr.]
(Buehlman; Davis) LUDWIG LLE-76
(219)

Famous Waltz In G [arr.] *see SUITE
OF WALTZES, A

Lullaby [arr.] *see AT END OF DAY
[arr.]

Scottish Folksong [arr.]
(Burton) string orch (gr. III) KJOS
sc SO-43F $3.00, set 43B $26.00
(220)

Serenade, Op. 11,Scherzo, [arr.]
(Dackow, Sandra) string orch (med)
LUDWIG STRO 55 $45.00   (221)

Symphony No. 1,Finale, [arr.]
(Carlin) 1.1.2.1.alto sax.tenor
sax. 2.2.2.0. timp,perc,pno,
strings CARLIN sc $4.00, set
$38.00, pts $1.50, ea.   (222)

Symphony No. 1, [excerpt]
(Applebaum, Samuel; Ployhar, James)
(themes [arr.]) set BELWIN
C000181 $25.00   (223)

Symphony No.1: Themes [arr.]
(Frost, Robert S.) string orch,opt
pno [2'15"] (gr. II) sets KENDOR
$16.00, and up   (224)

Symphony No. 3, Op. 90,Third
Movement, [arr.]
(Herfurth, C. Paul) [4'20"] set
SHAWNEE J-86   (225)

Symphony No. 4,Third Movement, [arr.]
(Leidig, Vernon) 2.1.2+opt bass
clar.1.opt alto sax.opt tenor
sax. 2.3.3.1. timp,perc,strings
(gr. IV) set KJOS WO5B $30.00
(226)

Three Waltzes [arr.]
(Burton) string orch (gr. III) KJOS
sc SO-44F $3.00, set SO-44B
$24.00   (227)

Two Sarabandes [arr.]
(Burton) string orch (gr. IV) KJOS
set SO-45B $25.00, sc SO-45F
$3.00   (228)

Valse [arr.]
(Lacour) sc BILLAUDOT $15.00
contains also: Corelli,
Arcangelo, Sarabande [arr.];
Rameau, Jean-Philippe, Tambourin
[arr.]   (229)

BRANDENBURG CONCERTO NO. 1 [ARR.] see
Bach, Johann Sebastian

BRANDENBURG CONCERTO NO. 2: ALLEGRO
[ARR.] see Bach, Johann Sebastian

BRANDENBURG CONCERTO NO. 2 [ARR.] see
Bach, Johann Sebastian

BRANDENBURG CONCERTO NO. 4, FIRST
MOVEMENT [ARR.] see Bach, Johann
Sebastian

BRANDON, SEYMOUR (SY) (1945-   )
Celebration Dance
string orch CO OP $15.00   (230)

Gettysburg Portrait, For Narrator And
Orchestra
CO OP perf mat rent   (231)

Melting Pot Overture, For Narrator
And Orchestra
CO OP perf mat rent   (232)

Robin Hood Suite
string orch CO OP $20.00   (233)

BREEDON, DANIEL
Variations On "The Minstrel Boy"
3.2.2.2. 2.3.3.1. timp,perc,strings
[7'] (med diff) set SHAWNEE J-99
$40.00   (234)

BREUER, KARL GÜNTHER (1926-   )
Atonalyse I
string orch,clar/vln/vla solo
SIKORSKI sc 403P $11.95, solo pt
403 $3.95   (235)

BRIANNA see Lowden, Bob

BRICUSSE, LESLIE (1931-   )
Candy Man, The [arr.] (composed with
Newley, Anthony)
(Caponegro, John) string orch,opt
perc,opt pno [2'30"] (gr. II)
sets KENDOR $16.00, and up   (236)

BRIDGE AROUND THE WORLD, A [ARR.]
(Caponegro, John) string orch,opt
pno,narrator [3'30"] (gr. I) set
KENDOR 8187 $23.00, and up   (237)

BRIDGE OVER TROUBLED WATER [ARR.] see
Sounds Of Simon And Garfunkel, Vol.
I

BRIGHT STAR see Chase, Bruce

BRITISH GRENADIERS [ARR.]
(Richardson, Clive) 1+pic.1.2.1.2sax.
2.2.2.0. timp,perc,strings (med
easy) set KALMUS A6024 $13.50, and
up   (238)

BROADWAY JOE see Cunha

BROOKS, JOE
You Light Up My Life [arr.]
(Cerulli, Bob) string orch (easy)
CPP 4885YB4X $25.00   (239)

BROWN, CHRISTOPHER (ROLAND) (1943-   )
Rustic Dances
string orch (med easy) CHESTER
CH 55629 sc $7.75, pts $22.50
(240)

BRUCH, MAX (1838-1920)
Scottish Fantasy [arr.]
(Alshin, Harry A.) string orch
[2'35"] (gr. III) set KENDOR 9867
$24.00, and up   (241)

BRUDER MARTIN, [ARR.] see Mahler,
Gustav

BRUMLEBUFF II see Bakke, Ruth

BRUNI, ANTONIO BARTOLOMEO (1759-1821)
Scherzo in G minor, [arr.]
(Errante, Belisario) string orch
[4'] (gr. III) set MOSAIC M120
$20.00   (242)

Sicilienne And Gigue [arr.]
(Errante, Belisario) string orch
[5'] (gr. IV) set MOSAIC M130
$2.00   (243)

BRUYERES [ARR.] see Debussy, Claude

BRYANT, BOUDLEAUX
Rocky Top [arr.] (composed with
Bryant, Felice)
(Chase) string orch (med easy)
LEONARD-US 04849675 $18.00   (244)

BUCCI
Italian Folk Fantasy
(med diff) set WYNN 4392-5392
$48.00, and up   (245)

BUDDHA'S TEMPLE see Heilmann, Francis

BUFFALO GALS
(Davis, Albert O.) sets LUDWIG
BGS-106 $20.00, and up   (246)

BULL, JOHN (ca. 1562-1628)
Pavana [arr.] *see FITZWILLIAM SUITE

BUSY BOWS see Hubbell, Fred M.

BUTTERFLIES [ARR.] see Schaefer, C.
Grant

BUTTERFLY see Chase, Bruce

BUTZ, JOSEF
Festliche Musik *Op.51
string orch BUTZ 398 f.s.   (247)

BUXTEHUDE, DIETRICH (ca. 1637-1707)
Chaconne In E Minor [arr.]
(Hause, Robert) string orch (gr.
III) SHAWNEE J-142 $25.00   (248)

BYNG, F.D.
Eastern Pictures [arr.]
sc,pts LENGNICK f.s.   (249)

BYNG, F.D. (cont'd.)

Harlequinade [arr.]
sc,pts LENGNICK f.s.   (250)

BYRD, WILLIAM (1543-1623)
Fortune, My Foe [arr.] *see
FITZWILLIAM SUITE

C.P. TWO OH! see Petrone, John

C.R. MARCHANT SUITE FOR STRINGS see
Dawson, Ted

CABARET see String Orchestra Pak No. 4

CACAVAS, JOHN (1930-   )
Time Of Kings Overture, A
2.2.2.2.2sax. 4.3.3.1. timp,chimes,
perc,strings (med) set KALMUS
A6058 $15.00, and up   (251)

CADKIN, EMIL
Real People March, The [arr.] *see
Loose, William

CADUTA DE DECEM VIRI, LA: OVERTURE
[ARR.] see Scarlatti, Alessandro

CAGE AUX FOLLES, LA: SELECTIONS [ARR.]
see Herman, Jerry

CAHN, SAMMY (1913-1993)
Let It Snow [arr.] *see Styne, Jule

CAIX D'HERVELOIS, LOUIS DE
(ca. 1670-ca. 1760)
Deux Menuets [arr.]
(Rougeron) flexible instrumentation
sc,pts LEDUC AL 27183 f.s. (252)

CAJKOVSKIJ, PETR ILJIC
see TCHAIKOVSKY, PIOTR ILYICH

CALLIOPE, THE see Frost, Robert S.

CALS, MICHEL
Esquisses
RIDEAU   (253)

CAMERON, JAMES
White Knight And The Dragon, The
string orch (med easy) CHESTER
CH 55587 sc $7.25, pts $17.25
(254)

CAMP MEETIN' see Fletcher, Gary

CAMPFIRE SUITE
(Arnold, Alan) string orch,opt perc,
opt pno set FIDDLE $20.00   (255)

CAMPRA, ANDRÉ (1660-1744)
Passepied [arr.] *see SUITE OF
WALTZES, A

Rigaudon And Processional [arr.]
(Leidig, Vernon) (gr. II) set
HIGHLAND $28.00, and up   (256)

CAMPTOWN BLUEGRASS RACE [ARR.] see
Foster, Stephen Collins

CAMPTOWN RACES [ARR.] see Foster,
Stephen Collins

CANADIAN SUNSET [ARR.] see Heywood,
Eddie

CANDLE ON THE WATER see String
Orchestra Pak No. 5

CANDLE ON THE WATER [ARR.] see Kasha,
Al

CANDLELIGHT WALTZ see Chase, Bruce

CANDY CANE POLKA see Arnold, Alan

CANDY MAN, THE [ARR.] see Bricusse,
Leslie

CANON see Suben, Joel Eric

CANON [ARR.] see Pachelbel, Johann

CANON: THEME [ARR.] see Pachelbel,
Johann

CANTICLE, SOUNDS OF SILENCE [ARR.] see
Sounds Of Simon And Garfunkel, Vol.
II

CANZON [ARR.] see Froberger, Johann
Jakob

CANZONA see Schoonenbeek, Kees

CANZONA PER SONARE NO. 2 [ARR.] see
Gabrieli, Giovanni

CANZONETTA E BALLO FOR VIOLIN AND
STRING ORCHESTRA see Sanfilippo,
Margherita Marie

CAPITAN, EL [ARR.] see Sousa, John
Philip

CAPONEGRO, JOHN
Country Ragtime
string orch,perc,opt pno [2'30"]
(gr. II) sets KENDOR $16.00, and
up   (257)

Doodlin' Digits
string orch,opt pno [1'25"] (gr. I)
set KENDOR 8257 $19.00, and up
(258)

Highland Song
string orch,opt perc,opt pno
[2'40"] (gr. II) sets KENDOR
$16.00, and up   (259)

March Of The Bowmen
string orch,opt perc,opt pno
[2'10"] (gr. I) sets KENDOR
$14.00, and up   (260)

Rough Stuff
string orch,perc,opt pno [2'45"]
(gr. I) set KENDOR 8555 $19.00,
and up   (261)

CAPRICCIO ESPAGNOL [ARR.] see Rimsky-
Korsakov, Nikolai

CARILLON SUITE see Cruft, Adrian

CARLIN, SIDNEY
Prayer For America
1.1.2.0. 2.2.2.0. timp,perc,strings
CARLIN sc $3.00, sets $26.00, and
up   (262)

CARMEN: CHANGING OF THE GUARD, [ARR.]
see Bizet, Georges

CARMEN: HABANERA [ARR.] see Bizet,
Georges

CARMEN: PRELUDE, ACT IV, [ARR.] see
Bizet, Georges

CARMEN: SEGUIDILLA, [ARR.] see Bizet,
Georges

CARMEN SUITE [ARR.] see Bizet, Georges

CARMEN: THE TOREADOR SONG [ARR.] see
Bizet, Georges

CARMICHAEL, HOAGY (1899-1981)
Stardust [arr.]
(Ployhar) (gr. III) BELWIN 89321
$40.00   (263)

CARNIVAL SONG see Scott, Richard

CARNIVAL TIME see Townsend, Jill

CAROL OF THE BELLS [ARR.]
(Arnold, Alan) string orch,opt perc,
opt pno set FIDDLE $16.00   (264)

CAROUSAL see McLeod, James (Red)

CARR, BENJAMIN (1768-1831)
Petite Ouverture, Une [arr.]
(Dennison) 1.2.2.1. 2.0.0.0. timp,
strings KALMUS A6730 sc $8.00,
set $12.00   (265)

CARROLL, JAMES
Liturgy
string orch (gr. III) BELWIN
BSO 00060 $40.00   (266)

CARROLL COUNTY see Niehaus, Leonard

CARTE POSTALE NO. 1: LILLE OCTOBRE 1984
see Lancen, Serge

CASCADE see Frost, Robert S.

CASTELLANA see Chagrin, Francis

CASUS BELLI see Boysen, Andrew

CATS AND DOGS see Stephan, Richard

CAT'S CRADLE see Goldsmith, Owen

CATS: MEMORY [ARR.] see Lloyd Webber,
Andrew

CATS: SELECTIONS [ARR.] see Lloyd
Webber, Andrew

CAUCASIAN SKETCHES: PROCESSION OF THE
SARDAR [ARR.] see Ippolitov-Ivanov,
Mikhail Mikhailovich

CAUVIN, A.
A La Maniere De Stravinsky
see Trois Pieces Pour Orchestra
D'enfants

Dans Le Style De Mozart
see Trois Pieces Pour Orchestra
D'enfants

Dans Le Style D'une Danse De La
Renaissance
see Trois Pieces Pour Orchestra
D'enfants

Trois Pieces Pour Orchestra D'enfants
CHOUDENS f.s.
contains: A La Maniere De
Stravinsky; Dans Le Style De
Mozart; Dans Le Style D'une
Danse De La Renaissance   (267)

CAVALRY MARCH see Gould, Morton

CECHVALA, AL
Bagatelle for Strings
string orch [2'15"] (gr. II)
CONCERT W J-161 $22.00   (268)

Sarabande And Musette
string orch (med easy) sets WYNN
6013-7013 $18.00, and up   (269)

CELEBRATION see Daniels, Melvin L.

CELEBRATION [ARR.] see Dvořák, Antonín

CELEBRATION DANCE see Brandon, Seymour
(Sy)

CELEBRATION SUITE see Missal, Joshua M.

CELESTIAL CALENDAR see Hodkinson,
Sydney P.

CENTENNIAL OVERTURE see Hofeldt,
William

CEREMONIAL OCCASION *CCU
(Friend, Howard C.) 1.1.2.1. 2.3.3.0.
timp,perc,pno,strings (med diff)
sc,pts BOSWORTH f.s.   (270)

CERULLI, BOB
Four Dances For String Orchestra
string orch [4'15"] (gr. II)
CONCERT W J-159 $22.00   (271)

Spanish Serenade
string orch [2'30"] (gr. II)
CONCERT W J-166 $20.00   (272)

CHABRIER, [ALEXIS-] EMMANUEL
(1841-1894)
España, [arr.]
(Carter, A.) 2.2.3.1. 2.3.3.0.
timp,perc,pno,strings (med diff)
sc,pts BOSWORTH f.s.   (273)

CHACONNE IN E MINOR [ARR.] see
Buxtehude, Dietrich

CHAGRIN, FRANCIS (1905-1972)
Castellana
1.1.1.1. 1.1.1.0. opt perc,opt pno,
strings sc,pts NOVELLO 09.0019.02
f.s.   (274)

Renaissance Suite
string orch,opt woodwind quar [8']
NOVELLO sc 09.0021.04.00 f.s.,
pts 09.0021.04.06 f.s.   (275)

CHAIKOVSKII, PETR IL'ICH
see TCHAIKOVSKY, PIOTR ILYICH

CHAILLY, LUCIANO (1920-   )
Studio Per Un'orchestra Di Ragazzi
2.2.2.2. 2.2.2.0. harp,strings
[10'] sc BSE 1025 f.s., perf mat
rent   (276)

CHANSON D'AUTREFOIS see Rougeron,
Philippe

CHANSON DE METELOTS [ARR.] see
Schumann, Robert (Alexander)

CHANSON DU NORD [ARR.] see Schumann,
Robert (Alexander)

CHANT D'ESPOIR see Dachez

CHANT DU BERCEAU [ARR.] see Schumann,
Robert (Alexander)

CHANUKAH HAPPENING see Bender, Mitchell

CHAPTER ONE see Nunez, Carold

CHARADES see Swayne, Giles

CHARIOTS OF FIRE [ARR.] see Vangelis

CHARPENTIER, MARC-ANTOINE
   (ca. 1634-1704)
   Te Deum [arr.] *see Beethoven,
      Ludwig Van, Hymne A La Joie
      [arr.]
   see Beethoven, Ludwig van, Hymne A
      La Joie [arr.]

CHASE, BRUCE
   Adios Amigos [arr.]
      string orch (easy) LEONARD-US
      04620080 $16.00   (277)

   Apache Pass
      string orch (easy) set LEONARD-US
      08720366 $25.00   (278)

   Barnyard Bash
      string orch (easy) LEONARD-US
      04620170 $16.00   (279)

   Beaver Valley
      string orch (gr. I) LAKES $14.00
                                 (280)

   Blue Grass Ball
      string orch,pno,opt perc (gr. III)
      set KJOS GS02 $15.00   (281)

   Blue Ridge Boogie
      string orch (easy) LEONARD-US
      04620211 $16.00   (282)

   Bluegrass Bingo
      string orch (easy) LEONARD-US
      04620216 $16.00   (283)

   Bright Star
      string orch (gr. I) set LAKES
      $14.00, and up   (284)

   Butterfly
      string orch (gr. I) LAKES $14.00
                                 (285)

   Candlelight Waltz
      string orch (easy) set LAKES
      $14.00, and up   (286)

   Cornpone County
      string orch (gr. III) LAKES $17.50
                                 (287)

   Country Cousins
      string orch [2'] (easy) set
      LEONARD-US 04620365 $22.50 (288)

   Cross Country
      string orch set LAKES $14.00, and
      up   (289)

   Doctor Fiddlesticks
      string orch (easy) LEONARD-US
      04620450 $16.00   (290)

   Echo Canyon Polka
      string orch (gr. I) LAKES $14.00
                                 (291)

   Happy Hoedown [arr.]
      string orch (easy) LEONARD-US
      04620862 $16.00   (292)

   Holiday Bells
      string orch (gr. I) LAKES $14.00
                                 (293)

   Little Bow Peep
      string orch (gr. I) LAKES $14.00
                                 (294)

   Peanut Parade
      string orch (gr. I) set LAKES
      $14.00, and up   (295)

   Popcorn Polka
      string orch (easy) LEONARD-US
      08720368 $35.00   (296)

   Ragtime Fiddles
      string orch (easy) LEONARD-US
      4621890 $22.50   (297)

   Saludo
      string orch (easy) LEONARD-US
      04622003 $16.00   (298)

CHATEAU DU TEMPS PERDU [ARR.] see
   Meunier, Gérard

CHEERFUL EARFUL, A see Isaac, Merle
   John

CHEETHAM, JOHN EVERETT (1939-   )
   Three Binghams
      string orch (gr. V) SHAWNEE J-147
      $35.00   (299)

CHERISH [ARR.] see Kirkman, Terry

CHERRY BLOSSOM SONG [ARR.]
   (Magnusson, Daniel) string orch,pno
      CARLIN sc $3.00, set $17.00, and up
                                 (300)

CHIAPANECAS see Isaac, Merle John

CHICKEN REEL see Anderson, Leroy

CHILDREN'S FANTASIES [ARR.] see
   Schumann, Robert (Alexander)

CHIM-CHIM-CHER-EE [ARR.] see Sherman,
   Richard M.

CHIMES see Frost, Robert S.

CHISEL, THE see Frost, Robert S.

CHOPIN, FRÉDÉRIC (1810-1849)
   Chopin Portrait, A [arr.]
      (Arnold, Alan) string orch,opt
      perc,opt pno (theme from Etude
      No. 3) set FIDDLE $16.00   (301)

   Fantasie Impromptu: Theme [arr.]
      (Frost, Robert) string orch,opt pno
      [2'25"] (gr. II) sets KENDOR
      $16.00, and up   (302)

   Mazurka, MIN 211, [arr.]
      (Myers) string orch (gr. III) LAKES
      $17.50   (303)

   Memories Of Chopin [arr.]
      (McLeod, James) string orch,opt pno
      [4'10"] (gr. I) set KENDOR 8443
      $23.00, and up   (304)

   Polonaise in A flat, [arr.]
      (Sopkin) 2.2.2.2.3sax. 4.3.2.1.
      timp,drums,strings (med easy) set
      KALMUS A6035 $26.50, and up (305)

   Tristesse [arr.]
      (Lacour, Guy) 2.2+opt English
      horn.2+opt bass clar.0.2alto
      sax.opt tenor sax.opt baritone
      sax. 2.2.1.1. perc,gtr,opt acord,
      pno/harp/elec org,strings sc,pts
      BILLAUDOT f.s. contains also:
      Mozart, Wolfgang Amadeus, Premier
      Menuet [arr.]; Wagner, Richard,
      Lohengrin: Choeur Des Fiancailles
      [arr.]   (306)

CHOPIN PORTRAIT, A [ARR.] see Chopin,
   Frédéric

CHORAL [ARR.] see Schumann, Robert
   (Alexander)

CHORALE AND FANFARE [ARR.] see Vivaldi,
   Antonio

CHORALE PRELUDE, "IN DEEPEST NEED",
   [ARR.] see Bach, Johann Sebastian

CHOUCOUNE [ARR.]
   (Isaac) string orch (med easy) set
      WYNN 6275 $18.00, and up   (307)

CHRISTMAS ALBUM *CC7L
   (Stone, David) 2.1.3+bass clar.1.alto
      sax. 2.2.1.0. timp,2perc,pno,
      strings sets BOOSEY $24.00, and up
      may be performed by strings alone
                                 (308)

CHRISTMAS AROUND THE WORLD
   (Applebaum, Samuel; Gordon, Louis)
      string orch BELWIN sc $2.00, set
      $15.00   (309)

CHRISTMAS BOWS
   (Wieloszynski, Stephen) string orch,
      opt pno [1'50"] (gr. I) set KENDOR
      8205 $19.00, and up   (310)

CHRISTMAS CANTATA see Downes, Andrew

CHRISTMAS CANTATA: OVERTURE [ARR.] see
   Bach, Johann Sebastian

CHRISTMAS CAROLS, 17 [ARR.]
   (Adams, D.) string orch set ADAM 8501
      $25.00   (311)

CHRISTMAS CAROLS FOR STRINGS *CC8L
   (Caponegro, John) string orch (gr. I)
      sets KENDOR $22.00, and up (312)

CHRISTMAS CLASSICS
   (O'reilly, John) string orch,opt
      perc,opt winds (gr. II) ALFRED 3219
      $35.00
      contains: Bizet, Georges,
      Arlesienne, L': Suite No. 1,
      March Of The Three Kings [arr.];
      Handel, George Frideric, Messiah:
      Hallelujah Chorus [arr.];
      Tchaikovsky, Piotr Ilyich,
      Nutcracker Suite: March [arr.]
                                 (313)

CHRISTMAS COLLAGE
   (Mendelson, Manny) 2(pic).1.2+bass
      clar.1. 2.4.4.1. perc,pno,opt harp,
      elec bass,strings [4'20"] (gr. V)
      set ALMITRA $40.00   (314)

CHRISTMAS FESTIVAL, A
   (Gordon, Philip) 2.1.2.2.1.alto
      sax.tenor sax. 2.2.1.1. timp,perc,
      pno,strings [3'10"] (gr. II) sets
      KENDOR $32.00, and up   (315)
   (Gordon, Philip) string orch,opt
      perc,opt pno [3'10"] (gr. II) sets
      KENDOR $18.00, and up   (316)

CHRISTMAS KALEIDOSCOPE *CC14L
   (Frost, Robert) string orch,pno KJOS
      76 sc $7.95, pts $3.00, ea. (317)

CHRISTMAS MUSIC FOR STRINGS *CC7L
   (Grant, Francis; Donegan, Wilda)
      string orch,pno LUDWIG   (318)

CHRISTMAS REFLECTIONS [ARR.]
   (Frost, Robert) string orch (gr. I)
      KJOS set SO-76B $22.00, sc SO-76F
      $3.00   (319)

CHRISTMAS SARABANDE see Kovats, Daniel

CHRISTMAS SONG, THE [ARR.] see Torme,
   Melvin Howard (Mel)

CHRISTMAS SUITE, A
   (Arnold, Alan) string orch,opt perc,
      opt pno set FIDDLE $20.00 (320)

CHRISTMAS THROUGH THE CENTURIES
   (Applebaum, Samuel; Gordon, Louis)
      string orch BELWIN BS033 sc $3.50,
      set $15.00   (321)

CHRISTMAS-TIDE see Bourdon, Rosario

CHRISTMAS TREASURES [ARR.]
   (Rosenhaus) LEONARD-US 08720582
      $45.00   (322)

CHRISTMAS TREAT *CC7L
   (Bowden, Robert) 3.3.3.2. 4.3.3.1.
      timp,perc,harp,pno,strings (med
      diff) set SHAWNEE J-93 $50.00 (323)

CHRISTMAS VISIONS [ARR.]
   (Sayre) LEONARD-US 08720584 $45.00
                                 (324)

CIAIKOVSKI, PIETRO
   see TCHAIKOVSKY, PIOTR ILYICH

CID, LE: ARAGONAISE [ARR.] see
   Massenet, Jules

CIELITO LINDO [ARR.]
   (Clebanoff, Herman) string orch
      DORABET D-148 f.s.   (325)
   (Isaac) string orch (med easy) set
      WYNN 6273 $18.00, and up   (326)
   (Lang) 2.2.2.2.3sax. 4.3.3.0. timp,
      perc,harp,strings (med easy) set
      KALMUS A6005 $17.00, and up (327)

CINQ PIECES POUR BOULOGNE see Jolas,
   Betsy

CINQUANTAINE, LA [ARR.] see Marie,
   Gabriel

CIRCUS SUITE see Mistak

CITIZEN PATRIOT see Goodman, Stephen
   Kent

CLASSIC IMPRESSIONS
   (Herfurth, C. Paul) 2.1.2.2.opt alto
      sax.opt tenor sax. 2.2.2.0. timp,
      perc,pno,strings [4'] set SHAWNEE
      J-135 $40.00   (328)

CLASSIC SYMPHONY see Gerschefski, Edwin

CLASSICAL OVERTURE [ARR.] see Mozart,
   Wolfgang Amadeus

CLASSICAL REFLECTIONS see Feese,
   Francis L.

CLASSICAL SUITE see Rokos, K.W.

CLEBANOFF, HERMAN, EDITOR
   Four Latin Songs, For String
      Orchestra *CC4L
      string orch,pno DORABET sc $7.50,
      pts $2.00, ea. contains:Ay, Ay,
      Ay; Cielito Lindo; La Golondrina;
      La Paloma   (329)

CLEMENS, JACOBUS (CLEMENS NON PAPA)
   (ca. 1510-ca. 1556)
   Flemish Songs [arr.]
      (Brentlinger, Lee) string orch (gr.
      I) BELWIN CO 00192 $35.00 (330)

CLEMENS NON PAPA
   see CLEMENS, JACOBUS

CLEMENT, JACOBUS
   see CLEMENS, JACOBUS

CLEMENTI, MUZIO (1752-1832)
   Sonatina Accompagnamento, [arr.]
      (Clare, D.) string orch,pno solo,
      opt winds&perc (easy) sc,pts
      BOSWORTH f.s.   (331)

CLERGUE, J.
   Danse Rustique [arr.] *see DEUX
      DANSES

CLIMB EV'RY MOUNTAIN [ARR.] see
   Rodgers, Richard

CLOCK SYMPHONY see Haydn, [Franz] Joseph

CLOG DANCE see Pavey, Sidney

CLOVERLEAF see Frost, Robert S.

CLOWN, THE [ARR.] see Kabalevsky, Dmitri Borisovich

CLUSTER OF CAROLS
(Siennicki, Edmund) string orch (gr. II) set HIGHLAND $20.00. and up (332)

COAKLEY, DONALD
Bonavista Harbour [5'50"]
KERBY 27741 (333)

COCKSHOTT, GERALD WILFRED (1915-1979)
Maddermarket Suite
2.2.2.2. 2.1.0.0. timp,perc,strings [11'] NOVELLO sc 09.0026.05.00 f.s., pts 09.0026.05.06 f.s. (334)

COFFEE SONG, THE [ARR.] see Miles, Richard

COHAN, GEORGE MICHAEL (1878-1942)
You're A Grand Old Flag [arr.]
(Chase) string orch (easy) LEONARD-US 4622835 $22.50 (335)
(Isaac, Merle J.) string orch (gr. III) set HIGHLAND $29.00 (336)

COLEMAN, CHRISTOPHER
Ventricle Of Memory, The
string orch (med) TCAPUB sc $5.00, set $15.00, pts $.75, ea. (337)

COLEMAN, CY (1929-)
If My Friends Could See Me Now [arr.]
(Cerulli) (easy) CPP T1600IB7 $40.00 (338)

Sweet Charity Medley [arr.]
(Holcombe) (med diff) CPP CO135B6X $65.00 (339)

COLONIAL CHRISTMAS see Siennicki, Edmund John

COME LET US TO THE BAGPIPES SOUND [ARR.] see Bach, Johann Sebastian

COMPARSA, LA [ARR.] see Lecuona, Ernesto

CONCERT MARCH AND DANSE ANTIQUE [ARR.] see Mazas, Jacques-Fereol

CONCERT MARCH [ARR.] see Weber, Carl Maria von

CONCERT MINUET see Gerschefski, Edwin

CONCERT PIECE FOR STRINGS see Del Borgo, Elliot A.

CONCERT PIECES FOR YOUNG STRING ORCHESTRA
(Adams, Keith) string orch OXFORD 361070-1 sc $7.75, pts $3.00, ea.
contains: Grandfather's Clock, The [arr.]; Variations On A Nursery Tune [arr.]; We Wish You A Merry Christmas [arr.] (340)

CONCERT PIECES I *CC8L
(Stone, David) 2.1.3+bass clar.1.alto sax. 2.2.1.0. timp,2perc,pno, strings sets BOOSEY $24.00, and up may be performed by strings alone (341)

CONCERT PIECES II *CC8L
(Stone, David) 2.1.3+bass clar.1.alto sax. 2.2.1.0. timp,2perc,pno, strings sets BOOSEY $24.00, and up may be performed by strings alone (342)

CONCERTANTE FOR CLARINET AND STRING ORCHESTRA see Walker, G.

CONCERTI, OP. 8 NOS. 1, 3 AND 4 [ARR.] see Vivaldi, Antonio

CONCERTINO DES ENFANTS, FOR PIANO AND ORCHESTRA see Kont, Paul

CONCERTINO FOR 3 RECORDERS AND STRING ORCHESTRA see Bossler, Kurt

CONCERTINO FOR SOLO INSTRUMENT AND ORCHESTRA see Gunsenheimer, Gustav

CONCERTINO IN THE STYLE OF MOZART, [ARR.] see Millies, Hans

CONCERTO CONCITATO II see Leistner-Mayer, Roland

CONCERTO FOR FACULTY VS ORCHESTRA see Ployhar

CONCERTO FOR VIOLIN AND ORCHESTRA, OP. 61: THEMES, [ARR.] see Beethoven, Ludwig van

CONCERTO IN D MINOR [ARR.] see Bach, Johann Sebastian

CONCERTO ITALIANO [ARR.] see Vivaldi, Antonio

CONCERTO MADRIGALESCO see Vivaldi, Antonio

CONCERTO PIFFERARO, FOR FLUTE AND ORCHESTRA see Joubert, Claude-Henry

CONCERTO RUSTICO see Huszar, Lajos

CONDOR PASA, EL [ARR.] see Sounds Of Simon And Garfunkel, Vol. I

CONLEY, LLOYD EDGAR (1924-)
Diversion No. 4
string orch,pno (gr. III) BELWIN BSO 00058 $40.00 (343)

CONTI, BILL
Musical Highlights From "Rocky" [arr.]
(Lowden) CPP TB00038 $45.00 (344)

CONTRADANCE [ARR.] see Beethoven, Ludwig van

CONTRASTS see Frost, Robert S.

CONTRASTS FOR STRINGS see McLeod, James (Red)

CONTREDANSE ET RONDEAU [ARR.] see Mozart, Wolfgang Amadeus

CONVERGENCE see Nunez, Carold

COOMBES, DOUGLAS
Sinfonietta
2.2.2.2. 4.3.2.1. timp,perc,strings LINDSAY (345)

COOTS, JOHN FREDERICK (1897-)
Santa Claus Is Coming To Town [arr.]
(Cerulli, Bob) string orch (easy) CPP TO510SB4 $25.00 (346)

COPLAND, AARON (1900-1990)
Rodeo: Hoe Down
string orch sets BOOSEY $24.00, and up (347)

CORELLI, ARCANGELO (1653-1713)
Concerto Grosso, MIN 165, [arr.]
(Isaac) string orch (med diff) set WYNN 6283 $36.00, and up (348)

Corelli Sinfonia [arr.] (from Trio Sonata, Op. 4, No. 5)
(Halen, Walter) string orch,opt pno [3'35"] (gr. IV) sets KENDOR $17.00, and up (349)

Corelli Suite [arr.]
(Leidig) string orch (gr. II) set HIGHLAND $20.00, and up (350)

Folia, La [arr.]
(Alshin, Harry A.) string orch [3'55"] (gr. III) KENDOR 9845 f.s. (351)

Gigue, [arr.] (from Sonata No. 9)
(Goldsmith, Owen) string orch (med easy) BELWIN BSO 00073 $35.00 (352)

Prelude And Dance [arr.]
(Myers, Theldon) string orch (gr. III) LAKES $24.00 (353)

Preludio E Danzetta, [arr.]
(Livingston, Wayne) LYDIAN ORCH set $14.00, pts $.80, ea. (354)

Sarabande [arr.]
see Brahms, Johannes, Valse [arr.]

CORELLI SINFONIA [ARR.] see Corelli, Arcangelo

CORELLI SUITE [ARR.] see Corelli, Arcangelo

CORNPONE COUNTY see Chase, Bruce

COTTON CURTAIN, THE see Tillis, Frederick C.

COTTON-EYED JOE see Frost, Robert S.

COTTON-EYED JOE AND TURKEY IN THE STRAW [ARR.]
(Duncan, Craig) string orch (gr. III) KJOS sc SO-53F $5.00, set SO-53B $22.50 (355)

COUNTDOWN MARCH see Frost, Robert S.

COUNTRY COOKIN' see Fletcher, Gary

COUNTRY COUSINS see Chase, Bruce

COUNTRY DANCE [ARR.] see Weber, Carl Maria von

COUNTRY RAGTIME see Caponegro, John

COUPERIN, FRANÇOIS (LE GRAND) (1668-1733)
Folies Francaises Ou Les Dominos, Les: Suite No. 1 [arr.]
rec,fl,ob,clar,bsn,horn,strings sc, pts LEMOINE f.s. (356)

Folies Francaises Ou Les Dominos, Les: Suite No. 2 [arr.]
rec,fl,ob,clar,bsn,horn,strings sc, pts LEMOINE f.s. (357)

COVENTRY CAROL see Two Yuletide Carols

CRADLE SONG [ARR.] see Schubert, Franz (Peter)

CREPUSCULE [ARR.] see Friml, Rudolf

CRIMSON TRAIL see Frost, Robert S.

CRINOLINE AND LACE see Gould, Morton

CROSS COUNTRY see Chase, Bruce

CRUFT, ADRIAN (1921-1987)
Carillon Suite *Op.61a
1.1.1.1. 1.1.1.0. perc,pno,strings [7'] JOAD f.s. (358)

CRÜGER, JOHANN (1598-1662)
Now Thank We All Our God *see SONGS OF THANKSGIVING

CSARDAS, FOR VIOLIN AND STRING ORCHESTRA [ARR.] see Monti, Vittorio

CUI, CÉSAR ANTONOVICH (1835-1918)
Orientale [arr.]
(Isaac) (med) sets WYNN 4269-5269 $24.00, and up (359)

CUNHA
Broadway Joe
string orch (easy) set WYNN 6085 $14.00, and up (360)

CURTAIN RAISERS *CCU
(Osborne, Tony) string orch (gr. III) set BOOSEY $16.00 (361)

CZAR'S BRIDE, THE: DANCE [ARR.] see Rimsky-Korsakov, Nikolai

CZECH RUSTIC DANCE, [ARR.] see Smetana, Bedrich

CZERNY, CARL (1791-1857)
March in C, [arr.]
(Jurey, Edward) (easy) BELWIN CO 00198 $35.00 (362)

DACHEZ
Chant D'Espoir
flexible instrumentation sc,pts LEDUC AL 27411 f.s. (363)

DAMASE, JEAN-MICHEL (1928-)
Scherzando
2.2.2.2. 2.2.2.0. timp,perc,strings [2'30"] (from the series "feuilles vives") BILLAUDOT perf mat rent (364)

Suite in G
string orch [8'40"] sc,pts BILLAUDOT f.s. (365)

DAMNATION OF FAUST, THE: HUNGARIAN MARCH [ARR.] see Berlioz, Hector (Louis)

DANCE CONVERSATIONS see Frost, Robert S.

DANCE DIVERSIONS see Hurd, Michael

DANCE, GYPSY see Scott, Richard

DANCE OF THE DWARFS [ARR.] see Manhire, Wilson

DANCE OF THE WITCHES [ARR.] see Williams, John T.

DANCE SCENARIO see Del Borgo, Elliot A.

DANCE SUITE, A [ARR.] see Gervaise, Claude

DANCE SUITE IN D see Leighton, Kenneth

DANCERIES DE LA RENAISSANCE [ARR.] see
  Gervaise, Claude

DANCERS see Johansen, Bertil Palmar

DANCES OF POZSONY see Kocsar, Miklos

DANIELS, MELVIN L. (1931-   )
  Celebration
    3(pic).2(English horn).3.2.
    4.3.3.1. timp,perc,harp,strings
    [10'] (gr. V) SOUTHERN A-30 sc
    $7.50, set $55.00, pts $2.50, ea.
                                        (366)
  Fanfare And Arrayment
    (gr. III) KJOS sc WO-6F $5.00, set
    WO-6B $35.00   (367)
  Interlude
    string orch (gr. III) KJOS sc
    WSO-5F $4.00, set WSO-5B $25.00   (368)
  Rondo Caprice
    string orch,opt pno [1'50"] (gr. I)
    set KENDOR $19.00, and up   (369)
  Three Miniatures For Strings
    string orch (gr. II) KJOS sc WSO-3F
    $5.00, set WSO-3B $25.00   (370)

DANS LE STYLE DE MOZART see Cauvin, A.

DANS LE STYLE D'UNE DANSE DE LA
  RENAISSANCE see Cauvin, A.

DANSE DE COLOMBINE [ARR.] see Horvath,
  G.

DANUBE WAVES WALTZ [ARR.] see
  Ivanovici, Ion, Waves Of The Danube
  [arr.]

DANZA LUCUMI [ARR.] see Lecuona,
  Ernesto

DARK EYES [ARR.]
  (Lang, Philip) 2(pic).2.2.2.3sax.
  4.3.3.1. timp,perc,strings (med)
  set KALMUS A6020 $17.00, and up
                                        (371)

DAVE'S HERE see Radd, John

DAVIES, PETER MAXWELL (1934-   )
  Welcome To Orkney, A
    2.2.2.2. 2.3.3.0. timp,perc,strings
    sc BOOSEY $4.25   (372)

DAVIS, ALBERT OLIVER (1920-   )
  Pizzicato Pizzazz
    (med) LUDWIG LLE-73   (373)

DAVIS, KATHERINE K. (1892-1980)
  Little Drummer Boy [arr.]
    (Cerulli, Bob) (med easy) CPP
    2793LB7X $40.00   (374)

DAWSON, TED (1951-   )
  C.R. Marchant Suite For Strings
    string orch CAN.MUS.CENT.
    MI 1500 D272CR   (375)
  Weston Reflections
    2perc,strings CAN.MUS.CENT.
    MI 1500 D272WE   (376)

DAY BY DAY see String Orchestra Pak No.
  4

DAY IN TOWN, A see Hawkins, Malcolm

DEBUSSY, CLAUDE (1862-1918)
  Bruyeres [arr.]
    (Cheucle) 2.2.2.2.baritone sax.
    1.0.2.1. saxhorn, harp, strings
    LEMOINE perf mat rent   (377)
  Fille Aux Cheveux De Lin, La [arr.]
    (Cheucle) 2.2.2.2. 2.2.0.0. English
    horn/alto sax,timp,harp,strings
    LEMOINE perf mat rent   (378)
    (Siennicki, Edmund) "Girl With The
    Flaxen Hair, The [arr.]" string
    orch,vla solo (gr. III) set
    HIGHLAND $29.00   (379)
  Girl With The Flaxen Hair, The [arr.]
    see Fille Aux Cheveux De Lin, La
    [arr.]
  Soiree Dans Grenade [arr.]
    (Cheucle) 2.2.2.2.baritone sax.
    2.2.3.1. timp,harp/pno,strings,
    saxhorn LEMOINE perf mat rent
                                        (380)

DECK THE HALLS [ARR.]
  (Chase) string orch (easy) LEONARD-US
  4620400 $22.50   (381)

DECSENYI, JANOS (1927-   )
  Folksong
    sc,pts EMB 12362 f.s.   (382)
  Suite
    sc,pts EMB 3352 f.s.   (383)

DEFENDERS OF THE NATION [3'30"]
  (Frost, Robert S.) string orch,opt
  perc,opt pno (gr. II) set KENDOR
  9030 $24.00, and up   (384)

DEJA VU see Nunez, Carold

DEL BORGO, ELLIOT A. (1938-   )
  Concert Piece For Strings
    string orch [4'5"] (gr. II) set
    KENDOR 9005 $23.00, and up   (385)
  Dance Scenario
    string orch [3'40"] (gr. II) set
    KENDOR 9017 $23.00, and up   (386)
  Fantasia For Strings
    string orch (med easy) BELWIN
    BSO 00080 $35.00   (387)
  Petite Overture
    string orch [4'15"] (gr. II) set
    KENDOR 9355 $23.00, and up   (388)
  Rustic Dance
    string orch,opt pno [3'45"] (gr. I)
    set KENDOR 8561 $23.00, and up
                                        (389)
  Suite for Strings
    string orch,opt pno [5'30"] (gr.
    II) set KENDOR $22.00, and up   (390)
  Three Dances For Strings
    string orch [3'] (gr. II) set
    KENDOR 9595 $24.00, and up   (391)
  Triptych For Strings
    string orch [4'45"] (gr. II) set
    KENDOR 9635 $23.00, and up   (392)

DELFT, MARC VAN (1958-   )
  Ouverture "De Vier Temperamenten"
    *Op.5
    3.3.3.3. 4.3.3.1. timp,5perc,2harp,
    pno,cel,strings [10'] sc DONEMUS
    f.s.   (393)

DELIBES, LÉO (1836-1891)
  Pizzicati [arr.] (from Sylvia)
    (Isaac) string orch (med) set WYNN
    6297-7297 $18.00, and up   (394)
  Prelude And Mazurka [arr.] (from
    Coppelia)
    (Cobb, Ian) 3.2.2.1. 2.2.2.0. timp,
    3perc,pno,strings [6'] sc,pts
    NOVELLO 09.0539.09 f.s.   (395)

DELLO JOIO, NORMAN (1913-   )
  Suite For The Young: Two Pieces
    [arr.]
    (Prokes, Patricia) string orch (gr.
    II) MARKS $16.00   (396)

DENVER, JOHN
  see DEUTSCHENDORF, HENRY JOHN

DENZA, LUIGI (1846-1922)
  Funiculi Funicula [arr.]
    (Lang) 2.2.2.2.3sax. 4.3.2.0.
    drums,strings (med easy) set
    KALMUS A6034 $30.00, and up   (397)

DESERT NOEL see Scott, Richard

DESERTED BALLROOM, THE see Gould,
  Morton

DESLOGES
  Avec Quelques Airs Connus *see SIX
    PIECES FACILES
  Berceuse *see SIX PIECES FACILES
  Choral *see SIX PIECES FACILES
  Cloches De Paques, Les *see SIX
    PIECES FACILES

DESPORTES, YVONNE (1907-   )
  Neuf Images
    sc BILLAUDOT $23.50   (398)

DEURSEN, ANTON VAN (1922-   )
  Six Intermezzi
    string orch HARMONIA 2612 f.s.
                                        (399)

DEUTSCHENDORF, HENRY JOHN (JOHN DENVER)
  (1943-   )
  Annie's Song [arr.]
    (Feldstein, Sandy) string orch,opt
    pno,opt perc [3'] (easy) CHERRY
    CL3217 $25.00   (400)

DEUX DANSES
  2rec,2clar,gtr,pno,strings sc,pts
  LEMOINE f.s.
    contains: Clergue, J., Danse
    Rustique [arr.]; Ziberlin,
    François, Petite Gavotte [arr.]
                                        (401)

DEUX HYMNES [ARR.] see Beethoven,
  Ludwig van

DEUX MENUETS [ARR.] see Caix
  d'Hervelois, Louis de

DEUX PIECES DU QUINZIEME SIECLE [ARR.]
  3rec,ob,clar,bsn,trom,3gtr,strings
  sc,pts LEMOINE f.s.   (402)

DEUX PIECES LYRIQUES: VALSE ET MELODIE
  NORVEGIENNE [ARR.] see Grieg,
  Edvard Hagerup

DEUX PIECES: ROMANE ET MARCHE [ARR.]
  see Weber, Carl Maria von

DEVIL'S DREAM
  (Muller, J. Frederick) sets LUDWIG
  BGS-104 $20.00, and up   (403)

DEVOGEL, JACQUES (1926-   )
  Air Dithyrambique, For Trumpet And
    Orchestra
    (easy) sc,pts MARTIN $45.00   (404)
  Mignardise, For Saxophone And
    Orchestra
    (med easy) sc,pts MARTIN $45.00
                                        (405)
  Rondes Et Chansons
    [3'] sc,pts BILLAUDOT f.s.   (406)
  Suite Enfantine
    sc,pts BILLAUDOT f.s.   (407)

DIABELLI, ANTON (1781-1858)
  Andantino [arr.]
    see Beethoven, Ludwig van, Romance
    [arr.]

DIAMOND, NEIL (1941-   )
  Jazz Singer, The [arr.]
    (Gold, Marty) (gr. III) CHERRY
    580-07778 $35.00   (408)

DIDN'T WE ALMOST HAVE IT ALL [ARR.] see
  Masser, Michael

DIDO AND AENEAS: SUITE [ARR.] see
  Purcell, Henry

DIERCKS, JOHN HENRY (1927-   )
  Suite for Strings
    string orch [9'] (med) set SHAWNEE
    J-91 $15.00   (409)

DING DONG MERRILY ON HIGH see
  Feldstein, Saul (Sandy)

DIRRIWACHTER, WIM (1937-   )
  Greek Dances
    sc,pts BROEKMANS 1589 f.s.   (410)

DISCO-TINUED see Petrone, John

DISNEY ADVENTURE, A [ARR.]
  (Sayre) LEONARD-US 0872338 $45.00
                                        (411)

DISNEY SUPERTIME, A [ARR.]
  (Lowden) LEONARD-US 08720336 $50.00
                                        (412)

DITTERSDORF, KARL DITTERS VON
  (1739-1799)
  Allegro [arr.] (from Quartet In D)
    (Dasch) string orch FITZSIMONS
    F0554 set $12.00, sc $3.00, pts
    $2.00, ea.   (413)
  Concerto for Violoncello and
    Orchestra in D
    (Pulkert, Oldrich) ZINNEB ZI 21
    f.s.   (414)
  German Dance [arr.]
    (Isaac) string orch (med easy) set
    WYNN 6281 $14.00, and up   (415)

DIVA DE L'EMPIRE, LA see Satie, Erik

DIVERSION NO. 4 see Conley, Lloyd Edgar

DIVERTIMENTO FOR YOUNG PLAYERS see
  Mamlok, Ursula

DIVERTISEMENTS see Martino, Donald
  James

DIVISIONS ON A GROUND [ARR.] see
  Gibbons, Orlando

DO-RE-MI [ARR.] see Rodgers, Richard

DO YOU HEAR WHAT I HEAR [ARR.] see
  Regney, Noel

DOCTOR FIDDLESTICKS see Chase, Bruce

DODD, JIMMIE (1910-1964)
  Mickey Mouse March [arr.]
    (Jennings) string orch [2'30"] (med
    easy) LEONARD-US $30.00   (416)

DOERNBERG, MARTIN (1920-   )
  Kleine Ouverture
    string orch ZINNEB ZI 23 f.s. (417)

DOERNBERG, MARTIN (cont'd.)

Sonatina
  string orch ZINNEB ZI 24 f.s. (418)

DON GIOVANNI: OVERTURE [ARR.] see
  Mozart, Wolfgang Amadeus

DON QUIXOTE: "PAS DE DEUX", [ARR.] see
  Minkus, Léon (Fyodorovich) [Alois;
  Louis]

DONA NOBIS PACEM [ARR.]
  (Wieloszynski, Stephen) string orch,
  opt pno [2'] (gr. I) set KENDOR
  8255 $19.00, and up   (419)

DONDEYNE, DESIRE (1921-   )
  Symphonie Landaise
  [15'] sc,pts BILLAUDOT f.s.   (420)

DON'T BE CROSS [ARR.] see Zeller, Carl

DON'T CRY FOR ME, ARGENTINA [ARR.] see
  Lloyd Webber, Andrew

DOODLIN' DIGITS see Caponegro, John

DORIAN VARIATIONS see Israel, Brian

DOWN IN THE VALLEY
  (Davis, Albert O.) sets LUDWIG
  BGS-109 $20.00, and up   (421)

DOWNES, ANDREW (1950-   )
  Christmas Cantata *Op.4
  1.1.3.2. 3.3.0.0. timp,perc,
  strings,cor [15'] LYNWD sc $7.80,
  pts $9.00   (422)

DOWNLAND SUITE, A see Ireland, John

DOWNTOWN [ARR.] see Hatch, Tony
  (Anthony Peter)

DOZIER
  Without You [arr.]
  (Custer) (med diff) CPP 6964WB6X
  $55.00   (423)

DREAMS see Hanson, Jens

DROTTNINGHOLMSMUSIKEN: TRE SATSER
  [ARR.] see Roman, Johan Helmich

DUBOIS, PIERRE-MAX (1930-   )
  Avec Vivacite
  2.2.2.2. 2.2.2.0. timp,perc,strings
  [2'30"] (from the series
  "feuilles vives") BILLAUDOT perf
  mat rent   (424)

  Bebe Rose
  fl,opt rec,ob,clar,alto sax,horn/
  tenor sax,trp,opt timp,perc,opt
  gtr,opt pno,strings [3'30"] sc,
  pts BILLAUDOT f.s.   (425)

DUBOIS, THEODORE (1837-1924)
  Chaconne, [arr.]
  (Keuning, Hans P.) 2.2.2.0+opt bsn.
  2.2.0.0. strings HARMONIA 3635
  f.s.   (426)

DUELING JINGLE STRINGS [ARR.] see
  Pierpont, James

DUELING VIOLERS
  string orch set ADAM 8704 $15.00
                                 (427)

DUNCAN, S.
  In The Days Of Drake [arr.]
  see Newton, E., Shepherd In Love,
  The [arr.]

DUNHILL, THOMAS FREDERICK (1877-1946)
  Irish Boy, The [arr.]
  (Twinn, Sidney) string orch sc,pts
  LENGNICK f.s. contains also:
  Newton, E., Fanny's Delight
  [arr.]   (428)

  Morning Song [arr.]
  (Twinn, Sidney) string orch sc,pts
  LENGNICK f.s. contains also:
  Manhire, Wilson, Merry Haymakers
  [arr.]   (429)

DURAND, [MARIE-] AUGUSTE (1830-1909)
  Chaconne, [arr.]
  (Isaac, Merle J.) string orch (gr.
  III) set HIGHLAND $29.00   (430)

DURKO, ZSOLT (1934-   )
  Fantasy And Postlude
  sc EMB 10244 f.s.   (431)

DVORÁK, ANTONÍN (1841-1904)
  Bohemian Dance [arr.]
  (Leidig, Vernon) string orch (gr.
  II) set HIGHLAND $20.00, and up
                                 (432)

  Celebration [arr.]
  (Alshin, Harry) string orch (med)
  BELWIN BSO 00076 $35.00   (433)

DVORÁK, ANTONÍN (cont'd.)

  From The New World [arr.] (Symphony
  No. 9, Op. 95, [excerpt], [arr.])
  (Largo) sc,pts LENGNICK f.s.   (434)
  (Herfurth, C. Paul) 2.1.2.1.
  2.2.2.0. timp,perc,pno,strings
  (excerpts from movements 2 and 4)
  SHAWNEE sc $4.50, set $42.00
                                 (435)
  (Isaac) BELWIN CO00164 sc $5.00,
  set $30.00   (436)
  (Leidig, Vernon) (gr. III, (First
  Movement)) set HIGHLAND $37.00 (437)

  Humoresque, Op. 101, No. 1 [arr.]
  sc,pts LENGNICK f.s.   (438)

  Humoresque, Op. 101, No. 7 [arr.]
  sc,pts LENGNICK f.s.   (439)

  Indian Canzonetta [arr.] (from Violin
  Sonata In G Minor)
  (Alshin, Harry A.) string orch
  [3'30"] (gr. II) set KENDOR 9165
  $23.00, and up   (440)

  New World Theme [arr.]
  (Arnold, Alan) string orch,opt
  perc,opt pno set FIDDLE $16.00
                                 (441)

  Slavonic Dance [arr.]
  (Isaac) (med) sets WYNN 4268-5268
  $28.00, and up   (442)

  Slavonic Dances, Op. 46, Nos. 4 And 6
  [arr.]
  (Stone, David) 1.1.3.1. 2.2.1.0.
  timp,perc,pno,strings NOVELLO sc
  09.0038.09 f.s., pts 09.0039.07
  f.s.   (443)

  Sonatina Symfonicka, [arr.] (from
  Sonatina, Op.100)
  (Rokos; Arnell) 1.1.2.1. 2.2.1.0.
  perc,strings (med diff) sc,pts
  BOSWORTH f.s.   (444)

  Songs My Mother Taught Me [arr.]
  *Op.55,No.4
  sc,pts LENGNICK f.s.   (445)

  Symphony No. 6, [excerpt]
  (Golsmith, Owen) (med, Furiant
  [arr.]) BELWIN CO 00201 $45.00 (446)

  Symphony No. 7,Scherzo, [arr.]
  (Isaac) BELWIN CO00158 sc $5.00,
  set $30.00   (447)

  Symphony No. 8,Fourth Movement,
  [arr.]
  (Leidig, Vernon) (gr. III) set
  HIGHLAND $37.00   (448)

  Symphony No. 8,Finale, [arr.]
  (Dackow, Sandra) string orch (med)
  LUDWIG   (449)

  Symphony No. 9, Op. 95, [excerpt],
  [arr.]
  see From The New World [arr.]

DYKES, JOHN BACCHUS (1823-1876)
  Jesus, The Very Thought Of Thee
  [arr.]
  (Pinner, Dianne) string orch (gr.
  III) set TRN $20.00   (450)

DYLAN, ROBERT (BOB) (1941-   )
  Forever Young [arr.]
  (Graham) string orch LEONARD-US
  08720346 $35.00   (451)

E.T.: SELECTIONS [ARR.] see Williams,
  John T.

E.T.: THEME [ARR.] see Williams, John
  T.

EARLY ONE MORNING [ARR.] see Folk-Songs
  For Strings, Set 2

EASTERN PICTURES [ARR.] see Byng, F.D.

EASY STRING ORCHESTRA CLASSICS *CCU
  (Sanfilippo, M.) string orch HIGHLAND
  sc $6.00, pts $3.00, ea.   (452)

EASY STRING ORCHESTRA CLASSICS, BOOK 2
  (Sanfilippo) string orch (gr. II)
  HIGHLAND pno-cond sc $7.00, pts
  $3.50, ea.   (453)

EASY WINNERS RAG, THE [ARR.] see
  Joplin, Scott

ECCLES, JOHN
  Sonata in G minor, [arr.]
  (Lipkin, M.) string orch sc,pts
  BOSWORTH f.s.   (454)

ECHO CANYON POLKA see Chase, Bruce

ECHOES see Frost, Robert S.

EDELWEISS [ARR.] see Rodgers, Richard

EDER, HELMUT (1916-   )
  Froh Zu Sein Bedarf Es Wenig *Op.93
  2.1.1.0. 2.0.0.0. strings [10']
  DOBLINGER perf mat rent   (455)

EIRE
  (Shapiro, Marsha Chusmir) string orch
  (gr. II) set HIGHLAND $29.00   (456)

EL MANGO TANGO see Fletcher, Gary

ELEANOR RIGBY [ARR.] see Lennon, John

ELGAR, [SIR] EDWARD (WILLIAM)
  (1857-1934)
  Land Of Hope And Glory [arr.]
  MIDDLE CMK 211 f.s.   (457)
  (Barrie) string orch sc,pts CHESTER
  E9 f.s.   (458)

  Pomp And Circumstance [arr.]
  (Caponegro, John) string orch,opt
  perc (gr. I) sets KENDOR $14.00,
  and up   (459)

  Pomp And Circumstance March No. 4
  [arr.]
  (Isaac, Merle) 2.1.2+bass clar.1.
  2.2.2.1. timp,perc,strings [2']
  (gr. III) set TRN $50.00   (460)

  Salut D'amour [arr.]
  (McLeod, James) string orch,opt pno
  [2'15"] (gr. III) set KENDOR 9864
  $23.00, and up   (461)

  Six Easy Pieces, Op.22
  string orch (easy) sc,pts BOSWORTH
  f.s.   (462)

ELIJAH: SELECTIONS [ARR.] see
  Mendelssohn-Bartholdy, Felix

ELLEDGE, CHUCK
  Blue Mountain Pass
  string orch (gr. I) KJOS set
  GSO-20B $25.00, sc GSO-20F $3.00
                                 (463)

  Phantom Dance
  string orch (gr. I) KJOS set
  GSO-13B $22.00, sc GSO-13F $3.00
                                 (464)

  Summer's Rain
  (gr. II) KJOS set GO-103B $30.00,
  sc GO-103F $3.00   (465)

ELLINGTON, EDWARD KENNEDY (DUKE)
  (1899-1974)
  Sophisticated Ladies: Highlights
  [arr.]
  (Lowden) BELWIN 89338 sc $5.00, set
  $35.00   (466)

ELLMENREICH
  Spinning Song, The [arr.]
  (Curnow, James) string orch (gr.
  III) JENSON 502-19040 $24.00
                                 (467)

ELVEY, GEORGE JOB (1816-1893)
  Come Ye Thankful People *see SONGS
  OF THANKSGIVING

EMPEROR WALTZ [ARR.] see Strauss,
  Johann, [Jr.]

ENCHANTED CASTLE, THE [ARR.] see
  Glazunov, Alexander Konstantinovich

ENCORE, VOL.1 *CC11L
  (Ryden, William; Warsager, Sam)
  string orch (gr. III) BELWIN pno-
  cond sc EL 03411 $13.00, pts
  EL 03412-03416 $5.50, ea.   (468)

ENDLESS LOVE [ARR.] see Tunick,
  Jonathan

ENESCO, GEORGES (ENESCU) (1881-1955)
  Rumanian Rhapsody No. 1 [arr.]
  (Guenther, F.) 2.2.2.2.3sax.
  4.2.3.0. timp,perc,strings (med
  diff) set KALMUS A6026 $33.00,
  and up   (469)

ENGRAVINGS IN SOUND see Frost, Robert
  S.

ENSEMBLE TIME FOR STRINGS VOL. 2
  *CC14L
  (Siennicki, Edmund) string orch (gr.
  II) HIGHLAND sc $6.00, pts $3.00
                                 (470)

ENTERTAINER, THE [ARR.; see Joplin,
  Scott

ENTRANCE MARCH FROM ROSAMUNDE [ARR.]
see Schubert, Franz (Peter)

EPIGRAMME see Hummel, Bertold

EPISTLE SONATA [ARR.] see Mozart,
Wolfgang Amadeus

EPPING FOREST SUITE see Ticciati, Niso

EROTIK, [ARR.] see Grieg, Edvard
Hagerup

ERRANTE, BELISARIO ANTHONY (1920-   )
Perpetual Motion
1.1.2+bass clar.1.opt alto sax.opt
tenor sax. 2.2.2.1. timp,perc,
pno,strings [2'] (gr. II) set
MOSAIC M060 $26.00, and up   (471)

Prelude And Capriccio
[5'15"] (gr. IV) set MOSAIC M050
$32.00, and up   (472)

Scherzino
[3'] (gr. III) set MOSAIC M030
$26.00, and up   (473)

ESCHER, RUDOLF GEORGE (1912-1980)
Hylas
2.1.1.0. 0.0.0.0. 4perc,pno 4-
hands,6vln,4vcl [18'] sc DONEMUS
f.s., perf mat rent   (474)

ESPAÑA, [ARR.] see Chabrier, [Alexis-]
Emmanuel

ESPANA WALTZ [ARR.] see Waldteufel,
Emile

ESPECIALLY FOR STRINGS *CC20L
(Frost, Robert S.) string orch,pno
KJOS pts $3.95, ea., kbd pt $4.95,
sc $6.95   (475)

ESQUISSES see Cals, Michel

ESSENTIALS FOR STRINGS see Anderson,
Gerald

ESTEFAN, G.M.
Anything For You [arr.]
(Cerulli, Bob) (med easy) CPP
4573AB7X $40.00   (476)

ESTUDIANTINA WALTZ [ARR.] see
Waldteufel, Emile

EVENING IN ARABIA see Heilmann, Francis

EVENING PRAYER see Reinecke, Carl

EVENING SONG [ARR.] see Handel, George
Frideric

EVITA: HIGHLIGHTS [ARR.] see Lloyd
Webber, Andrew

EVOCATIONS see Koykkar, Joseph

FAIRY QUEEN, THE: PRELUDE [ARR.] see
Purcell, Henry

FAIRY QUEEN, THE: RONDEAU [ARR.] see
Purcell, Henry

FALL OF THE COUNCIL OF TEN, THE:
OVERTURE [ARR.] see Scarlatti,
Alessandro, Caduta De Decem Viri,
La: Overture [arr.]

FAME [ARR.] see Gore, Michael

FAMOUS AMERICAN SPIRITUALS
(Frost, Robert) string orch,opt pno
[2'50"] (gr. II) sets KENDOR
$16.00, and up   (477)

FANDANGO AND ALBORADO [ARR.] see
Rimsky-Korsakov, Nikolai

FANFARE AND ARRAYMENT see Daniels,
Melvin L.

FANFARE AND FRIPPERY see Stephan,
Richard

FANFARE, INTERLUDE AND FINALE see
Walker, Gwyneth

FANFARONDO see Gibson, John

FANNY'S DELIGHT [ARR.] see Newton, E.

FANTASIA AND FUGUE [ARR.] see Bach,
Johann Sebastian

FANTASIA FOR ORCHESTRA, ON A THEME BY
TARTINI see Bauernschmidt, Robert

FANTASIA FOR STRINGS see Del Borgo,
Elliot A.

FANTASIA FOR STRINGS [ARR.] see
Vivaldi, Antonio

FANTASIA ON "DULCIMER" see Spring,
Glenn

FANTASIE IMPROMPTU: THEME [ARR.] see
Chopin, Frédéric

FANTASIE WITH FUGUE, PLAIN AND
ACCOMPANIED, FOR VIOLIN AND
ORCHESTRA see Fischer, Irwin

FANTASY AND ALLEGRO see Myers, Robert

FANTASY AND POSTLUDE see Durko, Zsolt

FANTASY FOR DOUBLE ORCHESTRA see Raum,
Elizabeth

FAREWELL TO AMERICA [ARR.] see Strauss,
Johann, [Jr.]

FARKAS, FERENC (1905-   )
Music From Zanka
sc,pts EMB 13426 f.s.   (478)

Musica Serena
string orch sc,pts EMB 12615 $13.25
(479)

FARNABY, GILES (ca. 1560-1640)
Toye, A [arr.] *see FITZWILLIAM
SUITE

FASSERT, FRED
Barbara Ann [arr.]
(Jennings, Paul) string orch JENSON
592-02010 $30.00   (480)

FATINITZA MARCH [ARR.] see Suppe, Franz
von

FAURE, GABRIEL-URBAIN (1845-1924)
Berceuse, [arr.] (from Dolly Suite)
MIDDLE CMK 210 f.s.   (481)

FAUST, JAN (1908-   )
Tri Skladby *Op.22
string orch SUPRAPHON f.s. (482)

FEDERAL MARCH [ARR.] see Reinagle,
Alexander

FEESE, FRANCIS L. (1926-   )
Classical Reflections
string orch,opt pno (gr. II) set
YOUNG WORLD $22.00, and up (483)

Gemini
string orch set YOUNG WORLD $18.00,
and up   (484)

Jazz Moods
string orch,pno (gr. III) sets
YOUNG WORLD $18.00, and up (485)

Mosaics
string orch,opt winds (gr. III)
sets YOUNG WORLD $20.00, and up
(486)

Seasons
(gr. IV) set YOUNG WORLD CO 228
$42.00, and up   (487)

String Fever
string orch (gr. II) set YOUNG
WORLD YS227 $20.00, and up (488)

FELDSTEIN, SAUL (SANDY) (1940-   )
America Takes Note!
[2'30"] (gr. II) ALFRED 3193 $40.00
(489)

Ding Dong Merrily On High
string orch,opt pno,opt perc
[2'30"] (gr. I) ALFRED 3216
$25.00   (490)

FELICIANO, JOSE (1945-   )
Feliz Navidad [arr.]
(Rosenhaus) string orch (med)
LEONARD-US $35.00   (491)

FELIZ NAVIDAD [ARR.] see Feliciano,
Jose

FENIGSTEIN, VIKTOR
Five Orchestra Studies For Young
Strings
string orch sc,pts KUNZEL GM 118
$8.00   (492)

FESTIVAL FOR FIDDLERS see Frost, Robert
S.

FESTIVAL MARCH see Jepson, David W. see
McLeod, James (Red)

FESTIVAL OF HYMNS, A *CCU
(Severson, Paul; Ployhar, James)
2.2.2.0.sax. 1.3.2.0. timp,pno,

strings BELWIN sc $7.50, pts $2.95,
ea.   (493)

FESTIVAL POLKA see Kerr, Wallis

FESTIVE MARCH see Renesse, George van

FESTIVE MOODS see Quagenti, Samuel

FESTIVE SOUNDS OF HANUKAH
(Holcombe; Rothrock) MUSICIANS PUB
SOS-607A $35.00   (494)
(Holcombe; Rothrock) string orch set
MUSICIANS PUB SO-607B $15.00, and
up   (495)

FESTIVIDAD, LA see Scott, Richard

FESTLICHE MUSIK see Butz, Josef

FEYNE, BUDDY (1912-   )
Tuxedo Junction [arr.] (composed with
Johnson, William; Dash, Julian;
Hawkins, Erskine)
(Caponegro, John) string orch,opt
perc,opt pno [2'30"] (gr. II)
sets KENDOR $16.00, and up (496)

FIDDLE AND STOMP see McLeod, James
(Red)

FIDDLE FACTORY see Frost, Robert S.

FIDDLE FIDDLE FIDDLE see McLeod, James
(Red)

FIDDLE FROLICS see Gordon, Philip

FIDDLE RAGS see Halen, Walter J.

FIDDLE TUNES NO. 1 see Isaac, Merle
John

FIDDLE TUNES NO. 2 see Isaac, Merle
John

FIDDLE TUNES NO. 3 see Isaac, Merle
John

FIDDLER ON THE ROOF: OVERTURE [ARR.]
see Bock, Jerry

FIDDLER'S DANCE MEDLEY, A
(Alshin, Harry A.) string orch [5']
(gr. III) set KENDOR 9821 $24.00,
and up   (497)

FIDDLER'S SQUARE DANCE [ARR.]
(McLeod) string orch (gr. III) KJOS
set GSO-10B $25.00, sc GSO-10F
$3.00   (498)

FIDDLESTICKS see Niehaus, Leonard

FIDDLIN' FREDDIE see McLeod, James
(Red)

FIELD, JOHN (1782-1837)
Romanza [arr.] (from Concerto No. 2)
(Branson, D.) fl,pno,strings (med
easy) sc,pts BOSWORTH f.s. (499)

FIESTA MEXICANA see Quagenti, Samuel

FIFTY-NINTH STREET BRIDGE SONG, THE
[ARR.] see Sounds Of Simon And
Garfunkel, Vol. I

FILLE AUX CHEVEUX DE LIN, LA [ARR.] see
Debussy, Claude

FINLANDIA [ARR.] see Sibelius, Jean

FINTA GIARDINIERA, LA: OVERTURE [ARR.]
see Mozart, Wolfgang Amadeus

FIRE AND RAIN [ARR.] see Taylor, James

FIREFLY SKY see Niehaus, Leonard

FIRST DAY OF SPRING, THE see Anderson,
Leroy

FIRST NOEL, THE see Angels, Shepherds,
Christmas, Kings

FISCHER, IRWIN (1903-1977)
Fantasie With Fugue, Plain And
Accompanied, For Violin And
Orchestra
fl,ob,clar,harp,strings,vln solo
[10'] (med) AM.COMP.AL. perf mat
rent   (500)

Lament, For Violoncello And Orchestra
3.2.2.3. 4.3.3.1. timp,strings,vcl
solo [5'] (med) sc AM.COMP.AL.
$7.70, perf mat rent   (501)

Overture On An Exuberant Tone Row
3.2.2.2. 4.3.3.1. timp,strings [8']
(med) sc AM.COMP.AL. $18.40, perf
mat rent   (502)

FIT AS A FIDDLE see Niehaus, Leonard

FITZWILLIAM SUITE
(Gordon, Philip) 2.1.2.1.3sax.
2.2.1.1. timp,perc,strings (med
easy) KALMUS A6007 pno-cond sc
$3.00, set $16.50, and up
contains: Bull, John, Pavana
[arr.]; Byrd, William, Fortune,
My Foe [arr.]; Farnaby, Giles,
Toye, A [arr.]   (503)

FIVE CHRISTMAS CAROLS
(Willcocks, David) 2.2.2.2. 2.2.0.0.
timp,strings (med easy, alternate
scoring: string orch) OXFORD 48.007
sc $11.50, set $49.95, pts $4.00,
ea.   (504)

FIVE ORCHESTRA STUDIES FOR YOUNG
STRINGS see Fenigstein, Viktor

FLASHDANCE ... WHAT A FEELING [ARR.]
see Moroder, Giorgio

FLEDERMAUS, DIE: WALTZES [ARR.] see
Strauss, Johann, [Jr.]

FLEMISH SONGS [ARR.] see Clemens,
Jacobus (Clemens non Papa)

FLETCHER, GARY
Baroque Bouree
string orch [1'36"] (gr. II) LEE
S0316 $25.00   (505)

Blueberry Jam
string orch (gr. II) set BARNHS
130-2166-00 $26.00   (506)

Camp Meetin'
string orch [2'0"] (gr. II) LEE
S0317 $25.00   (507)

Country Cookin'
string orch [1'24"] (gr. II) LEE
S0311 $25.00   (508)

El Mango Tango
string orch LEE S0305 $25.00   (509)

Gallant Gavotte
string orch [1'56"] (gr. II) LEE
S0310 $25.00   (510)

Goin' Bowin'
string orch [2'34"] (gr. I) set
BARNHS 130-2187-00 $26.00   (511)

Hop, Skip And Jump
string orch [1'34"] (gr. I) set
BARNHS 130-2132-00 $26.00   (512)

Joggin' Tune
string orch [1'52"] (gr. II) set
BARNHS 130-2188-00 $26.00   (513)

Lil' Grits
string orch LEE S0303 $25.00   (514)

Mistletoe Memories
string orch [1'52"] (gr. II) LEE
S0313 $25.00   (515)

Moonlight Sleigh Ride
string orch [2'23"] (gr. II) LEE
S0315 $25.00   (516)

Overture For Strings
string orch [5'15"] (gr. III) set
BARNHS 130-2131-00 $30.00   (517)

Perpetual Motion
string orch [1'48"] (gr. II) LEE
S0314 $25.00   (518)

Pizza-Taco
string orch LEE S0301 $25.00   (519)

Rococo Rondo
string orch LEE S0306 $25.00   (520)

Roll'n
string orch LEE S0308 $25.00   (521)

Scherzo On American Themes
string orch [3'36"] (gr. III) set
BARNHS 130-2158-00 $30.00   (522)

Semiquaver Serenade
string orch [1'18"] (gr. II) LEE
S0312 $25.00   (523)

Two-Horse Open Sleigh
string orch LEE S0307 $25.00   (524)

FLETCHER, PERCY EASTMAN (1879-1932)
Folk Tune And Fiddle Dance
string orch [9'] KALMUS A7390 sc
$8.00, set $12.50, pts $2.50, ea.
                                   (525)

FLING FOR STRINGS see Frost, Robert S.

FLOR
Intonation And Rhythm
string orch,pno sc,pts BOSTON 13951
$10.00   (526)

FLORESTINA [ARR.] see Markham, Lee

FLOWERS IN THE VALLEY, THE [ARR.] see
Folk-Songs For Strings, Set 1

FOGERTY, J.C.
Proud Mary [arr.]
(Cerulli, Bob) string orch (med
easy) CPP 5758PB4X $25.00   (527)

FOLIA, LA [ARR.] see Corelli, Arcangelo

FOLIES FRANCAISES OU LES DOMINOS, LES:
SUITE NO. 1 [ARR.] see Couperin,
François (le Grand)

FOLIES FRANCAISES OU LES DOMINOS, LES:
SUITE NO. 2 [ARR.] see Couperin,
François (le Grand)

FOLK SONG CONCERT OVERTURE see Rokos,
K.W.

FOLK SONG VARIATIONS [ARR.] see
Kabalevsky, Dmitri Borisovich

FOLK SONGS AND DANCES *CCU
(Stone, David) 2.0.2.0. 0.2.0.0. pno,
strings (med easy) set BOOSEY
$30.00, and up optional parts for
additional winds and percussion are
available   (528)

FOLK-SONGS FOR STRINGS, SET 1
(Auton, John) string orch OXFORD
361144-9 sc $8.75, pts $2.00, ea.
contains: Afton Water [arr.];
Flowers In The Valley, The
[arr.]; My Love, She's But A
Lassie Yet [arr.]; Strawberry
Fair [arr.]   (529)

FOLK-SONGS FOR STRINGS, SET 2
(Auton, John; Auton Christine) string
orch OXFORD 361137-6 sc $6.75, pts
$2.00, ea.
contains: Early One Morning [arr.];
Tarpaulin Jacket, The [arr.];
Vicar Of Bray, The [arr.]; Ye
Banks And Braes [arr.]   (530)

FOLK-SONGS FOR STRINGS, SET 3
(Auton, John; Auton Christine) string
orch OXFORD 361167-8 sc $7.75, pts
$2.00, ea.
contains: Bluebells Of Scotland,
The [arr.]; Bobby Shaftoe [arr.];
Good Sword And A Trusty Hand, A
[arr.]; King Arthur Ruled The
Land [arr.]   (531)

FOLK SONGS OF THE MOUNTAINS
(Shapiro, Marsha Chusmir) string orch
[4'] (gr. II) SHAWNEE J-153 $25.00
                                   (532)

FOLK SONGS OF THE ORIENT
(Shapiro, Marsha Chusmir) string orch
[6'45"] (gr. II) CONCERT W J-157
$27.00   (533)

FOLK SONGS OF THE WEST
(Shapiro, Marsha Chusmir) string orch
(gr. II) SHAWNEE J-143 $25.00   (534)

FOLK TUNE AND FIDDLE DANCE see
Fletcher, Percy Eastman

FOLKSONG see Decsenyi, Janos

FOLLAS, RONALD
Variations On A Quaker Hymn
2.2.2.2. 4.3.3.1. timp,perc,strings
SOUTHERN $35.00   (535)

FOR A SUMMER'S DAY see Knight, Sally

FORBES, PATRICK (1920-   )
Miniature Suite
1.1.2.1. 2.2.1.0. timp,perc,pno,
strings (med easy) sc,pts
BOSWORTH f.s.   (536)

FOREVER YOUNG [ARR.] see Dylan, Robert
(Bob)

FORREST, JIMMY
Night Train [arr.]
(Caponegro, John) string orch,opt
perc,opt pno [2'20"] (gr. II)
sets KENDOR $16.00, and up (537)

FORSSMARK, KARL A.
Lyric Poem
1.1.2.1. 2.2.3.0. timp,strings
[2'25"] (gr. III) SHAWNEE J-148
$25.00   (538)

Summer Night
[6'45"] (med diff) set SHAWNEE J-82
$15.00   (539)

FOSTER, DAVID
St. Elmo's Fire: Love Theme [arr.]
(Cerulli, Bob) (easy) CPP 5231LB7X
$40.00   (540)

FOSTER, STEPHEN COLLINS (1826-1864)
Camptown Bluegrass Race [arr.]
(McLeod, James) string orch (gr.
II) sets KENDOR $16.00, and up
                                   (541)

Camptown Races [arr.]
(Chase) string orch (easy) LEONARD-
US 4620238 $22.50   (542)

Oh, Susanna [arr.]
(Muller, J. Frederick) sets LUDWIG
BGS-103 $20.00, and up   (543)
(Richardson, Clive) 2+
pic.1.2.1.2sax. 2.2.2.0. perc,
strings (med easy) set KALMUS
A6009 $14.50, and up   (544)

Songs Of Stephen Foster, Part 1
[arr.]
(Caponegro, John) string orch,opt
perc,opt pno [2'40"] (gr. I) set
KENDOR 8615 $23.00, and up (545)

FOUR BACH DANCES [ARR.] see Bach,
Johann Sebastian

FOUR CENTURIES FOR STRINGS see Gordon,
Philip, Editor

FOUR COUNTRY DANCES [ARR.] see
Beethoven, Ludwig van

FOUR DANCES FOR STRING ORCHESTRA see
Cerulli, Bob

FOUR LATIN SONGS, FOR STRING ORCHESTRA
see Clebanoff, Herman, Editor

FOUR MINIATURES see Pettersen, Nancy

FOUR MOVEMENTS FOR STRING ORCHESTRA see
Ovanin, Nikola Leonard

FOUR SEASONS: SPRING, AUTUMN, WINTER
[ARR.] see Vivaldi, Antonio,
Concerti, Op. 8 Nos. 1, 3 And 4
[arr.]

FOUR SHORT PIECES see Stevens, Halsey

FOUR SONGS FROM HUNGARY [ARR.]
(Alshin, Harry) string orch [3'45"]
PRESSER 116-40026 sc $1.50, set
$15.00, pts $1.00, ea.   (546)

FOUR STUDIES see Turok, Paul Harris

FREEDMAN, MAX C. (1893-1962)
Rock Around The Clock [arr.]
(Jennings) string orch [2'30"] (med
easy) LEONARD-US $30.00   (547)

FREISCHUTZ, DER: CHORUS OF HUNTSMEN
[ARR.] see Weber, Carl Maria von

FREISCHÜTZ, DER: PEASANT WALTZ AND
MARCH [ARR.] see Weber, Carl Maria
von

FRENCH DANCE SUITE, [ARR.] see
Marchand, Louis

FRIDAY NIGHT see Nunez, Carold

FRIDAYS, SATURDAYS see Townsend, Jill

FRIML, RUDOLF (1879-1972)
Bohemian Dance [arr.]
see Zilcher, P., Spanish Serenade
[arr.]

Crepuscule [arr.] *Op.36,No.2
sc,pts LENGNICK f.s.   (548)

Orange Blossoms [arr.]
sc,pts LENGNICK f.s.   (549)

Suite Mignonne [arr.]
sc,pts LENGNICK f.s.   (550)

FRITZ KREISLER ALBUM NO. 1 [ARR.] see
Kreisler, Fritz

FRITZ KREISLER ALBUM NO. 2 [ARR.] see
Kreisler, Fritz

FROBERGER, JOHANN JAKOB (1616-1667)
Canzon [arr.]
(Frost, Robert) string orch KJOS sc
SO-47F $3.00, set SO-47B $22.50
contains also: Kindermann, Johann
Erasmus, Fuga [arr.]   (551)

FROH ZU SEIN BEDARF ES WENIG see Eder,
Helmut

FROHLICHER ANFANG, VOL. 5:
ORCHESTERSCHULE FÜR VERSCHIEDENE
INSTRUMENTE see Biedermann-
Klimesch, Gretl

FROM A SONATA [ARR.] see Beethoven, Ludwig van

FROM THE NEW WORLD [ARR.] see Dvořák, Antonín

FROST, ROBERT S. (1942-   )
Alpha Beta Alpha
  string orch (gr. I) LAKES $14.00
                                      (552)

Calliope, The
  string orch,opt pno [1'30"] (gr. II) set KENDOR $16.00, and up
                                      (553)

Cascade
  (med easy) set SHAWNEE J-130 $16.00
                                      (554)

Chimes
  string orch (gr. II) sets KENDOR $16.00, and up
                                      (555)

Chisel, The
  string orch set LAKES $16.00, and up
                                      (556)

Cloverleaf
  string orch (gr. I) KJOS set SO-51B $21.00, sc SO-51F $3.00   (557)

Contrasts
  string orch set SOUTHERN $20.00
                                      (558)

Cotton-Eyed Joe
  string orch set SOUTHERN $20.00
                                      (559)

Countdown March
  string orch (gr. I) set LAKES $16.00, and up
                                      (560)

Crimson Trail
  string orch (gr. I) KJOS sc SO-46F $3.00, set SO-46B $22.50   (561)

Dance Conversations
  string orch set SOUTHERN $16.00
                                      (562)

Echoes
  string orch set LAKES $14.00, and up
                                      (563)

Engravings In Sound
  string orch SOUTHERN SO-49 sc $3.00, set $20.00, pts $1.25, ea.
                                      (564)

Festival For Fiddlers
  string orch SOUTHERN $20.00   (565)

Fiddle Factory
  string orch,opt pno [2'10"] (gr. I) set KENDOR 8263 $27.00   (566)

Fling For Strings
  string orch [2'] (med easy) set SHAWNEE J-89 $10.00   (567)

Half And Half
  string orch set SOUTHERN $16.00
                                      (568)

Highland Dance
  string orch (easy) set LAKES $16.00, and up
                                      (569)

Immigration Trail
  string orch (gr. I) set LAKES $14.00, and up
                                      (570)

Lucky Charm
  string orch LAKES   (571)

Main Street March
  string orch (gr. I) KJOS set SO-75B $22.00, sc SO-75F $3.00   (572)

Movin' Along
  string orch (gr. I) KJOS sc SO-48F $3.00, set SO-48B $22.50   (573)

My Favorite Ice Cream Is Chocolate
  string orch,opt pno [2'20"] (gr. II) sets KENDOR $16.00, and up
                                      (574)

Odds And Ends
  string orch,opt pno [2'40"] (gr. I) sets KENDOR $14.00, and up   (575)

120 Allegro Parkway
  string orch (gr. I) LAKES $14.00
                                      (576)

Pair Of Soks, A
  2perc,pno,strings SOUTHERN SO-46 sc $5.00, set $25.00, pts $1.25, ea.
                                      (577)

Peppermint Polka
  string orch,opt pno [1'30"] (gr. I) sets KENDOR $14.00, and up   (578)

Petit Traineau, Le
  string orch,opt pno, sleigh bells [1'20"] (gr. I) sets KENDOR $14.00, and up
                                      (579)

Pineapple Upside-Down Cakewalk
  string orch (gr. III) KJOS set SO-50B $25.00, sc SO-50F $3.00
                                      (580)

FROST, ROBERT S. (cont'd.)

Prom Night
  string orch (gr. I) LAKES $14.00
                                      (581)

Pyramids
  string orch set SOUTHERN $16.00
                                      (582)

River City Variations
  string orch,opt pno [8'] (gr. II) set KENDOR 9435 $24.00, and up
                                      (583)

Rocky Mountain Switchback
  string orch [2'20"] (med) set SHAWNEE J-90 $12.00   (584)

Sombrero, El
  string orch (easy) set LAKES $14.00, and up   (585)

Splish Splash
  string orch (med easy) set SHAWNEE J-132 $15.00   (586)

Spring Break And Fiesta
  string orch [3'30"] set SHAWNEE J-139 $17.00   (587)

Star Valley Suite
  string orch set SOUTHERN $20.00
                                      (588)

Strings In Review
  string orch,opt perc,opt pno [2'45"] (gr. I/gr. II) sets KENDOR $14.00, and up   (589)

Syncopation
  string orch,perc [1'30"] (gr. II) KJOS set SO-52B $25.00, sc SO-52F $3.00   (590)

Timberline Trails
  string orch,opt pno [2'20"] (gr. I) sets KENDOR $14.00, and up   (591)

Tumbleweed
  string orch SOUTHERN $16.00   (592)

Two Persuasions
  string orch SOUTHERN $15.00   (593)

Wasatch Boulevard
  string orch,opt pno [2'35"] (gr. I) sets KENDOR $20.00, and up   (594)

Whistler, The
  string orch,opt pno [1'40"] (gr. I) set KENDOR 8855 $19.00, and up   (595)

Wishing Well, The
  string orch,opt pno [2'] (gr. I) set KENDOR 8857 $19.00, and up   (596)

FROSTY THE SNOW MAN [ARR.] see Nelson, Steve

FUGA [ARR.] see Kindermann, Johann Erasmus

FUGAL CONCERTO FOR FLUTE, OBOE AND STRING ORCHESTRA see Holst, Gustav

FUGUES, TWO [ARR.] see Bach, Johann Sebastian

FUM, FUM, FUM see Ryden, William

FUN AND GAMES see Townsend, Jill

FUNERAL MARCH OF A MARIONETTE [ARR.] see Gounod, Charles François

FUNICULI FUNICULA [ARR.] see Denza, Luigi

FUNKY FINGERS see Mosier, Kirt N.

FUNKY MONKEY AND FRIENDS see Jones

FÜR ELISE [ARR.] see Beethoven, Ludwig van

GABRIEL-MARIE
see MARIE, GABRIEL

GABRIELI, ANDREA (1510-1586)
Ricercare, [arr.]
  4rec,2clar,strings sc,pts LEMOINE f.s.   (597)

GABRIELI, GIOVANNI (1557-1612)
Canzona Per Sonare No. 2 [arr.]
  (Kovats, Daniel) string orch set LAKES $20.00, and up   (598)

GALAXY 11, 820 see Thomas, Augusta Read

GALIMATHIAS MUSICUM [ARR.] see Mozart, Wolfgang Amadeus

GALLANT GAVOTTE see Fletcher, Gary

GALLIARD
Tanzun [arr.]
  (Fishburn; Luman) string orch [3'] (gr. III) TRN $30.00   (599)

GALOP see McLeod, James (Red)

GARDEN STREET RAG see Isaac, Merle John

GARDENS OF GRANADA see Moreno Torroba, Federico

GASSER, ULRICH (1950-   )
Vier Stucke Zur Passions Und Weihnachtszeit
  1-3fl,opt ob,opt clar,strings [12'] RICORDI-GER SY 2397 perf mat rent
                                      (600)

GAVOTTE AND MARCH [ARR.] see Handel, George Frideric

GAVOTTE AND MUSETTE [ARR.] see Bach, Johann Sebastian

GAVOTTES NOS. 1 AND 2 [ARR.] see Bach, Johann Sebastian

GEESON, DENIS
Vintage Western
  (easy) sc,pts BOSWORTH f.s.   (601)

GEMINI see Feese, Francis L.

GEORGIA CAKEWALK [ARR.] see Mills, Frederick Allen (Kerry)

GERMAN DANCE [ARR.] see Beethoven, Ludwig van see Dittersdorf, Karl Ditters von see Mozart, Wolfgang Amadeus

GERSCHEFSKI, EDWIN (1909-   )
Classic Symphony *Op.4a
  string orch [23'] (med) sc AM.COMP.AL. $15.30, perf mat rent
                                      (602)

Concert Minuet *Op.4c
  1.1.2.1.3sax. 4.2.0.1. timp,strings [3'] (med) sc AM.COMP.AL. $3.85, perf mat rent   (603)

Nocturne, Op. 42, No. 2
  2.3.2.2. 4.3.3.0. perc,harp/pno, strings [4'] (med easy) sc AM.COMP.AL. $11.45   (604)

Pastorale, Op. 4b
  2.2.2.2. 2.2.0.0. timp,strings [3'] (med) sc AM.COMP.AL. $3.85, perf mat rent   (605)

GERSHWIN, GEORGE (1898-1937)
American In Paris, An [arr.]
  (Jennings) string orch [2'30"] (med easy) LEONARD-US $30.00   (606)

Porgy And Bess: Selections [arr.]
  (Sayre) LEONARD-US 08720196 $50.00
                                      (607)

Rhapsody In Blue [arr.]
  (Curnow, James) string orch (gr. III) JENSON 502-18010 $30.00   (608)

GERVAISE, CLAUDE (fl. ca. 1550)
Dance Suite, A [arr.]
  (White, Richard) opt ob,3clar,bsn, opt trom,opt perc,strings sc,pts NOVELLO 09.0067.02 f.s.   (609)

Danceries De La Renaissance [arr.]
  4rec,2clar,2gtr,strings sc,pts LEMOINE f.s.   (610)

GESUALDO TRIPTYCH see Suben, Joel Eric

GETTYSBURG PORTRAIT, FOR NARRATOR AND ORCHESTRA see Brandon, Seymour (Sy)

GIAMMARIO, MATTEO
Three Movements In Baroque Style
  string orch set MUSICIANS PUB SO-205 $15.00, and up   (611)

GIBB, STEVE
She Believes In Me [arr.]
  (Odrich) (with optional piano solo) CHERRY 6575 $35.00   (612)

GIBBONS, ORLANDO (1583-1625)
Divisions On A Ground [arr.]
  (Myers) string orch (gr. III) LAKES $20.00   (613)

GIBBS, ALAN
Petite Suite
  1.1.2.1. 1.1.1.0. timp,perc,opt pno,strings (med diff) sc,pts BOSWORTH f.s.   (614)

GIBSON, JOHN
  Fanfarondo
    (med diff) SHAWNEE set $28.00, pts
    $.75, ea.   (615)

GIFT OF CHRISTMAS, THE [ARR.]
  (Chase) LEONARD-US 04620762 $16.00
                                           (616)

GILLET
  Passepied, [arr.]
    (Chase) string orch [2'] (easy) set
    LEONARD-US 04621810 $22.50 (617)

GILLIS, DON E. (1912-1978)
  Peachtree Promenade (from Atlanta
  Suite)
    2(pic).2.2.2.3sax. 4.3.3.0. timp,
    perc,strings (med easy) set
    KALMUS A6018 $31.50, and up (618)

  Tango Lullaby
    2.2.2+bass clar.2.opt 3sax.
    0.0.0.0. perc,pno/cel,strings
    (med easy) set KALMUS A6017
    $32.50, and up   (619)

GIORGIO'S LAMENT see Scott, Richard

GIRL WITH THE FLAXEN HAIR, THE [ARR.]
  see Debussy, Claude, Fille Aux
  Cheveux De Lin, La [arr.]

GITANERIAS [ARR.] see Lecuona, Ernesto

GLAZUNOV, ALEXANDER KONSTANTINOVICH
  (1865-1936)
  Enchanted Castle, The [arr.]
    (Starr) string orch (gr. IV) KJOS
    set SO-57B $30.00, sc SO-57F
    $5.00   (620)

  Meditation [arr.]
    (Elledge) string orch (gr. V) KJOS
    set GSO-11B $25.00, sc GSO-11F
    $3.00   (621)

GLIÈRE, REINHOLD MORITZOVICH
  (1875-1956)
  Russian Sailors' Dance [arr.]
    (Errante) set HIGHLAND $28.00, and
    up   (622)

GLINKA, MIKHAIL IVANOVICH (1804-1857)
  Life For The Czar, A [arr.]
    (Dasch) FITZSIMONS F0503 set
    $25.00, sc $6.50, pts $3.00, ea.
                                      (623)

  Polka [arr.] *see MOSTLY TCHAIKOVSKY

GLORIA AND ALLELUIA [ARR.] see Saint-
  Saëns, Camille

GLORIA: THEMES [ARR.] see Vivaldi,
  Antonio

GLOW WORM [ARR.] see Lincke, Paul

GLUCK, CHRISTOPH WILLIBALD, RITTER VON
  (1714-1787)
  Alceste: Overture, [arr.]
    (Arnell; Rokos) (med diff) sc,pts
    BOSWORTH f.s.   (624)

  Iphigenia In Aulis: Two Pieces [arr.]
    see Iphigenie En Aulide: Two Pieces
    [arr.]

  Iphigenie En Aulide: Two Pieces
  [arr.]
    (Isaac, Merle) "Iphigenia In Aulis:
    Two Pieces [arr.]" 2.1.2+bass
    clar.1.alto sax.tenor sax.
    2.2.2.1. timp,perc,strings [3']
    (contains: Enchanted Gardens;
    Petite Ballet) set LUDWIG LLE-70
    $38.00, and up   (625)

  Iphigenie En Tauride: Choeur Des
  Pretresses [arr.]
    see Bach, Johann Sebastian,
    Gavottes Nos. 1 And 2 [arr.]

  Musette From "Armide" [arr.] *see
    MUSETTE AND DANCE

GOD BLESS THE U.S.A. [ARR.] see
  Greenwood, Lee

GOD REST YE MERRY GENTLEMEN see Angels,
  Shepherds, Christmas, Kings

GOD REST YE MERRY GENTLEMEN [ARR.]
  (Elledge) string orch (gr. I) KJOS
    set SO-60B $22.00, sc SO-60F $3.00
                                      (626)
  (Frost, Robert S.) string orch,opt
    pno [2'40"] (gr. II) sets KENDOR
    $16.00, and up   (627)

GOIN' BAROQUE see Petrone, John

GOIN' BOWIN' see Fletcher, Gary

GOLDSMITH, JERRY (1929-   )
  Gremlins: Highlights [arr.]
    (Rosenhaus, Steven) string orch
    (gr. II) sc,pts JENSON 502-07010
    $24.00   (628)

GOLDSMITH, OWEN
  Afternoon Waltz
    string orch (gr. II) BELWIN
    BSO 00062 $35.00   (629)

  Baroque Bagatelle, A
    string orch,opt kbd (med) BELWIN
    BSO 00078 $35.00   (630)

  Cat's Cradle
    string orch (gr. II) BELWIN
    BSO 00063 $35.00   (631)

  Nordic Legend, A
    string orch (gr. II) BELWIN
    BSO 00064 $40.00   (632)

  Old Carousel, The
    string orch (gr. II) BELWIN
    BSO 00061 3500   (633)

  Someday
    string orch,pno (gr. II) BELWIN
    BSO 00065 $40.00   (634)

GOLONDRINA, LA [ARR.]
  (Clebanoff, Herman) string orch
    DORABET D-150 f.s.   (635)

GOOD SWORD AND A TRUSTY HAND, A [ARR.]
  see Folk-Songs For Strings, Set 3

GOOD TIDINGS OF GREAT JOY see Holcombe,
  Bill

GOODMAN, STEPHEN KENT
  Citizen Patriot
    [2'45"] (gr. IV) CONCERT W J-165
    $40.00   (636)

GORDON, PHILIP (1894-1983)
  Fiddle Frolics
    string orch [2'] PRESSER 116-40024
    set $22.50, sc $2.50, pts $1.50,
    ea.   (637)

GORDON, PHILIP, EDITOR
  Four Centuries For Strings *CC12L
    string orch,opt pno sc,pts FISCHER,
    C 04616-04622 f.s.   (638)

GORE, MICHAEL
  Fame [arr.]
    (Holcombe) orch (med easy) LEONARD-
    US 04792381 $20.00   (639)

  I Sing The Body Electric [arr.]
    (Holcombe) string orch (med easy)
    LEONARD-US 04849300 $18.00   (640)
    (Marsh) orch (med easy) LEONARD-US
    04793174 $20.00   (641)

GOSSEC, FRANÇOIS JOSEPH (1734-1829)
  Rosine [arr.]
    (Keuning, Hans P.) 2.2.2.0+opt
    2bsn. 2.2.0.0. strings sc,pts
    HARMONIA 3635 f.s.   (642)

GOULD, MORTON (1913-   )
  Cavalry March
    2.2(English horn).2.2. 4.3.3.1.
    perc,gtr,pno,harp,strings (med
    easy) set KALMUS A6017 $32.50,
    and up   (643)

  Crinoline And Lace
    2(pic).2.2.2+contrabsn.3sax.
    4.3.2.0. perc,harp,strings (med
    easy) set KALMUS A6046 $31.50,
    and up   (644)

  Deserted Ballroom, The
    1.1.2+bass clar.1. 2.3.3.0. chimes,
    drums,xylo,strings (med easy) set
    KALMUS A6045 $28.00, and up (645)

  Pirouette
    2+pic.2.2.2.3sax. 4.3.2.0. perc,
    strings (med easy) set KALMUS
    A6039 $31.50, and up   (646)

GOUNOD, CHARLES FRANÇOIS (1818-1893)
  Funeral March Of A Marionette [arr.]
    (McLeod, James) string orch,opt pno
    [3'15"] (gr. III) KENDOR 9824
    f.s.   (647)

GRANADOS, ENRIQUE (1867-1916)
  Spanish Dance No. 3 [arr.]
    (Errante, Belisario) [2'30"] (gr.
    IV) set MOSAIC M010 $26.00, and
    up   (648)

GRAND EVENEMENT [ARR.] see Schumann,
  Robert (Alexander)

GRANDFATHER'S CLOCK, THE [ARR.] see
  Concert Pieces For Young String
  Orchestra

GRANT, W. PARKS (1910-   )
  Instrumental Motet
    string orch [8'] (med) sc
    AM.COMP.AL. $4.60, perf mat rent
                                      (649)

  Quiet Piece, A *Op.47b
    [6'] (med) sc AM.COMP.AL. $12.25,
    perf mat rent   (650)

  Suite No. 1
    string orch [11'] (med) sc
    AM.COMP.AL. $7.70, perf mat rent
                                      (651)

  Suite No. 2
    string orch [12'] (med) sc
    AM.COMP.AL. $9.15, perf mat rent
                                      (652)

GRASSHOPPERS see Mamlok, Ursula

GREATEST LOVE OF ALL, THE [ARR.] see
  Masser, Michael

GREEK DANCES see Dirriwachter, Wim

GREEN, W.
  Playful Rondo [arr.]
    (Frost, Robert S.) string orch,opt
    pno SOUTHERN SO-50 sc $3.00, set
    $20.00, pts $1.25, ea.   (653)

GREEN MOUNTAIN OVERTURE, A see Stevens,
  Halsey

GREENSLEEVES [ARR.]
  (Clebanoff, Herman) string orch
    DORABET D-149 f.s.   (654)
  (Hermann, Ralph) string orch (gr.
    III) LAKES $17.50   (655)

GREENWOOD, LEE
  God Bless The U.S.A. [arr.]
    (Lowden) LEONARD-US 04500430 $30.00
                                      (656)
    (Lowden) string orch (med easy)
    LEONARD-US 04849207 $20.00   (657)

GREETING TO AMERICA see Strauss,
  Johann, [Jr.]

GREMLINS: HIGHLIGHTS [ARR.] see
  Goldsmith, Jerry

GRÉTRY, ANDRÉ ERNEST MODESTE
  (1741-1813)
  Opera Ballet [arr.]
    (Gordon, Philip) 1.1.2.1. 2.2.2.1.
    timp,perc,strings (easy) KALMUS
    A6023 pno-cond sc $2.00, set
    $15.50, and up   (658)

  Tambourin [arr.] *see BAROQUE SUITE
    NO. 1

GRIEG, EDVARD HAGERUP (1843-1907)
  Allegretto Quasi Andantino [arr.]
    (from Sonata, Op. 5)
    (Dasch) string orch FITZSIMONS
    F0553 set $12.00, sc $3.00, pts
    $2.00, ea.   (659)

  Deux Pieces Lyriques: Valse Et
  Melodie Norvegienne [arr.]
    fl,ob,2clar,bsn,2horn,strings sc,
    pts LEMOINE f.s.   (660)

  Erotik, [arr.]
    (Isaac, Merle J.) string orch
    BELWIN sc $2.00, set $12.00 (661)

  In The Hall Of The Mountain King
    [arr.] (from Peer Gynt Suite No.
    1)
    (Carlin) 1.1.2.1.alto sax.tenor
    sax. 2.2.2.0. timp,perc,pno,
    strings CARLIN sc $4.00, set
    $38.00, pts $1.50, ea.   (662)

  March Of Homage [arr.]
    (Isaac, Merle) set TRN $20.00 (663)

  March Of The Dwarfs [arr.]
    see Zur Der Zwerge [arr.]

  Norwegian Dances Nos. 2 And 3 [arr.]
    (Isaac) BELWIN C000156 sc $4.00,
    set $25.00   (664)

  Quatre Morceaux Lyriques [arr.]
    (Lacour, Guy) 2.2+opt English
    horn.2+opt bass clar.0.2alto
    sax.opt tenor sax.opt baritone
    sax. 2.2.1.1. perc,gtr,opt acord,
    pno/harp/elec org,strings [6'5"]
    sc,pts BILLAUDOT f.s.   (665)

  Sailor's Song [arr.]
    (Myers, Theldon) string orch (gr.
    II) LAKES $16.00   (666)

  Suite, [arr.]
    (Stegen, Harro) string orch ZINNEB
    ZI 25 f.s.   (667)

  Three Norwegian Pieces [arr.] (from
    Op. 17)
    (Tomlinson, Geoffrey) string orch

GRIEG, EDVARD HAGERUP (cont'd.)

[3'] sc,pts NOVELLO 09.0543.07
f.s.   (668)

Zur Der Zwerge [arr.]
(Grantham, William) "March Of The
Dwarfs [arr.]" [4'45"] (med) set
SHAWNEE J-123 $25.00   (669)

GRIER, JON
Allegretto Animoso
string orch (gr. III) BELWIN
BSO 00070 $40.00   (670)

GRIESHABER, REINHARD (1949-   )
Zehn Kleine Stucke
string orch ZINNEB ZI 27 f.s.   (671)

GRIFFIN, MERV
Hour With The Game Shows, An [arr.]
(Cerulli, Bob) CPP CO159B7X $45.00
                                        (672)

GRISEY, GERARD (1946-   )
Manifestations, No. 1: Pour Echapper
A La Television
2fl,2clar/2sax,2perc,2gtr,8vln/
6vln&2vla,4vcl,opt db, 4
solfeggisti sc RICORDI-FR R.2237
f.s.   (673)

Manifestations, No. 2: Pour Trouver
Le Silence
2fl,2clar/2sax,2perc,2gtr,8vln/
6vln&2vla,4vcl,opt db, 4
solfeggisti sc RICORDI-FR R. 2235
f.s.   (674)

Manifestations, No. 3: Pour Obtenir
Une Aire De Jeux
2fl/2clar,2clar/2sax,2perc,4gtr,
8vln/6vln&2vla,4vcl, 4
solfeggisti sc RICORDI-FR R.2258
f.s.   (675)

GROTE SPEELBOECK VOOR KLEINE MENSEN,
HET see Keuning, Hans P.

GRUBER, FRANZ XAVER (1787-1863)
Silent Night [arr.]
(Shaffer, David) string orch (gr.
II) LAKES $16.00   (676)
see Stille Nacht [arr.]

Stille Nacht [arr.]
(Curnow, James) "Silent Night
[arr.]" string orch (easy) JENSON
502-19020 $24.00   (677)
(Davis; Custer) LEONARD-US 08720629
$35.00   (678)

GRUSIN, DAVID
On Golden Pond: Theme [arr.]
(Lowden) LEONARD-US 04501087 $25.00
                                        (679)

GUIDEPOST, THE [ARR.] see Schubert,
Franz (Peter), Wegweiser, Der
[arr.]

GUNSENHEIMER, GUSTAV (1934-   )
Concertino For Solo Instrument And
Orchestra
[10'15"] sc,pts VOGT f.s.   (680)

GURLITT, CORNELIUS (1820-1901)
Little Suite [arr.]
(Errante, Belisario) string orch,
pno (gr. II) MOSAIC M140   (681)

GUSTAFSON, DWIGHT LEONARD (1930-   )
Prayer
string orch [3'] (gr. II) CONCERT W
J-162 $20.00   (682)

GYPSY BARON WALTZES [ARR.] see Strauss,
Johann, [Jr.]

GYPSY CARNIVAL see Bauernschmidt,
Robert

GYPSY MELODIES [ARR.]
(Errante, Belisario) string orch,pno
[2'] (gr. II) set MOSAIC M080
$15.00, and up   (683)

GYPSY MOON [ARR.]
(Alshin, Harry A.) string orch
[1'20"] (gr. III) set KENDOR 9825
$19.00, and up   (684)

GYPSY RONDO see Scott, Richard

GYROWETZ, ADALBERT (JIROVEC)
(1763-1850)
Symphony No. 12,First Movement
(Luse, Michael) string orch (gr.
III) set YOUNG WORLD S0230
$20.00, and up   (685)

Symphony No. 12,Finale
(Wippler, Harold) string orch (gr.
III) set YOUNG WORLD $25.00, and
up   (686)

GYROWETZ, ADALBERT (JIROVEC) (cont'd.)

Symphony No. 12, Minuet
(Wippler, Harold) string orch (gr.
III) set YOUNG WORLD $18.00, and
up   (687)

HABANERA [ARR.] see Bizet, Georges

HALEN, WALTER J. (1930-   )
Fiddle Rags
string orch [2'30"] (gr. IV)
CONCERT W J-156 $22.00   (688)

Stick Horse Parade
(med easy) set SHAWNEE J-134 $10.00
                                        (689)

HALF AND HALF see Frost, Robert S.

HAMILTON, FRED
Memoire De Montreal
string orch,opt drums,opt pno (gr.
III) set YOUNG WORLD $22.00, and
up   (690)

HAMLISCH, MARVIN F. (1944-   )
Ordinary People: Theme [arr.]
(Lowden) (based on the Pachelbel
Canon) LEONARD-US 04501100 $25.00
                                        (691)

Themes From Ice Castles [arr.]
(Cerulli, Bob) (med easy) CPP
2625TB7X $40.00   (692)
(Cerulli, Bob) string orch CPP
2617TB4X $25.00   (693)

HAND ME DOWN MY WALKIN' CANE [ARR.]
(Forsblad, Leland) string orch,perc,
opt pno [1'55"] (gr. II) set KENDOR
9137 $19.00, and up   (694)

HANDEL, GEORGE FRIDERIC (1685-1759)
Air Con Variazioni [arr.]
see Handel For Strings

Allegro [arr.] (from Sonata No. 3)
(Dasch) string orch FITZSIMONS
F0555 set $12.00, sc $3.00, pts
$2.00, ea.   (695)
(Metcalf) string orch set BELWIN
BS053 $20.00   (696)
see Handel For Strings

Allegro Moderato [arr.] (from
Concerto Grosso No. 10)
(Clebanoff) string orch [2'30"]
DORABET sc $2.00, set $16.00, and
up, pts $1.25, ea.   (697)

Bourree, [arr.]
see Handel For Strings

Bourree, MIN 110, [arr.]
(Borowski) string orch sc,pts
BOSWORTH f.s.   (698)

Concerto Grosso, Op. 6, No. 1,
[excerpt]
(Dackow, Sandra) string orch
[2'45"] (med, Allegro [arr.])
LUDWIG STRO-31 $30.00   (699)

Courante in G, [arr.] (from The Third
Collection Of Clavichord Pieces)
(Cechvala) string orch set BELWIN
BS054 $20.00   (700)

Evening Song [arr.]
(Applebaum, Samuel; Ployhar, James)
1.1.2.1.2sax. 2.2.1.1. perc,
strings set BELWIN CO00176 $20.00
                                        (701)

Fugue, MIN 161, [arr.]
(Applebaum, Samuel; Ployhar, James)
set BELWIN C000177 $30.00   (702)

Gavotte And March [arr.] (from Trio
Sonata In D)
(Errante, Belisario) string orch
(gr. II) set MOSAIC M150 $20.00 (703)

Gavotte, MIN 3, [arr.]
(Borowski) string orch sc,pts
BOSWORTH f.s.   (704)

Gigue (from Concerto Grosso, Op. 6
No. 2)
(Applebaum, Samuel; Ployhar, James)
1.1.2.1.2sax. 2.2.1.1. perc,
strings BELWIN   (705)

Handel Celebration, A [arr.]
(Isaac) set BELWIN C000178 $35.00
                                        (706)

Handel For Strings
(Applebaum, Samuel; Gordon, Louis)
string orch set BELWIN BS000056
$25.00
contains: Air Con Variazioni

HANDEL, GEORGE FRIDERIC (cont'd.)

[arr.]; Allegro [arr.];
Bourree, [arr.]; Saraband,
[arr.]   (707)

Handel In Miniature [arr.]
string orch (med easy) CHESTER
CH.55627 sc $7.25, pts $16.50   (708)

Handel Suite, A [arr.]
(Isaac) set BELWIN CO178 $35.00
                                        (709)

Handel Suite [arr.]
(Leidig) string orch (gr. II) set
HIGHLAND $20.00, and up   (710)

Handel's Air, For Trumpet And
Orchestra [arr.]
(Stephens) (gr. II) set HIGHLAND
$37.00   (711)

Hornpipe [arr.]
(Borowski) string orch sc,pts
BOSWORTH f.s.   (712)

Judas Maccabaeus: Choeurs Et Marche
[arr.]
3rec,2fl,2clar,alto sax,gtr,strings
sc,pts LEMOINE f.s.   (713)

Larghetto , [arr.] (from Concerto No.
12)
(Anderson; Rokos) (easy) sc,pts
BOSWORTH f.s.   (714)

Larghetto, MIN1, [arr.]
(Bauernschmidt) string orch (med
easy) sets WYNN 6300-7300 $14.00,
and up   (715)

Largo, MIN 155, [arr.]
(Borowski) string orch sc,pts
BOSWORTH f.s.   (716)

Menuetto From Alcina [arr.] *see
BAROQUE SUITE O. 1

Menuetto From The Royal Fireworks
[arr.] *see BAROQUE SUITE NO. 2

Messiah: And The Glory Of The Lord
[arr.]
(Frost, Robert S.) string orch,opt
pno [3'45"] (gr. III) set KENDOR
$22.00, and up   (717)

Messiah: Hallelujah Chorus [arr.]
sc,pts CHESTER CH 55739 $16.50 (718)
(Frost, Robert) string orch,opt pno
[4'15"] (gr. IV) sets KENDOR
$19.00, and up   (719)
*see CHRISTMAS CLASSICS

Minuet, [arr.] (from Berenice)
(Borowski) string orch sc,pts
BOSWORTH f.s.   (720)

Minuet, MIN 154, [arr.]
(Bauernschmidt, R.L.) LYDIAN ORCH
set $14.00, pts $.80, ea.   (721)

Musette [arr.]
(Borowski) string orch sc,pts
BOSWORTH f.s.   (722)

Occasional Suite, An, [arr.]
(Siennicki, Edmund J.)
2(pic).2.2.2. 4.2.3.1. timp,perc,
opt pno,strings sets LUDWIG
LLE-67 f.s.   (723)

Overture in D minor, [arr.] (from
Concerto Grosso, Op. 3, No. 5)
(Isaac, Merle J.) (gr. III) set
HIGHLAND $37.00   (724)

Passacaglia, MIN 2, [arr.]
(Zinn, William) string orch
EXCELSIOR f.s.   (725)

Rejouissance, La [arr.]
(Frazer, Alan) MIDDLE CMK 207 f.s.
                                        (726)

Riccardo: March [arr.]
(Applebaum, Samuel; Ployhar, James)
set BELWIN C000173 $20.00   (727)

Rigaudon, [arr.]
(Hughes-Jones, L.) 1.2.2.1.
2.2.2.0. timp,opt pno,strings
(med easy) sc,pts BOSWORTH f.s.
                                        (728)

Royal Fireworks Music: Selections
[arr.]
(Frost) string orch (gr. III) LAKES
$20.00   (729)

Royal Fireworks Music: Suite [arr.]
(Stone, David) 2.2.2.1. 2.2.0.0.
timp,pno,strings sc,pts NOVELLO
09.0072.09 f.s.   (730)

HANDEL, GEORGE FRIDERIC (cont'd.)

Saraband, [arr.] (from Concerto For
Oboe In G Minor)
(Farago) string orch set BELWIN
BS052 $20.00   (731)
see Handel For Strings

Saraband, MIN 156, [arr.]
(Borowski) string orch sc,pts
BOSWORTH f.s.   (732)

Saraband, MIN 166, [arr.]
(Myers, Theldon) string orch set
LAKES $17.50, and up   (733)

Sarabande And Bourree [arr.]
(Isaac) string orch (med easy) set
WYNN 6293-7293 $14.00, and up
                                    (734)

Scipio: March [arr.]
(Applebaum, Samuel; Ployhar, James)
set BELWIN C000174 $20.00   (735)

See The Conquering Hero Comes [arr.]
(Applebaum, Samuel; Ployhar, James)
set BELWIN C000175 $20.00   (736)

Sonata No. 3, [arr.]
(Isaac) string orch (med) set WYNN
6285 $14.00, and up   (737)

Two Handel Marches [arr.]
(Isaac, Merle) [3'5"] (gr. III) set
LUDWIG LLE-77 $39.00, and up (738)

Water Music: Bourree And Hornpipe
[arr.]
(Rougeron, Philippe) sc,pts LEDUC
f.s.   (739)

Water Music: Hornpipe [arr.]
MIDDLE CMK 213 f.s.   (740)

Water Music: Minuets I And II [arr.]
(Wystraete) flexible
instrumentation sc,pts LEDUC
AL 27192 f.s.   (741)

HANDEL CELEBRATION, A [ARR.] see
Handel, George Frideric

HANDEL FOR STRINGS see Handel, George
Frideric

HANDEL IN MINIATURE [ARR.] see Handel,
George Frideric

HANDEL SUITE, A [ARR.] see Handel,
George Frideric

HANDEL SUITE [ARR.] see Handel, George
Frideric

**HANDEL'S AIR, FOR TRUMPET AND ORCHESTRA
[ARR.]** see Handel, George Frideric

HANSEL UND GRETEL [ARR.] see
Humperdinck, Engelbert

HANSON, JENS (1935-   )
Dreams
string orch [12'] CAN.MUS.CENT.
                                    (742)

HANUKKAH HOLIDAY [ARR.]
(Caponegro, John) string orch,opt pno
[1'45"] (gr. I) set KENDOR 8295
$19.00, and up   (743)

HAPPY BIRTHDAY VARIATIONS
(Hermann, Ralph) string orch set
LAKES $17.50, and up   (744)

HAPPY HOBO, THE see Bowles, Richard W.

HAPPY HOEDOWN [ARR.] see Chase, Bruce

HAPPY WANDERER [ARR.] see Moller,
Friedrich W.

HARK, THE HERALD ANGELS SING see
Angels, Shepherds, Christmas, Kings

HARLEQUINADE [ARR.] see Byng, F.D.

HATCH, TONY (ANTHONY PETER) (1939-   )
Downtown [arr.]
(Graham) string orch LEONARD-US
08720380 $35.00   (745)

HAUGLAND, A. OSCAR (1922-   )
Modal Suite
string orch set HOA $20.00   (746)

Nocturne
string orch set HOA $12.00   (747)

HAUNTING HOUR, THE [ARR.]
(Hughes, Ed) (gr. I) set HIGHLAND
$31.00   (748)

HAVE, WILLEM TEN
Allegro Brillant [arr.] *Op.19
string orch sc,pts BOSWORTH f.s.
                                    (749)

HAVE, WILLEM TEN (cont'd.)

Capriccio, Op. 24, [arr.]
string orch sc,pts BOSWORTH f.s.
                                    (750)

Concerto, Op. 30, [arr.]
string orch sc,pts BOSWORTH f.s.
                                    (751)

**HAVE YOURSELF A MERRY LITTLE CHRISTMAS
[ARR.]**
(Cerulli, Bob) CPP TI720HB7 $40.00
                                    (752)

HAWKINS, MALCOLM
Day In Town, A
sc,pts UNITED MUS f.s.   (753)

HAY, GEORGE
Silhouettes [arr.]
sc,pts LENGNICK f.s.   (754)

HAYDN, [FRANZ] JOSEPH (1732-1809)
Allegretto [arr.] (from String
Quartet In G)
(Clebanoff) string orch DORABET sc
$2.00, set $16.00, and up, pts
$1.25, ea.   (755)

Best Of Haydn, The
(Applebaum, Samuel; Paradise, Paul)
string orch BELWIN EL3201-3206 sc
$10.00, pts $3.95, ea.   (756)

Clock Symphony (Symphony No. 101,
[excerpt], [arr.])
(Isaac) string orch (med easy) set
WYNN 6290 $14.00, and up   (757)

Poule Symphony, La (Symphony No. 83,
Minuet, [arr.])
(Rogers, David) string orch,pno
CARLIN sc $3.00, sets $17.00, and
up   (758)

St. Anthony Chorale [arr.]
(Dackow, Sandra) string orch [2']
(easy) LUDWIG STRO-30 $25.00
                                    (759)

Sinfonia Semplice [arr.]
(Bauernschmidt) [6'25"] (gr. III)
SHAWNEE J-152 $50.00   (760)

Sinfonietta in C, [arr.] (from
Baryton Trios)
(Bauernschmidt, Robert) [8'] (med)
set SHAWNEE J-87 $35.00   (761)

Surprise Symphony
see Symphony No. 94, Minuet, [arr.]

Symphony No. 3,Finale, [arr.]
(Isaac, Merle J.) (gr. III) set
HIGHLAND $28.00, and up   (762)

Symphony No. 82, Minuet, [arr.]
(Rougeron) flexible instrumentation
sc,pts LEDUC AL 27191 f.s.   (763)

Symphony No. 83,Minuet, [arr.]
see Poule Symphony, La

Symphony No. 88,Finale, [arr.]
(Isaac) (med diff) set WYNN
4277-5277 $28.00, and up   (764)
(Isaac) string orch (med diff) set
WYNN 6299-7299 $18.00, and up
                                    (765)

Symphony No. 94, [excerpt]
(Dackow, Sandra) string orch (easy,
Andante [arr.]) LUDWIG STRO-43
$45.00   (766)

Symphony No. 94, Minuet, [arr.]
(Lacour, Guy) "Surprise Symphony"
2.2+opt English horn.2+opt bass
clar.0.2alto sax.opt tenor
sax.opt baritone sax. 2.2.1.1.
perc,gtr,opt acord,pno/harp/elec
org,strings sc,pts BILLAUDOT f.s.
contains also: Monteverdi,
Claudio, Sinfonia Et Toccata
[arr.] (from Orfeo)   (767)

Symphony No. 101, [excerpt], [arr.]
see Clock Symphony

Two Minuets *see THREE CLASSICAL
PIECES

HAYDN SEEK see Petrone, John

HEDGES, ANTHONY JOHN (1931-   )
Prelude And Fugue For Fun
string orch (med easy) CHESTER
CH 55611 sc $7.25, pts $16.50
                                    (768)

HEILIGE NACHT *CC17U
(Burkhart, F.) string orch DOBLINGER
sc 07 505 f.s., pts 07 506 f.s.
                                    (769)

HEILMANN, FRANCIS
Buddha's Temple
string orch,perc,pno [2'25"] (very
easy) set HEILNN $21.00, and up
                                    (770)

2fl,2clar,2alto sax,2trp,trom,perc,
pno,strings [2'25"] (very easy)

HEILMANN, FRANCIS (cont'd.)

set HEILNN $27.00, and up   (771)

Evening In Arabia
2fl,2clar,2alto sax,2trp,trom,perc,
pno,strings [2'55"] (med easy)
set HEILNN $27.00, and up   (772)

Magic Music Box
2fl,2clar,2alto sax,2trp,trom,perc,
pno 4-hands,strings [1'45"]
(easy) set HEILNN $27.00, and up
                                    (773)
string orch,perc,pno 4-hands
[1'45"] (easy) set HEILNN $21.00,
and up   (774)

Open String Rock
perc,pno,strings [2'] (easy) set
HEILNN $21.00, and up   (775)

Picnic In The Park
2fl,2clar,2alto sax,2trp,trom,perc,
pno,strings [2'30"] (easy) set
HEILNN $27.00, and up   (776)
string orch,perc,pno [2'30"] (easy)
set HEILNN $21.00, and up   (777)

Rockin' Easy
2fl,2clar,2alto sax,2trp,trom,perc,
pno,strings [2'] (easy) set
HEILNN $27.00, and up   (778)
string orch,perc,pno [2'] (easy)
set HEILNN $21.00, and up   (779)

Symphonic Miniature, For Violin And
Orchestra
2fl,2clar,2alto sax,2trp,trom,perc,
pno,strings,vln solo [3'55"]
(orch. parts easy; solo violin
part difficult) set HEILNN
$27.00, and up   (780)

Symphonic Miniature, For Violin And
String Orchestra
string orch,pno,perc,vln solo
[3'55"] (orch. part easy; solo
violin part difficult) set HEILNN
$21.00, and up   (781)

Western Rider
string orch,perc,pno,gtr [2']
(easy) set HEILNN $21.00, and up
                                    (782)
2fl,2clar,2alto sax,2trp,trom,perc,
pno,gtr,strings [2'] (easy) set
HEILNN $27.00, and up   (783)

Winter Fun
string orch,perc,pno [1'45"] (easy)
set HEILNN $21.00, and up   (784)

HELLEM, MARK
Russian Peasant Dance
string orch (gr. III) KJOS set
SO-64B $25.00, sc SO-64F $3.00
                                    (785)

HELLO [ARR.] see Richie, Lionel

HEMEL, OSCAR VAN (1892-1981)
Divertimento
1.0.1.0. 0.1.0.0. pno,strings,
(without vla or db) sc DONEMUS
f.s.   (786)

HENLEY, LARRY
Wind Beneath My Wings, The [arr.]
(composed with Silbar, Jeff)
(Jennings, Paul) string orch JENSON
592-23040 $30.00   (787)

HENRY, CHARLES (1909-   )
Jazz Suite No. 1 [arr.]
2rec,2clar,3sax,strings sc,pts
LEMOINE f.s.   (788)

Jazz Suite No. 2 [arr.]
2rec,2clar,3sax,strings sc,pts
LEMOINE f.s.   (789)

Mandarin Swing [arr.]
(Guelis, Alain) 1.1.1.1. 4.2.3.0.
timp,glock,xylo,perc,2harp,
strings LEMOINE perf mat rent
                                    (790)

**HENRY MANCINI FOR STRINGS, VOL. 1
[ARR.]** see Mancini, Henry

**HENRY MANCINI FOR STRINGS, VOL. 2
[ARR.]** see Mancini, Henry

HERBERT, VICTOR (1859-1924)
Toyland [arr.]
(Arnold, Alan) string orch,opt
perc,opt pno set FIDDLE $16.00
                                    (791)

HERMAN, JERRY (1933-   )
Cage Aux Folles, La: Selections
[arr.]
(Lang) LEONARD-US 04500742 $45.00
                                    (792)

We Need A Little Christmas [arr.]
(Rosenhaus) string orch (med easy)
LEONARD-US 04849885 $20.00   (793)

HERMANN, RALPH J. (1914-   )
    Hoe Down For Young Dancers
        string orch (gr. III) LAKES $17.50
                                                (794)

HERVELOIS, CAIX D'
    see CAIX D'HERVELOIS, LOUIS DE

HE'S GONE AWAY [ARR.]
    (Clebanoff, Herman) string orch
        DORABET D-143 f.s.   (795)

HEYWOOD, EDDIE (? -1989)
    Canadian Sunset [arr.]
        (Applebaum) string orch CHERRY
        24038 $15.00   (796)

HIBBARD, WILLIAM (1939-   )
    Sinfonia On Expanding Matrices
        string orch [8'] (diff) sc
        AM.COMP.AL. $13.80   (797)

HIGGINS, JAMES
    Perpetual Motion
        string orch,opt pno (gr. III)
        BELWIN CO 00189 $35.00   (798)

HIGH LOW FUN see Hubbell, Fred M.

HIGH PLACES see Mauldin, Michael

HIGHLAND DANCE see Frost, Robert S.

HIGHLAND SONG see Caponegro, John

HIRSCH
    Concerto Grosso
        (med easy) sets WYNN 4331-5331
        $28.00, and up   (799)

HODDINOTT, ALUN (1929-   )
    Hommage A Chopin *Op.107,No.2
        3(pic).2.2+bass clar.2. 4.3.3.1.
        timp,3perc,harp,strings [12']
        UNIV.CR perf mat rent   (800)

    Quodlibet On Welsh Nursery Tunes
        3(pic).2.3.2. 4.3.3.1. timp,3perc,
        harp,pno,strings [12'] study sc
        UNIV.CR P66717 f.s., perf mat
        rent   (801)

    Welsh Dances No. 3 *Op.123
        3(pic).2+English horn.2+bass
        clar.2+contrabsn. 4.3.3.1. timp,
        2perc,harp,strings [14'] study sc
        UNIV.CR P02801 f.s., perf mat
        rent   (802)

HODKINSON, SYDNEY P. (1934-   )
    Celestial Calendar
        string orch [12'] (med easy) AMP
                                                (803)

HOE DOWN FOR YOUNG DANCERS see Hermann,
    Ralph J.

HOEDOWN see Pettersen, Nancy

HOFELDT, WILLIAM (1951-   )
    Centennial Overture
        (gr. III) KJOS set O-1060B $35.00,
        sc O-1060F $3.00   (804)

    Lullaby
        string orch (gr. III) KJOS set
        WSO-2B $25.00, sc WSO-2F $3.00
                                                (805)

    Nocturne
        string orch (gr. IV) KJOS set
        SO-81B $25.00, sc SO-81F $3.00
                                                (806)

HOFFMEISTER, FRANZ ANTON (1754-1812)
    German Dance *see THREE CLASSICAL
        PIECES

HOLCOMBE, BILL
    Good Tidings Of Great Joy
        MUSICIANS PUB SOS-604 $40.00 (807)

HOLD ON TO THE NIGHTS [ARR.] see Marx

HOLDRIDGE, LEE ELWOOD (1944-   )
    Moonlighting: Theme [arr.]
        (Jankowski, Chris) string orch (gr.
        III) JENSON 502-13020 $30.00
                                                (808)

HOLIDAY BELLS see Chase, Bruce

HOLIDAY FESTIVAL OF LIGHTS, A see Ward,
    Norman

HOLIDAY FOR ORCHESTRA see Mitchell, Rex

HOLIDAY FOR STRINGS [ARR.] see Rose,
    David

HOLLY AND THE IVY, THE see Two Yuletide
    Carols

HOLST, GUSTAV (1874-1934)
    Fugal Concerto For Flute, Oboe And
        String Orchestra *Op.40,No.2
        string orch,2vln/fl&ob soli NOVELLO
        sc 09.0542.09 f.s., pts
        12.0060.07 f.s.   (809)

HOLST, GUSTAV (cont'd.)
    Jupiter, Bringer Of Jollity [arr.]
        (Leidig) (gr. III) set HIGHLAND
        $28.00, and up   (810)

    Jupiter: Themes [arr.]
        sc,pts CHESTER CH 55730 $16.50
                                                (811)

HOMAGE TO BACH see Levenson, David

HOME FOR THE HOLIDAYS [ARR.] see Allen,
    Robert

HOMMAGE A CHOPIN see Hoddinott, Alun

HOMMES ET PAYS NOUVEAUX [ARR.] see
    Schumann, Robert (Alexander)

HOOD, BARBARA W.
    Redstone Jive And Green Mountain
        Blues
        string orch (gr. I) set HIGHLAND
        $20.00, and up   (812)

HOOKED ON CLASSICS
    (Clark, Louis; Burden, James)
        2(pic).2.2.2. 4.3.3.1. timp,perc,
        strings set BRADLEY $75.00   (813)

HOP, SKIP AND JUMP see Fletcher, Gary

HOPAK [ARR.] see Mussorgsky, Modest
    Petrovich

HORNER, JAMES
    Somewhere Out There [arr.] (composed
        with Mann, Barry; Weil, Cynthia)
        (Lowden) LEONARD-US 04501500 $30.00
                                                (814)
    (Rosenhaus) string orch LEONARD-US
        04849700 $20.00   (815)
    (Vosbein) LEONARD-US 08720388
        $35.00   (816)

HORNPIPE [ARR.] see Handel, George
    Frideric

HORSE AND BUGGY see Anderson, Leroy

HORVATH, G.
    Danse De Colombine [arr.]
        sc,pts LENGNICK f.s.   (817)

HOUR WITH THE GAME SHOWS, AN [ARR.] see
    Griffin, Merv

HOYLAND, VICTOR (1945-   )
    Xingu
        3.0.3.0. 3.3.3.0. 4perc,cel,vibra,
        harp,strings, children's voices
        [30'] UNIVER. perf mat rent (818)

HUBBELL, FRED M.
    Busy Bows
        2.1.2.1.alto sax.tenor sax.
        2.3.2.1. perc,pno,strings [2'15"]
        set LUDWIG LLE-69 $34.00, and up
                                                (819)

    High Low Fun
        string orch (gr. II) set HIGHLAND
        $29.00   (820)

    Ladybug On A Carousel
        string orch (gr. I) set HIGHLAND
        $20.00, and up   (821)

HUGHES-JONES, LLIFON (1918-   )
    Langdon Overture
        (med easy) sc,pts BOSWORTH f.s.
                                                (822)

    Two Preludes
        1.1.2.1. 1.0.0.0. strings (med
        easy) sc,pts BOSWORTH f.s.   (823)

HULTGREN, RALPH
    Aussie Hoedown
        string orch (gr. I) set HIGHLAND
        $29.00   (824)

    Waltzing Wombat, The
        string orch [1'40"] (gr. II)
        CONCERT W J-164 $20.00   (825)

    Warrior, The
        string orch (easy) set LAKES
        $14.00, and up   (826)

HUMMEL, BERTOLD (1925-   )
    Epigramme *Op.69a
        string orch [12'] PETERS perf mat
        rent   (827)

HUMORESQUE, OP. 101, NO. 1 [ARR.] see
    Dvořák, Antonín

HUMORESQUE, OP. 101, NO. 7 [ARR.] see
    Dvořák, Antonín

HUMPERDINCK, ENGELBERT (1854-1921)
    Hansel Und Gretel [arr.]
        (Siennicki, Edmund) string orch
        (gr. III) HIGHLAND $29.00   (828)

HUNGARIAN MARCH, [ARR.] see Berlioz,
    Hector (Louis)

HUNGARIAN MEMORIES [ARR.]
    (Kohut) (gr. II) set HIGHLAND $37.00
                                                (829)

HUNGARIAN RHAPSODIE NO.2 [ARR.] see
    Liszt, Franz

HUNT, THE, [ARR.] see Vivaldi, Antonio

HURD, MICHAEL (1928-   )
    Dance Diversions
        2.2.2.2. 2.2.2.0. timp,perc,strings
        [15'] sc,pts NOVELLO 09.0541.00
        f.s.   (830)

    Little Suite
        string orch sc,pts NOVELLO
        09.0569.00 f.s.   (831)

HUREL, PHILIPPE (1955-   )
    Premiere Improvisation A Raphaele
        3.2.3.2. 2.2.0.0. 4perc,strings
        [4'] BILLAUDOT perf mat rent
                                                (832)

HUSZAR, LAJOS
    Concerto Rustico
        string orch sc,pts EMB 13308 f.s.
                                                (833)
    Serenata Concertante, For Flute And
        String Orchestra
        string orch,fl solo sc,pts EMB
        13307 f.s.   (834)

HVOSLEF, KETIL (1939)
    Suite For School Orchestra
        1.1.1.1. 0.0.0.0. strings NORGE
                                                (835)

HYACINTHE CONCERTO, FOR CLARINET AND
    STRING ORCHESTRA see Joubert,
    Claude-Henry

HYLAS see Escher, Rudolf George

HYMN AND FINALE [ARR.] see Bach, Johann
    Sebastian

HYMNE A LA JOIE [ARR.] see Beethoven,
    Ludwig van

HYMNE [ARR.] see Vangelis

HYMNS, 17 [ARR.] *CCU
    (Adams, D.) string orch set ADAM 8705
    $28.00   (836)

I DREAMED A DREAM [ARR.] see Schonberg,
    Claude-Michel

I GET AROUND [ARR.] see Wilson, Brian

I HEARD IT THROUGH THE GRAPEVINE [ARR.]
    see Whitfield, Norman

I JUST CALLED TO SAY I LOVE YOU [ARR.]
    see Morris, Stevland (Stevie
    Wonder)

I JUST CAN'T STOP LOVING YOU [ARR.] see
    Jackson, Michael

I PLAY! WHAT DO YOU PLAY...? see
    Rixmann, Gerd, Ich Spiele! Was
    Spielst Du...?

I SING THE BODY ELECTRIC [ARR.] see
    Gore, Michael

I WANT TO HOLD YOUR HAND [ARR.] see
    Lennon, John

I WHISTLE A HAPPY TUNE see String
    Orchestra Pak No. 5

ICH SPIELE! WAS SPIELST DU...? see
    Rixmann, Gerd

ICICLES see Arnold, Alan

IF I WERE A RICH MAN [ARR.] see Bock,
    Jerry

IF MY FRIENDS COULD SEE ME NOW [ARR.]
    see Coleman, Cy

IL EST NE, LE DIVIN ENFANT [ARR.] see
    Two French Carols

ILE AUX LUMIERES, L', FOR VIOLIN AND
    STRING ORCHESTRA see Reverdy,
    Michele

ILG, STEVE
    Three Teaching Pieces For Strings
        string orch [8'45"] (med easy) set
        SHAWNEE J-96 $12.00   (837)

I'M GETTING SENTIMENTAL OVER YOU [ARR.]
see Washington, Ned

IMMER KLEINER [ARR.] see Schreiner,
Alexander

IMMIGRATION TRAIL see Frost, Robert S.

IMPRAVADA see Shaffer, David

IN DULCI JUBILO see Angels, Shepherds,
Christmas, Kings

IN THE DAYS OF DRAKE [ARR.] see Duncan,
S.

IN THE HALL OF THE MOUNTAIN KING [ARR.]
see Grieg, Edvard Hagerup

INDIAN CANZONETTA [ARR.] see Dvořák,
Antonín

INSTRUMENTAL MOTET see Grant, W. Parks

INTERNATIONAL DIXIELAND JAMBOREE
(Holcombe, Bill) MUSICIANS PUB
SOS-907A $30.00   (838)

INTERNATIONAL STRINGS
(Caponegro, John) string orch,opt
perc,opt pno,opt narrator [6'15"]
(gr. I) sets KENDOR $20.00, and up
(839)

INTO THE FERMENT, FOR INSTRUMENTAL
SOLOISTS AND SCHOOL ORCHESTRA see
Macmillan, James

INTONATION AND RHYTHM see Flor

INVERNO, L': FIRST MOVEMENT, [ARR.] see
Vivaldi, Antonio, Concerto, Op. 8,
No. 4,First Movement, [arr.]

INVERNO, L': SECOND AND THIRD MOVEMENTS
[ARR.] see Vivaldi, Antonio,
Concerto, Op. 8, No. 4,Second
Movement,Third Movement, [arr.]

IOLANTHE: FANFARE AND MARCH [ARR.] see
Sullivan, [Sir] Arthur Seymour

IPHIGENIA IN AULIS: TWO PIECES [ARR.]
see Gluck, Christoph Willibald,
Ritter von, Iphigenie En Aulide:
Two Pieces [arr.]

IPHIGENIE EN AULIDE: TWO PIECES [ARR.]
see Gluck, Christoph Willibald,
Ritter von

IPHIGENIE EN TAURIDE: CHOEUR DES
PRETRESSES [ARR.] see Gluck,
Christoph Willibald, Ritter von

IPPOLITOV-IVANOV, MIKHAIL MIKHAILOVICH
(1859-1935)
Caucasian Sketches: Procession Of The
Sardar [arr.]
(Isaac) BELWIN C000157 sc $5.00,
set $30.00   (840)

IRELAND, JOHN (1879-1962)
Downland Suite, A
string orch [16'] (gr. IV) JENSON
502-04020 $40.00   (841)

IRISH BOY, THE [ARR.] see Dunhill,
Thomas Frederick

ISAAC, MERLE JOHN (1898-   )
Boogie Bass No. 1
see Steppin' Out

Cheerful Earful, A
[4'] (gr. II) set TRN $25.00, and
up   (842)
string orch [4'] (gr. II) set TRN
$22.00, and up   (843)

Chiapanecas
string orch (med easy) set WYNN
6278 $14.00, and up   (844)

Fiddle Tunes No. 1
string orch (med) sets WYNN
6270-7270 $18.00, and up   (845)

Fiddle Tunes No. 2
string orch (med) set WYNN 6279
$18.00, and up   (846)

Fiddle Tunes No. 3
string orch (med) set WYNN 6280
$18.00, and up   (847)

Garden Street Rag
see Steppin' Out

Lively Waltz, The
see Steppin' Out

Mexican Serenade
string orch (med easy) set WYNN
6272 $18.00, and up   (848)

ISAAC, MERLE JOHN (cont'd.)

Springtime Suite
string orch [6'30"] (gr. II) set
TRN $22.00, and up   (849)

Steppin' Out
string orch (gr. III) set HIGHLAND
$33.00
contains: Boogie Bass No. 1;
Garden Street Rag; Lively
Waltz, The   (850)

ISRAEL, BRIAN (1951-1986)
Dorian Variations
string orch [4'30"] sc,pts LUDWIG
STRO 18 f.s.   (851)

Sinfonietta
LUDWIG LLE-74   (852)

ISRAEL SINGS [ARR.]
(Byers, Betty) string orch (gr. III)
set HIGHLAND $31.00   (853)

ITALIAN FOLK FANTASY see Bucci

ITALIAN MEDLEY
(McLeod, James) string orch,opt pno
[3'10"] (gr. II) sets KENDOR
$16.00, and up   (854)

IT'S CHRISTMAS TIME [ARR.]
(Custer, Calvin) CPP C0157B7X $65.00
(855)

IVANOVICI, ION (1845-1902)
Danube Waves Waltz [arr.]
see Waves Of The Danube [arr.]

Waves Of The Danube [arr.]
(McLeod, James) "Danube Waves Waltz
[arr.]" string orch,opt pno
[3'45"] (gr. II) sets KENDOR
$20.00, and up   (856)
(Sopkin) 2.2.2.2.3sax. 4.3.3.1.
timp,perc,harp,strings (med easy)
set KALMUS A6021 $16.50, and up   (857)

I'VE HAD THE TIME OF MY LIFE [ARR.] see
Previte, Frank

JACKSON, MICHAEL
I Just Can't Stop Loving You [arr.]
(Chase, Bruce) string orch (gr.
III) JENSON 502-09010 $30.00
(858)

JAECKER, FRIEDRICH
Zwei Stücke: Fragment; Metamorphose
sc,pts BOSSE 157 f.s.   (859)

JASTRZEBSKA, ANNA (1950-   )
Miligram For Strings
string orch NORGE   (860)

JAZZ MOODS see Feese, Francis L.

JAZZ PIZZICATO, [ARR.] see Anderson,
Leroy

JAZZ SINGER, THE [ARR.] see Diamond,
Neil

JAZZ SUITE NO. 1 [ARR.] see Henry,
Charles

JAZZ SUITE NO. 2 [ARR.] see Henry,
Charles

JE TE VEUX see Satie, Erik

JEPSON, DAVID W.
Festival March
3.2.2.2. 4.2.3.1. timp,perc,opt
pno,strings OXFORD sc 365071-1
$15.75, pts 380087-X $35.00   (861)

JESSE POLKA
(Isaac) (med easy) sets WYNN
4267-5267 $28.00, and up   (862)

JESSEL, LEON (1871-1942)
Parade Of The Wooden Soldiers [arr.]
(McLeod, James) string orch,opt pno
[3'10"] (gr. II) set KENDOR
$20.00, and up   (863)

JESU, JOY OF MAN'S DESIRING [ARR.] see
Bach, Johann Sebastian

JESUS, THE VERY THOUGHT OF THEE [ARR.]
see Dykes, John Bacchus

JINGLE BELL ROCK [ARR.] see Beal,
Joseph Carleton

JINGLE BELLS? see Ryden, William

JIROVEC, VOJTECH MATEJ
see GYROWETZ, ADALBERT

JOEL, WILLIAM MARTIN (BILLY)
(1949-   )
Best Of Billy Joel, The [arr.]
(Sayre) LEONARD-US 04500700 $45.00
(864)

JOGGIN' see Senob, Carl

JOGGIN' TUNE see Fletcher, Gary

JOHANSEN, BERTIL PALMAR (1954-   )
Dancers
3.0.2.0. 2.2.2.0. timp,perc,strings
[8'30"] NORGE   (865)

JOLAS, BETSY (1926-   )
Cinq Pieces Pour Boulogne
[10'] SALABERT   (866)
2.1.2.1.sax. 1.1.1.0. timp,2perc,
pno,strings [10'] SALABERT perf
mat rent   (867)

JONES
Funky Monkey And Friends
string orch (gr. III) BOOSEY   (868)

JONES, LLIFON HUGHES
see HUGHES-JONES, LLIFON

JOPLIN, SCOTT (1868-1917)
Easy Winners Rag, The [arr.]
(Frazer, Alan) MIDDLE RW2 f.s.   (869)

Entertainer, The [arr.;
(Cheucle) 2.3.2.2. 2.2.3.1. strings
LEMOINE perf mat rent   (870)

Maple Leaf Rag [arr.]
(Cheucle) 2.3.2.2. 2.2.3.0. strings
LEMOINE perf mat rent   (871)

Peacherine Rag [arr.]
(Frazer, Alan) MIDDLE RW1 f.s.   (872)

Ragtime Dance [arr.]
(Higgins, James) string orch (med)
BELWIN BSO 00071 $40.00   (873)

Ragtime Favorites For Strings [arr.]
(Zinn, William) string orch BELWIN
sc 11633 $11.00, pts 11634-11638
$4.50, ea.   (874)

Sting, The: Music [arr.]
(Hamlisch; Muller) string orch
BELWIN V 114 sc $3.50, set $15.00
(875)

Sting, The: Selections [arr.]
(Hamlisch; Cacavas) BELWIN V 111 sc
$4.00, set $25.00   (876)

String Along With Scott [arr.]
(Silverman) string orch,gtr,pno
PRESSER 494-01463-71 sc $16.00,
kbd pt $7.00, pts $5.00, ea.   (877)

JOSEPHS, WILFRED (1927-   )
Concerto for Orchestra, Op. 89
3(pic).3(English horn).3(bass
clar).3. 3.3.3.0. 3perc,harp,pno,
strings [11'] NOVELLO perf mat
rent   (878)

JOSE'S BLUES see Sabien, Randel

JOSHUA
(Sabien, Randel) perc,strings sets
ETOILE $15.00, and up   (879)

JOUBERT, CLAUDE-HENRY
Au Bal Masque
string orch [7'] sc,pts BILLAUDOT
f.s.   (880)

Concerto Pifferaro, For Flute And
Orchestra
(med easy) sc,pts MARTIN $65.00
(881)

Hyacinthe Concerto, For Clarinet And
String Orchestra
string orch,clar solo (med easy)
sc,pts MARTIN $65.00   (882)

JUBILEE see Latham, William Peters

JUDAS MACCABAEUS: CHOEURS ET MARCHE
[ARR.] see Handel, George Frideric

JUNE [ARR.] see Tchaikovsky, Piotr
Ilyich

JUPITER, BRINGER OF JOLLITY [ARR.] see
Holst, Gustav

JUPITER: THEMES [ARR.] see Holst,
Gustav

JUVENES see Berge, Sigurd

KABALEVSKY, DMITRI BORISOVICH
(1904-1987)
Clown, The [arr.]
(Wieloszynski, Stephen) string
orch,opt pno [1'45"] (gr. II) set
KENDOR $23.00, and up   (883)

Folk Song Variations [arr.] *Op.51,
No.3-4
(Thurston, Richard) string orch
(gr. III) SOUTHERN SO-48 sc
$5.00, set $25.00, pts $1.25, ea.
(884)

KADDISH see McBeth, William Francis

KANDER, JOHN (1927)
New York, New York: Theme [arr.]
(Whitney) (easy) CPP TO450TB7
$40.00   (885)

KARG-ELERT, SIGFRID (1877-1933)
Aria And Fughetta [arr.]
(Rhoads) string orch (med) set
SHAWNEE J-133 $17.00   (886)

KARLIN, FREDERICK JAMES (1936-)
Nightingale Sang In Berkeley Square,
A [arr.]
(Vosbein) LEONARD-US 08720274
$35.00   (887)

KASHA, AL (1937-)
Candle On The Water [arr.]
(Kerr) string orch (easy) LEONARD-
US 04841475 $15.00   (888)

KERN, JEROME (1885-1945)
Show Boat [arr.]
string orch LEONARD-US 06024040
$20.00   (889)

Show Boat: Highlights [arr.]
(Applebaum; Gordon) string orch
CHERRY 24040 $20.00   (890)

Way You Look Tonight, The [arr.]
(Vosbein) LEONARD-US 08720362
$35.00   (891)

KERR, WALLIS
Festival Polka
string orch (gr. I) SOUTHERN SO-43
sc $3.00, set $16.00, pts $1.25,
ea.   (892)

KERSTSUITE see Keuning, Hans P.

KETÈLBEY, ALBERT WILLIAM (1875-1959)
Persian Market Swing, [arr.]
(Naylor, F.) 2(pic).2.3(alto clar
in E flat).2.2alto sax.tenor sax.
4.3.3.0. perc,gtr,strings (med
easy) sc,pts BOSWORTH f.s. (893)

KEUNING, HANS P. (1926-)
Grote Speelboeck Voor Kleine Mensen,
Het
2S rec,A rec,2vln,vcl,pno HARMONIA
1219 f.s.   (894)

Kerstsuite
2S rec,A rec,2vln,vcl,pno HARMONIA
1288 f.s.   (895)

KEUNING, KEN
Royal Processional
string orch (gr. I) KJOS set SO-71B
$22.00, sc SO-71F $3.00   (896)

Sailor's Song
string orch (gr. II) KJOS set
SO-72B $22.00, sc SO-72F $3.00
(897)

San Francisco Suite
string orch (gr. III) set YOUNG
WORLD SO229 $20.00, and up (898)

Strings In Concert
string orch (gr. I) set YOUNG WORLD
YS227 $20.00, and up   (899)

Sweet Jazz Suite
string orch (gr. III) set YOUNG
WORLD SO224 $20.00, and up (900)

KINDER SUITE see Levin, Rami

KINDERMANN, JOHANN ERASMUS (1616-1655)
Fuga [arr.]
see Froberger, Johann Jakob, Canzon
[arr.]

KINDERSINFONIE see Reinecke, Carl

KING, BEN
Stand By Me [arr.] (composed with
Stoller, Michael Endore; Lieber,
Jerry)
(Custer) set LEONARD-US 04797225
$25.00   (901)

KING AND I, THE: SELECTIONS [ARR.] see
Rodgers, Richard

KING ARTHUR RULED THE LAND [ARR.] see
Folk-Songs For Strings, Set 3

KING COTTON [ARR.] see Sousa, John
Philip

KING'S MUSICIANS, THE [ARR.] see Lully,
Jean-Baptiste (Lulli)

KIRK, THERON WILFORD (1919-)
Latham Suite
string orch [9'] OXFORD 92.706 sc
$12.00, pts $2.00, ea.   (902)

KIRKMAN, TERRY
Cherish [arr.]
(Whitney) (easy) CPP 2618CB7X
$40.00   (903)

KIRKPATRICK
Away In A Manger [arr.]
(Coombes, Douglas) 2fl,2clar,2horn,
glock,strings LINDSAY   (904)

KLEINE NACHTMUSIK, EINE: MENUETT [ARR.]
see Mozart, Wolfgang Amadeus

KLEINE OUVERTURE see Doernberg, Martin

KLOTMAN, ROBERT (1918-)
Two Moods In 3-4 Time
(gr. II) KJOS set GO-101B $30.00,
sc GO-101F $3.00   (905)

KNIGHT, SALLY
For A Summer's Day
string orch (easy) CHESTER CH 55621
sc $7.75, pts $27.00   (906)

Strawberry Fair
string orch (easy) CHESTER CH 55624
sc $7.75, pts $21.00   (907)

KOCH, ERLAND VON (1910-)
Arioso And Furioso
sc,pts NORDISKA f.s.   (908)

KOCHER, CONRAD (1786-1872)
For The Beauty Of The Earth *see
SONGS OF THANKSGIVING

KOCSAR, MIKLOS (1933-)
Dances Of Pozsony
sc,pts EMB 12348 f.s.   (909)

KOKAI, REZSÖ (1906-1962)
Little Recruiting Dance
sc,pts EMB 1274 f.s.   (910)

KOKOMO [ARR.] see Love, Mike

KONT, PAUL (1920-)
Concertino Des Enfants, For Piano And
Orchestra
1.1.3.1. 0.0.0.0. strings,pno solo
[15'] DOBLINGER perf mat rent
(911)

KORN, PETER JONA (1922-)
Adagietto *Op.23
ZINNEB ZI 26 f.s.   (912)

Romanza Concertante, For Oboe And
Orchestra *Op.84
ZINNEB ZI 18 f.s.   (913)

KOSCIELNY, JOHN
Suite For Strings
(Epperson, Gordon) string orch set
LUDWIG STRO-20 $24.00, and up (914)

KOVATS, DANIEL
Christmas Sarabande
string orch (gr. III) LAKES $17.50
(915)

Santa's Super Sleigh
string orch (gr. IV) LAKES $24.00
(916)

Winter's Sunshine
string orch (gr. III) set LAKES
$17.50, and up   (917)

KOYKKAR, JOSEPH
Evocations
3(pic).2.2+bass clar.2. 4.3.3.1.
timp,perc,pno,strings (gr. III)
BELWIN CO 00191 $55.00   (918)

KRAFT, KARL (1908-1978)
Partita in D
string orch [8'] sc,pts SCHWANN
S2024 f.s.   (919)

KREISLER, FRITZ (1875-1962)
Fritz Kreisler Album No. 1 [arr.]
(Isaac, Merle; Goldberg, Milton)
string orch (gr. III) set
HIGHLAND $31.00   (920)

Fritz Kreisler Album No. 2 [arr.]
(Isaac, Merle; Goldberg, Milton)
string orch (gr. III) set
HIGHLAND $31.00   (921)

KÜCHLER, FERDINAND
Concertino, Op. 12, [arr.]
(med diff) sc,pts BOSWORTH f.s.
(922)

Concertino, Op. 15, [arr.]
string orch,opt pno&winds (med
diff) sc,pts BOSWORTH f.s. (923)

KUHLAU, FRIEDRICH (1786-1832)
Concertino for Piano and String
Orchestra in C, [arr.]
(Grieshaber) string orch,pno solo
ZINNEB ZI 7 f.s.   (924)

KULESHA, GARY (1953-)
Youth Orchestra Exercises
3(pic).1.2.1. 2.2.3.0. 2perc,pno,
strings CAN.MUS.CENT.   (925)

KURPIE FOLK SONG see Urbaniak, Michal

LADY BETTY COCHRAN'S MINUET [ARR.] see
Newton, E.

LADYBUG ON A CAROUSEL see Hubbell, Fred
M.

LAMENT, FOR VIOLONCELLO AND ORCHESTRA
see Fischer, Irwin

LANCEN, SERGE (1922-)
Carte Postale No. 1: Lille Octobre
1984
2.2+opt English horn.2+opt bass
clar.0.2alto sax.opt tenor
sax.opt baritone sax. 2.2.1.1.
perc,gtr,opt acord,pno/harp/elec
org,strings [3'10"] sc,pts
BILLAUDOT f.s.   (926)

LAND OF HOPE AND GLORY [ARR.] see
Elgar, [Sir] Edward (William)

LAND OF LIBERTY
(Frost, Robert S.) 2.1.2.1. 2.2.1.1.
timp,2perc,opt pno,strings [2'30"]
(gr. II) set KENDOR 10075 $25.00,
and up   (927)
(Frost, Robert S.) string orch,opt
pno [2'30"] (gr. II) sets KENDOR
$16.00, and up   (928)

LANDOWSKI, MARCEL (1915-)
Pour Les Orchestrades
4.2.2.2. 4.4.3.1. 3perc,harp,pno,
strings [15'] SALABERT sc f.s.,
pts f.s.   (929)

LANGDON OVERTURE see Hughes-Jones,
Llifon

LAREDO [ARR.] see Williams, Clifton

LARGHETTO , [ARR.] see Handel, George
Frideric

LARGHETTO, MINI, [ARR.] see Handel,
George Frideric

LATHAM, WILLIAM PETERS (1917-)
Jubilee
(med diff) set SHAWNEE J-131 $45.00
(930)

LATHAM SUITE see Kirk, Theron Wilford

LATIN AMERICAN ALBUM *CCU
(Stone, David) 2.0.2.0. 0.2.0.0. pno,
strings (med easy) set BOOSEY
$33.00, and up optional parts for
additional winds and percussion are
available   (931)

LATIN AMERICANA, [ARR.] *CCU
(Naylor, Frank) 2fl,2clar,2trp,perc,
pno,strings (med diff) sc,pts
BOSWORTH f.s.   (932)

LAUGHING SONG see Rafter, Leonard

LAWRANCE, BRUCE
Space Travellers
string orch (easy) CHESTER CH 55631
sc $7.25, pts $27.25   (933)

LECLAIR, JEAN MARIE (1697-1764)
Theme And Extension [arr.]
(Bauernschmidt, Robert) [3'15"]
(med) set SHAWNEE J-84 $18.00
(934)

LECUONA, ERNESTO (1896-1963)
Comparsa, La [arr.]
(Gould, Morton) 2.2.3+bass
clar.1.2sax. 2.3.3.1. perc,harp,
cel,strings (med) set KALMUS
A6726 $22.00, and up   (935)

Danza Lucumi [arr.]
(Guenther) 2(pic).2.2.2.2sax.
4.3.3.1. perc,harp,strings,vln

LECUONA, ERNESTO (cont'd.)

    solo (med easy) set KALMUS A6457
    $22.00, and up   (936)

    Gitanerias [arr.] (from Andalucia
    Suite)
    (Gould, Morton) 2.2.2+bass
    clar.1.4sax. 2.3.3.1. perc,harp,
    cel,gtr,strings (med diff) set
    KALMUS A6721 $30.00, and up (937)

LEFEBVRE, CLAUDE (1931-   )
  Tourbillonnements
    2.1.2.1. 2.2.2.0. 3perc,strings
    [5'] SALABERT sc f.s., pts f.s.
                                  (938)

LEGEND, [ARR.] see Tchaikovsky, Piotr
  Ilyich

LEGRAND, MICHEL (1932-   )
  Umbrellas Of Cherbourg: Highlights
    [arr.]
    (Muller) CHERRY 24005 $20.00 (939)

LEHAR, FRANZ (1870-1948)
  Merry Widow, The: Selections [arr.]
    (Isaac) string orch (gr. III) set
    HIGHLAND $20.00, and up   (940)

LEIGH, MITCH (1928-   )
  Man Of La Mancha: Selections [arr.]
    (Lang, Philip) (gr. III) CHERRY
    580-03765 $35.00   (941)

LEIGHTON, KENNETH (1929-1988)
  Dance Suite In D *Op.53
    3.2.2.2. 4.3.3.1. timp,3perc,
    strings [15'] NOVELLO sc
    09.0097.04.00 f.s., pts
    09.0097.04.06 f.s.   (942)

LEISTNER-MAYER, ROLAND (1945-   )
  Concerto Concitato II
    string orch ZINNEB ZI 17 f.s. (943)

LENNON, JOHN (1940-1980)
  Eleanor Rigby [arr.] (composed with
    McCartney, [John] Paul)
    MIDDLE MK 18 f.s.   (944)

  I Want To Hold Your Hand [arr.]
    (Rosenhaus) string orch [3'] (med)
    LEONARD-US $35.00   (945)

  Michelle [arr.] (composed with
    McCartney, [John] Paul)
    (Caponegro, John) string orch,opt
    perc,opt pno [3'50"] (gr. II)
    sets KENDOR $16.00, and up (946)
    (Lowden) string orch LEONARD-US
    04849826 $20.00   (947)

  Ob-La-Di, Ob-La-Da [arr.] (composed
    with McCartney, [John] Paul)
    MIDDLE MK 14 f.s.   (948)

  Penny Lane [arr.] (composed with
    McCartney, [John] Paul)
    MIDDLE MK 19 f.s.   (949)

  When I'm Sixty-Four [arr.] (composed
    with McCartney, [John] Paul)
    MIDDLE MK 15 f.s.   (950)

  Yellow Submarine [arr.] (composed
    with McCartney, [John] Paul)
    MIDDLE MK 16 f.s.   (951)

  Yesterday [arr.] (composed with
    McCartney, [John] Paul)
    MIDDLE MK 13 f.s.   (952)
    (Riggio, Donald) string orch,opt
    pno,opt perc (gr. II) sc,pts
    JENSON 502-25010 $20.00   (953)

LENTO AND ALLEGRETTO [ARR.] see Sor,
  Fernando

LEONCAVALLO, RUGGIERO (1858-1919)
  Mattinata [arr.]
    (Carlin, Sidney) string orch,pno
    CARLIN sc $3.00, sets $17.00, and
    up   (954)

LEROY ANDERSON FOR STRINGS [ARR.] see
  Anderson, Leroy

LET IT SNOW [ARR.] see Styne, Jule
  (Jules Stein)

LET THE EARTH RESOUND, [ARR.] see
  Purcell, Henry

LET THE RIVER RUN [ARR.] see Simon,
  Carly

LEVENSON, DAVID
  Homage To Bach
    string orch (gr. V) KJOS set SO-67B
    $28.00, sc SO-67F $3.00   (955)

LEVIN, RAMI (1954-   )
  Kinder Suite
    string orch (easy) TCAPUB sc $5.00,
    set $15.00, pts $.75, ea.   (956)

LIFE FOR THE CZAR, A [ARR.] see Glinka,
  Mikhail Ivanovich

LIGHT CAVALRY OVERTURE [ARR.] see
  Suppe, Franz von

LIGHT UP THE ORCHESTRA *CC10U
  (Applebaum, Samuel; Ployhar)
    1.1.2.1.alto sax.tenor sax.
    2.2.1.1. timp,perc,pno,strings
    BELWIN sc $7.50, pts $2.95, ea.,
    kbd pt $4.00   (957)

LIL' GRITS see Fletcher, Gary

LINCKE, PAUL (1866-1946)
  Glow Worm [arr.]
    (Gould, Morton) 2.2.2.1.4sax.
    2.3.3.0. perc,harp,gtr,strings
    (med easy) set KALMUS A6025
    $32.00, and up   (958)

LINCOLN
  Repasz Band [arr.]
    (McLeod) string orch [3'] (gr. III)
    TRN $30.00   (959)

LINDBERGH JUBILEE see Bencriscutto,
  Frank Peter Anthony

LIONEL RICHIE IN CONCERT [ARR.] see
  Richie, Lionel

LISZT, FRANZ (1811-1886)
  Arbre De Noel, L' [arr.]
    fl,2clar,3sax,bsn,strings sc,pts
    LEMOINE f.s.   (960)

  Hungarian Rhapsodie No.2 [arr.]
    (McLeod, James) string orch (gr.
    III) set HIGHLAND $29.00   (961)

  Preludes, Les, [arr.]
    (Leidig, Vernon) 2.1.2.1.opt alto
    sax.opt tenor sax. 2.3.3.1. timp,
    perc,strings (gr. IV) set KJOS
    WO4B $35.00   (962)

LISZT CHRISTMAS SUITE [ARR.]
  (Leidig, Vernon) string orch (gr.
    III) set HIGHLAND $20.00, and up
                                 (963)

LITTLE BIT OF...TIME...SPACE, A see
  Adler, Samuel Hans

LITTLE BOW PEEP see Chase, Bruce

LITTLE BROWN JUG
  (Davis, Albert O.) sets LUDWIG
    BGS-107 $20.00, and up   (964)

LITTLE DRUMMER BOY [ARR.] see Davis,
  Katherine K.

LITTLE KLEZMER MUSICK, A [ARR.]
  (Alshin, Harry A.) string orch,opt
    perc,opt pno [3'20"] (gr. II) set
    KENDOR 9223 $23.00, and up (965)

LITTLE RECRUITING DANCE see Kokai,
  Rezsö

LITTLE SPRING MUSIC, A [ARR.] see
  Vivaldi, Antonio, Concerto, Op. 8,
  No. 1, [arr.]

LITTLE SUITE see Hurd, Michael

LITTLE SUITE [ARR.] see Gurlitt,
  Cornelius

LITTLE SUMMER MUSIC, A [ARR.] see
  Vivaldi, Antonio, Concerto, Op. 8,
  No. 2, [arr.]

LITTLE WINTER MUSIC, A [ARR.] see
  Vivaldi, Antonio, Concerto, Op. 8,
  No. 4, [arr.]

LITURGICAL MUSIC [ARR.] see
  Tchaikovsky, Piotr Ilyich

LITURGY see Carroll, James

LIVELY WALTZ, THE see Isaac, Merle John

LIVINGSTON, JAY HAROLD (1915-   )
  Silver Bells [arr.] (composed with
    Evans, Raymond Bernard)
    (Frost, Robert S.) string orch,opt
    pno [2'45"] (gr. I) sets KENDOR
    $14.00, and up   (966)
    (Lowden, Bob) (gr. II) WARNER
    575-30020 $30.00   (967)
    (Whitney, John) CPP 2792SB7X $20.00
                                 (968)

LIVRE DES PROGRESSIONS, VOL. 2 see
  Tosi, Daniel

LLANOS see Mauldin, Michael

LLOYD WEBBER, ANDREW (1949-   )
  Cats: Memory [arr.]
    sc,pts CHESTER CH 55675 $16.50
                                 (969)
    (Lang) string orch LEONARD-US
    04801478 $20.00   (970)

  Cats: Selections [arr.]
    (Lowden) LEONARD-US 04499886 $45.00
                                 (971)
  Don't Cry For Me, Argentina [arr.]
    (Rosenhaus) string orch LEONARD-US
    08720382 $35.00   (972)
  Evita: Highlights [arr.]
    (Lowden) MCA 00120093 $45.00 (973)

  Memory [arr.]
    (Chase) string orch (med easy)
    LEONARD-US 04849512 $18.00 (974)
    (Lowden) LEONARD-US 04500900 $28.50
                                 (975)
  Music Of The Night, The [arr.]
    (Lowden) string orch set LEONARD-US
    $20.00   (976)

  Phantom Of The Opera, The: Selections
    [arr.]
    (Custer) LEONARD-US 04501215 $55.00
                                 (977)
  Symphonic Selections [arr.]
    (Chase) LEONARD-US 04502000 $45.00
                                 (978)

LOEWE, FREDERICK (1904-1988)
  Tribute To Lerner And Loewe, A [arr.]
    (Rosenhaus) LEONARD-US 08720210
    $45.00   (979)

LOHENGRIN: CHOEUR DES FIANCAILLES
  [ARR.] see Wagner, Richard

LOHENGRIN: ELSA'S PROCESSION TO THE
  CATHEDRAL [ARR.] see Wagner,
  Richard

LONDONDERRY AIR [ARR.]
  (Hermann, Ralph) string orch (gr.
    III) set LAKES $17.50, and up (980)
  (Muller, J. Frederick) sets LUDWIG
    BGS-105 $20.00, and up   (981)

LOOSE, WILLIAM
  Real People March, The [arr.]
    (composed with Cadkin, Emil)
    (Caponegro, John) string orch,opt
    pno,opt perc [2'30"] (gr. II)
    sets KENDOR $16.00, and up (982)
    (Caponegro, John) 1.1.2.1.alto
    sax.tenor sax. 2.2.1.1. 2perc,opt
    pno,strings [2'30"] (gr. II) sets
    KENDOR $24.00, and up   (983)

LOVE, MIKE
  Kokomo [arr.] (composed with Melcher,
    Terry; Mckenzie, Scott)
    (Graham) string orch LEONARD-US
    08720200 $35.00   (984)

LOVE WILL CONQUER ALL [ARR.] see
  Richie, Lionel

LOWDEN, BOB
  Brianna
    string orch,opt pno [1'45"] (gr. I)
    KENDOR 8186 f.s.   (985)

  Pizz-A-Plenty
    string orch,opt pno [1'10"] (gr. I)
    KENDOR 8510 f.s.   (986)

LOWERING THE FLAG [ARR.] (from Concert
  In The Park)
    (Dardess, B.) string orch,opt pno
    [2'45"] (gr. I) BOOSEY sc $6.00,
    set $25.00, pts $2.50, ea.   (987)

LUCIO SILLA: OVERTURE [ARR.] see
  Mozart, Wolfgang Amadeus

LUCK O' THE IRISH
  (Frost, Robert) string orch,opt pno
    [3'30"] (gr. II) sets KENDOR
    $20.00, and up   (988)

LUCKY CHARM see Frost, Robert S.

LULLABY see Hofeldt, William

LULLY, JEAN-BAPTISTE (LULLI)
  (1632-1687)
  Amour Malade, L': Suite [arr.]
    4rec,2gtr,strings sc,pts LEMOINE
    f.s.   (989)

  Bourgeois Gentilhomme, Le: Overture
    [arr.]
    (Seay, Albert) string orch,pno/hpsd
    [5'30"] sc,pts LUDWIG STRO 19
    f.s.   (990)

  Gavotte, [arr.]
    (Isaac) string orch (med easy) set
    WYNN 6276 $14.00, and up   (991)

LULLY, JEAN-BAPTISTE (LULLI) (cont'd.)

King's Musicians, The [arr.]
(Seay, Albert) 2.2.2.2. 4.2.3.1.
timp,perc,strings [12'] set
LUDWIG LLE-71 $40.00, and up
(992)

Roland: Chaconne
(Hitchcock, H. Wiley) 2fl,strings
[6'] PETERS P66648 $6.00   (993)

LYRIC POEM see Forssmark, Karl A.

M TO THE THIRD POWER see Nunez, Carold

MCBETH, WILLIAM FRANCIS (1933-   )
Kaddish
3.2.3.2. 4.3.2.1. timp,perc,strings
[7'] set SOUTHERN $30.00   (994)

MACDOWELL, EDWARD ALEXANDER (1861-1908)
To A Wild Rose [arr.]
(Curnow, James) string orch (gr.
III) JENSON 502-20040 $30.00
(995)

MCKAY, GEORGE FREDERICK (1899-1970)
Sinfonia No. 1
(gr. II) WARNER 575-10023 $30.00
(996)

MCLEOD, JAMES (RED) (1912-   )
Andante Grazioso
string orch,opt pno [3'50"] (gr. I)
set KENDOR 8155 $19.00, and up
(997)

Andantino Cantabile
string orch,opt pno [3'] (gr. I)
set KENDOR 8156 $19.00, and up
(998)

Carousal
string orch [3'] (gr. II) TRN
$30.00   (999)

Contrasts For Strings
string orch,opt pno [3'25"] (gr. I)
set KENDOR 8235 $19.00, and up
(1000)

Festival March
string orch (gr. I) KJOS set
GSO-15B $22.00, sc GSO-15F $3.00
(1001)

Fiddle And Stomp
string orch,opt pno [2'20"] (gr.
II) set KENDOR $16.00, and up
(1002)

Fiddle Fiddle Fiddle
string orch,opt perc,opt pno (gr.
II) sets KENDOR $14.00, and up
(1003)

Fiddlin' Freddie
string orch (gr. II) sets KENDOR
$16.00, and up   (1004)

Galop
string orch,pno (gr. II) set TRN
$20.00   (1005)

San Sebastian
string orch,opt pno [2'45"] (gr.
IV) set KENDOR 9865 $24.00, and
up   (1006)

Serenata, La
string orch,opt pno [3'40"] (gr. I)
set KENDOR 8357 $19.00, and up
(1007)

Trinidad
string orch,opt pno,opt claves,opt
maracas, opt. Quijada, Opt. Guiro
[3'50"] (gr. III) set KENDOR 9925
$23.00, and up   (1008)

Waltz Etude
string orch,pno (gr. II) set TRN
$20.00   (1009)

Waltz Giocoso
string orch,opt pno [3'30"] (gr. I)
set KENDOR 8835 $19.00, and up
(1010)

MACMILLAN, JAMES (1959-   )
Into The Ferment, For Instrumental
Soloists And School Orchestra
[15']
2.2.2.2. 4.2.3.1. timp,perc,
strings,fl solo,ob solo,clar
solo,bsn solo,horn solo,trp
solo,trom solo,perc solo,harp
solo,2vln soli,vla solo,vcl
solo,db solo
UNIVER. perf mat rent   (1011)

MADAMA BUTTERFLY [ARR.] see Puccini,
Giacomo

MADDERMARKET SUITE see Cockshott,
Gerald Wilfred

MADISON'S MARCH [ARR.] see Reinagle,
Alexander

MADRID KID see Niehaus, Leonard

MADSEN, TRYGVE (1940-   )
Play
see Spill

Spill
"Play" 2.0.2.0. 0.2.0.0. timp,perc,
pno,db [2'] MUSIKK   (1012)

MAGIC MUSIC BOX see Heilmann, Francis

MAGIC OF LEROY ANDERSON, THE [ARR.] see
Anderson, Leroy

MAGNIFICAT [ARR.] see Vivaldi, Antonio

MAHLER, GUSTAV (1860-1911)
Bruder Martin, [arr.] (from Symphony
No.1)
(Rokos; Simpson) 2.1.2.1. 2.2.1.0.
timp,perc,strings (diff) sc,pts
BOSWORTH f.s.   (1013)

Moods Of Mahler's First Symphony
[arr.]
(Leidig, Vernon) (gr. III) set
HIGHLAND $37.00   (1014)

Song Of A Wayfarer [arr.]
(Goldsmith, Owen) string orch (med)
BELWIN BSO 00079 $35.00   (1015)

Symphony No. 1,Second Movement,
[arr.]
(Dackow, Sandra) string orch
[3'18"] (med) LUDWIG STRO-46
$45.00   (1016)

Symphony No. 3,Finale, [arr.]
(Leidig, Vernon) 2.1.2.1.alto
sax.tenor sax. 2.3.3.1. timp,
perc,strings [7'] (gr. III) KJOS
set WO-8B $35.00, sc WO-8F $3.00
(1017)

MAIN STREET MARCH see Frost, Robert S.

MALAGUENA see String Orchestra Pak No.
4

MAMLOK, URSULA (1928-   )
Divertimento For Young Players
2.0.2.1. 3.2.2.1. timp,perc,strings
[7'] (med easy) AM.COMP.AL. perf
mat rent   (1018)

Grasshoppers
3.2.2.3. 2.2.3.1. perc,strings [7']
(diff) sc AM.COMP.AL. $19.15
(1019)

MAN OF LA MANCHA: SELECTIONS [ARR.] see
Leigh, Mitch

MANCINI, HENRY (1924-   )
Henry Mancini For Strings, Vol. 1
[arr.] *CC11L
(Zinn, William) string orch BELWIN
sc EL 03596 $17.50, pts
EL 03597-03601 $5.50, ea. (1020)

Henry Mancini For Strings, Vol. 2
[arr.] *CC10L
(Zinn, William) string orch BELWIN
sc EL 03613 $17.50, pts
EL 03614-03618 $5.50, ea. (1021)

Moon River [arr.]
(Gold) (med) CPP $40.00   (1022)

Peter Gunn [arr.]
(Custer) (med easy) CPP 1470PB6X
$55.00   (1023)

Pink Panther, The [arr.]
(Custer) (med easy) CPP 2739PB6X
$55.00   (1024)

Thorn Birds, The: Theme [arr.]
(Rosenhaus, Steven) string orch
(gr. III) JENSON 502-20010 $20.00
(1025)

MANDARIN SWING [ARR.] see Henry,
Charles

MANDEL, JOHNNY ALFRED (1925-   )
Shadow Of Your Smile, The [arr.]
(from The Sandpiper)
(Sayre, Chuck) CPP TO410SB6 $55.00
(1026)

MANHIRE, WILSON
Dance Of The Dwarfs [arr.]
see Newton, E., Lady Betty
Cochran's Minuet [arr.]

Merry Haymakers [arr.]
see Dunhill, Thomas Frederick,
Morning Song [arr.]

MANIFESTATIONS, NO. 1: POUR ECHAPPER A
LA TELEVISION see Grisey, Gerard

MANIFESTATIONS, NO. 2: POUR TROUVER LE
SILENCE see Grisey, Gerard

MANIFESTATIONS, NO. 3: POUR OBTENIR UNE
AIRE DE JEUX see Grisey, Gerard

MAPLE LEAF RAG [ARR.] see Joplin, Scott

MARCH FROM "LOVE FOR THREE ORANGES"
[ARR.] see Prokofiev, Serge

MARCH FROM "MUSIC FOR CHILDREN" [ARR.]
see Prokofiev, Serge

MARCH GRANDE see Shaffer, David

MARCH OF HOMAGE [ARR.] see Grieg,
Edvard Hagerup

MARCH OF THE BOWMEN see Caponegro, John

MARCH OF THE DWARFS [ARR.] see Grieg,
Edvard Hagerup, Zur Der Zwerge
[arr.]

MARCH OF THE SIAMESE CHILDREN see
String Orchestra Pak No. 4

MARCH TO THE SCAFFOLD [ARR.] see
Berlioz, Hector (Louis)

MARCH TRIUMPHANT [ARR.] see Rusch

MARCHAND, LOUIS (1669-1732)
French Dance Suite, [arr.]
(Bauernschmidt, R.L.) LYDIAN ORCH
set $14.00, pts $.80, ea.   (1027)

MARCHE [ARR.] see Prokofiev, Serge

MARCHE MILITAIRE [ARR.] see Schubert,
Franz (Peter)

MAREZ OYENS, TERA DE (1932-   )
Divertimento
S rec,A rec,timp,Orff inst,gtr, 3
fiddles, tenorgamba sc DONEMUS
f.s.   (1028)

MARIANINA [ARR.]
(Magnusson, Daniel) string orch,pno
CARLIN sc $3.00, set $17.00, and up
(1029)

MARIE, GABRIEL (1852-1928)
Cinquantaine, La [arr.]
(Isaac) string orch (med easy) set
WYNN 6289 $18.00, and up   (1030)

MARKHAM, LEE
Florestina [arr.]
sc,pts LENGNICK f.s.   (1031)

Moorland And Torland [arr.]
sc,pts LENGNICK f.s.   (1032)

MARKS, JOHNNY D. (1909-1985)
Rockin' Around The Christmas Tree
Medley [arr.]
(Caponegro, John) string orch,opt
perc,opt pno [3'10"] (gr. I) sets
KENDOR $16.00, and up   (1033)

Rudolph-Holly Jolly Christmas Medley
[arr.]
(Caponegro, John) string orch,opt
perc,opt pno [2'15"] (gr. I) sets
KENDOR $16.00, and up   (1034)

MARRIAGE OF FIGARO: MON COEUR SOUPIRE
[ARR.] see Mozart, Wolfgang Amadeus

MARRIAGE OF FIGARO: OVERTURE, [ARR.]
see Mozart, Wolfgang Amadeus

MARRIAGE OF FIGARO: WEDDING PROCESSION
[ARR.] see Mozart, Wolfgang Amadeus

MARSH
Pizzicato Di Blue
string orch (med easy) sets WYNN
6080-7080 $14.00, and up   (1035)

Texas, Our Texas [arr.]
(Guenther) SOUTHERN $25.00   (1036)
(Wright) string orch SOUTHERN
$25.00   (1037)

MARTINI, [PADRE] GIOVANNI BATTISTA
(1706-1784)
Gavotte, [arr.]
sc,pts EMB 12838 f.s.   (1038)

MARTINI, GIOVANNI
see MARTINI, JEAN PAUL EGIDE

MARTINI, JEAN PAUL EGIDE
(SCHWARZENDORF) (1741-1816)
Gavotte, [arr.]
(Isaac) string orch (med easy) set
WYNN 6271 $18.00, and up   (1039)

MARTINO, DONALD JAMES (1931-   )
Divertisements [7']
2.2.2.2. 2.2.2.0. 2perc,pno,
strings
sc,pts DANTALIAN DSE 106 $40.00

MARTINO, DONALD JAMES (cont'd.)

                              (1040)

MARX
  Hold On To The Nights [arr.]
    (Gold) [4'10"] ALFRED 3421 $35.00
                         (1041)

MASQUES see Arel, Bülent

MASSENET, JULES (1842-1912)
  Angelus And Bohemian Festival [arr.]
    (from Scenes Pittoresques)
    (Leidig, Vernon) (gr. III) set
    HIGHLAND $39.00   (1042)

  Cid, Le: Aragonaise [arr.]
    (Isaac, Merle J.) string orch (gr.
    III) set HIGHLAND $29.00   (1043)

MASSER, MICHAEL (1941-   )
  Didn't We Almost Have It All [arr.]
    (Cerulli, Bob) (easy) CPP 2803DB7X
    $45.00   (1044)

  Greatest Love Of All, The [arr.]
    (Whitney) (med easy) CPP 5724GB6X
    $55.00   (1045)

MASSEUS, JAN (1913-   )
  Concertino for Accordion and
    Orchestra, Op. 62
    2.2.2.2. 2.2.2.1. timp,2perc,
    strings,acord solo [18'] DONEMUS
    perf mat rent   (1046)

MASTERPIECE, THE [ARR.] see Mouret,
  Jean Joseph

MASTERS IN THIS HALL [ARR.]
  (Frost, Robert S.) string orch,opt
    pno [1'] (gr. II) set KENDOR 9235
    $19.00, and up   (1047)

MATCH POINT see Walker, Gwyneth

MATCHMAKER see String Orchestra Pak No.
  5

MATESKY, RALPH (1913-1979)
  Odyssey In Strings, Vol. 2
    string orch,pno BELWIN EL 02347-53
    sc $7.50, pts $3.95, kbd pt $5.00
                          (1048)

MATTHEW'S MARCH see Shapiro, Marsha
  Chusmir

MATTINATA [ARR.] see Leoncavallo,
  Ruggiero

MATZ, RUDOLF (1901-   )
  Divertimento
    string orch set DOMINIS $23.00
                         (1049)
  Young String Players
    string orch set DOMINIS $19.00
                         (1050)

MAULDIN, MICHAEL
  High Places
    (gr. IV) KJOS set WO-10B $38.00, sc
    WO-10F $3.00   (1051)

  Llanos
    [4'] (gr. III) KJOS set GO-104B
    $35.00, sc GO-104F $3.00   (1052)

MAW, NICHOLAS (1935-   )
  Summer Dances
    3(pic).3.3.3. 4.3.3.1. timp,perc,
    pno,strings [24'] sc FABER F0712
    f.s., perf mat rent   (1053)

MAXWELL DAVIES, PETER
  see DAVIES, PETER MAXWELL

MAZAS, JACQUES-FEREOL (1782-1849)
  Concert March And Danse Antique
    [arr.] *Op.38
    (Isaac, Merle J.) string orch,pno
    BOURNE sc $4.50, set $22.50, and
    up   (1054)

MEACHAM
  American Patrol [arr.]
    (Caponegro, John) string orch,opt
    perc (gr. I) sets KENDOR $14.00,
    and up   (1055)
    (Sopkin) 1.1.2.1.3sax. 2.3.2.1.
    perc,strings (med easy) set
    KALMUS A6028 $28.00, and up
                          (1056)

MEDITATION [ARR.] see Glazunov,
  Alexander Konstantinovich

MEISTERSINGER, DIE: MARCH OF THE
  MEISTERSINGERS [ARR.] see Wagner,
  Richard

MEISTERSINGER, DIE: OVERTURE [ARR.] see
  Wagner, Richard

MELTING POT OVERTURE, FOR NARRATOR AND
  ORCHESTRA see Brandon, Seymour (Sy)

MEMOIRE DE MONTREAL see Hamilton, Fred

MEMORIES OF CHOPIN [ARR.] see Chopin,
  Frédéric

MEMORIES OF COVENT GARDEN [ARR.] see
  Strauss, Johann, [Jr.]

MEMORY see String Orchestra Pak No. 4

MEMORY [ARR.] see Lloyd Webber, Andrew

MENDELSSOHN, L.
  Polish, [arr.]
    (Turner) (easy) sc,pts BOSWORTH
    f.s.   (1057)

MENDELSSOHN-BARTHOLDY, FELIX
  (1809-1847)
  Barcarolle in G minor, [arr.]
    2rec,fl,2clar,2gtr,strings sc,pts
    LEMOINE f.s.   (1058)

  Elijah: Selections [arr.]
    (Adams, D.) string orch set ADAM
    8611 $20.00   (1059)

  Romances Sans Paroles, Deux [arr.]
    (Lacour) sc BILLAUDOT 576-00420
    $15.75   (1060)

  Sinfonia No. 9,Scherzo, [arr.]
    (Frost, Stephen) string orch
    [3'30"] (med diff) set SHAWNEE
    J-88 $10.00   (1061)

MENUET DU SEXTUOR, OP. 71 [ARR.] see
  Beethoven, Ludwig van

MENUETTS 1 & 2 AND GIGUE [ARR.] see
  Bach, Johann Sebastian

MERLE, JOHN
  see ISAAC, MERLE JOHN

MERRY GO RONDO see Anderson, Gerald

MERRY HAYMAKERS [ARR.] see Manhire,
  Wilson

MERRY WIDOW, THE: SELECTIONS [ARR.] see
  Lehar, Franz

MESSIAH: AND THE GLORY OF THE LORD
  [ARR.] see Handel, George Frideric

MESSIAH: HALLELUJAH CHORUS [ARR.] see
  Handel, George Frideric

METCALF, LEON V.
  Allegro
    string orch BELWIN BSO 00035 sc
    $3.50, set $15.00   (1062)

MEUNIER, GÉRARD (1928-   )
  Chateau Du Temps Perdu [arr.]
    (Cheucle) 1.1.1.0. 0.1.0.0. vibra,
    harp/pno,strings LEMOINE perf mat
    rent   (1063)

  Princesses [arr.]
    (Cheucle) 1.1.1.0.alto sax.
    0.1.0.0. perc,harp,strings
    LEMOINE perf mat rent   (1064)

MEXICAN SERENADE see Isaac, Merle John

MEYER, RICHARD
  On Walden Pond
    string orch (gr. III) set HIGHLAND
    $29.00   (1065)

MEYLAN, RAYMOND
  Assonances
    2.2.2.2. 1.0.0.0. strings PAN sc
    1105 f.s., pts 1105A f.s. (1066)

MICHAEL JACKSON SPECTACULAR, A
  (Rosenhaus, Steven) 2.1.2.1. 4.3.3.1.
    timp,perc,strings (gr. III) sc,pts
    JENSON 503-13010 $40.00   (1067)

MICHELLE [ARR.] see Lennon, John

MICKEY MOUSE MARCH [ARR.] see Dodd,
  Jimmie

MICRO FUGUE see Siennicki, Edmund John

MIGNARDISE, FOR SAXOPHONE AND ORCHESTRA
  see Devogel, Jacques

MIKADO, THE: BEHOLD THE LORD HIGH
  EXECUTIONER [ARR.] see Sullivan,
  [Sir] Arthur Seymour

MILES, RICHARD (1916-   )
  Coffee Song, The [arr.]
    (Stephen, Richard) string orch,opt
    pno [3'] (gr. II) sets KENDOR
    $16.00, and up   (1068)

MILIGRAM FOR STRINGS see Jastrzebska,
  Anna

MILLER, LEWIS MARTIN (1933-   )
  Overture To Tartuffe
    2(pic).2.2.2. 4.2.3.0. timp,perc,
    strings sets LUDWIG LLE-64
    $34.00, and up   (1069)

  Overture To The School For Wives
    2+pic.2.2.2. 4.2.3.0. timp,perc,
    strings [4'15"] (med diff) set
    SHAWNEE J-128 $38.00   (1070)

MILLIES, HANS
  Concertino In The Style Of Mozart,
    [arr.]
    (Rokos, K.W.) string orch,opt
    winds&timp (med diff) sc,pts
    BOSWORTH f.s.   (1071)

MILLS, FREDERICK ALLEN (KERRY)
  (1869-1948)
  Georgia Cakewalk [arr.]
    (Isaac) string orch (med easy) set
    WYNN 6291-7291 $14.00, and up
                         (1072)
  Red Wing [arr.]
    (Fishburn, Kathy; Luman, Virginia)
    string orch (gr. II) set TRN
    $20.00   (1073)
    (Isaac) (med) set WYNN 4278-5278
    $28.00, and up   (1074)
    (Isaac) string orch (med) set WYNN
    6400-7400 $18.00, and up (1075)
    (McLeod, James) string orch (gr.
    II) sets KENDOR $16.00, and up
                         (1076)
  Whistlin' Rufus [arr.]
    (McLeod, James) string orch,opt pno
    [1'50"] (gr. III) set KENDOR 9938
    $24.00, and up   (1077)

MINIATURE SUITE see Forbes, Patrick

MINKUS, LÉON (FYODOROVICH) [ALOIS;
  LOUIS] (1826-1917)
  Don Quixote: "Pas De Deux", [arr.]
    (Naylor, F.) 1.1.2.1. 2.2.3.0.
    perc,pno,strings (diff) sc,pts
    BOSWORTH f.s.   (1078)

MINOR VARIATIONS see Shapiro, Marsha
  Chusmir

MINUET GRACIEUSE [ARR.] see Zilcher, P.

MINUET IN G [ARR.] see Beethoven,
  Ludwig van

MINUETTO ANTICO see Quagenti, Samuel

MINUETTO [ARR.] see Bolzoni, Giovanni

MIRROR IT see Åm, Magnar

MISERABLES, LES: SELECTIONS [ARR.] see
  Schonberg, Claude-Michel

MISS MCCLOUD'S REEL [ARR.]
  (McLeod, James) string orch (gr. III)
    set HIGHLAND $29.00   (1079)

MISSAL, JOSHUA M. (1915-   )
  Celebration Suite
    string orch (gr. III) KJOS set
    GSO-17B $25.00, sc GSO-17F $3.00
                         (1080)

MISSION, THE [ARR.] see Williams, John
  T.

MISTAK
  Circus Suite
    string orch (gr. II) set HIGHLAND
    $29.00   (1081)

MR. ROBERTS: SUITE see Waxman, Franz

MISTLETOE MEMORIES see Fletcher, Gary

MITCHELL, REX (1929-   )
  Holiday For Orchestra
    2.2.3.2. 4.4.3.1. timp,perc,strings
    [5'] (med diff) set SHAWNEE J-127
    $35.00   (1082)

  Starflight Overture
    2(pic).2.2+bass clar.2. 4.3.2.1.
    timp,perc,strings sets LUDWIG
    LLE-65 $37.50, and up   (1083)

MIXTUNES I *CCU
  (Foxley, Simon) string orch,opt pno
    (gr. II) set BOOSEY $16.00 (1084)

MODAL SUITE see Haugland, A. Oscar

MODERN CHRISTMAS CLASSICS
  (Caponegro, John) string orch,perc,
    opt pno [5'20"] (gr. II) sets
    KENDOR $22.00, and up   (1085)

MOLDAU, THE, [ARR.] see Smetana,
  Bedrich

MOLDAU, THE: COUNTRY WEDDING [ARR.] see
  Smetana, Bedrich

MOLLER, FRIEDRICH W.
Happy Wanderer [arr.]
string orch sc,pts BOSWORTH f.s.
(1086)

(Rokos, K.W.) 1.1.2.1. 1.1.1.0.
timp,strings (easy) sc,pts
BOSWORTH f.s. (1087)

MONAR, A.J.
Joyous Morn, A *see TWO PIECES FOR
STRING ORCHESTRA

MONTEVERDI, CLAUDIO (ca. 1567-1643)
Sinfonia Et Toccata [arr.]
see Haydn, [Franz] Joseph, Symphony
No. 94, Minuet, [arr.]

MONTI, VITTORIO
Csardas, For Violin And String
Orchestra [arr.]
(Fishburn; Luman) string orch,vln
solo [6'] (gr. V) TRN $40.00
(1088)
Monti Csardas, The [arr.]
(McLeod) string orch KJOS set
GSO-19B $25.00, sc GSO-19F $3.00
(1089)

MONTI CSARDAS, THE [ARR.] see Monti,
Vittorio

MOODS [ARR.] see Bartók, Béla

MOODS OF A SHAKER HYMN [ARR.]
(Alshin, Harry) string orch [3'] (gr.
II) set KENDOR 9295 $23.00, and up
(1090)
MOODS OF MAHLER'S FIRST SYMPHONY [ARR.]
see Mahler, Gustav

MOODS OF RACHMANINOFF [ARR.] see
Rachmaninoff, Sergey Vassilievich

MOON RIVER [ARR.] see Mancini, Henry

MOONLIGHT SLEIGH RIDE see Fletcher,
Gary

MOONLIGHTING: THEME [ARR.] see
Holdridge, Lee Elwood

MOORLAND AND TORLAND [ARR.] see
Markham, Lee

MOORLAND FIDDLERS see Wood, Arthur

MORE see String Orchestra Pak No. 5

MORE CHRISTMAS CAROLS FOR STRINGS
[ARR.]
(Caponegro, John) string orch (gr. I)
set KENDOR 8465 $24.00, and up
(1091)
MORENO TORROBA, FEDERICO (1891-1982)
Gardens Of Granada
2(pic).1.2.1.2sax. 2.2.3.0. perc,
harp,strings (med easy) set
KALMUS A6027 $14.50, and up
(1092)
MORNING SONG [ARR.] see Dunhill, Thomas
Frederick

MORODER, GIORGIO
Flashdance ... What A Feeling [arr.]
(Rosenhaus) string orch LEONARD-US
04849175 $18.00 (1093)

MORRIS, STEVLAND (STEVIE WONDER)
(1950-   )
I Just Called To Say I Love You
[arr.]
(Whitney) (easy) CPP 3025IB7X
$40.00 (1094)

MOSAICS see Feese, Francis L.

MOSIER, KIRT N.
Funky Fingers
string orch (gr. II) KJOS set
SO-83B $22.00, sc SO-83F $3.00
(1095)
MOSS, PIOTR (1949-   )
Poem for Violoncello and Orchestra
2.2.2.2. 1.1.1.0. perc,strings,vcl
solo [7'] sc,pts BILLAUDOT f.s.
(1096)
MOSTLY TCHAIKOVSKY
(Alshin, Harry A.) string orch (gr.
II) KENDOR 9297 f.s. [3'25]
contains: Glinka, Mikhail
Ivanovich, Polka [arr.];
Tchaikovsky, Piotr Ilyich, In
Church [arr.]; Tchaikovsky, Piotr
Ilyich, Mazurka [arr.];
Tchaikovsky, Piotr Ilyich,
Russian Song [arr.] (1097)

MOURET, JEAN JOSEPH (1682-1738)
Masterpiece, The [arr.]
(Cerulli, Bob) (gr. II) WARNER
575-30017 $30.00 (1098)
(Lowden, Bob) (gr. III) WARNER
575-40022 $30.00 (1099)

Rondeau [arr.] *see BAROQUE SUITE
NO. 1

MOURET, JEAN JOSEPH (cont'd.)

Rondo, [arr.]
(Leidig) (theme from Masterpiece
Theatre) set HIGHLAND $20.00, and
up (1100)

MOUSSORGSKY, MODEST PETROVITCH
see MUSSORGSKY, MODEST PETROVICH

MOVIN' ALONG see Frost, Robert S.

MOZART, LEOPOLD (1719-1787)
Sleigh Ride [arr.] *see THREE
CHRISTMAS CLASSICS

MOZART, WOLFGANG AMADEUS (1756-1791)
Adagio Favorito [arr.]
(deRubertis) string orch FITZSIMONS
F0551 set $12.00, sc $3.00, pts
$2.00, ea. (1101)

Air And Variation [arr.]
see Three Pieces By Mozart

Allegro [arr.] (from Sonata Facile)
(Riggio, Donald) string orch (gr.
III) JENSON 502-19060 $30.00
(1102)
Andante, [arr.] (from Quintet, K.
614)
(easy) sc,pts BOSWORTH f.s. (1103)

Best Of Mozart, The [arr.]
(Applebaum, Samuel; Paradise, Paul)
string orch BELWIN sc EL 03242
$17.50, pts EL 03243-03247 $5.50,
ea. (1104)

Classical Overture [arr.]
(Applebaum, Samuel; Ployhar, James)
set BELWIN CO00180 $25.00 (1105)

Concerto No. 1 for Violin and
Orchestra, [arr.]
(Rokos, K.W.) string orch,opt
winds,timp (diff) sc,pts BOSWORTH
f.s. (1106)

Contredanse Et Rondeau [arr.] (from
Divertimento, K. 213)
(Dackow, Sandra) string orch (easy)
LUDWIG STRO 49 $30.00 (1107)

Divertimento No. 4, [arr.]
(Klotman, Robert) 2.1.2.1.opt alto
sax. 2.2.1.1. pno,strings (gr.
II) BELWIN CO 00188 $40.00 (1108)

Don Giovanni: Overture [arr.]
(Isaac) BELWIN CO00160 sc $5.00,
set $30.00 (1109)

Epistle Sonata [arr.]
(Davison) string orch sc,pts
BOSWORTH f.s. (1110)

Finta Giardiniera, La: Overture
[arr.]
(Lacour, Guy) 2.2+opt English
horn.2+opt bass clar.0.2alto
sax.opt tenor sax.opt baritone
sax. 2.2.1.1. perc,gtr,opt acord,
pno/harp/elec org,strings sc,pts
BILLAUDOT f.s. contains also:
Schubert, Franz (Peter), Marche
Militaire [arr.] (1111)

Galimathias Musicum [arr.] *K.32
(Maasz, G.) sc,pts PELIKAN PE 941
f.s. (1112)

German Dance [arr.]
(Caponegro, John) string orch,opt
pno [2'] (gr. I) sets KENDOR
$14.00, and up (1113)
*see MUSETTE AND DANCE

Kleine Nachtmusik, Eine: Menuett
[arr.]
(Lacour, Guy) "Petite Musique De
Nuit: Menuet [arr.]" sc,pts
BILLAUDOT f.s. contains also:
Mozart, Wolfgang Amadeus,
Marriage Of Figaro: Mon Coeur
Soupire [arr.], "Noces De Figaro:
Mon Coeur Soupire [arr.]" (1114)

Lucio Silla: Overture [arr.]
(Dackow, Sandra) string orch
[3'30"] (med) LUDWIG STRO-41
$35.00 (1115)

Marriage Of Figaro: Mon Coeur Soupire
[arr.]
see Mozart, Wolfgang Amadeus,
Kleine Nachtmusik, Eine: Menuett
[arr.]

Marriage Of Figaro: Overture, [arr.]
(Isaac, Merle J.) 2.2.3.2. 2.2.2.0.
timp,strings BELWIN sc $4.00, set
$25.00 (1116)

MOZART, WOLFGANG AMADEUS (cont'd.)

Marriage Of Figaro: Wedding
Procession [arr.]
(Errante, Belisario) [3'] (gr. III)
set MOSAIC M020 $26.00, and up
(1117)
(Kindler) 2.2.2.2. 2.2.1.0. timp,
strings (easy) set KALMUS A6053
$15.00, and up (1118)

Minuet, [arr.] (from Quintet In C)
(Dasch) string orch FITZSIMONS
F0558 set $12.00, sc $3.00, pts
$2.00, ea. (1119)

Minuet, K. 24, [arr.]
(Rokos, K.W.) (easy) sc,pts
BOSWORTH f.s. (1120)

Mozart In Miniature [arr.]
(Forbes) string orch (med easy)
CHESTER CH 55572 sc $7.25, pts
$16.50 (1121)

Noces De Figaro: Mon Coeur Soupire
[arr.] *see Mozart, Wolfgang
Amadeus, Kleine Nachtmusik, Eine:
Menuett [arr.]

Petite Musique De Nuit: Menuet [arr.]
see Kleine Nachtmusik, Eine:
Menuett [arr.]

Petits Riens, Les [arr.]
(Fodor, A.) 2fl.2ob,strings sc,pts
EMB 12301 f.s. (1122)
(Gordon, Philip) string orch,opt
pno PRESSER 116-40020 set $15.00,
pts $1.00, ea., sc $5.00 (1123)

Premier Menuet [arr.]
see Chopin, Frédéric, Tristesse
[arr.]

Rondo, [arr.] (from Divertimento No.
17)
(Isaac, Merle J.) string orch (gr.
III) set HIGHLAND $20.00, and up
(1124)
(Sheinberg) string orch (gr. IV)
SHAWNEE J-141 $9.00 (1125)

Serenade No. 9,Finale, [arr.]
(Dackow, Sandra) string orch
[3'45"] ("Posthorn", med) LUDWIG
STRO-34 $40.00 (1126)

Sonatina No. 6, [arr.]
(Rosen) string orch (gr. IV) KJOS
set SO-49B $30.00, sc SO-49F
$3.00 (1127)

Song From "Don Giovanni" [arr.]
see Three Pieces By Mozart

Spring Rondo, [arr.]
(Collins, A.) 2fl,2rec,strings,opt
winds&timp (med diff) sc,pts
BOSWORTH f.s. (1128)

Suite 1772, [arr.]
(Rokos, K.W.) string orch,opt
winds&timp (diff) sc,pts BOSWORTH
f.s. (1129)

Symphony in G minor,First Movement,
[arr.]
(Isaac, Merle J.) 2.2.3.2. 2.2.2.0.
timp,perc,strings BELWIN sc
$5.00, set $30.00 (1130)

Symphony in G minor, Minuet, [arr.]
(Isaac, Merle J.) BELWIN sc $4.00,
set $20.00 (1131)

Symphony No. 10 in G, [arr.]
(Dackow, Sandra) string orch (med)
LUDWIG STRO 51 $30.00 (1132)

Symphony No. 12 in G, K. 110,First
Movement, [arr.]
(Dackow, Sandra) string orch
[4'35"] (med) LUDWIG STRO-40
$30.00 (1133)
(Isaac) (med) set WYNN 4270 $28.00,
and up (1134)
(Isaac) string orch (med) set WYNN
6274 $18.00, and up (1135)

Symphony No. 15 in G, K. 124,Fourth
Movement, [arr.]
(Isaac) string orch (med) set WYNN
6287 $18.00, and up (1136)

Symphony No. 25 in G minor,First
Movement, [arr.]
(Matesky, Ralph) (gr. IV) set
HIGHLAND $48.00 contains also:
Symphony No. 25 in G minor,Second
Movement, [arr.] (1137)

Symphony No. 25 in G minor,Second
Movement, [arr.]
see Symphony No. 25 in G minor,
First Movement, [arr.]

MOZART, WOLFGANG AMADEUS (cont'd.)

Symphony No. 25 in G minor,Third
Movement, [arr.]
(Matesky, Ralph) (gr. III) set
HIGHLAND $32.00, and up contains
also: Symphony No. 25 in G minor,
Fourth Movement, [arr.]   (1138)

Symphony No. 25 in G minor,Fourth
Movement, [arr.]
see Symphony No. 25 in G minor,
Third Movement, [arr.]

Symphony No. 29,First Movement,
[arr.]
(Frost, Robert S.) string orch
[7'40"] (gr. IV) set KENDOR 9907
$24.00, and up   (1139)

Symphony No. 40,First Movement,
[arr.]
(Rokos, K.W.) 2.2.2.2. 2.0.0.0.
strings (diff) sc,pts BOSWORTH
f.s.   (1140)

Symphony No. 40: Themes [arr.]
(Frost, Robert) string orch,opt pno
[3'15"] (gr. III) sets KENDOR
$19.00, and up   (1141)

Third Position Waltz [arr.] *see
SUITE OF WALTZES, A

Three Pieces By Mozart
(Auton, John; Auton, Christine)
string orch OXFORD 365968-9 sc
$6.25, pts $1.50, ea.
contains: Air And Variation
[arr.]; Song From "Don
Giovanni" [arr.]; Waltz [arr.]
(1142)

Turkish March [arr.]
(Isaac) string orch (med easy) set
WYNN 6295-7295 $14.00, and up
(1143)
(McLeod) string orch (gr. III) KJOS
set GSO-5B $25.00, sc GSO-5F
$3.00   (1144)

Waltz [arr.]
see Three Pieces By Mozart

MOZART IN MINIATURE [ARR.] see Mozart,
Wolfgang Amadeus

MRS. MADISON'S MINUET [ARR.] see
Reinagle, Alexander

MRS. ROBINSON [ARR.] see Sounds Of
Simon And Garfunkel, Vol. II

MÜLLER, J. FREDERICK
Valse Moderne
(Fink, Lorraine) string orch (med)
SHAWNEE set $9.00, pts $.75, ea.
(1145)

MÜLLER, J. FREDERICK, EDITOR *CC10L
String Orchestra Classics
string orch,pno LUDWIG sc SOC-47K
$8.00, kbd pt SOC-47J $4.00, pts
$3.00, ea.   (1146)

MULTIPLES see Stahmer, Klaus H.

MUSETTA'S WALTZ SONG [ARR.] see
Puccini, Giacomo

MUSETTE AND DANCE
(Klotman, Robert) 2.1.2.1.opt alto
sax. 2.2.1.1. timp,pno,strings (gr.
II) BELWIN CO 00196 $45.00
contains: Gluck, Christoph
Willibald, Ritter von, Musette
From "Armide" [arr.]; Mozart,
Wolfgang Amadeus, German Dance
[arr.]   (1147)

MUSETTE [ARR.] see Handel, George
Frideric

MUSIC FOR CHILDREN, VOL. 2 [ARR.] see
Bartók, Béla

MUSIC FOR CHILDREN, VOL. 2 [ARR.]
*CC8L
(McAlister) 1(pic).1(English
horn).1.1. 1.1.1.0. perc,strings
KALMUS A6324 sc $25.00, set $25.00,
perf mat rent contains 8 pieces by
Shostakovich and Kabalevsky (1148)

MUSIC FOR STRINGS AND KEYBOARD see
Purcell, Henry

MUSIC FOR YOUNG STRINGS, VOL. 1
(Spatz, Alice) string orch (med easy)
set SHAWNEE J-124 $10.00   (1149)

MUSIC FOR YOUNG STRINGS, VOL. 2
(Spatz, Alice) string orch (med) set
SHAWNEE J-126 $12.00   (1150)

MUSIC FROM ZANKA see Farkas, Ferenc

MUSIC OF THE NIGHT, THE [ARR.] see
Lloyd Webber, Andrew

MUSIC OMNIBOOK *CC16L
(Rimer, Robert H.; Siennicki, Edmund
J.) pts are available for fl, ob,
clar, bsn, alto sax, tenor sax,
horn, trp, cornet, trom, baritone
horn, tuba, perc, strings LUDWIG
f.s.   (1151)

MUSIC SCHOOL INTRODUCES ITSELF, A, VOL.
10 see Roeder, Toni, Musikschule
Stellt Sich Vor, Eine, Vol. 10

MUSICA SERENA see Farkas, Ferenc

MUSICAL BUFFET OF ALL-TIME FAVORITES, A
*CCUL
(McLeod) string orch,pno KJOS GL118
sc $8.95, pts $3.45, ea.   (1152)

MUSICAL HIGHLIGHTS FROM "ROCKY" [ARR.]
see Conti, Bill

MUSIKSCHULE STELLT SICH VOR, EINE, VOL.
10 see Roeder, Toni

MUSIQUE AU FEUTRE BLEU see Werner,
Jean-Jacques

MUSSORGSKY, MODEST PETROVICH
(1839-1881)
Hopak [arr.]
(Alshin, Harry) string orch (med)
BELWIN BSO 00074 $35.00   (1153)

Pictures At An Exhibition: The Great
Gate Of Kiev [arr.]
(Reibold) FITZSIMONS F0501 set
$45.00, sc $6.50, pts $2.00, ea.
(1154)

MY FAVORITE ICE CREAM IS CHOCOLATE see
Frost, Robert S.

MY FAVORITE THINGS [ARR.] see Rodgers,
Richard

MY HEART EVER FAITHFUL [ARR.] see Bach,
Johann Sebastian

MY LOVE, SHE'S BUT A LASSIE YET [ARR.]
see Folk-Songs For Strings, Set 1

MY WILD IRISH ROSE [ARR.] see Olcott,
Chauncey

MYERS, ROBERT (1941-   )
Fantasy And Allegro
string orch,vibra (med) TCAPUB sc
$8.00, set $25.00, pts $.75, ea.
(1155)

MYERS, THELDON (1927-   )
Unicorn, The
string orch set LAKES $20.00, and
up   (1156)

MYSTERIEUX ET INTENSE see Pinchard, Max

NABUCCO: OVERTURE [ARR.] see Verdi,
Giuseppe

NATIONAL EMBLEM MARCH [ARR.] see
Bagley, E.E.

NELHYBEL, VACLAV (1919-   )
Bohemian Suite
string orch [6'30"] CHRI ABC 30 sc
$2.50, set $22.00   (1157)

NELSON, STEVE
Frosty The Snow Man [arr.]
(Chase) string orch (easy) LEONARD-
US 04620690 $16.00   (1158)
(Holcombe) set LEONARD-US 04792274
$25.00   (1159)
(Holcombe) string orch set LEONARD-
US 04849200 $20.00   (1160)
(Rosenhaus) string orch LEONARD-US
08720204 $35.00   (1161)

NEUF IMAGES see Desportes, Yvonne

NEW RIVER TRAIN, THE [ARR.]
(Forsblad, Leland) string orch,opt
perc,opt pno [2'15"] (gr. I) set
KENDOR 8475 $19.00, and up   (1162)

NEW WORLD THEME [ARR.] see Dvořák,
Antonín

NEW YORK, NEW YORK: THEME [ARR.] see
Kander, John

NEWTON, E.
Belinda's Rigadoon [arr.]
see Zilcher, P., Minuet Gracieuse
[arr.]

NEWTON, E. (cont'd.)

Fanny's Delight [arr.]
see Dunhill, Thomas Frederick,
Irish Boy, The [arr.]

Lady Betty Cochran's Minuet [arr.]
(Twinn, Sidney) string orch sc,pts
LENGNICK f.s. contains also:
Manhire, Wilson, Dance Of The
Dwarfs [arr.]   (1163)

Shepherd In Love, The [arr.]
(Twinn, Sidney) string orch sc,pts
LENGNICK f.s. contains also:
Duncan, S., In The Days Of Drake
[arr.]   (1164)

NIEHAUS, LEONARD
Apron Strings
string orch,opt perc,opt pno
[2'30"] (gr. I) set KENDOR 8157
$19.00, and up   (1165)

Bow Ties
string orch,opt pno [3'] (gr. I)
set KENDOR 8182 $19.00, and up
(1166)

Bows And Arrows
string orch,opt perc,opt pno
[2'30"] (gr. I) set KENDOR 8185
$19.00, and up   (1167)

Carroll County
string orch,opt pno,opt perc
[3'55"] (gr. II) KENDOR 8962 f.s.
(1168)

Fiddlesticks
string orch,opt perc,opt pno
[2'30"] (gr. I) set KENDOR 8265
$19.00, and up   (1169)

Firefly Sky
string orch,opt pno,opt perc
[2'45"] (gr. I) set KENDOR 8268
$19.00, and up   (1170)

Fit As A Fiddle
string orch [2'25"] (gr. II) set
BARNHS 130-2133-00 $26.00   (1171)

Madrid Kid
string orch,opt perc,opt pno
[2'30"] (gr. I) set KENDOR 8400
$19.00, and up   (1172)

Rainbows
string orch,opt perc,opt pno
[2'30"] (gr. I) set KENDOR 8535
$19.00, and up   (1173)

Royalwood Overture
string orch,opt perc,opt pno [5']
(gr. II) set KENDOR 9437 $23.00,
and up   (1174)

String Beans
string orch,opt pno,opt perc
[2'15"] (gr. I) set KENDOR 8667
$19.00, and up   (1175)

String Fever
string orch [2'30"] (gr. II) set
BARNHS 130-2134-00 $26.00   (1176)

Stringumajig
string orch,opt perc,opt pno
[2'25"] (gr. I) KENDOR f.s.
(1177)

Theme and Variations
string orch,opt perc,opt pno
[2'55"] (gr. I) set KENDOR 8728
$19.00, and up   (1178)

Vagabond Strings
string orch,opt pno,opt perc
[2'20"] (gr. II) set KENDOR 9735
$19.00, and up   (1179)

NIGHT AT THE SYMPHONY, A *CCU
(McLeod, James) string orch KJOS
GL120 sc $9.95, pts $3.95, ea.
(1180)

NIGHT IN VIENNA, A *CCU
(McLeod) string orch,pno KJOS GL119
sc $9.95, pts $3.95, ea.   (1181)

NIGHT TRAIN [ARR.] see Forrest, Jimmy

NIGHTINGALE SANG IN BERKELEY SQUARE, A
[ARR.] see Karlin, Frederick James

NOBODY KNOWS THE TROUBLE I'VE SEEN
[ARR.]
(Alshin, Harry) string orch [2'45"]
(gr. II) set KENDOR 9318 $19.00,
and up   (1182)

NON PAPA, JACOBUS CLEMENS
see CLEMENS, JACOBUS

NORDIC LEGEND, A see Goldsmith, Owen

NORTH COUNTRY HOEDOWN see Stephan,
Richard

NORWEGIAN DANCES NOS. 2 AND 3 [ARR.]
see Grieg, Edvard Hagerup

NUNEZ, CAROLD
Bluegrass Country
string orch [3'30"] (med easy) set
SHAWNEE J-85 $15.00   (1183)

Chapter One
string orch (gr. III) KJOS set
SO-82B $25.00, sc SO-82F $3.00
(1184)

Convergence
string orch (gr. V) KJOS set SO-69B
$28.00, sc SO-69F $3.00   (1185)

Deja Vu
string orch [4'45"] (gr. III)
CONCERT W J-155 $22.00   (1186)

Friday Night
string orch [4'25"] (gr. IV)
SHAWNEE J-151 $25.00   (1187)

M To The Third Power
string orch [3'] set SHAWNEE J-138
$15.00   (1188)

NURSERY RHYME OVERTURE see Blake,
Howard

NUTCRACKER: SUITE [ARR.] see
Tchaikovsky, Piotr Ilyich

NUTCRACKER SUITE: DANCE OF THE SUGAR
PLUM FAIRY [ARR.] see Tchaikovsky,
Piotr Ilyich

NUTCRACKER SUITE: MOTHER GINGER [ARR.]
see Tchaikovsky, Piotr Ilyich

NUTCRACKER SUITE: RUSSIAN DANCE [ARR.]
see Tchaikovsky, Piotr Ilyich

NUTCRACKER SUITE: TREPAK [ARR.] see
Tchaikovsky, Piotr Ilyich

NUTCRACKER SUITE: WALTZ [ARR.] see
Tchaikovsky, Piotr Ilyich

NUTCRACKER: THEMES [ARR.] see
Tchaikovsky, Piotr Ilyich

OB-LA-DI, OB-LA-DA [ARR.] see Lennon,
John

OCCASIONAL SUITE, AN, [ARR.] see
Handel, George Frideric

OCEAN STAR A DREAMING SONG see Bedford,
David

ODDS AND ENDS see Frost, Robert S.

ODYSSEY IN STRINGS, VOL. 2 see Matesky,
Ralph

OFFENBACH, JACQUES (1819-1880)
Offenbach Melodies [arr.]
(McLeod) string orch (gr. III) set
HIGHLAND $20.00, and up   (1189)

Orpheus In The Underworld: Finale
[arr.]
(Dackow, Sandra) string orch,opt
perc [2'10"] (easy) LUDWIG
STRO-45 $50.00   (1190)

OFFENBACH MELODIES [ARR.] see
Offenbach, Jacques

OH, SUSANNA [ARR.] see Foster, Stephen
Collins

OKLAHOMA see String Orchestra Pak No. 5

OKLAHOMA: SELECTIONS [ARR.] see
Rodgers, Richard

OLCOTT, CHAUNCEY (1858-1932)
My Wild Irish Rose [arr.]
(Leidig, Vernon) (gr. I) set
HIGHLAND $31.00   (1191)

OLD CAROUSEL, THE see Goldsmith, Owen

OLD SCOTTISH MELODY [ARR.]
(Wiley) [2'14"] (gr. III) set TRN
$35.00   (1192)

OLIVER: OOM-PAH-PAH [ARR.] see Bart,
Lionel

OLYMPIC FANFARE AND THEME [ARR.] see
Williams, John T.

ON GOLDEN POND: THEME [ARR.] see
Grusin, David

ON THE STEPPES OF CENTRAL ASIA [ARR.]
see Borodin, Alexander Porfirievich

ON TOP OF OLD SMOKEY [ARR.]
(Clebanoff, Herman) string orch
DORABET D-145 f.s.   (1193)

ON WALDEN POND see Meyer, Richard

120 ALLEGRO PARKWAY see Frost, Robert
S.

OPEN STRING ROCK see Heilmann, Francis

OPERA BALLET [ARR.] see Grétry, André
Ernest Modeste

ORANGE BLOSSOMS [ARR.] see Friml,
Rudolf

ORCHALA, FOR VIOLONCELLO AND STRING
ORCHESTRA see Thirault, Marc-Didier

ORCHESTRA EXPERIENCE, THE *CCU
1.1.2.1.alto sax.tenor sax. 2.2.2.0.
perc,strings BELWIN FDL 814-834 sc
$7.50, pts $2.95, ea.   (1194)

ORDINARY PEOPLE: THEME [ARR.] see
Hamlisch, Marvin F.

ORIENTALE [ARR.] see Cui, César
Antonovich

ORPHEUS IN THE UNDERWORLD: FINALE
[ARR.] see Offenbach, Jacques

OUR DIRECTOR [ARR.] see Bigelow, F.E.

OUVERTURE "DE VIER TEMPERAMENTEN" see
Delft, Marc van

OVANIN, NIKOLA LEONARD (1911-   )
Four Movements For String Orchestra
string orch [9'45"] (med) set
SHAWNEE J-92 $14.00   (1195)

Poem for String Orchestra
string orch [6'30"] (med) set
SHAWNEE J-129 $16.00   (1196)

OVER THE RAINBOW [ARR.] see Arlen,
Harold

OVERTURE 1812 [ARR.] see Tchaikovsky,
Piotr Ilyich

OVERTURE FOR CHRISTMAS, AN see Benoy,
A.W.

OVERTURE FOR STRINGS see Fletcher, Gary

OVERTURE ON AN EXUBERANT TONE ROW see
Fischer, Irwin

OVERTURE TO TARTUFFE see Miller, Lewis
Martin

OVERTURE TO THE SCHOOL FOR WIVES see
Miller, Lewis Martin

OYENS, TERA DE MARZ
see MAREZ OYENS, TERA DE

PACHELBEL, JOHANN (1653-1706)
Canon [arr.]
(Gordon, Philip) PRESSER 116-40022
sc $3.00, set $20.00, pno-cond sc
$1.50, pts $1.00, ea.   (1197)

Canon: Theme [arr.]
(Caponegro, John) string orch,opt
pno [2'55"] (gr. II) set KENDOR
$17.00, and up   (1198)

PADILLA, JOSÉ (1889-1960)
Relicario, El [arr.]
(Isaac) (gr. III) set HIGHLAND
$28.00, and up   (1199)

PAGANINI, NICCOLO (1782-1840)
Variations On The 24th Caprice [arr.]
(Alshin, Harry) string orch (gr.
IV) set HIGHLAND $29.00   (1200)

PAIR OF SOKS, A see Frost, Robert S.

PALOMA, LA [ARR.]
(Clebanoff, Herman) string orch
DORABET D-151 f.s.   (1201)

PAPP, LAJOS (1935-   )
Scherzo
string orch sc,pts EMB 6664 f.s.
(1202)

PARADE OF THE WOODEN SOLDIERS [ARR.]
see Jessel, Leon

PARALLEL WORLDS see Tanenbaum, Elias

PASSACAGLIA AND FUGUE IN C MINOR [ARR.]
see Bach, Johann Sebastian

PASTEL see Vercken, François

PAT-A-PAN [ARR.] see Two Songs For The
Holidays

PATAPAN see Ryden, William

PATAPAN [ARR.]
(Day, Neil) 2.1.2.1. 0+baritone
horn.2.2.0. perc,strings [4']
(easy) UNIV.CR sc P68501 f.s., pts
P68502 f.s.   (1203)

PAVEY, SIDNEY
Clog Dance
2.1.3.1.3rec. 2.2.1.0. perc,pno,
strings (easy) sc,pts BOSWORTH
f.s.   (1204)

Russian Dance
(easy) sc,pts BOSWORTH f.s. (1205)

Variations On A French Theme
3.1.2.1.3rec. 2.2.1.0. timp,perc,
pno,strings (easy) sc,pts
BOSWORTH f.s.   (1206)

Windmills
2.1.3.1.2rec. 2.2.1.0. timp,perc,
pno,strings (easy) sc,pts
BOSWORTH f.s.   (1207)

PEACHERINE RAG [ARR.] see Joplin, Scott

PEACHTREE PROMENADE see Gillis, Don E.

PEANUT PARADE see Chase, Bruce

PENNY LANE [ARR.] see Lennon, John

PEPPERMINT POLKA see Frost, Robert S.

PERPETUAL MOTION see Errante, Belisario
Anthony see Fletcher, Gary see
Higgins, James

PERPETUAL MOTION [ARR.] see Bohm, Carl

PERSIAN MARCH [ARR.] see Strauss,
Johann, [Jr.]

PERSIAN MARKET SWING, [ARR.] see
Ketèlbey, Albert William

PETER GUNN [ARR.] see Mancini, Henry

PETIT TRAINEAU, LE see Frost, Robert S.

PETITE MUSIQUE DE NUIT: MENUET [ARR.]
see Mozart, Wolfgang Amadeus,
Kleine Nachtmusik, Eine: Menuett
[arr.]

PETITE OUVERTURE, UNE [ARR.] see Carr,
Benjamin

PETITE OVERTURE see Del Borgo, Elliot
A.

PETITE SUITE see Gibbs, Alan

PETITE SUITE FOR STRINGS
(Whear, Paul W.) string orch sets
LUDWIG STRO-3 $20.00, and up (1208)

PETITE SUITE: INTERMEZZO [ARR.] see
Borodin, Alexander Porfirievich

PETITE SUITE SUR UN CHORAL [ARR.] see
Bach, Johann Sebastian

PETITS RIENS, LES [ARR.] see Mozart,
Wolfgang Amadeus

PETRONE, JOHN
Also Sprach Whatshisname
1.1.2+bass clar.1. 2.2.2.1. 2perc,
gtr,strings (based on Richard
Strauss' "Also Sprach
Zarathustra") set LUDWIG CAR-104
$20.00   (1209)

C.P. Two Oh!
1.1.2+bass clar.1. 2.2.2.1. 2perc,
gtr,strings (based on theme from
"Chopin Prelude, Op. 20") set
LUDWIG CAR-103 $20.00   (1210)

Disco-Tinued
2.1.2+bass clar.1. 2.2.2.1. perc,
pno,gtr,strings (based on theme
from Schubert's "Unfinished
Symphony") set LUDWIG CAR-105
$20.00   (1211)

Goin' Baroque
1.1.2+bass clar.1. 2.2.2.1. 2perc,
opt gtr,strings (based on theme
from Bach's "Italian Concerto")
set LUDWIG CAR-102 $20.00   (1212)

PETRONE, JOHN (cont'd.)

Haydn Seek
1.1.2+bass clar.1. 2.2.2.1. 2perc,
opt gtr,strings (based on theme
from Haydn's "Surprise Symphony")
set LUDWIG CAR-101 $20.00   (1213)

PETTERSEN, NANCY
Four Miniatures
string orch (gr. III) BELWIN
BSO 00075 $35.00   (1214)

Hoedown
perc,pno,strings (gr. III) BELWIN
CO 00187 $30.00   (1215)

Symphonic Tribute
(med) BELWIN CO 00202 $50.00 (1216)

PHANTOM DANCE see Elledge, Chuck

PHANTOM OF THE OPERA, THE: SELECTIONS
[ARR.] see Lloyd Webber, Andrew

PICCADILLY, LE see Satie, Erik

PICKIN' PLEASURE see Ployhar

PICNIC IN THE PARK see Heilmann,
Francis

PICTURES AT AN EXHIBITION: THE GREAT
GATE OF KIEV [ARR.] see Mussorgsky,
Modest Petrovich

PIERPONT, JAMES (1822-1893)
Dueling Jingle Strings [arr.]
(Dabczynski, Andrew) string orch,
opt pno, opt rhythm instrument
[2'15"] (gr. III) BOOSEY sc
$8.00, set $30.00, pts $2.50, ea.
(1217)

Tintinabulations [arr.]
(Punwar, Katherine W.) 2.2.2.2.alto
sax.tenor sax. 3.3.3.1. 2perc,
strings [4'15"] (gr. III) KJOS
set O-1057B $38.00, sc O-1057F
$5.00   (1218)

PINCHARD, MAX (1928-   )
Mysterieux Et Intense
2.2.2.2. 0.0.0.0. vibra,strings
[3'] (from the series "feuilles
vives") BILLAUDOT perf mat rent
(1219)

PINEAPPLE UPSIDE-DOWN CAKEWALK see
Frost, Robert S.

PINK PANTHER, THE [ARR.] see Mancini,
Henry

PIRATE DANCE see Anderson, Leroy

PIRATES OF PENZANCE, THE: OVERTURE
[ARR.] see Sullivan, [Sir] Arthur
Seymour

PIRATES OF PENZANCE, THE: THREE PIECES
[ARR.] see Sullivan, [Sir] Arthur
Seymour

PIROUETTE see Gould, Morton

PIZZ-A-PLENTY see Lowden, Bob

PIZZA-TACO see Fletcher, Gary

PIZZICATI [ARR.] see Delibes, Léo

PIZZICATO DI BLUE see Marsh

PIZZICATO PIZZAZZ see Davis, Albert
Oliver

PLAY see Madsen, Trygve, Spill

PLAY A SIMPLE MELODY [ARR.] see Berlin,
Irving

PLAYFUL RONDO [ARR.] see Green, W.

PLOYHAR
Concerto For Faculty Vs Orchestra
(med easy) set WYNN 4018-5018
$22.00, and up   (1220)

Pickin' Pleasure
BELWIN CO 00184 sc $4.00, set
$25.00   (1221)

PLUCKY AND BOWDIDDLE see Ward, Norman

POET AND PEASANT OVERTURE [ARR.] see
Suppe, Franz von

POLISH, [ARR.] see Mendelssohn, L.

POLLY-WOLLY-DOODLE [ARR.]
(Richardson, Clive) 2.1.2.1.2sax.
2.2.2.0. timp,drums,strings (med
easy) set KALMUS A6033 $26.50, and
up   (1222)

POMP AND CIRCUMSTANCE [ARR.] see Elgar,
[Sir] Edward (William)

POMP AND CIRCUMSTANCE MARCH NO. 4
[ARR.] see Elgar, [Sir] Edward
(William)

PONGRACZ, ZOLTAN (1912-   )
Three Little Pieces
sc,pts EMB 5860 f.s.   (1223)

POPCORN POLKA see Chase, Bruce

PORGY AND BESS: SELECTIONS [ARR.] see
Gershwin, George

PORTNOFF, LEO
Concertino, Op. 13, [arr.]
string orch,opt winds&timp (med
easy) sc,pts BOSWORTH f.s.   (1224)

POSTCARDS GREETINGS see Takacs, Jenö,
Postkartengrusse

POSTKARTENGRUSSE see Takacs, Jenö

POUDRE D'OR see Satie, Erik

POULE SYMPHONY, LA see Haydn, [Franz]
Joseph

POUR LES ORCHESTRADES see Landowski,
Marcel

POUR LES TRILLES ET LES NOTES REPETEES
see Werner, Jean-Jacques

PRAGUE STUDENTS' MARCH see Smetana,
Bedrich

PRAYER see Gustafson, Dwight Leonard

PRAYER FOR AMERICA see Carlin, Sidney

PRAYER OF THANKSGIVING *see SONGS OF
THANKSGIVING see Songs Of
Thanksgiving

PRELUDE AND CAPRICCIO see Errante,
Belisario Anthony

PRELUDE AND DANCE [ARR.] see Corelli,
Arcangelo

PRELUDE AND FUGUE FOR FUN see Hedges,
Anthony John

PRELUDE AND FUGUE FOR YOUNG STRINGS see
Sebesky, Gerald John

PRELUDE AND MAZURKA [ARR.] see Delibes,
Léo

PRELUDE AND POLKA [ARR.] see
Shostakovich, Dmitri

PRELUDE TO A CEREMONY see Taylor,
Herbert F.

PRELUDE TO A SUMMER'S DAWN see Presser,
William Henry

PRELUDES, LES, [ARR.] see Liszt, Franz

PRELUDIO E DANZETTA, [ARR.] see
Corelli, Arcangelo

PREMIER MENUET [ARR.] see Mozart,
Wolfgang Amadeus

PREMIERE IMPROVISATION A RAPHAELE see
Hurel, Philippe

PRESSER, WILLIAM HENRY (1916-   )
Prelude To A Summer's Dawn
[5'30"] TENUTO 196-00004 sc $5.00,
set $25.00, pts $1.00, ea. (1225)

PRESTO PIZZICATO [ARR.] see Böhm, Georg

PREVITE, FRANK
I've Had The Time Of My Life [arr.]
(Cerulli, Bob) string orch CPP
2874TB4X $25.00   (1226)
(Cerulli, Bob) (easy) CPP 2874TB7X
$45.00   (1227)

PRINCE IGOR: POLOVTSIAN DANCE, [ARR.]
see Borodin, Alexander Porfirievich

PRINCESSES [ARR.] see Meunier, Gérard

PROKOFIEV, SERGE (1891-1953)
Gavotte, [arr.]
string orch (med) set WYNN 6282
$14.00, and up   (1228)

March From "Love For Three Oranges"
[arr.]
(McLeod) string orch (gr. IV) KJOS
set GSO-4B $22.00, sc GSO-4F
$3.00   (1229)

March From "Music For Children"
[arr.]
(Levenson) string orch (gr. IV)

PROKOFIEV, SERGE (cont'd.)

KJOS set SO-70B $25.00, sc SO-70F
$3.00   (1230)

Marche [arr.]
(Gearhart, Livingston) (med diff)
SHAWNEE set $20.00, pts $.75, ea.
(1231)

Promenade And March [arr.]
(Myers, Theldon) string orch (gr.
IV) LAKES $24.00   (1232)

Romeo And Juliet: The Montagues And
The Capulets [arr.]
(Siennicki, Edmund) (gr. IV) set
HIGHLAND $37.00   (1233)

PROM NIGHT see Frost, Robert S.

PROMENADE AND MARCH [ARR.] see
Prokofiev, Serge

PROUD MARY [ARR.] see Fogerty, J.C.

PUCCINI, GIACOMO (1858-1924)
Madama Butterfly [arr.]
(Zinn, William) string orch
EXCELSIOR sc $6.00, set $35.00,
pts $1.50, ea.   (1234)

Musetta's Waltz Song [arr.] (from La
Boheme)
(McLeod) string orch (gr. II) set
HIGHLAND $20.00, and up   (1235)

PURCELL, HENRY (1658 or 59-1695)
Air And Rondo [arr.]
(Rowley) 1.1.1.1. 1.1.1.0. timp,
strings (easy) set KALMUS A6050
$11.50, and up   (1236)

Bell Anthem, The [arr.]
(De Valve) string orch [4'30"] (gr.
III) BOURNE $28.50   (1237)

Dido And Aeneas: Suite [arr.]
(Wienandt, Elwyn) string orch (gr.
II) SOUTHERN SO-47 sc $3.00, set
$20.00, pts $1.25, ea.   (1238)

Fairy Queen, The: Prelude [arr.]
(Clebanoff, Herman) string orch
DORABET D-139 f.s.   (1239)

Fairy Queen, The: Rondeau [arr.]
(Clebanoff, Herman) string orch
DORABET D-140 f.s.   (1240)

Let The Earth Resound, [arr.]
1.1.2.1. 2.2.1.0. timp,strings
(easy) sc,pts BOSWORTH f.s. (1241)

Music For Strings And Keyboard
(Dart, Thurston) string orch,kbd
sc,pts NOVELLO 12.0403.03 f.s.
(1242)

Purcell In Miniature [arr.]
(Forbes) string orch (easy) CHESTER
CH 55625 sc $7.25, pts $19.75
(1243)

Rondo, [arr.] (from The Moor's
Revenge)
(Curnow, James) string orch (gr.
III) JENSON 502-18020 $30.00
(1244)

Sonata in F, [arr.]
(Klotman, Robert) string orch (gr.
III, The Glorious) BELWIN
BSO 00059 $45.00   (1245)

Suite in G
string orch [5'20"] sc,pts
BILLAUDOT f.s.   (1246)

Suite in G minor, [arr.]
(Rafter, L.) (diff) sc,pts BOSWORTH
f.s.   (1247)

Suite No. 1 in D, [arr.]
(Rafter, L.) 1.1.2.1. 2.2.1.0.
timp,strings (diff) sc,pts
BOSWORTH f.s.   (1248)

Tempest, The: Overture [arr.]
(Errante, Belisario) string orch
[3'] (gr. III) set MOSAIC M100
$20.00, and up   (1249)

Trumpet Tune [arr.] *see BAROQUE
SUITE NO. 2

Two Seventeenth Century Dances [arr.]
(Frost) string orch (gr. II) KJOS
set SO-77B $22.00, sc SO-77F
$3.00   (1250)

PURCELL IN MINIATURE [ARR.] see
Purcell, Henry

PURVIS, STANLEY H.
Snow Chimes
string orch,triangle,opt pno
[3'30"] (gr. I) set KENDOR 8605
$19.00, and up   (1251)

PYGMIES II, FOR NARRATOR AND ORCHESTRA
see Schelle, Michael

PYRAMID DANCE, FROM "GOLDILOCKS" see
Anderson, Leroy

PYRAMIDS see Frost, Robert S.

QUAGENTI, SAMUEL
Ballet Scenes
BELWIN sc $2.00, set $12.00   (1252)

Festive Moods
BELWIN sc $2.00, set $12.00   (1253)

Fiesta Mexicana
BELWIN sc $2.00, set $12.00   (1254)

Minuetto Antico
BELWIN sc $2.00, set $12.00   (1255)

QUATRE MORCEAUX LYRIQUES [ARR.] see
Grieg, Edvard Hagerup

QUIET PIECE, A see Grant, W. Parks

QUITTEZ PATEURS [ARR.] see Two French
Carols

QUODLIBET ON WELSH NURSERY TUNES see
Hoddinott, Alun

RACHMANINOFF, SERGEY VASSILIEVICH
(1873-1943)
Moods Of Rachmaninoff [arr.]
(Leidig, Vernon) (gr. II) set
HIGHLAND $39.00   (1256)

Variations On A Paganini Theme [arr.]
(Leidig, Vernon) (gr. III) set
HIGHLAND $37.00   (1257)

RADD, JOHN
Dave's Here
perc,strings sets ETOILE $15.00,
and up   (1258)

String-A-Ling
perc,strings sets ETOILE $15.00,
and up   (1259)

RADETZKY MARCH [ARR.] see Strauss,
Johann, [Sr.]

RAFTER, LEONARD
Laughing Song
1.1.2.1. 2.2.1.0. timp,perc,pno,
strings,treb cor (med diff) sc,
pts BOSWORTH f.s.   (1260)

RAGTIME DANCE [ARR.] see Joplin, Scott

RAGTIME FAVORITES FOR STRINGS *CCU
string orch BELWIN 11633-11638 sc
$7.50, pts $2.95, ea.   (1261)

RAGTIME FAVORITES FOR STRINGS [ARR.]
see Joplin, Scott

RAGTIME FIDDLES see Chase, Bruce

RAGTIME PARADE [ARR.] see Satie, Erik

RAINBOWS see Niehaus, Leonard

RAMEAU, JEAN-PHILIPPE (1683-1764)
Gavotte, [arr.]
string orch (med) set WYNN
6296-7296 $14.00, and up   (1262)

Tambourin [arr.]
see Brahms, Johannes, Valse [arr.]

RASKIN, EUGENE (1909-   )
Those Were The Days [arr.]
(McLeod, James) string orch,opt pno
[2'15"] (gr. II) sets KENDOR
$16.00, and up   (1263)

RASPBERRY RAMBLE see Siennicki, Edmund
John

RAUM, ELIZABETH (1945-   )
Fantasy For Double Orchestra
[13'] (for junior and senior
orchestras each consisting of
.2222 2231., timp, perc, harp,
str) CAN.MUS.CENT.   (1264)

REAL PEOPLE MARCH, THE [ARR.] see
Loose, William

RED CARPET, THE see Wiggins, Arthur M.

RED WING [ARR.] see Mills, Frederick
Allen (Kerry)

REDSTONE JIVE AND GREEN MOUNTAIN BLUES
see Hood, Barbara W.

REFLETS SUR FEUILLES see Sauguet, Henri

REGNEY, NOEL
Do You Hear What I Hear [arr.]
(composed with Shayne, Gloria)
(Barker) string orch LEONARD-US
00024018 $24.00   (1265)
(Cerulli) CHERRY 27217 $17.50
(1266)

(Lowden, Robert) 2.2.2+bass
clar.2.2alto sax.tenor
sax.baritone sax. 2.3.3.1. timp,
perc,strings CHERRY 27216 $25.00
(1267)
(Riggio, Donald) string orch,opt
pno,opt perc (gr. II) JENSON
502-04010 $20.00   (1268)

REINAGLE, ALEXANDER (1756-1809)
Federal March [arr.]
(Dennison) 1(pic).2.2.1. 2.0.0.0.
timp,strings KALMUS A6731 sc
$5.00, set $12.00   (1269)

Madison's March [arr.]
(Dennison) 1.2.2.1. 2.0.0.0. timp,
strings KALMUS A6729 sc $5.00,
set $12.00   (1270)

Mrs. Madison's Minuet [arr.]
(Dennison) 1.2.2.1. 2.0.0.0. timp,
strings KALMUS A6732 sc $5.00,
set $12.00   (1271)

REINECKE, CARL (1824-1910)
Evening Prayer *Op.88,No.9
string orch (gr. IV) sc,pts JTL
GS68 $6.60, and up   (1272)

Kindersinfonie *Op.239
pno 4-hands, 7 children's
instruments
KALMUS A5789 sc $10.00, set $18.00,
perf mat rent   (1273)
ZIMMER.   (1274)

REJOUISSANCE, LA [ARR.] see Handel,
George Frideric

RELICARIO, EL [ARR.] see Padilla, José

REMENYI, A.
Six Movements For Chamber Ensemble
sc,pts EMB 13465 f.s.   (1275)

RENAISSANCE SUITE see Chagrin, Francis

RENESSE, GEORGE VAN
Festive March
2S rec,A rec,2vln,vcl,pno 4-hands
HARMONIA 2827 f.s.   (1276)

REPASZ BAND [ARR.] see Lincoln

RESNICK, ARTIE
Under The Boardwalk [arr.] (composed
with Young, Kenny)
(Rosenhaus) string orch LEONARD-US
08720206 $35.00   (1277)

RETURN OF THE JEDI: EWOK CELEBRATION
[ARR.] see Williams, John T.

RETURN OF THE JEDI: HIGHLIGHTS [ARR.]
see Williams, John T.

RETURN OF THE JEDI: PARADE OF THE EWOKS
[ARR.] see Williams, John T.

REVERDY, MICHELE (1943-   )
Ile Aux Lumieres, L', For Violin And
String Orchestra
string orch,vln solo [10'] SALABERT
sc f.s., pts f.s.   (1278)

RHAPSODY IN BLUE [ARR.] see Gershwin,
George

RHOADS, WILLIAM EARL (1918-   )
Tres Baladas
1.1.3.1. 2.2.1.1. perc,strings (gr.
III) SHAWNEE J-136 $32.00 (1279)

Tres Danzas De Mexico
(gr. IV) set TRN $62.00, and up
(1280)

RICCARDO: MARCH [ARR.] see Handel,
George Frideric

RICHARD RODGERS PORTRAIT, A [ARR.] see
Rodgers, Richard

RICHIE, LIONEL
Ballerina Girl [arr.]
(O'reilly, John) string orch,opt
perc,opt winds [3'] (med easy)
CHERRY CL3220 $35.00   (1281)

RICHIE, LIONEL (cont'd.)

Hello [arr.]
sc,pts CHESTER CH 55729 $16.50
(1282)
(Riggio, Donald) string orch,opt
pno,opt perc (gr. II) sc,pts
JENSON 502-08010 $20.00   (1283)

Lionel Richie In Concert [arr.]
(Rosenhaus, Steven) 2.1.2.1.
4.3.3.1. timp,perc,strings (gr.
III) sc,pts JENSON 503-12010
$40.00   (1284)

Love Will Conquer All [arr.]
(Feldstein, Sandy) string orch,opt
pno,opt perc [3'] (med easy)
CHERRY CL3218 $25.00   (1285)

Truly [arr.]
(Riggio, Donald) string orch,opt
pno,opt perc (gr. III) JENSON
502-22020 $20.00   (1286)

RIDE OF THE VALKYRIES [ARR.] see
Wagner, Richard

RIEDING, OSCAR
Concerto, Op. 34, [arr.]
string orch sc,pts BOSWORTH f.s.
(1287)
Concerto, Op. 35, [arr.]
string orch,opt winds&timp (med
easy) sc,pts BOSWORTH f.s.   (1288)

RIENZI: OVERTURE [ARR.] see Wagner,
Richard

RIGAUDON AND PROCESSIONAL [ARR.] see
Campra, André

RIGAUDON, [ARR.] see Handel, George
Frideric

RILEY, DENNIS (1943-   )
Allegro
string orch [5'] (med easy)
AM.COMP.AL. perf mat rent   (1289)

RIMSKY-KORSAKOV, NIKOLAI (1844-1908)
Capriccio Espagnol [arr.]
(Dackow, Sandra) string orch (med)
LUDWIG STRO-53 $55.00   (1290)

Czar's Bride, The: Dance [arr.]
(Barnes) string orch BELWIN BS039
sc $3.50, set $15.00   (1291)

Fandango And Alborado [arr.]
(Isaac, Merle J.) [2'20"] (gr. III)
set HIGHLAND $37.00   (1292)

Russian Easter Overture [arr.]
(Dackow, Sandra) string orch (med)
LUDWIG STRO 57 f.s.   (1293)

Sadko: Song Of India [arr.]
(Frost, Robert) string orch (gr.
II) sets KENDOR $16.00, and up
(1294)

Sarabande And Courante, [arr.]
(Barnes, Clifford P.) string orch
BELWIN sc $2.00, set $12.00
(1295)

Scheherazade: Third Movement Theme
[arr.]
(Frost, Robert S.) string orch,opt
pno [1'30"] (gr. II) sets KENDOR
$16.00, and up   (1296)

Slava [arr.]
(Dackow, Sandra) string orch (med)
LUDWIG STRO 56 $45.00   (1297)

Snow Maiden, The: Dance Of The
Tumblers [arr.]
(Dackow, Sandra) string orch,opt
pno set LUDWIG STRO-25 $25.00
(1298)

RIPE FOR PLUCKING see Shulman, Alan M.

RIVER CITY VARIATIONS see Frost, Robert
S.

RIXMANN, GERD
I Play! What Do You Play...?
see Ich Spiele! Was Spielst Du...?

Ich Spiele! Was Spielst Du...?
"I Play! What Do You Play...?"
parts available for sop rec, alto
rec, bass rec, fl, ob, clar, bn,
trp, trb, gt, vln, vcl, db, pno
pts ZIMMER. $2.25, ea.   (1299)

ROBIN HOOD SUITE see Brandon, Seymour
(Sy)

ROCK AROUND THE CLOCK [ARR.] see
Freedman, Max C.

ROCKIN' A ROUND see Siennicki, Edmund
John

ROCKIN' AROUND THE CHRISTMAS TREE
   MEDLEY [ARR.] see Marks, Johnny D.

ROCKIN' EASY see Heilmann, Francis

ROCKING STRINGS, THE see Ward, Norman

ROCKY MOUNTAIN SWITCHBACK see Frost,
   Robert S.

ROCKY TOP [ARR.] see Bryant, Boudleaux

ROCOCO RONDO see Fletcher, Gary

ROCOCO SYMPHONY, [ARR.] see Stamitz,
   Johann Wenzel Anton

RODEO: HOE DOWN see Copland, Aaron

RODGERS, RICHARD (1902-1979)
   Climb Ev'ry Mountain [arr.]
      (Chase) string orch [2'] (med easy)
      LEONARD-US $25.00   (1300)

   Do-Re-Mi [arr.]
      (Chase) string orch (easy) LEONARD-
      US 04620440 $22.50   (1301)

   Edelweiss [arr.]
      (Forsblad) string orch LEONARD-US
      04842600 $15.00   (1302)

   King And I, The: Selections [arr.]
      (Lowden) LEONARD-US 08720198 $45.00
                                  (1303)

   My Favorite Things [arr.]
      (Chase) string orch (easy) LEONARD-
      US 04621530 $16.00   (1304)

   Oklahoma: Selections [arr.]
      (Rosenhaus) LEONARD-US 08720208
      $50.00   (1305)

   Richard Rodgers Portrait, A [arr.]
      (Chase) LEONARD-US 04501325 $45.00
                                  (1306)

   Sound Of Music, The: Title Song
      [arr.]
      LEONARD-US 00348877 $38.50   (1307)
      (Chase) string orch [2'20"] (easy)
      set LEONARD-US 04622164 $22.50
                                  (1308)

   Surrey With The Fringe On Top, The
      [arr.]
      (Chase) string orch (easy) LEONARD-
      US 08720161 $25.00   (1309)

   You'll Never Walk Alone [arr.]
      LEONARD-US 06024034 $20.00 (1310)

RODRIGUEZ, MATOS
   Comparsita, La *see TWO SOUTH
      AMERICAN TANGOS [aRR.]

ROEDER, TONI
   Music School Introduces Itself, A,
      Vol. 10
      see Musikschule Stellt Sich Vor,
      Eine, Vol. 10

   Musikschule Stellt Sich Vor, Eine,
      Vol. 10
      (Fink, Siegfried) "Music School
      Introduces Itself, A, Vol. 10"
      ZIMMER. 2149 perf mat rent (1311)

ROKOS, K.W.
   Classical Suite
      (easy) sc,pts BOSWORTH f.s. (1312)

   Folk Song Concert Overture
      string orch,opt winds&timp (easy)
      sc,pts BOSWORTH f.s.   (1313)

ROLAND: CHACONNE see Lully, Jean-
   Baptiste (Lulli)

ROLL'N see Fletcher, Gary

ROMAN, JOHAN HELMICH (1694-1758)
   Drottningholmsmusiken: Tre Satser
      [arr.]
      (Genetay, Claude) [8'] GEHRMANS sc
      6530P f.s., pts 6530S f.s. (1314)

ROMANCE AND STAMPING see Zempleni, L.

ROMANCE [ARR.] see Beethoven, Ludwig
   van

ROMANCES SANS PAROLES, DEUX [ARR.] see
   Mendelssohn-Bartholdy, Felix

ROMANZA [ARR.] see Field, John

ROMANZA CONCERTANTE, FOR OBOE AND
   ORCHESTRA see Korn, Peter Jona

ROMBERG, BERNHARD (1865-1913)
   Symphonie Burlesque
      trp,perc,pno,strings without vla
      [8'] pts BILLAUDOT f.s.   (1315)

ROMEO AND JULIET: THE MONTAGUES AND THE
   CAPULETS [ARR.] see Prokofiev,
   Serge

RONDES ET CHANSONS see Devogel, Jacques

RONDO CAPRICE see Daniels, Melvin L.

ROSAMUNDE: BALLET MUSIC NO. 1 [ARR.]
   see Schubert, Franz (Peter)

ROSE, DAVID (1919-1990)
   Holiday For Strings [arr.]
      (Riggio, Donald) string orch (gr.
      II) sc,pts JENSON 502-08020
      $20.00   (1316)

ROSENHAUS
   Sea Song Suite
      string orch LEONARD-US 04802031
      $20.00   (1317)

ROSES FROM THE SOUTH [ARR.] see
   Strauss, Johann, [Jr.]

ROSINE [ARR.] see Gossec, François
   Joseph

ROSSINI, GIOACCHINO (1792-1868)
   Barber Of Seville: Overture [arr.]
      (Isaac) (med diff) set WYNN 4271
      $48.00, and up   (1318)

   Sonata, No. 1, [arr.]
      (Wright, Carla) string orch (gr. V)
      SOUTHERN SO-44 sc $7.50, set
      $37.50, pts $2.50, ea.   (1319)

   William Tell: Overture [arr.]
      (McLeod, James) string orch,opt pno
      [1'55"] (gr. V) sets KENDOR
      $20.00, and up   (1320)

   William Tell: Overture, Finale [arr.]
      (Dackow, Sandra) string orch,opt
      pno [3'50"] set LUDWIG STRO-23
      $25.00   (1321)

ROUGERON, PHILIPPE (1928-   )
   Chanson D'Autrefois
      flexible instrumentation sc,pts
      LEDUC AL 27212 f.s.   (1322)

ROUGH STUFF see Caponegro, John

ROUND DANCE [ARR.] see Schubert, Franz
   (Peter)

ROYAL FIREWORKS MUSIC: SELECTIONS
   [ARR.] see Handel, George Frideric

ROYAL FIREWORKS MUSIC: SUITE [ARR.] see
   Handel, George Frideric

ROYAL PROCESSIONAL see Keuning, Ken

ROYALWOOD OVERTURE see Niehaus, Leonard

RUDOLPH-HOLLY JOLLY CHRISTMAS MEDLEY
   [ARR.] see Marks, Johnny D.

RUMANIAN RHAPSODY NO. 1 [ARR.] see
   Enesco, Georges (Enescu)

RUSCH
   March Triumphant [arr.]
      (Spinosa) string orch (gr. II) KJOS
      set SO-61B $22.00, sc SO-61F
      $3.00   (1323)

   Trinal Contrasts [arr.]
      (Spinosa) string orch (gr. III)
      KJOS set SO-62B $25.00, sc SO-62F
      $3.00   (1324)

RUSSIAN AIR, OP. 107, NO. 3 [ARR.] see
   Beethoven, Ludwig van

RUSSIAN DANCE see Pavey, Sidney

RUSSIAN EASTER OVERTURE [ARR.] see
   Rimsky-Korsakov, Nikolai

RUSSIAN FOLK SONG NO. 7 [ARR.]
   (Applebaum; Ployhar) BELWIN CO 00185
   sc $4.00, set $25.00   (1325)

RUSSIAN PEASANT DANCE see Hellem, Mark

RUSSIAN SAILORS' DANCE [ARR.] see
   Glière, Reinhold Moritzovich

RUSSIAN THEME, OP. 107, NO. 7 [ARR.]
   see Beethoven, Ludwig van

RUSTIC DANCE see Del Borgo, Elliot A.

RUSTIC DANCES see Brown, Christopher
   (Roland)

RYDEN, WILLIAM
   Fum, Fum, Fum
      string orch,opt pno [3'] (gr. III)
      BOURNE B24024 sc $4.50, set
      $22.50, and up   (1326)

   Jingle Bells?
      string orch [2'45"] (gr. III)
      BOURNE $22.50   (1327)

RYDEN, WILLIAM (cont'd.)

   Patapan
      string orch (gr. III) BOURNE
      B240911 sc $4.50, set $22.50, and
      up   (1328)

SABIEN, RANDEL
   Jose's Blues
      perc,strings sets ETOILE $15.00,
      and up   (1329)

SADKO: SONG OF INDIA [ARR.] see Rimsky-
   Korsakov, Nikolai

SAILOR'S SONG see Keuning, Ken

SAILOR'S SONG [ARR.] see Grieg, Edvard
   Hagerup

ST. ANTHONY CHORALE [ARR.] see Haydn,
   [Franz] Joseph

SAINT-SAËNS, CAMILLE (1835-1921)
   Gloria And Alleluia [arr.] (from
      Christmas Oratorio)
      (Hubbell, Fred) string orch (gr.
      III) set HIGHLAND $29.00   (1330)
      (Isaac) (med easy) set WYNN 4272
      $28.00, and up   (1331)

   Minuet, Op. 56, [arr.]
      (Keuning, Hans P.) 2.2.2.0+opt
      2bsn. 2.2.0.0. strings sc,pts
      HARMONIA 3639 f.s.   (1332)

   Samson And Delilah: Bacchanale [arr.]
      (Isaac) 2.2.3.1.alto sax.tenor sax.
      2.2.2.1. timp,perc,strings BELWIN
      CO00166 sc $4.00, set $25.00
                                  (1333)

   Symphony No. 3 in C, [excerpt],
      [arr.]
      (Dackow, Sandra) string orch,opt
      pno [3'5"] (poco adagio) set
      LUDWIG STRO-24 $15.00   (1334)

SALLINEN, AULIS (1935-   )
   Variations for Orchestra *Op.8
      2.2.2.2. 2.2.2.0. marimba,strings
      sc NOVELLO 2970-90 $19.00, perf
      mat rent   (1335)

SALUDO see Chase, Bruce

SALUT D'AMOUR [ARR.] see Elgar, [Sir]
   Edward (William)

SALUTE TO FREEDOM [ARR.]
   (McLeod) string orch KJOS set GSO-7B
   $25.00, sc GSO-7F $5.00   (1336)

SALUTE TO THE LADY
   (Heilmann, Francis) 2fl,2clar,2alto
   sax,2trp,trom,perc,pno,strings
   [2'45"] (med easy) set HEILNN
   $27.00, and up   (1337)

SAMMARTINI
   Concerto for Recorder and String
      Orchestra in F
      string orch,rec solo sc,pts SCHOTTS
      CON 195 $16.95   (1338)

SAMSON AND DELILAH: BACCHANALE [ARR.]
   see Saint-Saëns, Camille

SAN FRANCISCO SUITE see Keuning, Ken

SAN SEBASTIAN see McLeod, James (Red)

SANDPAPER SYMPHONY see Shaffer, David

SANFILIPPO, MARGHERITA MARIE
   (1927-   )
   Canzonetta E Ballo For Violin And
      String Orchestra
      string orch,vln solo (gr. III) set
      HIGHLAND $20.00, and up   (1339)

SANTA CLAUS IS COMING TO TOWN [ARR.]
   see Coots, John Frederick

SANTA'S SUPER SLEIGH see Kovats, Daniel

SARABANDE AND BOURREE [ARR.] see
   Handel, George Frideric

SARABANDE AND COURANTE, [ARR.] see
   Rimsky-Korsakov, Nikolai

SARABANDE AND MUSETTE see Cechvala, Al

SARABANDE [ARR.] see Bach, Johann
   Sebastian see Corelli, Arcangelo

SATIE, ERIK (1866-1925)
  Diva De L'Empire, La
    2.1.1.1. 1.1.1.0. perc,strings
    [2'30"] SALABERT perf mat rent
                                        (1340)

  Je Te Veux
    2.1.2.1. 2.2.3.0. perc,strings [5']
    SALABERT perf mat rent   (1341)

  Piccadilly, Le
    string orch [5'] SALABERT perf mat
    rent   (1342)

  Poudre D'Or
    2.1.2.1. 2.1.3.0. perc,strings [7']
    SALABERT perf mat rent   (1343)

  Ragtime Parade [arr.]
    (Siennicki, Edmund) string orch
    (gr. III) set HIGHLAND $29.00
                                        (1344)

SAUGUET, HENRI (1901-1989)
  Reflets Sur Feuilles
    1.1.2.1. 1.1.1.0. timp,perc,harp,
    strings [2'30"] (from the series
    "feuilles vives") BILLAUDOT perf
    mat rent   (1345)

SCARBOROUGH FAIR [ARR.]
  (Clebanoff, Herman) string orch
    DORABET D-152 f.s.   (1346)
  (Myers) string orch (gr. III) LAKES
    $20.00   (1347)
  see Sounds Of Simon And Garfunkel,
    Vol. II

SCARLATTI, ALESSANDRO (1660-1725)
  Caduta De Decem Viri, La: Overture
    [arr.]
    (Goldsmith, Owen) "Fall Of The
    Council Of Ten, The: Overture
    [arr.]" string orch,pno (gr. III)
    BELWIN BSO 00069 $40.00   (1348)

  Fall Of The Council Of Ten, The:
    Overture [arr.]
    see Caduta De Decem Viri, La:
      Overture [arr.]

SCHAEFER, C. GRANT
  Butterflies [arr.]
    sc,pts LENGNICK f.s.   (1349)

SCHAFER, M.
  see SCHAFER, R. MURRAY

SCHAFER, R.
  Schulerstreichorchester, Das, Vol. 1
    string orch DOBLINGER 07 503 f.s.
                                        (1350)
  Schulerstreichorchester, Das, Vol. 2
    string orch DOBLINGER 07 504 f.s.
                                        (1351)

SCHAFER, R. MURRAY (1933-   )
  Train
    perf sc BERANDOL BER 1727 $2.00
                                        (1352)

SCHEHERAZADE: THIRD MOVEMENT THEME
  [ARR.] see Rimsky-Korsakov, Nikolai

SCHEIDT, SAMUEL (1587-1654)
  Symphonies, Three [arr.]
    4rec,2clar,strings sc,pts LEMOINE
    f.s.   (1353)

SCHELLE, MICHAEL (1950-   )
  Pygmies II, For Narrator And
    Orchestra
    3.2.2.2. 4.2.3.1. timp,perc,pno/
    cel,strings,narrator [15'] (med)
    sc AM.COMP.AL. $17.65, perf mat
    rent   (1354)

SCHERZANDO see Damase, Jean-Michel

SCHERZINO see Errante, Belisario
  Anthony

SCHERZO ON AMERICAN THEMES see
  Fletcher, Gary

SCHONBERG, CLAUDE-MICHEL
  I Dreamed A Dream [arr.]
    (Holcombe) LEONARD-US 04793323
    $25.00   (1355)
    (Holcombe) string orch (med easy)
    LEONARD-US 04849325 $20.00   (1356)

  Miserables, Les: Selections [arr.]
    (Lowden) LEONARD-US 04500768 $45.00
                                        (1357)

SCHOONENBEEK, KEES (1947-   )
  Canzona
    2harp/2synthesizer,2pno,2elec org,
    strings [10'] sc DONEMUS f.s.,
    perf mat rent   (1358)

SCHOSTAKOWITSCH, DMITRI
  see SHOSTAKOVICH, DMITRI

SCHREINER, ALEXANDER (1901-1987)
  Immer Kleiner [arr.]
    (Howard; Davis) LUDWIG LLE-144
                                        (1359)

SCHREINER, ALEXANDER (cont'd.)

  Worried Drummer, The [arr.]
    (Osterling; Davis) LUDWIG LLE-84
                                        (1360)

SCHUBERT, FRANZ (PETER) (1797-1828)
  Adagio, [arr.] (from Quartet, Op.
    125, No. 1)
    (Dasch) string orch FITZSIMONS
    F0552 set $12.00, sc $3.00, pts
    $2.00, ea.   (1361)

  Allegretto [arr.]
    (Errante, Belisario) string orch
    (gr. III) set HIGHLAND $20.00,
    and up   (1362)

  Andantino And Allegretto [arr.]
    (Errante, Belisario) string orch
    [3'] sc,pts LUDWIG STRO 21 f.s.
                                        (1363)

  Ave Maria [arr.]
    see Beethoven, Ludwig van, Romance
    [arr.]

  Best Of Schubert, The [arr.]
    (Paradise, Paul) string orch BELWIN
    sc EL 03417 $17.50, pts
    EL 03418-03422 $5.50, ea.   (1364)

  Contra Dance [arr.] *see TWO COUNTRY
    DANCES

  Cradle Song [arr.]
    see Schubert Suite

  Entrance March From Rosamunde [arr.]
    see Schubert Suite

  Flowing Stream, The [arr.] *see
    SUITE OF WALTZES, A

  Guidepost, The [arr.]
    see Wegweiser, Der [arr.]

  Marche Militaire [arr.]
    MIDDLE CMK 212 f.s.   (1365)
    see Mozart, Wolfgang Amadeus, Finta
    Giardiniera, La: Overture [arr.]

  Rosamunde: Ballet Music No. 1 [arr.]
    (Dackow, Sandra) string orch
    [2'30"] (med) LUDWIG STRO-44
    $40.00   (1366)

  Round Dance [arr.]
    see Schubert Suite

  Scherzo, [arr.] (from Octet, D. 803)
    (Roper, Neville) 2.1.2.1. 2.2.3.0.
    timp,2perc,opt pno,strings [6']
    sc,pts BOSWORTH f.s.   (1367)

  Schubert Suite
    (Errante, Belisario) string orch,
    pno set MOSAIC $20.00, and up
    contains: Cradle Song [arr.];
    Entrance March From Rosamunde
    [arr.]; Round Dance [arr.]
                                        (1368)

  Serenade [arr.] *see Beethoven,
    Ludwig Van, Hymne A La Joie
    [arr.]
    see Beethoven, Ludwig van, Hymne A
    La Joie [arr.]

  Symphony No. 5,Minuet, [arr.]
    MIDDLE CMK 214 f.s.   (1369)

  Symphony No. 8, [arr.]
    (Carlin) "Unfinished Symphony
    [arr.]" 1.1.2.1.alto sax.tenor
    sax. 2.2.2.0. timp,perc,pno,
    strings CARLIN sc $4.00, set
    $38.00, pts $1.50, ea.   (1370)
    (Frost, Robert S.) "Unfinished
    Symphony [arr.]" string orch,opt
    pno [2'35"] (gr. II, %t[excerpt]
    [arr.]) set KENDOR $17.00, and up
                                        (1371)
  Unfinished Symphony *see Symphony
    No. 8 in B Minor, D. 759

  Unfinished Symphony [arr.]
    see Symphony No. 8, [arr.]

  Wegweiser, Der [arr.]
    (Grantham, William) "Guidepost, The
    [arr.]" [4'30"] (med) set SHAWNEE
    J-97 $16.00   (1372)

SCHUBERT SUITE see Schubert, Franz
  (Peter)

SCHULERSTREICHORCHESTER, DAS, VOL. 1
  see Schafer, R.

SCHULERSTREICHORCHESTER, DAS, VOL. 2
  see Schafer, R.

SCHUMANN, ROBERT (ALEXANDER)
  (1810-1856)
  Album Pour La Jeunesse: Petite Suite
    No. 1 [arr.]
    2rec,2fl,2clar,alto sax,gtr,pno,
    strings sc,pts LEMOINE f.s.

SCHUMANN, ROBERT (ALEXANDER) (cont'd.)
                                        (1373)

  Chanson De Metelots [arr.]
    see Suite Pour La Jeunesse [arr.]

  Chanson Du Nord [arr.]
    see Suite Pour La Jeunesse [arr.]

  Chant Du Berceau [arr.]
    see Suite Pour La Jeunesse [arr.]

  Children's Fantasies [arr.]
    (Alshin, Harry A.) string orch,opt
    pno [6'] (gr. II) set KENDOR 8965
    $23.00, and up   (1374)

  Choral [arr.]
    see Suite Pour La Jeunesse [arr.]

  Grand Evenement [arr.]
    see Suite Pour La Jeunesse [arr.]

  Hommes Et Pays Nouveaux [arr.]
    see Suite Pour La Jeunesse [arr.]

  Suite Pour La Jeunesse [arr.]
    (Lacour, Guy) 2.2+opt English
    horn.2+opt bass clar.0.2alto
    sax.opt tenor sax.opt baritone
    sax. 2.2.1.1. perc,gtr,opt acord,
    pno/harp/elec org,strings sc,pts
    BILLAUDOT f.s.
    contains: Chanson De Metelots
    [arr.]; Chanson Du Nord [arr.];
    Chant Du Berceau [arr.]; Choral
    [arr.]; Grand Evenement [arr.];
    Hommes Et Pays Nouveaux [arr.]
                                        (1375)

  Symphony No. 4,Finale, [arr.]
    (Leidig) set HIGHLAND $28.00, and
    up   (1376)

SCHÜTT, EDUARD (1856-1933)
  Serenade D'Arlequin [arr.]
    sc,pts LENGNICK f.s.   (1377)

SCHWANDA: POLKA [ARR.] see Weinberger,
  Jaromir

SCIOSTAKOVIC, DMITRI
  see SHOSTAKOVICH, DMITRI

SCIPIO: MARCH [ARR.] see Handel, George
  Frideric

SCOTT, RICHARD
  Alpine Holiday
    string orch,opt pno,opt gtr, or
    autoharp [1'50"] (gr. I) set
    KENDOR 8115 $23.00, and up (1378)

  Baile En La Calle
    string orch,opt pno [2'15"] (gr. I)
    set KENDOR $14.00, and up   (1379)

  Carnival Song
    string orch,opt pno [4'] (gr. I)
    set KENDOR 8195 $23.00, and up
                                        (1380)

  Dance, Gypsy
    string orch,opt pno [3'10"] (gr.
    II) set KENDOR 9015 $23.00, and
    up   (1381)

  Desert Noel
    string orch,opt perc,opt pno
    [3'40"] (gr. I) set KENDOR 8253
    $23.00, and up   (1382)

  Festividad, La (from The Mexican
    Suite)
    string orch,opt pno [3'40"] (gr. I)
    set KENDOR 8355 $23.00, and up
                                        (1383)
  Giorgio's Lament (from Gypsy Fantasy)
    string orch,opt pno [4'] (gr. I)
    set KENDOR 8278 $19.00, and up
                                        (1384)
  Gypsy Rondo (from Gypsy Fantasy)
    string orch,opt perc,opt pno [3']
    (gr. II) set KENDOR 9128 $23.00,
    and up   (1385)

  Siesta Dulce (from The Mexican Suite)
    string orch,opt pno [4'5"] (gr. I)
    set KENDOR $14.00, and up   (1386)

  Songs Of The Trail
    string orch,opt pno,opt perc [3']
    (gr. II) KENDOR 9485 f.s.   (1387)

  Tango Corto, Un (from The Mexican
    Suite)
    string orch,opt pno [3'35"] (gr. I)
    set KENDOR 8805 $23.00, and up
                                        (1388)
  Tanya's Waltz (from Gypsy Fantasy)
    string orch,opt pno [3'15"] (gr. I)
    set KENDOR 8725 $23.00, and up
                                        (1389)

SCOTTISH FANTASY [ARR.] see Bruch, Max

SCOTTISH FOLKSONG [ARR.] see Brahms,
  Johannes

SEA SONG SUITE see Rosenhaus

SEASHORE FESTIVAL see Siennicki, Edmund John

SEASONAL STRINGS [ARR.]
  (Higgins, Jim) string orch,opt pno
  [2'30"] (gr. III) set KENDOR 9868
  $23.00, and up   (1390)

SEASONS see Feese, Francis L.

SEASON'S GREETINGS *CC12L
  (Klevenow, Spencer; Pierce, Ransford)
  string orch BIG3 f.s.   (1391)

SEASON'S GREETINGS
  (Dickson, Richard) string orch,pno
  [4'] (gr. III) CONCERT W J-63
  $26.00   (1392)

SEBESKY, GERALD JOHN (1941-   )
  Prelude And Fugue For Young Strings
  string orch [2'50"] (gr. I) SHAWNEE
  J-150 $22.00   (1393)

SECUNDA, SHOLOM (1894-1974)
  Tango De La Luna
  2(pic).2.2.2.opt 3sax. 4.3.3.0.
  timp,perc,strings (med easy) set
  KALMUS A6016 $30.00, and up
                                    (1394)
SEE THE CONQUERING HERO COMES [ARR.]
  see Handel, George Frideric

SEITZ, FRIEDRICH (1848-1918)
  Concerto, Op. 15, [arr.]
  string orch sc,pts BOSWORTH f.s.
                                    (1395)

  Concerto, Op. 22, [arr.]
  string orch sc,pts BOSWORTH f.s.
                                    (1396)

SEMIQUAVER SERENADE see Fletcher, Gary

SENAILLE, JEAN BAPTISTE (1687-1730)
  Allegro [arr.] (from Sonata No. 4)
  (Errante, Belisario) string orch
  sets LUDWIG STRO-17 $20.00, and
  up   (1397)

  Allegro Spiritoso [arr.]
  (Higgins, James) string orch,opt
  pno (gr. III) BELWIN CO 00190
  $35.00   (1398)
  *see BAROQUE SUITE NO. 1

SENOB, CARL
  Joggin'
  string orch (gr. III) BELWIN
  BSO 00068 $35.00   (1399)

SEPARATE LIVES [ARR.] see Bishop, Stephen

SEPTEMBER SONG see String Orchestra Pak No. 5

SEQUENCES AND BURLESQUE see Tillis, Frederick C.

SERENADA see Urbaniak, Michal

SERENADE [ARR.] see Schubert, Franz (Peter)

SERENADE D'ARLEQUIN [ARR.] see Schütt, Eduard

SERENADE FOR STRINGS: THEMES FROM THE FIRST MOVEMENT [ARR.] see Tchaikovsky, Piotr Ilyich

SERENADE FOR STRINGS: WALTZ [ARR.] see Tchaikovsky, Piotr Ilyich

SERENADE NO. 2, OP. 63: WALTZ [ARR.] see Volkmann, Robert

SERENATA, LA see McLeod, James (Red)

SERENATA CONCERTANTE, FOR FLUTE AND STRING ORCHESTRA see Huszar, Lajos

SERLY, TIBOR (1900-1978)
  String Symphony In Four Cycles
  string orch PEER sc 61334-766
  $8.00, set 61333-767 $50.00
                                    (1400)

SEVILLA [ARR.] see Albéniz, Isaac

SHADOW OF YOUR SMILE, THE [ARR.] see Mandel, Johnny Alfred

SHAFFER, DAVID
  Impravada
  string orch [2'58"] (gr. II) BARNHS
  130-2186-00 $26.00   (1401)

  March Grande
  string orch (gr. II) LAKES $16.00
                                    (1402)
  Sandpaper Symphony
  string orch (gr. I) set LAKES
  $16.00, and up   (1403)

SHAFFER, DAVID (cont'd.)
  Westminster Prelude And Fugue
  string orch (gr. II) set LAKES
  $16.00, and up   (1404)

  Wonder Waltz
  string orch [1'10"] (gr. I) BARNHS
  130-2130-00 $26.00   (1405)

SHAPIRO, MARSHA CHUSMIR
  Asia Minor
  string orch (gr. II) KJOS set
  SO-78B $25.00, sc SO-78F $3.00
                                    (1406)
  Matthew's March
  string orch (gr. I) KJOS set SO-55B
  $25.00, sc SO-55F $3.00   (1407)

  Minor Variations
  string orch (gr. II) set HIGHLAND
  $29.00   (1408)

  Shores Of Biscayne Bay, The
  string orch (gr. I) KJOS set SO-56B
  $25.00, sc SO-56F $3.00   (1409)

  Variations On A Ground
  string orch (gr. II) KJOS set
  SO-63B $25.00, sc SO-63F $3.00
                                    (1410)
SHE BELIEVES IN ME [ARR.] see Gibb, Steve

SHEAR DELIGHTS
  (Niehaus, Lennie) string orch,opt
  perc,opt pno [2'15"] (gr. I) set
  KENDOR 8564 $19.00, and up   (1411)

SHENANDOAH [ARR.]
  (Clebanoff, Herman) string orch
  DORABET D-153 f.s.   (1412)
  (Davis, Albert O.) 2.1.2.1. 2.3.2.1.
  timp,perc,strings sets LUDWIG
  LLE-66 $22.00, and up   (1413)
  (Niehaus, Lennie) string orch,opt pno
  [3'35"] (gr. I) set KENDOR 8565
  $19.00, and up   (1414)
  (Shaffer, David) string orch (easy)
  set LAKES $16.00, and up   (1415)

SHEPHERD IN LOVE, THE [ARR.] see Newton, E.

SHERMAN, RICHARD M.
  Chim-Chim-Cher-Ee [arr.] (composed
  with Sherman, Robert B.)
  (Chase) string orch (easy) LEONARD-
  US 08720163 $25.00   (1416)

SHORES OF BISCAYNE BAY, THE see Shapiro, Marsha Chusmir

SHOSTAKOVICH, DMITRI (1906-1975)
  Ballet Suite No. 1: Polka, Waltz,
  Galop [arr.]
  (Isaac) set BELWIN CO167 $45.00
                                    (1417)
  Prelude And Polka [arr.]
  (Alshin, Harry) string orch [4'10"]
  (gr. III) set KENDOR 9862 $23.00,
  and up   (1418)

SHOW BOAT [ARR.] see Kern, Jerome

SHOW BOAT: HIGHLIGHTS [ARR.] see Kern, Jerome

SHULMAN, ALAN M. (1915-   )
  Ripe For Plucking
  string orch [4'30"] set ASTA
  196-00064 $28.00   (1419)

SIBELIUS, JEAN (1865-1957)
  Finlandia [arr.]
  (Carlin) 1.1.2.1.alto sax.tenor
  sax. 2.2.2.0. timp,perc,pno,
  strings CARLIN sc $4.00, set
  $38.00, pts $1.50, ea.   (1420)

SICILIENNE AND GIGUE [ARR.] see Bruni, Antonio Bartolomeo

SICILIENNE [ARR.] see Bach, Johann Sebastian

SIENNICKI, EDMUND JOHN (1920-   )
  Blue Jean Jacket
  string orch (easy) set LAKES
  $14.00, and up   (1421)

  Bounce A Round
  string orch [2'] (gr. I) LUDWIG
  STRO-39 $25.00   (1422)

  Bowin' And Scrapin'
  string orch (gr. I) set HIGHLAND
  $20.00, and up   (1423)

  Chaconne
  string orch (med) LUDWIG STRO-27
                                    (1424)
  Colonial Christmas
  (gr. III) set HIGHLAND $37.00
                                    (1425)

SIENNICKI, EDMUND JOHN (cont'd.)
  Micro Fugue
  string orch [2'] set LUDWIG STRO-22
  $20.00, and up   (1426)

  Raspberry Ramble
  string orch (gr. III) set LAKES
  $17.50, and up   (1427)

  Rockin' A Round
  string orch LUDWIG STRO-26   (1428)

  Seashore Festival
  string orch (easy) set LAKES
  $16.00, and up   (1429)

  Suite No. 2
  string orch set HIGHLAND $20.00,
  and up   (1430)

  Suite No. 3
  string orch (gr. II) set HIGHLAND
  $29.00   (1431)

  Sunshine In G
  string orch (gr. I) set LAKES
  $14.00, and up   (1432)

  Two Tunes For Fiddlin'
  string orch (gr. I) set HIGHLAND
  $20.00, and up   (1433)

SIESTA DULCE see Scott, Richard

SILENT NIGHT [ARR.] see Gruber, Franz
  Xaver see Gruber, Franz Xaver,
  Stille Nacht [arr.]

SILHOUETTES [ARR.] see Hay, George

SILVER BELLS [ARR.] see Livingston, Jay Harold

SIMON, CARLY
  Let The River Run [arr.]
  (Cerulli, Bob) CPP 1649LBX $40.00
                                    (1434)
SIMON, PAUL
  Sound Of Silence, The
  sc,pts CHESTER CH 55734 $16.50
                                    (1435)
SIMPLE GIFTS [ARR.]
  (Chase) string orch (easy) LEONARD-US
  08720165 $25.00   (1436)
  (Heilmann, Francis) 2fl,2clar,2alto
  sax,2trp,trom,perc,pno,strings [2']
  (easy) set HEILNN $27.00, and up
                                    (1437)
  (Heilmann, Francis) string orch,perc,
  pno [2'10"] (easy) set HEILNN
  $21.00, and up   (1438)
  (Shapiro, Marsha Chusmir) [2'50"]
  (gr. II) KJOS set 0-1056B $30.00,
  sc 0-1056F $3.00   (1439)

SIMPLE SQUARE DANCE see Straub, Dorothy

SIMPLE SYMPHONY see Vlak, K.

SINFONIA ET TOCCATA [ARR.] see Monteverdi, Claudio

SINFONIA ON EXPANDING MATRICES see Hibbard, William

SINFONIA PICCOLA see Suslin, Viktor

SINFONIA SEMPLICE [ARR.] see Haydn, [Franz] Joseph

SINGING STRINGS *CC8L
  string orch sc,pts BOSWORTH f.s.
                                    (1440)
SIX EASY PIECES, OP.22 see Elgar, [Sir] Edward (William)

SIX INTERMEZZI see Deursen, Anton van

SIX MOVEMENTS FOR CHAMBER ENSEMBLE see Remenyi, A.

SIX PIECES FACILES
  sc,pts BILLAUDOT f.s.
  contains: Arnold, Gitans Quittent
  Le Village, Les; Arnold, Sapin De
  Noel, Le; Desloges, Avec Quelques
  Airs Connus; Desloges, Berceuse;
  Desloges, Choral; Desloges,
  Cloches De Paques, Les   (1441)

SKATERS, THE [ARR.] see Waldteufel, Emile

SKETCHES ON A THEME BY THOMAS TALLIS [ARR.] see Tallis, Thomas

SKIP TO MY LOU [ARR.]
  (Clebanoff, Herman) DORABET D-141
  f.s.   (1442)

SKOLA PRO SMYCCOVY ORCHESTR see Bartovsky, Josef

SLAVA [ARR.] see Rimsky-Korsakov, Nikolai

SLAVONIC DANCE [ARR.] see Dvořák, Antonín

SLAVONIC DANCES, OP. 46, NOS. 4 AND 6 [ARR.] see Dvořák, Antonín

SLEEPING BEAUTY, THE: WALTZ [ARR.] see Tchaikovsky, Piotr Ilyich

SMETANA, BEDRICH (1824-1884)
Czech Rustic Dance, [arr.]
(Rokos) 1.1.2.1.alto sax.tenor sax. 2.2.1.0. timp,pno,strings (med easy) sc,pts BOSWORTH f.s. (1443)

Moldau, The, [arr.]
(Rokos) "Vltava, [arr.]" 2.1.2.2. 2.2.1.0. timp,perc,strings (med diff) sc,pts BOSWORTH f.s. (1444)

Moldau, The: Country Wedding [arr.]
(Dackow, Sandra) string orch [1'48"] (med) LUDWIG STRO-37 $30.00 (1445)

Prague Students' March
(Rokos) (med easy) sc,pts BOSWORTH f.s. (1446)

Vltava, [arr.]
see Moldau, The, [arr.]

SMITH
Apogees
string orch BOURNE B238535 sc $4.50, set $22.50, and up (1447)

SMITH, CLAUDE THOMAS (1932-   )
Symphonic Rhythms And Scales
JENSON 253-18010 sc $9.95, pts $3.95, ea. (1448)

Symphonic Techniques For Band And Orchestra
JENSON 253-20010 sc $12.95, pts $3.95, ea. (1449)

SMITH, JOHN STAFFORD (1750-1836)
Star-Spangled Banner, The [arr.]
(Dackow, Sandra) string orch [1'] (easy) LUDWIG STRO-36 $10.00 (1450)
(Frackenpohl) sets LUDWIG QSM-340 $20.00, and up (1451)
(McLeod) string orch (gr. III) KJOS set GSO-6B $18.00, sc GSO-6F $3.00 (1452)

SNOW CHIMES see Purvis, Stanley H.

SNOW MAIDEN, THE: DANCE OF THE TUMBLERS [ARR.] see Rimsky-Korsakov, Nikolai

SNOWMAN, THE: WALKING IN THE AIR [ARR.] see Blake, Howard

SOIREE DANS GRENADE [ARR.] see Debussy, Claude

SOMBRERO, EL see Frost, Robert S.

SOMEDAY see Goldsmith, Owen

SOMEWHERE OUT THERE [ARR.] see Horner, James

SONATA FROM DIE BANKELSANGERLIEDER [ARR.]
(Kovats, Daniel) string orch (gr. IV) set LAKES $20.00, and up (1453)

SONATINA ACCOMPAGNAMENTO, [ARR.] see Clementi, Muzio

SONATINA SYMFONICKA, [ARR.] see Dvořák, Antonín

SONG AND DANCE see Washburn, Robert Brooks

SONG FROM "DON GIOVANNI" [ARR.] see Mozart, Wolfgang Amadeus

SONG OF A WAYFARER [ARR.] see Mahler, Gustav

SONGS AND DANCES *CCU
(Foxley, Simon) string orch,opt pno (gr. II) set BOOSEY $13.00 (1454)

SONGS MY MOTHER TAUGHT ME [ARR.] see Dvořák, Antonín

SONGS OF CHANUKAH [ARR.]
(Errante, Belisario) [4'30"] (gr. III) set MOSAIC M040 $26.00, and up (1455)

SONGS OF CROATIA
(Alshin, Harry) string orch [3'30"] BOSTON sc,pts $10.00, sc $4.00, pts $1.75, ea. (1456)

SONGS OF EARLY AMERICA [ARR.]
(Errante, Belisario) string orch,pno [9'] (gr. II) set MOSAIC M090 $20.00, and up (1457)

SONGS OF STEPHEN FOSTER, PART 1 [ARR.] see Foster, Stephen Collins

SONGS OF THANKSGIVING
(Frost, Robert S.) string orch,opt pno (gr. I) sets KENDOR $18.00, and up
contains: Prayer Of Thanksgiving; Crüger, Johann, Now Thank We All Our God; Elvey, George Job, Come Ye Thankful People; Kocher, Conrad, For The Beauty Of The Earth (1458)

SONGS OF THE OLD WEST
(Rothrock, Carson) string orch set MUSICIANS PUB IS-109 $12.00, and up (1459)

SONGS OF THE TRAIL see Scott, Richard

SOPHISTICATED LADIES: HIGHLIGHTS [ARR.] see Ellington, Edward Kennedy (Duke)

SOR, FERNANDO (1778-1839)
Lento And Allegretto [arr.]
(Sharp, James L.) (med diff) SHAWNEE set $21.00, pts $1.00, ea. (1460)

SORELLA, LA [ARR.] see Borel-Clerc, Charles

SOUND OF MUSIC, THE: TITLE SONG [ARR.] see Rodgers, Richard

SOUND OF SILENCE, THE see Simon, Paul

SOUNDS FROM SCOTLAND
(Barrie) string orch (easy) CHESTER CH 55724 sc $7.75, pts $18.75 (1461)

SOUNDS OF SIMON AND GARFUNKEL, VOL. I
(Lowden, Bob) WARNER 575-40031 $30.00
contains: Bridge Over Troubled Water [arr.]; Condor Pasa, El [arr.]; Fifty-Ninth Street Bridge Song, The [arr.] (1462)

SOUNDS OF SIMON AND GARFUNKEL, VOL. II
(Lowden, Bob) (gr. III) WARNER 575-40034 $30.00
contains: Canticle, Sounds Of Silence [arr.]; Mrs. Robinson [arr.]; Scarborough Fair [arr.] (1463)

SOUSA, JOHN PHILIP (1854-1932)
Capitan, El [arr.]
(McLeod, James) string orch,opt pno [2'20"] (gr. III) set KENDOR 9810 $19.00, and up (1464)

King Cotton [arr.]
(Fennell, Frederick) [2'40"] CHURCH 125-40042 set $27.50, pno-cond sc $3.00, pts $1.00, ea. (1465)
(McLeod, James) string orch,opt pno [2'45"] (gr. III) set KENDOR 9842 $24.00, and up (1466)

Stars And Stripes Forever, The [arr.]
(Isaac, Merle) 2+pic.1.2+bass clar.1.alto sax.tenor sax. 2.2.2.1. timp,perc,pno,strings [3'30"] (gr. IV) set TRN $40.00 (1467)

SPACE TRAVELLERS see Lawrance, Bruce

SPANISH DANCE [ARR.] see Bohm, Carl

SPANISH DANCE NO. 3 [ARR.] see Granados, Enrique

SPANISH MEDLEY [ARR.]
(McLeod, James) string orch,opt pno [3'50"] (gr. IV) set KENDOR $22.00, and up (1468)

SPANISH SERENADE see Cerulli, Bob

SPANISH SERENADE [ARR.] see Zilcher, P.

SPANISH SONGS AND DANCES, [ARR.] *CCU
(Naylor, Frank) 2fl,2clar,2trp,perc, pno,strings (med diff) sc,pts BOSWORTH f.s. (1469)

SPILL see Madsen, Trygve

SPINNING SONG, THE [ARR.] see Ellmenreich

SPINOSA, FRANK
Sinfonietta
(Rusch) string orch (gr. I) KJOS set SO-59B $25.00, sc SO-59F $5.00 (1470)

SPIRIT OF CHRISTMAS, THE *CC8L
(Curnow, Jim) JENSON 244-19010 sc $7.95, pts $1.95, ea. (1471)

SPLENDOR OF STRINGS, THE *CC20L
(Wikstrom, Thomas) string orch sc,pts FISCHER,C 04725-04730 f.s. (1472)

SPLISH SPLASH see Frost, Robert S.

SPRING, GLENN
Fantasia On "Dulcimer"
string orch (gr. II) BELWIN BSO 00067 $40.00 (1473)

SPRING BREAK AND FIESTA see Frost, Robert S.

SPRING, FROM THE FOUR SEASONS [ARR.] see Vivaldi, Antonio, Concerto, Op. 8, No. 1, [arr.]

SPRING RONDO, [ARR.] see Mozart, Wolfgang Amadeus

SPRINGTIME SUITE see Isaac, Merle John

ST. ELMO'S FIRE: LOVE THEME [ARR.] see Foster, David

STAHMER, KLAUS H. (1941-   )
Multiples
(Fink, Siegfried) (Musical Workshop, Vol. 3) ZIMMER. 2014 $6.50 (1474)

STAMITZ
Concerto for Viola and String Orchestra in D, [arr.]
(Grant) string orch,vla solo sets LUDWIG STRO-16 f.s. (1475)

STAMITZ, JOHANN WENZEL ANTON (1717-1757)
Rococo Symphony, [arr.] (Symphony, Op. 5, No. 5, [arr.])
(Arnell; Rokos) 1.1.2.1. 2.2.1.0. timp,strings (diff) sc,pts BOSWORTH f.s. (1476)

Symphony, Op. 5, No. 5, [arr.]
see Rococo Symphony, [arr.]

STAND BY ME [ARR.] see King, Ben

STAR-SPANGLED BANNER, THE [ARR.] see Smith, John Stafford

STAR VALLEY SUITE see Frost, Robert S.

STARDUST [ARR.] see Carmichael, Hoagy

STARFLIGHT OVERTURE see Mitchell, Rex

STARS AND STRIPES FOREVER, THE [ARR.] see Sousa, John Philip

STATIPIZZIGLISSIC see Thomas, Augusta Read

STEELE, HELEN (1904-   )
America Our Heritage
(Ades, Hawley) (med easy) SHAWNEE set $10.00, pts $.75 (1477)

STEIN, JULES
see STYNE, JULE (JULES STEIN)

STEPHAN, RICHARD
Cats And Dogs
string orch (gr. II) KJOS set SO-74B $22.00, sc SO-74F $3.00 (1478)

Fanfare And Frippery
string orch (gr. IV) set LAKES $30.00, and up (1479)

North Country Hoedown
string orch [1'50"] (gr. II) sets KENDOR $16.00, and up (1480)

Two Sets Of Rounds
string orch,opt pno (gr. I) set KENDOR 8785 $23.00, and up (1481)

STEPPIN' OUT see Isaac, Merle John

STEVENS, HALSEY (1908-1989)
Four Short Pieces
1.1.2.1. 2.1.0.0. timp,perc,strings [7'] (med) sc AM.COMP.AL. $11.45, perf mat rent (1482)

Green Mountain Overture, A
2.2.2.2. 4.3.3.1. timp,perc,strings [6'] (med) sc AM.COMP.AL. $19.05, perf mat rent (1483)

STICK HORSE PARADE see Halen, Walter J.

STILL, WILLIAM GRANT (1895-1978)
Bells, School Orchestra Version
2(pic).2(English horn).2.1.2alto sax.tenor sax. 4.3.3.1. timp, perc,harp,pno,cel,strings [6'] MCA perf mat rent (1484)

STILL AS THE NIGHT [ARR.] see Bohm, Carl

STILL, STILL, STILL [ARR.]
(Chase) string orch (easy) LEONARD-US
08720167 $25.00   (1485)

STILLE NACHT [ARR.] see Gruber, Franz
Xaver

STING, THE: MUSIC [ARR.] see Joplin,
Scott

STING, THE: SELECTIONS [ARR.] see
Joplin, Scott

STRAUB, DOROTHY
Simple Square Dance
string orch,opt pno [1'] (gr. I)
BOOSEY sc $5.00, set $20.00, set
$2.50, ea.   (1486)

Summer Stomp
string orch,opt drums,opt pno
[1'30"] (gr. I) BOOSEY sc $5.00,
set $20.00, pts $2.50, ea. (1487)

STRAUSS, EDUARD (1835-1916)
Bahn Frei Polka [arr.]
(Isaac) string orch (med) set WYNN
6288 $18.00, and up   (1488)

STRAUSS, JOHANN, [SR.] (1804-1849)
Radetzky March [arr.] *Op.228
(Isaac) (med) set WYNN 4274 $28.00,
and up   (1489)
(Naylor, Frank) 1.1.2.1. 2.2.3.0.
timp,perc,pno,strings (med easy)
sc,pts BOSWORTH f.s.   (1490)

STRAUSS, JOHANN, [JR.] (1825-1899)
Annen Polka [arr.] *Op.117
(Naylor, Frank) 1.1.2.1. 2.2.3.0.
timp,perc,pno,strings (med easy)
sc,pts BOSWORTH f.s.   (1491)

Emperor Waltz [arr.]
(Applebaum, Samuel; Ployhar, James)
BELWIN CO000183 sc $4.00, set
$25.00   (1492)

Farewell To America [arr.]
(Cohen, Jerome) 1+pic.2.2.2.
4.2.3.0. timp,glock,2perc,harp/
pno,strings [7'30"] OXFORD sc
97.719 $18.00, set 97.719-70
$68.00   (1493)

Fledermaus, Die: Waltzes [arr.]
(Isaac) string orch (gr. III) set
HIGHLAND $20.00, and up   (1494)

Greeting To America
(Cohen, Jerome) 1+pic.2.2.2.
4.2.3.0. timp,2perc,strings,opt
harp [7'30"] (winds may be
reduced to 1.1.2.1. 2.2.1.0.)
OXFORD sc 97.718 $18.00, set
97.718-70 $68.00   (1495)

Gypsy Baron Waltzes [arr.]
(Isaac, Merle J.) string orch (gr.
III) set HIGHLAND $29.00 (1496)

Memories Of Covent Garden [arr.]
*Op.329
(Naylor, Frank) 2.1.2.1. 2.2.3.0.
timp,perc,pno,strings (med easy)
sc,pts BOSWORTH f.s.   (1497)

Persian March [arr.] *Op.289
(Naylor, Frank) 1.1.2.1. 2.2.3.0.
perc,pno,strings (med easy) sc,
pts BOSWORTH f.s.   (1498)

Roses From The South [arr.] *Op.388
(Isaac, Merle J.) string orch (gr.
III) set HIGHLAND $29.00 (1499)
(Naylor, Frank) 1.1.2.1. 2.2.3.0.
timp,perc,pno,strings (med easy)
sc,pts BOSWORTH f.s.   (1500)

Strauss In Three-Quarter Time [arr.]
(Lang, Philip) 2.1.2.1.3sax.
2.2.1.0. timp,perc,strings (med
easy) set KALMUS A6003 $14.50,
and up   (1501)

Thunder And Lightning [arr.] *Op.324
(Isaac) (med diff) set WYNN 4273
$28.00, and up   (1502)
(Naylor, Frank) 1.1.2.1. 2.2.3.0.
timp,perc,pno,strings (med easy)
sc,pts BOSWORTH f.s.   (1503)

Vienna Life [arr.]
(Zinn, William) string orch set
EXCELSIOR $10.00   (1504)

STRAUSS, RICHARD (1864-1949)
All Souls' Day [arr.]
see Allerseelen [arr.]

Allerseelen [arr.]
(Davis, Albert Oliver) "All Souls'
Day [arr.]" 2(pic).2.2+opt bass
clar.2. 4.3.3.1. perc,strings
[7'] sc,pts LUDWIG 68 f.s. (1505)

STRAUSS, RICHARD (cont'd.)

Zueignung [arr.]
(Goldsmith, Owen) string orch,pno
(med easy) BELWIN BSO 00077
$35.00   (1506)

STRAUSS IN THREE-QUARTER TIME [ARR.]
see Strauss, Johann, [Jr.]

STRAVINSKY, IGOR (1882-1971)
Two Moods [arr.]
(Myers) string orch (gr. III) LAKES
$17.50   (1507)

STRAWBERRY FAIR see Knight, Sally

STRAWBERRY FAIR [ARR.] see Folk-Songs
For Strings, Set 1

STRING-A-LING see Radd, John

STRING ALONG WITH SCOTT [ARR.] see
Joplin, Scott

STRING BEANS see Niehaus, Leonard

STRING FEVER see Feese, Francis L. see
Niehaus, Leonard

STRING ORCHESTRA CLASSICS see Müller,
J. Frederick, Editor

STRING ORCHESTRA PAK NO. 1 *CC6L
string orch (med easy) LEONARD-US
04849001 $36.00   (1508)

STRING ORCHESTRA PAK NO. 2 *CC6L
string orch (med easy) LEONARD-US
04849006 $36.00   (1509)

STRING ORCHESTRA PAK NO. 3 *CC6L
string orch (med easy) LEONARD-US
04849011 $36.00   (1510)

STRING ORCHESTRA PAK NO. 4
string orch (med easy) LEONARD-US
04849016 $36.00
contains: Cabaret; Day By Day;
Malaguena; March Of The Siamese
Children; Memory; Sunrise, Sunset
(1511)

STRING ORCHESTRA PAK NO. 5
string orch (med easy) LEONARD-US
04849021 $36.00
contains: Candle On The Water; I
Whistle A Happy Tune; Matchmaker;
More; Oklahoma; September Song
(1512)

STRING QUARTET NO. 2: NOCTURNE [ARR.]
see Borodin, Alexander Porfirievich

STRING SERENADES *CCU
(Henderson, Kenneth; Stoutamire,
Albert) string orch LAKES pno-cond
sc $5.00, pts $3.00, ea.   (1513)

STRING SYMPHONY IN FOUR CYCLES see
Serly, Tibor

STRINGS AND FRIENDS *CCU
2.1.2.1. 1.2.1.1. perc,strings BELWIN
EL2944-2960 sc $7.50, pts $2.95,
ea.   (1514)

STRINGS ARE FUN *CCU
string orch,pno BELWIN EL2772-2776
pts $2.95, ea., kbd pt $5.00 (1515)

STRINGS GO TO THE MOVIES *CC10L
(Brockner, Charles) strings,pno,
drums,gtr CHERRY 580-08450-08459 sc
$9.95, pts $2.95, ea.   (1516)

STRINGS IN CONCERT see Keuning, Ken

STRINGS IN REVIEW see Frost, Robert S.

STRINGUMAJIG see Niehaus, Leonard

STUDIO PER UN'ORCHESTRA DI RAGAZZI see
Chailly, Luciano

STYNE, JULE (JULES STEIN) (1905-   )
Let It Snow [arr.] (composed with
Cahn, Sammy)
(Caponegro, John) string orch,perc,
opt pno [2'5"] (gr. II) sets
KENDOR $18.00, and up   (1517)

SUBEN, JOEL ERIC (1946-   )
Canon
string orch [2'] (med easy)
AM.COMP.AL. sc $4.60, pts $1.00,
ea.   (1518)

Gesualdo Triptych
string orch [5'] (med) AM.COMP.AL.
sc $7.25, pts $1.00, ea.   (1519)

SUITE 1772, [ARR.] see Mozart, Wolfgang
Amadeus

SUITE ENFANTINE see Devogel, Jacques

SUITE FOR SCHOOL ORCHESTRA see Hvoslef,
Ketil

SUITE FOR STRINGS see Koscielny, John

SUITE FOR THE YOUNG: TWO PIECES [ARR.]
see Dello Joio, Norman

SUITE FROM "THE GIFT" see Albert,
Thomas Russell

SUITE MIGNONNE [ARR.] see Friml, Rudolf

SUITE OF MUSIC BY ROYALTY [ARR.]
(Maganini, Quinto) sc,pts MUSICUS
f.s.   (1520)

SUITE OF WALTZES, A
(Alshin, Harry A.) string orch (gr.
III) set KENDOR 9905 $24.00, and up
[3'30]
contains: Brahms, Johannes, Famous
Waltz In G [arr.]; Campra, André,
Passepied [arr.]; Mozart,
Wolfgang Amadeus, Third Position
Waltz [arr.]; Schubert, Franz
(Peter), Flowing Stream, The
[arr.]   (1521)

SUITE POUR LA JEUNESSE [ARR.] see
Schumann, Robert (Alexander)

SULLIVAN, [SIR] ARTHUR SEYMOUR
(1842-1900)
Iolanthe: Fanfare And March [arr.]
(Leidig) (gr. III) KJOS set WO-7B
$35.00, sc WO-7F $3.00   (1522)

Mikado, The: Behold The Lord High
Executioner [arr.]
sc,pts CHESTER CH 55731 $16.50
(1523)

Pirates Of Penzance, The: Overture
[arr.]
(Irving, W.H.) 2.2.2.2. 4.2.3.1.
timp,perc,pno,strings NOVELLO sc
09.0167.09.00 f.s., pts
09.0167.09.06-07 f.s.   (1524)

Pirates Of Penzance, The: Three
Pieces [arr.]
string orch (med easy) CHESTER sc
$7.25, pts $25.25   (1525)

Suite, [arr.]
(Cox-Ife) 1.1.2.1. 2.2.2.0. timp,
opt pno,strings (diff) sc,pts
BOSWORTH f.s.   (1526)

SULTAN'S POLKA, THE [ARR.] see Albert,
Eugène Francis Charles d'

SUMMER [ARR.] see Vivaldi, Antonio,
Concerto, Op. 8, No. 2, [arr.]

SUMMER DANCES see Maw, Nicholas

SUMMER NIGHT see Forssmark, Karl A.

SUMMER SKIES see Anderson, Leroy

SUMMER STOMP see Straub, Dorothy

SUMMER'S RAIN see Elledge, Chuck

SUNRISE, SUNSET see String Orchestra
Pak No. 4

SUNRISE, SUNSET [ARR.] see Bock, Jerry

SUNSHINE IN G see Siennicki, Edmund
John

SUPERMAN: THEME [ARR.] see Williams,
John T.

SUPERSTAR STRINGS FOLIO, VOL. 1 *CCU
(Higgins; Lavender; Jennings;
Wisniewski) string orch,pno,drums
JENSON sc $14.95, kbd pt $6.95, pts
$5.95, ea.   (1527)

SUPPE, FRANZ VON (1819-1895)
Fatinitza March [arr.]
(Naylor, Frank) 2(pic).2.3.2.2alto
sax.tenor sax. 4.3.3.0. perc,
strings (med easy) sc,pts
BOSWORTH f.s.   (1528)

Light Cavalry Overture [arr.]
(Isaac) string orch (med easy) set
WYNN 6294-7294 $18.00, and up
(1529)

Poet And Peasant Overture [arr.]
(McLeod, James) string orch,opt pno
[5'40"] (gr. IV) set KENDOR
$23.00, and up   (1530)

SURFIN' U.S.A. [ARR.] see Berry, Chuck

SURPRISE SYMPHONY see Haydn, [Franz]
Joseph, Symphony No. 94, Minuet,
[arr.]

THIRAULT, MARC-DIDIER
Orchala, For Violoncello And String
Orchestra
string orch,vcl solo sc,pts
BILLAUDOT f.s.   (1577)

THOMAS
Gavotte, [arr.]
(Isaac) string orch (med easy) set
WYNN 6277 $14.00, and up   (1578)

THOMAS, AUGUSTA READ (1964-   )
Galaxy 11, 820
string orch (easy) TCAPUB sc $4.00,
set $12.00, pts $.75, ea.   (1579)

Statipizziglissic
string orch (easy) TCAPUB sc $5.00,
set $18.00, pts $.75, ea.   (1580)

Waltz
string orch (easy) TCAPUB sc $4.00,
set $12.00, pts $.75, ea.   (1581)

THOMAS-MIFUNE, WERNER
Walzer-Collage II
string orch sc,pts SCHOTTS CON 200
$8.75   (1582)

THORN BIRDS, THE: THEME [ARR.] see
Mancini, Henry

THOSE WERE THE DAYS [ARR.] see Raskin,
Eugene

THREE BINGHAMS see Cheetham, John
Everett

THREE CHINESE SCENES see Alshin, Harry

THREE CHRISTMAS CLASSICS
(Siennicki, Edmund) string orch (gr.
III) set HIGHLAND $33.00
contains: Bach, Johann Sebastian,
Jesu, Joy Of Man's Desiring
[arr.]; Bach, Johann Sebastian,
Sheep May Safely Graze [arr.];
Mozart, Leopold, Sleigh Ride
[arr.]   (1583)

THREE CLASSICAL PIECES *CC3L
(Gange, Kenneth) 2.1.3.1. 1.2.1.0.
strings (easy) sc,pts BOSWORTH f.s.
contains: Beethoven: Minuet and
Trio; Hoffmeister, F.A.: German
Dance; Haydn: Two Minuets   (1584)

THREE CZECH SONGS
(Cechvala, Al) string orch SOUTHERN
set $10.00, sc $2.50, pts $.75, ea.
(1585)

THREE DANCES FOR STRINGS see Del Borgo,
Elliot A.

THREE LITTLE PIECES see Pongracz,
Zoltan

THREE MINIATURES FOR STRINGS see
Daniels, Melvin L.

THREE MINUTES CONCERTO see Beurden,
Bernard van

THREE MOVEMENTS IN BAROQUE STYLE see
Giammario, Matteo

THREE NORWEGIAN PIECES [ARR.] see
Grieg, Edvard Hagerup

THREE PIECES BY MOZART see Mozart,
Wolfgang Amadeus

THREE PIECES FROM THE 18TH CENTURY
(Anderson, Kenneth) string orch sc,
pts BOSWORTH f.s.   (1586)

THREE SHIPS FOR CHRISTMAS
(Day, Neil) 2.1.3.1. 0+baritone
horn.2.2.0. perc,strings [8'] (med
easy) UNIV.CR sc P68401 f.s., pts
P68402 f.s.   (1587)

THREE SONGS FOR CHANUKAH [ARR.]
(Shapiro, Marsha Chusmir) string orch
(gr. II) KJOS set SO-65B $28.00, sc
SO-65F $3.00   (1588)

THREE SPANISH CHRISTMAS CAROLS [ARR.]
(Hellem, Mark) string orch (gr. III)
KJOS set SO-65B $25.00, sc SO-65F
$3.00   (1589)

THREE TEACHING PIECES FOR STRINGS see
Ilg, Steve

THREE WALTZES [ARR.] see Brahms,
Johannes

THUNDER AND LIGHTNING [ARR.] see
Strauss, Johann, [Jr.]

TICCIATI, NISO (1924-   )
Epping Forest Suite
(easy) sc,pts BOSWORTH f.s. (1590)

TILLIS, FREDERICK C. (1930-   )
Cotton Curtain, The
1.1.2.1. 4.3.2.1. timp,perc,strings
[5'] (med easy) sc AM.COMP.AL.
$16.10, perf mat rent   (1591)

Sequences And Burlesque
string orch [6'] sc AM.COMP.AL.
$9.15, perf mat rent   (1592)

TIMBERLINE TRAILS see Frost, Robert S.

TIME OF KINGS OVERTURE, A see Cacavas,
John

TINTINABULATIONS [ARR.] see Pierpont,
James

TO A WILD ROSE [ARR.] see MacDowell,
Edward Alexander

TO THE RISING SUN [ARR.] see Torjussen,
T.

TOMASI, H.
Minuet, [arr.]
2rec,fl,ob,2clar,2sax,strings sc,
pts LÉMOINE f.s.   (1593)

TOMORROW WILL BE CHRISTMAS [ARR.] see
Two Songs For The Holidays

TORJUSSEN, T.
To The Rising Sun [arr.] *Op.4,No.1
sc,pts LENGNICK f.s.   (1594)

TORME, MELVIN HOWARD (MEL) (1925-   )
Christmas Song, The [arr.]
(Jennings) string orch [2'30"] (med
easy) LEONARD-US $30.00   (1595)
(Lowden) LEONARD-US 4500015 $28.50
(1596)

TOSI, DANIEL
Livre Des Progressions, Vol. 2
orch,jr cor,opt electronic tape
SALABERT   (1597)

TOUCHING GRACE, WE PRINCES THREE see
Angels, Shepherds, Christmas, Kings

TOURBILLONNEMENTS see Lefebvre, Claude

TOURDION [ARR.]
(Hare) sc,pts CHESTER CH 55664 $16.50
(1598)

TOWNSEND, JILL
Carnival Time
string orch (med easy) CHESTER
CH 55716 sc $7.75, pts $23.70
(1599)

Fridays, Saturdays
string orch CHESTER sc $6.75, pts
$35.00   (1600)

Fun And Games
string orch CHESTER sc $6.75, pts
$35.00   (1601)

TOY SYMPHONY see Arnold, Malcolm

TOYLAND [ARR.] see Herbert, Victor

TRACK, GERHARD (1934-   )
Symphonic March
2(pic).2.2.2. 4.2.3.1. timp,perc,
strings (gr. IV) set KJOS WO2B
$35.00   (1602)

TRAIN see Schafer, R. Murray

TRAVELS IN STYLE *CCU
(Osborne, Tony) string orch (gr. III)
set BOOSEY $16.00   (1603)

TRAVIATA, LA: MEDLEY OF WALTZES [ARR.]
see Verdi, Giuseppe

TRES BALADAS see Rhoads, William Earl

TRES DANZAS DE MEXICO see Rhoads,
William Earl

TRI SKLADBY see Faust, Jan

TRIBUTE TO LERNER AND LOEWE, A [ARR.]
see Loewe, Frederick

TRINAL CONTRASTS [ARR.] see Rusch

TRINIDAD see McLeod, James (Red)

TRIPTYCH FOR STRINGS see Del Borgo,
Elliot A.

TRISTESSE [ARR.] see Chopin, Frédéric

TRITOGNO see Andriessen, Jurriaan

TROIS FRANCAIS EN AMERIQUE
2rec,2clar,2sax,strings sc,pts
LEMOINE f.s.
contains: Jacob, [Dom] Clement,
Blues [arr.]; Thiriet, Maurice,
Plantation Song [arr.]; Wiener,
Jean, Spiritual [arr.]   (1604)

TROIS PIECES POUR ORCHESTRA D'ENFANTS
see Cauvin, A.

TRULY [ARR.] see Richie, Lionel

TSCHAIKOWSKY, PJOTR ILJITSCH
see TCHAIKOVSKY, PIOTR ILYICH

TUMBLEWEED see Frost, Robert S.

TUNES FOR MY STRING ORCHESTRA *CCU
(Nelson, Sheila) string orch,opt pno
(gr. I) set BOOSEY $15.25   (1605)

TUNICK, JONATHAN (1938-   )
Endless Love [arr.]
(Holcombe) (med easy) LEONARD-US
0489100 $20.00   (1606)
(Holcombe) string orch (med easy)
LEONARD-US 0489110 $15.00   (1607)

TURKISH MARCH [ARR.] see Mozart,
Wolfgang Amadeus

TUROK, PAUL HARRIS (1929-   )
Four Studies
orch,opt cor SCHIRM.G set $45.00,
cor pts,set $15.00, sc $4.00, pts
$1.50   (1608)

TURTLE DOVE, THE [ARR.]
(Myers, Theldon) string orch (med
easy) set LAKES $17.50, and up
(1609)

TUXEDO JUNCTION [ARR.] see Feyne, Buddy

TV SPECTACULAR
(Curnow, James) JENSON 593-23010
$45.00   (1610)

TWENTIANA
(Ades, Hawley) (med) SHAWNEE set
$25.00, pts $.75, ea.   (1611)

TWINKLE, TWINKLE LITTLE FUGUE see
Weinstangel, Sasha

TWO BACH MINUETS, [ARR.] see Bach,
Johann Sebastian

TWO BRITISH AIRES [ARR.]
(Chase) string orch (easy) LEONARD-US
08720169 $25.00   (1612)

TWO BY BERLIN see Berlin, Irving

TWO CHRISTMAS FAVORITES
(Frost, Robert) string orch,opt pno
[2'40"] (gr. I) sets KENDOR $16.00,
and up   (1613)

TWO COUNTRY DANCES
(Frost, Robert S.) string orch,opt
pno (gr. III) KENDOR 9928 f.s.
[3'30]
contains: Arne, Thomas Augustine,
Jig [arr.]; Schubert, Franz
(Peter), Contra Dance [arr.]   (1614)

TWO FOLK SONGS [ARR.]
(Wells, Dorothy) string orch,opt pno
(gr. I) SOUTHERN SO-45 sc $3.00,
set $16.00, pts $1.25, ea.   (1615)

TWO FRENCH CAROLS
(Hastings, Ross) string orch,opt pno
BOURNE sc $2.50, set $17.50, and up
contains: Il Est Ne, Le Divin
Enfant [arr.]; Quittez Pateurs
[arr.]   (1616)

TWO GUITARS [ARR.]
(McLeod, James) string orch (gr. III)
set HIGHLAND $29.00   (1617)

TWO HANDEL MARCHES [ARR.] see Handel,
George Frideric

TWO HEBREW MELODIES [ARR.]
(Niehaus, Lennie; Leidig, Vernon)
string orch (gr. I) set HIGHLAND
$20.00, and up   (1618)

TWO-HORSE OPEN SLEIGH see Fletcher,
Gary

TWO IRISH FOLKSONGS [ARR.]
(Chase) string orch [2'] (med easy)
LEONARD-US $25.00   (1619)

TWO MADRIGALS
(Cheyette, I.) [4'30"] KERBY 694C set
$15.00, sc $1.50   (1620)

TWO MOODS [ARR.] see Stravinsky, Igor

TWO MOODS IN 3-4 TIME see Klotman,
Robert

TWO PERSUASIONS see Frost, Robert S.

TWO PIECES [ARR.] see Bartók, Béla

TWO PIECES FOR STRING ORCHESTRA
(Rhoads, William) string orch set
SHAWNEE J-137 $18.00

contains: Biehl, E., Evening
Prayer, An [arr.]; Monar, A.J.,
Joyous Morn, A [arr.]   (1621)

TWO PIECES FOR YOUNG ORCHESTRA [ARR.]
(Applebaum) BELWIN CO 00186 sc $4.00,
set $25.00   (1622)

TWO PIECES FOR YOUNG STRINGS see
Beecher, Kirk

TWO PRELUDES see Hughes-Jones, Llifon

TWO SARABANDES [ARR.] see Brahms,
Johannes

TWO SETS OF ROUNDS see Stephan, Richard

TWO SEVENTEENTH CENTURY DANCES [ARR.]
see Purcell, Henry

TWO SONGS FOR CHANUKAH [ARR.]
(Arnold, Alan; Ward, Norman) string
orch,opt perc,opt pno set FIDDLE
$16.00   (1623)

TWO SONGS FOR THE HOLIDAYS
(Jurey, Edward) (med easy) BELWIN
CO 00199 $35.00
contains: Pat-A-Pan [arr.];
Tomorrow Will Be Christmas [arr.]
                                         (1624)

TWO SOUTH AMERICAN TANGOS [ARR.]
(Isaac, Merle J.) (gr. III) set
HIGHLAND $37.00
contains: Rodriguez, Matos,
Comparsita, La; Villoldo, A.G.,
Choclo, El   (1625)

TWO TUNES FOR FIDDLIN' see Siennicki,
Edmund John

TWO YULETIDE CAROLS
(Frost, Robert S.) string orch,opt
pno (gr. II) sets KENDOR $16.00,
and up
contains: Coventry Carol; Holly And
The Ivy, The   (1626)

UKRAINIAN CAROL [ARR.]
(Pettersen, Nancy) string orch,pno/
harp (med easy) BELWIN BSO 00081
$35.00   (1627)

UKRAINIAN FOLK SONGS [ARR.]
(Dackow, Sandra) string orch (easy)
LUDWIG STRO-35 $30.00   (1628)

ULTAN, LLOYD (1929-   )
Wakonda Sketch
2.1.3.1. 2.2.2.1. strings [7']
(med) sc AM.COMP.AL. $5.40, perf
mat rent   (1629)

UMBRELLAS OF CHERBOURG: HIGHLIGHTS
[ARR.] see Legrand, Michel

UNDER THE BOARDWALK [ARR.] see Resnick,
Artie

UNDER THE DOUBLE EAGLE [ARR.] see
Wagner, Josef

UNFINISHED SYMPHONY [ARR.] see
Schubert, Franz (Peter), Symphony
No. 8, [arr.]

UNICORN, THE see Myers, Theldon

UP AND BACK A DOUBLE see Auton, John

URBANIAK, MICHAL
Kurpie Folk Song
string orch CAMERICA CAM0135 $25.00
                                         (1630)
March
string orch CAMERICA CAM0134 $25.00
                                         (1631)
Serenada
string orch CAMERICA CAM0133 $25.00
                                         (1632)

VAGABOND STRINGS see Niehaus, Leonard

VALSE [ARR.] see Brahms, Johannes

VALSE MODERNE see Müller, J. Frederick

VANGELIS
Chariots Of Fire [arr.]
(Reilly, Jim) (gr. II) WARNER
575-40058 $30.00   (1633)

VANGELIS (cont'd.)

Hymne [arr.]
(Curnow, James) string orch (gr.
III) JENSON 502-08030 $24.00
                                         (1634)

VANHAL, JOHANN BAPTIST
see WANHAL, JOHANN BAPTIST

VANHALL, JAN KRTITEL
see WANHAL, JOHANN BAPTIST

VARIATIONEN UBER EIN THEMA VON HANDEL
see Baumann, Herbert

VARIATIONS ON A FOLK MELODY [ARR.]
(Alshin, Harry) (med diff) BELWIN
CO 00197 $45.00   (1635)

VARIATIONS ON A FRENCH THEME see Pavey,
Sidney

VARIATIONS ON A GROUND see Shapiro,
Marsha Chusmir

VARIATIONS ON A NURSERY TUNE [ARR.] see
Concert Pieces For Young String
Orchestra

VARIATIONS ON A PAGANINI THEME [ARR.]
see Rachmaninoff, Sergey
Vassilievich

VARIATIONS ON A QUAKER HYMN see Follas,
Ronald

VARIATIONS ON THE 24TH CAPRICE [ARR.]
see Paganini, Niccolo

VARIATIONS ON "THE MINSTREL BOY" see
Breedon, Daniel

VELLONES, PIERRE (1889-1939)
Aventure De Babar, Une: Suite No. 1
[arr.]
fl,ob,2clar,bsn,2horn,strings sc,
pts LEMOINE f.s.   (1636)

Aventure De Babar, Une: Suite No. 2
[arr.]
fl,ob,2clar,bsn,2horn,strings sc,
pts LEMOINE f.s.   (1637)

VENTRICLE OF MEMORY, THE see Coleman,
Christopher

VERACINI, FRANCESCO MARIA (1690-1768)
Gigue, [arr.]
(Isaac) string orch (med) set WYNN
6286 $18.00, and up   (1638)

Sonata in E minor,Second Movement,
[arr.]
(Isaac, Merle J.) string orch (gr.
III) set HIGHLAND $29.00   (1639)

VERCKEN, FRANÇOIS (1928-   )
Pastel
2.2.2.2. 2.2.2.0. timp,vibra,
strings [3'] (from the series
"feuilles vives") BILLAUDOT perf
mat rent   (1640)

VERDI, GIUSEPPE (1813-1901)
Aida: Ballet Music [arr.]
(Isaac) BELWIN CO 00159 sc $5.00,
set $35.00   (1641)

Nabucco: Overture [arr.]
(Dackow, Sandra) [4'20"] (med) set
LUDWIG LLE-80 $65.00, and up
                                         (1642)
Traviata, La: Medley Of Waltzes
[arr.]
(McLeod, James) string orch (gr.
III) set HIGHLAND $29.00   (1643)

VICAR OF BRAY, THE [ARR.] see Folk-
Songs For Strings, Set 2

VIENNA LIFE [ARR.] see Strauss, Johann,
[Jr.]

VIER STUCKE ZUR PASSIONS UND
WEIHNACHTSZEIT see Gasser, Ulrich

VIJF NUMMERS see Vriend, Huub de

VILLOLDO, A.G.
Choclo, El *see TWO SOUTH AMERICAN
TANGOS [aRR.]

VINTAGE WESTERN see Geeson, Denis

VITAVA, [ARR.] see Smetana, Bedrich,
Moldau, The, [arr.]

VIVA VIVALDI [ARR.] see Vivaldi,
Antonio

VIVALDI, ANTONIO (1678-1741)
Autumn: Allegro, [arr.]
see Concerto, Op. 8, No. 3, [arr.]

VIVALDI, ANTONIO (cont'd.)

Autumn [arr.] *see BAROQUE SUITE NO.
2
see Concerto, Op. 8, No. 3, [arr.]

Chorale And Fanfare [arr.]
(Alshin, Harry A.) string orch
[2'55"] (gr. III) set KENDOR 9795
$23.00, and up   (1644)

Concerti, Op. 8 Nos. 1, 3 And 4
[arr.]
(Leidig) "Four Seasons: Spring,
Autumn, Winter [arr.]" string
orch (gr. II) set HIGHLAND
$20.00, and up   (1645)

Concerto for 2 Violins and String
Orchestra in D minor, MIN 210,
[arr.]
(Wright) string orch,2vln soli
SOUTHERN $37.50   (1646)

Concerto for 2 Violins and String
Orchestra in G, MIN 164, [arr.]
(Wright) string orch,2vln soli
SOUTHERN $37.50   (1647)

Concerto Grosso, F.IX no. 2, in G,
[arr.]
(Matesky, Ralph) RICORDI-IT RR 2120
set $19.00, sc $4.75, pts $1.00,
pno red $1.75   (1648)

Concerto in C minor, MIN 212,
[excerpt], [arr.]
(Clebanoff, Herman) string orch
(Largo [arr.]) DORABET D-137 f.s.
                                         (1649)
Concerto in G, MIN 213, [excerpt],
[arr.]
(Clebanoff, Herman) string orch
(Allegro [arr.]) DORABET D-138
f.s.   (1650)

Concerto Italiano [arr.]
(Alshin, Harry) string orch (gr.
IV) set HIGHLAND $29.00   (1651)

Concerto Madrigalesco
string orch SCHOTT 71 U0166 sc
$7.75, pts $1.75   (1652)

Concerto, Op. 8, No. 1, [arr.]
(Alshin, Harry) "Little Spring
Music, A [arr.]" string orch
BOSTON sc,pts $10.00, sc $4.25,
pts $1.75, ea.   (1653)
(Riggio, Donald) "Spring, From The
Four Seasons [arr.]" string orch
(gr. II) sc,pts JENSON 502-19010
$24.00   (1654)

Concerto, Op. 8, No. 2, [arr.] (from
The Four Seasons)
(Alshin, Harry) "Little Summer
Music, A [arr.]" string orch
BOSTON sc,pts $10.00, sc $4.25,
pts $1.75, ea.   (1655)
(Riggio, Donald) "Summer [arr.]"
string orch (gr. III) JENSON
502-19080 $30.00   (1656)

Concerto, Op. 8, No. 3, [arr.]
(Alshin, Harry A.) "Autumn [arr.]"
string orch [2'35"] (gr. III)
sets KENDOR $17.00, and up   (1657)
(Frazer, James) "Autumn: Allegro,
[arr.]" ([excerpt]) MIDDLE
CMK 208 f.s.   (1658)

Concerto, Op. 8, No. 4,First
Movement, [arr.]
(Bauernschmidt) "Inverno, L': First
Movement, [arr.]" (med) sets WYNN
4307-5307 $28.00, and up   (1659)

Concerto, Op. 8, No. 4,Second
Movement,Third Movement, [arr.]
(Bauernschmidt) "Inverno, L':
Second And Third Movements
[arr.]" (med) sets WYNN 4308-5308
$36.00, and up   (1660)

Concerto, Op. 8, No. 4, [arr.]
(Alshin, Harry) "Little Winter
Music, A [arr.]" string orch
BOSTON sc,pts $10.00, sc $4.25,
pts $1.75, ea.   (1661)

Fantasia For Strings [arr.]
(Alshin, Harry A.) string orch
[2'20"] (gr. III) set KENDOR 9820
$19.00, and up   (1662)

Four Seasons: Spring, Autumn, Winter
[arr.]
see Concerti, Op. 8 Nos. 1, 3 And 4
[arr.]

Gloria: Themes [arr.]
(Alshin, Harry A.) string orch,opt
pno [2'20"] (gr. III) set KENDOR
$21.00, and up   (1663)

VIVALDI; ANTONIO (cont'd.)

Hunt, The, [arr.] (from The Four
   Seasons)
   (Rokos) 2.1.2.1. 2.2.2.0. timp,
   strings (easy) sc,pts BOSWORTH
   f.s.   (1664)

Inverno, L': First Movement, [arr.]
   see Concerto, Op. 8, No. 4,First
   Movement, [arr.]

Inverno, L': Second And Third
   Movements [arr.]
   see Concerto, Op. 8, No. 4,Second
   Movement,Third Movement, [arr.]

Little Spring Music, A [arr.]
   see Concerto, Op. 8, No. 1, [arr.]

Little Summer Music, A [arr.]
   see Concerto, Op. 8, No. 2, [arr.]

Little Winter Music, A [arr.]
   see Concerto, Op. 8, No. 4, [arr.]

Magnificat [arr.]
   (Alshin, Harry A.) string orch
   [1'30"] (gr. II) set KENDOR 9745
   $23.00, and up   (1665)

Spring, From The Four Seasons [arr.]
   see Concerto, Op. 8, No. 1, [arr.]

Summer [arr.]
   see Concerto, Op. 8, No. 2, [arr.]

Viva Vivaldi [arr.]
   (Goldsmith, Owen) string orch (gr.
   I) BELWIN BSO 00057 $30.00 (1666)

VLAK, K. (1938-   )
   Simple Symphony
   MOLENAAR 03175007 f.s.   (1667)

VOLGA BOATMAN SWING, THE
   (Caponegro, John) string orch,opt
   perc,opt pno [2'10"] (gr. I/gr. II)
   sets KENDOR $14.00, and up (1668)

VOLKMANN, ROBERT (1815-1883)
   Serenade No. 2, Op. 63: Waltz [arr.]
   (Dasch) string orch FITZSIMONS
   F0560 set $12.00, sc $3.00, pts
   $2.00, ea.   (1669)

VOLKSMELODIEN AUS FRANKREICH
   (Lilienfeld, Francois) sc PAN 1103
   f.s.   (1670)

VOLKSMELODIEN AUS SCHOTTLAND, KANADA
   UND DER SCHWEIZ
   (Lilienfeld, Francois) sc PAN 1102
   f.s.   (1671)

VOSS, CARL
   Symphony for Strings
   string orch (gr. IV) KJOS set
   SO-66B $25.00, sc SO-66F $3.00
                               (1672)

VRIEND, HUUB DE (1954-   )
   Vijf Nummers
   variable instrumentation [24'] sc
   DONEMUS f.s., perf mat rent (1673)

WABASH CANNONBALL [ARR.]
   (McLeod, James "Red") 2(opt
   pic).1.2.1. 2.2.1.1. opt perc,opt
   pno,strings [2'20"] (gr. IV/gr. V)
   sets KENDOR $24.00, and up (1674)
   (McLeod, James "Red") string orch,opt
   perc,pno [2'20"] (gr. IV/gr. V)
   sets KENDOR $17.00, and up (1675)
   (Rosenhaus) string orch (med easy)
   LEONARD-US 04849875 $20.00 (1676)

WAGNER, JOSEF (1856-1908)
   Under The Double Eagle [arr.]
   (Naylor, F.) 1+pic.2.3.2.alto
   sax.tenor sax. 2.3.3.0. perc,
   strings (med easy) sc,pts
   BOSWORTH f.s.   (1677)

WAGNER, RICHARD (1813-1883)
   Lohengrin: Choeur Des Fiancailles
   [arr.]
   see Chopin, Frédéric, Tristesse
   [arr.]

   Lohengrin: Elsa's Procession To The
   Cathedral [arr.]
   (Kohut, Daniel) (gr. II) set
   HIGHLAND $37.00   (1678)

   Meistersinger, Die: March Of The
   Meistersingers [arr.]
   (Dackow, Sandra) string orch
   [1'45"] (easy) LUDWIG STRO-32
   $30.00   (1679)

WAGNER, RICHARD (cont'd.)

   Meistersinger, Die: Overture [arr.]
   (Rokos) 2+pic.2.3.1. 2.2.3.1. timp,
   4perc,strings [6'] sc,pts
   BOSWORTH f.s.   (1680)

   Ride Of The Valkyries [arr.]
   (Carlin) 1.1.2.1.alto sax.tenor
   sax. 2.2.2.0. timp,perc,pno,
   strings CARLIN sc $4.00, set
   $38.00, pts $1.50, ea.   (1681)

   Rienzi: Overture [arr.]
   (Dackow, Sandra) string orch
   [7'10"] (med) LUDWIG STRO-38
   $55.00   (1682)

   Tannhauser: Entrance And March Of The
   Guests [arr.]
   (Dackow, Sandra) string orch (med)
   LUDWIG STRO-50 $40.00   (1683)

WAKONDA SKETCH see Ultan, Lloyd

WALDTEUFEL, EMILE (1837-1915)
   Espana Waltz [arr.]
   (Isaac) string orch (med easy) set
   WYNN 6292-7292 $14.00, and up
                               (1684)

   Estudiantina Waltz [arr.,]
   (Isaac) string orch (med) sets WYNN
   6269-7269 $18.00, and up   (1685)

   Skaters, The [arr.]
   (Arnold, Alan) string orch,opt
   perc,opt pno set FIDDLE $16.00
                               (1686)

   Syncopated Skaters [arr.]
   (McLeod, James) string orch,pno
   [4'20"] (gr. III) set KENDOR 9908
   $24.00, and up   (1687)

WALK ON BY [ARR.] see Bacharach, Burt
   F.

WALKER, G.
   Anthony Gell Suite
   (med diff) sc,pts BOSWORTH f.s.
                               (1688)

   Concertante For Clarinet And String
   Orchestra
   string orch,clar solo (diff) sc,pts
   BOSWORTH f.s.   (1689)

WALKER, GWYNETH (1947-   )
   Fanfare, Interlude And Finale
   2.1.1.1. 2.2.0.0. timp,strings
   [11'] WALKER MUS. PRO. sc
   $175.00, pts rent   (1690)

   Match Point
   2.2.2.2. 4.2.3.0. 3perc,strings
   [6'] WALKER MUS. PRO. sc $150.00,
   pts rent   (1691)

   Symphony For Young String Players
   string orch [8'] WALKER MUS. PRO.
   sc $10.00, pts $10.00, ea. (1692)

WALTZ see Thomas, Augusta Read

WALTZ [ARR.] see Mozart, Wolfgang
   Amadeus

WALTZ ETUDE see McLeod, James (Red)

WALTZ GIOCOSO see McLeod, James (Red)

WALTZ MEDLEY
   (Heilmann, Francis) 2fl,2clar,2alto
   sax,2trp,trom,perc,pno,strings
   [2'30"] (easy) set HEILNN $27.00,
   and up   (1693)
   (Heilmann, Francis) string orch,perc,
   pno [2'30"] (easy) set HEILNN
   $21.00, and up   (1694)

WALTZ MEMORIES
   (Heilmann, Francis) 2fl,2clar,
   2soprano sax,2trp,trom,perc,pno,
   strings [2'10"] (easy) set HEILNN
   $27.00, and up   (1695)
   (Heilmann, Francis) string orch,perc,
   pno [2'10"] (easy) set HEILNN
   $21.00, and up   (1696)

WALTZING MATILDA [ARR.]
   (Hultgren, Ralph) string orch (gr. I)
   set HIGHLAND $29.00   (1697)

WALTZING WOMBAT, THE see Hultgren,
   Ralph

WALZER-COLLAGE II see Thomas-Mifune,
   Werner

WANHAL, JOHANN BAPTIST (JAN KRTITEL)
   (1739-1813)
   Concerto for Piano and Orchestra in C
   (Csurka; Vigh) sc,pts EMB 13552
   f.s.   (1698)

WARD, NORMAN
   Blades And Ice
   string orch,opt perc,opt pno set
   FIDDLE $16.00   (1699)

   Holiday Festival Of Lights, A
   string orch,opt perc,opt pno set
   FIDDLE $16.00   (1700)

   Plucky And Bowdiddle
   string orch,opt perc,opt pno set
   FIDDLE $16.00   (1701)

   Rocking Strings, The
   string orch,opt perc,opt pno set
   FIDDLE $16.00   (1702)

   Zoo Folk
   string orch,opt perc,opt pno set
   FIDDLE $20.00   (1703)

WARP NINE see Whitney

WARRIOR, THE see Hultgren, Ralph

WASATCH BOULEVARD see Frost, Robert S.

WASHBURN, ROBERT BROOKS (1928-   )
   Song And Dance
   string orch [5'] sets BOOSEY
   $12.00, and up   (1704)

WASHINGTON, NED (1901-   )
   I'm Getting Sentimental Over You
   [arr.] (composed with Bassman,
   George)
   (Sopkin) 2.2.2.2.3sax. 0.0.0.0.
   timp,perc,strings (med easy) set
   KALMUS A6037 $12.50, and up (1705)

WATER MUSIC: BOURREE AND HORNPIPE
   [ARR.] see Handel, George Frideric

WATER MUSIC: HORNPIPE [ARR.] see
   Handel, George Frideric

WATER MUSIC: MINUETS I AND II [ARR.]
   see Handel, George Frideric

WAVES OF THE DANUBE [ARR.] see
   Ivanovici, Ion

WAXMAN, FRANZ (1906-1967)
   Mr. Roberts: Suite
   [2'24"] FIDELIO   (1706)

WAY YOU LOOK TONIGHT, THE [ARR.] see
   Kern, Jerome

WAYFARING STRANGER [ARR.]
   (Clebanoff, Herman) string orch
   DORABET D-142 f.s.   (1707)
   (Myers, Theldon) string orch (gr. IV)
   LAKES $20.00   (1708)

WE NEED A LITTLE CHRISTMAS [ARR.] see
   Herman, Jerry

WE THREE KINGS [ARR.]
   (Heilmann, Francis) string orch,pno,
   perc [2'50"] (easy) set HEILNN
   $21.00, and up   (1709)

WE WISH YOU A MERRY CHRISTMAS [ARR.]
   (Curnow, James) string orch (easy)
   JENSON 502-23020 $30.00   (1710)
   (Wieloszynski, Stephen) string orch,
   opt pno [2'15"] (gr. I) set KENDOR
   8845 $19.00, and up   (1711)
   see Concert Pieces For Young String
   Orchestra

WEBBER, ANDREW LLOYD
   see LLOYD WEBBER, ANDREW

WEBER, CARL MARIA VON (1786-1826)
   Concert March [arr.]
   (Isaac) (med) set WYNN 4276-5276
   $22.00, and up   (1712)
   (Isaac) string orch (med) set WYNN
   6298-7298 $14.00, and up   (1713)

   Country Dance [arr.]
   (Isaac) string orch (med) set WYNN
   6284 $14.00, and up   (1714)

   Deux Pieces: Romane Et Marche [arr.]
   2rec,fl,2clar,alto sax,2gtr,strings
   sc,pts LEMOINE f.s.   (1715)

   Freischutz, Der: Chorus Of Huntsmen
   [arr.]
   (Dackow, Sandra) string orch
   [1'20"] (easy) LUDWIG STRO-29
   $30.00   (1716)

   Freischütz, Der: Peasant Waltz And
   March [arr.]
   (Carter, Anthony) 2.2.3.1. 2.2.3.1.
   timp,3perc,opt pno,strings [4']
   sc,pts BOSWORTH f.s.   (1717)

WEGWEISER, DER [ARR.] see Schubert,
   Franz (Peter)

WEINBERGER, JAROMIR (1896-1967)
Schwanda: Polka [arr.]
(Stone, David) 1.1.2+bass
clar.1.alto sax.tenor sax.
2.2.1.0. timp,perc,opt pno,
strings sets BOOSEY HHS 82
$26.00, and up   (1718)

WEINSTANGEL, SASHA (1947-   )
Twinkle, Twinkle Little Fugue
1.1.1.1. 1.1.1.0. drums,strings
[7'] CAN.MUS.CENT. MI 1200 W424T
(1719)

WELCOME TO ORKNEY, A see Davies, Peter
Maxwell

WELSH DANCES NO. 3 see Hoddinott, Alun

WERDIN, EBERHARD (1911-   )
Balletto
2fl,drums,strings [22'] sc,pts
SCHWANN S2362 f.s.   (1720)

WERNER, JEAN-JACQUES (1935-   )
Musique Au Feutre Bleu
2.0.3.0.sax. 1.0.0.0. perc,acord,
pno,2gtr,strings [6'] BILLAUDOT
perf mat rent   (1721)

Pour Les Trilles Et Les Notes
Repetees
2.2.2.2. 2.2.2.0. timp,perc,harp,
strings [4'] (from the series
"feuilles vives") BILLAUDOT perf
mat rent   (1722)

WESTERA, A.
Bambino
sc,pts BROEKMANS 767 f.s. (1723)

WESTERN RIDER see Heilmann, Francis

WESTMINSTER PRELUDE AND FUGUE see
Shaffer, David

WESTON REFLECTIONS see Dawson, Ted

WHEN I FALL IN LOVE [ARR.] see Young,
Victor

WHEN I'M SIXTY-FOUR [ARR.] see Lennon,
John

WHEN THE SAINTS GO MARCHING IN
(Caponegro, John) string orch,opt
perc,opt pno [1'35"] (gr. I/gr. II)
sets KENDOR $14.00, and up (1724)

WHISTLER, THE see Frost, Robert S.

WHISTLIN' RUFUS [ARR.] see Mills,
Frederick Allen (Kerry)

WHITE KNIGHT AND THE DRAGON, THE see
Cameron, James

WHITFIELD, NORMAN
I Heard It Through The Grapevine
[arr.] (composed with Strong,
Barrett)
(Cerulli, Bob) (med easy) CPP
2410IB7X $40.00   (1725)

WHITNEY
Warp Nine
(easy) CPP 0225WB7X $40.00 (1726)

WIGGINS, ARTHUR M. (1920-   )
Red Carpet, The
2+pic.2.2+opt bass clar.2. 4.3.3.1.
timp,perc,strings (gr. IV) BELWIN
CO 00194 $50.00   (1727)

WILLIAM TELL: OVERTURE [ARR.] see
Rossini, Gioacchino

WILLIAM TELL: OVERTURE, FINALE [ARR.]
see Rossini, Gioacchino

WILLIAMS, CLIFTON (1923-1976)
Laredo [arr.]
(Astwood, Michael) 2+pic.2.3+bass
clar.2. 4.3.3.1. timp,perc,
strings (gr. IV) SOUTHERN A-34 sc
$7.50, set $50.00, pts $2.50. ea.
(1728)

WILLIAMS, JOHN T. (1932-   )
Dance Of The Witches [arr.]
(Curnow, James) string orch (gr.
III) JENSON 502-04040 $30.00
(1729)

E.T.: Selections [arr.]
(Cacavas) 3.2.4.2.4sax. 4.3.3.1.
timp,perc,opt pno,strings MCA
00120095 $45.00   (1730)
(Erickson) 2.2.3.2. 4.3.3.1. timp,
perc,strings MCA 00120096 $30.00
(1731)

E.T.: Theme [arr.]
(Ployhar) MCA 00120094 $30.00
(1732)

Mission, The [arr.]
(Curnow, James) string orch (gr.
III) JENSON 502-13010 $30.00
(1733)

WILLIAMS, JOHN T. (cont'd.)

Olympic Fanfare And Theme [arr.]
(Riggio, Donald) 2.1.2.1. 4.3.3.1.
timp,perc,strings (gr. III) sc,
pts JENSON 503-15010 $36.00
(1734)

Return Of The Jedi: Ewok Celebration
[arr.]
(Riggio, Donald) string orch (gr.
II) JENSON 502-05010 $20.00
(1735)

Return Of The Jedi: Highlights [arr.]
(Rosenhaus, Steven) (gr. II) JENSON
503-18010 $40.00   (1736)

Return Of The Jedi: Parade Of The
Ewoks [arr.]
(Riggio, Donald) (gr. III) JENSON
503-16010 $40.00   (1737)

Superman: Theme [arr.]
(Rothrock, Carson) (gr. III) WARNER
575-10036 $35.00   (1738)

WILSON, BRIAN
I Get Around [arr.]
(Cerulli, Bob) string orch (easy)
CPP $25.00   (1739)

WIND BENEATH MY WINGS, THE [ARR.] see
Henley, Larry

WINDMILLS see Pavey, Sidney

WINTER FUN see Heilmann, Francis

WINTER MORN, [ARR.] see Tchaikovsky,
Piotr Ilyich

WINTER WONDERLAND [ARR.] see Bernard,
Felix

WINTER'S SUNSHINE see Kovats, Daniel

WISHING WELL, THE see Frost, Robert S.

WITHOUT YOU [ARR.] see Dozier

WONDER, STEVIE
see MORRIS, STEVLAND

WONDER WALTZ see Shaffer, David

WONDERFUL WORLD OF STRINGS: THE
ROMANTIC PERIOD *CC13L
(Matesky, Ralph) string orch sc,pts
FISCHER,C 04659-04664 f.s. (1740)

WOOD, ARTHUR
Moorland Fiddlers
2.2.2.2.3sax. 2.2.3.0. timp,perc,
strings (med easy) set KALMUS
A6032 $30.00, and up   (1741)

WOODARD, JAMES (1929-   )
American Folk Ballad
string orch MMB f.s.   (1742)

WORRIED DRUMMER, THE [ARR.] see
Schreiner, Alexander

XINGU see Hoyland, Victor

YE BANKS AND BRAES [ARR.] see Folk-
Songs For Strings, Set 2

YELLOW ROSE OF TEXAS, THE
(Davis, Albert O.) sets LUDWIG
BGS-110 $20.00, and up   (1743)

YELLOW SUBMARINE [ARR.] see Lennon,
John

YESTERDAY [ARR.] see Lennon, John

YORKSHIRE BALLAD see Barnes, James

YOU LIGHT UP MY LIFE [ARR.] see Brooks,
Joe

YOU'LL NEVER WALK ALONE [ARR.] see
Rodgers, Richard

YOUNG, VICTOR (1900-1956)
When I Fall In Love [arr.]
(Custer) LEONARD-US 08720159 $35.00
(1744)

YOUNG STRING PLAYERS see Matz, Rudolf

YOU'RE A GRAND OLD FLAG [ARR.] see
Cohan, George Michael

YOUTH ORCHESTRA EXERCISES see Kulesha,
Gary

YULETIDE GREETING, A [ARR.]
(Higgins, Jim) string orch,opt pno
[4'] (gr. III) KENDOR 9945 f.s.
(1745)

YULETIME STRING ALBUM *CCU
(Balent, Andy) string orch LEE SO309
$25.00   (1746)

ZEHN KLEINE STUCKE see Grieshaber,
Reinhard

ZELLER, CARL (1842-1898)
Don't Be Cross [arr.]
(Naylor, Frank) 1.1.2.1. 2.2.2.0.
perc,pno,strings (easy) sc,pts
BOSWORTH f.s.   (1747)

ZEMPLENI, L.
Romance And Stamping
perc,strings sc,pts EMB 13615 f.s.
(1748)

ZIBERLIN, FRANÇOIS
Petite Gavotte [arr.] *see DEUX
DANSES

ZILCHER, P.
Minuet Gracieuse [arr.]
(Twinn, Sidney) string orch sc,pts
LENGNICK f.s. contains also:
Newton, E., Belinda's Rigadoon
[arr.]   (1749)

Spanish Serenade [arr.]
(Twinn, Sidney) string orch sc,pts
LENGNICK f.s. contains also:
Friml, Rudolf, Bohemian Dance
[arr.]   (1750)

ZOO FOLK see Ward, Norman

ZUEIGNUNG [ARR.] see Strauss, Richard

ZUR DER ZWERGE [ARR.] see Grieg, Edvard
Hagerup

ZWEI STÜCKE: FRAGMENT; METAMORPHOSE see
Jaecker, Friedrich

Publisher Directory

The list of publishers which follows contains the code assigned for each publisher, the name and address of the publisher, and U.S. agents who distribute the publications. This is the master list for the Music-In-Print series and represents all publishers who have submitted information for inclusion in the series. Therefore, all of the publishers do not necessarily occur in the present volume.

Code	Publisher	U.S. Agent
A COEUR JOIE	Éditions A Coeur Joie Les Passerelles, BP 9151 24 avenue Joannès Masset F-69263 Lyon cédex 09 France	
A MOLL DUR	A Moll Dur Publishing House	
A-R ED	A-R Editions, Inc. 801 Deming Way Madison, WI 53717	
AAP	Edition AAP (Audio Attic Productions) Aas-Wangsvei 8 N-1600 Fredrikstad Norway	
ABC	ABC Music Co.	BOURNE
ABER.GRP.	The Aberbach Group 988 Madison Avenue New York, NY 10021	
ABERDEEN	Aberdeen Music, Inc. 170 N.E. 33rd Street Fort Lauderdale, FL 33334	PLYMOUTH
ABINGDON	Abingdon Press P.O. Box 801 Nashville, TN 37202	
ABRSM	Associated Board of the Royal Schools of Music 14 Bedford Square London WC1B 3JG England	PRESSER
ACADEM	Academia Music Ltd. 16-5, Hongo 3-Chome Bunkyo-ku Tokyo, 113 Japan	KALMUS,A
ACCURA	Accura Music P.O. Box 4260 Athens, OH 45701-4260	
ACORD	Edizioni Accordo	CURCI
ACSB	Antigua Casa Sherry-Brener, Ltd. of Madrid 3145 West 63rd Street Chicago, IL 60629	
ADAM	D. Adams Music P.O. Box 8371 Asheville, NC 28814	
ADD.PRESS	Addington Press	ROYAL
ADD.-WESLEY	Addison-Wesley Publishing Co., Inc. 2725 Sand Hill Road Menlo Park, CA 94025	
AEOLUS	Aeolus Publishing Co. 60 Park Terrace West New York, NY 10034	
AGAPE	Agape	HOPE
AHLINS	Ahlins Musikförlag Box 26072 S-100 41 Stockholm Sweden	

Code	Publisher	U.S. Agent
AHN	Ahn & Simrock Sonnenstraße 19 D-8 München Germany	
AKADDV	Akademische Druck- und Verlagsanstalt Schönaugasse 6 A-8010 Graz Austria	
AKADEM	Akademiska Musikförlaget Sirkkalagatan 7 B 41 SF-20500 Abo 50 Finland	
ALBERSEN	Muziekhandel Albersen & Co. Groot Hertoginnelaan 182 NL-2517 EV Den Haag Netherlands	DONEMUS
ALBERT	J. Albert & Son Pty. Ltd. 139 King Street Sydney, N.S.W. Australia 2000	
ALBERT	J. Albert & Son - U.S.A. 1619 Broadway New York, NY 10019	
ALCOVE	Alcove Music	WESTERN
ALEX.HSE.	Alexandria House 468 McNally Drive Nashville, TN 37211	
ALFRED	Alfred Publishing Co. 16380 Roscoe Blvd. P.O. Box 10003 Van Nuys, CA 91410	
ALKOR	Alkor Edition	FOR.MUS.DIST.
ALLANS	Allans Music Australia Ltd. Box 513J, G.P.O. Melbourne 3001 Australia	PRESSER
ALLOWAY	Alloway Publications P.O. Box 25 Santa Monica, CA 90406	
ALMITRA	Almitra	KENDOR
ALMO	Almo Publications	CPP-BEL
ALPEG	Alpeg	PETERS
ALPHENAAR	W. Alphenaar Kruisweg 47-49 NL-2011 LA Haarlem Netherlands	
ALPUERTO	Editorial Alpuerto Caños del Peral 7 28013 Madrid Spain	
ALSBACH	G. Alsbach & Co. P.O. Box 338 NL-1400 AH Bussum Netherlands	
ALSBACH&D	Alsbach & Doyer	

Code	Publisher	U.S. Agent
AM.COMP.ALL.	American Composers Alliance 170 West 74th Street New York, NY 10023	
AM. GEHR	American Guild of English Handbell Ringers, Inc.	LORENZ
AM.INST.MUS.	American Institute of Musicology	FOSTER
AM.MUS.ED.	American Music Edition 263 East Seventh Street New York, NY 10009	PRESSER (partial)
AMADEUS	Amadeus Verlag Bernhard Päuler Am Iberghang 16 CH-8405 Winterthur Switzerland	FOR.MUS.DIST
	American String Teachers Association see ASTA	
AMICI	Gli Amici della Musica da Camera Via Bocca di Leone 25 Roma Italy	
AMP	Associated Music Publishers 225 Park Avenue South New York, NY 10003	LEONARD-US (sales) SCHIRM.G (rental)
AMPHION	Éditions Amphion 12, rue Rougemont F-75009 Paris France	
AMS PRESS	AMS Press, Inc. 56 East 13th Street New York, NY 10003	
AMSCO	AMSCO Music Publishing Co.	MUSIC
AMSI	Art Masters Studios, Inc. 2710 Nicollet Avenue Minneapolis, MN 55408	
ANDEL	Edition Andel Madeliefjeslaan, 26 B-8400 Oostende Belgium	
ANDERSONS	Anderssons Musikförlag Sodra Forstadsgatan 6 Box 17018 S-200 10 Malmö Sweden	
ANDRE	Johann André Musikverlag Frankfurterstraβe 28 Postfach 141 D-6050 Offenbach-am-Main Germany	
ANDPR	Andrea Press 75 Travis Road Holliston, MA 01746	
ANDREU	Andreu Marc Publications 611 Broadway, Suite 615 New York, NY 10012	MUSIC SC.
ANERCA	Anerca Music 35 St. Andrew's Garden Toronto, Ontario M4W 2C9 Canada	
ANFOR	Anfor Music Publishers (Div. of Terminal Music Supply) 1619 East Third Street Brooklyn, NY 11230	MAGNA D
ANGLO	Anglo-American Music Publishers 4 Kendall Avenue Sanderstead Surrey, CR2 0NH England	

Code	Publisher	U.S. Agent
ANTARA	Antara Music Group 468 McNally Drive Nashville, TN 37211	
ANTICO	Antico Edition P.O. Box 1, Moretonhampstead Newton Abbot Devon TQ13 8UA England	BOSTON EMC
APM	Artist Production & Management	VIERT
APNM	Association for Promotion of New Music 2002 Central Avenue Ship Bottom, NJ 08008	
APOGEE	Apogee Press	WORLD
APOLLO	Apollo-Verlag Paul Lincke Weihergarten 5 6500 Mainz Germany	
ARCADIA	Arcadia Music Publishing Co., Ltd. P.O. Box 1 Rickmansworth Herts WD3 3AZ England	
ARCANA	Arcana Editions Indian River Ontario K0L 2B0 Canada	
ARCO	Arco Music Publishers	WESTERN
ARGM	Editorial Argentina de Musica & Editorial Saraceno Beunos Aires, Argentina	PEER
ARIAD	Ariadne Buch- und Musikverlag Schottenfeldgasse 45 A-1070 Wien Austria	
ARION	Coleccion Arion	MEXICANAS
ARION PUB	Arion Publications, Inc. 4964 Kathleen Avenue Castro Valley, CA 94546	
ARISTA	Arista Music Co. 8370 Wilshire Blvd. Beverly Hills, CA 90211	CPP-BEL
ARNOLD	Edward Arnold Series	NOVELLO
ARS NOVA	Ars Nova Publications 121 Washington San Diego, CA 92103	PRESSER
ARS POLONA	Ars Polona Krakowskie Przedmieś cie 7 Skrytka pocztowa 1001 PL-00-950 Warszawa Poland	
ARS VIVA	Ars Viva Verlag Weihergarten D-6500 Mainz 1 Germany	EUR.AM.MUS.
ARSIS	Arsis Press 1719 Bay Street SE Washington, DC 20003	PLYMOUTH
ARTHUR	J. Arthur Music The University Music House 4290 North High Street Columbus, OH 43214	
ARTIA	Artia Prag Ve Smečkách 30 Praha 2 Czech Republic	
	Artist Production & Management see APM	

Code	Publisher	U.S. Agent
ARTRANSA	Artransa Music	WESTERN
ASCHERBERG	Ascherberg, Hopwood & Crew Ltd. 50 New Bond Street London W1A 2BR England	
ASHBOURN	Ashbourne Publications 425 Ashbourne Road Elkins Park, PA 19117	
ASHDOWN	Edwin Ashdown Ltd.	BRODT
ASHLEY	Ashley Publications, Inc. P.O. Box 337 Hasbrouck Heights, NJ 07604	
ASPEN	Aspen Grove Music P.O. Box 977 North Hollywood, CA 91603	
ASSMANN	Hermann Assmann, Musikverlag Franz-Werfel-Straße 36 D-6000 Frankfurt 50 Germany	
	Associated Board of the Royal Schools of Music see ABRSM	
	Associated Music Publishers see AMP	
	Association for Promotion of New Music see APNM	
ASTA	American String Teachers Association 2740 Spicewood Lane Bloomington, IN 47401	PRESSER
ATV	ATV Music Publications 6255 Sunset Boulevard Hollywood, CA 90028	CHERRY
	Audio Attic Productions see AAP	
AUG-FOR	Augsburg Fortress Publishers 426 South Fifth Street P.O. Box 1209 Minneapolis, MN 55440	
AULOS	Aulos Music Publishers P.O. Box 54 Montgomery, NY 12549	
AUTOGR	Autographus Musicus Ardalavägen 158 S-124 32 Bandhagen Sweden	
AUTRY	Gene Autry's Publishing Companies	CPP-BEL
AVANT	Avant Music	WESTERN
BAGGE	Jacob Bagge	STIM
BANK	Annie Bank Muziek P.O. Box 347 1180 AH Amstelveen Netherlands	
BANKS	Banks Music Publications The Old Forge Sand Hutton York YO4 1LB England	INTRADA
BARDIC	Bardic Edition 6 Fairfax Crescent, Aylesbury Buckhamshire, HP20 2ES England	PRESSER
BÄREN.	Bärenreiter Verlag Heinrich Schütz Allee 31-37 Postfach 100329 D-3500 Kassel-Wilhelmshöhe Germany	FOR.MUS.DIST.

Code	Publisher	U.S. Agent
BARNHS	C.L. Barnhouse 205 Cowan Avenue West P.O. Box 680 Oskaloosa, IA 52577	
BARON,M	M. Baron Co. P.O. Box 149 Oyster Bay, NY 11771	
BARRY-ARG	Barry & Cia Talcahuano 860, Bajo B Buenos Aires 1013-Cap. Federal Argentina	BOOSEY
BARTA	Barta Music Company	JERONA
BASART	Les Éditions Internationales Basart	GENERAL
BASEL	Musik-Akademie der Stadt Basel Leonhardsstraße 6 CH-4051 Basel Switzerland	
BAUER	Georg Bauer Musikverlag Luisenstraße 47-49 Postfach 1467 D-7500 Karlsruhe Germany	
BAVTON	Bavariaton-Verlag München Germany	ORLANDO
	Mel Bay Publications see MEL BAY	
BEACON HILL	Beacon Hill Music	LILLENAS
BEAUDN	Stuart D. Beaudoin 629 Queen Street Newmarket, Ontario Canada L3Y 2J1	
BEAUT	Beautiful Star Publishing, Inc. 3 Thrush Lane St. Paul, MN 55127-2613	
BECKEN	Beckenhorst Press P.O. Box 14273 Columbus, OH 43214	
BEECHWD	Beechwood Music Corporation 1750 Vine Street Hollywood, CA 90028	WARNER
BEEK	Beekman Music, Inc.	PRESSER
BEIAARD	Beiaardschool Belgium	
BELAIEFF	M.P. Belaieff Kennedyallee 101 D-6000 Frankfurt-am-Main 70 Germany	PETERS
	Centre Belge de Documentation Musicale see CBDM	
BELLA	Bella Roma Music 1442A Walnut Street Suite 197 Berkeley, CA 94709	
BELMONT	Belmont Music Publishers P.O. Box 231 Pacific Palisades, CA 90272	
BELWIN	Belwin-Mills Publishing Corp. 15800 N.W. 48th Avenue P.O. Box 4340 Miami, FL 33014	CPP-BEL PRESSER (rental)
BENJ	Anton J. Benjamin Werderstraße 44 Postfach 2561 D-2000 Hamburg 13 Germany	PRESSER

Code	Publisher	U.S. Agent
BENNY	Claude Benny Press 1401½ State Street Emporia, KS 66801	
BENSON	John T. Benson P.O. Box 107 Nashville, TN 37202-0107	
BERANDOL	Berandol Music Ltd. 110A Sackville Street Toronto, Ontario M5A 3E7 Canada	
BERBEN	Edizioni Musicali Berben Via Redipuglia 65 I-60100 Ancona Italy	PRESSER
BERGMANS	W. Bergmans	BANK
BERKLEE	Berklee Press Publications	LEONARD-US
BERLIN	Irving Berlin Music Corp. 29 W. 46 Street New York, NY 10036	
BERNOUILLI	Ed. Bernouilli	DONEMUS
BESSEL	Éditions Bessel & Cie	BREITKOPF-W
BEUSCH	Éditions Paul Beuscher Arpège 27, Boulevard Beaumarchais F-75004 Paris France	
BEZIGE BIJ	De Bezige Bij	DONEMUS
BIELER	Edmund Bieler Musikverlag Thürmchenswall 72 D-5000 Köln 1 Germany	
BIG BELL	Big Bells, Inc. 33 Hovey Avenue Trenton, NJ 08610	
BIG3	Big Three Music Corp.	CPP-BEL
BILLAUDOT	Éditions Billaudot 14, rue de l'Echiquier F-75010 Paris France	PRESSER
BIRCH	Robert Fairfax Birch	PRESSER
BIRNBACH	Richard Birnbach Musikverlag Aubinger Straße 9 D-8032 Lochheim bei München Germany	
BIZET	Bizet Productions and Publications	PRESSER
BMI	Broadcast Music, Inc. 320 West 57th Street New York, NY 10019	
	Boccaccini and Spada Editori see BSE	
BOCK	Fred Bock Music Co. P.O. Box 333 Tarzana, CA 91356	ANTARA
BODENS	Edition Ernst Fr. W. Bodensohn Dr. Rumpfweg 1 D-7570 Baden-Baden 21 Germany see also ERST	
BOEIJENGA	Boeijenga Muziekhandel Kleinzand 89 NL-8601 BG Sneek Netherlands	
BOELKE-BOM	Boelke-Bomart Music Publications Hillsdale, NY 12529	JERONA

Code	Publisher	U.S. Agent
BOETHIUS	Boethius Press 3 The Science Park Aberystinyth Dyfed SY23 3AH Wales	
BOHM	Anton Böhm & Sohn Postfach 110369 Lange Gasse 26 D-8900 Augsburg 11 Germany	
BOIL	Casa Editorial de Musica Boileau Provenza, 287 08037 Barcelona Spain	
BOIS	Bureau De Musique Mario Bois 17 Rue Richer F-75009 Paris France	
BOMART	Bomart Music Publications	BOELKE-BOM
BONART	Bonart Publications	CAN.MUS.CENT.
BONGIOVANI	Casa Musicale Francesco Bongiovani Via Rizzoli 28 E I-40125 Bologna Italy	
BOONIN	Joseph Boonin, Inc.	EUR.AM.MUS.
BOOSEY	Boosey & Hawkes Inc. 24 East 21st Street New York, NY 10010	
	Boosey & Hawkes Rental Library 52 Cooper Square New York, NY 10003-7102	
BOOSEY-CAN	Boosey & Hawkes Ltd. 279 Yorkland Boulevard Willowdale, Ontario M2J 1S7 Canada	BOOSEY
BOOSEY-ENG	Boosey & Hawkes Music Publishers Ltd. 295 Regent Street London W1 R 8JH England	BOOSEY
BORNEMANN	Éditions Bornemann 15 rue de Tournon F-75006 Paris France	KING,R PRESSER
BOSSE	Gustav Bosse Verlag Von der Tann Straße 38 Postfach 417 D-8400 Regensburg 1 Germany	EUR.AM.MUS.
BOSTON	Boston Music Co. 9 Airport Drive Hopedale, MA 01747	
BOSTON EMC	Boston Early Music Center see Early Music Shop of New England	
BOSWORTH	Bosworth & Company, Ltd. 14-18 Heddon Street, Regent Street London W1 R 8DP England	BRODT
BOTE	Bote & Bock Hardenbergstraße 9A D-1000 Berlin 12 Germany	PRESSER
BOURNE	Bourne Co. 5 W. 37th Street New York, NY 10018-6232	
BOWDOIN	Bowdoin College Music Press Department of Music Bowdoin College Brunswick, ME 04011	

Code	Publisher	U.S. Agent
BOWM	Bowmaster Productions 3351 Thornwood Road Sarasota, FL 33581	
BRCONT.MUS.	British And Continental Music Agencies Ltd.	EMI
BRADLEY	Bradley Publications 80 8th Avenue New York, NY 10011	CPP-BEL
BRANCH	Harold Branch Publishing, Inc. 95 Eads Street West Babylon, NY 11704	
BRANDEN	Branden Press, Inc. 17 Station Street P.O. Box 843 Brookline Village, MA 02147	
BRASS PRESS	The Brass Press 136 8th Avenue North Nashville, TN 37203-3798	
BRATFISCH	Musikverlag Georg Bratfisch Hans-Herold-Str. 23 D-95326 Kulmbach Germany	PRESSER
BRAUER	Les Éditions Musicales Herman Brauer 30, rue St. Christophe B-1000 Bruxelles Belgium	
BRAUN-PER	St. A. Braun-Peretti Hahnchenpassage D-53 Bonn Germany	
BRAVE	Brave New Music	SON-KEY
BREITKOPF-L	Breitkopf & Härtel (Leipzig)	
BREITKOPF-LN	Breitkopf & Härtel	
BREITKOPF-W	Breitkopf & Härtel Walkmühlstraβe 52 Postfach 1707 D-6200 Wiesbaden 1 Germany	SCHIRM.G (rental)
BRENNAN	John Brennan Music Publisher Positif Press Ltd. 130 Southfield Road Oxford OX4 1PA England	ORGAN LIT
BRENT	Michael Brent Publications, Inc. P.O. Box 1186 Port Chester, NY 10573	CHERRY
BRENTWOOD	Brentwood Publishing Group Inc. P.O. Box 19001 Brentwood, TN 37027	
BRIDGE	Bridge Music Publishing Co. 1350 Villa Street Mountain View, CA 94042	
BRIGHT STAR	Bright Star Music Publications	WESTERN
	British and Continental Music Agencies Ltd. see BR.CONT.MUS.	
	Broadcast Music, Inc. see BMI	
BROADMAN	Broadman Press 127 Ninth Avenue, North Nashville, TN 37234	
BRODT	Brodt Music Co. P.O. Box 9345 Charlotte, NC 28299-9345	

Code	Publisher	U.S. Agent
BROEKMANS	Broekmans & Van Poppel B.V. van Baerlestraat 92-94 NL-1071 BB Amsterdam Netherlands	
BROGNEAUX	Éditions Musicales Brogneaux 73, Avenue Paul Janson B-1070 Bruxelles Belgium	
BROOK	Brook Publishing Co. 3602 Cedarbrook Road Cleveland Heights, OH 44118	
BROUDE,A	Alexander Broude, Inc.	PLYMOUTH
BROUDE BR.	Broude Brothers Ltd. 141 White Oaks Road Williamstown, MA 01267	
	Broude Brothers Ltd.-Rental Dept. 170 Varick St. New York, NY 10013	
BROWN	Brown University Choral Series	BOOSEY
BROWN,R	Rayner Brown 2423 Panorama Terrace Los Angeles, CA 90039	WESTERN COMP.LIB
BROWN,WC	William C. Brown Co. 2460 Kerper Boulevard Dubuque, IA 52001	
BRUCK	Musikverlag M. Bruckbauer "Biblioteca de la Guitarra" Postfach 18 D-7953 Bad Schussenried Germany	
BRUCKNER	Bruckner Verlag Austria	PETERS (rental)
BRUZZI	Aldo Bruzzichelli, Editore Borgo S. Frediano, 8 I-50124 Firenze Italy	MARGUN
BSE	Boccaccini and Spada Editori Via Francesco Duodo, 10 I-00136 Roma Italy	PRESSER
BUBONIC	Bubonic Publishing Co. 706 Lincoln Avenue St. Paul, MN 55105	
BUDAPEST	Editio Musica Budapest (Kultura) P.O.B. 322 H-1370 Budapest Hungary see also EMB	BOOSEY PRESSER (partial)
BUDDE	Rolf Budde Musikverlag Hohenzollerndamm 54A D-1000 Berlin 33 Germany	
BUGZY	Bugzy Bros. Vocal Athletics P.O. Box 900 Orem, UT 84057	MUSICART
BUSCH	Hans Busch Musikförlag Stubbstigen 3 S-18147 Lidingö Sweden	
BUSCH,E	Ernst Busch Verlag Schlossstrasse 43 D-7531 Neulingen-Bauschlott Germany	
BUTZ	Dr. J. Butz Musikverlag Postfach 3008 5205 Sankt Augustin 3 Germany	

Code	Publisher	U.S. Agent
CAILLARD	Edition Philippe Caillard 5 bis rue du Château-Fondu 78200 Fontenay-Mauvoisin France	
CAILLET	Lucien Caillet	SOUTHERN
CAMBIATA	Cambiata Press P.O. Box 1151 Conway, AR 72032	
CAMBRIA	Cambria Records & Publishing P.O. Box 374 Lomita, CA 90717	
CAMBRIDGE	Cambridge University Press The Edinburgh Building Shaftesbury Road Cambridge CB2 2RU England	
CAMERICA	Camerica Music 535 Fifth Avenue, Penthouse New York, NY 10017	CPP-BEL
CAMPUS	Campus Publishers 713 Ellsworth Road West Ann Arbor, MI 48104	
CAN.MUS.CENT.	Canadian Music Centre 20 St. Joseph Street Toronto, Ontario M4Y 1J9 Canada	
CAN.MUS.HER.	Canadian Musical Heritage Society Patrimoine Musical Canadien P.O. Box 262, Station A Ottawa, Ontario K1N 8V2 Canada	
CANAAN	Canaanland Publications	WORD
CANT DO	Cantate Domino Editions de musique Rue du Sapin 2a C.P. 156 2114 Fleurier Switzerland	
CANTANDO	Cantando Forlag Bj. Bjørnsonsgt. 2 D N-4021 Stavanger Norway	
CANTORIS	Cantoris Music P.O. Box 162004 Sacramento, CA 95816	
CANYON	Canyon Press, Inc. P.O. Box 447 Islamorada, FL 33036	KERBY
CAPELLA	Capella Music, Inc.	BOURNE
CAPPR	Capital Press	PODIUM
CARABO	Carabo-Cone Method Foundation 1 Sherbrooke Road Scarsdale, NY 10583	
CARISCH	Carisch S.p.A. see Nuova Carisch	
CARLAN	Carlanita Music Co.	LEONARD-US (sales) SCHIRM.G (rental)
CARLIN	Carlin Publications P.O. Box 2289 Oakhurst, CA 93644	
CARLTON	Carlton Musickverlag	BREITKOPF-W
CARUS	Carus-Verlag	FOSTER
CATHEDRAL	Cathedral Music Maudlin House Westhampnett Chichester West Sussex PO18 0PB, England	
	Catholic Conference see U.S.CATH	
CAVATA	Cavata Music Publishers, Inc.	PRESSER
CAVELIGHT	Cavelight Music P.O. Box 85 Oxford, NJ 07863	
CBC	Cundey Bettoney Co.	FISCHER,C
CBDM	CeBeDeM Centre Belge de Documentation Musicale rue d'Arlon 75-77 B-1040 Bruxelles Belgium	
CCMP	Colorado College Music Press 14 E. Cache La Poudre Colorado Springs, CO 80903	
CEL	Celesta Publishing Co. P.O. Box 560603, Kendall Branch Miami, FL 33156	
	Centre Belge de Documentation Musicale see CBDM	
	Éditions du Centre Nationale de la Recherche Scientifique see CNRS	
CENTO	Centorino Productions P.O. Box 4478 West Hills, CA 91308	
CENTURY	Century Music Publishing Co. 263 Veterans Boulevard Carlstadt, NJ 07072	ASHLEY
CENTURY PR	Century Press Publishers	
CESKY HUD.	Cesky Hudebni Fond Parizska 13 CS-110 00 Praha 1 Czech Republic	BOOSEY (rental) NEW W
CHANT	Éditions Le Chant du Monde 23, rue Royale F-75008 Paris France	
CHANTERL	Éditions Chanterelle S.A. Postfach 103909 D-69 Heidelberg Germany	BÄREN.
CHANTRY	Chantry Music Press, Inc. Wittenberg University P.O. Box 1101 Springfield, OH 45501	AUG-FOR
CHAPLET	Chaplet Music Corp.	PARAGON
CHAPPELL	Chappell & Co., Inc. 1290 Avenue of the Americas New York, NY 10019	LEONARD-US
CHAPPELL-CAN	Chappell Music Canada Ltd 85 Scarsdale Road, Unit 101 Don Mills, Ontario M3B 2R2 Canada	LEONARD-US
CHAPPELL-ENG	Chappell & Co. Ltd. Printed Music Division 60-70 Roden Street Ilford, Essex IG1 2AQ England	LEONARD-US

Code	Publisher	U.S. Agent
CHAPPELL-FR	Chappell S.A. 25, rue d'Hauterville F-75010 Paris France	LEONARD-US
CHAR CROS	Charing Cross Music, Inc. 1619 Broadway, Suite 500 New York, NY 10019	
CHARTER	Charter Publications, Inc. P.O. Box 850 Valley Forge, PA 19482	PEPPER
CHENANGO	Chenango Valley Music Press P.O. Box 251 Hamilton, NY 13346	
CHERITH	Cherith Publishing Co.	INTRADA
CHERRY	Cherry Lane Music Co. 110 Midland Avenue Port Chester, NY 10573	CPP-BEL
CHESTER	Chester Music 8-9 Frith Street London W1V 5TZ England	SCHIRM.G
CHILTERN	Chiltern Music see Cathedral Music	
CHOIR	Choir Publishing Co. 564 Columbus Street Salt Lake City, UT 84103	
CHORAG	Choragus Box 1197 S-581 11 Linköping Sweden	
CHORISTERS	Choristers Guild 2834 West Kingsley Road Garland, TX 75041	LORENZ
CHOUDENS	Édition Choudens 38, rue Jean Mermoz F-75008 Paris France	PRESSER
CHRI	Christopher Music Co. 380 South Main Place Carol Stream, IL 60188	PRESSER
CHRIS	Christophorus-Verlag Herder Hermann-Herder-Straße 4 D-7800 Freiburg Breisgau Germany	
CHURCH	John Church Co.	PRESSER
CJC	Creative Jazz Composers, Inc. 1240 Annapolis Road Odenton, MD 21113	
CLARION	Clarion Call Music	SON-KEY
CLARK	Clark and Cruickshank Music Publishers	BERANDOL
CLASSV	Classical Vocal Reprints P.O. Box 20263 Columbus Circle Station New York, NY 10023	
CLIVIS	Clivis Publicacions C-Còrsega, 619 Baixos Barcelona 25 Spain	
CMP	CMP Library Service MENC Historical Center/SCIM Music Library/Hornbake University of Maryland College Park, MD 20742	
CNRS	CNRS Editions 20-22 rue Saint-Amand F-75015 Paris France	SMPF
CO OP	Co-op Press RD2 Box 150A Wrightsville, PA 17368	
COBURN	Coburn Press	PRESSER
CODERG	Coderg-U.C.P. sàrl 42 bis, rue Boursault F-75017 Paris France	
COLE	M.M. Cole Publishing Co. 919 North Michigan Avenue Chicago, IL 60611	
COLEMAN	Dave Coleman Music, Inc. P.O. Box 230 Montesano, WA 98563	
COLFRANC	Colfranc Music Publishing Corp.	KERBY
COLIN	Charles Colin 315 West 53rd Street New York, NY 10019	
COLOMBO	Franco Colombo Publications	CPP-BEL PRESSER (rental)
	Colorado College Music Press see CCMP	
COLUM UNIV	Columbia University Music Press 562 West 113th Street New York, NY 10025	SCHIRM.EC
COLUMBIA	Columbia Music Co.	PRESSER
COLUMBIA PIC.	Columbia Pictures Publications see CPP	
COMBRE	Consortium Musical, Marcel Combre Editeur 24, Boulevard Poissonnière F-75009 Paris France	PRESSER
COMP.FAC.	Composers Facsimile Edition	AM.COMP.AL.
COMP.LIB.	Composer's Library Editions	PRESSER
COMP-PERF	Composer/Performer Edition 2101 22nd Street Sacramento, CA 95818	
COMP.PR.	The Composers Press, Inc.	OPUS
COMPOSER'S GR	Composer's Graphics 5702 North Avenue Carmichael, CA 95608	
CONCERT	Concert Music Publishing Co. c/o Studio P-R, Inc. 16333 N.W. 54th Avenue Hialeah, FL 33014	CPP-BEL
CONCERT W	Concert Works Unlimited	SHAWNEE
CONCORD	Concord Music Publishing Co.	ELKAN,H
CONCORDIA	Concordia Publishing House 3558 South Jefferson Avenue St. Louis, MO 63118-3968	
CONGRESS	Congress Music Publications 100 Biscayne Boulevard Miami, FL 33132	
CONSOL	Consolidated Music Publishers, Inc. 33 West 60th Street New York, NY 10023	
CONSORT	Consort Music, Inc. (Division of Magnamusic Distributors) Sharon, CT 06069	
CONSORT PR	Consort Press P.O. Box 50413 Santa Barbara, CA 93150-0413	

Code	Publisher	U.S. Agent
CONSORTIUM	Consortium Musical	PRESSER
	Consortium Musical, Marcel Combre Editeur see COMBRE	
CONTINUO	Continuo Music Press, Inc.	PLYMOUTH
	Editorial Cooperativa Inter-Americana de Compositores see ECOAM	
COPPENRATH	Musikverlag Alfred Coppenrath Postfach 11 58 D-84495 Altötting Germany	
COR PUB	Cor Publishing Co. 67 Bell Place Massapequa, NY 11758	
CORMORANT	Cormorant Press P.O. Box 169 Hallowell, ME 04347	PLYMOUTH
CORONA	Edition Corona-Rolf Budde Hohenzollerndamm 54A D-1 Berlin 33 Germany	
CORONET	Coronet Press	PRESSER
COROZINE	Vince Corozine Music Publishing Co. 6 Gabriel Drive Peekskill, NY 10566	
COSTALL	Éditions Costallat 60 rue de la Chaussée d'Antin F-75441 Paris Cedex 09 France	PRESSER
COVENANT	Covenant Press 3200 West Foster Avenue Chicago, IL 60625	
COVENANT MUS	Covenant Music 1640 East Big Thompson Avenue Estes Park, CO 80517	
CPP	Columbia Pictures Publications 15800 N.W. 48th Avenue Miami, FL 33014	CPP-BEL
CPP-BEL	CPP-Belwin Music 15800 N.W. 48th Avenue Miami, FL 33014	
CRAMER	J.B. Cramer & Co., Ltd. 23 Garrick Street London WC2E 9AX England	CPP-BEL
CRANZ	Éditions Cranz 30, rue St.-Christophe B-1000 Bruxelles Belgium	
	Creative Jazz Composers see CJC	
CRES.-NETH	Uitgeverij Crescendo	DONEMUS
CRESCENDO	Crescendo Music Sales Co. P.O. Box 395 Naperville, IL 60540	FEMA
CRESPUB	Crescendo Publications, Inc. 6311 North O'Connor Road #112 Irving, TX 75039-3112	
CRITERION	Criterion Music Corp. P.O. Box 660 Lynbrook, NY 11563	
CROATICA	Croatian Music Institute	DRUS.HRVAT.SKLAD

Code	Publisher	U.S. Agent
CRON	Edition Cron Luzern Zinggentorstraße 5 CH-6006 Luzern Switzerland	
CROWN	Crown Music Press 4119 North Pittsburgh Chicago, IL 60634	BRASS PRESS (partial)
	Cundey Bettoney Co. see CBC	
CURCI	Edizioni Curci Galleria del Corso 4 I-20122 Milano Italy	
CURTIS	Curtis Music Press	KJOS
CURWEN	J. Curwen & Sons	LEONARD-US SCHIRM.G (rental)
CZECH	Czechoslovak Music Information Centre Besedni 3 CS-118 00 Praha 1 Czech Republic	BOOSEY (rental)
DA CAPO	Da Capo Press, Inc. 233 Spring Street New York, NY 10013	
	Samfundet til udgivelse at Dansk Musik see SAMFUNDET	
DANE	Dane Publications 1657 The Fairway, Suite 133 Jenkintown, PA 19046	
DANTALIAN	Dantalian, Inc. Eleven Pembroke Street Newton, MA 02158	
DAVIMAR	Davimar Music M. Productions 159 West 53rd Street New York, NY 10019	
DAYBRK	Daybreak Productions	ALEX.HSE.
DE MONTE	De Monte Music F-82240 Septfonds France	
DE SANTIS	Edizioni de Santis Viale Mazzini, 6 I-00195 Roma Italy	
DEAN	Roger Dean Publishing Co. 345 West Jackson Street, #B Macomb, IL 61455-2112	LORENZ
DEIRO	Pietro Deiro Publications 133 Seventh Avenue South New York, NY 10014	
DELRIEU	Georges Delrieu & Cie Palais Bellecour B 14, rue Trachel F-06000 Nice France	SCHIRM.EC
DENNER	Erster Bayerischer Musikverlag Joh. Dennerlein KG Beethovenstraße 7 D-8032 Lochham Germany	
DESC	Descant Publications	INTRADA
DESERET	Deseret Music Publishers P.O. Box 900 Orem, UT 84057	MUSICART

Code	Publisher	U.S. Agent
DESHON	Deshon Music, Inc.	CPP-BEL PRESSER (rental)
DESSAIN	Éditions Dessain Belgium	
DEUTSCHER	Deutscher Verlag für Musik Walkmühlstr. 52 D-6200 Wiesbaden 1 Germany	BREITKOPF-W
DEWOLF	DeWolfe Ltd. 80/88 Wardour Street London W1V 3LF England	DONEMUS
DIAPASON	The Diapason Press Dr. Rudolf A. Rasch P.O. Box 2376 NL-3500 GJ Utrecht Netherlands	
DIESTERWEG	Verlag Moritz Diesterweg Hochstraße 31 D-6000 Frankfurt-am-Main Germany	
	Dilia Prag see DP	
DIP PROV	Diputacion Provincal de Barcelona Servicio de Bibliotecas Carmen 47 Barcelona 1 Spain	
DITSON	Oliver Ditson Co.	PRESSER
DOBER	Les Éditions Doberman-Yppan C.P. 2021 St. Nicholas, Quebec G0S 3L0 Canada	BOOSEY
DOBLINGER	Ludwig Doblinger Verlag Dorotheergasse 10 A-1011 Wien I Austria	FOR.MUS.DIST.
DOMINIS	Dominis Music Ltd. Box 11307, Station H Ottawa Ontario K2H 7V1 Canada	
DONEMUS	Donemus Foundation Paulus Potterstraat 14 NL-1071 CZ Amsterdam Netherlands	PRESSER
DOORWAY	Doorway Music 2509 Buchanan Street Nashville, TN 37208	
DORABET	Dorabet Music Co. 170 N.E. 33rd Street Ft. Lauderdale, FL 33334	PLYMOUTH
DORING	G.F. Döring Musikverlag Hasenplatz 5-6 D-7033 Herrenburg 1 Germany	
DORN	Dorn Publications, Inc. P.O. Box 206 Medfield, MA 02052	
DOUBLDAY	Doubleday & Co., Inc. 501 Franklin Avenue Garden City, NY 11530	
DOUGLAS,B	Byron Douglas	CPP-BEL
DOVEHOUSE	Dovehouse Editions 32 Glen Avenue Ottawa, Ontario K1S 2Z7 Canada	
DOVER	Dover Publications, Inc. 31 East 2nd Street Mineola, NY 11501	ALFRED
DOXO	Doxology Music P.O. Box M Aiken, SC 29802	ANTARA
DP	Dilia Prag	BÄREN.
DRAGON	Dragon Music Co. 28908 Grayfox Street Malibu, CA 90265	
DREIK	Dreiklang-Dreimasken Bühnenund Musikverlag D-8000 München Germany	ORLANDO
DRK	DRK Music Co. 111 Lake Wind Rd. New Canaan, CT 06840	
DRUS.HRVAT. SKLAD.	Društvo Hrvatskih Skladatelja Berislavićeva 9 Zagreb Croatia	
DRUSTVA	Edicije Drustva Slovenskih Skladateljev Trg Francoske Revolucije 6 Ljubljana Slovenia	NEW W
DRZAVNA	Drzavna Zalozba Slovenije	DRUSTVA
DUCHESS	Duchess Music Corp.	MCA PRESSER (rental)
DUCKWORTH	Gerald Duckworth & Co., Ltd. 43 Gloucester Crescent London, NW1 England	
DUMA	Duma Music Inc. 580 Alden Street Woodbridge, NJ 07095	
DUN	Dunstan House P.O. Box 1355 Stafford, VA 22555	ANTARA
DUNV	Dunvagen Music Publishers, Inc. 853 Broadway, Rm. 1105 New York, NY 10003	SCHIRM.G
DURAND	Durand & Cie 215, rue du Faubourg St.-Honoré F-75008 Paris France	PRESSER
DUTTON	E.P. Dutton & Co., Inc. 201 Park Avenue South New York, NY 10003	
DUX	Edition Dux Arthur Turk Beethovenstraße 7 D-8032 Lochham Germany	DENNER
DVM	DVM Productions P.O. Box 399 Thorofare, NJ 08086	
EAR.MUS.FAC.	Early Music Facsimiles P.O. Box 711 Columbus, OH 43216	
	Early Music Shop of New England 65 Boylston Street Brookline, MA 02146	
	East West Publications see WP	
EARTHSNG	Earthsongs 220 N.W. 29th Corvallis, OR 97330	

Code	Publisher	U.S. Agent
EASTMAN	Eastman School of Music	FISCHER,C
EBLE	Eble Music Co. P.O. Box 2570 Iowa City, IA 52244	
ECK	Van Eck & Zn.	DONEMUS
ECOAM	Editorial Cooperativa Inter-Americana de Compositores Casilla de Correa No. 540 Montevideo Uruguay	PEER
EDI-PAN	Edi-Pan	DE SANTIS
EDUTAIN	Edu-tainment Publications (Div. of the Evolve Music Group) P.O. Box 20767 New York, NY 10023	
EERSTE	De Eerste Muziekcentrale Flevolaan 41 NL-1411 KC Naarden Netherlands	
EGTVED	Edition EGTVED P.O. Box 20 DK-6040 Egtved Denmark	FOSTER
EHRLING	Thore Ehrling Musik AB Linnegatan 9-11 Box 5268 S-102 45 Stockholm Sweden	
EIGEN UITGAVE	Eigen Uitgave van de Componist (Composer's Own Publication)	DONEMUS
ELITE	Elite Edition	SCHAUR
ELKAN,H	Henri Elkan Music Publisher P.O. Box 279 Hastings On Hudson, NY 10706	
ELKAN&SCH	Elkan & Schildknecht Vastmannagatan 95 S-113 43 Stockholm Sweden	
ELKAN-V	Elkan-Vogel, Inc. Presser Place Bryn Mawr, PA 19010	
ELKIN	Elkin & Co., Ltd	PRESSER
EMB	Editio Musica Budapest P.O.B. 322 H-1370 Budapest Hungary see also BUDAPEST	BOOSEY PRESSER
EMEC	Editorial de Musica Española Contemporanea Ediciones Quiroga Alcalá, 70 Madrid 9 Spain	
EMERSON	Emerson Edition Windmill Farm Ampleforth York YO6 4HF England	EBLE GROVE KING,R WOODWIND PRESSER
EMI	EMI Music Publishing Ltd. 127 Charing Cross Road London WC2H 0EA England	INTER.MUS.P.
ENGELS	Musikverlag Carl Engels Nachf. Auf dem Brand 3 D-5000 Köln 50 (Rodenkirchen) Germany	
ENGSTROEM	Engstroem & Soedering Palaegade 6 DK-1261 København K Denmark	PETERS
ENOCH	Enoch & Cie 193 Boulevard Pereire F-75017 Paris France	PRESSER SCHIRM.G (rental-partial)
ENSEMB	Ensemble Publications P.O. Box 98, Bidwell Station Buffalo, NY 14222	
ENSEMB PR	Ensemble Music Press	FISCHER,C
EPHROS	Gershon Ephros Cantorial Anthology Foundation, Inc	TRANSCON.
ERDMANN	Rudolf Erdmann, Musikverlag Adolfsallee 34 D-62 Wiesbaden Germany	
ERES	Edition Eres Horst Schubert Hauptstrasse 35 Postfach 1220 D-2804 Lilienthal/Bremen Germany	
ERICKSON	E.J. Erickson Music Co. 606 North Fourth Street P.O. Box 97 St. Peter, MN 56082	
ERIKS	Eriks Musikhandel & Förlag AB Karlavägen 40 S-114 49 Stockholm Sweden	
ERST	Erstausgaben Bodensohn see also BODENS	
ESCHENB	Eschenbach Editions 28 Dalrymple Crescent Edinburgh, EH9 2NX Scotland	PRESSER
ESCHIG	Éditions Max Eschig 215 rue du Faubourg Saint-Honoré F-75008 Paris France	PRESSER

	Editorial de Musica Española
	   Contemporanea
	  see EMEC	

	Union Musical Española see UNION ESP	
ESSEX	Clifford Essex Music	MUSIC-ENG
ESSO	Van Esso & Co.	DONEMUS
ETLING,F	Forest R. Etling see HIGHLAND	
ETOILE	Etoile Music, Inc. Publications Division Shell Lake, WI 54871	MMB

EULENBURG	Edition Eulenburg	EUR.AM.MUS.
		  (miniature
		  scores)

EUR.AM.MUS.	European American Music Corp. P.O. Box 850 Valley Forge, PA 19482	
EWP	East West Publications	MUSIC
EXC.MH	Excellent Music Holland Postbus 347 1180 AH Amstelveen Netherlands	
EXCELSIOR	Excelsior Music Publishing Co.	PRESSER

Code	Publisher	U.S. Agent
EXPO PR	Exposition Press 325 Kings Highway Smithtown, NY 11787	
FABER	Faber Music Ltd. 3 Queen Square London WC1N 3AU England	LEONARD-US (sales) SCHIRM.G (rental)
FAIR	Fairfield Publishing, Ltd.	PRESSER
FAITH	Faith Music	LILLENAS
FALLEN LEAF	Fallen Leaf Press PO 10034-N Berkeley, CA 94709	
FAR WEST	Far West Music	WESTERN
FARRELL	The Wes Farrell Organization	LEONARD-US
FAZER	Musik Fazer P.O. Box 169 SF-02101 Espoo Finland	PRESSER
FEEDBACK	Feedback Studio Verlag Gentner Strasse 23 D-5 Köln 1 Germany	BÄREN.
FEIST	Leo Feist, Inc.	PRESSER
FELDMAN,B	B. Feldman & Co., Ltd	EMI
FEMA	Fema Music Publications P.O. Box 395 Naperville, IL 60566	
FENETTE	Fenette Music Ltd.	BROUDE,A
FENTONE	Fentone Music Ltd. Fleming Road, Earlstrees Corby, Northants NN17 2SN England	PRESSER
FEREOL	Fereol Publications Route 8, Box 510C Gainesville, GA 30501	
FEUCHT	Feuchtinger & Gleichauf Niedermünstergasse 2 D-8400 Regensburg 11 Germany	
FIDDLE	Fiddle & Bow 7 Landview Drive Dix Hills, NY 11746	HHP
FIDELIO	Fidelio Music Publishing Co. 39 Danbury Avenue Westport, CT 06880-6822	
FIDULA	Fidula-Verlag Johannes Holzmeister Ahornweg, Postfach 250 D-5407 Boppard/Rhein Germany	HARGAIL
FILLMH	Fillmore Music House	FISCHER,C
FINE ARTS	Fine Arts Press 2712 W. 104th Terrace Leawood, KS 66206	ALEX.HSE.
FINN MUS	Finnish Music Information Center Runeberginkatu 15 A SF-00100 Helsinki 10 Finland	
FISCHER,C	Carl Fischer, Inc. 62 Cooper Square New York, NY 10003	
FISCHER,J	J. Fischer & Bro.	BELWIN PRESSER (rental)
FISHER	Fisher Music Co.	PLYMOUTH

Code	Publisher	U.S. Agent
FITZSIMONS	H.T. FitzSimons Co., Inc. 18345 Ventura Boulevard P.O. Box 333, Suite 212 Tarzana, CA 91356	ANTARA
FLAMMER	Harold Flammer, Inc.	SHAWNEE
FMA	Florilegium Musicae Antiquae	HÄNSSLER
FOETISCH	Foetisch Frères Rue de Bourg 6 CH-1002 Lausanne Switzerland	SCHIRM.EC
FOG	Dan Fog Musikforlag Grabrodretorv 7 DK-1154 København K Denmark	
FOLEY,CH	Charles Foley, Inc.	FISCHER,C PRESSER (rental)
FORBERG	Rob. Forberg-P. Jurgenson, Musikverlag Mirbachstraße 9 D-5300 Bonn-Bad Godesberg Germany	PETERS
FOR.MUS.DIST.	Foreign Music Distributors 13 Elkay Drive Chester, NY 10918	
FORLIVESI	A. Forlivesi & C. Via Roma 4 50123 Firenze Italy	
FORNI	Arnaldo Forni Editore Via Gramsci 164 I-40010 Sala Bolognese Italy	OMI
FORSTER	Forster Music Publisher, Inc. 216 South Wabash Avenue Chicago, IL 60604	
FORSYTH	Forsyth Brothers Ltd. 126 Deansgate Manchester M3 2GR England	
FORTEA	Biblioteca Fortea Fucar 10 Madrid 14 Spain	
FORTISSIMO	Fortissimo Musikverlag Margaretenplatz 4 A-1050 Wien Austria	
	Fortress Press	AUG-FOR
FOSTER	Mark Foster Music Co. 28 East Springfield Avenue P.O. Box 4012 Champaign, IL 61820-1312	
	Foundation for New American Music see NEWAM	
FOUR ST	Four Star Publishing Co.	CPP-BEL
FOXS	Sam Fox Publishing Co. 5276 Hollister Avenue Suite 251 Santa Barbara, CA 93111	PLYMOUTH (sales) PRESSER (rental)
FRANCAIS	Éditions Françaises de Musique	PRESSER
FRANCE	France Music	AMP
FRANCIS	Francis, Day & Hunter Ltd.	CPP-BEL
FRANG	Frangipani Press	ALFRED
FRANK	Frank Music Corp.	LEONARD-US SCHIRM.G (rental-partial)

Code	Publisher	U.S. Agent
FRANTON	Franton Music 4620 Sea Isle Memphis, TN 38117	
FREDONIA	Fredonia Press 3947 Fredonia Drive Hollywood, CA 90068	SIFLER
FREEMAN	H. Freeman & Co., Ltd.	EMI
FROHLICH	Friedrich Wilhelm Fröhlich Musikverlag Ansbacher Straße 52 D-1000 Berlin 30 Germany	
FUJIHARA	Fujihara	
FURORE	Furore Verlag Johannesstrasse 3 3500 Kassel Germany	TONGER
FURST	Fürstner Ltd.	BOOSEY
GAF	G.A.F. and Associates 1626 E. Williams Street Tempe, AZ 85281	
GAITHER	Gaither Music Company	ALEX.HSE.
GALAXY	Galaxy Music Corp.	SCHIRM.EC
GALLEON	Galleon Press 17 West 60th St. New York, NY 10023	BOSTON
GALLERIA	Galleria Press 170 N.E. 33rd Street Fort Lauderdale, FL 33334	PLYMOUTH
GALLIARD	Galliard Ltd. Queen Anne's Road Southtown, Gt. Yarmouth Norfolk England	GALAXY
GARLAND	Garland Publishing, Inc. 717 5th Avenue, #2500 New York, NY 10022-8101	
GARZON	Éditions J. Garzon 13 rue de l'Échiquier F-75010 Paris France	
GEHRMANS	Carl Gehrmans Musikförlag Odengatan 84 Box 6005 S-102 31 Stockholm Sweden	BOOSEY
GEMINI	Gemini Press Music Div. of the Pilgrim Press Box 390 Otis, MA 01253	PRESSER
GENERAL	General Music Publishing Co., Inc. 145 Palisade Street Dobbs Ferry, NY 10522	BOSTON
GENERAL WDS	General Words and Music Co.	KJOS
GENESIS	Genesis	PLYMOUTH
GENTRY	Gentry Publications P.O. Box 570567 Tarzana, CA 91356	ANTARA
GERIG	Musikverlage Hans Gerig Drususgasse 7-11 (Am Museum) D-5000 Köln 1 Germany	BREITKOPF-W
GIA	GIA Publications 7404 South Mason Avenue Chicago, IL 60638	
GILBERT	Gilbert Publications 4209 Manitou Way Madison, WI 53711	

Code	Publisher	U.S. Agent
GILLMAN	Gillman Publications P.O. Box 155 San Clemente, CA 92672	
GILPIN	Gilpin-McPheeters Publishing	INTRADA
GLOCKEN	Glocken Verlag Ltd. 12-14 Mortimer Street London W1N 8EL England	EUR.AM.MUS.
GLORY	Glory Sound Delaware Water Gap, PA 18327	SHAWNEE
GLOUCHESTER	Glouchester Press P.O. Box 1044 Fairmont, WV 26554	HEILMAN
GM	G & M International Music Dealers 1225 Candlewood Hill Road Box 2098 Northbrook, IL 60062	
GOLDEN	Golden Music Publishing Co. P.O. Box 383 Golden, CO 80402-0383	
GOODLIFE	Goodlife Publications	CPP-BEL
GOODMAN	Goodman Group (formerly Regent, Arc & Goodman)	WARNER LEONARD-US (choral)
GOODWIN	Goodwin & Tabb Publishing, Ltd.	PRESSER
GORDON	Gordon Music Co. Box 2250 Canoga Park, CA 91306	
GORNSTON	David Gornston	FOX,S
GOSPEL	Gospel Publishing House 1445 Boonville Avenue Springfield, MO 65802	
GRAHL	Grahl & Nicklas Braubachstraße 24 D-6 Frankfurt-am-Main Germany	
GRANCINO	Grancino Editions 15020 Burwood Dr. Lake Mathews, CA 92370 Grancino Editions 2 Bishopswood Road London N6 4PR England Grancino Editions Schirmerweg 12 D-8 München 60 Germany	
GRAS	Éditions Gras 36 rue Pape-Carpentier F-72200 La Flèche (Sarthe) France	SOUTHERN
GRAY	H.W. Gray Co., Inc.	CPP-BEL PRESSER (rental)
GREENE ST.	Greene Street Music 354 Van Duzer Street Stapleton, NY 10304	
GREENWOOD	Greenwood Press, Inc. 88 Post Road West P.O. Box 5007 Westport, CT 06881	WORLD
GREGG	Gregg International Publishers, Ltd. 1 Westmead, Farnborough Hants GU14 7RU England	

Code	Publisher	U.S. Agent
GREGGMS	Gregg Music Sources P.O. Box 868 Novato, CA 94947	
	Gregorian Institute of America see GIA	
GROEN	Muziekuitgeverij Saul B. Groen Ferdinand Bolstraat 6 NL-1072 LJ Amsterdam Netherlands	
GROSCH	Edition Grosch Phillip Grosch Bahnhofstrasse 94a D-8032 Gräfelfing Germany	THOMI
GROVEN	Eivind Grovens Institutt for Reinstemming Ekebergveien 59 N-1181 Oslo 11 Norway	
GUARANI	Ediciones Musicals Mundo Guarani Sarmiento 444 Buenos Aires Argentina	
GUILYS	Edition Guilys Case Postale 90 CH-1702 Fribourg 2 Switzerland	
GUNMAR	Gunmar Music, Inc. see Margun/Gunmar Music, Inc.	JERONA
HA MA R	Ha Ma R Percussion Publications, Inc. 333 Spring Road Huntington, NY 11743	BOOSEY
HAMBLEN	Stuart Hamblen Music Co. 26101 Ravenhill Road Canyon Country, CA 91351	
HAMELLE	Hamelle & Cie 175 rue Saint-Honoré F-75040 Paris Cedex 01 France	KING,R PRESSER SOUTHERN
HAMPE	Adolf Hampe Musikverlag Hohenzollerndamm 54A D-1000 Berlin 33 Germany	BUDDE
HAMPTON	Hampton Edition	MARKS
HANSEN-DEN	Wilhelm Hansen Musikforlag Bornholmsgade 1,1 1266 Copenhagen K Denmark	SCHIRM.G
HANSEN-ENG	Hansen, London see CHESTER	
HANSEN-FIN	Edition Wilhelm Hansen, Helsinki	SCHIRM.G
HANSEN-GER	Edition Wilhelm Hansen, Frankfurt	SCHIRM.G
HANSEN-NY	Edition Wilhelm Hansen-Chester Music New York Inc. New York, NY	SCHIRM.G
HANSEN-SWED	Edition Wilhelm Hansen see NORDISKA	SCHIRM.G
HANSEN-US	Hansen House Publications, Inc. 1824 West Avenue Miami Beach, FL 33139-9913	
HÄNSSLER	Hänssler-Verlag Röntgenstrasse 15 Postfach 1230 D-7312 Kirchheim/Teck Germany	ANTARA
HARGAIL	Hargail Music Press P.O. Box 118 Saugerties, NY 12477	CPP-BEL
HARMONIA	Harmonia-Uitgave P.O. Box 210 NL-1230 AE Loosdrecht Netherlands	FOR.MUS.DIST.
HARMS,TB	T.B. Harms	WARNER
HARMUSE	Harmuse Publications 529 Speers Road Oakville, Ontario L6K 2G4 Canada	
HARP PUB	Harp Publications 3437-2 Tice Creek Drive Walnut Creek, CA 94595	
HARRIS	Frederick Harris Music Co., Ltd. 529 Speers Road Oakville, Ontario L6K 2G4 Canada	HARRIS-US
HARRIS-US	Frederick Harris Company, Ltd. 340 Nagel Drive Buffalo, NY 14225-4731	
HARRIS,R	Ron Harris Publications 22643 Paul Revere Drive Woodland Hills, CA 91364	ALEX.HSE.
HART	F. Pitman Hart & Co., Ltd.	BRODT
HARTH	Harth Musikverlag Karl-Liebknecht-Straße 12 D-701 Leipzig Germany	PRO MUSICA
HASLINGER	Verlag Carl Haslinger Tuchlauben 11 A-1010 Wien Austria	FOR.MUS.DIST.
HASTINGS	Hastings Music Corp.	CPP-BEL
HATCH	Earl Hatch Publications 5008 Aukland Ave. Hollywood, CA 91601	
HATIKVAH	Hatikvah Publications	TRANSCON.
HAWK	Hawk Music Press 668 Fairmont Avenue Oakland, CA 94611	
HAYMOZ	Haydn-Mozart Presse	EUR.AM.MUS.
	Hebrew Union College Sacred Music Press see SAC.MUS.PR.	
HEER	Joh. de Heer & Zn. B.V. Muziek-Uitgeverij en Groothandel Rozenlaan 113, Postbus 3089 NL-3003 AB Rotterdam Netherlands	
HEIDELBERGER	Heidelberger	BÄREN.
HEILMAN	Heilman Music P.O. Box 1044 Fairmont, WV 26554	
HEINN	Heilmann Publications P.O. Box 18180 Pittsburgh, PA 15236	
HEINRICH.	Heinrichshofen's Verlag Liebigstraße 16 Postfach 620 D-26354 Wilhelmshaven Germany	PETERS
HELBING	Edition Helbling Kaplanstraße 9 A-6021 Neu-Rum b. Innsbruck Austria	

Code	Publisher	U.S. Agent
HELBS	Helbling Edition Pffäfikerstraβe 6 CH-8604 Voketswil-Zürich Switzerland	
HELICON	Helicon Music Corp.	EUR.AM.MUS.
HELIOS	Editio Helios	FOSTER
HENDON	Hendon Music	BOOSEY
HENKLE	Ted Henkle 5415 Reynolds Street Savannah, GA 31405	
HENLE	G. Henle Verlag Forstenrieder Allee 122 Postfach 71 04 66 D-81454 München 71 Germany G. Henle USA, Inc. P.O. Box 1753 2446 Centerline Industrial Drive St. Louis, MO 63043	
HENMAR	Henmar Press	PETERS
HENN	Editions Henn 8 rue de Hesse Genève Switzerland	
HENREES	Henrees Music Ltd.	EMI
HERALD	Herald Press 616 Walnut Avenue Scottdale, PA 15683	
HERITAGE	Heritage Music Press	LORENZ
HERITAGE PUB	Heritage Music Publishing Co.	CENTURY
HEUGEL	Heugel & Cie 175 rue Saint-Honoré F-75040 Paris Cedex 01 France	KING,R PRESSER SOUTHERN
HEUWEKE.	Edition Heuwekemeijer & Zoon Postbus 289 NL-1740 AG Schagen Netherlands	PRESSER
HHP	Hollow Hills Press 7 Landview Drive Dix Hills, NY 11746	
HIEBER	Musikverlag Max Hieber KG Postfach 330429 D-80064 München Germany	
HIGH GR	Higher Ground Music Publishing	ALEX.HSE.
HIGHGATE	Highgate Press	SCHIRM.EC
HIGHLAND	Highland/Etling Music Co. 1344 Newport Avenue Long Beach, CA 90804	
HILD	Hildegard Publishing Co. Box 332 Bryn Mawr, PA 19010	
HINRICHSEN	Hinrichsen Edition, Ltd.	PETERS
HINSHAW	Hinshaw Music, Inc. P.O. Box 470 Chapel Hill, NC 27514	
HINZ	Hinz Fabrik Verlag Lankwitzerstraβe 17-18 D-1000 Berlin 42 Germany	
HIRSCHS	Abr. Hirschs Forlag Box 505 S-101 26 Stockholm Sweden	GEHRMANS

Code	Publisher	U.S. Agent
HISPAVOX	Ediciones Musicales Hispavox Cuesta Je Santo Domingo 11 Madrid Spain	
HLH	HLH Music Publications 611 Broadway, Suite 615 New York, NY 10012	MUSIC SC.
HOA	HOA Music Publisher 756 S. Third Street Dekalb, IL 60115	
HOFFMAN,R	Raymond A. Hoffman Co. c/o Fred Bock Music Co. P.O. Box 333 Tarzana, CA 91356	ANTARA
HOFMEISTER	VEB Friedrich Hofmeister, Musikverlag, Leipzig Karlstraβ 10 D-701 Leipzig Germany	
HOFMEISTER-W	Friedrich Hofmeister Musikverlag, Taunus Ubierstraβe 20 D-6238 Hofheim am Taunus Germany	
HOHLER	Heinrich Hohler Verlag	SCHNEIDER,H
	Hollow Hills Press see HHP	
HOLLY-PIX	Holly-Pix Music Publishing Co.	WESTERN
HONG KONG	Hong Kong Music Media Publishing Co., Ltd. Kai It Building, 9th Floor 58 Pak Tai Street Tokwawan, Kowloon Hong Kong	
HONOUR	Honour Publications	WESTERN
HOPE	Hope Publishing Co. 380 South Main Place Carol Stream, IL 60188	
HORNPIPE	Hornpipe Music Publishing Co. 400 Commonwealth Avenue P.O. Box CY577 Boston, MA 02215	
HUEBER	Hueber-Holzmann Pädagogischer Verlag Krausstraße 30 D-8045 Ismaning, München Germany	
HUG	Hug & Co. Flughofstrasse 61 CH-Glattbrugg Switzerland	EUR.AM.MUS
HUGUENIN	Charles Huguenin & Pro-Arte Rue du Sapin 2a CH-2114 Fleurier Switzerland	
HUHN	W. Huhn Musikalien-Verlag Jahnstraβe 9 D-5880 Lüdenshied Germany	
HULST	De Hulst Kruisdagenlaan 75 B-1040 Bruxelles Belgium	
HUNTZINGER	R.L. Huntzinger Publications	WILLIS
HURON	Huron Press P.O. Box 2121 London, Ontario N6A 4C5 Canada	

Code	Publisher	U.S. Agent
ICELAND	Iślenzk Tónverkamidstöd Iceland Music Information Centre Freyjugata 1 P.O. Box 978 121 Reykjavik Iceland	
IISM	Istituto Italiano per la Storia della Musica Academia Nazionale di Santa Cecilia Via Vittoria, 6 I-00187 Roma Italy	
IMB	Internationale Musikbibliothek	BÄREN.
IMC	Indiana Music Center 322 South Swain P.O. Box 582 Bloomington, IN 47401	
IMPERO	Impero-Verlag Liebigstraβe 16 D-2940 Wilhelmshavn Germany	PRESSER (partial)
INDEPENDENT	Independent Publications P.O. Box 162 Park Station Paterson, NJ 07513	
INDIANA	Indiana University Press 601 N. Morton Street Bloomington, IN 47404-3797	
INST ANT	Instrumenta Antiqua, Inc. 2530 California Street San Francisco, CA 94115	
INST.CO.	The Instrumentalist 200 Northfield Road Northfield, IL 60093-3390	
	Institue Of Stringed Instruments Guitar & Lute see ISI	
	Editorial Cooperativa Inter-Americana de Compositores see ECOAM	
INTERLOCH	Interlochen Press	CRESCENDO
INTERNAT.	International Music Co. 5 W. 37th Street New York, NY 10018	
INTER.MUS.P.	International Music Publications Woodford Trading Estate Southend Road Woodford Green, Essex IG8 8HN England	
	Internationale Musikbibliothek see IMB	
INTERNAT.S.	International Music Service P.O. Box 66, Ansonia Station New York, NY 10023	
INTRADA	Intrada Music Group P.O. Box 1240 Anderson, IN 46015	
IONA	Iona Music Publishing Service P.O. Box 8131 San Marino, CA 91108	
IONE	Ione Press	SCHIRM.EC
IRIS	Iris Verlag Hernerstraβe 64A Postfach 100.851 D-4350 Recklinghausen Germany	
IROQUOIS PR	Iroquois Press P.O. Box 2121 London, Ontario N6A 4C5 Canada	

Code	Publisher	U.S. Agent
	Iślenzk Tónverkamidstöd see ICELAND	
ISI	Institute of Stringed Instruments, Guitar & Lute Poststraβe 30 4 Düsseldorf Germany	SANDVOSS
	Aux Presses d'Isle-de-France see PRESSES	
ISR.MUS.INST.	Israel Music Institute P.O. Box 3004 61030 Tel Aviv Israel	PRESSER
ISR.PUB.AG.	Israel Publishers Agency 7, Arlosoroff Street Tel-Aviv Israel	
ISRAELI	Israeli Music Publications, Ltd. 25 Keren Hayesod Jerusalem 94188 Israel	PRESSER
	Istituto Italiano per la Storia della Musica see IISM	
J.B.PUB	J.B. Publications 404 Holmes Circle Memphis, TN 38111	
J.C.A.	Japan Composers Association 3-7-15, Akasaka Minato-Ku Tokyo Japan	
JACKMAN	Jackman Music Corp. P.O. Box 900 Orem, UT 84057	MUSICART
JAPAN	Japan Federation of Composers Shinanomachi Building 602 33 Shinanomachi Shinjuku-Ku Tokyo Japan	
JAREN	Jaren Music Co. 9691 Brynmar Drive Villa Park, CA 92667	
JASE	Jasemusiikki Ky Box 136 SF-13101 Håmeenlinna 10 Finland	
JAZZ ED	Jazz Education Publications P.O. Box 802 Manhattan, KS 66502	
JEANNETTE	Ed. Jeannette	DONEMUS
JEHLE	Jehle	HÄNSSLER
JENSON	Jenson Publications, Inc. 7777 W. Bluemound Road Milwaukee, WI 53213	LEONARD-US
JERONA	Jerona Music Corp. P.O. Box 5010 Hackensack, NJ 07606-4210	
JOAD	Joad Press 4 Meredyth Road London SW13 0DY England	FISCHER,C (rental-partial)
JOBERT	Editions Jean Jobert 76, rue Quincampoix F-75003 Paris France	PRESSER

Code	Publisher	U.S. Agent
JOHNSON	Johnson Reprint Corp. 757 3rd Avenue New York, NY 10017	
JOHNSON,P	Paul Johnson Productions P.O. Box 2001 Irving, TX 75061	
JOSHUA	Joshua Corp.	SCHIRM.G
JOY	Joy Music Press	INTRADA
JRB	JRB Music Education Materials Distributor	PRESSER
JUNNE	Otto Junne GmbH Sendlinger-Tor-Platz 10 D-8000 München Germany	
JUS-AUTOR	Jus-Autor Sofia, Bulgaria	BREITKOPF-W
JUSKO	Jusko Publications	WILLIS
KAHNT	C.F. Kahnt, Musikverlag Kennedyallee 101 6000 Frankfurt 70 Germany	PETERS
KALLISTI	Kallisti Music Press 810 South Saint Bernard Street Philadelphia, PA 19143-3309	
KALMUS	Edwin F. Kalmus P.O. Box 5011 Boca Raton, FL 33431	CPP-BEL (string and miniature scores)
KALMUS,A	Alfred A. Kalmus Ltd. 38 Eldon Way, Paddock Wood Tonbridge, Kent TN12 6BE England	EUR.AM.MUS.
KAMMEN	J. & J. Kammen Music Co.	CENTURY
KAPLAN	Ida R. Kaplan 1308 Olivia Avenue Ann Arbor, MI 48104	
KARTHAUSE	Karthause Verlag Panzermacherstrasse 5 D-5860 Iserlohn Germany	
KAWAI	Kawai Gafuku	JAPAN
KAWE	Edition KaWe Brederodestraat 90 NL-1054 VC Amsterdam 13 Netherlands	KING,R
KAY PR	Kay Press 612 Vicennes Court Cincinnati, OH 45231	
KELTON	Kelton Publications 1343 Amalfi Drive Pacific Palisades, CA 90272	
KENDALE	Kendale Company 6595 S. Dayton Street Englewood, CO 80111	
KENDOR	Kendor Music Inc. Main & Grove Streets P.O. Box 278 Delevan, NY 14042	
KENSING.	Kensington Music Service P.O. Box 471 Tenafly, NJ 07670	
KENYON	Kenyon Publications	LEONARD-US
KERBY	E.C. Kerby Ltd. 198 Davenport Road Toronto, Ontario M5R IJ2 Canada	LEONARD-US BOOSEY (rental)

Code	Publisher	U.S. Agent
KIMM	Kimmel Publications, Inc. P.O. Box 1472 Decatur, IL 62522	HOPE
KINDRED	Kindred Press	HERALD
KING,R	Robert King Sales, Inc. Shovel Shop Square 28 Main Street, Bldg. 15 North Easton, MA 02356	
KING'S	King's Music Redcroft, Bank's End Wyton, Huntingdon Cambridgeshire PE17 2AA England	
KIRK	Kirkland House	LORENZ
KISTNER	Fr. Kistner & C.F.W. Siegel & Co. Adrian-Kiels-Straße 2 D-5000 Köln 90 Germany	CONCORDIA
KJOS	Neil A. Kjos Music Co. 4382 Jutland Drive Box 178270 San Diego, CA 92117-0894	
KLIMENT	Musikverlag Johann Kliment Kolingasse 15 A-1090 Wien 9 Austria	
KNEUSSLIN	Edition Kneusslin Amselstraße 43 CH-4059 Basel Switzerland	FOR.MUS.DIST.
KNOPF	Alfred A. Knopf 201 East 50th Street New York, NY 10022	
KNUF	Frits Knuf Uitgeverij Rodeheldenstraat 13 P.O. Box 720 NL-4116 ZJ Buren Netherlands	PENDRGN
KODALY	Kodaly Center of America, Inc. 1326 Washington Street West Newton, MA 02165	SUPPORT
KON BOND	Kon. Bond van Chr. Zang- en Oratoriumverenigingen	DONEMUS
KONINKLIJK	Koninklijk Nederlands Zangersverbond	DONEMUS
KOPER	Musikverlag Karl-Heinz Köper Schneekoppenweg 12 D-3001 Isernhagen NB/Hannover Germany	
KRENN	Ludwig Krenn Verlag Neulerchenfelderstr. 3-7 A-1160 Wien Austria	
KROMPHOLZ	Krompholz & Co Spitalgasse 28 CH-3001 Bern Switzerland	
KRUSEMAN	Ed. Philip Kruseman	DONEMUS
KUNZEL	Edition Kunzelmann Grutstrasse 28 CH-8134 Adliswil Switzerland	FOR.MUS.DIST.
KYSAR	Michael Kysar 1250 South 211th Place Seattle, WA 98148	
LAB	Editions Labatiaz Case Postale 112 CH-1890 St. Maurice Switzerland	

Code	Publisher	U.S. Agent
LAKES	Lake State Publishers P.O. Box 1593 Grand Rapids, MI 49501	
LAMP	Latin-American Music Pub. Co. Ltd. 8 Denmark Street London England	
LAND	A. Land & Zn. Muziekuitgevers	DONEMUS
LANDES	Landesverband Evangelischer Kirchenchöre in Bayern	HÄNSSLER
LANG	Lang Music Publications P.O. Box 11021 Indianapolis, IN 46201	
LANSMAN	Länsmansgarden PL-7012 S-762 00 Rimbo Sweden	
	Latin-American Music Pub. Co. Ltd. see LAMP	
LARK	Lark Publishing	INTRADA
LATINL	The Latin American Literary Review Press 2300 Palmer St. Pittsburgh, PA 15218	
LAUDA	Laudamus Press	INTRADA
LAUDINELLA	Laudinella Reihe	FOSTER
LAUMANN	Laumann Verlag Alter Gartenweg 14 Postfach 1360 D-4408 Dülmen Germany	
LAUREL	Laurel Press	LORENZ
LAURN	Laurendale Associates 15035 Wyandotte Street Van Nuys, CA 91405	
LAVENDER	Lavender Publications, Ltd. Borough Green Sevenoaks, Kent TN15 8DT England	
LAWSON	Lawson-Gould Music Publishers, Inc. 250 W. 57th St., Suite 932 New York, NY 10107	ALFRED
LEA	Lea Pocket Scores P.O. Box 138, Audubon Station New York, NY 10032	EUR.AM.MUS.
LEAWOOD	Leawood Music Press	ANTARA
LEDUC	Alphonse Leduc 175 rue Saint-Honoré F-75040 Paris Cedex 01 France	KING,R PRESSER (rental)
LEE	Norman Lee Publishing, Inc. Box 528 Oskaloosa, IA 52577	BARNHS
LEEDS	Leeds Music Ltd. MCA Building 2450 Victoria Park Avenue Willowdale, Ontario M2J 4A2 Canada	MCA PRESSER (rental)
LEMOINE	Henry Lemoine & Cie 17, rue Pigalle F-75009 Paris France	PRESSER
LENGNICK	Alfred Lengnick & Co., Ltd. Purley Oaks Studios 421a Brighton Road South Croydon, Surrey CR2 6YR England	

Code	Publisher	U.S. Agent
LEONARD-ENG	Leonard, Gould & Bolttler 60-62 Clerkenwell Road London EC1M 5PY England	
LEONARD-US	Hal Leonard Music 7777 West Bluemound Road Milwaukee, WI 53213	
LESLIE	Leslie Music Supply P.O. Box 471 Oakville, Ontario L6J 5A8 Canada	BRODT
LEUCKART	F.E.C. Leuckart Nibelungenstraße 48 D-8000 München 19 Germany	
LEXICON	Lexicon Music P.O. Box 2222 Newbury Park, CA 91320	ALEX.HSE.
LIBEN	Liben Music Publications 1191 Eversole Road Cincinnati, OH 45230	
LIBER	Svenska Utbildningsförlaget Liber AB Utbildningsförlaget, Centrallagret S-136 01 Handen Stockholm Sweden	
LICHTENAUER	W.F. Lichtenauer	DONEMUS
LIED	VEB Lied der Zeit Musikverlag Rosa-Luxemburg-Straße 41 D-102 Berlin Germany	
LIENAU	Robert Lienau, Musikverlag Hildegardstr. 16 D-10715 Berlin Germany	PETERS
LIGA	Liga de Compositores de Musica de Concierto de Mexico, A.C. Dolores 2 3er Piso Apartado Postal M-2904 06050 Mexico 1, D.F. Mexico	
LIGHT	Light of the World Music	INTRADA
LILLENAS	Lillenas Publishing Co. P.O. Box 419527 Kansas City, MO 64141	
LINDSAY	Lindsay Music 23 Hitchin Street Biggleswade, Beds SG18 8AX England	PRESSER
LINDSBORG	Lindsborg Press P.O. Box 737 State Road 9 South Alexandria, VA 46001	ANTARA
LINGUA	Lingua Press P.O. Box 3416 Iowa City, IA 52244	
LISTER	Mosie Lister	LILLENAS
LITOLFF,H	Henry Litolff's Verlag Kennedy Allee 101 Postfach 700906 D-6000 Frankfurt 70 Germany	PETERS
LITURGICAL	Liturgical Music Press St. Johns Abbey Collegeville, MN 56321	
LLUQUET	Guillermo Lluquet Almacen General de Musica Avenida del Oeste 43 Valencia Spain	

Code	Publisher	U.S. Agent
	London Pro Musica Edition see LPME	
LONG ISLE	Long Island Music Publishers	BRANCH
LOOP	Loop Music Co.	KJOS
LORENZ	Lorenz Corporation 501 East Third Street P.O. Box 802 Dayton, OH 45401-9969	
LPME	The London Pro Musica Edition 15 Rock Street Brighton BN2 1NF England	MAGNA D
LUCKS	Luck's Music Library P.O. Box 71397 Madison Heights, MI 48071	
LUDWIG	Ludwig Music Publishing Co. 557-67 East 140th Street Cleveland, OH 44110-1999	
LUNDEN	Edition Lundén Bromsvagen 25 S-125 30 Alvsjö Sweden	
LUNDMARK	Lundmark Publications 811 Bayliss Drive Marietta, GA 30067	SUPPORT
LUNDQUIST	Abr. Lundquist Musikförlag AB Katarina Bangata 17 S-116 25 Stockholm Sweden	
LYCHE	Harald Lyche Postboks 2171 Stromso N-3003 Drammen Norway	WALTON (partial)
LYDIAN ORCH	Lydian Orchestrations 31000 Ruth Hill Road Orange Cove, CA 93646	SHAWNEE
LYNWD	Lynwood Music Photo Editions 2 Church St. West Hagley West Midlands DY9 0NA England	
LYRA	Lyra Music Co. 133 West 69th Street New York, NY 10023	
MAA	Music Associates of America 224 King Street Englewood, NJ 07631	
MACNUTT	Richard Macnutt Ltd. Hamm Farm House Withyham, Hartfield Sussex TN7 4BJ England	
	Mac Murray Publications see MMP	
MAGNA D	Magnamusic Distributors Route 49 Sharon, CT 06069	
MALCOLM	Malcolm Music Ltd.	SHAWNEE
MANNA	Manna Music, Inc. 22510 Stanford Avenue Suite 101 Valencia, CA 91355	
MANNHEIM	Mannheimer Musikverlag Kunigundestraße 4 D-5300 Bonn 2 Germany	
MANU. PUB	Manuscript Publications 120 Maple Street Wrightsville, PA 17368	

Code	Publisher	U.S. Agent
MAPA MUNDI	Mapa Mundi—Music Publishers 72 Brewery Road London N7 9NE England	SCHIRM.EC
MARBOT	Edition Marbot GmbH Mühlenkamp 43 D-2000 Hamburg 60 Germany	PEER
MARCHAND	Marchand, Paap en Strooker	DONEMUS
MARGUN	Margun/Gunmar Music, Inc. 167 Dudley Road Newton Centre, MA 02159	JERONA
MARI	E. & O. Mari, Inc. 38-01 23rd Avenue Long Island City, NY 11105	
MARK	Mark Publications	CRESPUB
MARKS	Edward B. Marks Music Corp. 1619 Broadway New York, NY 10019	LEONARD-US (sales) PRESSER (rental)
MARSEG	Marseg, Ltd. 18 Farmstead Road Willowdale, Ontario M2L 2G2 Canada	
MARTIN	Editions Robert Martin 106, Grande rue de la Coupée F-71009 Charnay-les-Macon France	PRESSER
MASTER	Master Music	CRESPUB
MASTERS	Masters Music Publications P.O. Box 810157 Boca Raton, FL 33481-0157	
MAURER	J. Maurer Avenue du Verseau 7 B-1020 Brussel Belgium	
MAURRI	Edizioni Musicali Ditta R. Maurri Via del Corso 1 (17R.) Firenze Italy	
MAYHEW	Kevin Mayhew LTD. Rattlesden Bury St. Edmunds Suffolk IP30 0SZ England	
MCA	MCA and Mills/MCA Joint Venture Editions 1755 Broadway, 8th Floor New York, NY 10019	LEONARD-US (sales) PRESSER (rental)
MCAFEE	McAfee Music Corp.	CPP-BEL
MCGIN-MARX	McGinnis & Marx 236 West 26th Street, #11S New York, NY 10001	
MDV	Mitteldeutscher Verlag Thalmannplatz 2, Postfach 295 D-4010 Halle — Saale Germany	PETERS
MEDIA	Media Press P.O. Box 250 Elwyn, PA 19063	
MEDICI	Medici Music Press 5017 Veach Road Owensboro, KY 42301-9643	
MEDIT	Mediterranean	GALAXY
MEL BAY	Mel Bay Publications, Inc. P.O. Box 66 Pacific, MO 63069	

Code	Publisher	U.S. Agent
MELE LOKE	Mele Loke Publishing Co. Box 7142 Honolulu, Hawaii 96821	HIGHLAND (continental U.S.A)
MELODI	Casa Editrice Melodi S.A. Galleria Del Corso 4 Milano Italy	
MENC	Music Educators National Conference Publications Division 1902 Association Drive Reston, VA 22091	
MERCATOR	Mercator Verlag & Wohlfahrt (Gert) Verlag Köhnenstraβe 5-11 Postfach 100609 D-4100 Duisberg 1 Germany	
MERCURY	Mercury Music Corp.	PRESSER
MERIDIAN	Les Nouvelles Éditions Meridian 5, rue Lincoln F-75008 Paris 8 France	
MERION	Merion Music, Inc.	PRESSER
MERRYMOUNT	Merrymount Music, Inc.	PRESSER
MERSEBURGER	Merseburger Verlag Motzstraβe 13 D-3500 Kassel Germany	
METRO	Metro Muziek Uilenweg 38 Postbus 70 NL-6000 AB Weert Netherlands	
METROPOLIS	Editions Metropolis Van Ertbornstraat, 5 B-2108 Antwerpen Belgium	
MEULEMANS	Arthur Meulemans Fonds Charles de Costerlaan, 6 2050 Antwerpen Belgium	
MEXICANAS	Ediciones Mexicanas de Musica Avenida Juarez 18 Mexico City Mexico	PEER
MEZ KNIGA	Mezhdunarodnaya Kniga 39, Dimitrov St. Moscow 113095 Russia	
MIDDLE	Middle Eight Music	CPP-BEL
MILLER	Miller Music Corp.	CPP-BEL
MILLS MUSIC	Mills Music Jewish Catalogue	TRANSCON. PRESSER (rental)
MINKOFF	Minkoff Reprints 8 rue Eynard CH-1211 Genève 12 Switzerland	OMI
MIRA	Mira Music Associates 199 Mountain Road Wilton, CT 06897	
	Mitteldeutscher Verlag see MDV	
MJQ	M.J.Q. Music, Inc. 1697 Broadway #1100 New York, NY 10019	FOX,S

Code	Publisher	U.S. Agent
MMB	MMB Music, Inc. Contemporary Arts Building 3526 Washington Avenue St. Louis, MO 63103-1019	
MMP	Mac Murray Publications	MUS.SAC.PRO.
MMS	Monumenta Musica Svecicae	STIM
MOBART	Mobart Music Publications	JERONA
MOD ART	Modern Art Music	SON-KEY
MODERN	Edition Modern Musikverlag Hans Wewerka Elisabethstraβe 38 D-8000 München 40 Germany	
MOECK	Hermann Moeck Verlag Postfach 143 D-3100 Celle 1 Germany	EUR.AM.MUS.
MOLENAAR	Molenaar's Muziekcentrale Industrieweg 23 Postbus 19 NL-1520 AA Wormerveer Netherlands	GM
MONDIAL	Mondial-Verlag KG 8 rue de Hesse Genève Switzerland	
MONTEVERDI	Fondazione Claudio Monteverdi Via Ugolani Dati, 4 1-26100 Cremona Italy	
MORAVIAN	Moravian Music Foundation	CPP-BEL BOOSEY BRODT PETERS
MORN.ST.	Morning Star Music Publishers 2117 59th St. St. Louis, MO 63110-2800	
MOSAIC	Mosaic Music Corporation	BOSTON
MÖSELER	Karl Heinrich Möseler Verlag Hoffman-von-Fallersleben-Straβe 8-10 Postfach 1661 D-3340 Wolfenbüttel Germany	
MOSER	Verlag G. Moser Kirschweg 8 CH-4144 Arlesheim Switzerland	
MOWBRAY	Mowbray Music Publications Saint Thomas House Becket Street Oxford OX1 1SJ England	PRESSER
MSM	MSM Music Publishers	BRODT
MT.SALUS	Mt. Salus Music 709 East Leake Street Clinton, MS 39056	
MT.TAHO	Mt. Tahoma	BROUDE,A
MÜLLER	Willy Müller, Süddeutscher Musikverlag Marzgasse 5 D-6900 Heidelberg Germany	
MUNSTER	Van Munster Editie	DONEMUS
MURPHY	Spud Murphy Publications	WESTERN
MUS.ANT.BOH.	Musica Antiqua Bohemica	SUPRAPHON
MUS.ART	Music Art Publications P.O. Box 1744 Chula Vista, CA 92010	

Code	Publisher	U.S. Agent
MUS.PERC.	Music For Percussion, Inc. 17 West 60th Street New York, NY 10023	
MUS.RARA	Musica Rara Le Traversier Chemin de la Buire F-84170 Monteux France	
	Musica Russica 　　see RUSSICA	
MUS.SAC.PRO	Musica Sacra et Profana P.O. Box 7248 Berkeley, CA 94707	
MUS.SB	Music Service Bureau 1645 Harvard St. NW Washington, D.C. 20009-3702	
MUS.SUR	Musica del Sur Apartado 5219 Barcelona Spain	
MUS.VERA	Musica Vera Graphics & Publishers 350 Richmond Terrace 4-M Staten Island, NY 10301	ARISTA
MUS.VIVA	Musica Viva 262 King's Drive Eastbourne Sussex, BN21 2XD England	
MUS.VIVA.HIST.	Musica Viva Historica	SUPRAPHON
MUSIA	Musia	PETERS
MUSIC	Music Sales Corp. Executive Offices 225 Park Avenue South New York, NY 10003 Music Sales Corp. (Rental) 5 Bellvale Road Chester, NY 10918	
MUSIC BOX	Music Box Dancer Publications Ltd.	PRESSER
	Music Educators National Conference 　　see MENC	
MUSIC-ENG	Music Sales Ltd. Newmarket Road Bury St. Edmunds Suffolk IP33 3YB England	MUSIC
MUSIC INFO	Muzicki Informativni Centar—ZAMP Ulica 8 Maja 37 P.O. Box 959 Zagreb Croatia	BREITKOPF-W
MUSIC SC.	Musical Score Distributors 611 Broadway, Suite 615 New York, NY 10012	
MUSIC SEV.	Music 70, Music Publishers 170 N.E. 33rd Street Fort Lauderdale, FL 33334	
	Société d'Éditions Musicales Internationales 　　see SEMI	PLYMOUTH
MUSICART	Musicart West P.O. Box 1900 Orem, UT 84059	
MUSICIANS PUB	Musicians Publications P.O. Box 7160 West Trenton, NJ 08628	
MUSICO	Musico Muziekuitgeverij	DONEMUS
MUSICPRINT	Musicprint Corporation P.O. Box 20767 New York, NY 10023	

Code	Publisher	U.S. Agent
MUSICUS	Edition Musicus P.O. Box 1341 Stamford, CT 06904	
MUSIKAL.	Musikaliska Konstföreningen Aarstryck, Sweden	WALTON
MUSIKHOJ	Musikhojskolens Forlag ApS	EUR.AM.MUS
MUSIKINST	Verlag das Musikinstrument Klüberstraβe 9 D-6000 Frankfurt-am-Main Germany	
MUSIKK	Musikk-Huset A-S P.O. Box 822 Sentrum 0104 Oslo 1 Norway	
MUSIKWISS.	Musikwissenschaftlicher Verlag Wien Dorotheergasse 10 A-1010 Wien 1 Austria	FOR.MUS.DIST (Bruckner & Wolf)
	Eerste Muziekcentrale 　　see EERSTE	
MUZYKA	Muzyka Publishers 14 Neglinnaya Street 103031 Moscow Russia	
MYRRH	Myrrh Music	WORD
MYRTLE	Myrtle Monroe Music 2600 Tenth Street Berkeley, CA 94710	
NAGELS	Nagels Verlag	
NATIONAL	National Music Publishers 16605 Townhouse Tustin, CA 91680	ANTARA
NEUE	Verlag Neue Musik An der Kolonnade 15 Postfach 1306 D-1080 Berlin Germany	FOR.MUS.DIST
NEW HORIZON	New Horizon Publications	TRANSCON.
	New Music Edition 　　see NME	
NEW MUSIC WEST	New Music West P.O. Box 7434 Van Nuys, CA 91409	
NEW VALLEY	New Valley Music Press of Smith 　　College Sage Hall 49 Northampton, MA 01063	
NEW W	New World Enterprises of Montrose, 　　Inc. 2 Marisa Court Montrose, NY 10548	
NEWAM	Foundation for New American Music	LUCKS
NGLANI	Edition Nglani Box 871 Merrifield, VA 22116-2871	
NIEUWE	De Nieuwe Muziekhandel	DONEMUS
NIPPON	Nippon Hosu	PRESSER
NL	NL Productions Inc.	PLUCKED ST
N.LIGHT	Northlight Music Inc.	SCHIRM.G
NME	New Music Edition	PRESSER
NO.AM.LIT.	North American Liturgy Resources Choral Music Department 10802 North 23rd Avenue Phoenix, AZ 85029	

Code	Publisher	U.S. Agent
NOBILE	Nobile Verlag Aixheimer Straße 26 D-7000 Stuttgart 75 Germany	
NOETZEL	Noetzel Musikverlag Liebigstraße 16 Postfach 620 D-2940 Wilhelmshavn Germany	PETERS
NOMOS	Edition Nomos	BREITKOPF-W
NOORDHOFF	P. Noordhoff	DONEMUS
NORDISKA	AB Nordiska Musikförlaget Nybrogatan 3 S-114 34 Stockholm Sweden see also HANSEN-SWEDEN	
NORGE	Norsk Musikkinformasjon Toftesgatan 69 N-0552 Olso 5 Norway	
NORK	Norske Komponisters Forlag Gjernesvegen 24 N-5700 Voss Norway	
NORRUTH	Norruth Music Publishers	MMB
NORSK	Norsk Musikforlag AS Karl Johansgaten 39 P.O. Box 1499 Vika N-0116 Oslo 1 Norway	
	Northlight Music Inc. see N. LIGHT	
NORTHRIDGE	Northridge Music, Inc. 7317 Greenback Lane Citrus Heights, CA 95621	CPP-BEL
NORTON	W.W. Norton & Co., Inc. 500 Fifth Avenue New York, NY 10003	
	Norwegian Music Information Center see NORGE	
NOSKE	A.A. Noske	DONEMUS
NOTERIA	Noteria S-590 30 Borensberg Sweden	STIM
NOTON	Noton Kolltjernvn. 11 P.O. Box 1014 N-2301 Hamar Norway	
NOVA	Nova Music Ltd. Goldsmid Mews 15a Farm Road Hove Sussex BN3 1FB England	SCHIRM.EC
NOVELLO	Novello & Co., Ltd. Newmarket Road Bury St. Edmunds Suffolk IP33 3YB England	SHAWNEE MUSIC (rental)
NOW VIEW	Now View	PLYMOUTH
	Nuova Carisch s.r.l. Via M.F. Quintiliano, 40 20138 Milano Italy	
NYMPHEN	Edition Nymphenburg Unterföhring, Germany	PETERS
OAK	Oak Publications	MUSIC

Code	Publisher	U.S. Agent
OCTAVA	Octava Music Co. Ltd.	WEINBERGER
OECUM	Oecumuse 52a Broad St. Ely, CB7 4AH England	CANTORIS
OISEAU	Éditions de L'Oiseau-Lyre Les Remparts Boite Postale 515 MC-98015 Monaco Cedex	MAGNA D OMI
OJEDA	Raymond J. Ojeda 98 Briar Road Kentfield, CA 94904	
OKRA	Okra Music Corp.	SEESAW
OLIVIAN	Olivian Press	ARCADIA
OLMS	G. Olms Verlag Hagentorwall 7 D-3200 Hildesheim Germany	
OMI	OMI — Old Manuscripts & Incunabula P.O. Box 6019, FDR Station New York, NY 10150	
ONGAKU	Ongaku-No-Tomo Sha Co. Ltd. Kagurazaka 6-30, Shinjuku-ku Tokyo 162 Japan	PRESSER
OPUS	Opus Music Publishers, Inc. 1318 Chicago Avenue Evanston, IL 60201	
OPUS-CZ	Opus Ceskoslavenske Hudobne Vydaratelstro Mlynske nivy 73 827 99 Bratislava Slovak Republic	BOOSEY (rental)
OR-TAV	Or-Tav Music Publications Israel Composers League P.O. Box 3200 113, Allenby Street Tel-Aviv Israel	
ORGAN	Organ Music Co.	WESTERN
ORGAN LIT	Organ Literature Foundation 45 Norfolk Road Braintree, MA 02184	
ORGMS	Organmaster Music Series 282 Stepstone Hill Guilford, CT 06437	
ORION MUS	Orion Music Press P.O. Box 145, University Station Barrien Springs, MI 49104	OPUS
ORLANDO	Orlando Musikverlag Kaprunerstraße 11 D-8000 München 21 Germany	
ORPHEUM	Orpheum Music 10th & Parker Berkeley, CA 94710	
OSTARA	Ostara Press, Inc.	WESTERN
ÖSTER	Österreichischer Bundesverlag Schwarzenberg Platz 5 A-1010 Wien Austria	
OSTIGUY	Editions Jacques Ostiguy Inc. 12790 Rue Yamaska St. Hyacinthe, Quebec Canada J2T 1B3	

Code	Publisher	U.S. Agent
OSTNOR	Φstnorsk Musikkforlag Nordre Langgate 1 B N-9950 Vardφ Norway	
OTOS	Otos Edizioni Musicali Via Marsillo Ficino, 10 I-50132 Firenze Italy	
OUVRIERES	Les Éditions Ouvrières 12, Avenue Soeur-Rosalie F-75621 Paris Cedex 13, France	KING,R
OXFORD	Oxford University Press 7-8 Hatherly Street London SW1P 2QT England	
OXFORD	Oxford University Press 200 Madison Avenue New York, NY 10016	
PACIF	Pacific Publications	INTRADA
PAGANI	O. Pagani & Bro., Inc. c/o P. Deiro Music 289 Bleeker Street New York, NY 10014	
PAGANINI PUB	Paganiniana Publications, Inc. 1 T.F.H. Plaza 3rd & Union Avenue Neptune City, NJ 07753	
PAIDEIA	Paideia Editrice	BÄREN.
PALLMA	Pallma Music Co.	KJOS
PAN	Editions Pan Schaffhauserstraβe 280 Postfach 176 CH-8057 Zürich Switzerland	PRESSER
PAN AM	Pan American Union	PEER
PAN F	Edition Pan of Finland Vihertie 56C 01620 Vantaa Finland	
PANTONH	Panton Radlická 99 CS-150 00 Praha 5 Czech Republic	NEW W
PARACLETE	Paraclete Press P.O. Box 1568 Hilltop Plaza, Route 6A Orleans, MA 02653	
PARAGON	Paragon Music Publishers	CENTURY
PARAGON ASS.	Paragon Associates	ALEX.HSE.
PARIS	Uitgeverij H.J. Paris	DONEMUS
PARKS	Parks Music Corp.	KJOS
PASTORALE	Pastorale Music Company 235 Sharon Drive San Antonio, TX 78216	
PASTORINI	Musikhaus Pastorini AG Kasinostraβe 25 CH-5000 Aarau Switzerland	
PATERSON	Paterson's Publications, Ltd. 8-10 Lower James Street London W1R 3PL England	MUSIC
	Patrimoine Musical Canadien see CAN.MUS.HER.	

Code	Publisher	U.S. Agent
PAVAN	Pavane Publishing P.O. Box 2931 San Anselmo, CA 94979	INTRADA
PAXTON	Paxton Publications Sevenoaks, Kent, England	PRESSER
PECK	Pecktackular Music 3605 Brandywine Drive Greensboro, NC 27410	
PEER	Peer Southern Concert Music 810 Seventh Avenue New York, NY 10019	PRESSER
PEER MUSIK	Peer Musikverlag GmbH Muhlenkamp 43 Postfach 602129 D-2000 Hamburg Germany	PEER
PEG	Pegasus Musikverlag Liebig Straβe 16 Postfach 620 D-2940 Wilhelmshaven Germany	PETERS
PELIC.C	Pelican Cay Publications	PLYMOUTH
PELIKAN	Musikverlag Pelikan	EUR.AM.MUS.
PEMBROKE	Pembroke Music Co., Inc.	FISCHER,C
PENADES	José Penadés En Sanz 12 Valencia Spain	
PENDRGN	Pendragon Press R.R. 1, Box 159 Stuyvesant, NY 12173-9720	
PENGUIN	Penguin Books 120 Woodbine Street Bergenfield, NJ 07621	
PENN STATE	Penn State Press The Pennsylvania State University Barbara Building, Suite C University Park, PA 16802-1003	
PENOLL	Penoll Goteberg, Sweden	STIM
PEPPER	J.W. Pepper And Son, Inc. P.O. Box 850 Valley Forge, PA 19482	
PERF.ED.	Performers' Editions	BROUDE BR.
PERFORM	Perform Our Music Leuven, Belgium	PEER
PERMUS	Permus Publications P.O. Box 02033 Columbus, OH 43202	
PETERER	Edition Melodie Anton Peterer Brunnwiesenstraβe 26 Postfach 260 CH-8409 Zürich Switzerland	
PETERS	Edition Peters C.F. Peters Corp. 373 Park Avenue South New York, NY 10016	
	Edition Peters Postfach 746 D-7010 Leipzig Germany	
	C.F. Peters Musikverlag Postfach 700851 Kennedyallee 101 D-6000 Frankfurt 70 Germany	

Code	Publisher	U.S. Agent
	Peters Edition Ltd. Bach House 10-12 Baches Street London N1 6DN England	
PETERS,K	Kermit Peters 1515 90th Street Omaha, NE 68124	
PETERS,M	Mitchell Peters 3231 Benda Place Los Angeles, CA 90068	
PFAUEN	Pfauen Verlag Adolfsallee 34 Postfach 471 D-6200 Wiesbaden Germany	
PHILH	Philharmonia	EUR.AM.MUS. (miniature scores)
PHILIPPO	Editions Philippo	ELKAN-V
PHOEBUS	Phoebus Apollo Music Publishers 1126 Huston Drive West Mifflin, PA 15122	
PIEDMONT	Piedmont Music Co.	PRESSER (rental)
PILES	Piles Editorial de Musica Archena 33y Yatova, 4 Apartado 8.012 E-46080 Valencia Spain	
PILLIN	Pillin Music	WESTERN
PILLON	Pillon Press	THOMAS
PIONEER	Pioneer Music Press	MUSICART
PIPER	Piper Music Co. P.O. Box 1713 Cincinnati, OH 45201	LIBEN
PLAINSONG	Plainsong & Medieval Music Society Catherine Harbor, Hon. Sec. c/o Turner 72 Brewery Road London N7 9NE England	
PLAYER	Player Press 139-22 Caney Lane Rosedale, NY 11422	
PLENUM	Plenum Publishing Corp. 233 Spring Street New York, NY 10013	DA CAPO
PLESNICAR	Don Plesnicar P.O. Box 4880 Albuquerque, NM 87106	
PLOUGH	Plough Publishing House Rifton, NY 12471	
PLUCKED ST	Plucked String P.O. Box 11125 Arlington, VA 22210	
PLYMOUTH	Plymouth Music Co., Inc. 170 N.E. 33rd Street P.O. Box 24330 Fort Lauderdale, FL 33334	
PODIUM	Podium Music, Inc. 360 Port Washington Boulevard Port Washington, NY 11050	
POLSKIE	Polskie Wydawnictwo Muzyczne Al. Krasinskiego 11a PL31-111 Krakow Poland	PRESSER

Code	Publisher	U.S. Agent
POLYPH MUS	Polyphone Music Co.	ARCADIA
POLYPHON	Polyphon Musikverlag	BREITKOPF-W
PORT.MUS.	Portugaliae Musicae Fundaçao Calouste Gulbenkian Avenida de Berna 45 P-1093 Lisboa Codex Portugal	
	Postif Press Ltd. see BRENNAN	
POST	Posthorn Press	INTRADA
POWER	Power and Glory Music Co. 6595 S. Dayton St. Englewood, CO 80111	SON-KEY
PRAEGER	Praeger Publications 383 Madison Avenue New York, NY 10017	
PRB	PRB Productions 963 Peralta Avenue Albany, CA 94706-2144	
PREISSLER	Musikverlag Josef Preissler Postfach 521 Bräuhausstraβe 8 D-8000 München 2 Germany	
PRELUDE	Prelude Publications 150 Wheeler Street Glouchester, MA 01930	
PRENTICE	Prentice-Hall, Inc. Englewood Cliffs, NJ 07632	
PRESSER	Theodore Presser Co. Presser Place Bryn Mawr, PA 19010	
PRESSES	Aux Presses d'Isle-de-France 12, rue de la Chaise F-75007 Paris France	
PRICE,P	Paul Price Publications 470 Kipp Street Teaneck, NJ 07666	
PRIMAVERA	Editions Primavera	GENERAL
PRINCE	Prince Publications 1125 Francisco Street San Francisco, CA 94109	
PRO ART	Pro Art Publications, Inc.	CPP-BEL
PRO MUSICA	Pro Musica Verlag Karl-Liebknecht-Straβe 12 Postfach 467 D-7010 Leipzig Germany	
PRO MUSICA INTL	Pro Musica International 130 Bylor P.O. Box 1687 Pueblo, CO 81002	
PROCLAM	Proclamation Productions, Inc. Orange Square Port Jervis, NY 12771	
PROGRESS	Progress Press P.O. Box 12 Winnetka, IL 60093	
PROPRIUS	Proprius Musik AB Vartavagen 35 S-115 29 Stockholm Sweden	
PROSVETNI	Prosvetni Servis	DRUSTVO
PROVIDENCE	Providence Music Press 251 Weybosset St. Providence, RI 02903	

Code	Publisher	U.S. Agent
PROVINCTWN	Provincetown Bookshop Editions 246 Commercial Street Provincetown, MA 02657	
PROWSE	Keith Prowse Music Publishing Co. 138-140 Charing Cross Road London, WC2H 0LD England	INTER.MUS.P
PRUETT	Pruett Publishing Co. 2928 Pearl Boulder, CO 80301-9989	
PSALTERY	Psaltery Music Publications P.O. Box 11325 Dallas, TX 75223	KENDALE
PSI	PSI Press P.O. Box 2320 Boulder, CO 80306	
PURIFOY	Purifoy Publishing P.O. Box 30157 Knoxville, TN 37930	JENSON
PUSTET	Verlag Friedrich Pustet Gutenbergstraße 8 Postfach 339 D-8400 Regensburg 11 Germany	
PYRAMINX	Pyraminx Publications	ACCURA
QUEEN	Queensgate Music 120 Dowanhill Street Glasgow G12 9DN Scotland	
QUIROGA	Ediciones Quiroga Alcalá, 70 28009 Madrid Spain	PRESSER
RAHTER	D. Rahter Werderstraße 44 D-2000 Hamburg 13 Germany	PRESSER
RAMSEY	Basil Ramsey Publisher of Music	INTRADA
RARITIES	Rarities For Strings Publications 11300 Juniper Drive University Circle Cleveland, OH 44106	
RAVEN	Raven Press 1185 Avenue of the Americas New York, NY 10036	
REAL	Real Musical Carlos III, no. 1 28013 Madrid, Spain	
RECITAL	Recital Publications, Ltd. P.O. Box 1697 Huntsville, TX 77342-1697	
	Regent, Arc & Goodman see GOODMAN	
REGENT	Regent Music Corp. 488 Madison Avenue 5th Floor New York, NY 10022	LEONARD-US
REGINA	Regina Verlag Schumannstraße 35 Postfach 6148 D-6200 Wiesbaden 1 Germany	
REGUS	Regus Publisher 10 Birchwood Lane White Bear Lake, MN 55110	
REIMERS	Edition Reimers AB Box 15030 S-16115 Bromma Sweden	PRESSER

Code	Publisher	U.S. Agent
REINHARDT	Friedrich Reinhardt Verlag Missionsstraße 36 CH-4055 Basel Switzerland	
REN	Les Editions Renaissantes	EUR.AM.MUS.
RENK	Musikverlag Renk "Varia Edition" Herzog-Heinrich-Straße 21 D-8000 München 2 Germany	
RESEARCH	Research Publications, Inc. Lunar Drive Woodbridge, CT 06525	
RESTOR	Restoration Press	THOMAS
REUTER	Reuter & Reuter Förlags AB Box 26072 S-100 41 Stockholm Sweden	
RHODES,R	Roger Rhodes Music, Ltd. P.O. Box 1550, Radio City Station New York, NY 10101	
RICHMOND	Richmond Music Press, Inc. P.O. Box 465 Richmond, IN 47374	
RICHMOND ORG.	The Richmond Organization see also TRO	PLYMOUTH
RICORDI-ARG	Ricordi Americana S.A. Cangallo, 1558 1037 Buenos Aires Argentina	LEONARD-US BOOSEY (rental)
RICORDI-BR	Ricordi Brasileira S.A. R. Conselheiro Nebias 773 1 S-10-12 Sao Paolo Brazil	LEONARD-US BOOSEY (rental)
RICORDI-CAN	G. Ricordi & Co. Toronto Canada	LEONARD-US BOOSEY (rental)
RICORDI-ENG	G. Ricordi & Co. Ltd. The Bury, Church Street Chesham, Bucks HP5 1JG England	LEONARD-US BOOSEY (rental)
RICORDI-FR	Société Anonyme des Éditions Ricordi	LEONARD-US BOOSEY (rental)
RICORDI-GER	G. Ricordi & Co. Gewürzmühlstraße 5 D-8000 München 22 Germany	LEONARD-US BOOSEY (rental)
RICORDI-IT	G. Ricordi & Co. Via Salomone 77 I-20138 Milano Italy	LEONARD-US BOOSEY (rental)
RIDEAU	Les Éditions Rideau Rouge 24, rue de Longchamp F-75116 Paris France	PRESSER SCHIRM.G
RIES	Ries & Erler Charlottenbrunner Straße 42 D-1000 Berlin 33 (Grunewald) Germany	
RILEY	Dr. Maurice W. Riley Eastern Michigan University 512 Roosevelt Boulevard Ypsilanti, MI 48197	
ROBBINS	Robbins Music Corp.	CPP-BEL PRESSER (rental)

Code	Publisher	U.S. Agent
ROBERTON	Roberton Publications The Windmill, Wendover Aylesbury, Bucks, HP22 6JJ England	PRESSER
ROBERTS,L	Lee Roberts Music Publications, Inc. P.O. Box 225 Katonah, NY 10536	
ROBITSCHEK	Adolf Robitschek Musikverlag Graben 14 (Bräunerstraße 2) Postfach 42 A-1011 Wien Austria	
ROCHESTER	Rochester Music Publishers, Inc. 358 Aldrich Road Fairport, NY 14450	ACCURA
RODEHEAVER	Rodeheaver Publications	WORD
ROLLAND	Rolland String Research Associates 404 E. Oregon Urbana, IL 61801	BOOSEY
RONCORP	Roncorp, Inc. P.O. Box 724 Cherry Hill, NJ 08003	
RONGWEN	Rongwen Music, Inc.	BROUDE BR.
ROSSUM	Wed. J.R. van Rossum	ZENGERINK
ROUART	Rouart-Lerolle & Cie	SCHIRM.G
ROW	R.D. Row Music Co.	FISCHER,C
ROYAL	Royal School of Church Music Addington Palace Croydon, Surrey CR9 5AD England Associated Board of the Royal Schools of Music see ABRSM	
ROYAL,TAP.	Royal Tapestry 50 Music Square West Suite 500A Nashville, TN 37203	ALEX.HSE.
ROZSAVÖ.	Rozsavölgi & Co.	BUDAPEST
RUBANK	Rubank, Inc. 16215 N.W. 15th Avenue Miami, FL 33169	LEONARD-US
RUBATO	Rubato Musikverlag Hollandstraße 18 A-1020 Wien Austria	DONEMUS
RUH,E	Emil Ruh Musikverlag Zürichstraße 33 CH-8134 Adliswil - Zürich Switzerland	
RUMAN.COMP.	Uniunea Compozitorilor din R.S. România (Union of Rumanian Composers) Str. C. Escarcu No. 2 Bucureşti, Sector 1 Rumania	
RUSSICA	Musica Russica 27 Willow Lane Madison, CT 06443	
RUTGERS	Rutgers University Editions	JERONA
RYDET	Rydet Music Publishers P.O. Box 477 Purchase, NY 10577	
SAC.MUS.PR.	Sacred Music Press of Hebrew Union College One West Fourth Street New York, NY 10012	TRANSCON.

Code	Publisher	U.S. Agent
SACRED	Sacred Music Press	LORENZ
SACRED SNGS	Sacred Songs, Inc.	WORD
SALABERT	Francis Salabert Éditions 22 rue Chauchat F-75009 Paris France	LEONARD-US (sales) SCHIRM.G (rental)
SAMFUNDET	Samfundet til udgivelse af Dansk Musik Valkendorfsgade 3 DK-1151 Kobenhavn Denmark	PETERS
SAN ANDREAS	San Andreas Press 3732 Laguna Avenue Palo Alto, CA 94306	
SANJO	Sanjo Music Co. P.O. Box 7000-104 Palos Verdes Peninsula, CA 90274	
SAUL AVE	Saul Avenue Publishing Co. 4172 Fox Hollow Drive Cincinnati, OH 45241-2939	
SANTA	Santa Barbara Music Publishing P.O. Box 41003 Santa Barbara, CA 93140	
SAVGOS	Savgos Music Inc. P.O. Box 279 Elizabeth, NJ 07207	
SCARECROW	The Scarecorw Press, Inc. 52 Liberty Street P.O. Box 656 Metuchen, NJ 08840	
SCHAUM	Schaum Publications, Inc. 2018 East North Avenue Milwaukee, WI 53202	
SCHAUR	Richard Schauer, Music Publishers 67 Belsize Lane, Hampstead London NW3 5AX England	PRESSER
SCHEIDT	Altonaer Scheidt-Ausgabe	HÄNSSLER
SCHERZANDO	Muziekuitgeverij Scherzando Lovelingstraat 20-22 B-2000 Antwerpen Belgium	
SCHIRM.EC	E.C. Schirmer Music Co. 138 Ipswich Street Boston, MA 02215-3534	
SCHIRM.G	G. Schirmer, Inc. (Executive Offices) 257 Park Avenue South, 20th Floor New York, NY 10010 G. Schirmer Rental Performance Dept. P.O. Box 572 5 Bellvale Road Chester, NY 10918	LEONARD-US (sales)
SCHMIDT,H	Musikverlag Hermann Schmidt Berliner Straße 26 D-6000 Frankfurt-am-Main 1 Germany	
SCHMITT	Schmitt Music Editions	CPP-BEL
SCHNEIDER,H	Musikverlag Hans Schneider Mozartstraße 6 D-8132 Tutzing Germany	
SCHOLA	Editions Musicales de la Schola Cantorum Rue du Sapin 2A CH-2114 Fleurier Switzerland	PRESSER

Code	Publisher	U.S. Agent
SCHOTT	Schott & Co. Ltd. Brunswick Road Ashford, Kent TN23 1DX England	EUR.AM.MUS.
SCHOTT-FRER	Schott Frères 30 rue Saint-Jean B-1000 Bruxelles Belgium	EUR.AM.MUS.
SCHOTT,J	Schott & Co. #301,3-4-3 Iidabashi, Chiyoda-ku Tokyo 102 Japan	EUR.AM.MUS.
SCHOTTS	B. Schotts Söhne Weihergarten 5 Postfach 3640 D-6500 Mainz Germany	EUR.AM.MUS.
SCHROTH	Edition Schroth Kommandatenstrasse 5A D-1 Berlin 45 Germany	BÄREN.
SCHUBERTH	Edward Schuberth & Co., Inc.	CENTURY
SCHUBERTH,J	J. Schuberth & Co. Rothenbaumchaussee 1 D-2000 Hamburg 13 Germany	
SCHUL	Carl L. Schultheiß Denzenbergstraße 35 D-7400 Tübingen Germany	
SCHULZ.FR	Blasmusikverlag Fritz Schulz Am Märzengraben 6 D-7800 Freiburg-Tiengen Germany	
SCHWANN	Musikverlag Schwann	PETERS
SCHWEIZER.	Schweizerischer Kirchengesangbund Markusstrasse 6 CH-2544 Bettlach Switzerland	FOSTER
SCOTT	G. Scott Music Publishing Co.	WESTERN
SCOTT MUSIC	Scott Music Publications	ALFRED
SCOTUS	Scotus Music Publications, Ltd. see Eschenbach	ESCHENB
SCREEN	Screen Gems Columbia Pictures	WARNER
SDG PR	SDG Press 170 N.E. 33rd Street Ft. Lauderdale, FL 33334	PLYMOUTH
SEAMONT	Seamont International	INTRADA
SEESAW	Seesaw Music Corp. 2067 Broadway New York, NY 10023	
SELMER	Selmer Éditions 18, rue de la Fontaine-au-Roi F-75011 Paris France	
SEMI	Société d'Editions Musicales Internationales	PEER
SENART	Ed. Maurice Senart 22 rue Chauchat F-75009 Paris France	SCHIRM.G
SEPT	September Music Corp. 250 W. 57th Street New York, NY 10019	

Code	Publisher	U.S. Agent
SERENUS	Serenus Corp. 145 Palisade Street Dobbs Ferry, NY 10522	
SERVANT	Servant Publications P.O. Box 8617 840 Airport Boulevard Ann Arbor, MI 48107	
SESAC	Sesac, Inc. 10 Columbus Circle New York, NY 10019	
SHALL-U-MO	Shall-U-Mo Publications P.O. Box 2824 Rochester, NY 14626	
SHAPIRO	Shapiro, Bernstein & Co., Inc. 10 East 53 Street New York, NY 10022	PLYMOUTH
SHATTINGER	Shattinger Music Co. 1810 S. Broadway St. Louis, MO 63104	
SHAWNEE	Shawnee Press, Inc. 49 Waring Drive Delaware Water Gap, PA 18327-1099	MUSIC
SHEPPARD	John Sheppard Music Press	EUR.AM.MUS.
	Antigua Casa Sherry-Brener, Ltd. see ACSB	
SIDEMTON	Sidemton Verlag	BREITKOPF-W
SIFLER	Paul J. Sifler 3947 Fredonia Drive Hollywood, CA 90068	
SIGHT & SOUND	Sight & Sound International 3200 South 166th Street Box 27 New Berlin, WI 53151	
SIJN	D. van Sijn & Zonen Banorstraat 1 Rotterdam Netherlands	
SIKORSKI	Hans Sikorski Verlag Johnsallee 23 Postfach 132001 D-2000 Hamburg 13 Germany	LEONARD-US
SIMROCK	Nicholas Simrock Lyra House 37 Belsize Lane London NW3 5AX England	PRESSER
SINGSPIR	Singspiration Music The Zondervan Corp. 1415 Lake Drive S.E. Grand Rapids, MI 49506	
SIRIUS	Sirius-Verlag	PETERS
SKAND.	Skandinavisk Musikforlag Gothersgade 9-11 DK-1123 København K. Denmark	
SLATKINE	Slatkine Reprints 5 rue des Chaudronniers Case 765 CH-1211 Genève 3 Switzerland	
SLOV.AKA.	Slovenska Akademija Znanosti in Umetnosti Trg Francoske Revolucije 6 Ljubljana Slovenia	DRUSTVO

Code	Publisher	U.S. Agent
SLOV.HUD.FOND.	Slovenský Hudobný Fond Fucikova 29 811 02 Bratislava Slovak Republic	BOOSEY (rental)
SLOV.MAT	Slovenska Matica	DRUSTVO
SMITH PUB	Smith Publications-Sonic Art Editions 2617 Gwynndale Avenue Baltimore, MD 21207	
SMPF	SMPF, Inc. 16 E. 34th St., 7th Floor New York, NY 10016	
SOC.FR.MUS.	Société Française de Music	TRANSAT.
	Society for the Preservation & Encouragement of Barber Shop Quartet Singing in America see SPEBSQSA	
SOC.PUB.AM.	Society for the Publication of American Music	PRESSER
	Société d'Éditions Musicales Internationales see SEMI	
	Society of Finnish Composers see SUOMEN	
SOLAR	The Solar Studio 178 Cowles Road Woodbury, CT 06798	
SOLID	Solid Foundation Music	SON-KEY
SOMERSET	Somerset Press	HOPE
SON-KEY	Son-Key, Inc. P.O. Box 31757 Aurora, CO 80041	
SONANTE	Sonante Publications P.O. Box 74, Station F Toronto, Ontario M4Y 2L4 Canada	
SONOS	Sonos Music Resources, Inc. P.O. Box 1510 Orem, UT 84057	
SONSHINE	Sonshine Productions	LORENZ
SONZOGNO	Casa Musicale Sonzogno Via Bigli 11 I-20121 Milano Italy	PRESSER
SOUTHERN	Southern Music Co. 1100 Broadway P.O. Box 329 San Antonio, TX 78292	
SOUTHERN PUB	Southern Music Publishing Co., Pty. Ltd. Sydney, Australia	PEER
SOUTHWEST	Southwest Music Publications Box 4552 Santa Fe, NM 87501	
SPAN.MUS.CTR.	Spanish Music Center, Inc. 4 Division Street P.O. Box 132 Farmingville, NY 11738	
SPEBSQSA	Society for the Preservation & Encouragement of Barber Shop Quartet Singing in America, Inc. 6315 Third Avenue Kenosha, WI 53143-5199	
SPIRE	Spire Editions	FISCHER,C WORLD
SPRATT	Spratt Music Publishers 17 West 60th Street, 8th Fl. New York, NY 10023	PLYMOUTH

Code	Publisher	U.S. Agent
ST.GREG.	St. Gregory Publishing Co. 64 Pineheath Road High Kelling, Holt Norfolk, NR25 6RH England	ROYAL
ST. MARTIN	St. Martin Music Co., Inc.	ROYAL
STAFF	Staff Music Publishing Co., Inc. 170 N.E. 33rd St. Ft. Lauderdale, FL 33334	PLYMOUTH
STAINER	Stainer & Bell Ltd. P.O. Box 110, Victoria House 23 Gruneisen Road London N3 1DZ England	SCHIRM.EC
STAMON	Nick Stamon Press 4280 Middlesex Drive San Diego, CA 92116	
STAMPS	Stamps-Baxter Music Publications Box 4007 Dallas, TX 75208	SINGSPIR
STANDARD	Standard Music Publishing, Inc.	
STANGLAND	Thomas C. Stangland Co. P.O. Box 19263 Portland, OR 97280	
STEIN	Edition Steingräber Auf der Reiswiese 9 D-6050 Offenbach/M. Germany	
STILL	William Grant Still Music 22 S. San Francisco Street Suite 422 Flagstaff, AZ 86001-5737	
STIM	STIMs Informationcentral för Svensk Musik Sandhamnsgatan 79 Box 27327 S-102 54 Stockholm Sweden	
STOCKHAUS	Stockhausen-Verlag Kettenberg 15 D-5067 Kürten Germany	
	Stockhausen-Verlag, U.S. 2832 Maple Lane Fairfax, VA 22030	
STOCKTON	Fred Stockton P.O. Box 814 Grass Valley, CA 95945	
STRONG	Stronghold Publications	ALEX.HSE.
STUD	Studio 224	STUDIO
STUDIO	Studio P/R, Inc.	CPP-BEL
STYRIA	Verlag Styria Schönaugasse 64 Postfach 435 A-8011 Graz Austria	
SUECIA	Edition Suecia	STIM
SUISEISHA	Suiseisha Editions	ONGAKU
SUMMIT	Summit Music Ltd. 38 North Row London W1R 1DH England	
SUMMY	Summy-Birchard Co. 265 Secaucus Road Secaucus, NJ 07096-2037	LEONARD-US

Code	Publisher	U.S. Agent
SUOMEN	Suomen Säveltäjät ry (Society of Finnish Composers) Runeberginkatu 15 A SF-00100 Helsinki 10 Finland	
SUPPORT	Support Services 79 South Street P.O. Box 478 Natick, MA 01760	
SUPRAPHON	Supraphon Palackeho 1 CS-112 99 Praha1 Czech Republic	FOR.MUS.DIST. (rental) NEW W
	Svenska Utbildningsförlaget Liber AB see LIBER	
SVERIG	Sveriges Körförbund Box 38014 S-100 64 Stockholm, Sweden	
SWAN	Swan & Co. P.O. Box 1 Rickmansworth, Herts WD3 3AZ England	ARCADIA
SWAND	Swand Publications 120 North Longcross Road Linthicum Heights, MD 21090	
	Swedish Music Information Center see STIM	
SYMPHON	Symphonia Verlag	CPP-BEL
TAUNUS	Taunus	HOFMEISTER-W
TCAPUB	TCA Publications Teacher-Composer Alliance P.O. Box 6428 Evanston, IL 60204	
TECLA	Tecla Editions Preacher's Court, Charterhouse London EC1M 6AS England	
TEESELING	Muziekuitgeverij van Teeseling Buurmansweg 29B NL-6525 RV Nijmegen Netherlands	
TEMPLETN	Templeton Publishing Co., Inc.	SHAWNEE
TEMPO	Tempo Music Publications 3773 W. 95th Street Leawood, KS 66206	ALEX.HSE.
TEN TIMES	Ten Times A Day P.O. Box 230 Deer Park, L.I., NY 11729	
TENUTO	Tenuto Publications see also TRI-TEN	PRESSER
TETRA	Tetra Music Corp.	PLYMOUTH WESL (rental)
TFS	Things For Strings Publishing Co. P.O. Box 9263 Alexandria, VA 22304	
THAMES	Thames Publishing 14 Barlby Road London W10 6AR England	
THOMAS	Thomas House Publications P.O. Box 1423 San Carlos, CA 94070	INTRADA
THOMI	E. Thomi-Berg Musikverlag Bahnhofstraße 94A D-8032 Gräfelfing Germany	

Code	Publisher	U.S. Agent
THOMP.	Thompson Music House P.O. Box 12463 Nashville, TN 37212	
THOMPS.G	Gordon V. Thompson Music 85 Scarsdale Rd., Ste 104 Don Mills, Ontario M3B 2R2 Canada	OXFORD
TIEROLFF	Tierolff Muziek Centrale P.O. Box 18 NL-4700 AA Roosendaal Netherlands	
TISCHER	Tischer und Jagenberg Musikverlag Nibelungenstraße 48 D-8000 München 19 Germany	
TOA	Toa Editions	ONGAKU
TONGER	P.J. Tonger, Musikverlag Auf dem Brand 3 Postfach 501865 D-5000 Köln-Rodenkirchen 50 Germany	
TONOS	Editions Tonos Ahastraße 9 D-6100 Damstadt Germany	SEESAW
TOORTS	Muziekuitgeverij De Toorts Nijverheidsweg 1 Postbus 576 NL-2003 RN Haarlem Netherlands	
TRANSAT.	Éditions Musicales Transatlantiques 151, avenue Jean-Jaures F-75019 Paris France	PRESSER
TRANSCON.	Transcontinental Music Publications 838 Fifth Avenue New York, NY 10021	
TREKEL	Joachim-Trekel-Verlag Postfach 620428 D-2000 Hamburg 62 Germany	
TRI-TEN	Tritone Press and Tenuto Publications P.O. Box 5081, Southern Station Hattiesburg, MS 39401	PRESSER
TRIGON	Trigon Music Inc.	LORENZ
TRINITY	Trinity House Publishing	CRESPUB
TRIUNE	Triune Music, Inc.	LORENZ
TRN	TRN Music Publishers 111 Torreon Loop P.O. Box 1076 Ruidoso, NM 88345	
TRO	Tro Songways Service, Inc. 10 Columbus Circle New York, NY 10019 see also RICHMOND ORG.	PLYMOUTH
TROY	Troy State University Library Troy, AL 36081	
TUSKEGEE	Tuskegee Institute Music Press	KJOS
U.S.CATH	United States Catholic Conference Publications Office 1312 Massachusetts Avenue N.W. Washington, D.C. 20005	
UBER,D	David Uber Music Department Trenton State College Trenton, NJ 08625	
UFATON	Ufaton-Verlag	ORLANDO

Code	Publisher	U.S. Agent
UNICORN	Unicorn Music Company, Inc.	BOSTON
UNION ESP.	Union Musical Ediciones Carrera de San Jeronimo 26 Madrid 14 Spain	SCHIRM.G
UNISONG	Unisong Publishers	PRESSER
UNITED ART	United Artists Group	CPP-BEL PRESSER (rental)
UNITED MUS.	United Music Publishers Ltd. 42 Rivington Street London EC2A 3BN England	PRESSER
UNIV. ALA	University of Alabama Press Box 870380 Tuscaloosa, AL 35487-0380	
UNIV.CAL	University of California Press 2120 Berkeley Way Berkeley, CA 94720	
UNIV.CH	University of Chicago Press 5801 South Ellis Avenue Chicago, IL 60637	
UNIV.CR.	University College - Cardiff Press P.O. Box 78 Cardiff CF1 1XL, Wales United Kingdom	
UNIV.EVAN	University of Evansville Press P.O. Box 329 Evansville, IN 47702	
UNIV.IOWA	University of Iowa Press Iowa City, IA 52242	
UNIV.MIAMI	University of Miami Music Publications P.O. Box 8163 Coral Gables, FL 33124	PLYMOUTH
UNIV.MICRO	University Microfilms 300 North Zeeb Road Ann Arbor, MI 48106	
UNIV.MINN	University of Minnesota Press 2037 University Avenue S.E. Minneapolis, MN 55455	
UNIV.MUS.ED.	University Music Editions P.O. Box 192-Ft. George Station New York, NY 10040	
UNIV.NC	University of North Carolina Press P.O. Box 2288 Chapel Hill, NC 27514	
UNIV.OTAGO	University of Otago Press P.O. Box 56 Dunedin New Zealand	
UNIV.TEXAS	University of Texas Press P.O. Box 7819 Austin, TX 78712	
UNIV.UTAH	University of Utah Press Salt Lake City, UT 84112	
UNIV.WASH	University of Washington Press Seattle, WA 98105	
UNIVER.	Universal Edition Bösendorfer Straße 12 Postfach 130 A-1015 Wien Austria	EUR.AM.MUS.
	Universal Edition (London) Ltd. 2/3 Fareham Street, Dean Street London W1V 4DU England	EUR.AM.MUS.
UNIVERH	Universal Songs Holland Postbus 305 1200 AH Hilversum Netherlands	GM
UNIVERSE	Universe Publishers 733 East 840 North Circle Orem, UT 84057	PRESSER
UP WITH	Up With People 3103 North Campbell Avenue Tucson, AZ 85719	LORENZ
VAAP	VAAP 6a, Bolshaya Bronnaya St. Moscow 103670,GSP Russia	SCHIRM.G
VALANDO	Valando Music, Inc.	PLYMOUTH
VAMO	Musikverlag Vamö Leebgasse 52-25 Wien 10 Austria	
VAN NESS	Van Ness Press, inc.	BROADMAN
VANDEN-RUP	Vandenhoeck & Ruprecht Theaterstrasse 13 Postfach 3753 D-3400 Göttingen Germany	
VANDERSALL	Vandersall Editions	EUR.AM.MUS.
VANGUARD	Vanguard Music Corp. 357 W. 55th Street New York, NY 10019	
VER.HUIS.	Vereniging voor Huismuziek Utrechtsestraat 77 Postbus 350 NL-3041 CT Ijsselstein Netherlands	
VER.NED.MUS.	Vereniging voor Nederlandse Muziekgeschiedenis Postbus 1514 NL-3500 BM Utrecht Netherlands	
VEST-NORSK	Vest-Norsk Musikkforslag Postboks 4016, Dreggen N-5023 Bergen Norway	
VIERT	Viertmann Verlag Lübecker Straße 2 D-5000 Köln 1 Germany	
VIEWEG	Chr. Friedrich Vieweg, Musikverlag Nibelungenstraße 48 D-8000 München 19 Germany	LEONARD-US SCHIRM.G (rental)
VIKING	Viking Press, Inc. P.O. Box 4030 Church Street Station New York, NY 10261-4030	
VIOLA	Viola World Publications 14 Fenwood Road Huntington Station, NY 11746	
VOGGEN	Voggenrieter Verlag Viktoriastraße 25 D-5300 Bonn Germany	
VOGT	Musikverlag Vogt & Fritz Friedrich-Stein-Straße 10 D-8720 Schweinfurt Germany	
VOLK	Arno Volk Verlag	BREITKOPF-W
VOLKWEIN	Volkwein Brothers, Inc.	CPP-BEL

Code	Publisher	U.S. Agent
WADSWORTH	Wadsworth Publishing Co. 10 Davis Street Belmont, CA 94002	
WAGENAAR	J.A.H. Wagenaar Oude Gracht 109 NL-3511 AG Utrecht Netherlands	ELKAN,H
WAI-TE-ATA	Wai-te-ata Press Dept. of Music Victoria Univ. of Wellington P.O. Box 600 Wellington, New Zealand	
WALKER	Walker Publications P.O. Box 61 Arnold, MD 21012	
WALKER MUS.PRO.	Walker Music Productions 643 Oenoke Ridge New Canaan, CT 06840	
WALTON	Walton Music Corp.	PLYMOUTH
WARNER	Warner Brothers Publications, Inc. 265 Secaucus Road Secaucus, NJ 07096	CPP-BEL
	Warner-Chappell Music 810 Seventh Avenue New York, NY 10119	
WATERLOO	Waterloo Music Co. Ltd. 3 Regina Street North Waterloo, Ontario N2J 4A5 Canada	
WEHMAN BR.	Wehman Brothers, Inc. Ridgedale Avenue Morris County Mall Cedar Knolls, NJ 07927	
WEINBERGER	Josef Weinberger Ltd. 12-14 Mortimer Street London W1N 7RD England	BOOSEY CANTORIS BOCK
	Josef Weinberger Neulerchenfelderstrasse 3-7 A-1160 Wien Austria	
WEINTRAUB	Weintraub Music Co.	SCHIRM.G (rental)
WELT	Welt Musik Josef Hochmuth Verlage Hegergasse 21 A-1160 Wien Austria	
WESL	Wesleyan Music Press P.O. Box 1072 Fort George Station New York, NY 10040	
WESSMAN	Wessmans Musikforlag S-620 30 Slite Sweden	STIM
WESTEND	Westend	PETERS
WESTERN	Western International Music, Inc. 3707 65th Avenue Greeley, CO 80634	
WESTMINSTER	The Westminster Press 925 Chestnut Street Philadelphia, PA 19107	
WESTWOOD	Westwood Press, Inc. 3759 Willow Road Schiller Park, IL 60176	WORLD
WHITE HARV.	White Harvest Music Publications P.O. Box 1144 Independence, MO 64051	

Code	Publisher	U.S. Agent
WIDE WORLD	Wide World Music, Inc. Box B Delaware Water Gap, PA 18327	
WIEN BOH.	Wiener Boheme Verlag GmbH Sonnenstraße 19 D-8000 München 2 Germany	
WIENER	Wiener Urtext Edition	EUR.AM.MUS.
WILDER	Wilder	MARGUN
WILHELM	Wilhelmiana Musikverlag see HANSEN-GER	
	William Grant Still Music see STILL	
	Williams School of Church Music see WSCM	
WILLIAMSN	Williamson Music, Inc.	LEONARD-US
WILLIS	Willis Music Co. 7380 Industrial Road Florence, KY 41042	
WILLSHIRE	Willshire Press Music Foundation, Inc.	WESTERN
WILSHORN	Wilshorn	HOPE
WILSON	Wilson Editions 13 Bank Square Wilmslow SK9 1AN England	
WIMBLEDN	Wimbledon Music Inc. 1888 Century Park East Suite 10 Century City, CA 90067	
WIND MUS	Wind Music, Inc. 153 Highland Parkway Rochester, NY 14620	KALMUS,A
WINGERT	Wingert-Jones Music, Inc. 2026 Broadway P.O. Box 419878 Kansas City, MO 64141	
WISCAS	Wiscasset Music Publishing Company Box 810 Cambridge, MA 02138	
WOITSCHACH	Paul Woitschach Radio-Musikverlag Grosse Friedberger Strasse 23-27 D-6000 Frankfurt Germany	
WOLF	Wolf-Mills Music	WESTERN
WOLLENWEBER	Verlag Walter Wollenweber Schiffmannstrasse 4 Postfach 1165 D-8032 Gräfelfing vor München Germany	FOR.MUS.DIST
WOODBURY	Woodbury Music Co. 33 Grassy Hill Road P.O. Box 447 Woodbury, CT 06798	PRESSER (rental-partial)
WOODWARD	Ralph Woodward, Jr. 1033 East 300 South Salt Lake City, UT 84102	
WOODWIND	Woodwind Editions P.O. Box 457, Station K Toronto, Ontario Canada M4P 2G9	
WORD	Word, Incorporated 3319 West End Avenue Suite 200 Nashville, TN 37203	
WORD GOD	The Word of God Music	SERVANT

Code	Publisher	U.S. Agent
WORLD	World Library Publications, Inc. 3815 Willow Road P.O. Box 2701 Schiller Park, IL 60176	
WORLDWIDE	Worldwide Music Services P.O. Box 995, Ansonia Station New York, NY 10023	
WSCM	Williams School of Church Music The Bourne Harpenden England	
WYE	WYE Music Publications	EMERSON
WYNN	Wynn/Music Publications P.O. Box 739 Orinda, CA 94563	
XYZ	Muziekuitgeverij XYZ P.O. Box 338 NL-1400 AH Bussum Netherlands	
YAHRES	Yahres Publications 1315 Vance Avenue Coraopolis, PA 15108	
YBARRA	Ybarra Music P.O. Box Box 665 Lemon Grove, CA 92045	
YORKE	Yorke Editions 31 Thornhill Square London N1 1BQ England	SCHIRM.EC
YOUNG WORLD	Young World Publications 10485 Glennon Drive Lakewood, CO 80226	
	Yugoslavian Music Information Center see MUSIC INFO	
ZALO	Zalo Publications & Services P.O. Box 913 Bloomington, IN 47402	FRANG
ZANIBON	G. Zanibon Edition Piazza dei Signori, 44 I-35100 Padova Italy	
ZEN-ON	Zen-On Music Co., Ltd. 3-14 Higashi Gokencho Shinjuku-ku Tokyo 162 Japan	EUR.AM.MUS MAGNA D
ZENEM.	Zenemukiado Vallalat	BOOSEY GENERAL
ZENGERINK	Herman Zengerink, Urlusstraat 24 NL-3533 SN Utrecht Netherlands	
ZERBONI	Edizioni Suvini Zerboni Via Quintiliano 40 I-20138 Milano Italy	BOOSEY (rental)
ZIMMER.	Musikverlag Zimmermann Gaugrafenstraße 19-23 Postfach 940183 D-6000 Frankfurt-am-Main Germany	
ZIMMER.PUBS.	Oscar Zimmerman Publications 4671 State Park Highway Interlochen, MI 49643-9527	
ZINNEB	Zinneberg Musikverlag	LEUCKART
	The Zondervan Corp. see SINGSPIR	

Code	Publisher	U.S. Agent
ZURFLUH	Éditions Zurfluh 73, Boulevard Raspail F-75006 Paris France	PRESSER

Advertisements

Index to Advertisers

New for Orchestra from G. Schirmer, Inc.

Stephen Albert
Wind Canticle (1991) .... 14'
Clarinet; 2222/4200/timp/hp.pf/str

George Antheil
Lithuanian Night .... 4'
str

Tom Sawyer Overture .... 7'
2+pic.2+ca.2+bcl.2+cbn/4331/timp.3perc/pf/str

John Corigliano
Troubadours .... 21'
Guitar; 2(pic)12(bcl)0/0000/3perc/pf/str; offstage: ob.2bn/2hn

Richard Danielpour
City Lights (1992) .... ca. 10'
3(pic)2+ca.3(bcl)3(cbn)/4331/timp.4perc/hp.pf(cel)/str

Piano Concerto No. 2 (1993) .... 31'
Piano; 2(pic).2(ca).2+bcl.2(cbn)/4330/timp.3perc/hp/str

Song of Remembrance (1991) .... 14'
3(pic).2(ca).3(bcl).3(cbn)/4431/timp.4perc/hp.amp pf(cel)/str

Philip Glass
The "Low" Symphony (1992) .... 42'
2+pic.22+E♭cl+bcl.2/4331/4perc/hp.pf/str

Morton Gould
The Jogger and the Dinosaur (1992) .... 22'
Narrator(rapper); 2(pic)121/2221/2perc/str

String Music (1993) .... 30'
str

Marvin Hamlisch
Anatomy of Peace (1991) .... 30'
Child's voice; Chorus; 3(pic)2+ca.3(bcl)3(cbn)/4431/2timp.
4perc/cel/str

John Harbison
Concerto for Oboe (1991) .... 20'
Oboe; 2(pic)02+bcl(asx)3(cbn)/2221/timp.3perc/hp/str

Concerto for Cello (1994) .... 22'
Cello; 3(pic)23(bcl)3/4230/timp.4perc/hp.cel(pf)/str

The Most Often Used Chords (1993) .... 18'
2222/2200/timp.perc/hp.pf(cel)/str

Symphony No. 3 (1991) .... 21'
3(pic)3(ca)3(bcl)3(cbn)/4331/timp.4perc/pf/str

Aaron Jay Kernis
Colored Field (1994) .... 40'
English horn; 3(pic)23(E♭cl,bcl)2(cbn)/432+btbn1/timp.3perc/
egtr.eb.hp.pf/str

New Era Dance (1992) .... 6'
2+pic.22(E♭cl+bcl)2(opt police whistles)/4331/timp.4 perc/
pf(syn+police whistle)/str

Symphony No. 2 (1991) .... ca 23'
2(pic).3(ca).3(bcl).3(cbn)/4441/timp.4perc/pf(cel).hp/str

Leon Kirchner (b. 1919)
Music for Cello and Orchestra (1992) .... 18'
Cello; 3(pic)3+ca.2+bcl.2+cbn/4331/timp.3perc/pf(cel)/str

Peter Lieberson
Concerto for Viola (1993) .... 26'
Viola; 2(pic)1+ca.22/2221/timp/str

World's Turning (1991) .... 18'
4(2pic).2+ca.3(bcl).2(cbn)/4331/timp.perc.hp/str

Kirke Mechem
Songs of the Slave (1993) .... 31'
Bass-baritone; Chorus; 3333/4331/timp.4perc/hp/str

Gian Carlo Menotti
Llama de Amor Viva (1991) .... 10'
Baritone; Chorus; 2+pic.2+ca.2+bcl.2/4331/timp.2perc/hp.pf/str

Robert Xavier Rodríguez
Máscaras (1993) .... 18'
Cello; 2(pic)2(ca)2(E♭cl+bcl)2/2210/timp.2perc/hp.pf/str

Piñata (1991) .... 5'
2+pic.22.asx.2/4331/timp.3perc/hp.pf/str

Gunther Schuller
And They All Played Ragtime (1992) .... ca 20'
2+pic.2+ca.4(2bcl+cbcl).3(cbn)/4331/timp.4perc/pf(cel+syn)/str

Concerto for Violin No. 2 (1991) .... 26'
Violin; 3(pic)3(ca)3(bcl)3(cbn)/4331/timp.4perc/hp.pf(cel)/str

The Past is in the Present (1994) .... 25'
4(pic).3+ca.3+bcl.3+cbn/543+btbn.1/timp/2hp.pf(cel)/str

Of Reminiscences and Reflections (1993) .... 15'
4(2pic,afl)4(2ca)4(2bcl)4(cbn)/6441/timp.5perc/hp.pf(cel)/str

Ritmica-Melodica-Armonica (1993) .... ca 15-20'
3333/4331/timp.2perc/hp.pf/str

Bright Sheng
Arrows to the Page (1992) .... ca 5'
2(pic)+pic.2+ca.2+E♭cl(bcl).2+cbn/43(pic tpt)31/4perc/hp.pf/str

Fragments from 'The Song of Majnun' (1992) .... 18'
Small and large choruses; Soprano, Tenor;
2(2pic.afl).1(ca).1(bcl).1(cbn)/2110/2perc.hp.pf/str

Roberto Sierra
Concierto Evocativo (1991) .... 17'
Horn; str

A Joyous Overture (1991) .... ca 5'
2+pic.222/4321/timp.2perc/str

Tropicalia (1991) .... 23'
2+pic.2+ca.2+bcl.2+cbn/4331/timp.4perc/pf(cel).hp/str

Igor Stravinsky
Jeu de cartes .... 21'
2222/4231/timp.perc/str [*available in the US only*]

Tan Dun
Death and Fire: Dialogue with Paul Klee (1992) .... 27'
2(2pic)+pic(afl).2.2+bcl.2+cbn/4331/4perc/hp/str

Orchestral Theatre II: Re (1992) .... 17'
Bass; audience; 0+3pic.2+ca.2+bcl.2/4331/4perc/hp/str
(two conductors)

Michael Tilson Thomas
From the Diary of Anne Frank .... ca 35'
Narrator; 2+pic.2+ca.2+bcl.2+cbn/4331/timp.3perc/hp.pf/str

Joan Tower
Concerto for Orchestra (1991) .... 30'
3(pic).2+ca.3(E♭cl+bcl).3(cbn)/4331/timp.3perc/hp.pf/str

Concerto for Violin (1992) .... 19'
Violin; 2222/2210/timp.2perc/str

Stepping Stones: A Ballet (1993) .... 25'
2(pic)222/4220/2perc/hp.pf(cel)/str

For the Uncommon Woman (Fourth Fanfare) (1992) .... 5'
2(pic)222/4331/timp.3perc/str

For **perusal** materials:
G. Schirmer Promotion Department

257 Park Ave South, 20th floor
New York, NY 10010
Phone: 212 254-2100 Fax: 212 254-2013

For **performance** materials:
**G. Schirmer Rental and
Performance Department**
5 Bellvale Road
Chester, NY 10918
Phone: 914 469-2271 Fax: 914 469-7544

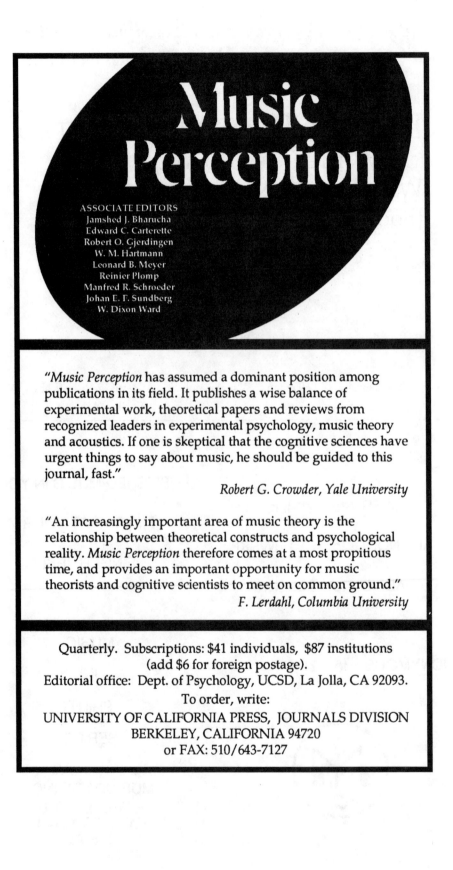

New and Forthcoming Books From
The Music Library Association

MLA INDEX SERIES

No. 25: **Analyses of Nineteenth- and Twentieth-Century Music, 1940-85,** compiled by Arthur B. Wenk, 1987. ISBN 0-914954-36-9; $29.00

No. 26: **Opera Performances in Video Format: A Checklist of Commercially Released Performances,** by Charles Croissant, 1992. ISBN 0-914954-43-1; $15.00

No. 27: **The Works of Robert Valentine: A Thematic Catalog,** compiled by J. Bradford Young. (to be published in early 1993).

MLA TECHNICAL REPORTS SERIES

No. 16: **Authority Control in Music Libraries: Proceedings of the Music Library Association Preconference, March 5, 1985,** edited by Ruth Tucker, 1989. ISBN 0-914954-22-3; $22.00

No. 17: **Planning and Caring for Library Audio Facilities,** edited and with a preface by James P. Cassaro, 1989. ISBN 0-914954-38-5; $20.00

No. 18: **Careers in Music Librarianship,** compiled by Carol Tatian, 1990. ISBN 0-914954-41-5; $19.00.

No. 19: **In Celebration of Revised 780: Music in the Dewey Decimal Classification, Edition 20,** compiled by Richard Wursten, 1990. ISBN 0-914954-42-3; $20.00

No. 20: **Space Utilization in Music Libraries,** compiled by James P. Cassaro, 1992. ISBN 0-914954-44-X; $30.00

No. 21: **Archival Information Processing for Sound Recordings,** by David H. Thomas, 1992. ISBN 0-914954-45-8; $33.00.

SPECIAL PUBLICATIONS

Cumulative Five-Year Index to the MUSIC CATALOGING BULLETIN. (to be issued in late 1992).

Music Cataloging Decisions, As Issued by the Music Section, Special Materials Cataloging Division, Library of Congress in the MUSIC CATALOGING BULLETIN through December 1991, indexed and edited by Betsy Gamble, 1992. ISBN 0-914954-39-3; $24.00.

Music Librarianship in America; Papers of a Symposium Held October 5-7, 1989, to Honor the Establishment of the Richard F. French Chair in Music Librarianship at Harvard University, edited by Michael Ochs, 1991. $22.00 (available exclusively through the Music Library Association).

Available from library booksellers or from
The Music Library Association, P.O. Box 487D, Canton, MA 02021.
Membership information is also available from the same address.
MLA members receive a 10% discount on all publications.
Institutions requesting billing will be charged for handling.